AUTOMOTIVE TECHNOLOGY

A Systems Approach

Jack Erjavec ■ Robert Scharff

DELMAR PUBLISHERS INC.®

NOTICE TO THE READER

Publisher does not warrant or guarantee any of the products described herein or perform any independent analysis in connection with any of the product information contained herein. Publisher does not assume, and expressly disclaims, any obligation to obtain and include information other than that provided to it by the manufacturer.

The reader is expressly warned to consider and adopt all safety precautions that might be indicated by the activities described herein and to avoid all potential hazards. By following the instructions contained herein, the reader willingly assumes all risks in connection with such instructions.

The publisher makes no representations or warranties of any kind, including but not limited to, the warranties of fitness for particular purpose or merchantability, nor are any such representations implied with respect to the material set forth herein, and the publisher takes no responsibility with respect to such material. The publisher shall not be liable for any special, consequential or exemplary damages resulting, in whole or in part, from the readers' use of, or reliance upon, this material.

Cover photo by Bruce Parker/PARKER PRODUCTIONS
Automotive parts courtesy of NAPA Auto Parts, Universal Auto Parts, and Cottman

Step-by-Step photos by Michael A. Gallitelli, Metroland Photo

DELMAR STAFF
Executive Editor: Michael A. McDermott
Administrative Editor: Vernon R. Anthony
Developmental Editor: Mary Ormsbee Clyne
Project Editor: Eleanor Isenhart
Production Coordinator: Teresa Luterbach
Senior Design Supervisor: Susan C. Mathews
Art Supervisor: John Lent

For information, address Delmar Publishers Inc.
3 Columbia Circle, PO Box 15015
Albany, New York 12212-5015

Copyright © 1992 by Delmar Publishers Inc.

All rights reserved. No part of this work covered by the copyright hereon may be reproduced or used in any form or by any means— graphic, electronic, or mechanical, including photocopying, recording, taping, or information storage and retrieval systems— without written permission of the publisher.

10 9 8 7 6 5 4

Printed in the United States of America
Published simultaneously in Canada by Nelson Canada
a division of The Thomson Corporation

Library of Congress Cataloging in Publication Data

Erjavec, Jack.
    Automotive technology : a systems approach / Jack Eriavec. Robert Scharff.
      p.   cm.
    Includes index.
    ISBN 0-8273-6292-7 (textbook-LTI edition)
    1. Automobiles. 2. Automobiles—Maintenance and repair.
  I. Scharff. Robert. II. Title.
TL205.E74   1992   91-33026
629.222—dc20   CIP

CONTENTS

Contents for
Photo Sequences xii

Preface xiv

SECTION ONE   Automotive Technology

CHAPTER 1

The Automotive Industry 2
Introduction 2 ■ Job Classifications 6 ■ Related Career Opportunities 8 ■ Working as an Automotive Technician 9 ■ Training for a Career in Automotive Service 10 ■ ASE Certification 10

CHAPTER 2

Practicing Safety in the Shop 16
Personal Safety 16 ■ Tool and Equipment Safety 18 ■ Work Area Safety 22 ■ Manufacturer's Warnings and Government Regulations 24

CHAPTER 3

Automotive Systems 28
Design Evolution 29 ■ Modern Unitized Construction 30 ■ Modern Body-Over-Frame Construction 30 ■ Body Shapes 30 ■ Modern Power Plants 32 ■ The Electronic Revolution 32 ■ Building Modern Vehicles 33 ■ The Basic Engine 34 ■ Mechanical Systems 36 ■ Drivetrain 41 ■ Running Gear 46 ■ Preventive Maintenance 48

CHAPTER 4

Shop Tools 54
Measuring Systems 54 ■ Engine Measuring Tools 54 ■ Hand Tools 65 ■ Power Tools 73 ■ Service Manuals 76 ■ Case Study 78

iv   Contents

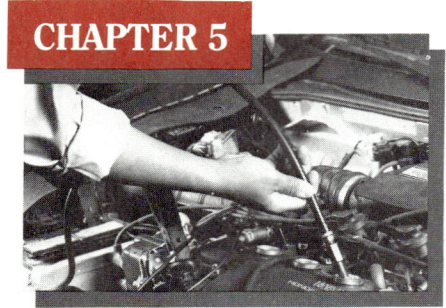

CHAPTER 5

Diagnostic Equipment 81

Electrical Fundamentals 81 ■ Measuring Electricity 82 ■ Ignition System Test Equipment 87 ■ Compression and Vacuum Testers 92 ■ Fuel System Test Equipment 97 ■ Exhaust Analyzer 98 ■ Microcomputer Scan Tools 99 ■ Engine Analyzer 100

SECTION TWO   Engines

CHAPTER 6

Automotive Engines 104

Engine Classifications 105 ■ Four-Stroke Gasoline Engines 106 ■ Two-Stroke Gasoline Engines 108 ■ Characteristics of Four-Stroke Engine Design 109 ■ Gasoline Engine Systems 113 ■ Engine Measurement and Performance 113 ■ Engine Identification 116 ■ Engine Diagnostics 116 ■ Oil Pressure Testing 117 ■ Cylinder Power Balance Testing 117 ■ Evaluating the Engine's Condition 118 ■ Noise Diagnosis 119 ■ Other Engine Designs 121 ■ Case Study 124

CHAPTER 7

Engine Disassembly 127

Preparing the Engine for Removal 127 ■ Lifting an Engine 127 ■ Engine Disassembly and Inspection 128 ■ Cleaning Engine Parts 134 ■ Crack Repair 141 ■ Case Study 143

CHAPTER 8

Short Blocks 146

Cylinder Blocks 146 ■ Cylinder Block Reconditioning 148 ■ Installing Core Plugs 153 ■ Crankshaft 155 ■ Crankshaft Inspection and Rebuilding 157 ■ Installing Main Bearings and Crankshaft 163 ■ Piston and Piston Rings 167 ■ Installing Pistons and Connecting Rods 169 ■ Case Study 172

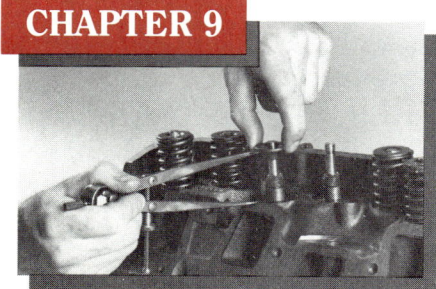

CHAPTER 9

Cylinder Heads and Valves 175

Combustion Chamber 176 ■ Intake and Exhaust Valves 178 ■ Aluminum Cylinder Heads 181 ■ Resurfacing Cylinder Heads 183 ■ Grinding Valves 186 ■ Valve Guide Reconditioning 188 ■ Reconditioning Valve Seats 193 ■ Valve Stem Seals 197 ■ Assembling the Cylinder Head 200 ■ Case Study 204

CHAPTER 10

Camshafts and Valve Trains 207

Camshaft 207 ■ Camshaft and Valve Train Inspection 213 ■ Installing the Camshaft 220 ■ Installing the Cylinder Head and Valve Train 221 ■ Installing the Timing Components 223 ■ Case Study 227

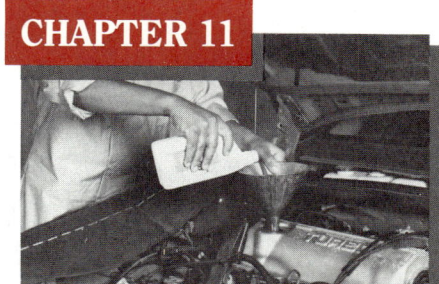

CHAPTER 11

Lubricating and Cooling Systems 230

Lubrication 230 ■ Lubricating Systems 233 ■ Oil Pump Inspection and Service 239 ■ Installing the Oil Pump 242 ■ Cooling Systems 243 ■ Cooling System Servicing 255 ■ Case Study 262

CHAPTER 12

Intake and Exhaust Systems 265

The Air Induction System 265 ■ Exhaust System Components 274 ■ Exhaust System Service 280 ■ Turbochargers and Superchargers 283 ■ Case Study 291

CHAPTER 13

Engine Sealing and Reassembly 295

Fasteners 295 ■ Gaskets 301 ■ Adhesives, Sealants, and Other Chemical Sealing Materials 306 ■ Oil Seals 309 ■ Engine Reassembly 311 ■ Installing the Engine 315 ■ Case Study 316

SECTION THREE Electricity

CHAPTER 14

Basics of Electrical and Electronic Systems 320

Basics of Electricity 320 ■ Conductors and Insulators 321 ■ Electromagnetism Basics 339 ■ Basics of Electronics 342 ■ Integrated Circuits 344 ■ Operation of Microprocessors 345 ■ Protecting Electronic Systems 350 ■ Batteries 351 ■ Conventional Design Battery 351 ■ Low-Maintenance and Maintenance-Free Batteries 353 ■ Battery Voltage and Capacity 354 ■ Battery Rating Methods 355 ■ Factors Affecting Battery Life 355 ■ Safety Procedures 356 ■ Routine Inspections 357 ■ Routine Cleaning 357 ■ Battery Testing 358 ■ Battery Charging 361 ■ Jump-Starting 362 ■ Case Studies 362

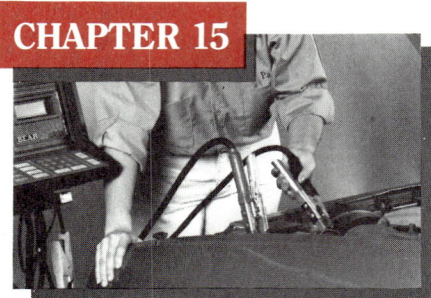

CHAPTER 15

Starting and Charging Systems 365

Starting System—Design and Components 365 ■ Override Clutches 372 ■ Control Circuit 373 ■ Starting System Testing 374 ■ Alternating Current Charging Systems 380 ■ Preliminary Checks 389 ■ Alternator Service 393 ■ Case Study 394

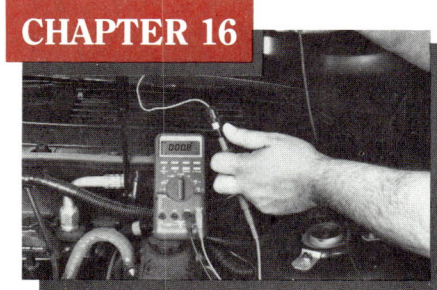

CHAPTER 16

Lighting Systems 397

Headlights 397 ■ Interior Light Assemblies 401 ■ Rear Exterior Light Assemblies 403 ■ Light Bulbs 406 ■ Lighting Maintenance 412 ■ Case Study 412

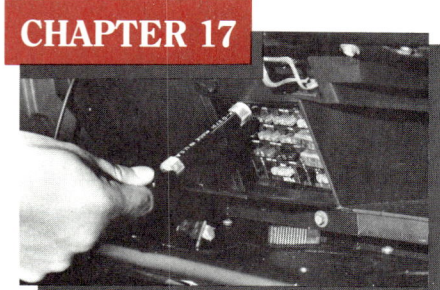

CHAPTER 17

Electrical Instruments and Accessories 415

Instrument Gauges 415 ■ Instrument Panels 416 ■ Basic Information Gauges 418 ■ Indicators and Warning Devices 420 ■ Electrical Accessories 424 ■ Case Studies 436

SECTION FOUR Engine Performance

CHAPTER 18

Ignition Systems 439

Ignition Timing 440 ■ Basic Circuitry 441 ■ Ignition Components 442 ■ Spark Timing Systems 445 ■ Advantages of Electronic Ignition 447 ■ Electronic Switching Systems 448 ■ Electronic Ignition System Operation 453 ■ Computer-Controlled Ignition System Operation 455 ■ Distributorless Ignition System Operation 457 ■ Case Study 459

CHAPTER 19

Ignition System Service 462

Visual Inspection 462 ■ Electrical Test Procedures 467 ■ Individual Component Testing 477 ■ Replacing Breaker Points 486 ■ Checking Dwell 486 ■ Setting Ignition Timing 487 ■ Distributorless System Service 488 ■ Knock Sensors 488 ■ Case Study 488

CHAPTER 20

Fuel Systems 492

Gasoline 492 ■ Fuel Performance 493 ■ Basic Fuels 495 ■ Gasoline Additives 495 ■ Diesel Fuel 496 ■ Alternative Fuels 497 ■ Fuel Delivery System 498 ■ Electronic Fuel System 515 ■ Case Study 516

CHAPTER 21

Fuel Injection 519

Gasoline Fuel Injection 519 ■ Throttle Body Versus Port Injection 520 ■ System Sensors 524 ■ Electronic Control Computer 527 ■ Fuel Injectors 527 ■ Idle Speed Control 529 ■ Continuous Injection Systems 530 ■ Servicing Fuel Injection Systems 535 ■ EFI System Component Checks 536 ■ Injector Cleaning 541 ■ Injector Replacement 542 ■ Idle Adjustment 542 ■ CIS Checks and Tests 544 ■ High-Pressure Diesel Fuel Injection 547 ■ Diesel Fuel System Components 548 ■ Diesel Electronic Control 554 ■ Case Study 555

CHAPTER 22

Carburetors 558

Carburetion 558 ■ Venturi 558 ■ Throttle Plate 560 ■ Basic Carburetor Circuits 560 ■ Additional Carburetor Control 567 ■ Types of Carburetors 569 ■ Variable Venturi Carburetors 570 ■ Feedback Carburetor Systems 571 ■ Carburetor Diagnosis and Adjustment 574 ■ Case Study 579

viii   Contents

CHAPTER 23

Emission Control Systems 582

PCV Systems 583 ■ Exhaust Gas Recirculating (EGR) Systems 585 ■ EGR Valves and Systems Testing 588 ■ EGR System Troubleshooting 591 ■ Air Temperature Emission Control 591 ■ Spark Advance Systems 595 ■ Air Injection Systems 596 ■ Secondary Air System 597 ■ Secondary Air System Troubleshooting 599 ■ Catalytic Converters 600 ■ Evaporative Emission Control System 600 ■ Case Studies 603

CHAPTER 24

Computerized Engine Controls 606

System Functions 606 ■ System Components 607 ■ Principal Sensors 609 ■ Computer Outputs and Actuators 613 ■ System Operation 614 ■ Logical Troubleshooting 616 ■ Isolating Computerized Engine Control Problems 617 ■ Case Study 625

SECTION FIVE   Manual Transmissions and Transaxles

CHAPTER 25

Clutches 628

Operation 628 ■ Clutch Service Safety Precautions 634 ■ Clutch Maintenance 634 ■ Clutch Problem Diagnosis 636 ■ Clutch Service 637 ■ Case Study 638

CHAPTER 26

Manual Transmissions and Transaxles 641

Transmission versus Transaxle 641 ■ Gears 642 ■ Transmission/Transaxle Design 645 ■ Synchronizers 648 ■ Gearshift Mechanisms 650 ■ Transmission Power Flow 652 ■ Five-Speed Overdrive 654 ■ Transaxle Power Flows 655 ■ Final Drive Gears and Overall Ratios 658 ■ Case Study 659

CHAPTER 27

Manual Transmission/Transaxle Service 661

Lubricant Check 661 ■ Diagnosing Problems 662 ■ Transmission/Transaxle Removal 664 ■ Cleaning and Inspection 665 ■ Reassembly/Reinstallation of Transmission/Transaxle 668 ■ Case Study 668

Contents   ix

CHAPTER 28

Drive Axles and Differentials 671

Front-Wheel-Drive (FWD) Axles 671 ■ Types of CV Joints 671 ■ Front-Wheel-Drive Applications 675 ■ CV Joint Service 675 ■ Preventive Maintenance 678 ■ Operation of U-Joints 684 ■ Types of U-Joints 686 ■ Diagnosis of Drive Shaft and U-Joint Problems 688 ■ Differentials 689 ■ Limited Slip Differentials 695 ■ Axle Shafts 697 ■ Servicing the Differential 702 ■ Diagnosing Differential Noises 705 ■ Case Study 706

SECTION SIX   Automatic Transmissions and Transaxles

CHAPTER 29

Automatic Transmissions and Transaxles 710

Torque Converters 710 ■ Lockup Torque Converters 714 ■ Planetary Gears 717 ■ Planetary Gear Controls 720 ■ Planetary Gear Trains 723 ■ Chrysler Transaxle Power Flows 724 ■ General Motors THM 200-4R Transmission 727 ■ Ravigneaux Gear Train 731 ■ Ford ATX Transaxle 732 ■ Ford ATX Operation 733 ■ Ford Automatic Overdrive Transmission 737 ■ Hydraulic Systems 739 ■ Pumps 741 ■ Valve Body 741 ■ Valves 742 ■ Pressure Regulator Valve 744 ■ Governor Assembly 747 ■ Hydraulic Circuits 748 ■ Shift Solenoids 756 ■ Continuous Variable Transmission 758 ■ Case Study 760

CHAPTER 30

Automatic Transmission/Transaxle Service 763

Automatic Transmission Fluid 764 ■ Gear Selector Linkage Check 766 ■ Throttle Cable Linkage Check 768 ■ Band Adjustment 769 ■ Vacuum Modulator Service 769 ■ Governor Service 770 ■ Road Testing 770 ■ Diagnosing Accurately 770 ■ Pressure Testing 770 ■ Case Study 772

CHAPTER 31

Four- and All-Wheel Drive 775

4WD Versus AWD 775 ■ Four-Wheel-Drive Systems 775 ■ Transfer Case 777 ■ Locking/Unlocking Hubs 779 ■ Conventional 4WD Operating Modes 780 ■ 4WD Passenger Cars 782 ■ Servicing 4WD Vehicles 783 ■ All-Wheel-Drive Systems 786 ■ Case Study 788

x Contents

SECTION SEVEN Suspensions

CHAPTER 32

Tires and Wheels 792

Wheels 792 ■ Tires 793 ■ Tire/Wheel Runout 805 ■ Tire/Wheel Assembly Service 806 ■ Case Study 811

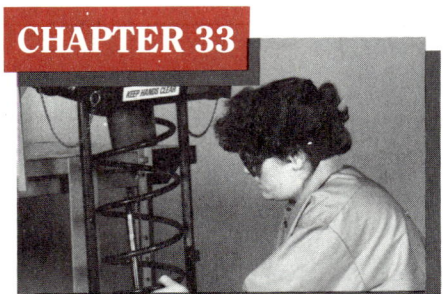

CHAPTER 33

Suspension Systems 814

Suspension System Components 814 ■ MacPherson Strut Suspension Components 823 ■ Independent Front Suspension 824 ■ General Front-Suspension Inspection 828 ■ Front-Suspension Component Servicing 829 ■ Rear-Suspension Systems 832 ■ Live-Axle Rear Suspension Systems 832 ■ Semi-Independent Suspension 834 ■ Independent Suspension 836 ■ Electronically Controlled Suspensions 839 ■ Servicing Electronic Suspension Components 843 ■ Active Suspensions 844 ■ Sonar Road Surface Sensing 846 ■ Case Study 846

CHAPTER 34

Steering Systems and Wheel Alignment 849

Manual Steering Systems and Their Components 849 ■ Manual Steering Service Procedures 857 ■ Power Steering 860 ■ Power-Steering Diagnosis 865 ■ General Conventional Power-Steering Checks 865 ■ Power-Steering System Servicing 867 ■ Electronically-Controlled Power-Steering Systems 867 ■ Four-Wheel Steering System 869 ■ Principles of Wheel Alignment 875 ■ Alignment Procedures 879 ■ Rear Alignment 885 ■ Four-Wheel-Drive Vehicle Alignment 887 ■ Case Study 888

SECTION EIGHT Brakes

CHAPTER 35

Brake Systems 892

Friction 892 ■ Principles of Hydraulic Brake Systems 894 ■ Hydraulic Brake System Components 896 ■ Hydraulic Tubes and Hoses 901 ■ Hydraulic System Safety Switches and Valves 902 ■ Drum and Disc Brake Assemblies 904 ■ Hydraulic System Service 905 ■ Pushrod Adjustment 910 ■ Hydraulic-Assist Power Brakes 911 ■ Testing the Hydro-Boost 911 ■ Powermaster Hydraulic Booster 912 ■ Anti-Lock Brake Systems 913 ■ Types of ABS Systems 914 ■ Integrated ABS System Components 914 ■ Integrated System Operation 916 ■ Non-Integrated ABS Systems 918 ■ Diagnosis and Testing 920 ■ Automatic Stability (Traction) Control 920 ■ Case Study 921

CHAPTER 36

Drum Brakes 923

Drum Brake Operation 923 ■ Drum Brake Components 923 ■ Drum Brake Designs 926 ■ Road Testing Brakes 932 ■ Drum Brake Inspection 934 ■ Brake Shoes and Linings 940 ■ Wheel Cylinder Inspection and Servicing 942 ■ Drum Parking Brakes 944 ■ Integral Parking Brakes 946 ■ Case Study 949

CHAPTER 37

Disc Brakes 952

Disc Brake Components and Their Functions 953 ■ Rear Disc/Drum (Auxiliary Drum) Parking Brake 956 ■ Rear Disc Parking Brakes 957 ■ Service Precautions 957 ■ General Caliper Inspecting and Servicing 958 ■ Rotor Inspecting and Servicing 966 ■ Case Study 967

SECTION NINE Passenger Comfort

CHAPTER 38

Heating and Air Conditioning 970

Ventilation System 970 ■ Automotive Heating Systems 971 ■ Heating System Service 974 ■ Theory of Automotive Air Conditioning 974 ■ The Air Conditioning System and Its Components 974 ■ Air-Conditioning Systems and Controls 981 ■ Maintenance Precautions 986 ■ Refrigerant Safety Precautions 987 ■ Air Conditioner Testing and Servicing Equipment 988 ■ Diagnostic and Troubleshooting Procedures 996 ■ Temperature Control Systems 996 ■ Electrical System Inspection 999 ■ Case Study 999

CHAPTER 39

Other Safety and Security Equipment 1003

Safety Glass 1003 ■ Restraint Systems 1005 ■ Servicing the Air Bag System 1012 ■ Energy-Absorber Safety Bumpers 1014 ■ Security and Antitheft Devices 1015 ■ Other Electronic Equipment 1018 ■ Case Study 1022

Appendix A Decimal and Metric Equivalents ... 1025

Appendix B Abbreviations 1027

Glossary 1031

Index 1041

PHOTO SEQUENCES

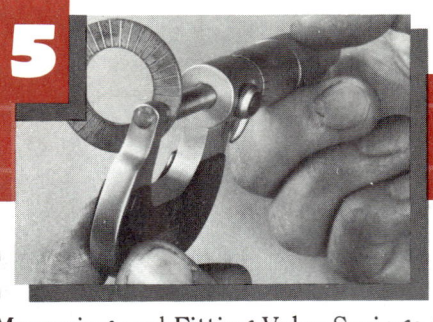
5. Measuring and Fitting Valve Springs/201

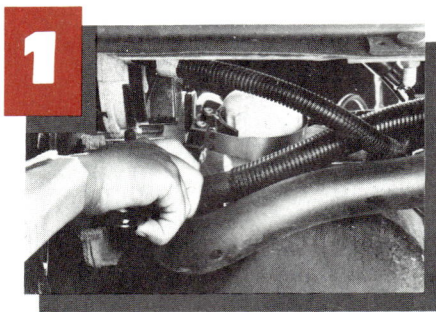
1. Changing the Oil and Oil Filter/49

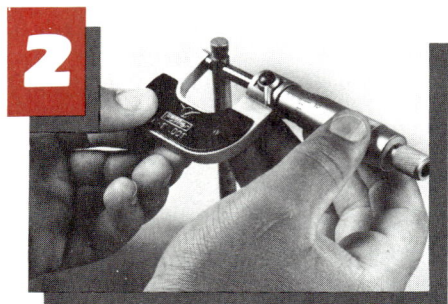
2. Using a Micrometer/57

3. Conducting a Compression Test/93

4. Checking Main Bearing Clearance with Plastigage/165

6. Replacing a Timing Belt on an OHC Engine/225

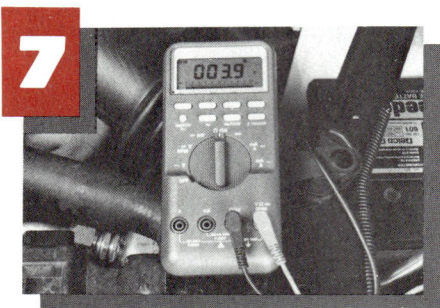
7. Using a DVOM to Measure Voltage, Current, and Resistance/337

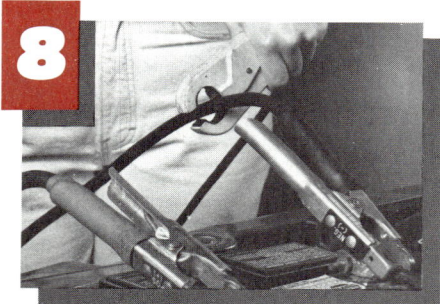
8. Using a Volt and Amp Tester to Test the Battery and the Starting and Charging Systems/377

9. Removing and Replacing Various DIS Components/489

Photo Sequences   **xiii**

Checking the Fuel Pressure on a PFI System/511

Removing and Replacing a Fuel Injector on a PFI System/543

Installing and Aligning a Clutch Disc/639

Removing and Replacing a CV-joint Boot/679

Performing an Automatic Transmission Fluid and Filter Change/767

Dismounting and Mounting a Tire on a Wheel Assembly/803

Removing and Replacing a MacPherson Strut/833

Adjusting Rear Drum Parking Brake/947

Removing and Replacing Brake Pads/961

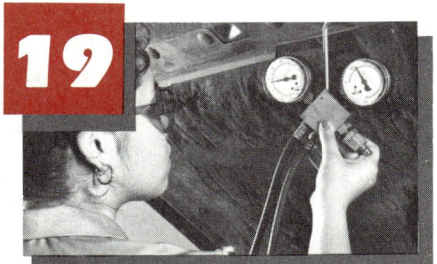

Evacuating and Recharging an A/C System with a Recycling and Charging Station/993

PREFACE

Today's vehicles are complex and each new model will be even more so. Mandatory environmental, safety and economy standards require continual engineering changes. New materials, changes in systems and microcomputers have turned automotive technology in completely new directions.

You are entering the field of automotive service at a very exciting time, a time of broad challenge and great opportunity. You will need to gain knowledge and develop skills that were unheard of by your predecessors. While this should not be alarming, it does present a challenge. The goal of this book is not to teach you the trade. It is meant to prepare you to gain the most from each of your learning experiences. Look through it for a while and you will find that it provides detailed coverage of basic skills and knowledge. While this book has broad coverage of automotive technology, it may not always contain all information that you will study. It will be supplemented by other publications as you progress to more complex and specialized subjects.

Historically, schools have expected students to study. The students' reluctance to do so is widely known. A successful student is a prepared student. The amount of learning is in direct relationship to the amount of preparation the student does.

Since we do not want to make study a burden and yet we want you to be a successful student, we suggest that you use this book in the following way. Your instructor may or may not give you a reading assignment before each lesson but you will usually know what it is about. Set aside some time and read the applicable text. If you do not understand everything, do not be alarmed. Make a note of what you do not understand so that you will have a list of what questions to ask. Remember, read for interest.

You will find questions at the end of each chapter. Try to answer them. If you are uncertain of the answers, check the text. Write down questions to ask your instructor. The more you participate by asking questions, the more you will learn and the more you will please your instructor. It is his or her job to teach you but you can help them more than you can imagine by being prepared and by being an active participant.

It is also a good idea to review each session by re-reading the material that was covered. Frequently, additional learning can be accomplished by this practice. We are personally interested in your future in the Automotive Service Industry and wish you the best of luck in the program that you are undertaking. Your diligence and dependability can result in much needed professionalism for the industry and a rewarding career for you.

Pat J. Santangelo, President, and Bert Kearns, National Training Director

❏ FEATURES OF THE TEXT

Learning how to maintain and repair today's automobiles can be a daunting endeavor. To guide the readers through this complex material, we have built in a series of features that will ease the teaching and learning processes.

Photo Sequences

Step-by-Step photo sequences have been prepared carefully to illustrate practical shop techniques. The sequences focus on techniques that are common, need-to-know service and maintenance procedures. The exceptional photos prepared especially for this text give students a clean, detailed image of what to look for when they perform these procedures.

Color Insert

The color insert shows sixteen pages of full-color cutaways and functional details from the eight ASE systems. Many of these up-to-date illustrations are gathered from industry and show the details of system operation.

PROCEDURES

This feature gives detailed, step-by-step instructions for important service and maintenance procedures. Because these hands-on procedures are so important to developing good shop skills and meeting ASE competencies, this feature appears often, and the detail is thorough.

CASE STUDIES

Case Studies highlight our emphasis on logical troubleshooting. At the end of each chapter, a service problem is outlined, and then a technician's solution is described, giving the student a worked-out example of logical troubleshooting. The *Tech Manual* provides many open-ended case studies for more practice.

USING SERVICE MANUALS

Using service manuals can be a confusing and time-consuming task. Therefore, we have included this feature as a way to familiarize the reader with the information available in this important resource. Throughout the text, students will read tips and instructions on how to locate the information they need. In the *Tech Manual*, students will practice recording and analyzing service manual data.

SHOP TALK

These features are sprinkled throughout each chapter to give common-sense advice on service and maintenance procedures.

CUSTOMER CARE

Creating a professional image is an important aspect of shaping a career in automotive technology today. The customer care tips were written to encourage professional integrity. They give advice on educating customers and keeping them satisfied.

CAUTIONS AND WARNINGS: Instructors often tell us that shop safety is their most important concern. Cautions and warnings appear frequently in every chapter to alert students to important safety concerns.

SUPPLEMENTS

The *Automotive Technology* package offers a full complement of supplements to keep instructors up to date in the classroom.

TECH MANUAL This student Tech Manual gives hands-on, practical shop experience. It contains hundreds of shop activities and interactive job sheets, with practice in troubleshooting, using diagnostic charts, and using service manuals. Service manual report sheets, open-ended case studies, review questions and ASE prep tests reinforce hands-on learning.

INSTRUCTOR'S GUIDE This comprehensive guide provides teaching hints, answers to review questions and *Tech Manual* questions, transparency masters, and guidelines for using the *Tech Manual*. A unique *Crossover Guide* is included to help make the switch from your current text to *Automotive Technology*.

TEST BANK More than 2,000 questions, including sample ASE tests, are available on hard copy or disk. The computerized version is designed for easy tailoring and contains graphics.

TRANSPARENCIES Full-color reproductions from the color insert and from the text have been chosen for their usefulness in the classroom.

❏ ACKNOWLEDGMENTS

We gratefully acknowledge the contributions of the following text reviewers.
Dimas Albert, Hartnell College, Salinas, CA
James E. Blackburn, Portland Community College, Portland, OR
Stephen M. Carr, Johnson County Community College, Overland Park, KS
Clemmon Childress, Fischer Technical institute, Virginia Beach, VA
Henry Chiulli, New England Institute of Technology, Warwick, RI
Robert F. Davis, Texas State Technical Institute, Waco, TX
Patrick L. Devlin, Montgomery College, Rockville, MD
Thomas A. Donaldson, Lincoln Land Community College, Springfield, IL
Roger Donovan, Illinois Central College, East Peoria, IL
Ronald D. Finney, Indiana Vocational-Technical College, Indianapolis, IN
Laurence S. Gaff, TAD Technical Institute, Chelsea, MA
James Helmle, Milwaukee Area Technical College, Milwaukee, WI
Barry A. Hollembeak, Denver Automotive and Diesel College, Denver, CO
Henry L. Jarvis, Glendale Community College, Glendale, AZ
Michael Kozenko, Vale Technical Institute, Blairsville, PA
Alan K. Krieg, Pima Community College, Tucson, AZ
Terry Laverty, Lincoln Technical Institute, Cloverdale, IN
Roy Marks, Owens Technical College, Toledo, OH
Leslie Macaulay, Portland Community College, Portland, OR
Dennis W. Meyers, Texas State Technical Institute, Waco, TX
Paul Myshaniuk, Lakeland College, Vermillion Campus, Alberta, Canada
Gabriel F. Perry, Truckee Meadows Community College, Reno, NV
Robert J. Prediger, Fairview College, Fairview Alta, Alberta, Canada
Fred Raadsheer, BCIT, Burnaby, British Columbia, Canada
Charles Rockwood, Ventura College, Ventura, CA
Edward Szczepanski, Erie Community College, Williamsville, NY
Don R. Wier, Cummins Mid-States Power, Inc., Indianapolis, IN
Sidney W. Wilson, Arizona Automotive Institute, Glendale, AZ
A.B. Winchester, DeKalb Area Technical Institute, Clarkston, GA

We also acknowledge the following individuals from Columbus State Community College's automotive maintenance technology department, who provided valuable assistance in preparing the step-by-step photos in this text.

Bill Ackley	Dave Slater
Chuck Frieze	Rez Talbert
Rusty Gillman	Bill Warner
Tadashi Nakamura	

The following individuals were also instrumental in producing the step-by-step photos.

Michael Gallitelli, photographer	John Flores, model
Dino Petrocelli, photographer's assistant	Robert Jones, model
Connie Cittadino, model	Maureen McDermott, model
Rosemary Flores, model	

SECTION 1

AUTOMOTIVE TECHNOLOGY

Chapter 1   **The Automotive Industry**
Chapter 2   **Practicing Safety in the Shop**
Chapter 3   **Automotive Systems**
Chapter 4   **Shop Tools**
Chapter 5   **Diagnostic Equipment**

The automotive service industry faces severe challenges in the coming years. Rapidly changing technology has revolutionized the way vehicles are built, operated, and serviced.

Many automotive systems bare little resemblance to their counterparts of ten or twenty years ago. Electronic computer controls are now standard on nearly every system from engines and ignitions to brakes and transmissions. Many service personnel that have not kept pace with these changes have left or been forced out of the industry. Career opportunities for skilled ASE certified service technicians have never been greater.

The material covered in Section 1 explains these career opportunities. It presents a short overview of modern automotive systems. Finally, it outlines important safety practices and describes the uses of common shop tools, equipment, and modern diagnostic equipment.

WE ENCOURAGE
PROFESSIONALISM

THROUGH TECHNICIAN
CERTIFICATION

1 THE AUTOMOTIVE INDUSTRY

Objectives

■ Understand the modern automotive industry as a global industry. ■ Explain the importance of autotronics and how modern computer technology has changed the way vehicles are built and serviced. ■ Explain why the need for automotive service is increasing. ■ Describe the major types of businesses that employ automotive service technicians. ■ List some of the many job classifications open to personnel with a background in automotive technology. ■ Describe the characteristics of a good service technician employee. ■ Explain the role ASE now plays within the automotive service industry. ■ Describe the requirements for ASE certification as an automotive technician and master auto technician.

American society is built around the idea of personal transportation. Our workforce is basically one of commuters. Many people spend hours each week traveling to and from work. The drive-through lanes at banks and fast-food restaurants are often busier than the service counters inside. We drive to centralized malls to shop, see a motion picture, or dine out. Our leisure time often involves travel. We think little of driving hundreds of miles to beaches, ski resorts, theme parks, or historical sites.

The concept of the family car is quickly evolving into the reality of one car for every licensed driver in America. There are now 85 passenger cars in the United States for every 100 licensed drivers. In fact, there is one passenger car for every 1.8 people. This is the highest ratio of cars to population in the world (Table 1-1).

It is easy to see why the automotive industry is second only to the food industry in its contribution to the American economy. Manufacturing, selling, and servicing these vehicles is an incredibly large, diverse, and expanding industry.

❑ INTRODUCTION

Once dominated by America's "big three" auto makers—General Motors, Ford Motor Company, and Chrysler Corporation—the auto industry is now a global industry. Auto makers from Japan, Germany, Sweden, and other European and Asian countries compete vigorously with U.S. companies for domestic and foreign sales (Table 1-2).

Several Japanese and Asian manufacturers operate assembly plants in the United States and Canada. A number of joint car building arrangements exists between the U.S. and foreign manufacturers. Under these joint agreements, vehicles are assembled from components built both in the U.S. and overseas.

This market competition and mutual cooperation has resulted in an extremely wide selection of vehicles from which to choose. It has also created new challenges in the service industry as technicians must handle an increasing variety of operating systems.

The Technology Boom

The same electronic microchip technology responsible for the boom in affordable personal computers (PCs), calculators, VCRs, compact disc players, and other electronic equipment has also revolutionized the way modern auto systems operate and are serviced.

Electronic circuits and computers are now the cornerstones of an education in automotive servicing. This merging of high-technology and vocational and technical education has replaced the old auto shop with the new autotronics classroom. The term autotronics combines the words automotive and electronics. It is the study of electronic technology as it is used on automobiles. Computers and electronics have brought sweeping changes to automotive maintenance and repair. In addition to mastering the mechanical skills needed to remove, repair, and replace faulty or damaged components, today's technician must also understand electronics and computer operation.

The Automotive Industry

TABLE 1-1	PASSENGER CAR COUNT OF SELECT COUNTRIES	
Country	Passenger Cars (Millions)	People Per Passenger Car
United States	140.1	1.8
Canada	25.3	2.3
Germany	31.3	2.4
Italy	22.3	2.5
France	21.2	2.6
United Kingdom	17.4	3.2
Spain	9.7	4.1
Japan	28.6	4.3
Brazil	10.0	15.4
Mexico	5.0	17.6
USSR	9.2	31.0
China	0.79	1345.0

TABLE 1-2	TODAY'S FOREIGN CARS AND THEIR ORIGINS
Vehicle	Exporting Country
Acura	Japan
Audi/Porsche	Germany
BMW	Germany
Honda	Japan
Hyundai	Korea
Infiniti	Japan
Isuzu	Japan
Jaguar	Great Britain
Lexus	Japan
Mazda	Japan
Mercedes-Benz	Germany
Mitsubishi	Japan
Nissan	Japan
Saab	Sweden
Sterling	Great Britain
Subaru	Japan
Toyota	Japan
Volkswagen	Germany
Volvo	Sweden
Yugo	Yugoslavia

Computers and electronic devices now control many aspects of engine operation. They control ignition timing, fuel injection, air intake, emission control, and other engine functions related to performance, fuel economy, and operating efficiency.

Electronic controls can also be used to activate shifting in automatic transmissions, eliminate brake lockup in anti-lock braking systems, or control four-wheel steering systems for precise handling and vehicle maneuverability. The ride characteristics of some suspension systems are also electronically set, monitored, and adjusted. The amount of electronics used on cars and trucks is increasing dramatically with each model year. Consider these projections for the 1990s and beyond.

- In 1991, about 20% of all functions on new cars were controlled by electronics. By 1995, this figure will jump to over 80%.
- By the year 2000, the cost of electronics in the average car will be twice the 1991 value.
- The 24-, 36-, and 48-volt electrical systems will become standard as more on-board functions are being powered by electric motors instead of the engine.
- By the year 2000, anti-lock braking systems (ABS), now an option on many vehicles, will become standard equipment on virtually all cars.
- Vehicles will use three different computers to control functions. One will control engine and transmission/transaxle. One will control instrumentation and interior functions, including climate control. A third one will combine suspension, steering, and anti-lock brakes.
- Vehicle diagnostic systems will anticipate breakdowns, contact emergency road service, and guide technicians through the repair process.
- By the year 2000, some model vehicles will have light-emitting surfaces integrated into the glass. Others will have multiple video cameras to view the area all around the car to eliminate blind spots and an infrared system to provide good vision at night and in bad weather.
- Ceramic materials, which are lighter and more heat resistant than metals, will serve dozens of uses in engines and related systems.
- Electronic mufflers will analyze engine noise in the exhaust pipe and generate anti-noise, a sound wave exactly 180° out of phase with the offending noise. The original noise and mirror-image anti-noise cancel out each other when they meet. The result is a soundless exhaust system.
- Engine component status monitors will give a continuous account of what is happening in the engine. This will alert the driver to any potential malfunctions.
- Intelligent cruise control devices will combine throttle control with limited radar braking. It will keep safe distances between moving cars. These devices are expected to be in use in most new cars within the next twenty years.

The Need for Quality Service

As vehicles become more complex, the need for qualified service technicians becomes greater. Servicing today's electronic systems and components requires specialized training and new diagnostic equipment (Figure 1-1).

Lack of training and the reluctance to invest in new, sometimes very expensive, equipment has forced many mechanics out of the repair industry. The number of career opportunities in auto servicing and related fields

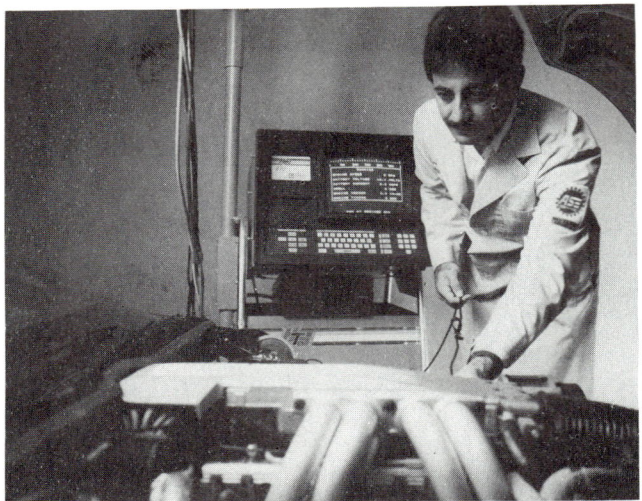

Figure 1-1 Sophisticated diagnostic equipment is required to service today's automotive systems. *Courtesy of Environmental Systems Products*

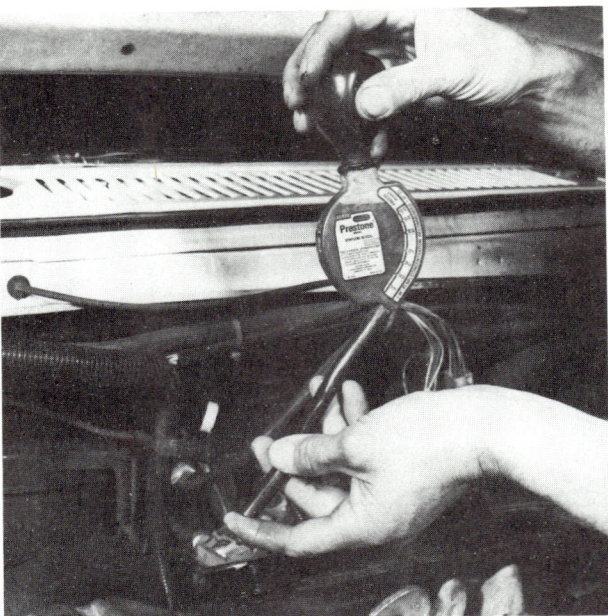

Figure 1-2 Regular preventive maintenance is important in keeping electronic control systems operating smoothly. This coolant is being checked for strength.

has never been greater for those willing to study and learn this new technology.

Good diagnostic skills are especially important. Technicians who can accurately pinpoint problems the first time the vehicle is brought into the shop will be in great demand. The high cost of electronic components and many mechanical parts has made the "hit-and-miss" method of repair too expensive. Too often, mechanics who do not understand how to properly troubleshoot an electronic system will automatically replace its most expensive component—the computer module. This often translates into a very expensive misdiagnosis. Computers are highly reliable. The problem usually is caused by a faulty (and less expensive) sensor, a poor electrical connection, or a malfunctioning mechanical component within the system.

The Need for On-going Service

The use of electronics and computer controls has not eliminated the need for routine service and scheduled maintenance (Figure 1-2). In fact, it has made it more important than ever. An electronic control system cannot clean a fouled spark plug, clogged fuel injector, or corroded battery terminal. It cannot tighten loose belts, change weak or dirty coolant, or change engine oil. Simple problems such as these can set off a chain of events in an engine control system.

The computer, its sensors, and control devices may attempt to compensate for a problem by adjusting other aspects of engine operation. As a result, the engine still runs reasonably well, but overall performance and efficiency is lowered. Electronic controls are designed to help a well-maintained vehicle to operate effectively. They are not designed as repair systems.

Simple maintenance procedures are usually performed according to a schedule recommended by the vehicle manufacturer. Scheduled preventive maintenance normally includes oil and filter changes, coolant and lubrication service, replacement of belts and hoses, and tune-up service, such as replacing spark plugs and worn electrical parts. Failure to follow specified preventive maintenance procedures may affect the warranty offered on new vehicles. For example, a claim filed for a defective engine may be refused if the owner does not have a written record proving oil changes were performed at required intervals.

Increased Vehicle Age

Until quite recently, it was common practice for many motorists to purchase a new vehicle every three years. With a reasonable down payment, the purchase could be financed over this period. The owner enjoyed the advantages of driving a new vehicle. Chances of major breakdowns and repairs were greatly reduced. Also, a better trade-in value was possible.

However, the steady increase in the purchase price of new vehicles has eliminated this option for many buyers. A vehicle is now a major, long-term investment. Payment plans of five or six years are now quite common. Even with extended financing, the down payment on a vehicle can be substantial.

The result of these economic pressures is that motorists are keeping their vehicles longer and driving them more miles. The average age of on-the-road automobiles ranges from four to seven years. This trend towards an older average vehicle age shows no signs of reversing.

Older vehicles generate the majority of major repair and overhaul work performed in dealership and independent garage service bays. The days when a service department or station could survive repairing older vehicles with little or no electronic equipment are over. Older vehicles finding their way into shops today can be quite sophisticated in terms of electronic technology.

Emissions and Fuel Economy Requirements

Environmental and safety concerns are two more reasons the need for vehicle service is increasing. Most states now have laws that require periodic inspections of passenger vehicles. In many cases, vehicles must pass exhaust emission and safety inspections before vehicle registration can be renewed. A vehicle that fails these inspections must be brought up to the required standards at the owner's expense.

In order to meet federal regulations governing emissions control and minimum fuel mileage standards, vehicles are now equipped with emission control devices, such as positive crankcase ventilation (PCV), exhaust gas recirculation (EGR), and catalytic converter systems. These systems require periodic maintenance or replacement in order to function properly. Service guidelines for these systems are often mandated by law.

Career Opportunities

Qualified service technicians are needed by many types of automotive businesses.

Dealerships

New car dealerships (Figure 1-3) are a major employer of service technicians and related automotive personnel. The dealership is the major link between the vehicle manufacturer and the customer.

Dealerships are privately-owned businesses. A franchised dealership is one that has signed a contract with a particular auto manufacturer to sell and service a particular line of vehicles. Many dealerships now sign contracts with more than one manufacturer—usually one domestic and one import line.

The sales and service policies of the dealership are usually set by the manufacturer. Service performed while the vehicle is under warranty is usually performed by dealerships or authorized service centers.

Auto manufacturers have been taking an increasing role in securing service business for their dealerships. Extended warranties and service plans are designed to channel repair and maintenance work to the dealerships. Manufacturers provide special diagnostic equipment designed specifically for their vehicles. They stress the compatibility of their replacement parts and actively promote their service personnel as the most qualified to work on their products.

Working for a dealership backed by a major auto maker can have many advantages. Technical support, equipment, and the opportunity for on-going training are usually excellent. However, being tied into one or two particular model lines may limit the scope of your servicing expertise.

WARRANTIES Before discussing career opportunities in independent service shops and other outlets, a closer look at a subject related to dealerships is in order—warranties. A warranty provides repair cost protection to the owner of a vehicle. It is an agreement by the auto manufacturer to have its authorized dealers repair, replace, or adjust certain parts if they become defective. The defects must occur under normal use of the vehicle during the warranty coverage period. There are basically two types of warranties: those initiated by the manufacturer and those mandated by federal and state laws.

The parts covered and the length of coverage of a manufacturer-initiated warranty may vary. Typically, a manufacturer provides several kinds of warranty coverages. For instance, there is often a basic coverage warranty that covers the complete vehicle for the first year or 12,000 miles, whichever comes first. Additional warranties may cover the power train, battery, safety restraint systems, the body, or other components of the vehicle. These warranties extend the coverage on particular items beyond the basic coverage warranty. On these warranties, a certain amount of money, called the deductible, must be paid by the owner. The manufacturer covers whatever costs are incurred beyond that deductible. Charges covered by some warranties, such as on batteries, are often pro-rated. This means that the percentage of the charge covered by the manufacturer decreases according to the length of time the vehicle has been in service.

FEDERAL WARRANTIES Two government-mandated warranties are the Federal Emissions Defect Warranty and the Federal Emissions Performance Warranty. The Federal Emissions Defect Warranty ensures the owner that the vehicle meets applicable emissions regulations and that the vehicle's emission control system is free from defects in materials and workmanship. The Federal Emissions Performance Warranty covers a vehicle if it is registered in a state where the state or local

Figure 1-3 Dealerships sell and service vehicles made by a specific auto manufacturer.

Figure 1-4 Full-service gasoline stations are one type of independent service shop.

Figure 1-5 Many major retail store chains sell auto parts and offer limited service and installation work.

government has an inspection and maintenance program that meets the Environmental Protection Agency's (EPA) requirements. If the vehicle is properly maintained by the owner and it fails an EPA-approved emissions test, one of the manufacturer's dealers will repair any of the covered parts of the vehicle's emission control system. Additional warranties may be applicable in certain states, such as those required in California. Always check the owner's manual for specific warranty information.

Independent Service Shops

Independent service shops (Figure 1-4) are shops that service all types of vehicles. Some shops may develop a particular area of expertise, such as imports or certain domestic lines. Often this specialization spreads by word of mouth or reputation. These shops outnumber dealerships by six to one. They are the largest source of service technician employment. As the name states, an independent service shop is not associated with any particular model line of vehicles.

An independent shop may range in size from a two-bay garage employing two to four people, to a multiple-bay service center employing twenty to thirty people. It may rival even the largest dealerships in the diagnostic equipment used and training available. Working in an independent shop may present constant diagnostic and servicing challenges and lead to a well-rounded technical background.

Many independent shops are started by technicians eager to be their own boss and run their own business.

Store-Associated Shops

Many large chain stores that sell automotive parts often offer certain types of automotive services, such as brake, exhaust system, electrical system, and wheel and tire work (Figure 1-5).

Specialty Service Shops

Specialty service shops are shops that specialize in areas such as engine rebuilding, transmission/transaxle overhauling, and brake, exhaust, cooling, emissions, and electrical work.

The number of specialty shops that service and repair only one or two systems of the automobile has steadily increased over the past ten to twenty years. Service technicians employed by such shops have the opportunity to become very good in one particular area of vehicle service and repair.

Fleet Service and Maintenance

Any company that operates more than several vehicles faces an on-going vehicle service and preventive maintenance problem. While small fleets often employ the services of an independent shop or freelance service technician to do this work, larger companies usually have their own preventive maintenance and repair organizations.

Car rental companies, overnight delivery services, and taxi cab companies are three good examples of businesses that usually staff their own service departments. Many career opportunities are available in this segment of the auto service industry.

JOB CLASSIFICATIONS

The automobile industry offers numerous types of employment for people with a sound understanding of auto systems. Not all jobs involve hands-on service and diagnostic testing.

Service Technician

The most important and popular career choice in the automotive industry is the service technician (Figure 1-6). The service technician assesses vehicle problems, performs all necessary diagnostic tests, and competently repairs or replaces faulty components. The skills to do this job are based on a sound understanding of auto technology, on-the-job experience, and continuous training in new technology as it is introduced by auto manufacturers.

Skilled service personnel are now referred to as technicians. There is a good reason for this. Mechanic stresses the ability to repair and service mechanical

A

B

Figure 1-6 Service technicians perform all types of (A) diagnostic and (B) general repair work.

systems. While this skill is still absolutely needed, it is only part of the service technician's overall job. Today's vehicles require mechanical knowledge plus an understanding of electronics, hydraulics, and pneumatics.

Service technicians must be skilled in all areas of automotive maintenance and repair. The National Institute for Automotive Service Excellence (ASE) has established a certification program for automotive, heavy-duty truck, auto body repair, and engine machine shop technicians. This certification system combines voluntary testing with on-the-job experience to confirm that technicians have the skills needed to work on today's more complex vehicles. ASE recognizes two distinct levels of service capability—the automotive technician and the master auto technician. The master auto technician is certified by ASE in all major automotive systems (Figure 1-7). The automotive technician may have certification in only several areas. More information on ASE and the certification process is given at the end of this chapter.

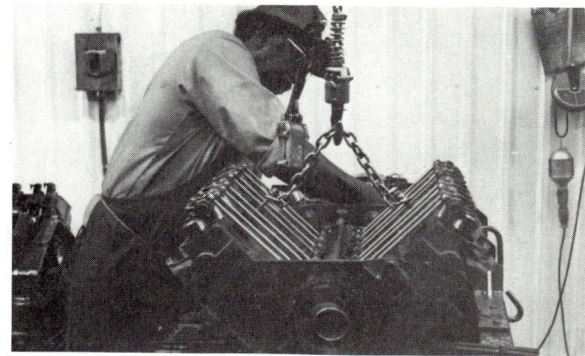

Figure 1-7 Master technicians have proven their ability to work on the most complex repair jobs, such as engine rebuilding.

Specialty Technician

The automotive specialty technician concentrates on servicing a single system of an automobile, such as electrical, brakes, or transmission (Figure 1-8). These specialties require advanced and continuous training in that particular field. Specialty technicians often are certified by ASE in one or more service areas.

Service Writer

The person who greets customers at a service center is the service writer or service advisor. The service writer must have a good knowledge of automobiles plus a sound understanding of the automotive parts aftermarket. A friendly attitude and the ability to deal with people effectively are important. Customers discuss their automotive problems and needs with the service writer. The service writer then consults the service technician on the vehicle's diagnosis and prepares a detailed cost estimate for the customer.

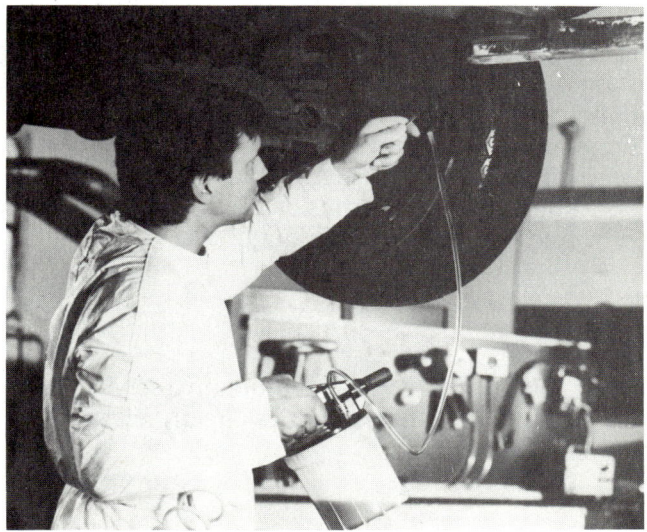

Figure 1-8 Specialty technicians repair only one system on the vehicle, such as brakes.

Figure 1-9 Correctly identifying and ordering replacement parts is a crucial step in the repair process.

Parts Manager

The parts manager (Figure 1-9) is in charge of ordering all replacement parts for the repairs the shop performs. The ordering and timely delivery of parts is extremely important if the shop is to operate smoothly and on schedule. Delays in obtaining parts or omitting a small but crucial part from the initial parts order can cause frustrating hold-ups for both the service technicians and customers.

Most dealerships and large independent service shops maintain a set inventory of commonly-used parts, such as filters, belts, hoses, and gaskets. The parts manager is responsible for maintaining this inventory.

Thoroughness, attention to detail, and the ability to work with people face-to-face and over the phone are a must for a parts manager.

Service Manager

The service manager oversees the entire service operation of a large dealership or independent shop. Customer concerns and complaints are usually handled through the service manager. One must have good human relations skills as well as a sound automotive background.

In a dealership, the service manager makes certain the auto manufacturers' policies concerning warranties, service procedures, and customer relations are carried out. The service manager normally coordinates on-going training programs and keeps all other shop personnel informed and working together.

❑ RELATED CAREER OPPORTUNITIES

In addition to careers in automotive service, there are many other job opportunities directly related to the automotive industry.

Parts Distribution

Few people are aware of the complexity and operation of what is generally called the automotive aftermarket. The automotive aftermarket refers to the network of businesses that supplies replacement parts and services to independent service shops, specialty repair shops, car and truck dealerships, fleet and industrial operations, and the general buying public.

The traditional automotive aftermarket distribution system begins with the manufacturer of the parts. Vehicle manufacturers and independent parts manufacturers sell and supply parts to approximately 1,000 warehouse distributors throughout the United States. These warehouse distributors (WDs) carry substantial inventories of many part lines.

Warehouse distributors serve as large distribution centers or parts hubs. In turn, WDs sell and supply parts to auto wholesalers. In the aftermarket industry, parts wholesalers are commonly known as jobbers.

Jobbers sell parts and supplies to independent shops and other service outlets. They also sell to the general public interested in doing their own repair work. Many jobbers operate machine shops that offer another source of employment for skilled technicians.

Jobbers or parts stores can be independently owned and operated. They can also be part of a larger national chain (Figure 1-10). Auto manufacturers have also set up their own parts distribution systems to their dealerships and authorized service outlets. Parts manufactured by the original vehicle manufacturer are called original equipment manufacturer or OEM parts.

Opportunities for employment exist at all levels in the parts distribution network, from warehouse distributors to the counter-people at local jobber outlets (Figure 1-11). The rising number of parts available on

Figure 1-10 Many auto parts stores are part of a national organization with outlets across the country.

Figure 1-11 Jobbers perform a valuable service in the parts distribution system. There are many careers available in parts management.

the aftermarket has made the jobs of WDs and parts store personnel more challenging and complex.

Marketing and Sales

Companies that manufacture vehicles and aftermarket parts for the service industry are constantly searching for the most knowledgeable people available to represent and sell their products. For example, a sales representative working for an aftermarket parts manufacturer specializes in the company's product line, such as brake, suspension, or engine parts. The sales representative works with WDs, jobbers, and service shops to ensure their parts are being sold and installed correctly. They also help coordinate service clinics and supply support materials to ensure everyone using their products is properly trained and informed.

Other Opportunities

Other career possibilities open to those with a sound automotive background include insurance company claims adjusters and auto body shop technicians. Claims adjusters appraise damage to vehicles involved in accidents and estimate the cost of repair work. Auto body shop technicians repair sheet metal damage, certain mechanical systems, and auto frame damage on vehicles involved in accidents.

The automotive industry is extremely diverse and capable of supporting tens of thousands of interesting careers with unlimited opportunity for advancement. Many people working in related automotive fields such as sales and parts distribution began their careers as service technicians. In this text, we will concentrate on this area of the service industry.

☐ WORKING AS AN AUTOMOTIVE TECHNICIAN

Becoming a successful automotive service technician requires good training, desire, and commitment. It also requires the willingness to fulfill the responsibilities of an employee and to work together with other technicians and personnel to make the organization successful.

Employer-Employee Relationships

Becoming a valuable worker requires more than learning job skills. When you begin a job, you enter into a business transaction with your employer. A business transaction is an exchange of things of value. When you become an employee, you sell your time, skills, and efforts. Your employer pays you for these resources.

Employer Obligations

Both parties in a business transaction have responsibilities. The obligations of an employer to a worker include the following.

INSTRUCTION AND SUPERVISION You should be told what is expected of you on the job. There should be a supervisor who can observe your work and tell you if it is satisfactory.

CLEAN, SAFE PLACE TO WORK An employer should provide a clean and safe work area as well as adequate facilities for personal clean-up.

WAGES You should know how much you are to be paid before accepting a job. Your employer should pay you on designated paydays.

FRINGE BENEFITS When you are hired, you should be advised about any benefits, in addition to wages, that you can expect. Fringe benefits usually include paid vacations and employer contributions to health insurance and retirement plans.

OPPORTUNITY AND FAIR TREATMENT Opportunity means that you are given a chance to succeed and possibly advance within the company. Fair treatment means that all employees are treated equally, without prejudice or favoritism.

Employee Obligations

On the other side of this business transaction, employees have responsibilities to their employers. Your obligations as a worker include the following.

REGULAR ATTENDANCE A good employee is reliable. Businesses cannot operate successfully unless their workers are on the job.

FOLLOWING DIRECTIONS As an employee, you are part of a team. Doing things your way may not serve the best interests of the business.

RESPONSIBILITY Be willing to answer for your work-related obligations and your conduct.

PRODUCTIVITY Remember, you are paid for your time as well as your skills and effort. You have a duty to use time on the job as effectively as possible.

ATTITUDE With a positive attitude, you increase your value beyond your skills and time. Your attitude can have a positive effect on other employees.

LOYALTY Last but not least, loyalty is expected by any employee. Being loyal means that you act in the best interests of your employer, both on and off the job. Another word for loyalty is trustworthiness.

Getting Along at Work

In addition to your obligations to an employer, you also will have certain responsibilities toward your fel-

Figure 1-12 Keeping the customer informed and satisfied is the responsibility of everyone involved in the service industry.

low workers. You will be a member of a team. Teamwork means cooperating with, and caring about, other workers. An important strength of a valuable employee is the ability to work in harmony with fellow employees. You also should strive for harmonious relations with your supervisors and with those you supervise.

Customer Relations

The automotive service industry, led by ASE and other trade organizations, is constantly working to improve the public's perception of the industry and to increase the self-esteem of the technicians, owners, and managers of repair facilities.

Good customer relations begin at the service technician level (Figure 1-12). Learn to listen and communicate clearly. Be polite and organized, particularly when dealing with customers on the telephone.

Respect the vehicles you work on. They are a major investment in the lives of your customers. Always use fender covers and return the vehicle to the owner in a clean, undamaged condition.

Finally, explain the repair process to the customer in understandable terms. Make repair estimates as precisely as possible. No one likes surprises, particularly when substantial amounts of money are involved.

To help you develop your customer relation skills, special customer care tips appear throughout this text. They contain sound advice you can share with customers on personal car care. They also give you advice on how to conduct business in a courteous, professional manner.

❑ TRAINING FOR A CAREER IN AUTOMOTIVE SERVICE

Most young adults interested in a career in auto servicing now receive training in formal school settings—secondary, post secondary, vocational/technical, or community colleges, both private and public. To help these schools keep pace with the rapidly changing technology and equipment needed for training and maintaining a curriculum that meets the service industry's needs, many auto manufacturers now work with these schools through their own cooperative programs. These apprenticeship-type programs blend work experience in the real world with formal training at local schools. Programs vary, but generally the manufacturer provides specific product training curriculum, test equipment, vehicles, and components to participating schools and on-the-job training at local dealerships.

The course in which you are using this text is probably the first—and most important—step in your training. In this course you will learn the basics of how automobiles operate and how they are serviced.

A general course in automotive technology just scratches the surface of the possible service applications and techniques with which a service technician must become familiar.

Training in automotive technology and service does not end upon graduation from the training school or apprenticeship program. The professional auto technician must constantly learn. Car manufacturers, aftermarket parts manufacturers, and independent publishers are always producing new training materials to keep technicians informed on how to service the next generation of cars and trucks.

In addition, technical clinics are often sponsored by car manufacturers, aftermarket parts manufacturers, and parts dealers. Reading trade magazines and publications is also an excellent way to stay informed and up to date. A competent technician takes advantage of every opportunity to acquire updated information concerning the latest in automotive technology.

❑ ASE CERTIFICATION

As mentioned earlier, ASE has worked for years to improve the quality of auto repair and the image of the profession through the voluntary testing and certification of automotive service technicians. Nearly 300,000 ASE certified technicians now work in independent garages, dealerships, service stations, fleets, tire, collision repair, and specialty shops. ASE certification offers customers a concrete indication of the competency of a technician as well as the repair shop's commitment to quality service. Shops that employ ASE certified technicians display the ASE blue seal of excellence.

To become ASE certified, a technician must pass one or more tests that stress diagnostic and repair problems. Eight different tests are offered in automotive repair. They are as follows.

1. Engine repair
2. Automatic transmission/transaxle

TABLE 1-3 ASE TEST SPECIFICATIONS*

ENGINE REPAIR (TEST A1)

Content Area	Questions in Test	Percentage of Test
A. General Engine Diagnosis	18	22.5%
B. Cylinder Head and Valve Train Diagnosis and Repair	17	21.0%
C. Engine Block Diagnosis and Repair	16	20.0%
D. Lubrication and Cooling Systems Diagnosis and Repair	10	12.5%
E. Ignition System Diagnosis and Repair	7	9.0%
F. Fuel and Exhaust Systems Diagnosis and Repair	7	9.0%
G. Battery and Starting System Diagnosis and Repair	5	6.0%
Total	80	100.0%

AUTOMATIC TRANSMISSION/TRANSAXLE (TEST A2)

Content Area	Questions in Test	Percentage of Test
A. General Transmission/Transaxle Diagnosis	15	37.5%
B. Transmission/Transaxle Maintenance and Adjustment	4	10.0%
C. In-Vehicle Transmission/Transaxle Repair	9	22.5%
D. Off-Vehicle Transmission/Transaxle Repair	12	30.0%
1. Removal, Disassembly, and Assembly	(2)	
2. Oil Pump and Converter	(2)	
3. Gear Train, Shafts, Bushings, and Case	(3)	
4. Friction and Reaction Units	(5)	
Total	40	100.0%

MANUAL TRANSMISSIONS AND DRIVE AXLES (TEST A3)

Content Area	Questions in Test	Percentage of Test
A. Clutch Diagnosis and Repair	6	15.0%
B. Transmission Diagnosis and Repair	8	20.0%
C. Transaxle Diagnosis and Repair	9	22.5%
D. Drive (Half) Shaft and Universal Joint Diagnosis and Repair	6	15.0%
E. Rear Axle Diagnosis and Repair	8	20.0%
1. Ring and Pinion Gears	(3)	
2. Differential Case Assembly	(2)	
3. Limited Slip Differential	(1)	
4. Axle Shafts	(2)	
F. Four-Wheel-Drive Component Diagnosis and Repair	3	7.5%
Total	40	100.0%

SUSPENSION AND STEERING (TEST A4)

Content Area	Questions in Test	Percentage of Test
A. Steering Systems Diagnosis and Repair	9	22.5%
1. Steering Columns and Manual Steering Gears	(2)	
2. Power-Assisted Steering Units	(4)	
3. Steering Linkage	(3)	
B. Suspension Systems Diagnosis and Repair	13	32.5%
1. Front Suspensions	(6)	
2. Rear Suspensions	(5)	
3. Miscellaneous Service	(2)	
C. Wheel Alignment Diagnosis, Adjustment, and Repair	13	32.5%
D. Wheel and Tire Diagnosis and Repair	5	12.5%
Total	40	100.0%

TABLE 1-3 ASE TEST SPECIFICATIONS* (CONTINUED)

BRAKES (TEST A5)

Content Area	Questions in Test	Percentage of Test
A. Hydraulic System Diagnosis and Repair	11	27.5%
1. Master Cylinders	(4)	
2. Fluids, Lines, and Hoses	(2)	
3. Valves and Switches	(3)	
4. Bleeding, Flushing, and Leak Testing	(2)	
B. Drum Brake Diagnosis and Repair	7	17.5%
C. Disc Brake Diagnosis and Repair	11	27.5%
D. Power Assist Units Diagnosis and Repair	4	10.0%
E. Miscellaneous Diagnosis and Repair	5	12.5%
F. Anti-Lock Brake System Diagnosis and Repair	2	5.0%
Total	40	100.0%

ELECTRICAL SYSTEMS (TEST A6)

Content Area	Questions in Test	Percentage of Test
A. General Electrical System Diagnosis	10	20.0%
B. Battery Diagnosis and Service	5	10.0%
C. Starting System Diagnosis and Repair	5	10.0%
D. Charging System Diagnosis and Repair	6	12.0%
E. Lighting Systems Diagnosis and Repair	6	12.0%
1. Headlights, Parking Lights, Taillights, Dash Lights, and Courtesy Lights	(3)	
2. Stoplights, Turn Signals, Hazard Lights, and Back-up Lights	(3)	
F. Gauges, Warning Devices, and Driver Information Systems Diagnosis and Repair	7	14.0%
G. Horn and Wiper/Washer Diagnosis and Repair	3	6.0%
H. Accessories Diagnosis and Repair	8	16.0%
1. Body	(4)	
2. Miscellaneous	(4)	
Total	50	100.0%

HEATING AND AIR-CONDITIONING (TEST A7)

Content Area	Questions in Test	Percentage of Test
A. A/C System Diagnosis and Repair	11	27.5%
B. Refrigeration System Component Diagnosis and Repair	10	25.0%
1. Compressor and Clutch	(4)	
2. Evaporator, Condenser, Receiver/Drier, Etc.	(6)	
C. Heating and Engine Cooling Systems Diagnosis and Repair	5	12.5%
D. Operating Systems and Related Controls Diagnosis and Repair	14	35.0%
1. Electrical	(7)	
2. Vacuum/Mechanical	(4)	
3. Automatic and Semi-Automatic Temperature Controls	(3)	
E. Refrigerant Recovery, Recycling, and Handling		
Total	40	100.0%

ENGINE PERFORMANCE (TEST A8)

Content Area	Questions in Test	Percentage of Test
A. General Engine Diagnosis	19	24.0%
B. Ignition System Diagnosis and Repair	16	20.0%

TABLE 1-3 ASE TEST SPECIFICATIONS* (CONTINUED)
ENGINE PERFORMANCE (TEST A8)

Content Area	Questions in Test	Percentage of Test
C. Fuel, Air Induction, and Exhaust Systems Diagnosis and Repair	21	26.0%
D. Emissions Control Systems Diagnosis and Repair	19	24.0%
1. Positive Crankcase Ventilation	(1)	
2. Spark Timing Controls	(3)	
3. Idle Speed Controls	(3)	
4. Exhaust Gas Recirculation	(4)	
5. Exhaust Gas Treatment	(2)	
6. Inlet Air Temperature Controls	(2)	
7. Intake Manifold Temperature Controls	(2)	
8. Fuel Vapor Controls	(2)	
E. Engine-Related Service	2	2.5%
F. Engine Electrical Systems Diagnosis and Repair	3	2.5%
1. Battery	(1)	
2. Starting System	(1)	
3. Charging System	(1)	
Total	80	100.0%

*The 5-year Recertification Test will cover the same content areas as those listed. However, the number of questions in each content area of the Recertification Test will be reduced by about one-half.

3. Manual transmissions and drive axles
4. Suspension and steering
5. Brakes
6. Electrical systems
7. Heating and air conditioning
8. Engine performance (driveability)

The content of each of these tests is summarized in Table 1-3. ASE also offers certification programs for engine machinists, body and paint technicians, and heavy-duty truck technicians.

After passing at least one exam and providing proof of two years of hands-on work experience, the technician becomes ASE certified. Retesting is necessary every five years to remain certified. A technician who passes one examination receives an automotive technician shoulder patch. The master auto technician patch is awarded to service technicians who successfully pass testing in all eight ASE designated areas. See Figure 1-13.

Each certification test consists of 40 to 80 multiple-choice questions. The questions are written by a panel of technical service experts, including domestic and import vehicle manufacturers, repair and test equipment and parts manufacturers, working automotive technicians, and automotive instructors. All questions are pretested and quality-checked on a national sample of technicians before they are included in actual tests. Many test questions force the student to choose between two distinct repair methods. Questions similar to this Technician A/Technician B format are included in the review questions at the end of each chapter in this text.

A   B

Figure 1-13 ASE certification shoulder patches worn by (A) automotive technicians and (B) master auto technicians.

As mentioned, ASE certification requires that you have two or more years of full-time hands-on working experience as an automotive technician. You may receive credit for one of the two-year hands-on experience requirement by substituting relevant formal training in one, or a combination, of the following.

- High school training. Three full years of training, either in automotive repair or in body repair and refinishing, may be substituted for one year of work experience.
- Post-high school training. Two full years of post-high school training in a public or private trade school, technical institute, community or four-

year college, or in an apprenticeship program may be counted as one year of work experience.
- Short courses. For shorter periods of post-high school training, you may substitute two months of training for one month of work experience.

You may receive full credit for the two-year hands-on work experience requirement by satisfactorily completing a three- or four-year bona fide apprenticeship program.

To have your training considered as a substitute for work experience, you will need a copy of a transcript of courses, a statement of training, or a certificate showing satisfactory completion of apprenticeship. Documents should show length of training (hours or weeks). ASE reserves the right to evaluate all requests for substitution of training and to grant such credit as may be appropriate. Work experience other than as an automobile technician also may be credited toward fulfillment of the two-year experience requirement where, in the judgment of ASE, the nature of the substitute experience so warrants.

The knowledge and skills needed to pass the tests follows.

BASIC TECHNICAL KNOWLEDGE What is it? How does it work? This requires knowing what is in a system and how the system works. It also calls for knowing the procedures and precautions to be followed in making repairs and adjustments.

REPAIR KNOWLEDGE AND SKILL What is a likely source of a problem? How do you fix it? This requires you to understand and to apply generally-accepted procedures and precautions in disassembly, assembly, and reconditioning operations and in making major inspections and adjustments. It also calls for an ability to use service manuals and the precision tools of the trade.

TESTING AND DIAGNOSTIC KNOWLEDGE AND SKILL How do you find what is wrong? How do you determine the effectiveness of work done? This requires that you be able to recognize the existence of a problem and to use generally available measuring and testing equipment to diagnose the difficulty. You also must be able to trace the effects of a particular condition and efficiently find the cause of a particular set of symptoms.

For further information on the ASE certification program, write: National Institute for Auto Service Excellence (ASE), 13505 Dulles Technology Drive, Herndon, VA 22071.

Summary

- The modern auto industry is a global industry involving vehicle and parts manufacturers from many countries.
- Autotronics is the study of electronic technology as it is used on automobiles. Electronic computer controls are found on many auto systems, such as engines, ignition systems, transmissions, steering systems, and suspensions. The use of electronics in automobiles is increasing rapidly.
- The increasing complexity of vehicles, the increasing age of vehicles on the road, and the need to comply to federal laws concerning emission control and mileage are three reasons the need for quality service technicians is increasing.
- Preventive maintenance is extremely important in keeping today's electronically-controlled systems in good working order.
- New car dealerships, independent service shops, specialty service shops, fleet operators, and many other businesses are in great need of qualified service technicians.
- A solid background in auto technology may be the basis for many other types of careers within the industry. Some examples are parts management, collision damage appraisal, sales, and marketing positions.
- Besides learning technical and mechanical skills, service technicians must learn to work as part of a team. As an employee, you will have certain responsibilities to both your employer and customers.
- Customer relations is an extremely important part of doing business. Professional, courteous treatment of customers and their vehicles is a must.
- Training in auto technology is available from many types of secondary and vocational and technical schools. Auto manufacturers also have cooperative programs with schools to ensure graduates understand modern systems and the equipment to service them.
- The National Institute for Automotive Service Excellence (ASE) actively promotes professionalism within the industry. Its certification program for automotive technicians and master auto technicians helps guarantee a high level of quality service.
- The ASE certification process involves both written tests and credit for on-the-job experience. Testing is available in eight separate areas of auto technology. Certification in engine machining, heavy-duty truck servicing, auto body painting, and collision repair is also offered.

Review Questions

1. Give three examples of how the automotive industry has evolved into a global industry.
2. Define the term autotronics. Explain its effect on the auto service industry.
3. List at least five different types of businesses that hire service technicians. Describe the types of

work these businesses handle and the advantages and disadvantages of working for them.
4. List some of the responsibilities of both employee and employer in maintaining a good working relationship.
5. Explain the role of ASE in the auto service industry and the ASE certification process of service technicians.
6. Repair work performed on vehicles still under manufacturer's warranty is usually performed by _____ .
   a. independent service shops
   b. dealerships
   c. specialty shops
   d. either a or b
7. Which of the following businesses perform work on only one or two automotive systems?
   a. dealerships
   b. independent service shops
   c. specialty shops
   d. fleet service departments
8. Whose job is it to prepare the cost estimate for a customer?
   a. service manager
   b. parts manager
   c. master auto technician
   d. service writer
9. Technician A says that the Federal Emissions Performance Warranty is applicable only in certain states. Technician B says it is applicable for the entire U.S. Who is correct?
   a. Technician A
   b. Technician B
   c. Both A and B
   d. Neither A nor B
10. In which of the following areas could an automotive technician become a specialist?
    a. brakes
    b. electrical system
    c. transmission
    d. all of the above
11. A technician must have a minimum of _____ year(s) of hands-on work experience to get ASE certification.
    a. one
    b. two
    c. three
    d. four
12. A technician who passes all eight ASE automotive certification tests is certified as a(n) _____ .
    a. automotive technician
    b. master auto technician
    c. service manager
    d. parts manager
13. Technician A says that battery warranties are often pro-rated. Technician B says that battery warranties are never pro-rated. Who is correct?
    a. Technician A
    b. Technician B
    c. Both A and B
    d. Neither A nor B
14. Wholesale auto parts stores that sell aftermarket parts and supplies to service shops and the general public are called _____ .
    a. warehouse distributors
    b. mass merchandisers
    c. jobbers
    d. freelancers
15. On-going technical training and support is available from _____ .
    a. aftermarket parts manufacturers
    b. auto manufacturers
    c. jobbers
    d. all of the above

2 PRACTICING SAFETY IN THE SHOP

Objectives

■ Understand the vital importance of safety and accident prevention in the automotive shop. ■ Know the principles of personal safety, including protective eyeware, clothing, gloves, shoes, and hearing protection. ■ Explain proper tool and equipment safety procedures. ■ Know how to maintain a safe work area, including handling vehicles in the shop and venting carbon monoxide gases. ■ Know the laws and safe handling practices used with hazardous waste materials, including the right-to-know laws.

Safety and accident prevention must be the top priority in all automotive service shops and businesses. The potential for serious accidents exists in many areas.

Vehicles and many components are very heavy, and parts often fit tightly together. Many components become hot during operation and high fluid pressures can build up inside the cooling system, fuel system, or battery. Batteries contain highly corrosive and potentially explosive acids. Fuels and cleaning solvents are flammable. Exhaust fumes are poisonous. Dust and vapors generated during many repairs can also be harmful.

Good safety practices eliminate these potential dangers. A careless attitude and poor work habits invite disaster. Shop accidents can cause serious injury, temporary or permanent disability, and death.

Safety is a very serious matter. Both employer and employees must cooperate together to establish a safety program that protects the health and welfare of all who work in the shop.

This chapter contains many guidelines concerning personal, work area, tool and equipment, and hazardous material safety. In addition to these rules, special warnings have been used throughout this book to alert you to situations where carelessness could result in personal injury. Finally, follow all safety guidelines given in specific service manuals and technical literature. They are there for your protection.

☐ PERSONAL SAFETY

Personal safety relates to the precautions you take to protect yourself from injury. It involves wearing protective gear, dressing for safety, and handling tools and equipment correctly.

EYE PROTECTION The eyes are sensitive to nearly all types of foreign matter, such as dust, vapors, metal shavings, and liquids.

Grinding and other operations generate tiny particles that are thrown off at very high speeds. Gases and liquids escaping a ruptured hose or fuel line fitting can be projected considerable distances under great force. Dirt and sharp bits of corroded metal can easily fall down into your eyes when working under a vehicle.

Eye protection should be worn whenever you are exposed to these risks. It is good practice to wear safety glasses at all times in the shop. There are many types of eye protection available (Figure 2-1). The lenses must be made of safety glass. They must offer some sort of side protection. Regular prescription glasses do not offer sufficient protection. Select safety glasses that fit well and feel comfortable. Develop the habit of putting eye protection on and leaving it on.

If chemicals such as battery acid, fuel, or solvents enter your eyes, flush them continuously with clean water until medical help is obtained.

CLOTHING Clothing should be durable, comfortable, and well-fitted. Loose, baggy clothing can get caught on moving parts and machinery. Neck ties should not be worn. Many service technicians prefer to wear coveralls or shop coats to protect their personal clothing. Cut-offs and short pants are inappropriate for shop work.

SHOES Service work involves the handling of many heavy objects that could be accidentally dropped onto

Practicing Safety in the Shop 17

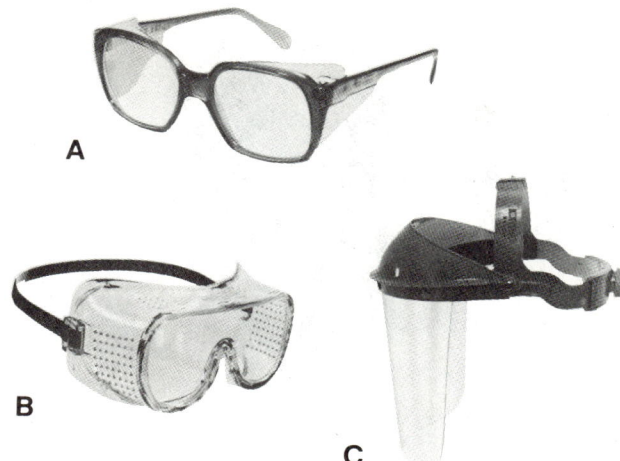

Figure 2-1 (A) Safety glasses; (B) splash goggles; (C) face shield. *Courtesy of Goodson Shop Supplies*

feet and toes. Always wear steel-tipped safety shoes with non-slip soles. Athletic shoes, street shoes, and sandals are inappropriate in the shop.

GLOVES Good hand protection is often overlooked. A scrape, cut, or burn can seriously impair your ability to work for many days. A well-fitted pair of heavy work gloves should be worn during operations such as grinding and welding, or when handling caustic chemicals or high-temperature components.

EAR PROTECTION Exposure to very loud noise levels for extended periods of time can lead to ear damage and hearing loss. Air wrenches, engines run on dynomometers, and vehicles running in enclosed areas can all generate annoying and harmful levels of noise. Simple ear plugs or earphone-type protectors (Figure 2-2) should be worn in constantly noisy environments.

HAIR AND JEWELRY Long hair and loose, hanging jewelry can create the same type of hazard as loose-fitting clothing. They can become caught on moving engine parts and machinery. Tie up long hair securely behind your head or cover it with a cap.

Remove all rings, watches, bracelets, and neck chains. These items can easily be caught on moving parts, causing serious injury.

LIFTING AND CARRYING Knowing the proper way to lift heavy materials is important. You should always lift and work within your ability and seek help from others when you are not sure you can handle the size or weight of the material or object. Even small, compact auto parts can be surprisingly heavy or unbalanced. Always examine the lifting task before beginning. When lifting any object, follow these steps.

1. Place your feet close to the load and properly positioned for balance.
2. Keep your back and elbows as straight as possible. Bend your knees until your hands reach the best place for getting a strong grip on the load (Figure 2-3).
3. If the part or component is stored in a cardboard box, be certain the box is in good condition. Old, damp, or poorly-sealed boxes will tear or otherwise fail. A heavy object could tear through the side or bottom of the container, causing injury or damage.
4. Grasp the object or container firmly. Do not attempt to change your grip as you move the load.
5. Keep the object close to your body and lift by straightening your legs. Use your leg muscles, not back muscles.
6. When changing direction of travel, do not twist your body. Turn your whole body, including your feet.
7. When placing the object on a shelf or counter, do not bend forward. Place the edge of the load on the surface and slide it forward. Be careful not to pinch your fingers.
8. When setting down a load, bend your knees and keep your back straight. Do not bend forward—this strains the back muscles.

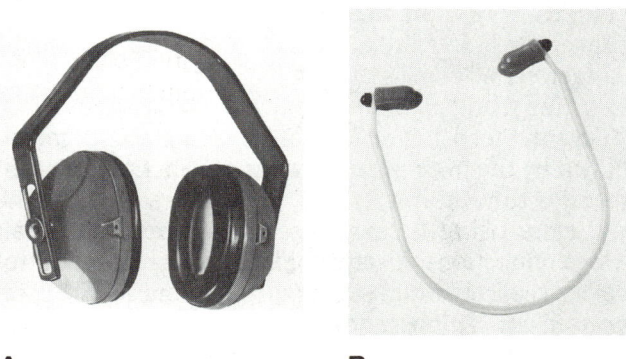

Figure 2-2 Typical (A) ear muffs and (B) ear plugs. *Courtesy of Willson Safety Products, Inc.*

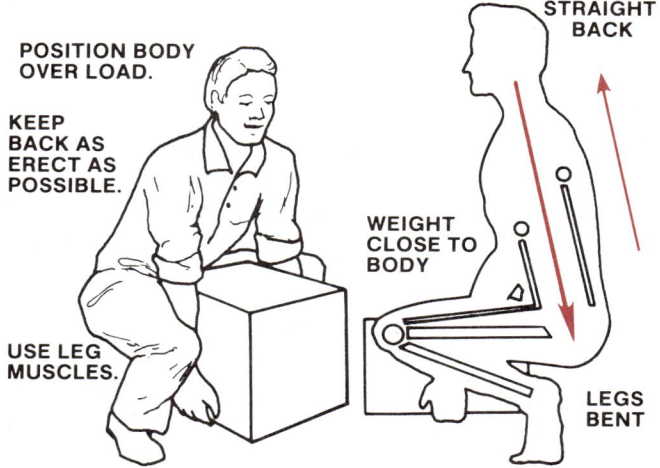

Figure 2-3 Use your leg muscles—never your back—when lifting any heavy load.

9. Use blocks to protect your fingers when picking up or lowering heavy objects to the floor.

OTHER PERSONAL SAFETY WARNINGS Never smoke while working on any vehicle or machine in the shop.

Proper conduct can help prevent accidents. Horseplay is not fun when it sends someone to the hospital. Such things as air nozzle fights, creeper races, or practical jokes do not have any place in the shop.

A welding helmet or welding goggles with the proper shade lens must be worn when welding. These will protect the eyes and face from flying molten pieces of steel and harmful light rays.

To prevent serious burns, avoid contact with hot metal parts such as the radiator, exhaust manifold, tail pipe, catalytic converter, and muffler.

When working with a hydraulic press, make sure that hydraulic pressure is applied in a safe manner. It is generally wise to stand to the side when operating the press. Always wear safety glasses.

Store all parts and tools properly by putting them away neatly where people will not trip over them. This practice not only cuts down on injuries, it also reduces time wasted looking for a misplaced part or tool.

☐ TOOL AND EQUIPMENT SAFETY

The automotive technician must observe the following shop tool and equipment safety guidelines.

HAND TOOL SAFETY Careless use of simple hand tools such as wrenches, screwdrivers, and hammers account for many shop accidents that could be prevented.

Keep all hand tools grease-free and in good condition. Tools that slip can cause cuts and bruises. If a tool slips and falls into a moving part, it can fly out and cause serious personal injury.

Use the proper tool for the job. Wrong tools can damage parts, the tool itself, or cause injury. Do not use broken or bent tools.

Be careful when using sharp or pointed tools that can slip and cause injury. Do not place sharp tools, or other sharp objects, in your pockets. They can stab or cut your skin, ruin automotive upholstery, or scratch a painted panel. If a tool is supposed to be sharp, make sure it is sharp. Dull tools can be more dangerous than sharp tools.

POWER TOOL SAFETY Power tools are operated by an outside source of power, such as electricity, compressed air, or hydraulic pressure. Safety around power tools is very important. Serious injury can result from carelessness. Always wear safety glasses when using power tools.

Make sure that the tool is properly grounded and check the wiring for cracks in the insulation, as well as

Figure 2-4 Safety guards in position on a bench grinder. *Courtesy of Snap-on Tools Corp.*

for bare wires. Also, when using electrical power tools, never stand on a wet or damp floor. Disconnect electrical power before performing any service on the machine or tool. Before plugging in any electric tool, make sure the switch is off to prevent serious injury. When you are through using the tool, turn it off and unplug it. Never leave a power tool unattended when it is running. If you leave, turn off the machine.

When using power equipment on small parts, never hold the part in your hand. Always mount the part in a bench vise or use vise grip pliers. Do not attempt to use a machine or tool beyond its stated capacity or for operations requiring more than the rated horsepower of the tool.

When working with larger power tools—like bench or floor equipment—check the machines for signs of damage and proper adjustments before using them. Place all safety guards in position (Figure 2-4). A safety guard is a protective cover over a moving part designed to prevent injury. Wear safety glasses or a face shield. Make sure everyone and all parts are clear before starting the machine. Keep hands and clothing away from the moving parts. Never overreach. Maintain a balanced stance to avoid slipping.

COMPRESSED AIR EQUIPMENT SAFETY Compressed air is pressurized and directed through hoses to perform work. Compressed air is used to inflate tires, apply paint, and drive tools. Compressed air can be dangerous when it is not used properly.

When using compressed air, safety glasses or a face shield are needed. Particles of dirt and pieces of metal, blown by the high-pressure air, can penetrate the skin or get into your eyes.

Before using a compressed air system, check all hose connections. Always hold the air nozzle or control device securely when starting or shutting off the compressed air. A loose nozzle can whip suddenly and cause serious injury. Never point an air nozzle at anyone. Do not use compressed air to blow dirt from clothes or hair. Do not use compressed air to clean the floor or workbench.

Never spin bearings with compressed air. If the bearing is damaged, one of the steel balls might come loose and cause serious injury. Damage to the bearing can also result.

Finally, pneumatic tools must be operated at the pressure recommended by the manufacturer.

LIFT SAFETY Raising a vehicle on a lift or a hoist requires specific care. Adapters and hoist plates must be positioned correctly on twin post and rail-type lifts to prevent damage to the underbody of the vehicle. There are specific lift points to use where the weight of the vehicle is evenly supported by the adapters or hoist plates. The correct lift points can be found in the vehicle's service manual. Figure 2-5 shows typical locations for frame and unibody cars. These diagrams are for illustration only. Always follow the manufacturer's instructions. Before operating any lift or hoist, carefully read the owner's manual and understand all the operating and maintenance instructions.

WARNING: Never use a lift or jack to move something heavier than it is designed for. Always refer to the rated tonnage before using a lift or jack. If a jack is rated for 2 tons, do not attempt to use it for a job requiring 5 tons. It is dangerous for both the technician and the vehicle.

Before driving a vehicle over a lift, position the arms and supports to provide unobstructed clearance. Do not hit or run over lift arms, adapters, or axle supports. This could damage the lift, vehicle, or tires.

Position the lift supports to contact at the vehicle manufacturer's recommended lifting points. Raise the lift until the supports contact the vehicle. Check supports for secure contact with the vehicle. Raise the lift to the desired working height.

Make sure the vehicle's doors, hood, and trunk are closed prior to raising the vehicle. Never raise a car with passengers inside.

WARNING: When working under a car, the lift should be raised high enough for the lift's locking device to be engaged.

After lifting a vehicle to the desired height, always lower the unit onto mechanical safeties. Note that with some vehicles, the removal (or installation) of components can cause a critical shift in the center of gravity and result in raised vehicle instability. Refer to the vehicle manufacturer's service manual for recommended procedures when removing vehicle components.

Make sure tool trays, stands, and so forth are removed from under the vehicle. Release locking devices as per instructions before attempting to lower the lift. Loosen convertible top latches before raising the vehicle on a lift.

Be very careful with pick-up trucks and four-wheel-drive vehicles. Never raise a four-wheel-drive vehicle on a frame contact lift.

JACK AND JACK STAND SAFETY An automobile can be raised off the ground by a hydraulic jack (Figure 2-6). Jack stands, also called safety stands, are important safety devices used with a jack or a hoist (Figure 2-7). Jack stands are supports of different heights that sit on the floor. They are placed under a sturdy chassis member, such as the frame or axle housing.

Often, the jack is removed after the jack stands are set in place. This eliminates a hazard, such as a jack handle sticking out into a walkway. A jack handle that

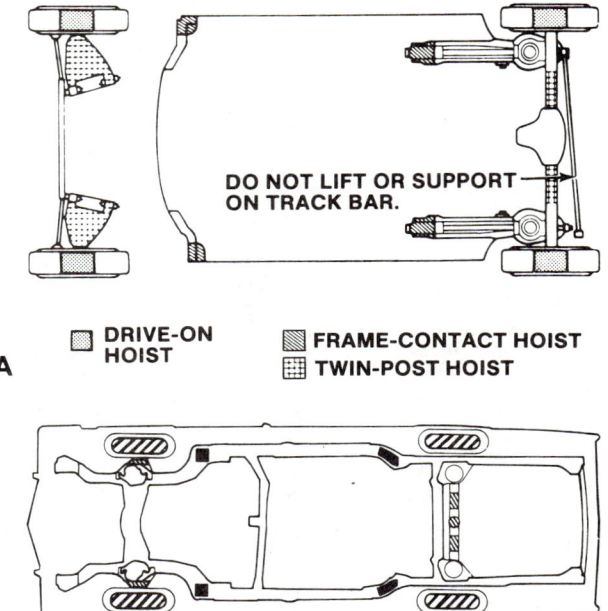

Figure 2-5 Typical lift points for (A) unibody and (B) frame/body vehicles.

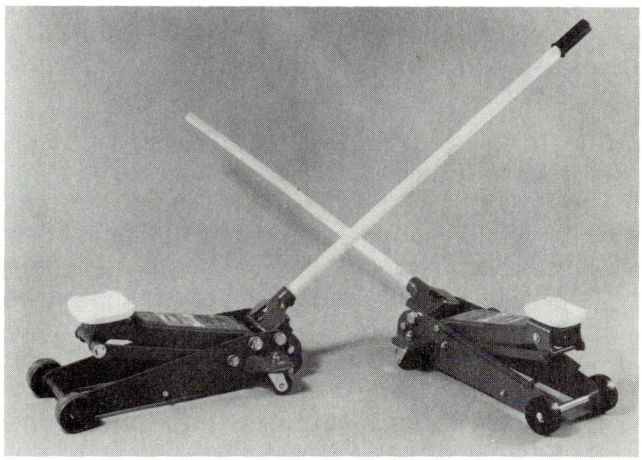

Figure 2-6 Typical hydraulic jacks. *Courtesy of Blackhawk Automotive, Inc.*

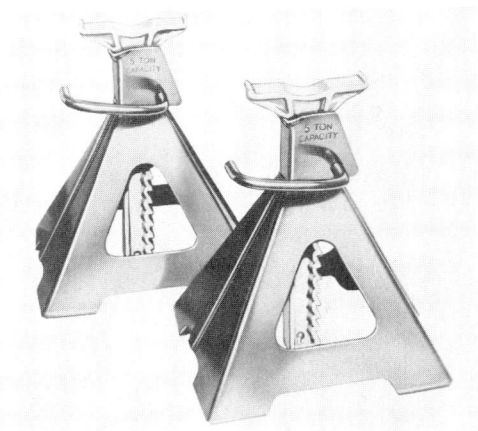

Figure 2-7 Jack stands are used in combination with jacks and hoists. *Courtesy of Lincoln, St. Louis*

Figure 2-9 Cranes can also be used to remove an engine. *Courtesy of Tool Division—SPX Corp.*

Figure 2-8 Using a chain hoist to lift an engine. *Courtesy of Tool Division—SPX Corp.*

is bumped or kicked can cause a tripping accident or cause the vehicle to fall. To safely operate jacks and jack stands never use a jack by itself to support an automobile. Always use a jack stand with the jack, as a safety precaution. Make sure the jack stands are properly placed under the vehicle.

CHAIN HOIST AND CRANE SAFETY Heavy parts of the automobile, such as engines, are removed by using chain hoists (Figure 2-8), or cranes (Figure 2-9). Another term for a chain hoist is chain fall. Cranes often are called cherry pickers.

To prevent serious injury, chain hoists and cranes must be properly attached to the parts being lifted. Always use bolts of sufficient strength to attach the hoist to the object being lifted. Attach the lifting chain or cable to the system that is to be removed. Have the instructor check the attachment. Place the chain hoist or crane directly over the assembly that is to be removed. Before lifting, secure the chain or cable.

CLEANING EQUIPMENT SAFETY Parts cleaning is necessary in all repair shops. The process for cleaning automotive engine parts can be divided into four basic categories.

Chemical cleaning relies primarily on some type of chemical action to remove dirt, grease, scale, paint, or rust (Figure 2-10). A combination of heat, agitation, mechanical scrubbing, or washing may also be used in the process to aid in removing surface contaminants. Chemical cleaning equipment includes small parts

Figure 2-10 Hot tank used for chemical cleaning. *Courtesy of Kansas Instruments, Inc.*

Figure 2-11 Complete thermal cleaning system. *Courtesy of Bayco, Inc.*

washers, hot/cold tanks, pressure washers, spray washers, and salt baths.

Thermal cleaning relies exclusively on heat to bake off or oxidize surface contaminants (Figure 2-11). Thermal cleaning leaves an ash residue on the surface that must be subsequently removed by an additional cleaning process such as airless shot blasting or spray washing. Thermal cleaning equipment includes conventional ovens and open flame ovens.

Abrasive cleaning relies on physical abrasion to clean the surface. This includes everything from a wire brush to glass bead blasting, airless steel shot blasting, abrasive tumbling, and vibratory cleaning (Figure 2-12). Chemical in-tank solution sonic cleaning might also be included here because it relies on the scrubbing action of ultrasonic sound waves to dislodge surface contaminants.

Steam cleaning uses hot water vapor strengthened with chemical cleaning agents to remove both the

Figure 2-13 Open steam cleaning was once a popular means of cleaning engines.

by-products of petroleum and water-soluble soils (Figure 2-13). After the steam cleaning is completed, all surfaces are then flushed with clean water from a high-pressure washer and air dried.

There are several reasons why the use of steam cleaning has declined very rapidly in recent years. Environmental considerations require that steam cleaning must be performed in a closed loop. That is, the runoff from the cleaning process can no longer be carried off in a public sewer system or on the ground. The runoff must be contained within the steam-cleaning system.

Steam cleaning usually must be done in an uncongested portion of the shop or in a separate building. Care must be taken to protect surrounding painted surfaces and exposed skin that could come into contact with the steam's heat and chemicals. In addition, care must also be taken when working on the slippery floor that this process creates.

Another hazard associated with steam cleaning is the danger of electrical shock if the machine is not properly grounded.

Figure 2-12 Heads undergoing abrasive cleaning in a steel shot blaster. *Courtesy of Kansas Instruments, Inc.*

Finally, steam cleaning is very labor intensive. Most shops cannot justify the labor cost for using open steam cleaning.

VEHICLE OPERATION When the customer turns the vehicle over for service, certain safe shop operations must be considered. For example, when moving a car in the work area, first test the brakes. Then, buckle the safety belt. Use extreme care when driving a car in the shop. Make sure no one is under another car, that the way is clear, and that there are no tools or parts under the car before you start the engine.

When taking a road test, observe all traffic laws. Drive only as far as is necessary to check the automobile. Never make jackrabbit starts, turn corners too quickly, or drive faster than conditions allow.

If the engine must be running while working on the car, block the wheels to prevent the car from moving. Place the transmission lever into park for automatic transmissions or in neutral for manual transmissions. Set the emergency brake. Never stand in front of or behind a running vehicle.

Operate the engine only in a well-ventilated area to avoid the danger of poisonous carbon monoxide (CO) in the engine exhaust. If the shop is equipped with a tail pipe exhaust system to remove CO from the garage (Figure 2-14), use it. If not, use the direct piping to the outside method or a mechanical ventilation system.

❏ WORK AREA SAFETY

It is very important that the work area be kept safe. All surfaces should be kept clean, dry, and orderly. Any oil, coolant, or grease on the floor can cause slips that could result in serious injuries. To clean up oil, be sure to use a commercial oil absorbent. Keep all water off the floor. Remember, water is a conductor of electricity. Aisles and walkways should be kept clean and wide enough for safe clearance. Provide for adequate work space around any machines. Also, keep workbenches clean and orderly.

Figure 2-14 Removing carbon monoxide.

Space heaters used in some shops can also be a serious source of CO and therefore should be periodically inspected to make sure they are adequately vented and do not become blocked. Proper ventilation is very important in areas where volatile solvents and chemicals are used. A volatile liquid is one that vaporizes very quickly.

Keep a list of up-to-date emergency telephone numbers clearly posted next to the telephone. These numbers should include a doctor, hospital, and fire and police departments. Also, the work area should have a first-aid kit for treating minor injuries. Facilities for flushing the eyes should also be in or near the shop area.

Gasoline is a highly flammable volatile liquid. For this reason, always keep gasoline or diesel fuel in an approved safety can and never use it to wash hands or tools. Oily rags should also be stored in an approved metal container. When these oily, greasy, or paint-soaked rags are left lying about or are stored improperly, they are prime candidates for spontaneous combustion, that is, fires that start by themselves.

Check to be sure that all drain covers are snugly in place. Open drains can cause toe, ankle, and leg injuries.

Handle all solvents (or any liquids) with care to avoid spillage. Keep all solvent containers closed, except when pouring. Extra caution should also be used when transferring flammable materials from bulk storage (Figure 2-15). Otherwise, static electricity can

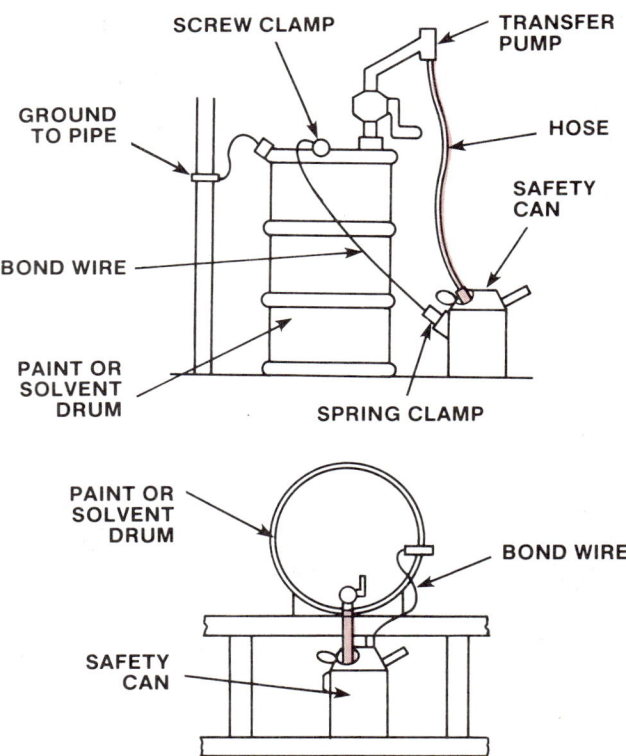

Figure 2-15 Safe methods of transferring flammable materials from bulk storage. *Courtesy of Du Pont Co.*

Practicing Safety in the Shop

Figure 2-16 Store combustible materials in approved safety cabinets. *Courtesy of Sherwin-Williams Co.*

build up enough to create a spark that could cause an explosion. Discard or clean all empty solvent containers. Solvent fumes in the bottom of these containers are prime ignition sources. Do not light matches or smoke near flammable solvents and chemicals, including battery acids. Solvents and other combustible materials must be stored in approved and designated storage cabinets or rooms (Figure 2-16). Storage rooms should have adequate ventilation.

Know where the fire extinguishers are and what types of fires they put out (Table 2-1). A multi-purpose dry chemical fire extinguisher will put out ordinary combustibles, flammable liquids, and electrical fires. In case of a gasoline fire, do not put water on it. The water will just spread the fire. Use a fire extinguisher to smother the flames. Remember, during a fire, never

TABLE 2-1 GUIDE TO EXTINGUISHER SELECTION

	Class of Fire	Typical Fuel Involved	Type of Extinguisher
Class A Fires (green)	**For Ordinary Combustibles** Put out a class A fire by lowering its temperature or by coating the burning combustibles.	Wood Paper Cloth Rubber Plastics Rubbish Upholstery	Water*[1] Foam* Multipurpose dry chemical[4]
Class B Fires (red)	**For Flammable Liquids** Put out a class B fire by smothering it. Use an extinguisher that gives a blanketing, flame-interrupting effect; cover whole flaming liquid surface.	Gasoline Oil Grease Paint Lighter fluid	Foam* Carbon dioxide[5] Halogenated agent[6] Standard dry chemical[2] Purple K dry chemical[3] Multipurpose dry chemical[4]
Class C Fires (blue)	**For Electrical Equipment** Put out a class C fire by shutting off power as quickly as possible and by always using a nonconducting extinguishing agent to prevent electric shock.	Motors Appliances Wiring Fuse boxes Switchboards	Carbon dioxide[5] Halogenated agent[6] Standard dry chemical[2] Purple K dry chemical[3] Multipurpose dry chemical[4]
Class D Fires (yellow)	**For Combustible Metals** Put out a class D fire of metal chips, turnings, or shavings by smothering or coating with a specially designed extinguishing agent.	Aluminum Magnesium Potassium Sodium Titanium Zirconium	Dry powder extinguishers and agents only

*Cartridge-operated water, foam, and soda-acid types of extinguishers are no longer manufactured. These extinguishers should be removed from service when they become due for their next hydrostatic pressure test.

Notes:
(1) Freeze in low temperatures unless treated with antifreeze solution, usually weighs over 20 pounds, and is heavier than any other extinguisher mentioned.
(2) Also called ordinary or regular dry chemical. (sodium bicarbonate)
(3) Has the greatest initial fire-stopping power of the extinguishers mentioned for class B fires. Be sure to clean residue immediately after using the extinguisher so sprayed surfaces will not be damaged. (potassium bicarbonate)
(4) The only extinguishers that fight A, B, and C classes of fires. However, they should not be used on fires in liquefied fat or oil of appreciable depth. Be sure to clean residue immediately after using the extinguisher so sprayed surfaces will not be damaged. (ammonium phosphates)
(5) Use with caution in unventilated, confined spaces.
(6) May cause injury to the operator if the extinguishing agent (a gas) or the gases produced when the agent is applied to a fire is inhaled.

open doors or windows unless it is absolutely necessary; the extra draft will only make the fire worse. A good rule is to call the fire department first and then attempt to extinguish the fire. Standing 6 to 10 feet from the fire, hold the extinguisher firmly in an upright position. Aim the nozzle at the base and use a side-to-side motion, sweeping the entire width of the fire. Stay low to avoid inhaling the smoke. If it gets too hot or too smoky, get out. Remember, never go back into a burning building for anything.

Keep customers' vehicles away from immediate work areas to prevent them from being damaged while waiting to be worked on. Never allow customers into the shop's work areas.

☐ MANUFACTURER'S WARNINGS AND GOVERNMENT REGULATIONS

The solvents and other chemical products used in an auto repair shop carry warning and caution information that must be read and understood by all users. Likewise, all federal (including Occupational Safety and Health Administration [OSHA], Mine Safety and Health Administration [MSHA], and National Institute for Occupational Safety and Health [NIOSH]), state, and local safety regulations must be fully understood, and strictly observed.

Many auto service procedures generate what are known as hazardous wastes. Dirty solvents and liquid cleaners are a good example. Every employee in the shop is protected by right-to-know laws concerning these materials. These laws started with the Occupational Safety and Health Administration (OSHA). OSHA's Hazard Communication Standard was published in 1983. This document was originally intended for chemical companies and manufacturers that require employees to handle potentially hazardous materials in the workshop. Since then, the majority of states have enacted their own right-to-know laws. The federal courts have decided that these regulations should apply to all companies, including auto servicing professions.

The general intent of right-to-know laws is for employers to provide their employees with a safe working place as it relates to hazardous materials. Specifically, there are three areas of employer responsibility.

First, all employees must be trained about their rights under the legislation, the nature of the hazardous chemicals in their workplace, the labeling of chemicals, and the information about each chemical posted on material safety data sheets (MSDS). These sheets (Figure 2-17) are available from product manufacturers. They detail the chemical composition and precautionary information for all products that can present a health or safety hazard. Employees must be familiar-

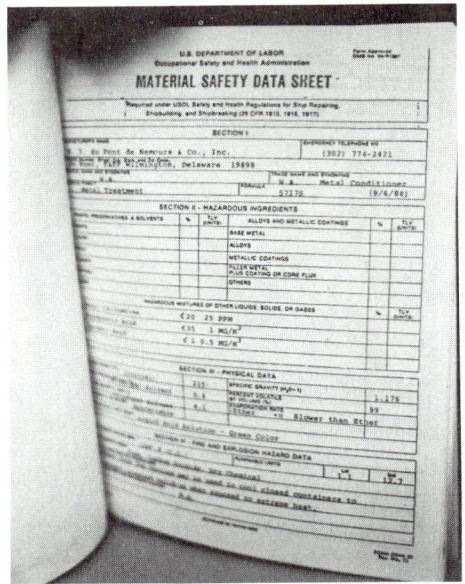

Figure 2-17 Material safety data sheets are an important part of employee training. *Courtesy of Storm Vulcan Co.*

ized about the general uses, protective equipment, accident or spill procedures, and any other information regarding the safe handling of the hazardous material. This training must be given to employees annually and provided to new employees as part of their job orientation. The Canadian equivalents to MSDS are called workplace hazardous materials information systems (WHMIS).

Secondly, all hazardous materials must be properly labeled, indicating what health, fire, or reactivity hazard it poses and what protective equipment is necessary when handling each chemical. The manufacturer of the hazardous waste materials must provide all warnings and precautionary information, which must be read and understood by the user before application. Attention to all label precautions is essential for the proper use of the chemical and for prevention of hazardous conditions. A list of all hazardous materials used in the shop must be posted for the employees to see.

Finally, shops must maintain documentation on the hazardous chemicals in the workplace, proof of training programs, records of accidents or spill incidents, satisfaction of employee requests for specific chemical information via the MSDS, and a general right-to-know compliance procedure manual utilized within the shop.

WARNING: *When handling any hazardous waste material, be sure to wear the proper safety equipment (Figure 2-18) covered under the right-to-know law. Follow all required procedures correctly. This includes the use of approved respirator equipment.*

Hazardous waste as determined by the Environmental Protection Agency (EPA) must be in the form of

Figure 2-18 Wear proper safety equipment when handling hazardous waste. *Courtesy of Du Pont Co.*

Figure 2-19 Many automotive shops hire full-service haulers for hazardous waste removal. *Courtesy of Du Pont Co.*

"solid" material, but the EPA includes many liquids in this definition. Waste is considered hazardous if it is on the EPA list of known harmful materials or has one or more of the following characteristics.

- Ignitability. If it is a liquid with a flash point below 140 degrees Fahrenheit or a solid that can spontaneously ignite.
- Corrosivity. If it dissolves metals and other materials or burns the skin.
- Reactivity. Any material that reacts violently with water or other materials or releases cyanide gas, hydrogen sulfide gas, or similar gases when exposed to low pH acid solutions. This also includes material that generates toxic mists, fumes, vapors, and flammable gases.
- EP toxicity. Materials that leach one or more of eight heavy metals in concentrations greater than 100 times primary drinking water standard concentrations.

Complete EPA lists of hazardous wastes can be found in the Code of Federal Regulations. It should be noted that no material is considered hazardous waste until the shop is finished using it and ready to dispose of it.

WARNING: *The shop is ultimately responsible for the safe disposal of hazardous wastes, even after the waste leaves the shop. Be sure that any hauling contract is in writing. Leave nothing to chance. In the event of an emergency hazardous waste spill, contact the National Response Center (1-800-424-8802) immediately. Failure to do so can result in a $10,000 fine, a year in jail, or both.*

Many shops use full-service haulers to remove hazardous waste from the property (Figure 2-19). Besides hauling the hazardous waste away, the hauler will also take care of all the paperwork, deal with the various government agencies, and advise the shop on how to recover the disposal costs.

Good housekeeping is essential in a workplace where materials containing asbestos such as brake pads and some engine gaskets are handled. All asbestos waste must also be disposed of in accordance with OSHA and EPA asbestos regulations. An industrial vacuum equipped with multiple-stage, high-efficiency filters and housing to work on brakes should be used for removing accumulations of asbestos dust and waste. During the removal of vacuum bags, an approved respirator should be worn. Never use compressed air or dry sweeping for cleaning. Water or other dust suppressants should be applied to the floor if brooms are used to clean it.

Good personal hygiene practices are important in minimizing exposure to asbestos dust and other hazardous wastes.

- Do not smoke.
- Wash before eating.
- Shower after work.
- Change to work clothes upon arrival at work, and change from work clothes after work. Work clothing should not be taken home.

OSHA and the EPA have other strict rules and regulations that help to promote safety in the auto shop. These are described throughout the text where applicable.

Summary

- Dressing safely in the shop is very important. This includes snug-fitting clothing, eye and ear protec-

tion, protective gloves, strong shoes, and caps to cover long hair.
- When choosing eye protection, make sure it has safety glass and offers side protection.
- When shop noise exceeds safe levels, protect your ears by wearing ear plugs or ear muffs.
- Safety while using any tool is a must, particularly power tools. Before plugging in a power tool, make sure the power switch is off. Disconnect the power before doing any servicing of the tool.
- Always observe all relevant safety rules when operating a vehicle lift or hoist. Jacks, jack stands, chain hoists, and cranes can also cause injury if not operated safely.
- Steam cleaning must be done in an uncongested area. Due to environmental considerations and because it is so labor intensive, its use has declined recently.
- Use care whenever it is necessary to move a vehicle in the shop. Carelessness and horseplay can lead to a damaged vehicle and serious injury.
- Carbon monoxide gas is a poisonous gas present in engine exhaust fumes. It must be properly vented from the shop using tail pipe hoses or other reliable methods.
- Adequate ventilation is also necessary when working with any volatile solvent or material.
- Gasoline and diesel fuel are highly flammable and should be kept in approved safety cans. Never light matches near any combustible materials.
- It is important to know when to use each of the various types of fire extinguishers. When fighting a fire, aim the nozzle at the base and use a side-to-side sweeping motion.
- Right-to-know laws began in 1983 and are designed to protect employees who must handle hazardous wastes on the job. The EPA lists many materials as hazardous, provided they have one or more of the following characteristics: ignitability, corrosivity, reactivity, and EP toxicity.
- Material safety data sheets contain important chemical information and must be furnished to all employees annually. New employees should be given the sheets as part of their job orientation.
- All asbestos waste should be disposed of according to OSHA and EPA regulations.

Review Questions

1. At what point is a material considered hazardous?
2. Where in the shop should a list of emergency telephone numbers be posted?
3. When should eye protection be worn?
4. How should a class B fire be extinguished?
5. Where can complete EPA lists of hazardous wastes be found?
6. Safety glasses should have _____.
   a. side protection
   b. shatter-proof lenses
   c. comfortable fit
   d. all of the above
7. Gasoline is _____.
   a. highly volatile and flammable
   b. an excellent tool cleaner
   c. an excellent hand cleaner
   d. all of the above
8. Technician A says it is not necessary to wear shoes with non-slip soles in the shop, but Technician B says it is. Who is correct?
   a. Technician A
   b. Technician B
   c. Both A and B
   d. Neither A nor B
9. Technician A does steam cleaning in a building separate from the shop. Technician B does it in an uncongested part of the shop. Who is correct?
   a. Technician A
   b. Technician B
   c. Both A and B
   d. Neither A nor B
10. Which type of parts cleaning method leaves an ash residue that must be removed by further cleaning?
    a. chemical
    b. abrasive
    c. thermal
    d. steam
11. Federal right-to-know laws concern _____.
    a. auto emission standards
    b. hazards associated with chemicals used in the workplace
    c. employee benefits
    d. hiring practices
12. Which of the following is/are important when working in the automotive shop?
    a. Use the proper tool for the job.
    b. Avoid loose-fitting clothes.
    c. Wear steel-tipped shoes.
    d. All of the above.
13. Which exhaust gas from automobiles is considered dangerous?
    a. carbon dioxide
    b. carbon monoxide
    c. nitrogen
    d. both a and b
14. Which of the following is not recommended to extinguish flammable liquid fires?
    a. foam
    b. carbon dioxide
    c. water
    d. dry chemical

15. Technician A says that some machines can be routinely used beyond their stated capacity. Technician B says that a power tool can be left running unattended if the technician puts up a power on sign. Who is correct?
    a. Technician A
    b. Technician B
    c. Both A and B
    d. Neither A nor B
16. If a substance dissolves metals and other materials, or burns the skin, it is said to possess _____ .
    a. toxicity
    b. reactivity
    c. ignitability
    d. corrosivity
17. Technician A ties his long hair behind his head while working in the shop. Technician B covers her long hair with a brimless cap. Who is correct?
    a. Technician A
    b. Technician B
    c. Both A and B
    d. Neither A nor B
18. Technician A uses compressed air to blow dirt from his clothes and hair. Technician B says this should not be done. Who is correct?
    a. Technician A
    b. Technician B
    c. Both A and B
    d. Neither A nor B
19. Protective gloves should be worn when _____ .
    a. welding
    b. grinding metal
    c. working with caustic cleaning solutions
    d. all of the above
20. Jack stands are used _____ .
    a. with a jack or hoist
    b. in place of a jack or hoist
    c. under sturdy chassis members
    d. both a and c

3 AUTOMOTIVE SYSTEMS

Objectives

- Explain some of the forces and events that have influenced the development of the automobile over the past twenty-five years.
- Explain the difference between unitized and body-over-frame vehicles.
- Describe the manufacturing process used in a modern automated automobile assembly plant.
- List the basic systems that make up an automobile and name their major components and functions.
- Explain the importance of preventive maintenance, and give at least six examples of preventive maintenance procedures performed on automobiles.

Much about the automobile has changed since the first horseless carriage ventured out on American streets. In 1896, the year when both Henry Ford and Ransom Eli Olds test drove their first gasoline-powered vehicles, the automobile looked more like the horse-drawn carriages it was destined to replace than the vehicles now rolling off assembly lines (Figure 3-1). Ninety percent of the cars were open bodies as late as 1919. It was not until 1939 that running boards began disappearing. Most early vehicles had a rear-mounted engine with a carriage-style body. These high-wheeled carriage bodies were well suited for traveling on America's dirt roads. As America and the automobile adapted to each other, the automobile slowly evolved into a sturdy, dependable, and comfortable machine (Figure 3-2). The basic structure of the automobile has changed very little over the years.

Most cars still use a gasoline engine to drive two or more wheels that maintain contact between the vehicle and the road. A steering system is used to control the direction of the car. A brake system is used to slow and halt the movement of the vehicle. A suspension system absorbs road shocks and helps to maintain control on bumpy roads. The components of these major systems are mounted on a steel frame and the frame is clad with body panels that give the vehicle its shape and protect the occupants from inclement weather, airborn matter, and collision injury.

The components and processes used to activate these systems are technologically light-years ahead of

Figure 3-1 The modern automobile has changed greatly from the days of the first horseless carriages.

Automotive Systems

Figure 3-2 The 1925 Pierce Arrow, like most older cars, had the same basic systems found on today's cars.

Figure 3-3 Today's automobile is the result of almost 100 years of innovation. *Courtesy of General Motors Corp.*

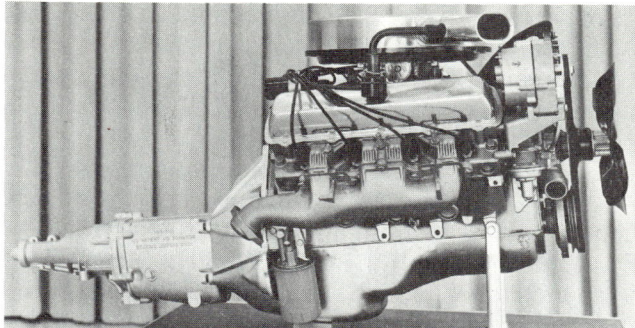

Figure 3-4 The 1965 Oldsmobile 442 engine. *Courtesy of General Motors Corp.*

those used on Ford's and Olds' early models (Figure 3-3). Almost 100 years of innovations and refinements have gone into transforming the slow, unreliable, user-hostile vehicles of the early 1900s into vehicles that travel at speeds in excess of 200 mph, operate trouble-free for thousands of miles, and provide amenities that even the rich had not dreamed of in 1896.

The most dramatic changes have occurred during the past 25 years. By the mid-1960s, the automobile had become overweight, oversized, and flexed a lot of muscle under the hood. Gas-guzzling engines with over 400 cubic inches of displacement, producing 300 horsepower or more, were the norm. For example, in 1965, the Oldsmobile 442 sported a 400 cubic inch V-8 engine, a 4-barrel carburetor, and dual exhaust (Figure 3-4). The power package developed 345 horsepower. However, 1965 also saw the passing of congressional legislation in which the federal government limited the levels of fuel and exhaust emissions. Automotive manufacturers had to produce cleaner-burning engines.

The various emission control systems that were developed and added to the automobile over the next ten years put a damper on the performance output of the big power plants of the 1960s. Compression ratios were lowered. Air/fuel mixtures became leaner. Unleaded gasoline was introduced. Exhaust gases were diverted into the intake manifold. Catalytic converters were added, which increased exhaust back pressures, decreasing volumetric efficiency. Horsepower and torque values began to drop.

Outside forces in the 1970s continued to shape the development of today's automobile. An oil embargo by Arab nations in 1973 caused the price of gasoline to quadruple and force the American car owner to realize that gasoline and other non-renewable resources were limited. Car buyers demanded a car that was not only kind to the atmosphere but one that also efficiently used our limited natural resources.

In 1975, Congress passed the Corporate Average Fuel Economy (CAFE) standards that required auto makers to not only manufacture clean-burning engines, but also to equip their vehicles with engines that burned gasoline efficiently. Under the CAFE standards, various models from each manufacturer were tested for the number of miles they could be driven on a gallon of gas. The fuel efficiencies of these vehicles were averaged together to arrive at a corporate average. A manufacturer that does not meet CAFE standards for a given model year faces heavy fines.

❏ DESIGN EVOLUTION

Through the 1960s and early 1970s, virtually all American automobiles were manufactured with the following design characteristics.

- Body-over-frame construction
- Rear drive
- Independent front suspension
- Symmetrical design

In the mid 1970s, foreign car manufacturers were already offering small, fuel-efficient vehicles to the American market. When gasoline prices skyrocketed, cars and light trucks from Japan and Europe began selling in the United States in unprecedented numbers.

To meet this foreign challenge, domestic auto makers adopted many of the designs and features introduced to America by foreign manufacturers.

In 1977, most cars used a perimeter-type frame. They averaged around 4500 pounds, used 18 gauge mild steel, and were still conventional in design. By

1978, modern unitized construction was used on American-made cars. Body weight began to decrease, thinner gauge metal was used, and the first American-made transverse engine, front-wheel-drive, strut suspension cars were introduced.

By 1981, unibodies were used in almost half the American-made cars. Today, all but a small handful of domestic cars produced are unibodies constructed of 24-gauge high-strength steel. Average vehicle weight is approximately 3,000 pounds. MacPherson struts, rack-and-pinion steering, and front-wheel drive are standard features on many vehicles.

☐ MODERN UNITIZED CONSTRUCTION

Modern or completely unitized design is sometimes called third generation unitized construction, although it is the first true unitized design found in modern domestic vehicles. A unibody has no separate frame (Figure 3-5). It is a stressed hull structure in which each of the components supplies structural support and strength to the entire vehicle.

The major advantage of unibody vehicles is that they tend to be more tightly constructed because the major parts are all welded together. This design characteristic helps protect the occupants during a collision. However, it causes damage patterns that differ from those of body-over-frame vehicles. Rather than localized damage, the stiffer sections used in unibody design tend to transmit and distribute impact energy throughout more of the vehicle.

☐ MODERN BODY-OVER-FRAME CONSTRUCTION

In the body-over-frame construction, the frame is the vehicle's foundation. The body and all major parts of a vehicle are attached to the frame. It must provide

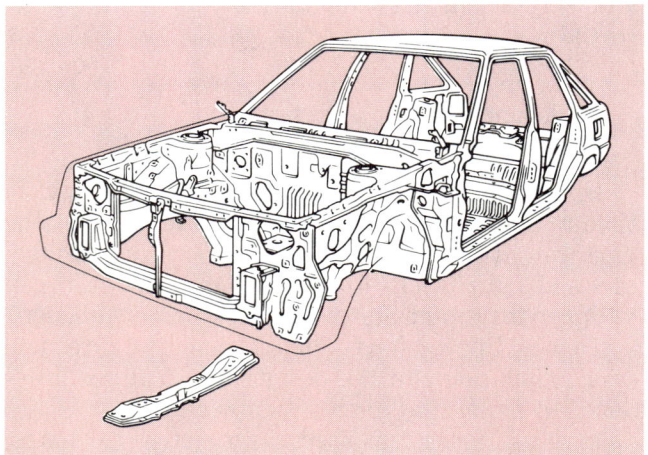

Figure 3-5 Structure of a typical unibody vehicle. *Courtesy of Toyota Motor Corp.*

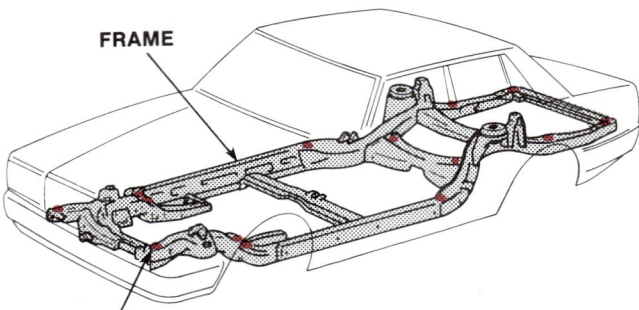

Figure 3-6 Location of rubber biscuits or mounts. *Courtesy of Toyota Motor Corp.*

the support and strength needed by the assemblies and parts attached to it. The frame must also be strong enough to keep the other car parts in alignment should a collision occur.

The conventional frame is an independent, separate component, because it is not welded to any of the major units of the body shell. The body is generally bolted to the frame and large, specially designed rubber or mounts are placed between the frame and body structure to reduce noise and vibration from entering the passenger compartment (Figure 3-6). Quite often, two layers of rubber are used in the mounting pads to provide a smoother ride. In higher priced vehicles, a shock absorber is mounted between the body and the rear frame, which serves to minimize vibrations when the car is traveling at high speeds.

Today, the strong steel frame side members are normally made of U-shaped channel sections or box-shaped sections. Cross members of the same material reinforce the frame and provide support for the wheels, engine, and suspension systems. Various brackets, braces, and openings are provided to permit installation of the many parts that make up the automotive chassis.

Modern body-over-frame designs are still used on many of today's pick-up trucks, full-size vans, and some full-size passenger cars.

☐ BODY SHAPES

Various methods of classifying vehicles exist—by engine type, body/frame construction, fuel consumption structure, and type of drive. The classifications most common to consumers are the use of body shape, seat arrangement, and number of doors.

Six basic body shapes are used today.

1. Sedan. A vehicle with front and back seats that accommodates four to six persons is classified as either a two- or four-door sedan (Figure 3-7).
2. Hardtop. A vehicle with front and back seats, a hardtop is generally characterized by a lack of door or B pillars (Figure 3-8). It can also be classified as either a two- or four-door hardtop.

Automotive Systems

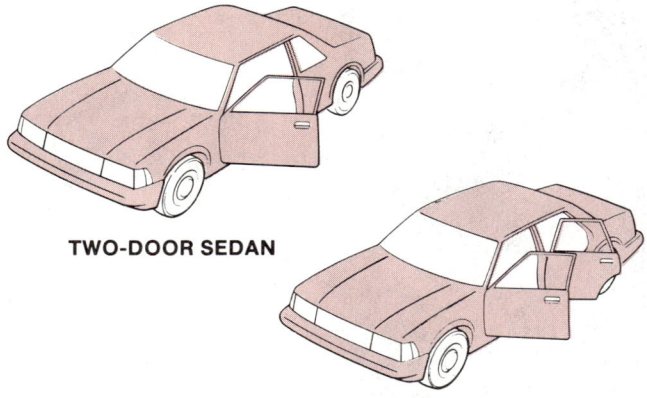

Figure 3–7 Typical sedan body shapes.

Figure 3–8 Typical hardtop body shapes.

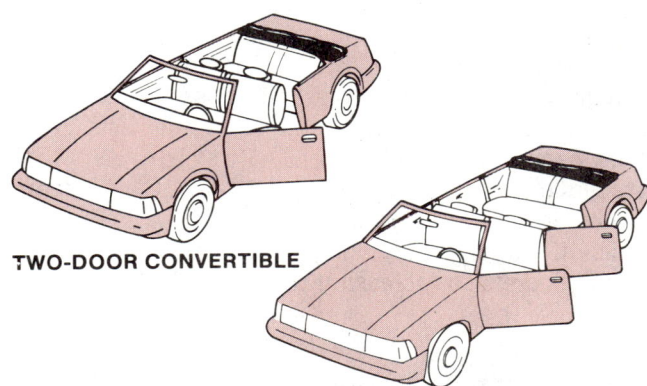

Figure 3–9 Typical convertible body shapes.

3. Convertible top. After an absence from the domestic market for several years, the convertible top made a comeback in 1985. Today's convertible top vehicle has a vinyl roof that can be raised or lowered (Figure 3–9). Like a hardtop, a convertible top has no door pillars and, depending on the make, can be purchased with or without a back

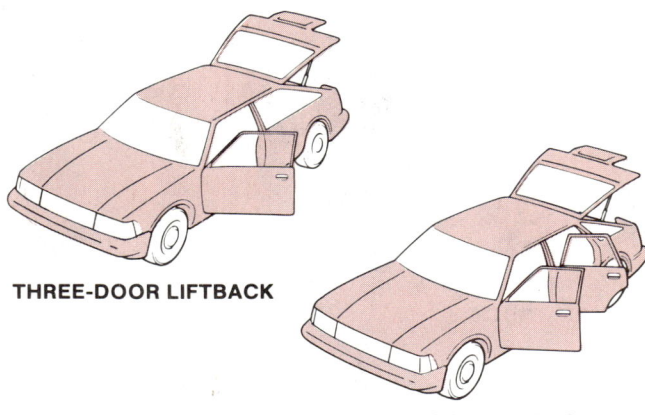

Figure 3–10 Typical liftback or hatchback body shapes.

window. It is available in two- and four-door models.

4. Liftback or hatchback. The distinguishing feature of this vehicle is its rear luggage compartment, which is an extension of the passenger compartment. Access to the luggage compartment is gained through an upward opening hatch-type door (Figure 3–10). The vehicle comes in three- and five-door models.

5. Station wagon. A station wagon (Figure 3–11) is characterized by its roof, which extends straight back for the length of the vehicle, allowing a spacious interior luggage compartment in the rear. The rear door, which can be opened in various ways depending on the model, provides access to the luggage compartment. Station wagons come in three- and five-door models and have space for up to nine passengers.

6. Utility or multi-purpose vehicles. This new classification of vehicles covers a range of body designs (Figure 3–12). They are available in two-wheel drive, four-wheel drive (4×4), or all-wheel drive. Pick-up truck body designs are available with

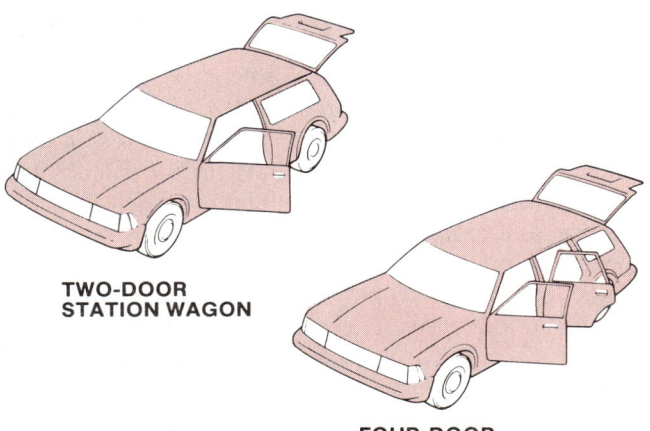

Figure 3–11 Typical station wagon body shapes.

32 Section 1   Automotive Technology

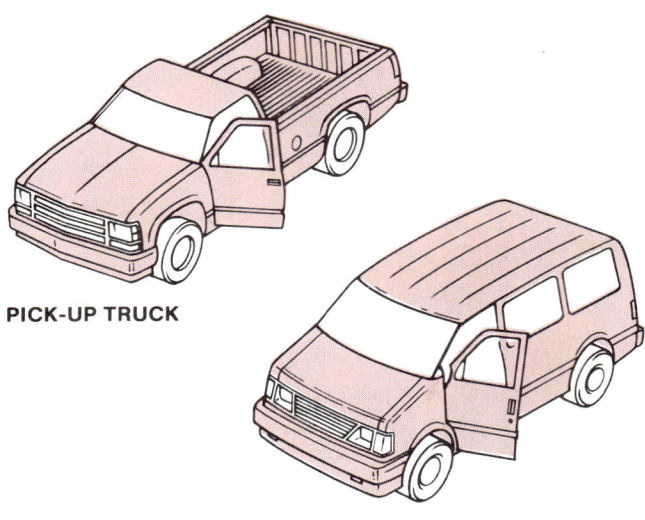

Figure 3-12   Typical sports vehicle body shapes.

Figure 3-13   The Quad 4 is an example of the highly efficient engines developed in the late 1980s. *Courtesy of General Motors Corp.*

standard cab designs, with extended cab areas (some have added seats in back of the front seat), and some with open or closed pick-up spaces. Sports vehicles appeal to the outdoor enthusiast who wants both road and off-road applications. Vans are considered sports vehicles for family use.

❏ MODERN POWER PLANTS

In the move to produce more efficient vehicles, V-8s were passed over in favor of small, four-cylinder engines. Some holdovers from the automobile's infancy—like carburetors and ignition breaker points—were shelved. Fuel injection systems and electronic ignition systems became characteristics of the maturing automobile.

By the mid-1980s the American automobile had gained a measure of self-control over emissions and fuel efficiency via microprocessors (computers) and related electronics. Fuel and air were carefully monitored and consumed in proportions that optimized the performance of the smaller engine while minimizing the production of harmful pollutants.

After a prolonged period of economic growth in the 1980s, the demand for power performance is once again a shaping force in automotive developments. However, this time the industry is responding with sophistication and responsibility. Electronic sensors are used to monitor consumption, performance, and emissions. Computerized engine control systems control air and fuel delivery, ignition timing, emission systems operation, and a host of other related operations. The result is a clean-burning, fuel-efficient, and powerful engine. An example of this is Oldsmobile's Quad 4 (Figure 3-13). This engine is a four-cylinder power plant with four valves per cylinder. It is multi-port, fuel-injected, and has double overhead cams. The high-output version has a compression ratio of 10 to 1 and develops 180 horsepower.

❏ THE ELECTRONIC REVOLUTION

The most influential catalyst in the recent evolution in automobile design is microcomputers. Not only are engine support systems subjected to control by on-board computers, every other major system on a car has some sort of electronic control or assist.

The revolution in construction materials and computer technology is continuing. Engine designs are becoming so sophisticated that some emission control systems are no longer necessary. Electronics are being integrated into more and more components. New composite materials are being used for engine parts. Steel body panels are being replaced with plastic parts that are glued to a space frame (Figure 3-14). Experiments are being conducted to create an engine that can run efficiently and reliably on alcohol-based fuels. Developments are also increasing the possibility that other

Figure 3-14   All exterior panels on this van are bonded to a space frame with adhesives. *Courtesy of General Motors Corp.*

engine types—such as two-stroke engines, Stirling engines, solar-powered engines, and battery-powered electronic motors—may all be used to power future automobiles.

❑ BUILDING MODERN VEHICLES

There has also been a technology revolution in the way vehicles are manufactured. The basic principles of assembly line production introduced by Henry Ford in 1914 still hold true. However, much of the labor is performed by computer-controlled robotics systems. Workers now spend the majority of their time monitoring these systems and performing constant quality control checks and tests.

The following sections describe the assembly techniques used at a state-of-the-art domestic assembly plant. It features just-in-time delivery of parts and materials. Inventory and parts handling costs are kept to a minimum. All handling of parts and materials is fully automated and computer controlled (Figure 3-15).

Automated guided vehicles (AGVs) move the vehicle bodies through the assembly process. The AGVs are guided by electrical impulses from grids laid in the concrete floor of the plant. Robotic welders also communicate electronically, signalling each other as to when to move and work. The entire assembly process is highly orchestrated and extremely precise. A typical car body shell may contain 840 different welds made by 225 robots. The welds must be within 1/25 inch of their target.

The entire assembly process is run by a system known as programmable logic control (PLC). This system does not simply give orders. It monitors conditions and adjusts the plant's rhythm accordingly. If there are problems, it pinpoints them. It recalls past problems and recommends corrections. It also controls maintenance. It takes about a day and a half to complete a vehicle on this line. This is not a production speed record. Quality measures, including extensive corrosion protection, have slowed things down. The assembly process begins with the just-in-time delivery of the engine, transaxle, suspension components, electrical system, and some inner body parts from the manufacturer's component divisions and original equipment manufacturer (OEM) suppliers. As these are fed into the system, the stamping department is making outer body panels—roofs, hoods, deck lids, fenders, quarter panels—from coils of two-sided galvanized steel. The stampings are monitored constantly for thickness, fit, and finish. Quality reports are issued hourly.

The unwelded body panels are assembled together on a locating fixture on an AGV that moves it through the welding process. First, the body goes through a welding robogate where an initial 70 welds are made in 44 seconds. This is where some of the safety features built into the vehicle begin—like the side door guard beams. The body then moves to other stations for another 760 welds. The entire welding process takes 11.5 minutes.

The body then is taken off the AGV and put on a special conveyor system that moves it through the paint shop. Separated by four-foot spaces, the bodies move through the assembly process. The body is washed first with phosphate and then a bonding agent. The entire body is then dropped into an electrodeposition dip. This is a process involving the use of an electrical charge to coat the body with corrosion-resistant primer. A sealer is then applied and the body is baked for an hour at 350 degrees Fahrenheit.

The body then moves through a neon-bright preparation booth. Here technicians inspect the body for flaws and hand sand any minor surface imperfections. Next, it is given an alcohol bath and passed through rotating ostrich feather dusters. (Ostrich feathers do not create static electricity that would attract dirt and lint to the body.)

Next, the body moves into one of two color booths. Here, the body is electrically grounded. A charge of 80,000 volts of electricity is applied to the body as a paint ball rotates as fast as 30,000 rpm, discharging the paint onto the sedan. There is no mist or paint flying in the air. The body just changes color as the electrical charge attracts the paint to the body. It takes 1.5 minutes to apply the color coat.

The color coat is baked dry, then the clear coat is applied and baked. The baking process is vital as the color and clear coats will not air dry. The total time in the paint shop is 10 hours out of the total assembly time of 36 hours per car.

A technician stands at a computer console to monitor the paint shop. With the aid of the computer, the technician can quickly pinpoint bodies that require special attention and pull them out of the line.

Figure 3-15 Modern vehicle assembly lines use computer-controlled robotics systems. *Courtesy of General Motors Corp.*

A small transponder mounted under the front of the body electronically tells every station in the department all about the car. It tells what color the car should be, whether it is a two-door or four-door, what engine is to be installed, and what options are required. It is all part of the PLC.

After the paint shop, the doors are removed and the body and doors are sent separately to the trim shop. The doors are taken off so the interior and instrument panel can be installed.

Meanwhile, on the engine line, the engine for the vehicle is having the transaxle, wiring, hoses, and exhaust system attached. The front and rear subassemblies with suspension components are put together on a jig. Then the power train is dropped into place. The term power train is often used to describe both the engine and the drivetrain.

As part of the general assembly process, the body goes to glass installation for the windshield, backlight, and rear quarter windows. Meanwhile, glass is installed in the doors. Finally, weather-protection seals are applied to the doors and they are reattached to the original body. At this point all components meet at the so-called marriage point. Here, the bodies meet the appropriate power train and subassemblies, which are on carts with hydraulic lifts. They are raised to be attached to the bodies. Workers remove locator pins and replace them with bolts to attach mechanical components to the body. The vehicle then moves down the line for tires, wheels, moldings, and bumpers. It then hits the roll-off point where monitors make sure standards are met. The cars are driven to a station where headlights are aimed and wheels aligned.

Finally, at the last station, a web of umbilical cords from a computer are hooked to appropriate points on the car for a 30-point systems check—electrical, gauges, lights, engine performance, transaxle performance, and steering. Finally, if all quality checks are met, the vehicle is moved out to the holding lot for shipment to a dealership.

❑ THE BASIC ENGINE

In a passenger car or truck, the engine provides the power to drive the wheels through the transmission—usually by a clutch or torque converter—and driving axle. All automobile engines, both gasoline and diesel, are classified as internal combustion engines because the combustion or burning that creates heat energy takes place inside the engine. These systems require an air/fuel mixture that arrives in the combustion chamber with exact timing and an engine constructed to withstand the temperatures and pressures created by thousands of fuel droplets burning.

The following descriptions apply to gasoline engines (Figure 3-16). Diesel engines share the same major parts, but they do not use a spark to ignite an air/fuel mixture.

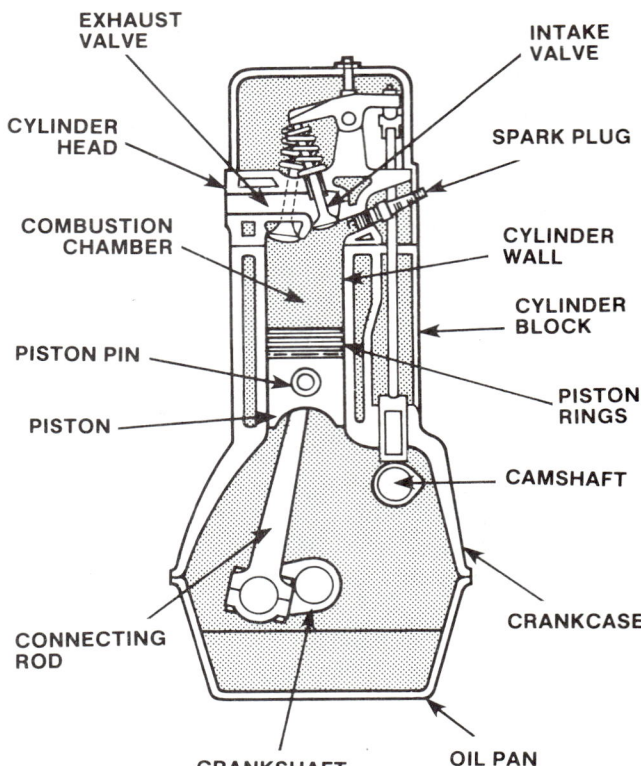

Figure 3-16 Basic parts of a reciprocating piston gasoline engine.

Cylinder Block

The biggest part of the engine is the cylinder block, which is also called an engine block (Figure 3-17). The cylinder block is a large casting of metal that is drilled with holes to allow for the passage of lubricants and coolant through the block and provide spaces for movement of mechanical parts. The block contains the cylinders, which are round passageways fitted with pistons. The block houses or holds the major mechanical parts of the engine.

Figure 3-17 The cylinder block is the foundation of the engine.

Cylinder Head

The cylinder head fits on top of the cylinder block to close off and seal the top of the cylinder. The combustion chamber is an area into which the air/fuel mixture is compressed and burned. The cylinder head contains all or most of the combustion chamber. The cylinder head also contains ports, which are passageways through which the air/fuel mixture enters and burned gases exit the cylinder.

Valve Train

A valve train is a series of parts used to open and close the intake and exhaust ports. A valve is a movable part that opens and closes a passageway. A camshaft controls the movement of the valves (Figure 3-18), causing them to open and close at the proper time.

Piston

The burning of air and fuel occurs between the cylinder head and the top of the piston. The piston is a can-shaped part closely fitted inside the cylinder. In an engine with a four-stroke cycle, the piston has four strokes or movements: intake, compression, power, and exhaust. On the intake stroke, the piston moves downward, and a charge of air/fuel mixture is introduced into the cylinder. As the piston travels upward, the air/fuel mixture is compressed in preparation for burning. When the piston returns to the top of the cylinder, combustion occurs, and forces the piston downward on its power stroke. When it reciprocates, or moves upward again, the piston pushes the burned gases out of the cylinder.

Connecting Rods and Crankshaft

The reciprocating motion must be converted to rotary motion before it can drive the wheels of a vehicle.

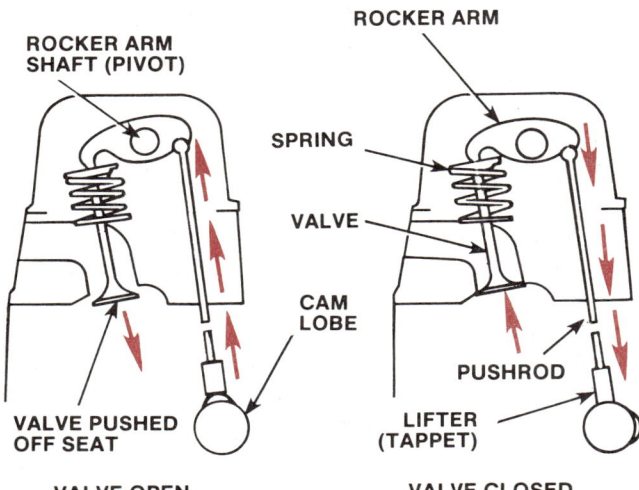

Figure 3-18 The valve train opens and closes the intake and exhaust ports.

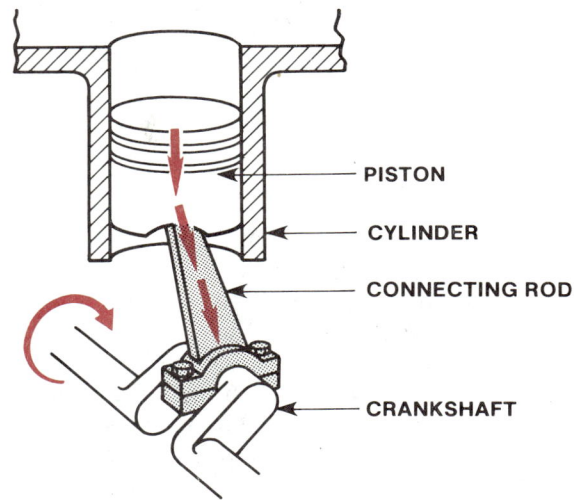

Figure 3-19 The crankshaft changes reciprocating motion to rotary motion.

As shown in Figure 3-19, this conversion is achieved by linking the piston to a crankshaft with a connecting rod. The upper end of the connecting rod moves with the piston as it moves up and down in the cylinder. The lower end of the connecting rod is attached to the crankshaft and moves in a circle. The end of the crankshaft is connected to the transmission to continue the power flow through the drivetrain and to the wheels.

Manifolds

A manifold is metal ductwork assembly used to direct the flow of gases to or from the combustion chambers. To separate manifolds, metal fixtures attach to the cylinder head (Figure 3-20). The intake manifold delivers a mix of outside air and fuel vapor to the intake ports. The exhaust manifold mounts over the exhaust ports and carries exhaust gases away from the cylinders. The design of the manifolds has a critical effect on volumetric efficiency, or how easily an engine breathes. An engine that can gulp down more air per intake stroke burns more fuel, making more power than an engine that does not breathe as efficiently.

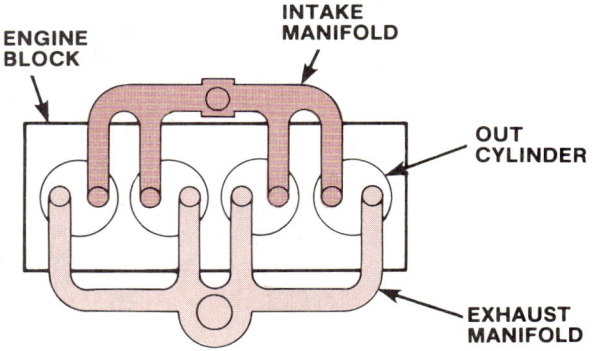

Figure 3-20 Manifolds direct gases in and out of the combustion chambers.

◻ MECHANICAL SYSTEMS

The following sections present a brief explanation of the systems used in modern vehicles and their basic functions.

Lubrication System

The moving parts of an engine need constant lubrication to prevent premature wear and the buildup of frictional heat to dangerous levels. Friction is the resistance to motion that occurs when two objects rub against each other.

Motor or engine oil is the lubricating fluid used. Several quarts of oil are stored in an oil pan bolted to the bottom of the engine block. When the engine is operating, an oil pump draws oil from the pan and forces it through a network of oil galleries. These galleries are small passageways that direct the lubricating oil to the moving components of the engine, particularly the crankshaft, connecting rods, and cylinder walls.

Oil from the pan or sump is run through an oil filter before passing to other sections of the engine (Figure 3-21). The filter removes dirt and metal particles from the oil so they will not harm precision machined and matched engine parts. Regular replacement of the lubrication system oil filter and oil is an important preventive maintenance requirement.

Cooling System

The burning of the air/fuel mixture in the combustion chambers of the engine produces high amounts of heat. If left unchecked, this heat could damage and warp metal engine parts. To avoid this, engines are equipped with a cooling system (Figure 3-22).

The most common method used to cool an engine is to circulate a liquid coolant through the engine block and cylinder head. Liquid cooling is preferable to air cooling because it is less noisy and is better able to maintain a constant temperature at the cylinders. It also lets the engine operate more efficiently and makes a ready supply of hot coolant available to operate a heater for the passage compartment.

A cooling system is made up of the following components.

- Pump. Circulates the cooling liquid through the system. The liquid is a mixture of water and antifreeze that is referred to as coolant.
- Water jackets. Cored passages in the cylinder block and cylinder head that carry the coolant around the cylinder's combustion chambers.
- Radiator. Transfers the coolant's heat to the outside air as the coolant flows through its tubes.
- Fan. A device that pulls cool outside air through the fins of the radiator to help cool the coolant.
- Pressure cap. Maintains a pressure in the system to raise the boiling point of the coolant. Also provides relief from excess pressure or vacuum.
- Hoses. Connect the components of the system to one another.
- Thermostat. Blocks off circulation in the system until a preset temperature is reached to speed engine warmup. Also, keeps engine temperature to a predetermined level.
- Temperature indicator. Warns the driver in case of overheating.

Fuel System

The fuel system supplies a combustible mixture of gasoline and air to the engine's cylinders. To do this, the fuel system must store the fuel, deliver fuel to the metering devices, atomize and mix the fuel with air, and vary the proportion of fuel-to-air to satisfy the many load requirements of the engine.

The fuel system uses several components to accomplish these tasks. A fuel tank stores the gasoline in liquid form. Fuel lines carry the liquid from the tank to the other parts of the system. A pump moves the gasoline from the tank. A filter removes dirt or other harm-

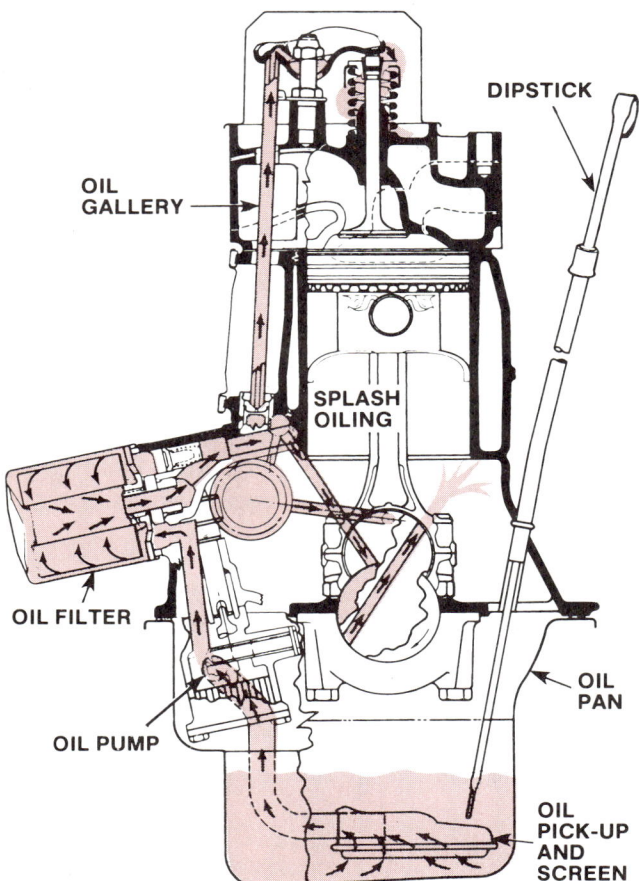

Figure 3-21 The lubrication system distributes oil throughout the engine. *Courtesy of Buick Motor Division—GMC*

Automotive Systems 37

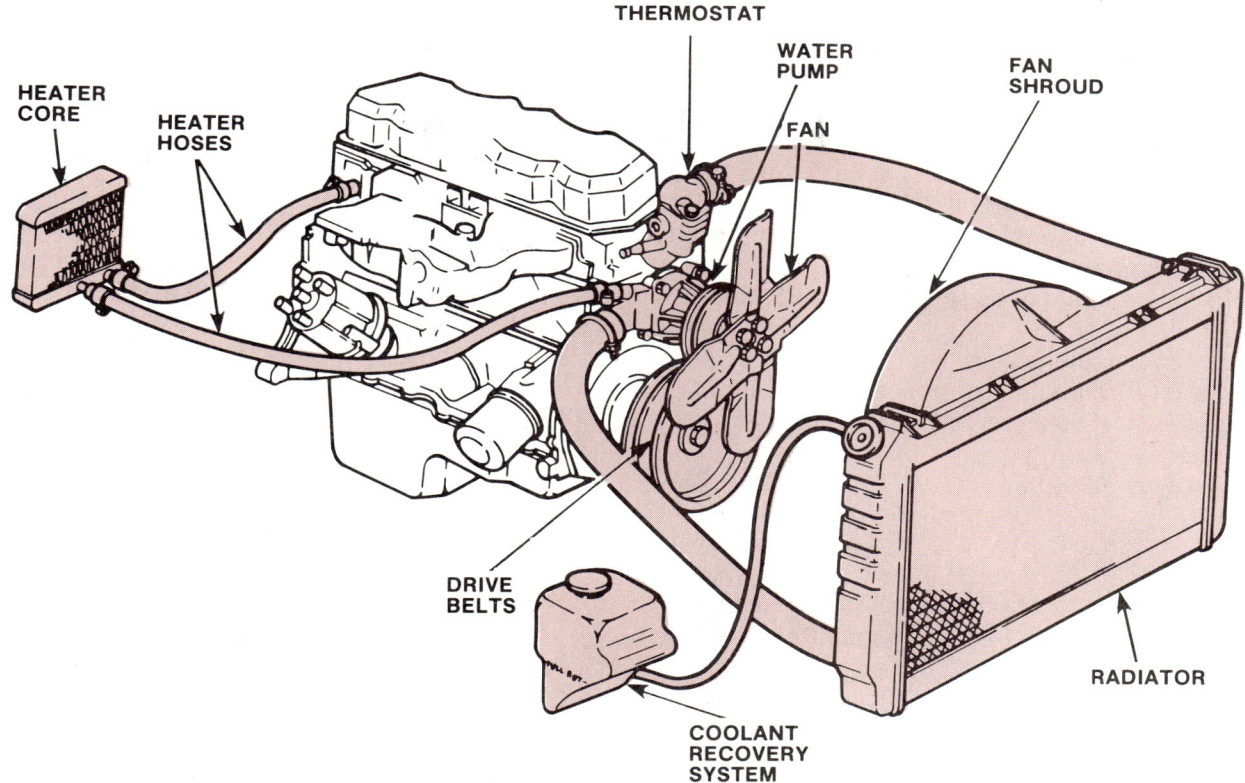

Figure 3-22 Typical automotive cooling system. *Courtesy of Buick Motor Division—GMC*

ful particles that might be in the fuel. A fuel pressure regulator keeps the pressure below a specified level. Fuel injectors or a carburetor mix the liquid gasoline with air for delivery to the cylinders after the air has passed through an air filter. An intake manifold directs the air/fuel mixture to each of the cylinders. The components of a typical fuel system are shown in Figure 3-23.

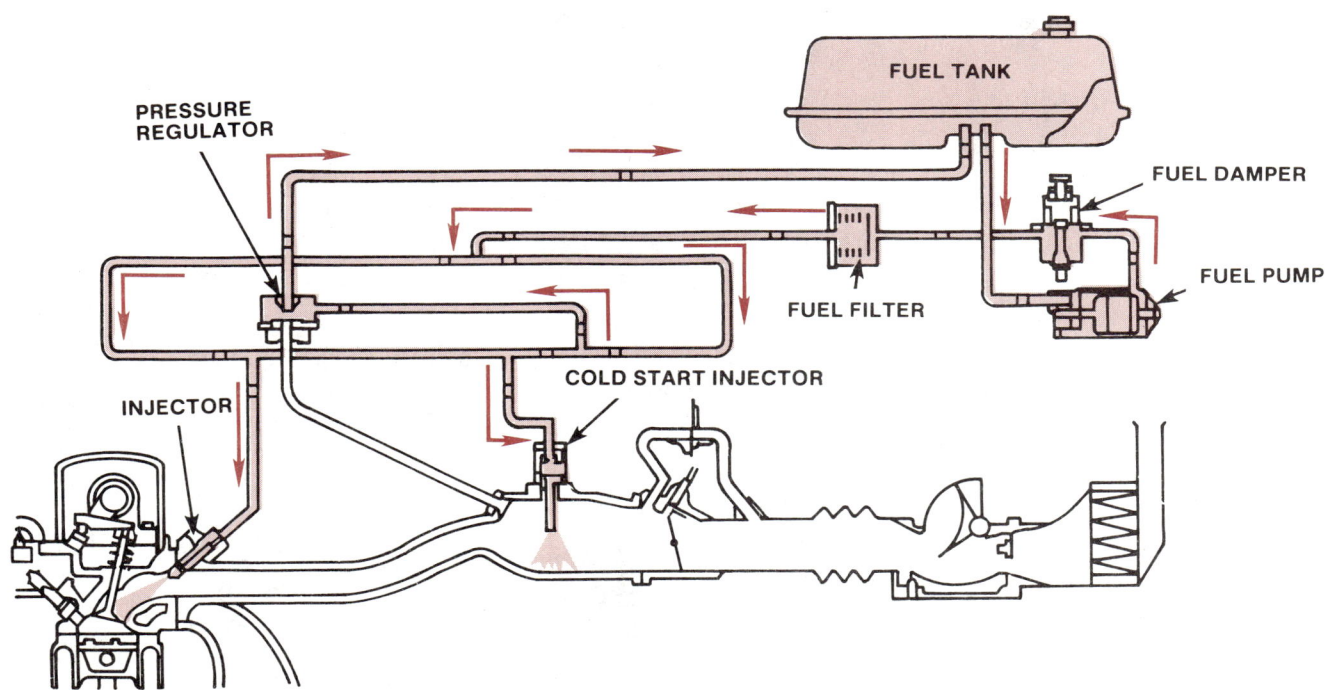

Figure 3-23 Parts of a fuel system.

Emission Control System

Car manufacturers are required by the federal government to produce cars that emit less than a certain amount of pollutants. Some of the major vehicle emissions that are harmful to individual health and to the environment are hydrocarbons (HC), carbon monoxide (CO), and oxides of nitrogen (NO_x). The Environmental Protection Agency establishes emissions standards that limit the amount of these pollutants that a vehicle can emit.

Car manufacturers have equipped their engines with a variety of emission control devices and systems. A list of the most common follows.

- Positive crankcase ventilation (PCV) system. Draws fuel and oil vapors from the crankcase and introduces them into the intake air to be burned.
- Evaporative emission controls (EEC) system. Draws fuel vapors from the fuel tank and the carburetor bowl and introduces them into the intake air to be burned.
- Exhaust gas recirculation (EGR) system. Introduces exhaust gases into the intake air to reduce the formation of oxides of nitrogen in the combustion chamber.
- Catalytic converter. Burns hydrocarbons and carbon monoxide in the exhaust stream. Also breaks down oxides of nitrogen into harmless nitrogen and oxygen.
- Air injection system. Introduces fresh air into the exhaust stream to cause a second burning of the hydrocarbons in the exhaust.
- Early fuel evaporation (EFE) system. Warms intake air to reduce the condensation of fuel on the walls of the intake manifold and to speed the warmup of the vehicle.

Exhaust System

As each piston reaches its top dead center position on its exhaust stroke, the burned air/fuel mixture, or exhaust, is forced out of the combustion chamber and into the exhaust manifold. From the manifold the gases travel on to the other parts of the exhaust system (Figure 3-24). The exhaust system is designed to channel toxic exhaust fumes away from the passenger compartment, to quiet the sound of the exhaust pulses, and to burn or catalyze emissions in the exhaust. A typical exhaust system contains the following components.

- exhaust manifold and gasket
- exhaust pipe, seal, and connector pipe
- intermediate pipes
- catalytic converter
- muffler
- resonator
- tail pipe
- heat shields
- clamps, gaskets, and hangers

On some engines, the exhaust system performs several other functions. Some vehicles have a stove on the exhaust manifold that is used to heat the incoming air. A hot-air pipe or hose leads up from the manifold to the air cleaner snorkel and carries heated air to mix with the normal intake air.

Some engines use manifold heat to warm a section of the intake manifold. An exhaust crossover passage directs exhaust under the intake manifold, warming

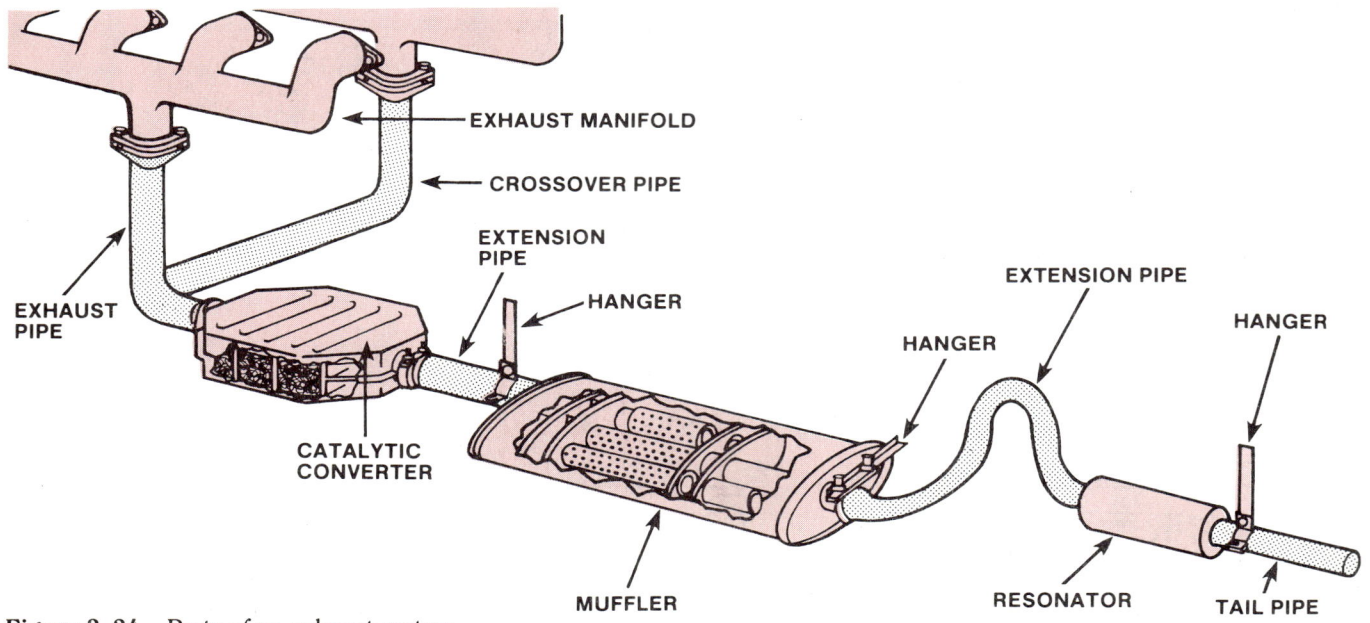

Figure 3-24 Parts of an exhaust system.

Automotive Systems 39

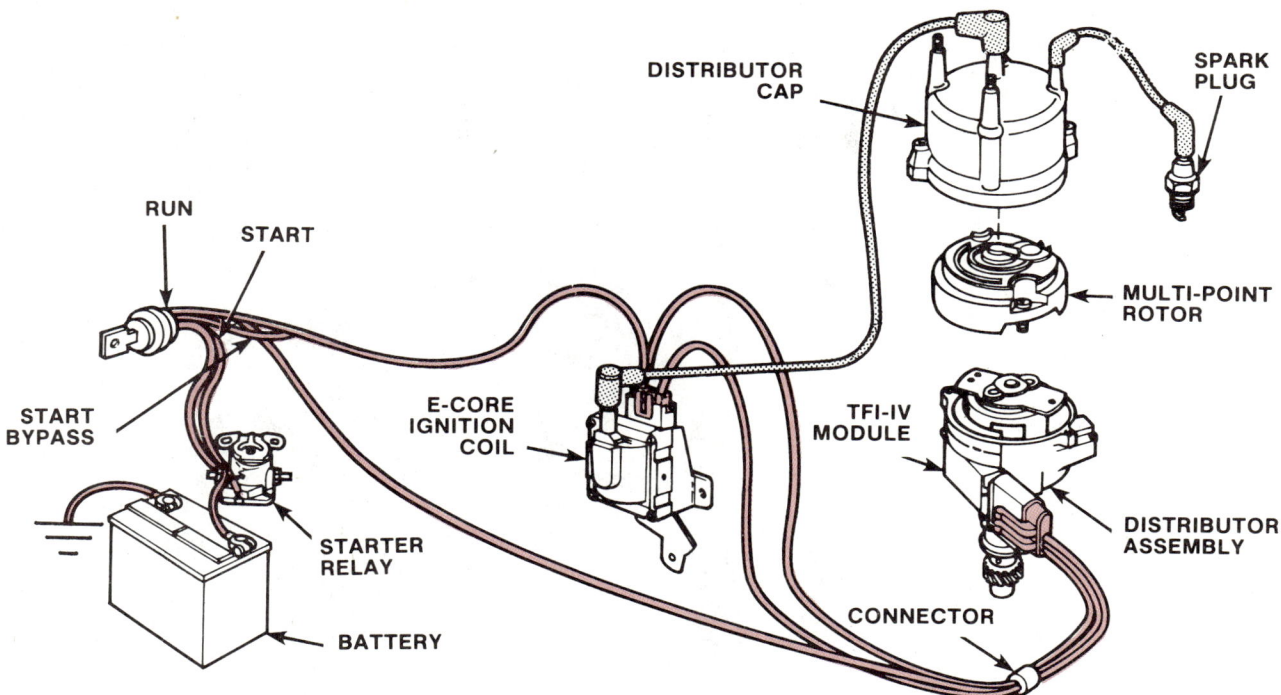

Figure 3-25 The ignition system generates the necessary electrical spark. *Courtesy of Ford Motor Co.*

the air/fuel charge. This improves cold engine operation.

Electrical and Electronic Systems

Automobiles have many circuits that carry electrical current from the battery to individual components. The total electrical system includes such major subsystems as the ignition system, starting system, charging system, and the lighting and other electrical systems.

Ignition System

After the air/fuel charge has been delivered to the cylinder and compressed by the piston, it must be ignited. A gasoline engine uses an electrical spark to ignite the mixture. Generating this spark is the role of the ignition system (Figure 3-25).

The electricity necessary to create the spark is generated by a coil. The coil transforms the low voltage of the battery into a burst of 20,000 to 100,000 volts. The generation of this surge of high voltage must be timed to arrive at the cylinder at just the right moment during the piston's compression stroke. On many engines, the motion of the piston and the rotation of the crankshaft is monitored by a crankshaft position sensor. The sensor electronically tracks the position of the crankshaft and relays that information to an ignition control module. Based on input from the crankshaft position sensor, and, in some systems, the electronic engine control computer, the ignition control module then turns the battery current to the coil on and off at just the precise time so that the voltage surge arrives at the cylinder at the right time.

The voltage surge from the coil must be distributed to the correct cylinder since only one cylinder is fired at a time. In some systems, this is the job of the distributor. The distributor is driven by a gear on the crankshaft at one half of the crankshaft speed. It transfers the high-voltage surges from the coil to high-tension spark plug wires in the correct firing order.

The spark plug wires deliver the voltage surges to the spark plugs, which are screwed into the cylinder head. The voltage jumps across a space between two electrodes on the end of each spark plug and a spark is created. This spark causes the air/fuel mixture in the combustion chamber to ignite.

Many ignition systems do not have a distributor. Instead, these systems have several coils—one for each pair of spark plugs (Figure 3-26). When a coil is activated by the electronic control module, the voltage surge is sent directly to two spark plugs, which fire simultaneously. One spark plug fires during the compression stroke of a cylinder and the other fires during the exhaust stroke and is wasted. In this way, the electronic control module controls both the timing and the distribution of the coil's spark-producing voltage.

Starting and Charging Systems

The starting system initiates engine operation (Figure 3-27). When the ignition key is turned to the start position, a small amount of current flows from the battery to a solenoid or relay switch. When activated, this switch closes another electrical circuit that allows full battery voltage to reach the starter motor. The

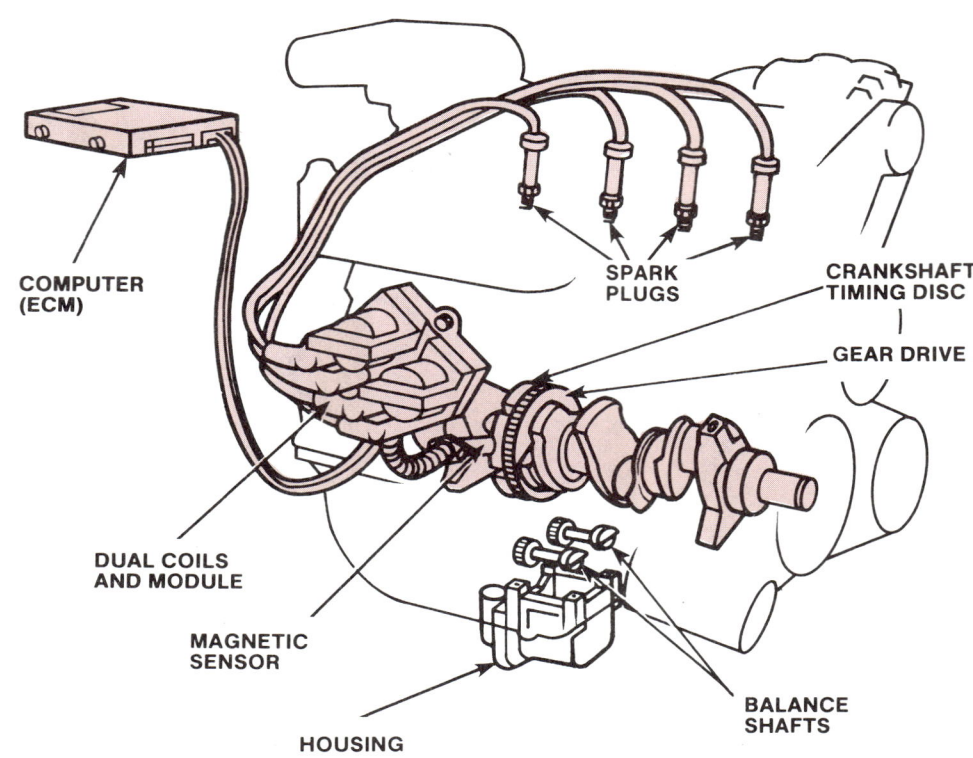

Figure 3-26 Typical distributorless ignition system.

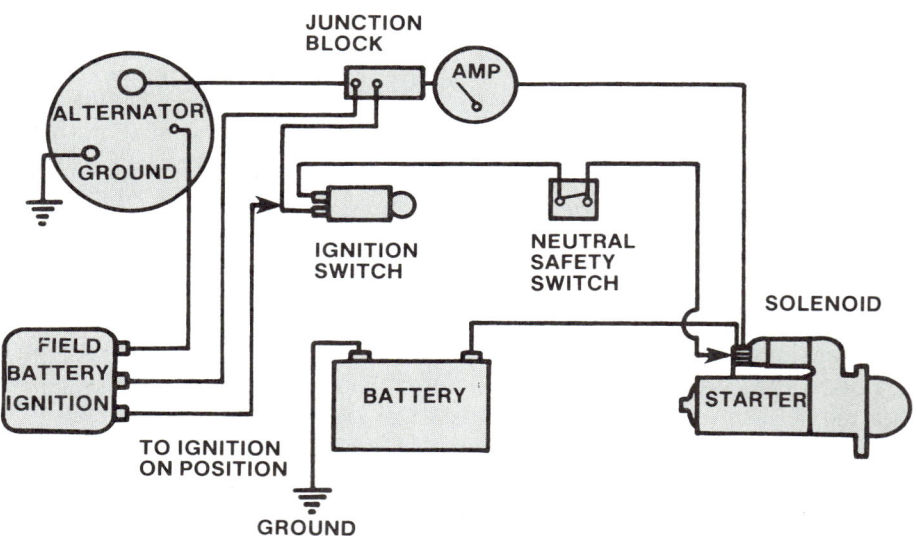

Figure 3-27 Schematic of a typical starting system.

starter motor then turns the flywheel mounted on the rear of the crankshaft that starts all engine parts in motion. The ignition system provides a spark that ignites the air/fuel mixture. Once this is started, the ignition key is turned to the on position. From this point on, the engine is self-sustaining until the ignition key is turned off, cutting ignition spark power.

The charging system maintains the battery's state of charge and provides electrical power for the ignition system, air-conditioner, heater, lights, radio, and all electrical accessories when the engine is running.

In addition to the battery, the charging system includes the alternator or generator, voltage regulator, indicator light, and the necessary wiring (Figure 3-28).

Turned by a drive belt driven by the engine crankshaft, the charging unit—either the generator or, most likely, an alternator—converts mechanical energy into electrical energy. When the electrical current flows into the battery, the battery is said to be charging. When the current flows out of the battery, the battery is said to be discharging.

Electronic Engine Controls (EEC)

An electronic engine control system is an assembly of electronic and electromechanical components that

Automotive Systems   **41**

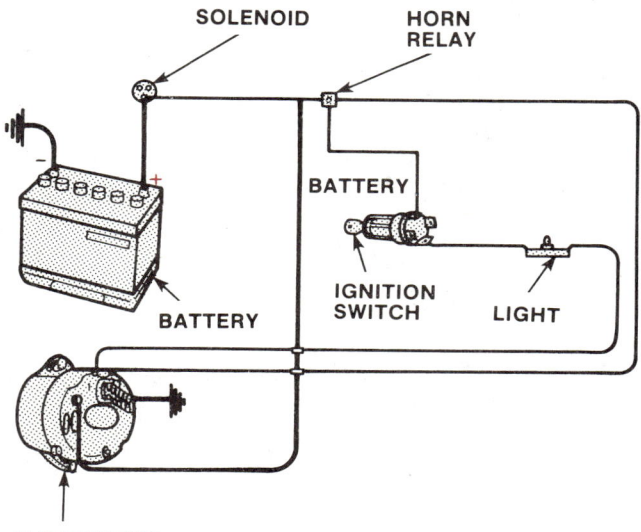

Figure 3-28 Typical charging system circuit.

continuously monitor engine operation to meet emission, fuel economy, and driveability requirements. Electronic control systems have three main types of components: input sensors, a microprocessor or computer, and output devices (Figure 3-29). The computer analyzes data from the input sensors and then directs the output devices to alter engine systems operation accordingly. The use of electronic engine controls have given the automotive manufacturer the capability to meet federal government regulations by controlling various engine systems accurately. In addition, electronic control systems have fewer moving parts than old style mechanical and vacuum controls. Therefore, the engine and other support systems can maintain their calibration almost indefinitely.

As an added advantage, an electronic control system is very flexible. Because it uses microcomputers, it can be modified through programming changes to meet a variety of different vehicle engine combinations or calibrations. Critical quantities that determine an engine's performance can be changed easily by changing data that is stored in the system's computer memory.

DRIVETRAIN

The drivetrain is made up of all components that transfer power from the engine to the driving wheels of the vehicle. The exact components used in a vehicle's drivetrain depend on whether the vehicle is equipped with rear-wheel drive, front-wheel drive, or four-wheel drive (Figure 3-30).

Power flow through the drivetrain of a rear-wheel-drive vehicle passes through the clutch or torque converter, manual or automatic transmission, and the

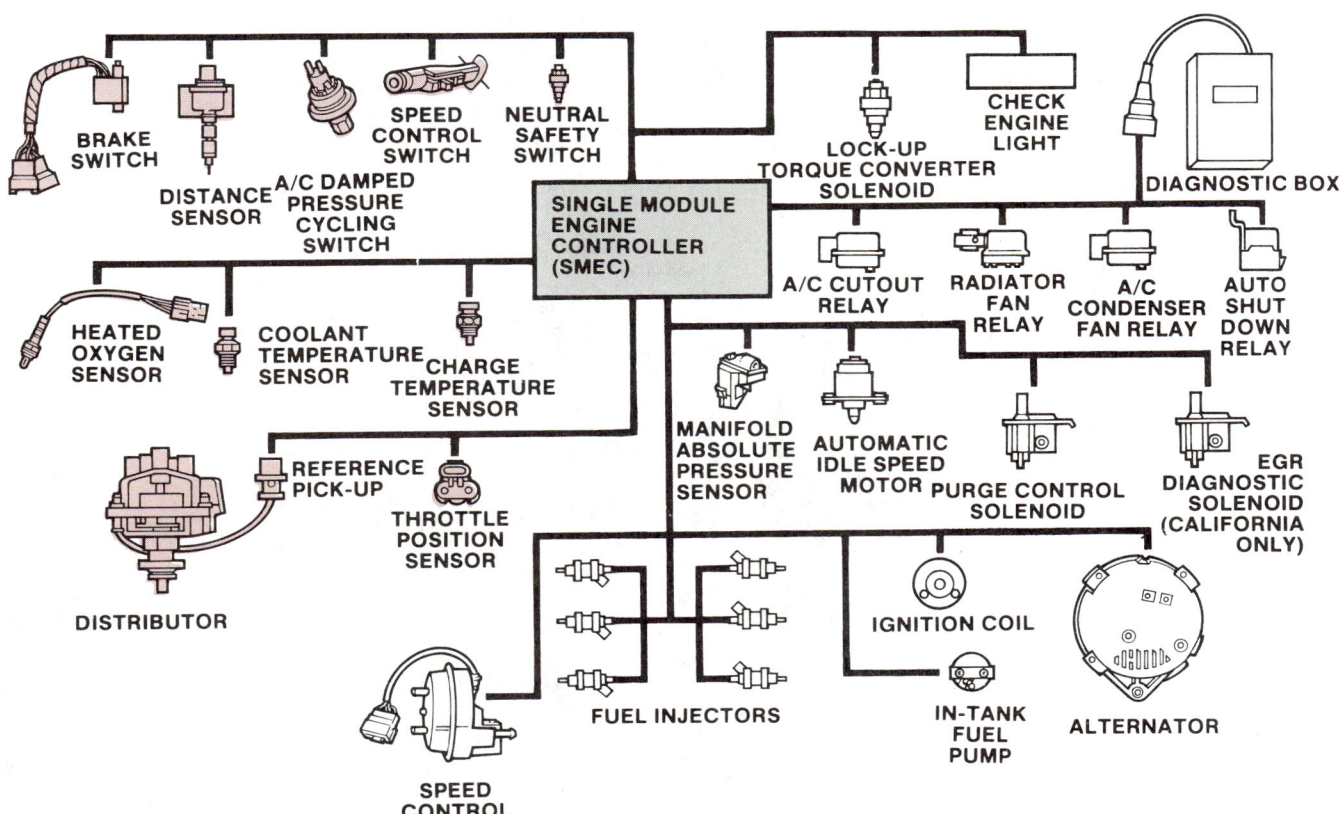

Figure 3-29 Electronic control systems rely on input sensors, central processing computers, and output devices. *Courtesy of Chrysler Motors*

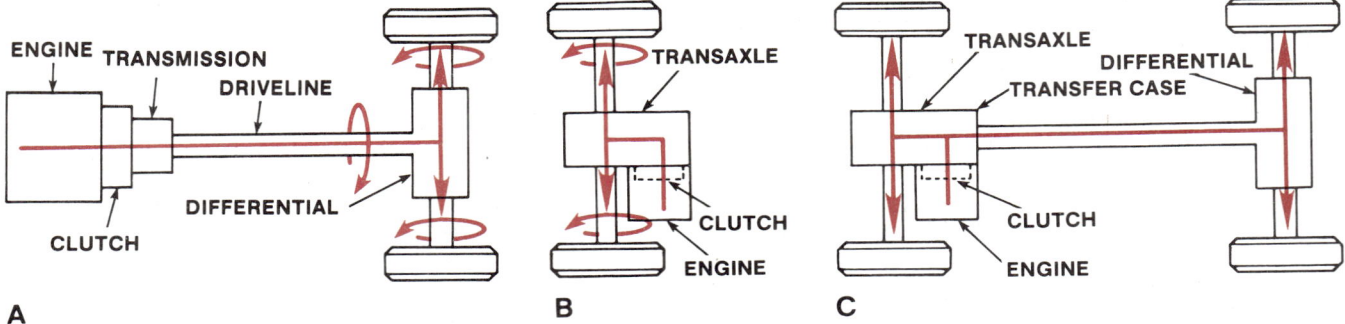

Figure 3-30 Typical drivetrains (A) rear-wheel drive, (B) front-wheel drive, and (C) four-wheel drive.

driveline (drive shaft assembly). Then it goes through the rear differential, the rear-driving axles, and onto the rear wheels.

Power flow through the drivetrain of a front-wheel-drive vehicle passes through the clutch or torque converter, manual or automatic transaxle, front-driving axles, and onto the front wheels.

Four-wheel-drive, or all-wheel-drive, vehicles combine features of both rear- and front-wheel-drive systems so that power can be delivered to all wheels either on a permanent or on-demand basis.

Clutches

Clutches are used on vehicles with manual transmissions/transaxles. The clutch is used to mechanically connect the engine's flywheel to the transmission/transaxle input shaft (Figure 3-31). It does this through the use of a special friction plate that is splined to the input shaft. When the clutch is engaged, the friction plate contacts the flywheel, transferring power through the plate to the input shaft.

When stopping, starting, and shifting from one gear to the next, the clutch is disengaged by pushing in the clutch pedal. This moves the clutch plate away from the flywheel. Power flow to the transmission stops. The drive can then shift gears without damaging the transmission or transaxle. Slowly releasing the clutch reengages the clutch, and power flow resumes.

Manual Transmissions

A manual or standard transmission houses a number of individual gearsets that can produce different gear ratios (Figure 3-32). These gear ratios provide the driver with a selection of speed- and power- (torque-) producing ranges. A typical manual transmission has four or five forward gear ranges, neutral, and reverse.

The driver selects the desired range by disengaging the clutch and moving a shift lever to the required

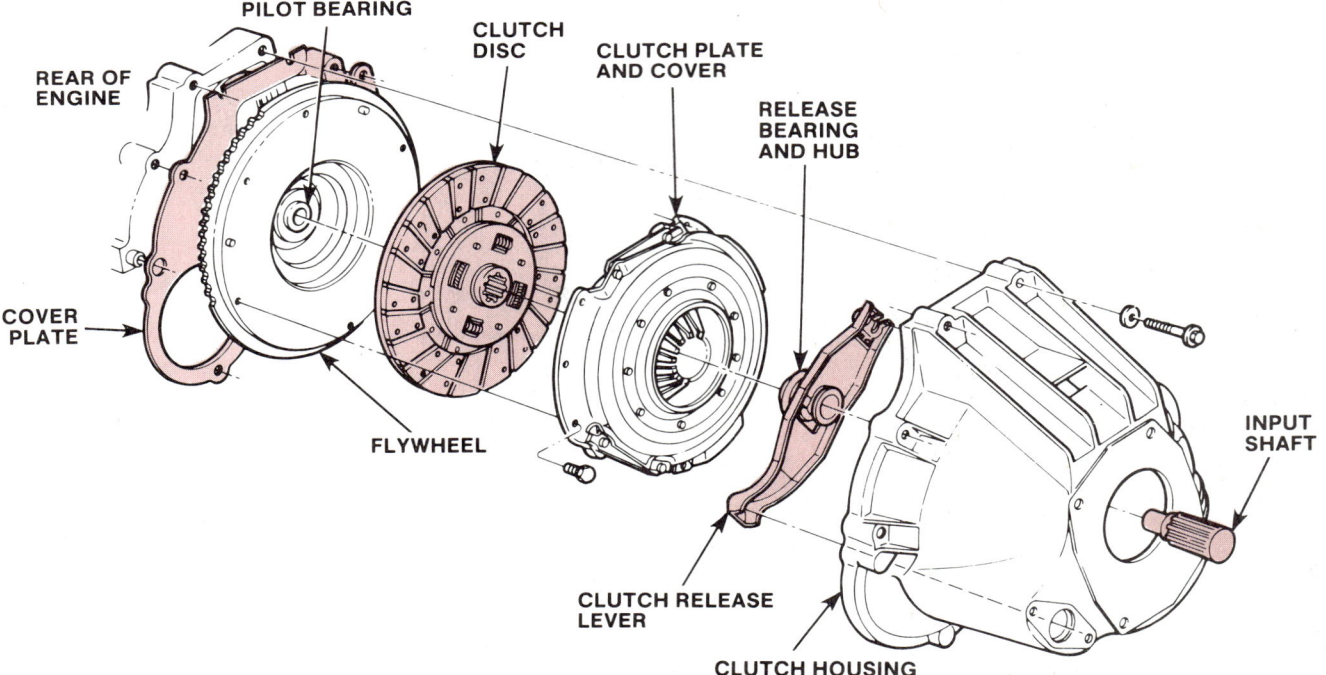

Figure 3-31 Parts of a clutch assembly. *Courtesy of Ford Motor Co.*

Automotive Systems 43

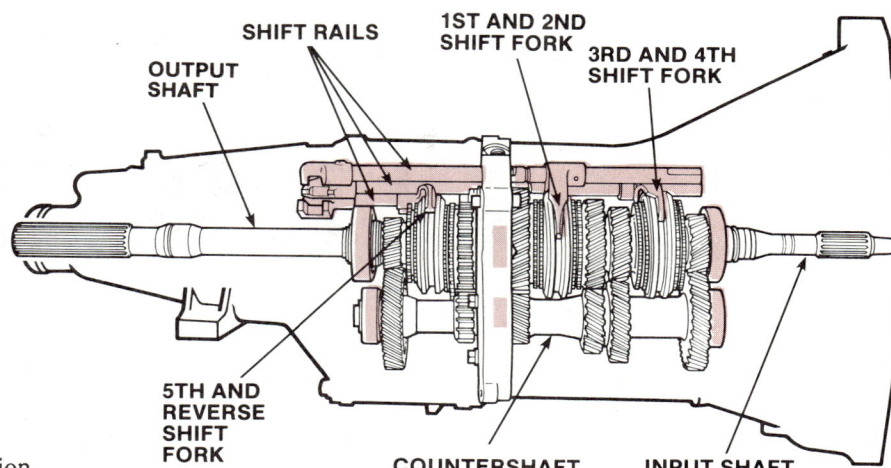

Figure 3-32 Typical manual transmission.

position. This action slides the required gearsets into mesh so the desired output shaft rotation speed is produced.

Automatic Transmissions

An automatic transmission eliminates the use of a mechanical clutch and shift lever. In place of a clutch, it uses a fluid coupling called a torque converter to transfer power from the engine flywheel to the transmission input shaft. The torque converter allows for smooth transfer of power at all engine speeds (Figure 3-33).

Shifting in an automatic transmission is controlled by either a hydraulic system or an electronic system. In hydraulic systems, an intricate network of valves and

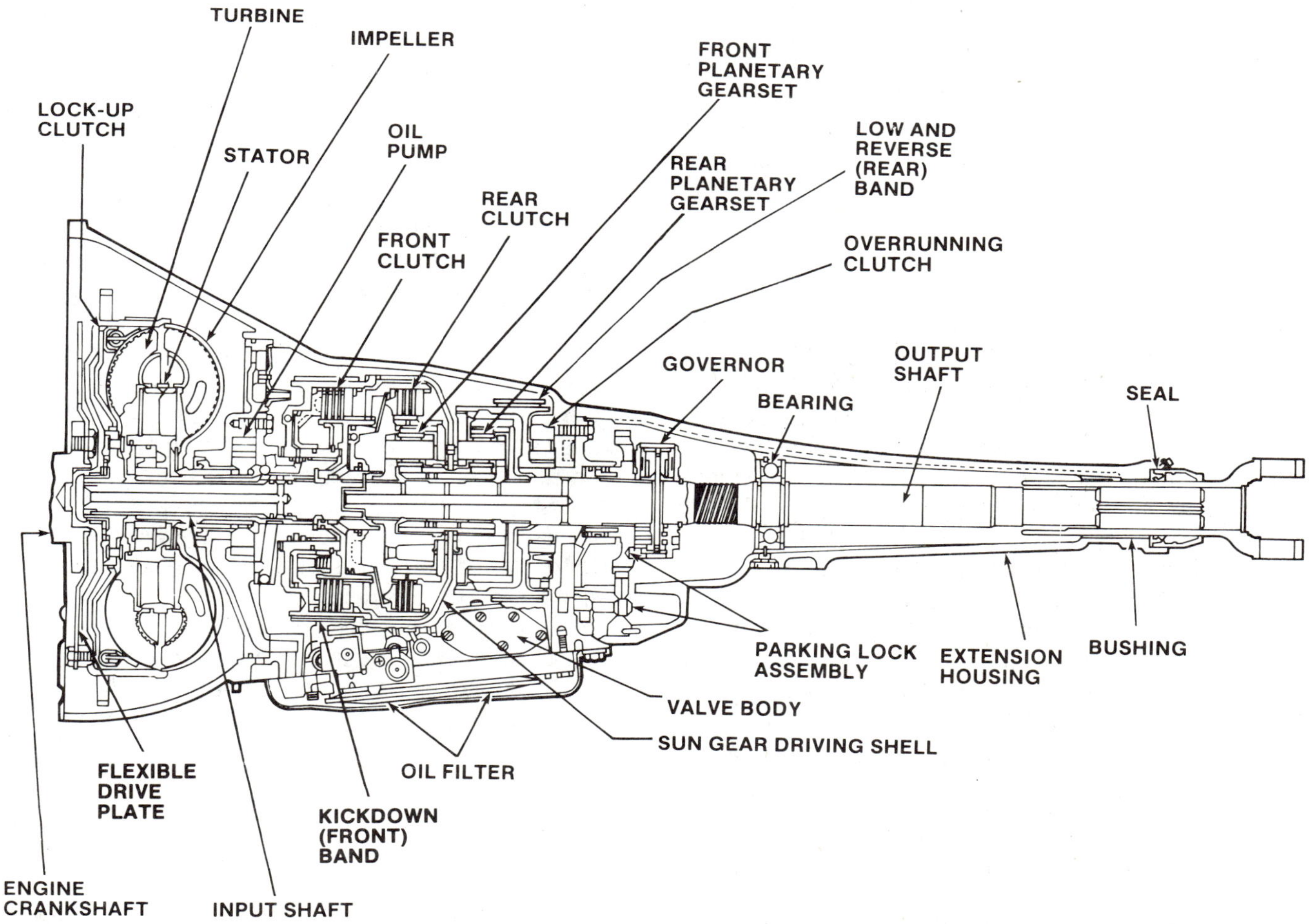

Figure 3-33 Typical torque converter and automatic transmission. *Courtesy of General Motors Corp.*

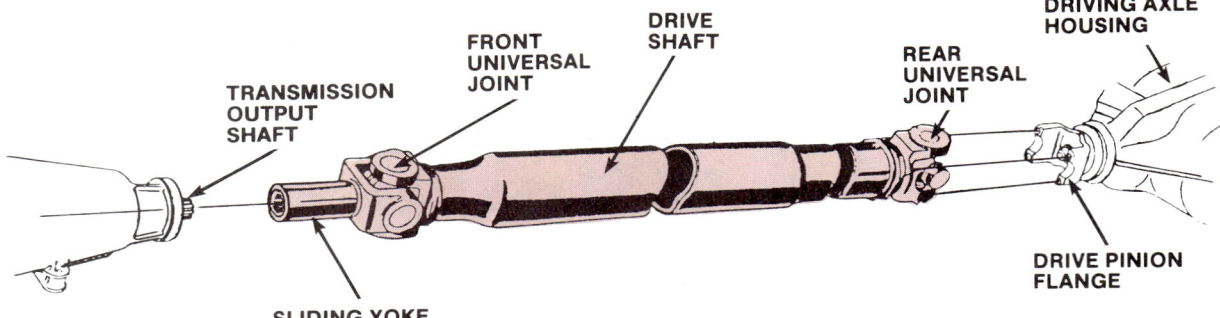

Figure 3-34 Output power from the transmission is connected to the differential in the drive axle housing by a drive shaft.

other components use hydraulic pressure to control the operation of planetary gearsets. These gearsets generate the three or four forward speeds, neutral, park, and reverse gears normally found on automatic transmissions. Newer electronic shifting systems use electric solenoids to control shifting mechanisms. Electronic shifting is precise and can be varied to suit certain operating conditions.

Driveline

Drivelines are used on rear-wheel-drive vehicles and four-wheel-drive vehicles. They connect the output shaft of the transmission with the differential gearing in the rear axle housing (Figure 3-34).

A driveline consists of a hollow drive or propeller shaft that is connected to the transmission and rear differential using universal joints. These U-joints allow the drive shaft to ride up and down with the rear suspension, preventing damage to the shaft.

Differential

On rear-wheel-drive vehicles, the drive shaft from the transmission is turning perpendicular to the forward motion of the vehicle. The differential gearing in the rear axle housing changes the side-to-side rotation of the drive shaft to the front-rear rotation parallel with the rotation of the rear wheels. It then passes this power flow on to the rear axles and wheels (Figure 3-35).

The differential also performs two other important jobs. It multiplies the torque of the power it receives from the drive shaft by providing a final gear reduction. Also, it divides this power between the left and right driving axles and wheels in such a way that a differential wheel speed is possible. This means one wheel can turn faster than the other when going around turns.

Driving Axles

Driving axles are solid steel shafts that transfer differential torque to the driving wheels. A separate axle shaft is used for each driving wheel. The driving axles and part of the differential are enclosed in an axle

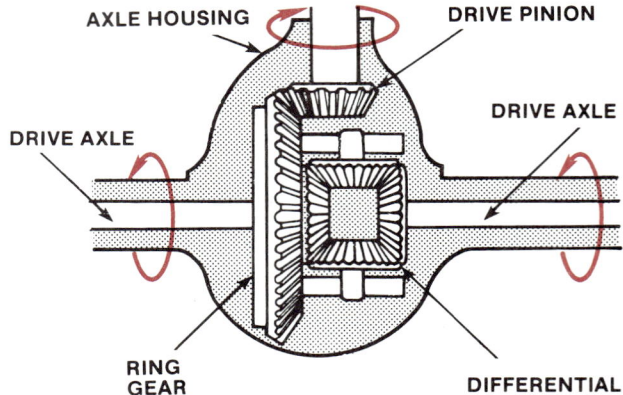

Figure 3-35 Rear differential components.

housing that protects and supports these parts. Figure 3-36 shows a housing and axle setup for a rear-wheel-drive automobile.

Each driving axle is connected to the side gears in the differential. The inner, or differential, ends of the axles are splined to fit into the side gears. As the side gears are turned, the axles to which they are splined turn at the same speed.

At their outer or wheel ends, the axles are attached to the driving wheels. For attachment to a wheel, the outer end of each axle has a flange mounted to it. A flange is a rim for attaching one part to another part. To hold the wheel in place against the flange, studs are used. Studs are threaded shafts, resembling bolts without heads. One end of the stud is screwed or pressed into the flange. The wheel fits over the studs and a nut, called the lug nut, is tightened over the open end of the stud. This holds the wheel in place.

The inner end of each axle is supported by the differential carrier. The outer end of the axle shaft is supported by a bearing inside the axle housing. A bearing supports and holds a rotating part in place. This bearing, called the axle bearing, allows the axle to rotate smoothly inside the axle housing.

Transaxles

Transaxles are used on front-wheel-drive vehicles. A transaxle combines the transmission gearing and the

Automotive Systems   45

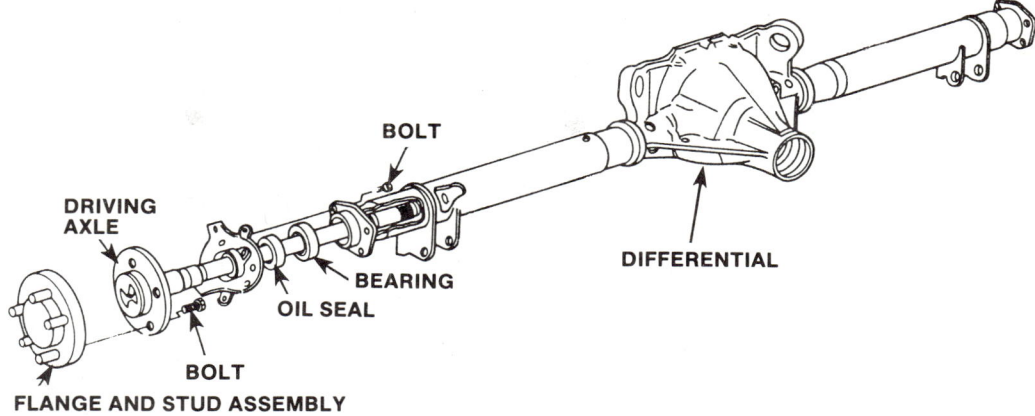

Figure 3-36 Housing and axle setup for a rear-wheel-drive automobile.

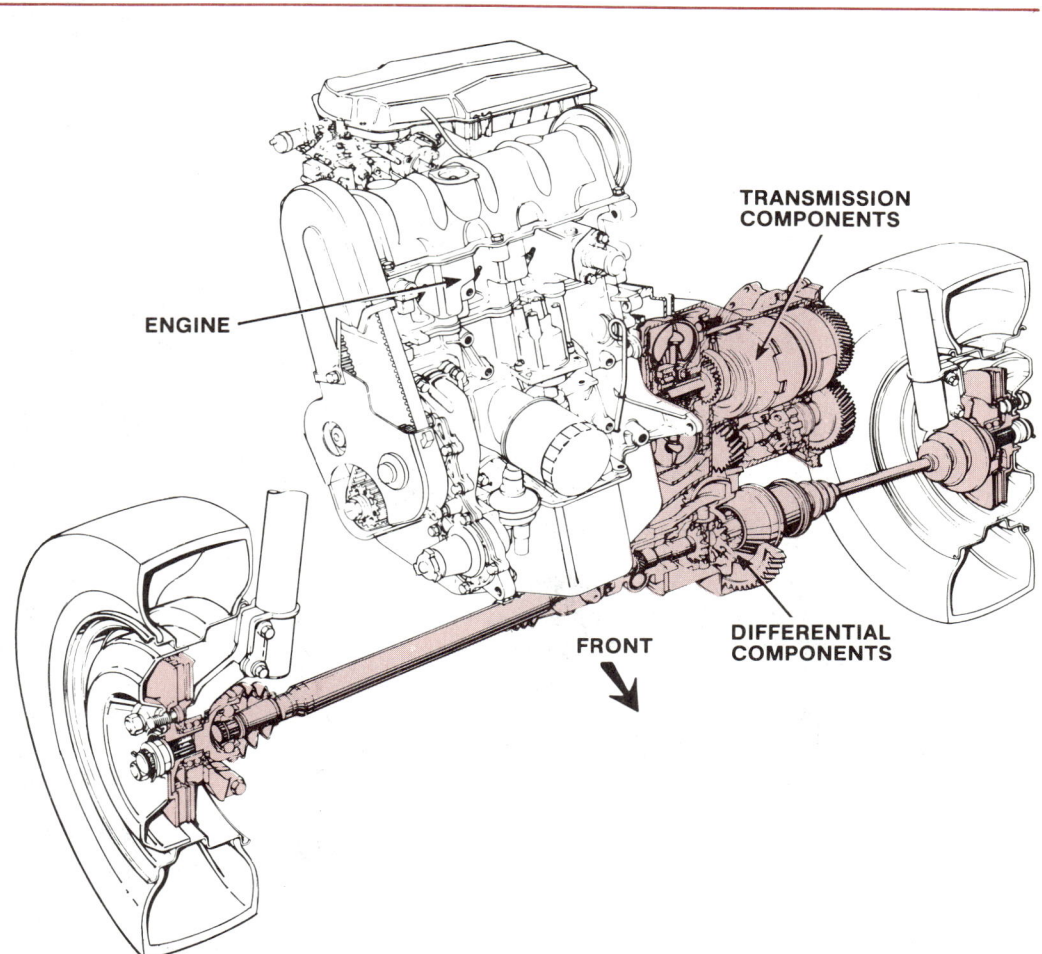

Figure 3-37 Some manufacturers place the entire driveline in the front of the vehicle. *Courtesy of Chrysler Corp.*

differential gearing into a single unit (Figure 3-37). The gearsets in the transaxle generate the required gear ratios and pass the power flow onto the differential. The differential gearing in the transaxle creates the final gear reduction and splits the power flow between the left and right front drive axles.

Driving axles on front-wheel-drive cars protrude from the sides of the transaxle. These axles can be hollow or solid. The outer end of the axles are fitted to the hubs of the drive wheels. Constant velocity joints mounted on each end of the drive axles allow for steering and suspension (up-and-down) motion without affecting the power flow to the wheels.

Four-Wheel-Drive Systems

Four-wheel- or all-wheel-drive vehicles combine features of rear-wheel-drive transmissions and front-wheel-drive transaxles. Additional transfer case gearing splits the power flow between a differential driving the front wheels and a rear differential that drives the rear wheels. This transfer case gearing can be contained in a housing bolted directly to the transmission/transaxle, or it can be located at some point in the driveline running to the rear differential of the vehicle.

❏ RUNNING GEAR

The running gear consists of components that are used to control the vehicle. The running gear includes the suspension system, the steering system, the braking system, and the wheels and tires.

Suspension System

The suspension system on the automobile includes such components as the springs, shock absorbers, MacPherson struts, torsion bars, axles, and connecting linkages. These components are designed to support the body and frame, the engine, and the drivelines. Without these systems, the comfort and ease of driving the vehicle would be reduced. Figure 3-38 illustrates some of the components that are used in a suspension system.

Springs and torsion bars are used to support the axles of the vehicle. The two types of springs commonly used are the leaf spring and the coil spring (Figure 3-39).

Torsion bars are made of long spring steel rods. One end of the rod is connected to the frame, while the other end is connected to the movable parts of the axles. As the axles move up and down, the rod twists and acts as a spring.

Shock absorbers slow down the upward and downward movement of the vehicle. This action occurs when the car goes over a rough road.

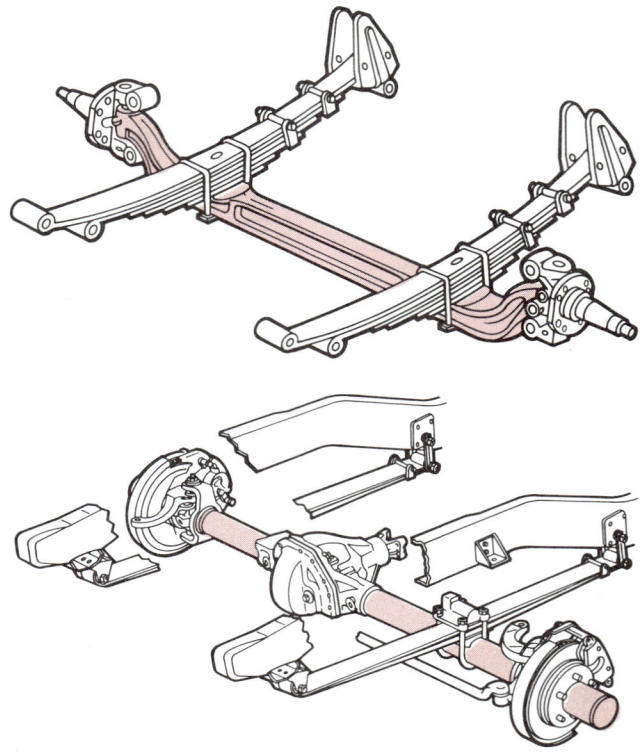

Figure 3-39 Leaf springs help support the rear axles on some systems.

Steering System

A steering system allows the control of the direction of the vehicle. A steering system includes the steering wheel, steering gear, steering shaft, and steering linkage.

There are two types of steering gears in use on today's vehicles: a rack-and-pinion gear and a recirculating ball gear (Figure 3-40). The rack-and-pinion

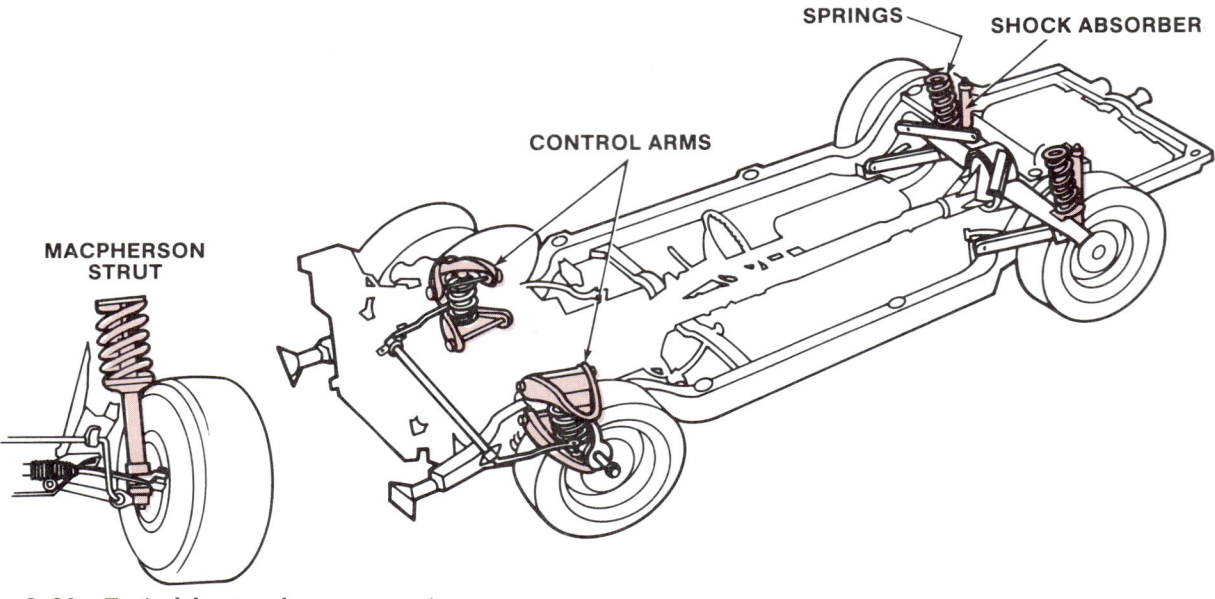

Figure 3-38 Typical front and rear suspension system.

Automotive Systems 47

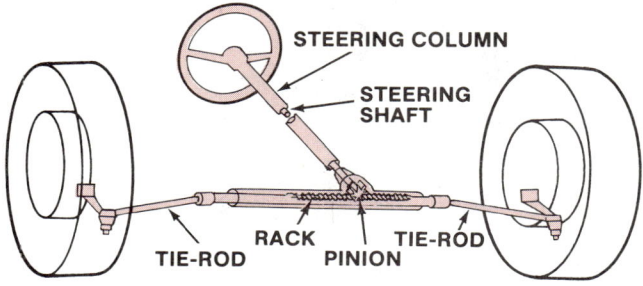
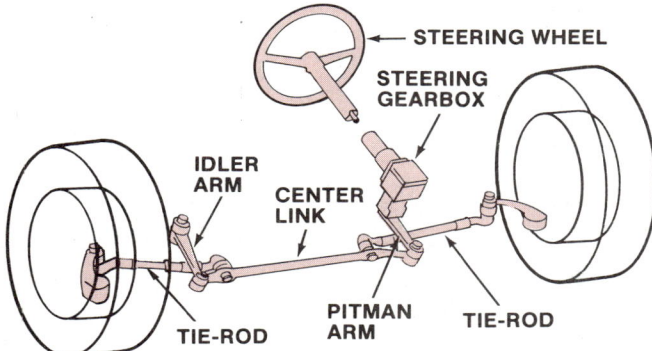

Figure 3-40 Common steering systems.

gear is used most commonly on modern cars. The recirculating ball gear is normally used only on heavy vehicles, such as large pickup trucks, station wagons, and full-size luxury cars.

Steering gears provide a gear reduction to make turning the wheels easier. On all but some light subcompact and compact models, the steering gear is also power assisted to ease the effort of turning the wheels. In a power-assisted system, a pump provides hydraulic fluid under pressure to the steering gear. A spool valve directs fluid to one side or the other of the steering gear to assist the operator in turning the wheels.

Some new vehicles have four-wheel steering. Some systems use a mechanical gearbox directly linked to the front steering gear to turn the rear wheels. Other systems use a second power steering gearbox that is computer controlled. In a low-speed turning mode, the rear wheels turn in the opposite direction of the front wheels to reduce the turning radius. When turning the wheels at high speeds, the rear wheels turn in the same direction as the front wheels so that the back wheels follow the front wheels in quick lane changes and other high-speed maneuvers.

Brakes

Automobiles are stopped by activating the brake system (Figure 3-41). Brakes, which are located at each wheel, utilize friction to slow and stop the automobile.

The brakes are activated when the vehicle operator depresses a brake pedal. The brake pedal is connected to a plunger in a master cylinder, which is filled with hydraulic fluid. The force exerted by the plunger on the hydraulic fluid is transferred through brake hoses and lines to the four brake assemblies.

The two types of brakes used on automobiles are drum brakes and disc brakes. Many automobiles use a combination of the two types: disc brakes at the front wheels and drum brakes at the rear wheels.

Most vehicles have power-assisted brakes. A brake booster uses manifold vacuum to increase the pressure applied to the plunger in the master cylinder. This lessens the amount of pressure that must be applied to the brake pedal by the operator and increases the responsiveness of the brake system.

Wheels and Tires

The only contact a vehicle has with the road is its tires. Tires are made of rubber and other materials and are filled with air to cushion the ride of the automobile.

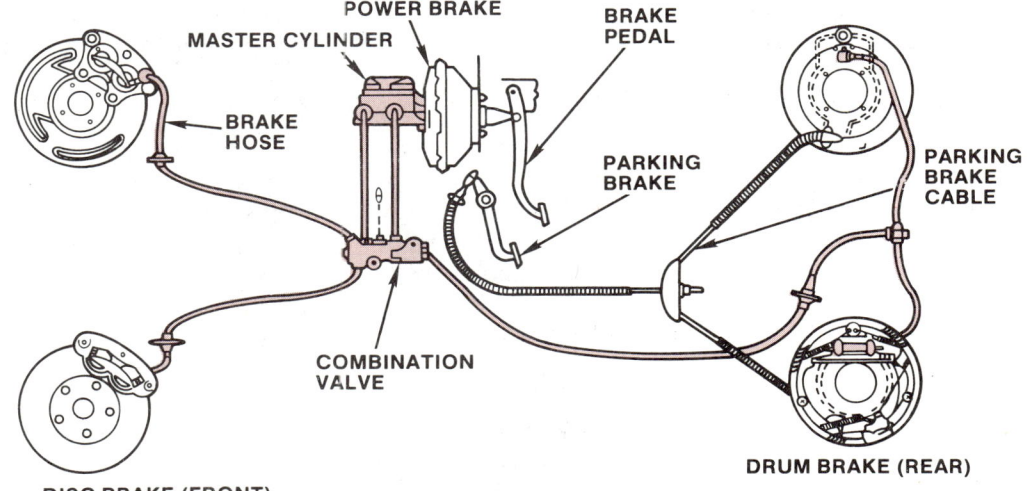

Figure 3-41 Many automobiles feature a combination of drum and disc brakes.

CUSTOMER MAINTENANCE SCHEDULE B

Follow Maintenance Schedule B if, generally, you drive your car on a daily basis for several miles and NONE OF THE DRIVING CONDITIONS SHOWN IN SCHEDULE A APPLY TO YOUR DRIVING HABITS.

PERFORM AT THE MONTHS OR DISTANCES SHOWN, WHICHEVER OCCURS FIRST.									
	MILES (000)	7.5	15	22.5	30	37.5	45	52.5	60
	KILOMETERS (000)	12	24	36	48	60	72	84	96
EMISSION CONTROL SERVICE									
Change engine oil and oil filter (every 6 months) or 7500 miles, whichever occurs first		X	X	X	X	X	X	X	X
TURBOCHARGED ENGINES (Four Cylinder)	Replace spark plugs			(X)		X		(X)	X
	Change oil and filter	EVERY 5,000 MILES (8,000 km) OR 6 MONTHS, WHICHEVER OCCURS FIRST							
ALL ENGINES									
Replace spark plugs					X				X
Inspect accessory drive belt(s)					X				X
Replace EGR vacuum solenoid and filter—Six cylinder engine only									X
Check/lube exhaust control valve (5.8L)		(X)			(X)		(X)		(X)
Change crankcase emission filter (if so equipped)					X				X
Replace air cleaner filter (1)					X				X
Check/clean choke linkage (5.8L only)					X				X
Replace engine coolant (every 36 months) OR					X				X
Check engine coolant protection, hoses and clamps		ANNUALLY							
GENERAL MAINTENANCE									
Check exhaust heat shields					X				X
Lube steering and/or suspension					X				X

(1) If operating in severe dust, ask your dealer for proper replacement intervals.

(X) All items with either an "X" or an "(X)" code are required to be performed in all states except California. For vehicles sold in California, only "X" items are REQUIRED to be performed. However, Ford recommends that you also perform maintenance on items designated by a "(X)" in order to achieve best vehicle operation.

Figure 3-42 Typical preventive maintenance schedule.

Wheels are made of metal and are bolted to the axles or spindles. Wheels hold the tires in place. Wheels and tires come in many different sizes. Their sizes must be matched to one another and to the automobile.

❏ PREVENTIVE MAINTENANCE

Preventive maintenance (PM) involves performing certain service jobs on a vehicle on a regularly scheduled basis, before there is any sign of trouble. Regular inspection and routine maintenance can prevent major breakdowns and expensive repairs. It also keeps customers' vehicles running efficiently and safely.

A recent survey of 2,375 vehicles conducted during National Car Care Month found that more than 90% needed some form of repair or service work. The vehicles were inspected for exhaust emissions, fluid levels, tire pressure, and other safety features. The results indicated that 34% of the cars failed due to restricted air filters, 27% for worn belts, 26% for clogged PCV filters, 14% for worn hoses, 20% for bad batteries, battery

PHOTO SEQUENCE 1

CHANGING THE OIL AND OIL FILTER

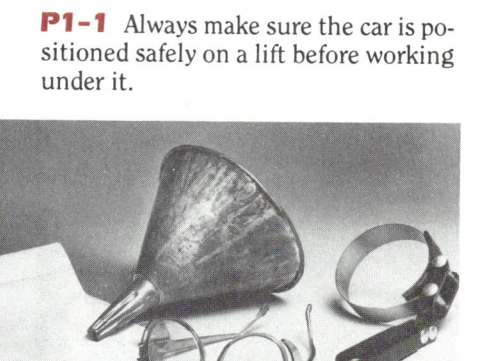

P1-1 Always make sure the car is positioned safely on a lift before working under it.

P1-2 The tools and other items needed to change the engine's oil and oil filter are rags, a funnel, an oil filter wrench, safety glasses, and a wrench for the drain plug.

P1-3 Place the oil drain pan under the drain plug before beginning to drain the oil.

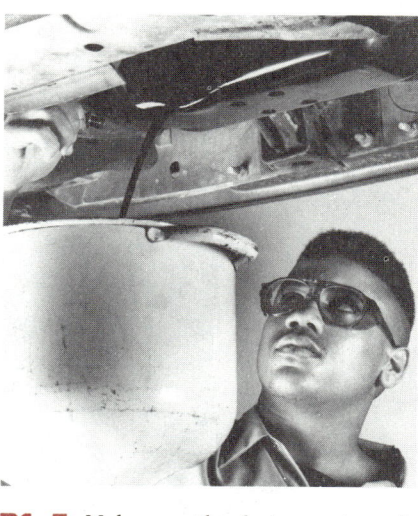

P1-4 Loosen the drain plug with the appropriate wrench. After the drain plug is loosened, quickly remove it so that the oil can freely drain from the pan.

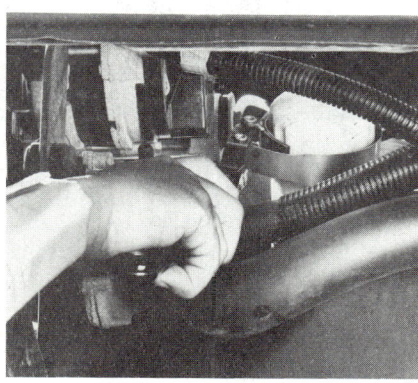

P1-5 Make sure the drain pan is positioned so that it can catch all of the oil.

P1-6 While the oil is draining, use an oil filter wrench to loosen and remove the oil filter.

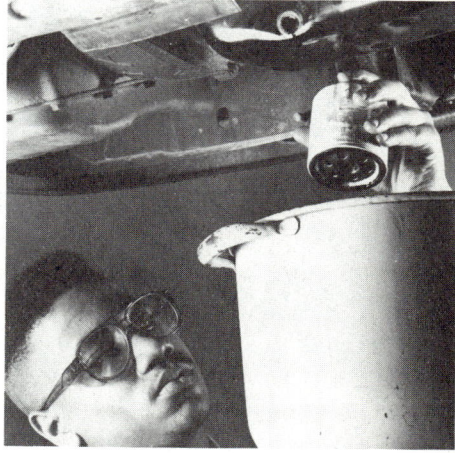

P1-7 Place the old filter in the drain pan so it can drain. Then discard the filter according to local regulations.

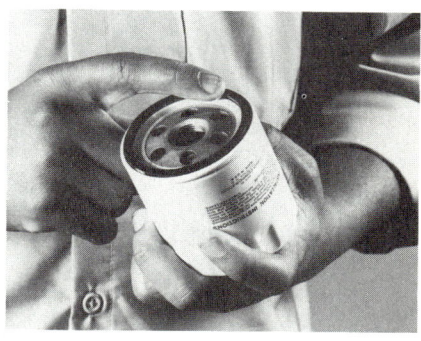

P1-8 After wiping the oil filter sealing area on the engine, apply a coat of clean engine oil on the new filter's seal.

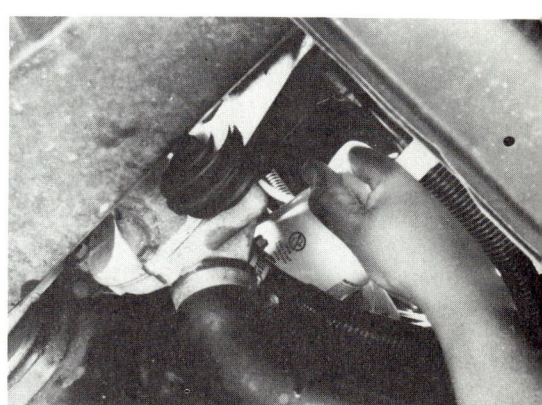

P1-9 Hand-tighten the filter to the block. Oil filters should be tightened according to the directions given on the filter.

(continued)

49

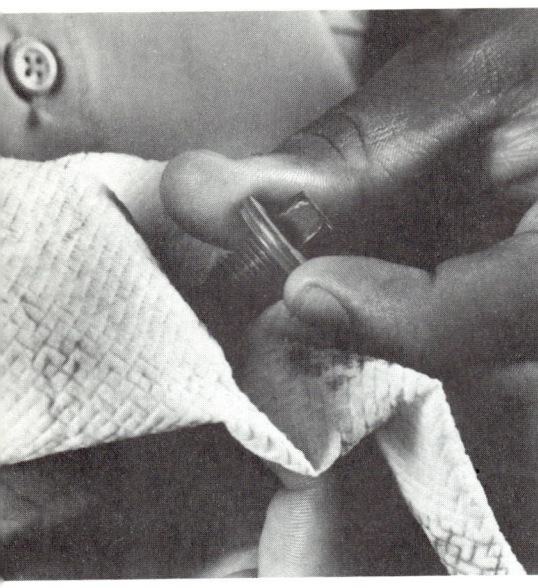

P1-10 Prior to reinstalling the drain plug, wipe off its threads and sealing surface with a clean rag.

P1-11 The drain plug should be tightened according to the manufacturer's recommendations. Overtightening can cause thread damage, while undertightening may result in oil leakage.

P1-12 With the oil filter and drain plug installed, lower the car to the ground and remove the oil filler cap.

P1-13 Carefully pour the oil into the engine. The use of a funnel usually keeps oil from spilling on the engine.

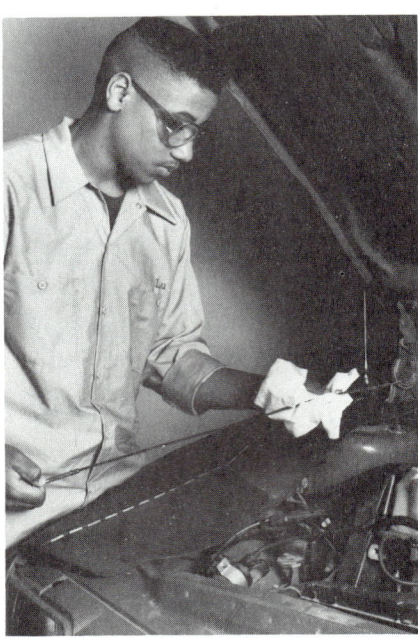

P1-14 After the recommended amount of oil has been put in the engine, check the oil level.

P1-15 Start the engine and allow it to reach operating temperature. While the engine is running, check the engine for oil leaks. Extra attention should be given to the seal of the oil filter. If there is evidence of a leak, turn off the engine and correct the problem.

P1-16 After the engine has been turned off, recheck the oil level and correct it if necessary. ■

cables, or terminals. In the fluid and cooling system inspection, 39% failed due to bad or contaminated transmission or power steering fluid, 36% for worn out engine oil, 28% for inadequate cooling system protection, and 8% for faulty radiator caps. In the safety category, 50% failed due to worn or improperly inflated tires, 32% for inoperative headlights or brake lights, and 14% for worn wipers.

Professional service technicians stress preventive maintenance to their customers. The basis for a particular vehicle's PM program is outlined in the owner's or maintenance manual provided by the manufacturer. These booklets list recommended service intervals and specific fluid, air pressure, and other vital requirements.

A typical example of preventive maintenance inspection, adjustment, and service intervals is given in Figure 3-42. Technicians should also question the vehicle owner as to specific driving habits and conditions that may affect PM service intervals. For example, vehicles subject to low mileage and local driving conditions may require more frequent oil changes due to the more rapid accumulation of condensation and unburned fuel in the oil. Oil change intervals as short as 3 months or 3,000 miles are sometimes recommended. The steps involved in changing engine oil and filter are illustrated in Photo Sequence 1, included in this chapter.

Most manufacturers also specify more frequent service intervals for vehicles used to tow a trailer, or those that operate in extremely dusty or unusual conditions.

The following PM checks should also be performed at the suggested time intervals to help ensure safe, dependable vehicle operation.

Whenever refueling

- Check the engine oil level.
- Check the windshield washer fluid level.
- Look for low or under-inflated tires.

At least monthly

- Check the tire pressure. (Check tires when cold, not after a long drive.)
- Check the coolant in the coolant recovery reservoir.
- Check the operation of all exterior lights, including the brake lights, turn signals, and hazard warning flashers.

At least twice a year (for example, every spring and fall)

- Check windshield washer spray and wiper operation. Check and replace worn wiper blades.
- Check for worn tires and loose wheel lug nuts.
- Check pressure in spare tire.
- Check headlight alignment.
- Check muffler, exhaust pipes, and clamps.
- Inspect the lap/shoulder belts for wear.
- Check radiator, heater, and air-conditioning hoses for leaks or damage.

At least once a year

- Lubricate all hinges and all outside key locks.
- Lubricate the door rubber weatherstrips.
- Clean the body water drain holes.
- Check the air-conditioning system before the warm weather season.
- Check the power steering fluid level.
- Check the brake fluid level.
- Check the battery connections.
- Lubricate the transmission controls and linkage.

While operating the vehicle

- Note any changes in the sound of the exhaust or any smell of exhaust fumes in the vehicle.
- Check for vibrations in the steering wheel. Notice any increased steering effort or looseness in the steering wheel.
- Notice if the vehicle constantly turns slightly or pulls to one side of the road.
- When stopping, listen and check for strange sounds, pulling to one side, increased brake pedal travel, or hard to push brake pedal.
- If any slipping or changes in the operation of your transmission occurs, check the transmission fluid level.
- Check for fluid leaks under the vehicle. (Water dripping from the air-conditioning system after use is normal.)
- Check an automatic transmission's park function.
- Check the parking brake.

Summary

- Dramatic changes to the automobile have occurred over the last two decades, including the addition of emission control systems, more fuel efficient and cleaner burning engines, and lighter body weight.
- In addition to being lighter than body-over-frame vehicles, unibodies offer better occupant protection by distributing impact forces throughout the vehicle.
- There are six basic vehicle body shapes: sedan, hardtop, convertible, liftback or hatchback, station wagon, and sports or multi-purpose vehicles.
- Today's computerized engine control systems regulate such things as air and fuel delivery, ignition timing, and emissions. The result is a combination of fuel efficiency and power previously unattainable on vehicles.
- In modern automated and computer-controlled domestic vehicle assembly plants, automatic guided vehicles move the vehicle bodies through the assembly process. Conditions in the plant are

- constantly monitored and adjusted by programmable logic control, which also controls maintenance operations.
- All automobile engines are classified as internal combustion, because the burning that creates heat energy occurs inside the engine. Diesel engines share the same major parts as gasoline engines, but they do not use a spark to ignite the air/fuel mixture.
- The cooling system maintains proper engine temperatures. Liquid cooling is more efficient than air cooling and is more commonly used.
- The lubrication system distributes motor oil throughout the engine. This system also contains the oil filter necessary to remove dirt and other foreign matter from the oil.
- The fuel system is responsible not only for fuel storage and delivery, but also for atomizing and mixing it with the air in the correct proportion.
- The exhaust system has a three-fold purpose: channel toxic exhaust away from the passenger compartment, quiet the exhaust pulses, and burn the emissions in the exhaust.
- The total electrical system of an automobile includes the ignition, starting, charging, and lighting systems. Electronic engine controls regulate these systems very accurately through the use of microcomputers.
- Modern automatic transmissions use a computer to match the demand for acceleration with engine speed, wheel speed, and load conditions. It then chooses the proper gear ratio and, if necessary, initiates a gear change.
- The running gear is critical to controlling the vehicle. It consists of the suspension system, braking system, steering system, and wheels and tires.
- Preventive maintenance involves regularly scheduled service on a vehicle to keep it operating efficiently and safely. Professional technicians should stress its importance to the customer.

Review Questions

1. Under the CAFE standards, what are vehicles tested for?
2. Describe the basic unitized vehicle.
3. Define internal combustion.
4. In addition to the battery, what does the charging system include?
5. What preventive maintenance checks should be made whenever the vehicle is refueled?
6. Which of the following was not a result of the emission control systems that were added to automobiles in the 1970s?
   a. leaner air/fuel mixtures
   b. catalytic converters
   c. higher compression ratios
   d. lower horsepower
7. Automatic transmissions replace the clutch with a _____ to transfer power from the flywheel to the transmission input shaft.
   a. differential
   b. U-joint
   c. torque converter
   d. constant velocity joint
8. Technician A stresses the need for preventive maintenance to customers, while Technician B downplays its importance. Who is correct?
   a. Technician A
   b. Technician B
   c. Both A and B
   d. Neither A nor B
9. How many basic vehicle body shapes are used today?
   a. three
   b. four
   c. five
   d. six
10. Technician A says that the best diagnostic tool for the modern automobile is the technician's two ears. Technician B says that your ears are not adequate to correctly diagnose today's sophisticated engines. Who is correct?
    a. Technician A
    b. Technician B
    c. Both A and B
    d. Neither A nor B
11. Which type of engine is classified as internal combustion?
    a. gasoline
    b. diesel
    c. both a and b
    d. neither a nor b
12. What is the function of the valve train?
    a. close off and seal the top of the cylinder
    b. house the major parts of the engine
    c. convert reciprocating motion to rotary motion
    d. open and close the intake and exhaust ports
13. Technician A says that liquid cooling an engine is preferable to air cooling. Technician B says that air cooling lets the engine operate more efficiently. Who is correct?
    a. Technician A
    b. Technician B
    c. Both A and B
    d. Neither A nor B
14. An engine is experiencing trouble generating the electrical spark needed to ignite the air/fuel mixture. Technician A says the problem is probably in the starting system, while Technician B says the ignition system is most likely at fault. Who is correct?
    a. Technician A
    b. Technician B
    c. Both A and B
    d. Neither A nor B

15. Which emission control system introduces exhaust gases into the intake air to reduce the formation of oxides of nitrogen in the combustion chamber?
    a. evaporative emission controls
    b. exhaust gas recirculation
    c. air injection
    d. early fuel evaporation
16. Technician A says that late-model vehicles use a conventional generator as the charging unit. Technician B says an alternating current generator is used on late-model vehicles. Who is correct?
    a. Technician A
    b. Technician B
    c. Both A and B
    d. Neither A nor B
17. Technician A says that a transaxle is used in combination with a drive shaft in front-wheel-drive vehicles. Technician B says the transaxle eliminates the need for a drive shaft. Who is correct?
    a. Technician A
    b. Technician B
    c. Both A and B
    d. Neither A nor B
18. Which of the following is not part of the running gear?
    a. differential
    b. steering
    c. suspension
    d. brakes
19. Which of the following PM checks should be made most often?
    a. coolant in the coolant recovery reservoir
    b. operation of all exterior lights
    c. engine oil level
    d. spare tire pressure
20. Technician A says that water dripping from the air-conditioning system often after use indicates a problem in the system, but Technician B says that such dripping is normal. Who is correct?
    a. Technician A
    b. Technician B
    c. Both A and B
    d. Neither A nor B

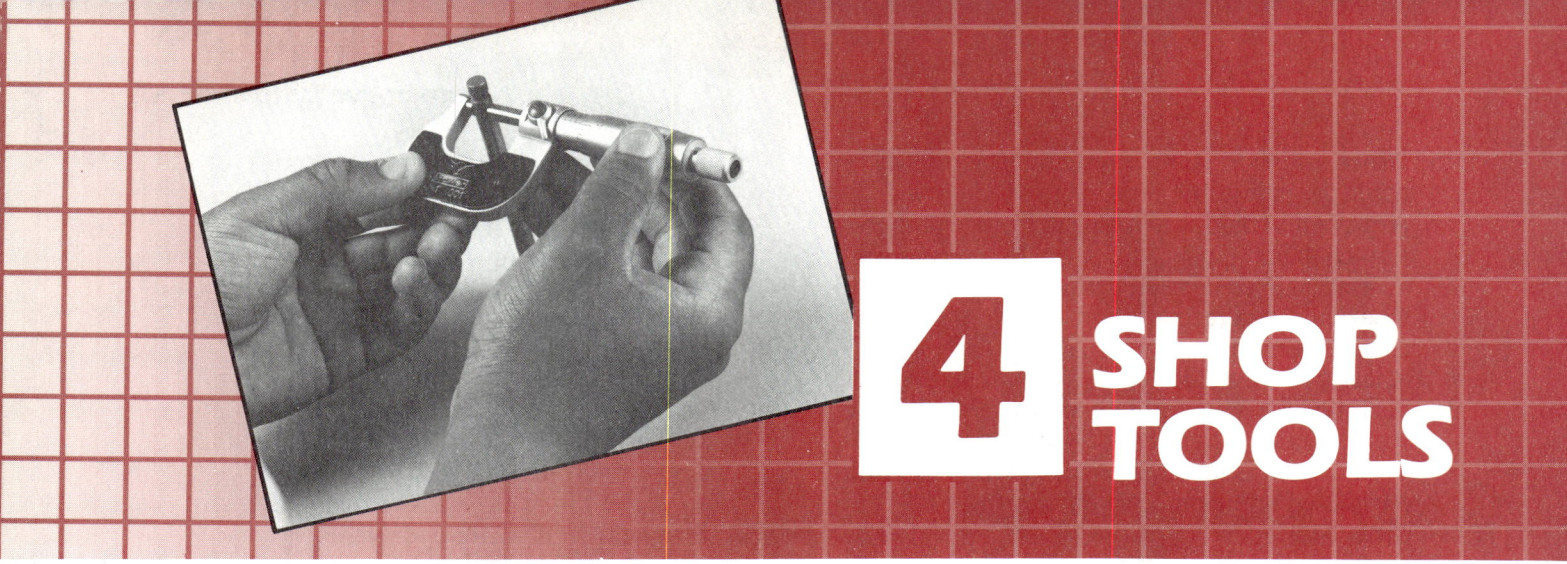

4 SHOP TOOLS

Objectives

- List the basic units of measure for length, volume, and mass in the two measuring systems.
- List the various mechanical measuring tools used in the automotive shop.
- Describe the proper procedure for using a micrometer to measure.
- List some of the common hand tools used in auto repair.
- Describe the use of common pneumatic, electrical, and hydraulic power tools found in an automobile service department.

Repairing the modern automobile requires the use of various tools. Many of these tools are common hand and power tools often used every day by a professional repair technician. Other tools are very specialized and are only for specific repairs on specific systems and/or vehicles. This chapter will present some of the more commonly used hand and power tools that every technician must be familiar with. Since units of measurement play such an important part in tool selection and in diagnosing automotive problems, this chapter begins with a presentation of measuring systems. A description of some important measuring tools follows.

❑ MEASURING SYSTEMS

Two systems of weights and measures now exist side by side in the United States—the United States customary systems (UCS) and the international system (SI). The UCS is commonly known as the English system, while the international system is normally called the metric system.

The basic unit of linear measurement in the UCS is the inch. The basic unit of linear measurement in the SI, or metric system, is the meter. The meter is easily broken down into smaller units, such as the centimeter (1/100 meter) and millimeter (1/1000 meter).

All units of measurement in the metric system are related to each other by the factor of 10. Every metric unit can be multiplied or divided by the factor of 10 to get larger units (multiples) or smaller units (submultiples). This makes the metric system much easier to use than the English system (Figure 4-1). There is much less chance of a math error using the metric system.

The United States passed the Metric Conversion Act in 1975 in an attempt to push American industry and the general public toward acceptance of the metric system. While the general public has been slow to drop the customary measuring system of inches, gallons, and pounds, many industries, led by the automotive industry, are now predominantly metric.

All import vehicles, and now many domestics, are built to metric standards. Service technicians must be able to measure and work with these units of measurement. The following are some common equivalents between the two systems.

1 meter (m) = 39.37 inches (in.)
1 centimeter (cm) = 0.3937 inch
1 millimeter (mm) = 0.03937 inch
1 inch = 2.54 centimeters
1 inch = 25.4 millimeters

❑ ENGINE MEASURING TOOLS

Engine work requires very close measurements, often in ten thousandths (0.0001) inch or thousandths (0.001) millimeter. Accurate measurements to this high standard of precision can only be made through the use of measuring devices especially designed to show these very small differences in size.

Measuring tools are precise and delicate instruments. In fact, the more precise they are, the more delicate they are. They should be handled with great care. Never pry, strike, drop, or force these instruments. They might be damaged beyond usability.

Precision measuring instruments, especially micrometers, are extremely sensitive to rough handling. Clean them before and after every use. All measuring operations must be performed on parts that are room temperature. Never measure parts that are still warm from machining operations.

Shop Tools

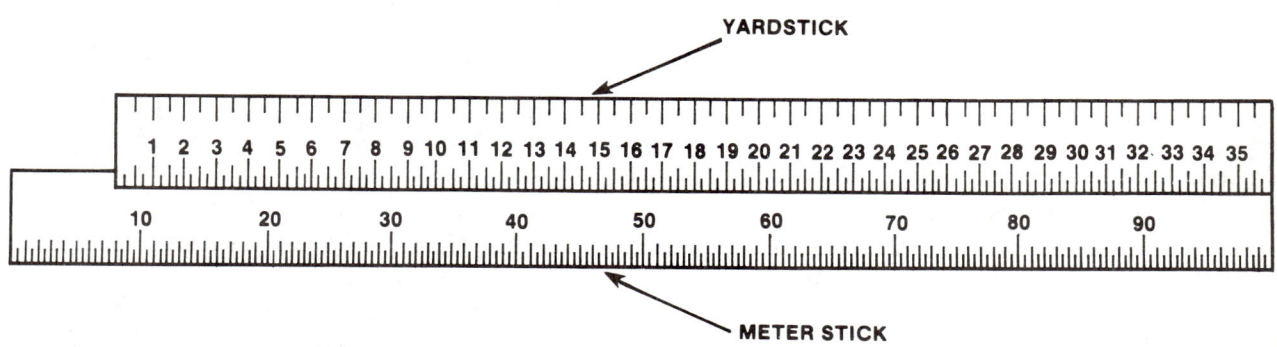

Figure 4-1 A meter stick is made of 1,000 increments known as millimeters.

> **SHOP TALK**
>
> Check measuring instruments regularly against known good equipment. This is done to ensure that they are operating properly and capable of accurate measurement. Always refer to the appropriate service manual or other reference material for the correct specifications before performing any service or diagnostic procedures. The close tolerances in current vehicles make using the correct specifications and taking accurate measurements more important than ever. A difference of even a fraction of an inch is crucial in delicate engine work.

Machinist's Rule

The machinist's rule looks very much like an ordinary ruler. Each edge of this basic engine measuring tool is divided into increments based on a different scale. As shown in Figure 4-2, a typical machinist's rule based on the English system of measurement may have scales based on 1/8-, 1/16-, 1/32-, and 1/64-inch intervals.

English system machinist rules are also available based on decimal intervals. These are typically divided into 1/10-, 1/50-, and 1/100-inch (0.1, 0.02, and 0.01) increments. Decimal machinist rules are very helpful when measuring dimensions that are specified in decimal fractions; they make such measurments much easier.

Of course, machinist rules are also available based on the metric measuring system. Metric rules are usually divided into 0.5-mm and 1-mm increments. As stated earlier, the metric system is based on a decimal system of measurement.

Dial Caliper

The dial caliper (Figure 4-3) is a versatile measuring instrument capable of taking inside, outside, depth, and step measurements. UCS calipers commonly measure dimensions from 0 inches to 6 inches. Metric dial calipers typically measure from 0 mm to 150 mm in

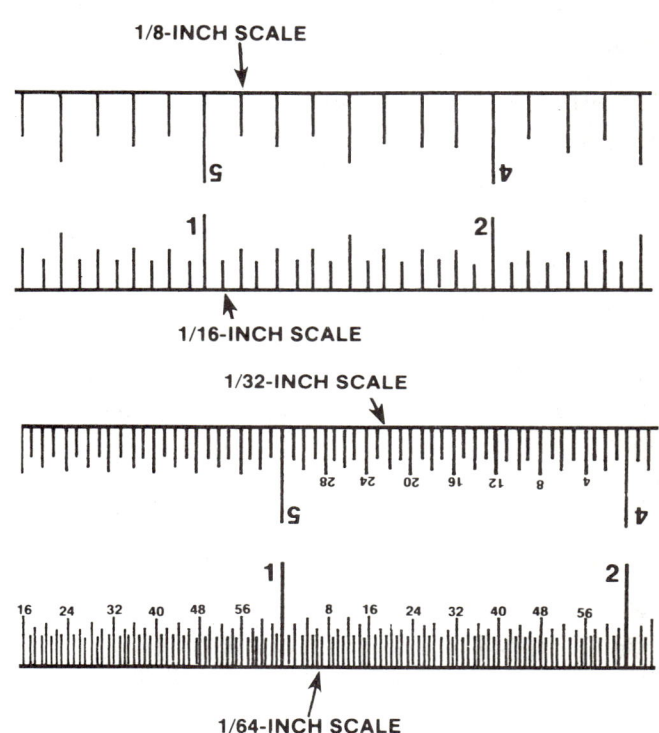

Figure 4-2 Typical machinist's rule graduations.

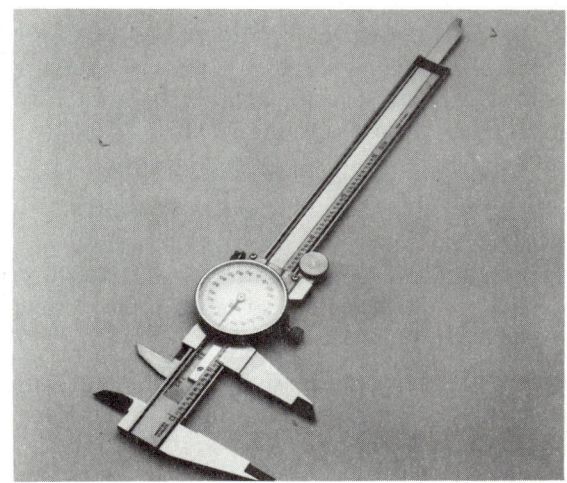

Figure 4-3 Typical dial caliper. *Courtesy of Central Tools, Inc.*

increments of 0.02 mm. The dial caliper features a depth scale, bar scale, dial indicator, inside measurement jaws, and outside measurement jaws.

The bar scale of an English system dial caliper is divided into one-tenth (0.1) inch graduations. The dial indicator is divided into one-thousandth (0.001) inch graduations. Therefore, one revolution of the dial indicator needle equals one-tenth inch on the bar scale. (One hundred-thousandths inch equals one-tenth inch.)

The metric dial caliper is similar in appearance to the United States (inch reading) model. However, the bar scale is divided into 2-mm increments. Additionally, on the metric dial caliper, one revolution of the dial indicator needle equals 2 mm.

Both English and metric dial calipers use a thumb-operated roll knob for fine adjustment. When you use a dial caliper, always move the measuring jaws backward and forward to center the jaws in the work. Make sure that the caliper jaws lay flat on the work. If the jaws or the work are tilted in any way, you will not obtain an accurate measurement. However, although dial calipers are precision measuring instruments, they are only accurate to plus or minus two-thousandths (± 0.002) inch. The factors that limit dial caliper accuracy include jaw flatness and feel. Micrometers are better suited to measuring tasks that require extreme precision.

Micrometers

The micrometer is used to measure the outside diameter of a shaft and the inside diameter of a hole. Both outside and inside micrometers are calibrated and read in the same manner. Both are operated so that the measuring points exactly contact the surfaces being measured.

The major components and markings of a micrometer include the frame, anvil, spindle, locknut, sleeve, sleeve numbers, sleeve long line, thimble marks, thimble, and ratchet (Figure 4-4). Micrometers are calibrated in either inch or metric graduations and are available in a range of sizes. The proper procedure for measuring with an inch-graduated outside micrometer is outlined in Photo Sequence 2, included in this chapter.

Reading a Metric Outside Micrometer

The metric micrometer is read in the same manner as the inch-graduated micrometer, except that the graduations are in the metric system of measurement. Readings are obtained as follows.

- Each number on the sleeve of the micrometer represents 5 millimeters (mm) or 0.005 meter (m)(Figure 4-5A).
- Each of the ten equal spaces between each number, with index lines alternating above and below the horizontal line, represents 0.5 mm or five tenths of

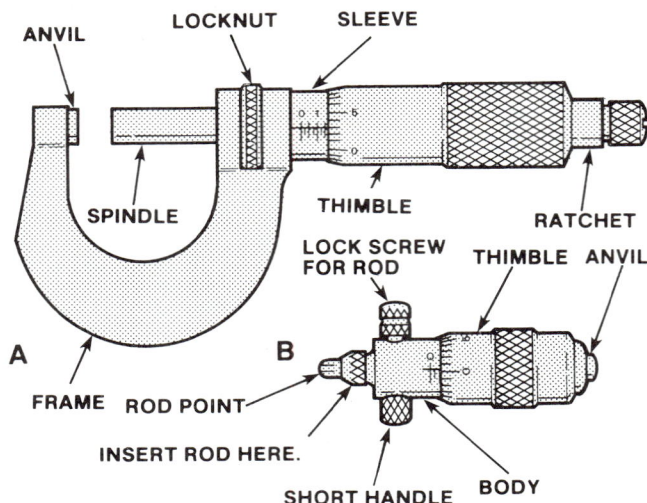

Figure 4-4 Major components of (A) an outside and (B) an inside micrometer.

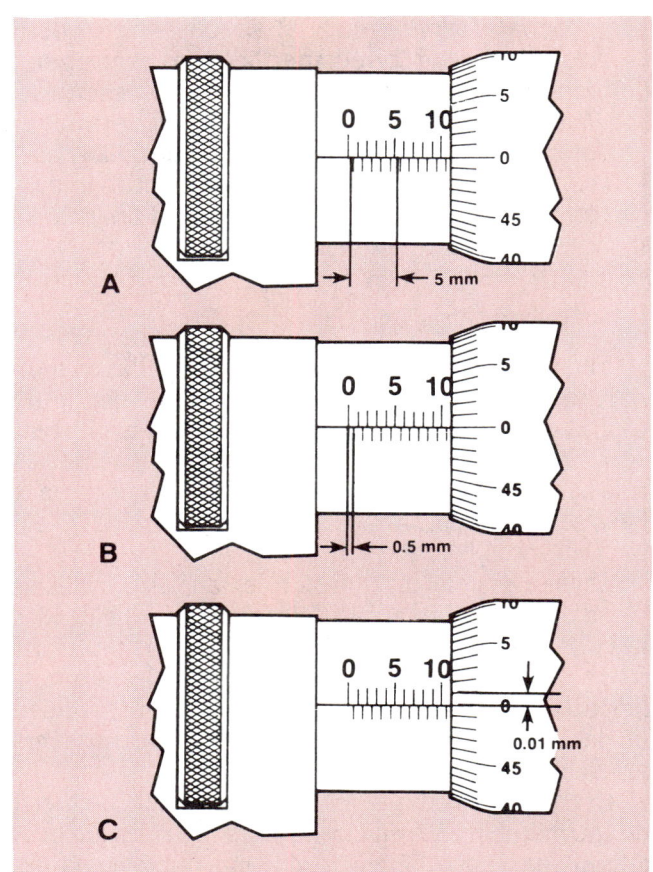

Figure 4-5 Reading a metric micrometer: (A) 5 mm; (B) 0.5 mm; (C) 0.01 mm.

a mm. One revolution of the thimble changes the reading one space on the sleeve scale or 0.5 mm (Figure 4-5B).
- The beveled edge of the thimble is divided into 50 equal divisions with every fifth line numbered 0, 5, 10 . . . 45. Since one complete revolution of the

PHOTO SEQUENCE 2

❏ **USING A MICROMETER**

P2-1 Micrometers can be used to measure the diameter of many objects. By measuring the stem of a valve in two places, the wear of the stem can be determined.

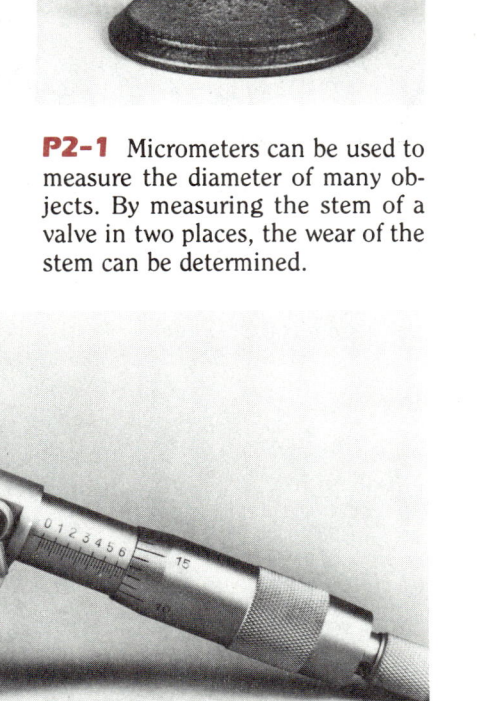

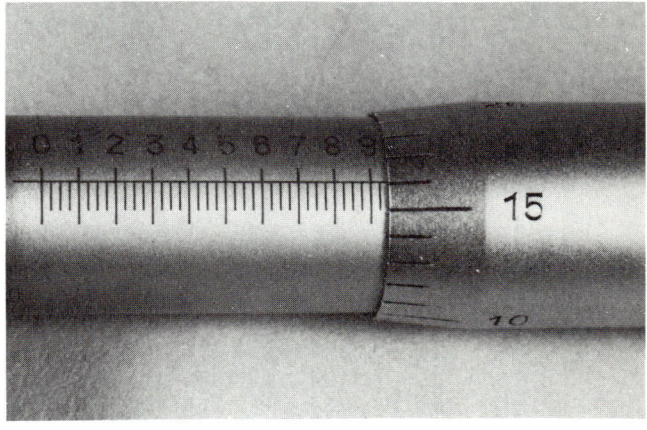

P2-3 The graduations on the sleeve each represent 0.025 inch. To read a measurement on a micrometer, begin by counting the visible lines on the sleeve by 0.025.

P2-4 The graduations on the thimble assembly define the area between the lines on the sleeve. The number indicated on the thimble is added to the measurement shown on the sleeve.

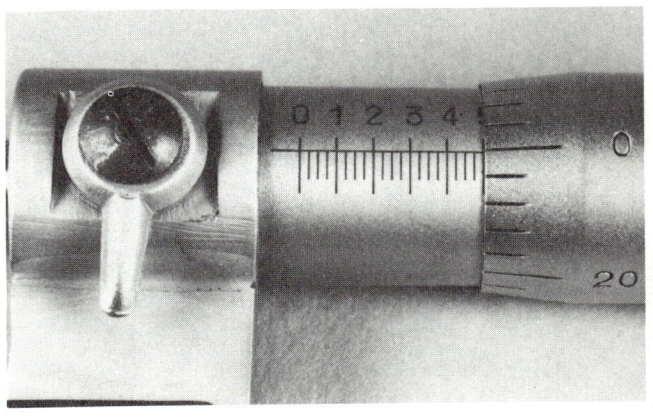

P2-2 Because the diameter of the stem is less than one inch, a 0-to-1-inch micrometer is used.

P2-5 Micrometer reading of 0.500 inch.

(continued)

57

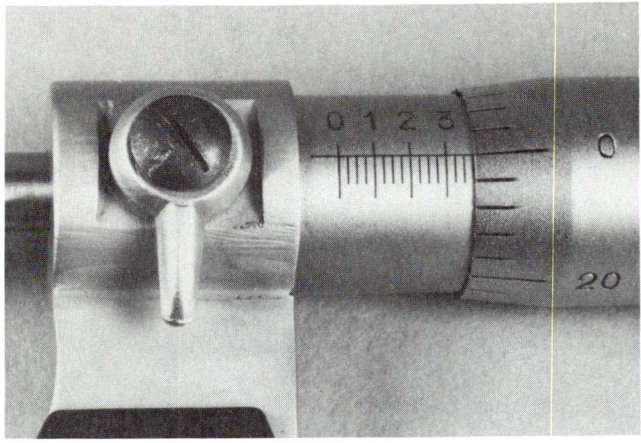

P2-6 Micrometer reading of 0.375 inch.

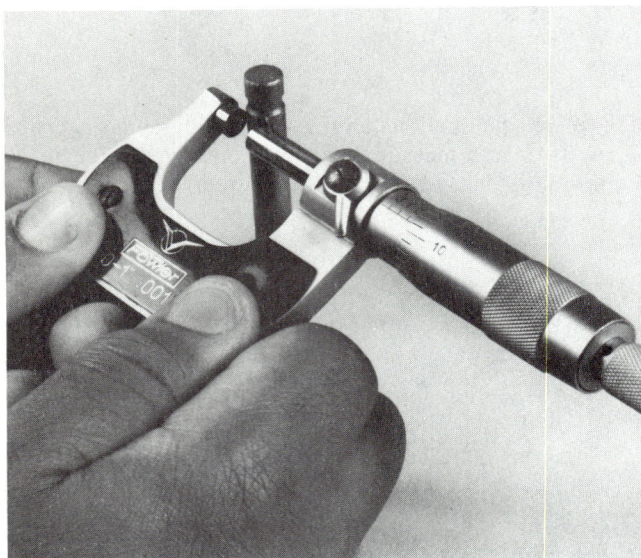

P2-7 Normally little stem wear is evident directly below the keeper grooves. To measure the diameter of the stem at that point, close the micrometer around the stem.

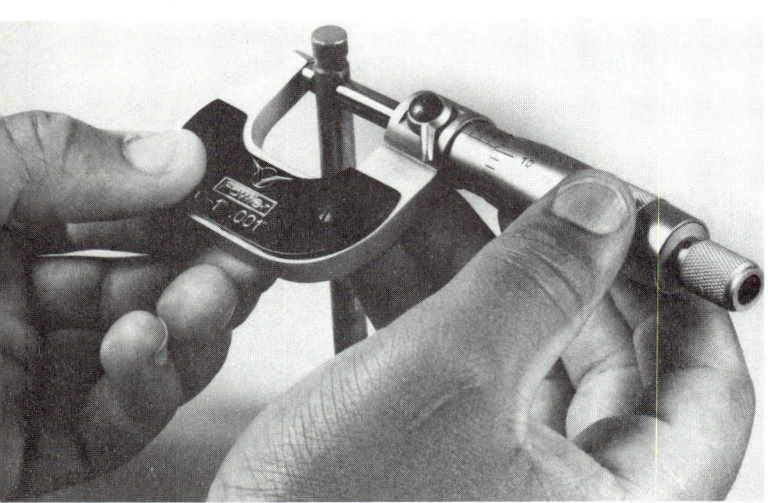

P2-8 To get an accurate reading, slowly close the micrometer until a slight drag is felt while passing the valve in and out of the micrometer.

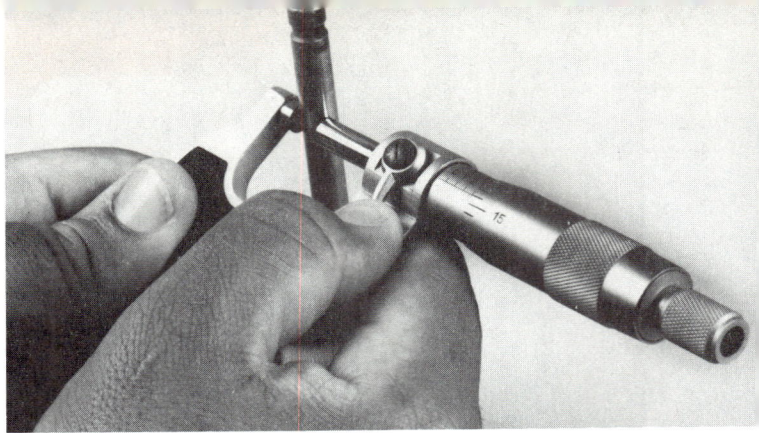

P2-9 To prevent the reading from changing while you move the micrometer away from the stem, use your thumb to activate the lock lever.

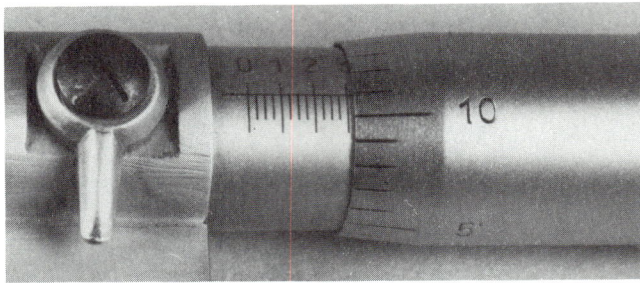

P2-10 This reading (0.311 inch) represents the diameter of the valve stem at the top of the wear area.

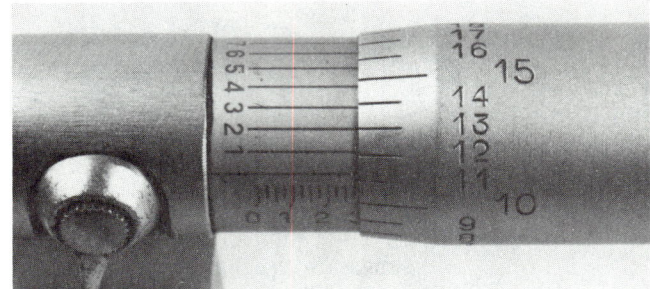

P2-11 Some micrometers are able to measure in 0.0001 inch. Use this type of micrometer if the specifications call for this type of accuracy. Note that the exact diameter of the valve stem is 0.3112 inch.

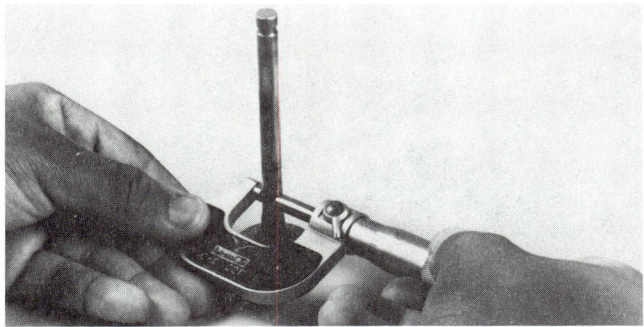

P2-12 Most valve stem wear occurs above the valve head. The diameter here should also be measured. The difference between the diameter of the valve stem just below the keepers and just above the valve head represents the amount of valve stem wear. ■

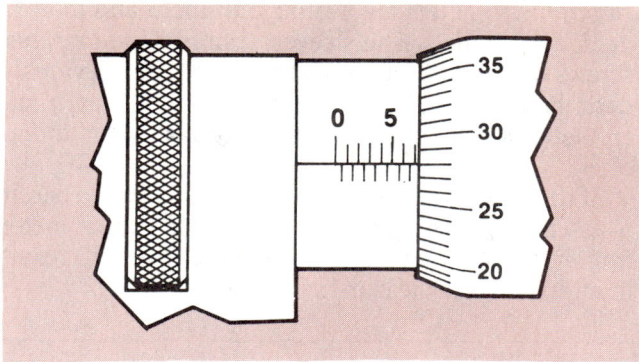

Figure 4-6 The total reading on this micrometer is 7.28 mm.

thimble advances the spindle 0.5 mm, each graduation on the thimble is equal to 1/50 of 0.5 mm or one hundredth of a millimeter (Figure 4-5C).

As with the inch-graduated micrometer, the three separate readings are added together to obtain the total reading (Figure 4-6).

PROCEDURES
Using a Metric Outside Micrometer

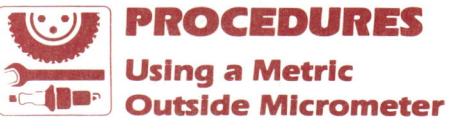

1. Read the largest number on the sleeve that has been uncovered by the thimble. In the illustration it is 5, which means the first number in the series is 5 mm.
2. Count the number of lines past the number 5 that the thimble has uncovered. In the example, this is 4. Since each space is equal to 0.5 mm, 4 spaces equal 4 × 0.5 or 2 mm. This added to the figure obtained in step 1 gives 7 mm.
3. Read the graduation line on the thimble that coincides with the horizontal line of the sleeve scale and add this to the total obtained in step 2. In the example, the thimble scale reads 28 or 0.28 mm. This added to the 7 mm from step 2 gives a total reading of 7.28 mm.

Using an Outside Micrometer

To measure small objects using an outside micrometer, open the jaws of the tool and slip the object to be measured between the spindle and anvil. While holding the object against the anvil, turn the thimble using the thumb and forefinger until the spindle contacts the object. Never clamp the micrometer tightly. Use only enough pressure on the thimble to allow the work to just fit between the anvil and spindle. For a correct measurement, the object must slip through the micrometer with only a very light resistance. When a satisfactory adjustment has been made, lock the micrometer (if so equipped). Read the measurement

Figure 4-7 Using a digital micrometer.

scale. Be careful not to change the setting if the tool is not equipped with a lock. Figure 4-7 shows a digital outside micrometer in use.

To measure larger objects such as a piston, hold the frame of the micrometer and slip it over the work while adjusting the thimble. It is important to slip the micrometer back and forth over the work until you feel a very light resistance, while at the same time rocking the tool from side to side to make certain the spindle cannot be closed any farther (Figure 4-8). These steps should be taken with any precision measuring device to ensure correct measurements.

Measurements will be reliable if the micrometer is calibrated correctly. To calibrate a micrometer, close the micrometer over a micrometer standard. If the reading differs from that of the known micrometer standard, then the micrometer will need adjustment.

Reading an Inside Micrometer

Inside micrometers (Figure 4-9) are used to measure bore or hole sizes. To use an inside micrometer,

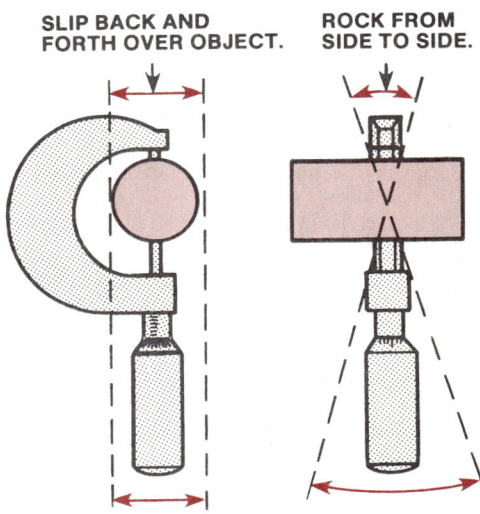

Figure 4-8 Slip the micrometer when measuring larger objects.

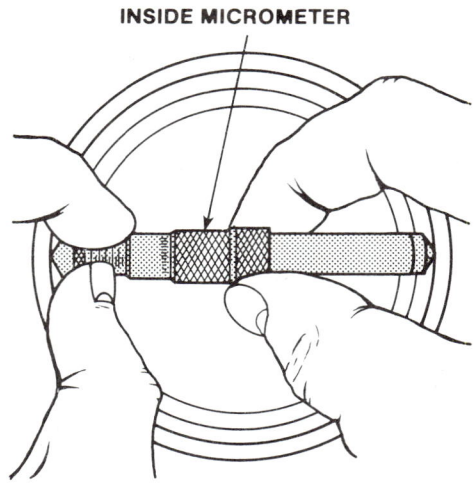

Figure 4-9 Obtaining a precise measurement with an inside micrometer.

place it inside the bore or hole and extend the measuring surfaces until each end touches the bore's surface. If the bore is large, it might be necessary to use an extension rod to increase the micrometer's range. These extension rods come in various lengths. The inside micrometer is read in the same manner as an outside micrometer.

To obtain a precise measurement in either inch or metric graduations, keep the anvil firmly against one side of the bore and rock the inside micrometer back and forth and side to side. This ensures that the micrometer fits in the center of the work with the correct amount of resistance. As with the outside micrometer, this procedure will require a little practice until you get the feel for the correct resistance and fit of the tool.

Reading a Depth Micrometer

The depth micrometer (Figure 4-10) is used to measure the distance between two parallel surfaces. Depth micrometers are available in inch- and metric-graduated models. The sleeves, thimbles, and ratchet screws operate in the same manner as the previously described inside and outside micrometers. Depth micrometers are read in the same way as other micrometers.

If the depth micrometer is used with a gauge bar, it is essential to keep both the bar and the micrometer from rocking. Any movement of either part will result in an inaccurate measurement.

> **SHOP TALK**
>
> Follow these tips for taking care of a micrometer.
> - Always clean the micrometer before using it.
> - Do not touch measuring surfaces.
> - Store the tool properly. The spindle face should not touch the anvil face, or a change in temperature might spring the micrometer.
> - Clean the micrometer after use. Wipe it clean of any oil, dirt, or dust using a lint-free cloth.
> - Do not drop the tool. It is a sensitive instrument and must be handled with care.
> - Check the calibration weekly. If it drops at any time, check it immediately.

Telescoping Gauge

Telescoping gauges (Figure 4-11) are used for measuring bore diameters and other clearances. They may also be called snap gauges. They are normally offered in sizes ranging from fractions of an inch through 6 inches. Each gauge consists of two telescoping plungers, a handle, and a lock screw. Telescoping gauges are usually used with an outside micrometer.

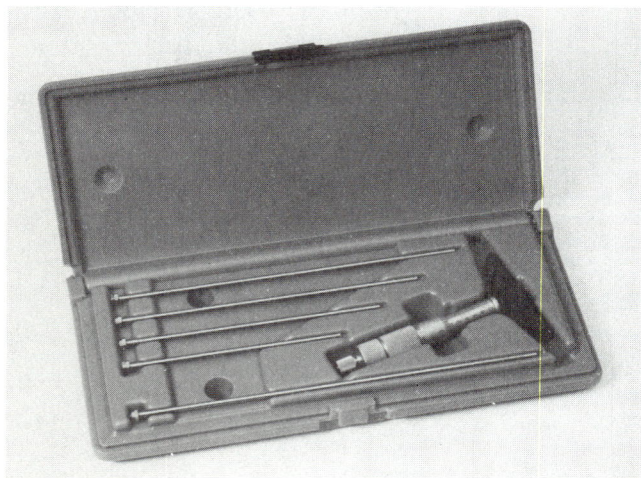

Figure 4-10 Typical depth micrometer. *Courtesy of Central Tools, Inc.*

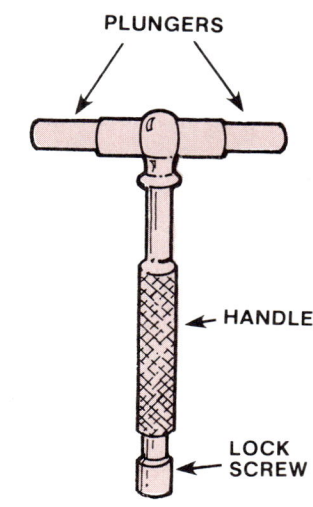

Figure 4-11 Typical telescoping gauge.

Shop Tools   61

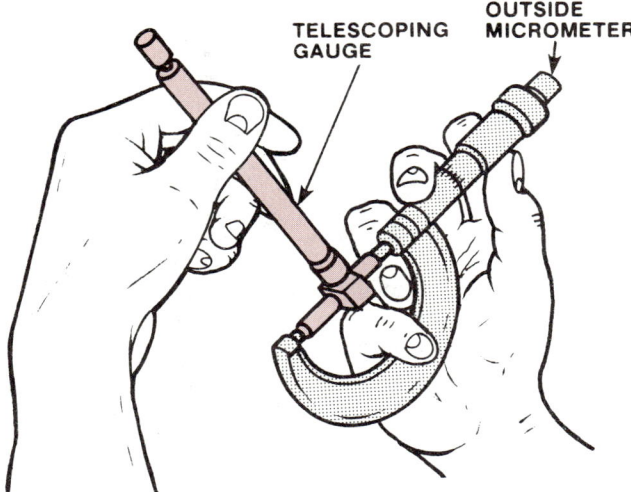

Figure 4-12 Measuring a telescoping gauge with a micrometer.

To use the telescoping gauge, insert it into the bore and loosen the lock screw. This will allow the plungers to snap against the bore. Lock the screw in place before removing. Then, the telescoping gauge is measured using a micrometer (Figure 4-12).

Small Hole Gauge

The small hole gauge functions in the same manner as the telescoping gauge. It is expanded in a bore, then measured with an outside micrometer (Figure 4-13). Like the telescoping gauge, the small hole gauge consists of a lock, handle, and an expanding end. It expands or retracts by turning the gauge handle. The small hole gauge is commonly used to determine the diameter of valve guides.

Feeler Gauge

The feeler gauge is a thin strip of metal of known and closely controlled thickness. Several of these metal

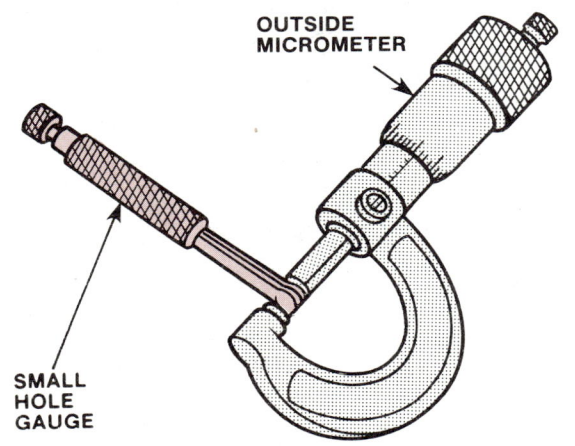

Figure 4-13 Measuring a small hole gauge with a micrometer.

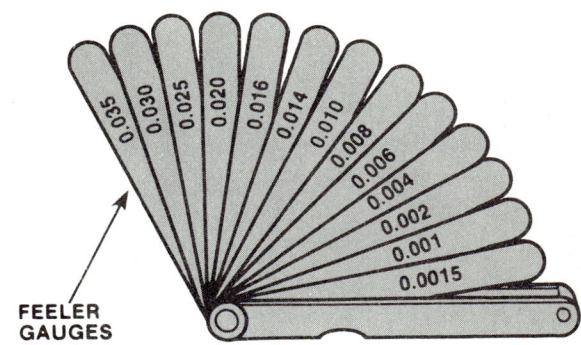

Figure 4-14 Typical feeler gauge pack.

strips are often combined into a multiple measuring instrument that pivots in a manner similar to a pocket knife (Figure 4-14). The desired thickness gauge can be pivoted away from others for convenient use. A steel feeler gauge pack usually contains leaves of 0.002- to 0.010-inch thickness (in steps of 0.001 inch) and leaves of 0.012- to 0.024-inch thickness (in steps of 0.002 inch).

The feeler gauge can be used by itself to measure piston ring side clearance, piston ring end gap, connecting rod side clearance, crankshaft end play, and other similar procedures. The feeler gauge can also be used with a precision straightedge to measure main bearing bore alignment and cylinder head/block warpage (Figure 4-15).

Radius Gauge

A radius gauge (Figure 4-16) is used to check the crankshaft fillet radii at the edge or side of the rod and main bearing journals to make sure they are the same size as specified in the service manual. They can be used to measure the radii of the grooves and the external or internal fillets (round corners).

Screw Pitch Gauge

The use of a screw pitch gauge (Figure 4-17) provides a quick and accurate method of checking the

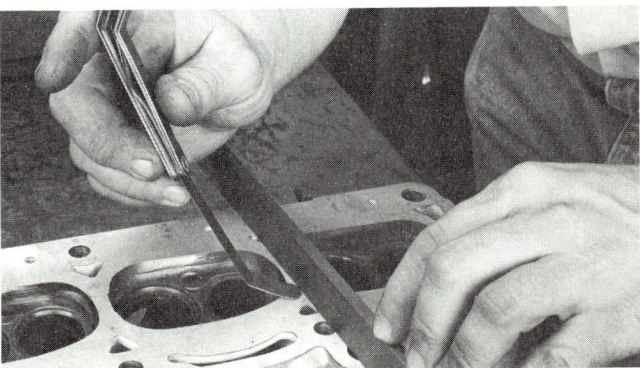

Figure 4-15 Using a feeler gauge and precision straightedge to check for warpage. *Courtesy of Fel-Pro, Inc.*

Figure 4-16 A set of radius gauges. *Courtesy of Goodson Shop Supplies*

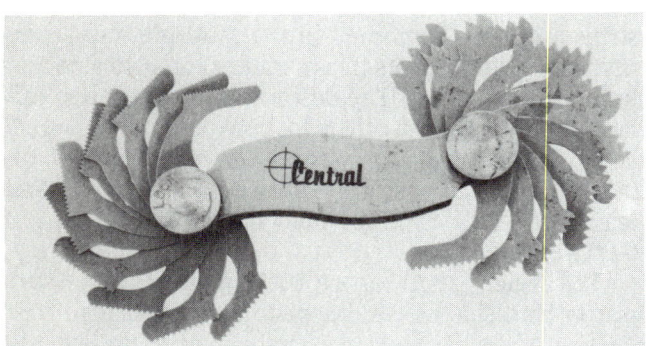

Figure 4-17 Typical screw pitch gauge. *Courtesy of Central Tools, Inc.*

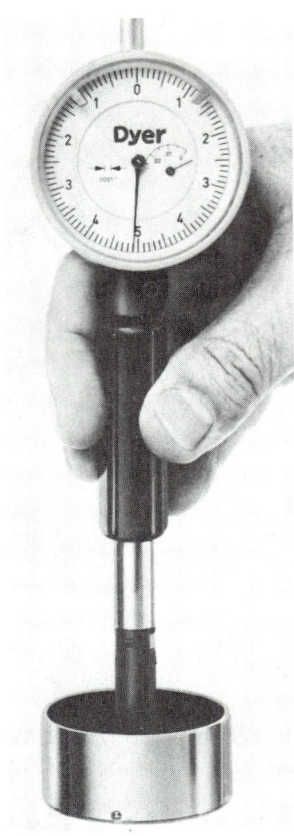

Figure 4-18 Typical dial indicator. *Courtesy of The Dyer Co.*

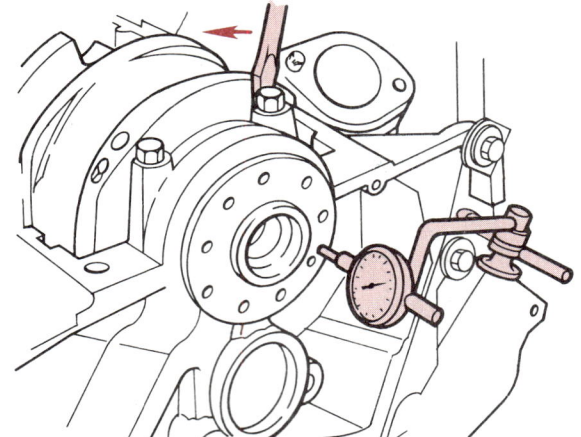

Figure 4-19 Using a dial indicator to measure crankshaft end play.

threads per inch (pitch) of a fastener. The leaves of this measuring tool are marked with the various pitches. Just match the teeth of the gauge with the threads of the fastener and the correct pitch can be read directly from the leaf.

Screw pitch gauges are available for the various types of fastener threads used in the automotive industry: American National coarse and fine threads, metric threads, International Standard threads, and Whitworth threads.

Dial Indicator

The dial indicator (Figure 4-18) is calibrated in 0.001-inch (one-thousandth inch) increments. Metric dial indicators are also available. Both types are used to measure movement. Common uses of the dial indicator include measuring valve lift, journal concentricity, flywheel or brake rotor runout, gear backlash, and crankshaft end play. Dial indicators are available with various face markings and measurement ranges to accommodate many measuring tasks.

To use a dial indicator, position the indicator rod against the object to be measured. Then, push the indicator toward the work until the indicator needle travels far enough around the gauge face to permit movement to be read in either direction (Figure 4-19). Zero the indicator needle on the gauge. Always be sure that the range of the dial indicator is sufficient to allow the amount of movement required by the measuring operation. For example, do not use a 1-inch indicator on a component that will move 2 inches.

Valve Seat Runout Gauge

The valve seat runout gauge, also called a concentricity gauge, is similar to the dial indicator. It features a gauge face divided into 0.001-inch (one-thousandth inch) increments, an arbor that centers the instrument in the valve guide bore, and an indicator bar that can be adjusted so that it bears on the valve seat (Figure

Figure 4-20 Typical valve seat runout gauge. *Courtesy of Central Tools, Inc.*

4-20). The tool is then slowly rotated around the circumference of the valve seat to check its concentricity (runout).

Cylinder Bore Dial Gauge

The cylinder bore dial gauge is used to determine cylinder bore size, out-of-round, and taper. These three measurements, in addition to main bearing saddle alignment, provide basic information about the condition of the cylinder block.

Cylinder bore dial gauges are read in the same way that a dial indicator is read. As with the inside micrometer and telescoping gauge, the cylinder bore micrometer must be rocked to obtain the correct measurement.

The parts of the cylinder bore dial gauge include the handle, guide blocks, lock, indicator contact, and dial indicator (Figure 4-21). Various indicator contacts can be installed to measure several bore sizes with one gauge.

Cylinder bores do not always wear in a perfectly round pattern. One side of the cylinder wall usually wears more than the other. For this reason, cylinder roundness must be determined (Figure 4-22). To measure out-of-round, measure the cylinder bore at uniform depth in three directions: front/rear, right/left, and diagonally (Figure 4-23). Then, the smallest reading obtained from the cylinder is subtracted from the largest reading. The resulting figure is cylinder bore out-of-round. By measuring the bore at the top of the ring travel, it is possible to determine the maximum cylinder wear.

Another cylinder bore gauge that is used to check cylinder taper and out-of-roundness is shown in Figure 4-24. The cylinder diameter can also be determined when used with a micrometer.

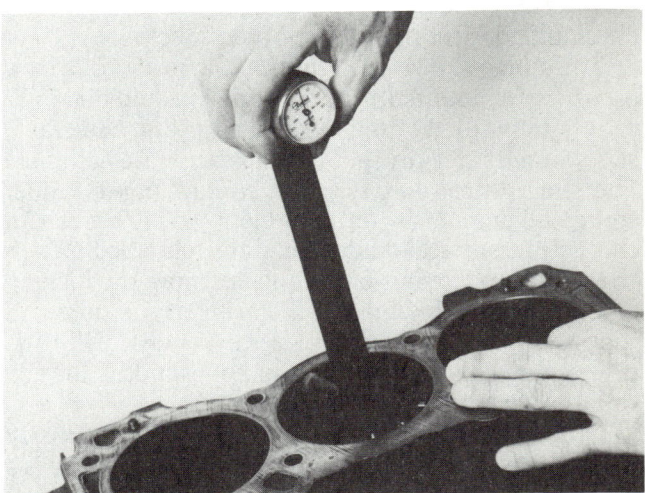

Figure 4-22 Determining cylinder roundness using a cylinder bore dial gauge. *Courtesy of Central Tools, Inc.*

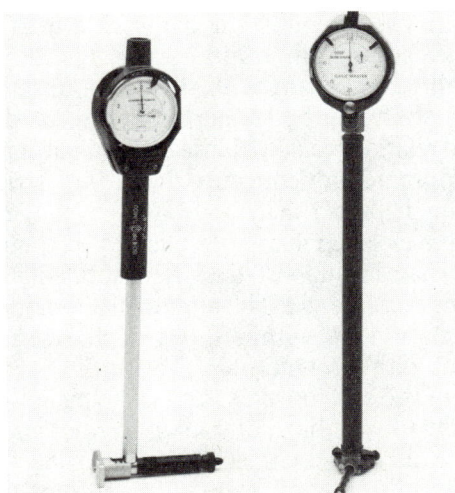

Figure 4-21 Typical cylinder bore dial gauges. *Courtesy of Goodson Shop Supplies*

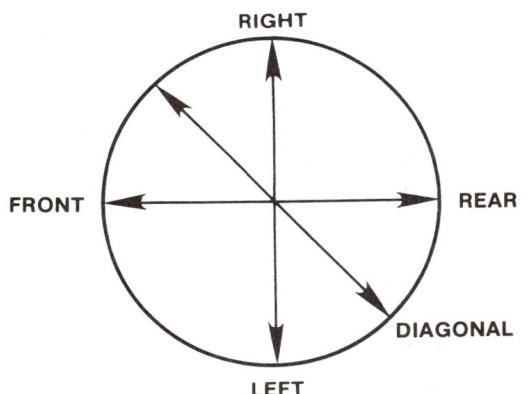

THE DIFFERENCE BETWEEN THE LARGEST AND SMALLEST DIAMETERS EQUALS OUT-OF-ROUND.

Figure 4-23 Recommended directions for measuring cylinder out-of-roundness.

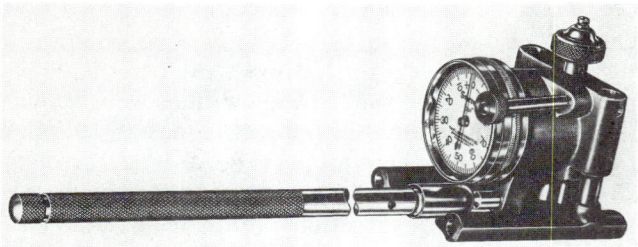

Figure 4-24 Another common type of cylinder bore dial gauge. *Courtesy of L. S. Starrett Company*

Out-of-Roundness Gauge

The present-day thin-wall bearing insert is designed to assure complete contact between the bearing back and saddle bore. A properly assembled bearing insert will, therefore, conform exactly to the contour of the saddle bore, making it imperative that the saddle bore is a perfect circle. Special gauges are available for checking connecting rod out-of-roundness.

The gauge shown in Figure 4-25 consists of a base on which is mounted a thousandths reading dial indicator and on the bottom a positive locking adjustable slide, which is readily set to the approximate hole size. The sliding head has two line contact points under spring tension insuring alignment at all times. All contacting surfaces and points are hardened. When checking a rod for out-of-roundness, move the locking adjustable slide to suit the diameter of the bore and then set the dial indicator at zero. The dial will then give a plus or minus reading in thousandths for any variation in the rod diameter.

Out-of-roundness can be checked by using an inside micrometer. However, the out-of-roundness gauge is a much quicker and easier method.

Aligning Bar

An aligning bar is an excellent tool for checking the alignment of the crankcase saddle bores (Figure 4-26). With the bearings removed, insert the aligning bar into the full length of the crankcase and tighten the bearing caps. If the bar can then be turned by hand using a short bar (12 inches) for leverage, the saddle bores are

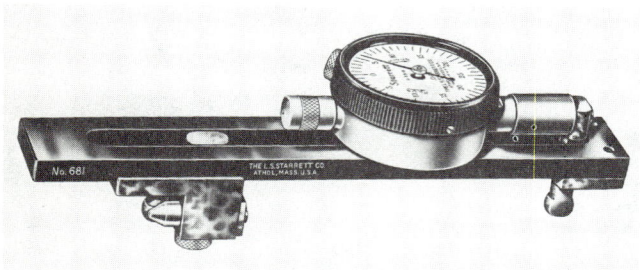

Figure 4-25 Typical out-of-roundness gauge. *Courtesy of L. S. Starrett Company*

Figure 4-26 Checking crankcase saddle bore alignment with an aligning bar. *Courtesy of Sunnen Products Co.*

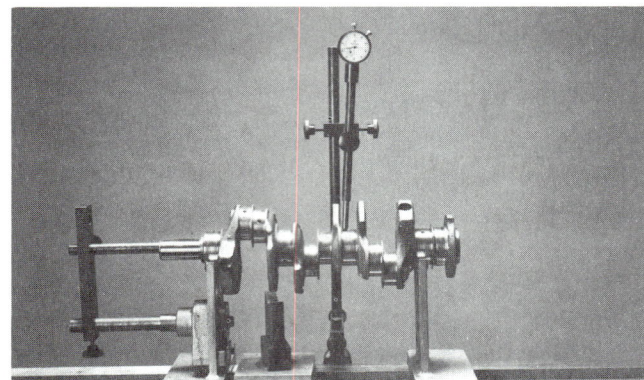

Figure 4-27 Using V-blocks and a dial indicator to check crankshaft alignment. *Courtesy of Perfect Circle/Dana*

in alignment. If the aligning bar will not turn, the saddle bores are out of alignment.

V-Blocks

The use of V-blocks and a dial indicator is the recommended method for checking crankshaft alignment (Figure 4-27). With the front and rear main journals in the V-blocks, the dial indicator is used to check the center main journal.

On short crankshafts with three or four main journals, the shaft can be supported and rotated on the front and rear journals, with the dial indicator registering the alignment or concentricity at the vertical centerline on the other main journals. On longer shafts having five or seven main journals, it is recommended that the shaft be supported at the intermediate mains to prevent possible sag. The alignment from journal to journal should be within 0.001 inch, with overall alignment within 0.002 inch.

Each of the end journals is checked by moving one of the V-blocks to the center main journal and taking the dial reading on the unsupported journal. A strip of paper should be placed in each V to prevent the journals from becoming scratched. It is also important to check the nose of the crankshaft for runout.

Torque-Indicating Wrench

The fact that practically every vehicle and engine manufacturer publishes a list of torque recommendations is ample proof of the importance of using the proper amounts of torque when tightening nuts or cap screws on bearing caps and other engine parts.

Several types of torque-indicating wrenches are available. One of the most popular is the dial type (Figure 4-28). Any one of these will enable the technician to duplicate the pressure used when the engine was assembled originally, thereby duplicating conditions of tightness and stress that the manufacturer has found to be the most desirable (Figure 4-29).

Bearing caps that are too tight will distort the bearings, causing excessive wear and incorrect oil clearance, which often results in rapid wear of other engine parts due to the altered oil clearance between parts.

Insufficient torque can result in out-of-round bores with less horizontal than vertical clearance and subsequent failure due to side contact. In extreme cases of inadequate bolt torque, bolt and rod or cap breakage can result, causing major engine failure.

> ### SHOP TALK
>
> The torque wrench, as already noted, has long been the standard tool for tightening bolts and nuts that clamp parts together. Torque is actually the twisting force used to turn a fastener (bolt or nut) against friction (between threads and between fastener head and component surface). It is a fact that up to 90% of the torque is used up by friction. The remaining 10% is used to clamp parts together. Therefore, clamping forces can vary significantly over a single cylinder head or other engine component.
>
> Because new high tech engines are designed with extremely close tolerances, it is not surprising that torque alone is no longer adequate for proper service procedures. Torque/angle measurement of fastener installations is a method of clamping parts together that ensures like fasteners will exert the same clamp force without deviation from one fastener to the next. Without proper clamping forces, distortion of cylinder bores and bearing bores can occur as well as leaking head gaskets. The torque/angle method first specifies a low threshold torque on the fastener to move components in close touch. Torque is least affected by fastener friction at these low values. The fasteners are then turned through a specified angle. The clamping force of each fastener will then be consistent.
>
> The unit shown in Figure 4-30 is a precision, microprocessor-controlled torque/angle meter that makes sure fasteners are tightened to true clamp load specifications consistently and easily.

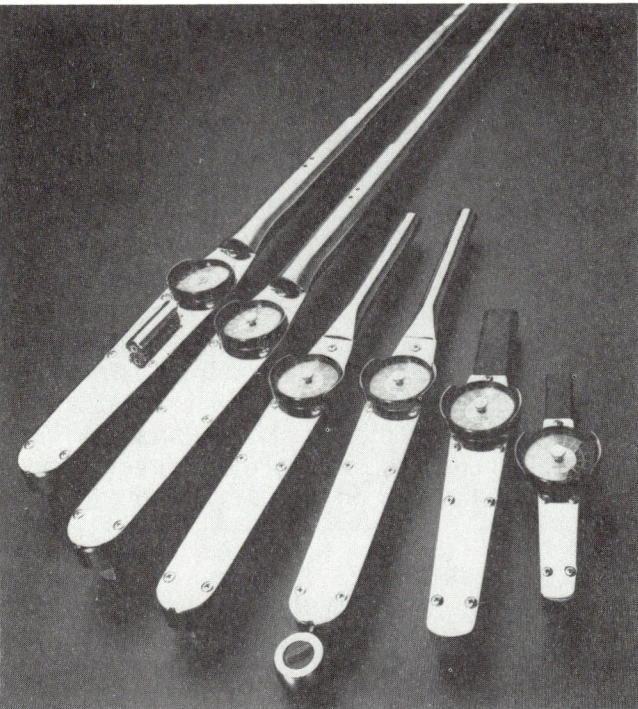

Figure 4-28 Dial-type torque-indicating wrenches. *Courtesy of Central Tools, Inc.*

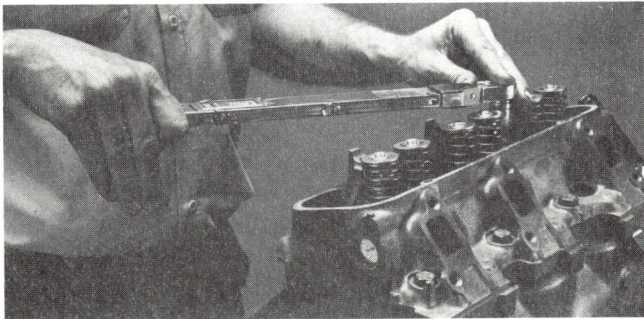

Figure 4-29 Using a torque-indicating wrench. *Courtesy of Perfect Circle/Dana*

☐ HAND TOOLS

There are many repair tasks that do not lend themselves to the use of power tools. For those jobs, the automobile technician must have suitable hand tools. Most service departments and garages require their technicians to buy their own hand tools. A set of master technician's hand tools and tool chest are shown in Figure 4-31.

Wrenches

A complete collection of wrenches is indispensable for the technician. A well-equipped technician will

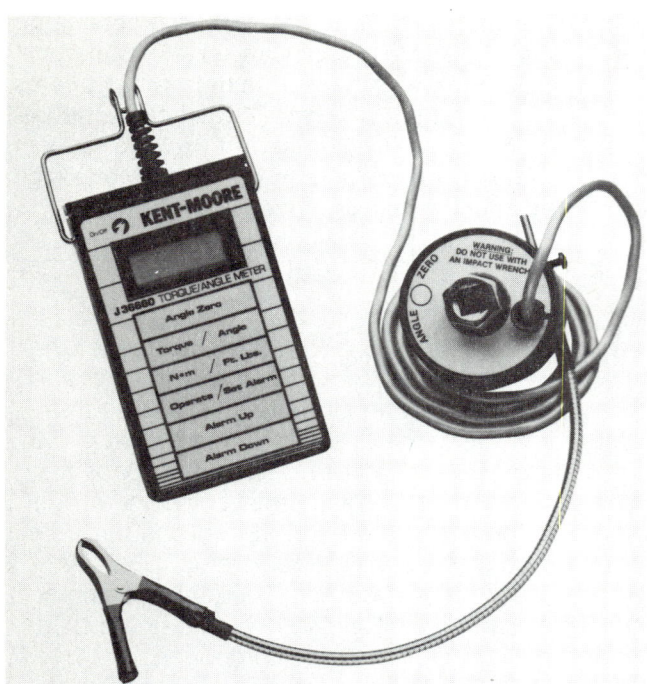

Figure 4-30 Typical precision torque/angle meter. *Courtesy of Kent-Moore Corp.*

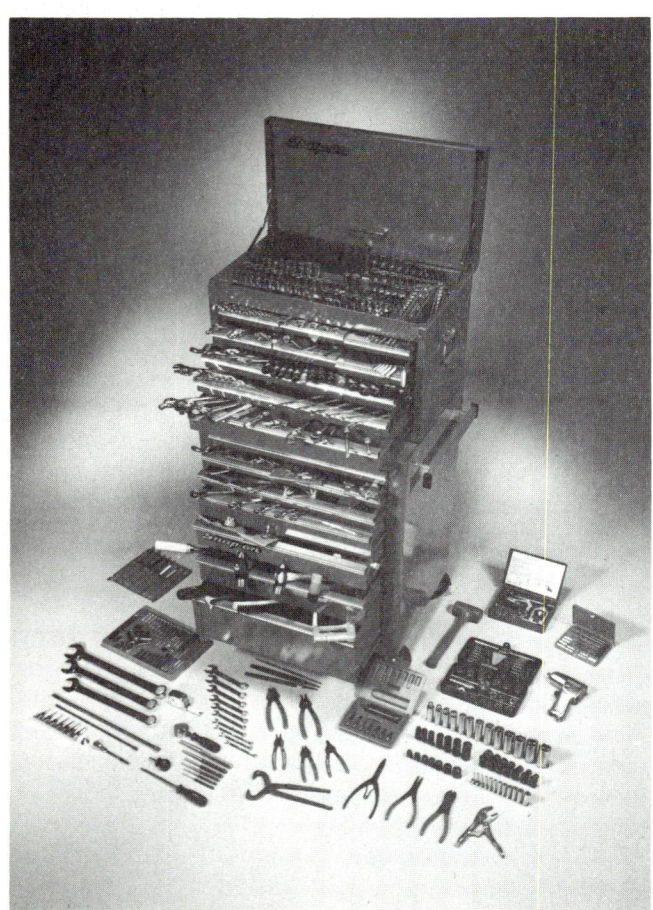

Figure 4-31 Professional set of automotive hand tools. *Courtesy of Snap-on Tools Corp.*

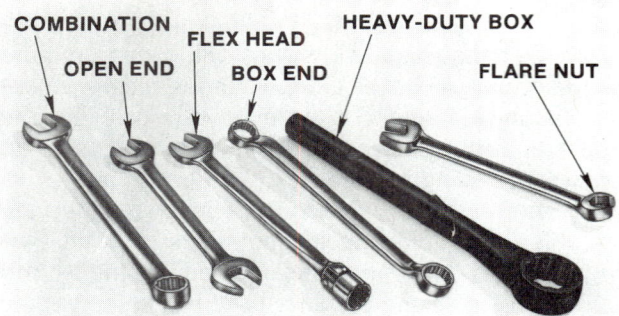

Figure 4-32 Wrench assortment. *Courtesy of Snap-on Tools Corp.*

have both metric and SAE wrenches in a variety of sizes and styles (Figure 4-32).

The word wrench means twist. A wrench is a tool for twisting and/or holding bolt heads or nuts. The width of the jaw opening determines its size. For example, a 1/2-inch wrench has a jaw opening (from face to face) of 1/2 inch. The size is actually slightly larger than its nominal size so that the wrench fits around a nut or bolt head of equal size.

SHOP TALK

Metric and SAE wrenches are not interchangeable. For example, a 9/16-inch wrench is 0.02 inch larger than a 14-millimeter nut. If the 9/16-inch wrench is used to turn or hold a 14-millimeter nut, the wrench will probably slip. This may cause rounding of the points of the nut and possibly skinned knuckles as well.

OPEN-END WRENCHES The jaws of the open-end wrench (Figure 4-33) allow the wrench to slide around bolts or nuts where there might be insufficient clear-

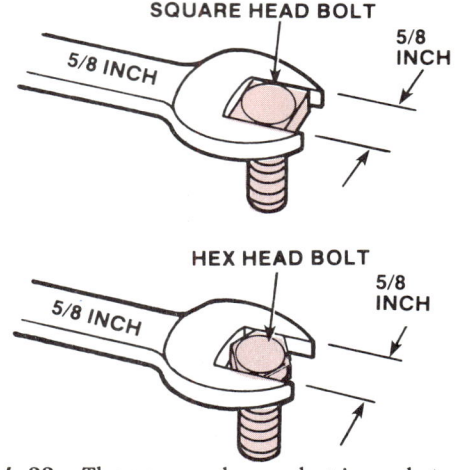

Figure 4-33 The open-end wrench grips only two faces of a fastener.

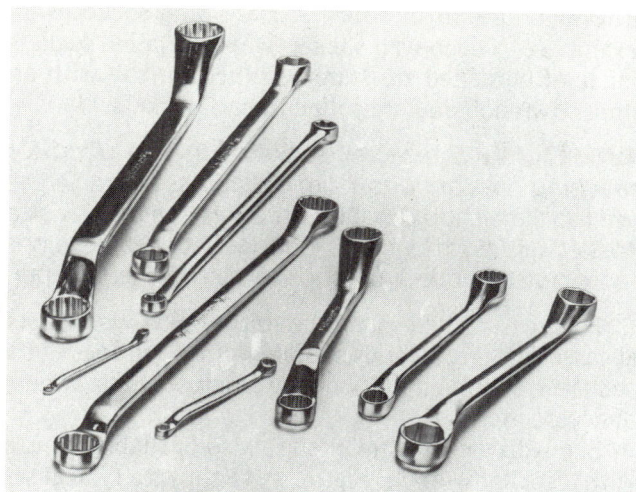

Figure 4–34 Box-end wrenches are closed to provide better holding power. *Courtesy of Snap-on Tools Corp.*

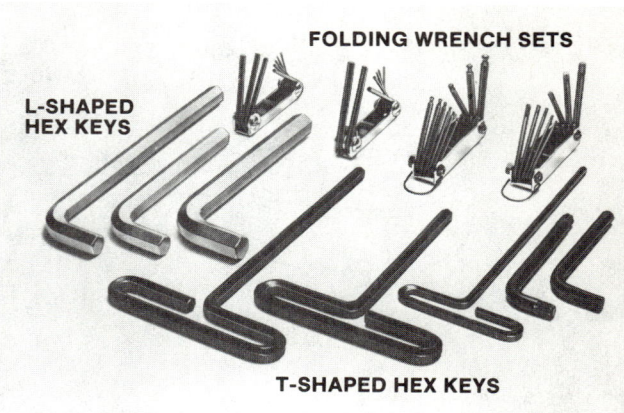

Figure 4–36 Typical Allen wrench set. *Courtesy of Snap-on Tools Corp.*

ance above or on one side of the nut to accept a box wrench.

BOX-END WRENCHES The end of the box-end wrench is boxed or closed rather than open (Figure 4–34). The jaws of the wrench fit completely around a bolt or nut, gripping each point on the fastener. The box-end wrench is not likely to slip off a nut or bolt. It is safer than an open-end wrench.

COMBINATION WRENCHES The combination wrench has an open-end jaw on one end and a box-end on the other. Both ends are the same size. Every auto technician should have two sets of wrenches: one for holding and one for turning. The combination wrench is probably the best choice for the second set. It complements either open-end or box-end wrench sets.

ADJUSTABLE WRENCHES An adjustable wrench has one fixed jaw and one movable jaw. The wrench opening can be adjusted by rotating a helical adjusting screw that is mated to teeth in the lower jaw. Because this type of wrench does not firmly grip a bolt's head, it is likely to slip. Adjustable wrenches should be carefully used and only when necessary. Be sure to put all of the turning pressure on the fixed jaw (Figure 4–35).

ALLEN WRENCHES Set screws are used to fasten door handles, instrument panel knobs, and even brake calipers. A set of hex head wrenches, or Allen wrenches (Figure 4–36), should be in every technician's tool box.

SOCKET WRENCHES In many situations, a socket wrench is much safer, faster, and easier to use than an open-end or box-end wrench. Some applications absolutely require one.

The basic socket wrench set consists of a ratchet handle and several barrel-shaped sockets. The socket fits over and around a given size bolt, nut, or wrench (Figure 4–37). Inside, it is shaped like a box-end

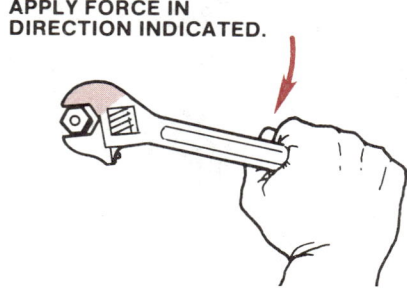

Figure 4–35 Pull the adjustable wrench so that the force bears against the fixed jaw.

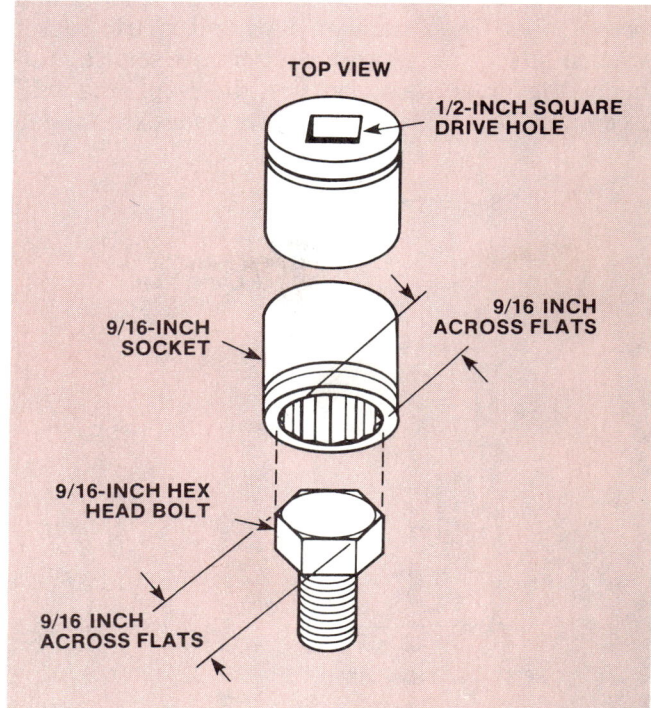

Figure 4–37 The size of a socket is the same as the bolt or nut size it fits.

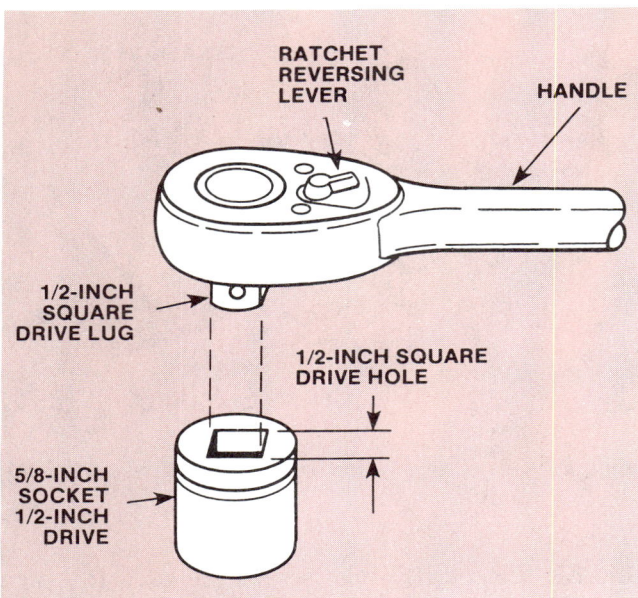

Figure 4-38 The socket drive size is equal to the diameter of the handle lug.

fit over bolt ends or studs. A spark plug socket is an example of a deep-well socket. Heavier walled sockets made of hardened steel are designed for use with an impact wrench and are called impact sockets.

CAUTION: Deep-well sockets are also good for reaching nuts or bolts in limited access areas. Deep-well sockets should not be used when a regular size socket will do the job. The longer socket develops more twist torque and tends to slip off the fastener.

Figure 4-40 shows a number of socket wrench set accessories. Accessories multiply the usefulness of a socket wrench. A good socket wrench set has a variety of accessories.

Screwdriver attachments are also available for use with a socket wrench. Figure 4-41 shows a typical set of screwdriver attachments and three specialty sockets. These socket wrench attachments are very handy when

wrench. Sockets are available in 6, 8, or 12 points. The top side of a socket has a square hole that accepts a square lug on the socket handle (Figure 4-38). One handle fits all the sockets in a set. The size of the lug (3/8 inch, 1/2 inch, and so on) indicates the drive size of the socket wrench. On better quality handles, a spring-loaded ball in the square lug fits into a depression in the socket. This ball holds the socket to the handle.

Sockets are available in various sizes, lengths, and bore depths. Both standard SAE and metric socket wrench sets are necessary for automotive service. Normally, the larger the socket size, the deeper the well. Deep-well sockets (Figure 4-39) are made extra long to

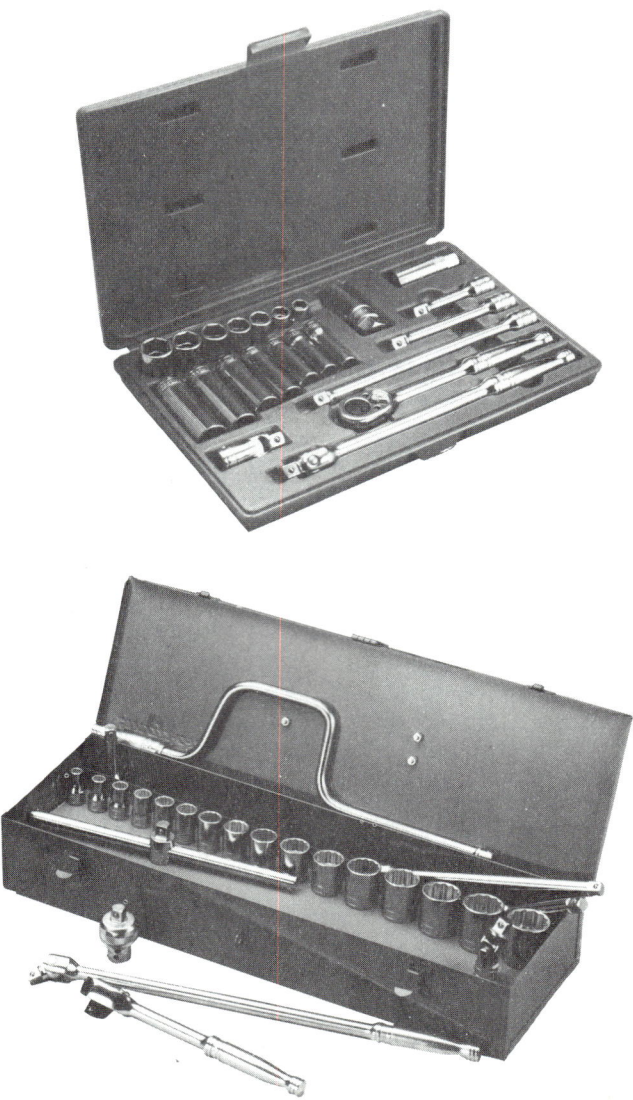

Figure 4-39 Deep-well sockets fit over bolt ends and studs.

Figure 4-40 Typical 3/8-inch and 1/2-inch socket wrench sets. *Courtesy of Snap-on Tools Corp.*

Shop Tools   69

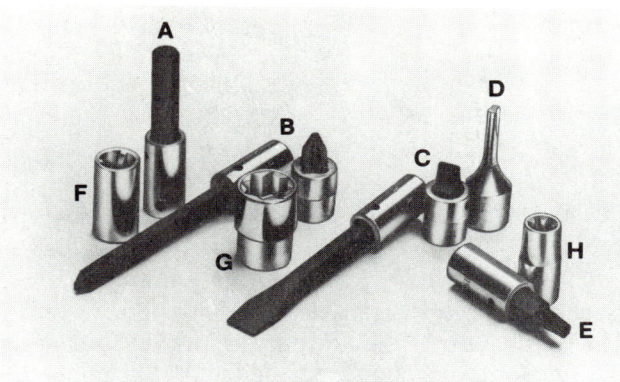

Figure 4-41 Typical screwdriver attachment set, including (A) hex driver, (B) Phillips driver, (C) flat tip driver, (D) clutch head driver, (E) Torx driver, (F) three wing socket, (G) double square socket, and (H) Torx socket. *Courtesy of Snap-on Tools Corp.*

a fastener cannot be loosened with a regular screwdriver. The leverage given by the ratchet handle is often just what it takes to break a stubborn screw loose.

Screwdrivers

A variety of threaded fasteners used in the automotive industry are driven by a screwdriver. Each fastener requires a specific kind of screwdriver, and the well-equipped technician will have several sizes of each (Figure 4-42).

All screwdrivers, regardless of the type of fastener they were designed for, have several things in common. The size of the screwdriver is determined by the length of the shank or blade. The size of the handle is important, too. The larger the handle diameter, the better grip it has and the more torque it will generate when turned. Screwdriver handles should also be insulated from the blade and made with a material that does not conduct electricity.

SHOP TALK

A screwdriver should not be used as a chisel, punch, or pry bar. Screwdrivers were not made to withstand blows or bending pressures. When misused in such a fashion, the tips will wear, become rounded, and tend to slip out of the fastener. Its usefulness is impaired, and a defective tool is also a dangerous tool.

STANDARD TIP SCREWDRIVERS A slotted screw accepts a screwdriver with a standard tip. The standard tip screwdriver is probably the most common type (Figure 4-43). It is useful for turning carriage bolts, machine screws, and sheet metal screws.

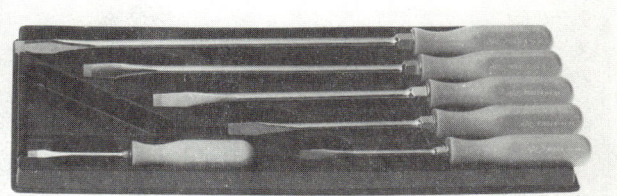

Figure 4-42 The prepared technician keeps several sizes of screwdrivers on hand. *Courtesy of Stanley Works*

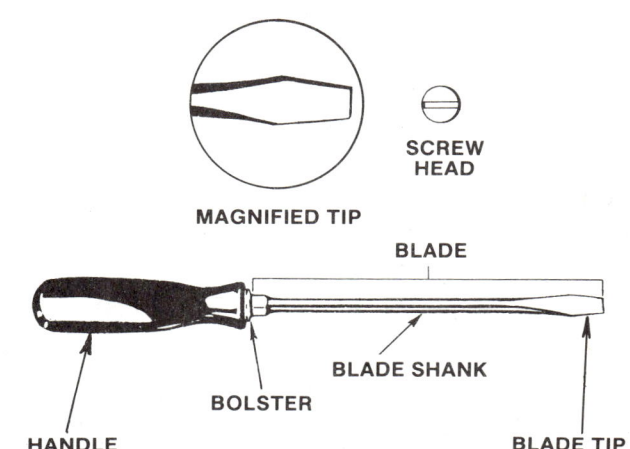

Figure 4-43 The standard tip screwdriver fits slotted head screws.

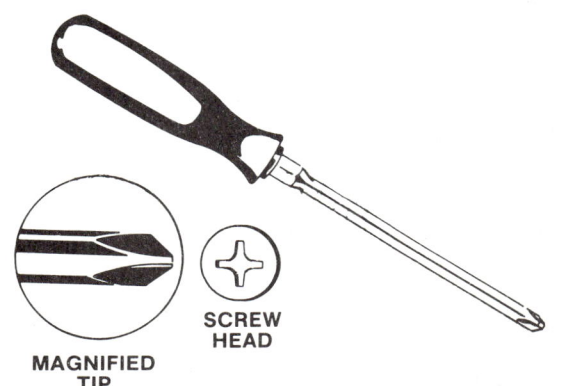

Figure 4-44 The tip of a Phillips screwdriver has four prongs that help prevent slippage of the fastener.

PHILLIPS SCREWDRIVERS The tip of a Phillips screwdriver has four prongs that fit the four slots in a Phillips head screw (Figure 4-44). This type of fastener is used very often in the automotive field. Not only does it look nicer than the slot head screw, but it also is easier to install. The four surfaces enclose the screwdriver tip so that there is less likelihood that the screwdriver will slip off the fastener.

SPECIALTY SCREWDRIVERS A number of specialty fasteners have been replacing the slot and Phillips

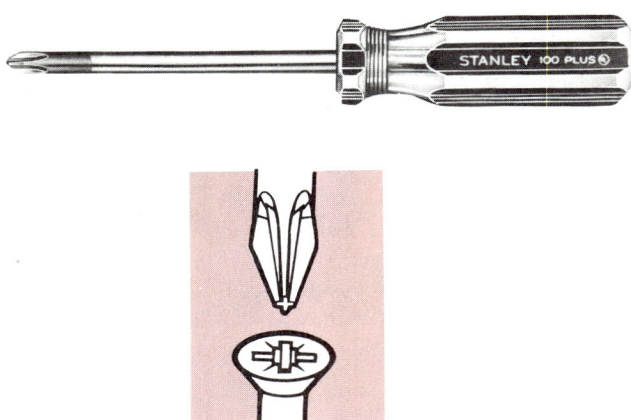

Figure 4-45 The Posidriv screwdriver is similar to a Phillips. *Courtesy of Stanley Works*

head screws. This new breed of fasteners is designed to improve transfer of torque from the screwdriver to the fastener, to slip less, and to offer some tamper resistance.

The Posidriv® screwdriver is like a Phillips but with a tip that is flatter and blunter (Figure 4-45). The squared tip grips the screw's head and slips less than a Phillips screwdriver. The Torx® fastener is used to secure headlight assemblies, mirrors, and luggage racks. Not only does the six-prong tip provide greater turning power and less slippage (Figure 4-46), but the Torx fastener also provides a measure of tamper resistance.

Pliers

Pliers are an all-around gripping tool used for working with wires, clips, and pins. The auto technician must own several types: standard pliers for common parts and wires, needle nose for really small parts, and large adjustable pliers for large items and heavy-duty work.

COMBINATION PLIERS Combination pliers (Figure 4-47) are the most common type of pliers and are

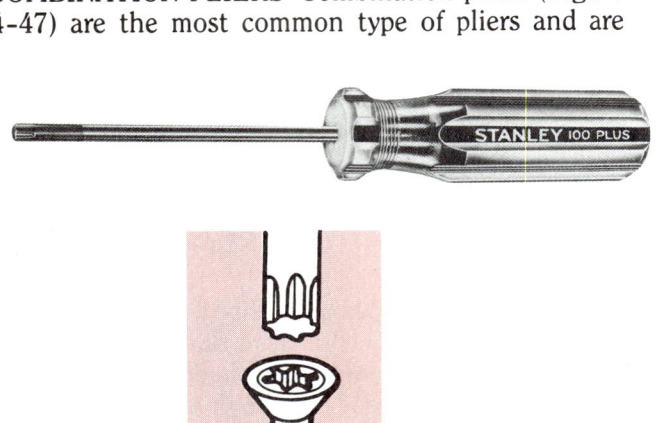

Figure 4-46 Torx screwdrivers feature a six-prong tip. *Courtesy of Stanley Works*

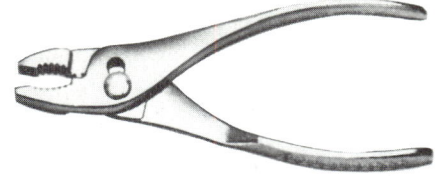

Figure 4-47 Combination, or slip-joint, pliers. *Courtesy of Snap-on Tools Corp.*

frequently used in many kinds of automotive repair. The jaws have both flat and curved surfaces for holding flat or round objects. Also called slip-joint pliers, the combination pliers have many jaw-opening sizes. One jaw can be moved up or down on a pin attached to the other jaw to change the size of the opening.

ADJUSTABLE PLIERS Adjustable pliers, commonly called channel locks (Figure 4-48), have a multi-position slip joint that allows for many jaw-opening sizes.

NEEDLE NOSE PLIERS Needle nose pliers have long tapered jaws (Figure 4-49). They are indispensable for grasping small parts or for reaching into tight spots. Many needle nose pliers also have wire cutting edges and a wire stripper.

LOCKING PLIERS Locking pliers, or vise grips, are similar to the standard pliers, except that they can be locked closed with a very tight grip (Figure 4-50). They are extremely useful for holding parts together. They are also useful for getting a firm grip on a badly rounded fastener on which wrenches and sockets are no longer effective. Locking pliers come in several sizes and jaw configurations for use in many auto repair jobs.

DIAGONAL CUTTING PLIERS Diagonal cutting pliers, or cutters, are used to cut electrical connections, cotter pins, and other wires on an automobile. Jaws on these pliers have extra-hard cutting edges (Figure 4-51).

Figure 4-48 Adjustable pliers. *Courtesy of Snap-on Tools Corp.*

Shop Tools

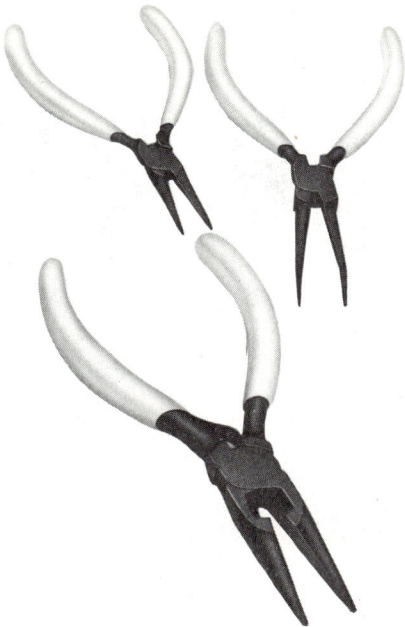

Figure 4-49 Needle nose pliers. *Courtesy of Snap-on Tools Corp.*

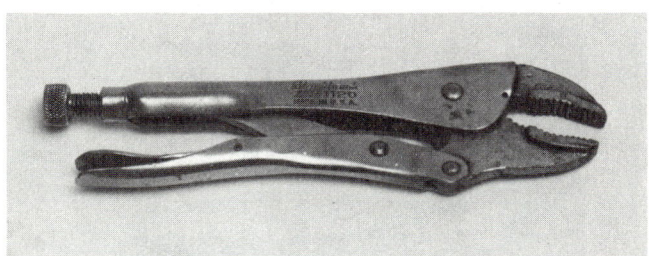

Figure 4-50 Locking pliers, or vise grips, can be locked closed.

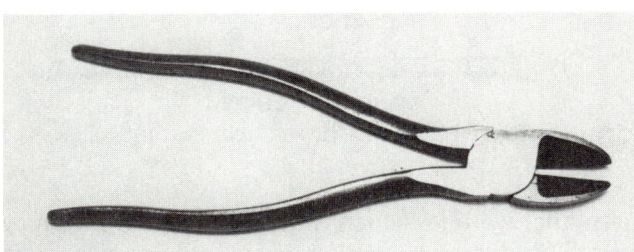

Figure 4-51 Diagonal cutting pliers.

SNAP RING PLIERS Snap ring, or lock ring, pliers generally consist of a linkage that permits the jaw to stay parallel throughout their operating range (Figure 4-52). The jaw surface is usually serrated (notched or toothed) to prevent slipping.

RETAINING RING PLIERS Retaining ring pliers are identified by their pointed tips that engage holes in retaining rings (Figure 4-53). Retaining ring pliers are also available in sets with interchangeable jaws.

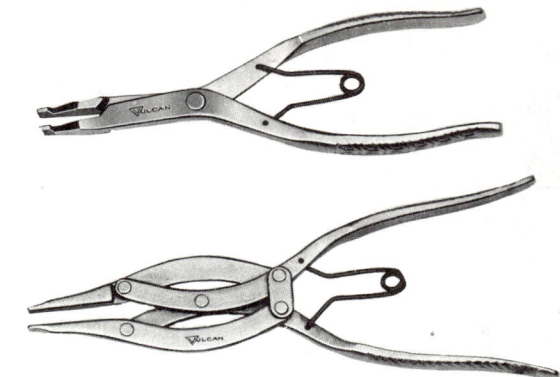

Figure 4-52 Snap ring pliers.

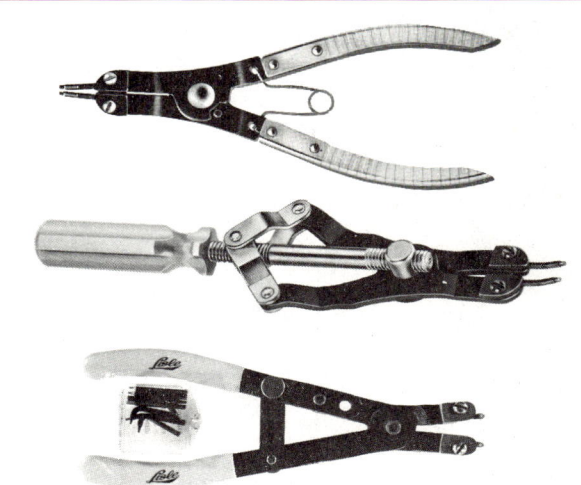

Figure 4-53 Retaining ring pliers.

Hammers

Hammers are identified by the material and weight of the head. There are two groups of hammer heads: steel and soft face (Figures 4-54 and 4-55). The heads of steel-face hammers are made from high-grade alloy steel. The steel is deep forged and heat treated to a suitable degree of hardness. Soft-face hammers have a surface that yields when it strikes an object. Soft-face hammers are preferred when machined surfaces and precision are involved or when marring a finish is undesirable. For example, a brass hammer is used to drive in gears or shafts.

Taps and Dies

The hand tap is a small tool used for hand cutting internal threads (Figure 4-56). An internal thread is cut on the inside of a part, such as a thread on the inside of a nut. This tap is also used for cleaning and restoring threads previously cut.

Hand-threading dies (Figure 4-57) are the opposite of taps because they cut external (outside) threads on bolts, rods, and pipes rather than internal threads. Dies are made in various sizes and shapes, depending on the

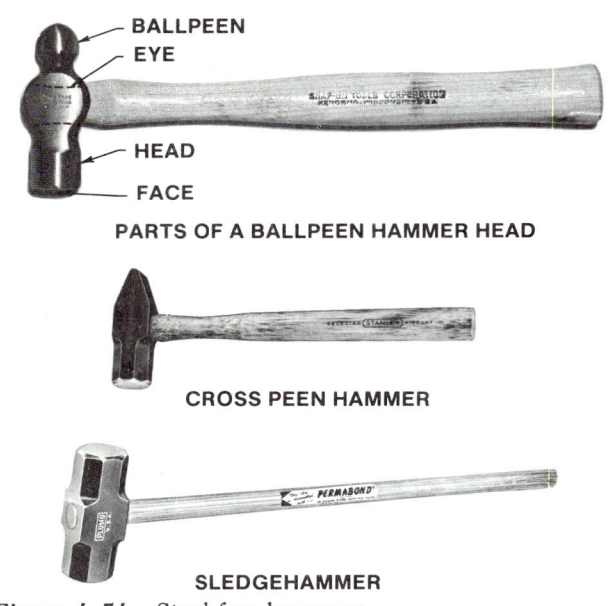

Figure 4-54 Steel-face hammers.

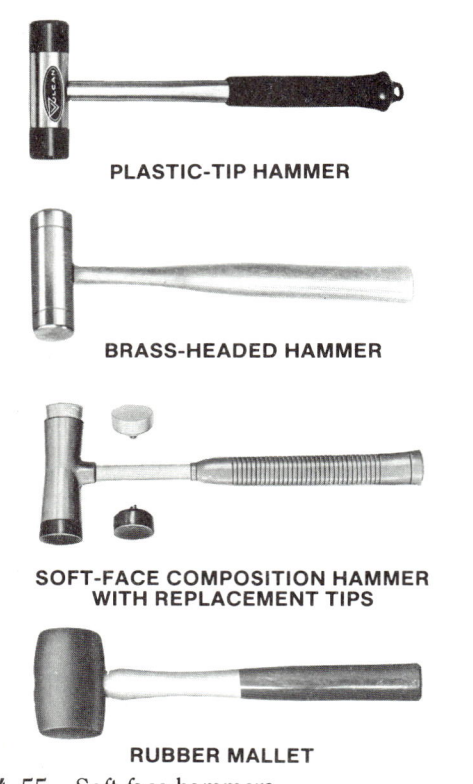

Figure 4-55 Soft-face hammers.

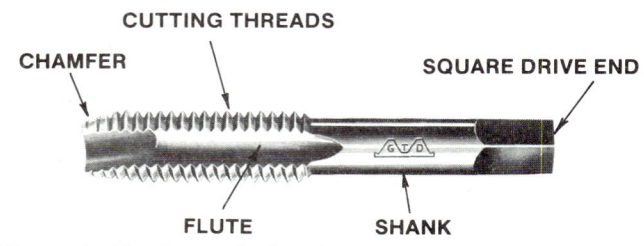

Figure 4-56 Parts of a hand tap.

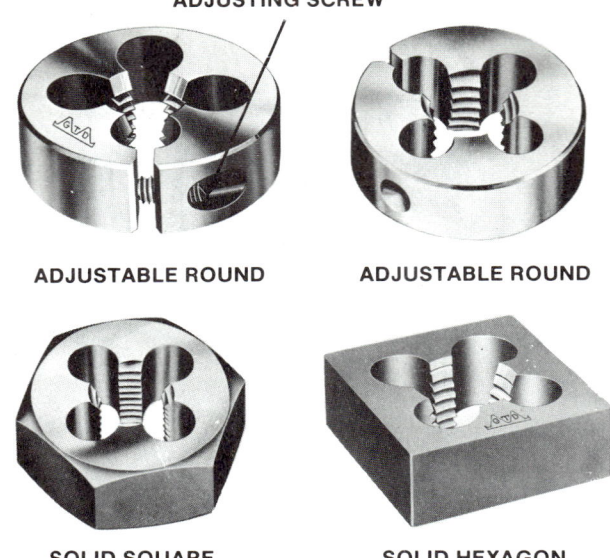

Figure 4-57 Common die shapes.

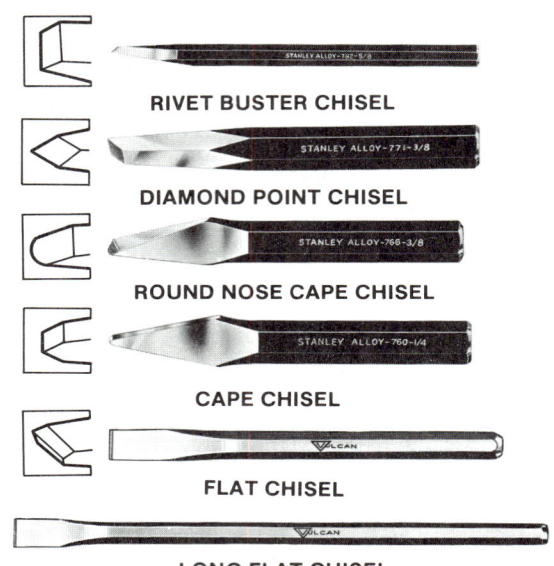

Figure 4-58 Chisels and their correct cutting edges.

particular work for which they are intended. Dies may be solid (fixed size), split on one side to permit adjustment, or have two halves held together in a collet that provides for individual adjustments. Dies fit into holders called die stocks.

Chisels and Punches

Chisels (Figure 4-58) are used to cut metal by driving them with a hammer. Automotive technicians use a variety of chisels for cutting sheet metal, shearing off rivet and bolt heads, splitting rusted nuts, and chipping metal.

Punches (Figure 4-59) are used for driving out pins, rivets, or shafts; aligning holes in parts during assem-

Shop Tools

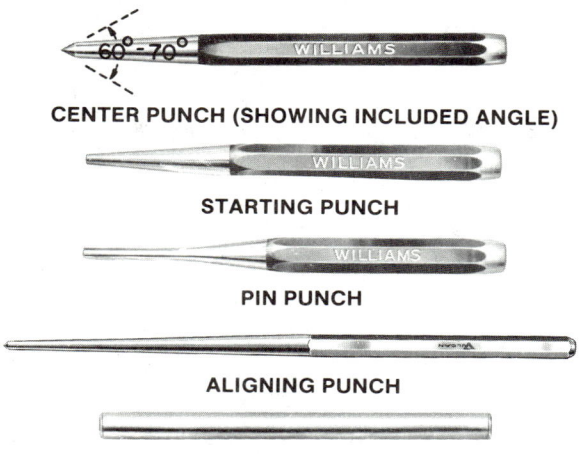

Figure 4-59 Punches are designated by point diameter and punch shape.

bly; and marking the starting point for drilling a hole. Punches are designated by their point diameter and punch shape.

Rust, corrosion, and prolonged heat can cause automotive fasteners, such as cap screws and studs, to become stuck. A box wrench or socket is used to loosen cap screws. A special gripping tool is designed to remove studs. However, if the fastener breaks off, special extracting tools and procedures must be employed.

Removers

Several stud removers are shown in Figure 4-60. These tools are also used to install studs. Stud removers have a hardened, knurled, or grooved eccentric roller or jaws that grip the stud tightly when operated. Stud removers/installers may be turned by a socket wrench drive handle.

Screw Extractors

Extractors are used on screws and bolts that are broken off below the surface. Twist drills, fluted extrac-

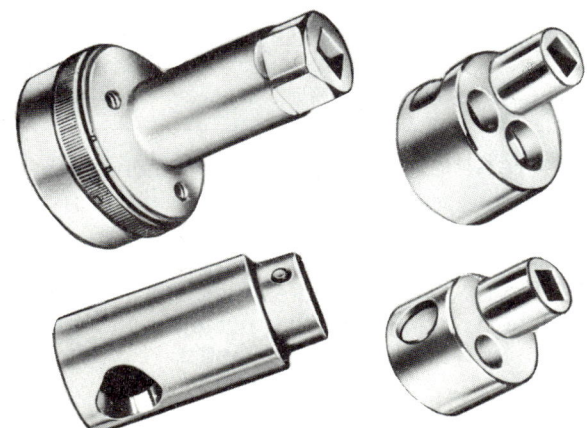

Figure 4-60 Various stud removers.

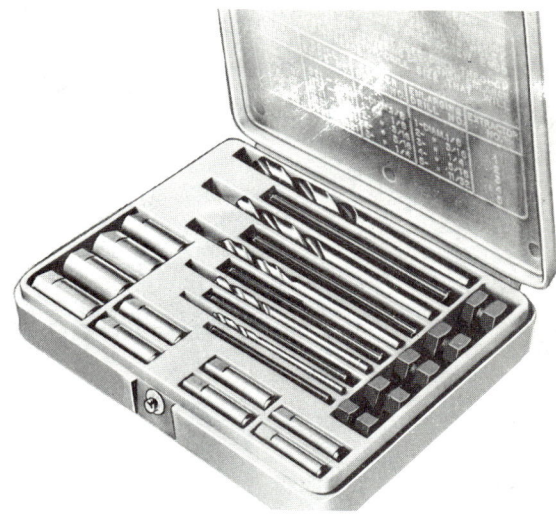

Figure 4-61 Screw extractor set.

tors, and hex nuts are included in a screw extractor set (Figure 4-61). This type of extractor lessens the tendency to expand the screw or stud that has been drilled out by providing gripping power along the full length of the stud.

Tubing Tools

Tubing made from steel, copper, aluminum, and plastic is used frequently on the automobile. During service work, tubing often needs to be repaired or replaced. Tubing tools are made for such tasks as cutting, deburring, flaring, swaging, bending, and removing fittings. Figure 4-62 illustrates some of these tools.

Gear and Bearing Puller

Many precision gears and bearings have a slight interference fit (press-fit) when installed on a shaft or a housing. The press-fit allows no motion between parts and, therefore, prevents wear. The removal of gears and bearings must be done carefully. Prying or hammering can break or bind the parts. A puller with the proper jaws and adapters should be used when applying force to remove gears and bearings. Using proper tools, the force can be applied with a slight and steady motion. Various gears and bearing puller styles and sizes are shown in Figure 4-63.

❑ POWER TOOLS

Power tools make a technician's job easier. They operate faster and with more torque than hand tools. However, power tools require greater safety measures. Power tools do not stop unless they are turned off. Power is furnished by either air (pneumatic), electricity, or hydraulic fluid. Power also offers extra cleaning capability in the way of special cleaning tools.

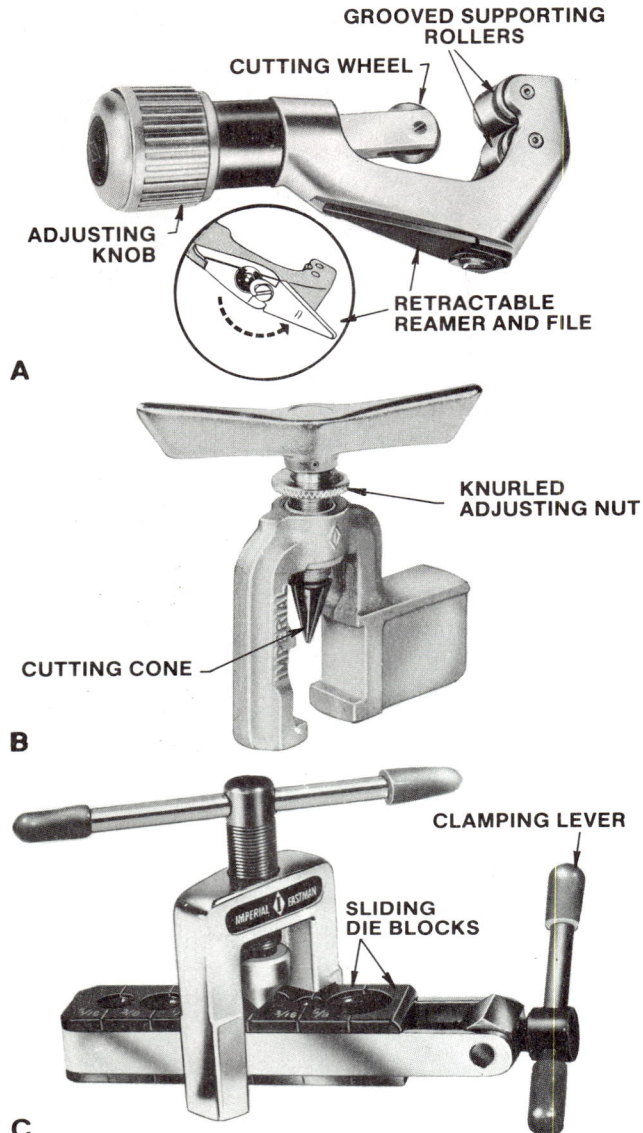

Figure 4-62 Common tubing tools: (A) tubing cutter, (B) deburring tool, and (C) single-lap flaring tool.

> ### SHOP TALK
>
> Safety is critical when using power tools. Carelessness or mishandling of power tools can cause serious injury. Do not use a power tool without obtaining permission from your instructor. Be sure you know how to operate the tool properly before using it. Prior to using a power tool, read the instructions carefully.

IMPACT WRENCHES An impact wrench (Figure 4-64) is a portable hand-held reversible wrench. A heavy-duty model can deliver up to 450 foot-pounds of torque. When triggered, the output shaft, onto which the impact socket is fastened, spins freely at 2,000 to 14,000 rpm, depending on the wrench's make and

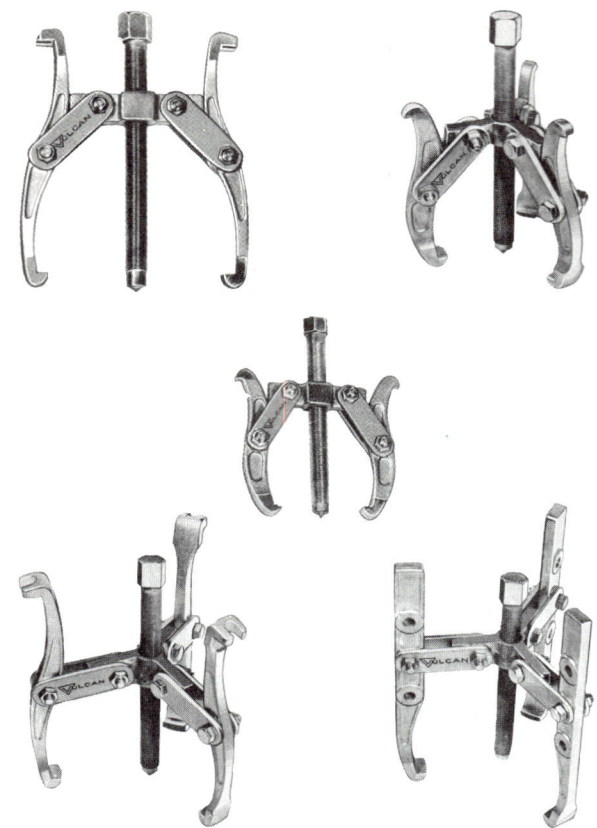

Figure 4-63 Various gear and bearing pullers.

model. When the impact wrench meets resistance, a small spring-loaded hammer, which is situated near the end of the tool, strikes an anvil attached to the drive shaft onto which the socket is mounted. Each impact moves the socket around a little until torque equilibrium is reached, the fastener breaks, or the trigger is released.

> ### SHOP TALK
>
> When using an air impact wrench, it is important that only impact sockets and adapters are used. Other types of sockets and adapters, if used, might shatter and fly off, endangering the safety of the operator and others in the immediate area.

AIR RATCHET WRENCHES An air ratchet wrench, like the hand ratchet, has a special ability to work in hard-to-reach places. Its angle drive reaches in and loosens or tightens where other hand or power wrenches just cannot work (Figure 4-65). The air wrench looks like an ordinary ratchet but has a fat handgrip that contains the air vane motor and drive mechanism.

AIR DRILLS They are usually available in 1/4-, 3/8-, and 1/2-inch sizes and operate in much the same manner as an electric drill, but they are smaller and

Shop Tools 75

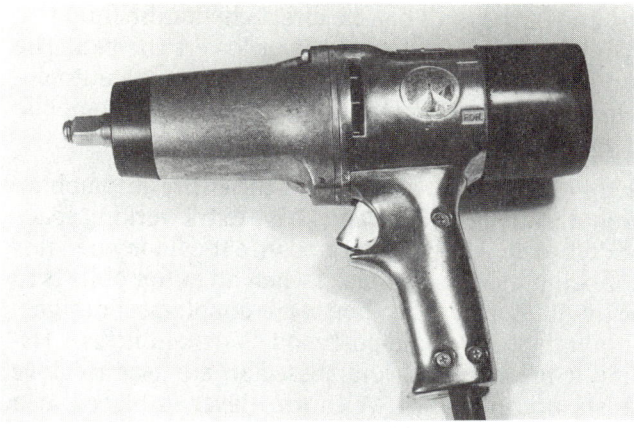

Figure 4-64 Typical impact wrench.

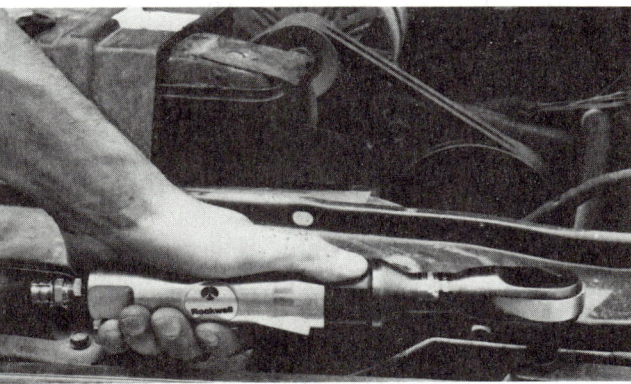

Figure 4-65 Using an air ratchet wrench.

Figure 4-66 Using a pneumatic drill.

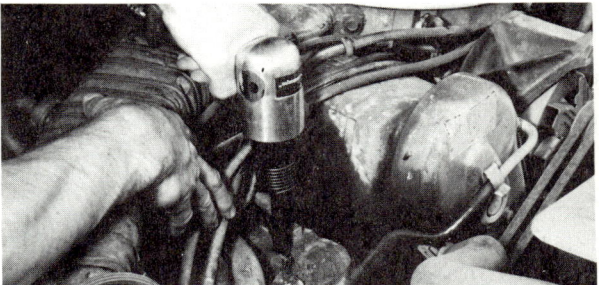

Figure 4-67 The air chisel is a very versatile tool.

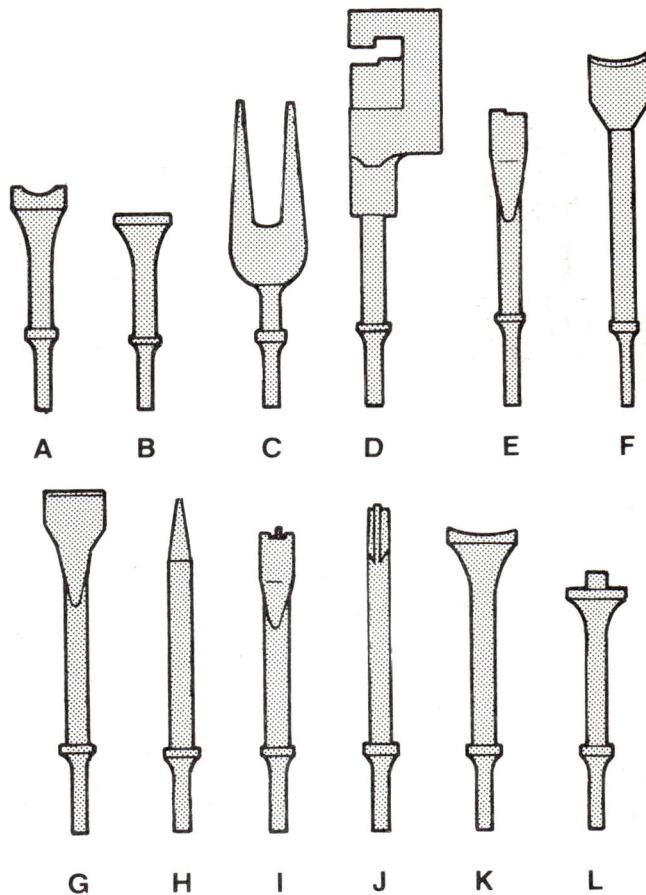

Figure 4-68 Air chisel accessories: (A) universal joint and tie-rod tool; (B) smoothing hammer; (C) ball joint separator; (D) panel crimper; (E) shock absorber chisel; (F) tail pipe cutter; (G) scraper; (H) tapered punch; (I) edging tool; (J) rubber bushing splitter; (K) bushing remover; and (L) bushing installer.

lighter. This compactness makes them a great deal easier to use for drilling operations in auto work (Figure 4-66).

AIR CHISELS OR HAMMERS Of all auto air tools, the air chisel or hammer (Figure 4-67) is one of the most useful. Used with the accessories illustrated in Figure 4-68, this tool will perform many different operations.

- Universal joint and tie-rod tool. It helps to shake loose stubborn universal joints and tie-rod ends.
- Ball joint separator. The wedge action breaks apart frozen ball joints.
- Shock absorber chisel. Quick work of the roughest jobs is made without the usual bruised knuckles and lost time. It easily cracks frozen shock absorber nuts.

- Tail pipe cutter. The cutter slices through mufflers and tail pipes.
- Tapered punch. Driving frozen bolts, installing pins, and punching or aligning holes are some of the many uses for this accessory.
- Rubber bushing splitter. Old bushings can be opened up for easy removal.
- Bushing removal. This accessory is designed to remove all types of bushings. The blunt edge pushes but does not cut.
- Bushing installer. The installer drives all types of bushings to the correct depth. A pilot prevents the tool from sliding.

BLOWGUN One way to use compressed air from a pneumatic hose is with a blowgun (Figure 4-69). A blowgun snaps into one end of the hose and directs airflow when a button is pressed. Before using a blowgun, be sure it has not been modified to eliminate air-bleed holes on the side. Blowguns are used for blowing off parts during cleaning. Never point a blowgun at yourself or someone else.

BENCH GRINDER This electric power tool is generally bolted to a workbench. A bench grinder is classified by wheel size. Six- to ten-inch wheels are the most common in auto repair shops. Three types of wheels are available with this bench tool.

- Grinding wheel. For a wide variety of grinding jobs from sharpening cutting tools to deburring.
- Wire wheel brush. Used for general cleaning and buffing, removing rust and scale, paint removal, deburring, and so forth.
- Buffing wheel. For general purpose buffing, polishing, light cutting, and finish coloring operations.

TROUBLE LIGHT Adequate light is necessary when working under and around automobiles. A trouble light can be hand-held or hung in a convenient location. It is insulated to protect the user. Trouble lights use either a bulb or fluorescent tube. The bulb or tube is surrounded by a cage or enclosed in clear plastic to prevent accidental breaking. The light has a long cord for freedom of movement in the shop area.

FLOOR JACK A floor jack is a portable tool on wheels that is used to raise an automobile. A control lever at the end of the long handle directs hydraulic fluid to a cylinder, which in turn raises or lowers the pad. The pad is a portion of the jack that contacts the automobile. Always use jack stands to support the automobile after it has been raised by a jack.

HOIST The lift, or hoist, raises the entire automobile. This allows the technician to have extra working space underneath. A hoist is lowered into the floor when it is not being used and is raised when an automobile is to be lifted. Most modern hoists are double-post designs, although some single-post models remain in use. Hydraulic pressure and compressed air are used to move hoists up and down. A control lever is placed at a convenient location near the hoist.

PRESSES Many automotive jobs require the use of powerful force to assemble or disassemble parts that are press-fit together. Removing and installing piston pins, servicing rear axle bearings, pressing brake drum and rotor studs, and transmission assembly work are just a few of the examples. Presses can be hydraulic, electric, air, or hand driven. Capacities range up to 150 tons of pressing force, depending on the size and design of the press. Smaller arbor and C-frame presses can be bench or pedestal mounted (Figure 4-70), while high capacity units are free-standing or floor mounted (Figure 4-71).

❏ SERVICE MANUALS

One of the most important tools of the trade is the service manual. The publications that should be available to automotive technicians follow.

AUTO MANUFACTURER'S SERVICE MANUALS The main source of repair and specification information for any car, van, or truck is the manufacturer. Service manuals are published each year for every vehicle built.

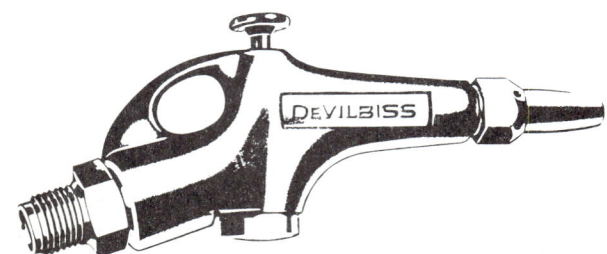

Figure 4-69 Typical blowgun. *Courtesy of DeVilbiss Co.*

Figure 4-70 Small bench-mounted, manually operated arbor press. *Courtesy of Auto Electric Supplier and Equipment Co.*

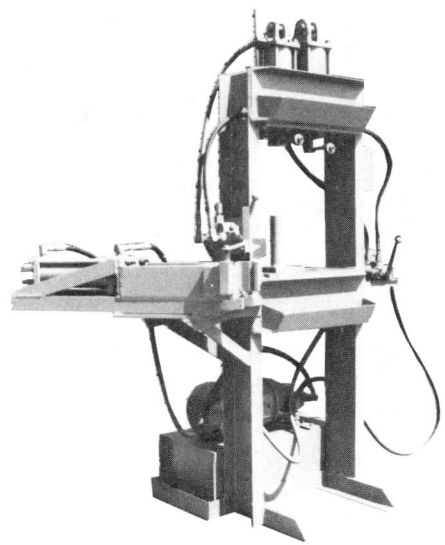

Figure 4–71 Typical heavy-duty electro shop press. *Courtesy of LS Industries.*

These manuals are written in technical language for professional technicians.

Because of the enormous amount of information, some manufacturers publish more than one manual per year per car model. They may be separated into sections such as chassis, suspension, steering, emission controls, fuel systems, brakes, basic maintenance and tuneup, engine, transmission, body, and so on (Figure 4–72).

When complete information with step-by-step testing, repair, and assembly procedures is desired, nothing can match the auto manufacturers' repair manuals. They are the most reliable because they cover all repairs, adjustments, specifications, detailed diagnostic procedures, and special tools required. They can be purchased directly from the automobile manufacturer.

TABLE OF CONTENTS

1 GENERAL SECTION	1–1 Specifications
	1–2 * * * * * * * * * * * *
	1–3 General Information
	1–4 Pre-Delivery Inspection
	1–5 Periodic Maintenance Services
	1–6 Special Tools
2 ENGINE SECTION	2–1 Emission Control System and Vacuum Fitting
	2–2 On-Car Services
	2–3 Engine
	2–4 Engine Lubrication System
	2–5 Engine Cooling System
	2–6 Carburetor
	2–7 * * * * * * * * * * * *
	2–8 Fuel System
	2–9 Exhaust System
	2–10 Clutch
	2–11 Engine and Transmission Mounting System
3 TRANSMISSION AND DIFFERENTIAL SECTION	3–1 Manual Transmission and Differential
	3–2 * * * * * * * * * * * *
	3–3 Transmission Control System
	3–4 4WD System
4 MECHANICAL COMPONENTS SECTION	4–1 Suspension
	4–2 Wheels and Axles
	4–3 Steering System
	4–4 Brakes
	4–5 Pedal System and Control Cables
	4–6 Heater and Ventilator
	4–7 * * * * * * * * * * * *
5 BODY SECTION	5–1 Body and Exterior
	5–2 Doors and Windows
	5–3 Seats, Seat Belts, and Interior
	5–4 Instrument Panel
6 ELECTRICAL SECTION	6–1 Engine Electrical System
	6–2 Body Electrical System
	6–3 Wiring Diagram and Troubleshooting

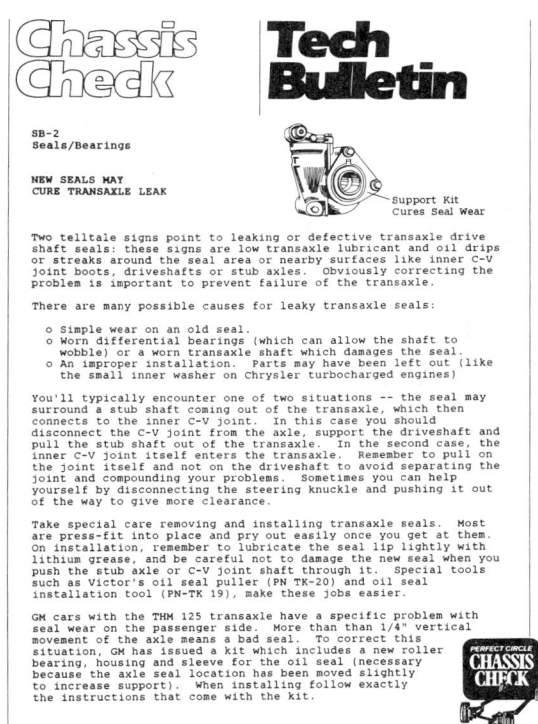

Figure 4–72 Service manuals are separated into sections. *Courtesy of Subaru of America*

To help you learn how to use service manuals effectively, you will see service manual tips throughout this text.

Since numerous technical changes occur on specific vehicles each year, manufacturers' service manuals need to be constantly updated. Updates are published as service bulletins that show the changes in specifications and repair procedures during the model year (Figure 4–73). These changes do not appear in the service manual until the next year. The car manufacturer provides these bulletins to dealers and repair facilities on a regular basis.

Automotive manufacturers also publish a series of technician reference books. The publications provide general instructions on all their current vehicles for accomplishing service and repair with their tested, effective techniques.

AFTERMARKET SUPPLIERS' GUIDES AND CATALOGS Many of the larger parts manufacturers have excellent guides on the various parts that they manufacture or supply. They also provide updated service bulletins on their products.

GENERAL AND SPECIALTY REPAIR MANUALS These are published by independent companies rather than the manufacturers. However, they pay for and get

Chassis Check

Tech Bulletin

SB-2
Seals/Bearings

NEW SEALS MAY
CURE TRANSAXLE LEAK

Two telltale signs point to leaking or defective transaxle drive shaft seals: these signs are low transaxle lubricant and oil drips or streaks around the seal area or nearby surfaces like inner C-V joint boots, driveshafts or stub axles. Obviously correcting the problem is important to prevent failure of the transaxle.

There are many possible causes for leaky transaxle seals:

- o Simple wear on an old seal.
- o Worn differential bearings (which can allow the shaft to wobble) or a worn transaxle shaft which damages the seal.
- o An improper installation. Parts may have been left out (like the small inner washer on Chrysler turbocharged engines)

You'll typically encounter one of two situations -- the seal may surround a stub shaft coming out of the transaxle, which then connects to the inner C-V joint. In this case you should disconnect the C-V joint from the axle, support the driveshaft and pull the stub shaft out of the transaxle. In the second case, the inner C-V joint itself enters the transaxle. Remember to pull on the joint itself and not on the driveshaft to avoid separating the joint and compounding your problems. Sometimes you can help yourself by disconnecting the steering knuckle and pushing it out of the way to give more clearance.

Take special care removing and installing transaxle seals. Most are press-fit into place and pry out easily once you get at them. On installation, remember to lubricate the seal lip lightly with lithium grease, and be careful not to damage the new seal when you push the stub axle or C-V joint shaft through it. Special tools such as Victor's oil seal puller (PN TK-20) and oil seal installation tool (PN-TK 19), make these jobs easier.

GM cars with the THM 125 transaxle have a specific problem with seal wear on the passenger side. More than than 1/4" vertical movement of the axle means a bad seal. To correct this situation, GM has issued a kit which includes a new roller bearing, housing and sleeve for the oil seal (necessary because the axle seal location has been moved slightly to increase support). When installing follow exactly the instructions that come with the kit.

Figure 4–73 Service bulletins are issued to provide the latest repair procedures and other changes. *Courtesy of Perfect Circle/Dana*

most of their information from the car maker. They contain component information, diagnostic steps, repair procedures, and specifications for several car makes in one book. Information is usually condensed and is more general in nature, depending on which manual is used. The condensed format allows for more coverage in less space and therefore is not always specific. They also can contain several years of models as well as several car makes in one book.

FLAT-RATE MANUALS Flat-rate manuals contain figures dealing with the length of time a specific repair is supposed to require. Usually they contain a parts list with approximate or exact parts prices. They are excellent for making estimates of costs and are published by manufacturers and independents.

The same information available in the service manuals and bulletins is also available on compact disc-read only memory systems (CD-ROM). A single compact disc can hold a quarter million pages of text. One great advantage of this system is that it makes accessing the right information much easier and quicker. The manufacturer sends monthly update discs that not only contain the most recent service bulletins but also engineering and field service fixes. Other sources of up-to-date technical information are trade magazines and trade associations.

CASE STUDY

Case 1

The word diagnosis is commonly used in automotive textbooks and service manuals. However, it is a term that is seldom explained. It is more than following a series of interrelated steps in order to find the solution to a specific condition. Diagnosis is a way of looking at systems that are not functioning the way they should and finding out why. It is knowing how the system should work and deciding whether it is working correctly. Through an understanding of the purpose and operation of the car's systems, a technician can accurately diagnose problems.

Most good diagnosticians use the same basic diagnostic procedure. Because of its logical approach, this procedure can quickly lead a technician to the cause of a problem. Accurate diagnostics include the following steps.

1. Gather information about the condition or problem.
2. Verify that the condition exists.
3. Thoroughly define what the problem is and when it occurs.
4. Determine the possible causes of the problem.

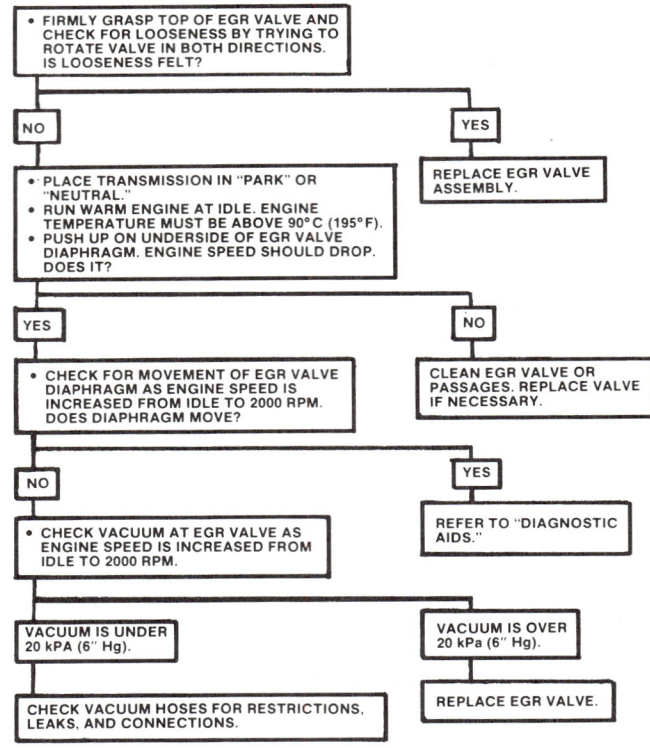

Figure 4-74 Typical diagnostic chart or tree. *Courtesy of General Motors Corp.*

5. Isolate the problem by general testing.
6. Test to pinpoint the cause of the problem.
7. Repair the problem and verify the repair.

Most service manuals contain diagnostic charts that help technicians pinpoint the cause of the problem (Figure 4-74). The steps of diagnostic charts or trees are designed to be followed in order.

These charts contain the most probable causes of a particular problem and simple tests that lead to the exact cause.

Summary

- Repairing the modern automobile requires the use of many different hand and power tools. Units of measurement play a major role in tool selection. Therefore, it is important to be knowledgeable in not only the UCS system, but also the increasingly used metric system of measurement.
- Engine measuring tools must operate to very high standards of precision. They should be handled with care at all times, and cleaned before and after every use.
- The micrometer can be used to measure the outside diameter of shafts and the inside diameter of

holes. It is calibrated in either inch or metric graduations.
- Telescoping gauges are designed to measure bore diameters and other clearances. They are usually used with an outside micrometer. Small hole gauges are used in the same manner as the telescoping gauge, usually to determine valve guide diameter.
- The screw pitch gauge provides a fast and accurate method of measuring the threads per inch (pitch) of fasteners. This is done by matching the teeth of the gauge with the fastener threads and reading the pitch directly from the leaf of the gauge.
- While out-of-roundness can be checked with an inside micrometer, an out-of-roundness gauge does the job better. To check a connecting rod, move the locking adjustable slide to suit the diameter of the bore, then set the dial indicator to zero. Then rotate the gauge within the bore. The dial will give a plus or minus reading in thousandths for any variation in the rod diameter.
- It is crucial to use the proper amount of torque when tightening nuts or cap screws on any part of a vehicle, particularly the engine. A torque-indicating wrench makes it possible to duplicate the conditions of tightness and stress recommended by the manufacturer.
- Metric and SAE size wrenches are not interchangeable. The well-equipped technician will have a variety of both types on hand.
- The handle of a screwdriver is important. The larger the diameter, the better grip and torque it will provide. A screwdriver, no matter what type, should never be used as a chisel, punch, or pry bar.
- The hand tap is used for hand cutting internal threads and for cleaning and restoring previously cut threads. Hand-threading dies cut external threads and fit into holders called die stocks.
- Carelessness or mishandling of power tools can cause serious injury. Safety measures are needed when working with such tools as impact and air ratchet wrenches, blowguns, bench grinders, lifts, hoists, and hydraulic presses.
- The main source of repair and specification information for any vehicle is the service manual issued by the manufacturer. Updates are published as service bulletins. These include changes made during the model year, which will not appear in the manual until the following year.
- Flat-rate manuals are ideal for making cost estimates. Published by manufacturers and independent companies, they contain figures showing how long specific repairs should take to complete, as well as a parts list with prices.
- Diagnosis means looking at a malfunctioning vehicle and finding the cause or causes of the problem. It requires a thorough understanding of the purpose and operation of the various automotive systems. Diagnostic charts found in service manuals can aid in this diagnosis.

Review Questions

1. How often should the calibration of a micrometer be checked?
2. List some common uses of the dial indicator.
3. What determines the size of a wrench?
4. Name the three types of wheels available for use with a bench grinder.
5. How do manufacturers show changes in vehicle specifications and repair procedures during the model year?
6. Which of the following wrenches is the best choice for turning a bolt?
   a. open-end
   b. box-end
   c. combination
   d. none of the above
7. Technician A sometimes uses a screwdriver as a chisel. Technician B sometimes uses a screwdriver as a pry bar. Who is correct?
   a. Technician A
   b. Technician B
   c. Both A and B
   d. Neither A nor B
8. Technician A says that a tap cuts external threads. Technician B says that a tap cuts internal threads. Who is correct?
   a. Technician A
   b. Technician B
   c. Both A and B
   d. Neither A nor B
9. Which of the following screwdrivers is like a Phillips but has a flatter and blunter tip?
   a. standard
   b. Torx
   c. Posidriv
   d. clutch head
10. Which of the following pliers is best for grasping small parts?
    a. adjustable
    b. needle nose
    c. retaining ring
    d. snap ring
11. Technician A uses a punch to align holes in parts during assembly. Technician B uses a punch to drive out rivets. Who is correct?
    a. Technician A
    b. Technician B
    c. Both A and B
    d. Neither A nor B
12. An extractor is used for removing broken _____.
    a. seals

b. bushings
c. pistons
d. bolts

13. Which of the following operations can the air chisel or hammer perform?
    a. bushing installation
    b. bushing removal
    c. shock absorber chisel
    d. all of the above

14. Technician A uses a blowgun to blow off parts during cleaning. Technician B uses a blowgun to clean off after working. Who is correct?
    a. Technician A
    b. Technician B
    c. Both A and B
    d. Neither A nor B

15. Always use jack stands to support a vehicle after it has been raised by a _____ .
    a. floor jack
    b. hoist
    c. hydraulic press
    d. all of the above

16. Technician A uses a dial caliper to take inside and outside measurements. Technician B uses a dial caliper to take depth measurements. Who is correct?
    a. Technician A
    b. Technician B
    c. Both A and B
    d. Neither A nor B

17. For a measurement that must be made within one ten-thousandth of an inch, Technician A uses a machinist's rule. For the same measurement, Technician B uses a standard micrometer. Who is correct?
    a. Technician A
    b. Technician B
    c. Both A and B
    d. Neither A nor B

18. Which of the following feeler gauge measurements requires the use of a precision straightedge as well?
    a. piston ring end gap
    b. connecting rod side clearance
    c. crankshaft end play
    d. cylinder head warpage

19. Technician A uses a 9/16-inch wrench to turn a 14-millimeter nut. Technician B uses a 9/16-inch wrench to hold a 14-millimeter nut. Who is correct?
    a. Technician A
    b. Technician B
    c. Both A and B
    d. Neither A nor B

20. When using an air impact wrench, Technician A uses only impact sockets and adapters. Technician B uses other types of sockets and adapters. Who is correct?
    a. Technician A
    b. Technician B
    c. Both A and B
    d. Neither A nor B

5 DIAGNOSTIC EQUIPMENT

Objectives

- Explain the basic elementary principles of electricity.
- Name the diagnostic tools and equipment commonly used in vehicle repair work.
- Describe the basic applications and operation of these tools.
- Explain the importance of trained technicians skilled in the use of electrical, electronic, and computerized test equipment.

As the trend toward electronic integration of ignition, fuel, and emission systems progresses, diagnostic test equipment must also reflect these changes. New tools and techniques have been developed to support diagnosis of electronic ignition systems, fuel injection systems, and computer engine controls.

Today's automotive technician must not only keep up with changes in automotive technology but must also stay informed of new testing procedures and the use of specialized diagnostic equipment. The successful repair shop must invest in the testing equipment and technical training necessary to troubleshoot today's electronic engine systems.

However, many testing devices used on pre-electronic-controlled vehicles are still important diagnostic tools. Not all performance problems are related to electronic control systems. Time-proven test procedures designed to check air and fluid pressures and basic electronical conditions are still a very vital part of modern vehicle service.

☐ ELECTRICAL FUNDAMENTALS

There is often confusion concerning the terms electrical and electronic. In this book, electrical and electrical systems will refer to wiring and electrical parts such as alternators, lights, and voltage regulators. Electronics will mean computers and other black box type items used to control engine and vehicle systems.

A basic understanding of electrical principles is essential to operate diagnostic tools and interpret their readings. Although the subject will be covered in greater detail in later chapters, an elementary overview of electricity and its principles is presented here.

Flow of Electricity

Understanding the structure of the atom is the first step in comprehending how electricity works. The following principles describe atoms, which are the building blocks of all materials.

- In the center of every atom is a nucleus.
- The nucleus contains positively-charged particles called protons and particles called neutrons that have no charge.
- Negatively-charged particles called electrons orbit around every nucleus.
- Every type of atom has a different number of protons and electrons, but each atom has an equal number of protons and electrons. Therefore, the total electrical charge of an atom is zero, or neutral.

In all atoms, the electrons are arranged in different orbits, called shells. Each shell contains a specific number of electrons. Figure 5-1A shows a copper atom. This atom has 29 electrons and 29 protons. The

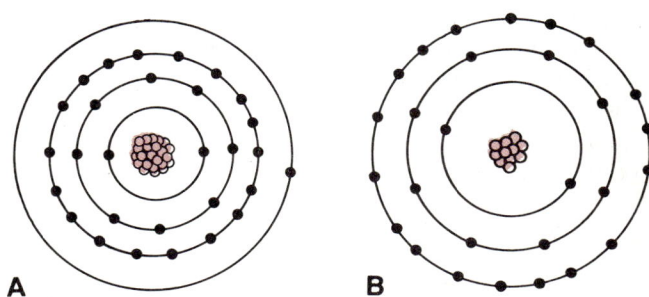

Figure 5-1 Electron arrangement of (A) a copper atom and (B) a nickel atom.

81

29 electrons are arranged in shells. Notice that the outer shell has only 1 electron. This outer shell needs 32 electrons to be completely full. This means that the 1 electron in the outer shell is loosely tied to the atom and can be easily removed.

Figure 5-1B shows a simplified drawing of a nickel atom. This atom contains 28 protons in the nucleus and 28 electrons arranged in shells. The third shell of any atom can contain only 18 electrons. In the nickel atom, the outer shell is completely filled. Therefore, its electrons are closely tied to the atom and cannot be removed easily.

The looseness or tightness of electrons is important in electrical theory. Electricity is caused by the flow of electrons from one atom to another. To create this flow, there must be a source of energy. Several kinds of energy are strong enough to force electrons away from atoms and begin the flow of electricity. In automobile electrical systems, the two energy sources used are chemical reaction and magnetism.

The vehicle's battery is its source of chemical energy. A chemical reaction in the battery produces a source of electrons that are then drawn from the battery. This process continues to provide electrons until the chemicals are exhausted. Fortunately, the vehicle's charging system replenishes the battery's supply of electrons so the chemical reaction can continue indefinitely.

Electricity and magnetism are also interrelated. One can be used to produce the other. Moving a wire (a conductor) through an already existing magnetic field (such as a permanent magnet) can produce current flow (electricity). This happens because the magnetic fields of the electrons in the wire react to the already existing magnetism. This process of producing electricity through magnetism is called induction. In a generator, the coil of wire is moved through the magnetic field. In an alternator, the magnetic field is moved through the coil of wire. In both cases, electrical flow is produced.

For electrical flow to occur (and continue), three things must be present: an excess of electrons in one place, a lack of electrons in another place, and a path between the two places.

A simple example of this process is shown in the battery and light arrangement in Figure 5-2.

The chemical reaction in a battery causes a lack of electrons at the positive (+) terminal and an excess at the negative (-) terminal. This creates an electrical imbalance, causing the electrons to flow through the path provided by the wire.

❑ MEASURING ELECTRICITY

Current is the number of electrons flowing past a given point in a given amount of time. This current, like the flow of water or any other substance, can be measured. When any substance flows, it meets resis-

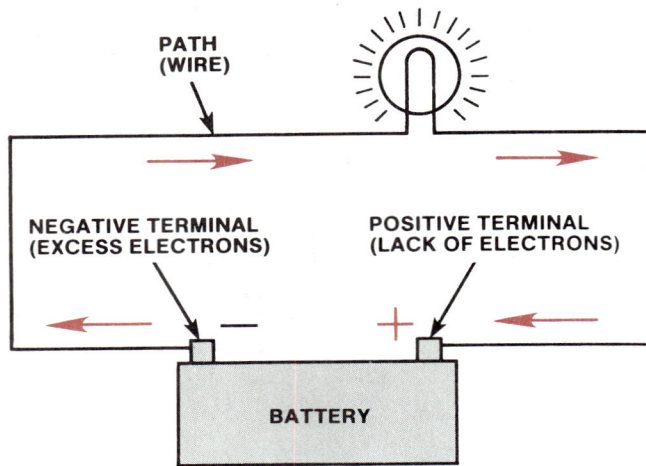

Figure 5-2 Electricity results from the flow of electrons from the negative side of the battery to the positive side.

tance. The resistance to electrical flow can be measured. Power is the rate at which work can be done. Forcing a current through a resistance is work. The power used in a circuit can also be determined. The following section explains the measurement of flow (current), resistance (ohms), pressure (voltage), and power (wattage).

Electrical Flow (Current)

The unit for measuring electrical current is the ampere, usually called an amp. The instrument used to measure electrical current flow in a circuit is called an ammeter.

In the flow of electricity, millions of electrons are moving past any given point at the speed of light. Also, the electrical charge of any one electron is extremely small. It takes millions of electrons to make a charge that can be measured. For these reasons, 1 ampere means that 6.25 billion billion electrons are flowing past a given point in 1 second.

There are two types of electrical flow, or current: direct current (DC) and alternating current (AC). In direct current, the electrons flow in one direction only. The example of the battery and light shown earlier is based upon direct current. In alternating current, the electrons change direction at a fixed rate.

Resistance

In every atom, the electrons resist being moved out of their shell. The amount of resistance depends on the type of atom. As explained earlier, in some atoms (such as those in copper) there is very little resistance to electron flow because the outer electron is loosely held. In other substances (such as nickel) there is more resistance to flow, because the outer electrons are tightly held.

The resistance to current flow produces heat. This heat can be measured to indicate the amount of resistance. A unit of measured resistance is called an ohm. Resistance can be measured by an instrument called an ohmmeter. Differing amounts of resistance are measured by changing scales (such as × 1, × 10, × 100) on the ohmmeter.

Pressure

In electrical flow, some force is needed to move the electrons between atoms. This force is the pressure that exists between the positive and negative points (the electrical imbalance). This force, also called electromotive force (EMF), is measured in units called volts. One volt is the amount of pressure (force) required to move 1 ampere of current through a resistance of 1 ohm. Voltage is measured by an instrument called a voltmeter.

Power

Electrical power, or the rate of work, is found by multiplying the amount of voltage by the amount of amperes flowing. Power is measured in watts. Although power measurements are rarely, if ever, needed in automotive servicing, knowing the power requirements of light bulbs, electric motors, and other components is sometimes useful when troubleshooting electrical systems.

Circuits

When electrons are able to flow along a path (wire) between two points, an electrical circuit is formed. An electrical circuit is considered complete when there is a path that connects the positive and negative terminals of the electrical source. Most automotive electrical circuits use the chassis as the path to the negative side of the battery. Electrical components have a lead that connects them to the chassis. These are called the chassis ground connections. In a complete circuit, the flow of electricity can be controlled and applied to do useful work, such as light a headlight or turn over a starter motor. Components that use electrical power put a load on the circuit and consume electrical energy.

Electrical test equipment is often used to troubleshoot problems in a particular circuit. Electrical problems are normally one of the following.

OPEN CIRCUIT An open circuit is one that has a break in the wire, often called a break in the circuit's continuity. Without a completed path, current cannot flow.

SHORTED CIRCUIT A shorted circuit is an accidental path of low resistance in the circuit. Since the short allows current to bypass part of the circuit's normal resistance or load, current flow increases and heat buildup can occur. Improper wiring or damaged insulation are the two major causes of short circuits.

GROUNDED CIRCUIT A grounded circuit is actually a shorted circuit that allows current to return to the ground before it has reached the circuit's load.

HIGH-RESISTANCE CIRCUIT This circuit offers increased resistance to current flow due to damage or corrosion buildup within the circuit. High-resistance circuits reduce current flow and prevent full voltage or current signals from reaching the proper points within the system.

With a basic understanding of electricity and simple circuits it is easier to understand the function and use of the electrical test equipment described in the following sections.

Circuit Testers

Circuit testers (Figure 5-3) are used to identify shorted and open circuits in any electrical circuit. Low-voltage testers are used to troubleshoot 6- to 12-volt circuits. High-voltage circuit testers diagnose primary and secondary ignition circuits.

A circuit tester, commonly called a test light, looks like a stubby ice pick. Its handle is transparent and contains a light bulb. A probe extends from one end of the handle and a ground clip and wire from the other end. When the ground clip is attached to a good ground and the probe touched to a live connector, the bulb in the handle will light up. If the bulb does not light, voltage is not available at the connector.

A self-powered circuit tester is called a continuity tester (Figure 5-4). It is used with the power off in the circuit being tested. It looks like a regular test light, except that it has a small internal battery. When the

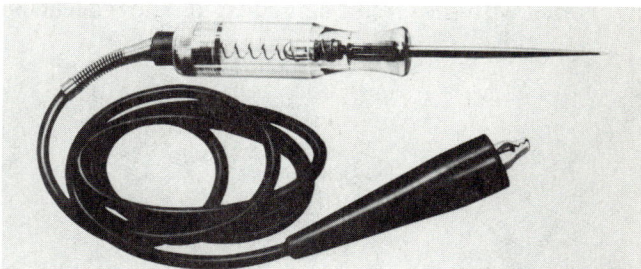

Figure 5-3 Typical circuit tester, commonly called a test light. *Courtesy of MAC Tools*

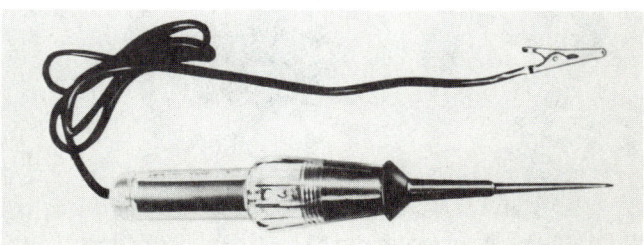

Figure 5-4 Typical self-powered circuit tester, commonly called a continuity tester. *Courtesy of MAC Tools*

ground clip is attached to the ground terminal of a component and the probe touched to the feed wire, the light will be illuminated if there is continuity in the circuit. If an open circuit exists, the light will not be illuminated.

Electrical Test Meters

Several meters are essential for testing and troubleshooting electrical systems. These are the voltmeter, ohmmeter, and ammeter.

VOLTMETER The voltmeter (Figure 5-5) measures the voltage available at any point in an electrical system. For example, it can be used to measure the voltage available at the battery. It can also be used to test the voltage available at the terminals of any component or connector. The voltage meter can also be used to test voltage drop across a relay, switch, or connector.

A voltmeter usually has two leads: a red positive lead and a black negative lead. The red lead should be connected to the positive (voltage side) circuit. The black should be connected to ground or to the negative side of the component. Voltage meters should always be connected across the circuit being tested. When connected in series, the high resistance of the meter will prevent proper operation of the component.

OHMMETER As mentioned earlier, an ohmmeter (Figure 5-6) measures resistance to current flow in a circuit. In contrast to the voltmeter, which uses the voltage available in the circuit, the ohmmeter is battery powered. The circuit being tested must be open. If the power is on in the circuit, the ohmmeter will be damaged.

The two leads of the ohmmeter are placed across or in parallel with the circuit being tested. The red lead is

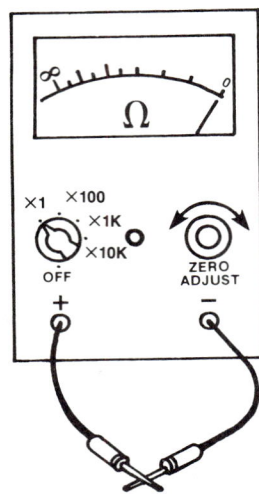

Figure 5-6 Typical ohmmeter.

placed on the positive side of the circuit and the black lead is placed on the ground or negative side of the circuit. The meter supplies voltage to the circuit and compares the voltage available on the positive side of the circuit with the voltage available at the negative side of the circuit. This voltage drop is used to determine the resistance in the circuit or component. The ohmmeter scale will read from 0 to infinity (∞). A 0 reading means there is no resistance in the circuit and may indicate a short in a component that should show a specific resistance. An infinity reading indicates a number higher than the meter can measure. This usually is an indication of an open circuit.

AMMETER As previously discussed, an ammeter (Figure 5-7) measures current flow in a circuit. Current is measured in amperes. Unlike the voltmeter and ohmmeter, the ammeter must be placed into the circuit or in series with the circuit being tested. Normally, this requires disconnecting the positive wire from the component and connecting the ammeter between them.

It is much easier to test current using an ammeter with an inductive pickup. The pickup clamps around

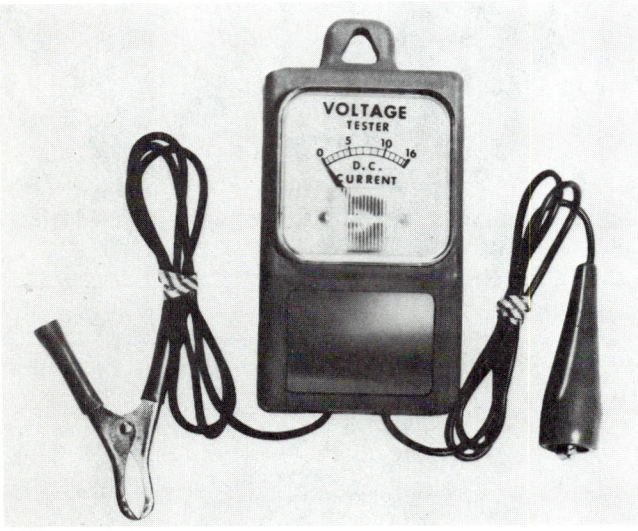

Figure 5-5 A voltmeter can be used to measure the voltage available at any point in an electrical system. *Courtesy of MAC Tools*

Figure 5-7 Typical ammeter. *Courtesy of MAC Tools*

Diagnostic Equipment

Figure 5-8 The volt/ampere tester is used for testing batteries and the starting and charging systems. *Courtesy of Sun Electric Corp.*

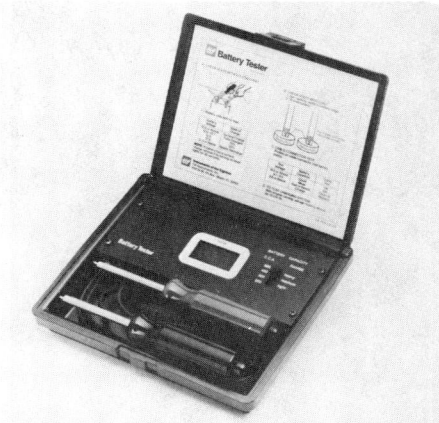

Figure 5-9 Typical battery tester. *Courtesy of TIF Instruments, Inc.*

Figure 5-10 The digital volt/ohmmeter can be used to test voltage and resistance. *Courtesy of Actron Manufacturing Co.*

the wire or cable being tested. The ammeter determines amperage based on the magnetic field created by the current flowing through the wire. This type of pickup eliminates the need to separate the circuit and insert the meter.

VOLT/AMPERE TESTER A volt/ampere tester (VAT), shown in Figure 5-8, is used to test batteries, starting systems, and charging systems. The tester contains a voltmeter, ammeter, and carbon pile. The carbon pile is a variable resistor. A knob on the tester allows the technician to vary the resistance of the pile. When the tester is attached to the battery, the carbon pile will draw current out of the battery. The ammeter will read the amount of current flowing. The resistance of the carbon pile must be adjusted to match the size of the battery. The smaller the battery, the lower the load.

Figure 5-9 shows a small battery tester. This battery tester does not have a carbon pile. However, it can be used to test open circuit voltage and to perform battery load tests on 6- and 12-volt batteries. It can also be used to check the condition of battery cables and connectors, and to check running voltage.

MULTIMETER It is not necessary for a technician to own separate voltmeters, ohmmeters, and ammeters. These meters are combined in a single tool called a multimeter. A multimeter is one of the most versatile tools used in diagnosing engine performance and electrical systems. The most basic multimeter is the digital volt/ohmmeter (DVOM). As its name implies, the DVOM tests both voltage and resistance (Figure 5-10).

Top-of-the-line multimeters are multi-functional. Most test—DC and AC—volts, ohms, and amperes. Usually there are several test ranges provided for each of these functions. In addition to these basic electrical tests, multimeters also test engine revolutions per minute (rpm), ignition dwell, diode condition, distributor conditions, frequency, and even temperature (Figure 5-11). Table 5-1 shows some of the many tests that can be performed with a multimeter.

Multimeters are available with either analog or digital displays. Analog meters (Figure 5-12) enjoyed wide popularity prior to the advent of electronic control systems. They are still favored by technicians who have used them for years and prefer the visual reference provided by a moving needle.

However, there are several drawbacks to using most analog-type meters for testing electronic control systems. Many electronic components require very precise test results. Digital meters can measure volts, ohms, or amperes in tenths and hundredths. Some have multiple test ranges that must be manually selected. Others

Figure 5-11 Typical multi-functional, low-impedance multimeter. *Courtesy of OTC Tool and Equipment Division of SPX Corp.*

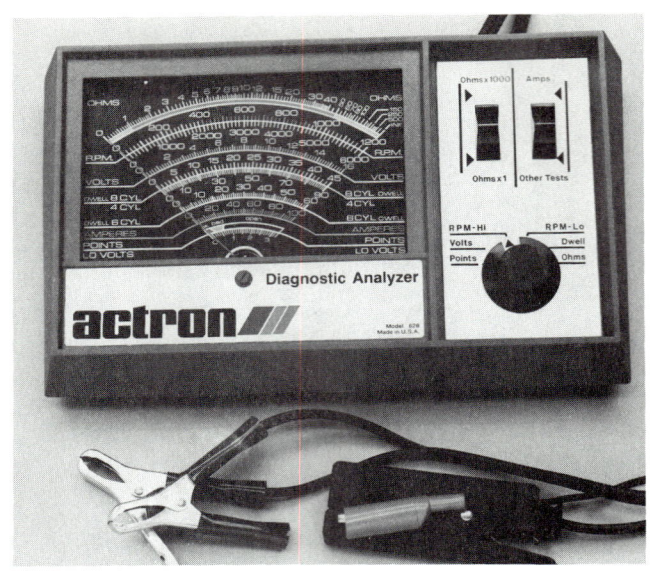

Figure 5-12 Analog multimeters provide a visual reference point in the form of the moving needle. *Courtesy of Actron Manufacturing Co.*

TABLE 5-1 ELECTRICAL TESTING WITH A MULTIMETER

System/Component	Measurement Type			
	Voltage Presence & Level	Voltage Drop	Current	Resistance
Charging System				
Alternators	•		•	
Regulators	•			
Diodes		•		•
Connectors	•	•		•
Starting System				
Batteries	•	•	•	
Starters		•	•	
Solenoids	•	•		•
Connectors		•		•
Interlocks	•			
Ignition System				
Coils	•			•
Connectors	•	•		•
Condensers				•
Contact set (points)	•			•
Distributor caps				•
Plug wires				•
Rotors				•
Magnetic pickup	•			•

Diagnostic Equipment 87

Figure 5-13 This multimeter has 18 test ranges. *Courtesy of TIF Instruments, Inc.*

are auto ranging. The multimeter shown in Figure 5-13 has 18 test ranges. For example, it can measure DC voltage readings as small as 1/10 millivolt or as high as 1000 volts.

Another problem with analog meters is their low internal resistance (input impedance). The low input impedance allows too much current to flow through circuits and should not be used on delicate electronic devices.

Digital meters, on the other hand, have a high input impedance, usually at least 10 megohms (10 million ohms). Metered voltage for resistance tests is well below 5 volts, reducing the risk of damage to sensitive components and delicate computer circuits.

One of the major problems with circuit checking is the vehicle's wiring harness. The introduction of breakout boxes (Figure 5-14) allows the technician to check voltage and resistance readings between specific points within the harness.

Figure 5-14 The wiring harness breakout box allows for detailed testing of individual circuits and components.

❏ IGNITION SYSTEM TEST EQUIPMENT

Some of the tools used to troubleshoot ignition systems have been in use for years. Others are relatively new, having been developed in response to electronic ignition systems.

Tach-Dwellmeter

A tool very commonly used for tune-up and engine diagnosis is the tach-dwellmeter (Figure 5-15). This meter is a combination tachometer and dwellmeter. A tachometer measures engine rpm. A dwellmeter measures the time a circuit is on. On ignition systems, the dwell time is the degree of crankshaft rotation during which the primary circuit is on. On older GM vehicles with the C-4 or computer command control carburetors, the dwellmeter can be used to measure the type of signal (rich or lean) going to the carburetor mixture control solenoid.

A typical tach-dwellmeter has three leads. Two heavy-duty leads connect the meter to the battery terminals. The third lead usually connects the meter to the distributor or tach terminal on the coil. As the breaker points or electronic control module turns the primary ignition system on and off, the tach-dwellmeter uses this signal to determine engine speed and dwell angle. The advances made in automotive electronics in recent years, however, have diminished the usefulness of the tach-dwellmeter.

Tachometers

Tachometers are still commonly used to measure engine speed. Like other meters, they are available in

Figure 5-15 Typical tach-dwellmeter. *Courtesy of Actron Manufacturing Co.*

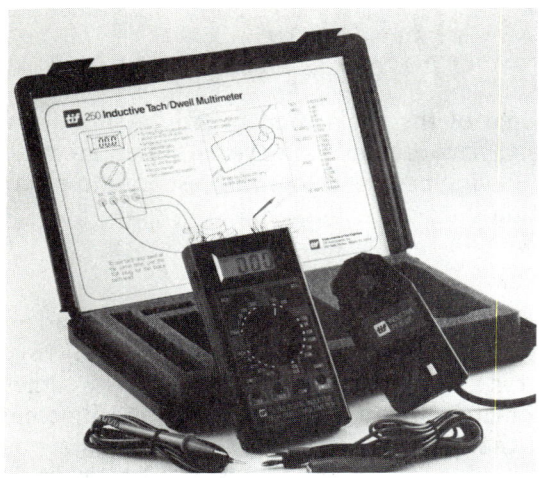

Figure 5-16 An inductive pick-up tachometer clamps over the spark plug wires for testing engine rpm. *Courtesy of TIF Instruments, Inc.*

analog and digital types. Digital are the most common. Tachometers are connected to the ignition system to monitor ignition pulses. These pulses are then converted to engine speed by the meter.

Several types of inductive pickup tachometers are now available that simplify rpm testing. The inductive tachometer shown in Figure 5-16 simply clamps over the number 1 spark plug wire. The digital display gives the engine rpm, based on the magnetic pulses created by the secondary voltage in the wire.

Another type of digital tachometer is the photoelectric tachometer (Figure 5-17). The photoelectric tachometer converts light pulses into rpm readings. This type of meter has an internal light source, powered either by an internal battery or by the car's battery. Reflective tape is applied to any rotating part of the engine, such as the crankshaft pulley. When the meter light is pointed at the revolving tape, a photoelectric eye in the meter reacts to the reflected light. The flashes of light are converted into electrical signals, which the meter uses to determine the engine rpm.

When electronic ignitions replaced breaker-point ignitions, magnetic pulse sensors were used to determine crankshaft position and rotational speed. The sensors were usually mounted over the harmonic balancer, the flywheel, or beside a crankshaft-mounted reluctor. As the mechanical components rotate, voltage pulses are magnetically induced in the sensor. An electronic control module monitors the voltage pulses to determine crankshaft position and engine speed.

Figure 5-18 illustrates a magnetic probe receptacle provided on the sensing device. This permits a probe to be placed in the receptacle and the electrical pulses to be remotely monitored. Figure 5-19 shows a digital

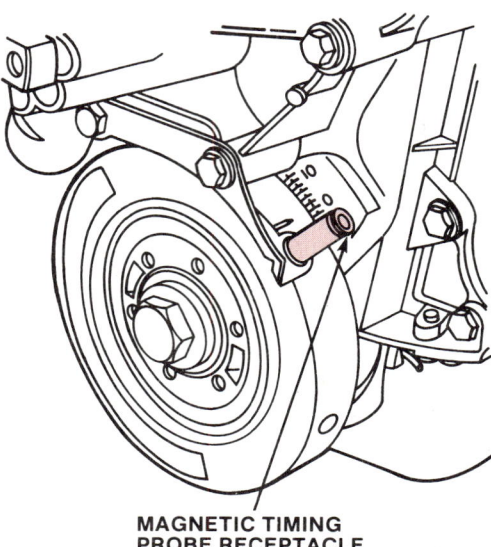

Figure 5-18 Location of the magnetic timing probe receptacle.

Figure 5-17 The photoelectric tachometer converts light pulses into rpm readings. *Courtesy of TIF Instruments, Inc.*

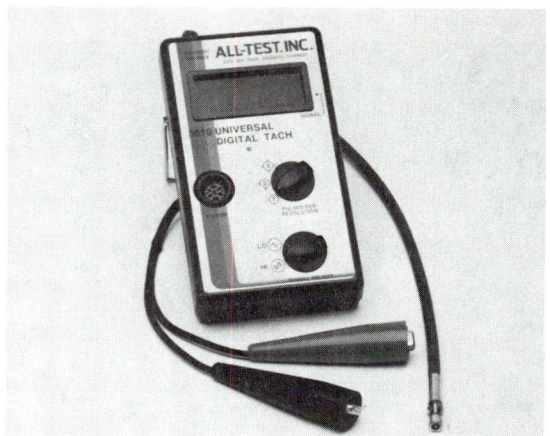

Figure 5-19 Digital tachometer with inductive probe. *Courtesy of All-Test, Inc.*

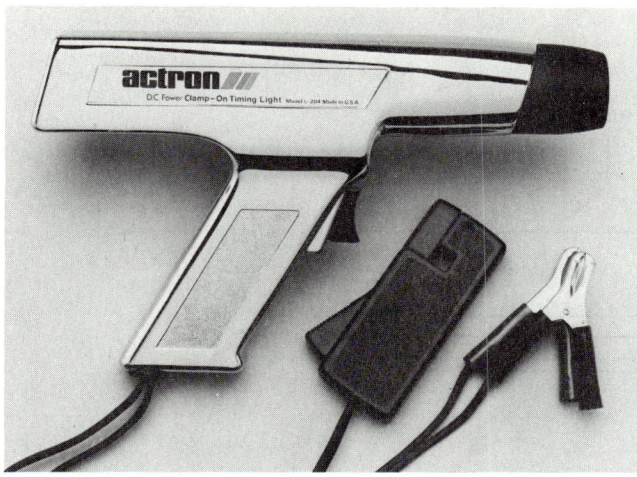

Figure 5-20 Timing light with inductive pick-up. *Courtesy of Actron Manufacturing Co.*

tachometer with a magnetic coil pick-up, or inductive probe. The tachometer counts the number of pulses and, based on the number of pulses generated per minute by the vehicle's crankshaft position sensor, determines the rpm.

Timing Light

A timing light (Figure 5-20) is an essential tool in tuning up most vehicles. A timing light is used to reveal when the spark plugs are firing in relation to the piston position. A timing light normally consists of a strobe light and three leads. Two of the leads connect to the car battery to power the strobe. The third lead (pick-up lead) connects to the number 1 spark plug wire. The pick-up lead on most newer timing lights have an inductive pick-up that clamps over the spark plug wire. Older timing lights have an adapter that must be placed between the spark plug wire and the spark plug. When the engine is turned on, the timing light will flash every time the number 1 plug fires.

CAUTION: Never pierce the spark plug wire to connect the pick-up lead when using a non-inductive timing light.

To check the ignition timing, the technician points the flashing timing light at the ignition timing marks. The timing marks (Figure 5-21) are located either in front of the engine on the harmonic balancer or crankshaft pulley or at the rear of the engine on the flywheel.

The timing marks consist of a pointer, line, or notch and a scale. The scale indicates degrees of crankshaft rotation. The scale usually has a zero reference mark that refers to the crankshaft position when the number 1 piston is at top dead center (TDC) on the compression stroke. On either side of the zero reference mark are marks spaced every 2 or 3 degrees. These marks indicate degrees of crankshaft rotation before top dead center (BTDC) and after top dead center (ATDC).

When the number 1 piston is at TDC on the compression stroke, the line or notch will line up with the zero reference mark on the timing plate. Usually an engine is timed so that the number 1 spark plug fires several degrees BTDC.

When the timing light is connected to the battery and the number 1 spark plug wire, it will flash every time the number 1 spark plug fires. When pointed at the timing marks, the strobe effect of the light will freeze the spinning timing mark as it passes the timing scale. In this way the technician can determine the ignition timing by observing the degree of crankshaft rotation BTDC or ATDC when the spark plug fires.

Base timing is checked at base, or curb, idle. Advanced timing is checked at a higher rpm specified by the vehicle manufacturer. As engine speed increases, the timing is advanced (either mechanically, by vacuum, or electronically). The actual amount of timing advance can be measured with an advance timing light (Figure 5-22).

The advance timing light has either a scale or meter that indicates degrees of timing advance. The advance knob on the light can be turned to delay the flash of the light. By pointing the flashing light at the timing marks and turning the dial until the timing marks appear to line up again at the base timing position, the dial will indicate the amount of timing advance.

A more versatile advanced timing light is the digital timing light. The timing light shown in Figure 5-23 electronically measures timing advance as the engine rpm is increased and displays timing advance on the LED display. This light flashes only when a trigger is squeezed, unlike most timing lights that flash all the time the engine is running. When the trigger is released, the LED displays engine rpm. This combined feature eliminates the need for a separate tachometer when setting timing.

Magnetic Timing Probe

The timing light is no longer necessary when tuning many cars. The magnetic probe receptacle on the crankshaft position sensor allows the ignition timing to be electronically monitored with a magnetic timing probe (Figure 5-24). Changes in the magnetic field create electrical pulses in the tip of the timing probe. These pulses are monitored by the timing meter to determine crankshaft position and ignition timing.

The only trick to using a magnetic timing probe is correcting the offset of the probe receptacle. The receptacle is usually situated on either side of the vehicle's coil pick-up. The degree of offset must be factored into the timing probe's reading or the timing readout will be inaccurate by that many degrees. The timing meter must be programmed for the degree of offset specified by the car manufacturer.

The magnetic timer shown in Figure 5-24 measures not only timing but engine rpm as well.

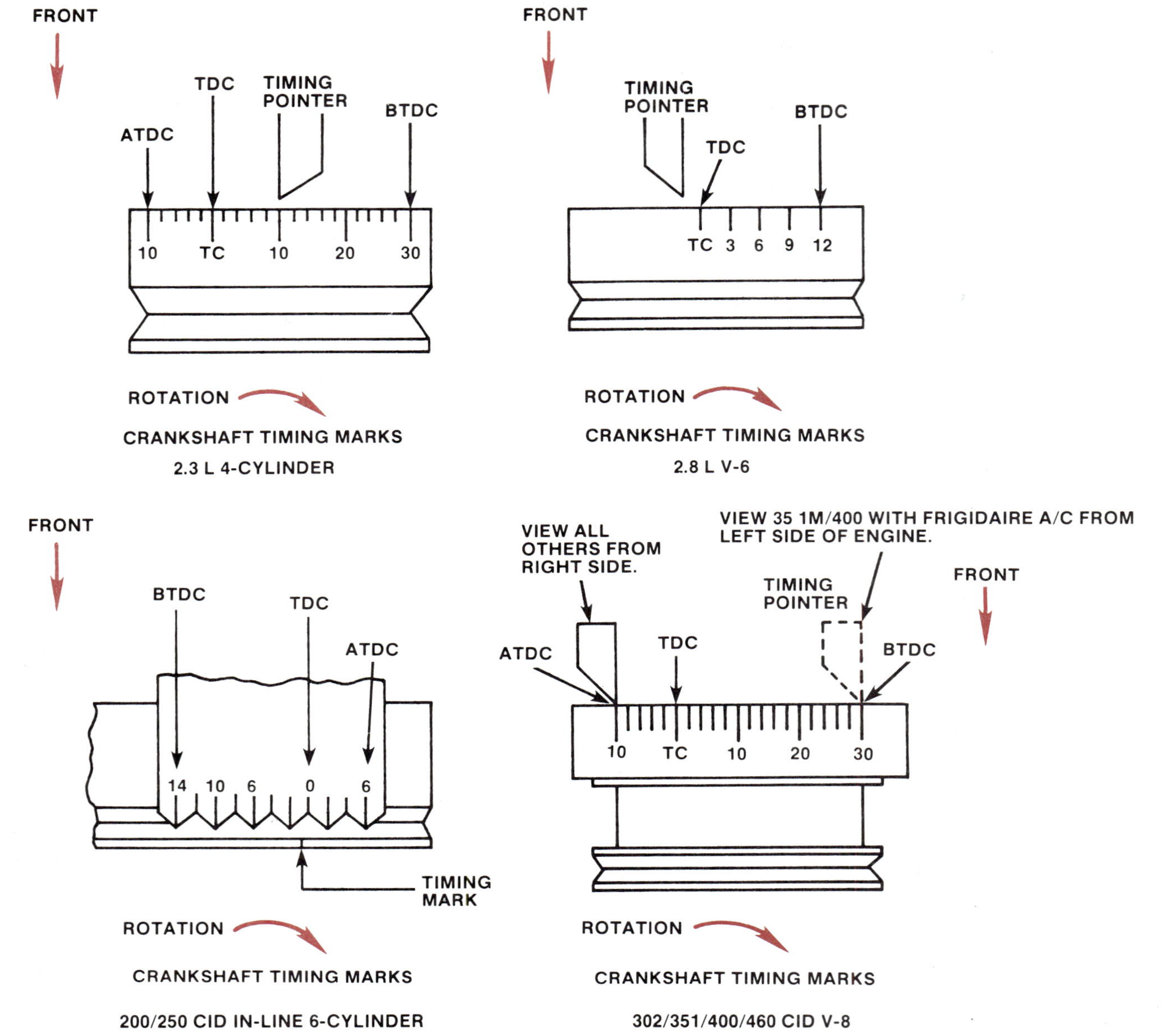

Figure 5-21 Typical timing marks.

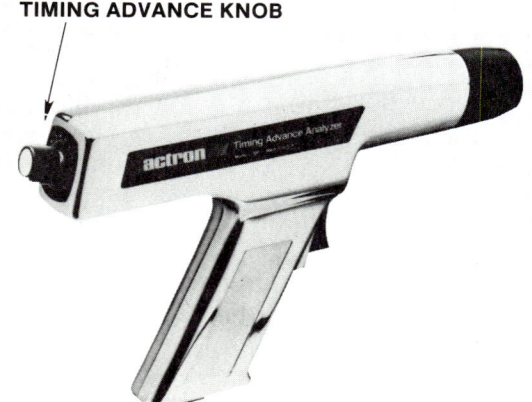

Figure 5-22 Advance timing light. *Courtesy of Actron Manufacturing Co.*

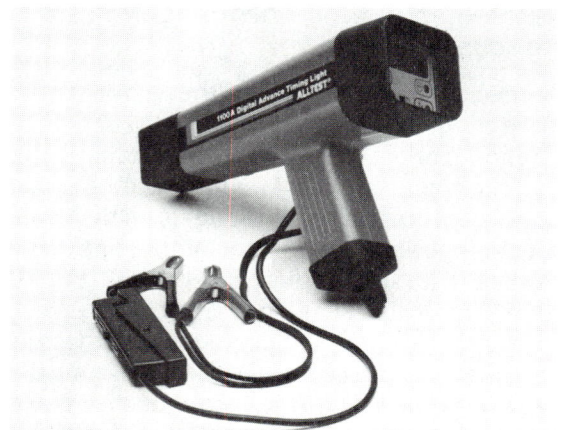

Figure 5-23 Digital timing light with LED display. *Courtesy of All-Test, Inc.*

Diagnostic Equipment 91

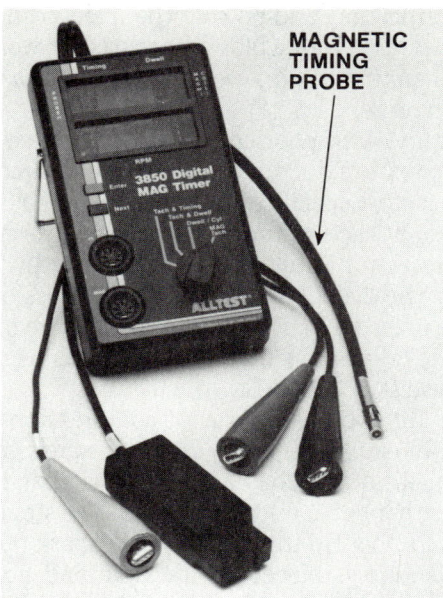

Figure 5-24 Ignition timing tester with a magnetic probe attachment. *Courtesy of All-Test, Inc.*

Electronic Ignition Module Tester

A defective electronic ignition module can cause a variety of problems. Some may be as obvious as a no-spark, no-start condition. Others may be only intermittent problems, such as a misfire at cruising speeds under certain load or temperature conditions. Tracing the source of intermittent problems to the ignition module can be difficult without an ignition module tester (Figure 5-25).

An electronic module ignition tester evaluates and determines if the module is operating within a given set of design parameters. It does so by simulating normal operating conditions while looking for faults in key components. A typical ignition module tester will perform the following tests.

- Shorted module test
- Cranking current test
- Key on/engine off current test
- Idle current test
- Cruise current test
- Cranking primary voltage test
- Idle primary voltage test
- Cruise primary voltage test

Some ignition module testers are also able to perform an ignition coil-spark test (actually firing the coil) and a distributor pick-up test.

Test selection is made by pushing the appropriate button. The module tester usually responds to these tests with a pass or fail indication.

Oscilloscope

The oscilloscope (Figure 5-26) was developed in the 1950s. It is still one of the most important troubleshooting tools for diagnosing electrical systems. Some of the tests that can be performed with an oscilloscope are shown in Table 5-2. The primary job of the oscilloscope is to convert the electrical signals of the ignition system into a visual image representing voltage changes over a specific period of time. This information is displayed on a CRT in the form of a continuous voltage line called a waveform pattern or trace (Figure 5-27).

Dual-trace oscilloscopes can display two different waveform patterns at the same time. For example, it is possible to view both the ignition system primary and secondary patterns on the same screen. Dual-trace oscilloscopes can also show how fuel-injector pulse width affects the oxygen sensor voltage signal, and other highly useful cause-and-effect electrical tests.

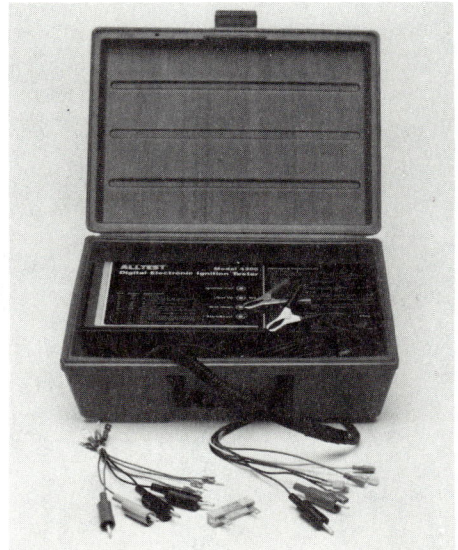

Figure 5-25 Typical electronic ignition module tester. *Courtesy of All-Test, Inc.*

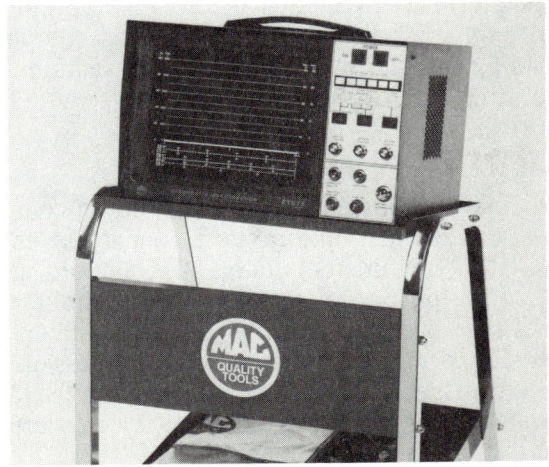

Figure 5-26 The oscilloscope is sometimes referred to as a tune-up scope. *Courtesy of Electro Specialties*

TABLE 5-2 IGNITION SYSTEM SCOPE TESTS

Breaker Point Systems	Electronic Systems
Cranking coil output	Cranking spark duration
Coil polarity	Coil polarity
Spark plug firing voltage	Spark plug firing voltage
Rotor air gap voltage drop	Rotor air gap voltage drop
Rotor register	Rotor register
Secondary circuit resistance	Secondary circuit resistance
Maximum coil output	Running spark duration
Secondary insulation	Secondary insulation
Spark plugs under load	Spark plugs under load
Coil and condenser	Coil condition
Cylinder timing accuracy	Cylinder timing accuracy
Breaker point dwell	Not applicable
Breaker point condition	Not applicable
Dwell variation	Dwell and dwell variation
Battery voltage	Battery voltage
Charging voltage	Charging voltage
Alternator condition	Alternator condition

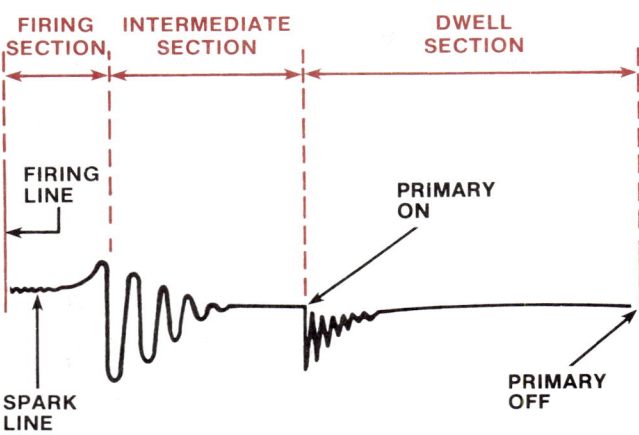

Figure 5-27 Typical oscilloscope waveform pattern.

☐ COMPRESSION AND VACUUM TESTERS

Compression and vacuum are two important indicators of engine condition. The following test equipment is used for measuring compression and vacuum, and for locating pressure and vacuum leaks.

Compression Gauge

Internal combustion engines depend on compression of the air/fuel mixture to maximize the energy potential of the air/fuel charge. The upward movement of the piston on the compression stroke compresses the air within the combustion chamber. The air/fuel mixture gets hotter as it is compressed. The hot mixture is easier to ignite, and when ignited it will generate much more power than the same mixture at a lower temperature.

If the combustion chamber leaks, some of the air/fuel mixture will escape when compressed, resulting in a loss of efficiency and power. The leaks could be the fault of burned valves, a blown head gasket, worn rings, a slipped timing chain, worn valve seats, a cracked head, and more.

An engine with poor compression (decreased compression pressure due to leaks) cannot be successfully tuned to factory specifications. That is why a compression check of each cylinder should be performed.

A compression gauge is used to check cylinder compression. The dial face on a typical compression gauge indicates pressure in both pounds per square inch (psi) and metric kilopascals (kPa). The range is usually 0 to 300 psi and 0 to 2100 kPa.

There are two basic types of compression gauges: the push-in gauge (Figure 5-28) and a screw-in gauge.

The push-in type has a short stem that is either straight or bent at a 45-degree angle. The stem ends in a tapered rubber tip that fits any size spark plug hole. The rubber tip is placed in the hole and held there while the engine is cranked through several compression cycles. Although simple to use, the push-in gauge will give an inaccurate reading if it is not held tightly in the hole.

The screw-in gauge has a long, flexible hose that ends in a threaded adapter. The flexible hose can reach into areas that are inaccessible with a push-in type. The adapters are changeable and come in several thread sizes to fit 10 mm, 12 mm, 14 mm, and 18 mm diameter holes. The adapters screw into the spark plug holes in place of the spark plugs. When installed properly, the gauge is leakproof and the technician's hands are free.

The better compression gauges have a vent valve that holds the highest pressure reading on the dial. Opening the valve releases the pressure when the test is complete. The steps for conducting a cylinder compression test are shown in Photo Sequence 3, included in this chapter.

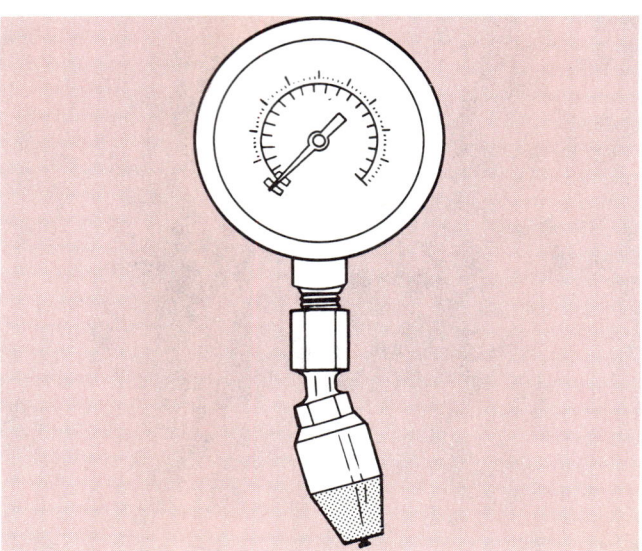

Figure 5-28 Push-in compression gauge.

PHOTO SEQUENCE 3

❑ CONDUCTING A COMPRESSION TEST

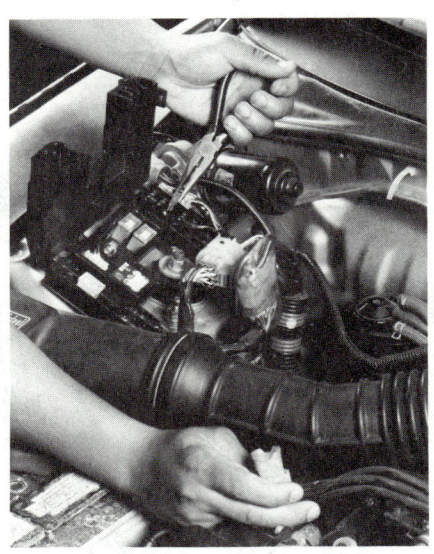

P3-1 Before conducting a compression test, disable the ignition and the fuel injection system (if the engine is so equipped).

P3-2 Prop the throttle plate into a wide open position. This will allow an unrestricted amount of air to enter the cylinders during the test.

P3-3 Remove all of the engine's spark plugs.

P3-4 Connect a remote starter button to the starter system.

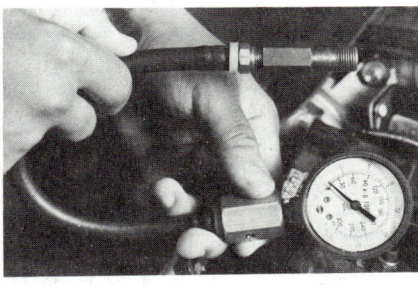

P3-5 Many types of compression gauges are available. The screw-in type tends to be the most accurate and easiest to use.

P3-6 Carefully install the gauge into the spark plug hole of the first cylinder.

P3-7 Connect a battery charger to the car. This will allow the engine to crank at consistent and normal speeds that are needed for accurate test results.

P3-8 Depress the remote starter button and observe the gauge's reading after the first engine revolution.

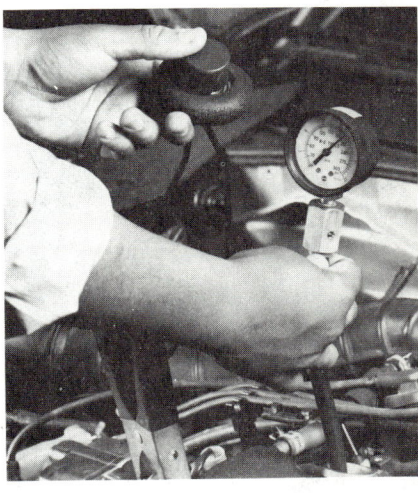

P3-9 Allow the engine to turn through four revolutions, and observe the reading after the fourth. The reading should increase with each revolution.

(continued)

P3-10 Readings observed should be recorded. After all cylinders have been tested, a comparison of cylinders can be made.

P3-11 Before removing the gauge from the cylinder, release the pressure from it using the release valve on the gauge.

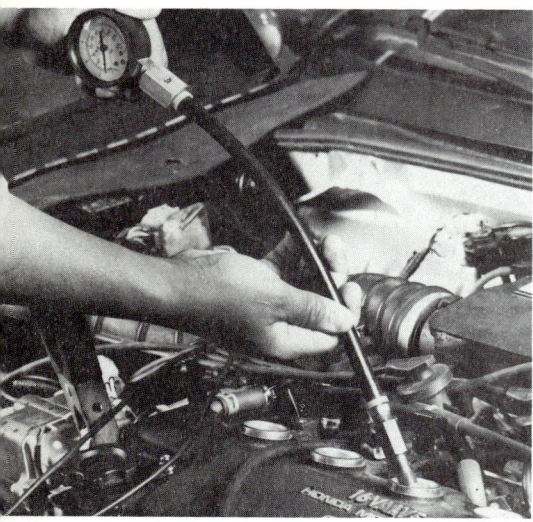

P3-12 Each cylinder should be tested in the same way.

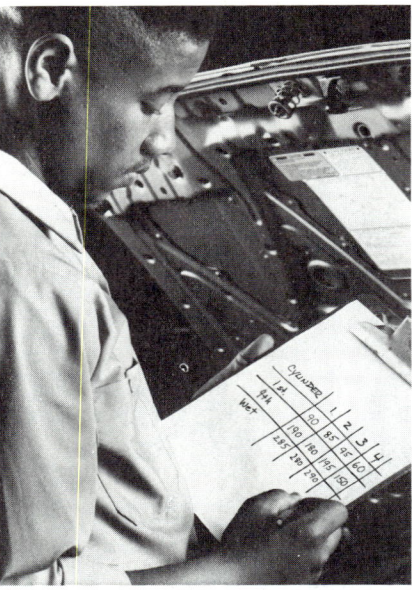

P3-13 After completing the test on all cylinders, compare them. If a cylinder is much lower than the others, continue testing that cylinder.

P3-14 Squirt a small amount of oil into the weak cylinder.

P3-15 Reinstall the compression gauge into that cylinder and conduct the test.

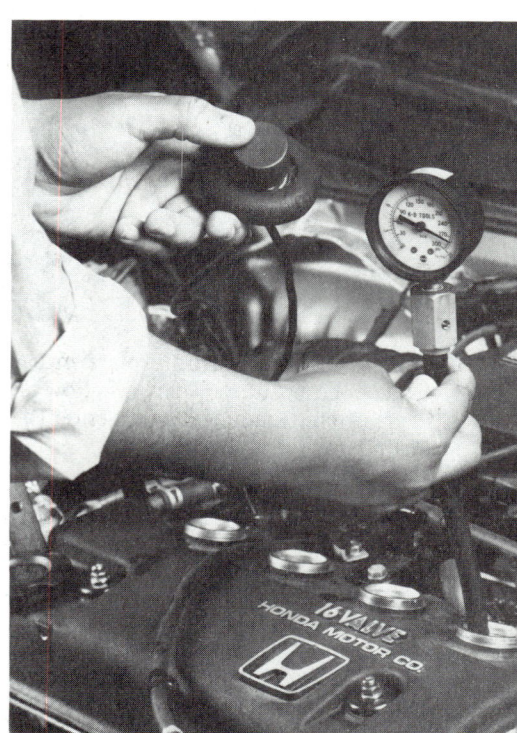

P3-16 If the reading increases with the presence of oil in the cylinder, the most likely cause of the original low readings was poor piston ring sealing. Using oil during a compression test is normally referred to as a wet test. ■

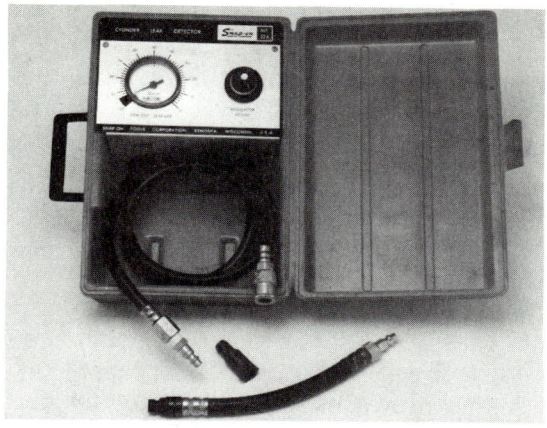

Figure 5-29 Typical cylinder leakage tester. *Courtesy of Snap-on Tools*

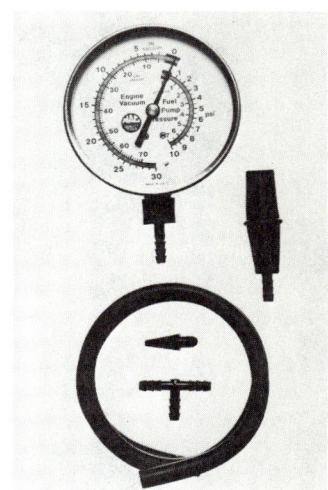

Figure 5-30 Vacuum gauge kit. *Courtesy of MAC Tools*

Cylinder Leakage Tester

If a compression test shows that any of the cylinders are leaking, a cylinder leakage test can be performed to measure the percentage of compression lost and help locate the source of leakage.

A cylinder leakage tester (Figure 5-29) applies compressed air to a cylinder through the spark plug hole. A threaded adapter on the end of the air pressure hose screws into the spark plug hole. Compressed air is provided from the shop compressed air system. A pressure regulator in the tester controls the pressure applied to the cylinder. An analog gauge registers the percentage of air pressure lost from the cylinder when the compressed air is applied. The scale on the dial face reads 0 to 100 percent.

A zero reading means that there is no leakage from the cylinder. Readings of 100 percent would indicate that the cylinder will not hold any pressure. The location of the compression leak can be found by listening and feeling around various parts of the engine. If a bad exhaust valve is responsible for the leakage, air can be felt leaving the exhaust system during the test. Air leaving the radiator would indicate a faulty head gasket or a cracked block or head. If the piston rings are bad, air will be heard leaving the crankcase or through the valve cover's breather cap. Most vehicles, even new cars, experience some leakage around the rings. Up to 20 percent is considered acceptable during the leakage test. When the engine is actually running, the rings will seal much better. However, there should be no leakage around the valves or the head gasket.

Vacuum Gauge

Measuring intake manifold vacuum is another way to diagnose the condition of an engine. Manifold vacuum is tested with a vacuum gauge (Figure 5-30). Vacuum is formed on a piston's intake stroke. As the piston moves down, it lowers the pressure of the air in the cylinder—if the cylinder is sealed. This lower cylinder pressure is called engine vacuum. If there is a leak, atmospheric pressure will force air into the cylinder and the resultant pressure will not be as low.

The vacuum gauge measures the difference in pressure between the intake manifold and the outside atmosphere. If the manifold pressure is lower than the atmospheric pressure, a vacuum exists. Vacuum is measured in inches of mercury (in./Hg) and in kiloPascals (kPa) or millimeters of mercury (mm/Hg).

A flexible hose on the gauge must be connected to a source of manifold vacuum, either on the manifold or the carburetor. Sometimes this requires removing a plug from the manifold and installing a special fitting.

The test is made with the engine cranking or running. A good vacuum reading is 15 to 20 in./Hg (50 to 65 kPa). However, be sure to consult the factory service manual for specifications.

Low or fluctuating readings can indicate many different problems. For example, a low, steady reading might be caused by retarded ignition or valve timing. A sharp vacuum drop at regular intervals might be caused by a burned intake valve.

Other conditions that can be revealed by vacuum readings follow.

- Stuck or burned valves
- Improper valve or ignition timing
- Weak valve springs
- Leaking intake manifold or EGR valve
- Uneven compression
- Worn rings or cylinder walls
- Leaking head gaskets
- Incorrect carburetor adjustments
- Restricted exhaust system
- Ignition defects

The vacuum gauge can also be used to test vacuum-operated components, such as a distributor vacuum advance mechanism or a thermal vacuum valve. A tee connector is used to connect the gauge in line with the system's vacuum hoses.

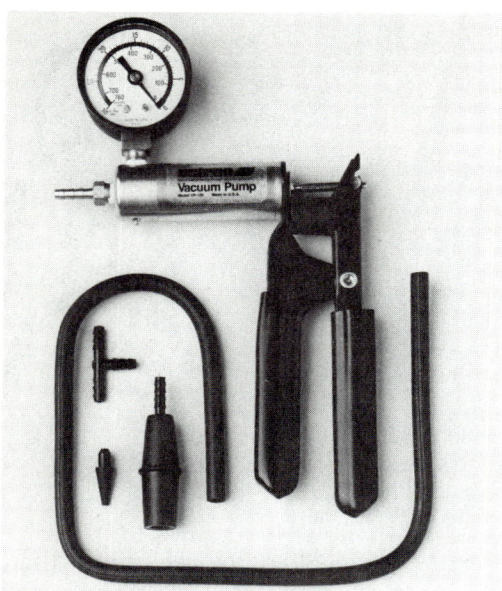

Figure 5-31 Typical vacuum pump with accessories. *Courtesy of Actron Manufacturing Co.*

Vacuum Pumps

Another tool used to test vacuum-actuated components is the vacuum pump (Figure 5-31). A vacuum pump consists of a hand pump, a vacuum gauge, and a length of rubber hose used to attach the pump to the component being tested. Tests with the vacuum pump can usually be performed without removing the component from the car.

When the handles of the pump are squeezed together, a piston in the pump body draws air out of the component being tested. The partial vacuum created by the pump is registered on the pump's vacuum gauge. The vacuum level needed to actuate a given component should be compared to the specifications given in the factory service manual.

The vacuum pump is also commonly used to locate vacuum leaks. This is done by connecting the vacuum pump to a suspect vacuum hose or component and applying vacuum. If the needle on the vacuum gauge begins to drop after the vacuum is applied, a leak exists somewhere in the system.

The following list shows some of the systems and components that can be tested with a vacuum pump.

1. Carburetor service
   a. Choke pull-off diaphragm
   b. Vacuum break diaphragm
2. Ignition system service
   a. Vacuum advance unit
   b. Vacuum retard unit
3. Computerized engine control system—vacuum transducer MAP sensor
4. Emission control system
   a. Thermal vacuum switch
   b. Vacuum control valve
   c. Heated air intake system
   d. EGR (exhaust gas recirculation) valve
5. Automatic transmission modulator valve

Vacuum Leak Detector

A vacuum or compression leak might be revealed by a compression check, a cylinder leak down test, or a manifold vacuum test. However, finding the location of the leak can be very difficult.

A simple, but time-consuming way to find leaks in a vacuum system is to check each component and vacuum hose with a vacuum pump. Simply apply vacuum to the suspected area and watch the gauge for any loss of vacuum.

The most technologically advanced method of leak detection is called an ultrasonic leak detector (Figure 5-32). Air rushing through a vacuum leak creates a high-frequency sound, higher than the range of human hearing. An ultrasonic leak detector is designed to hear the frequencies of the leak. When the tool is passed over a leak, the detector responds to the high-frequency sound by emitting a warning beep. Some detectors also have a series of LEDs that light up as the frequencies are received. The closer the detector is moved to the leak, the more LEDs light up or the faster the beeping occurs. This allows the technician to zero in on the leak. An ultrasonic leak detector can sense leaks as small as 1/500 inch and accurately locate the leak to within 1/16 inch.

An ultrasonic leak detector can also be used to detect compression leaks, bearing wear, and electrical arcing. It can also be used to diagnose fuel injector operation.

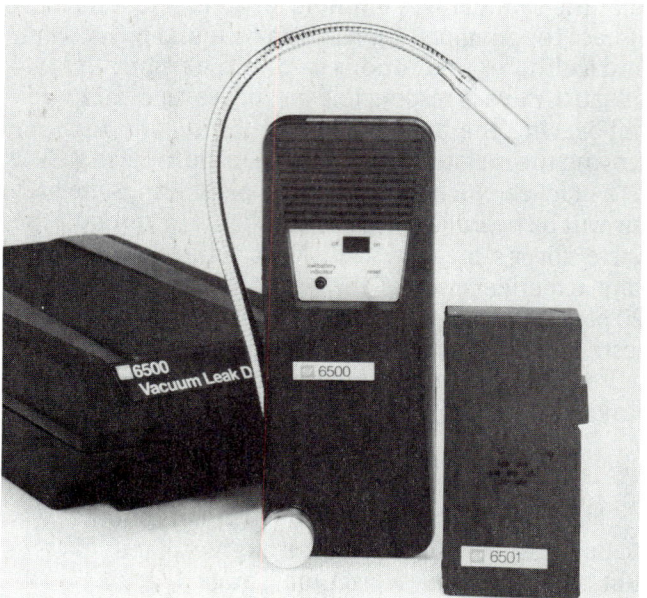

Figure 5-32 An ultrasonic leak detector picks up the sound frequencies of the leak. *Courtesy of TIF Instruments, Inc.*

Diagnostic Equipment

☐ FUEL SYSTEM TEST EQUIPMENT

Misadjusted or misfunctioning fuel system components will adversely affect engine performance. The following tools are used to test fuel system components.

Pressure Gauge

A pressure gauge (Figure 5-33) is needed to measure the pressure in the fuel system. This is particularly true in fuel-injected systems in which the discharge pressure of the fuel pump may be 35 to 70 psi. A drop in fuel pressure will reduce the fuel delivered to the injectors and result in a lean air/fuel mixture.

The pressure gauge can be used to check discharge pressure of fuel pumps, the regulated pressure of fuel injection systems, and injector pressure drop.

> **SHOP TALK**
>
> The fuel system on fuel-injected vehicles is highly pressurized. The pressure must be relieved before servicing any component in the fuel system.

Some fuel pressure gauges also have a valve and outlet hose for testing fuel pump discharge volume (Figure 5-34). The manufacturer's specification for discharge volume will be so many pints or liters of fuel in a certain number of seconds. Discharge volume testing is particularly applicable to carbureted engines.

Fuel Injector Cleaner

Clogged fuel injectors are becoming a much more common problem as the use of fuel injection systems

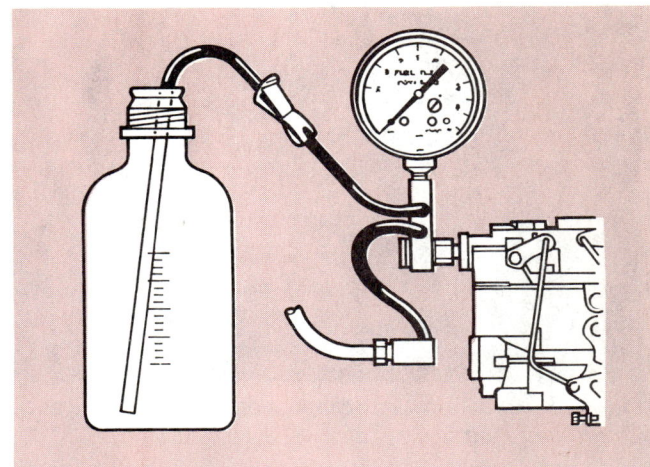

Figure 5-34 Checking fuel pump discharge volume.

increases. Clogged injectors are the result of inconsistencies in gasoline detergent levels and high sulfur content. When these sensitive injection systems become partially clogged, fuel flow is restricted. Spray patterns are altered, causing poor performance and reduced fuel economy.

The solution to a sulfated and plugged fuel injector is to clean it, not replace it. There are two kinds of fuel injector cleaners. One is a pressure tank (Figure 5-35). A mixture of solvent and unleaded gasoline is placed in the tank, following the manufacturer's instructions for mixing, quantity, and safe handling. The vehicle's fuel pump must be disabled and, on some vehicles, the fuel line must be blocked between the pressure regulator and the return line. Then, the hose on the pressure tank is connected to the service port in the fuel system. The in-line valve is then partially opened and the engine is started. It should run at approximately 2000

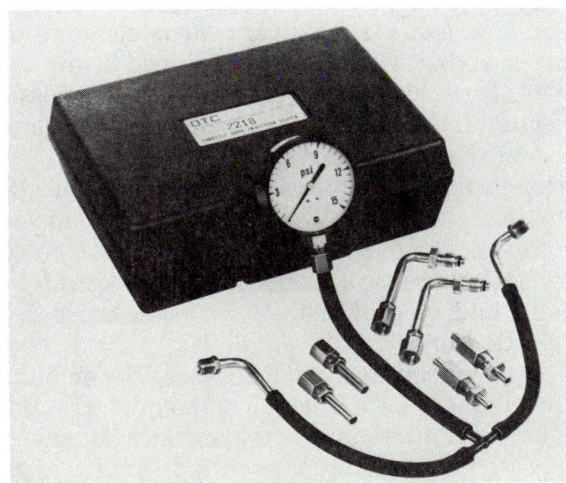

Figure 5-33 Fuel pressure gauge and various adapters. *Courtesy of OTC Tool and Equipment Division of SPX Corp.*

Figure 5-35 Pressurized tank used to clean fuel injectors. *Courtesy of OTC Tool and Equipment Division of SPX Corp.*

Figure 5-36 Throwaway canister of fuel injector cleaner. *Courtesy of Penray Co.*

rpm for about 10 minutes to clean the injectors thoroughly.

An alternative to the pressure tank is a pressurized canister (Figure 5-36) in which the solvent solution is premixed. Use of the canister-type cleaner is similar to this procedure, but does not require mixing or pumping.

The canister is connected to the injection system's service fitting, and the valve on the canister is opened. The engine is started and allowed to run until it dies. Then, the canister is discarded.

Fuel Injector Pulse Tester

The only accurate cylinder balance test when injectors are suspect is with a fuel injector pulse tester (Figure 5-37). This electronic tool fires individual fuel injectors in 1/2-second increments in three different ranges: 1 pulse of 500 milliseconds, 50 pulses of 10

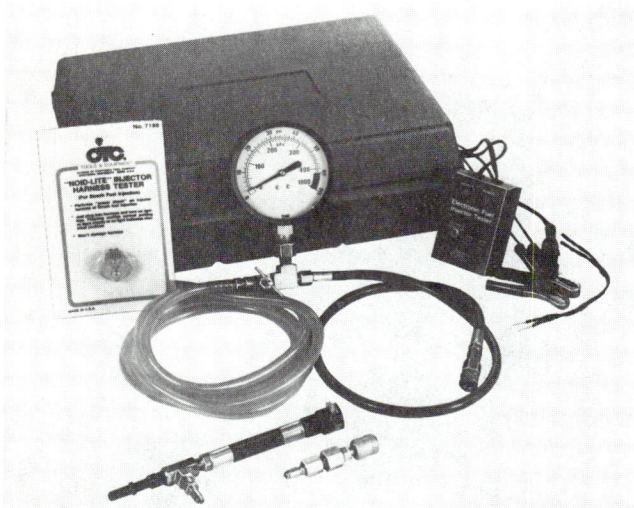

Figure 5-37 A fuel injector pulse tester monitors fuel pressure while the injector is pulsed by the tester's control box. *Courtesy of OTC Tool and Equipment Division of SPX Corp.*

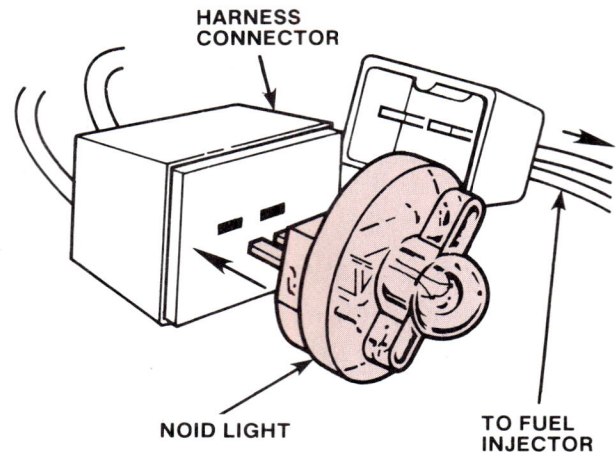

Figure 5-38 A noid light is used to check for voltage pulses at the fuel injector harness.

milliseconds, and 100 pulses of 5 milliseconds. While the injector is being pulsed, the technician will monitor pressure drop. Ideally, each injector should create the same pressure drop when activated for the same amount of time. Little or no pressure drop indicates a plugged or defective injector. Excessive pressure drop indicates an overly rich condition.

Injector Circuit Test Light

A special test light called a noid light is used to determine if a fuel injector is receiving its proper voltage pulse. The wiring harness connector is disconnected from the injector and the noid light is plugged into the connector (Figure 5-38). After disabling the ignition to prevent starting, the engine is cranked. The noid light should flash rapidly if the voltage signal is present. No flash usually indicates broken voltage supply wires or the injector is not properly grounded.

❑ EXHAUST ANALYZER

Federal laws require new cars and light trucks to meet specific emissions levels. State governments also passed laws requiring that car owners maintain their vehicles so that the emissions remained below an acceptable level. Most states require an annual emissions inspection to meet that goal. Therefore, most garages have an exhaust analyzer.

These exhaust analyzers are also valuable diagnostic tools. By monitoring the exhaust, a technician is able to look at the effects of the combustion process. Any defect can cause a change in exhaust quality. The amount and type of change serves as the basis of diagnostic work.

Early emission analyzers measured the amount of hydrocarbons (HC) and carbon monoxides (CO) in the exhaust. Hydrocarbons in the exhaust is raw, unburned fuel. Emissions analyzers measure HC in parts per million (ppm) or grams per mile (g/mi). Carbon monoxide is an odorless, toxic gas that is the product of incomplete combustion. CO is measured as a percent of the total exhaust.

An exhaust analyzer measures the emissions in the exhaust by infrared refraction. Two air samples—one from the exhaust pipe and one from the shop—are drawn into glass tubes in the analyzer. (Some analyzers have a sealed reference cell and do not require a fresh air sample.) An infrared beam shines through both tubes. As the beam passes through the exhaust sample, it bends, or refracts. The amount of refraction is determined by the level of impurities in the sample. The analyzer measures the amount of refraction and converts it into electrical signals to activate the HC and CO meters.

The level of HC and CO in the exhaust has always been an indication of engine performance. A high level of hydrocarbons could indicate a fouled spark plug, a defective spark plug wire, or a burned valve allowing unburned fuel vapor to enter the exhaust system. A high CO level indicates an excessively rich air/fuel mixture.

However, the advances in electronic spark control, fuel and air metering, and electronic integration of related systems, along with the development of very efficient catalytic converters, has reached a point where there is little HC and CO remaining in the exhaust. On most late-model cars, HC and CO levels alone are no longer a useful indicator of engine operation.

The manufacturers of emissions analyzers have responded by producing the four-gas exhaust analyzer. In addition to measuring HC and CO levels, a four-gas exhaust analyzer also monitors carbon dioxide (CO_2) and oxygen (O_2) levels in the exhaust. This diagnostic capability permits a technician to use the four-gas analyzer to diagnose the following conditions.

- Rich or lean mixtures (Table 5-3)
- Air pump malfunctions
- Catalytic converter malfunction
- Blown head gaskets
- Faulty carburetors or injectors
- Intake manifold leaks
- Leaking EGR valves
- Excessive misfire
- Excessive spark advance
- Leaks or restrictions in the exhaust system

❏ MICROCOMPUTER SCAN TOOLS

The introduction of computer-controlled ignition and fuel systems brought with it the need for tools capable of diagnosing and troubleshooting electronic control systems. There are a variety of microcomputer scan tools available today that do just that. A scan tool (Figure 5-39) is a microprocessor designed to communicate with the vehicle's on-board computer. Con-

TABLE 5-3 ANALYSIS OF FOUR-GAS EMISSIONS ANALYZER RESULTS

Gas Condition		With Catalytic Converter	Without Catalytic Converter
HC*	Over 110 ppm	Rich or lean	—
	Over 250 ppm	—	Rich or lean
CO	Over 3%	—	Rich
	Over 1%	Rich	—
O_2	Over 2%	Lean mixture	
	Under 1%	Rich mixture	
CO_2	Less than 10%	Rich mixture or misfire	

*HC readings can vary significantly depending on the age and condition of the engine, and the temperature of the engine.

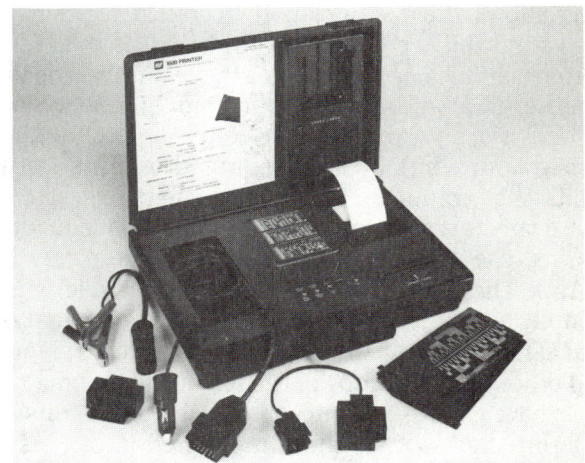

Figure 5-39 This scan tool has a coded identification card for each car model and a built-in printer. *Courtesy of TIF Instruments, Inc.*

nected to the computer module via model specific connectors, a scan tool will access trouble codes, run key-on and key-off tests to check system operations, and run tests that activate various engine controls. Trouble codes and test results are displayed on an LED screen, printed out on the scanner printer, or connected to an engine analyzer or PC monitor for data display.

A computer scan tool can derive its intelligence from one of several sources. Some scan tools have a programmable read-only memory (PROM) chip that contains all the information needed to diagnose specific model lines (usually GM, Ford, or Chrysler).

Other scanners use plug-in type software cartridges or optically-read plastic identification cards. A software cartridge or data card is needed for each make and

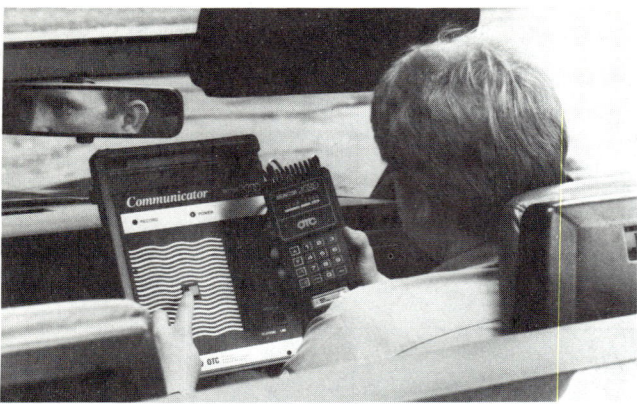

Figure 5-40 Using a scan tool during a road test. *Courtesy of OTC Tool and Equipment Division of SPX Corp.*

model vehicle. As new systems are introduced on new models, the replaceable PROM chip is updated or new software or data cards are made available.

Computer scan tools often do the same job as larger engine analyzers at a lower cost. It is also possible to use some scan tools during road testing (Figure 5-40). This allows the technician to record data from the on-board vehicle computer at the exact time an intermittent fault is occurring. After the test drive, the data is retrieved from the scan tool memory for analysis.

LED displays are generally only large enough to display four short lines of information. This feature limits the technician's ability to compare test data. However, most scan tools overcome this inadequacy by storing the test data in a random access memory (RAM). The scan tool then can be interfaced with a printer, personal computer, or larger engine analyzer that can retrieve the information stored in the memory and produce a hard copy of the test results. Some scan tools have a built-in printer so that the test results can be printed as soon as they are entered into the scan tool's memory.

❑ ENGINE ANALYZER

When performing a complete engine performance analysis, an engine analyzer keeps all of the necessary test equipment within easy reach. Although the term engine analyzer is often loosely applied to any multipurpose test meter, a complete engine analyzer will incorporate most, if not all, of the test instruments mentioned in this chapter. A state-of-the-art analyzer will do the work of the following tools.

- Compression gauge
- Pressure gauge
- Vacuum gauge
- Vacuum pump
- Tachometer
- Timing light/probe
- Voltmeter
- Ohmmeter
- Ammeter
- Oscilloscope
- Computer scan tool
- Emissions analyzer

With an engine analyzer, one can perform tests on the battery, starting system, charging system, primary and secondary ignition circuits, electronic control systems, the fuel system, the emissions systems, and the engine block. The analyzer is connected to these systems by a variety of leads, inductive clamps, probes, and connectors. The data received from these connections is processed by several microprocessors (computers) within the analyzer.

The microprocessors in some computerized engine analyzers are programmed with specifications pertaining to specific model vehicles. Diagnostic trouble codes have been loaded into the analyzer's memory circuits. Based on the input from the leads and connectors, the microprocessors will identify worn, misadjusted, or malfunctioning components in all major engine systems. The analyzer will logically deduce the probable cause of specific performance complaints and will prompt, or guide, the technician step by step through a troubleshooting procedure designed to verify and correct the problem.

Commands and specifications can be entered into the analyzer on the computer-like keyboard. Specifications, commands, and test results are displayed on the CRT screen. Some analyzers have adapted PC technology and display test results graphically on the CRT screen (Figure 5-41). The analyzer's printer will print out hard copies of the information that appears on the screen.

Most engine analyzers have both manual and automatic test modes. In the manual modes, any single test, such as cylinder compression or alternator current, can be performed. The manual test mode is useful when troubleshooting for a specific performance problem. The automatic test mode is useful when performing a general tune-up. When the automatic test mode is selected (usually by striking the appropriate command key on the analyzer's keyboard), specific tests are performed in a specific sequence automatically by the analyzer. Following is a typical test procedure that is performed when the analyzer is placed in the automatic test mode.

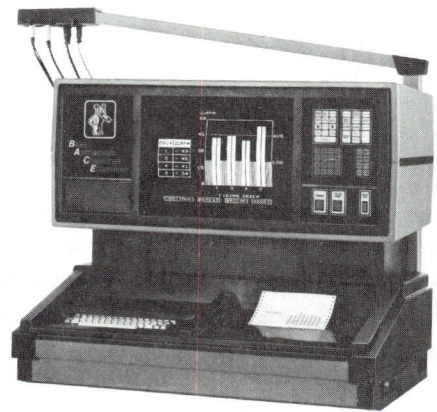

Figure 5-41 Engine analyzer with PC technology. *Courtesy of Bear Automotive Service Equipment Co.*

- Cranking voltage
- Relative compression
- Charging voltage
- Running voltage
- Primary circuit voltage
- Secondary circuit kilovoltage
- Dwell per cylinder
- Cylinder power balance

These tests give a basic performance analysis of the engine, starting system, charging system, and ignition system. Other engine analyzers have automatic test modes for specific systems (cranking, charging, timing, fuel system, primary ignition circuit/dwell, secondary ignition circuit/power analysis, and cylinder balance, and exhaust analysis).

Summary

- A basic understanding of electrical principles is essential to operating diagnostic tools and interpreting the readings. The flow of electricity is called current and is measured in amperes. There are two types of electrical flow: direct current (DC) and alternating current (AC).
- Resistance to current flow produces heat. The amount of resistance is measured in ohms.
- In a complete electrical circuit, the flow of electricity is controlled and applied to perform tasks such as lighting headlights and turning over the starter motor. Circuit testers are used to identify shorted and open circuits.
- Three important electrical test meters are the voltmeter, which measures the voltage available at any point in an electrical system; the ohmmeter, which measures resistance to current flow in a circuit; and the ammeter, which measures current flow in a circuit.
- A volt/ampere tester can be used to test batteries, starting systems, and charging systems. This tester contains a carbon pile, which is a variable resistor used to draw current out of the battery. The resistance of the carbon pile must be adjusted to match the battery size.
- The timing light is an essential tool for tuning up most vehicles. It reveals when the spark plugs are firing in relation to the piston position. Base timing is checked at base, or curb, idle. Advanced timing is checked at a higher rpm specified by the vehicle manufacturer.
- An electronic ignition module tester is capable of performing a series of tests to trace the source of ignition problems. Intermittent problems, such as misfire at cruising speeds under certain load or temperature conditions, can be difficult without the use of this tester.
- Compression is an important indicator of engine condition. Two types of compression gauges (push-in and screw-in) are available to test each cylinder for compression.
- Vacuum is another indicator of engine condition. The vacuum gauge measures the difference in pressure between the intake manifold and the outside atmosphere. If manifold pressure is lower, a vacuum exists.
- The vacuum pump is used to locate vacuum leaks. This can be time consuming. The most sophisticated method of finding the source of leaks is using an ultrasonic leak detector, which can sense leaks as small as 1/500 inch.
- Fuel system pressure is particularly important in fuel-injected systems. A pressure gauge can be used to check fuel pump discharge pressure, the regulated pressure of injection systems, and injector pressure drop.
- Even partially clogged fuel injectors can cause poor engine performance and reduced fuel economy. There are two types of injector cleaners available: a pressure tank and a canister-type cleaner.
- On most new cars, hydrocarbons (HC) and carbon monoxide (CO) are no longer a good indicator of engine operation. A four-gas exhaust analyzer is now used because it monitors carbon dioxide (CO_2) and oxygen (O_2) levels, in addition to HC and CO.
- Computer scan tools are often used instead of engine analyzers. Connected to the vehicle's on-board computer, a scan tool will access trouble codes, run key-on and key-off tests to check system operations, and run tests that activate various engine controls.
- A state-of-the-art engine analyzer does the work of the following tools: compression, pressure, and vacuum gauge; vacuum pump; tachometer; timing light/probe; voltmeter, ohmmeter, and ammeter; oscilloscope; computer scan tool; and exhaust analyzer. The engine analyzer points out the probable cause of a specific problem and guides the technician through a step-by-step troubleshooting procedure.

Review Questions

1. Name the two energy sources used in automobile electrical systems.
2. What are circuit testers used to identify?
3. Name the two basic types of compression gauges.
4. What tool is used to test manifold vacuum?
5. Define induction.
6. The center of an atom is known as the _____.
   a. shell
   b. proton
   c. nucleus
   d. neutron
7. Resistance is measured in _____.
   a. current

b. volts
   c. ohms
   d. watts
8. What type of circuit allows electricity to bypass part of the circuit's normal load?
   a. grounded
   b. open
   c. shorted
   d. none of the above
9. When using a voltmeter, Technician A connects it across the circuit being tested. Technician B connects the voltmeter in series with the circuit being tested. Who is correct?
   a. Technician A
   b. Technician B
   c. Both A and B
   d. Neither A nor B
10. Technician A uses a digital volt/ohmmeter to test voltage. Technician B uses the same tool to test resistance. Who is correct?
    a. Technician A
    b. Technician B
    c. Both A and B
    d. Neither A nor B
11. Recent advances in automotive electronics have lessened the usefulness of the _____.
    a. multimeter
    b. volt/ampere tester
    c. tach-dwellmeter
    d. magnetic timing probe
12. Which of the following tests can be performed only with some ignition module testers?
    a. idle current
    b. cruise primary voltage
    c. distributor pick-up
    d. key-on/engine-off current
13. Technician A says that a push-in compression gauge must be held tightly in the spark plug hole in order to get an accurate reading. Technician B says that the gauge must be held loosely in the hole. Who is correct?
    a. Technician A
    b. Technician B
    c. Both A and B
    d. Neither A nor B
14. When conducting a cylinder leakage test, Technician A says that 20 percent leakage around the rings means that the cylinder in question is defective. Technician B says that 20 percent leakage is considered acceptable. Who is correct?
    a. Technician A
    b. Technician B
    c. Both A and B
    d. Neither A nor B
15. Which of the following conditions can be revealed by vacuum readings?
    a. leaking intake manifold
    b. uneven compression
    c. restricted exhaust system
    d. all of the above
16. Technician A uses an ultrasonic leak detector to check bearing wear, and Technician B uses it to detect electrical arcing. Who is correct?
    a. Technician A
    b. Technician B
    c. Both A and B
    d. Neither A nor B
17. Technician A says that the only solution to a sulfated and plugged fuel injector is to replace it. Technician B says a sulfated and plugged fuel injector can be cleaned. Who is correct?
    a. Technician A
    b. Technician B
    c. Both A and B
    d. Neither A nor B
18. A computer scan tool can be used to retrieve codes much like a more expensive _____.
    a. fuel injector pulse tester
    b. exhaust analyzer
    c. engine analyzer
    d. digital volt/ohmmeter
19. When using a fuel injector pulse tester, Technician A says that little or no pressure drop indicates a plugged or defective injector. Technician B says that it indicates an overly rich condition. Who is correct?
    a. Technician A
    b. Technician B
    c. Both A and B
    d. Neither A nor B
20. It is much easier to test current using an ammeter with a(n) _____.
    a. continuity tester
    b. carbon pile
    c. inductive pick-up
    d. tachometer

SECTION 2 ENGINES

Chapter 6 Automotive Engines
Chapter 7 Engine Disassembly
Chapter 8 Short Blocks
Chapter 9 Cylinder Heads and Valves
Chapter 10 Camshafts and Valve Trains
Chapter 11 Lubricating and Cooling Systems
Chapter 12 Intake and Exhaust Systems
Chapter 13 Engine Sealing and Reassembly

A vehicle's engine is an extremely complex piece of precision-built machinery. A clear understanding of how this power plant controls the internal combustion process and generates usable power is essential before attempting any engine service.

Engine repair and rebuilding procedures are among the most demanding jobs performed by service technicians. Components must be handled with great care and assembled to exacting tolerances. Absolute cleanliness must be maintained. Bolt torque and sealing requirements must be met.

The information found in Section 2 explains all engine systems and components, including disassembly, inspection, repair, and reassembly procedures. It corresponds to materials covered on the ASE certification test on engine repair.

6 AUTOMOTIVE ENGINES

Objectives

- Describe the various ways in which engines can be classified.
- Explain what occurs during each stroke of a four-stroke engine cycle.
- Describe the performance differences between two-stroke and four-stroke engines.
- Outline the advantages and disadvantages of the in-line and V-type engine designs.
- Define important engine measurements and performance characteristics, including bore and stroke, displacement, compression ratio, engine efficiency, torque, and horsepower.
- Evaluate the engine's condition.
- List and describe nine abnormal engine noises.
- Outline the basics of diesel, rotary, and stratified engine operation.

Modern engines are highly engineered state-of-the-art power plants. These engines are designed to meet the special demands of the automobile buying public for achieving greater performance and fuel efficiency. The days of the heavy, cast-iron V-8 engine with its poor gas mileage are quickly drawing to a close. Today, these engines have been replaced by compact, high-tech, four-cylinder and V-6 power plants (Figure 6-1). Modern engine technology utilizes many extremely lightweight engine castings and stampings; non-traditional materials for power plant applications (for example, aluminum, magnesium, fiber-reinforced plastics); and fewer and smaller fasteners to hold things together, due to computerized joint designs that optimize loading patterns. Each of these newer engine designs has its own distinct personality, based on construction materials, casting configurations, and design optimizations that concern weight, power, manufacturing costs, and serviceability.

These modern engine technologies have created problems for the profession. Before examining how these problems might affect the technician, it is important to have a basic knowledge of engine design and operation (Figure 6-2).

A B

Figure 6-1 (A) Typical late-model four-cylinder engine and (B) typical V-6 engine. *Courtesy of General Motors Corp.*

Automotive Engines   105

❑ ENGINE CLASSIFICATIONS

Modern automotive engines can be classified in several ways depending on the following design features.

- Operational cycles. Most technicians will generally come in contact with only two- or four-stroke cycle engines. The most popular is the four-stroke engine (Figure 6-3).
- Number of cylinders. Current engine designs include 3-, 4-, 5-, 6-, 8-, and 12-cylinder engines.
- Cylinder arrangement. An engine can be flat (opposed), in-line, or V-type. Other more complicated designs have also been used.
- Valve train type. Engine valve trains can be either the overhead camshaft (OHC) type or the camshaft in-block overhead valve (OHV) type. It is also possible to use separate camshafts for intake and exhaust valves. Some late-model cars use dual overhead camshafts (DOHC). V-type engines may be equipped with four camshafts—two on each side.
- Valve arrangement. There are several types of valve arrangements as described later in this chapter.
- Ignition type. There are two types of ignition systems: spark and compression. In a spark ignition system, the air/fuel mixture is ignited by an electrical spark. Diesel engines, or compression ignition engines, have no spark plugs. An automotive diesel engine has a higher compression ratio than a spark ignition engine. The higher compression

Figure 6-2   (A) A V-6 gasoline engine and (B) a cutaway view of the same engine. *Courtesy of General Motors Corp.*

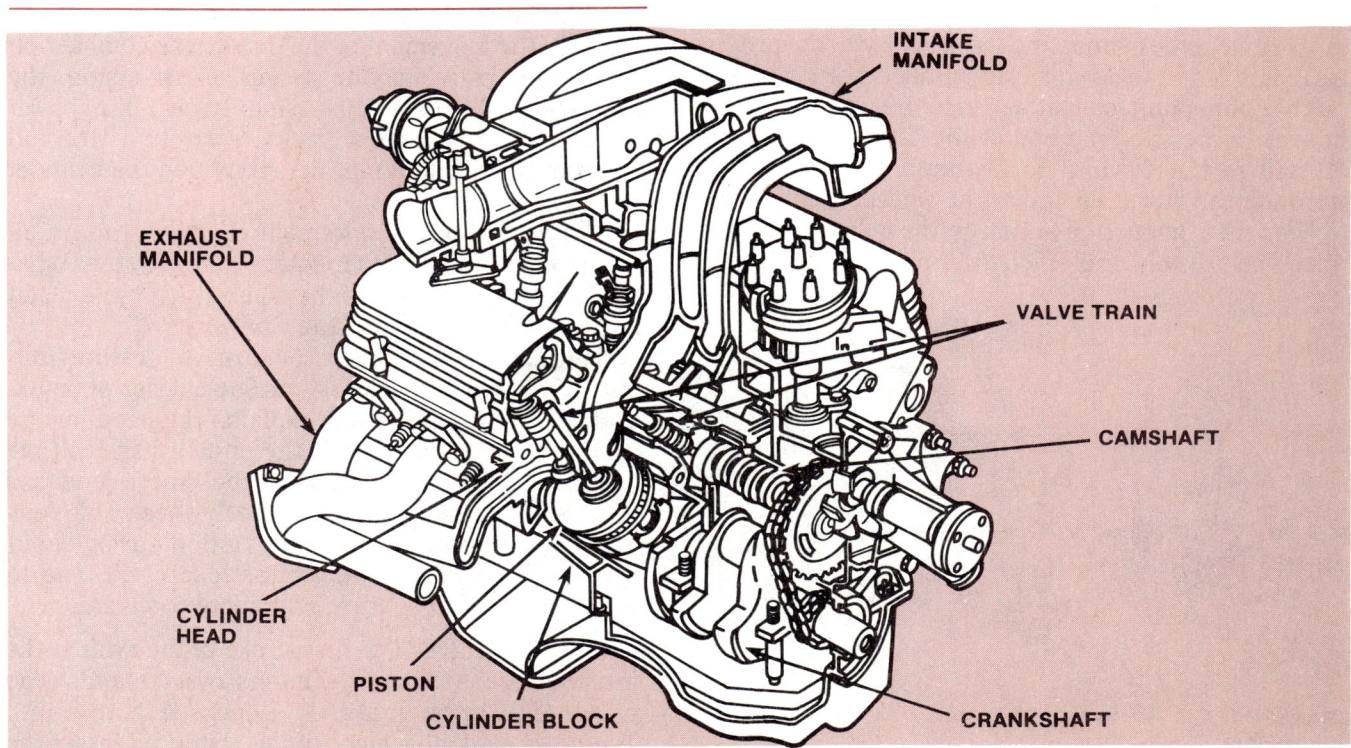

Figure 6-3   Major components of a four-stroke engine.

generates enough heat to ignite the air/fuel mixture for the power stroke.
- Cooling systems. There are both air-cooled and liquid-cooled engines in use. Most engines have liquid-cooling systems.
- Fuel systems. Fuel systems currently used in automobile engines include gasoline, diesel, and propane.

☐ FOUR-STROKE GASOLINE ENGINES

In a passenger car or truck, the engine provides the rotating power to drive the wheels through the transmission and driving axle. All automobile engines, both gasoline and diesel, are classified as internal combustion because the combustion or burning takes place inside the engine. These systems require an air/fuel mixture that arrives in the combustion chamber at the correct time and an engine constructed to withstand the temperatures and pressures created by the burning of thousands of fuel droplets.

The combustion chamber is the space between the top of the piston and cylinder head. It is an enclosed area in which the gasoline and air mixture is burned. The piston is a hollow metal tube with one end closed that moves up and down in the cylinder. This reciprocating motion is caused by the increase of pressure, due to combustion, in the cylinder.

The reciprocating motion must be converted to rotary motion before it can drive the wheels of a vehicle. This conversion is achieved by linking the piston to a crankshaft with a connecting rod (Figure 6-4). The upper end of the connecting rod moves with the piston as it moves up and down in the cylinder. The lower end of the connecting rod is attached to the crankshaft and moves in a circle. The end of the crankshaft is connected to the flywheel to continue the power flow through the drivetrain and to the wheels.

For the combustion action in the cylinder to take place completely and efficiently, precisely measured amounts of air and fuel must be combined in the right proportions. A fuel injection system, or in some cases a carburetor, makes sure that the engine gets exactly as much fuel and air as it needs for the many different conditions under which the vehicle must operate: starting, idling, accelerating, or cruising.

There are at least two valves at the top of each cylinder. The air/fuel mixture enters the combustion chamber through an intake valve and leaves (after having been burned) through an exhaust valve. The valves are accurately machined plugs that fit into machined openings. A valve is said to be seated or closed when it rests in its opening. When the valve is pushed off its seat, it opens.

A rotating camshaft, driven by the crankshaft, opens and closes the intake and exhaust valves. Cams are raised sections of the shaft with high spots called lobes. As the camshaft rotates, the lobes rotate and push the valve open by lifting it off its seat. Once the lobe on the cam rotates out of the way, the valve, forced by a spring, moves and reseats. The camshaft can be located either in the cylinder block or in the cylinder head.

In summary, the essentials for the complete combustion process include the following.

- Admit a proper mixture of air and fuel into the cylinder.
- Compress (squeeze) the mixture so it will burn better and deliver more power.
- Ignite and burn the mixture.
- Remove the burned gases from the cylinder so that the process can be completed and repeated.

With the action of the valves and spark plug properly timed to the movement of the piston, the combustion cycle takes place in four strokes of the piston: the intake stroke, the compression stroke, the power stroke, and the exhaust stroke. A stroke is the full travel of the piston either up or down in the cylinder bore.

The up-and-down movement of the piston on all four strokes is converted to rotary motion by the crankshaft. The four strokes of the combustion cycle result in two full revolutions of the crankshaft.

The piston is affected by combustion pressures during only about half a stroke or one-quarter of crankshaft revolution. This fact explains the need for the flywheel. For even though the engine has multiple cylinders, a certain amount of the power produced must be stored momentarily in the flywheel. This power is used to keep the piston in motion during about seven-eighths of the total four-stroke cycle, and to compress the fuel mixture just before combustion.

INTAKE STROKE The first stroke of the cycle is the intake stroke. As the piston moves away from top dead center (TDC), the intake valve opens (Figure 6-5A). The downward movement of the piston increases the volume of the cylinder above it. This reduces the pres-

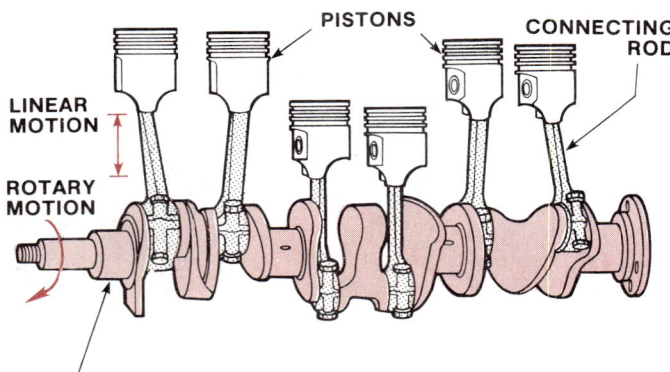

Figure 6-4 The reciprocating motion of the pistons is converted to rotary motion by the crankshaft.

Automotive Engines 107

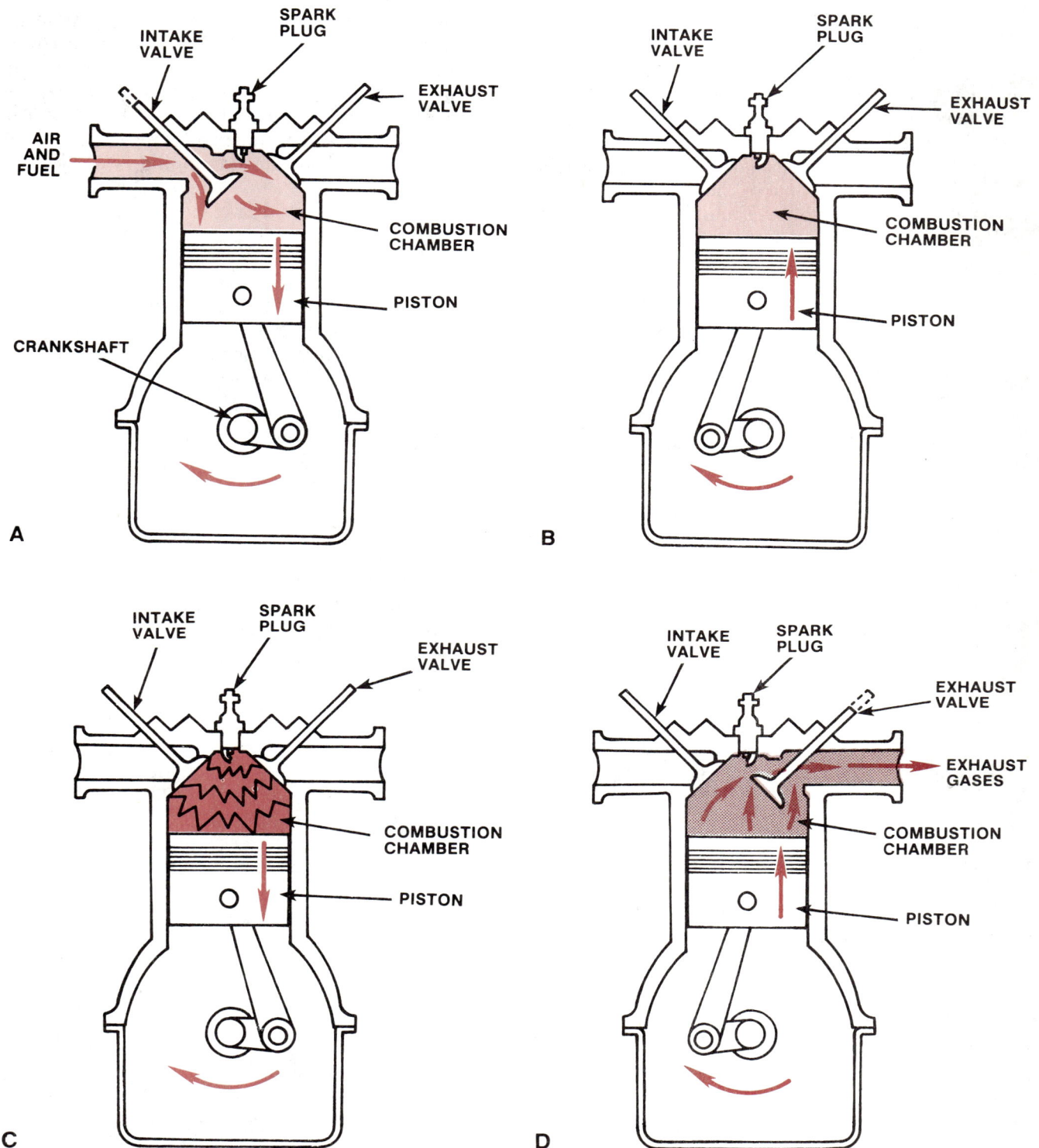

Figure 6–5 (A) Intake stroke, (B) compression stroke, (C) power stroke, and (D) exhaust stroke.

sure in the cylinder below atmospheric pressure. This reduced pressure, commonly referred to as engine vacuum, causes the atmospheric pressure to push a mixture of air and fuel through the open intake valve. (Some engines are equipped with a super- or turbocharger that pushes more air past the valve.) As the piston reaches the bottom of its stroke, the reduction in pressure stops and the intake of air/fuel mixture nearly ceases. But due to the weight and movement of the air/fuel mixture, it will continue to enter the cylinder until the intake valve closes. The delayed closing of the intake valve increases the volumetric efficiency of the cylinder by packing as much air and fuel into it as possible.

COMPRESSION STROKE The compression stroke begins as the piston starts to move from bottom dead center (BDC). The intake valve closes, trapping the air/fuel mixture in the cylinder (Figure 6-5B). Upward movement of the piston compresses the air/fuel mixture, thus heating it up. At TDC, the piston and cylinder walls form a combustion chamber in which the fuel will be burned. The volume of the cylinder with the piston at BDC compared to the volume of the cylinder with the piston at TDC determines the compression ratio of the engine.

POWER STROKE The power stroke begins as the compressed fuel mixture is ignited in the combustion chamber (Figure 6-5C). An electrical spark across the electrodes of a spark plug ignites the air/fuel mixture. The burning fuel rapidly expands, creating a very high pressure against the top of the piston. This drives the piston down toward BDC. The downward movement of the piston is transmitted through the connecting rod to the crankshaft.

EXHAUST STROKE The exhaust valve opens just before the piston reaches BDC on the power stroke (Figure 6-5D). Pressure within the cylinder causes the exhaust gas to rush past the open valve and into the exhaust system. Movement of the piston from BDC pushes most of the remaining exhaust gas from the cylinder. As the piston nears TDC, the exhaust valve begins to close as the intake valve starts to open. The exhaust stroke completes the four-stroke cycle. The opening of the intake valve begins the cycle again. This cycle occurs in each cylinder and is repeated over and over, as long as the engine is running.

☐ TWO-STROKE GASOLINE ENGINES

In the past, several imported vehicles have used two-stroke engines. As the name implies, this engine requires only two strokes of the piston to complete all four operations: intake, compression, power, and exhaust. As shown in Figure 6-6, this is accomplished as follows.

1. Movement of the piston from BDC to TDC completes both intake and compression (Figure 6-6A).
2. When the piston nears TDC, the compressed air/fuel mixture is ignited, causing expansion of the gases. Note that the reed valve is closed and the piston is blocking the intake port or fuel transfer passage (Figure 6-6B).
3. Expanding gases in the cylinder force the piston down, rotating the crankshaft. Downward move-

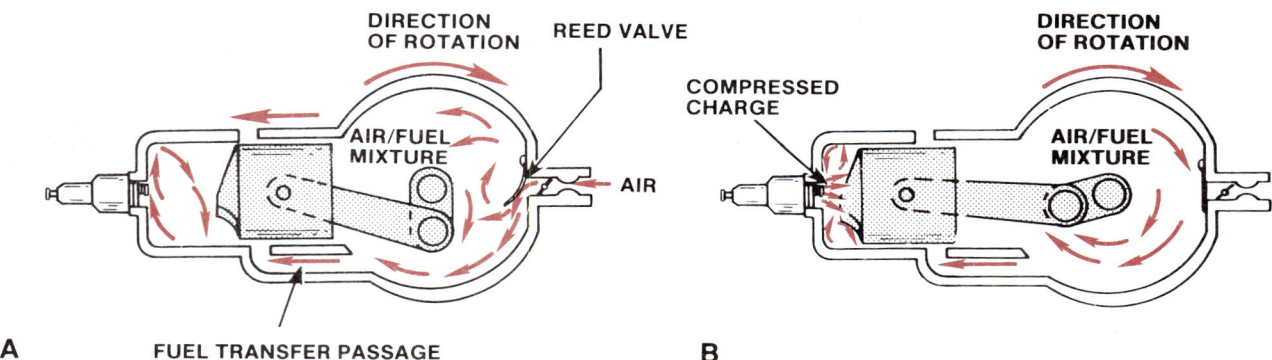

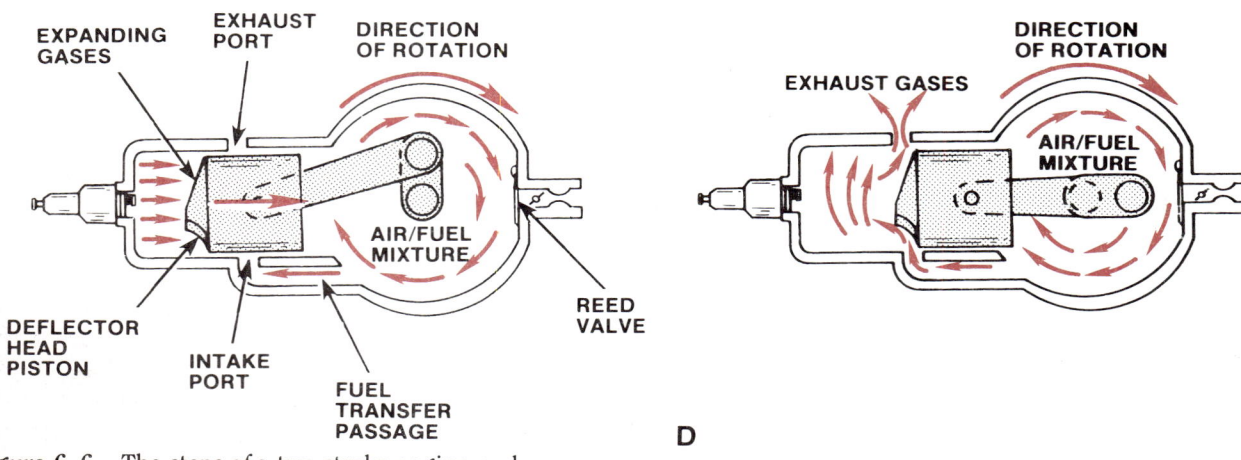

Figure 6-6 The steps of a two-stroke engine cycle.

ment of the piston compresses the air/fuel mixture in the crankcase (Figure 6-6C).
4. With the piston at BDC, the intake and exhaust ports are both open, allowing exhaust gases to leave the cylinder and air/fuel mixture to enter (Figure 6-6D).

Although the two-stroke-cycle engine is simple in design and lightweight because it lacks a valve train, it has never been seriously considered for automotive applications for several reasons. Poor cylinder scavenging and blowback prevent a two-stroke from breathing as efficiently as a four-stroke. Thus, fuel consumption is higher.

In recent years, however, thanks to a revolutionary pneumatic fuel injection system, there has been increased interest in the two-stroke engine. The injection system, which works something like a spray paint gun, uses compressed air to blow highly atomized fuel directly into the top of the combustion chamber. The system became the long sought-after answer to the fuel economy and emissions problems of the conventional two-stroke engine. Thus evolved the orbital two-stroke direct injection piston engine.

A small two-stroke can deliver as much horsepower as a larger displacement four-stroke engine because in a two-stroke combustion occurs every crankshaft revolution rather than every other revolution (Figure 6-7). That means a smaller displacement two-stroke engine can be used in the same vehicle application as a larger four-stroke engine. The improvement in fuel economy that the orbital engine has achieved is due in part to a number of mechanical design features in addition to its pneumatic direct injection fuel system.

One of these is the use of a three-cylinder engine block (Figure 6-8). Though the same direct injection technology can be used with a four-cylinder or a V-6, a three-cylinder block saves the weight, bulk, and manufacturing expense of an extra cylinder. The reduction in internal engine friction achieved by eliminating the fourth piston and the valve train is in itself worth a significant improvement in fuel economy.

Figure 6-8 A three-cylinder two-stroke orbital engine (left) puts out as much power as the much larger four-cylinder four-stroke.

Additional performance improvements are obtained in the orbital two-stroke design by using a high-turbulence combustion chamber that promotes rapid mixing at high and low loads. The engine also has an exhaust port scavenge flow control valve, which is controlled by the engine computer to increase low-speed torque and assist in emissions control. The valve can be partially closed to restrict the flow of exhaust out of the cylinder under certain operating conditions, creating an exhaust gas recirculation effect to reduce NO_x.

❏ CHARACTERISTICS OF FOUR-STROKE ENGINE DESIGN

Depending on the vehicle, either an in-line, V-type, slant, or opposed cylinder design can be used. The most popular designs are in-line and V-type engines.

IN-LINE ENGINES In the in-line engine design (Figure 6-9), the cylinders are all placed in a single row. There is one crankshaft and one cylinder head for all of the cylinders. The block is a single cast piece with all cylinders located in an upright position.

Figure 6-7 Cutaway of a two-stroke engine.

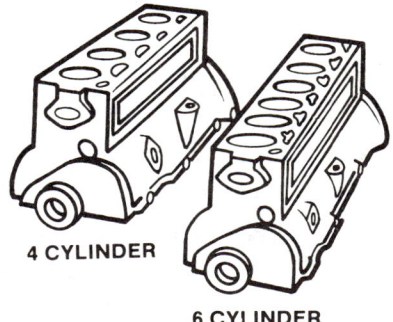

Figure 6-9 In-line engine designs.

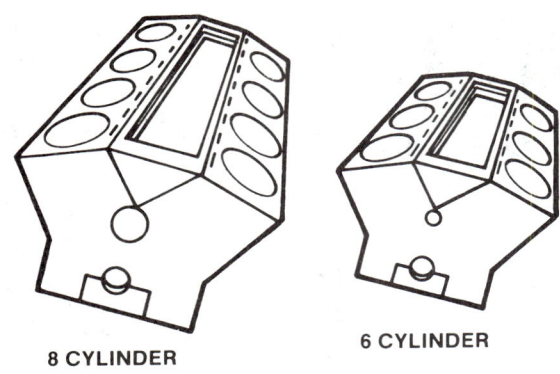

Figure 6-10   V-type engine designs.

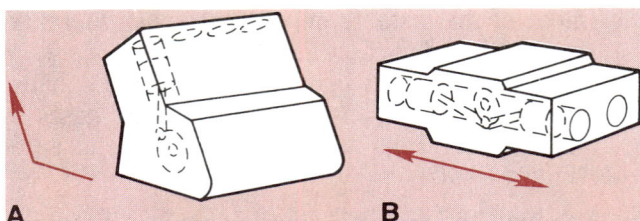

Figure 6-11   (A) Slant cylinder and (B) opposed cylinder engine designs.

In-line engine designs have certain advantages and disadvantages. They are easy to manufacture and to perform maintenance on. However, because the cylinders are positioned vertically, the front of the vehicle must be higher. This affects the aerodynamic design of the car. Aerodynamic design refers to the ease at which the car can move through the air. The front of the vehicle cannot be made lower as with other engines. This means that the aerodynamic design of the car cannot be improved easily.

V-TYPE ENGINES The V-type engine design has two rows of cylinders (Figure 6-10) approximately 90 degrees from each other. This is the angle in most V- or Y-configurations. However, other angles ranging from 60 to 90 degrees are used. This design utilizes one crankshaft that operates the cylinders on both sides of the vee. However, there are two cylinder heads on this type of engine.

One advantage of using a V-configuration is that the engine is not as vertically high as with the in-line configuration. The front of a vehicle can now be made lower. This design improves the outside aerodynamics of the vehicle. If eight cylinders are needed for power, a V-configuration makes the engine much shorter and more compact. Previously, some vehicles were equipped with an in-line eight-cylinder engine. The vehicle was hard to design around this long engine. The engine's long crankshaft also caused increased torsional vibrations in the engine.

SLANT CYLINDER ENGINES Another way of arranging the cylinders is in a slant configuration (Figure 6-11A). This is much like an in-line engine, except that the entire block has been placed at a slant. The slant engine was designed to reduce the distance from the top to the bottom of the engine. Vehicles using the slant engine can be designed more aerodynamically.

OPPOSED CYLINDER ENGINES In this design, two rows of cylinders are located opposite the crankshaft (Figure 6-11B). Opposed cylinder engines are used in applications where there is very little vertical room for the engine. For this reason, opposed cylinder designs are commonly used on vehicles that have the engine in

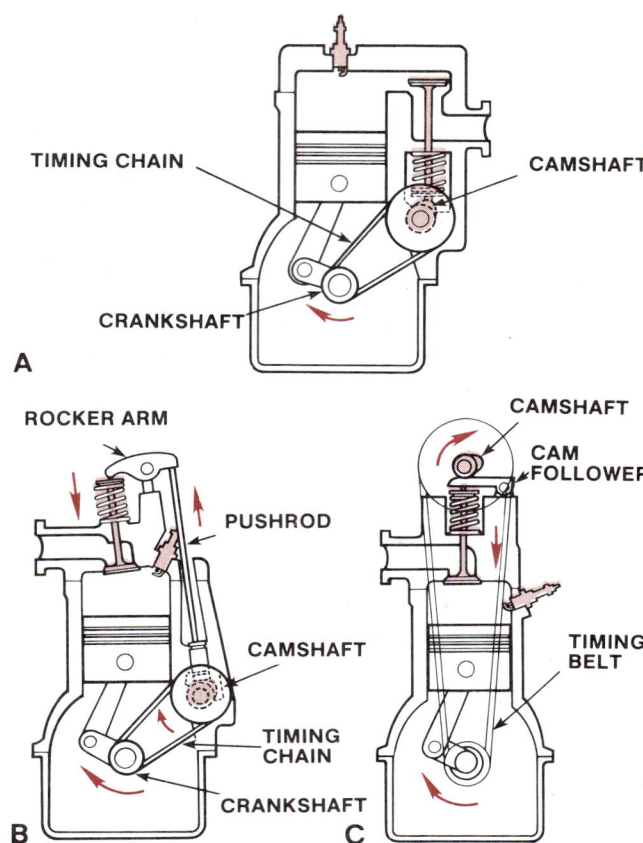

Figure 6-12   The three basic valve and camshaft placement configurations: (A) flathead or side valve, (B) overhead valve, and (C) overhead cam.

the rear. The angle between the two cylinders is typically 180 degrees. One crankshaft is used with two cylinder heads.

Valve and Camshaft Placement Configurations

Three basic valve and camshaft placement configurations of the four-stroke gasoline engines are used in automobiles (Figure 6-12).

FLATHEAD OR SIDE VALVE This was, at one time, a popular valve arrangement. It is not used today. A timing belt or chain, driven by the crankshaft, was used to rotate the camshaft. The valves were opened and closed directly by the camshaft.

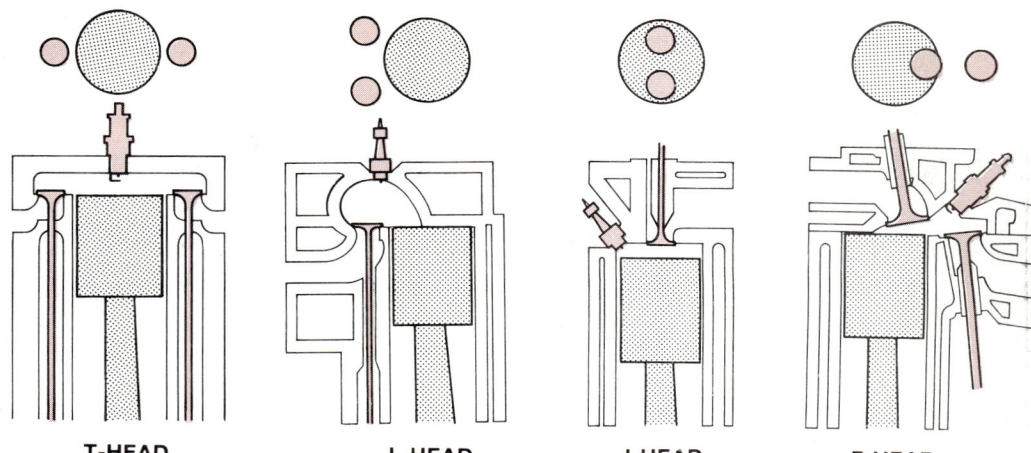

Figure 6-13 Other valve arrangements.

T-HEAD L-HEAD I-HEAD F-HEAD

OVERHEAD VALVE (OHV) As the name implies, the intake and exhaust valves on an overhead valve engine are mounted in the cylinder head and are operated by a camshaft located in the cylinder block. This arrangement requires the use of valve lifters, pushrods, and rocker arms to transfer camshaft rotation to valve movement. The intake and exhaust manifolds are attached to the cylinder head.

OVERHEAD CAM (OHC) An overhead cam engine also has the intake and exhaust valves located in the cylinder head. As the name implies, the cam is located in the cylinder head. In an overhead cam engine, the valves are operated directly by the camshaft through cam followers or tappets.

Valve Arrangement

As shown in Figure 6-13, there are several valve arrangements.

L-HEAD ENGINE DESIGN This engine type is characterized by having no moving parts contained in the cylinder head. The head serves only as the combustion chamber. The valves are located in the cylinder block beside each cylinder. The intake and exhaust manifolds mount to the cylinder block. This type of engine is not used in today's automobile.

I-HEAD ENGINE DESIGN I-head means the valves are directly above the piston (overhead valves). The valves are located in the cylinder head. The design allows air and fuel to move easily into and out of the cylinder with little restriction.

T-HEAD ENGINE DESIGN The T-head design has the valves located within the block. The difference between this design and the L-head design is that two camshafts are needed. Because of this extra expense, T-head designs have not been used in the automotive industry for many years.

F-HEAD ENGINE DESIGN This design is a combination of the I-head and the L-head designs. There are valves located in the head as well as in the block. It has some of the advantages of the L-head and I-head designs. However, the increased cost of parts is a disadvantage.

Valve and Camshaft Operation

In camshaft in-block overhead valve engines (Figure 6-14), the valves are operated by valve lifters and pushrods that are actuated by the camshaft. On overhead cam engines, the cam lobes operate the valves directly and there is no need for pushrods or lifters.

Cam lobes are oval shaped. The placement of the lobe on the shaft determines when the valve will open. Design of the lobe determines how far the valve will open and how long it will remain open in relation to piston movement.

The camshaft is driven by the crankshaft through gears, or sprockets, and a cogged belt, or timing chain. The camshaft turns at half the crankshaft speed and rotates one complete turn during each complete four-stroke cycle.

Engine Location

The engine is placed in one of two locations. In the vast majority of vehicles, it is located at the front of the vehicle, forward of the passenger compartment. Front-mounted engines can be positioned either longitudinally or transversely with respect to the vehicle.

The second engine location is a mid-mount position between the passenger compartment and rear suspension. Mid-mount engines are always transversely mounted. Each of these engine locations offers advantages and disadvantages. Typical engine locations and drivetrain configurations are illustrated in the color insert of the text.

FRONT ENGINE LONGITUDINAL In this type of vehicle, the engine, transmission, front suspension, and steering equipment are installed in the front body and the differential and rear suspension are installed in the rear body. Most front engine longitudinal vehicles are

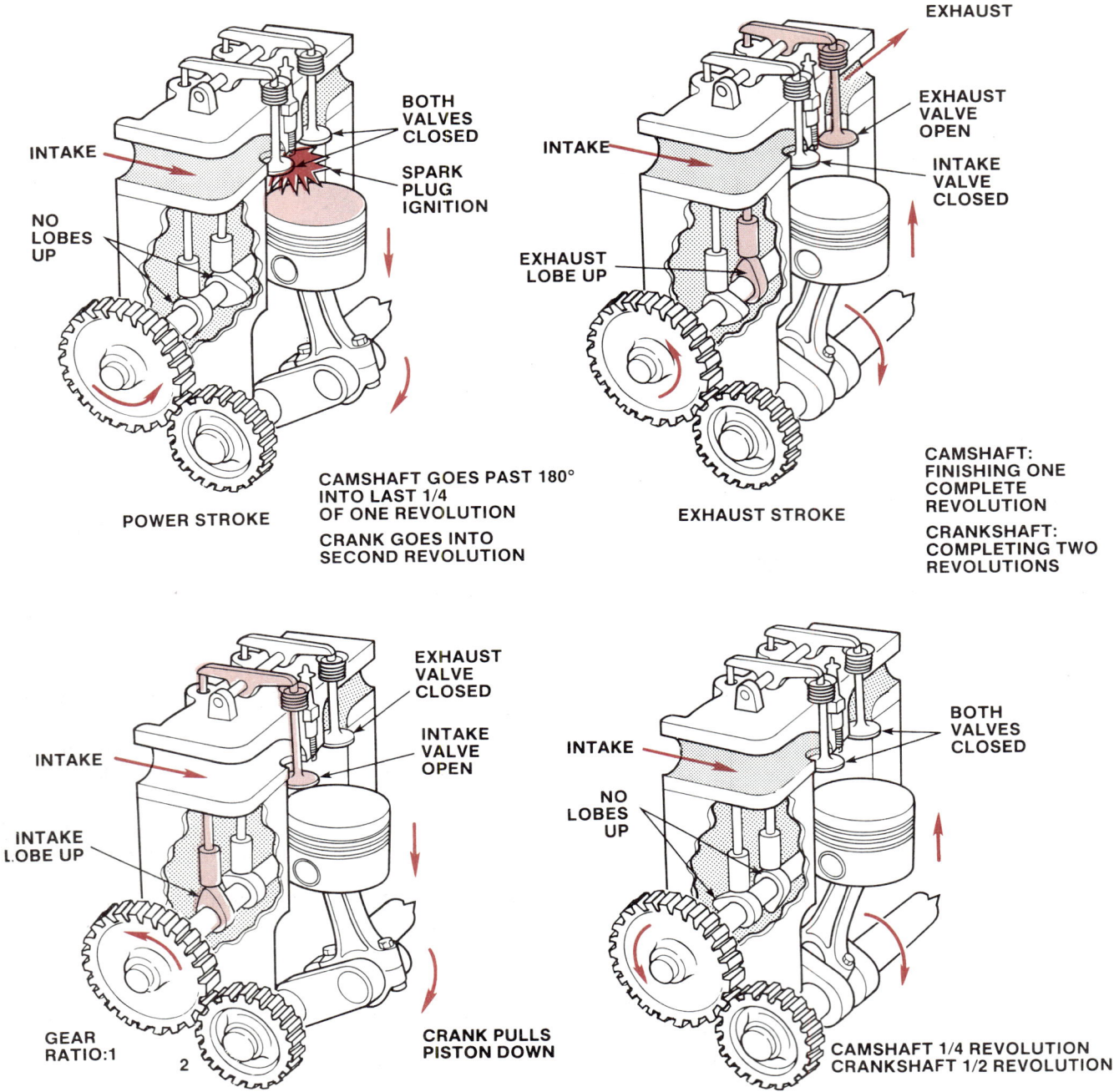

Figure 6-14 Valve operation in an overhead engine.

rear-wheel drive, but with the use of a transfer case four-wheel drive is also possible.

Vehicle weight is distributed more or less uniformly between the front and rear wheels, which lightens the steering force and equalizes the braking load. With this design, it is possible to independently remove and install the engine, propeller shaft, differential, and suspension. Longitudinally-mounted engines require large engine compartments. The need for a rear-drive propeller shaft and differential also cuts down passenger compartment space.

FRONT ENGINE TRANSVERSE Front engines that are mounted transversely sit sideways in the engine compartment. They are used with transaxles that combine transmission and differential gearing into a single compact housing fastened directly to the engine. Transversely-mounted engines/transaxles reduce the size of the engine compartment and overall vehicle weight. On front-wheel-drive vehicles, the need for a propeller shaft and rear differential is eliminated. On four-wheel-drive vehicles a propeller shaft and rear differential are needed.

Transversely-mounted front engines allow for downsized, lighter vehicles with increased interior space. However, most of the vehicle weight is toward the front of the vehicle. This places a greater load on front suspension and brakes.

MID-ENGINE TRANSVERSE In this design, the engine and drivetrain are positioned between the passenger compartment and rear axle. Mid-engine location is used in smaller, rear-wheel-drive, high-performance sports cars for several reasons. The central location of heavy components results in a center of gravity very near the center of the vehicle. This vastly improves steering and handling. Since the engine is not under the hood, the hood can be sloped downward, improving aerodynamics and increasing the driver's field of vision. However, engine access and cooling efficiency are reduced. A barrier is also needed to reduce the transfer of noise, heat, and vibration to the passenger compartment.

❏ GASOLINE ENGINE SYSTEMS

Besides the major power-generating system in the gasoline engine, there are, of course, several other systems essential to the engine operation.

AIR/FUEL SYSTEM This system ensures that the engine gets the right amount of both air and fuel needed for efficient operation. For many years air and fuel were mixed in a carburetor, which supplied the resulting mixture to the cylinder. Today, most late-model automobiles have a fuel injection system that replaces the carburetor but performs the same function.

IGNITION SYSTEM This system supplies a precisely timed spark to ignite the compressed air/fuel mixture in the cylinder at the end of the compression stroke. The firing order of the cylinders is determined by the engine manufacturer and can be found in the vehicle's service manual. Typical firing orders are illustrated in Figure 6-15.

LUBRICATION SYSTEM This system supplies oil to the various moving parts in the engine. The oil lubricates all parts that slide in or on other parts, such as the piston, bearings, crankshaft, and valve stems. The oil enables the parts to move easily so that little power is lost and wear is kept to a minimum. The lubrication system also helps transfer heat from one part to another for cooling.

COOLING SYSTEM This system is also extremely important. Coolant circulates in jackets around the cylinder and in the cylinder head. This removes part of the heat produced by the combustion of the air/fuel mixture and prevents the engine from being damaged by overheating.

① ② ③ ④ ⑤ ⑥
FIRING ORDER 1-5-3-6-2-4
6 CYLINDER

② ④ ⑥ ⑧ RIGHT BANK
① ③ ⑤ ⑦ LEFT BANK
FIRING ORDER 1-8-4-3-6-5-7-2
V-8

⑤ ③ ① RIGHT BANK
⑥ ④ ② LEFT BANK
FIRING ORDER 1-4-5-2-3-6
V-6

② ④ ⑥ ⑧ RIGHT BANK
① ③ ⑤ ⑦ LEFT BANK
FIRING ORDER 1-8-7-2-6-5-4-3
V-8

① ② ③ ④ RIGHT BANK
⑤ ⑥ ⑦ ⑧ LEFT BANK
FIRING ORDER 1-5-4-8-6-3-7-2
V-8

① ② ③ ④
FIRING ORDER 1-3-4-2
1-2-4-3
4 CYLINDER

② ④ ⑥ RIGHT BANK
① ③ ⑤ LEFT BANK
FIRING ORDER 1-6-5-4-3-2
V-6

① ② ③ ④ RIGHT BANK
⑤ ⑥ ⑦ ⑧ LEFT BANK
FIRING ORDER 1-5-4-2-6-3-7-8
V-8

Figure 6-15 Common cylinder firing orders.

EXHAUST SYSTEM This system efficiently removes the burned gases and limits the noise produced by the engine. An important part of the exhaust system on many new engines is a turbocharger.

EMISSION CONTROL SYSTEM Several control devices, which are designed to reduce emission levels of combusted fuel, have been added to the engine. Engine design changes, such as reshaped combustion chambers and altered tune-up specs, have also been implemented to help control the auto's smog-producing by-products. These devices and adjustments have reduced emissions considerably but have not changed automotive engine servicing and rebuilding to a great extent.

❏ ENGINE MEASUREMENT AND PERFORMANCE

Some engine measurements and performance characteristics that a technician should be aware of follow.

BORE AND STROKE The bore of a cylinder is simply its diameter measured in inches (in.) or millimeters (mm). The stroke is the length of the piston travel between TDC and BDC. Between them, bore and stroke determine the displacement of the cylinders (Figure 6-16). When the bore of the engine is larger than its stroke, it is said to be oversquare. When the stroke is larger than the bore, the engine is said to be undersquare.

Generally, an oversquare engine will deliver high rpm, such as for automobile use. An undersquare or long-stroke engine will deliver good low end torque, such as an engine for a truck or tractor. The crank throw is the distance from the crankshaft's main bear-

Section 2 Engines

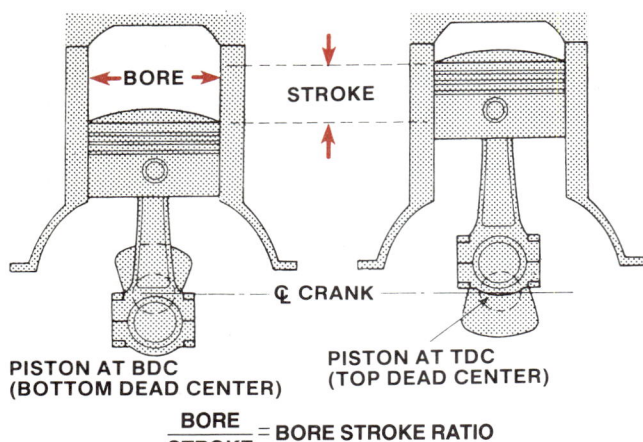

Figure 6-16 The bore and stroke of a cylinder.

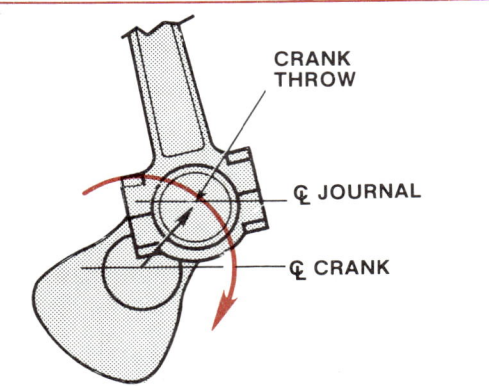

Figure 6-17 The stroke of an engine is equal to twice the crank throw.

ing centerline to the crankshaft throw centerline. The stroke of any engine is twice the crank throw (Figure 6-17).

DISPLACEMENT Displacement is the volume of the cylinder between the TDC and BDC positions of the piston. It is usually measured in cubic inches, cubic centimeters, or liters (Figure 6-18). The total displacement of an engine (including all cylinders) is a rough indicator of its power output. Displacement can be increased by opening the bore to a larger diameter or by increasing the length of the stroke. Total displacement is the sum of displacements for all cylinders in an engine. Cubic inch displacement (CID) may be calculated as follows.

$$CID = \pi \times R^2 \times L \times N$$

where π = 3.1416
R = bore radius or bore diameter/2
L = length of stroke
N = number of cylinders

Example: Calculate the cubic inch displacement (CID) of a six-cylinder engine with a 3.7-in. bore and 3.4-in. stroke.

$$CID = 3.1416 \times 1.85^2 \times 3.4 \times 6$$
$$CID = 219.66$$

Most of today's engines are described by their metric displacement. Cubic centimeters and liters are determined by using metric measurements in the displacement formula.

Example: Calculate the metric displacement of a four-cylinder engine with a 78.9-mm stroke and a 100-mm bore.

2479 cubic centimeters (cc) = 2.5 liters (L)

Larger, heavier vehicles are provided with large displacement engines. Large displacement engines produce more torque than smaller displacement engines. They also consume more fuel. Smaller, lighter vehicles can be adequately powered by lower displacement engines that use less fuel.

COMPRESSION RATIO The compression ratio is a measure of how much the air and fuel mixture will be compressed. The compression ratio is defined as the ratio of the volume in the cylinder above the piston when the piston is at BDC to the volume in the cylinder above the piston when the piston is at TDC. The compression ratio is shown in Figure 6-19. The formula for calculating the compression ratio is as follows.

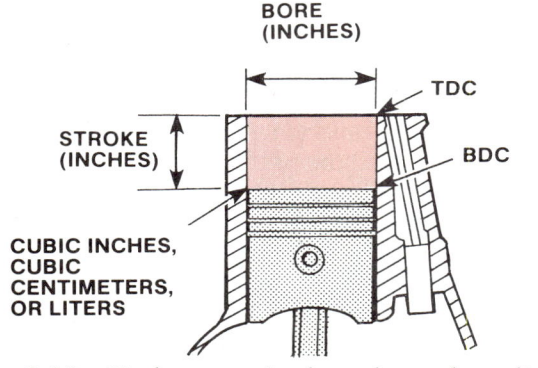

Figure 6-18 Displacement is the volume the cylinder holds between TDC and BDC.

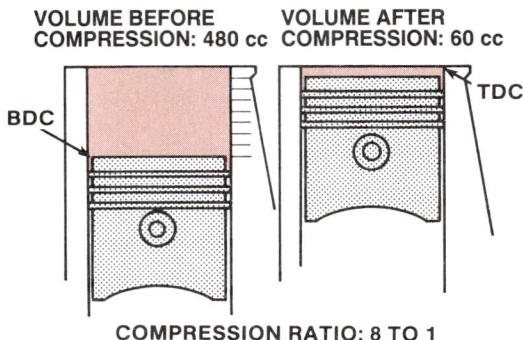

Figure 6-19 Compression ratio measures the amount the air and fuel have been compressed.

$$\frac{\text{volume above the piston at BDC}}{\text{volume above the piston at TDC}}$$

or

$$\frac{\text{total cylinder volume}}{\text{total combustion chamber volume}}$$

In many engines, the top of the piston is even or level with the top of the cylinder block at TDC. The combustion chamber volume is in the cavity in the cylinder head above the piston. This is modified slightly by the shape of the top of the piston. The combustion chamber volume must be added to each volume stated in the formula to give accurate results.

Example: Calculate the compression ratio if the total piston displacement is 45 cubic inches and the combustion chamber volume is 5.5 cubic inches.

$$\frac{45 + 5.5}{5.5} = \text{compression ratio}$$

$$9.1 \text{ to } 1 = \text{compression ratio}$$

(Be sure to add the combustion chamber volume to the piston displacement to get the total cylinder volume.)

The higher the compression ratio, the more power an engine theoretically can produce. Also, as the compression ratio increases, the heat produced as the piston rises on its compression stroke also increases. Gasoline with a low octane rating may explode rather than burn. This can lead to preignition. The higher a gasoline's octane rating, the less likely it is to explode.

Ideally, ignition should occur so that maximum pressure is produced slightly after the piston reaches TDC on the power stroke. The compression ratio of an engine must be suited to the type of fuels available. In other words, as compression ratio increases, the octane rating of the gasoline also should be increased to prevent abnormal combustion.

ENGINE EFFICIENCY Engine efficiency is a measure of the relationship between the amount of energy put into the engine and the amount of available energy from the engine. For understanding basic engine principles, efficiency is defined as follows.

$$\text{efficiency} = \frac{\text{output energy}}{\text{input energy}} \times 100$$

Other types of engine efficiencies of interest to the automotive engine technician include mechanical efficiency, volumetric efficiency, and thermal efficiency. They are expressed as a ratio of input (actual) to output (maximum or theoretical). Efficiencies are expressed as percentages. They are always less than 100%. The difference between the efficiency and 100% is the percentage lost during the process. For example, if there were 100 units of energy put into the engine and 28 units came back, the efficiency would be equal to 28%. This would mean that 72% of the energy received was wasted or lost.

TORQUE AND HORSEPOWER Torque is a turning or twisting force. The engine crankshaft applies torque that is transmitted through the drivetrain to turn the driving wheels of the vehicle. Horsepower is the rate at which torque is produced.

Engines produce power by turning a crankshaft in a circular motion. To convert terms of force applied in a straight line to force applied in a circular motion, the formula is torque = force × radius.

Example: A 10-pound force applied to a wrench 1 foot long will produce 10 pound-feet (lb-ft) of torque. Imagine that the 1-foot-long wrench is connected to a shaft. If 1 pound of force is applied to the end of the wrench, 1 pound-foot of torque is produced. Ten pounds of force applied to a wrench 2 feet long will produce 20 pound-feet of torque (Figure 6–20).

The technically correct torque measurement is stated in pound-feet (lb-ft). However, it is rather common to state torque in terms of foot-pounds (ft-lb). In the metric or SI system, torque is stated in Newton-meters (N·m) or kilogram-meters (kg-m).

If the torque output of an engine at a given speed (rpm) is known, horsepower can be determined by the following formula.

$$HP = (\text{torque} \times \text{rpm}) \div 5{,}252$$

where HP = horsepower
rpm = revolutions per minute

An engine produces different amounts of torque based on the rotational speed of the crankshaft and other

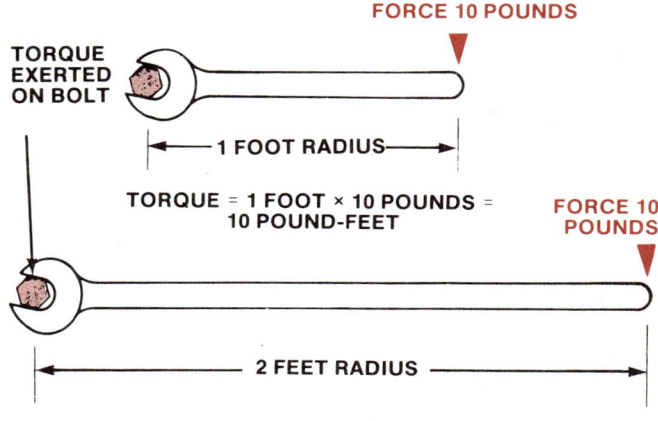

Figure 6–20 Force applied to a wrench produces torque.

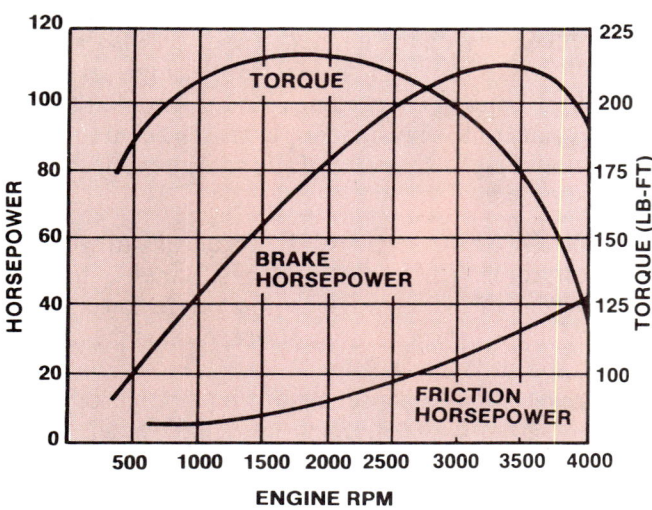

Figure 6–21 The relationship between horsepower and torque.

factors. A mathematical representation, or graph, of the relationship between horsepower and torque in one engine is shown in Figure 6-21.

This graph shows that torque drops off above about 1,700 rpm. Brake horsepower increases steadily until about 3,500 rpm. Then it drops. The third line on the graph indicates horsepower needed to overcome the resistance to movement of engine internal parts against each other. This resistance is known as friction.

Complete engine specifications can usually be found in service manuals as shown in Figure 6-22.

GENERAL SPECIFICATIONS	
DISPLACEMENT	1.9L
NUMBER OF CYLINDERS	1-4
BORE AND STROKE	
1.9L	82 x 88 (3.23 x 3.46)
FIRING ORDER	1-3-4-2
OIL PRESSURE (HOT 2000 RPM)	240-450 kPa (35-65 PSI)
DRIVE BELT TENSION	178-311 (40-70 Lb-Ft)
CYLINDER HEAD AND VALVE TRAIN ① ②	
COMBUSTION CHAMBER VOLUME (cc)	EFI-HO 55 ± 1.6
VALVE GUIDE BORE DIAMETER	EFI 39.9 ± 0.8
Intake	13.481-13.519mm (0.531-0.5324 in.)
Exhaust	13.481-13.519mm (0.531-0.532 in.)
VALVE GUIDE I.D.	
Intake and Exhaust	8.063-8.094 N•m (.3174-.3187 in.)
VALVE SEATS	
Width — Intake & Exhaust	1.75-2.32mm (0.069-0.091 in.)
Angle	45°
Runout (T.I.R.)	0.076mm (0.003 in.) MAX.
Bore Diameter (Insert Counterbore Diameter)	
Intake	(EFI-HO) 43.763mm (1.723 in.) MIN.
	43.788mm (1.724 in.) MAX.
	(EFI) 39.940 mm (1.572 in.) MIN
	39.965 mm (1.573 in.) MAX.
Exhaust	(EFI-HO) 38.263mm (1.506 in.) MIN.
	38.288mm (1.507 in.) MAX.
	(EFI) 34.940 mm (1.375 in.) MIN.
	39.965 mm (1.573 in.) MAX.
GASKETS SURFACE FLATNESS	0.04mm (0.0016 in.)/26mm (1 in.)
	0.08mm (0.003 in.)/156mm (6 in.)
	0.15mm (0.006 in.) Total
HEAD FACE SURFACE FINISH	0.7/2.5 0.8 (28/100 .030)
VALVE STEM TO GUIDE CLEARANCE	
Intake	0.020-0.069mm (0.0008-0.0027 in.)
Exhaust	0.046-0.095mm (0.0018-0.0037 in.)
VALVE HEAD DIAMETER	
Intake	42.1-41.9mm (1.66-1.65 in.)
Exhaust	37.1-36.9mm (1.50-1.42 in.)
VALVE FACE RUNOUT	
LIMIT	Intake & Exhaust .05mm (0.002 in.)
VALVE FACE ANGLE	45.6°
VALVE STEM DIAMETER (Std.)	
Intake	8.043-8.025mm (0.3167-0.3159 in.)

Figure 6–22 Service manuals contain engine specifications. *Courtesy of Ford Motor Co.*

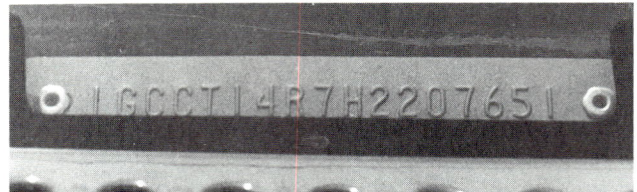

Figure 6–23 The VIN is visible through the driver's side of the windshield.

❑ ENGINE IDENTIFICATION

To determine the correct specifications of an engine, the automotive technician must know the vehicle identification number (VIN). The VIN is a code of seventeen numbers and letters stamped on a metal tab that is riveted to the instrument panel close to the windshield (Figure 6-23).

> **USING SERVICE MANUALS**
>
> Normally, information used to identify the size of an engine is given at the beginning of the section covering that particular manufacturer.

The adoption of the seventeen number and letter code became mandatory beginning with 1981 vehicles. The standard VIN of the United States National Highway Transportation and Safety Administration Department of Transportation is being used by all manufacturers of vehicles both domestic and foreign.

By referring to the VIN, much information about the vehicle can be determined (Figure 6-24). An engine serial number is also stamped on many blocks (Figure 6-25). Its location varies among different makes. The manufacturer's manual will tell you where to look for it. The engine code generally is found beside the serial number. A typical engine code might be DZ or MO. These letters indicate the horsepower rating of the engine, whether it was built for an automatic or manual transmission, and other important details. The engine code will help you determine the correct tune-up specifications for a particular engine.

Casting numbers are often mistaken for serial numbers and engine codes. Manufacturers use a casting number to identify major engine parts on the assembly line.

❑ ENGINE DIAGNOSTICS

In the previous chapter, different types of test equipment were discussed. Many of these tested the mechanical condition of an engine, such as the wet and dry compression, cylinder leakage, and engine vacuum. In addition to these, two other common tests can be performed to evaluate the condition of an engine and to identify any problem areas. The cylinder

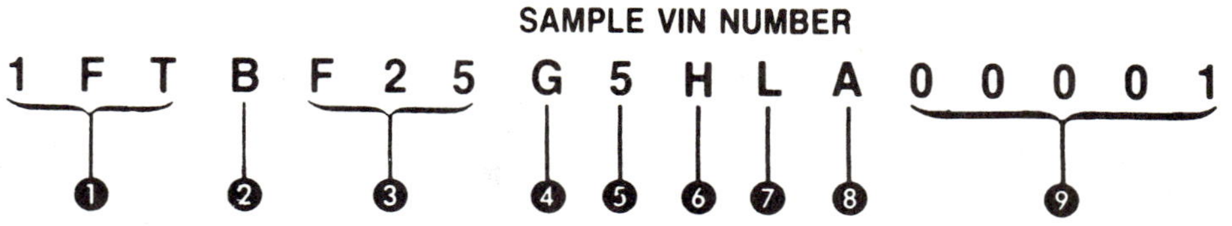

Automotive Engines   117

SAMPLE VIN NUMBER

1 F T B F 2 5 G 5 H L A 0 0 0 0 1

1. POSITION 1, 2, AND 3—MANUFACTURER, MAKE, AND TYPE (WORLD MANUFACTURER IDENTIFIER)
2. POSITION 4—BRAKE SYSTEM
3. POSITION 5, 6, AND 7—MODEL OR LINE, SERIES, CHASSIS, CAB OR BODY TYPE
4. POSITION 8—ENGINE TYPE
5. POSITION 9—CHECK DIGIT
6. POSITION 10—MODEL YEAR
7. POSITION 11—ASSEMBLY PLANT
8. POSITION 12—CONSTANT A UNTIL SEQUENCE NUMBER 99,999 IS REACHED, THEN CHANGES TO A CONSTANT B AND SO ON.
9. POSITION 13 THROUGH 17—SEQUENCE NUMBER—BEGINS AT 00001

Figure 6-24   The VIN provides a great deal of information.

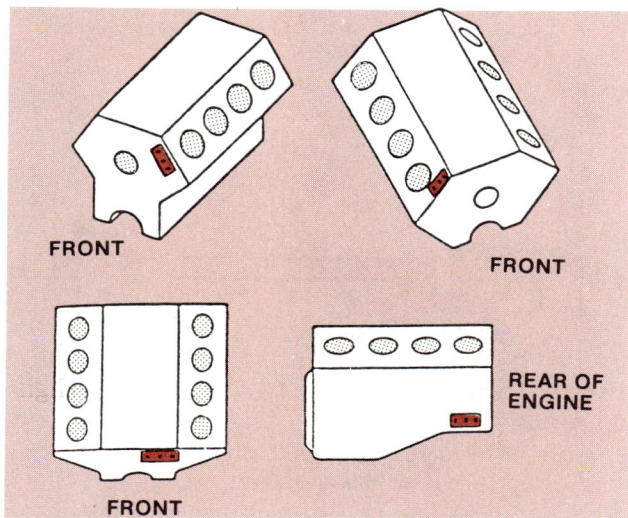

Figure 6-25   Common engine serial number locations.

power balance test checks the efficiency of individual cylinders. The results of this test are often used in conjunction with the results of compression and cylinder leakage tests.

Unlike other engine tests, an oil pressure test does not test a cylinder's ability to seal. It is used to determine wear on the engine's parts. Excessive clearances, often the result of wear, between a shaft and its bearings will have an affect on oil pressure. The oil pressure test is performed with an oil pressure gauge and measures the pressure of the oil while it is circulating through the engine. The pressure of the oil depends upon the efficiency of the oil pump and the clearances it travels through.

USING SERVICE MANUALS

Whenever you test oil pressure, be sure to refer to the service manual to find out the required conditions for the test and the desired pressure readings.

❑ OIL PRESSURE TESTING

Loss of performance, excessive engine noise, and poor starting can all result from abnormal oil pressures. An insufficient amount of pressure may also cause premature wear on rotating parts. An oil pressure tester is a gauge with a high-pressure hose attached to it. The scale of the gauge typically reads from 0 to 100 psi. The hose is connected to the engine block in a place where oil pressure can be measured (usually where the oil pressure indicator light sensor is screwed into the block).

To conduct the test, simply follow the guidelines given in the service manual and observe the gauge. The pressure is read when the engine is at normal operating temperatures and at a fast idle speed. Low oil pressures can be caused by a worn oil pump, excessive wear on the crankshaft or camshaft and their bearings, a plugged oil pick-up screen, or a weak or broken oil pressure relief valve. High oil pressure is normally caused by restrictions in the oil passages.

❑ CYLINDER POWER BALANCE TESTING

The cylinder power balance test is useful in determining if a cylinder or bank of cylinders is producing its share of engine power. Ideally, all the cylinders should be doing the same amount of work, and changes in engine rpm should be about equal as each cylinder is shorted out. Unequal cylinder power can mean a problem in the cylinders themselves, as well as the rings, valves, intake manifold, head gasket, fuel system, or ignition system.

The power balance test is performed quickest and easiest using an engine analyzer, because the spark plugs can be controlled with push buttons. Changes are measured in rpm drop. Keep in mind that the push-button numbers refer to the cylinder firing order, not the cylinder number designation. For example, when testing an engine with a firing order of 1-3-4-2, pushing the first button shorts out the number 1 cylinder, pushing the second button shorts out the number 3 cylinder, and so on.

Test Precautions

On some computer-controlled or fuel-injected engines, certain components must be disconnected before attempting the power balance test. Because of the wide variations from manufacturer to manufacturer, consult the vehicle's service manual for specific instructions.

If the engine being tested has an exhaust gas recirculation (EGR) system, added precautions must be taken. If the system is valve controlled, disconnect the vacuum or electrical connection to the EGR valve. This will prevent the valve from cycling due to vacuum changes when the cylinders are shorted out. For engines with a floor jet EGR system, the power balance test cannot be performed accurately because of the possibility of the unburned fuel mixture being sent back into the cylinders. The compression test is the recommended alternative in such cases.

Care must be taken when performing the power balance test on vehicles with catalytic converters. To prevent unburned fuel from building up in the converter, short each spark plug for less than 15 seconds, then allow the engine to run for another 30 seconds before shorting another one.

Performing the Test

The standard power balance test is fairly simple. If the engine has an air/fuel mixture feedback control or O_2 sensor (Figure 6-26A), disconnect and plug either the air pump hose going to the catalytic converter or the downstream hose between the air switching valve and the check valve. On some Ford models, the air switching valve can routinely have up to 10% leakage, in which case both hoses must be disconnected and plugged. If the engine does not have an air/fuel mixture feedback control or O_2 sensor (Figure 6-26B), disconnect and block the air pump on the valve side.

Override the controls of the electric cooling fan by jumper wiring the controls so that the fan runs constantly. If the fan cannot be bypassed, disconnect it. Be careful that the engine does not overheat during the test.

Connect the engine analyzer's leads, referring to the equipment's instruction manual for specific instructions.

Turn on the engine and let it reach its normal operating temperature before beginning the test. Engine speed should be stabilized at approximately 1,000 rpm. When a cylinder is shorted, note any drop in rpm or manifold vacuum.

As each cylinder is shorted out, a noticeable drop in engine speed should occur. Little or no decrease in rpm indicates a weak cylinder. If all the readings are fairly

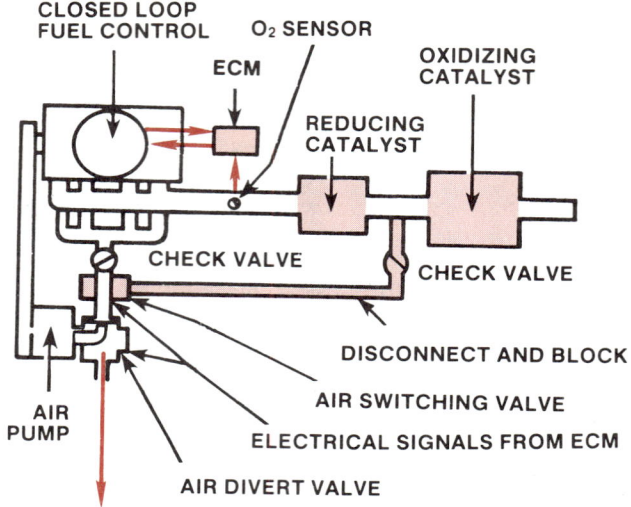

A

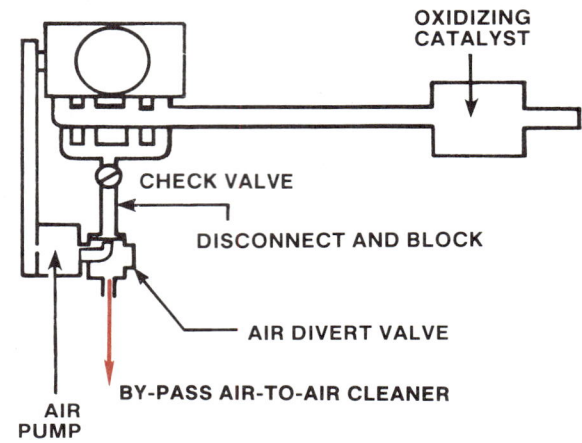

B

Figure 6-26 The procedure for conducting a cylinder power balance test differs, depending on whether the engine (A) has an air/fuel mixture feedback control or (B) does not have an air/fuel mixture feedback control.

close to each other, the engine is in sound mechanical condition. If a reading in one or more cylinders differs greatly from the rest, there is a problem. Further testing should be done to determine if the problem is purely mechanical, or if it is in the ignition or fuel system.

☐ EVALUATING THE ENGINE'S CONDITION

Once the compression tests (including the leakage test), vacuum tests, and power balance tests are performed, the technician should be ready to start evaluating the engine's condition. For example, an engine with good relative compression but high cylinder leakage past the rings is typical of a high-mileage engine that is worn out. Other symptoms include excessive blowby, lack of power, poor performance, and reduced fuel economy.

If these same compression and leakage conditions are noted on an engine with comparatively low mileage, the problem is most likely that the piston rings are stuck and not expanding properly. If such is the case, try treating the engine with a combustion chamber cleaner, oil treatment, or engine flush. If this effort proves futile, the only other remedy requires a complete engine disassembly.

A cylinder that has poor compression but minimal leakage indicates a valve train problem. Under these circumstances, a valve might not be opening at the right time, might not be opening enough, or might not be opening at all. This condition can be confirmed on engines with a pushrod-type valve train by pulling the rocker covers and watching the valves operate while the engine is cycled. If one or more valves fail to move, either the lifters are collapsed or the cam lobes are worn. If all of the cylinders have low compression with minimal leakage, the most likely cause is incorrect valve timing.

If compression and leakage are both good, but the power balance test revealed weak cylinders, the cause of the problem is outside the combustion chamber. Assuming there are no ignition or fuel problems, check for broken, bent, or worn valve train components, collapsed lifters, leaking intake manifold, or excessively leaking valve guides. If the latter is suspected, squirt some oil on the guides. If they are leaking, blue smoke will be seen in the exhaust.

❏ NOISE DIAGNOSIS

More often than not, a malfunction in the engine will reveal itself first as an unusual noise. This can happen before the problem affects the driveability of the vehicle. Problems such as loose pistons, badly worn rings or ring lands, loose piston pins, worn main bearings and connecting rod bearings, loose vibration damper or flywheel, and worn or loose valve train components all produce telltale sounds. Of course, unless the technician has experience in listening to and interpreting engine noises, it can be very hard to distinguish one from the other.

> **CUSTOMER CARE**
>
> When attempting to diagnose the cause of abnormal engine noise, it may be necessary to temper the enthusiasm of a customer who thinks they have pinpointed the exact cause of the noise using nothing more than their own two ears. While the owner's description may be helpful (and should always be asked for), it must be stressed that one person's "rattle" can be another person's "thump." You are the professional. The final diagnosis is up to you. If the customer has been proven correct in their diagnosis, make it a point to tell them so. Everyone feels better about dealing with an automotive technician who listens to them.

When correctly interpreted, engine noise can be a very valuable diagnostic aid. For one thing, a costly and time-consuming engine teardown might be avoided. Always make a noise analysis before doing any repair work. This way, there is a much greater likelihood that only the necessary repair procedures will be done. Careful noise diagnosis also reduces the chances of ruining the engine by continuing to use the vehicle despite the problem.

WARNING: Be very careful when listening for noises around moving belts and pulleys at the front of the engine. Keep the end of the hose or stethoscope probe away from moving parts. Physical injury can result if the hose or stethoscope is pulled inward or flung outward by moving parts.

Using a Stethoscope

Some engine sounds can be easily heard without using a listening device, but others are impossible to hear unless amplified. A stethoscope or rubber hose (as mentioned earlier) is very helpful in locating engine noise by amplifying the sound waves. It can also distinguish between normal and abnormal noise. The procedure for using a stethoscope is simple. Use the metal prod to trace the sound until it reaches its maximum intensity. Once the precise location has been discovered, the sound can be better evaluated. A sounding stick, which is nothing more than a long, hollow tube, works on the same principle, though a stethoscope gives much clearer results.

Common Noises

Following are examples of abnormal engine noises, including a description of the sound, its likely cause, and ways of eliminating it. An important point to keep in mind is that insufficient lubrication is the most common cause of engine noise. For this reason, always check the oil level first before moving on to other areas of the vehicle. Some noises are more pronounced on a cold engine because clearances are greater when parts are not expanded by heat. Remember that aluminum and iron expand at different rates as temperatures rise. For example, a knock that disappears as the engine warms up probably is piston slap or knock. An aluminum piston expands more than the iron block, allowing the piston to fit more closely as engine temperature rises.

RING NOISE This sound can be heard during acceleration as a high-pitched rattling or clicking in the upper part of a cylinder. It can be caused by worn rings or cylinders, broken piston ring lands, or insufficient ring tension against the cylinder walls. Ring noise is corrected by replacing the rings, pistons, or sleeves or reboring the cylinders.

PISTON SLAP This is a common sound when the engine is cold. It often intensifies when the vehicle accelerates. When a piston slaps against the cylinder wall, the result is a hollow, bell-like sound. Piston slap is caused by worn pistons or cylinders, collapsed piston skirts, misaligned connecting rods, excessive piston-to-cylinder wall clearance, or lack of lubrication, resulting in worn bearings. Correction requires either replacing the pistons, reboring the cylinder, replacing or realigning the rods, or replacing the bearings. Shorting out the spark plug of the affected cylinder might quiet the noise.

PISTON PIN KNOCK Piston pin knock is a sharp, metallic rap that can sound more like a rattle if all the pins are loose. It originates in the upper portion of the engine and is most noticeable when the engine is hot and at idle. Piston pin knock is caused by a worn piston pin, piston pin boss, or piston pin bushing or lack of lubrication, resulting in worn bearings. To correct it, either install oversized pins, replace the boss or bushings, or replace the piston.

RIDGE NOISE This noise is less common but very distinct. As a piston ring strikes the ridge at the top of the cylinder, the result is a high-pitched rapping or clicking noise that becomes louder during deceleration (Figure 6-27).

There can be more than one reason for the ridge interfering with the ring's travel. For one thing, if new rings are installed without removing the old ridge, the new rings will contact the ridge and make a noise. Also, if the piston pin is very loose or the connecting rod has a loose or burned-out bearing, the piston will go high enough in the cylinder for the top ring to contact the ridge. Thus, in order to eliminate ridge noise, remove the old ring ridge and replace the piston pin or piston.

ROD-BEARING NOISE The result of worn or loose connecting rod bearings, this noise is heard at idle as well as at speeds over 35 mph. Depending on how badly the bearings are worn, the noise can range from a light tap to a heavy knock or pound. Shorting out the spark plug of the affected cylinder can lessen the noise, unless the bearing is extremely worn. In this case, shorting out the plug will have no effect. Rod-bearing noise is caused by a worn bearing or crankpin, a misaligned rod, or lack of lubrication, resulting in worn bearings. To correct it, service or replace the crankshaft, realign or replace the connecting rods, and replace the bearings.

MAIN OR THRUST BEARING NOISE A loose crankshaft main bearing produces a dull, steady knock, while a loose crankshaft thrust bearing produces a heavy thump at irregular intervals. The thrust bearing noise might only be audible on very hard acceleration. Both of these bearing noises are usually caused by worn bearings or crankshaft journals. To correct the problem, replace the bearings or crankshaft.

TAPPET NOISE Tappet noise is characterized by a light, regular clicking sound that is more noticeable when the engine is idling. It is the result of excessive clearance in the valve train. The clearance problem area is located by inserting a feeler gauge between each lifter and valve, or between each rocker arm and valve tip, until the noise subsides. Tappet noise can be caused by improper valve adjustment, worn or damaged parts, dirty hydraulic lifters, or lack of lubrication. To correct the noise, adjust the valves, replace any worn or damaged parts, or clean or replace the lifters.

ABNORMAL COMBUSTION NOISES Preignition and detonation noises are caused by abnormal engine combustion. For instance, detonation knock or ping is a noise most noticeable during acceleration with the engine under load and running at normal temperature. Excessive detonation can be very harmful to the engine. It is often caused by advanced ignition timing or substantial carbon buildup in the combustion chambers that increases combustion pressure. Carbon deposits that get so hot they glow will also preignite the air/fuel mixture, causing detonation. Another possible cause is fuel whose octane is too low. Detonation knock can usually be cured by removing carbon deposits from the combustion chambers with a rotary wire brush as well as recommending the use of a higher octane gasoline. A malfunctioning EGR valve can also cause detonation and even rod knock.

Sometimes abnormal combustion combines with other engine parts to cause noise. For example, rumble is a term that is used to describe the knock or noise

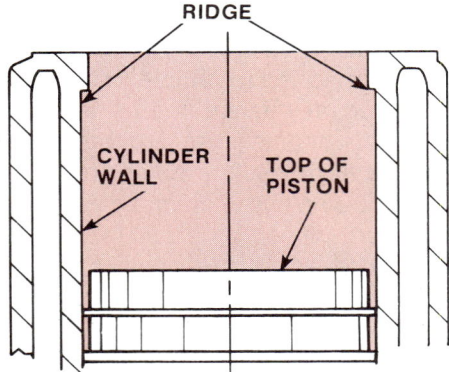

Figure 6-27 When the piston strikes the ridge at the top of the cylinder, a high-pitched rapping or clicking sound is made.

resulting from another form of abnormal ignition. Rumble is a bending vibration of the crankshaft and connecting rods that is caused by multi-surface ignition. Rumble is a form of preignition in which several flame fronts occur simultaneously from overheated deposit particles. Multi-surface ignition causes a tremendous sudden pressure rise near top dead center. It has been reported that the rate of pressure rise during rumble is five times the rate of normal combustion.

A loose vibration damper causes a heavy rumble or thump in the front of the engine that is more apparent when the vehicle is accelerating from idle under load or is idling unevenly. A loose flywheel causes a heavy thump or light knock at the back of the engine, depending on the amount of play and the type of engine. Both of these problems are corrected either by tightening or replacing the damper or flywheel.

❑ OTHER ENGINE DESIGNS

The gasoline-powered, internal combustion piston engine has been the primary automotive power plant for many years and probably will remain so for years to come. Present-day social requirements and new technological developments, however, have necessitated searches for ways to modify or replace this time-proven workhorse. This portion of the chapter takes a brief look at seven most likely contenders, and how they work. These seven engines are diesel, rotary (Wankel), stratified charge, and electric.

Diesel Engines

Diesel engines represent tested, proven technology with a long history of success. Invented by Dr. Rudolph Diesel, a German engineer, and first marketed in 1897, the diesel engine is now the dominate power plant in heavy-duty trucks, construction equipment, farm equipment, buses, and marine applications.

During the late 1970s and early 1980s, many predicted small diesel engines would replace gasoline engines in many passenger vehicles. However, stabilized gas prices and other factors dampened the enthusiasm for diesels in these markets. The use of diesel power plants in passenger cars and light trucks is now limited to several manufacturers.

Diesel engines (Figure 6-28) and gasoline-powered engines share several similarities. They have a number of components in common, such as the crankshaft, pistons, valves, camshaft, and water and oil pumps. They both are available in four-stroke combustion cycle models. However, the diesel engine and four-stroke compression-ignition engine are easily recognized by the absence of the conventional ignition components found on gasoline engines. Instead of relying on a spark for ignition, a diesel engine uses the heat produced by compressing air in the combustion chamber to ignite the fuel. The engine systems used in diesel-driven vehicles are essentially the same as those used in gasoline types.

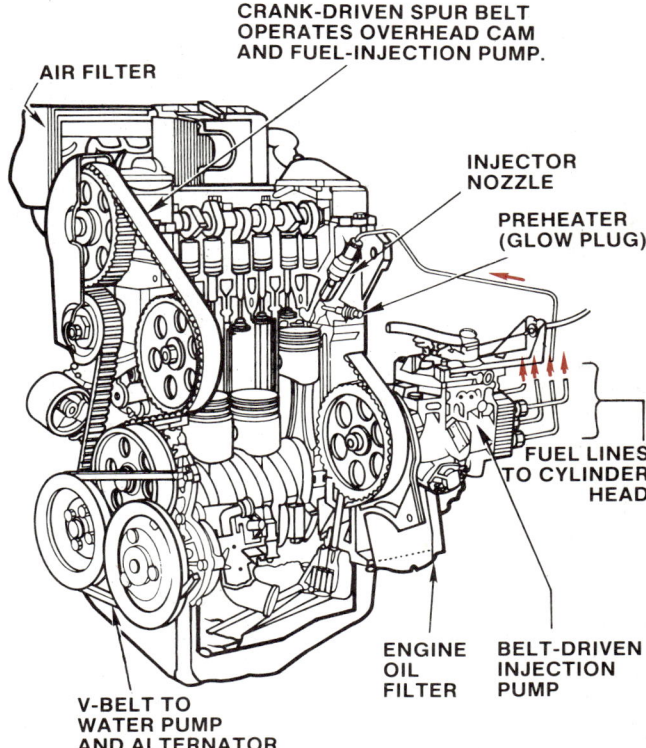

Figure 6-28 Typical four-stroke diesel engine.

Figure 6-29 shows one cycle of a four-stroke diesel engine operation. Fuel injection is used with all diesel engines. Injectors spray pressurized fuel into the cylinders as the piston is completing its compression stroke. The heat of the compressed air ignites the fuel and begins the power stroke.

Glow plugs are used only to warm the combustion chamber when the engine is cold. Cold starting is impossible without these plugs because even the high-compression ratios cannot heat cold air sufficiently for combustion.

Diesel combustion chambers are different from gasoline combustion chambers because diesel fuel burns differently. Three types of combustion chambers are used in diesel engines: open combustion chamber, precombustion chamber, and turbulence combustion chamber. The open combustion chamber has the combustion chamber located directly inside the piston. Diesel fuel is injected directly into the center of the chamber. The shape of the chamber and the quench area produces turbulence. The precombustion chamber is a smaller, second chamber connected to the main combustion chamber. On the power stroke, fuel is injected into the small chamber. Combustion is started there and then spreads to the main chamber. This design allows lower fuel injection pressures and simpler injection systems on diesel engines.

122   Section 2   Engines

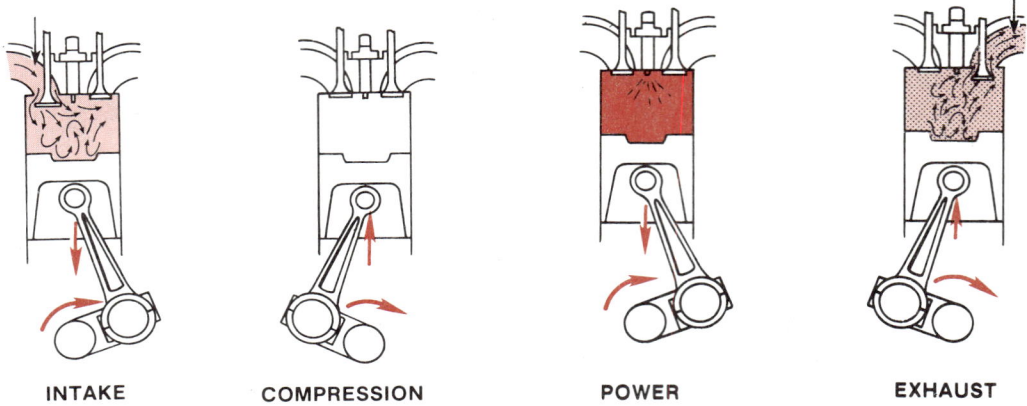

Figure 6-29 Four-stroke diesel engine cycle.

INTAKE   COMPRESSION   POWER   EXHAUST

The turbulence combustion chamber is designed to create an increase in air velocity or turbulence in the combustion chamber. The fuel is injected into the turbulent air and burns more completely. The prechambers on a diesel engine head must be properly indexed with the head and correctly installed (Figure 6-30). They must be perfectly flush (not above or below) with the cylinder head. Failure to follow this will cause the head gasket to fail.

Table 6-1 compares the gasoline and diesel four-stroke-cycle engines. Remember that diesel engines are also available in two-stroke-cycle models (Figure 6-31).

Rotary Engine

The rotary engine, or Wankel engine, is somewhat similar to the standard piston engine in that it is a

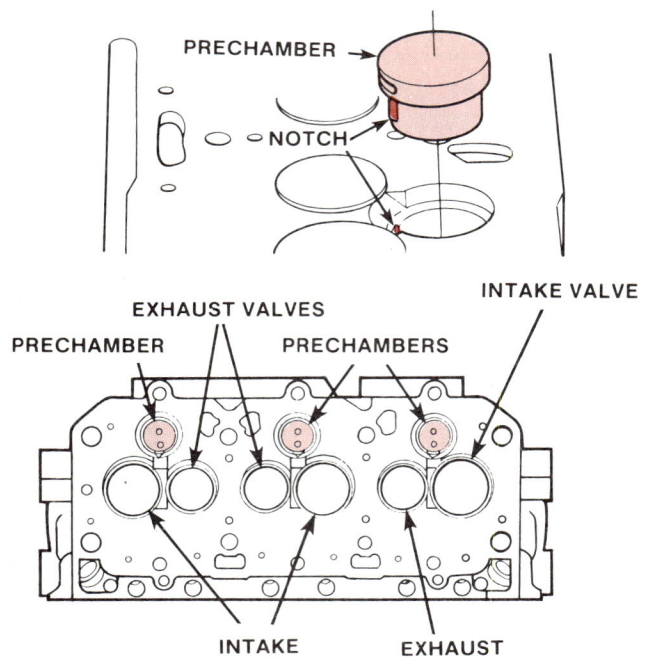

Figure 6-30 Correctly installed diesel prechambers.

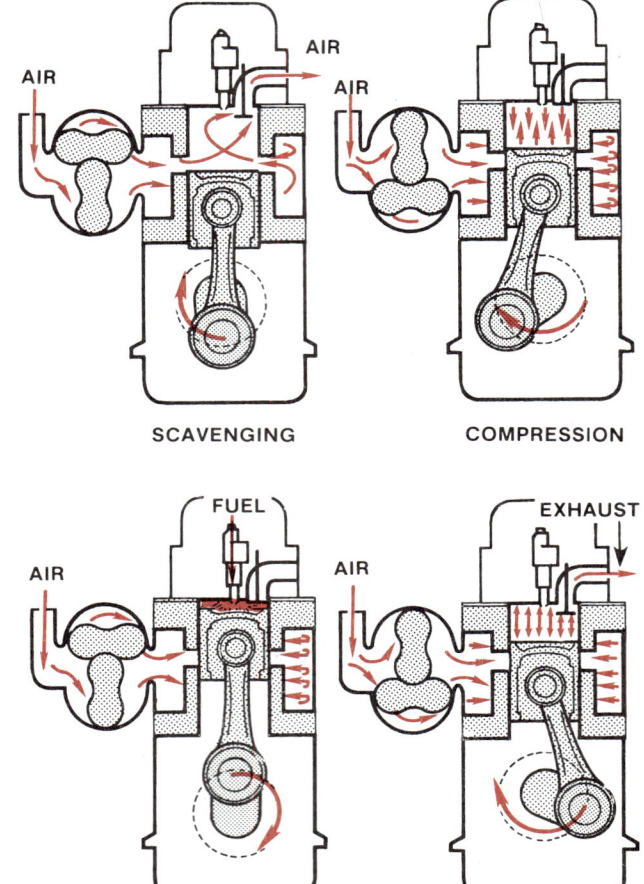

Figure 6-31 Two-stroke diesel engine cycle.

four-cycle, spark ignition, internal combustion engine. Its mechanical design, however, is quite different. For one thing, the rotary engine uses a rotating motion rather than a reciprocating motion. In addition, it uses ports rather than valves for controlling the intake of the air/fuel mixture and the exhaust of the combusted charge.

As shown in Figure 6-32 the heart of a rotary engine is a roughly triangular rotor that "walks" around a

TABLE 6-1 COMPARISON BETWEEN GASOLINE AND DIESEL ENGINES

	Gasoline	Diesel
Intake	Air/fuel	Air
Compression	8-10 to 1 130 psi 545°F	13-25 to 1 400-600 psi 1,000°F
Air/fuel mixing point	Carburetor or before intake valve with fuel injection	Near TDC by injection
Combustion	Spark ignition	Compression ignition
Power	464 psi	1,200 psi
Exhaust	1,300°-1,800°F CO = 3%	700°-900°F CO = 0.5%
Efficiency	22-28%	32-38%

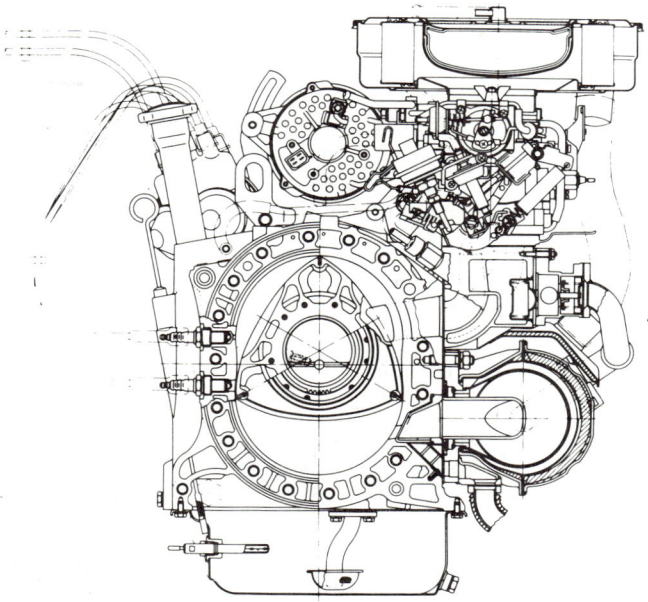

Figure 6-32 Typical rotary engine.

smaller, rigidly mounted gear. The rotor is connected to the crankshaft through additional gears in such a manner that for every rotation of the rotor the crankshaft revolves three times. The tips of the triangular rotor move within the housing and are in constant contact with the housing walls. As the rotor moves, the volume between each side of the rotor and the housing walls continually changes.

Referring to Figure 6-33, when side A of the rotor is in position 1, the intake port is uncovered and the

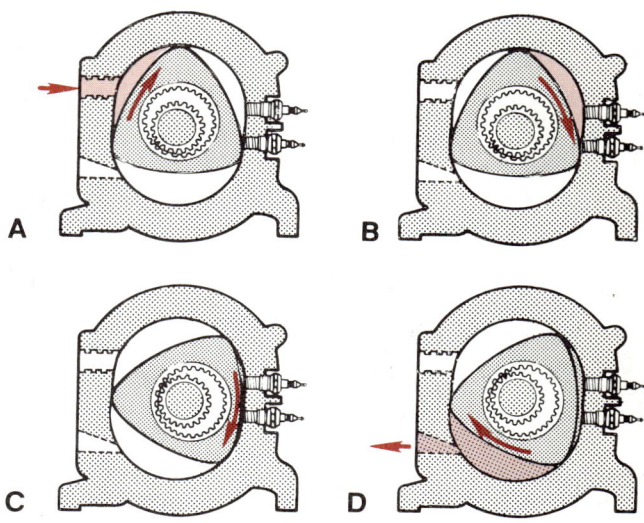

Figure 6-33 Rotary engine cycle.

air/fuel mixture is entering the upper chamber. As the rotor moves to position B, the intake port closes and the upper chamber reaches its maximum volume. When full compression has reached position C, the two spark plugs fire, one after the other, to start the power stroke. At position D, rotor side A uncovers the exhaust port and exhaust begins. This cycle continues until position 1 is reached where the chamber volume is at minimum and the intake cycle starts once again.

The fact that the rotating combustion chamber engine is small and light for the amount of power it produces makes it attractive for use in automobiles. Using this small, lightweight engine can provide the same performance as a larger engine. But, the rotary engine, at present, cannot compete with the piston gasoline on durability, exhaust emission control, and economy.

Stratified Charge Engine

The stratified charge engine (Figure 6-34) combines the features of both the gasoline and diesel engines. It differs from the conventional gasoline engine in that the air/fuel mixture is deliberately stratified to produce a small rich mixture at the spark plug while providing a leaner, more efficient and cleaner burning main mixture. In addition, the air/fuel mixture is swirled for more complete combustion.

Referring to position A in Figure 6-35, on the intake stroke a large amount of very lean mixture is drawn through the main intake valve to the main combustion chamber. At the same time, a small amount of rich mixture is drawn through the auxiliary intake valve into the precombustion chamber. At the end of the compression stroke in position B, the spark plug fires the rich mixture in the precombustion chamber. As the rich mixture ignites, it in turn ignites the lean mixture in the main chamber. The lean mixture minimizes the formation of carbon monoxide during the power stroke

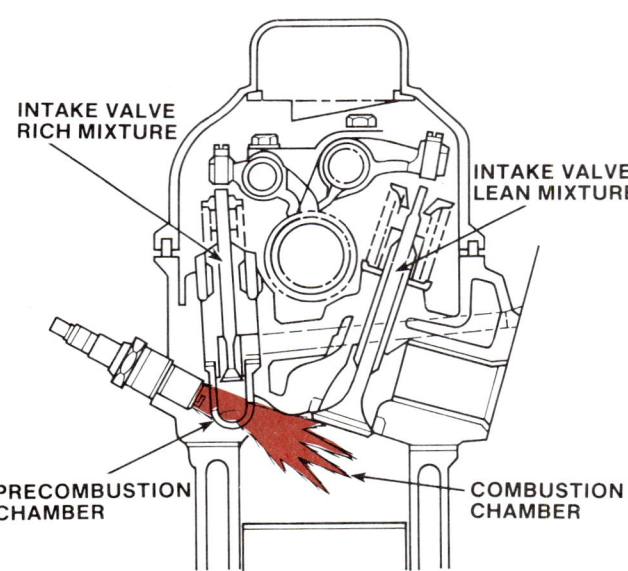

Figure 6-34 Typical stratified charge engine.

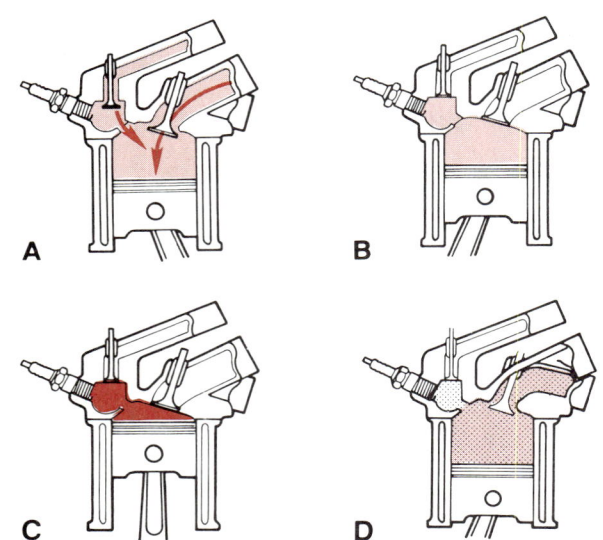

Figure 6-35 Four-stroke cycle of a stratified charge engine.

(position C). In addition, the peak temperature stays low enough to minimize the formation of oxides of nitrogen, and the mean temperature is maintained high enough and long enough to reduce hydrocarbon emissions. During the exhaust stroke (position D) the hot gases exit through the exhaust valve.

A great deal of automobile engineering research, especially by Japanese and European manufacturers, is being done on these engines. In fact, the Honda CVCC engine uses a stratified charge design. This engine uses a third valve to release the initial charge. The stratified charge combustion chamber has three important advantages. It produces good part-load fuel economy. It can run efficiently on low-octane fuel. It appears to produce low exhaust emissions.

Electric Motors

In the early days of the automobile, electric cars outnumbered gasoline cars. The electric motor is quiet, has little or no emissions and few moving parts. It starts well in the cold, is simple to maintain, and does not burn petroleum products to operate. Its disadvantages are limited speed, power, and range as well as the need for heavy, costly batteries. Experimental vehicles employing solar-charged batteries are being considered as sources of automotive power.

Case 1

A customer complains that the engine has a rough idle and does not have as much power as it used to. Also, the customer says that the engine is difficult to start when it is cold and runs better while cruising at highway speeds. Upon examining the car, it is found that it has a four-cylinder engine with nearly 65,000 miles on it. Driving the car verifies the customer's complaint.

Diagnosis begins with a visual inspection that reveals only that the car has been well-maintained. Because there is an endless list of possible causes for these problems, the first test is for engine vacuum. With the vacuum gauge connected to the manifold and the engine at idle speed, the gauge's needle constantly drops from a normal reading to 10 in. hg. The rhythm of the drop matches the rhythm of the idle. The behavior of the gauge indicates a probable problem in one cylinder.

To verify this, a cylinder power balance test is conducted. The results show an engine speed drop of 100-125 rpm when cylinders 1, 2, and 4 are shorted, and a drop of only 10 rpm when cylinder 3 is shorted. Based on this test, cylinder 3 is identified as having the problem.

To identify the exact fault, further testing is required. The spark plugs are removed and inspected. All look normal, including cylinder 3. Next, a compression test is taken. All cylinders have normal readings. A cylinder leakage test is then conducted and it too shows normal conditions. The results of the power balance, compression, and cylinder leakage tests lead to the conclusion that the cause has to be in the valve train. Something is preventing a valve from opening.

Removing the cam cover for a visual inspection leads to the discovery of the fault: the intake lobe for cylinder 3 on the camshaft is severely worn. A replacement of the camshaft and matching lifter will correct the problem. The worn lobe only affects the opening of the valve and does not prevent it from sealing, which is why the compression and cylinder leakage test results were normal. Cylinder power and vacuum are affected by the valve not opening fully.

Summary

- Automotive engines are classified several ways, depending on such design features as operational cycles, number of cylinders, cylinder arrangement, valve train type, valve arrangement, ignition type, cooling system, and fuel system.
- The basis of automotive gasoline engine operation is the four-stroke cycle. This includes the intake stroke, compression stroke, power stroke, and exhaust stroke. The four strokes require two full crankshaft revolutions.
- The most popular engine designs are the in-line (in which all the cylinders are placed in a single row) and V-type (which features two rows of cylinders). The slant design is much like the in-line, but with the entire block placed at a slant. Opposed cylinder engines use two rows of cylinders located opposite the crankshaft.
- The two basic valve and camshaft placement configurations currently in use on four-stroke engines are the overhead valve and overhead cam. A third type, the flathead or side valve, was once popular but is no longer in use.
- Bore is the diameter of a cylinder and stroke is the length of piston travel between top dead center (TDC) and bottom dead center (BDC). Together these two measurements determine the displacement of the cylinder, which is the volume the cylinder holds between the TDC and BDC positions of the piston.
- Compression ratio is a measure of how much the air and fuel have been compressed. The higher the compression ratio is, the more power an engine can produce. The compression ratio of an engine must be suited to the fuel available. As compression ratio increases, the octane rating of the fuel must increase to prevent abnormal engine combustion.
- Horsepower is the rate at which torque is produced by an engine. The torque is then transmitted through the drivetrain to turn the driving wheels of the vehicle.
- The vehicle identification number, or VIN, is used to identify correct engine specifications. It is stamped on a metal tab that is riveted to the instrument panel.
- An oil pressure test measures the pressure of the engine oil as it circulates throughout the engine. This test is very important because abnormal oil pressures can cause a host of problems, including poor performance and premature wear.
- The cylinder power balance test reveals if all the cylinders are doing an equal amount of work; if not, there is either a mechanical problem or trouble in the fuel or ignition system. This test is performed easiest on an engine analyzer. As each cylinder is shorted out, a noticeable drop in engine speed should occur.
- An engine malfunction often reveals itself as an unusual noise. When correctly interpreted, engine noise can be a very helpful diagnostic aid. A stethoscope is good not only for locating and amplifying noises, but in distinguishing between those that are normal and those that require attention.
- Abnormal engine combustion can cause preignition and detonation noises. Detonation knock or ping is most noticeable during acceleration with the engine under load. Though this can be very harmful to the engine, it can usually be cured by removing carbon deposits from the combustion chambers and using a higher octane gasoline.
- Instead of relying on a spark for ignition, diesel engines use the heat produced by compressing air in the combustion chamber to ignite the fuel. Three types of combustion chambers are used in diesel engines: open, precombustion, and turbulence.
- Features of both the gasoline and diesel engine are found in the stratified charge engine. Its major advantages are good part-load fuel economy, low exhaust emissions, and an ability to operate on low-octane fuel.
- In addition to the diesel and stratified charge, other automotive engines that may figure prominently in the future include the rotary or Wankel, and electric.

Review Questions

1. What occurs in the combustion chamber of a four-stroke engine?
2. Name the four strokes of a four-stroke cycle engine.
3. As an engine's compression ratio increases, what should happen to the octane rating of the gasoline?
4. What test can be performed to check the efficiency of individual cylinders?
5. Describe tappet noise.
6. Which of the following statements about engines is not true?
   a. The engine provides the rotating power to drive the wheels through the transmission and driving axle.
   b. Only gasoline engines are classified as internal combustion.
   c. The combustion chamber is the space between the top of the piston and the cylinder head.

d. For the combustion in the cylinder to take place completely and efficiently, air and fuel must be combined in the right proportions.
7. Which stroke in the four-stroke cycle begins as the compressed fuel mixture is ignited in the combustion chamber?
   a. power stroke
   b. exhaust stroke
   c. intake stroke
   d. compression stroke
8. What is compression ratio?
   a. diameter of the cylinder
   b. cylinder arrangement
   c. the amount the air/fuel mixture is compressed
   d. none of the above
9. When a customer refers to the engine component that opens and closes the intake and exhaust valves, Technician A believes the customer is referring to the camshaft. Technician B thinks the component in question is the intake manifold. Who is correct?
   a. Technician A
   b. Technician B
   c. Both A and B
   d. Neither A nor B
10. A two-stroke engine is normally equipped with a _____.
    a. valve train
    b. piston
    c. reed valve
    d. all of the above
11. Technician A says the L-head engine design is characterized by the use of two camshafts. Technician B says an L-head design means that the valves are located directly above the piston. Who is correct?
    a. Technician A
    b. Technician B
    c. Both A and B
    d. Neither A nor B
12. What is piston slap?
    a. grooves on the side of the piston
    b. force applied to the piston
    c. noise made by the piston when it contacts the cylinder wall
    d. a high-pitched clicking that becomes louder during deceleration
13. Which engine system removes burned gases and limits noise produced by the engine?
    a. exhaust system
    b. emission control system
    c. ignition system
    d. air/fuel system
14. Technician A measures engine displacement in cubic centimeters, while Technician B measures it in cubic inches. Who is correct?
    a. Technician A
    b. Technician B
    c. Both A and B
    d. Neither A nor B
15. The stroke of an engine is _____ the crank throw.
    a. half
    b. twice
    c. four times
    d. equal to
16. Technician A calculates compression ratio with the following formula.
    $$\frac{\text{volume above the piston at BDC}}{\text{volume above the piston at TDC}}$$
    Technician B calculates compression ratio with the following formula.
    $$\frac{\text{total cylinder volume}}{\text{total combustion chamber volume}}$$
    Who is correct?
    a. Technician A
    b. Technician B
    c. Both A and B
    d. Neither A nor B
17. When performing a cylinder power balance test, Technician A says that the push-button numbers on the engine analyzer refer to cylinder number designation. Technician B says they refer to cylinder firing order. Who is correct?
    a. Technician A
    b. Technician B
    c. Both A and B
    d. Neither A nor B
18. A vehicle is producing a sharp, metallic rapping sound originating in the upper portion of the engine. It is most noticeable during idle. Technician A diagnoses the problem as piston pin knock, while Technician B says the problem is most likely a loose crankshaft thrust bearing. Who is correct?
    a. Technician A
    b. Technician B
    c. Both A and B
    d. Neither A nor B

7 ENGINE DISASSEMBLY

Objectives

- Prepare an engine for removal.
- Explain what is involved in lifting an engine.
- Describe how to disassemble and inspect an engine.
- Name the three basic cleaning processes.
- Identify the different types of cleaning equipment.

Careful diagnostics will determine if a vehicle's starting or operating problem is caused by the engine itself or by one of its support systems, such as the ignition or air/fuel system. When the engine is the source of the problem, or its components are broken or excessively worn, it normally needs to be rebuilt or overhauled. While some engine repairs can be made with the engine still in the vehicle, most require its removal.

Once an engine is removed from the vehicle, it must be disassembled and its parts properly cleaned using acceptable methods. Always refer to the service manual before beginning engine removal and disassembly. Procedures and safety precautions can vary greatly from model to model.

❑ PREPARING THE ENGINE FOR REMOVAL

It is often desirable to clean the engine and engine compartment before beginning the engine removal. If steam cleaning, always follow EPA regulations.

CAUTION: Extreme care must be taken to avoid damaging electronic and fuel injection components during steam or other cleaning procedures. Cover susceptible components with plastic bags and avoid direct contact with steam, water, or other cleaning agents.

Once cleaned, certain engine components must be disconnected or removed. The cooling system must be drained, and other steps taken to prepare the engine for lifting. Again, always follow the specific steps in the vehicle's service manual. A typical procedure for preparing an engine for removal is outlined in the Tech Manual that accompanies this text.

CUSTOMER CARE

Make sure your hands, shoes, and clothing are clean before getting into a customer's car. Disposable seat and floor coverings should be used to help protect the interior.

❑ LIFTING AN ENGINE

To lift an engine out of its compartment use either a canvas hoist (Figure 7-1) and chain, which consists of

Figure 7-1 A canvas hoist is ideal for lifting engines.

127

128 Section 2 Engines

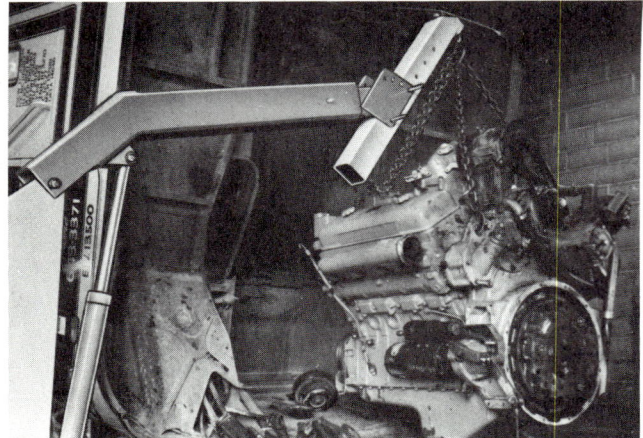

Figure 7-2 Lifting an engine out of its compartment. *Courtesy of Tool Division—SPX Corp.*

gears that provide the necessary mechanical advantage to do the lifting, or a mobile crane, frequently called a cherry picker, that uses hydraulic power to do the lifting.

To lift an engine attach a pulling sling or chain (Figure 7-2) to the engine. Some engines have eye plates for use in lifting. If they are not available, the sling must be bolted to the engine. The sling attaching bolts must be large enough to support the engine and must thread into the block a minimum of 1-1/2 times the bolt diameter. Connect the chain hoist or mobile crane to the pulling cable. Check the engine to be sure that everything is disconnected.

Raise the engine slightly and make certain that the sling attachments are secure. Carefully lift the engine out of its compartment. Be sure that the engine does not bind or damage any compartment component during this procedure.

Lower the engine close to the floor so it can be transported to the desired location. If you have not already disconnected the transmission and torque converter or clutch from the engine, do so now. The torque converter must remain with the transmission when the engine is removed. A C-clamp or bar clamp will prevent the converter from dropping out of the bell housing.

Raise the engine and position it next to an engine stand. Mount the engine to the engine stand with bolts. Most stands use a plate with several holes or adjustable arms. The engine must be supported by at least four bolts that fit solidly into the engine. Once the pulling cable or chain is removed from the engine, the engine can be disassembled.

SHOP TALK

When lifting a transverse-mounted engine with front-wheel drive (Figure 7-3), most service manuals recommend removing the engine and transaxle assembly as a unit. The transaxle can be separated from the engine once it has been lifted out of the vehicle. In this case, the drive axles must be disconnected from the transaxle. It is wise to employ a transverse engine support bar before attempting to remove this type of engine (Figure 7-4).

☐ ENGINE DISASSEMBLY AND INSPECTION

Before engine disassembly, be sure the engine is securely bolted to an engine stand or sitting on blocks. Go slowly and visually inspect each part for any signs of damage. Look for excessive wear on the moving parts. Check all parts for signs of overheating, unusual wear, and chips. Look for signs of gasket and seal leakage. A disassembled engine is shown in Figure 7-5.

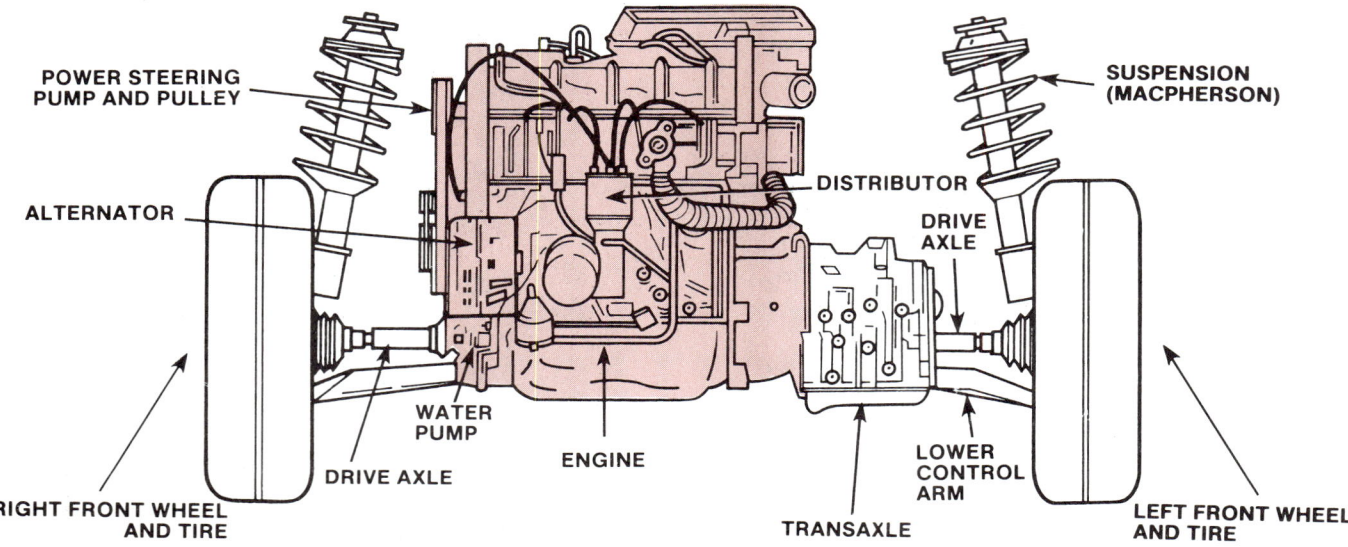

Figure 7-3 Transverse-mounted front-wheel-drive engine.

Figure 7-4 A transverse engine support bar provides the necessary support when removing the lower driveline cradle on a front-wheel-drive vehicle. *Courtesy of Tool Division—SPX Corp.*

The following engine teardown of both cylinder head and block can be considered typical. Exact details will vary slightly depending on the style and type of engine. For instance, in some engines, the overhead camshaft is mounted directly in the cylinder head. In other engines, it is located in a separate housing that is mounted on the cylinder head. The camshaft housing is unbolted from the cylinder head. The bearing caps must be removed in order to remove a camshaft mounted to the cylinder head.

Although general methods of parts removal and procedures to inspect the various engine components are given in later chapters of this book, the vehicle's OEM service manual is always the final word.

> **USING SERVICE MANUALS**
>
> Look up the specific model car and engine prior to disassembling the engine.

Cylinder Head Removal

The first step in disassembly of an engine is usually the removal of the intake and exhaust manifolds. On some in-line engines, the intake and exhaust manifolds are often removed as an assembly and are not disconnected from each other unless a problem exists that would require disassembly.

> **SHOP TALK**
>
> It is important to let an aluminum cylinder head cool completely before removing it.

To start cylinder head removal, remove the valve cover or covers and disassemble the rocker arm components. When removing the rocker assembly, remember that each has a different disassembly procedure. It is best to check the manufacturer's manual for specific procedures.

After removing the rocker arm and pushrods, check the rocker area for sludge. Excessive buildup can indicate a poor oil change schedule and is a signal to look for similar wear patterns on other components.

When removing the cylinder head, keep the pushrods and rocker arms or rocker arm assemblies in exact order if they will be reused (Figure 7-6). These parts are wear-mated to each other and should be reassembled in the same position on the camshaft. Use an organizing tray or label the parts with a felt-tipped marker to keep them together and labeled accurately. Check lifters for a dished bottom or scratches, which indicate poor rotation.

The cylinder head bolts are loosened one or two turns each, working from the center of the cylinder head outward (Figure 7-7). This procedure prevents the distortion that can occur if bolts are all loosened at once. The bolts are then removed, again following the center-outward sequence. With the bolts removed, the cylinder head can be lifted off (Figure 7-8). The cylinder head gasket should be saved to compare with the new head gasket during reassembly.

On standard overhead valve engines, remove the timing cover. With certain engines this may require removing the oil pan. The harmonic balancer or vibration damper usually must also be removed. This usually requires a special puller designed for the purpose (Figure 7-9).

The camshaft can now be carefully removed (Figure 7-10). Support the camshaft during removal to avoid dragging lobes over bearing surfaces, which would damage bearings and lobes. Do not bump cam lobe edges, which can cause chipping. Some engines might require the removal of the thrust plate before taking out the camshaft.

After the camshaft has been removed, visually examine the camshaft for any obvious defects—rounded lobes, edge wear, galling, and the like. If either the camshaft or lifters are worn at all, both should be replaced. Do not install old valve lifters with a new camshaft. Do not install new valve lifters on a used camshaft.

Cylinder Head Disassembly

On overhead cam engines, the camshaft must be removed before the cylinder head can be disassembled. Before tearing down the cam follower assembly, draw a diagram and use a felt-tipped marker to label the parts. Since the camshaft and followers are wear-mated parts, this will help insure that each one is returned to the same position.

If the cam has springs beneath it, there is 60 to 80 psi pressure against any spot with the cam lobe against the follower. Random removal of bearing caps can cause the cam to break or spring up, possibly striking the technician. Be sure to follow the automotive service manual for the correct procedure because it is

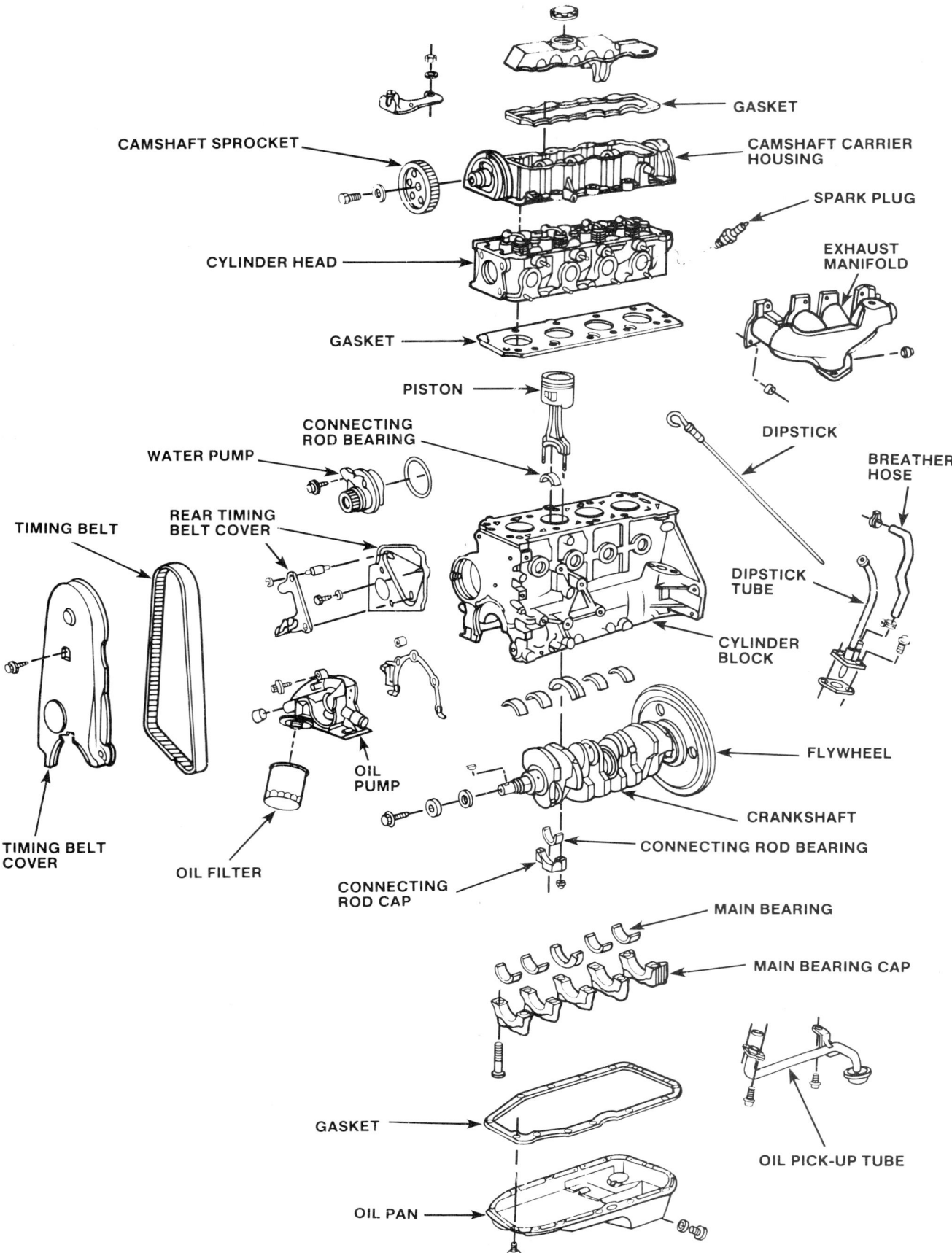

Figure 7-5 Disassembled engine.

Figure 7-6 Keep the rocker arm assemblies in exact order if they will be reused. *Courtesy of Perfect Circle/Dana*

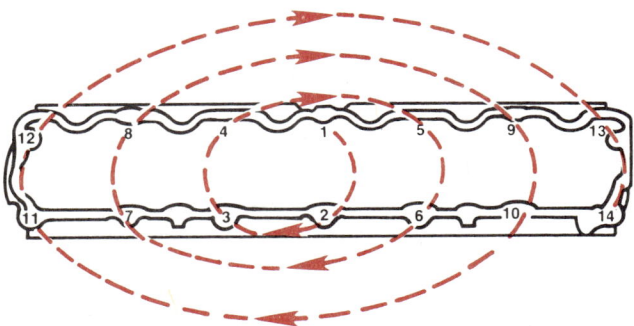

Figure 7-7 Cylinder head bolts are loosened from the center outward.

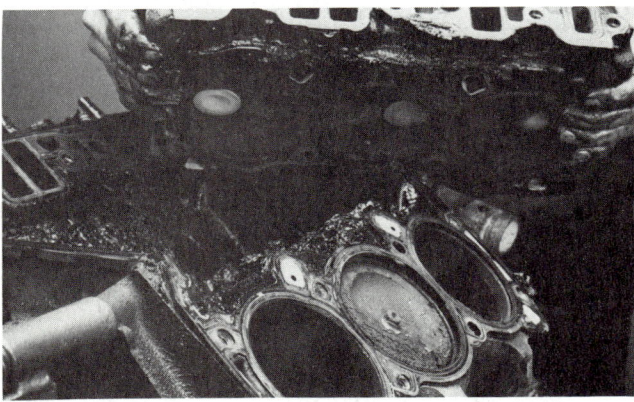

Figure 7-8 Cylinder head removal. *Courtesy of Perfect Circle/Dana*

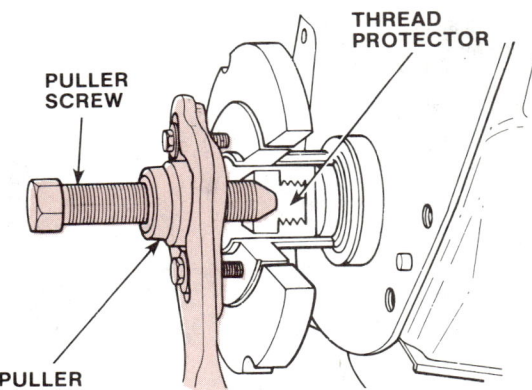

Figure 7-9 Using a special puller to remove the harmonic balancer or vibration damper.

Figure 7-10 Removing the camshaft from the engine block. *Courtesy of Perfect Circle/Dana*

Figure 7-11 Using a valve spring compressor. *Courtesy of Fel-Pro, Inc.*

Figure 7-12 Using a valve stem height gauge. *Courtesy of Perfect Circle/Dana*

different for the bucket-type lifter design and lash adjuster design.

Next, use a valve spring compressor to begin disassembling the valve train. This compressor will allow the technician to compress the valve springs and remove the keepers (Figure 7-11). With the valves still in the cylinder head, use a valve stem height gauge to measure the stem height for each valve and record it (Figure 7-12). This measurement will be needed dur-

Figure 7-13 File away the excess metal. *Courtesy of Perfect Circle/Dana*

ing reassembly to set the installed valve stem height.

Next, remove the valve oil seals and the valves. If a valve seems to be stuck in the guide, the tip might be peened over. If this is the case do not drive the valve through the guide. It could score or crack the valve guide or head. Raise the stem and file the excess metal until the stem slides through the guide easily (Figure 7-13).

While removing valves, look for signs of burning, pitting, cracks, grooves, scores, necking, or other signs of wear. These wear patterns signal other problems in the engine. Valves that cannot be refaced without leaving at least a 1/32-inch valve margin must be discarded. Also discard any valve that is badly burned, cracked, pitted, or shows signs of valve stem wear, bent valve stems, or damaged keeper grooves. Examine the backside of the intake valves. A black oily buildup in the neck and stem area indicates oil is entering the cylinder through the intake valve (Figure 7-14). Use this method to check for excessive oil consumption.

CUSTOMER CARE

When working on an engine, it is good practice to keep the customer informed of any unexpected problems.

Figure 7-14 Oily buildup on the backside of the intake valves.

Cylinder Block Disassembly

After the cylinder head has been removed, the cylinder block can be torn down. First, remove the oil pan if it was not removed previously. Then, remove the oil pump as directed in the service manual.

Continue the disassembly by removing the timing components. There are three different types of timing component assemblies: the chain and sprocket, the gear, and the timing belt and sprocket.

Often the chain and sprocket assembly and the timing belt and sprocket assembly both have tensioners and guides (Figure 7-15). All three types of timing mechanisms should be replaced as complete assemblies during an engine overhaul. The tensioners and guides wear and should be replaced as well.

Some OHC engines have complicated driving systems; so if you are unsure of the removal process, consult the proper engine repair manual. Inspect the sprockets for wear, cracks, and broken teeth. Inspect the timing gears for excessive backlash. Check the chain for slackness and wear.

Carefully scrape the cylinder ridge with a ridge removing tool. Rotate the tool clockwise with a wrench to remove the ridge (Figure 7-16). Do not cut too deeply, because it will leave an indentation in the bore. Remove just enough metal to allow the piston assembly to set properly.

If the ridge is too large, the new top rings will hit it and possibly break the ring lands. In this case, the

Figure 7-15 Tensioners and guides should be periodically checked for wear. *Courtesy of Perfect Circle/Dana*

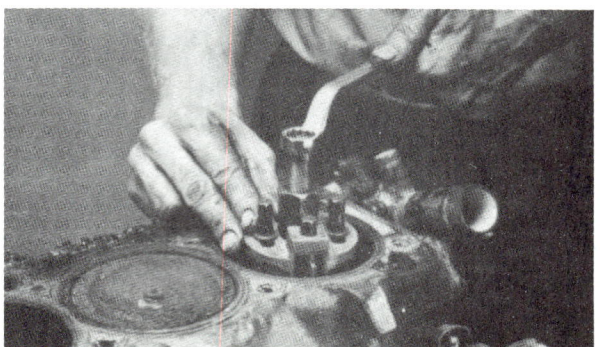

Figure 7-16 Remove the cylinder ridge with a ridge reamer. *Courtesy of Perfect Circle/Dana*

Engine Disassembly 133

Figure 7-17 Stamping the bearing caps. *Courtesy of Perfect Circle/Dana*

engine should be rebored. The ridge is formed at the top of the cylinder. Because the top ring stops traveling before it reaches the top of the cylinder, a ridge of unworn metal is left. Carbon also builds up above this ridge, adding to the problem.

After the ridge removing operation, wipe all the metal cuttings out of the cylinder. Use an oily rag to wipe the cylinder. The cuttings will stick to it.

Prior to removal of the piston and rod assembly, check all connecting rods and main bearing caps for correct position and numbering. If the numbers are not visible, use a center punch or number stamp to number them (Figure 7-17). Caps and rods should be stamped on the external flat surface. Remember that caps and rods must remain as a set.

To remove the piston and rod assemblies, position the crankshaft throw at the bottom of its stroke. Remove the connecting rod nuts and cap. Tap the cap lightly with a soft hammer or wood block to aid in cap removal. Cover the rod bolts with protectors to avoid damage to the crankshaft journals (Figure 7-18). Carefully push out the piston and rod assembly with the wooden hammer handle or wooden drift and support the piston by hand as it comes out of the cylinder. Be sure that the connecting rod does not damage the cylinder during removal. With bearing inserts in the rod and cap, replace the cap (numbers on same side) and install the nuts. (Store the piston and rod assembly properly.) Repeat the procedure for all other piston and rod assemblies.

Remove the flywheel or flex plate. Scribe marking the position of the crankshaft and flywheel or plate aids in reassembly. Remove the main bearing cap bolts and main bearing cap.

After removing the main bearing caps, carefully take out the crankshaft by lifting both ends equally to avoid bending and damage (Figure 7-19). Store the crankshaft in a vertical position to avoid damage.

Remove the main bearings and rear main oil seal from the block and the main bearing caps. Examine the bearing inserts for signs of abnormal engine conditions such as embedded metal particles, lack of lubrication, antifreeze contamination, oil dilution, uneven wear, and wrong or undersized bearings. Remember that keeping the main bearing caps in order is very important. The location and position of each main bearing cap should be marked. Inspect them for any unusual wear signs, and inspect the main bearing inserts for indications that they are over- or undersized. Also, carefully inspect the main journals on the crankshaft for damage (Figure 7-20).

The block cannot be thoroughly cleaned unless all core plugs and oil gallery plugs are removed. It is imperative that all plugs be removed to allow for a thorough cleaning. To remove cup-type freeze/core plugs, drive them in and then use a pair of channel lock pliers to pull them out. Flat-type plugs can be removed by drilling a hole near the center and then inserting a slide hammer to pull out the plug (Figure 7-21).

Figure 7-19 Lift the crankshaft out carefully. *Courtesy of Perfect Circle/Dana*

Figure 7-18 Install rod bolt protectors before removing the rod assembly from the block to prevent crankshaft damage. *Courtesy of Perfect Circle/Dana*

Figure 7-20 Inspect each crankshaft journal for damage and wear. *Courtesy of Perfect Circle/Dana*

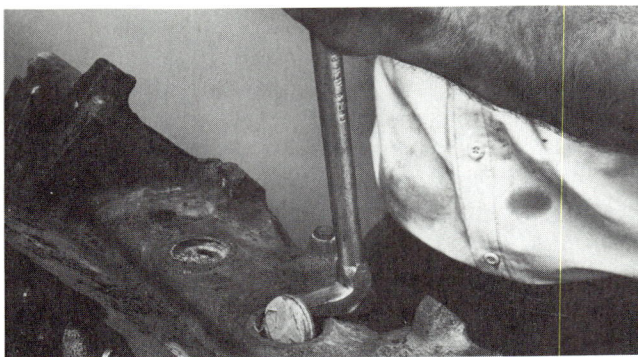

Figure 7-21 Removing a flat-type core plug. *Courtesy of Perfect Circle/Dana*

Sometimes removing threaded front and rear oil gallery plugs can be difficult. Using a drill and screw extractor can help. In some engines, the cup-type plug can be removed easily by using a slide hammer or by driving the plug out from the backside with a long rod.

> **SHOP TALK**
>
> Using heat to melt paraffin into the threads of oil plugs will make removal much easier. As the part is heated, it will expand and the paraffin will leak down between the threads. Because the paraffin provides a lubrication, you will be able to loosen the two parts. Hot paraffin burns, so wear gloves when handling it.

After the teardown, the cylinder head and block and their parts must be visually checked for cracks or other damage before they are cleaned as described in the next section. While inspecting the parts, check to see if the engine has ever been torn down before. To do this, inspect the bearings for undersizes and check to see if the bearings are the original ones. For instance, Ford's bearings are date coded. If the engine has been previously torn down, use caution because a mistake could have been made during the last rebuild. Check for correct sizing before ordering any parts.

☐ CLEANING ENGINE PARTS

When the block or cylinder head parts have been removed, they must be thoroughly cleaned (Figure 7-22). The cleaning method depends on the component to be cleaned and the type of equipment available. An incorrect cleaning method or agent can often be more harmful than no cleaning at all. For example, using caustic soda to clean aluminum parts will dissolve the part.

Only after all components have been thoroughly and properly cleaned can an effective inspection be made or proper machining be done.

Figure 7-22 From (A) grime to (B) shine.

Types of Soil Contaminants

The ability to understand specific soils that might be encountered is the first step toward saving valuable time and effort during the cleaning process. There are four categories of soil contaminants.

WATER-SOLUBLE SOILS The easiest soils to deal with fall under the category of water soluble. Water-soluble soils include dirt, dust, and mud.

ORGANIC SOILS Organic soils contain carbon and cannot be effectively removed with plain water. There are three distinct groupings of organic soils:

- Petroleum by-products derived from crude oil including tar, road oil, engine oil, gasoline, diesel fuel, grease, and engine oil additives.
- By-products of combustion including carbon, varnish, gum, and sludge.
- Coatings including such items as rust-proofing materials, gasket sealers and cements, paints, waxes, and sound-deadener coatings.

RUST Rust is the result of a chemical reaction that takes place when iron and steel are exposed to oxygen and moisture. Corrosion, like rust, results from a similar chemical reaction between oxygen and metal containing aluminum. If left unchecked, both rust and corrosion can physically destroy unprotected metal parts quite rapidly. In addition to metal destruction, rust also acts to insulate and prevent proper heat transfer inside the cooling system.

SCALE When water containing minerals and deposits is heated (as in the cooling system), suspended minerals and impurities tend to dissolve, settle out, and attach to the surrounding hot metal surfaces. This buildup of minerals and deposits inside the cooling system is known as scale. Over a period of time, scale can accumulate to the extent that passages become blocked, cooling efficiency is compromised, and metal parts start to deteriorate.

Cleaning with Chemicals

There are three basic processes for cleaning automotive engine parts. The first process that will be discussed is chemical cleaning.

This method of cleaning uses chemical action to remove dirt, grease, scale, paint, and/or rust.

WARNING: When working with any type of cleaning solvent or chemical, be sure to wear protective gloves and goggles and work in a well-ventilated area. Prolonged immersion of the hands in a solvent can cause a burning sensation. In some cases, a skin rash might develop. There is one caution to mention about all manufactured cleaning materials that cannot be overemphasized: Read the labels carefully before mixing or using. Before using, learn how to operate the equipment. The best way to learn is from someone who already knows the equipment. The next best way is to study the equipment manufacturer's operating instructions.

The most traditional line of defense against soils involves the use of cleaning chemicals. However, there is a major concern within the industry as to what chemicals to use. Chlorinated hydrocarbons and mineral spirits may have some health risks associated with their use through skin exposure and inhalation of vapors. Hydrocarbon cleaning solvents are also flammable. The use of a water-based nontoxic chemical can eliminate such risks. Those who prefer hydrocarbon solvents say solvents clean better than their water-based counterparts.

WARNING: Prior to using any chemical, read through all of the information given on the material safety data sheet (MSDS) or the Canadian workplace hazardous materials information systems sheets (WHMIS) for that chemical. Become aware of the health hazards presented by the various chemicals.

Hydrocarbon solvents are labeled hazardous or toxic and require special handling and disposal procedures. The makers of many water-based cleaning solutions claim their products are biodegradable. Once the cleaning solution has become contaminated with grease and grime, it too becomes a hazardous or toxic waste that can be subject to the same disposal rules as a hydrocarbon solvent. Because there is so much latitude in local disposal rules, some municipalities allow neutralized water-based biodegradable cleaning solutions to be dumped down the sewer. Others do not.

Another alternative to the liquid waste disposal problem is recycling. Some manufacturers offer waste-handling services. The old solvent is recycled by a distillation process to separate the sludge and contaminants. The solvent is then returned to service and the contaminants disposed of. Independent services for maintaining hot tanks and spray washers are also available.

The choice of any cleaning system must take into consideration the types of chemicals and solvents required for the process involved. With more stringent EPA and OSHA regulations, some chemicals are becoming increasingly harder (and more expensive) to dispose of.

Steam Cleaning

Steam cleaning was considered the best method of underhood cleaning. However, problems with the disposal of contaminated water have led to strict EPA regulations concerning open steam cleaning. Closed loop steam cleaning systems that filter out grease and dirt from the used water are now required by law in some areas.

Parts Washers

Parts washers (often called solvent tanks) are one of the most widely used and inexpensive methods of removing grease, oil, and dirt from the metal surfaces of a seemingly infinite variety of automotive components and engine parts. A typical washer setup (Figure 7-23) might consist of a tank to hold a given volume of solvent cleaner and some method of applying the solvent. These methods include soaking, soaking and agitation, solvent streams, and spray gun applicators. Because the solvent cleaners used in most parts washers are highly susceptible to evaporation and fuming, parts washers are restricted to operate only at cold or room temperatures.

Soak Tanks

There are two types of soak tanks: cold and hot. Cold soak tanks are commonly used to clean carburetors, throttle bodies, and aluminum parts. A typical cold soak unit consists of a tank to hold the cleaner and a

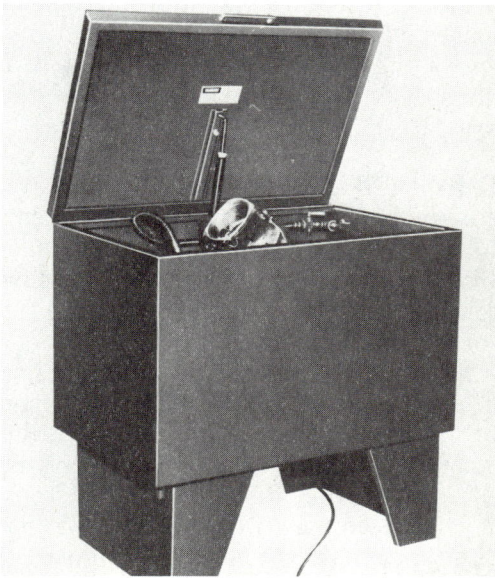

Figure 7-23 Typical parts washer. *Courtesy of Kansas Instruments, Inc.*

136 Section 2 Engines

Figure 7-24 Typical cold soak tank.

basket to hold the parts to be cleaned (Figure 7-24). After soaking with or without gentle agitation is complete, the parts are removed, flushed with water, and blown dry with compressed air.

Cleaning time is short, about 20 to 30 minutes, when the chemical cleaner is new. The time becomes progressively longer as the chemical ages. Agitation by raising and lowering the basket (usually done mechanically) will reduce the soak period to about 10 minutes. Some more elaborate tanks are agitated automatically.

Hot soak tanks are actually heated cold tanks. The source of heat is either electricity, natural gas, or propane. The electrical elements are inside the hot tank but are shielded from the solution. The gas heating elements are located outside and underneath the tank. The solution inside the hot tanks usually ranges from 160 to 200 degrees Fahrenheit. Most tanks are generally large enough to hold an entire engine block and its related parts.

Hot tanks use a simple immersion process that relies on a heated chemical to lift the grease and grime off the surface. Liquid or parts agitation may also be used to speed up the job. Agitation helps shake the grime loose and also helps the liquid penetrate blind passageways and crevices in the part (Figure 7-25). Generally speaking, it takes one to several hours to soak most parts clean.

Hot Spray Tanks

Because of the EPA regulations against open steam cleaning, the spray tank has become more popular. The hot spray tank resembles a large automatic dishwasher and is designed to remove organic and rust soils from a variety of automotive parts (Figure 7-26). In addition to parts being bathed and soaked as in the hot soak method, spray washers add the benefit of moderate pressure cleaning. In a typical spray cabinet, linear or circular configurations of spray nozzles apply the hot alkaline-based solution from all directions ensuring more effective cleaning. With some spray washers, the part sits on a turntable that rotates so liquid can be divided at every surface. As the soil is dislodged, it is washed away by the continuous streams of cleaner.

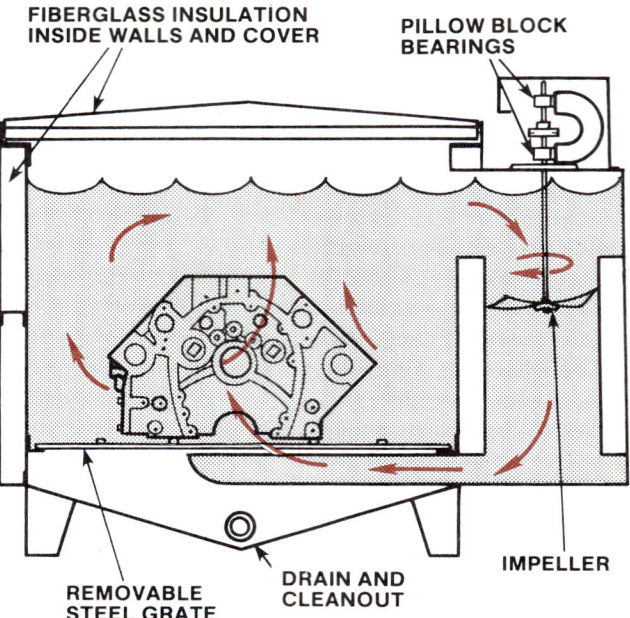

Figure 7-25 Hot soak tanks rely on agitating action to remove grime.

Figure 7-26 Hot spray tanks do a good job of initial post-machining cleanup. *Courtesy of Bayco, Inc.*

Using a hot jet spray washer can cut cleaning time to less than 10 minutes. Normally, a caustic soda or a strong soap solution is used as the cleaning agent. The speed of this system, along with lower operating costs, makes it popular with many machine shop owners.

SHOP TALK

Caustic soda, also known as sodium hydroxide, can be a very dangerous irritant to the eyes, skin, and mucous membranes. These chemicals should be used and handled with care. Because of the accumulation of heavy metals, it is considered a hazardous waste material and must be disposed of in accordance with EPA guidelines.

Engine Disassembly

Figure 7-27 Typical pass-through spray washer. *Courtesy of Peterson Machine Tool, Inc.*

Figure 7-28 Typical thermal cleaning oven.

Spray washers are often used to preclean engine parts prior to disassembly. A pass-through spray washer (Figure 7-27) is fully automatic once the parts have been loaded, and the cabinet prevents the runoff from going down the drain or onto the ground (which is not permitted in many areas because of local waste disposal regulations). Spray washers are also useful for post-machining cleanup to remove machine oils and metal chips. Most use low-pressure (50 psi) spray nozzles to wash parts clean, although some spray washers (called power washers) use high pressure (80 to 180 psi or higher) to blast surfaces clean.

Regardless of the chemical cleaning method used, periodic cleaning or replacement of the chemicals and solid material filters is necessary. Failure to "sweeten" or maintain the proper chemical concentration of the cleaner not only reduces cleaning effectiveness but also increases operating costs and labor time as well. Also, the surface of the tank should be skimmed (preferably when cold) daily or weekly to remove any oil, grease, or scum that has accumulated at the surface.

Thermal Cleaning

The second basic process for cleaning engine parts is thermal cleaning. This process relies on heat to bake off or oxidize dirt and other contaminants.

Thermal cleaning ovens (Figure 7-28), especially the pyrolytic type, have become increasingly popular. The main advantage of thermal cleaning is a total reduction of all oils and grease on and in blocks, heads, and other parts. The high temperature inside the oven (generally 650 to 800 degrees Fahrenheit) oxidizes all the grease and oil leaving behind a dry, powdery ash on the parts. The ash must then be removed by shot blasting or washing. The parts come out dry, which makes subsequent cleanup with shot blast or glass beads easier because the shot will not stick.

Figure 7-29 Typical convection oven. *Courtesy of Bayco, Inc.*

Ovens come in two basic varieties. A convection oven (Figure 7-29) is like a kiln. It uses indirect heat to bake the parts. By heating the part all the way through, the inside and outside are baked clean. Cycle times for a convection oven can run from 2 to 6 hours or more depending on the size of the oven and the load (larger loads take longer to reach baking temperature). Cleaning is still required afterward, which can be done by shot blasting or a hot spray washer.

Pyrolytic ovens (Figure 7-30) impinge a flame directly on the surface of the parts to sear off the contaminants. These ovens are also called open- or direct-flame ovens. Pyrolytic ovens rotate the parts on a rotisserie-like device to allow heat dissipation throughout the component, regardless of its configuration.

Pyrolytic oven action is similar to that of a self-cleaning kitchen oven. The cleaning cycle time is generally 1 to 4 hours, including cooling time. The smoke from the burning process is burnt in an afterburner, leaving carbon dioxide as the exhaust gas that is emitted.

Figure 7-30 Pyrolytic ovens use a direct flame. *Courtesy of Am/Pro Machinery, Inc.*

> **SHOP TALK**
>
> A slow cooling rate is recommended to prevent distortion that could be caused by unequal cooling rates within complex castings.

One of the major attractions of cleaning ovens is that they offer a more environmentally-acceptable process than chemical cleaning. But, although there is no solvent or sludge to worry about with an oven, the ash residue that comes off the cleaned parts must still be handled according to local disposal regulations. In some areas, steel shot can be thrown in the regular trash. In others, it must be treated as a hazardous waste if lead is present in the residue.

TABLE 7-1 COMMON MEDIA USED AS ABRASIVE CLEANERS*

Media	Available Sizes	Use/Result
Glass beads	8 to 10 sizes; from 30 to 440 mesh; also many special graduations	Blending, light deburring, peening, general cleaning, texturing. Non-contaminating. Peening media for nonmetal removal cleaning (holds tolerances). Retains critical part dimensions.
Aluminum oxide grit	10 to 12 sizes; from 16 to 325 mesh	Fast-cutting, matte finish. Do not use if etching is not wanted.
Aluminum shot	10 to 12 sizes; from 8 to 200 mesh	Primarily for cleaning aluminum. Gives bright or satin finish; expensive.
Stainless steel shot	6 to 8 sizes; from 16 to 325 mesh	Cleaning or peening parts where residual iron could be a problem; expensive.
Ceramic shot	6 to 10 sizes; from 12 to 320 mesh	Cleaning or peening hard metals.
Salt	10 to 60 mesh	Good cleaning for all soils. No residue, inexpensive, but it can only be used once.
Nut shells crushed	6 sizes; wide-band screening	Cleaning, very light deburring. Good for fragile parts.
Garnet	6 to 8 sizes; wide-band screening from 16 to 325 mesh	Noncritical cleaning, cutting, texturing. Noncontaminating for brazing steel and stainless steel.
Crushed glass	5 sizes; wide-band screening from 30 to 400 mesh	Fast-cutting, low-cost, short-life, abrasive. Noncontaminating.
Silicon carbide	36 to 220 mesh	Extremely fast cutting.
Steel shot	12 or more sizes; close graduation from 8 to 200 mesh	General-purpose, rough cleaning foundry operations, etc. Peening.
Steel grit	12 or more sizes; close graduation from 10 to 325 mesh	Rough cleaning, coarse textures.
Plastic chips	3 sizes; fine, medium, coarse definite size particles	Cleaning, light deburring.
Sand	10 to 50 mesh	General cleaning. Good for all soils.

*Courtesy of Zero Manufacturing Company

The maintenance procedure given in the owner's manual must be followed if the ovens are to operate properly.

Abrasive Cleaners

The third process used to clean engine parts involves the use of abrasives. Most abrasive cleaning machines are used in conjunction with other cleaning processes (such as an oven, hot tank, or spray washer) rather than as a primary cleaning process itself. Parts must be dry and grease-free when they go into an abrasive blast machine. Otherwise, the shot or beads will stick. Table 7-1 lists the media used in abrasive cleaners and the resulting finishing results.

Abrasive Blaster

Airless shot and grit blasters are used best on parts that will be machined after they have been cleaned (Figure 7-31). Two basic types of media are available: shot and grit. Shot is round; grit is angular in shape (Figure 7-32). Steel shot and glass beads are used primarily for cleaning operations where etching or material removal is not desired. Steel shot and glass beads are also used for peening the surfaces of certain parts. Peening is a process of hammering on the surface of a part. This packs the molecules tighter thereby increasing the part's resistance to fatigue and stress.

Stainless steel shot can be used for cleaning or peening parts where residual iron left on the surface is not wanted. Ceramic shot, which is very hard, is used primarily for peening heat-treated and hard alloy steels where maximum strength is desired. Ceramic is also clean in that it leaves no residue on the surface. Ceramic shot lasts about as long as steel shot, but like stainless it is expensive. Salt is a good and inexpensive cleaner that leaves no residue, but it can only be used once.

Aluminum shot, by comparison, is soft and is used primarily to clean aluminum surfaces where a bright or satin finish is desired. Plastic is the softest material of all and is used for cleaning soft metals and plastics and

Figure 7-31 Typical airless shot blaster. *Courtesy of Am/Pro Machinery, Inc.*

A

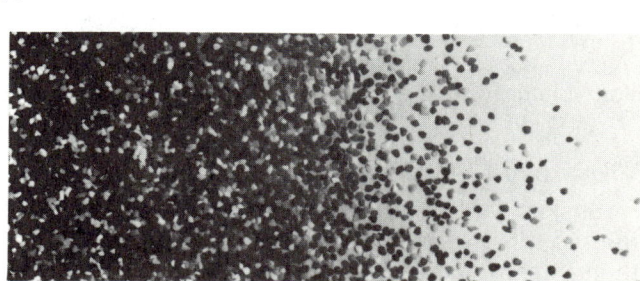

B

Figure 7-32 (A) Shot- and (B) grit-blasting media.

for jobs where shot retention poses a serious problem, such as inside an engine.

Grit is used primarily for aggressive cleaning jobs or where the surface of the material needs to be etched to improve paint adhesion. Steel grit and aluminum oxide are the two most common media for this purpose. Because grit cuts into the surface as it cleans, it removes dirt and scale faster than shot blasting or glass beading. But it also removes metal, leading to some change in tolerances. The beneficial effect of grit blasting is that it roughens the surface, leaving a matte finish to which paint or other surface treatments will stick better than a peened or polished surface. On the other hand, grit blasting is an abrasive process that chews out pits in the surface into which pollutants and blast residue can settle. This leads to stress corrosion unless the surface is painted or treated. The tiny crevices also focus surface stresses in the metal, which can lead to cracking in highly loaded parts. Because of that, grit should never be used for peening.

The type of media that is used for a given job depends on the job itself and the type of equipment. Steel shot is normally used with airless wheel blast equipment, which hurls the shot at the part with the centrifugal force of the spinning wheel. Used with air blast equipment, glass beads are blown through a nozzle by compressed air.

Parts Tumbler

A cleaning alternative that can save considerable labor when cleaning small parts such as engine valves is a tumbler. Various cleaning media can be used in a tumbler to scrub the parts clean. This saves considerable hand labor and eliminates dust. In some tumblers, all parts are rotated and tilted at the same time.

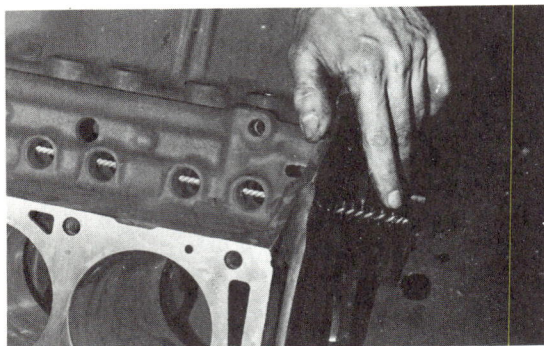

Figure 7-33 It is often necessary to remove the gallery plugs and hand clean the oil galleries.

Vibratory Cleaning

Shakers, as they are frequently called, use a vibrating tub filled with ceramic steel, porcelain, or aluminum abrasive to scrub parts clean. Most shakers flush the tub with solvent to help loosen and flush away the dirt and grime. The solvent drains out the bottom and is filtered to remove the sludge.

Cleaning by Hand

Some manual cleaning must be done in every rebuilding job. Regardless of the cleaning process used, it is usually necessary to remove galley plugs and hand clean the oil galleries (Figure 7-33). Another often neglected area is between the heat shield and the bottom of the intake manifold, where carbon and oil deposits collect. This shield should be removed before cleaning the manifold. Any residual dirt left in the engine after cleaning can lead to failure. Therefore, proper cleaning of all engine components is vital in the rebuilding process. Remove any surface irregularities with very fine, abrasive paper (Figure 7-34). Make sure to keep any dirt out of the cylinder bores. The special power scraper pad shown in action in Figure 7-35 is guaranteed not to remove any metal.

Carbon can be removed from parts using a twist-type wire brush driven by an electric or air drill motor. Using brushes can often be a time-consuming job. Some shops use a wire brush in addition to another cleaning method. Moving the drill motor in a light circular

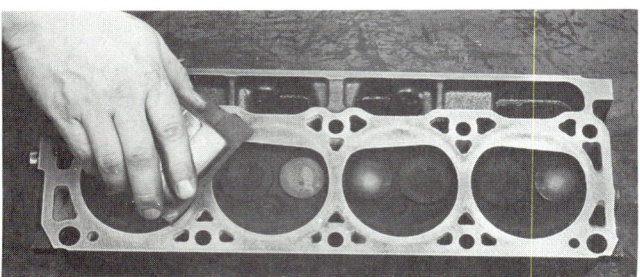

Figure 7-34 Removing surface irregularities from the cylinder block or heads with abrasive paper. *Courtesy of Perfect Circle/Dana*

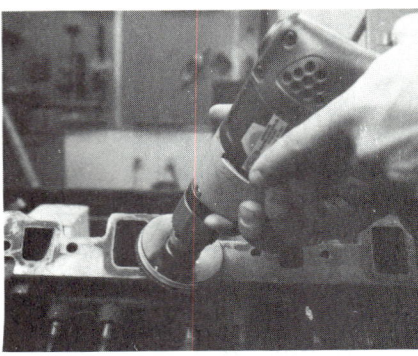

Figure 7-35 Using a power scraper pad will prevent any metal from being removed. *Courtesy of Goodson Shop Supplies*

motion against the carbon helps to crack and dislodge the carbon for easier wire brush cleaning.

Alternative Cleaning Methods

In this age of material handling sheets, right-to-know laws, and concerns over hazardous waste generation and disposal, it is impossible to ignore the fact that cleaning equipment manufacturers and chemical producers are currently under much pressure to find alternatives to the cleaning chemicals that are commonly being used. Three of the most popular alternatives to traditional chemical cleaning systems are ultrasonic cleaning, citrus chemicals, and salt baths.

Ultrasonic Cleaning

This cleaning process has been used for a number of years to clean small parts like jewelry, dentures, and medical instruments. Recently, however, the use of larger ultrasonic units has expanded into small engine parts cleaning (Figure 7-36). Ultrasonic cleaning utilizes high-frequency sound waves to create microscopic bubbles that burst into energy to loosen soil from parts. Because the tiny bubbles do all the work, the chemical content of the cleaning solution is minimized, making waste disposal less of a problem. At the present time, however, the initial cost and handling

Figure 7-36 Typical ultrasonic cleaning system. *Courtesy of Ramco Corp.*

capacity of ultrasonic equipment is its major disadvantage.

Citrus Chemicals

Some chemical producers are starting to develop citrus-based cleaning chemicals as a replacement for the more hazardous solvent and alkaline-based chemicals currently used. Because of their citrus origin, these chemicals are safer to handle, easier to dispose of, and even smell good. As to their effectiveness, preliminary results show a great deal of promise; however, cost is a factor. At the present time, citrus-based cleaners cost more to produce than conventional chemicals.

Salt Bath

The salt bath (Figure 7-37) is a unique process that uses high-temperature molten salt to dissolve organic materials including carbon, grease, oil, dirt, paint, and some gaskets. For cast iron and steel, the salt bath operates at about 700 to 850 degrees Fahrenheit. For aluminum or combinations of aluminum and iron, a different salt solution is used at a lower temperature (about 600 degrees Fahrenheit). The contaminants precipitate out of the solution and sink to the bottom of the tank where they must be removed periodically. The salt bath itself lasts indefinitely as long as the salt is maintained properly. Cycling times with a salt bath are fairly quick, averaging 20 to 30 minutes. Like a hot tank, the temperature of the salt bath is maintained continuously. Because of the high initial cost, the salt bath process is limited mainly to high-volume rebuilding shops. However, the disposal of contaminated salt waste can be as much of a problem as some caustics.

❏ CRACK REPAIR

Once engine parts have been cleaned and given a thorough visual inspection, actual repair work begins. If cracks in the metal casting were discovered during the inspection, they should be repaired or the part replaced.

Figure 7-37 The salt bath cleaning method is primarily used only by high-volume engine rebuilders. *Courtesy of Kolene Corp.*

Figure 7-38 Example of stress cracks.

Cracks in metal castings are the result of stress or strain in a section of the casting. This stress or strain finds a weak point in that section of the casting and causes it to distort or separate at that point (Figure 7-38). Such stresses or strains in castings can develop from the following.

- Pressure or temperature changes during the casting procedure may cause internal material structure defects, inclusion, or voids.
- Fatigue may result from fluctuating or repeated stress cycles. It might begin as small cracks and progress to larger ones under the action of the stress.
- Flexing of the metal may result due to its lack of rigidity.
- Impact damage may occur by a solid, hard object hitting a component.
- Constant impacting of a valve against a hardened seat may produce vibrations that could possibly lead to fracturing a thin-walled casting.
- Chilling of a hot engine by a sudden rush of cold water or air over the surface may happen.
- Excessive overheating is possible due to improper operation of an engine system.

No matter what caused the crack, it is important to relieve the stress at the point of distortion or cracking and then add more metal and move it in such a way as to close the crack. This can be accomplished by the cold process of pinning or the hot process of welding.

Detecting Cracks

With either method of repair, detecting a crack in a metal casting means not only finding that a crack exists but also determining the exact location and extent of the crack.

The three most common methods of crack detection follow.

1. Use a magnet and magnetic powder (frequently referred to as the magna flux process).

2. Use penetrant dye (developed specially for non-magnetic castings such as aluminum heads and blocks).
3. Pressurize the head or block with a pressure tester.

Furnace Welding Crack Repairs

Furnace welding is considered by many people to be the best way to repair cracks in a cast-iron head. By preheating the entire casting, the problem of stress cracks forming during the cooling-off period is eliminated. Heat welding, however, requires a good heat source and proficient welding skills. As a rule, this repair is conducted only by a specialist.

Repairing Aluminum Heads

Aluminum heads have become popular in recent years, primarily because of the weight savings they offer. However, there are many problems associated with an aluminum cylinder head. The typical shop is most likely to encounter the following problems.

- Cracks in the aluminum between the valve seat rings (Figure 7-39). These cracks, usually quite small, require close inspection to find. They very seldom leak and can be closed by a light peening. Some shops make no repairs to them.
- Bottomside cracks coming from the coolant passages. These cracks can be repaired by veeing out the damaged area and welding with an aluminum filler rod.
- Topside cracks across the main oil artery. These cracks, although not too common, are usually very visible (Figure 7-40). Most authorities recommend replacing the head completely if such a crack is found. The length of time required to make the repair is not reasonable. The labor cost is not worth the risk of possible failure and is higher than the cost of purchasing an uncracked core.
- Detonation damage can occur on any cylinder (Figure 7-41). Repairs can be made by welding and

Figure 7-40 The topside oil artery crack appeared when an oxyacetylene flame was passed over the casting. Carbon in the flame was trapped in the crack, highlighting it.

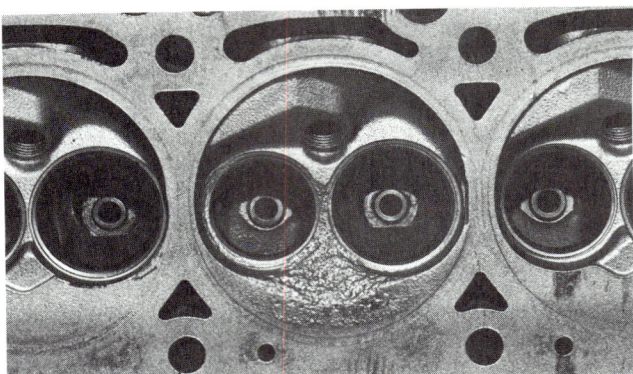

Figure 7-41 The effect of detonation on a combustion chamber.

Figure 7-42 Typical combustion chamber meltdown damage.

Figure 7-39 Cracks between the center two valve seat rings are common with aluminum heads.

  freehand machining with a rotary burr in a die grinder.
- Meltdown damage is a somewhat common occurrence on the high-swirl combustion chamber heads (Figure 7-42). Again, repairs can be made by welding and freehand machining.
- Coolant-related metal erosion. If damage around coolant passages is excessive, if the side of any

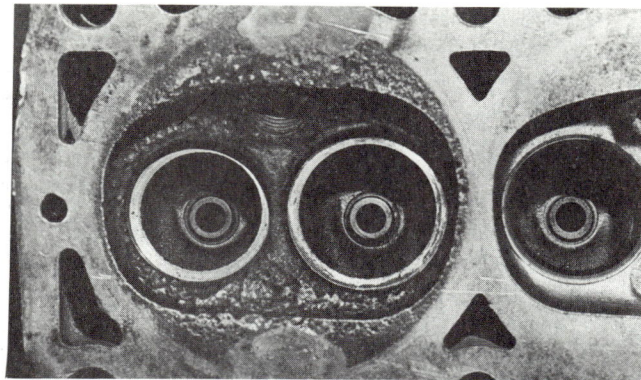

Figure 7-43 Severe coolant related damage can sometimes be repaired, but more often the head is replaced.

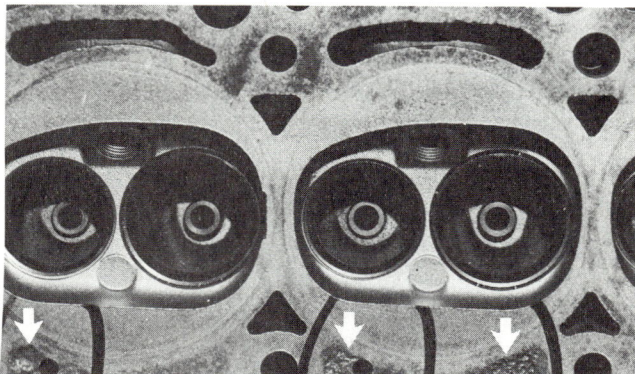

Figure 7-44 This type of coolant erosion damage can be fixed by welding and resurfacing.

valve seat has been exposed, or if the combustion chamber shows erosion, the head must be repaired or replaced (Figure 7-43). Coolant erosion such as shown in Figure 7-44 can be easily fixed by welding and resurfacing.

TIG welding is the preferred repair technique for aluminum heads (Figure 7-45). Welding aluminum is often considered difficult because it welds differently than iron or steel. When exposed to air, aluminum

Figure 7-45 A TIG-welded aluminum head repair.

forms an oxide coating on the surface that helps protect the metal against further corrosion. The oxide layer makes welding difficult because it interferes with fusing and weakens the weld. Cleaning the surface can remove the oxide. However, as soon as the metal is heated, it re-forms (unless the weld is bathed in a constant supply of inert gas).

CASE STUDY

Case 1

A four-cylinder engine is brought into the shop. The customer complains of excessive oil consumption and oil leaks. Compression and cylinder leakage tests indicate that the cylinders are sealing well and a power balance test indicates that all of the cylinders are producing about the same amount of power. Based on these results, the technician assumes the problem to be leaking valve seals. The initial plan is to replace the seals and regasket the engine.

It is odd that the engine has both of these problems. It has less than 50,000 miles on it. Not really sure if the problems are related, the technician proceeds to disassemble the engine. Upon removing the valve cover, large amounts of sludge are evident throughout the valve train. This is normally a sign that the engine has been neglected. However, a review of the files indicates that the oil has recently been changed. In fact, the car has been well-maintained. Is the sludging related to the oil consumption and leaks?

The oil pan is removed and additional sludge is found. The cylinder head is then removed from the block. The piston tops and the combustion chamber are covered with a thick black carbon coating. Is this buildup related to other problems?

The cylinder head is disassembled and each of the valve seals is found to be deteriorated. What could cause the deterioration of rubber parts, leaking gaskets, sludging, and carbon buildup in the cylinders? After careful thought, the technician pays attention to the parts taken off the engine during initial disassembly. A thorough inspection is made of the PCV system and it is discovered that the hose that connected the valve to the manifold is plugged solid. The valve is also found to be plugged.

The PCV system is designed to remove crankcase fumes and pressure from the crankcase. These fumes can cause rapid sludging of the oil and deterioration of rubber parts. Excessive crankcase pressure can cause leaks, as the pressure seeks to relieve itself. A faulty PCV valve can cause all of the problems exhibited by this engine. In fact, it is the cause of the problems.

The engine is resealed and new valve stem seals are installed. The engine is then installed with a new PCV valve and hose. Not only is the customer's complaint taken care of, but so is the cause of the problem.

Summary

- When preparing an engine for removal and disassembly, it is important to always follow the specific service manual procedures for the particular vehicle being worked on.
- A canvas hoist and chain or a cherry picker are needed to lift an engine out of its compartment. Mount the engine to an engine stand with a minimum of four bolts, or sit it securely on blocks.
- While an engine teardown of both the cylinder head and block is a relatively standard procedure, exact details vary among engine types and styles. The vehicle's service manual should be considered as the final word.
- An understanding of specific soil types can save time and effort during the engine cleaning process. The main categories of contaminants include water-soluble and organic soils, rust, and scale.
- Protective gloves and goggles should be worn when working with any type of cleaning solvent or chemical. Read the label carefully before using, as well as all of the information provided on material safety data sheets.
- Parts washers, or solvent tanks, are a popular and inexpensive means of cleaning the metal surfaces of many automotive components and engine parts. Regardless of the type of solvent used, it usually requires some brushing, scraping, or agitation to increase the cleaning effectiveness.
- Cold soak tanks are used to clean carburetors, throttle bodies, and aluminum parts. Hot soak tanks, which can accommodate an entire engine block, use a heated cleaning solution to boil out dirt. Hot heat spray washers have the added benefit of moderate pressure cleaning.
- Alternatives to chemical cleaning have emerged in recent years, including ultrasonic cleaning, salt baths, and citrus chemical cleaning. These methods are all growing in popularity.
- The main advantage of thermal cleaning is its total reduction of all oils and grease. The high temperatures inside the oven leave a dry, powdery ash on the parts. This is then removed by shot blasting or washing.
- Steel shot and glass beads are used for cleaning operations where etching or material removal are not desired. Grit, the other type of abrasive blaster, is used for more aggressive cleaning jobs.
- Some degree of manual cleaning is necessary in any engine rebuilding job. Very fine, abrasive paper should be used to remove surface irregularities. A twist-type wire brush driven by an electric or air drill motor is also helpful, though it can be time-consuming to work with.
- There are three common methods for detecting cracks in the metal casting of engine parts: using a magnet and magnetic powder, using penetrant dye (especially for aluminum heads and blocks), and pressurizing with a pressure tester.
- TIG welding is the preferred repair technique for aluminum cylinder heads. Because it reacts differently to heat than iron or steel, aluminum is considered a challenge to repair by welding.

Review Questions

1. What precautions should be taken when cleaning an engine prior to its removal?
2. What should be worn when working with any type of cleaning solvent or chemical?
3. Name the two types of thermal cleaning ovens.
4. What is the best way to repair cracks in a cast-iron head?
5. What welding method is preferred for repairing aluminum heads?
6. When lifting a transverse-mounted engine on a front-wheel-drive vehicle, Technician A removes the engine and transaxle as a unit. Technician B uses a transverse engine support bar. Who is correct?
   a. Technician A
   b. Technician B
   c. Both A and B
   d. Neither A nor B
7. Technician A uses a cherry picker to remove an engine from its compartment. Technician B uses a canvas hoist and chain to remove an engine from its compartment. Who is correct?
   a. Technician A
   b. Technician B
   c. Both A and B
   d. Neither A nor B
8. Upon inspection of a camshaft, the valve lifters are found to be worn. Technician A replaces the lifters only, while Technician B replaces the lifters and camshaft. Who is correct?
   a. Technician A
   b. Technician B
   c. Both A and B
   d. Neither A nor B
9. Technician A uses caustic soda to clean aluminum parts. Technician B uses caustic soda as the cleaning agent in a hot jet spray washer. Who is correct?
   a. Technician A
   b. Technician B
   c. Both A and B
   d. Neither A nor B

10. What do all organic soils contain?
    a. oil
    b. tar
    c. carbon
    d. nitrogen
11. Hydrocarbon solvents are _____ .
    a. flammable
    b. toxic
    c. both a and b
    d. neither a nor b
12. Technician A operates parts washers at room temperatures. Technician B operates parts washers at cold temperatures. Who is correct?
    a. Technician A
    b. Technician B
    c. Both A and B
    d. Neither A nor B
13. Failure to "sweeten" the cleaner in a hot spray tank will _____ .
    a. reduce cleaning effectiveness
    b. increase operating costs
    c. increase labor time
    d. all of the above
14. Which cleaning method uses high-frequency sound waves to create microscopic bubbles that loosen dirt from parts?
    a. ultrasonic
    b. salt bath
    c. thermal
    d. caustic
15. Technician A uses a fast cooling rate when working with thermal cleaning ovens, while Technician B uses a slow cooling rate. Who is correct?
    a. Technician A
    b. Technician B
    c. Both A and B
    d. Neither A nor B
16. Parts must be _____ when they go into an abrasive blast machine.
    a. wet
    b. dry
    c. grease-free
    d. both b and c
17. Technician A uses aluminum shot for peening heat-treated and hard alloy steels. Technician B uses ceramic shot for peening heat-treated and hard alloy steels. Who is correct?
    a. Technician A
    b. Technician B
    c. Both A and B
    d. Neither A nor B
18. Which of the following is best suited to cleaning small parts such as valves?
    a. shaker
    b. pyrolytic oven
    c. tumbler
    d. none of the above
19. Which method of crack detection is designed especially for aluminum heads and blocks?
    a. penetrant dye
    b. magna flux
    c. pressurizing
    d. both b and c
20. Technician A uses light peening to repair small cracks between aluminum head valve seat rings. Technician B repairs bottomside coolant passage cracks by welding. Who is correct?
    a. Technician A
    b. Technician B
    c. Both A and B
    d. Neither A nor B

8 SHORT BLOCKS

Objectives

■ List the engine components that make up a short block and briefly describe their operation. ■ Describe the major service and rebuilding procedures performed on cylinder blocks. ■ Explain crankshaft construction, inspection, and rebuilding procedures. ■ Explain the function of engine bearings, flywheels, and harmonic balancers. ■ Explain the common service and assembly techniques used in connecting rod and piston servicing. ■ Explain the purpose and design of the different types of piston rings. ■ Describe the procedure for installing pistons in their cylinder bores.

A basic short block assembly consists of the engine's cylinder block, crankshaft, crankshaft bearings, connecting rods, pistons and rings, and oil galley and core plugs (Figure 8-1). Related items also include the engine's flywheel and harmonic balancer. A short block may also include the engine's camshaft and timing gear. However, for the sake of organization, these components will be discussed in a later chapter.

☐ CYLINDER BLOCKS

The cylinder block comprises the lower section of the engine. It houses the areas where compression, ignition, and combustion of the air/fuel mixture take place (Figure 8-2). The upper section of the engine, known as the cylinder head, bolts on top of the cylinder block. In addition to covering the tops of the cylinder block bores, the head forms part of the combustion chamber and often contains the valve train components.

Figure 8-2 A V-6 cylinder block.

The cylinder block (Figure 8-3) is normally one piece, cast, and machined so that all the parts contained in it fit properly. They may be cast from several different materials: iron, aluminum or even plastic, which is being tested as a material for block construction.

The word cast, with regard to the engine block, refers to how it is made. To cast is to form molten metal into a particular shape by pouring or pressing it into a mold. This molded piece must then undergo a number of machining operations to make sure all the working surfaces are smooth and true. The top of the block must be perfectly smooth because the cylinder head will later be attached at this point. The base or bottom of the block must also be machined because the oil pan attaches here. All block sealing areas are also machined. The cylinder bores must be smooth and have the correct diameter to accept the pistons.

Figure 8-1 Basic short block assembly. *Courtesy of Jasper Engine and Transmission Exchange, Inc.*

Short Blocks 147

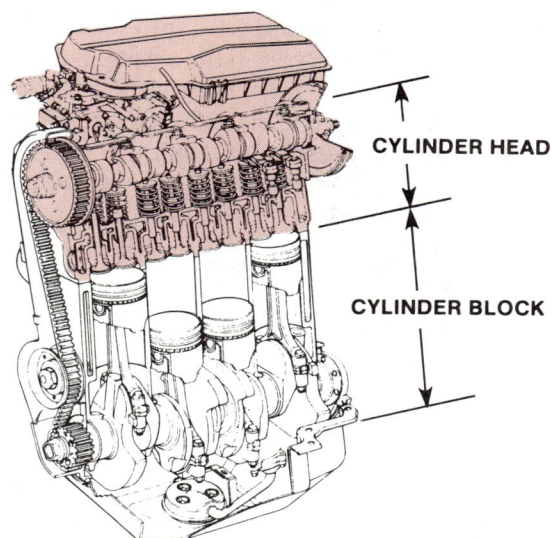

Figure 8-3 An engine can be divided into two main assemblies: the engine or cylinder block and the cylinder head.

The main bearing area of the block must be align bored to a diameter that will accept the crankshaft. Camshaft bearing surfaces must also be bored. The word bore means to drill or machine a hole. Align boring is a series of holes in a straight line.

Cast iron blocks offer great strength and controlled warpage due to heat. With the increased concern for improved gasoline mileage, however, car manufacturers are trying to make the vehicle lighter. One way to do this is to reduce the weight of the block. Aluminum is used for this purpose because it is a very light metal. Certain materials are added to the metal before it is poured into the mold. These materials are used to make the aluminum stronger and less likely to warp from the heat of combustion. Aluminum blocks normally have a sleeve or steel liner placed in them to serve as cylinder walls. Steel liners are placed in the mold before the metal is poured. After the metal is poured, the steel liner cannot be removed.

Silicon has also been added to the aluminum. Through a special process, called silicon-impregnation, the silicon is concentrated on the cylinder walls, eliminating the need for a steel liner. One problem with this design is that it requires the use of very high-quality engine oils. Because of owner neglect, this type of engine block does not usually survive its intended service life, and therefore is not widely used.

Lubrication and Cooling

The cylinder block contains a series of oil passages that allow engine oil from the oil pan to be pumped through the block and crankshaft and on to the cylinder head. The oil lubricates, cools, and cleans engine components (Figure 8-4).

Because engines are not 100% efficient, they generate heat. This heat must be removed from engine parts

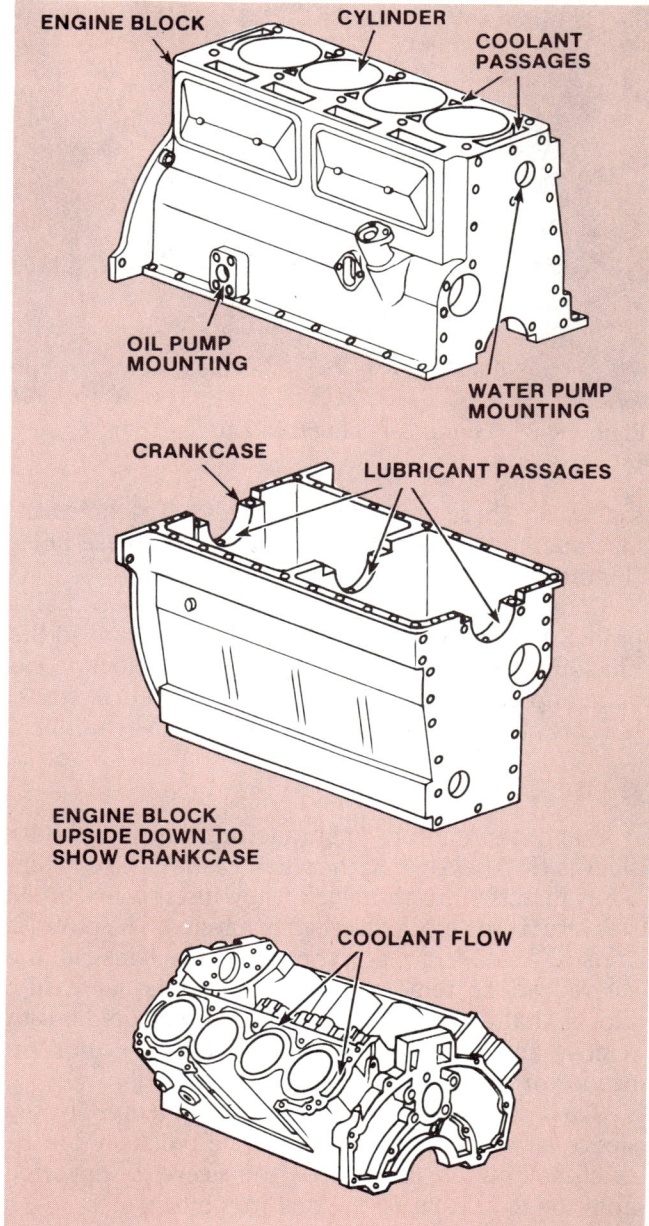

Figure 8-4 Oil and coolant passages in in-line and V-type engine blocks.

before it can cause damage. This is the job of the liquid coolant system. Water jackets are cast in the cylinder block around the cylinder bores. As shown in Figure 8-4, coolant circulates through these jackets to transfer heat away from these areas.

Core Plugs

All cylinder blocks use core plugs. These are also called freeze or expansion plugs. During the manufacturing process, sand cores are used. These cores are partly broken and dissolved when the hot metal is poured into the mold. However, holes have to be placed in the block to get the sand out of the internal pas-

148 Section 2 Engines

Figure 8-5 Typical core plug locations.

sageways. These are called core holes. The holes are machined and core plugs are placed into these holes (Figure 8-5).

Core plugs are made of soft metal. They can also protect the block from cracking. If the coolant in the block freezes, it will expand causing the block to expand and crack. Rather than having the block crack, the core plugs may pop out and possibly save the block.

Cylinder Sleeves

Some automobile manufacturers use cylinder sleeves (Figure 8-6). Rather than casting the cylinder bores directly into the block, they insert a machined sleeve after the block has been machined. The purpose of using a sleeve is that if the cylinder is damaged, the sleeve can be removed and replaced rather easily. Blocks that do not have sleeves must be bored out to remove any damage. After boring, larger pistons are needed or standard-sized sleeves are added.

There are two types of sleeves: wet and dry. The dry sleeve is pressed into a hole in the block. It can be machined quite thin because the sleeve is supported from top to bottom by the cast-iron block.

The wet sleeve is also pressed into the block. Coolant touches the center part of the sleeve. This is why it is called a wet sleeve. It must be machined thicker than the dry sleeve because it is supported only on the top and bottom. Seals must be used on the top and bottom of the wet sleeve to keep the coolant from leaking out. Wet sleeves are used on some larger diesel engines.

❏ CYLINDER BLOCK RECONDITIONING

Before any reconditioning or rebuilding work is started, threaded holes should be cleaned with the correct size tap to remove any and all burrs or dirt and to allow for proper bolt torquing (Figure 8-7). Use a bottoming tap in any blind holes. Chamfering or counterboring will eliminate thread pulls and jagged edges. All burrs and casting slag should be removed from inside the block with a high-speed grinder.

Deck Flatness

The top of the engine block, where the cylinder head mounts, is called the deck. To check deck warpage, use a precision straightedge and feeler gauge (Figure 8-8) to measure the deck in each direction. With the straightedge positioned diagonally across the deck, the amount of warpage is determined by the size of feeler gauge that fits into the gap between the deck and the straightedge.

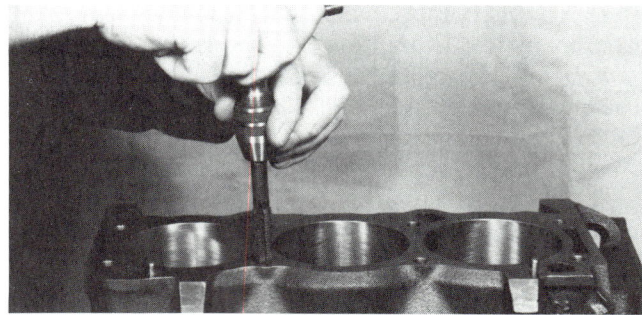

Figure 8-7 All threaded bores in the engine block should be cleaned with the correct size tap. *Courtesy of Perfect Circle/Dana*

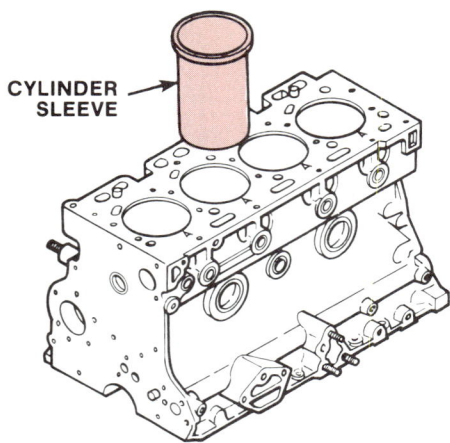

Figure 8-6 A cylinder sleeve is fitted into the bore to serve as a wear surface for the piston rings.

Figure 8-8 Checking for deck warpage with a straightedge and feeler gauge.

Figure 8-9 A dial indicator and arbor can also be used to check for deck warpage. *Courtesy of Goodson Shop Supplies*

> ### SHOP TALK
> Instead of using a straightedge and feeler gauge, many technicians prefer to make the warpage test with an arbor and gauge. Roll the dial indicator along the arbor and across the surface of the block. It can also be used to check the head for warpage (Figure 8-9).

Some engines have special sealing surface flatness requirements. Consult the manufacturer's specifications. If specifications are not available, use 0.003 inch per 6 inches, and no more than 0.006-inch maximum on any length. New or resurfaced tolerances are usually 0.001 inch. In most cases, if more than one head is used on an engine, all must be resurfaced an equal amount to maintain uniform compression and manifold alignment. If the gasket surface of the block is warped and not corrected, valve seat distortion will occur when the head is tightened to the block. Coolant and combustion leakage can also occur.

Two other reasons a technician might elect to resurface are to blend the sleeves into the deck surface after sleeving or to obtain uniform cylinder length for performance or blueprint work. Blocks can be refinished by broaching, milling, or grinding. Any of these methods is acceptable as long as the proper surface finish is obtained.

Cylinder Walls

Inspect the cylinder walls for scoring, roughness, or other signs of wear. Ring and cylinder wall wear can be accelerated by an abrasive environment. Abrasive particles that get between mated moving parts grind away at the adjoining surfaces and remove material from the parts. Abrasive particles can include metallic debris in the engine, which is a result of wear and nonmetallic dirt particles that entered the engine during operation or maintenance. The source of contamination should be located and corrected to avoid a recurrence of the problem.

> ### CUSTOMER CARE
> If the cause of the engine problem is customer neglect, inform the customer of this. Do so in an understanding way. Never make the customer feel stupid.

Piston ring, piston, and cylinder wall damage can also be caused by scuffing and scoring. Grooves cut in these parts act as passages for oil to bypass the rings and enter the combustion chamber. Scuffing and scoring occur when the oil film on the cylinder wall is ruptured, allowing metal-to-metal contact of the piston and rings on the cylinder wall. The heat generated causes momentary welding of the contacting parts. The reciprocating movement of the piston breaks these welds, cutting grooves in the ring faces, piston skirt, and cylinder wall. Cooling system hot spots, oil contamination, and fuel wash are significant causes of this problem.

A problem affecting the newer thin-wall engines is block distortion. Out-of-round cylinders break the face seal between the rings and cylinder wall permitting the passage of oil into the combustion chamber (Figure 8-10).

The cylinder heads and main bearing caps induce stresses in the block. These stresses must be duplicated when the cylinders are being oversized or bored, particularly if the block is of the thin-wall design. To accomplish this, the main bearing caps should be installed and torqued to specifications. Torque or deck plates should be bolted to the block to simulate the effect of the cylinder heads so that the bores will be round when the engine is assembled. Omission of these steps on some blocks will almost certainly cause distortion and oil consumption.

Cylinder Bore Inspection

Cylinder bore wear is not uniform (Figure 8-11). Maximum wear occurs at the top of the ring travel area.

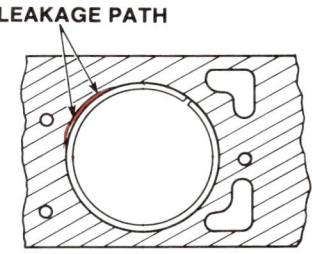

Figure 8-10 Checking for oil leakage past the piston rings.

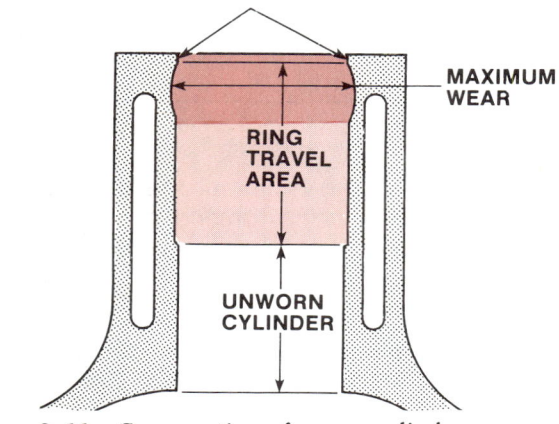

Figure 8-11 Cross section of a worn cylinder.

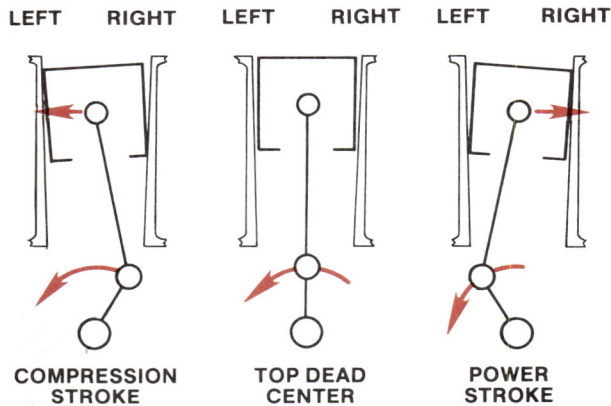

Figure 8-12 When piston slap occurs, the cylinder bore wears most at the top.

Pressure on the top ring is at a peak and lubrication at a minimum when the piston is at the top of its stroke. Shallow depressions form at the top of the cylinder on the thrust faces, giving the cylinder an oval shape at the top. A ridge of unworn material will remain above the upper limit of ring travel. Below the ring travel area, wear is negligible because only the piston skirt contacts the cylinder wall. Piston slap is one of the major causes of more wear at the top of the cylinder and less at the bottom (Figure 8-12).

There are several requirements for a properly reconditioned cylinder. It must be the correct diameter, have no taper or runout (out-of-round), and the surface finish must be such that the piston rings will seat to form a seal that will minimize blowby and control oil.

Taper is the difference in diameter between the cylinder bore at the bottom of the hole and the bore at the top of the hole—just below the ridge (Figure 8-13). Subtracting the smaller diameter from the larger one gives the cylinder taper. Some taper is permissible, but normally not more than 0.006 inch. If taper is less than 0.006 inch, it is possible to get by with just a re-ring job as opposed to reboring.

Cylinder out-of-roundness is the difference between the measurement parallel with the crank and the mea-

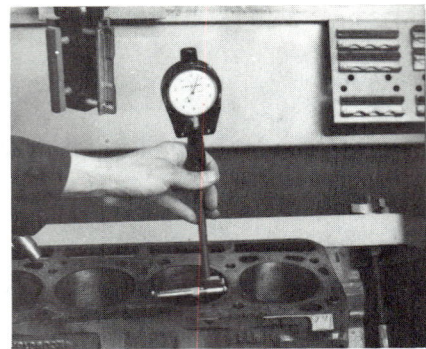

Figure 8-13 Cylinder taper is determined by measuring the diameter of the bore at the top of ring travel and comparing it to the diameter at the bottom of ring travel. *Courtesy of Goodson Shop Supplies*

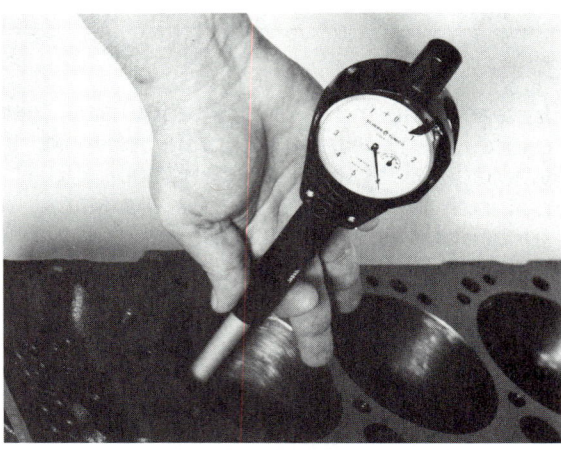

Figure 8-14 Measuring out-of-roundness with a dial bore gauge. *Courtesy of Atlas Engineering and Manufacturing, Inc.*

surement perpendicular to the crank (Figure 8-14). Out-of-roundness is measured at the top of the cylinder just below the ridge. Typically, the maximum allowable out-of-roundness is 0.0015 inch. Normally the diameter of a cylinder is measured with a dial bore gauge. A telescoping gauge (Figure 8-15) can also be used.

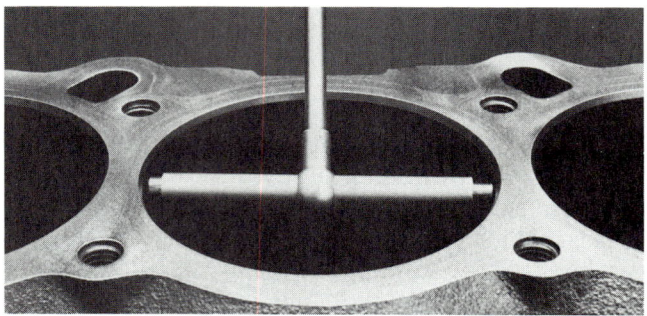

Figure 8-15 After the telescoping gauge has been expanded to fit the bore, it is measured with a micrometer. *Courtesy of Perfect Circle/Dana*

Cylinder Bore Surface Finish

The surface finish on a properly prepared cylinder wall acts as a reservoir for oil to lubricate the piston rings and prevent piston and ring scuffing primarily during break-in. Piston ring faces can be damaged and experience premature wear if the cylinder wall is too rough. A surface that is too smooth will not allow the rings to seat properly.

Obtaining the optimum cylinder surface finish is one of the most important operations of an engine overhaul because it is a primary factor in good oil control. There are probably almost as many theories on cylinder finishing as there are those on doing the work. Unfortunately, many of these theories are not supported by facts.

CYLINDER DEGLAZING If the inspection and measurements of the cylinder wall prove that surface conditions, the taper, and out-of-round are within acceptable limits, only the cylinder walls need to be deglazed. Combustion heat, engine oil, and piston movement combine to form a thin residue on the cylinder walls that is commonly called glaze.

CAUTION: Always wear eye protection when operating deglazing, honing, or boring equipment.

The two most common types of glaze breakers are shown in Figure 8-16. With either type, use an abrasive with about 220 or 280 grit. The driver end of the glaze breaker is installed in a slow-moving electric drill that operates at 300 to 500 rpm or in a honing machine. Various sizes of resilient-based hone-type brushes are available for honing and deglazing (Figure 8-17).

Deglazing residue and metal fragments adhering to the cylinder walls are abrasive and will quickly damage the rings, pistons, and cylinders if not removed. Using plenty of hot, soapy water, a stiff bristle brush, and a soft, lint-free cloth is the best way to clean the residue

Figure 8-16 Two types of glaze breakers. *Courtesy of K-Line Industries*

Figure 8-17 Using a resilient-based, hone-type brush, commonly called a ball hone.

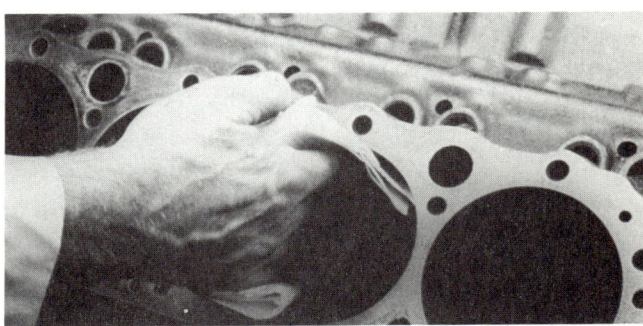

Figure 8-18 After honing, clean with soapy water and a soft, lint-free cloth. *Courtesy of TRW, Inc.*

(Figure 8-18). Then rinse the block with clear water and dry thoroughly. Lightly coat all machined areas of the engine with clean, light engine oil to prevent rust. Cylinder cleanliness can be checked by wiping them with a clean white cloth after oiling. The cylinder walls can be considered free of abrasive residue when the cloth remains clean.

SHOP TALK

If the cylinders have varnish deposits, they can be swabbed with lacquer thinner to remove the varnish. Should the cylinders be lightly scuffed or scratched, light honing is recommended. Also, remember to adhere to the engine manufacturer's instructions.

CYLINDER BORING When cylinder surfaces are badly worn or excessively scored or when a perfectly straight (no taper) cylinder is desired, a boring bar is needed to bore the cylinders for oversize pistons or sleeves. A boring bar leaves a pattern on the cylinder wall similar

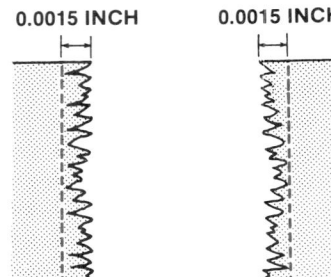

Figure 8-19 Typical bore pattern created by a boring bar.

to uneven screw threads (Figure 8-19). The tool causes surface fractures in the metal. These fractures generally extend to a depth of 0.0005 to 0.001 inch below the surface. This makes it necessary to finish hone after rough sizing the cylinder to remove fractured metal fragments so that the proper finish can be applied to the base metal and the bore can be opened to the proper size. This size is determined by the size of the replacement pistons and rings, which will be larger to accommodate the larger bore.

As shown in Figure 8-20, there are two types of boring machines: (A) stationary and (B) portable. Boring bars and boring-bar operators vary in their ability to make a good cylinder wall finish.

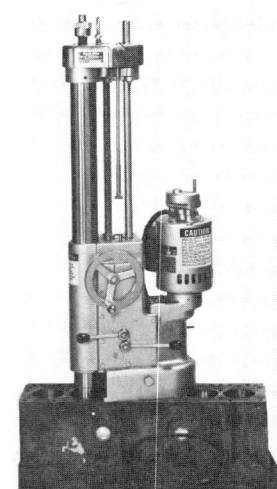

Figure 8-20 (A) Stationary and (B) portable boring machines. *Courtesy of Sunnen Products Co.*

CYLINDER HONING The honing operation after cylinder boring is vitally important to obtaining proper ring and cylinder seating. Failure to remove adequate stock (0.003-inch minimum) from the cylinders by honing can result in leaving traces of the boring bar's cutter markings. The torn and fragmented cylinder surface can retain a sufficient amount of lubrication to retard seating (wear-in) of the cylinder surface. Such a surface can only result in poor oil control, blowby, and a dissatisfied customer. Honing will leave the cylinder with the proper surface so that it will distribute oil, serve as an oil reservoir, and provide a place for worn metal and abrasive particles. At the same time, it must have sufficient flat areas or plateaus to act as a bearing surface on which an oil film can form (Figure 8-21).

A conventional rigid hone usually consists of two stones mounted opposite each other on a holder with guides located at right angles between them (Figure 8-22). The hone rotates at a selected speed. It also reciprocates in the cylinder either manually or automatically, depending on the type of equipment. Outward pressure is applied to the stones so they will remove stock from the cylinder while turning. Coolant, which is a special honing oil, flows over the stones and cylinder to regulate the temperature and flush out metallic and abrasive residue. It is necessary to select the proper stones to obtain the correct cylinder surface finish. Honing stones are classified by grit size, although honing equipment manufacturers can also

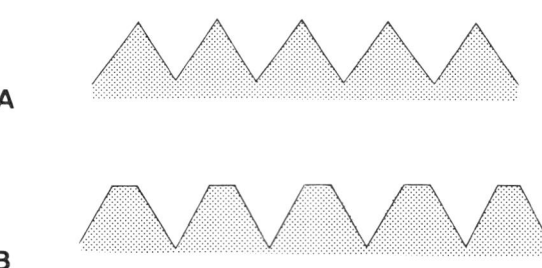

Figure 8-21 Comparison of (A) ridges and (B) plateaus on a honed cylinder surface.

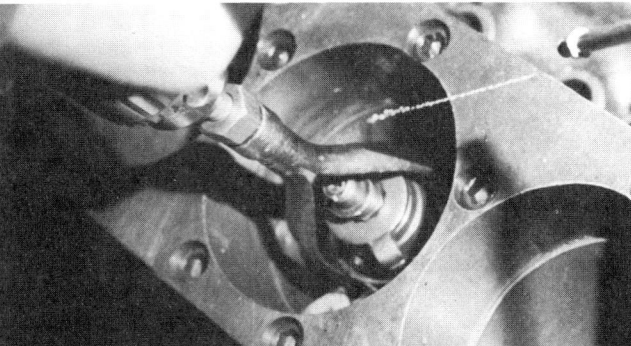

Figure 8-22 Using a rigid hone. *Courtesy of Sealed Power Corp.*

Short Blocks 153

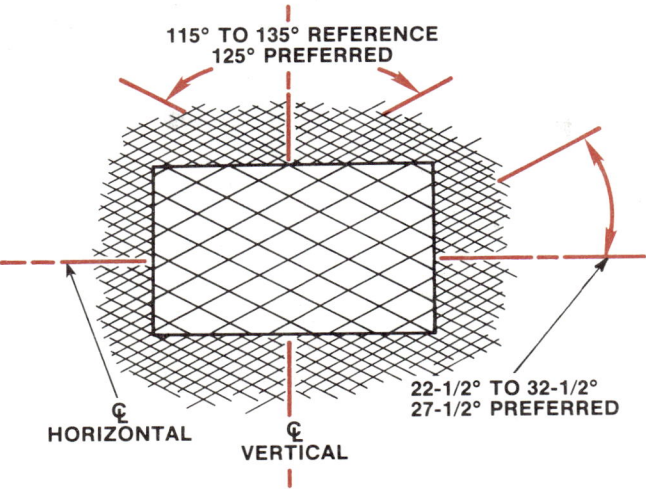

Figure 8-23 Ideal cylinder honing pattern. *Courtesy of Sealed Power Corp.*

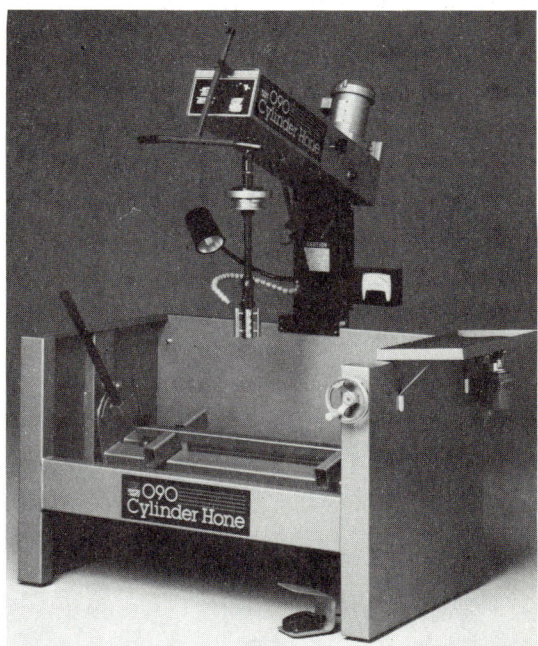

Figure 8-24 Automatic cylinder hone machine. *Courtesy of Kwik-Way Manufacturing Co.*

Figure 8-25 Torquing plates are fastened to the block during cylinder boring to prevent distortion. *Courtesy of Atlas Engineering and Manufacturing, Inc.*

have their own designation. The lower the grit number, the coarser the stone.

A honing stone has thousands of tiny cutting edges that leave a multitude of crisscross grooves in the cylinder wall (Figure 8-23). These cutting edges continually break away from a properly operated hone to expose new, sharp cutting edges. Millions of tiny diamond-shaped areas are generated during the honing process, which serve as lubricant reservoirs to maintain the oil film on which the piston rings ride. Ideally, these grooves cross at 50 degree angles, though anything in the 20- to 60-degree range is acceptable.

Cylinder hone machines are available in manual and automatic models (Figure 8-24). The major advantage of the automatic type is that it allows the machine operator to dial in the exact crosshatch angle required in both the upper and lower stops of the bore.

Torquing plates are usually fastened to the cylinder block to equalize or prevent twist and distortion, while honing or boring a cylinder (Figure 8-25). When honing, be sure to keep a good flow of honing oil.

Engines with cylinder walls too thin for boring, engines with oversize pistons, and engines with only one damaged cylinder can be reconditioned by sleeving. Sleeving involves boring the cylinder oversize, then installing a thin metal liner. The inside diameter of the sleeve is then bored, usually to the original or standard piston size. This procedure can be used in one or all of the engine's cylinders. Figure 8-26 shows two methods used to install a cylinder sleeve.

❏ INSTALLING CORE PLUGS

Old core and oil galley plugs are normally removed and replaced as part of cylinder block reconditioning. To install new core or soft plugs in the block, always use a nonhardening gasket sealer and the proper installation tool (Figure 8-27). It is important that the proper size and type are used. Check a service manual for the proper replacement numbers. Brass core plugs are often recommended because they will not rust.

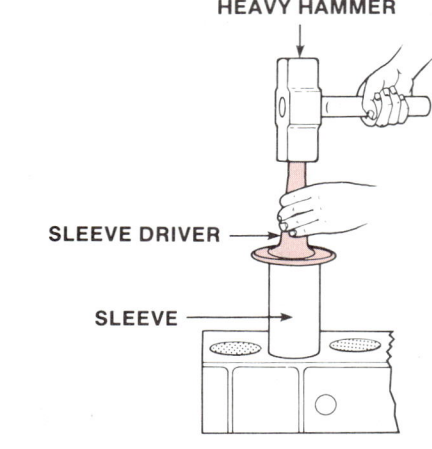

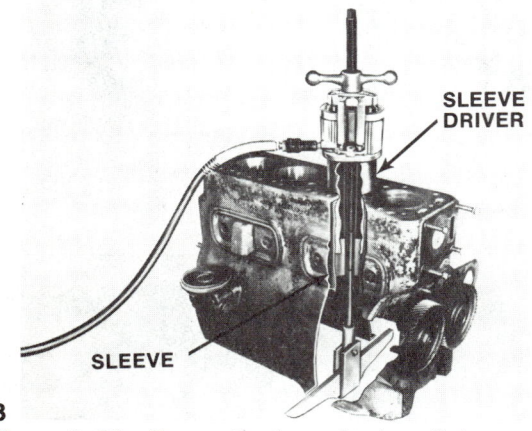

Figure 8-26 Two methods used to install sleeves: (A) driving and (B) pressing. *Courtesy of Goodson Shop Supplies*

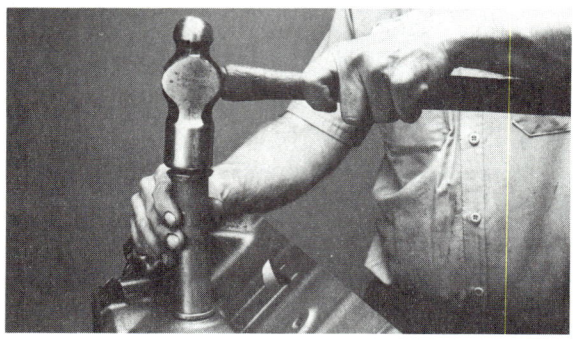

Figure 8-27 Steps in installing core plugs. *Courtesy of Goodson Shop Supplies*

Prior to installing a core plug, the plug bore should be inspected for any damage that would interfere with the proper sealing of the plug. If the bore is damaged, it will be necessary to true the surface by boring for the next specified oversize plug. Oversize (OS) plugs are identified by the OS stamped in the flat located on the cup side of the plug.

Coat the plug or bore lightly with an oil-resistant (oil galley) or water-resistant (cooling jacket) sealer. The three basic core plugs are installed as follows.

DISC- OR DISHED-TYPE This type fits in a recess in the engine casting with the dished side facing out (Figure 8-28A). With a hammer, hit the disc in the center of the crown and drive the plug into the bore until just the crown becomes flat. In this way the plug will expand properly and give a good tight fit.

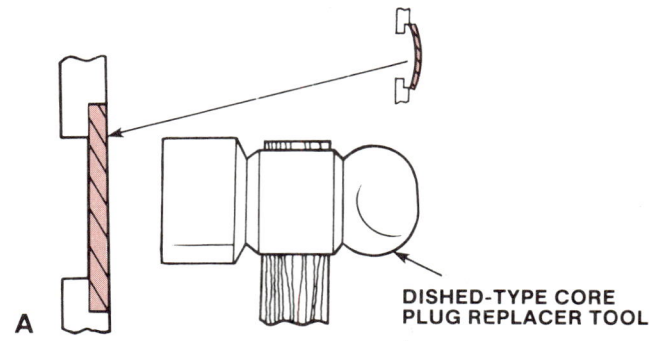

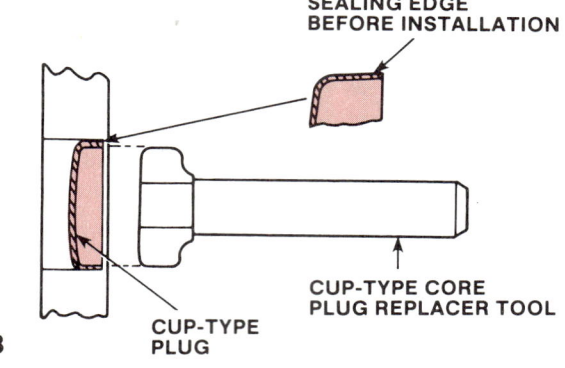

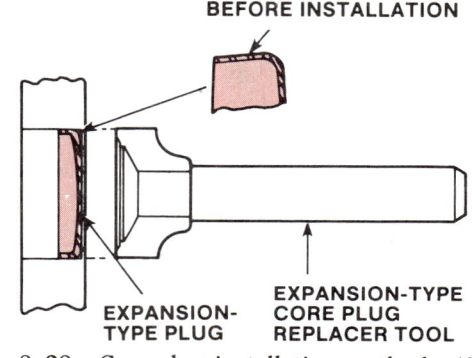

Figure 8-28 Core plug installation methods: (A) dished, (B) cup, and (C) expansion.

CUP-TYPE This type of plug is installed with the flanged edge outward (Figure 8-28B). The maximum diameter of this plug is located at the outer edge of the flange. The flange on cup-type plugs flares outward with the largest diameter at the outer (sealing) edge. The flanged (trailing) edge must be below the chamfered edge of the bore to effectively seal the plugged bore. If the core plug replacing tool has a depth seating surface, do not seat the tool against a nonmachined (casting) surface.

EXPANSION-TYPE This type of plug is installed with the flanged edge inward (Figure 8-28C). The maximum diameter of this plug is located at the base of the flange with the flange flaring inward. When installed, the trailing (maximum) diameter must be below the chamfered edge of the bore to effectively seal the plugged bore. As was the case with a cup-type, if the core plug replacing tool has a depth seating surface, do not seat the tool against a nonmachined (casting) surface.

❏ CRANKSHAFT

Crankshafts (Figure 8-29) are generally made of cast iron, forged cast steel, or nodular iron, and then machined. At the centerline of the crankshaft are the main bearing journals (Figure 8-30). These journals must be machined to a very close tolerance because the weight and movement of the crankshaft will be supported at these points. The number of main bearings is determined by the design of the engine. V-block engines generally have fewer main bearings than an in-line engine with the same number of cylinders. This is because the V-block engine uses a shorter crankshaft. Offset from the crankshaft centerline are the connecting rod bearing journals. The degree of offset and the number of journals are determined by engine design. An in-line six cylinder engine will have six connecting rod journals. A V-8 engine will have only four. Each journal will be connected to two connecting rods, one from each side of the V. The connecting rod journal is also called the crank pin. This area is machined

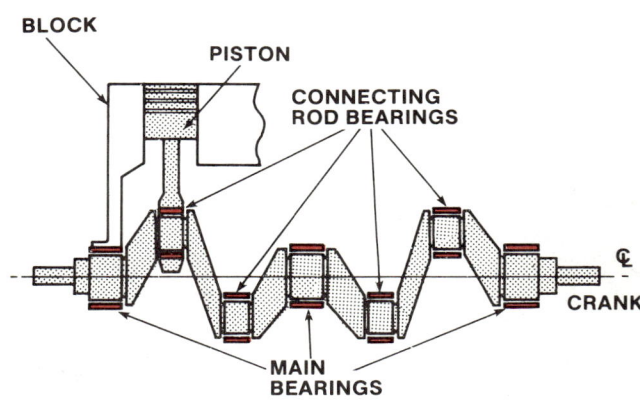

Figure 8-30 Crankshaft bearing and journal locations.

to a very close tolerance just like the main bearing journal. The machining of the main and rod bearing journals must have a very smooth surface at the bearing area. The bearings must fit tightly enough to eliminate noise but must also have a clearance between them and their bearings for an oil film of 0.0015 inch and 0.002 inch to form. This is usually checked by the use of plastigage that is available at most jobber stores.

The crankshaft does not turn directly on the bearings. It turns on a film of oil trapped between the bearing surface and the journal surface (Figure 8-31). This oil is supplied by the engine's oil pump. Should the crankshaft journals become out of round, tapered, or scored, the oil film will not form properly and the journal will contact the bearing surface. This causes early bearing or crankshaft failure. The main and rod bearings are generally made of lead-coated copper or tin and aluminum. Both of these are softer material than that used to form the crankshaft. By using the soft material, any wear will appear first on the bearings. Early diagnosis of bearing failure most often will spare the crankshaft and only the bearings will need to be replaced.

Figure 8-29 Typical crankshaft.

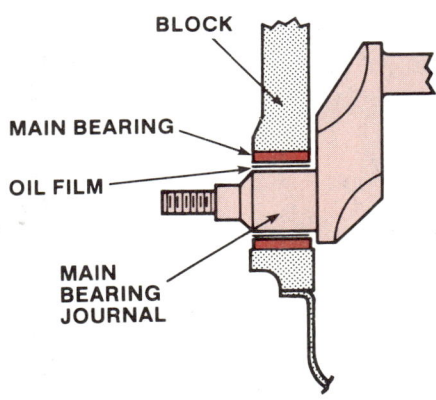

Figure 8-31 The crankshaft rotates on oil film between the bearing and journal.

156 Section 2 Engines

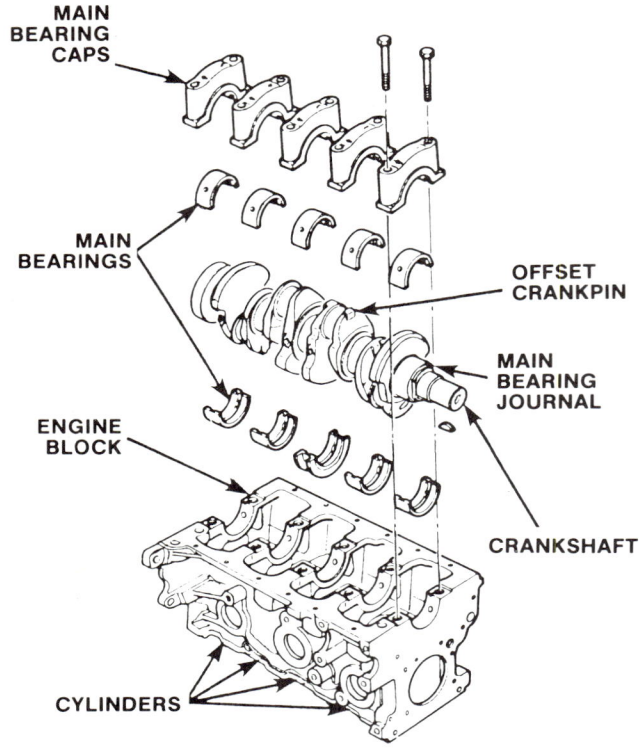

Figure 8-32 Bearings surround the journals in a crankshaft assembly.

As mentioned, the connecting rod journals are offset from the centerline of the crankshaft. This puts weight and piston pressure off center on the crankshaft. To balance this for smooth engine operation, counterweights must be added to the crankshaft. These weights are cast as part of the crankshaft and are positioned opposite the connecting rod journals.

Bearings surround each journal and are fed oil under pressure (Figure 8-32). In order for the oil to reach these bearings, oil passages must be drilled into the crankshaft. Each main bearing receives oil under pressure from the pump. Each main bearing journal will have a hole drilled into it with a connecting hole or holes leading to one or more rod bearing journals. In this way, all bearing journals receive oil under pressure to protect both the bearing and the journal. The crankshaft configuration determines the engine block design, or the positioning of the connecting rod journals around the centerline (₵) of the crankshaft (Figure 8-33).

The crankshaft has two distinct ends (Figure 8-34). One is called the flywheel end and, as its name implies, this is where the flywheel is connected to it. The front end or belt drive end of the crankshaft contains a threaded snout or is drilled and tapped. This is for attaching a vibration damper.

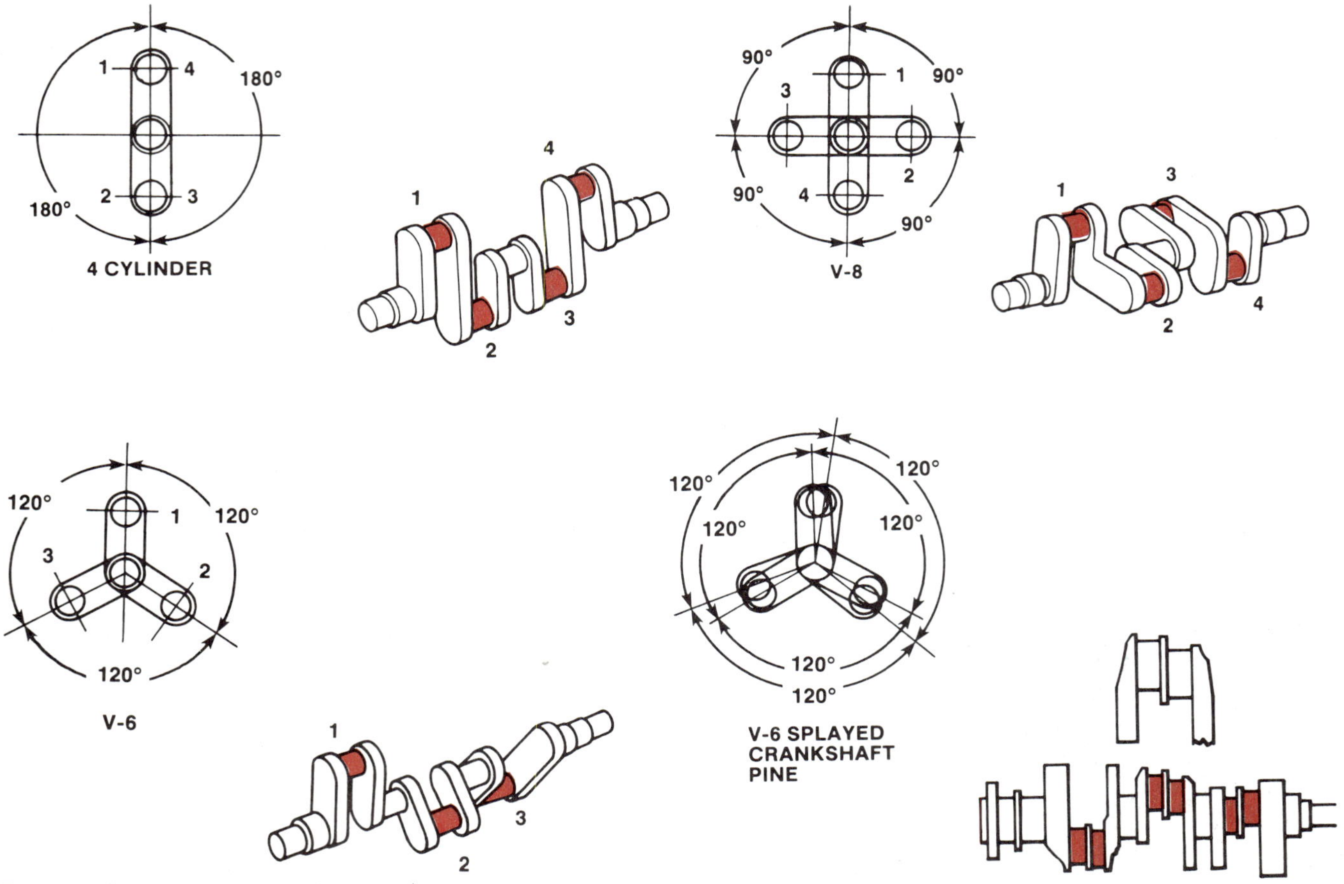

Figure 8-33 Various crankshaft configurations.

Short Blocks

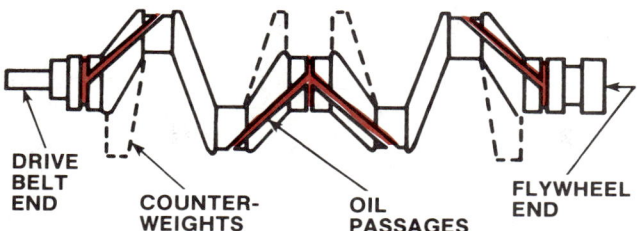

Figure 8-34 A crankshaft has two distinct ends: drive belt and flywheel.

CAUTION: Never lay down a crankshaft. It can warp out of shape or become bent. It should not be stored without proper support in the middle. Remember that all engine parts must be carefully stored.

Vibration Damper

The purpose of the vibration damper is to dampen crankshaft vibration. The crankshaft experiences a back-and-forth or twisting motion each time a cylinder fires. The force applied to the crankshaft can be more than two tons. This causes the crank to momentarily twist and snap back. The vibration damper (Figure 8-35) consists of a center section, which is attached to the crankshaft. Surrounding the center section is a strip of rubber-like material. Attached to the material is a grooved counterweight. As the crankshaft twists, the center section (A) applies a force to the material. The material must then apply this force to the counterweight (C). The weight is snapped in the direction of the crankshaft rotation to counterbalance the crankshaft connecting rod journal snapping back against the force due to ignition B. The back-and-forth movement of the crankshaft is counterbalanced by the back-and-forth movement of the vibration damper, and the engine runs smoothly.

Flywheel

The flywheel also adds to the smooth running of the engine by applying a constant moving force to carry the crankshaft from one firing stroke to the next. This is called inertia. Because of its large diameter, the flywheel makes a convenient point for the starter to connect to the engine. The large diameter supplies good gear reduction for the starter, making it easy for the starter to turn the engine against its compression. The surface of a flywheel may be used as part of the clutch. On an engine that drives an automatic transmission, a flex plate is used. The automatic transmission torque converter provides the weight required to attain flywheel functions.

Balancer Shafts

The crankshaft is one of the main sources of engine vibration because its shape makes it inherently out of balance as it rotates. On some engines a balancer shaft (Figure 8-36) is employed to reduce vibration.

In its basic form, the balancer shaft is fitted with counterweights designed to mirror the throws on the crankshaft. It is driven directly by the crankshaft but in the opposite direction. As the engine turns, the two out-of-balance shafts mutually cancel out any vibrations.

☐ CRANKSHAFT INSPECTION AND REBUILDING

Examine the crankshaft carefully. Check for the following.

- Are the vibration damper and flywheel mounting surfaces eroded or fretted?

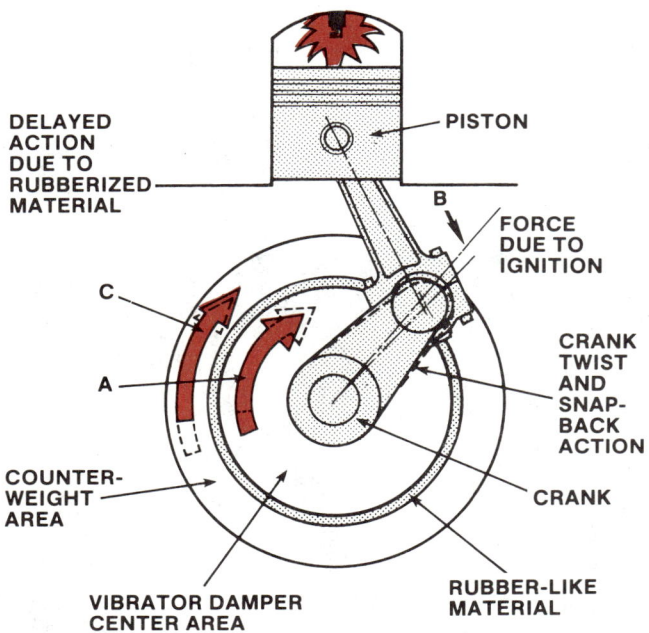

Figure 8-35 Typical vibration damper.

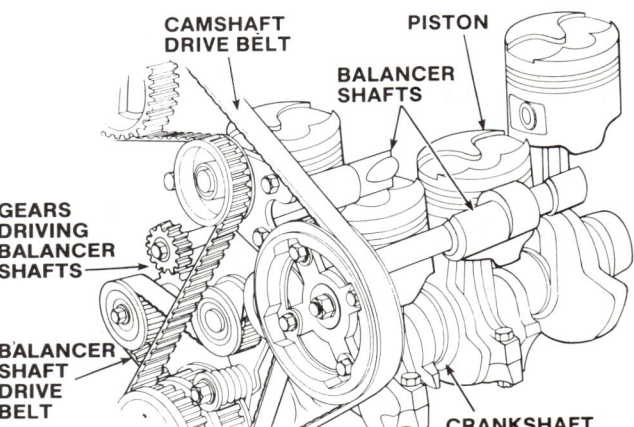

Figure 8-36 Balancer shaft location.

- Are there indications of damage from previous engine failures?
- Do any of the journal diameters show signs of heat checking or discoloration from high operating temperatures?
- Are any of the sealing surfaces deeply worn, sharply ridged, or scored?
- Are there any signs of surface cracks or hardness distress?

If any or all of these conditions are present, document the area(s) of concern on the repair order and mark the areas for further evaluation.

To measure the rod journal (often called a throw or crank pin) diameter, use an outside micrometer (Figure 8-37). A micrometer can also be used to measure the journals for out-of-roundness and taper (Figure 8-38). Taper is measured from one side of the journals to the other. The maximum taper is 0.001 inch.

Compare these measurements to specifications and establish wear limits to determine the undersize the crankshaft is to be reground. Mark the repair order and the crankshaft to indicate the undersizing requirements and reference source for making these determinations. Generally, rebuilt crankshafts are used for replacement. Be sure that they meet specifications.

> **USING SERVICE MANUALS**
> Crankshaft specifications can be found in the engine specification section of a service manual.

Checking Crankshaft Saddle Alignment

Figure 8-39 is an exaggerated illustration of crankcase housing bores out of alignment. If the engine is operated with a warped housing centerline, the crankshaft will inflict heavy false loads on one side of the main bearings. Depending upon the direction of the bowing or warpage of the main bearing housing bores, any side of the main bearings can become distressed. Engine blocks that are not severely warped can be repaired by an operation called line boring, a machining operation in which the main bearing housing bores are rebored to standard size and in perfect alignment (Figure 8-40).

To check the alignment of the crankshaft saddle bore, place an accurately ground arbor into the saddles (Figure 8-41). It should be 0.001 inch less in diameter

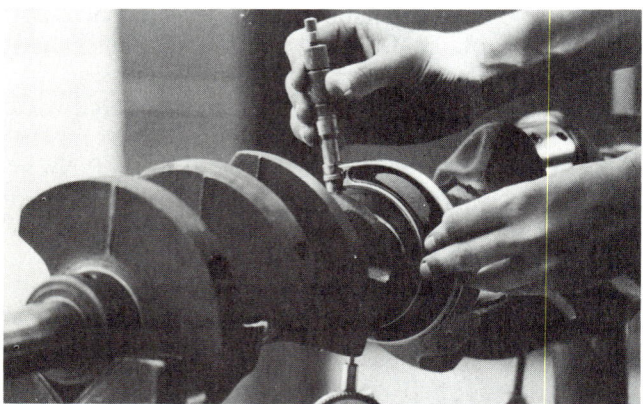

Figure 8-37 Measuring the connecting rod journal with a micrometer.

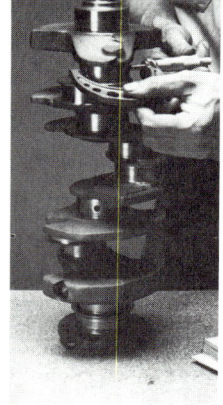

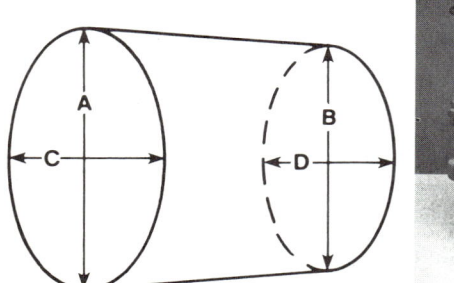

Figure 8-38 Checking for out-of-roundness and taper. *Courtesy of Perfect Circle/Dana*

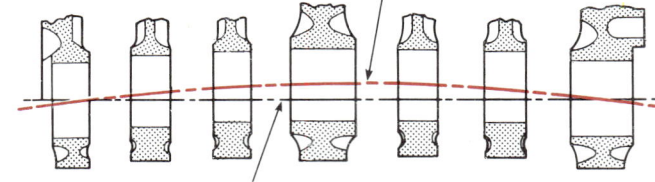

Figure 8-39 Exaggerated view of crankcase housing misalignment.

Figure 8-40 An engine block in a line boring machine.

Short Blocks 159

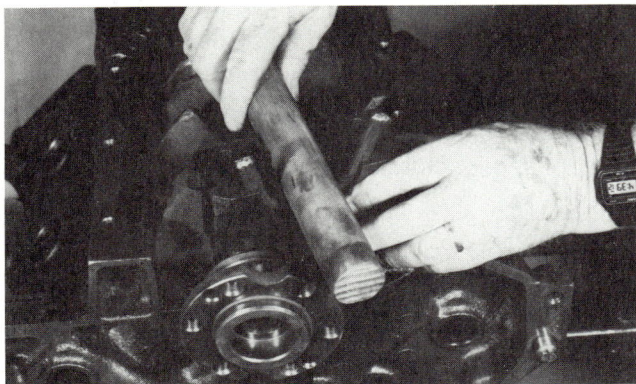

Figure 8-41 Checking crankshaft saddle bore alignment. *Courtesy of J. P. Industries, Inc.*

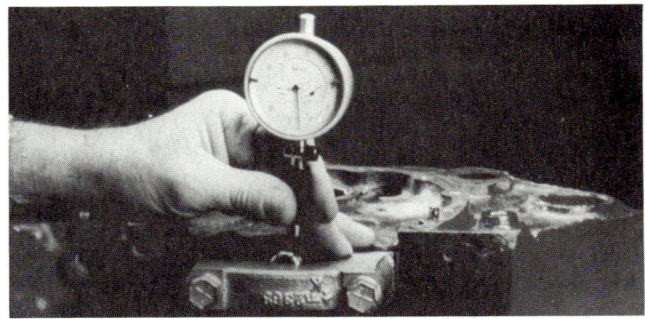

Figure 8-43 Main bearing saddles can be checked for out-of-roundness with a dial bore gauge. *Courtesy of Perfect Circle/Dana*

than the low limit of the saddle bore specification and a little longer than the crankshaft. After the arbor is in position, assemble the main bearing caps without their bearings and tighten the cap bolts to the recommended torque specification. Rotate the arbor using a bar approximately 1 foot long. If it will not turn, one or more of the bores might be out-of-round. The condition must be corrected before the engine is assembled.

If a proper arbor is not available, saddle alignment can be checked with a metal straightedge (Figure 8-42). Place the straightedge in the saddles as shown. Using a feeler gauge that is half the maximum specified oil clearance, try to slide the feeler under the straightedge. If this can be done at any saddle, the saddles are out of alignment and the block must be line-bored. Repeat this procedure at two other parallel positions in the saddles.

Out-of-roundness of the saddles can also be checked by bolting on the main bearing caps and checking each bore with a dial bore gauge or an out-of-roundness indicator (Figure 8-43).

Checking Crankshaft Straightness

To evaluate the alignment or straightness of the crankshaft, the check should be made with the shaft supported on the main bearing journals, not on the centers of the crankshaft. The recommended location for supporting the crankshaft is on the end main bearing journals.

The journal supports should be a matched pair of well-maintained V-blocks. V-blocks made with roller bearings can introduce erroneous values due to bearing tolerances and clearances. Consequently, the best practice is to avoid the roller type of V-blocks unless they are a calibrated set. Once the crankshaft is located in the V-blocks, select and position the indicator for measuring the alignment/bow of the crankshaft. The selected indicator should have an accuracy of no less than 0.001 inch per full scale deflection. Position the indicator at the 3 o'clock position on the center main bearing journal (Figure 8-44).

Set the indicator at 0 (zero) and turn the crankshaft through one complete 360-degree rotation. The total deflection of the indicator, the amount greater than zero plus the amount less than zero, is the total indicator reading (TIR). Bow is 50 percent of the TIR (Figure 8-45). The bow indication at this bearing establishes the bow of the crankshaft. Compare the bow of the

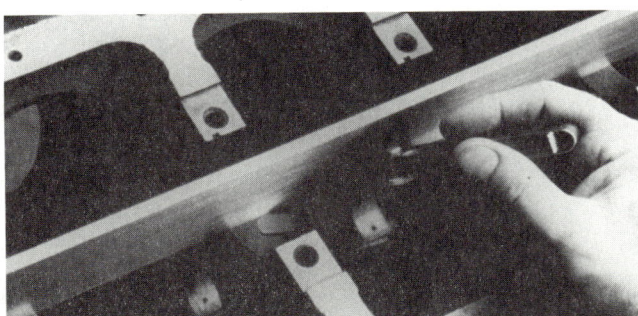

Figure 8-42 Checking bore alignment with a straightedge and feeler gauge. *Courtesy of TRW, Inc.*

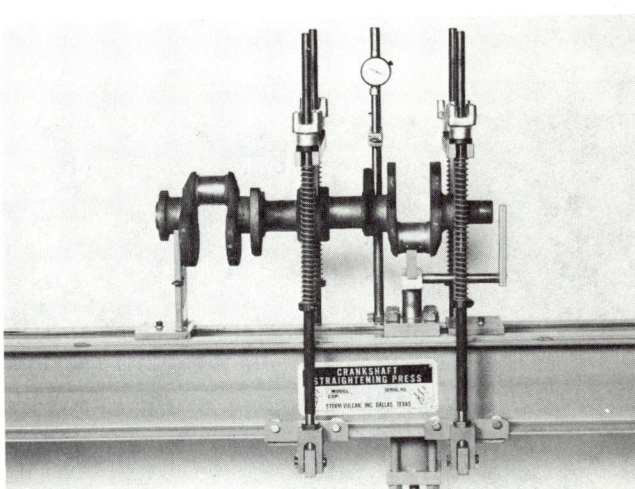

Figure 8-44 Checking the crankshaft for straightness. *Courtesy of Storm Vulcan, Inc.*

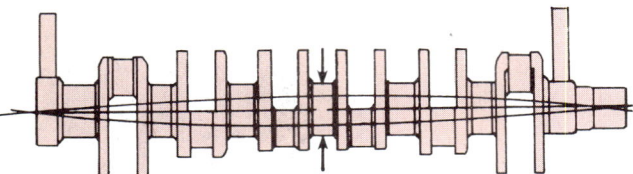

Figure 8-45 Evaluating alignment bow.

crankshaft to the acceptable alignment/bow specifications. Accept or reject as appropriate.

Checking Crankshaft Clearance and End Play

Clearance and end play should be checked before teardown is completed. The clearance check is made with a feeler gauge (Figure 8-46). The end play is checked with a dial gauge (Figure 8-47). Both checks should be within the specified limits given in the service manual.

Flywheel Inspection

Check the runout of the flywheel and carefully inspect its surface. Replacement or resurfacing may be required. When checking the flywheel in a vehicle with automatic transmission, it must be done with the torque converter bolted to the flex plate.

With both manual shift or automatic transmissions, inspect the flywheel for a damaged or worn ring gear. Remember that improper flywheel runout can cause vibrations, poor clutch action, and clutch slippage.

> **USING SERVICE MANUALS**
>
> Procedures and specifications for checking a flywheel or flex plate will be found in the engine or transmission section of most service manuals.

Crankshaft Bearings

Bearings are used to carry the critical loads created by crankshaft movement. They are a major wear item in the engine and require close inspection. Main bearings support the crankshaft journals that rest in the cylinder block. Connecting rod bearings are installed between the crankshaft and connecting rods.

The great majority of modern bearings are known as insert bearings. This name is derived from the fact that the bearing is made as a self-contained part and then inserted into the bearing housing. This type provides many advantages, including relative ease of replacement, greater variety of bearing materials, controlled lining thickness, and improved structure. Bearing thickness can be measured with a micrometer.

There are two types of insert bearings. Precision insert bearings are manufactured to close tolerances so that no further sizing is required at the time of assembly into the engine. Resizable insert bearings are manufactured with an extra-thick lining of bearing material on the inside diameter. This permits the bearing to be machined to any desired size up to and including standard size.

There are two basic designs of insert bearings (Figure 8-48). A full round (one piece) bearing is used in bores that allow the shaft's journals to be inserted into the bearing, such as with a camshaft. A split (two halves) bearing is used where the bearing must be assembled around the journal with the bearing hous-

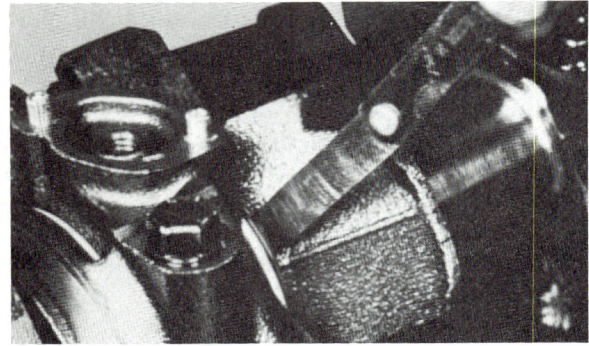

Figure 8-46 Checking crankshaft clearance with a feeler gauge. *Courtesy of Federal Mogul Corp.*

Figure 8-47 Checking crankshaft end play with a dial indicator. *Courtesy of Perfect Circle/Dana*

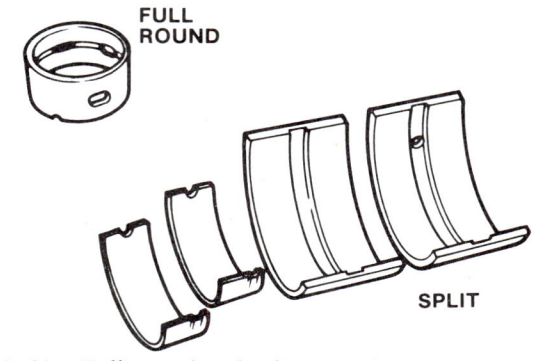

Figure 8-48 Full-round and split insert bearings.

ing being of two parts also, including a cap that holds the assembly together. Connecting rod bearings are split type.

The straight shell bearing and the flanged thrust bearing are two other configurations found in an automotive engine. The flanged thrust bearing provides the same support as the straight shell bearing, but also controls any horizontal movement or end play of the shaft. The connecting rod and most main bearings utilize the straight shell design. The flange bearing is used in the thrust position of the block. Most thrust main bearings are double flanged.

Bearing Spread

Most main and connecting rod bearings are manufactured with spread. Bearing spread means the distance across the outside parting edges of the bearing insert is slightly greater than the diameter of the housing bore. To position a bearing half that has spread, it must be snapped into place by a light forcing action (Figure 8-49). This assures positive positioning against the total bore and assists in subsequent assembly work by keeping the bearing halves in place.

Bearing Crush

Each half of a split bearing is made so it is slightly greater than an exact half. This can be seen quite easily when a half is snapped into place in its housing. The parting faces extend a little beyond the seat (Figure 8-50). This extension (as little as 0.001 inch) is called crush.

When the two bearing halves are assembled and the housing cap tightened, the crush sets up a radial pressure on the bearing halves so they are forced tightly into the housing bore.

Bearing Locating Devices

Engine bearings must be provided with some means to keep them from rotating or shifting sideways in their housings. There are a number of approaches to the problem with the specific design utilized being established by the original equipment manufacturer. The most common design is the locating lug. As shown in Figure 8-51, this consists of a protruding lug at the parting face of the bearing that nests into a slot in the housing that has been machined out to receive it.

Another approach is the locating dowel illustrated in Figure 8-52. The dowel can be located on the housing or on the back of the bearing, with the dowel hole located in the mating part. In some cases, there is a dowel hole in both parts, with the dowel inserted as a separate piece.

A third design, which is not commonly used, utilizes a flathead screw. It is secured to the housing through a hole in the crown of the bearing.

Oil Grooves

Providing an adequate oil supply to all parts of the bearing surface, particularly in the load area, is an absolute necessity. In many cases, this is accomplished by the oil flow through the bearing oil clearance. In other cases, however, engine operating conditions are such that this oil distribution method is inadequate. When this occurs, some type of oil groove must be added to the bearing. Some oil grooves are used to assure an adequate supply of oil to adjacent engine parts by means of oil throw-off.

Although oil grooves vary in size and shape, it has been found that a single groove works the best. A few typical oil grooves are shown in Figure 8-53.

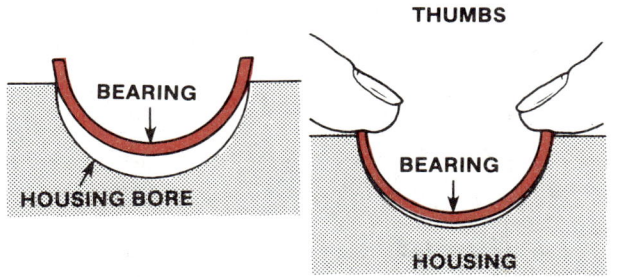

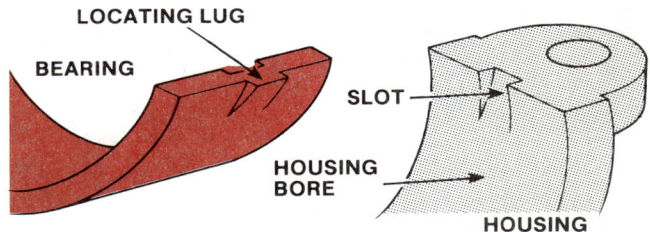

Figure 8-51 The locating lug fits into the slot in the housing.

Figure 8-49 Spread requires a bearing to be lightly snapped into place.

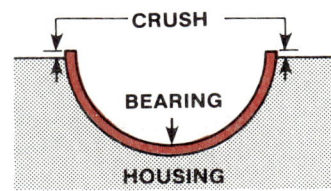

Figure 8-50 Crush assures good contact between the bearing and the housing.

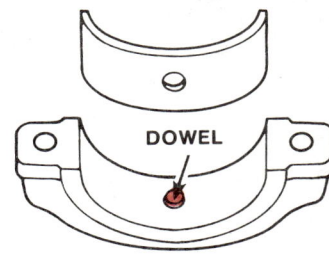

Figure 8-52 The locating dowel fits into the corresponding hole in the mating part.

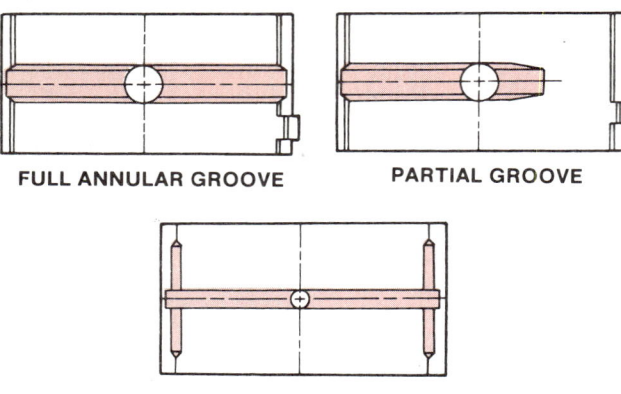

Figure 8-53 Typical bearing oil grooves.

Oil Holes

Oil holes are designed to allow the oil flowing through the engine block galleries to enter the bearing oil clearance space. Connecting rod bearings receive oil from the main bearings by means of rifled oilways in the crankshaft. Oil holes are also used to meter the amount of oil supplied to other parts of the engine. For example, oil spurt holes in connecting rods are often used to direct oil for the purpose of lubricating the cylinder walls. Oil spurt holes are also sometimes used in the bearing caps of the crankshaft main bearing (Figure 8-54). When the bearing is equipped with an

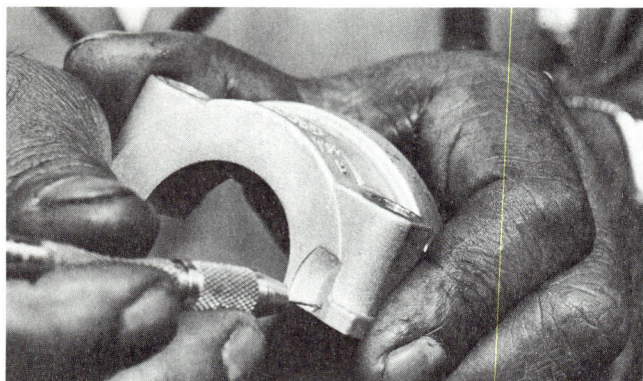

Figure 8-54 Oil holes are often used in the main bearing cap to lubricate the camshaft.

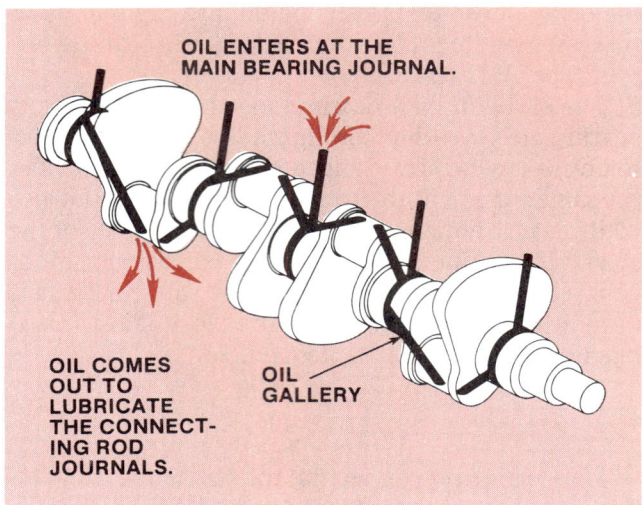

Figure 8-55 Crankshaft lubrication.

oil groove, the oil hole normally is in line with the groove.

The size and location of oil holes is critical. Thus, when replacement bearings are installed, care must be exercised to be sure that the oil hole matches the original equipment specifications. In addition to oil inlet holes, crankshafts are drilled with all the necessary passages (Figure 8-55) for lubrication.

Oil Clearance

Maintaining a specific oil clearance is critical to proper bearing operation. Many times, when wear on internal engine components such as the crankshaft is negligible, the proper oil clearance specifications can be restored with the installation of standard size replacement bearings. However, if the crankshaft is worn to the point where the installation of standard size bearings will result in excessive oil clearance space, a bearing with a thicker wall must be used to compensate. Although these bearings are thicker, they are known as undersize because the journals and crankpins of the crankshaft are smaller in diameter. In other words, they are under the standard size.

SHOP TALK

Worn crankshaft journals have the same effect on oil pressure as worn bearings. When they are worn, they will not give uniform oil clearance.

Undersize bearings are available in 0.001-inch or 0.002-inch sizes for shafts that are uniformly worn by that amount. Undersize bearings are also available in thicker sizes, such as 0.010 inch, 0.020 inch, and 0.030 inch, for use with crankshafts that have been refinished (or reground) to one of these standard undersizes.

Short Blocks   163

Figure 8-56 Polishing the journals will help determine if grinding is needed. *Courtesy of Perfect Circle/Dana*

SHOP TALK

If the journals measure within specifications but visual pits and gouges exist, polish the worst journal to determine whether or not grinding is necessary (Figure 8-56). If polishing the journal achieves smoothness, then grinding is probably not necessary. If the crankshaft does not have to be reground, check it for straightness.

Bearing Failure and Inspection

As shown in Figure 8-57, bearings can fail due to a wide variety of reasons. Dirt infiltration and oil starvation are the major reasons for bearing failure. Insufficient or excessive crush is also a common cause. Problems in other engine components, such as bent or twisted crankshafts or connecting rods, or out-of-shape journals, can also cause bearings to wear irregularly.

A complete listing of bearing related problems, their symptoms, probable causes, and remedies is given in the Tech Manual that accompanies this textbook.

❑ INSTALLING MAIN BEARINGS AND CRANKSHAFT

When selecting a new main bearing, remember that it must match the crankshaft journal diameter and main bearing housing size. If the crankshaft has been ground undersize, the main bearings will also have to be undersize. Similarly, if the housing bores have been machined oversize by align boring or align honing, the bearings must take up this space. Bearing size is usual-

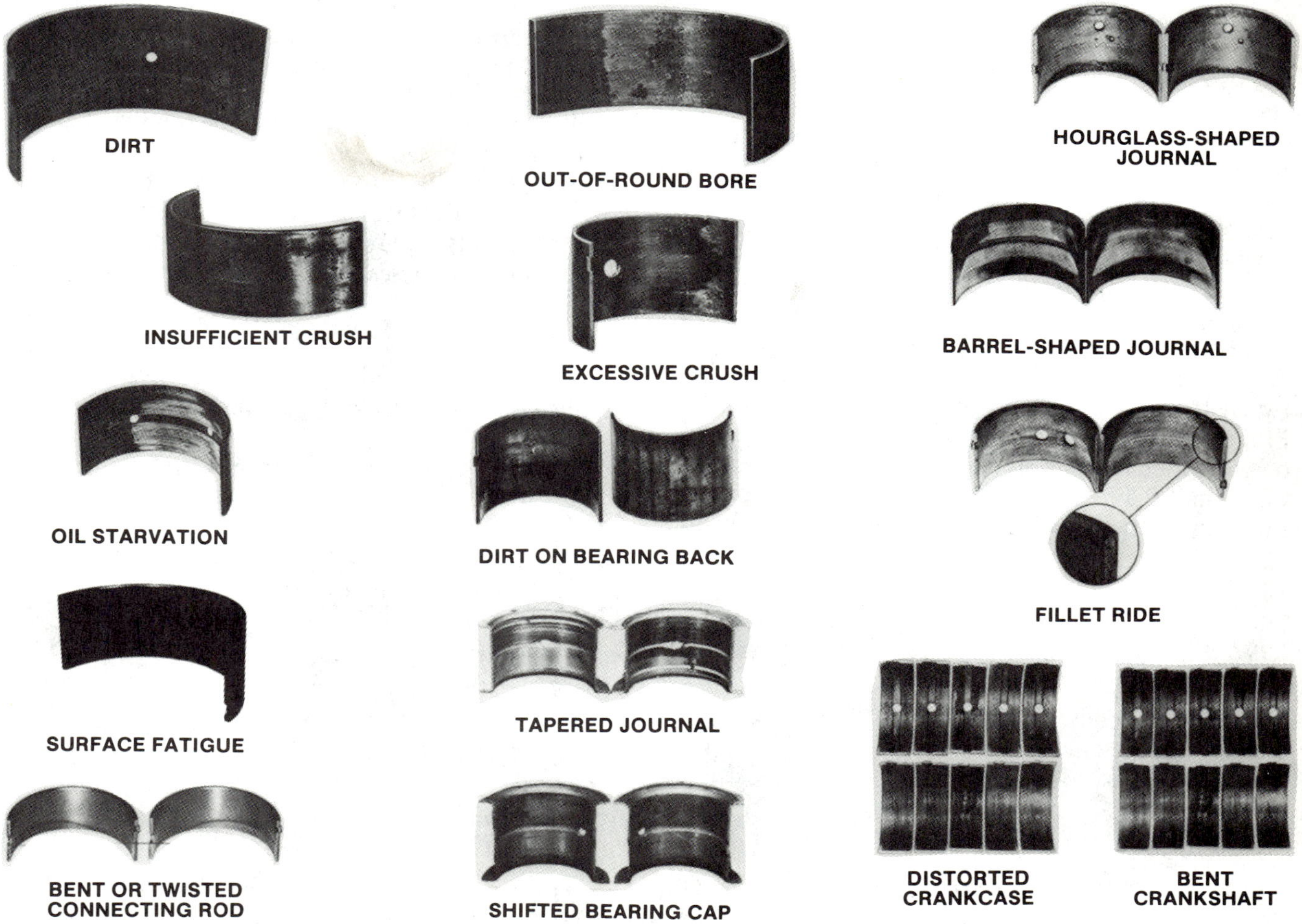

Figure 8-57 Common forms of bearing distress. *Courtesy of J. P. Industries, Inc.*

Figure 8-58 Crankshaft in main bearing saddles with the main bearings installed.

ly marked on the bearing box and on the back of the bearing.

Consult the engine manufacturer's service literature for the exact engine buildup procedures. When the bearings are ready to be installed in the main bearing bores, make sure the bore is clean and dry before installing the bearing halves into place (Figure 8-58). Use a clean, lint-free cloth to wipe the bearing back and bore surface. Be certain that nothing is placed between the bearing back and the surface of the housing bore.

Put the new main bearing inserts into each of the main bearing caps and into the cylinder block housings. Be sure to wipe the caps and housings perfectly clean and dry first. Make sure all holes align (Figure 8-59). The backs of the main bearing inserts should never be oiled or greased. Place the crankshaft in the block on the new main bearing inserts and arrange the main bearing caps in the correct order and direction over the crankshaft. Follow the factory markings or use those made during disassembly.

The next step is to measure the oil clearance between the crankshaft and the main bearing inserts. Proper lubrication and cooling of the bearing depend on correct crankshaft oil clearances. Scored bearings, worn crankshaft, excessive cylinder wear, stuck piston rings, and worn pistons can result from too small an oil clearance. If the oil clearance is too great, the crankshaft might pound up and down, overheat, and weld itself to the insert bearings.

Plastigage is fine, plastic string used to measure the oil clearance between the insert bearing and the crankshaft. The soft plastic string is relatively long and has a small diameter. The procedure for checking bearing clearance with plastigage is outlined in Photo Sequence 4 included in this chapter.

One side of the plastigage has clearance stripes for U.S. standard measurements. The other side has stripes for measuring clearance in metric measurements. The string can be purchased to measure different clearance ranges. Usually, only the smallest clearance range is necessary for reassembly work. Plastigage designed to measure wide clearances can be used for troubleshooting worn engines.

It is also possible to measure the end play with a feeler gauge by prying the crankshaft rearward and measuring the clearance between the cap and the counterweight with a blade. Insert the feeler gauge at several locations around the rear thrust bearing face. If end play is uniform at all locations and the measurements are within specifications, the end play is correct.

If the end play is within the specified limits, the job is done. If the end play is too large or too small, the main bearing with the thrust surface must be exchanged for one with a thicker or thinner thrust surface. If the engine has thrust washers or shims, thicker or thinner washers or shims must be used.

Most engines require the installation of main bearing seals during the final installation of the crankshaft. Always follow the recommended procedures for installing these seals, as given in the service manual. More details about these seals will be given in a later chapter.

Connecting Rod

The connecting rod is used to transmit the pressure applied on the piston to the crankshaft (Figure 8-60).

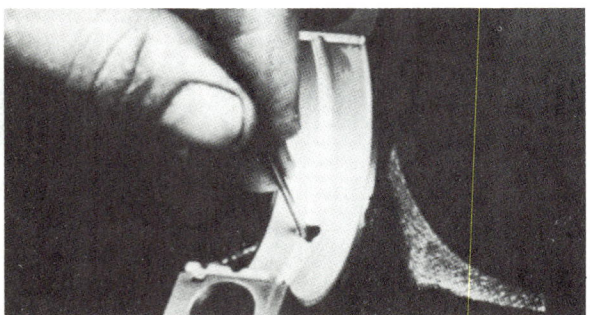

Figure 8-59 Align the oil holes in the bearings with those in the saddle. *Courtesy of Federal Mogul Corp.*

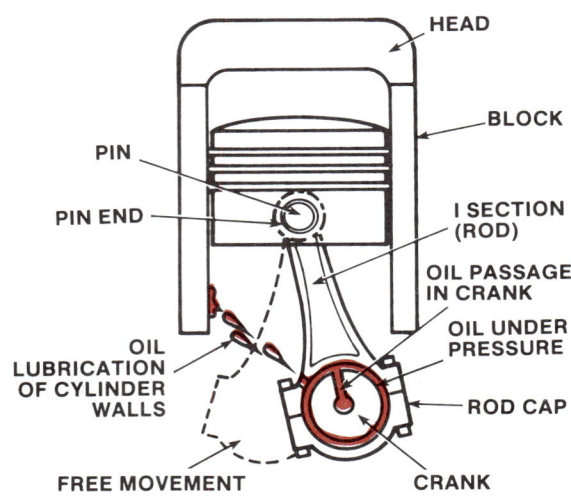

Figure 8-60 Typical connecting rod.

PHOTO SEQUENCE 4

☐ CHECKING MAIN BEARING CLEARANCE WITH PLASTIGAGE

P4-1 Checking main bearing clearance begins with mounting the engine block upside down on an engine stand.

P4-2 Install main bearings into bores, being careful to properly seat them.

P4-3 Wipe the bearings with a clean lint-free rag.

P4-4 Wipe the crankshaft journals with a clean rag.

P4-5 Carefully install the crankshaft into the bearings. Try not to allow the crankshaft to move on the bearing surfaces.

P4-6 Place a piece of plastigage on the journal. The piece should fit between the radii of the journal.

(continued)

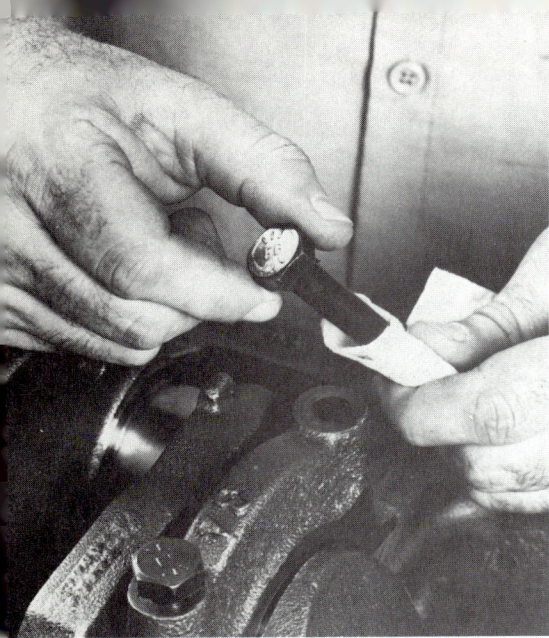

P4-7 Install the main caps in their proper locations and directions. Wipe the threads of the cap bolts with a clean rag.

P4-8 Install the cap bolts and tighten them according to the manufacturer's recommendations.

P4-9 Remove the main caps and observe the spread of the plastigage. If the gage did not spread, try again with a larger gage.

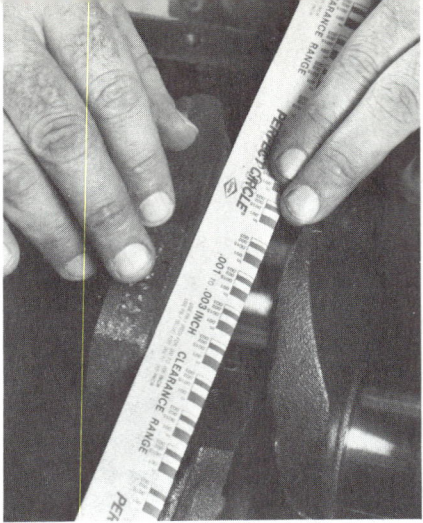

P4-10 Compare the spread of the gage with the scale given on the plastigage container. Compare the clearance with the specifications.

P4-11 Carefully scrape the plastigage off the journal surface.

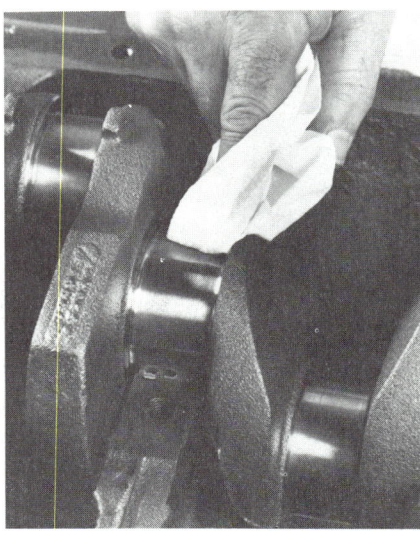

P4-12 Wipe the journal clean with a rag.

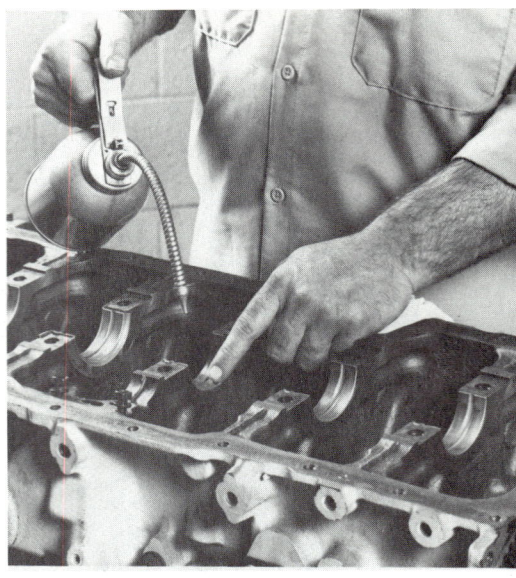

P4-13 If the clearance was within the specifications, remove the crankshaft and apply a good coat of fresh engine oil to the bearings.

P4-14 Reinstall the crankshaft and apply a coat of oil to the journal surfaces.

P4-15 Reinstall the main caps and tighten according to specifications. ■

The rod must be very strong and at the same time be kept as light as possible. Connecting rods are generally forged from high-strength steel, or are made of nodular steel or cast iron. The center section is made in the form of an I for maximum strength with minimum weight. The small end or piston pin end is made to accept the piston pin, which connects the piston to the connecting rod. The rod must be free to move back and forth as the crankshaft rotates. The piston pin can be a pressed fit in the piston and free fit in the rod. When this is the case, the small end of the rod will be fitted with a bushing. The pin can also be a free fit in the piston and pressed fit in the rod. In this case no bushings are used. The pin simply moves in the piston using the piston hole as a bearing surface. A third mounting allows the pin to move freely in both the piston and the rod. This design requires the use of clips or caps to prevent the pin from moving out against the cylinder walls.

The larger end of the rod is used to attach the connecting rod to the crankshaft. This end is made in two pieces. The upper half is part of the rod. The lower half is called the rod cap and is bolted to the rod. The connecting rod and its cap are manufactured as a unit and must always be kept together. During production, the rod caps are either machined off the rod or are scribed and broken off. The large crankshaft end of the rod is fitted with bearing half shells made of the same material as the main bearings (Figure 8-61). As mentioned earlier in the chapter, the crankshaft has oil passages that lead to the crank pins for lubricating the rod bearings. Some connecting rods have a hole drilled through the big end to the bearing area. The bearing insert might have a hole, which will align with this drilling. This hole is used to supply oil for lubricating and cooling the piston skirt. When the rod is properly installed, the oil hole should be pointing to the major thrust area of the cylinder wall.

❑ PISTON AND PISTON RINGS

The piston forms the lower portion of the combustion chamber. The force of the expanding air/fuel mixture at the time of ignition is exerted against the head or dome of the piston. This force then pushes the piston down in the cylinder. The force applied to the piston can be as high as 2-1/2 tons. Therefore, the piston must be very strong.

In the past, pistons were made primarily of cast iron or a mixture of iron and steel. They were strong, but also heavy. Due to advances in aluminum technology, most modern pistons are made of lighter weight aluminum or aluminum alloys.

Hypereutectic pistons are cast from an aluminum alloy containing up to 20% silicon. The silicon adds exceptional strength and durability to the metal. Higher strength means thinner side walls can be used, reducing piston weight. Hypereutectic pistons are very scuff resistant and less prone to ring groove, skirt, and pin bore wear. They offer excellent heat resistance and reduce thermal expansion so they can be installed to tight tolerances. This improves cold sealing and reduces operating noise. Hypereutectic pistons are now OEM equipment on many engines and are recommended replacement equipment for engines with scuffing and/or detonation problems. Passenger cars and light trucks with turbochargers or high output or severe duty operation also benefit from hypereutectic pistons.

The top of the piston is called the head or dome. Just below the dome on the side of the piston is a series of grooves. The grooves are used to contain the piston rings. The high parts between the grooves are called ring lands. Below the grooves, as shown in Figure 8-62, there is a bore, or hole, which is used for the piston pin, sometimes called the wrist pin. This hole is not always centered in the piston. It can be offset to one side. Piston pin offset is toward the major thrust side of the piston, the side that will contact the cylinder wall during the power stroke. By offsetting the pin, piston slap caused by the piston changing direction in the cylinder is eliminated.

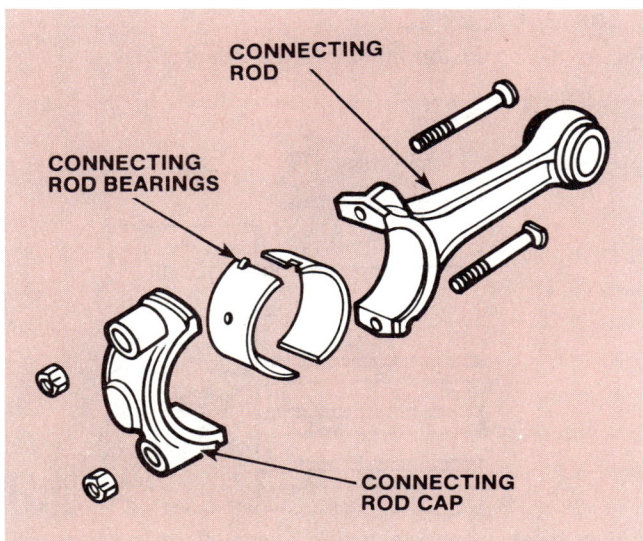

Figure 8-61 Connecting rod assembly with a bearing insert.

SHOP TALK

The term piston slap or bang is used to describe the noise made by the piston when it contacts the cylinder wall. This noise is usually heard only in older, high-mileage engines that have worn pistons or cylinder walls.

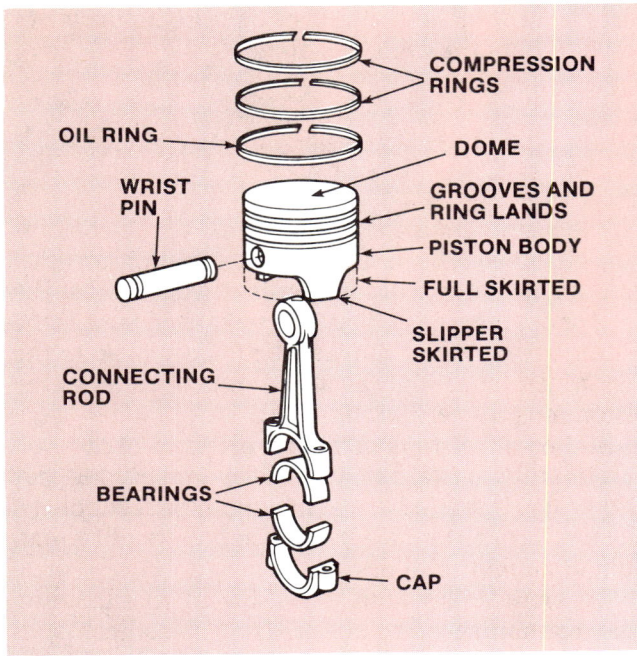

Figure 8-62 Piston and connecting rod assembly.

Piston Rings

Piston rings are used to fill the expansion gap between the piston and cylinder wall. It is the piston rings that seal the combustion chamber at the piston.

Piston rings, which are available in several coatings, must serve three functions. They must seal the combustion chamber at the piston. They must remove oil from the cylinder walls to keep oil from reaching the upper cylinder where it will be burned. They must also carry heat from the piston to the cylinder walls to help cool the piston.

There are two basic ring families: compression rings and oil control rings. In most modern automobile engines, pistons are fitted with two compression rings and one oil control ring (Figure 8-63). The compression rings are found in the two upper grooves closest to the piston head. The oil ring is fitted to the groove just above the wrist pin.

Compression Rings

The compression rings form the seal between the piston and cylinder walls (Figure 8-64). They are designed to use combustion pressure to force the ring against the cylinder wall and against the bottom edge of the ring groove. The top ring is the primary seal with

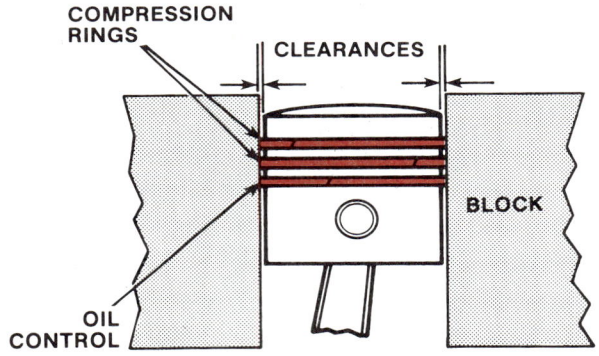

Figure 8-63 Piston fitted into the cylinder bore.

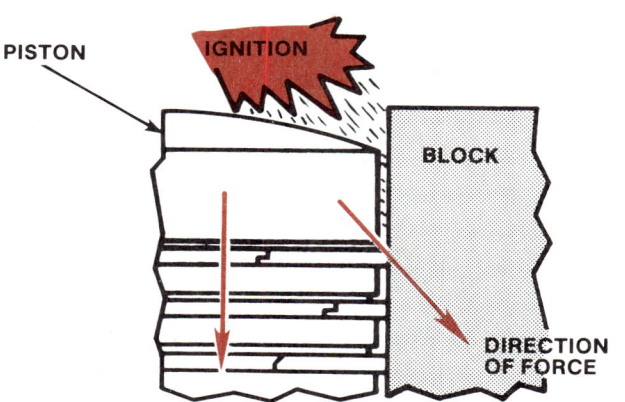

Figure 8-64 The combustion rings use combustion pressure to push themselves against the cylinder walls and form a better seal.

To ensure that the piston is installed correctly and the offset is on the proper side, the top of the piston will have a mark. The most common mark is a notch, machined into the top edge of the piston. This mark must always face the timing chain end of the engine when the piston is installed. The base of the piston, the area below the piston pin, is called the piston skirt. The area from just below the bottom ring groove to the tip of the skirt is the piston thrust surface.

There are two basic types of piston skirts: the slipper type and the full skirt. The full skirt is used primarily in truck and commercial engines. The slipper type is used for automobile engines. The slipper-type skirt allows the piston enough thrust surface for normal operation and has the advantage of allowing the piston to be lighter. This design also cuts down on piston expansion because there is less material to hold heat.

When an engine is designed, piston expansion determines how much piston clearance will be needed in the cylinder bore. Too little clearance will cause the piston to bind at operating temperatures. Too much will cause piston slap. The normal piston clearance for an engine, using slipper skirted pistons, is about 0.001 to 0.002 inch. This clearance is measured cold between the piston skirt and the cylinder wall. The piston clearance also supplies a space for piston lubrication.

USING SERVICE MANUALS

Piston clearance is normally found in the engine specifications table at the beginning of the engine section in a service manual.

the second ring used to seal any small amount of pressure which may reach it.

During the power stroke, the pressure caused by the expanding air/fuel mixture is applied between the inside of the ring and the piston groove. This forces the ring into full contact with the cylinder walls. The same force is applied to the top of the ring forcing it against the bottom of the ring groove. The combination of combustion pressure and the compression ring join together to form a tight ring seal.

Compression rings are generally made of cast iron. They come in a number of variations in cross section design. Most compression rings have a coating on their face, which aids the wear-in process. Wear-in is the time needed for the rings to conform to the shape and surface of the cylinder wall. Typical soft coatings are graphite, phosphate, iron oxide, and molybdenum. Some compression rings have a hard coating, such as chromium.

Oil Control Rings

Oil is constantly being applied to the cylinder walls. The oil is used for lubrication as well as to clean the cylinder wall of carbon and dirt particles. This oil bath also aids cooling the piston. Controlling this oil is the primary function of the oil ring. The two most common types of oil rings are the segmented oil ring and the cast-iron oil ring. Both types of rings are slotted so that excess oil from the cylinder wall can pass through the ring. The oil ring groove of the piston is also slotted. After the oil passes through the ring, it can then pass through the slots in the piston and return to the oil sump through the open section of the piston.

Segmented oil rings are made of three pieces: an upper and lower scraper rail and an expander. The scrapers and expanders are made of spring steel. Segmented oil rings are a free-fit design. This means that the expander is larger than the diameter of the cylinder. They must be carefully compressed when installed. The expander is used to form a tight seal of the scrapers at the cylinder walls.

☐ INSTALLING PISTONS AND CONNECTING RODS

Once the crankshaft is in place, the next installation task is the piston and connecting rod assemblies. First, lay out the piston assemblies in order from the front to the rear of the engine. Check the marks on the connecting rod caps to make sure they are matched. Check the pistons to make sure they are installed on the connecting rods in the correct direction. Various markings are used to identify the positioning of pistons and connecting rods. Some of the more common markings are shown in Figure 8-65. Always check the manufacturer's service manual for exact component directions.

The insert bearings for the connecting rods, like those for the main bearings, must be the correct size. If the crankshaft has been machined undersize, matching rod bearing inserts must be installed. The size of the bearing inserts is printed on the box they come in and is stamped on the backs of the bearings (Figure 8-66).

Snap the new connecting rod bearing inserts into the connecting rods and rod caps. Make sure the tang on the bearing fits snugly into the matching notch

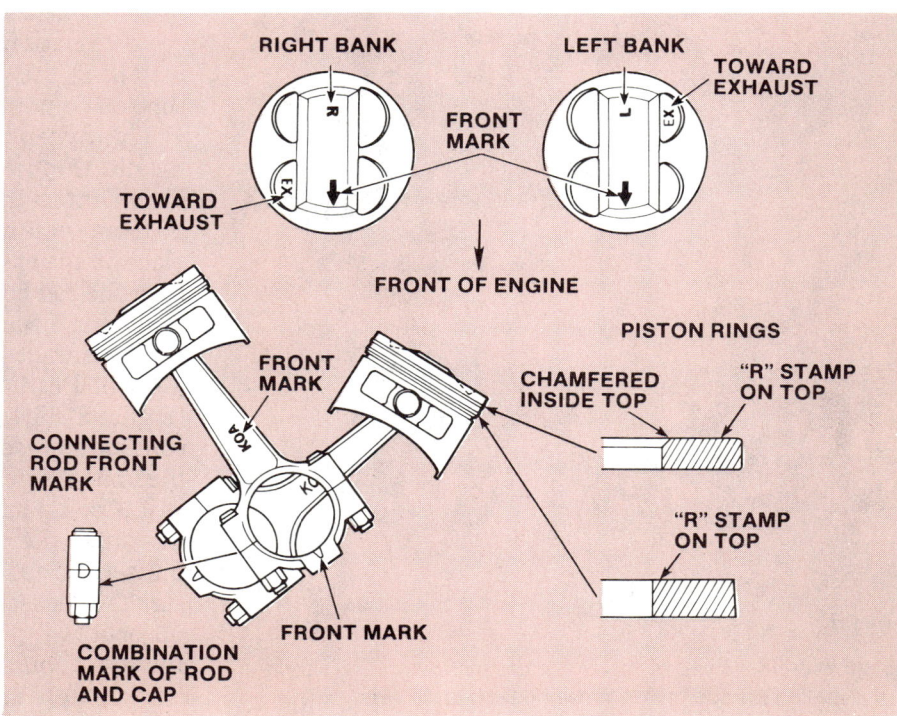

Figure 8-65 Common piston and connecting rod identification marks.

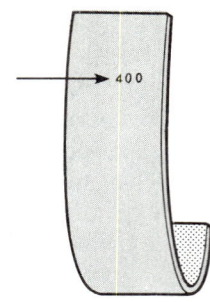

Figure 8-66 The connecting rod bearing size is marked on the back of the bearing.

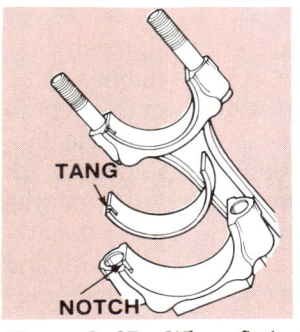
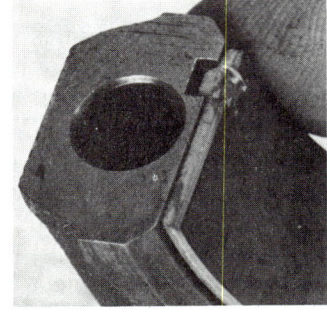

Figure 8-67 When fitting a bearing into the connecting rod, make sure the bearing tang is fully seated in the notch of the rod.

(Figure 8-67). Also make certain the con-rod and piston move freely (Figure 8-68).

The piston and rod can be assembled in the block in the following manner. Insert a new piston ring into the cylinder. Use the head of the piston to position the ring

Figure 8-68 Prior to installing the piston and rod assembly, make sure the piston moves freely on its wrist pin.

so that it is square with the cylinder wall. In slightly worn cylinders that will not be resized, position the ring below the ring travel area. When the cylinders have been refinished and have zero taper, the location of the ring is not critical. Next, use a feeler gauge to check the end gap (Figure 8-69A). Compose the end-gap specifications with the measured gap. Correct as needed. Check the instructions on the piston ring box for correct installation. Normally, the gaps of the piston rings are staggered to prevent them from being in line with each other. Piston rings are installed easily with a ring expander.

Before attempting to install the piston/con-rod assembly in the cylinder bore, place rubber or aluminum protectors or boots over the threaded section of the rod bolts (Figure 8-69B). This will help to prevent bore and crankpin damage.

Lightly coat the piston, rings, rod bearings, cylinder wall, and crankpin with a light engine oil (Figure 8-69C). Some technicians submerge the piston in a large can of clean engine oil before it is installed. Also, be sure to coat the cylinder wall with oil.

Fit the piston and ring into the cylinder bore by using a ring compressor tool (Figure 8-69D). This tool is expanded to fit around the piston rings. The steps on the tool are positioned downward. It is tightened with an Allen wrench to compress the piston rings. When the rings are fully compressed, the tool will not compress any further. The piston will fit snugly, but not tightly.

Rotate the crankshaft until the crankpin is at its lowest level (BDC). Then place the piston/rod assembly into the cylinder bore until the steps on the ring compressor contact the cylinder block deck (Figure 8-69E). Make sure that the piston reference mark is in correct relation to the front of the engine. Also, when installing the assembly, make certain that the rod threads do not touch or damage the crankpin.

Lightly tap on the head of the piston with a mallet handle (Figure 8-69F) or block of wood until the piston enters the cylinder bore. Push the piston down the bore while making sure the connecting rod fits into place on the crankpin. Remove the protective covering from the rod bolts.

A drop of anaerobic thread-locking compound is good insurance against a loose rod cap nut (Figure 8-69G). Position the matching connecting rod cap (Figure 8-69H) and finger tighten the rod nuts. Make sure the connecting rod blade and cap markings are on the same side. Gently tap each cap with a plastic mallet as it is being installed to properly position and seat it.

Torque the rod nuts to the specifications given in the service manual. When torquing the nuts, make sure the socket does not interfere with the bearing cap rib or it will give a false reading. Lifting the socket slightly should alleviate this problem. Rotate the crankshaft to check for binding after each connecting

Short Blocks 171

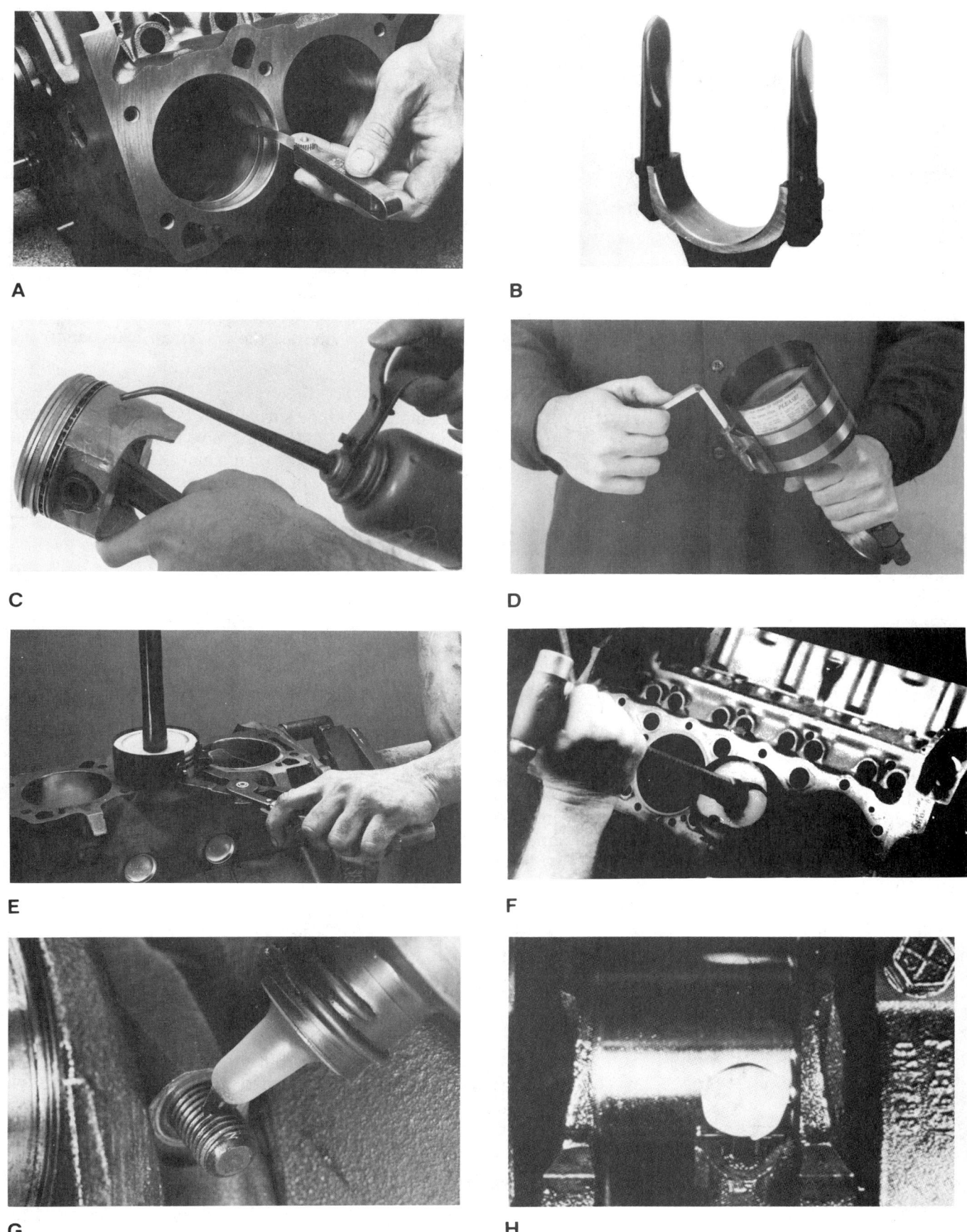

Figure 8-69 Steps in installing the piston and rod assembly in the block.

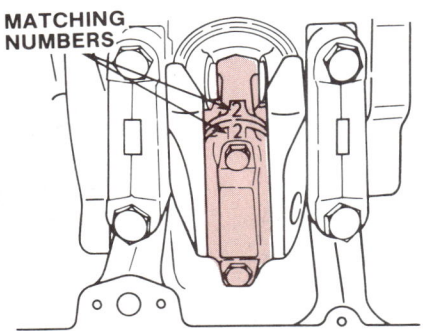

Figure 8-70 Typical markings used to match a connecting rod cap with a rod.

rod is tightened to the crankshaft. Repeat the piston/rod assembly procedure for each assembly. Remember that connecting rods are numbered for easy identification and proper assembly (Figure 8-70).

When all the pistons and rods have been installed, the connecting rod side clearance can be measured (Figure 8-71). The side clearance is the amount of clearance between the crankshaft and the side of the connecting rod. Side clearance is measured by inserting a feeler gauge between the crankshaft and connecting rod side or between the two connecting rods. The clearance determines the amount of oil throw-off from the connecting rod bearings. The clearance can be increased by removing the connecting rod and grind-

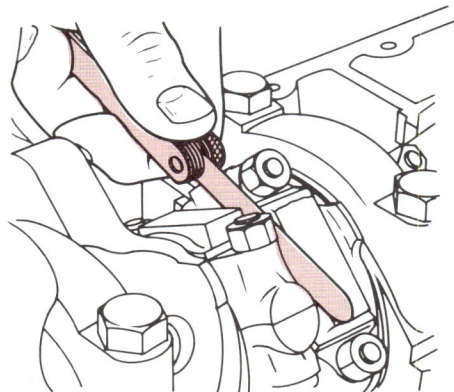

Figure 8-71 Measuring connecting rod side clearance.

Figure 8-72 Lubricate the crankshaft both during and after assembly.

ing material off the sides. If the clearance is too great, the connecting rods might have to be replaced.

Be sure to coat the crankshaft assembly with clean bearing lubricant or clean engine oil (Figure 8-72).

SHOP TALK

Most expert technicians recommend that the bearing oil clearance of the connecting rod be checked against a manual's specifications. To do this, put a small strip of plastigage on the rod cap insert and hold it in place while positioning the insert on the connecting rod. Install the rod cap nuts and torque them to specifications. Remove the nuts and remove the cap. Compare the flattened plastic string to the plastigage package just as was done for the main bearings.

 ## CASE STUDY

Case 1

A car is brought into the shop just 2000 miles after the owner rebuilt the engine. The shop is asked to diagnose the cause of excessive blue exhaust smoke and oil consumption and fouled spark plugs. Responding to questions, the customer indicates that she has rebuilt many engines before and never had this problem. She also has receipts for the parts she installed and the machining she had done to the engine. All of the parts were high-quality, and the machining was done by a reputable machine shop.

To verify the problem, a cylinder leakage test is conducted. The results indicate excessive leakage past the piston rings. To determine what went wrong during the rebuild, further questioning is needed. Assembly procedures are reviewed. No steps were apparently missed. New piston rings were sized to the freshly-honed cylinder walls and the resultant ring end gap is within specifications. The ring gaps were also staggered in the way recommended by the manufacturer. The work order from the machine shop showed that the cylinders were honed to a 30 RMS surface finish and the resultant size was 3.751 inches. The pistons are measured to be approximately 3.749 inches. The 0.002-inch clearance is within specifications.

Further examination of the receipts reveal the problem. The customer had originally intended to install cast-iron piston rings. But while the block was in the machine shop, she bought a set of molybdenum rings. Although these rings have advantages over cast rings, they are not best for this block. Molybdenum rings require a smooth cylinder wall finish; typically, a finish of 10 to 15 RMS is recommended. The rougher cylinder wall finish intended for cast-iron rings wore off the molybdenum coating, allowing oil to leak past the rings. This is the cause of the smoke, oil consumption, and spark plug fouling.

Summary

- The basic short block assembly consists of the cylinder block, crankshaft, crankshaft bearings, connecting rods, pistons and rings, and oil galley and core plugs. Related items include the flywheel and harmonic balancer.
- The cylinder block houses the areas where compression, ignition, and combustion occur. To protect the block from cracking due to expansion, core plugs are inserted during the manufacturing process.
- Cylinder bore wear is not uniform. Maximum wear occurs at the top of the ring travel area. A properly reconditioned cylinder must be of the correct diameter, have no taper or runout, and have a surface finish such that the piston rings will seat to form a seal that minimizes blowby and controls oil.
- Glaze is the thin residue that forms on cylinder walls due to a combination of heat, engine oil, and piston movement. Eye protection is a must when deglazing, as well as when honing and boring a cylinder.
- Freeze plugs and oil galley plugs are normally removed and replaced as part of cylinder block reconditioning. The three basic core plugs are the disc- or dished-type, cup-type, and expansion-type.
- The crankshaft turns on a film of oil trapped between the bearing surface and the journal surface. The journals must be smooth and highly polished.
- The flywheel adds to an engine's smooth running by applying a constant moving force to carry the crankshaft from one firing stroke to the next. The flywheel surface may be used as part of the clutch.
- Important crankshaft checks include saddle alignment, straightness, clearance, and end play. When replacement is necessary, a rebuilt crankshaft can be used as long as it meets specifications.
- Bearings carry the critical loads created by crankshaft movement. Most bearings used today are insert bearings, which are self-contained parts inserted into the bearing housing.
- Maintaining a specific oil clearance is critical to proper bearing operation. If the crankshaft is so worn that using standard size bearings will result in excessive oil clearance space, then so-called undersize bearings are needed.
- Today's aluminum pistons are lightweight, yet strong enough to withstand combustion pressure. Because of the tendency of aluminum to expand, steel struts are cast into aluminum pistons to help hold the heat and control expansion.
- Piston rings are used to fill the expansion gap between the piston and cylinder wall. Most of today's vehicle engines are fitted with two compression rings and one oil control ring.
- When installing a piston and connecting rod assembly, various markings can be used to make sure the installation is correct. Always check the service manual for exact locations.
- Connecting rod side clearance, the amount of clearance between the crankshaft and the side of the connecting rod, is an important measurement. It determines the amount of oil throw-off from the bearings. It is measured with a feeler gauge.

Review Questions

1. Rather than casting the cylinder bores directly into the block, what do some vehicle manufacturers use?
2. What is the deck?
3. Where does maximum cylinder bore wear occur?
4. What type of insert bearing is manufactured with an extra-thick lining of bearing material on the inside diameter?
5. What is the function of compression rings?
6. Most pistons used today are made from _____ .
   a. cast iron
   b. aluminum
   c. ceramic
   d. none of the above
7. Core plugs _____ .
   a. are also called expansion plugs
   b. are used in all cylinder blocks
   c. protect the block from cracking
   d. all of the above
8. Technician A says the maximum amount of cylinder out-of-roundness allowed in most cases is

0.0015 inch. Technician B says that cylinder out-of-roundness is permissible up to 0.015 inch. Who is correct?
a. Technician A
b. Technician B
c. Both A and B
d. Neither A nor B

9. The maximum amount of cylinder taper normally allowed is _____.
a. 0.0015 inch
b. 0.006 inch
c. 0.015 inch
d. 0.06 inch

10. Technician A says that a cylinder wall with too smooth a surface will prevent the piston rings from seating properly. Technician B says a cylinder wall can never be too smooth. Who is correct?
a. Technician A
b. Technician B
c. Both A and B
d. Neither A nor B

11. Technician A says that cylinder deglazing is not necessary if the cylinder out-of-roundness is within acceptable limits. Technician B says glaze should always be removed from the cylinder walls. Who is correct?
a. Technician A
b. Technician B
c. Both A and B
d. Neither A nor B

12. Technician A installs a cup-type core plug with its flanged edge outward. Technician B installs a cup-type core plug with its flanged edge inward. Who is correct?
a. Technician A
b. Technician B
c. Both A and B
d. Neither A nor B

13. Each half of a split bearing is made so it is slightly greater than an exact half. What is this extension called?
a. spread
b. crush
c. both a and b
d. neither a nor b

14. The connecting rod journal is also called the _____.
a. balancer shaft
b. vibration damper
c. plastigage
d. crankpin

15. Technician A uses a micrometer to measure the connecting rod journal for taper. Technician B uses a micrometer to measure the connecting rod journal for out-of-roundness. Who is correct?
a. Technician A
b. Technician B
c. Both A and B
d. Neither A nor B

16. Technician A uses line boring to repair engine blocks that are not severely warped. Technician B uses line boring to repair engine blocks that are severely warped. Who is correct?
a. Technician A
b. Technician B
c. Both A and B
d. Neither A nor B

17. Technician A checks crankshaft clearance with a feeler gauge, while Technician B uses a dial gauge. Who is correct?
a. Technician A
b. Technician B
c. Both A and B
d. Neither A nor B

18. _____ main and connecting rod bearings are manufactured with spread.
a. All
b. Most
c. Very few
d. No

19. Technician A says the size and location of engine oil holes is unimportant, provided there are a sufficient number of them. Technician B says the size and location of engine oil holes is critical. Who is correct?
a. Technician A
b. Technician B
c. Both A and B
d. Neither A nor B

20. Which type of oil ring is slotted so that excess oil can pass through it?
a. cast-iron
b. segmented
c. both a and b
d. neither a nor b

9 CYLINDER HEADS AND VALVES

Objectives

- Describe the location and function of an engine's cylinder head, valves, and related valve parts.
- Describe the types of combustion chamber shapes found on modern engines.
- Explain the procedures involved in reconditioning cylinder heads, valve guides, valve seats, and valve faces.
- Explain the steps in cylinder head and valve reassembly.

The cylinder head mounts on top of the cylinder block to form the top portion of the engine. The cylinder head (Figure 9-1) is made of cast iron or aluminum. On overhead valve engines, the cylinder head contains the valves, valve seats, valve guides, valve springs, rocker arm supports, and a recessed area that makes up the top portion of the combustion chamber. On overhead cam engines, the cylinder head contains these items, plus the supports for the camshaft and camshaft bearings.

Both overhead valve and overhead cam cylinder heads contain passages that match passages in the cylinder block. These passages allow coolant to circulate in the head. The cylinder head also contains tapped holes in the combustion chamber to accept the spark plugs.

The surface of the head that contacts the block must be perfectly smooth. This area must contain the force of the burning air/fuel mixture. To aid in the sealing, a gasket is placed between the head and block. This gasket is called the head gasket. It is made of special material that can withstand high temperatures, high pressures, and the expansion of the metals around it. The head also serves as the mounting point for the intake and exhaust manifolds and contains the intake and exhaust ports.

Intake and exhaust ports must be cast into the cylinder head. These ports are made so the air and fuel can pass through the cylinder head into the combustion chamber. One port is normally used for each valve. However, ports are sometimes combined because of space. These ports are called siamese ports (Figure 9-2). Siamese ports can be used because each cylinder uses the port at a different time. Cross flow ports are used on some engines and have the intake and exhaust ports on the opposite sides.

Large openings cast into the cylinder head allow coolant to pass through the head (Figure 9-3). Coolant must circulate throughout the cylinder head so excess heat can be removed. The coolant flows from passages in the cylinder block through the head gasket and into

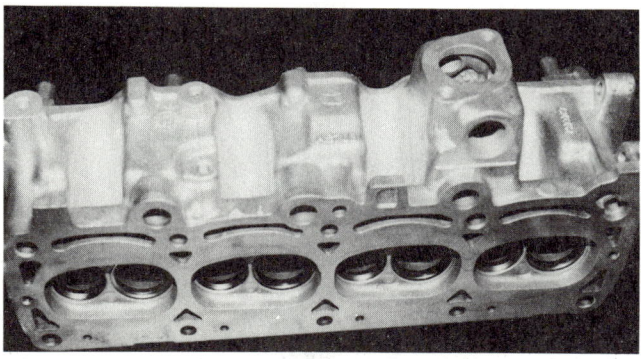

Figure 9-1 Most of the other engine parts attach to the cylinder head.

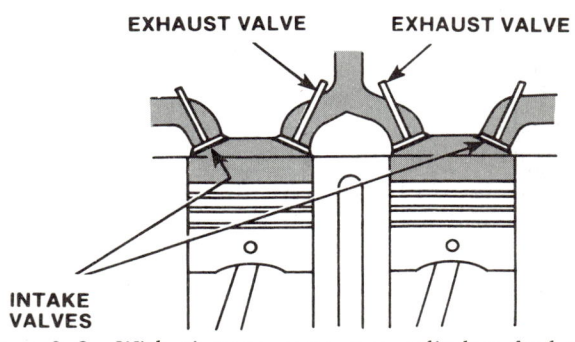

Figure 9-2 With siamese ports, two cylinders feed the same exhaust port.

175

Figure 9-3 Coolant passages are cast into the cylinder head.

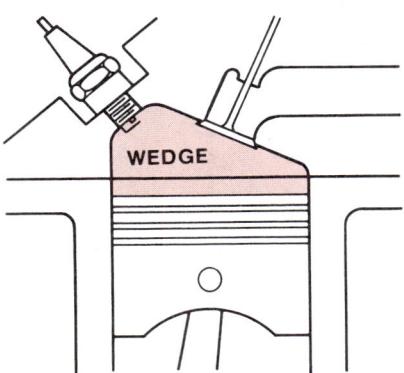

Figure 9-4 Typical wedge combustion chamber.

the cylinder head. The coolant then passes back to other parts of the cooling system.

COMBUSTION CHAMBER

The performance of an engine, its fuel efficiency, and the level of pollutants in the exhaust all depend to a large extent on the shape of the combustion chamber. An efficient combustion chamber must be compact to minimize the surface area of the walls through which heat is lost to the engine's cooling system. The point of ignition (the nose of the spark plug) should be at the center of the combustion chamber. This also has the advantage of minimizing the flame path, or the distance from the spark to the furthermost point in the chamber. The shorter the flame path, the more progressive and even the combustion of the air/fuel mixture.

Manufacturers have designed several different shapes of combustion chambers in attempts to approach these ideals. Before looking at the popular combustion chamber designs, there are two terms that should be defined.

1. Turbulence is a very rapid movement of gases. Turbulence causes better combustion because the air and fuel are mixed better.
2. Quenching is the cooling of gases by pressing them into a thin area. The area in which gases are thinned is called the quench area.

Wedge Chamber

In the wedge-type combustion chamber, the spark plug is located at the wide part of the wedge (Figure 9-4). As the piston comes up on the compression stroke, the air/fuel mixture is squashed in the quench area. The quench area causes the air and fuel to be mixed thoroughly before combustion. This helps to improve the combustion efficiency of the engine. Spark plugs are positioned to allow for rapid and even combustion. When the spark occurs, a flame front moves from the spark plug outward. The wedge-shaped combustion chamber is also called a turbulence-type combustion chamber. On newer model cars, the quench area has been reduced, which helps reduce exhaust emissions.

Hemispherical Chamber

The hemispherical combustion chamber gets its name from the chamber shape. Hemi is defined as half, and spherical means circle. The combustion chamber is shaped like a half circle. This type of chamber is also called the hemi-head. The piston top forms the base of the hemisphere, and the valves are inclined at an angle of 60 to 90 degrees to each other with the spark plug positioned centrally between them (Figure 9-5).

This design has several advantages. The flame path from the spark plug to the piston head is short, which gives efficient burning. The cross flow arrangement of the inlet and exhaust valves allows for a relatively free flow of gases into and out of the chamber. Yet, the shape of the chamber also creates some turbulence to ensure a thorough mixing of the fuel and air. The result is that the engine can breathe deeply, meaning that it can draw in a large volume of gas for the space available and give a high power output.

The hemispherical combustion chamber is considered a nonturbulence-type combustion chamber. Little turbulence is produced in this type chamber. The air/fuel mixture is compressed evenly on the compression

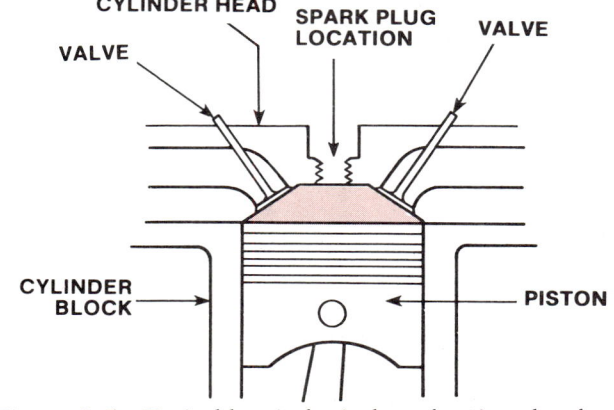

Figure 9-5 Typical hemispherical combustion chamber.

Cylinder Heads and Valves

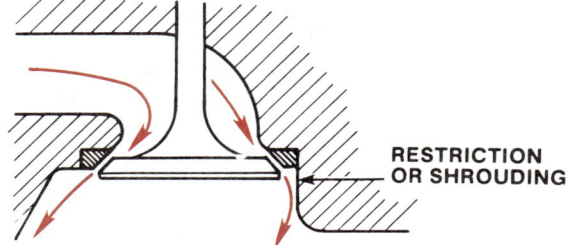

Figure 9-6 Shrouding is a restriction in the flow of intake gases caused by the shape of the combustion chamber.

stroke. The spark plug is located directly between the valves. Combustion radiates evenly from the spark plug, completely burning the air/fuel mixture.

One of the more important advantages of the hemispherical combustion chamber is that air and fuel can enter the chamber very easily. The wedge combustion chamber restricts the flow of air and fuel to a certain extent. This is called shrouding. Figure 9-6 shows the valve very close to the side of the combustion chamber, which causes the air and fuel to be restricted. Volumetric efficiency is reduced. Hemispherical combustion chambers do not have this restriction. Hemispherical combustion chambers are used on many high-performance applications. This is especially true when large quantities of air and fuel are needed in the cylinder.

Some engines use a domed piston. This type of piston has a quench area to improve turbulence (Figure 9-7). Several variations of this design are used today by different engine manufacturers.

Swirl Chamber

A swirl combustion chamber uses a compound curve port design to cause the air/fuel mixture to swirl in a corkscrew pattern to improve combustion. The swirl effect is the result of the intake port design, port location in the combustion chamber, and shape of the chamber itself. As the piston comes up on the compression stroke, this agitation of the air/fuel mixture continues and is compounded by compression (Figure

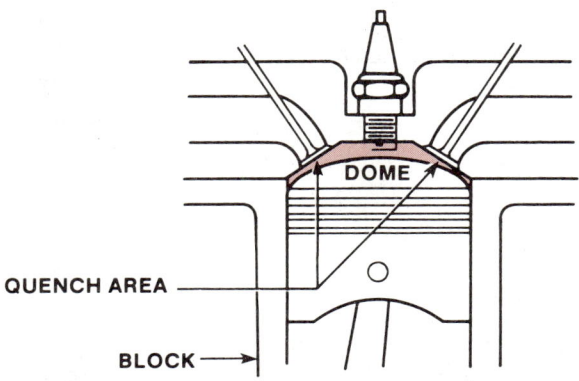

Figure 9-7 Domed pistons improve turbulence by producing a quench area.

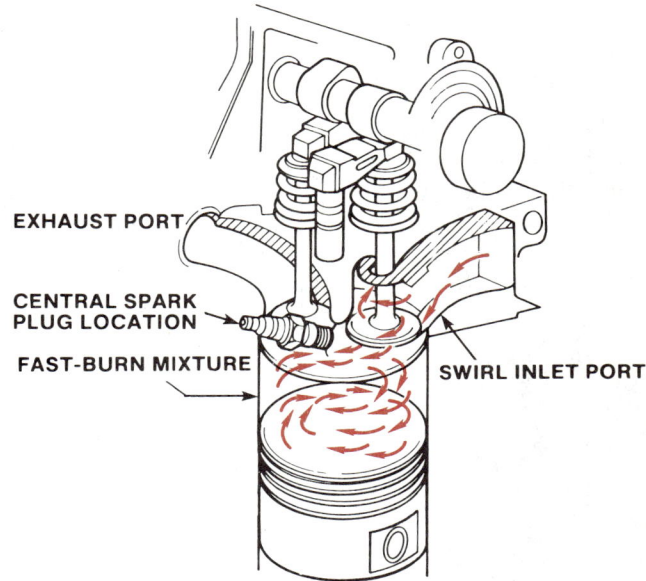

Figure 9-8 Typical swirl combustion chamber.

9-8). This swirl action provides better fuel economy and lower exhaust emissions since fewer unburned hydrocarbons enter the exhaust system. A comparison of the swirl and hemispherical combustion chambers is shown in Figure 9-9.

Chamber-in-Piston

In this design, the valves are positioned vertically in the top of the cylinder head and are generally set flush with the face of the head (Figure 9-10). The spark plug is set to one side, midway between the inlet and exhaust valves. It is sometimes inclined a little away from the vertical.

In some designs, the inlet valve is well recessed into the inlet port and may even have a shroud on the head. Opening the inlet valve ensures a strong swirl and thorough mixing of the incoming charge of gases. The rim of the bowl in the piston head creates some squish. As the piston reaches the top of its stroke, some of the combustion gases around the rim are forced into the bowl itself, producing enough turbulence to minimize knocking.

A   B

Figure 9-9 (A) Swirl and (B) hemispherical combustion chambers.

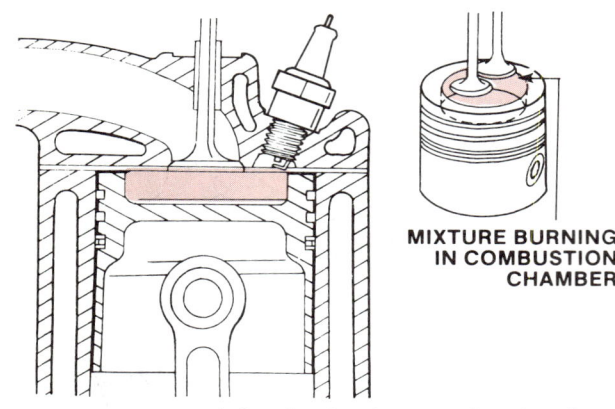

Figure 9-10   Typical chamber-in-piston combustion chamber.

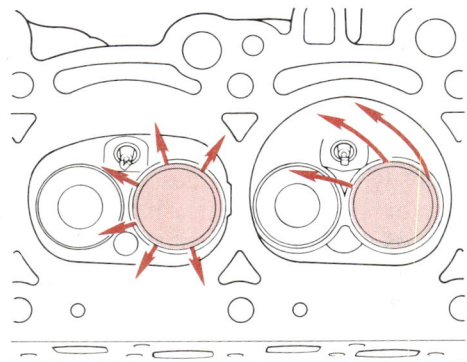

Figure 9-11   (A) Standard uniform flow and (B) fast-burn, tangential-flow combustion chambers.

An advantage of this shape is that because the combustion chamber lies in the piston itself, it remains hot. This helps to ensure the complete vaporization of combustion gases under light load, which, in turn, ensures smooth combustion.

Fast-Burn Combustion Chamber

A fast-burn combustion chamber is used on certain four-cylinder engines to improve their efficiency (Figure 9-11). Faster combustion is achieved by directing airflow tangentially through the intake valves to create turbulence. Fast-burn combustion chambers also decrease potential engine knock. With less potential for knock, compression ratios can be increased without increasing fuel octane requirements.

❏ INTAKE AND EXHAUST VALVES

Every cylinder of a four-stroke cycle engine contains at least one intake valve to permit the air/fuel mixture to enter the cylinder and one exhaust valve to allow the burned exhaust gases to escape. The intake and exhaust valves, along with the cylinder head gasket, must also seal the combustion chamber (Figure 9-12).

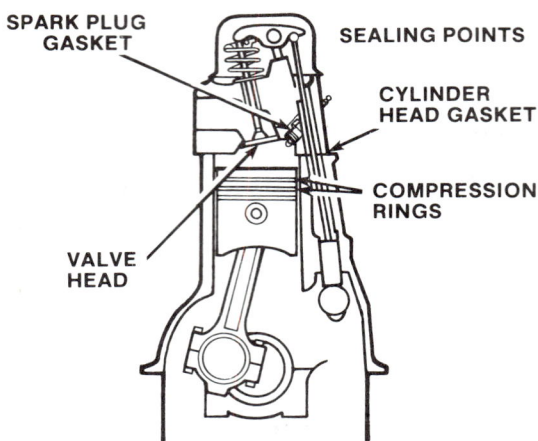

Figure 9-12   Sealing points of a typical engine.

The type of valve used in automotive engines is called a poppet. This is derived from the popping action of the valve as it opens and closes. A poppet valve has a round head with a tapered face, a stem that is used to guide the valve, and a slot that is machined at the top of the stem for the valve spring retainers.

The head of the valve is the large diameter end and is used to seal the intake or exhaust port. This seal is made by the valve face contacting the valve seat. The valve face is the tapered area machined on the head of the valve. The angle of this taper is determined by the design and manufacturer of the engine. The taper will vary from one engine family to another and may vary between intake and exhaust valves in the same engine. The area between the valve face and the head of the valve is called the margin. The margin allows for some machining of the valve face, which is sometimes necessary to restore its finish, and allows the valve an extra capacity to hold heat.

The intake and exhaust valve heads are different diameters. The intake valve is the larger of the two (Figure 9-13). The size or diameter of the valves is determined by the engine design. As mentioned, the stem guides the valve during its up-and-down movement and serves to connect the valve to its spring

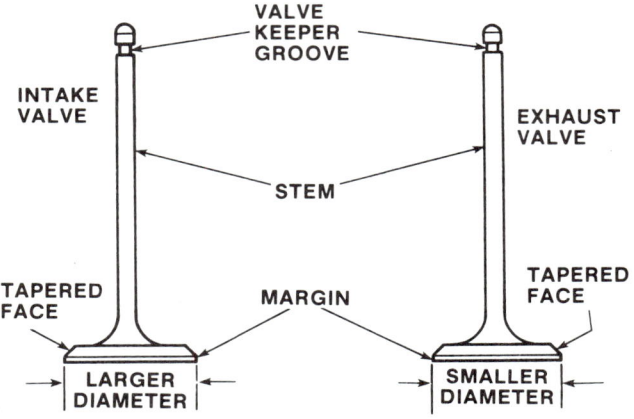

Figure 9-13   Valve nomenclature.

through its valve spring retainers and keepers. The stem rides in a guide that is either machined into the head (integral type) or pressed into the head (insert type) as a separate replaceable part.

The valve seat is the area of the cylinder head contacted by the face of the valve. The seat may be machined in the head (integral type) or it may be pressed in (insert type) like the valve guide. The valves found in today's engines are made from special high-strength steel or ceramic that is highly heat resistant. Heat resistance is very critical for exhaust valves because they must withstand working temperatures of between 1500 to 4000 degrees Fahrenheit. Heat resistance is much less of a problem for intake valves because they receive extra cooling from the fuel mixture during the intake stroke.

There are two ways for the exhaust valve to cool. First, when the valve face is in contact with its seat, the heat from the valve will be transferred to the cylinder head, which is liquid cooled. The second is through the valve stem to the valve guide and again to the cylinder head. To aid in this second method of heat transfer, some exhaust valve stems are hollow. This hollow section is filled with sodium (Figure 9-14). Sodium is a silver-white alkaline metallic chemical element that transfers heat much better than steel.

WARNING: Never cut open any sodium-filled valves. Sodium will burn violently when it contacts water.

The valve seat area must be hard enough to withstand the constant closing of the valve and supply good heat transfer. Due to corrosive products found in the exhaust gas, the seats must be highly resistant to corrosion. When the cylinder head material meets these requirements, the seats are machined directly into it. When it does not, the seats are then made of material that will meet the requirements and the seats are pressed into the head.

The following are the important valve components found in a four-stroke engine.

VALVE GUIDES Valve guides are the parts that support the valves in the head. They are machined to a fit of a few thousandths of an inch clearance with the

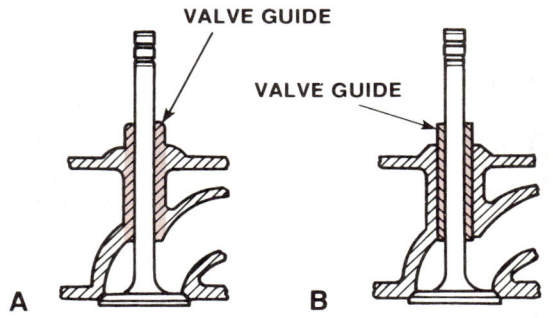

Figure 9-15 (A) Integral and (B) removable valve guides.

valve stem. This close clearance is important for the following reasons.

- It keeps the lubricating oil from being drawn into the combustion chamber past the intake valve stem during the intake stroke.
- It keeps exhaust gases from leaking into the crankcase area past the exhaust valve stems during the exhaust stroke.
- It keeps the valve face in perfect alignment with the valve seat.

Valve guides can be cast integrally with the head, or they can be removable (Figure 9-15). Removable valve guides usually are press-fit into the head.

VALVE SPRINGS, RETAINERS, AND SEALS The valve assembly is completed by the spring, retainer, and seal. Before the spring and the retainer fit into place, a seal is placed over the valve stem. The seal acts like an umbrella to keep oil from running down the valve stem and into the combustion chamber. The spring, which keeps the valve in a normally closed position, is held in place by the retainer. The retainer locks onto the valve stem with two wedge-shaped parts that are called valve keepers. Some engines utilize a single valve spring per valve (Figure 9-16A). Others use two or three springs (Figure 9-16B). Often the

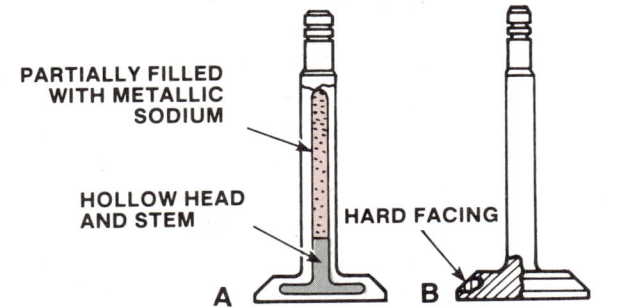

Figure 9-14 (A) Sodium-filled valve and (B) hard-faced valve.

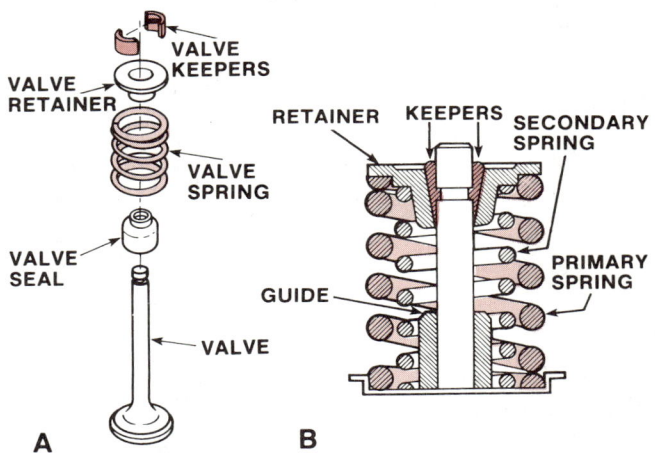

Figure 9-16 Two types of valve spring assemblies: (A) single spring and (B) reverse wound secondary spring.

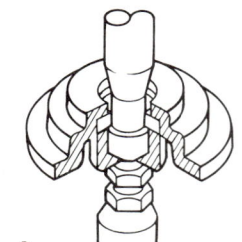 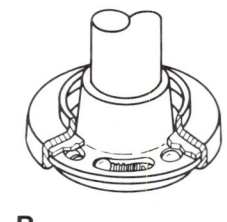

Figure 9-17 (A) Release and (B) positive valve rotators.

second or third spring is a flat spring called a damper which is designed to control spring vibrations.

VALVE ROTATORS It is common in heavy-duty applications to use mechanisms that cause the exhaust valves to rotate. The purpose is to keep carbon from building up between the valve face and seat. This could hold the valve partially open, causing it to burn. The release-type rotator (Figure 9-17A) releases the spring tension from the valve while it is open. The valve will then rotate from engine vibration. The positive rotator (Figure 9-17B) is a two-piece valve retainer that has a flexible washer between the two pieces. A series of balls, between the retainer pieces, roll on a machined ramp as pressure is applied and released from the opening and the closing of the valve. The movement of the balls up and down the ramps causes the valve to rotate.

Multivalve Engines

Some newer engines use multivalve arrangements. Automotive engineers have long been obsessed with the idea of additional valves in the cylinder head. It all started in 1918 with the dual-valve Pierce Arrow. This was one of the first cars to use four valves per cylinder as a way to enhance gas flow and increase horsepower.

Multivalve can be three valves per cylinder (Figure 9-18) or four valves (Figure 9-19) per cylinder. This means that a four-cylinder car can have either twelve valves (two intakes and one exhaust) or sixteen valves

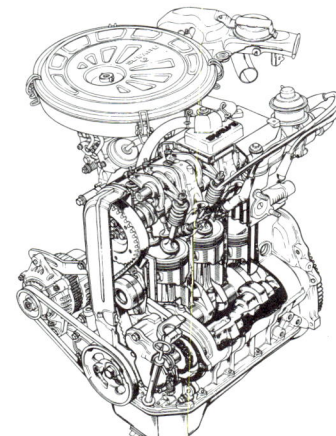

Figure 9-18 Single overhead camshaft engine with two intake valves and one exhaust valve for each cylinder.

Figure 9-19 Cutaway view of a multivalve arrangement with four valves per cylinder.

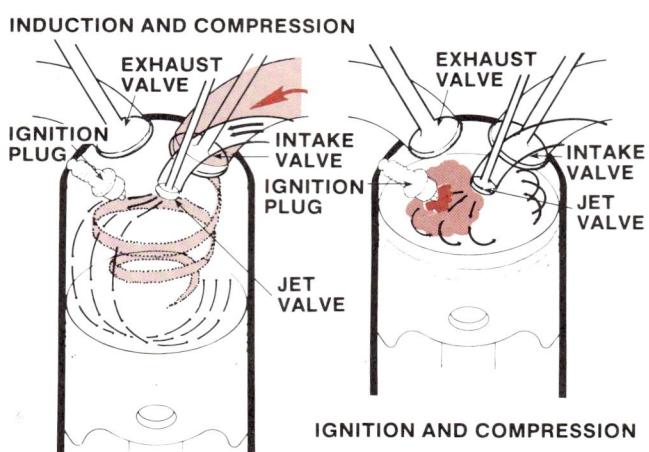

Figure 9-20 How a jet valve operates in a multivalve engine.

(two intakes and two exhausts). A six-cylinder engine can have either eighteen or twenty-four valves. An eight-cylinder engine can have twenty-four or thirty-two valves. To aid in combustion, some multivalve arrangements feature a jet valve (Figure 9-20). Air from the carburetor throttle plate is directed to the jet valve (a smaller intake valve) at lower engine speeds. This results in a swirling action in the combustion chamber and increased turbulence. The location of the air inlet above the throttle plate allows very little air to enter the passage to the jet valve at higher engine speeds and greater throttle openings. In all multivalve engines, the heads are of the cross flow design (Figure 9-21).

Replacing the conventional single intake and single exhaust valve with two intake and one or two exhaust valves increases the area of the intake and exhaust ports. Thus, multivalve engines have a more complete combustion, which reduces the chances of misfire and detonation. This results in enhanced fuel efficiency, cleaner exhaust, and increased power output. A related

Cylinder Heads and Valves   181

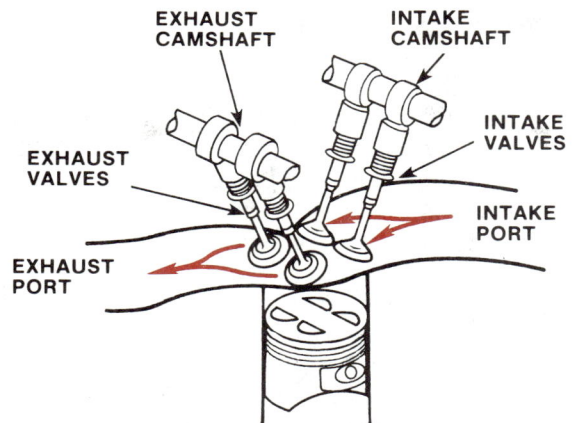

Figure 9-21 Typical cross flow pattern used in multivalve engines.

point is intake velocity, which is easier to keep high with small multiple ports than a large single passage. This fast-moving intake charge promotes good torque production during low- and mid-range rpm operation. The smaller valves naturally have less mass than big ones, so mechanical inertia is reduced, making a higher engine speed possible before valve float occurs. The more times the cylinder can be filled and evacuated per second, the more horsepower can be obtained.

Because increased gas velocity is the main benefit of a four-valve cylinder head, the technology works best at high engine speeds. Unfortunately, multiple-valve technology is also inhibited by manifold constrictions and exhaust back pressure. This is the reason some manufacturers are researching new engine blocks that feature a one-piece cast cylinder head and block. The lack of cylinder head bolts allows a highly efficient manifold that maximizes the effect of multivalve design.

The benefits of multivalves are offset to some extent, however, by a more complicated camshaft arrangement. The easiest way to actuate four valves per cylinder is with dual overhead camshafts (Figure 9-22).

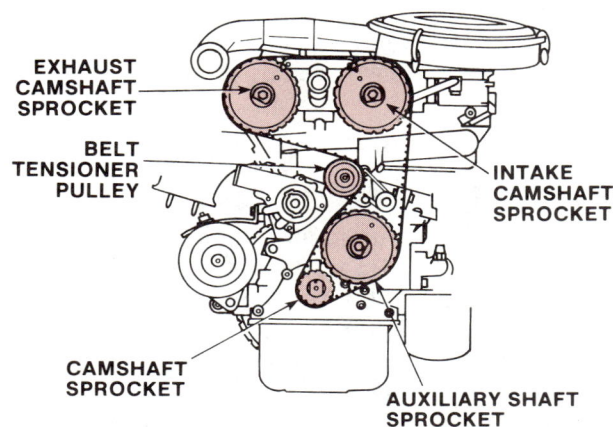

Figure 9-22 Typical dual overhead camshaft (DOHC) configuration.

These are sometimes difficult to lubricate. The cam drive is even more complicated with V-power plants. Most are using a single overhead cam per cylinder bank, with some kind of lever arm actuating the opposite bank of valves.

The high revolution rate inherent to multivalve engine design puts a premium on balancing techniques. Four-cylinder engines without balance shafts tend to be prone to high shaking forces. To overcome this problem, some multivalve engines use relatively long connecting rods to reduce angular changes during a piston stroke, a solution that has only been partially successful in the past. Using lightweight materials in the manufacturing of the piston rod assembly also contributes to the solution.

☐ ALUMINUM CYLINDER HEADS

Aluminum heads have become popular primarily because a typical aluminum head weighs roughly half as much as an iron head. Eliminating anywhere from 20 to 40 pounds of weight is a plus for fuel economy, but it has its drawbacks.

Attempts to lower overall engine weight have resulted in many lightweight cylinder head designs. One major problem with thin-walled, lightweight heads is cracking (Figure 9-23). These heads have also created head gasket sealing problems in the spark plug cooling port area (Figure 9-24). Head resurfacing when there is

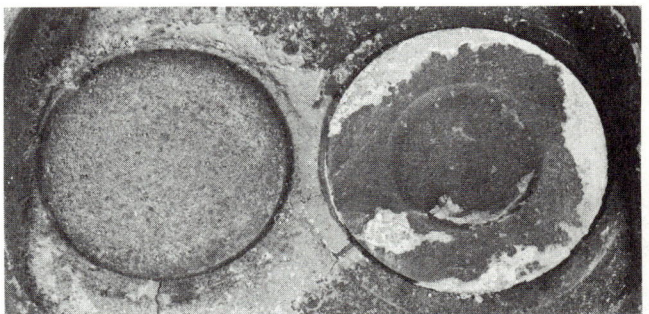

Figure 9-23 Lightweight heads are prone to cracking. This can lead to a recessed exhaust valve seat.

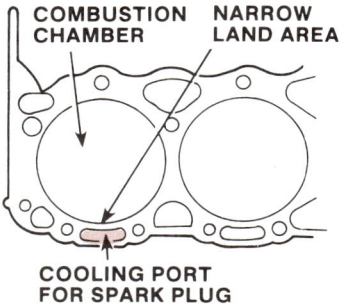

Figure 9-24 Before installing a rebuilt lightweight head, check the gasket-to-casting fit around the cooling port areas.

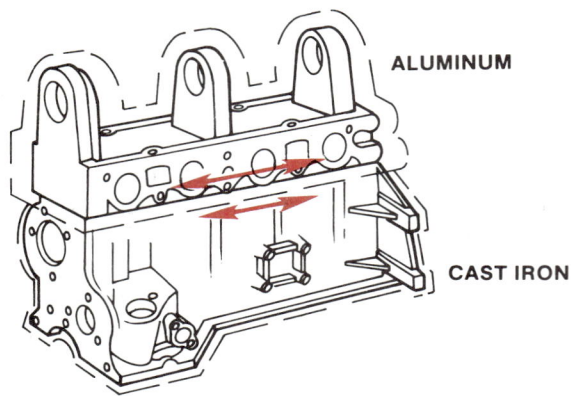

Figure 9-25 Aluminum expands and contracts almost twice as much as cast iron.

an existing core shift causes the narrow land area to move inward toward the combustion chamber and reduce gasket contact. Coolant can then leak into the cylinder. Before installing a lightweight head, carefully check this area for proper head gasket fit and possible hairline cracks. Aluminum expands and contracts almost twice as much as cast iron in response to temperature changes (Figure 9-25). This creates a number of problems. When an aluminum head is mated to an iron block (which most are), the difference in thermal expansion between head and block creates a great deal of scrubbing stress on the head gasket. Unless the gasket is engineered to take such punishment, leakage and premature gasket failure can result.

Increased thermal expansion and stress can also lead to cracking. The most crack-prone areas in the head are usually the areas around the valve seats. High combustion temperatures and the constant pounding of the valve against its seat often cause cracking between the intake and exhaust seats or just under the exhaust seat. If the seats are not machined to very close tolerances and installed properly, cracking is virtually guaranteed.

The difference in thermal expansion between aluminum and iron creates a lot of stress throughout the head. The head wants to expand in all directions at once as it heats up, but the head bolts keep it from going sideways or lengthwise. The only place left to go is up, so the head tends to bow up in the middle.

Lack of rigidity in the head itself is another factor to consider and one that can contribute to other problems in an engine. Aluminum is not as strong as cast iron. Consequently, the head provides less top end support for the block. This can allow more distortion in the upper cylinder bore area, affecting combustion sealing, blowby, and ring life. Using deck plates when boring the block can help minimize some of the distortion that will occur after the head is torqued down. Aluminum cylinder head bolts should never be loosened or tightened when the metal is hot. Stresses from torque changes can cause the head to warp.

In engines with overhead cams and aluminum heads, the cam journals often run in machined bores in the head itself. Aluminum makes a fairly good bearing material. It is soft and provides good imbedability to foreign particles. But it lacks the support and rigidity of a conventional steel-backed bearing in an iron saddle. Because of this, overhead cam bores in such heads typically experience more flex than their cast-iron counterparts. The result is usually accelerated wear and egg-shaped bores. If the head overheats and warps, alignment through the cam bores is destroyed. In some instances, the misalignment can be so bad the cam will not turn once the head is unbolted from the engine. Since many aluminum heads lack serviceable cam bearings and, in many instances, enough metal for boring and sleeving (repair sleeves are generally unavailable anyway), the only cure short of replacing the head is to machine out the cam bores and install a cam with oversized journals.

Aluminum has another drawback—porosity. The casting process sometimes leaves microscopic pores in the metal, which can weep oil or coolant. In most instances, the problem is cosmetic only in that it does no real harm. But the customer may not agree. To him or her a wet spot on the outside of a cylinder head looks like a leak.

If these shortcomings are not enough, aluminum is also highly vulnerable to electrolysis corrosion within the cooling system. Whenever two different metals such as aluminum and iron are in contact with one another it creates a battery-like condition in which the lesser of the two metals is eaten away. The lesser metal in this case is aluminum, and the only way to prevent such corrosion is to use an antifreeze with the right kind of corrosion inhibitors and to change it regularly. Unfortunately, many motorists do not follow this bit of advice, so by the time a technician sees the head it can be severely corroded.

With so many shortcomings it makes one wonder why the auto manufacturers use aluminum at all. The weight savings apparently exceed all other trade-offs, so it looks as if aluminum is here to stay. This is good for the aftermarket because it means more aluminum head work for those who can do it correctly.

Reconditioning Aluminum Cylinder Heads

Warpage in an aluminum cylinder head is usually the result of overheating (low coolant, uneven coolant circulation within the head, a too lean fuel mixture, and incorrect ignition timing).

Alignment of the cam bores in an overhead cam head must be checked with either a straightedge and feeler gauge (Figure 9-26) or with a dial indicator. If off by more than 0.002 to 0.003 inch, corrective action is required.

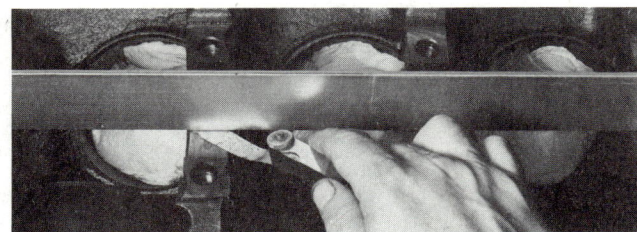

Figure 9-26 Checking cam bore alignment with a straightedge and feeler gauge.

CUSTOMER CARE

Explain to the customer the reasons why a cylinder head will warp. An informed customer is more likely to be a satisfied one.

SHOP TALK

Although specifications vary according to the application, traditionally, the maximum acceptable limit for cast-iron heads is 0.005 inch. Aluminum is not as forgiving, so 0.002 inch to 0.003 inch is a more realistic upper limit.

Although align boring and the installation of oversized cam bearings in the head or a cam with oversized journals might restore alignment in the cam bores, a badly warped head might be too far gone to allow the face to be resurfaced. Removing metal from the face of the head also alters the valve train geometry, which limits the amount of aluminum that can be removed.

Aluminum cylinder heads can be straightened through the use of heat and special clamping fixtures. Some manufacturers recommend that warped heads not be straightened, and instead should be replaced. Always follow the recommendations of the manufacturer.

SHOP TALK

Some engine rebuilding shops have ovens that can be used to straighten aluminum heads. Do not attempt to straighten a head without using an oven or without proper guidance.

☐ RESURFACING CYLINDER HEADS

There are three reasons for resurfacing the deck surface of a cylinder head.

1. To make the surface flat so that the gasket seals properly
2. To raise the compression ratio
3. To square the deck to the main bores

As engines undergo heating and cooling cycles over their life span, certain components tend to warp. This is especially true of cylinder heads. By using a precision straightedge or flatness bar and feeler gauge, the amount of warpage can be easily measured. While the manufacturers' specifications should always be checked, maximum head warpage for cast-iron limits are generally recognized as follows.

- In-line 6-cylinder—0.006 inch
- In-line 4-cylinder—0.004 inch
- V-6—0.003 inch
- V-8—0.004 inch
- Aluminum heads—0.002 to 0.003 inch

SHOP TALK

Some manufacturers allow aluminum heads to warp more than cast iron before recommending replacement.

The deck surface should be checked both across the head as well as lengthwise. Be sure to also check flatness of the intake and exhaust manifold mounting surface on the head. In general, maximum deformation allowed here is 0.004 inch.

In addition to warpage inspection, check for dents, scratches, and corrosion around water passages. This is especially important on aluminum heads. Heads that are deformed beyond specifications must be surfaced. The finished surface, however, should not be too smooth. It must be rough enough to provide "bite," but not enough to cause a poor seal and leakage.

Surface Finish

No cylinder head surface, no matter how it appears, is perfectly smooth. When viewed in cross section (Figure 9-27), a surface consists of a series of peaks and valleys. A special instrument, called a profilometer, incorporates a stylus that moves across the area to be checked. It is used to check surface roughness and to measure the distance between the peaks and valleys (Figure 9-28). It calculates the average value, which is about one-third of the peak-to-valley depth.

The unit of measurement used when checking surface finish is the microinch. One microinch is equal to one-millionth (0.000001) of an inch. Average surface finish can be expressed using either the RMS (root mean square) or AA (arithmetic average) methods. RMS readings are approximately 11 percent higher than AA readings. For all practical purposes this difference is negligible when checking machine finish.

184 Section 2 Engines

Figure 9-27 Cross section of a cylinder head surface.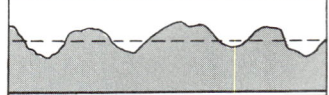

Figure 9-28 Measuring head surface roughness with a profilometer.

> ### SHOP TALK
>
> A profilometer is the ideal instrument to measure cylinder head surface finish; however, it is expensive. Another way to measure surface finish is to use a specimen block kit. This kit contains a set of blocks that have various microinch roughnesses. By using a fingernail to compare the finish on the head with the many blocks in the kit, it is possible to estimate the head surface smoothness.

For proper head gasket seating, a cylinder head surface finish range of 60 to 120 microinches is generally recommended. This finish consists of shallow scratches and small projections that allow for gasket support and sealing of voids. A surface finish greater than 120 microinches is too rough. Such a finish has scratches and projections that allow only the gasket to be supported at a few points. Even with the head bolts torqued to proper specifications, there is improper loading on the gasket bore flange leading to leaking combustion gases.

Four different types of machines—belt surfacer, milling, broaching, and grinding—can be used in resurfacing operations.

WARNING: Before attempting to operate any surfacing machine, be sure to become familiar with and follow all the cautions and warnings given in the machine's operation manual. Also, when operating these machines, you must wear safety glasses, goggles, or a face shield.

Belt Surfacers

Belt surfacers resemble belt sanders. These machines are easy to set up and operate. An operator

A

B

Figure 9-29 (A) Typical belt surfacer and (B) how it is used.

merely places the part to be surfaced on the belt. A restraint rail helps keep the part positioned (Figure 9-29). Some machines have air-operated holddown fixtures.

Resurfacing quality depends on operator skill and factors such as belt condition, machine horsepower, and the holddown pressure applied.

Milling Machines

Milling machines (Figure 9-30) cut away thin layers of metal to create a level, properly finished surface

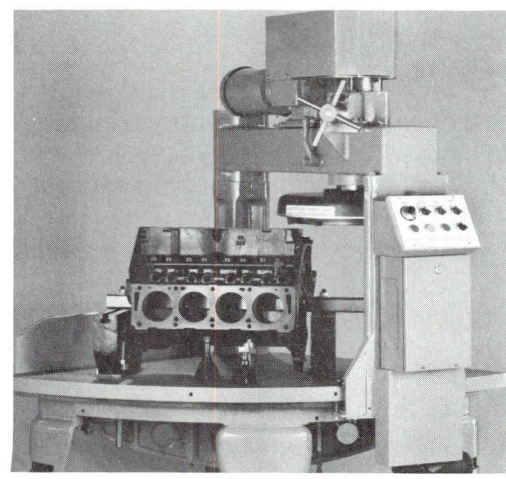

Figure 9-30 Typical milling machine. *Courtesy of Storm Vulcan, Inc.*

Figure 9-31   Milling an aluminum cylinder head.

(Figure 9-31). Cutters remove up to 0.050 inch per pass. Both rough and finish cuts are usually made to create the desired finish. Milling requires operator skill. However, machine maintenance is low. A good variety of surface finishes are possible.

Broaching Machines

Broaching machines use an underside rotary cutter or broach (Figure 9-32). A block, cylinder head, or intake manifold is held in an inverted position as the broach passes underneath. A mirror setup is needed to inspect the work in progress.

Figure 9-32   Typical broaching machine. *Courtesy of Winona Van Norman Machine Co.*

Surface Grinders

Surface grinders use a grinding wheel to remove metal stock (Figure 9-33). They set up and operate similarly to milling machines. Grinding wheels must be sharp. A dull wheel will simply polish, not cut, the surface.

Stock Removal Guidelines

The amount of stock removed from the head gasket surface must be limited. Excessive surfacing can lead to problems in the following areas.

Engine's Clearance Volumes

It might be necessary to measure and adjust the size of an engine's clearance volumes. Clearance volume is the volume of the combustion chamber plus the volume of the cylinder when the piston is at TDC.

Measuring the clearance volume is called cc-ing the cylinder head. This is done with the valves and spark plugs installed. The cylinder head is mounted upside down, and a glass or plastic plate is installed over the combustion chamber. A graduated container called a burette is used to fill the combustion chamber with thin oil. The oil is poured through a hole in the plate, as shown in Figure 9-34. The amount of oil that enters the combustion chamber is noted by observing the cubic centimeter (cc) markings on the burette. The number of cc's used is equal to the clearance volume (in cubic centimeters) for this cylinder.

The clearance volumes for an engine can be adjusted in several ways. They may be reduced by surfacing the cylinder head. This, of course, reduces all the clearance volumes for that cylinder head. Individual clearance volumes can be increased by grinding the valve seats to sink the valves and by grinding and polishing metal from the combustion chamber surface. Either method can be employed to equalize all the clearance volumes and adjust them to the manufacturer's specifications.

Figure 9-33   Typical surface grinder.

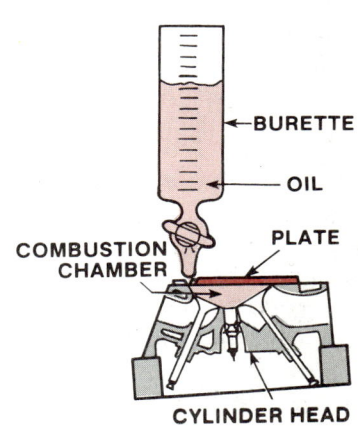

Figure 9-34   Cc-ing a cylinder head to find the combustion volume.

Compression Ratio

Standard engine rebuilding procedures can affect the engine's compression ratio in a number of ways.

Boring the block oversize changes the swept volume and the compression ratio. Generally speaking, the compression ratio increases at the same percentage that the displacement increased. Boring an engine 0.060 inch oversize will increase the displacement 9 cubic inches or slightly more than 3%. Assuming the replacement piston has the same compression height as the original, the initial 9.0:1 compression ratio will be increased by 3.0% to 9.27:1. As a rule of thumb, there is a 2% increase at 0.030 inch oversize, a 4% increase at 0.060 inch and a 6% increase at 0.125 inch. With today's gas, anything more than 9.0:1 is suspect without a detonation sensor.

Decking the block changes the compression ratio. Removing 0.010 inch from the deck surface of an engine with a 4-inch bore, 76-cc head, 0.060-inch head gasket, 0.080-inch deck height would raise the compression ratio by 0.14:1.

Resurfacing the head also increases the compression ratio. Though the effect varies for every type and size of chamber, a good rule of thumb is that when a head is surfaced 0.010 inch, the chamber is reduced by 1.50 cc for a 60-cc head and by 2.50 cc for a 90-cc head. This will increase the compression ratio by about 0.141:1 to 0.20:1, depending on the specific head configuration and actual swept volume.

Variations in head gasket thicknesses affect the compression ratio. There can be as much as 0.040 inch difference between various types and brands of gaskets. For instance, changing from a soft-faced to a steel or copper shim gasket can increase the compression ratio by as much as 0.50:1.

The piston itself can have an effect on the compression ratio. Replacing a dished piston with a flat top will increase the compression ratio significantly. Using the wrong piston with a particular chamber will raise or lower the compression ratio. The difference of 10 cc in chamber size can have a dramatic effect on the compression ratio and might require the use of a different piston.

Fortunately, most aftermarket suppliers either deck or destroke their oversize pistons to enable the technician to reduce or maintain the compression ratio instead of increasing it. These pistons should be used whenever available.

Piston/Valve Interference and Misalignment

When the block or head is surfaced, the piston-to-valve clearance during the overlap period becomes less. To prevent the valves from making contact with the piston, a minimum of 0.070 inch piston-to-valve clearance is recommended.

Surfacing can also cause valve tips, rocker arms, and pushrods to be dimensioned closer to the camshaft. This causes a change in rocker arm geometry and can also cause hydraulic lifters to bottom out.

When metal is removed from the block or heads on a V-type OHV engine, the heads will be positioned closer to the crankshaft. This downward movement will cause the intake manifold to fit differently between the heads. As a result, ports might be mismatched and manifold bolts might not line up. In order to return the intake manifold to its original alignment, corrective machining on the manifold is required.

GRINDING VALVES

Valve grinding or refacing is done by machining a fresh, smooth surface on the valve faces and stem tips. Valve faces suffer from burning, pitting, and wear caused by opening and closing millions of times during the life of an engine. Valve stem tips wear because of friction from the rocker arms.

Before grinding, inspect each valve face for burning and each stem tip for wear. Replace any valves that are badly burned or worn. Reusable valves are cleaned by soaking them in solvent, which will soften the carbon deposits. The deposits are then removed with a wire buffing wheel. Once the deposits are removed, the valve can be resurfaced. The face is reconditioned prior to grinding the valve tip.

Valves can be refaced on either grinding (Figure 9-35) or cutting (Figure 9-36) machines. Although both can reface valves and smooth and chamfer valve stem ends, the traditional grinding method of refacing is still the most popular. Larger valve grinder machines are capable of doing valve train reconditioning tasks such as refacing certain types of rocker arms and other repair jobs described in this chapter. There are also computerized valve refacing grinder machines.

Figure 9-35 Grinder-type valve resurfacer. *Courtesy of Sunnen Products Co.*

Cylinder Heads and Valves   187

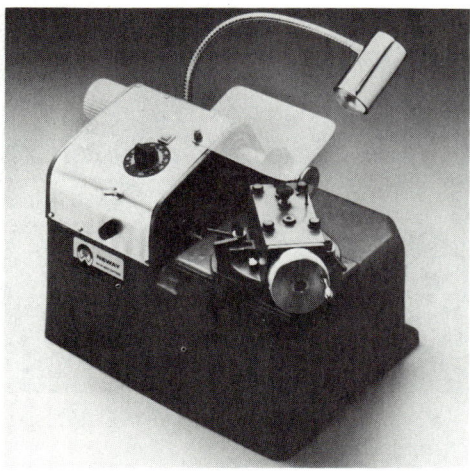

Figure 9-36 Cutter-type valve resurfacer. *Courtesy of Neway Manufacturing, Inc.*

> **USING SERVICE MANUALS**
>
> Specifications for valve angles are normally listed in the engine specifications section of a service manual.

To start the valve grinding operation, chuck the valve as close as possible to the valve head to eliminate stem flexing from wheel pressure (Figure 9-37). Set the grinding angle according to the desired angle. Take light cuts using the full grinding wheel width (Figure 9-38). Make sure coolant is striking the contact point between the valve face and grinding wheel. Remove only enough metal to clean up the valve face. A knifelike edge will burn easily or might cause pre-ignition (Figure 9-39). As a general rule, it is not advisable to grind a valve face to a point where the margin is reduced by more than 25% or to where it is less than 0.045 inch on the exhaust and 0.030 inch on the intake valves.

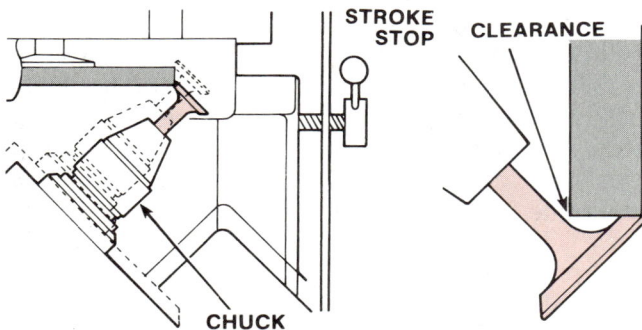

Figure 9-37 Once the grinder is set up, the valve is secured in the chuck, the correct angle is set, and the proper stroke is set. Be sure there is clearance between the edge of the stone and the valve.

Figure 9-38 Light cutting on a valve. *Courtesy of Sioux Tools, Inc.*

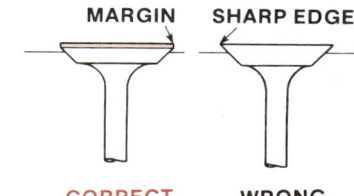

Figure 9-39 A sharp edge on the valve face is not recommended.

After grinding, check valve head runout. Use a dial indicator on the valve margin and rotate the valve while it is still in the chuck. Valve runout should not exceed 0.002 inch total indicated reading (TIR). The face should not show any chatter marks or unground areas. After grinding, examine the valve face for cracks. Sometimes fine cracks are visible only after grinding. Sometimes they occur during grinding due to inadequate coolant flow or excessive wheel pressure.

WARNING: Always wear eye protection when operating any type of grinding equipment.

If an interference angle is to be used, the grinder is set 1/2 to 1 degree less than the standard 30- or 45-degree face angle. Always consult the manufacturer's specifications to determine whether an interference angle is to be used. Grinding an interference angle produces a face angle close to 29 or 44 degrees. For the valve to seat properly, the face angle cannot be less than 29 or 44 degrees (Figure 9-40).

Once the face is ground, the valve tip might also need to be ground. This is best determined by placing the valve in the cylinder head to check the stem height. Using the manufacturer's specifications, determine whether and to what extent the tip must be ground. As shown in Figure 9-41, the tip is ground using a stemming stone that has been dressed. Just like the facing stone, the stemming stone is dressed with a diamond tool. The valve is secured in a V-holder and clamp, and a coolant is used to cool the valve tip and remove grit during grinding.

The valve tip is ground so that it is exactly square with the stem. Because valve tips have hardened surfaces that are up to 0.030 inch in depth, only 0.010 inch can be removed during grinding. If more than

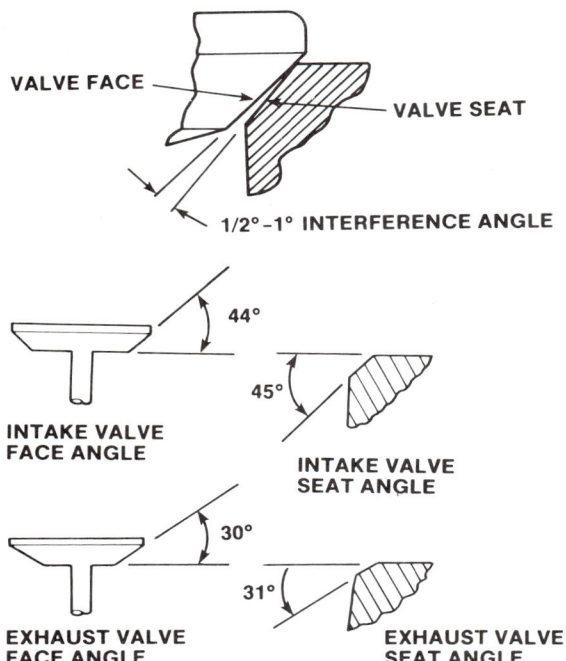

Figure 9-40 The difference between the seat angle and the valve face angle is known as the interference angle.

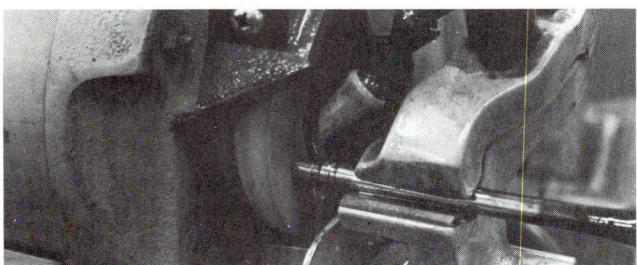

Figure 9-41 Grinding a valve tip. *Courtesy of Sioux Tools, Inc.*

0.010 inch is removed from the tip, the valve must be replaced. Also, if too much material is removed from the valve tip, there might be interference between the rocker arm and spring retainer or valve rotator. Follow the manufacturer's specifications for the allowable limits.

There is little basic difference in the refacing procedures for a grinder and cutter machine. In fact, most of the guidelines given for grinding a valve face are the same for cutting. Actually, the only difference is in the cutting tool—a grind wheel or a cutting tool such as shown in Figure 9-42.

SHOP TALK

Some valve refacing equipment requires a procedure that is the reverse of the one just given in the text. That is, the valve tip is dressed and chamfered before it is refaced. If this is not done

Figure 9-42 Cutting to reface a valve. *Courtesy of Neway Manufacturing, Inc.*

on this type of equipment, the valve face will be ground off center. Follow the equipment manufacturer's instructions for procedures and sequences.

Material removed from the valve face and valve seat increases the amount of valve stem length on the spring side of the cylinder head when the valve is seated. If excessive, this could cause the hydraulic lifter plunger to bottom out and prevent the valve from being fully seated when it is closed.

Grinding material from the stem tip will generally correct any stem height problems and will center the hydraulic lifter plunger. Do not remove more material from the valve stem than the maximum allowed in the vehicle's service manual. If the valve stem height is greater than the acceptable amount plus the maximum amount allowed to be ground off the stem, this indicates that the valve or seat should be replaced.

❏ VALVE GUIDE RECONDITIONING

Valve guide problems can be lumped into one of three basic categories: inadequate lubrication, valve geometry problems, and wrong valve stem-to-guide clearance.

Inadequate lubrication can be caused by oil starvation in the upper valve train due to low oil pressure, obstructed oil passages, improper operation of pushrods, and using the wrong type of valve seal. Insufficient lubrication results in stem scuffing, rapid stem and guide wear, possible valve sticking, and ultimately valve failure due to poor seating and over-heating.

Geometry problems include an incorrectly installed valve height, off-square springs, and rocker arm tappet screws or rocker arms that push the valve sideways every time it opens. This causes uneven guide wear, leaving an egg-shaped hole. The wear leads to increased stem-to-guide clearance, poor valve seating, and premature valve failure.

As for valve stem-to-guide clearance, a certain minimum amount is needed for lubrication and thermal expansion of the valve stem. Exhaust valves require more clearance than intakes because they run hotter. Clearance should also be close enough to prevent a buildup of varnish and carbon deposits on the stems, which could cause sticking. Insufficient clearance, however, can lead to rapid stem and guide wear, scuffing, and sticking, which prevents the valve from seating fully. This, in turn, causes the valve to run hot and burn.

If the clearance is too great, oil control will be a serious problem. Contrary to what some technicians might think, oil can be drawn past both the intake and exhaust guides. Though oil consumption is more of a problem with sloppy or worn intake guides because the guides are constantly exposed to vacuum, oil can also be pulled down the exhaust guides by suction created in the exhaust port. The outflow of hot exhaust creates a venturi effect as it exits the exhaust port, creating enough vacuum to draw oil down a worn guide (Figure 9-43).

Some guides might have internal rifling or spiral grooves to improve oil retention. These are usually used with exhaust valves and on diesel engines or dry fuel engines, such as those built to run on propane.

The antiseize and antiwear characteristics of bronze generally enable a bronze guide to last two to five times longer than a cast-iron guide. Unfortunately, bronze guides are more expensive so their use in original equipment applications is limited. Bronze is also a more difficult material to machine so tooling does not last as long with bronze as it does with cast iron. Because of these drawbacks, bronze guides are commonly used only as aftermarket replacements.

Bronze inserts provide better thermal conductivity than cast iron, allowing the valves to run cooler and last longer. Bronze also has a lower coefficient of friction and retains oil better than cast iron. This allows closer stem-to-guide clearances for improved valve stem cooling and reduced oil consumption.

Knurling

Knurling is one of the fastest techniques for restoring the inside diameter (ID) dimensions of a worn valve guide. The process raises the surface of the guide ID by plowing tiny furrows through the surface of the metal (Figure 9-44). As the knurling tool cuts into the guide, metal is raised or pushed up on either side of the indentation. This effectively decreases the ID of the guide hole. A burnisher is used to press the ridges flat and is then used to shave off the peaks of these ridges to produce the proper-sized hole and restore the correct guide-to-stem clearance.

Knurling can be done with either a tap-type knurling tool or a wheel-type or roller knurler (Figure 9-45).

One of the main advantages of knurling is that it does not change the centerline of the valve stem appreciably, so it reduces the amount of work necessary to reseat the valve. Knurling also allows a rebuilder to reuse the old valve if wear is within acceptable limits, helping to reduce rebuilding costs. In spite of its speed and simplicity, knurling is not a cure for restoring badly worn guides to their original condition.

Opinions vary as to how much wear is acceptable for knurling. Most automotive experts seem to agree that the maximum amount of acceptable wear ranges from 0.004 to 0.007 inch.

Some technicians do not consider knurling to be a long-term repair because it restores only a portion of the original surface. As the raised ridges are worn, wear accelerates and clearances become excessive. This occurs long before it would have if the entire ID of the guide had been restored.

Another consideration with knurling is that guides do not wear evenly from top to bottom. They wear the least in the middle and the most toward either end. The tapered wear pattern means a knurling tool will do the

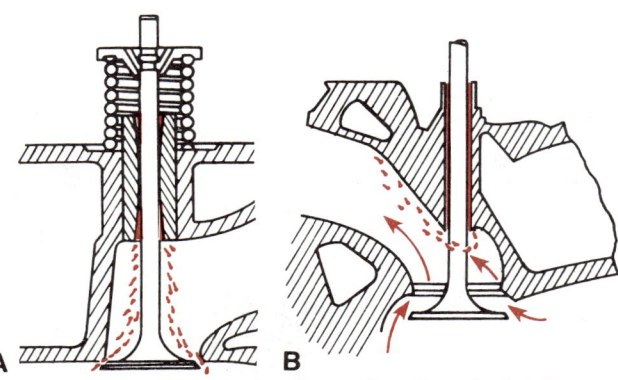

Figure 9-43 (A) Worn intake guides allow the intake vacuum to suck oil down the guide, and (B) worn exhaust guides can do the same.

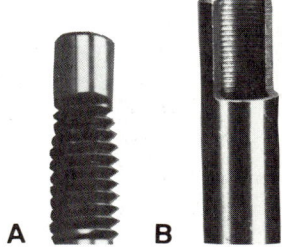

Figure 9-44 (A) Typical tap-type knurling tool tip and (B) the cut it makes. *Courtesy of Goodson Shop Supplies.*

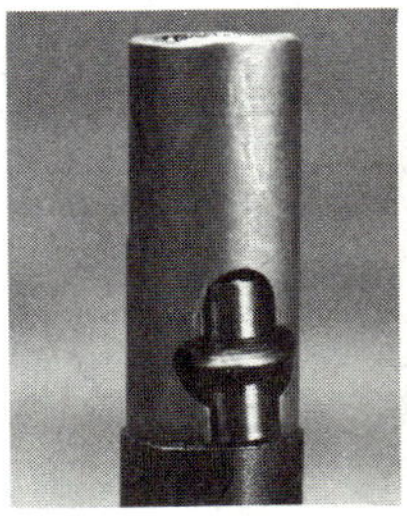

Figure 9-45 Wheel-type or roller knurling tool. *Courtesy of Sunnen Products Co.*

least where it is needed the most—toward the ends. Knurling a bell-mouthed guide, therefore, only succeeds in restoring the middle section of the guide. Excessive clearance might remain at either end. This has the same effect as shortening the valve guide: it decreases stem cooling and can encourage wobbling.

Reaming and Oversized Valves

Reaming is used to repair worn guides by increasing the guide hole size to take an oversize valve stem or by restoring the guide to its original diameter after installing inserts or knurling. Standard oversizes are 0.003, 0.005, 0.006, 0.010, 0.013, and 0.015. In some cases, other sizes also may be available. Be sure to check their availability before doing any machining.

When reaming (Figure 9-46), limit the amount of metal removed per pass to 0.005 inch. Always reface the valve seat after the valve guide has been reamed and use a suitable scraper to break the sharp corner (ID) at the top and bottom of the valve guide.

The advantage of reaming for an oversized valve is that the finished product is totally new. The guide is straight, the valve is new, and the clearance is accurate. The use of oversized valve stems is generally considered to be superior to knurling. Yet, like knurling, it is relatively quick and easy. The only tool that is required is a reamer. The valve centerline is maintained so the work required to finish the seat is reduced. However, since reaming requires the use of new valves, it can be more expensive on an engine with many worn guides. Its use is also limited to heads where the guides are not worn beyond the limits of the maximum oversize valve that is available. Because of these limitations, many technicians prefer more cost-effective alternatives such as guide liners, inserts, or replacement guides.

Thin-Wall Guide Liners

The thin-wall guide liners repair technique offers a number of important advantages and is also popular with many production engine rebuilders (PERs) as well as smaller shops. It provides the benefits of a bronze guide surface (better lubricity, wear, and tighter clearances). It can be used with either integral or replaceable guides (cast iron or bronze). It is faster, easier, and cheaper than installing new guides in heads with replaceable or integral guides, and it maintains guide centering with respect to the seats.

Thin-wall guide liners are manufactured from a phosphor-bronze or silicon-aluminum-bronze material. The popular liner size is the 0.502-inch universal guide. This liner has a 0.502-inch outside diameter (OD), and its ID varies from 0.312 to 0.375 inch. These liners can be cut to almost any length. They are designed for a 0.002- to 0.0025-inch press fit. A tight fit is essential for proper heat transfer to the head and to prevent the liner from working loose.

The liners are installed by first boring out (Figure 9-47) the original guides to 0.030-inch oversize with a special piloted boring tool (Figure 9-48A) pressed into the guide using a driver and air hammer (Figure 9-48B). On guides not precut to length, the excess must be milled off before finishing (Figure 9-48C). The liner is then wedged in place and sized in a single operation by passing a ball broach down through it

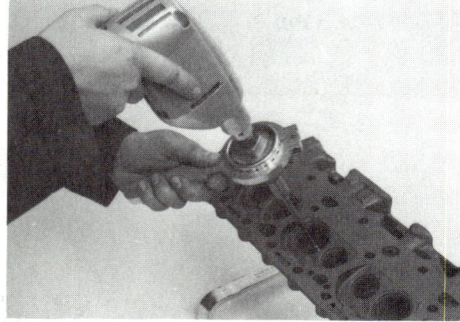

Figure 9-46 Reaming valve guides. *Courtesy of Goodson Shop Supplies*

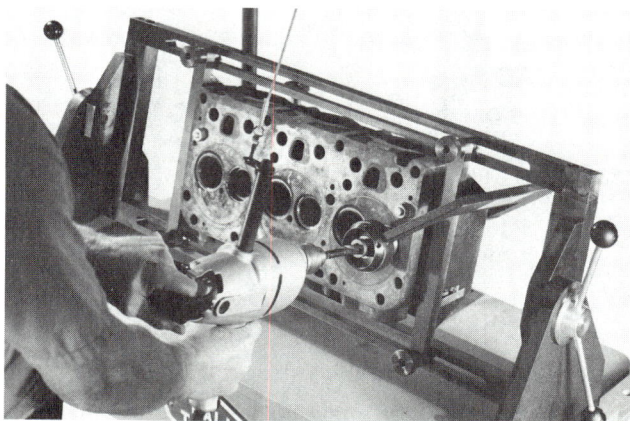

Figure 9-47 Two setups for boring out old and worn guides. *Courtesy of Hall-Toledo, Inc.*

Cylinder Heads and Valves

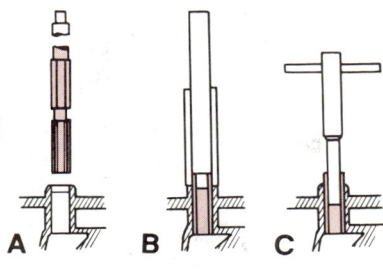

Figure 9-48 Bronze guide liner installation: (A) boring the guide to oversize; (B) installing the liner; and (C) trimming the liner.

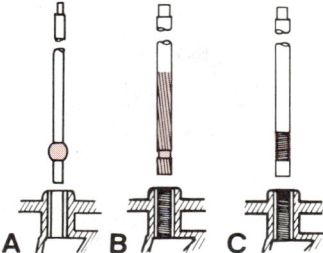

Figure 9-49 ID finishes used for guides: (A) ball broach; (B) ream; and (C) spiral.

(Figure 9-49A). This eliminates the need to ream it to size and assures a tight fit between the liner and guide. If a ream finish is desired (Figure 9-49B), it can be obtained by lubricating the reamer with a bronze-lube and then running it through the guide. For closer than normal stem-to-guide clearance, spiraling or knurling is suggested for added lubrication (Figure 9-49C).

The only trick to using liners is to make sure the hole is round and the correct size. If the hole is distorted excessively or if it is too large, the liner will not fit properly and will cause problems. Running a ball broach or a roller burnishing tool down the liner helps compensate for hole distortion and presses the liner for a tight fit.

Valve Guide Replacement

Replacing the entire valve guide is another repair option possible on cylinder heads with replaceable guides. However, pressing out the old guides and installing new ones can be difficult with some aluminum heads where the interference fit is considerable. Cracking the head or galling the guide hole is always a risk.

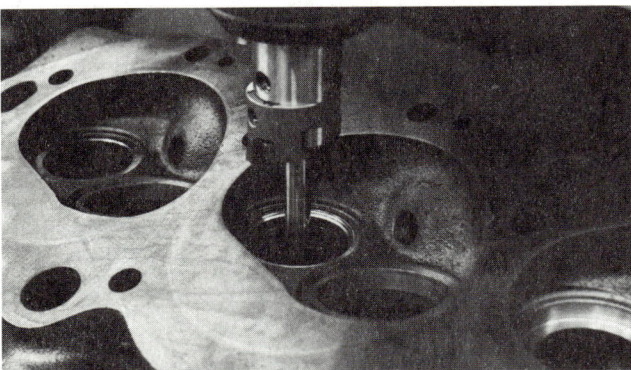

Figure 9-50 Boring out an integral guide.

One recommendation is to preheat the heads in an oven prior to guide removal and to lubricate dry liners before driving them out.

> ### SHOP TALK
>
> An oven should be used to bring the head to 250 degrees Fahrenheit. Guides can be difficult to remove after heating to 500 degrees. A torch should never be used because it can burn through the head. Localized heating can also induce considerable distortion.

INTEGRAL GUIDES To replace integral guides, bore (Figure 9-50) or drive (Figure 9-51) the old guide out and drive a thin-wall replacement guide into the hole. Many shops use a seat and guide machine for this process (Figure 9-52), although it can be done with portable equipment. Drive the replacement guides in cold with approximately 0.002-inch press fit. Use an assembly lube to prevent galling. It is necessary to keep the centerline of the guide concentric with the valve seat so that the rocker arm-to-valve stem contact area is not disturbed (Figure 9-53).

Occasionally, a new guide will not be concentric with the valve seat. Install a new seat to correct the

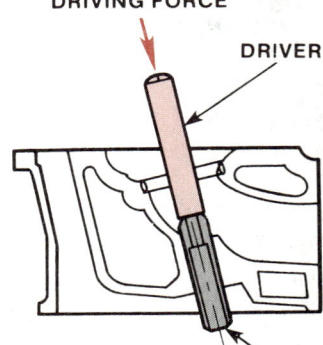

Figure 9-51 Driving out an integral guide.

Figure 9-52 Valve seat and guide machine. *Courtesy of Kwik-Way Manufacturing Co.*

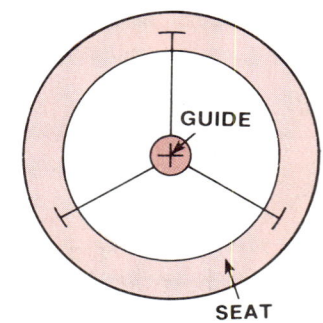

Figure 9-53 The centerline of the guide should be concentric with the seat.

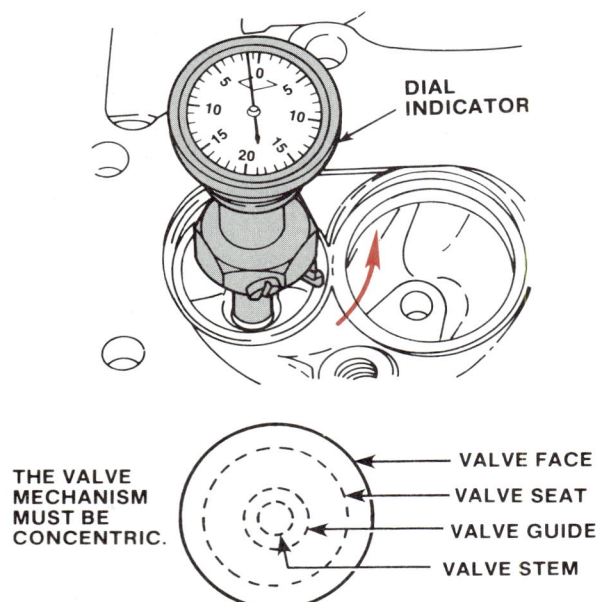

Figure 9-54 Checking valve seat concentricity.

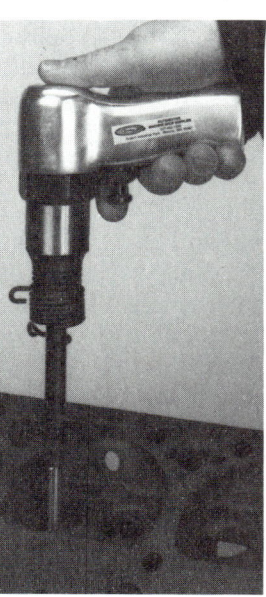

Figure 9-55 Installing new guides (A) with a press and driver and (B) with an air hammer. *Courtesy of TRW, Inc. and Goodson Shop Supplies*

problem and check the concentricity of the valve seat with a concentricity gauge (Figure 9-54).

INSERT GUIDES To press out an old valve guide, place a proper-sized driver so that its end fits snugly into the guide. The shoulder on the driver must also be slightly smaller than the OD of the guide, so that it will go through the cylinder head. Use a heavy ball peen hammer to drive the pressed guide out of the cylinder head.

Pressing or driving out and installing new guides is not difficult, but there is always the danger of breaking the guide or tearing up the guide hole in the head. Cast-iron guides in particular have a tendency to gall aluminum heads. Once the hole is damaged, it must be bored out and an oversized guide installed—assuming one is available to fit the application. New guides should be chilled prior to installation because of the needed interference fit between the guide and head. Chilling them in a freezer or with dry ice works well. Lubricant also helps to prevent galling.

When installing new guides, be careful not to damage them. Use a press and the same driver that was used to remove the old guide. Align the new guide and press straight down (Figure 9-55A), not at an angle. An air hammer (Figure 9-55B) and special driver can also be used to install new guides.

At least one engine manufacturer uses guides that are cut off at an angle on the combustion chamber end. Others may also be found to have guides cut at an angle at one end or the other. No attempt should be made to press or drive against the angled end.

Find the correct amount of guide protrusion. Guide height is important to avoid interference with the valve spring retainer. The guide must also fit the hole tightly or it can work loose. The manufacturer's specifications give the correct valve guide installed height, but it is good practice to measure how far the old guides stick out of the cylinder head and to use this measurement as a reference. As each guide is installed, the technician should measure the installed height with a scale (Figure 9-56). After the new guides have been installed, insert a valve. Check for any stem interference.

Valve guide honing is ideal for sizing both integral and insert guides. Very close tolerances, ± 0.002 inch,

Cylinder Heads and Valves

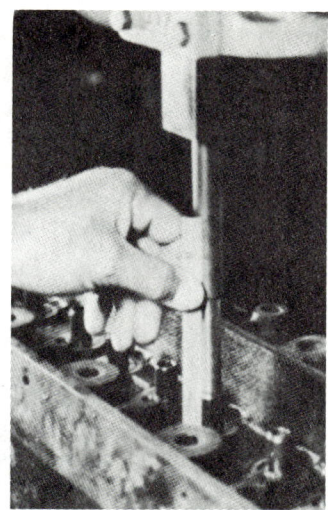

Figure 9-56 Measuring guide protrusion. *Courtesy of TRW, Inc.*

can be obtained with this process. With reaming, for example, it is difficult to have any clearance closer than 0.005 inch. These close tolerances give better oil control and heat dissipation.

One of the main drawbacks of replacing guides is that it changes the valve centerline, particularly when drilling out heads with integral guides. This can sometimes lead to seat refinishing problems if the centerline has moved too far off center.

☐ RECONDITIONING VALVE SEATS

The most critical sealing surface in the valve train assembly is between the face of the valve and its seat in the cylinder head when the valve is closed. Leakage between these surfaces reduces the engine's compression and power and can lead to valve burning. To insure proper seating of the valve, the valve seat must be correct width (Figure 9-57), correct location on the valve face, and concentric with the guide (less than 0.002 inch runout).

The ideal seat width for automotive engines is 1/16 inch for intake valves and 3/32 inch for exhaust valves. Maintaining this width is important to insure proper sealing and heat transfer. However, when an existing seat is refinished to make it smooth and concentric, it also becomes wider.

Wide seats cause problems. Seating pressure drops as seat width increases. Less force is available to crush carbon particles that stick to the seats, and seats run cooler, allowing deposits to build up on them.

The seat should contact the valve face 1/32 inch from the margin of the valve. When the engine reaches operating temperature, the valve expands slightly more than the seat. This moves the contact area down the valve face. Seats that make too low of a contact with the valve face might lose partial contact at normal operating temperatures.

Like valve guides, there are two types of valve seats—integral and insert. Integral seats are part of the casting. Insert seats are pressed into the head and are always used in aluminum cylinder heads.

Valve seats can be reconditioned or repaired by one of two methods, depending on the seat type—machining a counterbore to install an insert seat, or grinding, cutting, or machining an integral seat.

Before starting seat work, carefully check the seats for cracks (Figure 9-58). Cracked integral seats sometimes can be repaired by installing inserts, if the crack is not too deep. Cracked insert seats must be replaced. Check insert seats for looseness with a small pry bar (Figure 9-59). Replace if movement is noted.

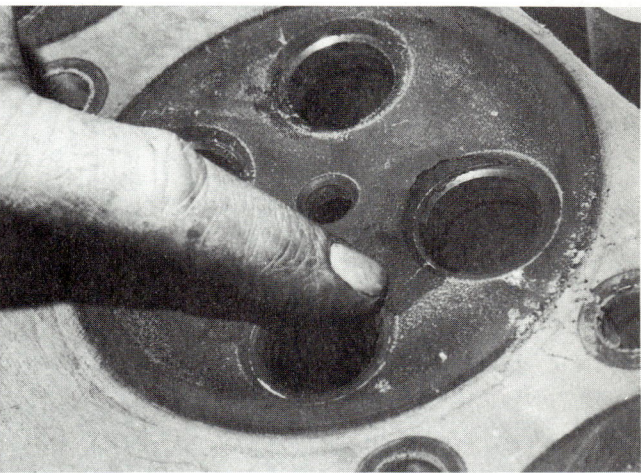

Figure 9-58 Checking the seat for cracks.

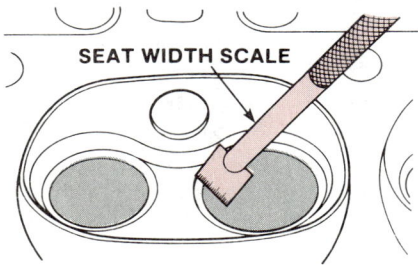

Figure 9-57 Checking valve seat width.

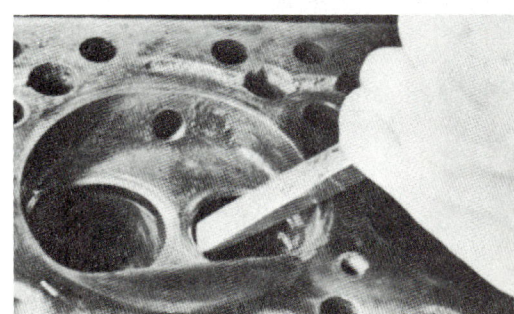

Figure 9-59 Use a small pry bar to check insert seats for looseness. *Courtesy of TRW, Inc.*

Installing Valve Seat Inserts

The following steps outline a typical insert valve seat removal and replacement.

PROCEDURES
Insert Valve Seat Removal and Replacement

1. To remove the damaged insert, use a puller (Figure 9-60) or a pry bar (Figure 9-61).
2. After removal, clean up the counterbores or recut it to accommodate oversized inserts (Figure 9-62).
3. Insert the counterboring pilot into the valve guide. Then mount the base and ball shaft assem-

Figure 9-63 Mounting the base and ball shaft assembly to the gasket face angle of the head. *Courtesy of Hall-Toledo, Inc.*

bly to the gasket face angle of the cylinder head (Figure 9-63).
4. Use an outside micrometer to accurately expand the cutterhead to a predetermined size of the counterbore (Figure 9-64). Remember that the counterbore should have a slightly smaller ID than the OD of the insert to provide for an interface fit.
5. Place the valve insert counterboring tool over the pilot and ball-shaft assembly. Preset the depth of the valve seat insert at the feed screw. A magnetic ring is often used to trap the dust created when counterboring valve seats (Figure 9-65).
6. Cut the insert by turning the stop-collar until it reaches the preset depth (Figure 9-66). Use a lubricant on the cutters for a smoother finish.
7. To install the insert, heat the head in a parts cleaning oven to approximately 350 to 400 degrees Fahrenheit. Chill the insert in a freezer or with dry ice before installation.

WARNING: Wear the proper gloves when handling dry ice.

Figure 9-60 Using a puller to remove a damaged insert seat. *Courtesy of TRW, Inc.*

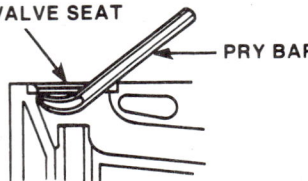

Figure 9-61 Using a pry bar to remove a damaged insert seat.

Figure 9-62 Counterbores can be cleaned or recut to accommodate oversized inserts. *Courtesy of TRW, Inc.*

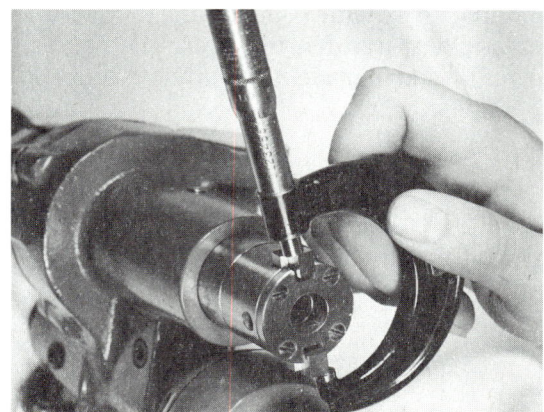

Figure 9-64 Using an outside micrometer to expand a cutterhead. *Courtesy of Hall-Toledo, Inc.*

Cylinder Heads and Valves   195

Figure 9-65 A magnetic ring is ideal for collecting grinding dust. *Courtesy of Goodson Shop Supplies*

Figure 9-66 Cutting the insert. *Courtesy of Hall-Toledo, Inc.*

8. Press the seat with the proper interference fit using a driver (Figure 9-67).
9. When the installation is complete, the edge around the outside of the insert is staked as shown in Figure 9-68. By doing so, the inserts will be secured more effectively in the counterbore.

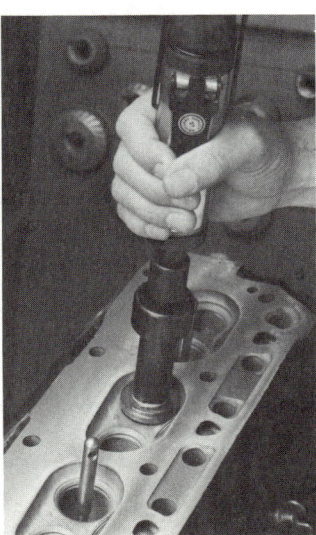

Figure 9-67 Seat the insert firmly in the cylinder head. *Courtesy of Sunnen Products Co.*

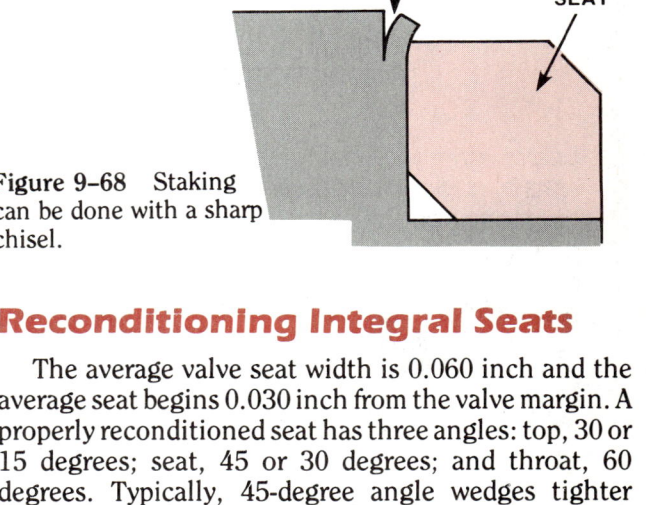

Figure 9-68 Staking can be done with a sharp chisel.

Reconditioning Integral Seats

The average valve seat width is 0.060 inch and the average seat begins 0.030 inch from the valve margin. A properly reconditioned seat has three angles: top, 30 or 15 degrees; seat, 45 or 30 degrees; and throat, 60 degrees. Typically, 45-degree angle wedges tighter than the 30-degree seat, so it is used more often. Using three angles maintains the correct seat width and sealing position on the valve face (Figure 9-69). Correct sealing pressure and heat transfer from the valve through the seat are also affected. Always check service manual specifications for valve seat angles and valve face-to-seat contact amounts. As stated earlier, contact is usually 1/16 inch for intake valves and 3/32 inch for exhaust valves (Figure 9-70). Maintaining proper seat overhang is also required. This overhang is usually 1/64 inch for all valves.

Integral valve seats can be reconditioned by grinding, cutting, or machining.

Grinding Valve Seats

When grinding a valve seat, it is very important to select and use the correct size pilot and grind stone.

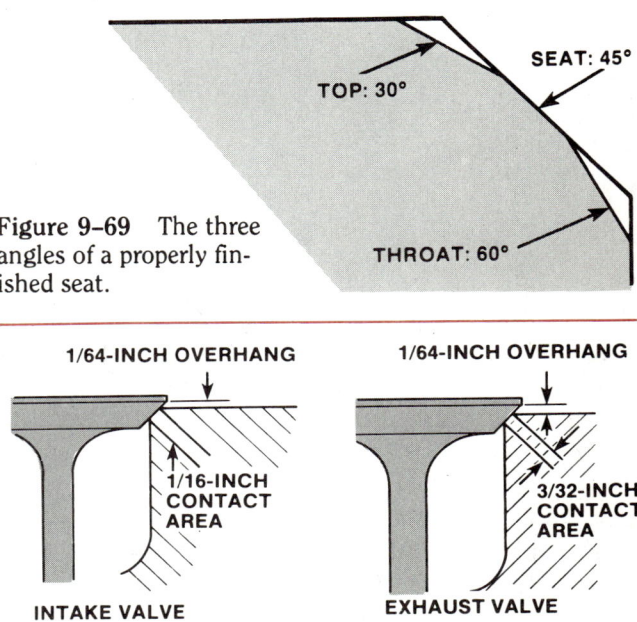

Figure 9-69 The three angles of a properly finished seat.

Figure 9-70 Proper valve overhang.

Hard seats use a soft stone and soft seats (cast iron) use a harder stone. The stone must be properly dressed and cutting oil used to aid in grinding.

> **SHOP TALK**
>
> Before grinding, many technicians clean the seats by placing a piece of fine emery cloth between the stone and the seat and giving the surface a hard rub. This will help prevent contamination of the seat grinding stone with any oil or carbon residue that might be present on the valve seat. Such contamination could cause glazing.

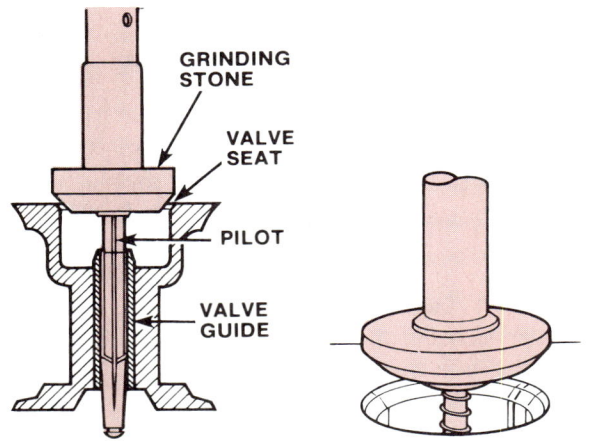

Figure 9-71 Inserting a pilot shaft into the valve guide in preparation for grinding.

The grinding wheel is positioned and centered by inserting a properly sized pilot shaft into the valve guide (Figure 9-71). All valve guide service must be completed before installing the pilot.

The seat is ground by continually raising and lowering the grinder unit on and off the seat at a rate of approximately 120 times per minute (Figure 9-72). Grinding should only continue until the seat is clean and free of defects.

After the seat is ground, valve fit is checked using machinist dye. The valve face is coated with dye, installed in its seat, and slightly rotated. The valve is then removed and the dye pattern on the valve face and valve seat inspected.

If the valve face and seat are not contacting each other evenly, or if the contact line is too high, the seat must be reground with the same stone used initially to correct the condition. If the line is too low or the width is not correct, the seat must be reground with stones of different angles (Figure 9-73).

Cutting Valve Seats

Cutting valve seats differs from grinding only in the equipment used (Figure 9-74). Hardened valve seat cutters replace grinding wheels for seat finishing. The basic seat cutting procedures are the same as those for grinding.

Machining Valve Seats

As stated earlier in this chapter, a valve system rebuilding machine such as the one shown in Figure

Figure 9-72 Grinding the seat. *Courtesy of Hall-Toledo, Inc.*

Figure 9-74 Cutting a valve seat. *Courtesy of Neway Manufacturing, Inc.*

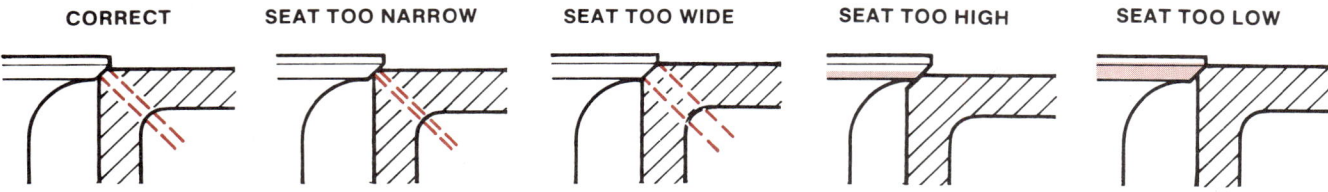

Figure 9-73 The fit of the valve in the seat should be checked carefully.

Cylinder Heads and Valves

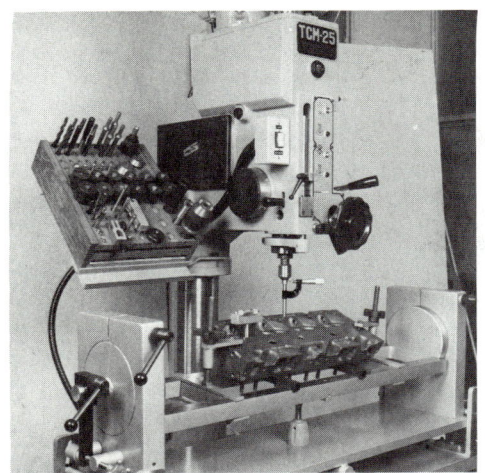

Figure 9-75 Typical valve system rebuilding machine. *Courtesy of Peterson Machine Tool, Inc.*

9-75 can be used to install valve guides and to machine valve seats. Some have optional seat cutters that make three-angle cuts. The cutters are set to the proper diameter. Once set, they machine the seat as well as the top and throat angles. Two primary advantages of these cutters over other methods are high speed and precision.

❏ VALVE STEM SEALS

Valve stem seals (Figure 9-76) are used on many engines to control the amount of oil allowed between the valve stem and guide. The stems and guides will scuff and wear excessively if they do not have enough lubrication. Too much oil produces heavy deposits that build up on the intake valve and hard deposits at the head end of the exhaust valve stem. Worn valve stem seals can increase the oil consumption by as much as 70%.

There are basically two types of seals. Positive seals fit tightly around the top of the stem and scrape oil off the valve as it moves up and down. Deflector, splash, or umbrella-type seals ride up and down on the valve stems to deflect oil away from the guides.

Figure 9-76 A valve stem seal on a guide.

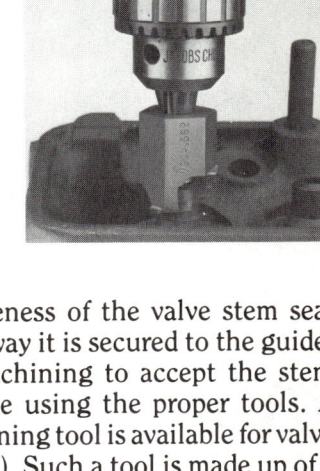

Figure 9-77 Typical valve guide machining tool. *Courtesy of Goodson Shop Supplies*

The ultimate effectiveness of the valve stem seal depends entirely on the way it is secured to the guide. Many guides require machining to accept the stem seals. This must be done using the proper tools. A special valve guide machining tool is available for valve seal cutting (Figure 9-77). Such a tool is made up of a cutter and pilot, with sizes that vary according to the valve stem diameter and desired guide OD. The pilot is inserted into the guide, and the cutting tool machines the top of the guide.

Installing Positive Valve Seals

To install a positive valve seal (Figure 9-78), place the plastic sleeve in the kit over the end of the valve stem (Figure 9-79). This will protect the seal as it

Figure 9-78 Positive valve seal designs. *Courtesy of Goodson Shop Supplies*

Figure 9-79 The plastic sleeve goes over the end of the valve stem before the seal is slipped over the guide. *Courtesy of Fel-Pro, Inc.*

Figure 9-80 Push the seal down until it touches the top of the valve guide. *Courtesy of Fel-Pro, Inc.*

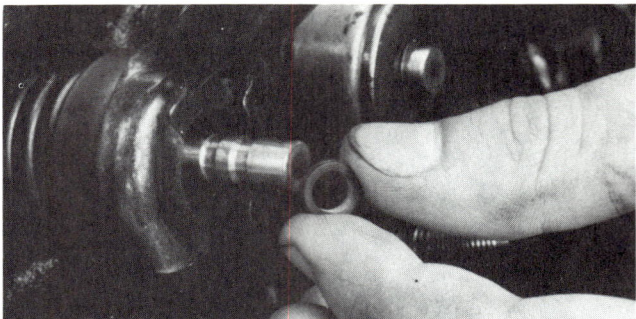

Figure 9-82 Installing an O-ring. *Courtesy of Fel-Pro, Inc.*

slides over the keeper grooves. Lightly lubricate the sleeve. If it extends more than 1/16 inch below the lower keeper groove, you might want to remove the sleeve and cut off the excess length for easier removal. Carefully place the seal on the cap over the valve stem and push the seal down until it touches the top of the valve guide (Figure 9-80). At this point, the installation cap can be removed and placed on the next valve. A special installation tool can be used to finish pushing the seal over the guide until the seal is flush with the top of the guide.

Installing Umbrella-Type Valve Seals

An umbrella-type seal is installed on the valve stem before the spring is installed. It is pushed down on the valve stem until it touches the valve guide boss (Figure 9-81). It will be positioned correctly when the valve first opens.

Installing O-Rings

When installing O-rings, use engine oil to lightly lubricate the O-ring. Then install it in the lower groove of the lock section of the valve stem (Figure 9-82). Make sure that the O-ring is not twisted.

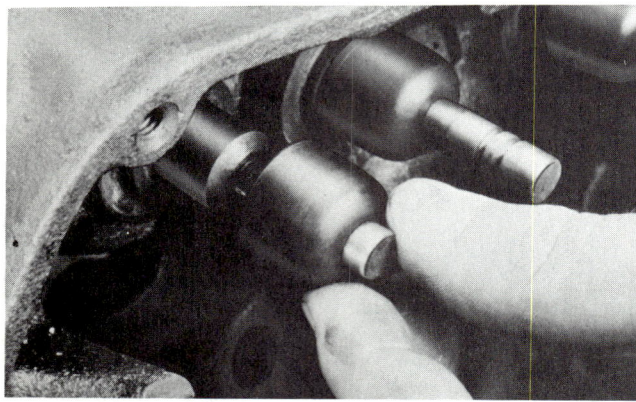

Figure 9-81 Installing an umbrella valve seal. *Courtesy of Fel-Pro, Inc.*

Valve Spring

The valve spring performs two functions. It closes the valve and maintains valve train contact during the opening and closing of the valve. Insufficient spring pressure can lead to valve bounce and breakage. Too much pressure can also lead to valve breakage. Figure 9-83 shows the components that make up a valve spring assembly.

The common designs of valve springs are illustrated in Figure 9-84. A problem that valve springs might have is spring surge. As the name implies, spring surge is the violent extending motion of the coils resulting in abnormal oscillation. The uniform pitch type is used

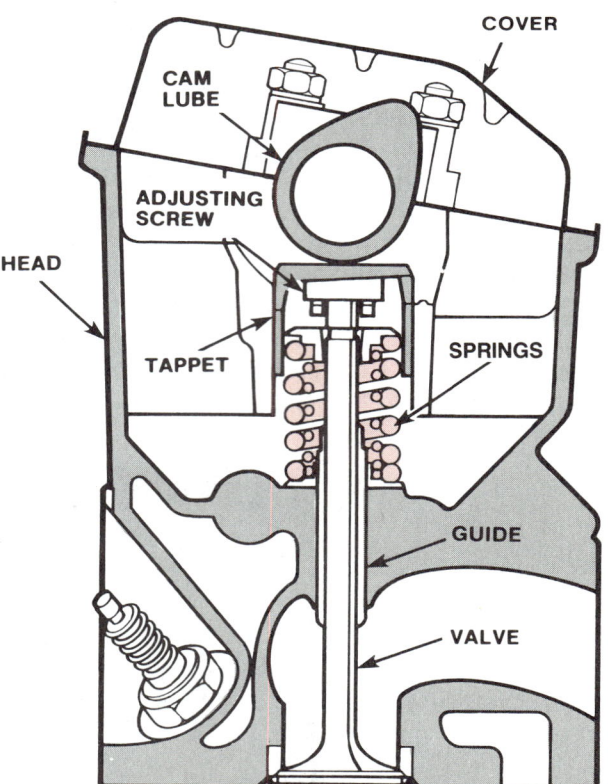

Figure 9-83 The valve spring is compressed between the valve spring seat on the cylinder head and the spring retainer.

Cylinder Heads and Valves

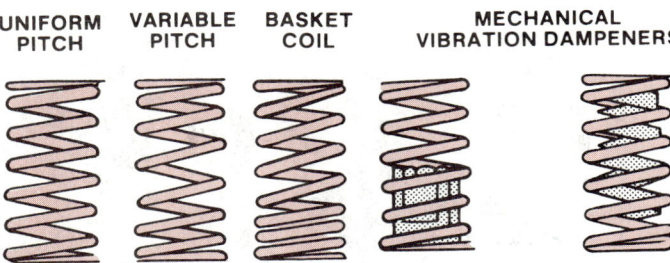

Figure 9-84 Common valve spring designs.

where surge is usually not encountered. The other designs represent different approaches to surge control. Mechanical spring surge dampers depend on friction to control surge. Therefore, it is advisable to replace them at the same time the springs are replaced. Always install the closely wound coils of a basket coil-type spring toward the head end of the valve. Mechanical surge and vibration dampers should also be installed toward the head end of the valve. To dampen spring vibrations and increase total spring pressure, some engine manufacturers use a reverse wound secondary spring inside the main spring.

Spring surge can occur when the springs are weak, the installed spring height is improper, or engine speeds are excessive. Whatever the cause, the occurrence of spring surge is visually apparent. The ends of the springs will look smooth or polished due to their rotation during operation. If left alone and not corrected, spring surge can cause damage to the valve train. For example, the self-rotation of the valve springs causes a grinding action between the valve face and seat. As a result, the face will wear down and the seat will recess. Continued operation with spring surge can also cause the springs to break.

The high stresses and temperatures imposed on valve springs during operation cause them to weaken and sometimes break. Rust pits will also cause valve spring breakage. To determine if the spring can be reused, the following tests should be performed.

FREESTANDING HEIGHT TEST Line up all the springs on a flat surface and place a straightedge across the tops (Figure 9-85). Free length should be within 1/16 inch of OE specifications. Throw away any spring that is not within specifications.

Figure 9-85 Freestanding spring height test. *Courtesy of Perfect Circle/Dana*

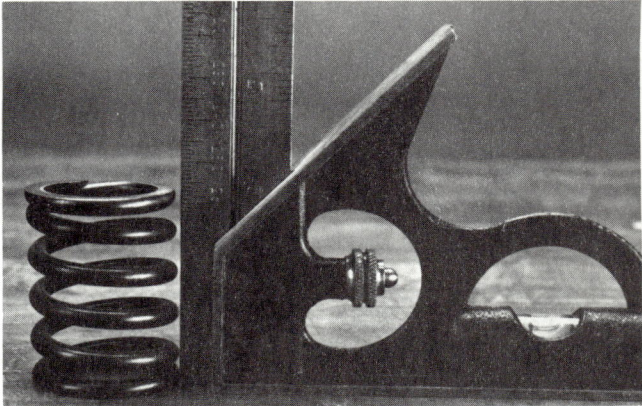

Figure 9-86 Spring squareness test. *Courtesy of Perfect Circle/Dana*

SPRING SQUARENESS TEST A spring that is not square will cause side pressure on the valve stem and abnormal wear. To check squareness, set a spring upright against a square (Figure 9-86). Turn the spring until a gap appears between the spring and the square. Measure the gap with a feeler gauge. If the gap is more than 0.060 inch, the spring should be replaced.

OPEN/CLOSE SPRING PRESSURE TEST Use a spring tester to check for open and close spring pressure. Close pressure guarantees a tight seal. The open pressure overcomes valve train inertia and closes the valve when it should close. Service manuals list spring pressure specifications according to spring height (Figure 9-87). The proper procedure for testing valve spring tension is given in Photo Sequence 5, which is included in this chapter. Low spring pressure may allow the valve to float during high speed operation. Excessive spring tension may cause premature valve train wear. Any spring that does not meet specifications should be replaced.

Valve Spring Retainers and Keepers

Valve spring retainers and valve keepers hold the valve spring and valve in place. The retainer holds the spring in line with the valve stem. A worn retainer will

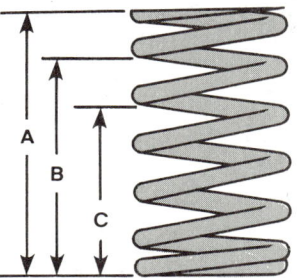

Figure 9-87 Valve spring height terminology: (A) free height, (B) valve closed spring height, and (C) valve open spring height.

allow the spring to move away from the centerline of the valve. This will affect valve operation because spring tension on the valve will not be evenly distributed. Each retainer should be carefully inspected for cracks, since a cracked retainer may result in serious damage to the engine. The inside shape of most retainers is a cone which matches the outside shape of the keepers. This must be a good fit, in order for the keepers to stay in their grooves on the valve stem.

The valve stem grooves should match the inside shape of the keepers. Some valves have multiple keeper grooves. Others have only one. All of the valve stem grooves should be inspected for damage and fit by inserting a keeper in them. Both the retainers and keepers should be carefully inspected for damage. If a defect is found, they should be replaced.

Valve Rotators

Most rotators impart positive rotation to the valve during each valve cycle and improve valve life two to five times, and in some cases, even more. In normal operation, rotators will continue to function for more than 100,000 miles and require no maintenance. However, when valves are refaced or replaced at high mileage, the rotators should be replaced because they cannot be visually inspected accurately. Whether or not they rotate when held in the hand is no indication of their function in the engine. While rotation can only be checked in a running engine, uneven wear patterns (Figure 9-88) develop at the valve stem tip if the rotators are not functioning properly.

Several types of rotators are available, but the most commonly used are the following.

- Ball type. This employs two small balls and slight ramp. Each ball moves down its ramp to turn the rotator sections in a positive direction as the valve opens (Figure 9-89).
- Spring-loaded type. In this design, the spring starts to move down as the valve opens. The spring-loaded rotator can rotate the valve in either direction (Figure 9-89).
- Free type. This rotator permits a momentary release of the spring tension from the valve during opening so that the valve is free to rotate (Figure 9-90). The action does not cause positive valve rotation. Engine vibration and turbulence of gases

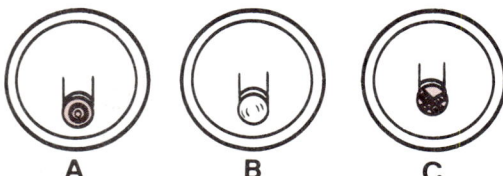

Figure 9-88 (A) An even pattern means the rotator is functioning properly, while (B) no pattern and (C) a partial pattern means the rotator should be replaced and the rotation checked.

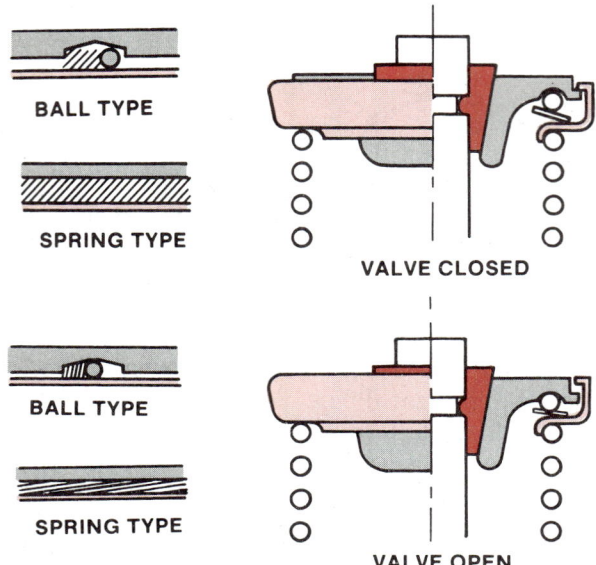

Figure 9-89 Ball-type and spring-type valve rotators.

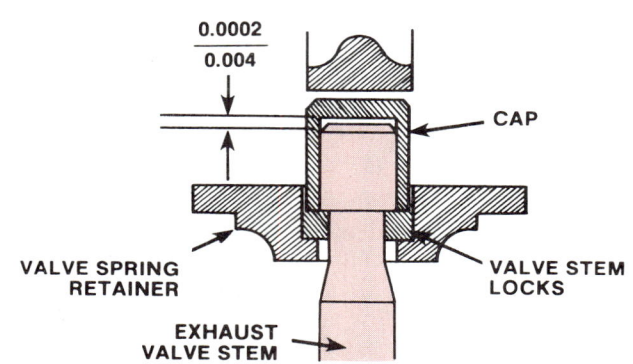

Figure 9-90 Free-type valve rotator.

contribute to valve rotation during the time the valve is free to rotate.

☐ ASSEMBLING THE CYLINDER HEAD

Before a cleaned or reconditioned cylinder head is reassembled and installed, there are two critical measurements that must be carefully checked: the installed stem height and the installed spring height.

Installed stem height is determined by measuring the distance between the spring seat and stem tip. Since this measurement directly influences rocker arm geometry and installed spring height, accuracy and precision are important. This is especially true when the valve or valve seat has been ground. There are a number of tools that can be used to obtain an accurate stem height reading. These include a depth micrometer, vernier caliper, and telescoping gauge (Figure 9-91). There are several specially designed stem height gauges available (Figure 9-92). Use these as directed by their manufacturers.

PHOTO SEQUENCE 5

☐ MEASURING AND FITTING VALVE SPRINGS

P5-1 Prior to installing the valve and fitting valve springs, all other head work should be completed.

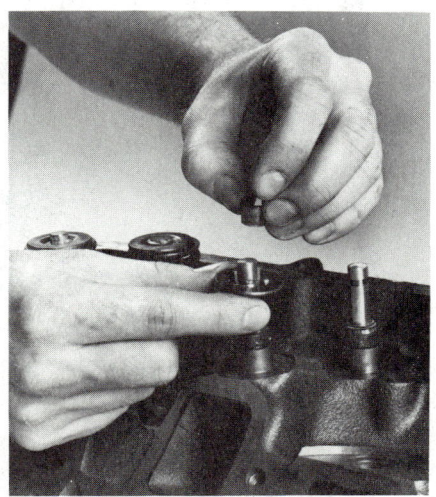

P5-2 Install the valve into its proper valve guide.

P5-3 Install the valve retainer and keepers. Without the spring, these must be held in place.

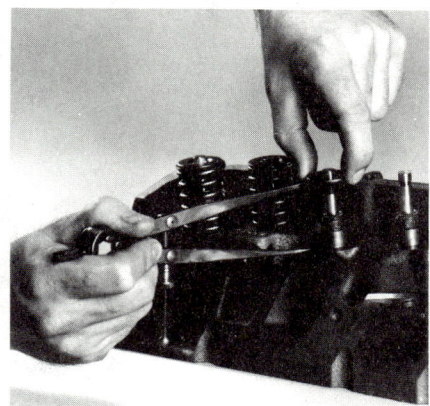

P5-4 While pulling up on the retainer, measure the distance between the bottom of the retainer and the spring pad on the cylinder head with a divider.

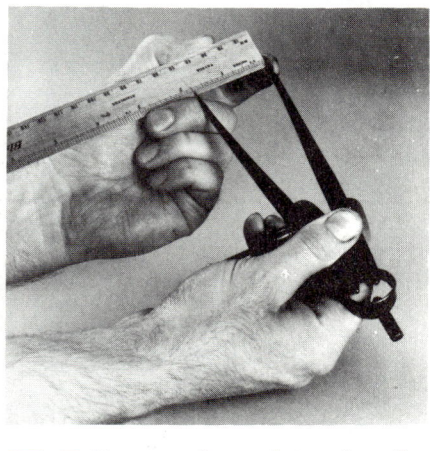

P5-5 Use a scale to determine the measurement expressed by the divider.

P5-6 Compare this measurement with the specifications given in the service manual for installed spring height.

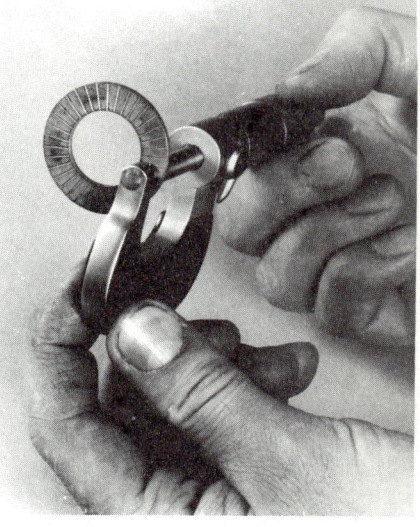

P5-7 If measured installed height is greater than the specifications, a valve shim must be placed under the spring to correct the difference.

P5-8 Spring tension must be checked at the installed spring height; therefore, if a shim is to be used, insert it under the spring on the valve spring tension gauge.

(continued)

201

P5-9 Compress the spring into the installed height by pressing down on the tester's lever.

P5-10 The tension gauge will reflect the pressure of the spring when compressed to the installed or valve closed height. Compare this reading to the specifications.

P5-11 Now compress the spring to the open height specification. Use the rule on the gauge or a scale to measure the compressed height.

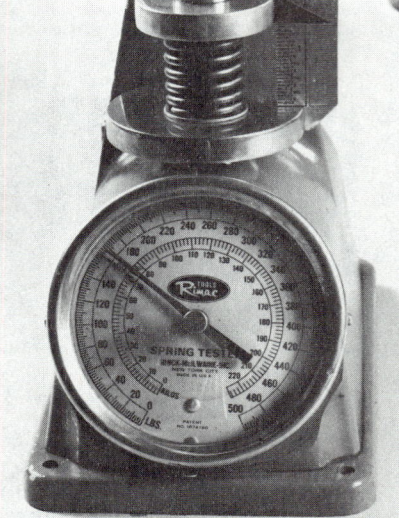

P5-12 Compare this reading to specifications. Any pressure outside the pressure range given in the specifications indicates that the spring should be replaced. After the tension and height have been checked, the spring can be installed on the valve stem. ■

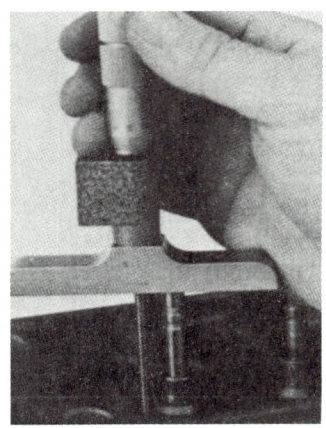

Figure 9-91 Stem height can be measured using (A) a depth micrometer, (B) a vernier caliper, or (C) a telescoping gauge. *Courtesy of TRW, Inc.*

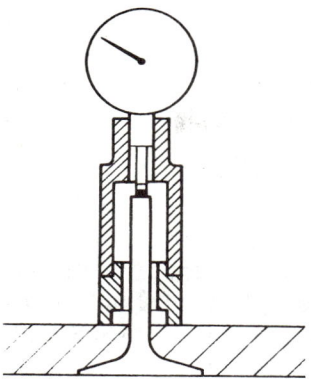

Figure 9-92 Special stem height gauges. *Courtesy of Goodson Shop Supplies*

USING SERVICE MANUALS

Stem height specifications are often not available in service manuals. As a guide for assembly, record the stem heights for all valves during disassembly.

Another specification can be used that corresponds directly to installed stem height—installed spring height. Installed spring height is measured from the spring seat to the underside of the retainer when it is assembled with keepers and held in place. This measurement, which can be made by using a set of dividers or scales, telescoping gauge, or spring height gauge, should be taken only after valve and seat work is completed, valves are installed in their guides, and retainers and keepers are assembled.

By comparing the measurement to factory specs, it is possible to determine the needed increase in installed stem height. For example, if the installed spring height for an exhaust valve is 1.600 inches, and the measurement is 1.677 inches the increase in spring height is 0.077 inch. This means installed stem height also has been increased by 0.077 inch.

Adjustments to valve spring height can be made with the aid of valve spring inserts, otherwise known as spring shims. Even though valve shims come in only three standard thicknesses—0.060, 0.030, and 0.015 inch—using combinations of different shims gives the correct amount of compensation (within 0.005 or 0.010 inch).

SHOP TALK

A 0.060-inch shim may increase spring pressure by 12 pounds, whereas 0.030-inch and 0.015-inch shims increase pressure by 6 and 3 pounds.

By comparing spring height to specifications, the desired amount of spring tension correction can be easily determined. For example, if spring height is 0.180 inch and the specifications call for 0.149 inch, a 0.030 shim (0.149 + 0.030 = 0.179) would be needed. If more than one shim is required, place the thickest one next to the spring—not the head. If one side of the shim is serrated or dimpled, place that side over the valve stem and onto the spring seat. There are two words of caution.

1. If the springs have close-spaced coils, the close end should be placed next to the head.
2. If the spring has an OD that is slightly tapered, the end with the greater diameter should be facedown.

SHOP TALK

Valve keepers should be replaced in pairs. If a new keeper is mated with a used one, the spring retainer may cock and break off the valve tip or allow the assembly to come apart.

With the valve inserted into its guide, position the valve spring inserts, valve spring, and retainer over the valve stem. Using a valve spring compressor, compress the spring just enough to install the valve keepers into their grooves (Figure 9-93). Excess pressure may cause the retainer to damage the oil seal. Release the spring compressor and tap the valve stem with a rubber mallet to seat the keepers. When doing this, the valve will open slightly. To prevent damage to the valves, never tap the stems with the cylinder head lying flat on the bench. Turn the head on its side or raise it off the bench.

CAUTION: If the keepers are not fully seated, the spring assembly could fly apart and cause personal injury (or serious damage to the engine if it occurred while the engine was running). For these reasons, it is good practice to assemble the valves with the retainers facing a wall and to wear eye protection.

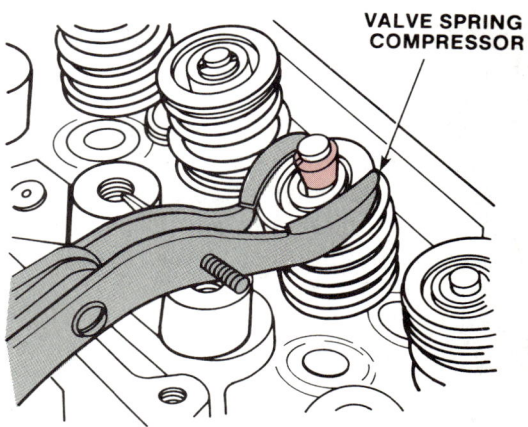

Figure 9-93 Compress the spring just enough to install the keepers.

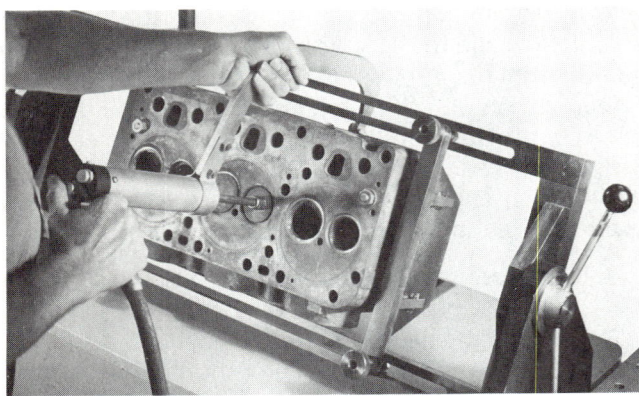

Figure 9-94 Air-operated valve spring compressor. *Courtesy of Hall-Toledo, Inc.*

Valve spring compressors are available in different designs for different applications. The most commonly used compressor is hand-operated. There are two different hand-operated designs: a universal tool with interchangeable jaws and a compressor specifically designed for OHC engines. This compressor allows for positive contact on the retainer without removing the camshaft. Another type of spring compressor is air-operated (Figure 9-94). Air-operated spring compressors are typically found in high-volume engine rebuilding shops.

Case 1

While traveling in a late-model car, a family's car engine overheats. Water is added to the radiator. Then the car is taken to a service station to be diagnosed and repaired. Simple tests reveal that a heater hose has split and is leaking coolant. The hose is replaced and new coolant added to the system. With the car repaired, the family continues on their trip.

After driving only a short while, smoke is noticed coming out of the tailpipe. Soon the engine shakes violently whenever it is placed in a load condition. The driver turns the car around and heads back to the shop that fixed the leak. Upon arrival, the driver says that the technician must have knocked something loose or broken something while replacing the hose. The technician doubts this, but agrees to take another look.

A cylinder power balance test would verify this, but it cannot be conducted because of the erratic idle. Instead, the spark plugs are removed and inspected. All look normal except for plug #2, which looks newer than the rest. A comparison test is taken and cylinder #2 has very low dry and wet readings. Then a cylinder leakage test is conducted. Cylinder #2 has excessive leakage and air can be felt leaving the exhaust pipe.

These test results lead to the conclusion that the engine is running on one less cylinder because an exhaust valve is not sealing. The customer still feels that the technician did something wrong but agrees to allow the technician to remove the cylinder head for further diagnosis. As soon as the head is off the block, the problem is identified. The exhaust valve seat for cylinder #2 came loose from the head and is preventing the valve from closing. The technician then explains that this undoubtedly happened when the engine overheated, due to the expansion of the metal. The customer is satisfied with the explanation and allows the technician to correct the problem. The family is able to continue their trip.

Summary

- Aluminum cylinder heads have grown in popularity recently due to their light weight. However, the thermal expansion characteristics of aluminum can lead to problems such as leaking and cracking. The natural porosity of aluminum is another negative factor. Despite such obvious drawbacks, however, it appears that aluminum cylinder heads are here to stay.
- An efficient combustion chamber must be compact in order to minimize heat loss. Popular combustion chamber designs include the wedge, hemispherical, swirl, chamber-in-piston, and fast-burn varieties.
- Every cylinder of a four-stroke engine contains at least one intake valve (for the air/fuel mixture to enter the cylinder) and one exhaust valve (for the burned gases to escape). The type of valve used in automotive engines is known as a poppet, which is characterized by a popping action as the valve opens and closes.
- Multivalve engines feature either three or four valves per cylinder, which means more complete combustion and reduced misfire and detonation. These benefits are offset to some extent by a more complicated camshaft arrangement.
- The means of resurfacing the deck surface of a cylinder head include grinding, milling, belt surfacing, and broaching.
- The amount of stock removed from the cylinder head gasket surface must be limited. Excessive surfacing can create problems in the engine's clearance volume and compression ratio, not to mention piston/valve interference and misalignment.
- The two surfaces of a valve that are reconditioned by grinding are the face and the tip. Valves can be refaced on grinding or cutting machines, with the traditional grinding method still the most popular.

In general, do not grind a valve face to the point where the margin is reduced by more than 25%, or to where it is less than 0.045 inch on the exhaust and 0.030 inch on the intake valves.
- One of the fastest methods for restoring the inside diameter dimensions of a worn valve guide is knurling. This process does not change the centerline of the valve stem very much, so it reduces the work needed to reseat the valve. Reaming repairs worn guides by increasing the guide hole size to take an oversize valve stem or by restoring the guide to its original dimension after knurling or installing inserts.
- Pressing out an old valve guide to install a new one can be difficult on some aluminum heads where the interference fit is considerable. Preheating the head in an oven prior to guide removal and lubricating the liners before driving them out can make the job easier.
- To assure proper seating of a valve, the seat must be the correct width, in the correct location on the valve face, and concentric with the guide. The ideal seat width for automotive engines is 1/16 inch for intake valves and 3/32 inch for exhaust valves.
- When grinding a valve seat, choosing the correct size pilot and stone is important. For soft seats such as cast iron, use a hard stone. For hard seats, a soft stone is needed. An overhang (the area of the face between the contact area and the margin) of 1/64 inch is required for both the intake and exhaust valves.
- Valve stem seals are used to control the amount of oil between the valve stem and guide. Too much produces deposits, while insufficient lubrication leads to excessive wear. The effectiveness of a valve stem seal depends on the way it is secured to the guide.
- The valve spring closes the valve and also maintains the valve train contact during the opening and closing of the valve. To determine if a spring needs to be replaced, three tests are valuable: freestanding height, spring squareness, and open/close spring pressure.
- Two critical measurements that must be made before a cylinder head is reassembled and installed are installed stem height and installed spring height. The first of these is determined by measuring the distance between the spring seat and stem tip. The latter is measured by the spring seat to the underside of the retainer when it is assembled with keepers and held in place.

Review Questions

1. Despite its obvious drawbacks, why do auto manufacturers use aluminum to make cylinder heads?
2. Define valve margin.
3. What usually causes warpage in an aluminum cylinder head?
4. What is one microinch equal to?
5. Why do some technicians not consider knurling a long-term repair?
6. Which of the following can be reconditioned by grinding?
   a. valve face
   b. valve tip
   c. both a and b
   d. neither a nor b
7. Which of the following is not true of knurling?
   a. It is one of the fastest techniques for restoring the ID dimensions of a worn valve guide.
   b. It reduces the amount of work necessary to reseat the valve.
   c. It is useful for restoring badly worn guides to their original condition.
   d. None of the above.
8. According to most experts, what is the maximum amount of acceptable wear for knurling?
   a. 0.005 to 0.009 inch
   b. 0.006 to 0.008 inch
   c. 0.004 to 0.007 inch
   d. 0.003 to 0.006 inch
9. To insure proper seating of the valve, the valve seat must be _____ .
   a. correct width
   b. correct location on the valve face
   c. concentric with the guide
   d. all the above
10. When grinding valve seats, _____ .
    a. a pilot shaft is inserted into the valve guide
    b. a hard stone should be used on a hard seat
    c. a soft stone should be used on a soft seat
    d. all of the above
11. If the valve face and valve seat do not contact each other evenly after grindings, _____ .
    a. regrind with the same stone
    b. regrind with stones of different angles
    c. discard cylinder head
    d. none of the above
12. Technician A says that bronze valve guides retain oil better than cast-iron ones. Technician B says that cast-iron valve guides are better at retaining oil. Who is correct?
    a. Technician A
    b. Technician B
    c. Both A and B
    d. Neither A nor B
13. Technician A says that positive valve stem seals fit tightly around the top of the stem. Technician B says that positive stem seals scrape oil off the valve as it moves up and down. Who is correct?
    a. Technician A
    b. Technician B

c. Both A and B
   d. Neither A nor B
14. When adjusting spring height, Technician A places the thickest shim next to the spring. Technician B places the thickest shim furthest away from the spring. Who is correct?
    a. Technician A
    b. Technician B
    c. Both A and B
    d. Neither A nor B
15. Which type of combustion chamber is considered to be nonturbulent?
    a. wedge
    b. hemispherical
    c. both a and b
    d. neither a nor b
16. Technician A uses a profilometer to measure cylinder head surface finish. Technician B uses a specimen block kit. Who is correct?
    a. Technician A
    b. Technician B
    c. Both A and B
    d. Neither A nor B
17. Which type of surfacing machine uses underside rotary cutters?
    a. milling
    b. broaching
    c. belt
    d. grinding
18. Technician A says it is not necessary to measure valve stem height unless the valves have been replaced. Technician B says the valve stem height should be measured whenever any valve work has been done. Who is correct?
    a. Technician A
    b. Technician B
    c. Both A and B
    d. Neither A nor B
19. _____ is the cooling of gases by pressing them into a thin area.
    a. Turbulence
    b. Shrouding
    c. Reaming
    d. Quenching
20. Technician A uses a 30-degree stone for topping a 45-degree valve seat. Technician B uses a 60-degree stone for topping a 45-degree valve seat. Who is correct?
    a. Technician A
    b. Technician B
    c. Both A and B
    d. Neither A nor B

10 CAMSHAFTS AND VALVE TRAINS

Objectives

- Describe the function, operation, and location of the camshaft.
- Identify the parts of the valve train and the different mechanisms.
- Inspect the camshaft, valve train, and timing components.
- Describe the four types of camshafts.
- Describe how to install a camshaft and its bearings.
- Explain the factors involved in camshaft/crankshaft timing.

The camshaft and valve train work together to open and close the intake and exhaust valve of the engine. This interaction must be precisely timed for the engine to breathe properly and burn fuel efficiently.

CAMSHAFT

A camshaft is a shaft (Figure 10-1) with a cam for each exhaust and intake valve, each one placed to allow for the proper timing of each valve. A cam is a device that changes rotary motion into reciprocating motion. Each cam has a high spot or cam lobe that controls the opening of the valves. The height of the lobe is proportional to the amount the valve will open. Some camshafts may also be equipped with an eccentric to operate the fuel pump and a gear to drive the distributor and oil pump. Some diesel engines utilize lobes for fuel injectors, fuel injection pumps, or air starting valves.

The camshaft can be located in either the cylinder block or in the cylinder head. If the camshaft is in the block (Figure 10-2), it is positioned above the crankshaft, and the valves are opened through lifters, pushrods, and rocker arms. As the cam lobe rotates, it pushes up on the lifter, which lifts up the pushrod, moving one end of the rocker arm up while the other end pushes the valve down to open it. As the cam rotates, the valve spring forces the valve to close and maintains the contact between the valve and the rocker arm, thereby keeping the pushrod and the lifter in contact with the rotating cam. Engines with the camshaft in the engine block and the valves in the cylinder head are referred to as overhead valve (OHV) engines.

Overhead camshaft (OHC) engines have the camshaft mounted in or on the cylinder head (Figure 10-3). OHC engines have no need for pushrods. As the camshaft rotates, the cams ride directly above the valves. The lobes open the valves by either directly depressing the valve or by depressing the valve through the use of a cam follower, rocker arm, or bucket-type tappet. The closing of the valves is still the responsibility of the valve springs.

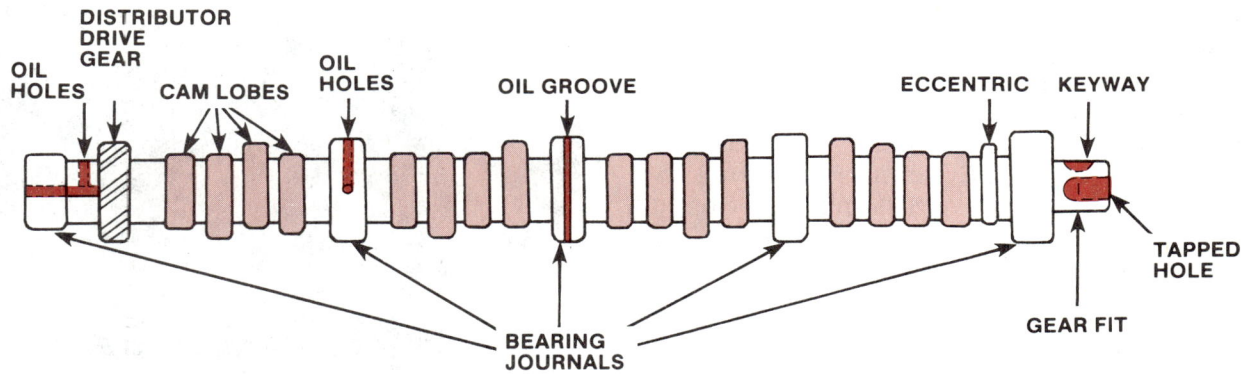

Figure 10-1 Parts of a camshaft.

208   Section 2   Engines

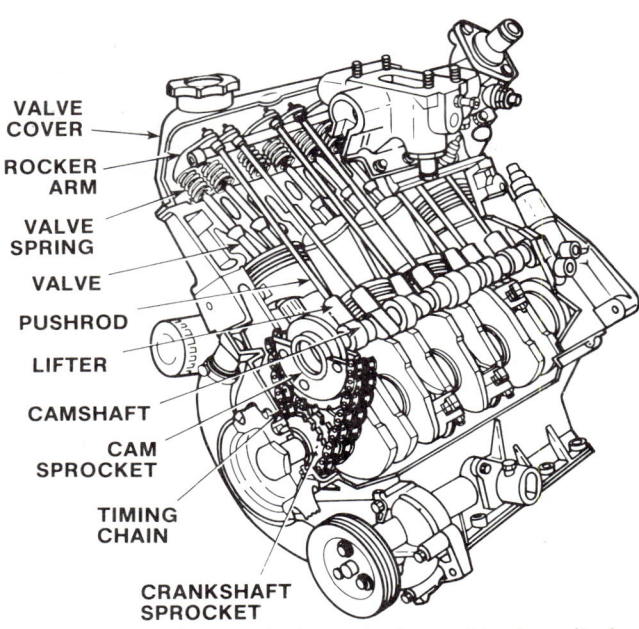

Figure 10-2   The camshaft may be located in the cylinder block.

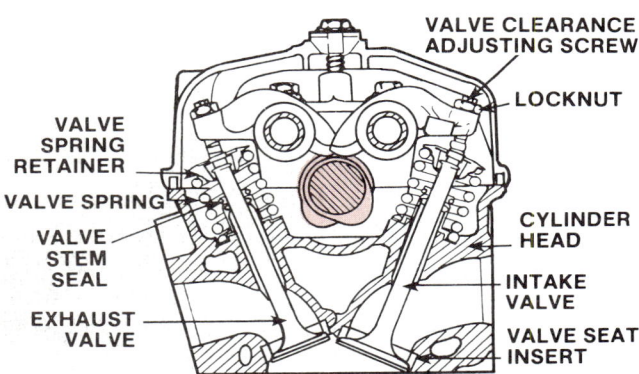

Figure 10-3   On OHC engines, the camshaft is located in or on the cylinder head.

An advantage of the overhead camshaft engine is that through the elimination of the pushrod and, on some engines, the valve lifter, the inertia of the valve train is lower and there is less deflection in the system. Valve float is less likely to occur in OHC engines because they have fewer valve train parts and, therefore, less inertia. Inertia is best defined as the tendency of an object to continue moving in the same direction without a direct force applied to it. The heavier the object is and the greater its speed, the higher the inertia force will be. The OHC arrangement also allows for more precise control of valve opening and closing times.

Camshaft Bearings

The camshaft is supported by several friction-type bearings, or bushings. They are designed as one piece and are typically pressed into the camshaft bore in the

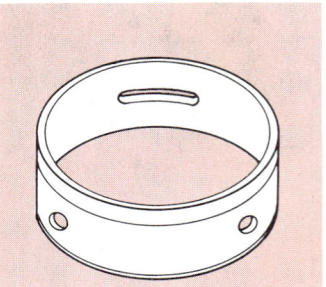

Figure 10-4   The typical camshaft bearing is a full round design.

cylinder head or block (Figure 10-4). Some OHC engines use split bearings to support the camshaft. Camshaft bearings are normally replaced during engine rebuilding. The old bearings should be inspected for signs of unusual wear that may indicate an oiling or bore alignment problem.

Cam bearings are normally press fit into the block using a bushing driver and hammer (Figure 10-5). This procedure is illustrated in the Tech Manual that accompanies this textbook.

Some overhead camshafts do not have bearing inserts. The bores in the aluminum casting serve as a bearing surface. On others, the camshaft bearings might be split two-piece inserts or the full-round type. When installing full round bearings, a special type of puller tool such as the one shown in Figure 10-6 is required. Using this tool, it is possible to pull out the old bearings and push in new ones. Be sure to follow the manufacturer's directions when using this tool.

CAUTION: *The use of a standard bushing driver and hammer is not recommended because aluminum bearing supports are very easily damaged or broken. This can result in expensive head replacement.*

After the cam bearings have been installed, the oil hole in the bearings should be checked for proper alignment with those in the block or head. This will ensure correct lubrication and oil supply in vital engine areas. Proper alignment can be checked by inserting a wire through the holes or by squirting oil into the holes. If the oil does not run out, the holes are misaligned. This procedure should be repeated with each bearing.

Figure 10-5   Installing a cam bearing using a hammer and driving tool. *Courtesy of Sealed Power Corp.*

Camshafts and Valve Trains 209

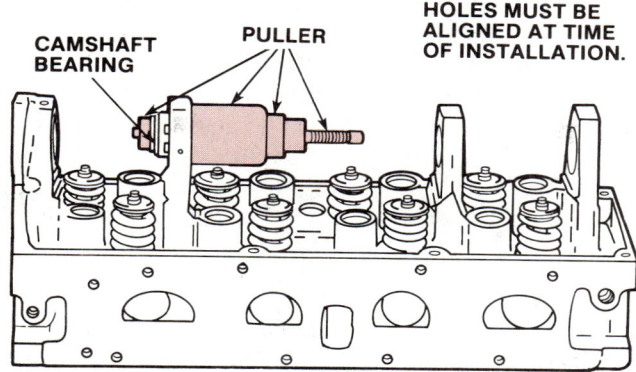

Figure 10-6 A puller is needed to install full-round bearings.

Valve Lifters

Valve lifters, sometimes called cam followers or tappets, follow the contour or shape of the cam lobe. Lifters are either mechanical (solid) or hydraulic. Solid valve lifters provide for a rigid connection between the camshaft and the valves. Hydraulic valve lifters provide for the same connection but use oil to absorb the shock that results from the movement of the valve train. Although both types function the same, solid lifters have certain disadvantages when compared to hydraulic lifters.

Hydraulic lifters (Figure 10-7) are designed to automatically compensate for the effects of engine temperature. Changes in temperature cause valve train components to expand and contract. Hydraulic lifters are designed to automatically maintain a direct connection between valve train parts.

Solid lifters (Figure 10-8) do not have this built-in feature and require a clearance between the parts of the valve train. This clearance allows for expansion of the components as the engine gets hot. Periodic adjustment of this clearance must be made. Excessive clearance might cause a clicking noise. This clicking noise is also an indication of the hammering of valve train parts against one another, which will result in reduced camshaft and lifter life.

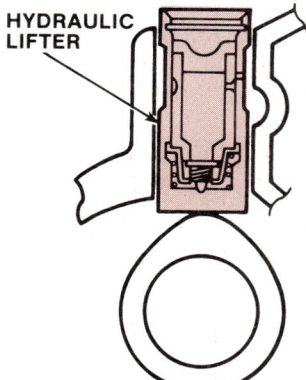

Figure 10-7 Hydraulic valve lifter.

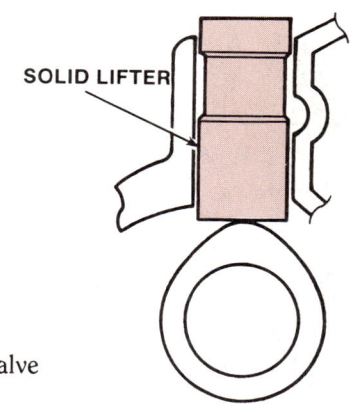

Figure 10-8 Solid valve lifter.

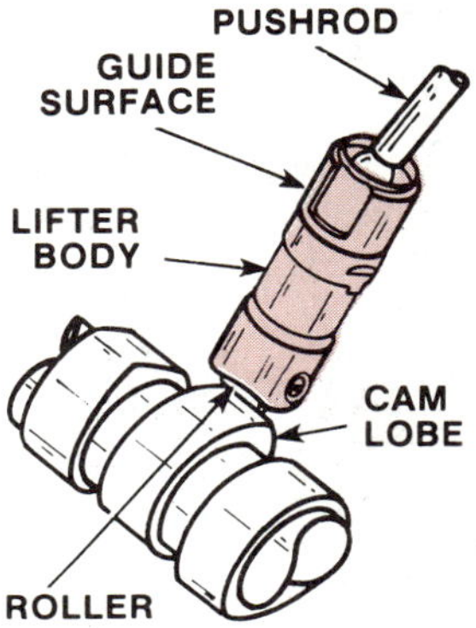

Figure 10-9 Typical roller lifter.

In an effort to reduce the friction—and the resulting power loss—from the lifter rubbing against the cam lobes, engine manufacturers often use roller-type hydraulic lifters. Roller lifters (Figure 10-9) are manufactured with a large roller on the camshaft end of the lifter. The roller acts like a wheel and allows the lifter to follow the cam lobe contour better than a flat-type lifter with reduced friction between the contacting surfaces. Friction is reduced by the lifter rolling along the surface of the cam lobe as opposed to rubbing along it.

Operation of Hydraulic Lifters

A typical hydraulic lifter contains ten parts. There is a plunger, oil metering valve disc, pushrod seat, retaining ring, valve disc or ball, check valve retainer, check valve spring, retainer clip, and plunger return spring all housed in a hardened iron body (Figure 10-10).

When the lifter is resting on the base circle of the cam (not on the lobe), the valve is closed and the plunger spring inside the lifter maintains a zero clearance in the valve train. Oil is pumped by the oil pump from the oil pan, to the oil filter, main bearings, camshaft bearings, and from there to the oil feed holes of the valve lifter bore. That is, pressurized oil enters the lifter and flows through the plunger. Oil flow continues through the lifter until it is filled. The pressure of the oil seals the oil in the lifter by forcing down the check valve inside the lifter (Figure 10-11). The oil between the plunger and the check valve forms a rigid

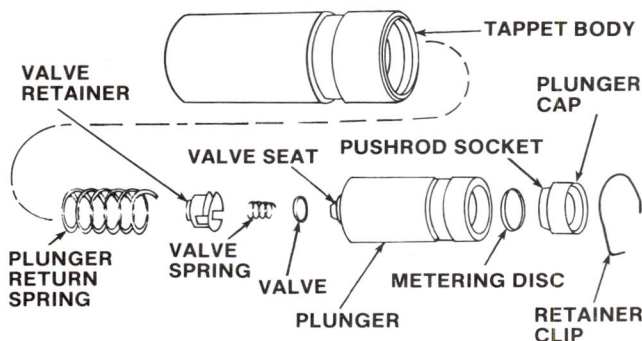

Figure 10-10 Exploded view of hydraulic valve lifter.

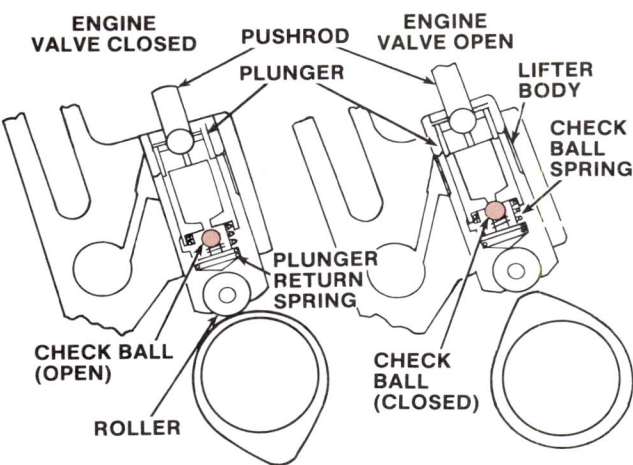

Figure 10-11 Hydraulic roller-type valve lifter with the valve closed and the valve open.

connection between the lifter and the pushrod. The position of the plunger inside the lifter is determined by the force of the pushrod on the plunger.

As the valve train grows from heat, clearance is reduced so the plunger is held lower in the lifter. As the cam lobe turns, the lifter's oil feed hole is no longer lined up with the feed in the block. New supplies of oil are not available until the lifter returns to the lower part of its bore. Also, the amount of force on the plunger increases as new forces result from the opening of the valve against the pressure of the valve spring. This new pressure causes the plunger to depress slightly. This allows a small amount of oil to leak out. This leaking out of oil is called leakdown.

Leakdown is defined as the relative movement of the plunger with respect to the lifter body after the check valve is seated by the pressurized oil. When the cam rotates and the lifter returns to the base of the cam, oil again can enter the lifter. At this point, the oil fills the lifter, and the lifter is ready to open the valve again.

If the lifter is unable to fill with oil or if it does not leak down the proper amount, a noise will be heard when the engine is running. Quite often light tapping noises are referred to as lifter noises. Not always is the lifter at fault. There are other causes for similar sounding engine noises, such as worn cam lobes, stuck valve, broken valve spring, insufficient lubrication between the rocker arm and the pushrod or valve, or a loose rocker arm assembly. All of these problems relate to the opening and closing of the valves and will take on the rhythm of valve operation. Careful listening and troubleshooting will help determine if the cause of the noise is a lifter or one of the other possible problems.

Pushrods

Pushrods are designed to be the connecting link between the rocker arm and the valve lifter; they are either solid or hollow. On certain engines, the pushrods have a hole in the center to allow oil to pass from the hydraulic lifter to the upper portion of the cylinder head. Some are designed to have small convex balls on both ends. These balls ride inside the lifter and the rocker arm.

Rather than having a convex ball, the end of the pushrod on solid lifters is concave. This end then fits into a ball on the rocker arm. Figure 10-12 shows examples of different types of pushrod ends. Pushrods are used only on engines that have the camshaft placed within the block. Overhead camshafts do not need pushrods.

PUSHROD GUIDE PLATES In some engines, pushrod guide plates are used to limit side movement of the pushrods. The guides hold the pushrods in alignment with the rocker arms. When the pushrods pass through holes in the cylinder head or intake manifold, guide plates are not needed.

Rocker Arms

Rocker arms are designed to do two things. They change the direction of the cam lifting force and provide a certain mechanical advantage during valve lifting. As the lifter and pushrod move upward, the rocker arm pivots at the center point (Figure 10-13). This causes a change in direction on the valve side. This change in direction causes the valve to open downward.

On some engines, it may be important to open the valve more than the actual lift of the cam lobe. This can be done by changing the distance from the pivot point to the ends of the rocker arm. The difference in length from the valve end of the rocker arm and the center of the pivot point (shaft or stud) compared to the pushrod

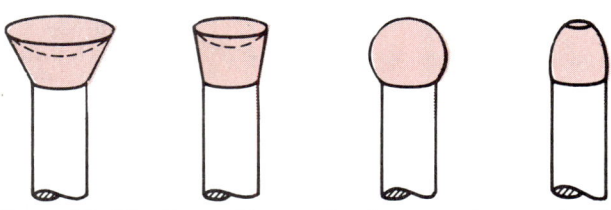

Figure 10-12 Several types of ends are used on pushrods.

Camshafts and Valve Trains   211

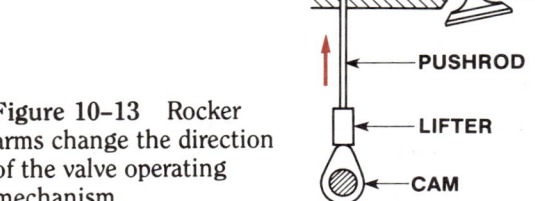
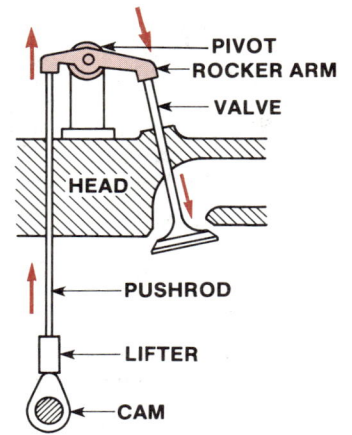

Figure 10-13 Rocker arms change the direction of the valve operating mechanism.

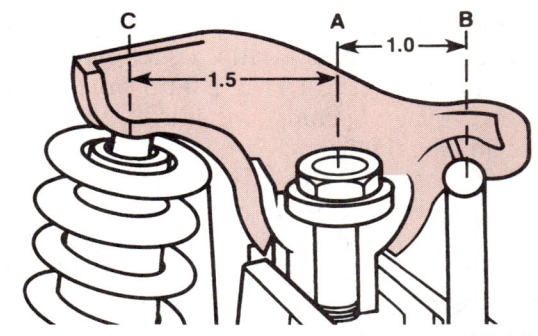

Figure 10-14 Rocker arm ratio is determined by the distance from (A) the rocker pivot to (B) the contact points of the pushrod and (C) the valve stem tip.

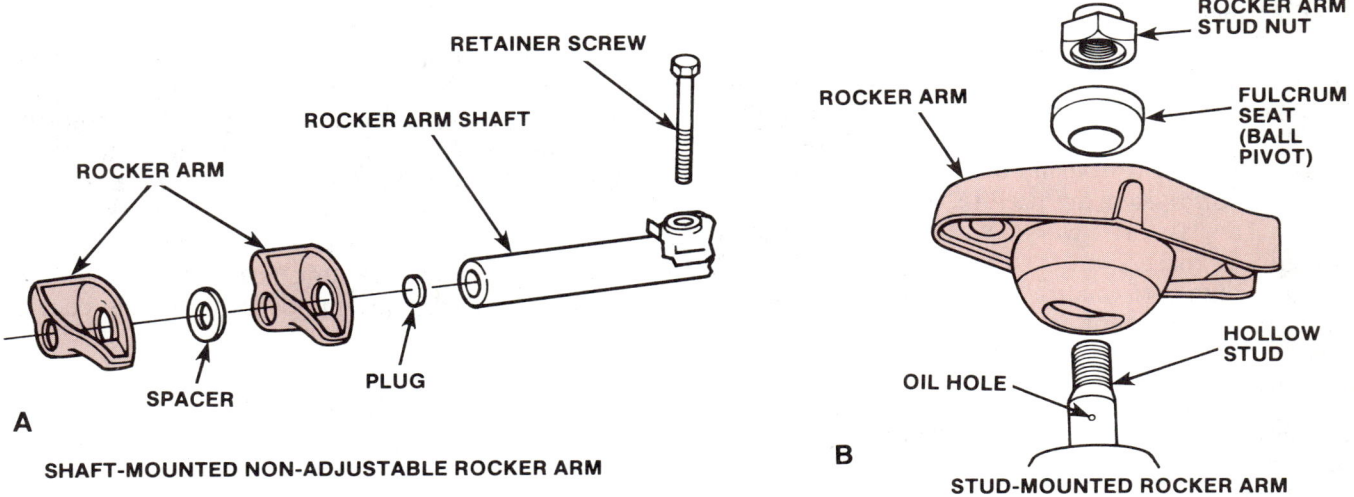

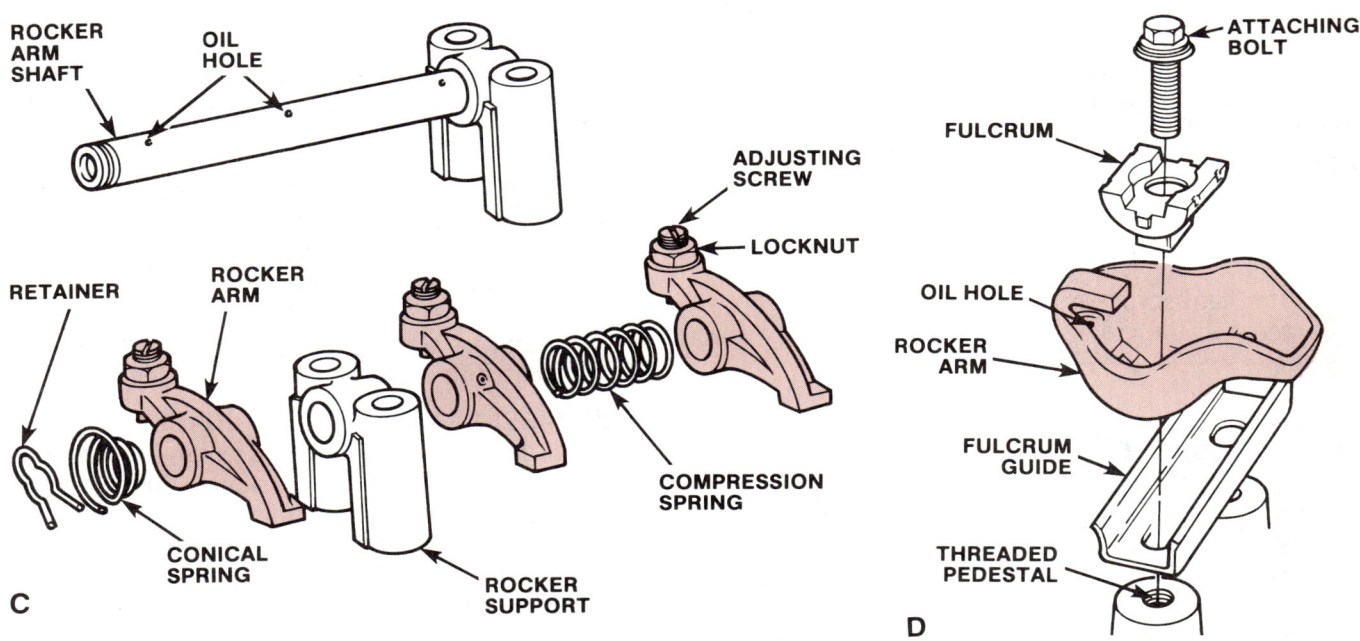

Figure 10-15 Various rocker arm mountings: (A) shaft-mounted nonadjustable; (B) stud-mounted; (C) shaft-mounted adjustable; and (D) pedestal-mounted.

or cam end of the rocker arm and the pivot point (shaft or stud) is expressed as a ratio. Usually, rocker arm ratios range from 1:1 to 1:1.75. A ratio larger than 1:1 results in the valve opening farther than the actual lift of the cam lobe (Figure 10-14).

Rocker arms are designed and mounted in several ways (Figure 10-15). Some are designed to fit on a rocker arm shaft. Springs, washers, individual rocker arms, and bolts are used in this type of assembly. Other rocker arms are placed on studs that are mounted directly in the cylinder head.

Some overhead camshaft engines use rocker arms in such a way that the camshaft rides directly on top of the rocker arm. Other overhead camshaft engines do not use rocker arms and the camshaft rides directly on top of the valves.

Rocker arms are manufactured of steel, aluminum, or cast iron. The most common for current use are the stamped steel variety (Figure 10-16). They are lightweight, strong, and inexpensive to manufacture. They usually pivot on a stud and ball.

Cast-iron rockers are used in large, low-speed engines. They almost always pivot on a common shaft. Aluminum rockers, on the other hand, are generally used on high-performance applications and frequently pivot on needle bearings.

Timing Mechanisms

On a four-stroke cycle engine, the camshaft is driven by the crankshaft at half the speed of the engine. This is accomplished through the use of a camshaft drive gear or drive sprocket that is twice as large as the crankshaft sprocket. For every two complete turns of the crankshaft, the camshaft turns once. Because the camshaft rotates at half the speed of the crankshaft and because the exhaust and intake valves are each opened only once during the four strokes, there is a cam lobe for each exhaust valve and a lobe for each intake valve on the camshaft.

> **SHOP TALK**
>
> The cam sprocket or gear has twice as many teeth as the crankshaft sprocket or gear.

Figure 10-16 Stamped steel rocker arms.

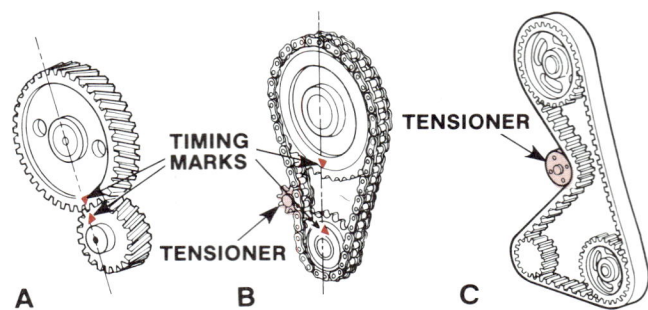

Figure 10-17 Timing drive mechanisms: (A) gear drive, (B) chain drive, and (C) belt drive.

The following are the basic configurations for driving the camshaft.

GEAR DRIVE A gear on the crankshaft meshes directly with another gear on the camshaft (Figure 10-17A). The gear on the crankshaft is usually made of steel. The gear on the camshaft may be steel for heavy-duty applications, or it may be made of aluminum or pressed fiber when quiet operation is a major consideration. The gears are helical in design. Helical gears are used because they are stronger and also tend to push the camshaft backward during operation to help control thrust.

CHAIN DRIVE Sprockets on the camshaft and the crankshaft are linked by a continuous chain (Figure 10-17B). The sprocket on the crankshaft is usually made of steel. The sprocket on the camshaft may be steel for heavy-duty applications. When quiet operation is a major consideration, an aluminum sprocket with nylon covering on the teeth is used. There are two common types of timing chains. One is a silent link-type chain that is used in standard and light-duty applications. The other is the roller link chain, which is used in heavy-duty applications. The roller link chain may have a single or double row of links.

BELT DRIVE Sprockets on the crankshaft and the camshaft are linked by a continuous neoprene belt (Figure 10-17C). The belt has square-shaped internal teeth that mesh with teeth on the sprockets. The timing belt is reinforced with nylon or fiberglass to give it strength and prevent stretching. This drive configuration is limited to overhead camshaft engines.

TIMING BELT AND CHAIN TENSIONERS Many engines with chain-driven and all engines with belt-driven camshafts employ a tensioner. The tensioner pushes against the belt or chain to keep it tight. This serves to keep it from slipping on the sprockets, provide more precise valve timing, and compensate for component stretch and wear.

TIMING MARKS The camshaft and the crankshaft must always remain in the same relative position to each other. They must also be in the proper initial

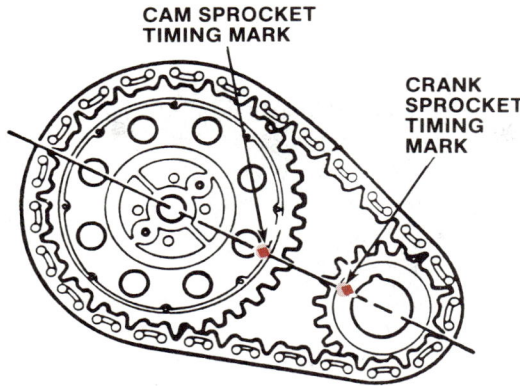

Figure 10-18 Timing mark alignment.

relation to each other. This initial position between the two shafts is designated by marks called timing marks. To obtain the correct initial relationship of the components, the corresponding marks are aligned at the time of assembly (Figure 10-18).

AUXILIARY CAMSHAFT FUNCTIONS The camshaft, driven by the crankshaft, drives other engine components. On gasoline engines, the oil pump and the distributor are usually driven from a common gear that is machined into the camshaft. The fuel pump can also be driven by the camshaft. This is usually accomplished by machining an extra lobe or eccentric on the camshaft to operate the pump.

> **USING SERVICE MANUALS**
>
> Normally, camshaft timing marks are shown in the engine section of a service manual, under the heading of Timing Belt or Chain R&R.

Variable Valve Timing

The absolute best valve timing for an engine varies with engine rpm. This means valve timing set to produce smooth idling may not deliver top performance at high engine speeds. And an engine timed to produce maximum horsepower at higher speeds will idle poorly, if at all.

For this reason, the valve timing in most vehicles is a compromise between these two extremes. For most vehicles, this does not pose a problem. On high-performance vehicles, however, some top end performance is lost in order to maintain a workable idle speed.

Automotive manufacturers are now developing systems that vary valve timing, depending on engine speed (rpm).

In one system a computer monitors engine speed. At high speeds it activates a solenoid. This solenoid activates a special hydraulic device that allows the camshaft to rotate on its drive sprocket. As the camshaft rotates, timing is advanced. When engine speed drops, the device allows the camshaft to return to its normal position.

In a second system, the intake camshafts are not solidly mounted to their drive sprockets. Instead a special spiral sleeve allows the camshaft and sprocket to move in relation to each other. As the camshaft and sprocket rotate against each other on the sleeve, the camshaft timing is either advanced or delayed.

Oil pressure is used to manipulate the position of the sleeve to provide the proper relationship between the camshaft and crankshaft. A computer-controlled solenoid determines what this relationship should be based on engine speed and other operating factors.

A third system operates on an entirely different principle. In this system, computer-controlled solenoids are used to bring the rocker arms into contact with a second set of high-performance camshaft lobes. At low speed the valves are opened and closed by the standard lobes on the camshaft.

At high speeds, the solenoids are activated, raising the rocker arms slightly. This brings them into contact with the second set of performance lobes on the camshaft. These lobes are machined to increase valve lift, duration, and overlap. The result is more power.

Although not presently in widespread use, variable valve timing will become more common, particularly on high-performance engines.

☐ CAMSHAFT AND VALVE TRAIN INSPECTION

A valve will operate only as well as its actuating parts. This includes the timing gears, chain or belt, sprockets, camshaft, lifters, pushrods, and rocker arm assemblies. For good valve life, each of these must be checked and replaced if worn or damaged.

When making an inspection, each valve train component should be carefully checked. Use the following guidelines when inspecting the components.

1. Individually mounted rocker arm assemblies
   - Check for loose mounting stud and nut or bolt.
   - Check for plugged oil feed in the rocker arm.
2. Pushrods: Check for bent pushrods.
3. Valve spring assembly—with or without damper spring: Check for broken or damaged parts.
4. Retainer and keepers—both two-piece and one piece: Check for proper seating of keeper in the stem grooves and in the retainer.
5. Overhead cam follower arm and lash adjuster assemblies
   - Check for broken or severely damaged parts.
   - Check for soft lash adjuster by using hand pressure on rocker arm while it is on the base circle of the camshaft.
6. Camshaft
   - Check for plugged oil feed.

Figure 10-19 (A) Steel camshaft and roller followers in good condition; (B) badly burned and worn camshaft bearing bores.

- Check for correct cam lift.
- Check for broken or severely worn areas.
- Check for soft lash adjuster.

7. Check the timing belt, sprockets, and related component.

Camshaft

After the camshaft has been cleaned and a visual inspection has been made, check each lobe for scoring, scuffing, fractured surface, pitting, and signs of abnormal wear (Figure 10-19).

Premature lobe and lifter wear is generally caused by metal-to-metal contact between the cam lobe and lifter bottom due to inadequate lubrication (Figure 10-20). The nose will be worn from the cam lobes, and the lifter bottoms will be worn to a concave shape or may be worn completely away. This type of failure usually begins within the first few minutes of operation. It is the result of insufficient lubrication or use of an oil that does not meet the engine manufacturer's requirements for viscosity and API service grade.

There are several methods of measuring cam lobes for wear, but the two most popular are the dial indicator and outside micrometer.

The dial indicator test for worn cam lobes should be conducted with the camshaft in the engine. Check the lift of each cam lobe (Figure 10-21) in consecutive order and make a note of the readings. Be sure that the pushrod is in the valve lifter socket. Install the dial indicator so that the cup-shaped adapter fits onto the end of the pushrod and is in the same plane as the pushrod movement (Figure 10-22). Connect a remote starter switch into the starting circuit. With the ignition switch off, bump the crankshaft over until the lifter is on the base circle of the camshaft lobe. At this point, the pushrod will be in its lowest position. Put the dial indicator at zero. Continue to rotate the crankshaft slowly until the pushrod is in its fully raised position (highest indicator reading). Compare the total lift recorded on the indicator with specifications. If the lift on any lobe is below the specified service limits, the camshaft and lifters operating on the worn lobe(s) must be replaced. Any lifter showing pitting or having its contact face worn flat or concave must also be replaced.

To compare the cam lobe height with an outside micrometer, the camshaft must be removed from the engine. Place the micrometer in position to measure from the heel to the nose of the lobe and again 90 degrees from the original measurement. Record the measurement for each intake and exhaust lobe. Any variation in heights indicates wear. Also check the measurements taken against the manufacturer's cam lobe heights.

Measure each camshaft journal in several places with a micrometer to determine if it is worn excessively. If any journal is 0.001 inch or more below the manufacturer's prescribed specifications, it should be replaced.

The camshaft should also be checked for straightness with a dial indicator. Place the camshaft on V-blocks. Position the dial indicator on the center bearing journal and slowly rotate the camshaft (Figure 10-23). If the dial indicator shows runout (a 0.002 inch deviation), the camshaft is not straight. A bent camshaft must be replaced.

Valve Lifters

All engines that have mechanical lifters use some method of adjustment to bring valve lash (clearance) back into specification. There are four basic methods for lash adjustment: rocker arm with adjustable pivots,

Figure 10-20 Badly worn camshaft.

Camshafts and Valve Trains   215

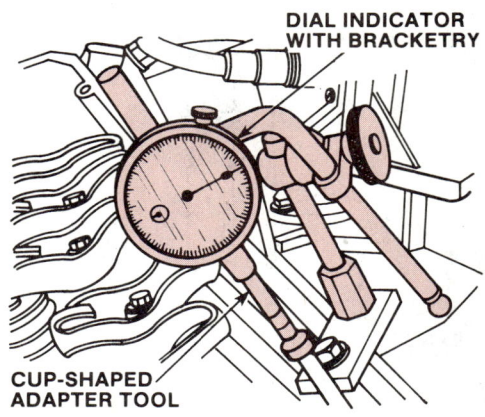

Figure 10-22 Checking camshaft lobe using a dial indicator.

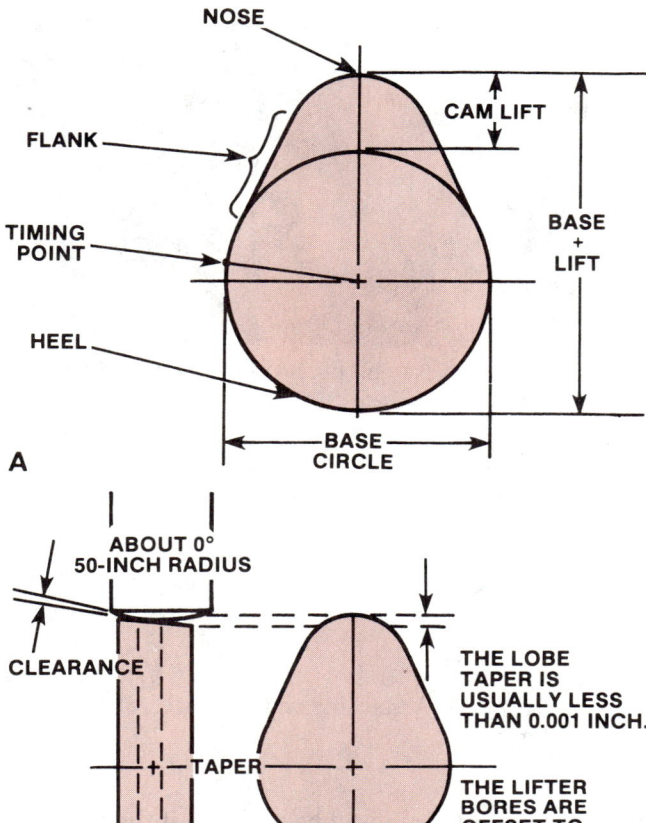

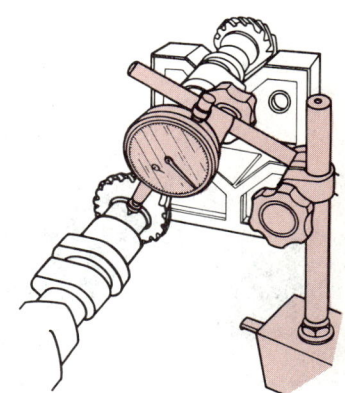

Figure 10-23 Checking camshaft straightness using a dial indicator.

Figure 10-21 (A) Cam lobe nomenclature; (B) correct camshaft pattern; (C) determining cam lobe lift.

adjustable pushrods, rocker arms with adjustable screws, and adjustable cam follower (using some type of adjustable screw or replaceable shim).

Of these four adjustment types, the first two methods are typically associated with OHV engines. The other two adjustment procedures—rocker arms with adjustment screws and adjustable cam followers—are commonly found on OHC designs.

When inspecting mechanical lifters, carefully check their bottoms and pushrod sockets. Wear, scoring, or pitting makes their replacement necessary.

Technically, the normal wear of the valve lifters is referred to as adhesive or galling wear. This is a result of two solid surfaces (camshaft lobe and lifter face) that are in rubbing contact. The two surfaces tend to weld together. This process is considered normal wear between the cam lobe and lifter. Fortunately, proper lubrication retards this process. However, excessive loading will negate the beneficial effects of the lubricant and accelerate the wear process. Examples of excessive loading would be incorrectly matched valve springs (too much spring pressure), old lifters on a new camshaft, or new lifters on an old camshaft.

If a camshaft and lifters are going to be reused, the lifters must remain with their respective lobes. Worn valve lifters and improper camshaft installation are common causes of camshaft/lifter failure. Figure 10-24 shows the ideal contact between the crowned lifter bottom and the tapered cam lobe.

The normal wear path is off center with no edge contact between the lifter and the lobe. The taper on the cam lobe and the spherical radius of the lifter bottom are specifically designed to result in an offset contact pattern causing the lifter to rotate. The spin-

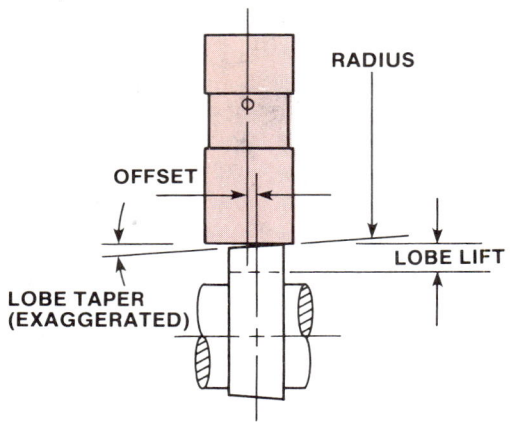

Figure 10-24 Ideal contact between the crowned lifter bottom and the tapered cam lobe.

Figure 10-25 An example of lobe and lifter interference. *Courtesy of TRW, Inc.*

Figure 10-26 An example of cam lobe edge wear. *Courtesy of TRW, Inc.*

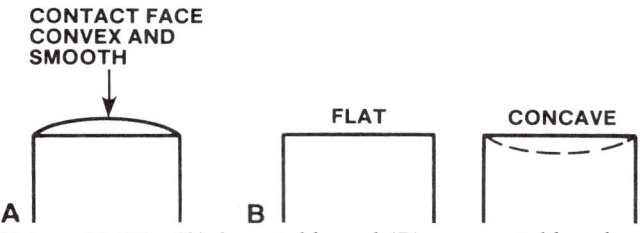

Figure 10-27 (A) Acceptable and (B) unacceptable valve lifter bottoms.

ning lifter reduces the sliding friction as well as equalizes the load around the lifter bottom.

Interference occurs primarily in engines originally equipped with a separate cam sprocket spacer (used to control end clearance). The problem develops when a replacement sprocket with a built-in spacer is installed without removing the original spacer. This forces the camshaft rearward, allowing the lobes to strike adjacent lifters, chipping the edges of both (Figure 10-25). Interference will also develop if sprocket bolts are not tightened properly or if the cam sprocket/engine block thrust surfaces are worn excessively.

Edge wear on cam lobes occurs when used lifters are installed with a new camshaft (Figure 10-26). The bottoms of used lifters are often flat or slightly concave due to previous wear. As a consequence, the lifters will contact the lobe along a narrow band at the lobe's edge. This tends to create high contact forces and rapid wear results. The cam shown in the right portion of the illustration displays a normal wear pattern.

Malfunctioning hydraulic lifters can cause valves to burn or break. Whenever the valve train is disturbed, the hydraulic lifters should be removed, disassembled, cleaned, and checked. They should be kept in sequence during removal so that they can be put back in the same place. Lifters should be replaced if the bottoms are worn or pitted or if a new camshaft is installed. Lifter bottoms, generally, are spherical (Figure 10-27).

To inspect, disassemble each lifter separately, but make sure not to intermix any parts because they are selectively fitted. Any time hydraulic lifters are removed, the varnish and deposits should be carefully removed from the lifter bores in the engine block, and the galleries should be flushed with pressurized oil to clear any dirt from the holes that feed the lifters. This latter step is of utmost importance because the act of removing the lifters will normally deposit some dirt right where the feed holes break into the bores. If this is not flushed out, the first oil fed to the newly installed lifter will contain this dirt, and trouble might develop immediately.

After cleaning, check the lifter's leakdown with a leakdown tester (Figure 10-28). Lifter (tappet) leakdown rate is important. If the tappets leak down too quickly, noisy operation will result. When diagnosis indicates no cause for noisy tappet operation, the condition can sometimes be remedied by checking the lifter leakdown rate and replacing all lifters that are outside specifications.

Pushrods

The pushrod fits between the valve lifter and the rocker arm to transmit cam action to the valves. During inspection, some pushrods may be found to have a groove worn in the area in which they pass through the cylinder head, and some may have tip wear. Also, the

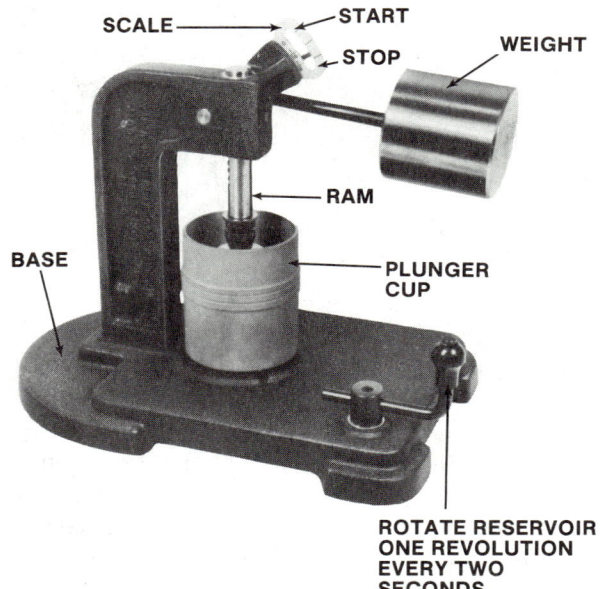

Figure 10-28 The hydraulic tappet leakdown tester uses a special fluid to check lifter leakdown rate. *Courtesy of Kent-Moore Corp.*

Rocker Arms

The rocker arm converts the upward movement of the valve lifter into a downward motion that opens the valve. Rocker arms also permit valves to be angled.

Rocker arms are lubricated in various ways. In some, engine oil is forced up around the outside of the cap screw that holds the bracket in place. On some overhead valve V-type engines, oil reaches the rocker arm assembly through a drilled passage in the cylinder head and rocker arm shaft bracket (Figure 10-30).

Possibly the most popular method of supplying oil to the rocker arms is through the pushrods. Some pushrods are hollow and function as part of the lubricating system for the rocker arm assembly (Figure 10-31). Oil flows under pressure from the block through a hole in the valve lifter and up through the pushrod to the rocker arm. No oil will get to the rocker arms if these pushrods are plugged. Look through each pushrod to make sure the oil flow passage is clear.

Rocker arms are made of cast iron, cast aluminum, or stamped steel. Cast adjustable rocker arms are attached to a rocker arm shaft that is mounted on the

ends of the pushrods should be checked for nicks, grooves, roughness, or signs of excessive wear.

Bent pushrods can be the result of valve timing, valve sticking, or improper valve adjustment. Bent or broken pushrods indicate interference in the valve train. Common causes are the use of incorrect valve springs or an installed height less than specified, which can cause coil bind. Also, insufficient valve-to-piston clearance can cause a collision between the valve and piston at high engine speeds.

The pushrods can be visually checked for straightness while they are installed in the engine by rotating them with the valve closed. With the pushrods out of the engine, they can be checked for straightness by rolling them over a flat surface such as a surface plate. If a pushrod is not straight, it will appear to hop as it is rolled. However, the most accurate way to check for straightness is by using a dial indicator (Figure 10-29). If more than 0.003 TIR is found, the pushrod is not straight and should be replaced.

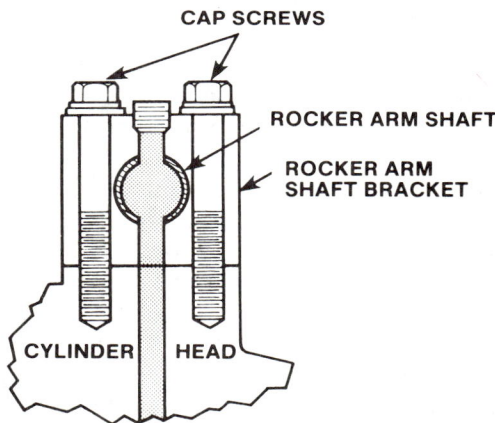

Figure 10-30 The rocker arm shaft is lubricated by the oil supply drilled into the rocker arm bracket.

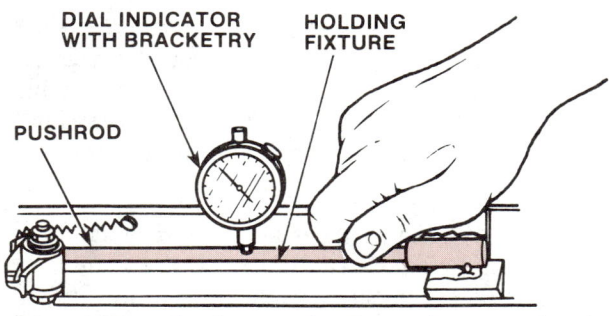

Figure 10-29 Checking pushrod straightness with a dial indicator.

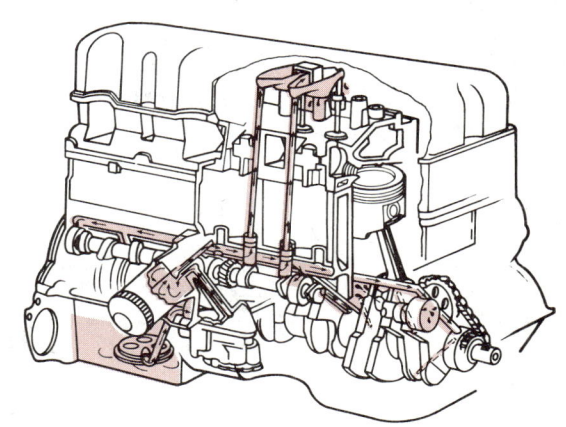

Figure 10-31 Some pushrods are hollow in order to carry oil to the upper reaches of the valve train.

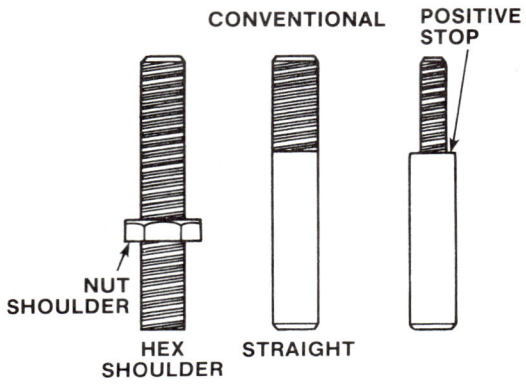

Figure 10-32 Three types of rocker arm studs.

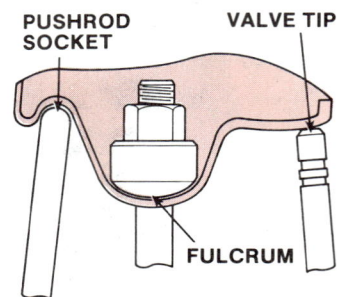

Figure 10-34 Rocker arm wear spots.

head by rocker arm brackets. Although a cast rocker arm can be resurfaced, a stamped nonadjustable rocker arm that is worn must be replaced.

Even though some cast rocker arms are still in use, most domestic engines are equipped with an independent stamped rocker arm assembly for each valve and no rocker arm shaft is used. Rather, the rocker arm is mounted to a stud which is either pressed or threaded into the cylinder head (Figure 10-32) and must be replaced if worn, bent, broken, or loose. On some engines, the studs are drilled for an oil passage to the rocker arms. Make sure oil can pass through before installing the cylinder head on the block. Replacement press-in studs are available in standard sizes and oversizes. The standard size is used to replace damaged or worn studs and the oversizes are used for loose studs.

Inspect the rocker shaft assembly for wear, especially at points that contact the valve stem and pushrod. The fit between the cast rocker arm and the rocker shaft is checked by measuring the outside diameter of the shaft and comparing it to the inside diameter of the rocker arm. Excessive clearance requires replacement of the rocker arm or the rocker shaft, or both. Another wear point that should be checked is the pivot area of the rocker arm to rocker shaft (Figure 10-33). Other rocker arm wear points are shown in Figure 10-34.

Excessive wear of the valve pad occurs when the rocker arm repeatedly strikes the valve tip in a hammer-like fashion. It is able to strike the valve tip in this way when valve train clearance, or lash, is excessive. Excessive valve lash can occur in several ways. For example,

it occurs when mechanical lifters are not adjusted properly or when hydraulic lifters are not working properly. In addition, worn rocker arm valve pads can result when there is insufficient lubrication. Proper lubrication transfers heat away from the valve pad and reduces the metal-to-metal contact. This will keep valve pad wear to a minimum.

Another problem associated with rocker arms is breakage due to interference in the valve train. Other rocker problems are shown in Figure 10-35.

Timing Components

The timing belt (or chain) and crankshaft/camshaft sprockets should be inspected and replaced if damaged or worn. This inspection should include a timing chain deflection check. To conduct this test, simply depress the chain at its midway point between the gears and measure the amount that the chain can be deflected. If the deflection measurement exceeds specifications, the timing chain and gears should be replaced.

Timing Gear Backlash

A gear with cracks, spalling, or excessive wear on the tooth surface is an indication of improper backlash (either insufficient or excessive). With excessive backlash, operation will be noisy because the teeth will make violent impact contact. This overloading when coupled with the normal valve train loads causes accelerated tooth wear and often breakage. Insufficient backlash places a bind on the gears. Also, it generates high contact forces that can rupture the lubrication film between the teeth, causing spalling and wear.

To determine gear backlash, install a dial indicator and bracketry on the cylinder block (Figure 10-36). Check the backlash between the camshaft gear and the crankshaft gear with a dial indicator at six equally-spaced teeth. Hold the gear firmly against the block while making the check. Refer to specifications in the vehicle's service manual for the backlash limits.

Rubber Timing Belt

Stripped/broken rubber belt failure is commonly due to insufficient tensioning, extended service life (belts should be checked for cracking around 50,000 to 60,000 miles), abusive operation, or worn tensioners. Loose timing belts will jump across the teeth of the

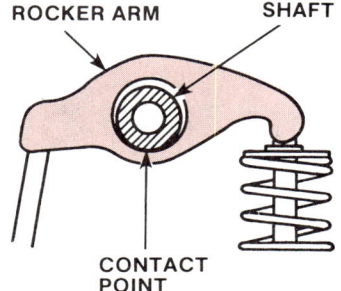

Figure 10-33 A common area of wear is the rocker arm to rocker shaft pivot point.

Camshafts and Valve Trains 219

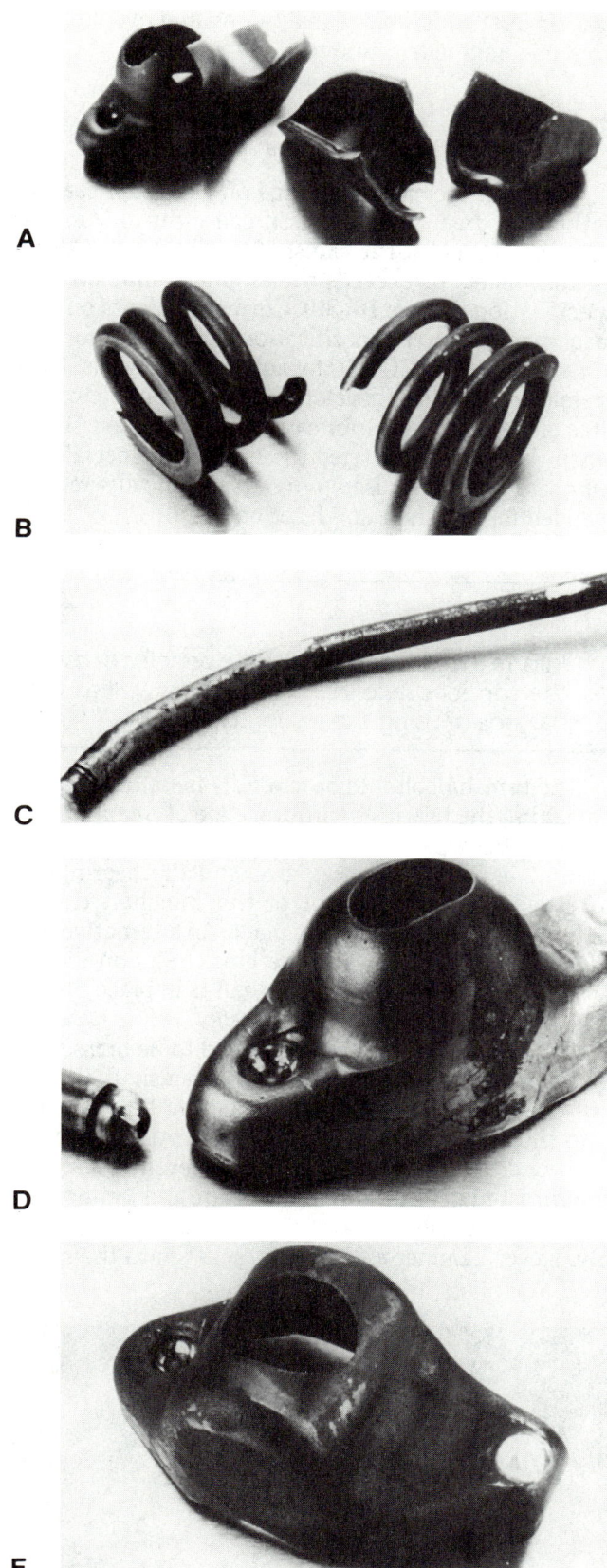

Figure 10-35 Common rocker arm and pushrod problems: (A) broken rocker arm; (B) broken valve spring; (C) broken or bent pushrod; (D) worn pushrod end/ball socket; (E) worn rocker arm pad.

Figure 10-36 Checking timing gear backlash. *Courtesy of TRW, Inc.*

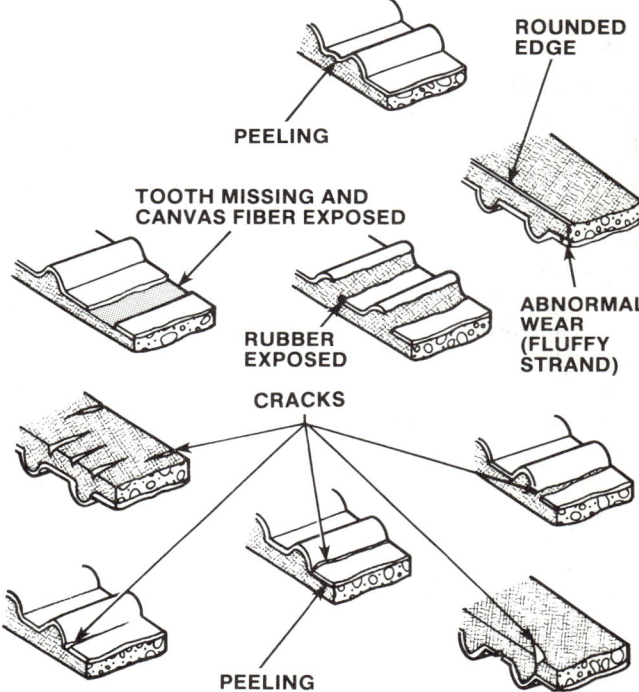

Figure 10-37 Various forms of timing belt wear.

timing sprockets causing shearing of the belt teeth. Localized tensile overloads from over-revving the engine can lead to belt breakage. Also, belts on those engines equipped with adjustable tensioners should be checked for wear whenever a belt is retensioned. In addition, check for cord separation and cracks on all surfaces (Figure 10-37). If the belts are damaged, they should be replaced.

SHOP TALK

The condition of a rubber timing belt can frequently be checked by the fingernail test. Press your fingernail into the hardened backside of the belt. If no impression is left, the belt is too hard, caused by overheating and aging.

Camshaft/Crankshaft Timing

For the valves to open and close in correct relation to the position of the crankshaft, the camshaft must be timed to the crankshaft. This means that the two shafts must be assembled so the cam lobes open the valves at a precise time in relation to the position of the piston and crankshaft. In the typical valve timing diagram shown in Figure 10-38, which shows the relation to crankshaft rotation, the intake valve starts to open at 21 degrees when the piston has reached top dead center (TDC) and remains open until it has traveled 51 degrees past bottom dead center (BDC). The number of degrees between the valve's opening and closing is called intake valve duration time.

The exhaust stroke begins at 53 degrees before BDC and continues until 15 degrees after TDC, or a total exhaust valve duration time of 200 degrees of crankshaft rotation. Although both power and compression time are approximately the same, there is a period of time when both the exhaust and intake valves are open, which is known as the valve overlap.

Overlap is critical to exhaust gas scavenging and the development of proper cylinder pressure. A camshaft with a lot of overlap helps scavenge the cylinders at high engine speeds for improved efficiency. However, since both valves are open for a longer period of time, low rpm cylinder pressure tends to drop. The amount of overlap, since it has an effect on cylinder pressure, is also a factor in determining overall engine efficiency and exhaust emissions. Valve timing and overlap vary from one engine to another.

❑ INSTALLING THE CAMSHAFT

To install the camshaft, wipe off each cam bearing with a lint-free cloth, then spread clean oil on the bearings. Also coat the camshaft (and lifters) with an oil that meets or exceeds the engine manufacturer's specification (Figure 10-39). Current grades of oil that meet manufacturer's specifications are SF/SG for gasoline engines and CC/CD for automotive diesels. Most premature cam wear develops within the first few minutes of operation. Prelubrication helps to prevent this when the engine is started the first time. Special prelubricants can be used only if specifically recommended for camshaft and lifter break-in.

> **CUSTOMER CARE**
>
> Inform the customer about the benefits of using the correct grade of engine oil, as well as the hazards of using the wrong type.

The camshaft should be carefully installed to avoid damaging the bearings with the edge of a cam lobe or journal. Be especially careful to keep it straight to prevent it from cutting or grooving the bearings. A threaded bolt in the front of the camshaft can be helpful in guiding the cam in place. An alternative is to install the camshaft while the block rests on its end (Figure 10-40). When the camshaft is in place, install the thrust plate and the timing gear.

A camshaft timing gear may need to be pressed off and a replacement pressed on the camshaft (Figure 10-41). This is done prior to installing the camshaft into the block. Be sure to align the thrust plate with the woodruff key during removal to prevent damage to the thrust plate. Both the thrust plate and timing gear must then be aligned with the woodruff key for assembly. Never hammer a gear or sprocket onto the shaft.

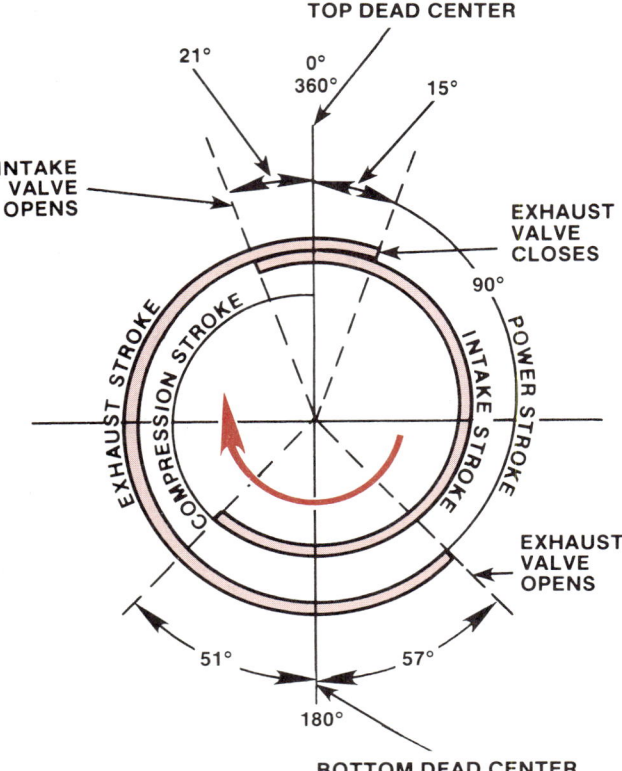

Figure 10-38 Typical valve timing diagram.

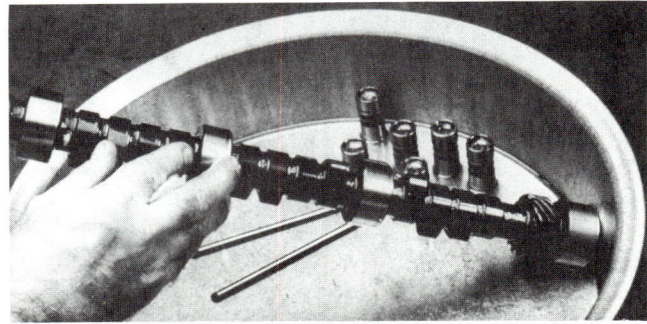

Figure 10-39 Coating the camshaft with oil. *Courtesy of TRW, Inc.*

Camshafts and Valve Trains   221

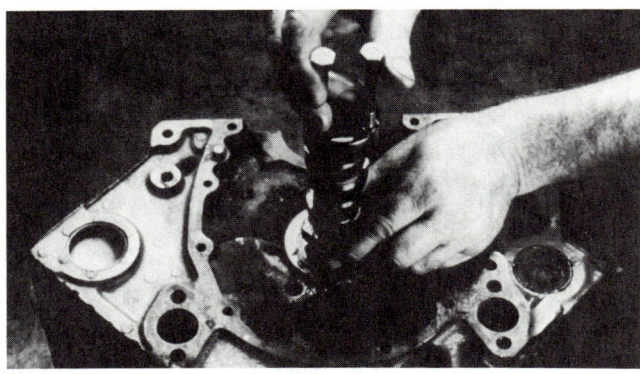

Figure 10–40 Installing the camshaft with the block on end. *Courtesy of TRW, Inc.*

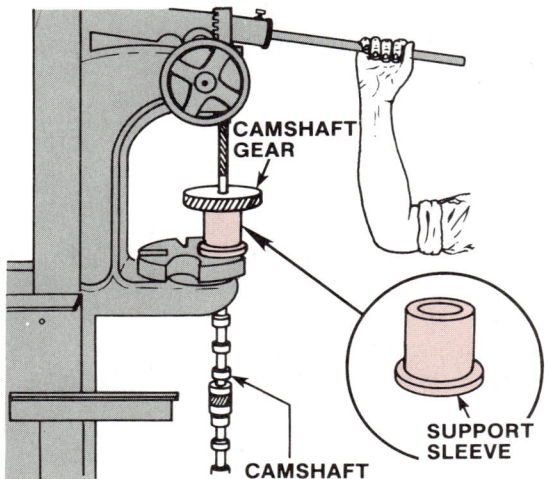

Figure 10–41 When pressing a camshaft timing gear on or off the shaft, always use the correct size sleeve.

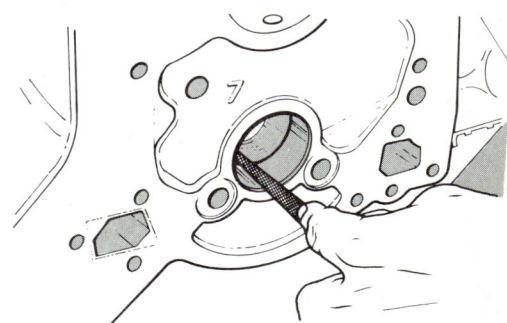

Figure 10–42 Hand scraping a journal with a bearing scraper. *Courtesy of Perfect Circle/Dana*

Heat all metal and aluminum gears on a hot plate 200 to 300 degrees Fahrenheit. Be sure to install the gear while it is still hot to ensure ease of installation. The above step does not apply to fiber gears. These gears should be carefully installed. Press the camshaft into the gear and be sure to keep the gear square and aligned with the keyway at all times.

Once the shaft is completely in the block, the shaft should be able to be turned by hand. If the cam does not turn, binding might be the cause. Binding is the result of a damaged bearing, a nick on the cam's journal, or a slight misalignment of the block journals. When the problem is determined as well as which bearings are tight, hand scraping the journal might be necessary to clear up the problem (Figure 10–42). This can be done with an old camshaft where the end journal is cut for scraper grooves, a broken piston ring, or a bearing scraper.

Camshaft End Play

Before proceeding to the next step in the reassembly, check to be sure that the clearance between the camshaft boss (or gear) and the backing plate is within manufacturer's specifications. Make this check with a feeler gauge. Install shims behind the thrust plate or reposition the camshaft gear and retest the end play. In some cases, adjustment is made by replacing the thrust plate. To check end play, use a dial indicator setup. Be sure the camshaft end play is not more than recommended in the service manual.

☐ INSTALLING THE CYLINDER HEAD AND VALVE TRAIN

As mentioned several times, the valve train includes everything between the camshaft and valve. In the majority of domestic engines, it includes the lifter, pushrod, rocker arm, and rocker support. Once the basic assembly procedure is complete, the lower and upper portions of the engine can be reassembled. The first step in doing this is to sort out the cylinder head bolts. Many engines use head bolts of different lengths (Figure 10–43). The service manual usually identifies where the long and short bolts go. The threads of the bolts should be thoroughly cleaned and then lightly lubricated with oil or antiseize compound.

The head gasket should be positioned on the block and checked for fit. The cylinder head is then placed in position on the block, and the bolts are inserted into the bolt holes.

Cylinder head bolts must be tightened in the correct order and to the proper amount of torque. A typical tightening sequence (Figure 10–44) is usually provided in the service manual. The chart shows which bolt should be tightened first, second, and third. Most cylinder heads are tightened in a sequence that starts in the middle then moves out to the ends. The bolts are generally tightened in two or three stages. If the final torque is 100 foot-pounds, the bolts may first be tightened at 35 foot-pounds. Some manufacturers recommend that the head bolts be retorqued after the engine has been run and is hot.

When assembling the block and head, make sure the dowel pins are in place and the head and block are

222 Section 2 Engines

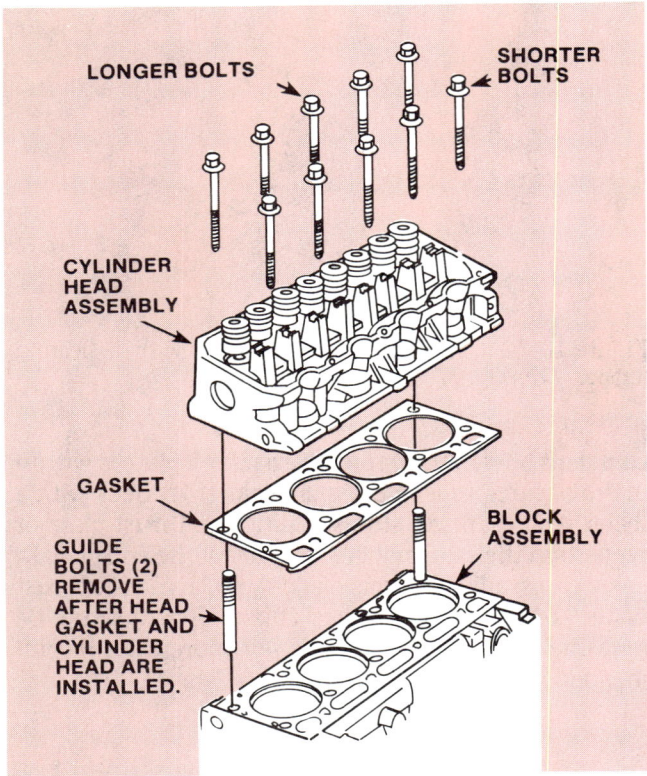

Figure 10-43 Head bolts are different lengths in some engines.

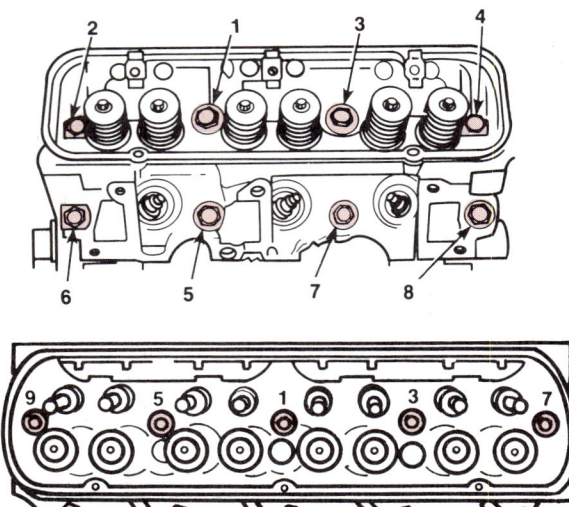

Figure 10-44 Examples of head bolt tightening sequences.

properly aligned. Threaded bolts entering the coolant jackets should be coated with nonhardening gasket sealant.

Before inserting the pushrods, apply a small drop of prelube to eliminate any metal-to-metal contact on start-up. Liberally coat the rocker arms with clean SF/SG grade oil. Then insert the rods and the rocker

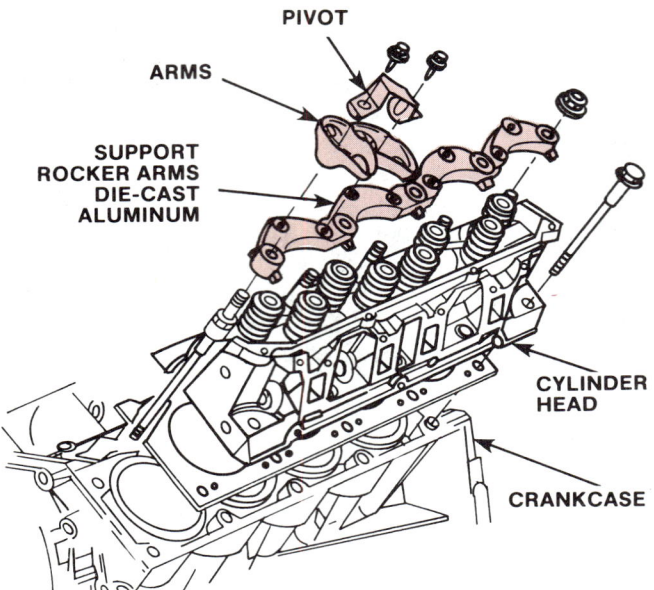

Figure 10-45 Typical rocker arm assembly.

arms (Figure 10-45). Most modern domestic engines use positive stop rocker arm adjustments. This means that when torquing the rocker arms to spec, the plunger is positioned into the lifter, giving correct lifter adjustment. This cannot happen if the lifter has been hand primed before installation. Therefore, it is not recommended that new lifters be primed before installation. This can damage the valve train components.

SHOP TALK

Some engines have rocker arms designated for right- or left-hand positions. They must be installed in the correct locations for proper pushrod alignment. Note the location of the pushrod socket to determine position.

If the metal was removed by machining from the gasket surface of either the block or head, it will affect the valve train geometry by lengthening the linkage. On engines with nonadjustable rocker arms, removal of more than 0.010 inch of material must be compensated for by shimming up the rocker arm assembly supports or by using shorter pushrods.

Adjustable tappets, or cam followers, have been on the automotive scene for years. An early design featured the tappet sitting on top of the cam lobe with a threaded adjusting device directly under the valve tip.

Many of today's overhead cam engines utilize an adjustment screw. One side of the screw is flat and rests against the valve tip, and the other side is tapered and fits underneath the follower (Figure 10-46). By threading the screw in or out of the follower, the gap between

Camshafts and Valve Trains 223

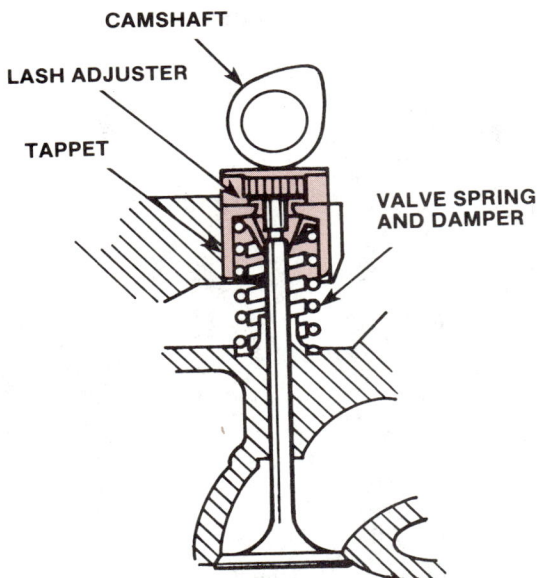

Figure 10-46 Some overhead cam engines feature a cam follower with an adjustment screw.

the cam lobe surface and the top of the follower is made larger or smaller. The screw must be adjusted one complete turn at a time to keep the flat side against the valve tip. If necessary, install a different size adjustment screw to get proper clearance for turning.

Valve lash, on some engines, is adjusted with an adjusting nut on the valve tip end of the rocker arm. The lash or clearance is checked by inserting a feeler gauge between the valve tip and the adjusting nut (Figure 10-47). Installed valve stem height is critical to avoid incorrect valve train geometry and to correctly set valve lash.

Some overhead cam engines have an adjustment disc or shim between the cam lobe surface and the follower. To adjust clearance, a special tool and magnet must be used. To correct excessive clearance, a thicker disc or shim is added. If reduced clearance is the problem, a thinner disc or shim must be installed.

Static valve adjustment is required after an engine has been rebuilt to ensure proper engine starting and prevent damage to the valves caused by the pistons hitting the valves. Normally, if the valves are adjusted accurately, no further valve adjustment is required unless the cylinder heads are retightened. All valve adjustments should be made only within the limits prescribed in the manufacturer's vehicle service manual (Figure 10-48). The service manual is the best source of information on the latest in cylinder head design (Figure 10-49).

❏ INSTALLING THE TIMING COMPONENTS

During most engine rebuilds, a completely new timing assembly is usually installed. If wear exists on any component, replacement of the entire assembly is necessary. Wear in the chain, gears, or sprockets means a timing lag, which results in poor engine performance.

If the camshaft is mounted in the cylinder block, it can be installed after the piston assemblies have been put in place. Each camshaft lobe and each bearing journal is lubricated with assembly lubricant. The camshaft is then carefully pushed into the cylinder block, as discussed earlier in this chapter. Next, the lifters are lubricated and installed in their bores on top of the camshaft lobes.

With either a cylinder block or cylinder head mounted camshaft, the camshaft drive must be installed so that the camshaft and crankshaft are in time with each other. Both sprockets are held in position by a key or possibly a pin. There are factory timing marks on the crankshaft gear or sprocket and on the camshaft gear or sprocket (Figure 10-50). In some timing arrangements, the timing adjustment is on the crankshaft pulley damper. An overhead cam drive, which is belt-driven, can have several idler gears or pulleys with timing marks (Figure 10-51). The timing marks on all the gears must be positioned according to the manufacturer's instructions. The timing chain or belt is generally installed with the gears in their correct positions.

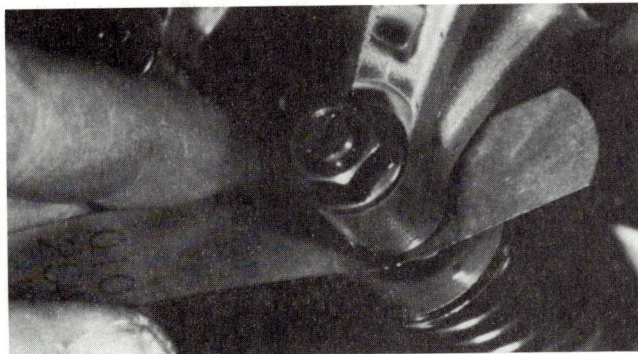

Figure 10-47 Checking clearance with a feeler gauge.

Figure 10-48 Always adjust the lifters according to the engine manufacturer's specifications. *Courtesy of TRW, Inc.*

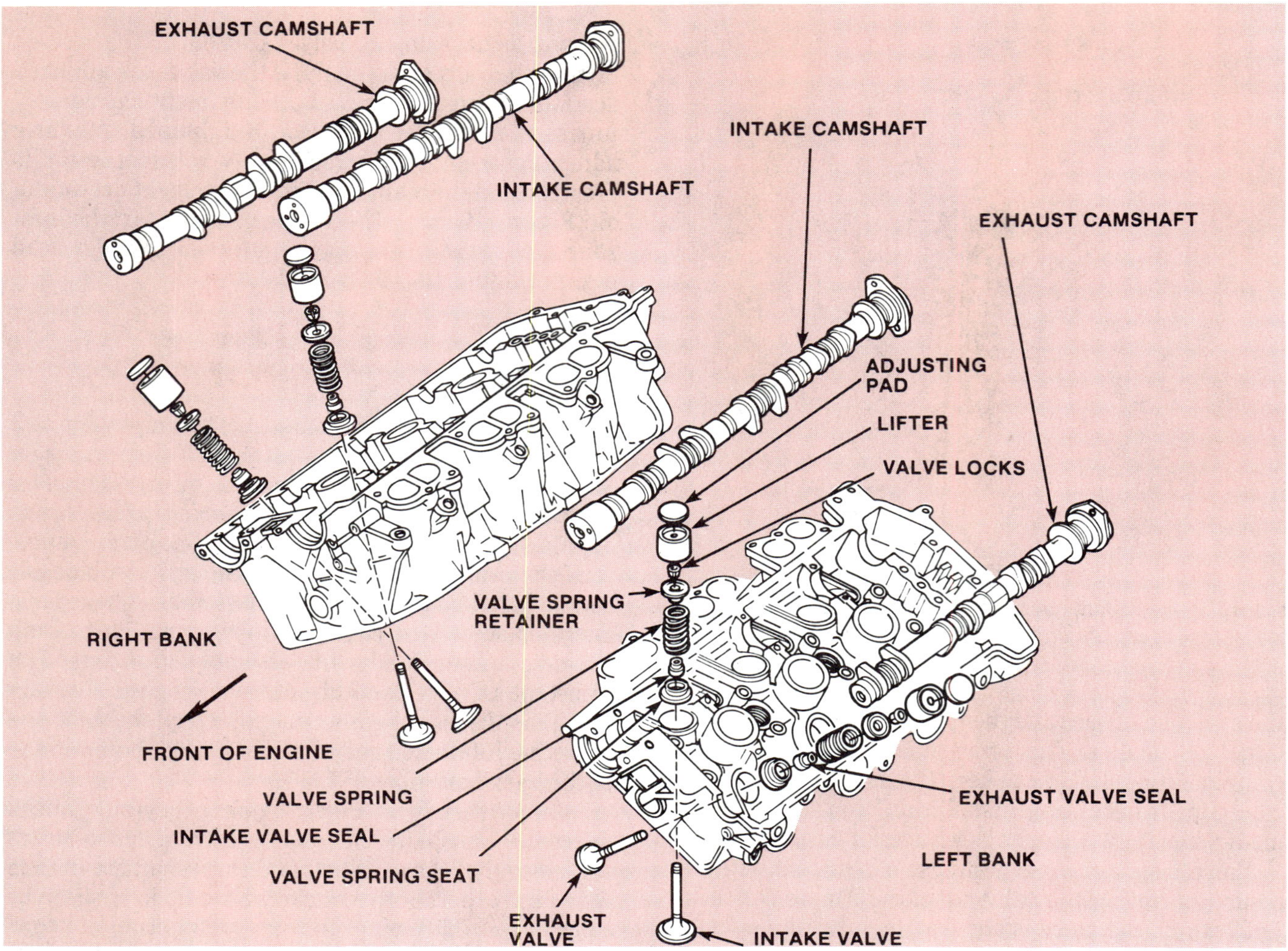

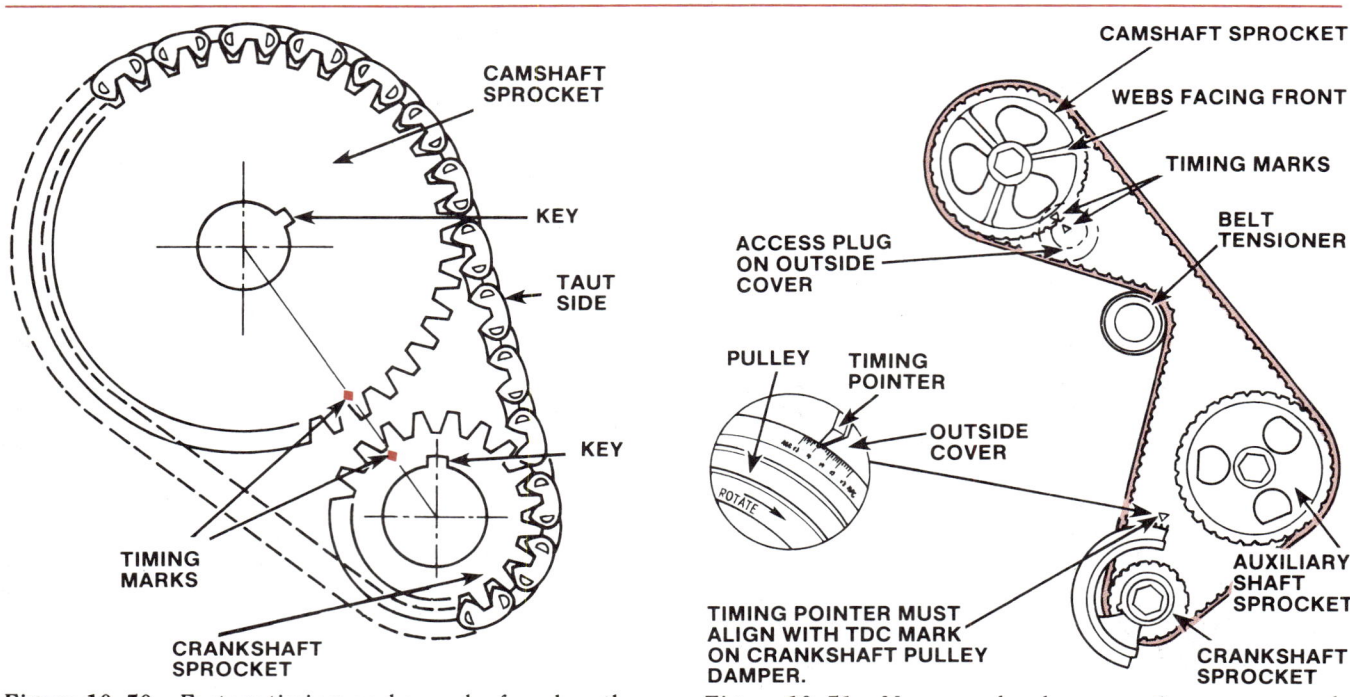

Figure 10-49 Dual overhead camshaft and four-valve per cylinder head design.

Figure 10-50 Factory timing marks can be found on the camshaft and crankshaft sprockets.

Figure 10-51 Many overhead cam engines use several idler gears or pulleys.

PHOTO SEQUENCE 6

☐ REPLACING A TIMING BELT ON AN OHC ENGINE

P6-1 Disconnect the negative cable from the battery prior to beginning to remove and replace the timing belt.

P6-2 Carefully remove the timing cover, be careful not to distort or damage it while pulling it up. With the cover removed, check the immediate area around the belt for wires and other obstacles. If some are found, move them out of the way.

P6-3 Align the timing marks on the camshaft's sprocket with the mark on the cylinder head. If the marks are not obvious, use a paint stick or chalk to clearly mark them.

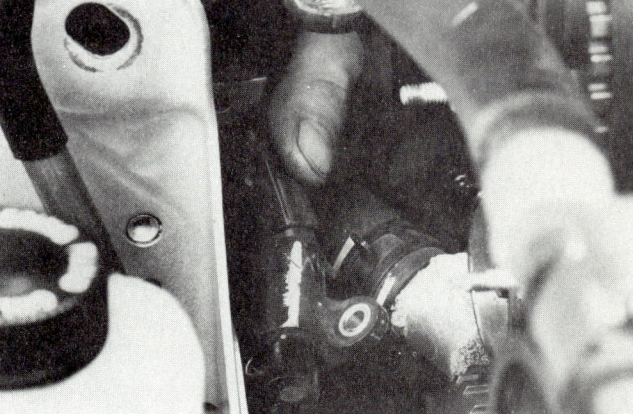

P6-4 Carefully remove the crankshaft timing sensor and probe holder.

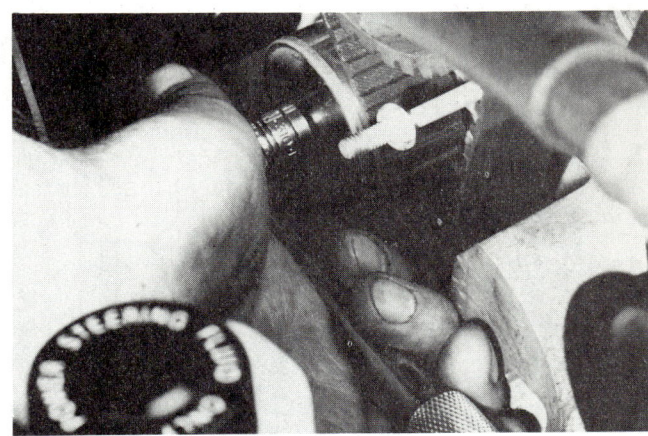

P6-5 Loosen the adjustment bolt on the belt tensioner pulley. It is normally not necessary to remove the tensioner assembly.

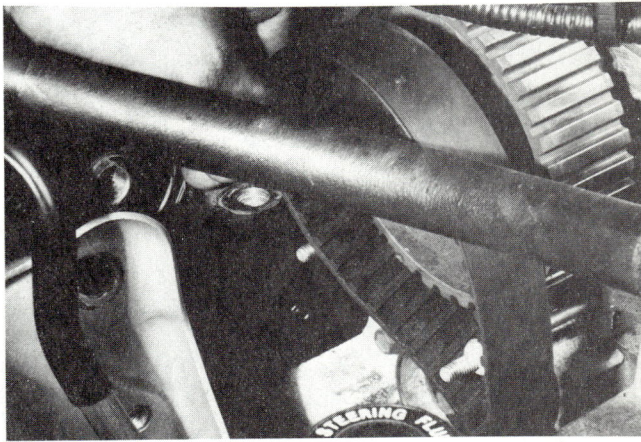

P6-6 Slide the belt off the camshaft sprocket. Be careful not to allow the crankshaft pulley to rotate while doing this.
(continued)

225

P6-7 To remove the belt from the engine, the crankshaft pulley must be removed. Then the belt can be slipped off the crankshaft sprocket.

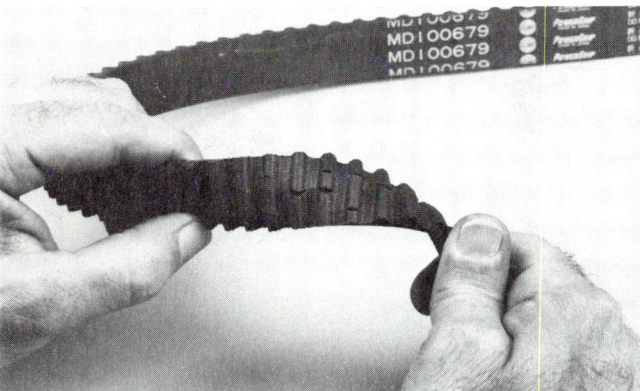

P6-8 After the belt has been removed, inspect it for cracks and other damage. Cracks will become more obvious if the belt is twisted slightly. Any defects in the belt indicate that it must be replaced.

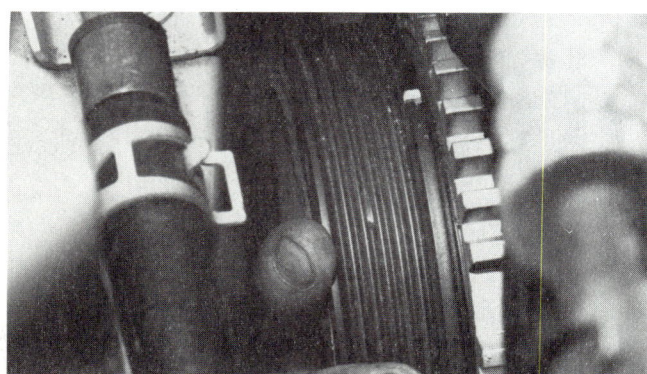

P6-9 To begin reassembly, place the belt around the crankshaft sprocket. Then reinstall the crankshaft pulley.

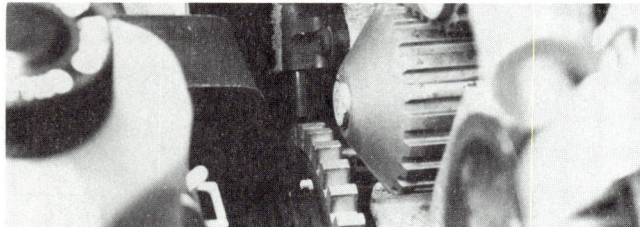

P6-10 Make sure the timing marks on the crankshaft pulley are lined up with the marks on the engine block. If they are not, **carefully rock the crankshaft** until the marks are lined up.

P6-11 With the timing belt fitted onto the crankshaft sprocket and the crankshaft pulley tightened in place, the crankshaft timing sensor and probe can be reinstalled.

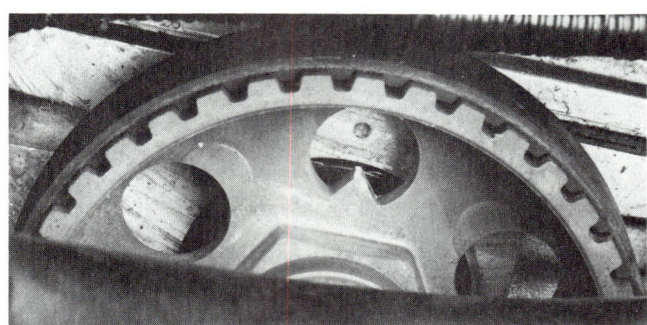

P6-12 Align the camshaft sprocket with the timing marks on the cylinder head. Then wrap the timing belt around the camshaft sprocket and allow the belt tensioner to put a slight amount of pressure on the belt.

P6-13 Adjust the tension as described in the service manual. Then rotate the engine two complete turns. Recheck the tension.

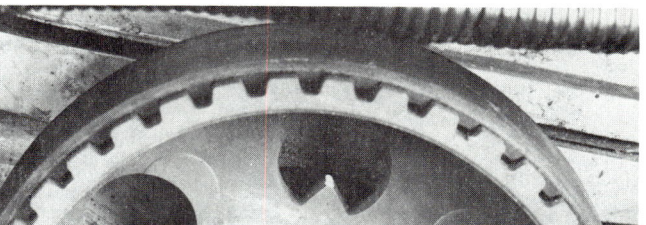

P6-14 Rotate the engine through two complete turns again, then check the alignment marks on the camshaft and the crankshaft. Any deviation needs to be corrected before the timing cover is reinstalled. ∎

The chain is installed on the crankshaft sprocket first, then around the camshaft sprocket. Never wind a chain onto the sprockets. Also, a screwdriver, pry bar, or hammer should never be used to force a chain into position. Prying or pounding on the chain will damage the links causing the chain to stretch and fail. Carefully place the chain on the sprockets and install the entire assembly as a unit by pressing both sprockets on evenly, keeping the keyways aligned. Use a sleeve and tap gently into place keeping the sprockets parallel and aligned.

When installing a timing belt, be sure to align the sprocket timing marks properly and adjust belt tension to the manufacturer's specifications. For more information, see Photo Sequence 6, which is included in this chapter.

SHOP TALK

As the valve train and timing system become more and more complex, the service manual becomes a must. This can be noted in Figure 10-52, which shows the crankshaft and camshaft timing belt installation for the dual overhead camshaft (DOHC) and four valves per cylinder design.

CASE STUDY

Case 1

A four-cylinder DOHC engine has just been rebuilt. During the initial running of the engine, it runs quite rough. This is normal until everything gets seated. However, the condition becomes worse the more the engine runs. Slight adjustments to the ignition timing do not help the condition. A visual inspection reveals nothing loose or disconnected. Each hose and wire is traced to make sure it is connected to the proper fitting and terminal.

Because it seems that the engine is running on only three cylinders, a cylinder leakage test is performed. The results indicate excessive leakage past the #4 intake valve. In an attempt to visually locate the problem, the intake cam cover is removed. A look at the camshaft reveals that the #4 intake lobe is worn. This was a new camshaft. Was it defective? Was it not hardened properly? Did something else cause this?

Further visual inspection reveals that the shim used to set valve lash was not fully seated in its cup. The edge of the shim was working like a knife, cutting off the metal from the lobe. The initial rough

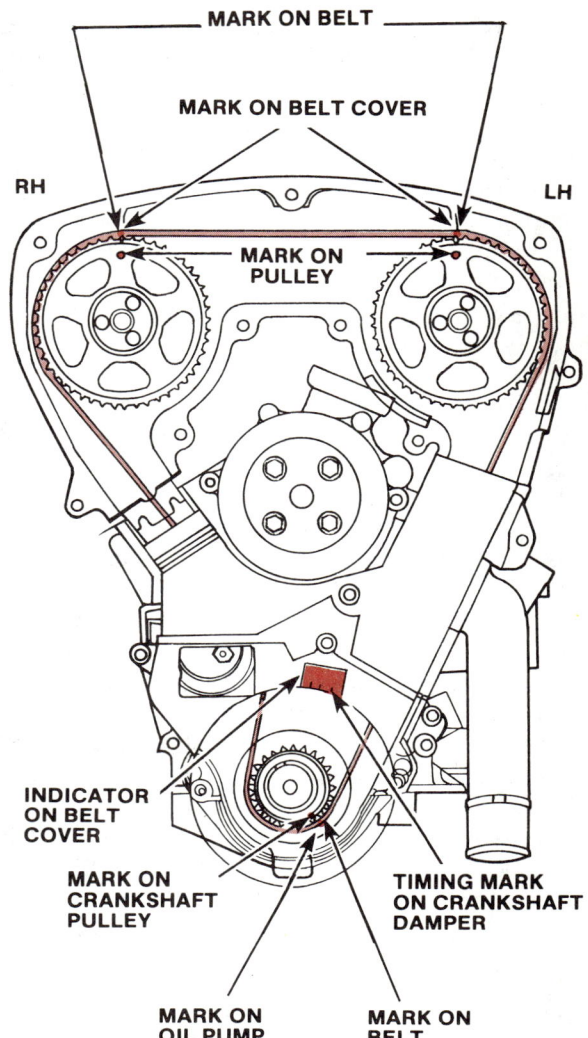

Figure 10-52 Crankshaft and camshaft timing belt installation for a dual overhead cam engine.

running of the engine was caused by the shim preventing the valve from fully closing. The condition worsened as the lobe was cut away.

The oil was changed and a new camshaft and shim were installed to correct the problem.

Summary

- A cam changes rotary motion into reciprocating motion. The part of the cam that controls the opening of the valves is the cam lobe. The closing of the valves is the responsibility of the valve springs.
- The camshaft is supported in the cylinder block by friction-type bearings, or bushings, which are typically pressed into the camshaft bore in the block or head. Camshaft bearings are normally replaced during engine rebuilding.
- Solid valve lifters provide for a rigid connection between the camshaft and the valves. Hydraulic

valve lifters do the same but use oil to absorb the shock resulting from movement of the valve train. Roller lifters are used to reduce friction and power loss.
- Lifter noises do not necessarily mean the lifter is at fault. Other causes for light tapping noise in the engine include worn cam lobes, a stuck valve, a broken valve spring, insufficient lubrication between the rocker arm and the pushrod or valve, or a loose rocker arm assembly. Careful troubleshooting is required to determine the source of the noise.
- Pushrods are the connecting link between the rocker arm and the valve lifter. They can be either solid or hollow. Pushrods are used only on engines that have the camshaft in the block.
- On a four-stroke cycle engine, the camshaft is driven by the crankshaft at half the engine speed. This is accomplished by a camshaft drive gear or drive sprocket that is twice as large as the crankshaft sprocket.
- A valve will operate only as well as its actuating parts, including the timing gears, chain or belt and sprockets, camshaft, lifters, pushrods, and rocker arm assemblies. When making an inspection, each valve train component should be carefully checked.
- The two most popular ways of measuring cam lobes for wear are the dial indicator and outside micrometer. The dial indicator test should be conducted with the camshaft in the engine. When using an outside micrometer, the camshaft must be out of the engine.
- All engines with mechanical lifters have some method of adjustment to bring valve lash (clearance) back into specification. Rocker arms with adjustable pivots and adjustable pushrods are found on OHV engines. Rocker arms with adjustable screws and adjustable cam followers are part of OHC engines.
- The rocker arm converts the upward movement of the valve lifter into a downward motion to open the valve. It also permits the valves to be angled. Most domestic engines have an independent stamped rocker arm assembly for each valve, rather than a cast rocker arm.
- The timing belt or chain and crankshaft/camshaft sprockets should be inspected and replaced if damaged or worn. This inspection should include a timing chain deflection check.
- For the valves to open and close in correct relation to the crankshaft position, the camshaft must be timed to the crankshaft. The number of degrees between the intake valve's opening and closing is known as intake valve duration time.
- The period of time when both the exhaust valve and intake valve are open is known as valve overlap. Overlap is critical to exhaust gas scavenging and proper cylinder pressure. It is also a factor in determining overall engine efficiency and exhaust emission.
- Most premature cam wear develops within the first few minutes of operation. Prelubrication with the proper oil (SF/SG for gasoline engines and CC/CD for diesel) or approved assembly lubricant can help prevent this from occurring.
- During most engine rebuilds, a completely, new timing assembly is installed. When installing a timing belt, be sure to align the sprocket timing marks properly and adjust the belt tension to the manufacturer's specifications.

Review Questions

1. Where is the camshaft mounted on overhead camshaft engines?
2. What is used in some engines to limit side movement of the pushrods?
3. Name the two most popular methods of measuring cam lobe wear.
4. Define galling wear.
5. How can pushrods be visually checked for straightness while installed in the engine?
6. What device in the valve train changes rotary motion into reciprocating motion?
   a. eccentric
   b. cam
   c. bushing
   d. mandrel
7. Technician A says that valve float is less likely to occur in OHC engines. Technician B says that valve float is less likely to occur in OHV engines. Who is correct?
   a. Technician A
   b. Technician B
   c. Both A and B
   d. Neither A nor B
8. After installing cam bearings, Technician A checks that the oil holes in the bearings are properly aligned with those in the block by squirting oil into the holes. Technician B checks for proper alignment by inserting a wire through the holes. Who is correct?
   a. Technician A
   b. Technician B
   c. Both A and B
   d. Neither A nor B
9. What type of valve lifter automatically compensates for the effects of engine temperature?
   a. hydraulic
   b. solid
   c. roller
   d. all of the above
10. Technician A conducts the dial indicator test for worn cam lobes with the camshaft in the engine. Technician B conducts this test with the cam-

shaft removed from the engine. Who is correct?
a. Technician A
b. Technician B
c. Both A and B
d. Neither A nor B

11. Technician A says a bent camshaft can be repaired, but Technician B says it must be replaced. Who is correct?
a. Technician A
b. Technician B
c. Both A and B
d. Neither A nor B

12. What converts the upward movement of the valve lifter into a downward motion to open the valve?
a. pushrod
b. tappet
c. rocker arm
d. cam lobe

13. If the timing chain deflection measurement exceeds specifications, what should be done?
a. replace the timing chain
b. replace the timing gears
c. both a and b
d. neither a nor b

14. Timing gear backlash is determined by means of a dial indicator and _____.
a. outside micrometer
b. inside micrometer
c. vernier caliper
d. bracketry

15. A camshaft with _____ overlap helps scavenge the cylinders at high engine speeds for improved efficiency.
a. no
b. very little
c. half the normal amount of
d. a lot of

16. Technician A says that the engine must be removed to replace a timing belt on a transversely-mounted engine. Technician B says the procedures given in a service manual should be followed whenever a timing belt is being replaced. Who is correct?
a. Technician A
b. Technician B
c. Both A and B
d. Neither A nor B

17. Technician A uses SF/SG oil to coat the camshaft and lifters on a gasoline engine. Technician B uses CC/CD oil to coat the camshaft and lifters on a gasoline engine. Who is correct?
a. Technician A
b. Technician B
c. Both A and B
d. Neither A nor B

18. Which of the following statements is incorrect?
a. Cylinder head bolts must be tightened to the proper amount of torque.
b. Most cylinder head bolts are tightened in a sequence that starts on one end.
c. On some engines, the head bolts are retorqued after the engine has been run and is hot.
d. Many engines use head bolts of different lengths.

19. On engines with nonadjustable rocker arms, removal of more than _____ inch of metal from the gasket surface of either the block or head must be compensated for by shimming up the rocker arm assembly supports.
a. 0.10
b. 0.010
c. 0.001
d. 0.50

20. Technician A uses a pry bar to force the timing chain into position on its sprockets. Technician B uses a screwdriver to force the timing chain into position on its sprockets. Who is correct?
a. Technician A
b. Technician B
c. Both A and B
d. Neither A nor B

11 LUBRICATING AND COOLING SYSTEMS

Objectives

- Name and describe the components of a typical lubricating system.
- Inspect, service, and install an oil pump.
- Describe the crankcase ventilation system.
- Explain oil service and viscosity ratings.
- List and describe the components of the cooling system.
- Describe the operation of the cooling system.
- Describe the function of the water pump, radiator, pressure radiator caps, and thermostats in the cooling system.
- Test and service components of the cooling system.

Proper operation of the engine's lubricating and cooling systems is important to its well-being. If an engine does not supply oil or coolant to itself, all the work done by the technician on the components of the engine will be quickly destroyed.

☐ LUBRICATION

An engine's lubricating system must perform several important functions. It must hold an adequate supply of oil to cool, clean, lubricate, and seal the engine. It must also remove contaminants from the oil, and deliver oil to all necessary areas of the engine.

Oil Types

Engine oils are carefully formulated to reduce the adverse effects of engine operation. An effective engine oil should possess these important properties.

- Prompt circulation through the engine lubrication system
- Provide lubrication without foaming
- Reduce friction and wear
- Prevent rust and corrosion
- Provide cooling for engine parts
- Keep internal engine parts clean

To provide all these properties, modern engine oil contains many additives. Because of these additives, choosing the correct oil for each engine application can be a difficult task. However, the American Petroleum Institute (API) has developed service ratings that greatly simplify oil selection.

The API classifies engine oil as standard or S-class for passenger cars and light trucks and as commerical or C-class for heavy-duty commercial applications. Additionally, various grades of oil within each class are further classified alphabetically according to their ability to meet the engine manufacturers' warranty specifications (Table 11-1).

SHOP TALK

Among lubrication engineers, the designations S and C do not stand for standard and commercial vehicles respectively. The letters refer to the type of ignition that each engine utilizes. S is for gasoline engines that employ spark ignition. C is for compression ignition systems utilized by diesels.

In addition to oil additives, oil viscosity is equally important in selecting an engine oil. The viscosity is affected by its temperature. For example, hot oil flows faster than cold. Since the rate of oil flow through the lubrication system is crucial for maintaining proper lubrication levels, viscosity is an important factor. Add to this the fact that the engine operates under a wide range of temperatures, and viscosity becomes even more important.

To standardize oil viscosity ratings, the Society of Automotive Engineers (SAE) has established an oil viscosity classification system that is accepted throughout the industry. This system is a numeric rating in which the higher viscosity, or heavier weight oils, receive the higher numbers. For example, an oil classified as an SAE 50 weight oil is heavier and flows slower than an SAE 10 weight oil. Heavyweight oils are best

Lubricating and Cooling Systems

	TABLE 11-1 API GASOLINE ENGINE DESIGNATION
SC	Service typical of gasoline engines in 1964 through 1967. Oil designed for this service provides control of high and low temperature deposits, wear, dust, and corrosion in gasoline engines.
SD	Service typical of gasoline engines in 1968 through 1970. Oils designed for this service provide more protection against high and low temperature deposits, wear, rust, and corrosion in gasoline engines. SD oil can be used in engines requiring SC oil.
SE	Service typical of gasoline engines in automobiles and some trucks beginning in 1972. Oil designed for this service provides more protection against oil oxidation, high temperature engine deposits, rust, and corrosion in gasoline engines. SE oil can be used in engines requiring SC or SD oil.
SF	Service typical of gasoline engines in automobiles and some trucks beginning with 1980. SF oils provide increased oxidation stability and improved antiwear performance over oils that meet API designation SE. It also provides protection against engine deposits, rust, and corrosion. SF oils can be used in engines requiring SC, SD, or SE oils.
SG	Service typical of gasoline automobiles and light-duty trucks, plus CC classification diesel engines beginning in the late 1980s. SG oils provide the best protection against engine wear, oxidation, engine deposits, rust, and corrosion. It can be used in engines requiring SC, SD, SE, or SF oils.

CUSTOMER CARE

Use of the proper grade oil should be recommended to all customers. Highlight the benefits of using it.

suited for use in high-temperature regions. Low-weight oils work best in low temperature operations.

To meet the needs of the average motorist who might not want to change oils seasonally, oil manufacturers have developed multiviscosity oils. These oils carry a combined classification such as 10W-30. This classification means that the oil has a weight of 10 at ambient air temperature. Once the engine builds up heat, the oil actually thickens to a weight of 30. An oil of this type allows easy starting in cold weather and adequate protection in all operating temperatures.

The SAE classification (Table 11-2) and the API rating are usually indicated on top of an oil can (Figure 11-1). Selecting oils that specifically meet or exceed the manufacturer's recommendations and maintaining a regular oil change schedule is instrumental in obtaining maximum service life from an engine.

SHOP TALK

Using the incorrect grade or type of oil in an engine can cause a variety of problems. For example, the wrong viscosity oil can cause either an oil consumption problem or a low oil pressure problem, depending upon the weather and driving conditions. Using an oil with the incorrect service rating can result in inadequate protection for engine bearings and other moving engine parts. Always consult the engine manufacturer's recommendations to make certain the engine is using the correct grade and type of oil.

Figure 11-1 API designation and SAE rating.

TABLE 11-2 SAE GRADES OF MOTOR OIL		
Lowest Atmospheric Temperature Expected	Single-Grade Oils	Multigrade Oils
32° F (0° C)	20, 20W, 30	10W-30, 10W-40, 15W-40, 20W-40, 20W-50
0°F (-18° C)	10W	5W-30, 10W-30, 10W-40, 15W-40
-15° F (-26° C)	10W	10W-30, 10W-40, 5W-30
Below -15° F (-26° C)	5W*	*5W-20, 5W-30

*SAE 5W and 5W-20 grade oils are not recommended for sustained high-speed driving.

Two new terms have entered the oil field: energy-conserving and synthetic oil. Engine oils that are classified as energy-conserving or fuel-saving are designed to reduce friction, which in turn reduces fuel consumption. Friction modifiers and other additive changes are used to achieve this result. Energy-conserving oil is identified as such on the top of the oil can.

The introduction of synthetic motor oils dates back to World War II. It is often described as the oil of the future. Synthetic oils are manufactured in a laboratory rather than pumped out of the ground and refined. They offer a variety of advantages over natural oils including better fuel economy, stability over a wide range of temperatures and operating conditions, and longevity. They are more costly than natural oil.

> **CUSTOMER CARE**
>
> When changing oil or doing any work on an automobile, use fender covers and do not leave fingerprints on the exterior of the car. If oil or grease gets on the car, clean it off.

Oil Consumption

Excessive oil consumption can be a result of external and internal leaks, faulty accessories, piston rings, and valve guides. Internal leaks (Figure 11-2), which usually result in oil burning, are usually more difficult to diagnose.

To start an oil consumption diagnosis, examine the engine thoroughly for external leaks. These leaks can occur at the valve cover gasket, camshaft expansion plug, oil filter, front and rear oil seals, oil pan gasket, fuel pump gasket, and timing gear cover.

Even the smallest oil leak can cause major oil consumption. Three drops of oil lost externally every 100 feet amounts to 3 quarts every thousand miles. External leaks occur under normal and abnormal crankcase pressure.

Figure 11-2 Indication of internal oil leak condition. *Courtesy of Perfect Circle/Dana*

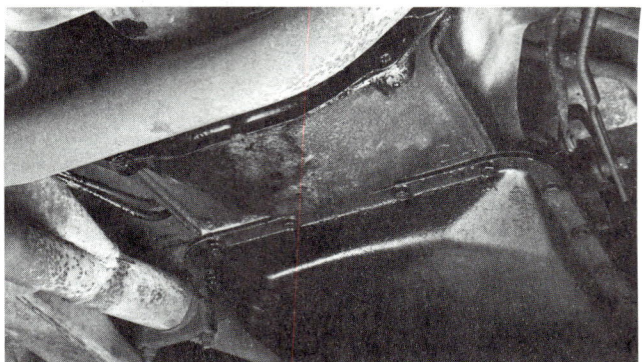

Figure 11-3 Fresh oil on the clutch housing or oil pan usually indicates a leak. *Courtesy of Perfect Circle/Dana*

Normal crankcase pressure will cause oil leaks at gasket or past metal-to-metal joints which are in direct contact with oil. Worn seals, faulty gaskets, and loose cover or housing bolts could be the problem. Fresh oil on the clutch housing, oil pan (Figure 11-3), fuel pump, edges of valve covers, external oil lines, distributor shaft housing, base or crankcase filler tube, or at the bottom of the timing gear or chain cover usually indicates a leak close to that point.

As shown in Figure 11-4, check for proper oil pressure at the sending unit passage with an externally-mounted mechanical oil pressure gauge (as opposed to relying on an OE installed dash-mounted gauge). To insure accurate test results, follow the car manufacturer's pretest recommendations and compare your readings to the minimum/maximum oil pressure specification listed in the manual. Low oil pressure readings can be attributed to internal component wear, pump-related problems, a low oil level, or oil viscosity that is too low. Conversely, a pressure reading that is too high could be caused by an overfilled crankcase, too high of an oil viscosity, the wrong pump (remote but possible, especially if the pump has been replaced), or a faulty pressure relief valve.

When crankcase pressure is abnormally high, oil is forced out through joints that normally would not leak. Pressure develops when the crankcase ventilator inlet becomes clogged, when blowby becomes excessive, or

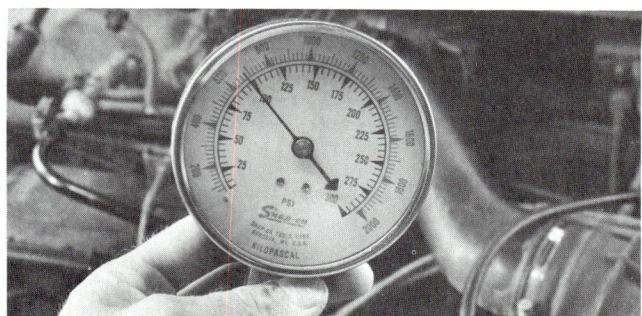

Figure 11-4 Typical mechanical oil pressure gauge. *Courtesy of Snap-On Tools Corp.*

Lubricating and Cooling Systems   233

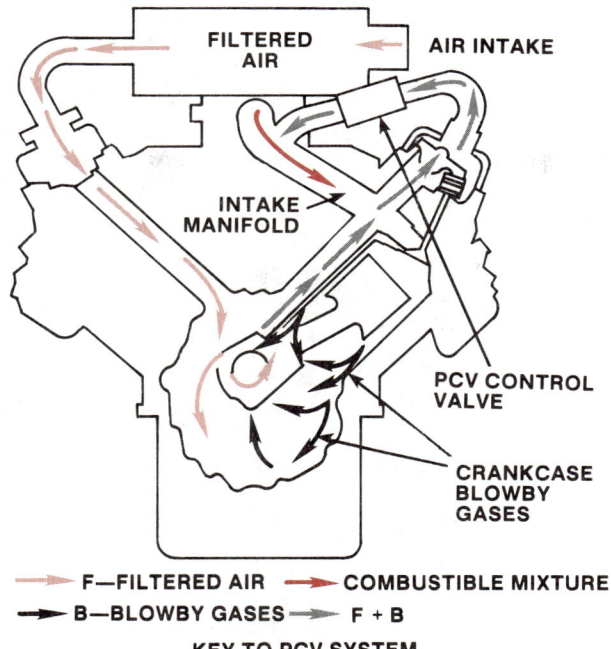

Figure 11-5 Operation of a PCV system.

> **SHOP TALK**
>
> Internal leaks are frequently the result of aluminum intake manifolds on V-6 and V-8 engines because aluminum often does not seal as well as cast iron. If an unacceptable amount of warpage is found, removing and milling the manifold is necessary.

Most oil consumption problems, as shown in Figure 11-6, can be corrected by proper servicing of the engine.

☐ LUBRICATING SYSTEMS

The main components of a typical lubricating system (Figure 11-7) are described here.

OIL PUMP The oil pump is the heart of the lubricating system. Just as the heart in the human body circulates blood through the veins, the oil pump circulates oil through the engine.

OIL PUMP PICKUP The oil pump pickup is a line from the oil pump to the oil stored in the oil pan (Figure 11-8). It usually contains a filter screen, which is submerged in the oil at all times. The screen serves to keep large particles from reaching the oil pump. This screen should be cleaned any time the oil pan is removed.

OIL PAN OR SUMP The oil pan attaches to the crankcase or block. It serves as the reservoir for the engine's lubricating oil. It is designed to hold all the oil necessary to lubricate the engine when it is running, plus a reserve. The oil pan helps to cool the oil through its contact with the outside air.

PRESSURE RELIEF VALVE Since the oil pump is a positive displacement pump, an oil pressure relief valve

when a positive crankcase ventilation (PCV) valve is malfunctioning. The latter system provides a continuous flow of fresh air through the crankcase to inhibit formation of corrosive contaminants (Figure 11-5). It is important that the correct replacement valve is installed because each is designed for a particular engine's operating characteristics. Use of the wrong valve can cause oil consumption, as well as other problems. If the PCV valve or connecting hoses become clogged, excessive pressure will develop in the crankcase, which might force oil into the air cleaner or cause it to be sucked into the intake manifold. This problem can be prevented by maintenance of the system and replacement of the PCV valve as recommended by the vehicle manufacturer.

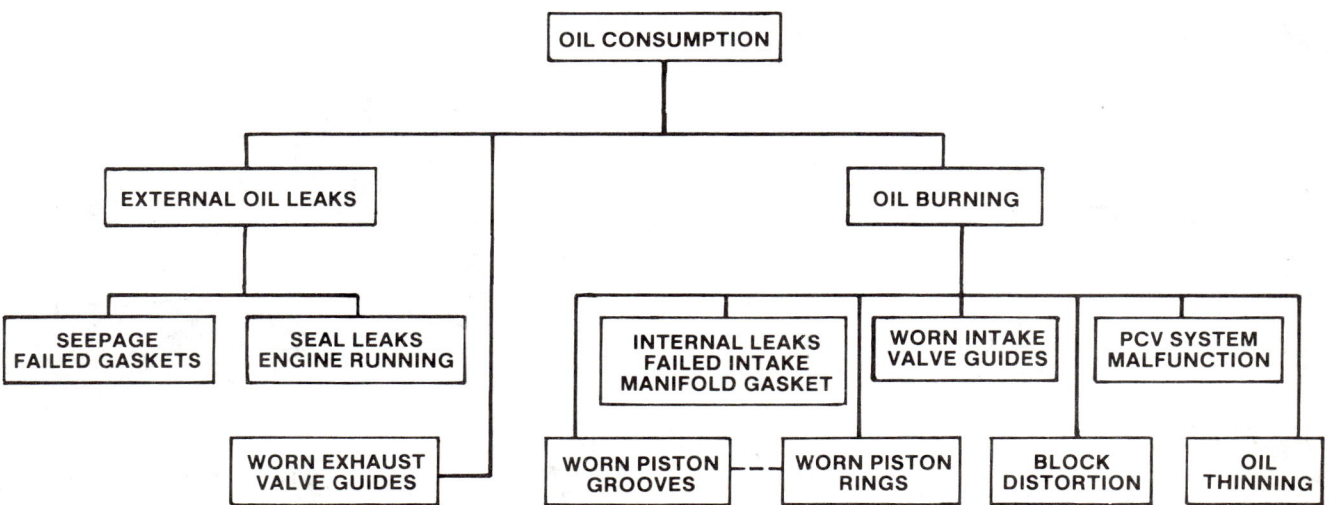

Figure 11-6 Common oil consumption problems and their causes.

234 Section 2 Engines

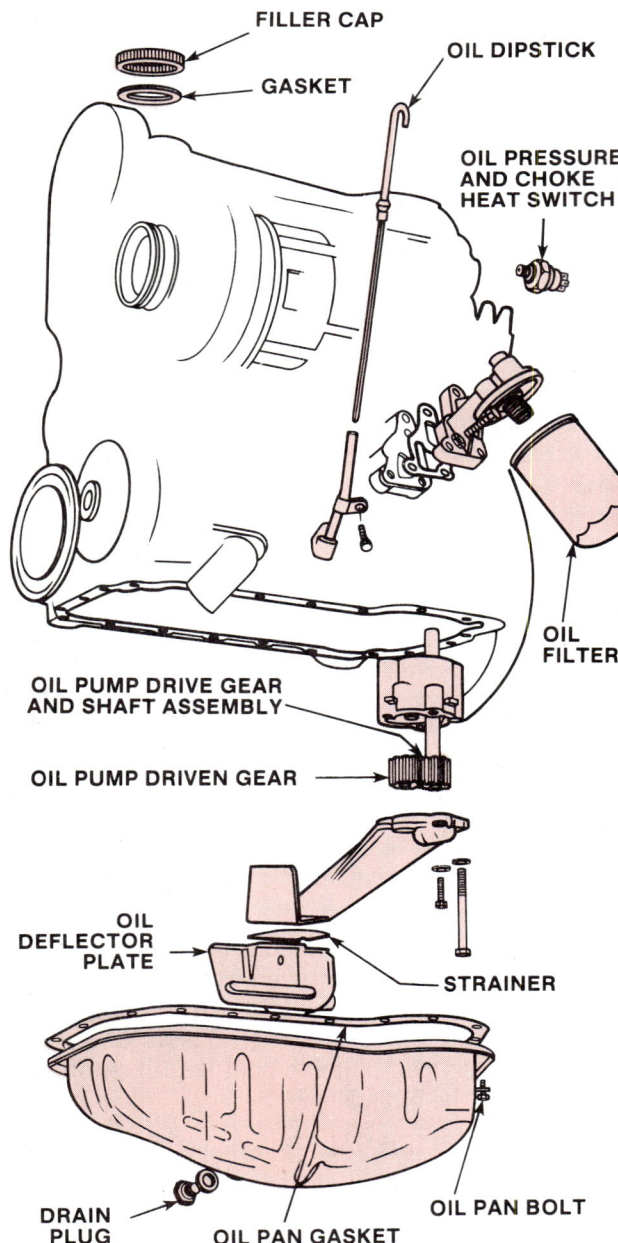

Figure 11-7 Components of a typical lubricating system.

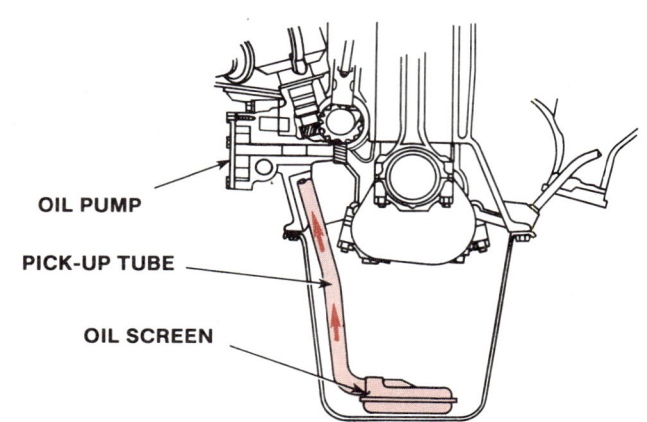

Figure 11-8 Oil pump pickup.

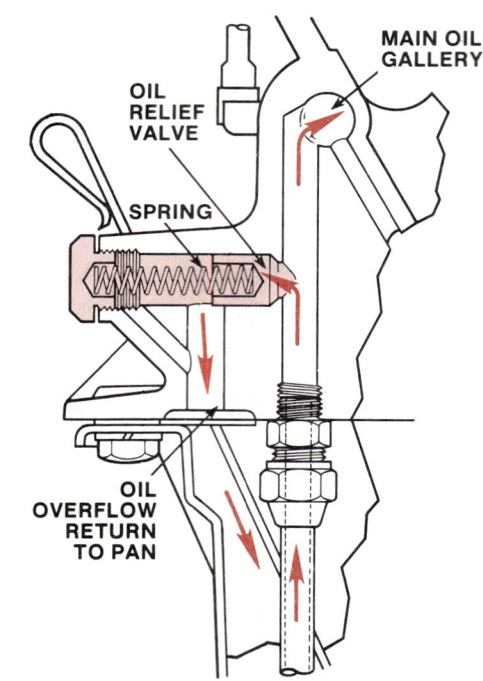

Figure 11-9 Oil pressure relief valve.

(Figure 11-9) is included in the system to prevent excessively high system pressures from occurring as engine speed is increased. Once oil pressures exceed a preset limit, the spring-loaded pressure relief valve opens and allows the excess oil to by-pass the rest of the system and return directly to the sump.

OIL FILTER Under pressure from the oil pump, oil flows through a filter (Figure 11-10) to remove any impurities that might have become suspended in the oil in the sump. This is necessary so impurities will not

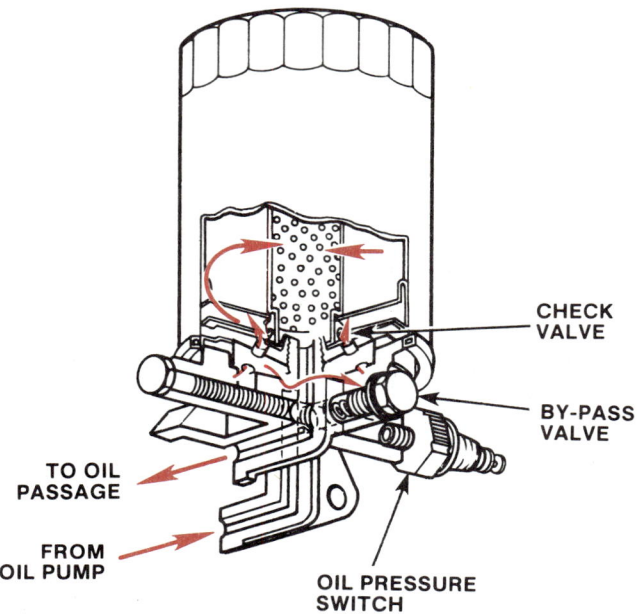

Figure 11-10 Typical oil filter circuit.

Lubricating and Cooling Systems

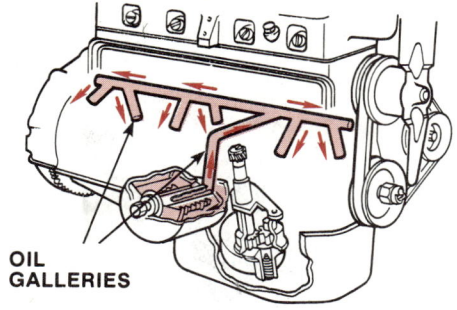

Figure 11-11 Oil galleries.

circulate through the engine and cause premature wear. Filtering also increases the usable life of the oil. Oil filters are equipped with a by-pass valve to allow oil to by-pass the filter when the filter is clogged.

ENGINE OIL PASSAGES OR GALLERIES From the filter, the oil then flows into the engine oil galleries (Figure 11-11). These galleries consist of interconnecting passages that have been drilled completely through the engine block during manufacturing. The outside ends of the passages are then blocked off so the oil can be routed through these galleries to various parts of the engine internally, including the engine bearings. The crankshaft also contains oil passages (oilways) to route the oil from the main bearings to the connecting rod bearing surfaces (Figure 11-12).

ENGINE BEARINGS Since oil is delivered to the engine bearings by an oil gallery, an oil hole is machined in the bearing for alignment with the oil gallery in the engine block. In this manner, the bearing oil clearance space receives a constant supply of oil. In addition, many engine bearings are manufactured with an oil groove to help distribute the oil over the surface of the bearing. Oil grooving the main bearing also aids the flow of oil to the connecting rod bearings in the engine. Once the oil has been used by the bearing, it flows out of the oil clearance space and is replenished by a fresh supply of oil under pressure from the engine oil pump. This oil is then splashed or thrown off the bearing surface by the spinning motion of the rotating engine part. This splashed oil then lubricates many other parts of the engine, such as the cylinder walls and pistons.

CRANKCASE VENTILATION Crankcase ventilation is necessary because pressure can build in the crankcase due to combustion pressure. This pressure passes the piston rings. Piston rings do not provide a complete positive seal of the combustion area and some combustion gases reach the oil pan. These gases can contaminate the oil and apply unwanted pressure to gaskets and seals.

OIL PRESSURE INDICATOR This system can be in the form of a gauge, which indicates the engine oil pressure at all times, or it can be a warning light that will come on whenever the engine is running with insufficient oil pressure. The warning light is the most common oil pressure indicator.

OIL SEALS AND GASKETS These are used throughout the engine to prevent both external and internal oil loss. The most common materials used for sealing are synthetic rubber, soft plastics, fiber, and cork. In critical areas these materials might be bonded to a metal.

DIPSTICK The dipstick is used to measure the level of oil in the oil pan. The end of the stick is marked to indicate when the engine oil level is correct. It has a mark to indicate the need to add oil to the system.

OIL COOLERS Some engines, such as diesel engines or turbocharged engines, use an oil cooler. Most look like a small radiator mounted near the front of the engine. Heat is removed from the oil as air flows through the cooler core. Normal maximum engine oil temperature is considered to be 250 degrees Fahrenheit. Hot oil combined with oxygen breaks down (oxidizes) and forms carbon and varnish. The higher the temperature, the faster these deposits build. An oil cooler helps keep the oil at its normal operating temperature.

Oil Pumps

The oil pump is usually located in the oil pan. Its function is to supply lubricating oil to the various moving parts in the engine. To do this, two things are necessary: volume and pressure. The pump is designed to have more than adequate volume and pressure under all operating conditions. Both volume and pressure are directly related to the bleed-off through the clearances at the various parts of the engine. Engine bearing clearances have the greatest effect on oil flow.

Increased clearances reduce the resistance to oil flow and, consequently, increase the volume of oil circulating through the engine. At the same time, they cause pressure throughout the operating range to decrease. The excess flow capacity of the pump is a safety measure to ensure lubrication of vital parts as the

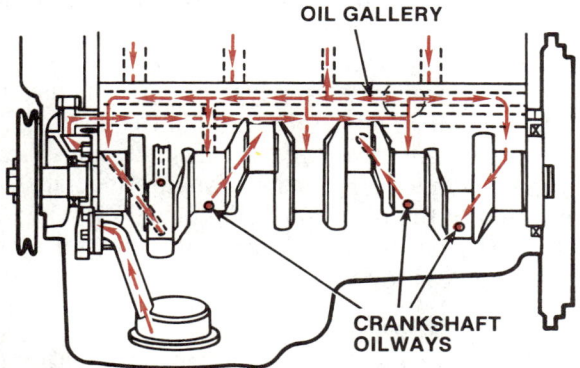

Figure 11-12 Oil passages in block and crankshaft.

engine wears. Too much oil pressure is seldom a problem. Too little oil pressure can cause oil starvation in those pressure lubricated parts more distant from the pump.

Engine oil pressure is also dependent upon oil viscosity, or the internal flow resistance of oil, and is temperature related. A high-viscosity oil has more flow resistance than a low-viscosity oil. As already mentioned, viscosity decreases as the temperature increases. For this reason, oil pressure is higher in a cold engine than it is when the engine reaches its normal operating temperature.

Types of Oil Pumps

The most commonly used oil pumps are the rotor and gear types. Both are positive displacement pumps. That is, a fixed volume of oil passes through the pump with each revolution of its drive shaft. This is because the gears or rotors form a near perfect mechanical seal as they mesh. They trap fixed volumes of oil inside the pump and push it out. Output volume is proportional to pump speed. As engine rpm increases, pump output also increases. Oil pumps usually rotate at camshaft speed, since in most engines the oil pump and distributor drive are connected.

A typical automotive rotor-type oil pump (Figure 11-13) consists of a four-lobe inner rotor and a five-lobe outer rotor, driven by the inner rotor. As the turning rotor lobes unmesh, oil is drawn in from the pan. Oil is trapped between the lobes, cover plate, and top of the pump cavity and moved to the outlet where the meshing lobes force the oil out. Output per revolution depends upon rotor diameter and thickness.

Gear pumps (Figure 11-14) consist of a drive gear connected to the input shaft and a driven gear. The drive gear turns the driven gear. Both gears trap oil between their teeth and the pump cavity wall, moving it from the inlet to the outlet. Output volume per

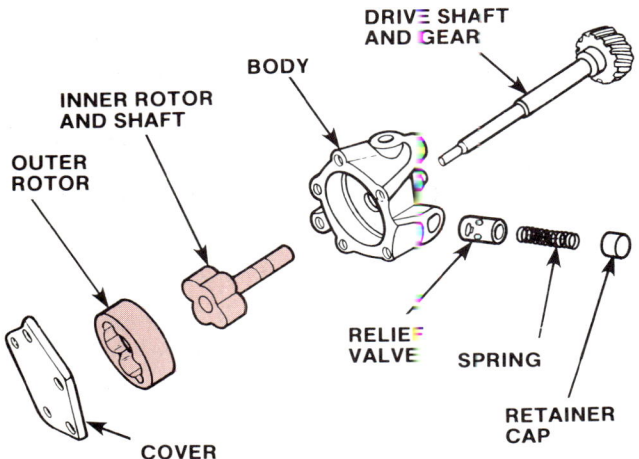

Figure 11-13 The rotor oil pump.

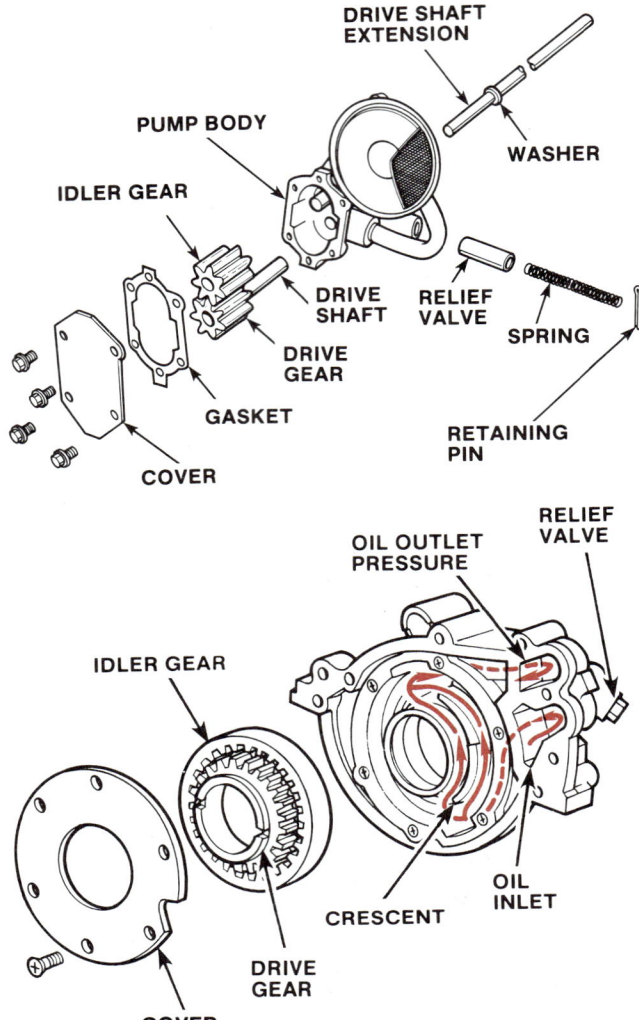

Figure 11-14 Two popular types of gear-driven oil pumps.

revolution depends upon gear length and tooth depth. Another style of gear-type oil pump uses an idler gear with internal teeth that spins around the drive gear. In this style of pump, often called a crescent or trochoidal type, the gears are eccentric. That is, as the larger gear turns, it walks around the smaller, moving the oil in the space between.

The rotor type moves a greater volume of oil than a gear type because there is more room inside the open lobe of the outer rotor than there is room between the teeth of the gears of a gear-type pump. This means a greater volume of oil is sent through the engine.

Oil pumps are driven off the camshaft, some directly, others indirectly, by means of an intermediate shaft connected to the distributor (Figure 11-15). On a few engines the oil pump housing is an integral part of the timing gear cover.

Pressure Regulation

Some means must also be provided to control the maximum oil pressure. The faster the pump turns, the

Lubricating and Cooling Systems

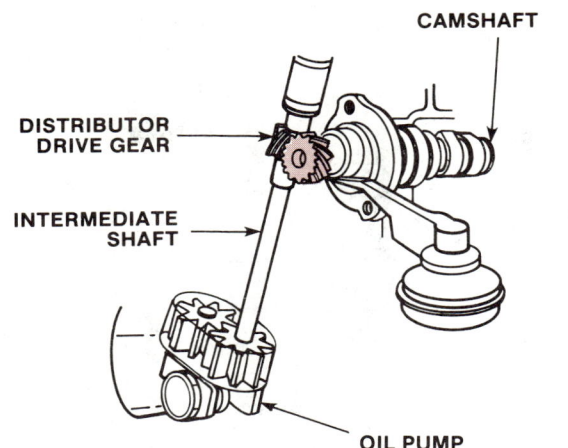

Figure 11-15 Gear on the end of this camshaft drives the distributor.

Oil Pressure Indicators

All automotive vehicles are equipped with either an oil pressure gauge or a low-pressure indicator light. An oil pressure indicator warns the driver of low oil pressure. The gauges are either mechanically or electrically operated.

In a mechanical system, oil travels up to the back of the gauge where a springy, flexible, hollow tube, called a Bourdon tube, uncoils as the pressure increases. A needle attached to the Bourdon tube moves over a scale to indicate the oil pressure.

Most pressure indicators found in vehicles today are electrically controlled (Figure 11-17). An oil pressure sensor is screwed into an oil gallery. As oil passes through an oil pressure sender (Figure 11-18), it moves a diaphragm, which is connected to a variable resistor. This resistor lowers the amount of current passing through the circuit. A gauge on the dashboard reacts to the amount of current and moves a needle over a scale to indicate the oil pressure.

greater the pressure becomes. Therefore, a pressure-regulating valve is installed. Different types of designs are used. However, their function remains the same. The valve is loaded with a closely calibrated spring that allows oil to bleed off at a given pressure. If the engine manufacturer decides that a 50 psi oil pressure is desirable in the engine, the pressure-regulating valve will not allow the pressure to go beyond 50 psi. When the pressure on the output side of the pump reaches this point, it presses against either a check valve, a ball, or a plunger, forcing it to unseat and allow oil to by-pass and return to either the inlet side of the pump or to the crankcase.

Figure 11-16A is a cutaway of an oil pump showing the pressure-regulating valve in the closed position. Figure 11-16B is the same pump with the valve in the open position. Note how the oil can flow through the end of the plunger to the by-pass and return to the inlet side of the pump. The plunger works within its bore with very little clearance. Therefore, it can be seen that foreign material entering this area can jam or hinder the operation of the pressure-regulating valve.

On most engines made in recent years there is an oil filtering system somewhere on the output side of the pump. In some cases the filter is attached right to the pump. In other cases, it is attached in various locations depending on the manufacturer.

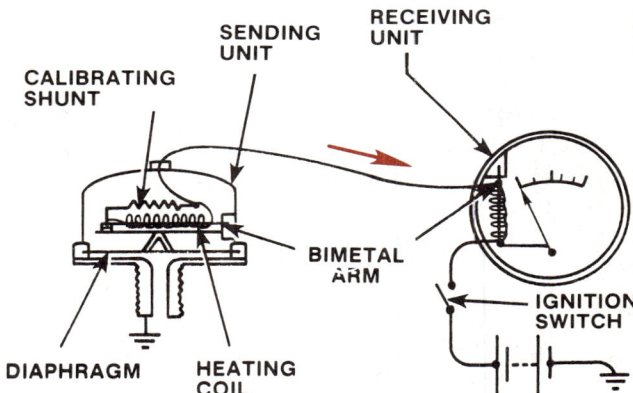

Figure 11-17 Schematic of an electric oil pressure indicator.

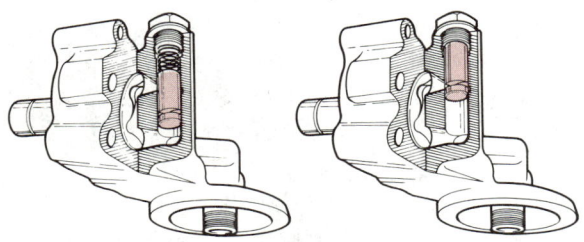

Figure 11-16 Cutaway of an oil pump showing the pressure-relief regulating valve in the (A) closed position and (B) in the open position. *Courtesy of TRW, Inc.*

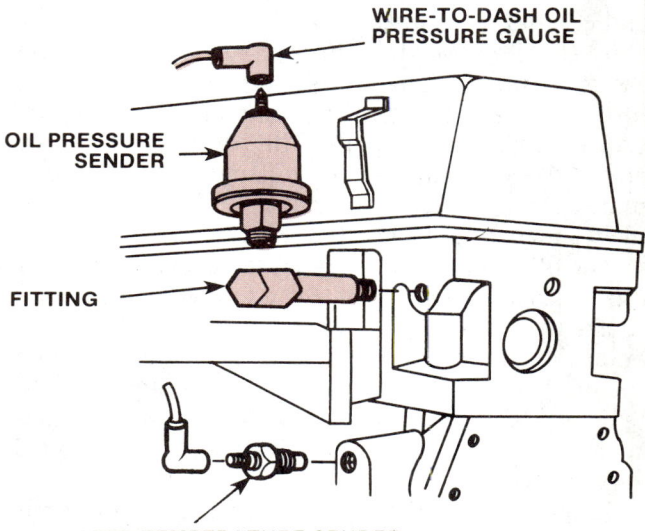

Figure 11-18 Oil pressure gauge sender.

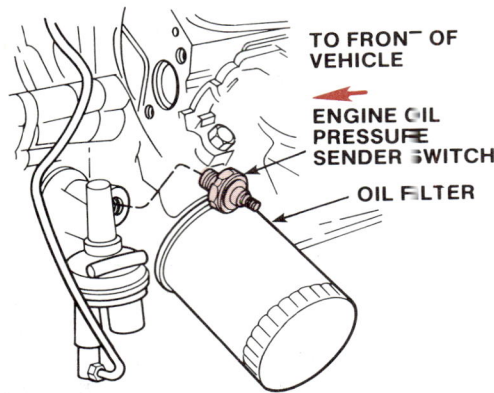

Figure 11-19 Oil pressure sender switch.

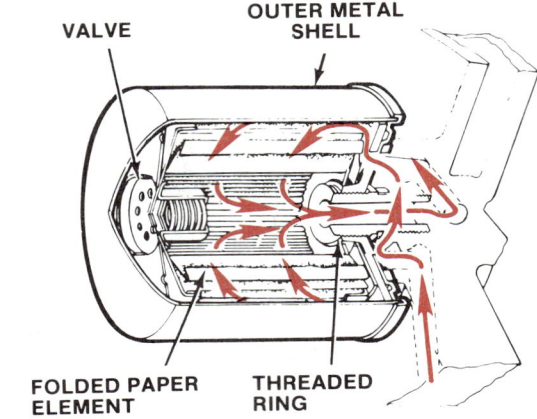

Figure 11-20 Oil flow through the filter.

In vehicles equipped with a warning light system, a diaphragm is connected to a sender switch or sensor. Under normal conditions, the sender switch is open. When oil pressure falls below the level necessary for safe operation, the reduction of pressure causes the diaphragm to move and close the sender switch (Figure 11-19), completing the electrical circuit. When this occurs, electricity flows and turns on the warning light on the dashboard.

Some late-model vehicles are equipped with an electronic oil level indicator. When the oil level in the oil pan drops below a predetermined level, a sensor allows for the oil level indicator circuit to be complete and the warning lamp lights.

Oil Filters

As stated previously, all oil leaving the oil pump is directed to the oil filter. The oil flows through the filter, then on to lubricate the engine. No unfiltered oil flows through the engine. This insures that very small particles of dirt and metal carried by the oil will not reach the close-fitting engine parts. The filter element and container are made as a unit, with a seal at the point the filter assembly contacts the block. The filter assembly threads directly onto the main oil gallery tube, eliminating external oil leaks and the possibility of pressurized oil leakage. The oil from the pump enters the filter can on the outside of the element, passes through the element of the filter and into the main gallery (Figure 11-20).

The filter unit itself is a disposable metal container filled with a special type of treated paper or other filter substance (cotton, felt, and the like) that catches and holds the oil's impurities. It is usually mounted on an adapter that bolts to the engine block (Figure 11-21). Since there are several types of filter designs, always consult the vehicle manual for the one recommended for the engine.

In recent years, the trend toward smaller filters has prompted the development of dual filtration systems (two separate filters in series) by some aftermarket companies. Dual filtration systems are common on heavy-duty trucks but are a relatively new development for automobiles.

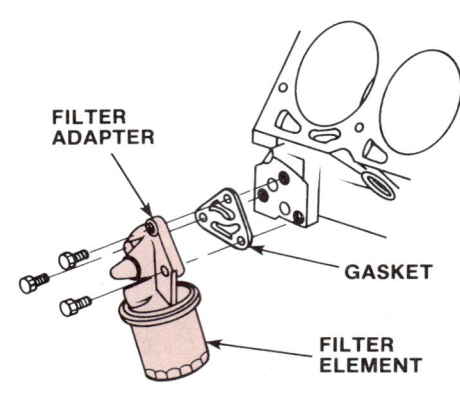

Figure 11-21 The oil filter is usually mounted on an adapter that bolts to the engine block.

Oil Filtration Systems

Two types of oil filtration systems are commonly used. The full flow type is used on most engines today (Figure 11-22). All of the oil going to the engine

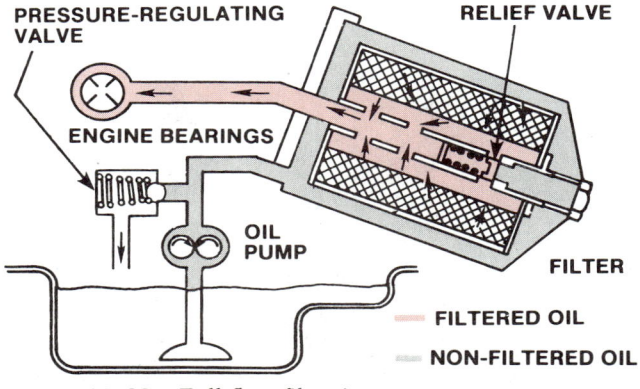

Figure 11-22 Full flow filtration system.

Lubricating and Cooling Systems 239

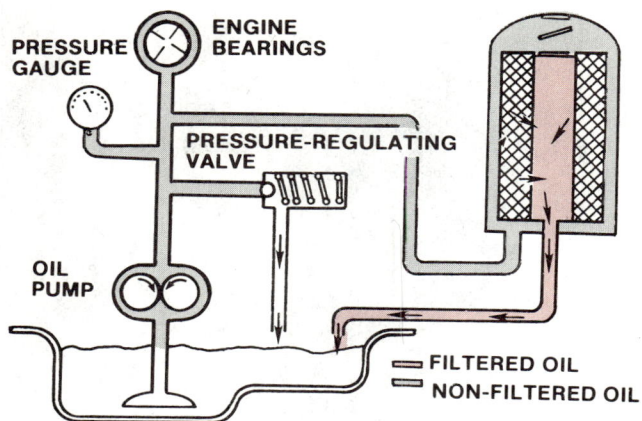

Figure 11-23 By-pass filtration system.

Figure 11-24 Defective sending unit.

Figure 11-25 Plugged oil pickup screen.

bearings goes through the filter first. However, should the filter become plugged, the relief valve contained in the filter will open and allow oil to by-pass and go directly to the bearings. This provides the bearings and the rest of the engine with necessary, though unfiltered, lubrication. The by-pass system is the least complex type of filtration. In Figure 11-23, note that on the output side of the pump the oil is fed directly to the engine bearings, the pressure-regulating valve, and the oil filter. The filtered oil is then returned to the oil pan. The oil is not filtered before it is sent to the bearings. Should the filter become plugged, no oil will flow through it. The oil that is not used in the engine bearings will be by-passed through the pressure-regulating valve.

SHOP TALK

In the by-pass system, approximately 90% of the oil is pumped directly to the engine bearings and other moving parts, then drains back to the oil pan. The remaining 10% of the oil is diverted into the filter housing. It is cleaned as it passes through the filter cartridge and out through the orifice to the sump.

☐ OIL PUMP INSPECTION AND SERVICE

Many technicians install a new or rebuilt oil pump (depending on the type) on each engine they rebuild. Integral pumps must be rebuilt. Bolt-on or nonintegral pumps can be rebuilt or replaced. If the old pump is to be reused, it should be carefully inspected for wear and thoroughly cleaned.

If the oil pressure tests low during diagnostic checks, any number of problems could be the cause. Some examples follow.

- Worn or damaged oil pump
- Defective sending unit (Figure 11-24)
- Weak or damaged pressure relief valve spring
- Plugged oil pick-up screen (Figure 11-25)
- Relief valve stuck in the open position
- Excessive oil dilution
- Buildup of sludge and dirt (Figure 11-26)
- Excess bearing clearances (crankshaft and camshaft)
- Air leak on the suction side of the oil pump (Figure 11-27). Since the air is compressible, it will cause the indicator to fluctuate and, in some cases, can cause the pressure-regulator valve to hammer back and forth. Under prolonged operation this can cause the valve to fail. It can also cause oil aeration, foaming, marginal lubrication, and failure of engine parts. Care should be exercised to make

Figure 11-26 Sludge and dirt buildup.

Figure 11-27 Air leak on the oil pump's suction side.

sure that all parts on the suction side of the pump fit tightly and that there is no place for air leakage. Air leakage often comes from cracked seams in the pickup tube.

Even though the oil pump is probably the best lubricated part of the engine, it is lubricated before the oil passes through the filter. As a result, it is subject to premature failure caused by foreign material entering the close tolerance area. Foreign particles can cause three kinds of trouble in a pump.

1. Fine abrasive particles gradually wear the surfaces, causing a reduction in efficiency.
2. Hard particles larger than the clearances can cause scoring and raising of metal as they pass through, finally resulting in seizure.
3. Large particles that cannot pass through will physically lock up the pump.

Of course, when the pump seizes or locks up, the intermediate or drive shaft is twisted off or sheared (Figure 11-28).

During normal operation the pick-up by-pass valve seats on the cross strap (Figure 11-29). When there is a demand for a large quantity of oil and the oil is cold and thick, the valve will unseat and allow the oil to by-pass the screen and go directly into the pump. Of course, if the pump screen becomes plugged, the by-pass valve will be open during the majority of the time the engine

Figure 11-28 Sheared drive shaft.

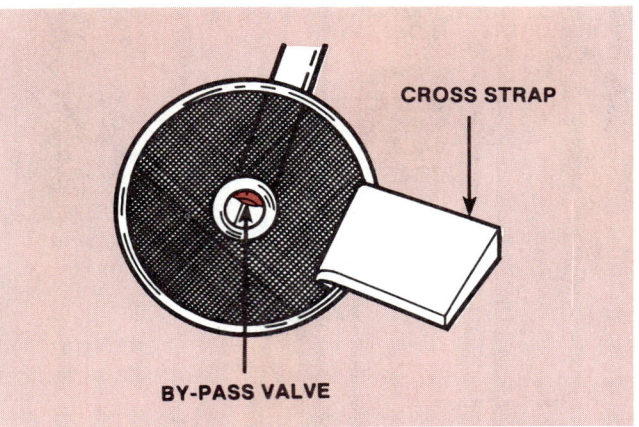

Figure 11-29 Pickup screen with cross strap bent out of position to show the by-pass valve.

is in operation. As the oil rushes through the by-pass valve, it can create a vortex in the oil pan. This could draw up debris that is either floating in the oil or lying in the bottom of the pan.

To thoroughly inspect the oil pump, it must be disassembled. Carefully remove the pressure relief valve and note the direction in which it is pointing so it can be reinstalled in its proper position (Figure 11-30). If the relief valve is installed backwards, the pump will not be able to build up pressure.

Before disassembling the pump, mark the gear teeth so they can be reassembled with the same tooth indexing (Figure 11-31). Some pumps have the gears or

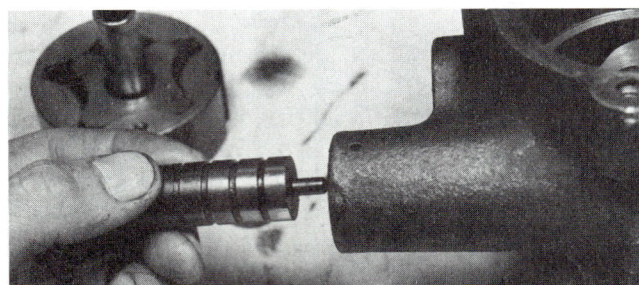

Figure 11-30 Remove pressure relief valve and note direction in which it is pointing.

Figure 11-31 Mark the gear teeth so they can be reassembled with the same indexing.

rotors marked when they are manufactured. Once all the serviceable parts have been removed, clean them and dry them off with compressed air.

> ### USING SERVICE MANUALS
> Correct oil pump disassembly instructions are given in the oil pump unit of the engines section of a service manual.

After the pump has been disassembled and cleaned, inspect the pump gears or rotors for chipping, galling, pitting, or signs of abnormal wear. Examine the housing bores for similar signs of wear. If any part of the housing is scored or noticeably worn, replace the pump as an entire assembly.

Check the mating surface of the pump cover for wear. If the cover mating surface is worn, scored, or grooved, replace the pump. Use a feeler gauge and straightedge to determine the cover flatness. The service manual gives the maximum and minimum acceptable feeler gauge thicknesses for the cover. If the cover is excessively worn, grooved, or scratched, it should be replaced.

Use an outside micrometer to measure the diameter and thickness of the outer rotor (Figure 11-32). The inner rotor's thickness should also be checked with an outside micrometer. If these dimensions are less than the specified amount given in the service manual, the rotors must be replaced.

With rotor-type pumps, assemble the rotors back into the pump body. Use a feeler gauge to check the clearance between the outer rotor and pump body (Figure 11-33). If the manufacturer's specifications are not available, replace the pump or rotors if the measured clearance is greater than 0.012 inch.

After checking the outer rotor-to-pump housing clearance, position the inner and outer rotor lobes so they face each other. Measure the clearance between

Figure 11-33 Checking clearance between the outer rotor and pump body.

Figure 11-34 Measuring clearance between the inner and outer rotor lobes.

them with a feeler gauge (Figure 11-34). A clearance of more than 0.010 inch is unacceptable.

On a gear-type pump, it is important to measure the clearance between the gear teeth and pump housing. Take several measurements at various locations around the housing (Figure 11-35) and compare the readings. If the clearance at any point exceeds 0.005 inch, replace the pump as an assembly.

On both gear or rotor oil pumps, place a straightedge across the pump housing and measure the clearance between the straightedge and gears (Figure

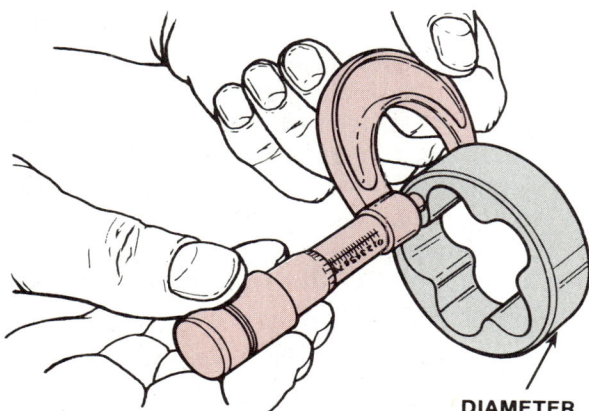

Figure 11-32 Measuring the outer rotor with an outside micrometer.

Figure 11-35 Taking several measurements around the housing.

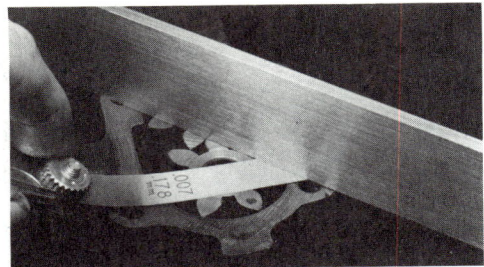

Figure 11-36 Measuring clearance between a straightedge and gears.

11-36). To insure an accurate reading, make sure the housing surface is clean and free of residual gasket material and that the gears are bottomed in the bore. The desired end play clearance should not exceed 0.003 inch.

If the pump uses a hexagonal drive shaft, inspect the pump drive and shaft to make sure the corners are not rounded. Check the drive shaft-to-housing bearing clearance by measuring the OD of the shaft and the ID of the housing bearing.

The gasket that is used to seal the end housing is also designed to provide the proper clearance between the gears and end plate. Consequently, do not substitute another gasket or make a gasket to replace the original one. If a precut gasket was not originally used, seal the end housing with a thin bead of anaerobic sealing material.

Inspect the relief valve spring for a collapsed or worn condition. Check the relief valve spring tension according to specifications for the specific engine. Also check the relief valve piston for scores and free operation in its bore.

The pick-up screen and pump drive (Figure 11-37) should be replaced when an engine is rebuilt. The screen and drive must be properly positioned. This is important to avoid oil pan interference and to ensure that the pick-up is always submerged in oil. To make the oil pump pick-up tube installation easier, there are several types of drivers available that are suitable for

Figure 11-37 Pickup screen and pump drive.

Figure 11-38 Manual installation of pump pick-up tube. *Courtesy of Goodson Shop Supplies*

use with air-powered equipment or with a light mallet (Figure 11-38).

On integral pumps, the timing case and gear thrust plate might also be worn. This will limit pump efficiency due to excess clearance. Replace them as necessary.

❏ INSTALLING THE OIL PUMP

Whether the pump is an integral or nonintegral type, it can be driven by a gear on the camshaft or by an extension shaft from the distributor. Care must be taken to make sure the gear or extension is engaged properly. Also, regardless of the type of pump, both should be primed before assembly. This can be done by submerging the pump in oil or by packing the pump with lightweight assembly lube, petroleum jelly, or oil. Rotate the pump shaft to distribute the oil within the pump body. In the case of a typical distributor-driven oil pump, the installation should be performed in the following manner.

1. Position the intermediate drive shaft into the distributor socket. With the shaft firmly seated, the stop on the shaft should touch the roof of the crankcase. Remove the shaft and position the stop as necessary.

2. With the stop properly positioned, insert the intermediate drive shaft into the oil pump. Install the pump and shaft as an assembly. Do not attempt to force the pump into position if it will not seat readily. The drive shaft hex might be misaligned with the distributor shaft. To align, rotate the intermediate drive shaft into a new position. Tighten the oil pump attaching screws to torque specifications.

3. Clean and install the oil pump inlet tube and screen assembly.

The installation of a typical camshaft-driven oil pump is as follows (Figure 11-39).

1. Apply suitable sealant to the pump and to the block interface.

Lubricating and Cooling Systems

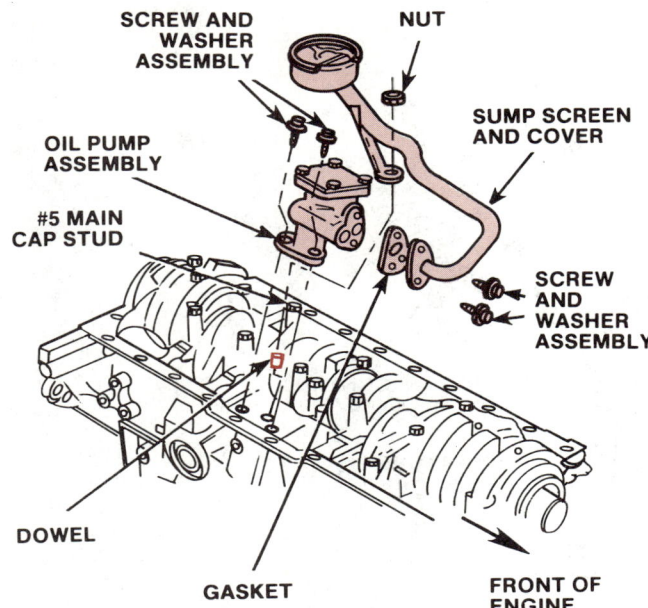

Figure 11-39 Camshaft-driven oil pump installed.

2. Install the pump to the full depth and rotate it back and forth slightly to ensure proper positioning and alignment through the full surface of the pump and the block machined interface surfaces.
3. Once installed, tighten the bolts or screws. The pump must be held in a fully seated position while installing bolts or screws (Figure 11-40).

SHOP TALK

The instructions here for the installation of either type of pump are general. Specific installation directions, as well as oil priming instructions (if necessary), can be found in the service manual.

Figure 11-40 Position and align the pump on the block. Tighten the mounting bolts uniformly. *Courtesy of TRW, Inc.*

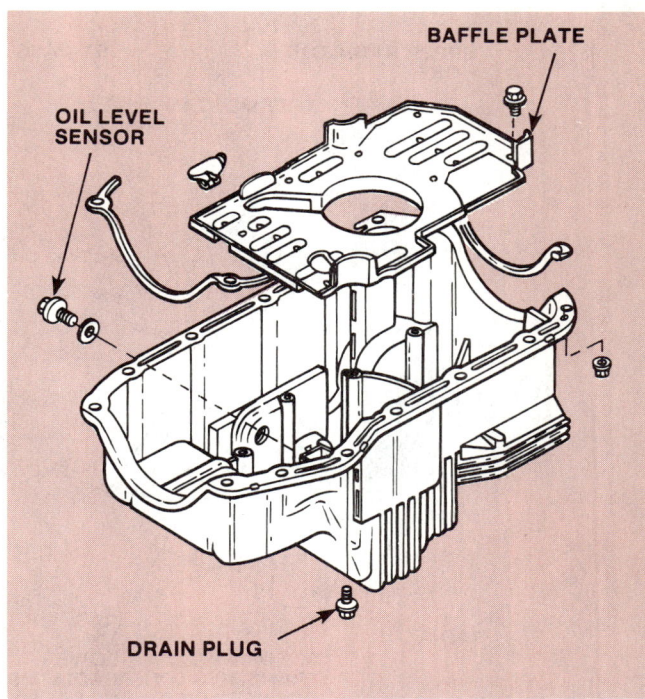

Figure 11-41 Oil pan assembly with baffle plate.

There are some components that can be considered part of the lubrication system that help to assist in increasing engine performance. In newer engines, the baffle assembly (Figure 11-41) is one of these components. It is used to restrict oil movement in the oil sump. Uncontrolled movement can allow the oil to mix with air.

◻ COOLING SYSTEMS

Today's internal combustion engines generate a tremendous amount of heat. This heat is created when the fuel and air mixture ignites inside the engine's combustion chamber. Metal temperatures around the combustion chamber can run as high as 1000 degrees Fahrenheit. To prevent the overheating of cylinder walls, pistons, valves, and other engine parts by these extreme temperatures, it is necessary to dispose of this heat.

Two basic types of cooling systems are utilized by automotive manufacturers: liquid-cooled and air-cooled systems.

Liquid-Cooled System

By far, the most popular and efficient method of engine cooling is the liquid-cooled system (Figure 11-42). In this system, heat is removed from around the combustion chambers by a heat-absorbing liquid (coolant) circulating inside the engine. This liquid is pumped through the engine and, after absorbing the heat of combustion, flows into the radiator where the heat is transferred to the atmosphere. The cooled liquid

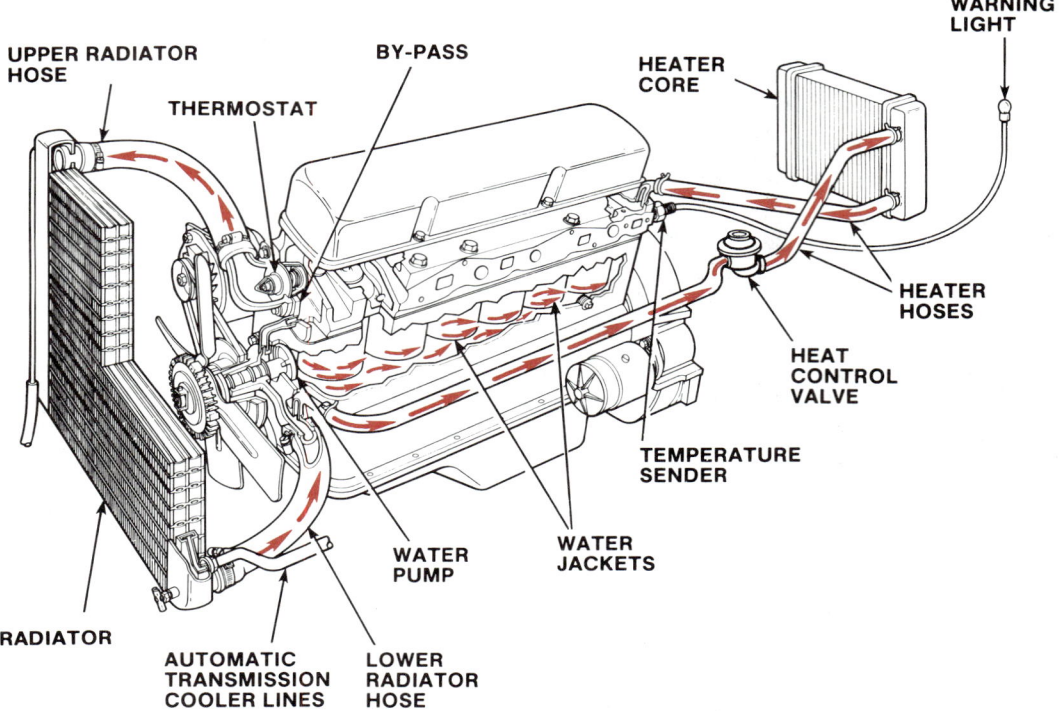

Figure 11-42 Major components of a typical liquid-cooling system. Arrows indicate the coolant flow.

is then returned to the engine to repeat the cycle. Excessive cooling capacity can decrease engine efficiency. Therefore, systems are designed to keep engine temperatures within a range where they provide peak performance.

The technical definition of a thermostat is a temperature-responsive coolant flow control valve. The engine thermostat controls the temperature and amount of coolant entering the radiator. While the engine is cold, the thermostat remains closed, allowing coolant to circulate only inside the engine, by-passing the radiator. This by-pass circulation of coolant allows the engine to warm up uniformly and eliminates hot spots. When the coolant reaches the opening temperature of the thermostat, the thermostat begins to open and to allow the flow of coolant to the radiator. The hotter the coolant gets, the more the thermostat opens, allowing more coolant to flow through the radiator. Once the coolant has passed through the radiator and has given up its excess heat, it reenters the water pump. Here it is again pushed through the engine passages surrounding the combustion chambers to pick up excess heat and start the cycle once again.

Coolant

The fluid used as coolant today is a mixture of water and ethylene glycol-based antifreeze/coolant. Water alone has a boiling point of 212 degrees Fahrenheit and a freezing point of 32 degrees Fahrenheit at sea level. A mixture of 67% antifreeze and water will raise the boiling point of the mixture to 235 degrees Fahrenheit and lower the freezing point to -92 degrees Fahren-

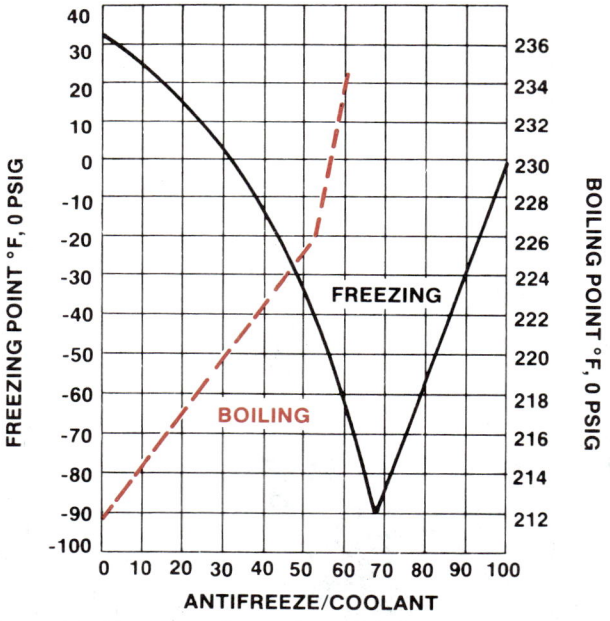

Figure 11-43 The relationship of the percentage of antifreeze in the coolant to the coolant's freezing and boiling points.

heit. As can be seen in Figure 11-43, antifreeze in excess of 67% will actually raise the freezing point of the mixture. This chart also indicates why antifreeze that is stored outside a service station might be very hard to pour at temperatures below 0 degrees Fahrenheit. The normal mixture used is a 50/50 solution of water and antifreeze/coolant.

Lubricating and Cooling Systems

CUSTOMER CARE

Customers ought to be told that although ethylene glycol-based antifreeze is advertised as permanent, this simply means it should not boil away like earlier nonpermanent (alcohol) types. By no means does permanent mean that it should not be replaced. The antifreeze/coolant contains various rust and foam inhibitors that wear out. A system should be drained, flushed, and filled every two years to keep it intact.

Most cooling systems today use an expansion or recovery tank. Cooling systems with expansion tanks are called closed-cooling systems. They are designed to hold any coolant that passes through the pressure cap when the engine is hot. As the engine warms up, the coolant expands. This eventually causes the pressure cap to release. The coolant passes to an expansion tank. When the engine is shut down, the coolant begins to shrink. Eventually, the vacuum spring inside the pressure cap opens and the coolant in the expansion tank is drawn back into the cooling system.

Recovery tanks have markings indicating where coolant levels should be when the car is running and when it is not (Figure 11-44). To check coolant levels on a car without a recovery tank, remove the radiator cap (when the engine is cold) and see if the coolant is up to where it should be. If there are no markings, coolant should be covering the radiator core. If the coolant level is low after repeated filling, there is probably a leak in the cooling system.

WARNING: When working on the cooling system, remember that at operating temperature the coolant is extremely hot. Touching the coolant or spilling the coolant can cause serious body burns. Never remove the radiator cap when the engine is hot.

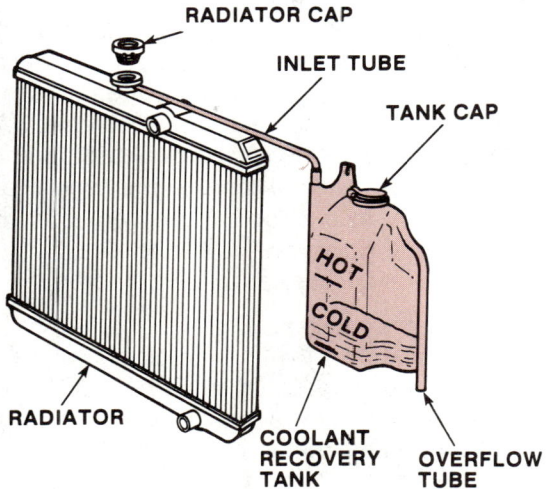

Figure 11-44 Coolant recovery system with coolant levels marked on recovery tank.

Water Pump

The heart of the cooling system is the water pump. Its job is to move the coolant efficiently through the system. Most automotive applications drive the pump via the V-belt drive. Some vehicles may drive the pump off of the camshaft or the gear train. No matter how these units are driven, they all basically work the same way. The pumps are of the centrifugal design (Figure 11-45), with a rotating paddle wheel type impeller to move the coolant. The shaft is mounted in the water pump housing and rotates on bearings. The pump contains a seal to keep the coolant from passing through it. At the drive end, the exposed end, a pulley is mounted to accept the belt. The pulley is driven by the crankshaft. The pump housing usually includes the mounting point for the lower radiator hose.

When the engine is started, the pump impeller pushes the water from its pumping cavity into the engine block. When the engine is cold, the thermostat is closed. This stops the coolant from reaching the top of the radiator. In order for the water pump to circulate the coolant through the engine during warm-up, a by-pass passage is added below the thermostat, which leads back to the water pump. This passage must be kept free to eliminate hot spots in the engine during warm-up. It also allows hot coolant to pass through the valve, which will open the thermostat when it reaches the proper temperature.

Radiator

The radiator is basically a heat exchanger, transferring heat from the engine to the air passing through it. The radiator itself is a series of tubes and fins that expose the heat from the coolant to as much surface

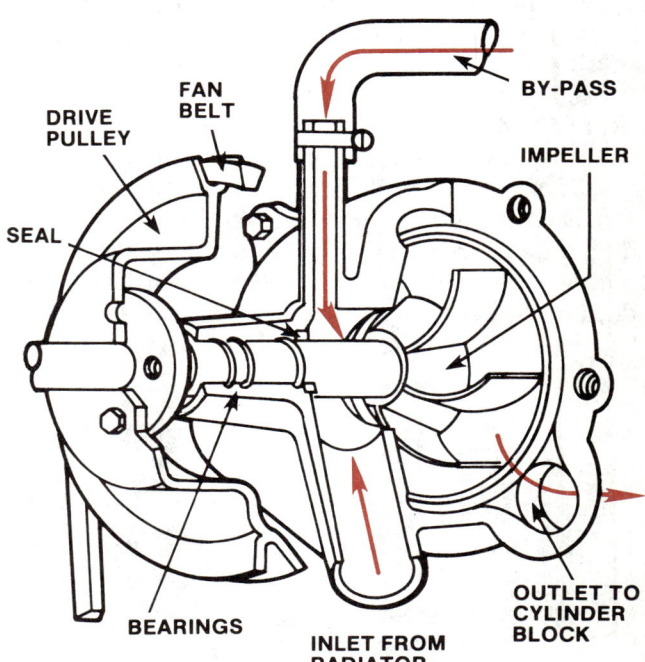

Figure 11-45 Impeller-type water pump.

area as possible, thus maximizing the potential of the heat being transferred to the passing air. The inlet tank on the radiator contains a baffle to distribute and de-aerate the coolant, thus increasing the efficiency of the unit.

Factors influencing the efficiency of the radiator are the basic design of the radiator, the area and thickness of the radiator core exposed to the cooling air, the amount of coolant going through the radiator, and the temperature of the cooling air.

The major factor that will increase a radiator's efficiency is increasing the difference between the temperature of the coolant and the outside air flowing through it. This can be done only by raising the temperature of the coolant. Doing this permits the use of a smaller radiator or the use of the same size radiator to cool a larger engine. This is the primary reason manufacturers have been specifying higher start-to-open temperatures for thermostats and higher pressure ratings for radiator pressure caps.

The radiator is usually based on one of these two designs: cross flow or down flow. In a cross flow radiator (Figure 11-46A), coolant enters on one side, travels through tubes, and collects on the opposite side. In a down flow radiator (Figure 11-46B), coolant enters the top of the radiator and is drawn downward by gravity. Cross flow radiators are seen most often on large-engine or late-model cars because all the coolant flows through the fan air stream, which provides maximum cooling.

There are two types of radiator core construction: honeycomb or cellular type (Figure 11-47A) and tube and fin (Figure 11-47B). There also are two radiator core construction materials used—the conventional copper/brass, soft solder coolers (Figure 11-48A) and the vacuum-brazed, aluminum cores cinched to nylon tanks (Figure 11-48B).

The aluminum type is thin, lightweight, and cost effective from the manufacturer's standpoint. (The initial price of aluminum is below that of copper.) For these reasons, aluminum core radiators are being used more and more on newer model vehicles.

Most radiators feature petcocks or plugs that allow a technician to drain coolant from the system. Coolant is added to the system at the radiator cap or the recovery tank depending on the type of system being used.

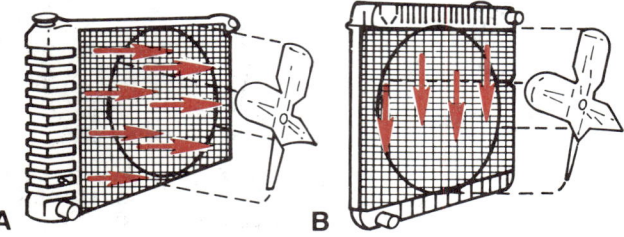

Figure 11-46 Two radiator designs: (A) cross flow and (B) down flow.

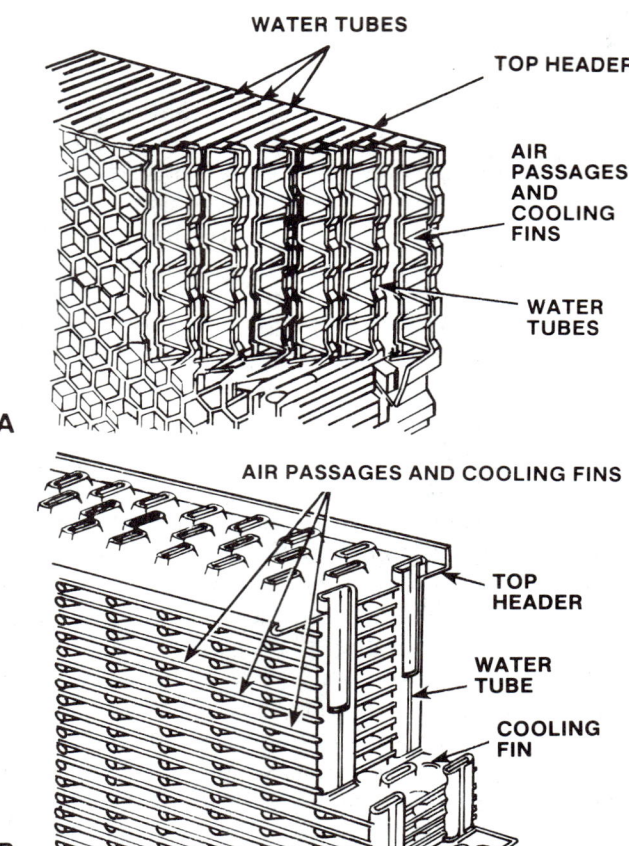

Figure 11-47 Two types of radiator core construction: (A) honeycomb or cellular and (B) tube and fin. *Courtesy of Ford Motor Co.*

RADIATOR PRESSURE CAPS At one time, the radiator cap was simply designed to keep the coolant (water and alcohol combination in the early days of motoring) from splashing out of the radiator. Today, it still serves that purpose, but it also does much more. Today radiator caps are equipped with pressure springs and atmospheric vents. The cap allows for an increase of pressure in the radiator, which raises the boiling point of the coolant. For every pound of pressure put on the coolant, the boiling point is raised about 3-1/4 degrees Fahrenheit. Today's caps normally are designed to hold between 14 and 17 pounds per square inch (psi). When pressures exceed this, the seal between the cap and the radiator filler neck opens and allows the excessive pressure to vent into a coolant recovery tank or out onto the ground via an overflow tube.

The three basic pressure cap designs are:

1. Constant pressure type (Figure 11-49A). The lower seal or pressure valve is held closed by a spring until the coolant gets hot enough to build enough pressure to open it within the preset pressure range. Pressure builds gradually as the coolant becomes hot.

2. Pressure vent type (Figure 11-49B). The lower seal or pressure valve is held closed as with the con-

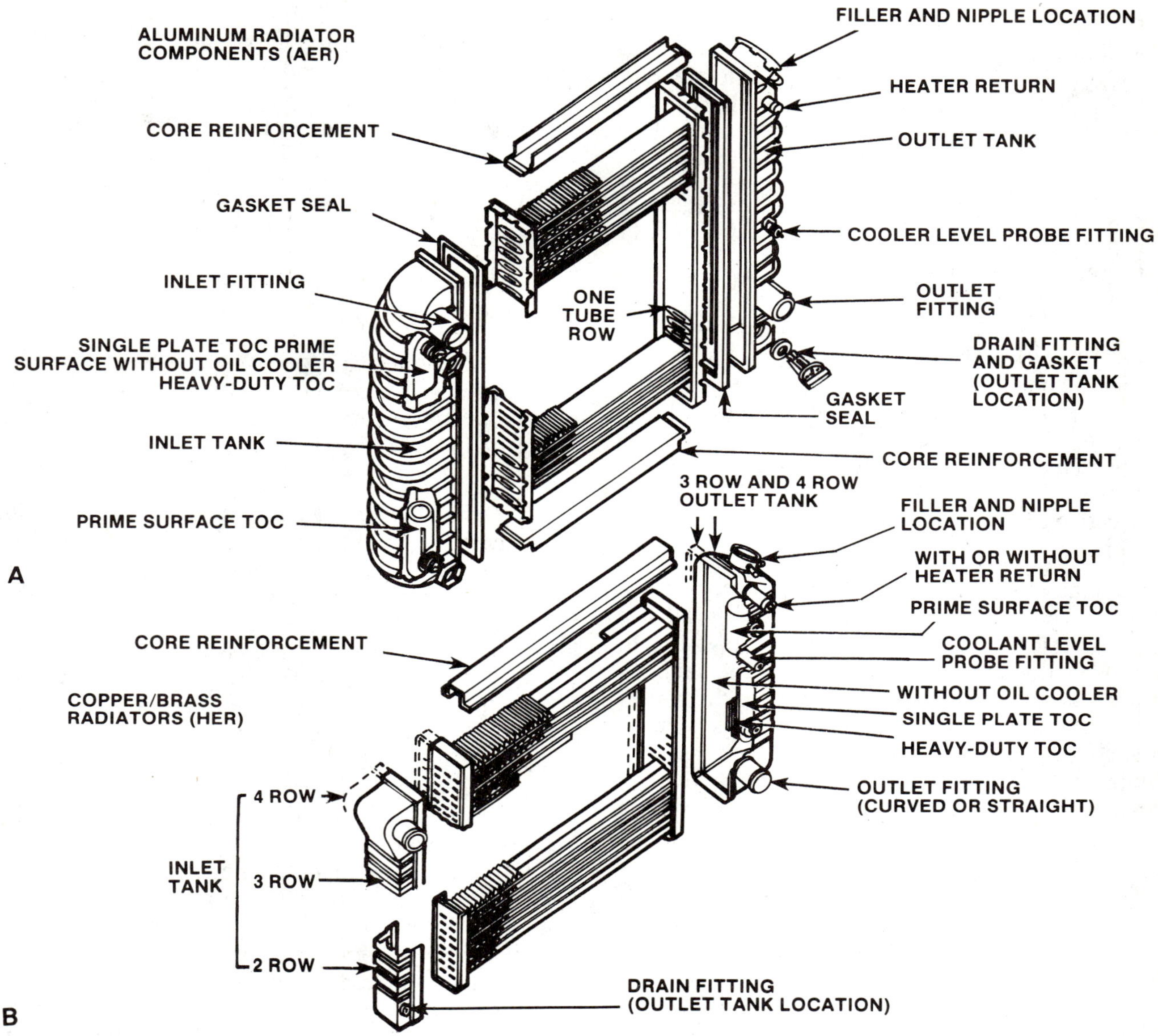

Lubricating and Cooling Systems 247

Figure 11-48 Types of radiator core materials: (A) aluminum and (B) copper/brass. *Courtesy of Harrison Radiator, Division of General Motors Corp.*

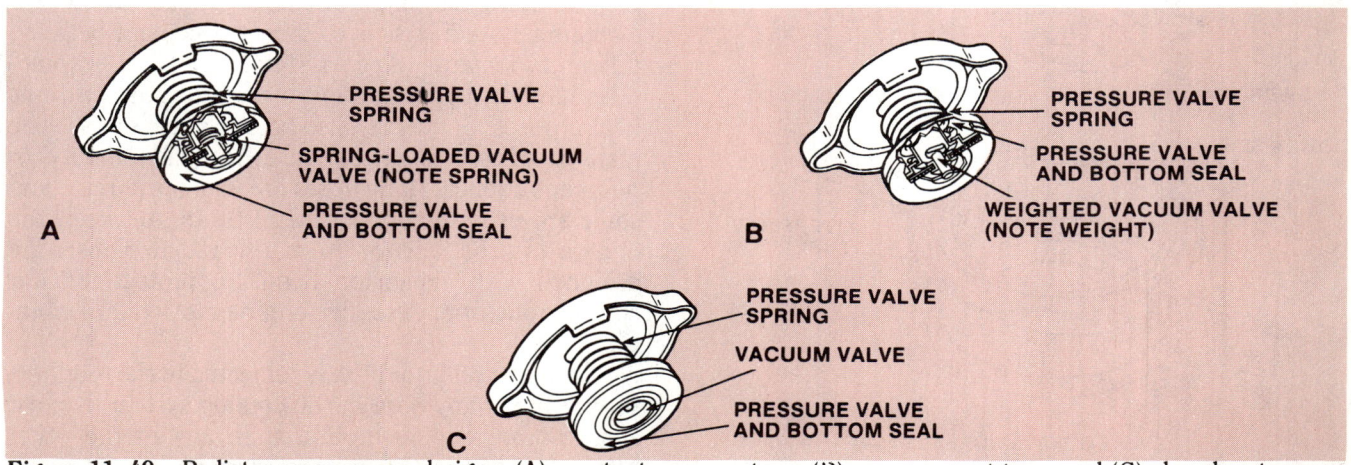

Figure 11-49 Radiator pressure cap designs: (A) constant pressure type; (B) pressure vent type; and (C) closed system type.

stant pressure type. The vacuum release valve installed in the pressure valve is held open by a weight. The cap is open to atmospheric pressure through the vacuum release valve until the coolant gets hot enough to cause a surge of coolant or steam to hit it, causing it to close to atmospheric pressure. From this point, the pressure vent cap works in the same way as the constant pressure cap.

3. Closed system type (Figure 11-49C). These caps operate in the same manner as the constant pressure caps except that they are designed for a closed system. The closed design keeps the cooling system full at all times without losing coolant due to expansion or overflow. On closed systems, coolant is added to the reservoir instead of to the radiator. The radiator caps are not designed to be removed. Late-model cars use this type of radiator cap, and accessory kits are available to install them in other cars.

All radiator caps are designed to meet SAE standards for safety. This standard specifies that there shall be a detent or safety stop position allowing pressure to escape from the system without allowing the hot coolant to blow out of the radiator's neck onto the person opening the cap. Only after all pressure has been relieved should the cap be removed from the filler neck (Figure 11-50). A lever or push button may be employed in the cap to relieve the pressure prior to removal.

Cap specifications require that the cap must not leak below the low limit of the pressure range and must open above the high limit of the range. (Radiator cap pressures: a 4-pound cap, 3.5 pounds; 7-pound cap, 6.8 pounds; 13- or 14-pound cap, 12.16 pounds; and a 15- or 16-pound cap, 14.18 pounds.) Pressure caps should always be tested for the proper pressure release level and checked for gasket cracking, brittleness, or deterioration each time the antifreeze is changed or when any routine cooling system maintenance is performed.

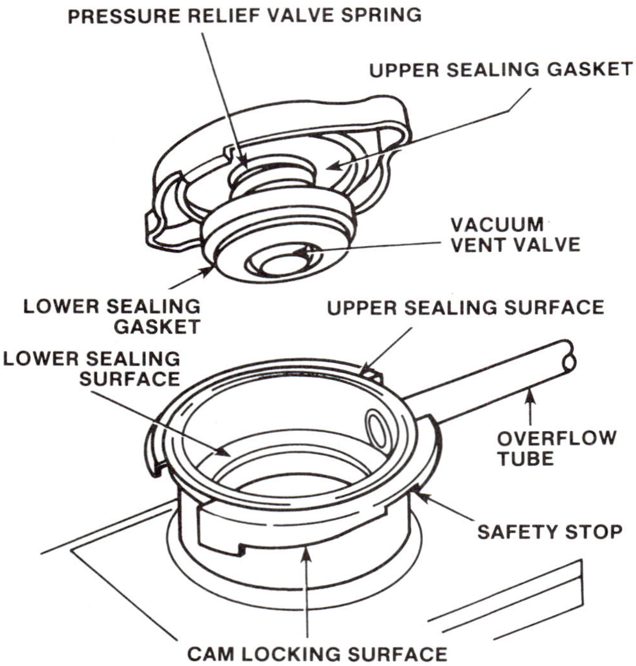

> **SHOP TALK**
>
> Always refer to application charts or a service manual when replacing a pressure cap to make sure that a cap in the same pressure range as the original equipment cap is used.

WATER OUTLET The water outlet is the connection between the engine and the upper radiator hose through which hot coolant from the engine is pumped back into the radiator. The water outlet has been called a gooseneck, elbow, inlet, outlet, or thermostat housing. Generally, it covers and seals the thermostat and, in some cases, includes the thermostat by-pass.

Most water outlets are made of cast iron, cast aluminum, or stamped steel. Most domestic car manufacturers have specified cast iron. Most import cars feature a cast aluminum outlet. The stamped steel outlet has become popular on newer cars because of weight reduction.

Internal corrosion, because of the lack of rust inhibitors in antifreeze, contributes to the passive failure of water outlets. Cast iron water outlets are more resistant to this type of corrosion than stamped steel or cast aluminum outlets. A more common factor contributing to the failure of the water outlet is the uneven torquing down of the water outlet mounting bolts, which can cause a mounting ear to break off. When this happens, the outlet will not seal and must be replaced.

HOSES As already mentioned, the primary function of a cooling system hose is to carry the coolant between different elements of the system. Nearly all automobiles have an upper and lower radiator hose and two heater hoses. Some may also have a by-pass hose. The majority of cooling system hoses are made of butyl or neoprene rubber. Many hoses are wire reinforced, and some are used to connect metal tubing between the engine and the radiator. Normally, radiator hoses are designed with expansion bends to protect radiator connections from excessive engine motion and vibration.

The upper radiator hose is subjected to the roughest service life of any hose in the cooling system. It must absorb more engine motion than any of the other hoses. It is exposed to the coolant at its hottest stage, plus it is insulated by the hood during hot soak periods.

Figure 11-50 Parts of a radiator pressure cap assembly. *Courtesy of Chrysler Corp.*

These conditions make the upper hose the most probable to fail.

Normally, hoses begin to deteriorate on the inside. Pieces of deteriorated hose will circulate through the system until they find a place to rest. This place is usually the radiator core, causing clogging. Any external bulging or cracking of hoses is a definite sign of failure. Hoses will become either very soft and spongy or very hard and brittle when their life is near the end. When one hose fails, all of the others should be carefully inspected.

Nearly all original equipment radiator hose is of the molded, curved design. Aftermarket products may be of this type or of a wire inserted flex type. This flex-type hose allows greater vehicle coverage per part number, but may not be designed for some cars that require radical bends and shapes. Lower radiator hoses are normally wire reinforced to prevent collapse due to the suction of the water pump.

All cooling system hoses are basically installed the same way. The hose is clamped onto inlet-outlet nipples on the radiator, water pump, and heater. Figure 11-51 illustrates the four most common types of hose clamps.

Most new cars today come from the factory equipped with clamps that are simply spring steel wires that exert the pressure necessary to seal a connection after being stretched over the joint.

Twin wire clamps use a bolt to tighten a metal band or wire. The bolt sometimes tends to be unnecessarily strong and can be difficult to remove. Perhaps the best clamp, overall, is the worm-drive clamp, which uses a simple screwdriver for tightening and loosening. The notched band will not cut the hose as a wire can. A worm-drive also will not distort the pressure applied to the hose end when it is tightened.

Thermostat

The automotive thermostat functions somewhat like a typical home thermostat. It attempts to control the engine's operating temperature by routing the coolant either to the radiator or through the by-pass or sometimes by a combination of both.

Thermostats have developed right along with the automobile engine. As greater horsepower was developed, more heat had to be removed from the engine. This meant increased water pump speeds and increased water pressure. The modern thermostat is composed of a specially formulated wax and powdered metal pellet, which is tightly contained in a heat-conducting copper cup equipped with a piston inside a rubber boot. Heat causes the wax pellet to expand, forcing the piston outward, which opens the valve of the thermostat. The pellet senses temperature changes and opens and closes the valve to control coolant temperature and flow. Today's thermostats are also designed to slow down coolant flow when they are open. This helps to prevent overheating which can result from the coolant moving too quickly, through the engine, to absorb enough heat.

While the thermostat might be situated in several locations, the most common spot is at the front of the engine on top of the engine block (Figure 11-52). The heat element fits into a recess in the block where it will be exposed to hot coolant. The top of the thermostat is then covered by the water outlet housing, which holds it in place and provides a connection to the upper radiator hose.

There are two basic types of thermostats on the market today. Both function in the same manner, but each has distinct differences.

The reverse poppet thermostat (Figure 11-53A) opens against the flow of the coolant from the water pump. The coolant, under water pump pressure, is used to help the reverse poppet thermostat stay closed when cool to prevent leakage. The valve is self-aligning and also self-cleaning.

The balanced sleeve thermostat (Figure 11-53B) eliminates pressure shocks by allowing pressurized coolant to circulate around all of its working parts. By reducing pressure shocks, it provides coolant temperature stability during the most difficult operating conditions.

The thermostat permits fast warm-up of the engine after it has been started (Figure 11-54A). Slow warm-up causes moisture condensation in the combustion

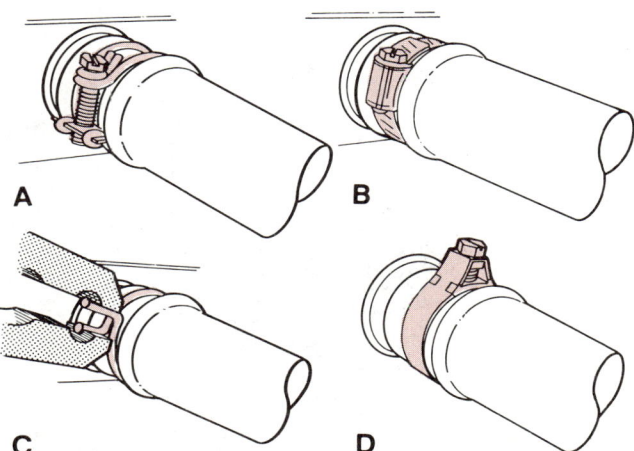

Figure 11-51 Common types of hose clamps: (A) twin wire; (B) worm-drive; (C) spring; and (D) screw tower.

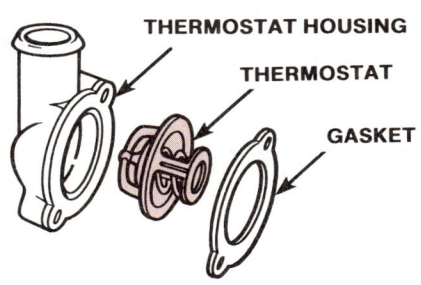

Figure 11-52 Parts of a thermostat.

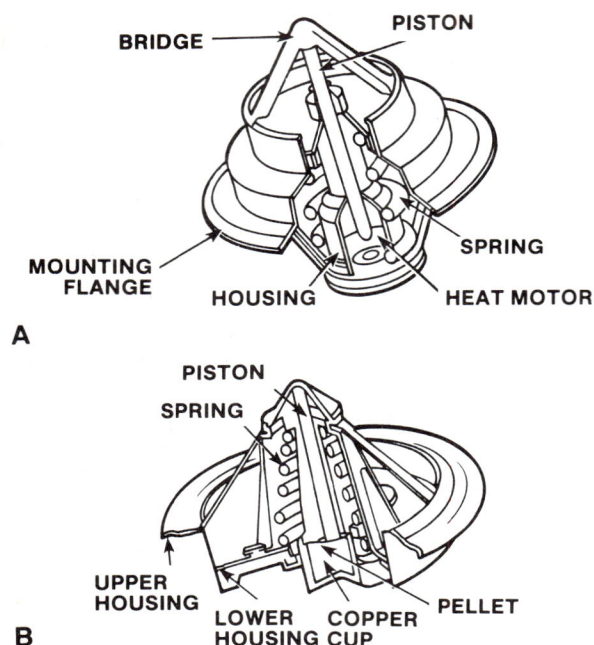

Figure 11-53 Types of thermostats: (A) reverse poppet; (B) balanced sleeve.

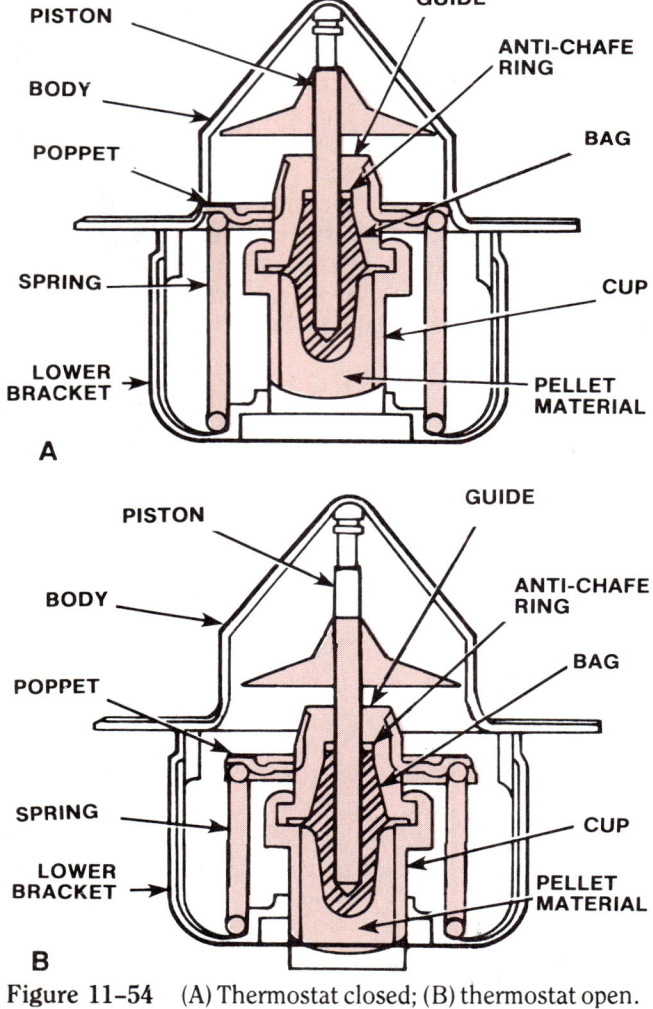

Figure 11-54 (A) Thermostat closed; (B) thermostat open.

chambers, which finds its way into the crankcase and causes sludge formation. The thermostat keeps the coolant above a designated minimum temperature required for efficient engine performance. Most engines are equipped with a coolant by-pass, either outside the engine block or built into the casting. Some thermostat models are equipped with a by-pass valve that shuts off the engine by-pass after warm-up, forcing all coolant to flow to the radiator.

Thermostats must start to open at a specified temperature (Figure 11-54B)—normally 3 degrees Fahrenheit above or below its temperature rating. It must be fully opened at about 20 degrees Fahrenheit above the "start to open" temperature. They must also permit the passage of a specified amount of coolant when fully open and leak no more than a specified amount when fully closed.

When replacing the thermostat, be sure to use the same temperature thermostat as was used for original equipment. The thermostat should always be checked when performing routine cooling system maintenance.

Some cooling systems employ a two-stage thermostat. This thermostat is designed to control engine temperature more precisely by reducing peak temperatures during the critical warm-up periods. This type of thermostat contains two valves: a main valve and subvalve (Figure 11-55). The subvalve begins to open at above 175 degrees Fahrenheit and permits a limited amount of cooling during warm-up. This prevents peak temperature hot spots. The main valve begins to open at 192 or 195 degrees Fahrenheit. Both valves remain open up to 212 degrees Fahrenheit and both close at about 175 degrees Fahrenheit.

Belt Drives

Belt drives (Figure 11-56) have been used for more than 60 years. V-belts and serpentine belts (multiple-ribbed belts) are used to drive water pumps, power steering pumps, air-conditioning compressors, alternators, and emission control pumps (Figure 11-57). The flexibility of belt drives has allowed many inexpensive improvements in the modern automobile.

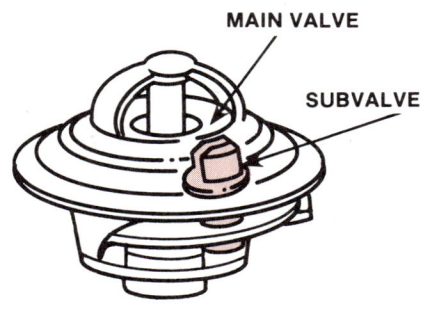

Figure 11-55 Two-stage thermostat. *Courtesy of Ford Motor Co.*

Lubricating and Cooling Systems   251

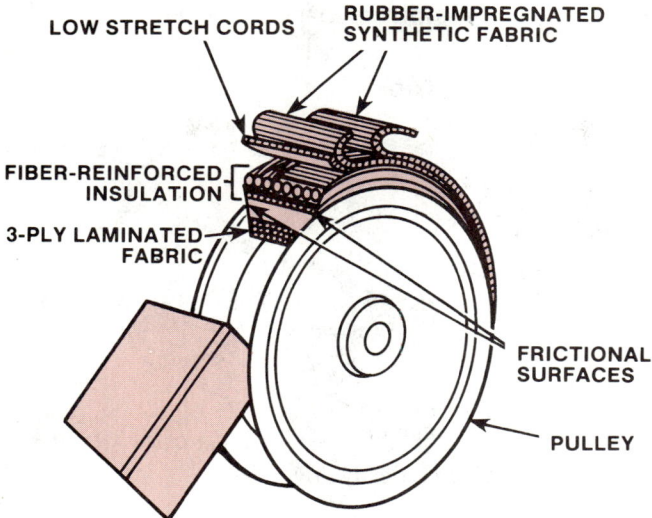

Figure 11-56 V-belt. *Courtesy of Chrysler Corp.*

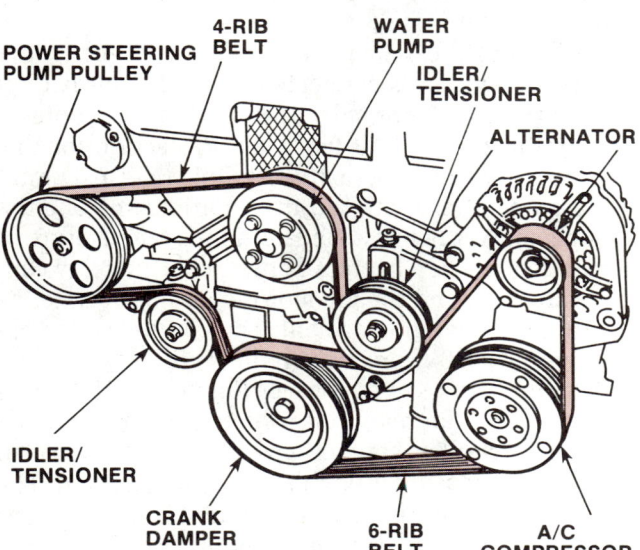

Figure 11-57 Single belts can drive many components.

The belt system is popular for a number of reasons. It is very inexpensive and quiet when compared to chains and gears. It is also very easy to repair. Because the belts are flexible, they will absorb some shock loads and cushion shaft bearings from excessive loads.

The biggest problem with belt drives is that they are neglected. Typically, no one makes an effort to check these vital links until they begin to make noise or break. Additional requirements have been put on these belts and have tended to cause a few more problems with them. As engines began developing more horsepower, heavy-duty fans and water pumps were necessary. This placed more tension on the drive belt. Greater output requirements from charging systems meant more load on the belts. The advent of air-conditioning units added the greatest impact load to the belt because of the magnetic clutch operation that engages

the unit at any engine speed. But even with all these changes, the belt continues to be the primary method for power take-offs on the automotive engine.

Heat is the number one enemy of belts. Belts tend to overcure due to excessive heat. This causes the rubber to harden and crack. Excessive heat usually comes from slippage. Slippage can normally be attributed to lack of proper belt tension or oily conditions. When slippage occurs heat not only overcures the belt, it also travels through the drive pulley and down the shaft to the support bearing. On some occasions these bearings might be damaged if the slippage is allowed to continue. As a V-belt wears, it begins to ride deeper in the pulley groove. This reduces its tension and promotes slippage. As this is a normal occurrence, periodic adjustment of belt tensions should be expected.

Serpentine belts are kept under constant tension by an idler pulley or tensioner. This pulley is designed to compensate for belt stretch and to keep a proper amount of tension on the belt.

Many drive units consist of two matched belts that run over parallel pulleys. If one pulley or belt should wear excessively, although the belts may be the same length, problems can arise because of the wear. The belts will run at slightly different speeds, thus one will be constantly slipping. Matched belts should always be replaced in pairs so they wear together, thus maintaining the same length to prevent slippage and problems.

USING SERVICE MANUALS

Proper belt tightening procedures and specifications are given in the specification section of most service manuals.

Fans and Fan Clutches

As mentioned earlier, the efficiency of the cooling system is based on the amount of heat that can be removed from the system and transferred to the air. Without air, the system cannot be very efficient. At highway speeds, the ram air through the radiator should be sufficient to maintain proper cooling. At low speeds and idle, the system needs additional air. This air is delivered by a fan.

The design of fans varies with the air requirements of the engine's cooling system. Diameter, pitch, and the number of blades can be varied to attain the needed flow. Fans are usually shrouded to maintain efficiency by causing all of the flow to pass through the radiator. This shrouding also allows the fan to be placed relatively far from the radiator, thus allowing the engine to be set back in the car while the radiator is left near the front of the vehicle.

Five- or six-blade fans are usually found on air-conditioned cars. A four-blade fan is standard on non-air-conditioned cars. Fans may be made of steel, nylon,

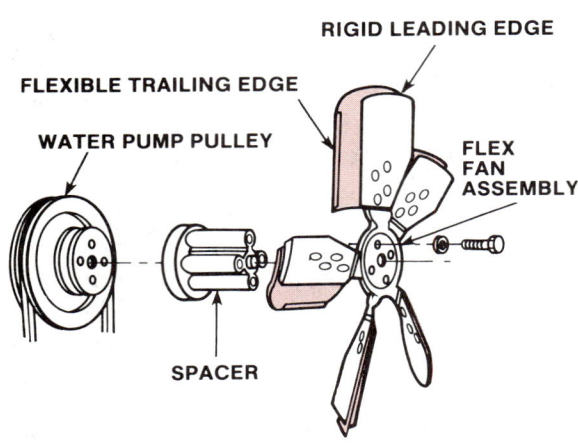

Figure 11-58 Flexible fan features.

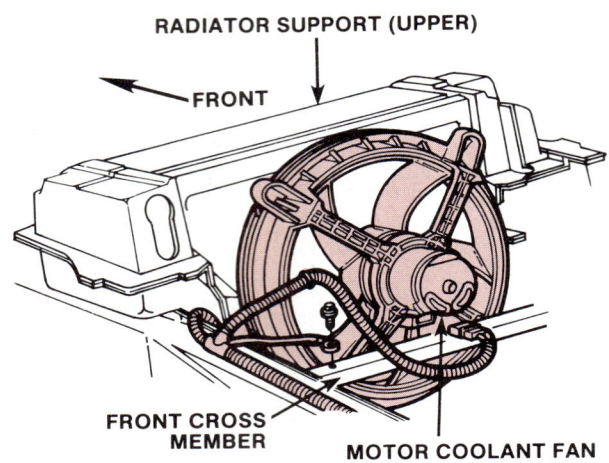

Figure 11-60 Electrically driven fan.

or fiberglass, and are precisely balanced to prevent water pump bearing and seal damage. Since fan air is usually only necessary at idle and low speed operation, various design concepts are used to limit the fan's operation at higher speeds. Horsepower is required to turn the fan. Therefore, the fan has an effect on the available horsepower to the drive wheels, as well as affecting the fuel economy of the vehicle. Fans are also very noisy at high speeds, adding to driver fatigue and total vehicle noise.

In an effort to overcome these problems, some vehicle manufacturers use flexible blades or flex-blades (Figure 11-58) that bend or change pitch based on engine speed. That is, at slower speeds the blade pitch is at the maximum (Figure 11-59A). As engine speed increases (Figure 11-59B), the blade pitch decreases as does the horsepower losses and noise levels.

In most late-model applications, to save power and reduce the noise level, the conventional belt-driven, water-pump-mounted engine coolant fan has been replaced with an electrically driven fan (Figure 11-60). This fan and motor are mounted to the radiator shroud and are not connected mechanically or physically to the engine. The 12-volt, motor-driven fan is electrically controlled by either, or both, of two methods: an engine coolant temperature switch or sensor and the air-conditioner switch.

Following the schematic in (Figure 11-61A), the cooling fan motor is connected to the 12-volt battery supply through a normally open (NO) set of contacts (points) in the cooling fan relay. Protection for this circuit is provided by a fusible link (F/L). During normal operation, with the air conditioner off and the engine coolant below a predetermined temperature of approximately 215 degrees Fahrenheit, the relay contacts are open and the fan motor does not operate.

Should the engine coolant temperature exceed approximately 230 degrees Fahrenheit, the engine coolant temperature switch closes (Figure 11-61B). This energizes the fan relay coil, which in turn closes the relay contacts. The contacts provide 12 volts to the fan motor if the ignition switch is in the on position. The 12-volt supply for the relay coil circuit is independent of the 12-volt supply for the fan motor circuit. The coil circuit is from the on terminal of the ignition switch, through a fuse in the fuse panel, and to ground through the relay coil and temperature sensor.

Should the air-conditioner select switch be turned to any cool position, regardless of engine temperature, a circuit is completed through the relay coil to ground through the select switch. This action closes the relay contacts to provide 12 volts to the fan motor. The fan then operates as long as the air-conditioner and ignition switches are on.

There are many variations of electric cooling fan operation. Some provide a cool-down period whereby the fan continues to operate after the engine has been stopped and the ignition switch is turned off. The fan stops only when the engine coolant falls to a predetermined safe temperature, usually about 210 degrees Fahrenheit. In some systems, the fan does not start when the air-conditioner select switch is turned on unless the high side of the air-conditioning (A/C) system is above a predetermined safe temperature.

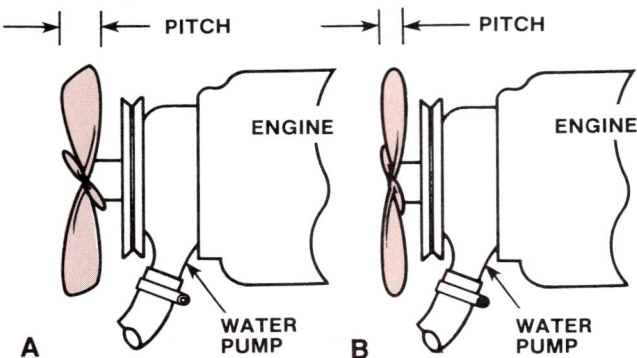

Figure 11-59 Flex fan: (A) extreme pitch at low speed; (B) reduced pitch at high speed.

Lubricating and Cooling Systems 253

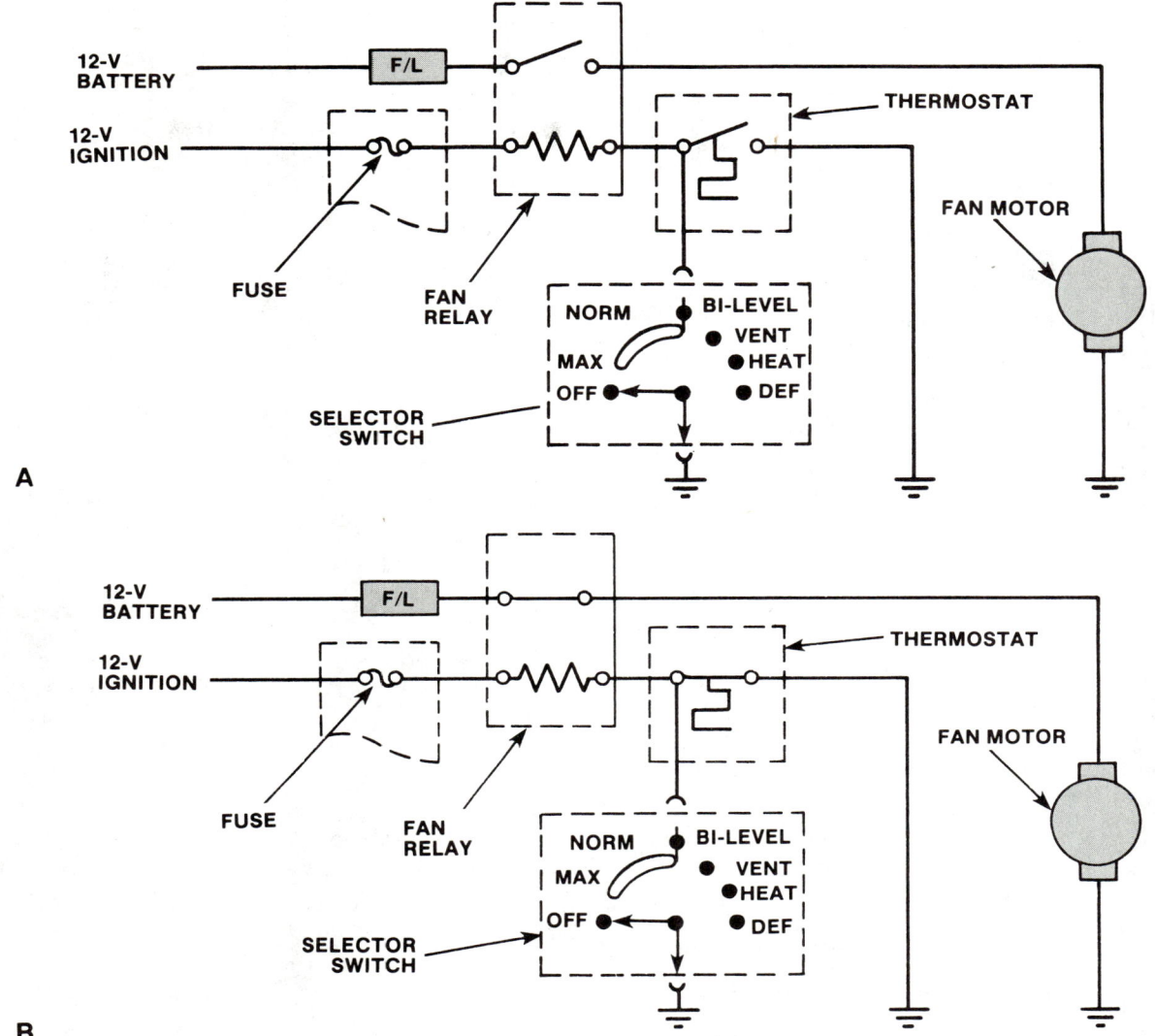

Figure 11-61 (A) Electric engine cooling fan schematic; (B) with the temperature sensor closed, the relay will be energized, completing the circuit to the fan motor.

WARNING: The engine electric cooling fan can come on at any time without warning even if the engine is not running. For this reason, it is always wise to remove the negative terminal from the battery while working around an electric cooling fan.

Another way of controlling fan noise and horsepower loss is by the use of a fan clutch. This is a unit that couples the fan to the drive pulley (usually on the water pump shaft). The basic principle of the clutch is that it slips at high speeds, thus it is not turning at full engine speed.

Cooling fans may be speed-controlled or temperature-controlled. The obvious advantage of the temperature-controlled unit is the fact that it knows when air is needed to cool the system. A silicone fluid couples the fan blade drive plate to a driven disc via a series of annular grooves in the two pieces (Figure 11-62). The fluid fills these grooves and drives the fan until the differential torque between the fan and the drive disc causes the fluid to shear or slip. The unit has a bimetallic element that senses the air temperature behind the radiator. This bimetal is calibrated to open and close a valve in the clutch that dispenses the silicone at particular temperatures. When the fluid is returned to its reservoir, the unit free wheels the fan until more cooling is required. Tests have proven that maximum cooling is necessary less than 10% of the time. Therefore, a temperature-controlled fan clutch saves fuel and reduces noise 90% of the time, while it still has the capability of doing the job the other 10% of the time.

Water Jackets

Hollow passages in the block and cylinder heads surround the areas closest to the cylinders and combustion chambers (Figure 11-63). Coolant flow through the block and head can be in one of the following ways.

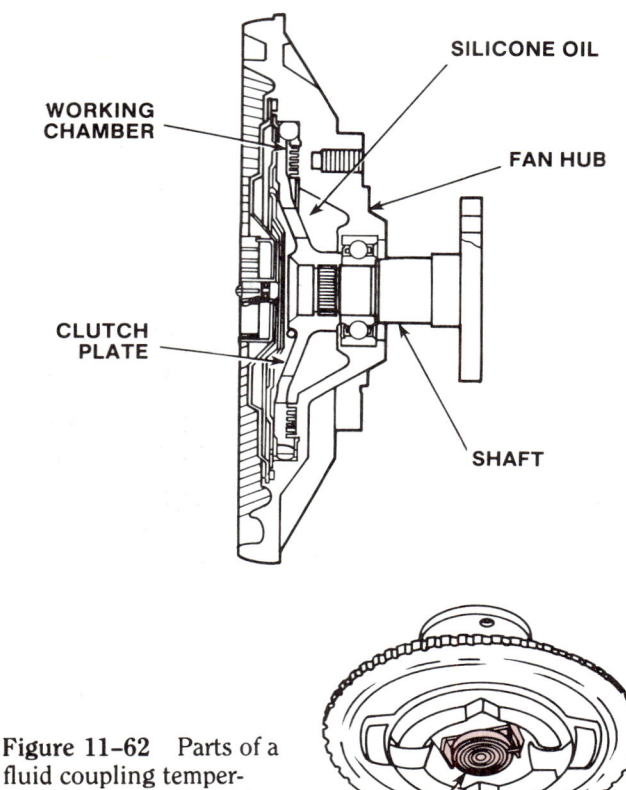

Figure 11-62 Parts of a fluid coupling temperature-controlled fan drive. *Courtesy of Chrysler Corp.*

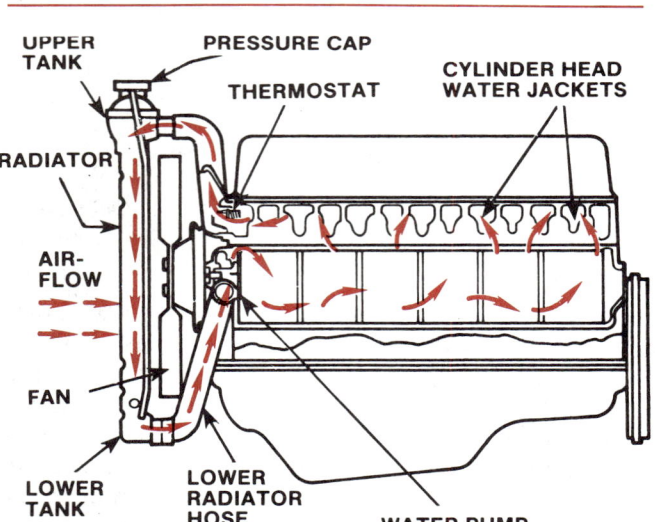

Figure 11-63 Cooling system circulates coolant through the engine.

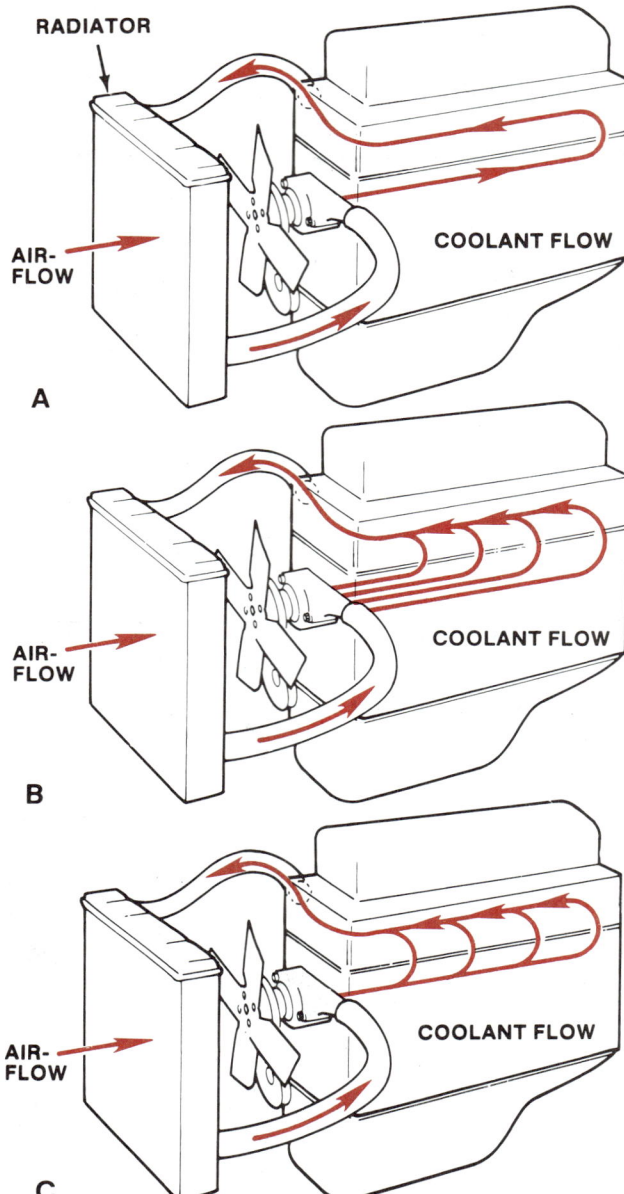

Figure 11-64 Coolant flow through the engine block and cylinder head: (A) series flow system; (B) parallel flow system; (C) series parallel flow system.

SERIES FLOW SYSTEM In this system (Figure 11-64A), the coolant flows around all the cylinders on each bank as it flows to the rear of the block. Large main coolant passages at the rear of the block direct the coolant through the head gasket and to the head.

PARALLEL FLOW SYSTEM In this system (Figure 11-64B), coolant flows into the block under pressure, then crosses the gasket to the head through main coolant passage openings beside each cylinder.

SERIES-PARALLEL FLOW SYSTEM This system (Figure 11-64C) uses a combination of series and parallel flow systems. The cooling passages inside the engine are designed so that the whole system can be drained and that there are no pockets in which steam can form. Any steam that develops must be able to go directly to the top of the radiator, in order for the cooling system to function properly.

Included in the water jackets are soft plugs and a block drain plug. The soft plugs and drain are usually removed during engine teardown. New ones are installed during reassembly.

Lubricating and Cooling Systems

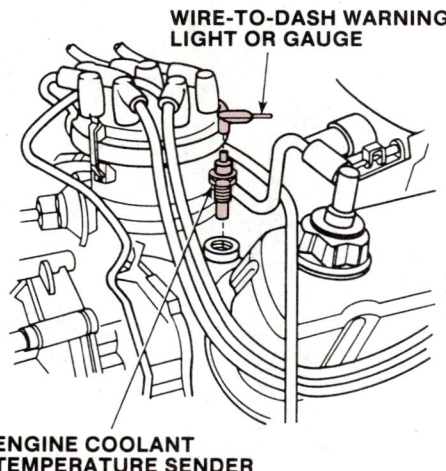

Figure 11-65 Coolant temperature sender or sensor.

Temperature Indicator

Coolant temperature indicators are mounted in the dashboard to alert the driver of an overheating condition. It consists of a temperature gauge and a light. A temperature sensor is screwed into a threaded hole in the water jacket (Figure 11-65). A schematic of an electric temperature gauge including a voltage limiter is shown in Figure 11-66. Besides indicating coolant temperatures to the driver, temperature sensors play a vital role on today's computer-controlled engine control systems.

Heater System

A hot liquid passenger heater is part of the engine cooling system. Heated coolant flows from the engine block or head through the heater hoses and a heater control valve to a small heater core, or radiator, located in a hollow container on either side of the fire wall. Air is directed or blown over the hot heater core, and the heated air flows into the passenger compartment. Movable doors can be controlled to blend cool air with heated air for more or less heat.

Oil Cooler

Radiators for vehicles with automatic transmissions have a sealed heat exchanger, or form of radiator, located in the coolant outlet tank. Metal or rubber hoses carry hot automatic transmission fluid to the heat exchanger. The coolant passing over the sealed heat exchanger cools the fluid, which is then returned to the transmission. Cooling the transmission fluid is essential to the efficiency and durability of an automatic transmission.

Air-Cooled System

As mentioned at the beginning of this chapter, a few engines use a cooling system that employs air rather than liquid as the medium to transfer heat from the engine components to the atmosphere (Figure 11-67). Cylinders and heads have fins and are enclosed in a shroud to control airflow. Fins expose more of the surface area to airflow for better heat dissipation. Ducts and shrouds direct the airflow over the engine components, especially over the hotter cylinder head area. A belt-driven or electric blower provides the means for airflow. Fresh air is taken in and heated air expelled into the atmosphere. A thermostat connected to a control valve or door regulates airflow to control engine temperature.

☐ COOLING SYSTEM SERVICING

The cooling system must function as a system. It must also be inspected and serviced as a system. Replacing one damaged part while leaving others dirty or clogged will not increase system efficiency. Service the entire system to ensure good results.

Service involves both the visual inspection of parts and connections and pressure testing to detect the

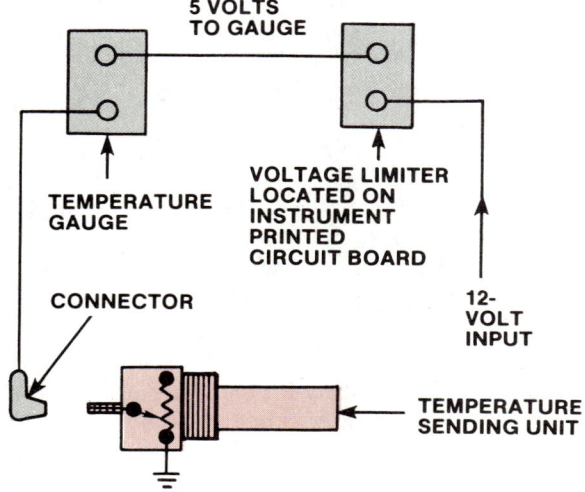

Figure 11-66 Schematic of an electric temperature gauge. *Courtesy of Ford Motor Co.*

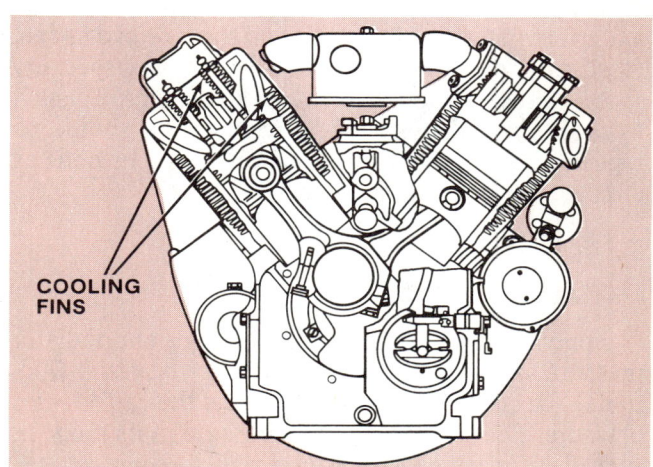

Figure 11-67 Cross section of a V-type air-cooled engine.

presence of internal or external leaks. Guidelines for inspection and pressure testing of the cooling system are given in the Tech Manual that accompanies this textbook.

The following is a list of places to check for a suspected leak in the cooling system. Although this list is not all inclusive, it does present the most common areas in which a leak can occur.

External Leakage
- Radiator leak
- Loose hose clamp
- Hose leak
- Faulty radiator cap
- Dented radiator inlet or outlet tube
- Leak in heater connection
- Water pump leak through weep hole
- Cracked or porous water pump housing
- Water core leak
- Loose core hole plug in cylinder block
- Cracked thermostat housing
- Leak at water temperature sending unit
- Cylinder head bolts loose or tightened unevenly
- Warped or cracked cylinder head
- Heater control valve leak
- Cracked cylinder block
- Damaged gasket or dry gasket if engine has been stored
- Coolant reservoir or hose leak

Internal Leakage
- Faulty head gasket
- Cracked head
- Cracked block
- Transmission fluid cooler leak

Repairing Radiators

Most radiator leak repairs require the removal of the radiator from the vehicle. The coolant must be drained and all hoses and oil cooler lines disconnected. Bolts holding the radiator are then loosened and removed.

The actual radiator repair procedures depend on the material from which it is made and the type of damage. Most radiator repairs are made by radiator specialty shops whose technicians have knowledge of such work. If the radiator is badly damaged, it should be replaced and the installation of a new one be done as directed by the manufacturer.

Testing the Radiator Pressure Cap

Apply the proper cap testing adapter and radiator pressure cap to the tester head. Pump the tester (Figure 11-68) until the pressure valve of the cap releases pressure. The cap should hold pressure in its range as indicated on the tester gauge dial for one minute. If it doesn't, replace it. Remove the cap from the tester

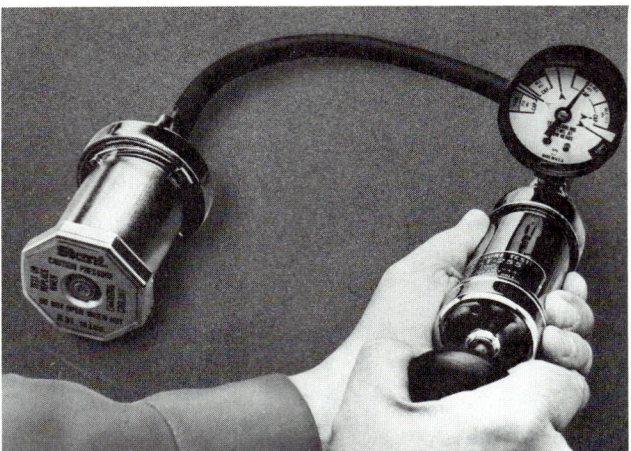

Figure 11-68 Testing a radiator cap with radiator leaks.

and visually inspect the condition of the cap's pressure valve and upper and lower sealing gaskets. If the gaskets are hard, brittle, or deteriorated, the cap will not hold the proper pressure. It should be replaced with a new cap in the same pressure range.

WARNING: The radiator cap should never be removed when the cap or radiator is hot to the touch. The radiator should first be allowed to cool, or force cool it by lightly spraying water on the radiator core. When the cap is cool to the touch and the engine is shut off, release the pressure with the safety lever or push button (if the cap is so equipped) or use a cloth over the cap and turn it counterclockwise one-quarter turn to the filler neck safety stop. Carefully watch for any liquid or steam loss around the ring of the cap and from the radiator overflow tube. Let the cap remain in this position until all pressure subsides. In this position, the pressure valve is lifted from the bottom sealing seat in the filler neck. When all evidence of discharge ends, use a cloth to cover the cap, press it down to pass the cap's ears over the safety stops, and continue to turn counterclockwise to remove the cap.

Testing the Thermostat

There are several ways to test the opening temperature of a thermostat. First, do not remove the thermostat from the engine. Remove the radiator pressure cap from a cold or cool radiator and insert a thermometer. Start the engine and let it warm up. Watch the thermometer and the surface of the coolant. When the coolant begins to flow, this indicates that the thermostat has started to open. The reading on the thermometer indicates the opening temperature of the thermostat. If the engine is cold and coolant circulates, this indicates the thermostat is stuck open and must be replaced.

Secondly, if the thermostat is removed from the engine after the coolant has been drained, suspend the

Lubricating and Cooling Systems   257

Figure 11-69 Testing a thermostat's opening temperature by submerging it in water.

thermostat completely submerged in a small container of water so that it does not touch the bottom (Figure 11-69). Place a thermometer in the water so that it does not touch the container and only measures water temperature. Heat the water. When the thermostat valve barely begins to open, read the thermometer. This is the opening temperature of this particular thermostat. If the valve stays open after the thermostat is removed from the water, the thermostat is defective and must be replaced.

Several types of commercial testers are available. When using such a tester be sure to follow the manufacturer's instructions.

SHOP TALK

If a vehicle overheats and there is no evidence of previous water loss and the radiator pressure cap is holding the proper pressure, chances are very good that the thermostat is defective.

If a thermostat is more than two years old, or if there is any doubt about its operation, replace it. Markings on the thermostat normally indicate which end should face toward the radiator. Regardless of the markings, the sensored end always must be installed toward the engine.

When replacing the thermostat also replace the gasket that seals the thermostat in place and is positioned between the water outlet casting and the engine block. Generally, these gaskets are made of a composition fiber material and are die-cut to match the thermostat opening and mounting bolt configuration of the water outlet. Thermostat gaskets generally come with or without an adhesive backing. The adhesive backing of gaskets holds the thermostat securely centered in the mounting flange, leaving both hands of the technician free to align and bolt the thermostat securely in place. With the adhesive-backed gasket holding the thermostat in place, it will not drop out or become misaligned. This provides for a tight seal and also prevents breaking the mounting flange of the water outlet during installation.

Checking and Replacing Hoses

Carefully check all cooling hoses for leakage, swelling, and chafing. Also change any hose that feels mushy or extremely brittle when squeezed firmly (Figure 11-70). Be especially watchful for signs of splits when hoses are squeezed. These splits have a habit of bursting wide open under pressure. Also look for rust stains around the clamps. Rust stains indicate that the hose is leaking, possibly because the clamp has eaten into the hose. Loosen the clamp, slide it back, and check for cuts.

Do not overlook the small by-pass hose on some models. It is located between the water pump and engine block. Also check the lower radiator hose very carefully. This hose contains a coiled wire lining to keep it from collapsing during operation. If the wire loses tension, the hose can partially collapse at high speed and restrict coolant flow. This results in a very elusive overheating problem.

CUSTOMER CARE

Technicians should do their customers a favor and remind them that all cooling hoses should be changed every two to four years.

When replacing a hose, drain the coolant system below the level that is being worked on. Use a knife to cut off the old hose (Figure 11-71) and loosen or cut the old clamp. Slide the old hose off the fitting. If the hose is stuck, do not pry it off. You could possibly damage the inlet/outlet nipple or the attachment between the end of the hose and the bead. Carefully cut the stuck hose off its fitting.

Clean off any remaining hose particles with a wire brush or emery cloth. The fitting should be clean when

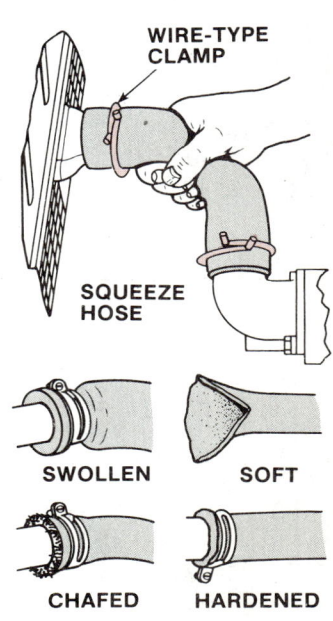

Figure 11-70 Defects in hoses.

258 Section 2 Engines

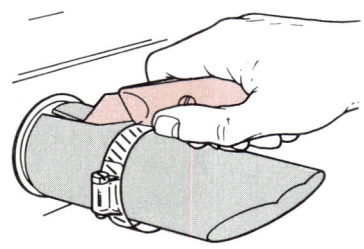

Figure 11-71 Cutting off an old hose.

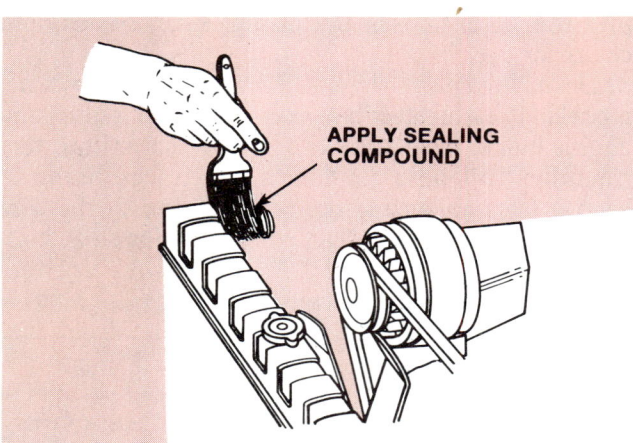

Figure 11-72 Applying sealing compound.

installing the new hose. Burrs or sharp edges could cut into the hose tube and lead to premature failure.

Coat the surface with a sealing compound (Figure 11-72). Place the new clamps on each end of the hose before positioning the hose. Do not reuse old spring-type clamps, even if they look good. Slide the clamps to about 1/4 inch from the end of the hose after it is properly positioned on the fitting (Figure 11-73). Tighten the clamp securely. Do not overtighten.

It is a good idea to readjust the clamp of a newly installed coolant hose after a brief run-in period. The hose end does not contract and expand at the same rate as the metal of the inlet/outlet nipple it is attached to. Rubber coolant hose, warmed by the hot coolant and hot engine, will expand. The clamp compresses the rubber around the hose end and sets it. When the engine cools, the fitting contracts more than the rubber, and the hose will not be as secure. This can result in cold leaks of coolant at the inlet/outlet nipple when the engine is cool. Retightening the clamp eliminates the problem.

Water Pump Service

The majority of water pump failures are attributed to leaks of some sort. When the pump seat fails, coolant will begin to seep out of the weep hole in the casting. This is an early indicator of trouble. The seals may simply wear out due to abrasives in the cooling system, or some types of seals crack due to thermal shock such as adding cold water to an overheated engine. Obviously, the addition of cold coolant to an extremely hot engine can also cause other internal parts to fail.

Other failures can be attributed to bearing and shaft problems and an occasional cracked casting. Water pump bearing or seal failure can be caused by surprisingly small out-of-balance conditions that are difficult to spot. Look for the following.

- A bent fan. A single bent blade will cause problems.
- A piece of fan missing.
- A cracked fan blade. Even a small crack will prevent proper flexing.
- Fan mounting surfaces that are not clean or flush.
- A worn fan clutch.

To check a water pump, start the engine and listen for a bad bearing, using a mechanic's stethoscope (Figure 11-74) or rubber tubing. Place the stethoscope or hose on the bearing or pump shaft. If a louder than normal noise is heard, the bearing is defective.

WARNING: *Whenever working near a running engine, keep your hands and clothing away from the moving fan, pulleys, and belts. Do not allow the stethoscope or rubber tubing to be caught by the moving parts.*

There is another test that can be performed with the engine off and the fan belt and shroud removed. Grasp

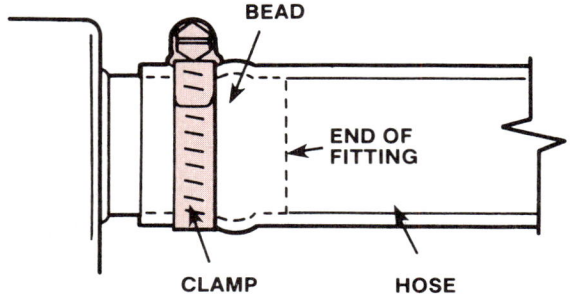

Figure 11-73 New clamps should be placed immediately after the bead of the fitting.

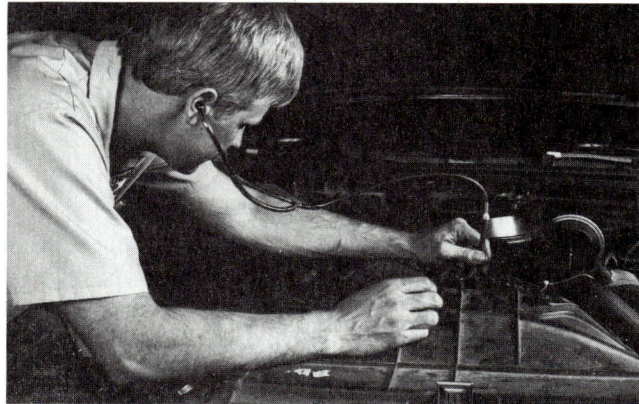

Figure 11-74 A stethoscope can help locate a bad bearing. *Courtesy of Perfect Circle/Dana*

Lubricating and Cooling Systems

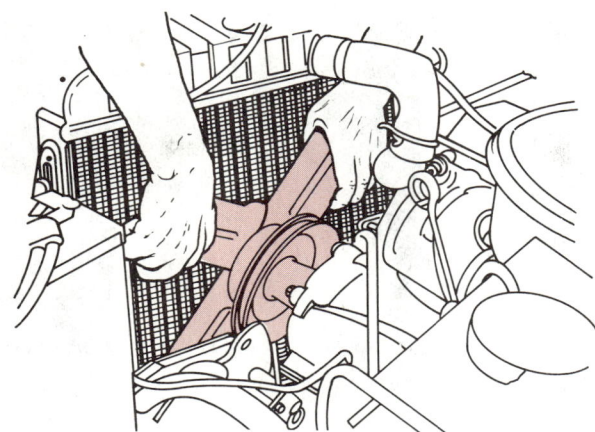

Figure 11-75 Checking water pump bearings. *Courtesy of Chrysler Corp.*

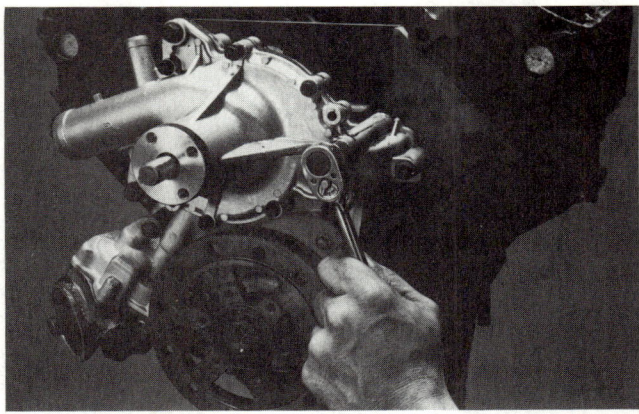

Figure 11-76 Installing a water pump. *Courtesy of Perfect Circle/Dana*

the fan and attempt to move it in and out and up and down (Figure 11-75). More than 1/16 inch of movement indicates worn bearings that require water pump replacement.

To determine whether the water pump is allowing for good circulation, warm up the engine and run it at idle speed. Squeeze the upper hose connection with one hand and accelerate the engine with the other hand. If a surge on the hose is felt, the pump is working.

Any air being sucked into the cooling system is certain to have a detrimental effect. It cuts down pumping efficiency and causes both rusting and wear at a rate approximately three times above normal. To test for aeration, have the engine fully warmed up, all hose connections tight, and the coolant level up to normal. Attach one end of a small hose to the radiator overflow pipe and put the other end into a jar of water. Run the engine at a fast idle. If a steady stream of bubbles appears in the jar of water, this means that air is getting into the cooling system.

Check first for a cylinder gasket leak by running a compression test. If two adjacent cylinders test low, the gasket is bad. Otherwise, there is an air leak somewhere else in the cooling system.

Replacing the Water Pump

When replacing a water pump, it is necessary to drain the cooling system. Any components—belts, fan, fan shroud, shaft spacers, or viscous drive clutch—should be removed to make the pump accessible. Most pumps are attached to the cylinder block as shown in Figure 11-76. Loosen and remove the bolts in a criss-cross pattern from the center outward. Insert a rag into the block opening and scrape off any remains of the old gasket.

WARNING: When working on the coolant system, for example, replacing the water pump or thermostat, a certain amount of coolant will spill on the floor. The antifreeze in the coolant causes it to be very slippery. Always immediately wipe up any coolant that spills to reduce or eliminate the chance of injury.

When replacing a water pump, apply a coating of good waterproof sealer to a new gasket and place it in position on the water pump. Coat the other side of the gasket with sealer, and position the pump against the engine block until it is properly seated. Install the mounting bolts and tighten them evenly in a staggered sequence to the torque specifications with a torque wrench. Careless tightening could cause the pump housing to crack. Check the pump to make sure it rotates freely.

Checking Fans and Fan Clutches

Fan operation can be checked by spinning the fan by hand. A noticeable wobble or any blade that is not in the same plane as the rest indicates that replacement is in order. The fan can also be checked by removing it and laying it on a flat surface. If it is straight, all the blades should touch the surface. Never attempt to straighten a damaged cooling fan. Bending it back into shape might seem easier (and cheaper) than replacing it, but doing so is risky. Whenever metal is bent, it is weakened. Bending creates microscopic stress cracks that spread throughout the metal. Repeated bending or stress eventually leads to fatigue failure. Cooling fans are especially vulnerable to this type of failure. Their vulnerability is due to the high rotational speeds at which they operate and the centrifugal forces and loading they experience.

Any condition that causes the fan blades to run untrue can produce enough vibration and overload to knock out the water pump bearing and break the shaft. Obviously, the farther out from the pump bearing the fan blade is located, the more severe will be the effect of the blade being mounted in a crooked position. Almost all cars equipped with an air conditioner also have a fan clutch, which locates the fan blades several inches out from the flange on the pump shaft. This amounts to an outboard weight of approximately 6 pounds and creates a terrific strain on the pump shaft if it is not running in perfect alignment and balance.

Both types of fan clutches—torque drive or thermostat and controlled viscous drive—use a fluid-filled chamber (usually silicone) to turn the fan. Obviously, loss of the drive fluid will render the fan useless. In thermostat-type units, a defective thermostat spring or binding in the clutch plates will also cause problems and prevent the fan from speeding up as the engine gets hotter. The result is overheating and boiling over.

One of the simplest checks to make is to visually inspect the fan clutch for signs of fluid loss. Oily streaks radiating outward from the hub shaft means fluid has leaked out past the bearing seal.

Most fan clutches offer a slight amount of resistance if turned by hand when the engine is cold. They offer drag when the engine is hot. If the fan freewheels easily hot or cold, replace the clutch.

Another check that should be made is to push the tip of a fan blade in and out. Any visible looseness in the shaft bearing means the fan clutch should be replaced.

Fan blades are balanced at the time of manufacture but can be bent if handled carelessly. Likewise, fan clutches are machined very accurately to run true. However, rough handling at the time of pump replacement causes nicks and dents on the mounting faces. This can cause the fan blade to be installed crookedly. Serious trouble might follow soon after the car is back in service. Therefore, technicians should be cautioned to handle fan clutches and blades with care and to file away any nicks, burrs, or dents someone else might have caused. Obviously, if any fins have been broken off the fan clutch, it must be replaced.

SHOP TALK

Damaged fan shrouds can usually be repaired if the damage is not severe. Polyethylene and polypropylene plastics can be hot-air or airless welded. Fiberglass can be glued with epoxy. The important rule here is never leave a fan shroud off. The shroud is needed to help the fan work at peak efficiency and leaving it off will affect the fan's efficiency.

Checking Belts

If a belt breaks, at best the fan stops spinning and the coolant does not cool down efficiently. At worst, the water pump stops, the coolant does not circulate, and, eventually, the engine overheats.

Belts, like hoses, are made of elastic rubber compounds. Although they are extremely sturdy, they are primarily designed for transmitting power. Even the best belts last only an average of four years. Advise the

Figure 11-77 Drive belt defects. *Courtesy of Chrysler Corp.*

customer to replace all belts every four years, regardless of how they look.

Fortunately, belt problems are easily discovered either by visual inspection for cracks, splits, glazing, or oil soakage (Figure 11-77), or by the screech of slippage. As stated earlier in the chapter, the coolant fan belt is part of a multibelt arrangement. In servicing a multibelt setup, it is very important to replace all of the belts when one set is bad.

The mounting brackets on alternators, power-steering pumps, and air compressors are designed to be adjustable so that proper tension can be maintained on these belts. Some of these brackets have a hole or slot to allow the use of a pry bar or wrench when adjusting. Some automobiles require the fan, fan pulley, and other accessory drive belts to be removed to gain access to belts needing replacement. After replacing a belt, make sure it is adjusted properly. To do so use a pry bar, where possible, to move the accessory so there is tension on the belt (Figure 11-78). Tighten all bolts and nuts to keep the tension. Then check the belt's tension with a belt tension gauge (Figure 11-79). Bring the belt to the manufacturer's recommended tension.

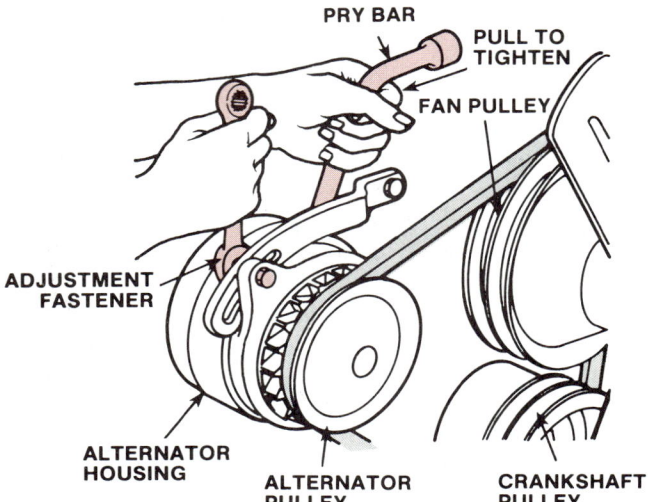

Figure 11-78 Adjusting tension of a drive belt. *Courtesy of Chrysler Corp.*

Lubricating and Cooling Systems

Figure 11-79 Checking fan belt tension. *Courtesy of TRW, Inc.*

> **SHOP TALK**
>
> *It is never advisable to pry a belt onto a pulley. Obtain enough slack so the belt can be slipped on without damaging either the V-belts or a pulley. Some power-steering pumps have a 1/2-inch drive socket to aid in adjusting belts to the proper tension without prying against any accessory.*

After installation of the new belts, the engine should be run for 10 to 15 minutes to allow belts to seat and reach their initial stretch condition. Modern steel-strengthened V-belts do not stretch much after the initial run-in, so the retensioning should be done very carefully with an accurate gauge. Recheck the tension again after 5,000 miles.

Misalignment of the V-pulleys reduces the belt's service life and brings about rapid V-pulley wear, which causes thrown belts and screech. Undesirable side or end thrust loads can also be imposed on pulley or pump shaft bearings. The more wrap a belt has around a pulley, the easier it is to transmit full power. A small pulley causes more belt flexing; therefore it will crack and be ruined sooner.

It is important to check alignment by using a straightedge. Pulleys should be in alignment within 1/16 inch per foot of the distance across the face of the pulleys.

Flushing Cooling Systems

Rust and scale will inevitably form in any cooling system. When they do, there are a few vulnerable places they can attack. One happens to be the main seal in the water pump, which keeps coolant away from the bearing and its lubricant. If grit is allowed to erode the seal, the bearing will be the next item to go. Coolant leaking from the water pump's vent hole is evidence of seal failure.

Whenever coolant is changed—and especially before a water pump is replaced—a thorough reverse flushing or back flushing should be performed. Before this flushing is done, chemical cleaners can be added to the cooling system to help dissolve rust and scale deposits. Two types of cleaners are commonly used for this purpose.

Heavy-duty cooling system cleaners consist of powdered phosphoric acid. The thermostat must be removed to prevent damage before heavy-duty cleaners are used. After use, a chemical neutralizer (baking soda) is put into the system to neutralize any remaining phosphoric acid before flushing.

WARNING: Always wear proper clothing and eye protection when using coolant additives to remove silicate and calcium deposits. They might be very corrosive. Be careful not to inhale fumes when pouring the powdered cleaner into the radiator. If powder gets on your skin, wash the area immediately.

Liquid-cooling system cleaners consist of a milder solution of phosphoric acid dissolved in water and mixed with detergent. Liquid cleaners can be used without removing the thermostat. The flushing procedure removes the cleaning solution.

Reverse flushing is the procedure of forcing clean liquid backwards through the cooling system. This carries away rust, scale, corrosion, and other contaminants. A flushing gun that operates on compressed air is used to force clean water and air through the system (Figure 11-80).

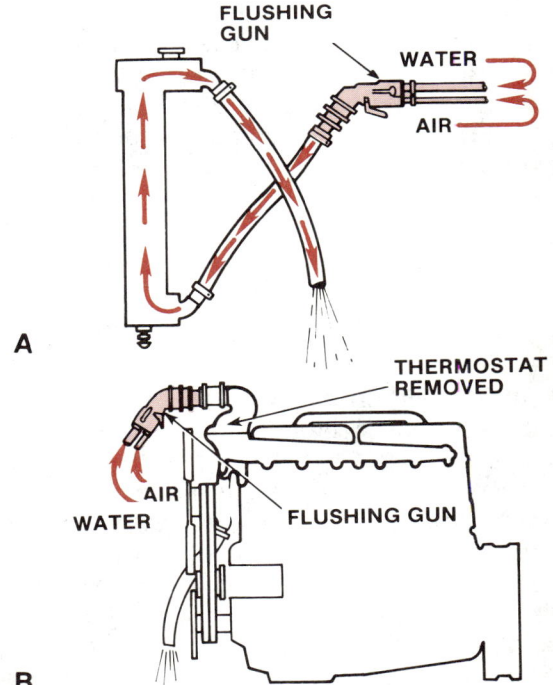

Figure 11-80 (A) Reverse flushing the radiator with shop air and water with a special flushing gun; (B) reverse flushing head and block. *Courtesy of Chrysler Corp.*

Refilling and Bleeding

After the cooling system has been cleaned, refill the system with new coolant mixed to the recommended strength. Be sure all the flushing water is out of the radiator and evacuated from the engine block before refilling.

The cooling system must be bled to insure there are no air pockets in the coolant. Air in the system can reduce cooling ability and lead to water pump and other component damage.

Each vehicle has its own specific bleeding procedure. In many cases, the system is filled and the radiator cap is left off. The engine is then run until the thermostat opens and the coolant circulates. Trapped air bubbles escape through the opened radiator.

Other bleeding procedures are more involved. They may require the connection of special bleeder hoses to air bleed valves located on the radiator or other components. Air is bled through the valves as the system is filled. Always follow the bleeding steps outlined in the vehicle's service manual.

CUSTOMER CARE

Many additives, inhibitors, and quick-fix remedies are available for use in the automotive cooling system. These include, but are not limited to, stop leak, water pump lubricant, engine flush, and acid neutralizers. Explain to your customers that extreme caution should be exercised when using any additive in the cooling system. Tell them to read the label directions and precautions in order to know in advance the end results of any additive used. For example, caustic solutions must never be used in aluminum radiators. Alcohol-based remedies should never be used in any cooling system.

CASE STUDY

Case 1

A late-model minivan's engine overheats while going up a mountain road. It is a very hot day so water is added to the radiator and the trip continues. After driving 30 miles, the engine overheats again. Again water is added. The engine is allowed to cool for an hour while the owner eats. After about 30 miles of driving, the engine overheats again. This time the van is taken to a service station to be diagnosed and repaired. It is late in the day and the owner agrees to stay overnight at a local motel. A fresh supply of water is added to the radiator and the owner drives about a mile to the motel.

In the morning the owner adds water to the system. The van is brought back to the service station for diagnosis. It is obvious that the engine is overheating and there is a loss of fluid. There is no need to verify the customer's complaint. A visual inspection shows little water in the radiator but no signs of external leakage is found. The oil level is found to be a little high and the oil appears to be thin.

A radiator tester is attached to the system and there is no sign of pressure or coolant leakage. The operation of the water pump is to be checked next. However, this test cannot be done because the engine will not start. The starter cannot turn the engine over. A quick check of the battery reveals that it is fully charged. Careful thought suggests that the problem is hydrostatic lock-up. This is a condition where a liquid fills the cylinder. Since a liquid cannot be compressed, the liquid prevents the piston from moving up.

To verify this, the spark plugs are removed. All plugs looked normal except cylinder #5. It is wet with water. With the plugs out, the engine is cranked by the starter motor and water comes gushing out of the cylinder. The exact cause of the internal leak will be best identified by tearing down the engine. During disassembly, a crack in the engine block is found. This crack allowed the coolant to pass from a coolant passage in the block into the cylinder.

This leak was not detected by the radiator pressure test because when the engine is cold, little, if any, coolant leaks through the crack. The crack grows larger as the engine becomes hotter, allowing the cylinder to rapidly fill when it is hot. A new short block is put in the van and the problem is corrected.

Summary

- An engine's lubrication system must perform several important functions: hold an adequate supply of oil to cool, clean, lubricate, and seal the engine; remove contaminants from the oil; and deliver oil to all necessary areas of the engine. The API has developed two basic classifications for engine oils: S class for passenger cars and light trucks and C class for heavy-duty commercial applications. The SAE has standardized oil viscosity ratings. API and SAE classifications are stamped on top of the oil can.

- Excessive oil consumption can be a result of external and internal leaks, faulty accessories, piston rings, and valve guides. Internal leaks, which usually result in oil burning, are usually more difficult to diagnose.

- The main components of a typical lubrication system are: an oil pump, oil pump pick-up, oil pan, pressure relief valve, oil filter, engine oil passages,

Lubricating and Cooling Systems 263

- engine bearings, crankcase ventilation, oil pressure indicator, oil seals and gaskets, dipstick, and oil coolers.
- The purpose of the oil pump is to supply oil to the various moving parts in the engine. The most commonly used stock pumps are the rotor and gear type. Both are positive displacement pumps. Because the faster the pump turns the greater the pressure becomes, a pressure-regulating valve is installed to control the maximum oil pressure. All automotive vehicles are equipped with either an oil pressure gauge or a low-pressure indicator light. The gauges are either mechanically or electrically operated.
- All oil leaving the oil pump is directed to the oil filter. The filter is a disposable metal container filled with a special type of treated paper or other filter substance that catches and holds the oil's impurities. Two types of oil filtration systems are commonly used: full flow and by-pass.
- After an engine is rebuilt, a new or rebuilt oil pump is often installed. Integral pumps must be rebuilt. Bolt-on or nonintegral pumps can be rebuilt or replaced. If the old pump is to be reused, it should be carefully inspected for wear and thoroughly cleaned.
- Two basic types of cooling systems are utilized by automotive manufacturers: liquid-cooled systems and air-cooled systems. The most popular and efficient method of engine cooling is the liquid-cooled system.
- The fluid used as coolant today is a mixture of water and ethylene glycol-based antifreeze/coolant. Closed-cooling systems are cooling systems with an expansion or recovery tank. The function of the water pump is to move the coolant efficiently through the system. The radiator transfers heat from the engine to the air passing through it. The radiator is usually one of two designs: cross flow or down flow. The thermostat attempts to control the engine's operating temperature by routing the coolant either to the radiator or through the by-pass or sometimes a combination of both.
- V-belts and multiple-ribbed belts (called serpentine belts) are used to drive water pumps, power steering pumps, air-conditioning compressors, alternators, and emission control pumps. The fan delivers additional air to the radiator to maintain proper cooling at low speeds and idle. Since fan air is usually only necessary at idle and low speed operation, various design concepts are used to limit the fan's operation at higher speeds.
- The hollow passages in the block and cylinder heads through which coolant flows may be arranged as a series flow system, a parallel flow system, or a series-parallel flow system. Included in the water jackets are soft plugs and a block drain plug. A temperature indicator is mounted in the dashboard to alert the driver of an overheating condition. A hot liquid passenger heater is part of the engine cooling system. Radiators for vehicles with automatic transmissions have a sealed heat exchanger located in the coolant outlet tank.
- The basic procedure for testing a vehicle's cooling system includes inspecting the radiator filler neck, inspecting the overflow tube for dents and other obstructions, testing for external leaks, and testing for internal leaks. Most radiator leak repairs require removing the radiator from the vehicle.
- The pressure cap should hold pressure in its range as indicated on the tester gauge dial for one minute. A thermostat can be tested in the engine or after it is removed. If a thermostat is more than two years old, or if there is any doubt about its operation, replace it.
- Hoses should be checked for leakage, swelling, and chafing. Any hose that feels mushy or extremely brittle or shows signs of splitting when it is squeezed should be replaced. The majority of water pump failures are attributed to leaks of some sort. Other failures can be attributed to bearing and shaft problems and an occasional cracked casting.
- Fan operation can be checked by spinning the fan by hand. A noticeable wobble or any blade that is not in the same plane as the rest indicates that replacement is in order. The fan can also be checked by removing it and laying it on a flat surface. If it is straight, all the blades will touch the surface. Never attempt to repair a damaged fan; replace it. One of the simplest ways to check a fan clutch is to visually inspect it for signs of fluid loss.
- Belt problems are easily discovered by visual inspection or by the screech of slippage. When a new belt is installed, it should be properly adjusted.
- Whenever coolant is changed, a thorough reverse flushing or back flushing should be performed.

Review Questions

1. What is the major factor that will increase a radiator's efficiency?
2. What is indicated by an abnormal amount of water being emitted from the exhaust?
3. Describe the simple test used to determine whether the water pump is causing good circulation.
4. How is the oil pump driven?
5. What is the name of the component in the lubrication system that prevents excessively high system pressures from occurring as engine speed increases?
6. Which of the following is a function of the engine's lubrication system?
    a. Hold an adequate supply of oil
    b. Remove contaminants from the oil

c. Deliver oil to all necessary areas of the engine
d. All of the above

7. Technician A says that the gear pump pumps a greater volume of oil than a rotor pump. Technician B says that engine oil pressure is dependent upon oil viscosity. Who is correct?
   a. Technician A
   b. Technician B
   c. Both A and B
   d. Neither A nor B

8. Technician A says that most pressure indicators found in vehicles today are electronically controlled. Technician B says that most engines made in recent years have an oil filtering system somewhere on the input side of the pump. Who is correct?
   a. Technician A
   b. Technician B
   c. Both A and B
   d. Neither A nor B

9. Which type of oil filtration system is used on most engines today?
   a. by-pass
   b. independent
   c. full flow
   d. shunt

10. Which of the following could cause low oil pressure during diagnostic checks?
    a. plugged oil pick-up screen
    b. excessive oil dilution
    c. both a and b
    d. neither a nor b

11. Technician A uses a feeler gauge and straight-edge to determine the pump cover flatness. Technician B uses an outside micrometer to measure the diameter and thickness of the outer rotor. Who is correct?
    a. Technician A
    b. Technician B
    c. Both A and B
    d. Neither A nor B

12. Technician A says that the API classification S stands for standard passenger cars. Technician B says that the API classification C stands for vehicles with compression ignition. Who is correct?
    a. Technician A
    b. Technician B
    c. Both A and B
    d. Neither A nor B

13. Technician A says that the American Petroleum Institute has established an oil viscosity classification system. Technician B says that higher viscosity oils receive the higher rating numbers. Who is correct?
    a. Technician A
    b. Technician B
    c. Both A and B
    d. Neither A nor B

14. Which of the following is designed to greatly reduce friction?
    a. SE oil
    b. CC oil
    c. energy-conserving oil
    d. synthetic oil

15. In most automotive applications, the water pump is driven by the _____ .
    a. gear train
    b. belt
    c. crankshaft
    d. impeller

16. Which of the following statements is incorrect?
    a. When replacing a hose, drain the coolant system below the level that is being worked on.
    b. A thermostat that is more than two years old should be replaced.
    c. Spring-type hose clamps should not be reused, even if they look good.
    d. It is not possible to tell if a coolant hose is working correctly simply by starting the engine and feeling the hose.

17. Technician A says that, if a vehicle overheats, but there is no evidence of previous water loss and the radiator pressure cap is holding the proper pressure, chances are very good that there is a defective water pump. Technician B replaces matched drive belts in pairs. Who is correct?
    a. Technician A
    b. Technician B
    c. Both A and B
    d. Neither A nor B

18. When must a thermostat be fully opened?
    a. 3 degrees Fahrenheit above its temperature rating
    b. 3 degrees Fahrenheit above or below its temperature rating
    c. 20 degrees Fahrenheit above the start to open temperature
    d. 20 degrees Fahrenheit below the start to open temperature

19. In which type of system does coolant flow into the engine block under pressure, then cross the head gasket to the head through the main coolant passage openings beside each cylinder?
    a. parallel flow
    b. balanced flow
    c. series flow
    d. all of the above

20. Most fan clutches will offer a lot of drag when the engine is _____ .
    a. cold
    b. hot
    c. turned by hand
    d. both a and c

12 INTAKE AND EXHAUST SYSTEMS

Objectives

- Explain the function and components of the air induction system, including ductwork, air cleaner/filters, and intake manifolds.
- Describe how the engine generates vacuum and how this vacuum is used to operate and control many vehicle systems.
- Inspect and troubleshoot vacuum and air induction systems.
- Explain the function of exhaust system components, including exhaust manifold, gaskets, exhaust pipe and seal, catalytic converter, muffler, resonator, tailpipe, and clamps, brackets, and hangers.
- Properly perform an exhaust system inspection, and service and replace exhaust system components.
- Explain the function and operation of a turbocharger.
- Inspect a turbocharger, and describe some common turbocharger problems.
- Explain supercharger operation, and identify common supercharger problems.

An internal combustion engine requires air to operate. This air supply is drawn into the engine by the vacuum created during the intake stroke of the pistons. The air is mixed with fuel and delivered to the combustion chambers. Controlling the flow of air and the air/fuel mixture is the job of the air induction system.

☐ THE AIR INDUCTION SYSTEM

Prior to the introduction of emission control devices, the air induction system was quite simple. It consisted of an air cleaner housing mounted on top of the engine with a filter inside the housing. Its function was to filter dust and grit from the air being drawn into the carburetor.

Modern air induction systems filter the air and do much more. The introduction of emission standards and fuel economy standards encouraged the development of intake air temperature controls. Figure 12-1 shows a typical thermostatic air cleaner housing with a vacuum motor and temperature sensor. These components draw air warmed by the exhaust manifold into the engine during cold start-up and warm-up.

The air intake system on a modern fuel injected engine is much more complicated (Figure 12-2). Ducts channel cool air from outside the engine compartment to the throttle body. The air filter has moved to a position below the top of the engine to allow for an aerodynamic body design. Electronic meters measure airflow, temperature, and density. Heat riser tubes

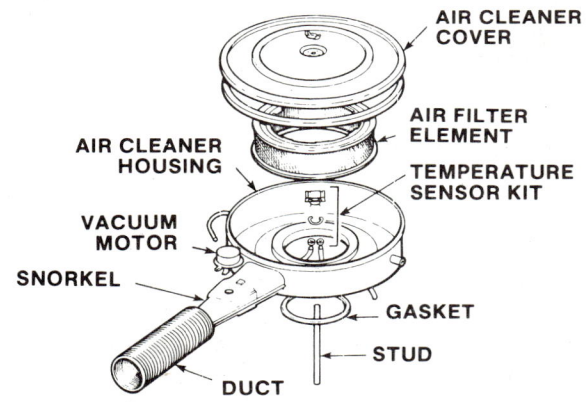

Figure 12-1 Typical air cleaner assembly.

warm the intake air during cold weather warm-up. Pulse air systems provide fresh air to the exhaust stream to oxidize unburned hydrocarbons in the exhaust. These components allow the air induction system to perform the following functions.

- Provide the air that the engine needs to operate
- Filter the air to protect the engine from wear
- Monitor air temperature flow and density for more efficient combustion and reduction of hydrocarbon (HC) and carbon monoxide (CO) emissions
- Control the amount of air flowing into the engine
- Operate in conjunction, with the positive crankcase ventilation (PCV) system to burn the crankcase fumes in the engine
- Provide air for some air injection systems

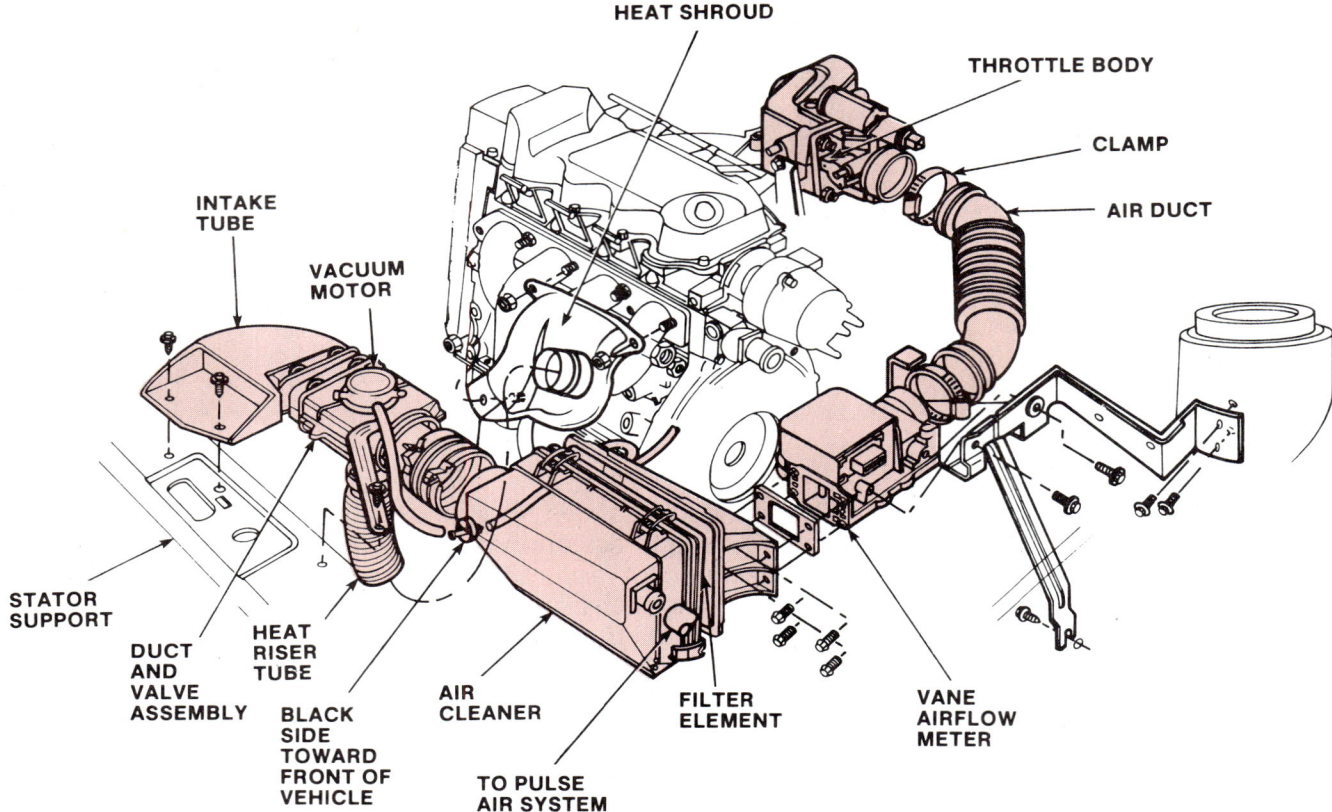

Figure 12-2 Typical air induction system for engines equipped with throttle body fuel injection.

Air Intake Ductwork

Figure 12-3 shows a typical air intake system. Cool air is drawn through the fresh air tube from the leading edge of the engine compartment and routed through a preheat assembly, the air cleaner, and into the carburetor. In a fuel injection system, air usually passes through an air filter and airflow meter before entering a throttle body.

It is important to make sure that the intake ductwork is properly installed and all connections are airtight—especially those between an airflow sensor or remote air cleaner and the carburetor or fuel injection throttle body. Generally metal or plastic ducts are used where engine heat is not a problem. Special paper-metal ducts or all-metal ones are used when they will be exposed to high engine temperatures.

Air Cleaner/Filter

The primary function of the air filter is to prevent airborne contaminants and abrasives from entering into the engine with the air/fuel mixture. Without proper filtration, these contaminants can cause serious damage and appreciably shorten engine life. Remember that all incoming air must pass through the filter element before entering the engine.

The air filter unit used on most cars and light-duty trucks is located inside the air cleaner housing, which can be mounted directly to a flange on the carburetor air horn, the fuel injection throttle body, or the intake manifold (on diesel engines). On late-model automobiles and trucks, it is often also mounted in a remote location on the engine or engine compartment to reduce overall engine height (Figure 12-4). In such cases, the air cleaner unit is connected to the air horn, throttle body, or manifold by an air transfer tube or duct.

The air cleaner assembly also helps muffle noise caused by airflow through the carburetor and intake valve operation. On late-model cars, the air cleaner assembly provides a control and mixing function. Incoming air is maintained at a constant temperature of about 100 degrees Fahrenheit to help reduce emissions and improve engine performance. The air cleaner also provides filtered air to the positive crankcase ventilation (PCV) emission control system and provides engine compartment fire protection in the event of backfire.

Air Filter Design

Air filters are available in two basic designs. Light-duty (standard) air filters are usually made of pleated paper or oil-wetted polyurethane. Heavy-duty air filters have an oil-wetted polyurethane outer cover over a dry paper element. The polyurethane effectively traps larger dirt particles on its surface. The finer particles

Intake and Exhaust Systems   267

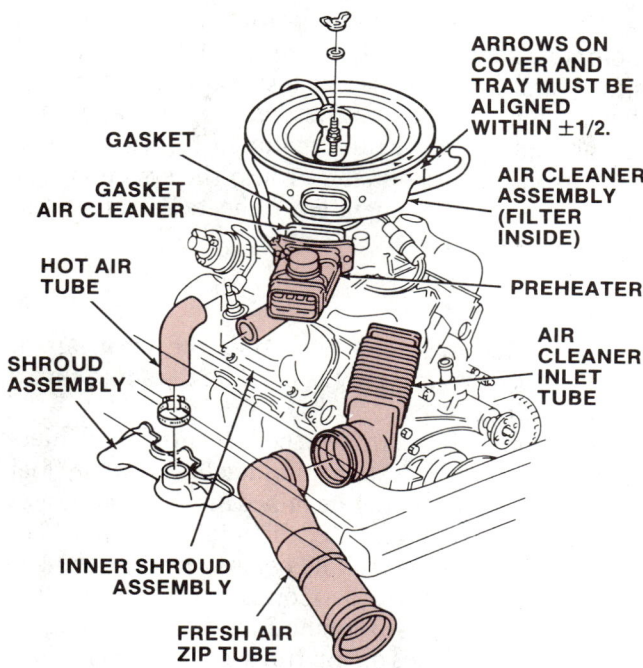

Figure 12-3 Typical air induction system for carburetor-equipped engines.

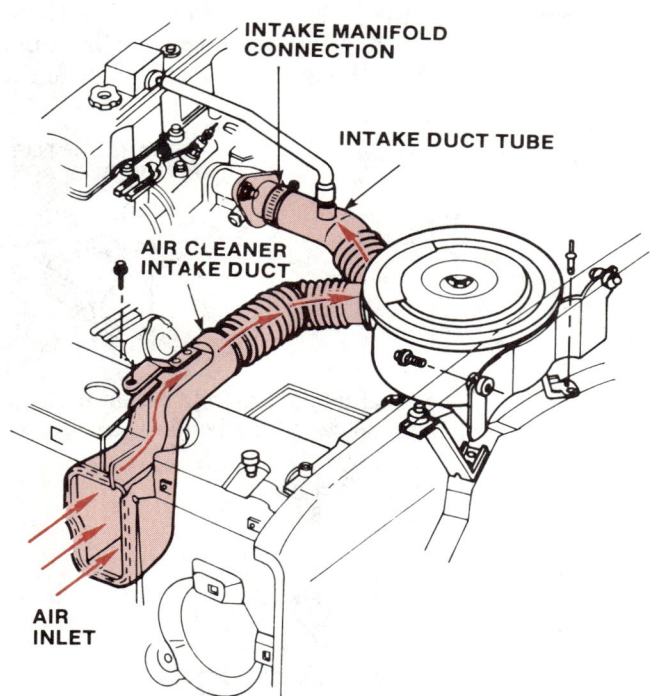

Figure 12-4 Ducts are used on remote air cleaners.

that pass through the polyurethane are trapped by the paper media. The polyurethane outer cover can be removed, cleaned, and reinstalled. This extends filter life.

When selecting a new air filter keep these design features in mind (Figure 12-5).

- Fine mesh screen on the inside reduces the possibility of fire hazards caused by engine backfire.

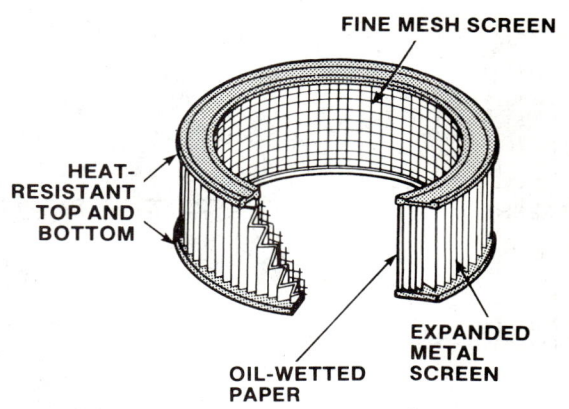

Figure 12-5 Automotive air filter design features.

- Heat-resistant plastisol on the top and bottom with special sealing beads provides a positive dust seal.
- Oil-wetted resin-impregnated paper provides long-lasting filter efficiency.
- Wire or expanded metal outer screen adds construction strength and protects against accidental paper damage during handling and shipping.

Air Filter Servicing

If the air filter becomes very dirty, the dirt will partially block the flow of air into the fuel charging assembly (Figure 12-6). Without enough air, the engine will constantly burn a rich air/fuel mixture. The use of extra fuel means poor fuel economy, and the reduced airflow can cause lack of power.

The engine manufacturer's recommended air filter replacement interval is usually specified in the vehicle owner's service manual. However, replacement of the air filter might be required on a more frequent schedule if the vehicle is subjected to continuous operation in an extremely dusty or severe off-the-road environment.

Certain types of heavy-duty air filters can be cleaned and reused. These filters have a heavy paper media encased in an element with metal end caps. Generally, reusable heavy-duty air filter elements should be replaced with a new element after six cleanings, or once a year.

Thermostatic Air Cleaners

Thermostatic air cleaners are now used on carbureted and throttle body fuel injection engines to heat the intake air when needed. Warm combustion air improves fuel evaporation leading to cleaner burning and therefore lower emissions.

These systems mix air that has been heated by a heat stove (shroud) on the exhaust manifold with cooler outside air to heat the intake air to an ideal combustion temperature (Figure 12-7).

If the heated air inlet door sticks open, heated air cannot reach the engine. The cold air that enters the

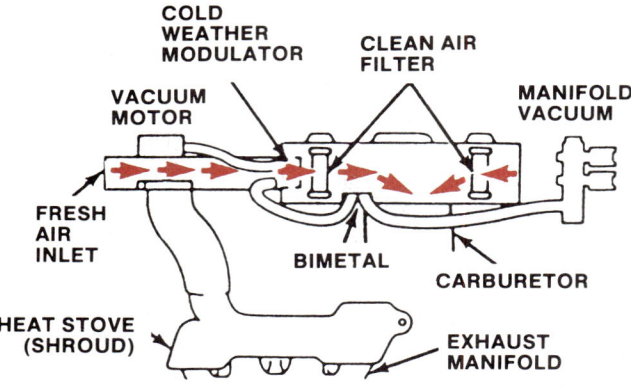

CLEAN AIR FILTER ALLOWS THE REQUIRED AMOUNT OF AIR TO ENTER THE ENGINE.

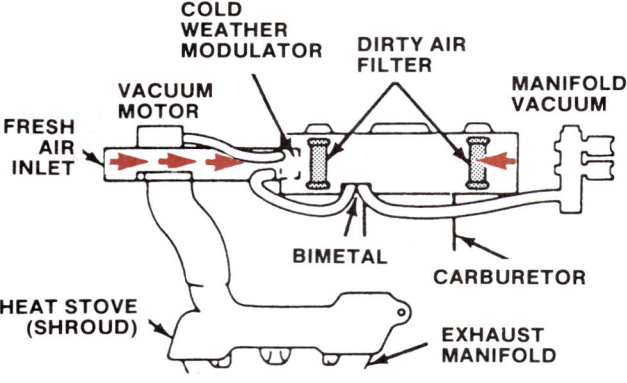

DIRTY AIR FILTER PREVENTS THE REQUIRED AMOUNT OF AIR FROM ENTERING THE ENGINE.

Figure 12-6 Restricted airflow within the induction system caused by a dirty air filter.

engine will not allow the fuel to vaporize completely. Liquid fuel will not ignite as easily as fuel that is vaporized.

A bimetal temperature sensor is used to monitor air temperature within the air cleaner housing. When the temperature is too low, the sensor signals a vacuum motor to close a door in the cold air intake snorkel and route warm air from the exhaust manifold stove into the assembly. If the intake air becomes too warm, the sensor signals the vacuum motor to reopen the door and introduce cold outside air into the system. Complete details on the operation of heated air inlet systems are given in a later chapter.

Intake Manifolds

The intake manifold distributes the clean air or air/fuel mixture as evenly as possible to each cylinder of the engine.

On carbureted and throttle body (central) fuel injection systems the intake manifold delivers an air/fuel mixture. The air and fuel are mixed in the carburetor or throttle body and then enter the intake manifold. The design of the intake manifold helps to prevent condensation and assists in the vaporization of the air/fuel mixture (Figure 12-8). Smooth and efficient engine performance depends on mixtures entering each cylinder that are uniform in strength, quality, and degree of vaporization. This is partly the job of the intake manifold. Ideally, the air/fuel mixture is completely vaporized when it goes into the combustion chamber. Complete vaporization requires high temperature, but high temperature decreases the volumetric efficiency of the

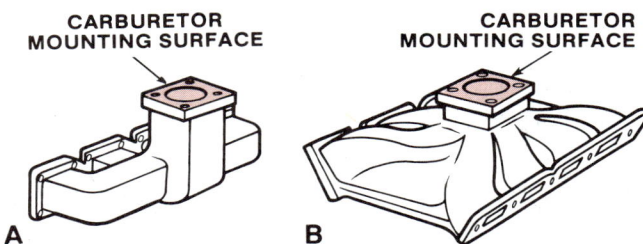

Figure 12-8 (A) Typical intake manifold design used on in-line engines; (B) typical design used on V-type engines.

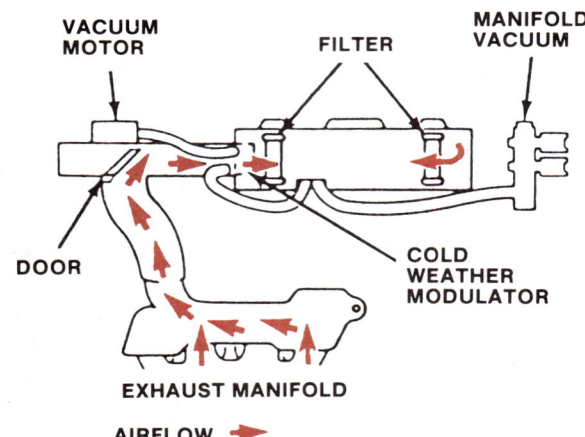

Figure 12-7 Heated air intake system operation.

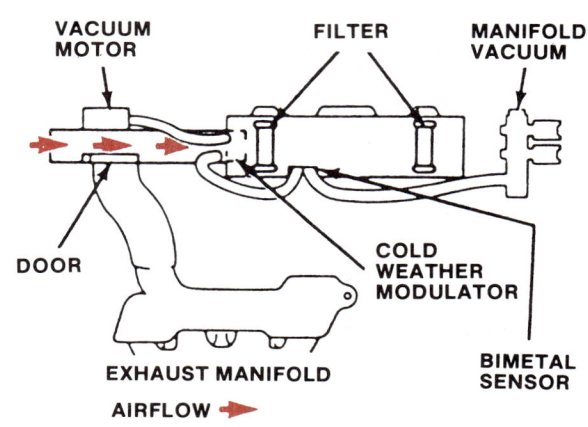

engine. Therefore, the best alternative is to introduce an air/fuel mixture into the manifold that is vaporized above the point where fuel particles will be deposited on the manifold and below the point where excess heat results in power losses.

On port fuel injection and diesel injection systems the intake manifold delivers only clean air to the cylinders. Fuel is introduced into the combustion chamber by the individual fuel injectors. There are many new intake manifold designs for ported gasoline fuel injection. They are often referred to as tuned intake manifolds because they have been redesigned to deliver the most equal amounts of airflow to each cylinder that is possible (Figure 12-9).

Intake manifolds are of cast-iron or die-cast aluminum construction. Aluminum manifolds reduce engine weight. A few are cast integrally with the cylinder head.

Manifolds can be either wet or dry. Wet manifolds have coolant passages cast directly into the manifold. Dry manifolds do not have cooling passages. Some intake manifolds have an integrally cast water crossover passage. This allows coolant to flow through a passage below the carburetor and warm the incoming air/fuel mixture.

Manifold design varies greatly depending on engine types. For example, on four-cylinder engines, the intake manifold has either four runners or two runners that break into four near the cylinder head (Figure 12-10). On in-line six-cylinder engines, there are either six runners or three that branch off into six near the cylinder head. On V-configuration engines (V-6 and V-8), both open and closed intake manifolds are made. Open intake manifolds have an open space between the bottom of the manifold and the valve lifter valley.

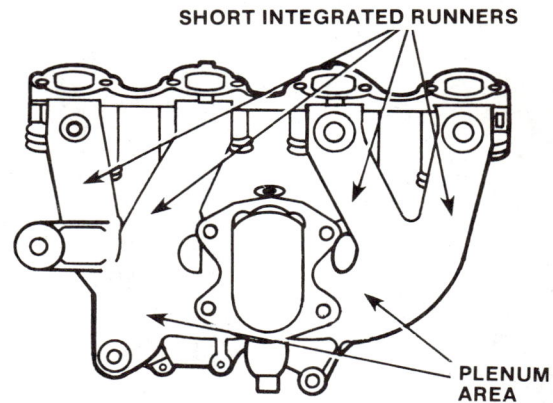

Figure 12-10 The intake manifold on an in-line four-cylinder engine.

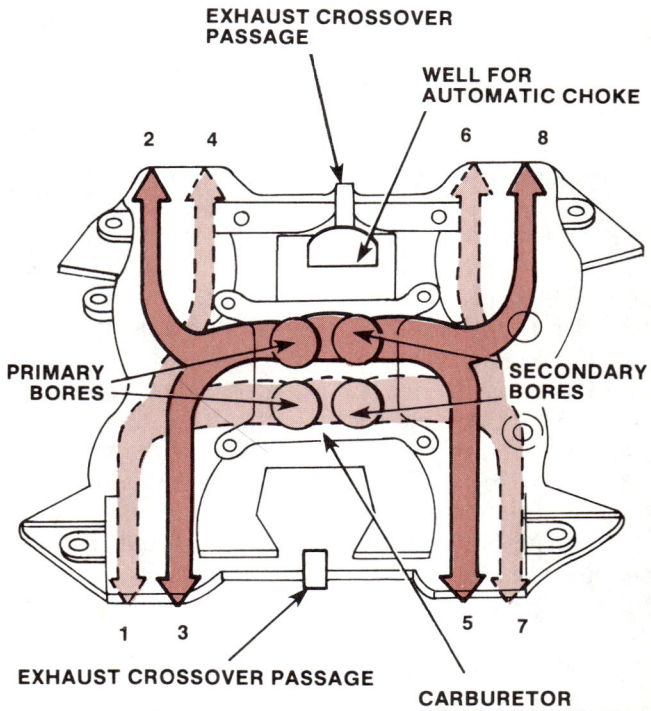

Figure 12-11 V-8 engine intake manifold. Note how cylinders are fed from carburetor boxes. Exhaust crossover passage provides heat for improved fuel vaporization and prevents carburetor icing.

Closed intake manifolds act as the cover to the lifter valley.

On some manifolds, there is an exhaust crossover passage (Figure 12-11). This passage allows the exhaust from one side of the engine to cross over through the intake manifold to the other side to be exhausted. The exhaust crossover provides heat to the base of the carburetor to improve the vaporization of the fuel while the engine is warming up. On many engines, the exhaust crossover is also used to provide automatic choke heat. On in-line engines the heat riser valve also directs heat to the base of the carburetor. Some engines use an

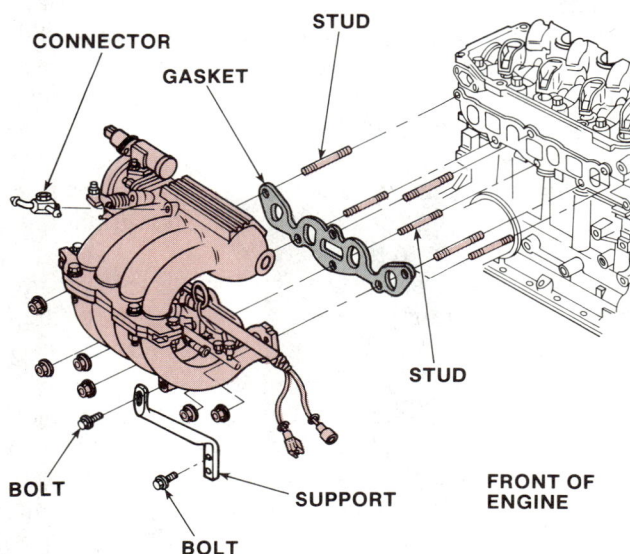

Figure 12-9 This type of tuned intake manifold, used with ported fuel injection, gives a more equal amount of air to each cylinder.

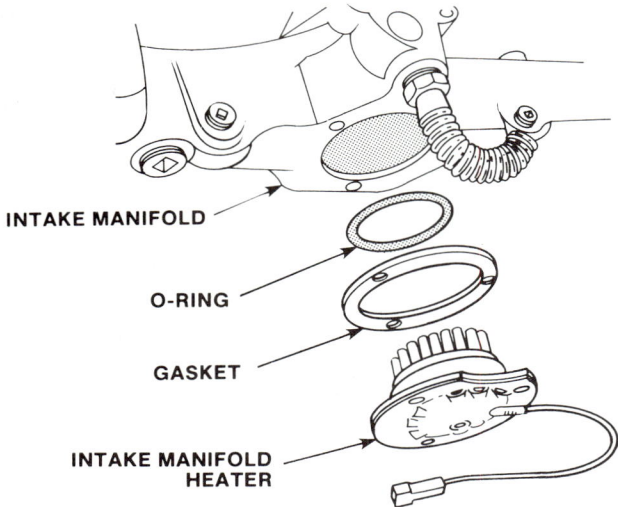

Figure 12-12 Intake manifold for an in-line engine with electric heater.

electric grid or heater located under the carburetor to improve vaporization and reduce icing (Figure 12-12).

Intake manifolds for V-type engines may include coolant connecting passages between cylinder heads. Some include a provision for mounting the thermostat and thermostat housing. In addition, connections to the intake manifold in some vehicles provide the necessary vacuum source for exhaust gas recirculation valves (EGR), automatic transmission vacuum modulators, distributor vacuum advance units, thermostatic air cleaners, power brakes, and heater and air-conditioning airflow control doors. Other devices include manifold absolute pressure sensors, manifold air temperature sensors, knock sensors, and exhaust gas recirculation passages.

Vacuum Systems

The vacuum created in the intake manifold is used to operate many systems, such as emission controls, brake boosters, parking brake releases, headlight doors, heater/air conditioners, and cruise controls. Vacuum is applied to these systems through a system of hoses and tubes, which can become quite elaborate.

Vacuum Basics

The term vacuum refers to a pressure level that is lower than the earth's atmospheric pressure at any given altitude. The higher the altitude, the lower the atmospheric pressure.

Vacuum is measured in relation to atmospheric pressure. Atmospheric pressure is the pressure exerted on every object on earth and is caused by the weight of the surrounding air. At sea level, the pressure exerted by the atmosphere is 14.7 psi (absolute). Most pressure gauges ignore atmospheric pressure and read zero under normal conditions. But, the usual measure of vacuum is in in. Hg instead of psi. Other units of measurement for vacuum seen on automotive service gauges are kilopascals and bars. Normal atmospheric pressure at sea level is about 1 bar or 100 kilopascals.

Vacuum in any four-stroke engine is created by the downward movement of the piston during the intake stroke. With the intake valve open and the piston moving downward, a partial vacuum is created within the cylinder and intake manifold. A pressure lower than atmospheric is formed by the sudden increase in cylinder volume caused by the downward movement of the piston. The air passing the intake valve does not move fast enough to fill the cylinder, thereby causing the lower pressure. This partial vacuum is continuous in a multi-cylinder engine, since at least one cylinder is always at some stage of its intake cycle.

The amount of vacuum created is partially related to the positioning of the choke (on carbureted vehicles) and to the throttle plates. The throttle plate not only admits air or air/fuel into the intake manifold, it also helps to control the amount of vacuum available during engine operation. At closed throttle idle, the vacuum available is usually between 15 to 22 inches. At a wide-open throttle acceleration, the vacuum can drop to zero.

Increased Vacuum Controls

The intake manifold on early engines simply connected the carburetor to the engine. It did not have any auxiliary vacuum plugs or connections.

From the 1920s to the early 1970s, a single vacuum line was normally found. It either operated the vacuum advance of the distributor or the windshield wipers.

Since the 1970s, there has been an explosion in the number of systems using vacuum control. In fact, vacuum systems used on today's vehicles are probably more complicated than most electrical systems used during the 1970s. The use of electronic engine controls have further complicated the vacuum system. Where once a vacuum line may have run from a carburetor to the exhaust gas recirculation valve, it now goes from the carburetor to a computer-controlled vacuum relay solenoid and then to the valve.

In addition to being used to draw filtered air into the engine, vacuum is typically used to control these systems.

- Fuel Induction System. Certain vacuum-operated devices are added to carburetors and some central fuel-injection throttle bodies to ease engine start-up, warm-and-cold engine driveaway, and to compensate for air conditioner load on the engine.
- Emission Control System. While some emission control output devices are solenoid or linkage controlled, many operate on vacuum. This vacuum is

usually controlled by solenoids that are opened or closed, depending on electrical signals received from the electronic control assembly (ECA). The PCV valve is an important part of the air induction system. It delivers gases at normal cruise speeds when the engine can best handle them. Other systems use switches that are controlled by engine coolant temperature, such as a ported vacuum switch (PVS), or by ambient air such as a temperature vacuum switch (TVS).

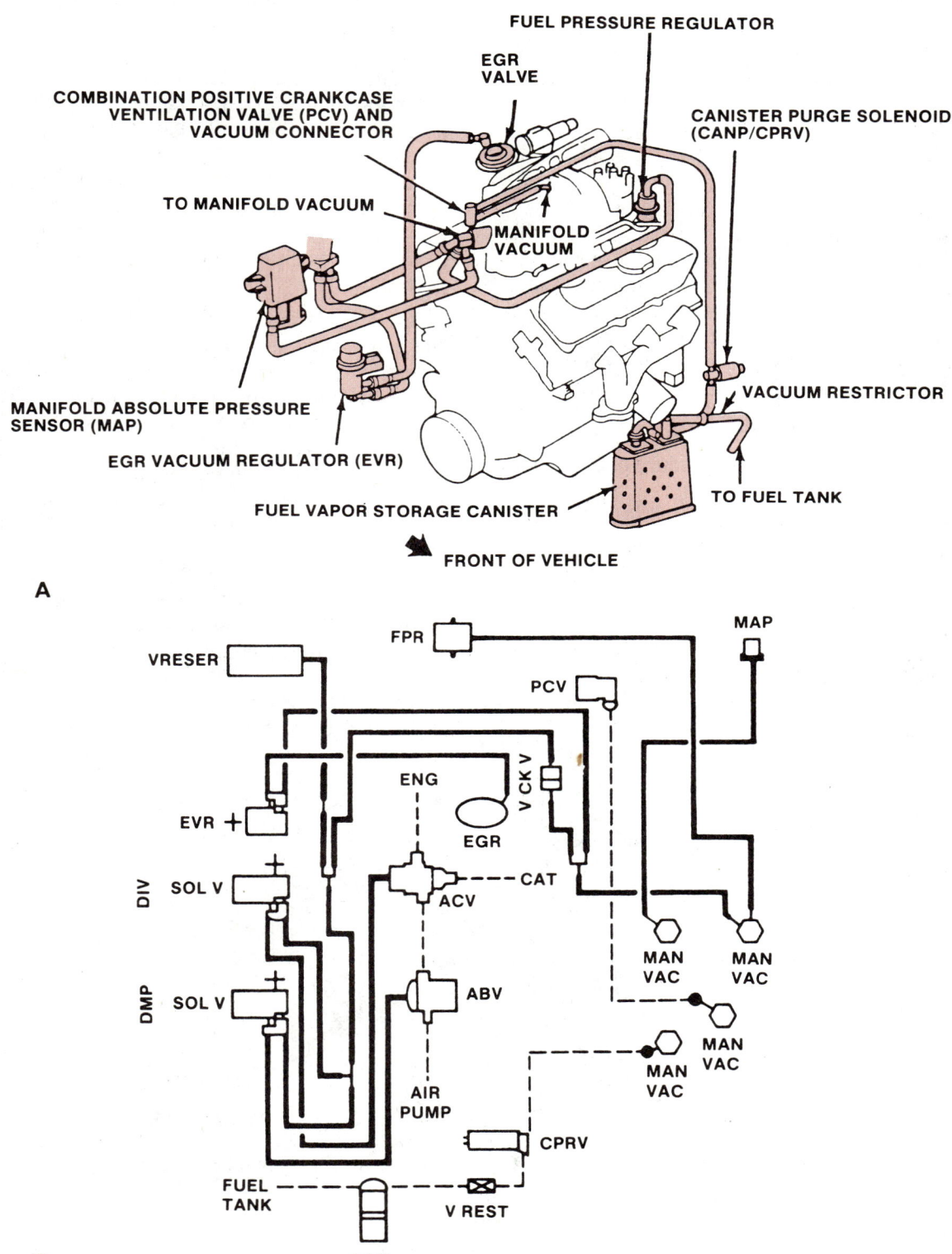

Figure 12-13 (A) New style line-drawn vacuum schematic; (B) old style vacuum schematic.

- Accessory Controls. Engine vacuum is used to control operation of certain accessories, such as air conditioner/heater systems, power brake boosters, speed-control components, automatic transmission vacuum modulators, and so on.

Vacuum Schematic

An engine emissions vacuum schematic is required on all domestic and import vehicles. It is located on an underhood decal. This schematic shows the vacuum hose routings and vacuum source for all emissions-related equipment. The vacuum schematic shown in Figure 12-13A is a new-style line-drawing schematic that shows the relationship and position of components as they are mounted on the engine. This new type of schematic is easier to understand than the flat-plane road-map vacuum schematics used in the past (Figure 12-13B). It is important to remember that these schematics only show emission system vacuum equipment. Hose routing and equipment positions for vacuum devices not related to emissions equipment can be found in the service manual.

Diagnosis and Troubleshooting

Vacuum system problems can produce or contribute to the following driveability symptoms.

- Stalls
- No start (cold)
- Hard start (floods hot)
- Backfire (deceleration)
- Rough idle
- Poor acceleration
- Rich or lean stumble
- Overheating
- Detonation, or knock or pinging
- Rotten eggs exhaust odor
- Poor fuel economy

As a routine part of problem diagnosis, a technician suspecting a vacuum problem should first

- Inspect vacuum hoses for improper routing or disconnections (engine decal identifies hose routing).
- Look for kinks, tears, or cuts in vacuum lines.
- Check for vacuum hose routing and wear near hot spots, such as exhaust manifold or the EGR tubes.
- Make sure there is no evidence of oil or transmission fluid on vacuum hose connections. (Valves can become contaminated by oil getting inside).
- Inspect vacuum system devices for damage (dents in cans; by-pass valves; broken nipples on VCV or PVS valves; broken "tees" in vacuum lines, and so on).

Broken or disconnected hoses allow vacuum leaks that admit more air into the intake manifold than the engine is calibrated for. The most common result is a rough running engine due to the leaner air/fuel mixture created by the excess air.

Kinked hoses can cut off vacuum to a component, thereby disabling it. For example, if the vacuum hose to the exhaust gas recirculation valve is kinked, vacuum cannot be used to move the diaphragm. Therefore, the valve will not open.

To check vacuum controls, refer to the vehicle manufacturer's service manual for the correct location and identification of components. Typical locations of vacuum-controlled components are shown in Figure 12-14.

Remember, when troubleshooting the system, the underhood decal shows routing for emission equip-

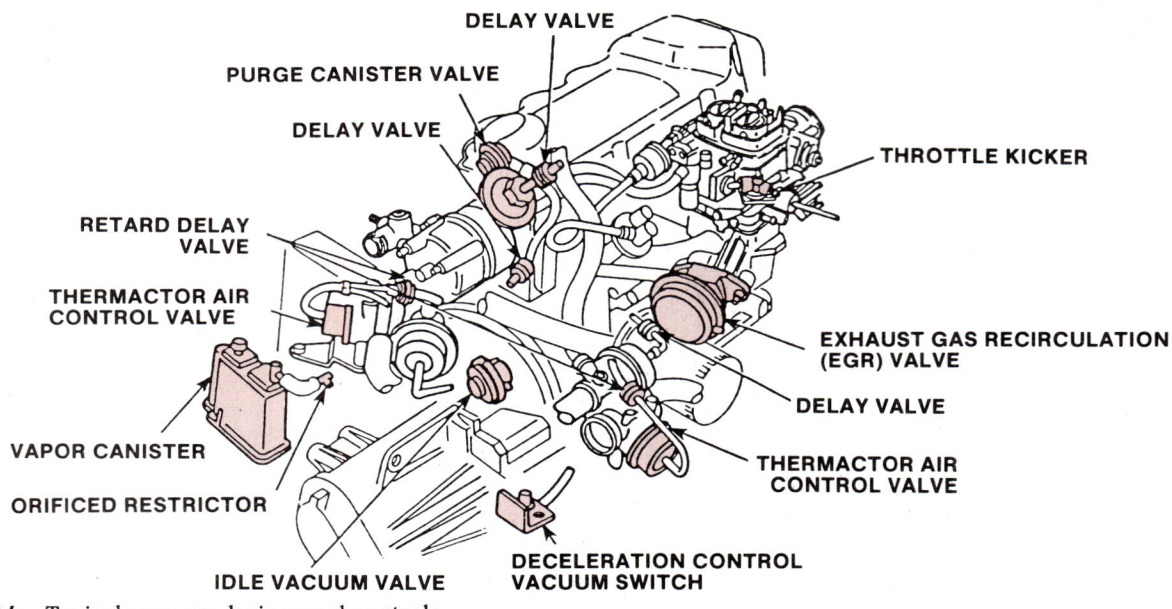

Figure 12-14 Typical vacuum devices and controls.

Intake and Exhaust Systems 273

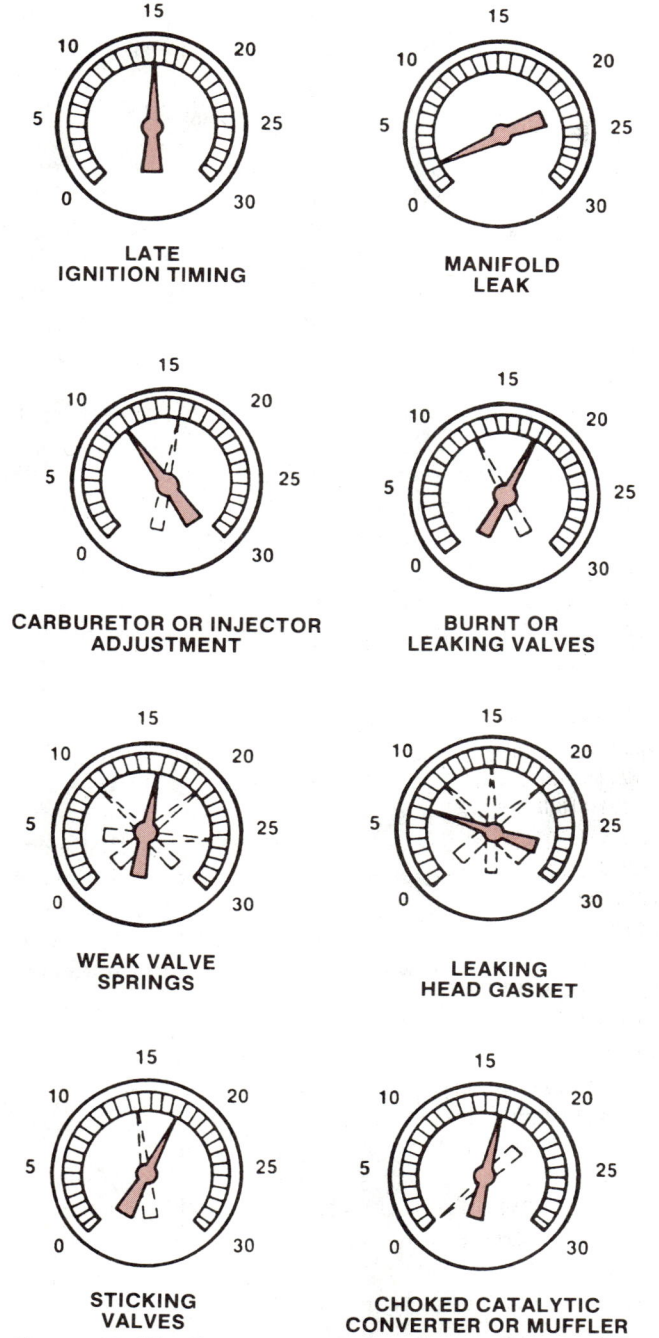

Figure 12-15 Common vacuum gauge readings and the conditions they indicate.

provide a seal between the nylon connector and the component connection (nipple). In recent years, many domestic car manufacturers have been using ganged steel vacuum lines.

Vacuum Test Equipment

Until the introduction of the computerized engine analyzer, the vacuum gauge was one of the most important engine diagnostic tools used by service technicians. With the gauge installed according to manufacturer's instruction and the engine warm and idling properly, watch the action of the gauge's needle. A healthy engine will give a steady, constant vacuum reading between 17 and 22 in. Hg. On some four- and six-cylinder engines, however, a reading of 15 inches is considered acceptable. With high-performance engines, a slight flicker of the needle can also be expected. Keep in mind that the gauge reading will drop about 1 inch for each 1,000 feet above sea level. Figure 12-15 shows some of the common readings and what engine malfunctions they indicate.

As shown in Figure 12-16, a hand-held vacuum pump/gauge is used to test vacuum-actuated valves and motors. If the component does not operate when the proper amount of vacuum is applied, it should be serviced or replaced.

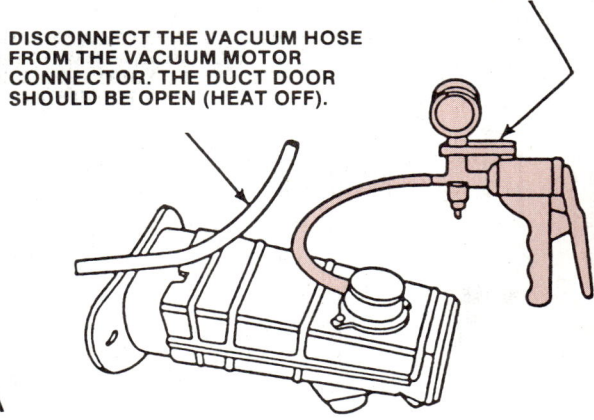

A

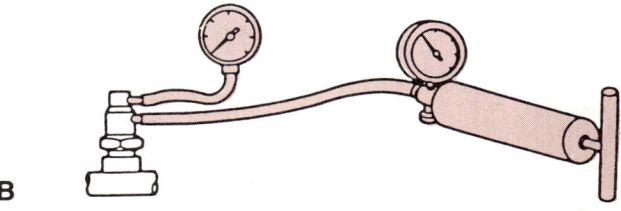

B

Figure 12-16 (A) Hand-operated vacuum pump being used to test an air cleaner vacuum motor; (B) two-port/four-port VCV or PVS test.

ment vacuum hoses only. Vacuum lines for brakes, accessories, and other equipment must not, however, be overlooked. Tears and kinks in these lines can also affect engine operation.

Any defective hoses should be replaced one at a time to avoid misrouting. OEM equipped vacuum lines are installed in a harness consisting of 1/8-inch or larger outer diameter and 1/16-inch inner diameter nylon hose with bonded nylon or rubber connectors. Occasionally, a rubber hose might be connected to the harness. The nylon connectors have rubber inserts to

EXHAUST SYSTEM COMPONENTS

The various components of the typical exhaust system include the following.

- Exhaust manifold
- Exhaust pipe and seal
- Catalytic converter
- Muffler
- Resonator
- Tail pipe
- Heat shields
- Clamps, brackets, and hangers

All the parts of the system are designed to conform to the available space of the vehicle's undercarriage and yet be a safe distance above the road.

WARNING: When inspecting or working on the exhaust system, remember that its components get very hot when the engine is running and contact with them could cause a severe burn. Also, always wear safety glasses or goggles when working under a vehicle.

Exhaust Manifold

The exhaust manifold (Figure 12-17) is a bank of pipes that collects the burnt gases as they are expelled from the engine's cylinders and directs them to the exhaust pipe. Exhaust manifolds for most vehicles are made of cast- or nodular-iron. Some newer, smaller passenger vehicles have stamped, heavy-gauge sheet metal or stainless steel units. The manifold unit has one port for each cylinder.

In-line engines have one exhaust manifold. V-type engines have an exhaust manifold on each side of the engine. An exhaust manifold will have either three, four, or six passages (depending on the type of engine) at one end. These passages blend into a single passage at the other end, which connects to an exhaust pipe. From here, the flow of exhaust gases continues to the back of the car.

V-type engines may be equipped with a dual exhaust system that consists of two almost identical, but individual systems in the same vehicle (Figure 12-18). Dual exhaust systems are excellent when designed into the vehicle by the manufacturer, who usually specifies them only for large displacement engines. The dual system is seldom very useful on smaller engines.

Exhaust systems are designed for particular engine-chassis combinations. Exhaust system length, pipe size, and silencer are designed to make use of the tuning effect of the gas column resonating within the exhaust system. Tuning occurs when the exhaust pulses are emptied into the manifold between the pulses of other cylinders. Proper tuning of the exhaust manifold tubes can actually create a vacuum that helps to draw exhaust gases out of the cylinder, improving volumetric efficiency. Separate, tuned exhaust headers (Figure 12-19) can also improve efficiency by preventing the exhaust flow of one cylinder from interfering

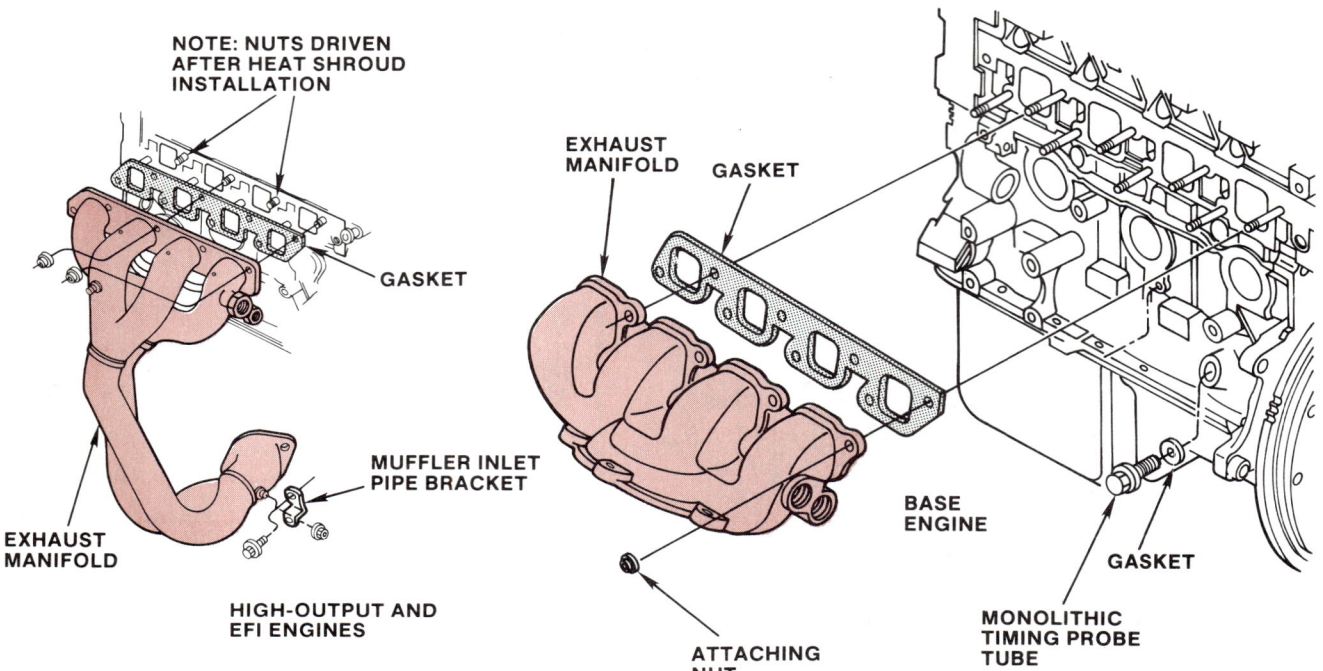

Figure 12-17 Exhaust manifold designs for an in-line engine.

Intake and Exhaust Systems

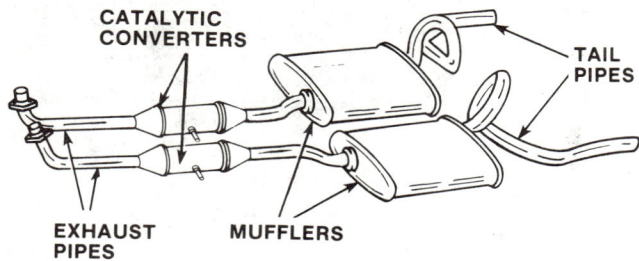

Figure 12-18 Dual exhaust system.

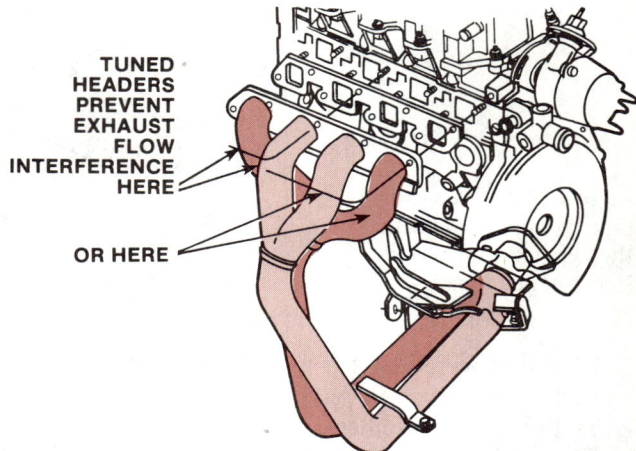

Figure 12-20 Tuned exhaust headers in a four-cylinder engine designed to prevent flow interference.

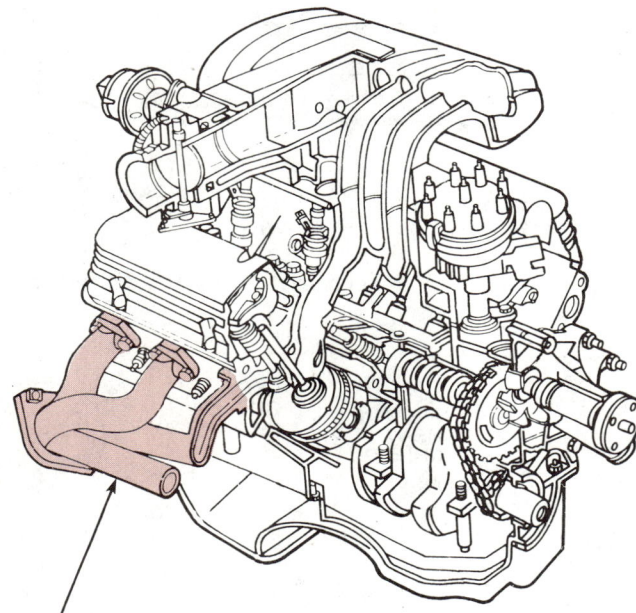

Figure 12-19 Efficiency can be improved with tuned exhaust headers.

with the exhaust flow of another cylinder. Cylinders next to one another may release exhaust gas at about the same time. When this happens, the pressure of the exhaust gas from one cylinder can interfere with the flow from the other cylinder (Figure 12-20). With separate headers, the cylinders are isolated from one another, interference is eliminated, and the engine breathes better. The problem of interference is especially common with V-8 engines. V-6 engines have less of an exhaust overlap problem.

Four-cylinder engines often have an exhaust overlap problem with the first and second or third and fourth cylinders. While the overlap is usually not as severe as with a V-8 engine, the result is quite noticeable. Half of the engine's cylinders are affected.

Exhaust Pipe and Seal

The exhaust pipe is metal pipe—either aluminized steel, stainless steel, or zinc-plated heavy-gauge steel—that runs under the vehicle between the exhaust manifold.

Some type of emission control, such as an exhaust gas recirculation (EGR) valve, early fuel evaporation (EFE) valve, or a heat riser valve, is usually mounted between the exhaust manifold and the exhaust pipe. In an electronic engine-control system, an oxygen sensor is installed in the exhaust pipe. This device is used to sense the amount of oxygen in the exhaust gas and to send signals to an electronic control unit to change the mixture of air and fuel being delivered to the engine.

Intermediate, or connecting, zinc-plated steel or stainless steel pipes are used at any point past the exhaust pipe to join the exhaust system components (Figure 12-21).

SHOP TALK

The exhaust manifold gasket seals the joint between the head and exhaust manifold. Many new engines are assembled without exhaust manifold gaskets. This is possible because new manifolds are flat and fit tightly against the head without leaks. During use, the exhaust manifolds go through many heating/cooling cycles. This causes stress and some corrosion in the exhaust manifold. Removing the manifold will usually distort the manifold slightly so it is no longer flat enough to seal without a gasket. Exhaust manifold gaskets are normally used to eliminate leaks when exhaust manifolds are reinstalled. When replacing exhaust manifold gaskets, be sure to follow the manufacturer's instructions.

Catalytic Converters

The catalytic converter (CC) has been the biggest change in exhaust systems over the years. It was added in the mid-1970s to reduce emissions, but car makers

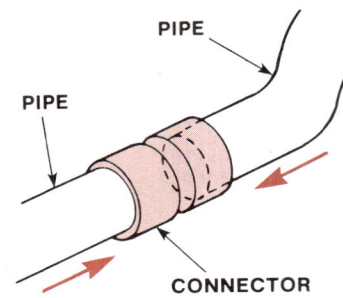

Figure 12-21 Exhaust pipe coupling connecting the exhaust pipe with the intermediate pipe.

quickly discovered that it also did part of the job of silencing the exhaust. As a result, mufflers have become lighter and simpler.

The catalytic converter is located ahead of the muffler in the exhaust system. The extreme heat in the converter oxidizes the exhaust that flows out of the engine. A catalyst is a substance that causes a chemical reaction in other elements without actually becoming a part of the chemical change itself and without being used up or consumed in the process. An automotive CC is a device that uses catalysts to cause a change in the elements of the waste exhaust gases as they pass through the exhaust system.

The catalyst elements used in catalytic converters are platinum, palladium, and rhodium. These elements are used alone or in combination to change the undesirable CO, HC, and NO_x into harmless water vapor, CO_2, N, and O_2 (Figure 12-22).

There are several types of catalytic converters. The most common follow.

PELLET CATALYTIC CONVERTER Uses hundreds of small beads that act as the catalyst agent (Figure 12-23A).

MONOLITHIC CATALYTIC CONVERTER Uses a ceramic block shaped like a honeycomb or beehive that is coated with a special chemical that helps the converter act on the exhaust gases (Figure 12-23B).

THREE-WAY CONVERTER The dual-bed type (Figure 12-24) treats all three controlled emission gases. It oxidizes HC and CO by adding oxygen and reduces NO_x by removing oxygen from the nitrogen oxides.

MINICATALYTIC CONVERTER Provides a close coupled converter that is either built in the engine exhaust

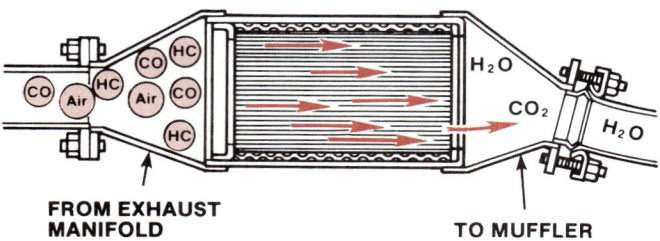

Figure 12-22 How a conventional catalytic converter works.

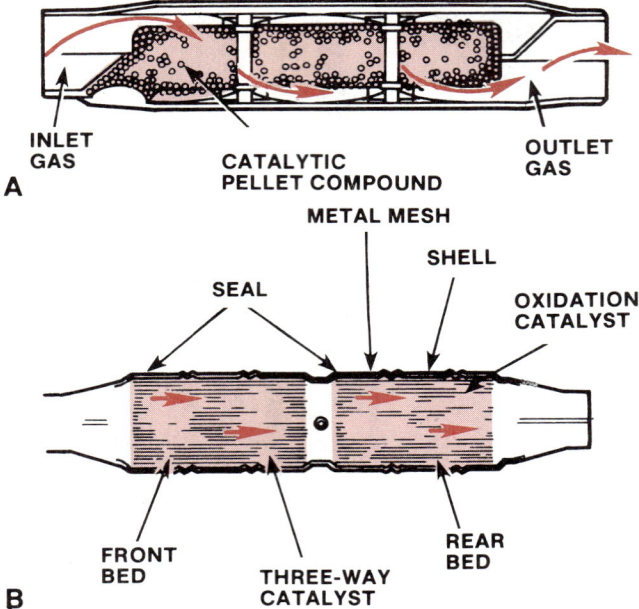

Figure 12-23 (A) Pellet catalytic converter; (B) monolithic catalytic converter.

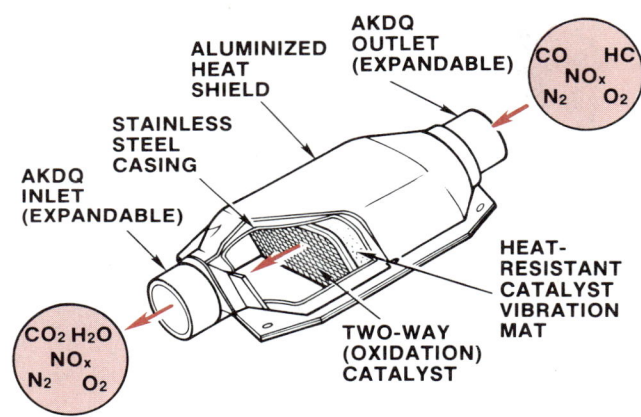

Figure 12-24 Three-way or dual-bed converter.

manifold or located next to it (Figure 12-25). It is primarily used as a second converter.

PARTICULATE OXIDIZER CATALYTIC CONVERTER Uses a monolithic element, located between the exhaust manifold and turbocharger, to react to the particulates of a diesel engine (Figure 12-26). Particulates are solid particles of carbon-like soot that are emitted from the diesel engine as black smoke.

> **SHOP TALK**
>
> Because of constant change in EPA catalytic converter removal and installation requirements, check with the CC manufacturer or EPA for the latest data regarding replacement.

Intake and Exhaust Systems   **277**

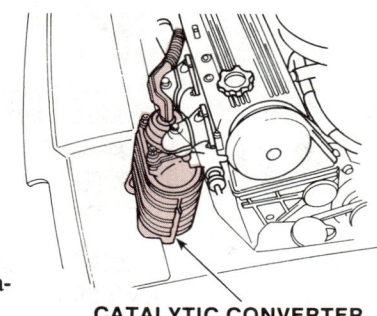

Figure 12-25 Minicatalytic converter.

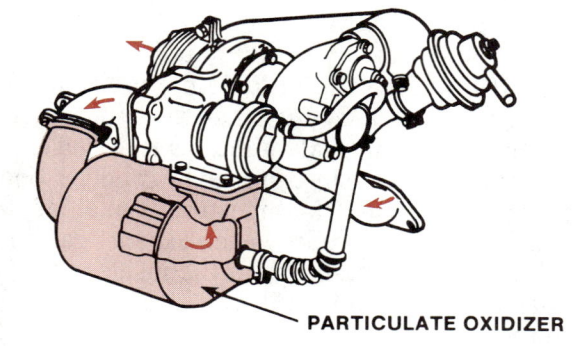

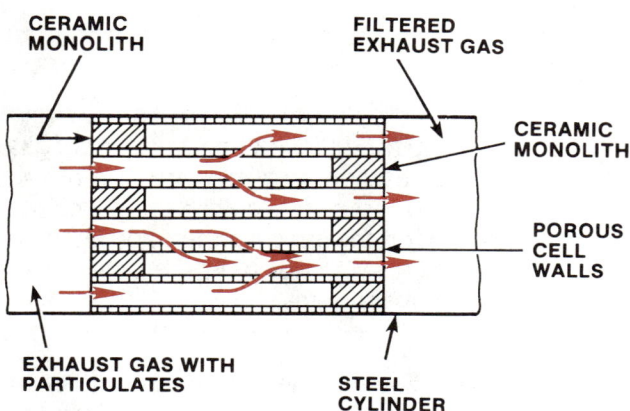

Figure 12-26 Particulate catalytic converter.

The converter is normally a trouble-free emission and exhaust control device, but two things can damage it. One is leaded gasoline. Lead coats the catalyst and renders it useless. The difficulty of obtaining leaded gasoline has reduced this problem. The other is overheating. If raw fuel enters the exhaust because of a fouled spark plug or leaky exhaust valve, the temperature of the converter will soar. This can melt the ceramic honeycomb or pellets inside, causing a severe or complete exhaust blockage.

CUSTOMER CARE

To avoid converter overheating, advise customers to use unleaded fuel only. They should also avoid prolonged idling (20 minutes or more) or coasting with the ignition turned off. Running on very low fuel levels may also cause a misfire that can overload the converter.

Follow these precautions in the shop and on test drives. In addition, avoid prolonged engine compression measurement or spark jump testing. They can allow fuel to collect in the converter. When needed, perform these tests as rapidly as possible.

A plugged converter produces the characteristic symptoms of an exhaust restriction: loss of power at high speeds, stalling after starting (if totally blocked), a drop in engine vacuum as engine rpm increases, or sometimes popping or backfiring at the carburetor.

Converter efficiency usually requires special test equipment. The best way to check the operation of a catalytic converter is with a four-gas infrared exhaust analyzer. When testing the condition of CC, carefully follow the directions given in the manufacturer's service manual.

Another way to test a converter is to use a hand-held digital pyrometer, an electronic device that measures heat. By touching the pyrometer probe to the exhaust pipe just ahead of and just behind the converter, it is possible to read an increase of at least 100 degrees as the exhaust gases pass through the converter. If the outlet temperature is the same or lower, nothing is happening inside the converter. Do not be quick to condemn the converter. To do its job efficiently, the converter needs a steady supply of oxygen from the air pump. A bad pump, faulty diverter valve or control valve, leaky air connections, or faulty computer control over the air injection system could be preventing the needed oxygen from reaching the converter.

Once a CC is determined faulty, replacement is usually best. There are two types of replacement. Installation kits (Figure 12-27) include all necessary components for the installation. There are also direct-fit catalytic converters (Figure 12-28).

SHOP TALK

Under no circumstances should the converter be removed and replaced with a straight piece of pipe (a test pipe). This practice is illegal for the professional auto mechanic.

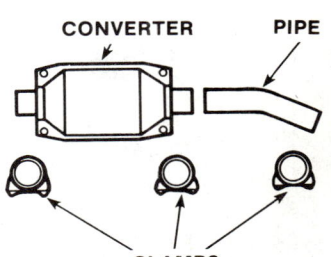

Figure 12-27 Catalytic converter installation kit.

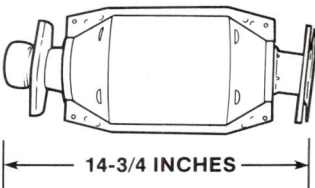

Figure 12-28 Direct fit catalytic converter replaces original equipment with no modification to the exhaust system.

Mufflers

The muffler is a cylindrical or oval-shaped component, generally about 2 feet long, mounted in the exhaust system about midway or toward the rear of the car. It consists of a series of baffles, chambers, tubes, and holes to break up, cancel out, or silence the pressure pulsations that occur each time an exhaust valve opens.

Two types of mufflers are commonly used on passenger vehicles (Figure 12-29). Reverse-flow mufflers change the direction of the exhaust gas flow through the inside of the unit. This is the most common type of muffler found on passenger cars. Straight-through mufflers permit exhaust gases to pass through a single tube. The tube has perforations that tend to break up pressure pulsations. They are not as quiet as the reverse-flow type.

Though mufflers still reduce noise as the exhaust gases pulse through them, there have been several important changes in recent years in their design. Most of these changes have been centered at reducing weight and emissions, improving fuel economy, and simplifying assembly. Many also affect the technician who repairs or replaces the system. These changes include the following.

NEW MATERIALS More and more mufflers are being made of aluminized and stainless steel. Car designers, trying to make exhaust systems lighter, sometimes call for thinner metal for some components.

> ### SHOP TALK
> Remember that stainless steel pipe tends to break rather than rust out. It might take some tact to explain to the customers why a cracked pipe that does not look rusted is actually worn out. Also, if low-quality components are used where the car had stainless or aluminized steel, you are likely to end up with a premature rust-out and an unhappy customer.

DOUBLE-WALL DESIGN Retarded engine ignition timing that is used on many small cars tends to make the exhaust pulses sharper. Many small cars now use a double-wall exhaust pipe to better contain the sound and reduce pipe ring.

REAR-MOUNTED MUFFLERS More and more often, the only space left under the car for the muffler is at the very rear. This means that the muffler runs cooler than before and is more easily damaged by condensation in the exhaust system. This moisture, combined with nitrogen and sulfur oxides in the exhaust gas, forms acids that rot the muffler from the inside out. Many mufflers are being produced with drain holes drilled in to them.

> ### CUSTOMER CARE
> Many customers do not always like the drain holes because they allow a small amount of gas and noise to escape, but they are one of the cheapest and most effective ways to fight corrosion. Explain this to your customers and let them make the choice. Do not plug the drain holes with a sheet metal screw.

BACK PRESSURE Even a well-designed muffler will produce some back pressure in the system. Back pressure reduces an engine's volumetric efficiency, or ability to "breathe." Excessive back pressure caused by defects in a muffler or other exhaust system part can slow or stop the engine. However, a small amount of back pressure can be used intentionally to allow a slower passage of exhaust gases through the catalytic converter. This slower passage results in more complete conversion to less harmful gases.

ELECTRONIC MUFFLERS Basically, sensors and microphones pick up the pattern of the pressure waves an engine emits from its exhaust pipe (Figure 12-30). This data is analyzed by a computer. A mirror-image pattern of pulses is instantly produced and sent to speakers mounted near the exhaust outlet. Contra-waves are created that cancel out the noise. Electronic mufflers have been introduced in heavy-duty truck applications, and several manufacturers suggest that they be used on some passenger vehicles by the mid-1990s.

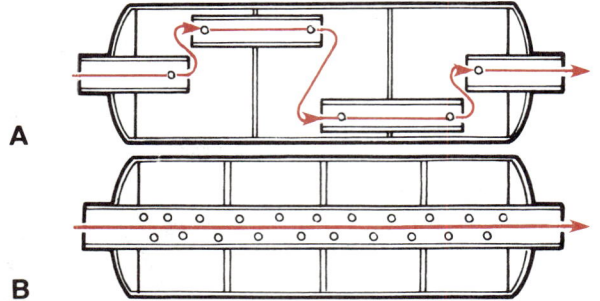

Figure 12-29 (A) Reverse-flow muffler; (B) straight-through muffler.

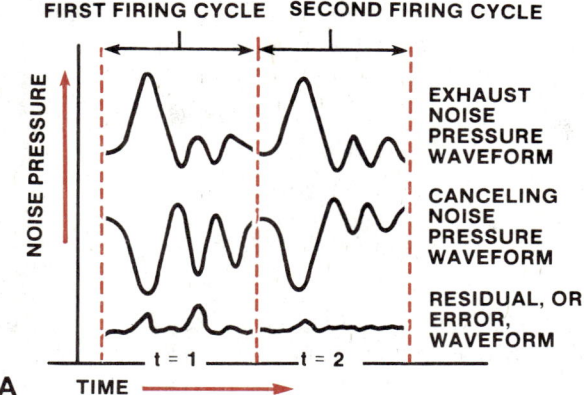

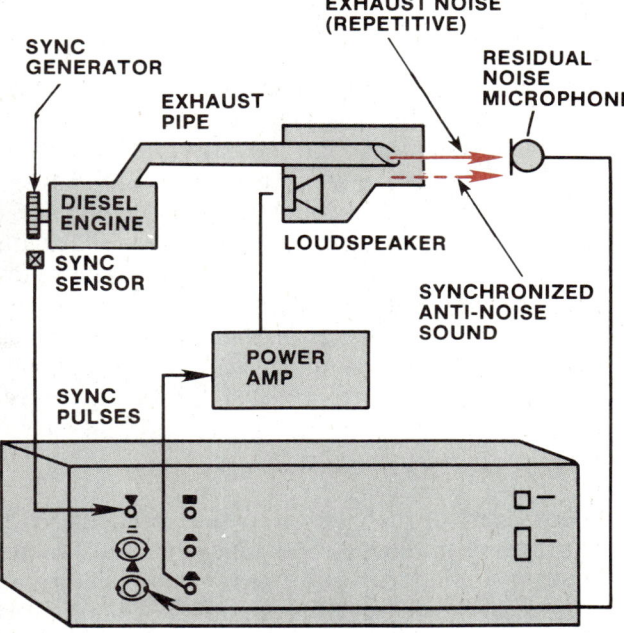

Figure 12-30 (A) An electronic muffler might seem far-fetched, but the production of a mirror image, out-of-phase waveform can cancel out sound. (B) Schematic shows how sensors, microphones, and speakers are teamed up to alternate noise.

Resonator

On some vehicles, there is an additional muffler, known as a resonator or silencer, to further reduce the sound level of the exhaust. This is located toward the end of the system and generally looks like a smaller, rounder version of a muffler. The resonator is constructed like a straight-through muffler and is connected to the muffler by an intermediate pipe.

Because of vehicle manufacturers' concern with weight and cost, resonators have been eliminated on nearly all model cars. On cars equipped with a resonator, the resonator can be located in the middle of the tail pipe. In fact, the resonator on some cars is an integral part of the tail pipe, forming a one-piece unit.

Intake and Exhaust Systems   279

If one or the other is damaged, the entire unit must be replaced.

Tail Pipe

The tail pipe is the end of the pipeline carrying exhaust fumes to the atmosphere beyond the back end of the car. In most cases, the tail pipe opens at the rear of the vehicle below the rear bumper. In some cases, it opens at the side of the vehicle just ahead of or just behind the rear wheel. Decorative tail pipe exhaust extensions in either chrome or black are available (Figure 12-31). Most extensions are fastened to the tail pipe with double-lock screws. The downward exhaust spout deflects gases down and away from the vehicle.

Heat Shields

Heat shields are used to protect vehicle parts from the heat of the exhaust system and catalytic converter (Figure 12-32). They are usually made of pressed or perforated sheet metal.

Clamps, Brackets, and Hangers

Clamps, brackets, and hangers are used to properly join and support various exhaust system components

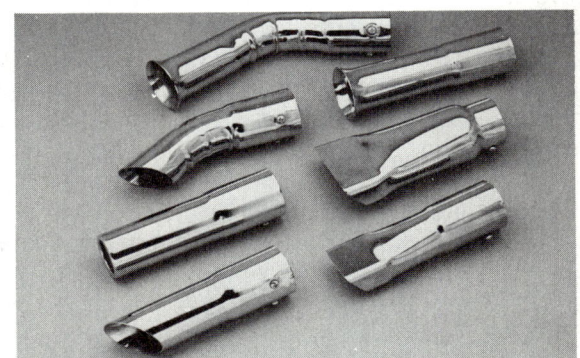

Figure 12-31 Decorative exhaust extensions.

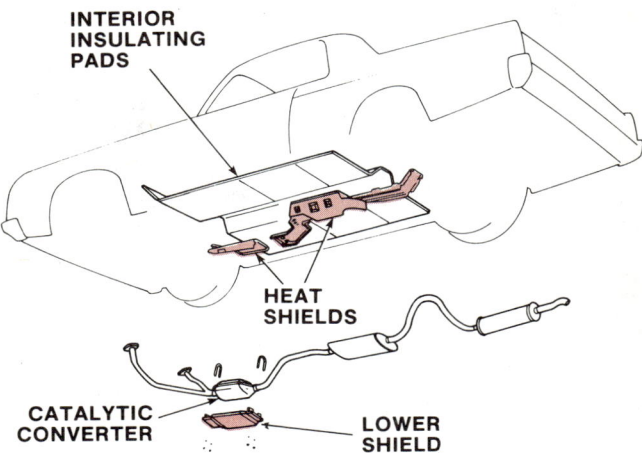

Figure 12-32 Location of heat shields.

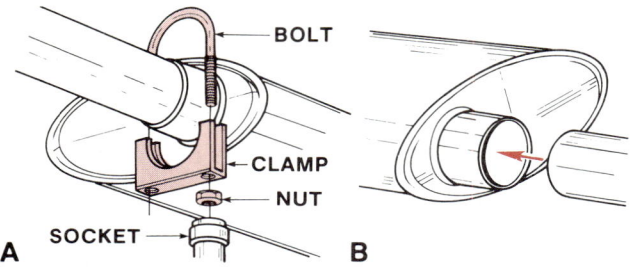

Figure 12-33 (A) One pipe slides inside the other. (B) Clamps secure exhaust system parts to each other.

as well as to help isolate noise by preventing its transfer through the frame or body to the passenger compartment. Clamps help to secure exhaust system parts to one another. The pipes are formed in such a way that one slips inside the other (Figure 12-33). This design makes a close fit. A U-type clamp usually holds this connection tight. Another important job of clamps and brackets is to hold pipes to the bottom of the vehicle.

New hanger arrangements have been necessary due to automobile design. For instance, transverse mounted engines rock back and forth on their mounts, instead of rocking from side to side. Without some sort of hinge in the exhaust system, this rocking motion would cause the tail pipe to move up and down—as much as a foot or two on some cars.

Various types of hangers are available. Some exhaust systems are supported by doughnut-shaped rubber rings between hooks on the exhaust component and on the frame or car body. Others are supported at the exhaust pipe and tail pipe connections by a combination of metal and reinforced fabric hanger (Figure 12-34). Both the doughnuts and the reinforced fabric allow the exhaust system to vibrate without breakage that could be caused by direct physical connection to the vehicle's frame.

Exhaust system pipes can be welded together. Welding, of course, is a process in which heat is used to melt metal and allow the molten portions to flow together. When cooled, a welded joint is as strong as, or sometimes stronger than, a single piece of metal. A welding torch can also be used to cut exhaust system pipes.

WARNING: Do not attempt to use welding equipment without proper training and safety equipment. The light caused by welding can cause permanent eye damage or even blindness. Furthermore, the heat from welding can ignite fuel vapors or damage parts.

Some OE is a fully welded exhaust system. By welding instead of clamping, car makers save the weight of overlapping joints as well as that of clamps.

EXHAUST SYSTEM SERVICE

Exhaust system components are subject to both physical and chemical damage. Any physical damage to an exhaust system part that causes a partially restricted or blocked exhaust system usually results in loss of power or backfire up through the throttle plate(s). In addition to improper engine operation, a blocked or restricted exhaust system causes increased vehicle noise and air pollution. Leaks in the exhaust system caused by either physical or chemical (rust) damage could result in illness, asphyxiation, or even death. Remember that vehicle exhaust fumes can be very dangerous to one's health.

Exhaust System Inspection

Most parts of the exhaust system, particularly the exhaust pipe, muffler, and tail pipe, are subject to rust, corrosion, and cracking. Broken or loose clamps and hangers can allow parts to separate or strike the road surface. Rough roads and rocks thrown by the wheels can also damage parts.

WARNING: During all exhaust inspection and repair work, wear safety glasses or equivalent eye protection.

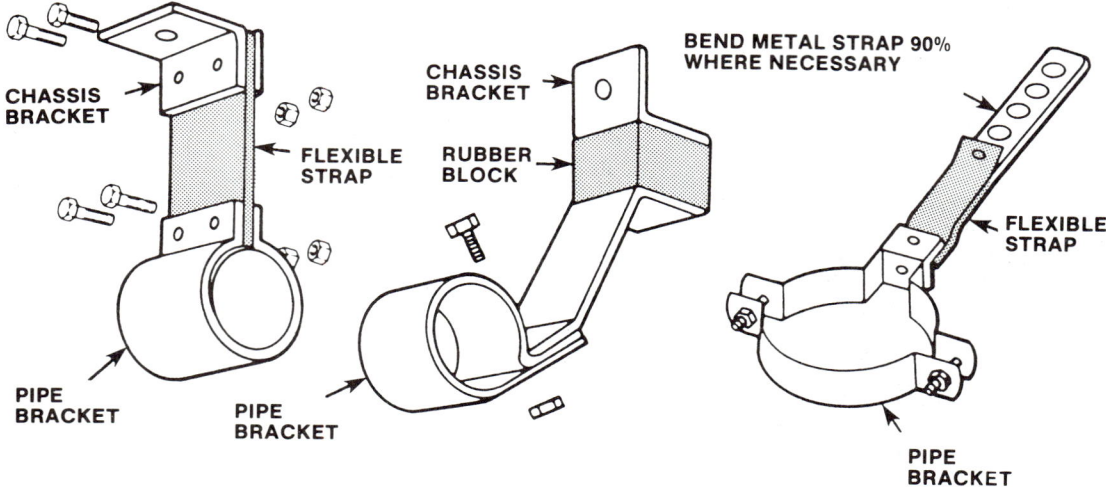

Figure 12-34 Various exhaust clamp assemblies.

Intake and Exhaust Systems 281

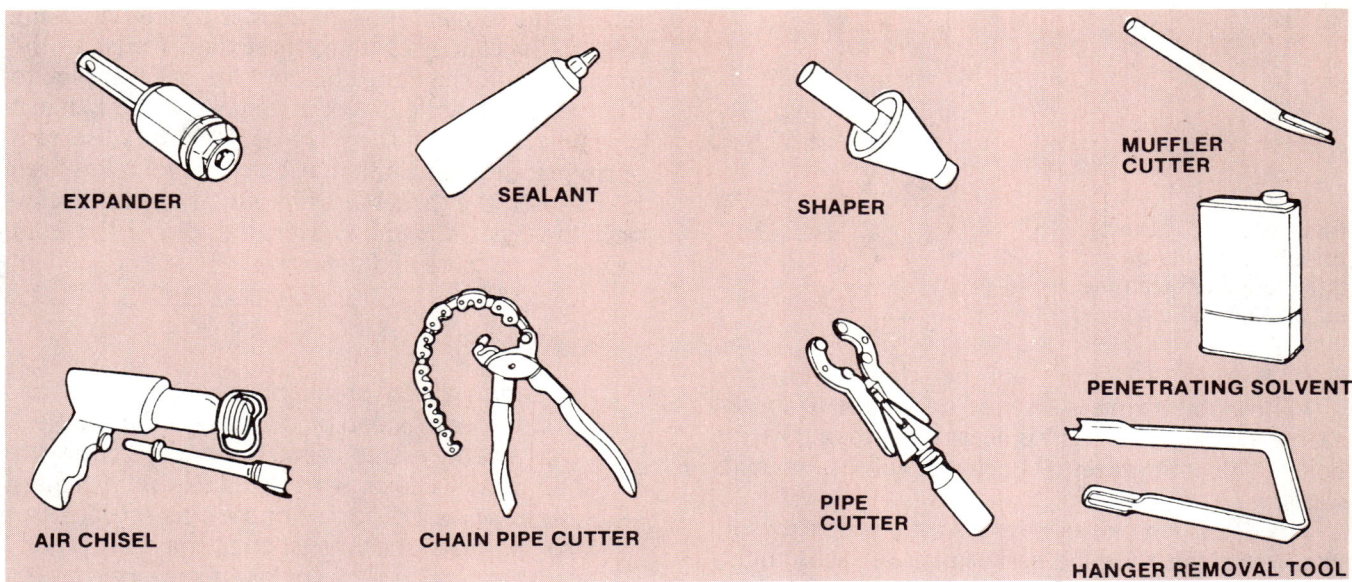

Figure 12-35 Special tools required for exhaust work.

Complete exhaust system inspection and testing procedures are given in the Tech Manual that accompanies this textbook. Any inspection should include listening for hissing or rumbling that indicates the presence of a leak. An on-lift inspection should pinpoint any of the following types of damage.

- Holes, road damage, separated connections, and bulging muffler seams
- Kinks and dents
- Discoloration, rust, soft corroded metal, etc.
- Torn, broken, or missing hangers and clamps
- Loose tail pipes or other components
- Bluish or brownish catalytic converter shell indicating overheating

The system should also be tested for blockage and restrictions using a vacuum gauge and tachometer.

Before beginning work on the system, be sure it is cool to the touch. Disconnect the battery ground to avoid short-circuiting the electrical system. Soak all rusted nuts, bolts, etc., in a good quality penetrating oil. Finally, check the system for critical clearance points so they can be maintained when new components are installed.

Replacing Exhaust System Components

Most exhaust system servicing involves the replacement of parts. When replacing exhaust system components, it is important that original equipment parts (or their equivalent) are used to ensure proper alignment with other parts in the system and provide acceptable exhaust noise levels. When replacing only one component in an exhaust system, it is not always necessary to take off the parts behind it.

Exhaust system component replacement might require the use of special tools (Figure 12-35) and welding equipment.

Exhaust Manifold and Exhaust Pipe Servicing

As mentioned, the manifold itself rarely causes any problems. On occasion, an exhaust manifold will warp because of excess heat. A straightedge and feeler gauge can be used to check the machined surface of the manifold.

Another problem—also the result of high temperatures generated by the engine—is a cracked manifold. This usually occurs after the car passes through a large puddle and cold water splashes on the manifold's hot surface. If the manifold is warped beyond manufacturer's specifications or is cracked, it must be replaced. Also, check the exhaust pipe for signs of collapse. If there is damage, repair it. These repairs should be done as directed in the vehicle's service manual.

REPLACING LEAKING GASKETS AND SEALS The most likely spots for leaking gaskets and seals are between the exhaust manifold and the cylinder head and between the exhaust pipe and the exhaust manifold (Figure 12-36).

When installing exhaust gaskets, carefully follow the recommendations on the gasket package label and instruction forms. Read through all installation steps before beginning. Take note of any of the original equipment manufacturer's recommendations in service manuals that could affect engine sealing. This is especially important when working with aluminum components. Manifolds warp more easily if an attempt is made to remove them while still hot. Remember heat expands metal, making assembly bolts more difficult to remove and easier to break.

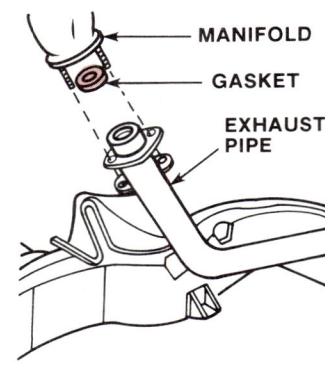

Figure 12-36 Leaking gaskets and seals are often found between the exhaust manifold and pipe.

Follow the torque sequence in reverse to loosen each bolt. Then repeat the process again to remove the bolts. This minimizes the chance of components warping.

Any debris left on the sealing surfaces increases the chance of leaks. A good gasket remover will quickly soften the old gasket debris and adhesive for quick removal. Carefully remove the softened pieces with a scraper and a wire brush. Be sure to use a nonmetallic scraper when attempting to remove gasket material from aluminum surfaces.

Inspect the manifold for irregularities that might cause leaks, such as gouges, scratches, or cracks. Replace any parts that are cracked or badly warped. This will insure proper sealing of the manifold.

Due to high heat conditions, it is important to retap and redie all threaded bolt holes, studs, and mounting bolts. This procedure insures tight, balanced clamping forces on the gasket. Lubricate the threads with a good high-temperature antiseize lubricant. Use a small amount of contact adhesive to hold the gasket in place. Align the gasket properly before the adhesive dries. Allow the adhesive to dry completely before proceeding with manifold installation.

Install the bolts finger tight. Tighten the bolts in three steps—one-half, three-quarters, and full torque—following the torque tables in the service manual or gasket manufacturers' instructions. Torquing is usually begun in the center of the manifold, working outward in an X pattern.

To replace a damaged exhaust pipe, begin by supporting the converter to keep it from falling. Carefully remove the oxygen sensor if there is one. Remove any hangers or clamps holding the exhaust pipe to the frame. Unbolt the flange holding the exhaust pipe to the exhaust manifold. When removing the exhaust pipe, check to see if there is a gasket. If so, discard it and replace it with a new one. Once the joint has been taken apart, the gasket loses its effectiveness. Disconnect the pipe from the converter and pull the front exhaust pipe loose and remove it.

SHOP TALK

An easy way to break off rusted nuts is to tighten them instead of loosening them. Sometimes a badly rusted clamp or hanger strap will snap off with ease. Sometimes the old exhaust system will not drop free of the body because a large part is in the way, such as the rear end or the transmission support. Use a large cold chisel, pipe cutter, hacksaw, muffler cutter, or chain cutter to cut the old system at convenient points to make the exhaust assembly smaller.

Although most exhaust systems use a slip joint and clamps to fasten the pipe to the muffler, a few use a welded connection. If the vehicle's system is welded, cut the pipe at the joint with a hacksaw or pipe cutter (Figure 12-37). The new pipe need not be welded to the muffler. An adapter, available with the pipe, can be used instead. When measuring the length for the new pipe, allow at least 2 inches for the adapter to enter the muffler. If the pipe has to be expanded, it could be done as shown in Figure 12-38.

CAUTION: Be sure to wear work gloves to prevent cutting your hands on rusted metal parts.

The old exhaust pipe might be rusted into the muffler or converter opening. Attempt to collapse the old pipe by using a cold chisel or slitting tool and a hammer (Figure 12-39). While freeing the pipe, try not to damage the muffler inlet. It must be perfectly round to accept the new pipe.

Slide the new pipe into the muffler (some lubricant might be helpful). Attach the front end to the manifold.

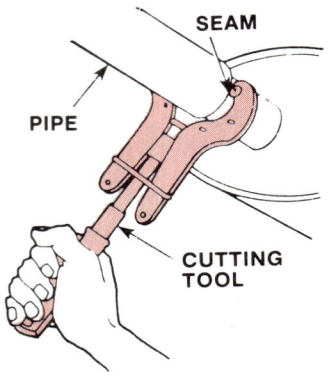

Figure 12-37 Cutting an exhaust pipe with a pipe cutter.

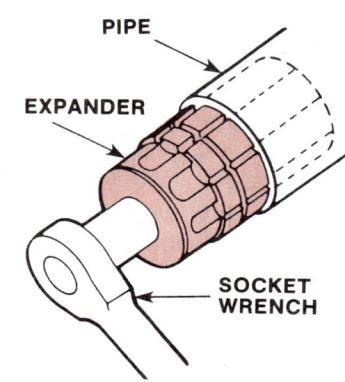

Figure 12-38 Expanding an exhaust pipe with an expander tool.

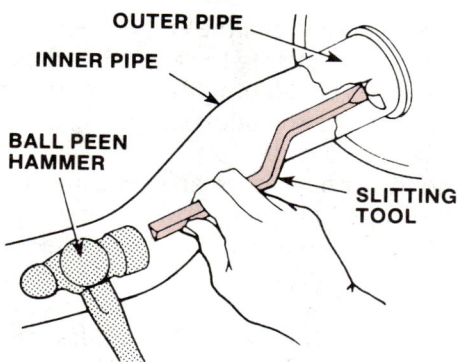

Figure 12-39 Removing a rusted-on muffler.

The pipe must fit at least 1-1/2 inches into the converter or muffler. A new gasket must be used at the manifold, as previously described. Before tightening the connectors, check the system for alignment. When it is properly aligned, tighten the clamps.

When removing the exhaust pipe, be careful with the emission controls. If the vehicle is equipped with a mechanical heat riser valve, it should be sprayed with graphite oil. Also be sure that the counterweight is in balance (Figure 12-40). To do this, use pliers to move the counterweight and valve shaft slowly and carefully. Graphite oil is applied liberally during this process until the shaft moves freely and easily.

SHOP TALK

Graphite oil is a thin lubricant containing graphite particles. After the engine starts, the oil will burn off. The graphite, an excellent dry lubricant, will remain.

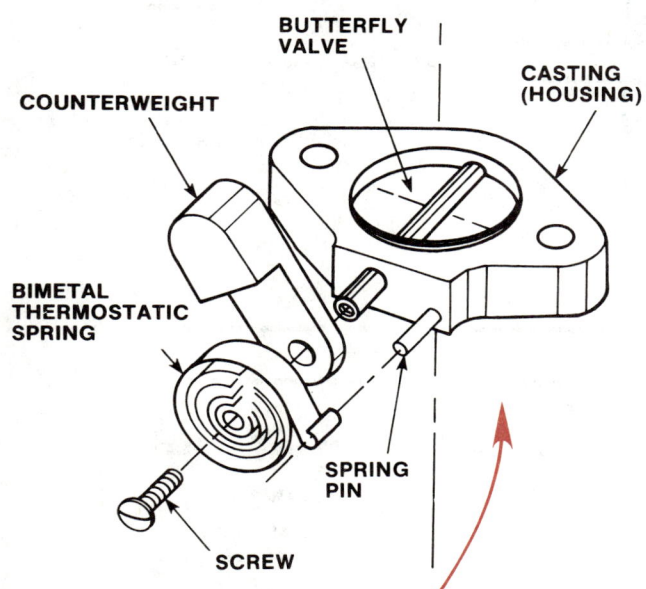

Figure 12-40 Mechanical heat riser valve.

CAUTION: Be sure no exhaust part comes into direct contact with any section of the body, fuel lines, fuel tank, or brake lines.

☐ TURBOCHARGERS AND SUPERCHARGERS

The power generated by the internal combustion engine is directly related to the compression force exerted on the air/fuel mixture. In other words, the greater the compression (within reason), the greater the output of the engine.

Two approaches can be used to increase engine compression. One is to modify the internal configuration of the engine to increase the basic compression ratio. This has been accomplished in many ways including the use of such things as domed or high top pistons, altered crankshaft strokes, or changes in the shape and structure of the combustion chamber design.

Another, less expensive way to increase mixture compression (and engine power) without physically changing the shape of the combustion chamber is to simply increase the quantity of the intake charge. By pressurizing the intake mixture before it enters the cylinder, more air and fuel molecules can be packed into the combustion chamber. Keep in mind that any time the amount of the air/fuel mix that enters the cylinder is increased, there is a substantial increase in power.

The two processes of artificially increasing the amount of airflow into the engine are known as turbocharging and supercharging.

Turbocharger Operation

Turbochargers are used to increase engine power by compressing (or densifying) the air that goes into the engine's combustion chambers. Increased power comes from the additional fuel that the denser air accommodates. Today, turbochargers are the most popular method of increasing engine compression.

The turbocharger does not require a mechanical connection between the engine and the pressurizing pump to compress the intake gases. Instead, it relies on the rapid expansion of hot exhaust gases exiting the cylinders to spin turbine blades (hence the name turbocharger). Because exhaust gas is a waste product, the energy developed by the turbine is said to be free since it theoretically does not rob the engine of any of the power it helps to produce.

A typical turbocharger, usually called a turbo, consists of the following components (Figure 12-41).

- Turbine or hot wheel
- Shaft
- Compressor or cold wheel
- Waste gate valve

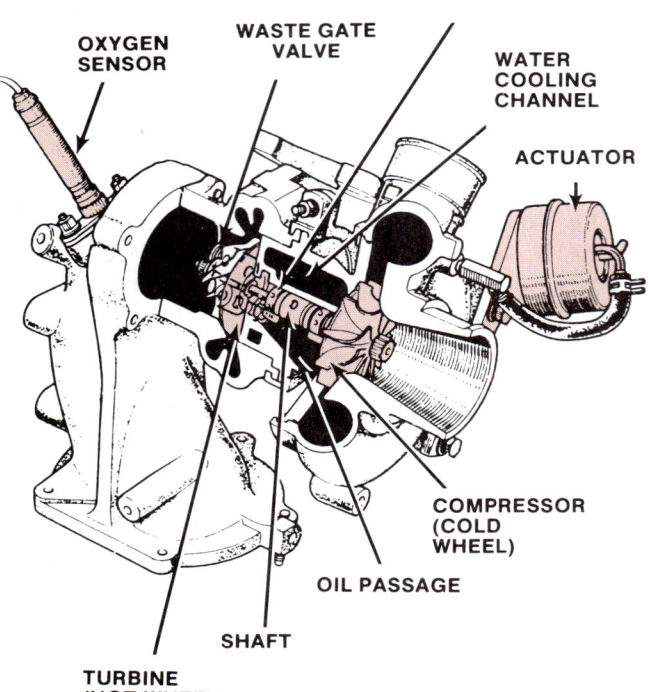

Figure 12-41 Cross section of a turbocharger shows the turbine wheel, the compressor wheel, and their connecting shaft. *Courtesy of Toyota Motor Corp.*

- Actuator
- Center housing and rotating assembly (CHRA). This component contains the bearings, shaft, turbine seal assembly, and compressor seal assembly.

The turbocharger is located to one side of the engine, usually close to the exhaust manifold. An exhaust pipe runs between the engine exhaust manifold and the turbine housing to carry the exhaust flow to the turbine wheel (Figure 12-42). Another pipe connects the compressor housing intake to an injector throttle body or a carburetor.

Inside the turbocharger, an exhaust-driven turbine wheel (hot wheel) is attached via a shaft to an intake compressor wheel (cold wheel). Each wheel is encased in its own spiral-shaped housing that serves to control and direct the flow of exhaust and intake gases. The shaft that joins the two wheels rides on bearings (generally the free-floating type). These bearings are part of a bearing lubrication and rotational housing cartridge assembly.

The air compressing process starts when exhaust gas enters the turbine housing. When the engine's speed and load are high enough (generally above 2000 rpm), the force of the exhaust flow is directed through a nozzle against the side of the turbine wheel. As the hot gases hit the turbine wheel causing it to spin, the specially curved turbine fins direct the air toward the center of the housing where it exits. This action creates a flow called a vortex. Once the turbine starts to spin, the compressor wheel (shaped like a turbine wheel in reverse) also starts to spin. This causes air to be drawn into the center where it is caught by the whirling blades of the compressor and thrown outward by centrifugal force. From there the air exits under pressure through the remainder of the induction system on its way to the cylinder.

Under normal atmospheric conditions, air is drawn into the engine at a maximum of 14.7 psi at sea level. A turbocharged engine, however, is capable of pressurizing the intake charge above and beyond nature's limits. Turbo boost is the term used to describe the positive

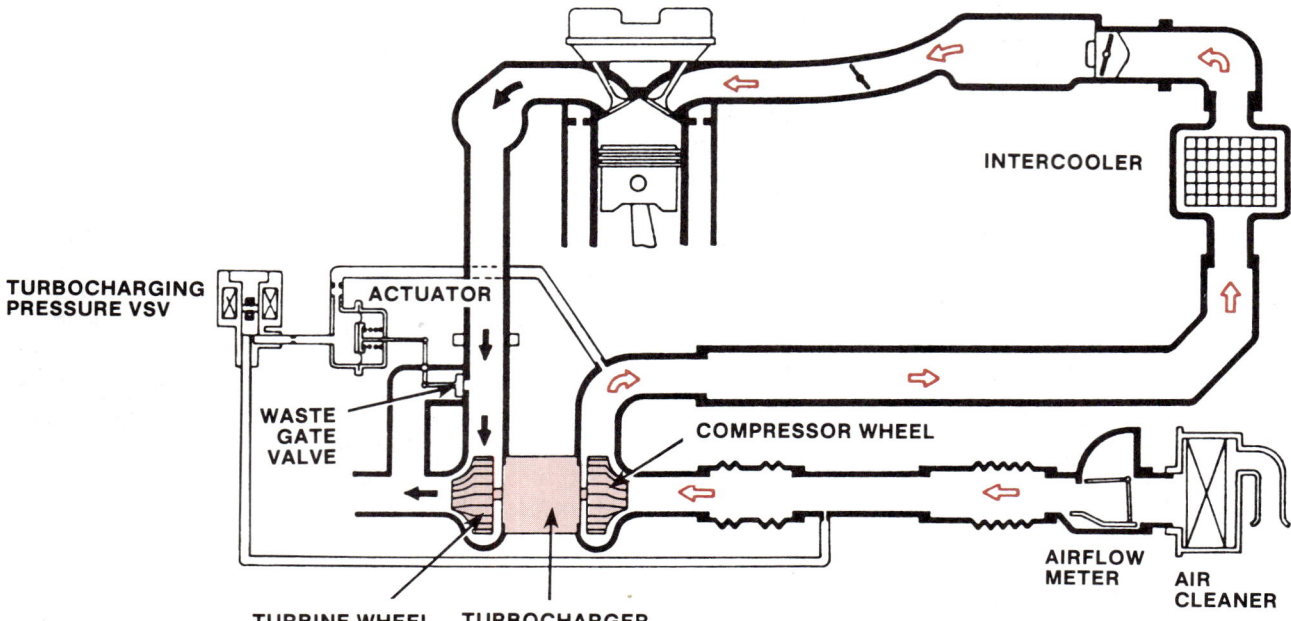

Figure 12-42 Exhaust gas and airflow in a typical turbocharger system. *Courtesy of Toyota Motor Corp.*

pressure increase created by a turbocharger. For example, 10 psi of boost means the air is being fed into the engine at 24.7 psi (14.7 psi atmospheric plus 10 pounds of boost).

WASTE GATE VALVE High engine output can be achieved through turbocharging. But if the turbocharged air pressure becomes too high, knocking occurs and output actually decreases. To prevent this, the turbocharger uses a waste gate valve. This valve allows a certain amount of exhaust gas to bypass the turbine once the ideal turbocharged air pressure is exceeded. The waste gate is usually operated by an actuator that senses the air pressure in the induction system. When the pressure becomes too high, the actuator opens the waste gate valve. The flow of exhaust gas reaching the turbine decreases. This reduces turbine and compressor wheel speed. The result is a drop in turbocharged air pressure.

INTERCOOLER The intercooler cools the turbocharged air before it reaches the combustion chamber. Cooling the air makes it denser. It also lowers the temperature produced in the combustion chamber. These factors help reduce engine knock and increase engine output. Intercoolers are like radiators in that heat from the air passing through it is removed and dissipated to the atmosphere. Intercoolers can be air or water cooled.

LUBRICATING SYSTEM Most turbochargers are lubricated by pressurized and filtered engine oil which is line-fed to the unit's oil inlet. The oil drains back to the engine (by gravity) through a separate line.

CAUTION: Lack of lubrication and oil lag are major causes of turbocharger failure.

A turbocharger should never be operated under engine load conditions with less than 30 psi oil pressure. A turbocharger is much more sensitive to a limited oil supply than an engine, due to the high rotational speed of the shaft and the relatively small area of the bearing surfaces. Oil pressure and flow lag during engine starting can have detrimental effects on the turbocharger bearings. During normal engine starting, this should not be a problem. There are, of course, abnormal starting conditions. Oil lag conditions will most often occur during the first engine start after an engine oil and filter change, when the lubricating oil system is empty. Before the engine is put under load and the turbo activated, the engine should be run for 3-5 minutes at idle to prevent oil starvation to the turbo, thereby preventing premature bearing failure. Similar conditions can also exist if an engine has not been operated for a prolonged period of time. Engine lube systems have a tendency to bleed down. Before allowing the engine to start, the engine should be cranked over until a steady oil pressure reading is observed. This is called priming the lubricating system. The same starting procedure should be followed when starting an engine in cold weather. The engine oil can be congealed and take a longer period of time to flow. Turbocharger bearing damage can occur if the oil delay is in excess of 30 seconds, and much sooner if the engine is accelerated much beyond low idle rpm.

SHOP TALK

When oil leakage is noted at the turbine end of the turbocharger, always check the turbocharger oil drain tube and the engine crankcase breathers for a restricted condition. When a sludged engine oil condition is found, it is mandatory that the engine oil and oil filters are changed, using the factory recommended lubricating oil. Correct as necessary before working on the turbocharger.

CUSTOMER CARE

Explain to customers the oiling needs of a turbocharger and the need for special attention during starting and turning off the engine.

SPARK-RETARD SYSTEM Retarding spark timing is an often used method of controlling detonation on turbocharged engine systems. Unfortunately, any time the ignition is permanently retarded to prevent detonation, power is lost, fuel economy suffers, and the engine tends to run hotter. Because of these trade-offs, most systems use knock-sensing devices to retard timing only when detonation is detected.

COMPUTER-CONTROLLED SYSTEM The design capacity of the turbocharger depends on engine size and type, which is determined by the vehicle manufacturer. Control devices limit the amount of boost to prevent detonation and engine damage. In fact, some turbocharging systems on computer-controlled vehicles use an electronic control unit to operate the waste gate control valve through sensor signals.

USING SERVICE MANUALS

General service procedures for turbocharger systems are normally in a separate section of service manuals. Individual inputs and outputs that are part of the electronic control system are covered in the engine control section of the manual.

Turbocharger Inspection

To inspect a turbocharger, start the engine and listen to the sound the turbo system makes. As a technician becomes more familiar with this characteristic sound, it will be easier to identify an air leak between the compressor outlet and engine or an exhaust leak between engine and turbo by the presence of a higher pitched sound. If the turbo sound cycles or changes in intensity, the likely causes are a plugged air cleaner or loose material in the compressor inlet ducts or dirt buildup on the compressor wheel and housing.

> **SHOP TALK**
>
> Usually within each manufacturer's series, there are several sizes and shapes to fit various engine requirements. This chapter will use typical units to explain the procedures necessary for proper inspection, troubleshooting, and service. Use the manufacturer's service manual for exact details.

After listening, check the air cleaner for a dirty element. Next, with the engine stopped, remove the ducting from the air cleaner to turbo and look for dirt buildup or damage from foreign objects. Check for loose clamps on the compressor outlet connections and check the engine intake system for loose bolts, and leaking gaskets. Then, disconnect the exhaust pipe and look for restrictions or loose material. Examine the engine exhaust system for cracks, loose nuts, or blown gaskets. Rotate the turbo shaft assembly. Does it rotate freely? Are there signs of rubbing or wheel impact damage?

Visually inspect all hoses, gaskets, and tubing for proper fit, damage, and wear. Do not underestimate the importance of a broken or deteriorated hose in a system that depends on vacuum and pressure for proper operation. Check the low pressure, or air cleaner, side of the intake system for vacuum leaks. Propane is good for checking potential leak areas. Infrared analyzers are an excellent means of determining if there is a vacuum leak and where it is located.

On the pressure side of the system you can check for leaks by using soapy water. After applying the soap mixture, look for bubbles to pinpoint the source of the leak.

Leakage in the exhaust system upstream from the turbine housing will also affect turbo operation. If exhaust gases are allowed to escape prior to entering the turbine housing, the reduced temperature and pressure will cause a proportionate reduction in boost and an accompanying loss of power. If the waste gate does not appear to be operating properly (too much or too little boost), check to make sure the connecting linkage is operating smoothly and not binding. Also, check to make sure the pressure sensing hose is clear and properly connected.

> **SHOP TALK**
>
> Specialty shops normally rebuild turbochargers. Because of the needed balance and sealing of the units, automotive technicians do not rebuild the units. Most repair shops do not have the equipment needed.

WASTE GATE SERVICE If the waste gate is not operating properly, boost pressure can be either too little or too much. Waste gate malfunctions can usually be traced to carbon buildup, which keeps the unit from closing or causes it to bind. A defective diaphragm or leaking vacuum hose can result in an inoperative waste gate. But, before condemning the waste gate, check the ignition timing, the spark-retard system, vacuum hoses, and (if used) the knock sensor, the oxygen sensor, and the computer to be sure each is operating properly.

When testing or checking the waste gate and its control, always carefully follow the procedures given in the vehicle or turbo manufacturer's service manual.

CAUTION: When removing carbon deposits from turbine and waste gate parts, never use a hard metal tool or sandpaper. Remember that any gouges or scratches on these metal parts can cause severe vibration or damage to the turbocharger. To clean these parts, use a soft brush and a solvent.

Common Turbocharger Problems

The turbocharger, with proper care and servicing, will provide years of reliable service. Most turbocharger failures are caused by lack of lubricant, ingestion of foreign objects, or contamination of lubricant.

Refer to Table 12-1 and the service manual for the symptoms of turbocharger failures and a summary of causes and recommended remedies.

Turbo-Lag

Increases in horsepower are normally evidenced by an engine's response to quick opening of the throttle. The lack of throttle response is felt with some of today's turbocharged systems, because the exhaust gas requires a little time to build enough energy to spin the blower up to speed. In today's engine horsepower race, the exhaust-gas-driven turbochargers, which became popular in the late 1970s, are being challenged by new alternatives, including bigger engines, multivalve power plants, and direct-drive supercharged engines. To overcome such problems as turbo-lag, excess heat, and preignition or knock, turbocharger manufacturers have a new generation of turbos (Figure 12-43). The variable nozzle turbine (VNT) has greatly improved the turbo-lag traditionally associated with turbochargers. Turbo lag occurs when the turbocharger is unable to meet the immediate demands of the engine. The power

Intake and Exhaust Systems

TABLE 12-1 TURBOCHARGER TROUBLESHOOTING GUIDE

Condition	Possible Causes Code Numbers	Remedy Description by Code Numbers

Engine lacks power	1, 4, 5, 6, 7, 8, 9, 10, 11, 18, 20, 21, 22, 25, 26, 27, 28, 29, 30, 37, 38, 39, 40, 41, 42, 43	1. Dirty air cleaner element
		2. Plugged crankcase breathers
		3. Air cleaner element missing, leaking, not sealing correctly; loose connections to turbocharger
		4. Collapsed or restricted air tube before turbocharger
		5. Restricted-damaged crossover pipe, turbocharger to inlet manifold
		6. Foreign object between air cleaner and turbocharger
		7. Foreign object in exhaust system (from engine, check engine)
		8. Turbocharger flanges, clamps, or bolts loose.
		9. Inlet manifold cracked; gaskets loose or missing; connections loose
		10. Exhaust manifold cracked, burned; gaskets loose, blown, or missing
		11. Restricted exhaust system
		12. Oil lag (oil delay to turbocharger at start-up)
		13. Insufficient lubrication
		14. Lubricating oil contaminated with dirt or other material
		15. Improper type lubricating oil used
		16. Restricted oil feed line
		17. Restricted oil drain line
		18. Turbine housing damaged or restricted
		19. Turbocharger seal leakage
		20. Worn journal bearings
		21. Excessive dirt buildup in compressor housing
		22. Excessive carbon buildup behind turbine wheel
		23. Too fast acceleration at initial start (oil lag)
		24. Too little warm-up time
		25. Fuel pump malfunction
		26. Worn or damaged injectors
		27. Valve timing
		28. Burned valves
		29. Worn piston rings
		30. Burned pistons
		31. Leaking oil feed line
		32. Excessive engine pre-oil
		33. Excessive engine idle
		34. Coked or sludged center housing
		35. Oil pump malfunction
		36. Oil filter plugged
		37. Oil-bath-type air cleaner:
		  • Air inlet screen restricted
		  • Oil pullover
		  • Dirty air cleaner
		  • Oil viscosity low
		  • Oil viscosity high
		38. Actuator damaged or defective
		39. Waste gate binding
		40. Electronic control module or connector(s) defective
		41. Waste gate actuator solenoid or connector defective
		42. EGR valve defective
		43. Alternator voltage incorrect
		44. Engine shut off without adequate cool-down time
		45. Leaking valve guide seals
		46. Low oil level

Black smoke	1, 4, 5, 6, 7, 8, 9, 10, 11, 18, 20, 21, 22, 25, 26, 27, 28, 29, 30, 37, 38, 39, 40, 41, 43	
Blue smoke	1, 2, 4, 6, 8, 9, 17, 19, 20, 21, 22, 32, 33, 34, 37, 45	
Excessive oil consumption	2, 8, 15, 17, 19, 20, 29, 30, 31, 33, 34, 37, 45	
Excessive oil turbine end	2, 7, 8, 17, 19, 20, 22, 29, 30, 32, 33, 34, 45	
Excessive oil compressor end	1, 2, 4, 5, 6, 8, 19, 20, 21, 29, 30, 33, 34, 45	
Insufficient lubrication	8, 12, 14, 15, 16, 23, 24, 31, 34, 35, 36, 44, 46	
Oil in exhaust manifold	2, 7, 17, 18, 19, 20, 22, 29, 30, 33, 34, 45	
Damaged compressor wheel	3, 4, 6, 8, 12, 15, 16, 20, 21, 23, 24, 31, 34, 35, 36, 44, 46	
Damaged turbine wheel	7, 8, 12, 13, 14, 15, 16, 18, 20, 22, 23, 24, 25, 28, 30, 31, 34, 35, 36, 44, 46	
Drag or bind in rotating assembly	3, 6, 7, 8, 12, 13, 14, 15, 16, 18, 20, 21, 22, 23, 24, 31, 34, 35, 36, 44, 46	
Worn bearings, journals, bearing bores	6, 7, 8, 12, 13, 14, 15, 16, 23, 24, 31, 35, 36, 44, 46	
Noisy	1, 3, 4, 5, 6, 7, 8, 9, 10, 11, 12, 13, 14, 15, 16, 18, 20, 21, 22, 23, 24, 31, 34, 35, 36, 37, 44, 46	
Sludged or coked center housing	2, 11, 13, 14, 15, 17, 18, 24, 31, 35, 36, 44, 46	

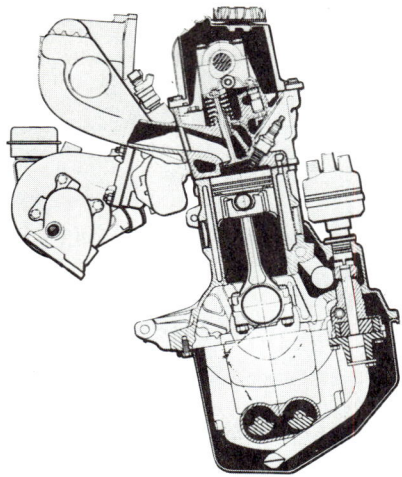

Figure 12-43 Cross sectional view of a VNT turbocharger.

from the engine temporarily lags behind the need. VNT units allow the turbine to accelerate quicker than the conventional turbos thereby reducing the lag time.

Replacing a Turbocharger

If the turbocharger is faulty it can be replaced with a new or rebuilt unit. Always follow the exact replacement procedure given in the service manual.

Once the new or rebuilt unit is installed, the turbo should be started up as described in the following section.

TURBO START-UP AND SHUTDOWN Oil supply to a turbocharger's shaft bearings is, as mentioned previously, critical to long life for this high-speed component. After replacement of a turbocharger, or after an engine has been unused or stored, there can be a considerable lag after engine start-up before the oil pressure is sufficient to deliver oil to the turbo's bearings. To prevent the problem, which can lead to premature turbo failure, follow these simple steps:

1. When installing a new or remanufactured turbocharger, make certain that the oil inlet and drain lines are clean before connecting them.
2. Be sure the engine oil is clean and at the proper level.
3. Fill the oil filter with clean oil.
4. Leave the oil drain line disconnected at the turbo and crank the engine without starting it until oil flows out of the turbo drain port.
5. Connect the drain line, start the engine, and operate it at low idle for a few minutes before running it at higher speeds.

> **CUSTOMER CARE**
>
> Remind your customer not to immediately stop the engine after pulling a trailer or driving at a high speed or uphill. Idle the engine for 20 to 120 seconds, depending on the severity of the driving conditions. Remember the turbocharger will continue to rotate after the engine oil pressure has dropped to zero, which can cause bearing damage. Avoid sudden racing or acceleration after starting a cold engine. Allow at least 30 seconds for the oil to flow. Stress the importance of proper lube oil and filter change intervals. Check the service manual.

Contaminated oil can cause sludge buildups within the turbo. Check the oil drain outlet for sludge buildup with the oil drain line removed. Failure to follow these steps can result in bearing failure on the turbo's main shaft. Remember, shaft rotation speed on modern turbochargers can easily exceed 2,000 revolutions per second, so momentary oil flow interruption is likely to lead to turbocharger failure.

Superchargers

Supercharging fascinated auto engineers even before they decided to steer with a wheel instead of a tiller. The 1906 American Chadwick sported a supercharger, followed by a variety of American and European efforts. Supercharged Dusenbergs, Hispano-Suizas, and Mercedes-Benzes were giants among luxury-car marques, as well as winners on the race tracks in the 1920s and '30s. Then, after World War II, supercharging started to fade, though both Ford and American Motors sold supercharged passenger cars into the late 1950s. However, after being displaced first by larger V-8 engines, then by exhaust-driven turbochargers, the supercharger has started to make a comeback with 1989 models. Some automobile manufacturers are offering superchargers as an alternative to the turbo (Figure 12-44).

Figure 12-44 A supercharger installed on a V-6 engine.

Intake and Exhaust Systems 289

> **USING SERVICE MANUALS**
> Service procedures for supercharger systems are normally in a separate unit of a service manual.

Supercharger Operation

Superchargers are air pumps connected directly to the crankshaft by a belt. They improve horsepower and torque by pumping extra air into the engine in direct relationship to crankshaft speed. This positive connection yields instant response, in contrast to turbochargers, which must overcome inertia and spin up to speed as the flow of exhaust gas increases.

Figure 12-45 illustrates the flow of the air through the supercharger. The air comes in through the remote-mounted air cleaner and the mass airflow meter, which are not shown. It goes through the air intake charge throttle body assembly, then passes through the supercharger inlet plenum assembly, which is bolted to the back of the supercharger.

The air is inducted into the bottom of the supercharger, pressurized by the spinning rotors, and exits through the top of the supercharger by the way of the

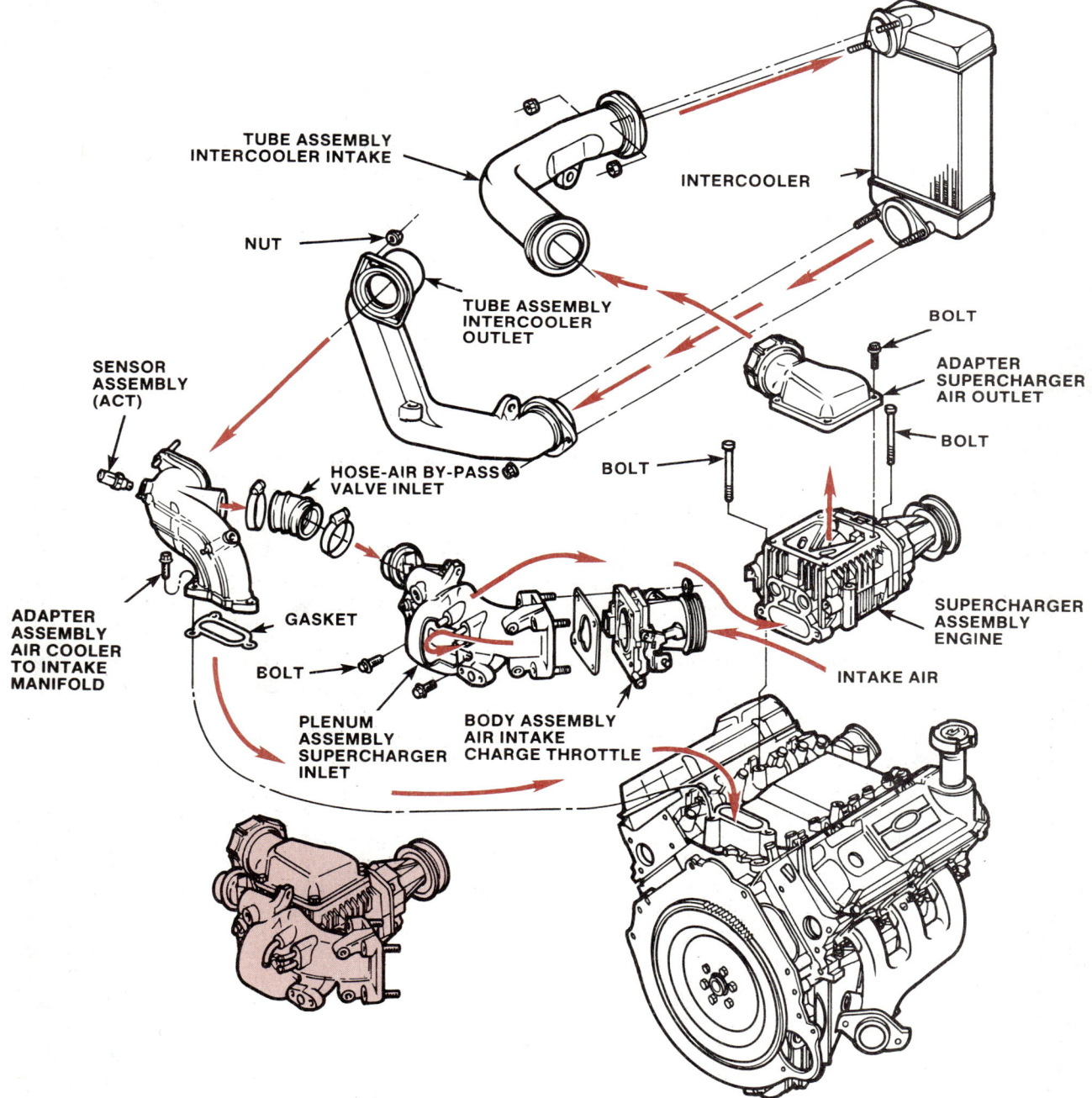

Figure 12-45 Airflow through a supercharger assembly into the engine.

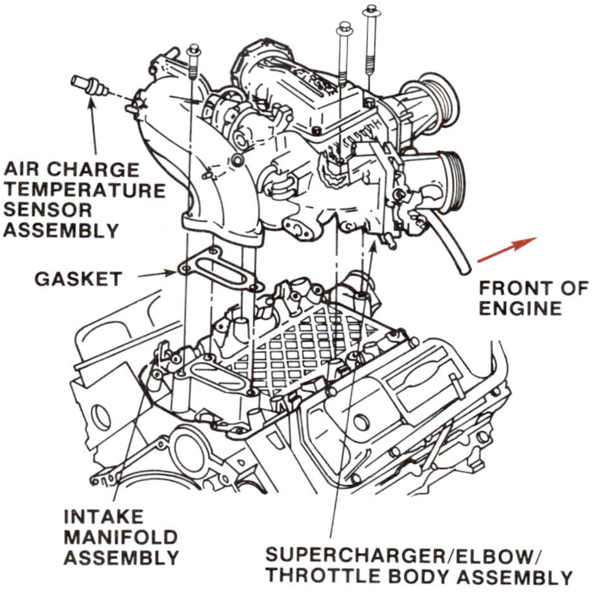

Figure 12-46 The supercharger and throttle plate assembly are mounted to the intake manifold.

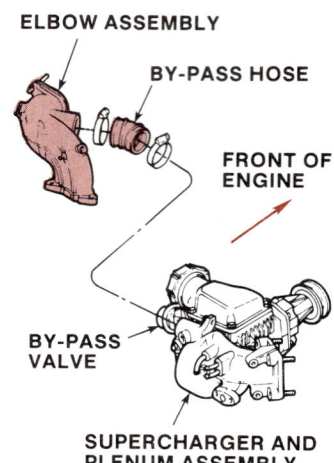

Figure 12-47 Supercharger by-pass hose and intake elbow.

air outlet adapter. The compression of the air by the supercharger also results in it being heated. Since cooler, denser air is desired for increased power, the heated air is routed through the air-to-air intercooler. The upper tube assembly carries the air into the top of the intercooler, and it exits through the outlet tube assembly at the bottom. The intercooler is quite efficient and can decrease the temperature of the air by 150 degrees Fahrenheit.

This cooled air then passes through to the intake manifold adapter assembly, which is bolted to the rear of the intake manifold (Figure 12-46). The intake manifold is a plenum rather than a runner design, since the pressure allows the air to be efficiently routed to the individual cylinders without the use of separate runners. When the intake valves open, the air is forced into the combustion chambers where it is mixed with fuel delivered by the port-mounted fuel injectors.

Notice that the system also incorporates a by-pass, which branches off from the upper portion of the air cooler to the intake manifold adapter assembly. This by-pass (Figure 12-47) is designed to allow the supercharger to idle along when the extra power is not needed. The by-pass routes any excess air in the intake manifold back through the supercharger inlet plenum assembly, allowing the engine to run, in effect, normally aspirated.

The by-pass incorporates a simple vacuum motor that regulates the amount of air to be by-passed according to the power demands placed upon the engine. As the engine's power demands increase, the vacuum motor modulates a butterfly valve to progressively close off the by-pass and route more of the air to the intake manifold, thereby increasing boost. With the by-pass completely closed, boost can reach about 12 psi.

Unlike a turbocharger, the supercharger does not require a waste gate to limit boost and prevent a potentially damaging overboost condition. Since the speed of the supercharger is directly linked to the engine speed, its pumping power is limited by the rpm of the engine itself rather than revolutions produced by exhaust gases. Supercharger boost is therefore directly controlled through the opening and closing of the throttle.

Supercharger Designs

While there have been a number of supercharger designs on the market over the years, the most popular is the Roots type. The pair of three lobed rotor vanes in the Roots supercharger is driven by a belt from the crankshaft. The lobes force air into the intake manifold. Boost is roughly proportional to engine speed. In a typical system, a valve allows the engine computer to by-pass the supercharger when boost is not needed. An airflow meter helps the fuel-injection system meter the correct quantity of gas, and the intercooler reduces intake air temperature for greater efficiency.

The key to the supercharger's operation, of course, is primarily the design of the rotors. Some Roots-type superchargers use straight-lobe rotors that result in uneven pressure pulses and, consequently, relatively high noise levels. Therefore, the supercharger used with most of today's engines employs a helical design for the two rotors. The helical design evens out the pressure pulses in the blower and reduces noise. It was found that a 60-degree helical twist works best for equalizing the inlet and outlet volumes.

Another benefit of the helical rotor design is it reduces carryback volumes—air that is carried back to the inlet side of the supercharger because of the unavoidable spaces between the meshing rotors—which represents a loss of efficiency. Although some designs result in a carryback volume of only 1.2% of supercharger displacement, it still adds to the compressor noise level by generating pressure pulses in the inlet system. To help minimize the noise problem, some

Intake and Exhaust Systems 291

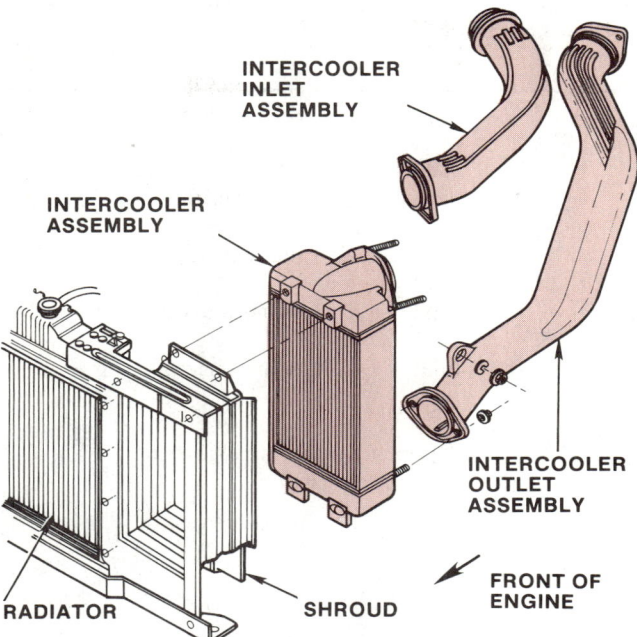

Figure 12–48 A typical intercooler system.

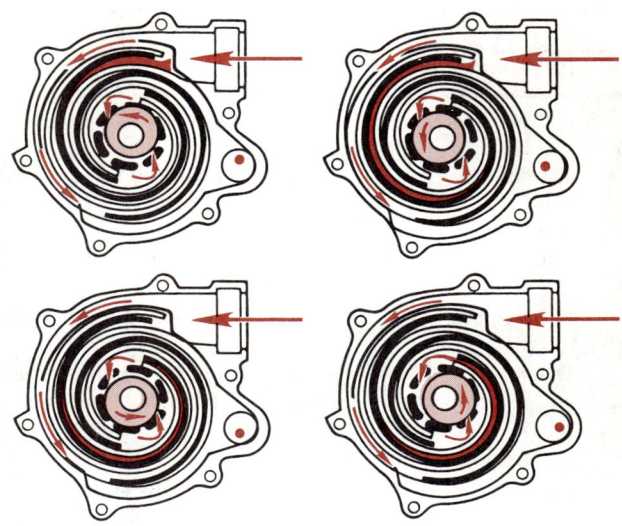

Figure 12–49 Operation of a G-Lader type supercharger.

manufacturers milled pulsation chambers into the casing, resulting in about a 6-decibel noise reduction across the supercharger's operating range. The rotors are held in a proper relationship to each other by timing gears. They are supported by ball bearings in the front and needle roller bearings in the back. The needle bearings are greased for life. The ball bearings are generally lubricated by gear oil and a plug is provided for periodic checks of the oil level at the ball bearings. The oil is a synthetic base specifically produced for high-speed use. When servicing the gear case, it is very important to keep out dirt and moisture.

The intercooler (Figure 12–48) in the supercharging system extracts excess heat from the air. By cooling the air in this manner, its density and consequently its oxygen content, results in increased power output for a given boost pressure. The air-to-air intercooler is located next to the conventional cooling radiator.

To handle the higher operating temperatures imposed by supercharging, an engine oil cooler is usually built into the engine system. This water-to-oil cooler is generally mounted between the engine front cover and oil filter.

As mentioned earlier, boost can be added during selected conditions. That is, superchargers can be enhanced with electrically operated clutches and by-pass valves. These allow the same computer that controls fuel and ignition to kick the boost on and off precisely as needed, resulting in far greater efficiency than a full-time supercharger.

Another popular supercharger design, especially in Europe, is the so-called G-Lader supercharger, which is based on a 1905 French design. As shown in Figure 12–49, spiral ramps in both sides of the rotor intermesh with similar ramps in the housing. Unlike most superchargers, the rotor of the G-Lader does not spin on its axis, rather it moves around an eccentric shaft. This motion draws in air, squeezes it inward through the spiral, which compresses it, then forces it through ducts in the center into the engine. Airflow is essentially constant, so intake noise is lower than that of a Roots blower. Because there is only a slight wiping motion between the spiral and housing, wear is minimal, too.

The current G-Lader design supercharger seems most effective for small displacement engines. The cost of supercharging and turbocharging is similar when each is installed in a production vehicle. A comparison of supercharger and turbocharger operations is given in Table 12–2.

Supercharger Problems

Many of the problems and their remedies given for turbochargers hold good for superchargers. There are also problems that are associated specifically with the supercharger. Refer to the service manual for the symptoms of supercharger failure and a summary of causes and recommended remedies.

Case 1

A customer's high-mileage, mid-80s car has a tendency to run hotter than it used to. It seems to be using more gas and has less power. There are no service records for the car and based on the overall condition of the car, it is determined that the car was not well-maintained. A visual inspection is performed and nothing abnormal is found. However, when the technician removes the air-

TABLE 12-2 COMPARISON OF SUPERCHARGER VS TURBOCHARGER

	Supercharger	Turbocharger
Efficiency loss	Mechanical friction	Increased exhaust back pressure
Packaging	Belt driven	Major revisions required to package—new exhaust manifold
Lube system	Self-contained	Uses engine oil and coolant
System noise	Pressure pulsation and gear noise	High frequency whine and waste gate
Durability	Not proven in significant OEM automotive applications	In use by OEMs, improvements being made
Performance	30% to 40% power increase over naturally aspirated	30% to 40% power increase over naturally aspirated
	Better low end torque	No loss of horsepower to operate
	No lag—dramatic improvement in start-up and passing acceleration, particularly with automatic transmission	
Temperatures		Increased underhood temperatures

filter assembly to visually check the action of the carburetor, the smell of raw fuel is evident. Careful inspection reveals no fuel leaks. The engine is started so the carburetor and fuel lines can be observed. A small amount of fuel sprays out the top of the carburetor each time the throttle is opened. This is probably the cause for the gas smell. But what is causing the fuel to spray out? Is this related to the original complaint?

Diagnosis continues with a vacuum test. At idle, the engine has 17 in. Hg. When the engine speed is raised to 1500 rpm and held there, the vacuum gauge climbs to 19 in. Hg then starts to drop. This normally indicates excessive exhaust back pressure. A collapsed exhaust pipe or plugged converter could be the problem. A plugged exhaust will cause fuel to spray out of the carburetor and it will cause poor gas mileage and poor overall performance.

To determine the location of the exhaust restriction, the catalytic converter is removed and the same vacuum test performed. This time the gauge reacts normally. The restriction in the exhaust is the converter. It is plugged. Replacing the converter will correct the problem. However, the cause of the plugging is still unknown.

A look at the fuel filler assembly reveals the cause of the problem. The owner has enlarged the nozzle opening to accommodate leaded fuel nozzles. The lead in this type fuel will clog a converter. This is explained to the customer and a new fuel filler neck and converter is installed.

Summary

- The air induction system allows a controlled amount of clean, filtered air to enter the engine. Cool air is drawn in through a fresh air tube. It passes through a preheater and air cleaner before entering the carburetor or fuel injection throttle.
- The intake manifold distributes the air or air/fuel mixture as evenly as possible to each cylinder, helps to prevent condensation, and assists in the vaporation of the air/fuel mixture. Intake manifolds are made of cast iron or die cast aluminum. They can be either wet or dry. That is, they may or may not have coolant passages cast in them. Some manifolds have an exhaust crossover passage.
- The vacuum created in the intake manifold operates many systems such as emission controls, brake boosters, heater/air conditioners, cruise controls, and more. Vacuum is applied through an elaborate system of hoses, tubes, and relays. A diagram of emission system vacuum hose routing is located on the underhood decal. Loss of vacuum can create many driveability problems.
- A vehicle's exhaust system carries away gases from the passenger compartment, cleans the exhaust emissions, and muffles the sound of the engine. Its components include the exhaust manifold, exhaust pipe, catalytic converter, muffler, resonator, tail pipe, heat shields, clamps, brackets, and hangers.
- The exhaust manifold is a bank of pipes that collects the burned gases as they are expelled from the engine cylinders and directs them to the exhaust

- pipe. Engines with all the cylinders in a row have one exhaust manifold. V-type engines have an exhaust manifold on each side of the engine. The exhaust pipe runs between the exhaust manifold and the catalytic converter.
- The catalytic converter uses the catalysts palladium and rhodium to change the exhaust gases CO, HC, and NO_x into water vapor, CO_2, N, and O_2. The most common types of converters are the pellet, monolythic, three-way, particulate oxidizer catalytic converter, and the minicatalytic converter.
- The muffler consists of a series of baffles, chambers, tubes, and holes to break up, cancel out, and silence pressure pulsations. Two types commonly used are the reverse-flow and the straight-through mufflers.
- Some vehicles have an additional muffler called a resonator to further reduce the sound level of the exhaust. The tail pipe is the end of the pipeline carrying exhaust fumes to the atmosphere beyond the back end of the car. Heat shields protect vehicle parts from exhaust system heat. Clamps, brackets, and hangers join and support exhaust system components.
- Exhaust system components are subject to both physical and chemical damage. The exhaust can be checked by listening for leaks and by visual inspection. Most exhaust system servicing involves the replacement of parts.
- Two approaches can be used to increase engine compression. One is to modify the internal configuration of the engine to increase the basic compression ratio. The less expensive way is to increase the quantity of the intake charge. The two processes of artifically increasing the amount of airflow into the engine are known as turbocharging and supercharging.
- The turbocharger does not require a mechanical connection between the engine and pressurizing pump to compress the intake gases. Instead, it relies on the rapid expansion of hot exhaust gases exiting the cylinder to spin turbine blades.
- A typical turbocharger consists of a turbine (or hot wheel), shaft, compressor (or cold wheel), turbine housing, compressor housing, and center housing and rotating assembly. A waste gate manages turbo output by controlling the amount of exhaust gas that is allowed to enter the turbine housing. Turbo boost is the positive pressure increase created by a turbocharger.
- Most turbochargers are lubricated by pressurized and filtered engine oil which is line-fed to the unit's oil inlet. Some turbocharged engines are equipped with an intercooler which is designed to cool the compressed air from the turbocharger.
- Retarding spark timing is an often used method of controlling detonation on turbocharged engine systems. Most systems use knock-sensing devices to retard timing only when detonation is detected. Some systems use an electronic control unit to operate the waste gate control valve through sensor signals.
- If the turbo sound cycles or changes in intensity, the likely causes are a plugged air cleaner or loose material in the compressor inlet ducts of dirt build-up on the compressor wheel and housing. Most turbocharger failures are caused by one of the following reasons: lack of lubricant, ingestion of foreign objects, or contamination of lubricant. Turbo lag occurs when the turbocharger is unable to meet the immediate demands of the engine.
- Superchargers are air pumps connected directly to the crankshaft by a belt. The positive connection yields instant response and pumps air into the engine in direct relationship to crankshaft speed.
- The most popular supercharger design is the Roots type. Another supercharger design is the G-Lader supercharger.

Review Questions

1. What can be used to check for leaks on the pressure side of a turbocharger system?
2. What advantages are there to preheating combustion air?
3. Name three functions of the intake manifold.
4. What is the best way to check the operation of a catalytic converter?
5. Name two likely spots for leaking gaskets and seals.
6. Which of the following statements is not a basic function of a vehicle's exhaust system?
   a. carry away poisonous gases from the passenger compartment
   b. muffle the sound of the engine
   c. enhance carburetor performance
   d. clean exhaust emissions
7. Which of the following are functions of a modern air cleaner assembly?
   a. provide filtered air to the PCV emission control system
   b. provide engine compartment fire protection in the event of a backfire
   c. meter, mix, and warm incoming air
   d. all of the above
8. Technician A says a vacuum leak results in less air entering the engine and a richer air/fuel mixture. Technician B says a vacuum leak allows more air to enter the engine causing a leaner air/fuel mixture. Who is correct?
   a. Technician A
   b. Technician B
   c. Both A and B
   d. Neither A nor B
9. Technician A says that vacuum hose routing for the entire vehicle is illustrated on the underhood

decal. Technician B says this decal illustrates emission system routing only. Who is correct?
a. Technician A
b. Technician B
c. Both A and B
d. Neither A nor B

10. Before replacing any exhaust system component, Technician A soaks all old connections with a penetrating oil. Technician B checks the old system's routing for critical clearance points. Who is correct?
a. Technician A
b. Technician B
c. Both A and B
d. Neither A nor B

11. A vehicle's manifold is warped beyond the manufacturer's specifications. Technician A replaces it. Technician B rebuilds it. Who is correct?
a. Technician A
b. Technician B
c. Both A and B
d. Neither A nor B

12. Technician A says the exhaust manifold gasket seals the joint between the exhaust manifold and the exhaust pipe. Technician B says that a resonator helps to reduce exhaust noise. Who is correct?
a. Technician A
b. Technician B
c. Both A and B
d. Neither A nor B

13. Technician A says that a catalytic converter breaks down HC and CO to relatively harmless by-products. Technician B says that using leaded gasoline or allowing the converter to overheat can destroy its usefulness. Who is correct?
a. Technician A
b. Technician B
c. Both A and B
d. Neither A nor B

14. Which of the following is not characteristic of a turbocharger?
a. used to increase engine power by compressing the air that goes into the combustion chambers
b. usually located close to the exhaust manifold
c. utilizes an exhaust-driven turbine wheel
d. requires a mechanical connection between the engine and the pressurizing pump to compress the intake gases

15. Ten psi of turbo boost means that air is being fed into the engine at _____ when the engine is operating at sea level.
a. 10 psi
b. 10.7 psi
c. 14.7 psi
d. 24.7 psi

16. What manages turbo output by controlling the amount of exhaust gas entering the turbine housing?
a. waste gate
b. turbine seal assembly
c. hot wheel
d. cold wheel

17. Technician A says a turbocharger can be operated at an oil pressure as low as 20 psi. Technician B says a turbocharger should not be operated at an oil pressure any lower than 30 psi. Who is correct?
a. Technician A
b. Technician B
c. Both A and B
d. Neither A nor B

18. What is the first step in turbocharger inspection?
a. Check the air cleaner for a dirty element.
b. Open the turbine housing at both ends.
c. Start the engine and listen to the system.
d. Remove the ducting from the air cleaner to turbo and examine the area.

19. Which of the following statements concerning superchargers is incorrect?
a. Superchargers must overcome inertia and spin up to speed as the flow of exhaust gas increases.
b. Superchargers do not require a waste gate to limit boost.
c. A by-pass is designed into the system to allow the supercharger to idle along when extra power is not needed.
d. Superchargers improve horsepower and torque.

20. Technician A uses sandpaper to remove carbon deposits from turbocharger waste gate parts. Technician B uses a hard metal scraper. Who is correct?
a. Technician A
b. Technician B
c. Both A and B
d. Neither A nor B

13 ENGINE SEALING AND REASSEMBLY

Objectives

- Explain the principles and precautions of working with various automotive fasteners.
- Explain the purpose of the various gaskets used to seal an engine.
- Identify the major gasket types and their uses.
- Explain general gasket installation procedures.
- Describe the methods of sealing the timing cover and rear main bearing.
- Reassemble a torndown engine including core plugs, bearings, crankshaft, camshaft, pistons, connecting rods, timing components, cylinder head, valvetrain components, oil pump, oil pan, and timing covers.
- Identify the methods of prelubricating a rebuilt engine.
- Install a rebuilt engine in a vehicle and observe the correct starting and break-in procedures.

Effectively sealing conventional gasoline and diesel engines means several things.

- Keep the low-pressure liquids in the cooling system away from the cylinders and lubricating oil.
- Prevent both internal and external oil leaks.
- Suppress and muffle noise.

❏ FASTENERS

New assembly methods have eliminated the need for many automotive fasteners. Ironically, however, nearly as many new fastener applications have arisen for those that have been replaced. Nuts and bolts remain an excellent means of holding engine parts together. For parts that must be disassembled and reassembled, there is no substitute for these fasteners. On the other hand, they are probably the most neglected of all mechanical devices. Depending on the application, they are also potentially the most dangerous.

Many types and sizes of fasteners are used in the automotive industry. Each fastener is designed for a specific purpose and specific conditions that are encountered in vehicle operation. One of the most popular type of fastener is the threaded fastener. Threaded fasteners include bolts, nuts, screws, and similar items that allow the technician to install or remove parts easily (Figure 13-1).

When replacing fasteners, the technician should observe the following precautions.

- Always use the same number of fasteners as originally used by the OEM.

Figure 13-1 Many different threaded fasteners are used on the automobile engine. *Courtesy of Botts Auto Parts Co.*

- Always use the same diameter, length, number of threads, type, and grade of fasteners as used by the OEM.
- Always observe the OEM's recommendation for tightening sequence, tightening steps (increments), and torque values given in the service manual.
- Never reuse a cotter pin.
- Always replace stretched fasteners or fasteners with damaged threads.
- Always use the correct washers and pins as specified by the OEM.

A number of terms have been used over the years to identify the various types of threads. Some of these have been replaced with new terms. The terms most

295

commonly employed in the automotive trade—the United States Standard (USS), the American National Standard (ANS), and the Society of Automotive Engineers Standard (SAE)—have all been replaced by the Unified National Series. The Unified National Series consists of four basic classifications.

- Unified National Coarse (UNC or NC)
- Unified National Fine (UNF or NF) (SAE)
- Unified National Extrafine (UNEF or NEF)
- Unified National Pipe Thread (UNPT or NPT)

The two common metric threads are coarse and fine and can be identified by the letters SI (Systeme International d'Unites or International System of Units) or ISO (International Standards Organization).

Bolt Usage

To identify the type of threads on a bolt, bolt terminology must be defined. The bolt has several parts (Figure 13-2). The bolt head is used to torque or tighten the bolt. A socket or wrench fits over the head, which enables the bolts to be tightened. Common U.S. Customary (USC) and metric sizes for bolt heads in-

TABLE 13-1 STANDARD BOLT HEAD SIZES

Common English (U.S. Customary) Head Sizes	Common Metric Head Sizes
Wrench Size (inches)	Wrench Size (millimeters)
3/8	9
7/16	10
1/2	11
9/16	12
5/8	13
11/16	14
3/4	15
13/16	16
7/8	17
15/16	18
1	19
1-1/16	20
1-1/8	21
1-3/16	22
1-1/4	23
1-5/16	24
1-3/8	26
7/16	27
1-1/2	29
	30
	32

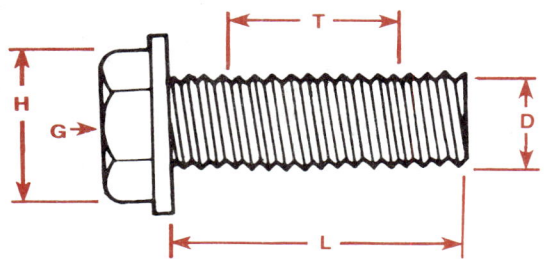

H = HEAD
G = GRADE MARKING (BOLT STRENGTH)
L = LENGTH (INCHES)
T = THREAD PITCH (THREAD/INCH)
D = NOMINAL DIAMETER (INCHES)

A

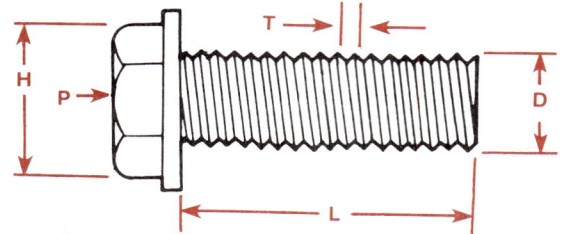
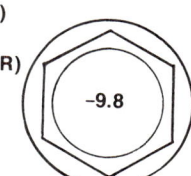

H = HEAD
P = PROPERTY CLASS (BOLT STRENGTH)
L = LENGTH (MILLIMETERS)
T = THREAD PITCH (THREAD/MILLIMETER)
D = NOMINAL DIAMETER (MILLIMETER)

B

Figure 13-2 (A) English and (B) metric bolt terminology.

clude those given in Table 13-1. The sizes are given in fractions of an inch and in millimeters.

WARNING: Although some of USC and metric head sizes are very close, never use a metric wrench or socket for USC bolts, or vice versa. Tool slippage may cause injury or damage the bolt head.

Bolt diameter is the measurement across the major diameter of the threaded area or across the bolt shank. The thread pitch of a bolt in the English system is determined by the number of threads there are in one inch of threaded bolt length and is expressed in number of threads per inch. The thread pitch in the metric system is determined by the distance in millimeters between two adjacent threads. To check the thread pitch of a bolt or stud, a thread pitch gauge is used. Gauges are available in both English and metric dimensions. Bolt length is the distance measured from the bottom of the head to the tip of the bolt. The bolt's tensile strength, or grade, is the amount of stress or stretch it is able to withstand. The type of bolt material and the diameter of the bolt determine its tensile strength. In the English system, the tensile strength of a bolt is identified by the number of radial lines (grade marks) on the bolt head. More lines mean higher ten-

Engine Sealing and Reassembly

TABLE 13-2 STANDARD BOLT STRENGTH MARKINGS

SAE Grade Markings	⬡	⬡ (3 lines)	⬡ (4 lines)	⬡ (5 lines)	⬡ (6 lines)
Definition	No lines: unmarked indeterminate quality SAE grades 0-1-2	3 Lines: common commercial quality Automotive and AN bolts SAE grade 5	4 Lines: medium commercial quality Automotive and AN bolts SAE grade 6	5 Lines: rarely used SAE grade 7	6 Lines: best commercial quality NAS and aircraft screws SAE grade 8
Material	Low carbon steel	Med. carbon steel tempered	Med. carbon steel quenched and tempered	Med. carbon alloy steel	Med. carbon alloy steel quenched and tempered
Tensile Strength	65,000 psi	120,000 psi	140,000 psi	140,000 psi	150,000 psi

sile strength (Table 13-2). In the metric system, tensile strength of a bolt or stud can be identified by a property class number on the bolt head (Figure 13-3). The higher the number, the greater the tensile strength.

It is very important to be familiar with the standard bolt indication measurements and grade markings. All bolts in the same connection must be of the same grade. Otherwise, they will not perform equally. Likewise, nuts are graded to match their respective bolts (Table 13-3). For example, a grade 8 nut must go with a grade 8 bolt. If a grade 5 nut was used instead, a grade 5 connection would result. The grade 5 nut cannot carry the loads expected of the grade 8 bolt. Look for the nut markings which are usually located on one side. Grade 8 and critical applications require the use of

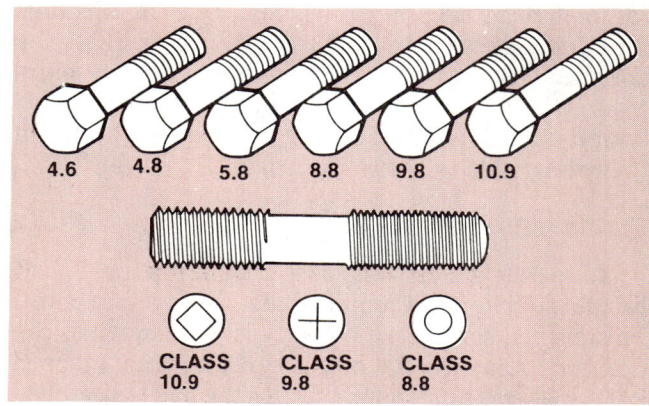

Figure 13-3 The grade of metric bolts and studs is marked by a property class number.

TABLE 13-3 STANDARD NUT STRENGTH MARKING

Inch System		Metric System	
Grade	Identification	Class	Identification
Hex Nut Grade 5	3 Dots	Hex Nut Property Class 9	Arabic 9
Hex Nut Grade 8	6 Dots	Hex Nut Property Class 10	Arabic 10
Increasing dots represent increasing strength.		Can also have blue finish or paint dab on hex flat. Increasing numbers represent increasing strength.	

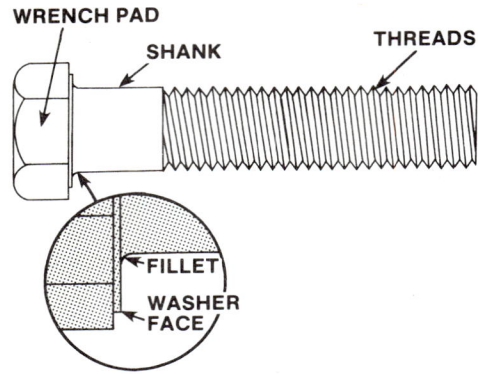

Figure 13-4 Bolt fillet detail.

fully hardened flat washers. They do not dish out like soft wrought washers that cause loss of clamp load.

Bolt heads can pop off because of fillet damage. The fillet is the smooth curve where the shank flows into the bolt head (Figure 13-4). Scratches in this area introduce stress to the bolt head, causing failure. The bolt head can be protected by removing any burrs around the edges of holes. Also, place flat washers with their rounded, punched side against the bolt head and their sharp side to the work surface.

Torque Principles

All metals are elastic. Elasticity means that a bolt can be stretched and compressed up to a certain point. This elastic, spring-like property is what provides the clamping force when a bolt is threaded into a tapped hole or when a nut is tightened. As the bolt is stretched a few thousandths of an inch, clamping force or holding power is created due to the bolt's natural tendency to return to its original length.

Like a spring, the more a bolt is stretched, the tighter it becomes. However, a bolt can be stretched too far. This is obvious when the grip on the wrench feels "mushy." At this point, the bolt can no longer safely carry the load it was designed to support.

If a bolt is stretched into yield, it takes a permanent set and never returns to normal (Figure 13-5). The bolt will continue to stretch more each time it is used, just like a piece of taffy that is stretched until it breaks.

Proper use of torque will avoid this yield condition. Torque values are calculated with a 25% safety factor below the yield point. There are some fasteners, however, that are torqued intentionally just barely into a yield condition, although not far enough to create the classic soda bottle shape. This type of fastener, known as a torque-to-yield (T-T-Y) bolt, will produce 100% of its intended strength, compared to 75% when torqued to normal values. These fasteners, however, should not be reused, unless otherwise specified by the manufacturer. Consult the OEM's specifications and the gasket set instructions for bolt reuse. Some aftermarket gasket manufacturers make the decision easy for the technician by including new T-T-Y bolts.

Table 13-4 gives standard bolt and nut torque specifications. If the manufacturer's torque specifications are available, follow them precisely. If a T-T-Y bolt is replaced with a new bolt of identical grade but torqued to a value found in a regular torque table, the clamping force produced will be at least 25% less. This is one reason many manufacturers are replacing OEM bolts with the next higher grade. As an example, a grade 8 bolt torqued properly to its 25% safety factor produces as much, if not more, clamping force than a grade 5 bolt at 100% with no safety factor.

The grade and surface condition, whether plated or nonplated, dry or lubricated, oil or antiseize, cut threads or rolled, straight shank or reduced, affects the torque/tension relationship and causes the performance of the connection to change. Because torque is actually a combination of both tension and torsion, it is also a function of friction. The bolt head or nut, whichever is being rotated, produces friction as it is turned, as do the threads when they gall together under the pressure of being in tension. Tests have proven that 90% of work energy is consumed by friction. Friction must first be overcome before any true work is done. For example, stretching the bolt must first be overcome. To compensate for surface variations, the following formula may be used to approximate the required torque.

$$T = FDC \div 12$$

where T = Torque in pound-feet
       F = Friction factor (torque coefficient)
       D = Bolt diameter in inches
       C = Bolt tension required in pounds

Table 13-5 gives the friction factor (F) for various surfaces and the percentage of torque required.

Nonplated bolts have a rougher surface than plated finishes. Therefore, it takes more torque to produce the same clamping force as on a plated bolt, even with one-third less friction. Add a lubricant and the torque might be as much as two-thirds lower.

Figure 13-5 These bolts have been torqued past their yield points. Note the classic soda bottle effect.

Engine Sealing and Reassembly

TABLE 13-4 STANDARD BOLT AND NUT TORQUE SPECIFICATIONS

Size Nut or Bolt	Torque (foot-pounds)	Size Nut or Bolt	Torque (foot-pounds)	Size Nut or Bolt	Torque (foot-pounds)
1/4-20	7-9	7/16-20	57-61	3/4-10	240-250
1/4-28	8-10	1/2-13	71-75	3/4-16	290-300
5/16-18	13-17	1/2-20	83-93	7/8-9	410-420
5/16-24	15-19	9/16-12	90-100	7/8-14	475-485
3/8-16	30-35	9/16-18	107-117	1-8	580-590
3/8-24	35-39	5/8-11	137-147	1-14	685-695
7/16-14	46-50	5/8-18	168-178		

TABLE 13-5 COMPENSATION FOR VARIOUS SURFACES

Surface	Friction Factor	Percentage of Torque Change Required
Dry, unplated steel	0.20	Use standard torque value shown.
Cadmium plating	0.15	Reduce standard torque 25%.
Zinc plating	0.21	Increase standard torque 10%.
Aluminum	0.15	Reduce standard torque 25%.
Stainless steel	0.30	Increase torque 50%.
Supertanium Special alloy steel	0.20	

TABLE 13-6 FRICTION FACTORS (F) AND TORQUE REDUCTIONS FOR LUBRICATED SURFACES ON ALLOY STEEL BOLTS

Lubricant	Friction Factor	Percentage of Torque Reduction Required
Collodial copper	0.11	Reduce standard torque 45%.
Never-seize	0.11	Reduce standard torque 45%.
Grease	0.12	Reduce standard torque 40%.
Moly-cote (molybdenum disulphite)	0.12	Reduce standard torque 40%.
Heavy oils	0.12	Reduce standard torque 40%.
Graphite	0.14	Reduce standard torque 30%.
White lead	0.15	Reduce standard torque 25%.

Most printed torque values are for dry, plated bolts. Lubricants are beneficial when working with engines. They provide smoother surfaces and more consistent and evenly loaded connections. They also help reduce thread galling.

Reusing a dry nut will produce a connection with decreasing clamp force each time it is used. Nut threads are designed to collapse slightly to carry the bolt load. If dry nuts are reused, increased thread galling will result each time the nuts are reused at the same torque.

Lubrication of fasteners is recommended for consistency (Table 13-6). However, be sure to lubricate all the bolts with the same lubricant. Some lubricants are more slippery than others, which affects torque values. Lubricate the bolt, never the hole. Otherwise, the bolt may merely be tightening against the oil in the hole.

If a bolt with a reduced shank diameter (for example, a connecting rod bolt) is specified by the OEM, never replace it with a standard, straight shank bolt. A reduced shank diameter bolt looks "dog-boned." Its function is to reduce the stress on the threads by transferring it to the shank. A standard bolt under similar conditions would break very quickly at the threads.

Rolled threads are 30% stronger than cut threads. They also offer better fatigue resistance because there are no sharp notches to create stress points.

Studs are used to prevent continued damage to tapped holes by remaining in place at one end while the other end does the remainder of the work for future use. If a bolt or stud breaks in a tapped hole, the threads will become damaged from the shock of the breakage. The hole must then be retapped to reshape the damaged threads and assure even torque. Tapped holes in aluminum alloys should always be strengthened with thread inserts. Manufacturers do not add them during assembly because of cost and labor time. However, they are necessary for repeated maintenance.

Some manufacturers recommend a torque-turn method for cylinder head bolts. This is a very accurate approach. It works for standard bolts and nuts as well. If the work thickness is no more than four times the bolt's diameter, snug the nut lightly against the work and rotate it one-third of a turn (120 degrees). If the work is between four to eight times the diameter, rotate the nut a half turn (180 degrees). This will produce a very reliable clamp load that is much higher than can be achieved just by torquing. Other variables will not affect the results.

Keep the following points in mind.

1. Visually inspect the bolts.
   - Threads must be clean and undamaged. Discard all bolts that are not acceptable.
   - Use liquid sealant or engine oil on the threads and seating face of the cylinder head bolts to prevent seizure from rust and corrosion. This is particularly important for an aluminum block or head. Use sealant on those bolts that hold in coolant or oil.
   - Install bolts in their proper holes.
   - Run a nut over the bolt's threads by hand. Discard it if any binding occurs.
   - Clean bolt and cylinder block threads with a thread chaser or tap (Figure 13-6).
2. Apply a light coat of 10W engine oil to threads and bottom face of bolt head. A sealer is required for a bolt that enters a water jacket (Figure 13-7). This will stop coolant seepage around the bolt threads. Seeping coolant could get in the oil or cause corrosion that might damage parts, resulting in engine failure.
3. Tighten bolts in the recommended sequence. This is important to prevent warpage of the cylinder head or other parts.
   - Use an accurate torque wrench.
   - Tighten bolts to the recommended torque in steps and proper sequence.
4. If bolt heads are not tight against the surface, the bolts should be removed and washers installed.
5. Make sure the bolt is the proper length and it is not too long.

Bolt hole threads in the engine block will often pull up, leaving a raised edge around the hole (Figure 13-8). If the block has been resurfaced, the threads might run up to the surface. In either case, the bolt holes should be cleaned by chamfering and the threads cleaned with an appropriate size bottoming tap. Always repair damaged threads to assure proper bolt performance.

Many different nuts are used by the automotive industry. Beware of hexagon (hex) nut rotation on power wrenches. It is deceptively easy to place a bolt into a yield condition within seconds. Impact wrenches are the worst offenders. Friction is needed to prevent the nut from spinning. If the nut is lubricated, there is no friction left to stop the impact wrench from hammering the nut past the bolt's yield point or stripping the threads.

SHOP TALK

Impact wrenches should only be used to loosen nuts and bolts. Use other power or hand tools to tighten them. Final tightening should always be done with a torque wrench.

Smaller air-powered speed wrenches do not produce the severe force of impact wrenches and are much safer to use.

A rule of thumb about lock washers: If the connection did not come with one, do not add one. Lock washers are extremely hard and tend to break under severe pressure (Figure 13-9).

Thread Repair

A common fastening problem is threads stripping inside an engine block, cylinder head, or other struc-

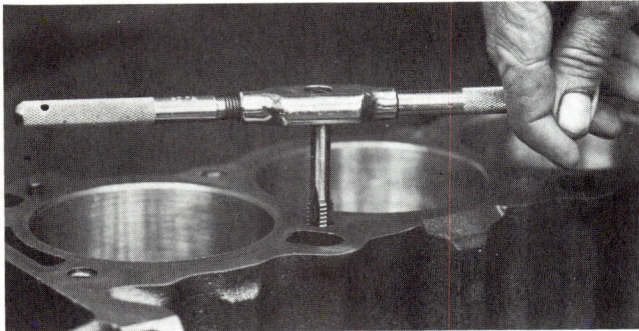

Figure 13-6 Cleaning bolt holes with a tap. *Courtesy of JP Industries, Inc.*

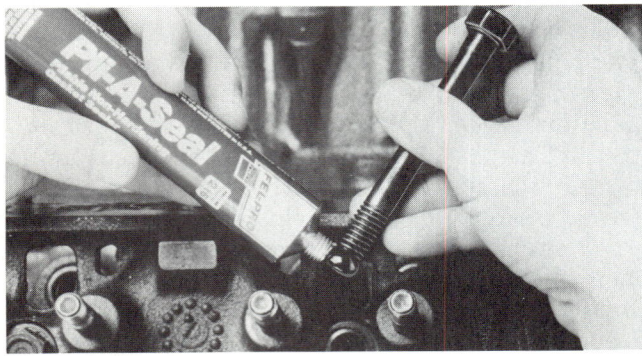

Figure 13-7 If a bolt enters the coolant passages, coat it with a flexible sealer. *Courtesy of Fel-Pro, Inc.*

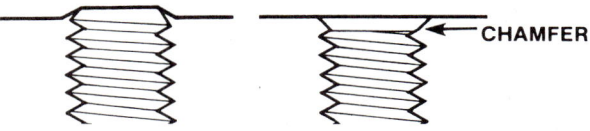

Figure 13-8 Bolt hole threads can pull up, leaving a raised edge. Also, if the block has been resurfaced, the threads might run up to the surface. In either case, the hole must be chamfered.

Engine Sealing and Reassembly 301

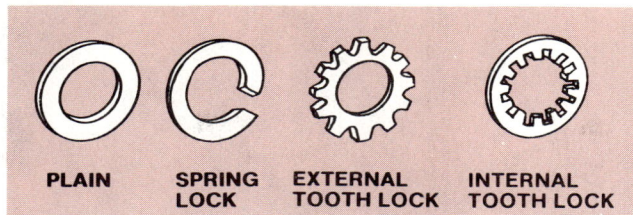

Figure 13-9 Types of lock washers.

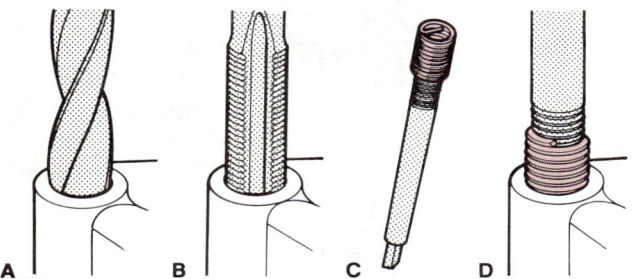

Figure 13-10 Steps in the installation of a helically-coiled threaded insert. (A) Drill the damaged threads and clean all metal chips out of the hole. (B) Tap new threads in the hole using the specified tap. The thread depth should exceed the length of the bolt. (C) Install the insert on the mandrel provided in the installation kit. Bottom it against the tang. (D) Lubricate the insert with oil and thread it into the hold until flush with the surface. Use a punch or side-cutters to break off the tang.

ture. This problem is usually caused by torque that is too high or by incorrectly threading the bolt into the hole. Rather than replacing the block or cylinder head, the threads can be replaced by the use of threaded inserts. Several threaded inserts are available. The helically-coiled insert is the most popular. Figure 13-10 shows the proper procedure for installing this type of threaded insert. Always follow the directions given with the insert kit.

❏ GASKETS

Gaskets are used predominantly to prevent gas or liquid leakage between two parts that are bolted together (Figure 13-11). In addition to the sealing function mentioned earlier, gaskets also serve as spacers, wear insulators, and vibration dampers.

As a spacer, the gasket serves as a shim between two joined engine components, such as the fuel pump lever and cam. It also helps compensate for manufacturing or rebuilding tolerances in the cylinder head. In the wear insulator function, the gasket material is softer than the separated components. This allows for alternating expansion and contraction with less friction, thus preventing fretting or brinelling of machined surfaces. Keep in mind that the vibration damper function does not apply to liquid sealants that are used without a gasket and allow a metal-to-metal seal.

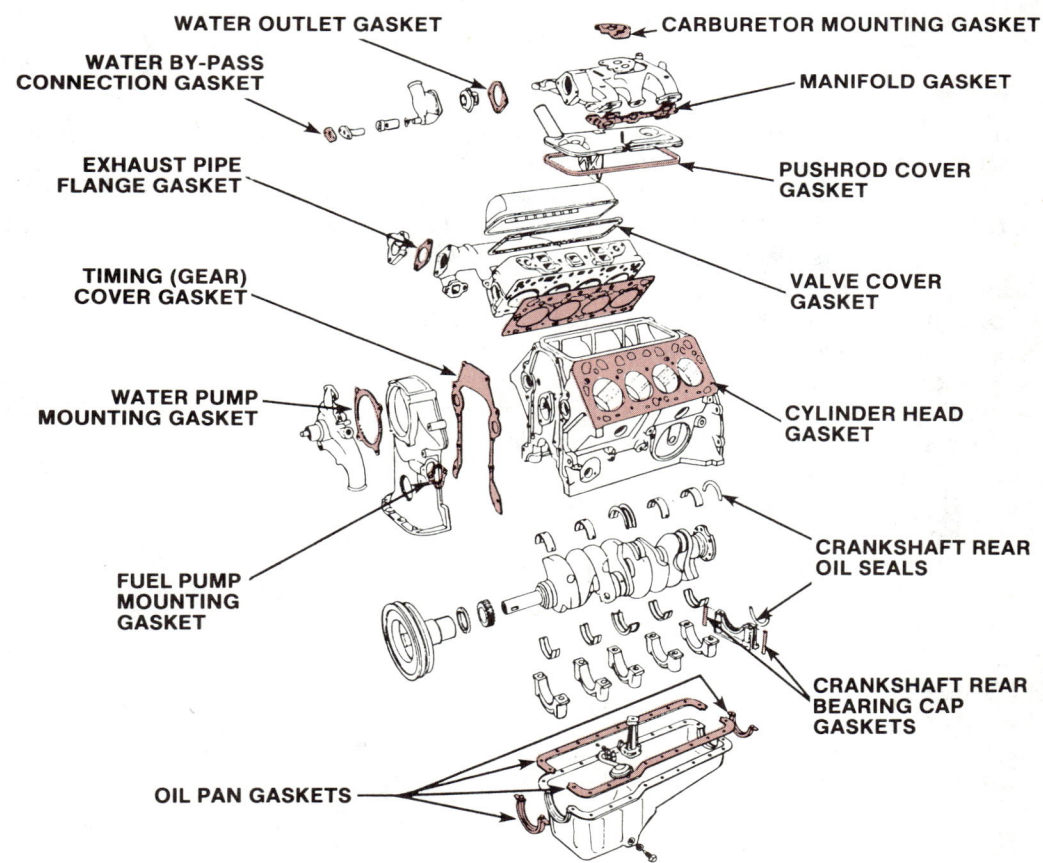

Figure 13-11 Typical engine gasket and seal locations.

There are three basic classifications of engine gaskets.

- Hard gaskets are steel, stainless steel, copper, or a combination metal enclosure with a compressible and heat-resistant clay/fiber compound sandwiched inside. Gaskets in this class are cylinder head gaskets, exhaust manifold gaskets, and some intake manifold gaskets.
- Soft gaskets consist of soft, flexible materials such as cork, rubber, a combination of cork/rubber, rubber-coated steel, paper, and other compressed fiber materials. Newer materials, sometimes called gaskets-in-a-tube, include silicone gaskets and anaerobics. Soft gaskets are often used on valve covers, oil pans, rocker covers, pushrod covers, water pumps, thermostat housing, timing covers, and inspection plates.

  Silicone gasketing is available in three grades. The black is for general purpose; blue is for special applications; and red is for high-temperature requirements. Most mechanics use silicone gasketing to aid sealing in notches or dovetails.
- Sealants and adhesives generally come in liquid form to be applied to all metal gaskets such as beaded steel-type cylinder head gaskets and intake manifold gaskets. It dries into a flexible, nonhardening sealant to help prevent leaks of oil, water, gasoline, air pressure, or vacuum. It is also useful as an antiseize for threads on bolts, studs, and fittings.

Gasket Materials

Historically, with heavy-wall all-cast-iron engines, most gasket materials and constructions were similar, if not identical. Most engine applications were inherently forgiving. One key to the auto industry's success in achieving late-model engine performance goals has been the development of gaskets specifically designed to seal the new engines. This includes exhaust-flange gaskets as well as exhaust rings—areas most subject to severe stresses of temperature and pressure. These new sealing products have been highly engineered for virtually all critical areas of application in dozens of different engine designs. Inappropriate substitution of non-OE-equivalent products in servicing or rebuilding them is not sufficient as it might have been in the past.

Another major change in gasket technology today is the elimination of asbestos. Although the automotive industry has voluntarily cut back the use of asbestos, the EPA has banned its use in all manufactured products after 1994. The irony is that asbestos is such an excellent gasket material that were it not for health liability issues, there would be no reason to replace it with anything else. It offers good strength and chemical resistance, and it is cheap compared to other materials. But the physical properties that make asbestos

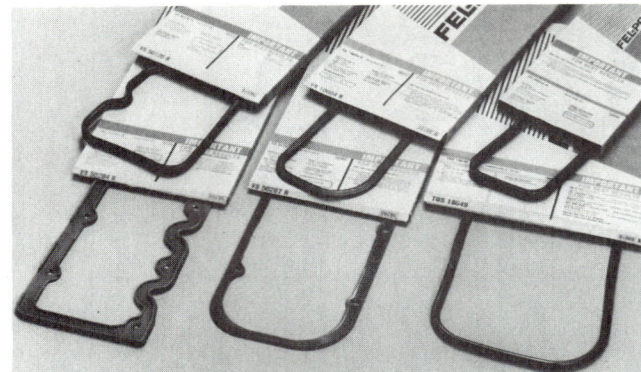

Figure 13-12 Molded silicone rubber gaskets designed for use with late-model engines. *Courtesy of Fel-Pro, Inc.*

such a good gasket fiber also make it a hazardous substance to those who work with it.

Most late-model engines are equipped with premium gaskets made of space-age materials, such as molded silicone rubber (Figure 13-12) and cut plastic gaskets with silicone sealing beads. Advanced gasketing technology incorporating flexible graphite cores, specialized surface coatings, new asbestos-free materials, elastomeric beading, reinforced cork products, wire-ring combustion seals, flat-plate hoop-strength constructions, and many other gasket design innovations all are different technological approaches by different OE suppliers to reach the same goal. That goal is long-term leak-free joints. The new gaskets have entirely different properties than traditional gasketing materials (asbestos, rubber, cork, and the like) that influence many critical design features including gasket thickness, compressibility, no-retorque characteristics, near-zero creep, greatly improved corrosion resistance, and superior thermal properties in sealing at temperatures exceeding 1000 degrees Fahrenheit.

General Gasket Installation Procedures

The following general instructions will serve as a helpful guide for installing gaskets. Because there are many different gasket materials and designs, it is impossible to list directions for every type of installation in this chapter. Remember to follow any special directions provided on the important instruction sheets packed with most gasket sets (Figure 13-13). These will give you additional tips on replacing the gaskets on the engine.

USING SERVICE MANUALS

Special procedures for installing gaskets are found in the section that covers the part to be fastened to the engine block or cylinder head.

Engine Sealing and Reassembly

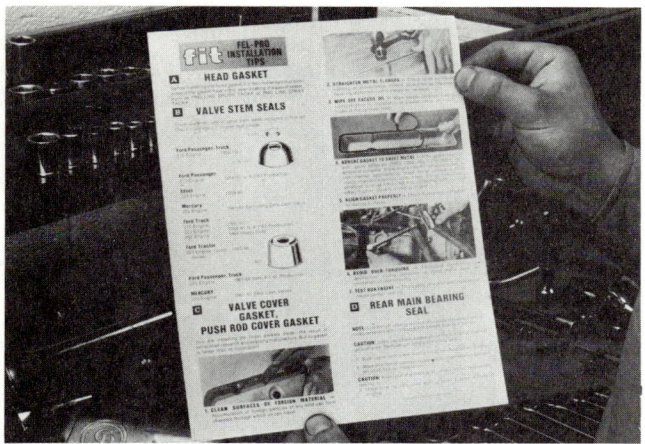

Figure 13-13 Follow the directions provided with the gasket set. *Courtesy of Fel-Pro, Inc.*

1. Never reuse old gaskets. Even if the old gasket appears to be in good condition, it will never seal as well as a new one. The old gasket has been exposed to high combustion temperatures and pressures, hot oil or coolant, and might have worn or damaged sealing surfaces. It also has been compressed by bolt torquing to fit the parts it has been sealing. It will not be able to re-form itself to create another good seat.
2. Handle new gaskets carefully. Be careful not to damage the new gaskets before placing them on the engine. Any bend or crease in the gasket material is a potential weak spot that might cause a leak after installation. This is especially true of the composition-type gaskets used on many cylinder heads and manifolds. If any attempt is made to straighten a bent or distorted gasket, it could fracture the gasket and create a weak spot. Protect the new gaskets by keeping them in their package until installation.

USING SERVICE MANUALS

Always refer to the specific engine and engine part section of the service manual for the recommended procedures for using sealants.

3. Use gasket sealants only when they are absolutely necessary. The hot, oily environment of an engine can cause some chemical sealants to react adversely with the binding compound in composition-type gaskets, causing the gasket to deteriorate and leak.

SHOP TALK

Many technicians tend to use too much sealant on gaskets. Do not make this mistake. Because sealants have less strength than gasket materials, they create weaker joints. They also can prevent some gasket material from doing what it is supposed to do—soak up oil and swell to make a tight seal.

4. Cleanliness is essential. New gaskets seal best when used on clean surfaces. Thoroughly clean all mating surfaces of dirt, oil deposits, rust, old sealer, and gasket material. If any foreign substances remain, they can create a path for leaks. Scraping away the old gasket is not an easy job, but it is essential to assure a leak-free seal. When using a hand gasket scraper on aluminum parts, be very careful not to scratch the softer metal surfaces (Figure 13-14).
5. Use the right gasket in the right position. Always compare the new gasket to the component mating surfaces to make sure that it is the right gasket (Figure 13-15). Comparing the new gasket with the original is another way to confirm that you are using the correct part. Check that all bolt holes, dowel holes, pushrod openings, coolant, and lubrication passages line up perfectly with the gasket.

Figure 13-14 Use care when scraping off an old gasket, particularly on aluminum surfaces. *Courtesy of Victor/Dana*

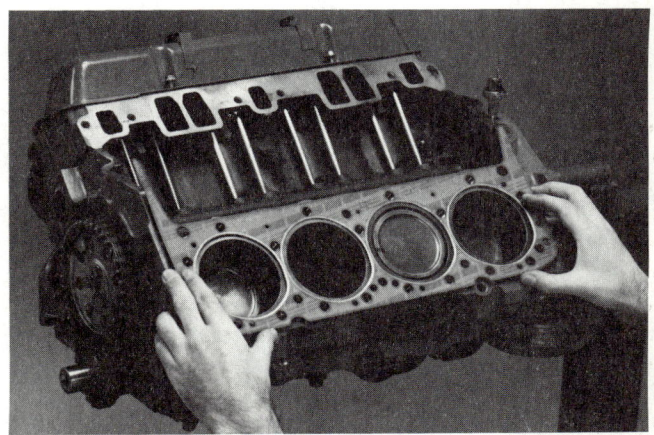

Figure 13-15 Checking a head gasket for proper fit. *Courtesy of Fel-Pro, Inc.*

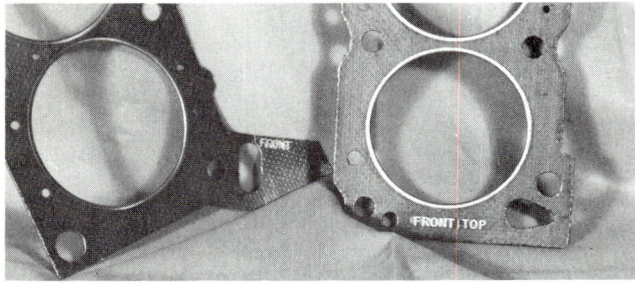

Figure 13-16 Some gaskets have installation directions stamped on them. *Courtesy of JP Industries, Inc.*

Some gaskets will have directions such as top, front, or this side up stamped on one surface (Figure 13-16). Remember to follow these instructions exactly when putting the gasket in place. An upside-down or reversed gasket can easily cause loss of oil pressure, overheating, and engine failure.

Cylinder Head Gaskets

Cylinder head gaskets are the most sophisticated type of gasket. They also have the most demanding job to do. When first starting an engine in cold weather, parts near the combustion chamber might be subfreezing. Then, after only a few minutes of engine operation, these same parts might reach 400 degrees Fahrenheit. The inner edges of the cylinder head gasket are exposed to combustion flame temperatures from 2000 to 3000 degrees Fahrenheit.

Pressures inside the combustion chamber also vary tremendously. On the intake stroke, a vacuum or low pressure exists in the cylinder. Then, after combustion, pressure peaks of approximately 1,000 psi occur. This extreme change from suction to high pressure happens in a fraction of a second.

Cylinder head gaskets, under these conditions, must simultaneously do the following.

- Seal intake stroke vacuum, combustion pressure, and the flame in the combustion chamber.
- Prevent coolant leakage, resist rust, corrosion and, in many cases, meter coolant flow.
- Seal oil passages through the block and head while resisting chemical action.
- Allow for lateral and vertical head movement as the engine heats and cools.
- Be flexible enough to seal minor surface warpage while being stiff enough to maintain adequate gasket compression.
- Fill small machining marks that could lead to serious gasket leakage and failure.
- Withstand forces produced by engine vibration.

Bimetal Engine Requirements

Another problem that head gaskets must face is the differing expansion rates of aluminum/cast-iron com-

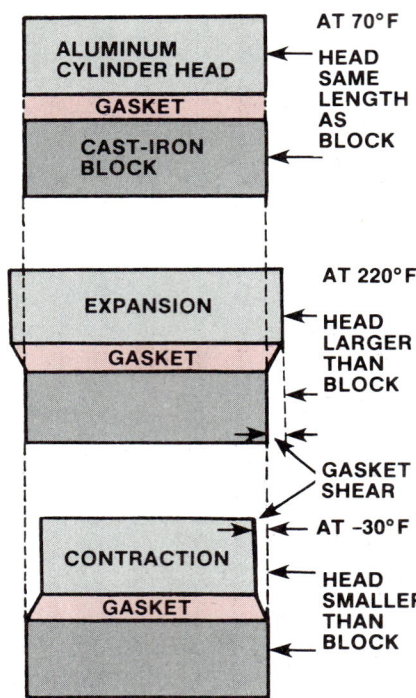

Figure 13-17 Thermal growth characteristics of bimetal engines.

bination engines (Figure 13-17). Aluminum has a coefficient of thermal expansion two to three times greater than steel, depending on the alloy. This creates scrubbing action on a head gasket as the engine goes from cold to hot and back again. If the surface of the aluminum head has been roughly machined, it can grab and tear the head gasket facing material. To prevent this, slippery nonstick surface coatings and other materials are applied, by the manufacturer, to the gaskets to create the needed lubrication between the head and gasket. Graphite is a natural lubricant, so graphite-faced gaskets are not coated.

Today's bimetal engines with thin-wall castings experience more movement and flexing between the head, block, and cylinder bores, which means a more rigid gasket is often needed. This can be accomplished by using different facing materials, changing the design and loading of the combustion flanges, or by using silicone beading to increase sealing loads in critical areas.

The latest generation of aftermarket gaskets includes a bead sealant that increases clamping pressure around troublesome areas. Another common and desirable gasket design today is the no-retorque type. Older gasket designs, such as the steel-faced sandwich and perforated core, require the cylinder head of an engine to be retorqued 300 to 500 miles after it has been rebuilt. These gaskets take a set after initial engine operation and relax to the point where retorquing is needed to restore the clamping force. The extra labor and expense of retorquing a cylinder head gasket makes the repair more expensive than no-retorque designs in the long run. The no-retorque design retains a higher level of clamping force. Therefore, no retorquing is needed.

> **CUSTOMER CARE**
>
> If a head gasket that requires retorquing has been installed, explain the importance of doing this to the customer.

Impression Testing

The carbon impression paper technique is growing in popularity as a means of checking the effectiveness of the head gasket seal. Start by cutting a piece of carbon impression paper to about the size of the gasket and follow these steps.

1. Place the paper on top of the old gasket installed on the engine block.
2. Reinstall the cylinder head.
3. Tighten the head bolts to the recommended torque and in the proper sequence.
4. Remove the cylinder head.
5. Inspect the impression left on the paper (Figure 13-18). Dim or weak lines indicate poor gasket contact due to a warped block or head.

Manifold Gaskets

There are three types of manifold gaskets—the intake manifold, exhaust manifold (Figure 13-19), and the combination intake and exhaust (Figure 13-20). Each type of manifold gasket has its own sealing characteristics and problems. Therefore, be sure to follow the manufacturer's instructions when installing.

> **USING SERVICE MANUALS**
>
> Refer to the manifold unit in the engine section of the service manual for specific instructions on the installation of manifold gaskets.

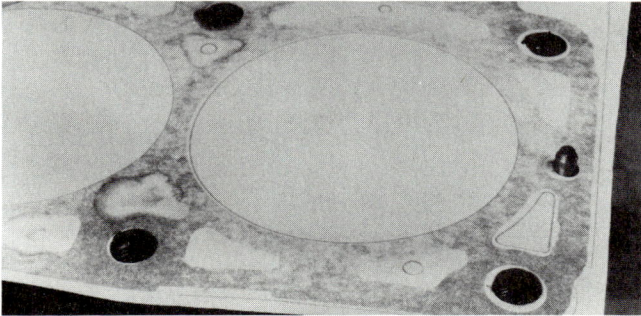

Figure 13-18 Dim or weak lines on the carbon paper indicate poor surface gasket. *Courtesy of Victor/Dana*

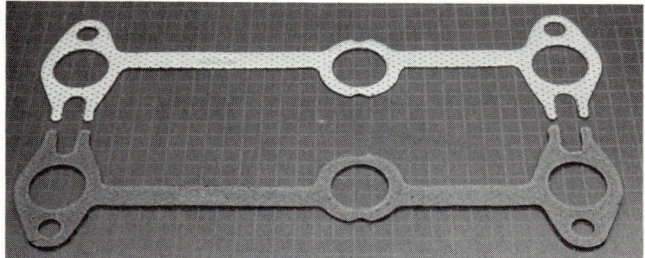

Figure 13-19 Typical exhaust manifold gaskets. *Courtesy of Fel-Pro, Inc.*

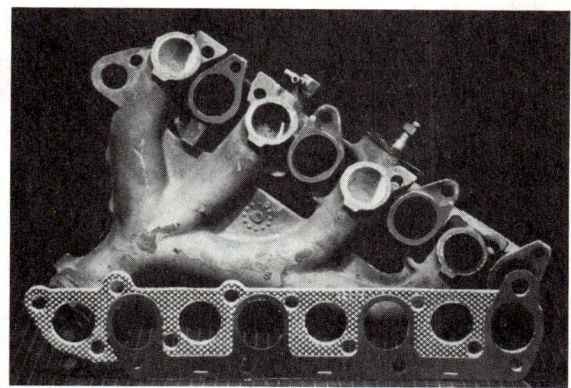

Figure 13-20 Combination intake/exhaust manifold gasket. *Courtesy of Fel-Pro, Inc.*

Valve Cover Gaskets

Valve cover gaskets have an increasingly difficult job in today's high-temperature engines. They must seal between a steel or aluminum (or molded plastic) stamping and a cylinder head surface that might not be machined. The valve cover does not seal by pressure. The bolts that attach the cover to the cylinder head are usually widely spaced. It might appear that almost any gasket could do the job. But the gasket must also withstand high temperatures and the caustic action of acids in the oil.

To provide an effective seal, a valve cover gasket must conform to flange distortion. At the same time, it must provide good crush and split resistance to limit torque loss and provide chemical and heat resistance for long-term sealing. The most commonly used material is a blend of cork and rubber particles. The quality of the materials is crucial when using cork/rubber gaskets, because a low-quality cork/rubber mixture can develop leakage after a fairly short period of operation. Another popular valve cover material is made of synthetic rubber. Whether it is a cork/rubber or synthetic rubber gasket, it must be a perfect fit (Figure 13-21).

Oil Pan Gaskets

The oil pan gasket seals the joint between the oil pan and the bottom of the block (Figure 13-22). In

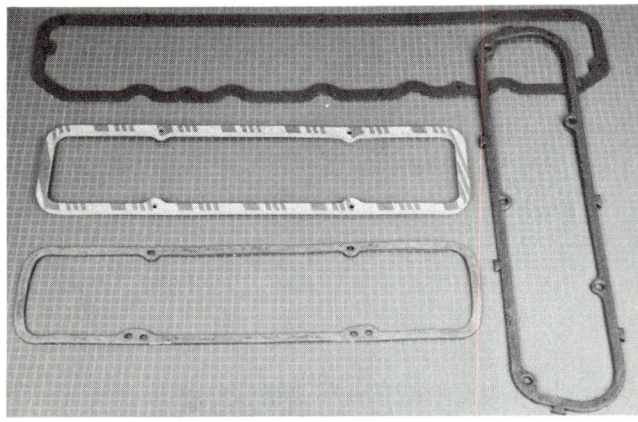

Figure 13-21 The two primary valve cover gasket materials are synthetic rubber and cork/rubber. *Courtesy of Fel-Pro, Inc.*

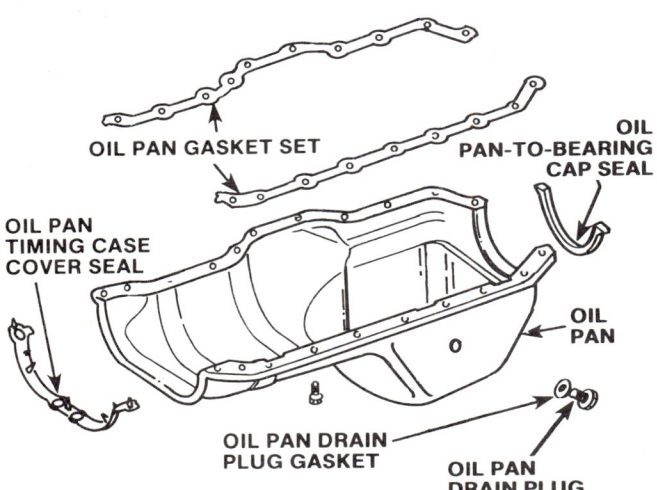

Figure 13-22 Oil pan gaskets and seals.

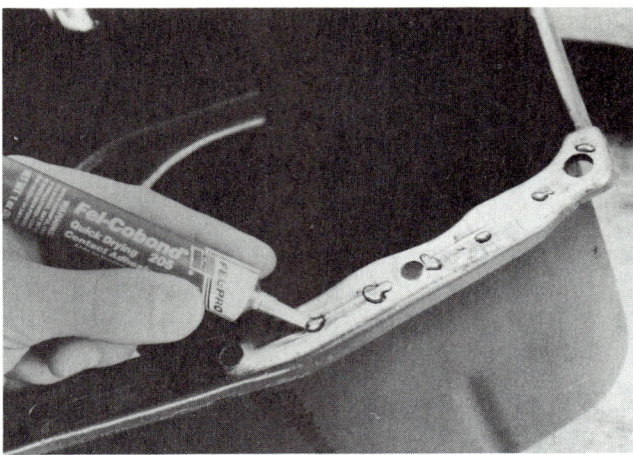

Figure 13-23 Applying adhesive to the oil pan flange will prevent the gasket from moving and will provide a positive seal. *Courtesy of Fel-Pro, Inc.*

many cases, the oil pan gasket might also seal the bottom of the timing cover and the lower section of the rear main bearing cap.

It is difficult to locate oil pan gasket leaks. They might be in areas not immediately seen, making the oil pan gasket one of the most ignored gaskets on an engine. Oil leaks might be blamed on other gaskets or seals rather than the oil pan gasket.

Like valve cover gaskets, the oil pan gasket must resist hot, thin engine oil. Oil pans are usually made of stamped steel, but with a stronger gasket flange. Because of the added weight and splash of crankcase oil, the pan has many assembly bolts closely spaced. As a result, the clamping force on the oil pan gasket is great. The gasket is thinner and must resist crushing.

Oil pan gaskets, which are similar to valve covers, are made of several types of material. A commonly used material is synthetic rubber, known for its long-term sealing ability. It is tough, durable, and resists hot engine oil. Synthetic rubber gaskets are easy to remove, so the sealing surfaces need less cleanup.

Carefully follow the recommendations on the gasket package label and instruction forms. Read through all the installation steps before beginning. Take note of any of the original equipment manufacturer's recommendations that could affect engine sealing. Before installing the oil pan, make sure its flange is flat. The gasket should be mounted with a few dabs of quick-drying contact adhesive (Figure 13-23). Carefully align the gasket before the adhesive dries. Wait until the adhesive is dry before installing the pan. Tighten the oil pan bolts to the recommended torque specification and sequence given in the service manual.

❏ ADHESIVES, SEALANTS, AND OTHER CHEMICAL SEALING MATERIALS

There are a number of chemicals that can be used to reduce labor and insure a good seal. Many gasket sets include a label with the proper chemical recommendation for use with that gasket set. Some even include sealers in the sets when the original equipment manufacturer used a sealer to replace a gasket and a gasket cannot be manufactured for that application. They also include sealers in some sets where gasket unions need a sealant to assure a good seal.

SHOP TALK

Chemical adhesives and sealants give added holding power and sealing ability where two parts are joined. Sealants usually are added to threads where fluid contact is frequent. Chemical thread retainers are either aerobic (cures in the presence of air) or anaerobic (cures in the absence of air). These chemical products are used in place of lock washers.

Of course, there are numerous locations in an engine where precut or premolded gaskets can benefit from the services of a chemical sealant. For example, to seal the intake manifold on a V-type engine, it is important to place a dab of silicone in the corners. The same can be said about the front cover-to-oil-pan joint, rear bearing cap seals, and valley pan manifold installations.

Adhesives

Quick-drying contact adhesive is designed for bonding cork, rubber, fiber, and metal gaskets in place prior to assembly. Gasket adhesives form a tough bond when used on clean, dry surfaces. Adhesives do not aid the sealing ability of the gasket. They are meant only to hold gaskets in place during component assembly. Use small dabs; they will dry quicker for fast installation. Do not assemble components until the adhesive is completely dry. Most adhesives are ideal for use on gasket applications such as valve covers, pushrod covers, manifold and manifold end seals, and oil pan and oil pan end seals (Figure 13-24).

Sealants

General-Purpose Sealants

General-purpose sealers (sometimes called chemical positioning agents) come in liquid form and are available in a brush type (known as brush tack) and an aerosal type (known as spray tack). General purpose sealers (Figure 13-25) form a tacky, flexible seal when applied in a thin, even coat that aids in gasket sealing by helping to position the gasket during assembly. The chemicals in a general-purpose sealant will not upset the designed performance of most mechanical gaskets. The possible exception to this is that sealant manufacturers do not recommend their use on rubber parts. These sealants are nonhardening and can cause rubber gaskets to slip.

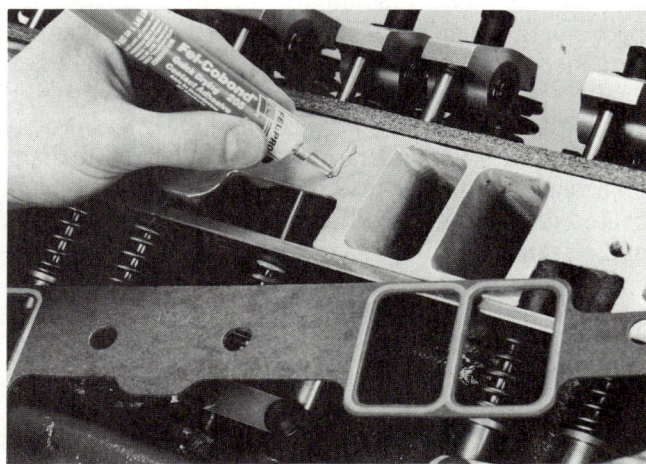

Figure 13-24 Holding an intake manifold gasket in place with contact adhesive. *Courtesy of Fel-Pro, Inc.*

A

B

Figure 13-25 Applying (A) brush-type and (B) aerosol-type general-purpose sealant. *Courtesy of Fel-Pro, Inc.*

CAUTION: *Never use a hard-drying sealant (such as shellac) on gaskets. It will make future disassembly extremely difficult and might damage the gasket material.*

Flexible Sealants

Flexible sealants are most often used on threads of bolts that go into fluid passages. They are nonhardening sealers that fill voids, preventing the fluid from running up the threads. They resist the chemical attack of lubricants, synthetic oils, detergents, antifreeze, gasoline, and diesel fuel.

Silicone Formed-in-Place Sealants

Silicone gasketing can be used to replace conventional paper, cork, and cork/rubber gaskets. It is generally for use on oil pans, valve covers, thermostat housing, timing covers, water pumps, and other such installations. Room temperature vulcanizing (RTV) silicone sealing products are the best known of the formed-in-place (FIP) gasket products.

Today's RTV aerobic silicone formulations are impervious to most automotive fluids, extremely resistant to oil, oxygen-sensor safe, exhibit outstanding flexibility (a necessary feature on modern bimetal engines),

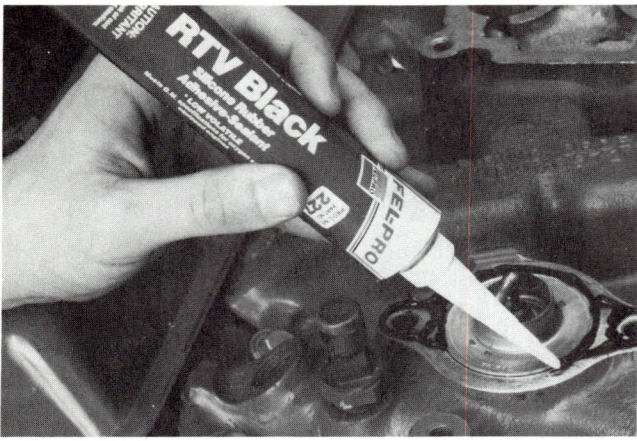

Figure 13-26 When using RTV silicone, assemble the joint as soon as possible before the RTV begins to cure. *Courtesy of Fel-Pro, Inc.*

and adhere well to a broad range of materials that include plastics, metal, and glass.

To use RTV silicone, make sure the mating surfaces are free of dirt, grease, and oil. Apply a continuous 1/8-inch bead on one surface only (preferably the cover side). Make sure to circle all bolt holes. Adjust the shape before a skin forms (in about 10 minutes) as shown in Figure 13-26. Remove excess RTV silicone with a dry towel or paper towel. Press the parts together. Do not slide the parts together—this will disturb the bead. Tighten all retaining bolts to the manufacturer's specified torque. Cure time is approximately 1 hour for metal-to-metal joints and can take up to 24 hours for 1/8-inch gaps.

WARNING: The uncured rubber contained in RTV silicone gasketing irritates the eyes. If any gets in your eyes, immediately flush with clean water or eyewash. If the irritation continues, see a doctor.

Anaerobic Formed-in-Place Sealants

These formed-in-place materials are used for thread locking as well as gasketing (Figure 13-27). As a re-

Figure 13-27 Anaerobic sealant is used as a formed-in-place gasket, as well as a retaining compound. *Courtesy of Fel-Pro, Inc.*

taining compound, they are mostly used to hold sleeves, bearings, and locking screw nuts in place where there is a high exposure to vibration.

CAUTION: Never use a sealant or formed-in-place gasket material on exhaust manifolds.

The major difference between aerobic and anaerobic sealants other than their method of curing is their gap-filling ability. Typically, 0.050 inch (3/64 inch) is the absolute limit of any anaerobic's gap-filling material. Some are only designed to seal 0.005- to 0.010-inch gaps. Anaerobic sealers are intended to be used between the machined surfaces of rigid castings, not on flexible stampings.

> ### SHOP TALK
> Once hardened, a good anaerobic bond is unbelievably tenacious and can withstand high temperatures. Therefore, care must be taken in selection. They tend to be highly specialized and not readily interchangeable. For example, there are various levels of thread-locking products that range from medium-strength antivibration agents to high-strength, weld-like retaining compounds. The inadvertent use of the wrong product could make future disassembly an impossibility. Check the label to be certain that anaerobic material will suit the purpose of the application.

Hylomar

Hylomar, which stands for high temperature (hy), low cost (lo), Marston (mar) product, is neither an RTV nor an anaerobic. It is a combination of polyurethene paste and silica (not silicone) flakes mixed with methylene chloride solvent. When Hylomar is clamped in a joint, the silica flakes interlock and encapsulate the plastic paste, effectively shielding it from heat, liquids, and contaminants that might otherwise dissolve it. Because Hylomar never hardens or cures, the center remains soft and pliable—like an armor-plated sponge.

As a sealing supplement, Hylomar sticks to virtually any surface, it resists all fluids (including gasoline), and has a claimed temperature range of 60 to more than 600 degrees Fahrenheit. In addition, if a Hylomar-coated gasket is set down wrong, it can be peeled off and reseated without damage.

Antiseize Compounds

Antiseize compound prevents dissimilar metals from reacting with one another and seizing (Figure 13-28). This chemical-type material is used on many fasteners, especially those used with aluminum parts. Be sure to follow the manufacturer's recommendations on the use of this compound.

Engine Sealing and Reassembly   **309**

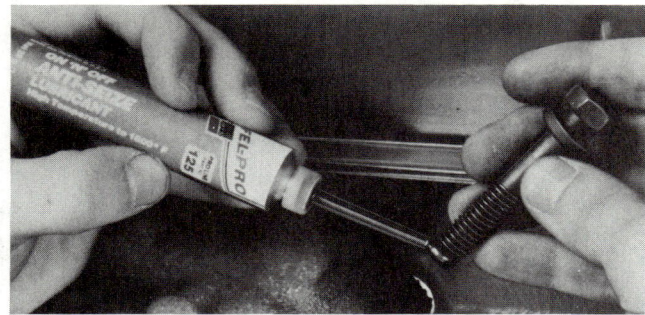

Figure 13-28 Using a high-temperature antiseize compound. *Courtesy of Fel-Pro, Inc.*

❏ OIL SEALS

The job of seals is to keep oil and other vital fluids from escaping around a rotating shaft. They are pressed into stationary bores in the crankshaft and timing gear cover and generally consist of a metal casing to which a synthetic rubber sealing element is bonded.

Timing Cover Oil Seals

An oil seal prevents oil from leaking out around the crankshaft at the front of the engine. The seal is usually located in the timing cover. It seals on the shaft hub of the harmonic balancer pulley hub or on the crankshaft. Sometimes this seal will wear a groove in the shaft or hub. A replacement seal will not be reliable if it is installed on the worn shaft. It can only seal properly on a smooth surface.

If the balancer shaft or pulley hub has a groove, it might have to be replaced, a new sleeve installed, or welded and ground to its original size and finish. To replace the sleeve, use a rebuilder replacement set that includes a sleeve, new front seal, anaerobic sealant, and any other gasket components required to seal the timing cover assembly (Figure 13-29). The sleeve will cover the groove in the balancer shaft or pulley hub and provide a new sealing surface for the front oil seal.

To install the remaining oil cover seals, follow the gasket manufacturer's instructions.

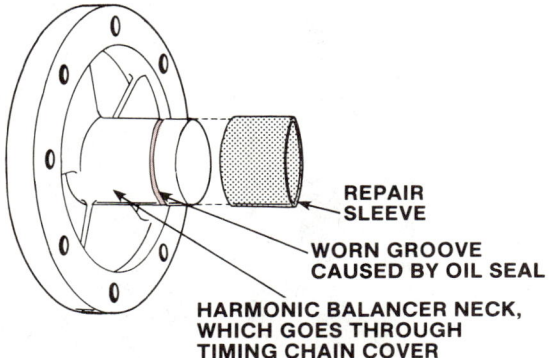

Figure 13-29 Replacement sleeves are available for the harmonic balancer pulley hub.

Rear Main Bearing Seals

Always make it a practice to replace oil seals on re-ring or overhaul jobs to avoid the chance of costly do-overs. This is a simple, inexpensive operation when the engine is torn down, but a costly and time-consuming job when seals start to leak after assembly.

Rear main bearing seals keep oil from leaking at the crankshaft around the rear main bearing. There are two basic types of constructions: wick- or rope-type packing and molded synthetic rubber.

Wick- or rope-type packings are common on many older engines (Figure 13-30). Molded synthetic rubber lip-type seals are used on many newer engines. They do

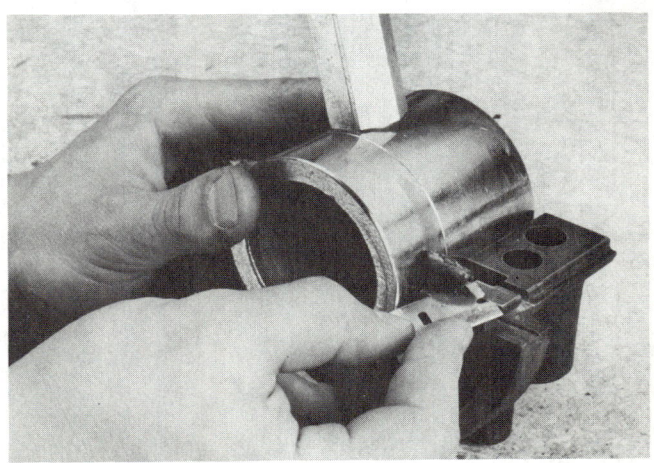

Figure 13-30 Installing wick- or rope-type seals. *Courtesy of Fel-Pro, Inc.*

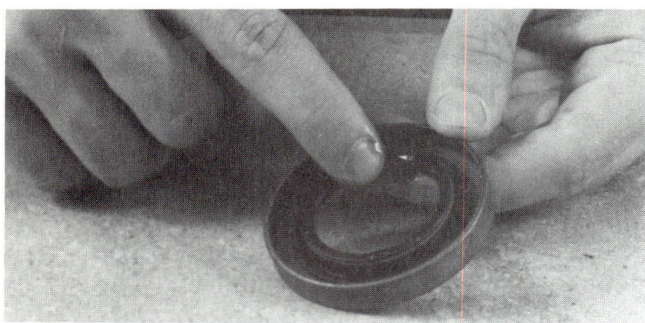
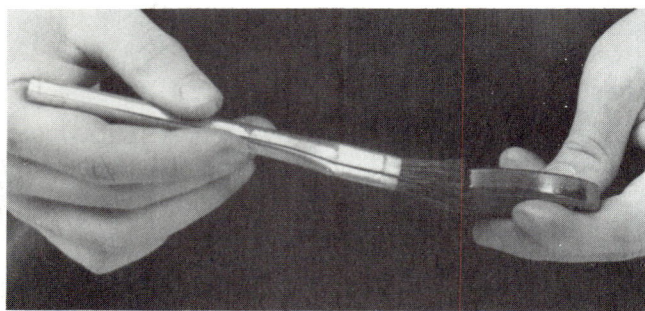

Figure 13-31 Installing a one-piece rubber crankshaft seal. *Courtesy of JP Industries, Inc.*

a good job of sealing even when there is some eccentricity in the shaft, as long as the surface of the shaft is very smooth. Synthetic rubber seals may sometimes be retrofitted to some older engines that have wick seals, but only if the seals are offered as an option by the sealing manufacturer.

Three types of synthetic rubber are used for rear main bearing seals. Polyacrylate is commonly used because it is tough and abrasion resistant, with moderate temperature resistance to 350 degrees. Silicone synthetic rubber has a greater temperature range, but it has less resistance to abrasion and is more fragile than polyacrylate. Silicone seals must be handled carefully during installation to avoid damage. Viton has the abrasion resistance of polyacrylate and the temperature range of silicone, but is the most expensive of the synthetic types. The synthetic rubber seals may be one piece (Figure 13-31) or two piece (Figure 13-32).

No matter what the construction of the seal is, always check the shaft for smoothness. Shafts should be free of nicks and burrs to assure long oil seal life. Carefully remove any roughness with a very fine emery cloth and then clean the shaft thoroughly. The shaft should have a highly polished appearance and a smooth feel. Also, be sure to check and clean the oil slinger and oil return channel in the bearing cap.

Other Seals

Different parts of the engine have different sealing requirements. Some gaskets must seal pressure, others must seal vacuum. Some seal hot oil and others hot antifreeze. Some gaskets seal joints under flexible flanges, others seal joints between fairly rigid flanges held together with large mounting bolts. The construction of each gasket matches its sealing requirement. Choose the correct gasket or sealing material to insure that proper sealing is achieved.

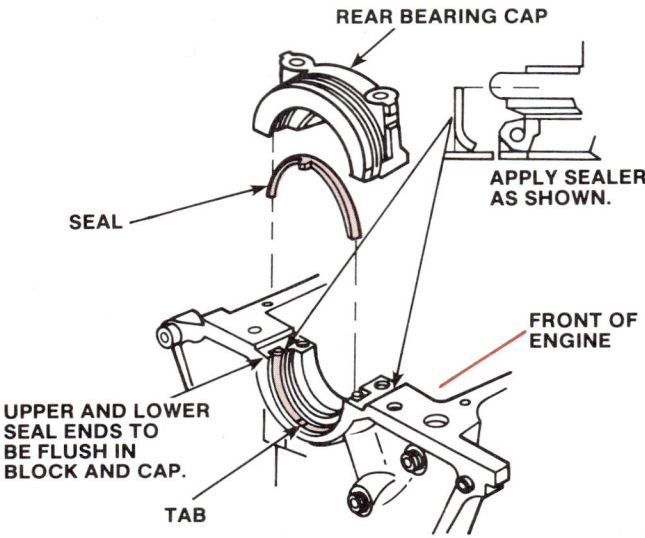

Figure 13-32 Typical two-piece rubber seal.

Engine Sealing and Reassembly   311

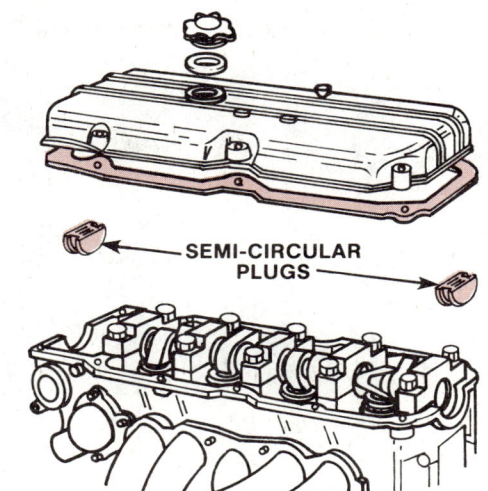

Figure 13-33 Typical OHC cover seals.

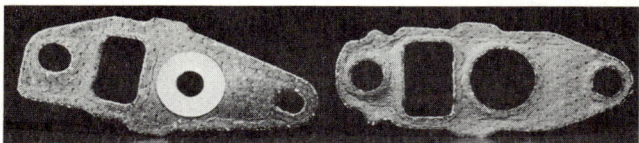

Figure 13-35 Typical EGR valve gaskets. *Courtesy of Fel-Pro, Inc.*

Some overhead cam engines, for example, have solid, one-piece cam bearings and cam bearing supports. It is necessary to have a semicircular notch in the front and back of the head for machining the cam bearing bore or saddle at the factory (Figure 13-33). The notch is sealed with molded synthetic rubber semicircular plugs. These plugs can deteriorate in time, taking a set. They should be replaced anytime a cam cover gasket is replaced.

Most gasket sets for V-type engines include manifold end strip seals. They seal the joint between the manifold ends and the block (Figure 13-34). Molded rubber and cork/rubber are materials often used for end strip seals. Some have self-adhesive backings to aid in installation. The corner joints where the end strip seals meet the intake manifold gaskets should be sealed with a small amount of RTV silicone. This insures a complete seal all around the manifold.

The exhaust gas recirculation (EGR) valve recirculates some of the exhaust gases back into the engine, reducing NO_x emissions by lowering the combustion temperature. The EGR valve gasket (Figure 13-35) seals the valve and, in some applications, regulates the flow of exhaust by a specifically sized hole in the gasket. Choosing the correct gasket for this application is critical because a one-size-fits-all gasket could change the exhaust gas flow and, as a result, change the performance of the engine.

The carburetor mounting gasket, located between the carburetor and the manifold, prevents vacuum and fuel leaks. Hotter running late-model engines require thicker carburetor mounting gaskets to help insulate the carburetor from engine heat. High-quality carburetor mounting gaskets use ferrules at the bolt holes, which help prevent carburetor base distortion that could damage the casting, as well as bind throttle plates and cause fuel leaks. Spacers are used in some engine applications for emission control systems or heat insulation for the carburetor. The carburetor spacer is located between the carburetor and the manifold, with the space gasket mounted underneath the spacer.

Many overhead cam (OHC) engine designs allow replacement of individual seals at the front of the engine. Figure 13-36 illustrates the typical timing sealing arrangement. Although it might save money to purchase only the parts that are needed, most technicians replace all of them.

❏ ENGINE REASSEMBLY

When reassembling the components of a torn down engine, the assembly sequence is essentially the re-

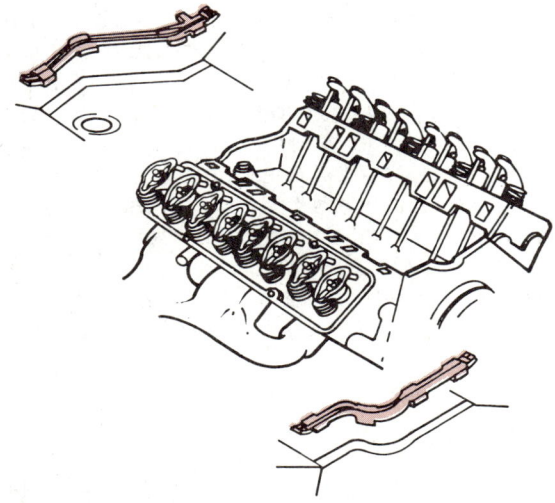

Figure 13-34 Intake manifold end strip seals.

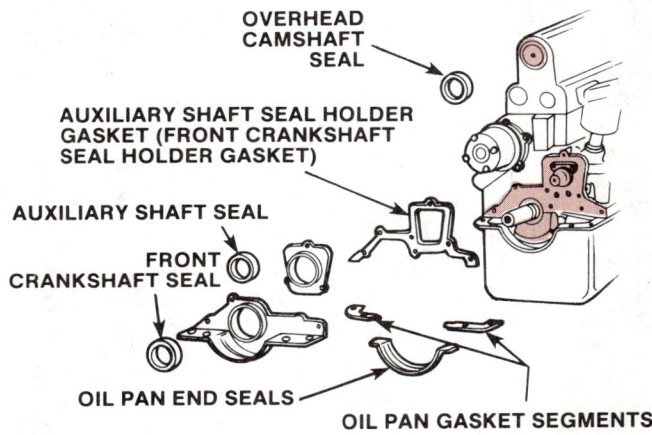

Figure 13-36 Typical OHC timing cover gasket arrangement.

verse of the tear down sequence outlined in a previous chapter. Details can be found in the chapters dealing with the assembly of major engine parts. It should be noted that some technicians prefer to install the camshaft prior to the crankshaft in pushrod type engines.

Final Reassembly Steps

The steps in final engine assembly involve installing various engine covers, prelubing the engine, and installing manifolds and related items that mount directly to the engine assembly.

INSTALL THE TIMING COVER When replacing the timing cover, remove the old gaskets and seals from the timing cover and engine block. If the timing cover extends over the front lip of the oil pan, the front portion of the oil pan gasket will be exposed. With a sharp knife or razor blade, carefully cut off the front exposed portion of the oil pan gasket.

Install the new seal using a press, seal driver, or hammer and a clean block of wood (Figure 13-37). When installing the seal, be sure to support the cover underneath to prevent damage. Apply a light coating of adhesive on the timing cover and position the gasket on the cover. Some manufacturers recommend that a sealant be used on both surfaces. Check the service manual and gasket instructions. Finally, mount the timing cover and torque the bolts to specifications.

INSTALL THE VIBRATION DAMPER Install the vibration damper by carefully pounding on it, or using a special installation tool. In most cases, the damper is installed until it bottoms out against the oil slinger and the timing sprocket. If in doubt, install the water pump and pulley and pound the damper into place until its pulley aligns with the water pump pulley. It is advisable to use the installation tool, because pounding on the damper can cause stress on the crank thrust bear-

Figure 13-37 Installing a timing cover seal. *Courtesy of Fel-Pro, Inc.*

Figure 13-38 When checking the valve cover for flatness, a hammer can be used to tap down any distorted bolt holes. *Courtesy of Fel-Pro, Inc.*

ing surface. It is best to stand the engine block on end and support the crankshaft if the damper must be pounded on.

Some vibration dampers are not pressed-fit on the crankshaft. Be sure to install the large washer behind the damper-retaining bolt on these engines. Otherwise, the damper might fly off, causing damage and a safety hazard.

INSTALL THE VALVE COVER To install the valve cover, first make sure the cover's sealing flange is flat (Figure 13-38), then apply contact adhesive to the valve cover's sealing surfaces in small dabs. Mount the valve cover gasket on the valve cover and align it in position. If the gasket has mounting tabs, use them in tandem with the contact adhesive. Allow the adhesive to dry completely before mounting the valve cover on the cylinder head. Torque the mounting bolts to specifications.

SHOP TALK

Many technicians install the water pump at this point or wait until the engine is back in the vehicle. When installing a water pump, apply a coating of good waterproof sealer to a new gasket and place it in position on the water pump. Coat the other side of the gasket with sealer and position the pump against the engine block until it is properly seated. Install the mounting bolts and tighten them, in a staggered sequence, to specifications with a torque wrench. Careless tightening could cause the pump housing to crack. Check the pump to make sure it rotates freely.

Prelubrication Check

There are several ways to prelubricate, or prime, an engine. One method is to drive the oil pump with an

Engine Sealing and Reassembly   313

Figure 13-39 Using an electric drill to prelubricate an engine. *Courtesy of Perfect Circle/Dana*

electric drill. With most engines, it is possible to make a drive that can be chucked in an electric drill motor to engage the drive on the oil pump. Insert the fabricated oil pump drive extension into the oil pump through the distributor drive hole. Drive the oil pump with the electric drill (Figure 13-39) and observe the rocker arms on the engine. Set the valve cover(s) on the engine to prevent oil splash. After running the oil pump for several minutes, remove the valve cover and see whether there is any oil flow to the rocker arms. If oil gets to the rocker arms, the lubrication system is full of oil and operating properly. If no oil is observed at the rocker arm area, there is a problem either with the pump, with an alignment of an oil hole in a bearing, or perhaps a plugged gallery.

CAUTION: *A great deal of care must be taken when using an electric drill to prime an engine. An rpm that is too fast could damage the oil pump internally.*

Using a prelubricator (Figure 13-40), which consists of an oil reservoir attached to a continuous air supply, is the best method of prelubricating an engine with oil under pressure without running it. When the reservoir is attached to the engine and the air pressure turned on, the prelubricator will supply the engine lubrication system with oil under pressure.

The engine prelubricator provides three important benefits. It prelubricates the engine after an overhaul to assure adequate lubrication from the moment the engine is turned over. It helps determine the need for engine bearing replacement by showing the amount of oil leakage through the existing bearings. Finally, it monitors the effectiveness of the repair job by showing the amount of leakage through the replacement bearings.

If the prelubrication check indicates the overhaul was performed properly, continue with final reassembly.

INSTALL OIL PAN Before installing the oil pan gasket, check the flanges for warpage. Use a straightedge or lay the pan, flange side down, on a flat surface with a flashlight underneath it to spot uneven edges. Check particularly around bolt holes. Minor distortions can be corrected with a hammer and block of wood (Figure 13-41). If the flanges are too bent to be repaired in this manner, the pan should be replaced. Once it has been determined that the flanges are flat, install the oil pan with a new gasket. Finally, fill the engine with the proper grade oil.

INSTALL INTAKE MANIFOLD The intake manifold gasket seals the joint between the intake manifold and the cylinder head. To be sure the gasket will seal, check its fit (Figure 13-42). This will insure proper sealing of the manifold. On steel shim-type gaskets, it is necessary to put a thin and even coat of positioning sealer around the vacuum port openings and a small bead of RTV silicone around the coolant openings. Install the intake manifold with a new gasket and tighten the fastening bolts to the recommended torque specification.

INSTALL THE THERMOSTAT AND WATER OUTLET HOUSING In frost-free areas of the country, some

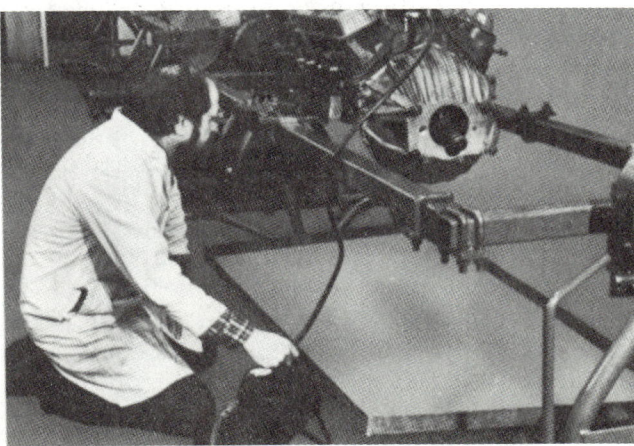

Figure 13-40 Priming an engine with a prelubricator. *Courtesy of Federal Mogul Corp.*

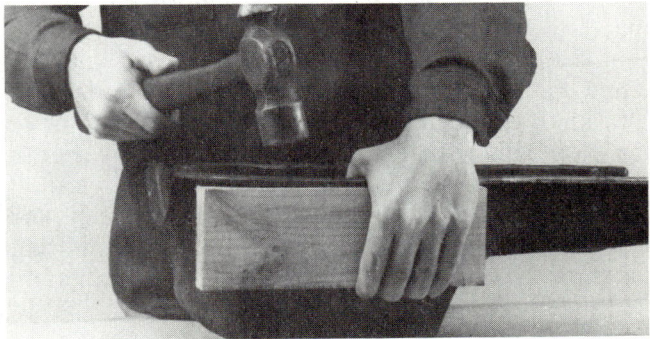

Figure 13-41 Straightening distorted oil pan flanges. *Courtesy of JP Industries, Inc.*

Figure 13-42 Checking for proper fit of the intake manifold gasket. *Courtesy of Fel-Pro, Inc.*

people neglect their cooling systems and do not use coolant. Many of today's automobiles have aluminum heads and must be run with anticorrosion additives, like those found in coolant. Aluminum water outlet housings are not very durable when used with water alone. Install the thermostat with the temperature sensor facing into the block. If the thermostat is installed upside down, the engine will overheat.

> **CUSTOMER CARE**
>
> Advise the customer about the need to change coolant every 2 years. Stress the importance of the anticorrosion additives in coolant.

INSTALL THE FUEL PUMP Most late-model engines are equipped with an electric fuel pump. However, some still use mechanical pumps, as do many older engines. If the engine has a mechanical pump, install the pump with its gasket. Prior to installation, turn the engine over until the fuel pump eccentric is at its lowest position in relation to the pump. Failure to do this makes it difficult to install the pump. Then tighten the pump's attaching bolts.

PAINT THE ENGINE A good paint job is an important part of a professional engine overhaul. It is easier to paint the engine when it is completely assembled. Exhaust manifolds should not be painted, so paint the engine before they are installed. Apply a thin layer of grease to exhaust gasket surfaces and carburetor or throttle body gasket surfaces. This makes it easier to remove paint from these areas. Spray one light coat of paint. Wait until it becomes tacky to the touch, and then spray the second coat. Spraying the second coat after the first coat becomes tacky will prevent runs and promote better paint coverage.

SPIN TEST THE ENGINE If the test equipment is available, always use a run-on stand to spin test rebuilt engines following assembly. The engine is spun at 600 rpm with oil pressure. Major problems can be spotted using this test. Compression and oil pressure can be checked. Cam, rod, and main bearings can be visually checked for excessive bearing oil leakage. Valve adjustment can be performed. And, lifter rotation can be checked.

When a dynamometer is used for spin testing (Figure 13-43), break in the engine at 10% load. When running an engine on a dyno at high rpm, a remote control should be used so the operator will not be injured if an engine part should fail.

INSTALL EXHAUST MANIFOLD After the block assembly is painted, install the exhaust manifold(s). Tighten the bolts in the center of the manifold first to prevent cracking it. If there are dowel holes in the exhaust manifold that align with dowels in the cylinder head, make sure that these holes are larger than the dowels. If the dowels do not have enough clearance because of the buildup of foreign material, the manifold will not be able to expand properly, and may crack. Tighten the individual manifold-to-engine bolts first. Then, tighten the bolts where the two parts meet. Some in-line engines use a combined intake and exhaust manifold gasket.

INSTALL FLYWHEEL OR FLEX PLATE Reinstall the engine sling. Raise the engine into the air on a suitable lift, and remove the engine stand mounting head. Set the assembled engine on the floor and support it with blocks of wood while attaching the flywheel (standard transmission vehicles). Be sure to use the right flywheel bolts and lock washers. These bolts have very thin heads and the lock washers are thin. If normal bolts or washers are used, they may cause interference with the clutch disc or the torque converter. Make sure that the bolts are properly torqued.

INSTALL CLUTCH PARTS Install the clutch, if the vehicle has a manual transmission. Check to see that the transmission input shaft pilot bushing or bearing, in the hole at the rear of the crankshaft, is installed and in good condition. If the bushing must be removed, use a puller. On vehicles with pilot bearings, a trick that sometimes works is to pack the cavity behind the bearing with grease, and then insert the largest bolt that will fit into the ID of the bearing. Pound on the bolt to force out the bearing.

Using a clutch-aligning tool, or an old transmission input shaft, align the clutch disc. Then, tighten the disc and clutch pressure plate to the flywheel. Be careful to install the disc in the right direction. There should be a marking on it that says flywheel side. Then install the bell housing if it was removed from the transmission.

INSTALL TORQUE CONVERTER On cars equipped with automatic transmissions, it is a good practice to

Engine Sealing and Reassembly 315

Figure 13-43 When possible, spin test the engine on a dynamometer before installing it in the vehicle. *Courtesy of Clayton Dynamometer, Inc.*

replace the transmission's front pump seal. If the transmission was removed from the car with the engine, reinstall it on the engine now.

Make sure that the torque converter is correctly engaged with the transmission's front pump. The drive lugs on the converter should be felt engaging the transmission front pump gear. Failure to correctly install the converter can result in damage to the transmission front pump.

INSTALL MOTOR MOUNTS The motor mount bolts may be installed loosely on the block. The bolts are left loose during engine installation so that the mounts can be more easily aligned with the front mount brackets. Make sure the mounts are in good condition.

❏ INSTALLING THE ENGINE

Installing a computer-controlled engine with a modern emissions system into the engine compartment of a front-wheel-drive vehicle can be a complex task requiring special procedures. Very often engine system specialists may be needed to perform the various tasks involved in the installation of a rebuilt engine.

The Tech Manual that accompanies this textbook outlines the general procedures for engine installation. Referring to the vehicle's service manual is absolutely essential for this procedure.

Starting Procedure

Set the valves, carburetor, and ignition timing as accurately as possible before starting the engine. The engine can be fine-tuned after it has been started and goes through the break-in test by using an engine analyzer or diagnostic tester. However, it is wise to time the ignition distributor before attempting to start the engine even though it is not the final adjustment.

WARNING: An engine that is not in correct time might backfire when it is first started. If this happens when there is a fuel leak, a fire might start and cause burns. Also, be sure to connect the exhaust pipes ventilation system to prevent a dangerous buildup of carbon monoxide when the engine is running.

To adjust the ignition distributor, mark the crankshaft pulley notch or TDC mark and the timing cover pointer on the TDC mark with a dab of white paint. Turn the crankshaft until the number 1 piston, coming up on the compression stroke, aligns the TDC mark with the pulley or pointer. Watch the rocker arms on number 1 cylinder. TDC on the compression stroke is just after the intake arm closes and before the exhaust arm opens. The exhaust valve is closed when the marks are aligned. Install the distributor with the rotor pointing to the mark on the body that indicates number 1 position. It might be necessary to turn the rotor about 15 degrees away from the mark and wiggle the rotor slightly to engage the intermediate drive shaft or oil pump drive. Once the distributor base slides into solid contact with the block or manifold mounting, align the reference marks and tighten the mounting bolt slightly. You will have to check the ignition timing later, so do not completely tighten at this time.

> **USING SERVICE MANUALS**
>
> Ignition timing specifications and the guidelines for setting timing are given in the tune-up specification section of the service manual.

When the engine is in time, fill the gasoline tank with several gallons of fresh gasoline. Have an associate crank the engine. It will take some time for fuel to be pumped from the tank to the engine. When the engine gets fuel, it will try to start. Once it does start, set the throttle to an engine speed of approximately 1500 rpm. Truck engines should be one-third throttle. When the engine coolant reaches normal operating temperature, turn off the engine. Recheck carburetor or injector adjustments, ignition timing, and valve clearance. Look for any coolant or oil leaks. After these checks run the engine at fast idle during the warm-up period to assure adequate initial lubrication for the piston rings, pistons, and camshaft.

Break-In Procedure

To prevent engine damage after it has been rebuilt or completely overhauled and to insure good initial oil control and long engine life, the proper break-in procedure must be followed. Make a test run at 30 mph and accelerate at full throttle to 50 mph. Repeat the acceleration cycle from 30 to 50 mph at least ten times. No further break-in is necessary. If traffic conditions will not permit this procedure, accelerate the engine rapidly several times through the intermediate gears during the check run. The objective is to apply a load to the engine for short periods of time and in rapid succession soon after engine warm-up. This action thrusts the piston rings against the cylinder wall with increased pressure and results in accelerated ring seating.

> **CUSTOMER CARE**
>
> After the engine has been totally checked over, return it to the owner with the following instructions:
> 1. Drive the vehicle normally but avoid sustained high speed during the first 500 miles (break-in period).
> 2. Check the oil level frequently during the break-in period. It is not unusual to use 1 or 2 quarts of oil during this time.
> 3. The oil and oil filter will need to be changed at the end of the break-in time.
> 4. All cylinder head and intake manifold bolts will need to be retorqued.
> 5. The fuel injectors or carburetor adjustments will need to be checked.
> 6. The valve adjustments and ignition timing will also need to be checked.

CASE STUDY

Case 1

A car with a four-cylinder OHC engine is towed back to the shop. It was recently in the shop because of overheating. The head was milled and a new head gasket installed. This time, the engine will not run. The technician attempts to start the engine and finds that it turns over faster than normal. Black powder is discovered on the timing belt cover and the front of the engine during a visual inspection. The powder is obviously from the timing belt. The timing belt cover is removed to examine the belt. More than half of the teeth are worn off.

A new belt was installed when the head gasket was replaced. Therefore, it is unlikely that the belt has failed on its own. To determine the cause of the failure, attempts are made to turn the camshaft. Only with a great amount of effort would the camshaft turn. This explains why the belt is worn. And the worn belt explains why the engine turns over faster than normal with the starter motor.

To determine what has caused the camshaft to be so hard to turn, the cam cover is removed. There is no sign of oil around the camshaft or followers. Both the camshaft and followers have a blue tint to them, indicating that they had been overheated. The technician remembers that the oil pressure was checked after the head was reinstalled and it was good. Why is there no oil to the camshaft now? After removing the timing belt, oil pressure was again checked by cranking the engine with the starter motor. Oil pressure is still good.

Still not sure of the cause of the problem, the technician removes the head to visually inspect the valve train and oil passages. During disassembly, the head gasket is inspected, and the cause of the problem is discovered. The gasket has been blocking off an oil feed hole from the engine block to the cylinder head. During the original repair, the technician failed to check the gasket against the block surface. Blocking this oil feed prevented oil from flowing into the cylinder head. This resulted in damage to the cam bearings and caused the problem.

The technician apologizes to the customer and explains what has gone wrong. The correct head gasket and new camshaft, cam bearings, followers, and timing belt are installed. This corrects the problem.

Summary

- Threaded fasteners, including bolts, nuts, and screws, allow easy installation and removal of parts. It is very important to be familiar with the standard bolt indication measurements and grade markings. Likewise, nuts are graded to match their respective bolts.
- Elasticity means that a bolt can be stretched a certain amount and, when the stretching load is reduced, return to its original size. Yield means that a stretched bolt takes a permanent set and never returns to normal. Proper use of torque will prevent a yield condition.
- When threads inside a block or head are stripped, they can be replaced by the use of threaded inserts. While several types are available, the helically-coiled insert is the most popular.
- Gaskets serve as sealers, spacers, wear insulators, and vibration dampeners. Engine gaskets are generally classified as either hard or soft. Today's gaskets are specifically designed to seal the new engine designs, and thus must cope with severe temperature and pressure stresses.
- General recommendations for installing gaskets include the following: never reuse old ones; handle new ones carefully, especially the composition-type; use sealants properly; thoroughly clean all mating surfaces; and use the right gasket in the right position.
- Cylinder head gaskets on today's bimetal engines have a demanding job to do. The no-retorque head gasket retains a high level of clamping force. A good way to check the effectiveness of a head gasket seal is with a carbon impression test.
- Contact adhesive bonds cork, rubber, fiber, and metal gaskets in place. It does not aid in sealing. Its only purpose is to hold the gasket securely during component assembly.
- General purpose sealers aid in gasket sealing without upsetting the designed performance of most mechanical gaskets. Hard-drying sealants such as shellac should never be used on gaskets because they will make future disassembly very difficult.
- Flexible sealant is often used on bolt threads that go into fluid passages. Silicone gasketing, of which RTV is the best known, is used on oil pans, valve covers, thermostat housing, timing covers, and water pumps. Anaerobic formed-in-place sealants are used for both thread locking and gasketing.
- Oil seals keep oil and other vital fluids from escaping around a rotating shaft. Oil seals should always be replaced on re-ring or overhaul jobs as insurance against costly do-overs.
- The steps in final engine assembly involve installing various engine covers, prelubing the engine, and installing manifolds and related items that mount directly to the engine assembly. The best method of prelubricating an engine under pressure without running it is to use a prelubricator, which consists of an oil reservoir attached to a continuous air supply.
- Whenever possible, use a run-on stand to spin test a rebuilt engine following assembly. This can detect problems in major areas such as compression and oil pressure. When using a dynamometer for spin testing, break in the engine at 10% load.
- Time the ignition before attempting to start a reassembled engine. This will prevent backfire. Be sure to connect the exhaust pipes ventilation system to prevent a dangerous buildup of carbon monoxide.
- A proper break-in procedure is necessary to ensure good initial oil contact and long engine life. Make a test run at 30 mph and accelerate at full throttle to 50 mph. Repeat this acceleration cycle from 30 to 50 mph at least ten times to achieve accelerated ring seating.

Review Questions

1. How is bolt length measured?
2. What does it mean when a bolt is stretched into yield?
3. Name some applications of hard gaskets.
4. Where are flexible sealers most often used?
5. Other than their method of curing, what is the major difference between aerobic and anaerobic sealants?
6. Which of the following performs the vital task of sealing the engine?
   a. gaskets
   b. seals
   c. fasteners
   d. all of the above
7. Technician A uses a metric wrench on USC bolts. Technician B uses a metric socket on USC bolts. Who is correct?

a. Technician A
b. Technician B
c. Both A and B
d. Neither A nor B

8. Which of the following statements is incorrect?
   a. All metals are elastic.
   b. Proper use of torque will avoid a yield condition.
   c. Torque is a function of friction.
   d. Cut bolt threads are 30% stronger than rolled threads.

9. Technician A uses an impact wrench to tighten nuts and bolts. Technician B uses an impact wrench to loosen nuts and bolts. Who is correct?
   a. Technician A
   b. Technician B
   c. Both A and B
   d. Neither A nor B

10. Technician A uses soft gaskets on valve covers. Technician B uses soft gaskets on water pumps. Who is correct?
    a. Technician A
    b. Technician B
    c. Both A and B
    d. Neither A nor B

11. Technician A reuses old gaskets if they appear to be in good condition. Technician B never reuses old gaskets. Who is correct?
    a. Technician A
    b. Technician B
    c. Both A and B
    d. Neither A nor B

12. Which gasket is one of the most ignored on an engine?
    a. valve cover
    b. cylinder head
    c. exhaust manifold
    d. oil pan

13. Technician A uses chemical thread retainers in place of lock washers. Technician B says that chemical thread retainers cannot be used as a substitute for lock washers. Who is correct?
    a. Technician A
    b. Technician B
    c. Both A and B
    d. Neither A nor B

14. Hylomar is _____ .
    a. an anaerobic
    b. an RTV
    c. both a and b
    d. neither a nor b

15. Which of the following statements is incorrect?
    a. In a pushrod type engine, the camshaft can be installed prior to the crankshaft.
    b. Some vibration dampeners are not pressed-fit on the crankshaft.
    c. Most gasket sets for V-type engines include manifold end strip seals.
    d. Wick- or rope-type packing rear main bearing seals are common on late-model engines.

16. Coolant should be changed _____ .
    a. once a year
    b. every two years
    c. every three years
    d. every five years

17. Technician A spray paints the exhaust manifold. Technician B paints the exhaust manifold with a brush. Who is correct?
    a. Technician A
    b. Technician B
    c. Both A and B
    d. Neither A nor B

18. After assembling and installing an engine, when is it best to time the ignition distributor?
    a. after the engine has been run a few minutes
    b. after the vehicle has been driven a few miles
    c. immediately following proper break-in
    d. before starting the engine

19. When replacing fasteners, Technician A uses twice the number originally used by the OEM. Technician B uses half the number originally used by the OEM. Who is correct?
    a. Technician A
    b. Technician B
    c. Both A and B
    d. Neither A nor B

20. The proper engine break-in procedure is _____ .
    a. a test run at 30 mph
    b. a test run at 10 mph and acceleration to 30 mph
    c. a test run at highway speed
    d. a test run at 30 mph and acceleration to 50 mph

SECTION 3 ELECTRICITY

Chapter 14 Basics of Electrical and Electronic Systems
Chapter 15 Starting and Charging Systems
Chapter 16 Lighting Systems
Chapter 17 Electrical Instruments and Accessories

A vehicle cannot operate without a properly working electrical system. Electricity provides the all-important spark for combustion, plus power for starting, lighting and signalling, instrumentation, safety devices, and many other accessories. Modern ignition and computerized engine control systems all depend on a vast array of electrical components, sensors, and intricate circuitry. Although modern test equipment can simplify working with these systems, understanding electrical principles, component operation, circuit design, and testing procedures is now absolutely essential to the success of an automotive technician.

The material covered in Section 3 matches the content areas of the ASE certification test on electrical systems.

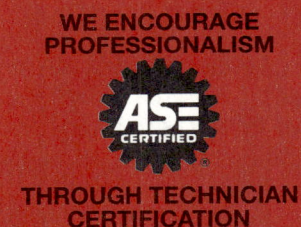

WE ENCOURAGE PROFESSIONALISM

THROUGH TECHNICIAN CERTIFICATION

14 BASICS OF ELECTRICAL AND ELECTRONIC SYSTEMS

Objectives

- Use Ohm's law to determine voltage, current, and resistance. ■ List the basic types of electrical circuits.
- Name the various electrical components and their uses in electrical circuits. ■ Describe the different kinds of automotive wiring. ■ Read electrical automotive diagrams. ■ Perform troubleshooting procedures using meters, test lights, and jumper wires. ■ Explain the principles of magnetism and electromagnetism.
- Explain the advantages of using electronic control systems. ■ Describe how semiconductors, diodes, and transistors work. ■ Explain the function of sensors and actuators. ■ Summarize the function of a binary code. ■ Name the various memory systems used in automotive microcomputers. ■ Identify the proper procedures to safeguard electronic systems. ■ Explain the basics of batteries. ■ Describe the basic parts of an automotive battery. ■ Compare conventional and maintenance-free batteries.
- Explain battery safety, maintenance, and testing.

The electrical and electronic systems are critical parts of any automobile. In addition to playing a vital role in starting the vehicle and providing power for lighting and other auxiliary safety systems, these systems must also provide power to the sophisticated controls now found on engine, brake, suspension, emission, steering, and other automotive systems. To operate accurately, these controls need well-maintained, properly functioning electrical and electronic systems.

◻ BASICS OF ELECTRICITY

Understanding components and their functions is absolutely essential to proper automobile servicing. There is no intent to scare you with this statement. The intent instead is to emphasize the need for you to understand the purpose of each component and signal, and to reinforce knowledge you already possess. An elementary overview of electricity and its principles was presented in a previous chapter as an aid to understanding the use of electrical diagnostic equipment.

Ohm's Law

A simple electrical circuit is a resistor connected to a voltage source by conductors. The resistor could be a fog light, the voltage source could be a battery, and the conductor could be a copper wire (Figure 14-1).

In any electrical circuit, current (I), resistance (R), and voltage (E) work together in a mathmatical relationship. This relationship is expressed in a basic law of

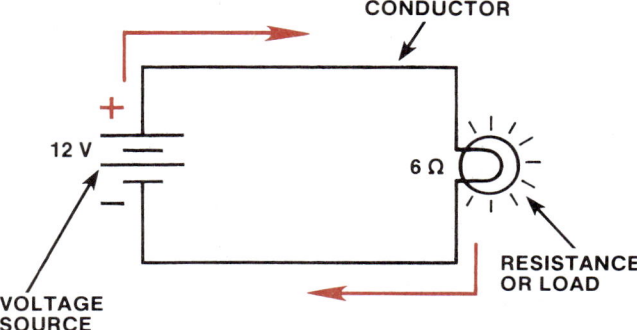

Figure 14-1 A simple circuit consists of a voltage source, conductors, and a resistance or load.

electricity—Ohm's law. Ohm's law can be applied to the entire circuit or to any part of a circuit. When any two factors are known, the third factor can be found by using Ohm's law. Following is the formula.

$$E = I \times R$$

That is, the voltage (E) in a circuit is equal to the current (I) in amperes multiplied by the resistance (R) in ohms. A second way to express it follows.

$$I = \frac{E}{R}$$

The current (amperage) in a circuit equals the voltage divided by the resistance (in ohms). A third way to express it follows.

320

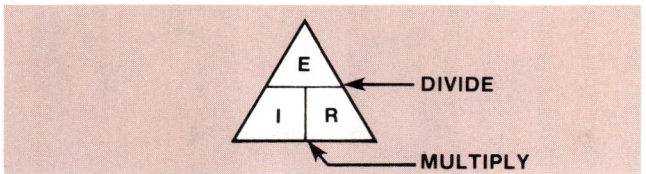

Figure 14-2 Ohm's law states that voltage (E) = amperage (I) × resistance (R).

$$R = \frac{E}{I}$$

The resistance of a circuit (in ohms) equals the voltage divided by the current (in amperes). One easy method of remembering these equations is by using the triangle method shown in Figure 14-2.

It is extremely important for all service technicians to understand Ohm's law. It explains how an increase or decrease in voltage, resistance, or current will affect a circuit.

For example, if the fog light in Figure 14-1 has a 6-ohm resistance, how many amperes does it use to operate? Since all passenger cars and light trucks now operate using a 12-volt storage battery, and you know two of the factors in the fog light circuit, it is simple to solve for the third.

$$I \text{ (unknown)} = \frac{E \text{ (12 volts)}}{R \text{ (6 ohms)}}$$
$$I = \frac{12}{6}$$
$$I = 2 \text{ amperes}$$

In a clean, well-wired circuit, the fog lights will draw 2 amperes of current. But what would happen if resistance in the circuit increases due to corroded or damaged wire or connections?

For example, if corroded connections add 2 ohms of resistance to the fog light circuit, the amount of current reaching the lights decrease as follows.

$$I = \frac{12}{6 + 2} = \frac{12}{8}$$
$$I = 1.5 \text{ amperes}$$

If the lights are designed to operate at 2 amperes, this decrease to 1.5 amperes will cause them to burn dimly. Cleaning the corrosion away, or installing new wires and connectors will eliminate this increased resistance and restore proper current flow.

Power

Another useful formula is one used to find the power of an electrical circuit expressed in watts.

$$P = E \times I$$

That is, power (P) in watts equals the voltage (E) multiplied by the current (I) in amperes (Figure 14-3).

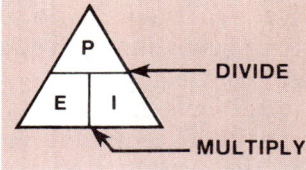

Figure 14-3 Watt's law states that wattage (P) = voltage (E) × amperage (I).

This is known as Watt's law. Power is measured in watts. Looking back at the example of the fog light circuit, we can calculate the power or heat generated by the fog light.

$$P = 12 \text{ volts} \times 2 \text{ amperes}$$
$$P = 24 \text{ watts}$$

The normal fog light generates 24 watts of power, while the corroded fog light circuit produces the following.

$$P = 12 \text{ volts} \times 1.5 \text{ amperes}$$
$$P = 18 \text{ watts}$$

This reduction in power or heat explains the decrease in bulb brightness.

❏ CONDUCTORS AND INSULATORS

Controlling and routing the flow of electricity requires the use of materials known as conductors and insulators.

Conductors are materials with a low resistance to the flow of current. Remember, if the number of electrons in the outer shell or ring of an atom is less than 4, the force holding them in place is weak. The voltage needed to move these electrons and create current flow is relatively small. Most metals, such as copper, silver, and aluminum are excellent conductors. When the number of electrons in the outer ring are greater than 4, the force holding them in orbit is very strong, and very high voltages are needed to dislodge them.

These materials are known as insulators. They resist the flow of current. Thermal plastics are the most common electrical insulators used today. They can resist heat, moisture, and corrosion without breaking down.

WARNING: *Your body is an excellent conductor of electricity. Remember this when working on a vehicle's electrical system. Always observe all electrical safety rules.*

Wire insulation should always be in good condition. Broken, frayed, or damaged insulation that exposes live wires can cause shorts, grounds, and other problems. It also creates a safety hazard. Replace all damaged insulation.

Copper wire is by far the most popular conductor used in automotive electrical systems. Wire wound inside of electrical units, such as ignition coils and generators, usually has a very thin baked-on insulating coating. External wiring often is covered with a plastic-type insulating material that is highly resistant to environmental factors like heat, vibration, and moisture. Where flexibility is required, the copper wire may consist of a large number of very small strands of wire.

The resistance of a uniform, circular copper wire depends on the length of the wire, the diameter of the wire, and the temperature of the wire. If the length is doubled, the resistance between the wire ends is doubled. The longer the wire, the greater the resistance. If the diameter of a wire is doubled, the resistance for any given length is cut in half. The larger the wire's diameter, the lower the resistance.

In any circuit, the smallest wire that will not cause excessive voltage drop is used to minimize cost.

The other important factor affecting the resistance of a copper wire is temperature. As the temperature increases, the resistance increases. The effects of temperature are very important in the design of electrical equipment. Excessive resistance caused by normal temperature increases can hurt the performance of the equipment.

Heat is developed in any wire carrying current because of the resistance in the wire. If the heat becomes excessive, the insulation will be damaged. Resistance occurs when electrons collide as current flows through the conductor. These collisions cause friction which in turn generates heat.

Circuits

A complete electrical circuit exists when electrons flow along a path between two points. In a complete circuit, resistance must be low enough to allow the available voltage to push electrons between the two points. Most automotive circuits contain four basic parts.

1. Power sources, such as a battery or alternator that provides the energy needed to create electron flow.
2. Conductors, such as copper wires that provide a path for current flow.
3. Loads, which are devices that use electricity to perform work, such as light bulbs, electric motors, or resistors.
4. Controllers, such as switches or relays that direct the flow of electrons.

There are also three basic types of circuits used in automotive and all types of electrical circuits. They are series circuits, parallel circuits, and series-parallel circuits. Each circuit type has its own characteristics regarding amperage, voltage, and resistance.

Series Circuits

A series circuit consists of one or more resistors connected to a voltage source with only one path that the electrons can follow. For example, a simple series circuit consists of a resistor (2 ohm in this example)

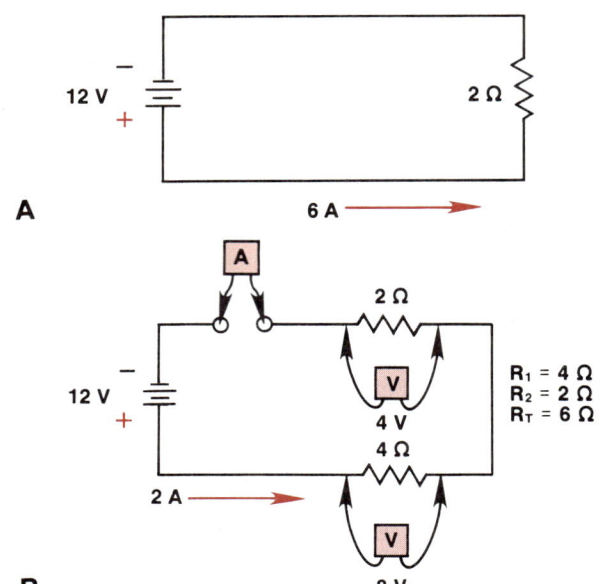

Figure 14–4 In series circuits, the same amount of current flows through each resistor.

connected to a 12-volt battery (Figure 14-4A). The current can be determined from Ohm's law.

$$I = \frac{E}{R} = \frac{12}{2} = 6 \text{ amperes}$$

Another series circuit may contain a 2-ohm resistor and a 4-ohm resistor connected to a 12-volt battery (Figure 14-4B). The word series is given to a circuit in which all the current that flows through one resistor also flows through other resistors. In a series circuit, the total circuit resistance is equal to the sum of all the individual resistors. In this circuit, the total circuit resistance is $4 + 2 = 6$ ohms. The current from Ohm's law is $I = E/R = 12/6 = 2$ amperes.

Ohm's law can be used to determine the voltage drop across the 2-ohm resistor. Thus, $E = IR = 2 \times 2 = 4$ volts. For the 4-ohm resistor, $E = 2 \times 4 = 8$ volts. These values are called voltage drops. The sum of all voltage drops in the circuit must equal the source voltage, or $4 + 8 = 12$ volts.

An ammeter connected anywhere in this circuit will read 2 amperes, and a voltmeter connected across each of the resistors will read 4 volts and 8 volts, as shown in Figure 14-4B.

SHOP TALK

When testing and troubleshooting an electrical circuit, voltage drop is usually measured. Voltage must be present for amperage to flow through a resistor (load). Voltage is dropped across each resistor that it pushes amperage through. To determine the voltage drop across any resistor, simply use Ohm's law.

A series circuit is characterized by the following three facts.

1. The current is determined by total resistance and is constant throughout the circuit.
2. The voltage drops across each resistor are different if the resistance values are different.
3. The sum of the voltage drops equals the source voltage.

Parallel Circuits

A parallel circuit provides two or more different paths for the current to flow through. Each path has separate resistors (loads) and operates independently of the other paths. Current can flow through more than one resistor at a time.

A parallel circuit is characterized by the following three facts.

1. Total circuit resistance is always lower than the smallest resistor.
2. The current through each resistor will be different if the resistance values are different.
3. The sum of the separate currents equals the total circuit current.

Consider the circuit shown in Figure 14-5. A 2-ohm and a 4-ohm resistor are connected to a 12-volt battery. The resistors are in parallel with each other, since the battery voltage (12 volts) appears across each resistor. The current through each resistor, often called a branch of the circuit, can be determined from Ohm's law. For the 2-ohm resistor, $I = E/R = 12/2 = 6$ amperes. For the 4-ohm resistor, $I = 12/4 = 3$ amperes. The total circuit current supplied by the battery is $6 + 3 = 9$ amperes.

A method of determining the value of circuit resistance when two resistors are in parallel is to divide the product of their ohm value by the sum of their ohm values.

$$\frac{2 \text{ ohms} \times 4 \text{ ohms}}{2 \text{ ohms} + 4 \text{ ohms}} = \frac{8}{6} = 1.3 \text{ ohms}$$

Series-Parallel Circuits

In a series-parallel circuit, both series and parallel combinations exist in the same circuit.

A series-parallel is illustrated in Figure 14-6. The 6- and 3-ohm resistors are in parallel with each other and together are in series with the 2-ohm resistor.

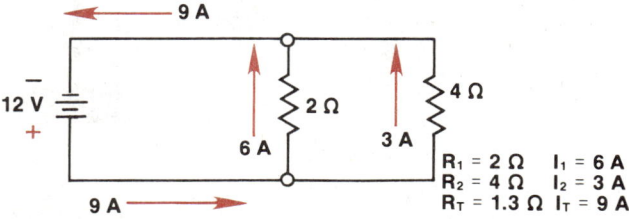

Figure 14-5 In a parallel circuit there are several paths for the current to flow through.

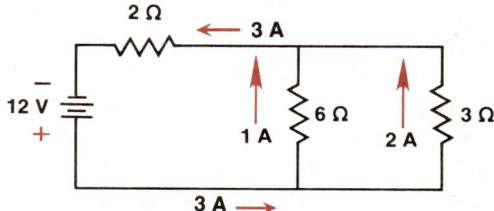

Figure 14-6 In a series-parallel circuit both series and parallel combinations exist for current flow.

The total current in this circuit is equal to the voltage divided by the total resistance. The total resistance can be determined as follows. The 6- and 3-ohm parallel resistors in Figure 14-6 are equivalent to a 2-ohm resistor, since $6 \times 3/6 + 3 = 2$. This equivalent 2-ohm resistor added in series to the other 2-ohm resistor gives a total circuit resistance of 4 ohms ($2 + 2 = 4$ ohms). The total current, therefore, is $I = 12/4 = 3$ amperes. Thus, in series-parallel circuits, the sum of the currents, flowing in the parallel resistors, must equal that of the series resistors' current.

With 3 amperes flowing through the 2-ohm resistor connected nearest to the battery, the voltage drop across this resistor is $E = IR = 3 \times 2 = 6$ volts, leaving 6 volts across the 6- and 3-ohm resistors. The current through the 6-ohm resistor is $I = E/R = 6/6 = 1$ ampere, and through the 3-ohm resistor is $I = 6/3 = 2$ amperes. The sum of these two current values must equal the total circuit current or $1 + 2 = 3$ amperes.

Grounding the Load

In the illustrations used to explain series, parallel, and series-parallel circuits, the return wire from the load or resistor connects directly to the negative terminal of the voltage source (battery). If this were the case in a vehicle, there would be literally dozens of wires connected to the negative battery terminal.

To avoid this, auto manufacturers use a wiring style that involves using the vehicle's metal frame components as part of the return circuit. As shown in Figure 14-7, the load is grounded directly to the metal frame. The metal frame then acts as the return wire in the

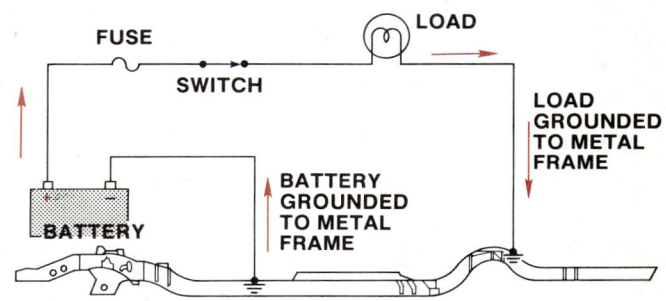

Figure 14-7 In most vehicles, the metal frame, engine block, or transmission case is used as a source of ground to complete the circuit back to the battery.

circuit. Current passes from the battery, through the load, and into the frame. The frame is connected to the negative terminal of the battery through the battery's ground wire. This completes the circuit.

An electrical component, such as an alternator is often mounted directly to the engine block, transmission case, or frame. This direct mounting effectively grounds the component without the use of a separate ground wire. In other cases, however, a separate ground wire must be run from the component to the frame or another metal part to ensure a sound return path. The increased use of plastics and other nonmetallic materials in body panels and engine parts has made electrical grounding more difficult. To assure good grounding back to the battery, some manufacturers now use a network of common grounding terminals and wires (Figure 14-8).

Circuit Components

Automotive electrical circuits contain a number of different types of electrical devices. The more common components are outlined in the following sections.

Resistors

As shown in the explanation of simple circuit design, resistors are used to limit current flow (and thereby voltage) in circuits where full current flow and voltage are not needed. Resistors are devices specially constructed to introduce a measured amount of electrical resistance into a circuit. In addition, some other components use resistance to produce heat and even light. An electric window defroster is a specialized type of resistor that produces heat. Electric lights are resistors that get so hot they produce light.

Resistors in common use in automotive circuits are of three types: fixed value, stepped or tapped, and variable.

Fixed value resistors are designed to have only one rating, which should not change. These resistors are used to control voltage such as in an automotive ignition system.

Tapped or stepped resistors are designed to have two or more fixed values, available by connecting wires to the several taps of the resistor. Heater motor resistor packs, which provide for different fan speeds, are an example of this type of resistor.

Variable resistors are designed to have a range of resistances available through two or more taps and a control. Two examples of this type of resistor are rheostats and potentiometers. Rheostats have two connections, one to the fixed end of a resistor and one to a sliding contact with the resistor. Turning the control moves the sliding contact away from or toward the fixed end tap, increasing or decreasing the resistance. Potentiometers have three connections, one at each end of the resistance and one connected to a sliding contact with the resistor. Turning the control moves the sliding contact away from one end of the resistance, but toward the other end.

Another type of variable resistor is the thermistor. This resistor is designed to change in values as its temperature changes. Although most resistors are carefully constructed to maintain their rating within a few ohms through a range of temperatures, the thermistor is designed to change its rating. Thermistors are used to provide compensating voltage in components or to determine temperature. As a temperature sender, the thermistor is connected to a voltmeter calibrated in degrees. As the temperature rises or falls, the resistance also changes. This changes the reading on the meter.

Circuit Protective Devices

When overloads or shorts in a circuit cause too much current to flow, the wiring in the circuit heats up, the insulation melts, and a fire can result, unless the circuit has some kind of protective device. Fuses, fuse links, maxi-fuses, and circuit breakers are designed to provide protection from high current. They may be used singularly or in combination.

FUSES There are three basic types of fuses in automotive use: cartridge, blade, and ceramic (Figure 14-9). The cartridge fuse is found on most older domestic cars

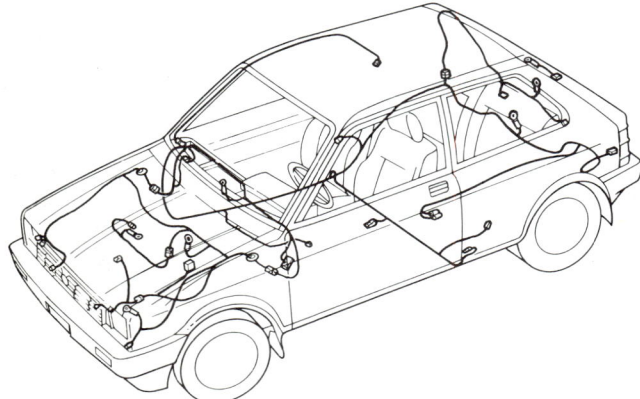

Figure 14-8 Some vehicles use a network of grounding wires and terminals to assure good ground in all electrical circuits. *Courtesy of Subaru of America*

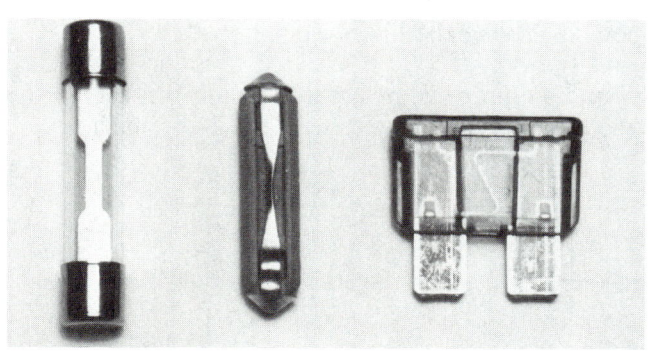

Figure 14-9 (A) Cartridge fuse, (B) ceramic fuse, and (C) blade fuse.

Basics of Electrical and Electronic Systems

and a few imports. It is composed of a strip of low melting metal enclosed in a glass or transparent plastic tube. To check, look for a break in the internal wire or metal strip. Discoloration of the glass cover or glue bubbling around the metal end caps is an indication of overheating. Late-model domestic vehicles and many imports use blade or spade fuses. To check the fuse, pull it from the fuse panel and look at the fuse element through the transparent plastic housing. Look for internal breaks and discoloration. The ceramic fuse is used on many European imports. The core is a ceramic insulator with a conductive metal strip along one side. To check, look for a break in the contact strip on the outside of the fuse. All fuse types can be checked with a circuit tester or multimeter.

Fuses are rated by the current at which they are designed to blow. A three-letter code indicates the type and size of the fuses. Blade fuses have codes ATC or ATO. All glass SFE fuses have the same diameter, but the length varies with the current rating. Ceramic fuses are available in two sizes, code GBF (small) and the more common code GBC (large). The ampere rating is also embossed on the insulator. Codes such as AGA, AGW, and AGC indicate the length and diameter of the fuse. Fuse lengths in each of these series is the same, but the current rating can vary. The code and the current rating is usually stamped on the end cap.

The current rating for blade fuses is indicated by the color of the plastic case (Table 14-1). In addition, it is usually marked on the top. The insulator on ceramic fuses is color coded to indicate different current ratings.

> ### CUSTOMER CARE
>
> Advise your customers to carry an assortment of spare fuses in the car's glove compartment. It is difficult to know when one will blow. Also, show the customer how to borrow a fuse from a less critical circuit. For example, it is possible to do without power for the radio or air conditioner, if a fuse is needed for the headlights or brake lights. Make certain, however, that the fuse borrowed and later replaced has the same current rating. Remember that a blown fuse must always be replaced with the correct rated fuse, in type, size, and current capacity.

Fuses are located in a box or panel (Figure 14-10), usually under the dashboard, behind a panel in the foot well, or in the engine compartment. Fuses are generally numbered, and the main components abbreviated. On late-model cars there may be icons or symbols indicating which circuits they serve. This identification system is covered in more detail in the owner's and service manuals.

Sometimes it is necessary to protect a device in a portion of a circuit even though the entire circuit is protected by a fuse in the fuse panel. This is done by installing an in-line fuse in the wire that carries the electricity to the device. These fuse-installations are primarily used on accessories that are very sensitive to power surges, such as radios and compact disc players. They are also used with add-on units like driving lights and power antennas. Normally these fuses are close to the units they protect.

There are several types of in-line fuse carriers. One of the most popular and easiest to install is shown in Figure 14-11.

TABLE 14-1 TYPICAL COLOR CODING OF PROTECTIVE DEVICES

Blade Fuse Color Coding

Ampere Rating	Housing Color
4	pink
5	tan
10	red
15	light blue
20	yellow
25	natural
30	light green

Fuse Link Color Coding

Wire Link Size	Insulation Color
20 GA	blue
18 GA	brown or red
16 GA	black or orange
14 GA	green
12 GA	gray

Maxi-fuse Color Coding

Ampere Rating	Housing Color
20	yellow
30	light green
40	amber
50	red
60	blue

> ### SHOP TALK
>
> To calculate the correct fuse rate, remember Watt's law: watts divided by volts equals amperes. Therefore, if installing a 55 watt accessory, such as a pair of fog lights, divide 55 by the battery voltage (12 volts) to find out how much current the circuit has to carry. Since $55 \div 12 = 4.58$, the current is approximately 5 amperes. To allow for current surges, the fuse should be slightly higher than the normal current flow. In this case, an 8- or 10-ampere fuse would do the job.

FUSE LINKS Fuse or fusible links are used in circuits where maximum current controls are not so critical.

326 Section 3   Electricity

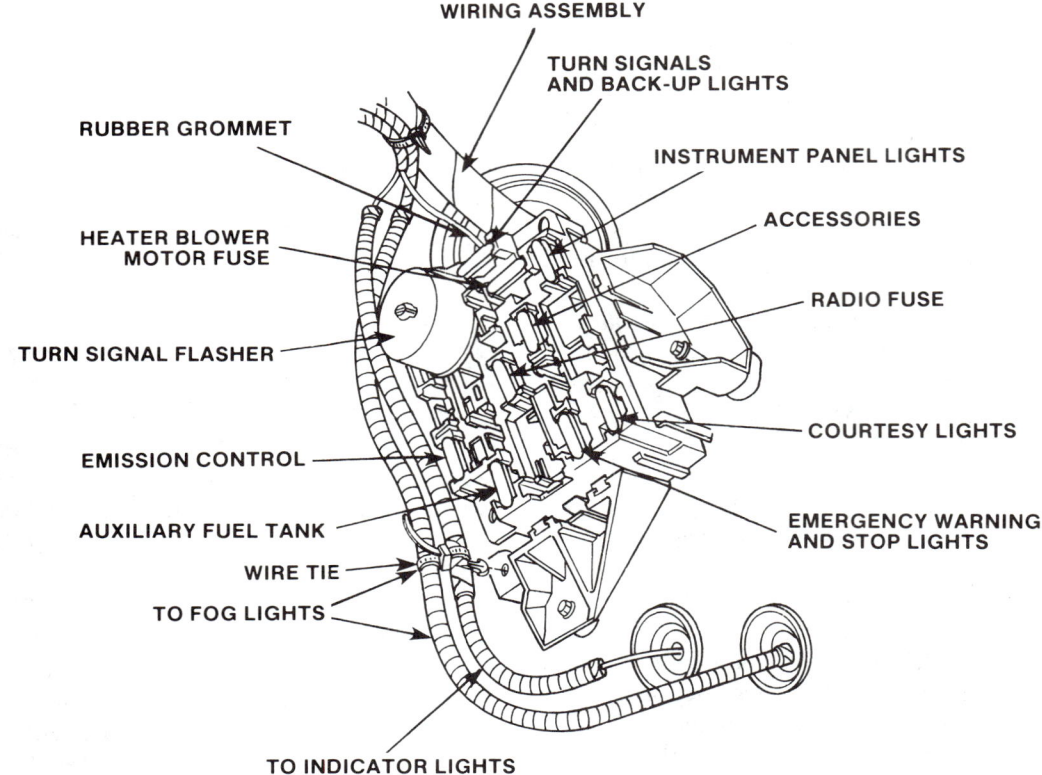

Figure 14-10 Typical fuse box or panel.

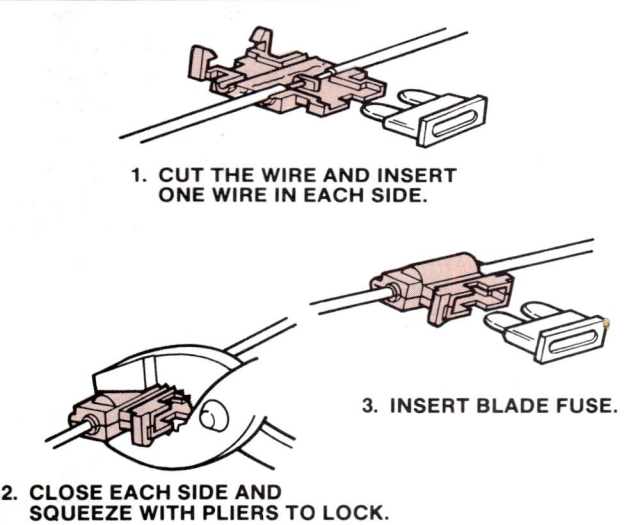

Figure 14-11 In-line blade fuse carrier.

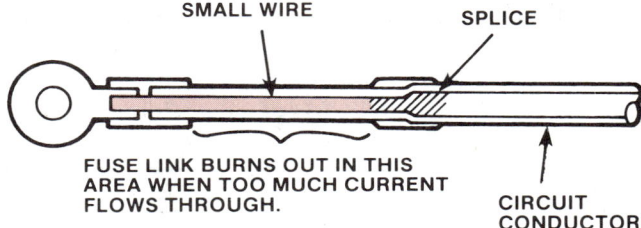

Figure 14-12 Typical fuse link.

They are often installed in the positive battery lead that powers the ignition switch and other circuits that are live with the key off. These are normally found in the engine compartment near the battery. Fusible links are also used in similar situations when it would be awkward to run wiring from the battery, to the fuse panel, and back to the load.

The fuse link (Figure 14-12) is a short length of small guage wire installed in a conductor. Because the fuse link is a lighter gauge of wire than the main conductor, it melts and opens the circuit before damage can occur in the rest of the circuit. Fuse link wire is covered with a special insulation that bubbles when it overheats, indicating that the fuse link has melted. If the insulation appears good, pull lightly on the wire. If the fuse link stretches, the wire has melted. Of course, when it is hard to determine if the fuse link is burned out, perform a continuity check with a test light or an ohmmeter.

CAUTION: Do not mistake a resistor wire for a fuse link. The resistor wire is generally longer and is clearly marked "Resistor—do not cut or splice."

When replacing fuse links, first cut the protected wire where it is connected to the fuse link. Then, tightly crimp or solder a new eyelet fusible link of the same rating as the link it is replacing (Figure 14-13). Since the insulation on the manufacturer's fuse links is flame proof, never fabricate a fuse link from ordinary wire because the insulation may not be flame proof.

Basics of Electrical and Electronic Systems

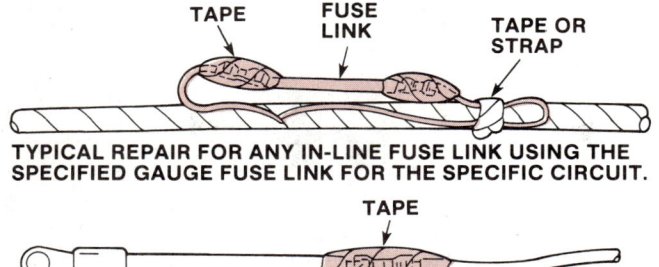

Figure 14-13 Typical fuse link repair.

WARNING: Always disconnect the battery ground cable prior to servicing any fuse link.

MAXI-FUSES A number of new electrical systems use maxi-fuses in place of traditional fusible links. Maxi-fuses look and operate like two-prong, blade or spade fuses, except they are much larger and can handle more current. (Typically, a maxi-fuse is four to five times larger.) Maxi-fuses are located in their own underhood fuse block.

Maxi-fuses are easier to inspect and replace than fuse links. To check a maxi-fuse, look at the fuse element through the side transparent colored plastic housing. If there is a break in the element, the maxi-fuse has blown. To replace it, pull it from its fuse box or panel. Always replace a blown maxi-fuse with a new one having the same ampere rating.

Another advantage of maxi-fuses is that they allow the vehicle's electrical system to be broken down into smaller circuits that are easy to diagnose and repair. For example, in some vehicles a single fusible link controls one-half or more of all circuitry. If it burns out, many electrical systems are lost. By replacing this single fusible link with several maxi-fuses, the number of systems lost due to a single fuse failure is drastically reduced. This makes it easy to pinpoint the source of trouble.

CIRCUIT BREAKERS Some circuits are protected by circuit breakers (abbreviated c.b. in a fuse chart or service manual). They can be fuse panel mounted or in-line. Like fuses, they are rated in amperes.

Each circuit breaker conducts current through an arm made of two types of metal bonded together (bimetal arm). If the arm starts to carry too much current, it heats up. As one metal expands faster than the other, the arm bends, opening the contacts. Current flow is broken. A circuit breaker can be cycling (Figure 14-14) or noncycling.

In the cycling type, the bimetal arm will begin to cool once the current to it is stopped. Once it returns to its original shape, the contacts are closed and power is restored. If the current is still too high, this cycle of breaking the circuit will be repeated. In this case the problem should be found and repaired.

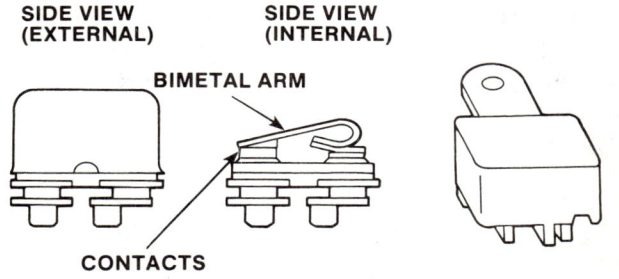

Figure 14-14 Cycling circuit breaker.

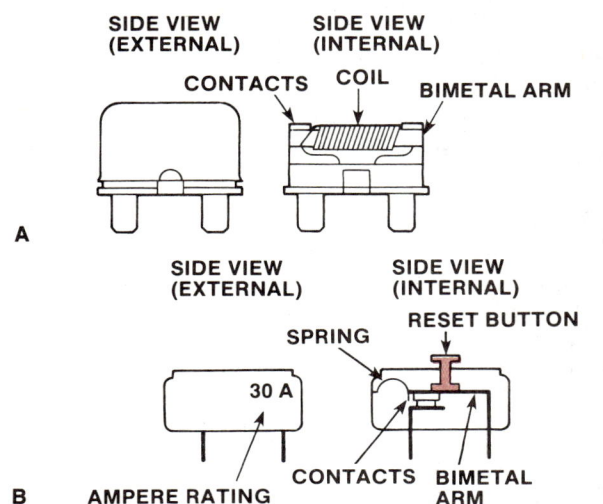

Figure 14-15 Resetting noncycling circuit breakers by (A) removing power from the circuit and (B) depressing a reset button.

Cycling circuit breakers are generally used in circuits that are prone to occasional overloads. These include devices such as power windows, in which a jammed or sticking window can overwork the motor. In this situation a circuit breaker prevents the motor from burning out.

In automotive work, two types of noncycling circuit breakers are used. One is reset by removing the power from the circuit. There is a coil wrapped around a bimetal arm (Figure 14-15A). When an overcurrent exists and the contacts open, a small current passes through the coil. This current through the coil is not enough to operate a load, but it does heat up both the coil and the bimetal arm. This keeps the arm in the open position until power is removed. The other is reset by depressing a reset button. A spring pushes the bimetal arm down and holds the contacts together (Figure 14-15B). When an overcurrent condition exists and the bimetal arm heats up, the bimetal arm bends enough to overcome the spring and the contacts snap open. The contacts stay open until the reset button is pushed and the contacts snap together again.

Voltage Limiter

Some instrument panel gauges are protected against heavy voltage fluctuations that could damage the gauges or give erroneous readings. A voltage limiter restricts voltage to the gauges to approximately 5 volts. The limiter contains a heating coil, a bimetal arm, and a set of contacts. When the ignition is in the on or accessory position, the heating coil heats the bimetal arm, causing it to bend and open the contacts. This action results in voltage from both the heating coil and the circuit. When the arm cools down to the point that the contacts close, the cycle is repeated. The rapid opening and closing of the contacts produces a pulsating voltage at the output terminal averaging about 5 volts.

Switches

Electrical circuits are usually controlled by a switch of some type. Switches do two things. They control on/off, and they direct the flow of current in a circuit. Switches can be under the control of the driver or can be self-operating through a condition of the circuit, the vehicle, or the environment.

Contacts in a switch can be of several types, each named for the job they do or the sequence in which they work. A hinged-pawl switch (Figure 14-16) is the simplest type of switch. It either makes or breaks the current in a single conductor or circuit. It is a single-pole, single-throw (SPST) switch. The throw refers to the number of output circuits, and the pole refers to the number of input circuits made by the switch.

Another type of SPST switch is the momentary contact switch shown in Figure 14-17. The spring-loaded contact on this switch keeps it from making the circuit except when pressure is being applied to the button. A horn switch is of this type. Because the

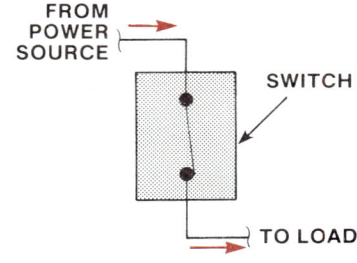

Figure 14-16 SPST hinged-pawl switch diagram.

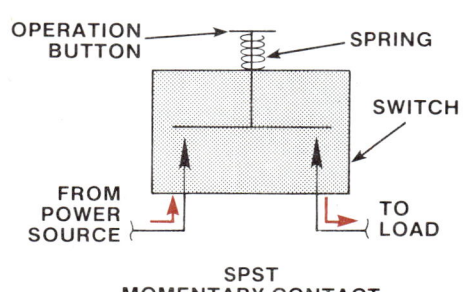

Figure 14-17 SPST momentary contact switch diagram.

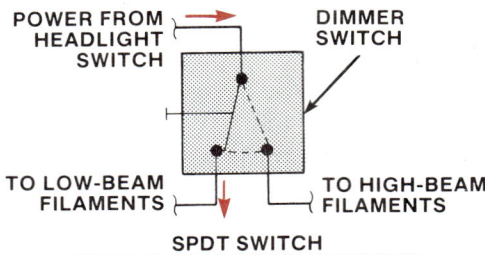

Figure 14-18 SPDT headlight dimmer switch.

spring holds the contacts open, the switch has a further designation: normally open. In the case where the contacts are held closed except when the button is pressed, the switch is designated normally closed.

Single-pole, double-throw switches have one wire in and two wires out. Figure 14-18 shows an SPDT hinged-pawl switch that feeds either the high-beam or low-beam headlight circuit. The dotted lines in the symbol show movement of the switch pawl from one contact to the other.

Switches can be designed with a great number of poles and throws. The transmission neutral start switch shown in Figure 14-19, for instance, has two poles and six throws and is referred to as a multiple-pole, multiple-throw (MPMT) switch. It contains two movable wipers that move in unison across two sets of terminals. The dotted line shows that the wipers are mechanically linked, or ganged. The switch closes a circuit to the starter in either P (park) or N (neutral) and to the back-up lights in R (reverse).

Most switches are combinations of hinged-pawl and push-pull switches, with different numbers of poles and throws. Some special switches are required, however, to satisfy the circuits of modern automobiles. A mercury switch is sometimes used to detect motion in a component, such as the one used in the engine compartment to turn on the compartment light.

Mercury is a very good conductor of electricity. In the mercury switch, a capsule is partially filled with mercury (Figure 14-20). In one end of the capsule are two electrical contacts. The switch is attached to the hood or luggage compartment lid. Normally, the mercury is in the end opposite to the contacts. When the lid is opened, however, the mercury flows to the con-

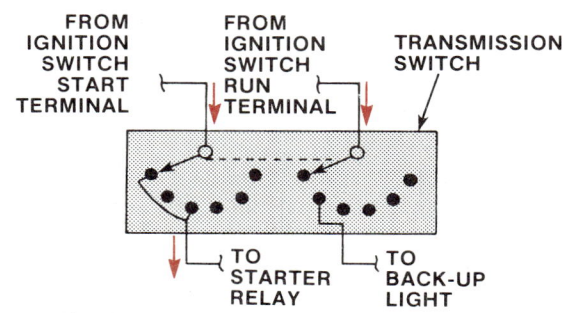

Figure 14-19 MPMT neutral start safety switch.

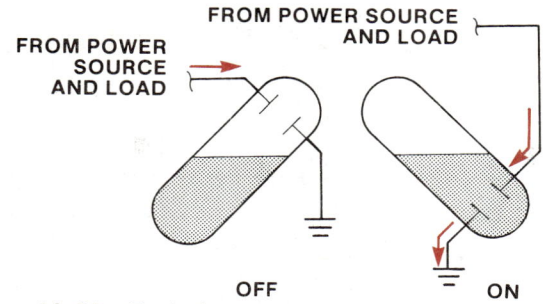

Figure 14-20 Typical mercury switch.

tact end and provides a circuit between the electrical contacts.

A temperature-sensitive switch usually contains a bimetallic element heated either electrically or by some component where the switch is used as a sensor. When engine coolant is below or at normal operating temperature, the engine coolant temperature sensor is in its normally open condition. If the coolant exceeds the temperature limit, the bimetallic element bends the two contacts together and the switch is closed to the indicator on the instrument panel. Other applications for heat-sensitive switches are time delay switches and flashers.

Relays

A relay is an electric switch that allows a small amount of current to control a much larger one. It consists of a control circuit and a power circuit (Figure 14-21). When the control circuit switch is open, no current flows to the coil, so the windings are de-energized. When the switch is closed, the coil is energized, turning the soft iron core into an electromagnet and drawing the armature down. This closes the power circuit contacts, connecting power to the load circuit. When the control switch is opened, the current stops flowing in the coil, the electromagnet disappears, and the armature is released, which breaks the power circuit contacts.

Solenoids

Solenoids are also electromagnets with movable cores used to translate electrical current flow into mechanical movement. They can also close contacts, acting as a relay at the same time.

Capacitors (Condensers)

Capacitors are constructed from two or more sheets of electrically conducting material with a nonconducting or dielectric (anti-electric) material placed between them and conductors connected to the two sheets.

If a battery is connected to the two plates of a capacitor as shown in Figure 14-22, electrons will be pushed up the wires from the battery's negative post and will distribute themselves along the negative plate of the capacitor. At the same time, electrons will be attached to the positive post of the battery and pulled down the wire from the negative plate of the capacitor. The combination of the electrons being pushed and pulled will charge the capacitor.

If the circuit is now broken, the capacitor remains charged until a circuit is completed between the two plates. If the charge is routed through a voltmeter, the brief discharge as the capacitor charge is neutralized gives the same voltage potential as the battery that charged it.

Since current from the battery flowed into the capacitor only until it was charged and then stopped, it is said that direct current cannot flow through a capacitor. Although alternating current does not flow through the capacitor either, its flow through the circuit is not stopped by the capacitor. Since current flows into and out of a capacitor only until it is charged, and since alternating current switches before a capacitor can be charged in either direction, the effect is the same as connecting a solid conductor in the line.

Automotive capacitors are normally encased in metal. The grounded case provides a connection to one set of conductor plates and an insulated lead connects to the other set.

Variable capacitors are called trimmers or tuners and are rated very low in capacity because of the reduced size of their conducting plates. For this reason, they are only used in very sensitive circuits such as radios and other electronic applications.

Wiring

Electrical wires are used to conduct electricity to operate the electrical and electronic devices in a vehi-

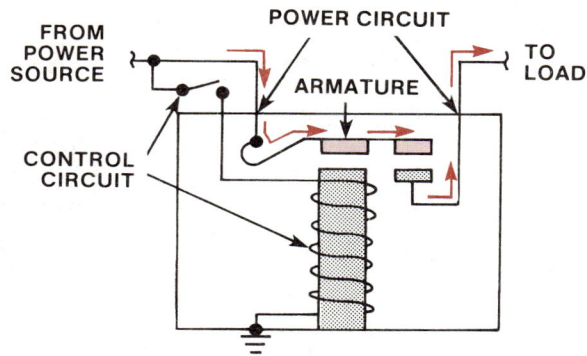

Figure 14-21 Typical electrical relay design.

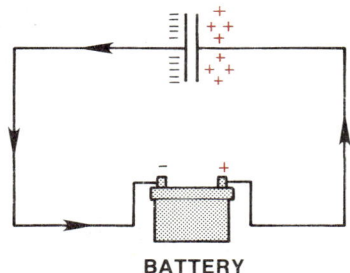

Figure 14-22 Charging a capacitor.

cle. There are two basic types of wires used: solid and stranded. Solid wires are single-strand conductors. Stranded wires are made up of a number of small solid wires twisted together to form a single conductor. Stranded wires are generally used as conductors in light, charging, and most accessory systems. On-board electronic computers use specially-shielded, twisted cable for protection from unwanted induced voltages that interfere with computer functions. In addition, some solid state components use printed circuits.

The current-carrying capacity and the amount of voltage drop in an electrical wire are determined by its length and gauge (size). The wire sizes are established by the Society of Automotive Engineers (SAE), which is the American wire gauge (AWG) system. Sizes are designed by a numbering system ranging from number 0 to 20, with number 0 being the largest and number 20 the smallest in a cross-sectional area (Table 14-2). Most of the current vehicle wiring ranges from number 10 to 18 with 12-volt battery cables usually being at least number 4 gauge. Domestic vehicle manufacturers have used metric wire sizing in their electrical schematics for a number of years.

Automotive wiring is also classified as primary and secondary. Primary wiring carries low voltage to all the electrical systems of the vehicle except to ignition secondary systems. Secondary wire, also called high tension cable, has extra thick insulation to carry high voltage from the vehicle's ignition coil to the spark plugs. The conductor itself is designed for low currents. The battery cable, as mentioned earlier, is a large gauge wire capable of carrying high currents from the battery to the starter.

The selection of the correct gauge primary wire of heavy enough gauge is very important for automotive low voltage wiring to assure safe and reliable performance. When gauge primary wire is too small, a voltage drop occurs due to electrical resistance. The two factors that should always be considered in selecting an adequate gauge primary wire are the total amperage the circuit carries and the total length of wire used in each circuit, including the return. Allowance for the return circuits, including grounded returns, has been computed in Table 14-3. The length of cable should be determined by totaling both wires on a two-wire circuit.

Wires are commonly grouped together in harnesses. A single-plug harness connector may form the connections for four, six, or more circuits. Harnesses and harness connectors help organize the vehicle's electrical system and provide a convenient starting point for tracking and testing many circuits. Most major wiring harness connectors are located in a vehicle's dash or fire wall area (Figure 14-23).

Printed Circuits

Many modern electronic components use printed circuit boards (Figure 14-24). A printed circuit board is made of thin sheets of nonconductive plastic onto which conductive metal such as copper has been deposited. Parts of the metal are then etched or eaten away by acid. The remaining metal lines form the conductors for the various circuits on the board. A printed circuit board can hold many complex circuits in a very small area. The circuit board can be connected to power supply or ground wiring through the use of plug-in connectors mounted on the circuit board.

There are several precautions that should be observed when working on a printed circuit.

TABLE 14-2 WIRE GAUGE SIZES

Metric Size (mm²)	Wire Size	Ampere Capacity
0.5	20	4
0.8	18	6
1.0	16	8
2.0	14	15
3.0	12	20
5.0	10	30
8.0	8	40
13.0	6	50
19.0	4	60

TABLE 14-3 WIRE SIZE AND LENGTH

Total Approximate Circuit Amperes 12 V	Wire Gauge (for Length in Feet)								
	3	5	7	10	15	20	25	30	40
1.0	18	18	18	18	18	18	18	18	18
1.5	18	18	18	18	18	18	18	18	18
2	18	18	18	18	18	18	18	18	18
3	18	18	18	18	18	18	18	18	18
4	18	18	18	18	18	18	18	16	16
5	18	18	18	18	18	18	18	16	16
6	18	18	18	18	18	18	16	16	16
7	18	18	18	18	18	18	16	16	14
8	18	18	18	18	18	16	16	16	14
10	18	18	18	18	16	16	16	14	12
11	18	18	18	18	16	16	14	14	12
12	18	18	18	18	16	16	14	14	12
15	18	18	18	18	14	14	12	12	12
18	18	18	18	16	16	14	12	12	10
20	18	18	18	16	16	14	12	10	10
22	18	18	18	16	16	12	12	10	10
24	18	18	18	16	16	12	12	10	10
30	18	18	16	16	14	10	10	10	10
40	18	18	16	14	12	10	10	8	8	6
50	16	14	12	12	10	10	8	8	6
100	12	12	10	10	6	6	4	4	4
150	10	10	8	8	4	4	2	2	2
200	10	8	8	6	4	4	2	2	1

Note: 18 AWG as indicated above this line could be 20 AWG electrically. 18 AWG is recommended for mechanical strength.

Basics of Electrical and Electronic Systems 331

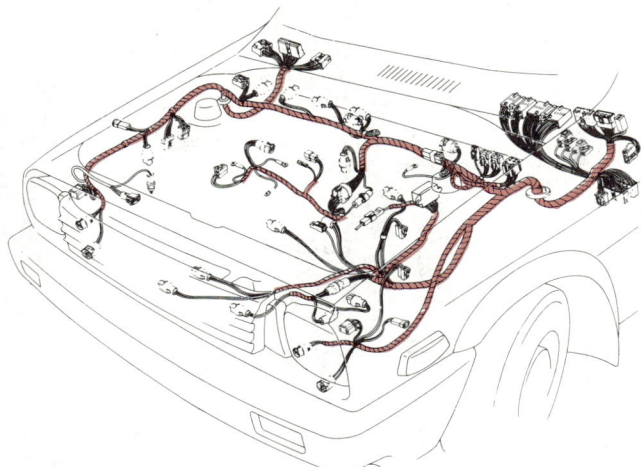

Figure 14-23 Typical front wiring harness connections. *Courtesy of Subaru of America*

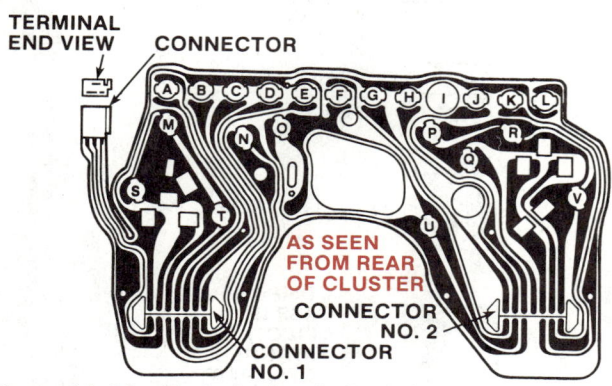

Figure 14-24 Typical printed circuit board.

1. Never touch the surface of the board. Dirt, salts, and acids on your fingers can etch the surface and set up a resistive condition. It is possible to knock out an entire section of the dash with a fingerprint.
2. The copper conductors can be cleaned with a commercial cleaner or by lightly rubbing an eraser across the surface.
3. The printed circuit board is damaged very easily because it is very thin. Be careful when plugging in bulbs. Do not tear the surface. Handle printed circuits with care.

An advantage of printed circuits is their high degree of reliability. In addition, they allow the instrument panels, for example, to be pulled back and worked on with the entire circuit layed out and functional.

Electrical Wiring Diagrams

Wiring diagrams, sometimes called schematics, are used to show how circuits are constructed. A typical service manual contains dozens of wiring diagrams vital to the diagnosis and repair of the vehicle.

A wiring diagram does not show the actual position of the parts on the vehicle or their appearance, nor does it indicate the length of the wire runs between components. It usually indicates the color of the wire's insulation, and sometimes the wire gauge size. Typically the primary wire insulation is color coded as shown in Table 14-4. The first letter in a combination of letters usually indicates the base color. The second letter usually refers to the strip color (if any). Tracing a circuit through a vehicle is basically a matter of following the colored wires.

Many different symbols are also used to represent components such as resistors, batteries, switches, transistors, and many other items. Some of these symbols have already been shown earlier in the chapter. Other common symbols are shown in Figure 14-25. As shown in the interior wiring diagram illustrated in Figure 14-26, components are also labeled. This manual uses letter/number codes next to the part. Other manuals use different systems.

Wiring diagrams can become quite complex. To avoid this, most diagrams usually illustrate only one distinct system, such as the backup light circuit, oil pressure indicator light circuit, or wiper motor circuit. In more complex ignition, electronic fuel injection, and computer control systems, a diagram may be used to illustrate only part of the entire circuit.

USING SERVICE MANUALS

Keep in mind that electrical symbols are not standardized throughout the automotive industry. Different manufacturers may have different methods of representing certain components, particularly the less common ones. Always refer to the symbol reference charts, wire

TABLE 14-4 COMMON WIRE COLOR CODES

Color	Abbreviations		
Aluminum	AL		
Black	BLK	BK	B
Blue (Dark)	BLU DK	DB	DK BLU
Blue (Light)	BLU LT	LB	LT BLU
Brown	BRN	BR	BN
Glazed	GLZ	GL	
Gray	GRA	GR	G
Green (Dark)	GRN DK	DG	DK GRN
Green (Light)	GRN LT	LG	LT GRN
Maroon	MAR	M	
Natural	NAT	N	
Orange	ORN	O	ORG
Pink	PNK	PK	P
Purple	PPL	PR	
Red	RED	R	RD
Tan	TAN	T	TN
Violet	VLT	V	
White	WHT	W	WH
Yellow	YEL	Y	YL

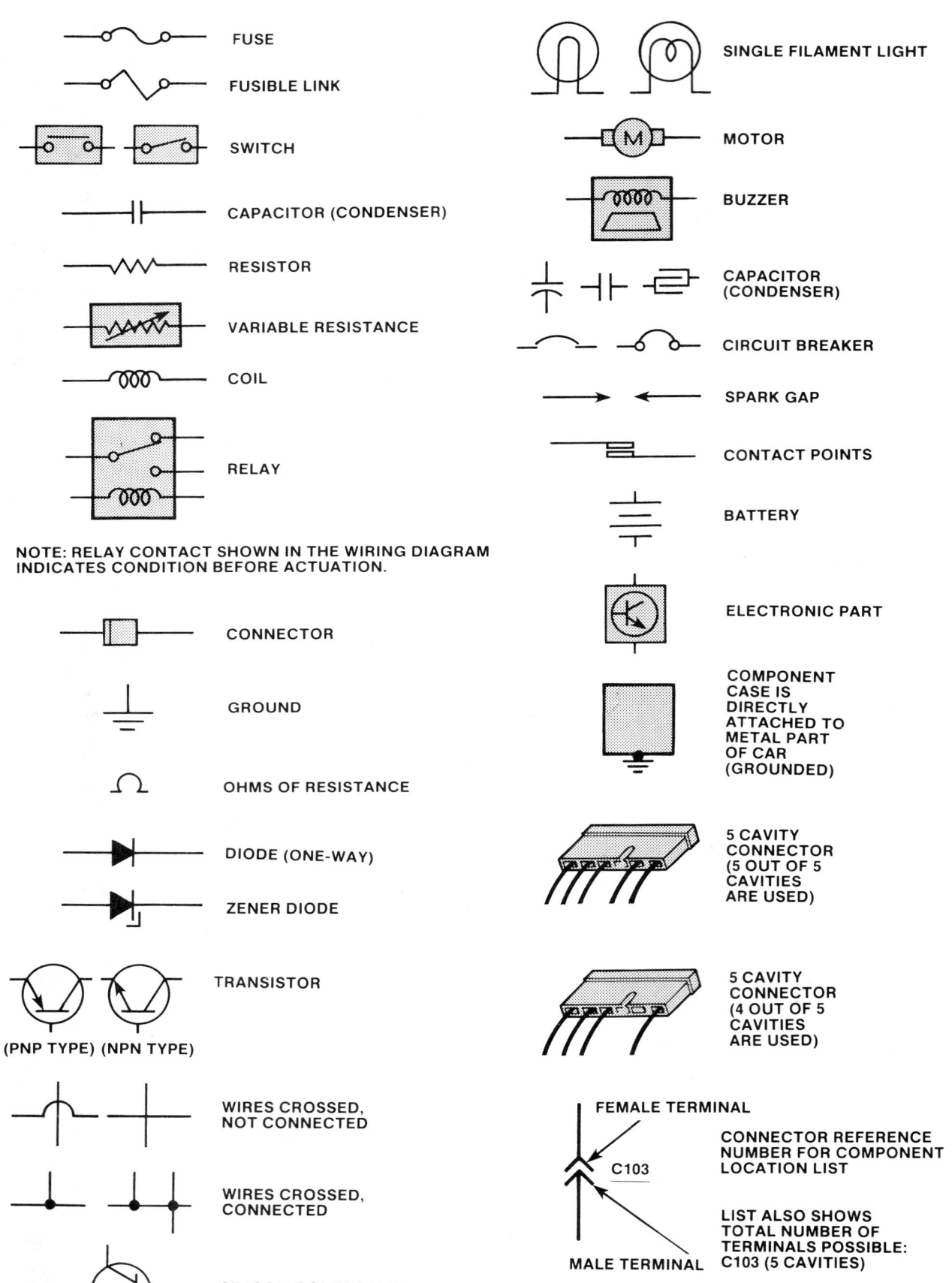

Figure 14-25 Common electrical symbols used on wiring diagrams.

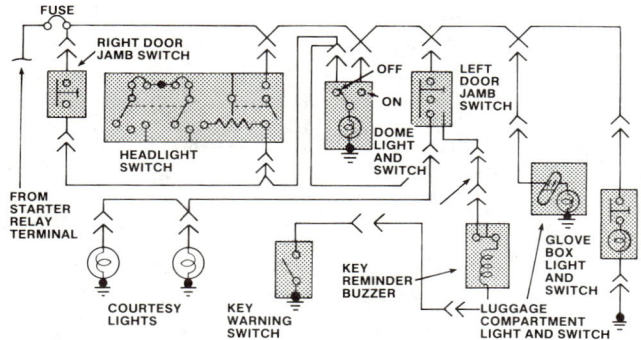

Figure 14-26 Wiring diagram of starting and ignition system. Harness connections are keyed to Figure 14-23. *Courtesy of Subaru of America*

color code charts, and abbreviation tables listed in the vehicle's service manual to avoid confusion when reading wiring diagrams. Also, most diagrams are designed to be read from left to right, top to bottom, just as you would a book.

Test Meter Use

Test meters include the voltmeter, the ammeter, and the ohmmeter. These should be used along with jumper wires, test lights, and variable resistors (piles) in the diagnosis of electrical circuit problems.

Voltmeters

Voltmeters are always connected into a circuit in parallel—never in series with the circuit. Voltmeters can be used to insure that battery voltage is sufficient and that this same voltage is reaching the electrical components of the circuit.

Consider a simple circuit (Figure 14-27). If there is 12 volts available at the battery, and the switch is closed, there should also be 12 volts available at each light. If, for example, less than 12 volts is indicated, there would be a high resistance somewhere. The lights would light, but not as strongly as they would with 12 volts.

The loss of voltage due to resistance in wires, connectors, and loads is called voltage drop. Voltage drop is checked using a voltmeter.

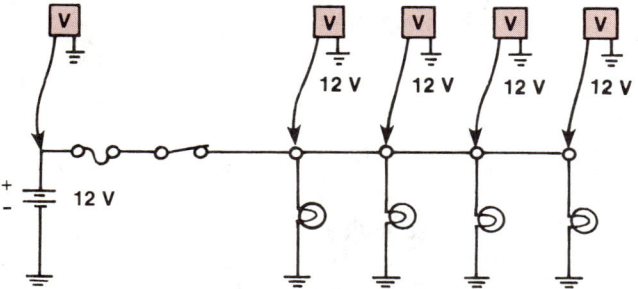

Figure 14-27 Checking a circuit using a voltmeter.

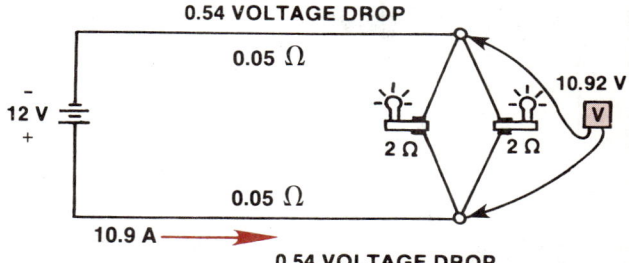

Figure 14-28 Wire resistance results in a slight voltage drop in the circuit.

Figure 14-28 illustrates two headlights connected to a 12-volt battery using two copper wires. Each copper wire has a resistance of 0.05 ohm. Each headlight has a resistance of 2 ohms. As you can see, the two headlights are wired parallel so their effective resistance is

$$\frac{2 \text{ ohms} \times 2 \text{ ohms}}{2 \text{ ohms} + 2 \text{ ohms}} = 1 \text{ ohm}$$

The total circuit resistance is

1 ohm + 0.05 ohm + 0.05 ohm = 1.1 ohms

The current in the circuit is

$$I = \frac{E}{R} = \frac{12}{1.1} = 10.9 \text{ amperes}$$

The voltage drop in each wire is

$$E = I \times R$$
$$E = 10.9 \times 0.05 = 0.54 \text{ V}$$

This means there is a 1.08 voltage drop for both wires. When the total voltage drop of the wires is subtracted from the 12-volt source voltage, 10.92 volts remain for the headlights to light them.

Without resistance in the copper wires, the headlights receive 12 amperes. With resistance, the current flow was reduced to 10.9 amperes. Any circuit wiring must have resistance values low enough to allow enough voltage to the load for proper operation.

The maximum allowable voltage loss due to voltage drops across wires, connectors, and other conductors in an automotive circuit is 10% of the system voltage. So, in an automotive electrical system powered by a 12-volt battery, this maximum loss is 1.2 volts.

A voltmeter can also be used to check for proper circuit grounding. For example, consider the lighting circuit shown in Figure 14-27. If the voltmeter reading indicates full voltage at the lights, but no lighting is seen, the bulbs or sockets could be bad or the ground connection is faulty.

An easy way to check for a defective bulb is to replace it with one known to be good. You can also use an ohmmeter to check for electrical continuity through the bulb.

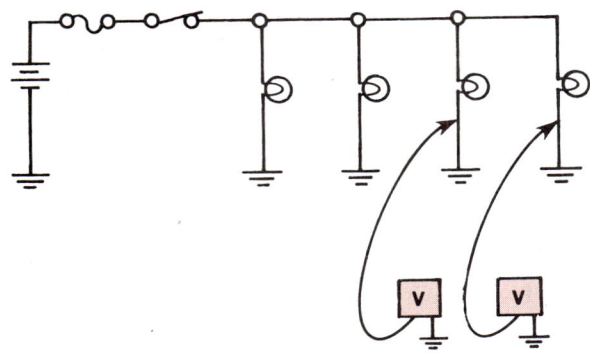

Figure 14-29 Using a voltmeter to check for open grounds.

If the bulbs are not defective, the problem lies in either the light sockets or ground wires. Connect the voltmeter to the ground wire and a good ground as shown in Figure 14-29. If the light socket is defective, there would be no voltage through the lights and the voltmeter would read 0 volts. If the socket was not defective, but the ground wire was broken or disconnected, the voltmeter would read very close to 12 volts.

Ammeters

Ammeters are always connected into a circuit in series—never in parallel with the circuit. This means that a wire must always be disconnected in order to connect the ammeter.

Because ammeters are built in very low internal resistance, connecting them in series does not add any appreciable resistance to the circuit. An accurate measurement of the current flow can be taken.

For example, assume that a circuit normally draws 5 amperes and is protected by a 6-ampere fuse. The customer's complaint indicates that the circuit draws in excess of 6 amperes constantly blowing the 6-ampere fuse. A short exists somewhere in the circuit (Figure 14-30). Mathematically, each light should draw 1.25 amperes ($5 \div 4 = 1.25$). Disconnect all lights by removing them from their sockets. Close the switch, and read the ammeter. With the load disconnected, the meter should read 0 amperes. If there is any reading, the wire between the fuse block and the disconnect is shorted to ground.

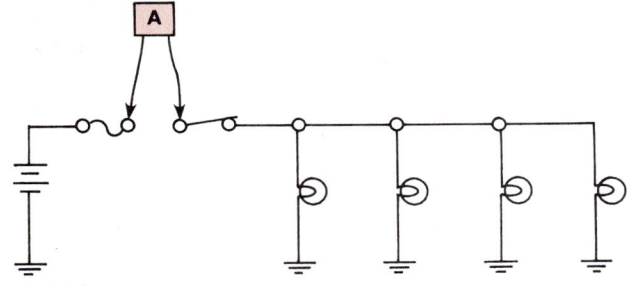

Figure 14-30 Checking a circuit using an ammeter.

When each light is reconnected in sequence, the reading should increase 1.25 amperes. Now, connect the second. The reading should be 2.5 amperes (1.25 + 1.25 = 2.5).

If, when making any connection, the reading is higher than expected, the problem is in that part of the light circuit.

When testing, always use a fuse. Never by-pass the fuse with a wire. The fuse should be rated at no more than 50% higher capacity than specifications. This offers circuit protection and provides enough amperage for testing. After the problem is found and corrected, be sure to replace the original specification fuse for maximum circuit protection.

Ohmmeters

Ohmmeters are used to test circuit continuity and resistance with no power applied. In other words, the circuit or component to be tested must first be disconnected from the power source (Figure 14-31). Connecting an ohmmeter into a live circuit usually results in damage to the meter.

Ohmmeters are also used to trace and check wires or cables. Assume that one wire of a four-wire cable is to be found. Connect one probe of the ohmmeter to the known wire at one end of the cable and touch the other probe to each wire at the other end of the cable. A meter needle deflection indicates the correct wire. Using this same method, you can check a suspected defective wire. If the meter needle deflects, the wire is sound. If it does not, the wire is defective (open). If the wire is sound, continue checking by connecting the probe to other leads. Any deflection of the meter needle indicates that the wire is shorted to one of the other wires and that the harness is defective.

Volt-Ohmmeter

This combination meter is very useful for all types of diagnostics. It is capable of measuring exact amounts of voltage and resistance at any point in a circuit.

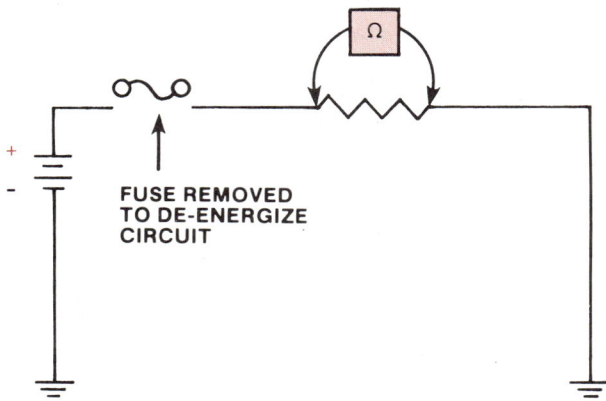

Figure 14-31 Measuring resistance using an ohmmeter. Note that the circuit fuse is removed to de-energize the circuit.

Basically, there are two types of volt-ohmmeters available: the analog and digital. Analog meters use a sweeping needle to indicate the measurement. This type meter is commonly used on normal automotive electrical circuits. A digital volt-ohmmeter (DVOM) is used on electronic circuitry. This type meter displays the measurement in numerical or digital form. Most DVOMs are of high impedance, which is a requirement for use on most computerized and other sensitive electronic equipment.

The proper methods for using a DVOM to measure voltage, amperage, and resistance are shown in Photo Sequence 7, which is included in this chapter.

Test Lights

There are two types of test lights commonly used in diagnosing electrical problems, the non-powered and powered test light. Non-powered test lights are used to check for available voltage. With the wire lead connected to ground and the tester's probe at a point of voltage, the light turns on (Figure 14-32A). The brightness of the light is determined by the amount of voltage present at that point. A powered test light is used to check for continuity. Hooked across a circuit or component, the light turns on if the circuit is complete. A powered test light should only be used if the power for the circuit or component has been disconnected (Figure 14-32B).

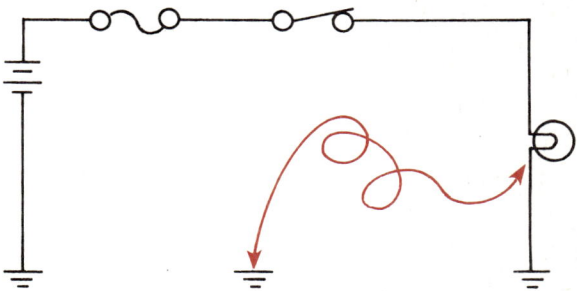

Figure 14-33 Using a jumper wire to test for an open ground.

Jumper Wires

These are used to by-pass individual wires, connectors, or components. By-passing a component or wire helps to determine if that part is faulty (Figure 14-33). If the problem is no longer evident after the jumper wire is installed, the part by-passed is normally faulty. Technicians typically have jumper wires of various lengths, usually some of the wires have a fuse or circuit breaker in them to protect the circuits being tested.

Troubleshooting Circuits

Troubleshooting procedures involve using meters, test lights, and jumper wires to determine if any part of the circuit is open, grounded, or shorted. An open circuit consists of a break or interruption in the circuit such as a wire that has come loose, or a slip connection that is not making contact (Figure 14-34A). A short to ground occurs whenever any part of the wiring circuit inadvertently is touching the vehicle frame (Figure 14-34B). A short occurs when two or more wires contact each other and by-pass part of the circuit's normal load (Figure 14-34C).

An ammeter and a voltmeter connected in a circuit at the different locations shown in Figure 14-35, should give readings as indicated when no part of the circuit is open, grounded or shorted. The meter readings indicated can be verified by Ohm's law.

If any part of the circuit opens, the ammeter reads zero current. If the open occurs in the 1-ohm resistor, a voltmeter connected from C to ground reads zero. However, if the resistor is open and the voltmeter is connected to points B and C, the reading is 12 volts. The reason is that the battery, ammeter, voltmeter, 2-ohm resistor, and 3-ohm resistor are all connected together to form a series circuit. The resistors have very little effect on the circuit, and only reduce the current flow through the high resistance voltmeter a negligible amount, hence the pointer deflects to indicate 12 volts.

To illustrate this type of 12-volt meter reading further, if the 2-ohm resistor were to become open instead of the 1-ohm resistor, a voltmeter connected from point C to ground would indicate 12 volts. The 1-ohm resistor in series in the high resistance of the

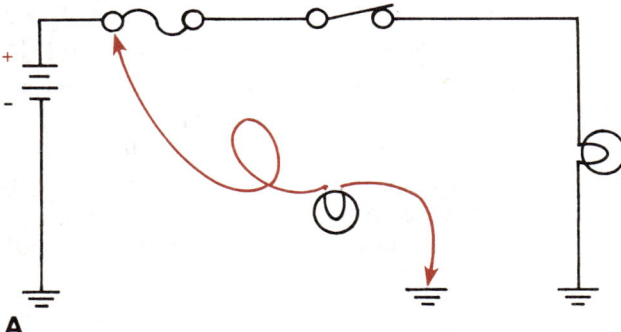

A

CIRCUIT IS DISCONNECTED AT POINT OF TEST.

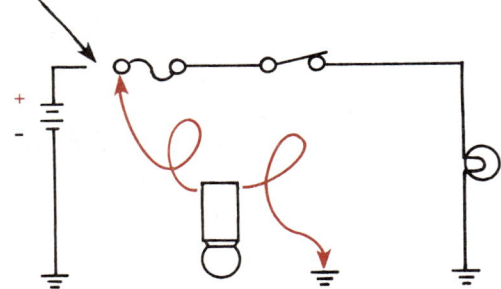

B

Figure 14-32 (A) Testing a circuit using a non-powered test light, and (B) testing with a powered test light. With powered test lights, the circuit must be de-energized.

336 Section 3 Electricity

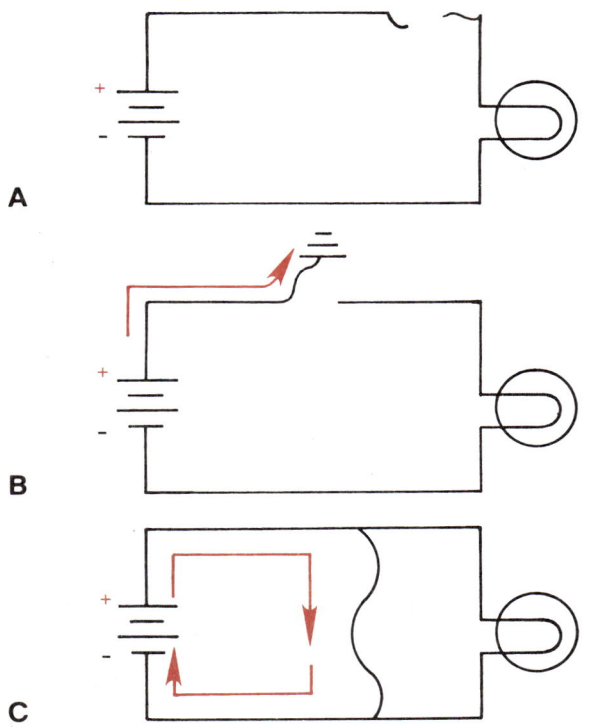

Figure 14-34 (A) Open, (B) grounded, and (C) shorted circuits are three common electrical circuit problems.

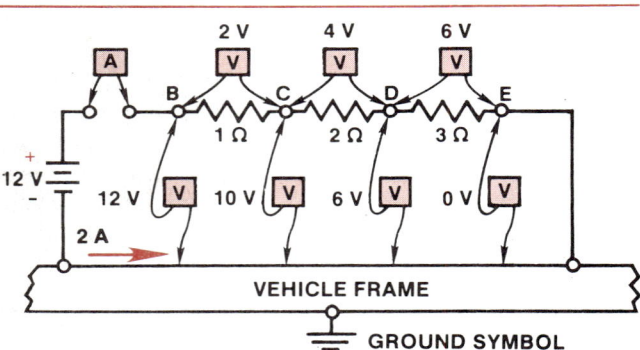

Figure 14-35 Sample circuit being tested with voltmeter and ammeter.

voltmeter has negligible effect. If an open should occur between point E and ground, a voltmeter connected from points B, C, D, or E to ground reads 12 volts. A voltmeter connected across any one of the resistors, from B to C, C to D, or D to E, will read zero volts, because no voltage drop occurs with no current flow as indicated by a zero reading on the ammeter.

If the 2-ohm resistor becomes completely shorted, the ammeter reads 3 amperes, since I = E/R = 12/1 + 3 = 3 amperes.

If point D becomes grounded, the ammeter reads I = 12/3 = 4 amperes. No current flows through the 3-ohm resistor.

These examples illustrate how a voltmeter and ammeter may be used to check for defects in a circuit. An ohmmeter also may be used to measure the values of each resistor. A high reading indicates an open or poor contact inside the resistor, and a low or zero reading indicates a partial or complete short circuit.

Repairing Connecting and Wiring

Many automotive electrical problems can be traced to faulty wiring. Loose or corroded terminals, frayed, broken, or oil soaked wires, and faulty insulation are the most common causes. Wires, fuses, and connections should be checked carefully during troubleshooting. Keep in mind that the insulation does not always appear to be damaged when the wire inside is broken. Also a terminal may be tight and yet be corroded.

Wire end terminals are connecting devices. They are generally made of tin-plated copper and come in many shapes and sizes. They may be either soldered or crimped in place.

When installing a terminal, select the appropriate size and type terminal. Be sure it is suitable for the unit connecting post or prongs and it has enough current carrying capacity for the circuit. Also, make sure it is heavy enough to endure normal wire flexing and vibration. Ring terminals should be used for critical applications or where heavy vibration occurs. Because they completely encircle the post, they will not fall off if the connection loosens. Figure 14-36 shows how to crimp a terminal. Be sure to use the proper crimping tool and to follow the tool manufacturer's instructions.

CAUTION: *Do not crimp a terminal with the cutting edge of a pair of pliers. While this method may crimp the terminal, it also weakens it.*

Figure 14-37 shows how to prepare a lip type terminal for soldering. Once the terminal and wire are prepared as shown, solder the lips and wire with rosin core solder. Do not use acid core solder. It creates corrosion and can damage electronic components. Keep soldering iron contact on the terminal to a minimum since it tends to melt the insulation.

Figure 14-38 shows how to solder a barrel-type terminal. Notice the stripped wire must be tinned. Tinning a wire means coating it with a thin layer of solder. The wire is then inserted into the barrel. The

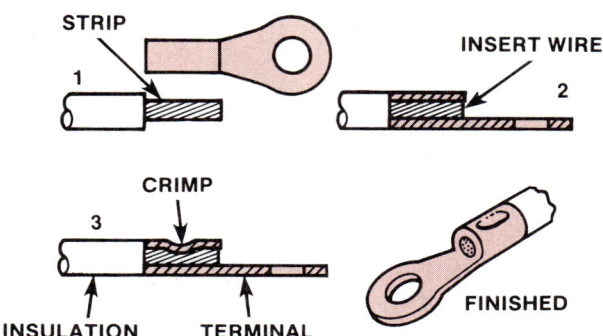

Figure 14-36 Proper method of crimping a wire to a terminal.

PHOTO SEQUENCE 7

☐ USING A DVOM TO MEASURE VOLTAGE, CURRENT, AND RESISTANCE

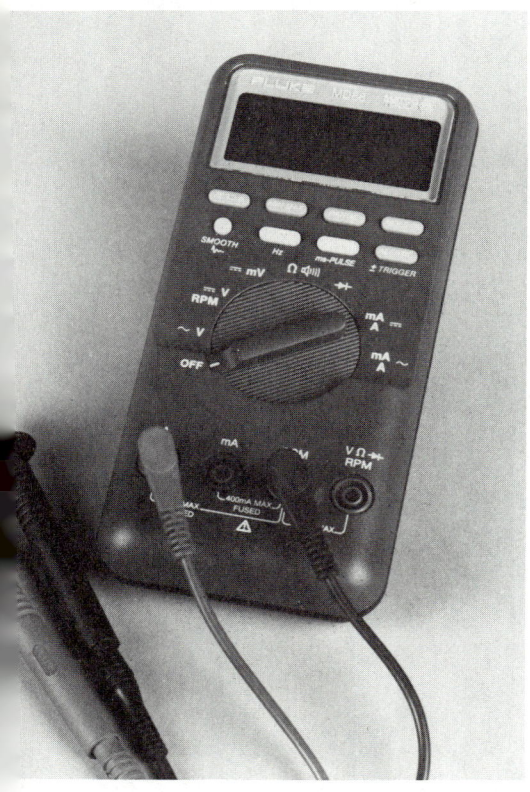

P7-1 DVOM with multiple scales and standard positive (red) and negative (black) leads.

P7-2 To test voltage, the meter should be placed in the appropriate voltage scale.

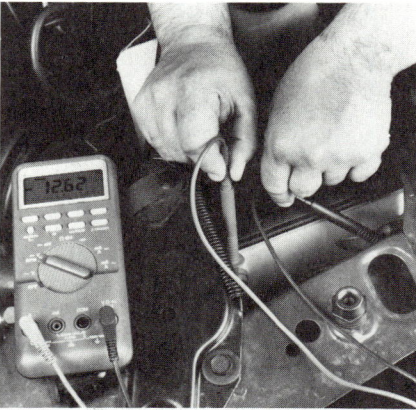

P7-3 Battery voltage is read by holding the red lead to the battery's positive terminal and the black lead to the negative terminal.

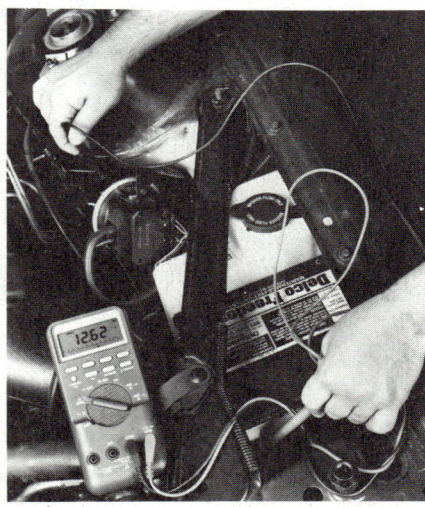

P7-4 System voltage is checked by placing the red lead on the positive battery terminal and the black lead to a chassis ground. If system voltage is less than battery voltage, resistance is present in the battery's ground connection.

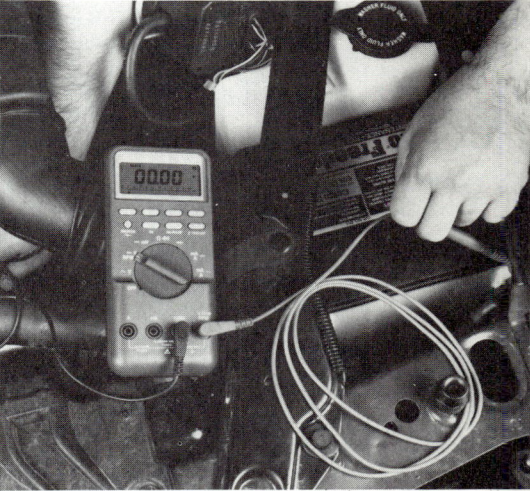

P7-5 Any resistance in the battery's ground connection will appear as a voltage drop between the negative terminal of the battery and the point where the negative cable attaches to the chassis. The amount of voltage drop will equal the difference between battery and system voltage.

P7-6 This voltage drop can also be determined by measuring the resistance of the cable's battery connection to ground. To measure resistance, the meter should be switched to read ohms and the meter zeroed according to the manufacturer's recommendations.

(continued)

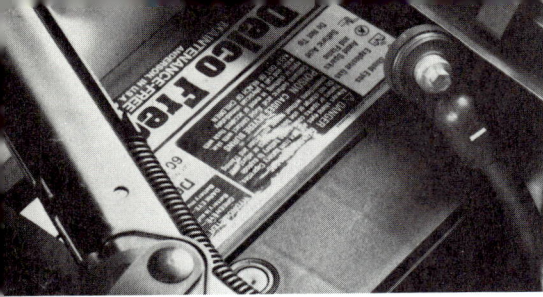

P7-7 Prior to making any resistance check, the item checked must be disconnected from its power source. Therefore, the negative cable must be disconnected for this test.

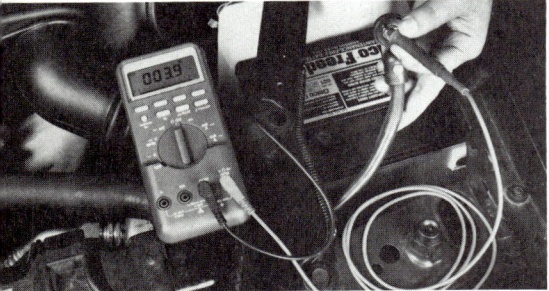

P7-8 Measure the resistance of the cable. Note that although some resistance is present, it did not cause a voltage drop. Larger amounts of resistance will and should be corrected.

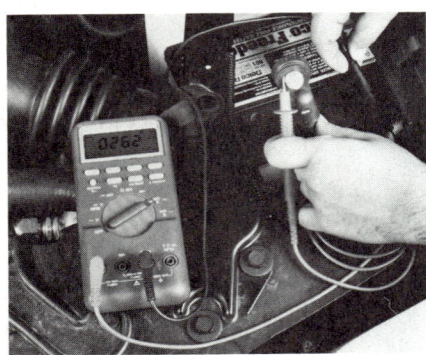

P7-9 A slight amount of resistance in the ground cable will cause some current to flow. To measure current, switch the meter to the appropriate ampere scale. Place the meter in series with the tested circuit. Note the position of the leads in the photo.

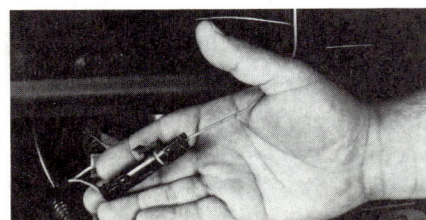

P7-10 Normally the ammeter is connected into a circuit at a wire connector. The connector shown is for the underhood light.

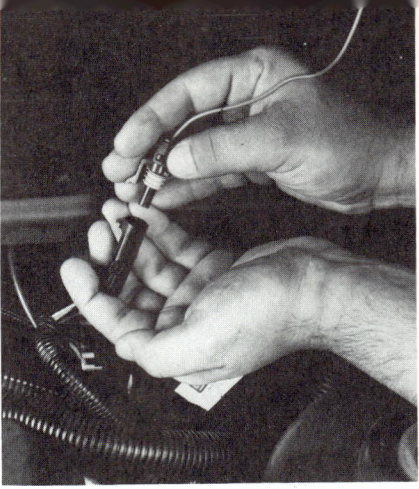

P7-11 With the battery negative cable reinstalled on the battery, disconnect the circuit connector. This causes an open circuit and the light goes out.

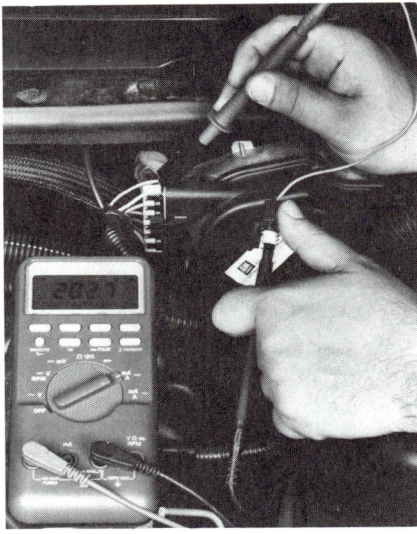

P7-12 By connecting the meter in series with the circuit, the light turns back on and the meter measures the current of the circuit.

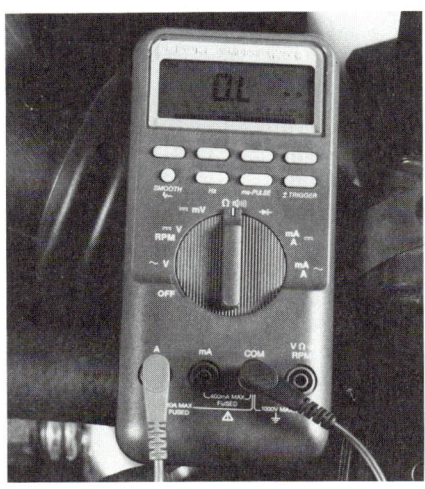

P7-13 Disconnect the meter leads from the circuit and switch the meter to the resistance scale.

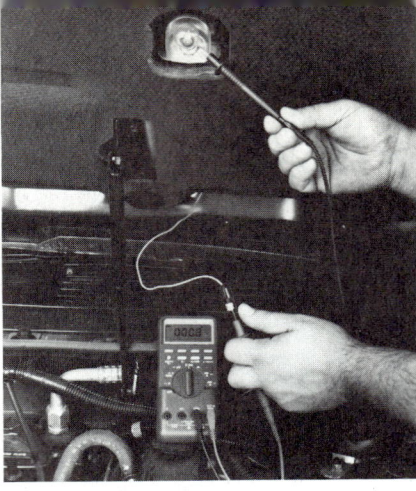

P7-14 To measure the resistance of the circuit, connect the meter leads across the circuit (from the connector to the ground). Make sure the connector is disconnected when doing this.

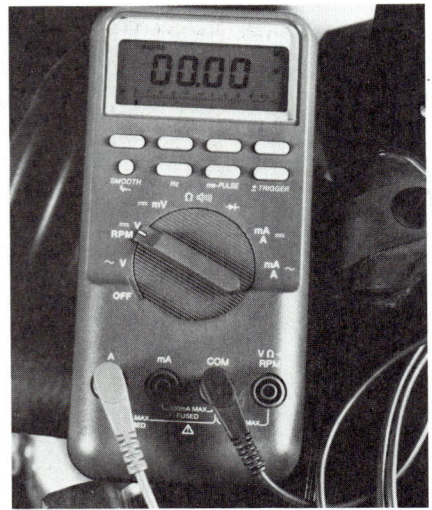

P7-15 To measure the voltage drop of the circuit, reconnect the circuit connector and set the meter to the appropriate voltage scale.

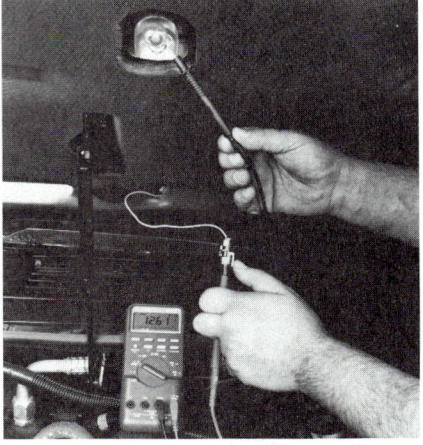

P7-16 By inserting the red lead into the circuit connector and the black lead to the lamp's ground, the voltage drop of that circuit is measured. ∎

Basics of Electrical and Electronic Systems

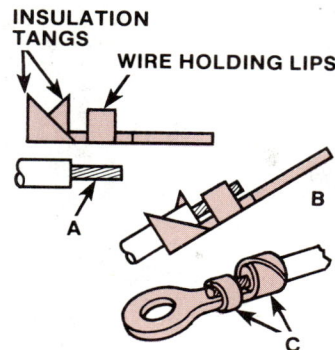

Figure 14-37 Preparing a lip-type terminal and wire for soldering.

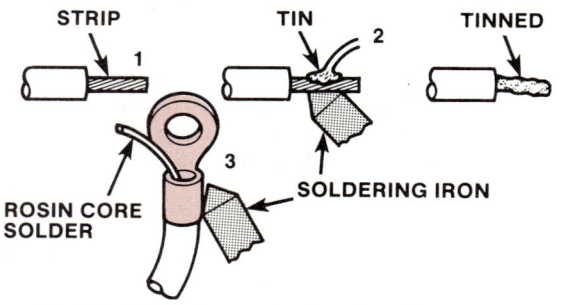

Figure 14-38 Soldering a wire to a barrel-type terminal.

barrel may be crimped if desired. Then the barrel is heated with the iron and the solder is held against the end of the barrel. Allow the solder to melt, flow into the barrel, and bond to both the barrel and wire.

All copper wire joints should be soldered. Some car makers, however, use aluminum in their wiring. Aluminum cannot be soldered. Care must be taken to ensure a good electrical contact and freedom from corrosion. Follow manufacturer's guidelines and use repair kits when available.

Never pull on wires to separate connectors. This can create an intermittent contact later and cause much trouble which is hard to track. Use special tools designed for separating connectors.

Never reroute wires when making repairs. Rerouting wires can result in induced voltages in nearby components. These stray voltages can interfere with the function of electronic circuits.

Dielectric grease is used to moisture proof and to protect connections from corrosion. Some car manufacturers suggest using petroleum jelly to protect connection points.

CUSTOMER CARE

Many electrical wire repairs require splices. But if you have to make multiple splices in a single wiring harness, make sure you stagger your splices. The end result will look much neater, and it will reduce the risk of unwanted wire-to-wire contact, which could result in a comeback repair.

☐ ELECTROMAGNETISM BASICS

Electricity and magnetism are related. One can be used to create the other. Current flowing through a wire creates a magnetic field around the wire. Moving a wire through a magnetic field creates current flow in the wire.

Many automotive components, such as alternators, ignition coils, starter solenoids, and magnetic pulse generators operate using principles of electromagnetism.

Fundamentals of Magnetism

Although almost everyone has seen magnets at work, a simple review of magnetic principles is in order to ensure a clear understanding of electromagnetism.

A substance is said to be a magnet if it has the property of magnetism—the ability to attract such substances as iron, steel, nickle, or cobalt. These are called magnetic materials.

A magnet has two points of maximum attraction, one at each end of the magnet. These points are called poles, with one being designated the North pole and the other the South pole (Figure 14-39A). When two

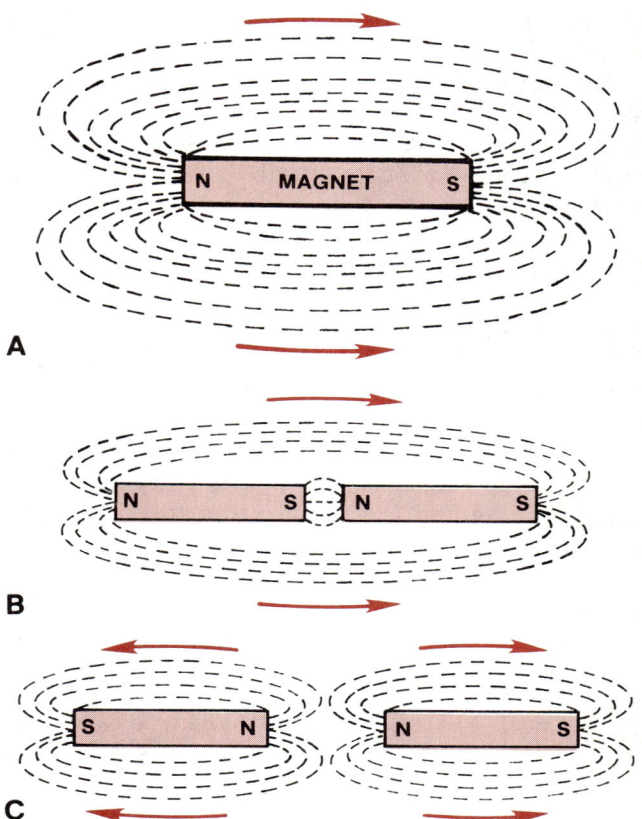

Figure 14-39 (A) In a magnet, lines of force emerge from the North pole and travel to the South pole before passing through the magnet back to the North pole. (B) Unlike poles attract, while (C) similar poles repel each other.

magnets are brought together, opposite poles attract (Figure 14-39B), while similar poles repel each other (Figure 14-39C).

A magnetic field, called a field of flux, exists around every magnet. The field consists of imaginary lines along which a magnetic force acts. These lines emerge from the North pole and enter the South pole, returning to the North pole through the magnet itself. All lines of force leave the magnet at right angles to the magnet. None of the lines cross each other. All lines are complete.

Magnets can occur naturally in the form of a mineral called magnetite. Artificial magnets can also be made by inserting a bar of magnetic material inside a coil of insulated wire and passing a heavy direct current through the coil. This principle is very important in understanding certain automotive electrical components. Another way of creating a magnet is by stroking the magnetic material with a bar magnet. Both methods force the randomly arranged molecules of the magnetic material to align themselves along North and South poles (Figure 14-40).

Artificial magnets can be either temporary or permanent. Temporary magnets are usually made of soft iron. They are easy to magnetize but quickly lose their magnetism when the magnetizing force is removed. Permanent magnets are difficult to magnetize, but once magnetized they retain this property for very long periods.

The earth is in fact a very large magnet, having a North and South pole, with lines of magnetic force running between them as in any other magnet. This is why a compass always aligns itself to straight north and south.

In 1820, a simple experiment discovered the existence of a magnetic field around a current-carrying wire. When a compass was held over the wire, its needle aligned itself at right angles to the wire (Figure 14-41). The lines of magnetic force are concentric circles around the wire. The density of these circular lines of force is very heavy near the wire and decreases farther away from the wire. As is also shown in Figure 14-41, the polarity of a current-carrying wire's magnetic field changes depending on the direction the current is flowing through the wire.

Remember, these magnetic lines of force or flux lines do not move or flow around the wire. They simply have a direction as shown by their effect on a compass

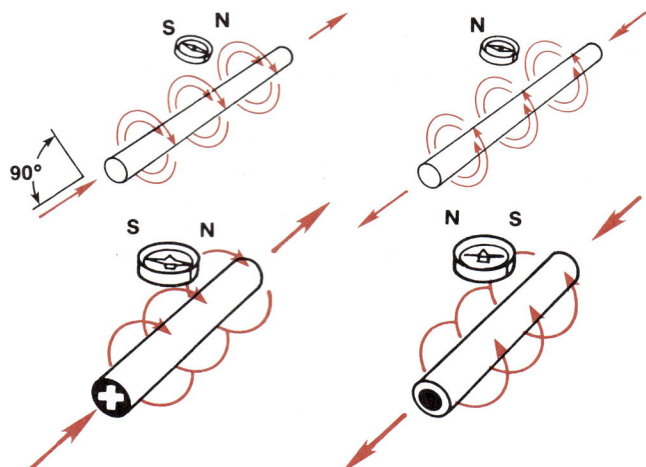

Figure 14-41   When current is passed through a conductor such as wire, magnetic lines of force are generated around the wire at right angles to the direction of the current flow.

needle. These lines of force are always at right angles to the conducting wire.

FLUX DENSITY   The more flux lines, the stronger the magnetic field at that point. Increasing current will increase flux density. Also, two conducting wires lying side by side carrying equal currents in the same direction create a magnetic field equal in strength to one conductor carrying twice the current. Adding more wires increases the magnetic effect proportionally (Figure 14-42).

COILS   Looping a wire into a coil concentrates the lines of force inside the coil. The resulting magnetic field is the sum of all the single-loop magnetic fields added together (Figure 14-43). The overall effect is the same as placing many wires side by side, each carrying current in the same direction.

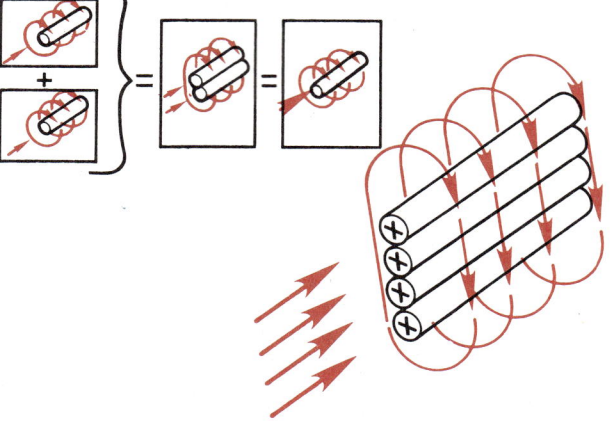

MAGNETIC FIELDS ADD TOGETHER.

Figure 14-42   Increasing the number of conductors carrying current in the same direction increases the strength of the magnetic field around them.

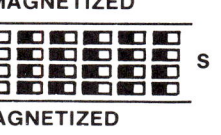

Figure 14-40   Molecular arrangement of unmagnetized and magnetized iron.

Basics of Electrical and Electronic Systems 341

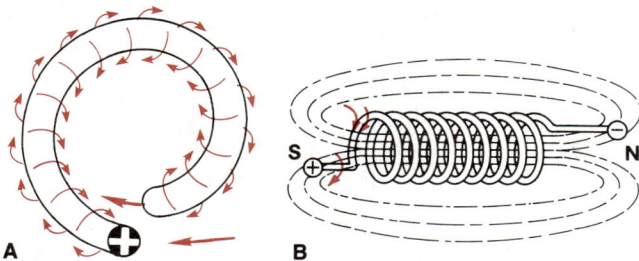

Figure 14-43 (A) Forming a wire loop concentrates the lines of force inside the loop. (B) The magnetic field of a wire coil is the sum of all the single-loop magnetic fields.

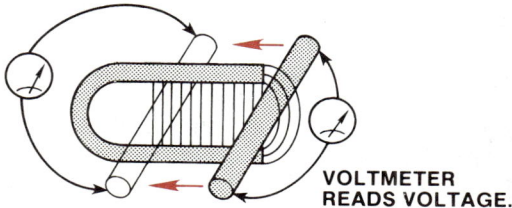

Figure 14-45 Moving a conductor so it cuts across the magnetic lines of force induces a voltage in the conductor.

Magnetic Circuits and Reluctance

Just as current can only flow through a complete circuit, the lines of flux created by a magnet can only occupy a closed magnetic circuit. The resistance that a magnetic circuit offers to a line of flux is called reluctance. Magnetic reluctance can be compared to electrical resistance.

Reconsider the wire coil shown in Figure 14-43. The air inside the coil has very high reluctance and limits the magnetic strength produced. However, if an iron core is placed inside the coil, magnetic strength increases tremendously. This is because the iron core has a very low reluctance (Figure 14-44).

When a coil is wound around an iron core in this manner, it becomes a usable electromagnet. The strength of the magnetic poles in an electromagnet is directly proportional to the number of turns of wire and the current flowing through them.

The equation for an electromagnetic circuit is similar to Ohm's law for electrical circuits. It states that the number of magnetic lines is proportional to the ampere-turns divided by the reluctance. To summarize:

- Field strength increases if current through the coil increases.
- Field strength increases if the number of coil turns increases.
- If reluctance increases, field strength decreases.

Induced Voltage

Now that we have explained how current can be used to generate a magnetic field, it is time to examine the opposite effect of how magnetic fields can produce electricity.

Figure 14-45 shows a straight piece of conducting wire with the terminals of a voltmeter attached to both ends. If the wire is moved across a magnetic field, the voltmeter registers a small voltage reading. A voltage has been induced in the wire.

It is important to remember that the conducting wire must cut across the flux lines to induce a voltage. Moving the wire parallel to the lines of flux does not induce voltage.

The wire need not be the moving component in this setup. Holding the conducting wire still and moving the magnetic field at right angles to it also induces voltage in the wire. In fact, this is the exact setup used in a vehicle's alternator. A magnetic field is made to cut across stationary conductors to produce voltage and current.

The wire or conductor becomes a source of electricity and has a polarity or distinct positive and negative end. However, this polarity can be switched depending on the relative direction of movement between the wire and magnetic field (Figure 14-46). This is why an alternator produces alternating current.

The magnitude of the induced voltage depends on four factors.

- The stronger the magnetic field, the stronger the induced voltage.
- The faster the field is being cut, the more lines of flux are cut and the stronger the voltage induced.
- The greater the number of conductors, the greater the voltage induced.

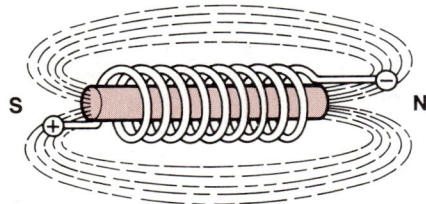

Figure 14-44 Placing a soft iron core inside a coil greatly reduces the reluctance of the coil and creates a usable electromagnet.

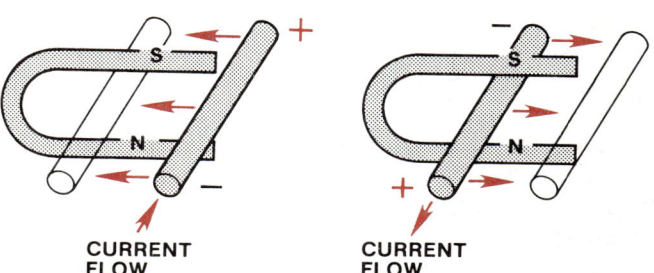

Figure 14-46 The polarity of the induced voltage depends on the direction in which the conductor moves as it cuts across the magnetic field.

- The closer the conductor(s) and magnetic field are to right angles (perpendicular) to one another, the greater the induced voltage.

The importance of electromagnetism and induced voltage is clearly seen in chapters dealing with starting, charging, ignition, and electronic control systems.

BASICS OF ELECTRONICS

Computerized engine controls and other features of today's cars would not be possible if it were not for electronics. For purposes of clarity, let us define electronics as the technology of controlling electricity. Electronics has become a special technology beyond electricity. Transistors, diodes, semiconductors, integrated circuits, and solid-state devices are all considered to be part of electronics rather than just electrical devices. But keep in mind that all the basic laws of electricity apply to electronic controls.

SHOP TALK

Although electrons in a circuit actually flow from negative to positive (the electron theory of current flow), many automotive electrical diagrams continue to assume that current flow is from positive to negative (the conventional theory of current flow). When examining an actual electrical diagram, always take care to determine which current flow theory is being used, because this can make a major difference in the operation of electronic components. Normally, full chassis or system wiring diagrams are based on the conventional theory of current flow, and internal component wiring schematics are based on the electron theory.

Semiconductors

A semiconductor is a material or device that can function as either a conductor or an insulator, depending on how its structure is arranged. Semiconductor materials have less resistance than an insulator but more resistance than a conductor. Some common semiconductor materials include silicon (Si) and germanium (Ge).

In semiconductor applications, materials have a crystal structure. This means that their atoms do not lose and gain electrons as the atoms in conductors do. Instead, the atoms in these semiconductor materials share outer electrons with each other. In this type of atomic structure, the electrons are tightly held and the element is stable.

Because the electrons are not free, crystals cannot conduct current. These materials are called electrically inert materials. In order to function as semiconductors, a small amount of trace element must be added.

The addition of these traces, called impurities, allows the material to function as a semiconductor. The type of impurity added determines what type of semiconductor will be produced.

N-Type Semiconductors

N-type semiconductors have loose, or excess, electrons. They have a negative charge. This enables them to carry current. N-type semiconductors are produced by adding an impurity with five electrons in the outer ring (called pentavalent atoms). Four of these electrons fit into the crystal structure, but the fifth is free. This excess of electrons produces the negative charge. Figure 14-47 shows an example.

P-Type Semiconductors

P-type semiconductors are positively charged materials. This enables them to carry current. P-type semiconductors are produced by adding an impurity with three electrons in the outer ring (trivalent atoms). When this element is added to silicon or germanium, the three outer electrons fit into the pattern of the crystal, leaving a hole where a fourth electron would fit. This hole is actually a positively charged empty space. This hole carries the current in the P-type semiconductor. Figure 14-48 shows an example of a P-type semiconductor.

HOLE FLOW Understanding how semiconductors carry current without losing electrons requires understanding the concept of hole flow. The holes in a P-type semiconductor, being positively charged, attract electrons. Although the electrons cannot be freed from their atom, they can rearrange their pattern and fill a hole in a nearby atom. Whenever this happens, the electron leaves a hole. This hole in turn is filled by another electron, and the process continues. The electrons move toward the positive side of the structure, and the holes move to the negative side. This is the principle by which semiconductors carry current.

Semiconductor Uses

Because semiconductors have no moving parts, they seldom wear out or need adjustment. Semicon-

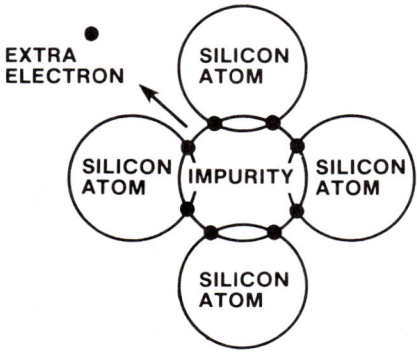

Figure 14-47 Atomic structure of N-type silicon semiconductor.

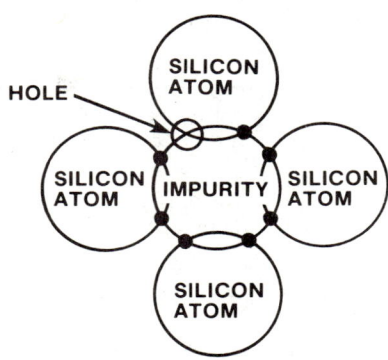

Figure 14-48 Atomic structure of P-type silicon semiconductor.

ductors, or solid-state devices, are also small, require little power to operate, are reliable, and generate very little heat. For all these reasons, semiconductors are being used in many applications.

Diodes and Transistors

Because a semiconductor can function as both a conductor and an insulator, it is very useful as a switching device. How a semiconductor functions depends upon the way current flows (or tries to flow) through it. Two common semiconductor devices are diodes and transistors.

Diodes

The diode is the simplest semiconductor device. It is formed by joining P-type semiconductor material with N-type semiconductor material. The point at which the two materials are joined is called the junction (Figure 14-49A).

A diode allows current to flow in one direction, but not in the opposite direction. Therefore, it can function as a switch, acting as either conductor or insulator, depending on the direction of current flow.

One application of diodes is in the alternator, where they function as a one-way valve for current flow. All charging systems, whether alternators or generators, produce alternating current. In the generator, current was rectified (changed from AC to DC) by a rotating commutator and a set of brushes. In the alternator, current is rectified by the use of diodes. The diodes are arranged so that current can leave the alternator in one direction only (as direct current).

When the electric current from the alternator is applied to the N side of the diode, the current (with its flowing electrons) pushes electrons in the N side toward the junction. These electrons cross the junction and fill holes in the P side. When this happens, electrons flow through the P side and out into the circuit. The diode is now functioning as a conductor. Figure 14-49B shows an example.

If alternator current is applied to the P side of the diode, the incoming electrons tend to fill the holes in the P side atoms. This stabilizes the P side, making it

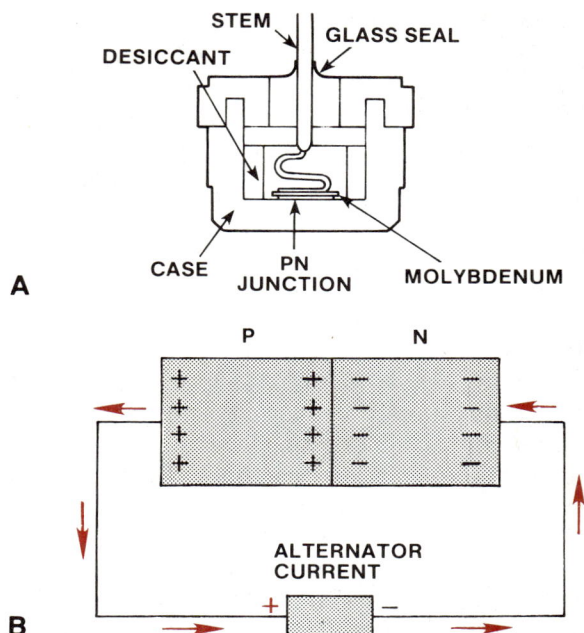

Figure 14-49 (A) Cross-sectional view of diode construction. Materials may vary in different diodes. (B) Current flow through a diode acting as a conductor. *Courtesy of General Motors Corp.*

an excellent insulator. At the same time, excess electrons in the N side are pulled out by the positive pull from the other side of the alternator circuit. This makes the N side into an excellent insulator. The entire diode is now functioning as an insulator, and current cannot flow through. Figure 14-50 shows an example. When the diode is used in this way, current can flow out of the alternator and into the battery in only one direction.

A variation of the diode is the zener diode. This device functions like a standard diode until a certain voltage is reached. When the voltage level reaches this point, the zener diode allows current to flow in the reverse direction. Zener diodes are often used in electronic voltage regulators.

Transistors

A transistor is an electronic device produced by joining three sections of semiconductor materials.

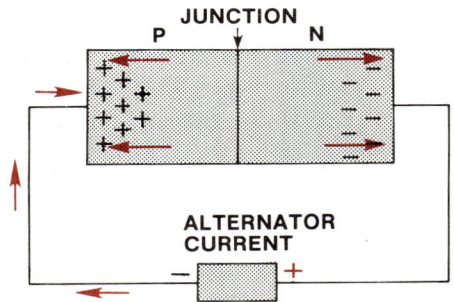

Figure 14-50 Current flow blocked by a diode acting as an insulator.

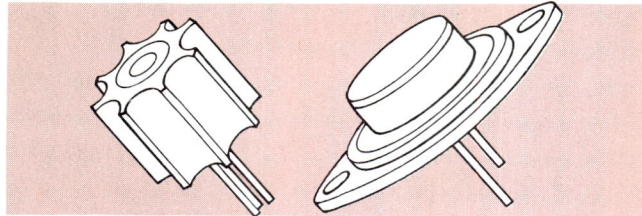

Figure 14-51   Typical transistors.

Like the diode, it is very useful as a switching device, functioning as either a conductor or an insulator. Figure 14-51 shows two designs of transistors, which come in many different sizes and types.

A transistor resembles a diode with an extra side. It can consist of two P-type materials and one N-type material or two N-type materials and one P-type material. These are called PNP and NPN types. In both types, junctions occur where the materials are joined. Figure 14-52 shows a PNP junction transistor in a circuit. Notice that each of the three sections has a lead connected to it. This allows any of the three sections to be connected to the circuit. The center section is called the base.

Transistors can function as insulators, as shown in Figure 14-53A. As long as the switch is open and no current is flowing into the center N section, the transistor is blocking current flow in the circuit. The junctions are thus acting as insulators.

However, if the switch is closed and current is applied to the center N section, the transistor changes functions. The incoming electrons destabilize the center section and both outside sections. This makes all of them conductors (Figure 14-53B).

An NPN-type transistor functions in the same manner, except that current flows out of the center P section instead of into it. The basic operation remains the same.

A very small amount of current applied to the center section (base) of a transistor can control a much larger amount of current flowing through the entire transistor. This fact allows transistors to be used as signal amplifiers in radios, stereos, calculators, home computers, and computerized engine controls.

Semiconductor Circuits

One transistor or diode is limited in its ability to do complex tasks. However, when many semiconductors

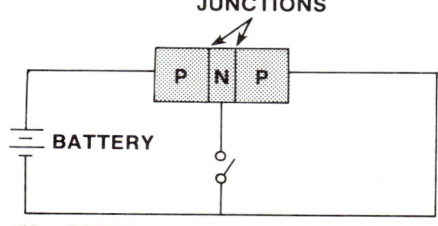

Figure 14-52   PNP junction transistor.

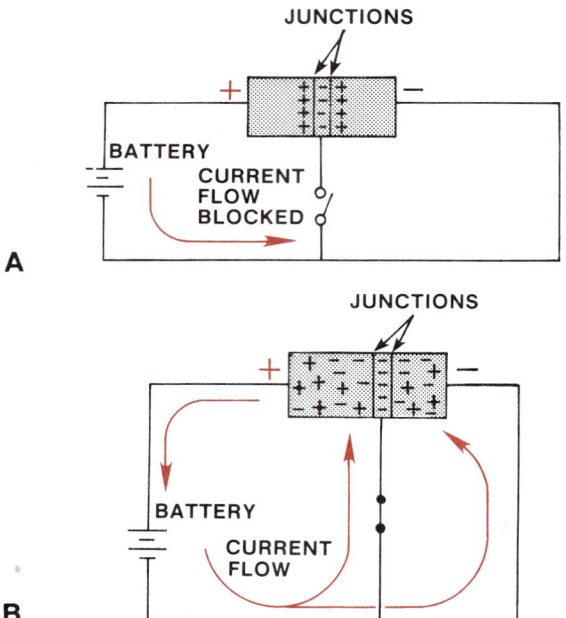

Figure 14-53   (A) Transistor acting as insulator. (B) Transistor acting as a conductor.

are combined into a circuit, they can perform complex functions. An example of this is the electronic voltage regulator.

The heart of the electronic regulator is a zener diode. As mentioned, the zener diode has the ability to conduct in the reverse direction without damage. The zener diode used in regulators is doped so that it conducts in reverse once the maximum battery voltage has been achieved.

Figure 14-54 shows a typical transistorized regulator circuit in simplified form. When the voltage of the vehicle's system rises above the maximum battery voltage, the diode conducts and permits current to flow to the base of transistor 1. This turns the transistor on, which in turn switches off transistor 2. Transistor 2 is in control of field current for the alternator. With it off, no field current can flow, thus shutting off the alternator until the voltage level drops below specification. Transistor 2 is acting like a switch turning field current on then off as the system voltage rises and falls above and below the specified voltage. This occurs many times a second and cannot be measured with a standard voltmeter. The thermistor in the upper left of the diagram gives the temperature voltage change necessary to keep the battery charged in cold weather. An actual voltage regulator would have many additional parts, such as capacitors to protect the regulator from voltage surges. These systems can use conventional electronic components or integrated circuits.

❏ INTEGRATED CIRCUITS

An integrated circuit is simply a large number of diodes, transistors, and other electronic components

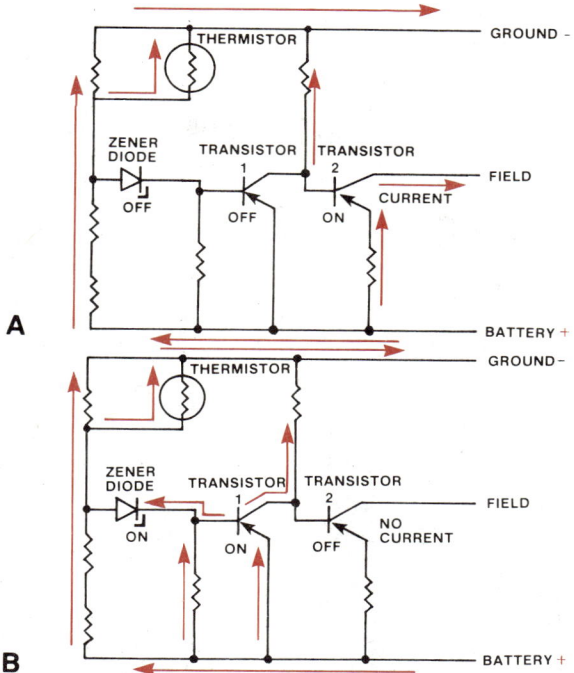

Figure 14-54 (A) Voltage regulator operation when battery is charging. (B) Voltage regulator operation when maximum battery voltage is exceeded.

such as resistors and capacitors, all mounted on a single piece of semiconductor material (Figure 14-55). This type of system has a tremendous size advantage. It is extremely small. Circuitry that used to take up entire rooms can now fit into a pocket. The principles of semiconductor operation remain the same in integrated circuits—only the size has changed.

The increasingly small size of integrated circuits is very important to automobiles. This means that electronics is no longer confined to the simple tasks such as rectifying alternator current. Enough transistors, diodes, and other solid-state components can be installed in a car to make logic decisions and issue commands to other areas of the engine. This is the foundation of computerized engine control systems.

Figure 14-55 This circuit board contains many integrated circuits and chips. This board is typical of those used in many automotive applications. *Courtesy of Kysor/Cadillac Corp.*

Basics of Electrical and Electronic Systems 345

☐ OPERATION OF MICROPROCESSORS

The microprocessor has taken over many of the tasks in cars and trucks that were formerly performed by vacuum, electromechanical, or mechanical devices. When properly programmed, they can carry out explicit instructions with blinding speed and almost flawless consistency.

A typical electronic control system is made up of sensors, actuators, and related wiring that is tied into a central processor called a microprocessor or microcomputer (a smaller version of a computer).

Sensors

All sensors perform the same basic function. They detect a mechanical condition (movement or position), chemical state, or temperature condition and change it into an electrical signal that can be used by the computer to make decisions. The microcomputer makes decisions based on information it receives from sensors (Figure 14-56). Each sensor used in a particular system has a specific job to do (for example, monitor throttle position, vehicle speed, manifold pressure). Together these sensors provide enough information to help the computer form a complete picture of vehicle operation. Even though there are a variety of different sensor designs, they all fall under one of two operating categories: reference voltage sensors or voltage generating sensors.

Reference voltage (Vref) sensors provide input to the computer by modifying or controlling a constant, predetermined voltage signal. This signal, which can have a reference value from 5 to 9 volts, is generated and sent out to each sensor by a reference voltage regulator located inside the processor. The term processor is used to describe the actual metal box that houses the computer and its related components. Because the computer knows that a certain voltage value has been sent out, it can indirectly interpret things like motion, temperature, and component position, based on what comes back. For example, consider the operation of the throttle position sensor (TPS). During acceleration (from idle to wide-open throttle), the computer monitors throttle plate movement based on the changing reference voltage signal returned by the TPS. (The TPS is a type of variable resistor known as a rotary potentiometer that changes circuit resistance based on throttle shaft rotation.) As TPS resistance varies, the computer is programmed to respond in a specific manner (for example, increase fuel delivery or alter spark timing) to each corresponding voltage change.

Most sensors presently in use are variable resistors or potentiometers. They modify a voltage to or from the computer, indicating a constantly changing status that can be calculated, compensated for, and modified. That is, most sensors simply control a voltage signal

346 Section 3 Electricity

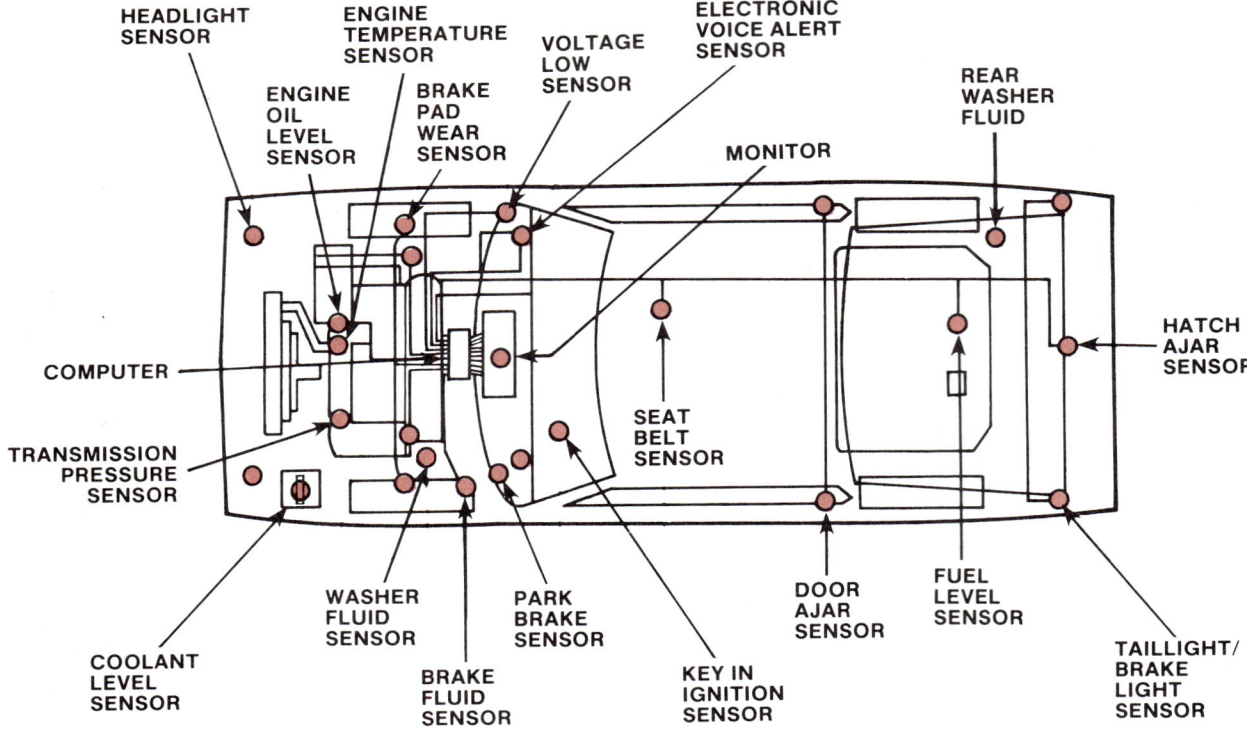

Figure 14-56 Principal automotive sensors and their locations. *Courtesy of Toyota Motor Corp.*

from the computer. When varying internal resistance of the sensor allows more or less voltage to ground, the computer senses a voltage change on a monitored signal line. The monitored signal line may be the output signal from the computer to the sensor (one and two-wire sensors), or the computer may use a separate return line from the sensor to monitor voltage changes (three-wire sensors).

While most sensors are variable resistance/reference voltage, there is another category of sensors—the voltage generating devices. These sensors include components like the Hall-effect switch, oxygen sensor (zirconium dioxide), and knock sensor (piezoelectric), which are capable of producing their own input voltage signal. This varying voltage signal, when received by the computer, enables the computer to monitor and adjust for changes in the computerized engine control system.

In addition to variable resistors, two other commonly used reference voltage sensors are switches and thermistors. Switches provide the necessary voltage information to the computer so that vehicles can maintain the proper performance and driveability. Thermistors are special types of resistors that convert tempera-

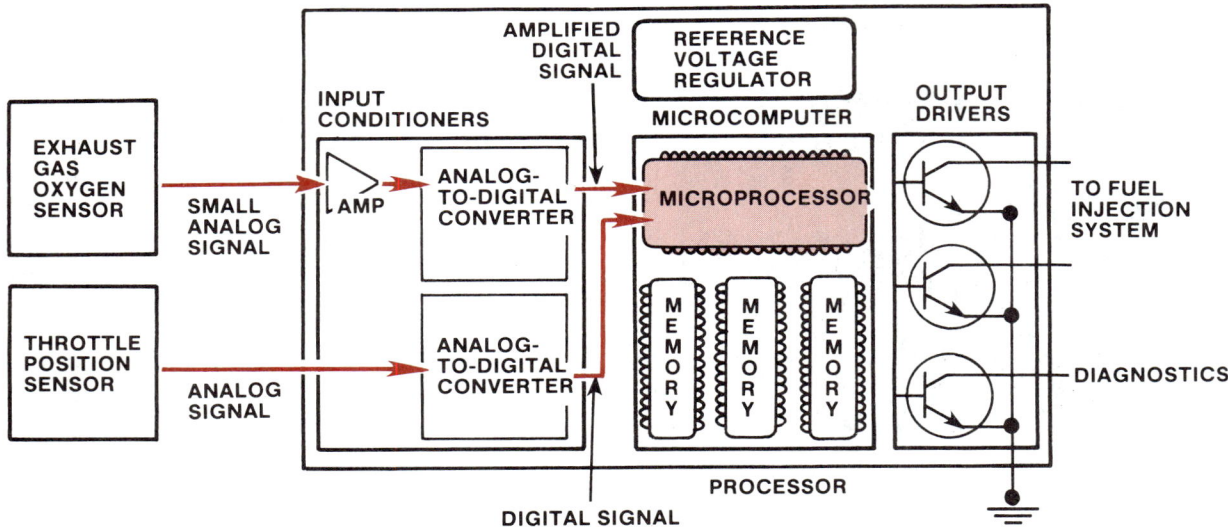

Figure 14-57 How an incoming signal from sensors travels through the microprocessor and its output.

ture into a voltage. Regardless of the type of sensors used in electronic control systems, the computer is incapable of functioning properly without input signal voltage from sensors (Figure 14-57).

Communication Signals

Most input sensors are designed to produce a voltage signal that varies within a given range (from high to low, including all points in between). A signal of this type is called an analog signal (Figure 14-58). Unfortunately, the computer does not understand analog signals. It can only read a digital binary signal, which is a signal that has only two values—on or off.

To overcome this communication problem, all analog voltage signals are converted to a digital format by a device known as an analog-to-digital converter (A/D converter). The A/D converter is located in a section of the processor called the input signal conditioner. Not all sensors produce analog signals, however. Some sensors like the Hall-effect switch produce a digital or square wave signal that can go directly to the microcomputer as input. The term square wave is used to describe the appearance of a digital circuit after it has been plotted on a graph. The abrupt changes in circuit condition (on and off) result in a series of horizontal and vertical lines that connect to form a square-shaped pattern.

The A/D converter changes a series of digital signals to a binary number made up of 1s and 0s. Voltage above a given value converts to 1, and zero voltage converts to 0 (Figure 14-59). Each 1 or 0 represents a bit of information. Eight bits equal a byte (sometimes referred to as a word). All communication between the microprocessor, the memories, and the interfaces is in binary code, with each information exchange being in the form of a byte.

To get an idea of how binary coding works, let us see how signals from the coolant temperature sensor (CTS) are processed by the microcomputer. The CTS is a type of thermistor (negative coefficient to be exact) that controls a reference signal based on temperature

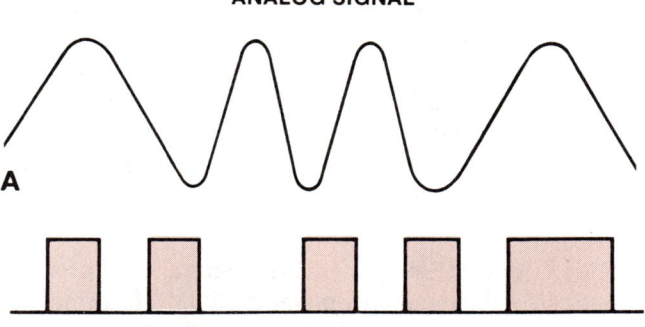

Figure 14–58 Graphic illustration comparing analog and digital voltage signals. *Courtesy of General Motors Corp.*

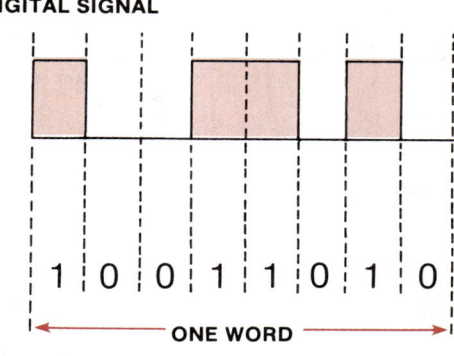

Figure 14-59 Each zero (0) and one (1) represents a bit of information. When eight bits are combined in specific sequence, they form a byte or word that makes up the basis of a computer's language. *Courtesy of General Motors Corp.*

changes (the higher the coolant temperature, the lower the resistance and vice versa). Upon receiving the CTS's analog signals, the input conditioner immediately groups each signal value into predetermined voltage range and assigns a numeric value to each range. In our example, use the following ranges and numeric values: 0-2 volts = 1, 2-4 volts = 2, and 4-5 volts = 3 (assuming a Vref of 5 volts). If you are wondering where these ranges and numeric values come from, they are written into the computer's memory by a human programmer at the time of the computer's development.

When the CTS is hot, its resistance is low and the modified voltage signal it sends back falls into the high range (4-5 volts). Upon entering the A/D converter, the voltage value is assigned a numeric value of three (based on our ranges above) and is ready for further translation into a binary code format.

Without going into the finer points of binary numbering, the number 3 in binary is expressed as 11 (Figure 14-60). To the thousands of tiny transistors and diodes that act as the on/off switches inside digitally oriented microprocessor, 11 instructs the computer to turn on or apply voltage to a specific circuit for a predetermined length of time (based on its program). Table 14-5 illustrates how binary numbers can be converted into decimal or base ten numbers. Note how the right-hand binary number equals one and the left number equals eight.

In addition to A/D conversion, some voltage signals require amplification before they can be relayed to the microcomputer. To perform this task, an input conditioner known as an amplifier is used to strengthen weak voltage signals.

After input has been generated, conditioned, and passed along to the microcomputer, it is ready to be processed for the purposes of performing work or displaying information. The portion of the microcomputer that receives sensor input and handles all calcula-

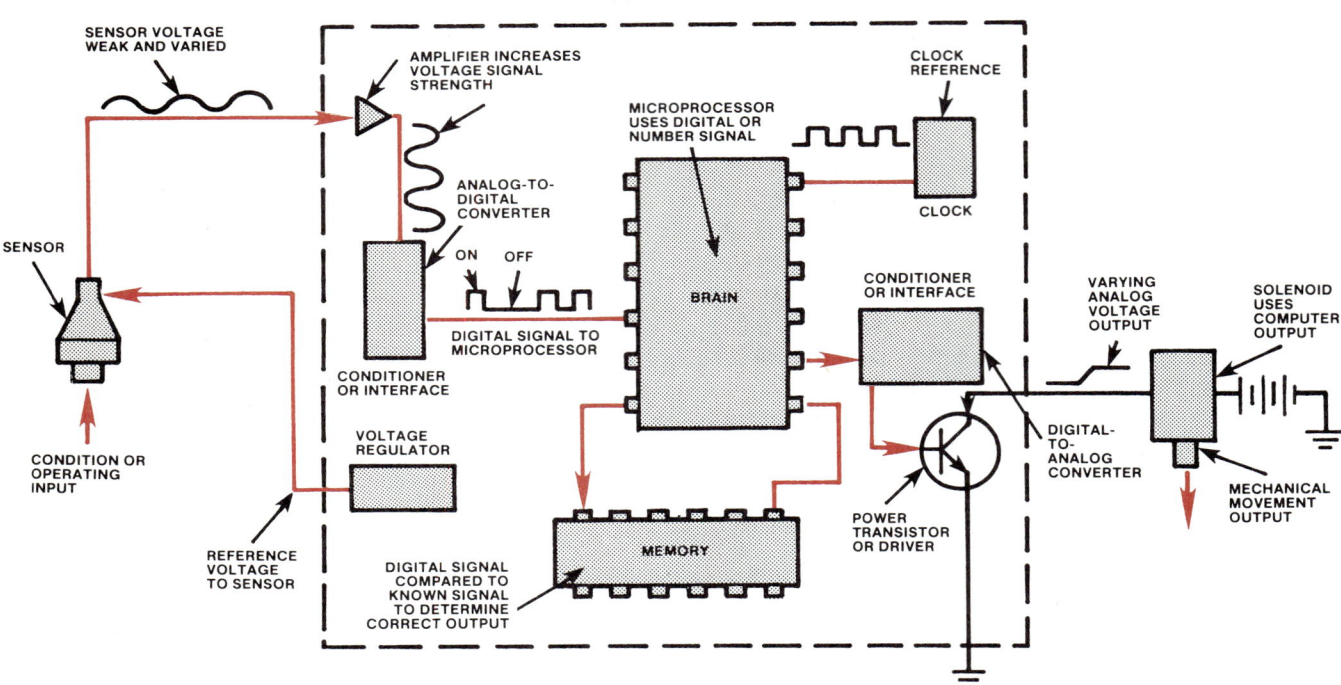

Figure 14-60 Here is an example of how digital voltage signals relay information. After receiving the digital signal and converting it to a binary format, the information is then displayed in a numerical form that is easily understood. *Courtesy of General Motors Corp.*

tions (makes decisions) is called the microprocessor. In order for the microprocessor to make the most informed decisions regarding system operation, sensor input is supplemented by the memory. Together, the microprocessor and memory make up the microcomputer portion of the processor.

Memories

A computer's memory holds the programs and other data, such as vehicle calibrations, which the microprocessor refers to in performing calculations. To the microcomputer, the program is a set of instructions or procedures that it must follow. Included in the program is information that tells the microprocessor when to retrieve input (based on temperature, time, etc.), how to process the input, and what to do with it once it has been processed.

The microprocessor works with memory in two ways: it can read information from memory or change information in memory by writing in or storing new information (Figure 14-61). To write information in memory, each memory location is assigned a number (written in binary code also) called an address. These addresses are sequentially numbered, starting with zero, and are used by the microprocessor to retrieve data and write new information into memory. During processing, the microcomputer often receives more data than it can immediately handle. In these instances, some information has to be temporarily stored or written into memory until the microprocessor needs it.

When ready, the microprocessor accesses the appropriate memory location (address) and is sent a copy of what is stored. By sending a copy, the memory retains the original information for future use.

There are basically three types of memory used in automotive microcomputers today (Figure 14-62). They are read only memory, programmable read only memory, and random access memory.

READ ONLY MEMORY (ROM) Permanent information is stored in read only memory (ROM). Information in ROM cannot be erased, even if the system is turned off or the microcomputer is disconnected from the battery. As the name implies, information can only be read from ROM.

TABLE 14-5 BINARY NUMBER CODE

Decimal Number	Binary Number Code 8 4 2 1	Binary to Decimal Conversion
0	0000	= 0 + 0 = 0
1	0001	= 0 + 1 = 1
2	0010	= 2 + 0 = 2
3	0011	= 2 + 1 = 3
4	0100	= 4 + 0 = 4
5	0101	= 4 + 1 = 5
6	0110	= 4 + 2 = 6
7	0111	= 4 + 2 + 1 = 7
8	1000	= 8 + 0 = 8

Basics of Electrical and Electronic Systems   349

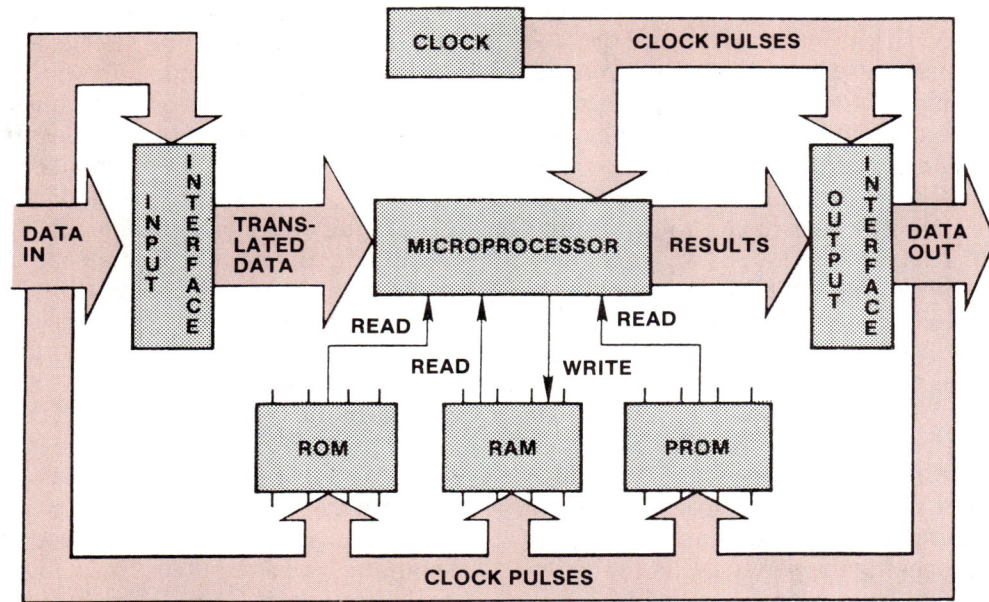

Figure 14-61   Interaction of the microprocessor and its support systems and memory banks. *Courtesy of General Motors Corp.*

When making decisions, the microprocessor is constantly referring to the stored information and the input from sensors. By comparing information from these sources, the microcomputer makes informed decisions.

PROGRAMMABLE READ ONLY MEMORY (PROM) The PROM differs from the ROM in that it plugs into the computer and is more easily removed and reprogrammed or replaced with one containing a revised program. It contains program information specific to different vehicle model calibrations.

RANDOM ACCESS MEMORY (RAM) The RAM is used during computer operation to store temporary information. The microcomputer can write, read, and erase information from RAM in any order, which is why it is called random. One characteristic of RAM is when the ignition key is turned off and the engine is stopped, information in RAM is erased. RAM is used to store information from the sensors, the results of calculations, and other data that is subject to constant change.

There are currently two other versions of RAM in use: volatile and non-volatile. A volatile RAM, usually called keep alive memory (KAM) has most of the features of RAM. Information can be written into KAM, and can be read and erased from KAM. Unlike RAM, information in KAM is not erased when the ignition key is turned off and the engine is stopped. However, if battery power to the processor is disconnected, information in KAM is erased.

A non-volatile RAM does not lose its stored information if its power source is disconnected. Vehicles with digital display odometers usually store mileage information in a non-volatile RAM.

Actuators

After the microprocessor has assimilated the information and the tools used by it to process this information it sends output signals to control devices called actuators. These actuators which are solenoids, switches, relays, or motors physically act or carry out a decision the computer has made.

Actually, actuators are electromechanical devices that convert an electrical current into mechanical action. This mechanical action can then be used to open and close valves, control vacuum to other components, or open and close switches. When the microcomputer receives an input signal indicating a change in one or more of the operating conditions, the microcomputer determines the best strategy for handling the conditions. The microcomputer then controls a set of actuators to achieve a desired effect or strategy goal. In order

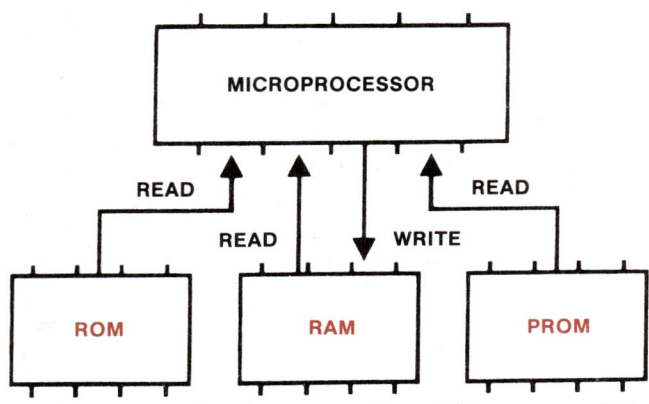

Figure 14-62   The three memories within a computer. *Courtesy of General Motors Corp.*

for the computer to control an actuator, it must rely on a component called an output driver.

Output drivers are also located in the processor (along with the input conditioners, microprocessor, and memory) and operate by the digital commands issued by the microcomputer. Basically, the output driver is nothing more than an electronic on/off switch that the computer uses to control the ground circuit of a specific actuator.

To illustrate this relationship, let us suppose the computer wants to turn on the engine's cooling fan. Once it makes a decision, it sends a signal to the output driver that controls the cooling fan relay (actuator). In supplying the relay's ground, the output driver completes the power circuit between the battery and cooling fan motor and the fan operates. When the fan has run long enough, the computer signals the output driver to open the relay's control circuit (by removing its ground), thus opening the power circuit to the fan.

For actuators that cannot be controlled by a solenoid, relay, switches or motors, the microcomputer must turn its digitally coded instructions back into an analog format via a digital-to-analog converter.

Displays can be controlled directly by the microcomputer. They do not require digital-to-analog conversion or output drivers because they contain circuitry that decodes the microprocessor's digital signal. The decoded information is then used to indicate such things as vehicle speed, engine rpm, fuel level, or scan tool values. Common types of electronic readout devices used as displays include light-emitting diodes (LED), liquid crystal display (LCD), and vacuum fluorescent display (VFD).

Power Supply

The microcomputer also contains a power supply that provides the various voltages required by the microprocessor and an internal clock that provides the clock pulse, which in turn controls the rate at which sensor readings and output changes are made. Also contained are protection circuits that safeguard the microprocessor from interference caused by other systems in the vehicle and diagnostic circuits that monitor all inputs and outputs and signal a warning light (check engine) if any values go outside the specified parameters.

Complete specific information concerning the use of computers (microprocessors) in various automotive electronic systems is presented in later chapters.

❏ PROTECTING ELECTRONIC SYSTEMS

The last thing a technician wants to do when a vehicle comes into the shop for repair is create problems. This is especially true when it comes to electronic components. It is a must to be aware of the proper ways to protect automotive electrical systems and electronic components during storage and repair.

The computer operates on very low voltage, and there needs to be a word said on static electricity, which can generate up to 25,000 volts. Simply touching the computer case is not likely to damage the computer, but it is always a good idea to be careful. Never touch the electrical contacts on any other electrical part. Before touching a computer, whether removing or replacing it, always touch a good ground with your finger. This safely discharges any static electricity. Some technicians even attach a metal wire or chain around their wrist and connect the other end to a good ground. When parts inside a computer are being replaced, such as a PROM module, this is a good idea.

Avoid touching bare metal contacts. Oils from the skin can cause corrosion and poor contacts.

The sensor wires that connect to the computer should never be rerouted. The resulting problem may be impossible to find. When replacing this wiring, always check the service manual and follow the routing instructions.

Accidentally touching a metal clip lead or test probe between metal terminals can cause a short circuit. Expensive computer modules or sensors can be destroyed instantly, without warning, by incorrect testing procedures.

If the code indicates a problem with the oxygen sensor, extra caution is required. The oxygen sensor wire carries a very low voltage and must be isolated from other wires. If it is not, nearby wires could add more induced voltage. This gives false data to the computer and can result in a driveability problem. Some car makers use a foam sleeve around the oxygen sensor wire for this purpose. Do not allow grease, lubricants, or cleaning solvents of any kind to touch the sensor end or the electrical connector plug. Apply the manufacturer's special anti-seize compound to the threads before installing the sensor.

Avoid jump starting whenever possible. The discharged battery can explode or you can create voltage spikes that could damage electronic components. This is true of both the car you are trying to start and the car providing the jump. However, if you must jump start a car, observe these safety precautions. Connect positive terminal to positive terminal on the batteries, connect the negative terminal of the good battery to a ground other than the ground terminal of the bad battery. If you use another car for the jump, make sure the two vehicles are not touching each other. Make sure every electrical device in the car, including the dome light, is turned off before connecting the batteries. Only after the hook-ups are properly made should you turn the key in the dead car to get it started. Once the dead car is running, remove all jumper connections before turning on any electrical devices.

Computer diagnostic tests can be performed using a scan tool. Connect the tool to the diagnostic connector. Follow the sequence given in the service manual or the scanning tool's instruction manual. The trouble codes are displayed on the scan tool readout.

Remove any computer module that could be affected by welding, hammering, grinding, sanding, or metal straightening. Be sure to protect the removed computer equipment by wrapping it in a plastic bag to shield it from moisture and dust.

Many test procedures require that electrical power or ground be supplied to the circuit being tested. Avoid grounding powered circuits with metal tools. Avoid touching live electrical leads to grounded metal parts of the automobile. Personal injury from sparks may result, or the unit being tested may be damaged or destroyed.

Be careful not to damage connectors and terminals when removing electronic components. Some may require special tools to remove them.

When procedures call for connecting test leads, or wires, to electrical connections, use extreme care and follow the manufacturer's instructions. Identify the correct test terminals before attempting to connect test leads.

The charging system, including the battery, must remain in good operating condition. If the electrical system falls below 12 volts, the computer may not work properly. However, low voltage does not damage the computer. If there are more than 15 volts, the computer may be damaged and must be replaced.

When checking a computerized ignition system, use a high impedance digital meter. The computer may be damaged by using an analog (needle type) meter. Do not connect the meter directly to the computer. Use part of the circuit. Do not connect jumper wires across a sensor unless the service manual tells you to do so. This could damage the computer.

❑ BATTERIES

The storage battery is the heart of a vehicle's electrical and electronic systems. It plays an important role in the operation of the starting, charging, ignition, and accessory circuits.

The storage battery converts electrical current generated by the alternator into chemical energy, then stores that energy until it is needed. When switched into an external electrical circuit, the battery's chemical energy is converted back to electrical energy.

A vehicle's battery has three main functions. It provides voltage and serves as a source of current for starting, lighting, and ignition. It acts as a voltage stabilizer for the entire electrical system of the vehicle. And, finally, it provides current whenever the vehicle's electrical demands exceed the output of the charging system.

There are four types of batteries in use today. They are the conventional, the low maintenance, the maintenance-free, and the sealed maintenance-free battery.

❑ CONVENTIONAL DESIGN BATTERY

The storage battery consists of grids, positive plates, negative plates, separators, elements, electrolyte, a container, cell covers, vent plugs, and cell containers (Figure 14-63). The grids form the basic framework of the battery plates. In a conventional battery, the grids are made of lead alloyed with approximately 5% antimony for strength. Each grid holds the active materials of the plate within its borders.

A positive plate consists of a grid filled with lead peroxide as its active material. Lead peroxide (PbO_2) is a dark brown, crystalline material. Its high degree of porosity allows the liquid electrolyte to penetrate freely.

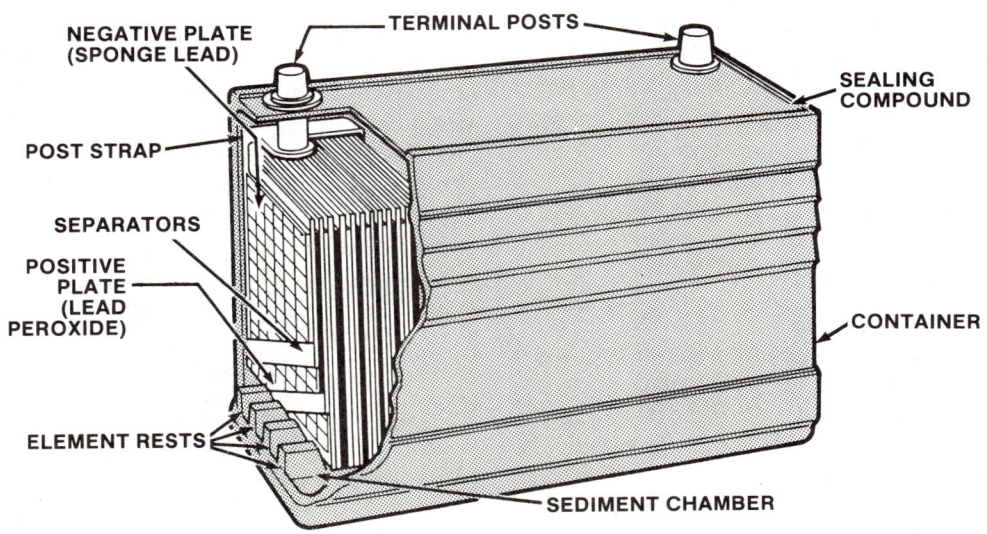

Figure 14-63 Components of a typical conventional storage battery.

The material pasted onto the grids of the negative plates is sponge lead (Pb). This porous gray lead allows the electrolyte to penetrate freely.

Elements and Cells

Each battery contains a number of elements. An element is a group of positive and negative plates. A group of plates, all positive or negative, are welded to a post strap. The positive and negative groups are then interlaced so the plates alternate. A separator is placed between the plates, to prevent contact, which would cause the plates to lose their stored energy. A further separator requirement is that the electrolyte must flow easily back and forth between the plates. Everything from wood to porous rubber has been used as a separator, but sheets of porous fiberglass or polyethylene are now most popular. The post straps extend up to provide terminals for connecting one element of a cell to another.

When the element is placed inside the battery case and immersed in electrolyte, it becomes a cell. Each cell has an open circuit voltage approximately 2.1 volts, so a 12-volt storage battery has 6 cells and an actual open circuit voltage of 12.6 volts.

Electrolyte and Specific Gravity

As mentioned, the lead peroxide and sponge lead that fill the element plates are the active materials in the battery. However, these materials cannot become active until they are immersed in electrolyte, a liquid composed of water and sulfuric acid (H_2SO_4).

The sulfuric acid of the electrolyte supplies sulfate, which chemically reacts with both the lead and lead peroxide to release electrical energy. In addition, the sulfuric acid is the carrier for the electrons inside the battery between the positive and negative plates.

The electrolyte of a fully charged battery is usually about 64% water and 36% sulfuric acid. This corresponds to a specific gravity of 1.270. Specific gravity is the weight of a given volume of any liquid divided by the weight of an equal volume of water. Pure water has a specific gravity of 1.000, while battery electrolyte should have a specific gravity of 1.260 to 1.280 at 80 degrees Fahrenheit (26.7 degrees Centigrade). In other words, the electrolyte of the battery is 1.260 to 1.280 times as heavy as water.

Discharging and Charging

Remember, a chemical reaction between active materials on the positive and negative plates and the acid in the electrolyte produces electrical energy. When a battery discharges, lead in the lead peroxide of the positive plate combines with the sulfate radical (SO_4) to form lead sulfate ($PbSO_4$).

A similar reaction takes place at the negative plate. In this plate, lead (Pb) of the negative active material

TABLE 14-6 ELECTROLYTE SPECIFIC GRAVITY AS RELATED TO CHARGE

Specific Gravity	Percent of Charge
1.265	100%
1.225	75%
1.190	50%
1.155	25%
1.120 or lower	discharged

combines with sulfate radical (SO_4) to also form lead sulfate ($PbSO_4$), a neutral and inactive material. Thus, lead sulfate forms at both types of plates as the battery discharges.

As the chemical reaction occurs, the oxygen from the lead peroxide and the hydrogen from the sulfuric acid combine to form water (H_2O). As discharging takes place, the acid in the electrolyte is used up and replaced with water.

Consequently, the specific gravity of the electrolyte decreases as it is discharged. This is why measuring the specific gravity of the electrolyte with a tool known as a hydrometer can be a good indicator of how much charge a battery has lost. Table 14-6 lists specific gravity readings for cells in various stages of charge with respect to its ability to crank an engine over at a temperature of 80 degrees Fahrenheit.

The recharging process is the reverse of the discharging process. Electricity from an outside source such as the vehicle's alternator, generator, or a battery recharger is forced into the battery. The lead sulfate ($PbSO_4$) on both plates separates into lead (Pb) and sulfate (SO_4). As the sulfate (SO_4) leaves both plates, it combines with hydrogen in the electrolyte to form sulfuric acid (H_2SO_4). At the same time, the oxygen (O_2) in the electrolyte combines with the lead (Pb) at the positive plate to form lead peroxide (PbO_2). As a result, the negative plate returns to its original form of lead (Pb), and the positive plate reverts to lead peroxide (PbO_2).

An unsealed battery gradually loses water due to its conversion into hydrogen and oxygen gases, which escape into the atmosphere through the vent caps. If the lost water is not replaced, the level of the electrolyte falls below the tops of the plates. This results in a high concentration of sulfuric acid in the electrolyte and also permits the exposed material of the plates to dry and harden. In this situation, premature failure of the battery is certain. The electrolyte level in the battery must be checked frequently.

Casing Design

The container or shell of the battery is usually a one-piece, molded assembly of hard rubber or plastic. The case has a number of individual cell compartments. A number of cell connectors are used to join all cells of a battery in series.

The top of the battery is encased by a cell cover. The cover may be a one-piece design, or the cells might have their own individual covers. On conventional-design batteries, the cover must have vents.

The vent holes provide access into the cells for servicing them with electrolyte or water and permit the escape of hydrogen and oxygen gases, which form during charging and discharging. Vent plugs or caps are used to close the openings in the cell cover.

WARNING: When lifting a plastic-cased battery, excessive pressure on the end walls could cause acid to spew through the vent caps, resulting in personal injury. Lift with a battery carrier or with your hands on opposite corners.

Terminals

The battery has two external terminals: a positive (+) and a negative (-). These terminals are either two tapered posts or threaded studs on top of the case or two internally threaded connectors on the side (Figure 14-64). Some newer batteries have both types of terminals so that one battery fits either application. These terminals connect to either end of the series of elements inside the battery and have either a positive (+) or a negative (-) marking, depending on which end of the series they represent.

Tapered terminals have a given dimension in accordance with standards agreed upon by the Battery Council International (BCI) and Society of Automotive Engineers (SAE). This insures that all positive and negative cable clamp terminals would fit any corresponding battery terminal interchangeably, regardless of the battery's manufacturer. However, the positive terminal is slightly larger, usually around 11/16 inch in diameter at the top, while the negative terminal usually has a 5/8-inch diameter. This design minimizes the danger of installing the battery cables in reverse polarity.

Heat Shields

Many late-model vehicles employ a heat shield made of plastic or other materials to protect the battery from

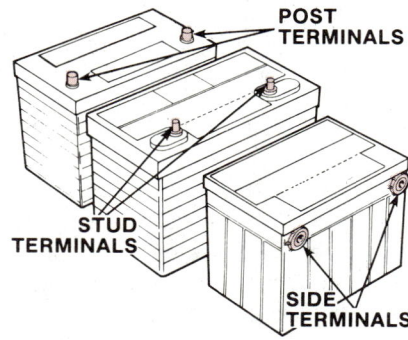

Figure 14-64 Types of battery terminals and their locations.

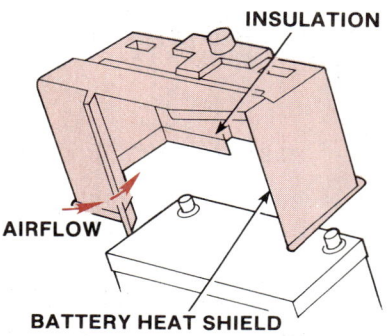

Figure 14-65 Many vehicles have a molded heat shield to protect the battery from high engine temperatures.

high underhood temperatures (Figure 14-65). While heat shields need not be removed for most routine testing and inspection jobs, they must be removed and correctly reinstalled during battery replacement.

☐ LOW-MAINTENANCE AND MAINTENANCE-FREE BATTERIES

The majority of batteries sold and installed in today's vehicles are either low-maintenance or maintenance-free designs. Low-maintenance batteries are still equipped with vent holes and caps, which allow water to be added to the cells. A low-maintenance battery will require additional water substantially less often than a conventional battery.

Maintenance-free batteries were introduced in 1972. They do not have holes or caps. They are equipped with small gas vents that prevent gas-pressure build-up in the case (Figure 14-66). Water is never added to maintenance-free batteries.

Both maintenance-free and low-maintenance batteries differ from conventional battery designs in two important ways: plate design and water use.

The most important difference is the materials used for the plate grids. As mentioned under the section on conventional battery design, antimony strengthens the grid alloy. In low-maintenance batteries, the amount of antimony is reduced to about 3%. In maintenance-free batteries, the antimony is eliminated and replaced by calcium or strontium. Reducing the amount of antimony or replacing it with calcium or strontium alloy reduces both the battery's internal heat and the amount of gassing that occurs during charging. Since these are the principal reasons for battery water loss, these changes reduce or eliminate the need to periodically add water. Reduced water loss also reduces terminal corrosion since the major cause of this corrosion is condensation from normal battery gassing. Additionally, nonantimony lead alloys have better conductivity, so a maintenance-free battery has about a 20% higher cold-cranking power rating than a comparably sized conventional battery.

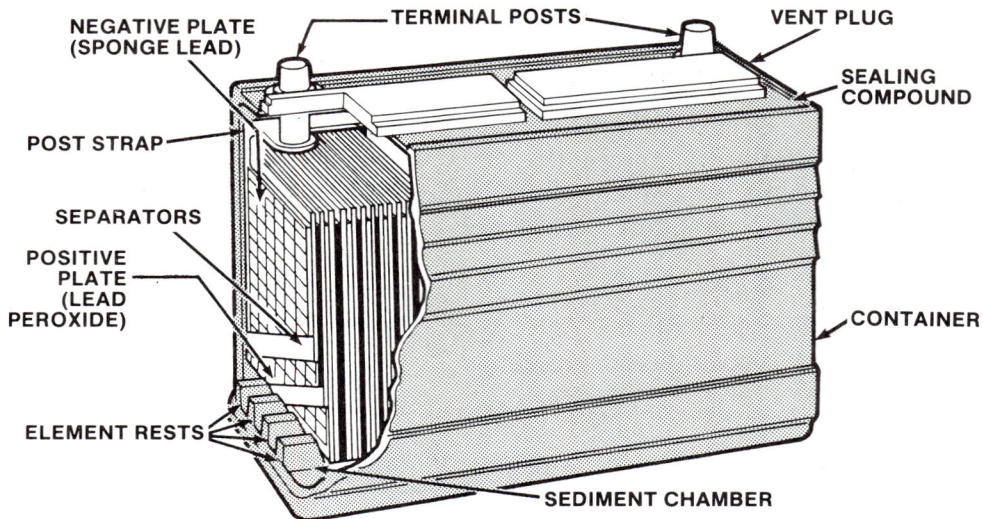

Figure 14-66 Construction of a maintenance-free battery.

The calcium battery is also more resistant to overcharging and its self-discharge rate is 20 to 30% lower. The tradeoff, however, is that calcium grids are not as well suited for deep cycling. In other words, if a calcium battery is run completely dead several times, its ability to deliver current can be diminished with each subsequent recharge.

> **CUSTOMER CARE**
>
> One good piece of advice you can give a customer is to remind him/her that just because it says maintenance-free on the side of the battery does not mean it can be ignored for the next five years. The battery should still be checked occasionally, battery terminals and case kept clean and tight, and the battery kept firmly mounted.

Recombination Batteries

Recently, several manufacturers have introduced completely sealed maintenance-free batteries. These new batteries do not require the gas vent used on other maintenance-free designs. Although these batteries are basically lead-acid voltage cells, a slight change in place and electrolyte chemistry virtually eliminates hydrogen generation.

During charging, a conventional or maintenance-free battery releases hydrogen at the negative plates and oxygen at the positive plates. Most of the hydrogen is released through electrolysis of the water in the electrolyte near the negative plates as the battery reaches full charge. In the new sealed maintenance-free batteries, the negative plates never reach a fully charged condition and therefore cause little or no release of hydrogen. Oxygen is released at the positive plates, but it passes through the separators and recombines with the negative plates.

The end result is virtually no gassing from the battery. Because the oxygen released by the electrolyte is forced to recombine with the negative plate, these batteries are often called recombination or recombinant electrolyte batteries.

Test and service requirements of sealed batteries are basically the same as for other maintenance-free, lead-acid batteries. Some manufacturers caution, however, that fast charging at high current rates might overheat the battery and cause damage. Always check the manufacturer's instructions for test specifications and charging rates before servicing.

❑ BATTERY VOLTAGE AND CAPACITY

The open-circuit voltage of a fully charged cell is roughly 2.1 volts in conventional batteries and 2.2 volts in some sealed maintenance-free batteries. The specific gravity of the electrolyte is roughly 1.270. A cell's voltage rating and specific gravity remain at these levels (when fully charged) regardless of the size of the cell. It is the fixed characteristics of the chemicals used in the battery and the strength of the electrolyte that determine this factor.

Cell size, state of charge, rate of discharge, battery condition and design, and electrolyte temperature all strongly influence the voltage of a cell during discharge. When cranking an engine over at 80 degrees Fahrenheit, the voltage of an average battery may be about 11.5 to 12 volts. At 0 degrees Fahrenheit, the voltage is significantly lower.

The concentration of acid in the electrolyte in the pores of the plates also affects battery voltage or discharge. As the acid chemically combines with the active materials in the plates and is used up, the voltage drops unless fresh acid from outside the plate moves in to take its place. As discharging continues, this outside acid becomes weaker, and sulfate saturates the plate material. It then becomes increasingly difficult for the chemical reaction to continue and as a result, voltage drops to a level no longer effective in delivering sufficient current to the electrical system.

Cold weather can create this same effect. Even the acid is not overly weak. At low temperatures, the viscosity of the electrolyte increases, making it more difficult for the acid to move freely into the plate pores and around the separators. This slows the rate of the chemical reaction and lowers battery voltage, limiting the output of the battery, especially at cranking rates.

Battery capacity is the ability to deliver a given amount of current over a period of time. It depends on the number and size of the plates used in the cells and the amount of acid used in the electrolyte.

BATTERY RATING METHODS

The Battery Council International (BCI) rates batteries according to reserve capacity and cold-cranking power. When replacing a battery, always refer to an application chart to select a battery with the correct BCI group number. Vehicle options, such as air conditioning and a number of major electrical accessories, may indicate the need for an optional heavy-duty battery with a higher rating. Remember, to handle cranking power and the vehicle's other electrical needs, the replacement unit should never have a lower rating than the original battery.

Reserve Capacity

A reserve capacity (RC) rating represents the approximate time in minutes it is possible to travel at night with battery ignition and minimum electrical load, but without a charging system in operation. The time in minutes is based on a current draw of 25 amperes while maintaining a minimum battery terminal voltage of 10.2 volts (12-volt batteries) at 80 degrees Fahrenheit. This rating represents the electrical load that must be supplied by the battery in the event of a charging system failure.

Cold Cranking

A cold-cranking amperes (CCA) rating specifies the minimum amperes available at 0 degrees Fahrenheit and at -20 degrees Fahrenheit. This rating allows cranking capability to be related to such significant variables as engine displacement, compression ratio, temperature, cranking time, condition of engine and electrical system, and lowest practical voltage for cranking and ignition. This rating indicates the amperes that a fully charged battery will maintain for 30 seconds without the terminal voltage falling below 7.2 volts for a 12-volt battery.

To provide enough starting power under adverse conditions, a 12-volt system generally requires 1 ampere for each cubic inch of engine displacement. In other words, a 350 cubic inch engine requires a battery with a cold-cranking rating of at least 350 amperes.

> **SHOP TALK**
>
> A rule of thumb that can be used when the ampere-hour rating cannot be determined is: Divide the cold-cranking rating at 0 degrees Fahrenheit by 2. The figure obtained in this manner equals the load that should be applied when making a battery capacity test, and is almost equal to the value of three times the ampere-hour rating of batteries that use the earlier rating system. An excellent service you can offer your customer is to help select the right type of battery based on the make of the vehicle and the customer's driving habits. In cold climates, putting in a larger battery with higher CCAs is a good idea, but do not get carried away. Reserve capacity and proper mounting are important, too.

FACTORS AFFECTING BATTERY LIFE

All storage batteries have a limited service life, but many conditions can decrease service life.

Improper Electrolyte Levels

With nonsealed batteries, water should be the only portion of the electrolyte lost due to evaporation during hot weather and gassing during charging. Maintaining an adequate electrolyte level is the basic step in extending battery life for these designs. When adding water to the cells, use distilled water when available or clean, soft water.

Fill each cell to just above the top of the plates. Underfilling causes a greater concentration of acid which deteriorates the plates' grids more rapidly.

Overfilling weakens the concentration of sulfuric acid (reduces the electrolyte's specific gravity), which reduces the efficiency of the battery.

Corrosion

Battery corrosion is commonly caused by electrolyte or electrolyte condensation

In either case, the sulfuric acid from the electrolyte corrodes, attacks, and can destroy not only connectors and terminals but holddown straps and the carrier box as well.

Corroded connections increase resistance at the battery terminals, which reduces the applied voltage to the vehicle's electrical system. The corrosion in the battery cover can also create a path for current which can allow the battery to slowly discharge. Finally, corrosion can destroy the holddown straps and carrier box, which can result in physical damage to the battery.

Overcharging

Batteries can be overcharged by either the vehicles charging system or a battery charger. In either case, the result is a violent chemical reaction within the battery that causes a loss of water in the cells. This can push active materials off the plates permanently reducing the capacity of the battery. Overcharging can also cause excessive heat, which can oxidize the positive plate grid material and even buckle the plates, resulting in a loss of cell capacity and early battery failure.

Undercharge/Sulfation

The vehicle's charging system might not fully recharge the battery due to excessive battery output, stop-and-go driving, or a fault in the charging system. In all cases, the battery operates in a partially discharged condition. A battery in this condition will become sulfated when the sulfate normally formed in the plates becomes dense, hard, and chemically irreversible. This occurs because the sulfate has been allowed to remain in the plates for a long period.

Sulfation of the plates causes two problems. First, it lowers the specific gravity levels and increases the danger of freezing at low temperatures. Secondly, in cold weather, a sulfated battery often fails to crank the engine because of its lack of reserve power.

Poor Mounting

Loose holddown straps or covers allow the battery to vibrate or bounce during vehicle operation. This can have several adverse effects. It can shake the active materials off the grid plates, severely shortening battery life. It can also loosen the plate connections to the terminals, cable connections, or even crack the battery case.

plates. Fortunately, the new envelope design found in many batteries reduces this problem.

☐ SAFETY PROCEDURES

The potential dangers caused by the sulfuric acid in the electrolyte and the explosive gases generated during battery charging require that battery service and troubleshooting be conducted under absolute safe working conditions. According to the National Society to Prevent Blindness, over 14,000 Americans suffered serious eye damage from acid in wet-cell batteries in a recent year.

WARNING: Always wear safety glasses or goggles when working with batteries no matter how small the job.

Sulfuric acid can also cause severe skin burns. If electrolyte contacts your skin or eyes, flush the area with water for several minutes. When eye contact occurs, force your eyelid open. Always have a bottle of neutralizing eyewash on hand and flush the affected areas with it. Do not rub your eyes or skin.

WARNING: Receive prompt medical attention if electrolyte contacts your skin or eyes. Call a doctor immediately.

When a battery is charging or discharging, it gives off quantities of highly explosive hydrogen gas. Some hydrogen gas is present in the battery at all times. Any flame or spark can ignite this gas, causing the battery to explode violently, propelling the vent caps at a high velocity and spraying acid in a wide area. To prevent this dangerous situation take these precautions.

- Do not smoke near the top of a battery. And never use a lighter or match as a flashlight.
- Remove wristwatches and rings before servicing any part of the electrical system. This helps to prevent the possibility of electrical arcing and burns.
- Even sealed, maintenance-free batteries have vents and can produce dangerous quantities of hydrogen if severely overcharged.
- Always disconnect the battery's ground cable when working on the electrical system or engine. This prevents sparks from short circuits and prevents accidental starting of the engine.
- Always operate charging equipment in well-ventilated areas. A battery that has been overworked should be allowed to cool down and let air circulate around it before attempting to jump start the vehicle. Most batteries have flame arresters in the caps to help prevent explosions, so make sure that the caps are tightly in place.
- Never connect or disconnect charger leads when the charger is turned on. This generates a dangerous spark.

- Never lay metal tools or other objects on the battery because a short circuit across the terminals can result.

Other battery and electrical system safety precautions follow.

- Always disconnect the battery ground cable before fast-charging the battery in the vehicle. Improper connection of charger cables to the battery can reverse the current flow and damage the alternator.
- When removing a battery from a vehicle, always disconnect the battery ground cable first. When installing a battery, connect the ground cable last.
- Never reverse the polarity of the battery connections. Generally, all vehicles use a negative ground. Reversing this polarity damages the alternator and circuit wiring. Another common cause of explosions is reversal of jumper cables. Remember to connect negative to negative and positive to positive.
- Never attempt to use a fast charger as a boost to start the engine.
- As a battery gets closer to being fully discharged, the acidity of the electrolyte is reduced, and the electrolyte starts to behave more like pure water. A dead battery may freeze at temperatures near 0 degrees Fahrenheit. Never try to charge a battery that has ice in the cells. Passing current through a frozen battery can cause it to rupture or explode. If ice or slush is visible or the electrolyte level cannot be seen, allow the battery to thaw at room temperature before servicing. Do not take chances with sealed batteries. If there is any doubt, allow them to warm to room temperature before servicing.
- As batteries get older, especially in warm climates and especially with lead-calcium cells, the grids start to grow. The chemistry is rather involved, but the point is that plates can grow to the point where they touch, producing a shorted cell. If you see a battery with normal fluid levels in five cells and one nearly dry cell, you are probably looking at a battery that has shorted one cell and turned its electrolyte into hydrogen gas.
- Always use a battery carrier or lifting strap (Figure 14-67) to make moving and handling batteries easier and safer.
- Acid from the battery damages a vehicle's paint and metal surfaces and harms shop equipment. Neutralize any electrolyte spills during servicing.

 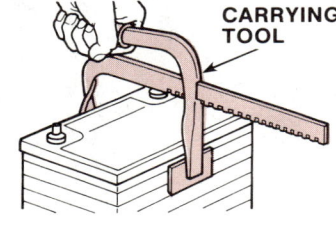

Figure 14-67 Use a lifting strap or carrier when carrying batteries. *Courtesy (left) of Johnson Controls Inc.*

❑ ROUTINE INSPECTIONS

As part of any tune-up procedure or electrical system work, always check the battery.

1. Visually inspect the battery cover and case for dirt and grease.
2. Check the electrolyte level.
3. Inspect the unit for cracks, loose terminal posts, and other signs of physical damage.
4. Check for missing cell plug covers and caps.
5. Inspect all cables for broken or corroded wires, frayed insulation, or loose or damaged connectors.
6. Visually check battery terminals, cable connectors, metal parts, holddowns, and trays for corrosion damage or buildup.
7. Check the heat shield for proper installation on vehicles so equipped.

❑ ROUTINE CLEANING

Before removing battery connectors or the battery itself for cleaning or other service, always neutralize accumulated corrosion on terminals, connectors, and other metal parts. Apply a solution of baking soda and water or ammonia and water (Figure 14-68).

Do not splash the corrosion onto the vehicle's paint, metal or rubber parts, or onto your hands and face. Be sure the solution cannot enter the battery cells. A stiff bristle brush is ideal for removing heavy buildup. Dirt and accumulated grease can be removed with a detergent solution or solvent.

After cleaning, rinse the battery and cable connections with clean water. Dry the components with a clean rag or low-pressure compressed air.

To clean the inside surfaces of the connectors and the battery terminals, remove the cables. Always begin with the ground cable. Spring-type cable connectors are removed by squeezing the ends of their prongs together with wide-jaw, vise-gripping, channel lock, or battery pliers. This pressure expands the connector so it can be lifted off the terminal post.

Figure 14-68 Cleaning and neutralizing acid corrosion using a solution of baking soda and water or water and ammonia.

SHOP TALK

It should be noted that disconnecting the battery on late-model cars removes some memory from the engine's computer and the car's accessories. Besides losing the correct time on its clock or the programmed stations on the radio, the car might run roughly. If this occurs, allow the engine to run for awhile before shutting it off.

For connectors tightened with nuts and bolts, loosen the nut using a box wrench or cable-clamp pliers. Using ordinary pliers or an open-end wrench can cause problems. These tools might slip off under pressure with enough force to break the cell cover or damage the casing.

Always grip the cable while loosening the nut. This eliminates unnecessary pressure on the terminal post that could break it or loosen its mounting in the battery. If the connector does not lift easily off the terminal when loosened, use a clamp puller to free it (Figure 14-69). Prying with a screwdriver or bar strains the terminal post and the plates attached to it. This can break the cell cover or pop the plates loose from the terminal post.

Once the connectors have been removed, open the connector using a connector-spreading tool. Neutralize any remaining corrosion by dipping it in a baking soda or ammonia solution. Next, clean the inside of the connectors and the posts using a wire brush with external and internal bristles (Figure 14-70).

Felt washers treated with corrosion-resistant compound can be installed over the terminals before reinstalling the cable connectors.

Begin reinstallation by correctly positioning the positive connector on its post. Do not overtighten any nuts or bolts since this could damage the post or connector. Finally, coat the connectors with petroleum jelly or battery anticorrosion paste or paint.

❏ BATTERY TESTING

Testing batteries is an important part of electrical system service. Poor and inaccurate tests can lead to serious problems and expensive and unneeded repairs. Depending on the design of the battery, state of charge and capacity can be determined in several ways: specific gravity tests, visual inspection of batteries with a built-in hydrometer, open circuit voltage tests, and the capacity test.

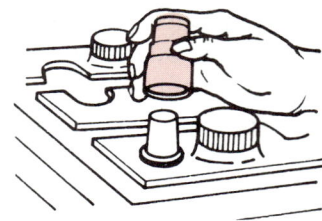

Figure 14-70 Combination external/internal wire brushes clean both terminals and inside cable connector surfaces.

Specific Gravity Tests

On unsealed battery designs, the specific gravity of the electrolyte can be measured to give a fairly good indication of the battery's state of charge. A hydrometer is used to perform this test (Figure 14-71). A basic battery hydrometer consists of a glass tube or barrel, rubber bulb, rubber tube, and a glass float or hydrometer with a scale built into its upper stem. The glass tube encases the float and forms a reservoir for the test electrolyte. Squeezing the bulb pulls electrolyte into the reservoir.

When filled with test electrolyte, the sealed hydrometer float bobs in the electrolyte. The depth to which the glass float sinks in the test electrolyte indicates its relative weight compared to water. The reading is taken off the scale by sighting along the level of the electrolyte.

If the hydrometer floats deep in the electrolyte, the specific gravity is low (Figure 14-72A). If the hydrometer floats shallow in the electrolyte, the specific gravity is high (Figure 14-72B).

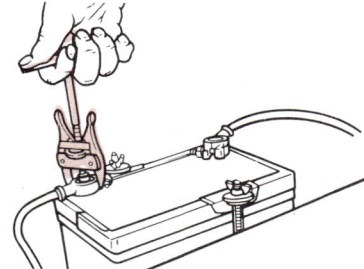

Figure 14-69 Battery pullers remove cables without damaging the terminal posts.

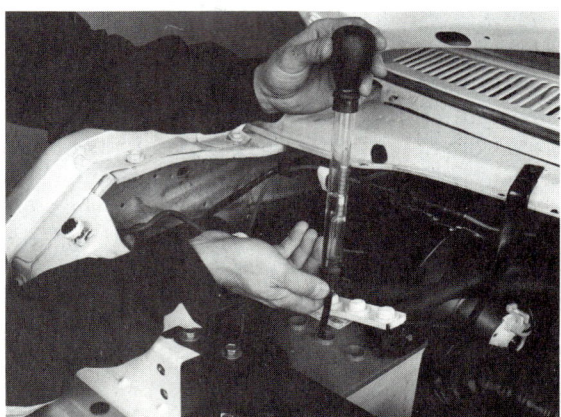

Figure 14-71 Check electrolyte strength using a hydrometer.

Basics of Electrical and Electronic Systems 359

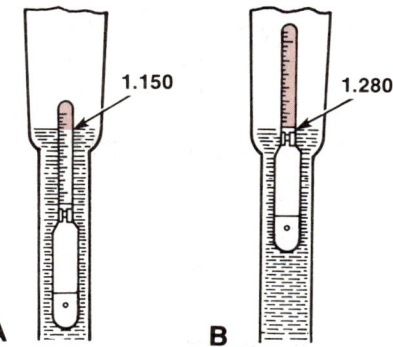

Figure 14-72 (A) When the scale sinks in the electrolyte, the specific gravity is low, (B) when it floats high, the specific gravity is high.

Temperature Correction

At extremely high and low electrolyte temperatures, it is necessary to correct the reading by adding or subtracting 4 points (0.004) for each 10 degrees Fahrenheit above or below the standard of 80 degrees Fahrenheit. Most hydrometers have a built-in thermometer to measure the temperature of the electrolyte (Figure 14-73). Hydrometer reading can be misleading if not adjusted. For example, a reading of 1.260 taken at 20 degrees Fahrenheit would be 1.260 - (6 × 0.004 or 0.024) = 1.236. This lower reading means the cell has less charge than indicated.

It is important to make these adjustments at high and low temperatures to determine the battery's true state of charge.

Interpreting Results

The specific gravity of the cells of a fully charged battery should be near 1.265 when corrected for electrolyte temperature. Table 14-6 shows the relationship between specific gravity and the state of charge of the cell.

Recharge any battery if the specific gravity drops below an average of 1.230. A specific gravity difference of more than 50 points between cells is a good indication of a defective battery in need of replacement.

Built-in Hydrometers

On many sealed maintenance-free batteries a special temperature-compensated hydrometer is built into the battery cover. A quick visual check indicates the battery's state of charge. The hydrometer has a green ball within a cage that is attached to a clear plastic rod. The green ball floats at a predetermined specific gravity of the electrolyte that represents about a 65% state of charge. When the green ball floats, it rises within the cage and positions itself under the rod. Visually, a green dot then shows in the center of the hydrometer (Figure 14-74). The built-in hydrometer provides a guide for battery testing and charging.

In testing, the green dot means the battery is charged enough for testing. If the green dot is not visible and has a dark appearance, it means the battery must be charged before the test procedure is performed.

While charging, the appearance of the green dot means that the battery is sufficiently charged. Charging can be stopped to prevent overcharging.

It is important when observing the hydrometer that the battery have a clean top to see the correct indication. A flashlight may be required in some poorly-lit

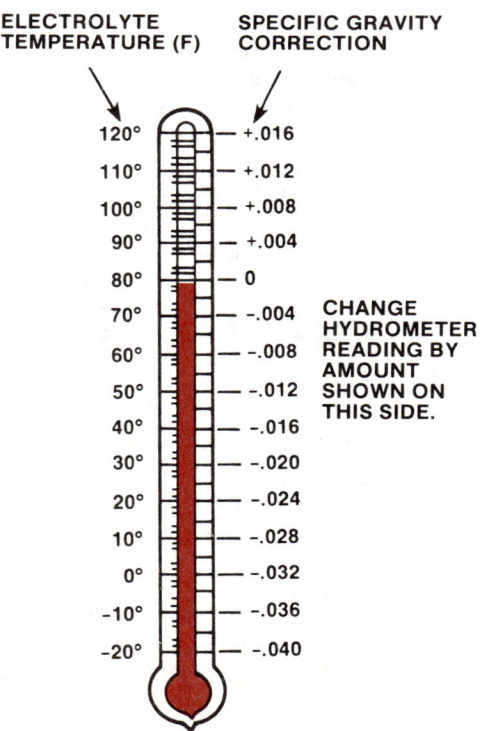

Figure 14-73 Hydrometers with thermometer correction scales make adjusting for electrolyte temperature easy.

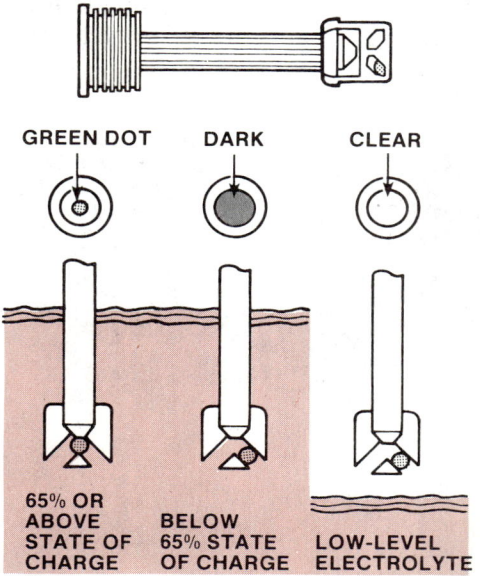

Figure 14-74 Design and operation of built-in hydrometers on maintenance-free sealed batteries.

areas. Always look straight down when viewing the hydrometer.

On some special applications, some hydrometers feature a red dot indication in addition to the green dot, dark, and clear appearances. The red dot means the battery is nearing complete discharge and must be charged before being used.

Complete hydrometer information on most batteries is printed on the label located on the top of the battery. By referring to this label, an accurate interpretation of the hydrometer appearance can be made.

Open Circuit Voltage Test

An open circuit voltage check can be used as a substitute for the hydrometer specific gravity test on maintenance-free sealed batteries with no built-in hydrometer. As the battery is charged or discharged, slight changes occur in the battery's voltage. So battery voltage with no load applied can give some indication of the state of charge.

The battery's temperature should be between 60 and 100 degrees Fahrenheit. The voltage must be allowed to stabilize for at least 10 minutes with no load applied. On vehicles with high drains (computer controls, clocks, and accessories that always draw a small amount of current), it may be necessary to disconnect the battery ground cable. On batteries that have just been recharged, apply a heavy load for 15 seconds to remove the surface charge. Then allow the battery to stabilize. Once voltage has stabilized, use a digital voltmeter to measure the battery voltage to the nearest one-tenth of a volt (Figure 14-75). Use Table 14-7 to interpret the results. As you can see, minor changes in battery open circuit voltage can indicate major changes in state of charge.

If the open circuit voltage test indicates a charge of below 75% of full charge, recharge the battery and perform the capacity test to determine battery condition.

TABLE 14-7	BATTERY OPEN CIRCUIT VOLTAGE AS AN INDICATOR OF STATE OF CHARGE
Open Circuit Voltage	State of Charge
12.6 or greater	100%
12.4 to 12.6	75-100%
12.2 to 12.4	50-75%
12.0 to 12.2	25-50%
11.7 to 12.0	0-25%
11.7 or less	0%

Capacity Test

The load or capacity test determines how well any type of battery, sealed or unsealed, functions under a load. In other words, it determines the battery's ability to furnish starting current and still maintain sufficient voltage to operate the ignition system.

The load or capacity test can be performed with the battery either in or out of the vehicle. The battery must be at or very near a full state of charge. Use the specific gravity test or open circuit voltage test to determine charge, and recharge the battery if needed before proceeding. For best results, the electrolyte should be as close to 80 degrees Fahrenheit as possible. Cold batteries show considerably lower capacity. Never load test a sealed battery if its temperature is below 60 degrees Fahrenheit.

On some batteries designed with side terminals, obtaining a sound connection can be a problem. The best solution is to screw in the appropriate manufacturer's adapter (Figure 14-76). If an adapter is not available, use a 3/8-inch coarse bolt with a nut on it. Bottom out the bolt. Back it off a turn. Then tighten the nut against the contact. Now, attach the lead to the nut.

CAUTION: Simply turning in a bolt does not do the job. The thread contact area is too small to carry enough current for the load test (or for battery charging).

When performing a battery load test, follow these guidelines.

1. An inductive pick-up must surround all of the wires from the battery's negative terminal.

Figure 14-75 Measuring open circuit voltage across battery terminals using a voltmeter.

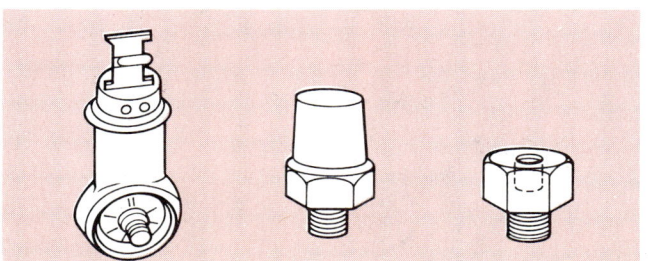

Figure 14-76 Adapters may be needed to test and charge batteries with side-mount terminals.

TABLE 14-8 MINIMUM LOAD TEST VOLTAGES AS AFFECTED BY TEMPERATURE

BATTERY TEMPERATURE (F)	MINIMUM TEST VOLTAGE
70°	9.6 volts
60°	9.5 volts
50°	9.4 volts
40°	9.3 volts
30°	9.1 volts
20°	8.9 volts
10°	8.7 volts
0°	8.5 volts

2. Observe the correct polarity and make sure the test leaks are making good contact with the battery posts.
3. If the tester is equipped with an adjustment for battery temperature, set it to the proper setting.
4. Turn the load control knob (if the tester is so equipped) to draw current at the rate of three times the battery's ampere-hour rating or one-half of its CCA rating.
5. Maintain the load for 15 seconds. Observe the tester's voltmeter.
6. Discontinue the load after 15 seconds of current draw.
7. At 70 degrees Fahrenheit or above or on testers which are temperature corrected, voltage at the end of 15 seconds should not fall below 9.6 volts. If the tester is not temperature corrected, use Table 14-8 to determine the adjusted minimum voltage reading for a particular temperature.

Interpreting Results

If the voltage reading exceeds the specification by a volt or more, the battery is supplying sufficient current with a good margin to safety. If the reading is right on the spec, the battery might not have the reserve necessary to handle cranking during low temperatures. If the battery was at 75% charge and fell right on the load specification, it is probably in good shape.

If the voltage reads below the temperature corrected minimum, continue to observe the voltmeter of the tester after removing the load. If it rises above 12.4, the battery is bad—it can hold a charge, but has insufficient cold-cranking amperes. The battery can be recharged and retested, but the results are likely to be the same.

If the voltage tests below the minimum and the voltmeter does not rise above 12.4 when the load is removed, the problem may only be a low state of charge. Recharge the battery and load test again.

If a volt-ampere tester is not available, the starter motor can be used as a loading device to conduct a capacity test. By observing a voltmeter before and after the starting motor has run, the condition of the battery can be determined. Connect the voltmeter across the battery. Make sure the ignition is disabled to prevent engine starting.

CAUTION: Electronic ignition systems might sustain damage during prolonged engine cranking unless properly disconnected. Refer to the vehicle's specific instructions if needed. One-time popular single cell checks such as cadmium-probe tests and the three-minute charge tests are seldom practiced today because they are not recommended for maintenance-free batteries.

❑ BATTERY CHARGING

Both fast- and slow-charging units are used to recharge batteries (Figure 14-77). Each has its advantages. Fast chargers are the most popular. They charge batteries at a higher rate or charge—usually 40 amperes for 12-volt batteries and 70 amperes for 6-volt batteries. At this rate fast chargers can recharge most batteries in about 1 hour. However, batteries must be

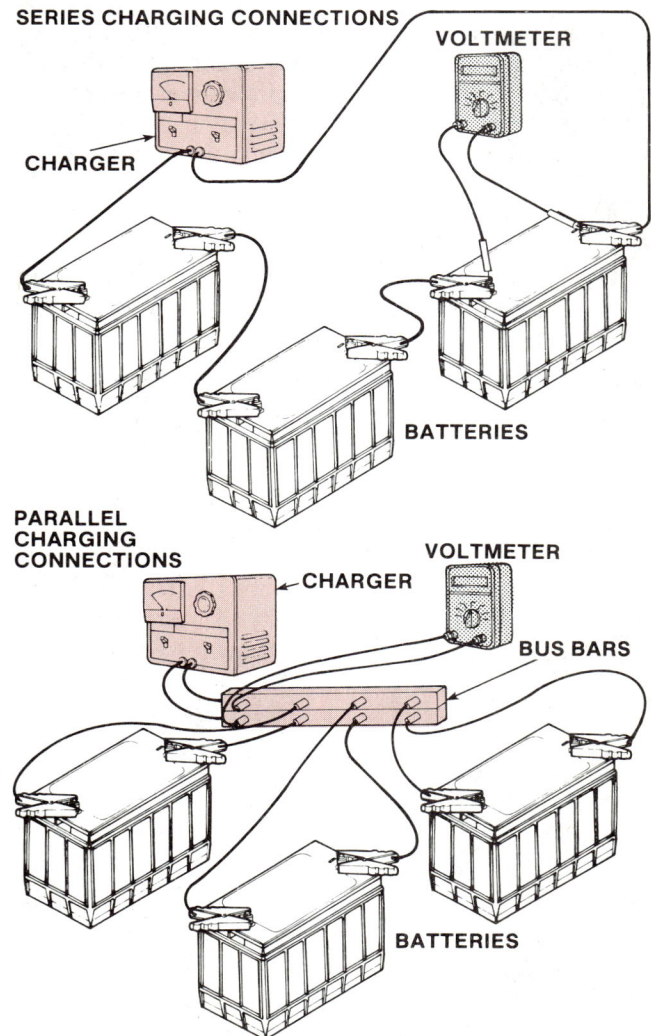

Figure 14-77 Battery charger connections. Always follow charger manufacturer directions.

in good condition to accept a fast charge. Sulfation on the plates of the battery can lead to excessive gassing, boiling, and heat buildup during fast-charging. Never fast-charge a battery that shows evidence of sulfation buildup or separator damage.

Slow types of trickle chargers provide low charging currents of about 5 to 15 amperes. Slow charging may require 12 to 24 hours but is the only safe way of charging sulfated batteries. In general, almost any battery can be charged at any current rate as long as excessive electrolyte gassing does not occur and the electrolyte temperature does not exceed 125 degrees Fahrenheit. However, when time is available, slow charging is the safest and easiest method to use. In fact, many fast chargers can be adjusted to provide slow charging.

Regardless of fast- or slow-charging rates, always begin by checking the electrolyte level when possible. Add water as needed to a conventional battery. Charging with electrolyte levels below the separators can damage the battery.

Perform charging in a well-ventilated area away from sparks and open flames. Always be sure the charger is off before connecting or disconnecting the leads to the battery. Remember to wear eye protection, and never attempt to charge a frozen battery.

All battery chargers have manufacturer specific characteristics and operating instructions that must be followed. When charging a battery in the vehicle, always disconnect the battery cables to avoid damaging the alternator or other electrical components. Complete details of charging procedures are given in the Tech Manual.

CAUTION: Do not exceed the manufacturer's battery charging limits. Also never charge the battery if the built-in hydrometer registers clear or light yellow. Replace the battery.

JUMP-STARTING

When it is necessary to jump-start a car with a discharged battery using a booster battery and jumper cables, follow the instructions shown in Figure 14-78

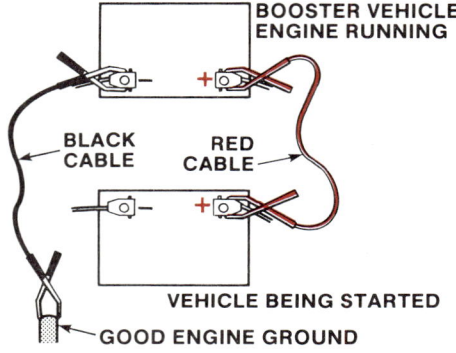

Figure 14-78 Proper setup and connections for boost (jump) starting a vehicle with a drained battery.

to avoid damaging the charging system or creating a hazardous situation. Always wear eye protection when making or breaking jumper cable connections.

CAUTION: Consult the manufacturer's service manual for procedures and precautions when jump-starting late-model vehicles with electronic control systems. Excessive battery voltages can damage sensitive electronic components.

CASE STUDIES
Case 1

A new car with under 5,000 miles on it has developed unusual electrical problems. For example, certain circuits do not work. These include the automatic door locks, the under-hood light, the automatic antenna, and the radio. What could be the problem?

Usually when multiple electrical circuits fail, this indicates the possibility of a burned electrical fusible link. Using the manufacturer's service manual, try to identify which fusible link is common to all of the circuits that are affected. Then check the appropriate fusible link for damage. It could be broken in the center, inside the wire insulation. A fusible link may also short out because the wiring harness rubs against the frame. If the link is found to be faulty, replace it, but also identify what caused it to be open, for example, a shorted wiring harness.

Case 2

A customer tells the technician that the fuse for the windshield wiper blows as soon as he replaces it and turns on the wipers.

The technician removes the fuse and observes that it is black inside. The technician knows that these symptoms indicate a short to ground and so substitutes a 12-volt test light for the blown fuse. With the test light in place, the technician disconnects the wiper motor (a mechanically grounded load component), turns the ignition switch on, and notes the status of the test light. Because the motor is disconnected, the circuit should be open and the test light is lit. The technician knows that the problem is not in the motor. The problem is a short to ground in the wiring that leads to the motor. The technician continues the search for the short by separating circuit connectors one at a time. He starts at the connector that is farthest from the test light and works toward the fuse panel. The light remains on when the technician unplugs the first connector so he knows that the short exists in some part of the circuit that is still intact. The light goes off when the technician unplugs the next connector one step closer to the fuse panel. The technician then realizes that the short is somewhere between the last two connectors unplugged because the test light indicates that there is no longer a path to ground. The technician visually inspects the wiring between the two connectors, discovers and repairs a bare spot in the wire that was contacting ground.

Summary

- For electrical flow to occur there must be an excess of electrons in one place, a lack of electrons in another, and a path between the two places.
- The mathematical relationship between current, resistance, and voltage is expressed in Ohm's law, E = IR, where voltage is measured in volts, current in amperes, and resistance in ohms.
- The mathematical relationship between current, voltage, and power is expressed in Watt's law, P = EI. Power is measured in watts or kilowatts (1,000 watts).
- Three basic types of circuits are used in automobile wiring systems: series circuits, parallel circuits, and series-parallel circuits.
- Electrical schematics are diagrams with electrical symbols that show the parts and how electrical current flows through the vehicle's electrical circuits. They are used in troubleshooting.
- An open circuit does not have a complete path for the current to flow through. A shorted circuit is one that allows electricity to flow past part of the normal load. A grounded circuit is a short circuit that allows current to return to the battery prematurely. A high-resistance problem in a circuit decreases the power available for the load.
- The strength of an electromagnet depends on the number of current carrying conductors, and what is in the core of the coil. Inducing a voltage requires a magnetic field producing lines of force, conductors that can be moved, and movement between the conductors and the magnetic field so that the lines of force are cut.
- Fuses, fuse links, maxi-fuses, and circuit breakers protect circuits against overloads. Switches control on/off and direct current flow in a circuit. A relay is an electric switch. A solenoid is an electromagnet that translates current flow into mechanical movement. Resistors limit current flow. Capacitors block DC and pass AC.
- The diode allows current to flow in one direction but not in the opposite direction. It is formed by joining P-type semiconductor material with N-type semiconductor material.
- A transistor resembles a diode with an extra side. There are PNP and NPN transistors. They are used as switching devices. A very small current applied to the base of the transistor controls a much larger current flowing through the entire transistor.
- Computers are electronic decision-making centers. Input devices called sensors feed information to the computer. The computer processes this information and sends signals to controlling devices.
- A typical electronic control system is made up of sensors, actuators, microcomputer, and related wiring.
- Most input sensors are variable resistance/reference types, switches, and thermistors.
- Microcomputer and its processors are the heart of the computerized engine controls.
- There are three types of computer memory used: ROM, PROM, and RAM.
- Output sensor or actuators are electromechanical devices that convert current into mechanical action.
- There are four types of batteries in use today: conventional, low-maintenance, maintenance-free, and sealed maintenance-free.
- The conventional battery consists of grids, positive plates, negative plates, separators, elements, electrolyte, a container, cell covers, vent plugs, and cell containers. Maintenance-free batteries have no holes or caps, but they do have gas vents. Sealed maintenance-free batteries do not require the gas vents used on other maintenance-free designs.
- Depending on the design of the battery, state of charge and capacity can be determined by several different test methods: specific gravity tests, built-in hydrometers, capacity test, alternative capacity test, and three-minute charge test.
- To charge a battery, a given charging current is passed through the battery for a period of time. Fast chargers are more popular, but slow charging is the only safe way to charge a sulfated battery.

Review Questions

1. What is the name for the formula E = IR?
2. In a series circuit, resistance is always _____ .
3. What kind of diagram is used to troubleshoot an electrical circuit?
4. An ammeter is always connected _____ with the circuit, while a voltmeter is connected in _____ with the circuit.
5. Variable capacitors are called _____ .
6. What is the process called in which a conductor cuts across a magnetic field and produces a voltage?
7. What are the major components of an electronic control system?
8. A _____ is the simplest type of semiconductor.
9. What kind of solder is used to repair electrical wiring?
10. What is the major difference between ROM and RAM memory in a microprocessor?

364 Section 3   Electricity

11. For electrical flow to occur, which of the following must be present?
    a. a difference in the quantity of electrons between two places
    b. a path between two places
    c. a battery
    d. both a and b
12. Technician A says that magnetism is a source of electrical energy in an automobile. Technician B says that chemical reaction is a source of electrical energy in an automobile. Who is correct?
    a. Technician A
    b. Technician B
    c. Both A and B
    d. Neither A nor B
13. Which of the following is not a type of information stored in ROM?
    a. strategy
    b. look-up tables
    c. sensor input
    d. none of the above
14. Technician A uses a test light to detect resistance. Technician B uses a jumper wire to test circuit breakers, relays, and lights. Who is correct?
    a. Technician A
    b. Technician B
    c. Both A and B
    d. Neither A nor B
15. Which type of resistor is commonly used in automotive circuits?
    a. fixed valve
    b. stepped
    c. variable
    d. all of the above
16. Technician A says that the cross sectional area in circular mils of a solid wire must be calculated in order to find its gauge. Technician B says the smaller the gauge number, the heavier the wire. Who is correct?
    a. Technician A
    b. Technician B
    c. Both A and B
    d. Neither A nor B
17. What is the first step when removing an old battery?
    a. Disconnect the ground cable.
    b. Remove the battery holddown straps and cover.
    c. Inspect and clean the area.
    d. Remove the heat shield.
18. Technician A says that some types of voltage sensors provide input to the computer by modifying or controlling a constant, predetermined voltage signal. Technician B says that another type of voltage sensor is a voltage generating sensor. Who is correct?
    a. Technician A
    b. Technician B
    c. Both A and B
    d. Neither A nor B
19. Which of the following statements concerning car batteries is untrue?
    a. A function of car batteries is to act as a voltage stabilizer for the entire electrical system of the vehicle.
    b. Car batteries convert chemical energy to electrical energy.
    c. A car battery is technically a storage battery.
    d. All of the above.
20. Technician A says that when current is applied to the base, the transistor shuts off. Technician B says that alternator current applied to the P side of the diode makes it an excellent conductor. Who is correct?
    a. Technician A
    b. Technician B
    c. Both A and B
    d. Neither A nor B

15 STARTING AND CHARGING SYSTEMS

Objectives

■ List the components of the starting system, starter circuit, and control circuit. ■ Explain the different types of magnetic switches and starter drive mechanisms. ■ Explain how a starter motor operates. ■ Perform starter system inspection and testing procedures using electrical test equipment. ■ Explain how AC charging systems work, and describe their advantages over DC charging systems. ■ Explain half- and full-wave rectification, and how they relate to alternator operation. ■ Identify the different types of AC voltage regulators. ■ Perform charging system inspection and testing procedures using electrical test equipment.

The vehicle's starting system is designed to turn or crank the engine over until it can operate under its own power. To do this, the starter motor receives electrical power from the storage battery. The starter motor then converts this energy into mechanical energy, which it transmits through the drive mechanism to the engine's flywheel.

The only function of the starting system is to crank the engine fast enough to run. The vehicle's ignition and fuel systems provide the spark and fuel for engine operation, but they are not considered components of the basic starting system.

☐ STARTING SYSTEM—DESIGN AND COMPONENTS

A typical starting system has six basic components and two distinct electrical circuits. The components are the battery, ignition switch, battery cables, magnetic switch (either electrical relay or solenoid), starter motor, and the starter safety switch.

The starter motor draws a great deal of electrical current from the battery. A large starter motor might require 200 to 300 amperes of current. This current flows through the heavy-gauge cables that connect the battery to the starter.

The driver controls the flow of this current using the ignition switch mounted (usually) on the steering column. However, if the cables were routed from the battery to the ignition switch and then on to the starter motor, the voltage drop caused by resistance in the cables and switch would be too great. To avoid this

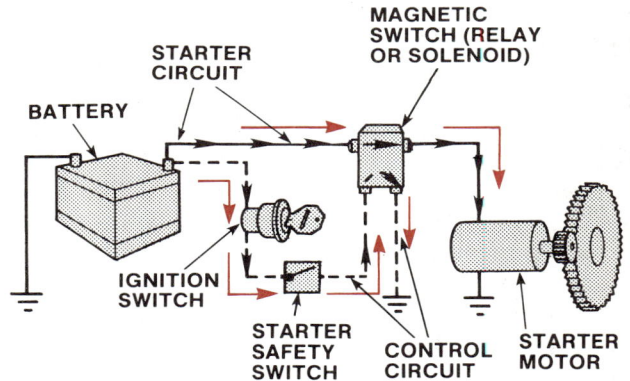

Figure 15-1 The major components and circuits of a typical starting system. The starter circuit is shown in a solid line. The control circuit is indicated by a dashed line.

problem, the system is designed with two connected circuits: the starter circuit and the control circuit. The starter circuit, indicated by the solid lines in Figure 15-1, carries the heavy current flow from the battery to the starter motor by way of the magnetic switch or solenoid. The control circuit, shown by the dashed lines in Figure 15-1, ties the ignition switch to the battery and magnetic switch so this heavy current flow can be conveniently controlled.

Starter Circuit

The starter circuit carries the high current flow within the system and supplies power for the actual engine cranking. Components of the starter circuit are the battery, battery cables, magnetic switch or solenoid, and the starter motor.

365

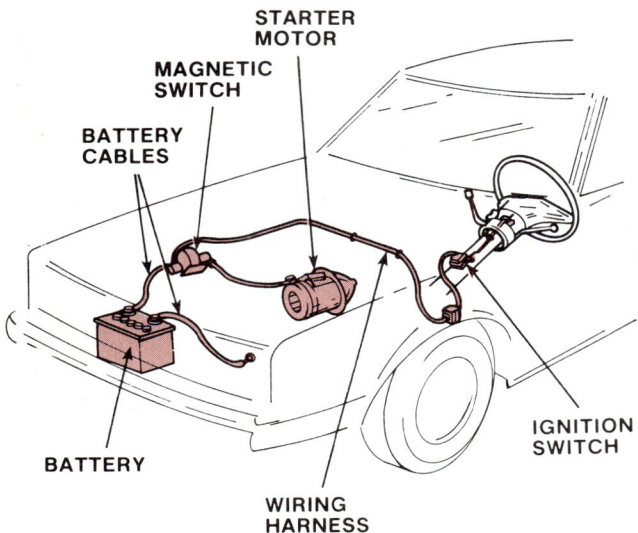

Figure 15-2 Basic battery cable and wiring connections in a typical starting system.

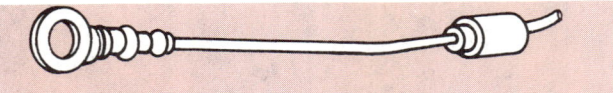
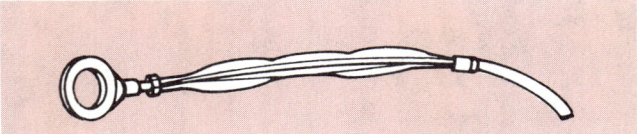

Figure 15-3 Example of a good and a burnt fusible link.

Battery and Cables

Many problems associated with the starting system can be solved by troubleshooting the battery and its related components.

The starting circuit requires two or more heavy-gauge cables (Figure 15-2). Two of these cables attach directly to the battery. One of these cables connects between the battery's negative terminal and an excellent ground. The other cable connects the battery's positive terminal with the magnetic switch or solenoid. On vehicles where the solenoid does not mount directly on the starter motor, two cables are needed. One runs from the positive battery terminal to the solenoid and the second from the solenoid to the starter motor terminal. In any case, these cables carry the necessary heavy current from the battery to the starter and from the starter back to the battery.

All cables must be in good condition. Corrosion on the cables act as a resistor and cause a voltage drop. Cables can be corroded by battery acid, and contact with engine parts and other metal surfaces can fray the cable insulation. Frayed insulation can cause a dead short that can seriously damage some of the electrical units of the vehicle. A short to ground is the cause of many dead batteries and can result in fire.

Cables must also be heavy enough to comfortably carry the required current load. Cranking problems can be created when undersized cables are installed. Some replacement cables use smaller-gauge wire encased in thick insulation, so the small gauge cables can look as heavy as the original equipment. In warm weather, with good connections and no extra current drawn from lights or accessories, an engine starts with smaller cables. But many starts must be done under conditions that are less than ideal. With undersized cables, the starter motor does not develop its greatest turning effort and even a fully charged battery might be unable to start the engine. Always check cable size during the general inspection of the system.

When checking cables and wiring, always check any fusible links in the wiring. Almost all vehicles are equipped with fusible links to protect the wiring from overloading. These links are different in construction than a fuse, but they operate in much the same way (Figure 15-3). The most common type is made of a wire with a special nonflammable insulation. Wire used to make fusible links is ordinarily two gauge sizes smaller than the wire in the circuit they are designed to protect. Often, when a fusible link is subjected to a current overload, the insulation will become charred and give the appearance of a failed link. This is not always a true indication. The best test is to disconnect the battery cables and connect an ohmmeter across the link to check for continuity.

The largest fusible link is usually located at the starter solenoid battery terminal. From this terminal, current is distributed to all parts of the vehicle. Another large fusible link joins this battery terminal to the main body harness and protects the complete wiring of the vehicle. It may be located in its own special holder or be attached directly to the starter relay terminal. When a link has failed, always troubleshoot the system and locate the cause before replacing the link.

Magnetic Switches

Every starting system contains some type of magnetic switch that enables the control circuit to open and close the starter circuit. This magnetic switch can be one of several designs.

SOLENOIDS The solenoid-actuated starter is by far the most common starter system used. As shown in the starter in Figure 15-4, the solenoid mounts directly on top of the starter motor.

In this type of starting system, the solenoid uses the electromagnetic field generated by its coil to perform two distinct jobs.

The first job is to push the drive pinion of the starter motor into mesh with the engine flywheel. This is its mechanical function. The second job is to act as an

Starting and Charging Systems

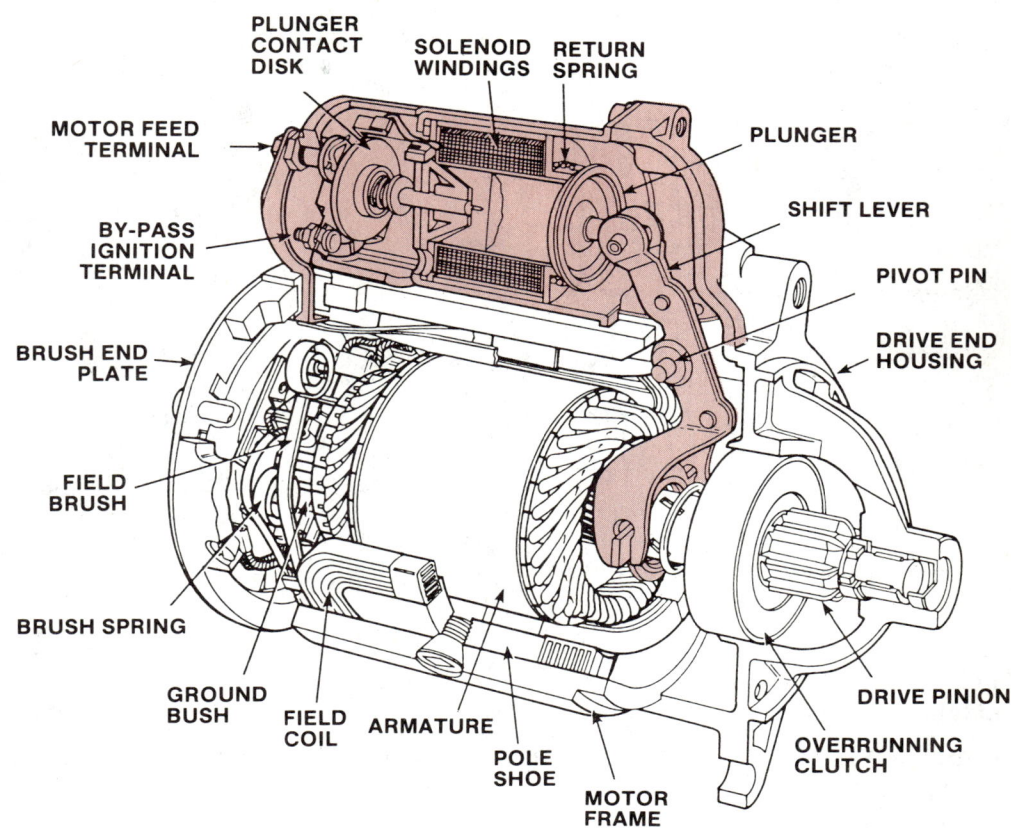

Figure 15-4 Example of a solenoid-actuated starter where the solenoid mounts directly to the starter motor.

electrical relay switch to energize the motor once the drive pinion is engaged. Once the contact points of the solenoid are closed, full current flows from the battery to the starter motor.

The solenoid assembly has two separate windings: a pull-in winding and a hold-in winding. The two windings have approximately the same number of turns but are wound from different size wire. Together these windings produce the electromagnetic force needed to pull the plunger into the solenoid coil. The heavier pull-in windings draw the plunger into the solenoid, while the lighter gauge windings produce enough magnetic force to hold the plunger in this position.

Both windings are energized when the ignition switch is turned to the start position. When the plunger disc makes contact with the solenoid terminals, the pull-in winding is deactivated. At the same time, the plunger contact disc makes the motor feed connection between the battery and the starting motor, directing full battery current to the field coils and starter motor armature for cranking power (Figure 15-5).

As the solenoid plunger moves, the shift fork also pivots on the pivot pin and pushes the starter drive pinion into mesh with the flywheel ring gear. When the starter motor receives current, its armature starts to turn. This motion is transferred through an overrunning clutch and pinion gear to the engine flywheel and the engine is cranked.

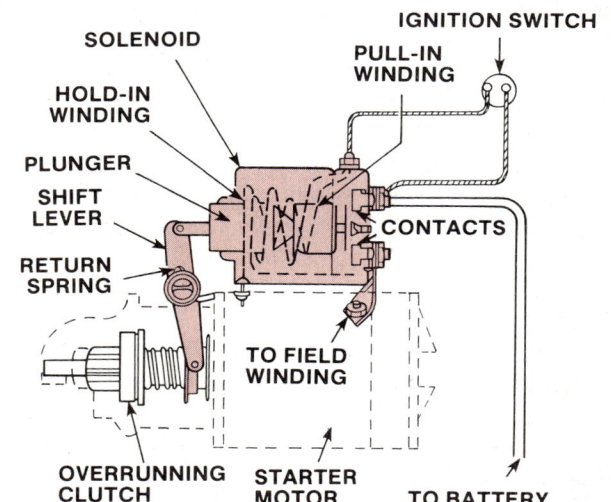

Figure 15-5 Solenoids operate using a heavy-gauge pull-in winding, and a light-gauge hold-in winding. The heavy-gauge pull-in winding generates a strong magnetic field to move the plunger. A light-gauge hold-in winding generates a weaker magnetic field to hold the plunger in position after it has moved and completed the starter circuit.

With this type of solenoid-actuated direct drive starting system, teeth on the pinion gear may not immediately mesh with the flywheel ring gear. If this occurs, a spring located behind the pinion compresses so that the solenoid plunger can complete its stroke. When the starter motor armature begins to turn, the

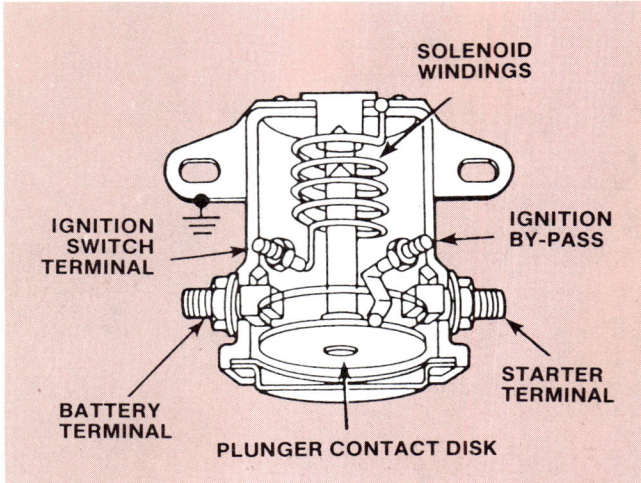

Figure 15-6 Cross-sectional view of a starter relay, which is actually a solenoid that is used to close an electrical circuit.

pinion teeth quickly line up with the flywheel teeth and the spring pressure forces them to mesh.

STARTER RELAYS Relays are the second major type of magnetic switch used. All positive engagement starters (described later in this chapter) use a relay in series with the battery cables to deliver the high current necessary through the shortest possible battery cables. Figure 15-6 shows a typical starter relay. It is very similar to the solenoid. However, it is not used to move the drive pinion into mesh. It is strictly an electrical relay or switch. When current from the ignition switch arrives at the ignition switch terminal of the relay, a strong magnetic field is generated in the coil of the relay. This magnetic force pulls the plunger contact disc up against the battery terminal and the starter terminal of the relay, allowing full current flow to the starter motor.

A secondary function of the starter relay is to provide an alternate electrical path to the ignition coil during cranking. This current flow by-passes the resistance wire (or ballast resistor) in the ignition primary circuit. This is done when the plunger disc contacts the ignition by-pass terminal on the relay. Not all systems have an ignition by-pass setup.

Some vehicles use both a starter relay and a starter motor mounted solenoid. The relay controls current flow to the solenoid, which in turn controls current flow to the starter motor. This reduces the amount of current flowing through the ignition switch. In other words, it takes less current to activate the relay than to activate the solenoid.

Basically, all the different starting systems in use today fit into one of three categories: the solenoid shift, solenoid shift with relay, or positive engagement with relay. Typical wiring diagrams for each type of system are shown in Figures 15-7 and 15-8.

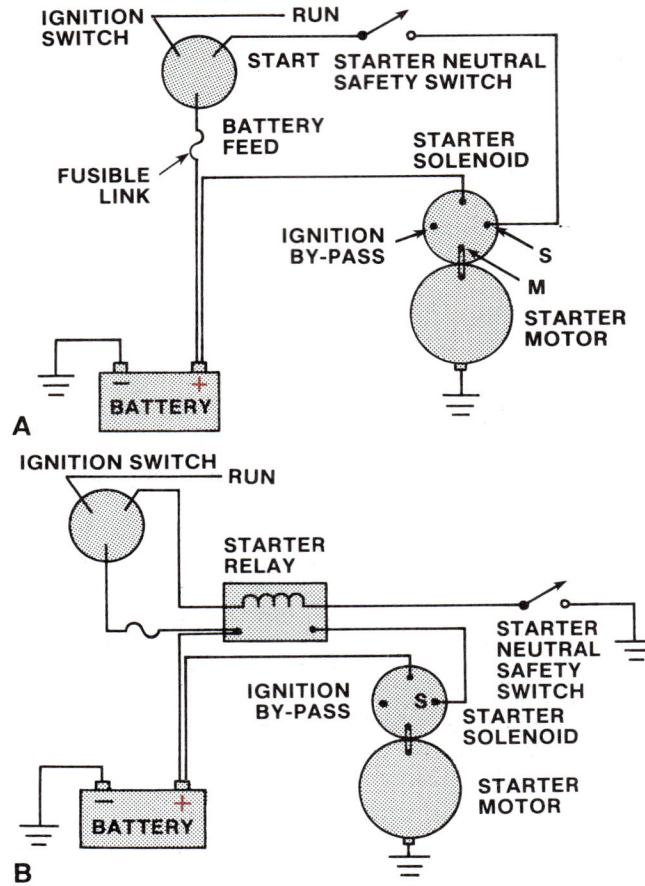

Figure 15-7 (A) Solenoid shift and (B) solenoid shift with starter relay starting systems.

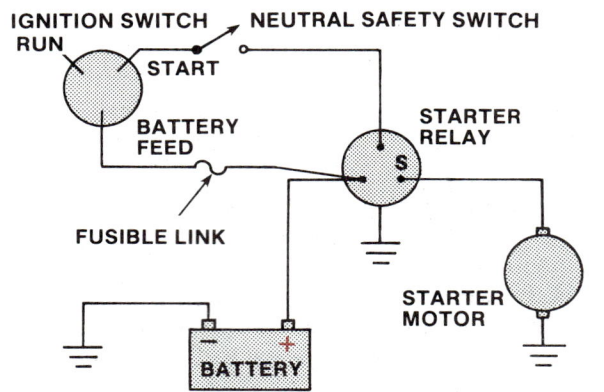

Figure 15-8 Starting relay with a positive engagement starter.

Starter Motors

The starting motor (Figure 15-4) converts the electrical energy from the battery into mechanical energy for cranking the engine. The starter is a special type of electric motor designed to operate under great electrical overloads and to produce very high horsepower.

Because of these design features, the starter can only operate for short periods of time without rest. The high current needed to operate the starter creates considerable heat, and continuous operation for any length of time causes serious heat damage to the unit. The starter must never operate for more than 30 seconds at a time and should rest for 2 minutes between these extended crankings. This permits the heat to dissipate without damage to the unit.

All starting motors are generally the same in design and operation. Basically the starter motor consists of a housing, field coils, an armature, a commutator and brushes, and end frames. The main difference between designs is in the drive mechanism used to engage the flywheel.

The starter housing or frame encloses the internal starter components and protects them from damage, moisture, and foreign materials. The housing supports the field coils and forms a path for the magnetism produced by the current passing through the coils.

The field coils and their pole shoes (Figure 15-9) are securely attached to the inside or the iron housing (Figure 15-10). The field coils are insulated from the housing but are connected to a terminal that protrudes through the outer surface of the housing.

The field coils and pole shoes are designed to produce strong stationary electromagnetic fields within the starter body as current is passed through the starter. These magnetic fields are concentrated at the pole shoe. Fields have a N or S magnetic polarity depending on the direction of current flow. The coils are wound around respective pole shoes in opposite directions to generate opposing magnetic fields.

The field coils connect in series with the armature winding through the starter brushes. This design permits all current passing through the field coil circuit to also pass through the armature windings.

The armature is the only rotating component of the starter. It is located between the drive and commutator end frames and the field windings. When the starter operates, the current passing through the armature produces a magnetic field in each of its conductors. The reaction between the armature's magnetic field and the magnetic fields produced by the field coils causes the armature to rotate. This is the mechanical energy that is then used to crank the engine.

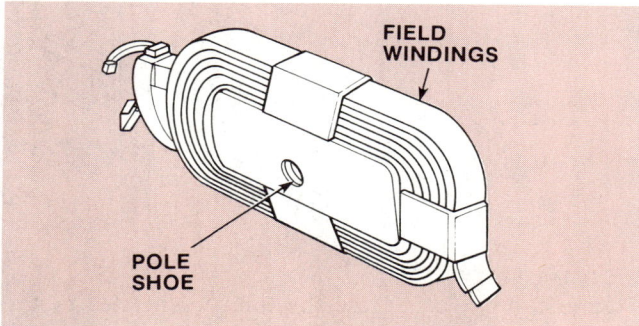

Figure 15-9 Example of a field coil and pole shoe.

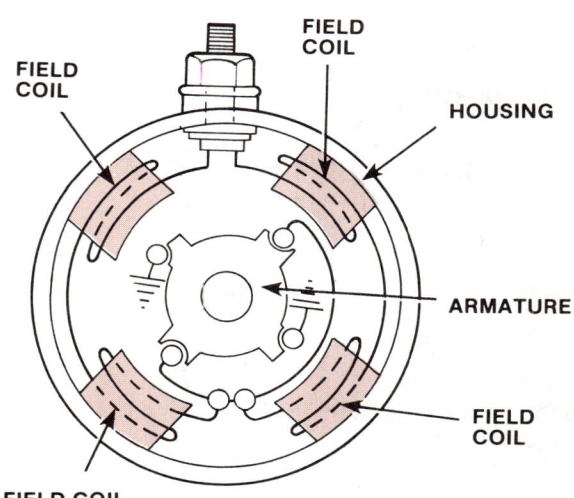

Figure 15-10 Cross-sectional view of a motor housing with field coils mounted to the inner housing walls.

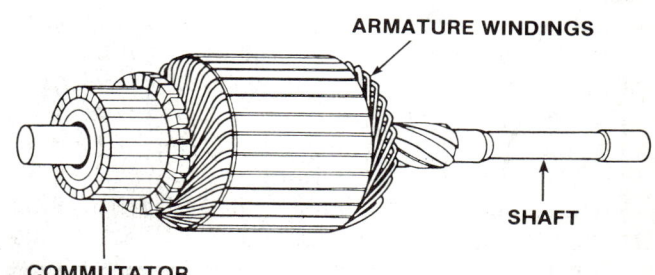

Figure 15-11 The armature's two main components, the commutator and the armature windings, are mounted to the armature shaft.

The armature has two main components: the armature windings and the commutator. Both mount to the armature shaft (Figure 15-11). The armature windings are not made of wire. Instead, heavy flat copper strips are used that can handle the heavy current flow. The windings are made of several coils of a single loop each. The sides of these loops fit into slots in the armature core or shaft, but they are insulated from it.

The coils connect to each other and to the commutator so that current from the field coils flows through all of the armature windings at the same time. This action generates a magnetic field around each armature winding, resulting in a repulsion force all around the conductor. This repulsion force causes the armature to turn.

The commutator assembly presses onto the armature shaft. It is made up of heavy copper segments separated from each other and the armature shaft by insulation. The commutator segments connect to the ends of the armature windings.

Most starter motors have two to six brushes that ride on the commutator segments and carry the heavy current flow from the stationary field coils to the rotating armature windings via the commutator segments.

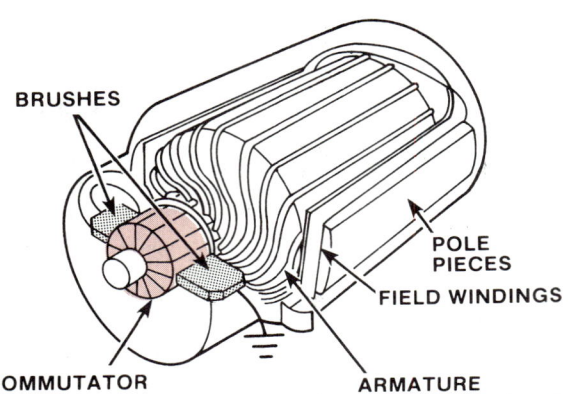

Figure 15-12 The location of the starter motor brushes and commutator.

The brushes mount on and operate in some type of holder which may be a pivoting arm design inside the starter housing or frame (Figure 15-12). However, in many starters the brush holders are secured to the commutator end frame. In both cases, the brush holder supports the brushes in position. Springs hold the brushes against the commutator with the correct pressure. Finally, alternate brush holders are insulated from the housing or end frame. Those in between the insulated holders are grounded.

The commutator end frame consists of a metal plate that bolts to the commutator end of the starter housing. It supports the commutator end of the armature with a bushing and often contains the brush holders that support the brushes.

Operating Principle

The starter motor converts electric current into torque or twisting force through the interaction of magnetic fields. It has a stationary magnetic field (created by passing current through the field coils) and a current-carrying conductor (the armature windings). When the armature windings are placed in this stationary magnetic field and current is passed through the windings, a second magnetic field is generated with its lines of force wrapping around the wire (Figure 15-13).

Since the lines of force in the stationary magnetic field flow in one direction across the winding, they combine on one side of the wire increasing the field strength but are opposed on the other side, weakening the field strength. This creates an unbalanced magnetic force, pushing the wire in the direction of the weaker field.

Since the armature windings are formed in loops or coils, current flows outward in one direction and returns in the opposite direction. Because of this, the magnetic lines of force are oriented in opposite directions in each of the two segments of the loop. When placed in the stationary magnetic field of the field coils, one part of the armature coil is pushed in one direction. The other part is pushed in the opposite direction. This causes the coil and the shaft to which it is mounted to rotate.

Each end of the armature windings are connected to one segment of the commutator. Carbon brushes are connected to one terminal of the power supply. The brushes contact the commutator segments conducting current to and from the armature coils.

As the armature coil turns through a half revolution, the contact of the brushes on the commutator causes the current flow to reverse in the coil. The commutator segment attached to each coil end has traveled past one brush and is now in contact with the other. In this way, current flow is maintained constantly in one direction, while allowing the segment of the rotating armature coils to reverse polarity as they rotate.

In a starter motor, many armature segments must be used (Figure 15-14). As one segment rotates past the stationary magnetic field pole, another segment immediately takes its place. The turning motion is made uniform and the torque needed to turn the flywheel is constant rather than fluctuating as it would be if only a few armature coils were used.

The number of coils and brushes may differ between starter motor models. The armature may be wired in series with the field coils (series motor); the field coils may be wired parallel or shunted across the armature

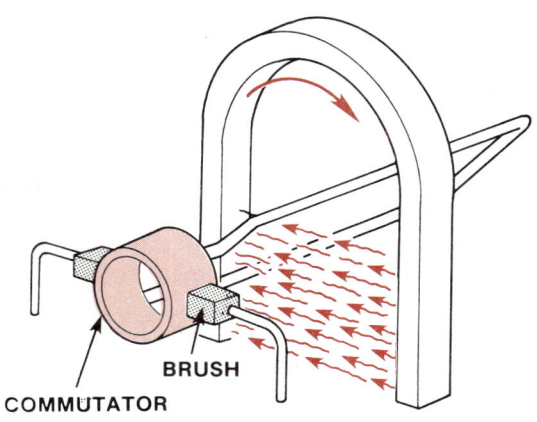

Figure 15-13 Simple motor operation.

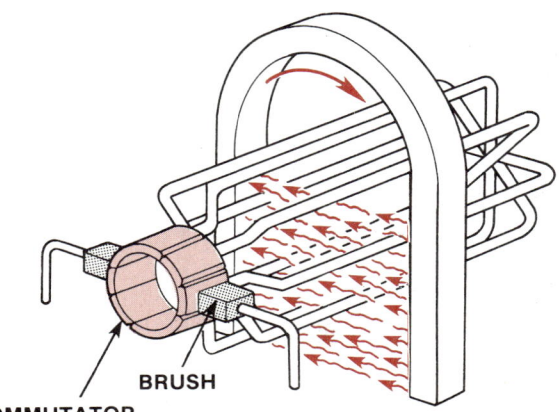

Figure 15-14 To increase the torque generated by the motor, many armature conductors and commutator segments are used.

Starting and Charging Systems

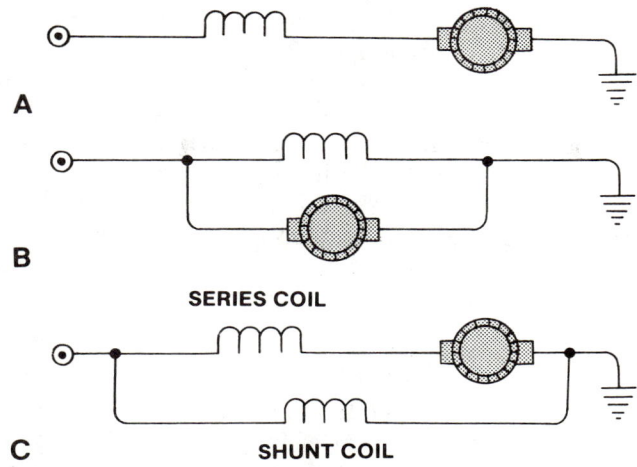

Figure 15-15 Starter motors are grouped according to how they are wired: (A) in series, (B) in parallel (shunt), or (c) a compound motor using both series and shunt coils.

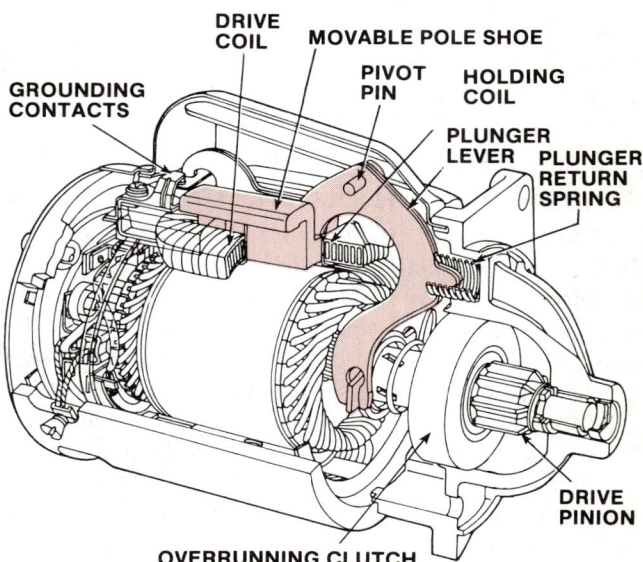

Figure 15-16 Typical positive engagement movable pole shoe starter.

(shunt motors); or a combination of series and shunt wiring may be used (compound motors) (Figure 15-15).

A series motor develops its maximum torque at start-up and develops less torque as speed increases. It is ideal for applications involving heavy starting loads.

Shunt motors develop considerably less start-up torque but maintain a constant speed at all operating loads. Compound motors combine the characteristics of good starting torque with constant speed. The compound design is particularly useful for applications in which heavy loads are suddenly applied. In a starter motor, a shunt coil is frequently used to limit the maximum free speed at which the starter can operate.

Drive Mechanisms

The area where starters differ most is in their drive mechanisms used to crank the engine. The solenoid-actuated direct drive system has already been explained earlier in this chapter.

Positive Engagement Movable Pole Shoe Drive

Positive engagement movable pole shoe drive starters (Figure 15-16) are mostly used by Ford. In this design, the drive mechanism is an integral part of the motor, and the drive pinion is engaged with the flywheel before the motor is energized.

When the ignition switch is moved to the start position, the system's starter relay closes, and full battery current is delivered to the starter. This current runs through the winding of the movable pole shoe and through a set of contacts to ground. This generates a magnetic force that pulls down the movable pole shoe. It also, using a lever action, forces the drive pinion to engage the flywheel ring gear using a lever action and opens the contacts. A small holding coil helps keep the movable shoe and lever assembly engaged during cranking. When the engine starts, an overrunning clutch prevents the flywheel from spinning the armature.

When the ignition switch is released from the start position, both the pole shoe and lever return to their original positions.

Solenoid-Actuated Gear Reduction Drive

Solenoid-actuated gear reduction-drive starters use a solenoid to engage the pinion with the flywheel and to close the motor circuit (Figure 15-17). The starter armature does not drive the pinion directly. Instead, it drives a small gear that is permanently meshed with a larger gear having a reduction ratio of 2:1 to 3.5:1, depending on the engine size. This design allows a small, high-speed motor to develop increased turning torque at a satisfactory cranking rpm. The solenoid and starter drive operation is basically the same as in solenoid-actuated direct drive systems.

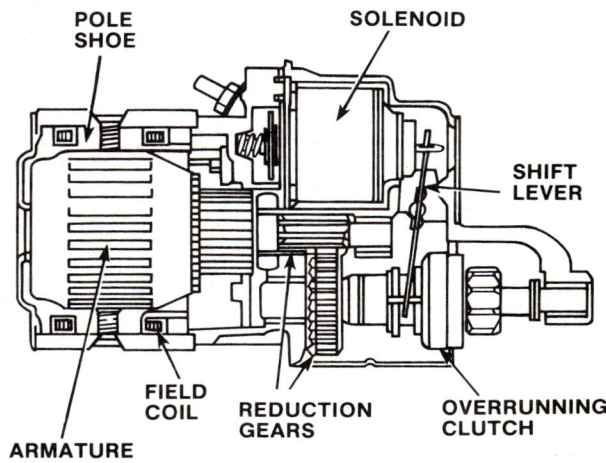

Figure 15-17 Typical gear reduction starter design.

While reduction starters are designed to deliver more cranking power using fewer amperes than ordinary starters, the reverse may be true if the gears wear or otherwise go bad. Increased starter noise is a sign that worn reduction gears may be a problem.

Permanent Magnet Starting Motors

The most recent change in starting motors has been in the use of permanent magnets rather than electromagnets as field coils. Electrically, this starter motor is simpler. It does not require current for field coils. Current is delivered directly to the armature through the commutator and brushes. Figure 15-18 shows this starter motor. With the exception of no electromagnets for the fields, this unit functions exactly as the other styles considered. Increased use of this style is expected in the future as production costs are greatly reduced. Maintenance and testing procedures are the same as for other designs. Notice the use of a planetary gear reduction assembly on the front of the armature. This allows the armature to spin with increased torque, resulting in improved starter cold-cranking performance. The starter design also results in reduced size and weight. Consequently, overall vehicle weight is lighter and fuel efficiency is enhanced. Reducing the overall size while keeping the torque high improves the adaptability of the unit in certain vehicles where space is at a premium. The unit still requires the use of a starting solenoid. It should also be noted that these units require special handling since the permanent magnet material is quite brittle and can be destroyed with a sharp blow or if the starter is dropped.

▢ OVERRIDE CLUTCHES

The overrunning clutch performs a very important job in protecting the starter motor. When the engine starts and runs, its speed increases. If the starter motor remained connected to the engine through the flywheel, the starter motor would spin at very high speeds, destroying the armature winding.

To prevent this, the starter must be disengaged from the engine as soon as the engine turns more rapidly than the starter has cranked it. However, with most

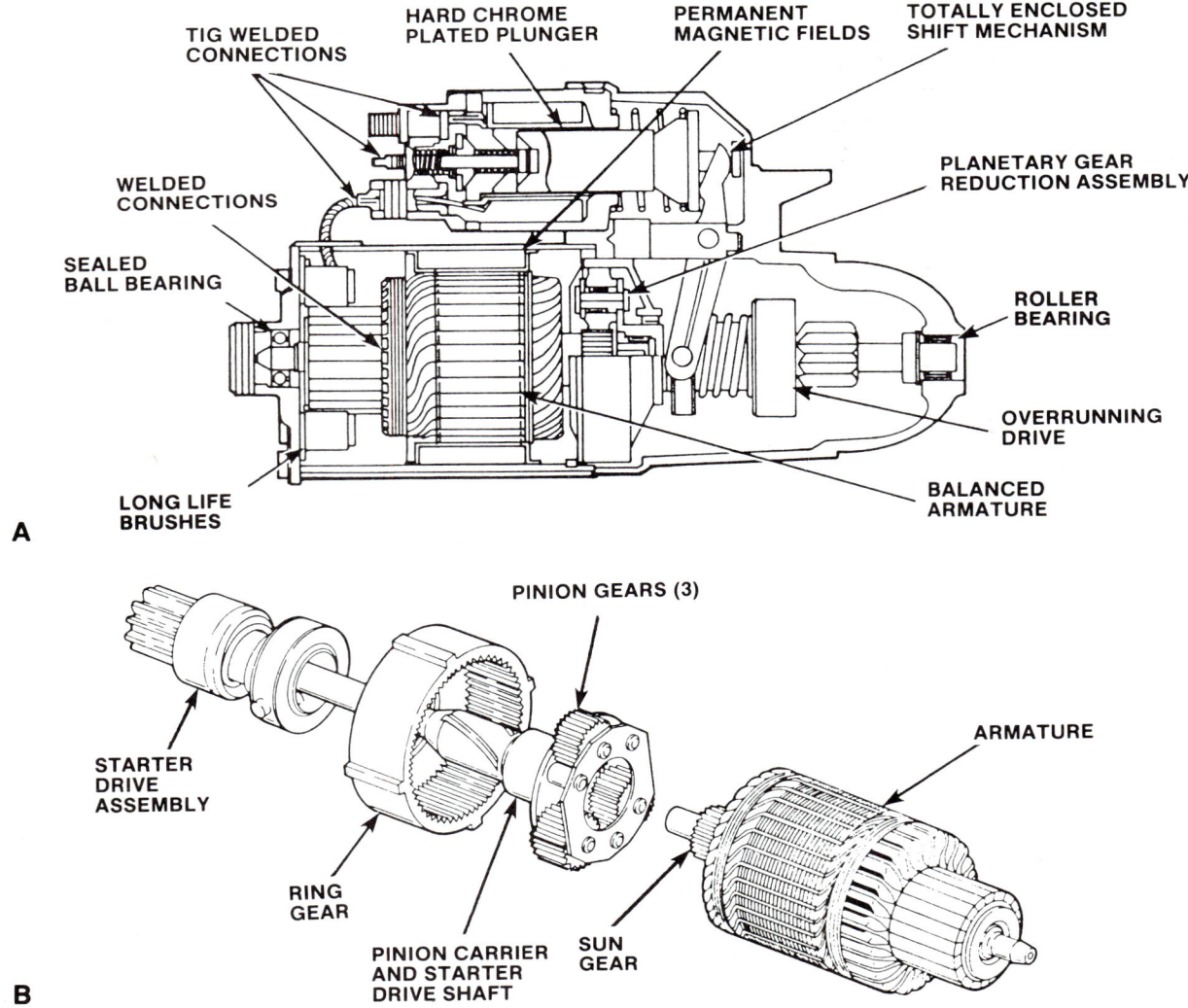

Figure 15-18 (A) Permanent magnet, planetary drive starter and (B) planetary gear construction details.

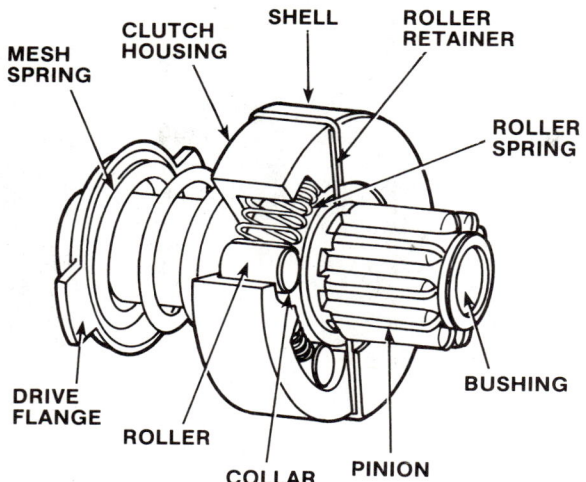

Figure 15-19 A sectional view of a typical overriding clutch.

starter designs the pinion remains engaged until electricity stops flowing to the starter. In these cases, an overriding clutch is used to disengage the starter. A typical overriding clutch is shown in Figure 15-19.

The clutch housing is internally splined to the starting motor armature shaft. The drive pinion turns freely on the armature shaft within the clutch housing. When the clutch housing is driven by the armature, the spring-loaded rollers are forced into the small ends of their tapered slots and wedged tightly against the pinion barrel. This locks the pinion and clutch housing solidly together, permitting the pinion to turn the flywheel and, thus, crank the engine.

When the engine starts (Figure 15-20) the flywheel spins the pinion faster than the armature. This releases the rollers, unlocking the pinion gear from the armature shaft. The pinion then overruns the armature shaft freely until being pulled out of the mesh without stressing the starter motor. Note that the overrunning clutch is moved in and out of mesh by the starter drive linkage.

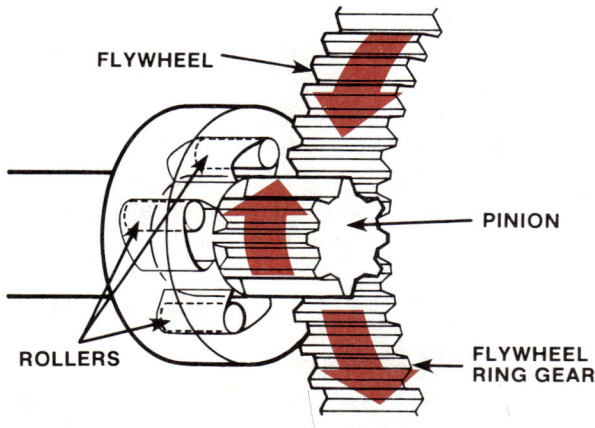

Figure 15-20 When the engine starts, the flywheel spins the pinion gear faster, which releases the rollers from the wedge.

☐ CONTROL CIRCUIT

The control circuit allows the driver to use a small amount of battery current to control the flow of a large amount of current in the starting circuit.

The entire circuit usually consists of an ignition switch connected through normal gauge wire to the battery and the magnetic switch (solenoid or relay). When the ignition switch is turned to the start position, a small amount of current flows through the coil of the magnetic switch, closing it and allowing full current to flow directly to the starter motor. The ignition switch performs other jobs besides controlling the starting circuit. It normally has at least four separate positions: accessory, off, on (run), and start.

Starting Safety Switch

The starting safety switch, often called the neutral safety switch, is a normally open switch that prevents the starting system from operating when the transmission is in gear. This eliminates the possibility of a situation that could make the vehicle lurch unexpectedly forward or backward. Safety switches are more commonly used with automatic transmissions, but are also used on manual transmission.

Starting safety switches can be located in either of two places within the control circuit. One location is between the igniton switch and the relay or solenoid (Figures 15-7A and 15-8). In this position, the safety switch must be closed before current can flow to the relay or solenoid. A second location for the safety switch is between the relay and ground (Figure 15-7B). The switch must be closed before current can flow from the relay to ground.

The safety switch used with an automatic transmission can be either an electrical switch or a mechanical device. Contact points on the electrical switch are only closed when the shift selector is in park or neutral (Figure 15-21). The switch can be mounted near the shift selector or on the transmission housing. The switch contacts are wired in series with the control circuit so that no current can flow through the relay or solenoid unless the transmisson is in neutral or park.

Mechanical safety switches for automatic transmissions are simply devices that physically block the movement of the ignition key when the transmission is in a gear (Figure 15-22). The ignition key can only be turned when the shift selector is in park or neutral.

The safety switches used with manual transmissions are usually electrical switches mounted near the gearshift lever or on the transmission housing. A clutch switch is a second type of safety switch used with manual transmissions. This electrical switch mounts on the floor or fire wall. Its contacts are closed only when the clutch pedal is fully depressed (Figure 15-23).

Section 3 Electricity

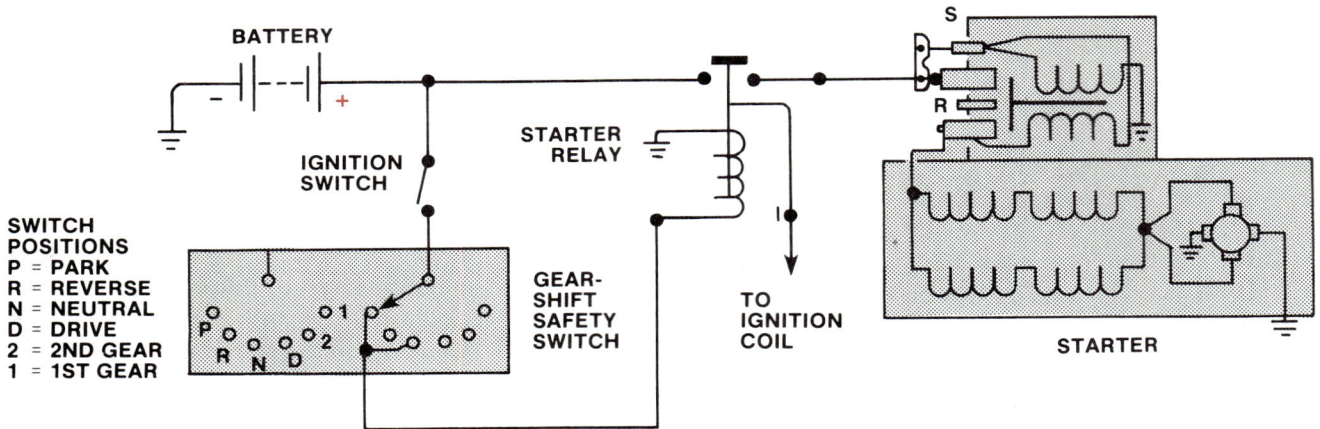

Figure 15-21 This starter safety switch must be closed before battery current can reach the starter relay.

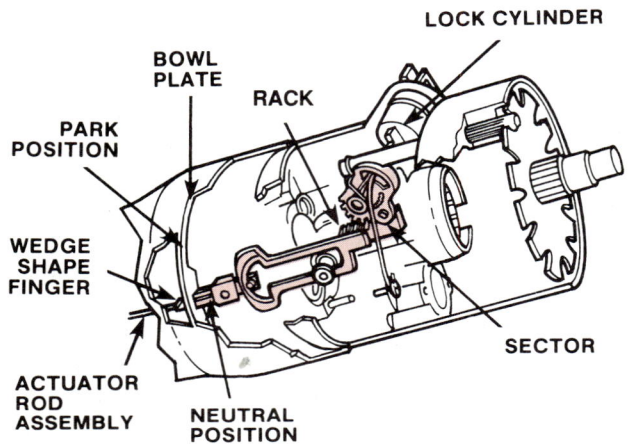

Figure 15-22 A mechanical device within the steering column blocks the movement of the ignition switch actuator rod when the transmission is in gear.

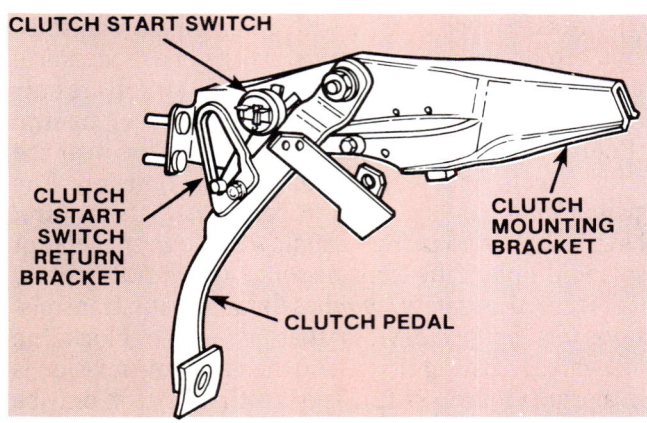

Figure 15-23 The clutch pedal must be fully depressed to close the clutch switch and complete the control circuit.

☐ STARTING SYSTEM TESTING

As mentioned earlier, the starter motor is a special type of electrical motor designed for intermittent use only. During testing, it should never be operated for more than 30 seconds without resting for 2 minutes to allow it to cool. Because the cranking motor is designed to operate under great overload for short periods of time, it provides high horsepower output for its small size.

Preliminary Checks

The cranking output obtained from the motor is also affected by the condition and charge of the battery, the wiring circuit, and the engine's cranking requirements.

The battery should be checked and charged as needed before testing. Be sure the battery is rated to meet or exceed the vehicle's manufacturer's recommendations. The voltage rating of the battery must also match the voltage rating of the starter motor.

Check the wiring for clean, tight connections. The starter motor may draw several hundred amperes or more during cranking. Loose or dirty connections will cause excessive voltage drop. Cables should also be checked for correct size.

Make certain the engine crankcase is filled with the proper weight oil as recommended by the vehicle manufacturer. Heavier than specified oil when coupled with low operating temperatures can drastically lower cranking speed to the point where the engine does not start.

Check the ignition switch for loose mounting, damaged wiring, sticking contacts, and loose connections. Check the wiring and mounting of the safety switch, if so equipped, and make certain the switch is properly adjusted. Check the mounting, wiring, and connections of the magnetic switch and starter motor. Also, be sure that the starter pinion is properly adjusted.

Safety Precautions

Almost all starting system tests must be performed while the starter motor is cranking the engine. However, the engine must not start and run during the test or the readings will be inaccurate.

To prevent the engine from starting, the ignition switch can be by-passed with a remote starter switch that allows current to flow to the starting system but not to the ignition system. On vehicles with the ignition starting by-pass in the ignition switch or the starter relay, the ignition must be disabled.

On standard ignition systems, disable the ignition by removing the secondary lead from the center of the distributor cap and grounding the lead. With electronic ignition systems or engine control systems, disconnect the wiring harness connector from the distributor.

During testing, be sure the transmission is out of gear during cranking and the parking brake is set. When servicing the battery, always follow safety precautions. Always disconnect the battery ground cable before making or breaking connections at the system's relay, solenoid, or starter motor.

Troubleshooting Procedures

A systematic troubleshooting procedure is essential when servicing the starting system. Consider the fact that nearly 80% of defective starters returned on warranty claims work perfectly when tested. This is often the result of poor or incomplete diagnosis of the starting and related charging systems. A summary of a systematic approach to starting system diagnosis is found in the Tech Manual that accompanies this textbook. Testing the starting system can be divided into area tests, which check voltage and current in the entire system, and more detailed pinpoint tests, which target one particular component or segment of the wiring circuit.

Battery Load Test (Area Test)

An engine that turns sluggishly when cranked is often not receiving sufficient voltage from the battery. The battery must be able to crank the engine under all load conditions while maintaining enough voltage to supply ignition current for starting. Perform a battery load test before performing any starting systems tests.

Cranking Voltage Test (Area Test)

The cranking voltage test measures the available voltage to the starter during cranking. To perform the test disable the ignition or use a remote starter switch to by-pass the ignition switch. Normally the remote starter switch is connected to the positive side of the battery and the starter terminal of the solenoid or relay (Figure 15-24). Refer to the service manual for specific instructions on the model car being tested. Connect the voltmeter's negative lead to a good chassis ground. Connect the positive lead to starter motor feed at the starter relay or solenoid. Compare the reading to the specifications given in the service manual. Normally, 9.6 volts is the minimum required.

Test Conclusions

If the reading is above specifications but the starter motor still cranks poorly, the starter motor is faulty. If the voltage reading is lower than specifications, a cranking current and circuit resistance tests should be performed to determine if the problem is caused by high resistance in the starter circuit or an engine problem.

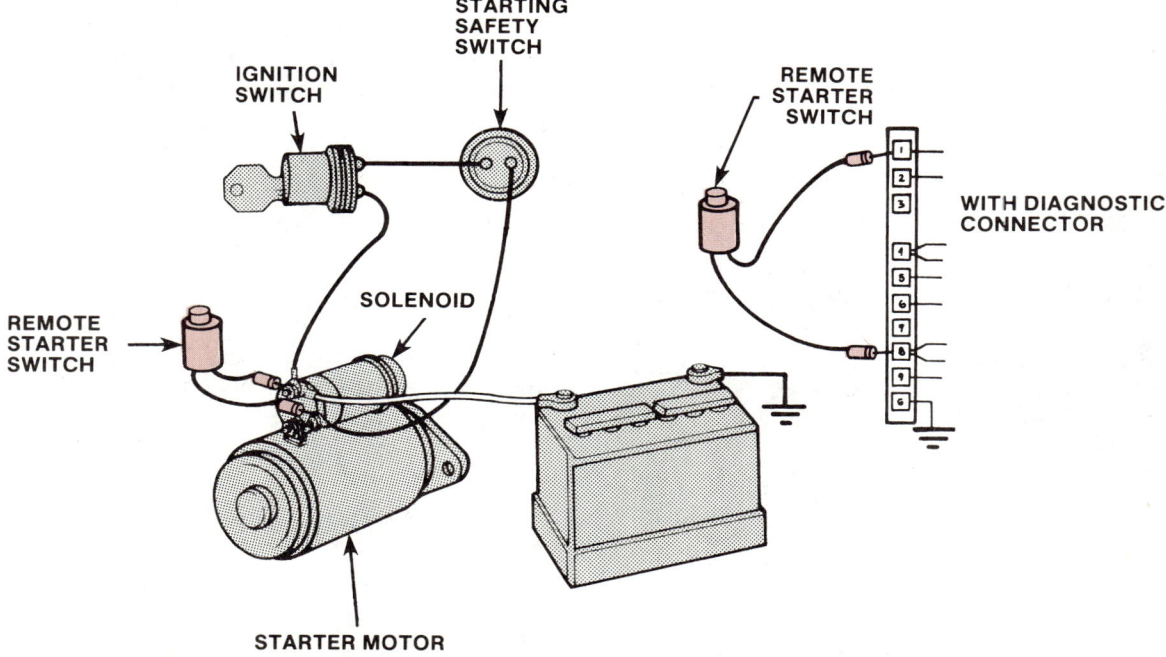

Figure 15-24 Using a remote starter switch to by-pass the control circuit and ignition system.

Cranking Current Test (Area Test)

The cranking current test measures the amount of current that the starter circuit draws to crank the engine. Knowing the amount of current draw helps to identify the cause of starter system problems. Photo Sequence 8, which is included in this chapter, outlines the procedure for conducting this test.

Nearly all starter current testers use an inductive pick-up (Figure 15-25) to measure the current draw. However, some earlier models were equipped with an ammeter that needed to be connected in series with the battery.

To conduct the cranking current test disable the ignition prior to testing. Follow the instructions given with the tester when connecting the test leads. Crank the engine for no more than 15 seconds. Observe the voltmeter. If the voltage drops below 9.6 volts, a problem is indicated. Observe the ammeter and compare the reading to specifications.

Test Conclusions

Normally the expected current draw is approximately equal to the cubic inch displacement of the engine. Table 15-1 summarizes the most probable causes of too low or high starter motor current draw. If the problem appears to be caused by excessive resistance in the system, conduct an insulated circuit resistance test.

Insulated Circuit Resistance Test

The complete starter circuit is made up of the insulated circuit and the bare ground circuit. The insulated circuit includes all of the high current cables and connections from the battery to the starter motor.

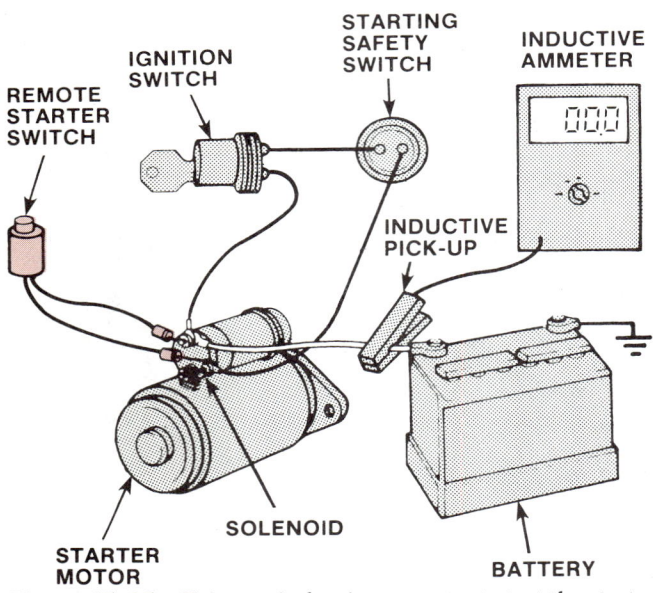

Figure 15-25 Using an inductive ammeter to test the starter current draw.

TABLE 15-1 RESULT OF CRANKING CURRENT TESTING

Problem	Possible Cause
Low current draw	Undercharged or defective battery. Excessive resistance in circuit due to faulty components or connections.
High current draw	Short in starter motor. Mechanical resistance due to binding engine or starter system component failure or misalignment.

To test the insulated circuit for high resistance disable the ignition or by-pass the ignition switch with a remote starter switch. Connect the positive (+) lead of the voltmeter to the battery's positive (+) terminal post or nut. By connecting the lead to the cable, the point of high resistance (cable-to-post connection) may be by-passed. Connect the negative (-) lead of the voltmeter to the starter terminal at the solenoid or relay. Crank the engine and record the voltmeter reading. If the reading is within specifications (usually 0.2 to 0.6 voltage drop), the insulated circuit does not have excessive resistance. Proceed to the ground circuit resistance test outlined in the next section. If the reading indicates a voltage loss above specifications, move the negative lead of the tester progressively toward the battery, cranking the engine at each test point. Normally, a voltage drop of 0.1 volt is the maximum allowed across a length of cable.

Test Conclusions

When a noticeable amount of voltage drop is observed, the trouble is located between that point and the preceding point tested. It is either a damaged cable or poor connection, an undersized wire, or possibly a bad contact assembly within the solenoid. Repair or replace any damaged wiring or faulty connections. Refer to Table 15-2 to find the maximum allowable voltage drops for the starter circuit.

Starter Relay By-pass Test

The starter relay by-pass test is a simple way to determine if the relay is operational. First, disable the ignition. Connect a jumper cable between the battery's

TABLE 15-2 MAXIMUM VOLTAGE DROPS

	6-volt	12-volt
Each cable	0.1	0.2
Each connection	0.1	0.1
Starter solenoid switch	0.3	0.3

PHOTO SEQUENCE 8

◻ USING A VOLT AND AMP TESTER TO TEST THE BATTERY AND THE STARTING AND CHARGING SYSTEMS

P8-1 Testing the battery and starting and charging systems begins with a visual inspection of the battery and its cables. Make sure they are clean and free of corrosion.

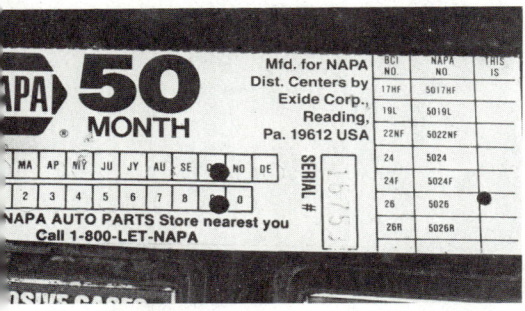

P8-2 The battery's label normally contains all of the information needed to test it. Locate the CCA rating of the battery on the label.

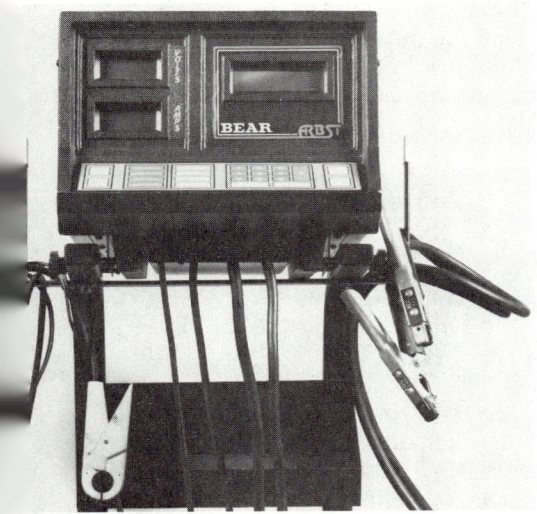

P8-3 A typical battery and starting and charging system tester.

P8-4 Testing begins with connecting the positive and negative tester leads to the battery.

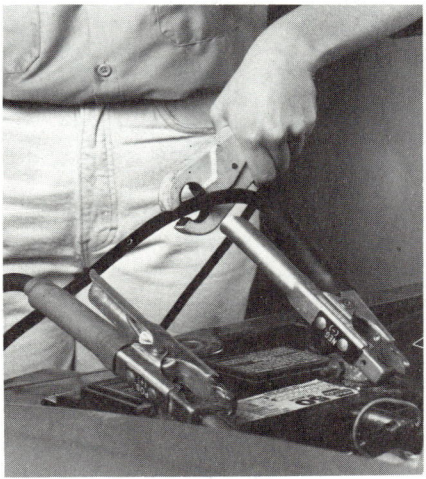

P8-5 When testing the battery, the tester's ampere pick-up probe must be installed around the tester's negative cable.

P8-6 The first test will measure the battery's capacity. For this test (known as the battery load test) both the voltage and amperage meters are observed.

P8-7 The tester puts a load or causes a current drain on the battery. The amount of load is determined by the battery's CCA rating. Some machines require the technician to manually set the load to an amount that draws one-half of the CCA rating. This tester automatically sets the load after the CCA is programmed into the tester and the load activation button is depressed.

P8-8 This battery checked out fine. Its voltage decreased to an amount above 9.6 volts while under a load of 156 amperes for 15 seconds.

(continued)

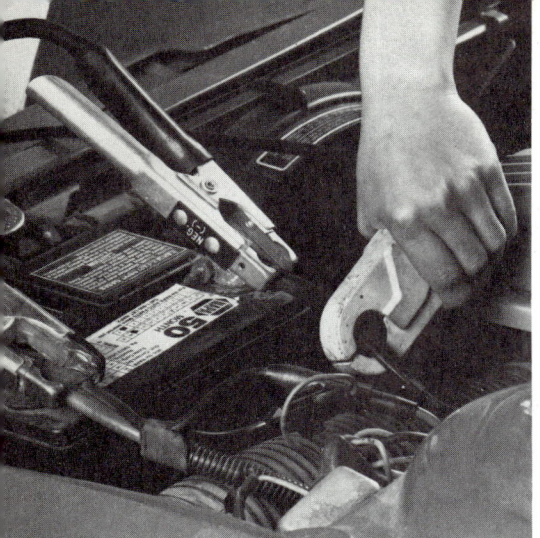

P8-9 To test the starting and charging systems, the ampere pick-up probe must be repositioned around the battery's negative cable.

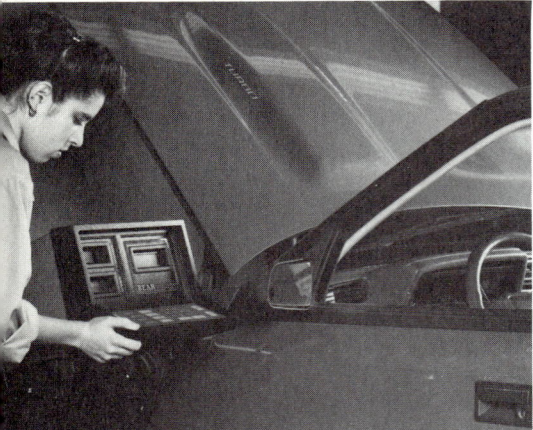

P8-10 To observe the tester's meters during this test, the tester should be placed where it can be easily seen from the driver's seat.

P8-11 Prior to testing the starting system, disable the ignition system.

P8-12 Turn the ignition key to allow the starter to rotate. Observe the readings on the tester. This starter drew 170 amperes and dropped voltage to 9.82 volts. These readings should be compared to the specifications given in the service manual.

P8-13 To test the charging system, it is recommended that engine speed be monitored. Therefore, connect a tachometer to the engine. Some testers, such as the one shown, are equipped with a tachometer that monitors ignition pulses at the battery.

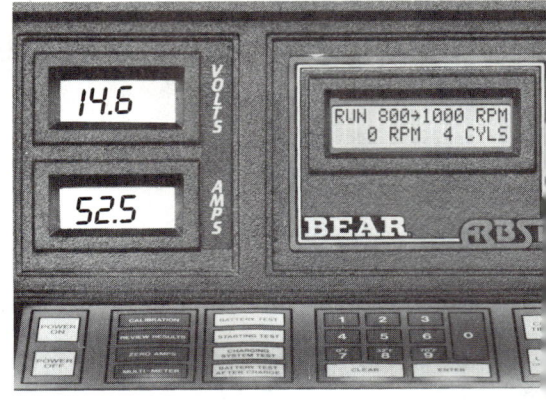

P8-14 At fast idle or 1500 rpm, the charging system will deliver a maximum amount of charge to the battery. This charging system is providing 14.6 volts at 52.5 amperes. Readings should be compared to specifications.

P8-15 If the readings are low, this may indicate that there is a fault in the charging system or that the battery is fully charged and not allowing the alternator to work at its peak. To determine the cause, the voltage regulator should be by-passed according to the procedures outlined in the service manual.

P8-16 With the regulator by-passed, this alternator increased its voltage output. This indicates that the regulator is regulating voltage output. The amperage reading is also well within specifications. Therefore, the charging system is functioning properly. ■

positive (+) terminal and the starter relay starter terminal. This by-passes the relay. Crank the engine.

Test Conclusions

If the engine cranks with the jumper installed and did not before the relay was by-passed, the starter relay is defective and should be replaced.

Ground Circuit Resistance Test

The ground circuit provides the return path to the battery for the current supplied to the starter by the insulated circuit. This circuit includes the starter-to-engine, engine-to-chassis, and chassis-to-battery ground terminal connections.

To test the ground circuit for high resistance, disable the ignition, or by-pass the ignition switch with a remote starter switch. Refer to Figure 15-26 for the proper test connections. Crank the engine and record the voltmeter reading.

Test Conclusions

Good results would be less than 0.2 voltage drop for a 12-volt system. Voltages in excess of these indicate the presence of a poor ground circuit connection, resulting from a loose starter motor mounting bolt, a poor battery ground terminal post connector, or a damaged or undersized ground system wire from the battery to the engine block. Isolate the cause of excessive voltage drop in the same manner as recommended in the insulated circuit resistance test by moving the positive (+) voltmeter lead progressively back toward the battery. If the ground circuit tests out satisfactorily and a starter problem exists, move on to the control circuit test.

Control Circuit Test

The control circuit test examines all the wiring and components used to control the magnetic switch, whether it is a relay, solenoid acting as a relay, or a starter motor-mounted solenoid.

High resistance in the solenoid switch circuit reduces the current flow through the solenoid windings, which can cause improper functioning of the solenoid. In some cases of high resistance, it may not function at all. Improper functioning of the solenoid switch generally results in the burning of the solenoid switch contacts, causing high resistance in the starter motor circuit.

Check the vehicle wiring diagram, if possible, to identify all control circuit components. These normally include the ignition switch, safety switch, the starter solenoid winding, or a separate relay.

To perform the test, disable the ignition system. Connect the positive meter lead to the battery's positive terminal and the negative meter lead to the starter switch terminal on the solenoid or relay. Crank the engine and record the voltmeter reading.

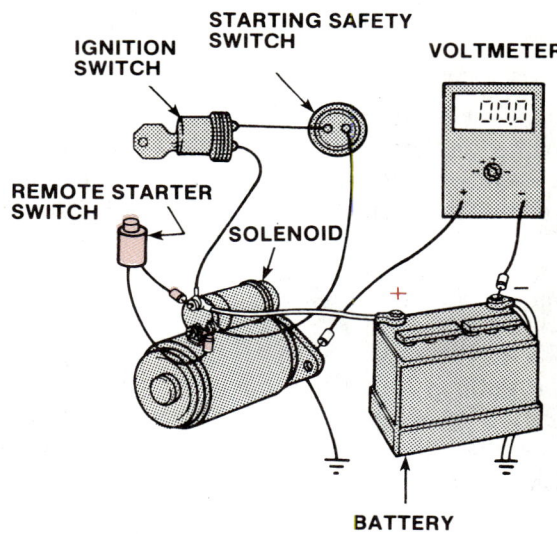

Figure 15-26 Setup for testing the resistance of the ground circuit.

Test Conclusions

Generally, good results would be less than 0.5 volt, indicating that the circuit condition is good. If voltage reads more than 0.5 volts, it is usually an indication of excessive resistance. However, on certain vehicles, a slightly higher voltage loss may be normal.

Identify the point of high resistance by moving the negative test lead back toward the battery's positive lead, eliminating one wire or component at a time (Figure 15-27).

A reading of more than 0.1 volt across any one wire or switch is usually an indication of trouble. If a high reading is obtained across the safety switch used on automatic transmissions, check the adjustment of the switch according to the manufacturer's service manual. Clutch-operated safety switches cannot be adjusted. They must be replaced.

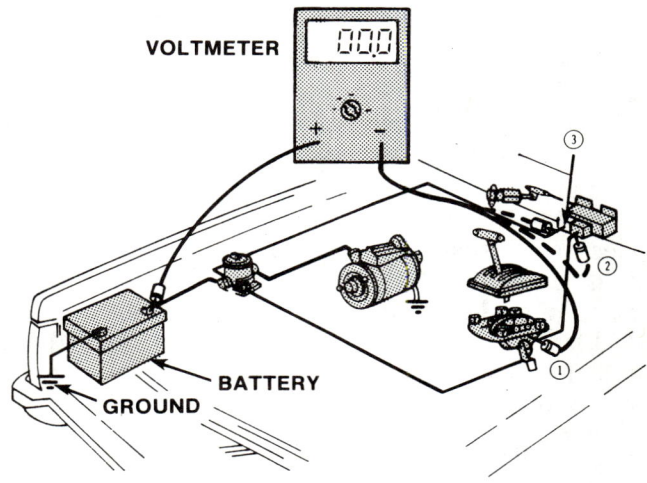

Figure 15-27 Typical test points to use when checking control circuit resistance.

Testing Starter Drive Components

This test detects a slipping starter drive without removing the starter from the vehicle. First, disable the ignition or by-pass the ignition switch with a remote starter switch. Turn the ignition switch to start and hold it in this position for several seconds. Repeat the procedure at least three times to detect an intermittent condition.

Test Conclusions

If the starter cranks the engine smoothly, this is an indication of acceptable starter drive. If the engine stops cranking and the starter spins noisely at high speed, the drive is slipping and should be replaced.

If the drive is not slipping, but the engine is not being cranked, inspect the flywheel for missing or damaged teeth. Remove the starter from the vehicle and check its drive components. Inspect the pinion gear teeth for wear and damage. Test the overrunning clutch mechanism. If good, the overriding clutch should turn freely in one direction, but not in the other. A bad clutch turns freely in both directions or not at all. If a drive locks up, it can destroy the starter by allowing the starter to spin at 15 times engine speed.

The weak point in the movable pole starter is the pole shoe that pulls in toward the armature to engage the starter. This starter requires a minimum of 10.5 volts and about 300 amperes to operate. Otherwise, it simply clicks and does not engage.

As a movable pole starter wears, the pivot bushing sometimes hangs up and prevents the movable pole shoe from being pulled down. When this happens, the starter spins but fails to engage the flywheel.

A similar problem can occur on solenoid-actuated starters. If the solenoid is too weak to overcome the force of the return springs, the starter does not operate.

□ ALTERNATING CURRENT CHARGING SYSTEMS

The charging system converts the mechanical energy of the engine into electrical energy. During cranking, the battery supplies all of the vehicle's electrical energy. However, once the engine is running, the charging system is responsible for producing enough energy to meet the demands of all the loads in the electrical system, while also recharging the battery (Figure 15-28). With more and more cars featuring electronic steering, brakes, suspension, transmissions, and air-conditioning systems—not to mention traditional items like wipers, lights, and horn—the demands on the charging system are great.

For many years, the automotive charging systems produced direct current, or DC, using a belt-driven generator that operated like a typical electric motor. In a DC generator a conductor (armature) spins inside a

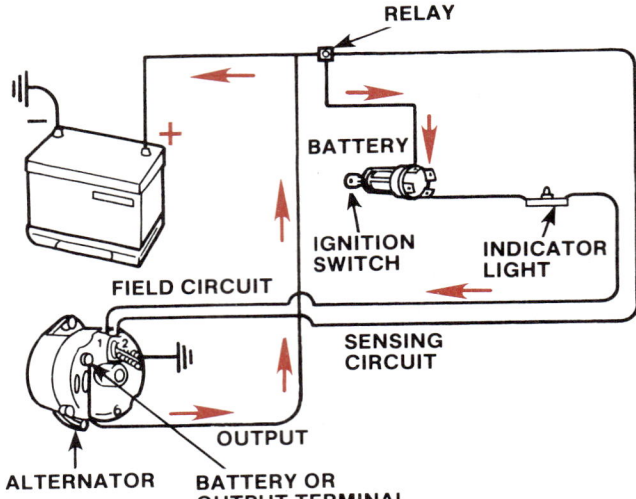

Figure 15-28 Component and current flow in an AC charging system.

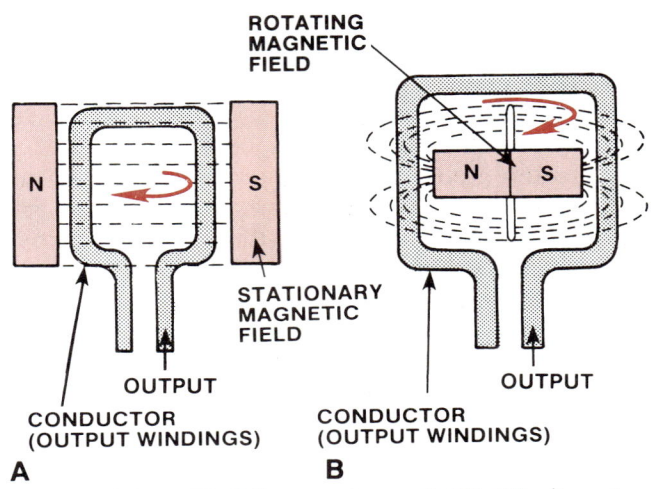

Figure 15-29 (A) DC generator and (B) AC alternator construction.

stationary magnetic field (Figure 15-29A). This induces an output voltage in the conductors. If this principle is unclear, magnetic induction is discussed in an earlier chapter.

These DC charging systems offered limited voltage output, particularly at low speeds or idle. For this reason, alternating current, or AC, charging systems were developed and are now universally used. Unlike the generators they replaced, alternators are compact, lightweight, and efficient at all engine speeds.

Alternators use a design that is basically the reverse of a generator. In an alternator, a spinning magnetic field rotates inside stationary conductors (Figure 15-29B). As the spinning north and south poles of the magnetic field pass the conducting wires, they induce voltage that first flows in one direction and then in the opposite direction. Because automotive electrical systems operate on direct current, this alternating current

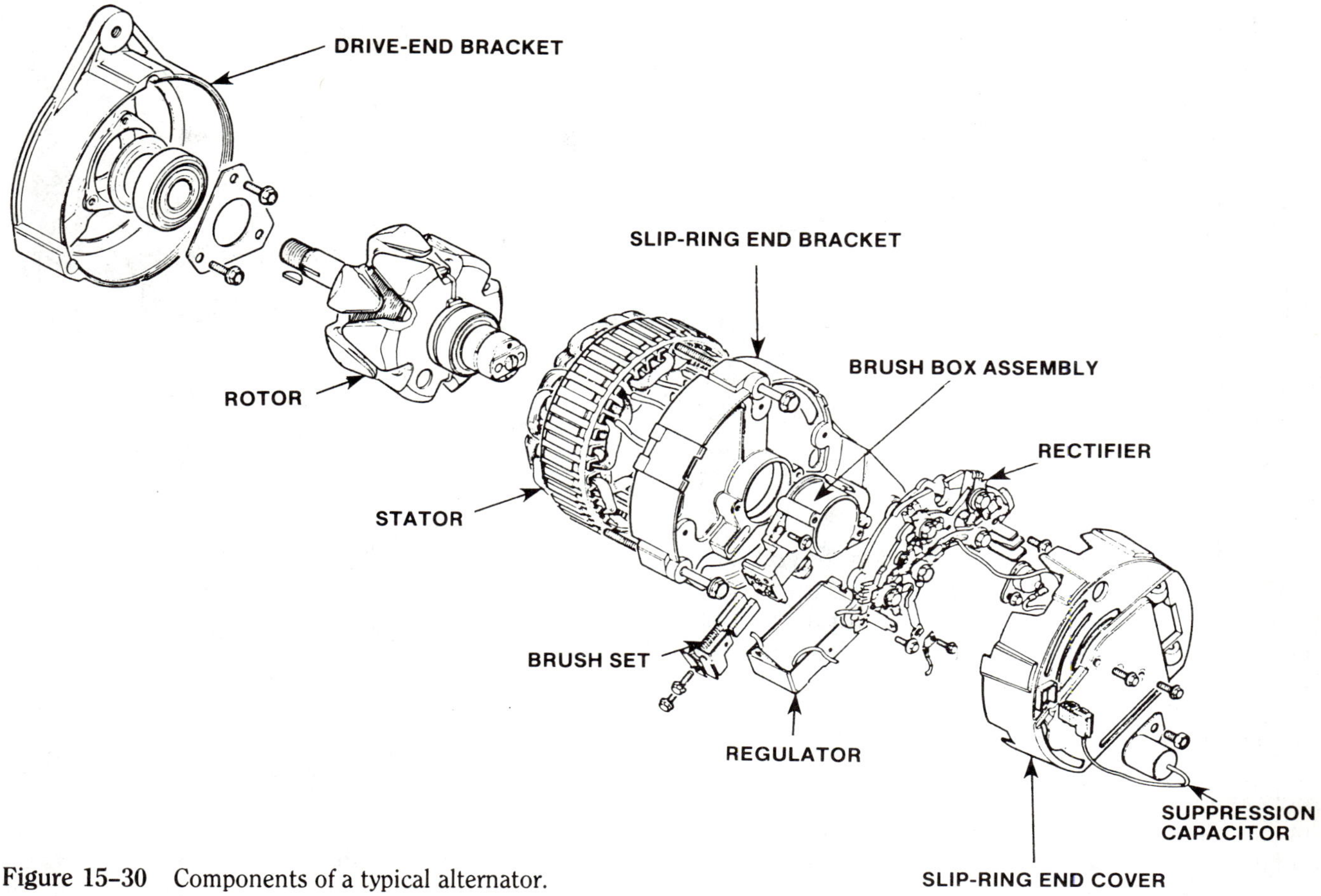

Starting and Charging Systems

Figure 15-30   Components of a typical alternator.

must be changed or rectified into direct current. This is done using an arrangement of diodes that will be explained later in the chapter.

Alternator Construction

Figure 15-30 illustrates the major parts of an alternator.

Rotor

The rotor assembly consists of a drive shaft, coil, and two pole pieces (Figure 15-31). A pulley mounted on the shaft end allows the rotor to be spun by a belt driven from the crankshaft pulley.

The rotor produces the alternator's rotating magnetic field. The coil is simply a series of conductive windings wrapped around an iron core. The core is located between the two pole pieces. The magnetic field is generated by passing a small amount (4.0 to 6.5 amperes) of current through the coil windings. As current flows through the coil, the core is magnetized and the pole pieces assume the magnetic polarity of the end of the core that they touch. Thus, one pole piece has a north polarity and the other has a south polarity. The extensions of the pole pieces, known as fingers, form the actual magnetic poles. A typical rotor has fourteen poles, seven north and seven south, with the

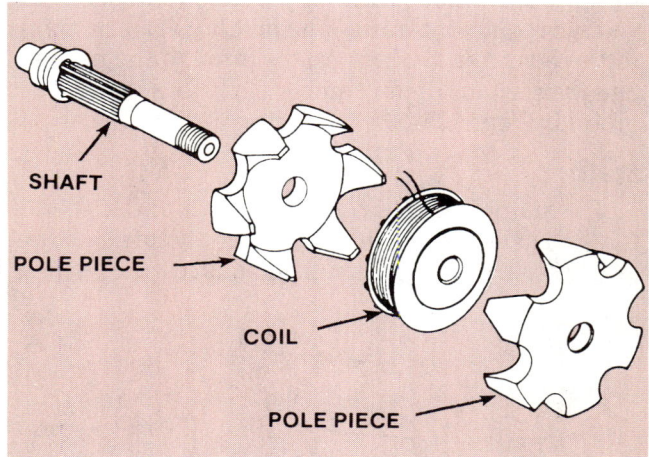

Figure 15-31   The rotor is made up of a coil, pole pieces, and a shaft.

magnetic field between the pole pieces moving from the N poles to the adjacent S poles (Figure 15-32).

Slip Rings and Brushes

Current to create the magnetic field is supplied to the coil from one of two sources, the battery, or when the engine is running, the alternator itself. In either case, the current is passed through the alternator's

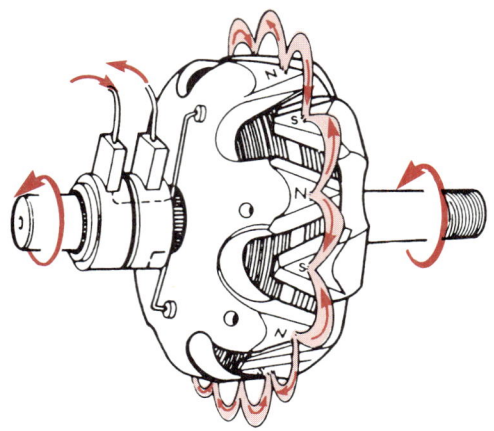

Figure 15-32 The magnetic field moves from the N poles, or fingers, to the S poles.

voltage regulator before being applied to the coil. The voltage regulator varies the amount of current supplied. Increasing field current through the coil increases the strength of the magnetic field. This, in turn, increases alternator voltage output. Decreasing the field voltage to the coil has the opposite effect. Output voltage decreases.

Slip rings and brushes conduct current to the rotor. Most alternators have two slip rings mounted directly on the rotor shaft. They are insulated from the shaft and each other. Each end of the field coil connects to one of the slip rings. A carbon brush located on each slip ring carries the current to and from the field coil. Current is transmitted from the field terminal of the voltage regulator through the first brush and slip ring to the field coil. Current passes through the field coil and the second slip ring and brush before returning to ground (Figure 15-33).

Stator

The stator is the stationary member of the alternator. It is made up of a number of conductors, or wires, into which the magnetic field induces the voltage.

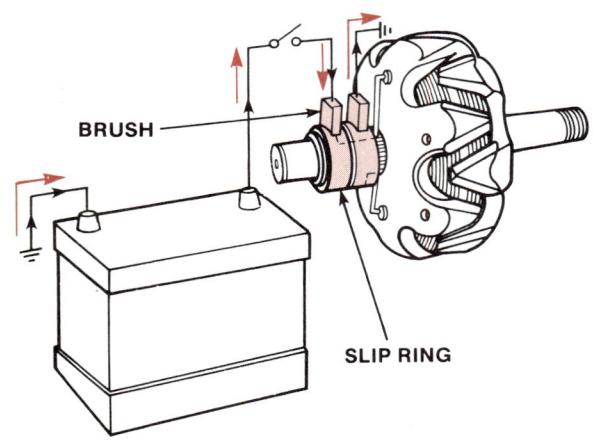

Figure 15-33 Current is carried by the brushes to the rotor windings via the slip rings.

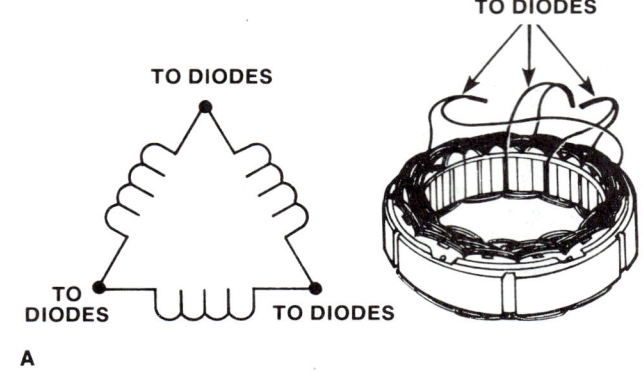

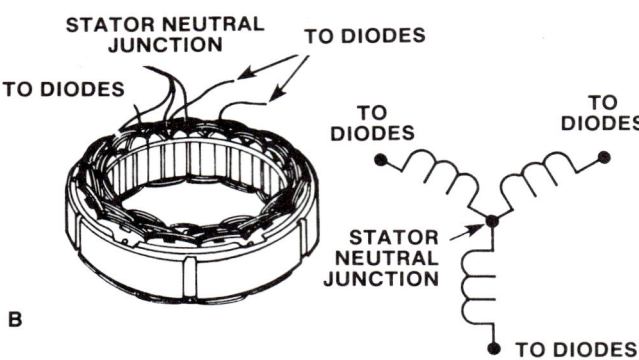

Figure 15-34 (A) Delta and (B) wye wound stators.

Most alternators use three windings to generate the required amperage output. They are placed in slightly different positions so their electrical pulses are staggered in either a delta configuration or a wye configuration (Figure 15-34). The delta winding received its name because its shape resembles the greek letter delta, Δ. The wye winding resembles the letter Y. Alternators use one or the other. Usually, lower output alternators use the wye configuration, while higher output alternators use delta.

The rotor fits inside the stator (Figure 15-35). A small air gap between the two allows the magnetic field of the rotor to energize all of the stator windings at the same time. The generation of AC can be quite high if needed.

Alternating current produces first a positive pulse and then a negative pulse. This sine wave can be represented on an oscilloscope (Figure 15-36). Notice that the complete waveforms start at zero, go positive, then drop to zero again before turning negative. The angle and polarity of the field coil fingers are what cause this sine wave in the stator. When the north pole magnetic field cuts across the stator wire, it generates a positive voltage within the wire. When the south polarity magnetic field cuts across the stator wire, a negative voltage is induced in the wire. A single loop of wire energized by a single north then a south results in a single-phase voltage. Remember that there are three stator windings overlapped. This produces the overlapping sine wave (Figure 15-37). This voltage, since it

Starting and Charging Systems 383

Figure 15-35 A small air gap exists between the spinning rotor and the stationary stator.

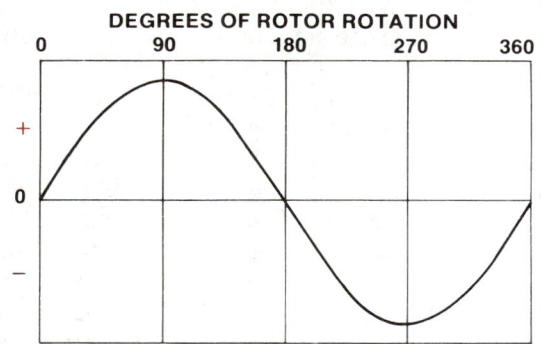

Figure 15-36 Sine wave from a stator, as displayed on an oscilloscope.

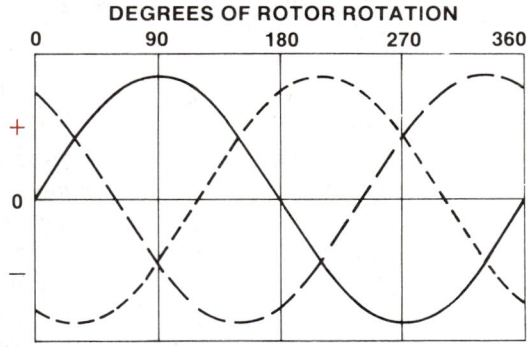

Figure 15-37 Three-phase sine wave.

was produced by three windings, is called three-phase voltage.

End Frame Assembly

The end frame assembly, or housing, is made of two pieces of cast aluminum. It contains the bearings for the end of the rotor shaft where the drive pulley is mounted. Each end frame also has built-in air ducts so

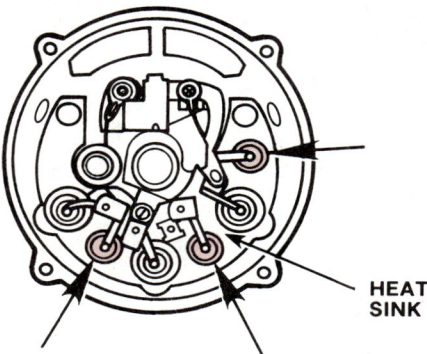

Figure 15-38 Three positive diodes mount directly onto the heat sink.

the air from the rotor shaft fan can pass through the alternator. Normally, a heat sink containing three positive rectifier diodes is attached to the rear end frame. Heat can pass easily from these diodes to the moving air (Figure 15-38). Three negative rectifier diodes are contained in the end frame itself. Because the end frames are bolted together and then bolted directly to the engine, the end frame assembly is part of the electrical ground path. This means that anything connected to the housing that is not insulated from the housing is grounded.

Alternator Operation

As mentioned earlier, alternators produce alternating current that must be converted, or rectified, to DC using diodes.

DC Rectification

Figure 15-39 shows that if AC runs through the diode, the negative pulses are blocked off to produce the scope pattern shown. If the diode is reversed, it blocks off current during the positive pulse and allows the negative pulse to flow (Figure 15-40). Because only half of the AC current pulses (either the positive or the negative) is able to pass, this is called half-wave rectification. This type of output would not be suitable in an automotive electrical system since current is available only half of the time.

By adding more diodes to the circuit, more of the AC is rectified. When all of the AC is rectified, full-wave rectification occurs.

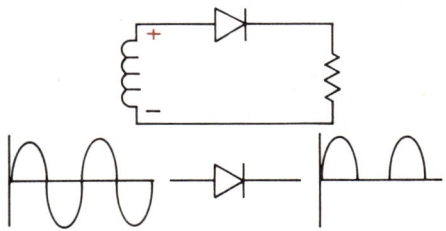

Figure 15-39 Half-wave rectification, diode positively biased.

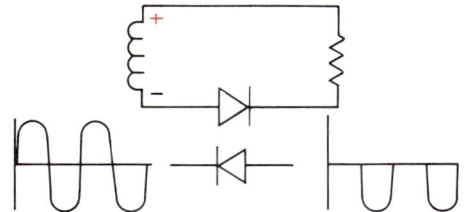

Figure 15-40 Half-wave rectification, diode negatively biased.

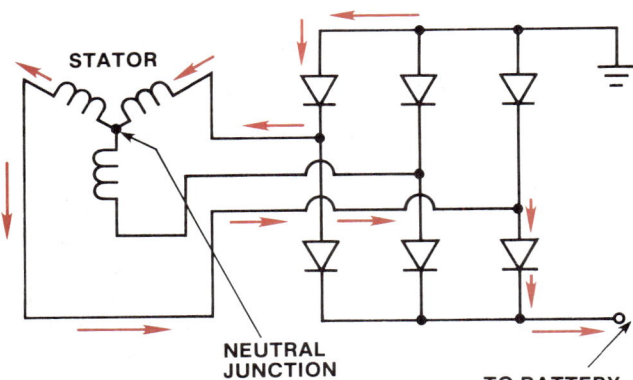

Figure 15-41 Wye stator wired to six diodes.

Full-wave rectification for stator windings requires another circuit with similar characteristics. Figure 15-41 shows a wye stator having two diodes attached to each winding. One diode is insulated, or positive, and the other is grounded, or negative. The center of the Y contains a common point for all windings. It can have a connection attached to it. It is called the stator neutral junction. At any time during the rotor movement, two windings are in series and the third coil is neutral and inactive. As the rotor revolves, it energizes the different sets of windings in different directions. However, the uniform result is that current in any direction through two windings in series produces the required DC for the battery.

The diode action does not change when the stator and diodes are wired into a delta pattern. Figure 15-42

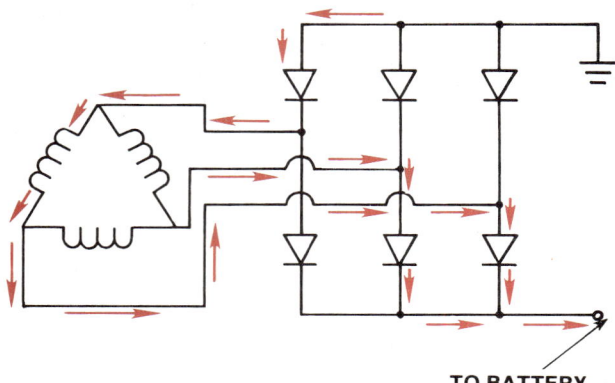

Figure 15-42 Delta stator wired to six diodes.

shows the major difference. Instead of having two windings in series, the windings are in parallel. Thus, more current is available from a delta wound alternator because the parallel paths allow more current to flow through the diodes. Nevertheless, the action of the diodes remains the same.

Voltage Regulation

A functioning alternator must be regulated to be efficient. A voltage regulator controls the amount of voltage produced by the alternator and thus the voltage level in the charging circuit. Without a voltage regulator, the battery would be overcharged and the voltage level in the electrical systems would rise to the point where lights would burn out and fuses and fusible links would blow. Controlling the voltage is particularly important for on-board computers and other digital equipment. Microprocessors and electronic sensors and switches are easily damaged by voltage spikes and high-voltage levels.

The regulation of the charging circuit is accomplished by varying the amount of field current flowing through the rotor. Output is high when the field current is high and low when the field current is low. The operation of the regulator is comparable to that of a variable resistor in series with the field coil (Figure 15-43). If the resistance the regulator offers is low, the field current is high and if the resistance is high, the field current is low. The amount of resistance in series with the field coil determines the amount of field current, the strength of the rotor's magnetic field, and thus the amount of alternator output. The resistance offered by the regulator varies according to charging system demands or needs. These needs are determined by the regulator as it interprets voltage and temperature inputs.

Voltage Input

Charging voltage is critically important to the process of fully charging the battery. If the charging voltage is only 11.5 volts, the battery nevers come all the way up on charge. Figure 15-44 shows what would happen to the vehicle system in this case. Not only does the entire vehicle operate at 11.5 volts, but current is being drawn from the battery instead of charging it. By raising the voltage of the alternator above the voltage of the battery (Figure 15-45), the alternator

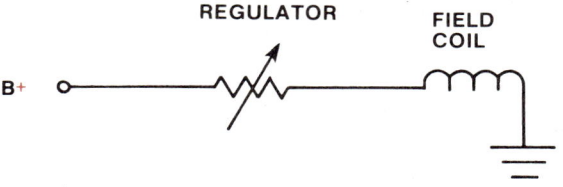

Figure 15-43 The voltage regulator acts like a variable resistor to control voltage.

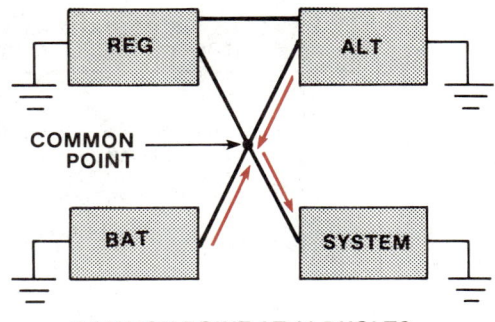

Figure 15-44 11.5 volts with current flowing out of the battery.

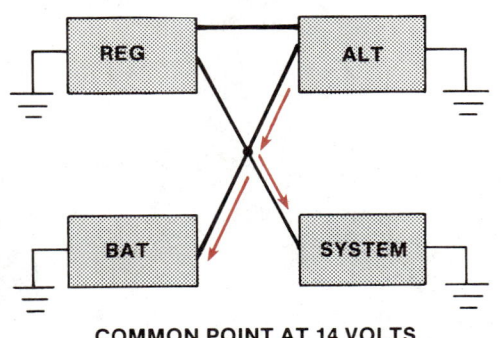

Figure 15-45 14 volts with current flowing into the battery.

now becomes the source of current for the vehicle and of current to charge the battery. Most regulators are set for a system voltage between 14.0 to 14.7 volts so that the charging voltage is slightly higher than the 12.6 volts of the battery. A full charge is insured.

In order to regulate the charging system, the regulator must have system voltage as an input. This voltage is also called sensing system voltage because the regulator is sensing system voltage. The regulator determines the need for charging current according to the level of the sensing voltage. When the sensing voltage is less than the regulator setting, the regulator increases the field current in order to increase the charging current. As sensing voltage rises, a corresponding decrease in field current and system output occurs. Thus, the regulator responds to changes in system voltage by increasing or decreasing charging current. For example, if a car is running down the road with no accessories on and a fully charged battery, the regulator senses a high system voltage because the battery is fully charged. So it maintains the charging voltage at a level sufficient enough to run the ignition system and to supply a 2- to 4-ampere trickle charge to the battery. If the headlights are turned on, the additional draw drops or loads the battery voltage down. When the regulator senses this reduced voltage through the sensing circuit, it reduces the field circuit resistance in order to increase the field current and, as a result,

Starting and Charging Systems

TABLE 15-3 REGULATOR TEMPERATURE VS. VOLTAGE

Temperature	Volts	
	Minimum	Maximum
20°F	14.3	15.3
80°F	13.8	14.4
140°F	13.3	14.0
Over 140°F	Less than 13.8	—

the charging current. This adjustment takes place in less than a second. Of course, turning off accessories reverses the process. In response to a system voltage rise, the regulator reduces field current and alternator output.

Temperature Input

Temperature is the second input to the regulator. All regulators are temperature compensated (Table 15-3), because the battery is less willing to accept a charge if it is cold. So, as the temperature goes down, the regulator raises the system voltage until it is at a level that the battery readily accepts. In this way, the battery can be brought up on charge quickly, even in very cold climates.

Regulator Circuits

There are basically two ways the regulator circuit is connected to the alternator. The A-circuit has a variable resistor wired between the field terminal of the alternator and ground. Field current is regulated by changing the resistance in the ground path as shown in Figure 15-46. This circuit is commonly used with solid-state regulators.

A B-circuit has the regulator variable resistor between the B+ feed and the field coil as shown in Figure 15-47. The field coil is grounded inside the alternator. The result is the same as it was in the A-circuit. B-circuits are often used with older electromagnetic voltage regulators.

Isolated Field Circuit

In an isolated field alternator, B+ and ground are picked up externally. It is usually easily identified

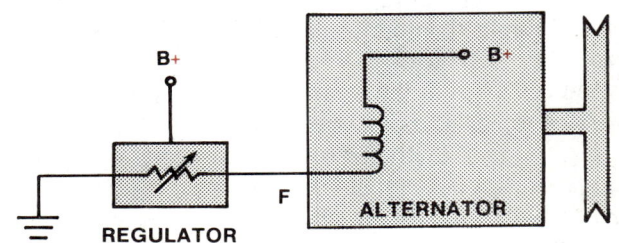

Figure 15-46 A-circuit.

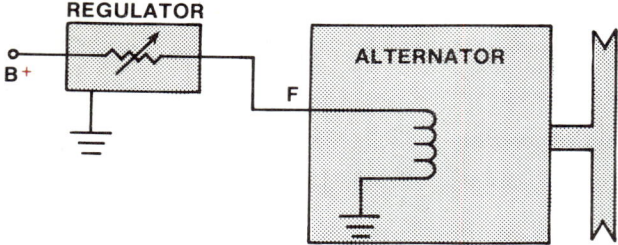

Figure 15-47 B-circuit.

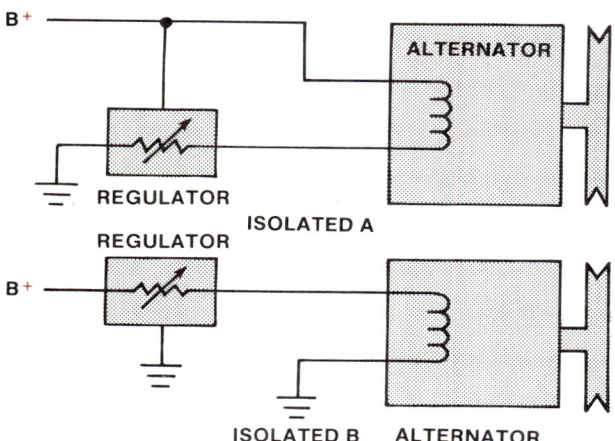

Figure 15-48 Isolated A- and B-circuits.

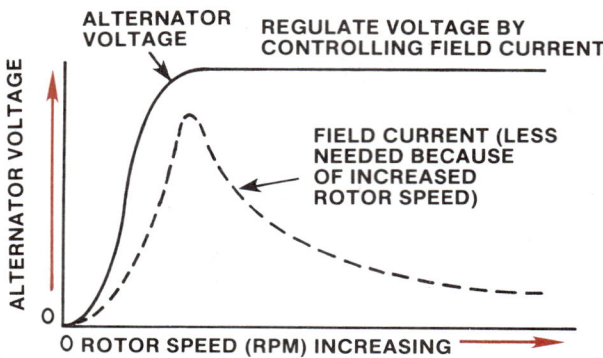

Figure 15-49 This chart shows the relationship between rotor speed, current in the field windings, and output voltage. As the rotor speed increases, field current is reduced to keep the regulated voltage controlled.

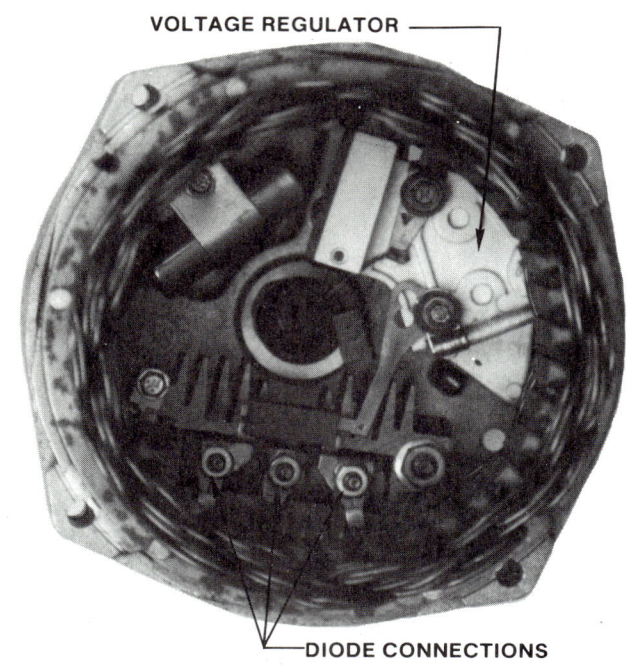

Figure 15-50 An alternator with an internally-mounted voltage regulator.

because it has two field wires attached to the outside of the alternator case. Isolated is another way of saying insulated or not connected. An isolated field alternator can have its regulator on either the ground (A-circuit) side or on the B+ (B-circuit) side. Both an isolated A-circuit and an isolated B-circuit are shown in Figure 15-48. Isolated field circuits are found mainly in Chrysler vehicles.

Voltage Regulator Design

All voltage regulators are designed to control the amount of current flowing through the field windings. The relationship between rotor speed, field current, and the regulated voltage is shown in Figure 15-49. In order to keep the regulated voltage controlled, the field current is reduced as the rotor speed increases.

Integrated circuit voltage regulators are now being used on many vehicles. This is the most compact regulator design. All of the control circuitry and components are located on a single silicon chip. The chip is sealed in a plastic module and mounted either inside or on the back of the alternator (Figure 15-50). Integrated circuit regulators are also nonserviceable and must be replaced if defective.

Figure 15-51 illustrates a solid-state integrated regulator. It mounts inside the alternator slip ring end frame along with the brush holder assembly. All voltage regulator parts are enclosed in a solid mold. The rectifier bridge contains the six diodes needed to change AC to DC that is then available at the output battery terminal. Field current is supplied through a diode trio, which is connected to the stator windings. Figure 15-52 illustrates the wiring diagram for this charging circuit.

FAIL-SAFE CIRCUITS To prevent simple electrical problems from causing high voltage outputs that can damage delicate electronic components, many voltage regulators contain fail-safe circuits.

A step-by-step explanation of how these circuits operate can be quite involved. It is sufficient to know what a fail-safe circuit does, not how it does it. If wire connections to the alternator become corroded or accidently disconnected, the regulator's fail-safe circuits may limit voltage output that might rise to dangerous

Starting and Charging Systems 387

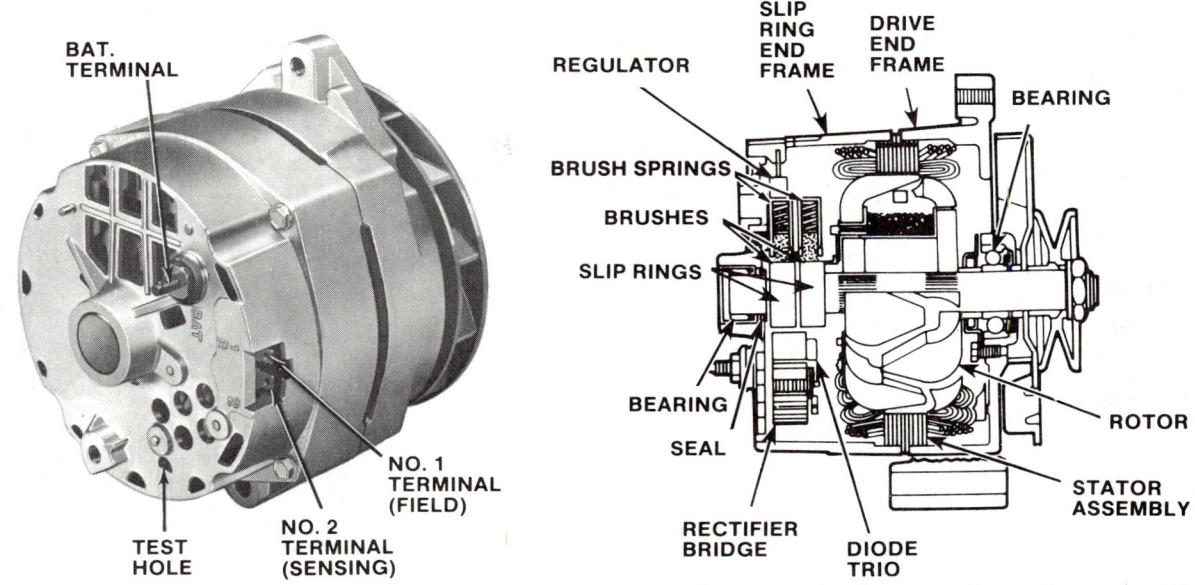

Figure 15-51 Component locations of an alternator with an internally-mounted voltage regulator. *Courtesy of General Motors Corp.*

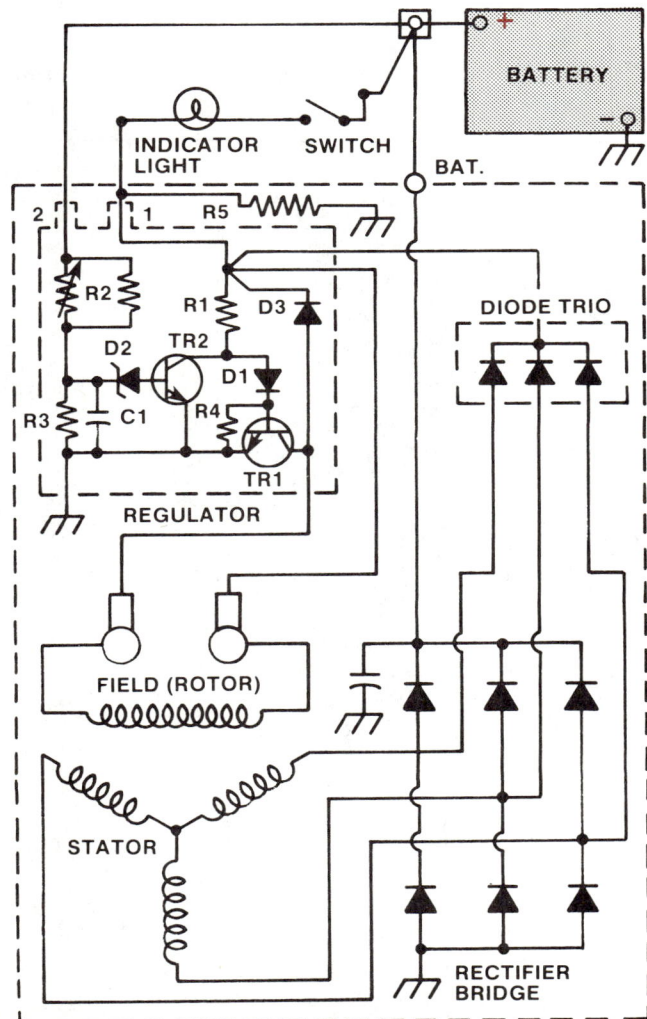

Figure 15-52 Charging circuit wiring diagram of the alternator shown in Figure 15-51. *Courtesy of Chrysler Motors*

levels. Under certain conditions the fail-safe circuits may prevent the alternator from charging at all. A fusible line in the fail-safe circuitry confines damage to the alternator. Delicate electronic components in other vehicle systems are not damaged.

Computer Regulation

On a growing number of late-model vehicles, a separate voltage regulator is no longer used. Instead the voltage regulation circuitry is located in the vehicle's electronic control module or unit (Figure 15-53). The module computer is used to control current to the field windings in the rotor.

This type of system does not control rotor field current by acting like a variable resistor. Instead, the computer switches or pulses field current on and off at a fixed frequency of about 400 cycles per second. By varying on-off times a correct average field current is produced to provide correct alternator output. At high engine speeds with little electrical system load, field circuit on time may be as low as 10%. At low engine speeds with high loads, the computer may energize the field circuit 90% of the time to generate the higher average field current needed to meet output demands.

A significant feature of this system is its ability to vary the amount of voltage according to vehicle requirements and ambient temperatures. This precise control allows the use of smaller, lighter, storage batteries. It also reduces the magnetic drag of the alternator, increasing engine output by several horsepower. Precise management of the charging rate can result in increased gas mileage and eliminate potential rough idle problems caused by parasitic voltage loss at low idling speeds. Most importantly, it allows the computer's diagnostic capabilities to be used in troubleshoot-

388 Section 3 Electricity

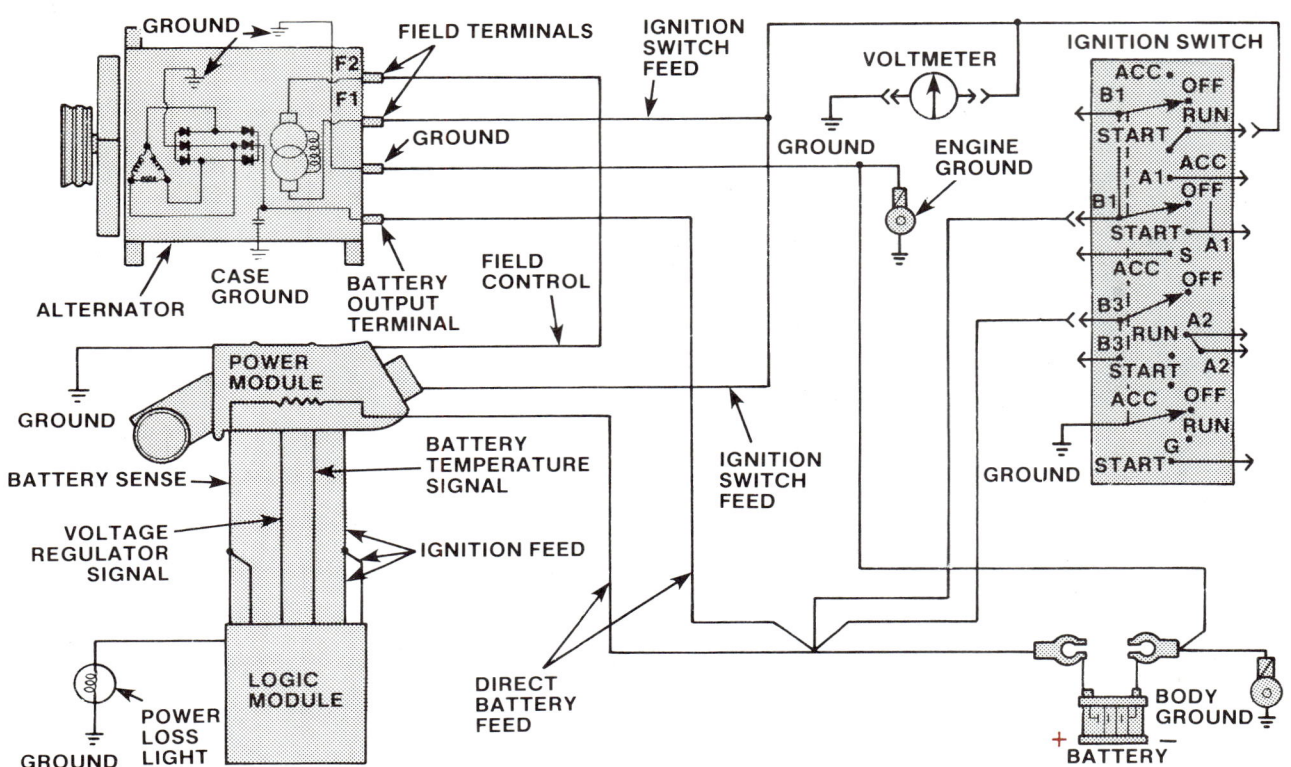

Figure 15-53 Wiring diagram of a charging system that uses the on-board computer system for voltage regulation control. *Courtesy of Chrysler Motors*

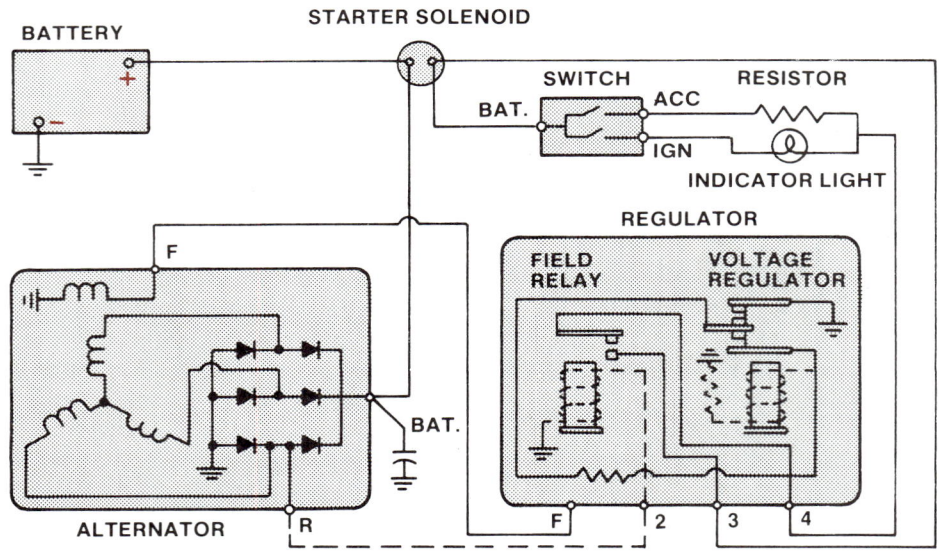

Figure 15-54 Older electromagnetically-controlled alternator that uses solenoid-controlled field and voltage relays.

ing charging system problems, such as low or high voltage outputs.

Older Voltage Regulator Designs

Older vehicles may be equipped with electromagnetic or partially transistorized voltage regulators. Electromagnetic regulators use two solenoid-operated contact point relays to control the charging circuit (Figure 15-54).

A field relay closes when the alternator begins to produce voltage. It allows a portion of the output current to energize the field coils. A second relay, known as the limiter, has two sets of contact points. When the lower set of contact points open, field current passes through a resistor, and gener-

Starting and Charging Systems

ated voltage decreases. When the possibility of excessive voltage exists during high speeds, the upper contact closes shutting off all current flow to the field windings.

Transistors can be used in place of the electromagnetic relays. Older transistorized voltage regulators often used an electromagnetic field relay and a transistorized voltage relay. As explained in previous sections, modern solid-state regulators are completely transistorized.

Indicators

It is very important to monitor charging system performance during the course of vehicle operation. Vehicles are equipped with an ammeter, voltmeter, and indicator light. These allow the driver to monitor the charging system.

Indicator Light

This is the simplest and most common method of monitoring alternator performance. When the charging system fails to supply sufficient current, the light turns on. However, when the ignition switch is first activated, the light also comes on. This is due to the fact that the alternator is not providing power to the battery and other electrical circuits. Thus, the only current path is through the ignition switch, indicator light, voltage regulator, part of the alternator, and ground, then back through the battery (see Figure 15-52). Once enough power is provided, the contact in the regulator changes. Only the battery, regulator, and alternator are in the circuit. With no current flowing through the indicator light, it goes out.

With the engine running, the indicator light comes on again if the electrical load is more than the alternator can supply. This occasionally happens when the engine is idling. If there are no problems, the light should go out as the engine speed is increased. If it does not, either the alternator or regulator is not working properly.

> **SHOP TALK**
>
> On late-model cars, the indicator light is often combined with the oil pressure warning light, and is usually labeled "engine." If this light turns on while the engine is running, either the alternator is not charging or the oil pressure is low—or both.

Voltmeter

Voltmeters indicate the amount of voltage across an electrical circuit. The voltmeter shown in Figure 15-53 measures battery voltage when the ignition switch is in the run position. A fully charged battery indicates just over 12 volts. As energy is taken from it, the battery's voltmeter reading drops. At the same time, the voltage regulator senses this and raises the charging voltage output to 14 volts or more. When the battery has been recharged, the alternator cuts back. The voltmeter now shows the fully charged battery voltage of just over 12 volts again. This on again, off again action of the alternator is constantly monitored by the voltmeter.

Ammeter

The ammeter is placed in series with the circuit to monitor current flow into or out of the battery (Figure 15-55). When the alternator is delivering current to the battery, the ammeter shows a positive (+) indication. When not enough current (or none at all) is being supplied, the result is a negative (−) indication. This is because the current flow is in the opposite direction, from the battery to the electrical system.

☐ PRELIMINARY CHECKS

The key in solving charging system problems is getting to the root of the trouble the first time. Once a customer drives away with the assurance that the problem is solved, another case of a dead battery is very costly—both in terms of a free service call and a damaged reputation. Add to this the many possible hours of labor trying to figure out why the initial repair failed,

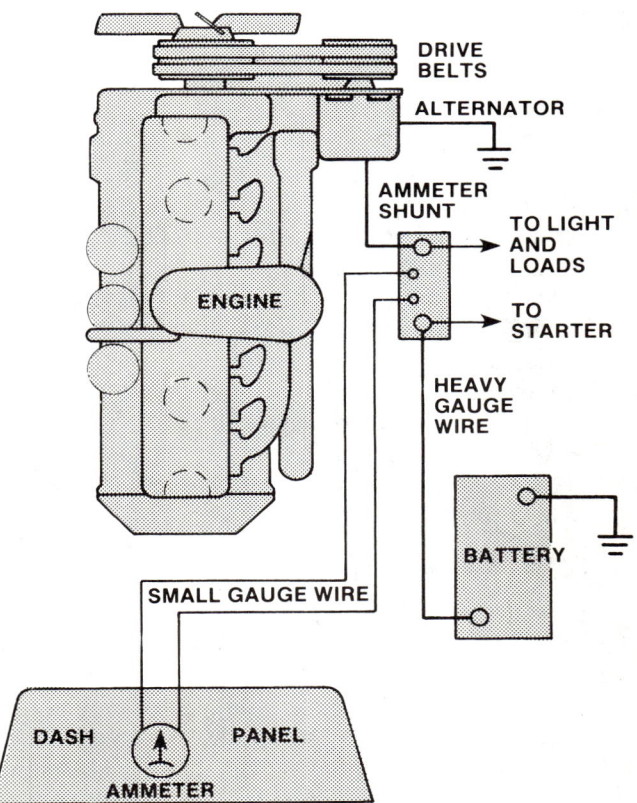

Figure 15-55 Typical circuit for an instrument panel-mounted ammeter.

and the importance of a correct initial diagnosis becomes all too clear.

When it comes to choosing equipment, the best tool to use for diagnosing the full spectrum of charging system problems is a charging-starting battery (CSB) analyzer. While a voltmeter helps in making intelligent decisions, the analyzer pinpoints the exact source of the trouble. Choose an analyzer that combines the functions of the carbon pile and separate meters to test the battery, alternator, regulator, and wiring.

Safety Precautions

Before beginning any work on the charging system, keep the following safety precautions in mind.

- Disconnect the battery ground cable before removing any leads from the system. Do not reconnect the battery ground cable until all wiring connections have been made.
- Avoid contact with the alternator output terminal. This terminal is hot (has voltage present) at all times when the battery cables are connected.
- Always make sure the ignition switch is off, except during actual test procedures.
- The alternator is not made to withstand a lot of force. Only the front housing is relatively strong. When adjusting belt tension, apply pressure to the front housing only to avoid damaging the stator and rectifier.
- Never operate the alternator without first connecting an external load to it. Failure to do so can cause extremely high voltage and possibly burn out the alternator.
- When installing a battery, be careful to observe the correct polarity. Reversing the cables destroys the diodes. Proper polarity must also be observed when connecting a booster battery: positive to positive and negative to ground.
- Always disconnect the battery ground cable before charging the battery. This greatly lessens the chance of flying sparks that could cause the battery to explode.
- Keep the tester's carbon pile off at all times, except during actual test procedures.
- Make sure all hair, clothing, and jewelry are kept away from moving parts.

Inspection

In addition to observing the ammeter, voltmeter, or indicator light, there are some common warning signs of charging system trouble. For example, a low state of battery charge often signals a charging problem, as does a noisy alternator. A detailed troubleshooting chart for charging systems is given in the Tech Manual that accompanies this textbook.

Many charging system complaints stem from easily repairable problems that reveal themselves during a visual inspection of the system. Remember to always look for the simple solution before performing more involved diagnostic procedures. Use the following inspection procedure when a problem is suspected.

PROCEDURES

Inspections

1. Before adjusting belt tension, check for proper pulley alignment. This is especially critical with serpentine belts.
2. Inspect the alternator drive belt. Loose drive belts are a major source of charging problems. If a belt does not have the proper tension, it might produce a loud squealing sound. Use a belt tension gauge to check the tension as shown in Figure 15-56. Keep in mind that different belts (V, cogged V, and multi-ribbed V) require different tensions. Always consult the manufacturer's specifications. In addition, check the belt for signs of fraying, cracking, or glazing, and replace if needed.
3. Inspect the battery. It might be necessary to charge the battery in order to restore it to a fully charged state. If the battery cannot be charged, it must be replaced. Also, make sure the posts and cable clamps are clean and tight, since a bad connection can cause reduced current flow.
4. Inspect all system wiring and connections. Many automotive electrical systems contain fusible links to protect against overloads. These are wires that melt at a lower temperature than the current-carrying wires they protect. Fusible links can blow like a fuse without being noticed. Also, look for a short circuit, an open ground, or high resistance in any of the circuits that could cause a problem that would appear to be in the charging system.

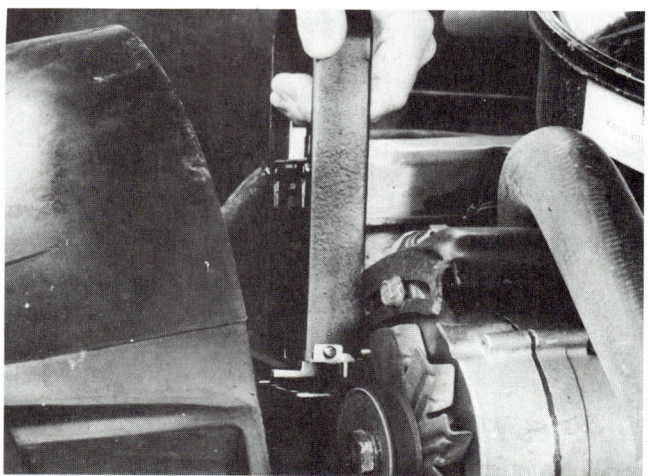

Figure 15-56 Using a tension gauge to check the tightness of an alternator's drive belt.

5. Inspect the alternator and regulator mountings for loose or missing bolts. Replace or tighten as needed.

> **SHOP TALK**
>
> Some late-model Chrysler engines require a torque reading to be taken when tension is applied to the alternator drive belt. This is especially important on the longer, multi-ribbed V belts.

If all preliminary visual checks come out positive, take a few moments to listen for noisy belts, bad bearings, or the whirring sound of a bad diode. If these checks also fail to produce anything, it is time to test the charging system.

General Test Procedure

On-car charging system tests are all basically the same. The major differences from model to model are the meter test points and the specifications. Keep in mind that not all vehicle manufacturers require all of these tests to be performed, while others suggest even more. During all of these tests, it is very important to refer to the vehicle manufacturer's specifications. Even the most accurate test results are no good if they are not matched against the correct specs. Before beginning, obtain a copy of the vehicle's service manual and keep it handy for reference. Also, while these tests are done most easily and accurately using a CSB analyzer, separate voltmeters and ammeters can be used if access to an analyzer is not possible.

CAUTION: All of the meter readings that follow apply to 12-volt DC systems. While it is possible to test 6-, 24-, and 32-volt systems, do not attempt to do so without first checking the specifications provided by the manufacturer of the vehicle or the charging system.

Voltage Output Test

To check charging system output, begin by recording battery open circuit voltage. To do so, connect the negative lead of the voltmeter to the negative battery cable clamp and the positive lead to the positive battery cable clamp. Note the voltage reading.

Next, start the engine and run it at the manufacturer's suggested rpm for this test. This is usually around 1500 rpm. With no electrical load, the charging voltage should be approximately 2 volts higher than the open circuit voltage. The exact acceptable range varies from model to model, but generally this reading will be between 13.5 to 15.0 volts.

A reading of less than 13.0 volts immediately after starting indicates a charging problem. No change in voltage between battery open circuit and charging voltage means the system is not producing voltage. A reading of 16 or more volts indicates overcharging. A faulty voltage regulator or control voltage circuit are the most likely causes.

If the unloaded charging system voltage matches specifications, test the loaded output. This involves increasing engine rpm slightly to 2000 rpm and turning on headlights, heaters, and other high-current consuming accessories. The charging system output when under heavy load should still be around 0.5 volt above battery open circuit voltage.

Current Output Test

The state of the charging system can also be checked by testing alternator current output. Exact test procedures vary according to the vehicle and alternator model. Some test procedures call for connecting an ammeter in series between the alternator output terminal and the positive battery terminal. A carbon pile regulator is then connected across the battery terminals. The engine is then operated at moderate speeds and the carbon pile adjusted to obtain maximum current output. This reading is compared against the rated output. Normally, readings greater than 10 amperes out of specifications indicate a problem.

When performing current output testing, the use of an inductive ammeter is highly recommended. An inductive ammeter eliminates the need to break battery connections. If you must break connections to hookup a regular ammeter, make certain you do not create an open circuit any time the alternator is generating current.

Other current output tests call for hooking up a voltmeter, ammeter, and carbon pile (Figure 15-57). With the engine running at a set speed, the carbon pile is adjusted to obtain a steady voltage reading. The ammeter is then read to record system current output. Always follow service manual procedures when conducting current output testing.

Regulator By-pass Test

If no or low voltage or current output is indicated, by-passing the voltage regulator by full-fielding the alternator will indicate if the alternator is bad. Once again, the exact procedure for full-fielding an alternator to make it produce maximum current varies according to the application, so check service manual procedures. On alternators where the terminals are not very accessible, jumper connections may be needed. Some new model alternators cannot be full fielded at all.

The usual procedure for full-fielding an A-circuit alternator is to ground the field terminal. On many internal regulator alternators, this is done by inserting a screwdriver through a special hole on the back of the unit (Figure 15-58). If the A-circuit alternator has two field terminals, ground one and feed battery positive voltage to the other to full-field the alternator. With

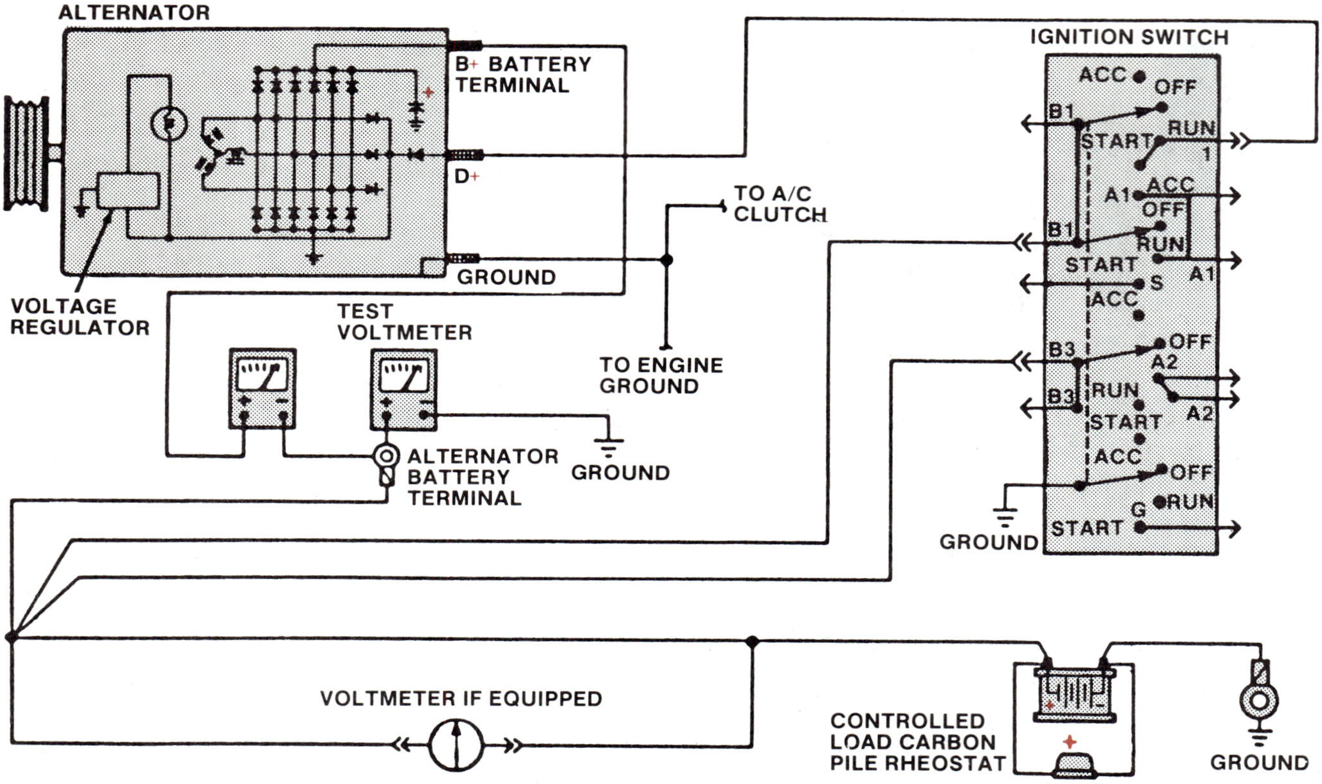

392 Section 3 Electricity

Figure 15-57 Ammeter, voltmeter, and carbon pile hook-up for a current output test on an alternator with an internal voltage regulator. *Courtesy of Chrysler Motors*

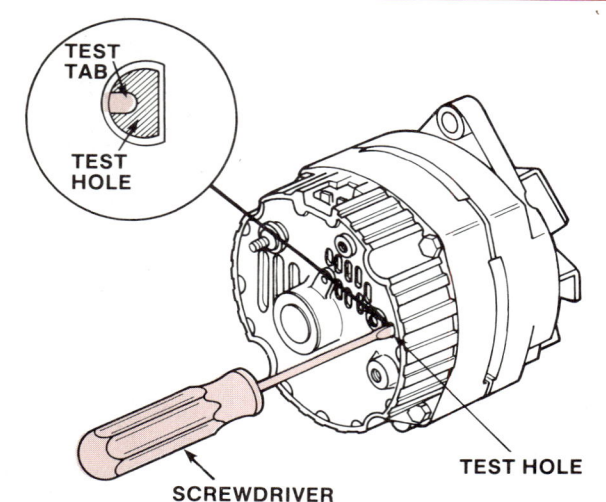

Figure 15-58 Grounding the field terminal with a screwdriver inserted into a special test hole on the back of the alternator.

B-circuit alternators, the alternator is full-fielded by connecting the field terminal to battery positive.

An A-circuit alternator has one carbon brush connected to positive battery voltage and the voltage regulator switches between field and negative to control output. With B-circuit systems, one brush is connected to battery negative and the regulator switches between field and positive to control output. If an A-circuit regulator loses positive voltage, the alternator will overcharge if the field coils still have power. If the A-circuit regulator loses its ground, the system will go dead.

In B-circuit alternators, the opposite is true. If a B-circuit system loses ground, it will overcharge. If it loses positive voltage, it will go dead.

If full-fielding an alternator suddenly brings charging system voltage or current output up to specifications, the voltage regulator, not the alternator is at fault. If charging output is still low or non-existent when full-fielding, the alternator is bad.

Oscilloscope Checks

Alternator output can also be checked using an oscilloscope. Figure 15-59 illustrates common alternator voltage patterns for good and faulty alternators. The correct pattern looks like the top of a picket fence. A regular dip in the pattern indicates that one or more of the coil windings is grounded or open, or that a diode in the rectifier circuit of a diode trio circuit has failed. Most battery/charging system testers also have a test function that detects faulty diodes.

Circuit and Ground Resistance

These tests measure voltage drop within the system wiring. They help pinpoint corroded connections or loose or damaged wiring.

Starting and Charging Systems

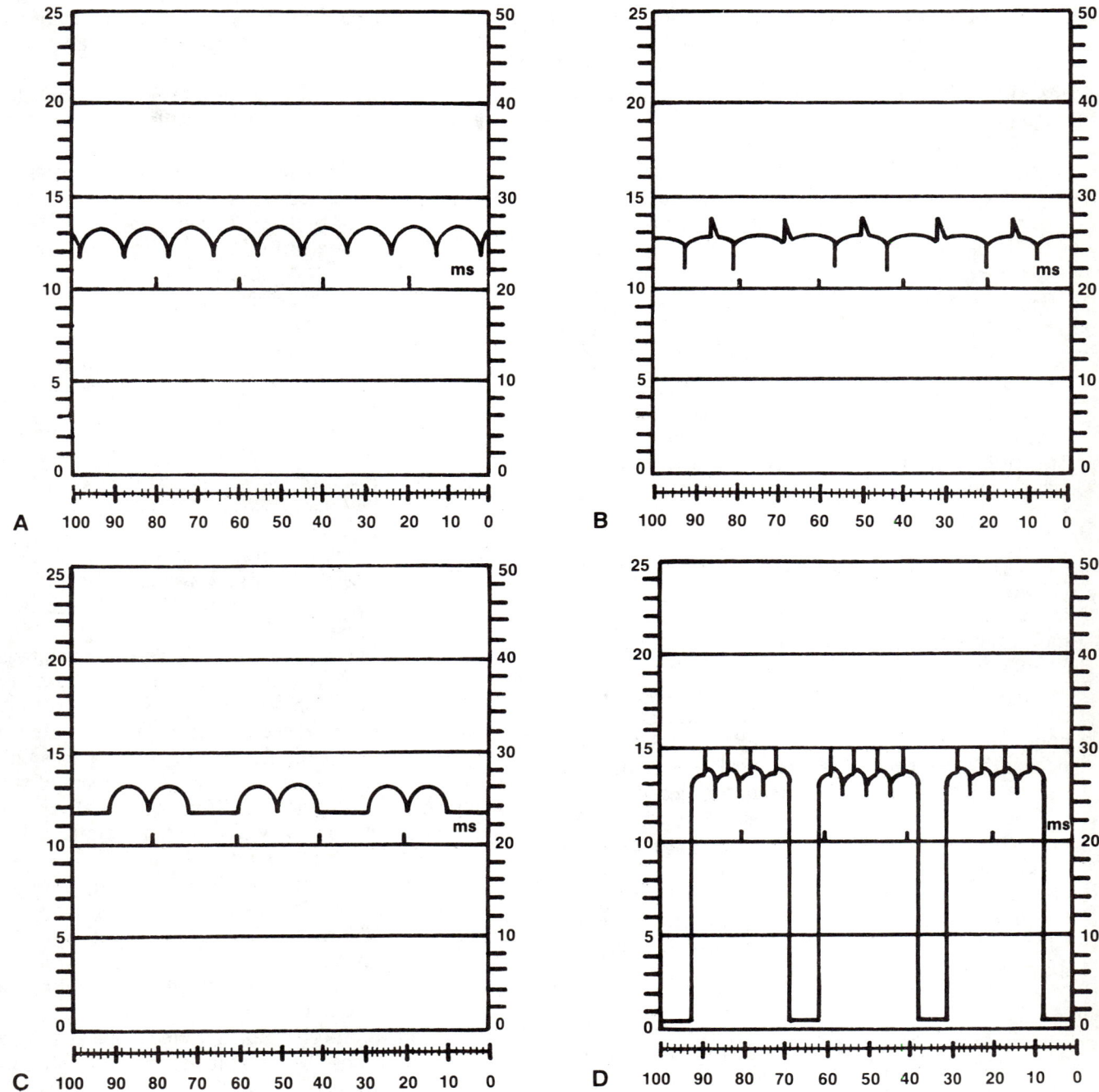

Figure 15-59 Alternator oscilloscope patterns: (A) good alternator under full load, (B) good alternator under no load, (C) shorted diode and/or stator winding under full load, and (D) open diode in diode trio.

Circuit resistance is checked by connecting a voltmeter to the positive battery terminal and the output, or battery terminal of the alternator. Ground resistance connections are the battery negative terminal and the alternator housing (ground). A voltage drop over 0.5 volt indicates high resistance in either circuit.

❏ ALTERNATOR SERVICE

A faulty alternator can be the result of many different types of internal problems. Diodes, stator windings, and field circuits may be open, shorted, or improperly grounded. The brushes or slip rings can become worn. The rotor shaft can become bent and the pulley can work loose or bend out of proper alignment.

After diagnosing a faulty alternator, many shops simply replace it with a new or rebuilt unit. Follow service manual procedures when removing and installing the alternator. Remember, improper connections to the alternator can destroy it.

Most alternator repair or rebuilding work is performed in specialty shops. Internal problems that cause alternator failure include open, shorted, or improperly grounded diodes, stator windings, or field circuits. Brushes and slip rings can also become worn. Rotor shafts and pulleys can become loose or bend out of alignment.

Follow service manual procedures for disassembling, inspecting, testing, and rebuilding alternators. Basic procedures for testing diodes and internal circuits are given in the Tech Manual that accompanies this textbook.

CASE STUDY

Case 1

A vehicle equipped with a solenoid actuated direct-drive starting system is towed into the shop. The owner complains that the starter does not crank the engine when the ignition switch is turned to the start position.

The technician performs a battery load test to confirm that the battery is in good working order. It is. The technician then tests for voltage to the M or motor terminal on the solenoid using a voltmeter. Voltage reading at the M terminal is 12.5 volts.

Because there is voltage at the M terminal of the solenoid, inspection of individual connections and components such as the starter safety switch are not needed at this time. They are obviously allowing current to pass through the insulated circuit.

The technician then performs a ground circuit check to verify that the ground return path is okay. It is. Since the insulated and ground circuits have checked out okay, the only other source of an open circuit is the starter motor. The technician can now confidently pull the starter motor from the vehicle for rebuilding or replacement.

Summary

- The starting system turns the engine over until it can operate under its own power. The system has two distinct electrical circuits: the starter circuit and the control circuit.
- The starter circuit carries high current flow from the battery, through heavy cables, to the starter motor.
- The control circuit uses a small amount of current to operate a magnetic switch that opens and closes the starter circuit.
- The ignition switch is used to control current flow in the control circuit.
- Solenoids and relays are the two types of magnetic switches used in starting systems. Solenoids use electromagnetic force to pull a plunger into a coil to close the contact points. Relays use a hinged armature to open and close the circuit.
- The starter motor is an electric motor capable of producing very high horsepower for very short periods.
- The drive mechanism of the starter motor engages and turns the flywheel to crank the engine for starting.
- An override clutch protects the starter motor from spinning too fast once the vehicle engine starts.
- Starting safety switches prevent the starting system from operating when the transmission is engaged.
- All starting system wiring must have clean, tight connections.
- During starter system testing, the ignition system must be by-passed or disabled so the vehicle does not start during cranking.
- Battery load, cranking voltage, cranking current, insulated circuit resistance, starter relay by-pass, ground circuit resistance, control circuit, and drive component tests are all used to troubleshoot the starting system.
- Modern vehicles use an alternator to produce electrical current in the charging system. Diodes in the alternator change or rectify the alternating current to direct current.
- A voltage regulator keeps charging system voltage above battery voltage. Keeping the alternator charging voltage above the 12.6 volts of the battery insures current flows into not out of the battery.
- Modern voltage regulators are completely solid-state devices that can be an integral part of the alternator or mounted to the back of the alternator housing. In some vehicles, voltage regulation is the job of the computer control module.
- Voltage regulators work by controlling current flow to the alternator field circuit. This varies the strength of the magnetic field, which in turn varies current output.
- The driver can monitor charging system operation with indicator lights.
- Problems in the charging system can be as simple as worn or loose belts, faulty connections, or battery problems.
- Circuit resistance, current output, voltage output, field current draw, and voltage regulator tests are all used to troubleshoot AC charging systems.

Review Questions

1. Which of the following is not part of the starter circuit?
   a. battery
   b. starting safety switch
   c. starter motor
   d. relay solenoid

2. Which of the following could result in a hard starting condition?

a. corroded battery cables
b. excessive CCA capacity
c. heavy-gauge battery cables
d. all of the above

3. Which of the following is not a member of the control circuit?
   a. ignition switch
   b. starter relay
   c. ballast resistor
   d. starting safety switch

4. Which of the following tests would be performed to check for high resistance in the battery cables?
   a. cranking voltage test
   b. insulated circuit resistance test
   c. starter relay by-pass test
   d. ground circuit resistance test

5. When the starter spins but does not engage the flywheel, which of the following may be true?
   a. defective starter drive
   b. excessive resistance in the control circuit
   c. a faulty starter relay
   d. all of the above

6. The usual cranking voltage specification is approximately _____ .
   a. 9.6 volts
   b. 10.5 volts
   c. 11.0 volts
   d. 12.65 volts

7. A cranking current test is performed, and the amperage is found to be less than specification. Technician A says that the starter is bad and that it should be replaced. Technician B insists on testing the resistance of the cables, grounds, and connections. Who is correct?
   a. Technician A
   b. Technician B
   c. Both A and B
   d. Neither A nor B

8. A control circuit test may uncover which of the following conditions?
   a. high resistance in the solenoid switch circuit
   b. defective starter relay
   c. loose battery cable connection
   d. short in the starter armature windings

9. An engine cranks slowly. Technician A says that a possible cause of the problem is poor starter circuit connections. Technician B says that a possible cause is incorrectly set ignition timing. Who is correct?
   a. Technician A
   b. Technician B
   c. Both A and B
   d. Neither A nor B

10. If a ground circuit test reveals a voltage drop of more than 0.2 volt, the problem may be _____ .
    a. a loose starter motor mounting bolt
    b. a poor battery ground terminal post connector
    c. a damaged battery ground cable
    d. all of the above

11. Which of the following components protects the starter motor from excessive turning speeds?
    a. sun gear
    b. drive pinion
    c. override clutch
    d. none of the above

12. A rotating magnetic field inside a set of conducting wires is a simple description of a _____ .
    a. DC generator
    b. AC alternator
    c. voltage regulator
    d. none of the above

13. What part of the alternator produces the rotating magnetic field?
    a. stator
    b. rotor
    c. brushes
    d. poles

14. Which type of stator winding produces higher alternator output?
    a. wye
    b. delta
    c. trio
    d. series

15. Slip rings and brushes _____ .
    a. mount on the rotor shaft
    b. conduct current to the rotor field coils
    c. are insulated from each other and the rotor shaft
    d. all of the above

16. The alternating current produced by the alternator is rectified into DC, or direct current, through the use of _____ .
    a. transistors
    b. electromagnetic relays
    c. diodes
    d. capacitors

17. Integrated voltage regulators _____ .
    a. contain all needed circuitry on a single silicone chip sealed in a plastic module
    b. mount to the back of or inside the alternator housing
    c. are unserviceable and must be replaced if defective
    d. all of the above

18. Voltage regulators or voltage regulator circuitry in the computer control module control alternator output by _____ .

a. using a variable resistor to vary current flow to the rotor field windings
   b. pulsing current flow to the rotor field windings on and off to create a correct average field current supply
   c. either a or b depending on the system
   d. neither a nor b

19. Technician A uses a current output test to check alternator output. Technician B uses a voltage output test to check output. Who is correct?
   a. Technician A
   b. Technician B
   c. Both A and B
   d. Neither A nor B

20. Technician A says that if alternator output rises to specifications when the alternator is full-fielded, the voltage regulator is faulty. Technician B says that this indicates an intermittent alternator problem. Who is correct?
   a. Technician A
   b. Technician B
   c. Both A and B
   d. Neither A nor B

21. Before adjusting alternator drive-belt tension, Technician A checks for proper pulley alignment. Technician B looks up the specified belt tension in the vehicle's service manual. Who is correct?
   a. Technician A
   b. Technician B
   c. Both A and B
   d. Neither A nor B

22. When checking alternator output using an oscilloscope, Technician A says the correct pattern resembles the rounded tops of a picket fence. Technician B says the correct pattern is a square sine-wave pattern. Who is correct?
   a. Technician A
   b. Technician B
   c. Both A and B
   d. Neither A nor B

23. A voltage drop over _____ indicates high resistance in either the circuit or ground wiring of the charging system.
   a. 0.1
   b. 0.2
   c. 0.5
   d. 1.0

16 LIGHTING SYSTEMS

Objectives

- Explain the operating principle of the various lighting systems.
- Understand the types of headlights and how they are controlled.
- Understand the functions of turn, stop and hazard warning lights.
- Know how backup lights operate.
- Replace headlights and other burned out bulbs.
- Explain how to aim headlights.
- Explain the purpose of auxiliary automotive lighting.
- Diagnose lighting problems.

The lighting system provides power to both exterior and interior lights. It consists of the headlights, parking lights, marker lights, taillights, courtesy lights, dome/map lights, instrument illumination or dash lights, coach lights (if so equipped), headlight switch, and various other control switches (Figure 16-1). Other lights such as vanity mirror lights, the underhood light, the glove box light, and the trunk compartment light are used on some vehicles and are also part of the lighting system.

Other lights which are not usually in the main lighting system are turn signal, hazard warning, backup, and stop lights. These lights, as well as the retractable headlight covers found on some vehicles, are operated by separate control circuits and are covered later in this chapter.

☐ HEADLIGHTS

Figure 16-2 is a typical service manual electrical schematic of a standard headlight system. Note that power on this main switch is supplied by the battery directly to the headlight portion of the switch and through a fuse in the fuse panel to the remainder of the switch. Although one of the functions of the headlight switch is to control the headlights, the switch has many other functions. For example, it may control operation of all exterior lights except turn signals, hazard warning, and stop lights.

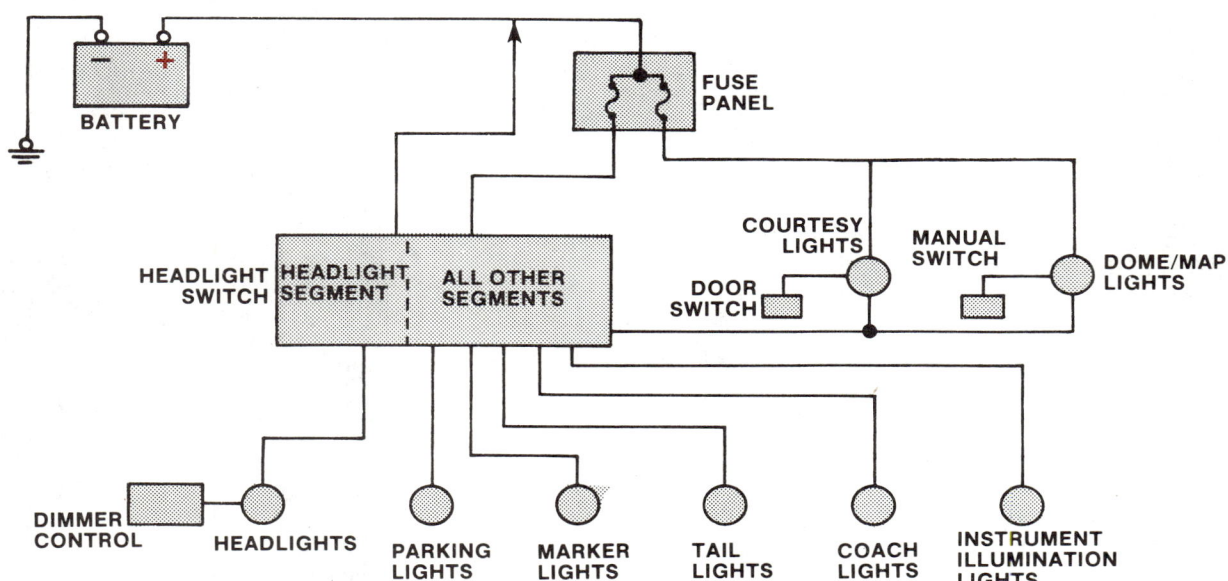

Figure 16-1 Basic automotive lighting system. *Courtesy of Ford Motor Co.*

397

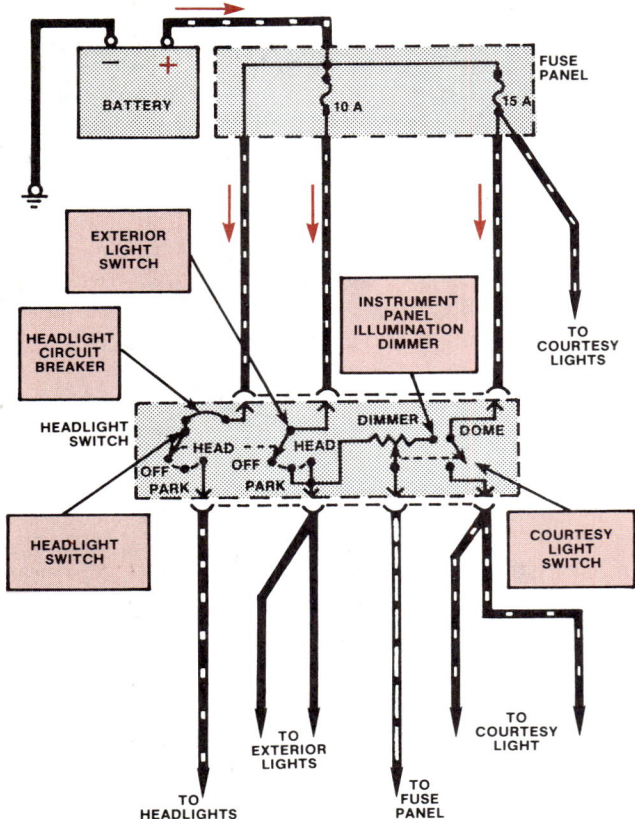

Figure 16-2 Electrical schematic of a standard headlight system. *Courtesy of Ford Motor Co.*

SHOP TALK

Canadian law requires that vehicles be equipped with daylight running lights (DRL) for added safety. The system uses the vehicle's high-beam lights. The control circuit is connected directly to the vehicle's ignition switch so the lights are on whenever the vehicle is running. The circuit is equipped with a module that reduces 12-volt battery voltage to approximately 6 volts. This voltage reduction allows the high beams to burn with less intensity and prolong light life. When the headlight switch is activated for night or poor weather driving, the module is deactivated and the lights burn with their regular intensity and brightness. Applying the parking brake will also disable the DRL systems.

Although the primary function of the headlight switch is the same from one car model to another, the operation, type, and design vary according to the particular lighting used on the vehicle. There are two basic types of headlight switches. The pull-out design has three positions: off, park, and head. Pulling a typical switch knob out to the park or first detent (knob catches at stop) illuminates all exterior lights except the headlights. Instrument panel lights are also illum-

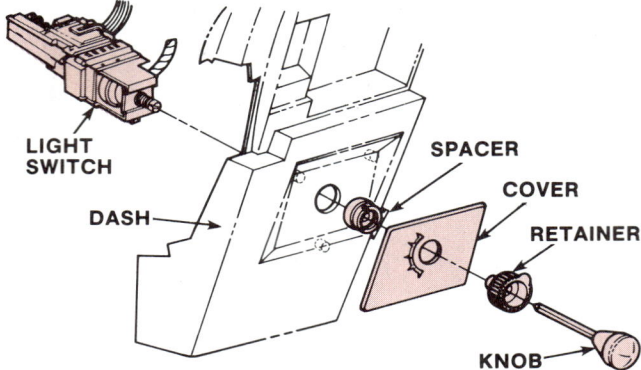

Figure 16-3 The rotary pull-out headlight switch mounts in the dash. A button is usually provided on the switch. When pressed, it releases the knob, after which the retainer and switch can also be removed. *Courtesy of Ford Motor Co.*

inated in this position. Pulling the head switch knob out to the head or second detent illuminates the headlights plus all of those lights illuminated in park position. In the switch shown in Figure 16-3, a dimmer rheostat controls the brightness of dash or instrument illumination lights. When the switch knob is rotated completely counterclockwise, the instrument panel illumination is at maximum brightness level. This position may also turn on the courtesy and dome/map lights. The second type of headlight switch is the push button design. The vehicle shown in Figure 16-4 has three lighting push button controls: off, park, and head. When the park button is pressed in, power is applied to all circuits except the headlights. When the headlight button is depressed, all of those lights illuminated in the park position are on. Some models have a three-position toggle switch, and not separate switches.

USING SERVICE MANUALS

One problem a technician often has is tracing a circuit through its various operational phases.

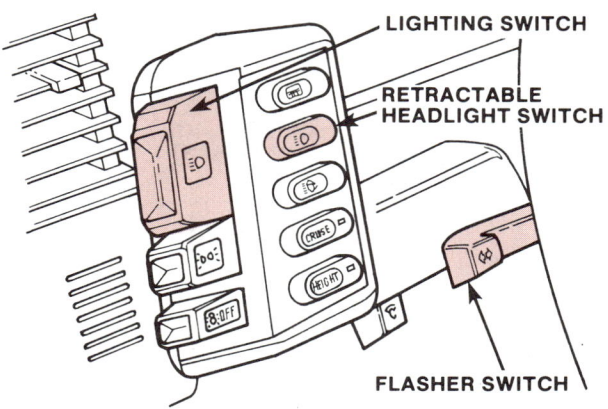

Figure 16-4 Typical push button headlight switch. *Courtesy of Toyota Motor Corp.*

Lighting Systems 399

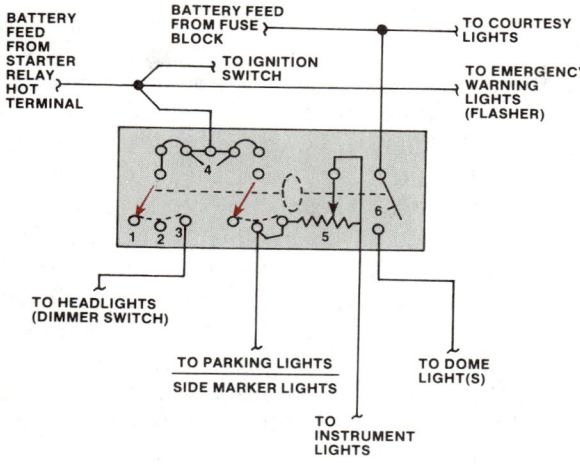

1—OFF
2—PARKING LIGHTS
3—HEADLIGHTS
4—CIRCUIT BREAKERS
5—VARIABLE RESISTOR
6—DOME LIGHT SWITCH

Figure 16-5 Schematic of a headlight switch (A) in the off position; (B) in the parking light position; and (C) in the on position. *Courtesy of Ford Motor Co.*

Figure 16-5 shows a headlight switch as it appears in a typical schematic. To understand how the switch operates, you must understand what is happening in the various switch positions.

Let us follow the current through the switch and see how it works. With the switch off, B+ flows through the common point (37Y) and is made available to the ignition switch and emergency light circuits. Notice that the circuit from the B+ common point is open through the switch's internal circuit breaker and the switch wiper, when the switch is in the off (#1) position (Figure 16-5A). As the switch is moved to the #2 position, current flows through the right circuit breaker and the wiper to the parking lights (Figure 16-5B). Notice that the left wiper is now connected to a vacant contact on the switch. The only light circuits powered are the park lights and the dashboard lights. As the switch is moved to the full on (#3) position, notice that current is available to the headlights and still flowing to the instrument panel and park lights (Figure 16-5C).

HEADLIGHT DIMMER SWITCH Headlights have both a high and low beam. Switching from high beam to low beam is controlled by a dimmer switch. Current truck models and earlier car models use a floor-mounted foot-operated dimmer switch (Figure 16-6A). Current car models use a multifunction steering column switch that may control the horn, turn signals, and the high and low beam headlight circuit (Figure 16-6B). Electrically, the dimmer switch is a simple two-position switch that controls the output of the headlight switch.

Some dimmer switches have the additional feature of being able to energize both the high and low beams even if the headlight switch is off. These circuits are usually referred to as flash to pass. By activating the dimmer, the entire headlight circuit has voltage applied to it and both sets of filaments light. In addition, the high beam indicator on the dash lights.

AUTOMATIC HEADLIGHT DIMMER The automatic headlight dimmer is a driver-controlled electronic device. It automatically switches the headlights from high to low beam in response to light from an approaching vehicle, or light from the taillights of a vehicle being overtaken. Major components of the system are a hi-lo beam photocell, an amplifier, a hi-lo beam relay, a dimmer switch, and a hi-lo beam range control.

When the switch is turned on, voltage is applied to both the hi-lo beam relay and the dimmer switch portion of the multi-function switch (Figure 16-7). If the dimmer switch is in the lo position, this voltage passes through the dimmer switch to the coil of the hi-lo beam

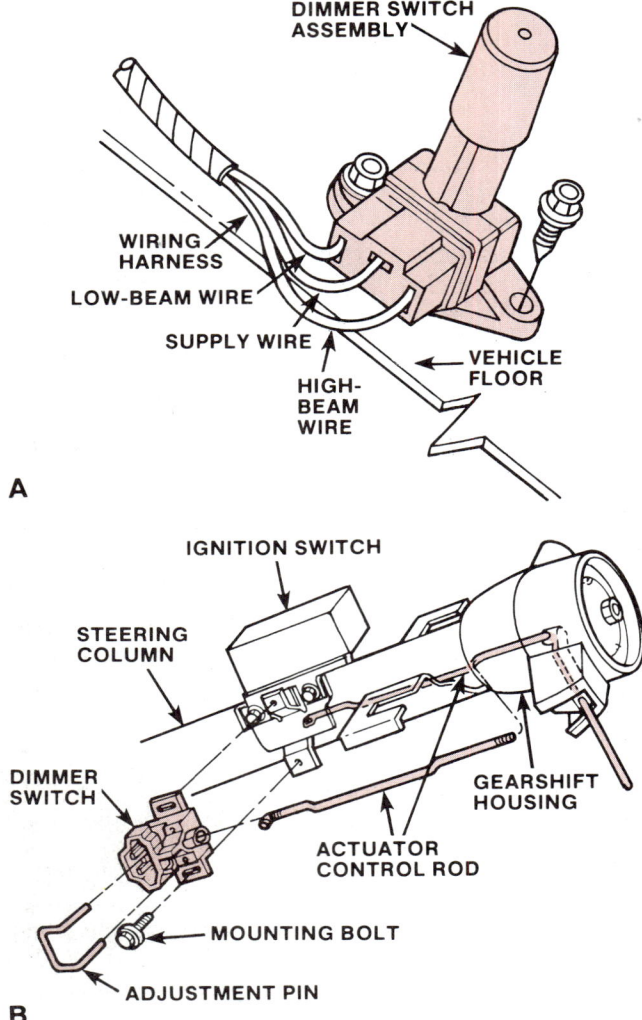

Figure 16-6 (A) Floor-mounted and (B) steering column headlight dimmer switches. *Courtesy of Ford Motor Co.*

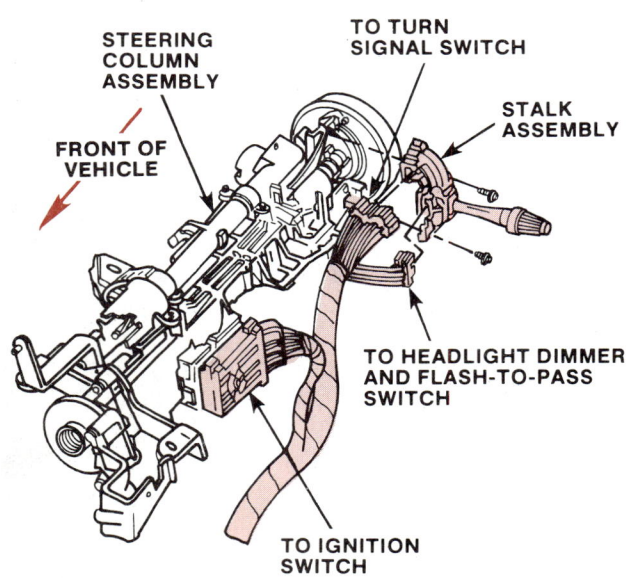

Figure 16-7 Typical multi-function switch.

relay. With battery voltage on one side and ground on the other side of the coil, the relay energizes. The headlight voltage then passes through the lo side relay contacts and only the lo-beam headlights are illuminated. If the dimmer switch is moved to the hi (or automatic) position, control of the hi-lo beam relay is switched to the hi-lo beam photocell amplifier. Power for the operation of the amplifiers is from the switch with additional circuit protection from a fuse. This same voltage is also applied to one side of the potentiometer in the hi-lo beam range control unit. The other side of the potentiometer is grounded. The voltage applied to the amplifier depends on the setting of the potentiometer. This voltage determines the sensitivity of the amplifier.

If the automatic dimmer system is not working, check to see if the hi and lo beams can be switched back and forth by using the dimmer switch. Make sure the hi-lo beam range control is in the off position. If the beams can be switched back and forth, the problem is definitely in the automatic dimmer system. If the beams cannot be switched, the problem may be in the multi-function switch or in the wiring.

If the problem is in the automatic dimmer circuit, make sure the hi-lo beam photocell amplifier lens is clean and the unit is properly adjusted. Refer to the appropriate service manual for adjustment procedures.

FLASH-TO-PASS SYSTEM The multi-function switch on some vehicles also contains a flash-to-pass switch that allows the driver to flash the high-beam headlights rapidly without using the main light switch.

When the multi-function switch lever is pulled towards the driver, the flash-to-pass switch contacts close. Current flows through the main light switch circuit breaker, the flash-to-pass switch contacts, and the high-beam headlights to ground. The high-beam headlights illuminate until the lever is released.

AUTOMATIC LIGHT SYSTEMS These systems provide light-sensitive automatic on-off control of the light normally controlled by the regular headlight switch. It consists of a light-sensitive photocell sensor/amplifier assembly and a headlight control relay. Turning the regular headlight switch on overrides the automatic system. In other words, automatic operation is not possible until the regular headlight switch is turned off.

In normal operation, the photocell sensor/amplifier, which is usually mounted under a group of perforated holes in the upper instrument panel pad or slotted holes in the defroster grille panel, is exposed to ambient light. As the light level decreases, the light sensor's resistance increases. When resistance increases to a preset amount, the amplifier applies power to the headlight coil relay. The headlights, exterior lights, and instrument illumination lights turn on. The lights remain on until the system is turned off or the ambient light level increases.

Lighting Systems   401

> **CUSTOMER CARE**
>
> If the customer's car is equipped with an automatic light control system, point out the location of the perforated holes or slots. Warn the customer not to place any items that may block light from the sensor/amplifier assembly. This causes erratic operation of the system. The photocell must always be exposed to outside light to function properly.

DELAYED-EXIT SYSTEM An automatic delayed-exit system is usually part of the automatic light operation (Figure 16-8). That is, the delayed-exit system keeps the lights operated by the automatic light system on for a preselected period of time after the ignition switch is turned off. It is turned on by the same switch that controls the automatic light switch system.

When the ignition switch is turned off, the delay system continues to energize the headlight relay. The exterior lights and instrument panel bulbs stay on for a few seconds or up to 5 minutes, depending on the setting selected by the driver. The driver typically selects the delayed-exit time period by rotating the autolight dial located behind the main light switch knob. Turning the dial clockwise increases the period of time that the lights stay on.

RETRACTABLE HEADLIGHT COVERS Some automobiles have retractable headlight covers or doors (Figure 16-9), which must be elevated before the headlights can serve their purpose.

These covers are powered by vacuum or electricity. Electrically-operated covers stay elevated when power is lost to the headlight cover motor because the motor needs electricity to turn the opposite direction and close the doors. The motors are equipped with a manual control which allows the covers to be elevated in the event of an electrical problem (Figure 16-10). Vacuum-operated covers are raised or lowered by the vacuum system in a car. In such a system, the intake manifold vacuum is stored in a reservoir that, when the light switch is turned off, allows a vacuum motor to close the

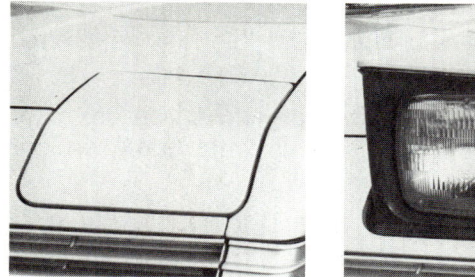

Figure 16-9 Retractable headlight covers are being used on a growing number of late-model cars. *Courtesy of General Motors Corp.*

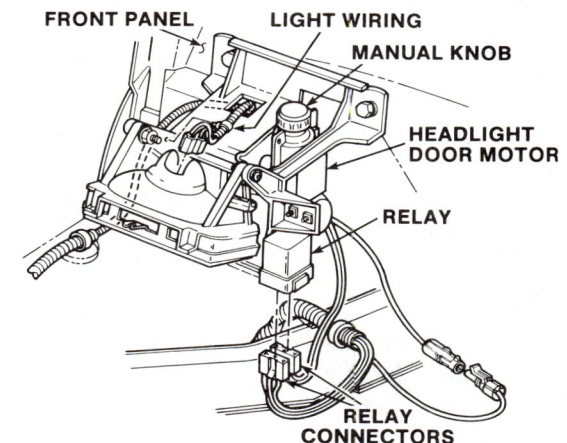

Figure 16-10 Electrically-operated headlight covers feature a manual control knob that allows the covers to be raised in the event of an electrical problem. *Courtesy of General Motors Corp.*

doors against spring pressure. Should the engine fail while the lights are on, spring pressure keeps the doors from closing.

❑ INTERIOR LIGHT ASSEMBLIES

The types and number of interior light assemblies used varies significantly from one vehicle to another. Following are the more common ones.

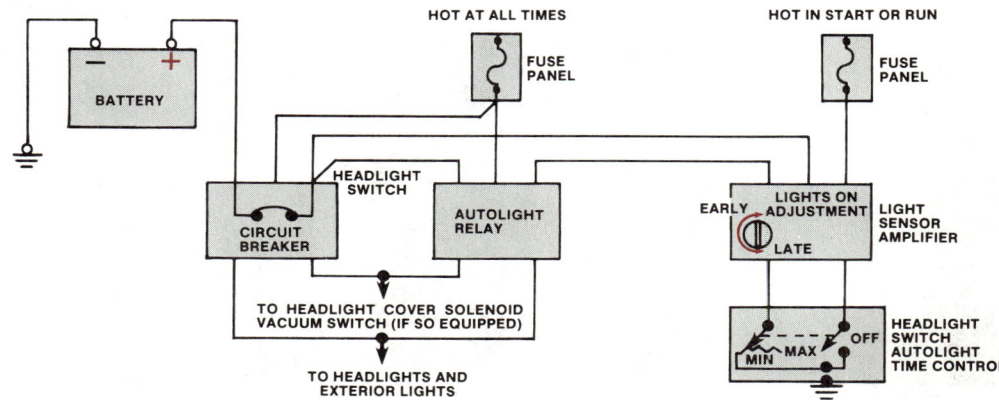

Figure 16-8 An automatic headlight dimmer circuit with a delayed-exit system. *Courtesy of Ford Motor Co.*

ENGINE COMPARTMENT LIGHT Opening the hood causes the engine compartment light mercury switch to close and light the underhood area.

GLOVE BOX LIGHT Opening the glove box door closes the glove box light switch contacts and the light comes on.

LUGGAGE COMPARTMENT LIGHT The light is mounted in the underside of the trunk deck lid in the luggage compartment.

TRUNK LID LIGHT Lifting the trunk lid causes the light mercury switch to close and the light comes on.

VANITY LIGHTS Piloting the sun visor and opening the vanity mirror cover causes the vanity light switch contacts to close and the light to come on.

COURTESY LIGHTS There are several types of courtesy lights. Some vehicles have courtesy lights that are in the door trim panels, under each side of the instrument panel, and in the center of the headlining. These are illuminated when the doors are opened or by rotating the headlight switch to the full counterclockwise position.

Front compartment foot well courtesy lights are mounted on the lower closeout panels at both ends of the instrument panel. The bulbs are accessible from under the instrument panel for replacement without removing other parts.

DOME/MAP LIGHT The dome/map light is shown in Figure 16-11. The two map lights are located on each side of the dome/map light housing. The map lights are operated independently of the dome light by two switches located at each map light housing. The dome light is actuated by turning the headlight switch control knob fully counterclockwise.

Power is supplied from the fuse block to the courtesy or dome/map light. The ground for the light is controlled by the position of the door switch. That is, these door switches are held in open position and do not provide for a ground circuit. When the door is opened, a spring pushes the switch closed to ground the circuit, and the dome/map or courtesy light comes on.

ILLUMINATED ENTRY SYSTEM This system assists vehicle entry during the hours of darkness by illuminating the door lock cylinder so it may be easily located for key insertion. The vehicle interior is also illuminated by the courtesy lights.

As illustrated in Figure 16-12, the system consists of four main components: electronic actuator module, illuminated door lock cylinder, door latch switch, and wiring harness.

Activation of the system is accomplished by raising the outside door handle or by pressing a code button on the keyless entry system. This action momentarily closes a switch mounted on the door latch mechanism, which completes the ground circuit of the electronic actuator module and switches the system on. The vehicle interior lights turn on, and both front door lock cylinders are illuminated by a ring of light around the area where the key enters. This illumination remains on for approximately 25 seconds, then automatically turns off. During this 25-second period, the system can be manually deactivated by turning the ignition switch to either run position.

The system is activated every time the outside front door handles are operated, whether the vehicle is locked or not. Opening the doors from the inside of the vehicle does not activate the system. If the outside door handle is held up indefinitely so that the latch switch is continuously closed, the system operates as normal and turns off after 25 seconds. At the completion of this cycle, if the door handle is still in the raised position, the system remains off, and it is impossible to activate the system from the other front door handle until the raised handle is returned to its normal position. This function is built into the logic circuitry of the system to

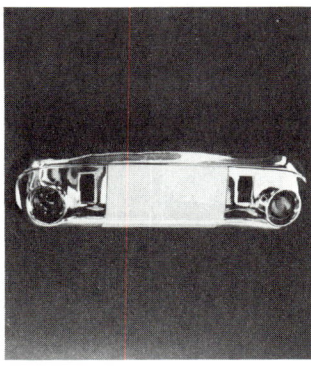

Figure 16-11 Typical dome/map light.

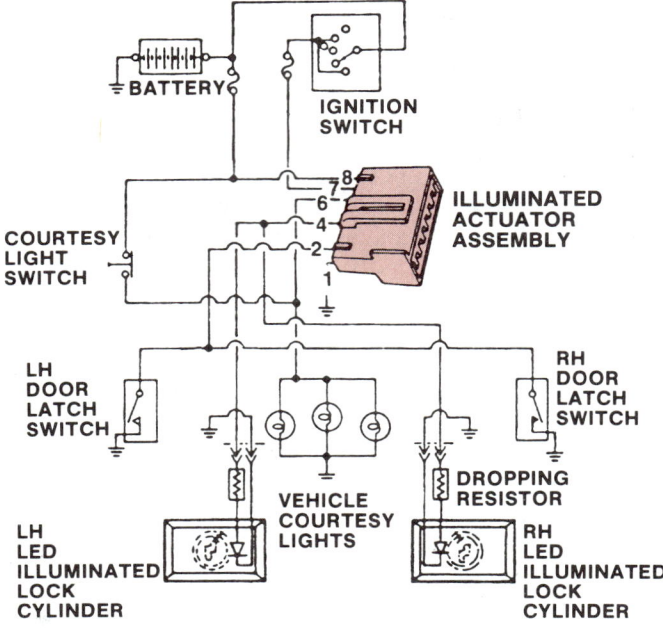

Figure 16-12 Illuminated lock electrical circuit. *Courtesy of Ford Motor Co.*

prevent battery discharge should the outside door handle be intentionally propped up or become jammed in any way.

Interior lights basically all operate the same. Whether the courtesy lights are on the door, under the seats, under the instrument panel, or on the rear interior quarter panels does not change how they are controlled. Also, whether the illumination lights are just behind the instrument panel or are also used in center consoles or door arm rests does not affect their operation. The only difference is the number of lights and variances in electrical wiring.

Interior and courtesy lights rarely give any trouble. However, if they do not operate, check the fuse, bulb, switch, and wiring.

☐ REAR EXTERIOR LIGHT ASSEMBLIES

The rear light assembly includes the taillights, turn signal/stop/hazard lights/high-mounted stop light, rear side marker lights, backup lights, and license plate lights (Figure 16-13). Taillights operate when the parking lights or headlights are turned on.

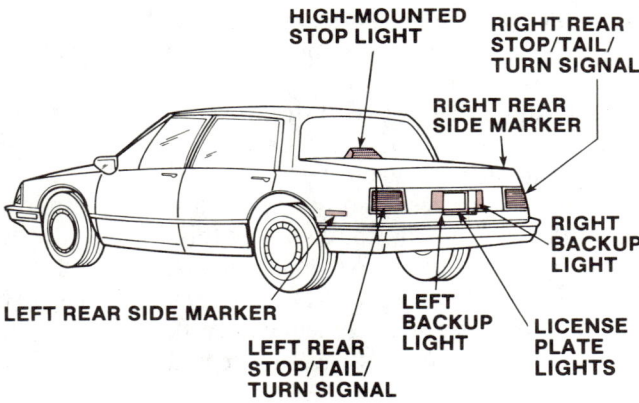

Figure 16–13 Typical rear light assembly.

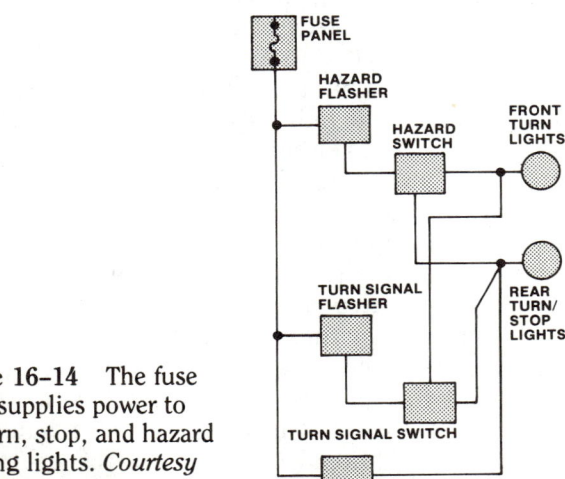

Figure 16–14 The fuse panel supplies power to the turn, stop, and hazard warning lights. *Courtesy of Ford Motor Co.*

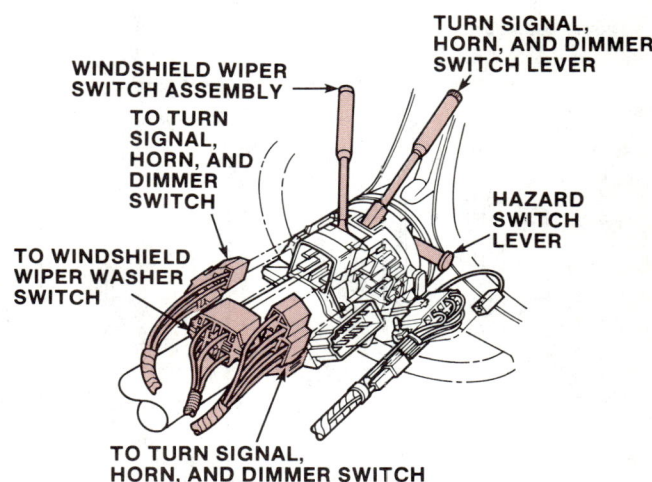

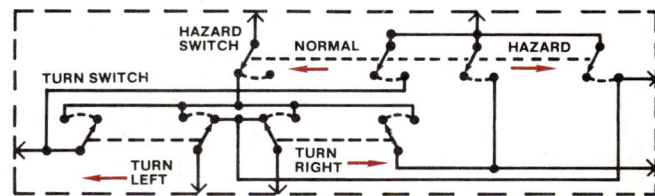

Figure 16–15 Typical turn signal and hazard multi-function switch. *Courtesy of Ford Motor Co.*

TURN, STOP, AND HAZARD WARNING LIGHT SYSTEMS Power for the turn (directional signal), stop, and hazard warning light systems is provided by the fuse panel (Figure 16-14). Each system has a switch that must close to turn on the applicable lights.

The turn signal and hazard light switches on many current vehicles are part of a multi-function switch (Figure 16-15). This switch also includes the horn and dimmer switches. On earlier models and some current light-duty truck models, these are separate switches. The directional and hazards controls are normally on the steering column. When the turn or directional signal switch is activated, only one set of the switch contacts are closed—left or right. However, when the hazard switch is activated, all contacts are closed and all turn signal lights and indicators flash in unison.

Some cars are equipped with cornering side lights, which are generally fed from the multi-function main switch. When the turn signal switch is activated, the cornering light on the appropriate side burns with a steady glow.

Side markers are connected in parallel with the feed circuit (from the headlight switch) that feeds the minor filaments of the front parking lights and rear taillights (Figure 16-16).

FLASHERS Flashers are components of both turn and hazard systems. They contain a temperature sensitive bimetallic strip and a heating element (Figure 16-17). The bimetallic strip is connected to one side of a set of contacts. Voltage from the fuse panel is connected to

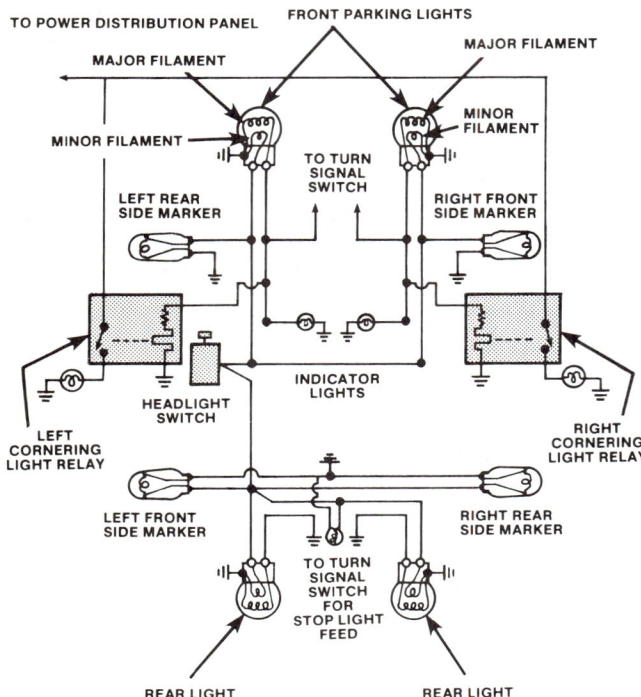

Figure 16-16 Typical side marker lighting system. *Courtesy of Ford Motor Co.*

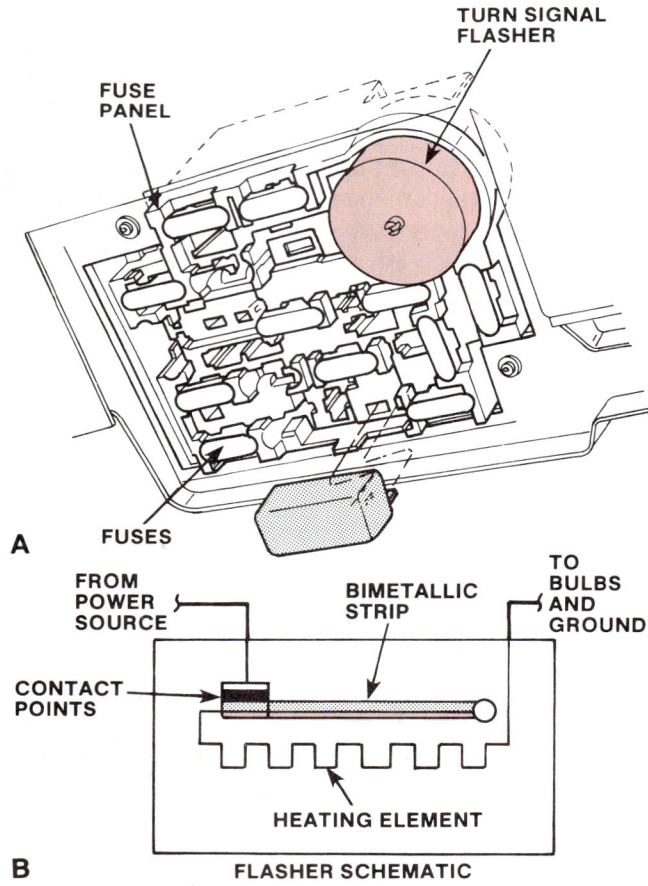

Figure 16-17 (A) A common location for flashes in the fuse panel. (B) Flashes contain a bimetallic strip, contact points, and a heating element. *Courtesy of Ford Motor Co.*

the other side. When the left turn signal switch is activated, current flows through the flasher unit to the turn signal bulbs. This current causes the heating element to emit heat, which in turn causes the bimetallic strip to bend and open the circuit. The absence of current flow allows the strip to cool and again close the circuit. This intermittent on/off interruption of current flow makes all left turn signal lights flash. Operation of the right turn is the same as the operation of the left turn signals.

Turn signal flashers are installed on the fuse panel on current car models and most current truck models. However, on earlier models this is not true. Hazard flashers are also mounted in various locations. Refer to the service manual for locations on the model being serviced.

A test light can be used to determine which flasher is used for the turn signals and which is used for the hazard warning light. An easier way is to turn on both the directionals and the hazards. This activates both flasher units. By removing one of the flashers, the affected circuit no longer flashes. Therefore, that flash unit controls that particular circuit. If the turn signals fail to operate and the fuse is good, the flasher has probably failed.

Occasionally, the flasher does not flash as fast as it once did, or it flashes faster. This is also cause for replacement. If it flashes too fast or too slowly, check for a burned-out bulb first.

A flasher features two or three prongs that plug into a socket. Just pull the flasher out of the socket and replace it with a new one.

Flashers are designed to operate a specific number of bulbs of a specific candlepower (brightness). If the candlepower of the turn signal bulbs are changed, or if additional bulbs are used (if a vehicle is hooked up to a trailer, for instance), a heavy-duty flasher must be used. This usually fits the socket without modifications.

STOP LIGHT SWITCH The stop lights are usually controlled by a stop light switch that is normally mounted on the brake pedal arm (Figure 16-18). Some cars are equipped with a brake or stop light switch mounted on the master cylinder, which closes when hydraulic pressure indicates in response to depressing the brake pedal. In either case, voltage is present at the stop light switch at all times. Depressing the brake pedal causes the stop light switch contacts to close. Current can now flow to the stop light filaments of the rear light assembly. These stay illuminated until the brake pedal is released.

In addition to the stop lights at the rear of the vehicle, all late-model cars have a high-mounted center stop light that provides an additional clear warning signal that the car is braking. Federal studies have shown the additional stop lights to be effective in reducing the number and severity of rear collisions.

Lighting Systems 405

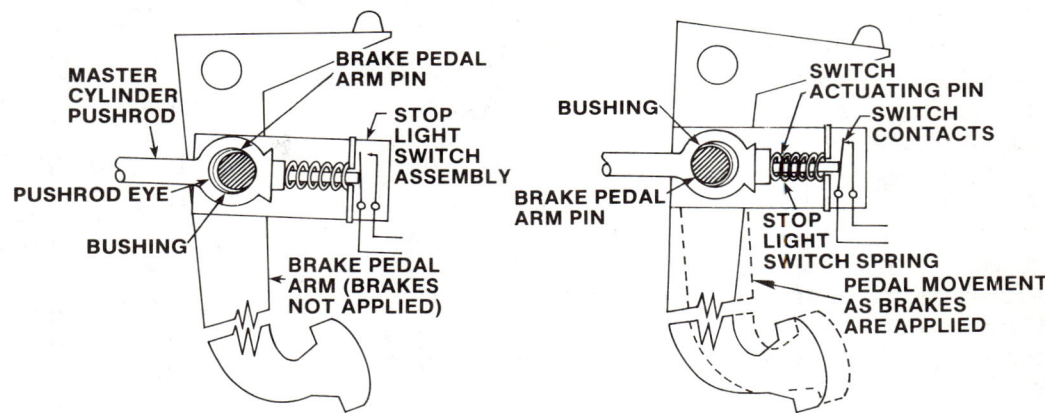

Figure 16-18 Typical brake pedal switch operation.

The high-mounted stop light is activated when current is applied to it from the stop light switch. It stays illuminated until the brake pedal is released. Kits are available to upgrade older cars with this important safety feature. Follow the kit manufacturer's instructions when installing a high-mounted stop light. When the contacts are closed, the stop light switch can also provide current to flow to the speed control amplifier, the anti-lock brake module, and the electric brake controller connector.

> ## USING SERVICE MANUALS
>
> In addition to the taillight system, the rear of vehicles have many other lighting circuits. Most cars have brake lights, run lights, turn signals, and backup lights. In addition, all vehicles produced since 1986 have collision avoidance lights. Let us look at these circuits (Figure 16-19) and see that their diagnosis is very simple once you are aware of how they appear in the service manual. Start with the brake lights. The easiest circuit to look at first is the three-bulb circuit found on many vehicles. The drawing shows a typical taillight circuit, which contains three separate filaments for each side of the rear of the vehicle. There is a separate filament for each function: brake, turn, and run. A constant source of fused B+ is made available to the brake switch. The brake switch is usually located on the brake pedal and is closed by pushing down on the brake pedal. B+ is now available to the bulbs, wired in parallel, at the rear of the vehicle. Releasing the brake pedal allows the spring-loaded normally-open (NO) switch to open and turn the brake lights off. This is a simple circuit that only requires a 12-volt test light or a voltmeter for diagnosis. The most common cause of failure are bulbs that burn out. Testing for B+ and ground at the bulb socket should verify the circuit. If B+ is not available at the socket, test for power at each connector, moving back toward the switch until it is found. Repair the open. Do not forget that the circuit is only hot if the brake pedal is depressed.

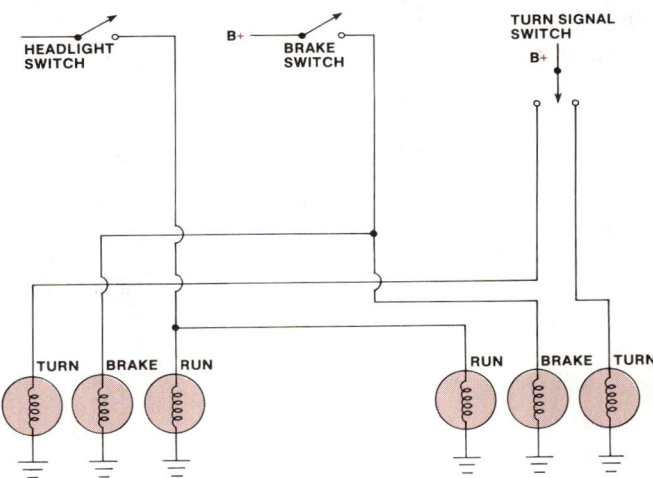

Figure 16-19 Typical three-bulb taillight circuit.

BACKUP LIGHTS When the vehicle is placed in reverse gear, backup lights are turned on to illuminate the area behind the vehicle. The major components in the system are the backup light switch and the lights.

Power for the backup light system is provided by the fuse panel. When the transmission is shifted to reverse, the backup light switch closes and power is provided to the backup lights. That is, anytime the transmission is in reverse, current flows from the fuse panel through the backup light switch to the backup lights. On many vehicles, the fuse which protects the backup light system is also the fuse which protects the turn signal system.

Various types of backup light switches are used depending on the type of transmission used on the vehicle. In general, vehicles with a manual transmission have a separate switch. Those with an automatic transmission use a combination neutral start/backup light switch. The combination neutral start/backup light switch used with automatic transmissions is actually two switches combined in one housing. In park or neutral, current from the ignition switch is applied through the neutral start switch to the starting system. In reverse, current from the fuse panel is applied through the backup light switch to the backup lights.

The backup light system is relatively easy to troubleshoot. On vehicles which use one fuse to protect both the turn signals and the backup lights, the fuse can be checked. If the backup lights are not working, check turn signal operation. If they work, the fuse is good. Check the power at the backup light switch input and the power at the switch outlet with the transmission in reverse. (Make sure the parking brake is set.)

If the switch is okay, or there is no power to the switch, check the wiring—especially the connectors. If the backup lights stay on when the transmission is not in reverse, suspect a short in the backup light switch.

LIGHT BULBS

There are several different types of light bulbs used in modern vehicles.

Headlight Bulbs

Most headlight systems consist of two or four sealed-beam tungsten headlight bulbs. On a two-headlight system, each headlight has two filaments, a high beam and a low beam (Figure 16-20). On the four-headlight system, the two outer headlights are of the two-filament type, and the two inner headlights have only one high-beam filament (Figure 16-21). In the vertical arrangement, the two upper lights are double filament. Until recently, all headlights were round, but recent styling developments created a need for rectangular light, which is more efficient and allows for more aerodynamic body styles.

CAUTION: *Sealed-beam lights are made of a single piece of molded glass and tungsten filaments that operate in an atmosphere of inert gas. The filaments quickly burn out if exposed to air.*

Some late-model cars use headlights that have a separate small light bulb enclosed in a reflector, with a separate lens in front. This type offers better light control and brightness when compared to sealed-beam types.

Halogen lights are commonly used as headlights. A halogen light contains a small quartz-glass bulb. Inside the bulb is a fuel filament surrounded by halogen gas. The small, gas-filled bulb fits within a larger metal reflector and lens element. A glass balloon sealed to the metal reflector allows the halogen bulb to be removed without danger of water or dirt damaging the optics

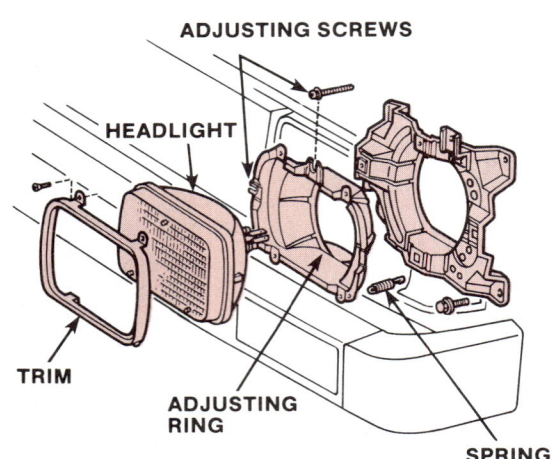

Figure 16-20 Typical two-headlight system. *Courtesy of Ford Motor Co.*

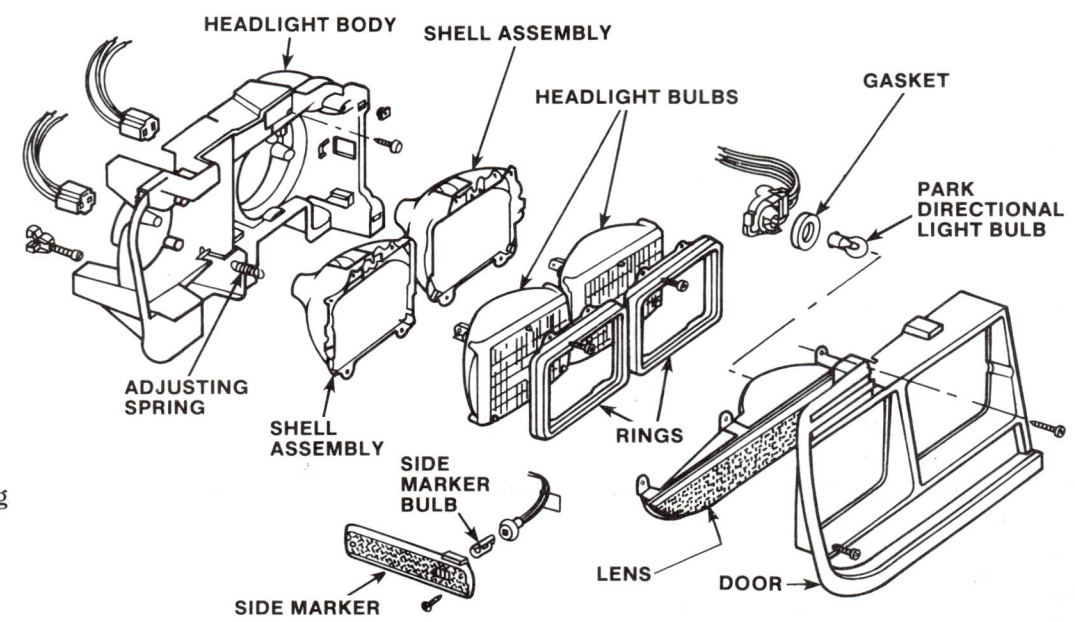

Figure 16-21 Mounting components for a typical four-headlight system. *Courtesy of General Motors Corp.*

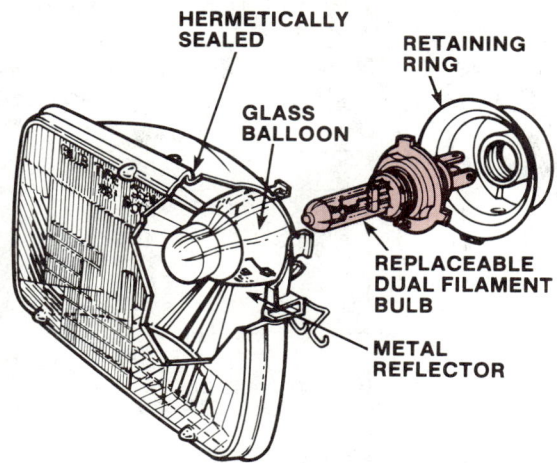

Figure 16-22 Replaceable-bulb halogen headlights are found on many import vehicles. While the conventional sealed-beam halogen is still most popular in the American market, the use of the European-style halogen headlight is on the increase.

within the light (Figure 16-22). The replaceable bulbs are removed by unplugging the electrical connector, twisting the retaining ring about 1/8 turn counterclockwise, then removing the bulb from its socket. The new bulb is installed by reversing this procedure (Figure 16-23). Sealed beam halogen lights are also available.

Halogen-sealed beams provide substantially more light on high beam to extend the driver's range of visibility for safer night driving. A halogen headlight puts out approximately twice the candlepower on high beam (150,000 vs. 75,000) as a conventional incandescent-sealed beam. On low beam, there is no difference in range between halogen and conventional incandescent-sealed beams. Both are limited by federal regulations (FMVSS 108) to a maximum of 20,000 candlepower output. Halogen bulbs do, however, produce a whiter light that helps improve visibility, last longer, and stay brighter. They also use less wattage for the same amount of light produced, which helps lessen the

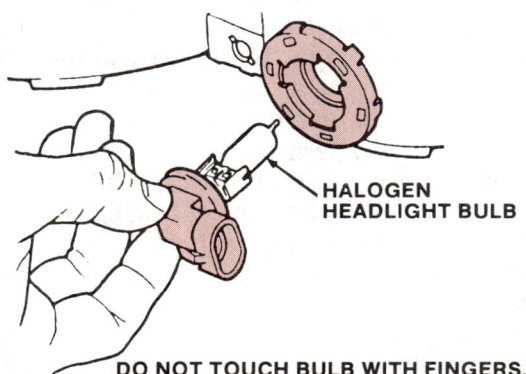

Figure 16-23 Installing a halogen bulb in its sealed enclosure. *Courtesy of Ford Motor Co.*

Lighting Systems 407

parasitic horsepower drain on the engine that is needed to drive the alternator.

CUSTOMER CARE

Both conventional sealed-beam halogen and the replaceable type are more expensive than incandescent-sealed beams. When helping a customer decide which type of replacement headlight should be used, point out the numerous advantages of either type of halogen and suggest upgrading to halogen if the vehicle currently has conventional incandescent-sealed beams. Discourage your customer from downgrading to cheaper replacement headlights if the vehicle currently has halogen.

There are various methods used to identify headlights, such as #1, #2, and the halogen marking molded into the front lens. Type #1 is high beam with two connections on the back. Type #2 is both hi/lo beam with three connections. A technician should be aware of their possible locations. Halogen headlights can be substituted for regular sealed beams, but it is suggested that this only be done in pairs. Some halogen headlight assemblies have replaceable bulbs and are not sealed beams. H1 and H2 quartz halogen are generally used in passenger vehicles.

CAUTION: *The halogen light bulb contains gas under pressure. The bulb may shatter if the glass envelope is cracked. Handle it carefully. Grasp the bulb only by its plastic base. Avoid touching the glass envelope. Skin oil can cause the bulb to shatter when turned on.*

Headlight Replacement

There can be slight variations in procedure from one model to another when replacing headlights. For instance, on some models the turn signal light assembly must be removed before the headlight can be replaced. Overall, however, the procedure does not differ much from the following typical instructions.

 **PROCEDURES**

Replacing Headlights

1. Remove the headlight bezel retaining screws. Remove the bezel. If necessary, disconnect the turn signal wires.
2. Remove the retaining ring screws from one or both lights.
3. Remove the retaining rings.
4. Remove the light from the housing. Disconnect the wiring connector from the back of the light.

5. Push the wiring connector onto the prongs at the rear of the new light.
6. Place the new light in the headlight housing. Position it so that the embossed number in the light lens is on the top.
7. Place the retaining ring over the light and install the retaining ring screws. Tighten them slightly.
8. Check the aim of the headlight and adjust it, if necessary.
9. Install the headlight bezel. Secure it with the retaining screws. Connect the turn signal wiring (if it was disconnected).

SHOP TALK

Some manufacturers recommend coating the prongs and base of a new sealed beam with dielectric grease for corrosion protection. Use an electrical lubricant approved by the manufacturer.

Headlight Adjustments

Headlights must be kept in adjustment to obtain maximum illumination. Sealed beams that are properly adjusted cover the correct range and afford the driver the proper nighttime view. Headlights that are out of adjustment can cause other drivers discomfort and sometimes create hazardous conditions.

Before adjusting or aiming to a vehicle's headlights, however, make the following inspections to ensure that the vehicle is level. Any one of the adverse conditions listed here can result in an incorrect setting.

- If the vehicle is heavily coated with snow, ice, or mud, clean the underside with a high-pressure stream of water. The additional weight can alter the riding height.
- Ensure that the gas tank is half full. Half a tank of gas is the only load that should be present on the vehicle.
- Check the condition of the springs or shock absorbers. Worn or broken suspension components affect the setting.
- Inflate all tires to the recommended air pressure levels. Take into consideration cold or hot tire conditions.
- Make sure that the wheel alignment and rear axle tracking path are correct before adjusting the headlights.
- After placing the vehicle in position for the headlight test, bounce the vehicle to settle the suspension. Stand on the bumper or push down on the front fender.

In order to properly adjust the headlights, headlight aim must be checked first. Various types of mechanical headlight aiming equipment are available commercial-

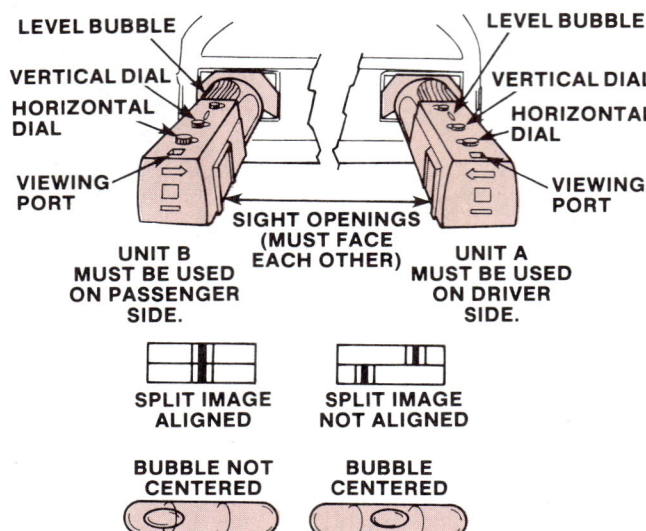

Figure 16-24 These popular mechanical headlight aiming units are mounted on the lights with suction cups. Horizontal adjustment is achieved by aligning split images in the viewer on each unit. Vertical adjustment is achieved by centering the level bubble on each unit. *Courtesy of Chrysler Corp.*

ly (Figure 16-24). These aimers use mirrors with split images, like split-image range finders on some cameras, and spirit levels to determine exact adjustment. When using any mechanical aiming equipment, follow the instructions provided by the equipment manufacturer. Where headlight aiming equipment is not available, headlight alignment can be checked by projecting the upper beam of each light upon a screen or chart at a distance of about 25 feet ahead of the headlight (Figure 16-25). The vehicle must be exactly perpendicular to the chart.

The chart should be marked in the following manner (Figure 16-26). First, measure the distance between the centers of the matching headlights. Use this measurement to draw two vertical lines on the screen with each line corresponding to the center of a headlight. Then, draw a vertical centerline halfway between the two vertical lines. Next, measure the distance from the floor to the centers of the headlights. Subtract 2 inches from this height and then draw a horizontal line on the screen at this new height.

With headlights on high beam, the hot spot of each projected beam pattern should be centered on the point of intersection of the vertical and horizontal lines on the chart. If necessary, adjust headlights vertically and laterally to obtain proper aim.

Headlight adjusting screws are provided to move the headlight within its shell assembly to obtain correct headlight aim. Lateral or side-to-side adjustment is accomplished by turning the adjusting screw at the side of the headlight (Figure 16-27). Vertical or up-and-down adjustment is accomplished by turning the screw

Lighting Systems   409

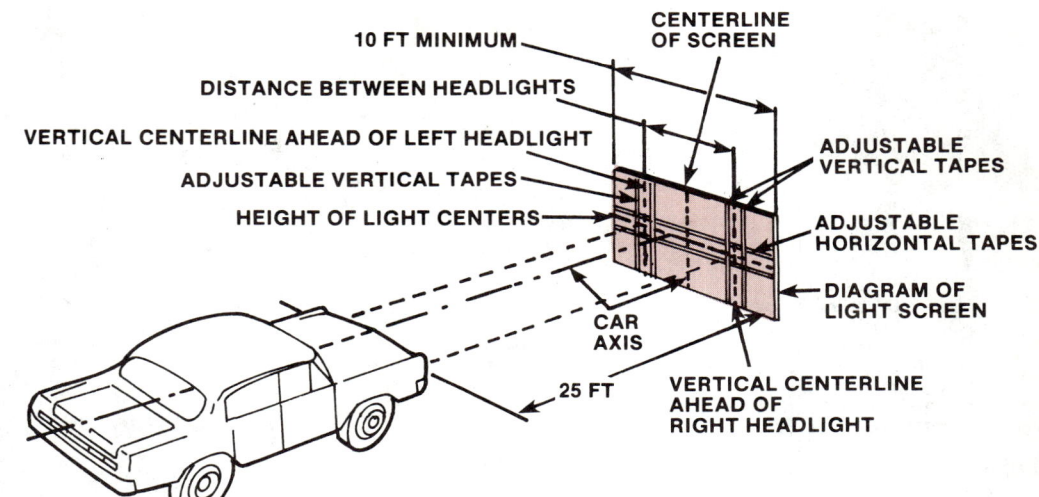

Figure 16-25 Checking headlight alignment without the luxury of aiming equipment.

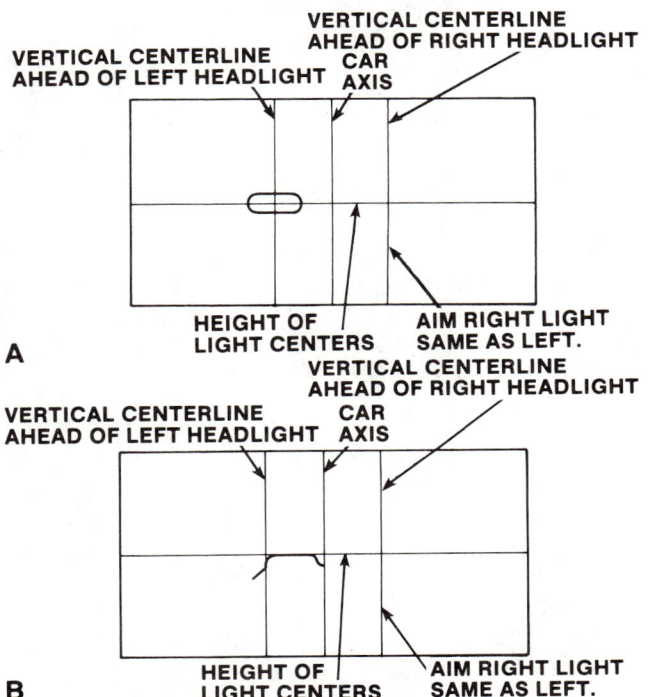

Figure 16-26 (A) Correct upper headlight beam alignment; (B) correct lower headlight beam alignment.

at the top of the headlight. Adjustments can be made without removing headlight bezels.

A properly aimed headlight normally does not need to be re-aimed after installation of a bulb. A burned out bulb should not be removed from the headlight reflector until just before a replacement bulb is to be installed. Removal of a bulb for an extended period of time may allow contaminants (dust, moisture, smoke) to enter the headlight body and affect the performance of the headlight. When servicing the headlight bulb, energize the bulb only while it is contained within the headlight body.

Other Bulbs

Bulbs used in most other lighting fixtures fit into sockets and are held in place by spring tension or mechanical force (Figure 16-28). Bulbs are coded with numbers for replacement purposes. Bulbs with different code numbers might appear physically similar but have different wattage ratings.

Light systems normally use one wire to the light, making use of the car body or frame to provide the ground back to the battery. Since many of the manufacturers have gone to plastic sockets and mounting

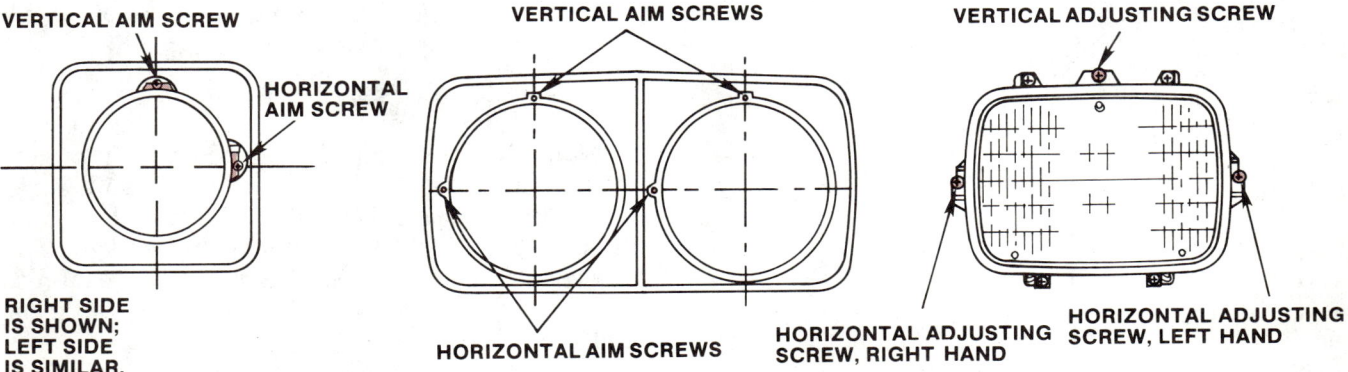

Figure 16-27 Headlight adjusting screws.

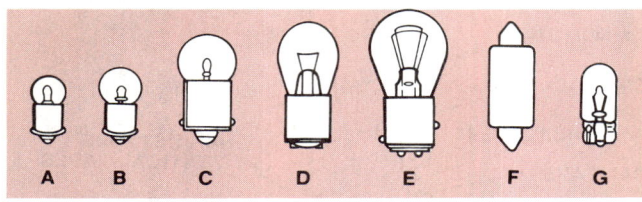

A,B MINIATURE BAYONET FOR INDICATOR AND INSTRUMENT LIGHTS
C — SINGLE CONTACT BAYONET FOR LICENSE AND COURTESY LIGHTS
D — DOUBLE CONTACT BAYONET FOR TRUNK AND UNDERHOOD LIGHTS
E — DOUBLE CONTACT BAYONET WITH STAGGERED INDEXING LUGS FOR STOP, TURN SIGNALS, AND BRAKE LIGHTS
F — CARTRIDGE TYPE FOR DOME LIGHTS
G — WEDGE BASE FOR INSTRUMENT LIGHTS

Figure 16–28 Common types of automotive bulbs.

plates (as well as plastic body parts) to reduce weight, many lights must now use two wires to provide the ground connection. Some double-filament lights use two hot wires and a third ground wire. That is, double-filament bulbs have two contacts and two wire connections to them if grounded through the base (Figure 16-29). If not grounded through the base of the bulb, a two-filament bulb has three contacts and three wires connected to it. Single-filament bulbs may be single- or double-contact types. Single-contact types are grounded through the bulb base, while double-contact, single-filament types have two wires—one live and the other a ground.

When replacing a bulb, inspect the bulb socket. If the socket is rusty or corroded, the socket or light assembly base should be replaced. Also, inspect the lens and gasket for damage while the lens is removed and replace any damaged part.

There are two basic construction designs for exterior lights: those in which the lens is removed and then the bulb removed from the front (Figure 16-30), and those in which the light assembly must first be removed then the socket from the back of the assembly, and finally the bulb from the socket (Figure 16-30B). Removing the lens from the latter type assembly could

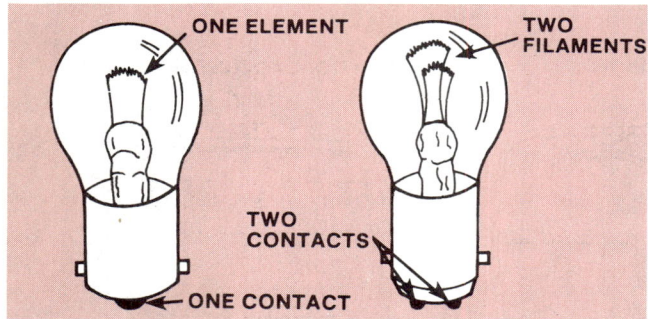

Figure 16–29 Single-filament bulbs are commonly used for license plate and side marker lights, while double-filament bulbs are ideal for front parking lights and taillights.

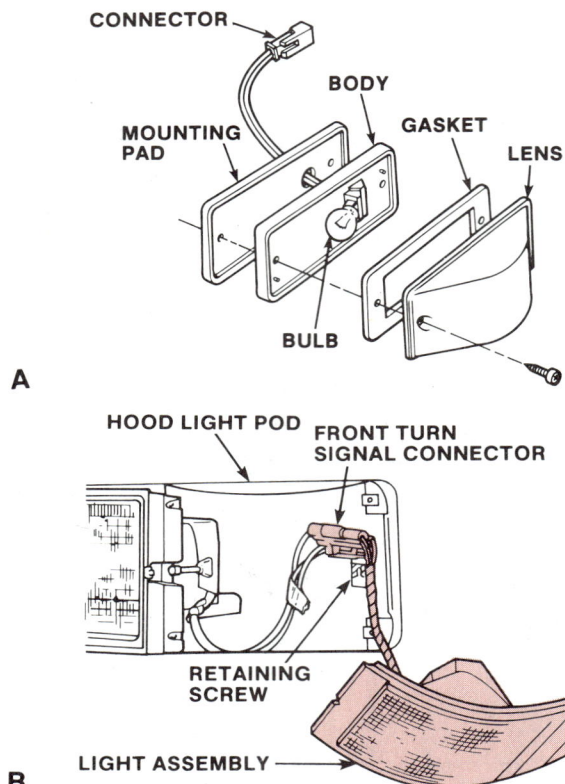

Figure 16–30 Two types of exterior lights: (A) the lens and bulb are removed from the front; (B) the light assembly is removed, then the socket is removed from the back of the assembly, then the bulb from the socket. *Courtesy of Navistar International Transportation Corp.*

cause serious damage to the reflector due to dust and other contaminants. Wiping the reflector surface to clean it can also seriously reduce the light's brightness. Therefore, do not remove the lens from light assemblies in which the socket and bulb are removed from the back of the assembly.

The bulbs are held in their sockets in a number of ways (Figure 16-31). Some bulbs are simply pushed into and pulled out of their sockets, and some are screwed in and out. To release a bayonet-style bulb from its socket, the bulb is pressed in and turned counterclockwise. The blade mount style is removed by pulling the bulb off the mounting tab, then turning the bulb and removing it from the retaining pin.

Auxiliary Lights

While the car's headlights are adequate in normal driving circumstances, some customers desire auxiliary lights for special conditions such as fog or extended night driving. In addition to the standard auxiliary fog, driving, and passing lights, there are off-road lights, worklights, rooflights, decklights, deckbars, and hand-held spotlights.

Auxiliary lights are easy to install when the manufacturer's instructions are carefully followed. The

Lighting Systems 411

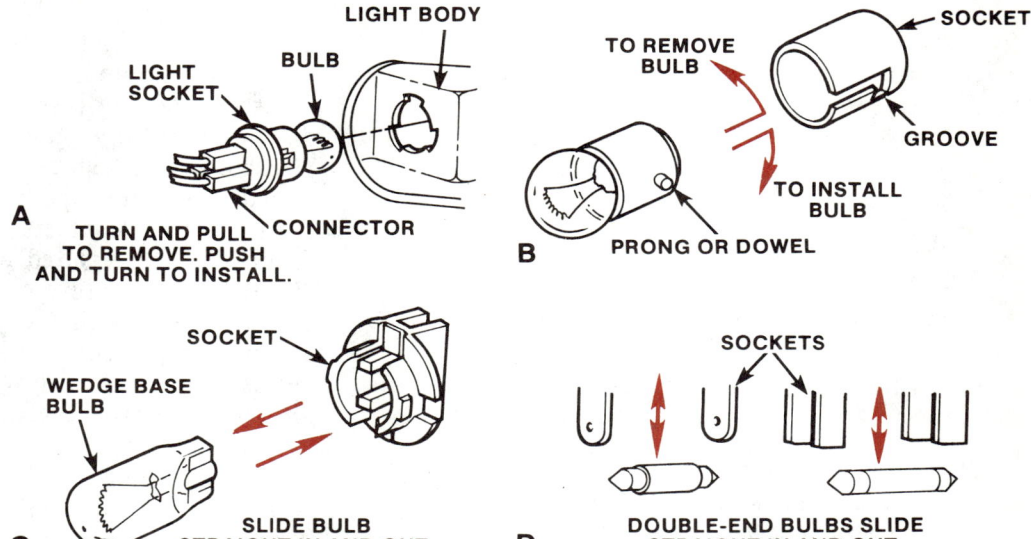

Figure 16-31 Methods of securing bulbs: (A) socket with lugs that lock into the light body; (B) prongs that are pushed in and turned; (C) wedge base is simply slid in and out; and (D) double-end are snapped in place. *Courtesy of Nissan Corp.*

mounting of auxiliary lights, of course, varies according to the type of lights being installed. For example, the ideal position for fog lights differs from that of driving and passing lights. Before beginning, remember that regulations involving auxiliary lights differ from state to state. For this reason, it is crucial that the technician be familiar with the state's regulations and adhere to them. These regulations are listed in the manual that accompanies this text or may be obtained from your state's department of transportation. Always follow all federal, state, and local laws when aiming headlights.

CUSTOMER CARE

If a customer is installing auxiliary lights, advise that the job is easier if a wiring kit is purchased along with the lights. A typical kit includes a switch and switch panel, 14-gauge wire, scotch lock connectors, solderless insulated terminals, sheet metal screws, wiring ties, fuse and fuse carrier, and a fuse box tap clip.

DRIVING AND PASSING LIGHTS Driving lights enhance the output of even the best factory headlights, affording the driver an additional margin of safety. Driving lights typically use an H3 or H4 quartz halogen bulb and a high-quality reflector and lens to project an intense, pencil-thin beam of light way down the road.

Proper aiming of the auxiliary lights is extremely important. Driving lights are used to supplement the high beams for greater distance and width. They should be used only in conjunction with the high beams. That is, driving lights should be wired so that they are off when the high beams are off. One way to do this is to supply the controlling switch with current from the high-beam circuit, rather than from a circuit that is live all the time. Passing lights are added to supplement the low beams and provide a more complete and uniform light pattern.

SHOP TALK

When adding auxiliary lights, make sure the alternator and wiring are heavy enough to handle the increased wattage. Installing a higher output may be recommended, especially if other electrical accessories are also being installed. The choice of wire size should be based on the load the wire will be powering.

FOG LIGHTS Light does not penetrate fog well at all. Focus a powerful beam of light at the fog and all the driver gets is a powerful glare back. To deal with that problem, fog lights use the same bulbs but, instead of trying to pierce the darkness, they attempt to sneak a flat, wide beam of light under the blanket of fog. This makes it important to mount them low, and to aim them low and parallel to the road. Also, because fog tends to reflect light back at the driver, some fog lights are equipped with yellow or amber lenses to reduce the discomfort caused by the glare.

While some vehicles have OEM fog lights, most are auxiliary lighting add-ons. Their circuits, however, are basically the same as drive lights (Figure 16-32). They involve a relay switch and the lights themselves. A relay is used because the amount of current that fog lights require, especially halogen ones, can be quite high. It is not unusual that they require as much as 25 amperes.

Fog lights are generally not wired directly from an unswitched battery power source. This would allow them to be left on with the vehicle off. Their high current draw would quickly drain the battery. The dash switch controls the current to one side of the relay's coil. A direct ground is supplied to the other side of the relay coil. With both battery voltage and ground ap-

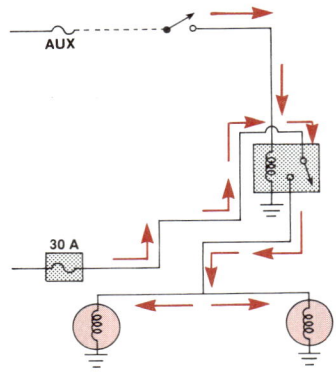

Figure 16-32 Typical auxiliary fog light circuit.

plied, current flows through the coil and a magnetic field develops. The field closes the contacts in the relay. Notice that one side of the contacts is connected to a fused source of battery voltage. The other side is connected to the fog lights, which are wired in parallel. Each filament has its own remote ground connection.

When adding fog lights, or any accessory, place the fuse as close to the source as possible. Picking up the power source under the hood is easy. There are many choices available. Solenoids, horn relays, and alternators are some of the common choices. An in-line fuse should be placed as close as is practical to this source. An overload or a short circuit would safely open the circuit protector and eliminate B+ for the entire circuit.

CAUTION: Fuse the circuit for the size of the wire. Overfusing and underwiring are two common problems that must be avoided. Also, keep in mind that amperage rating must be equal to or greater than the maximum electrical load the circuit is expected to carry. You can safely use a switch with more ampere capacity than the auxiliary lighting circuit requires, but never one with an underrated capacity.

Driving and fog lights have tremendous output and have correspondingly high electrical requirements. This means that the car should have an efficient charging system and a heavy-duty battery.

SHOP TALK

When replacing fog light bulbs, avoid touching the glass part of the new bulb assembly. Skin oil, present on even recently washed hands, remains on the glass. This oil prevents the bulb from dissipating heat. The increased heat inside the bulb causes the filament to burn out prematurely.

❏ LIGHTING MAINTENANCE

In addition to replacing all burnt out lights and bulbs, when a vehicle comes in for servicing, periodically check to see that all wiring connections are clean and tight, that light units are tightly mounted to provide a good ground, and that headlights are properly adjusted. Loose or corroded connections can cause a discharged battery, difficult starting, dim lights, and possible damage to the alternator and regulator. Often moisture gets into a bulb socket and causes corrosion of the electrical contacts and the bulb. Corrosive conditions can be repaired by using sandpaper on the affected areas. For severe cases, replace the socket and bulb. After any repair, always attempt to waterproof the assembly to prevent future problems. Cracked or broken assemblies are easily replaced. They are secured by attaching hardware that is normally readily accessible to the technician.

Another common electrical lighting problem is flickering lights (lights go on or off). The cause of this is usually a loose electrical connection or a circuit breaker that is kicking out because of a short. If all or several of the lights flicker, the problem is in a section of the circuit common to those lights. Check to see if the lights only flicker with the light switch in one position. For example, if the lights flicker only when the headlights are on high beam, check the components and wiring in the high-beam section of the circuit. If only one light flickers, the problem is in that section of the circuit. Check the bulb socket for corrosion. Also, make sure the bulb terminals are not worn. This could upset the electrical connection. If needed, replace the bulb socket and bulb.

➤ CASE STUDY

Case 1

The customer complains that the turn signals on his vehicle do not operate as they are supposed to, and they seldom cancel out properly. Turn signal circuits are frequent sources of difficulties. Their diagnosis, however, is not difficult and can usually be accomplished with just a 12-volt test light or a voltmeter. Look at the common circuits, starting first with the flasher. The flasher is actually a type of circuit breaker, which is an overload protection device designed to open the circuit because of heat developed from excessive current. Flashers are usually mounted in the fuse box and made up of a fixed contact and a movable bimetallic contact.

Look at the turn signal in Figure 16-33A. The diagram shows the inside of a turn signal switch for a two-bulb system. The turn signal switch determines whether one of the bulbs is used for turning or brake lighting. The rectangular bars on the diagram are stationary contacts that the circuit wires connect to. Each contact has one wire connected to it. The top connection is from the brake switch and is B+ if the brakes are applied. The middle row connections are for rear combination lights (combi-

Lighting Systems   413

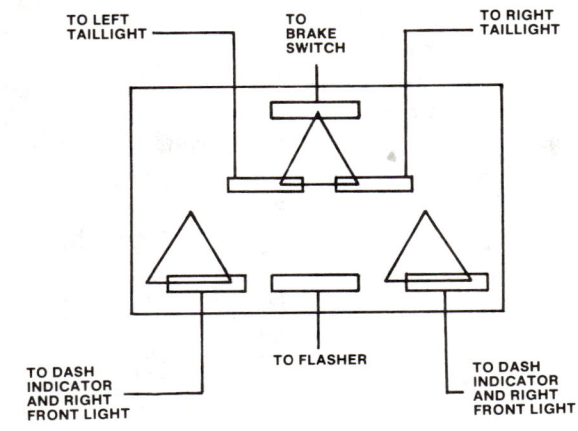

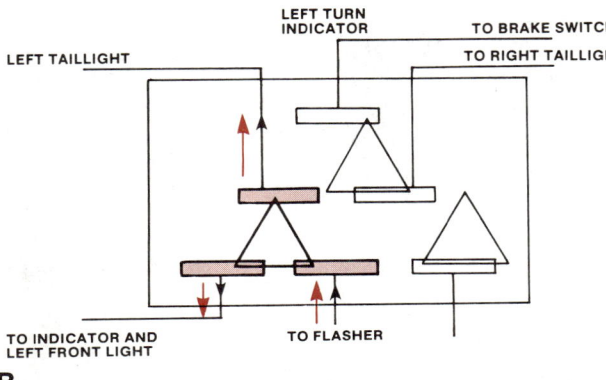

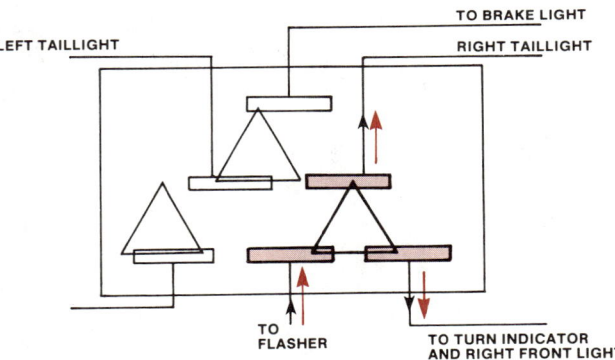

Figure 16-33 A turn signal switch (A) not in use, (B) with a left turn indicated, and (C) with a right turn indicated. *Courtesy of Ford Motor Co.*

nation brake/turn signal). The bottom row of connections is for the front lights, including the dash indicators, and the B+ coming from the flasher. The triangles drawn over the bars are a set of three movable conductive pads which connect the different bars together depending on the position of the switch. They are drawn in the no turn or neutral position. This allows B+ from the brake switch to activate both rear lights at the same time. Figure 16-33B shows the same switch in a left turn. Notice that the conductive pads or triangles have moved to the right. This allows the brake switch to only power the right taillight, while the flasher connection is now in contact with the left rear taillight and the left front/indicator lights. The right taillight is being operated as a brake light, while the left one is in a turn signal operation. Figure 16-33C shows the same switch in a right turn mode. Notice that the conductive pads have moved to the left and have connected the brake switch to the left taillight, while the right is now powered off of the turn signal flasher. This style of switch is very popular and normally is very durable. The most common problem encountered with the switch is usually mechanical rather than electrical. As the vehicle is driven around the corner, the cancelling mechanism must put the switch back into a neutral position so that both taillights can be used for brake warning. When this cancelling does not take place, the turn signal switch is normally replaced to correct the problem.

Summary

- The headlight switch controls the headlights and all other light systems, with the exception of the turn signals, hazard warning, and stop lights.
- Dimmer switches, located on either the steering wheel or the floor, permit the headlights to change from hi to lo beam and vice-versa.
- An automatic headlight dimmer circuit switches the headlights from hi to lo beam, in response to either light from an approaching vehicle or light from the taillights of a vehicle being overtaken.
- Depending on the make or model of the vehicle, courtesy lights can be found on the door, under the seats, under the instrument panel, on the rear interior quarter panels, or on the ceiling.
- The rear light assembly includes the taillights, turn signal/stop/hazard lights, high-mounted stop light, rear side marker lights, backup lights, and license plate lights. Taillights operate when the parking lights or headlights are on.
- Headlights must be kept in adjustment to obtain maximum illumination and vehicle occupant safety.
- Flashers are used in turn signal, hazard warning, and side marker light circuits.
- The backup light system illuminates the area behind the vehicle when it is put in reverse gear.
- Headlight systems consist of two or four sealed-beam tungsten or halogen headlight bulbs.

Review Questions

1. Name the two types of headlight switches.
2. When is the rear light assembly activated?
3. Where is the stop light switch normally mounted?
4. What lights are used to supplement the high beams?

5. What lights are used to supplement the low beams?
6. Which of the following is usually not included in the main lighting system?
   a. glove box light
   b. turn signals
   c. dome/map lights
   d. headlight switch
7. Which of the following is often controlled by a mercury switch?
   a. trunk light
   b. underhood light
   c. both A and B
   d. neither A nor B
8. The rear light assembly includes the _____.
   a. rear side marker lights
   b. taillights
   c. license plate light
   d. all of the above
9. Circuits that can energize both the high and low beams even if the headlight switch is off are known as _____ circuits.
   a. flash-to-pass
   b. mercury
   c. dimmer
   d. retractable
10. Technician A says that pulling out the regular headlight switch overrides the autolight/delayed exit system. Technician B says that pulling out the regular headlight switch has no effect on the autolight/delayed exit system. Who is correct?
    a. Technician A
    b. Technician B
    c. Both A and B
    d. Neither A nor B
11. Technician A handles halogen headlight bulbs by grasping the glass envelope. Technician B handles halogen headlight bulbs by grasping the plastic base. Who is correct?
    a. Technician A
    b. Technician B
    c. Both A and B
    d. Neither A nor B
12. Technician A adjusts a headlight side-to-side by turning the adjusting screw at the top of the headlight. Technician B makes the same adjustment by turning the adjusting screw at the side of the headlight. Who is correct?
    a. Technician A
    b. Technician B
    c. Both A and B
    d. Neither A nor B
13. Which of the following statements is incorrect?
    a. A blade mount style bulb is removed from its socket by pulling it off the mounting tab, then turning it and removing it from the retaining pin.
    b. Power for the hazard warning light system is provided by the fuse panel.
    c. Cornering side lights operate independently of the turn signals.
    d. None of the above
14. The stop light switch is normally mounted on the _____.
    a. instrument panel
    b. transmission
    c. brake pedal arm
    d. none of the above
15. Technician A says that the fuse which protects the backup light system is sometimes the same fuse which protects the turn signal system. Technician B says these two fuses are always separate. Who is correct?
    a. Technician A
    b. Technician B
    c. Both A and B
    d. Neither A nor B
16. The ideal position for fog lights _____.
    a. differs from state to state
    b. differs from that of driving and passing lights
    c. both A and B
    d. neither A nor B
17. Technician A uses a relay switch when installing auxiliary fog lights, but Technician B does not. Who is correct?
    a. Technician A
    b. Technician B
    c. Both A and B
    d. Neither A nor B
18. Technician A says that flickering vehicle lights can be caused by a circuit breaker that is kicking out due to a short. Technician B says that flickering vehicle lights can be caused by a loose electrical connection. Who is correct?
    a. Technician A
    b. Technician B
    c. Both A and B
    d. Neither A nor B

ELECTRICAL INSTRUMENTS AND ACCESSORIES

17

Objectives

- Know the purpose of gauges and how they function.
- Describe the two types of instrument panel displays.
- Know the basic operation of electric windshield wiper and washer systems.
- Explain the operation of power door locks, power windows, and power seats.
- Determine how well the defroster system performs.
- Understand how cruise or speed control operates and the differences of various systems.
- Consider the use and value of engine cooling fans.

Every automobile is equipped with a number of electrical instruments and accessories. The number and types of these systems and components varies significantly from vehicle model to model and year to year. Instrument gauges, lights and warning indicators provide valuable information to the driver concerning various systems in the automobile. These range from engine coolant temperature indications to fasten seat belt reminders. On the other hand, electrical accessories provide the driver with safety and warning devices such as windshield wipers, horns and speed controls and make driving more pleasant by offering such items as power seats, power windows, clocks, and radios.

☐ INSTRUMENT GAUGES

Gauges provide the driver with a scaled indication of the condition of a system. For example, the fuel tank is half full. Gauges that indicate a relative scale of values are known as analog instruments. Those that indicate an exact number for a measured quantity are known as digital instruments.

Two additional components are required besides the electrical gauge itself. These are instrument voltage regulators and sender units. Instrument voltage regulators (IVR) are used to stabilize and limit voltage for accurate instrument operation. Sender or sensor units change electrical resistance in response to changes or movements made by an external component. Movement may be caused by pressure against a diaphragm, heat, or motion of a float as liquid fills a fuel tank.

All gauges (analog or digital) require an input from either a sender or a sensor. However, with modern computer-controlled displays, the sensor's output is used in two ways. The engine control computer needs the same information as the electronic display, so the information passes through the computer first. It then goes on to the gauge.

Two types of electrical analog gauges are commonly used with sensor or sending units—magnetic and thermal.

Magnetic Gauges

There are several types of magnetic gauges. The simplest form is the ammeter type (Figure 17-1A). In this gauge, a permanent magnet attracts a ferrous indicator needle connected to a pivot point and holds it centered. An armature, or coil of wire, is wrapped around the base of the needle, near the pivot point. Current can flow through a conductor beneath the armature. When current flows, a magnetic field around the conductor induces magnetism in the armature. This magnetism opposes that of the permanent magnet. Attractive or repulsive magnetic forces cause the needle to swing left or right. The direction the needle swings depends on the direction of current flow in the conductor.

Figure 17-1B shows the magnetic bobbin gauge often used as an analog fuel indicator. In this type of gauge, the bobbin assembly creates a magnetic field. The pointer is attached to a magnet that reacts to the strength of that field. Changing current is again used to drive the gauge. The higher the level, temperature, or pressure, the more current flows in the gauge circuit. The current creates a magnetic field that moves the pointer.

In a typical example of the magnetic type of gauge, consider that a voltage of approximately 5 volts is applied by the IVR to each gauge circuit. By varying the

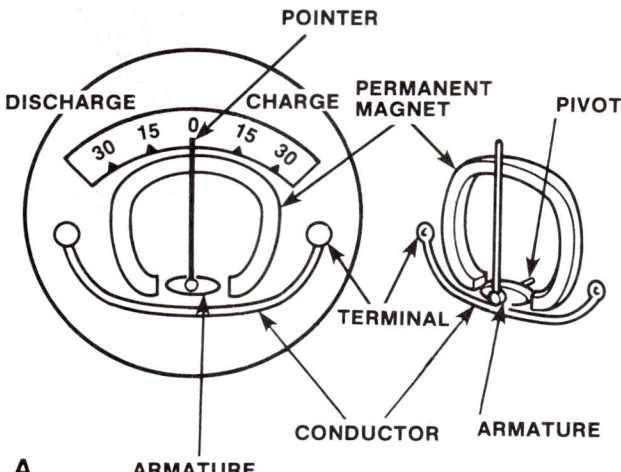

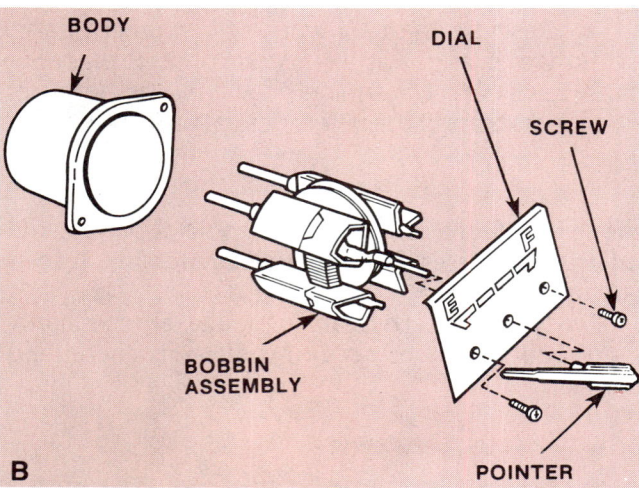

Figure 17-1 (A) Simple ammeter; (B) magnetic bobbin gauge. *Courtesy of Ford Motor Co.*

resistance in the sender, the current level reading on the gauge can be changed. The higher the resistance in the sender, the lower the current in the circuit, which is indicated by a smaller indicator movement on the gauge. As stated in Ohm's law: voltage (E) is equal to current (I) times resistance (R) or $E = IR$.

A balancing coil gauge also operates on principles of magnetic attraction and repulsion. However, a permanent magnet is not used. The base of the indicating arm is pivoted and includes an armature. Two coils are used to create magnetic fields (Figure 17-2).

A sending unit has a variable resistance. The two coils are connected so that electricity can flow through either one. When the resistance of a sending unit is low, the right-hand coil receives more current than the left-hand coil. More magnetism is created in the right-hand coil, attracting the armature. Thus, a gauge needle moves to the right.

When resistance of a sending unit is high, the left-hand coil receives more current. More magnetic force is created in the left-hand coil. A gauge needle swings to the left.

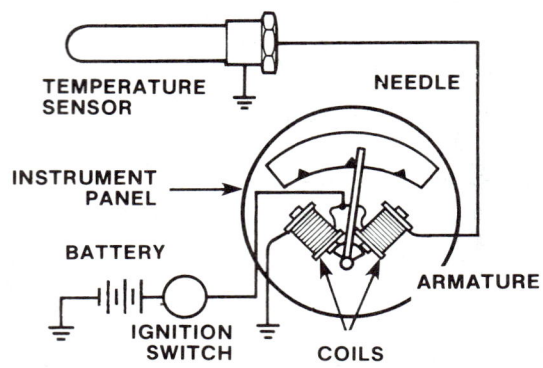

Figure 17-2 Balancing coil gauge. *Courtesy of Ford Motor Co.*

Thermal or Bimetallic Gauge

A thermal gauge operates through heat created by current flow (Figure 17-3). A variable-resistance sending unit causes different amounts of current to flow through a heating coil within a gauge. The heat acts on a bimetallic spring attached to a gauge needle. When more heat is created, the needle swings farther up the scale. When less heat is created, the needle moves down the scale.

☐ INSTRUMENT PANELS

In horse-and-wagon days, the dashboard really was a vertical board placed in front of the driver to protect from the mud slung up from horse hoofs just ahead. Today's dashboard is more properly called the instrument panel. It mounts an array of electrical gauges, switches, and controls all connected to mazes of wiring, printed circuitry, and air hoses beneath stylishly finished sheets of plastic or metal.

There are various instrument panel designs and layouts. The two basic types of instrument panel displays are analog and digital. In a traditional analog display (Figure 17-4), an indicator moves in front of a fixed scale to give variable readout. The indicator is often a needle, but it can also be liquid crystal or graphic display. A digital (or electronic) display uses numbers instead of a needle or graphic symbol. The advantage of analog displays is that they show relative change better than digital displays (Figure 17-5). Analog displays are useful when the driver must see something quickly and the exact reading is not important. For example, an analog tachometer shows the rise and fall of the engine speed better for shifting than a digital display. The driver does not need to know exactly how many rpm the engine is running. The most important thing is how fast the engine is reaching the red line on the gauge. A digital display is better for showing exact data such as miles or operating hours. Many speedometer-odometer combinations are examples of both analog (speed) and digital (distance).

Electrical Instruments and Accessories 417

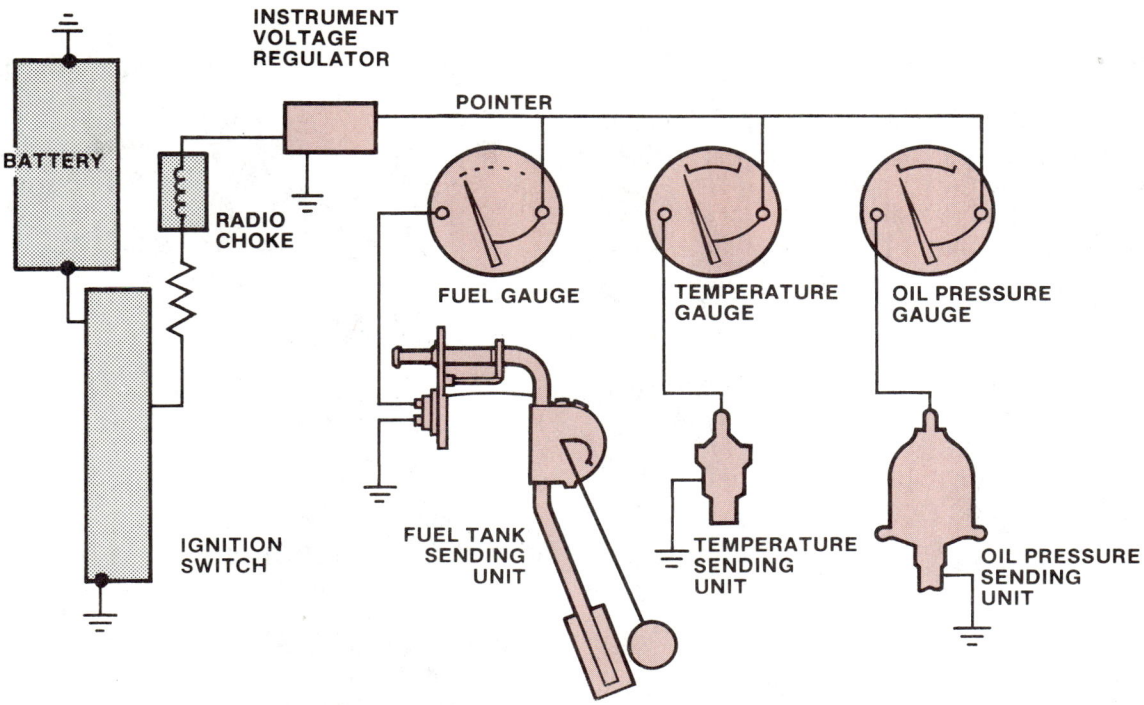

Figure 17-3 Typical bimetallic gauge system. *Courtesy of Ford Motor Co.*

A digital signal has only two states. It is either on or off. If a switch is turned on and off many times, the number of pulses can be counted. For example, a speed sensor can be made to turn on and off each time a wheel moves a certain distance. The number of pulses that are counted in a given period of time allows the computer to display the speed. The pulses can also be used by the computer to change the odometer reading.

There are three types of digital electronic displays used today. A description of each follows.

LIGHT-EMITTING DIODE (LED) These are used as either single indicator lights, or they can be grouped to show a set of letters or numbers. LED displays are commonly red, yellow, or green, and use more power than other displays. They can also be hard to see in bright light.

LIQUID CRYSTAL DIODE (LCD) These have become very popular for many uses, including watches, calcu-

Figure 17-5 A digital display.

lators, and dash gauges. They are made of sandwiches of special glass and liquid. A separate light source is required to make the display work. When there is no voltage, light cannot pass through the fluid. When voltage is applied, the light passes through the segment. LCDs do not like cold temperatures, and the action of the display slows down in cold weather. These displays are also very delicate, and must be handled with care. Any rough handling of the display can damage it.

Figure 17-4 A traditional analog display.

VACUUM FLUORESCENT These displays use glass tubes filled with argon or neon gas. The segments of the display are little fluorescent lights, like the ones in a fluorescent fixture. When current is passed through the tubes, they glow very brightly. These displays are both durable and bright.

The choice of either an analog or a digital display is a matter of designer or buyer preferences.

> **SHOP TALK**
>
> Most warning or instrument controls use International Standards Organization (ISO) symbols. These ISO automotive symbols were developed by this organization to provide easily recognizable symbols throughout the world. For instance, the fuel pump symbol is used to represent fuel. Other ISO symbols are illustrated in this chapter.

☐ BASIC INFORMATION GAUGES

The following gauges are found on almost every instrument panel—whether analog or digital. The detailed operation of some gauges is described in other chapters.

Speedometer

Until recently the speedometer was always considered a nonelectrical or mechanical gauge. The typical mechanical speedometer had a drive cable attached to a gear in the transmission that turns a magnet inside a cup-shaped metal piece (Figure 17-6). The cup is attached to a speedometer needle and held at zero by a hairspring (a fine wire spring). As the cable rotates faster with increasing speed, magnetic forces act on the cup and force it to rotate. The speedometer needle, attached to the cup, moves up the speed scale.

Electric speedometers are used in more and more cars. While there are several systems in use, one of the

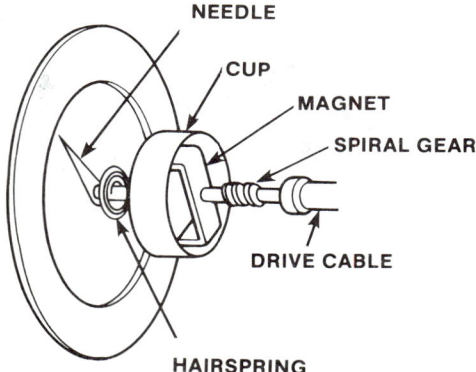

Figure 17-6 Typical conventional speedometer.

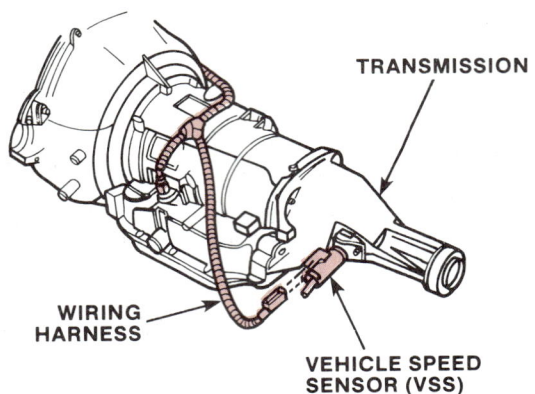

Figure 17-7 Transmission-mounted vehicle speed sensor (VSS).

most common types receives its speed information from the transmission-mounted eight-pole vehicle speed sensor (Figure 17-7). This speed signal is also used by other modules in the vehicle, including speed control, ride control module, the engine control module and others. In the event of a short or open in the system, check the connections for these other components.

For each 8000 pulses from the vehicle speed sensor (VSS), the speedometer electronics increment the trip and total odometers in miles. Speed is determined by taking the input pulse frequency (in Hertz) and dividing by 2.2 Hertz/mph. The circuit electronics are calibrated to drive the pointer to a location in proportion to the speed input frequency. That is, as the pulse rate increases, the speedometer records it on an analog display. This display may be limited to a maximum of 85 mph of 199 km/h.

Most digital speedometers display vehicle speeds from 0 to 85 mph or 199 km/h. If vehicle speed exceeds these values, the speedometer continues to display 85 mph or 199 km/h. Vehicle speed is displayed whether the vehicle is moving forward or backward.

A variation of the electric speedometer employs a permanent magnet generator. An electric signal is then sent from the generator sensor to a speed buffer and then to the speedometer.

Odometer

The odometer is a digital gauge that is usually driven by a spiral gear cut on the speedometer's magnet shaft. The odometer's numbered drums are geared so that any one drum finishes a complete revolution. The next drum to the left is turned one-tenth of a revolution (Figure 17-8).

Like the mechanical speedometer, the conventional odometer is giving way to the electrical type. Generally, the electric odometer receives its information from the VSS. Electrical odometers display seven digits, with the last digit in tenths of a unit. The odometer range is limited by the cluster memory space. The English units

Electrical Instruments and Accessories   419

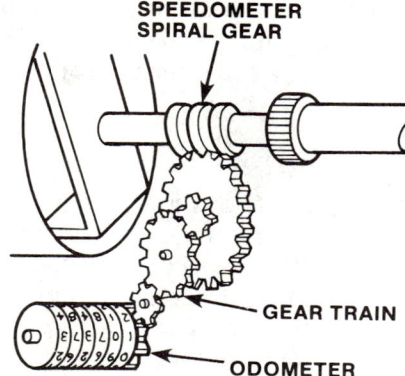

Figure 17-8 Odometer.

range from 000000.5 to 925691.9 miles. The display freezes at this value. In metric units, the range is from 000000.8 to 858993.4 km where the value rolls over to 000000.0 and continues accumulating up to 622113.6 km (the total distance is then the equivalent of 925691.9 total miles). The accumulated mileage value of the digital display odometer is stored in a non-volatile memory (ROM) that retains the mileage value even if the battery is disconnected.

Since the odometer records the number of miles a vehicle has traveled, federal law requires that the odometer, in any replacement speedometer, must register the same mileage as that registered on the removed speedometer. Therefore, if a speedometer has been replaced, set the odometer of the new one to match the old. The trip odometer may be reset whenever desired.

Other Gauges

Some other electrical gauges that are commonly used on vehicles follow.

OIL PRESSURE GAUGE This gauge indicates engine oil pressure. The oil pressure typically should be between 45 and 70 psi when the engine is running at a specified engine speed, with SAE 10W-30 oil, and at operating temperature. A lower pressure is normal at low idle speed.

The oil pressure switch determines whether or not current flows through the oil pressure gauge winding (Figure 17-9A). With low oil pressure (or with the engine shut off), the oil pressure switch is open and no current flows through the gauge winding. The needle points to L. With oil pressure above a specific limit, the switch closes and current flows through the gauge winding to ground. A resistor limits current flow through the winding and ensures that the needle points to about mid-scale with normal oil pressure.

COOLANT TEMPERATURE GAUGE This gauge indicates engine coolant temperature. It should normally indicate between 170 and 195 degrees Fahrenheit. Somewhat higher temperatures might occur under cer-

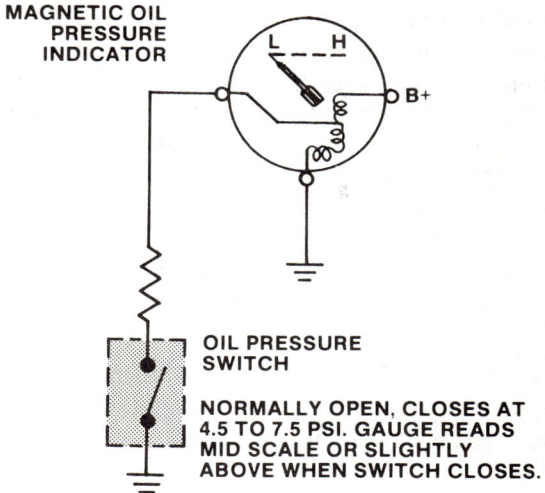

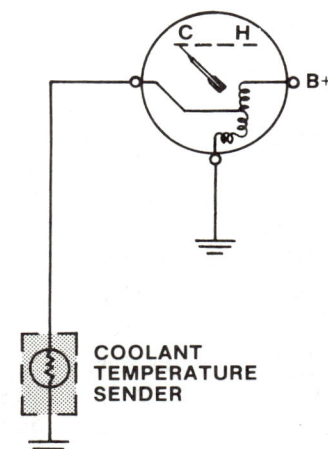

Figure 17-9 (A) Typical pressure indicator; (B) coolant temperature gauge; and (C) fuel indicating gauge.

tain conditions. Typically, the maximum allowable temperature is 210 degrees Fahrenheit.

The sender or sensor is a variable resistance such as a thermistor. It determines current flow through the temperature gauge winding (Figure 17-9B). With low coolant temperature, sender resistance is high and current flow is low. The needle points to C. As coolant temperature increases, sender resistance decreases and current flow increases. The needle moves toward H.

The temperature gauge on a digital panel is of the bar type with a set number of segments. The number of illuminated bars varies according to the voltage across the gauge sender. With low coolant temperature, sender resistance is high and few segments are turned on. As coolant temperature increases, sender resistance decreases and the number of illuminated segments increases.

FUEL LEVEL GAUGES These gauges indicate the fuel level in the fuel tank. It is a magnetic indicating system that can be found on either an analog (meter) or digital (bars) instrument panel.

The fuel sender unit is combined with the fuel pump assembly and consists of a variable resistor controlled by the level of an attached float in the fuel tank (Figure 17-9C). When the fuel level is low, resistance in the sender is low and movement of the gauge indicator dial or number of lit bars is minimal (from empty position). When the fuel level is high, the resistance in the sender is high and movement of the gauge indicator (from the empty position) or number of lit bars is greater.

In some fuel gauge systems, an anti-slosh/low fuel warning (LFW) module is used to reduce fuel gauge needle fluctuation caused by fuel motion in the tank and provide a low fuel warning when fuel reaches 1/8–1/16 full.

TACHOMETER The tachometer indicates engine rpm (engine speed). Figure 17-10 illustrates how the tachometer is connected. Electrical impulses from the coil are passed to the tachometer. The tachometer, using a balanced coil gauge, converts these impulses to rpm that can be read. The faster the engine rotates, the greater the number of impulses from the coil. Consequently, the greater the indicated rpm.

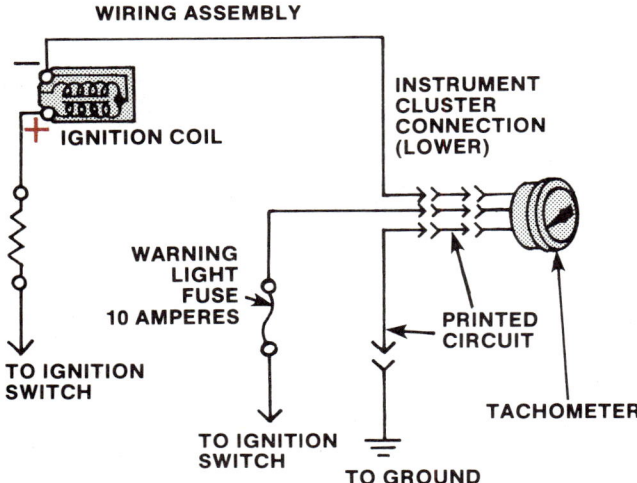

Figure 17-10 Typical tachometer circuit. *Courtesy of Ford Motor Co.*

In vehicles with digital instrumentation, the bar system is used with numbered segments. The numbers represent the engine's rpm times 1,000.

> **SHOP TALK**
>
> The bar gauge found in some digital displays can also be used to indicate trouble in the system. For example with one such system, diagnostic bars are displayed on a gauge when only the top and bottom two bar sections appear on the gauge. This can be an indication of a troubled signal or sender. Refer to diagnostic trouble bars given in the service manual.

CHARGING GAUGES These allow the driver to monitor the charging system. While a few cars use a voltmeter, most charging systems employ either an ammeter gauge or an indicator light. The ammeter gauge is placed in series with the battery and alternator. When the alternator is delivering current to the battery, the gauge displays a positive (+) indication. When the battery is not receiving enough current (or none at all) from the alternator, a negative (–) display is obtained.

☐ INDICATORS AND WARNING DEVICES

Indicator lights and warning devices are generally activated by the closing of a switch. With power from the fuse panel on the other side, the indicator light comes on to warn the driver that something in the system is not functioning properly or that a situation exists that must be corrected. Figure 17-11 shows the warning lights on a typical instrument panel. The function of some of the more common warning lights are given here.

AIR BAG READINESS LIGHT On vehicles equipped with air bags, the air bag readiness light lets the driver know the air bag system is working and ready to do its job. It lights briefly when the ignition is turned on. A malfunction in the air bag system causes the light to stay on continuously or to flash, or the light may not come on at all.

AIR SUSPENSION LIGHT Voltage is present at the air suspension indicator at all times. If an air suspension fault is present, the indicator illuminates.

FASTEN BELTS INDICATOR When the ignition is turned to run or start, the warning chime module applies voltage to illuminate the fasten belts indicator for six seconds, whether or not the driver's belt is buckled.

HIGH-BEAM LIGHT With the headlights turned on and the main light switch dimmer switch in the high-beam position, the indicator illuminates.

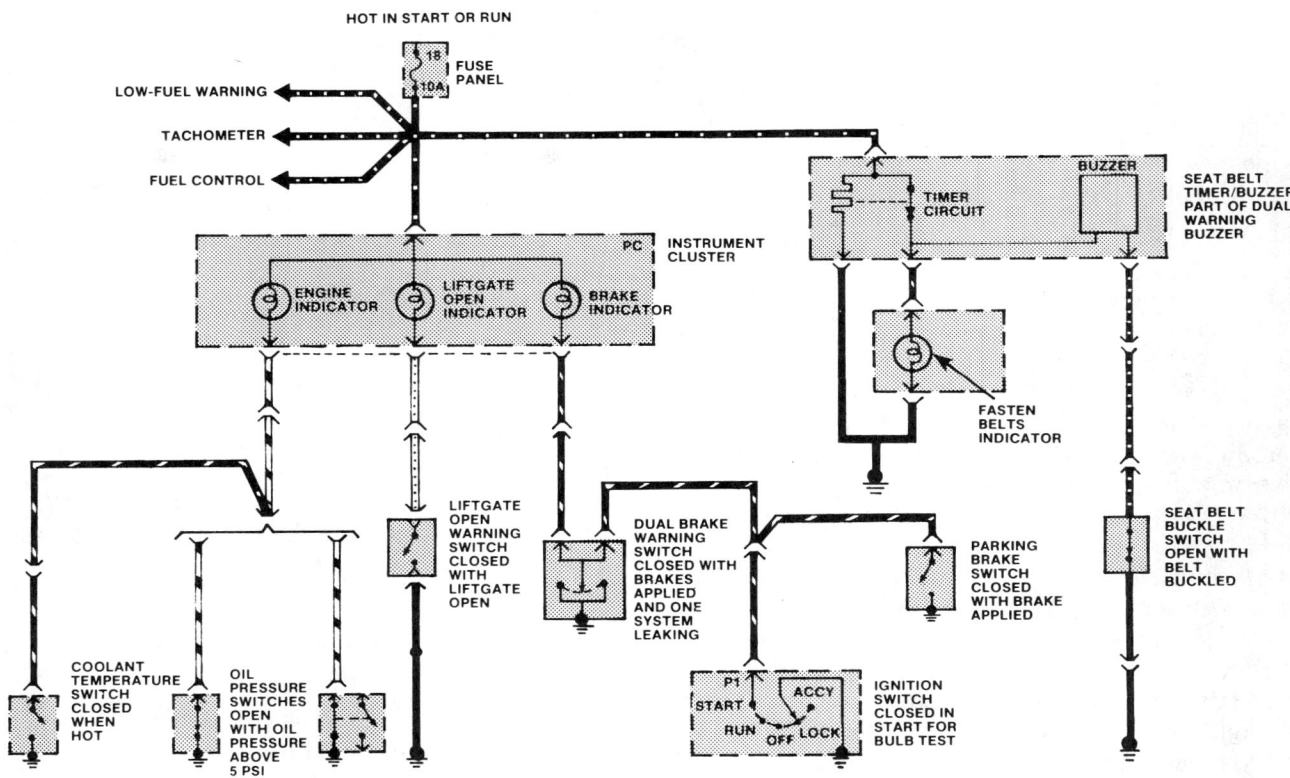

Figure 17-11 Typical warning indicators. *Courtesy of Ford Motor Co.*

LEFT AND RIGHT TURN INDICATORS With the multi-function switch in the left or right turn position, voltage is applied to circuit to illuminate the left or right turn indicator. The turn indicator flashes in unison with the exterior turn signal bulbs.

ANTI-LOCK LIGHT If an anti-lock brake system fault is present, the anti-lock brake module grounds the indicator circuit and the anti-lock light goes on.

RETRACTABLE HEADLIGHT This indicator light turns on only when the headlight raise/down motor is in operation. It comes on and lights for about one second when the headlights move up or down.

OIL TEMPERATURE WARNING LIGHT The warning light is provided for the purpose of preventing the overheating of torque converter fluid in case of repeated start-off operations in sand or on a snowy road, or when the car is operated at very low speed (near the stall speed) continuously under heavily-loaded conditions.

If the temperature of the fluid at the torque converter outlet exceeds a specified temperature, the warning light at oil temp illuminates and warns the driver of high oil temperature.

In such a case, the driver need not stop the car, but should avoid undue operation. The warning light goes out as the fluid temperature drops.

CHARGE INDICATOR LIGHT The light indicates the condition of the alternator and charging system. If there is something wrong with the alternator and charging system, the light comes on while the engine is running.

OIL PRESSURE INDICATOR LIGHT The light indicates whether or not the oil pump is feeding oil under normal pressure to various parts of the engine. The indicator light is operated by an oil pressure switch located in the engine's lubricating system.

STOP LIGHT WARNING LIGHT The light is controlled by the stop light checker. This checker consists of a reed switch and magnet coils, as shown in Figure 17-12. Under normal conditions, magnetic fields are generated in the magnet coils by the current flowing through each light while the stop light switch is on. These magnetic fields cancel each other because the coils turn in directions opposite to each other. As a result, the reed switch remains off, and the warning light is off. If either the left or right side stop light fails, current flows through only one magnet coil, and the resultant magnetic field causes the reed switch to turn on. Therefore, the warning light remains lighted as long as the brake pedal is depressed.

LAMP-OUT WARNING LIGHT The lamp-out warning module is a solid-state unit that is designed to measure small changes in voltage levels. An electronic switch in the module closes to complete a ground path for the indicator lights in the event of a bulb going out. The key to this system being able to detect one bulb out on

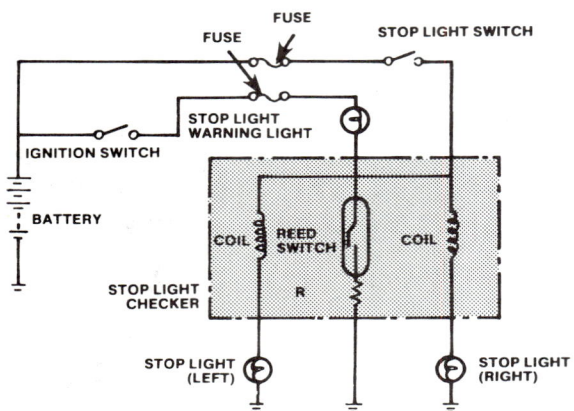

Figure 17-12 Stop light warning lamp, which alerts the driver whenever a stop (brake) light has failed. *Courtesy of General Motors Corp.*

a multi-bulb system is the use of the special resistance wires. With bulbs operating, the resistance wires provide 0.5 volt input to the light-out warning module. If one bulb in a particular system goes out, the input off the resistance wire drops to approximately 0.25 volt. The light-out warning module detects this difference and completes a ground path to the indicator light for the affected circuit.

BRAKE WARNING LIGHT When this light is lit, it is an indication that the parking brake is engaged.

BRAKE FLUID LEVEL WARNING LIGHT The light is connected to the brake fluid level sensor that is incorporated in the brake fluid reserve tank. If brake fluid decreases to less than the specified volume in the reservoir, the sensor is actuated and the light comes on while the engine is running.

LOW FUEL WARNING LIGHT This particular component monitors the fuel level. When it drops below a quarter full, an electronic switch in the module closes and power is applied to illuminate the low fuel indicator light.

CHECK ENGINE WARNING LIGHT This warning is provided for the purpose of indicating the condition of the vehicle's engine and its systems. If there is a fault in the system, the warning light comes on while the engine is running. Check engine lights may be triggered by oil pressure, coolant temperature, or by the engine control computer that monitors several engine systems and illuminates the warning light whenever it senses a fault.

DOOR LOCK INDICATOR LIGHT This indicator tells the driver if the door locks are engaged or not.

DOOR AJAR WARNING LIGHT When the ignition is turned on and if the doors are left open or are ajar, this light comes on.

REAR (OR FRONT) DEFROST INDICATOR LIGHT When this light is lit, the defroster or deicer is operating.

DRIVE INDICATOR LIGHT Some front-wheel/four-wheel-drive vehicles have a light, which when lit, indicates that the vehicle is in four-wheel-drive mode of operation.

Sound Warning Devices

Various types of tone generators, including buzzers, chimes, and voice synthesizers, are used to remind drivers of a number of vehicle conditions. These warnings can include fasten seat belts, air bag operational, key left in ignition, door ajar, and light left on. Figure 17-13 is a tone generator system schematic.

Graphic Displays

Graphic displays are translucent drawings or pictures of a vehicle. Lights operate to indicate problem locations. Figure 17-14 illustrates a typical graphic display.

DIAGNOSIS AND TESTING Items to be checked in a malfunctioning gauge or indicator system include the following.

- Fuses
- Indicator bulbs
- Detector switches (indicator systems)
- Sender units (gauge systems)
- IVR (gauge systems)
- Gauges (gauge systems)

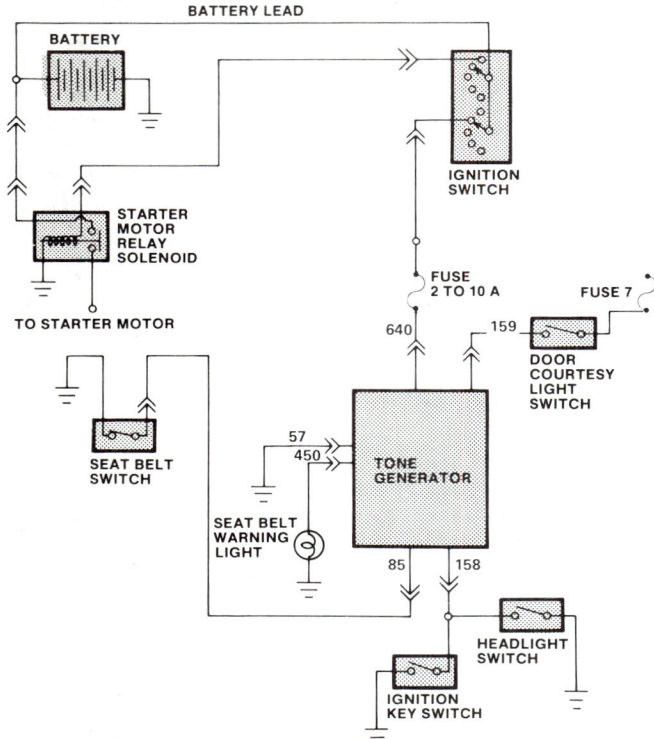

Figure 17-13 Tone generator warning system. *Courtesy of Ford Motor Co.*

Electrical Instruments and Accessories   423

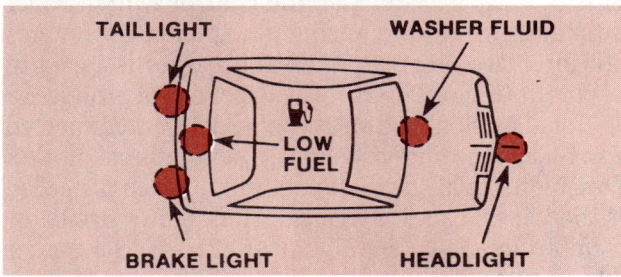

Figure 17-14 Graphic display warning system. *Courtesy of General Motors Corp.*

Service manuals contain detailed information on the diagnosis and testing of the affected system for a particular vehicle. Always refer to it before beginning to diagnose a circuit.

Driver Information Centers

The various gauges, warning devices, and comfort controls may be grouped together into a driver information center or instrument cluster. This information center may be simple (Figure 17-15) or it may be an all-encompassing cluster of information (Figure 17-16). The purpose of this message center is to keep the driver alert to the information provided by the system. The types and extent of information varies from one system to another.

In addition to standard warning signals, the information center may provide such vital data as fuel

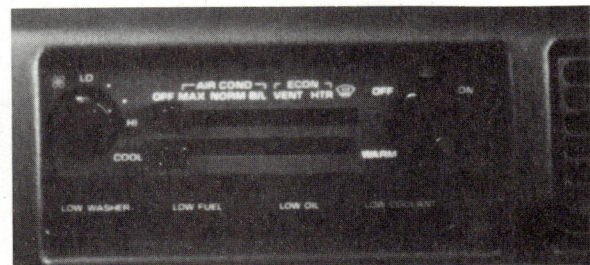

Figure 17-15 Simple driver information center air conditioner and heater controls, plus standard warning lamps for low windshield washer, fuel, and coolant levels. *Courtesy of Chrysler Corp.*

Figure 17-16 Full-scale driver information center. *Courtesy of General Motors Corp.*

range, average or instantaneous fuel economy, fuel used since reset, time, date, estimated time of arrival (ETA), distance to destination, elapsed time since rest, average car speed, percent of oil life remaining, and various engine-operating parameters. Some vehicles have separate data centers. For instance, the fuel data display (Figure 17-17) gives the driver such information as fuel economy, fuel used since last fill up, and the expected number of miles before more fuel is needed. The separate trip computer (Figure 17-18) reports such information to the driver as the time, distance traveled, average speed, stopwatch time, fuel range, average fuel economy, and instantaneous fuel economy.

Other electronic displays and controls can be found on today's vehicles.

STEERING WHEEL TOUCH CONTROLS Steering wheel touch controls are standard on many vehicles. Four or six large buttons are located conveniently in the steering wheel providing control over the more frequently used radio and heating/air conditioning functions. This provides the driver with fingertip controls where they are easy to use.

HEAD-UP DISPLAY (HUD) This system features visual images that are projected on the windshield by a

Figure 17-17 This fuel data display provides vacuum fluorescent displays of fuel data. *Courtesy of General Motors Corp.*

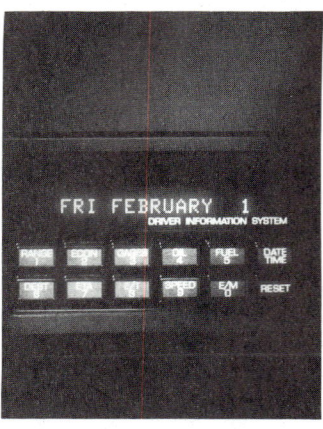

Figure 17-18 Trip computer reports time, distance traveled, average speed, stopwatch time, fuel range, average fuel economy, instantaneous fuel economy, and outside temperature. *Courtesy of General Motors Corp.*

Figure 17-19 The head-up display (HUD) can project the vehicle's speed onto the windshield, freeing the driver from looking down at the speedometer. *Courtesy of General Motors Corp.*

vacuum fluorescent light source to complement existing traditional in-dash (Figure 17-19). By projecting these images in the driver's peripheral field of view, it is not necessary for the driver to refocus attention or remove one's eyes from the road to obtain certain pertinent information. Among the images a HUD system may relate to the driver are vehicle speed, turn-signal indicators, low-fuel warning graphic, and a high-beam indicator.

❏ ELECTRICAL ACCESSORIES

Electrical accessories that make driving safer, easier, and more pleasant include windshield wipers/washers, power door locks, power trunk releases, illuminated entry systems, keyless door entry locks, power windows, power seats, power mirrors, rear-window defrosters and heated mirrors, moon or sun roof systems, radios, horns, clocks, cigarette lighters, and cruise controls, and engine cooling fans. Other automotive electric and electronic equipment such as radios and stereos, passive seat belts and air bags, and various auto security systems including keyless locks are described later in this book.

Windshield Wiper/Washer Systems

There are several types of windshield wiper systems. Both rear and front systems are commonly used. The wiper systems function to keep the windshield or back glass clear of rain, snow, and dirt. Headlight wipers are available that work in unison with conventional windshield wipers. There are two basic conventional systems commonly available. In the first system, the wiper motor has two speeds—low and high. In the other system a governor is added to the system to allow adjustment of the wiper interval period in addition to the low and high speeds. Both of these systems are with either a depressed or non-depressed park. In the depressed park system the blades drop down below the lower windshield molding. In non-depressed park the blades park at the lower moldings. The major components of a wiper system are the control switch, wiper motor and switch, and washer fluid pump. On systems with interval wipers, an interval governor is added to the circuit (Figure 17-20). The wiper motor produces a rotational motion, and an assembly of levers connected to an offset motor drive changes the rotational motion of the motor to an oscillation motion, which is needed for the wiper blades. A typical wiper motor oscillator assembly is shown in Figure 17-21. As the center motor rotates, the output is an oscillation motion.

When the wiper switch is moved to the low or high speed position, voltage from the fuse panel is applied through the wiper switch directly to the wiper motor on systems without interval wipers. Shutting off the switch cuts power to the wiper motor. However, the wiper motor park switch maintains power to the motor until it is in the park position.

On vehicles with interval wipers the low and high speed signals pass through the interval governor to the wiper motor. When the wiper switch is placed in the int position (interval), the signal is applied to an interval timer circuit in the governor. The time period

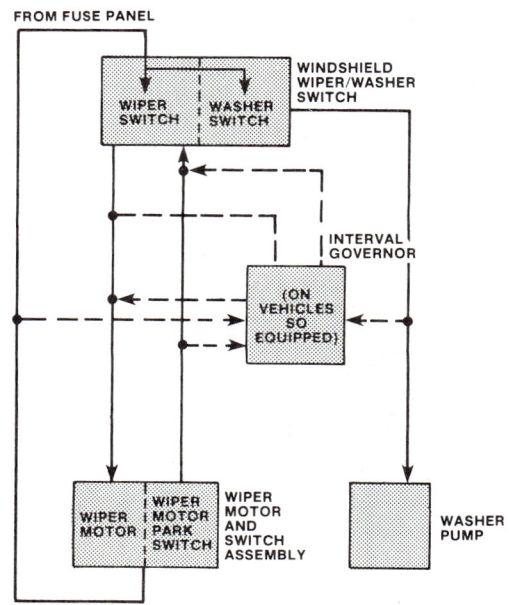

Figure 17-20 Windshield wiper/washer system. *Courtesy of Ford Motor Co.*

Electrical Instruments and Accessories 425

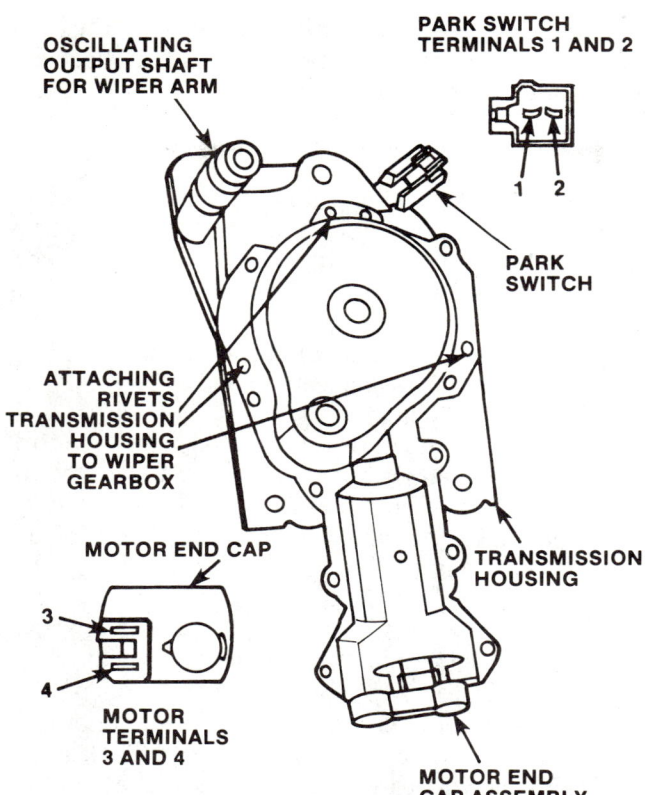

Figure 17-21 This oscillation mechanism is used to change rotational motion to oscillation motion on the windshield wiper motor. *Courtesy of General Motors Corp.*

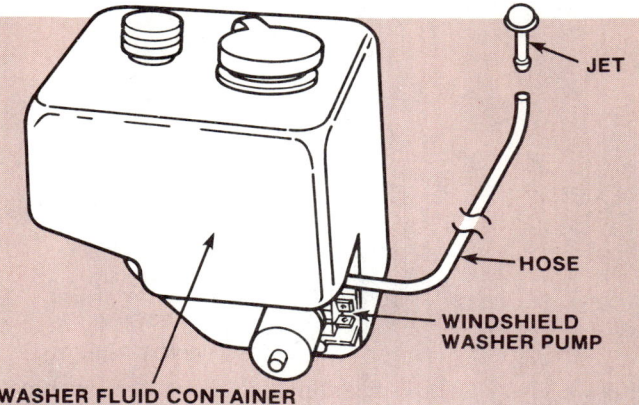

Figure 17-22 The windshield washer system uses a fluid container, a small washer pump, and hoses and nozzles (jets) to deliver the wash to the windshield. *Courtesy of Volkswagen of America, Inc.*

Figure 17-23 Headlight washer system. *Courtesy of General Motors Corp.*

of the interval is adjusted by a potentiometer in the wiper switch. The potentiometer is a variable resistor.

Speed-sensitive windshield wipers now are available and adjust wiper speed automatically to vehicle speed. Complete details on the operation and servicing of speed-sensitive wipers can be found in the service manual.

WASHER SYSTEM The washer pump (Figure 17-22) is operated by holding the washer switch in the activate position. On models with interval wipers this signal is also applied to the governor. If the wiper switch is in off or int, an interval override circuit in the governor causes the wipers to operate at low speed until the washer switch is released. Then the wipers operate for several more cycles and park or return to interval operation.

Vehicles are available with washers that help keep the integral headlight/foglight clean for maximum visibility (Figure 17-23). Headlight washer systems may operate from their own switch and pump or work from conventional windshield wiper systems.

A fluid washer nozzle is used on some cars for the front windshield washer system. The system consists of a fluid container, pump, fluid hoses and pipes, and nozzles or jets. When the operator turns on the washer, the small pump forces fluid through the hoses and pipes to the nozzle or jet by the windshield. The pump can be located either at the fluid container or wiper motor.

CUSTOMER CARE

It is good customer relations to advise the customer to check windshield washer fluid level periodically. If it is low, fill the washer reservoir with windshield washer fluid. It works better than plain water. Basically, the fluid is nothing more than a weak ammonia and water solution. Take a few minutes to show the customer where the reservoir is located and how the fluid should be added.

Some vehicles are equipped with a low fluid indicator. The washer fluid level switch closes when the fluid level in the reservoir drops below one quarter full. Closing of the switch allows power from the fuse panel to be applied to the indicator.

WINDSHIELD WIPER LINKAGE AND BLADES Several arms and pivot shafts make up the linkage used to transmit the oscillation motion at the motor to the windshield wipers. Figure 17-24 shows an example of the linkage. As the wiper motor oscillates, arm A moves from left to right. This moves arm B as well. As arm B

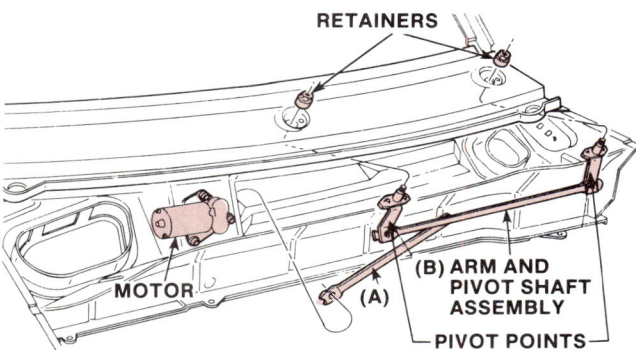

Figure 17-24 The oscillation motion from the wiper motor is transferred by a linkage system to the pivot points for the wipers. *Courtesy of Ford Motor Co.*

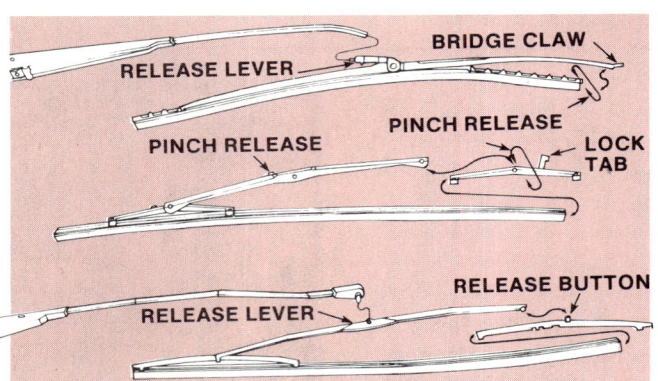

Figure 17-25 Various wiper blade attachment designs. *Courtesy of Chrysler Motors*

moves, it causes the two pivot points to oscillate. The windshield wipers are connected to the two pivot points.

The wiper arms and blades are attached directly to the two pivot points operated by the linkage and motor. The condition of wiper blades is critical to safe driving. If they are in poor condition, replace them. Figure 17-25 shows the various ways that wiper blades are attached to the wiper arms.

> **CUSTOMER CARE**
>
> After installing new wiper blades, be sure to warn the customer not to operate them on dry windows. The abrasive action caused by dirt and other deposits wear down the blades and reduce their effectiveness. For optimum performance in winter, blades specially designed for snow and ice can be purchased.

LIFTGATE WIPER/WASHER SYSTEM This system has an on/off switch to control power to the single speed wiper motor. The parking function is completed within the liftgate wiper motor and switch. Check the fuse or circuit breaker if any wiper/washer system is not working. If the wiper still does not work, trace the power flow through the system following the electrical schematic in the service manual.

Power Door Lock Systems

Although systems for automatically locking doors vary from one vehicle to another, the overall purpose is the same—to lock all outside doors. There are, however, several variations of door arrangements used that require slight differences in components from one system to another. As a safety precaution against being locked in a car due to an electrical failure, power locks can be manually operated.

When either the driver's or passenger's control switch is activated (either locked or unlocked), power from the fuse panel is applied through the switch to the door lock actuator motor. A rod that is part of the actuator moves up or down in the door latch assembly as required to lock or unlock the door. On some models the signal from the switch is applied to a relay that, when energized, applies an activating voltage to the door lock actuator. The door lock actuator consists of a motor and a built-in circuit breaker. On station wagon models with power door locks, the tailgate lock actuator is also controlled by the door lock switches. Station wagon models without power door locks can be equipped with a separate tailgate power lock system.

Most models use a control switch mounted in the door arm rest or in the door trim panel. However, some models use switches controlled by the front door push button locks (Figure 17-26).

While most power locks operate off the vehicle's electrical system, a few arrangements use the vacuum from the engine's intake manifold. This vacuum operates a small vacuum motor containing a spring-loaded diaphragm. A rod is connected between the diaphragm at one end and the locking mechanism at the other. When the driver's door is locked, vacuum is transferred to all locks causing rods to pull the latches closed. Opening the driver's lock releases the vacuum, and the springs force the diaphragms back and the locks open.

Power Trunk Release

The power trunk release system is a relatively simple electrical circuit that consists of a switch and a solenoid. Power to the switch is present any time the ignition switch is in run or accy. When the trunk release switch is pressed, voltage is applied through the switch to the solenoid. With battery voltage on one side and ground on the other, the trunk release solenoid energizes and the trunk latch releases to open the trunk lid.

Power door lock or trunk release systems rarely give trouble. Should a problem occur, check the following.

- If none of the locks work, check the circuit protection devices. If they are okay, check the wiring.

Electrical Instruments and Accessories   427

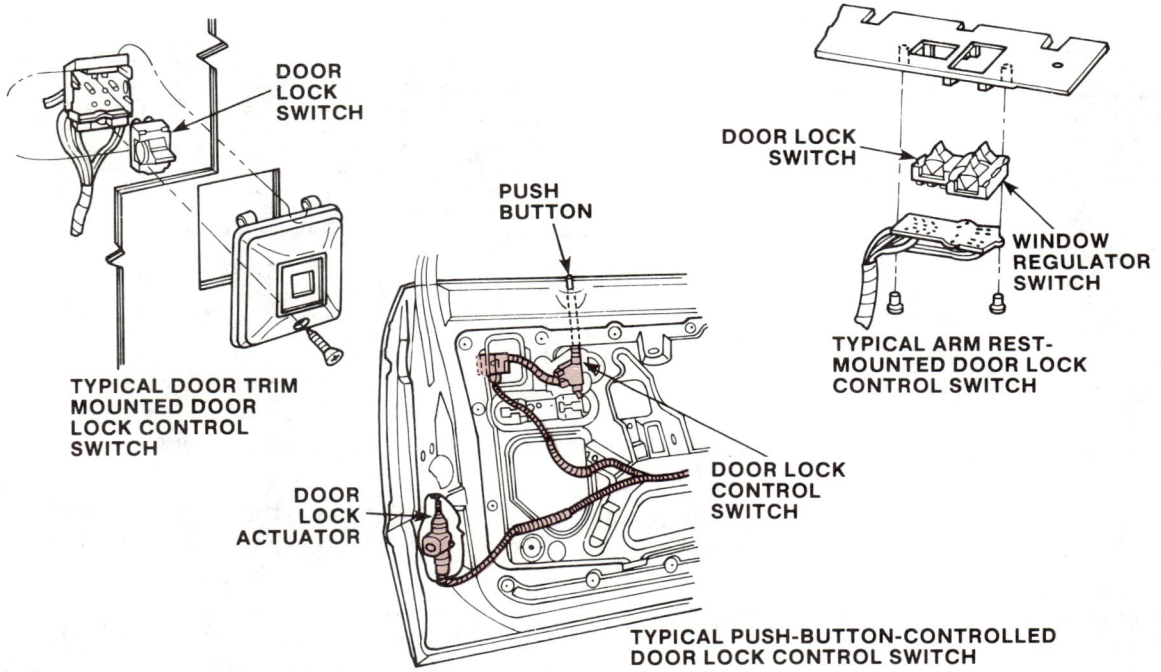

Figure 17-26 Typical door lock control switches. *Courtesy of Ford Motor Co.*

- If power locks operate to lock or unlock but not both, check the relays on vehicles so equipped. On vehicles without relays, check the wiring to and from the control switch on the side that is not working.
- If only one door lock does not operate, check the actuator for that door.
- If only one door lock switch does not work, perform a switch test as described in the service manual.
- If the trunk release does not work, check the fuse first. Then check for voltage through the switch with the ignition switch in run and the trunk release switch depressed. If the switch is okay, check for continuity through the trunk release solenoid to ground. If the solenoid is okay, check the wiring.

Power Windows

Obviously, the primary function of any power window system is to raise and lower windows. The systems do not vary significantly from one model to another. The major components of a typical system are the master control switch, individual window control switches, and the window drive motors. In addition, on four-door models, a window safety relay and in-line circuit breaker are also included.

The master control switch (Figure 17-27) provides overall system control. Power for the system comes directly from the fuse panel on two-door models and from an in-line circuit breaker on four-door models. The window safety relay used on four-door models prevents operation of the system if the ignition switch is not in run or accy. Power for the individual window

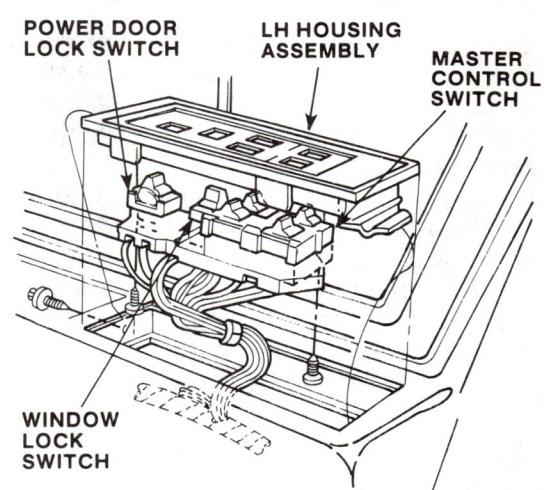

Figure 17-27 Typical power window master control switch. *Courtesy of Ford Motor Co.*

control switches comes through the master control switch.

Four-door model master control switches usually have four segments while two-door models have two segments (Figure 17-28). Each segment controls power to a separate window motor. Each segment actually operates as a separate independent switch. A window lock switch is included on four-door model master control switches. When open, this switch limits opening and closing of all windows to the master control switch. It is included as a safety device to prevent children from opening door windows without the driver knowing.

The first step in checking out a power window system is to determine whether the whole system is out

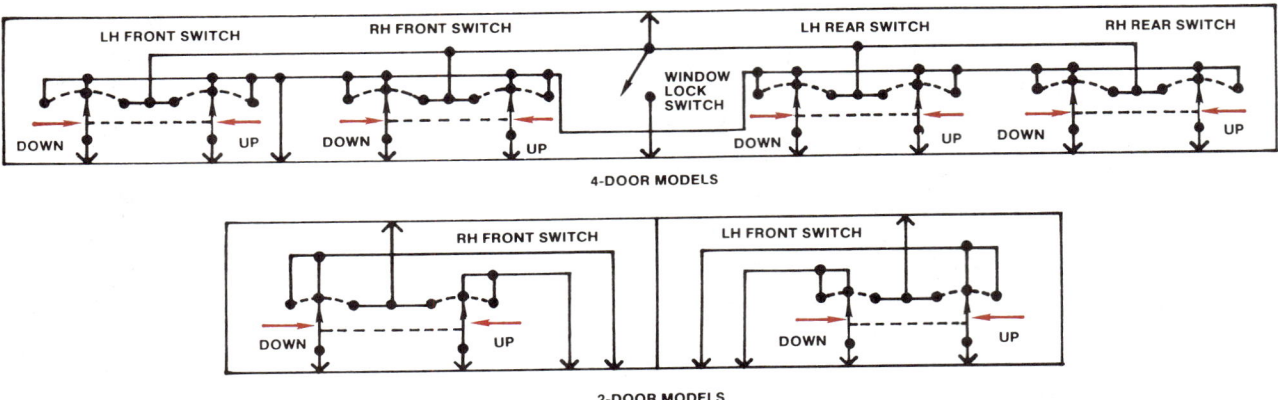

Figure 17-28 Power window master control switch electrical schematic. *Courtesy of Ford Motor Co.*

or just one or two portions. If the whole system is out, the problem can be isolated to fuses, circuit breakers or the master control switch. If only a portion of the system does not work, check the components used in the portion that is not working.

USING SERVICE MANUALS

Diagnosis and service is a very important part of the electrical accessory system. Use a standard troubleshooting procedure to find an electrical problem. For example, always verify the problem, read the schematic, look for possible causes, test for correct voltages, narrow the problem down to one circuit, find the cause, and correct the problem. Let us examine each power window component as it appears in a typical service manual schematic (Figure 17-29). Circuit breakers are generally used on power windows because they open if an overload occurs. Winter weather might freeze the window closed. Without a circuit breaker to open, the motor might be damaged trying to move the window against the ice. As the ice is removed, the breaker cools, closes, and allows future window operation. The motor is usually an insulated directional style that runs up or down, depending on the direction of the applied B+ and ground. The master switch has its own B+ source and is the ground for the entire system. Notice that the style of switch used at the window and the master control is basically the same. The switch allows B+ to be directed through the motor from the center terminal and then flow back through the other side of the switch. The window switch and master switch are actually wired in series. A problem with either switch affects motor operation. A dead motor can be diagnosed with a 12-volt light or voltmeter by first insuring that B+ is available to both switches. Moving the switches should switch the B+ from one side to the other. By connecting a test light across the switch, the presence of voltage and the switch itself can be checked. The motor is checked easily by jumping the terminals to B+ and ground. Reversing the connections should reverse the direction of the motor, raising and lowering the window. Corroded switch contacts generally indicate the presence of series resistance.

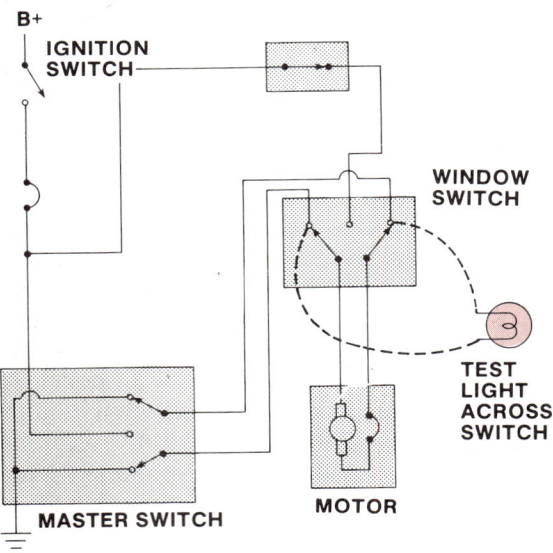

Figure 17-29 Typical power window service manual schematic. *Courtesy of Ford Motor Co.*

CAUTION: When installing electrical components, make certain they are properly fused. Wires must be insulated, kept from hot areas, and must be secured to prevent chafing. When passing through metal parts, install rubber grommets to protect the wires. Terminals should be clean and tight.

Power Seats

Power seats allow the driver or passenger to adjust the seat to the most comfortable position. The major components of the system are the seat control and the motors.

Power seats generally come in two configurations: four-way and six-way. In the four-way system the whole seat moves up or down, or forward and rearward. In the six-way system, the same movements are included plus the ability to adjust the height of the seat front or the seat rear. Generally, a four-way system is used on bench seats and a six-way system is used on split-bench seats. In addition, two different drives are used on the six-way system—rack and pinion and screw-drive. Electrically, the difference between the rack and pinion drive and the screw-drive is minimal.

Two motors are usually employed to make the adjustments on the four-way system, while three are used on a six-way system. The names of the motors easily identifies their function. To raise or lower the entire seat on a six-way system, both the front height and the rear height motors are operated together. The control motors themselves are generally two-directional motor assemblies that include a circuit breaker to protect against circuit overload if the control switch is held in the actuate position for long periods. A typical six-way motor rack and pinion system is shown in Figure 17-30. The four-way system and six-way screw-drive motor arrangements are similar.

Cars with on-board computers can store information about seat position. A seat can be returned to a preset

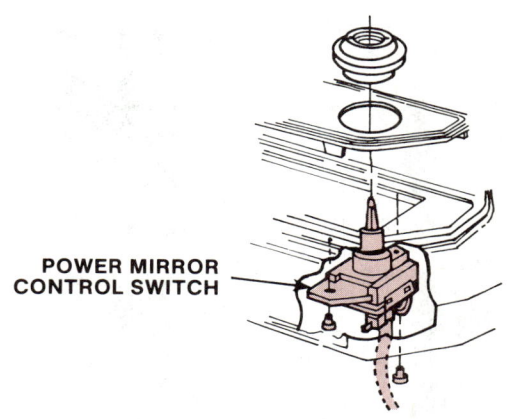

Figure 17-31 Power mirror control switch. *Courtesy of Ford Motor Co.*

position by depressing the memory switch. In addition, some power seats are heated to varying degrees depending on the driver's desires.

Power Mirror System

The power mirror system allows the driver to control both the lefthand and righthand outside rear view mirrors from one switch. The major components in the system are the joystick control switch and a dual motor drive assembly located in each mirror assembly.

Rotating the power mirror switch (Figure 17-31) to the left or right position selects one of the mirrors for adjustment. Now moving the joystick control up and down, or right and left moves the mirror to the desired position. The mirrors are moved by a dual motor drive assembly located behind the mirror glass (Figure 17-32).

Many new vehicles are being equipped with electrochromic inside rear-view and side-view mirrors. Requiring no electrical connections, these mirrors operate on the intensity of the glare in much the same manner as a pair of eyeglasses with photochromatic lens. When glare is heavy, the mirror darkens fully (down to 6% reflectivity) much the same as standard mirrors. But, when glare is mild, the electrochromic mirror provides a comfort zone. At this stage, the mirror gives 20% to 30% reflectivity. Glare is gone without

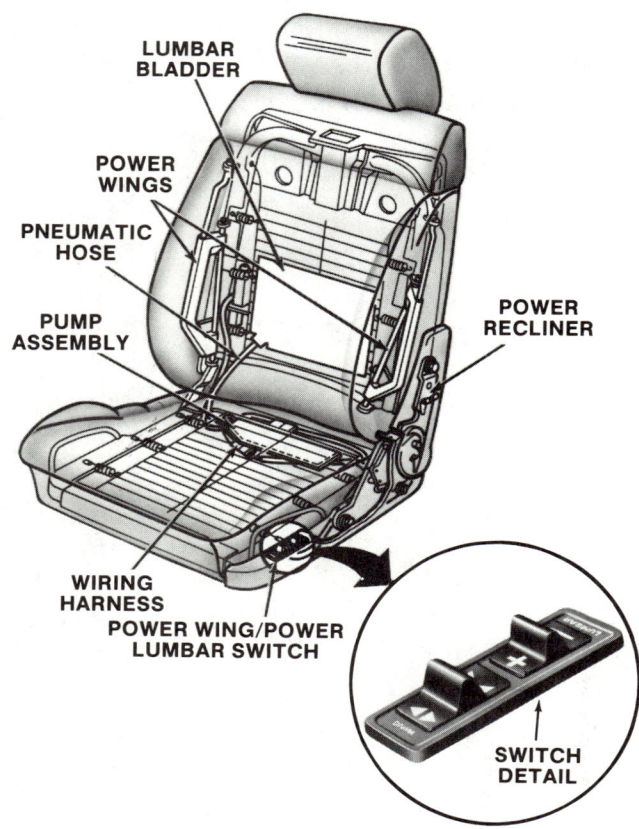

Figure 17-30 A six-way power seat assembly.

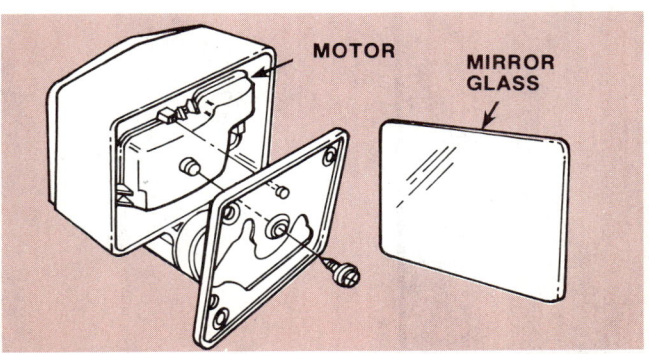

Figure 17-32 Power mirror motor switch. *Courtesy of General Motors Corp.*

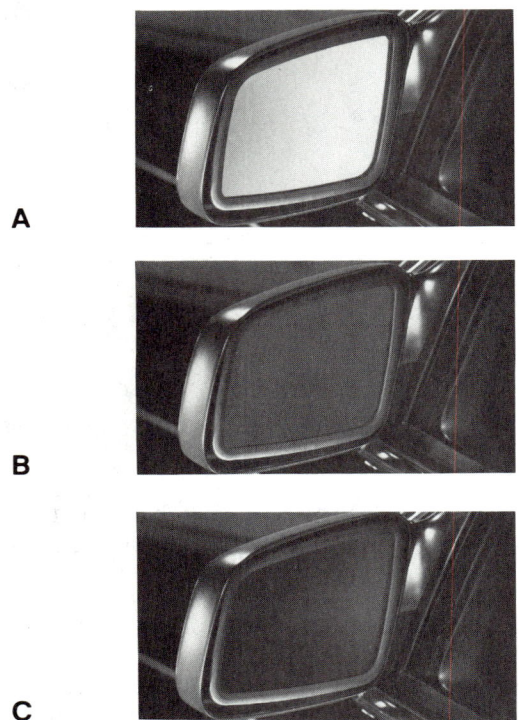

A

B

C

Figure 17-33 Operation of an electrochromic side-view mirror: (A) Daytime up to 85% reflectivity; (B) Mild glare from 20 to 30% reflectivity; and (C) High glare as low as 6% reflectivity. *Courtesy of Gentex Corp.*

impairing rear visibility. When glare subsides, the electrochromics change to the clear daytime state (Figure 17-33).

Rear- and Front-Window Defrosters and Heated Mirror System

The rear- and front-window defroster (also called a defogger or deicer) heats the rear-window surface to remove moisture and ice from the window. On some vehicles, the same control heats the outside mirrors.

The major components of a rear-window defroster are the deice switch relay assembly and the heating elements on the glass surfaces (Figure 17-34).

Pressing the rear-window defroster switch momentarily to the on position closes the on switch in the defroster switch relay assembly. The time delay circuit applies ground to one side of the relay coil and with battery voltage to the other side, the relay is energized. Battery voltage through the fuse link now flows through closed contacts of the relay to the rear-window defroster grid. On models with a heated mirror, the voltage through the relay contacts also flows through a separate fuse to the mirror heated grid.

After about 10 minutes, the time delay circuit opens the ground path to the coil and the coil de-energizes.

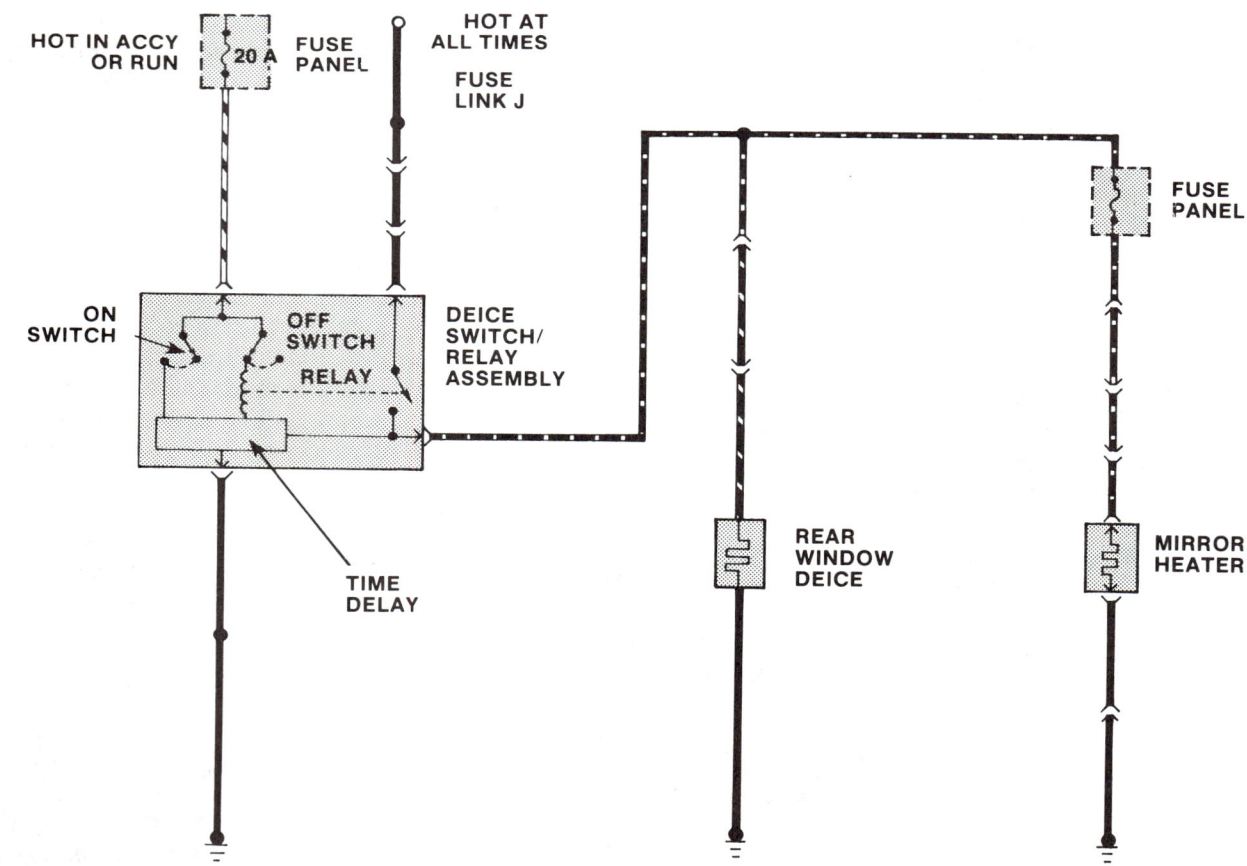

Figure 17-34 Defroster switch/relay assembly. *Courtesy of Ford Motor Co.*

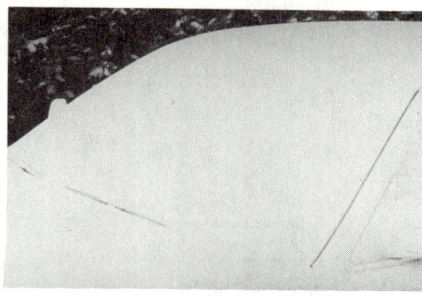

Figure 17-35 Heated windshields are capable of removing 1/10 inch of frost at 0 degrees Fahrenheit in just 2 to 3 minutes. *Courtesy of Ford Motor Co.*

This removes power from the system, and the grids cease to heat the glass surface. The time delay circuit prevents the system from remaining on during periods of extended driving. The system can also be shut off by momentarily moving the defroster switch to the off position.

Heater, or self-defrosting, front windshield systems are now offered as an option on a growing number of vehicles. These systems work like rear-window defrosters, heating the glass directly. Ice and frost are melted faster than with standard forced air systems (Figure 17-35). Rather than a wire grid that could hinder overall driver's vision, advanced glass making technology allows for a micro-thin metallic coating inside the windshield, where it is nearly undetectable.

The typical windshield defroster system is turned on by pressing a switch on the instrument panel. Once pushed on, the alternator output is redirected from the normal electrical system to the windshield circuit. All other electrical loads operate on battery power. When the alternator output is no longer going directly through the battery, the voltage regulator senses a drop in battery voltage and fully charges the alternator to between 30 and 90 volts. If the battery voltage drops below 11 volts, alternator output is directed to the battery, and the system is turned off. Some systems use a specially designed generator to provide the necessary power to operate the system without draining the battery. Check the defroster service manual for specific voltage details.

The defrost cycle generally lasts for about 4 minutes. After that, the alternator is switched to the normal charging operation controlled by the voltage regulator. If the windshield is not clear, the system can be selected again.

WARNING: The operating voltage of windshield defroster systems is high—between 30 and 90 volts. Be very careful when servicing or testing any parts or wiring. Do not pierce the insulation when checking the wire.

Moon (Sun) Roof System

The power moon roof or sun roof panel that is an option on some car models slides open or tilts up in the back to give the passenger compartment just the right amount of fresh air and natural light. With the roof tilted up, some moon roofs have a sliding louvered shade panel to block out bright rays and provide additional ventilation.

The major components of any roof panel system are a relay, control switch, sliding roof vent, and motor.

Power to the control switch is applied through a relay. The relay coil is energized only when the ignition switch is in accy or run. When the relay is energized, battery voltage can pass through the closed relay contacts to the control switch (Figure 17-36). This circuit is normally protected by the in-line circuit breaker.

When the two-position control switch is moved to the open position, battery voltage passes through the switch contacts into the motor terminals. The sun or moon roof begins to move back into a storage area between the headliner and the roof. The panel stops moving anytime the switch is released. Moving the switch to the close position reverses the power flow through the motor.

If the system is not operating, check the fuse and circuit breaker. If these are okay, check for power to the switch with the ignition switch in accy or run. If the voltage is present, the relay is okay. Check for power to the motor with the switch held in the open position. Refer to the service manual for additional diagnosis and testing information.

Horns/Clocks/Cigarette (Cigar) Lighter System

The function and operation of these systems are obvious. Circuits may vary from one model to another and from one year to another (Figure 17-37). However, the overall operation remains the same.

HORNS Most horn systems are controlled by relays. When the horn button, ring, or padded unit is depressed, electricity flows from the battery through a horn lead, into an electromagnetic coil in the horn relay to the ground. A small flow of electric current through the coil energizes the electromagnet, pulling a movable arm. Electrical contacts on the arm touch, closing the primary circuit and causing the horn to sound.

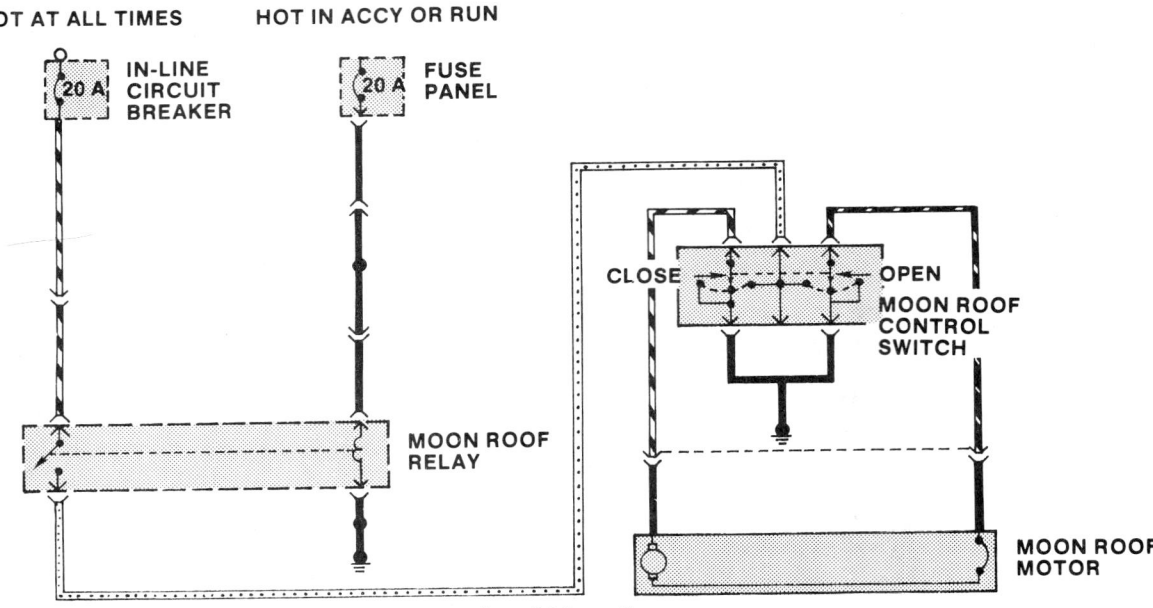

Figure 17-36   Typical moon roof system. *Courtesy of Ford Motor Co.*

Most light truck models and some import cars have the horn switch mounted in the steering wheel hub assembly. Many current car horn switches are now part of the multi-function or combination switch. This difference does not change the electrical operation of the horn system. Some vehicles are equipped with two horns. Each one is designed to emit a different tone. The purpose of a dual horn system is simply to provide a fuller sound. Figure 17-38 shows a typical dual horn assembly.

CLOCKS   The clock operates as a result of power from the fuse panel. Some clocks have additional functions. These are adequately discussed in the service manual and owner's guide for the particular vehicle being serviced.

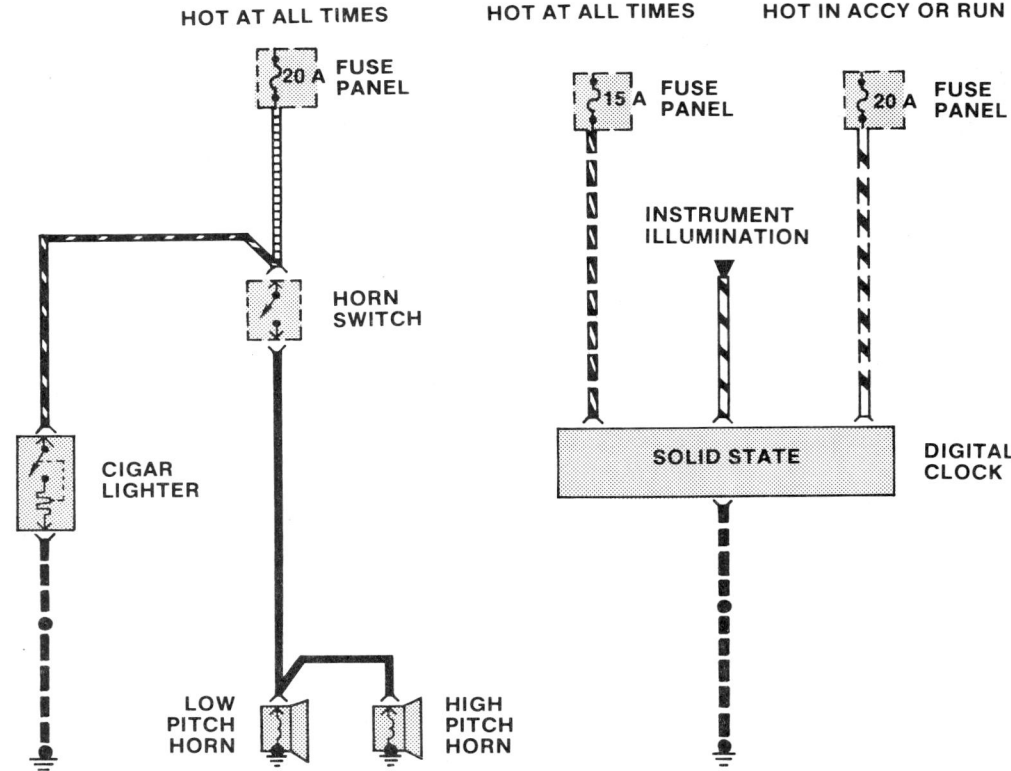

Figure 17-37   Typical horn/clock/cigar lighter circuit. *Courtesy of Ford Motor Co.*

Electrical Instruments and Accessories 433

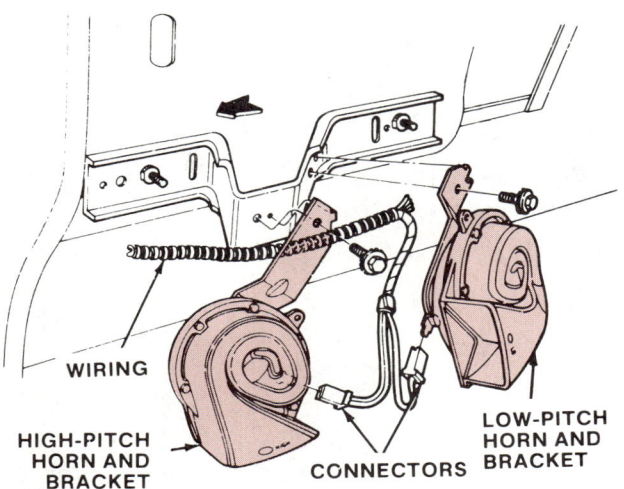

Figure 17-38 Typical dual horn assembly. *Courtesy of Chrysler Motors*

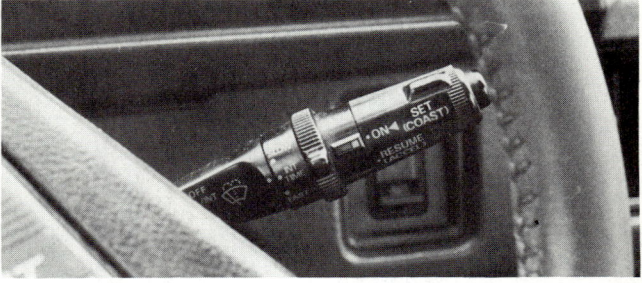

Figure 17-39 The cruise control switch is used to set or increase speed, resume speed, or turn the system off and on. *Courtesy of (top) General Motors Corp. and (bottom) Ford Motor Co.*

CIGARETTE LIGHTER The cigarette (cigar) lighter is a heating element that automatically releases itself from the pushed in position when the appropriate heat level is reached.

For an inoperative system, first check the fuse(s). If the fuse is good, make certain that power is present at the lighter receptacle. If power is present, the lighter unit is probably bad. Refer to the service manual for added troubleshooting information.

Cruise (Speed) Control System

Cruise or speed control systems are designed to allow the driver to maintain a constant speed (usually above 30 mph) without having to apply continual foot pressure on the accelerator pedal. Selected cruise speeds are easily maintained and speed can be easily changed. Several override systems also allow the vehicle to be accelerated, slowed, or stopped. Because of the constant changes and improvements in technology, each cruise control system may be considerably different. There are several types that are used, including the non-resume type, the resume type, and the electronic type.

When engaged, the cruise control components set the throttle position to the desired speed. The speed is maintained unless heavy loads and steep hills interfere. The cruise control is disengaged whenever the brake pedal is depressed. The common speed or cruise control system components function in the following manner.

- The cruise control switch is located on the end of the turn signal or near the center or sides of the steering wheel (Figure 17-39). There are usually several functions on the switch, including off-on, resume, and engage buttons. The switch is different for resume and non-resume systems.
- The transducer is a device that controls the speed of the vehicle. When the transducer is engaged, it senses vehicle speed and controls a vacuum source (usually the manifold). The vacuum source is used to maintain a certain position on a servo. The speed control is sensed from the lower cable and casing assembly attached to the transmission.
- The servo unit is connected to the throttle by a rod or linkage, a bead chain, or a bowden cable. The servo unit maintains the desired car speed by receiving a controlled amount of vacuum from the transducer. The variation in vacuum changes the position of the throttle. When a vacuum is applied, the servo spring is compressed and the throttle is positioned correctly. When the vacuum is released, the servo spring is relaxed and the system is not operating.
- There are two brake-activated switches. They are operated by the position of the brake. When the brake pedal is depressed, the brake release switch disengages the system. A vacuum release valve is also used to disengage the system when the brake pedal is depressed.

ELECTRICAL AND VACUUM CIRCUITS Figure 17-40 shows an electrical and vacuum circuit diagram. The system operates by controlling vacuum to the servo through various solenoids and switches.

ELECTRONIC CRUISE CONTROL COMPONENTS Cruise control can also be obtained by using electronic components rather than mechanical components. Depending upon the vehicle manufacturer, several additional components may be used.

The electronic control module (integrated circuitry) is used to control the servo unit. The servo unit is again used to control the vacuum which in turn controls the

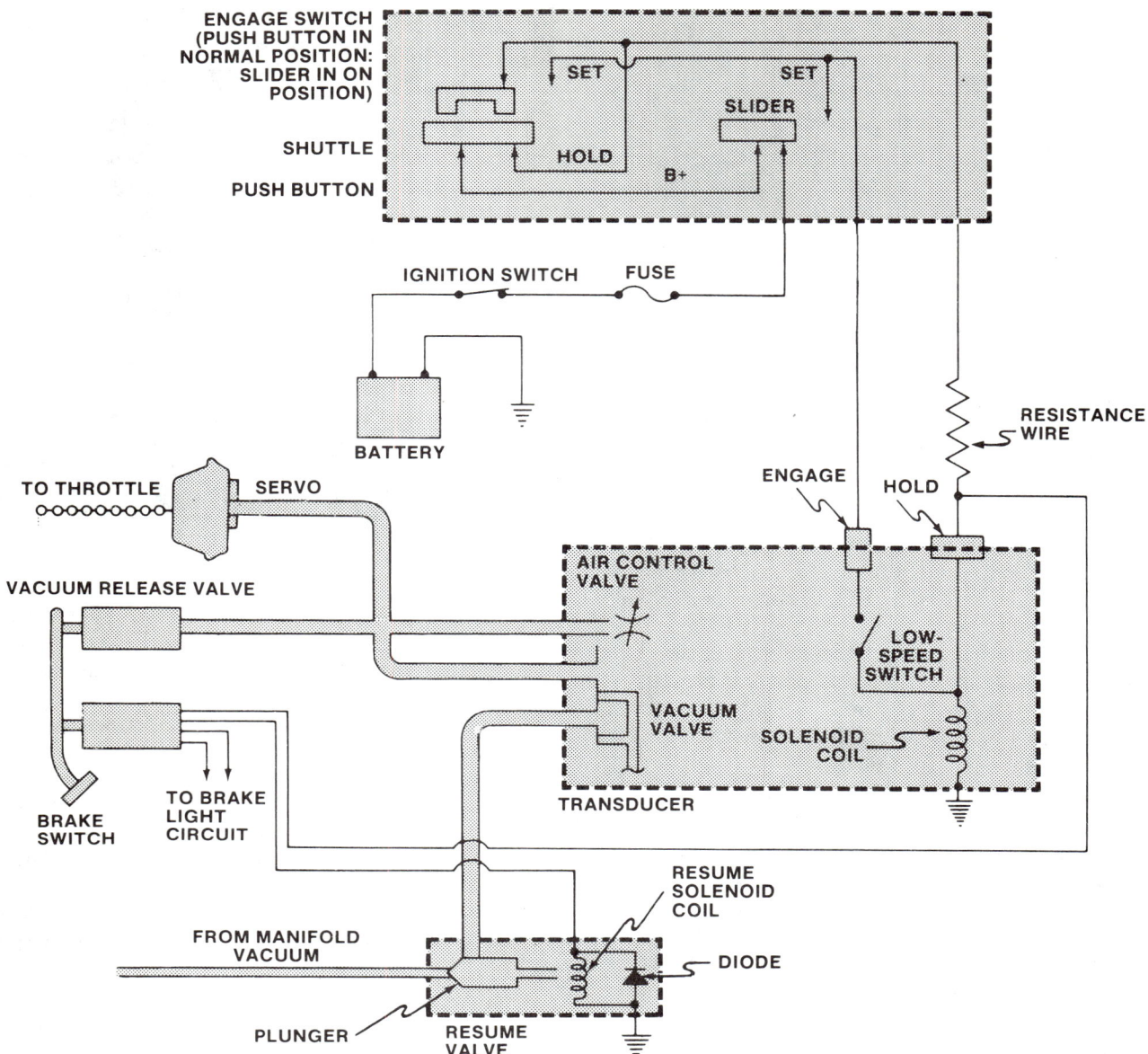

Figure 17-40 A cruise control circuit with vacuum and electrical systems. *Courtesy of General Motors Corp.*

throttle. The vehicle speed sensor (VSS) buffer amplifier is used to monitor or sense vehicle speed. The signal created is sent to the electronic control module. A generator speed sensor may also be used in conjunction with the VSS. The clutch switch is used on vehicles with manual transmissions to disengage the cruise control when the clutch is depressed. The accumulator is used as a vacuum storage tank on vehicles that have low vacuum during heavy load and high road speed.

Figure 17-41 shows how electronic cruise control components work together. The throttle position is controlled by the servo unit. The servo unit uses vacuum working against a spring pressure to operate an internal diaphragm. The servo unit vacuum circuit is controlled electronically by the controller.

The controller has several inputs that help determine how it will affect the servo. These inputs include a brake release switch (clutch release switch), a speedometer, buffer amplifier, or generator speed sensor, and a turn signal mode switch or speed control on the steering wheel (signal to control the cruise control).

Engine Cooling Fans

With the advent of transverse-mounted engines, electrical cooling fans found their way under the hood of the modern automobile. Today most new cars are equipped with an electric cooling fan. They offer advantages over the mechanical cooling fans because of their ability to move large amounts of air independent of engine speed. Their circuitry is very simple, especially on a vehicle that is not air-conditioned. Figure 17-42 shows an electric cooling fan circuit.

Air-conditioned vehicles, especially those with small engines, usually have additional circuitry to ensure

Electrical Instruments and Accessories 435

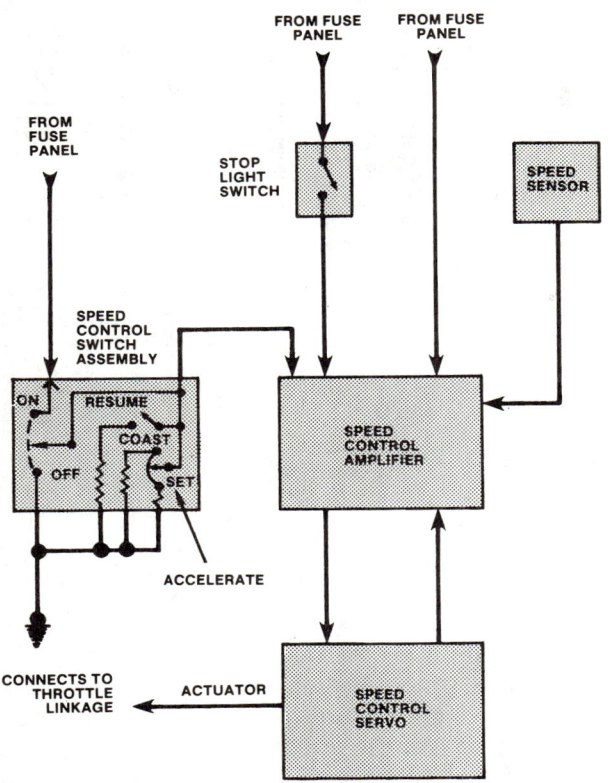

Figure 17-41 Electronic cruise control uses an electronic control module (controller) to operate a servo that controls the position of the throttle. *Courtesy of General Motors Corp.*

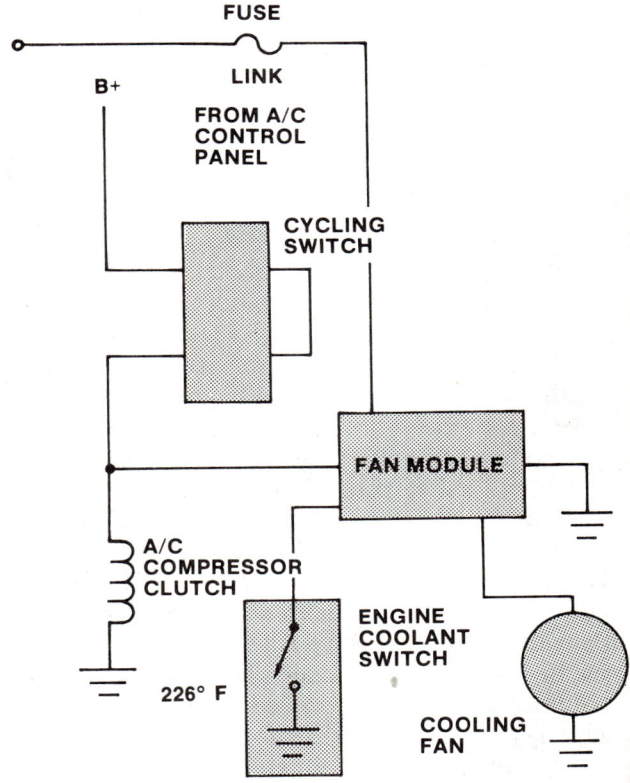

Figure 17-43 A system in which the compressor and fan are cycled at the same time.

that the cooling fan comes on when the compressor cycles on. Airflow through the condenser must be present for A/C to function correctly. With the condenser mounted in front of the radiator, the logical method of insuring airflow is to turn the cooling fan on as the A/C compressor cycles on. Most of the manufacturers follow one of two methods. Either they cycle the compressor and the fan at the same time as Figure 17-43 shows, or they cycle the fan on when A/C high side pressure reaches a predetermined level (Figure 17-44). In either case, this insures that airflow through the condenser keeps both the A/C and the engine cool.

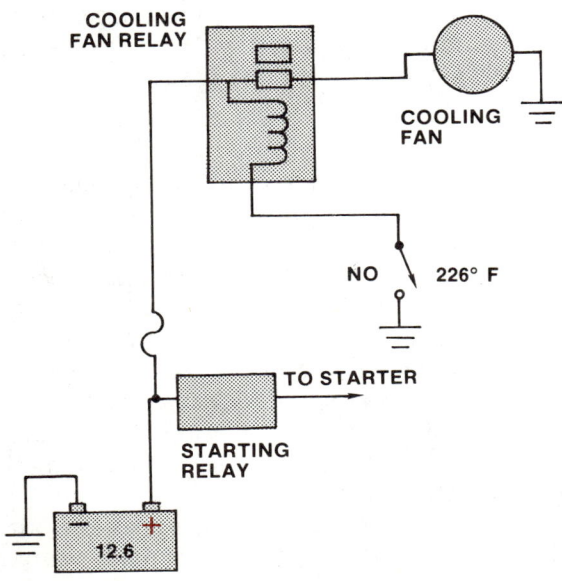

Figure 17-42 Cooling fan circuit, non-A/C equipped.

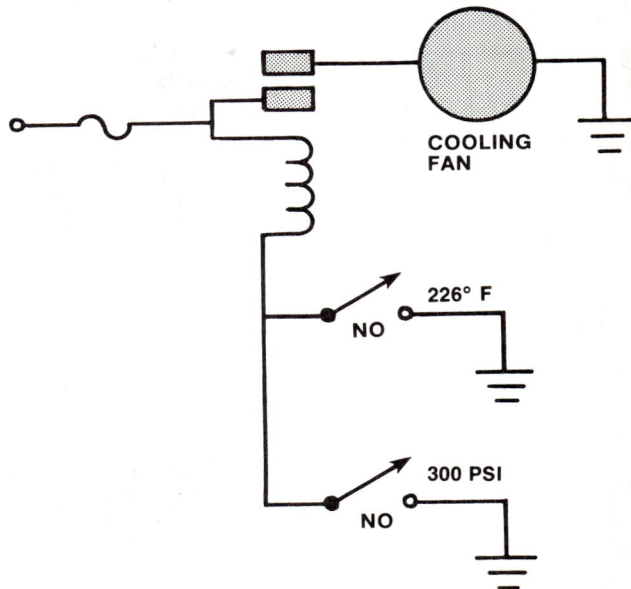

Figure 17-44 Cooling fan circuit with pressure switching.

CASE STUDY

Case 1

A customer complains that the horn does not operate.

To correct this situation, the technician must determine whether the horn system has a relay or not. Figure 17-45 shows a two-horn circuit without a relay. A fused B+ goes up the steering column to the horn button, which is normally open (NO). Closing the switch closes the circuit, bringing B+ down the column through the bulkhead connector to a common point where the two horns are connected in parallel. On the other side of the horn is a ground and the circuit is complete, a good example of a simple series-parallel circuit with one control. The circuit is easily diagnosed with a 12-volt test light, following the usual procedure of looking for B+ with the horn button pushed in. Correct diagnosis is important, especially because many horn switches are part of a multiple function switch, which is very costly. The same stalk on the steering column might be used for the horn, turn signals, windshield wipers, and cruise control. Make sure your diagnosis is correctly arrived at before you spend your customer's money. Power in at the switch and no power out with the button depressed would be the only reason to replace the switch unit.

Figure 17-46 shows an adaptation of the simple horn circuit. Notice that a fused B+ is run to the horn relay rather than to the switch. An NO relay is used. Notice that internally the relay coil receives B+ from the same fused source as the contacts do. The other end of the relay coil runs through the bulkhead connector and up into the steering column where an NO switch is located. Closing the switch grounds the relay coil, which develops a magnetic field, closing the contacts. The closed

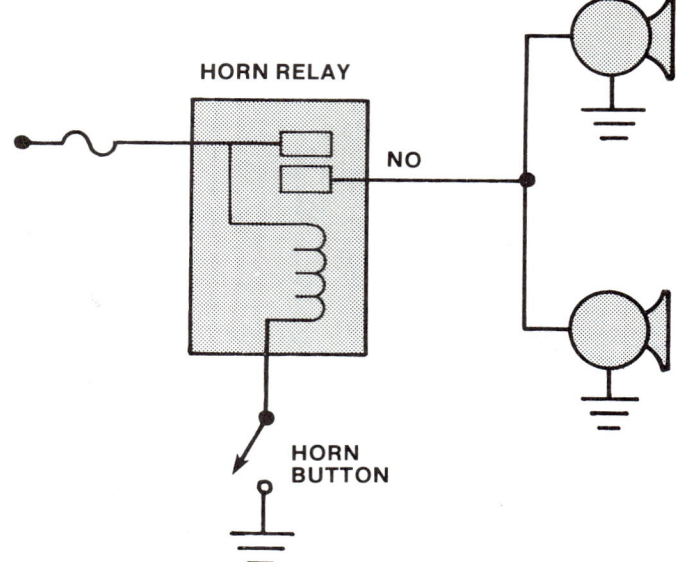

Figure 17-46 Horn circuit utilizing a relay.

contacts bring B+ over to the common point for the two horns, which are grounded. You can see that the circuit is slightly more complicated, but an excellent example of the use of a relay and ground side switching, which we have discussed before. Remember, any relay circuit must be diagnosed as two separate circuits wired in parallel. The relay coil is a separate circuit that needs a path for it to develop the magnetic field necessary to close the contacts. Closing the contacts allows current flow through the other circuit with the horns as the load. There are actually three loads in the previous example, two horns and the relay coil. Diagnose them separately, as you would any relay circuit, and you are less likely to make mistakes. Use a 12-volt test light with a wiring diagram to trace the power through the circuit.

CAUTION: Never replace a fuse with a higher capacity rating or by-pass it with a wire. The fuse of correct capacity must be in the circuit.

Summary

- Analog instrument gauges must have voltage regulators and senders or sensors in their circuit to function properly.
- Two types of electrical gauges are magnetic and thermal.
- The speedometer and odometer can operate on either an electrical or non-electrical principle.
- Indicators and warning devices generally operate as the result of a switch closing. They provide valuable information to the driver concerning the various system in the automobile.
- Lamps (lights), sound devices (chimes and buzzers), and graphic displays are popular warning systems.

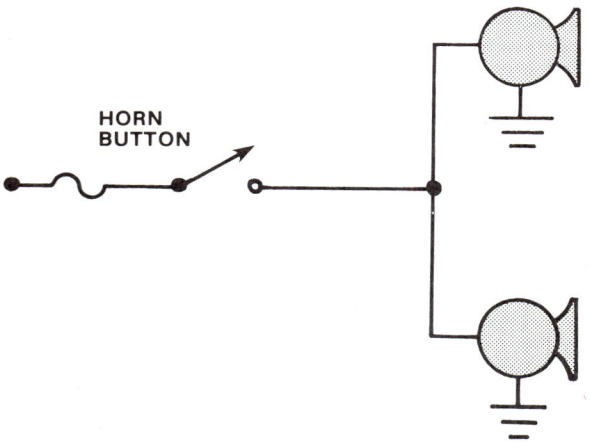

Figure 17-45 Two-horn circuit without relay.

- Instrument panels have two types of displays: analog and digital.
- There are three types of digital electronic displays: light-emitting diode (LED), liquid-crystal diode (LCD) and vacuum fluorescent.
- A printed circuit is composed of a film of plastic with small strips of copper. The electric current for various sections of the instrument panel run through these strips of copper. Lights, gauges, and indicators are plugged directly into the printed circuit board.
- The windshield wiper system uses several components. The windshield wiper motor is a permanent magnetic motor used to operate the windshield wipers. There is also a mechanism used to change the rotational motion of the motor to oscillation motion for the wipers. Each vehicle also uses mechanical linkage to connect the oscillation motion of the motor output to the wiper blades.
- A fluid washer nozzle and pump are used to pump cleaning fluid to the windshield.
- The power seats operate by using several motors on the bottom of the seats. The motors can operate in either direction. The switches, which are controlled by the operator, tell the motors which direction to turn.
- The deicer or defogger operates by using a switch, a timer to hold accessory on for a certain period of time, and a fuse panel.
- The horn circuit uses electricity from the battery, through the horn button, to the horn solenoid. A solenoid is also used to energize the horn.
- Cruise control is used to mechanically or electronically control the position of the throttle during highway operation. These systems help the operator to maintain a constant speed without having to apply foot pressure to the accelerator pedal. A cruise control switch is used to engage or disengage the system.
- There are several common parts used on cruise control systems. The servo is connected to the throttle linkage to control its position. It uses vacuum to move a wire or chain connected to the throttle mechanism. The transducer is used to control the vacuum sent to the servo. A brake-activated switch is used to disengage the system when the brakes are applied. The electrical circuit is used to control valves, which in turn control the vacuum to the transducer.
- Electronic cruise control systems use several additional parts. These include the electronic control module, a vehicle speed sensor (VSS), a clutch switch, and an accumulator used to store vacuum.

Review Questions

1. What is the simplest type of magnetic gauge?
2. What gauge indicates engine speed?
3. Name the three types of digital electronic displays used today.
4. What component in an electronic cruise control system is used to monitor or sense vehicle speed?
5. What component in a wiper system makes it possible to adjust the wiper interval period?
6. Technician A says that a common check on cruise control systems is to make sure all vacuum hoses are in good condition. Technician B says that a common check on cruise control is to make sure that the bead chain on the throttle linkage has no slack in it. Who is correct?
   a. Technician A
   b. Technician B
   c. Both A and B
   d. Neither A nor B
7. Which device on a cruise control system is used to adjust and control the position of the throttle?
   a. servo
   b. solenoid
   c. brake-activated switch
   d. transducer
   e. magnetic switch
8. Cruise control circuits operate by using _____.
   a. vacuum systems
   b. electrical systems
   c. mechanical systems
   d. all of the above
   e. none of the above
9. Technician A states horn buttons in circuits with relays are B+ switches. Technician B states horn buttons in circuits without relays are actually switches to ground. Who is correct?
   a. Technician A
   b. Technician B
   c. Both A and B
   d. Neither A nor B
10. Depressed park windshield wiper systems park the blades by generally _____.
    a. turning off B+ to the motor
    b. applying B+ to the motor
    c. ungrounding the switch
    d. reversing the motor direction
11. Rear defrosters generally have a relay with a timer. This allows _____.
    a. the defogger to operate for only a specific amount of time
    b. the defogger to function just until the rear window is clear
    c. the defogger to be independent of the ignition switch
    d. none of the above
12. The right front window does not function on a power window vehicle. Technician A states that the window motor might be insulated from ground causing the problem. Technician B states

that either the master or right door switch could be the problem. Who is correct?
a. Technician A
b. Technician B
c. Both A and B
d. Neither A nor B

13. On an air-conditioned vehicle the cooling fan does not turn off. A possible cause could be _____.
a. a grounded coolant temperature switch
b. an open relay
c. a grounded cooling fan motor
d. a burned out fuse link

14. Information that the trip computer can supply includes _____.
a. miles per gallon of fuel
b. miles to predetermined destination
c. estimated arrival time
d. all of the above

15. Technician A says that the odometer reports the total miles or kilometers the car has traveled. Technician B says the speedometer reports the miles or kilometers per hour the car is traveling. Who is correct?
a. Technician A
b. Technician B
c. Both A and B
d. Neither A nor B

16. The indicator needle on a speedometer is held to the zero position by _____.
a. magnetic force
b. the weight of the needle
c. the speedometer cable
d. a coiled spring

17. Power window systems use _____.
a. electric motors
b. permanent magnet motors
c. reversible motors
d. all of the above

18. The horn has _____.
a. vibrating contact points
b. a vibrating diaphragm
c. an electromagnet
d. all of the above

19. The oil pressure light stays on whenever the engine is running. The oil pressure has been checked and it meets specifications. Technician A says that a ground in the circuit between the indicator light and the pressure switch could be the cause. Technician B says that an open in the pressure switch could be the cause. Who is correct?
a. Technician A
b. Technician B
c. Both A and B
d. Neither A nor B

20. Which device on a cruise control system is used to control the amount of vacuum in the system?
a. servo
b. solenoid coil
c. brake-activated switch
d. transducer
e. none of the above

SECTION 4
ENGINE PERFORMANCE

Chapter 18 Ignition Systems
Chapter 19 Ignition System Service
Chapter 20 Fuel Systems
Chapter 21 Fuel Injection
Chapter 22 Carburetors
Chapter 23 Emission Control Systems
Chapter 24 Computerized Engine Controls

For efficient engine operation, the fuel and air to be burned must be accurately metered and delivered to the combustion chambers. The spark needed to ignite this mixture must be generated at precisely the correct moment. The gases and byproducts of combustion must be managed so they pose no threat to the driver or the environment.

These are the jobs of the ignition, fuel, and emission control systems. Although their jobs are simple in principle, these engine performance systems use some of the most technologically advanced equipment found on modern vehicles. They all use a network of input sensors and output devices and tie directly into the electronic engine control system. Mastery of these systems is necessary for the modern automotive technician.

The material in Section 4 matches the content areas of the ASE certification test on engine performance and sections of the test on engine repair.

WE ENCOURAGE
PROFESSIONALISM

THROUGH TECHNICIAN
CERTIFICATION

18 IGNITION SYSTEMS

Objectives

■ Name the major conditions of engine operation that have a bearing on ignition timing. ■ Name the two major electrical circuits used in ignition systems and their common components. ■ Identify the three major functions of an ignition system. ■ Describe the operation of ignition coils, spark plugs, and ignition cables. ■ Describe the various types of spark timing systems, including electronic switching systems and their related engine position sensors. ■ List at least two major advantages of electronic ignition over mechanical ignition systems. ■ Describe the operation of mechanical, first generation electronic, computer-controlled, and distributorless ignition systems.

Combustion in an automotive gasoline engine depends on three factors: sufficient air, sufficient fuel, and sufficient heat. The first two factors are controlled by the air induction and fuel systems. The third, heat, is generated by the ignition system.

The purpose of the ignition system is to supply properly timed, high-voltage surges to the spark plugs. Thus, the task that the ignition system must perform for each cylinder in the engine is actually two-fold. First, it must generate an electrical spark that has enough heat to ignite the air/fuel mixture in the combustion chamber. Secondly, it must time the arrival of the spark in the chamber to coincide with the compression stroke of the engine.

Combustion of the air/fuel mixture within the cylinder requires a short period of time, usually measured in thousandths of a second (milliseconds). However, during this short time, the spark must occur and ignite the mixture then continue until the entire mixture is ignited. Just as combustion is completed, maximum pressure is exerted against the piston top. For efficient engine operation, maximum pressure should occur about 10 degrees after top dead center (ATDC). Therefore, the delivery of the spark must be timed to arrive at some point before the piston reaches top dead center.

Attaining this ideal performance is complicated by the fact that the rate of combustion varies according to certain factors. Higher compression pressures tend to speed up combustion. Higher octane gasolines ignite less easily and require increased burning times. Increased vaporization and turbulence tend to decrease combustion times. Other factors, including intake air temperature, humidity, and barometric pressure, also affect combustion. Because these factors change the combustion rate, the optimum time for spark delivery varies with engine speed and load.

❑ IGNITION TIMING

Ignition timing refers to the precise time that spark occurs. Ignition timing is specified by referring to the #1 piston's position in relation to crankshaft rotation. External ignition timing marks can be located on engine parts and on a pulley or flywheel to indicate piston position (Figure 18-1). Vehicle manufacturers specify initial, or basic, ignition timing.

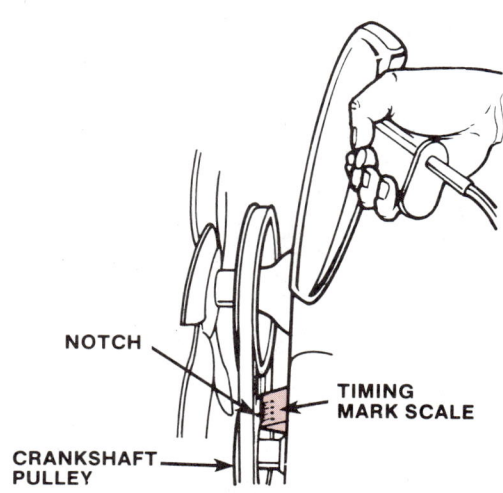

Figure 18-1 Reading ignition timing marks using a timing light.

When the marks are aligned at TDC, or 0, the piston in the number 1 cylinder is at TDC (compression stroke). Additional numbers on a scale indicate the number of degrees of crankshaft rotation before TDC (BTDC) or after TDC (ATDC). In a majority of engines, the initial timing is specified at a point between TDC and 20 degrees BTDC. A few manufacturers specified initial timing from 1 to 5 degrees ATDC for vehicles built during the 1970s.

If optimum engine performance is to be maintained, the ignition timing of the engine must be modified in accordance with these changes in conditions. Most ignition systems have methods for continually making these modifications. These methods are covered in greater detail later in this chapter. There are two major conditions of engine operation that have a bearing on ignition timing: engine speed (rpm) and load.

Engine RPM

At higher rpms, the crankshaft turns through more degrees in a given period of time. If combustion is to be completed by 10 degrees ATDC (power stroke), ignition timing must occur sooner or be advanced.

However, air/fuel mixture turbulence (swirling) increases with rpm. This causes the mixture to burn faster. Increased turbulence requires that ignition must occur slightly later or be slightly retarded.

These two factors must be balanced for best engine performance. Thus, while the ignition timing must be advanced as engine speed increases, the amount of advance must be diminished to some varying degree to compensate for increasing turbulence.

Engine Load

The load on an engine is the work it must do. Driving up hills or pulling extra weight increases engine load. Under load, the engine operates more slowly and less efficiently. A good indication of engine load is intake manifold vacuum.

Under light loads and with the throttle partially opened, a high vacuum exists in the intake manifold. The amount of air/fuel mixture drawn into the manifold and cylinders is small. On compression, this thin mixture produces less combustion pressure and combustion time is slow. To complete combustion by 10 degrees ATDC, ignition timing must be advanced.

Under heavy loads, when the throttle is opened fully, a larger mass of air/fuel mixture can be drawn in and the vacuum in the manifold is low. High combustion pressure and rapid burning results. In such a case, the ignition timing must be retarded to prevent complete burning from occurring before 10 degrees ATDC.

Firing Order

Up to this point, the primary focus of discussion has been ignition timing as it relates to any one cylinder. However, the function of the ignition system extends beyond timing the arrival of a spark to a single cylinder. It must perform this task for each cylinder of the engine in a specific sequence.

Each cylinder of an engine must produce power once in every 720 degrees of crankshaft rotation. Each must fire at its own appropriate time during that rotation. To make this possible, the pistons and rods are arranged in precise fashion. This is called the engine's firing order. The firing order is arranged to reduce rocking and imbalance in the engine that can be caused by the piston strokes. Thus, the firing order varies from engine to engine. Vehicle manufacturers simplify cylinder identification by numbering each cylinder (Figure 18-2). Regardless of the particular firing order used, the number 1 cylinder always starts the firing order, with the rest of the cylinders following in a fixed sequence.

The ignition system must be able to monitor the rotation of the crankshaft and the relative position of each piston in order to determine which piston is on its compression stroke. It must also be able to deliver a high-voltage surge to each cylinder at the proper time during its compression stroke. How the ignition system does these things depends on the type of system used.

❑ BASIC CIRCUITRY

All ignition systems consist of two interconnected electrical circuits: a primary (low voltage) circuit and a secondary (high voltage) circuit (Figure 18-3).

Depending on the exact type of ignition system, components in the primary circuit include the following.

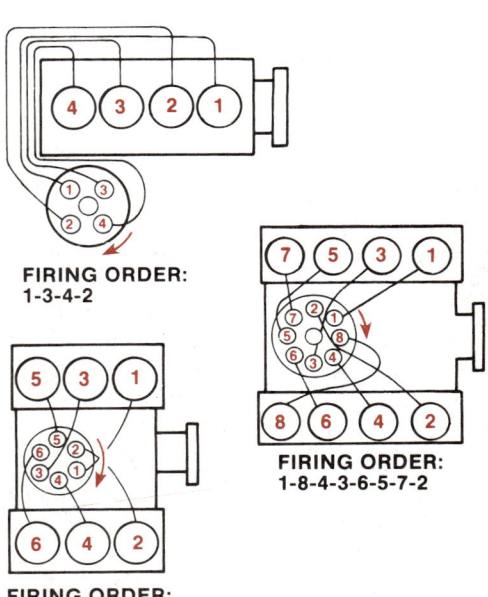

Figure 18-2 Examples of typical firing orders.

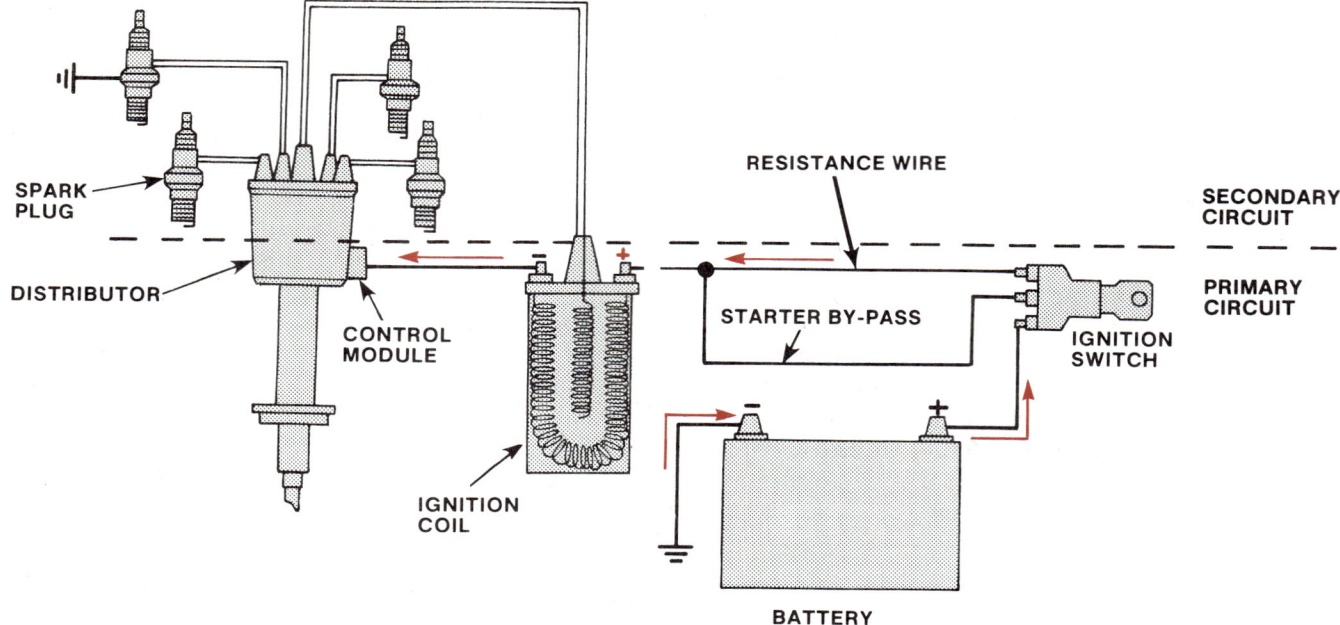

Figure 18-3 Ignition systems have a primary and secondary (high voltage) circuit.

- battery
- ignition switch
- ballast resistor or resistance wire (some systems)
- starting by-pass (some systems)
- ignition coil primary winding
- switching device or control module

The secondary circuit includes these components.

- ignition coil secondary winding
- distributor cap and rotor (some systems)
- ignition cables
- spark plugs

Primary Circuit Operation

When the ignition switch is in the on position, current from the battery flows through the ignition switch and primary circuit resistor to the primary winding of the ignition coil. From here it passes through some type of switching device and back to ground. The switching device can be electronically or mechanically controlled. The low-voltage current flow in the ignition coil's primary winding creates a magnetic field. The switching device or control module interrupts this current flow at predetermined times. When it does, the magnetic field in the primary winding collapses. This collapse generates a high-voltage surge in the secondary winding of the ignition coil. The secondary circuit of the system begins at this point.

Secondary Circuit Operation

The secondary circuit in the ignition systems carries high voltage to the spark plugs. The exact manner in which the secondary circuit delivers these high voltage surges depends on the system design. Until 1984 all ignition systems used some type of distributor to accomplish this job. However, in an effort to reduce emissions, improve fuel economy, and boost component reliability, many auto manufacturers are now using distributorless systems.

In a system using a distributor, such as that shown in Figure 18-3, high-voltage from the secondary winding passes through an ignition cable running from the coil to the distributor. The distributor then distributes the high-voltage to the individual spark plugs through a set of ignition cables. The distributor delivers the spark to match the compression stroke of the piston. The distributor may also have the capability of advancing or retarding ignition timing.

The newest type of ignition system is the distributorless, or direct ignition type. In these systems, the distributor is eliminated and spark distribution is controlled by the vehicle's computer.

Instead of a single ignition coil for all cylinders, each cylinder may have its own ignition coil, or two cylinders may share one coil. The coils are wired directly to the spark plug they control. An ignition control module, tied into the vehicle's computer control system, controls spark timing and advance. This module is typically located under the coil assembly. It may also be integrated into a special housing that contains most of the system's ignition parts.

❑ IGNITION COMPONENTS

All ignition systems share a number of common components. Some, such as the battery and ignition switch perform simple functions. The battery supplies low-voltage current to the ignition primary circuit. The current flows when the ignition switch is in the start or the run position. Full-battery voltage is always present at the ignition switch, as if it were directly connected to the battery.

Ignition Coils

To generate a spark to initiate combustion, the ignition system must deliver high-voltage to the spark plugs. Vehicles manufactured in recent years may require a voltage level between 30,000 and 60,000 volts to force a spark across the air gap of a spark plug. Since the battery typically delivers only 10 to 12 volts, a method of stepping up the voltage must be used. Multiplying battery voltage is the job of a coil.

The ignition coil is a pulse transformer. It transforms battery voltage into short bursts of high-voltage. As explained previously, when a wire is moved through a magnetic field, current is induced in the wire. The inverse of this principle is also true—when a magnetic field moves across a wire, current is induced in the wire.

If a wire is bent into loops forming a coil and a magnetic field is passed through the coil, an equal amount of voltage is generated in each loop of wire. The more loops of wire in the coil, the greater the total voltage induced.

Also, the faster the magnetic field moves through the coil, the higher the voltage induced in the coil. If the speed of the magnetic field is doubled, the voltage output doubles.

An ignition coil uses these principles and has two coils of wire wrapped around an iron core. The first, or primary, coil is normally composed of 100 to 150 turns of 20-gauge wire. This coil of wire conducts battery current. When a current is passing through the primary coil, it magnetizes the iron core. The secondary coil of wires may consist of 15,000 to 20,000, or more, turns of fine copper wire that is thinner than human hair. When battery current is applied to the primary coil, the magnetic field cuts across the windings of the secondary coil. This induces a voltage in the secondary coil.

It takes time for the coil to become fully magnetized or saturated. However, when the primary coil circuit is suddenly opened, the magnetic field collapses instantly. The sudden collapsing of the magnetic field produces a very high voltage in the secondary windings. It is this surge in voltage that pushes current across the gap of the spark plug. Figure 18-4 simplistically shows the coil's primary and secondary circuits.

The number of ignition coils used varies depending on the type of ignition system found on a vehicle. In most ignition systems with a distributor, only one ignition coil is used. Figure 18-5 shows a cutaway view of the type of ignition coil used in these systems. The high-voltage of the secondary winding is directed, by

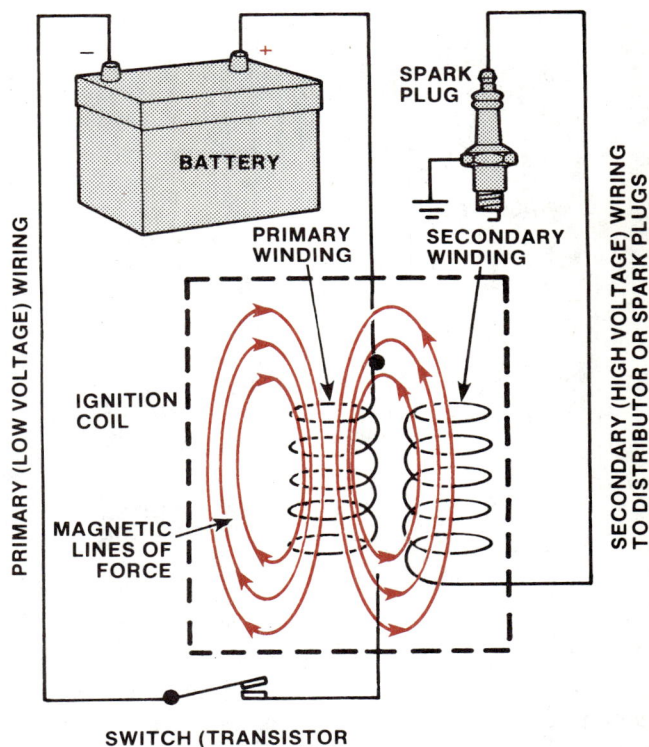

Figure 18-4 Current passing through the coil's primary winding creates magnetic lines of force that cut across and induce voltage in the secondary windings.

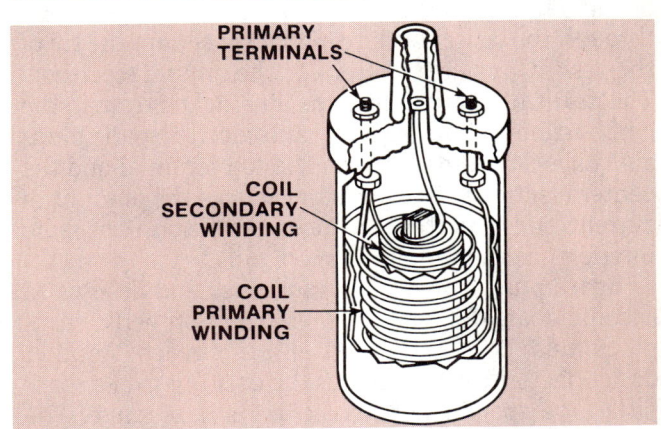

Figure 18-5 Cutaway view of a typical ignition coil.

the distributor, to the various spark plugs in the system. Therefore, there is one secondary circuit with a continually changing path.

While distributor systems have a single secondary circuit with a continually changing path, distributorless (DIS) systems have several secondary circuits, each with an unchanging path.

Spark Plugs

Every type of ignition system uses spark plugs. The spark plugs provide the crucial air gap through which

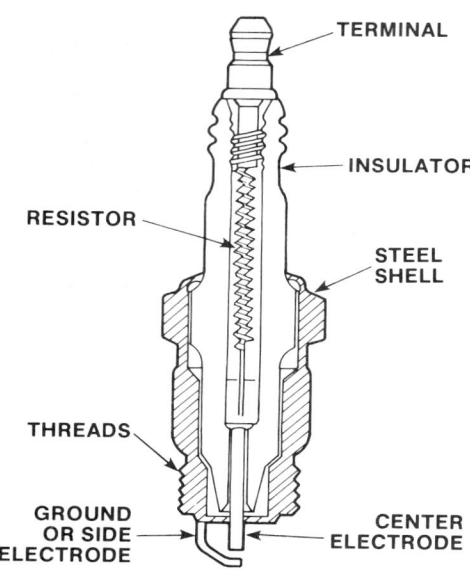

Figure 18-6 Components of a typical spark plug.

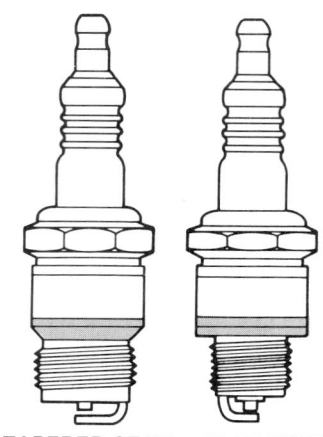

Figure 18-7 Spark plug seats: tapered versus flat.

the high-voltage from the coil flows across in the form of an arc. The three main parts of a spark plug are the ceramic core, or insulator, which acts as a heat conductor; a pair of electrodes, one insulated in the core and the other grounded on the shell; and a steel shell, which holds the ceramic core and electrodes in a gastight assembly and also contains threads for plug installation in the engine (Figure 18-6). A boot and cable are attached to the top of the plug. The current flows through the center of the plug and arcs from the tip of the center (or side) electrode to the ground electrode. The resulting spark ignites the air/fuel mixture in the combustion chamber. Most automotive spark plugs also have a resistor between the top terminal and the center electrode. This resistor reduces the amount of current and, therefore, reduces the amount of radio interference caused by the spark plug.

Spark plugs come in various sizes and designs to accommodate different engines. To fit properly, spark plugs must be of the proper size and reach. Another design factor that determines the usefulness of a spark plug for a specific application is its heat range. The desired heat range depends on the type of driving conditions the vehicle is subject to. Once a technician selects a spark plug with the correct size, reach, and heat range for a particular application, there is one more spark plug characteristic that must be checked and often adjusted—the spark plug air gap. Although the size, reach, and heat range of a spark plug are already determined by the manufacturer, the technician has the responsibility to properly gap the plug.

Size

Spark plugs are available in either 14-, or 18-millimeter diameters. All 18-millimeter plugs feature tapered seats that match similar seats in the cylinder head and need no gaskets. The 14-millimeter variety can have either a flat seat that requires a gasket, or a tapered seat that does not (Figure 18-7). The latter is found mainly in late-model applications. All spark plugs have a hex-shaped shell that accommodates a socket wrench for easy installation and removal. The 14-millimeter, tapered seat plugs have shells with a 5/8-inch hex; 14-millimeter gasketed and 18-millimeter tapered seat plugs have shells with a 13/16-inch hex.

Reach

One of the most important design differences among spark plugs is the reach, illustrated in Figure 18-8. This refers to the length of the shell from the contact surface at the seat to the bottom of the shell, including both threaded and nonthreaded sections. Reach is crucial so that the plug's air gap is in the correct position to produce the correct amount of heat. Installing plugs with too short a reach means that the electrodes are in a pocket and the arc is not able to ignite the air/fuel mixture. In addition, the exposed threads in the cylinder head accumulate carbon deposits. If the reach is too long, the exposed plug threads could get so hot that they ignite the air/fuel mixture at the wrong time, causing preignition.

Heat Range

Spark plugs are available in different heat ranges. A heat range indicates how well a spark plug can conduct

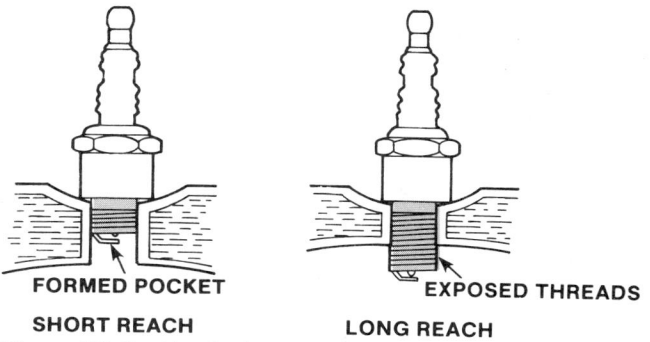

Figure 18-8 Spark plug reach: long versus short.

Ignition Systems 445

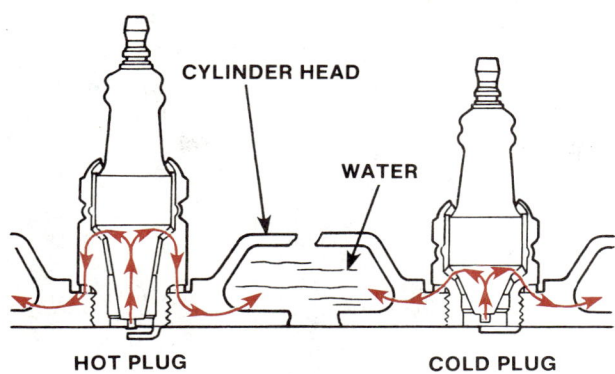

Figure 18-9 Spark plug heat range: hot versus cold.

heat away from the tip. A cooler plug transfers heat away from the tip rapidly, resulting in lower tip temperatures. A hotter plug transfers heat away slowly, resulting in higher tip temperatures (Figure 18-9). The shape of the porcelain insulator and its contact with the outer metal shell determines spark plug heat range.

Installing a plug with the correct heat range is important because the firing end must run hot enough to burn away fouling deposits while the engine is idling, yet cool enough at higher speed to prevent preignition and electrode wear. The heat range is indicated by a code imprinted on the side of the plug, usually on the porcelain insulator.

SHOP TALK

When spark plugs must be replaced, note the plug type specifications as recommended by the engine and plug manufacturers. These are recommendations only. For example, continuous heavy driving demands a much cooler plug than if the vehicle does a lot of stop-and-go driving.

Spark Plug Air Gap

The correct spark plug air gap is essential to achieve optimum engine performance and long plug life. A gap that is too wide (Figure 18-10) requires higher voltage to jump the gap. If the required voltage is greater than what is available, the result is misfiring. On the other hand, a gap that is too narrow requires lower voltages

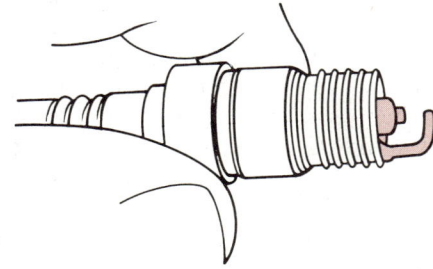

Figure 18-10 It is difficult for current to jump a gap this wide.

and leads to rough idle and prematurely burned electrodes, due to higher current flow. Always set the gap in accordance with the vehicle manufacturer's specifications. Electronic ignition systems utilize wider air gaps than older breaker point systems due to higher available voltages and leaner air/fuel mixtures of late-model engines.

Ignition Cables

Spark plug, or ignition cables make up the secondary wiring, which carries the high-voltage from the distributor or the multiple coils (DIS systems) to the spark plugs. Unlike the solid metal cores used many years ago, ignition cables contain fiber cores that act as a resistor in the secondary circuit. They cut down on radio and television interference, increase firing voltages, and reduce spark plug wear by decreasing current. Insulated boots on the ends of the cables strengthen the connections as well as prevent dust and water infiltration and voltage loss.

❑ SPARK TIMING SYSTEMS

To better understand the operation of electronic-controlled spark timing systems, it is helpful to first review how older, fully mechanical distributor timing systems worked (Figure 18-11).

Breaker Point Ignition

Breaker point ignition systems were used on vehicles for more than 60 years but were abandoned when automotive engineers sought ways to decrease emissions and increase fuel efficiency. The breaker point system performed three major functions.

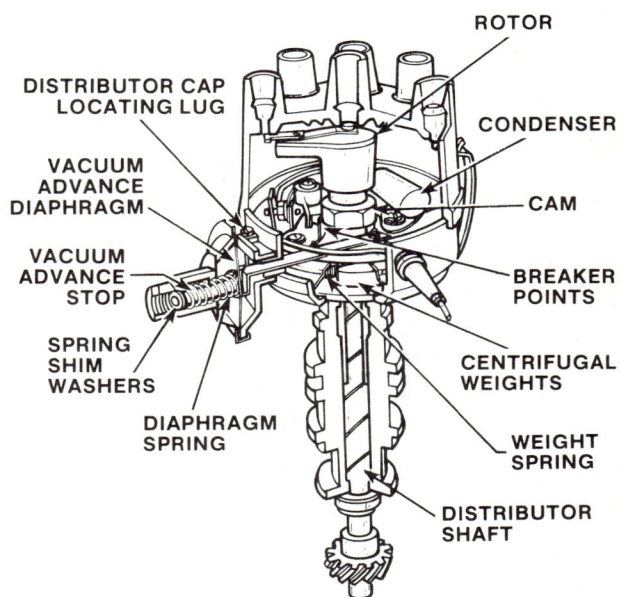

Figure 18-11 Typical nonelectronic distributor with mechanical timing advance units.

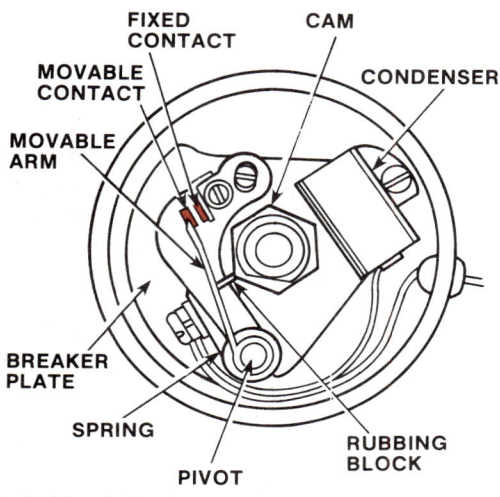

Figure 18-12 Older ignition systems used breaker points as the switching device in the primary circuit.

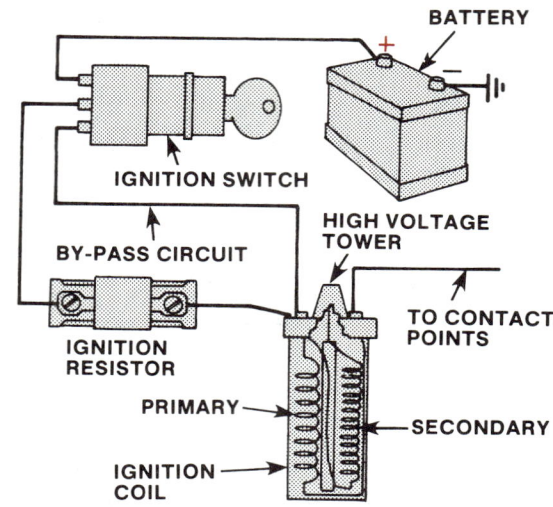

Figure 18-14 An ignition resistor bypass circuit controlled by the ignition switch.

SWITCHING DEVICE The distributor acted as a mechanical switch to turn the primary circuit on and off. The distributor's shaft, cam, breaker points, and condenser performed this function.

As shown in Figure 18-12, mechanical breaker, or contact, points are used as the primary circuit switching device. The breaker point assembly, which is mounted on the breaker plate inside the distributor, consists of a fixed contact, movable contact, movable arm, rubbing block, pivot, and spring. The fixed contact is grounded through the distributor housing, and the movable contact is connected to the negative terminal of the coil primary winding. As the cam is turned by the camshaft, the movable arm opens and closes, opening and closing the coil primary circuit.

Because voltage is still present at the movable arm when the breaker arms open, current could jump across the open point gap and damage the points. To prevent this from happening, a condenser (Figure 18-13) is attached to the movable arm. In this way, the voltage at the movable arm is retained by the condenser instead of transmitted across the gap.

A primary, or ballast, resistor is located in series between the battery and the primary coil winding and is responsible for maintaining the primary circuit voltage at the desired level (about 9 or 10 volts), thus preventing the contact points from burning due to high voltage. The ballast resistor could be either a separate unit or a specially made wire. During starting, a ballast resistor is by-passed to provide maximum current flow to the primary circuit (Figure 18-14).

TIMING ADJUSTER The distributor also mechanically adjusted the time the spark arrives at the cylinder through the use of two mechanisms: the centrifugal advance and the vacuum advance. In this way, it improved engine performance, fuel efficiency, and emission levels.

SPARK DISTRIBUTION As its name implies, the distributor mechanically distributed the spark so that it arrived at the correct moment in the compression stroke of each cylinder. The distributor's shaft, rotor, and cap performed this function.

Electronic or Solid State Ignition

From the fully mechanical breaker point setup, ignition technology first progressed to basic electronic or solid state ignitions. Breaker points were replaced with an electronic switching device. These electronic switching components are normally inside a separate housing known as a control module or control unit. These basic solid state electronic ignitions still relied on mechanical and vacuum advance mechanisms in the distributor.

As technology advanced, many manufacturers expanded the ability of the ignition control modules. For example, by tying a manifold vacuum sensor into the

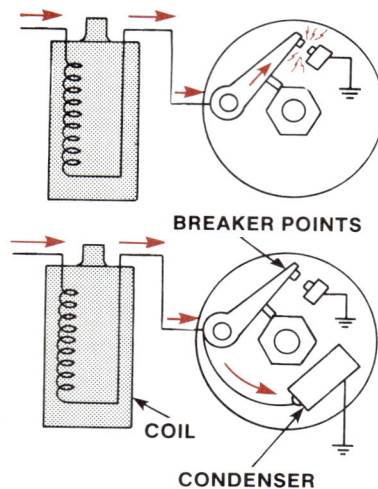

Figure 18-13 A condenser prevents current from jumping across the open point gap.

ignition module circuitry, the module could now detect when the engine was under heavy load and retard the timing automatically. Similar add-on sensors and circuits were designed to control: spark knock, start-up emissions, and altitude compensation. These innovations were a major step toward computer-controlled ignition systems, but none offered continuous spark timing control.

Computer-Controlled Electronic Ignition

Computer-controlled ignition systems are the latest generation of ignition systems used. They offer continuous spark timing control through a network of engine sensors and a central microprocessor. Based on its input, the central microprocessor or computer makes decisions regarding spark timing and signals the ignition module to fire the spark plugs accordingly.

Computer-controlled ignition systems may or may not use a distributor to distribute secondary voltage to the spark plugs. As mentioned earlier, distributorless systems use multiple coils and modules to generate and fire secondary voltages directly from the coil to the plug.

☐ ADVANTAGES OF ELECTRONIC IGNITION

Electronic ignition systems have many advantages over breaker point ignition systems.

Higher Secondary Voltages

Electronic ignition systems can carry the increased primary current needed to produce the higher secondary system voltages needed to ignite the leaner air/fuel mixtures used in modern vehicles.

The primary circuit in most breaker point systems carried 3.5 to 4.0 amperes. When the breaker points open, this current arcs between the points, electrolyzing and corroding the metal surface of the contacts. When primary current increases above 4 amperes, point life begins to decrease at an increased rate, resulting in a very limited point life (Figure 18-15A). Faster wearing points require extra maintenance and result in an ever decreasing dwell period, which in turn decreases the potential voltage induced in the secondary system.

Better High-Speed Performance

Another handicap of the old breaker point system is that as engine speed increases, the dwell time of the system decreases. This, in turn, decreases the output of the coil (Figure 18-15B). For the ignition coil to generate maximum secondary voltage, maximum primary current flow must be attained before the primary circuit is opened. This allows the magnetic field in the coil to reach full strength (saturation). In a breaker point system, the length of time the primary current is closed is controlled by the speed of the breaker cam. This period of time is called a dwell angle and is expressed in a number of degrees of distributor shaft rotation. For example, many V-8 engines have a dwell angle of 30 degrees during which time the points are closed and current builds in the coil primary. This dwell angle remains constant regardless of engine speed, but as engine rpm increases, the actual time the points are closed decreases. Any increase in engine speed above a specific rpm reduces the saturation time of the ignition coil, causing the available voltage to decrease.

This phenomenon is due to the fact that the current in the coil does not instantaneously reach its maximum value when the contact points close. Current in the coil must build for several milliseconds for this value to be reached. At 1000 rpm, the distributor shaft rotates once every 0.12 second. Of this time, the points are closed for 0.10 second, or 10 milliseconds, for every cylinder of an 8-cylinder engine. This is sufficient time for the primary current to build up to its maximum of just over 4 amperes. This time versus current relationship is shown in Figure 18-16.

When the engine speed increases to 2000 rpm, the time during which the points are closed for each plug firing is reduced to 5 milliseconds. A dwell period of 5 milliseconds allows the primary current to build to 3.8 amperes. At 3000 rpm, the dwell period drops to 3.3 milliseconds and the current to 3.2 amperes. The reduced saturation time weakens the secondary voltage, causing the spark plugs to misfire at high rpms. This increases exhaust emission and decreases fuel economy and engine performance.

An electronic ignition system, however, is not limited by a fixed dwell angle. The system's control unit can vary the on time of the primary circuit based on engine speed, load, and temperature. As the chart in Figure 18-16 shows, GM's high-energy ignition (HEI) system maintains a constant voltage level until reaching 3000 rpm. Because coil primary current levels are not limited by breaker points, low-resistance coils are used in the electronic ignition system. By decreasing the resistance in the primary circuit, the saturation

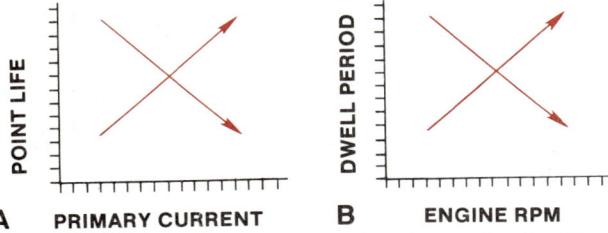

Figure 18-15 Disadvantages of breaker point ignitions: (A) point life decreases as primary current increases, and (B) dwell period drops as engine rpm increases.

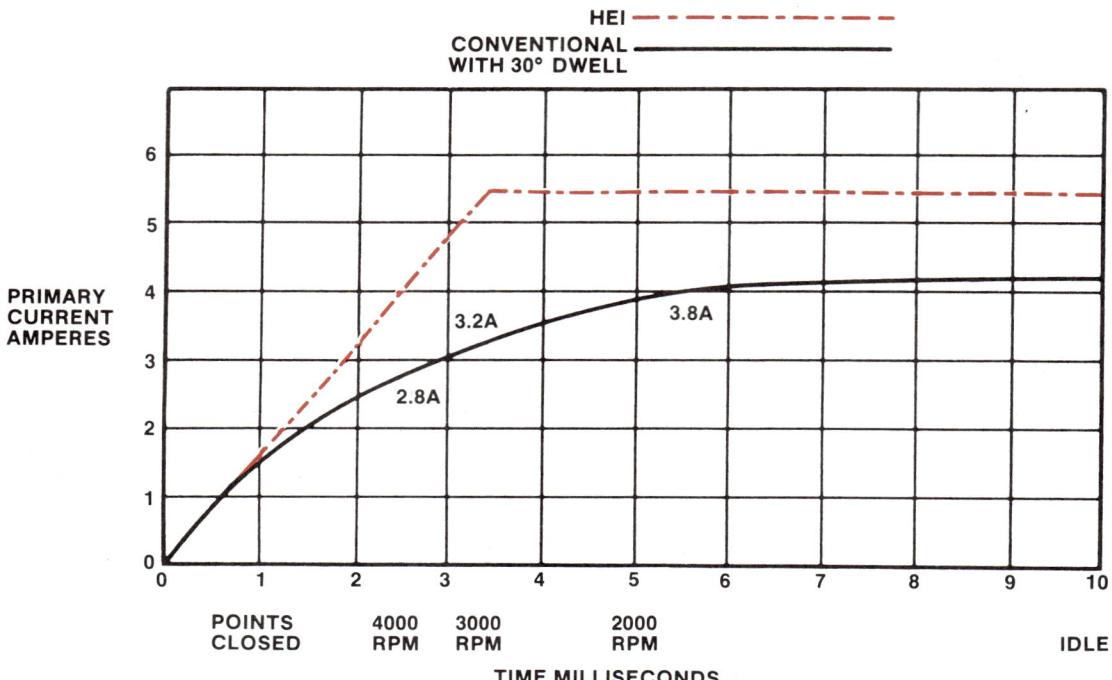

Figure 18-16 Current levels in GMs high-energy ignition system remain higher over a longer range of engine speeds when compared to breaker point systems.

time of the coil is greatly reduced. It takes 10 milliseconds for the current to reach maximum saturation in a coil with a resistance of 2.6 ohms. In a coil used in electronic ignition systems, the primary winding can have a resistance as low as 0.5 ohm. This allows full current to be reached in about 3.4 milliseconds. Because it takes less time to reach full current, coil saturation can be obtained at much higher engine speeds. For example, the HEI system developed by General Motors in 1974 is able to generate 35,000 volts at engine speeds above 3000 rpm. A typical engine breaker point system, on the other hand, develops a peak of 20,000 volts at 1000 rpm. Above this speed, the voltage drops off.

❏ ELECTRONIC SWITCHING SYSTEMS

Electronic ignition systems control the primary circuit, using an NPN transistor instead of breaker contact points. The transistor's emitter is connected to the negative (-) battery terminal (ground) and takes the place of the fixed contact point. The collector is connected to the negative (-) end of the coil primary circuit, taking the place of the movable contact point. When the triggering device supplies a small amount of current to the third transistor terminal (the center base), the collector and emitter act as if they are closed contact points (a conductor), allowing current to build up in the coil primary circuit. When the current to the base is interrupted by the triggering device, the collector and emitter act as an open contact (an insulator), interrupting the coil primary current. An example of how this works is shown in Figure 18-17, which is a simplified diagram of an electronic ignition system.

Engine Position Sensors

The time when the primary circuit must be opened and closed is related to the position of the pistons and

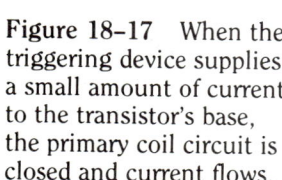

Figure 18-17 When the triggering device supplies a small amount of current to the transistor's base, the primary coil circuit is closed and current flows.

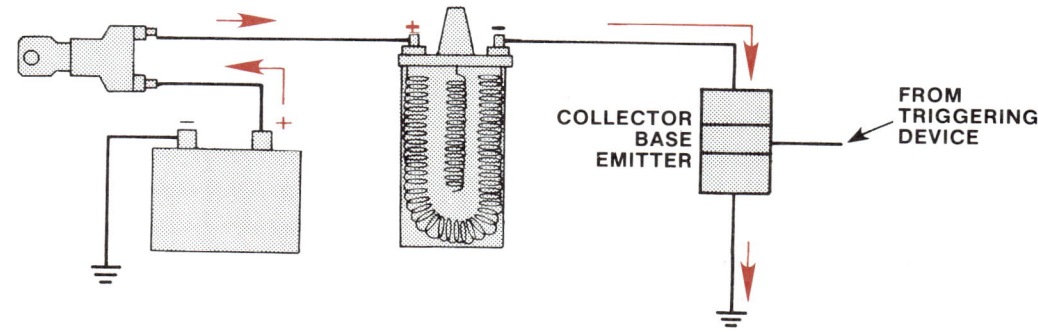

Ignition Systems

the crankshaft. Therefore, the position of the crankshaft is used to control the flow of current to the center base terminal of the switching transistor.

A number of different types of sensors are used to monitor the position of the crankshaft and control the flow of current to the center base terminal of the switching transistor. These engine position sensors and generators serve as triggering devices and include magnetic pulse generators, metal detection sensors, Hall-effect sensors, and photoelectric sensors.

The mounting location of these sensors depends on the design of the ignition system. All four types of sensors can be mounted on the distributor shaft, which is turned by the camshaft.

Magnetic pulse generators and Hall-effect sensors can also be located on the crankshaft (Figures 18-18 and 18-19). These sensors are also commonly used on DIS ignition systems. Both Hall-effect sensors and

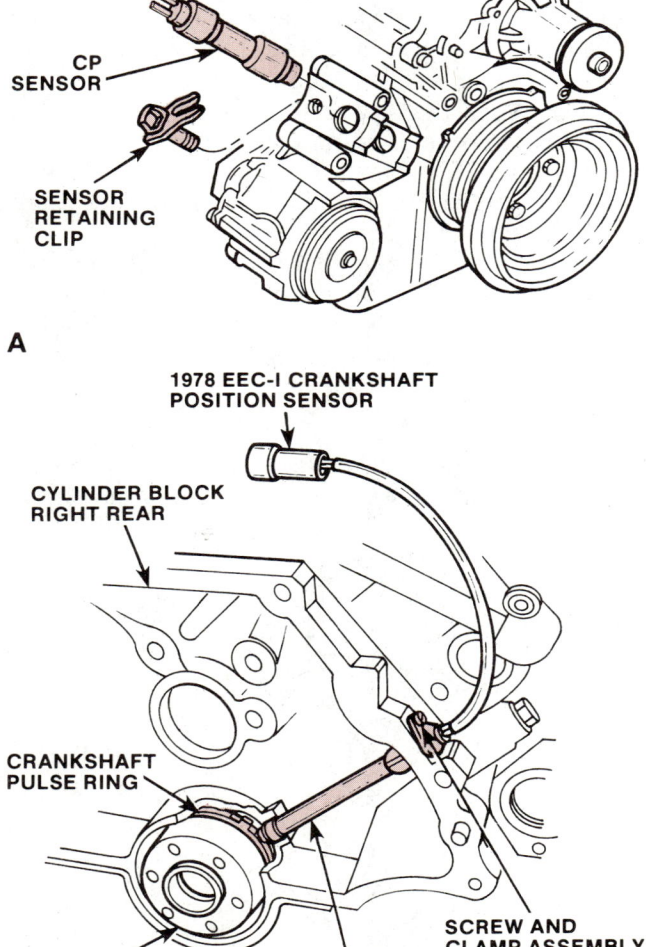

Figure 18-18 Magnetic pulse generator (A) front location (B) rear location.

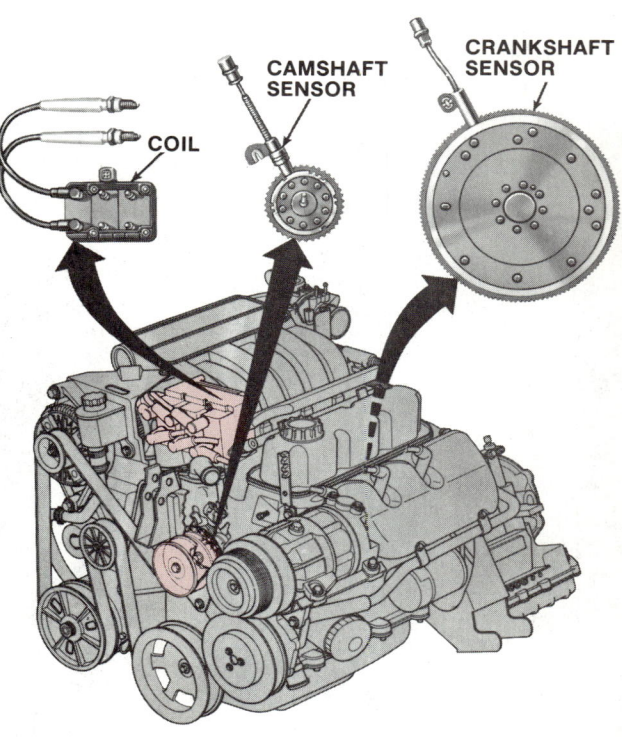

Figure 18-19 Hall-effect sensor location.

magnetic pulse generators can also be used as camshaft reference sensors to identify which cylinder is the next one to fire.

Magnetic Pulse Generator

Basically, a magnetic pulse generator consists of two parts: a timing disc and a pick-up coil. The timing disc may also be called a reluctor, trigger wheel, pulse ring, armature, or timing core. The pick-up coil, which consists of a length of wire wound around a weak permanent magnet, may also be called a stator, sensor, or pole piece. Depending on the type of ignition system used, the timing disc may be mounted on the distributor shaft, at the rear of the crankshaft (Figure 18-20), or on the crankshaft vibration damper (Figure 18-21).

The generator operates on basic electromagnetic principles. Remember that a voltage can only be induced when the magnetic field around the pick-up coil is moving. The rotating timing disc teeth produce the movement in the coil's magnetic field needed to induce voltage.

As the disc teeth approach the pick-up coil, they repell the magnetic field, forcing it to contact and concentrate around the pick-up coil (Figure 18-22A). Once the tooth passes by the pick-up coil, the magnetic field is free to expand or unconcentrate (Figure 18-22B), until the next tooth on the disc approaches.

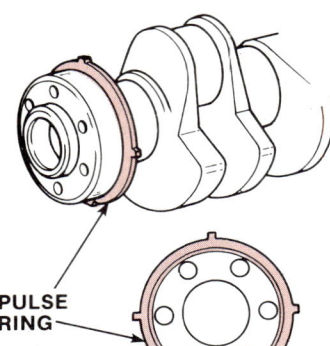

Figure 18-20 Pulse ring location at the rear of the crankshaft.

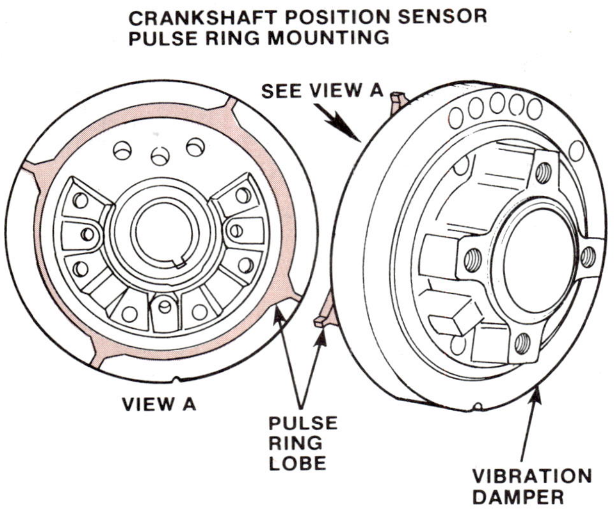

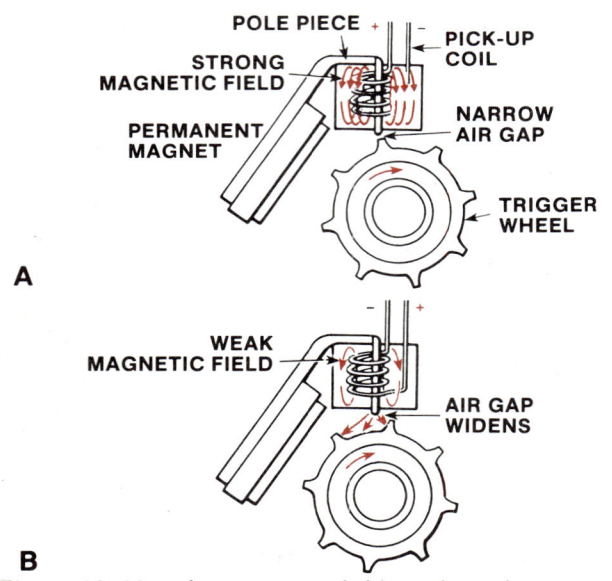

Figure 18-21 Pulse ring location on the vibration damper.

Figure 18-22 The magnetic field in the pole piece expands as the reluctor teeth approach and contracts as the teeth move away. This field movement induces voltage in the pick-up coil.

Approaching teeth concentrate the magnetic lines of force, while passing teeth allow them to expand. The moving lines of magnetic force cut across the winding of the pick-up coil, generating a voltage that is sent to the switching device in the primary circuit.

When a disc tooth is directly in line with the pick-up coil, the magnetic field is not expanding or contracting. Since there is no movement or change in the field, voltage at this precise moment drops to zero. At this point, the switching device (transistor) inside the ignition module reacts to the zero voltage signal by turning the ignition's primary circuit current off. As explained earlier, this forces the magnetic field in the primary coil to collapse, discharging a secondary voltage to the distributor or directly to the spark plug.

As soon as the tooth rotates past the pick-up coil, the magnetic field expands again and another voltage signal is induced. The only difference is that the polarity of the charge is reversed. Negative becomes positive or positive becomes negative. Upon sensing this change in current flow, the switching device turns the primary circuit back on and the process begins all over.

The slotted disc is mounted on the crankshaft, vibration damper, or distributor shaft in a very precise manner. When the disc teeth align with the pick-up coil, this corresponds to the exact time certain pistons are nearing TDC. This means the zero voltage signal needed to trigger the secondary circuit occurs at precisely the correct time.

The pick-up coil might have only one pole as shown in Figure 18-23. Other magnetic pulse generators have pick-up coils with two or more poles. The one shown in Figure 18-24 has as many poles as it has trigger teeth.

Metal Detection Sensors

Metal detection sensors are found on many early electronic ignition systems. They perform much like

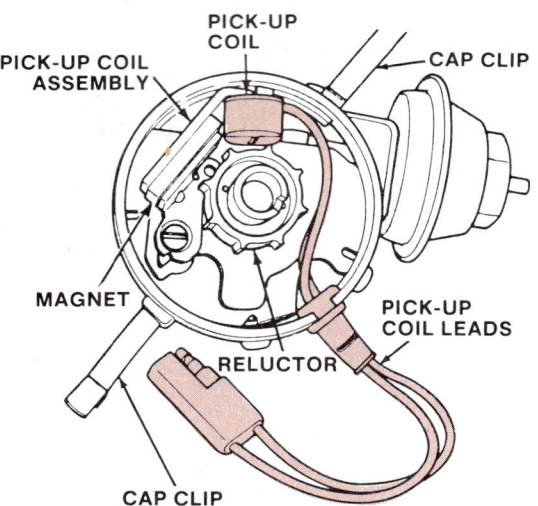

Figure 18-23 A magnetic pulse generator (pick-up coil) used on early Chrysler electronic ignition systems.

Ignition Systems

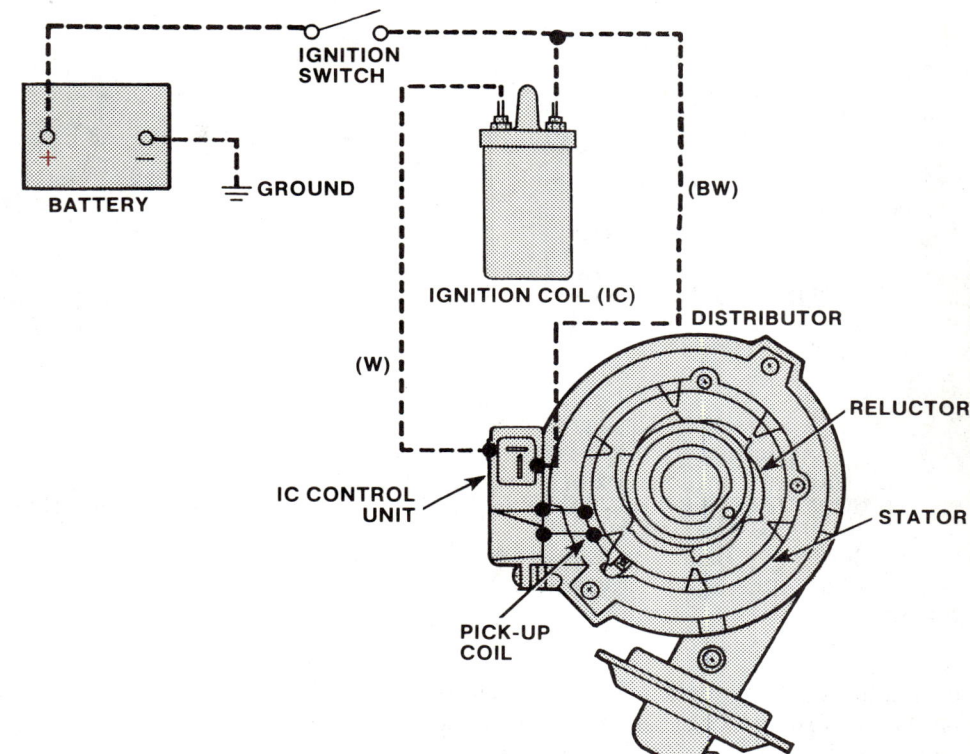

Figure 18-24 A magnetic pulse generator used in early Datsun electronic ignition systems. *Courtesy of Nissan Corp.*

the magnetic pulse generator described with one major difference.

A trigger wheel is pressed over the distributor shaft and a pick-up coil detects the passing of the trigger teeth as the distributor shaft rotates. However, unlike a magnetic pulse generator, the pick-up coil of a metal detection sensor does not have a permanent magnet. Instead, the pick-up coil is an electromagnet. A low level of alternating current is supplied to the coil by an electronic control unit, inducing a weak magnetic field around the coil. As the reluctor on the distributor shaft rotates, the trigger teeth pass very close to the coil (Figure 18-25). As the teeth pass in and out of the coil's magnetic field, the magnetic field builds and collapses, producing a corresponding change in the coil's voltage. The voltage changes are monitored by the control unit to determine crankshaft position.

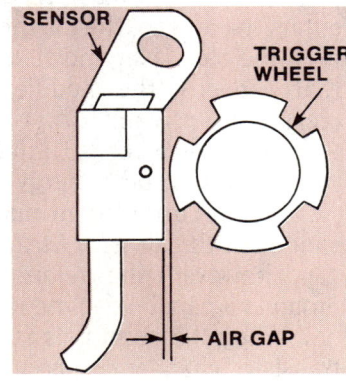

Figure 18-25 In a metal detecting sensor, the revolving trigger wheel teeth alter the magnetic field produced by the electromagnet in the pick-up coil.

Hall-Effect Sensor

Introduced in early 1982, the Hall-effect sensor or switch is now the most commonly used engine position sensor. There are several good reasons for this. Unlike a magnetic pulse generator, the Hall-effect sensor produces an accurate voltage signal throughout the entire rpm range of the engine. Furthermore, a Hall-effect switch produces a square wave signal that is more compatible with the digital signals required by on-board computers.

Functionally, a Hall switch performs the same tasks as a magnetic pulse generator. But the Hall switch's method of generating voltage is quite unique. It is based on the Hall-effect principle which states: If a current is allowed to flow through a thin conducting material, and that material is exposed to a magnetic field, voltage is produced.

The heart of the Hall generator is a thin semiconductor layer (Hall layer) derived from a gallium arsenate crystal. Attached to it are two terminals—one positive, and the other negative—that are used to provide the source current for the Hall transformation.

Directly across from this semiconductor element is a permanent magnet. It's positioned so that its lines of flux bisect the Hall layer at right angles to the direction of current flow. Two additional terminals, located on either side of the Hall layer, form the signal output circuit.

When current is passed through the Hall layer, a voltage is produced perpendicular to the direction of

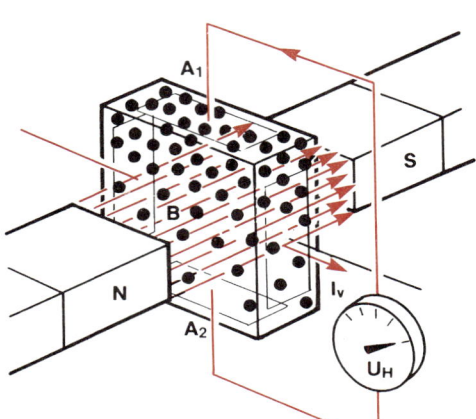

U_H = HALL VOLTAGE
B = MAGNETIC FIELD (FLUX DENSITY)
I_v = CONSTANT SUPPLY CURRENT
A_1, A_2 = HALL LAYER

Figure 18-26 In a Hall-effect sensor the electrons move perpendicular to the lines of magnetic flux and electrical current.

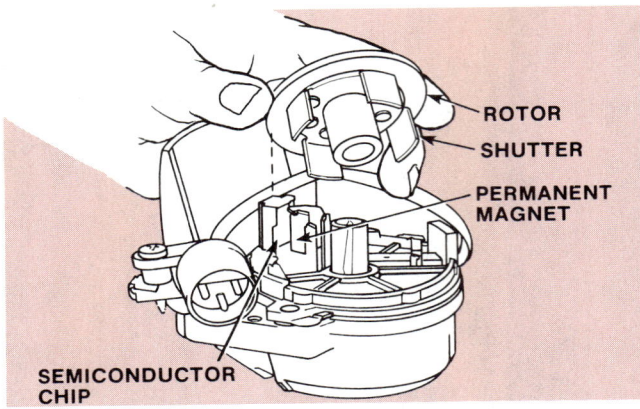

Figure 18-27 Example of a Hall-effect triggering device.

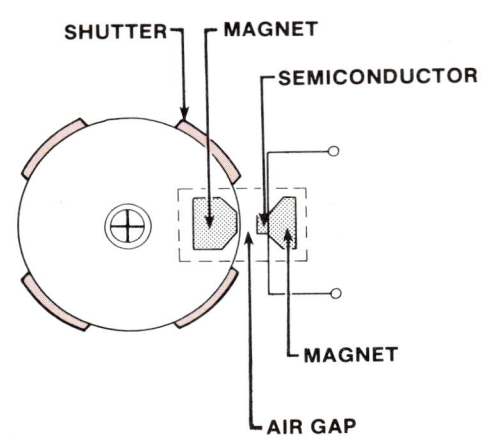

Figure 18-28 As the shutter wheel rotates with the distributor shaft, the shutters pass between the magnet and semiconductor, interrupting the Hall-effect voltage generation.

current flow and magnetic flux. The signal voltage that is produced is the direct result of the magnetic field's effect on electron flow. As the magnetic lines of force collide with the electrons in the supply current, current flow in the crystals is distorted and, as a result, electrons are deflected toward what becomes the negative Hall voltage terminal (Figure 18-26). It is this creation of an electron surplus at the Hall voltage terminal that results in the production of a weak voltage potential.

The Hall switch is described as being on any time the Hall layer is exposed to a magnetic field and a Hall voltage is being produced. However, before this signal voltage can be of any use, it has to be modified. After leaving the Hall layer, the signal is routed to an amplifier where it is strengthened and inverted so that the signal reads high when it is actually coming in low and vice versa. Once it has been inverted, the signal goes through a pulse-shaping device called a Schmitt trigger where it is turned into a clean square wave signal. After conditioning, the signal is sent to the base of a switching transistor that is designed to turn on and off in response to the signals generated by the Hall-effect switch assembly.

The shutter wheel is the last major component of the Hall switch. The shutter wheel consists of a series of alternating windows and vanes that pass between the Hall layer and magnet. The shutter wheel may be part of the distributor rotor (Figure 18-27) or be separate from the rotor.

The shutter wheel performs the same function as the timing disc on magnetic pulse generators. The only difference is with a Hall-effect switch there is no electromagnetic induction. Instead, the shutter wheel creates a magnetic shunt that changes the field strength through the Hall element. When a vane of the shutter wheel is positioned between the magnet and Hall element, the metallic vane blocks the magnetic field and keeps it from permeating the Hall layer. As a result, only a few residual electrons are deflected in the layer and Hall output voltage is low (Figure 18-28). Conversely, when a window rotates into the air gap, the magnetic field is able to penetrate the Hall layer, which in turn pushes the Hall voltage to its maximum range.

The points where the shutter vane begins to enter and begins to leave the air gap are directly related to primary circuit control. As the leading edge of a vane enters the air gap, the magnetic field is deflected away from the Hall layer and Hall voltage decreases. When that happens, the modified Hall output signal increases abruptly and turns the switching transistor on. Once the transistor is turned on, the primary circuit closes and the coil's energy storage cycle begins.

Primary current continues to flow as long as the vane is in the air gap. As the vane starts to leave the gap, however, the reforming Hall voltage signal prompts a parallel decline in the modified output signal. When the output signal goes low, the bias of the transistor changes. Primary current flow stops.

In summary, the ignition module supplies current to the coil's primary winding as long as the shutter wheel's vane is in the air gap. As soon as the shutter wheel moves away and the Hall voltage is produced, the control unit stops primary circuit current, high secondary voltage is induced, and ignition occurs.

In addition to ignition control, a Hall-effect switch can also be used to generate precise rpm signals (by determining the frequency at which the voltage rises and falls) and provide the sync pulse for sequential fuel ignition operation.

Photoelectric Sensor

A fifth type of crankshaft position sensor is the photoelectric sensor. The parts of this sensor include a light emitting diode (LED), a light sensitive phototransistor (photo cell), and a slotted disc called a light beam interrupter (Figure 18-29).

The slotted disc is attached to the distributor shaft. The LED and the photo cell are situated over and under the disc opposite of each other. As the slotted disc rotates between the LED and photo cell, light from the LED shines through the slots. The intermittent flashes of light are translated into voltage pulses by the photo cell. When the voltage signal occurs, the control unit turns the primary system on. When the disc interrupts the light and the voltage signal ceases, the control unit turns the primary system off, causing the magnetic field in the coil to collapse and sending a surge of voltage to a spark plug.

The photoelectric sensor sends a very reliable signal to the control unit, especially at low engine speeds. However, it has found very limited application on original equipment ignition systems.

❏ ELECTRONIC IGNITION SYSTEM OPERATION

The primary circuit of an electronic ignition system is controlled electronically by one of the sensors just described and an electronic control unit (module) that contains some type of switching device.

Primary Circuit Control

Figure 18-30 shows a basic electronic ignition system. The system consists of a distributor with a magnetic pulse pick-up unit and reluctor, an electronic control module, and a ballast resistor. As described earlier, when the tooth of the reluctor passes the pick-up, an electrical impulse is sent to the electronic module, which contains the switching transistor. The pulse signals the transistor to open the primary circuit, firing the plug. Once the plug stops firing, the transistor closes the primary coil circuit. The length of time that the transistor allows current flow in the primary ignition circuit is determined by the electronic circuitry in the control module. Some systems use a dual ballast resistor. A ceramic ballast resistor is mounted on the fire wall and has a 0.5-ohm resistance that maintains a constant primary current. The auxiliary ballast resistor uses a 5-ohm resistance to limit voltage to the electronic control unit.

There are some electronic ignition systems that do not require a ballast resistor. For instance, some control units directly regulate current flow in the coil primary. Hall-effect systems do not require ballast resistors either. The signal voltage is not changed by the speed of the distributor as it is in an inductive magnetic signal generating system.

Some systems can be enhanced with additional sensors that increase the control module's capabilities. The module shown in Figure 18-30 can be equipped with either a barometric pressure switch or vacuum switch. The barometric pressure switch enables the module to retard the ignition timing 3 to 6 degrees when the vehicle is operating at low elevations. The vacuum switch does the same if the engine is under hard acceleration or heavy load. Other modules have the ability to retard ignition timing during start-up or when engine knock is detected.

Timing Advance

As stated, basic electronic ignition systems still perform the timing advance function mechanically just like the older breaker point systems.

CENTRIFUGAL ADVANCE At idle, the firing of the spark plug usually occurs just before the piston reaches top dead center. At higher engine rpms, however, the spark must be delivered to the cylinder much earlier in the cycle to achieve maximum power from the air/fuel mixture since the engine is moving through the cycle more quickly. To change the timing of the spark in relation to rpm, the centrifugal advance mechanism is used (Figure 18-31).

This mechanism consists of a set of weights and springs connected to the distributor shaft and a dis-

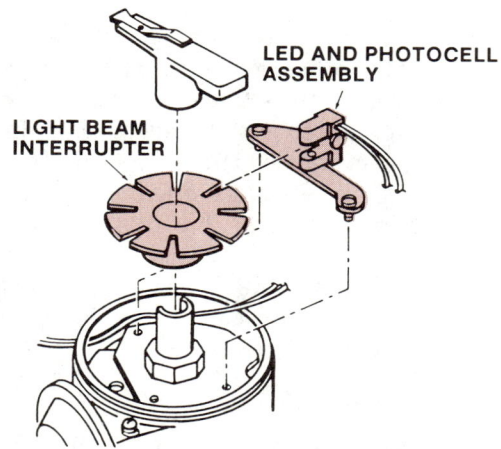

Figure 18-29 A photoelectric triggering device.

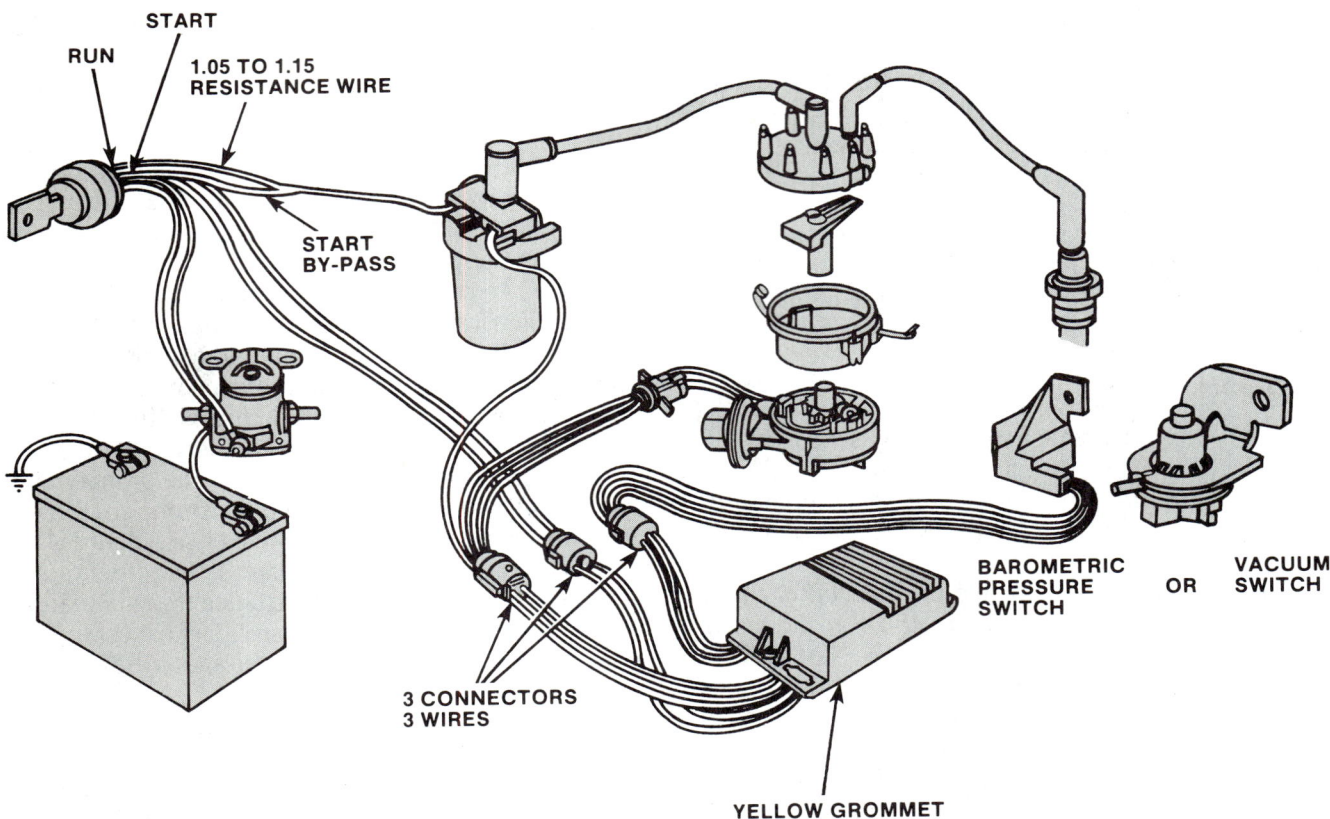

Figure 18-30 The Dura Spark II electronic ignition system. *Courtesy of Ford Motor Co.*

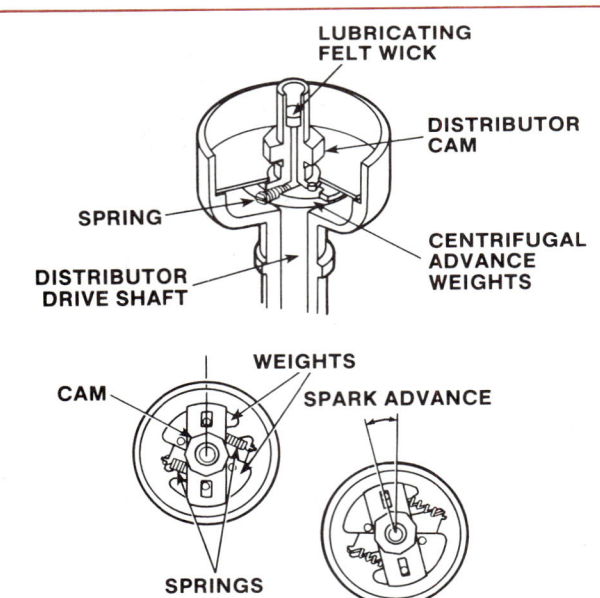

Figure 18-31 Typical centrifugal advance mechanism.

tributor armature assembly. During idle speeds, the springs keep the weights in place and the armature and distributor shaft rotate as one assembly. When speed increases, centrifugal force causes the weights to slowly move out against the tension of the springs. This allows the armature assembly to move ahead in relation to the distributor shaft rotation. The ignition's trigger-

ing device is mounted to the armature assembly. Therefore, as the assembly moves ahead, ignition timing becomes more advanced.

VACUUM ADVANCE During part-throttle engine operation, high vacuum is present within the intake manifold. To attain the highest possible power and economy, the arc must occur at the plugs even earlier in the cycle than is provided by a centrifugal advance mechanism.

The heart of the vacuum advance mechanism (Figure 18-32) is the spring-loaded diaphragm, which fits inside a metal housing and connects to a movable plate on which the pick-up coil is mounted. Vacuum is applied to one side of the diaphragm in the housing chamber while the other side of the diaphragm is open to the atmosphere. Any increase in vacuum allows atmospheric pressure to push the diaphragm. In turn, this causes the movable plate to rotate. The more vacuum present on one side of the diaphragm, the more atmospheric pressure is able to cause a change in timing. The rotation of the movable plate moves the pick-up coil so the armature develops a signal earlier. These units are also equipped with a spring that retards the timing as vacuum decreases.

Spark Distribution

The distributor cap and rotor receive the high voltage from the secondary winding via a high-tension

Ignition Systems 455

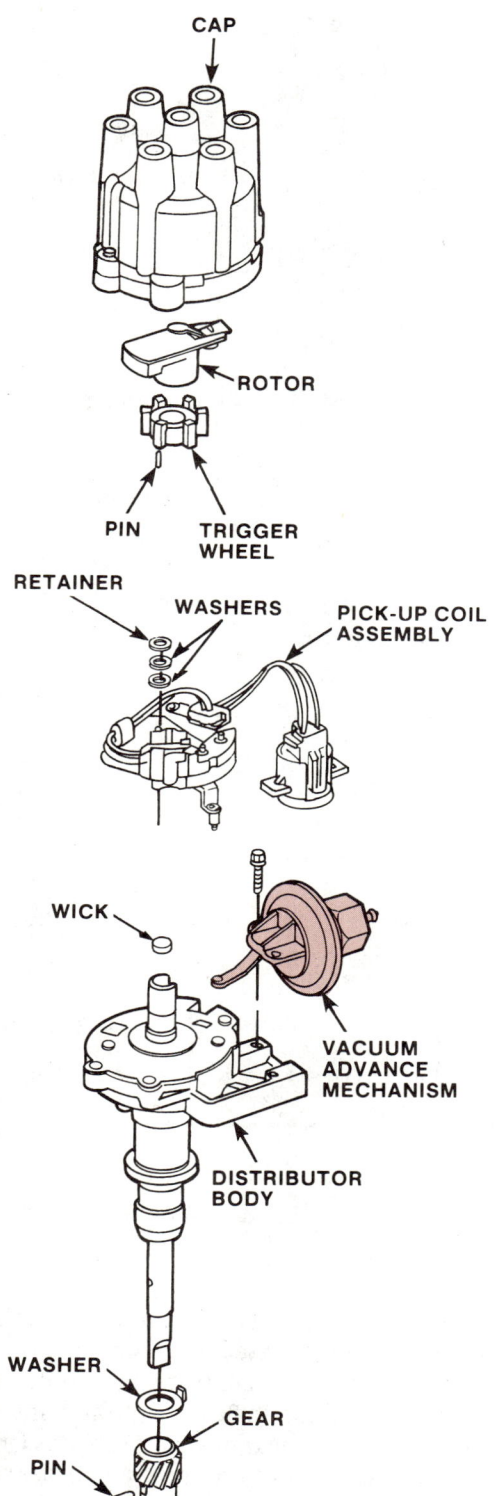

Figure 18-32 Typical vacuum advance mechanism.

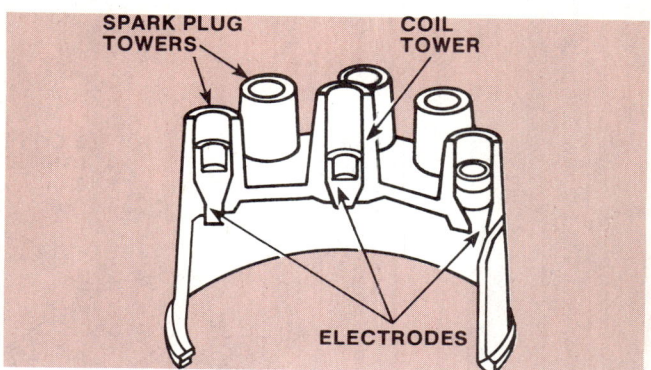

Figure 18-33 Cutaway view of a distributor cap.

wire. The voltage enters the distributor cap through the coil tower, or center terminal. The rotor then transports the voltage from the coil tower to the spark plug electrodes in the rim of the cap. The rotor mounts on the upper portion of the distributor shaft and rotates with it.

The distributor cap (Figure 18-33) is made from silicone plastic or similar material that offers protection from chemical attack. It is attached to the distributor housing with screws or spring-loaded clips. The coil tower contains a carbon insert that carries the voltage from the high-tension coil lead to the raised portion of the electrode on the rotor. Spaced evenly around the coil tower are the spark plug electrodes and towers, one for each plug.

An air gap of a few thousandths of an inch exists between the tip of the rotor electrode and the spark plug electrode in the cap. This gap is necessary in order to prevent the two electrodes from making contact. If they did make contact, both would wear out rapidly. It cannot be measured when the distributor is assembled, so the gap is usually described in terms of the voltage needed to create an arc between the electrodes.

❏ COMPUTER-CONTROLLED IGNITION SYSTEM OPERATION

Computer-controlled ignition systems (Figure 18-34) control the primary circuit and distribute spark in the same manner as other types of electronic ignition systems. The main difference between the systems is the elimination of any mechanical or vacuum advance devices from the distributor in the computer-controlled systems. In these systems, the distributor's sole purpose is to generate the ignition primary circuit switching signal and distribute the secondary voltage to the spark plugs. Timing advance is controlled by a microprocessor, or computer. In fact, some of these systems have even removed the primary switching function from the distributor by using a crankshaft position sensor. The distributor's only job is to distribute secondary voltage to the spark plugs.

Spark timing on these systems is controlled by a computer that continuously varies ignition timing to obtain optimum air/fuel combustion. The computer monitors the engine operating parameters with sensors. Based on this input, the computer signals an ignition module to collapse the primary switching cir-

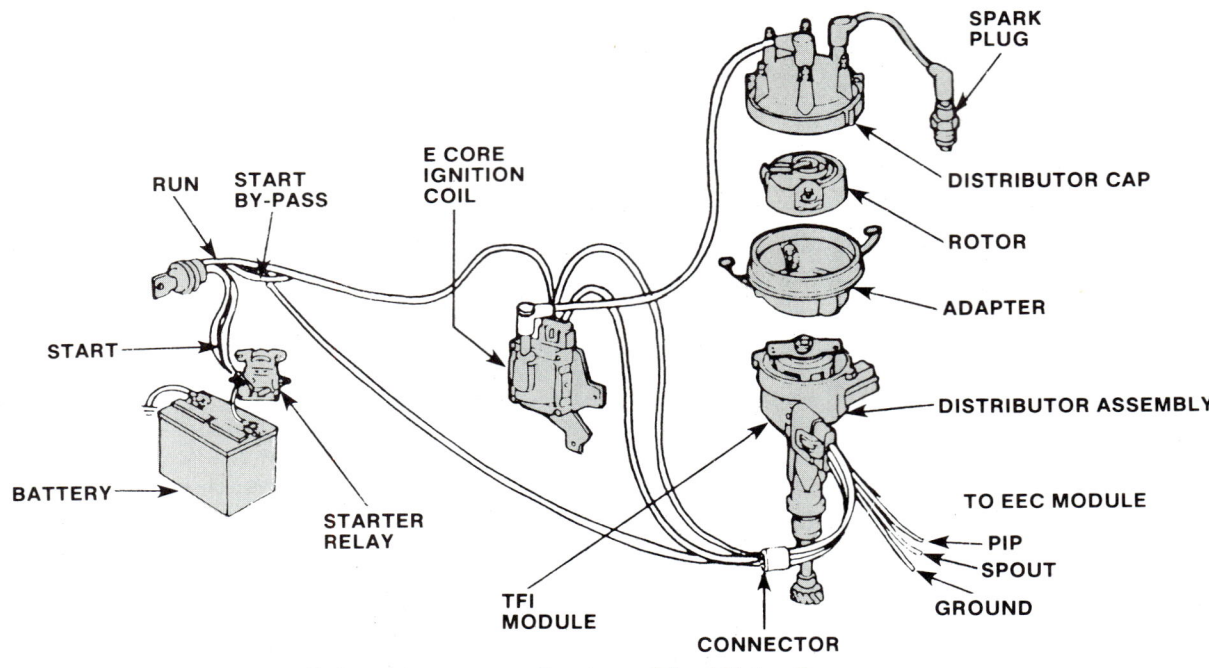

Figure 18-34 TFI-IV computer-controlled ignition system. *Courtesy of Ford Motor Co.*

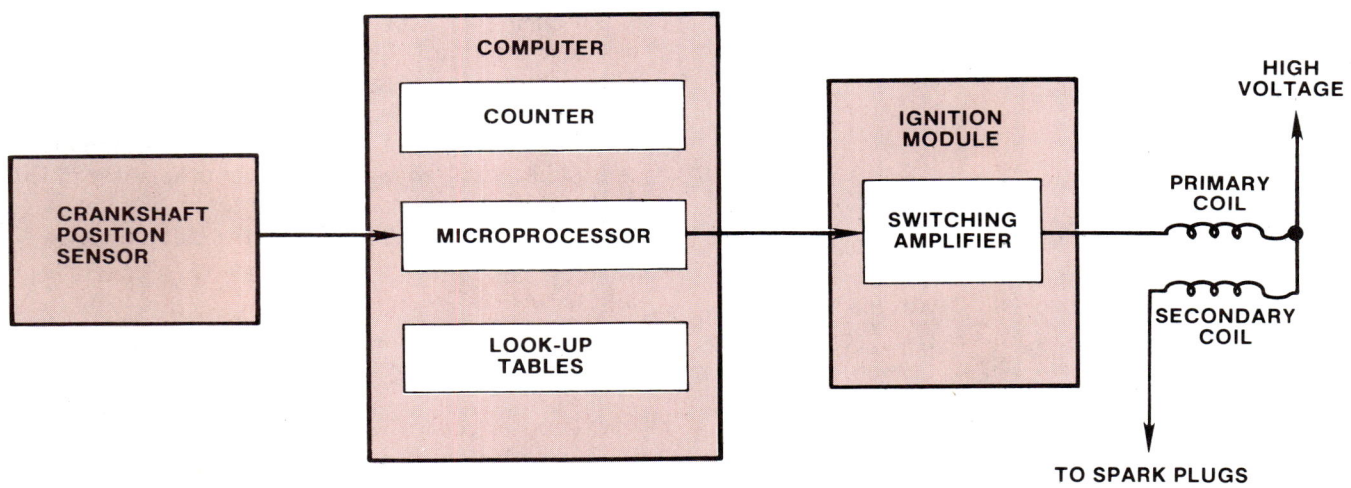

Figure 18-35 Typical engine timing control.

cuit, allowing the secondary circuit to fire the spark plugs (Figure 18-35).

The logic (hardware and software) in a computerized system's program selects the method of spark timing control. During engine starting, computer control is by-passed and the mechanical setting of the distributor controls spark timing. Once the engine is started and running, spark timing returns under the control of the computer control system. This scheme ensures that the vehicle starts regardless of whether the electronic control system is functioning or not.

The goal of computerized spark timing is to produce maximum engine power, top fuel efficiency, and minimum emissions levels under all types of operating conditions. The computer does this by continuously adjusting the timing of ignition in relation to piston's top dead center position. The computer determines the optimum spark timing based on certain engine operating conditions such as crankshaft position, engine speed, engine coolant temperature, and initial and operating manifold or barometric pressure. Once the computer receives input from these and other sensors, it compares the existing operating conditions to information permanently stored or programmed into its memory. The computer matches the existing conditions to a set of conditions stored in its memory, determines proper timing setting, and sends a signal to the ignition module that is responsible for firing the plug.

The computer continuously monitors existing conditions, adjusting timing to match what its memory tells it is the ideal setting for those conditions. It can do this very quickly, making thousands of decisions in a single second. The central control computer typically has the following types of information permanently programmed into it.

- Warm-up spark advance. This is used when the engine is cold, since a greater amount of advance is required while the engine warms up.
- Special spark advance. This is used to improve fuel economy during steady driving conditions.
- Spark advance due to barometric pressure. This is used when barometric pressure exceeds a preset calibrated value.

All of this information is then added together and the initial timing advance is subtracted to determine the final spark advance. The calibrated or programmed information in the computer is contained in what is called software look-up tables.

Ignition timing can also work in conjunction with the electronic fuel control system to provide emission control, optimum fuel economy, and driveability. They are all dependent on spark advance.

Many computer-controlled ignition systems have a self-diagnostic capability that aids in troubleshooting.

☐ DISTRIBUTORLESS IGNITION SYSTEM OPERATION

Distributorless ignition systems (Figure 18-36) perform all three functions of the distributor electronically. They control spark timing and advance in the same manner as the computer-controlled ignition systems. Yet the DIS is a step beyond the computer-controlled system because it also distributes spark electronically instead of mechanically. The distributor is completely eliminated from these systems.

The computer, ignition module, and position sensors combine to control spark timing and advance. The computer, as usual, is basically a master data interpreter collecting its information from a variety of input sensors. This input is used to selectively alter spark timing. The ignition module uses crank/cam sensor data to control the primary circuit of the coils. Remember that there is more than one coil in a distributorless ignition system. The ignition module synchronizes the coil firing sequence in relation to crankshaft position. Thus, the ignition module takes the place of the distributor.

The ignition module also adjusts spark timing below 400 rpm (for starting) and when the vehicle's control computer by-pass circuit becomes open or grounded. Depending on the exact DIS system, the ignition coils can be serviced as a complete unit or separately.

On those DIS systems that have one coil per plug, the electronic ignition module determines when each spark plug should fire and controls the on/off time of each plug's coil.

The systems with a coil for every two spark plugs also utilize an electronic ignition module, but they work on the waste spark method of spark distribution. Each of the coil secondary terminals are attached to a spark plug. Each coil fires the plugs at a pair of cylinders whose pistons rise and fall together. In all V-6s, the paired cylinders are 1 and 4, 2 and 5, and 3 and 6 (or 4 and 1 and 3 and 2 on 4-cylinder engines). With this arrangement, one cylinder of each pair is on its compression stroke while the other is on the exhaust stroke. Both cylinders get spark simultaneously, but only one spark generates power while the other is wasted out the exhaust. During the next revolution, the roles are reversed.

Due to the way the secondary coils are wired, when the induced voltage cuts across the primary and secondary windings of the coil, one plug fires in the normal direction—positive center electrode to negative side electrode—and the other plug fires just the reverse (side to center electrode). As shown in Figure 18-37,

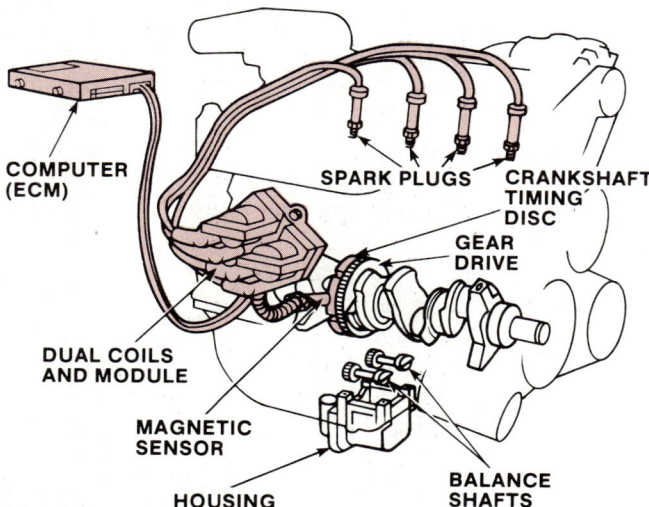

Figure 18-36 C-3 distributorless ignition system on GM 2.5-liter engine with a crankshaft sensor. *Courtesy of General Motors Corp.*

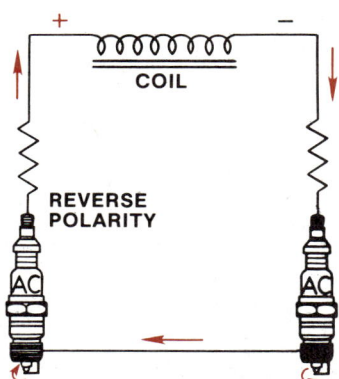

Figure 18-37 The manner in which two spark plugs are fired by a single ignition coil in DIS ignition system circuits.

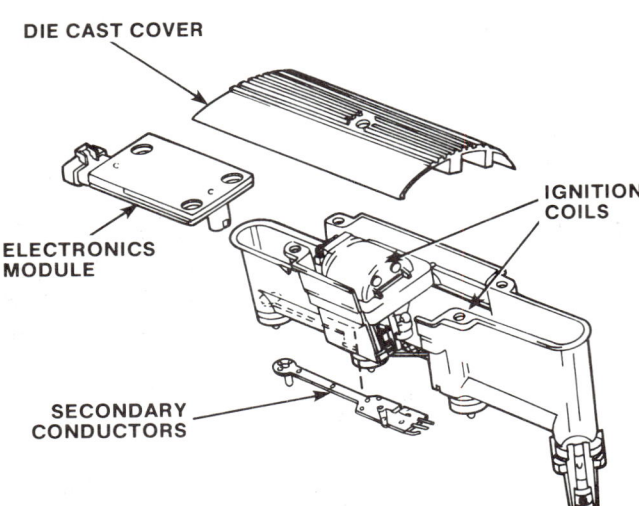

Figure 18-38 Integrated DIS with no secondary ignition cables.

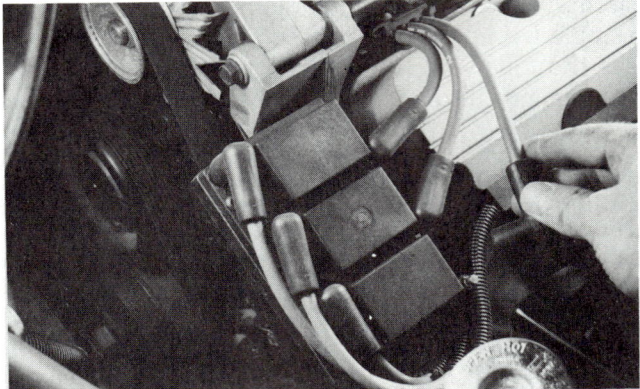

Figure 18-39 Coil pack for a V-6 engine. Each pack fires two spark plugs.

Figure 18-40 A V-6 engine coil pack with one coil for each cylinder.

both plugs fire simultaneously, completing the series circuit. Each plug always fires the same way on both the exhaust and compression strokes.

The coil is able to overcome the increased voltage requirements caused by reversed polarity and still fire two plugs simultaneously because each coil is capable of producing up to 60,000 volts. There is very little resistance across the plug gap on exhaust, so the plug requires very little voltage to fire, thereby providing its mate (the plug that is on compression) with plenty of available voltage.

Figure 18-38 shows a waste spark system in which the coils are mounted directly over the spark plugs so that no wiring between the coils and plugs is necessary. On other systems, the coil packs are mounted remote from the spark plugs. High-tension secondary wires carry high-voltage current from the coils to the plugs (Figure 18-39). Figure 18-40 shows a one-coil-per-plug DIS system.

Timing References

From a general operating standpoint, most distributorless ignition systems are similar. However, there are variations in the way different distributorless systems obtain a timing reference in regard to crankshaft and camshaft position.

Some engines use separate Hall-effect sensors to monitor crankshaft and camshaft position for the control of ignition and fuel injection firing orders. Others use a single Hall-effect switch mounted behind the harmonic balancer to determine both crankshaft and camshaft positioning.

Finally, some engines use a magnetic pulse generator setup. The reluctor or timing wheel is cast on the crankshaft and has seven machine slots on it, six of which are spaced exactly 60 degrees apart (if the engine is a 6-cylinder.) The seventh notch is located 10 degrees from the number six notch and is used to synchronize the coil firing sequence in relation to crankshaft position (Figure 18-41).

The magnetic sensor, which protrudes into the side of the block to within 0.050 in. (±0.020 in.) of the crankshaft reluctor, generates a small AC voltage each time one of the machined slots passes by.

By counting the time between pulses, the ignition module picks out the unevenly spaced seventh slot, which starts the calculation of the ignition coil sequencing. Once it has its bearings, the module is programmed to accept the AC voltage signals of the select notches for firing purposes.

When the system is working properly, there is no base timing to adjust and there are no moving parts to wear.

The development and spreading popularity of DIS is due to the automobile manufacturers constantly searching for new ways to reduce emissions, improve fuel economy, and boost component reliability.

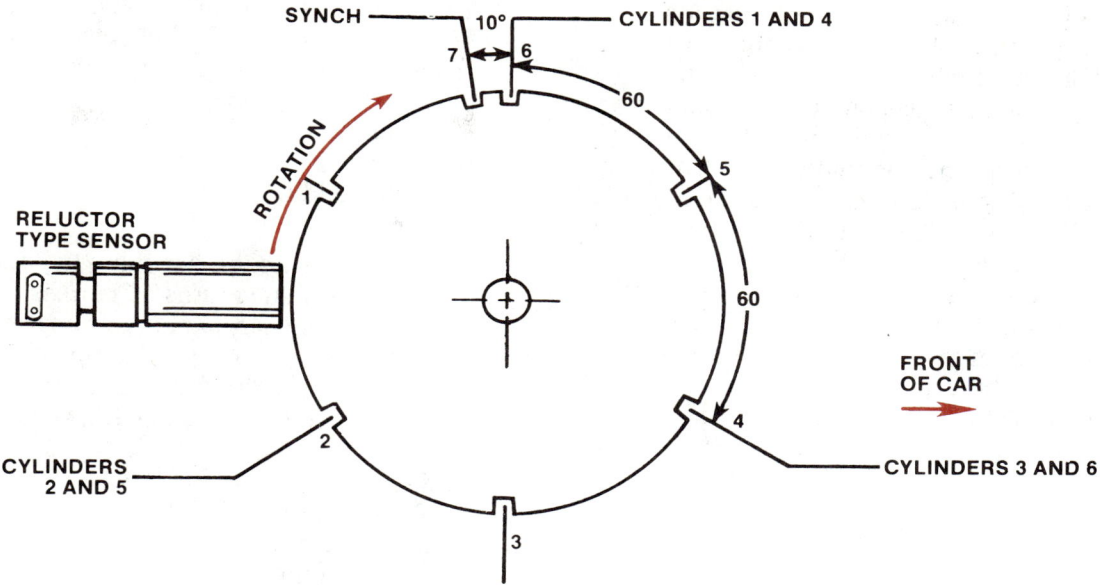

Figure 18-41 In a typical system, the AC voltage signal produced each time the magnetic pulse sensor passes notches 2, 4, and 6 triggers firing. The seventh notch references the coil firing sequence to the crankshaft position.

DIS offers advantages in production costs and maintenance considerations. By removing the distributor, the manufacturers realize a substantial savings in ignition parts and related machining costs. Also, by eliminating the distributor, they also do away with cracked caps, eroded carbon buttons, burned-through rotors, moisture misfire, base timing adjustments, and the like.

CASE STUDY

Case 1

A vehicle equipped with an early electronic ignition system is experiencing spark detonation (knocking) and erratic spark advance problems. The vehicle has 82,000 miles on it.

The technician checks the engine's base timing and finds it to be 5 degrees out of adjustment. The technician makes the adjustment, but it does not seem to hold steady. In fact, the problem still occurs on the test drive made immediately after the timing adjustment is made.

The technician then removes the distributor for closer inspection. The centrifugal advance mechanism appears to be in good order, but the technician notices shiny worn areas on the tangs of the distributor shaft's drive coupling. Wear on the tangs could mean the distributor shaft is not in proper mesh with the crankshaft. The technician replaces the worn drive coupling and reinstalls the distributor. After resetting initial timing, the problem of erratic advance disappears.

Summary

- The ignition system supplies high-voltage to the spark plugs to ignite the air/fuel mixture in the combustion chambers.
- The arrival of the spark is timed to coincide with the compression stroke of the piston. This basic timing can be advanced or retarded under certain conditions, such as high engine rpm or extremely light or heavy engine loads.
- The ignition system has two interconnected electrical circuits: a primary circuit and a secondary circuit.
- The primary circuit supplies low voltage to the primary winding of the ignition coil. This creates a magnetic field in the coil.
- A switching device interrupts primary current flow, collapsing the magnetic field and creating a high-voltage surge in the ignition coil secondary winding.
- The switching device used in electronic systems is an NPN transistor. Old ignitions use mechanical breaker point switching.
- The secondary circuit carries high voltage surges to the spark plugs. On some systems, the circuit runs from the ignition coil, through a distributor, to the spark plugs.
- The distributor may house the switching device plus centrifugal or vacuum timing advance mechanisms. Some systems locate the switching device outside the distributor housing.
- Ignition timing is directly related to the position of the crankshaft. Magnetic pulse generators and Hall-effect sensors are the most widely used engine position sensors. They generate an electrical signal

- at certain times during crankshaft rotation. This signal triggers the electronic switching device to control ignition timing.
- Direct ignition systems eliminate the distibutor. Each spark plug, or in some cases, pair of spark plugs, has its (their) own ignition coil. Primary circuit switching and timing control is done using a special ignition module tied into the vehicle control computer.
- Computer-controlled ignition eliminates centrifugal and vacuum timing mechanisms. The computer receives input from numerous sensors. Based on this data, the computer determines the optimum firing time and signals an ignition module to activate the secondary circuit at the precise time needed.

Review Questions

1. Under what condition is the ballast resistor in an ignition system's primary circuit by-passed?
2. Under light loads, what must be done to complete air/fuel combustion in the combustion chamber by the time the piston reaches 10 degrees ATDC?
3. At high engine rpm, what must be done to complete air/fuel combustion in the combustion chamber by the time the piston reaches 10 degrees ATDC?
4. How do DIS ignition systems differ from conventional breaker point and electronic ignition systems?
5. Explain the components and operation of a magnetic pulse generator.
6. What happens when the low-voltage current flow in the coil primary winding is interrupted by the switching device?
   a. The magnetic field collapses.
   b. A high-voltage surge is induced in the coil secondary winding.
   c. Both a and b.
   d. Neither a nor b.
7. Which of the following is a function of both breaker-point and electronic ignition systems?
   a. to generate sufficient voltage to force a spark across the spark plug gap
   b. to time the arrival of the spark to coincide with the movement of the engine's pistons
   c. to vary the spark arrival time based on varying operating conditions
   d. all of the above
8. Reach, heat range, and air gap, are all characteristics that affect the performance of which ignition system component?
   a. ignition coils
   b. ignition cables
   c. spark plugs
   d. breaker points
9. Technician A says all direct ignition systems use one coil for every spark plug. Technician B says some systems use one coil for every two spark plugs. Who is correct?
   a. Technician A
   b. Technician B
   c. Both A and B
   d. Neither A nor B
10. Technician A says the switching transistor in a DIS ignition system turns off current flow to the ignition coil primary winding whenever the pick-up coil is generating a voltage signal. Technician B says the transistor turns off current flow when the pick-up coil is not generating a voltage signal. Who is correct?
    a. Technician A
    b. Technician B
    c. Both A and B
    d. Neither A nor B
11. Which of the following components is not found in most electronic ignition systems?
    a. distributor cap
    b. condenser
    c. rotor
    d. spark plug
12. In an electronic ignition system, which of the following actually controls the primary coil current?
    a. breaker points
    b. pick-up coil
    c. reluctor
    d. transistor
13. Which of the following electronic switching devices is not equipped with a permanent magnet?
    a. magnetic pulse generator
    b. metal detection sensor
    c. Hall-effect sensor
    d. none of the above
14. Technician A says ignition systems equipped with Hall-effect sensors do not require a ballast resistor or resistance wire to regulate primary circuit current. Technician B says these systems do require resistance control in their primary circuit. Who is correct?
    a. Technician A
    b. Technician B
    c. Both A and B
    d. Neither A nor B
15. Modern ignition cables contain fiber cores that act as a _____ in the secondary circuit to cut down on radio and television interference and reduce spark plug wear.
    a. conductor
    b. resistor
    c. semiconductor
    d. heat shield

16. In DIS systems using one ignition coil for every two cylinders, Technician A says two plugs fire at the same time, with one wasting the spark on the exhaust stroke. Technician B says one plug fires in the normal direction (center to side electrode) and the other in reversed polarity (side to center electrode). Who is correct?
    a. Technician A
    b. Technician B
    c. Both A and B
    d. Neither A nor B
17. The magnetic field surrounding the pick-up coil in a magnetic pulse generator moves when the _____ .
    a. reluctor tooth approaches the coil
    b. reluctor tooth begins to move away from the pick-up coil pole
    c. reluctor is aligned with the pick-up coil pole
    d. both a and b
18. The pick-up coil in a magnetic pulse generator does not produce a voltage signal when
    a. a reluctor tooth approaches the coil.
    b. a reluctor tooth is aligned with the coil.
    c. a reluctor tooth begins to move away from the coil.
    d. the coil is midway between two reluctor teeth.
19. Which type of engine position sensor requires that its voltage signal be amplified, inverted, and shaped into a clean square wave signal?
    a. magnetic pulse generator
    b. metal detection sensor
    c. Hall-effect sensor
    d. photoelectric sensor
20. Which of the following electronic switching devices has a reluctor with wide shutters rather than teeth?
    a. magnetic pulse generator
    b. metal detection sensor
    c. Hall-effect sensor
    d. all of the above

19 IGNITION SYSTEM SERVICE

Objectives

- Perform a visual inspection of ignition system components, primary wiring, and secondary wiring to locate obvious trouble areas.
- Describe what an oscilloscope is, its scales and operating modes, and how it is used as a vital tool in ignition system troubleshooting.
- Identify and describe the major sections of primary circuit and secondary circuit trace patterns, including the firing line, spark line, intermediate area, and dwell zone.
- Describe the difference between fixed and variable dwell ignition systems.
- Perform cranking output, spark duration, coil polarity, spark plug firing voltage, rotor, secondary resistance, and spark plug load tests using the oscilloscope.
- Test individual ignition components using test equipment such as a voltmeter, ohmmeter, and test light.
- Service and install spark plugs.
- Test and set dwell (when possible) and ignition timing.

This chapter concentrates on testing ignition systems and their individual components. It must be stressed, however, that there are many variations in the ignition systems used by auto manufacturers. The tests covered in this chapter are those generally used as basic troubleshooting procedures. Exact test procedures and the ideal troubleshooting sequence will vary between vehicle makers and individual models. Always consult the vehicle's service manual when performing ignition system service.

Two important precautions should be taken during all ignition system tests.

1. Turn the ignition switch off before disconnecting any system wiring.
2. Do not touch any exposed connections while the engine is cranking or running.

◻ VISUAL INSPECTION

All ignition system diagnosis should begin with a visual inspection. The system should be checked for obvious problems.

- Disconnected, loose, or damaged secondary cables
- Disconnected, loose, or dirty primary wiring
- Loose distributor cap
- Damaged distributor cap or rotor
- Worn or damaged primary system switching mechanism
- Improperly mounted electronic control unit

Secondary and Primary Wiring Connections

Spark plug (ignition) and coil cables should be pushed tightly into the distributor cap and coil and onto spark plugs. Frayed or cracked secondary cables should be replaced. Figure 19-1 shows the various ways secondary cables are secured to the distributor cap.

Secondary cables must be connected according to the firing order. Refer to the manufacturer's service manual to determine the correct firing order and cylinder numbering (Figure 19-2).

White or grayish powdery deposits on secondary cables where they cross or near metal parts indicate faulty insulation. High-voltage electricity has burned collected dust. Such faulty insulation may produce a spark that sometimes can be heard and seen in the dark. An occasional glow around the spark plug cables, known as a corona effect, is not harmful.

Spark plug cables from consecutively firing cylinders should cross rather than run parallel to one another (Figure 19-3). Spark plug cables running parallel to one another can induce firing voltages in one another and cause the spark plugs to fire at the wrong time.

Primary ignition system wiring should be checked for tight connections, especially on vehicles with electronic- or computer-controlled ignitions. Electronic circuits operate on very low voltage. Resistance caused by corrosion or dirt can cause running prob-

Ignition System Service 463

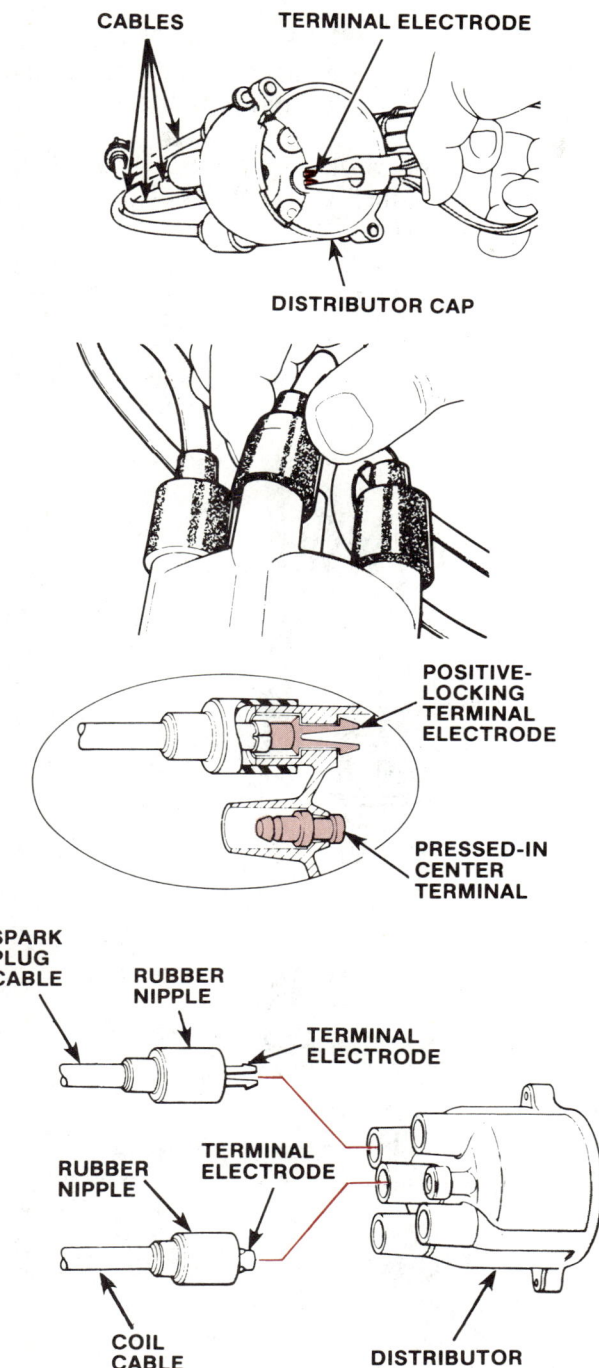

Figure 19-1 Removing and installing various distributor cap wires. *Courtesy of Chrysler Corp.*

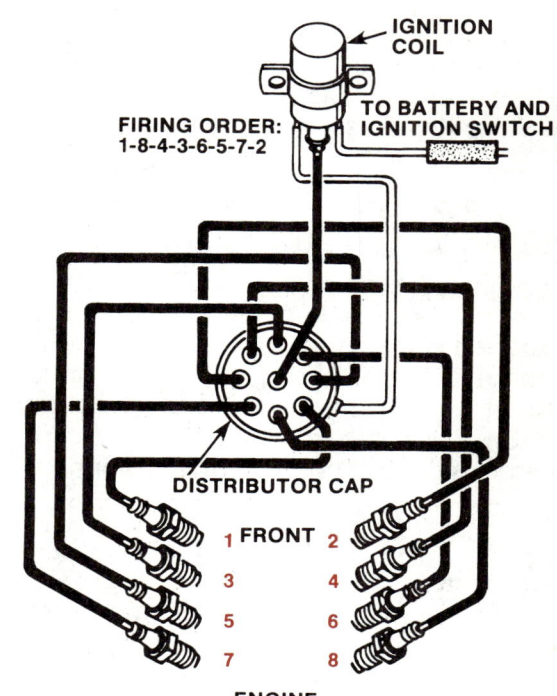

Figure 19-2 Example of firing order and ignition cable routing.

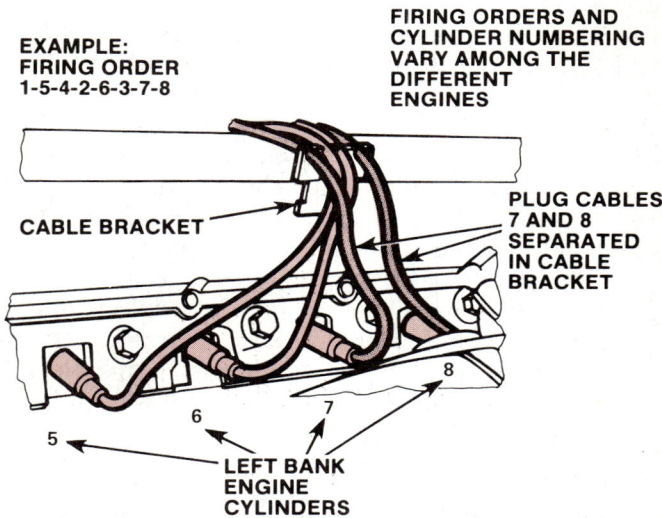

Figure 19-3 Routing spark plug cables to avoid inducing voltages. *Courtesy of Chrysler Corp.*

lems. Missing tab locks on wire connectors are often the cause of intermittent ignition problems due to vibration or thermal related failure.

Test the integrity of a suspect connection by tapping, tugging, and wiggling the wires while the engine is running. Be gentle. The object is to recreate an ignition interruption, not cause permanent circuit damage. With the engine off, separate suspect connectors and check them for dirt and corrosion. Clean the connectors according to the manufacturer's recommendations.

Many late-model vehicles require the use of a special dielectric grease on connector terminals. This grease seals the connections from outside elements.

Do not overlook the ignition switch as a source of intermittent ignition problems. A loose mounting rivet or poor connection can result in erratic spark output. To check the switch, gently wiggle the ignition key and connecting wires with the engine running. If the ignition cuts out or dies, the problem is located.

Check the battery connection to the starter solenoid. Remember, some vehicles use this connection as a voltage source for the coil. A bad connection can result in ignition interruption.

> **SHOP TALK**
>
> Any time you are faced with an intermittent or no-start problem on a General Motors HEI system, make sure you check the battery positive connection at the coil for a proper fit. Even if the connection looks good and feels tight, pull it apart and clean the terminals. After cleaning, lightly crimp the male end of the terminal to insure a good connection, then reconnect it.

Ground Circuits

Keep in mind that to simplify a vehicle's electrical system, auto makers use body panels, frame members, and the engine block as current return paths to the battery.

Unfortunately, ground straps are often neglected, or worse, left disconnected after routine service. With the increased use of plastics in today's vehicles, they may, mistakenly, be reconnected to a non-metallic surface. The result of any of these problems is that the current that was to flow through the disconnected or improperly grounded strap is forced to find an alternate path to ground. Sometimes the current attempts to back up through another circuit. This may cause the circuit to operate erratically or fail altogether. The current may also be forced through other components, such as wheel bearings or shift cables that are not meant to handle current flow causing them to wear prematurely.

Examples of bad ground circuit induced ignition failures include burnt ignition modules resulting from missing or loose coil ground straps, erratic performance caused by a poor distributor-to-engine block ground, and intermittent ignition operation resulting from a poor ground at the control module.

Electromagnetic Interference

Electromagnetic interference (EMI) can cause problems with the vehicle's on-board computer. EMI is produced when electromagnetic radio waves of sufficient amplitude escape from a wire or conductor. Unfortunately, an automobile's spark plug wires, ignition coil, and alternator coils all possess the ability to generate these radio waves. Under the right conditions, EMI can trigger sensors or actuators. The result may be an intermittent driveability problem that appears to be ignition system related.

To minimize the effects of EMI, check to make sure that sensor wires running to the computer are routed away from potential EMI sources. Rerouting a wire by no more than an inch or two may keep EMI from falsely triggering or interfering with computer operation.

Distributor Cap

The distributor cap should be properly seated on its base. All clips or screws should be tightened securely (Figure 19-4).

The distributor cap and rotor also should be removed for visual inspection. Physical or electrical damage is easily recognizable.

Electrical damage from high voltage can include corroded or burned metal terminals and carbon tracking inside distributor caps. Carbon tracking is the formation of a line of carbonized dust between distributor cap terminals or between a terminal and the dis-

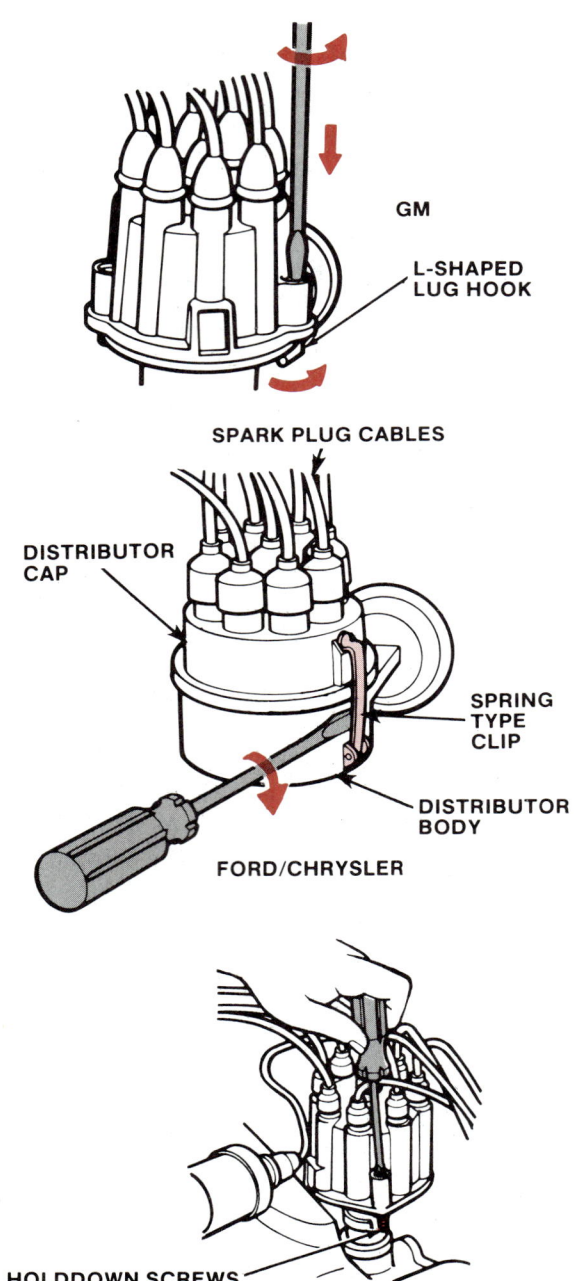

Figure 19-4 Distributor cap holddown devices. *Courtesy of Chrysler Corp.*

Ignition System Service   465

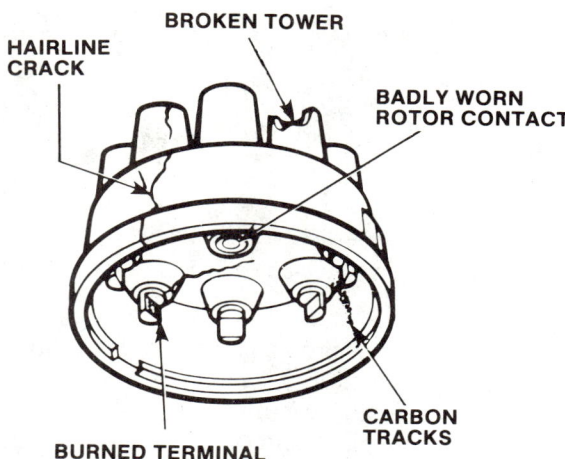

Figure 19-5 Types of distributor cap and rotor damage.

tributor housing. Carbon tracking indicates that high-voltage electricity has found a low-resistance conductive path over or through the plastic. The result is a cylinder that fires at the wrong time or a misfire. Check the outer cap towers and metal terminals for defects. Cracked plastic requires replacement of the unit. Damaged or carbon-tracked distributor caps or rotors should be replaced (Figure 19-5).

The rotor should be inspected carefully for discoloration, especially on vehicles with electronic ignition. Inspect the top and bottom of the rotor carefully for grayish, whitish, or rainbow-hued spots. Such discoloration indicates that the rotor has lost its insulating qualities. High-voltage is being conducted to ground through the plastic (Figure 19-6).

Timing Advance Mechanisms

Vacuum advance linkage should be attached securely. Disconnected linkage can cause stalling and dying.

Centrifugal advance mechanisms can be checked for free motion. Move the rotor on the distributor shaft clockwise and counterclockwise. The rotor should rotate in one direction approximately 1/4 inch, then spring back. If not, the centrifugal advance mechanism

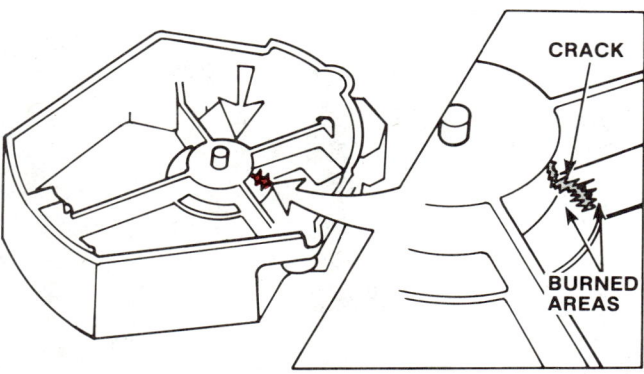

Figure 19-6 General Motors HEI distributor/rotor inspection. *Courtesy of General Motors Corp.*

might be binding or rusty. A lubricant might be necessary on advance mechanism pivots and rubbing surfaces.

Electronically-controlled advance mechanisms eliminate centrifugal and vacuum advance/retard mechanisms within the distributor. However, all wiring connections and parts should be thoroughly inspected for damage.

Primary Circuit Switches and Sensors

Several different types of switching systems are used to control current flow in the ignition's primary circuit.

Breaker Points

Older vehicles may be equipped with breaker point switching mechanisms. To inspect the mechanism, remove the distributor cap and rotor. Check the points and condenser to make sure they are securely fastened. Push the breaker points open with a screwdriver and check the condition of the contact surfaces (Figure 19-7). Badly oxidized (blackened) or pitted points should be replaced.

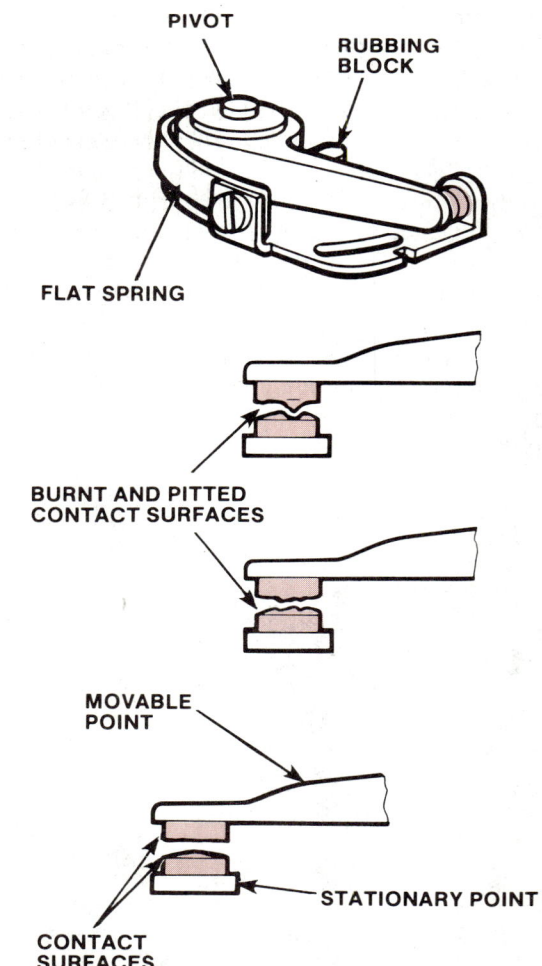

Figure 19-7 Breaker point inspection points.

Control Modules

Electronic and computer controlled ignitions use transistors as switches. These transistors are contained inside a control module housing that can be mounted to the distributor housing or remotely mounted on the vehicle's fire wall or other engine compartment surface. Control modules should be tightly mounted to clean surfaces. A loose mounting can cause a heat buildup that can damage and destroy transistors and other electronic components contained in the module. Some manufacturers recommend the use of a special heat-conductive silicone grease between the control unit and its mounting (Figure 19-8). This helps conduct heat away from the module, reducing the chance of heat related failure. During the visual inspection, check all electrical connections to the module. They must be clean and tight.

Sensors

The transistor in the control module is activated by a voltage pulse from an engine position sensor. In most modern ignition systems, this sensor is either a magnetic pulse generator or Hall-effect sensor. These types of sensors are mounted either on the distributor shaft or the crankshaft.

Magnetic pulse generators are relatively trouble free. The reluctor or pole piece is replaced only if it is broken or cracked. The pick-up coil wire leads can become grounded if their insulation rubs off when the vacuum advance mechanisms operate. Inspect these leads carefully (Figure 19-9). Position these wires so that they do not rub the switch plate as it moves.

Under unusual circumstances, the non-magnetic reluctor can become magnetized and upset the pick-up coil's voltage signal to the transistor. Use a steel feeler gauge to check for signs of magnetic attraction and replace the disc if the test is positive. On some systems, use a properly sized nonmagnetic feeler gauge to check the air gap between the coil and reluctor. Adjust the gap if it is out of specification.

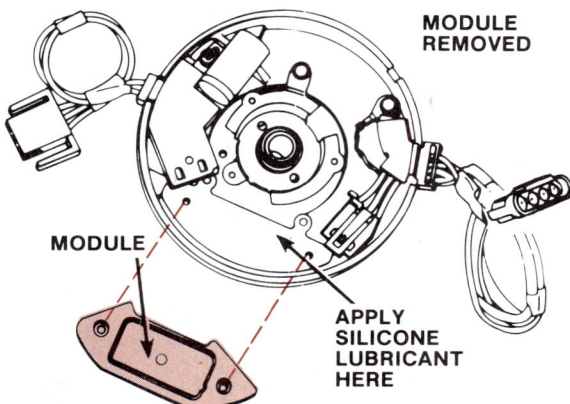

Figure 19-8 When replacing control modules some manufacturers specify to apply silicone lubricant to the mounting surface. *Courtesy of General Motors Corp.*

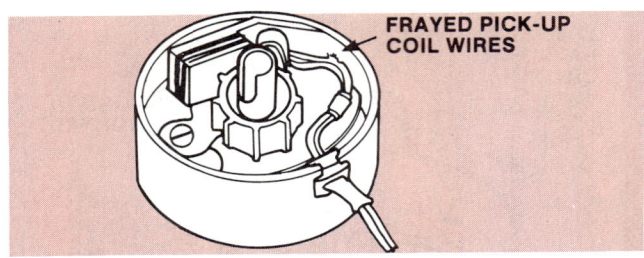

Figure 19-9 Inspect pick-up coil wiring for damage.

Hall-effect sensor problems are similar to those of magnetic pulse generators. Connecting wires that can move and rub as any vacuum advance mechanisms move the switch plate should be inspected (Figure 19-10). Also, check the condition of the distributor shaft drive coupling. Wear could effect the engine timing.

Distributorless Systems

On distributorless or direct ignition systems, visually inspect the secondary wiring connections at the

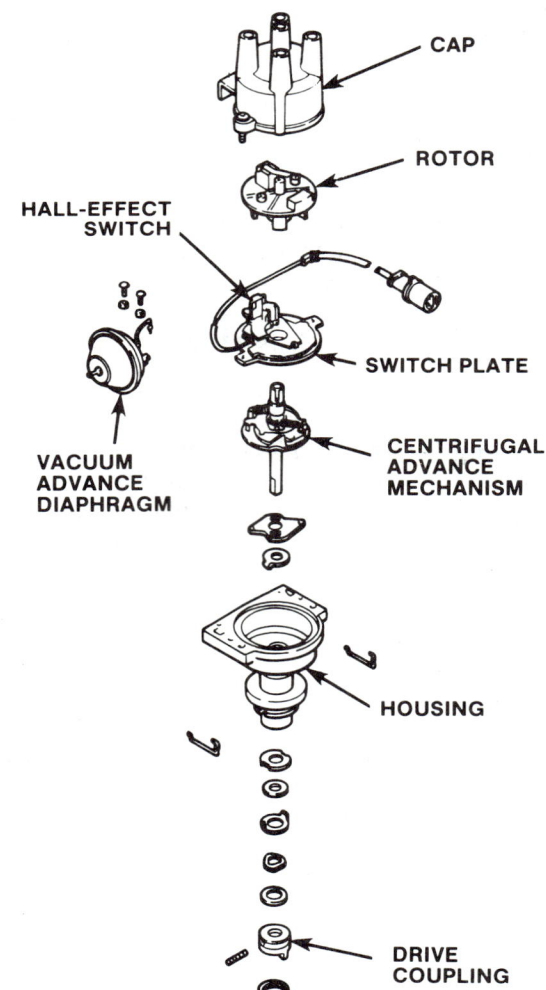

Figure 19-10 Hall-effect sensor and distributor system. *Courtesy of Chrysler Corp.*

Ignition System Service

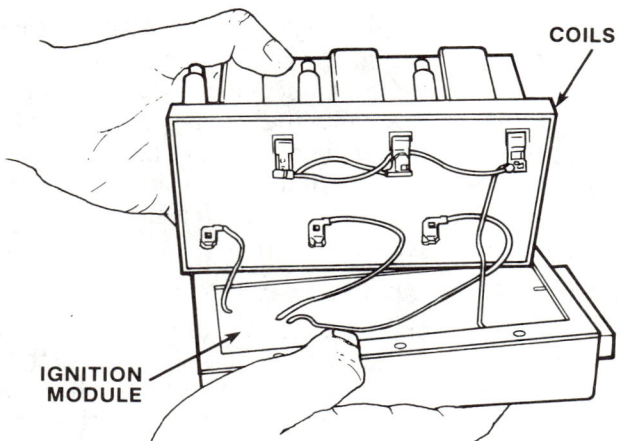

Figure 19-11 On distributorless systems check the wiring linking the coils to the ignition module.

individual coil modules. If a plug wire is loose, inspect the terminal for signs of burning. Check for terminal resistance and always remove and inspect the underside of the coil and the ignition module wires (Figure 19-11). A loose or damaged wire or bad plug can lead to carbon tracking of the coil. If this condition exists, the coil must be replaced.

If the visual inspection does not reveal obvious problems, test individual components and circuits in the next troubleshooting step.

❑ ELECTRICAL TEST PROCEDURES

It is impossible to accurately troubleshoot any ignition system without performing various electrical tests. Two pieces of test equipment, a digital volt-ohm-meter (multimeter) and an oscilloscope, are absolutely essential for diagnosing ignition problems.

Oscilloscope Testing

No discussion on ignition troubleshooting would be complete without a comprehensive discussion of oscilloscope use. The job of the oscilloscope is to convert the electrical signals of the ignition system into a visual image showing voltage changes over a given period of time. This information is displayed on a CRT screen in the form of a continuous voltage line called a pattern or trace. By studying the pattern, a technician can determine what is happening inside the ignition system.

The information on the design and use of oscilloscopes given in this text is general in nature. Always follow the oscilloscope manufacturer's specific instructions when connecting test leads or conducting test procedures.

Scales

On the face of the CRT screen is a voltage versus time graph (Figure 19-12). The waveform patterns are

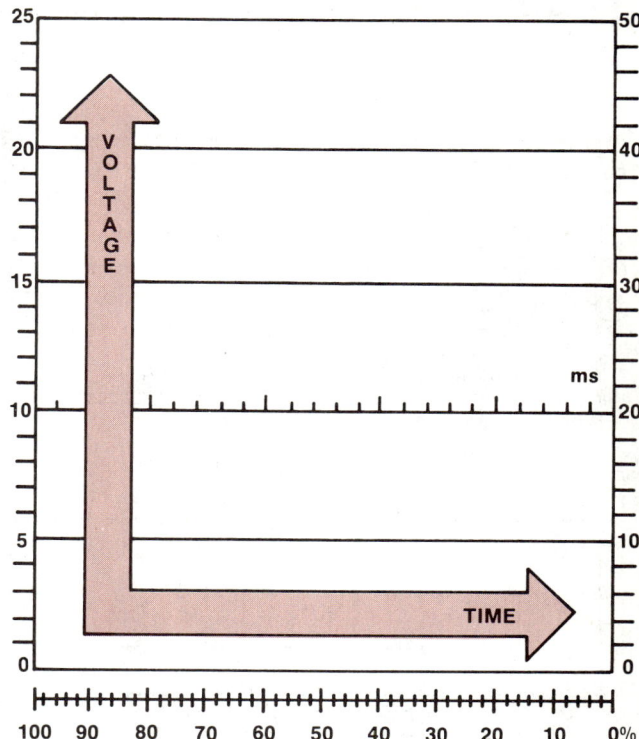

Figure 19-12 The oscilloscope actually plots a graph of voltage levels versus time.

displayed on the graph. The graph charts the changes in voltage and the time span in which the changes occur. The voltage versus time graph has four scales: two vertical scales (one on the left and one on the right), a horizontal percent of dwell scale, and a horizontal millisecond scale. The technician must select the proper scale for the test being conducted.

The left and right vertical scales measure voltage. The vertical scale on the left side of the graph is divided into increments of 1 kilovolt (1000 volts) and ranges from 0 to 25 kilovolts (kV). This scale is useful for testing secondary voltage. It can also be used to measure primary voltage by interpreting the scale in volts rather than kilovolts.

The vertical scale on the right side of the graph is divided into increments of 2 kilovolts and has a range of 0 to 50 kV. This scale is also used for testing secondary voltage. This scale can also be used to measure primary voltage in the 0 to 500 volt range.

The horizontal percent of dwell scale is located at the bottom of the scope screen. This scale is used for checking the dwell angle in both the primary and secondary circuits. The dwell scale is divided into increments of 2 percentage points and ranges from 0 to 100%.

The fourth scale—the millisecond scale—is a horizontal line that runs along the center of the voltage versus time graph. Depending on the test mode selected by the technician, the millisecond scale shows a range of 0 to 5 milliseconds (ms) or 0 to 25 millisec-

468 Section 4 Engine Performance

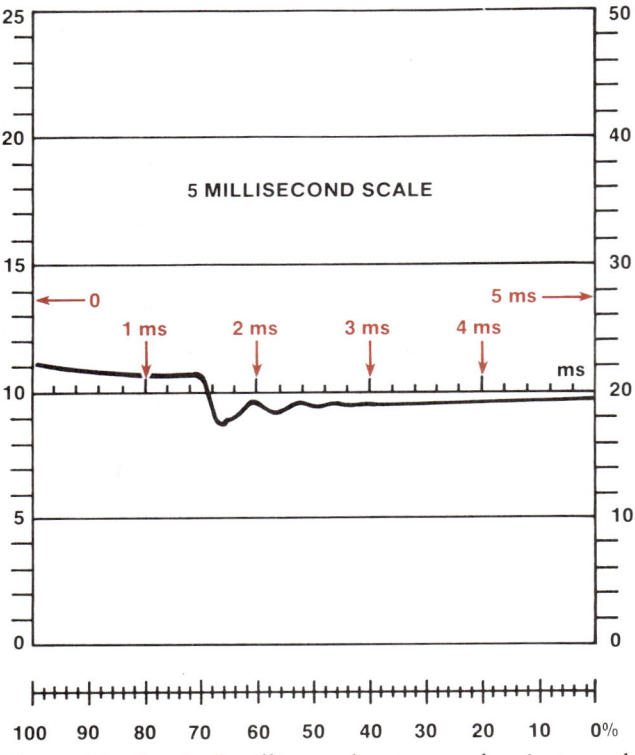

Figure 19-13 A 5-millisecond pattern showing spark duration.

onds. The 5 ms scale is often used to measure the duration of the spark (Figure 19-13). In the 25-millisecond mode, the complete firing pattern can normally be displayed.

An oscilloscope or scope displays voltage changes from left to right, similar to reading a book. So voltage lines or traces that appear on the left of the CRT screen occurred before those on the right. Oscilloscopes normally have four leads (Figure 19-14): primary pick-up that connects to the primary circuit, or negative terminal of the ignition coil; a ground lead that connects to a good engine ground; a secondary pick-up, which clamps around the coil's high tension wire; and a trigger pick-up, which clamps around the spark plug wire of the number 1 cylinder. The information received from these leads is translated into the scope pattern on the CRT screen.

Pattern Types and Phases

To monitor various phases of ignition system performance, a typical scope pattern is divided into three main sections: firing, intermediate, and dwell. Information received from specific testing in each one of these areas can be used to piece together a complete ignition picture.

Depending on the oscilloscope function selected by the technician, the scope can display the voltage versus time pattern for either the secondary or primary circuit. A typical secondary pattern is shown in Figure 19-15. A secondary pattern displays the following types of information.

- Firing voltage
- Spark duration
- Coil and condenser oscillations
- Transistor on/off switching or breaker point close and open
- Dwell and cylinder timing accuracy
- Secondary circuit accuracy

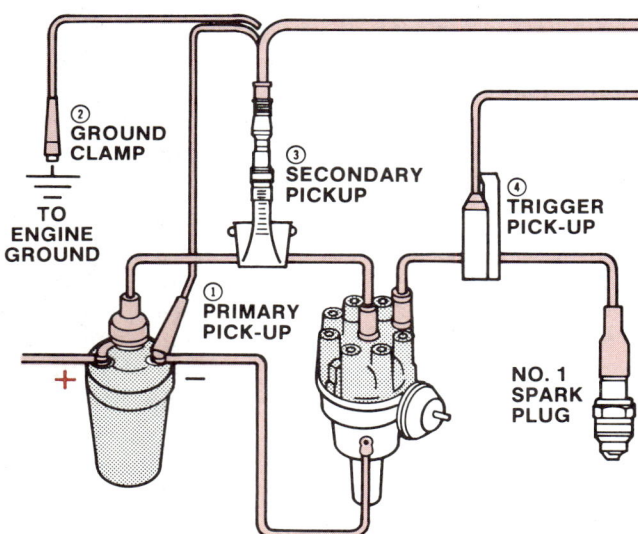

Figure 19-14 Typical oscilloscope pick-up connections to an ignition system.

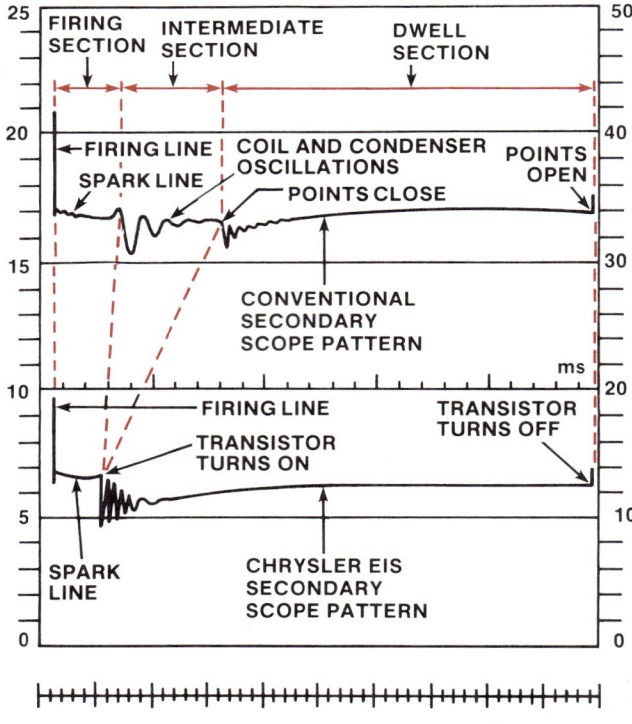

Figure 19-15 Comparison of typical breaker point and electronic-controlled ignition system secondary circuit patterns.

Ignition System Service   469

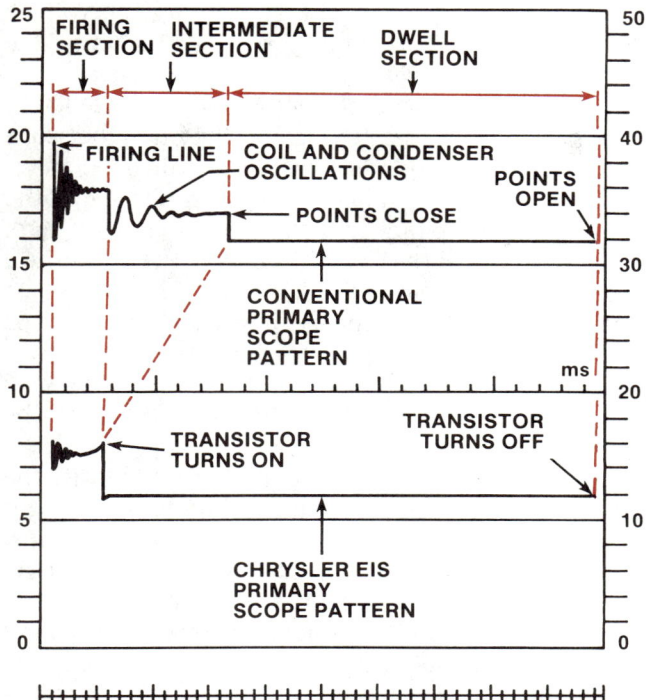

Figure 19-16 Comparison of typical breaker point and electronic-controlled ignition system primary circuit patterns.

A typical primary circuit pattern is shown in Figure 19-16. The primary scope pattern is used when secondary circuit connections are not possible. It is also useful for observing breaker point condition and action by non-electronic systems and for providing a means to observe dwell and cylinder timing problems.

Pattern Display Modes

The oscilloscope has several ways to display the voltage patterns of the primary and secondary circuits. When the display pattern is selected, the oscilloscope displays the patterns of all the cylinders in a row from left to right as shown in Figure 19-17. Each cylinder's ignition cycle is displayed in the engine's firing order. In the example shown in Figure 19-17 the firing order is 1, 8, 4, 3, 6, 5, 7, 2. The pattern begins with the spark line of the number 1 cylinder and ends with the firing line for the number 1 cylinder. This display pattern allows the technician to compare the voltage peaks for each cylinder.

A second choice of patterns is the raster pattern (Figure 19-18). A raster pattern stacks the voltage patterns of the cylinders one above the other. The number 1 pattern is displayed at the bottom of the screen and the rest of the cylinder's firing patterns are arranged above it in the engine's firing order.

In a raster pattern, the patterns for each cylinder are displayed across the width of the graph, also beginning with the spark line and ending with the firing line. This

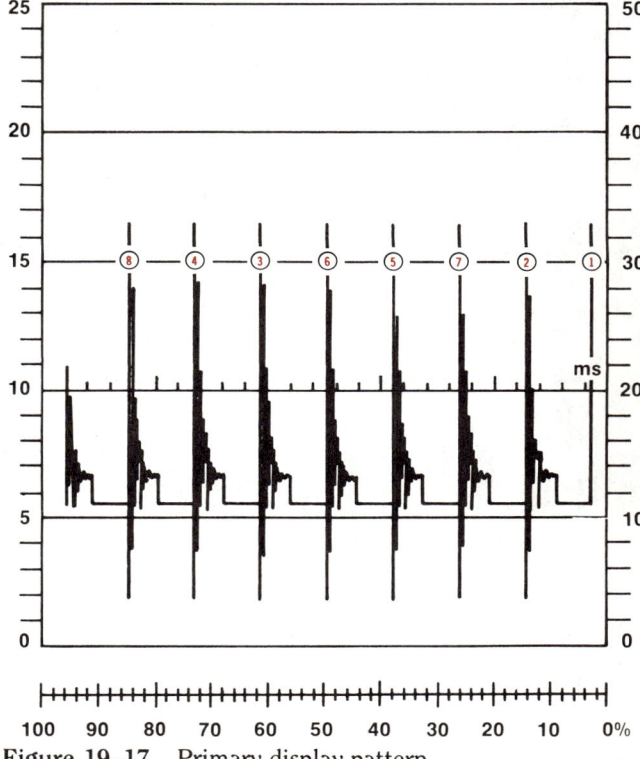

Figure 19-17 Primary display pattern.

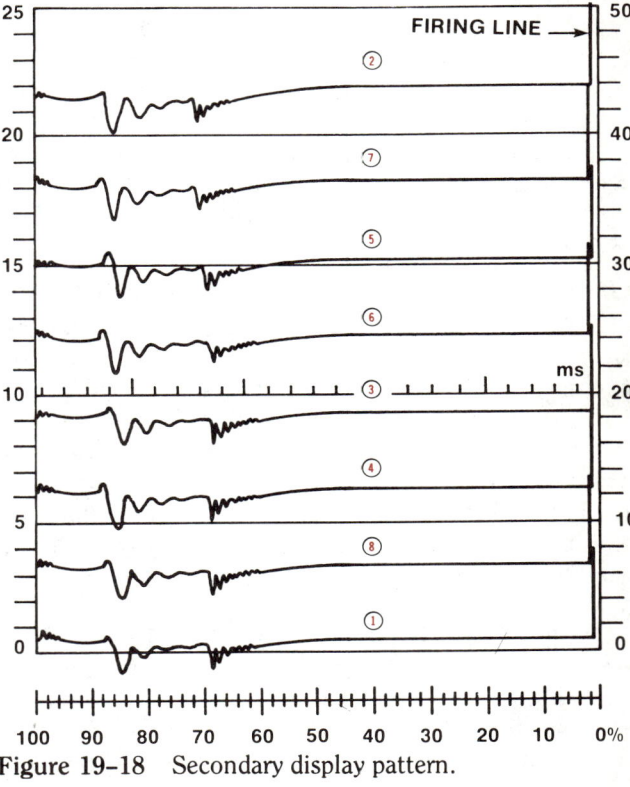

Figure 19-18 Secondary display pattern.

allows for a much closer inspection of the voltage and time trends than is possible with the display pattern.

All of the patterns for the cylinders can also be displayed in a superimposed pattern. A superimposed

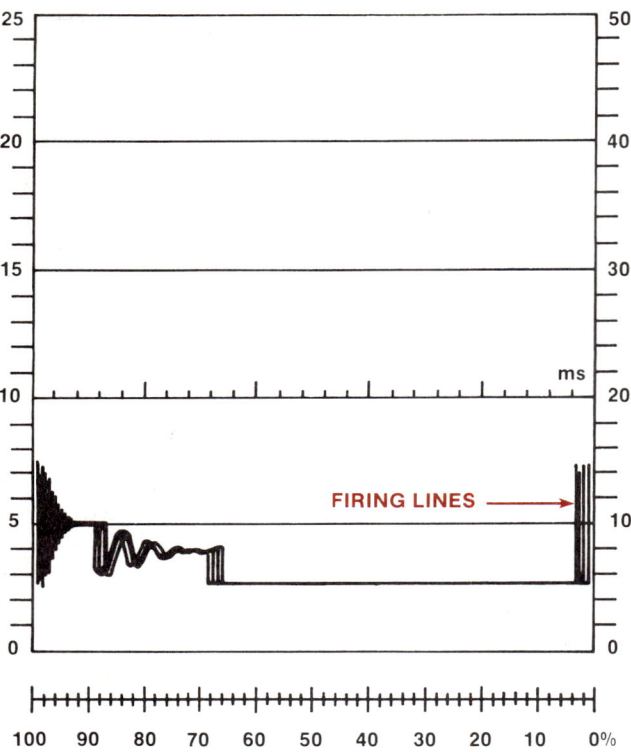

Figure 19-19 Primary superimposed pattern.

pattern displays all the patterns one on top of the other. Like the raster pattern, the superimposed voltage patterns are displayed the full width of the screen, beginning with the spark line and ending with the firing line.

A superimposed pattern allows a technician to detect variations of one cylinder's pattern from the others. A superimposed pattern for the primary circuits is shown in Figure 19-19.

Understanding Single Cylinder Patterns

The following section takes a closer look at the secondary circuit pattern (Figure 19-20). As shown, the firing line of the pattern appears at the left side of the CRT screen. An upward line signifies voltage. The firing line indicates the voltage needed to start the spark. The ignition coil's voltage pressure rises up to the point where it overcomes all electrical resistance in the secondary circuit. Typically, it requires around 10,000 volts to overcome this resistance and initiate a spark.

Keep in mind that cylinder conditions have an effect on this resistance. Leaner air/fuel mixtures increase the resistance and increase the required firing voltage.

Once secondary resistance is overcome, the spark jumps the plug gap, establishing current flow, and igniting the air/fuel mixture in the cylinder. The length of time the spark actually lasts is represented by the spark line portion of the pattern. The spark line begins at the firing line and continues tracing to the right until the coil's voltage drops below the level needed to keep current flowing across the gap.

In other words the spark is draining the voltage built up in the coil's secondary windings. As long as the coil has sufficient voltage, the spark continues.

Once coil voltage drops below the level needed to sustain the spark, the next major section of the scope trace pattern begins. This section is called the intermediate section or coil-condenser zone. It shows the remaining coil voltage as it dissipates or drops to zero. Remember, once the spark has ended, there is quite a bit of voltage stored in the ignition coil. The voltage remaining in the coil then oscillates or alternates back and forth within the primary circuit until it drops to zero. Notice that the lines representing the coil-condenser section steadily drop in height until the coil's voltage is zero.

The next section of the trace pattern begins with the primary circuit current on signal. It appears as a slight downward turn followed by several small oscillations. The slight downward curve occurs just as current begins to flow through the coil's primary winding. The oscillations that follow indicate the beginning of the magnetic field buildup in the coil. This curve marks the beginning of a period known as the dwell section or zone. The end of the dwell zone occurs when the primary current is turned off by the switching device (transistor or breaker points). The trace turns sharply upward at the end of the dwell zone. Turning the primary current off collapses the magnetic field in the coil and generates another high voltage spark for the next cylinder in the firing order. Remember, the primary current off signal is the same as the firing line for the next cylinder. The length of the dwell section represents the amount of time that current is flowing through the primary.

In general, most scope patterns look more or less like the one just described. The patterns produced by some systems have fewer oscillations in the intermediate section. Patterns may also vary slightly in the dwell section. The length of this section depends on when the control module turns the transistor on and off. Several variables may affect this timing. These variables can be categorized as follows.

1. fixed short dwell
2. fixed long dwell
3. variable dwell
4. current limiting

FIXED DWELL Older breaker point systems and some electronic ignition systems use a fixed dwell period. In a fixed dwell system, the number of dwell degrees remain the same during all engine speeds (Figure 19-21). So, if the engine has 30 degrees of dwell at idle, it should have 30 degrees of dwell at 2,000 rpm. This is not saying the actual amount of dwell time has remained the same. A fixed dwell of 30 degrees at 2,000 rpm gives the ignition coil only 1/4 the saturation time it has at 500 rpm. The oscilloscope should show

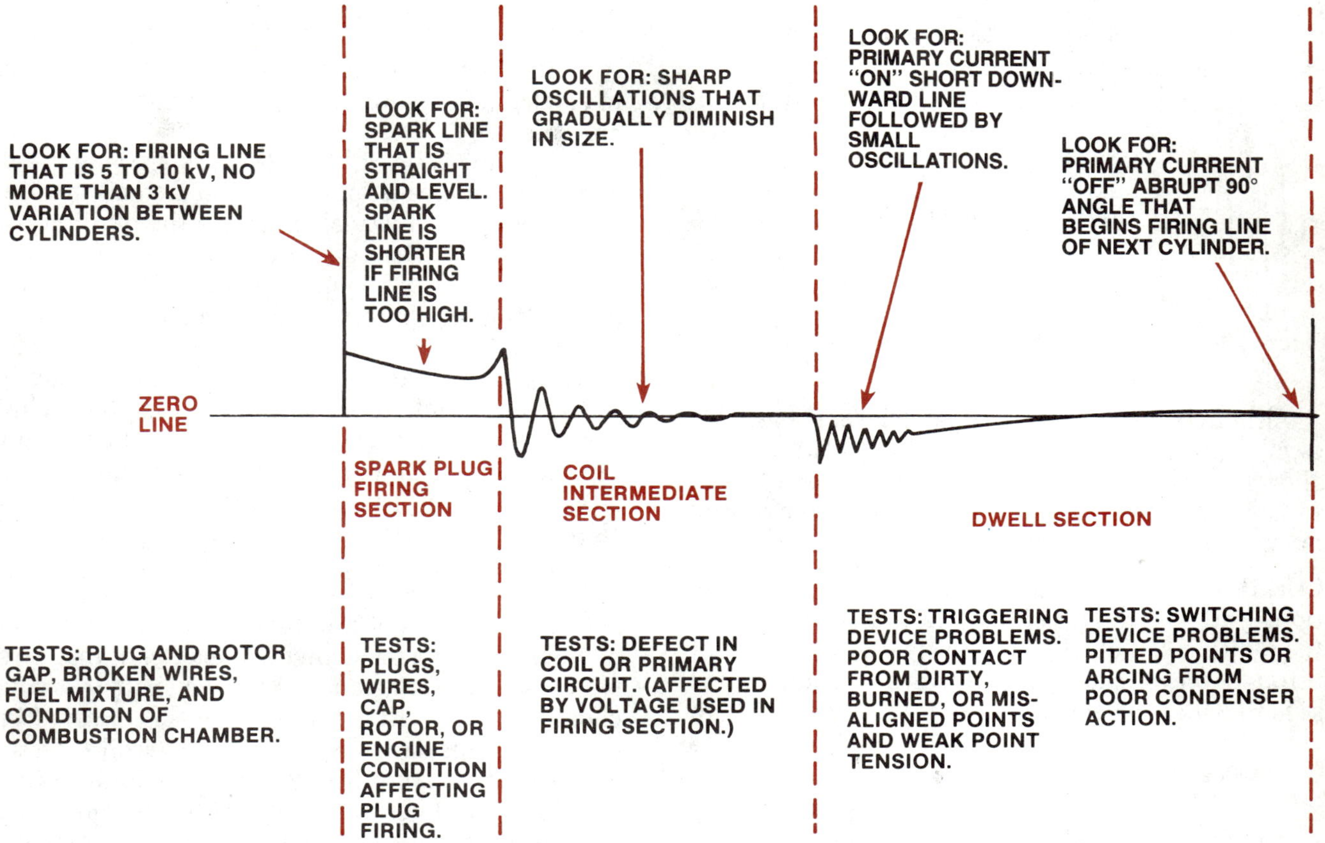

Ignition System Service   471

LOOK FOR: FIRING LINE THAT IS 5 TO 10 kV, NO MORE THAN 3 kV VARIATION BETWEEN CYLINDERS.

LOOK FOR: SPARK LINE THAT IS STRAIGHT AND LEVEL. SPARK LINE IS SHORTER IF FIRING LINE IS TOO HIGH.

LOOK FOR: SHARP OSCILLATIONS THAT GRADUALLY DIMINISH IN SIZE.

LOOK FOR: PRIMARY CURRENT "ON" SHORT DOWNWARD LINE FOLLOWED BY SMALL OSCILLATIONS.

LOOK FOR: PRIMARY CURRENT "OFF" ABRUPT 90° ANGLE THAT BEGINS FIRING LINE OF NEXT CYLINDER.

ZERO LINE

SPARK PLUG FIRING SECTION | COIL INTERMEDIATE SECTION | DWELL SECTION

TESTS: PLUG AND ROTOR GAP, BROKEN WIRES, FUEL MIXTURE, AND CONDITION OF COMBUSTION CHAMBER.

TESTS: PLUGS, WIRES, CAP, ROTOR, OR ENGINE CONDITION AFFECTING PLUG FIRING.

TESTS: DEFECT IN COIL OR PRIMARY CIRCUIT. (AFFECTED BY VOLTAGE USED IN FIRING SECTION.)

TESTS: TRIGGERING DEVICE PROBLEMS. POOR CONTACT FROM DIRTY, BURNED, OR MISALIGNED POINTS AND WEAK POINT TENSION.

TESTS: SWITCHING DEVICE PROBLEMS. PITTED POINTS OR ARCING FROM POOR CONDENSER ACTION.

Figure 19-20   Breakdown of a single cylinder secondary circuit pattern. *Courtesy of Sun Electric Corp.*

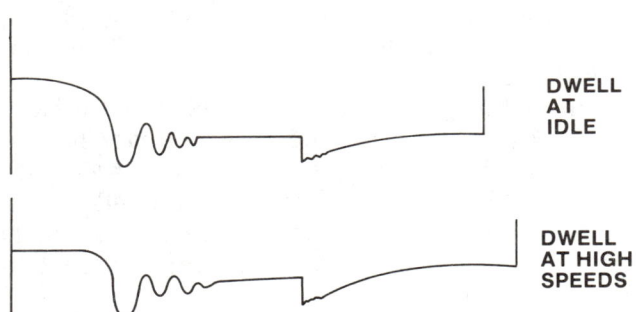

Figure 19-21   Pattern of a fixed dwell system at low and high engine speeds.

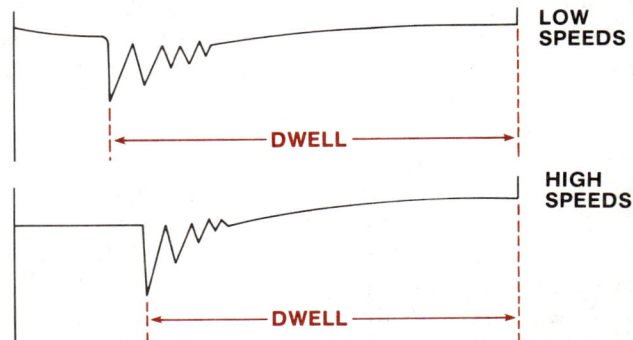

Figure 19-22   Speed reduces dwell slightly in this long dwell ignition system.

that the number of degrees or the percent of dwell remains the same as engine speed changes.

One exception to this rule is early Chrysler electronic ignition systems. These systems are characterized by a very long, distinctive dwell zone trace. The dwell zone begins just as the spark line ends. At higher engine speeds, the spark line increases slightly, forcing dwell to begin later (Figure 19-22). The change in dwell time is also slight, usually less than 5 degrees. This change in dwell has no effect on ignition timing because timing is controlled by switching off primary current. In these systems, the change takes place by increasing the spark duration and delaying the primary circuit on signal. Because this dwell change is so slight and has no effect on timing, this Chrysler system is commonly called a long fixed dwell system.

VARIABLE DWELL Most electronic ignition systems have a variable dwell function built into their control modules. In these systems, dwell changes significantly with engine speed. At idle and low rpm speeds, a short dwell provides enough time for complete ignition coil saturation (Figure 19-23A). The current on and current off signal appears very close to each other, usually less than 20 degrees.

As engine speed increases, the control module lengthens the dwell time (Figure 19-23B). This, of course, increases the available time for coil saturation.

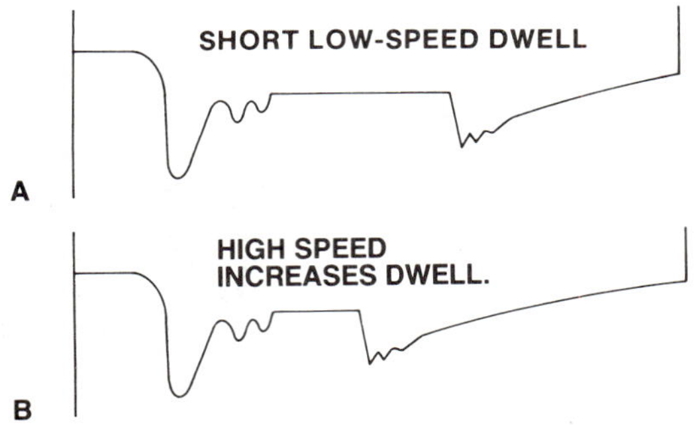

Figure 19-23 Example of variable dwell ignition system.

Although not common, it is possible for the variable dwell function of the control module to fail and still allow the vehicle to run. If testing indicates a lack of variable dwell on a system equipped with it, the control module must be replaced.

CURRENT LIMITING Many modern electronic ignitions feature current limiting. These systems saturate the ignition coil quickly by passing very high current through the primary winding for a fraction of one second. Once the coil is saturated, the need for high current is eliminated, and a small amount of current is used to keep the coil saturated. This type system extends coil life.

The point at which the control module cuts back from high to low current appears as a small blip or oscillation during the dwell section of the pattern (Figure 19-24). At very high engine speeds, this telltale blip may be missing, because the module keeps high current flow going to keep the coil continually saturated for fast firing.

At the opposite extreme, if the primary winding of the coil has developed excessive resistance or the coil is otherwise faulty, the cutback blip may never occur. This is because the primary winding never becomes fully saturated. Further testing of the coil would be needed to pinpoint the cause of the missing blip.

As with variable dwell, it is possible for the vehicle to run with the current limit function of the control module burned out or faulty. Again the blip would be missing from the trace.

CAUTION: Never touch the secondary wiring, cap, or coil if the current limiting blip is missing from the pattern of an ignition system that should have it. The secondary voltage available could easily exceed 100,000 volts.

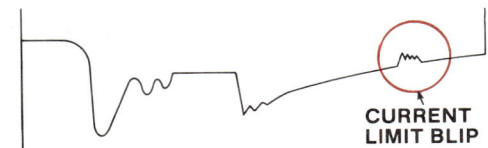

Figure 19-24 Pattern showing an ignition system limiting current during dwell.

Open Circuit Precautions

Precautions must be taken to prevent open circuits in an electronic ignition system during electrical test procedures.

This point is brought up because a common test performed on breaker point ignition systems involved seeing how much available voltage the ignition coil could produce. The coil wire was removed and the engine cranked or a plug wire was pulled with the engine running. Both procedures forced the ignition coil to produce its maximum output to try to overcome this massive resistance created in the circuit. Typically, the output would exceed 20,000 volts and the technician would have a good idea of what the coil was capable of producing under adverse conditions.

Open circuiting a modern ignition system, however, can damage the system. Features such as variable dwell and current limiting circuitry pull out all primary resistance if a spark does not occur. This causes tremendous amounts of current to flow through the primary circuit, producing an extremely high-voltage spark that must search out a path to ground. A frequent path to ground chosen by the spark is through the side of coil. This results in an insulation breakdown at the coil and a site where arcing to ground is likely to occur in the future.

To prevent these tremendous voltages from occurring during coil output testing, a special test plug is used when checking the coil voltage output (Figure 19-25). The test plug is connected to the coil wiring running to the distributor or to an ignition cable. A special grounding clip on the test plug is then connected to a good ground source.

The test plug looks like a spark plug, but it has a very large electrode gap. When the engine is cranked to check for voltage output, the ignition coil is forced to produce a higher voltage to overcome the added resistance created by the wide gap. Typically, about 35,000 volts is needed to fire the test plug. This is enough to stress the system without damaging it.

Coil Output Test

To safely perform a coil output test, proceed as follows.

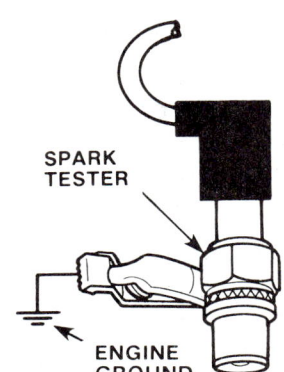

Figure 19-25 A test plug should be used to limit coil voltage output during testing.

Ignition System Service

1. Install the test plug in the coil wire or a plug wire if there is not a coil wire.
2. Set the oscilloscope on display and a voltage range of 50 kV.
3. Crank the engine over and note the height of the firing line.

The firing line should exceed 35 kV and be consistent. Lower than specified firing line voltages may indicate that the test plug did not fire. This could be the result of lower than normal available voltage in the primary circuit. The control module may have developed high internal resistance. The coil or coil cable may also be faulty. Further testing is needed to help pinpoint the problem.

Spark Duration Testing

Spark duration is measured in milliseconds, using the millisecond sweep of the oscilloscope. Most vehicles have a spark duration of approximately 1.5 milliseconds (Figure 19-26). A spark duration of approximately 0.8 millisecond is too short to provide complete combustion. A short spark also increases pollution and power loss. If the spark duration is too long (over approximately 2.0 milliseconds) the spark plug electrodes might wear prematurely. When the oscilloscope shows a long spark duration, it normally follows a short firing line which may indicate a fouled spark plug, low compression, or a spark plug with a narrow gap.

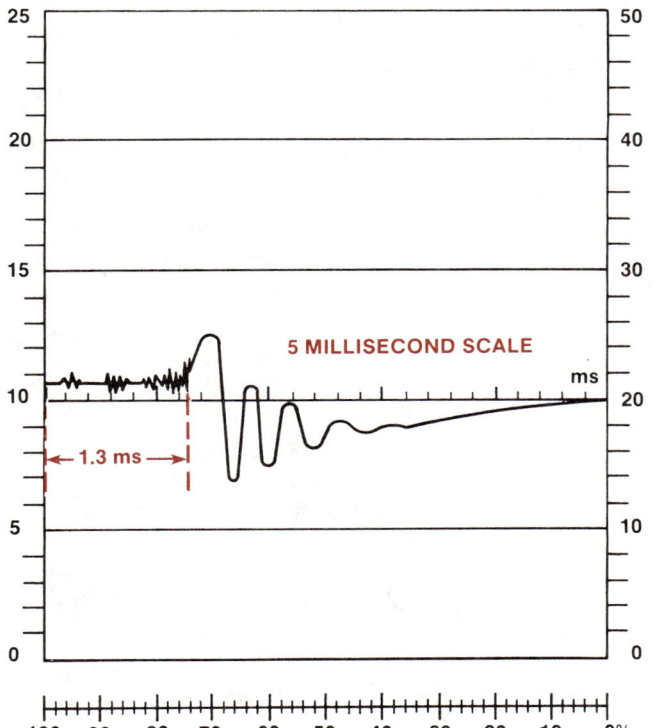

Figure 19-26 A 5-millisecond pattern showing a spark duration of 1.3 milliseconds during a cranking test.

Spark duration is normally measured two times—during engine cranking, and during engine running.

Cranking Test

When a vehicle is experiencing a no-start, or a hard start condition, perform a spark duration cranking test. This test also helps identify potential future problems by indicating a borderline condition. To perform the cranking test, do the following.

1. Disable the ignition system so the engine does not start. Different oscilloscope manufacturers recommend different methods of preventing engine startup during a cranking test. Always consult the scope manufacturer's instructions.
2. Set the pattern selector to the 5 millisecond position, the function selector to secondary, and pattern height control to the 0 to 25 kV scale.
3. Crank the engine and quickly note the spark duration.

Compare the recorded duration times to manufacturer's specifications. If spark duration is too short, look for causes of low coil output voltage. Start with a thorough examination of the primary system after checking for proper operation of the battery, starting, and charging systems. If these items appear to be working properly, search for sources of high primary circuit resistance.

Set the oscilloscope in the primary circuit position and check the height of the initial firing line oscillation. If a lower than normal height is observed, the most likely causes are a bad ballast resistor (where used), a poor control module ground, or loose, dirty, or corroded connectors in the primary circuit. Remember that a 1 volt loss in the primary circuit can result in a 1000-2000 volt loss in the secondary circuit.

Running Test

The running test measures spark duration while the engine is running at a specific rpm. To perform a running test on the oscilloscope, do the following.

1. Set the pattern selector to the 5 millisecond position, the function selector to secondary, and pattern height control to the 0 to 25 kV scale.
2. Start the engine and adjust the speed to 1000 rpm.
3. Note the spark duration.

Some oscilloscopes do not have a millisecond sweep. Instead, they are equipped with a percent of dwell scale. In that case, the percent of dwell must be converted to milliseconds. A conversion chart is given in Table 19-1. The table lists percent of dwell at various rpm and the corresponding spark duration in milliseconds. On oscilloscopes without a millisecond sweep, the pattern selector should be set to superimpose or raster when performing the spark duration cranking and running tests.

TABLE 19-1 CONVERTING PERCENT OF DWELL TO MILLISECONDS

	ms	600 rpm	1200 rpm	2400 rpm	Spark Duration
8 cylinder	0.5	2%	4%	8%	too short
	1.0	4%	8%	17%	minimum
	1.5	6%	13%	25%	average
	2.0	8%	17%	33%	too long
6 cylinder	0.5	1.5%	3%	6%	too short
	1.0	3%	6%	12%	minimum
	1.5	4.5%	9%	18%	average
	2.0	6%	12%	24%	too long
4 cylinder	0.5	1%	2%	4%	too short
	1.0	2%	4%	8%	minimum
	1.5	3%	6%	13%	average
	2.0	4%	8%	17%	too long

The raster pattern in Figure 19-27 is a secondary pattern of a 4-cylinder engine at 600 rpm. The spark duration is 3% of dwell, or 1.5 millisecond.

Coil Polarity

Less voltage is required to fire the spark plugs with proper coil polarity. If the coil polarity is reversed, 20 to 40% more voltage is needed to fire the spark plugs.

If the coil polarity is correct, the firing lines of the display pattern extends upward. If the polarity is reversed, the firing lines extend downward. If reverse polarity is indicated, check the coil primary connections. They are probably reversed.

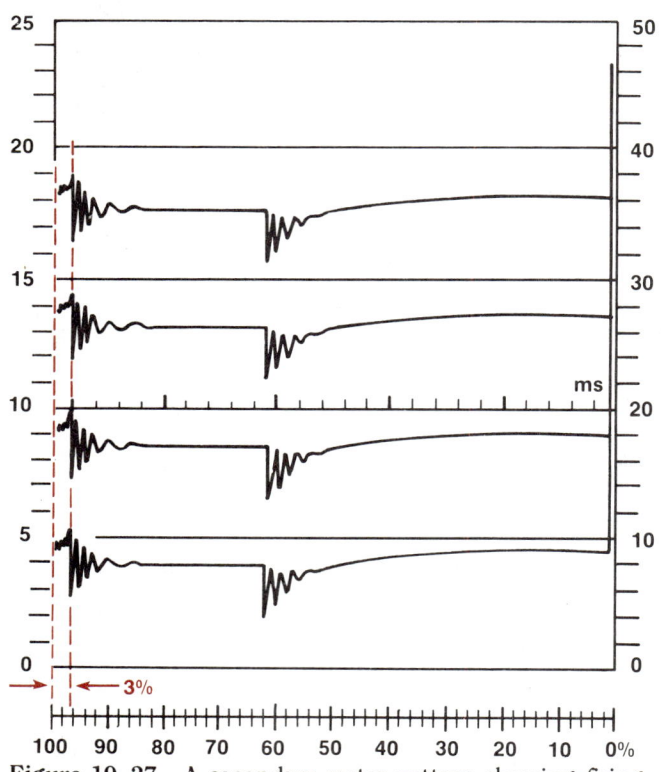

Figure 19-27 A secondary raster pattern showing firing duration as 3% of dwell.

Spark Plug Firing Voltage

The coil must generate sufficient voltage in the secondary system to overcome the total resistance in the secondary circuit and to establish a spark across the spark plug electrodes. On the oscilloscope, this spark plug firing voltage is seen as the highest line in the pattern. The firing voltage might be affected by the condition of the spark plugs or the secondary circuit, engine temperature, fuel mixture, and compression pressures. To test the spark plug firing voltage on an oscilloscope, observe the firing line of all cylinders for height and uniformity. The normal height of the firing voltages should be between 7 and 13 kV with no more than a 3 kV variation between cylinders.

If during the test, one or more of the firing voltages are uneven, low, or high, consult Table 19-2 for possible causes and corrections.

Rotor Air Gap Voltage Drop

When high firing voltages are present in one or more of the cylinders, perform a rotor air gap voltage drop test. The purpose of this test is to determine the amount of secondary voltage that is required to bridge the rotor gap.

SHOP TALK

Excessive rotor air gap can be caused by a bent distributor shaft or worn shaft bearings. Check shaft movement prior to testing the rotor air gap on the scope.

 **PROCEDURES**
Performing a Rotor Air Gap Voltage Drop Test

1. Set the pattern selector to the display position, the function selector to secondary, and the pattern height control to the 0 to 25 kV scale.

Ignition System Service 475

TABLE 19-2 FIRING LINE DIAGNOSIS

Condition	Probable Cause	Remedy
Firing voltage lines the same, but abnormally high	1. Retarded ignition timing 2. Fuel mixture too lean 3. High resistance in coil wire 4. Corrosion in coil tower terminal 5. Corrosion in distributor coil terminal	1. Reset ignition timing. 2. Readjust carburetor or check for vacuum leak. 3. Replace coil wire. 4. Clean or replace coil. 5. Clean or replace distributor cap.
Firing voltage lines the same, but abnormally low	1. Fuel mixture too rich 2. Breaks in coil wire causing arcing 3. Cracked coil tower causing arcing 4. Low coil output 5. Low engine compression	1. Readjust carburetor or check for plugged air filter. 2. Replace coil wire. 3. Replace coil. 4. Replace coil. 5. Determine cause and repair.
One or more, but not all firing voltage lines higher than the others	1. Idle mixture not balanced 2. EGR valve stuck open 3. High resistance in spark plug wire 4. Cracked or broken spark plug insulator 5. Intake vacuum leak 6. Defective spark plugs 7. Corroded spark plug terminals	1. Readjust idle mixture. 2. Inspect or replace EGR valve. 3. Replace spark plug wires. 4. Replace spark plugs. 5. Repair leak. 6. Replace spark plugs. 7. Replace spark plugs.
One or more, but not all firing voltage lines lower	1. Curb idle mixture not balanced 2. Breaks in plug wires causing arcing 3. Cracked coil tower causing arcing 4. Low compression 5. Defective or fouled spark plugs	1. Readjust idle mixture. 2. Replace spark plug wires. 3. Replace coil. 4. Determine cause and repair. 5. Replace spark plugs.
Cylinders not firing	1. Cracked distributor cap terminals 2. Shorted spark plug wire 3. Mechanical problem in engine 4. Defective spark plugs 5. Spark plugs fouled	1. Replace distributor cap. 2. Determine cause of short and replace wire. 3. Determine problem and correct. 4. Replace spark plugs. 5. Replace spark plugs.

2. Start the engine and adjust the speed to 1000 rpm.
3. Observe the height of the firing lines. Record the height and firing order number of any abnormal cylinder.
4. Shut the engine off.
5. Remove the spark plug wire of the abnormal cylinder from the distributor cap. Connect one end of the jumper lead to ground and the other end to the large portion of a grounding probe. Place the other end of the grounding probe in the distributor cap tower terminal.

SHOP TALK

Do not remove the spark plug wire from the distributor cap tower terminal while the engine is running. This causes an open circuit and might damage the ignition system components.

6. Start the engine and adjust the speed to 1000 rpm.
7. Observe the firing line of the abnormal cylinder previously recorded. There should be a drop in the firing voltage when using the grounding probe.

The observed voltage represents voltage needed to overcome the resistance in the coil wire and of the rotor air gap. The rotor air gap measurements should not exceed manufacturer's specifications. If during the test, the firing line remains high or drops to a level that does not meet manufacturer's specifications, the rotor or distributor cap might be defective. Visually inspect both and replace as necessary. A bent distributor shaft or worn shaft bushings will cause excessive rotor air gaps on about half the cylinders.

Rotor Register

The procedure for performing a rotor register test is very similar to that for performing a rotor air gap voltage drop test, except, in this test, vacuum is applied to the distributor vacuum advance unit with an external vacuum source.

SHOP TALK

If the vehicle is equipped with computer-controlled spark advance, consult the manufacturer's service manual for proper test procedures.

TABLE 19-3 TROUBLESHOOTING SPARK PLUGS

Symptom	Probable Cause	Remedy
ROTOR REGISTER TEST		
Difference between firing voltages is over 3 kV	1. Defective rotor 2. Defective distributor cap 3. Wrong vacuum advance unit used	1. Replace rotor. 2. Replace distributor cap. 3. Check manufacturer's part number, or use distributor tester to verify advance curve.
SECONDARY CIRCUIT RESISTANCE TEST		
High resistance in spark lines	1. Rotor tip burned 2. High resistance in the spark plug wire 3. Distributor cap segments burned 4. Faulty spark plug	1. Visually inspect. 2. Perform ohmmeter test. 3. Visually inspect. 4. Perform secondary resistance test using the grounding probe.
After grounding spark plug, abnormal spark lines appear normal	1. Faulty spark plug	1. Substitute spark plug.
After grounding spark plug, abnormal spark lines still show high resistance	1. Corroded distributor cap towers 2. Distributor cap segments burned 3. High resistance in the spark plug wires	1. Visually inspect. 2. Visually inspect. 3. Perform ohmmeter test.
All the spark lines show high resistance	1. Defective coil wire 2. Rotor tip burned	1. Perform ohmmeter test. 2. Visually inspect.
SPARK PLUGS UNDER LOAD TEST		
One or more of cylinders show a voltage rise over 4 kV	1. Spark plug gap too wide 2. Worn spark plug electrodes 3. Open or high resistance spark plug wire 4. Improper fuel mixture 5. Open spark plug resistor 6. Leakage in vacuum system	1. Check gap, then regap plug. 2. Replace the spark plug. 3. Perform ohmmeter test. 4. Adjust mixture. 5. Substitute spark plug. 6. Check for leaky vacuum hoses and diaphragms, or gaskets.
One or more cylinders show a voltage rise less than 3 kV or no voltage rise at all	1. Shorted spark plug wire 2. Broken spark plug insulator 3. Fouled spark plug 4. Low compression	1. Perform secondary insulation test. 2. Replace spark plug. 3. Clean or replace spark plug. 4. Perform compression test.
CYLINDER TIMING ACCURACY TEST		
Transistor turn off signals exceed specifications for engine being tested	1. Bent distributor shaft 2. Worn distributor bushings 3. Worn gear on distributor 4. Worn camshaft gear 5. Worn timing chain	1. Perform distributor test. 2. Perform distributor test. 3. Visually inspect. 4. Visually inspect. 5. Visually inspect.

PROCEDURES
Performing a Rotor Register Test

1. Set the pattern selector to the display position, the function selector to secondary, and the pattern height control to the 0 to 25 kV scale.
2. With the engine off, remove any spark plug wire from the distributor cap, except for the one connected to the trigger pick-up. Connect one end of the jumper lead to ground and the other end to the large portion of a grounding probe. Place the other end of the grounding probe in the distributor cap tower terminal.
3. Start the engine and adjust the speed to 1000 rpm.
4. Note the height of the firing line of the circuit connected to the grounding probe.
5. Using the external vacuum source, apply 16 to 22 inches of mercury to the distributor vacuum advance unit. Readjust the engine speed to maintain 1000 rpm.

6. Again, note the height of the firing lines of the circuit connected to the grounding probe. There should be no more than a 3 kV difference between the firing voltages observed in steps 4 and 6. If at any time during the test, the difference between the firing voltages is over 3 kV, see Table 19-3.

Secondary Circuit Resistance

Analysis of the spark line of a secondary pattern reveals the condition of the secondary circuit. The amount of resistance in the secondary circuit is indicated by the slope of the spark line. Excessive resistance in the secondary circuit causes the spark line to have a steep slope with a shorter firing duration. The excessive resistance restricts the current flow necessary to generate a good spark.

A good spark line should be relatively even and measure 2 to 4 kV in height. High resistance in the secondary circuit produces a firing line and spark line that are higher in voltage with shorter firing durations. If high resistance is shown during testing, see Table 19-3.

To pinpoint the cause of high resistance, use a grounding probe and jumper wire to bypass each component of the secondary circuit on all abnormal cylinders. Connect one end of the jumper lead to ground and the other end to the large portion of a grounding probe. Start the engine and adjust the speed to 1000 rpm. Touch each secondary connector with the point of the grounding probe and observe the spark lines.

If, after grounding, the abnormal spark lines appear normal, the part just bypassed is the cause of the problem. For further diagnosis, see Table 19-3.

While scanning the secondary circuit with the grounding probe, watch the firing lines on the scope. If there is an insulation break in the circuit, the firing lines decrease in height when the high secondary voltage arcs across to the probe.

> ### SHOP TALK
> When the voltage arcs across to the grounding probe, an electrical cracking sound might be heard or the spark might be visible.

Any insulated part of the secondary circuit can breakdown and leak. This includes the coil, coil wire and boots, distributor cap and terminals and spark plug wires and boots.

Spark Plugs Under Load

The voltage required to fire the spark plugs increases when the engine is under load. The voltage increase is moderate and uniform if the spark plugs are in good condition and properly gapped. However, if any unusual characteristics are displayed on the scope patterns when load is applied to the engine, the spark plugs are probably faulty. This condition is most evident in the firing voltages displayed on the scope. To test spark plug operation under load, note the height of the firing lines at idle speed. Then, quickly open and release the throttle (snap accelerate), and note the rise in the firing lines while checking the voltages for uniformity. A normal rise would be between 3 and 4 kV upon snap acceleration.

If during testing, one or more of the cylinders show a voltage rise of over 4 kV, or if one or more cylinders show a voltage rise less than 3 kV or no voltage rise at all, check Table 19-3.

Coil Condition

The energy remaining in the coil after the spark plugs fire gradually diminishes in a series of oscillations. These oscillations are observable in the intermediate sections of both the primary and secondary patterns. If the scope pattern shows an absence of normal oscillations in the intermediate section, check for a possible short in the coil by testing the resistance of the primary and secondary windings. The procedure is given later in the chapter.

❑ INDIVIDUAL COMPONENT TESTING

Electronic ignition systems have many characteristics unique to the system's manufacturer. It would be impossible in any one textbook to explain all the variations. However, the basic goal of any electrical troubleshooting procedure is always to identify electrical activity under a given set of circumstances. The manufacturer's service manual provides the technician with both the desired activity (specification) and the set of circumstances (procedures).

Tables 19-4 and 19-5 outline a procedure for quickly isolating an ignition related problem when an oscilloscope is not available. The first troubleshooting tree determines whether a spark is generated in the secondary system. If no spark is available, the second troubleshooting tree leads step by step through individual component tests until the problem is located.

The secret to component testing is to use good troubleshooting practices. Work systematically through a circuit, testing each wire, connector, and component. Do not jump around back and forth between components. The component inadvertently overlooked is probably the one causing the trouble. Checks must be made for available voltage, voltage output, resistance of wires and connectors, and available ground. Always compare the readings with specifications given in the manufacturer's service manual.

The following sections briefly outline common test procedures for individual system components. For ac-

478 Section 4 Engine Performance

TABLE 19-4 IGNITION SECONDARY QUICK CHECK CHART

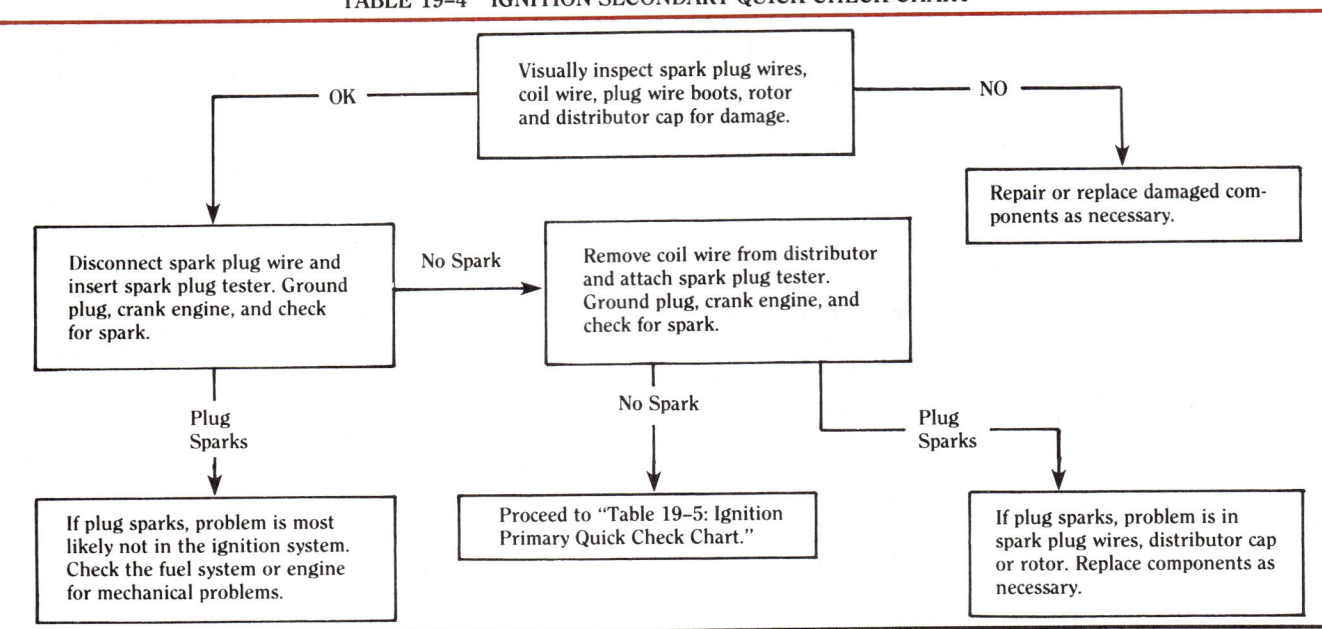

TABLE 19-5 IGNITION PRIMARY QUICK CHECK CHART

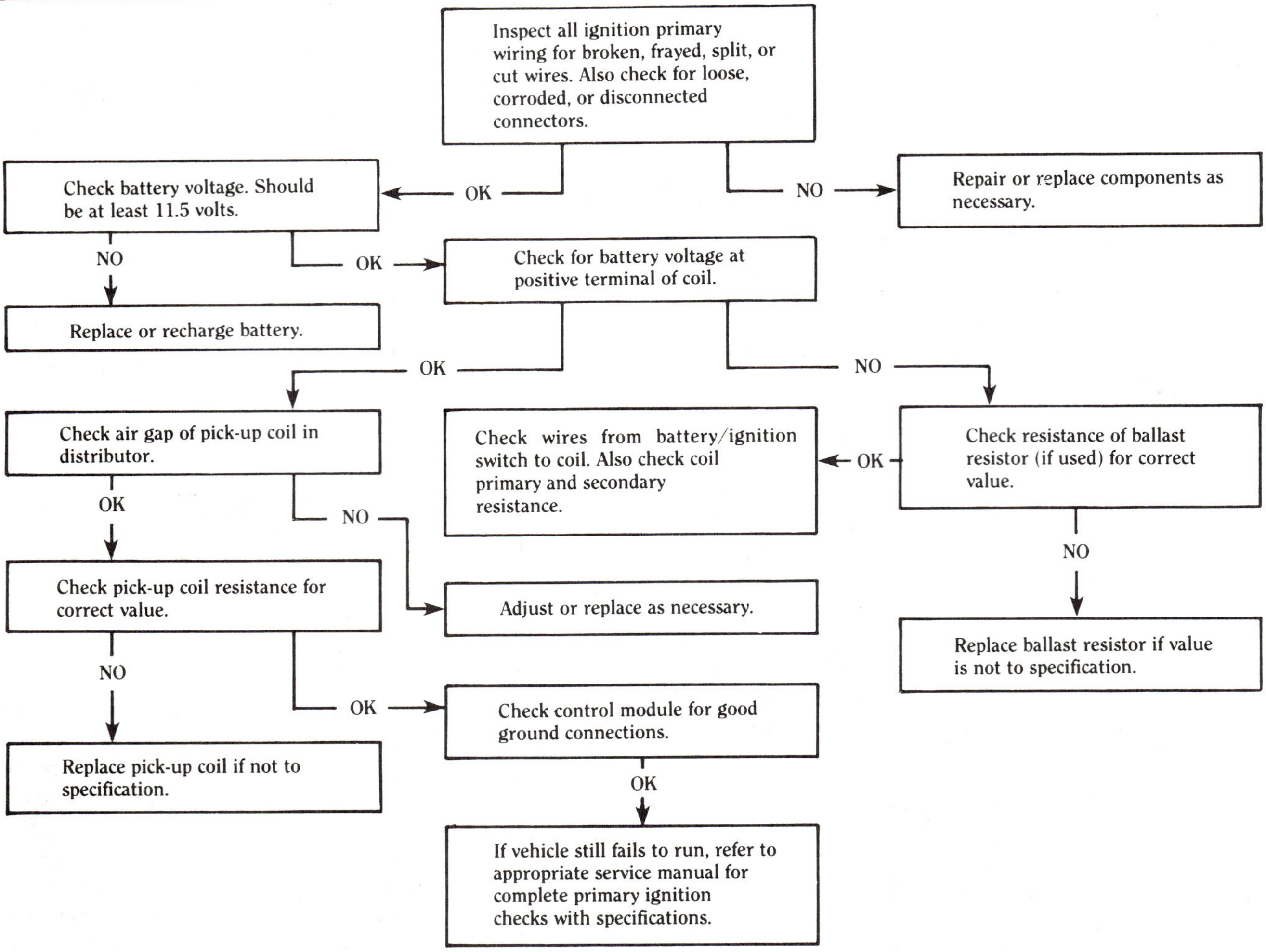

curate testing always refer to service manual wiring diagrams and testing instructions.

> ### USING SERVICE MANUALS
>
> Service manuals are indispensable when troubleshooting ignition problems. They contain such vital information as base and advance timing specifications, color coded wiring diagrams and terminal connector descriptions, and illustrations showing test connections for voltage, continuity, and resistance checks. The diagnostic charts found in the service manual are particularly helpful in troubleshooting ignition problems. Ignoring the valuable data contained in the ignition service section of these manuals can lead to many frustrating and costly service mistakes.

IGNITION SWITCH A faulty ignition switch or bad ignition switch wiring does not supply power to the ignition control module or ignition coil. The ignition system shown in Figure 19-28 has two wires connected to the run terminal of the ignition switch. One is connected to the module. The other is connected to the primary resistor and coil. The start terminal of the switch is also wired to the module.

You can check for voltage using either a 12-volt test light or a digital voltmeter. To use the test light method, turn the ignition key off and disconnect the wire connector at the module. Also, disconnect the S terminal of the starter solenoid to prevent the engine from cranking when the key is in the start position. Turn the key to the run position and probe the red wire connection to check for voltage (Figure 19-28A). Also check for voltage at the bat terminal of the ignition coil using the test light.

Next, turn the key to the start position and check for voltage at the white wire connector at the module and the bat terminal of the ignition coil.

To make the same test using a digital voltmeter, turn the ignition switch to the off position and install a small straight pin into the appropriate module wire as shown in Figure 19-28B. Connect the digital voltmeter's positive lead to the straight pin and ground the negative lead to the distributor base. Turn the ignition to the run or start position as needed and measure

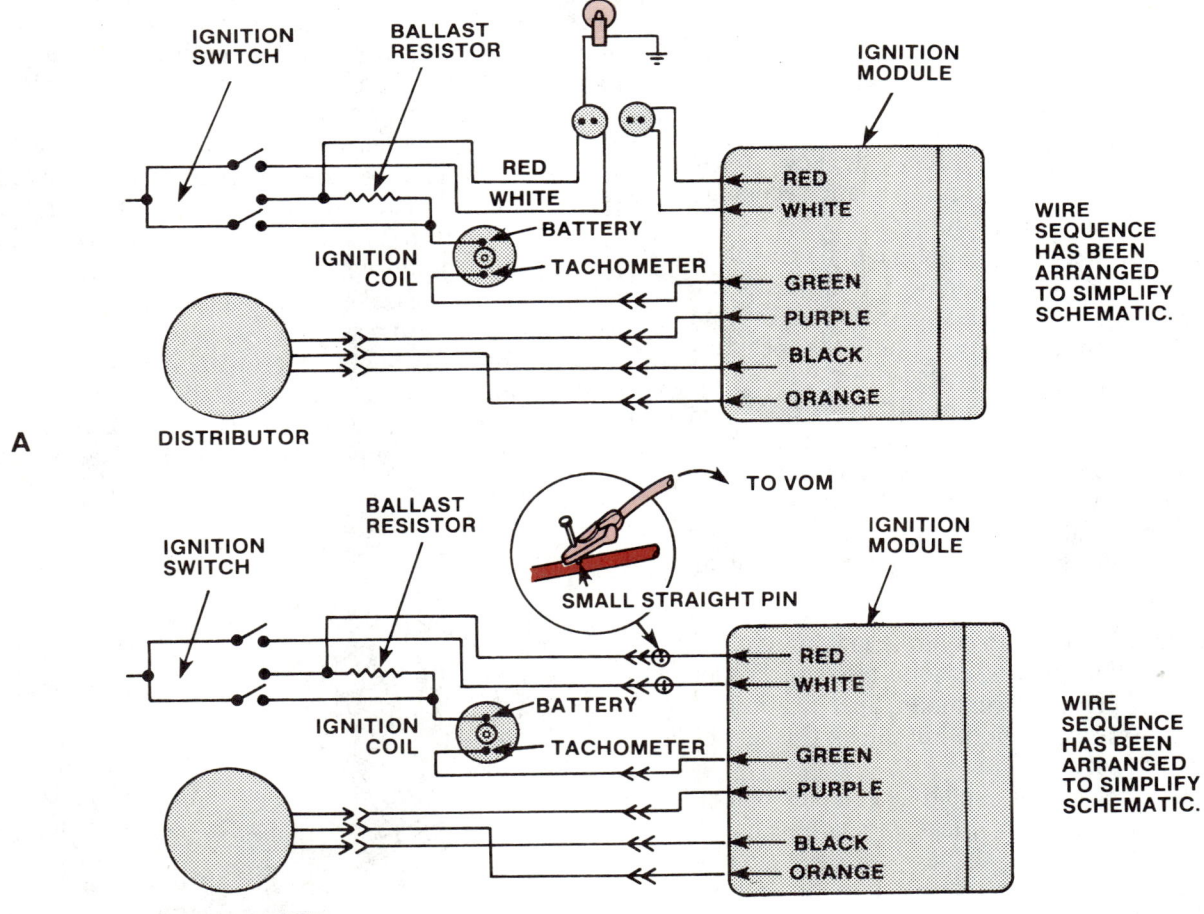

Figure 19-28 Testing for voltage at the ignition module to check ignition switch and wiring (A) test light method, and (B) digital. *Courtesy of Ford Motor Company*

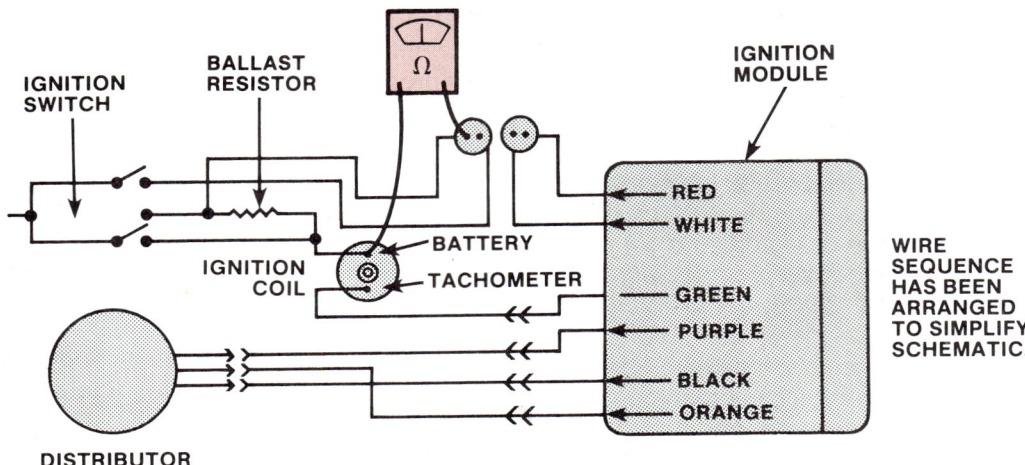

Figure 19-29 Checking primary (ballast) resistance. *Courtesy of Ford Motor Company*

voltage. Do not allow the straight pin to contact the engine or ground. Reading should be within 90% of battery voltage.

PRIMARY RESISTOR Measure the resistance of the primary (ballast) resistor using an ohmmeter. Remember, the key must be off when this test is performed or power in the circuit damages the meter. In the ignition system shown in Figure 19-29, ohmmeter leads are connected at the bat terminal of the coil and the wiring harness connector wire that join the red wire in the ignition module connector.

IGNITION COIL RESISTANCE With the key off, use the ohmmeter to measure the primary and secondary winding resistance of the ignition coil.

To measure primary coil resistance hook the ohmmeter across the bat (+) and tach (-) terminals of the ignition coil. Primary resistance usually ranges from less than 1 ohm to around 4 ohms. Check the specifications listed in the service manual.

To measure secondary coil resistance, hook the ohmmeter across the bat (+) terminal and the ignition coils center (high voltage) tower. Secondary resistance usually ranges from 7,000 to 13,000 ohms. Again, check service manual specifications. Also, check for breaks in the ignition coil insulation or oil leakage from its case.

PICK-UP COIL The pick-up coil of a magnetic pulse generator or metal detection sensor is also checked for proper resistance using an ohmmeter. Specifications of 400 to 800 ohms are common, but check the service manual specifications.

The oscilloscope can be used to check pick-up coil operation. The primary scope leads are connected to the pick-up coil leads. The scope is set on its lowest scale. When the distributor shaft is spun, an AC sine wave trace should appear on the CRT screen. The trace is not a true sine wave, but it should have both a positive and negative pulse.

Another method of measuring the pick-up coil's AC signal is with a simple voltmeter set on its low voltage scale. The meter registers AC voltage during cranking. Measure this voltage as close to the control module as possible to account for any resistance in the connecting wire from the pick-up coil to the module.

HALL-EFFECT SENSORS Most Hall-effect sensors can be tested by connecting a 12-volt battery across the plus (+) and minus (-) voltage (supply current) terminals of the Hall layer, and a voltmeter across the minus (-) and signal voltage terminals.

With the voltmeter hooked up, insert a steel feeler gauge or knife blade between the Hall layer and magnet (Figure 19-30). If the sensor is good, the voltmeter should read within 0.5 volt of battery voltage when the feeler gauge or knife blade is inserted and touching the magnet. When the feeler gauge or blade is removed, the voltage should read less than 0.5 volt.

It is often possible to observe the voltage levels of the Hall-effect sensor using an oscilloscope. Set the scope on its low scale primary pattern position and connect the primary positive lead to the Hall signal

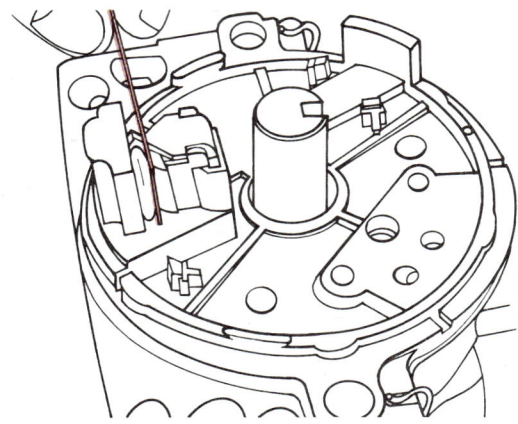

Figure 19-30 Test Hall-effect sensor operation with a steel feeler gauge.

Ignition System Service   481

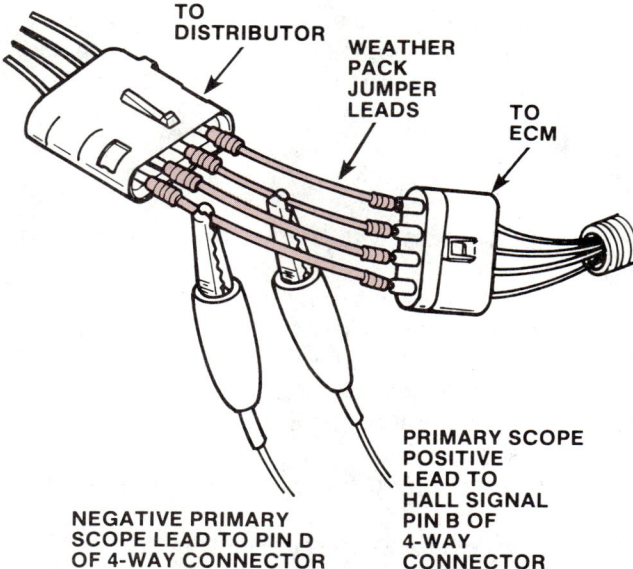

Figure 19-31 Connecting oscilloscope leads to late model GM Hall-effect sensor using weather pack jumper leads. *Courtesy of General Motors Corp.*

lead, using a weather pack jumper wire (Figure 19-31). The negative lead should connect to ground or the ground terminal at the sensor's connector.

With the engine running, the pattern should show a square wave pattern ranging from approximately 0 to 12 volts (Figure 19-32). If the range is out of specifications or distorted, replace the sensor.

CONTROL MODULE Use an ohmmeter to insure that the control module connection to ground is good. As shown in Figure 19-33, one lead of the meter is connected to the ground terminal at the module. The other is connected to a good engine ground. Zero resistance indicates good continuity in the ground circuit. Any resistance reading during this test is unacceptable.

The most effective method of testing for a defective control module is to use an ignition module tester. This electronic tester evaluates and determines if the module is operating within a given set of design parameters. It does so by simulating normal operating conditions while looking for faults in key components. A typical ignition module tester performs the following tests.

- Shorted module test
- Cranking current test
- Key on/engine off current test
- Idle current test
- Cruise current test
- Cranking primary voltage test
- Idle primary voltage test
- Cruise primary voltage test

Some ignition module testers are also able to perform an ignition coil-spark test (actually firing the coil) and a distributor pick-up test.

Test selection is made by pushing the appropriate button. The module tester usually responds to these tests with a pass or fail indication.

Unfortunately, many module testers are designed to troubleshoot specific makes and models of ignitions. Many shops find it impractical to have testers for every type of system they service.

Keep in mind that control modules are very reliable. They are also one of the most expensive ignition system components. So, if a module tester is not available, check out all other system components before condemning the control module.

Stress Testing Components

Often, an intermittent ignition problem only occurs under certain conditions such as extremes in heat or cold, or during rainy or humid weather. Careful questioning of the customer should lead to determining if

Figure 19-32 Square wave trace produced by properly operating Hall-effect sensor.

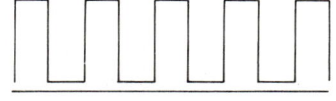

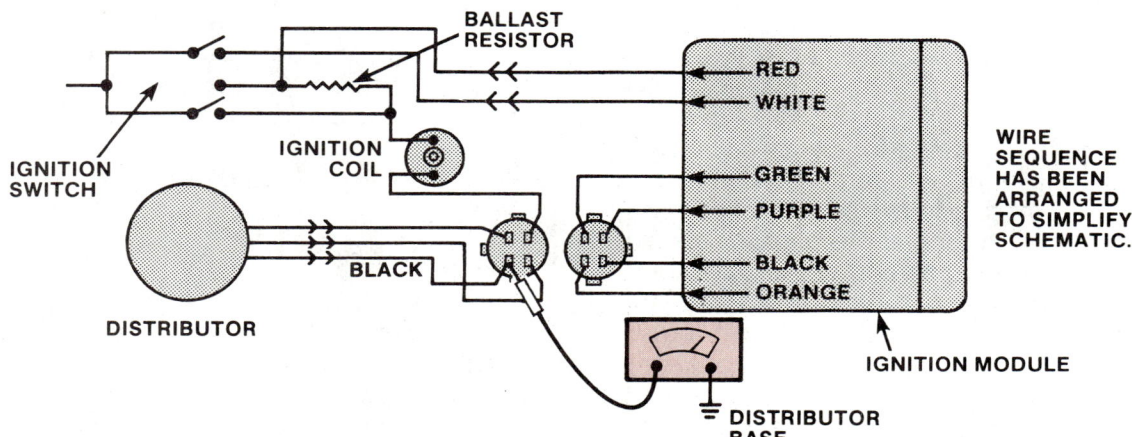

Figure 19-33 Using ohmmeter to check for proper control module grounding. *Courtesy of Ford Motor Company*

the problem is stress condition related. Does the problem occur on cold mornings? Does it occur when the engine is fully warmed up? Is it a rainy day problem? If the answer to any of these questions is positive, you can reproduce the same conditions in the shop during stress testing.

COLD TESTING With the scope on raster, cool major ignition components such as the control module, pickup coil, and major connections one at a time using a liquid cool-down agent.

CAUTION: *When using cool-down sprays, wear eye protection and avoid spraying your skin or clothing. Use extreme caution.*

After cooling a component, watch the pattern for any signs of malfunction, particularly in the dwell zone. If there is no sign of malfunction, cool down the next component after the first has warmed to normal operating temperature. Cooling (or heating) more than one component at a time provides inconclusive results.

HEAT TESTING To heat stress components, use a heat gun or hair dryer to direct hot air onto the component. Heat guns intended for stripping paint and other household jobs can become extremely hot and melt plastic, wire insulation, and other materials. Use a moderate setting and proceed cautiously. Look for changes in the dwell section of the trace, particularly in the variable dwell or current limiting areas. If connections appear to be the problem, disconnect them, clean the terminals, and coat them with dielectric compound to seal out dirt and moisture.

MOISTURE TESTING A wet stress test is performed by lightly spraying the components, coil and ignition cables, and connections with water. Do not flood the area, a light mist does the job. A scope set on raster or display helps pinpoint problems, but it is often possible to hear and feel the miss or stutter without the use of a scope. As with heat and cold testing, do not spray down more than one area at a time or results could be misleading. If you suspect a poor connection, clean and seal it, then retest it.

CUSTOMER CARE

The term tune-up essentially means adjusting the air/fuel mixture and setting the timing. Tamper-resistant carburetors, fuel injection systems, and electronic ignition eliminated these once common service procedures over a decade ago. Today, the computer-controlled system normally makes these adjustments. Unfortunately, your customers have probably not kept abreast of these changes. Many shop owners state that over half of the customers coming in for tune-ups still think their vehicles have breaker points.

So when a customer approaches you for a standard tune-up, it's the ideal time to explain in simple terms just how the vehicle operates and what is involved in a modern tune-up. These procedures should include these points.

- An initial test drive with the customer.
- Spark plug change.
- Compression test or dynamic compression test.
- Visual inspection of ignition system.
- Base timing check and idle speed check.
- Inspection of vacuum lines, air intake ducts, and PCV valve operation.
- Check operation of EGR valve and oxygen sensor.
- Pull computer trouble codes—if easily accessible.
- Replace air and fuel filters if the service interval is reached.
- Inspect all belts and hoses.
- Check fan operation.
- Inspect water pump seal.
- Service battery terminals and top all fluids.

Spark Plug Service

Spark plug service is a vital part of a complete engine tune-up. Vehicle manufacturers' recommendations for service intervals can range anywhere between 5,000 and 50,000 miles, depending on a variety of factors.

- The type of ignition system
- Engine design
- Spark plug design
- Vehicle operating conditions
- The type of fuel used
- Types of emission control devices used

Regardless of what other tools are used, a spark plug socket is essential for plug removal and installation. Spark plug sockets are available in two sizes: 3/16-inch (for 14-millimeter gasketed and 18-millimeter tapered-seat plugs) and 5/8-inch (for 14-millimeter tapered-seat plugs). They can be either 3/8- or 1/2-inch drive, and many feature an external hex so that they can be turned using an open end or box wrench.

PROCEDURES

Removing Spark Plugs

1. Remove the cables from each plug, being careful not to pull on the cables. Instead, grasp the boot and twist it off gently.
2. Using a spark plug socket and ratchet, loosen each plug a couple of turns.
3. Use compressed air to blow any dirt away from the base of the plugs.

4. Remove the plugs, making sure to remove the gasket as well (if applicable).

> ### SHOP TALK
> To save time and avoid confusion later, use masking tape to mark each of the cables with the number of the plug it attaches to.

Inspecting Spark Plugs

Once the spark plugs have been removed, it is important to "read" them (Figure 19-34). In other words, inspect them closely, noting in particular any deposits on the plugs and the degree of electrode erosion. A plug in good working condition can still have minimal deposits on it. They are usually light tan or gray in color. However, there should be no evidence of electrode burning, and the increase of the air gap should be no more than 0.001 inch for every 10,000 miles of engine operation. A plug that fits this description can be reinstalled after resetting the air gap to specifications.

It is possible to diagnose a variety of engine conditions by examining the firing end of the spark plugs. If an engine is in good shape, they should all look alike. Whenever plugs from different cylinders look differently, a problem exists somewhere in the engine or its systems. Following are examples of plug problems and how they should be dealt with.

COLD FOULING This condition is the result of an excessively rich air/fuel mixture. It is characterized by a layer of dry, fluffy black carbon deposits on the tip of the plug (Figure 19-35). Cold fouling is caused by a rich air/fuel mixture or an ignition fault causing the spark plug not to fire. If only one or two of the plugs show evidence of cold fouling, sticking valves are the likely cause. The plug can be used again, provided its electrodes are filed and the air gap is reset. Correct the cause of the problem before reinstalling or replacing the plugs.

Figure 19-35 Cold-fouled spark plug. *Courtesy of Denso Spark Plugs*

> ### SHOP TALK
> If cold fouling is present on a vehicle that operates a great deal at idle and low speeds, plug life can be lengthened by using hotter spark plugs.

WET FOULING When the tip of the plug is practically drowned in excess oil, this condition is known as wet fouling (Figure 19-36). In an overhead valve engine, the oil may be entering the combustion chamber past worn valve guides or valve guide seals. If the vehicle has an automatic transmission, a likely cause of wet-fouled plugs is a defective vacuum modulator that is allowing transmission fluid into the chamber. On high-mileage engines, check for worn rings or excessive cylinder wear. The best solution is to correct the problem and replace the plugs with the specified type.

SPLASH FOULING This condition occurs immediately following an overdue tune-up. Deposits in the combustion chamber, accumulated over a period of time due to misfiring, suddenly loosen when the temperature in the chamber returns to normal. During high-speed driving, these deposits can stick to the hot insulator and electrode surfaces of the plug. These deposits

Figure 19-34 Spark plug in good working order. *Courtesy of Denso Spark Plugs*

Figure 19-36 Wet-fouled spark plug. *Courtesy of Denso Spark Plugs*

can actually bridge across the gap, stopping the plug from sparking. Normally splash-fouled plugs can be cleaned and reused.

GAP BRIDGING A plug with a bridged gap is rarely seen in automobile engines. It occurs when flying carbon deposits within the combustion chamber accumulate over a long period of stop-and-go driving. When the engine is suddenly placed under a hard load, the deposits melt and bridge the gap, causing misfire. This condition is best corrected by replacing the plug.

GLAZING Under high-speed conditions, the combustion chamber deposits can form a shiny, yellow glaze over the insulator. When it gets hot enough, the glaze acts as an electrical conductor, causing the current to follow the deposits and short out the plug. Glazing can be prevented by avoiding sudden wide-open throttle acceleration after sustained periods of low-speed or idle operation. Because it is virtually impossible to remove glazed deposits, glazed plugs should be replaced.

OVERHEATING This condition is characterized by white or light gray blistering of the insulator. There may also be considerable electrode gap wear (Figure 19-37). Overheating can result from using too hot a plug, overadvanced ignition timing, detonation, a malfunction in the cooling system, an overly lean air/fuel mixture, using too-low octane fuel, an improperly installed plug, or a heat-riser valve that is stuck closed. Overheated plugs must be replaced.

TURBULENCE BURNING When turbulence burning occurs, the insulator on one side of the plug wears away as the result of normal turbulence in the combustion chamber (Figure 19-38). As long as the plug life is normal, this condition is of little consequence. However, if there is a larger than normal air gap, overheating can be the problem. In this case, check for all of the common causes of overheating discussed previously.

Preignition damage is caused by excessive engine temperatures. Preignition damage is characterized by melting of the electrodes, or chipping of the electrode

Figure 19-37 Condition of overheating spark plug. *Courtesy of Denso Spark Plugs*

Figure 19-38 Condition of spark plug after experiencing turbulence burning. *Courtesy of Denso Spark Plugs*

Figure 19-39 This plug shows evidence of preignition damage. *Courtesy of Denso Spark Plugs*

tips (Figure 19-39). When this problem occurs, look for the general causes of engine overheating, including overadvanced ignition timing, a burned head gasket, and using too-low octane fuel. Other possibilities include loose plugs or using plugs of the improper heat range. Do not attempt to reuse plugs with preignition damage.

A sure sign of reversed coil polarity damage is a slight dishing of the ground electrode. The center electrode does not normally wear badly. Misfiring and rough idling may also be present. In addition to reversal of the coil primary leads, older vehicles can experience reverse coil polarity damage by reversing the battery polarity.

SHOP TALK

It is a good idea to brush used spark plug electrodes with several strokes of a flat distributor point file or spark plug gauge file (Figure 19-40). This helps reduce the required firing voltage of the plug.

Ignition System Service

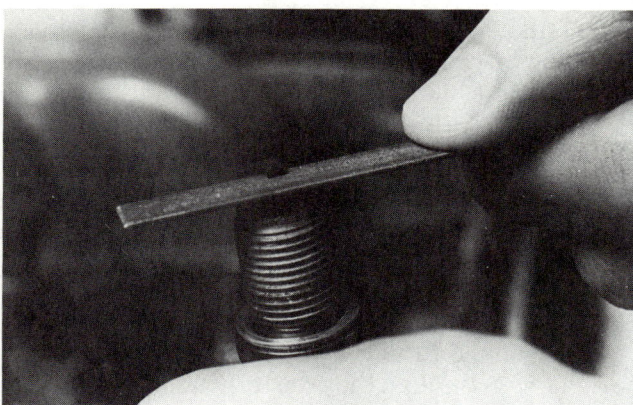

Figure 19-40 It may be helpful to file the electrodes clean.

Regapping Spark Plugs

Both new and used spark plugs must have their air gaps set to the engine manufacturer's specifications. Use an approved tool not only to measure the gap, but also to bend the side electrode to make the adjustment. The combination gauge and adjusting tool shown in Figure 19-41 is designed for use on new plugs only. This is because it utilizes flat gauges for the adjustment procedure. The gauges are mounted on the tool like spokes on a wheel. Above the gauges is an anvil, which is used to apply pressure to the electrode. On the opposite end of the tool is a curved seat. This seat performs two functions: it supports the plug shell during the procedure. It also compresses the ground electrode against the gauge, thus setting the air gap.

The tapered regapping tool is simply a piece of tapered steel with leading and trailing edges of different dimensions. Between these two points, the gauge varies in thickness. A scale, located above the gauge, indicates the thickness at any given point. When the gauge is slid between electrodes, it stops when the air gap size reaches the thickness on the gauge. The scale reading is made in thousandths of an inch. Adjusting slots are available to bend the ground electrode as needed to make the air gap adjustment.

In many instances, the electrodes on a used spark plug are no longer flat, thus rendering a flat gauge useless for regapping purposes. Instead, a round wire gauge is required. Combination round and flat feeler gauge sets are available. These multipurpose tools can be used to check air gaps, adjust contact points, bend electrodes, and file contact points and electrodes.

When regapping a spark plug, always check the air gap of a new spark plug before installing it. Never assume the gap is correct just because the plug is new. Do not try to reduce a plug's air gap by tapping the side electrode on a bench. Never attempt to set a wide gap, electronic ignition type plug to a small gap specification. Likewise, never attempt to set a small gap, breaker point ignition type plug to the wide gap necessary for electronic ignitions. In either case, damage to the electrodes results. Never try to bend the center electrode to adjust the air gap. This cracks the insulation.

PROCEDURES

Spark Plug Installation

1. Wipe dirt and grease from the plug seats with a clean cloth.
2. Be sure the gaskets on gasketed plugs are in good condition and properly placed on the plugs. If reusing a plug, install a new gasket on it. Be sure that there is only one gasket on each plug.
3. Adjust the air gap as needed.
4. Install the plugs and finger tighten. If the plugs cannot be installed easily by hand, the threads in the cylinder head may require cleaning with a thread-chasing tap. Be especially careful not to cross-thread the plugs when working with aluminum heads.
5. Tighten the plugs with a torque wrench, following the vehicle manufacturer's specifications, or the values listed in Table 19-6.

CAUTION: If thread lubricant is used, reduce the torque setting. Keep in mind that many spark plug manufacturers do not recommend the use of thread lubricant.

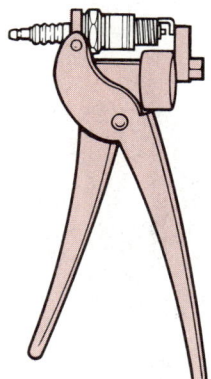

Figure 19-41 Combination spark plug gauge and adjusting tool.

TABLE 19-6	PLUG INSTALLATION TORQUE VALUES (IN FOOT-POUNDS)	
Plug Type	Cast-Iron Head	Aluminum Head
14-mm Gasketed	25 to 30	15 to 22
14-mm Tapered Seat	7 to 15	7 to 15
18-mm Tapered Seat	15 to 20	15 to 20

☐ REPLACING BREAKER POINTS

As already stated, one of the advantages of electronic systems is the elimination of breaker points. Breaker points require regular replacement typically at intervals of 10,000 to 12,000 miles. If no pitting of the contact point surfaces is evident, the condenser need not be replaced.

While used points can be filed and cleaned for reuse, this practice is not recommended. Most breaker points are made with specially hardened contact surfaces. When these surfaces are filed away, the points wear out very quickly. It is much more efficient to replace old points with a new set.

Most replacement breaker points are sold as preassembled sets, with the alignment and spring tension set at the factory. However, replacement points that come as two-piece units require alignment, as well as spring tension and dwell adjustment. Special spring scales are available to check the tension. Always compare the reading with the manufacturer's specifications. In most cases, the tension is adjusted by sliding the spring along its slot.

Point alignment is accomplished using a special tool. Be sure to bend only the stationary contact support, never the movable contact arm. Always clean and lubricate the distributor cam and breaker point rubbing block. Special grease is available for this purpose.

PROCEDURES

Setting Breaker Points

1. With the ignition off, remove the distributor cap and rotor (Figure 19-42).
2. Connect a remote starter switch and bump the engine with the starter motor until the rubbing block is exactly on a high point of the cam.
3. Slide a clean feeler gauge of the proper thickness between the points. It should slide between the contacts with a slight drag. Consult the manufacturer's specifications for proper gap dimension, and adjust accordingly. Make the adjustment by loosening the holddown screw and by shifting the position of the point assembly.
4. Tighten the holddown screw and recheck the gap. Make any further adjustments that may be necessary.

☐ CHECKING DWELL

As explained earlier, dwell is the amount of time current flows through the primary winding of the ignition coil. It is measured in terms of camshaft rotation using a tach-dwellmeter.

In a breaker point ignition system, dwell indicates the amount of time the points are closed. It is directly related to gap. If the gap is set correctly, the dwell reading matches specifications.

For example, if a four-cylinder engine has a dwell specification of 50 degrees, the points remain closed for 50 degrees and then open for 40 degrees (Figure 19-43). The 50 degrees and 40 degrees add up to 90 degrees of camshaft rotation between plug firings, with four firings every full 360 degrees rotation.

Measuring dwell is highly useful when setting and adjusting points. In electronic ignitions, dwell cannot be adjusted. However, a tach-dwellmeter can still be used to check the variable dwell function of the control module.

Figure 19-42 The first step in setting newly aligned breaker points is to remove the distributor cap and rotor.

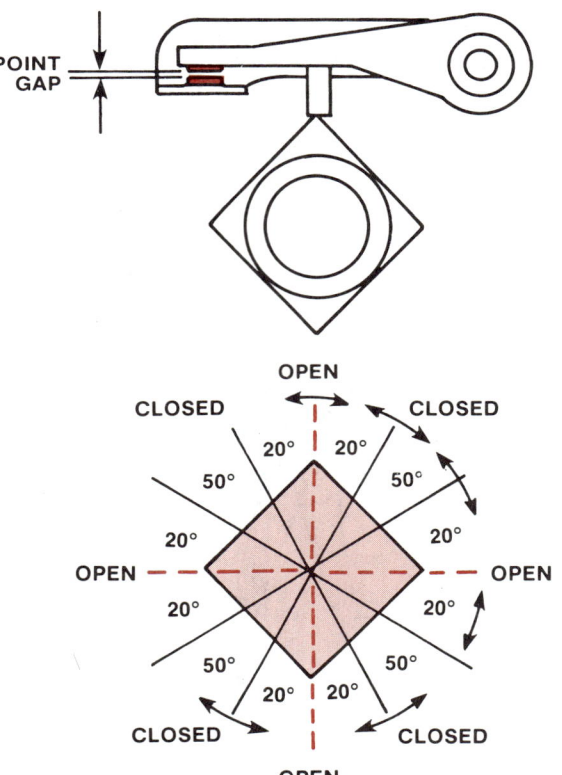

Figure 19-43 Typical four-cylinder engine dwell.

☐ SETTING IGNITION TIMING

Correct ignition timing depends on spark plug air gap, dwell (when adjustable), engine rpm (idle speed), and emission control devices.

Spark plug gap, idle speed, and dwell must be correct before setting ignition timing. Also, the engine must be at operating temperature.

Exact timing procedures vary between manufacturers and even between models made by the same manufacturer. Proper ignition timing procedures are listed on the underhood sticker that also details emission control instructions. Timing procedures are also found in the vehicle service manual. The following are some general points common to many systems.

- Base timing is normally checked and adjusted at idle speed or low engine speeds, such as 650 rpm. At this low speed, any mechanical advance mechanism is not activated and does not affect the base reading.
- Many systems require checking timing with the automatic transmission placed in drive. This is often abbreviated as DR on the instruction sticker.
- The vacuum advance mechanism must also be disabled so it does not affect the base reading. This is done by removing and plugging the vacuum advance line or hose from the manifold.
- In computer-controlled systems, the microprocessor controls ignition timing advance. To set correct base timing, the computer has to be eliminated from the timing control circuit. This is normally done by disconnecting the appropriate connector at the distributor. For example, Ford calls this connector the spout (spark out) connector. GM and other manufacturers have similar methods of disabling computer timing control. Setting base timing is very important in computer-controlled systems. If base timing is incorrect, the computer makes further adjustments based on incorrect data.

Making Base Timing Adjustments

Once you have obtained a base timing reading, compare it to manufacturer's specifications. For example, if the specification reads 10 degrees before top dead center (Figure 19-44A) and the reading found is 3 degrees before top dead center (Figure 19-44B) the timing is retarded or off by 7 degrees.

This means the timing must be advanced by 7 degrees to make it correct. To do this, rotate the distributor until the timing marks align at 10 degrees (Figure 19-45). Then retighten the distributor hold down bolt.

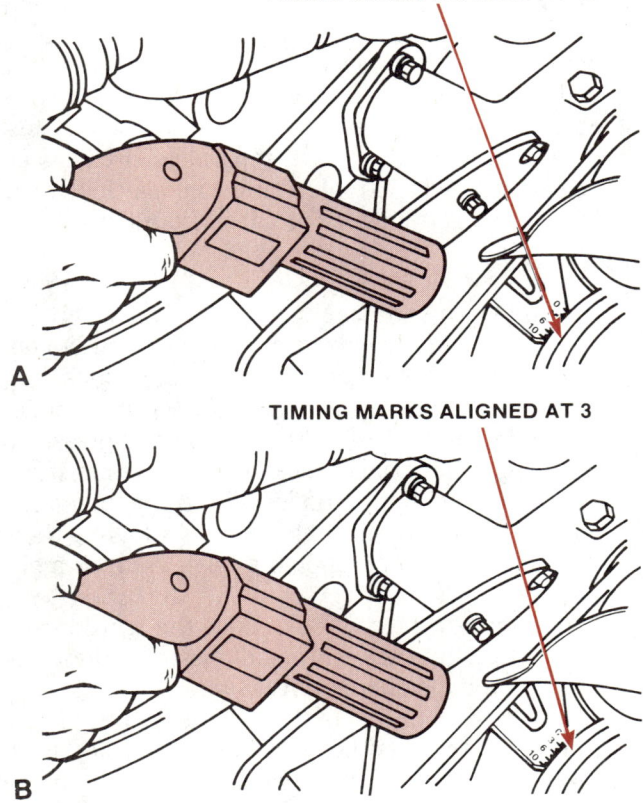

Figure 19-44 (A) Timing marks illuminated by a timing light at 10 degrees BTDC, and (B) timing marks at 3 degrees BTDC.

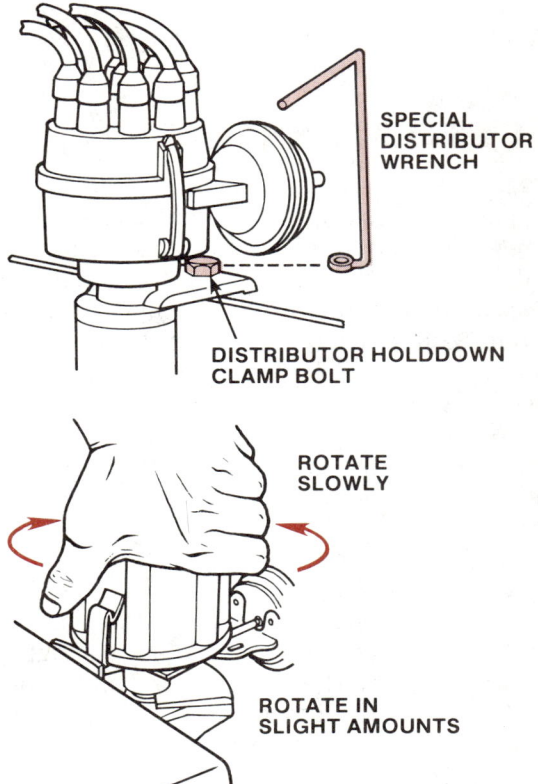

Figure 19-45 Turning the distributor to set timing. *Courtesy of Chrysler Corp.*

Checking Mechanical Advance Units

Mechanical or centrifugal units advance ignition timing in response to increases in engine speed. To check the operation of this unit, disable any vacuum advance system. Raise engine speed to 2000 rpm or speed specified in the service manual. Then shine the light on the vibration damper timing marks, and turn the timing knob on the advance timing light until the base timing reading of 10 degrees is again registering. Observe the reading on the timing meter of the timing light. It tells how many degrees the flash of light has been delayed. This meter reading should match the specified advance at that rpm level.

If the reading does not match up, the mechanical advance mechanism is faulty. The vacuum advance can be checked in the same manner. Use a hand-held vacuum pump to draw on the diaphragm until the vacuum specification is reached, and adjust the advance timing light until correct base timing is again registering. Once again, the amount of flash delay matches the amount of vacuum advance present.

Symptoms of overly advanced timing include pinging or engine knock. Insufficient advance or retarded timing at higher engine rpms could cause hesitation and poor fuel economy.

The normal test procedure is to compare vacuum and mechanical advance to manufacturer specifications at several different engine speeds.

❑ DISTRIBUTORLESS SYSTEM SERVICE

Standard test procedures using an oscilloscope, ohmmeter, and timing light can be used to diagnose problems in distributorless ignition systems. Keep in mind, however, that problems involving one cylinder may also occur in its companion cylinder that fires off the same coil. Some oscilloscopes require their pickups placed on each pair of cylinders to view all patterns. Special adapters are available to make these hookups less troublesome. Many newer engine analyzers with an oscilloscope use a single adapter that allows viewing of all cylinder patterns at one time.

Following the testing procedures outlined in the vehicle service manual for DIS systems and other computer-controlled ignition systems. Specific computer-generated trouble codes are designed to help troubleshoot ignition problems on computer-controlled-systems. Steps for the removal and inspection of coil packs and the ignition module are illustrated in Photo Sequence 9, which is included in this chapter.

❑ KNOCK SENSORS

Most computer-controlled systems use knock sensors to retard timing when the engine is experiencing pinging or knocking. Obviously, a faulty knock sensor produces problems that appear ignition system related.

CASE STUDY

Case 1

A customer complains that his vehicle runs poorly, misfiring, and losing power. He is embarrassed because he just performed his first ever preventive maintenance job on the vehicle—replacing spark plugs and ignition cables. He insists he did the job correctly. The problem must be somewhere else in the system.

Since the problem did not occur until after the customer worked on the vehicle, the technician begins troubleshooting by inspecting the plugs and cables. The job appears to be carefully and neatly done. The technician pulls a plug and inspects it. It is properly gapped, cleaned, and has been installed snugly, but not too tightly. The cables are not top quality but have been carefully and neatly installed and routed. Too neatly the technician suspects. At one point, three ignition cables have been wrapped together with several turns of electrical tape. It makes for a neat, tight appearance, but may be causing an inductive crossfire situation. The high secondary voltage in a firing plug's ignition cable may be inducing a voltage in the wire running parallel to it, causing it to fire a plug out of turn. The technician removes the tape and routes the wire according to service manual instructions. A test drive confirms this was the problem. Remember, neatly wrapped and routed plug wire may look nice, but engine performance problems could result.

Summary

- Sound wiring and connections are extremely important in modern electronic- and computer-controlled ignition systems. Loose connections, corrosion, and dirt can adversely affect performance.
- Many late-model vehicles use dielectric grease on connector terminals to seal out dirt and moisture.
- Wires, connections, and ignition components can be tested for intermittent failure by wiggling them or stress testing by applying heat, cold, or moisture.
- The oscilloscope can look inside the ignition system by giving the technician a visual representation of voltage changes over time.
- The trace patterns of the oscilloscope can be viewed in several different modes and scales. Both secondary and primary circuit patterns can be viewed.
- Trace patterns can be broken down into three main sections or zones: the firing section, intermediate section, and dwell section.

PHOTO SEQUENCE 9

☐ REMOVING AND REPLACING VARIOUS DIS COMPONENTS

P9-1 Late-model engines are equipped with different components than older models and are not equipped with some that were used for many years.

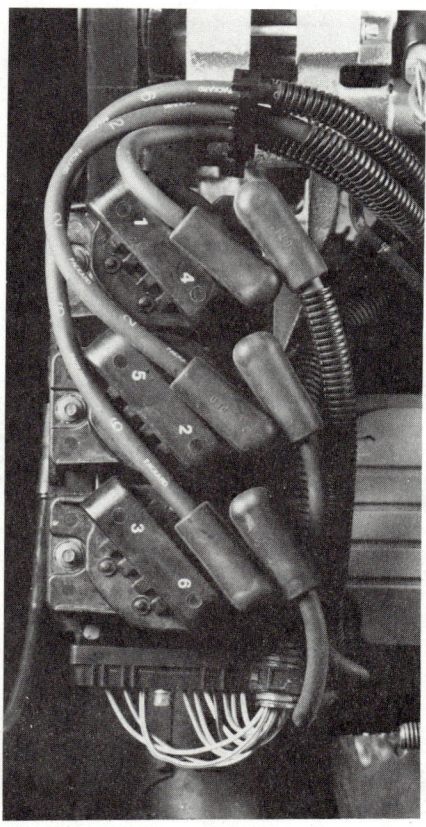

P9-2 This coil pack replaces the ignition coil and distributor assembly.

P9-3 Prior to removing or installing any electronic components, it is wise to disconnect the negative battery cable from the battery.

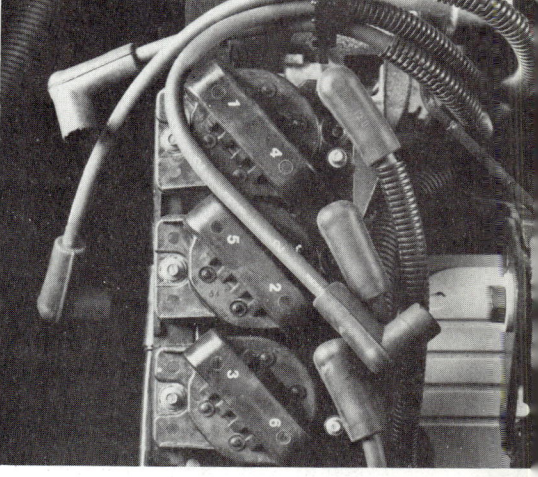

P9-4 The coil pack is removed by first disconnecting the spark plug wires from the coils. Prior to doing this, make sure their exact location is marked.

P9-5 Unbolt the assembly from the engine block.

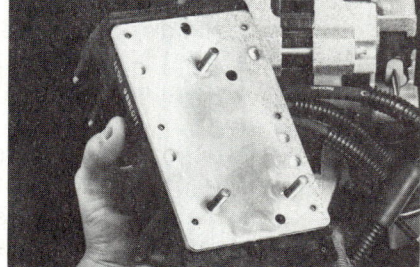

P9-6 The individual coils are bolted to the mounting plate that also houses the ignition module. If a coil or the module is to be replaced, unbolt it from the assembly. *(continued)*

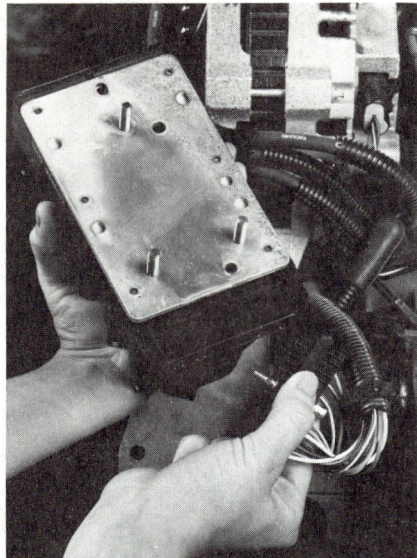

P9-7 Often, service of the assembly is done with the unit totally disconnected from the engine. To do this, loosen the remaining bolt on the electrical connector and pull the connector off the assembly. It is now free from the engine.

P9-8 Another integral part of the DIS system is the throttle position sensor (TPS).

P9-9 To remove this sensor and many other similar components, disconnect the electrical connector and loosen the assembly retaining bolts.

P9-10 Spark plug location has not changed on DIS engines. To disconnect the spark plug wires from the plugs, grasp the boot and twist while pulling off the wire.

P9-11 Spark plugs are removed in the normal manner with a spark plug socket and ratchet. ■

- The firing line and spark line of the firing section indicate firing voltage and spark duration.
- The intermediate section shows coil voltage dissipation.
- The dwell section shows the activation of primary coil current flow and primary coil current switch off. The primary current off signal is also the firing line for the next cylinder in the firing order.
- Dwell can be either fixed or variable. Variable dwell ignition systems gradually increase ignition dwell as engine speed increases.
- Ignition systems with current limiting, saturate the ignition coil very quickly with a very high current flow and then cut back or limit current flow to the small flow needed to maintain saturation. This system extends coil life.
- Precautions must always be taken to avoid open circuits during ignition system testing. A special test plug is used to limit coil output during testing.
- Spark duration should be at least 0.8 millisecond. The minimum acceptable spark duration can be computed in percent of dwell if the engine rpm is known.
- Firing voltages are normally between 7 and 13 kV with no more than 3 kV variation between cylinders.
- High secondary circuit resistance produces a higher than normal firing line.
- Individual ignition components are commonly tested for excessive internal resistance using an ohmmeter. A voltmeter or oscilloscope can also be used to monitor their operating voltages.
- Proper spark plug gapping and installation is very important to ignition system operation. Spark plug condition, such as cold fouling, wet fouling, and glazing is often a good indication of performance problems.
- Proper dwell and base timing are very important to ignition system operation. Although dwell is not adjustable on electronic systems, it still should be checked, particularly the operation of variable dwell.
- To properly set base timing, all mechanical, vacuum, or computer-controlled advance mechanisms must be temporarily disabled.

Review Questions

1. Name the three types of stress testing used to test for intermittent ignition component problems and list the procedures for conducting each type of test.
2. Outline the typical procedure for checking base timing including the steps taken to disable any

mechanical, vacuum, or computer-controlled advance systems.
3. Name the three types of trace pattern display modes used on an oscilloscope and give examples of when each mode is most useful.
4. List the common types of spark plug fouling and the typical problems each type of fouling indicates.
5. List at least two methods of checking the operation of Hall-effect sensors.
6. Upon inspection, a spark plug reveals a layer of dry, fluffy black carbon deposits on its tip. Technician A says the plug cannot be used again. Technician B says the plug can be cleaned and serviced, then reused. Who is correct?
   a. Technician A
   b. Technician B
   c. Both A and B
   d. Neither A nor B
7. On an oscilloscope, which section ends with the primary coil current off signal?
   a. intermediate
   b. dwell
   c. firing
   d. both a and b
8. The firing line on an oscilloscope pattern extends below the waveform. Technician A says the polarity of the coil is reversed. Technician B says the problem is fouled spark plugs. Who is correct?
   a. Technician A
   b. Technician B
   c. Both A and B
   d. Neither A nor B
9. The firing lines on an oscilloscope pattern are all abnormally low. Technician A says the problem is probably low coil output. Technician B says the problem could be an overly rich air/fuel mixture. Who is correct?
   a. Technician A
   b. Technician B
   c. Both A and B
   d. Neither A nor B
10. Technician A says that dielectric grease is used to seal dirt and moisture out of electrical terminals. Technician B says it is used to dissipate heat away from sensitive electrical components. Who is correct?
    a. Technician A
    b. Technician B
    c. Both A and B
    d. Neither A nor B
11. Which of the following ignition components have the ability to generate electromagnetic interference?
    a. spark plug wires
    b. alternator coil
    c. ignition coil
    d. all of the above
12. Leaner air/fuel mixtures, _____ .
    a. decrease the electrical resistance inside the cylinder and decrease the required firing voltage
    b. increase the electrical resistance inside the cylinder and increase the required firing voltage
    c. increase the electrical resistance inside the cylinder and decrease the required firing voltage
    d. have no measurable effect on cylinder resistance
13. The spark line of the trace pattern begins about _____ the way up the firing line.
    a. 1/8 to 1/4
    b. 1/4 to 1/3
    c. 1/2 to 3/4
    d. 3/4 to 7/8
14. Technician A says the vehicle does not run if the variable dwell function of the control module fails. Technician B says the vehicle may still run for a time before failing completely. Who is correct?
    a. Technician A
    b. Technician B
    c. Both A and B
    d. Neither A nor B
15. If the primary winding of the ignition coil develops excessive resistance, the current limiting blip on the dwell section of the pattern trace may _____ .
    a. disappear
    b. become more prominent
    c. shift to the intermediate section of the trace
    d. none of the above
16. During a cranking output test _____ .
    a. firing line voltage should exceed 20 kV
    b. firing line voltage should exceed 35 kV
    c. firing line voltage should exceed 50 kV
    d. the use of test plugs are not recommended
17. Most electronic ignition systems have a spark duration of approximately _____ .
    a. 0.5 millisecond
    b. 0.8 millisecond
    c. 1.5 milliseconds
    d. 2.5 milliseconds

20 FUEL SYSTEMS

Objectives

- Describe the four performance characteristics of gasoline.
- Describe the various types of gasoline and additives.
- Describe the different alternative fuels, including diesel.
- Define the fuel delivery system components and their functions, including the fuel tank, fuel lines, filters, and pump.
- Conduct inspecting and servicing procedures for a fuel system.
- Describe an electronic fuel system.

The automobile's fuel system is both simple and complicated. It is simple in the systems that transfer fuel to the engine and complex in the carburetor or fuel injector system that mixes fuel with air in the correct amounts and proportion to meet all needs of the engine.

This chapter focuses on the simple part of the fuel system. It covers the basic parts of the fuel delivery or transport system, including the fuel tank, lines, filters, and pump (Figure 20-1). The fuel transport portion of the system is very important in the operation of a gasoline driven vehicle. To fully understand the automotive fuel system, a knowledge of the performance of petroleum-based fuel used to power the engine is necessary. Although there are several different types of fuels, gasoline is the most commonly used motor fuel and is given primary consideration in this chapter. Diesel fuel and other alternative fuels are briefly discussed.

WARNING: *Extreme care should be used while working with any of the components of the fuel system. Gasoline is a very volatile and flammable substance. Do not expose it to an open flame, spark, or high heat. Disconnect the negative terminal of the battery before doing any task that releases gasoline from any part of the system. Use containers to catch the gasoline and cloths to wipe up the minor spills. Use a flashlight rather than a trouble light or drop light. Gasoline spilled on a hot bulb could cause the bulb to explode and ignite the gasoline. Never attempt to weld a fuel tank. Even when a fuel tank is empty, it can still contain enough gas fumes to cause an explosion if the fumes come in contact with a flame or excessive heat. Always keep a class B fire extinguisher nearby. It is specially intended for use on gasoline fires.*

❑ GASOLINE

Crude oil, as removed from the earth, is a mixture of hydrocarbon compounds ranging from gases to heavy tars and waxes. The crude oil can be refined into products such as lubricating oils, greases, asphalts, kerosene, diesel fuel, gasoline, and natural gas. Before its widespread use in the internal combustion engine of automobiles, gasoline was an unwanted byproduct of refining for oils and kerosene.

Two important factors affect the power and efficiency of a gasoline engine—compression ratio and detonation (abnormal combustion). The higher the compression ratio, the greater the engine's power output and efficiency. The better the efficiency, the less fuel consumed to produce a given power output. To have a high compression ratio requires an engine of greater structural integrity. Due to the use of low-octane unleaded gasoline in post-1975 models, compression ratios now generally range from 8:1 to 10:1. High performance cars may have higher compression ratios.

Normal combustion occurs gradually in each cylinder. The flame front (the edge of the burning area) advances smoothly across the combustion chamber until all the air/fuel mixture has been burned (Figure 20-2). Detonation occurs when the flame front fails to reach a pocket of mixture before the temperature in that area reaches the point of self-ignition. Normal burning at the start of the combustion cycle raises the temperature and pressure of everything in the cylinder. The last part of the air/fuel mixture is both heated and pressurized, and the combination of those two factors

Fuel Systems 493

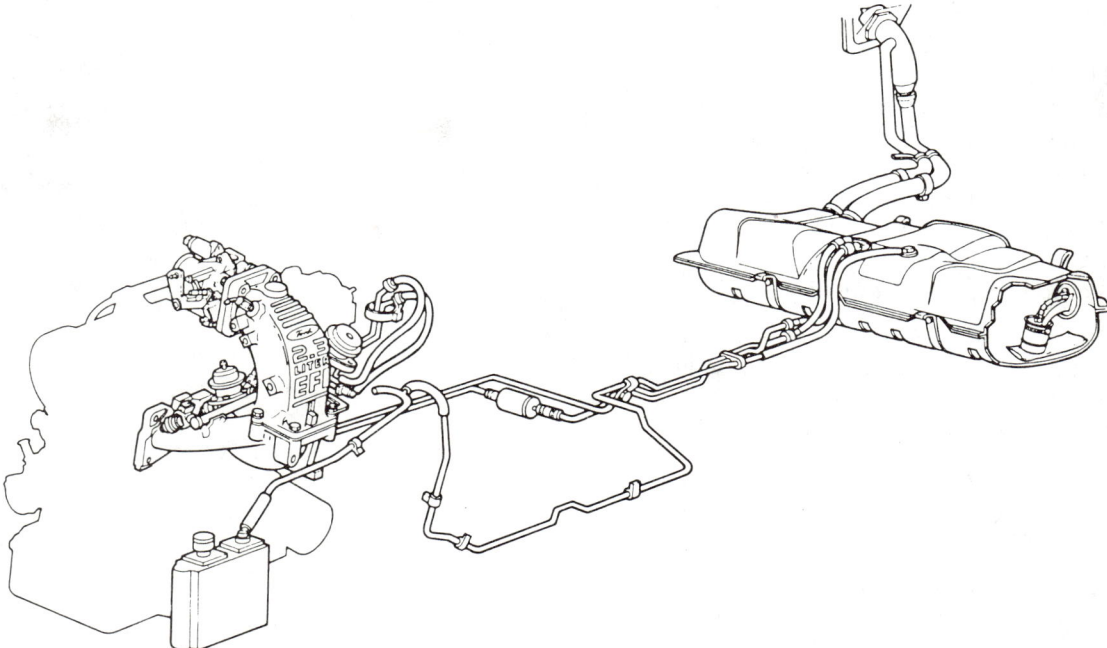

Figure 20-1 Typical fuel delivery system.

can raise it to the self-ignition point. At that moment, the remaining mixture burns almost instantaneously. The two flame fronts create a pressure wave between them that can destroy cylinder head gaskets, break piston rings, and burn pistons and exhaust valves. When detonation occurs, a hammering, pinging, or knocking sound is heard. But, when the engine is operating at high speed, these sounds cannot be heard because of motor and road noise.

☐ FUEL PERFORMANCE

Many of the performance characteristics of gasoline can be controlled in refining and blending to provide proper engine function and vehicle driveability. The major factors affecting fuel performance are antiknock quality, volatility, sulfur content, and deposit control.

Antiknock Quality

An octane number or rating was developed by the petroleum industry so the antiknock quality of a gasoline could be rated. The octane number is a measure of the fuel's tendency not to produce knock in an engine. The higher the octane number, the lesser the tendency to knock. By itself, the antiknock rating has nothing to do with fuel economy or engine efficiency.

Two commonly used methods for determining the octane number of motor gasolines are the motor octane number (MON) method and the research octane number (RON) method. Both use a laboratory single-cylinder engine equipped with a variable head and knock meter to indicate knock intensity. The test sample is used as fuel, and the engine compression ratio and air/fuel mixture are adjusted to develop a specified knock intensity. There are two primary standard reference fuels, isooctane and heptane. Isooctane does not knock in an engine, but is not used in gasoline because of its expense. Heptane knocks severely in an engine. Isooctane has an octane number of 100. Heptane has an octane number of zero.

A fuel of unknown octane value is run in the special test engine and the severity of knock is measured.

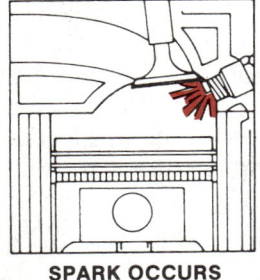
SPARK OCCURS

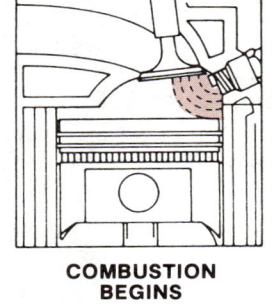
COMBUSTION BEGINS

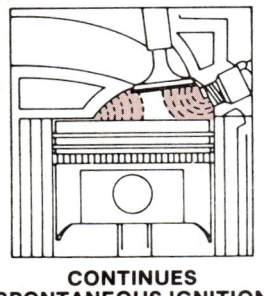
CONTINUES (SPONTANEOUS IGNITION)

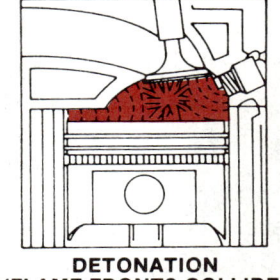
DETONATION (FLAME FRONTS COLLIDE)

Figure 20-2 The stages of combustion that lead to detonation.

Various proportions of heptane and isooctane are run in the test engine to duplicate the severity of the knock of the fuel being tested. When the knock caused by the heptane/isooctane mixture is identical to the test fuel, the octane number is established by the percentage of isooctane in the mixture. For example, if 85% isooctane and 15% heptane produce the same severity of knock as the fuel in question, the fuel is assigned an octane number of 85.

Factors that affect knock follow.

LEAN FUEL MIXTURE A lean mixture burns slower than a rich mixture. The heat of combustion is higher, which promotes the tendency for unburned fuel in front of the spark-ignited flame to detonate.

IGNITION TIMING OVERADVANCED Advancing the ignition timing induces knock. Slowing ignition timing suppresses knock.

COMPRESSION RATIO Compression ratio affects knock because cylinder pressures are increased with the increase in compression ratio.

VALVE TIMING Valve timing that fills the cylinder with more air/fuel mixture promotes higher cylinder pressures, increasing the chances for detonation.

TURBOCHARGING Turbocharging or supercharging forces additional fuel and air into the cylinder. This induces higher cylinder pressures and promotes knock.

COOLANT TEMPERATURE Hotspots in the cylinder or combustion chamber due to inefficient cooling or a damaged cooling system raise combustion chamber temperatures and promote knock.

CYLINDER-TO-CYLINDER DISTRIBUTION If an engine has poor distribution of the air/fuel mixture from cylinder to cylinder, the leaner cylinders could promote knock.

EXCESSIVE CARBON DEPOSITS The accumulation of carbon deposits on the piston, valves, and combustion chamber causes poor heat transfer from the combustion chamber. Carbon accumulation also artificially increases the compression ratio. Both conditions cause knock.

AIR INLET TEMPERATURE The higher the air temperature when it enters the cylinder, the greater the tendency to knock.

COMBUSTION CHAMBER SHAPE The optimum combustion chamber shape for reduced knocking is hemispherical with a spark plug located in the center (Figure 20-3). This hemi-head allows for faster combustion, allowing less time for detonation to occur ahead of the flame front.

OCTANE NUMBER Only when an engine is designed and adjusted to take advantage of the higher octane gasoline can the value of the fuel be obtained. Most modern engines are designed to operate efficiently with regular grade gasoline and do not require a high-octane premium grade.

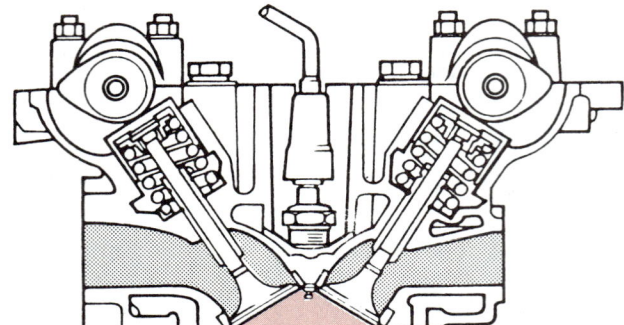

Figure 20-3 Cross section of a hemispherical combustion chamber.

Volatility

As stated earlier, gasoline is very volatile. It readily evaporates so its vapor adequately mixes with air for combustion. Only vaporized fuel supports combustion. To ensure complete combustion, complete vaporization must occur.

The volatility of gasoline affects the following performance characteristics or driving conditions.

COLD STARTING AND WARMUP A fuel can cause hard starting, hesitation, and stumbling during warmup if it does not vaporize readily. A fuel that vaporizes too easily in hot weather can form vapor bubbles in the fuel line and fuel pump, resulting in vapor lock or loss of performance.

TEMPERATURE Because a highly volatile fuel vaporizes at a lower temperature than a less volatile fuel, winter grade gasoline is more volatile than summer grade gasoline.

ALTITUDE Gasoline vaporizes more easily at high altitudes, so volatility is controlled in blending according to the elevation of the place where fuel is sold.

CARBURETOR ICING PROTECTION Carburetor icing is not as common in modern engines as in older engines. It can occur when ambient temperatures reach between 28 to 55 degrees Fahrenheit and the relative humidity rises above 65%. The humid air enters the carburetor and mixes with drops of fuel. When the fuel evaporates, it removes heat from the air and surrounding metal parts. When this occurs, the throttle temperature is rapidly lowered to below 32 degrees Fahrenheit (if the ambient temperature is within the range indicated), and condensing water vapor forms ice. The ice causes the engine to stall if it is idling during this phase.

CRANKCASE OIL DILUTION A fuel must vaporize well to prevent diluting the crankcase oil with liquid fuel. If parts of the gasoline do not vaporize, droplets of liquid break down the oil film on the cylinder wall, causing scuffing or scoring. The liquid eventually enters the crankcase oil and results in the formation of sludge, gum, and varnish accumulation as well as decreasing the lubrication properties of the oil.

DRIVEABILITY Poor vaporization can also affect the distribution of fuel from cylinder to cylinder since vaporized fuel travels farther and faster in the manifold.

Sulfur Content

Gasoline can contain some of the sulfur present in the crude oil. Sulfur content is reduced at the refinery to limit the amount of corrosion it can cause in the engine and exhaust system.

When the hydrogen in the hydrocarbon of the fuel is burned with air, one of the products of combustion is water. Water leaves the combustion chamber as steam but can condense back to water when passing through a cool exhaust system. When the engine is shut off and cools, steam condenses back to a liquid and forms water droplets. Steam present in crankcase blowby also condenses to water.

When the sulfur in the fuel is burned, it combines with oxygen to form sulfur dioxide. This sulfur dioxide can then combine with water to form highly corrosive sulfuric acid. This type of corrosion is the leading cause of exhaust valve pitting and exhaust system deterioration. With catalysts, the sulfur dioxide can cause the obnoxious odor of rotten eggs during vehicle warm-up. To reduce corrosion caused by sulfuric acid, the sulfur content in gasoline is limited to less than 0.01%.

Deposit Control

Several additives are put in gasoline to control harmful deposits, including gum or oxidation inhibitors, detergents, metal deactivators, and rust inhibitors.

❏ BASIC FUELS

For many years, lead compounds such as tetraethyl lead (TEL) and tetramethyl lead (TML) were added to gasoline to improve its octane ratings. However, since the mid-1970s, vehicles have been designed to run on unleaded gasoline only. Leaded fuels are no longer available as automotive fuels. The main reason for the change to unleaded gasoline was to provide a fuel for cars with special antipollution devices—catalytic converters. These systems must have unleaded fuel in order to work properly.

Because of the deactivating or poisoning effect lead has on the catalyst, gasolines are limited to a lead content of 0.06 gram per gallon. Since TEL or TML is not added to unleaded gasolines, the required octane number is obtained by blending compounds of the required octane quality. Methylcylopentadienyl manganese tricarbonyl (MMT) is a catalyst-compatible octane improver. Vehicles with catalytic converters are labeled at both the fuel gauge and fuel filler—unleaded fuel only.

❏ GASOLINE ADDITIVES

At one time, all a gasoline-producing company had to do to produce their product was pump the crude from the ground, run it through the refinery to separate the fractions, dump in a couple of grams of lead per gallon, and deliver the finished product to the service station. Of course, automobiles were much simpler then and what they burned was not very critical. As long as gasoline vaporized easily and did not cause the low compression engines to knock, everything was fine.

Times have changed. Today, refiners are under constant pressure to ensure that their product passes a series of rigorous tests for seasonal volatility, minimum octane, existent gum and oxidation stability as well as add the correct deicers and detergents to make the product competitive in a price-sensitive marketplace.

Gasoline additives—primarily used in unleaded types—have different properties and a variety of uses.

Anti-Icing or Deicer

Isopropyl alcohol is added seasonally to gasoline as an anti-icing agent to prevent gas line freeze-up in cold climates.

Metal Deactivators and Rust Inhibitors

These additives are used to inhibit reactions between the fuel and the metals in the fuel system that can form abrasive and filter-plugging substances.

Gum or Oxidation Inhibitors

During storage, harmful gum deposits can form due to the reaction of some gasoline components with each other and with oxygen. Oxidation inhibitors are added to promote gasoline stability. They help control gum, deposit formation, and staleness. Stale gasoline becomes cloudy and smells like paint thinner.

Gasoline must not leave excessive deposits, gums, or varnishes on engine parts exposed to fuel before and after combustion. An undesirable residue is gum, a sticky substance, which can harden into varnish as it absorbs heat and oxygen. Gum content is also influenced by the age of the gasoline and its exposure to oxygen and certain metals such as copper. If gasoline is allowed to evaporate, the residue left can form gum and varnish.

Gasoline must have as little gum residue as possible to prevent gum formation in the intake manifold, carburetor or fuel injectors, and on intake valve stems. Some gasolines contain aromatic amines and phenols to prevent formation of gum and varnish.

Detergents

The use of detergent additives in gasoline has been the subject of some public confusion. Detergent additives are designed to do only what their name implies—clean certain critical components inside the engine. They do not affect octane.

Ethanol

By far the most widely used gasoline additive today is ethanol, or grain alcohol. Ethanol's value as an octane enhancer becomes more apparent when considered in the context of the government-mandated phasedown of tetraethyl lead. Blending 10% ethanol into gasoline is seen as a comparatively inexpensive octane booster that results in an increase of 2.5 to 3 road octane points. One of the biggest arguments against the use of ethanol in gasoline is that it increases gasoline volatility. However, for gasoline with a normal volatility for the geographic region and the season, a 10% ethanol blend should not contribute to any driveability problems.

In addition to octane enhancement, ethanol blending keeps the carburetor or fuel injectors clean due to detergent additive packages found in most of the ethanol marketed. It also inhibits fuel system and injection corrosion due to additive packages and decreases carbon monoxide emissions at the tail pipe due to the higher oxygen content of blended fuel.

Ethanol-blended motor fuels are not, according to ethanol industry spokesmen, to be referred to as gasohol. That term stopped being used in the late 1970s because it conveys a negative image of what is intended as a modern octane enhancer and fuel extender.

Methanol

Methanol is the lightest and simplest of the alcohols and is also known as wood alcohol. It can be distilled from coal, but most of what is used today is derived from natural gas.

In the early 1980s, a few companies began selling a blend of 5% methanol in gasoline in the Northeast and Midwest. This showed that methanol plus anticorrosion co-solvents could compete in the motor fuel market as an octane enhancer. Today, both GM and Ford have working prototypes on the road that can burn any combination of fuel from nearly neat methanol (85% methanol with 15% gasoline) to straight gasoline. The key is a fuel line sensor that detects methanol concentration and adjusts spark timing and air/fuel mixture accordingly. The federal government is pushing for methanol acceptance through industry incentives and fleet-sponsored programs.

For now, however, many auto makers continue to warn motorists about using a fuel that contains more than 10% methanol and co-solvents by volume. Methanol is recognized as being far more corrosive to fuel system components than ethanol, and it is this corrosion that has auto makers concerned.

MTBE

Methyl tertiary butyl ether (MTBE) has become very popular in the past few years as an octane enhancer and supply extender because of excellent compatibility with gasoline. Current U.S. EPA restrictions on oxygenates limit MTBE in unleaded gasoline to 11% of volume. At that level, it increases pump octane (RM/2) by 2.5 points. However, it is usually found in concentrations of 7 to 8% of volume.

MTBE has found favor among refiner/suppliers and independent marketers alike because it is not nearly as sensitive to moisture as the other oxygenates, has virtually no effect on fuel volatility, and can be shipped through product pipelines whereas ethanol and methanol blends cannot.

MTBE's prime asset in today's market is that it increases octane while reducing carbon monoxide emissions at the tail pipe and does it at a cost that makes it very attractive to gasoline marketers across the country.

Possibly the only major drawback to MTBE is its effect on fuel system elastomers and plastics. Studies have shown that gasoline containing MTBE (like those containing methanol, ethanol, or higher levels of aromatics) can lead to some swelling of elastomers but, in general, most cars manufactured since 1980 should not be affected. Although oxygenated blends and high aromatic gasolines caused some problems with these materials when they first hit the market, the auto manufacturers were quick to respond with new compounds that resist the effects of these additives.

☐ DIESEL FUEL

Diesel fuel, like gasoline, is made from petroleum. However, at the refinery, the petroleum is separated into three major components: gasoline, middle distillates, and all remaining substances. Diesel fuel comes from the middle distillate group, which has properties and characteristics different from gasoline.

The shape of the fuel spray, turbulence in the combustion chamber, beginning and duration of injection, and the chemical properties of the diesel fuel all affect the power output of the diesel engine. The significant chemical properties of diesel fuel are described briefly in the following paragraphs.

Viscosity

Viscosity is a measure of a fluid's resistance to flow. Low viscosity fluids flow easily; high viscosity fluids do

An ASE patch is the sign of a professional. To become certified, you must have an understanding of technical theory and of accepted diagnostic and repair procedures. To maintain certification, you must keep up with an ever-changing technology.

Today's automobiles are complex machines made up of many complicated systems.
Courtesy of Chrysler Corporation

ENGINES

Modern automobile engines are basically the same as older ones. However, technological advances have resulted in many new engine designs, as well as the use of new materials in the manufacturing process.

Courtesy of Chevrolet Motor Division—GMC

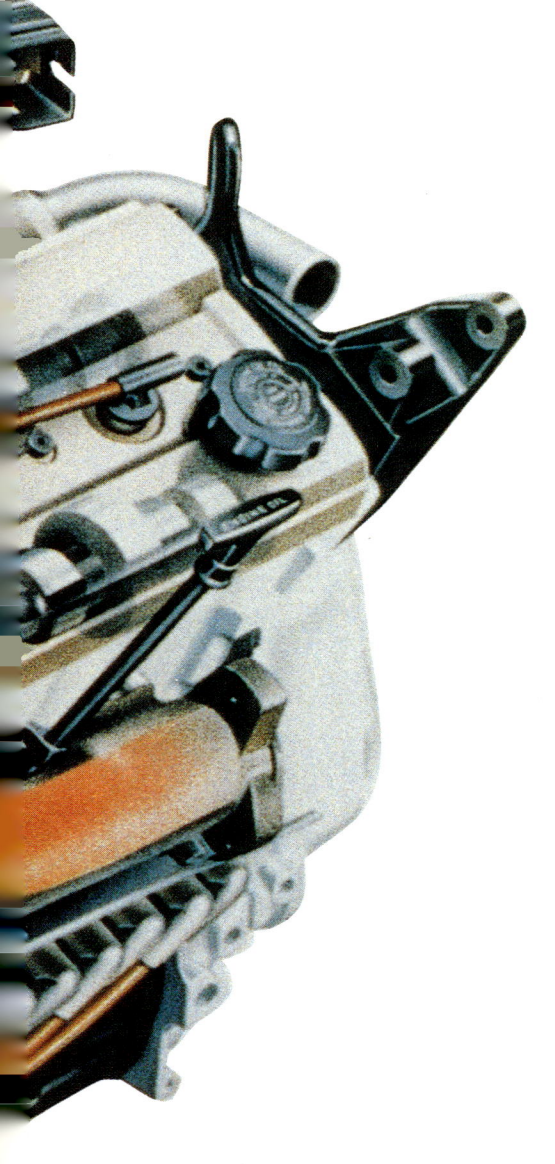

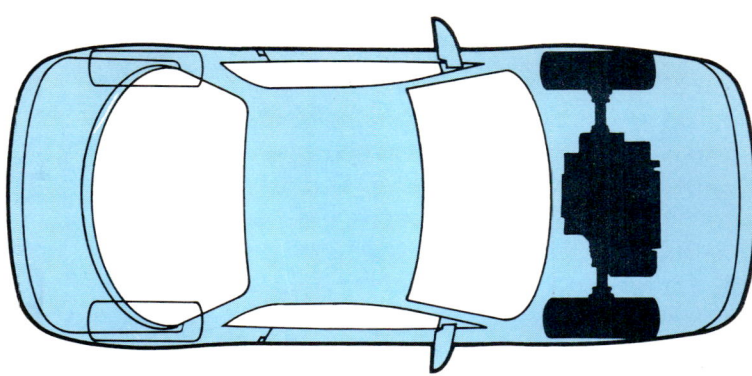

FRONT-WHEEL TRANSVERSE

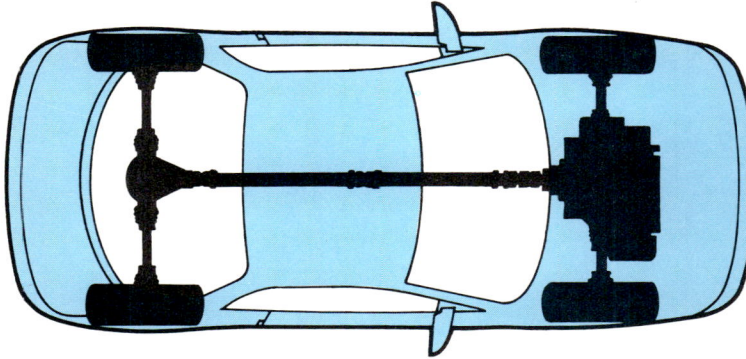

ALL-WHEEL TRANSVERSE

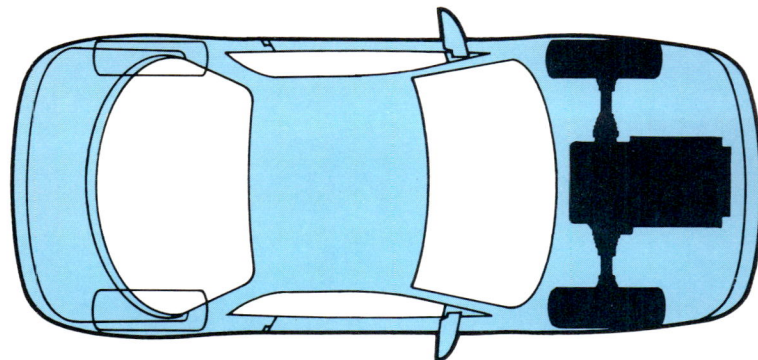

FRONT-WHEEL LONGITUDINAL

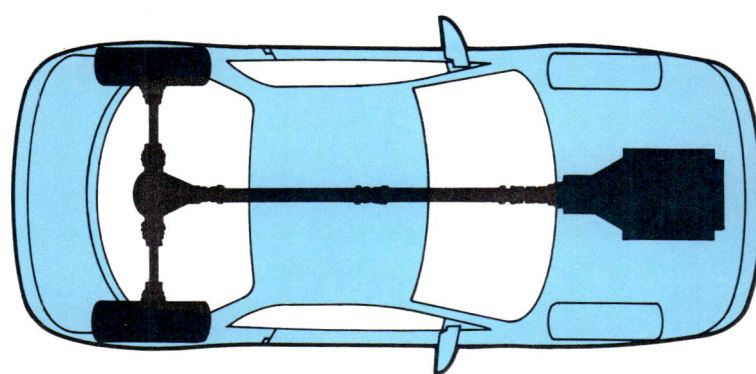

REAR-WHEEL LONGITUDINAL

Aerodynamics, fuel economy, and passenger safety and comfort have influenced the overall design of the automobile and the layout of the engine and its driveline.

ELECTRICAL SYSTEMS

Advances made in electronics have made the biggest impact on the industry. Microprocessors are used to control and monitor engine and driveline systems. Due to this electronic revolution, manufacturers have been able to produce cars that are more comfortable, safer, and more efficient.

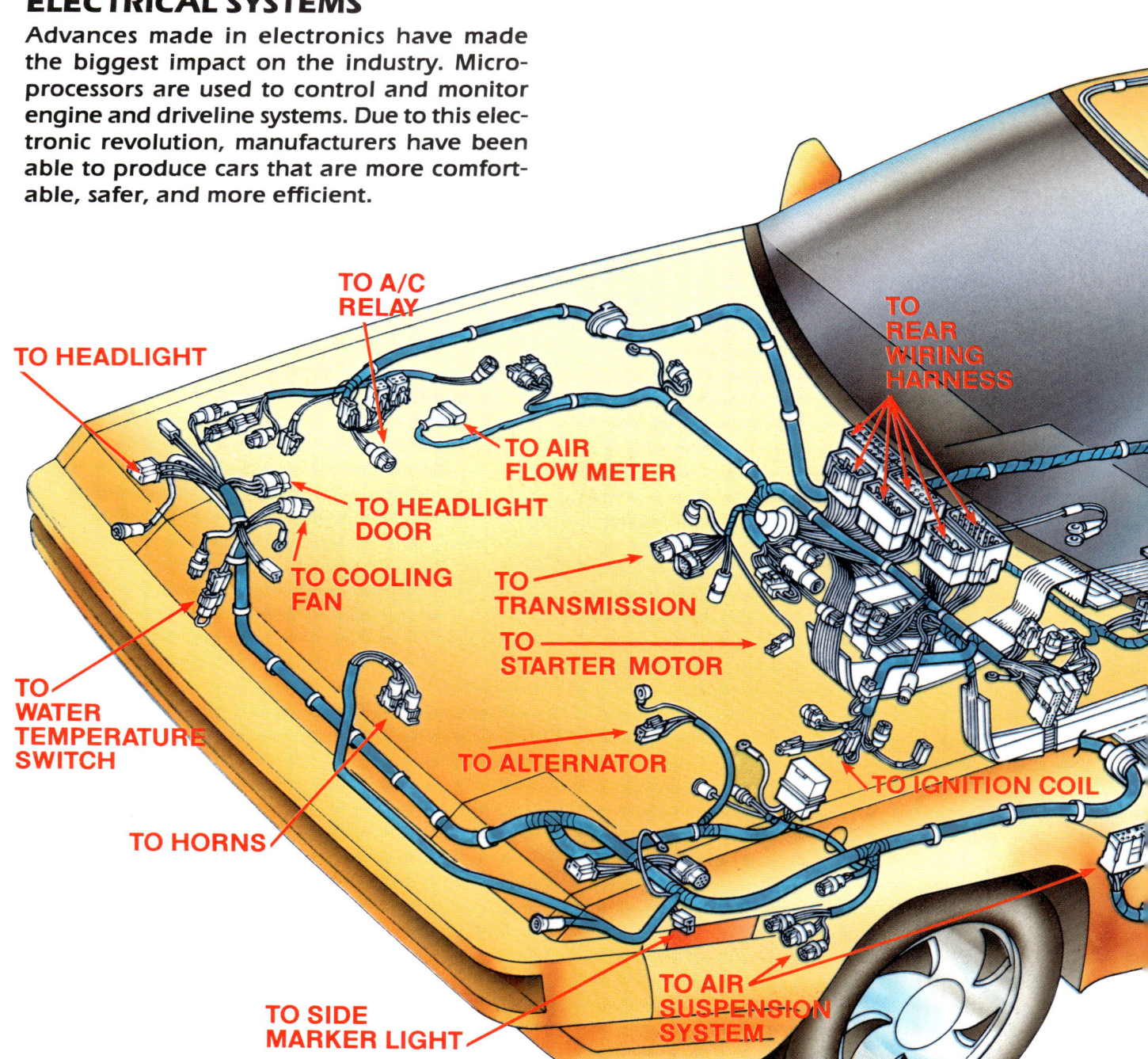

Diagnostic and repair procedures are rapidly changing. Electronics has introduced new terms and components, as well as new test equipment and procedures.

◀ TRUNK ELECTRICAL COMPONENTS

Courtesy of Cadillac Motor Car Division — GMC

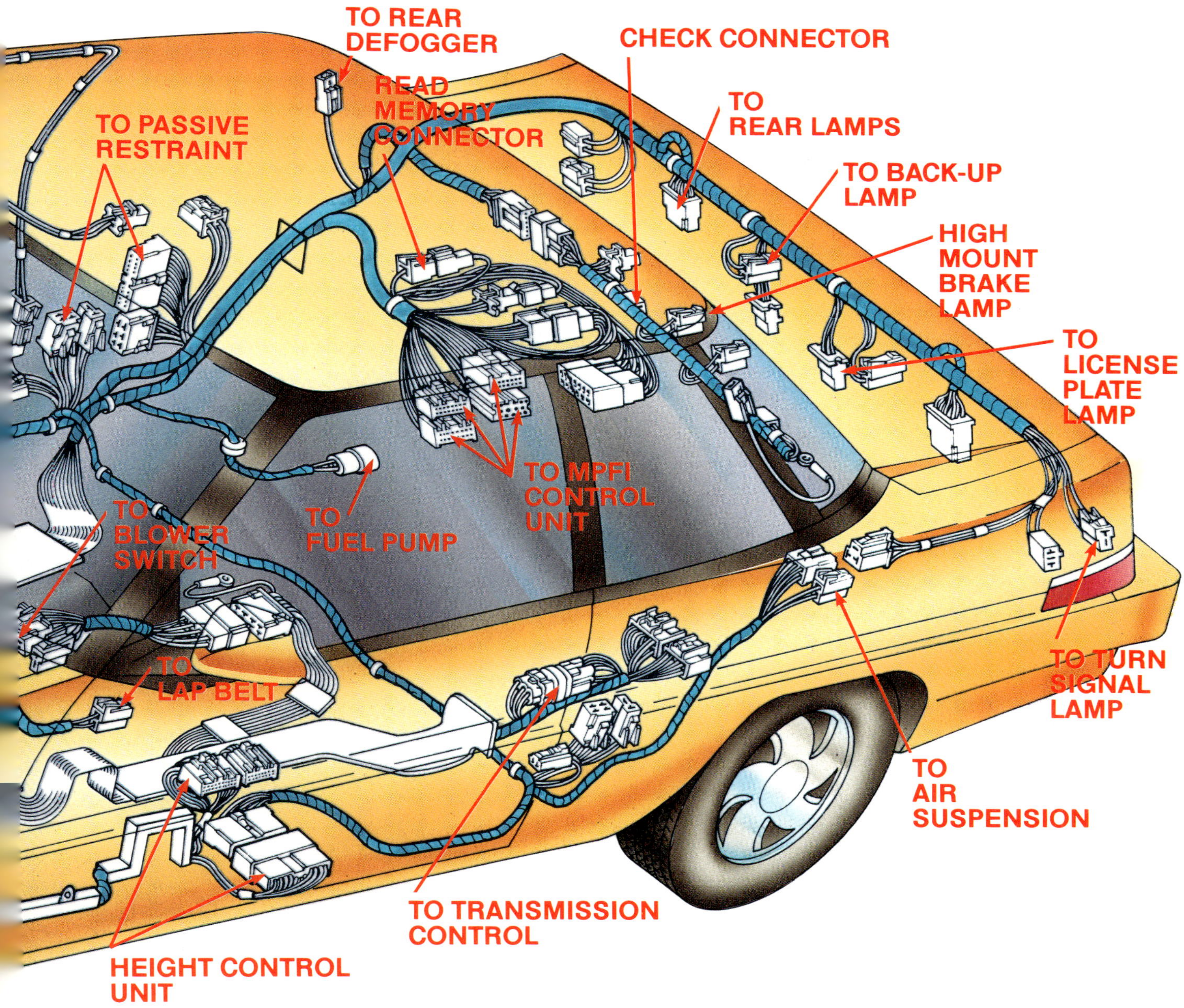

DIGITAL INSTRUMENT PANEL

Courtesy of Cadillac Motor Car Division—GMC

ANALOG INSTRUMENT PANEL

Courtesy of Ford Motor Company

ENGINE PEFORMANCE

No other major component of a car shows more evidence of the electronic revolution than the engine. A computer is used to integrate the various systems of the engine to ensure maximum efficiency.

Courtesy of Cleveland Institute of Electronics

Emission controls, the induction system, and the ignition circuit work together to improve driveability. Purely electronic systems have replaced many mechanical components, such as the distributor.

Courtesy of Ford Motor Company

Today's engines are much smaller than the engines of yesterday. Technology allows them to perform as well or better than the older-style engines. Many engines rely on superchargers or turbochargers for this performance.

Courtesy of Chevrolet Motor Division — GMC

Courtesy of Toyota Motor Corporation

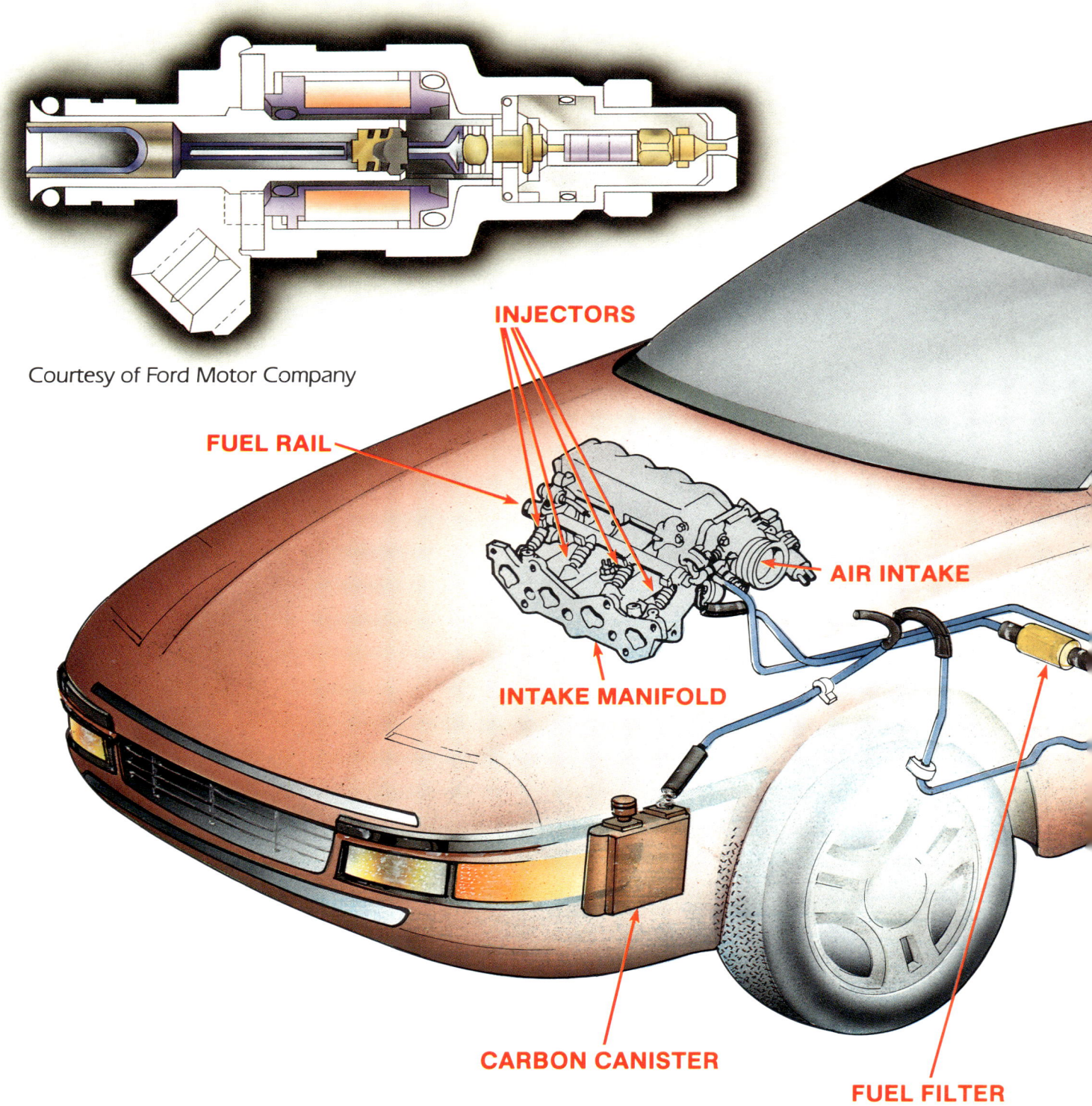

Courtesy of Ford Motor Company

INDUCTION SYSTEMS

Engine efficiency is affected by the induction system's ability to provide the correct air/fuel mixture under all conditions. Electronically-controlled fuel injection systems and tuned intakes provide this desired efficiency.

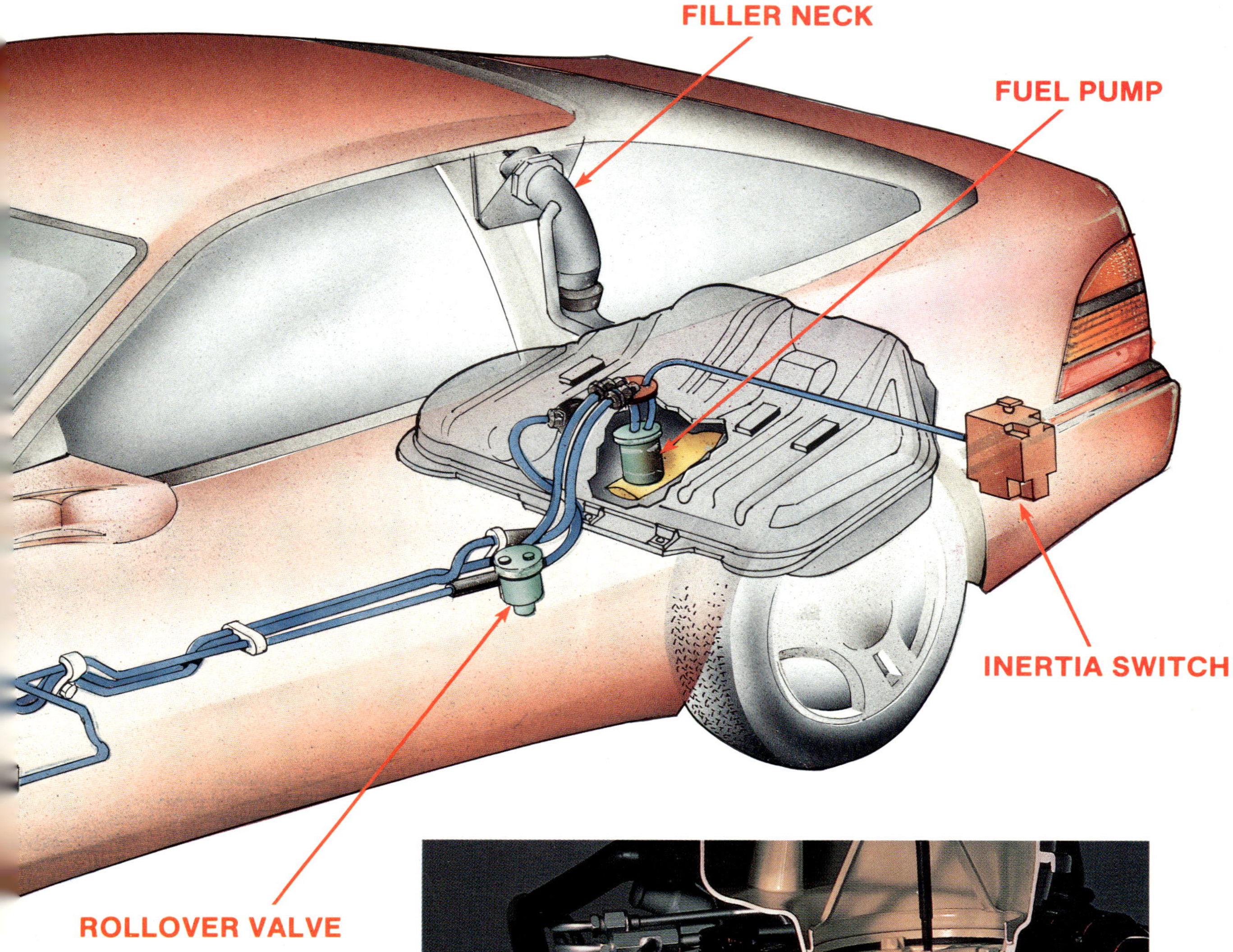

Courtesy of Cadillac Motor Car Division—GMC

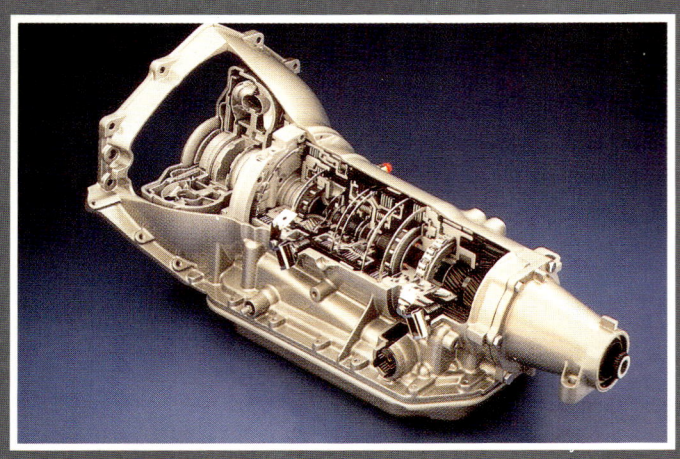

TRANSMISSIONS

Power from the engine is sent to the wheels by an efficient transmission. Both automatic and manually-shifted transmissions and transaxles have been modified to include additional speed gears and electronic controls to limit power loss.

Courtesy of General Motors Corporation

Courtesy of Toyota Motor Corporation

Courtesy of Chrysler Corporation

STEERING AND SUSPENSION SYSTEMS

Modifications to the car's steering and suspension systems permit aerodynamic styling and improve fuel economy by reducing the vehicle's weight.

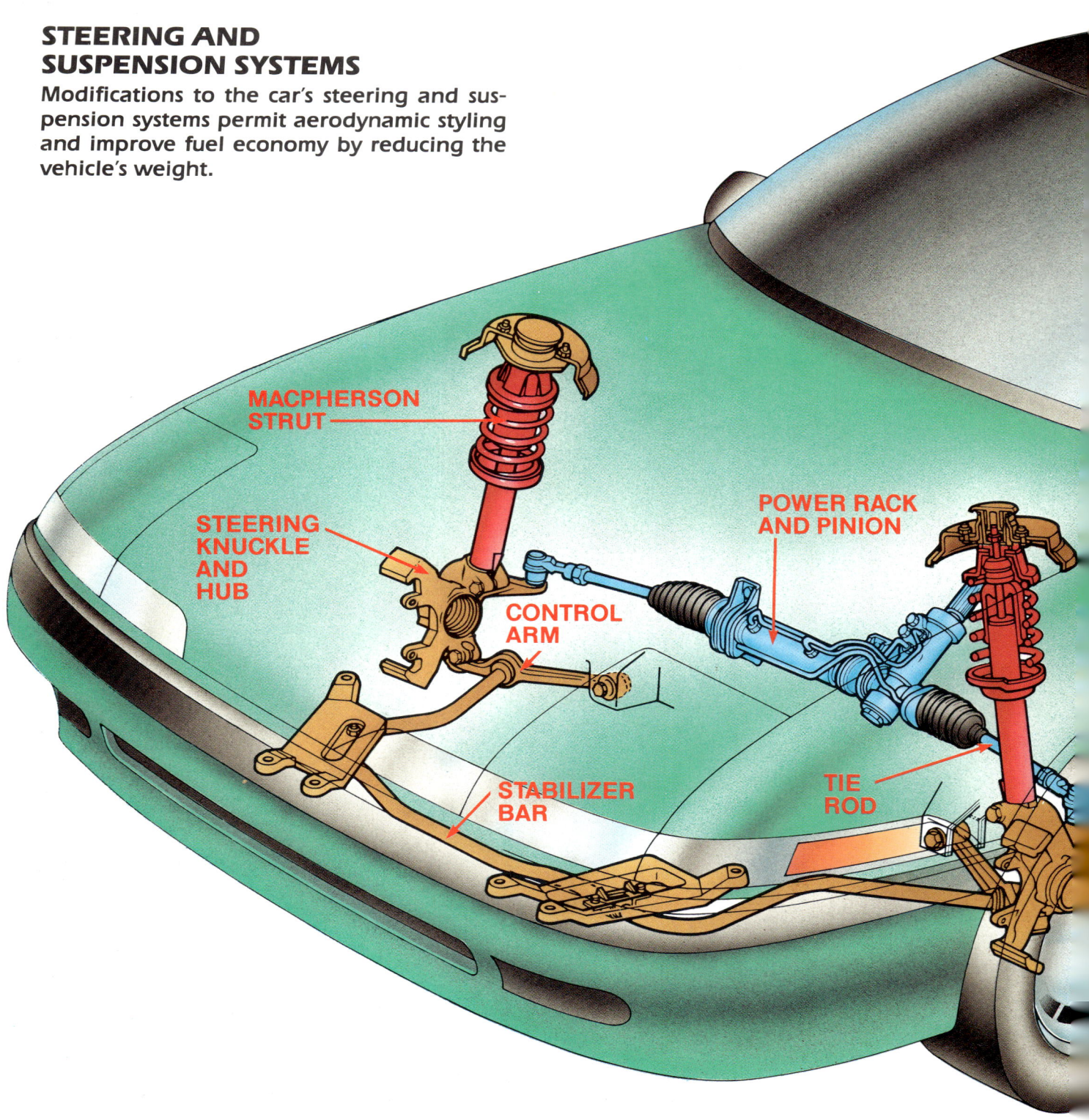

Electronic steering and suspension systems provide safety and comfort to passengers without sacrificing engine power.

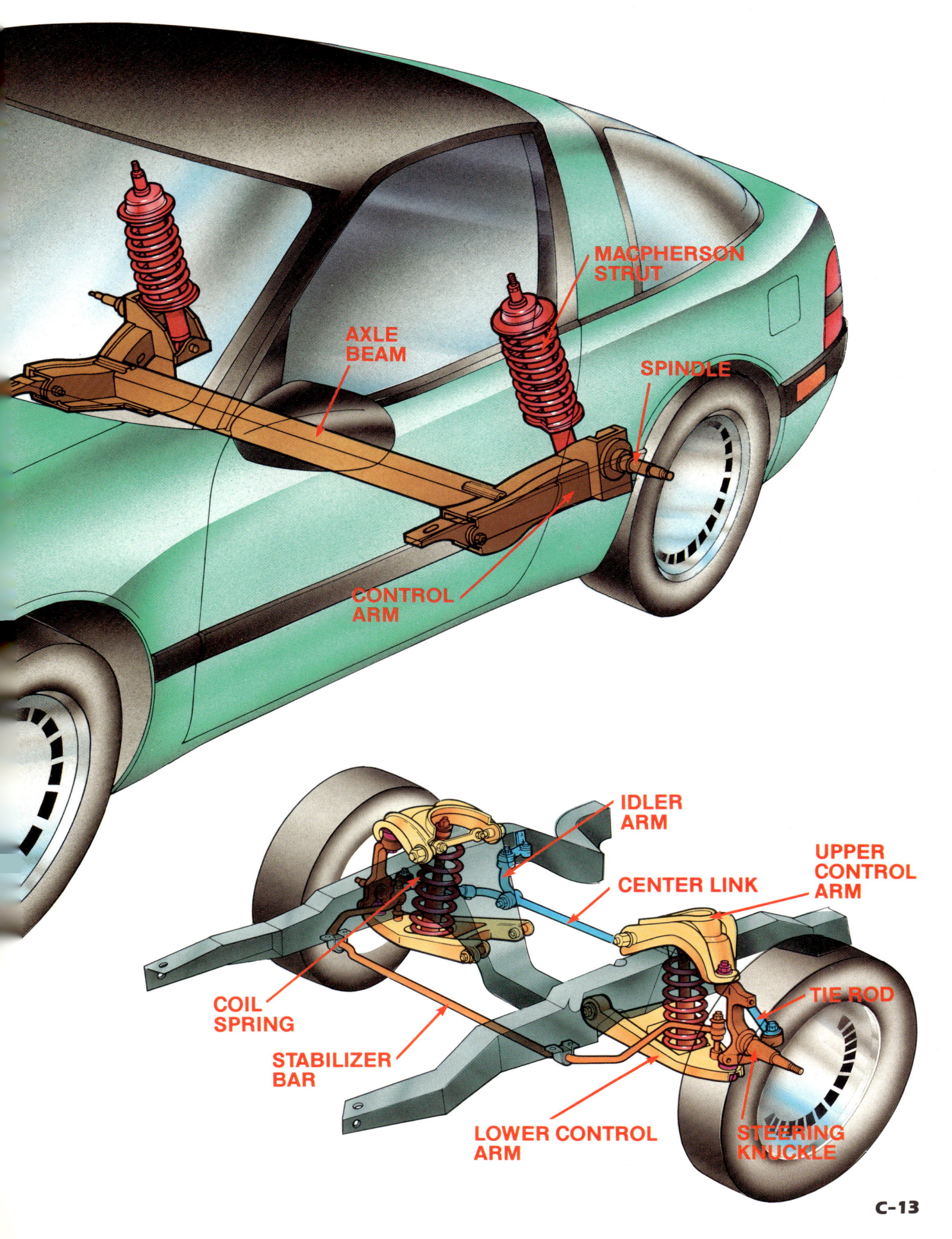

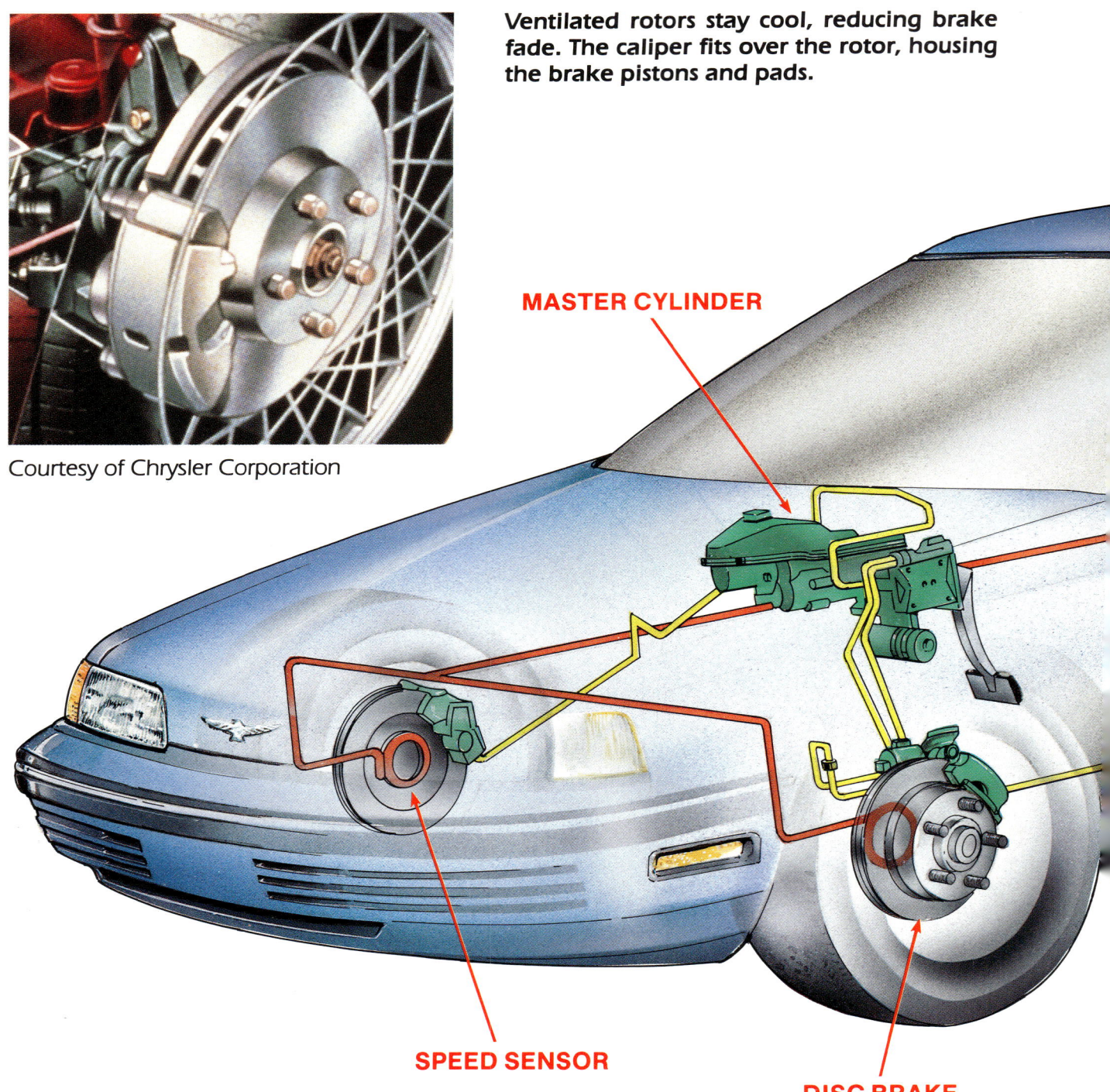

Ventilated rotors stay cool, reducing brake fade. The caliper fits over the rotor, housing the brake pistons and pads.

Courtesy of Chrysler Corporation

MASTER CYLINDER

SPEED SENSOR

DISC BRAKE

BRAKE SYSTEMS

Passenger safety has been a major focus of engineers. Today's cars are equipped with disc brakes on two or four wheels. The clamping power of this type of brake allows for quick and sure braking power, even after repeated use.

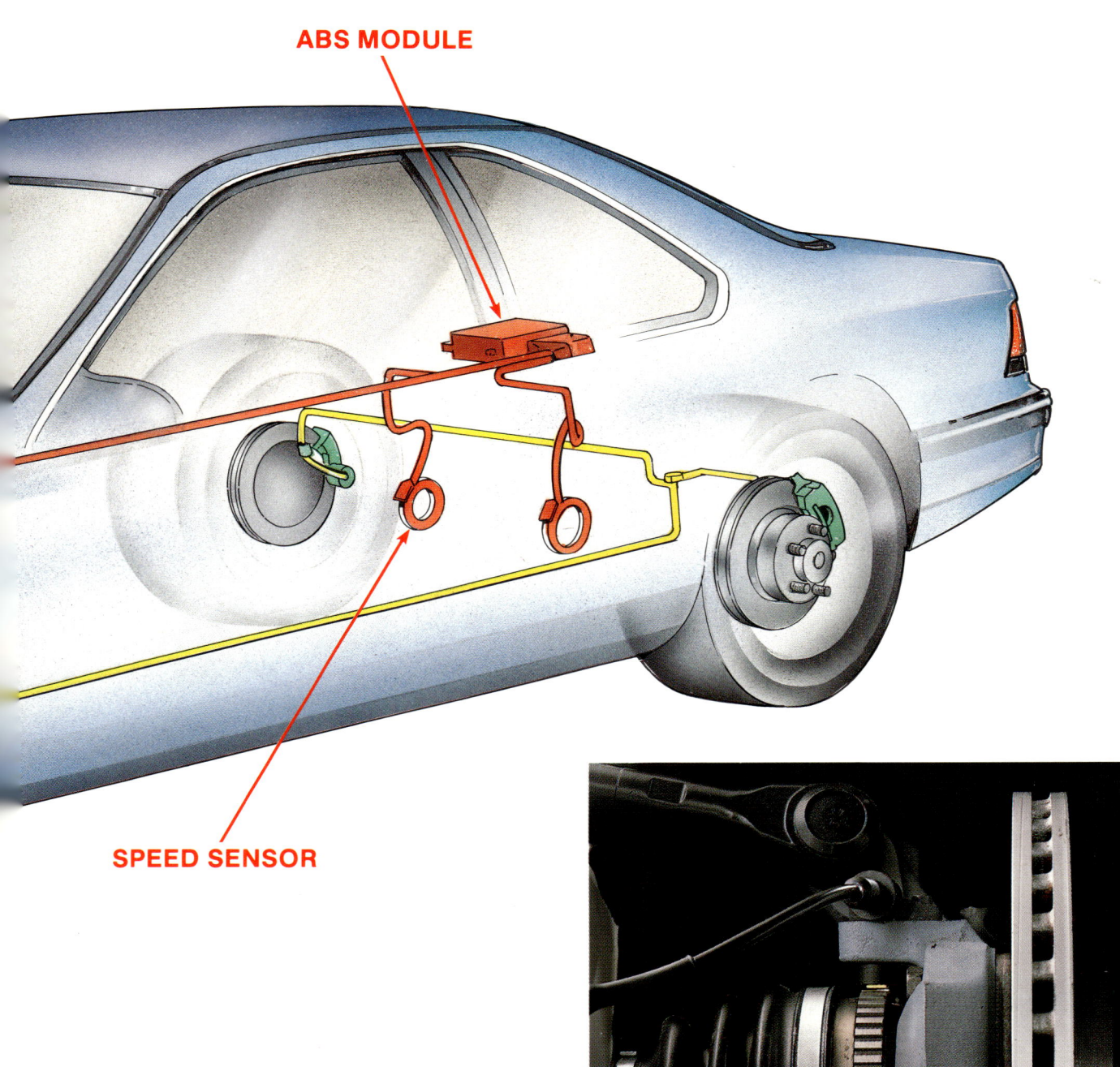

ABS MODULE

SPEED SENSOR

Many late-model vehicles are fitted with electronically-controlled anti-lock brake systems that increase the vehicles stability during hard braking.

Courtesy of Chrysler Corporation

HEATING SYSTEMS

New engine designs run at very high temperatures. Today's heater systems have been modified for this high heat and provide for quick passenger comfort in cold weather.

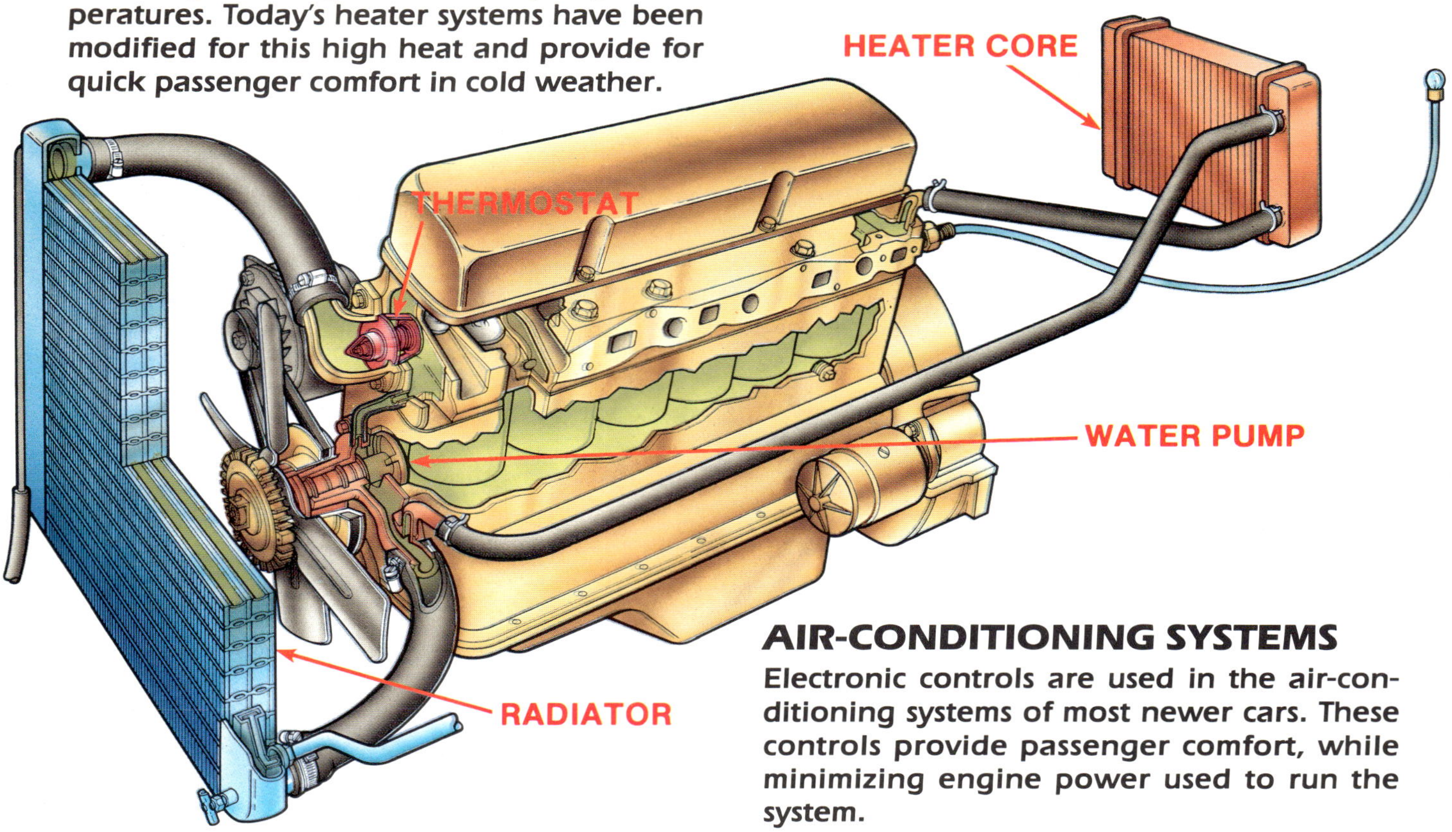

Labels: HEATER CORE, THERMOSTAT, WATER PUMP, RADIATOR

AIR-CONDITIONING SYSTEMS

Electronic controls are used in the air-conditioning systems of most newer cars. These controls provide passenger comfort, while minimizing engine power used to run the system.

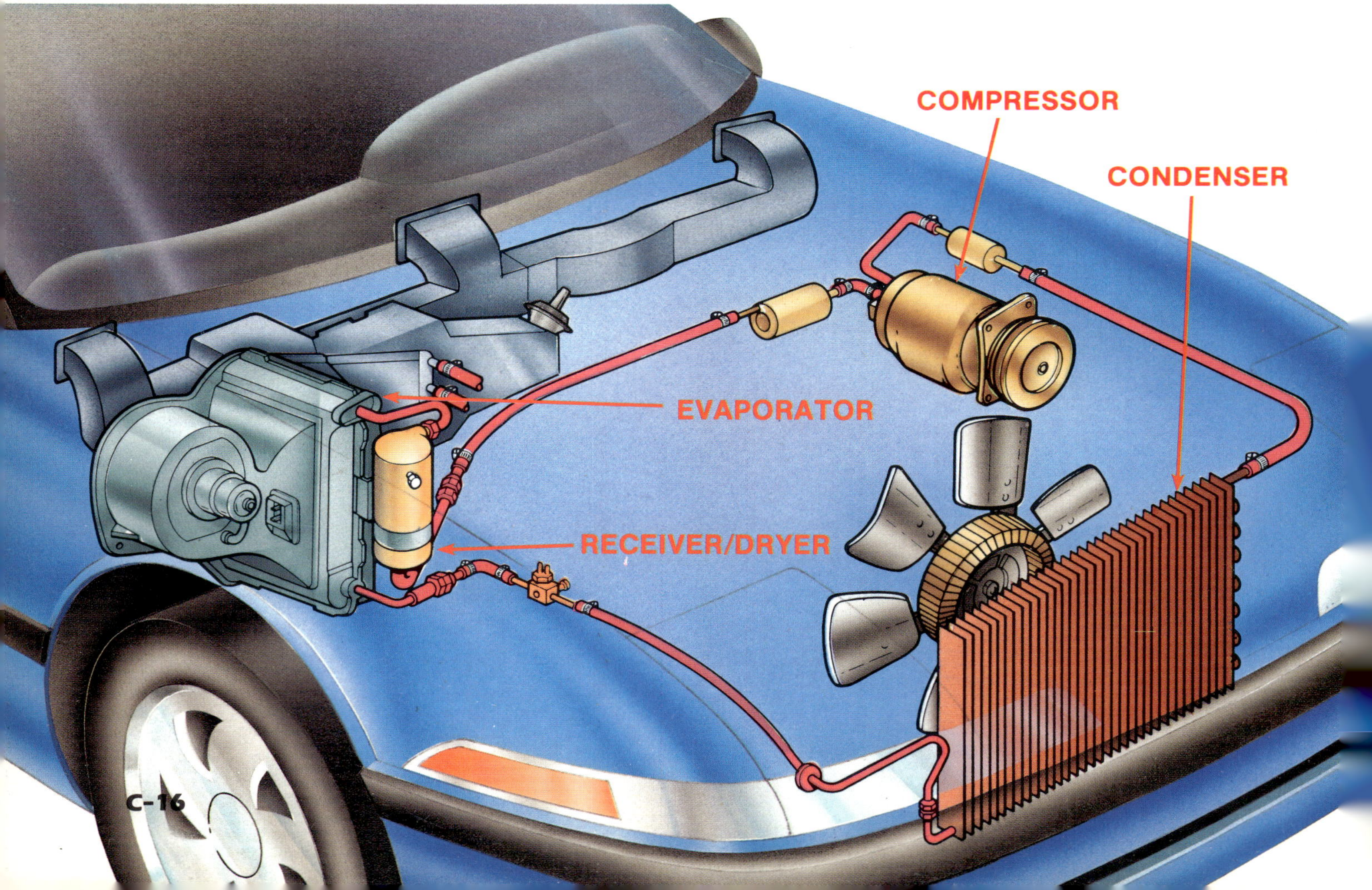

Labels: COMPRESSOR, CONDENSER, EVAPORATOR, RECEIVER/DRYER

Fuel Systems

not. Like most fluids, diesel fuel viscosity varies with temperature.

The viscosity of diesel fuel directly affects the spray pattern of the fuel into the combustion chamber and the fuel system components. Fuel with a high viscosity produces large droplets that are hard to burn. Fuel with a low viscosity sprays in a fine, easily burned mist. If the viscosity is too low, it does not adequately lubricate and cool the injection pump and nozzles.

Wax Appearance Point and Pour Point

Temperature affects diesel fuel more than it affects gasoline. This is because diesel fuels contain paraffin, a wax substance common among middle distillate fuels. As temperatures drop past a certain point, wax crystals begin to form in the fuel. The point where the wax crystals appear is the wax appearance point (WAP) or cloud point. The better the quality of the fuel, the lower the WAP. As temperatures drop, the wax crystals grow larger and restrict the flow of fuel through the filters and lines. Eventually, the fuel, which may still be liquid, stops flowing because the wax crystals plug a filter or line. As the temperature continues to drop, the fuel reaches a point where it solidifies and no longer flows. This is called the pour point. In cold climates it is recommended that a low-temperature pour point fuel be used.

Volatility

Gasoline is extremely volatile compared to diesel fuel. The amount of carbon residue left by diesel fuel depends on the quality and the volatility of that fuel. Fuel that has a low volatility is much more prone to leaving carbon residue. The small, high-speed diesels found in automobiles require a high-quality and highly volatile fuel because they cannot tolerate excessive carbon deposits. Large, low-speed industrial diesels are relatively unaffected by carbon deposits and can run on low-quality fuel.

Cetane Number or Rating

Diesel fuel's ignition quality is measured by the cetane rating. Much like the octane number, the cetane number is measured in a single-cylinder test engine with a variable compression ratio. The diesel fuel to be tested is compared to cetane, a colorless, liquid hydrocarbon that has excellent ignition qualities. Cetane is rated at 100. The higher the cetane number, the shorter the ignition lag time (delay time) from the point the fuel enters the combustion chamber until it ignites.

In fuels that are readily available, the cetane number ranges from 40 to 55 with values of 40 to 50 being most common. These cetane values are satisfactory for medium-speed engines whose rated speeds are from 500 to 1200 rpm and for high-speed engines rated over 1200 rpm. Low-speed engines rated below 500 rpm can use fuels in the above 30 cetane number range. The cetane number improves with the addition of certain compounds such as ethyl nitrate, acetone peroxide, and amyl nitrate. Amyl nitrate is commercially available for this purpose.

Diesel Fuel Grades

Minimum quality standards for diesel fuel grades have been set by the American Society for Testing Materials. Two grades of diesel fuels, Number 1 and Number 2, are used to fuel cars and trucks.

Number 2 diesel fuel is the most popular and widely distributed. Number 1 diesel fuel is less dense than Number 2, with a lower heat content. Number 1 diesel fuel is blended with Number 2 to improve starting in cold weather. In the winter, passenger car diesel is likely to be a mixture of Number 1 and 2 fuels. In moderately cold climates, the blend may be 90% Number 2 to 10% Number 1. In severe climates, the ratio may be as high as 50-50.

Diesel fuel economy can be expected to drop off during the winter months due to the use of Number 1 diesel in the fuel blend.

❏ ALTERNATIVE FUELS

Tighter federal, state, and local emissions regulations have led to a search for an alternative fuel. Many things are considered when determining the viability of an alternative fuel, including emissions, cost, fuel availability, fuel consumption, safety, engine life, fueling facilities, weight and space requirements of fuel tanks, and the range of a fully fueled vehicle. Currently, the major competing alternative fuels include ethanol, methanol, propane, and natural gas.

Ethanol and methanol were presented earlier under other gasoline additives. Propane is a petroleum-based pressurized fuel used as a liquid. It is a constituent of natural gas. Natural gas comes in two forms: compressed natural gas (CNG) and liquified natural gas (LNG).

LP-Gas

LP-gas (LP stands for liquefied petroleum) is a by-product of crude oil refining and it is also found in natural gas wells. Fuel grade LP-gas is almost pure propane with a little butane and propylene usually present. Because of its high propane content, many people simply refer to LP-gas as propane.

Propane burns clean in the engine and can be precisely controlled. Because it vaporizes at atmospheric temperatures and pressures, it does not puddle in the intake manifold. This means it emits less hydrocarbons and carbon monoxide. Emission controls on the engine can be simpler. Cold starting is easy, down to much below zero. At normal cold temperatures, the propane engine fires easily and produces power without surge or stumble.

One of the most noticeable differences between propane and gasoline is that propane is a dry fuel. It enters the engine as vapor. Gasoline, on the other hand, enters the engine as tiny droplets of liquid, whether it flows through a carburetor or is sprayed in through a fuel injector.

The propane fuel system is a completely closed system that contains a supply of pressurized LP-gas. Since the fuel is already under pressure, no fuel pump is needed. From the pressurized fuel tanks, the fuel flows to a vacuum filter fuel lock. This serves as a filter and a control allowing fuel to flow to the engine. Fuel flows to a converter or heat exchanger where it changes from a liquid to a gas. When the propane flows through the converter, it expands as it changes into a gas. The carburetor mixes gaseous propane with the gaseous air. Airflow into the engine is controlled by a butterfly valve in the venturi. Mixture is controlled by a fuel metering valve operated by a diaphragm, which is controlled by intake manifold pressure. The idle system is an air bleed, similar to a gasoline engine. In fact, except for the fact that the propane carburetor does not require a fuel bowl, the two carburetor types are basically the same.

Natural Gas

Vehicles have been designed with dual gasoline/CNG, diesel/CNG, and dedicated (single fuel) CNG engine applications. Natural gas vehicles offer several advantages over gasoline.

- The fuel costs less.
- It is the cleanest alternative fuel, generating up to 99% less carbon monoxide than gasoline, no particulates, almost no sulfur dioxide, and 85% less reactive hydrocarbons than gasoline.
- Natural gas vehicles are safer. The fuel tanks used for CNG are aluminum or steel cylinders with walls that are 1/2 to 3/4 inch thick. They can withstand severe crash tests, direct gunfire, dynamite explosions, and burning beyond any standard sheet metal gasoline tank. Because it is lighter than air, natural gas dissipates quickly. It also has a higher ignition temperature.
- It generally reduces vehicle maintenance since it burns cleanly. Oil changes may not be needed before 12,000 miles and spark plugs could last as long as 75,000 miles.
- Natural gas is abundant and readily available in the United States.

The chief disadvantage of CNG at present is its nonavailability to most users. Fuel facilities are needed in greater numbers than are currently in existence due to the relatively short range of CNG vehicles. The space taken by the CNG cylinders and their weight, about 300 pounds, also would be considered disadvantages in most applications.

❏ FUEL DELIVERY SYSTEM

The components of a typical fuel delivery system (Figure 20-4) are fuel tanks, fuel lines, fuel filters, and fuel pumps.

Fuel Tanks

Modern fuel tanks include devices that prevent vapors from leaving the tank. For example, to contain vapors and allow for expansion, contraction, and overflow that results from changes in the temperature, the fuel tank has a separate air chamber dome at the top. Another way to contain vapors is to use a separate internal expansion tank within the main tank (Figure 20-5). All fuel tank designs provide some control of fuel height when the tank is filled. Frequently, this is achieved by using vent lines within the filler tube or tank (Figure 20-6). With tank designs such as this, only 90% of the tank is ever filled, leaving 10% for expansion in hot weather. Some vehicles have an overfill limiting valve to prevent overfilling of the tank. If a

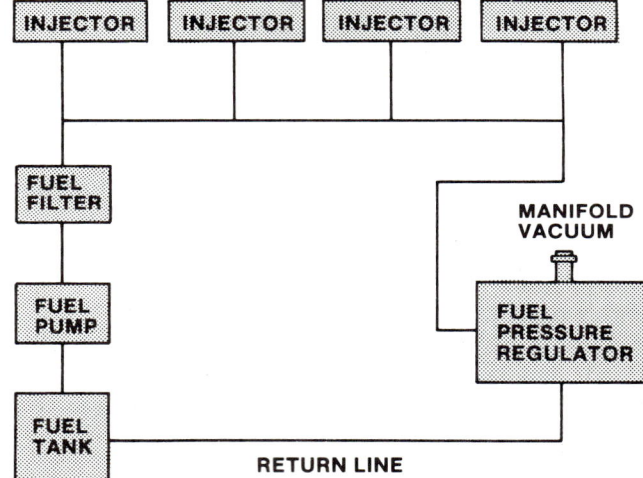

Figure 20-4   Typical fuel delivery system.

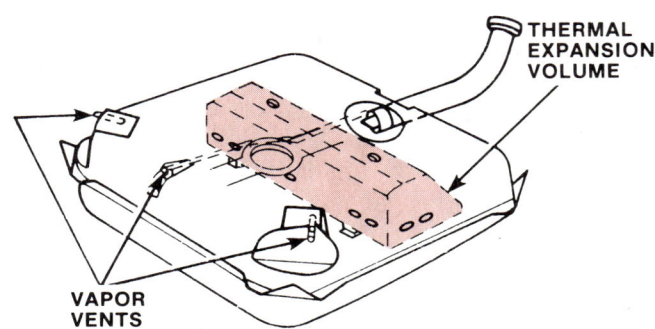

Figure 20-5   An internal expansion tank helps contain vapors in the fuel tank.

Fuel Systems 499

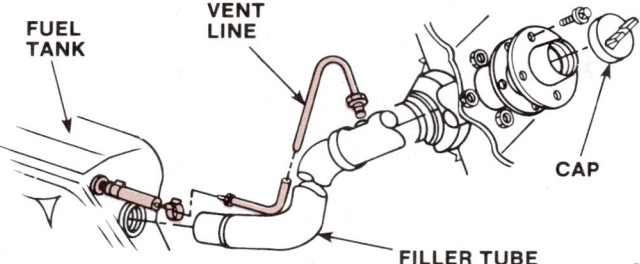

Figure 20-6 Vent lines within the fuel tank filler tube control the fuel level.

FUEL TANK IN REAR QUARTER PANEL

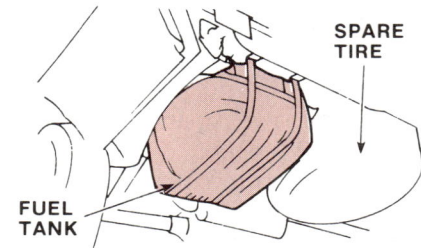

FUEL TANK UNDER TRUNK ON ONE SIDE

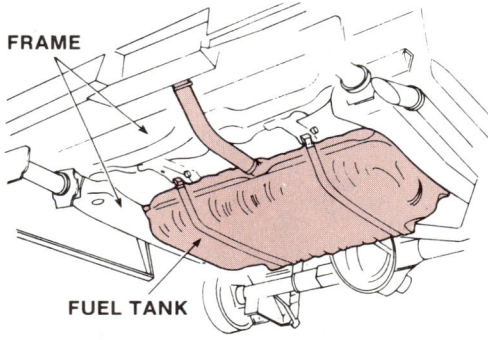

FUEL TANK INSIDE FRAME

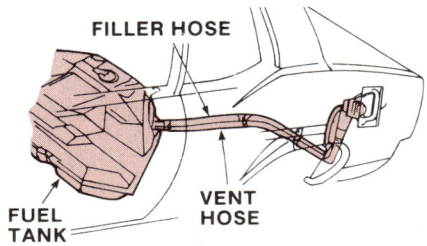

FUEL TANK UNDER SEAT

Figure 20-7 Common fuel tank locations.

tank is filled to capacity, it overflows whenever the temperature of the fuel increases.

Fuel tanks can be constructed of pressed corrosion-resistant steel, aluminum, or molded reinforced polyethylene plastic. Aluminum and molded plastic fuel tanks are becoming more common as manufacturers attempt to reduce the overall weight of the vehicle. Metal tanks are usually ribbed to provide added strength. Seams are welded, and heavier gauge steel is often used on exposed sections for added strength.

Most tanks have slosh baffles or surge plates to prevent the fuel from splashing around inside the unit. In addition to slowing down fuel movement, the plates tend to keep the fuel pick-up or sending assembly immersed in the fuel during hard braking and acceleration. The plates or baffles also have holes or slots in them to permit the fuel to move from one end of the tank to the other. Except for rear engine vehicles, the fuel tank in a passenger car is located in the rear of the vehicle for improved safety. Figure 20-7 illustrates the more common locations.

The fuel tank is provided with an inlet filler tube and cap. The location of the fuel inlet filler tube depends on the tank design and tube placement. It is usually positioned behind the filler cap or a hinged door in the center of the rear panel or in the outer side of either rear fender panel. Vehicles designed for unleaded fuel use have a restrictor in the filler tube that prevents the entry of the larger leaded fuel delivery nozzle at the gas pumps (Figure 20-8). The filler pipe can be a rigid one-piece tube soldered to the tank (Figure 20-9A) or a three-piece unit (Figure 20-9B). The three-piece unit has a lower neck soldered to the tank and an upper neck fastened to the inside of the body sheet metal panel.

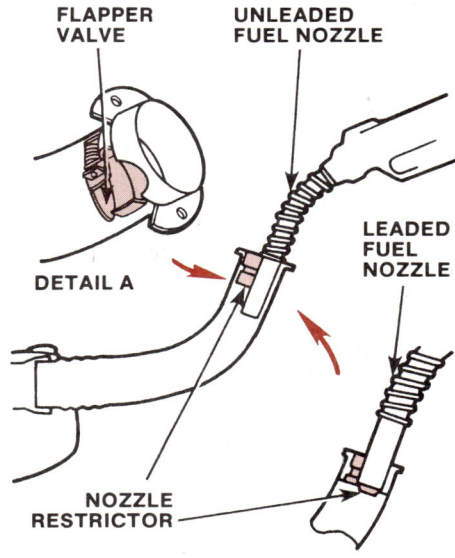

Figure 20-8 Cars requiring unleaded fuel have restrictors in the filler tube to allow only the insertion of smaller unleaded fuel pump nozzles.

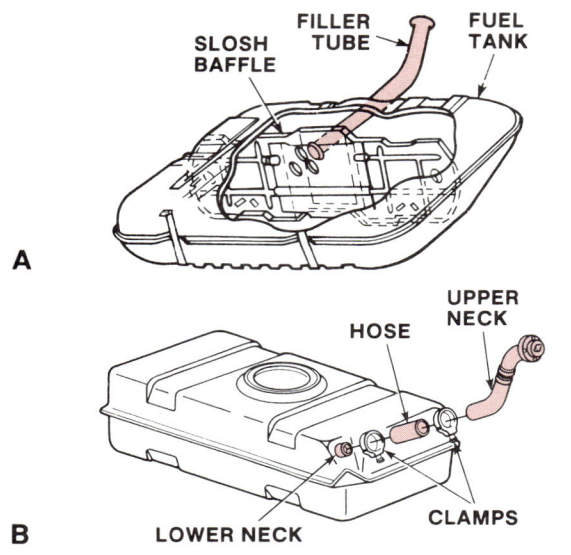

Figure 20-9 (A) One-piece and (B) three-piece filler tubes.

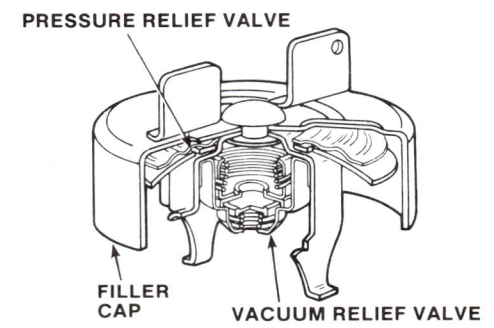

Figure 20-10 Pressure-vacuum relief filler caps.

Filler tube caps are nonventing and usually have some type of pressure-vacuum relief valve arrangement (Figure 20-10). Under normal operating conditions the valve is closed, but whenever pressure or vacuum is more than the calibration of the cap, the valve opens. Once the pressure or vacuum has been relieved, the valve closes. Most pressure caps have four anti-surge tangs that lock onto the filler neck to prevent the delivery system's pressure from pushing fuel out of the tank. By turning such a cap one-half turn, the tank pressure is released slowly and keeps pressure from blasting out of the tank all at once. Then, with another quarter turn, the cap can be removed.

Starting with the 1976 model year, a Federal Motor Vehicle Safety Standard (FMVSS 301) required a control on gasoline leakage from passenger cars and certain light trucks and buses, after they were subjected to barrier impacts and rolled over. Tests conducted under these severe conditions showed the most common gasoline leak path was the gasoline supply line from the fuel tank to the carburetor.

Most rollover leakage protection devices used on carburetor-equipped engines are variations of a basic one-way check valve. These protective check valves are usually installed in the fuel vapor vent line between the tank and the vapor canister and at the carburetor fuel feed or return line fitting (Figure 20-11). In some systems the check valve is part of the carburetor inlet fuel filter (Figure 20-12).

Under normal operation, the mechanical fuel pump pressure is sufficient to open the check valve and supply fuel to the engine. However, if the vehicle is

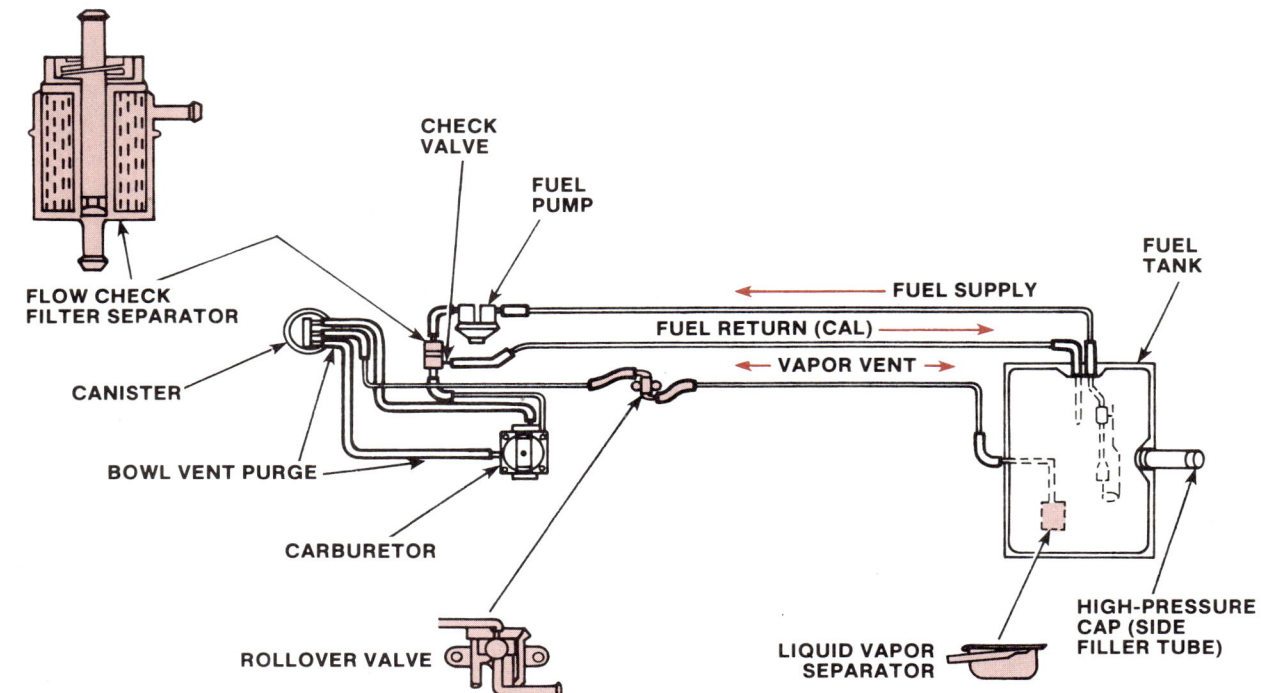

Figure 20-11 Rollover leakage protection devices.

Fuel Systems 501

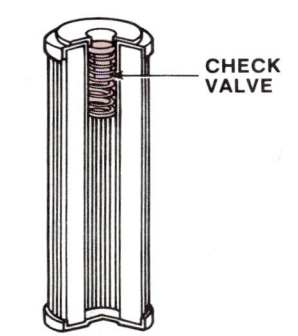

Figure 20-12 Fuel filter with built-in check valve.

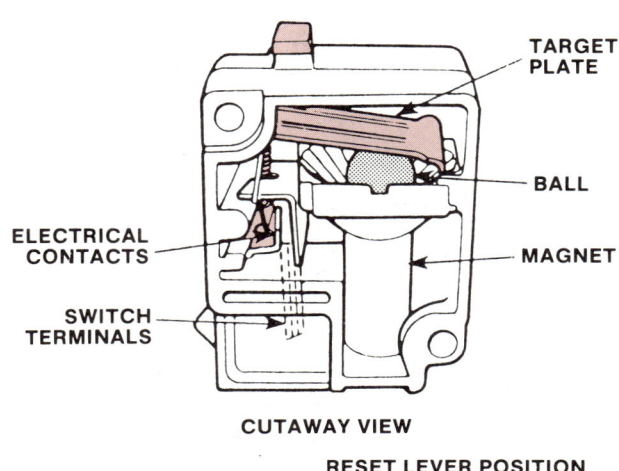

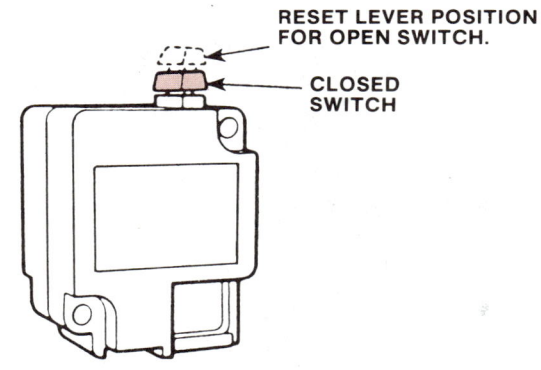

Figure 20-13 Inertia switch found on Ford vehicles.

involved in a rollover accident, fuel spills out of the carburetor, the engine stalls, and the fuel pump ceases to operate. This decreases fuel system pressure to the point where the check valve closes. This prevents fuel from reaching the carburetor where it would leak out.

A check valve might also be fitted in the fuel tank filler cap, and most caps' pressure-vacuum relief valve settings have been increased so that fuel pressure cannot open them in a rollover.

Many electric fuel pumps found on vehicles with fuel injection systems have an inertia switch that shuts off the pump if the vehicle is involved in a collision or rolls over. The Ford inertia switch (Figure 20-13) consists of a permanent magnet, a steel ball inside a conical ramp, a target plate, and a set of electrical contacts. The magnet holds the steel ball in the bottom of the conical ramp. In the event of a collision, the inertia of the ball causes it to break away from the magnet, roll up the conical ramp, and strike the target plate. The force of the ball striking the plate causes the electrical contacts in the inertia switch to open, cutting off power to the fuel pump. The switch has a reset button that must be depressed to close the contacts before the pump operates again.

Some fuel line systems contain a fuel return arrangement that aids in keeping the gasoline cool, thus reducing chances of vapor lock. The return system (Figure 20-14) consists of a special fuel pump equipped with an extra outlet fitting and necessary fuel line. The fuel return line generally runs next to the conventional fuel line (Figure 20-15), except that flow is in the opposite direction. The fuel return system allows a metered amount of cool fuel to circulate through the tank and fuel pump, thus reducing vapor bubbles caused by overheated fuel.

Some form of liquid vapor separator is incorporated into most modern vehicles to stop liquid fuel or bubbles from reaching the vapor storage canister or the engine crankcase (Figure 20-16). It can be located inside the tank, on the tank (Figure 20-17), or in fuel

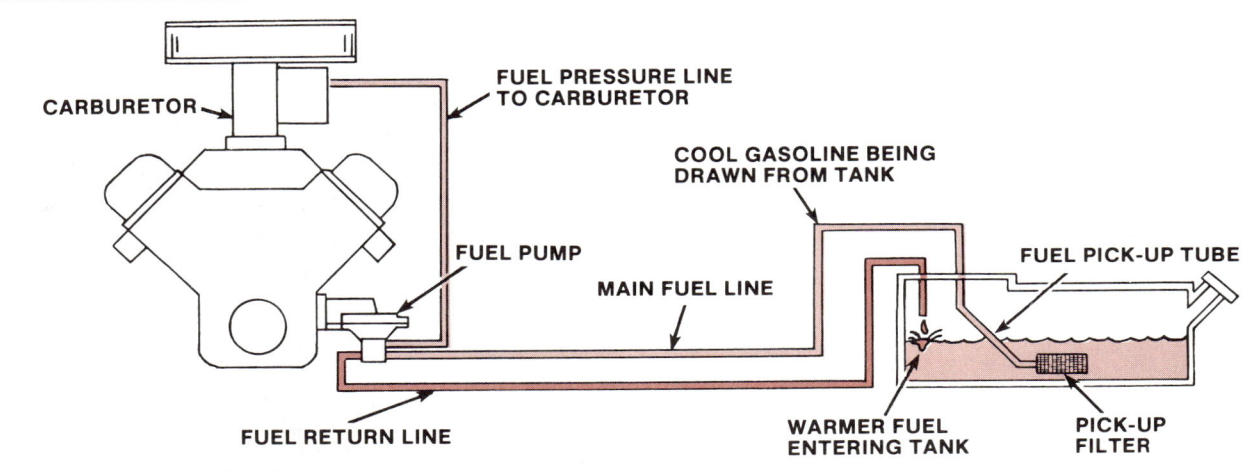

Figure 20-14 Typical fuel return system.

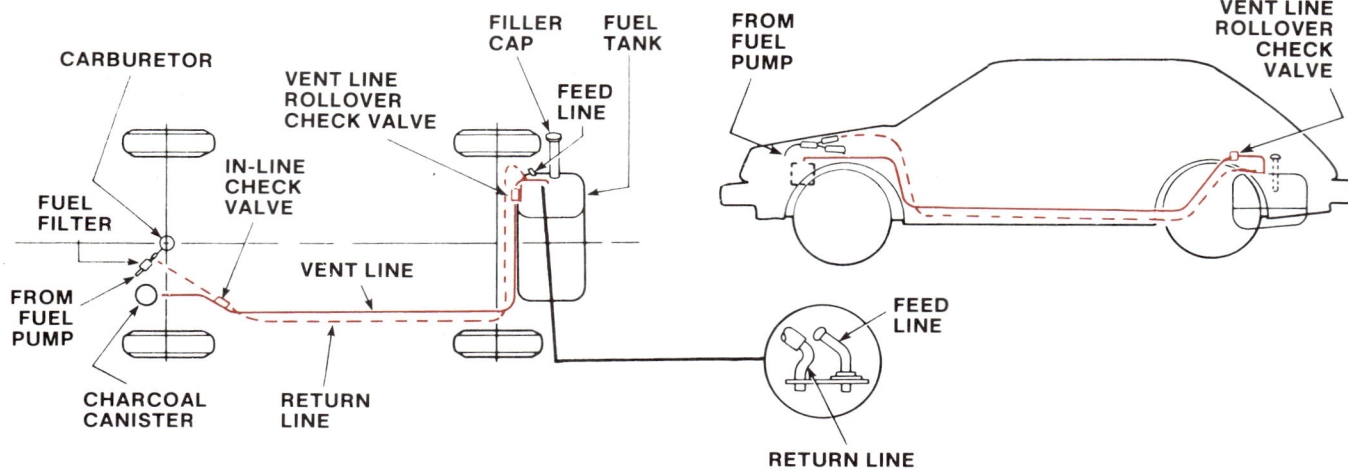

Figure 20-15   Parallel routing of the fuel return line and vapor line.

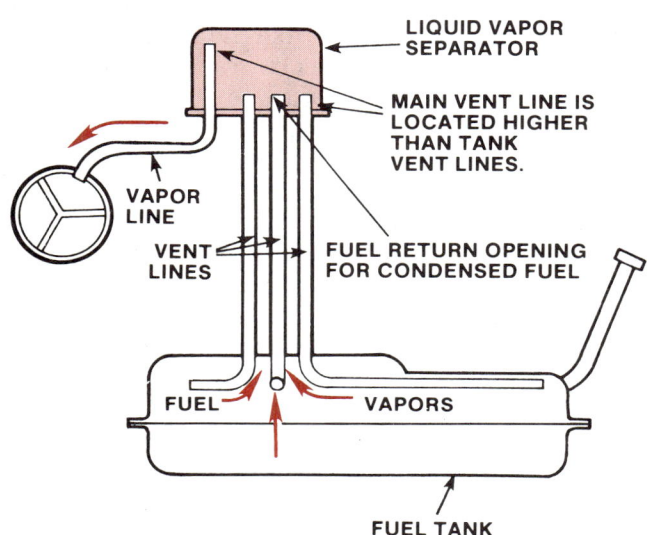

Figure 20-16   A fuel tank vapor separator allows some of the fuel vapors to condense back into liquid and return to the tank.

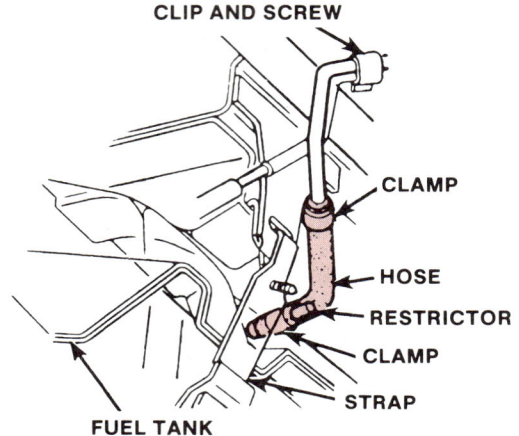

Figure 20-18   Vapor separator located in the fuel vent lines.

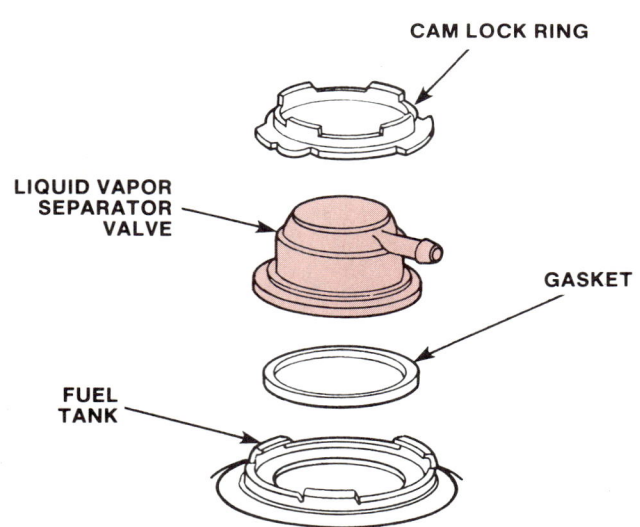

Figure 20-17   Vapor separator attached to the fuel tank.

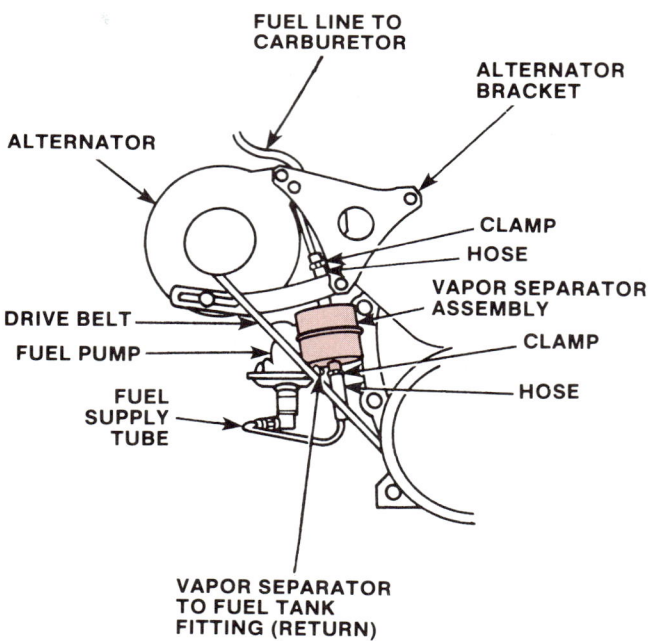

Figure 20-19   Vapor separator located near the fuel pump.

vent lines (Figure 20-18). It can also be located near the fuel pump (Figure 20-19). Check the service manual for the exact location of the liquid vapor separator and line routing.

Inside the fuel tank there is also a sending unit that includes a pick-up tube and float-operated fuel gauge (Figure 20-20). The fuel tank pick-up tube is connected to the fuel pump by the fuel line. Some electric fuel pumps are combined with the sending unit (Figure 20-21). The pick-up tube extends nearly, but not completely, all the way to the bottom of the tank. Rust, dirt, sediment, and water cannot be drawn up into the fuel tank filter, which can cause clogging. The ground wire is often attached to the fuel tank unit.

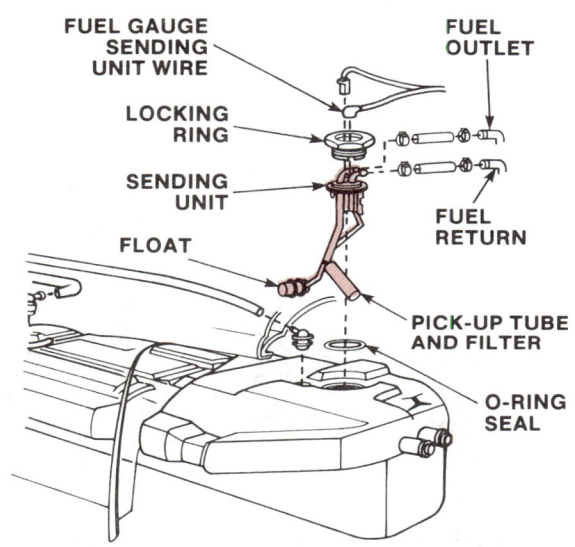

Figure 20-20 Fuel tank sending unit assembly.

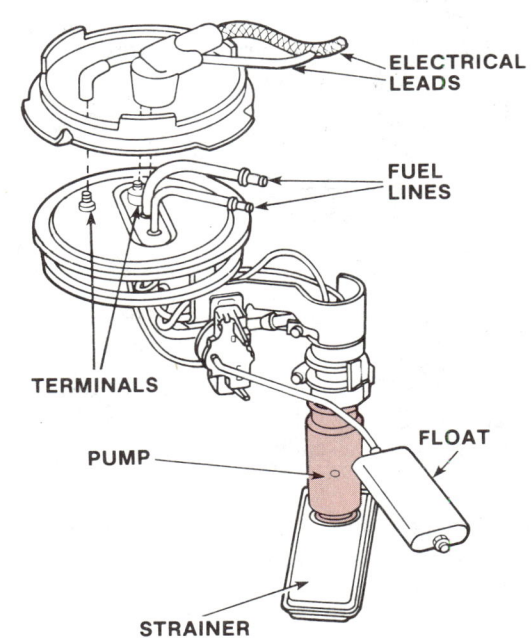

Figure 20-21 Combination electric fuel pump and sending unit.

Servicing the Fuel Tank

Leaks in the metal fuel tank can be caused by a weak seam, rust, or road damage. The best method of permanently solving this problem is to replace the tank. Another method is to remove the tank and steam clean or boil it in a caustic solution to remove the gasoline residue. After this has been done, the leak can be soldered or brazed by a specialty shop.

If the tank is leaking because of a puncture or small hole, it can be plugged by installing a sheet-metal screw with a neoprene washer. Holes in a plastic tank can sometimes be repaired by using a special tank repair kit. Be sure to follow manufacturer's instructions when doing the repair.

WARNING: Extreme care must be taken when using steam cleaning equipment or when washing with a caustic solution. Follow the manufacturer's instructions exactly. If the shop does not have steam cleaning or washing facilities, these services can be done by a radiator specialty shop. Do not use a steam cleaning procedure on a plastic tank. Because of the danger of explosion, leave gas tank welding to experts in repair shops that specialize in tank repair.

When a fuel tank is leaking dirty water or has water in it, the tank must be cleaned, repaired, or replaced.

 **PROCEDURES**

Replacing the Fuel Tank

1. Disconnect the negative terminal from the battery. Remove the tank filler cap, and drain the tank of all fuel.
2. Attach a piece of masking tape to the tank lines and hoses to insure correct reinstallation. Disconnect the vent lines and the wire connected to the sending unit.

CAUTION: Abide by local laws for the disposal of contaminated fuels. Be sure to wear eye protection when working under the vehicle.

3. Unfasten the filler from the tank. If it is a rigid one-piece tube, remove the screws around the outside of the filler neck near the filler cap. If it is a three-piece unit, remove the neoprene hoses after the clamp has been loosened.
4. Loosen the bolts holding the fuel tank straps to the vehicle (Figure 20-22) until they are about two threads from the end.

WARNING: Do not heat the bolts on the fuel tank straps in order to loosen them. The heat could ignite the fumes.

Holding the tank securely against the underchassis with one hand, remove the strap bolts and lower the tank to the ground. When lowering the

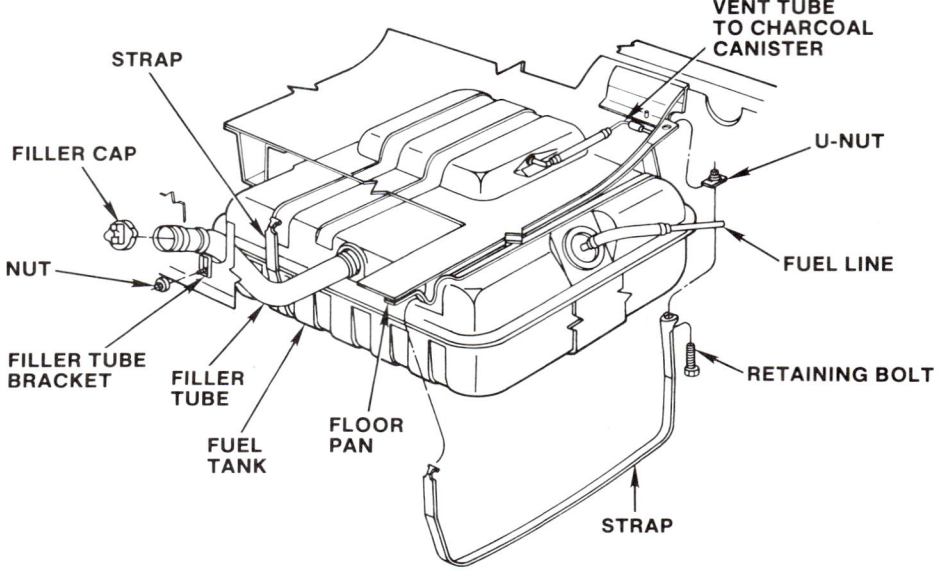

Figure 20-22 Fuel tank mounting components.

tank, make sure all wires and tubes are unhooked. Keep in mind that small amounts of fuel might still remain in the tank.

CAUTION: Use a drain pan to catch any spilled fuel or be sure to clean it up immediately.

5. To reinstall the new or repaired fuel tank, reverse the removal procedure. Be sure that all the rubber or felt tank insulators are in place. Then, with the tank straps in place, position the tank. Loosely fit the tank straps around the tank, but do not tighten them. Make sure that the hoses, wires, and vent tubes are connected properly. Check the filler neck for alignment and for insertion into the tank. Tighten the strap bolts and secure the tank to the car. Install all of the tank accessories (vent line, sending unit wires, ground wire, and filler tube). Fill the tank with fuel and check it for leaks, especially around the filler neck and the pick-up assembly. Reconnect the battery and check the fuel gauge for proper operation.

REMOVING AND REPLACING THE FUEL GAUGE SENDING UNIT The sending unit is held in the tank by either a retaining ring or screws. The easiest way to remove a sending unit retaining ring is to use a special tool designed for this purpose (Figure 20-23). This tool fits over the metal tabs on the retaining ring, and after about a quarter turn, the ring comes loose and the sender unit can be removed. If the special tool is not available, a drift punch or worn screwdriver and ball peen hammer usually do the job (Figure 20-24).

When removing the sending unit from the tank, be very careful not to damage the float arm, the float, or the fuel gauge sender. Check the unit carefully for any damaged components. Shake the float, and if fuel can

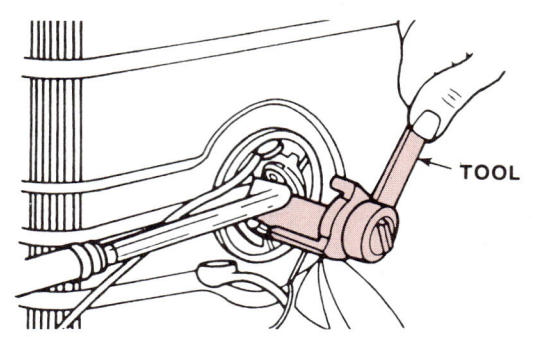

Figure 20-23 Using a special tool to remove the sending unit retaining ring.

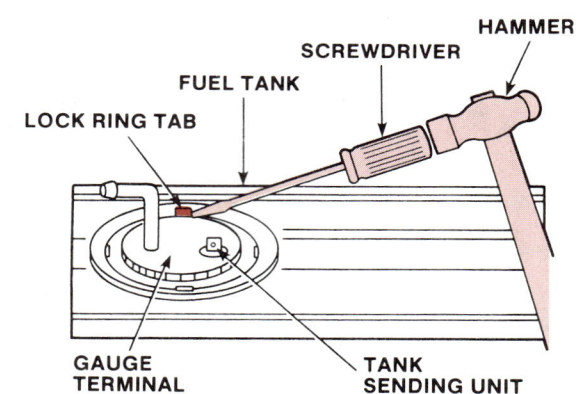

Figure 20-24 Using a dull screwdriver and ball peen hammer to remove the sending unit.

be heard inside it, replace it. Make sure the float arm is not bent. It is usually wise to replace the filter and O-ring before replacing the unit. Check the fuel gauge as described in the service manual. When reinstalling the pick-up pipe-sending unit, be very careful not to damage any of the components.

Fuel Lines

Fuel lines can be made of either metal tubing or flexible nylon or synthetic rubber hose. The latter must be able to resist gasoline. It must also be nonpermeable, so gas and gas vapors cannot evaporate through the hose. Ordinary rubber hose, such as that used for vacuum lines, deteriorates when exposed to gasoline. Only hoses made for fuel systems should be used for replacement. Similarly, vapor vent lines must be made of material that resist attack by fuel vapors. Replacement vent hoses are usually marked with the designation EVAP to indicate their intended use. The inside diameter of a fuel delivery hose is generally larger (5/16 to 3/8 inch) than that of a fuel return hose (1/4 inch).

Many fuel tanks have vent hoses to allow air in the fuel tank to escape when the tank is being filled with fuel. Vent hoses are usually installed alongside the filler neck.

The fuel lines carry fuel from the fuel tank to the fuel pump, fuel filter, and carburetor or fuel injection assembly. These lines are usually made of rigid metal, although some sections are constructed of rubber hose to allow for car vibrations. This fuel line, unlike filler neck or vent hoses, must work under pressure or vacuum. Because of this, the flexible synthetic hoses must be stronger. This is especially true for the hoses on fuel injection systems, where pressures reach 50 psi or more. For this reason, flexible fuel line hose must also have special resistance properties. Many auto manufacturers recommend that flexible hose only be used as a delivery hose to the fuel metering unit in fuel injection systems. It should not be used on the pressure side of the injector systems. This application requires a special high-pressure hose.

All fuel lines should occasionally be inspected for holes, cracks, leaks, kinks, or dents. Many fuel system troubles that occur in the lines are blamed on the fuel pump or carburetor. For instance, a small hole in the fuel line admits air but does not necessarily show any drip marks under the car. Air can then enter the fuel line, allowing the fuel to gravitate back into the tank. Then, instead of drawing fuel from the tank, the fuel pump sucks only air through the hole in the fuel line. When this condition exists, the fuel pump is frequently tested, and if there is insufficient fuel, it is considered faulty, when in fact there is nothing wrong with it. If a hole is suspected, remove the coupling at the tank and the pump and pressurize the line with air. The leaking air is easily spotted.

Since the fuel is under pressure, leaks in the line between the pump and carburetor or injectors are relatively easy to recognize. When a damaged fuel line is found, replace it with one of similar construction—steel with steel, and the flexible with nylon or synthetic rubber. When installing flexible tubing, always use new clamps. The old ones lose some of their tension when they are removed and do not provide an effective seal when used on the new line.

CAUTION: Do not substitute aluminum or copper tubing for steel tubing. Never use hose within 4 inches of any hot engine or exhaust system component. A metal line must be installed.

Fuel supply lines from the tank to the carburetor or injectors are routed to follow the frame along the underchassis of vehicles. Generally, rigid lines are used extending from near the tank to a point near the fuel pump. To absorb engine vibrations, the gaps between the frame and tank or fuel pump are joined by short lengths of flexible hose (Figure 20-25).

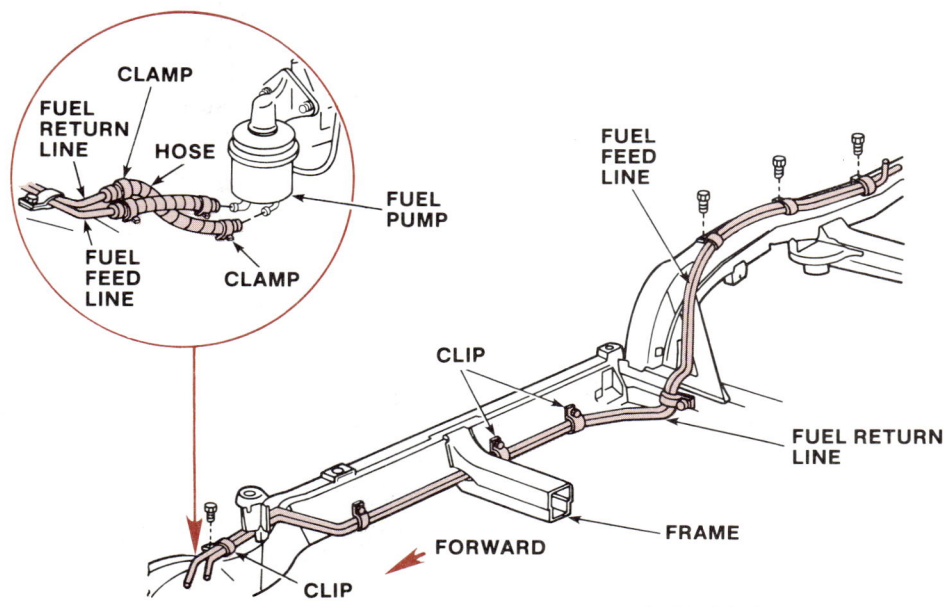

Figure 20-25 Gaps between the frame and tank or fuel pump are joined with flexible hose.

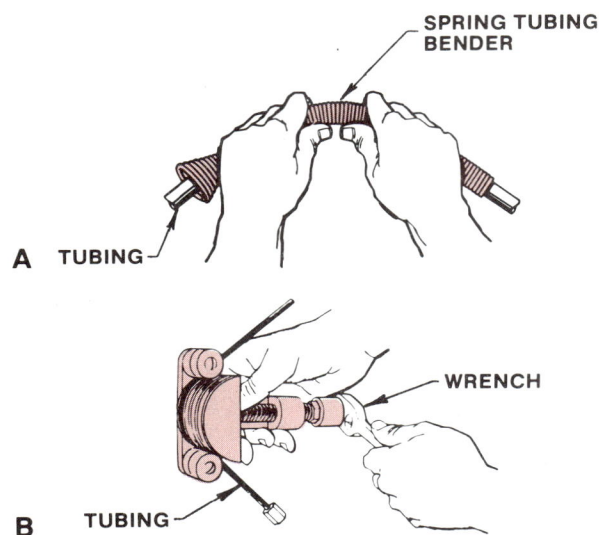

Figure 20-26 Two types of steel tubing bending tools.

Any damaged or leaking fuel line—either a portion or the entire length—must be replaced. To fabricate a new fuel line, select the correct tube and fitting dimension and start with a length that is slightly longer than the old line. With the old line as a reference, use a tubing bender to form the same bends in the new line as those that exist in the old. Although steel tubing can be bent by hand to obtain a gentle curve, any attempt to bend a tight curve by hand usually kinks the tubing. To avoid kinking, always use a bending tool like the ones shown in Figure 20-26.

The two most-used tubing fittings are the compression and the double-flare (Figure 20-27). The double-flare—which is the most common—is made with a special tool that has an anvil and a cone (Figure 20-28). The double-flaring process is performed in two steps. First, the anvil begins to fold over the end of the tubing. Then, the cone is used to finish the flare by folding the tubing back on itself, doubling the thickness, and creating two sealing surfaces.

The angle and size of the flare are determined by the tool. Careful use of the double-flaring helps to produce

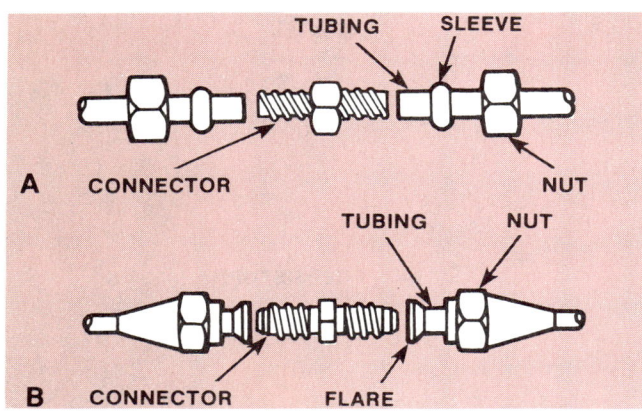

Figure 20-27 (A) Compression and (B) double-flare tubing fittings.

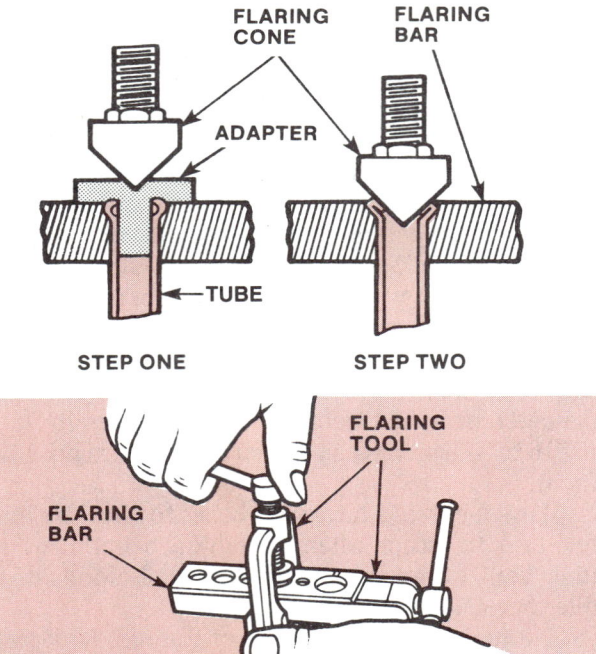

Figure 20-28 The double-flare tubing fitting is made with an anvil and cone.

strong, leakproof connections. Figure 20-29 shows other metal fuel line connections that are used by vehicle manufacturers.

The flare tool can also be used to make sure that nylon and synthetic rubber hoses stay in place. That is, to make sure the connection is secure, put a partial double-lip flare on the end of the tubing over which the hose is installed. This can be done quickly, with the proper flaring tool, by starting out as if it was going to be a double-flare, but stopping halfway through the procedure (Figure 20-30). This provides an excellent sealing ridge that does not cut into the hose. A clamp should be placed directly behind the ridge on the hose caused by the raised section on the metal line.

SHOP TALK

To insure a flexible fuel replacement hose is the right length, lay the old line alongside the new one. Then, with a sharp knife, cut the new line to the same length as the old one.

Nylon and synthetic rubber fuel line connectors are illustrated in Figure 20-31. Note that there are connectors available to combine rigid and flexible fuel lines. But if nylon or synthetic rubber fuel line is damaged, replace the entire line. Do not attempt to patch it or use a patched section.

There are a variety of clamps used on fuel system lines, including the spring and screw types (Figure

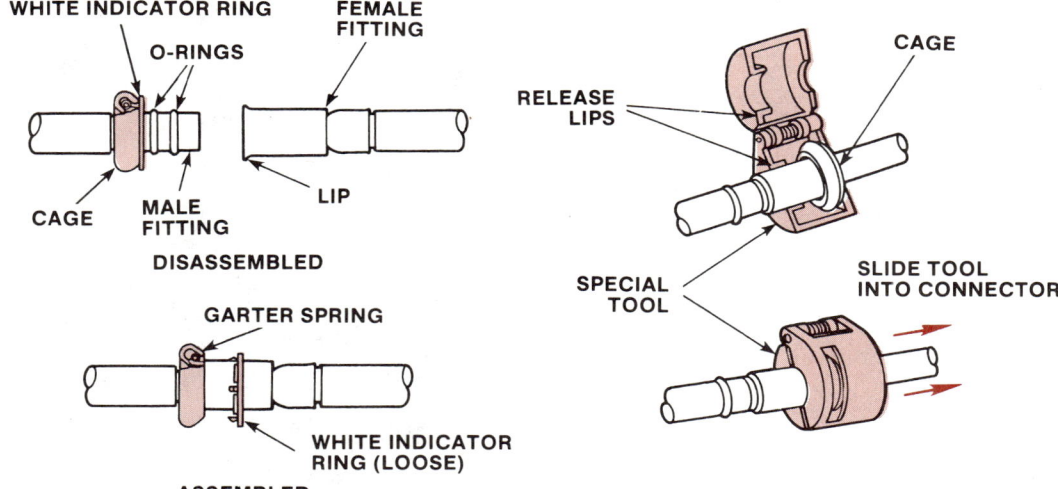

Figure 20-29 Common metal fuel line connections.

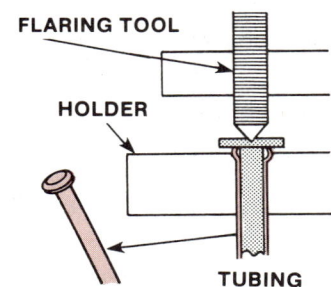

Figure 20-30 Using a flaring tool to secure hose connections.

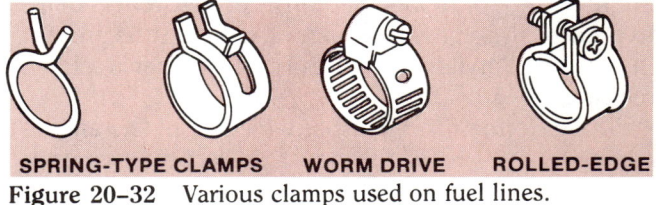

Figure 20-32 Various clamps used on fuel lines.

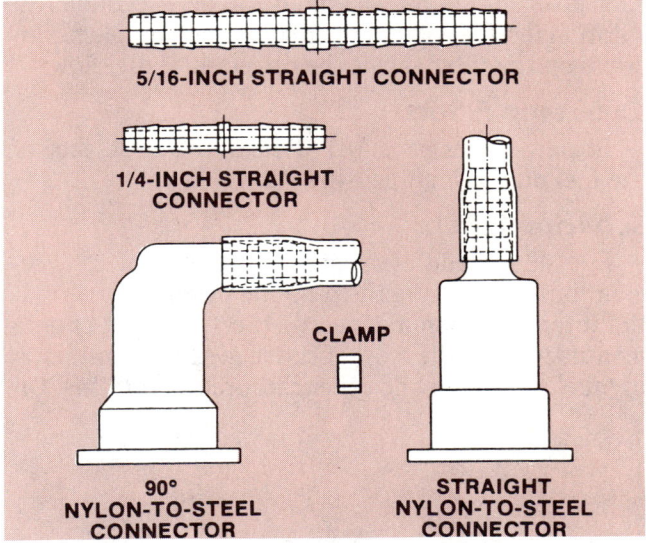

Figure 20-31 Nylon and synthetic rubber fuel line connectors.

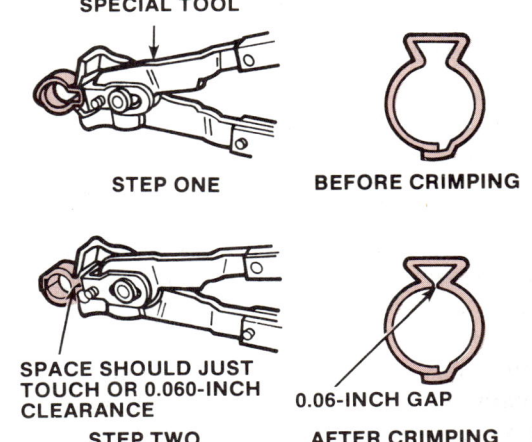

Figure 20-33 Crimp clamps require a special tool for installation.

20-32). The crimp clamps shown in Figure 20-33 are used most for metal tubing, but they require a special tool to install.

To control the rate of vapor flow from the fuel tank to the vapor storage tank, a plastic or metal restrictor may be placed in either the end of the vent pipe or in the vapor-vent hose itself. When the latter hose must be replaced, the restrictor must be removed from the old vent hose and installed in the new one.

Fuel Filters

Automobiles and light trucks usually have an in-tank strainer and a gasoline filter (Figure 20-34). The strainer, located in the gasoline tank, is made of a finely woven fabric. The purpose of this strainer is to prevent large contaminant particles from entering the fuel system where they could cause excessive fuel

508 Section 4 Engine Performance

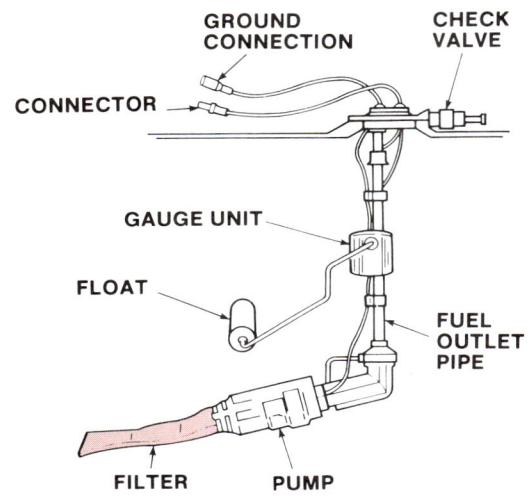

Figure 20-34 Most cars and light trucks have an in-tank strainer.

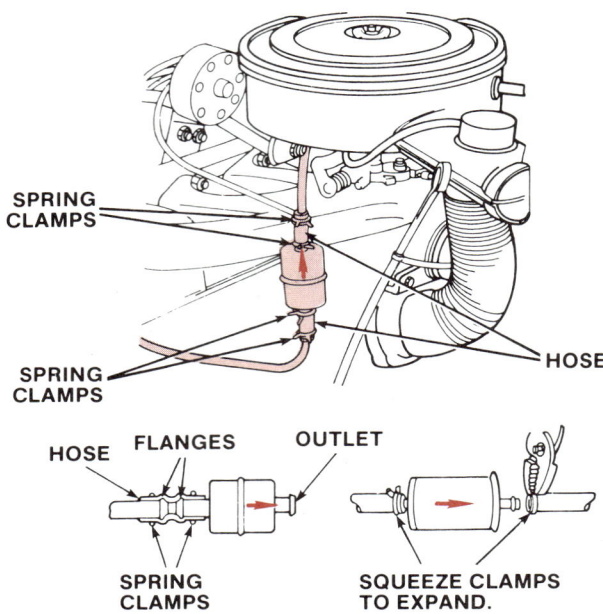

Figure 20-36 Installation of an in-line fuel filter.

pump wear or plug fuel metering devices. It also helps to prevent passage of any water that might be present in the tank. Servicing of the fuel tank strainer is seldom required.

The gasoline filter is usually located in the engine compartment and is the one this section examines because it is replaceable and might require service on a regular basis. The most common types of gasoline filters are in-carburetor filters, in-line filters, and out-pump filters.

In-Carburetor Filters

There are three basic types of in-carburetor gasoline filters. Pleated paper filters use pleated paper as the filtering medium. Paper elements are more efficient than screen-type elements, such as nylon or wire mesh, in removing and trapping small particles, as well as larger size contaminants. Sintered bronze filters are often referred to as a stone or ceramic filter. Screw-in filters are designed to screw into the carburetor fuel inlet. The fuel line attaches to a fitting on the filter. This filter has a magnetic element to remove metallic contamination before it reaches the carburetor (Figure 20-35).

In-Line Filters

This type of gasoline filter is installed in the fuel line (Figure 20-36). In carbureted engines, the in-line gas-

oline filter is usually installed between the fuel pump and the carburetor. In vehicles with a fuel injection system, the location of the fuel filter is determined by the manufacturer. Fitted with a pleated paper element, the in-line filter is sometimes installed as an extra protective measure. The optionally installed in-line filter then works in conjunction with the in-tank and in-carburetor gasoline filters. Because of its large capacity, an in-line filter is often the most economical solution to a fuel system's contamination problems. An arrow on the filter shows the direction of fuel flow.

Out-Pump Filters

Some vehicles have fuel filters in the outlet side of the fuel pump (Figure 20-37).

Servicing Filters

Fuel filters and elements are serviced by replacement only. Replacing the gasoline filter or element at the intervals recommended by the vehicle or engine manufacturer is the most effective method of minimizing fuel starvation and other carburetor problems. On

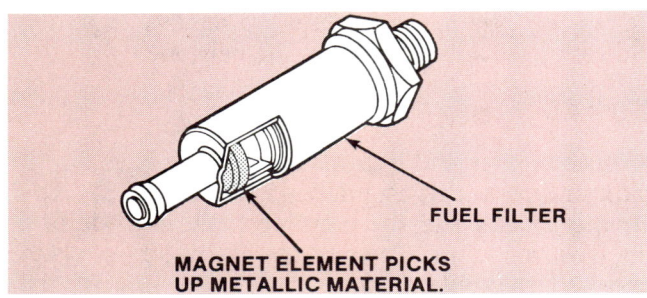

Figure 20-35 Screw-in fuel filter with magnetic element.

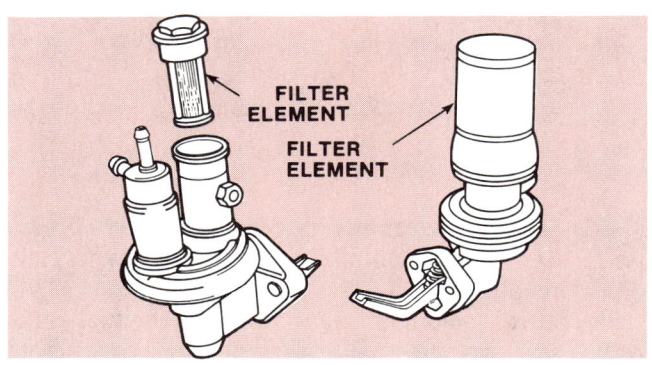

Figure 20-37 Out-pump fuel filter.

occasions when the fuel system has been subjected to excessive amounts of contaminants, more frequent filter changes may be required.

PROCEDURES
Replacing an In-Carburetor Filter

1. To remove the filter, remove the fuel line from the carburetor fuel inlet nut by using two wrenches, one to hold the inlet nut, the other to turn the fuel line fitting (Figure 20-38).
2. After disconnecting the fuel line, remove the inlet nut from the carburetor and discard the used filter. The inlet nut has a gasket that is loose or permanently attached. This gasket can usually be reused.

> **SHOP TALK**
>
> Take care not to lose the spring located behind the filter. The spring is required to seal the filter to the inlet nut.

3. Installation of the filter is accomplished by simply reversing the steps used to remove the used filter.

> **SHOP TALK**
>
> Be sure to properly start the inlet nut threads into the carburetor. If the threads are crossed, a fuel leak inevitably results.

4. Check fuel line connections for leaks with the engine running.

> **SHOP TALK**
>
> Most late-model automobiles have steel gasoline lines. Non-OE in-line gasoline filters can be installed using short rubber tubes and tangential screw hose clamps. There should be no bends in the rubber tubes after installation. After installing an in-line gasoline filter, start the engine and check for leaks.

Fuel Pumps

The fuel pump is the device that draws the fuel from the fuel tank through the fuel lines to the engine's carburetor or injectors. Basically, there are two types of fuel pumps: mechanical and electrical. The latter is the most commonly used today.

Mechanical Fuel Pumps

Mechanical fuel pumps have a synthetic rubber diaphragm inside the unit that is actuated by an eccentric located on the engine's camshaft (Figure 20-39). As the camshaft rotates during engine operation, a shaft or rocker arm in the pump is moved up and down or back and forth, depending on the fuel pump's position on the engine. This causes the diaphragm to move back and forth, drawing fuel from the fuel tank.

The mechanical fuel pump is located on the engine block near the front of the engine (Figure 20-40). Normally, it is a sealed unit that cannot be repaired. If the pump leaks from either the vent hole or from a

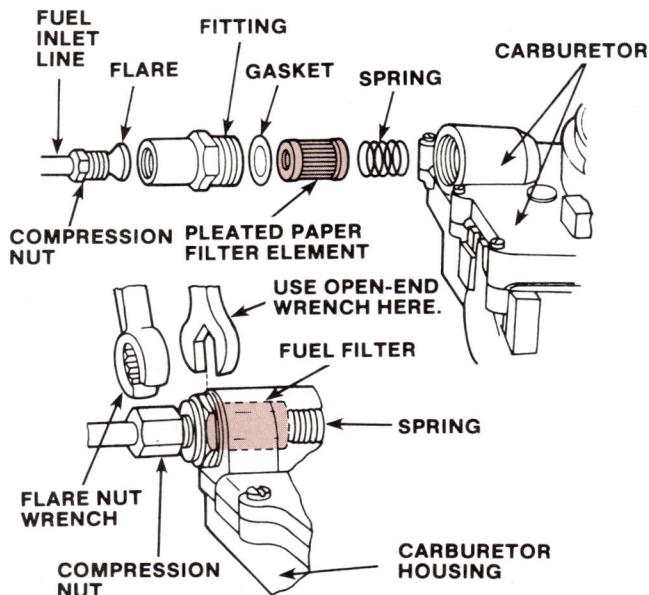

Figure 20-38 Two wrenches are needed to remove an in-carburetor filter.

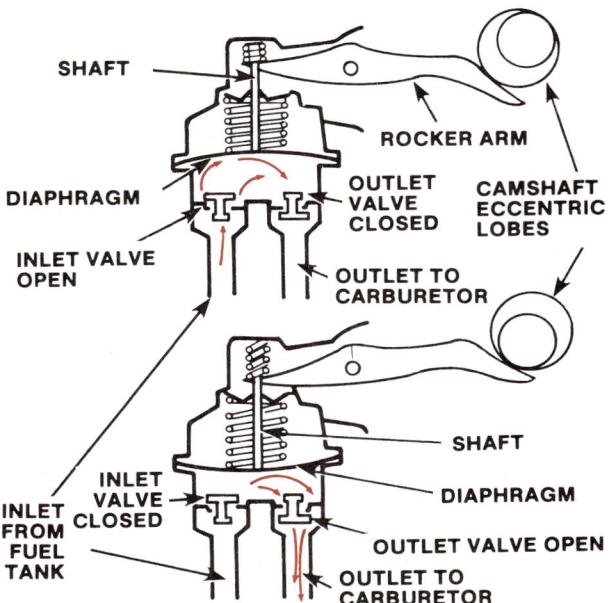

Figure 20-39 Mechanical fuel pump assembly.

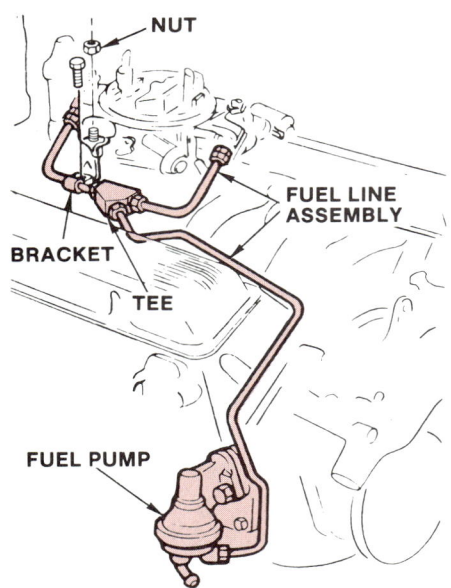

Figure 20-40 Mechanical fuel pump location on a V-8 engine.

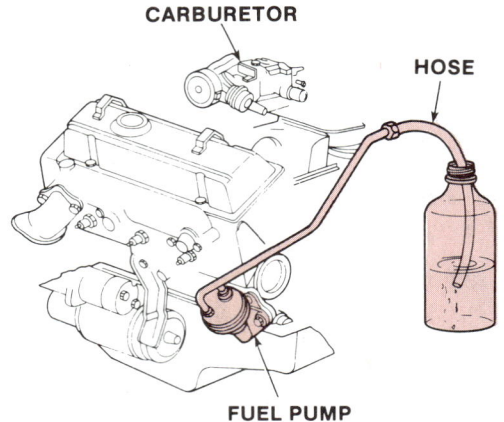

Figure 20-41 Measuring fuel pump discharge volume.

seam, it must be replaced. If engine performance indicates inadequate fuel, the pump, while mounted on the engine, should be tested for pressure and volume.

Incorrect fuel pump pressure and low volume (capacity of flow rate) are the two most likely fuel pump troubles that affect engine performance. Low pressure causes a lean mixture and fuel starvation at high speeds. Excessive pressure causes high fuel consumption and carburetor flooding. And, low volume causes fuel starvation at high speeds.

To determine that the fuel pump is in satisfactory operating condition, tests for both fuel pump pressure and fuel pump capacity (volume) should be performed. These tests are performed with the fuel pump installed on the engine and the engine at normal operating temperature and at idle speed.

SHOP TALK

Before making any tests, be sure the replaceable fuel filter has been changed within the recommended maintenance mileage interval. When in doubt, install a new filter.

The proper procedure for testing fuel pump pressure is shown in Photo Sequence #10, which is included in this chapter. These photos outline the steps to follow while performing the test on an engine with fuel injection. To conduct this test on specific fuel injection systems, refer to the service manual for instructions. When performing this test on carbureted engines, the pressure gauge is installed between the fuel filter and the carburetor fuel inlet. A tee fitting can be used to install the gauge.

SHOP TALK

Fuel pump pressure specifications are given by the manufacturer in pounds per square inch (psi) at a certain engine speed.

To measure fuel pump capacity or discharge volume, allow fuel to discharge from the pump into a graduated container (Figure 20-41) for the amount of time specified in the service manual. Compare the amount of fuel discharged with the specifications. Always follow the proper safety guidelines for handling and storing gasoline.

SHOP TALK

Manufacturer's specifications generally are given in terms of 1 pint of fuel delivered in a given number of seconds while the engine is at idle and also at a specified speed. Some manual specifications just state a good volume at cranking speed. This usually means a pint of fuel is delivered in 30 seconds or less at an engine speed of 500 rpm.

Figure 20-42 shows the common problems with a mechanical pump. To replace a mechanical fuel pump (Figure 20-43), remove the inlet and outlet lines at the pump. Use a plug to stop the flow of fuel from the tank. With the correct size socket wrench, remove the mounting bolts. Then, remove the pump from the engine. Clean the old gasket material from the engine block. Apply gasket sealer to the mounting surface on the engine and to the threads of the mounting bolts. Install the new gasket, then position the pump by tilting it either toward or away from the block to correctly place the lever against the cam. If the pump is driven by a pushrod, the rod must be held up to permit the rocker arm to go under it. When the pump is properly positioned, there should be an internal squeak-

PHOTO SEQUENCE 10

☐ CHECKING THE FUEL PRESSURE ON A PFI SYSTEM

P10-1 Many problems on today's cars can be caused by incorrect fuel pressure. Therefore, checking fuel pressure is an important step in diagnosing driveability problems.

P10-2 Prior to testing the injection system, a careful visual inspection of the injectors and fuel rail is necessary. Any sign of a fuel leak should be noted.

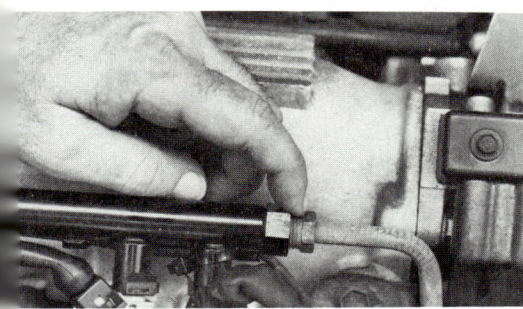

P10-3 The fuel supply line into the fuel rail is a likely point for leakage. Check the area around the fitting to make sure no leaks have occurred.

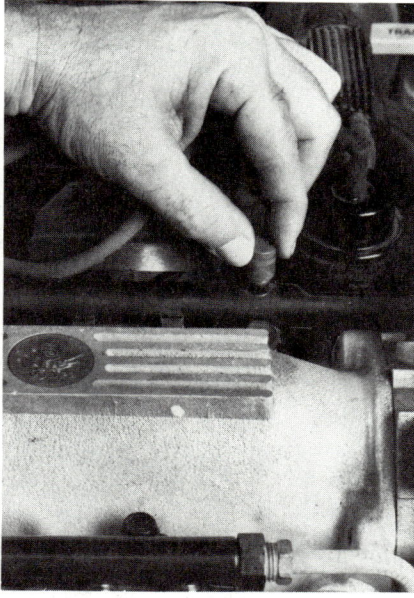

P10-4 Most fuel rails are equipped with a fitting that can be used to relieve pressure and to test pressure.

P10-5 To test fuel pressure, connect the appropriate pressure gauge to the fuel rail fitting.

P10-6 Connect a hand-held vacuum pump to the pressure regulator.

P10-7 Turn the ignition switch to the run position and observe the fuel pressure gauge. Compare the reading to specifications. A reading lower than normal indicates a faulty fuel pump or fuel delivery system.

P10-8 To test the fuel pressure regulator, create a vacuum at the regulator with the vacuum pump. Fuel pressure should decrease as vacuum increases. If pressure remains the same, the regulator is faulty. ■

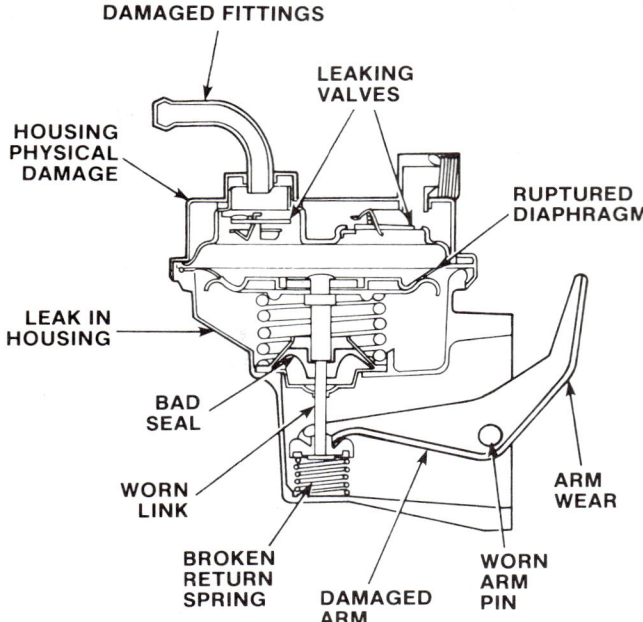

Figure 20-42 Common problems associated with a mechanical fuel pump.

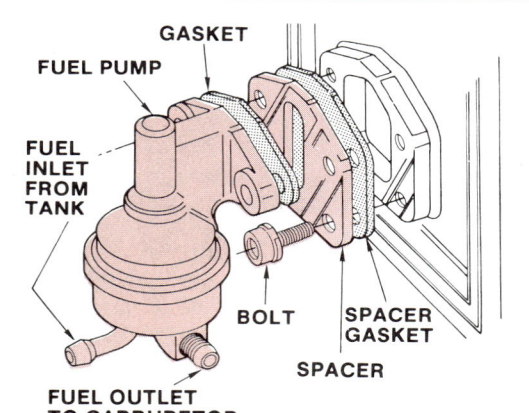

Figure 20-43 Removing a mechanical fuel pump.

ing noise with each movement of the pump. Tighten the mounting bolts firmly. Attach the inlet and outlet lines; start the engine; check for leaks.

Electric Fuel Pumps

Electric fuel pumps offer important advantages over mechanical fuel pumps. Because electric fuel pumps maintain constant fuel pressure, they aid in starting and reduce vapor lock problems.

The electric fuel pump can be located inside (Figure 20-44) or outside (Figure 20-45) the fuel tank. There are four basic types of electric fuel pumps: the diaphragm, plunger, bellows, and impeller or rotary. The in-tank electric pump is usually a rotary type. The diaphragm, plunger, and bellows type (Figure 20-46) are usually the demand style. That is, when the ignition is turned on, the pump begins operation. It shuts off automatically when the fuel line is pressurized. When there is a demand for more fuel, the electric pump provides more. When demand is lower, it pumps less, so proper fuel flow and pressure are constantly maintained. A typical wiring diagram for an electric fuel pump is shown in Figure 20-47.

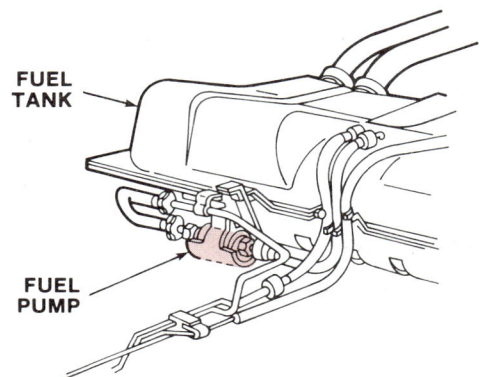

Figure 20-45 Electric fuel pump located outside the fuel tank.

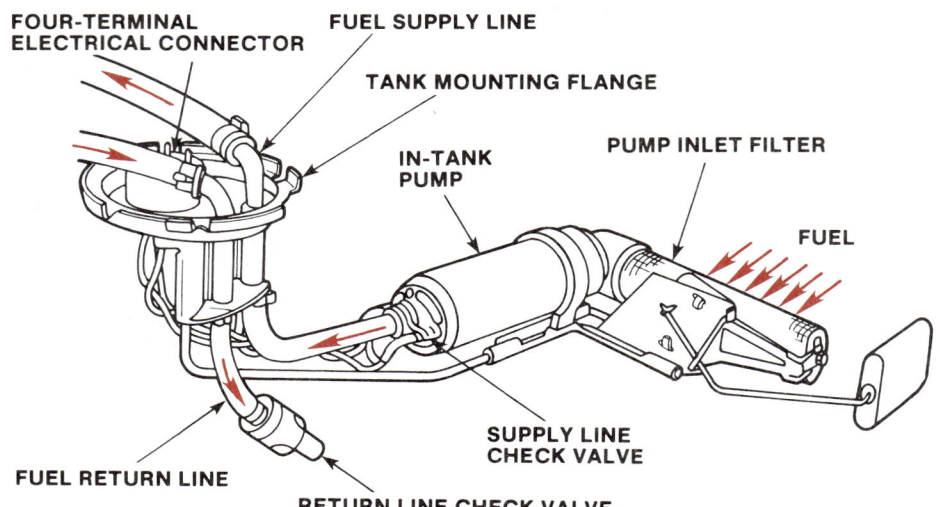

Figure 20-44 Electric fuel pump located inside the fuel tank.

Fuel Systems 513

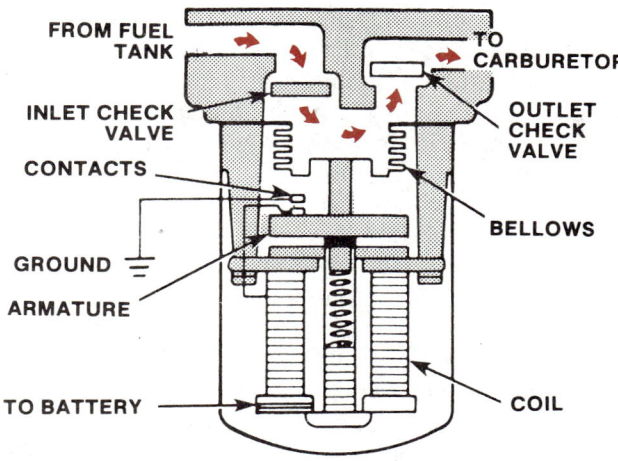

Figure 20-46 Bellows fuel pump.

TROUBLESHOOTING Problems in fuel systems using electric fuel pumps are usually indicated by improper fuel system pressure or a dead or inoperative fuel pump. A high pressure reading usually indicates either a faulty pressure regulator or an obstructed return line. To identify the cause, disconnect the fuel return line at the tank. Use a length of hose to route the returning fuel into an appropriate container. Start the engine and note the pressure reading at the engine. If fuel pressure is now within specifications, check for an obstruction in the in-tank return plumbing. The fuel reservoir check valve or aspirator jet might be clogged.

WARNING: The fuel supply lines remain pressurized for long periods of time after the engine is shut down. This pressure must be relieved before servicing of the fuel system begins. A valve is normally provided on the throttle body or fuel rail for this purpose.

If the fuel pressure still reads high with the return line disconnected from the tank, note the volume of fuel flowing through the line. Little or no fuel flow can indicate a plugged return line. Shut off the engine and connect a length of hose directly to the fuel pressure regulator return port to by-pass the return hose. Restart the engine and again check the pressure reading. If by-passing the return line brings the readings back within specifications, a plugged return line is the culprit. If pressure is still high, apply vacuum to the pressure regulator to see if that makes a difference. It should. If there is still no change, replace the faulty pressure regulator. If applying vacuum directly to the regulator lowers fuel pressure, the vacuum hose that controls the operation of the regulator might be plugged, leaking, or misrouted.

Low pressure, on the other hand, can be due to a clogged fuel filter, restricted fuel line, weak pump, leaky pump check valve, defective fuel pressure regulator, or dirty filter sock in the tank. It is possible to rule out filter and line restrictions as a cause of the problem by making a pressure check at the pump outlet. A higher reading at the pump outlet (at least 5 psi) means there is a restriction in the filter or line. If the reading at the pump outlet is unchanged, then either the pump is weak or is having trouble picking up fuel (clogged filter sock in the tank). Either way it is necessary to get inside the fuel tank. If the filter sock is gummed up with dirt or debris, it is also wise to clean out the tank when the filter sock is cleaned or replaced.

Another possible source of trouble is the pump check valve. Some pumps have one, others have two (positive displacement roller vane pumps). The purpose of the check valve is to prevent fuel movement through the pump when the pump is off so residual pressure remains at the injectors. This can be checked

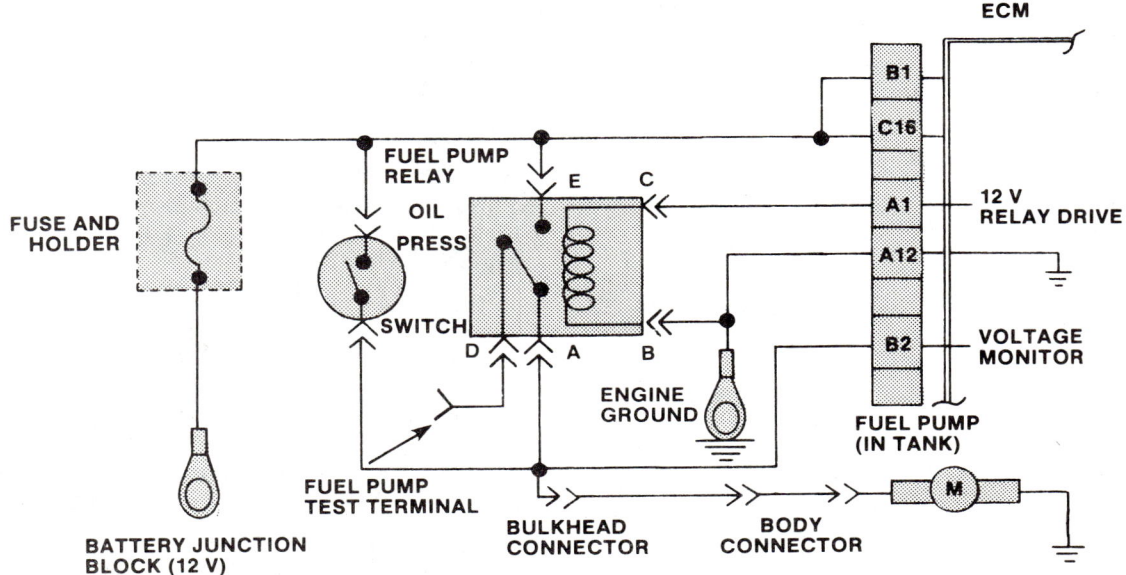

Figure 20-47 Typical wiring diagram for an electric fuel pump.

by watching the fuel pressure gauge after the engine is shut off.

Depending on the type of pump used, the check valve can also prevent the reverse flow of fuel and relieve internal pressure to regulate maximum pump output. Check valves can stick and leak. So, if a pump runs but does not pump fuel, a bad check valve is to blame. Unfortunately, the check valve is usually an integral part of the pump assembly, which is sealed at the factory. Therefore, if the check valve is causing trouble, the entire pump must be replaced.

When an engine fails to start because there is no fuel delivery, the first check is the fuel gauge. A gauge that reads higher than a half tank probably means there is fuel in the tank, but not always. A defective sending unit or miscalibrated gauge might be giving a false indication. Sticking a wire or dowel rod down the fuel tank filler pipe tells whether or not there is really fuel in the tank. If the gauge is faulty, repair or replace it.

Listen for pump noise. When the key is turned on, the pump should buzz for a couple of seconds to build system pressure. The pump is usually energized through an oil pressure switch (the purpose of which is to shut off the flow of fuel in case of an accident that stalls the engine). On most late-model cars with computerized engine controls, the computer energizes a pump relay when it receives a cranking signal from the distributor pick-up or crankshaft sensor. An oil pressure switch might still be included in the circuitry for safety purposes and to serve as a backup in case the relay or computer signal fails. Failure of the pump relay or computer driver signal can cause slow starting because the fuel pump does not come on until the engine cranks long enough to build up sufficient oil pressure to trip the oil pressure switch.

If a buzzing sound is not heard when the key is on or while the engine is being cranked, check for the presence of voltage at the pump electrical connectors. The pump might be good, but if it does not receive voltage and have a good ground, it does not run (Figure 20-48). To check the ground, connect a test light across the ground and feed wires at the pump to check for voltage, or use a voltmeter to read actual voltage and an ohmmeter to check ground resistance. The latter is the better test technique because a poor ground connection or low voltage can reduce pump operating speed and output. If the electrical circuit checks out but the pump does not run, the pump is probably bad and should be replaced.

No voltage at the pump terminal when the key is on and the engine is cranking indicates a faulty oil pressure switch, pump relay, relay driver circuit in the computer, or a wiring problem. Check the pump fuse to see if it is blown. Replacing the fuse might restore power to the pump, but until you have found out what caused the fuse to blow, the problem is not solved. The most likely cause of a blown fuse would be a short in the wiring between the relay and pump, or a short inside the oil pressure switch or relay.

A faulty oil pressure switch can be checked by bypassing it with a jumper wire. If that restores power to the pump and the engine starts, replace the switch. If an oil pressure switch or relay sticks in the closed position, the pump can run continuously whether the key is on or off, depending on how the circuit is wired.

To check a pump relay, use a test light to check across the relays and ground terminals. This tells if the relay is getting battery voltage and ground. Next, turn off the ignition, wait about 10 seconds, then turn it on. The relay should click and you should see battery voltage at the relay's pump terminal. If nothing happens, repeat the test checking for voltage at the relay terminal that is wired to the computer. The presence of a voltage signal here means the computer is doing its job but the relay is failing to close and should be replaced. No voltage signal from the computer indicates an opening in that wiring circuit or a fault in the computer itself.

WARNING: When testing an electric fuel pump, do not let fuel contact any electrical wiring. The smallest spark (electric arc) could ignite the fuel.

When replacing an electric pump, be sure that the new or rebuilt replacement unit meets the minimum requirements of pressure and volume for that particular vehicle. This information can be found in the service manual.

PROCEDURES

Replacing an Electric Fuel Pump

1. Disconnect the ground terminal at the battery.
2. Disconnect the electrical connectors on the electric fuel pump. Label the wires to aid in connecting it to the new pump. Reversing polarity on most pumps destroys the unit.

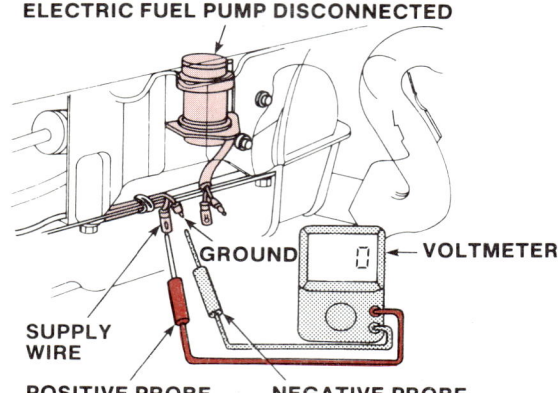

Figure 20-48 Checking for voltage and the condition of the ground to the electrical fuel pump.

3. Fuel and vapor lines should be removed from the pump. Label the lines to aid in connecting them to the new pump.
4. The inside tank pump can usually be taken out of the tank by removing the fuel sending unit retaining ring. However, it may be necessary to remove the fuel tank to get at the retaining ring. Removal of the fuel tank can be accomplished as described earlier in this chapter.
5. On a fuel pump that is outside of the tank, remove the bolts holding it in place. On in-tank models, loosen the retaining ring. Pull the pump and sending unit out of the tank (if they are combined in one unit) and discard the tank O-ring seal.
6. To remove the pump, twist off the filter sock, then push the pump up until the bottom is clear of the bracket. Swing the pump out to the side and pull it down to free it from the rubber fuel line coupler. The rubber sound insulator between the bottom of the pump and bracket and the rubber coupler on the fuel line are normally discarded because new ones are included with the replacement pump. Some pumps have a rubber jacket around them to quiet the pump. If this is the case, slip off the jacket and put it on the new pump.
7. Compare the replacement pump with the old one. If necessary, transfer any fuel line fittings from the old pump to the new one. Note the position of the filter sock on the pump so you can install a new one in the same relative position.
8. When inserting the new pump back into the sending unit bracket, be careful not to bend the bracket. Make sure the rubber sound insulator under the bottom of the pump is in place. Install a new filter sock on the pump inlet and reconnect the pump wires. Be absolutely certain you have correct polarity. Replace the O-ring seal on the fuel tank opening, then put the pump and sender assembly back in the tank and tighten the locking ring by rotating it clockwise. Some pump/sender assembly units are secured by bolts.
9. If the fuel was removed from the vehicle, replace it.

CAUTION: Avoid the temptation to test the new pump before reinstalling the fuel tank, by energizing it with a couple of jumper wires. Running the pump dry can damage it because the pump relies on fuel for lubrication and cooling.

10. Reconnect the electrical connectors.
11. Reconnect the ground terminal at the battery.
12. Start the engine and check all connections for fuel leaks.

CUSTOMER CARE
Never release a car from the shop after servicing a fuel pump without checking for fuel leaks. A leak could cause a very serious fire, but even if it does not, an angry customer has to bring the car back so that you can fix the leak.

ELECTRONIC FUEL SYSTEM

The basic function of an electronic engine control fuel delivery system is the same as the function of a conventional system just described in this chapter. The main difference is that control of the system is obtained through a power relay and computer. Electrically, the system consists of a fuel pump, an inertia switch, a fuel pump relay, a computer power relay, and a control computer (Figure 20-49).

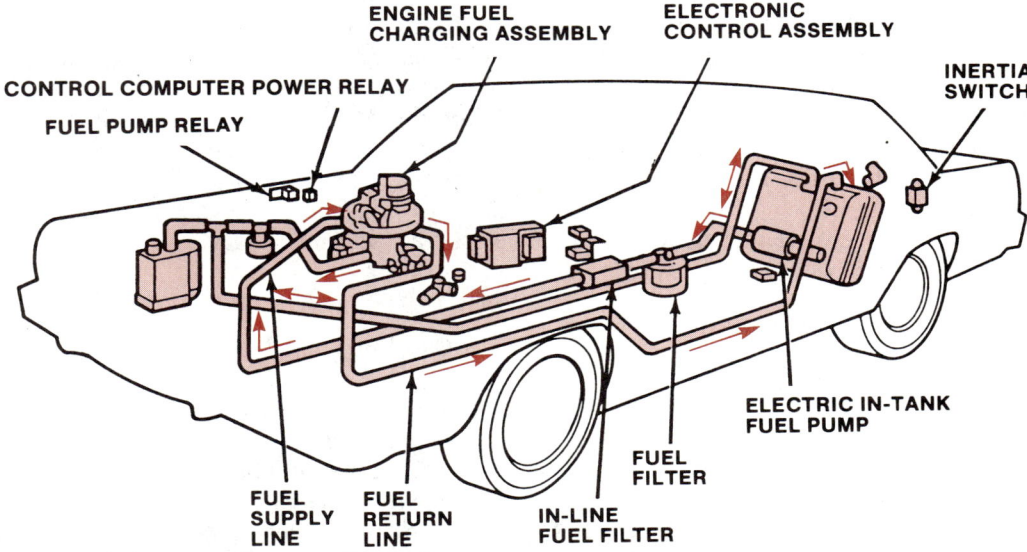

Figure 20-49 Typical electronically-controlled fuel system components.

516 Section 4 Engine Performance

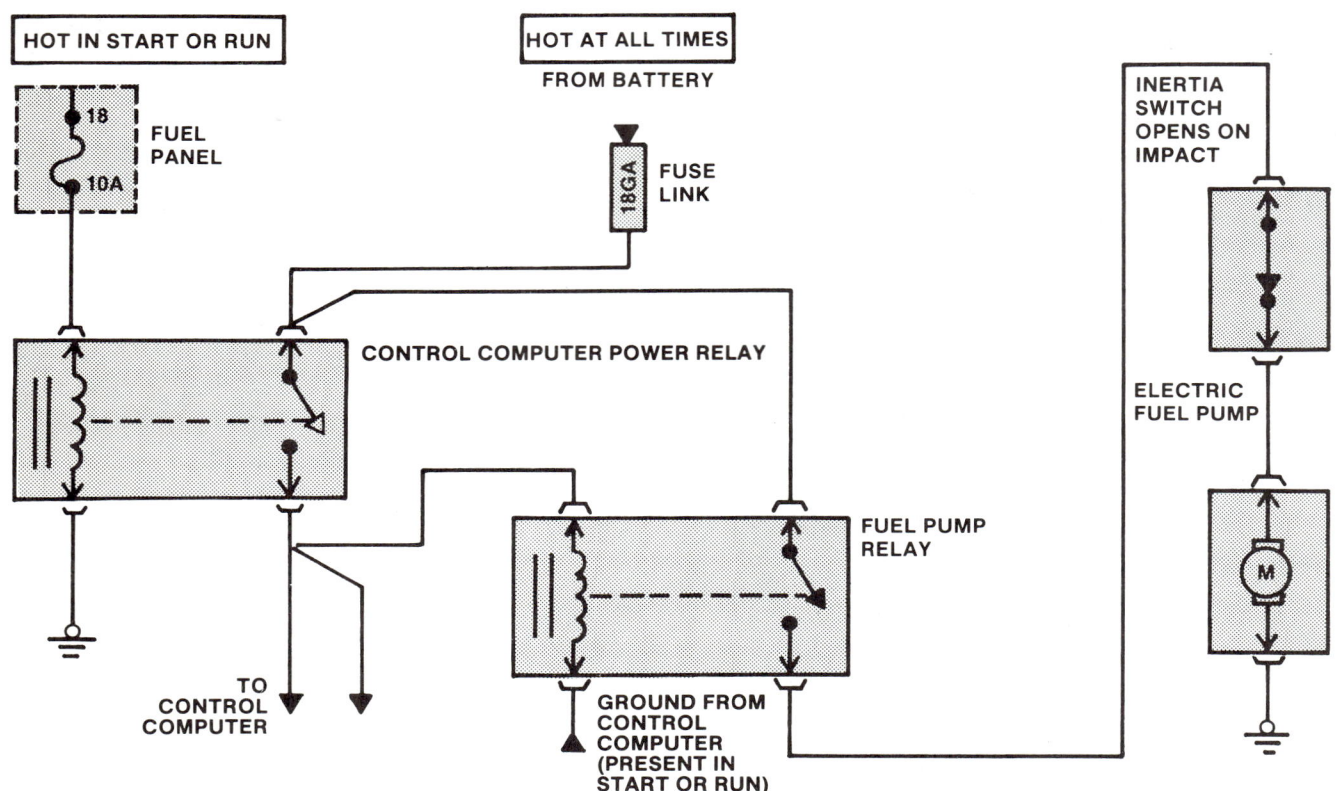

Figure 20–50 Electrical fuel delivery system wiring diagram.

When the ignition key is placed in the start or run position in a typical electronic system, the computer's power relay applies energizing voltage to the fuel pump relay. The ground path for the relay power circuit is through the computer. This ground path is present only when the ignition key is in start or run.

The computer controls operation of the fuel pump relay during the run mode by opening and closing the ground path to the relay coil (Figure 20-50). The computer also has a time-out feature that shuts off the fuel pump during a key on/engine off situation. Under a condition of engine flooding, the computer shuts off the injectors if the throttle position sensor (TPS) signals the wide-open throttle (WOT) valve during the crank mode. This allows the driver to start a flooded engine by using the same technique used on engines with a carburetor. Simply hold the accelerator pedal down while cranking the engine.

Detailed information concerning fuel delivery and control in electronic fuel injection systems is given in the next chapter.

 **CASE STUDY**

Case 1

A customer comes into the shop complaining about a hesitation problem. After taking a test drive with the customer in the car, the technician checks under the hood. He sees that the hot air duct between the exhaust manifold and the air cleaner is intact. The lines that route vacuum to the thermostatically-controlled air cleaner are in place, and the heat riser valve moves freely. He checks and finds that the rest of the vacuum lines are properly routed and connected.

So the technician removes the air cleaner and peers down the carburetor's throat while he works the throttle. He notes that the flow of gas is weak. The technician performs pressure and volume tests. The pressure is within the manufacturer's specifications, but the volume is low and large air bubbles are produced during the test. Because of the air bubbles the technician checks the flexible fuel hoses between the fuel pump and the fuel tank. He finds that one of the clamps has been tightened too much and a crack has resulted.

Summary

- Gasoline is made from crude oil.
- The major factors affecting fuel performance are antiknock quality, volatility, sulfur content, and deposit control.
- An octane number is a measure of a gasoline's burning quality.
- Two basic types of gasoline are used in vehicles: leaded and unleaded. The main reason unleaded

gasoline was introduced was to provide a fuel for cars with catalytic converters.
- Isopropyl alcohol is seasonally added to gasoline as an anti-icing agent. Oxidation inhibitors help control gum, deposit formation, and staleness. Metal deactivators and rust inhibitors reduce reactions between the fuel and the metals in the fuel system. Detergents clean certain critical components inside the engine. Ethanol and methanol are used as octane enhancers. MTBE is an active enhancer and supply extender.
- Diesel fuel is made from the middle distillates of crude oil.
- The significant chemical properties of diesel fuel are its wax appearance point, pour point, viscosity, volatility, and cetane number.
- Other alternate fuels include ethanol, methanol, propane, and natural gas.
- Because of its high propane content, LP-gas is often referred to as propane. Propane is a dry fuel, meaning that it enters the engine as a vapor. Gasoline, on the other hand, enters as tiny droplets of liquid.
- Natural gas costs less than gasoline. It is the cleanest alternative fuel. Therefore, it generally reduces vehicle maintenance. It is safe and abundant and readily available in the United States. The chief disadvantage at this time is its nonavailability to most users.
- Modern fuel tanks include devices that prevent vapors from leaving the tank. They have slash baffles or surge plates to prevent the fuel from splashing around. Each tank has an inlet filler tube and a nonvented cap. Rollover protection devices prevent gasoline from leaking out of the fuel tank in an accident. A liquid vapor separator stops liquid fuel or bubbles from reaching the vapor storage canister or the engine crankcase.
- The fuel lines carry fuel from the tank to the fuel pump, fuel filter, and carburetor or fuel injection metering pump. They are made of either metal tubing or flexible nylon or synthetic rubber hose.
- The three basic types of fuel filters are in-carburetor filters, in-line filters, and out-pump filters.
- Basically, there are two types of fuel pumps: mechanical and electrical. There are four basic types of electric fuel pumps: the diaphragm, plunger, bellows, and impeller (or rotary). Incorrect fuel pressure and low volume are the two most likely fuel pump troubles that affect engine performance.
- The control of an electronic fuel delivery system is obtained through a power relay and computer.

Review Questions

1. What rating is used as a measure of a diesel fuel's ignition quality?
2. Name the two forms of natural gas.
3. Name the components of a typical fuel delivery system.
4. Name the three basic types of in-carburetor gasoline filters.
5. Name the four basic types of electric fuel pumps.
6. Which of the following statements is false?
   a. An octane number is a measure of a fuel's tendency not to produce engine knock.
   b. Turbocharging deters knock.
   c. Both a and b
   d. Neither a nor b
7. Which of the following is the leading cause of exhaust valve pitting and exhaust system deterioration?
   a. gum
   b. oxidation
   c. sulfuric acid
   d. none of the above
8. Technician A says that the main reason unleaded gasoline was introduced was to provide a fuel for cars with catalytic converters. Technician B says that the main reason was to offset the effects of isopropyl alcohol in gasoline. Who is correct?
   a. Technician A
   b. Technician B
   c. Both A and B
   d. Neither A nor B
9. Which of the following is the most widely used gasoline additive today?
   a. ethanol
   b. MTBE
   c. methanol
   d. propane
10. Which of the following is known as wood alcohol?
    a. ethanol
    b. MTBE
    c. methanol
    d. propane
11. Which of the following is a major drawback to MTBE?
    a. It cannot be shipped through product pipelines.
    b. It causes elastomers and plastics to swell.
    c. Both a and b
    d. Neither a nor b
12. Which of the following is a measure of fluid's resistance to flow?
    a. wax appearance point
    b. pour point
    c. specific gravity
    d. none of the above
13. Which of the following statements is incorrect?
    a. Diesel fuel is more volatile than gasoline.
    b. Propane is a constituent of natural gas.

c. Propane burns clean in an engine.
d. High viscosity fuel is relatively hard to burn.

14. What percent of a modern fuel tank can ever be filled with fuel?
    a. 40%
    b. 60%
    c. 90%
    d. 100%
15. Technician A replaces any leaking metal fuel tank. Technician B steam cleans a leaking metal fuel tank and then solders or brazes it. Who uses the better method?
    a. Technician A
    b. Technician B
    c. Both A and B
    d. Neither A nor B
16. Technician A replaces a damaged steel fuel line with one made of synthetic rubber. Technician B replaces a damaged steel fuel line with another made of steel. Who is correct?
    a. Technician A
    b. Technician B
    c. Both A and B
    d. Neither A nor B
17. What component, located in the gasoline tank, prevents large contaminant particles from entering the fuel system?
    a. fuel filter
    b. diesel filter
    c. air filter
    d. strainer
18. A vehicle's engine performance indicates inadequate fuel, and a faulty fuel pump is suspected. Technician A tests the fuel pump for pressure and volume while mounted on the engine. Technician B removes the fuel pump to inspect it. Who is correct?
    a. Technician A
    b. Technician B
    c. Both A and B
    d. Neither A nor B
19. In a gasoline engine, _____ occurs when the flame front fails to reach a pocket of air/fuel mixture before the temperature in that area reaches the point of self-ignition.
    a. volatility
    b. carbon depositing
    c. detonation
    d. flaring
20. After a fuel pump is installed, an internal squeaking noise is heard with each movement of the pump. Technician A considers the noise to be normal. Technician B examines the pump for a defective or loose component. Who is correct?
    a. Technician A
    b. Technician B
    c. Both A and B
    d. Neither A nor B

21 FUEL INJECTION

Objectives

- Explain the principles of operation of a fuel injection system.
- List the advantages of fuel injection.
- Describe four methods of fuel injection.
- Explain the differences in point of injection in throttle body or port injection systems.
- Explain the design and function of EFI components.
- Explain the design and function of CIS components.
- Service fuel injection systems.
- Explain the basics of diesel fuel injection.

Fuel injection involves spraying or injecting fuel directly into the engine's intake manifold (Figure 21-1). Fuel injection, especially when it is electronically controlled, has several major advantages over carbureted systems. These include improved driveability under all conditions, improved fuel control, and an increase in engine efficiency and power. Gas mileage increases and there is a reduction in exhaust pollutant levels.

Although fuel injection technology has been around since the 1920s, several factors kept it from gaining widespread popularity until the 1980s. Cheap, plentiful fuel supplies and a lack of concern over engine emissions made the increased efficiencies of fuel injection more of a novelty than a necessity. Simple carburetor systems were less expensive, easier to repair, and provided adequate performance.

However, as carburetors evolved into more complex designs to meet increasing demand for fuel economy and emission standard laws, differences in price and complexity between mechanical fuel injection systems and carburetors decreased. The introduction of microcomputers in automotive applications greatly simplified fuel injection systems to the point where electronically controlled fuel injection has replaced carburetion on nearly all engines.

❏ GASOLINE FUEL INJECTION

There are many different gasoline fuel injection systems now being used on domestic and import vehicles. Most systems are one of four major types.

1. Electronic control throttle body injection (TBI)
2. Electronic control port fuel injection (PFI)
3. Mechanical control continuous injection systems (CIS)
4. Electronic control continuous injection systems (CIS-E)

Most electronic fuel injection systems only inject fuel during part of the engine's combustion cycle. The engine fuel needs are measured by intake airflow past a

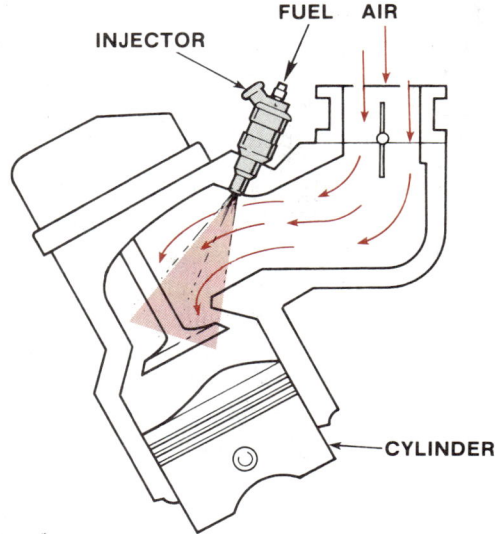

Figure 21-1 In a port fuel injection system, air and fuel are mixed in the intake manifold runners very close to the intake valve(s) of the combustion chamber.

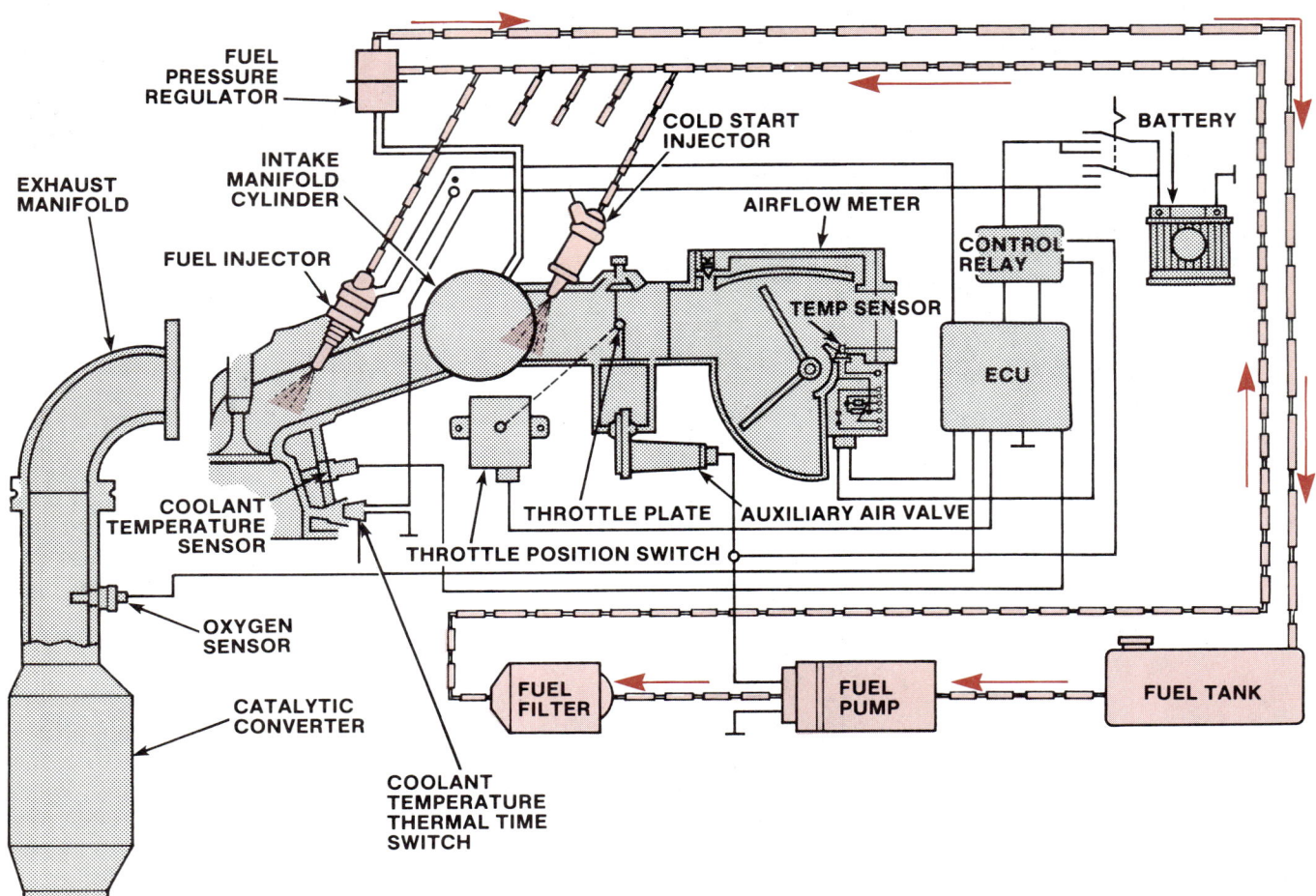

Figure 21-2 Components of a typical electronically controlled port fuel injection system.

sensor or by intake manifold pressure (vacuum). The airflow or manifold vacuum sensor converts its reading to an electrical signal and sends it to the engine control computer. The computer processes this signal (and others) and calculates the fuel needs of the engine. The computer then sends an electrical signal to the fuel injector or injectors. This signal determines the amount of time the injector opens and sprays fuel. This interval is known as the injector pulse width.

Most domestic electronic fuel injection systems are either throttle body or port injection systems. Throttle body injection systems have a throttle body assembly mounted on the intake manifold in the position usually occupied by a carburetor. The throttle body assembly usually contains one or two injectors.

On port fuel injection systems, fuel injectors are mounted in the intake manifold runners. One injector is directed at the back of each intake valve. Aside from the differences in injector location and number of injectors, operation of throttle body and port systems is quite similar with regard to fuel and air metering, sensors, and computer operation (Figure 21-2).

Continuous injection systems are used on many import vehicles. They deliver a steady stream of pressurized fuel into the intake manifold. In other words, the injectors do not pulse on and off as in port and throttle body systems. In CIS, the amount of fuel delivered is controlled by the rate of airflow entering the engine. An airflow sensor suspended in the path of the intake air controls movement of a plunger that alters fuel flow to the injectors. Technically, CIS is a mechanically controlled system. On early models, the only electrical component was the high pressure fuel pump. Later CIS systems added oxygen sensor feedback circuits and other electronic controls.

ELECTRONIC FUEL INJECTION SYSTEMS Electronic fuel injection (EFI) has proven to be the most precise, reliable, and cost effective method of delivering fuel to the combustion chambers of today's vehicles. EFI systems must provide the correct air/fuel ratio for all engine loads, speeds, and temperature conditions. To accomplish this, an EFI system uses a fuel delivery system, air induction system, input sensors, control computer, fuel injectors, and an idle speed control.

☐ THROTTLE BODY VERSUS PORT INJECTION

How fuel and air are handled within an EFI system depends on whether a throttle body or ported design is

Fuel Injection 521

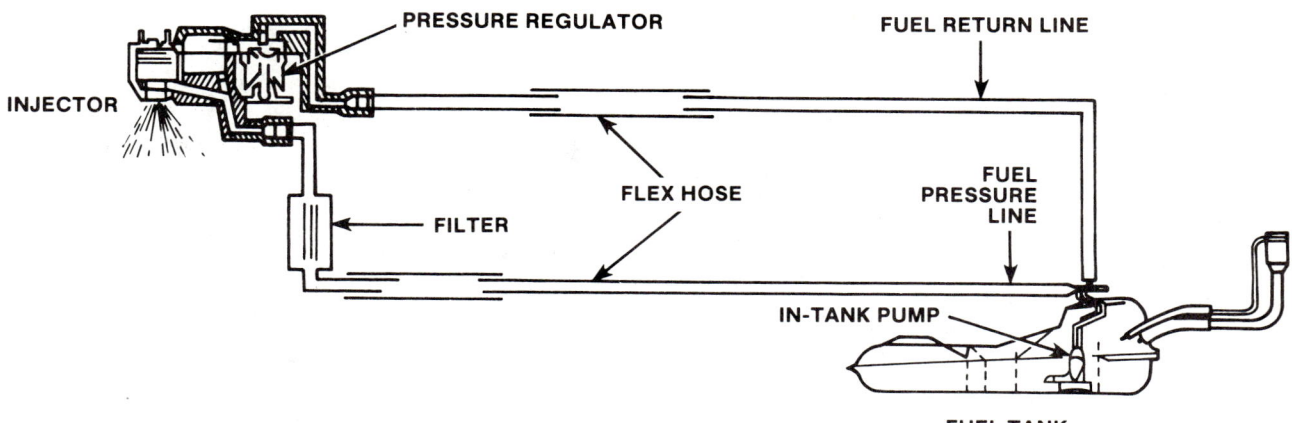

Figure 21-3 Components of a typical fuel circuit used in a throttle body fuel injection system.

used. However, there are some fuel system components common to both systems.

In a typical EFI fuel delivery system (Figure 21-3), fuel is drawn from the fuel tank by an in-tank or chassis-mounted electric fuel pump. Before it reaches the injectors, the fuel passes through a filter that removes dirt and impurities. A fuel line pressure regulator maintains a constant fuel line pressure that may be as high as 50 psi in some systems. This fuel pressure generates the spraying force needed to inject the fuel. Excess fuel not required by the engine passes through the fuel pressure regulator and returns to the fuel tank through a fuel return line.

Throttle Body Fuel Injection

For many auto manufacturers, throttle body injection (TBI) served as a stepping stone from carburetors to more advanced port fuel injection systems. TBI units were used on many engines during the 1980s and are still used on some engines. The throttle body unit is similar in size and shape to a carburetor, and like a carburetor, mount on the intake manifold (Figure 21-4). Fuel supply and return line service one or sometimes two fuel injectors. The injector(s) spray fuel down into a throttle body chamber leading to the intake manifold. The air/fuel mixture in the manifold feeds all cylinders.

TBI Operation

The basic TBI assembly consists of two major castings: a throttle body with a valve to control airflow and a fuel body to supply the required fuel. A fuel pressure regulator and fuel injector are integral parts of the fuel body (Figure 21-5). Also included as part of the assembly is a device to control idle speed and one to provide throttle valve positioning data.

The throttle body casting has ports that can be located above, below, or at the throttle valve depending on the manufacturer's design. These ports generate vacuum signals for the manifold absolute pressure sensor and for devices in the emission control system,

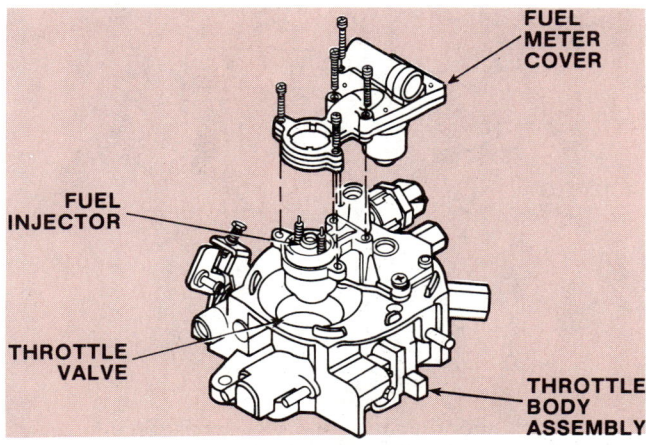

Figure 21-4 Parts of a throttle body injection unit.

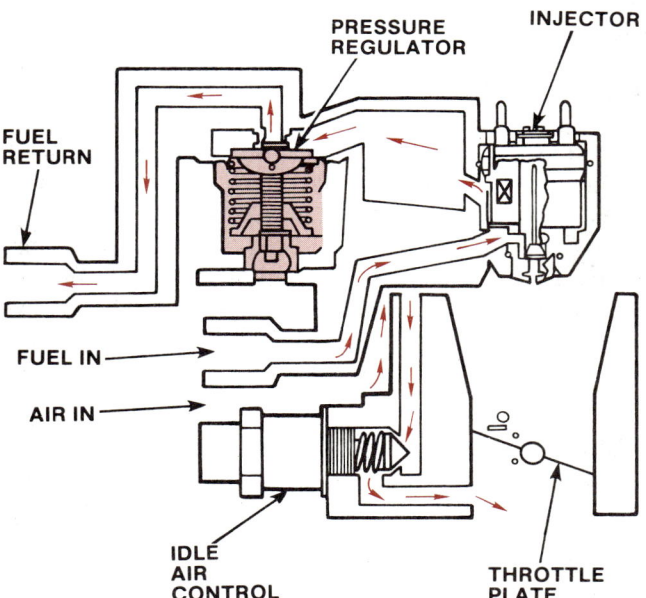

Figure 21-5 Fuel and airflow in a TBI injection system. The injector is a bottom fuel feed design. The idle air control allows air to bypass the throttle plate to regulate engine idle in all operating conditions.

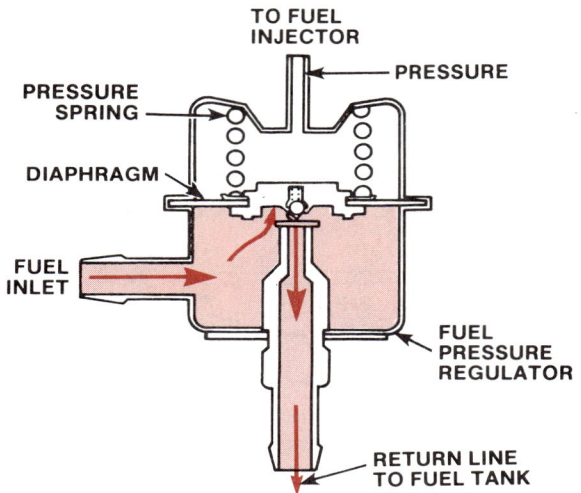

Figure 21-6 Operation of a diaphragm-operated fuel pressure regulator.

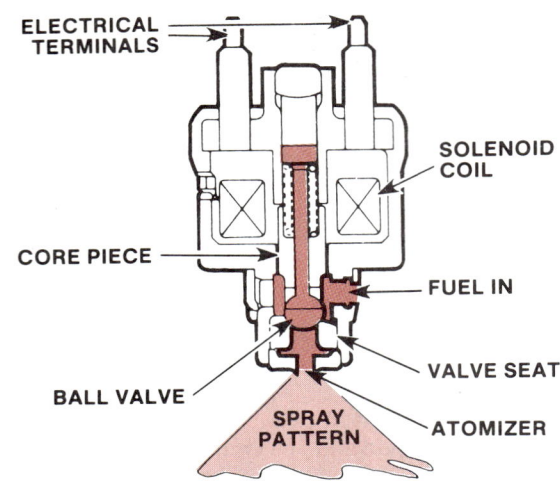

Figure 21-7 Solenoid-operated ball valve type fuel injector used in a TBI system. When electronically energized, the ball valve lifts off the valve seat, allowing fuel to spray into the throttle body housing.

such as the EGR valve, the canister purge system, and so on.

The fuel pressure regulator used on the throttle body assembly is similar to a diaphragm-operated relief valve (Figure 21-6). Fuel pressure is on one side of the diaphragm and air cleaner pressure is on the other side. The regulator is designed to provide a constant pressure on the fuel injector throughout the range of engine loads and speeds. If regulator pressure is too high, a strong fuel odor is emitted, and there is a chance that detonation could take place. On the other hand, regulator pressure that is too low results in poor engine performance.

The fuel injector is solenoid operated and pulsed on and off by the vehicle's electronic control computer. Remember, this computer is called by different names by different manufacturers. Electronic control unit (ECU) and electronic control module (ECM) are the most common names. In this chapter, the terms control computer and electronic control unit (ECU) are used interchangeably. Surrounding the injector inlet is a fine screen filter where the incoming fuel is directed. When the injector's solenoid is energized, a normally closed ball valve is lifted (Figure 21-7). Fuel under pressure is then injected at the walls of the throttle body bore just above the throttle plate. Excess fuel is returned to the fuel tank via the pressure regulator.

TBI Advantages

Throttle body systems provide improved fuel metering when compared to carburetors. They are also less expensive and simpler to service. Because they use a maximum of only two injectors, throttle body systems are considerably less expensive than port injection systems, which use an injector for each cylinder.

However, throttle body units are not as efficient as port systems. The disadvantages are primarily manifold related. Like a carburetor system, fuel is still not distributed equally to all cylinders, and a cold manifold may cause fuel to condense and puddle in the manifold. Like a carburetor, throttle body injection systems must be mounted above the combustion chamber level, which eliminates the possibility of tuning the manifold design for more efficient operation.

Port Fuel Injection

Port fuel injection (PFI) systems use one injector at each cylinder. They are mounted in the intake manifold near the cylinder head where they can inject a fine, atomized fuel mist as close as possible to the intake valve (Figure 21-8). Fuel lines run to each cylinder from a fuel manifold, usually referred to as a fuel rail. The fuel rail assembly on a PFI system of V-6 and V-8 engines usually consists of a left- and

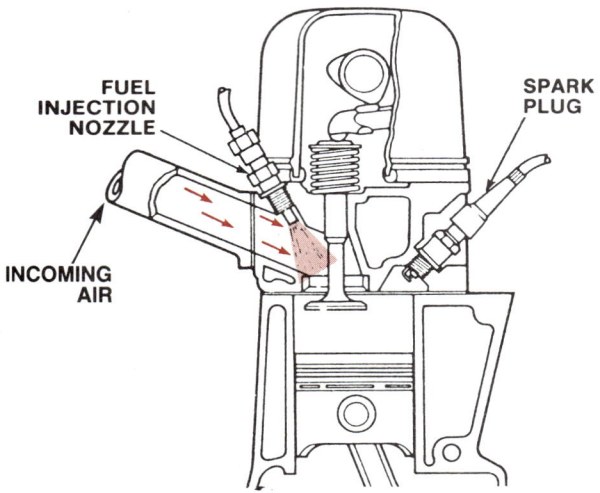

Figure 21-8 Port fuel injection systems use an injector at each cylinder.

Fuel Injection 523

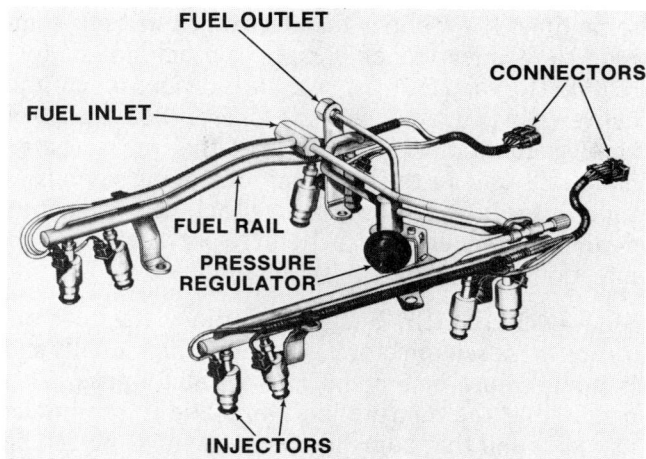

Figure 21-9 A fuel rail and injector wiring harness used to supply fuel and electrical power to the injectors on a port system. *Courtesy of General Motors Corp.*

Figure 21-11 Port injection systems often have tuned intake manifold runners to optimize low-speed power. *Courtesy of General Motors Corp.*

right-hand rail assembly. The two rails can be connected either by crossover and return fuel tubes or by a mechanical bracket arrangement. A typical fuel rail arrangement is shown in Figure 21-9. Fuel tubes crisscross between the two rails and the pressure regulator attaches to the back of one of the rails. Figure 21-10 shows a fuel rail on a transverse four cylinder engine. Since each cylinder has its own injector, fuel distribution is exactly equal. With little or no fuel to wet the manifold walls, there is no need for manifold heat or an early fuel evaporation system. Fuel does not collect in puddles at the base of the manifold. This means that the intake manifold passages can be tuned or designed for bettter low-speed power availability (Figure 21-11). The port type systems provide a more accurate and efficient delivery of fuel.

The throttle body in a port fuel injection system controls the amount of air that enters the engine as well as the amount of vacuum in the manifold. It also houses and controls the idle air control (IAC) motor

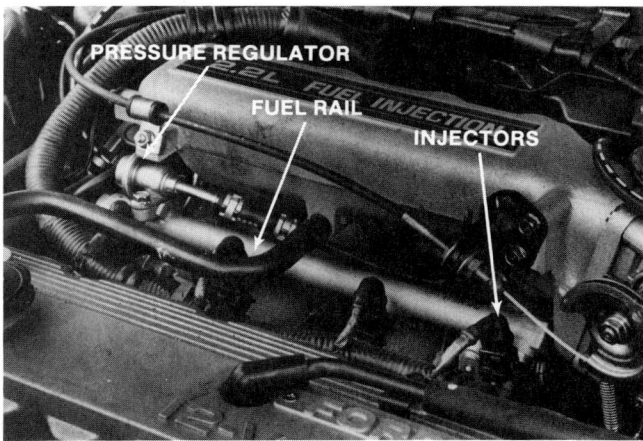

Figure 21-10 Fuel rail assembly found on a transverse four-cylinder engine.

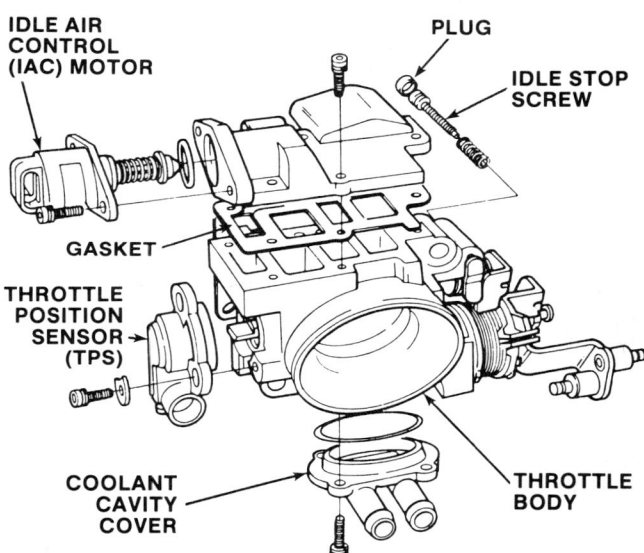

Figure 21-12 Throttle body assembly of a port fuel injection system.

and the throttle position sensor (TPS). The TPS enables the ECU to know where the throttle is positioned at all times.

The throttle body (Figure 21-12) is a single cast aluminum housing with a single throttle blade attached to the throttle shaft. The TPS and the IAC valve/motor are also attached to the housing. The throttle shaft is controlled by the accelerator pedal. The throttle shaft extends the full length of the housing. The throttle bore controls the amount of incoming air that enters the air induction system. A small amount of coolant is also routed through a passage in the throttle body to prevent icing during cold weather.

Port systems require an additional control system that throttle body injection units do not require. While throttle body injectors are mounted above the throttle plates and are not affected by fluctuations in manifold vacuum, port system injectors have their tips located in the manifold where constant changes in vacuum would affect the amount of fuel injected (at a given pulse width). To compensate for these fluctuations, port injection systems are equipped with fuel pressure regulators that sense manifold vacuum and continually adjust the fuel pressure to maintain a constant pressure drop across the injector tips at all times.

Port Firing Control

While all port injection systems operate using an injector at each cylinder, they do not fire the injectors in the same manner. Four firing systems used on domestic vehicles are grouped single fire, grouped double fire, simultaneous double fire, and sequential fire.

The terms grouped and simultaneous refer to how the injectors are connected within the system. Some systems fire the injectors in groups. Others fire them all together. The terms single and double fire refer to how many firings of each injector are used to make up the fuel charge for one combustion stroke.

GROUPED SINGLE FIRE In this type of system, injectors are split into two equal groups. The groups are fired alternately, with one group firing each engine revolution (Figure 21-13). Only one injector pulse is used for each combustion stroke.

Since only two injectors can be fired relatively close to the time when the intake valve is about to open, the fuel charge for the remaining cylinders must stand in the intake manifold for varying periods of time.

GROUPED DOUBLE FIRE This system also splits the injectors into two equal groups that alternately fire. But in this case, each group fires once each engine revolution. Two injector pulses make up each intake charge. This results in the air/fuel mixture remaining in the manifold for shorter periods of time.

SIMULTANEOUS DOUBLE FIRE This system fires all of the injectors at the same time, once each engine revolution. It offers ease in programming and relatively fast adjustments to the air/fuel mixture. The injectors are connected in parallel so the ECU develops just one signal for all injectors. They all open and close at the same time. It simplifies the electronics without compromising injection efficiency. The amount of fuel required for each four-stroke cycle is divided in half and delivered in two injections, one for every 360 degrees of crankshaft rotation. The fact that the intake charge must still wait in the manifold for varying periods of time is the system's major drawback. Simultaneous double fire systems are extremely popular with port injection.

SEQUENTIAL FIRE Sequential firing of the injectors means that each injector is controlled individually and is opened just before the intake valve opens. This means that the mixture is never static in the intake manifold and that adjustments to the mixture can be made almost instantaneously between the firing of one injector and the next.

Sequential firing is the most accurate and desirable method of regulating port injection.

❏ SYSTEM SENSORS

The ability of the fuel injection system to control the air/fuel ratio depends on its ability to properly time the injector pulses with the intake stroke of each cylinder and its ability to vary the injector on time, according to changing engine demands. Both tasks require the use of electronic sensors that monitor the operating conditions of the engine.

Airflow Sensors

In order to control the proportion of fuel to air in the air/fuel charge, the fuel system must be able to measure the amount of air entering the engine. Several sensors have been developed to do just that.

VOLUME AIRFLOW SENSOR The airflow sensor shown in Figure 21-14 measures airflow, or air volume. The sensor consists of a spring-loaded flap, potentiometer, damping chamber, backfire protection valve, and idle bypass channel. As air is drawn into the

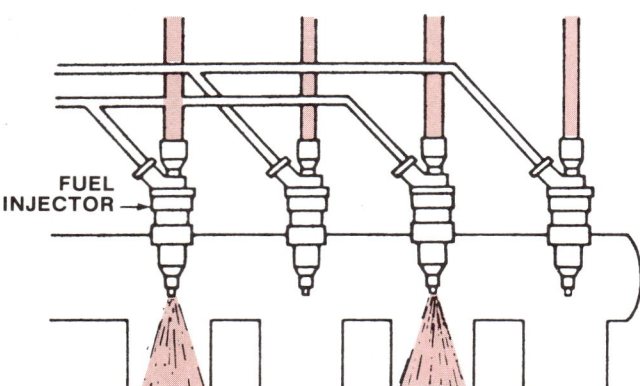

Figure 21-13   Grouped single-fire port injection.

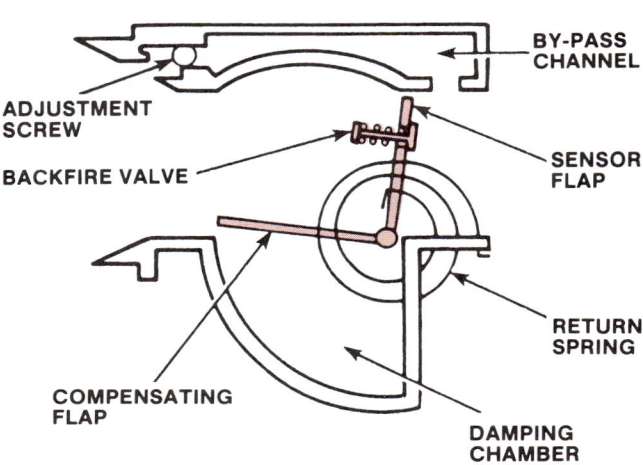

Figure 21-14   Typical airflow sensor.

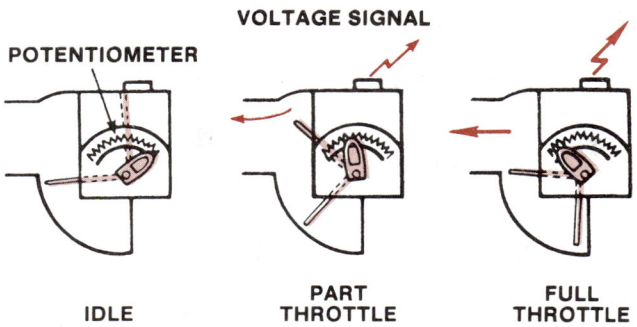

Figure 21-15 In a typical airflow sensor, the strength of the voltage signal produced by the potentiometer varies in response to the amount the sensor flap moves.

engine, the flap is deflected against the spring. A potentiometer, attached to the flap shaft, monitors the flap movement and produces a corresponding voltage signal (Figure 21-15). The strength of the signal increases as the flap opens. The signal voltage is relayed to the electronic control module.

DAMPING CHAMBER The curved shape of the airflow sensor is the damping chamber. The damping flap in this chamber is on the same shaft as the airflow sensing flap and is also about the same area. As a result, the damping flap smooths out any possible pulsations caused by opening and closing of the intake valves. Airflow measurement can be a steady signal, closely related to airflow as controlled by the movement of the flap.

BACKFIRE PROTECTION The airflow sensor flap provides for backfire protection with a spring-loaded valve. If the intake manifold pressure suddenly rises because of a backfire, this valve releases the pressure and prevents damage to the system.

IDLE BYPASS The airflow sensor assembly includes an extra air passage for idle, bypassing the airflow sensor plate. This is seen near the top of Figure 21-14. When the throttle is closed at idle, the opening and closing of intake valves can cause pulsations in the intake manifold. Without the idle bypass, such pulsations could cause the flap to shudder, resulting in an uneven air/fuel mixture. The idle bypass smooths the flow of the idle intake air, ensuring regular signals to the electronic control.

A second type of airflow sensor is shown in Figure 21-16. It works on a different operating principle. Air entering the airflow sensor assembly passes through vanes arranged around the inside of a tube. As the air flows through the vanes, it begins to swirl. The outer part of the swirling air exerts high pressure against the outside of the housing. There is a low-pressure area in the center.

The low-pressure area moves in a circular motion as the air swirls through the intake tube. Two pressure-sensing tubes near the end of the tube sense the low-

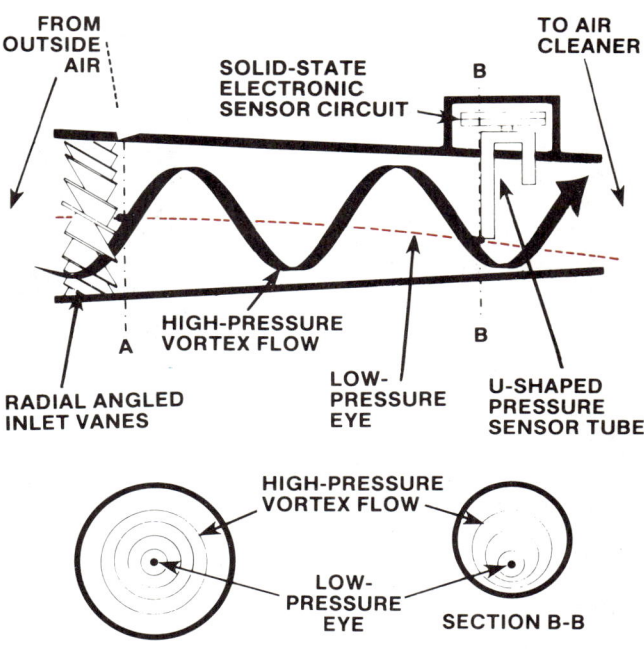

Figure 21-16 This airflow sensor uses special vanes to swirl the incoming air. It then measures the strength of the low-pressure swirl center to determine airflow volume.

pressure area as it moves around. An electronic sensor counts how many times the low-pressure area is sensed.

The faster the airflow, the more times the low-pressure area is sensed. This is translated into a signal that indicates to the combustion control computer how much air is flowing into the intake manifold.

Air Temperature Sensor

Cold air is denser (weighs more) than warm air. Cold, dense air can burn more fuel than the same volume of warm air because it contains more oxygen. This is why airflow sensors that only measure air volume must have their readings adjusted to account for differences in air temperature.

Most systems do this by using an air temperature sensor mounted in the throttle body of the induction system. The air sensor measures air temperature and sends an electronic signal to the control computer. The computer uses this input along with the air volume input in determining the amount of oxygen entering the engine.

In some early EFI systems, the incoming air is heated to a set temperature. In these systems an air temperature sensor is used to ensure this predetermined operating temperature is maintained.

Mass Airflow Sensor

A mass airflow sensor (Figure 21-17) does the job of a volume airflow sensor and an air temperature sensor.

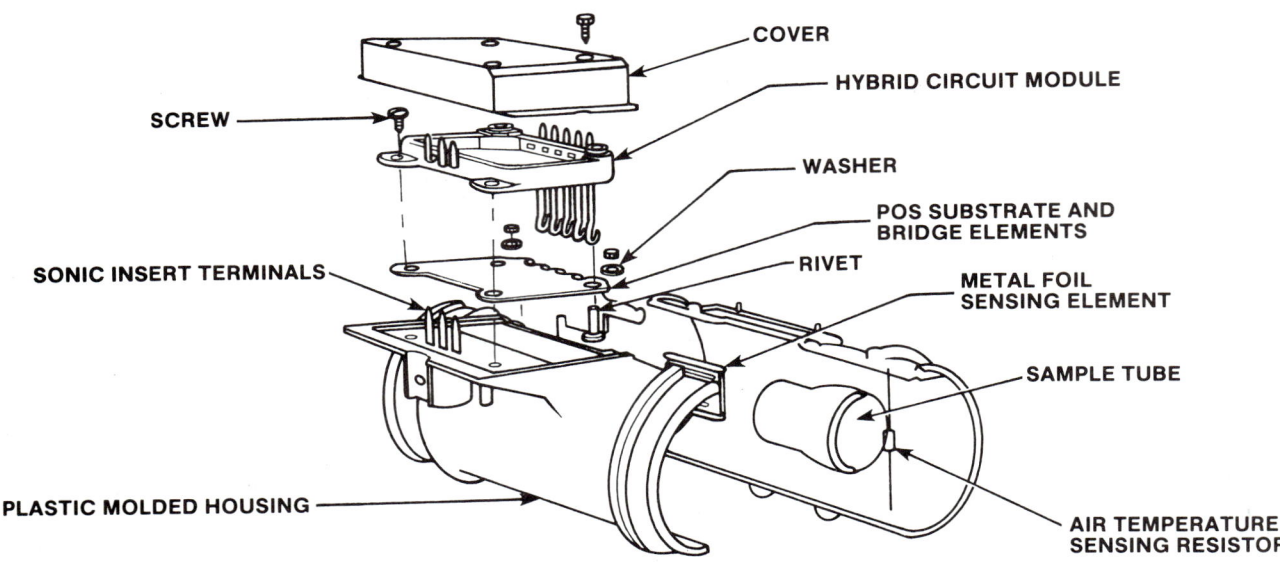

Figure 21-17 Components of a mass airflow sensor.

It measures air mass. The mass of a given amount of air is calculated by multiplying its volume by its density. As explained previously, the denser the air, the more oxygen it contains. Monitoring the oxygen in a given volume of air is important, since oxygen is a prime catalyst in the combustion process. From a measurement of mass, the electronic control unit adjusts the fuel delivery for the oxygen content in a given volume of air. The accuracy of air/fuel ratios is greatly enhanced when matching fuel to air mass instead of fuel to air volume.

The mass airflow sensor converts air flowing past a heated sensing element into an electronic signal. The strength of this signal is determined by the energy needed to keep the element at a constant temperature above the incoming ambient air temperature. As the volume and density (mass) of airflow across the heated element changes, the temperature of the element is affected and the current flow to the element is adjusted to maintain the desired temperature of the heating element. The varying current flow parallels the particular characteristics of the incoming air (hot, dry, cold, humid, high/low pressure). The electronic control unit monitors the changes in current to determine air mass and to calculate precise fuel requirements.

There are two basic types of mass airflow sensors: hot wire and hot film. In the first type, a very thin wire (about 0.2 mm thick) is used as the heated element. The element temperature is set at 100 degrees Celsius above incoming air temperature. Periodically, the wire is heated to approximately 1000 degrees Celsius for 1 second to burn off any accumulated dust and contaminants.

The second type uses a nickel foil sensor, which is kept 75 degrees Celsius above ambient air temperatures. It does not require a burn off period. Thus, it is potentially longer lasting than the hot wire type.

Manifold Absolute Pressure Sensor

Some EFI systems do not use airflow or air mass to determine the base pulse of the injector(s). Instead, the base pulse is calculated on manifold absolute pressure (MAP).

The MAP sensor measures changes in the intake manifold pressure that result from changes in engine load and speed. The pressure measured by the MAP sensor is the difference between barometric pressure (outside air) and manifold pressure (vacuum). At closed throttle, the engine produces a low MAP value. A wide-open throttle produces a high value. This high value is produced when the pressure inside the manifold is the same as pressure outside the manifold, and 100% of the outside air is being measured. This MAP output is the opposite of what is measured on a vacuum gauge. The use of this sensor also allows the control computer to adjust automatically for different altitudes.

The control computer sends a voltage reference signal to the MAP sensor. As the MAP changes, the electrical resistance of the sensor also changes. The control computer can determine the manifold pressure by monitoring the sensor output voltage. A high pressure, low vacuum (high voltage) requires more fuel. A low pressure, high vacuum (low voltage) requires less fuel. Like an airflow sensor, a MAP sensor relies on an air temperature sensor to adjust its base pulse signal to match incoming air density.

Other EFI System Sensors

In addition to airflow, air mass, or manifold absolute pressure readings, the control computer relies on input from a number of other system sensors. This input further adjusts the injector pulse width to match engine operating conditions. Operating conditions are communicated to the control computer by the following types of sensors.

COOLANT TEMPERATURE The coolant temperature sensor signals the electronic control unit when the engine needs cold enrichment, as it does during warm-up. This adds to the base pulse, but decreases to zero as the engine warms up.

THROTTLE POSITION The switches on the throttle shaft signal the electronic control unit for idle enrichment when the throttle is closed. These same throttle switches signal the electronic control unit when the throttle is near the wide-open position to provide full load enrichment.

ENGINE SPEED The ignition system sends a tachometer signal reference pulse corresponding to engine speed to the electronic control unit. This signal advises the electronic control unit to adjust the pulse width of the injectors for engine speed. This also times the start of the injection according to the intake stroke cycle.

CRANKING ENRICHMENT The starter circuit sends a signal for fuel enrichment during cranking operations even when the engine is warm. This is independent of any cold-start fuel enrichment demands.

ALTITUDE COMPENSATION As the car operates at higher altitudes, the thinner air needs less fuel. Altitude compensation in a fuel injection system is accomplished by installing a sensor to monitor barometric pressure. Signals from the barometric pressure sensor are sent to the ECU to reduce the injector pulse width (or reduce the amount of fuel injected).

COASTING SHUTOFF Coasting shutoff can be found on a number of control systems. It can improve fuel economy as well as reduce emissions of hydrocarbons and carbon monoxide. Fuel shutoff is controlled in different ways depending on the type of transmission (manual or automatic). The ECU makes a coasting shutoff decision based on a closed throttle as indicated by the throttle position or idle switch or on engine speed as indicated by the signal from the ignition coil. When the ECU detects that power is not needed to maintain vehicle speed, the injectors are turned off until the need for power exists again.

ADDITIONAL INPUT INFORMATION SENSORS Additional sensors are also used to provide the following information on engine conditions.

- Detonation
- Crankshaft position
- Camshaft position
- Timing of ignition spark
- Air conditioner operation
- Gearshift lever position
- Battery voltage
- Amount of oxygen in exhaust gases
- Emission control device operation

Figure 21-18 shows the typical inputs and outputs of an onboard computer (ECU) responsible for controlling the EFI system.

❑ ELECTRONIC CONTROL COMPUTER

The heart of the fuel injection system is the control computer, commonly called an electronic control unit or module. For consistency, the term ECU is used throughout this chapter. The ECU is a small computer that is usually mounted within the passenger compartment to keep it away from the heat and vibration of the engine. The ECU includes solid state devices, including integrated circuits and a microprocessor.

The ECU receives signals from all the system sensors, processes them, and transmits programmed electrical pulses to the fuel injectors. Both incoming and outgoing signals are sent through a wiring harness and a multiple-pin connector.

Electronic feedback in the ECU means the unit is self-regulating and is controlling the injectors on the basis of operating performance or parameters rather than on preprogrammed instructions. An ECU with a feedback loop, for example, reads signals from the oxygen sensor, varies the pulse width of the injectors, and again reads the signals from the oxygen sensor. This is repeated until the injectors are pulsed for just the amount of time needed to get the proper amount of oxygen into the exhaust stream. While this interaction is occurring, the system is operating in closed loop. When conditions, such as starting or wide open throttle, demand that the signals from the oxygen sensor be ignored, the system operates in open loop. During open loop, injector pulse length is controlled by set parameters contained in the ECU memory banks.

❑ FUEL INJECTORS

Fuel injectors are electromechanical devices that meter fuel so it can be sprayed into the intake manifold. Fuel injectors resemble a spark plug in size and shape. As mentioned earlier, they mount into the intake manifold runners (port systems) or throttle body housing (TBI systems). O-rings are used to seal the injector at the intake manifold, throttle body, and fuel rail mounting positions. These O-rings provide thermal insulation to prevent the formation of vapor bubbles and promote good hot start characteristics. They also dampen potentially damaging vibration.

When the injector is electrically energized, a solenoid-operated valve opens, and a fine mist of fuel sprays

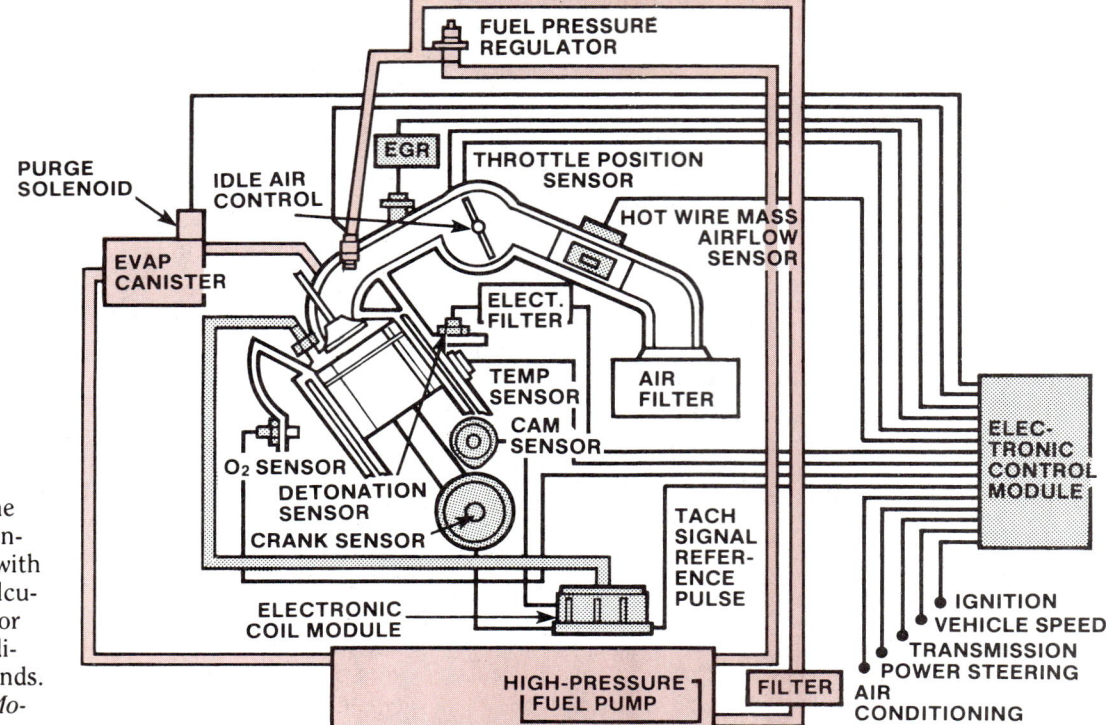

Figure 21-18 Input sensors from all engine systems supply the control computer (ECU) with the data needed to calculate the correct injector pulse for driving conditions and driver demands. *Courtesy of General Motors Corp.*

Figure 21-19 This fuel injector design is equipped with a nozzle or needle valve having a special ground pintle for precise fuel delivery control.

from the injector tip. Two different valve designs are commonly used.

The first consists of a valve body and a nozzle or needle valve that has a special ground pintle (Figure 21-19). A movable armature is attached to the nozzle valve, which is pressed against the nozzle body sealing seat by a helical spring. The solenoid winding is located at the back of the valve body.

When the solenoid winding is energized, it creates a magnetic field that draws the armature back and pulls the nozzle valve from its seat. When the solenoid is de-energized, the magnetic field collapses and the helical spring forces the nozzle valve back on its seat.

The second popular valve design uses a ball valve and valve seat. In this case, the magnetic field created by the solenoid coil pulls a plunger upward lifting the ball valve from its seat. Once again, a spring is used to return the valve to its seated or closed position.

Fuel injectors can be either top fuel feeding or bottom fuel feeding (Figure 21-20). Top feed injectors are primarily used in port injection systems that operate using high fuel system pressures. Bottom feed injectors are used in throttle body systems. Bottom feed injectors are able to use fuel pressures as low as 10 psi.

ELECTRICAL CONNECTORS Each fuel injector is equipped with a two-wire connector. The connector is often equipped with a spring clip that must be un-

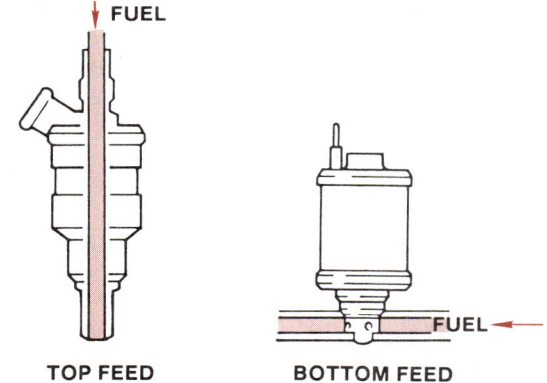

Figure 21-20 Examples of bottom and top feed injectors.

locked before the connector can be removed from the injector.

One wire of the connector supplies voltage to the injector. This voltage supply wire may connect directly to the fuse panel. Or it may connect to the ECU, which, in turn, connects to the fuse panel. In either case, a resistor at the fuse panel or ECU is used to reduce the 12-volt battery supply voltage to 3 volts or less.

The second wire of the connector is a ground wire. This ground wire is routed to the ECU. The ECU energizes the injector by grounding its electrical circuit. The pulse width of the injector equals the length of time the injector circuit is grounded. Typical pulse widths range from 1 millisecond to 10 milliseconds at full load. Port fuel injection systems having four, six, or eight injectors use a special wiring harness to simplify and organize injector wiring.

Cold Start Injectors

Many EFI systems are equipped with a separate cold start injector. The cold start injector delivers extra fuel while the cold engine is cranking. When the fuel pump is running, this extra injector is supplied with fuel under pressure. The colder the engine, the more extra fuel is injected during cranking. When the engine is warm, extra fuel is not injected.

The cold start injector is supplied with power from the starting circuit and is grounded through the thermal switch. The thermal switch is made of bimetal material that opens (switches off) the cold injector circuit once the engine coolant reaches a certain temperature. The length of time the cold injector circuit operates varies inversely with coolant temperature. In other words, as the coolant temperature goes up, the cold start injector on time decreases. The bimetal is also heated by windings in the thermal switch that allows the cold start injector to stay on for approximately 8 seconds at 68° coolant temperatures.

❏ IDLE SPEED CONTROL

In throttle body and port EFI systems, engine idle speed is controlled by bypassing a certain amount of airflow past the throttle valve in the throttle body housing. Two types of air bypass systems are used, auxiliary air valves and idle air control (IAC) valves. IAC valve systems are more common.

IAC Valves

The IAC system consists of an electrically-controlled stepper motor or actuator that positions the IAC valve in the air bypass channel around the throttle valve. The IAC valve is part of the throttle body casting (Figure 21-21). The control computer (ECU) calculates the amount of air needed for smooth idling based on input data such as coolant temperature, engine load, engine speed, and battery voltage. It then signals the actuator

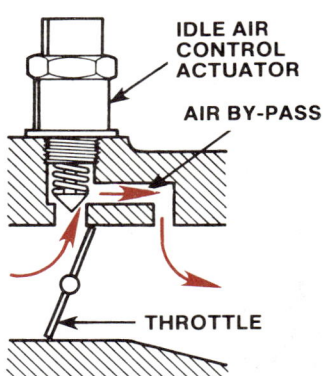

Figure 21-21 Components of an IAC system.

to extend or retract the idle air control valve in the air bypass channel.

If the engine speed is lower than desired, the ECU activates the motor to retract the IAC valve. This opens the channel and diverts more air around the throttle valve. If engine speed is higher than desired, the valve is extended and the bypass channel is made smaller. Air supply to the engine is reduced and engine speed falls.

During cold starts idle speed can be high as 2100 rpm to quickly raise the temperature of the catalytic converter for proper control of exhaust emissions. Idle speed that is attained after a cold start is controlled by the ECU. The ECU maintains idle speed for approximately 40 to 50 seconds even if the driver attempts to alter it by kicking the accelerator. After this preprogrammed time interval, depressing the accelerator pedal rotates the throttle position sensor (TPS) and signals the ECU to reduce idle speed.

Auxiliary Air Valve

The major difference between an IAC valve and an auxiliary air valve is that the auxiliary air valve is not controlled by the ECU. But like the IAC system, the auxiliary air valve provides additional air during cold engine starts and warm-up.

The auxiliary air valve consists of an air bypass channel or hose around the throttle valve, a movable plate or disc, and a heat sensitive bimetal strip. Figure 21-22 shows how an auxiliary air valve on a port injection system operates. When the plate opens the channel, extra air bypasses the throttle. Opening is controlled by the bimetal strip. As the bimetal heats up, it bends to rotate the movable plate, gradually blocking the opening. When the device is closed, there is no auxiliary airflow.

The bimetal strip is warmed by an electric heating element powered from the run circuit of the ignition switch. This bimetal element is not a switch, but a strip that moves the movable plate directly. The auxiliary air device is independent of the cold start injector. It is not controlled by the ECU but is continuously powered when the ignition key is set to the run position.

530 Section 4 Engine Performance

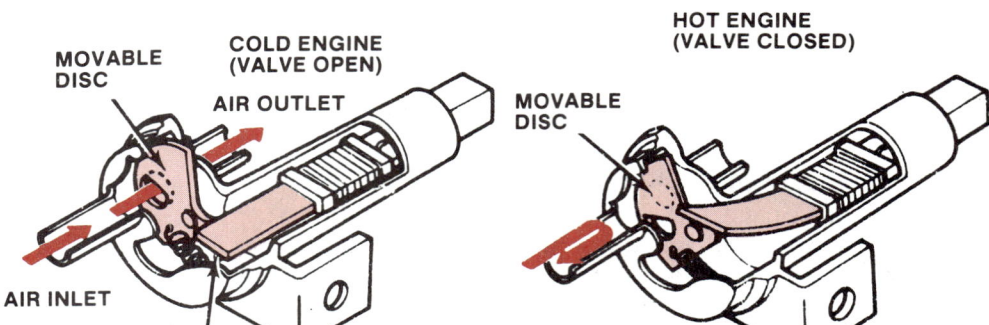

Figure 21-22 Operation of an auxiliary air valve. *Courtesy of Robert Bosch*

When the engine is cold, the passage opens for extra air when the engine starts. When the engine is running and still cold, the passage is open but the heater begins operating to close it gradually. If the engine is warm at start up, the passage is closed and normal air is delivered for idle.

☐ CONTINUOUS INJECTION SYSTEMS

Continuous injection systems (Figure 21-23) are the third major type of fuel injection used on modern engines. CIS is used almost exclusively on import vehicles. The basic technology for CIS was introduced in the early 1970s and has been continuously updated and refined. During the past twenty years, continuous injection systems have gained an excellent reputation for efficiency and reliability.

The major difference between CIS and electronically-controlled throttle body and port injection systems is the way in which the amount of fuel injected is controlled. In a CIS-equipped engine, the amount of fuel delivered to the cylinders is not varied by pulsing the injectors on and off. Instead CIS injectors spray fuel continuously. What does vary is the amount of fuel contained in the spray. CIS systems do this by maintaining a constant relative fuel system pressure and metering the amount of fuel fed to the injectors.

Basic Operation

Metering is done through a mixture control unit. This unit consists of an airflow sensor installed up-

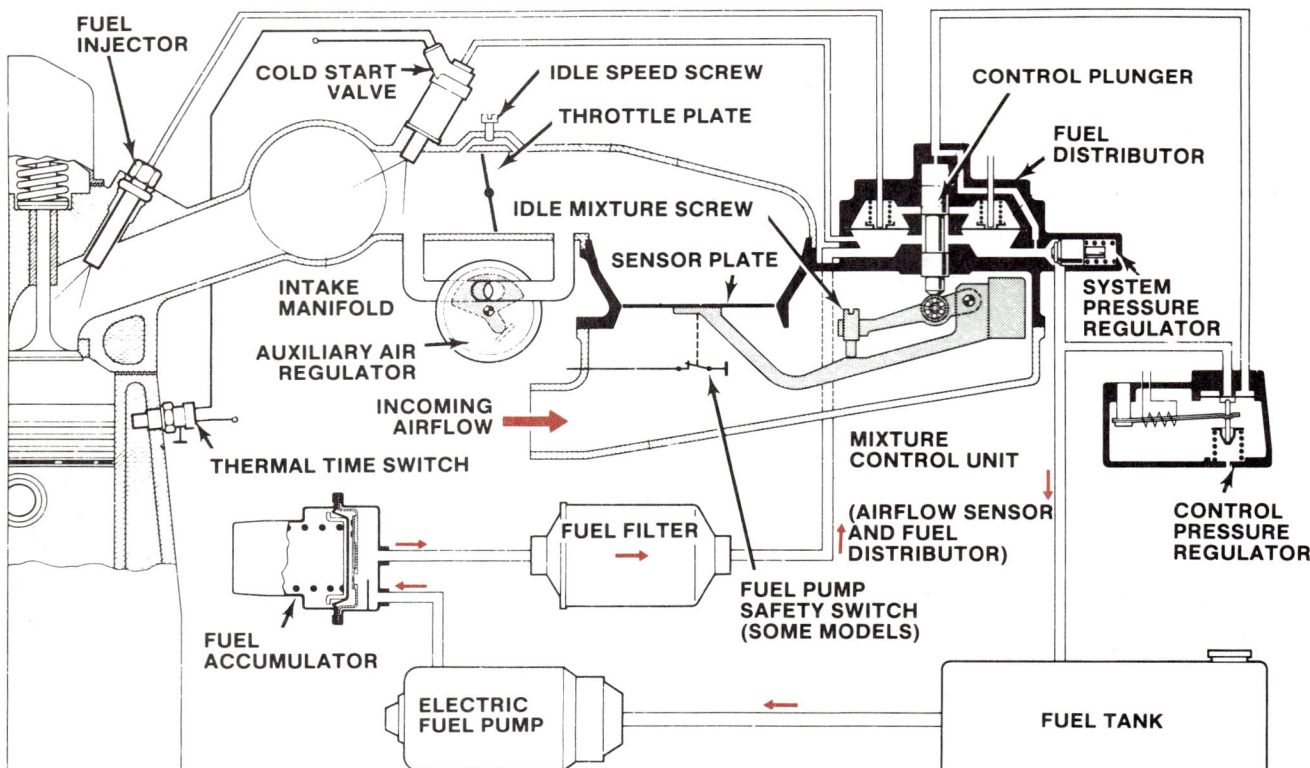

Figure 21-23 Components of a continuous injection system (CIS) that meters fuel mechanically. *Courtesy of Robert Bosch*

stream of the throttle valve and a special fuel distributor with fuel lines running to all injectors. A control plunger in the fuel distributor is mechanically linked to the airflow sensor plate by means of a lever. As the airflow sensor measures the volume of engine intake air, its plate moves. The lever transfers this motion to the control plunger in the fuel distributor. The plunger moves up or down changing the size of the fuel metering openings in the fuel lines. This increases or decreases the volume of fuel flowing to the injectors.

Air Delivery System

Air enters the system through the air filter and is measured by the airflow sensor. Airflow is controlled by the driver, using a regular throttle valve. The air flows through the intake manifold into the combustion chambers. In the system shown in Figure 21-24, the air enters beneath the airflow sensor plate, lifting the plate as it moves toward the throttle and intake manifold. This is known as an updraft system. In some CIS designs, movement of intake air presses down on the airflow sensor plate. This is called a downdraft system.

The sensor plate is located in an air venturi or funnel-shaped passage in the mixture control unit. Because of the shape of this venturi or funnel the airflow sensor rises farther (in an updraft system) when more air flows into the engine.

It is important to remember that any air entering the intake systems without passing the sensor plate interferes with the proper air/fuel mixture, causing the engine to run lean. The same holds true for all other types of injection systems. Proper operation of all systems depends on having no vacuum leaks.

Fuel Delivery System

The main components of the CIS fuel delivery system are the fuel tank, electronic fuel pump, prefeed pump (some systems only), fuel accumulator, fuel filter, fuel distributor, and fuel injectors.

As shown in Figure 21-23, fuel is drawn from the tank by the fuel pump. It passes through the fuel accumulator and filter before reaching the fuel distributor in the metering control unit.

FUEL TANK AND PUMP An electric fuel pump is mounted in or near the fuel tank. Some models use a prefeed pump to supply the main pump. This prefeed pump is located in the fuel tank or in-line upstream of the main pump. It helps prevent vapor lock in hot driving conditions.

FUEL ACCUMULATOR The fuel accumulator is needed to prevent a sudden rapid rise in fuel pressure inside the fuel distributor when the vehicle is being started. When the fuel pump is energized, the accumulator fills through a one-way reed valve. As it fills, the fuel compresses a diaphragm and spring until it reaches a preset stop. When the accumulator is full, fuel pressure in the system stabilizes. When the fuel pump is turned off, the accumulator maintains a rest pressure within the fuel system. This helps eliminate vapor lock in the fuel lines.

FUEL DISTRIBUTOR The fuel distributor consists of a fuel control unit, pressure regulating valves for each cylinder, and a system pressure regulator (Figure 21-25). The fuel control unit consists of a slotted metering cylinder. This cylinder contains the fuel control plunger. Part of the control plunger protrudes past the fuel distributor and rests on the airflow sensor lever.

Fuel flows through the slots in the fuel metering cylinder. There is one metering slot for each engine cylinder. Control plunger movement within the metering cylinder determines the amount of fuel released to the fuel injectors (Figure 21-26).

Each cylinder has its own pressure regulating valve. These valves maintain a constant pressure differential of approximately 1.5 psi on either side of the fuel metering slot. This pressure differential remains the same, regardless of the size of the slot opening. With-

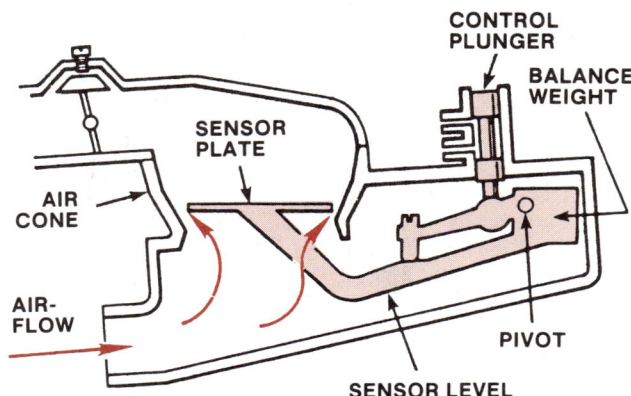

Figure 21-24 The CIS airflow sensor is coupled directly to the control plunger in the fuel distributor. This is an updraft air induction setup.

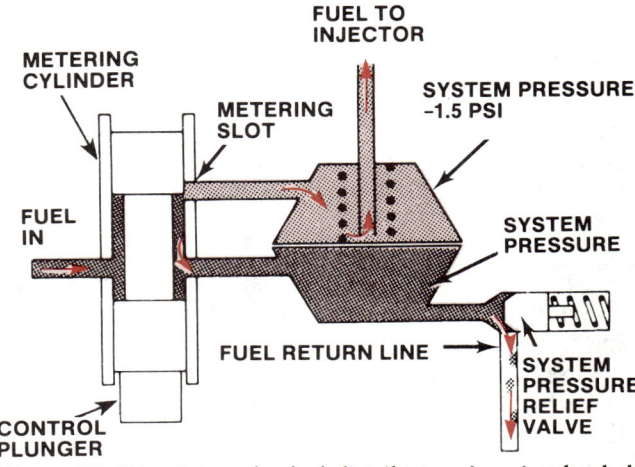

Figure 21-25 Parts of a fuel distributor. A spring-loaded regulator keeps fuel pressure delivered to the injectors 1.5 psi less than fuel system pressure. *Courtesy of Robert Bosch*

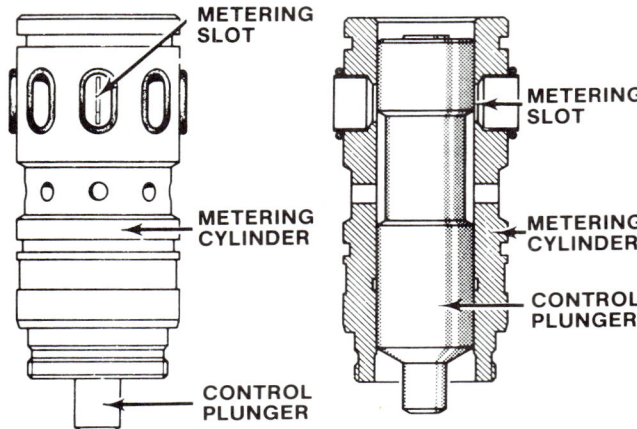

Figure 21-26 Fuel passes through metering slots in the metering cylinder and enters lines that carry it to the individual injectors. *Courtesy of Robert Bosch*

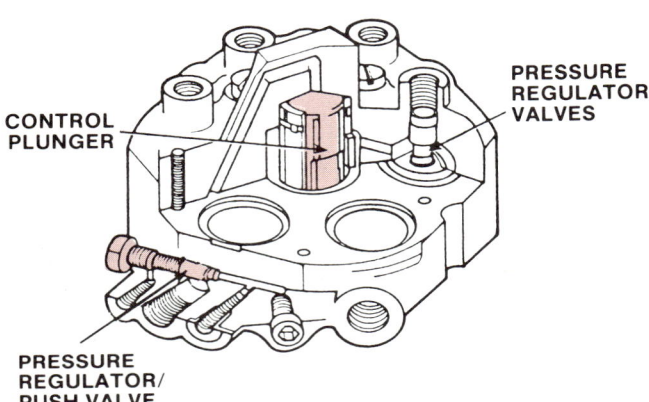

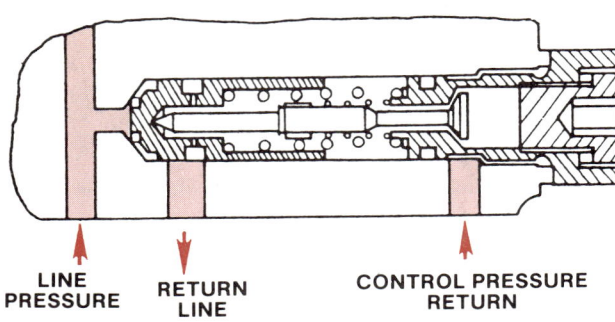

Figure 21-27 The fuel line system pressure regulator maintains a constant system pressure by venting excess fuel back to the fuel tank. It operates using a push valve.

Control Pressure Regulator

The airflow sensor lever is not the only mechanism that affects the position of the control plunger in the fuel distributor. A control pressure regulator (warm-up regulator) is also used to provide correct fuel pressure on top of the fuel control plunger. This helps regulate the engine air/fuel needs. A dampening restriction over the fuel control plunger also eliminates any fluctuations that may occur in the airflow sensor lever.

At normal operating temperature, the control pressure regulator maintains a constant control pressure of about 54 psi. During engine cold-starting and warm-up periods, the control pressure regulator reduces this pressure to about 7.3 psi. Less pressure above the fuel control plunger allows the sensor plate to open farther with the same airflow. This supplies more fuel to the cylinders to encourage engine warm-up. As the engine reaches operating temperature, the control pressure regulator gradually increases control pressure. This creates the air/fuel mixture.

When the engine is cold, a bimetallic strip exerts pressure against a spring-loaded valve, which causes the valve to open a fuel return passage in the control pressure regulator (Figure 21-28A). Fuel is allowed to return to the fuel tank, reducing fuel pressure above the control plunger in the fuel distributor.

As the engine warms, the bimetallic strip is heated by an electric heating coil. The strip gradually releases pressure on the spring, allowing the valve to close the

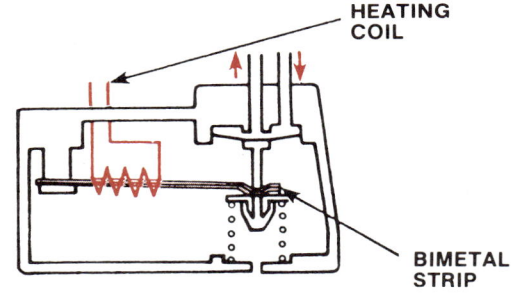

A COLD ENGINE—LOW CONTROL PRESSURE

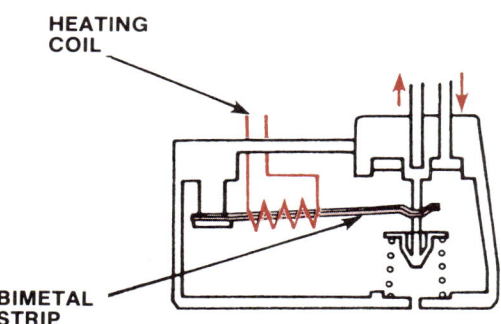

B WARM ENGINE—NORMAL CONTROL PRESSURE

Figure 21-28 The control pressure regulator reduces fuel pressure above the control plunger by venting additional fuel back to the fuel tank. The distributor can then meter more fuel to the injectors to help cold starting and warm-up.

out pressure regulating valves, the amount of fuel injected would not remain proportional to the size of the metering slot opening.

The fuel distributor also contains a pressure relief valve that regulates system pressure (Figure 21-27). Like the fuel pressure regulators used on EFI systems, this regulator maintains a constant system pressure by allowing excess fuel to return to the fuel tank via a return line.

Fuel Injection 533

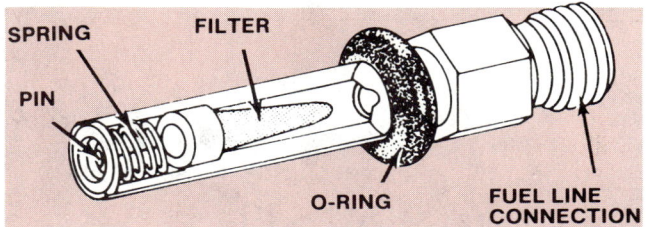

Figure 21-29 Typical CIS injector. *Courtesy of Robert Bosch*

fuel return passage. As the valve closes, control pressure gradually rises to normal (Figure 21-28B).

Depending on the vehicle, the control pressure regulator may have full-load enrichment and high altitude compensation, whereas some models use only the standard regulator.

FUEL INJECTORS CIS fuel injectors (Figure 21-29) open at a set fuel pressure. Once the engine is started, each injector continuously sprays finely atomized fuel into the intake port of the cylinder.

A vibrator pin or needle inside each injector helps break up and atomize the fuel. This vibrating action also helps keep the injectors from clogging. Clogging is much more common on TBI and PFI systems than on CIS-equipped engines.

When the engine is stopped, the pin and spring assembly seal off the injector to retain fuel pressure in the lines. This helps assure quick starting.

COLD START INJECTORS AND AUXILIARY AIR VALVES CIS systems are normally equipped with a cold start injector and auxiliary air valve system to control cold starting and engine idling. These systems operate similarly to the EFI systems discussed earlier in the chapter.

CUSTOMER CARE

Recommend the periodic inspection and replacement of fuel tubing and hoses to your customers. These items should be replaced at least every three years. Otherwise, particles from deteriorating rubber hoses may plug up injectors, fuel lines, and filters. While replacing a fuel filter is not a major repair, replacing damaged injectors is expensive.

Oxygen Control Feedback System

Continuous injection systems can be fitted with an oxygen sensor (sometimes called lambda sensor) for feedback control. The sensor is mounted in the exhaust manifold so it heats up rapidly when the engine is started.

Signals from the oxygen sensor are sent to the oxygen control unit. The ECU modifies the fuel flow in the mixture control unit so the engine operates on the proper ratio. The changing exhaust gas affects the oxygen sensor and it sends a signal in a closed loop through the mixture control unit to the engine (Figure 21-30).

The mixture control unit for system operation is shown in Figure 21-31. The lower chamber of each

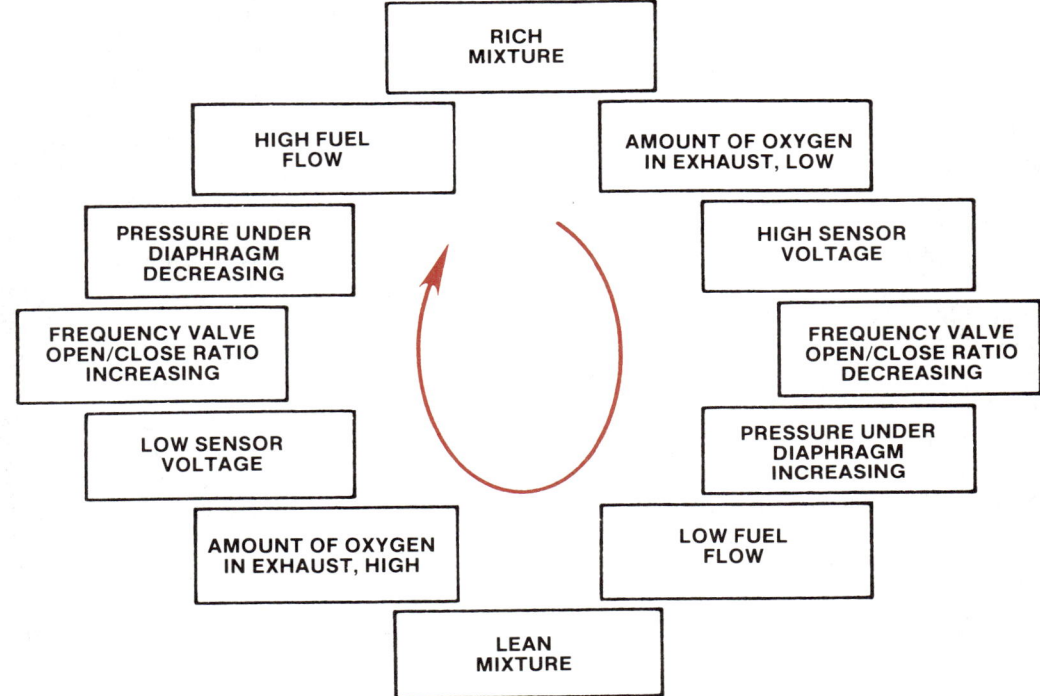

Figure 21-30 Closed loop operation refers to the way various components respond to each other to maintain optimum air/fuel proportioning.

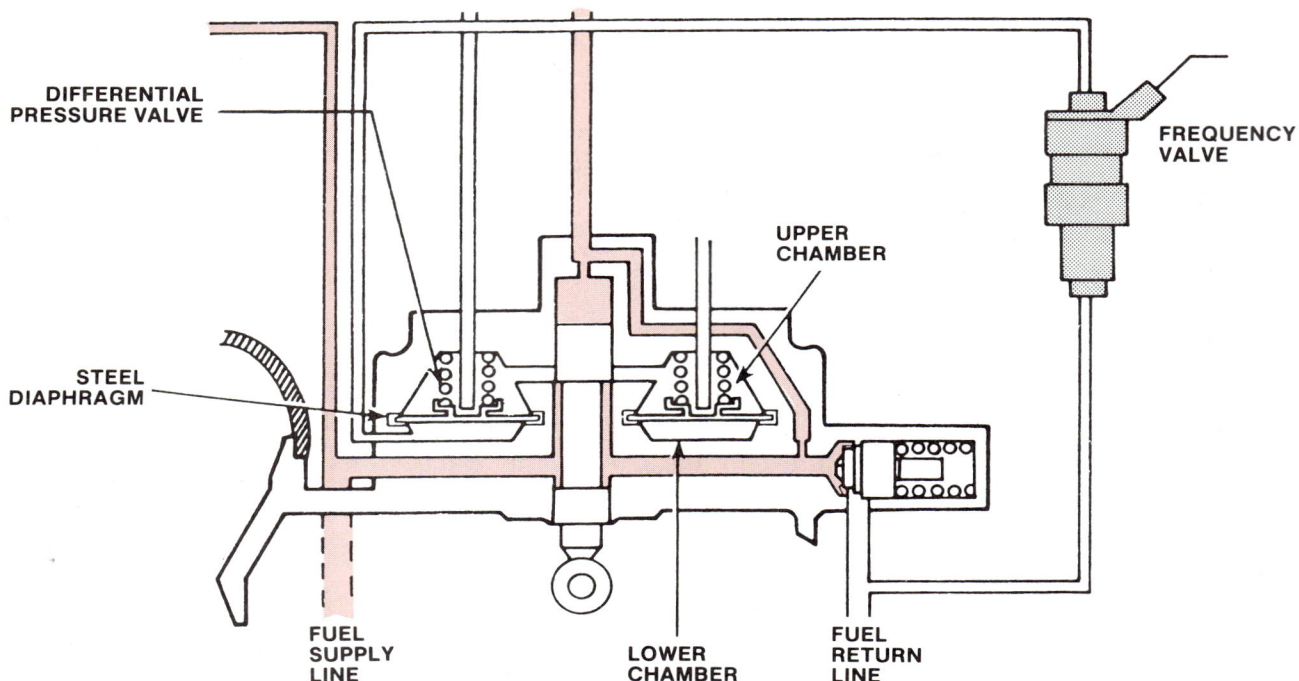

Figure 21-31 CIS mixture control unit.

differential pressure valve is provided with a bleed passage to the oxygen control valve.

The oxygen control valve (sometimes called a timing or frequency valve) operates on signals from the oxygen control unit. It opens and closes to allow more or less fuel to return to the tank through the fuel return. This is called dwell time. By reducing the pressure in the lower part of the differential pressure valve, fuel flow to the injector can be increased, enriching the mixture. Shortening the time that the oxygen control valve is open increases the pressure beneath the differential pressure valve diaphragm. This lessens the amount of fuel injected, leaning the mixture.

Based on a series of signals from the sensor from oxygen-rich to oxygen-lean, the control valve continually cycles from being open about 40% of the time to being open about 60% of the time averaging about 50%.

The oxygen control unit switches to open loop during conditions when the oxygen sensor is cold or when the engine is cold. This open loop operation holds the oxygen control valve open a fixed amount of time (around 60%). When testing the operation of the oxygen control unit and its control valve, it is possible to hear the change in sound caused by the change in open time.

Adjusting the carbon monoxide (CO) output level is accomplished by turning a mixture screw. If the mixture adjustment is covered with a tamper-proof plug, this plug must be drilled and removed from the mixture control unit. The oxygen (lambda) sensor wire can be disconnected and the exhaust sample taken at the pipe provided on the exhaust manifold. As an alternate procedure, the mixture is adjusted in closed loop, with oxygen sensor connected, using a dwellmeter. Additional details are provided on the underhood decal.

CIS-E Components

As mentioned earlier, CISs can also be equipped with certain electronic controls. They combine the benefits of a basic mechanically controlled fuel injection system with simple electronic controls for enrichment, cutoff, and closed loop feedback. Economy is improved through the use of minimum enrichment during warm-up and fuel cutoff during coast.

CIS-E uses an electrohydraulic actuator in the fuel distributor, which is controlled by an ECU (Figure 21-32). The ECU receives signals from the coolant temperature sensor, throttle switch, airflow sensor plate, and the oxygen or lambda sensor.

Like the basic CIS design, CIS-E has continuous injection, airflow sensing, and mechanical (hydraulic) control of basic metering. It has cold start provisions such as an auxiliary air device and cold start valve with a thermal time switch.

CIS-E differs from a basic CIS in three ways. First, the airflow sensor mechanism includes a potentiometer, which signals the position and movement of the plate for acceleration enrichment. Secondly, the system pressure regulator maintains a constant pressure. It also relieves electric fuel pump pressure and maintains pressure in the system for easy restarts by controlling return fuel flow from the fuel distributor. Finally, the electrohydraulic actuator is an electromagnetic differential pressure regulator on the fuel distributor. It operates a plate valve.

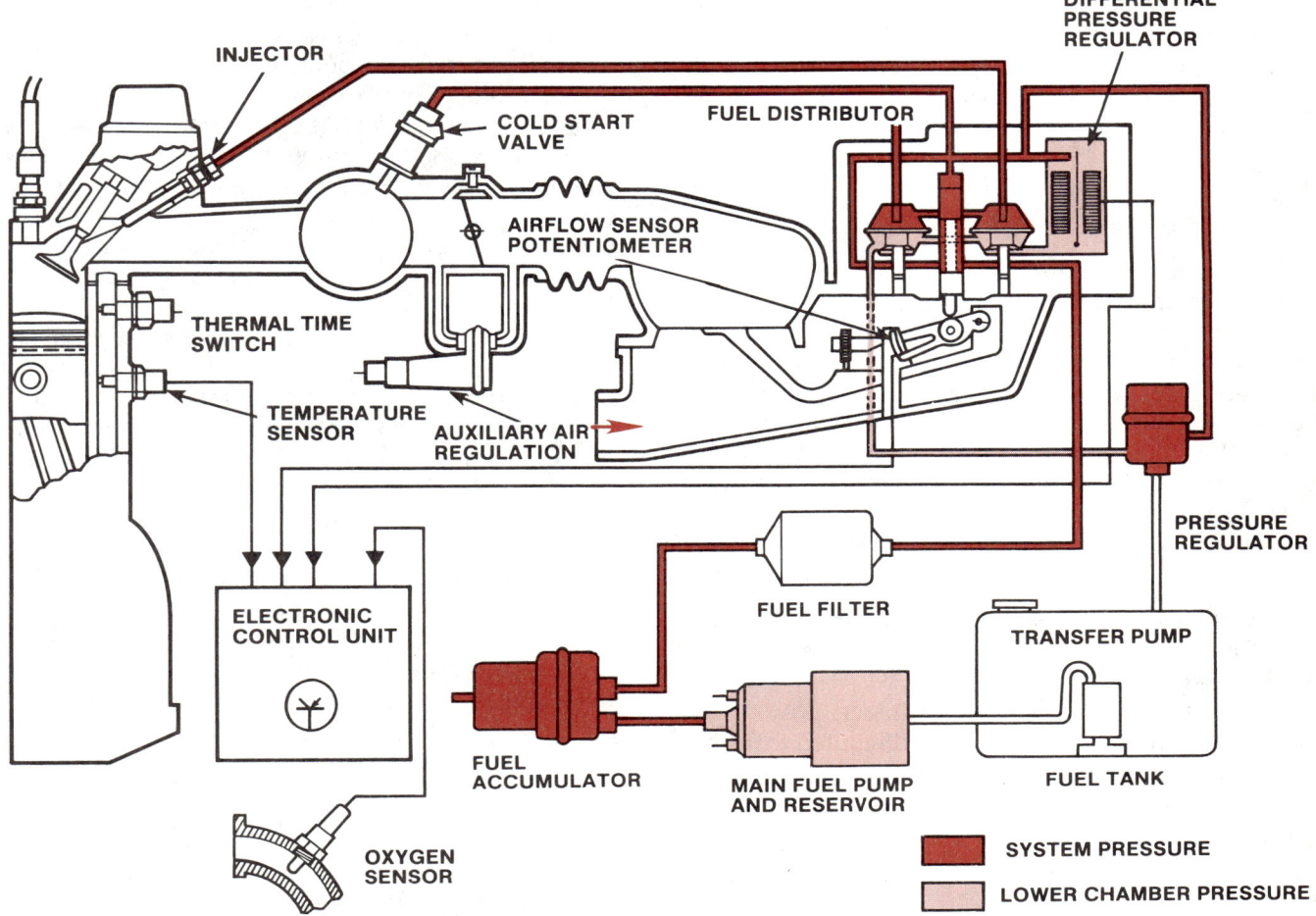

Figure 21-32 Schematic view of a CIS-E system.

System Operation

The system pressure regulator maintains a constant system of primary pressure. Constant system pressure is applied to the control plunger to counter the force of the airflow sensor mechanism. There is no control pressure and no control pressure regulator.

The electrohydraulic actuator provides enrichment reducing the pressure below the diaphragm of each differential pressure valve. This has the effect of increasing the pressure at each metering slit. In turn, this increases the amount of fuel delivered. For fuel cutoff during coasting or for rpm limitation, the electrohydraulic action is reversed. A decrease in the pressure at the metering slits cuts off delivery of fuel.

☐ SERVICING FUEL INJECTION SYSTEMS

Troubleshooting fuel injection systems requires systematic step-by-step test procedures. With so many interrelated components and sensors controlling fuel injection performance, a hit-or-miss approach to diagnosing problems can quickly become frustrating, time-consuming, and costly.

Most fuel injection systems are integrated into engine control systems. The self-test modes of these systems are designed to help in engine diagnosis. Unfortunately, when a problem upsets the smooth operation of the engine, many service technicians automatically assume that the computer (ECU) is at fault. But in the vast majority of cases, complaints about driveability, performance, fuel mileage, roughness, or hard starting or no-starting are due to something other than the computer itself (although many problems are caused by sensor malfunctions that can be traced using the self-test mode).

Before condemning sensors as bad, remember that weak or poorly operating engine components can often affect sensor readings and result in poor performance. For example, a sloppy timing chain, bad rings, or valves reduce vacuum and cylinder pressure, resulting in a lower exhaust temperature. This can affect the operation of a perfectly good oxygen or lambda sensor, which must heat up to approximately 600 degrees Fahrenheit before functioning in its closed loop mode.

A problem like an intake manifold leak can cause a sensor, the MAP sensor in this case, to adjust engine operation to less than ideal conditions.

One of the basic rules of electronic fuel injection servicing is that EFI cannot be adjusted to match the engine, you have to make the engine match EFI. In other words, make sure the rest of the engine is sound before condemning the fuel injection and engine control components.

Preliminary Checks

The best way to approach a problem on a vehicle with electronic fuel injection is to treat it as though it had no electronic controls at all. As the previous examples illustrate, any engine is susceptible to problems that are unrelated to the fuel system itself. Unless all engine support systems are operating correctly, the control system does not operate as designed.

Before proceeding with specific fuel injection checks and electronic control testing, be certain of the following.

- The battery is in good condition, fully charged, with clean terminals and connections.
- The charging and starting systems are operating properly.
- All fuses and fusible links are intact.
- All wiring harnesses are properly routed with connections free of corrosion and tightly attached.
- All vacuum lines are in sound condition, properly routed, and tightly attached.
- The PCV system is working properly and maintaining a sealed crankcase.
- All emission control systems are in place, hooked up and operating properly.
- The level and condition of the coolant/antifreeze is good and the thermostat is opening at the proper temperature.
- The secondary spark delivery components are in good shape with no signs of crossfiring, carbon tracking, corrosion, or wear.
- The base timing and idle speed are set to specifications.
- The engine is in good mechanical condition.
- The gasoline in the tank is of good quality and has not been substantially cut with alcohol or contaminated with water.

☐ EFI SYSTEM COMPONENT CHECKS

In any electronic throttle body or port injection system three things must occur for the system to operate.

1. An adequate air supply must be supplied for the air/fuel mixture.
2. A pressurized fuel supply must be delivered to properly operating injectors.
3. The injectors must receive a trigger signal from the control computer.

If all of these preliminary checks do not reveal a problem, proceed to test the electronic control system and fuel injection components.

Some older control systems require involved test procedures and special test equipment, but most newer designs have a self-test program designed to help diagnose the problem. These self-tests perform a number of checks on components within the system. Input sensors, output devices, wiring harnesses, and even the electronic control computer itself may be among the items tested.

The results of the testing are converted into two-digit trouble codes (Figure 21-33) that the technician may read using special test equipment, a test light, or an analog voltmeter. The meaning of trouble codes vary from manufacturer to manufacturer, year to year, and model to model, so it is important to have the appropriate service manuals.

Always remember that trouble codes only indicate the particular circuit in which a problem has been detected. They do not pinpoint individual components. So if a code indicates a defective lambda or oxygen sensor, the problem could be the sensor itself, the wiring to it, or its connector. Trouble codes are not a signal to replace components. They signal that a more thorough diagnosis is needed in that area.

The following sections outline general troubleshooting procedures for the most popular EFI and CIS designs in use today.

Air System Checks

In an injection system (particularly designs that rely on airflow meters or mass airflow sensors), all the air entering the engine must be accounted for by the air measuring device. If it is not, the air/fuel ratio becomes overly lean. For this reason, cracks or tears in the plumbing between the airflow sensor and throttle body are potential air leak sources that can affect the air/fuel ratio.

During a visual inspection of the air control system, pay close attention to these areas, looking for cracked or deteriorated ductwork. Also make sure all induction hose clamps are tight and properly sealed. Look for possible air leaks in the crankcase, for example, dipstick tube and oil filter cap. Any extra air entering the intake manifold through the PCV system is not measured either and can upset the delicately balanced air/fuel mixture at idle (Figure 21-34).

Airflow Sensors

When looking for the cause of a performance complaint that relates to poor fuel economy, erratic performance/hesitation or hard starting, make the following checks to determine if the airflow sensor (all types except CIS) is at fault. Start by removing the air intake duct from the airflow sensor to gain access to the sensor flap. Check for binding, sticking, or scraping by

Fuel Injection 537

Code	Circuit Affected or Possible Cause	Code	Circuit Affected or Possible Cause
12	No distributor reference pulses to the ECU. This code is not stored in memory and flashes only while the fault is present. Normal code with ignition on, engine not running.	34	Vacuum sensor or manifold absolute pressure (MAP) circuit. The engine must run up to 2 minutes at specified curb idle before this code sets.
13	Oxygen sensor circuit. The engine must run up to 4 minutes at part-throttle under road load before this code sets.	35	Idle speed control (ISC) switch circuit shorted. (Up to 70% TPS for over 5 seconds.)
14	Shorted coolant sensor circuit. The engine must run 2 minutes before this code sets.	41	No distributor reference pulses to the ECU at specified engine vacuum. This code stores in memory.
15	Open coolant sensor circuit. The engine must run 5 minutes before this code sets.	42	Electronic spark timing (EST) bypass circuit or EST circuit grounded or open.
21	Throttle position sensor (TPS) circuit voltage high (open circuit or misadjusted TPS). The engine must run 10 seconds at specified curb idle speed before this code sets.	43	Electronic spark control (ESC) retard signal for too long a time; causes retard in EST signal.
		44	Lean exhaust indication. The engine must run 2 minutes in closed loop and at part-throttle before this code sets.
22	Throttle position sensor (TPS) circuit voltage low (grounded circuit or misadjusted TPS). Engine must run 20 seconds at specified curb idle speed to set code.	45	Rich exhaust indication. The engine must run 2 minutes in closed loop and at part throttle before this code sets.
23	M/C solenoid circuit open or grounded.	51	Faulty or improperly installed calibration unit (PROM). It takes up to 30 seconds before this code will set.
24	Vehicle speed sensor (VSS) circuit. The vehicle must operate up to 2 minutes at road speed before this code sets.	53	Exhaust gas recirculation (EGR) valve vacuum sensor has seen improper EGR vacuum.
32	Barometric pressure sensor (BARO) circuit low.	54	Shorted M/C solenoid circuit or faulty ECU.

Figure 21-33 Common ECU trouble codes.

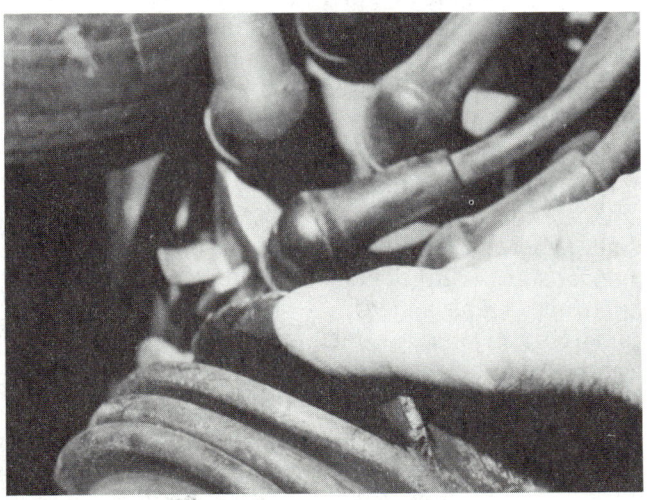

Figure 21-34 Checking for leaks in the air control system.

rotating the sensor flap (evenly and carefully) through its operating range. It should move freely, make no noise, and feel smooth. Next, turn the ignition on. Do not start the engine. Move the flap toward the open position. The electric fuel pump should come on as the flap is opened. If it does not, turn off the ignition, remove the sensor harness, and check for specific resistance values with an ohmmeter at each of the sensor's terminals.

On some models it is possible to check the resistance values of the potentiometer by moving the air flap, but in either case a service manual is needed to identify the various terminals and to look up resistance specifications.

On systems that use a mass airflow meter or manifold pressure sensor to measure airflow, other than checking for good electrical connections, there are usually no actual physical checks. However, a hand-held scan tool can be plugged into the diagnostic connector on some models to check for proper voltage values.

> ### SHOP TALK
>
> To quickly diagnose an intermittent failure of GM's hot film mass airflow meter (MAF), start the engine, let it idle, and lightly tap on the sensor with a plastic mallet or screwdriver handle. If the engine stalls, runs worse, or the idle quality improves while tapping on the sensor, the MAF meter is probably defective and should be replaced. Similiarly, if the engine does not start or idles poorly, unplug the MAF. If the engine starts or runs better with the sensor unplugged, the sensor is defective and should be replaced.

Throttle Body

Remove the air duct from the throttle assembly and check for carbon buildup inside the throttle bore and on the throttle plate. Soak a cloth with carburetor solvent and wipe the bore and throttle plate to remove light to moderate amounts of carbon residue. Also, clean the backside of the throttle plate. Then, remove the idle air control valve from the throttle body (if so equipped) and clean any carbon deposits from the pintle tip and the IAC air passage.

Fuel System Checks

If the air control system is in working order, move on to the fuel delivery system. It is important to always remember that fuel injection systems operate at high fuel pressure levels. This pressure must be relieved before any fuel line connections can be broken. Spraying gasoline (under a pressure of 35 psi or more) on a hot engine creates a real hazard when dealing with a liquid that has a flash point of minus 45 degrees Fahrenheit.

Follow the specific procedures given in the service manual when relieving the pressure in the fuel lines.

If the procedures are not available, a safe alternative procedure is to apply 20 to 25 inches of vacuum to the externally mounted fuel pressure regulator (with a hand vacuum pump connected to the manifold control line of the regulator), which bleeds fuel pressure back into the tank (Figure 21-35). If the vehicle does not have an externally mounted regulator, or a service valve or injector to energize, use a towel to catch excess fuel, while slowly breaking a fuel line connection. This method should only be used when all other possibilities have been tried.

CAUTION: *Dispose of the fuel-soaked rag in a fireproof container.*

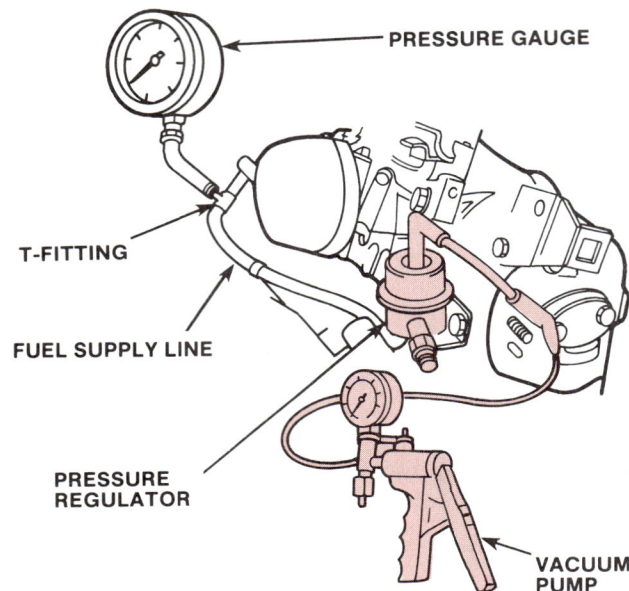

Figure 21-35 With an externally-mounted fuel pressure regulator, it's possible to bleed off system pressure into the fuel tank using a hand vacuum pump.

Fuel Delivery

When dealing with an alleged fuel complaint that is preventing the vehicle from starting, the first step (after spark, compression, etc., have been verified) is to determine if fuel is reaching the cylinders (assuming there is gasoline in the tank). Checking for fuel delivery is a simple operation on throttle body systems. Remove the air cleaner, crank the engine, and watch the injector for signs of a spray pattern. If a better view of the injector's operation is required, an ordinary strobe light does a great job of highlighting the spray pattern.

It is impossible to visually inspect the spray pattern and volume of port system injectors. However, an accurate indication of their performance can be obtained by performing simple fuel pressure and fuel volume delivery tests. See the service manual for details.

Low fuel pressure can cause a no-start or poor-run problem. It can be caused by a clogged fuel filter, a faulty pressure regulator, or a restricted fuel line anywhere from the fuel tank to the fuel filter connection.

If a fuel volume test shows low fuel volume, it can indicate a bad fuel pump or blocked or restricted fuel line. When performing the test, visually inspect the fuel for signs of dirt or moisture. These indicate the fuel filter needs replacement.

High fuel pressure readings will result in a rich-running engine. A restricted fuel return line to the tank or a bad fuel regulator may be the problem. To isolate the cause of high pressure, relieve system pressure and connect a tap hose to the fuel return line. Direct the hose into a container and energize the fuel pump. If fuel pressure is now within specifications, the fuel return line is blocked. If pressure is still high, the pressure regulator is faulty.

If the first fuel pressure reading is within specs, but the pressure slowly bleeds down, there may be a leak in the fuel pressure regulator, fuel pump check valve, or the injectors themselves. Remember, hard starting is a common symptom of system leaks.

Injector Checks

A fuel injector is nothing more than a solenoid-actuated fuel valve. Its operation is quite basic in that as long as it is held open and the fuel pressure remains steady, it delivers fuel until it is told to stop.

Because all fuel injectors operate in a similar manner, fuel injector problems tend to exhibit the same failure characteristics. The main difference is that in a TBI design, generally all cylinders suffer if the injectors malfunction, whereas in port systems the loss of one injector is not as crucial.

An injector that does not open causes hard starts on port-type systems and an obvious no-start on single-point TBI designs. An injector that is stuck partially open causes loss of fuel pressure (most noticeably after the engine is stopped and restarted within a short time period) and flooding due to raw fuel dribbling into the engine. In addition to a rich running engine, a leaking injector also causes the engine to diesel or run on when the ignition is turned off.

Checking Voltage Signals

When an injector is suspected as the cause of a problem, the first step is to determine if the injector is receiving a signal (from the control computer) to fire. Fortunately, determining if the injector is receiving a voltage signal is easy and requires simple test equipment. Unfortunately, the location of the injector's electrical connector can make this simple voltage check somewhat difficult. For example, on some recent Chevrolet 2.8 liter V-6 engines, the cover must be removed from the cast aluminum plenum chamber that is mounted over the top of the engine before the injector can be accessed (Figure 21-36).

Once the injector's electrical connector has been removed, check for voltage at the injector using an ordinary test light or a convenient noid light that plugs into the connector (Figure 21-37). After making the test connections, crank the engine. A series of rapidly flickering lights indicates the computer is doing its job and supplying voltage or a ground to open the injector.

When performing this test, make sure to keep off the accelerator pedal. On some models, fully depressing the accelerator pedal activates the clear flood mode, in which the voltage signal to the injectors is automatically cut off. Technicians unaware of this waste time tracing a phantom problem.

If sufficient voltage is present after checking each injector, check the electrical integrity of the injectors

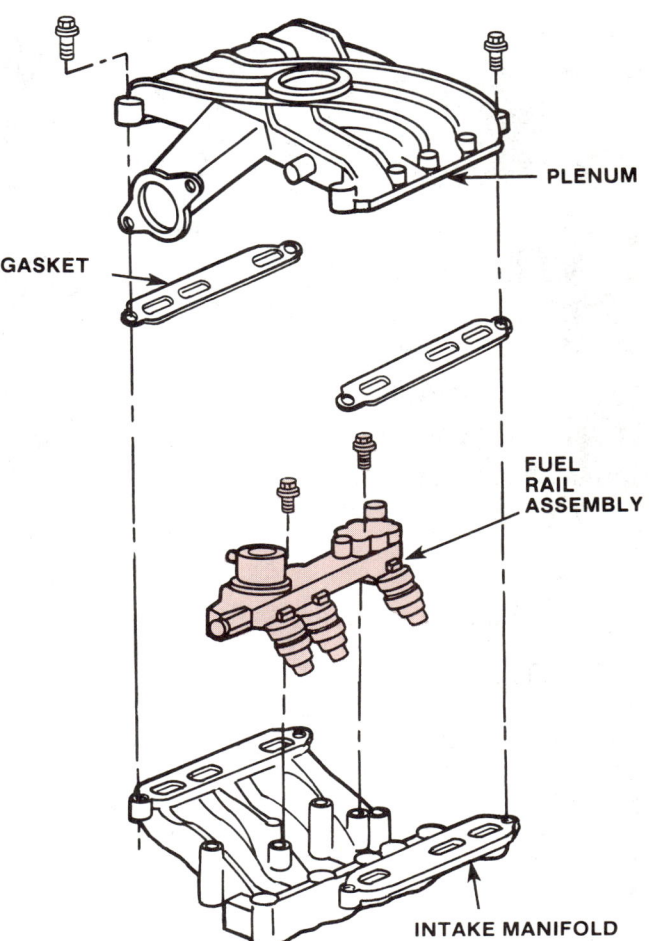

Figure 21-36 To access the injectors on a Chevy 2.8L V-6, the air plenum must be removed.

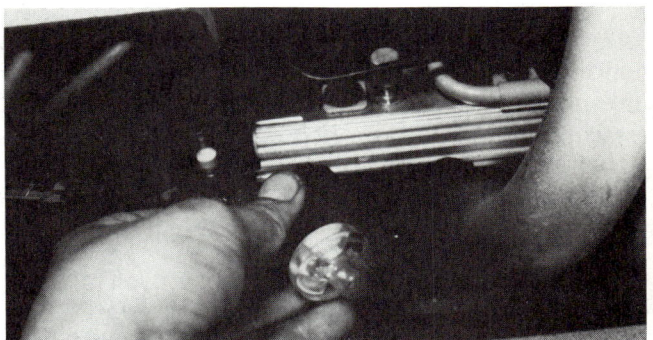

Figure 21-37 Checking for voltage at the injector using a noid light.

themselves. Use an ohmmeter to check each injector winding for shorts, opens, or excessive resistance. Compare resistance readings to the specifications found in the service manual.

Injector Balance Test

If the injectors are electrically sound, perform an injector pressure balance test. This test will help isolate a clogged or dirty injector.

Figure 21-38 Performing an injector pressure balance test.

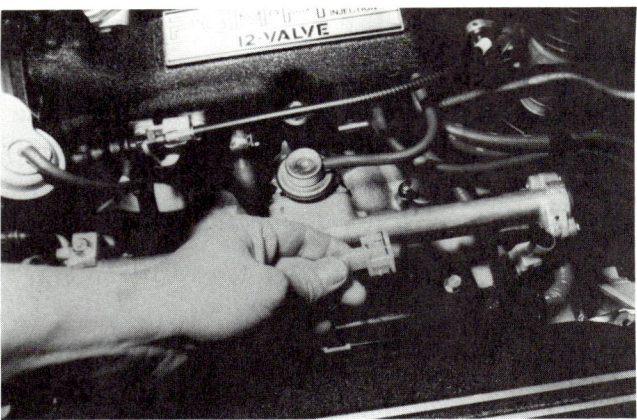

Figure 21-39 Peforming an injector power balance test.

To perform the test, an electronic injector pulse tester is used. Each injector is energized while observing a fuel pressure gauge to monitor the drop in fuel pressure. The tester is designed to safely pulse each injector for a controlled length of time. The tester is connected to one injector at a time (Figure 21-38). To prevent oil dilution, the electrical connectors to the other injectors are removed. The ignition is turned on until a maximum reading is on the pressure gauge. That reading is recorded and the ignition turned off. With the tester, activate the injector and record the pressure reading, after the needle has stopped pulsing. This same test is performed on each injector.

The difference between the maximum and minimum reading is the pressure drop. Ideally, each injector should drop the same amount when opened. A variation of 1.5 to 2 psi (10 kPa) or more is cause for concern. If there is no pressure drop or a low pressure drop, suspect a plugged injector. A higher than average pressure drop indicates a rich condition. If there are inconsistent readings, the nonconforming injectors either have to be cleaned or replaced.

Injector Power Balance Test

The injector pressure balance test is a good method of checking injectors on vehicles with no-start problems. When the vehicle runs, several other tests are possible. The injector power balance test is an easy method of determining if an injector is causing a miss.

To perform this test, first hook up a tachometer and fuel pressure gauge to the engine. Once all gauges are in place, start the engine and allow it to reach operating temperature. As soon as the idle stabilizes, unplug each injector one at a time (Figure 21-39). Note the rpm drop and pressure gauge reading. To ensure accurate test results on many electronic systems, it may be necessary to disconnect some type of idle air control device to prevent the computer from trying to compensate for the unplugged injector.

After recording the rpm and fuel pressure drop, reconnect the injector, wait until the idle stabilizes, and move on to the next one. Note the rpm and pressure drop each time. If an injector does not have much effect on the way the engine runs, chances are it is either clogged or electrically defective. It is a good idea to back up the power balance test with an injector resistance check, pressure balance test, or noid light check.

Alternative Checks

If the injector's electrical leads are difficult to access, an injector power balance test is hard to perform. As an alternative, start the engine and use a technician's stethoscope to listen for correct injector operation. A good injector makes a rhythmic clicking sound as the solenoid is energized and de-energized several times each second. If a clunk-clunk instead of a steady click-click is heard, chances are the problem injector has been found. Cleaning or replacement is in order. If a stethoscope is not handy, use a thin steel rod, wooden dowel, or fingers to feel for a steady on/off pulsing of the injector solenoid.

Another way to isolate an offending cylinder when injector access is limited is to perform the more traditional cylinder power balance test and disable the spark plugs instead of the injectors. (Remember to by-pass the idle air control.) Following the same warm-up and idle stabilizing procedures, watch the rpm drop and note any change in idle quality as each plug is shorted. If a lazy or dead cylinder is located, concentrate efforts on the portion of the fuel or ignition system pertaining to that cylinder (assuming, of course, no mechanical problems are present).

CAUTION: Any time cylinders are shorted during a power balance test, make the readings as quickly as possible. Prolonged operation of a shorted cylinder causes excessive amounts of unburned fuel to accumulate inside the catalytic converter and increase the risk of premature converter failure.

Oscilloscope Checks

An oscilloscope can be used to monitor the injector's pulse width and duty cycle when an injector-related problem is suspected. As covered earlier in the chapter, the pulse width is the time in milliseconds that the injector is energized. The duty cycle is the percentage of on-time to total cycle time.

To check the injector's firing voltage on the scope, a typical hookup involves connecting the scope's positive lead to the injector supply wire and the scope's negative lead to an engine ground. Even though these connections are considered typical, it is still a good idea to read the instruction manual provided with the test equipment before making connections.

With the scope set on the low voltage scale and the pattern adjusted to fill the screen, a square-shaped voltage signal should be present with the engine running or cranking (Figure 21-40). If the voltage pattern reads higher than normal, excessive resistance in the injector circuit is indicated. Conversely, a low-voltage trace indicates low-circuit resistance. If the pattern forms a continuous straight line, it means the injector is not functioning due to an open circuit somewhere in the injector's electrical circuit.

> **USING SERVICE MANUALS**
>
> Consult the service manual for pulse width and duty cycle specifications for the particular vehicle being worked on. The service manual also contains fault code diagnosis for a wide range of fuel injection system tests.

❑ INJECTOR CLEANING

Since a single injector can cost up to several hundred dollars, arbitrarily replacing injectors when they are not functioning properly, especially on multiport systems, can be an expensive proposition. If injectors are electrically defective, replacement is the only alternative. However, if the vehicle is exhibiting rough idle, stalling, slow or uneven acceleration, the injectors may just be dirty and require a good cleaning.

Before covering the typical cleaning systems available and discussing how they are used, several cleaning precautions are in order. First, never soak an injector in cleaning solvent. Not only is this an ineffective way to clean injectors, but it most likely destroys the injector in the process. Also, never use a wire brush, pipe cleaner, toothpick, or other cleaning utensil to unblock a plugged injector. The metering holes in injectors are drilled to precise tolerances. Scraping or reaming the opening result in a clean injector that is no longer an accurate fuel-metering device.

> **CUSTOMER CARE**
>
> After servicing a clogged injector, remove the fuel filter, open it up with a pipe cutter, slice the element with a razor blade, and examine the interior. If you find excessive rust particles or other contaminants, show the filter to the customer. Then recommend that the vehicle fuel tank be removed and cleaned and the fuel line blown out. If the customer declines the recommendation, make a big note on the repair order and customer receipt that his fuel filter replacement should be done more often than specified in the owner's manual. Showing the customer the evidence of contamination also justifies the repairs already made.

Always use an approved on-the-car cleaning system or injector cleaning bench to effectively clean clogged injectors. On-the-car cleaners are by far the most popular and practical method.

The basic premise of all injection cleaning systems is similar in that some type of cleaning chemical is run through the injector in an attempt to dissolve deposits that have formed on the injector's tip. The methods of

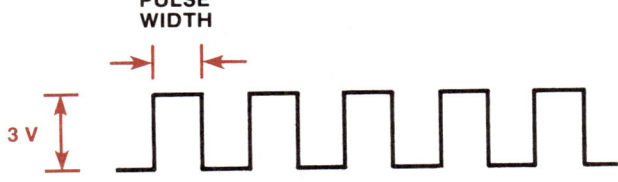

Figure 21-40 The trace pattern of the injector voltage pulse should be a square sine wave pattern.

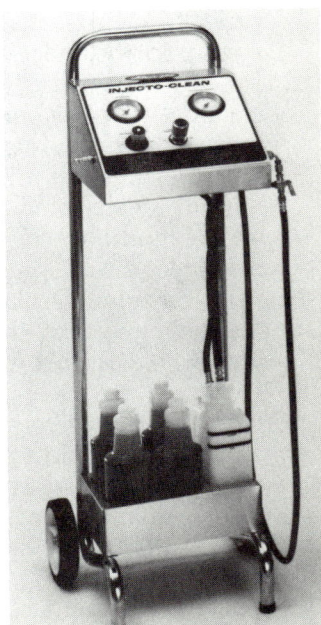

Figure 21-41 State-of-the-art fuel injector cleaning system.

applying the cleaner can range from single shot, pre-mixed, pressurized spray cans to self-mix, self-pressurized chemical tanks resembling bug sprayers. The pre-mixed, pressurized spray can systems are fairly simple and straightforward to use since the technician does not need to mix, measure, or otherwise handle the cleaning agent.

Other systems require the technician to assume the role of chemist and mix up a desired batch of cleaning solution for each application. The chemical solution then is placed in a holding container and pressurized by hand pump or shop air to a specified operating pressure.

The more advanced units feature electrically operated pumps neatly packaged in roll-around cabinets that are quite similar in design to an A/C charging station (Figure 21-41).

 **PROCEDURES**

Cleaning Injectors

1. Attach the cleaner's service hose to the fuel rail following the same procedure used when hooking up a fuel pressure gauge.
2. Disable the fuel pump as per the car manufacturer's instructions (for example, pull fuel pump fuse, disconnect lead at pump, etc.). Clamp off the fuel pump return line at the flex connection to prevent the cleaner from seeping into the fuel tank. For an extra margin of safety, clamp off the inlet line also.
3. Before starting the engine, open the cleaner's control valve one-half turn or so to prime the injectors and then start the engine.
4. If available, set and adjust the cleaner's pressure gauge to approximately 5 psi below the operating pressure of the injection system and let the engine run at 1000 rpm for 10 to 15 minutes or until the cleaning mix has run out. If the engine stalls during cleaning, simply restart it.
5. Run the engine until the recommended amount of fluid is exhausted and the engine stalls. Shut off the ignition, remove the cleaning setup, and reconnect the fuel pump.
6. After removing the clamping devices from around the fuel lines, start the car. Let it idle for 5 minutes or so to remove any leftover cleaner from the fuel lines.
7. On the more severely clogged cases, the idle improvement should be noticeable almost immediately. With more subtle performance improvements, an injector balance test verifies the cleaning results. Once the injectors are clean, recommend the use of an in-tank cleaning additive or a detergent-laced fuel.

> **SHOP TALK**
>
> If the fuel delivery system is equipped with a cold start injector, make sure it gets cleaned along with the primary injectors. This step is especially critical if the owner complains of cold starting problems.
>
> To effectively clean the cold start injector, hook up the cleaning system and remove the cold start injector from the engine. Open the control valve on the solvent containers and use an electronic triggering device to manually pulse the injector. Direct the spray into a suitable container. Pulse the injector until the spray pattern looks healthy.
>
> On models where the cold start injector is not readily accessible, check the fuel flow through the injector before and after the cleaning procedure. Pulse as necessary until the maximum flow through the injector is obtained.

☐ INJECTOR REPLACEMENT

Consult the vehicle's service manual for instructions on removing and installing injectors. Before installing the new one, always check to make sure the sealing O-ring is in place (Figure 21-42). Also, prior to installation, lightly lubricate the sealing ring with engine oil or automatic transmission fluid (avoid using silicone grease, which tends to clog the injectors) to prevent seal distortion or damage.

Photo Sequence 11, which is included in this chapter, outlines a typical procedure for removing and installing an injector. Always refer to the service manual for the exact procedure for the engine being serviced.

☐ IDLE ADJUSTMENT

In a fuel injection system, idle speed is regulated by controlling the amount of air that is allowed to by-pass

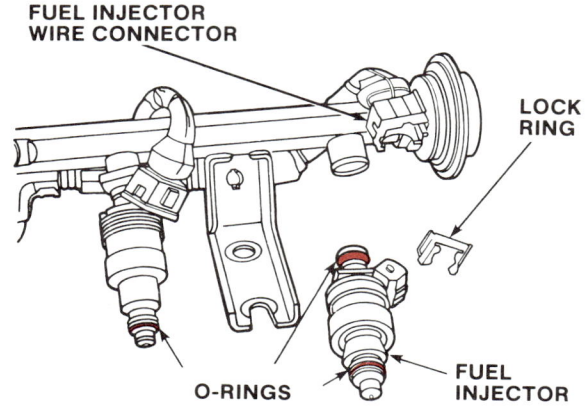

Figure 21-42 Before replacing an injector, inspect the sealing O-ring.

PHOTO SEQUENCE 11

☐ REMOVING AND REPLACING A FUEL INJECTOR ON A PFI SYSTEM

P11-1 Often an individual injector needs to be replaced. Random disassembly of components and improper procedures can result in damage to one of various systems located near the injectors.

P11-2 The injectors are normally attached to a fuel rail and inserted into the intake manifold or cylinder head. They must be positively sealed because high pressure fuel leaks can cause a serious safety hazard.

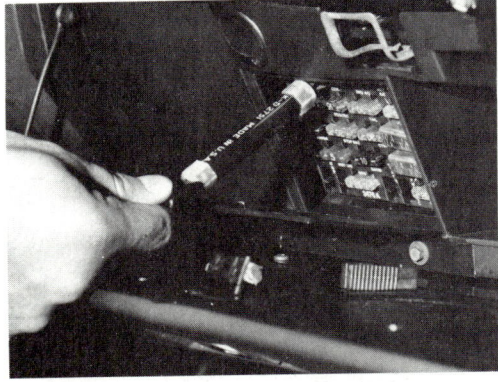

P11-3 Prior to loosening any fitting in the fuel system, the fuel pump fuse should be removed.

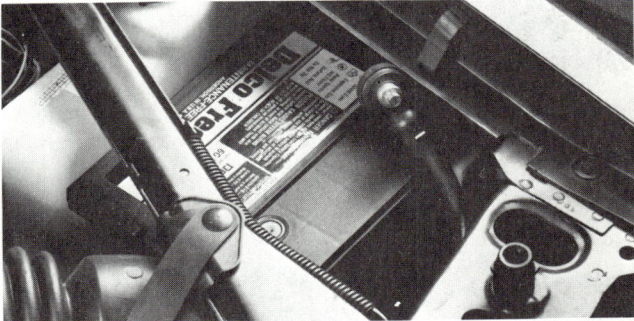

P11-4 As an extra precaution, many technicians disconnect the negative cable of the battery.

P11-5 To remove the fuel injector, the fuel rail must be able to move away from the engine. The rail holding brackets should be unbolted and the vaccum line to the pressure regulator disconnected.

P11-6 Disconnect the wiring harness to the injectors by depressing the center of the attaching wire clip.

(continued)

P11-7 The injectors are held to the fuel rail by a clip that fits over the top of the injector. An O-ring at the top and at the bottom of the injector seals the injector.

P11-9 Remove the clip from the top of the injector and remove the injector unit. Install new O-rings onto the new injector. Be careful not to damage the seals while installing them and make sure they are in their proper locations.

P11-11 Tighten the fuel rail hold down bolts according to the manufacturer's recommendations.

P11-8 Pull up on the fuel rail assembly. The bottom of the injectors will pull out of the manifold while the tops are secured to the rail by clips.

P11-10 Install the injector into the fuel rail and set the rail assembly into place.

P11-12 Reconnect all parts that were disconnected. Install the fuel pump fuse and reconnect the battery. Turn the ignition switch to the run position and check the entire system for leaks. After a visual inspection has been completed, conduct a fuel pressure test on the system. ■

---

the airflow sensor or throttle plates. When presented with a car that tends to stall, especially when coming to a stop, or idles too fast, look for obvious problems like binding linkage and vacuum leaks first. If no problems are found, go through the minimum idle checking/setting procedure described on the underhood decal. The instructions listed on the decal spell out the necessary conditions that must be met prior to attempting an idle adjustment. These adjustment procedures can range from a simple twist of a throttle stop screw (Figure 21-43) to more involved procedures requiring circumvention of idle air control devices, removal of casting plugs, or recalibration of the throttle position sensor. Specific idle adjustment procedures can also be found in the service manual.

The idle speed should always be adjusted before adjusting the air/fuel mixture. The mixture is adjusted by turning the mixture adjustment screw clockwise to decrease the by-pass air, which enriches the mixture. This also increases the CO in the exhaust. Backing out the mixture screw increases the by-pass air, leaning the mixture and reducing CO. Because some electronic fuel injection engines run so lean, the CO meter might not react to the mixture adjustment screw unless special enrichment procedures are followed. Instructions are usually given in the service manual for the particular application.

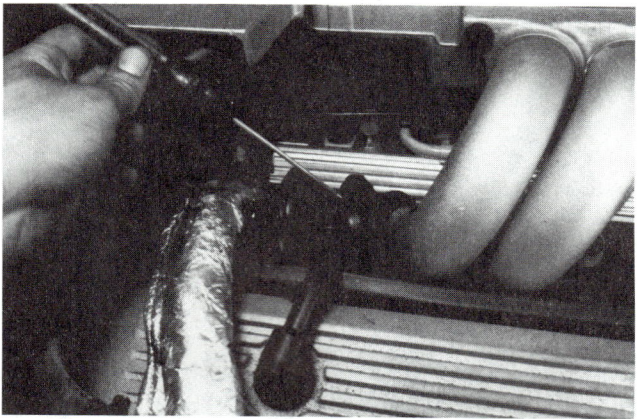

Figure 21-43 On many models, a tamper-proof idle stop screw plug must be removed before adjustments can be made.

❏ CIS CHECKS AND TESTS

Servicing mechanically controlled continuous injection systems requires the same logical approach and preliminary checks used in troubleshooting throttle body and port EFI systems. CISs are normally very reliable, and should not be blamed for a problem until the preliminary ignition and engine system checks given earlier have been completed.

Fuel Injection 545

The following service tips apply to most CIS vehicles in use today.

Difficult Cold Start

Often difficult cold starting is caused by a faulty cold start valve or thermal time switch. To test the thermal time switch, it is necessary to first make sure that the coolant is below 95 degrees Fahrenheit. Then, remove the coil high-tension wire from the distributor. Connect it to the ground. Unplug the connector from the cold start valve, attach a test light to the connector's terminals, then crank the engine. The light should go on for several seconds, then go out. In cases where this does not happen, the thermal time switch or its circuit is faulty.

Continuing to operate the starter on a car with a hot start relay causes the light to blink on and off at regular intervals. Before it is possible to check the cold start valve itself, it is necessary to make the fuel pump run constantly. On a typical model without air sensor wiring, remove the fuel pump relay and bridge the appropriate pair of relay board terminals with a fused jumper wire to energize the pump. (Refer to the vehicle service manual for proper terminals.)

Unplug the cold start valve's electrical connector. Remove the valve from the intake manifold, and place its nozzle end into a container. Connect a jumper between one of the valve's terminals and ignition coil terminal, and a second jumper between the valve's other terminal and ground. Turn the ignition on and look for a steady, cone-shaped fuel spray pattern. Shut the ignition off, wipe the nozzle, and watch it for a minute. No drops should appear.

Rough Running/Stalling

System pressure, idle mixture or speed, and a faulty air regulator are the common causes for rough running engines. As explained earlier, the auxiliary air regulator keeps rpm up while the engine is cold by providing a path for air to by-pass the throttle plate. A heating coil connected to the fuel pump and control pressure regulator circuit warms a bimetal strip. The deflection of the strip gradually closes the regulator's gate valve, cutting off the flow of extra air.

To test with the engine cold, unplug the electrical connector, start the engine and let it idle. Pinch either hose that is connected to the unit. Idle speed should decrease slightly. Plug the connector back in, and let the engine run until warm, then pinch either hose again. This time, there should be no change in idle rpm.

If the idle speed does slow down, remove the electrical connector and use a test light across the connector's terminals. If the light is on with the engine idling, the auxiliary air regulator is faulty.

Fuel Pressure Problems

As in EFI systems, CIS requires high fuel pressure to operate. Improper pressures or pressure leaks can cause a number of problems such as rough idling, stalling, surging or missing, or hard start problems.

A fuel pressure gauge of sufficient capacity is needed to make pressure checks. Use the gauge to check the three key pressures.

1. The system pressure provided by the fuel pump
2. The control pressure that opposes the airflow plate and controls the air/fuel ratio
3. The rest pressure, which can reveal the presence of a leak that allows the system to bleed down while the engine is shut off. Hot starting problems are the result.

Begin by checking system and control pressures. If the system pressure provided by the fuel pump matches specifications, make any changes needed in the control pressure by changing shims in the pressure relief valve.

To conduct a rest pressure test, begin by taking a pressure reading with the test valve open. After the system has reached control pressure, shut off the ignition and fuel pump then time any pressure drop. Although the specifications vary for different cars, a severe pressure drop is obvious and happens quickly—in under 5 minutes. To be sure, let the pressure drop for 20 minutes and compare the drop to specifications.

If the pressure drop is greater than allowed, repeat the test with the test valve closed. If the system now holds fuel pressure, the warm-up regulator is at fault. Replace it. If the pressure drop is the same as before, check the rest of the system.

The check valve in the fuel pump outlet is a likely culprit. Build up pressure in the system, shut off the pump and immediately pinch closed the fuel line from the pump outlet to the accumulator. If the system holds pressure, replace the fuel pump's check valve, which is available as a replacement part.

Another possible source of pressure leakage is the accumulator. Run the pump to build up control pressure in the system and then remove the screw from the back end of the accumulator. Insert a piece of wire in the hole to measure the depth inside the accumulator, with the pump running. If it is out of specifications, replace the accumulator.

If the check valve and accumulator are good, examine the O-ring seal in the pressure regulator relief valve. If it is nicked or deteriorated, fuel pressure does not hold.

Fuel Distribution Problems

Surging or missing can also be caused by unequal fuel distribution to the injectors. Ideally, CIS supplies all the cylinders with the same amount of fuel. If not, the symptoms are poor idle quality and part throttle performance. The procedure for measuring fuel volume delivered to each cylinder is normally outlined in the service manual and requires a special tool and two graduated measuring tubes. Refer to the manual whenever this test needs to be conducted.

If there is too much variation in fuel volume, swap the injectors of the two lines with the largest difference and repeat the test. If the same injector again flows too little fuel, it is faulty. On the other hand, if the same fuel line that supplied insufficient fuel in the first test does so again even though connected to a different injector, the problem can be found in the fuel distributor.

It is possible for the plunger in the fuel distributor to be worn or scored, allowing fuel to push past it rather than flowing to the injectors. If all else fails, remove the distributor. Then, carefully remove the plunger and inspect it. If there is any hint of damage, replace the fuel distributor and plunger assembly.

Airflow Sensor Adjustment

An airflow sensor plate that is off-center in its bore (Figure 21-44) can allow air to leak by, causing severe hot start problems.

Check the air sensor plate for drag by using a magnet on the plate bolt to move the air sensor plate up and down with the pump on. If there is drag, or if the plate does not appear to be concentric with the air cone, it should be centered. To do so, refer to the service manual for the proper procedure.

Idle and Air/Fuel Settings

The two basic adjustments made to the CIS are idle speed and the air/fuel mixture. To set the idle speed on a typical CIS setup, turn the screw next to the throttle plate linkage, which varies the size of a by-pass drilling. Counterclockwise equals faster (Figure 21-45).

Mixture is adjusted by turning a screw, which bears on the air sensor lever. A rubber plug is located between the fuel distributor and the air sensor cone, and

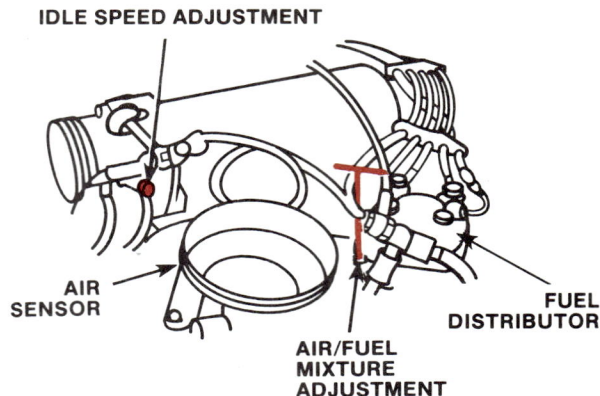

Figure 21-45 Location of the idle speed and air/fuel mixture screws in a CIS arrangement.

must be removed for access to the screw. Use a long, 3 mm Allen wrench to adjust. Clockwise richens the blend.

CIS-E Idle Control

In a CIS-E engine the control computer uses input signals to decide mixtures for different conditions. It controls idle speed with the idle-speed stabilizer, holding a higher speed for a colder engine and gradually slowing it down as the engine warms. Idle specifications are given in percent of dwell to rpm. Turning the idle screw, as on most domestic cars, does not change the idle speed. The idle stabilizer changes to correct it.

Idle speed is programmed into the computer and cannot be changed. Some systems include an increased idle setting when the air-conditioning is on to provide better compressor function and prevent stalls.

While the idle speed cannot be adjusted with an idle stabilizer, the dwell should be checked to see that it is within range. Changing the idle speed screw corrects incorrect dwell. Typical warm idle dwell is 30%. Note that figure is in percent, not in degrees. Most of the dwellmeters designed for use with older breaker point ignition systems are calibrated in degrees of distributor shaft rotation. To use these meters, convert the degree reading to a percentage, 360 degrees equals 100%.

If the idle speed is wrong and it is not possible to correctly adjust it, check the idle-speed stabilizer. If it works properly, the problem is in either the connecting wires or the computer itself. Remember, the air-conditioning can turn up the idle, but headlights, heater, and other alternator loads should not reduce it.

Additional CIS-E Checks

On CIS-E engines, a feedback circuit test is used to check the operation of the electromagnetic differential pressure regulator on the fuel distributor. Electromagnets are almost 100% efficient, so the current used is very small, measured in milliamperes. To check circuit current, a high-quality digital ammeter wired in

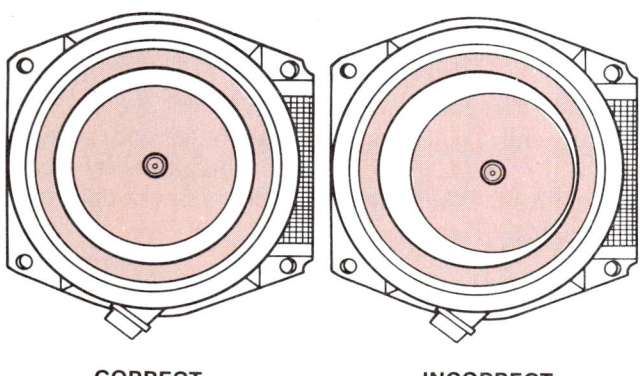

Figure 21-44 If an airflow sensor is off-center in its bore, air can leak by, causing a hot-start problem.

series and a special adapter for the regulator is needed. The key to whether the feedback system is working properly is whether the regulator current hunts back and forth. It may be necessary to hold the throttle open to 2000 rpm for a few seconds to warm the oxygen sensor.

Idle mixture adjustment on CIS-E is done through a hole in the fuel distributor/air flap housing using a long 3 mm Allen wrench. Connect an exhaust analyzer probe into the exhaust tap (which is generally covered with a blue cap). It is very critical to have a secure seal around the exhaust probe or the readings can be false. An exhaust leak can also fool the oxygen sensor into giving false lean readings and driving the system rich.

The key is to set both regulator current and exhaust CO in specifications. Some vehicle service procedures call for adjusting the mixture in closed loop by setting the parameters of the fluctuating current and checking against CO. Others call for unplugging the oxygen sensor (open loop), adjusting for CO, and checking against current fluctuation range. Obviously, these are two ways of doing the same thing. The service manuals list specifications for one method or the other.

☐ HIGH-PRESSURE DIESEL FUEL INJECTION

All diesel engines use a high-pressure fuel injection system that differs from gasoline fuel injection systems in several key areas.

The mechanical systems of a diesel engine and a gasoline engine are very similar, although diesel engine components are of heavier construction than those of a gasoline engine. The heavier construction in the diesel engine accommodates the highly compressed air pressures and the higher fuel injection pressures utilized by this type of engine.

The two types of engines also differ in their ignition and fuel metering systems. Ignition in a diesel engine takes place as the fuel is injected into the engine cylinder. The heat of the highly compressed air ignites the air/fuel charge without the help of an electrical spark. Therefore, the diesel engine does not have an electrical ignition system like that found on gasoline engines.

The output power of a diesel engine is directly proportional to the fuel charge injected into the combustion chamber. At an idle speed, a small fuel charge provides a very lean mixture (a high air/fuel ratio). As more fuel is injected, the mixture becomes rich, engine speed increases, and output power increases. The amount of fuel that can be injected is determined by the amount of air drawn into the engine on the intake stroke. In all types of diesel engines, however, the amount of fuel to be injected is limited by a governor. This device limits the air/fuel ratio for a diesel engine up to a maximum of 10 to 1 by weight. The air/fuel ratio of a typical gasoline engine is approximately 14.7 to 1 by weight.

Combustion Cycle

Combustion in a diesel engine occurs in four sequential stages or periods: the delay period, the uncontrolled burning period, the controlled burning period, and the after burning period (Figure 21-46). When the fuel is first injected into the combustion chamber, there is an initial delay as the fuel changes from a liquid state to a vapor or gas state. This liquid-to-vapor conversion is necessary so the fuel burns. The delay period is followed by a period of uncontrolled burning of the fuel already injected into the chamber. This period is followed by a controlled burning period as the injector continues to feed fuel into the combustion chamber. If and when the fuel injection stops, all the remaining fuel in the chamber continues to burn until it is con-

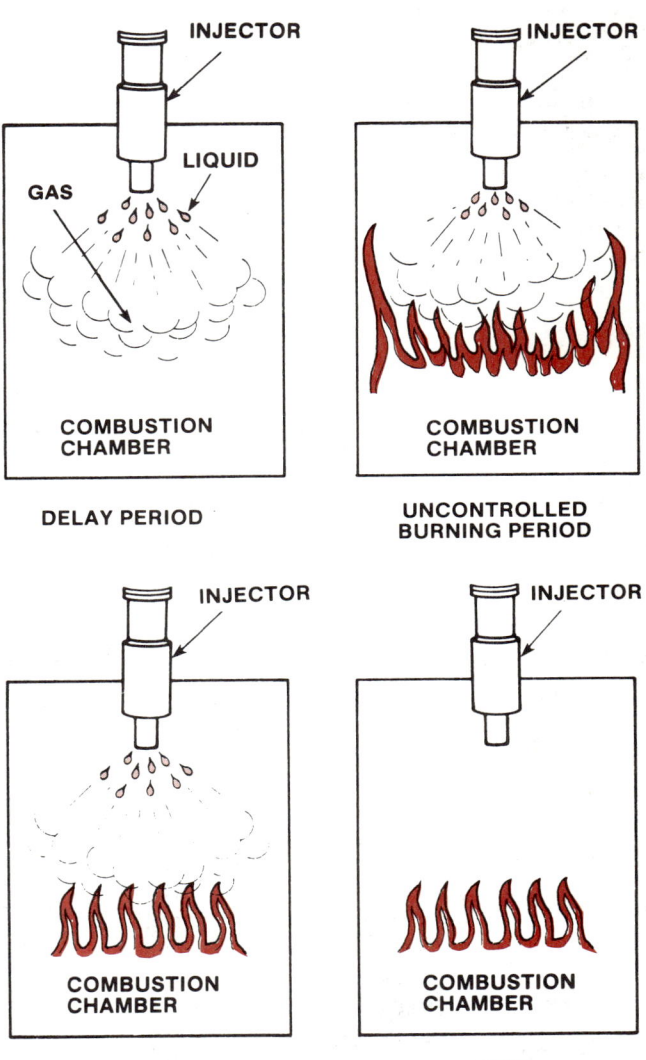

Figure 21-46 The four stages of diesel engine combustion.

sumed. This stage is known as the after burning period. In the diesel engine these periods of combustion simultaneously occur in different parts of the combustion chamber during injection.

The combustion of diesel fuel is not identical under all conditions. Combustion is affected by the following.

- Injector timing
- Length of time (or pulse width) of injection
- Position of injector nozzle
- Injection pressure
- Vaporization of fuel
- Distribution of fuel in the combustion chamber

The moment fuel is injected into the cylinder it is ignited. Therefore, the fuel injection pump utilized by the diesel engine system must inject the fuel at the precise instant when the piston is nearing the TDC position of its compression stroke.

❏ DIESEL FUEL SYSTEM COMPONENTS

The diesel fuel injection system contains the following components (Figure 21-47).

- fuel tank and pick-up unit
- fuel lines
- fuel pump system
- fuel filter
- water-in-fuel sensor (some systems)
- water-in-fuel separator (some systems)
- fuel heater (some systems)
- injection nozzles

Pump Assembly

A diesel engine fuel pump assembly or system combines most of the functions of a gasoline fuel injection or carburetor system, plus the timing functions of a spark ignition system. The assembly must be precise to meter fuel at high pressures. Several different types of pump systems are used.

DISTRIBUTOR PUMPS A distributor pump is the most popular pump design used on passenger vehicles. Some distributor pump designs are complete in one unit, housing a supply pump, governor, and injection pump. The supply pump draws the fuel from the fuel tank and delivers it to the distributor pump housing. The injection pump then increases the fuel pressure to the levels needed for combustion. The governor controls the speed of the engine.

A second type of distributor pump contains a transfer pump, governor, and injection pump within the

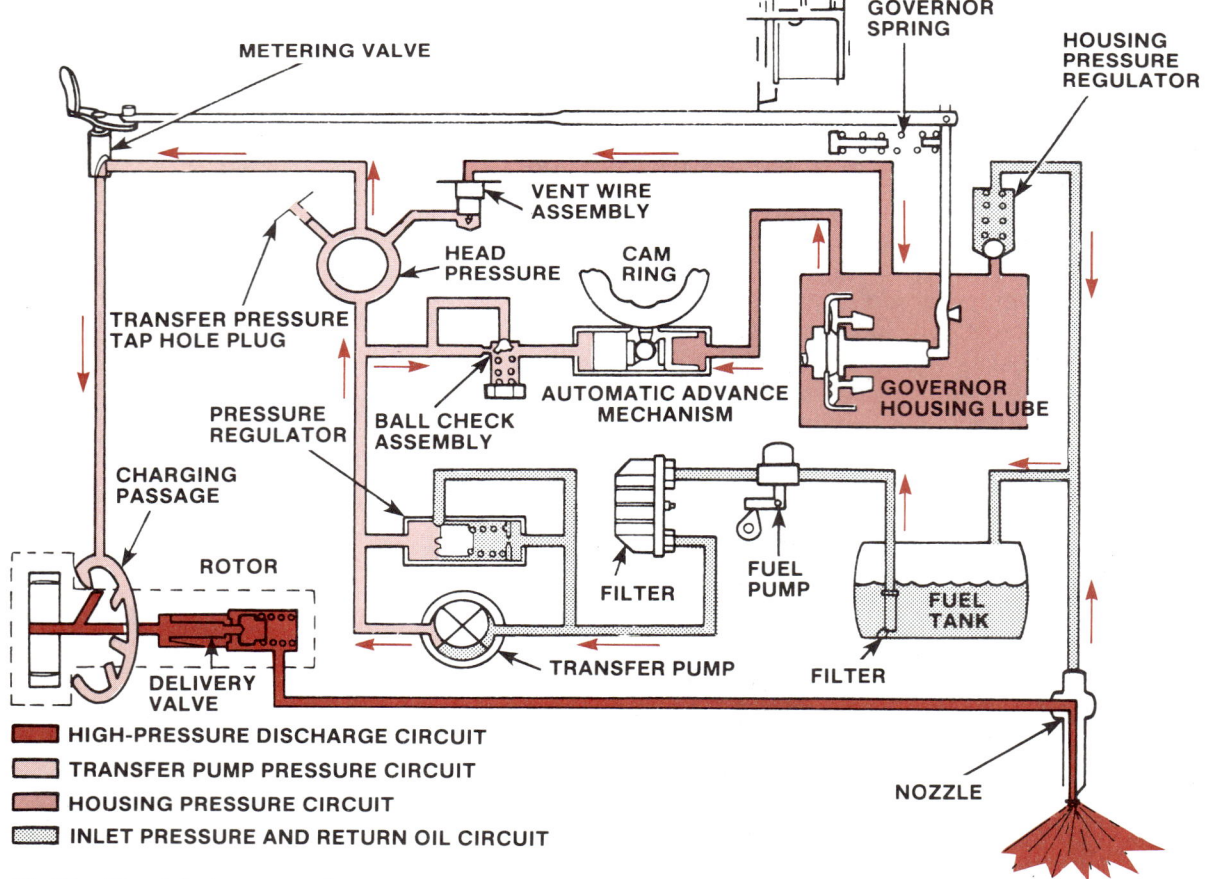

Figure 21-47 Diesel fuel system schematic.

Fuel Injection 549

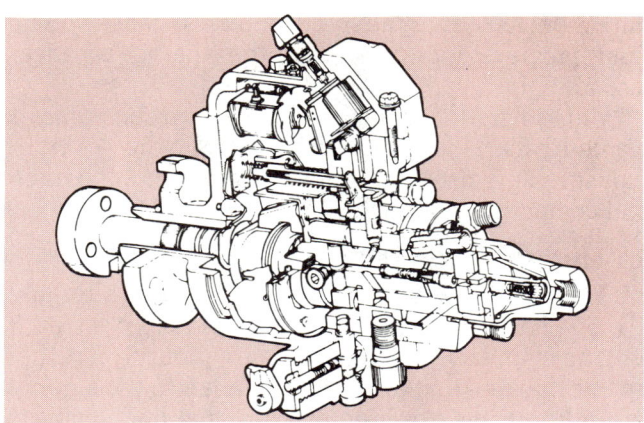

Figure 21-48 Distributor injection pump.

distributor pump housing. But it also uses an external supply pump to draw fuel from the tank and deliver it to the transfer pump. The transfer pump increases fuel pressure and passes the fuel on to the injection pump where it is further pressurized for injection into the combustion chamber.

IN-LINE PUMPS The second major type of pump used in diesel fuel injection systems is the in-line pump. Unlike the distributor pump, an in-line pump uses a separate injection pumping element for each cylinder.

Injection Pump Timing

The fuel injection pump used in the system is synchronized or timed to the engine's crankshaft by drive gears. The pump is designed to create or build up high fuel pressure (15,000 psi to as high as 30,000 psi) so that diesel fuel is injected into the combustion chamber as a fine mist or spray. The fuel spray rapidly evaporates when it encounters the high-pressure, high-temperature air charge in the combustion chamber and allows for ignition of the fuel. In order for the engine to operate smoothly, the following fuel injection conditions must exist.

- Pressure must be available at the precise instant of injection into the chamber.
- Injection rate must be equal for all cylinders so there are equal power pulses from each cylinder.
- Pressure must shut off at the precise instant to control the total amount of fuel to be injected.

Distributor Injection Pump

A typical distributor injection pump is illustrated in Figure 21-48. The pump is driven by the engine's crankshaft through the use of timing gears. The timing gears drive a rotor on the pump that is fitted into a close-tolerance bore in the hydraulic head of the pump. Drilled passageways to carry fuel are incorporated in both the pump rotor and hydraulic head. One type of

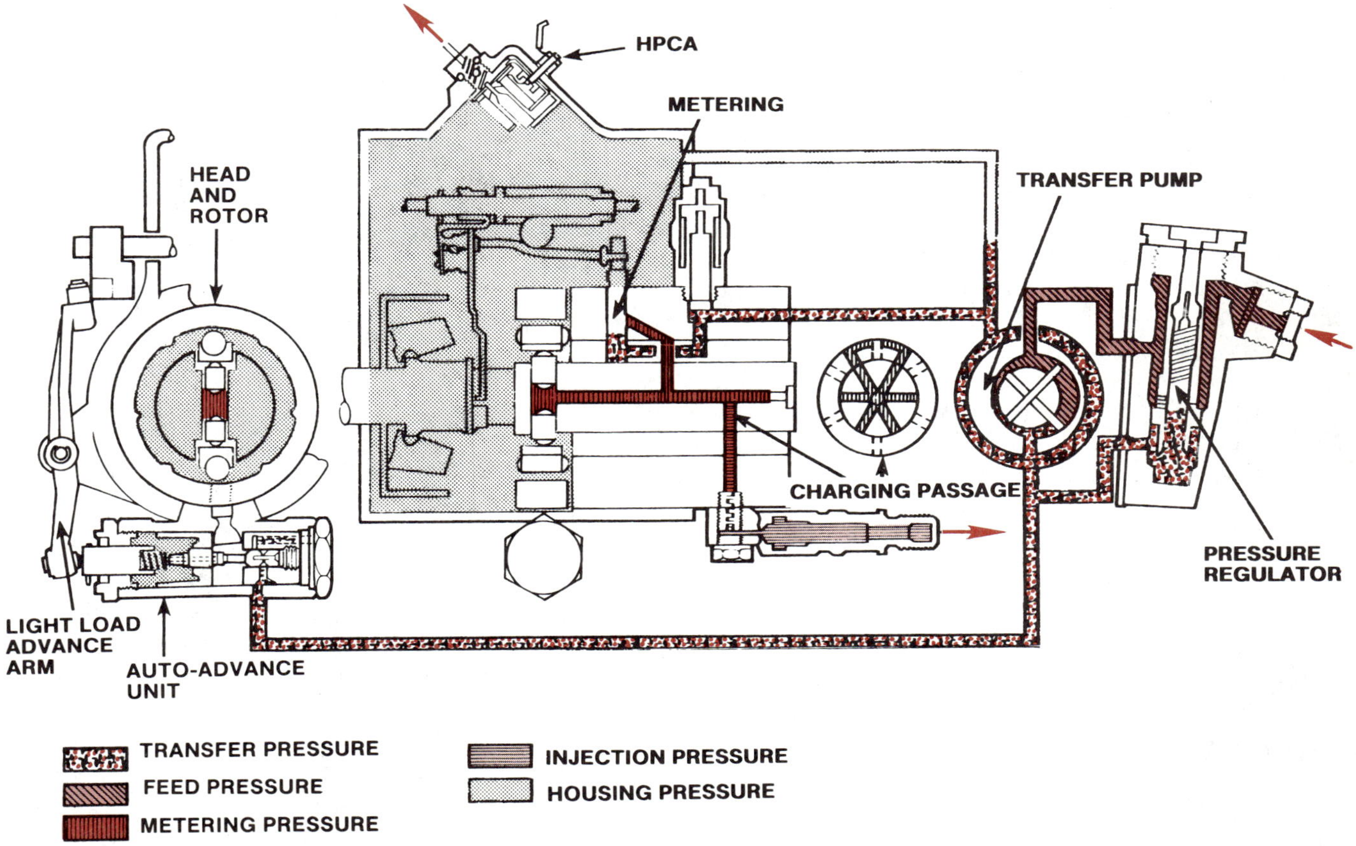

Figure 21-49 Cam plunger movement in a distributor injection pump.

pump uses two plungers that operate in a cross-drilled bore in the distributor rotor. Another type of pump uses only a single plunger. The two-plunger concept allows the plungers to move outward and opposite to each other when the pump chamber is filled with fuel. The plungers are forced together by internal cam lobes. When the plungers are together, they effectively reduce the chamber size and force the fuel into the injectors. Typical cam plunger movement in a distributor injection pump is shown in Figure 21-49.

Both the rotor and the hydraulic head have holes in their structure. As the rotor turns, the holes align with each other and allow fuel to flow between the rotor and the head. When the holes are misaligned, the fuel flow stops. The holes in both components are referred to as ports. Two types of ports are utilized: charging ports and discharging ports. When the charging ports are aligned, the pump chamber fills with fuel. When the discharging ports are aligned, fuel injection takes place.

A vane transfer pump draws and pushes fuel through passages in the hydraulic head to a fuel metering valve. The size of the opening in the metering valve is controlled by the accelerator pedal acting through a governor. A small opening in the valve is maintained at idle speed. Depressing the accelerator causes the valve opening to increase. When maximum engine speed is attained or an overspeed condition exists, the governor takes over and automatically begins to close the valve.

Fuel from the metering valve is routed to the charging ports on the distributor injection pump. As the fuel enters the pump, it forces the plungers outward or away from each other. At idle speed the metering valve is almost closed. Very little fuel is routed to the pump chamber. This forces the plungers slightly outward, partially charging the chamber. Depressing the accelerator pump causes more fuel to enter the chamber and forces the plungers farther apart. As the rotor turns, the charging ports on the rotor and the hydraulic head misalign, effectively closing the ports. Continued rotation of the rotor then aligns the discharge ports of both components. At this time, the plungers are forced or pushed inward by the rollers contacting the cam lobes. As the plungers move together, the fuel is forced out of the pump chamber into the fuel lines to the injectors. Fuel is prevented from dripping into the combustion chamber after the injection cycle by a delivery valve.

The quantity of fuel delivered by the distributor injection pump is directly proportional to the amount of fuel entering the pump chamber through the metering valve. Fuel injection timing is controlled by an internal time-advance mechanism. Timing is altered by rotating an internal cam ring in the rotor and head assembly. A pin in the auto-advance unit is connected to the internal cam and is located between a spring and piston. Fuel pressure from the transfer pump pushes the piston toward the spring and moves the pin. Movement of the pin moves the cam in an advance direction. As the engine speed increases, transfer pump fuel pressure increases, and the timing advances accordingly.

Unused injection fuel from the transfer pump is vented back to the fuel tank through the governor housing. It is also used to lubricate and cool the internal components of the distributor injection pump.

In-Line Injection Pump

The multicylinder in-line injection pump (Figure 21-50) has a plunger and barrel assembly for each engine cylinder. The assemblies are grouped together in one housing that resembles cylinders in the block of an in-line engine. A high-pressure fuel line connects each pump assembly to one injector. The pump delivers or pumps an equal amount of fuel on each stroke.

The in-line injection pump used on automotive diesel engines is lubricated with engine oil. The pump does not have a seal around the cam drive end bearing so the oil returns to the engine through the bearing.

Injection Nozzles

The fuel injection nozzle is designed to vaporize and direct the metered fuel into the combustion chamber. The injection pump forces the required fuel into the injection nozzle at the precise time it is needed. The design of the combustion chamber usually dictates the type of nozzle used, the droplet size, and the spray pattern required for optimum combustion in the given time frame and space. A typical injection nozzle is shown in Figure 21-51.

The typical injection nozzle has small openings so that the pressure can build up under some operating conditions. A spring-loaded needle valve in the injector nozzle keeps the opening of the nozzle closed until the pressure reaches the operating level. The fuel pressure opens the nozzle valve and the spring closes it. Fuel from the injection pump enters and pressurizes the fuel lines and the pressure chamber. When the force on the lift area is greater than the set spring force on the spindle, the needle valve lifts off its seat and rests with its upper shoulder against the face of the holder body. Fuel in a mist or spray-type pattern is then forced out into the combustion chamber. The pattern is determined by the type of tip used on the injector nozzle.

Only the tip of the injection nozzle protrudes into the combustion chamber. Two types of injector tips are used on diesel engines: the hole type and the pintle type. Open combustion chambers use the hole type (Figure 21-52), but it is also used on a few engines with divided combustion chambers. The pintle type tip (Figure 21-53) is used only on engines with a divided combustion chamber.

Governors

Gasoline engines are self-governing because the air entering the engine is controlled by the use of a car-

Fuel Injection 551

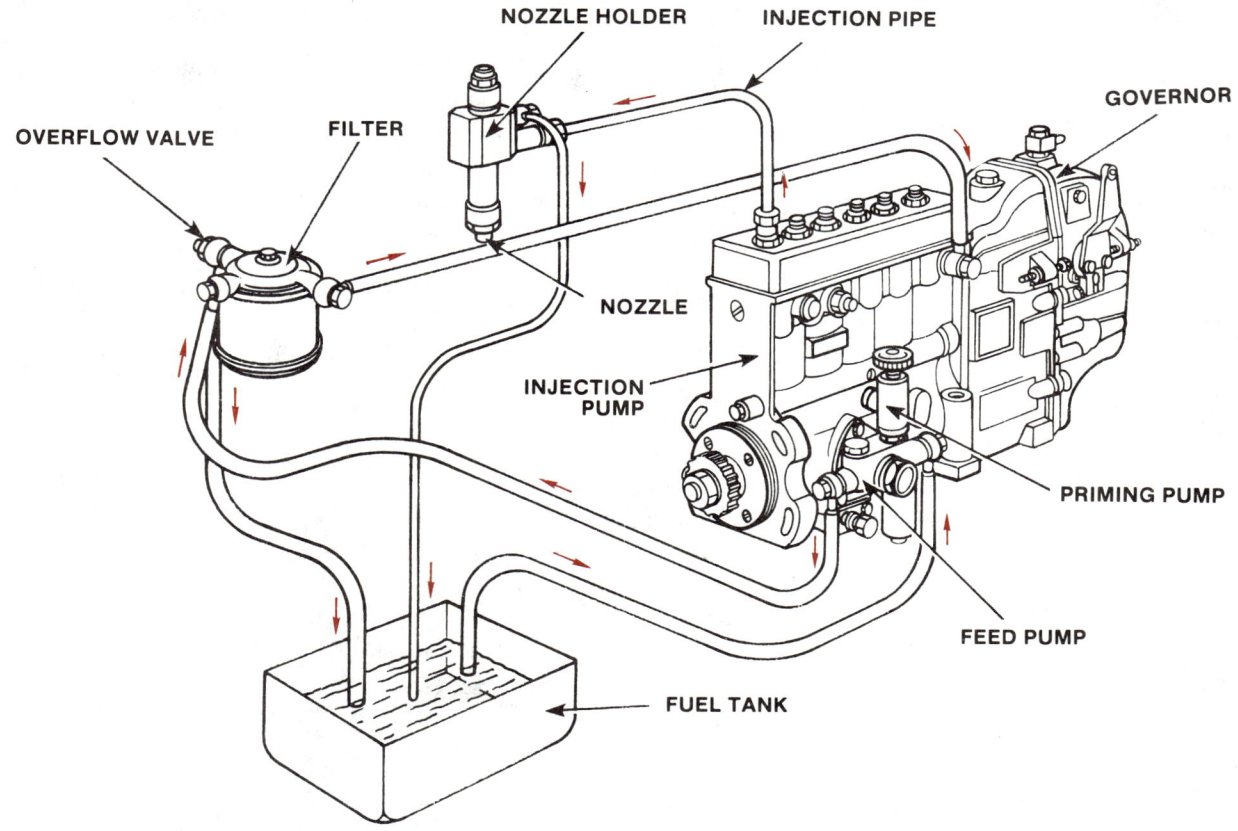

Figure 21-50 Typical in-line injection pump.

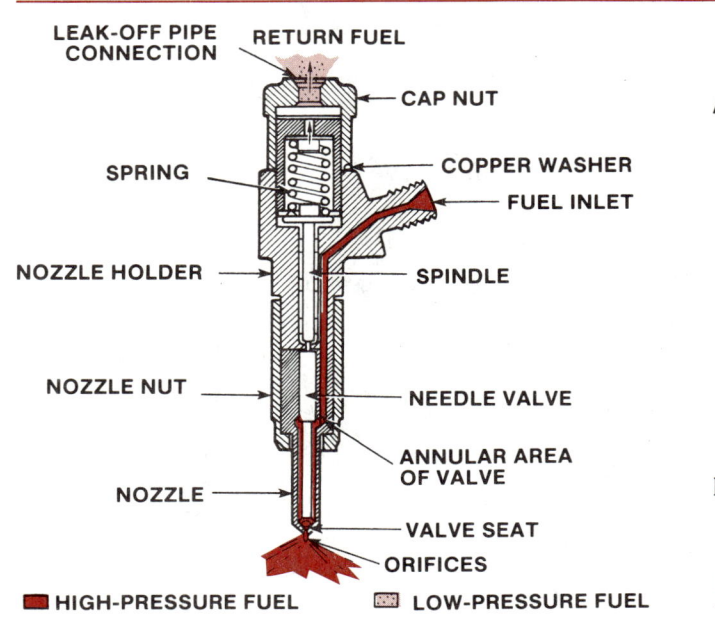

Figure 21-51 Parts of a diesel injection nozzle.

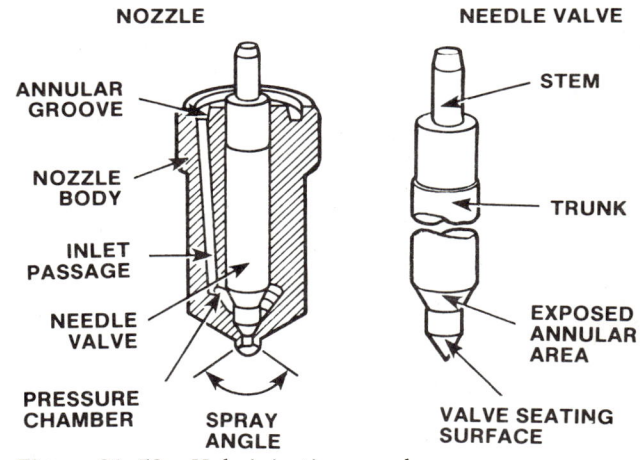

Figure 21-52 Hole injection nozzle.

buretor throttle valve or by the throttle body in a fuel injected system. The driver can change engine speed by manipulating the throttle pedal.

Because of this method, in most cases, the gasoline engine has no need for a governor. If such an engine is equipped with a governor mechanism, it is for the sole purpose of limiting the maximum road speed of the vehicle and the engine rpm to prevent engine abuse or avoid poor fuel economy.

The diesel engine, on the other hand, operates with an excessive amount of unthrottled air throughout its operating speed range. The fuel injection system is separately controlled from the airflow system. When a diesel engine is started, the air is unthrottled and remains so as the driver opens the fuel control mechanism or throttle linkage to allow the injection system to inject more fuel into the cylinders. Without some

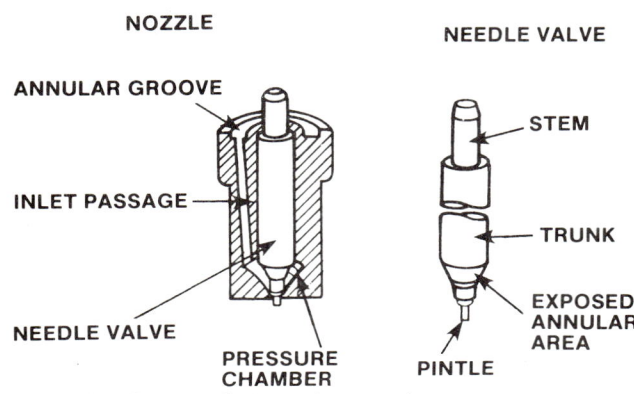

Figure 21-53 Pintle injection nozzle.

form of fuel control, the diesel engine can accelerate very rapidly and self-destruct, especially if the throttle were to be placed in the full-fuel position and left there with no mechanism to regulate the fuel input.

Therefore, a governor is required on diesel engines to regulate the fuel input and prevent engine stalling at the low-speed end and from overspeeding at the high-speed end. The governor controls the speed of the engine.

At minimum speed or idle, the governor controls pump injections so the engine gets just enough fuel to keep it running. At maximum rpm, the governor controls pump injection to limit fuel flow to keep the

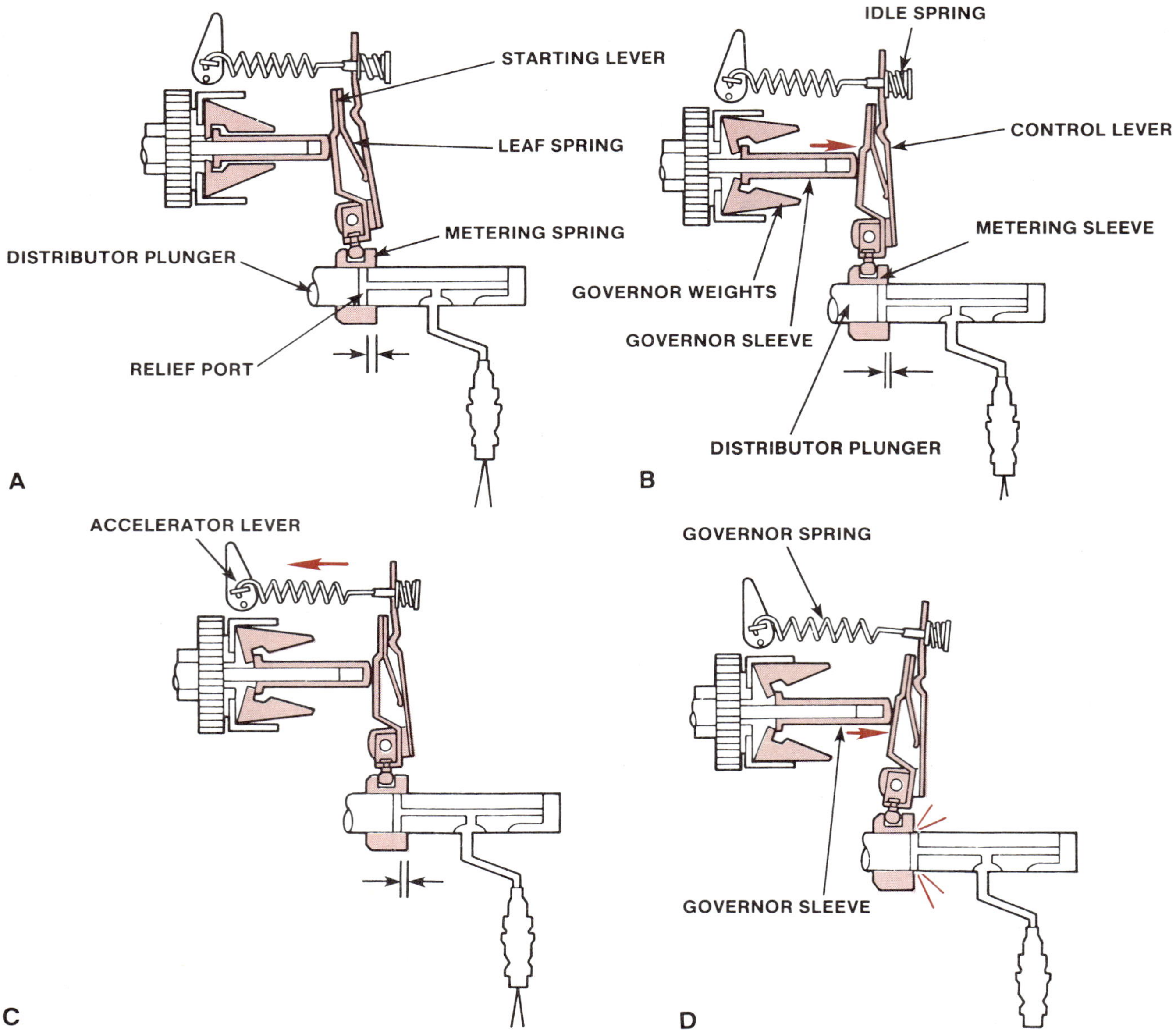

Figure 21-54 Governor operation in a diesel fuel injection system: (A) During starting, the metering sleeve is pushed farthest from bottom dead center, resulting in a longer injection period. (B) As engine speed increases, the weights push the governor sleeve to the right, which moves the metering sleeve to the left and shortens the injection period. (C) Depressing the accelerator moves the metering sleeve to the right, which causes more fuel to be injected. (D) Maximum engine speed is governed by limiting fuel delivery as during idle.

engine from overspeeding. At intermediate speeds, the pump responds to movements of the accelerator pedal so the driver can control car speed directly. During coasting, the governor can cut off fuel delivery for economy. See Figure 21-54 for the operation of a typical governor.

Starting Devices

Since diesel fuel does not vaporize or ignite as readily as gasoline, starting devices are required on diesel engines. These include glow plugs, fuel heaters, and engine block heaters.

Glow plugs (Figure 21-55), located in the combustion chamber, preheat the air and fuel during cranking (or prior to cranking depending on the system design). In colder climates, engine block heaters are used to heat the engine's coolant, which in turn keeps the cylinder block and head at a temperature suitable for starting purposes. A fuel heater preheats the fuel electrically before it reaches the filter. The heater, usually thermostatically controlled, is a resistance type designed to heat the fuel before it enters the filter. This reduces the possibility of wax plugging the filter, which usually occurs when the fuel temperature is 20 degrees Fahrenheit or lower.

A glow plug is a low-voltage heating element that is inserted into the precombustion chamber on the intake manifold. The plug is usually controlled by the ignition switch. However, other design applications might have a separate on-off switch within the passenger compartment. The glow plug is energized only until the air in the combustion chamber is adequately heated and can support ignition at start-up. The energized or heating period for a glow plug is directly dependent upon how fast the plug can heat up and what the ambient temperature of the combustion chamber is. Most glow plugs work off the car's 12-volt system.

A control module is the heart of the glow plug system (Figure 21-56). The module senses the en-

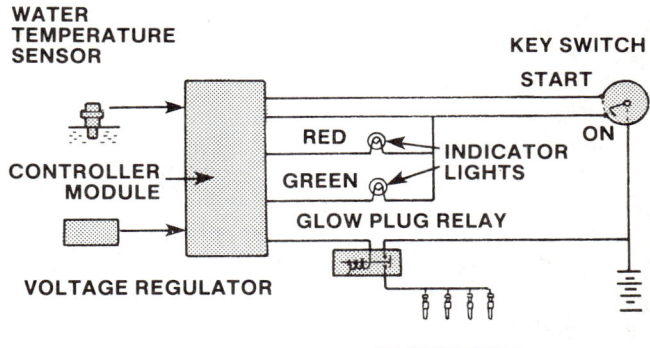

Figure 21-56 Electrical schematic of a glow plug system.

gine's coolant temperature and de-energizes the glow plugs when the coolant is sufficiently heated after start-up. Other design variations might use a cycling type of relay to pulse the glow plugs on and off. This type of system usually has a manual on-off switch to control the cycling relay.

Fuel Pick-up

The fuel pick-up is similar to the conventional gasoline pick-up, containing a fuel-level sending unit and a strainer. However, different features are added to accommodate the characteristics of diesel fuel and the diesel fuel system.

One type of pick-up unit uses a fuel pick-up filter (sock) and check valve assembly (Figure 21-57). The sock strains large particles, limits entry of water, and draws fuel from the bottom up to the pick-up tube, acting as a wick. A check valve is added to the sock. It is designed to open when the sock is restricted by wax or

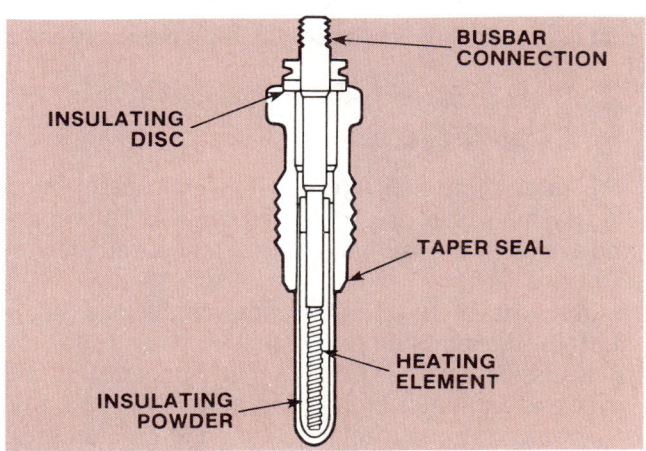

Figure 21-55 Cutaway view of a glow plug.

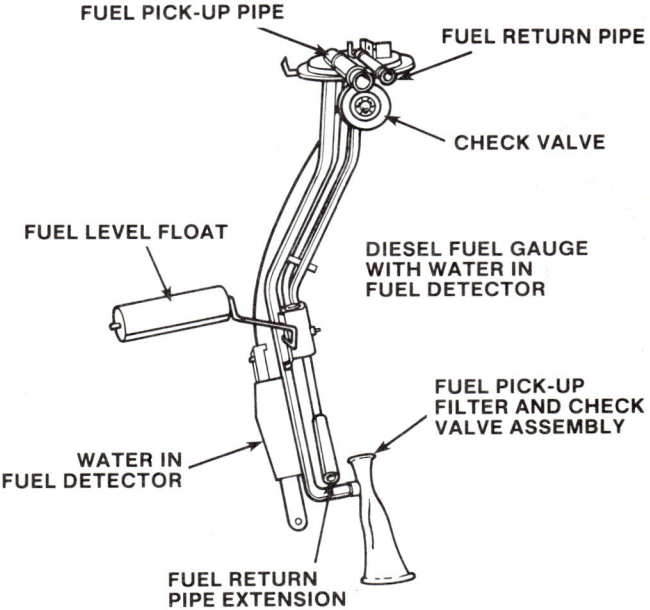

Figure 21-57 A combination fuel pick-up/fuel level indicator/water sensor.

ice, allowing the engine to run. This type of pick-up unit is usually equipped with a water-in-fuel sensor since the sock holds back only a certain amount of water before it passes and this system may not have a water-in-fuel separator.

Another type of pick-up unit places the fuel intake in contact with the bottom of the tank supported by several small nibs. Fuel going past the nibs accelerates, creating a pressure drop. This pressure drop attracts water. Water in the diesel fuel is drawn to the intake, accelerated, and forced through the nylon screen with the fuel. Using this type of pick-up unit necessitates a water-in-fuel separator to filter and eliminate the water. This pick-up unit also has low placement of the return line and a by-pass valve in the event the intake is clogged with wax or ice. With either pick-up unit, the tank must be at least one-quarter full for the by-pass valve to pick up fuel.

Fuel Filters

To protect the fuel injection system of a diesel engine, good filtration is essential. The clearances between injector parts require close control of solids in the fuel. To avoid erosion and wear, solids must not pass between closely mated injector parts. The primary filter, on the suction side of the transfer pump, protects the system from large solid contaminants. Most of the water in the fuel is also removed by this filter. The secondary filter is located between the transfer pump and the fuel injectors. Since the filter is located on the discharge side of the pump, the pressure drop across the secondary filter can be much higher than on a filter located on the suction side of the pump. This allows the secondary filter to be made in a compact size using a fine filtering media. This filter controls the size of particles allowed to pass into the fuel injectors. It also stops any water that might have passed through the primary filter.

Water Separators

A common diesel fuel problem is water in the fuel. Some vehicles are equipped with a water separator (Figure 21-58) in the fuel system. A fuel water separator works much like a filter, except that the element is replaced by a baffle. When contaminated fuel enters the separator, the heavier water settles at the bottom, while the light fuel rises to the top. A drain plug or petcock in the bottom of the separator allows the accumulated water to be drained periodically.

Fuel Lines

The fuel lines that carry the highly pressurized diesel fuel between the injection pump and fuel injectors are manufactured from special, thick-walled steel tubing (Figure 21-59). The steel fuel lines are always of the same length on a diesel engine so that each cylin-

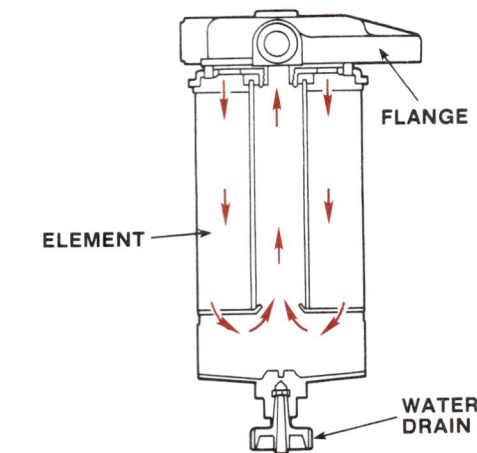

Figure 21-58 Diesel fuel filter/water separator.

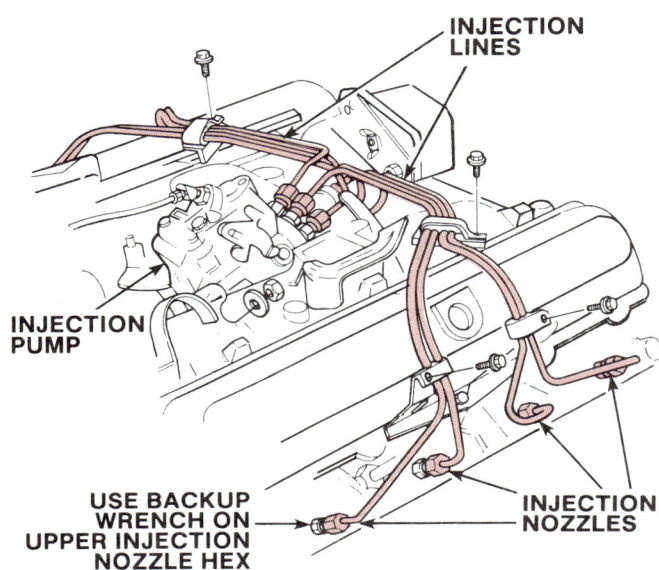

Figure 21-59 Routing of diesel injection fuel lines.

der receives an identical or equal fuel charge. During operation the steel fuel lines are completely full of fuel. If the fuel line contains 0.001 cc of fuel, 0.001 cc of fuel is delivered to the fuel injector because liquid diesel fuel does not compress under the high pump pressure.

☐ DIESEL ELECTRONIC CONTROL

Like gasoline fuel injection systems, diesel injection systems also use computer controls to monitor and activate various input (sensor) and output devices (Figure 21-60).

Input data includes engine rpm, vehicle speed, manifold absolute pressure (MAP), metering valve position, transmission gear position, coolant temperature, and brake and air conditioning operation.

The electronic control module or unit processes this data and signals various output devices to control

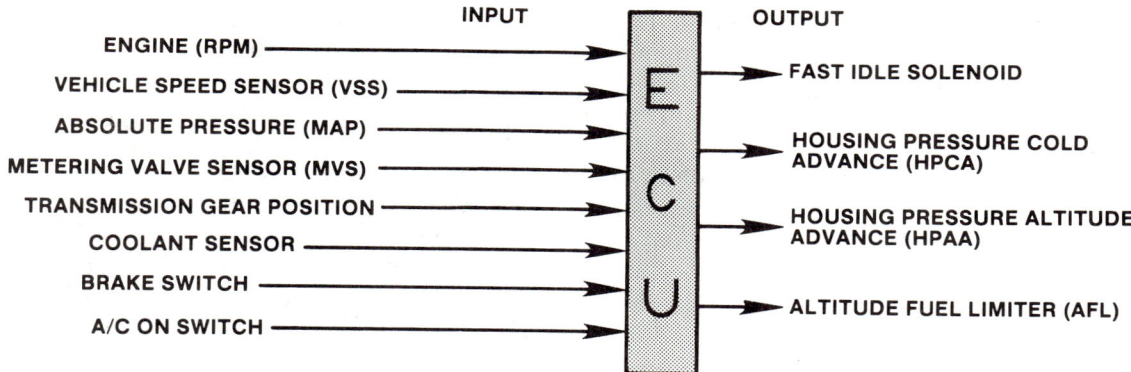

Figure 21-60 An electronic control system regulates the diesel fuel injection system.

engine performance and operation. These output devices include the following.

FAST IDLE SOLENOID The fast idle solenoid operates at temperatures below 100 degrees and above 248 degrees Fahrenheit. As the plunger of the solenoid moves, it increases spring pressure on the governor, thereby slightly increasing engine speed.

HOUSING PRESSURE COLD AND ALTITUDE ADVANCE These solenoid-operated mechanisms advance the fuel injection pump on a cold engine and at higher altitudes. This helps reduce engine noise and emissions.

ALTITUDE FUEL LIMITER This solenoid limits the travel of the metering valve at wide open throttle at altitudes above 4000 feet.

METERING VALVE SENSOR The variable resistor sensor sends a variable voltage signal to the ECU indicating metering valve position.

Case 1

A customer brings in a late-model GM automobile, with a 2.0L port fuel injected engine, and complains of poor performance and fuel economy. It is also mentioned that the service engine soon light had been on for some time.

Diagnosis of the problem begins with a visual inspection of the engine, including all hoses and wiring connectors. No problems are found.

Next, a scan tool is connected to the ECU and code 45 is retrieved from the computer's memory. The technician uses a code interpretation list to find a rich exhaust signal is coming from the oxygen sensor.

At first, the technician suspects a faulty oxygen sensor. By referring to the service manual, she finds that this code is set when the oxygen sensor signal to the control computer (ECU) is greater than 0.75 volt for 50 seconds and the system is in closed loop. Keep in mind that a faulty sensor is open, shorted, or has high resistance. An open sensor circuit or sensor would cause the engine to operate in open loop, not in closed loop. A short would cause high amperage, which would do physical damage to the wires and/or ECU. But, the visual inspection did not locate any damage. Excessive resistance in the circuit would cause voltages to be lower. The problem here is higher voltages. Therefore, it is unlikely that the problem is caused by a faulty sensor or sensor wiring harness. To locate the cause of the problem more testing is needed.

Following the appropriate troubleshooting tree, testing continues with the scan tool and reveals that the problem could be caused by an open in the ignition wiring, a saturated charcoal canister, a faulty MAP sensor or fuel pressure regulator, or by the improper use of RTV sealer. Detailed inspection and testing of these reveals the cause of the problem: a ruptured vacuum diaphragm in the fuel injection system's pressure regulator that allowed the excessive fuel pressure and a rich mixture.

The regulator is replaced, and the codes are cleared. The problem is corrected. To verify the repair, the technician runs the engine and observes the scan tool to make sure the engine went into closed loop and that no codes were set by the computer.

Summary

- There are two types of electronic fuel injection systems: throttle body and port injection. In the throttle body injection system, fuel is delivered to a central point. In the port injection system, there is one injector at each cylinder.
- Port injection systems use one of four firing systems: grouped single fire, grouped double fire, simultaneous double fire, or sequential fire.
- The electronic fuel injection system includes a fuel delivery system, system sensors, electronic control unit, and fuel injectors.

- The volume airflow sensor and mass airflow sensor determine the amount of air entering the engine. The MAP sensor measures changes in the intake manifold pressure that result from changes in engine load and speed.
- The heart of the fuel injection system is the electronic control unit. The ECU receives signals from all the system sensors, processes them, and transmits programmed electrical pulses to the fuel injectors.
- Two types of fuel injectors are currently in use: top feed and bottom feed. Top-feed injectors are used in port injection systems. Bottom-feed injectors are used in throttle body injection systems.
- Two methods are used to control idle speed on engines equipped with fuel injection: an auxiliary air valve and an idle speed solenoid.
- While some electronic control elements are being added to the basic system, continuous injection systems (CIS) meter fuel delivery mechanically not electronically.
- CIS injectors spray fuel constantly. They do not pulse on and off. The proper air/fuel mixture is attained by varying the amount of fuel delivered to the injectors.
- Continuous injection systems can be fitted with an oxygen sensor, or lambda sensor, for feedback control. Signals from the oxygen sensor are sent to the oxygen control unit. The oxygen control valve operates on signals from the oxygen control unit.
- Troubleshooting electronic fuel injection systems requires systematic step-by-step test procedures. Using a hit-or-miss approach can be frustrating, time-consuming, and costly.
- In any EFI system three things must occur. First, an adequate air supply must be supplied for the air/fuel mixture. Second, a pressurized fuel supply must be delivered to properly operating injectors. Finally, the injectors must receive a trigger signal from the control computer.
- When checking out the EFI, the air system should be checked first. Then, check the fuel system. The injectors are checked last. Servicing CIS requires the same logical approach and preliminary checks used in troubleshooting EFI systems.
- Diesel fuel injection systems operate under very high fuel and air pressures. The output power of a diesel engine is directly proportional to the fuel charge injected into the combustion chamber. A governor is used to limit the amount of fuel that can be injected. This limits engine speed and power output to levels that do not damage engine components.
- The injection pump is the heart of the diesel fuel injection system. The pump is driven off the engine's crankshaft to control injection timing. The pump is capable of generating the 15,000 to 30,000 psi fuel pressures needed and metering precise amounts of fuel to each injector.

Review Questions

1. Explain the major differences between throttle body fuel injection and port fuel injection systems.
2. What is meant by sequential firing of fuel injectors?
3. Describe the purpose of the idle speed solenoid and auxiliary air valve.
4. Describe the purpose of the manifold absolute pressure (MAP) sensor.
5. Describe the basic differences between gasoline fuel injection and diesel fuel injection systems.
6. Which of the following is not an advantage that fuel injection offers over carburetion?
   a. leaner air/fuel ratios
   b. better fuel economy
   c. no choke requirements
   d. lower engine torque
7. The length of time that an injector is energized is called _____ .
   a. intermittent system
   b. pulsed system
   c. injector pulse width
   d. open loop mode
8. Technician A says that most continuous injection systems in use today are electronically controlled. Technician B says that most continuous injection systems in use today are mechanically controlled. Who is correct?
   a. Technician A
   b. Technician B
   c. Both A and B
   d. Neither A nor B
9. Technician A says that electronic fuel injection must be adjusted to match the engine. Technician B says the engine must be made to match the EFI. Who is correct?
   a. Technician A
   b. Technician B
   c. Both A and B
   d. Neither A nor B
10. Technician A performs an injector pressure balance test by activating each injector with an electronic pulse tester. Technician B performs the same test by momentarily applying 12 volts to the injector terminals to activate the injector. Whose method is correct?
    a. Technician A
    b. Technician B
    c. Both A and B
    d. Neither A nor B
11. Bottom-feed injectors are used in _____ .

a. throttle body injection systems
   b. port injection systems
   c. both a and b
   d. neither a nor b
12. Technician A says that clogging of the injectors is more common on CIS. Technician B says that clogging of the injectors is more common on TBI. Who is correct?
    a. Technician A
    b. Technician B
    c. Both A and B
    d. Neither A nor B
13. Fuel tubing and hoses should be replaced at least every _____.
    a. year
    b. two years
    c. three years
    d. five years
14. Technician A says the CIS-E uses an airflow sensor, but Technician B says it does not. Who is correct?
    a. Technician A
    b. Technician B
    c. Both A and B
    d. Neither A nor B
15. An injector balance test produces a pressure drop variation of 2 psi. Technician A says this is acceptable and therefore no cause for concern. Technician B says it is a cause for concern. Who is correct?
    a. Technician A
    b. Technician B
    c. Both A and B
    d. Neither A nor B
16. As an alternative to an injector power balance test, Technician A uses a stethoscope to listen for correct operation. Technician B uses a thin steel rod for the same purpose. Who is correct?
    a. Technician A
    b. Technician B
    c. Both A and B
    d. Neither A nor B
17. Which of the following should be done as a preliminary step before attempting an idle adjustment of a fuel injection system?
    a. blocking the drive wheels
    b. connecting a tachometer
    c. checking and adjusting base ignition timing
    d. all of the above
18. An airflow sensor plate that is off-center in its bore can allow air to leak by, causing _____ problems.
    a. idling
    b. cold start
    c. hot start
    d. preignition
19. The governor on a diesel fuel injection system is responsible for _____.
    a. injection timing
    b. injection timing advance
    c. fuel metering
    d. both a and b
20. To relieve fuel pressure on an EFI car, Technician A connects a pressure gauge to the fuel rail. Technician B disables the fuel pump and runs the car until it dies. Who is correct?
    a. Technician A
    b. Technician B
    c. Both A and B
    d. Neither A nor B

22 CARBURETORS

Objectives

■ Describe the basic principles of carburetion. ■ Explain the purpose and operation of the different carburetor circuits. ■ Describe the various auxiliary carburetor controls. ■ Describe the different types of carburetors. ■ Recognize carburetor-related performance problems. ■ Explain how various carburetor adjustments are made.

The carburetor is a device used to mix, or meter, fuel with air in proportions that satisfy the energy demands of the engine in all phases of operation. Today's carburetor is a very complex mechanism (Figure 22-1). Some of the larger two- and four-barrel carburetors can have over 200 parts. These parts make up the metering systems and subsystems that are necessary for matching air and fuel delivery with engine performance demands. Each of these systems must be functional and properly adjusted if the engine is to operate efficiently.

Although fuel injection systems have replaced carburetion in most passenger cars and light trucks, there are many carbureted engines still on the road. Technicians must understand the principles of carburetion and how carburetors are constructed and operate before they can successfully diagnose and tune carbureted engines.

❑ CARBURETION

Carburetion is the enriching of a gas by combining it with a carbon-containing compound. The gas is usually air and the compound is a hydrocarbon fuel, usually gasoline. The three general stages involved in carburetion are metering, atomization, and vaporization.

Metering

Metering is another term for measuring. In the process of carburetion, fuel is metered into the airstream passing through the barrel of the carburetor. The mixture of air and fuel is called an emulsion. The ideal air/fuel ratio at which all the fuel blends with all the oxygen in the air is called the stoichiometric ratio. This ratio is about 14.7:1. If there is more fuel in the mixture it is called a rich mix. If there is less fuel it is called a lean mix. The amount of fuel metered into the airstream is varied in relation to the amount of air passing through the carburetor. Additional factors that influence the amount of fuel metered into the air include engine temperature, load and speed requirements, and the amount of oxygen in the exhaust stream.

Atomization

Atomization is the stage in which the metered fuel is broken down into tiny droplets as it is drawn into the airstream in the form of tiny droplets. The droplets of fuel are drawn out of passages called discharge ports.

Vaporization

The surface area of an atomized droplet is in contact with a relatively large amount of surrounding air. In addition, the venturi is a low-pressure area. These factors combine to create a fine mist of fuel below the venturi in the bore. This is called vaporization—the last stage of carburetion. It occurs below the venturi, in the intake manifold, and within the cylinder. Swirl, turbulence, and heat within the intake manifold and cylinder also enhance vaporization.

❑ VENTURI

Air is drawn into the engine by the intake stroke. As vacuum is created, it draws air through the carburetor and venturi into the engine.

A venturi is a streamlined restriction that partly closes the carburetor bore (Figure 22-2). Air is forced to speed up as it enters the venturi in order to pass

Carburetors 559

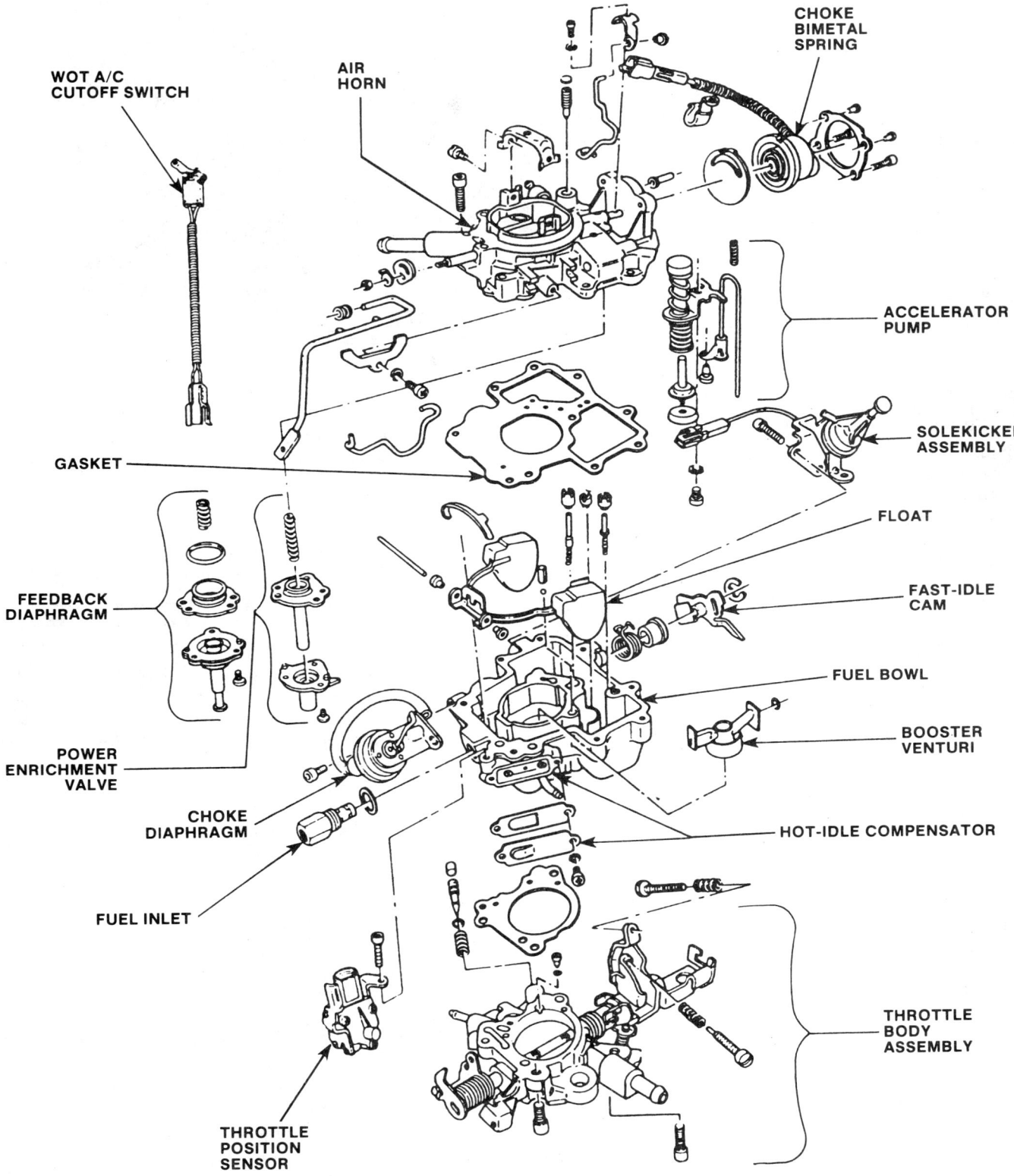

Figure 22-1 Typical carburetor.

through the restriction. This restriction causes an increase in vacuum. The vacuum is also present, to a lesser degree, below the major restricted area. As engine speed increases during acceleration, more air is drawn into the carburetor. As a result, venturi vacuum increases because the greater the velocity of air passing through the venturi, the greater the vacuum.

Venturi vacuum is used to draw in the correct amount of fuel through a discharge tube (Figure 22-3). As the air flows through the venturi, vacuum draws the

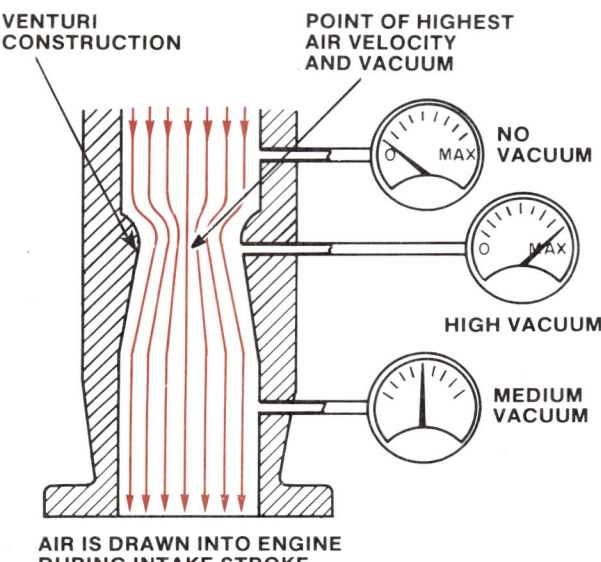

Figure 22-2 A venturi is a restriction in the path of air flow. A vacuum is produced at the point of greatest restriction.

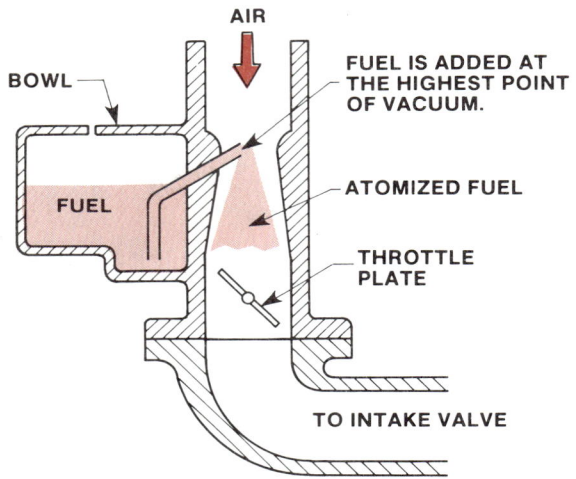

Figure 22-3 The vacuum that is produced at the venturi is used to draw in the fuel from the carburetor.

fuel from the carburetor bowl into the stream of air going into the engine. More fuel is drawn in as venturi vacuum increases, and less as the vacuum decreases.

❏ THROTTLE PLATE

The throttle plate controls the amount of air and fuel that flows through the carburetor into the engine. It is made of a circular disk and is placed directly in the flow of air and fuel, below the venturi. It is connected to the driver's throttle pedal so that it opens to a vertical position as the pedal is depressed. When the throttle plate is in this position, there is very little restriction of air and fuel. This is a maximum speed condition. As the driver's foot is removed, a spring closes the throttle plate. This restricts the amount of

Figure 22-4 The throttle plate is a circular disk attached to a center rod. As the rod is turned, the throttle plate opens and closes.

air and fuel going into the engine. This is a low speed condition. Figure 22-4 shows a throttle plate assembly.

❏ BASIC CARBURETOR CIRCUITS

Variations in engine speed and load demand different amounts of air and fuel (often in differing proportions) for optimum performance—and present complex problems for the carburetor. At engine idle speeds, for example, there is insufficient air velocity to cause fuel to be drawn from the discharge nozzle and into the airstream. Also, with a sudden change in engine speed, such as rapid acceleration, the venturi effect (pressure differential) is momentarily lost. Therefore, the carburetor must have special circuits or systems to cope with these situations. There are six basic circuits used on a typical carburetor.

1. Float
2. Idle and off-idle
3. Main metering
4. Full power (or power enrichment)
5. Accelerator pump
6. Choke

Float Circuit

The float circuit or fuel inlet system (Figure 22-5) of a typical carburetor consists of the fuel bowl, fuel inlet fitting, fuel inlet needle valve and seat, and the float. A fuel screen or filter is usually installed at the fuel inlet to prevent dirty fuel from mixing in the carburetor and causing a problem.

The float system stores fuel and holds it at a precise level as a starting point for uniform fuel flow. Fuel enters the carburetor through the inlet line and passes through an inlet filter to the inlet needle valve and seat. The incoming fuel is captured and stored in the reservoir or fuel bowl. The fuel bowl is normally an integral part of the main casting but can be a separate casting attached to the carburetor body with screws.

Carburetors 561

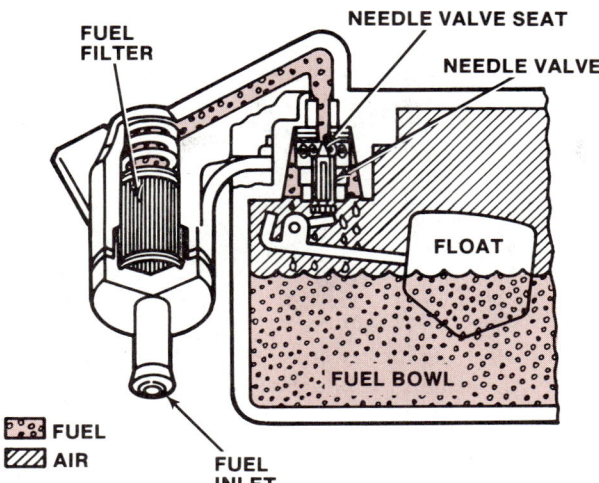

Figure 22-5 Fuel inlet system.

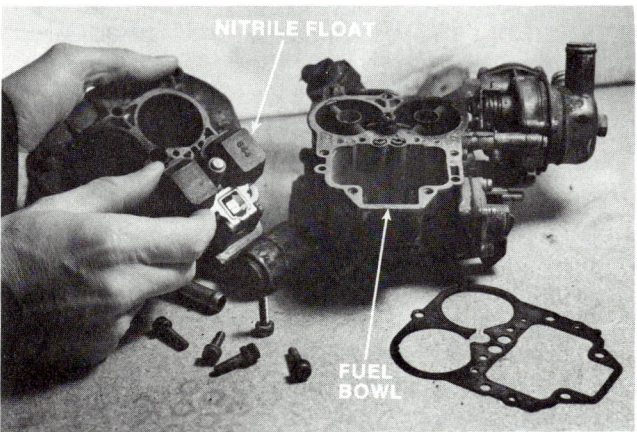

Figure 22-6 Nitrile rubber float assembly.

Carburetors with primary and secondary venturis might have two separate fuel bowls.

The level of the fuel in the bowl is maintained at a specified height by the rising and falling of the float in the fuel bowl. Early floats were made of brass stampings soldered into an airtight lung. Floats made of nitrile rubber (Figure 22-6), a closed cell material made of thousands of tiny hollow spheres, are used almost exclusively on domestic cars. Hollow plastic floats can also be found in carburetors.

As fuel enters the bowl, the float, which is connected to a hinged lever, rises and closes the inlet needle valve. With the needle valve closed, fuel is prevented from entering the carburetor. Fuel pressure against the inlet needle valve tends to force it open while the buoyancy of the float in the bowl tends to force it closed. This action establishes the precise fuel level for the carburetor. To prevent the float from bouncing and vibrating, a bumper spring is usually installed under the float or to a tang connected to the float.

The metering systems of a carburetor are designed to function properly only when the fuel level in the bowl is at a specific level. The specific level is adjusted with the carburetor partially disassembled on most models. However, it can be adjusted externally on some carburetors by turning a threaded inlet valve assembly.

The fuel bowl is vented internally to the air horn by a vent tube in the carburetor body. Prior to the introduction of emission controls, most primary fuel bowls were also vented to the atmosphere when the engine was at idle or turned off. Since the introduction of evaporative control systems, all fuel bowls are vented by a valve to a charcoal canister, which absorbs and stores fuel vapors. The vapors are returned to the engine when it is restarted.

Idle Circuit

At idle, the engine requires a richer air/fuel mixture than during normal cruising conditions. This is because residual exhaust gases remain in the combustion chambers during low-engine rpm and dilute the air/fuel charge. The idle circuit supplies the richer air/fuel mixture to operate the engine at idle and low speeds.

During idle conditions, there is not enough air entering the venturi to cause a vacuum to move the fuel. The throttle plate is almost all the way closed as shown in Figure 22-7. During this condition, there is a large vacuum below the throttle valve. This vacuum causes fuel to be drawn from the carburetor float bowl through internal passages to the idle port below the throttle plate. As fuel is drawn from the float bowl to the idle port, air is drawn in through an air-bleed passageway near the top of the carburetor. Only a small amount of air passes by the throttle plate. The end result is the richer air/fuel mixture needed for idle operation.

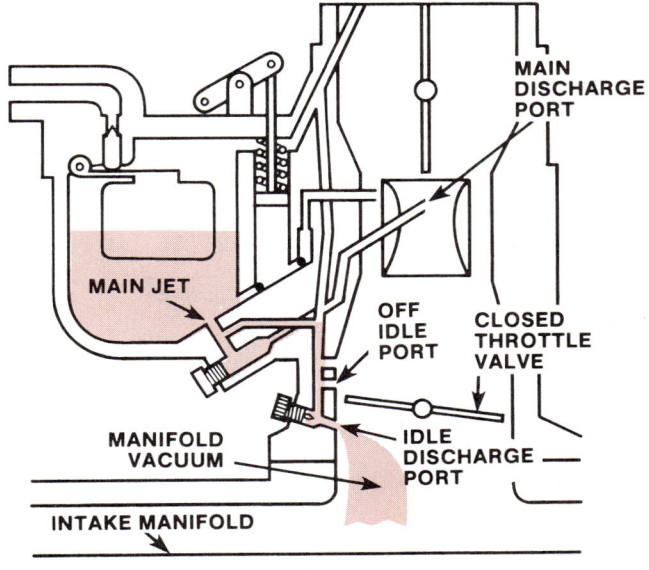

Figure 22-7 An idle discharge port draws fuel from the carburetor to allow the engine to run at idle.

As the throttle plate is opened during low-speed operation, a transfer slot located above the throttle plate is progressively exposed to vacuum and the air/fuel emulsion is also discharged from the transfer slot. The increased air/fuel mixture flow provides a smooth transition between idle and cruising modes of operation. Some carburetors have a series of holes called off-idle air passages, instead of a transfer slot. Like the transfer slot, the holes permit increased fuel delivery as the throttle opens. This is sometimes called an off-idle system.

On older carburetors there is an idle mixture needle valve. This valve is used to control or adjust the amount of air and fuel at idle. More current carburetors, however, have limiting caps on the idle mixture screws, which limit the amount of adjustment available. On newer carburetors, the idle mixture screws are sealed with steel plugs to eliminate all adjustment.

To improve idle quality when meeting emission standards, a variable air bleed idle system is used on some carburetors (Figure 22-8). In this system there are two idle air bleeds. One idle air bleed is installed normally in the air horn. An auxiliary idle air bleed is drilled into the lower skirt of the venturi. The air entering through the auxiliary passage is adjusted by an idle air adjusting screw. The screw is turned clockwise to enrich the idle mixture and counterclockwise to lean out the idle air/fuel mixture.

SHOP TALK

On most modern carburetors, the idle mixture is factory set and the adjustment screw is covered with a plate or plug. This ensures that the CO percentage in the exhaust meets emissions standards and prevents anyone from tampering with the factory setting. Earlier carburetors had an idle limiter cap attached to the idle mixture screw (Figure 22-9). The limiter cap also prevents the factory setting from being tampered with, but allows the idle mixture to be adjusted within a narrow range (about 3/4 of a turn).

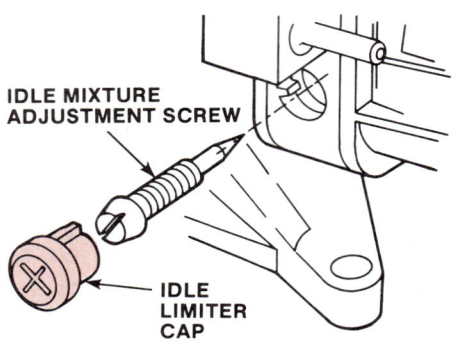

Figure 22-9 Idle limiter caps restrict the amount of adjustment allowed for the idle mixture.

Main Metering Circuit

The main metering circuit (Figure 22-10) comes into operation as engine speed increases. Opening the throttle plate past the idle position increases the air flowing through the venturi and creates enough vacuum to allow atmospheric pressure to force fuel through the main metering system and out the main fuel discharge nozzle, located in the center of the venturi. As engine speed is increased, the vacuum at the discharge nozzle increases.

This vacuum or pressure differential causes fuel to flow out of the fuel bowl, through the main metering jet, and into the main well. On most carburetors the

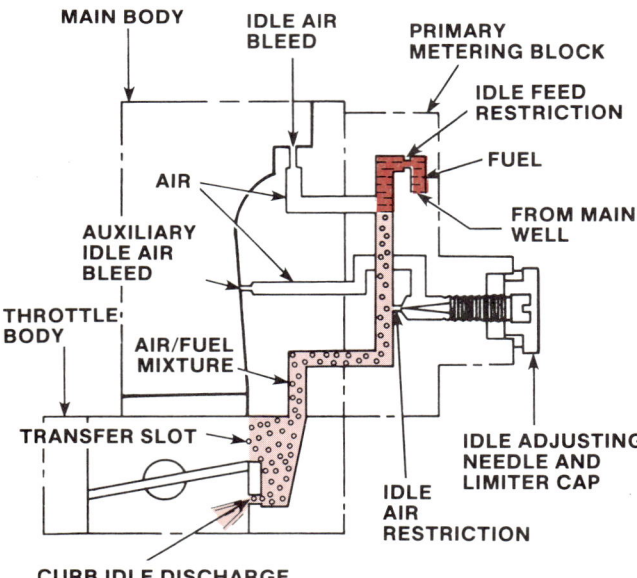

Figure 22-8 The idle discharge port and off-idle transfer slot supply fuel to the carburetor at low speeds.

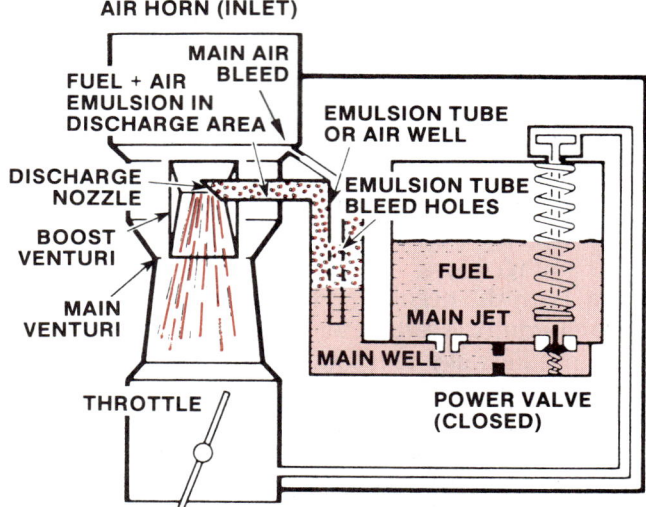

Figure 22-10 Air/fuel mixture routed to the venturi via the main metering circuit and discharge nozzle.

main well is vented through a precisely sized opening called the main well air bleed. The main well air bleed allows air to enter at the top of the main well. Air entering the calibrated main air bleed prevents a vacuum from developing in the main well. The air also allows for aeration of the fuel as it leaves the main well and travels up the well tube. This allows the fuel to be partially atomized as it travels toward the discharge nozzle.

Air flows through the bleeds because it draws air from the high-pressure area above the venturi and the main metering discharge nozzle is in the low-pressure venturi level.

As the air speed increases through the venturi, more fuel is drawn from the main well. This lowers the fuel level in the main well and exposes more air bleed openings in the main well tube. This causes extra air to enter the well tube, mix with the fuel, and dilute or lean the mixture. This action circumvents the richening effect caused by the increased carburetor airflow. If the fuel were not diluted as such, the air/fuel mixture would richen at high speed as the venturi vacuum increased faster than the engine's need for additional fuel.

Secondary Metering Systems

Some carburetors have more than one barrel or air horn. Each barrel has a throttle plate and main metering system (as well as other circuits). When all throttle plates open and close simultaneously, the carburetor is called a single stage carburetor.

Some carburetors have two stages, called primary and secondary stages. In the primary stage, one or two throttle plates operate normally as in a single stage carburetor. The secondary stage throttle plates, however, only open after the primary throttle plates have opened a certain amount. Thus, the primary stage controls off-idle and low cruising speeds and the secondary stage opens when high cruising speeds or loads require additional air and fuel. The added flow capacity raises the engine power output.

The secondary throttle plates can be opened mechanically or by a vacuum source. Mechanically actuated secondary throttle plates are opened by a tab on the primary throttle linkage. After the throttle primary plates open a set amount (usually 40 to 45 degrees), the tab engages the secondary throttle linkage, forcing the plates open (Figure 22-11). Vacuum-actuated secondaries have a spring-loaded diaphragm. Vacuum is supplied to the diaphragm from ports in the primary and secondary throttle bores. When the vacuum in the primary bore reaches a specific level, the vacuum supplied to the diaphragm overcomes the spring and opens the secondary throttle plates (Figure 22-12). The vacuum created in the secondary throttle bore increases the vacuum signal to the diaphragm, opening the secondary throttle valves still farther.

Power Enrichment Circuit

At wide open throttle, the engine needs a richer than normal air/fuel mixture. This mixture cannot be supplied by the main metering system. So, an additional fuel enrichment or full-power system is provided on most carburetors. The power enrichment system meters additional fuel into the mixture. This can be accomplished in several ways.

Metering Rods

In some carburetors, power enrichment is provided by metering rods placed in the main jets (Figure 22-13). The metering rods are actuated mechanically or by vacuum. When the throttle is not wide open (or nearly so), the throttle linkage keeps the rods in the jets, providing normal fuel flow. When the throttle is opened wide, either a mechanical link in the throttle linkage or vacuum-actuated lever lifts the rods out of the jets, enabling more fuel to be forced into the main well. The additional fuel flow richens the air/fuel mixture.

Power Valves

The power valve (Figure 22-14) is basically a vacuum-operated metering rod. It consists of a vacuum diaphragm or piston, a spring-loaded valve, and a metering rod inside an auxiliary fuel jet usually located in the bottom of the fuel bowl. A vacuum passageway

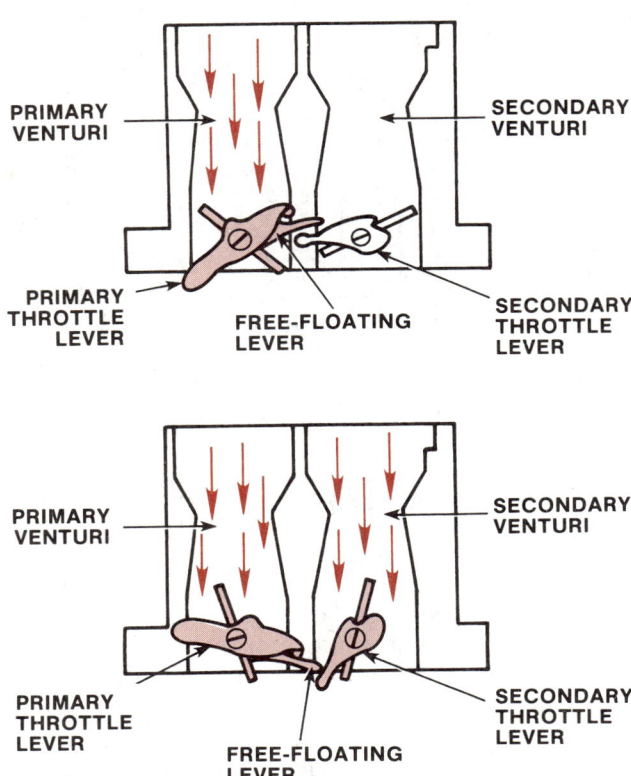

Figure 22-11 Mechanically actuated secondary throttle plates.

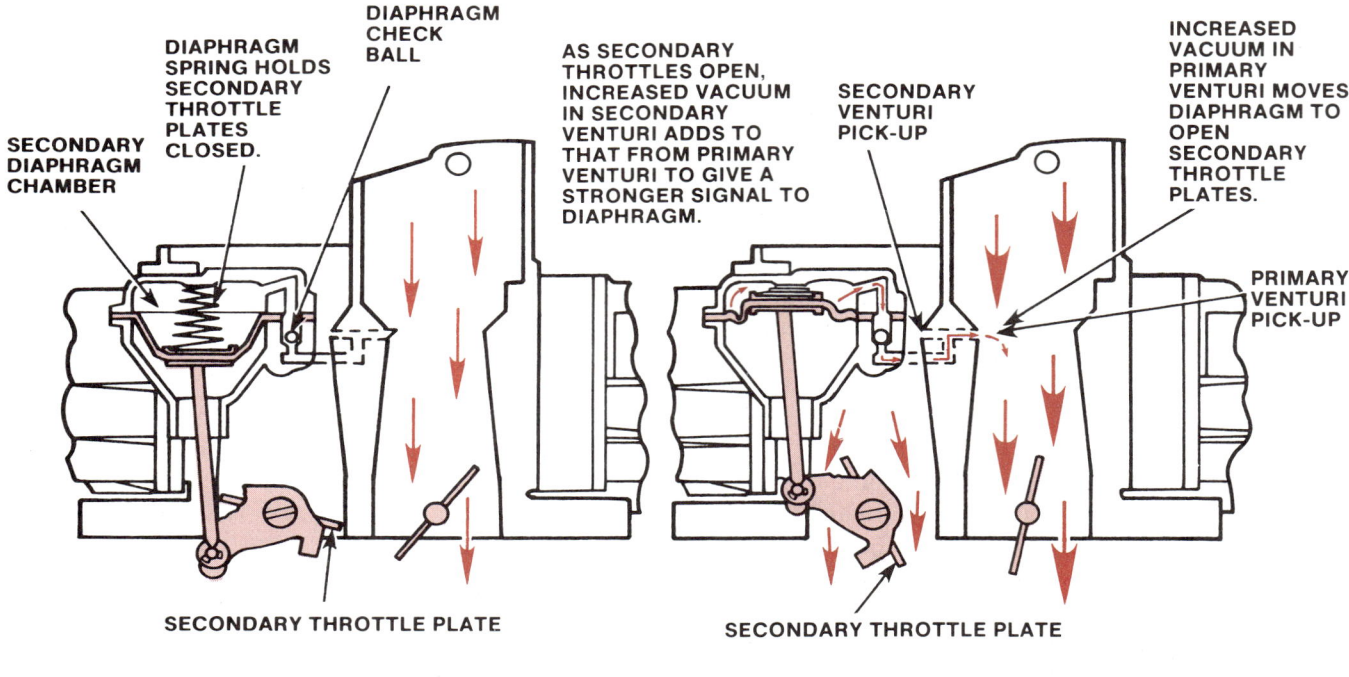

Figure 22-12 Vacuum-controlled secondary system.

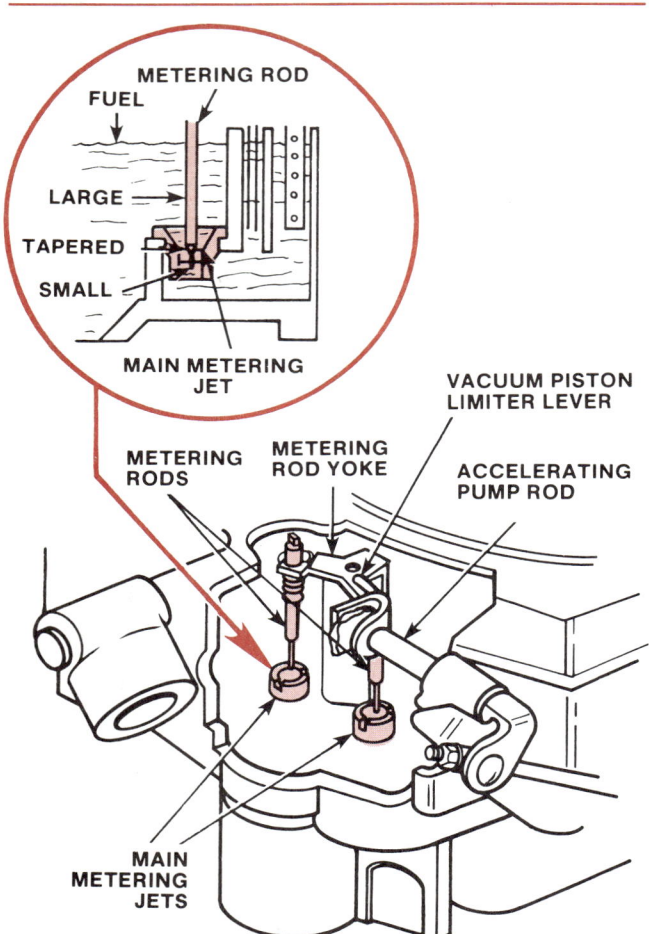

Figure 22-13 Some power systems consist of metering rods placed in the main jets.

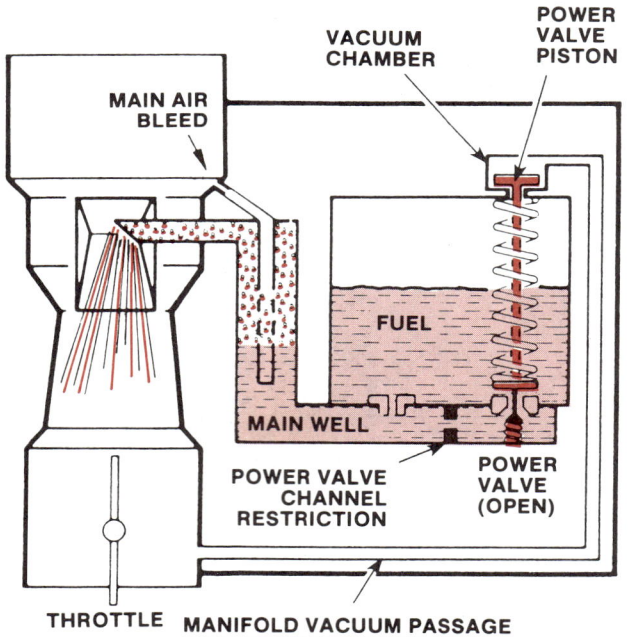

Figure 22-14 Power valve system.

machined into the main body casting supplies manifold vacuum to the diaphragm or piston. During idle and low cruising speeds, the vacuum holds the power valve closed. As engine speed and load increases and the vacuum signal drops to a specific level, the spring overcomes the vacuum and forces the power valve out of the jet. This increases the fuel flowing into the main well.

The power valve has been replaced or modified in today's feedback carburetor. In a feedback system, an electrical solenoid controls the metering fuel jets or idle air bleeds to regulate the air/fuel mixture. Feedback carburetors are discussed later in this chapter.

Accelerator Pump Circuit

The off-idle or transfer circuit discussed earlier allows the engine to be accelerated smoothly without hesitation or lags. However, during sudden acceleration, the engine experiences a momentary drop in power unless additional fuel is simultaneously introduced into the air charge.

During sudden acceleration the air flowing through the carburetor reacts almost immediately to each change in the throttle plate opening. However, since fuel is heavier than air, it has a slower response time. Fuel in the main metering system or idle system takes a fraction of a second to respond to the throttle opening. This lag in time creates a hesitation of fuel flow whenever the accelerator pedal is quickly depressed. The accelerator pump system solves this problem by mechanically supplying fuel until the other fuel metering systems are able to supply the proper mixture.

One type of accelerator pump (Figure 22-15) is the diaphragm type located in the bottom of the fuel bowl. Locating the pump in the bottom of the fuel bowl assures a more solid charge of fuel (fewer bubbles).

When the throttle is opened, the pump linkage, activated by a cam on the throttle lever, forces the pump diaphragm up. As the diaphragm moves up, the pressure forces the pump inlet check ball or valve onto its seat. This prevents the fuel from flowing back into the fuel bowl. At the same time, the pressure of the fuel

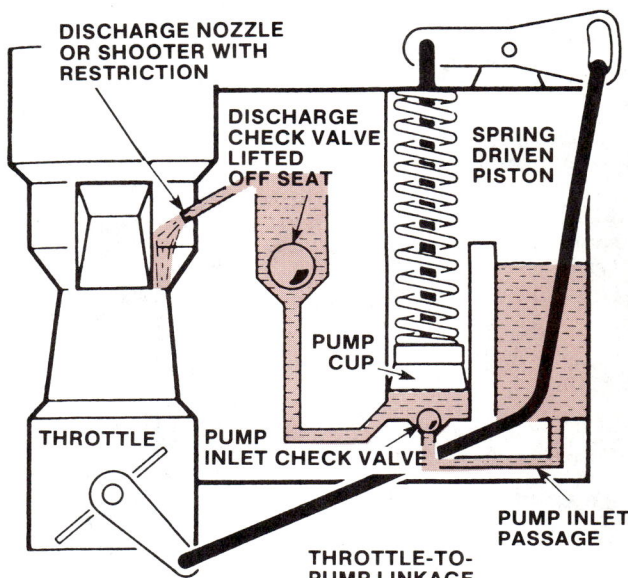

Figure 22-16 Plunger accelerator pump.

causes the discharge check ball or valve to raise and fuel is then discharged into the venturi.

As the throttle returns toward the closed position, the linkage returns to its original position and the diaphragm return spring forces the diaphragm down. The pump inlet check valve is moved off its seat and the diaphragm chamber is refilled with fuel from the fuel bowl.

Another common type of accelerator pump is shown in Figure 22-16. This type of pump uses a plunger rather than a diaphragm. As the throttle moves toward the open position, pressure from the plunger forces an inlet ball onto a check valve, sealing the inlet valve. At the same time, a ball is forced off the outlet check valve and fuel is discharged from the shooter nozzle. As the throttle moves back toward the closed position, the plunger retracts, allowing the inlet check valve to open and fuel to refill the pump.

Choke Circuit

A cold engine needs a very rich air/fuel mixture during cranking and start-up. Providing the rich mixture is the job of the choke circuit (Figure 22-17).

During a cold startup, the choke should be closed. This creates a very high vacuum level in the air horn below the choke plate. As the air pressure outside the carburetor forces its way into the low-pressure areas, it draws with it a rich air/fuel mixture. When the throttle plate is closed, the mixture is forced out through the idle port or ports below the throttle valve. If the throttle valve is opened to assist in starting the engine, additional ports are exposed to the low-pressure manifold pressure and additional fuel is forced into the air horn. After the engine starts, a leaner mixture can be used to keep the engine running. Therefore, the choke should

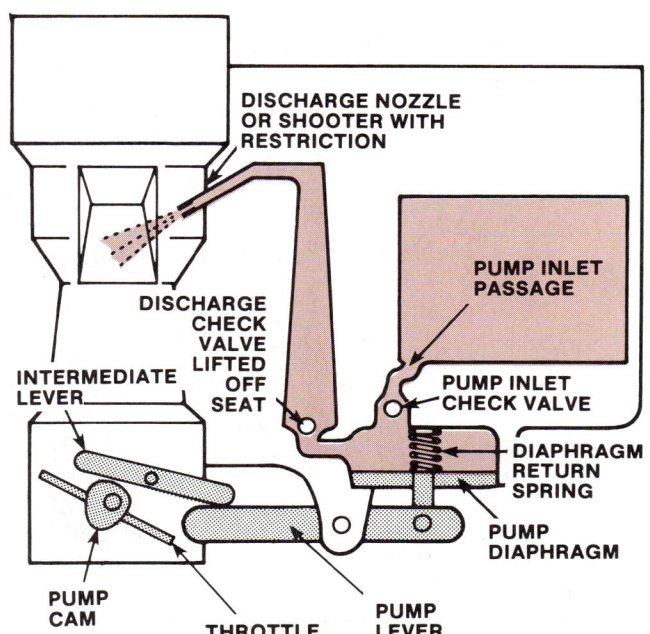

Figure 22-15 Diaphragm accelerator pump.

566 Section 4 Engine Performance

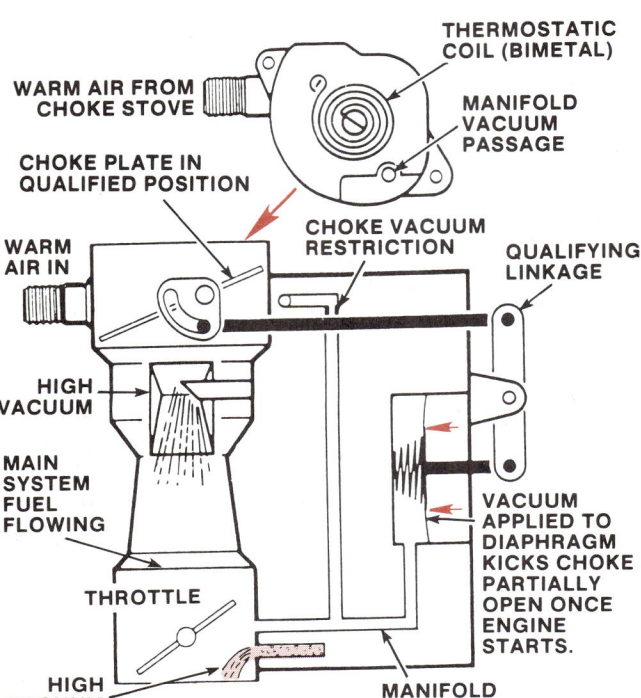

Figure 22-17 Choke system.

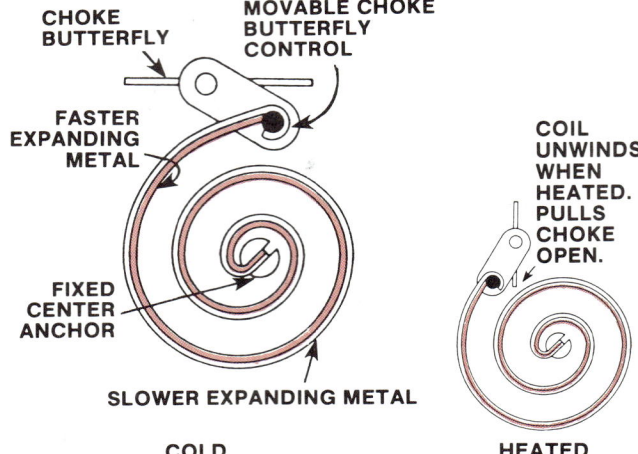

Figure 22-18 Principle of a bimetallic spring.

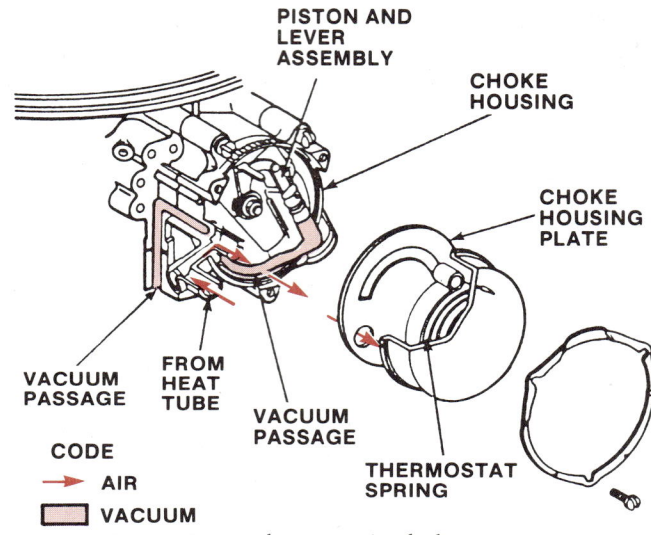

Figure 22-19 Integral automatic choke.

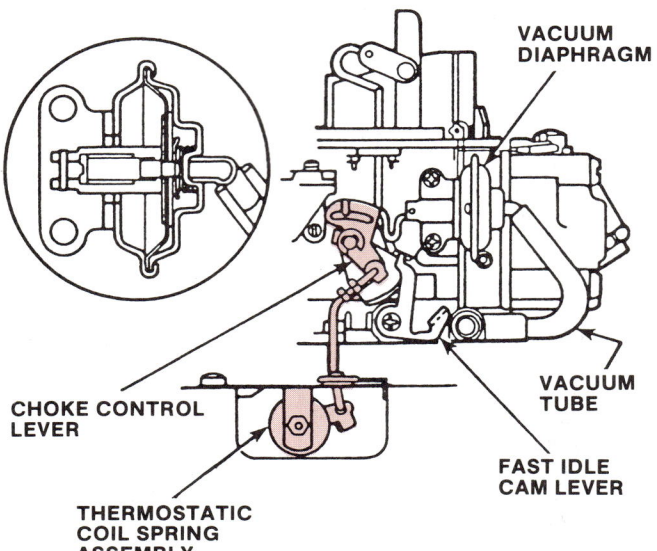

Figure 22-20 Divorced choke thermostatic element mounted in heat well.

be opened some to allow increased airflow. After the engine has warmed to normal operating temperatures, the choke should be opened completely to allow the throttle to control airflow and fuel metering.

Before the introduction of automatic chokes, the opening and closing of the choke plate was manually controlled by the driver. A choke cable was connected to a knob inside the passenger compartment on the dash. To close the choke, the driver simply pulled the knob out. As the engine warmed, the choke knob was gradually pushed in to open the choke.

Modern carbureted vehicles have an automatic choke that operates without any driver assistance. Being more sensitive to engine temperature, an automatic choke is more efficient.

The typical automatic choke has a bimetal coil called a thermostatic spring. When the coil is cold, it forces the choke plate closed. As the bimetal coil warms, it expands and pulls the choke plate open (Figure 22-18).

The bimetal coil can be mounted directly on the carburetor. This type is called an integral choke (Figure 22-19). The bimetal coil may also be mounted on the intake manifold or in a heat well in the exhaust heat passage of the intake manifold. This type is called a divorced or remote choke (Figure 22-20).

The integral choke normally has a heat source to warm the bimetal. The heat source might be hot air (Figure 22-21) or coolant. Many integral chokes also have an electrical heater to assist in warming the coil during warm weather or hot start-up. The bimetal coil

Carburetors

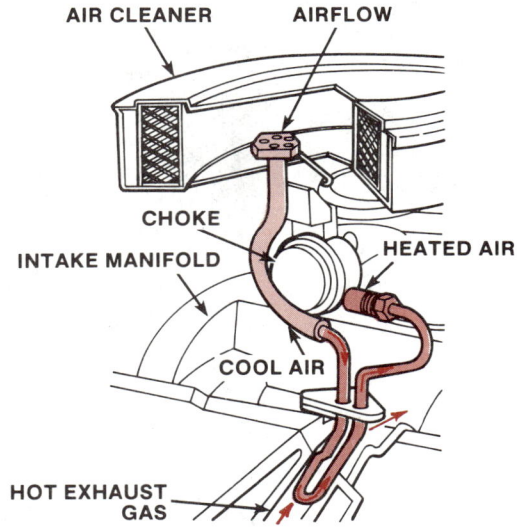

Figure 22-21 Hot air choke system.

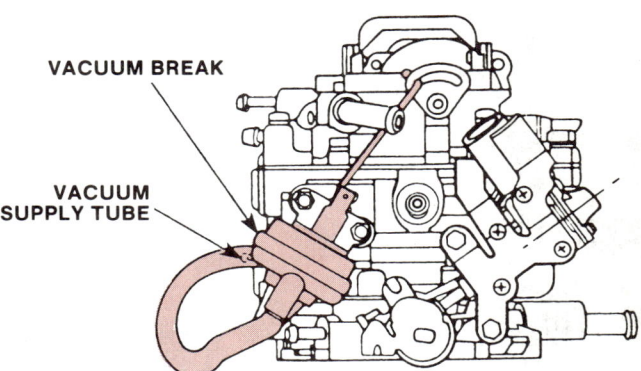

Figure 22-22 Vacuum break.

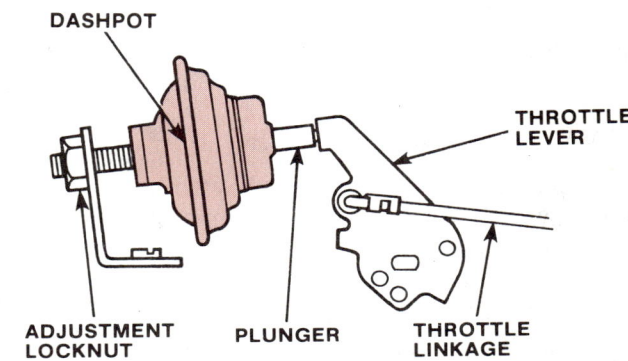

Figure 22-23 Typical carburetor dashpot installation.

on many feedback carburetors is heated solely by a solid state heating element. Voltage is usually provided to the heating element from the alternator circuit.

ADDITIONAL CARBURETOR CONTROL

To meet complex fuel economy and emission requirements, carburetors require the help of auxiliary controls. The following describes some of the more common assist devices you are likely to encounter when servicing a carburetor.

Choke Qualifier

Once the engine has started, a leaner mixture is needed. If the choke stays shut, the rich mixture floods the engine and causes stalling. Therefore, the automatic choke has a choke qualifying mechanism to open the choke plate slightly after the engine has started.

Many integral chokes have a vacuum piston in the choke housing that opens the choke slightly when manifold vacuum reaches a certain level (immediately after the engine starts). A vacuum passage in the carburetor supplies vacuum to the piston. When the piston retracts in its cylinder, a passage is opened in the housing, allowing warm air from the heat tube to circulate through the choke housing. This delays warming the bimetal coil until the engine is started.

Some integral chokes and all divorced chokes have a qualifying diaphragm (also called a choke pull-off diaphragm or vacuum break) instead of a vacuum piston (Figure 22-22). The diaphragm is connected to manifold vacuum, and when the engine starts, the diaphragm retracts, pulling the choke open. The amount of opening, or the distance between the upper edge of the choke plate and the side of the air horn, is called the qualifying dimension or setting. In some carbure-

tors, the pull-off diaphragm has a modulator spring that varies the qualifying setting based on ambient temperatures.

Dashpot

The dashpot (Figure 22-23) is used during rapid deceleration to retard the closing of the throttle. This allows a smooth transition from the main metering system to the idle system and prevents stalling due to an overly rich air/fuel mixture. It also controls the level of HC in the exhaust during deceleration.

The dashpot consists of a small chamber with a spring-loaded diaphragm and a plunger. A link from the throttle comes in contact with the dashpot plunger as the throttle closes. As the throttle linkage exerts force on the plunger, air slowly bleeds out of the diaphragm chamber through a small hole. This slows the closing action of the throttle plate.

Hot-Idle Compensator (HIC) Valve

When the engine is overheated, a hot-idle compensator opens an air passage to lean the mixture slightly (Figure 22-24). This increases idle speed to help cool the engine (by increased coolant flow) and to prevent excess fuel vaporization within the carburetor. The

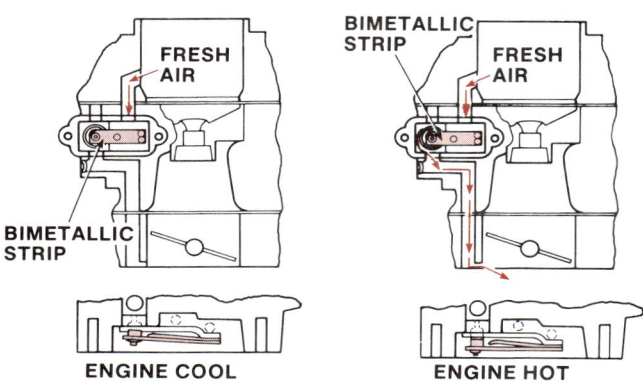

Figure 22-24 Hot-idle compensator operation: engine hot, valve open.

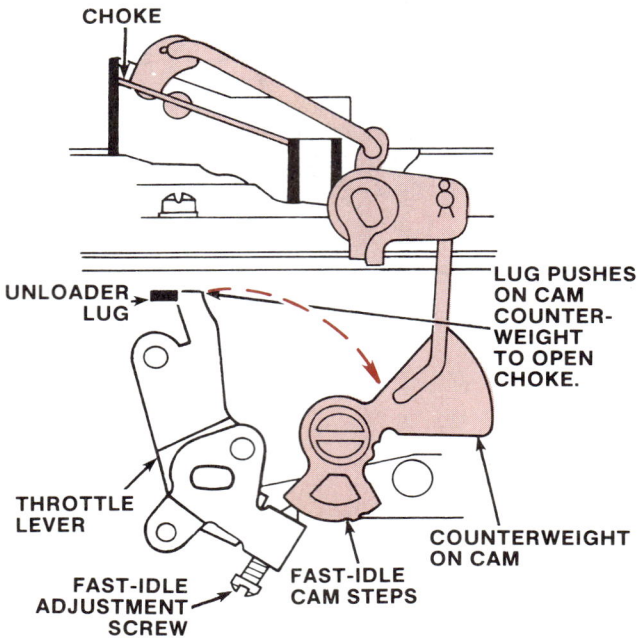

Figure 22-25 The choke unloader opens the choke any time the gas pedal is floored. Lug pushes on cam counterweight to open choke.

hot-idle compensator is a bimetal, thermostatically controlled air bleed valve.

Dual Vacuum Break

Some carburetors are equipped with a dual vacuum break system, which includes a primary diaphragm and a secondary diaphragm. The primary vacuum diaphragm opens the choke valve slightly as soon as the engine starts to keep the engine from overchoking and stalling. The secondary vacuum diaphragm, which is also attached to the choke lever, opens the choke valve slightly wider in warm weather or when a warm engine is being started.

Vacuum to the secondary diaphragm is controlled by a thermal vacuum switch or valve (TVV). The TVV releases vacuum to the secondary vacuum break when the engine reaches a certain temperature. This prevents a rich fuel mixture and the high emissions that result from starting a cold engine in warm weather or when a warm engine is started.

Choke Unloader

To be able to start a cold engine that has been flooded with gasoline, a choke unloader is required. The choke unloader (Figure 22-25) is throttle linkage actuated and opens the choke whenever the accelerator pedal is floored. At wide-open throttle, the partially opened choke allows additional air to lean out the mixture and reduce fuel flow.

Deceleration Valve

This valve (Figure 22-26) is designed to prevent backfire during deceleration as the fuel mixture becomes richer. The valve, which operates only during deceleration, is usually located between the intake manifold and the air cleaner. A typical valve has a cam-shaped diaphragm housing on one end. A control manifold-vacuum line is attached to a port under the diaphragm housing. The other end of the valve is connected by hoses to the intake manifold and air

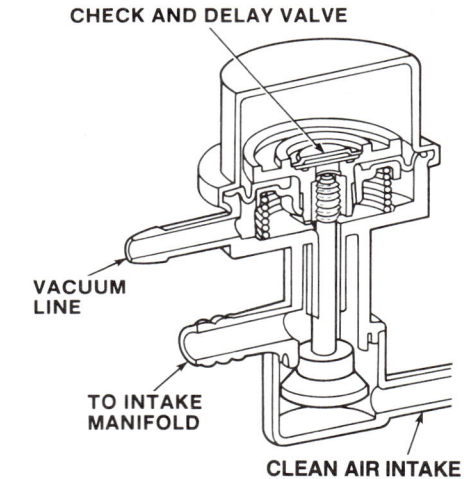

Figure 22-26 Deceleration valve.

cleaner. When deceleration causes an increase in manifold vacuum, the diaphragm opens the deceleration valve and allows air to pass from the air cleaner into the intake manifold, leaning the fuel mixture and preventing exhaust system backfire.

Throttle Position Solenoid

The throttle position solenoid is an electrical device used to control the position of the throttle plate (Figure 22-27). It can have several functions, depending on its application. When the basic function is to prevent dieseling, the solenoid is called a throttle stop solenoid or an idle stop solenoid. When the engine is started, the solenoid is energized and the plunger ex-

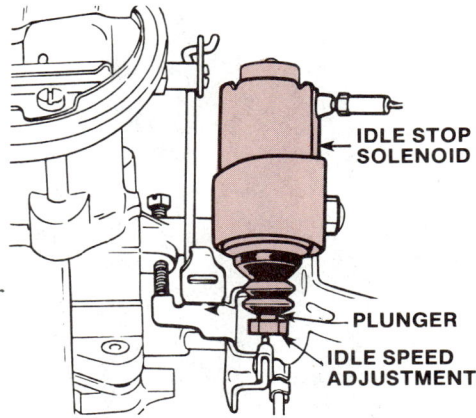

Figure 22-27 An idle stop solenoid is used to control the position of the idle setting when the ignition is turned off and on. *Courtesy of Echlin Manufacturing Co.*

tends, pushing against the throttle linkage. This forces the throttle plates open slightly to the curb idle position. When the ignition switch is turned off, the solenoid is de-energized and the plunger retracts. This allows the throttle plate to close completely, and it shuts off the air/fuel supply to prevent dieseling or run-on.

The throttle position solenoid is also used to increase the curb idle speed to compensate for extra loads on the engine. When this is its primary function, the solenoid might also be called an idle speed-up solenoid or a throttle kicker. This feature is most often used on cars with air conditioners. When the air conditioning is turned on, a relay energizes the solenoid so that the plunger extends farther, raising the idle rpm. This keeps the engine running at a higher speed, which is required to maintain a smooth idle speed and to ensure adequate emission control.

The throttle position solenoid is also used to control idle speed when the transmission is engaged. A relay in the park/neutral switch signals the solenoid to extend when the transmission is shifted into gear. This opens the throttle slightly to compensate for the increased load on the engine.

TYPES OF CARBURETORS

Many types of carburetors have been built in order to accommodate different load conditions, engine designs, and air/fuel requirements. Different carburetors feature different drafts, different numbers of barrels, different types of venturi, and different flow rates.

Carburetor Draft

Draft is defined as the act of pulling or drawing air. A carburetor's direction of draft is one way in which carburetors are classified. Most engines today have a downdraft carburetor that has air flowing vertically down into the engine. In the sidedraft carburetor, air flows through the carburetor in a horizontal direction. Many early sports cars used a sidedraft carburetor. Because it was placed on the side of the engine rather than on top, the engine compartment could be more streamlined. An updraft carburetor brings the air and fuel into the engine in an upward direction. Not many automobiles use this type, but they are used in forklifts and other industrial engine applications.

Carburetor Barrels

A carburetor barrel is a passageway or bore used to mix the air and fuel. It consists of the throttle plate, venturi, and air horn. A one-barrel carburetor is used on small engines that do not require large quantities of air and fuel.

A two-barrel carburetor has two throttle plates and two venturis. Figure 22-28 shows the throttle plates of a two-barrel carburetor. The area where the air comes into the carburetor is common on both barrels. A two-barrel carburetor is used on many newer small vehicles. These carburetors may have one barrel that is smaller in diameter than the other one.

Figure 22-29 shows a four-barrel carburetor. It has four barrels to mix the air and fuel. The engine operates on two barrels during most driving conditions. When more power is needed, the other two barrels add fuel to increase the amount of horsepower and torque produced by the engine.

Venturi Types

Carburetors are also categorized according to the type of venturi they use (Figure 22-30). The carburetor used on many small single-cylinder engines such as those used in gardening equipment has a single venturi.

The double (dual) venturi has an additional secondary or boost venturi. The bottom of the center (boost)

Figure 22-28 Carburetors are also classified by stating the number of barrels. This is a two-barrel carburetor.

Figure 22-29 A four-barrel carburetor has four barrels and four throttle plates.

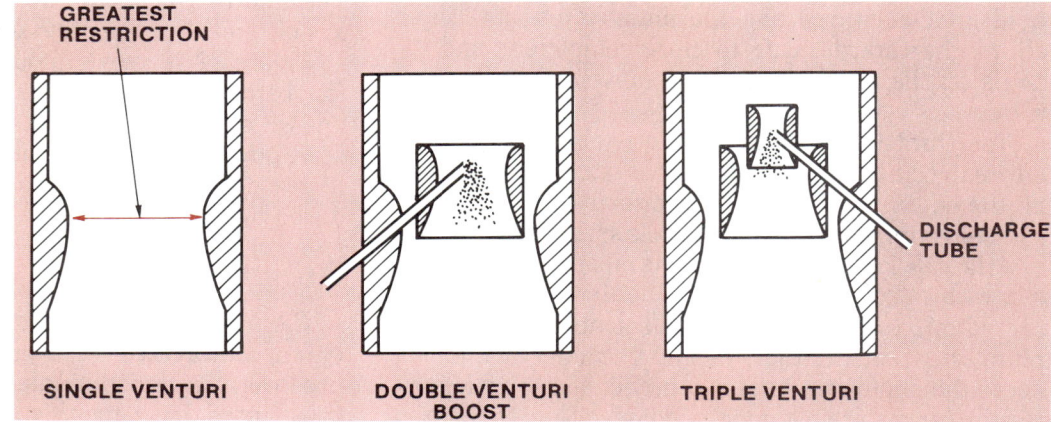

Figure 22-30 Carburetors have several types of venturis. One, two, and three venturis can be used. These can also be called boost venturis.

venturi is located at the greatest restriction area of the next larger venturi. This arrangement multiplies the vacuum developed in the venturi. The result is better vaporization and atomization and more control of fuel entering into the air stream. Thus, increasing the venturi effect increases the efficiency of the carburetor.

Even more control and atomization occur with a triple venturi design. The discharge tube feeds fuel into the smallest venturi for maximum control and atomization.

Some carburetors have a variable or changing venturi. As the throttle pedal is depressed, the venturi increases in size. The venturi decreases in size when the throttle pedal is released. Some American cars and several foreign cars used this type of carburetor.

❏ VARIABLE VENTURI CARBURETORS

A fixed venturi does not change shape and size to accommodate changing engine performance demands. Therefore, the speed of the air flowing through the venturi varies according to engine rpm and load. Because the vacuum in the venturi is the result of moving air, the amount of fuel drawn from the discharge nozzle varies as air velocity (and vacuum) in the venturi fluctuates. In some engine operating modes, the air speed, vacuum level, and fuel discharge are matched to the needs of the engine. At other times, the fuel discharge might be too little or too much. To compensate for the inadequacies of a fixed venturi, idle systems, power systems, and choke systems are needed to supplement the main metering system.

These assist systems are not necessary when a variable venturi is used. A variable venturi increases in size as engine demands increase. In this way, airflow speed through the venturi and the resulting pressure differential remains fairly constant. Thus, a variable venturi carburetor is also known as a constant velocity carburetor or a constant depression (vacuum) carburetor.

An example of a variable venturi carburetor is shown in Figure 22-31. The venturi valves are controlled by a

Carburetors 571

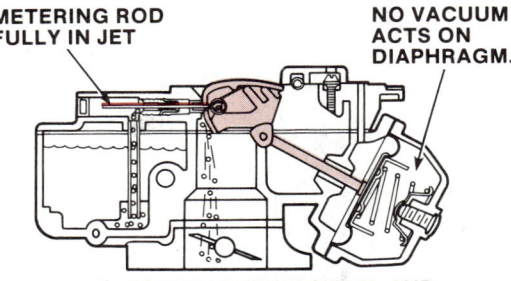

AT IDLE, VENTURI IS VERY SMALL AND METERING ROD REDUCES FUEL FLOW TO AIR HORN.

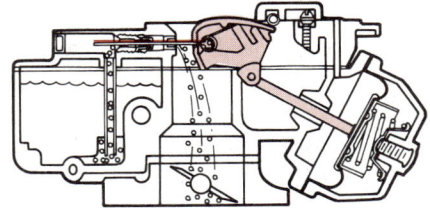

AT FAST IDLE, AIR HORN IS SLIGHTLY LARGER. MORE FUEL IS DRAWN INTO IT.

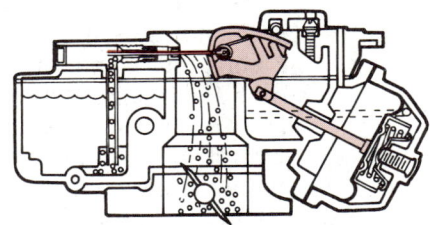

AT IMMEDIATE SPEED, STILL MORE FUEL AND AIR ARE DRAWN INTO THROAT.

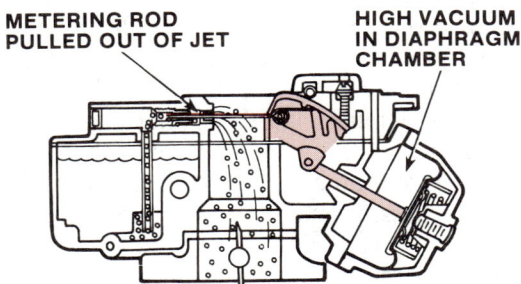

WITH WIDE-OPEN THROTTLE, VARIABLE VENTURI IS FULLY WITHDRAWN, AS IS METERING ROD.

Figure 22-31 Diaphragm controls variable venturis in this carburetor design.

vacuum diaphragm that receives vacuum from ports in the throttle bores between the venturi valves and the throttle plates. As the throttle plates open, vacuum in the throttle bore increases and the venturi valves open farther. As the valves open, tapered metering rods attached to the valves retract from metering jets in the sides of the throttle bores. This increases the size of the jet openings, allowing additional fuel to be drawn into the airstream so that the air/fuel ratio remains constant. By metering both the fuel and airflow simultaneously, better fuel economy and lower emissions are possible.

FEEDBACK CARBURETOR SYSTEMS

The latest type of carburetor system is the electronic feedback design, which provides better combustion by improved control of the air/fuel mixture.

The feedback carburetor was introduced following the development of the three-way catalytic converter. A three-way converter not only oxidizes HC and CO but also chemically reduces oxides of nitrogen (NO_x).

However, for the three-way catalyst to work efficiently, the air/fuel mixture must be maintained very close to a 14.7 to 1 ratio. If the air/fuel mixture is too lean, NO_x is not converted efficiently. If the mixture is too rich, HC and CO does not oxidize efficiently. Monitoring the air/fuel ratio is the job of the exhaust gas oxygen sensor (Figure 22-32).

An oxygen sensor (as its name implies) senses the amount of oxygen present in the exhaust stream. A lean mixture produces a high level of oxygen in the exhaust. A rich mixture produces little oxygen in the exhaust. The oxygen sensor, placed in the exhaust upstream from the catalytic converter, produces a voltage signal that varies in intensity in direct proportion to the amount of oxygen the sensor detects in the exhaust. If the oxygen level is high (a lean mixture), the voltage output is low. If the oxygen level is low (a rich mixture), the voltage output is high.

The electrical output of the oxygen sensor is monitored by an electronic control unit (ECU). This microprocessor is programmed to interpret the input signals from the sensor and in turn generate output signals to a mixture control device that meters more or less fuel into the air charge as it is needed to maintain the 14.7 to 1 ratio.

Whenever these components are working to control the air/fuel ratio, the carburetor is said to be operating in closed loop. Closed loop is illustrated in the schematic shown in Figure 22-33. The oxygen sensor is constantly monitoring the oxygen in the exhaust, and the control module is constantly making adjustments to the air/fuel mixture based on the fluctuations in the sensor's voltage output. However, there are certain

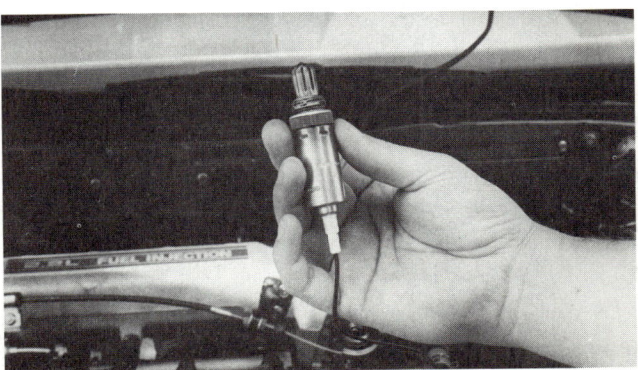

Figure 22-32 Exhaust gas oxygen sensor.

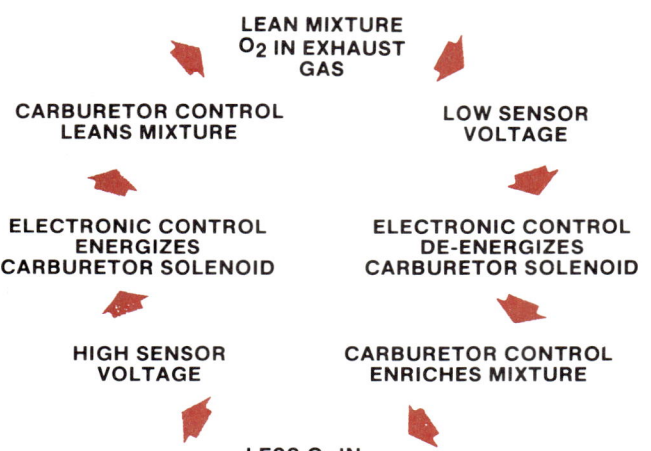

Figure 22-33 Closed loop operation.

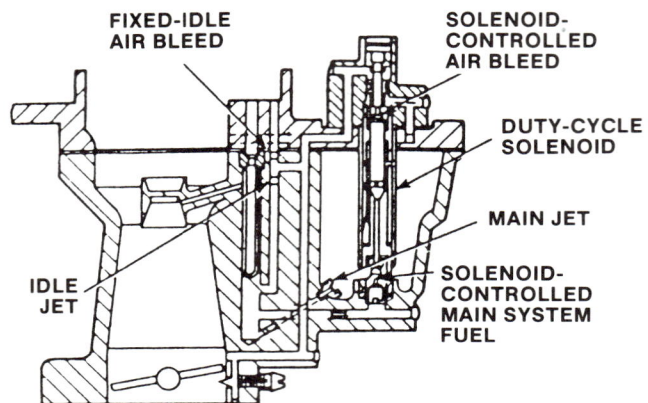

Figure 22-35 Electronic feedback carburetor.

conditions under which the control module ignores the signals from the oxygen sensor and does not regulate the ratio of fuel to air. During these times, the carburetor is functioning in a conventional manner and is said to be operating in open loop (the control cycle has been broken).

The carburetor operates in open loop until the oxygen sensor reaches a certain temperature (approximately 600 degrees Fahrenheit). The carburetor also goes into open loop when a richer than normal air/fuel mixture is required—such as during warm-up and heavy throttle application. Several other sensors are needed to alert the electronic control module of these conditions. A coolant sensor provides input relating to engine temperature. A vacuum sensor and a throttle position sensor indicate wide open throttle.

Early feedback systems used a vacuum switch to control metering devices on the carburetor. Closed loop signals from the electronic control module are sent to a vacuum solenoid regulator (Figure 22-34), which in turn controls vacuum to a piston and diaphragm assembly in the carburetor. The vacuum diaphragm and a spring above the diaphragm work together to lift and lower a tapered fuel metering rod that moves in and out of an auxiliary fuel jet in the bottom of the fuel bowl. The position of the metering rod in the jet controls the amount of fuel allowed to flow into the main fuel well.

The more advanced feedback systems use electrical solenoids on the carburetor to control the metering rods (Figure 22-35). These solenoids are generally referred to as duty-cycle solenoids or mixture control (M/C) solenoids. The solenoid is normally wired through the ignition switch and grounded through the electronic control module. The solenoid is energized when the electronic control module completes the ground. The control module is programmed to cycle (turn on and off) the solenoid ten times per second. Each cycle lasts 100 milliseconds. The amount of fuel metered into the main fuel well is determined by how many milliseconds the solenoid is on during each cycle. The solenoid can be on almost 100% of the cycle or it can be off nearly 100% of the time. The M/C solenoid can control a fuel metering rod, an air bleed, or both.

In the Carter thermo-quad carburetor shown in Figure 22-36, variable air bleeds control the air/fuel ratio. This carburetor contains two fuel supply sub-systems: the high-speed system and the low-speed system. The high-speed system meters fuel with a tapered metering rod positioned in the jet by the throttle. Fuel is metered into the main nozzle well where air from the feedback controlled variable air bleed is introduced. Since this

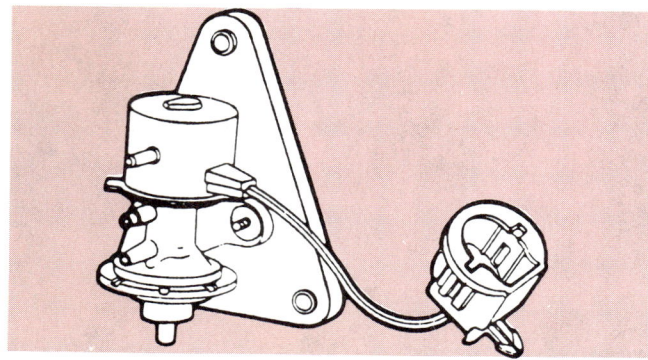

Figure 22-34 Remote-mounted fuel control solenoid.

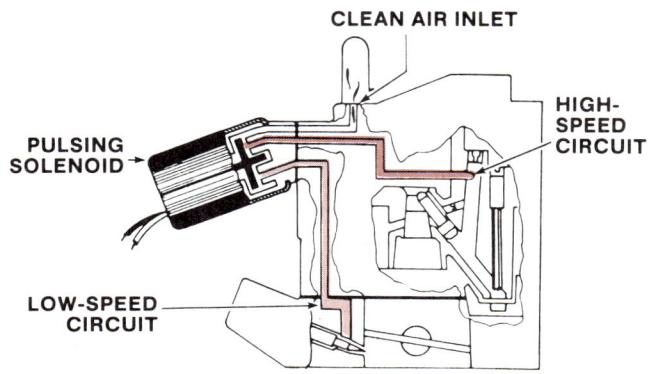

Figure 22-36 Thermo-quad with O_2 feedback.

air is delivered above the fuel level, it reduces the vacuum signal on the fuel thereby reducing the amount of fuel delivered from the nozzle.

The idle system is needed at times of low airflow through the venturi because there is insufficient vacuum at the nozzle to draw fuel into the airstream. After leaving the main jet, fuel is supplied to the idle system by the low-speed jet. It is then mixed with air from the idle by-pass, then accelerated through the economizer and mixed with additional air from the idle bleed before being discharged from the idle ports below the throttle. Air from the variable air bleed is introduced between the idle air bleed and idle port. This air reduces the vacuum signal on the low speed jet and consequently the amount of fuel delivered to the idle system.

The thermo-quad uses a mixture control or pulse solenoid to control the variable air bleeds. The solenoid has only two positions of operation: opened when energized to bleed air to both the high speed and low speed circuits or closed when de-energized, cutting off the air bleeds.

A less common method to control the air/fuel mixture is with a back suction system feedback. Figure 22-37 shows a variable venturi carburetor with an electric stepper motor rather than a duty-cycle solenoid. The back suction system consists of an electric stepper motor, a metering pintle valve, an internal vent restrictor, and a metering orifice. The stepper motor regulates the pintle movement in the metering orifice, thereby varying the area of the opening communicating control vacuum to the fuel bowl. The larger this area is, the leaner the air/fuel mixture is. Some of the control vacuum is bled off through the internal vent restrictor. The internal vent restrictor also serves to vent the fuel bowl when the back suction control pintle is in the closed position.

The 7200 VV carburetor was also produced with a feedback stepper motor that controls the main air bleed

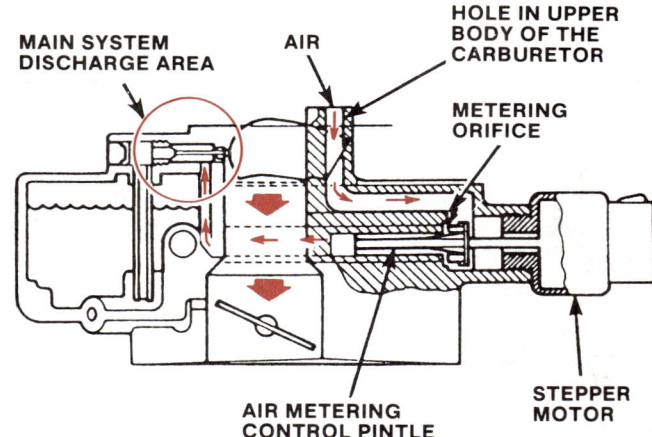

Figure 22-38 Air bleed feedback system.

(Figure 22-38). The stepper motor controls the pintle movement in the air metering orifice thereby varying the amount of air being metered into the main system discharge area. The greater the amount of air, the leaner the air/fuel mixture is. A hole in the upper body casting of the carburetor allows air from beneath the air cleaner to be channeled into the main system discharge area. The metered air lowers the metering signal at the main fuel metering jets.

Electronic Idle-Speed Control

In order to maintain federally mandated emission levels, it is necessary to control the idle speed. Most feedback systems operate in open loop when the engine is idling. To reduce emissions during idle, most feedback carburetors idle faster and leaner than non-feedback carburetors.

To adjust idle speed, many feedback carburetors have an idle speed control (ISC) motor that is controlled by an electronic control module. The ISC motor is a small, reversible, electric motor. It is part of an assembly that includes the motor, gear drive, and plunger (Figure 22-39). When the motor turns in one

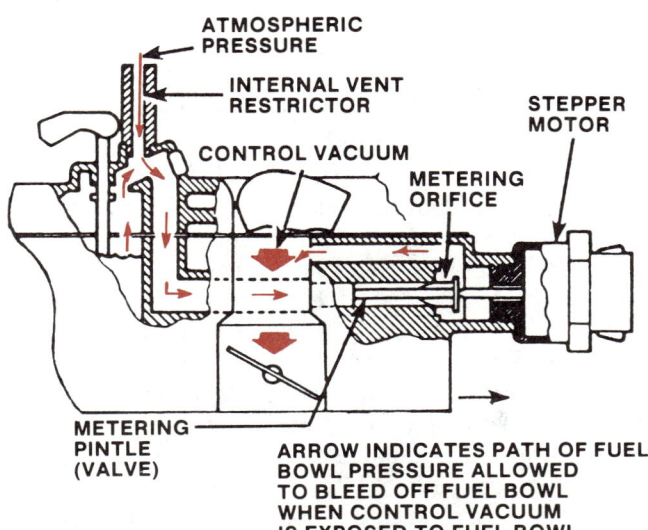

Figure 22-37 Back suction feedback system.

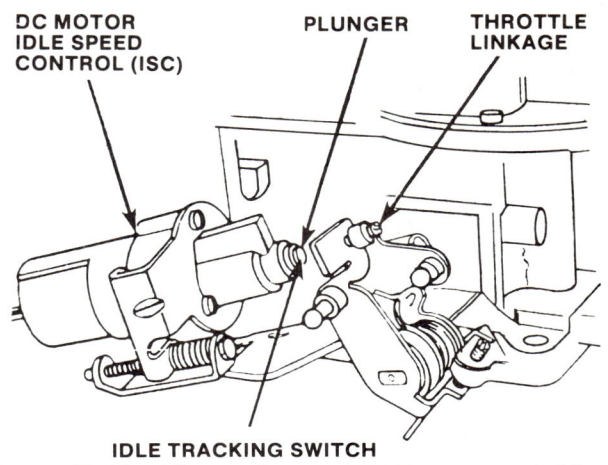

Figure 22-39 Idle speed control (ISC) motor assembly.

direction, the gear drive extends the plunger. When the motor turns in the opposite direction, the gear drive retracts the plunger. The ISC motor is mounted so that the plunger can contact the throttle lever. The ECU controls the ISC motor and can change the polarity applied to the motor's armature in order to control the direction it turns. When the idle tracking switch is closed (throttle closed), the ECU commands the ISC motor to control idle speed. The ISC provides the correct throttle opening for cold or warm engine idle.

The electronic control module receives input from various switches and sensors to determine the best idle speed. Some of the possible inputs follow.

- Engine coolant temperature sensor
- Air charge temperature (ACT) sensor
- Manifold absolute pressure (MAP) sensor
- Barometric pressure (BP) sensor
- Park/neutral or neutral gear switch
- Clutch engaged switch
- Power steering pressure switch
- A/C clutch compressor switch
- Idle tracking switch (ITS)

Based on the input signals from the system's sensors, the ECU increases the curb idle speed if the coolant is below a specific temperature, if a load (such as air conditioning, transmission, power steering) is placed on the engine, or when the vehicle is operated above a specific altitude.

During closed choke idle, the fast-idle cam holds the throttle blade open enough to lift the throttle linkage off the ISC plunger. This allows the ISC switch to open so that the ECU does not monitor idle speed. As the choke spring allows the fast-idle cam to fall away and the throttle returns to the warm idle position, the ECU notes the still low coolant temperature and commands a slightly higher idle speed.

As the engine warms up, the plunger is retracted by the electronic control module. If the A/C compressor is turned on, the ECU extends the plunger a certain distance to increase engine idle speed to compensate for the added load. When the throttle is opened and the lever leaves contact with the plunger, an idle tracking switch (ITS) in the end of the plunger signals the ECU. The electronic control module then fully extends the plunger where, upon contact with the lever (during deceleration), it acts as a dashpot, slowing the return of the throttle lever. When the engine is shut down, the plunger retracts, preventing the engine from dieseling. It then extends for the next engine startup.

In some systems, if the engine starts to overheat, the ECU commands a higher idle speed to increase coolant flow. Also, if system voltage falls below a predetermined value, the ECU commands a higher idle speed in order to increase alternator speed and output.

Normally, idle speed adjustments are not possible on carburetors with electronic idle speed control. Attempting to adjust idle speed by adjusting the ISC plunger screw results in the ECU moving the plunger to compensate for the adjustment. Idle speed does not change until the ISC motor uses up all of its plunger travel trying to compensate for the adjustment, at which point the system is completely out of calibration. When idle speed driveability problems occur, the ISC system is usually responding to or being affected by the problem, not causing it.

CUSTOMER CARE

Remember that the customer is not a technician. Listen to the customer's description and analysis of a problem, but do not accept the customer's conclusions without performing a test drive and the appropriate diagnostic test yourself. For instance, the average driver cannot detect a miss in one cylinder. While driving down the highway at 50-70 mph the car runs reasonably well, but when the driver pulls up to a stop signal and returns to an idle condition the engine idles roughly. So the driver brings the car to you complaining of a rough idle. Accepting that diagnosis without making your own and attempting to adjust the idle does more harm than good.

❏ CARBURETOR DIAGNOSIS AND ADJUSTMENT

The tuneup procedure of a late-model carbureted engine does not include as many carburetor adjustments as were once required, prior to the introduction of feedback carburetors and electronic engine controls. Idle mixture is factory set to meet precise emission control levels and is no longer an adjustable item. Idle speed is more often than not controlled by a computer and cannot be adjusted. About the only adjustment necessary on a properly operating carburetor is the fast-idle speed.

However, a malfunctioning carburetor can cause a variety of performance problems. Sometimes the problem is easily observed—such as a choke plate stuck open or an accelerating pump that is not pumping. Other problems require further testing.

A troubleshooting chart for carburetors is included in the Tech Manual. Use of the chart assumes that the engine is in good mechanical condition and properly tuned. Keep in mind that many ignition and carburetor problems have similar symptoms. An analysis of the engine's performance, using an engine analyzer with oscilloscope and exhaust analysis functions, help pinpoint the actual fault.

Some general test and adjustment procedures are given in the remainder of this chapter. However, for specific instructions and specifications, always refer to the manufacturer's service manual.

Carburetor Adjustments

Often a carburetor problem cannot be corrected without removing the carburetor from the engine and rebuilding it. Carburetor rebuilding goes beyond the scope of engine tune up. However, there are other tests and adjustments that can be made without removing the carburetor. Some of those procedures are given here.

Idle Speed Adjustment

As mentioned earlier, most vehicles with computer-controlled fuel systems have no provision for adjusting the idle speed. This is a function of the electronic control module. An idle speed that is not to specifications is a sign that a malfunction, such as an air leak, is occurring somewhere in one of the engine systems. Idle speed is checked using a tachometer.

If idle speed adjustment is possible on the carburetor, be sure to follow the manufacturer's instructions given on the emissions decal. Typical instructions might include the following.

1. Warm the engine to normal operating temperatures.
2. Make sure the choke plate is open and the throttle linkage is off fast-idle.
3. Set the parking brake and block the wheels.
4. Turn off all accessories (such as the air conditioner) and close the doors.
5. Shift the transmission into park, neutral, or drive.
6. Vehicles with feedback carburetion might also require that certain connectors be disconnected to keep the carburetor in open loop.

Then, while watching the tachometer, turn the idle-speed adjusting screw to adjust the idle rpm (Figure 22-40).

Fast-Idle Adjustment

Instructions for setting fast-idle speed are also contained on the emissions decal or in the manufacturer's

Figure 22-40   Adjusting the idle speed.

Figure 22-41   Adjusting a fast-idle screw.

service manual. Most carburetors have a fast-idle screw (Figure 22-41) that can be adjusted to correct the fast-idle speed. After satisfying any pretest conditions (such as A/C off or transmission in gear), place the specified step of the fast-idle cam on the adjusting screw. Turn the screw clockwise to increase rpm and counterclockwise to decrease rpm.

> **USING SERVICE MANUALS**
>
> Beside providing disassembly instructions, checks, tests, adjustments, and troubleshooting charts, carburetor service manuals offer tuning tips and methods for controlling fuel percolation.

Idle Mixture Adjustment

As stated earlier, idle mixture adjustments have been eliminated on the newer carburetors. On older carburetors that allow for idle mixture adjustment, a simple procedure is as follows.

1. Adjust the idle speed to the specified rpm.
2. Turn the mixture screws to obtain the smoothest idle.
3. Readjust the idle speed to specifications.
4. Repeat steps 2 and 3 until the engine idles smoothly at the correct engine rpm.
5. Turn the idle mixture adjustment screw in (in the lean direction) as far as possible without a loss of smoothness. Some procedures require leaning the mixture until there is a definite drop in rpm and loss of smoothness and then backing out the idle mixture screws one quarter.

Idle Adjustment Using Propane Enrichment Method

By the mid-1970s, the combination of catalytic converters and the very lean mixtures made it difficult to properly perform curb idle speed and mixture adjustments. However, these adjustments must be properly made to insure that emission control devices limit CO, HC, and NO_x to the specified levels. The solution was to use propane gas to assist in achieving correct idle settings.

When a controlled amount of propane is injected into the carburetor at idle, there is a direct correlation between the air/fuel ratio and engine rpm gain. If the rpm gain is less than the specifications found on the emissions control decal, the air/fuel ratio is too rich. If the rpm gain is more than specified, the air/fuel ratio is too lean.

Setting idle mixture using the artificial enrichment method requires a commercially available bottle of propane, a metering valve, a length of hose, and an adapter to connect the hose to the carburetor or air cleaner.

> **SHOP TALK**
>
> During the enrichment test, the propane tank must be upright to allow an even flow of gas. A practical and common way to do this is to hang the tank from the hood (Figure 22-42).

Although the propane injection method varies slightly from one manufacturer to another (check the service manual), the following procedure can be considered basic.

PROCEDURES
Adjusting the Idle—the Propane Injection Method

1. Apply the parking brake and block the wheels. Disconnect the automatic brake release and plug the vacuum connection.
2. Connect a tachometer to the engine.
3. Disconnect the fuel evaporative purge return hose at the engine and plug the connection.
4. Disconnect the fuel evaporative purge hose at the air cleaner and plug the nipple.
5. Disconnect the flexible fresh air tube from the air cleaner duct or adapter. Using a propane enrichment tool, insert the tool's hose approximately 3/4 inch of the way into the duct or fresh air tube. If necessary, secure the hose with tape and hold the bottle upright for an even flow of propane.
6. For vehicles equipped with an air injector system, revise the dump valve vacuum hoses.
    - For dump valves with two vacuum fittings, disconnect and plug the hoses.
    - For dump valves with one fitting, remove the hose at the dump valve and plug it. Connect a slave hose from the dump valve vacuum fitting to an intake manifold vacuum fitting.
7. Verify that the idle mixture limiter is set to the maximum rich position (counterclockwise against the stop). Correct if required.
8. Check the engine curb idle rpm (for A/C-off rpm). If necessary, reset to specification.
9. With the transmission in neutral, run the engine at approximately 2500 rpm for 15 seconds before each mixture check.
10. With the engine idling at normal operating temperature, place the transmission selector in the position specified for the mixture check. Gradually open the propane tool valve and watch for engine speed gain, if any, on the tachometer. When the engine speed reaches a maximum and then begins to drop off, note the amount of speed gain.
11. Compare the measured speed gain to the specified speed gain on the engine decal or specification sheet. If the idle rpm gain is not to specifications, adjust the mixture according to the reset rpm specification.
    - If the measured speed gain is higher than the speed gain specification, turn the mixture screw/limiter counterclockwise (rich) in equal amounts. Simultaneously repeat steps 8 through 10 until the measured speed rise meets the reset rpm specification.
    - If the measured speed gain is lower than the speed gain specification, turn the mixture screw/limiter clockwise (lean) in equal amounts. Simultaneously repeat steps 8 through 10 until the measured speed rise meets the reset rpm specification.

Choke Adjustments

A malfunctioning choke can cause a variety of performance problems, from no-start to missing and power loss at cruising speeds. These problems can be caused by choke stuck closed, choke stuck open, inoperative choke pull-off, or malfunctioning bimetal choke coil.

A visual inspection might identify the trouble spot quickly. Remove the air cleaner, making sure to label each vacuum hose as it is disconnected. If the engine is cold, the choke should be closed. Watch the choke plate as another technician cranks the engine. When the engine starts, the choke pull-off should open the

Figure 22-42 Propane tank hanging vertically during enrichment test.

choke slightly (about one quarter of an inch). As the engine warms, make sure that the bimetal coil slowly opens the choke to its fully-open position. The absence of one or more of these choke movements indicates the cause of a driveability problem.

Exact choke servicing and adjustment procedures vary with choke type and carburetor model. In fact, on today's electronically controlled vehicles, the electronic choke is sealed to prevent tampering and misadjusting. Operation of the heating element is checked with a digital volt-ohmmeter. Refer to the manufacturer's service manual for procedures and specifications.

Before making any choke adjustments, move its linkage by hand to be certain there is no binding or sticking in the linkage, shaft, or choke plate. Use an approved carburetor cleaner to remove any gum deposits that interfere with its operation.

Adjusting the Choke Index

If the choke housing permits adjustment of the choke setting, the choke can be adjusted to enrich or lean the air/fuel mixture. With an integral choke, manufacturers recommend specific alignment of the choke index marks. A mark on the plastic choke cover must be lined up with a mark on the metal choke housing or body. This initial choke setting usually provides adequate choke operation.

Check the thermostat housing index setting (Figure 22-43) against the specification on the engine decal or the vehicle's service manual.

For example, if the choke setting is specified as index, the index mark on the cap should be aligned with the center (index) notch on the housing. A specification of 1R, 2R, or 3R means that the cap index mark should be aligned with the housing marks 1, 2, or 3 notches to the right of the center notch. Specifications reading 1L, 2L, or 3L require positioning the index mark to the left of the center notch.

To adjust the choke setting, loosen the cap screws and the hot air or coolant tubes (if applicable). Turn the cap to realign the index mark with the specified notch on the housing. Then, retighten the tubes and screws.

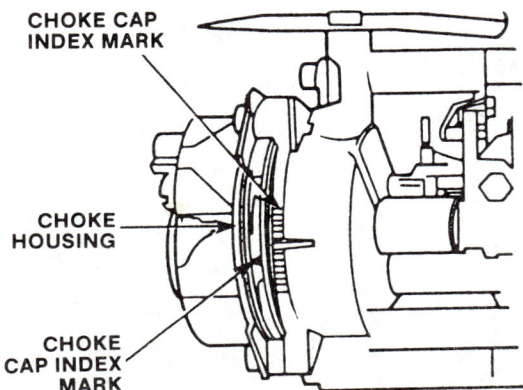

Figure 22-43 Choke index adjustment.

PROCEDURES

Divorced Choke Adjustment

1. Disconnect the choke rod from the choke plate and close the plate.
2. Move the rod up or down as directed in the service manual. Check whether or not the rod is above or below the hole in the check plate. The bottom of the rod should align with the top edge of the hole. With choke plates that use a sliding fit, the rod is usually set at the middle of the slot. However, always check the manufacturer's instructions.
3. Bend the choke rod to lengthen or shorten it as required.

CAUTION: Improper bending can cause the choke rod to bind.

4. Test for free movement between open and closed choke positions. There must not be any binding or interference.

CAUTION: Never attempt an adjustment on the thermostatic coil spring.

Choke Pulldown Adjustments

If the choke plate is not opening when the engine starts, check for a vacuum leak in the choke qualifying mechanism. If a diaphragm vacuum break is used, look for a cracked vacuum hose or loose hose connections. To check the diaphragm, remove the vacuum hose, and install a vacuum pump (Figure 22-44). Apply vacuum to the pump diaphragm. If the diaphragm does not hold vacuum or if the vacuum leaks down faster than the manufacturer specifies it should, the vacuum break should be replaced.

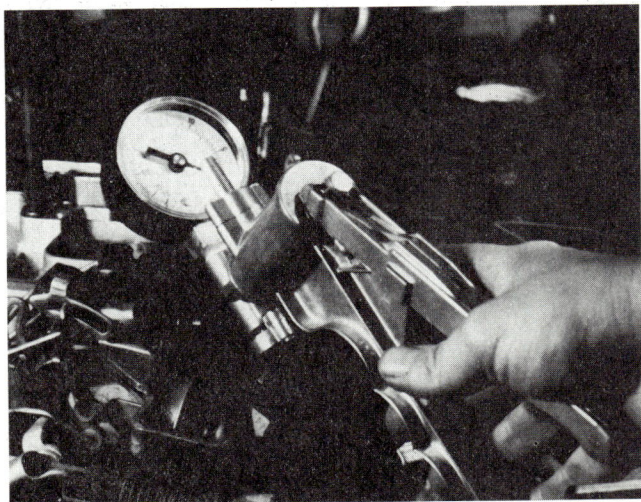

Figure 22-44 Checking vacuum break diaphragm with a vacuum pump.

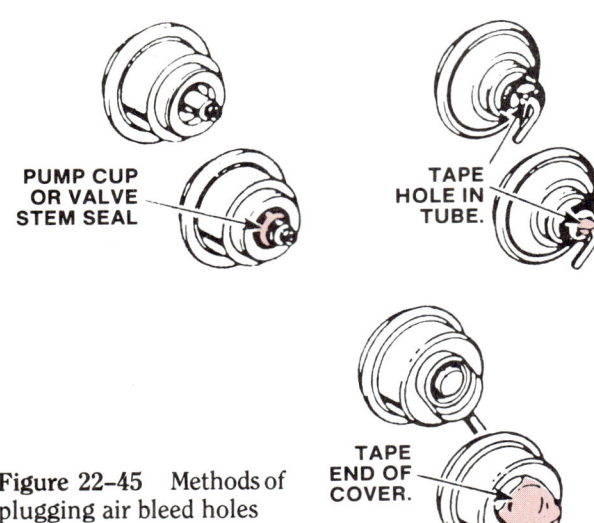

Figure 22-45 Methods of plugging air bleed holes prior to testing a vacuum break.

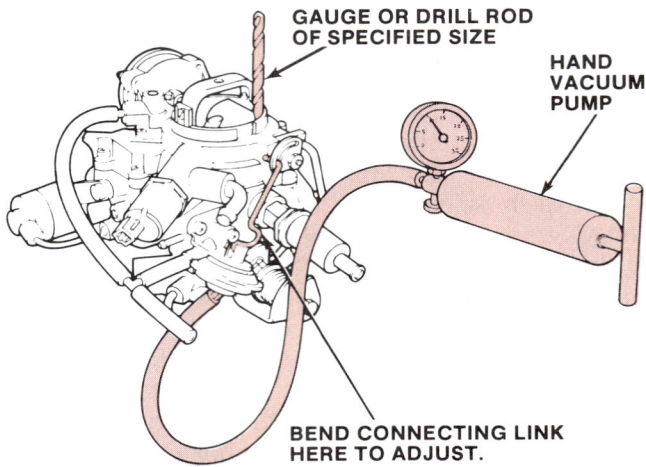

Figure 22-46 Choke pulldown adjustment.

SHOP TALK

Before many types of vacuum breaks can be tested with a vacuum pump, a bleed hole must be plugged. To do so, place your finger or a piece of tape over the bleed hole. Figure 22-45 shows several vacuum break styles with the recommended procedure for blocking the bleed hole prior to testing.

If the carburetor has a secondary vacuum break, test the thermal vacuum valve or choke vacuum thermal switch. Consult the manufacturer's service manual for temperature specifications. Connect a vacuum pump to the lower port and a vacuum gauge to the upper port. Apply the specified vacuum and alternately warm and cool the valve or switch. The valve should permit vacuum passage when the valve is warm, and block vacuum when the valve is cold.

If a vacuum piston is used to open the choke, remove the choke housing cap and inspect the piston and cylinder for carbon deposits. If the piston is sticking and not moving freely, remove the choke housing and clean the pull-off piston and vacuum passageways. Also, check the choke heat tube for carbon deposits. An exhaust leak in the area of the choke stove causes the carbon deposits. Locate and correct the problem.

If the engine runs rough initially after start-up, the choke might not be opening the specified amount. To check the qualifying dimension, apply the specified vacuum to the diaphragm, using a vacuum pump. Measure the clearance between the upper edge of the choke plate and the air horn wall, using a drill bit with a diameter equal to the specified dimension (Figure 22-46). To adjust the dimension, bend the choke linkage with a pair of pliers.

Choke Unloader Adjustment

The unloader can be adjusted following this procedure.

1. With the throttle plates wide open, close the choke plate as far as possible without forcing it.
2. Use a drill bit with a diameter equal to the specified unload dimension as a gauge. Place it between the upper edge of the choke valve and the air horn.
3. Bend the unloader tang on the throttle lever to obtain the dimension as listed in the specifications.

Checking the Accelerator Pump

If the accelerator pump is not operating properly, the engine hesitates when the accelerator pedal is depressed.

To check for accelerator pump operation, remove the air cleaner top. Make sure the actuating linkage is not binding. Using a flashlight, look down into the air horn while quickly moving the throttle linkage forward (Figure 22-47). Each time you do so, a stream or squirt of fuel from the discharge tube should be visible. If not,

Figure 22-47 Checking accelerator pump operation.

remove the air horn and service the accelerator pump following the specific procedures outlined in the manufacturer's service manual.

Float Adjustments

An improperly operating float system can result in a variety of performance problems: flooding, rich fuel mixture, lean fuel mixture, fuel starvation (no fuel), stalling, low-speed engine miss, and high-speed engine miss. Thus, a faulty float system can affect engine operations at all speeds.

On some carburetors, the fuel level in the fuel bowl can be checked without removing the air horn assembly from the carburetor. A gauge (Figure 22-48) is placed into the fuel bowl through a vent hole. The level of the fuel in the bowl is an indication of the float condition. Most carburetors, however, require that the air horn assembly be removed from the carburetor to inspect and adjust the float.

An error in float adjustment as small as 1/32 inch can change the air/fuel ratio sufficiently to make other carburetor adjustments difficult, if not impossible. Adjustments include the float level, float drop, float toe, and float adjustment. Since most do not require all four adjustments, check the vehicle's service manual or the rebuilding kit instruction sheet for the adjustment that must be performed.

PROCEDURES

Float Level Adjustment

1. Remove the upper body assembly (air horn assembly) and the upper body gasket. Install a new gasket before making the adjustment.
2. From cardboard, fabricate a gauge to the specified dimension following the specifications given in the service manual or rebuilding kit. Figure 22-49 shows a typical float gauge. Carburetor rebuilding kits often have these gauges included. Check the service manual for the exact dimensions.
3. With the upper body inverted, place the fuel level gauge on the cast surface of the upper body or gasket and measure the vertical distance from the surface and the bottom of the float. The service

Figure 22-48 Checking float level through a vent hole.

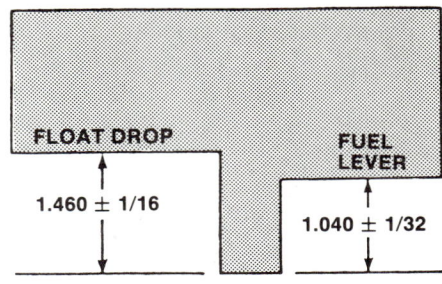

Figure 22-49 Float gauge.

manual notes the desired location of the gauge for this check.
4. To adjust, bend the float operating lever away from the fuel inlet needle to decrease the setting and toward the needle to increase the setting.
5. Check and adjust the float drop by turning the upper body over and allowing the float to drop.
6. Place the gauge into position and measure float drop.
7. Correct as needed, by bending the float's stop tab.
8. Reinstall the upper body assembly.

Some carburetors have a sight glass or plug in the fuel bowl that makes it possible to check the float level while the engine is operating. Float levels on these carburetors can be adjusted by an external screw or threaded inlet valve. Checking the fuel level on a carburetor with a sight glass not only aids in adjusting the float level but also in locating float problems.

Float Toe Adjustment

In addition to the float level and drop adjustments, some carburetors also have a float toe adjustment. To make this adjustment, the air horn is turned over (no gasket installed) and checked to make sure the float toes are flush with the air horn casting (Figure 22-50A). If the float has dimples (Figure 22-50B), measure from the dimples to the top of the gasket. In either case the float arm is bent to where it meets the float.

After making a toe adjustment, be sure to recheck the float level and drop to see if they have changed.

CASE STUDY

Case 1

A customer mentions that he noticed when checking the oil that the level has increased.

In response, the technician checks the oil by smelling it. The odor of gasoline in the oil leads the technician to check the fuel pump for a leak, but the pump is in good working order. The technician checks for an alternative cause. Realizing that a

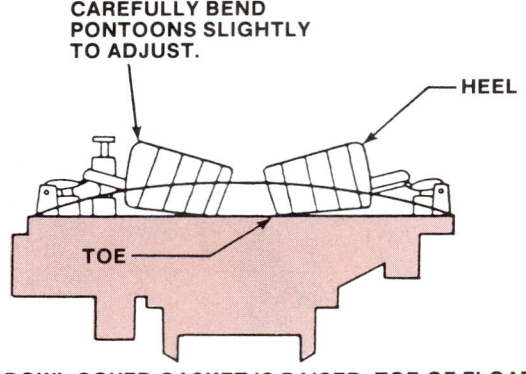

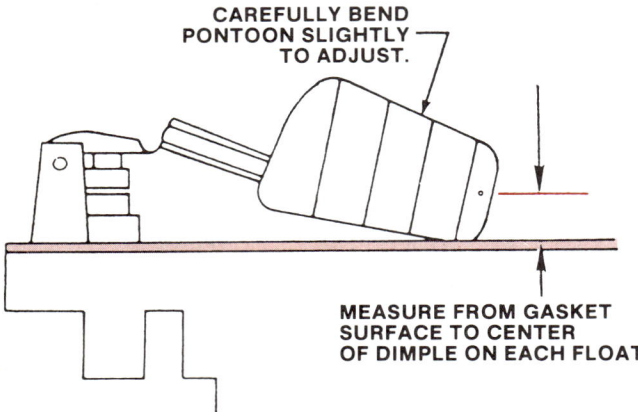

Figure 22-50 Checking float toe.

heavily choked engine will cause raw fuel to slip past the rings and into the crankcase area, the technician verifies that the choke is not adjusted properly by a visual inspection. The choke is readjusted according to the manufacturer's specifications. The oil and filter are changed. No further problems are reported.

Summary

- Carburetion means enriching a gas by combining it with a carbon-containing compound. Three general stages of carburetion are metering, atomization, and vaporization.
- A venturi is a streamlined restriction that partly closes the carburetor bore. This restriction causes an increase in vacuum.
- The flow of air and fuel through the carburetor is controlled by the throttle plate.
- There are six basic carburetor circuits: float, idle, main metering, full power, accelerator pump, and choke.
- The float system stores fuel and holds it at a precise level as a starting point for uniform fuel flow.
- The idle circuit supplies a richer air/fuel mixture to operate the engine at idle and low speeds.
- The main metering circuit comes into operation when the engine speed reaches about 1500 rpm or higher.
- The power system provides the engine with a richer air/fuel mixture at wide open throttle.
- The accelerator pump mechanically supplies extra fuel during sudden acceleration.
- The choke circuit provides a very rich mixture during cranking and start-up of a cold engine.
- Additional carburetor controls include the choke qualifier, dashpot, hot-idle compensator, dual vacuum break, choke unloader, deceleration valve, and throttle position solenoid.
- Carburetors are designed with different drafts, different numbers of barrels, different types of venturi, and different flow rates.
- The latest type of carburetor system is the electronic feedback design, which provides better combustion by control of the air/fuel mixture.
- About the only adjustment necessary on a properly operating carburetor is the fast-idle speed.
- A malfunctioning choke can cause a variety of performance problems, from no-start to missing and power loss at cruising speeds. If the accelerator pump is not operating properly, the engine hesitates when the accelerator pedal is depressed. An improperly operating float system can result in a variety of performance problems: flooding, rich fuel mixture, lean fuel mixture, fuel starvation (no fuel), stalling, low-speed engine miss, and high-speed engine miss.

Review Questions

1. Name the narrow passageway in a carburetor that speeds up the flow of intake air.
2. Name the component that speeds up the idle speed to compensate for the operation of the air conditioner.
3. A vacuum break is part of which carburetor system circuit?
4. Name the three general stages involved in carburetion.
5. What are the electrical solenoids used to control the metering rods on the more advanced feedback carburetor systems called?
6. On cold start-up which of the following is true?
   a. The throttle valve and the choke valve are closed.
   b. The throttle valve and the choke valve are open.
   c. The throttle valve is open and the choke valve is closed.
   d. The throttle valve is closed and the choke valve is open.

7. Which of the following draws air from the high-pressure area in the carburetor barrel above the venturi?
   a. idle air bleed
   b. accelerator pump system
   c. main air bleed
   d. choke
8. Which of the following statements about a vacuum break is true?
   a. The vacuum break is operated by ported vacuum.
   b. The vacuum break opens the choke after the engine has started.
   c. All integral chokes use a diaphragm vacuum break.
   d. All of the above.
9. Which of the following is used to speed up the opening of the choke?
   a. choke air modulator
   b. choke delay valve
   c. electric assist heating element
   d. all of the above
10. Which of the following components controls slow-idle speed?
    a. throttle stop solenoid
    b. idle mixture screw
    c. dashpot
    d. none of the above
11. On vehicles with catalytic converters, propane gas is injected into the carburetor to fine-tune which of the following adjustments?
    a. choke setting
    b. idle mixture
    c. fast-idle speed
    d. all of the above
12. Technician A says that an acceleration pump is necessary because the fuel pump cannot supply fuel rapidly enough when the throttle is suddenly opened. Technician B says that an acceleration pump is needed because the air/fuel mixture gets leaner when the throttle is suddenly opened. Who is correct?
    a. Technician A
    b. Technician B
    c. Both A and B
    d. Neither A nor B
13. During a discussion about carburetors with automatic chokes, Technician A says that some carburetors are designed to have hot water (radiator coolant) flowing through the choke housing. Technician B says that some carburetors are heated electrically. Who is correct?
    a. Technician A
    b. Technician B
    c. Both A and B
    d. Neither A nor B
14. Technician A says that a power valve is a vacuum-operated metering rod. Technician B says that the power valve controls the metering jets on a feedback carburetor. Who is correct?
    a. Technician A
    b. Technician B
    c. Both A and B
    d. Neither A nor B
15. Technician A says that a variable venturi carburetor is also known as a constant velocity carburetor. Technician B says that variable venturi carburetors are always computer-controlled. Who is correct?
    a. Technician A
    b. Technician B
    c. Both A and B
    d. Neither A nor B
16. Technician A says that a malfunctioning choke can cause power loss at cruising speeds. Technician B says that choke index marks are aligned integral chokes. Who is correct?
    a. Technician A
    b. Technician B
    c. Both A and B
    d. Neither A nor B
17. Technician A says that the float cannot be adjusted if there is not a threaded inlet valve assembly. Technician B says that all fuel bowls are vented by a valve to a charcoal canister. Who is correct?
    a. Technician A
    b. Technician B
    c. Both A and B
    d. Neither A nor B
18. Technician A says that a richer air/fuel mixture is needed for idle operation. Technician B says that some carburetors have a transfer slot instead of an idle port. Who is correct?
    a. Technician A
    b. Technician B
    c. Both A and B
    d. Neither A nor B
19. Technician A says that a very rich air/fuel mixture is needed during cold cranking and start-up. Technician B says that a rich mixture is needed at wide open throttle. Who is correct?
    a. Technician A
    b. Technician B
    c. Both A and B
    d. Neither A nor B
20. Which of the following describes the function of a dashpot?
    a. It opens an air passage to lean the mixture when the engine overheats.
    b. It is designed to prevent backfire during deceleration as the fuel mixture becomes richer.
    c. It is used during rapid deceleration to retard the closing of the throttle.
    d. None of the above

23 EMISSION CONTROL SYSTEMS

Objectives

■ Name and describe the three kinds of emissions being controlled in gasoline engines. ■ Name the three major types of emission control systems used on modern vehicles. ■ Describe the inspection and replacement of PCV system parts. ■ Explain the operation of the EGR valve and the function of the various EGR system controls. ■ Describe typical EGR system problems and EGR valve and system testing procedures. ■ Describe the function and operation of the two types of air injection systems. ■ Describe the secondary air system's operation and efficiency test. ■ Name the components of an evaporative emission control system. ■ Describe the testing of the canister and of the canister purge valve.

The three kinds of emissions that are being controlled in gasoline engines today are unburned hydrocarbons, carbon monoxide, and oxides of nitrogen.

Unburned hydrocarbons (HC) are particles, usually vapors, of gasoline that have not been fully burned. They are present in the exhaust and in crankcase vapors. Of course, any raw gas that evaporates out of the tank or carburetor is classed as HC.

Carbon monoxide (CO) is a poisonous chemical compound of carbon and oxygen. It forms in the engine when combustion is less than complete. CO is found in the exhaust principally, but can also be in the crankcase.

Oxides of nitrogen (NO_x; pronounced nox) are various compounds of nitrogen and oxygen, both present in the air used for combustion. They are formed in the cylinders during combustion and are part of exhaust gas.

The federal government has set standards for these pollutants. The exceptions to these standards are a few high-altitude western states and California. Because there is less oxygen at high altitudes to promote combustion, emission standards at high-altitudes are slightly less strict. California's standards allow less pollution than federal standards.

Automobile manufacturers have been working toward reduction of automotive air pollutants since the early 1950s, when emissions first were related to Los Angeles pollution. Governmental interest developed around the same time.

In late 1959, California established the first standards for automotive emissions. In 1967, the Federal Clean Air Act was amended to provide for federal standards to apply to motor vehicles.

The first source of emissions to be brought under control was the crankcase. Positive crankcase ventilation systems (PCV) to route these vapors back to the engine intake manifold were developed and incorporated into 1961 cars and light trucks sold in California. These systems were installed on all cars nationwide beginning with the 1963 models.

Control of unburned hydrocarbons and carbon monoxide in the engine exhaust was the next major development. An air injection reactor (AIR) system was built into cars and light trucks sold in California in 1966. Other systems, including the controlled combustion system (CCS), were developed and used nationwide in 1968. Further improvements in years following improved combustion to reduce hydrocarbon and carbon monoxide emissions.

Fuel vapors from the gasoline tank and the carburetor float bowl were brought under control with the introduction of evaporation control systems. These systems were first installed in 1970 model cars sold in California and in most domestic-made cars beginning with 1971 models.

Most vehicle manufacturers started to provide emission control systems that reduced oxides of nitrogen as early as 1970. The exhaust gas recirculation system used on some 1972 models was used extensively for 1973 models when federal standards for oxides of nitrogen took effect.

Present government goals call for a 98% reduction of unburned hydrocarbons, a 97% reduction of carbon monoxide, and a 90% reduction of oxides of nitrogen compared to precontrolled cars.

One of the most important developments for lowering emission levels has been the availability and use of unleaded gasolines. Beginning with 1971, cars have been designed to operate on unleaded fuels.

Removing lead from gasoline brings some immediate benefits. It eliminates the emission of lead particles from automobile's exhaust. It increases spark plug life—also important from an emission standpoint. It avoids formation of lead deposits in the combustion chambers that tend to increase hydrocarbon emissions.

The catalytic converter, a later development, provided a means for oxidizing the carbon monoxide and hydrocarbon emissions in the engine exhaust, a process that lowers the amount of these pollutants. Beginning with the 1975 model year, passenger cars and light trucks have been equipped with converters.

Three basic types of emission control systems are used in modern vehicles: precombustion, post-combustion, and evaporative control systems.

Most of the pollution control systems used today prevent emissions from being created in the engine, either during or before the combustion cycle. The common precombustion control systems are as follows.

- Positive Crankcase Ventilation (PCV). The PCV system removes pollutants that blow by the pistons into the crankcase and recirculates them into the induction system.
- Engine Modification Systems. These systems improve combustion and reduce HC-CO in the exhaust. They include a heated primary air system, air/fuel control changes, engine breathing refinements, and some spark timing controls.
- Exhaust Gas Recirculating (EGR) Systems. EGR reduces NO_x by diluting the air/fuel mixture with some exhaust gas, which does not burn.

Post-combustion control systems clean up the exhaust gases after the fuel has been burned. Secondary air or air injector systems put fresh air into the exhaust to reduce HC and CO to harmless water vapor and carbon dioxide by chemical (thermal) reaction with oxygen in the air. Catalytic converters help this process. Most catalysts now reduce NO_x as well as HC-CO.

The evaporative control system is a sealed system. It traps the fuel vapors (HC) that would normally escape from the fuel tank and carburetor into the air.

❑ PCV SYSTEMS

During the last part of the engine's combustion stroke, some unburned fuel and products of combustion—water vapor, for instance—leak past the engine's piston rings into the crankcase.

This leakage into the engine crankcase is called blowby. Blowby must be removed from the engine before it condenses in the crankcase and reacts with the oil to form sludge. Sludge, if allowed to circulate with engine oil, corrodes and accelerates wear of pistons, piston rings, valves, bearings, and other internal working parts of the engine. Blowby gases must also be removed from the crankcase to prevent premature oil leaks. Because these gases enter the crankcase by the pressure formed during combustion, they pressurize the crankcase. The gases exert pressure on the oil pan gasket and crankshaft seals. If the pressure is not relieved, oil is eventually forced out of these seals.

Because the air/fuel mixture in an engine never completely burns, blowby also carries some unburned fuel into the crankcase. If not removed, the unburned fuel dilutes the crankcase oil. When oil is diluted with gasoline, it does not lubricate the engine properly, which causes excessive wear.

Combustion gases that enter the crankcase are removed by a positive crankcase ventilation (PCV) system, which uses engine vacuum to draw fresh air through the crankcase. This fresh air, which dissipates the harmful gases, enters through the air filter or through a separate PCV breather filter located on the inside of the air filter housing. System operation is shown in Figure 23-1.

Because the vacuum supply for the PCV system is from the engine's intake manifold, the airflow through this system must be controlled in such a way that it varies in proportion to the regular air/fuel ratio being drawn into the intake manifold. Otherwise, the additional air that is drawn into the system would cause the air/fuel mixture to become too lean for efficient engine operation. Therefore, a PCV valve is placed in the flow just before the intake manifold to regulate the flow according to vacuum.

The positive crankcase ventilation system has two major functions. It prevents the emission of blowby gases from the engine crankcase to the atmosphere. These gases were once vented through a road draft tube. Now they are recirculated to the engine intake and burned during combustion. It also scavenges the crankcase of vapors that could dilute the oil and cause it to deteriorate or that could build undesirable pressure in the crankcase. Fresh air from the air cleaner mixes with these vapors and makes them flow to the intake.

The PCV system benefits the vehicle's driveability by eliminating harmful crankcase gases, reducing air pollution, and promoting fuel economy.

Note that an inoperative PCV system could shorten the life of the engine by allowing harmful blowby gases to remain in the engine, causing corrosion and accelerating wear.

PCV System Diagnosis and Service Procedures

No adjustments can be made to the PCV system. Service of the system involves a careful inspection,

584 Section 4 Engine Performance

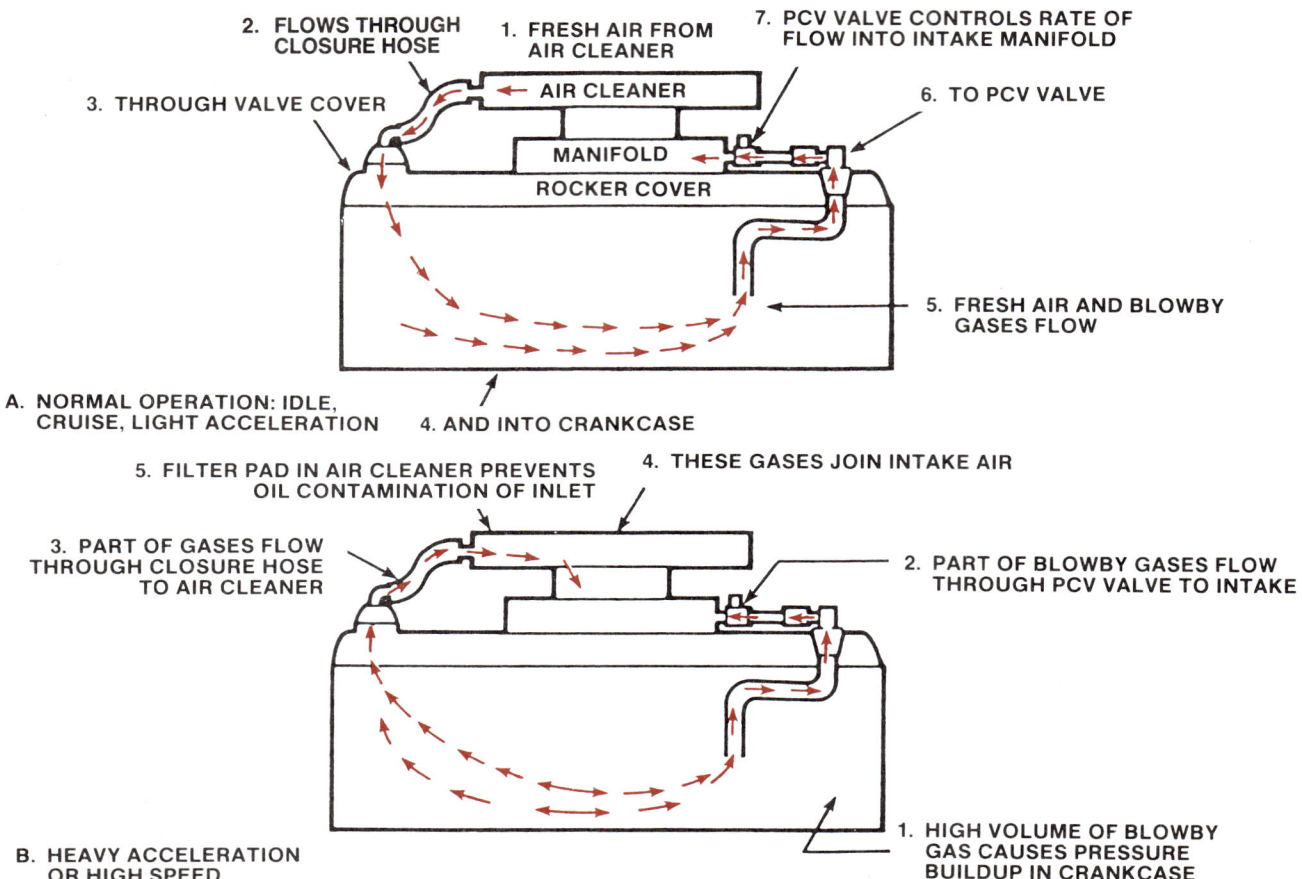

Figure 23-1 (A) Fresh airflow during normal operation: idle, cruise, and light acceleration; (B) during heavy acceleration or high speed.

operation, and replacement of faulty parts. When replacing a PCV valve, match the part number on the valve with the vehicle maker's specifications for the proper valve. If the valve cannot be identified, refer to the part number listed in the manufacturer's service manual.

The first step in PCV servicing is a visual inspection. As shown in Figure 23-2, the PCV valve can be located in several places. The most common location is in a rubber grommet in the valve or rocker arm cover (Figure 23-2A). It can be installed in the middle of the hose connections (Figure 23-2B), as well as installed directly in the intake manifold (Figure 23-2C).

Once the PCV valve is located, inspect the system by using the following procedure.

PROCEDURES

PCV System Inspection

1. Make sure all the PCV system hoses are properly connected and that they have no breaks or cracks.
2. Remove the air cleaner and inspect the carburetor or fuel injector air filter. Crankcase blowby can clog these with oil. Clean or replace such filters.
3. Check the crankcase inlet air filter, which is usually located in the air cleaner (Figure 23-3). As the filter does its job, it gets dirty. If it is oil soaked, it is a good indication that the PCV system is not working the way that it should. When the filter becomes so dirty that it restricts the flow of clean air to the crankcase, it can cause the same problems as a clogged PCV valve. So be sure to check this particular filter when checking the PCV system and replace it as necessary.
4. Inspect for dirt deposits that could clog the passages in the manifold or carburetor base. These deposits can prevent the system from functioning properly, even though the PCV valve, valve filter, and hoses might not be clogged.

Functional Checks of PCV Valve

A rough idling engine can signal a number of PCV valve problems, such as a clogged valve or a plugged hose. But before beginning the functional checks, double check the PCV valve part number to make certain the correct valve is installed. If the correct valve is being used, perform these functional checks.

1. Disconnect the PCV valve from the valve cover, intake manifold, or hose.

Emission Control Systems   585

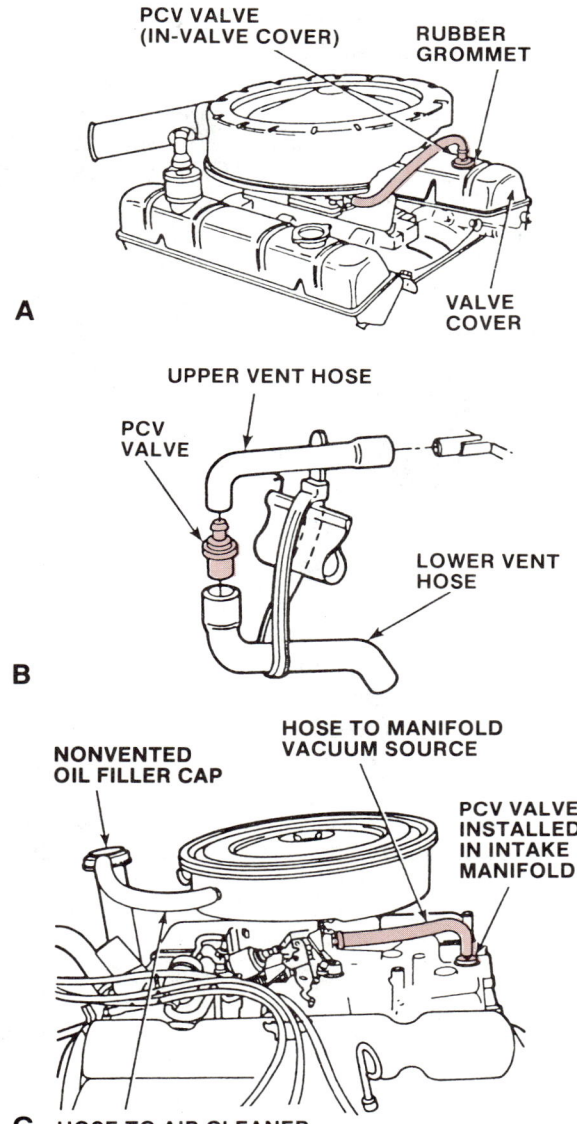

Figure 23-2 Various locations of the PCV valve.

2. Start the engine and let it run at idle. If the PCV valve is not clogged, a hissing is heard as air passes through the valve.
3. Place a finger over the end of the valve to check for vacuum. If there is little or no vacuum at the valve, check for a plugged or restricted hose. Replace any plugged or deteriorated hoses.
4. Turn off the engine and remove the PCV valve. Shake the valve and listen for the rattle of the check needle inside the valve. If the valve does not rattle, replace it.

Proper operation of the PCV system depends on a sealed engine. Remember that the crankcase is sealed by the dipstick, valve cover, gaskets, and sealed filler cap. If oil sludging or dilution is noted and the PCV system is functioning properly, check the engine for oil leaks and correct them to ensure that the PCV system functions as intended.

☐ EXHAUST GAS RECIRCULATING (EGR) SYSTEMS

Exhaust gas recirculating (EGR) systems reduce the amount of oxides of nitrogen emitted. The EGR system dilutes the air/fuel mixture with controlled amounts of exhaust gas. Since exhaust gas does not burn, this reduces the peak combustion temperatures. At lower combustion temperatures, very little of the nitrogen in the air combines with oxygen to form NO_x. Most of the nitrogen is simply carried out with the exhaust gases. For driveability/performance, it is desirable to have the EGR valve opening (and the amount of gas flow) proportional to the throttle opening. Driveability is also improved on most applications by shutting off the EGR when the engine is started up cold, at idle, and at full throttle. Since the NO_x control requirements vary

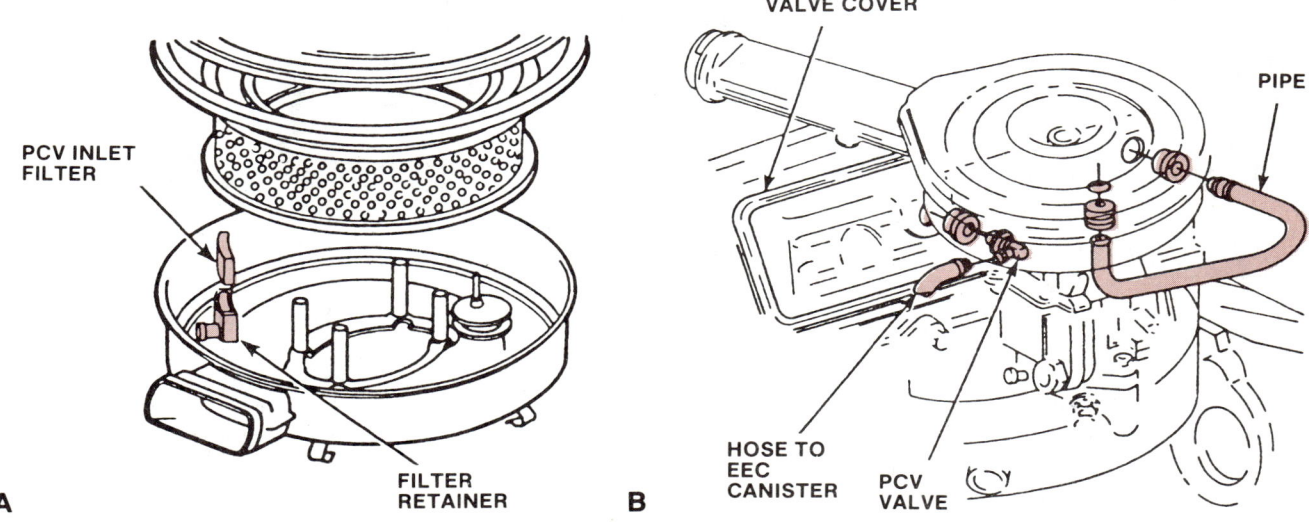

Figure 23-3 When inspecting the PCV system, check the PCV inlet filter in the air cleaner. *Courtesy of Ford Motor Co.*

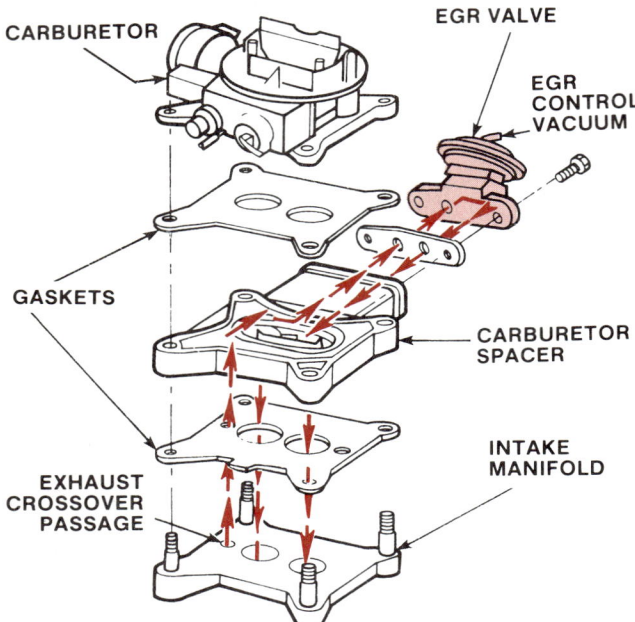

Figure 23-4 Typical vacuum-operated EGR valve.

on different engines, there are several different systems with various controls to provide these functions.

Most of these systems use a vacuum-operated EGR valve to regulate the exhaust gas flow into the intake manifold. Exhaust crossover passages under the intake manifold channel the exhaust gas to the valve. (Some in-line engines route the exhaust gas to the valve through an external tube.) Typical mounting of the EGR valve is either on a plate under the carburetor or directly on the manifold.

Figure 23-4 illustrates the basic valve design. The EGR valve is a vacuum-operated, flow control valve. On some systems, it is attached to a carburetor spacer. The carburetor spacer is sandwiched between the carburetor and intake manifold. Gaskets are used above and below the spacer to seal the EGR system and the carburetor-to-manifold air/fuel flow. A small exhaust crossover passage in the intake manifold admits exhaust gases to the spacer. These gases flow through the spacer to the inlet port of the EGR valve. Opening the EGR valve by control vacuum at the diaphragm allows exhaust gases to flow through the valve and back to another port of the spacer. Here, the exhaust gas mixes with the air/fuel mixture, leaving the carburetor and then entering the intake manifold. The effect is to dilute or lean-out the mixture so that it still burns completely but with a reduction in combustion chamber temperatures.

EGR valve control vacuum is from either of two sources (Figure 23-5). In the port vacuum system, a vacuum line connects the EGR valve to a slot port in the carburetor throttle body above the throttle plate. When the throttle plate is closed, no vacuum is transmitted. The port is exposed to increasing manifold vacuum as the throttle plate opens. The exhaust gas flow rate depends on manifold vacuum, throttle position, and exhaust gas back pressure. In a venturi vacuum system, the vacuum that controls the EGR valve is drawn from a port in the carburetor venturi. A vacuum amplifier is needed to boost this weak vacuum to operate the EGR valve. While the exhaust gas flow rate depends mainly on engine intake flow, it is also affected by intake vacuum and exhaust.

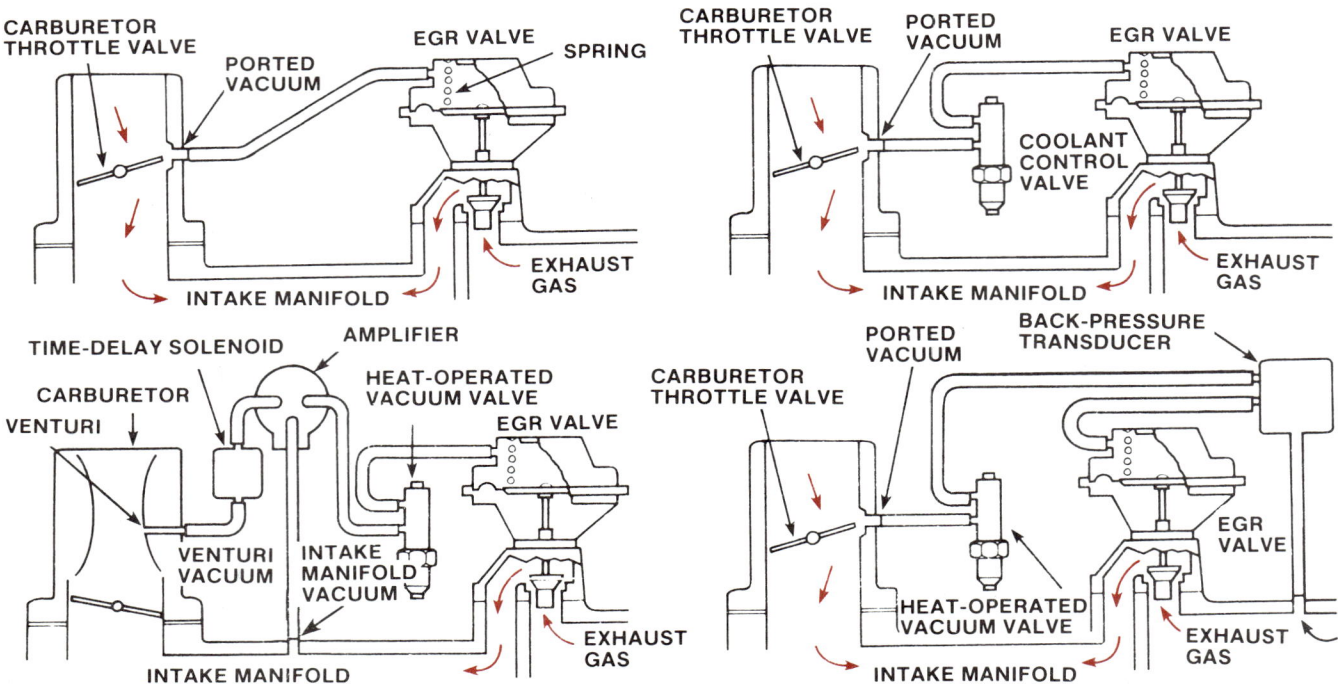

Figure 23-5 Two basic types of EGR systems are the port vacuum system and venturi vacuum system.

Emission Control Systems 587

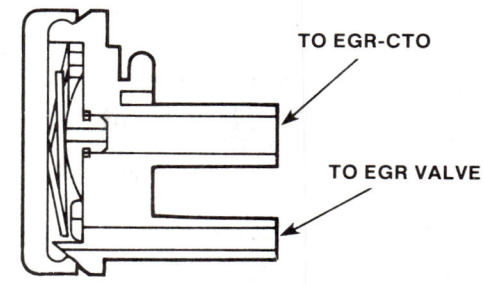

Figure 23-6 Thermal vacuum switch.

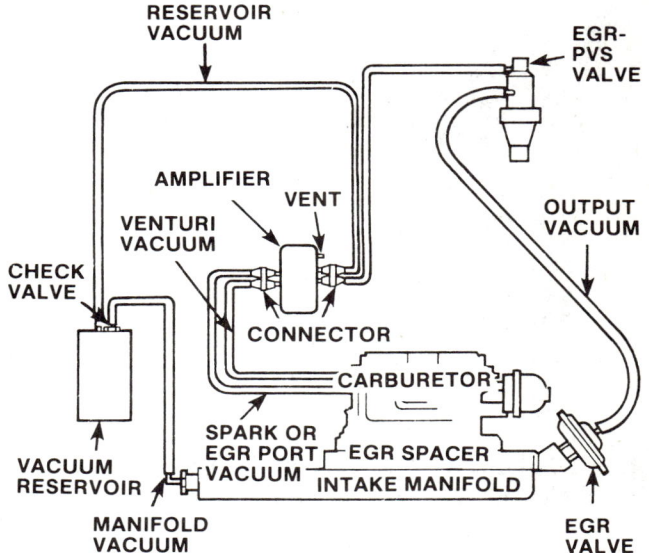

Figure 23-8 Venturi vacuum amplifier circuit.

The EGR system works when the engine reaches operating temperature or when the engine is operating under conditions other than idle or wide-open throttle. EGR systems include various functions that control the operation of the EGR valve. Some applications use cold engine EGR lockout and wide-open throttle EGR lockout. Basically, cold EGR lockout is necessary to keep the EGR valve closed during cold engine operation. Wide-open throttle EGR lockout might be required to keep the EGR valve closed when the engine is operating under maximum load. The following are various controls that relate directly to the EGR system.

THERMAL VACUUM SWITCH (TVS) The TVS senses the air temperature in the carburetor air cleaner to control vacuum to the EGR valve (Figure 23-6). When the engine reaches operating temperature, the TVS opens to supply vacuum to the EGR valve. This opens the EGR valve for exhaust gas recirculation.

PORTED VACUUM SWITCH (PVS) The PVS senses the coolant temperature to control vacuum to the EGR valve (Figure 23-7). The PVS operates in the same manner as the TVS, except it senses the coolant temperature instead of the air temperature. That is, the PVS function is to cut off vacuum to the EGR valve when the engine is cold and connect the vacuum to the EGR valve when the engine is warm.

VENTURI VACUUM AMPLIFIER (VVA) Some EGR systems use the VVA so that the carburetor venturi vacuum can control the EGR valve operation (Figure 23-8). Venturi vacuum is more desirable because it is in proportion to the airflow through the carburetor. Since the venturi vacuum is a relatively weak vacuum signal, the VVA converts it to a strong enough signal to operate the EGR valve. The VVA system uses manifold vacuum for strength and venturi vacuum for the control signal.

EGR DELAY TIMER CONTROL Some vehicles have an EGR delay system, which consists of an electrical timer that connects to an engine-mounted solenoid. Together, the purpose of the delay timer and solenoid is to prevent EGR operation for a predetermined amount of time after warm engine start-up. On cold engine start-ups, the TVS and PVS valves override the delay timer.

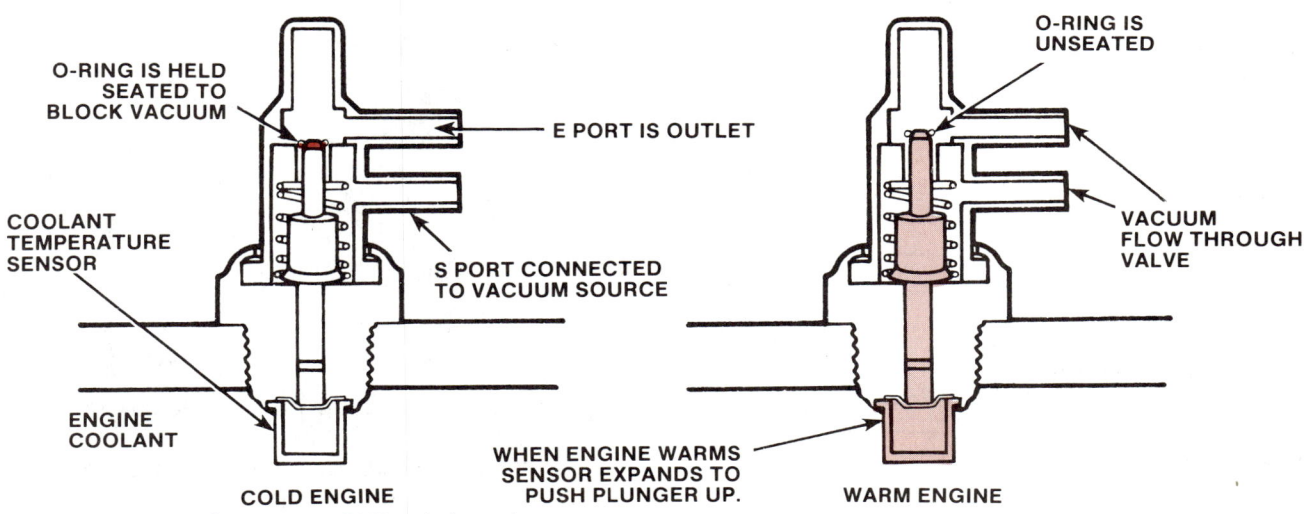

Figure 23-7 How the two-port PVS switch works.

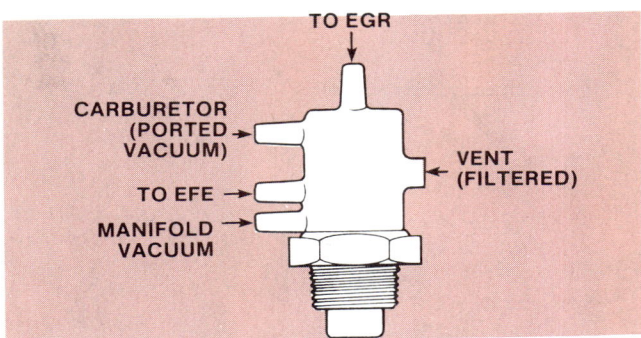

Figure 23-9 Early fuel evaporation/thermal vacuum switch.

EARLY FUEL EVAPORATION/THERMAL VACUUM SWITCH (EGR—EFE/TVS) In most common applications the EFE uses a valve that increases the exhaust gas flow under the intake manifold during cold engine operation through a crossover passage to heat up the incoming air/fuel charge (Figure 23-9). The EFE is vacuum-operated and controlled by a TVS that applies vacuum to the EFE valve when the coolant temperature is low. Once the engine reaches operating temperature, the TVS blocks off vacuum to the EFE and directs it to the EGR valve for EGR operation.

WIDE-OPEN THROTTLE VALVE (WOT) Some applications use the WOT valve where it is desirable to cut off EGR flow at wide-open throttle (Figure 23-10).

BACK PRESSURE TRANSDUCER This device can be used to modulate, or change, the amount the EGR valve opens. It controls the amount of air bleed in the EGR vacuum line according to the level of exhaust gas pressure, which is dependent on engine rpm. The EGR valve can be closed or partially opened at different engine speeds. Air bleed is stopped completely when the exhaust back pressure is high. Thus, maximum EGR occurs during normal acceleration, when back pressure is high. When back pressure decreases, the vacuum line bleed is reopened. This decreases the vacuum at the EGR valve, which then reduces the amount of exhaust gas recirculated. In the past, the back pressure transducer was a separate unit. Now it is incorporated into the design of the EGR valve itself.

These various EGR system controls represent some of the common controls currently used by automobile manufacturers. Control devices used in the various systems might have different labels but actually complete the same function within the EGR system. For further information on EGR system controls, it is advisable to consult the service manual that pertains to each vehicle being tested or serviced.

EGR System Diagnosis and Service

Manufacturers calibrate the amount of EGR gas flow for each engine. If there is too much or too little, it can cause performance problems by changing the engine breathing characteristics. Also, with too little EGR flow, the engine can overheat and detonate. Typical problems that show up in ported EGR systems follow.

- Rough idle. Possible causes are an EGR valve stuck open, PVS fails to close, dirt on the valve seat, or loose mounting bolts. Loose mounting causes a vacuum leak and a hissing noise.
- Surge, stall, or does not start. Probable cause is the valve stuck open.
- Detonation (spark knock). Any condition that prevents proper EGR gas flow can cause detonation. This includes a valve stuck closed, leaking valve diaphragm, restrictions in flow passages, EGR disconnected, or a problem in the vacuum source.
- Lead poisoning. The use of leaded gas can cause deposits on the seat and valve. This restricts flow, causing detonation and possibly overheating.
- Poor fuel economy. This is an EGR condition only if it relates to detonation or other symptoms of restricted or zero EGR flow.

☐ EGR VALVES AND SYSTEMS TESTING

Test the EGR valve by using a vacuum gauge or hand vacuum pump. Follow these procedures for using either piece of test equipment.

PROCEDURES
Using a Vacuum Gauge to Check Manifold Vacuum

1. Disconnect a vacuum line connected to an intake manifold port.
2. Put a vacuum gauge between the disconnected vacuum line and the intake manifold port.
3. Connect a tachometer.

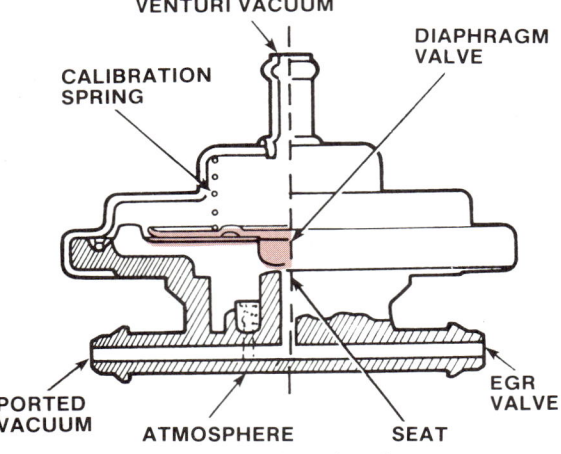

Figure 23-10 Wide-open throttle valve.

Figure 23-11 Reading from the manifold vacuum gauge should be above 16 inches mercury.

4. Start the engine and gradually increase speed to 2000 rpm with the transmission in neutral.
5. The reading from the manifold vacuum gauge (Figure 23-11) should be above 16 inches of vacuum. If not, there could be a vacuum leak or exhaust restriction. Before continuing to test the EGR, correct the problem of low vacuum.

 **PROCEDURES**
Using a Hand Vacuum Pump to Check the Operation of the EGR Valve

1. Check all vacuum lines for correct routing. Ensure that they are attached securely. Replace cracked, crimped, or broken lines.
2. With the engine at normal operating temperature, be certain there is no vacuum to the EGR valve at idle.
3. Install a tachometer.
4. On EFI engines (multi-point injection), disconnect the throttle air by-pass valve solenoid.
5. Remove the vacuum supply hose from the EGR valve port and plug the hose.
6. Observe the engine's idle speed. If necessary, adjust idle speed to the emission decal specification.
7. Slowly apply 5 to 10 inches of vacuum to the EGR valve vacuum port, using a hand vacuum pump. The idle speed should drop more than 100 rpm (the engine may stall), and then return to normal ($\pm$ 25 rpm) again when the vacuum is removed.
8. If the idle speed does not respond in this manner, replace the EGR valve.
9. If the EGR valve is operating properly, unplug and reconnect the EGR valve vacuum supply hose.
10. Reconnect the throttle air by-pass valve solenoid, if removed.

Electronic EGR Operation

On vehicles equipped with electronic engine control (EEC), the EGR valve within this system resembles

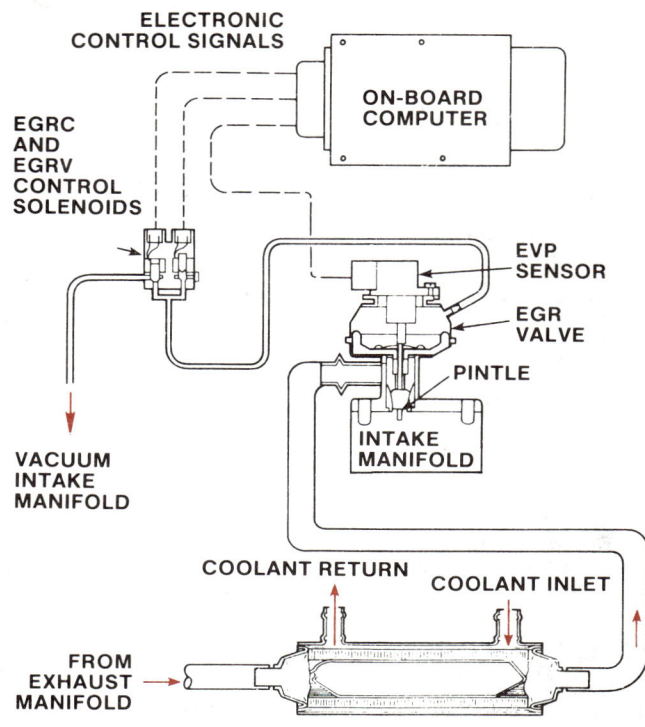

Figure 23-12 Typical EGR system used with an EEC. *Courtesy of Ford Motor Co.*

and is operated in a manner similar to the conventional EGR valves. This system uses sensors, solenoids, and an electronic control assembly to modulate and control EGR system components as shown in Figure 23-12. A pintle valve is often used in the valve to better control the flow rate of exhaust gases. A sensor mounted on the valve stem sends an electronic signal to the on-board computer, which in turn tells how far the EGR valve is opened. At this time, the EGR control solenoids (EGRV, EGRC) either maintain or alter the EGR flow, depending on engine operating conditions. Source vacuum is manifold vacuum and is applied or vented, depending on the computer commands. A cooler is frequently used to reduce exhaust gas temperatures, which enables the exhaust gas to flow better and in turn reduce the amount of detonation. Early EGR systems used an in-line cooler. Later systems use a cooler sandwiched between the EGR valve and carburetor spacer.

The EGRV/EGRC system is often controlled by two solenoids (Figure 23-13). The solenoids respond to voltage signals from the on-board computer. An EGR vent solenoid, or EGRV, normally an open vent solenoid valve, closes when it is energized (Figure 23-13A). An EGR control solenoid, or EGRC, normally a closed solenoid valve, opens when it is energized (Figure 23-13B).

Voltage signals from the on-board computer can trigger the solenoids to increase EGR flow by applying vacuum to the EGR valve, maintain EGR flow by trap-

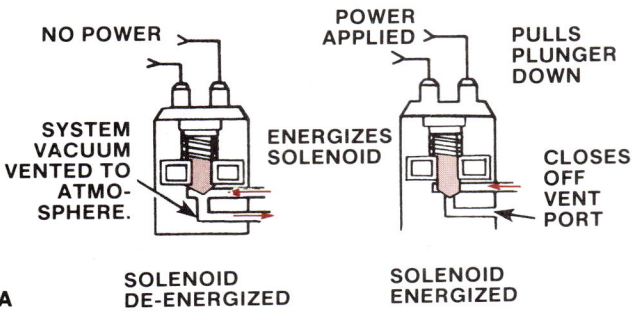

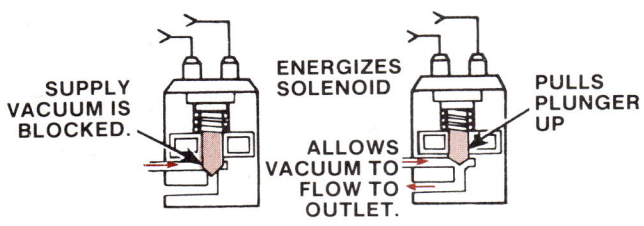

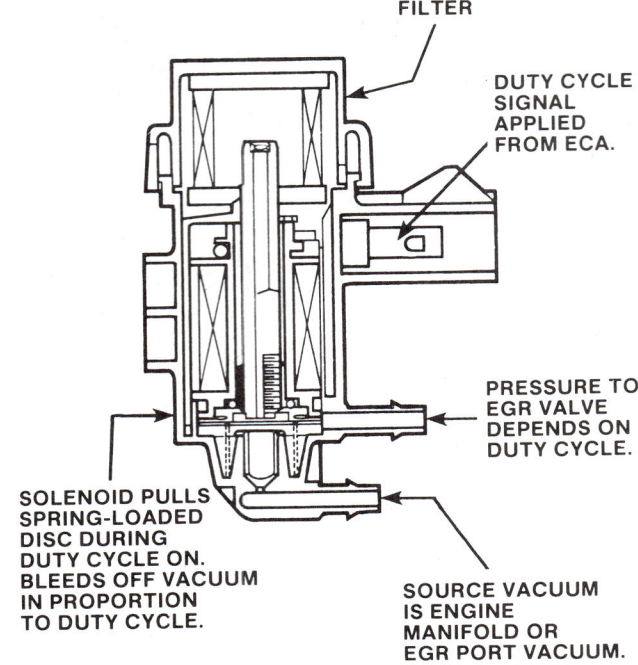

Figure 23-15 Electronic vacuum regulator (EVR) operation. *Courtesy of Ford Motor Co.*

Figure 23-13 EGRV/EGRC system is often controlled by two solenoids.

ping vacuum in the system, or decrease EGR flow by venting EGR vacuum.

In actual operation, both solenoids constantly shift between the three operating conditions mentioned as engine operating conditions change. If the on-board computer is doing its job, the solenoids click on and off. If not, there may be either a solenoid problem or an electronic control problem.

A schematic diagram of one of the more recent EGR emission control systems, the pressure feedback electronic (PFE) type, is shown in Figure 23-14. The electronic vacuum regulator (EVR) control applies, traps, or bleeds off vacuum to the EGR valve. That is, the vacuum to the EGR valve is supplied and controlled by the EVR instead of the EGRC and EGRV control solenoids. The EVR operates on a duty cycle output from the computer (Figure 23-15). The computer varies the rate of this cycle according to the signal it

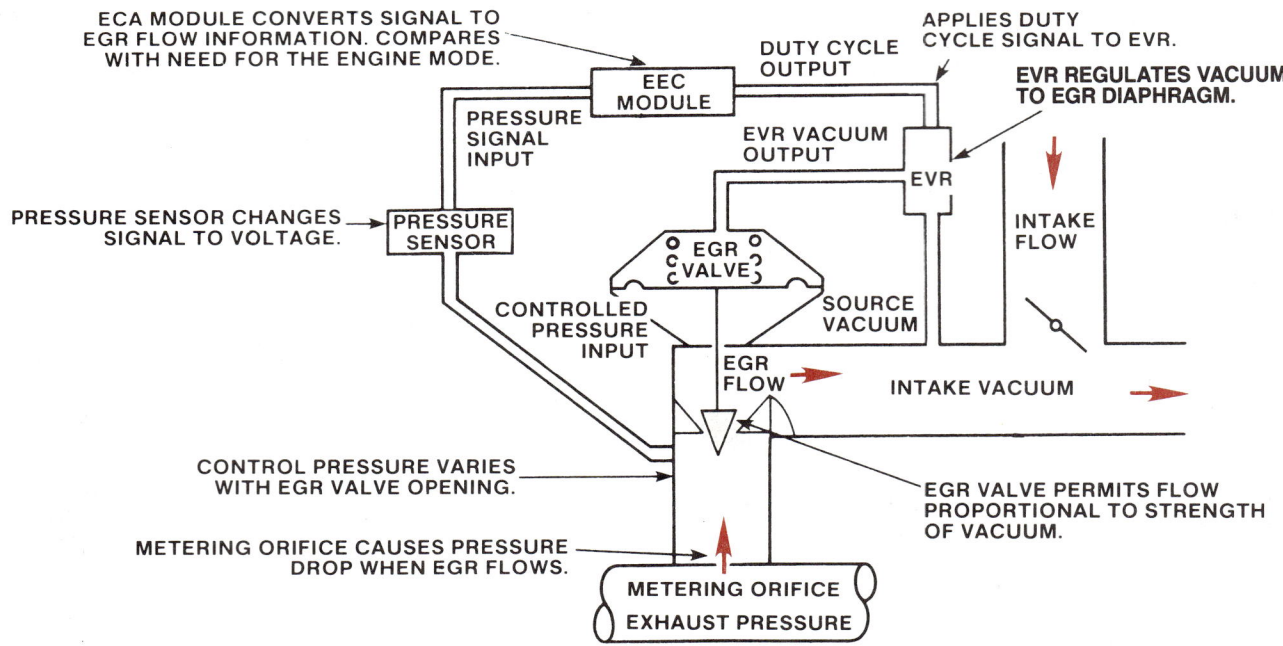

Figure 23-14 Functional schematic of a PFE-EVR system. *Courtesy of Ford Motor Co.*

receives from a sensor that monitors the control pressure between the metering orifice and the EGR valve pintle. There is also a similar system in which a sensor delivers a voltage signal proportional to the pintle opening instead of the control pressure.

The EGR system is activated only during part-throttle modes of operation and only when the engine is warm and running smoothly. For the EGR system to be enabled, the following conditions must be met.

- The engine must be warm. The engine coolant temperature (ECT) sensor must be sending a moderate- to low-voltage signal to the on-board computer.
- The throttle plate must be at a part-throttle position as sensed by the throttle plate (TP) sensor.
- Manifold absolute pressure (MAP) must be moderate as determined by the sensor and on-board computer.
- A calibrated length of time must have elapsed since start-up or cranking.

EGR SYSTEM TROUBLESHOOTING

Before attempting to troubleshoot or repair a suspected EGR system on a vehicle, the following conditions should be checked and be within specifications.

- Engine is mechanically sound.
- Injection system is operating properly.
- Mechanical-vacuum advance is properly adjusted (or the electronic advance system is operating properly).

If one or more of these conditions is faulty or operating incorrectly, perform the necessary tests and services to correct the problem before servicing the EGR system.

In all the closed loop electronic control EGR systems, the valve (by itself) functions the same as a ported EGR valve. Apart from the electronic control, the system can have all of the problems of any EGR system. Sticking valves, obstructions, and loss of vacuum produces the same symptoms as on non-EEC systems. If an electronic control component is not functioning, the condition is usually recognized by the computer. Check the service manual for instructions on how to use computer service codes. The EGRV and EGRC solenoids, or the EVR, should normally cycle on and off very frequently when EGR flow is being controlled (warm engine and cruise rpm). If they do not, it indicates a problem in the electronic control system or the solenoids. Generally, an electronic control failure results in low or zero EGR flow and might cause symptoms like overheating, detonation, and power loss.

Check the service manual for a summary of problems that can occur in an electronic EGR system, their possible causes, and suggested remedies. But before attempting any testing of the EGR system, visually inspect the condition of all vacuum hoses for kinks, bends, cracks, and flexibility. Replace defective hoses as required. Check vacuum hose routing. (See the underhood decal or the manufacturer's service manual for correct routing.) Correct any misrouted hoses.

> ### USING SERVICE MANUALS
> Service manuals have step-by-step instructions for inspecting the various emission control systems. They also provide the technician with troubleshooting flow charts that help the technician to logically pinpoint any problems in these systems. A student can learn more about these systems by studying these charts and reasoning through the repair process.

AIR TEMPERATURE EMISSION CONTROL

Hydrocarbon and carbon monoxide exhaust emissions are highest when the engine is cold. The introduction of warm combustion air improves the vaporization of the fuel in the carburetor, fuel injector body, or intake manifold. The three systems used on various gasoline engines to heat the inlet air and the air/fuel mixture are heated air inlet, manifold heat control valves, and early fuel evaporation (EFE) heaters.

Heated Air Inlet

A heated air inlet control (also called a thermostatic air cleaner) is used on gasoline engines with carburetion or central fuel injection. It is not used with turbocharging or ported fuel injection. This system controls the temperature of the air on its way to the carburetor or fuel injection body. By warming the air, it reduces HC and CO emissions by improved fuel vaporization and faster warm-up.

The principle components (Figure 23-16) and functions of a conventional air cleaner system follow.

- Heated air inlet duct. Directs air that has been warmed by the heat stove (shroud) on the manifold to the snorkel of the air cleaner.
- Air inlet door vacuum motor. Controls a flapper door inside the snorkel to admit manifold heated air, fresh air, or a mixture of both into the air cleaner.
- Air cleaner bimetal sensor. Regulates vacuum to the vacuum motor to determine the position of the air door. It is sensitive to air cleaner temperature.
- Cold weather modulator (CWM). Traps vacuum to the motor if manifold vacuum drops off due to the throttle opening while the air cleaner is cold.

The air cleaner bimetal sensor (Figure 23-17), which is installed in the air cleaner body or air horn,

592 Section 4 Engine Performance

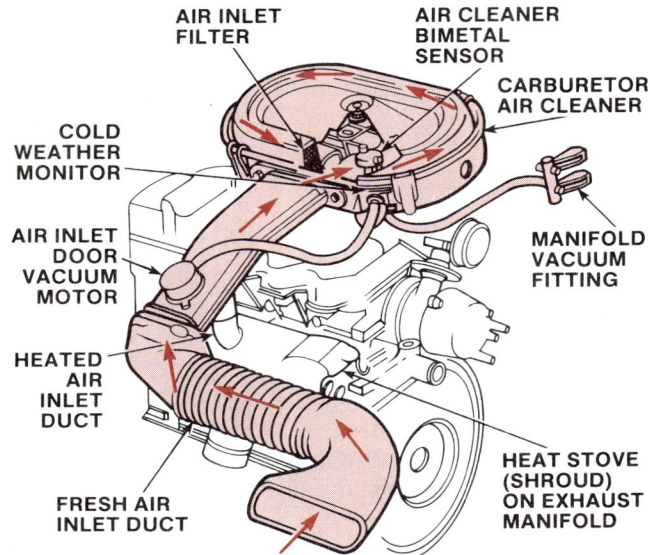

Figure 23-16 Typical heated air inlet system with conventional air cleaner.

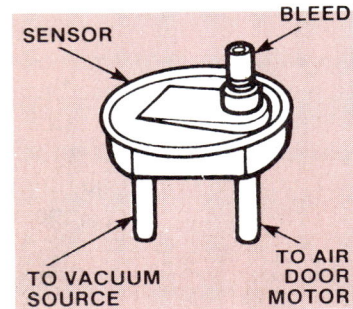

Figure 23-17 Air cleaner bimetal sensor.

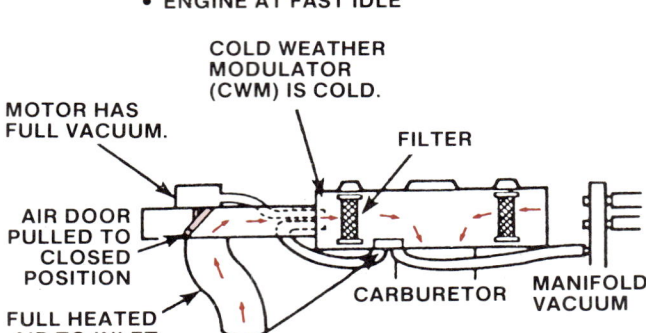

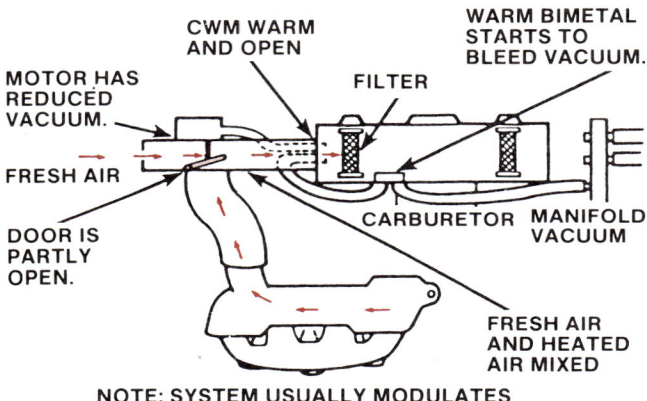

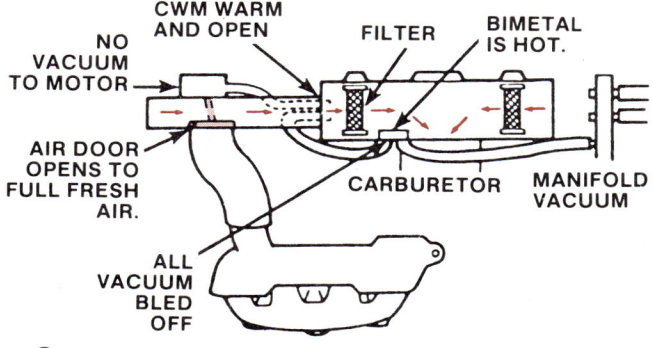

Figure 23-18 Air cleaner bimetal sensor at (A) cold start-up; (B) modulating partial warm-up; (C) hot engine/hot ambient air.

senses the air cleaner temperature. The sensing element is a bimetal spring, which is linked to a sensing valve. Depending on the calibration, the sensor can be set to operate at 75, 90, or 105 degrees Fahrenheit. It is what controls the operating modes shown in Figure 23-18. The sensor is calibrated to provide a specific output vacuum to the air door motor as it warms to its temperature setting. The calibration is based on 16 inches of source vacuum.

Some vacuum control systems use a retard delay valve instead of a cold weather modulator. The difference is that the retard delay valve traps the vacuum for a few seconds when the throttle opens. Its function is to prevent a change in the air door position if vacuum drops off because the throttle opens.

With a remote air cleaner, the functions are the same. As illustrated in Figure 23-19, however, the bimetal sensor is in the air horn assembly and the air inlet vacuum motor and door are in the air cleaner assembly instead of the inlet snorkel.

Troubleshooting the Heated Inlet Control System

In a modern gasoline engine, emission controls that have any effect on the mixture necessarily have an

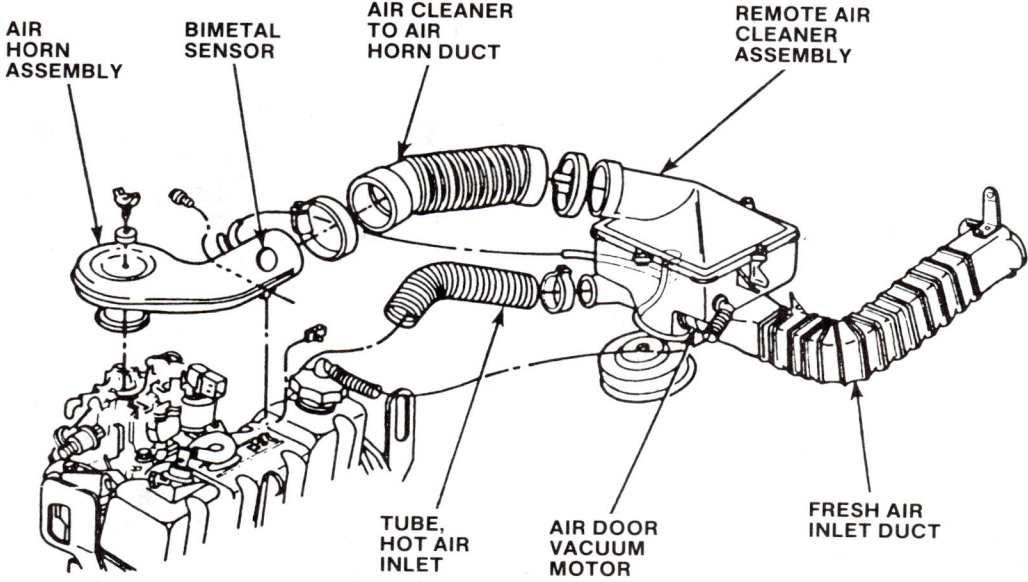

Figure 23-19 A heated air inlet system with a remote air cleaner.

effect on driveability, since all the systems are calibrated to operate as one integral system. Problems with the heated air inlet fall into the following groups.

- Obstructions to airflow, causing hard starting, performance problems, and poor fuel economy
- Vacuum loss, causing cold driveability problems since the system goes to full fresh air
- Air leaks, which by-pass the control and usually cause cold driveability problems
- Vacuum trap failure (CWM or retard delay valve), which causes stumble on cold acceleration because the engine suddenly gulps in cold air
- Failure to switch to fresh air, which can overheat the mixture and cause warm driveability problems and detonation

PROCEDURES
Heated Air Inlet System Inspection and Performance Test

1. Apply the parking brake and block the wheels.
2. Remove the air cleaner cover and element. Inspect the heated air duct for proper installation or damage. Service as required.
3. Remove components as necessary to ensure that the duct door is in the "open to fresh air" position. If the door is in the "closed to fresh air" position, check for binding and sticking. Service or replace as required.
4. Check the vacuum source and integrity of the vacuum hoses to the bimetal sensor, cold weather modulator (CWM), and vacuum motor.
5. Start the engine. If the duct door has moved to the "heat on" position (closed to fresh air), proceed to step 8. If the door stays in the "heat off" position (closed to warm air), place a finger over the bleed of the bimetal sensor. The air duct door must move rapidly to the "heat on" position. If the door does not fully move to this position, stop the engine and test the vacuum motor. Repeat this step with a new vacuum motor. The ambient air must be at least 60 degrees Fahrenheit during this test.
6. With the engine off, allow the bimetal sensor and CWM to cool.
7. Start and run the engine briefly (less than 15 seconds). The duct door should move to the "heat on" position. If the door does not move or moves only partially, replace the sensor. Cool the CWM and bimetal sensor.
8. Shut off the engine and observe the duct door:
   - Vehicles with a retard delay valve: Valve returns slowly to the "heat off" position (10 to 30 seconds).
   - Vehicles with CWM: Valve stays in the "heat on" position for at least 2 minutes. If less than 2 minutes, replace the CWM and repeat this step after cooling the CWM and bimetal sensor.

Manifold Heat Control Valves

The exhaust manifold heat control valve routes exhaust gases to warm the intake manifold when the engine is cold. This heats the air/fuel mixture in the intake manifold and improves vaporization. The result is reduced HC and CO emissions.

The two general types of valves are vacuum-operated and thermostat-operated. Some V-8 engines use a vacuum-operated valve, which is bolted between the left exhaust manifold and exhaust pipe. The vacuum diaphragm connects to the manifold vacuum through a

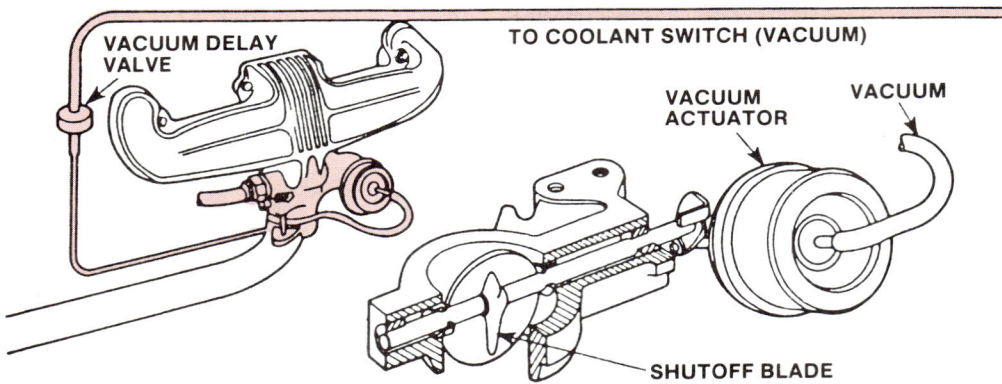

Figure 23-20 Power heat control valve.

ported vacuum switch (PVS). On EEC-controlled engines, the system also includes an electric solenoid-operated vacuum valve.

A thermostat-operated valve is used mostly on six-cylinder engines. It has the same function as the vacuum-operated valve. When the engine is cold, the thermostat closes the valve to block exhaust gas flow from the manifold, which forces the gas to flow up through the heat riser and then to the exhaust pipe. On a warm engine, the thermostat opens the valve to a position that seals off the heat riser passage. Exhaust gases flow directly to the exhaust pipe.

Some V-8 engines use a more complicated manifold heat control valve, which is called a power heat control valve (Figure 23-20). It works similarly to the vacuum-controlled valve. It is designed specifically to work with a minicatalyst and to preheat the air/fuel mixture for improved cold engine driveability. A vacuum actuator keeps the power heat control valve closed during warm-up. All right-side exhaust gas travels up through the intake manifold crossover to the left side of the engine. Then, all exhaust gas from the engine passes through a miniconverter just down from the left manifold. This converter warms up rapidly because it is small and close to the engine. Its rapid warm-up reduces exhaust emissions. As the engine and main converter warm up, a coolant-controlled engine vacuum switch (CCEVS) closes. This cuts vacuum to the actuator and allows the valve to open. Exhaust gas flows through both manifolds into the exhaust system and main converter.

PROCEDURES
Testing a Vacuum-Operated Valve

1. Inspect the valve for any abnormal condition (Figure 23-21). Repair or replace it as necessary.
2. Disconnect the hose from the PVS.
3. Apply 15 inches of vacuum to the vacuum motor diaphragm. Trap for 60 seconds. The valve must leak no more than 2 inches of vacuum in 60 seconds.

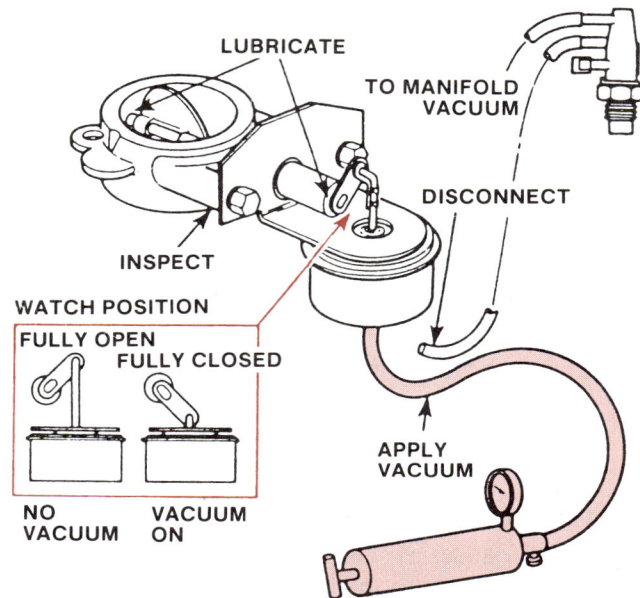

Figure 23-21 Testing a vacuum-operated valve.

4. Watch the position of the vacuum motor stem. It must go to the fully closed position with the vacuum on and to the fully open position when the vacuum is released.
5. If necessary, lubricate the shaft with a graphite lubricant.
6. If the valve and motor are all right, check the vacuum system. Look for a leaking or restricted hose. Repair as necessary. Check the hoses for proper routing.
7. If the valve closes with the engine started, let it warm. When the coolant warms, it should open.

Maintenance of a Vacuum-Operated Valve

Because of its location, the exhaust heat control valve can stick if the shaft is not serviced regularly with graphite lubricant or heat control solvent. Sticking closed can cause overheating, detonation, and hot performance problems. Sticking open can cause poor idle or poor performance cold. A vacuum loss usually

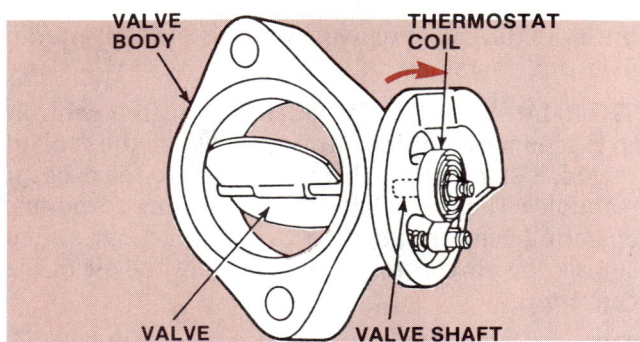

Figure 23-22 Inspect the valve and thermostat assembly for damage and lubricate the pivot.

causes the valve to be unable to open.

Thermostat-Operated Heat Control Valve

Although a thermostat-operated heat control valve is not as common as the vacuum type, some vehicles have them. To inspect and service this type of valve, proceed as follows.

1. Inspect the valve assembly for damage (Figure 23-22). Replace or repair it as necessary.
2. Turn the valve shaft by hand to see if it is free. It must turn freely and return to closed when cold.
3. Cool or heat the thermostat as required to check for proper opening or closing.
4. Lubricate the valve with a graphite lube.

Early Fuel Evaporation (EFE) Control

The early fuel evaporation (EFE) heater contains a resistance grid that heats the mixture from the primary venturi of the carburetor (Figure 23-23). Its purpose is the same as a manifold heat control valve: to improve vaporization in a cold engine. The heater operates for about the first 2 minutes, permitting leaner choke calibrations for improved emissions without cold driveability problems.

The basic EFE system is similar from one engine to the next. In addition to the grid heater, EFE has two other important components.

COOLANT TEMPERATURE SWITCH The EFE temperature switch or solenoid mounts to the engine,

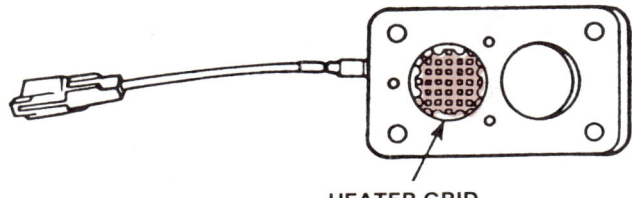

Figure 23-23 EFE heater resistance grid.

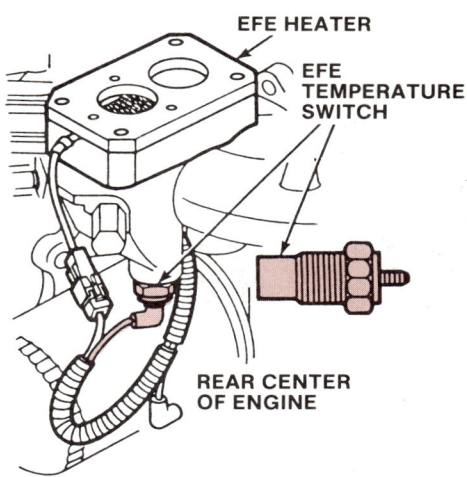

Figure 23-24 The EFE temperature switch is mounted in the engine.

usually on the bottom of the intake manifold (Figure 23-24). The switch is closed and provides a ground for the circuit when its temperature is below a specified temperature (generally between 130 to 150 degrees Fahrenheit). The switch opens as the engine coolant temperature goes above the specified temperature (see the service manual for the exact temperature).

EFE HEATER RELAY The temperature switch controls the EFE relay or valve. It powers the EFE heater when the temperature switch is cold and closed. After the engine has warmed up and the EFE is no longer needed, the relay de-energizes and the grid heater turns off. The EFE heater relay usually mounts on the body of the vehicle.

EFE HEATER CHECK An open circuit in EFE causes no heating of the mixture on a cold engine resulting in performance problems the first minute or two of cold operation. If the heater is powered continually for some reason, it can cause warm engine driveability problems and possibly overheating and detonation.

To perform a typical EFE electrical system check, use a 12-volt test light and jumper wires as needed for open-circuit testing. A service manual will provide the circuit checkpoints.

☐ SPARK ADVANCE SYSTEMS

Spark advance systems have been in use since the earliest gasoline engines. It was discovered that the proper timing of the ignition spark helped the engine to reduce exhaust emission and develop more power output. Throughout the years each car manufacturer developed slightly different spark timing controls according to engine requirements and emission standards for each model year, but the systems and devices all operate on the same principles.

☐ AIR INJECTION SYSTEMS

One of the earliest methods used to reduce the amount of hydrocarbons (HC) and carbon monoxide (CO) in the exhaust was by forcing fresh air into the exhaust system after combustion. This additional fresh air causes further oxidation and burning of the unburned hydrocarbons and carbon monoxide. The process is much like blowing on a dwindling fire. Oxygen in the air combines with the HC and CO to continue the burning that reduces the HC and CO concentrations. This allows them to oxidize and produce harmless water vapor and carbon dioxide.

The system can be equipped with or without an external air pump. Formal names of the pump systems include Air Injection Reaction (AIR) by General Motors, Thermactor Emission (TE) by Ford, Air Guard by American Motors, and Air Injection System by Chrysler. The nonpump systems are often identified on the underhood label by the terms pulse, aspirator, suction, or reed air injection.

Pump Type

A typical system with an air pump is shown in Figure 23-25. System components include the following.

AIR PUMP The air pump produces pressurized air that is sent to the exhaust manifold and to the catalytic converter. The air pump is driven by a belt from the crankshaft.

AIR CONTROL VALVE (OR AIR-SWITCHING VALVE) This vacuum-operated valve is used to route the air from the pump either to the exhaust manifold or to the catalytic converter. During engine warm-up, the valve directs the air into the exhaust manifold. Once the engine is warm, the extra air in the manifold would affect EGR operation, so the air control valve directs the air to the converter, where it aids the converter in oxidizing emissions.

THERMAL VACUUM SWITCH This switch controls the vacuum to the air control valve. When the coolant is cold, it signals the valve to direct air to the exhaust manifold. Then when the engine warms to normal operating temperature, the thermal vacuum switch signals the air control valve to reroute the air to the converter.

AIR BY-PASS VALVE (OR DIVERTER VALVE) This device is located between the air pump and the air control valve, or sometimes it is combined with the air control valve to make one component. The air by-pass valve diverts, or detours, air during deceleration. Excess air in an exhaust rich with fuel can produce a backfire or explosion in a muffler. A vacuum signal operates the by-pass valve during deceleration. Compressed air is diverted to the atmosphere.

ONE-WAY CHECK VALVES These valves allow air into the exhaust but prevent exhaust from entering the pump in the event the drive belt breaks. Their location in the system is behind the air control valve and before the exhaust manifold and catalytic converter.

HOSES AND NOZZLES These are necessary to distribute and inject the air.

Pulse Type (Nonpump Type)

This system uses the natural exhaust pressure pulses to pull air from the air cleaner into the catalytic converter.

The typical pulsed air system operates in the following manner. An air check valve and silencer (Figure 23-26) connects in-line between the air cleaner and the catalytic converter. When pressure in the exhaust system is greater than the pressure in the air cleaner, the reed valve (Figure 23-27) inside the air check valve

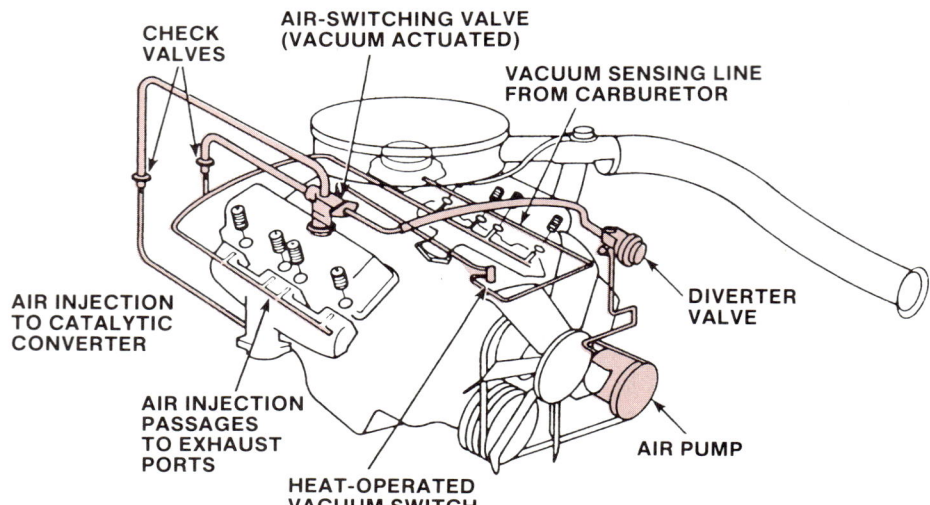

Figure 23-25 Engine-driven air pump type air injection system.

Emission Control Systems   597

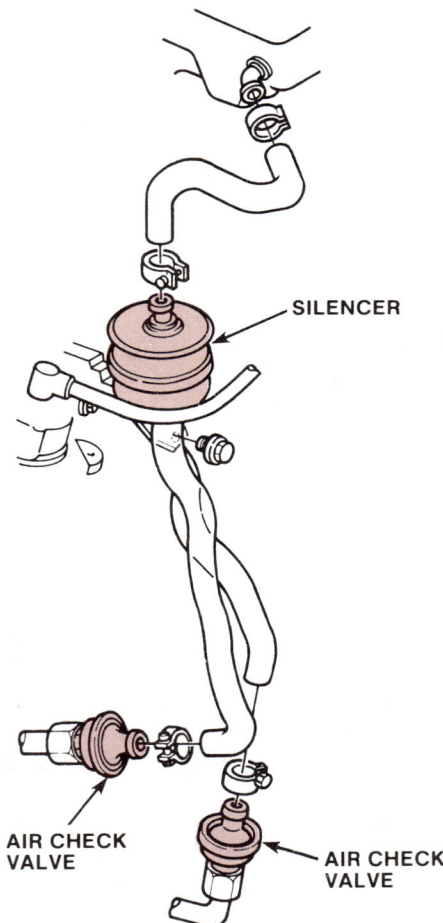

Figure 23-26 Typical pulse air system's check valves.

closes. When the pressure in the exhaust system is less than the pressure in the air cleaner, the reed valve opens and draws air into the catalytic converter. The incoming oxygen reduces the hydrocarbons and carbon monoxide content of the exhaust gases by continuing the combustion of unburned gases in the same manner as the conventional system (with an air pump).

Air injector systems rarely cause problems. If one should cause a difficulty, check the vehicle's service manual.

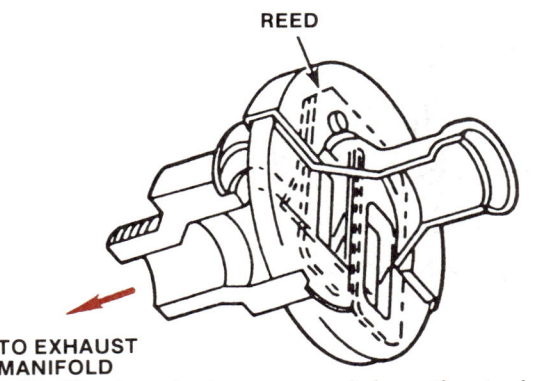

Figure 23-27 A reed valve opens and closes the air-check valve.

❏ SECONDARY AIR SYSTEM

The typical electronic secondary air system, like the conventional air injection system, consists of an air pump to a secondary air by-pass (SAB) valve, which directs the air either to the atmosphere or to the secondary air system (Figure 23-28). The major difference between the two systems is, of course, the on-board computer and diverter valve.

The air pump is driven by a belt on the front of the engine and supplies air to the system. Intake air passes through a centrifugal filter fan at the front of the pump where foreign materials are separated from the air by centrifugal force. In many systems, air flows from the pump to a secondary air by-pass (SAB) valve which directs the air either to the atmosphere or to the secondary air diverter (SAD) valve. The SAD valve directs the air either to the exhaust manifold or to the catalytic converter. Therefore, secondary airflow can be directed to three points.

1. Vented (or bypassed) to the atmosphere via the air filter.
2. Upstream to the exhaust manifold.
3. Downstream to the catalytic converter.

Both the SAB and SAD valves have solenoids that are controlled by the on-board computer. When either solenoid is energized by the computer, vacuum is applied to the SAB valve, secondary air is vented to the atmosphere. When no vacuum is applied to the SAD valve, secondary air (if present) is directed to the catalytic converter.

There are two check valves in the secondary air system. Secondary air must flow through a check valve before it reaches either the exhaust manifold or the catalytic converter. These check valves prevent the backflow of exhaust gases into the pump in the event of an exhaust backfire or if the pump drive belt fails.

By-pass Mode

In the by-pass mode, vacuum is not applied either to the SAB or the SAD valve and secondary air is vented to the atmosphere. Secondary air may be vented or by-passed due to a fuel-rich condition, when the on-board computer recognizes a problem in the system, or during deceleration. Secondary air is also typically by-passed during cold engine cranking and cold idle conditions.

When engine coolant temperature is below 55 degrees Fahrenheit at start-up, secondary air is automatically by-passed. The system maintains a by-pass mode of operation until the coolant temperature reaches 170 degrees Fahrenheit. The computer has an internal electronic timer that keeps track of the length of time since the engine was started. Secondary air is also maintained in the by-pass mode until a pre-set length of time has elapsed.

598 Section 4 Engine Performance

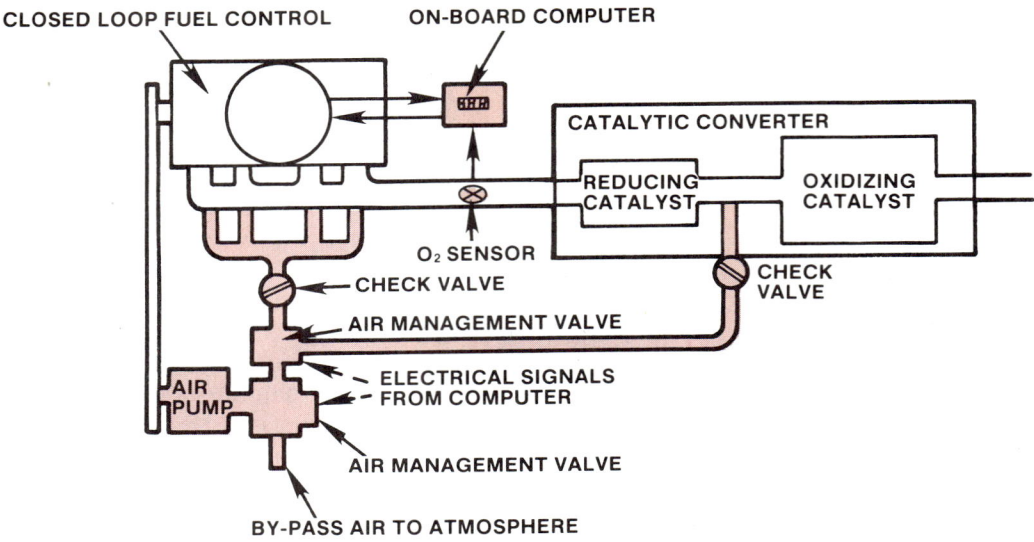

Figure 23-28 Typical secondary air system.

Upstream Mode

Figure 23-29 shows secondary air being routed through the SAB valve and the SAD valve to the exhaust manifold. The upstream mode is actuated when the computer senses a warm crank/start-up condition. The secondary airflow remains upstream for 1 to 3 minutes after start-up to help control emissions.

The air/fuel mixture at start-up is typically very rich. This rich mixture results in unburned HC and CO in the exhaust after combustion. By switching to the upstream mode, the hot HC and CO mix with the incoming secondary air and are burned up.

This reburning of HC and CO compounds causes the exhaust gases to get hotter, which in turn heats up the oxygen sensor. Therefore, switching to the upstream mode allows the electronic engine control system to switch to the closed loop operation sooner because the oxygen sensor is ready to function sooner.

The warm (and activated) oxygen sensor sends exhaust gas oxygen information to the computer. When the electronic engine control system is in the closed

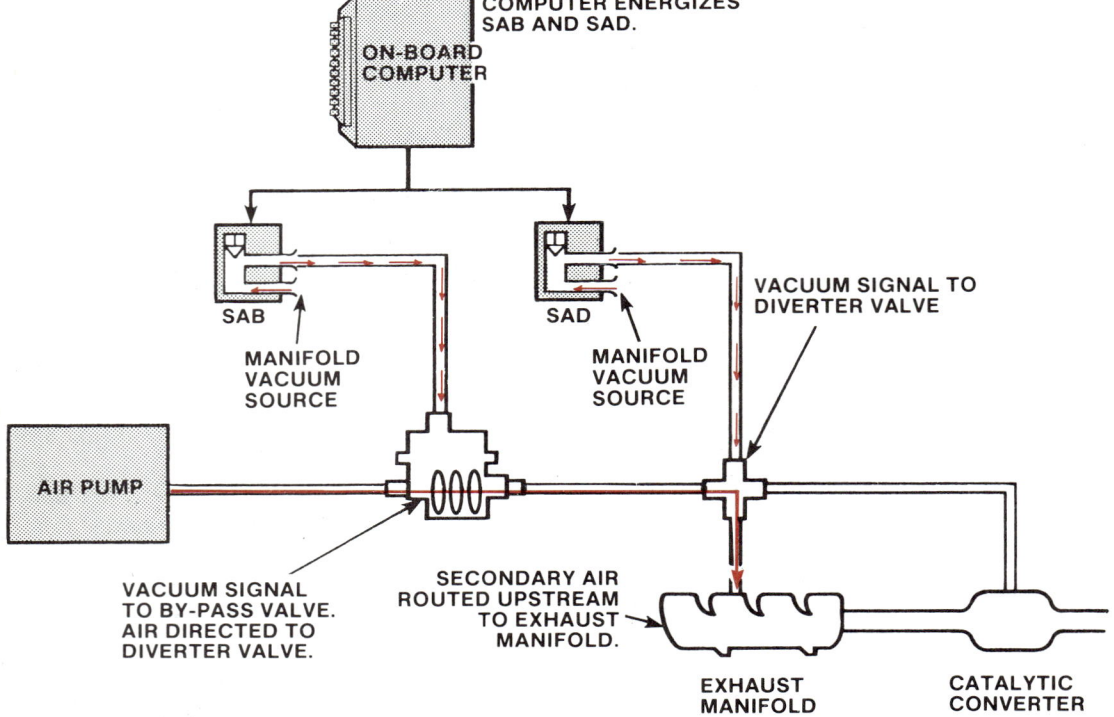

Figure 23-29 Secondary air system upstream mode of operation.

loop operation, the computer uses this information to adjust the air/fuel mixture.

It should be noted that the upstream mode of operation increases the oxygen level in the exhaust gases. The voltage signal from the oxygen sensor to the computer maintains a continuous low level. The computer interprets this signal as a continuous lean condition. That is, there is too much oxygen in the air/fuel mixture. It can readily be seen, then, that the upstream mode results in inaccurate exhaust gas oxygen measurements.

To solve this dilemma, the computer automatically switches to the open loop fuel control whenever the upstream mode is activated. It ignores the oxygen sensor input.

Downstream Mode

Figure 23-30 illustrates secondary air being routed through the SAB valve and the SAD valve to the catalytic converter. The secondary air system operates in the downstream mode during a majority of engine conditions.

The catalytic converter is most efficient at reducing NO_x when the air/fuel mixture is near stoichiometry (a chemically correct air/fuel mixture expressed by the ratio of 14.7:1). As already stated, the oxygen sensor has a big part in producing that optimum air/fuel mixture in the closed loop fuel control mode. When secondary air is diverted downstream, the oxygen sensor can provide accurate information about the level of oxygen in the exhaust gases to the computer. Therefore, the electronic engine control system can operate in the closed loop fuel control mode only when the secondary air system is diverted downstream.

After the engine has warmed up sufficiently, the air/fuel mixture tends to run lean, leaving fewer excess hydrocarbons remaining after combustion. Therefore, it is not necessary to run the secondary air system in the upstream mode of operation. The computer automatically switches the system to the downstream mode to allow the secondary air to mix with the exhaust gases inside the catalytic converter. The fresh secondary air diverted downstream assists the converter in reducing the NO_x emissions. NO_x emissions are also reduced by the closed loop mode.

☐ SECONDARY AIR SYSTEM TROUBLESHOOTING

Both the SAB valve and the SAD valve are operated by solenoids that are controlled by the computer. If no air (oxygen) enters the exhaust stream at the exhaust manifold or catalytic converter, HC and CO emission levels are too high. Air flowing to the exhaust manifold at all times can increase the temperature of the catalytic converter and cause damage to the catalyst. On the other hand, if air is flowing continuously to the catalytic converter, it can cause the converter to overheat during fuel rich operations. An electrical feature (open circuit) of the SAB valve diverts air to the atmosphere for all engine operations. Secondary air continuously flows to the catalytic converter if an open circuit occurs

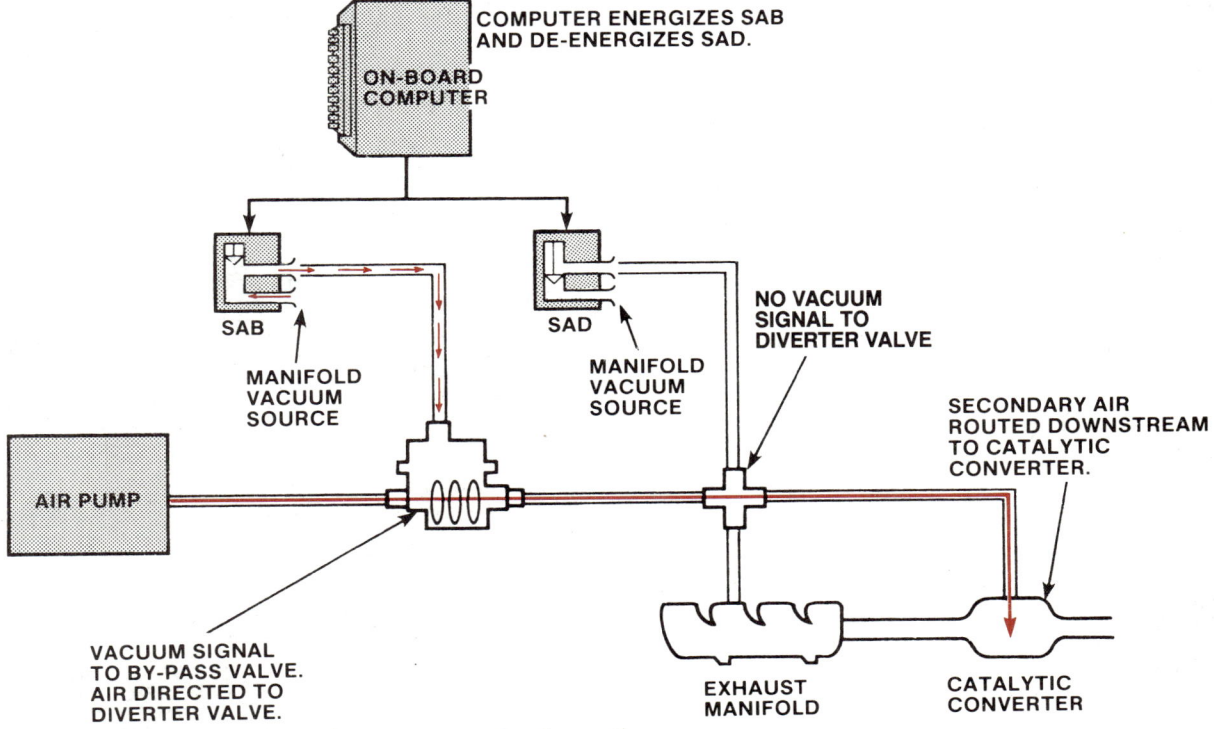

Figure 23-30 Secondary air system downstream mode of operation.

in the SAD valve. Mechanical failures in either or both of the valves can cause incorrect airflow to the exhaust manifold or the catalytic converter.

System Efficiency Test

Run the engine at idle with the secondary air system on (enabled). Using an exhaust gas analyzer, measure and record the oxygen (O_2) levels. Next, disable the secondary air system and continue to allow the engine to idle. Again, measure and record the oxygen level in the exhaust gases. The secondary air system should be supplying 2 to 5% more oxygen when it is operational (enabled).

❑ CATALYTIC CONVERTERS

Catalytic converters are the most effective devices for controlling exhaust emissions. Until 1975, car makers had done an effective job of controlling emissions by the use of other systems—auxiliary air injection systems, exhaust gas recirculation systems, and positive crankcase ventilation. But controlling emissions with these systems alone also meant lean mixtures and exotic ignition timing, which often severely penalized power and fuel economy. When catalytic converters were introduced, much of the emission control could be taken out of the engine and moved into the exhaust system. This change allowed manufacturers to retune the engine for better performance and improved fuel economy.

CUSTOMER CARE

You can assure your customer that a rotten egg odor is not necessarily an indication of a bad catalytic converter. On most vehicles, odor is caused by either high sulfur fuel (recommend switching brands of gasoline) or by an excessively rich or lean fuel mixture.

❑ EVAPORATIVE EMISSION CONTROL SYSTEM

The fuel evaporative emission control system reduces the amount of raw fuel vapors (HC) that are emitted into the air from the fuel tank and carburetor (if so equipped). While different manufacturers have slight variations and names for their evaporative emission control (EEC) systems they are very similar in operation. Since the first systems were used nationwide in the early 1970s, several refinements have been added (Figure 23-31). Current systems include the following components.

- A special filler design to limit the amount of fuel that can be put in the tank.
- A pressure/vacuum relief fuel tank cap instead of a plain vented cap (Figure 23-32).

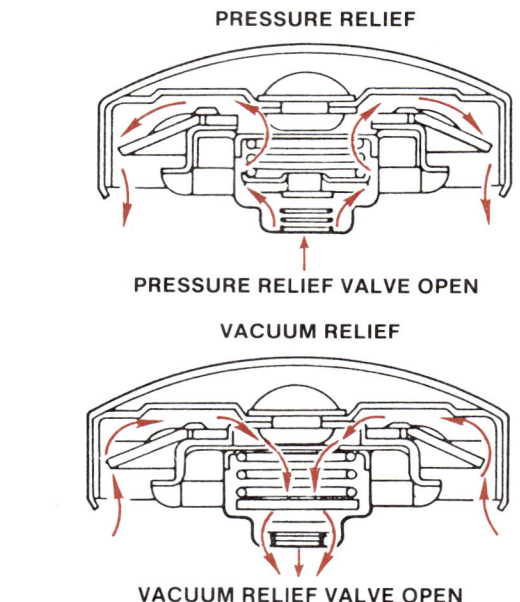

Figure 23-32 Sealed fuel tank cap.

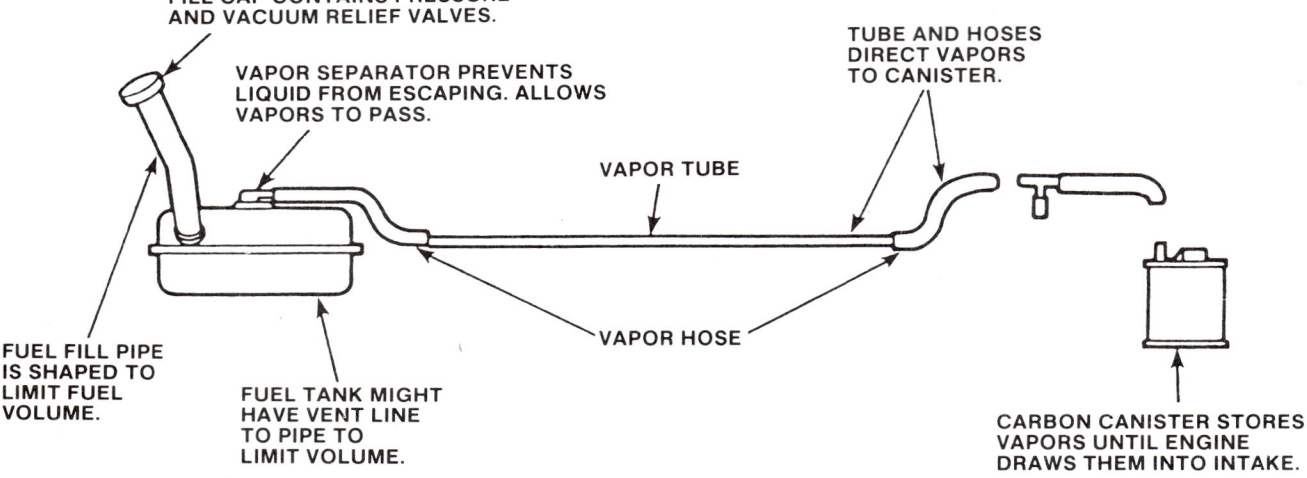

Figure 23-31 Typical evaporative emission control system.

Emission Control Systems **601**

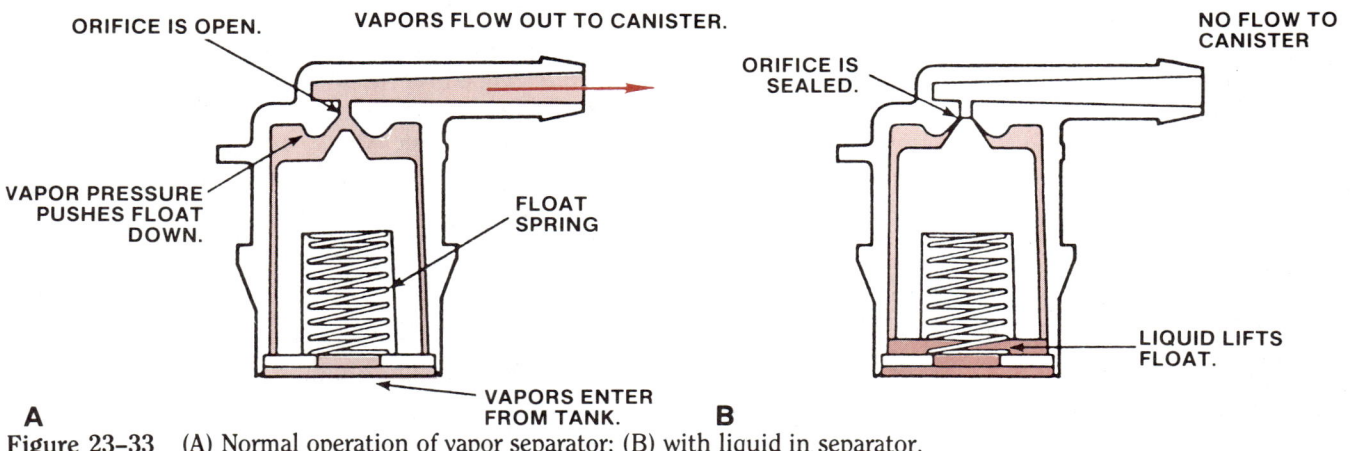

Figure 23-33 (A) Normal operation of vapor separator; (B) with liquid in separator.

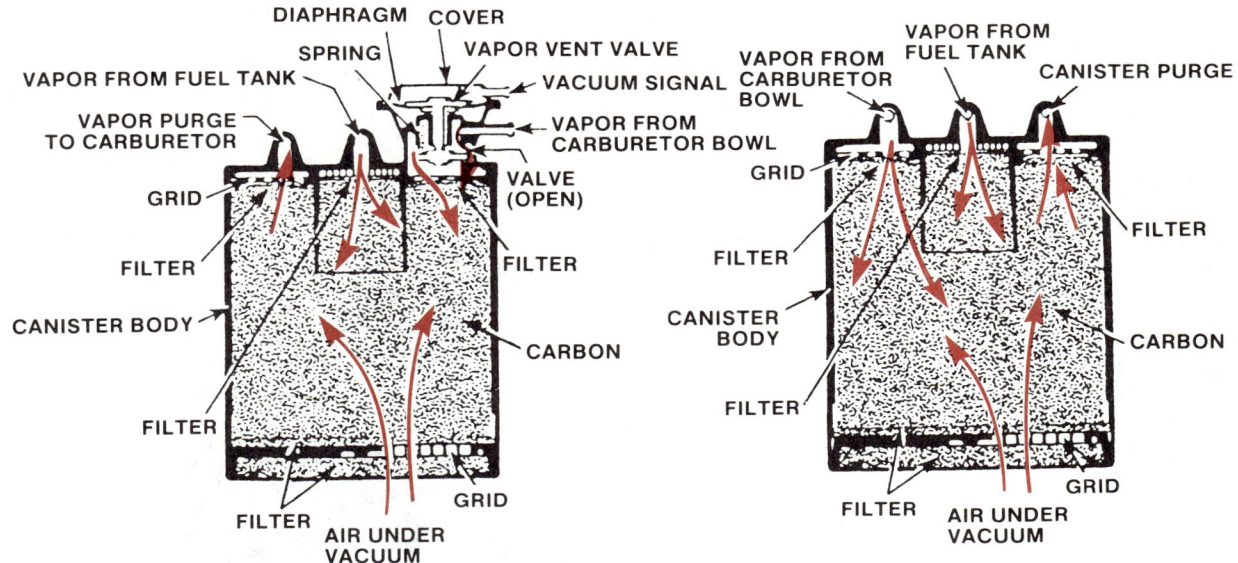

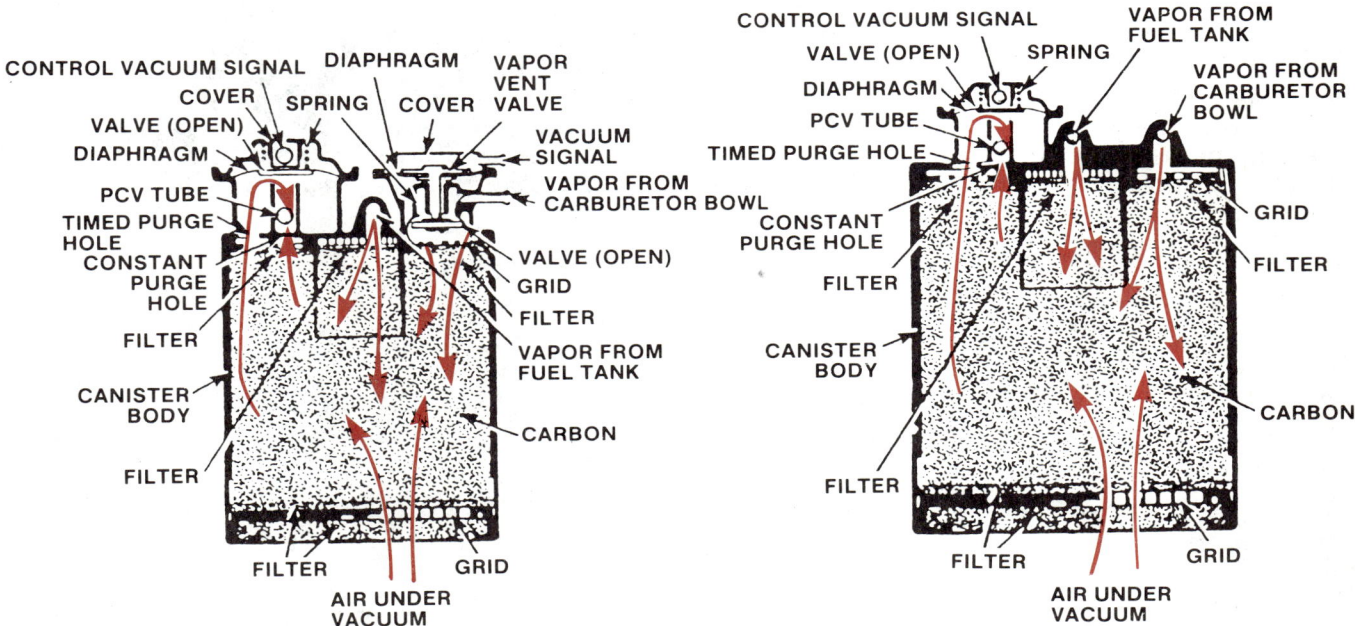

Figure 23-34 Various charcoal canister designs.

- A vapor separator in the top of the fuel tank (Figure 23-33). This device collects droplets of liquid fuel and directs them back into the tank.
- A domed fuel tank in which its upper portion is raised. Fuel vapors rise to this upper portion and collect.
- Check, or one-way, valves keep vapors confined. When an engine runs, vacuum- or electrically-operated valves open.
- Hoses and tubes connect parts of a vapor-recovery system. Special fuel/vapor rubber tubing must be used.

The most obvious part of the evaporative emission control system is the charcoal (carbon) canister in the engine compartment. This canister (Figure 23-34) is located in or near the engine compartment. Fuel vapors from the gas tank (and carburetor float bowl) are routed to and absorbed onto the surfaces of the canister's charcoal granules. When the vehicle is restarted, vapors are drawn by the vacuum into the carburetor or intake manifold to be burned in the engine. Canister purging varies widely with make and model. In some instances a fixed restriction allows constant purging whenever there is manifold vacuum. In others, a staged valve provides purging only at speeds above idle. Generally, the canister purge valve is normally closed. It opens the inlet to the purge outlet when vacuum is applied. Some units incorporate a thermal-delay valve so the canister is not purged until the engine reaches operating temperature. Purging at idle or with a cold engine creates other problems, such as rough running and increased emissions because of the additional vapor added to the intake manifold. Typical purge valve mountings are shown in Figure 23-35.

Canister purging may also be electronically controlled. The on-board computer enables a purge solenoid to initiate the purge cycle. The canister purge solenoid is mounted in-line between the canister and intake manifold. The purge solenoid is a normally closed solenoid. The on-board computer cycles the solenoid while the solenoid itself controls the release of fuel vapors trapped in the charcoal canister. When the solenoid is energized by the computer, the purge valve opens and allows the intake manifold vacuum to draw the trapped fuel vapors from the canister.

In the electronically-controlled canister, fuel vapors are purged only under the following conditions.

- After a predetermined length of time has elapsed following engine start-up.
- The engine coolant temperature sensor must indicate that engine temperature is within a predetermined range.
- The engine must be operated at stabilized, part-open throttle condition.
- The engine must be operating above a predetermined high rpm limit.

Normal service of the electronic fuel evaporative system consists of replacing the canister or canister filter at the manufacturer's suggested interval and replacing any worn or damaged hoses. Failure of the system to purge on command indicates a failed canister purge solenoid valve.

Canister Testing

Check the canister to make sure that it is not cracked or otherwise damaged (Figure 23-36). Also make certain that the canister filter is not completely saturated. Remember that a saturated charcoal filter can cause symptoms that can be mistaken for fuel system problems. Rough idle, flooding, and other con-

Figure 23-36 The canister should be checked for damage.

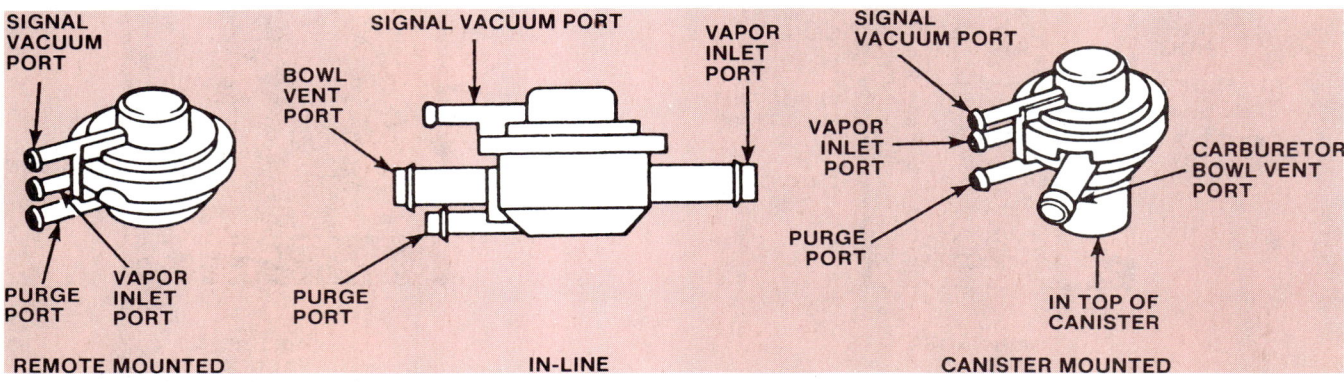

Figure 23-35 Typical purge valve mountings.

ditions can indicate a canister problem. A canister filled with liquid or water causes back pressure in the fuel tank. It can also cause richness or flooding symptoms during purge or start-up. (Some trucks have intentionally pressurized fuel tank systems. Check the calibration and engine decal before diagnosing.)

To test for saturation, unplug the canister momentarily during a diagnosis procedure and observe the engine's operation. If the canister is saturated, either it or the filter must be replaced depending on its design. That is, some models have a replaceable filter, others do not.

> **SHOP TALK**
>
> Sometimes a partially saturated canister can be evacuated by removing it from its mounting area (leaving the hoses connected), inverting it, and running the engine at high idle for 3 to 5 minutes. Be sure to replace the canister filter if it can be separated from the canister.

Testing the Canister Purge Valve

A vacuum leak in any of the evaporative emission components or hoses can cause starting and performance problems as can any engine vacuum leak. It can also cause complaints of fuel odor. Incorrect connection of the components can cause rich stumble or lack of purging (resulting in fuel odor). To conduct a vacuum-on, valve-open test consult the vehicle's service manual. Check the service manual for other common EEC system problems.

Float Bowl Vent Control

If a carburetor's float bowl does not vent properly, there can be flooding on start-up, especially if the vent fails to open with a hot carburetor. Flooding can also occur if vapors back up into the carburetor from the canister due to a failed thermal vent valve (TVV). A failed open carburetor bowl vent solenoid or vacuum/thermal bowl vent can cause suction in the fuel bowl during canister purging, resulting in lean driveability problems.

To test the fuel bowl vent or canister purge shutoff, follow the service manual procedure.

CASE STUDIES

Case 1

A customer complains of severe detonation. The technician checks all the EGR vacuum lines and finds them intact and properly routed.

The technician pushes the EGR valve stem against spring pressure. It moves freely and returns fully. With the engine at normal operating temperature, a helper opens the throttle enough to reach 2,500 rpm while the technician watches the EGR valve stem. When the throttle is released, the valve stem does not retract. The technician removes the hose and feels no vacuum when the engine is revved. Next, the technician pulls off the source line from the thermostatic vacuum switch and feels for vacuum. Because there is vacuum there but none gets to the valve with the engine warm, the technician replaces the thermostatic vacuum switch.

Case 2

A customer complains of a loud rapping or ticking noise (sounding similar to a rod knock) that seems to occur only during acceleration when the engine is cold.

When the technician pulls the vacuum line off the heat riser canister, the noise goes away. The technician replaces the vacuum check valve located between the vacuum switch and the heat riser vacuum motor.

Summary

- Unburned hydrocarbons, carbon monoxide, and oxides of nitrogen are three types of emissions being controlled in gasoline engines.
- Precombustion control systems prevent emissions from being created in the engine, either during or before the combustion cycle. Post-combustion control systems clean up exhaust gases after the fuel has been burned. The evaporative control system traps fuel vapors that would normally escape from the fuel tank and carburetor into the air.
- The PCV system removes blowby gases from the crankcase and recirculates them to the engine intake. The PCV system benefits the vehicle's driveability by eliminating harmful crankcase gases, reducing air pollution, and promoting fuel economy.
- The EGR system reduces the amount of NO_x emitted by the exhaust system by diluting the air/fuel mixture with controlled amounts of exhaust gas. The EGR valve may be controlled by a port vacuum system or a venturi vacuum system.
- The EGR valve can be tested with a vacuum gauge or a hand vacuum pump.
- In vehicles equipped with electronic engine controls, the EGR valve has a sensor that relays the position of its stem to the on-board computer. The computer signals two control solenoids, EGKV and EGRC, that either maintain or alter the EGR flow, depending on engine operating conditions.
- Air temperature emission control systems reduce HC and CO emissions in the exhaust. The heated

air inlet control system, used on all carbureted and central fuel injected engines, controls the inlet air temperature on the way to the carburetor or fuel injector body. The manifold heat control valve routes exhaust gases to warm the intake manifold when the engine is cold. This valve may be vacuum-operated or thermostat-operated. The early fuel evaporation (EFE) heater contains a resistance grid that heats the mixture before it enters the cylinders.
- The air injection system reduces the amount of HC and CO in the exhaust by forcing fresh air into the exhaust system after combustion. The system can be equipped with or without an external air pump.
- The secondary air system is a more complex electronic version of the air injection system. In its by-pass mode secondary air is vented to the atmosphere. In its upstream mode the air is directed to the exhaust manifold to aid in the burning of the HC and CO compounds. This also warms the oxygen sensor faster. Air is directed to the catalytic converter in the downstream mode.
- The secondary air system's SAB and SAD valves together control where secondary air is directed.
- The catalytic converter is the most effective device for controlling exhaust emissions.
- The fuel evaporative emission system reduces the amount of raw fuel vapors (HC) that are emitted into the air from the fuel tank and carburetor. Current systems include a special filler design, a pressure/vacuum relief fuel tank cap, a vapor separator, a domed fuel tank, check valves, hoses and tubes, and a charcoal canister.

Review Questions

1. Name the three types of emissions being controlled in gasoline engines.
2. Name the three basic types of emission control systems used in modern vehicles.
3. List three ways the PCV system benefits the vehicle's driveability.
4. Name three air temperature control systems.
5. Name the three modes of the secondary air system.
6. Which of the following is a post-combustion control system?
    a. exhaust gas recirculating (EGR) system
    b. catalytic converter
    c. both a and b
    d. neither a nor b
7. What is the leakage of unburned fuel and products of combustion into the engine crankcase called?
    a. blowby
    b. sludge
    c. both a and b
    d. neither a nor b
8. The exhaust gas recirculating system reduces what kind of emissions?
    a. HC
    b. CO
    c. NO_x
    d. all of the above
9. The vacuum used to control the EGR valve is taken from which of the following?
    a. a port in the carburetor throttle body above the throttle plate
    b. a port at the throat of the carburetor venturi
    c. both a and b
    d. neither a nor b
10. Which of the following causes detonation?
    a. an EGR valve stuck closed
    b. a leaking valve diaphragm
    c. restrictions in flow passages
    d. all of the above
11. Technician A says that the EGR vent solenoid is normally open. Technician B says that the EGR control solenoid is normally open. Who is correct?
    a. Technician A
    b. Technician B
    c. Both A and B
    d. Neither A nor B
12. Which of the following systems are used on gasoline engines to heat the inlet air and the air/fuel mixture?
    a. heated air inlet controls
    b. manifold heat control valves
    c. early fuel evaporation (EFE) heaters
    d. all of the above
13. Which of the following systems supplies fresh air to the exhaust system?
    a. pump air injection system
    b. pulse air injection system
    c. both a and b
    d. neither a nor b
14. A vehicle is experiencing flooding. Technician A says that the bowl vent valve has failed in the open position. Technician B says that the charcoal filter is saturated. Who is probably correct?
    a. Technician A
    b. Technician B
    c. Both A and B
    d. Neither A nor B
15. Which of the following are functions of the heated air inlet system?
    a. warming the inlet air
    b. improving fuel vaporization
    c. reducing HC and CO emissions
    d. all of the above
16. Technician A says that SAB valve directs secondary air either to the exhaust manifold or to the

catalytic converter. Technician B says that secondary air may be vented during deceleration. Who is correct?
   a. Technician A
   b. Technician B
   c. Both A and B
   d. Neither A nor B
17. Which of the following components is not a part of the early fuel evaporation (EFE) control system?
   a. power heat control valve
   b. resistance grid
   c. coolant temperature switch
   d. EFE relay
18. Which of the following devices delays the introduction of exhaust gases into the intake manifold until after the engine warms up?
   a. thermal vacuum switch
   b. ported vacuum switch
   c. delay timer control
   d. all of the above
19. Technician A says that the canister purge valve is normally open. Technician B says that the purge solenoid is normally open. Who is correct?
   a. Technician A
   b. Technician B
   c. Both A and B
   d. Neither A nor B
20. Technician A says that if secondary air flows continuously to the catalytic converter, the catalytic converter overheats during rich fuel operations. Technician B says that secondary air flows continuously to the catalytic converter if an open circuit occurs in the SAD valve. Who is correct?
   a. Technician A
   b. Technician B
   c. Both A and B
   d. Neither A nor B

24 COMPUTERIZED ENGINE CONTROLS

Objectives

- Explain the advantage of using computerized engine control systems. ■ Identify and explain computerized control system components. ■ Understand how a typical computerized engine control system operates. ■ Know the various memory systems used in automotive microcomputers. ■ Explain the operation of the various input and output sensors. ■ Explain what is meant by open loop and closed loop. ■ Know how to use computer logic and troubleshooting logic. ■ Understand self-diagnostic systems.

Computerized engine control systems present service technicians with a totally new way of troubleshooting performance problems. An on-board diagnostic capability allows the computer to aid the technician in pinpointing the source of many performance problems.

Because all manufacturers continually update, expand, and improve their computerized control systems, there are now hundreds of different domestic and import systems on the road today. Methods of reading on-board diagnostic data and troubleshooting systems can vary greatly between manufacturers and between model lines and years of the same manufacturer. That is why it is absolutely essential that the service manual be used during all diagnostic procedures.

Fortunately, manufacturers are moving toward standardizing certain aspects of their diagnostic systems. This includes a standard shape for the diagnostic connector into the system, and a standard format for the data that is read from the computer system. However, there will still be wide differences in how this data is used to troubleshoot the system.

❑ SYSTEM FUNCTIONS

In a computerized engine control system, four factors are carefully balanced to achieve maximum results with minimum waste.

EMISSIONS Factors that result in lower emissions follow.

- Air/fuel ratio held as closely to 14.7 to 1 as possible, allowing maximum catalytic converter efficiency.
- Emission control devices, such as EGR valve, carbon canister, and air pump, operated at high efficiency.
- Engine operated as efficiently as possible when cold and warmed up rapidly, reducing unburned hydrocarbon (raw gas) emissions.

MILEAGE Factors that result in increased mileage follow.

- Timing advanced as much as possible under all conditions.
- Air/fuel ratio kept as close to ideal (14.7 to 1 by weight) as possible.
- EGR valve positioned as accurately as possible.
- Lockup torque converter applied in manner to give more efficient operation.

PERFORMANCE (POWER AND DRIVEABILITY) Factors that result in improved engine performance follow.

- Timing and air/fuel ratio precisely controlled under all operating conditions.
- Control loop operation that enables the engine to make rapid changes to match changes in temperature, load, and speed.
- Engines that can be designed for higher power output and still meet mileage and emissions standards.

PROTECTION (DURABILITY) Factors that protect the engine follow.

- A system able to make changes in timing and air/fuel to compensate for excessive engine temperature or load.

Computerized Engine Controls 607

- A system able to retard ignition timing to eliminate engine knock (detonation).
- An engine that can warm up faster, with less engine wear from raw gas washing oil from the piston rings and getting into the crankcase to form sludge and varnish.

All these factors are especially important with today's smaller, harder working engines.

To control these factors under all modes of operation (start-up, warm-up, off-idle, cruising, and wide-open throttle), each manufacturer has developed computerized control systems that monitor engine performance, tailor fuel and spark delivery to match performance demands, and control emission systems to minimize the level of pollutants in the exhaust stream.

❑ SYSTEM COMPONENTS

The three basic components of a computer control system are the sensors, microcomputer (sometimes called a microprocessor, control module, or control unit), and actuators. Sensors supply the microcomputer with input on engine conditions. The microcomputer analyzes this data and calculates a response to these conditions. It then signals an output or actuator, such as a relay or solenoid, to adjust engine operation (Figure 24-1).

The sensors, actuators, and computer communicate through the use of electronic circuits. For example, when the incoming voltage signal from the coolant sensor tells the computer that the engine is getting hot, it generates an output command to turn on the electric cooling fan. The computer does this by grounding the relay circuit that controls the electric cooling fan. When the relay clicks on, the electric cooling fan starts to spin and cools the engine.

The engine control computer or microcomputer (Figure 24-2) has two basic types of memory. The first is random access memory (RAM). RAM is used to store data collected, by the sensors, the results of computer calculations, and other information that is constantly

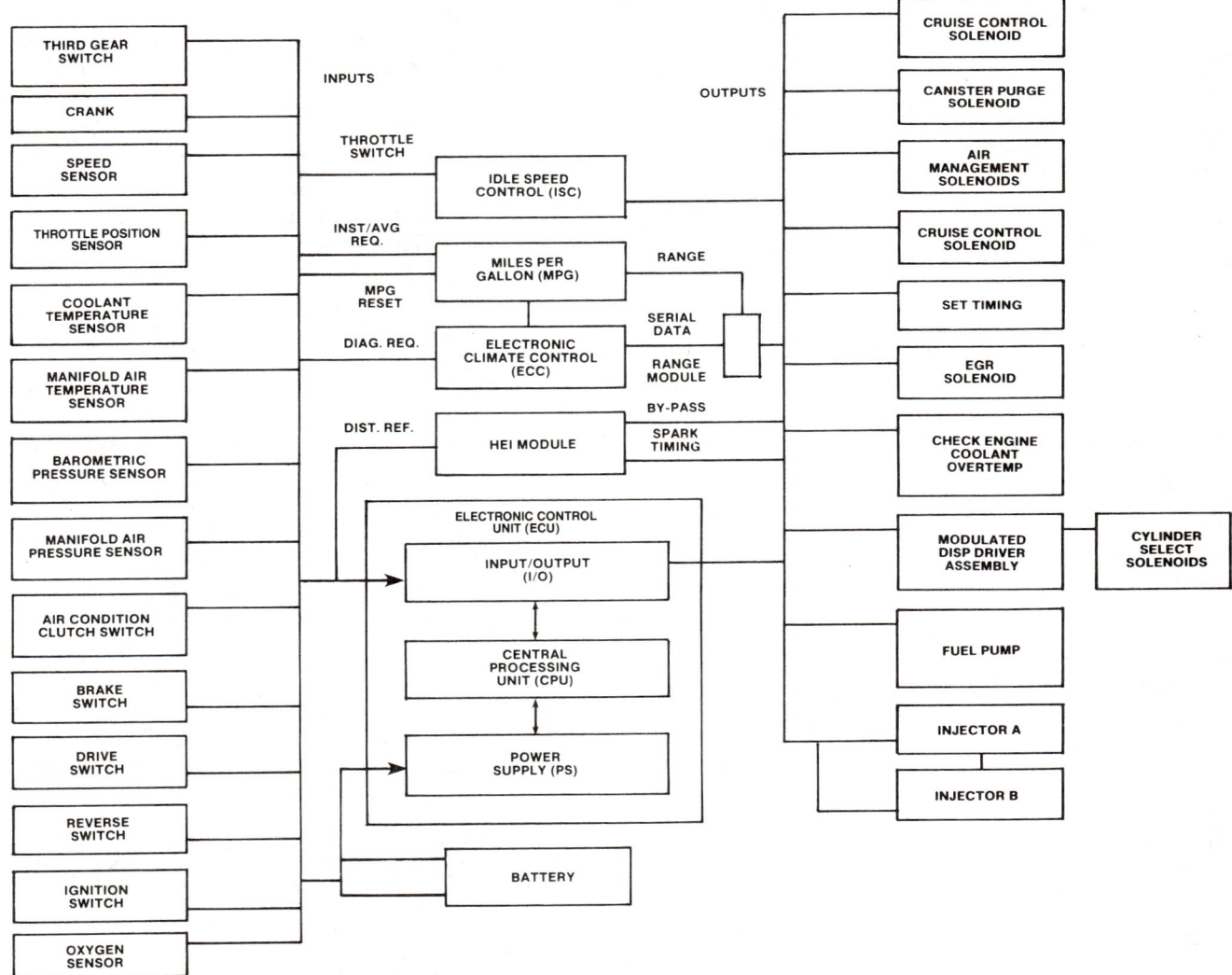

Figure 24-1 Typical computerized engine control system inputs and outputs. *Courtesy of* Counterman *magazine*

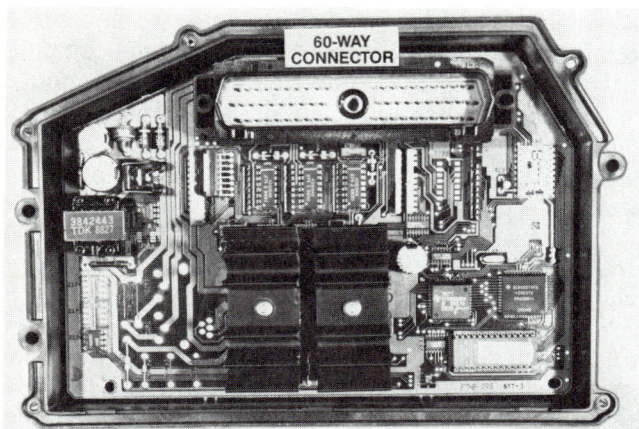

Figure 24-2 Typical engine control microcomputer or computer.

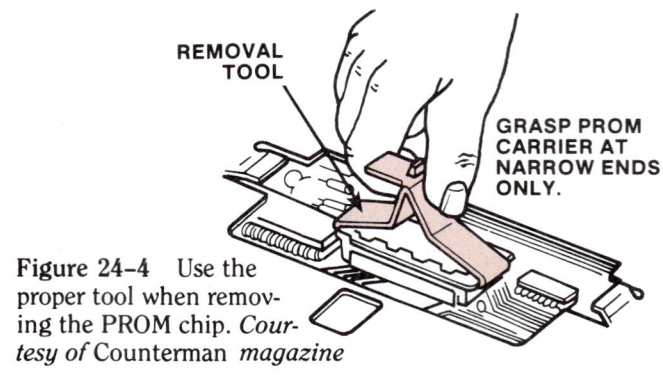

Figure 24-4 Use the proper tool when removing the PROM chip. *Courtesy of* Counterman *magazine*

changing during engine operation. Information in volatile RAM is erased when the ignition is turned off or when the power to the computer is disconnected. Nonvolatile RAM does not lose its data if its power source is disconnected.

The computer's permanent memory is stored in read only memory (ROM) or programmable read only memory (PROM). Like non-volatile RAM, ROM and PROM are not erased when the power source is disconnected. ROM and PROM are used to store computer control system strategy and look-up tables. PROM-integrated circuit chips are used in control computers on General Motors vehicles (Figure 24-3). These rectangular black chips have legs that plug into the computer circuitry. Changing the PROM chip recalibrates the fuel and ignition curves stored in the computer memory. PROM chips enable the same computer to be recalibrated for use in different applications.

When removing or installing a PROM chip, take care not to damage the chip. Always use a PROM removal tool (Figure 24-4) and never touch the legs of the PROM.

Two types of information stored in ROM are the system strategy and look-up tables. System adaptive strategy is a plan, created by engine designers and calibration engineers, for the timing and control of computer-controlled systems. In designing the best strategies, it is necessary to look at all the possible conditions an engine may encounter. It is then determined how the system should respond to these conditions. In other words, a strategy is a blueprint for how the system operates in order to reach a desired goal. The strategy goal may be increased power, improved mileage, lowered temperature, reduced emissions, or rapid warm-up. To do this, the ROM strategy includes all the equations and decision-making logic, and serves as a guide or plan in controlling engine operation. In order to be useful, the strategy requires additional data, which are obtained from the look-up tables.

The look-up tables (sometimes called maps) contain calibrations and specifications (Figure 24-5). Look-up tables indicate how an engine should perform. For example, a piece of information (a reading of 20 in. Hg) is received from the manifold absolute pressure (MAP) sensor. This information, plus information from the engine speed sensor, is compared to a table for spark advance. This preprogrammed table tells the computer what the spark advance should be for that throttle position and engine speed (Figure 24-6). The computer then modifies this spark advance value, by consulting other tables, with information concerning engine temperature and atmospheric pressure. To determine how much spark should be advanced, the microprocessor refers to a special look-up table called an adder. The adder indicates how much spark advance should be added with EGR gases flowing. Because these tables are stored in ROM, information in the look-up tables is retained when power to the microprocessor is turned off.

When making decisions, the microprocessor is constantly referring to three sources of information: the

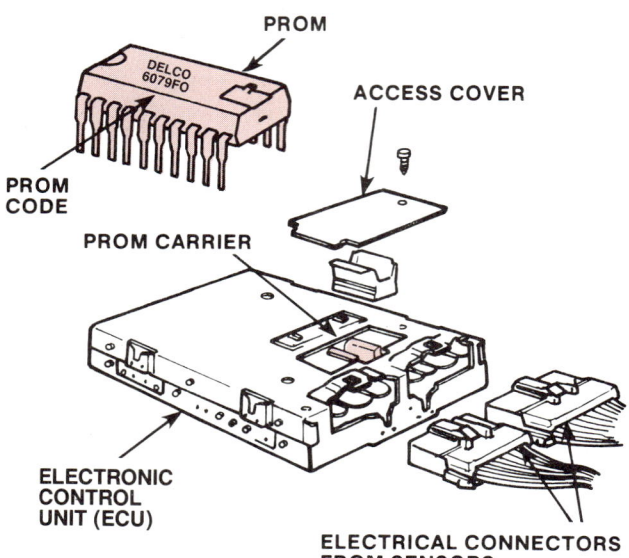

Figure 24-3 On GM computers, the PROM is replaceable. If the computer is replaced, the PROM must be removed from the old computer and installed in the replacement. *Courtesy of* Counterman *magazine*

Computerized Engine Controls 609

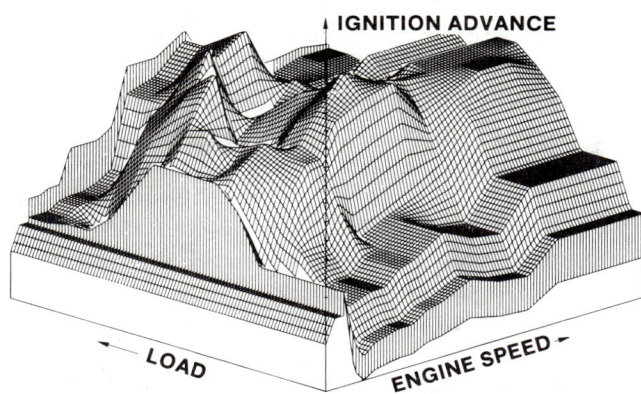

Figure 24-5 Graphic illustration of spark advance look-up table or map.

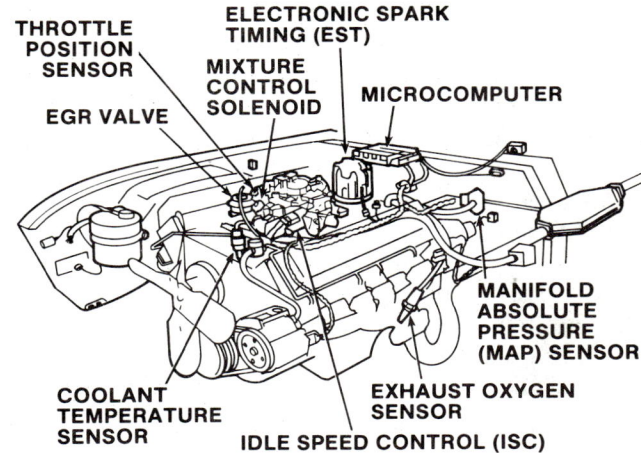

Figure 24-7 Typical location of major engine sensors and actuators. *Courtesy of General Motors Corp.*

look-up tables, system strategy, and the input from sensors. By comparing information from these sources, the microcomputer makes informed decisions.

☐ PRINCIPAL SENSORS

To monitor and adjust engine conditions, as already mentioned, the microcomputer uses a variety of sensors (Figure 24-7). The following represent the principal system sensors. It should be noted that these sensors are shared between the systems. For example, MAP sensor input is used to control fuel, ignition, EGR, emission system airflow, air intake, and idle speed systems. It is also important to remember that not all sensors are used on all vehicles. Some of these sensors perform essentially the same job in slightly different ways. The manufacturer's names for these devices may differ, but the description and operation of the sensors are basically the same. For specific application information, check the service manual.

AIR-CONDITIONING (A/C) DEMAND SENSOR This is a pressure switch that signals the computer control module that the A/C clutch is cycling. When the pressure switch is closed, a voltage signal is sent to the computer. The computer uses this data to help determine engine load and control engine idle speed. The timing on some engines can also be altered to prevent hesitation.

AIR TEMPERATURE SENSOR Also called air change or manifold air temperature sensor, this sensor is a thermistor. Its resistance decreases as manifold air temperature increases and increases as manifold air temperature decreases. The control module measures the voltage drop across the air temperature sensor and uses this input to help calculate fuel delivery. The input from this sensor may also be used to control the preheated air and early fuel evaporation systems.

In some vehicles, an ambient air temperature sensor is used to control the vehicle's automatic climate control system for passenger comfort.

BRAKES ON OR OFF This input signals the microprocessor to disengage the torque converter clutch. It can also lower idle speed.

BAROMETRIC PRESSURE (BARO) SENSOR This sensor alters the air/fuel mixture and timing controls, depending upon the altitude in which the car is being operated.

COOLANT TEMPERATURE SENSOR The coolant temperature sensor is very important. Its input is used to regulate many engine functions.

- Activating and deactivating the early fuel evaporation system.
- Controlling the open- and closed-loop feedback modes of the system. The coolant temperature sensor controls the air/fuel mixture (open loop)

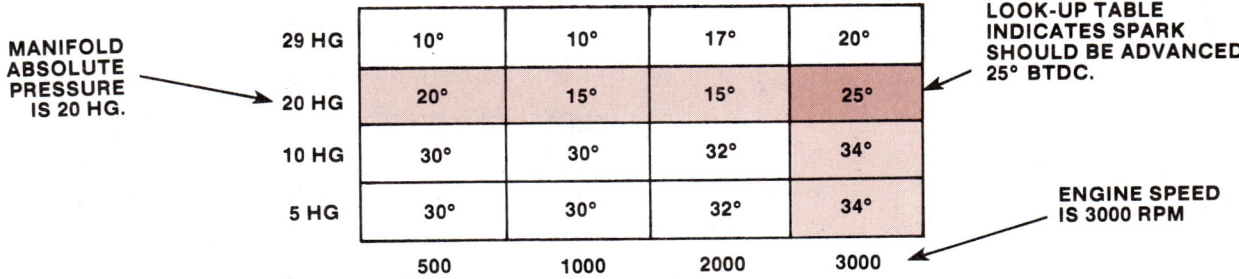

Figure 24-6 Example of base spark advance look-up table. *Courtesy of Ford Motor Co.*

until the engine is warm enough for the oxygen sensor to take over air/fuel mixture control (closed loop).
- Startup fuel enrichment on fuel-injected engines.
- Spark advance and retard. Spark advance is often limited until the engine reaches normal operating temperature.
- EGR flow, which is blocked while the engine is cold to improve driveability.
- Canister purge, which does not occur until the engine is warm.
- Throttle kicker or idle speed.
- Transmission torque converter clutch lockup.

The coolant temperature sensor (Figure 24-8) is usually located on the cylinder head or intake manifold. The sensor screws into the water jacket. On most systems, the coolant sensor is a variable resistance thermistor. On older systems, a switch coolant sensor may be used. This type of sensor may be designed to remain closed within a certain temperature range (55 to 235 degrees Fahrenheit, for example) or to open only when the engine is warm (125 degrees Fahrenheit or hotter).

Because of the coolant sensor's major role in triggering so many engine functions, a faulty sensor or sensor circuit can cause a variety of problems. The most common is the failure to switch to the closed-loop mode once the engine is warm. Other problems may include poor cold idling caused by no early fuel evaporation, heated air, or rich fuel mixture; stalling due to a rich mixture, retarded timing, or a slow idle speed; cold hesitation or stumble due to no EFE or EGR occurring too soon; or poor fuel mileage due to a rich mixture, open loop operation, or a retarded spark.

Coolant temperature sensor problems are often due to wiring faults or loose or corroded connectors rather than failure of the sensor itself. Correct operation of the sensor can also be upset by installing the wrong temperature range thermostat.

ENGINE POSITION SENSORS Engine position sensors tell the computer the speed of the engine and when the piston in each cylinder reaches top dead center (TDC). This input is used to set ignition timing and fuel injection delivery. Several distinct types of engine position sensors are used, but all communicate with the computer by generating a voltage signal. The sensor does this using a Hall-effect switch or electromagnetic induction. The engine position sensor may be called a distributor pick-up coil, crankshaft or camshaft position sensor, or a profile ignition pick-up sensor (Figure 24-9).

EGR DIAGNOSTIC SWITCH On some vehicles with port fuel injection systems that control EGR operation, an EGR diagnostic switch is used to tell the computer if the EGR is actually being applied when it is commanded to be applied.

EGR VACUUM DIAGNOSTIC CONTROL SWITCH Some cars include a vacuum-operated switch that is tied into the vacuum hose between the EGR valve and the EGR control solenoid. When vacuum is applied to the EGR valve, the switch closes. If the microcomputer detects a closed EGR diagnostic switch during starting, idle, or any other time, it has not commanded the EGR to be applied. It turns on the check engine light and sets a fault code in its diagnostic memory. If it sees an open switch during any time it has commanded the EGR to be applied, it turns on the check engine light and sets the same code.

EGR VALVE POSITION SENSOR Car manufacturers use a variety of sensors or switches to determine when the EGR valve is open. This information is used to adjust the air/fuel mixture. The exhaust gases introduced by the EGR valve into the intake manifold reduce the available oxygen and thus less fuel is needed in order to maintain low HC levels in the exhaust.

ENGINE SPEED SENSOR Similar to the engine position sensor, the information from this sensor may be used by the computer for determining timing (advance based on speed), fuel delivery, emission control, converter clutch operation, and idle speed.

HEATED WINDSHIELD MODULE This input tells the computer the heated windshield system is operating. This helps the computer accurately determine engine load and idle speed.

HIGH GEAR SWITCH This input tells the microcomputer when the car's automatic transmission is in high gear and allows the torque converter clutch to lock up.

KNOCK SENSOR The knock sensor tells the microprocessor that the engine is pinging. In turn, the microcomputer retards the timing (Figure 24-10). The

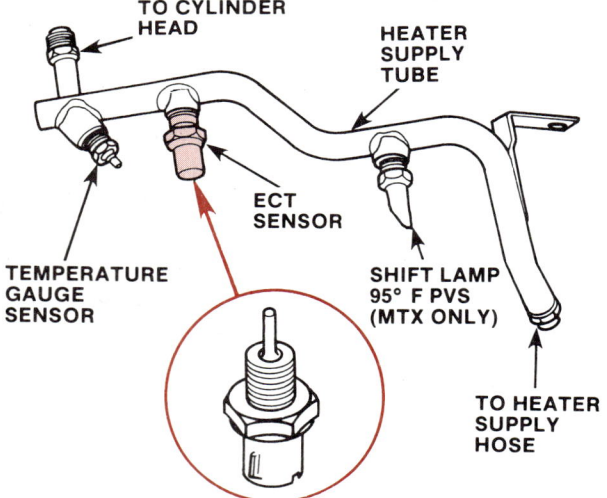

Figure 24-8 Typical engine coolant temperature (ECT) sensor. *Courtesy of Ford Motor Co.*

Computerized Engine Controls   611

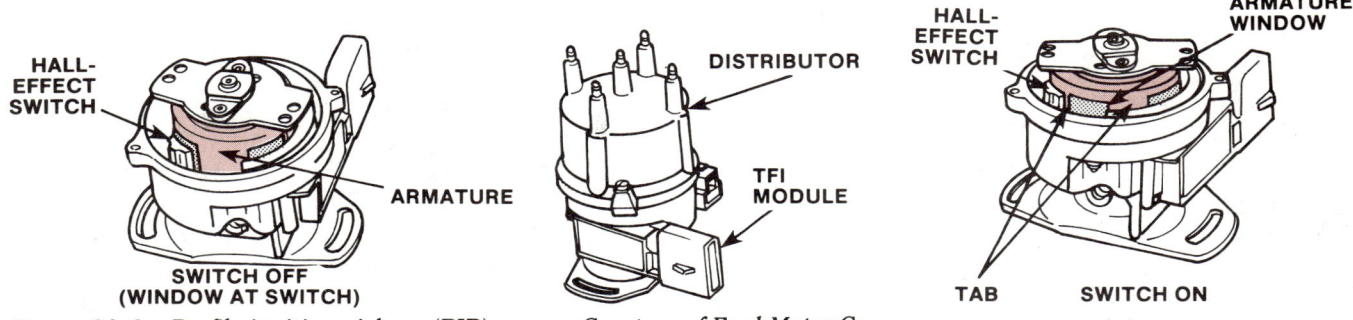

Figure 24-9 Profile ignition pick-up (PIP) sensor. *Courtesy of Ford Motor Co.*

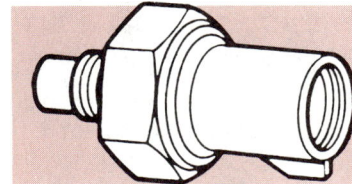

Figure 24-10 Typical location of knock sensor. *Courtesy of Ford Motor Co.*

knock sensor is a piezo-electric device that converts engine knock vibrations into a voltage signal. Some of the latest systems retard timing on an individual cylinder basis.

IDLE TRACKING SWITCH (ITS) In the body of the idle speed control motor assembly (used on some carbureted and fuel injected applications) is a normally closed switch. When the throttle is closed, the throttle lever presses against a plunger extending from the nose of the assembly. The pressure forces the plunger to move slightly back into the assembly and causes the switch to open. When the throttle is open, the switch closes again. The computer monitors the switch and can determine when the throttle is open or closed. It uses this information to function with the idle speed control (ISC) motor.

MANIFOLD ABSOLUTE PRESSURE (MAP) SENSOR The function of a MAP sensor is to sense air pressure or vacuum in the intake manifold. The computer uses this input as an indication of engine load to adjust the air/fuel mixture and spark timing (Figure 24-11). The MAP sensor reads vacuum and pressure through a hose connected to the intake manifold. A pressure-sensitive ceramic or silicon element and electronic circuit in the sensor generates a voltage signal that changes in direct proportion to pressure.

MAP sensors should not be confused with vacuum sensors or barometric pressure sensors. While a vacuum sensor reads the difference between manifold vacuum and atmospheric pressure, a MAP sensor measures manifold air pressure against a precalibrated absolute pressure. Because it bases its readings on preset absolute pressure, MAP sensor readings are not adversely altered by changes in operating altitudes or barometric pressure.

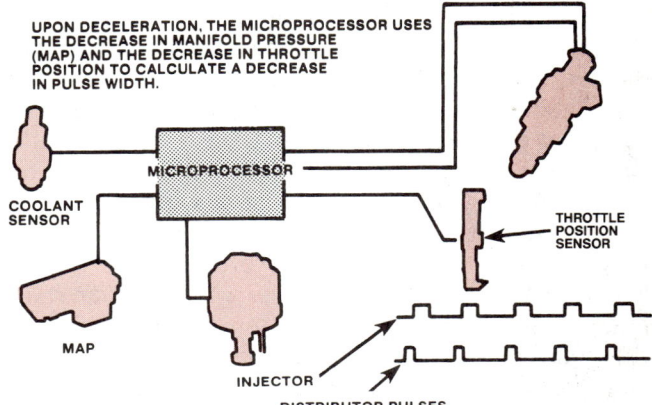

Figure 24-11 Computer-controlled fuel mixture is achieved through several sensors. To make the mixture leaner during deceleration, the microprocessor uses a decrease in MAP and a decrease in throttle position to shorten the open time (pulse width).

> **CUSTOMER CARE**
>
> It is a service to your customer to point out the vacuum hoses leading to MAP sensors. They should be checked at every tune-up. During winter months, the inside of the vacuum hoses should be checked for moisture buildup. Hoses can freeze and prevent the MAP from functioning.

MASS AIRFLOW (MAF) SENSOR This sensor measures the flow of air entering the engine. This measurement of airflow is a reflection of engine load (throttle opening and air volume and density). It is similar to the relationship of engine load to MAP or vacuum sensor signal. Since there are several types of MAFs (vane airflow, ultrasonic system and hot-wire), check the service manual for the one used.

NEUTRAL DRIVE/NEUTRAL GEAR SWITCH A neutral drive switch is used with automatic transmission vehicles to adjust idle speed due to the increased loading of an engaged transmission/transaxle. Vehicles with a manual transmission or transaxle use a neutral

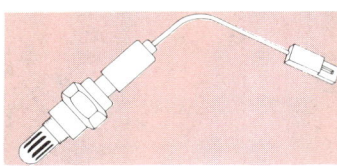

Figure 24-12 Exhaust gas oxygen sensor.

gear switch to inform the computer that the vehicle is out of gear.

OXYGEN SENSORS The exhaust gas oxygen sensor, or Lambda sensor as it is referred to on many import vehicles, is the key sensor in the closed-loop mode (Figure 24-12). Its input is used by the computer to maintain a balanced air/fuel mixture.

One type of oxygen sensor, made with a zirconium dioxide element, generates a voltage signal proportional to the amount of oxygen in the exhaust gas. It compares the oxygen content in the exhaust gas with the oxygen content of the outside air. As the amount of unburned oxygen in the exhaust gas increases, the voltage output of the sensor drops. Sensor output ranges from 0.1 volt (lean) to 0.9 volt (rich). A perfectly balanced air/fuel mixture of 14.7:1 produces an output of around 0.5 volt. When the sensor reading is lean, the computer enriches the air/fuel mixture to the engine. When the sensor reading is rich, the computer leans the air/fuel mixture.

Because the oxygen sensor must be hot to operate, some sensors are equipped with an internal heating element. This helps the sensor reach operating temperature more quickly and maintains temperature during periods of idling or low engine load.

A second type of oxygen sensor does not generate a voltage signal. Instead it acts like a variable resistor, altering a base voltage supplied by the control module. When the air/fuel mixture is rich, sensor resistance is low. When the mixture is lean, resistance increases. Variable-resistance oxygen sensors do not need an outside air reference. This eliminates the need for internal venting to the outside. They feature very fast warmup, and they operate at lower exhaust temperatures.

The normal life span of this important sensor is between 30,000 and 50,000 miles. Sensors can fail prematurely if they become clogged with carbon or solvents from the misuse of RTV silicone sealers. Older sensors may operate sluggishly as indicated by loss of power, rough idle, poor fuel mileage, or increased emissions.

The accuracy of the oxygen sensor reading can be affected by air leaks in the intake or exhaust manifold. A misfiring spark plug that allows unburned oxygen to pass into the exhaust also causes the sensor to give a false lean reading.

PRESSURE FEEDBACK EGR (PFE) The PFE sensor used in some vehicles is a pressure-sensing voltage divider (functions as a potentiometer) similar to the ones used as MAP and BP sensors. It senses exhaust

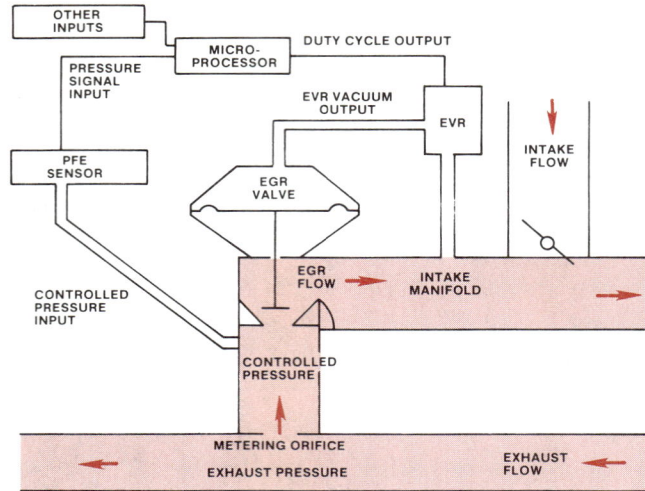

Figure 24-13 Circuit using pressure feedback EGR (PFE) sensor. *Courtesy of Ford Motor Co.*

pressure in a chamber just under the EGR valve pintle (Figure 24-13). This pressure causes the PFE to vary its output voltage signal to the computer. When the EGR valve is closed, the pressure in the sensing chamber is equal to exhaust pressure. When the EGR valve opens, pressure in this chamber drops because of the restricting orifice that lets exhaust into the sensing chamber from the exhaust system. The more the valve opens, the more the pressure drops. The PFE voltage signal tells the computer how far the EGR valve is open. The computer uses this information to fine tune its control of the electronic vacuum regulator (EVR), which controls vacuum to the EGR valve. This information also allows the computer to more accurately control air/fuel ratios and ignition timing.

POWER STEERING (PS) SWITCH This switch causes the microcomputer to raise the idle speed when the power steering is turned to lock. This prevents stalling when the automobile is engaged in tight turns or is being parked.

SYSTEM BATTERY VOLTAGE This voltage provides power for the system. Poor grounds can cause all or any part of the computer-controlled system to malfunction.

THROTTLE POSITION SENSOR (TPS) Engines with electronic fuel injection or feedback carburetions use a throttle position sensor to inform the computer about the rate or throttle opening and the relative throttle position (Figure 24-14). A separate idle switch or wide open throttle (WOT) switch may also be used to signal the computer when these throttle positions exist.

The TPS is a variable resistor that changes resistance as the throttle opens. As the throttle plate opens, the computer enriches the air/fuel mixture to maintain the proper air/fuel ratio.

The initial setting of the TPS is critical. The voltage signal the computer received is referenced to this set-

Computerized Engine Controls 613

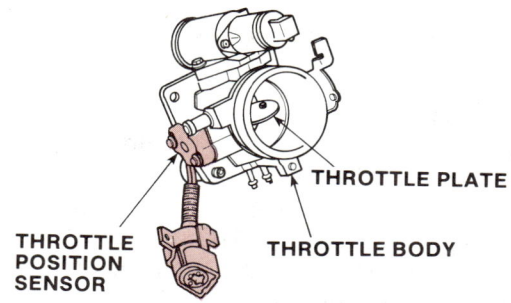

Figure 24-14 Throttle position sensor. *Courtesy of Ford Motor Co.*

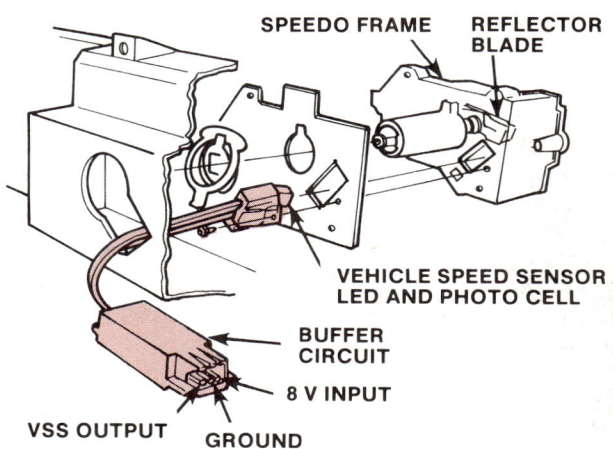

Figure 24-15 Vehicle speed sensor. *Courtesy of GM Product Service Training*

ting. Many service manuals list the initial TPS setting to the nearest one-hundredth volt, a clear indication of the importance of this setting.

The most common symptom of a bad or misadjusted TPS is hesitation or stumble during acceleration. The fuel mixture leans out because the computer does not receive the right signal telling it to add fuel as the throttle opens. Eventually, the oxygen sensor senses the problem and adjusts the mixture, but not before the engine stumbles.

VACUUM SENSOR Vehicles that do not have MAP or BARO sensors may use a vacuum sensor to provide engine load and speed change information. The vacuum sensor measures the difference between atmospheric pressure (outside air) and engine vacuum.

VEHICLE SPEED SENSOR This sensor tells the microcomputer the vehicle's speed in miles per hour (Figure 24-15). This input controls when the torque converter clutch locks up and also can be used to control EGR flow and canister purge.

SHOP TALK

The terms hardware and software are frequently used in descriptions of microcomputers and electronic control systems. Hardware refers to those parts of the system that are literally hard. It includes the parts of the system that can be seen and touched. Hardware includes the actual system components such as the sensors, actuators, microcomputers, the wiring, and the connectors between these components. In general, hardware cannot be changed once it is created. Modern electronic control systems also include software. Software is information, stored in microcomputer memory as tiny electrical signals. Software can be changed or modified, thus it is called soft. Software includes the information stored in microcomputer memory such as engine calibration information. Software also includes the programs that guide the microcomputer through each decision.

□ COMPUTER OUTPUTS AND ACTUATORS

Computer outputs are electronic signals to control devices or actuators. As mentioned earlier, these actuators perform mechanical movements or actions that change the operating conditions of the engine or vehicle. The major actuators in a computer-controlled engine include the following components.

AIR MANAGEMENT SOLENOIDS Air by-pass and diverter solenoids control the flow of air from the air pump to either the exhaust manifold (open loop) or the catalytic converter (closed loop).

CANISTER PURGE SOLENOID This solenoid controls when stored fuel vapors in the canister are drawn into the engine and burned. The computer only activates this solenoid valve when the engine is warm and above idle speed.

EGR FLOW SOLENOIDS EGR flow is controlled by a pair of electronically-controlled vacuum solenoids. One supplies manifold vacuum to the EGR valve when EGR is required. The second vents the vacuum when EGR is not required.

MIXTURE CONTROL SOLENOIDS In some carbureted engines, an electrical solenoid is used to operate the metering rods and idle air bleed valve in the carburetor.

FUEL INJECTORS These solenoid valves deliver the fuel spray in fuel-injected systems.

IDLE SPEED CONTROLS These actuators are small electric motors. On carbureted engines, this idle speed motor is mounted on the throttle linkage. On fuel-injected systems a stepper motor is used to control the amount of air by-passing the throttle plate.

OTHER SOLENOIDS Computer-controlled solenoids may also be used in the operation of cruise control systems, torque converter lockup clutches, automatic transmission shift mechanisms, and many other systems where mechanical action is needed.

IGNITION MODULE This is actually an electronic switching device triggered by a signal from the control computer.

MOTORS AND LIGHTS Using electrical relays, the computer is used to trigger the operation of electric motors such as the fuel pump, or various warning light or display circuits.

❏ SYSTEM OPERATION

Control loops are the cycles by which a process can be controlled by information received from input sensors, ROM, computer processing, and output of specific commands to control actuator devices.

The basic purpose of all computerized engine control loops is the same: to create an ideal air/fuel ratio, which allows the catalytic converter to operate at maximum efficiency, while giving the best mileage and performance possible and protecting the engine.

Closed Loop Mode

The closed loop mode is basically the same for any automotive system. Sensor inputs are sent to the computer; the computer processes them and sends commands to the output devices. The output devices adjust timing, air/fuel ratio, and emission control operation. The resulting engine operation affects the sensors, which send new messages to the computer, completing the cycle of operation. The complete cycle is called a closed loop.

Closed control loops are often referred to as feedback systems. This means that the sensors provide constant information, or feedback, on what is taking place in the engine. This allows the engine to make constant decisions and changes to output commands.

Open Loop Mode

When the engine is cold, most electronic engine controls go into what is called the open loop mode. In this mode, the control loop is not a complete cycle because the computer does not react to feedback information. Instead, the computer makes decisions based on preprogrammed information that allows it to make basic ignition or air/fuel settings and to disregard some sensor inputs. The open look mode is activated when a signal from the temperature sensor indicates that the engine temperature is too low for gasoline to properly vaporize and burn in the cylinders. Systems with oxygen sensors may also go into the open loop mode while idling, or at any time that the oxygen sensor cools off enough to stop sending a signal, and at wide open throttle.

Fail Safe or Limp-in Mode

Most computer systems also have what is known as the fail safe or limp-in mode. The limp-in mode is nothing more than the computer's attempt to take control of vehicle operation when input from one of its critical sensors–the MAP, throttle position, and coolant temperature sensor–has been lost. To be more specific, if the computer sees a problem with the input from any one of those devices, it either works with fixed values in place of the failed sensor input, or depending on which input was lost, it can also generate a modified value by combining two or more related sensor inputs.

To illustrate this last point, let us assume the MAP sensor stops working. Instead of an actual MAP measurement, the computer compensates by creating an artificial MAP signal from a combination of throttle position input and engine speed data. While this may not result in the most efficient operation, considering the alternatives, a modified MAP signal is better than no MAP signal at all. This allows the engine to run until the driver can reach a service location.

Spark Control Systems

In spark control systems, input to the computer usually consists of engine temperature, engine speed, and manifold vacuum. There may be other sensors for throttle position, incoming air temperature, or engine knocking (detonation).

The computer processes these inputs and advances or retards spark timing as required. This causes changes in engine operation, which sends new messages to the computer, continuing the control loop cycle. The computer can constantly adjust timing for maximum efficiency.

When the engine is cold, the spark control system is in the open loop and runs the engine on preprogrammed settings, disregarding sensors until the engine reaches normal operating temperature. Figure 24-16 shows a typical spark control system control

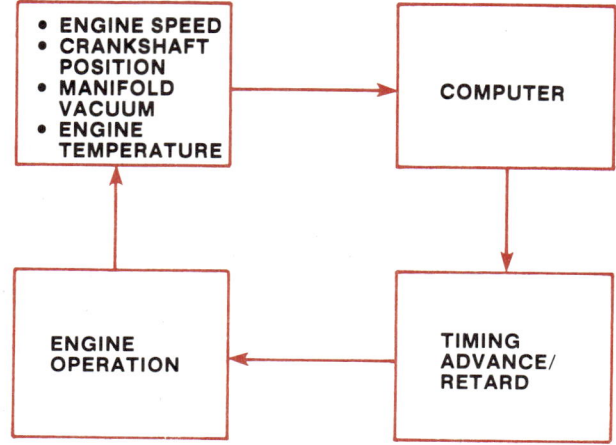

Figure 24-16   Typical spark control system control loop.

loop. This system is much more efficient than earlier spark control systems, such as those with vacuum and centrifugal advance mechanisms.

The advantage of the electronic spark control system is threefold. It compensates for changes in engine (and sometimes outside air) temperature. It makes changes at a rate many times faster than older systems. And finally, it has a feedback mechanism in which sensor readings allow it to complete its control loop and constantly compensate for changing conditions.

Fuel Control System

In carbureted fuel control systems, input to the computer come from sensors for manifold vacuum, engine temperature, and exhaust-gas oxygen. The computer processes this information and sends commands to the solenoid on the feedback carburetor, adjusting the air/fuel mixture entering the cylinder.

This electronic control is superior to the earlier carburetor system as it compensates for changes in the engine load, speed, and temperature much more quickly and accurately. It also constantly compensates for changes in air/fuel ratio, due to its control loop feature. Figure 24-17 shows a typical fuel control system control loop.

In fuel-injected systems, typical inputs to the computer are manifold pressure, throttle position, engine speed, crankshaft position, and engine temperature, inlet air temperature, and oxygen in the exhaust.

The computer processes these inputs and sends commands to the fuel injectors, telling them how long to stay open. This system controls air/fuel ratios much more precisely than any carburetor system. The constant sensor inputs and precise fuel control provide a very accurate air/fuel mixture. This fuel-injected system control loop is shown in Figure 24-18.

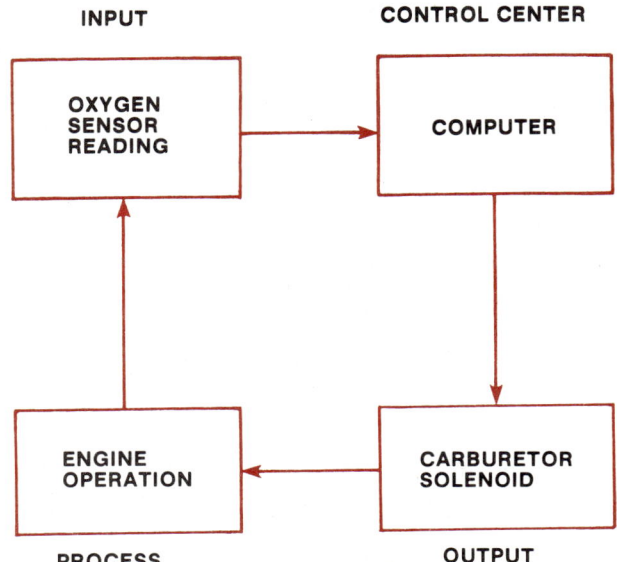

Figure 24-17 Typical carbureted engine fuel control system control loop.

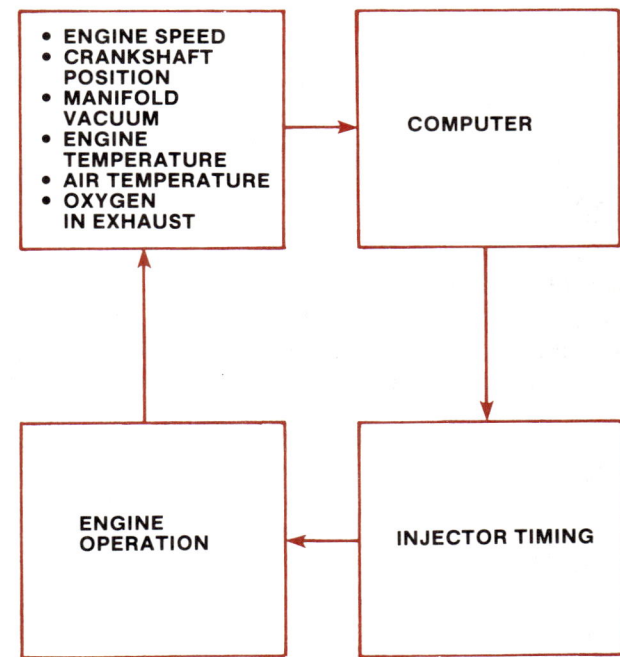

Figure 24-18 Typical fuel-injected engine control loop.

Emission Control System

Three main emission-controlled devices are controlled by the computer. These are the EGR valve, the air pump (thermactor), and the evaporative emissions canister. The computer keeps the level of the three major pollutants (CO, HC, and NO_x) at acceptably low levels.

Other emission control devices may be wholly or partly controlled by the computer. These include the thermostatic air cleaner, early fuel evaporation devices, and electric choke. Consult the appropriate service manual for exact applications.

Combined Spark/Fuel Emission Control Systems

Typical inputs to the spark and fuel control computer include the following.

- Engine temperature
- Engine speed
- Throttle position
- Manifold vacuum/manifold air pressure
- Inlet/charge air temperature
- Oxygen in exhaust
- Engine detonation (knock)
- EGR valve position

The computer processes this information and controls the following areas.

- Ignition timing
- Air/fuel ratio (carburetor or fuel injection)
- Air pump (thermactor) operation

- EGR valve operation
- Evaporative emissions canister purge

Control of Non-engine Functions

Some devices that are not directly connected to the engine are also controlled by the computer to ensure maximum efficiency.

For example, air conditioner compressor clutches can be turned on or off, depending on various conditions. One common control procedure turns off the compressor when the throttle is fully depressed. This allows maximum engine acceleration by eliminating the compressor load.

On some vehicles, the torque converter lock-up clutch is applied and released by a signal from the computer. The clutch is applied by transmission hydraulic pressure, which is controlled by electrical solenoids that are in turn controlled by the computer.

☐ LOGICAL TROUBLESHOOTING

The importance of logical troubleshooting cannot be overemphasized. The ability to diagnose a problem (to find its cause and its solution) is what separates the automotive technician from the parts changer.

There are two logics used when servicing electronic engine controls: computer logic and a technician's logical diagnosis.

Microcomputer Logic Flow

In order to control an engine system, the microcomputer makes a series of decisions. Decisions are made in a step-by-step fashion until a conclusion is reached. Generally, the first decision is to determine the engine mode. For example, to control air/fuel mixture the microcomputer first determines whether the engine is cranking, idling, cruising, or accelerating. Then, the microcomputer can choose the best system strategy for the present engine mode. In a typical example, sensor input indicates the engine is warm, rpm is high, manifold absolute pressure is high, and the throttle plate is wide open. The microcomputer determines the vehicle is under heavy acceleration, or wide-open throttle. Next, the microcomputer determines the goal to be reached. For example, with heavy acceleration, the goal is to create a rich air/fuel mixture. When operating in open loop fuel control, the microcomputer uses a look-up table similar to that shown in Figure 24-19. At wide-open throttle, with high manifold absolute pressure and coolant temperature of 170 degrees Fahrenheit, the table indicates the air/fuel ratio should be 13:1. That is, 13 pounds of air for every 1 pound of fuel. An air/fuel ratio of 13:1 creates the rich air/fuel mixture needed for heavy acceleration.

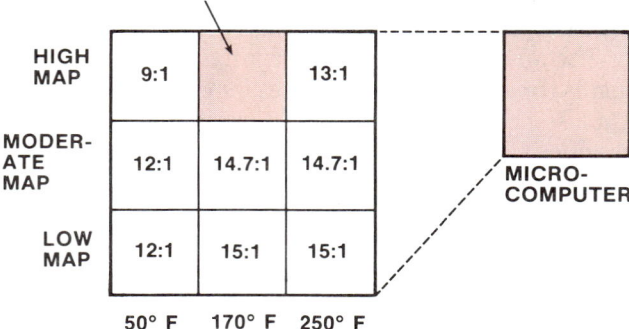

Figure 24-19 A typical look-up table for open loop fuel control.

In a final series of decisions, the microcomputer determines how the goal can be achieved. In our example, a rich air/fuel mixture is achieved by increasing fuel injector pulse width. The injector nozzle remains open longer and more fuel is drawn into the cylinder, providing the additional power needed.

Technician's Logical Diagnosis

The best automotive technicians use this same logical process to diagnose engine problems. When faced with an abnormal engine condition, they compare clues (such as meter readings, oscilloscope readings, visible problems) with their knowledge of proper conditions and discover a logical reason for the way the engine is performing. Logical diagnosis means following a simple basic procedure. Start with the most likely cause and work to the most unlikely. In other words, check out the easiest, most obvious solutions first before proceeding to the less likely, and more difficult, solutions. Do not guess at the problem or jump to a conclusion before considering all of the factors.

The logical approach has a special application to troubleshooting electronic engine controls. Always check all traditional nonelectronic engine control possibilities before attempting to diagnose the electronic engine control itself. For example, low battery voltage might result in faulty sensor readings. The distributor could also be sending faulty signals to the computer, resulting in poor ignition timing.

An additional problem that occurs when diagnosing any electronic part is that the part itself cannot be accurately tested. Most electronic parts are completely sealed and, because of complex, interlocking circuitry, cannot be checked at their input and output connections.

This problem can be overcome by using a logical procedure called the process of elimination. In other words, if every related part checks out okay, it must be the electronic part that is bad. This means thoroughly checking every component in a system, without assuming anything, as well as checking for such basic factors as proper current supply and good grounds.

CUSTOMER CARE

When a computer system component is replaced, it is possible that the vehicle runs poorly for a short time while the computer readjusts to the new component. This adjustment period usually lasts for about 5 miles, but if you do not explain this to your customers, they might blame you for the temporary poor performance (surging, high idle, hesitation).

One way to save your reputation and avoid this situation is to erase the memory or road test the vehicle (at least 5 miles) before releasing the vehicle to the customer. The computer's memory can be erased by disconnecting the battery or following the manufacturer's specific instructions. In some systems, for example, pulling the microprocessor fuse out for 10 seconds erases previously learned information without causing a complete power failure. This comes in handy, especially if your customer has an electronically tuned radio with a digital clock and preset channels that must be reprogrammed each time system power is lost.

This is also true of seat position, climate control settings, and other driver programmable options. Again while you must advise that he or she must reprogram these accessories, it would be better to record these settings before beginning the job and reprogram them before delivery.

❏ ISOLATING COMPUTERIZED ENGINE CONTROL PROBLEMS

Determining which part or area of an computerized engine control system is defective requires having a thorough knowledge of how the system works and following the logical troubleshooting process previously explained.

There are many variations in the operation of electronic engine controls. Therefore, always consult the specific applications chapters in the factory service manual before beginning any diagnosis and repair. However, here are some guidelines to follow.

Electronic engine control problems are usually caused by defective sensors and, to a lesser extent, output devices. The logical procedure in most cases is, therefore, to check the input sensors and wiring first, then the output devices and their wiring, and, finally the computer.

Most late-model computerized engine controls have self-diagnosis capabilities. A malfunction in any sensor, output device, or in the computer itself is stored in the computer's memory as a trouble code. Stored codes can be retrieved and the indicated problem areas checked further.

Systems without self-diagnostics must be checked out by the process of elimination. All possible causes of the problem that can be are tested. If the fault is not found, the components that cannot be tested may be malfunctioning or faulty.

Four methods can be used to check individual components.

VISUAL CHECKS This means looking for obvious problems. Any part that is burned, broken, cracked, corroded, or has any other visible problem must be replaced before continuing the diagnosis. Examples of visible problems include disconnected sensor vacuum hoses and broken or disconnected wiring.

OHMMETER CHECKS Most sensors and output devices can be checked with an ohmmeter. For example, Figure 24-20 shows an ohmmeter used to check a temperature sensor. Usually the ohmmeter reading is low on a cold engine and high or infinity on a hot engine. However, there are exceptions, so always check the service manual.

Output devices such as coils or motors can also be checked with an ohmmeter.

VOLTMETER CHECKS Many sensors, output devices, and their wiring can be diagnosed by checking the voltage to them, and in some cases, from them. Even some oxygen sensors can be checked in this manner.

SUBSTITUTION Substitution is the last resort when diagnosing a problem, but it can be necessary when there is no way to check the unit or if the checking procedure is inconclusive.

In most cases, a final check on the computer can be made only by substitution. Many vacuum, MAP, and barometric pressure sensors can only be checked by substitution. To substitute, replace the suspected part with a known good unit and recheck the system. If the system now operates normally, the original part is defective.

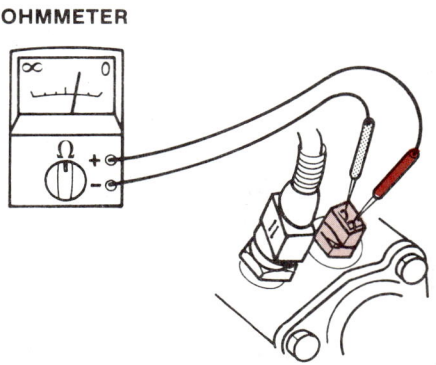

Figure 24-20 Checking a temperature sensor with an ohmmeter. *Courtesy of Toyota Motor Corp.*

SHOP TALK

Substitution can be an expensive way to test for problems since most parts suppliers do not allow electrical problems to be returned. To use this procedure, it is a good idea to build up a supply of known good parts such as ignition modules, electronic regulators, and computers to use as substitutes. These parts usually can be located at junkyards or body shops or from other sources.

Self-Diagnostic Systems

Today's computer-controlled systems are complicated. It would take endless amounts of time to diagnose these systems using precomputer control methods. For this reason, most computerized engine controls have self-diagnostic capabilities. By entering a self-test mode, the computer is able to evaluate the condition of the entire electronic engine control system, including itself. If problems are found, they are identified as either hard faults (on-demand) or intermittent failures. Each type of fault or failure is assigned a numerical trouble code that is stored in computer memory (Figure 24-21).

A hard fault means a problem has been found somewhere in the system at the time of the self-test. An intermittent problem, on the other hand, indicates a malfunction has occurred (for example, a poor connection causing an intermittent open or short), but is not present at the time of the self-test. As mentioned earlier in the chapter, non-volatile RAM allows intermittent faults to be stored for up to a specific number of ignition key on/off cycles. If the trouble does not reappear during that period, it is erased from the computer's memory.

There are various methods of assessing the trouble codes generated by the computer. Most manufacturers have diagnostic equipment designed to monitor and test the electronic components of their vehicles. Aftermarket companies also manufacture scan tools that have the capability to read and record the input and output signals passing to and from the computer. Another method of reading trouble codes is with an analog voltmeter. Some vehicles also flash trouble codes on dash lights or display them on CRT screens.

For each individual make and model, it is important that the technician consult the appropriate service manual to determine how trouble codes should be accessed and how to interpret the codes. The following sections give several examples of retrieving trouble codes, each using a different method.

Before reading self-diagnostic or trouble codes, do a visual check to make sure the problem is not a result of wear, loose connections, or vacuum hoses. Inspect the air cleaner, throttle body, or injection system. Do not forget the PCV system and vacuum hoses. Make sure the vapor canister is not flooded. Look at the wiring harnesses and connectors and the charging and alternator system. Also, check the connectors for signs of corrosion. The low level electrical signals in today's electronic circuits cannot tolerate the increased resistance caused by corrosion in contacts.

Unlocking Trouble Codes

Although parts in any computerized system are amazingly reliable, they do occasionally fail. Diagnostic charts in service manuals (Figure 24-22) help you through troubleshooting procedures in the proper order. Start at the top and follow the sequence down. There will be branches of the "tree"—yes or no, on or off, ok or not ok—to follow after making the check required in each step.

Tools to use when checking circuits, connections, sensors, and signals include the following.

- A digital VOM (volt/ohmmeter) with 10 megaohm impedance
- Dwell meter
- Tachometer
- Vacuum gauge and pump
- Scan tool analog VOM (used with some microcomputer systems)
- Service manuals with trouble code charts and diagnostic procedures

SENSOR TROUBLE CODES			
Sensor	Trouble Codes		
	GM	Ford	Chrysler
Oxygen (EGO)	13,44, 45,55	43,91, 92,93	21,51,52
Throttle Position (TPS)	21,22	23,53, 63,73	24
Engine Vacuum (MAP)	31,33,34	22,72	13,14
Barometric Pressure (BARO)	32	—	37
Coolant (ECT)	14,15	21,51,61	17,22
Knock	42,43	25	17 (some only)
Vehicle Speed (VSS)	24	—	15
Air Temperature (MAT, VAT, ACT)	23,25	24,54,64	23
Airflow (VAF, MAF)	33,34, 44,45	26,56, 66,76	—
EGR Valve (EGR, EVP)	—	31,32,33, 34,83,84	31

Figure 24-21 Different systems use different numerical codes to indicate problems. *Courtesy of* Counterman *magazine*

Computerized Engine Controls 619

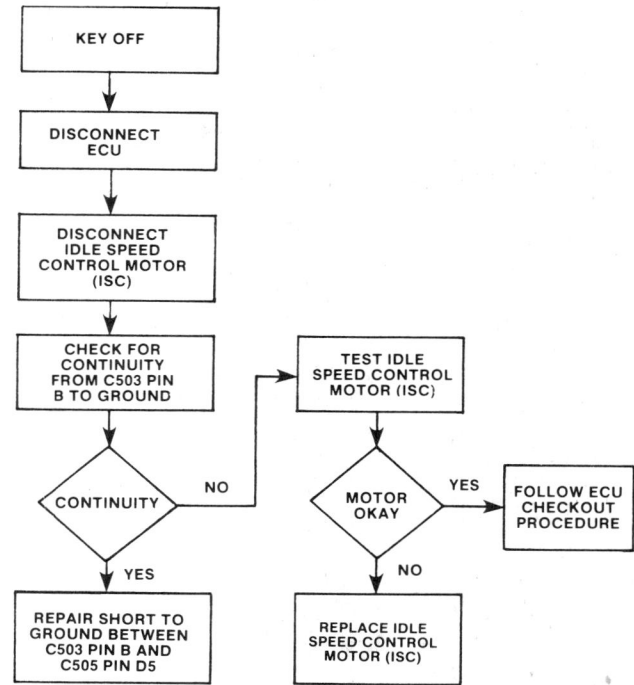

Figure 24-22 A diagnostic chart to be followed for a specific trouble code. *Courtesy of Chrysler Motors*

A spark tester, fuel pressure gauge, check engine light, a jumper wire with two alligator clips, and a nonpowered test light can also come in handy.

There are two things that would tell the driver there is a problem with some part of the computer system: the check engine, power loss, or service engine soon light, or the car simply does not start.

The check engine light (CEL) comes on normally for a few seconds when the key is turned on and during cranking. It should go off when the engine starts. The check engine light should not come back on unless the computer finds a problem. If it does come on, there is probably a trouble code stored in memory.

Self-diagnostic procedures and diagnostic or trouble codes differ with vehicle make and year. Each time the key is turned to the on position, the system does a self-check. The self-check makes sure that all of the bulbs, fuses, and electronic modules are working. If the self-test finds a problem, it might store a code for later servicing. It may also instruct the computer to turn on a trouble code light to show that service is needed.

General Motors' Systems

The main components of General Motors' CCC onboard diagnostic system include the electronic control module (ECM), a check engine or service engine soon warning light, and an assembly line communications link (ALCL). The check engine warning light serves two purposes (Figure 24-23). First, it is a signal to the vehicle operator that a detectable CCC failure has occurred. Secondly, it can also be used by a technician to aid in the location of system malfunctions.

Figure 24-23 GM's CCC system warning light.

To find the problem, you must perform a diagnostic circuit check to be sure the diagnostic system is working. Turn the ignition key on, but do not start the engine. If the check engine light does not come on, follow the diagnostic chart in the service manual. If the check engine light comes on, ground the diagnostic test terminal. This terminal is located on the ALCL connector (Figure 24-24). Connect pin A (A ground) to pin B (test terminal). Watch the check engine light to see if it displays code 12. Code 12 (think of it as 1, 2) is one flash, a short pause and two flashes (Figure 24-25). If the computer's diagnostic program is working properly, it flashes code 12 three times. If code 12 does not appear, follow the diagnostic chart in the manual. The system then displays any fault codes in the same manner.

Codes are identified through the flashing CEL as follows. The number of times the light flashes on before it pauses tells the number to which it refers. In other words, if the CEL flash like this: "on-off-on-off-on-off, pause," that means number 3 because it was on three times before it paused. If it flashed "on-off-on-off, pause," that means number 2. If it flashes "on-off, pause," that means number 1.

Because each code has two numbers to it, such as 12, 23, or 32, the flashes are read as a set. This means you always see two series of flashes separated by a pause: first number, pause, second number. As an example, a code 32 causes the light to go: "on-off-on-off-on-off" (it is on three times, which means the first number is 3), "pause, on-off-on-off" (it is on two times, which means the second number is 2). Together, they result in the number 32. The sequence repeats itself three times.

If the ECM has stored more than one trouble code, the codes flash starting with the lowest number code first and then work their way to the highest number code. For example, if the codes were 13 and 24, then 13 would flash first, then 24 would flash. Keep in mind that you have to watch closely while you do this.

If the ECM is good, the first code flashes when the connector is grounded and turn on the key is going to be twelve (12). This is the tachometer code. It is a normal condition when the key is on but the engine is

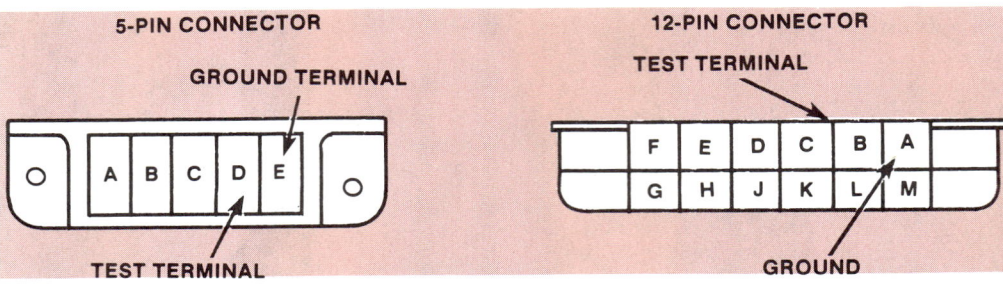

Figure 24-24 To initiate self-diagnostics, connect ground terminal and test terminal on ALCL connector.

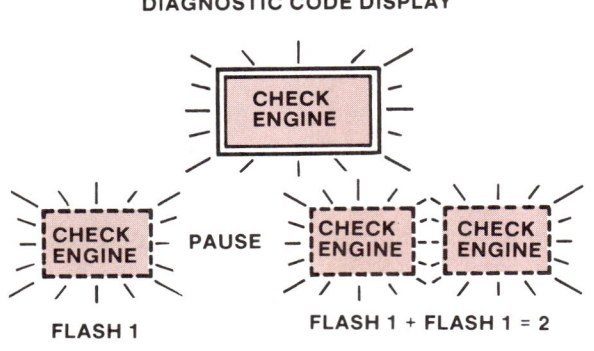

Figure 24-25 The check engine light signals the codes. Code 12 is a signal that the computer's diagnostic program is working properly. *Courtesy of General Motors Corp.*

not running. If a code 12 is not received, then there is something wrong in the ALDL or related circuits.

Once the codes have been identified, consult the service manual (Figure 24-26). Each code directs you to a specific troubleshooting tree. If you have a code, follow the tree exactly. Never try to skip a step, or you'll be certain to miss the problem. This is because, even though the codes may mean the same thing, how you trace the problems is different for different cars. This is one of the main reasons a manual for the car on which you are working is needed.

A hand-held scan tool (Figure 24-27) can be used by itself or in conjunction with CEL. When using a scan tool, follow the manufacturer's directions to the letter.

After correcting all faults or problems, clear the ECM memory of any current codes by pulling the ECM fuse at the fuse panel for 10 seconds. Then, to make sure the codes have cleared remove the test terminal ground, and set the parking brake. Put transmission in park, and run engine for 2 to 5 minutes. Watch the check engine light. If the light comes on again, ground the test lead and note the flashing trouble code. If no light comes on, check the codes recorded earlier, if any.

It is a good idea to give the vehicle a road test. Some parts such as the vehicle speed sensor do not show any problems with the engine just idling.

Chrysler's System

As far as basic system operation is concerned, Chrysler's engine control system is typical of most

Code 11 System "pass"
Code 13 RPM out of spec (normal idle)
Code 14 Profile ignition pickup erratic (continuous test)
Code 15 ROM test failed
Code 16 RPM too low (fuel lean test)
Code 22 MAP out of range
Code 23 TPS out of range
Code 25 Knock not sensed in test
Code 32 EGR not controlling
Code 34 No EGR flow
Code 36 Fuel always lean (at idle)
Code 44 Air management system inoperative
Code 45 Air always upstream
Code 46 Air not always bypassed
Code 48 Injectors imbalanced
Code 53 TPS input too high
Code 56 MAF (VAF) input too high
Code 61 ETC (coolant sensor) too low
Code 65 Electrical charging over voltage
Code 66 MAF (VAF) input too low
Code 67 Neutral drive switch—drive or accelerator on (engine off)
Code 73 No TPS change during "goose" test
Code 81 Thermactor air by-pass (TAB) circuit fault
Code 82 Thermactor air diverter (TAD) circuit fault
Code 87 Fuel pump circuit fault
Code 88 Throttle kicker circuit fault (5.0L)
Code 89 Exhaust heat control valve circuit fault
Code 91 Right EGO (oxygen sensor) always lean
Code 92 Right EGO always rich
Code 93 Right EGO cool down occurred
Code 97 RPM drop (with fuel lean) but right EGO rich
Code 98 RPM drop (with fuel rich) but right EGO lean

Figure 24-26 These are typical GM trouble codes. Check the service manual for information on a specific model. *Courtesy of General Motors Corp.*

Figure 24-27 Use of the hand-held scan tool for diagnostic testing.

Computerized Engine Controls   621

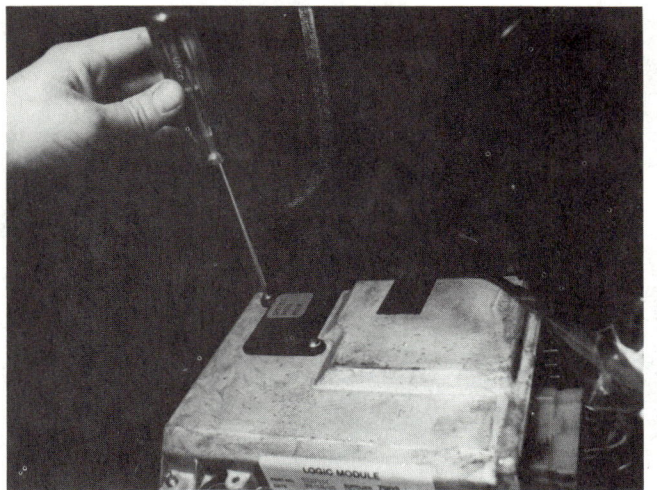

Figure 24-28   Logic module location.

Figure 24-29   Power module location.

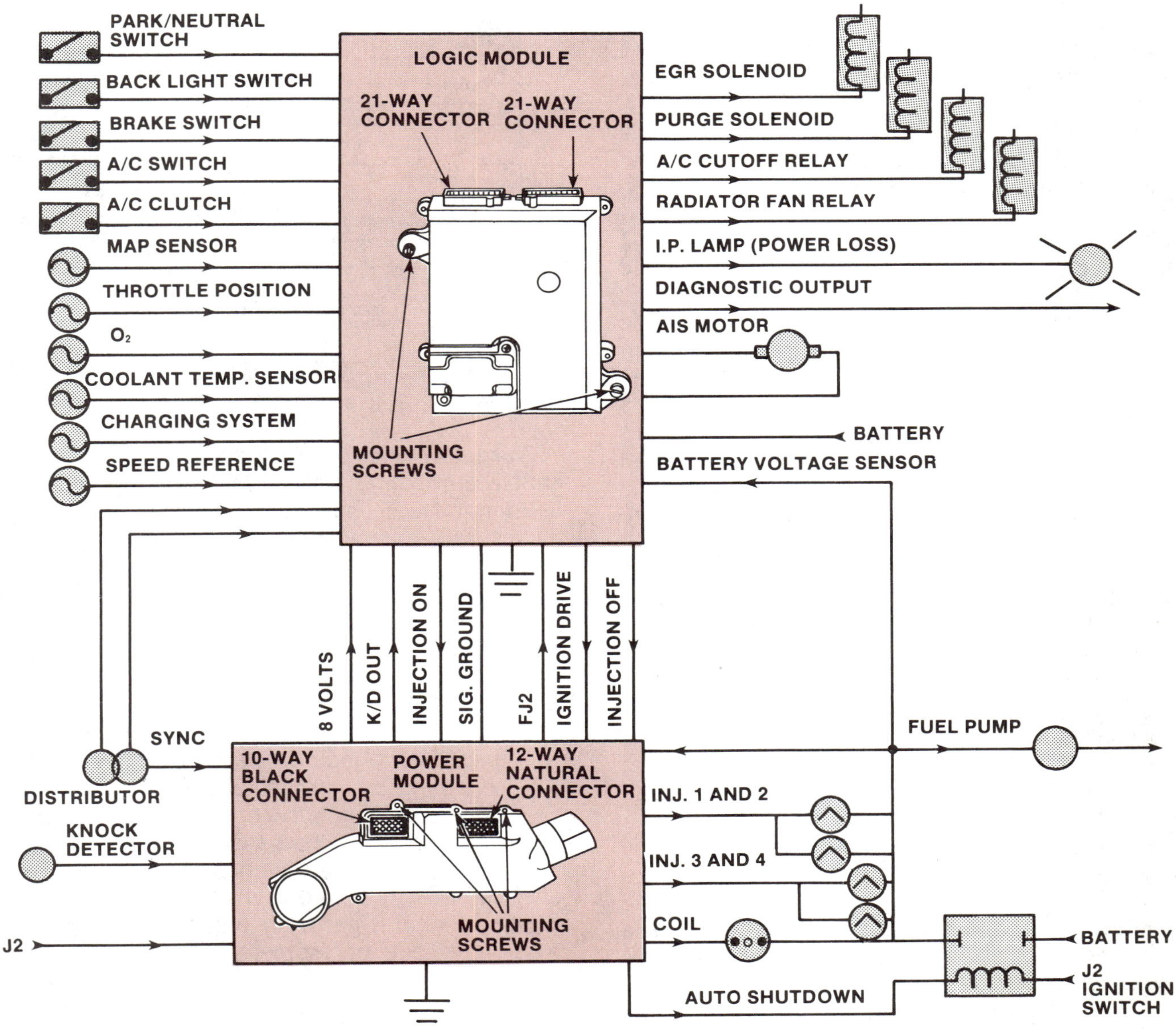

Figure 24-30   Chrysler's electronic engine control system with self-diagnosis.

computer-controlled designs. At the heart of Chrysler's computer-controlled system is a digital preprogrammed microprocessor known as the logic module (LM). From its location behind the right front kick pad (in the passenger compartment), the LM issues commands affecting fuel delivery, ignition timing, idle speed, and the operation of various emission control devices (Figure 24-28).

To accomplish all these tasks, the logic module operates in conjunction with a subordinate control unit called the power module (PM). The power module, located inside the engine compartment (Figure 24-29), is given the responsibility of controlling the injector and ignition coil ground circuit (based on the LM's commands). It is also in charge of supplying the ground to the automatic shutdown relay (ASD). The ASD relay controls the voltage supply to the fuel pump, logic module, injector, and coil drive circuits and is energized through the PM when the ignition switch is turned on.

Under normal operating conditions, the LM bases its decisions on information from several input devices (Figure 24-30).

From the information it receives, the logic module calculates the injector's pulse width, determines precise spark advance, maintains proper idle speed, governs turbo boost, controls the EGR and purge solenoids, and directs the operation of the electric cooling fan (among other things). When a computer-related failure occurs, the LM switches to a limp-in mode.

Chrysler has a simple method for checking trouble codes. Without starting the engine, turn the ignition key on and off three times within 5 seconds, ending with it on. The check engine or power loss light glows a short time to test the bulb, then starts flashing. Count the first set of flashes as tens. There is a half second pause before the light starts flashing again. This time count by ones. Add the two sets of flashes together to obtain the trouble code. For example, 3 flashes, a half second pause, followed by 5 flashes would be read as code 35. Watch carefully, because each trouble code is displayed only once. Look the code up in the service manual. This tells you which circuit to check. Once the trouble codes are flashed, the computer signals a code 55. If the light does not flash at all, there are no trouble codes stored. The problem could be a mechanical one, or the computer could be defective. Keep in mind that replacing the computer should be one of the last options. Check everything else first.

The same diagnostic or trouble code tests can be done using a scan tool. Connect the tool to the diagnostic connectors on the left fender apron. Follow the same sequence with the ignition key. The trouble codes are displayed on the scan tool readout. You can also check the circuits, switches, and relays with the scan tool. The service manual contains the troubleshooting trees (Figure 24-31) to continue your diagnosis of the problem.

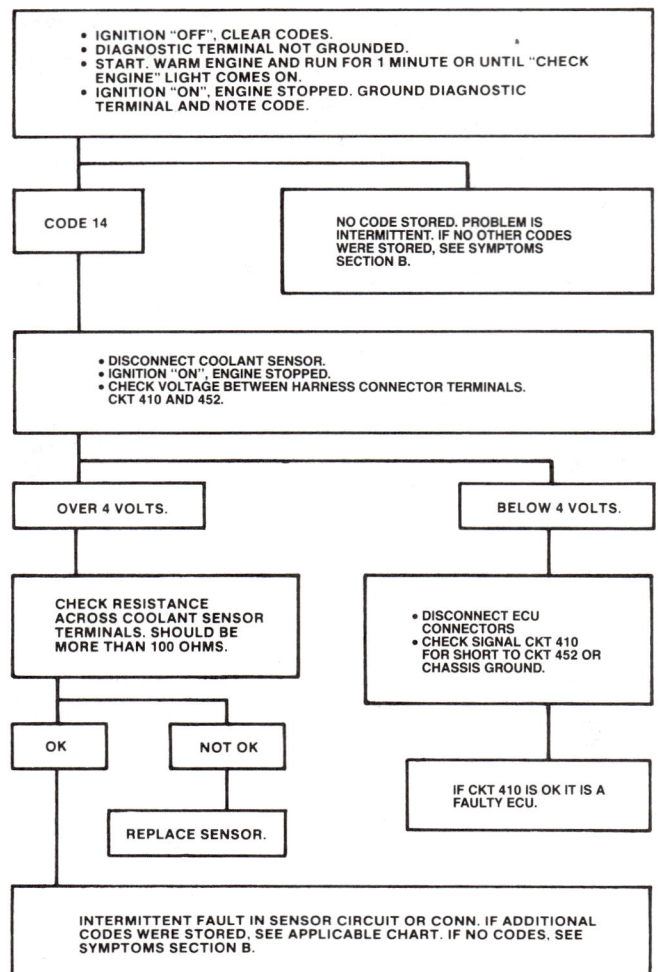

Figure 24-31 Typical manual troubleshooting tree.

A code 53 points to a problem with the logic module or SME controller. If a code 53 is received, turn off the ignition and recheck all electrical connections. Repeat the test procedure. If another code 53 is received, the module may be faulty.

Ford's System

> **USING SERVICE MANUALS**
>
> In this book we have described and illustrated service manual logic diagrams called tree charts. These so-called road maps are especially valuable in electronic service. However, the diagnostic procedure chart shown in Figure 24-32 for the Ford ECA is designed to make it easy to move quickly from one check to the next. The information is generally organized by system, trouble code, or test meter reading.

The main brain of the Ford's EEC-IV is a microcomputer unit called an electronic control assembly (ECA). Like the other computer-controlled systems discussed,

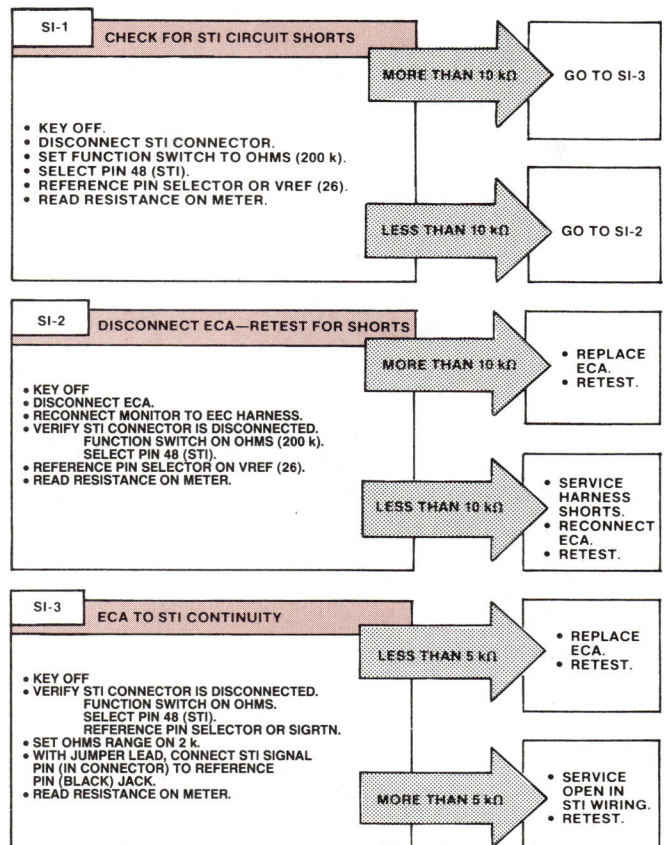

Figure 24-32 Typical service manual diagnostic procedure chart. *Courtesy of Ford Motor Co.*

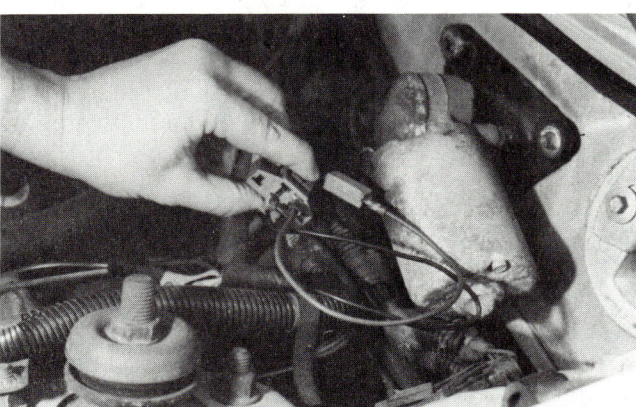

Figure 24-33 Self-test connectors are used to connect test equipment to the system's computer.

the ECA is endowed with self-diagnostic capabilities. By entering a mode known as self-test (Figure 24-33), the computer is able to evaluate the condition of the entire electronic system, including itself. If problems are found, they show up as either hard faults (on demand) or intermittent failures.

On 1988 and newer model vehicles, the diagnostic or trouble codes are displayed by the CEL on the instrument panel. The Ford self-test diagnostic procedure can be broken down into four parts.

Computerized Engine Controls 623

- Key on/engine off: checks system inputs for hard faults (malfunctions that occur during the self-test) and intermittent faults (malfunctions that occurred sometime prior to the self-test and were stored in memory).
- Computed ignition timing check: determines the ECA's ability to advance or retard ignition timing. This check is made while the self-test is activated and the engine is running.
- Engine running segment: checks system output for hard faults only.
- Continuous monitoring test (wiggle test): allows the technician to look for and set intermittent faults while the engine is running.

Within these four tests, there are six types of service codes. There are on-demand codes, keep-alive memory codes, separator codes, dynamic response codes, fast codes, and engine I.D. codes. To understand what you are dealing with when the codes start to display, a brief explanation of each type is necessary.

On-demand codes are used to identify hard faults. As mentioned earlier, a hard fault means that a system failure has been detected and is still present at the time of testing. The term on-demand simply means a technician is asking the computer if a problem exists right now. That is, the computer locates them while it is running its own self-test.

Keep-alive memory codes mean that a malfunction was noted sometime during the last 20 vehicle warm-ups but is not present now (if it were, it would be recorded as a hard fault). The continuous memory code comes on after an approximate ten second delay. Make the on-demand code repairs first. Once you have completed repairs, repeat the key on, engine off test. If all the parts are repaired correctly, a pass code of 11 should be received.

A separator code (10) indicates that the on-demand codes are over and the memory codes are about to begin. The separator code occurs as part of the key-on engine-off segment of the self-test only.

When a code 10 appears during the engine running segment of the self-test, it is referred to as a dynamic response code. The dynamic response code is a signal to the technician to goose the throttle momentarily so that the ECA can verify the operation of the throttle position (TP) and manifold absolute pressure (MAP) sensors. Failure to respond to the dynamic code within 15 seconds after it appears sets a code 77 (operator did not do goose test).

Fast codes are of no value to the service technician unless he happens to have a scan tool that is capable of reading them. They are designed for factory use and are transmitted about 100 times faster than even a scan or Ford's star tester can read. On the voltmeter, fast codes cause the needle to rapidly pulse between zero and three volts. On the scan tester, the LED light flickers. Although fast codes have no practical use in the service

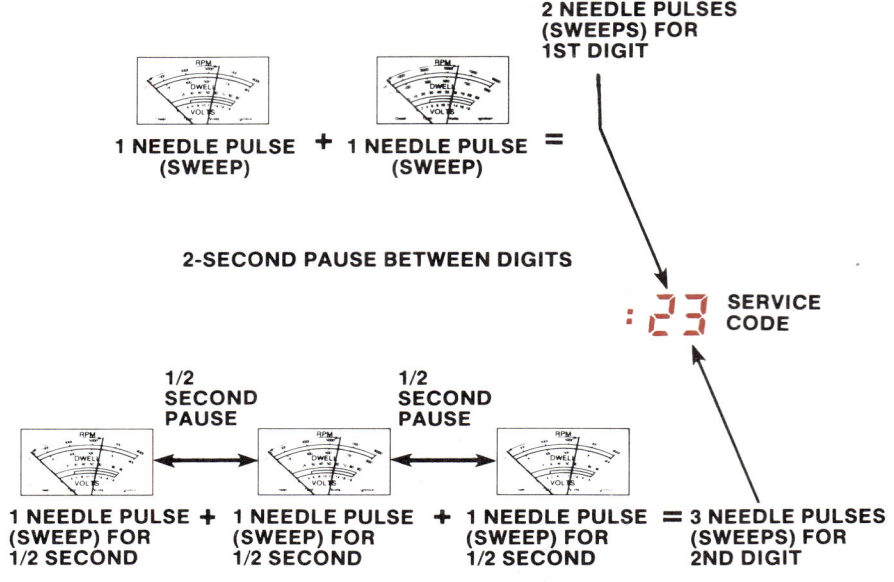

Figure 24-34 Reading an analog voltmeter and determining the service code.

bay, pay attention to when they occur so you know what is coming next. Fast codes appear twice during the entire self-test: once at the very beginning of the key-on/engine-off test (right before the on-demand codes) and again after the dynamic response code (prior to hard fault transmission).

Engine identification codes are used to tell automated assembly line equipment how many cylinders the engine has. Two needle pulses indicate a four-cylinder, three pulses a six-cylinder, and four pulses identify the engine as an eight-cylinder model. Engine I.D. codes appear at the beginning of the engine-running segment only.

Diagnostic codes can also be retreived using an analog volt-ohmmeter, a scan tool, or Ford star tester. When a service code is reported on the analog voltme-

ter for a function test, it represents itself as a pulsing or sweeping movement of the voltmeter (Figure 24-34). Therefore, a single-digit number of three is reported by three needle pulses (sweeps). However, as previously stated, a service code is represented by a two-digit number, such as 2-3. As a result, the self-test service code of 2-3 appears on the voltmeter as two needle pulses (sweeps). Then, after a two-second pause, the needle pulses (sweeps) three times. To activate the self-test mode, two jumper wires (about 6 inches long each) with male spade terminals and a voltmeter are needed (Figure 24-35).

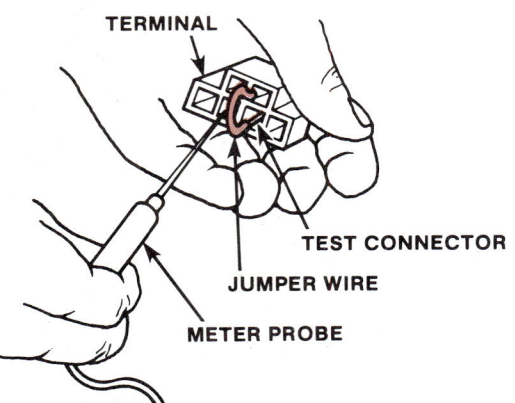

Figure 24-35 Checking a self-diagnostic connector with jumper wires and voltmeter probe.

CUSTOMER CARE

You have finished servicing the engine electronic control system and are ready to deliver the vehicle to the customer. This is a good time to make a final check of the electronic system. What you do not want to do is to release a car and then have the customer bring it back a few hours later because something is not right.

- Turn on the ignition. Does the check engine light stay on? If so, you go through the process of checking for diagnostic codes.
- If the CEL goes out, then listen to the engine. Does it sound normal? Do all the instruments and accessories work like they are supposed to?
- If everything seems okay here, take it for a test drive. Does it run right? Do all the systems work? Drive it for several miles, not

just around the block. Does the CEL come on? If there is a problem, it may take a few miles for the computer to detect it and store a code. This is why a customer often notices nothing for the first several miles after taking delivery of the car.
- If no problems show up by the time you have finished the test drive, it is a safe bet the car is okay.

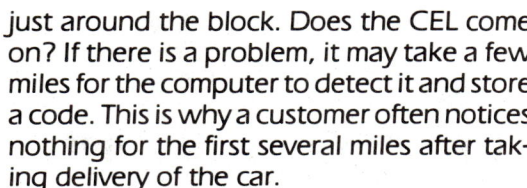

Case 1

Trouble code indicates that the computer is faulty (Chrysler code 53, Ford code 15, and General Motors code 54).

Computer modules seldom fail unless something on the vehicle puts an excess load on the unit. Therefore, you should never install a replacement computer without finding what caused it to fail. Otherwise, the replacement module could also be destroyed.

Once it has been determined that the computer should be replaced, follow these precautions.

1. Make sure that the ignition key is turned off.
2. Disconnect the battery ground cable and remove the fuse. It is necessary to eliminate all possibilities of static or stray voltage when you connect the new unit.
3. Disconnect the harness and remove the attaching bolts. Then, remove the computer unit.
4. Separate the multi-pin connector carefully from the computer itself, then remove the computer.
5. Some computers have removable calibration units that must be transferred to the new computer before installation.

Before installing the new computer, follow the step-by-step instructions for measuring the resistance between particular pins on the wiring harness. Computers rarely fail from internal problems. If any of the resistances do not match, test the subcircuits.

CAUTION: Static electricity, as mentioned earlier, can damage the calibration units. Do not open the package until you have grounded it and are ready to install it. Never touch the terminals on the part.

Summary

- The four major advantages of using electronic engine controls in a vehicle are better emissions, mileage, performance (power and driveability), and protection (durability).
- A typical electronic control system is made up of sensors, actuators, microcomputer, and related wiring.
- Most input sensors are variable resistance/reference types, switches, and thermistors.
- The microcomputer and its processors are the heart of the computerized engine control system.
- System strategy is a plan of how the computer will respond to all possible engine conditions. It is stored in the computer's permanent memory.
- The fail safe or limp-in mode allows the engine to operate if the computer loses a major input signal. The computer substitutes an input value for the lost sensor or input.
- Control loops are the cycles by which a process can be controlled by information received from input sensors, data computer processing, and out of specific commands to the output actuators.
- The three important control loops are the spark control system, fuel control system, and emission control system.
- Logical troubleshooting can involve either microcomputer logic flow, technician's logical diagnosis, or both.
- Electronic control components can be checked by visual inspection, ohmmeter and voltmeter checks, and by substitution of known good parts.
- Most computerized engine control systems have self-diagnostic capabilities. By entering a self-test mode, the microcomputer is able to evaluate the condition of the entire electronic engine control system, including itself.

 ## Review Questions

1. What advantages does the use of PROM chips offer?
2. What are self-diagnostics?
3. Describe the difference between an open and closed loop operation.
4. What devices may be involved in activating self-diagnosis and reading trouble codes?
5. Explain the use and importance of system strategy and look-up tables in the computerized control system.
6. When removing a PROM chip, Technician A uses a special removal tool. Technician B is careful not to touch the chip's legs. Who is correct?
   a. Technician A
   b. Technician B
   c. Both A and B
   d. Neither A nor B
7. Technician A says an oxygen sensor can be either a variable resistor or voltage-producing sensor. Technician B says an oxygen sensor is a thermistor sensor. Who is correct?
   a. Technician A
   b. Technician B

c. Both A and B
d. Neither A nor B

8. Technician A says that the oxygen sensor provides the major input during the open loop mode. Technician B says that the coolant temperature sensor controls open loop mode operation. Who is correct?
   a. Technician A
   b. Technician B
   c. Both A and B
   d. Neither A nor B

9. Which of the following inputs tells the microcomputer the make-up of the exhaust gas?
   a. MAP sensor
   b. high gear switch
   c. oxygen sensor
   d. throttle position sensor

10. All of the following statements about feedback control are correct except _____ .
    a. sensor input data are sent to the computer
    b. computer output is used to energize solenoids and other electrically-controlled devices
    c. the computer changes output in response to input data
    d. computer output signals are fed back into the computer as input data

11. Technician A says that electronic engine control problems are usually caused by defective sensors. Technician B says that most sensors and output devices can be checked with an ohmmeter. Who is correct?
    a. Technician A
    b. Technician B
    c. Both A and B
    d. Neither A nor B

12. Self-diagnostic systems provide _____ .
    a. computer codes that can be read on the dashboard
    b. computer codes that can be read on a tester
    c. both a and b
    d. neither a nor b

13. Technician A says that the power module in a Chrysler system is responsible for controlling the injector and ignition ground circuit. Technician B says that the logic module is responsible for supplying the ground to the automatic shutdown relay. Who is correct?
    a. Technician A
    b. Technician B
    c. Both A and B
    d. Neither A nor B

14. Technician A says that a code 11 on a Ford EEC-IV diagnostic system is referred to as a dynamic response code. Technician B says that a code 10 indicates that all the parts are repaired correctly. Who is correct?
    a. Technician A
    b. Technician B
    c. Both A and B
    d. Neither A nor B

15. A computer is capable of doing all of the following except _____ .
    a. receive input data
    b. process input data according to a program and monitor output action
    c. control the vehicle's operating conditions
    d. store data and information

16. The self-diagnostic feature of computer-controlled ignition systems displays _____ to identify trouble areas.
    a. trouble codes
    b. engine rpm
    c. torque specifications
    d. all of the above

17. Which of the following memory circuits is used to store trouble codes and other temporary information?
    a. read only memory
    b. programmed read only memory
    c. random access memory
    d. all of the above

18. When a sensor failure occurs in a computer control system, the computer enters a(n) _____ .
    a. fail safe or limp-in mode
    b. open loop mode of operation
    c. closed loop mode of operation
    d. none of the above

19. Which of the following are used to identify hard faults?
    a. on-demand codes
    b. keep-alive memory codes
    c. dynamic response codes
    d. fast codes

20. Technician A says that vehicles that do not have MAP or BARO sensors may use a vacuum sensor to provide engine load and speed change information. Technician B says that the vacuum sensor tells the microcomputer when vacuum is applied to the EGR valve. Who is correct?
    a. Technician A
    b. Technician B
    c. Both A and B
    d. Neither A nor B

SECTION 5
MANUAL TRANSMISSIONS AND TRANSAXLES

Chapter 25 Clutches
Chapter 26 Manual Transmissions and Transaxles
Chapter 27 Manual Transmission/Transaxle Service
Chapter 28 Drive Axles and Differentials

Transmissions/transaxles, drive axles, and differentials, perform the important task of manipulating the power produced by the engine and routing it to the driving wheels of the vehicle. Precision machined and fitted gearsets and shafts change the ratio of speed and power between the engine and drive axles. The flow of power is controlled through a manually-operated clutch and shift lever.

Transmission/transaxle service requires sound diagnostic skills plus the ability to work with intricate gearing and linkages. The material covered in Section 5 corresponds to the ASE certification test on manual drivetrain and axles.

25 CLUTCHES

Objectives

- Describe the various clutch components and their functions.
- Name and explain the advantages of the different types of pressure plate assemblies.
- Name the different types of clutch linkages.
- List the safety precautions that should be followed during clutch servicing.
- Explain how to perform basic clutch maintenance.
- Name the six most common problems that occur with clutches.
- Explain the basics of servicing a clutch assembly.

The clutch is located between the transmission and engine where it provides a mechanical coupling between the engine's flywheel and the transmission's input shaft. The driver operates the clutch through a linkage that extends from the passenger compartment to the bell housing (also called the clutch housing) between the engine and the transmission.

All manual transmissions require a clutch to engage or disengage the transmission. If the vehicle had no clutch and the engine was always connected to the transmission, the engine would stop every time the vehicle was brought to a stop. The clutch allows the engine to idle while the vehicle is stopped. It also allows for easy shifting between gears. (Of course, all of this applies to manual transaxles as well.)

The clutch engages the transmission gradually by allowing a certain amount of slippage between the input and the output shafts on the clutch. Figure 25-1 shows the components needed to do this: the flywheel, clutch disc, pressure plate assembly, clutch release bearing (or throwout bearing), and the clutch fork.

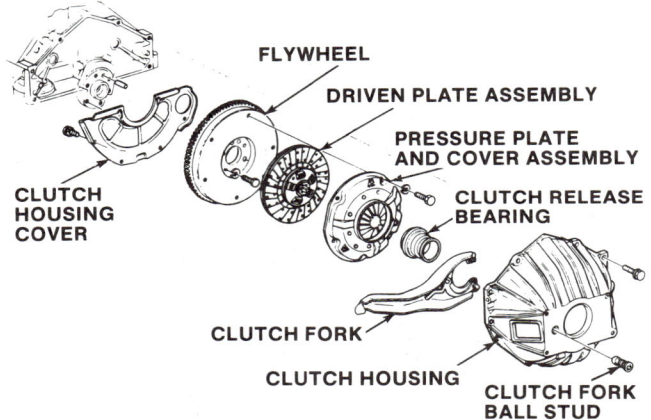

Figure 25-1 Major parts of a clutch assembly. *Courtesy of General Motors Corp.*

☐ OPERATION

The basic principle of engaging a clutch is demonstrated in Figure 25-2. The flywheel and the pressure plate are the drive or driving members of the clutch. The driven member connected to the transmission input shaft is the clutch disc, also called the friction disc. As long as the clutch is disengaged (clutch pedal depressed), the drive members turn independently of the driven member, and the engine is disconnected from the transmission. However, when the clutch is

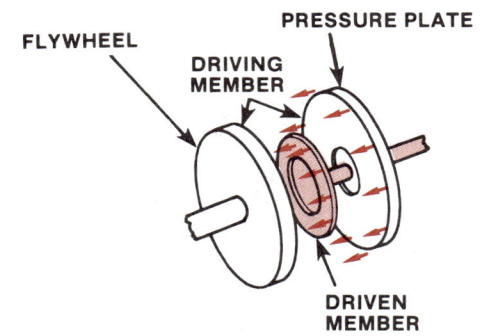

Figure 25-2 When the clutch is engaged, the driven member is squeezed between the two driving members. The transmission is connected to the driven member. *Courtesy of General Motors Corp.*

engaged (clutch pedal released), the pressure plate moves in the direction of the arrows and the clutch disc is bound between the two revolving drive members and forced to turn at the same speed.

Flywheel

The flywheel, an important part of the engine, is also the main driving member of the clutch. It is normally made of nodular cast iron, which has a high graphite content to lubricate the clutch engagement. The rear surface of the flywheel is a friction surface machined very flat to assure smooth clutch engagement. The flywheel has two sets of bolt holes drilled into it. The inner set is used to fasten the flywheel to the crankshaft, and the outer set provides a mounting place for the pressure plate assembly. A bore in the center of the flywheel and crankshaft holds the pilot bushing, which supports the front end of the transmission input shaft and maintains alignment with the engine's crankshaft. Sometimes a ball or roller needle bearing is used instead of a pilot bushing.

Clutch Disc

The clutch disc receives the driving motion from the flywheel and pressure plate assembly and transmits that motion to the transmission input shaft. The parts of a clutch disc are shown in Figure 25-3.

There are two types of friction facings. Molded friction facings are preferred because they withstand greater pressure plate loading force without damage. Woven friction facings are used when additional cushioning action is needed for clutch engagement. Until recently, the material that was molded or woven into facings was predominantly asbestos. Now, because of the hazards associated with asbestos, other materials such as paper-base and ceramics are being used instead. Particles of cotton, brass, rope, and wire are added to prolong the life of the clutch disc and provide torsional strength.

Grooves are cut across the face of the friction facings. This promotes clean disengagement of the driven disc from the flywheel and pressure plate; it also promotes better cooling. The facings are riveted to wave springs, also called cushioning springs, which cause the contact pressure on the facings to rise gradually as the springs flatten out when the clutch is engaged. These springs eliminate chatter when the clutch is engaged and also reduce the chance of the clutch disc sticking to the flywheel and pressure plate surfaces when the clutch is disengaged. The wave springs and friction facings are fastened to the steel disc.

The clutch disc has a flexible center to absorb such things as crankshaft vibration, abrupt clutch engagement, and driveline shock. Torsional coil springs allow the disc to rotate slightly in relation to the pressure plate while they absorb the torque forces. The number and tension of these springs is determined by engine torque and vehicle weight. Stop pins limit this torsional movement to approximately 3/8 inch.

Pressure Plate Assembly

The purpose of the pressure plate assembly is twofold. First, it must squeeze the clutch disc onto the flywheel with sufficient force to transmit engine torque efficiently. Second, it must move away from the clutch disc so that the clutch disc can stop rotating, even though the flywheel and pressure plate continue to rotate.

Basically, there are two types of pressure plate assemblies: those with coil springs and those with a diaphragm spring. Both types have a steel cover that bolts to the flywheel and acts as a housing to hold the parts together. In both, there is also the pressure plate, which is a heavy, flat ring made of cast iron. The assemblies differ in the manner they move the pressure plate toward and away from the clutch disc.

Coil Spring Pressure Plate Assembly

A coil spring pressure plate assembly, shown in Figure 25-4, uses coil springs and release levers to move the pressure plate back and forth. The springs exert pressure to hold the pressure plate tightly against the clutch disc. This forces the clutch disc against the flywheel. The release levers release the holding force of the springs. There are usually three of them. Each one has two pivot points. One of these pivot points attaches the lever to a pedestal cast into the pressure plate and the other to a release lever yoke bolted to the cover (Figure 25-5). The levers pivot on the pedestals and release lever yokes to move the pressure plate through its engagement and disengagement operations. To disengage the clutch, the release bearing pushes the inner ends of the release levers forward toward the flywheel. The release lever yokes act as fulcrums for the levers and the outer ends of the release levers move backward, pulling the pressure plate away from the clutch disc.

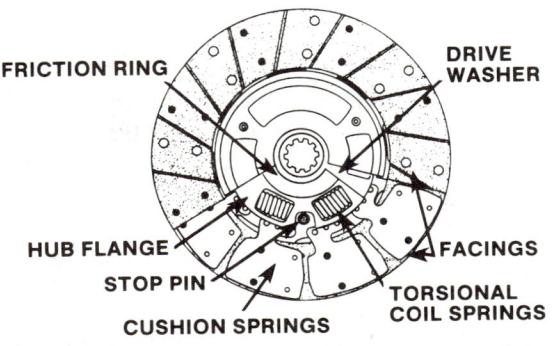

Figure 25-3 Parts of a clutch disc. *Courtesy of General Motors Corp.*

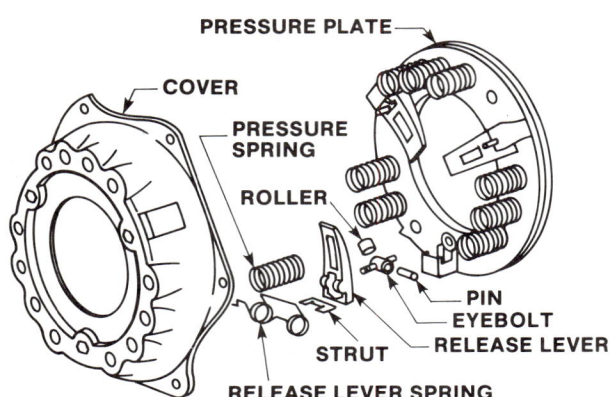

Figure 25-4 Parts of a coil spring pressure plate. *Courtesy of General Motors Corp.*

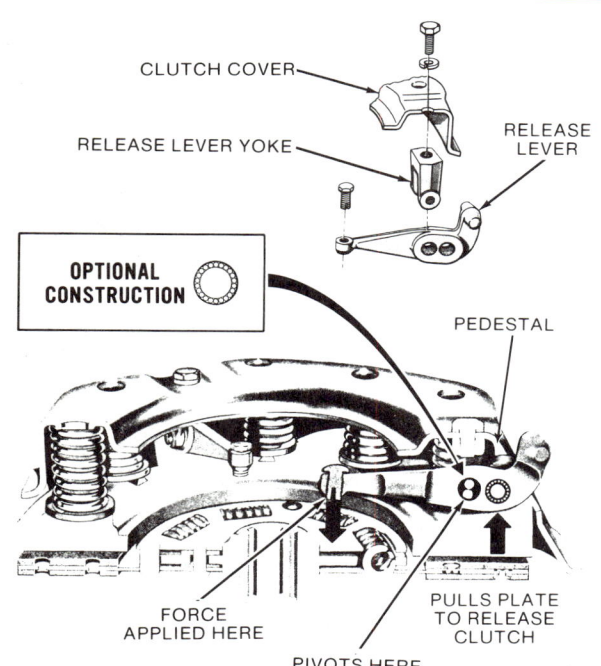

Figure 25-5 Release levers remove the coil spring's pressure on the pressure plate. *Courtesy of Ford Motor Co.*

This action compresses the coil springs and disengages the clutch disc from the driving members.

When the clutch is engaged, the release bearing moves backward toward the transmission. Without this force against the release levers, the coil springs are able to push the pressure plate and clutch disc against the flywheel with sufficient force to resist slipping.

Semicentrifugal Pressure Plate

A variation of the coil spring pressure plate is the semicentrifugal pressure plate. These assemblies increase or decrease the force holding the clutch disc against the flywheel according to engine speed. One design is the same as the coil spring pressure plate assembly except its release levers are weighted to take advantage of engine speed and centrifugal force (Fig-

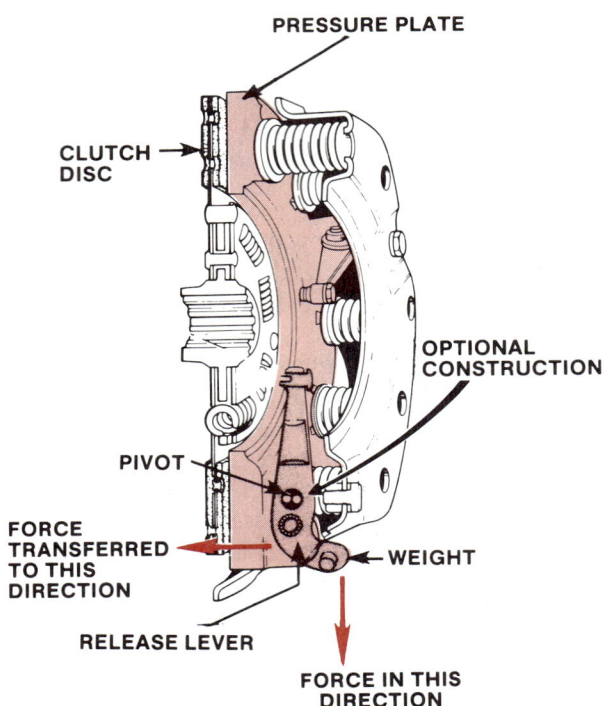

Figure 25-6 Semicentrifugal pressure plate. *Courtesy of Ford Motor Co.*

ure 25-6). Another type uses rollers between the release levers and the pressure plate cover. As engine speed increases, centrifugal force wedges the rollers between the cover and release levers and increases the plate loading of the clutch disc. Both designs permit the use of coil springs with less tension, since the pressure created from the centrifugal force compensates for the loss. Thus, less pedal effort is required to operate semicentrifugal pressure plate assemblies.

The following are common advantages of all pressure plate assemblies that use coil springs.

- They cleanly disengage the clutch at high engine speeds because of the high force exerted by the pressure plate springs.
- They offer great flexibility and can be used on various applications since the coil springs can be changed to increase or decrease pressure plate holding force.

Diaphragm Spring Pressure Plate Assembly

The diaphragm spring-type pressure plate assembly relies on a cone-shaped diaphragm spring between the pressure plate and the pressure plate cover to move the pressure plate back and forth. The diaphragm spring (sometimes called a Belleville spring) is a single, thin sheet of metal that works in the same manner as the bottom of an oil can. The metal yields when pressure is applied to it. When the pressure is removed, the metal springs back to its original shape. The center portion of the diaphragm spring is slit into numerous fingers that act as release levers (Figure 25-7).

Clutches   631

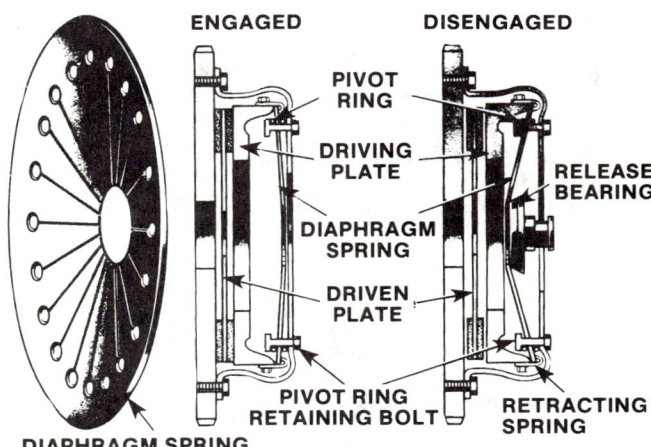

Figure 25-7 Diaphragm spring-type pressure plate assembly. *Courtesy of Chevrolet Motor Division—GMC*

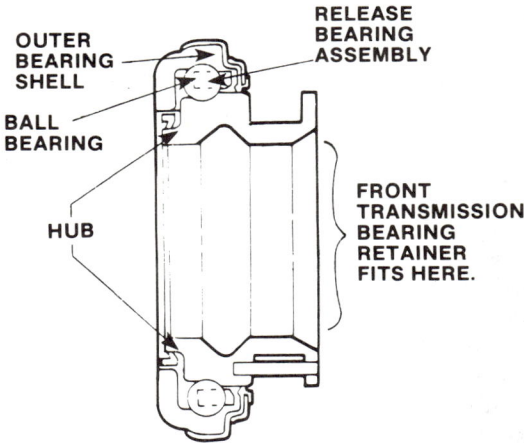

Figure 25-8 Typical clutch release bearing. *Courtesy of General Motors Corp.*

During clutch disengagement, these fingers are moved forward by the release bearing. The diaphragm spring pivots over the fulcrum ring (also called the pivot ring), and its outer rim moves away from the flywheel. The retracting springs pull the pressure plate away from the driven disc and disengage the clutch.

When the clutch is engaged, the release bearing and the fingers of the diaphragm spring move toward the transmission. As the diaphragm pivots over the pivot ring, its outer rim forces the pressure plate against the clutch disc so that the clutch is engaged to the flywheel.

Diaphragm spring pressure plate assemblies have the following advantages over other types of assemblies.

- Compactness
- Less weight
- Fewer moving parts to wear out
- Little pedal effort required from the operator
- Provide a balanced force around the pressure plate so that rotational unbalance is reduced.
- Clutch disc slippage is less likely to occur. Mileage builds because the force holding the clutch disc to the flywheel does not change throughout its service life.

Clutch Release Bearing

The clutch release bearing, also called a throwout bearing, is usually a sealed, prelubricated ball bearing (Figure 25-8). Its function is to smoothly and quietly move the pressure plate release levers or diaphragm spring through the engagement and disengagement process.

The release bearing is mounted on an iron casting called a hub, which slides on a hollow shaft at the front of the transmission housing. This hollow shaft, shown in Figure 25-9, is part of the transmission bearing retainer.

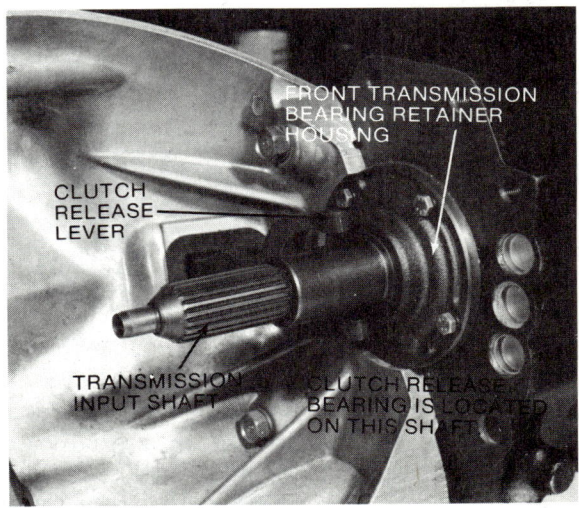

Figure 25-9 The clutch release bearing assembly slides on the hollow shaft of the front transmission bearing retainer housing.

To disengage the clutch, the release bearing is moved forward on its shaft by the clutch fork. As the release bearing contacts the release levers or diaphragm spring of the pressure plate assembly, it begins to rotate with the rotating pressure plate assembly. As the release bearing continues forward, the clutch disc is disengaged from the pressure plate and flywheel.

To engage the clutch, the release bearing slides to the rear of the shaft. The pressure plate moves forward and traps the clutch disc against the flywheel to transmit engine torque to the transmission input shaft. Once the clutch is fully engaged, the release bearing is normally stationary.

Rotating Release Bearing

Self-adjusting clutch linkages, used on many vehicles, apply just enough tension to the clutch control cable to keep a constant light pressure against the release bearing. As a result, the release bearing is kept in contact with the release levers or diaphragm spring of the rotating pressure plate assembly. The release bearing rotates with the pressure plate.

Clutch Fork

The clutch fork is a forked lever that pivots on a ball stud located in an opening in the bellhousing (Figure 25-10). The forked end slides over the hub of the release bearing and the small end protrudes from the bellhousing and connects to the clutch linkage and clutch pedal. The clutch fork moves the release bearing and hub back and forth during engagement and disengagement.

Clutch Linkage

The clutch linkage is a series of parts that connects the clutch pedal to the clutch fork. It is through the clutch linkage that the operator controls the engagement and disengagement of the clutch assembly smoothly and with little effort.

Clutch linkage can be mechanical or hydraulic. Mechanical clutch linkage can be divided into two types: shaft and lever linkage and cable linkage.

Shaft and Lever Linkage

The shaft and lever clutch linkage consists of the various shafts, levers, adjustable rods, and pivots that transmit clutch pedal motion to the clutch fork (Figure 25-11). A rod connects the clutch pedal to the lever and shaft assembly. When the upper lever is moved by the clutch pedal, the shaft rotates and moves the lower lever, which is connected to a pushrod that is attached to the clutch fork. The linkage assembly is located between the chassis and bellhousing, near the lower rear part of the engine block.

Cable Linkage

A cable linkage can perform the same controlling action as the shaft and lever linkage, but with fewer parts. The clutch cable system does not take up much room. It also has the advantage of flexible installation so it can be routed around the power brake and steering units. These advantages help to make it the most commonly used clutch linkage.

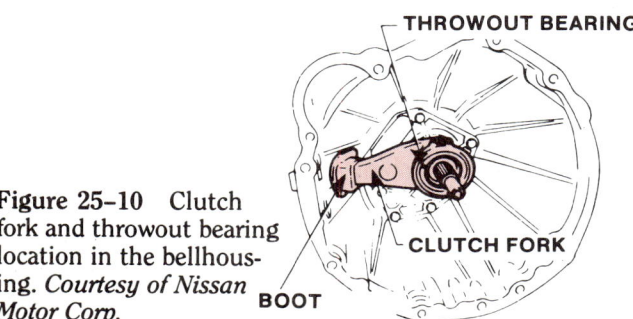

Figure 25-10 Clutch fork and throwout bearing location in the bellhousing. *Courtesy of Nissan Motor Corp.*

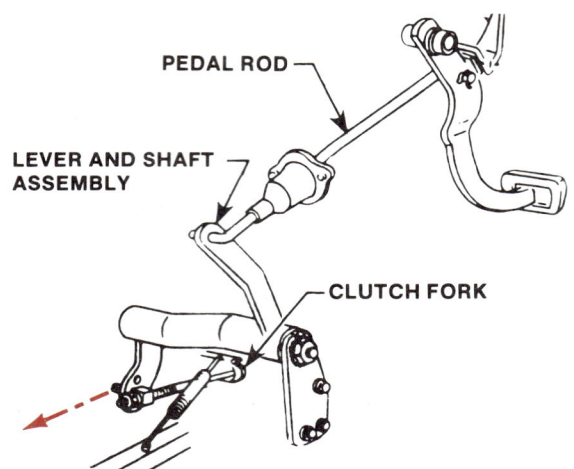

Figure 25-11 Shaft and lever clutch linkage. *Courtesy of Buick Motor Division—GMC*

The clutch cable (Figure 25-12) is made of braided wire. The upper end is connected to the top of the clutch pedal arm, and the lower end is fastened to the clutch fork. It is designed with a flexible outer housing that is fastened at the fire wall and the clutch housing.

When the clutch pedal is pushed to the disengaged position, it pivots on the pedal shaft and pulls the inner cable through the outer housing. This action moves the clutch fork forward to disengage the clutch. The pressure plate springs and springs on the clutch pedal provide the force to move the cable back when the clutch pedal is released.

SELF-ADJUSTING CLUTCH Self-adjusting clutch mechanisms monitor clutch pedal play and automatically adjust it when necessary.

Usually the self-adjusting clutch mechanism is a ratcheting mechanism located at the top of the clutch pedal behind the dash panel (Figure 25-13). The ratchet is designed with a pawl and toothed segment, and a pawl tension spring is used to keep the pawl in contact with the toothed segment. The pawl allows the toothed segment to move in only one direction in relation to the pawl.

The clutch cable is guided around and fastened to the toothed segment, which is free to rotate in one direction (backwards) independently of the clutch pedal. The tension spring pulls the toothed segment backwards.

When the clutch cable develops slack due to stretching and clutch disc wear, the cable is adjusted automatically when the clutch is released. The tension spring pulls the toothed segment backwards and allows the pawl to ride over to the next tooth. This effectively shortens the cable. Actually, the cable is not really shortened; but the slack has been reeled in by the repositioning of the toothed segment. This self-adjusting action takes place automatically during the clutch's operational life.

Clutches 633

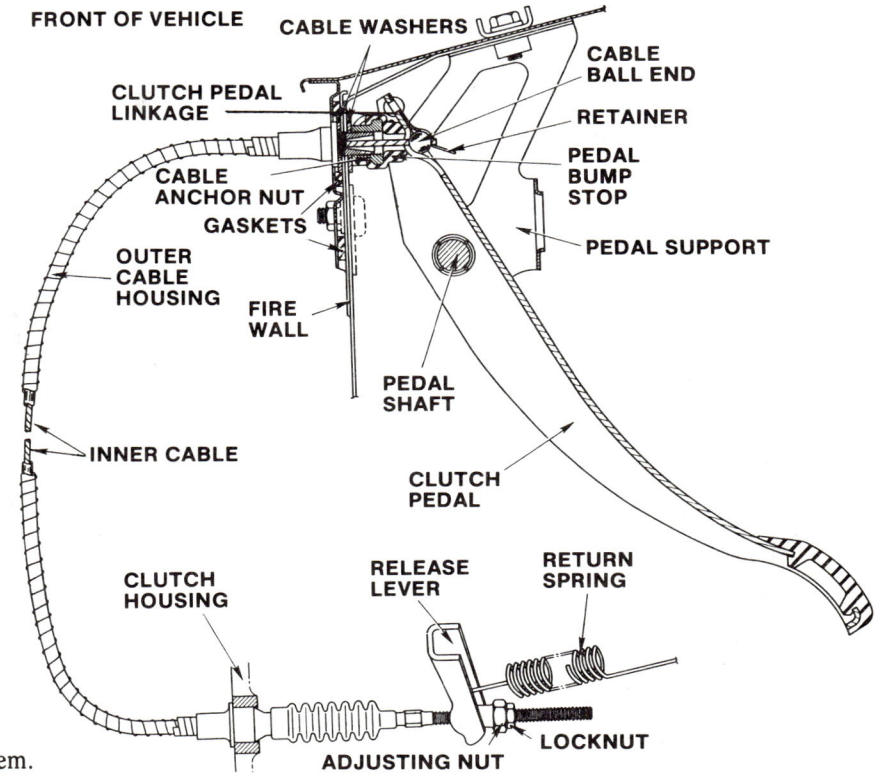

Figure 25-12 Typical clutch cable system.

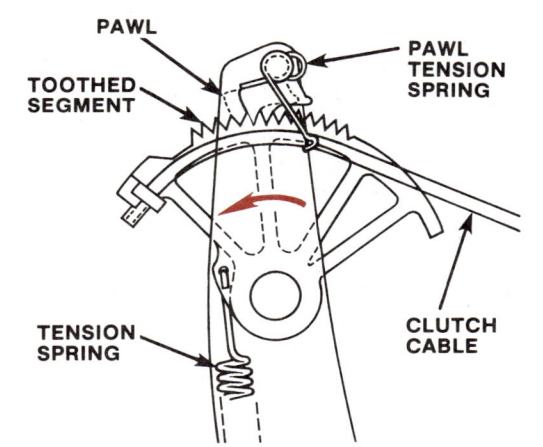

Figure 25-13 Ratchet-type automatic clutch adjusting mechanism. *Courtesy of Ford Motor Co.*

Hydraulic Clutch Linkage

Frequently, the clutch assembly is controlled by a hydraulic system (Figure 25-14). In the hydraulic clutch linkage system, hydraulic (liquid) pressure transmits motion from one sealed cylinder to another through a hydraulic line. Like the cable linkage assembly, the hydraulic linkage is compact and flexible. In addition, the hydraulic pressure developed by the master cylinder decreases required pedal effort and provides a precise method of controlling clutch operation.

A hydraulic clutch master cylinder is shown in Figure 25-15. Its pushrod moves the piston and primary cup to create hydraulic pressure. The snap ring re-

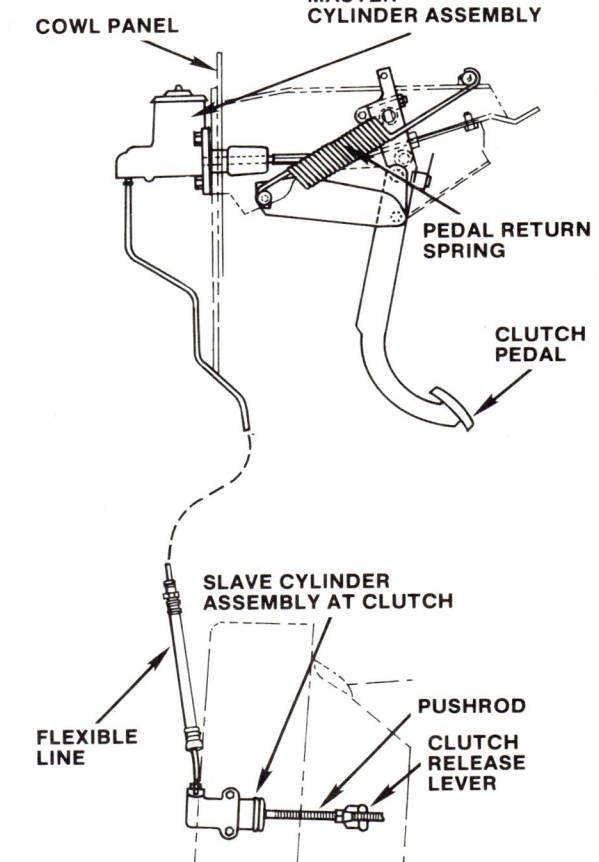

Figure 25-14 Typical hydraulic clutch linkage arrangement. *Courtesy of General Motors Corp.*

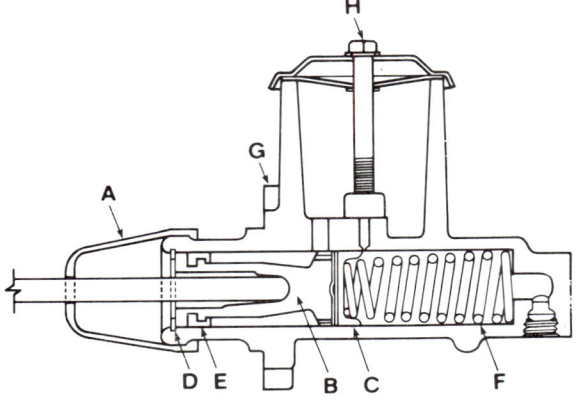

- A PUSHROD AND BOOT
- B PISTON
- C PRIMARY CUP
- D SNAP RING
- E SECONDARY CUP
- F PISTON RETURN SPRING
- G MASTER CYLINDER HOUSING
- H HYDRAULIC FLUID RESERVOIR AND BOLT

Figure 25-15 Parts of a hydraulic clutch master cylinder. *Courtesy of General Motors Corp.*

stricts the travel of the piston. The secondary cup at the snap ring end of the piston stops hydraulic fluid from dripping into the passenger compartment. The piston return spring holds the primary cup and piston in the fully released position. Hydraulic fluid is stored in the reservoir on top of the master cylinder housing.

The slave cylinder body has a bleeder valve to bleed air from the hydraulic system for efficient clutch linkage operation (Figure 25-16). The cylinder body is threaded for a tube and fitting at the fluid entry port. Rubber seal rings are used to seal the hydraulic pressure between the piston and the slave cylinder walls. The piston retaining ring is used to restrict piston travel to a certain distance. Piston travel is transmitted by a pushrod to the clutch fork. The pushrod boot keeps contaminants out of the slave cylinder.

When the clutch pedal is depressed, the movement of the piston and primary cup develops hydraulic pressure that is displaced from the master cylinder, through a tube, into the slave cylinder. The slave cylinder piston movement is transmitted to the clutch fork, which disengages the clutch.

When the clutch pedal is released, the primary cup and piston are forced back to the engaged position by the master cylinder piston return spring. External springs move the slave cylinder pushrod and piston back to the engaged position. Fluid pressure returns through the hydraulic tubing to the master cylinder assembly. There is no hydraulic pressure in the system when the clutch assembly is in the engaged position.

☐ CLUTCH SERVICE SAFETY PRECAUTIONS

When servicing the clutch, exercise the following precautions.

- Always wear eye protection when working underneath a vehicle.
- Remove asbestos dust only with a special, approved vacuum collection system or an approved liquid cleaning system.
- Never use compressed air or a brush to clean off asbestos dust.
- Follow all federal, state, and local laws when disposing of collected asbestos dust or liquid containing asbestos dust.
- Never work under a vehicle that is not raised on a hoist or supported by safety or jack stands.
- Use jack stands and special jacks to support the engine and transmission.
- Have a helper assist in removing the transmission.
- Be sure the work area is properly ventilated, or attach a ventilating hose to the vehicle's exhaust system when an engine is to be run indoors.
- Do not allow anyone to stand in front of or behind the automobile while the engine is running.
- Set the emergency brake securely and place the gearshift in neutral when running the engine of a stationary vehicle.
- Avoid touching hot engine and exhaust system parts. Whenever possible, let the vehicle cool down before beginning to work on it.

☐ CLUTCH MAINTENANCE

All clutches require checking and adjustment of linkage at regular intervals. Vehicles with external

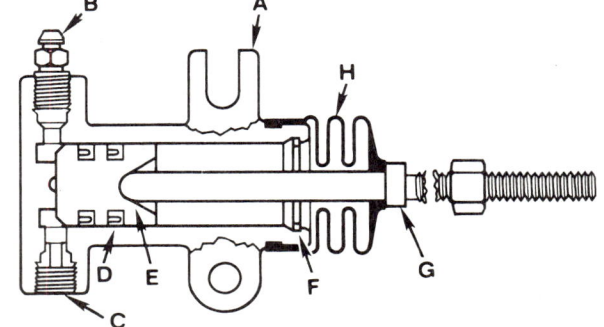

Figure 25-16 Parts of a clutch slave cylinder. *Courtesy of General Motors Corp.*

- A SLAVE CYLINDER BODY
- B BLEEDER VALVE
- C FLUID ENTRY PORT
- D PISTON SEAL RINGS
- E PISTON
- F PISTON RETAINING RING
- G PUSHROD
- H PUSHROD BOOT

clutch linkage require periodic lubrication. These maintenance procedures are explained in this section.

> **USING SERVICE MANUALS**
>
> Service manuals include adjustment procedures and instructions for clutch removal, inspection, installation, and troubleshooting. They may also offer information to aid in clutch release bearing distress analysis.

Clutch Linkage Adjustment

Except for systems with self-adjusting mechanisms, the release bearing should not touch the pressure plate release levers when the clutch is engaged (pedal up). Clearance between these parts prevents premature clutch plate, pressure plate, and release bearing wear. As the clutch disc wears and becomes thinner, this clearance changes.

Clearance can be assured by adjusting the clutch linkage so that the pedal has a specified amount of play, or free travel. Free travel is the distance a clutch pedal moves when depressed, before the clutch fork begins to move the release bearing.

To check pedal play, use a tape measure or ruler. Place the tape measure or ruler beside the clutch pedal and the end against the floor of the vehicle and note the reading (Figure 25-17). Then, depress the clutch pedal just enough to take up the pedal play and note the reading again. The difference between the two readings is the amount of pedal play.

Adjustment should be performed when pedal play is not correct or when the clutch does not engage or disengage properly. To adjust clutch pedal play, refer to the manufacturer's service manual for the correct procedure and adjustment point locations. Often pedal play can be increased or decreased by turning a threaded fastener located either under the dash at the clutch pedal or where the linkage attaches to the clutch fork.

Clean the linkage with a shop towel and solvent, if necessary, before checking it and replacing any damaged or missing parts or cables. Check hydraulic linkage systems for leaks at the clutch master cylinder, hydraulic hose, and slave cylinder. Then, adjust the linkage to provide the manufacturer's specified clutch pedal play.

External Clutch Linkage Lubrication

External clutch linkage should be lubricated at regular intervals, such as during a chassis lubrication. Refer to the vehicle's service manual to determine the proper lubricant. Many clutch linkages use the same chassis grease that is used for suspension parts and U-joints. Lubricate all the sliding surfaces and pivot points in the clutch linkage (Figure 25-18). The linkage should move freely after lubrication.

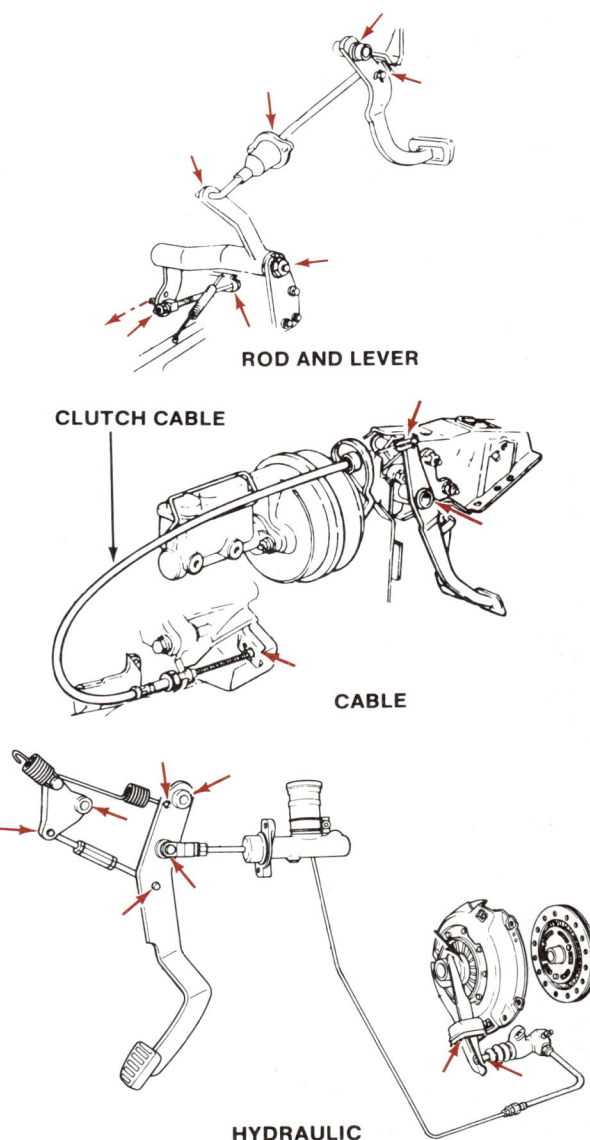

Figure 25-18 Clutch linkage lubrication points. *Courtesy of Buick Motor Division—GMC/Ford Motor Co./Nissan Motor Corp.*

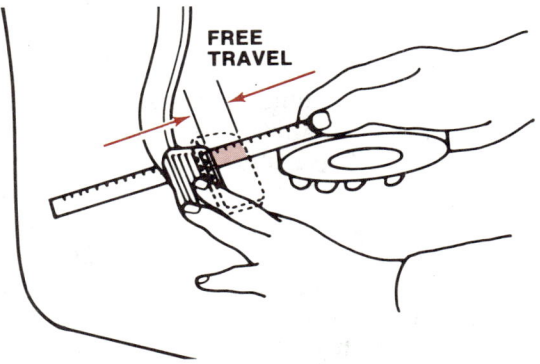

Figure 25-17 Checking clutch pedal play.

On vehicles with hydraulic clutch linkage, check the clutch master cylinder reservoir fluid level. It should be approximately 1/4 inch from the top of the reservoir. If it must be refilled, use approved brake fluid. Also, since the clutch master cylinder does not consume fluid, check for leaks in the master cylinder, connecting flexible line, and slave cylinder, if the fluid is low.

☐ CLUTCH PROBLEM DIAGNOSIS

Check and attempt to adjust the clutch pedal play before attempting to diagnose any clutch problems. If the friction lining of the clutch is worn too thin, the clutch cannot be adjusted successfully. The most common clutch problems are described here.

Slippage

Clutch slippage is a condition in which the engine overspeeds without generating any increase in torque to the driving wheels. It occurs when the clutch disc is not gripped firmly between the flywheel and the pressure plate. Instead, the clutch disc slips between these driving members. Slippage can occur during initial acceleration or subsequent shifts, but it is usually most noticeable in higher gears.

One way to check for slippage is by driving the vehicle. Normal acceleration from a stop and several gear changes indicate whether the clutch is slipping.

Slippage also can be checked in the shop. Check the service manual for correct procedures. A general procedure for checking clutch slippage follows. Be sure to follow the safety precautions stated earlier.

With the parking brake on, disengage the clutch. Shift the transmission into third gear, and increase the engine speed to about 2000 rpm. Slowly release the clutch pedal until the clutch engages. The engine should stall immediately.

If it does not stall within a few seconds, the clutch is slipping. Safely raise the vehicle and check the clutch linkage for binding, broken, or bent parts. If no linkage problems are found, the transmission and the clutch assembly must be removed so that the clutch parts can be examined.

> **SHOP TALK**
>
> Severe or prolonged clutch slippage causes grooving or heat damage to the pressure plate.

Clutch slippage can be caused by an oil-soaked or worn disc facing, warped pressure plate, weak diaphragm spring, or the release bearing contacting and applying pressure to the release levers.

Drag and Binding

If the clutch disc is not completely released when the clutch pedal is fully depressed, clutch drag occurs. Clutch drag causes gear clash, especially when shifting into reverse. It can also cause hard starting because the engine attempts to turn the transmission input shaft.

To check for clutch drag, start the engine, depress the clutch pedal completely, and shift the transmission into first gear. Do not release the clutch. Then, shift the transmission into neutral and wait 5 seconds before attempting to shift smoothly into reverse.

It should take no more than 5 seconds for the clutch disc, input shaft, and transmission gears to come to a complete stop after disengagement. This period, called the clutch spindown time, is normal and should not be mistaken for clutch drag.

If the shift into reverse causes gear clash, raise the vehicle safely and check the clutch linkage for binding, broken, or bent parts. If no problems are found in the linkage, the transmission and clutch assembly must be removed so that the clutch parts can be examined.

Clutch drag can occur as a result of a warped disc or pressure plate, a loose disc facing, a defective release lever, or incorrect clutch pedal adjustment that results in excessive pedal play.

Binding can result when the splines in the clutch disc hub or on the transmission input shaft are damaged or when there are problems with the release levers.

Chatter

A shaking or shuddering that is felt in the vehicle as the clutch is engaged is known as clutch chatter. It usually occurs when the pressure plate first contacts the clutch disc and stops when the clutch is fully engaged.

To check for clutch chatter, start the engine, depress the clutch completely, and shift the transmission into first gear. Increase engine speed to about 1500 rpm, then slowly release the clutch pedal and check for chatter as the pedal begins to engage. Do not release the pedal completely, or the vehicle might jump and cause serious injury. As soon as the clutch is partially engaged, depress the clutch pedal immediately and reduce engine speed to prevent damage to the clutch parts.

Usually clutch chatter is caused by liquid leaking onto the clutch and contaminating its friction surfaces. This results in a mirrorlike shine on the pressure plate or a glazed clutch facing. Oil and clutch hydraulic fluid leaks can occur at the engine rear main bearing seal, transmission input shaft seal, clutch slave cylinder, and hydraulic line. Other causes of clutch chatter include broken engine mounts, loose bellhousing bolts, and damaged clutch linkage.

During disassembly, check for a warped pressure plate or flywheel, a burned or glazed disc facing, and worn input shaft splines. If the chattering is caused by an oil-soaked clutch disc and no other parts are damaged, then the disc alone needs to be replaced. However, the cause of the oil leak must also be found and corrected.

Pedal Pulsation

Pedal pulsation is a rapid up-and-down movement of the clutch pedal as the clutch disengages or engages. This pedal movement usually is minor, but it can be felt through the clutch pedal. It is not accompanied by any noise. Pulsation begins when the release bearing makes contact with the release levers.

To check for pedal pulsation, start the engine, depress the clutch pedal slowly until the clutch just begins to disengage, and then stop briefly. Resume depressing the clutch pedal slowly until the pedal is depressed to a full stop.

On many vehicles, minor pulsation is considered normal. If pulsation is excessive, the clutch must be removed and disassembled for inspection.

Pedal pulsations can result from the misalignment of parts. Check for a misaligned bellhousing or a bent flywheel. Inspect the clutch disc and pressure plate for warpage. Broken, bent, or warped release levers also create misalignment.

> **CUSTOMER CARE**
>
> If you repair a vehicle with clutch slippage, tactfully inform the customer about the different poor driving habits that can cause this problem. These habits include riding the clutch pedal and holding the vehicle on an incline by using the clutch as a brake.

Vibration

Clutch vibrations, unlike pedal pulsations, can be felt throughout the vehicle, and they occur at any clutch pedal position. These vibrations usually occur at normal engine operating speeds (more than 1500 rpm).

There are other possible sources of vibration that should be checked before disassembling the clutch to inspect it. Check the engine mounts and the crankshaft damper pulley. Look for any indication that engine parts are rubbing against the body or frame.

Accessories can also be a source of vibration. To check them, remove the drive belts one at a time. Set the transmission in neutral, and securely set the emergency brake. Start the engine and check for vibrations. Do not run the engine for more than 1 minute with the belts removed.

If the source of vibration is not discovered through these checks, the clutch parts should be examined. Be sure to check for loose flywheel bolts, excessive flywheel runout, and pressure plate cover balance problems.

Noises

Many clutch noises come from bushings and bearings. Pilot bushing noises are squealing, howling, or trumpeting sounds that are most noticeable in cold weather. These bushing noises usually occur when the pedal is being depressed and the transmission is in neutral. Release bearing noise is a whirring, grating, or grinding sound that occurs when the clutch pedal is depressed and stops when the pedal is fully released. It is most noticeable when the transmission is in neutral, but it also can be heard when the transmission is in gear.

❑ CLUTCH SERVICE

A prerequisite for removing and replacing the clutch in a vehicle is removing the driveline or drive shafts and transmission or transaxle.

Removing the Clutch

After raising the vehicle on a hoist, clean excessive dirt, grease, or debris from around the clutch and transmission. Then, disconnect and remove the clutch linkage. Cable systems need to be disconnected at the transmission.

On rear-wheel-drive automobiles, remove the driveline and the transmission. In some cases the bellhousing is removed with the transmission. In others, it is removed after the transmission is removed.

On front-wheel-drive vehicles with transaxles, any parts that interfere with transaxle removal must be removed first. These parts might include drive axles, parts of the engine, brake and suspension system or body parts. Check the service manual for specific instructions.

The clutch assembly is accessible after the bellhousing has been removed. Use an approved vacuum collection system or an approved liquid cleaning system to remove asbestos dust and dirt from the clutch assembly.

Photo Sequence 12 outlines the typical procedure for replacing a clutch disc and pressure plate. Always refer to the manufacturer's recommendations for bolt torque specifications prior to reinstalling the assembly.

While disassembling the clutch, follow these guidelines.

- Check the bellhousing, flywheel, and pressure plate for signs of oil leaks.
- Carefully examine each part for wear, discoloration, and damage.
- Check the flywheel for signs of burning or excessive wear.

Figure 25-19 Check for pressure plate warpage. *Courtesy of Ford Motor Co.*

- When measuring the lining thickness of a bonded clutch disc, measure the total thickness of the facing or lining. To measure the wear of a riveted lining, measure the material above the rivet heads.
- Keep grease off the frictional surfaces of the clutch disc, flywheel, and pressure plate.
- Check the pressure plate surface for warpage by laying a straightedge across the surface and inserting a feeler gauge between the surface and the straightedge (Figure 25-19). Compare the measurement against the specifications given in the service manual.
- Check the release levers of the pressure plate for uneven wear or damage.
- Check the release bearing by turning it with your fingers and making sure it rotates freely.
- Check the clutch for damage.
- Lubricate the clutch fork pivot points, the inside of the release bearing hub, and the linkages.
- After the clutch assembly has been reinstalled, check the clutch pedal free travel.

CASE STUDY

Case 1

A customer brings in a car that develops a harsh scratching noise and becomes quite difficult to shift gears. The symptoms become more apparent when shifting into first gear.

Since trouble of this sort can be caused by a defective synchronization mechanism in the transmission as well as a problem with the clutch, a series of tests is called for. First, the technician disengages the clutch and shifts quickly from neutral to reverse in idling condition. If no gear noise resulted, the technician would know that there is sufficient disengagement of the clutch. But instead, gear noise does occur, so the technician performs the next test by shifting to reverse after 5 seconds of clutch disengagement. If no gear noise results, the technician knows that the transmission is defective or there is excessive clutch drag torque. Gear noise does occur, so the technician performs the next test by shifting between neutral and reverse several times, after having disengaged the clutch for 5 seconds. If no gear noise results, the technician knows that the problem is a stuck clutch disc. Since gear noise does occur, the technician knows that the clutch is not completely disengaging.

Summary

- The clutch, located between the transmission and the engine, provides a mechanical coupling between the engine flywheel and the transmission's input shaft. All manual transmissions and transaxles require a clutch.
- The flywheel, an important part of the engine, is also the main driving member of the clutch.
- The clutch disc receives the driving motion from the flywheel and pressure plate assembly and transmits that motion to the transmission input shaft.
- The twofold purpose of the pressure plate assembly is to squeeze the clutch disc onto the flywheel and to move away from the clutch disc so that the disc can stop rotating. There are basically two types of pressure plate assemblies: those with coil springs and those with a diaphragm spring.
- Semicentrifugal pressure plate assemblies use engine speed and centrifugal force to increase the plate loading of the clutch disc. In these assemblies, coil springs with less tension can be used, since the pressure created from the centrifugal force compensates for the loss.
- The clutch release bearing, also called a throwout bearing, smoothly and quietly moves the pressure plate release levers or diaphragm spring through the engagement and disengagement processes.
- The clutch fork moves the release bearing and hub back and forth. It is controlled by the clutch pedal and linkage.
- Clutch linkage can be mechanical or hydraulic. Mechanical linkage is divided into two types: shaft and lever linkage and cable linkage.
- The self-adjusting clutch is a clutch cable linkage that monitors clutch pedal play and automatically adjusts it when necessary.
- It is important that certain precautions are exercised when servicing the clutch. Clutch maintenance includes linkage adjustment and external clutch linkage lubrication.
- Slippage occurs when the clutch disc is not gripped firmly between the flywheel and the pressure plate. It can be caused by an oil-soaked or worn disc facing, warped pressure plate, weak diaphragm spring, or the release bearing contacting and applying pressure to the release levers.
- Clutch drag occurs if the clutch disc is not completely released when the clutch pedal is fully depressed. It can occur as a result of a warped disc or pressure plate, a loose disc facing, a defective release lever, or incorrect clutch pedal adjustment that results in excessive pedal play.
- Chatter is a shuddering felt in the vehicle when the pressure plate first contacts the clutch disc and it stops when the clutch is fully engaged. Usually chatter is caused when liquid contaminates the friction surfaces.

PHOTO SEQUENCE 12

☐ INSTALLING AND ALIGNING A CLUTCH DISC

P12-1 The removal and replacement of a clutch assembly can be completed while the engine is in or out of the car. The clutch assembly is mounted to the flywheel that is mounted to the rear of the crankshaft.

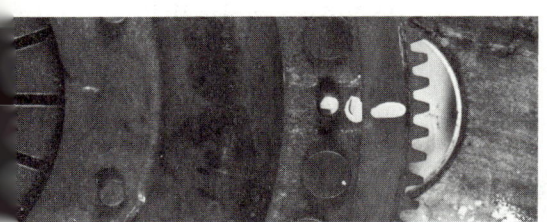

P12-2 Before disassembling the clutch, make sure alignment marks are present on the pressure plate and flywheel.

P12-3 The attaching bolts should be loosened before removing any of the bolts. With the bolts loosened, support the assembly with one hand while using the other to remove the bolts. The clutch disc will be free to fall as the pressure plate is separated from the flywheel. Keep it intact with the pressure plate.

P12-4 The surface of the pressure plate should be inspected for signs of burning, warpage, and cracks. Any faults normally indicate that the plate should be replaced.

P12-5 The surface of the flywheel should also be carefully inspected. Normally the flywheel surface can be resurfaced to remove any defects. The pilot bushing or bearing should also be inspected.

P12-6 The new clutch disc is placed into the pressure plate as the pressure plate is moved into its proper location. Make sure the disc is facing the correct direction. Most are marked to indicate which side should be seated against the flywheel surface.

P12-7 Install the pressure plate according to the alignment marks made during disassembly.

P12-8 Install the attaching bolts, but do not tighten. Then install the clutch alignment tool through the hub of the disc and the pilot bearing. This will center the disc on the flywheel.

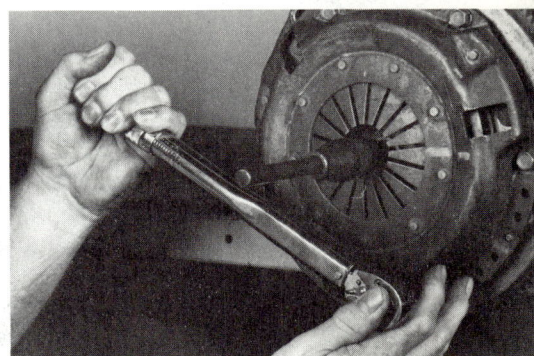

P12-9 With the disc aligned, tighten the attaching bolts according to the procedures outlined in the service manual. ■

- Pedal pulsation is a rapid up-and-down movement of the clutch pedal as the clutch disengages or engages. It results from a misalignment of parts.
- Clutch vibrations can be felt throughout the vehicle, and they occur at any clutch pedal position. Source of clutch vibrations include loose flywheel bolts, excessive flywheel runout, and pressure plate cover balance problems.

Review Questions

1. Name two types of friction facings.
2. List the two advantages of coil spring pressure plate assemblies.
3. What is another name for the diaphragm spring?
4. Name three types of clutch linkages.
5. What is used to measure clutch pedal play?
6. The clutch, or friction, disc is connected to the _____.
   a. engine crankshaft
   b. transmission input shaft
   c. transmission output shaft
   d. transmission counter shaft
7. Torsional coil springs in the clutch disc _____.
   a. cushion the driven disc engagement rear to front
   b. are the mechanical force holding the pressure plate against the driven disc and flywheel
   c. absorb the torque forces
   d. are located between the friction rings
8. Fulcrum rings are found in the _____.
   a. diaphragm pressure plate
   b. coil spring pressure plate
   c. driven disc between the friction facings
   d. release bearing
9. With the semicentrifugal pressure plate, _____.
   a. plate loading decreases with engine speed
   b. effective travel increases with an increase in engine speed
   c. plate loading increases with engine speed
   d. effective travel decreases with a decrease in engine speed
10. When a rotating release bearing is installed in a clutch assembly, the release bearing is _____.
    a. stationary when the clutch is fully engaged
    b. rotating when the clutch is fully engaged
    c. stationary when the engine is operating with clutch engaged
    d. stationary during clutch effective travel
11. When the clutch pedal is released on a hydraulic clutch linkage, the _____.
    a. master cylinder piston is released by spring tension
    b. master cylinder piston is released by hydraulic pressure
    c. slave cylinder is released by hydraulic pressure
    d. slave cylinder piston does not move
12. When the clutch is disengaged, the power flow stops at the _____.
    a. transmission input shaft
    b. driven disc hub
    c. pressure plate and flywheel
    d. torsion springs
13. Technician A says that the semicentrifugal pressure plate release levers are weighted for extra plate loading. Technician B says that the semicentrifugal pressure plate itself is weighted for extra plate loading. Who is correct?
    a. Technician A
    b. Technician B
    c. Both A and B
    d. Neither A nor B
14. Insufficient clutch pedal clearance results in _____.
    a. gear clashing while shifting transmission
    b. a noisy front transmission bearing
    c. premature release bearing failure
    d. premature pilot bearing failure
15. Technician A says that an oil-soaked clutch disc can cause clutch chatter. Technician B says that clutch chatter can be caused by loose bellhousing bolts. Who is correct?
    a. Technician A
    b. Technician B
    c. Both A and B
    d. Neither A nor B
16. When making a clutch adjustment, it is necessary to _____.
    a. measure clutch pedal free travel
    b. lubricate the clutch linkage
    c. check hydraulic fluid level
    d. place the transmission in reverse
17. Technician A says that clutch slippage is most noticeable in higher gears. Technician B says that clutch slippage is not noticeable in lower gears. Who is correct?
    a. Technician A
    b. Technician B
    c. Both A and B
    d. Neither A nor B
18. Technician A says that clutch drag can cause hard starting. Technician B says that clutch drag has no effect on starting. Who is correct?
    a. Technician A
    b. Technician B
    c. Both A and B
    d. Neither A nor B
19. The contact surface pressure plate contacts the _____.
    a. transmission mainshaft
    b. throwout bearing
    c. clutch disc
    d. flywheel

26 MANUAL TRANSMISSIONS AND TRANSAXLES

Objectives

■ Explain the design characteristics of the gears used in manual transmissions and transaxles.   ■ Explain the fundamentals of torque multiplication and overdrive.   ■ Describe the purpose, design, and operation of synchronizer assemblies.   ■ Describe the purpose, design, and operation of internal and remote gearshift linkages.   ■ Explain the operation and power flows produced in typical manual transmissions and transaxles.

The transmission or transaxle is a vital link in the power train of any modern vehicle. The purpose of the transmission or transaxle is to use gears of various sizes to give the engine a mechanical advantage over the driving wheels. During normal operating conditions, power from the engine is transferred through the engaged clutch to the input shaft of the transmission or transaxle. Gears in the transmission or transaxle housing alter the torque and speed of this power input before passing it on to other components in the power train. Without the mechanical advantage the gearing provides, an engine can generate only limited torque at low speeds. Without sufficient torque, moving a vehicle from a standing start would be impossible.

In any engine, the crankshaft always rotates in the same direction. If the engine transmitted its power directly to the drive axles, the wheels could be driven only in one direction. Instead, the transmission or transaxle provides the gearing needed to reverse direction so the vehicle can be driven backward.

☐ TRANSMISSION VERSUS TRANSAXLE

Vehicles are propelled in one of three ways: by the rear wheels, by the front wheels, or by all four wheels. The type of drive system used determines whether a conventional transmission or a transaxle is used.

Vehicles propelled by the rear wheels normally use a transmission. Transmission gearing is located within an aluminum or iron casting called the transmission case assembly (Figure 26-1). The transmission case assembly is attached to the rear of the engine, which is normally located in the front of the vehicle. A drive shaft links the output shaft of the transmission with

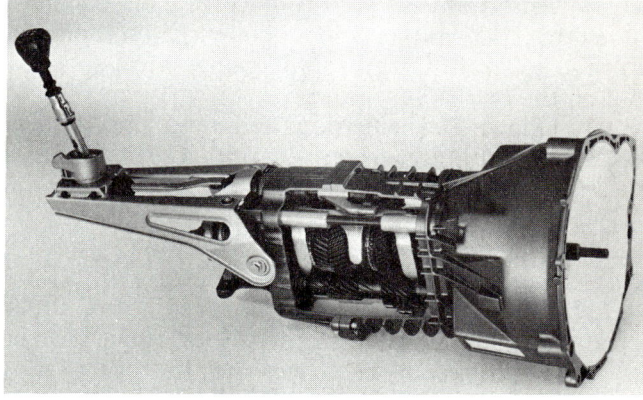

Figure 26-1 Typical five-speed manual transmission, with the mainshaft (speed) gears, countershaft cluster gears, and shaft forks visible through the case cutaway. *Courtesy of Ford Motor Co.*

the differential and drive axles located in a separate housing at the rear of the vehicle (Figure 26-2). The differential splits the driveline power and redirects it to the two rear drive axles, which then pass it onto the wheels. For many years, rear-wheel-drive systems were the conventional method of propelling a vehicle.

Front-wheel-drive vehicles are propelled by the front wheels. For this reason, they must use a drive design different from that of a rear-wheel-drive vehicle. The transaxle is the special power transfer unit commonly used on front-wheel-drive vehicles. A transaxle combines the transmission gearing, differential, and drive axle connections into a single case aluminum housing located in front of the vehicle (Figure 26-3). This design offers many advantages. One major advantage is the good traction on slippery roads due to the weight of

641

642 Section 5 **Manual Transmissions and Transaxles**

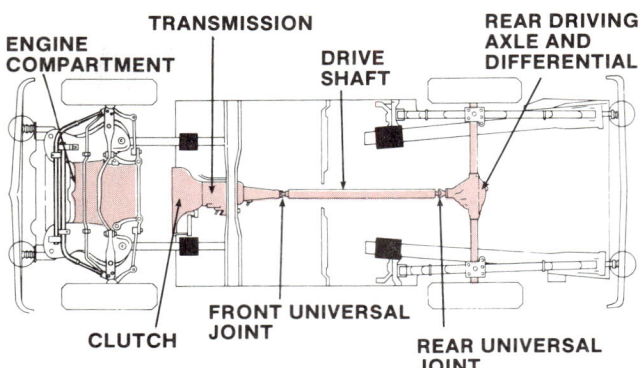

Figure 26-2 Location of typical rear-wheel-drive power train components. *Courtesy of Chrysler Corp.*

the power train components being directly over the driving axles of the vehicle.

Four-wheel-drive vehicles typically use a transmission and transfer case. The transfer case mounts on the side or back of the transmission. A chain or gear drive inside the transfer case receives power from the transmission and transfers it to two separate drive shafts. One drive shaft connects to a differential on the front drive axle. The other drive shaft connects to a differential on the rear drive axle.

Most manual transmissions and transaxles are constant mesh, fully synchronized units. Constant mesh means that regardless of the vehicle being stationary or moving, the gears within the unit are constantly in mesh. Fully synchronized means that the unit uses a mechanism of brass rings and clutches to bring rotating shafts and gears to the same speed before shifts occur. This promotes smooth shifting. In a vehicle equipped with a four-speed manual shift transmission or transaxle, all four forward gears are synchronized. Reverse gearing may or may not be synchronized, depending on the type of transmission/transaxle.

❏ GEARS

The purpose of a gear in a manual transmission or transaxle is to transmit rotating motion. Gears are normally mounted on a shaft, and they transmit rotating motion from one parallel shaft to another.

Gears and shafts can interact in one of three ways: the shaft can drive the gear; the gear can drive the shaft; or the gear can be free to turn on the shaft. In this last case, the gear acts as an idler gear.

Sets of gears can be used to multiply torque and decrease speed, increase speed and decrease torque, or transfer torque and leave speed unchanged.

Gear Design

Figure 26-4 illustrates the basic names of major gear tooth parts. Gear pitch is a very important factor in gear design and operation. Gear pitch refers to the number of teeth per given unit of pitch diameter. A simple way of determining gear pitch is to divide the number of teeth by the pitch diameter of the gear. For example, if a gear has 36 teeth and a 6-inch pitch diameter, it has a gear pitch of 6 (Figure 26-5). The important fact to remember is that gears must have the same pitch in order to operate together. A 5-pitch gear meshes only with another 5-pitch gear, a 6-pitch only with a 6-pitch, and so on.

Spur Gears

The spur gear is the simplest gear design used in manual transmissions and transaxles. As shown in Figure 26-6, spur gear teeth are cut straight across the edge parallel to the gear's shaft. During operation,

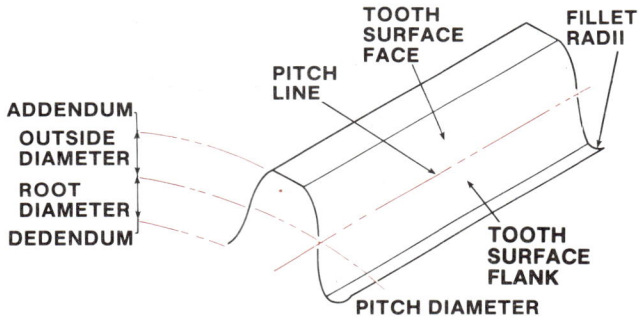

Figure 26-4 Basic names of major gear tooth parts.

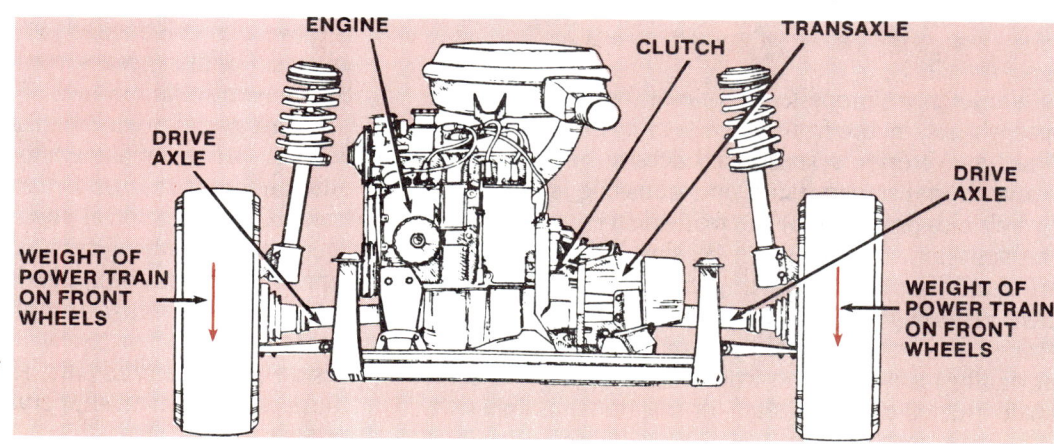

Figure 26-3 Location of typical front-wheel-drive power train components.

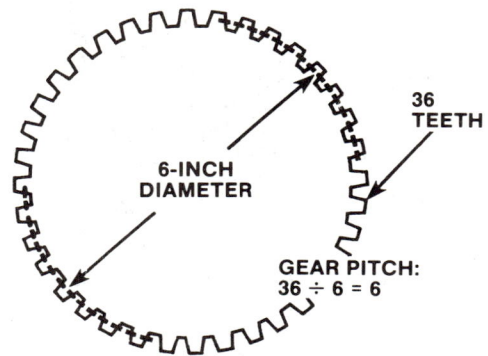

Figure 26-5 Determining gear pitch.

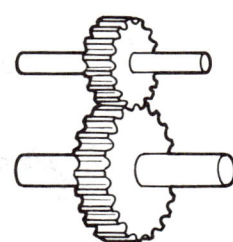

Figure 26-6 Spur gears have teeth cut straight across the gear edge, parallel to the shaft.

enmeshed spur gears have only one tooth in full contact at a time.

Its straight tooth design is the spur gear's main advantage. It minimizes the chances of popping out of gear, an important consideration during acceleration/deceleration and reverse operation. For this reason, spur gears are often used for the reverse gear.

The spur gear's major drawback is the clicking noise that occurs as teeth contact one another. At higher speeds, this clicking becomes a constant whine. Quieter gears, such as the helical design, are often used to eliminate this gear whine problem.

SHOP TALK

When a small gear is meshed with a much larger gear, as shown in Figure 26-6, the small gear is often called a pinion or pinion gear, regardless of its tooth design.

Helical Gears

A helical gear has teeth that are cut at an angle or are spiral to the gear's axis of rotation (Figure 26-7). This allows two or more teeth to mesh at the same time. This distributes tooth load and produces a very strong gear. Helical gears also run more quietly than spur gears because they create a wiping action as they engage and disengage the teeth on another gear. One disadvantage is that helical teeth on a gear cause the gear to move fore or aft on a shaft, depending on the direction of the angle of the gear teeth. This axial

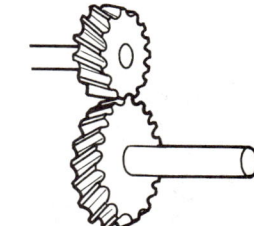

Figure 26-7 Helical gears have teeth cut at an angle to the gear's axis of rotation.

thrust must be absorbed by thrust washers and other transmission gears, shafts, or the transmission case.

Helical gears can be either righthanded or lefthanded, depending on the direction the spiral appears to go when the gear is viewed face-on. When mounted on parallel shafts, one helical gear must be righthanded and the other lefthanded. Two gears with the same direction spiral do not mesh in a parallel mounted arrangement.

External and Internal Gear Teeth

Spur and helical gears having teeth cut around their outer edge are called external gears. When the teeth of two external gears are meshed, the direction of rotation is reversed as the gears turn (Figure 26-8A). In other words, the driven or output gear rotates in the opposite direction of the drive or input gear.

An internal gear has teeth around its inside diameter. When an external gear and an internal gear are meshed and rotating, they do so in the same direction (Figure 26-8B).

Idler Gears

An idler gear is a gear that is placed between a drive gear and a driven gear. Its purpose is to transfer motion from the drive gear to the driven gear without changing the direction of rotation. It can do this because all three gears have external teeth (Figure 26-9).

Idler gears are used in reverse gear trains to reverse the directional rotation of the output shaft. In all forward gears the output shaft rotates in the opposite direction of the input shaft. With the placement of an idler gear in the reverse gearing, the input and output

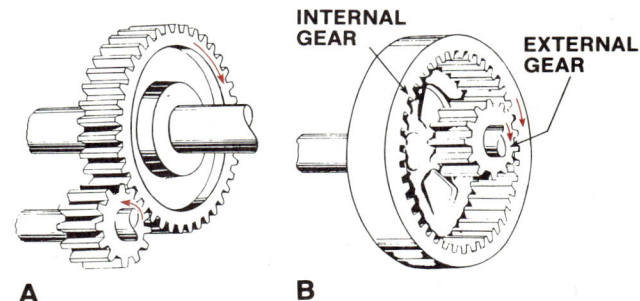

Figure 26-8 (A) Externally meshed gears rotate in opposite directions; (B) internally meshed gears rotate in the same direction.

Figure 26-9 An idler gear is used to transfer motion without changing rotational direction.

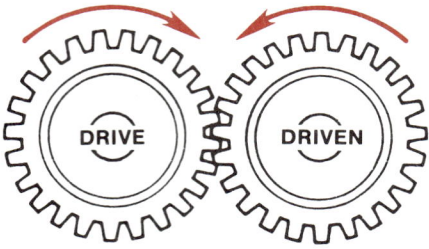

A   INPUT SPEED = OUTPUT SPEED

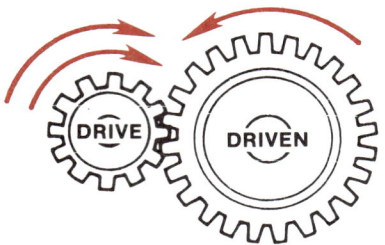

B   INPUT SPEED GREATER THAN OUTPUT SPEED

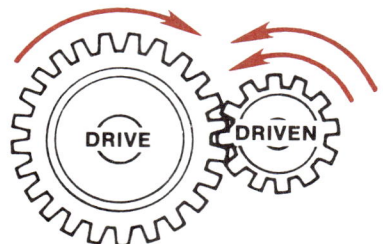

C   INPUT SPEED LESS THAN OUTPUT SPEED

Figure 26-10 (A) When gears of equal size are meshed, output speed equals input speed. (B) A small gear driving a large gear reduces output speed. (C) A large gear driving a small gear increases output speed. In all cases, the output gear rotates in the opposite direction of the input gear.

shafts now rotate in the same direction. This allows the vehicle drive wheels to turn backward.

Gear Ratios

As mentioned earlier, only gears with matching pitches can be meshed together. The speeds at which two meshed gears turn depend on the number of teeth on each gear. If both gears are the same size (same number of teeth), then the speed of both gears is equal (Figure 26-10A). If the driving gear is smaller (fewer teeth) than the driven gear, the speed of the driven (output) gear decreases (Figure 26-10B). However, when the driving gear is larger (more teeth) than the driven (output) gear, the speed of the driven gear increases (Figure 26-10C).

To calculate the speed of either gear, multiply the number of teeth of one gear by the speed of that gear. Divide that number by the number of teeth on the other gear.

For example, calculate the speed of the driven gear when the driving gear has 45 teeth and is rotating at 200 rpm, while the driven gear has 75 teeth. The formula follows.

$$\frac{\text{Teeth on driven gear}}{\text{Teeth on driving gear}} = \frac{\text{rpm of driving gear}}{\text{rpm of driven gear}}$$

Putting in the known data leads to

$$\frac{75}{45} = \frac{200}{x} \quad \text{therefore,}$$

$$x = \frac{45 \times 200}{75} = \frac{9000}{75}$$

$$x = 120 \text{ rpm of driven gear}$$

The input speed of 200 rpm is reduced to an output speed of 120 rpm. The relationship of input and output speeds is stated in a gear ratio. This gear ratio can be calculated in a number of ways depending on the data that is known. One method is to divide the speed of the driving (input) gear or shaft by the speed of the driven (output) gear or shaft. In the given example, this results in

$$\frac{200 \text{ rpm}}{120 \text{ rpm}} = 1.66\text{:gear ratio}$$

The gear ratio can also be found by dividing the number of teeth on the driven gear (d) by the number of teeth on the driving gear (D). Again, in the sample problem, this leads to

$$\frac{d}{D} = \frac{75 \text{ driven gear teeth}}{45 \text{ driving gear teeth}} = 1.66\text{:gear ratio}$$

This means the driven (output) gear is rotating 1.66 times slower than the driving (input) gear.

Speed Versus Torque

A rotating gear also produces a rotational force known as torque. Torque is calculated by multiplying the applied force by its distance from the centerline of rotation. A simple example of this law of physics is demonstrated whenever a torque wrench is used. As shown in Figure 26-11, when a force of 10 pounds is applied perpendicular to the centerline of the bolt's rotation at a distance 1 foot from this centerline, 10 foot-pounds of torque are generated at the centerline of rotation. The torque wrench acts as a lever to apply this force.

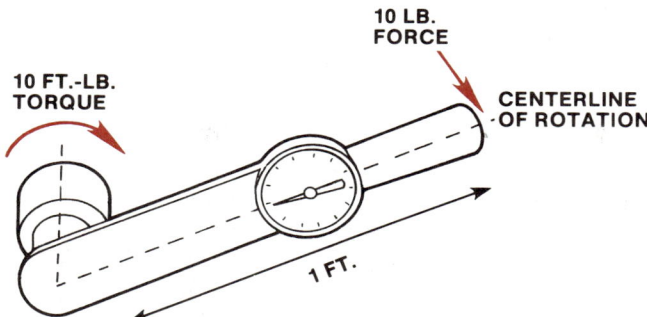

Figure 26-11 A torque wrench is a good example of how rotational force or torque is generated.

Meshed gears use this same leverage principle to transfer torque. If two gears in mesh have the same number of teeth, they rotate at the same speed, and the input gear transfers an equal amount of torque to the output gear (Figure 26-12A).

It has already been explained that when a driven gear is larger than its driving gear, output speed decreases. But how is torque affected?

Figure 26-12B illustrates a small gear with 12 teeth driving a large gear with 24 teeth. This results in a gear ratio of 2:1 with the output speed being half of the input speed.

In this example, torque at the input shaft of the driving gear is 10 foot-pounds. The distance from the centerline of this input shaft to the gear teeth is 1 foot.

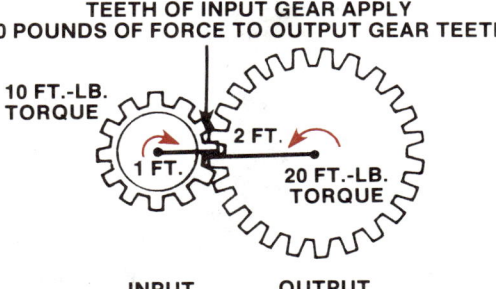

Figure 26-12 Gear teeth are actually a series of levers used to transfer torque. (A) If gears are the same size, output torque equals input torque. (B) When the input gear is smaller than the output gear, output torque increases.

Manual Transmissions and Transaxles 645

This means the driving gear transfers 10 pounds of force to the teeth of the larger driven gear. The distance between the teeth of the driven gear and the centerline of its output shaft is 2 feet. This means the torque at the output shaft is 10 pounds × 2 feet, or 20 foot-pounds. Torque has doubled.

The amount of torque increase from a driving gear to a driven gear is directly proportional to the speed decrease. When speed is halved, torque doubles.

Review the previous example. With a gear ratio of 1.66:1, the driven gear is rotating 1.66 times slower than the driving gear, but it is producing 1.66 times the torque of the driven gear. If torque at the driving gear input is 100 foot-pounds, torque at the driven gear output is 1.66 × 100 foot-pounds, or 166 foot-pounds.

Most manual transmission gearing is speed reducing/torque increasing. In some transmissions, the top gear is a 1:1 gear ratio where speed and torque are transferred directly from the input to the output shaft. In most cases, the top gear is an overdrive gear combination. This means it is a speed-increasing/torque-reducing gearing.

Overdrive gear ratios are stated using a decimal point, such as 0.85:1. This means that for every 0.85 times the input shaft rotates, the output shaft rotates one complete revolution. However, output torque is only 0.85 of input torque. This is because speed and torque are opposite.

Reverse Gear Ratios

Reverse gear ratios involve two driving gears and two driven gears:

- the input gear is driver #1
- the idler gear is driven #1
- the idler gear is also driver #2
- the output gear is driven #2
- the output gear is driven #2

If the input gear has 20 teeth, the idler gear 28 teeth, and the output gear 48 teeth, the calculations for determining reverse gear ratio are as follows.

$$\text{Reverse gear ratio} = \frac{\text{driven \#1} \times \text{driven \#2}}{\text{driver \#1} \times \text{driver \#2}}$$
$$= \frac{28 \times 48}{20 \times 28}$$
$$= \frac{1344}{560}$$
$$= 2.40$$

☐ TRANSMISSION/ TRANSAXLE DESIGN

The internal components of a transmission or transaxle consist of a parallel set of metal shafts on which meshing gearsets of different ratios are mounted (Figure 26-13). By moving the shift lever, gear ratios can

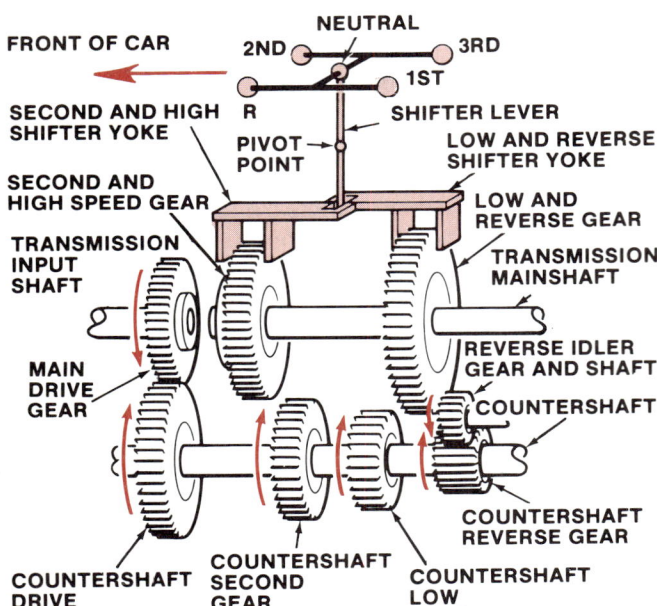

Figure 26-13 Simplified view of major transmission shafts and gearsets in a three-speed transmission.

be selected to generate different amounts of output torque and speed.

The gears are mounted or fixed to the shafts in a number of ways. They can be internally splined or keyed to a shaft. Gears can also be manufactured as an integral part of the shaft. Gears that must be able to freewheel around the shaft during certain speed ranges are mounted to the shaft using bushings or bearings.

The shafts and gears are contained in a transmission or transaxle case or housing. The components of this housing include the main case body, side or top cover plates, extension housings, and bearing retainers (Figure 26-14). The metal components are bolted together with gaskets providing a leak-proof seal at all joints. The case is filled with transmission fluid to provide constant lubrication and cooling for the spinning gears and shafts.

Transmission Features

Although they operate in a similar fashion, the layout, components, and terminology used in transmissions and transaxles are not exactly the same.

A transmission has three specific shafts: the input shaft, the countershaft gear, and the mainshaft or output shaft (Figure 26-15). The clutch gear is an integral part of the transmission's input shaft and always rotates with the input shaft.

The countershaft gear is actually several gears machined out of a single piece of steel. The countershaft gear may also be called the countergear or cluster gear. The countershaft gear mounts on roller bearings on the countershaft. The countershaft is pinned in place and does not turn. Washers control the amount of end play of the unit in the transmission case (Figure 26-16).

The main gears on the mainshaft or output shaft transfer rotation from the countershaft gears to the output shaft. The main gears are also called speed gears. They are mounted on the output shaft using roller bearings. Speed gears freewheel around the output shaft until they are locked to it by the engagement of their shift synchronizer unit (Figure 26-17).

Power flows from the transmission input shaft to the clutch gear. The clutch gear meshes with the large countergear of the countershaft gear cluster. This cluster gear is now rotating. Since the cluster gear is meshed with the speed gears on the mainshaft, the speed gears are also turning.

There can be no power output until one of the speed gears is locked to the mainshaft. This is done by activating a shift fork, which moves its synchronizer to engage the selected speed gear to the mainshaft. Power travels along the countershaft gear until it reaches this selected speed gear. It then passes through this gear

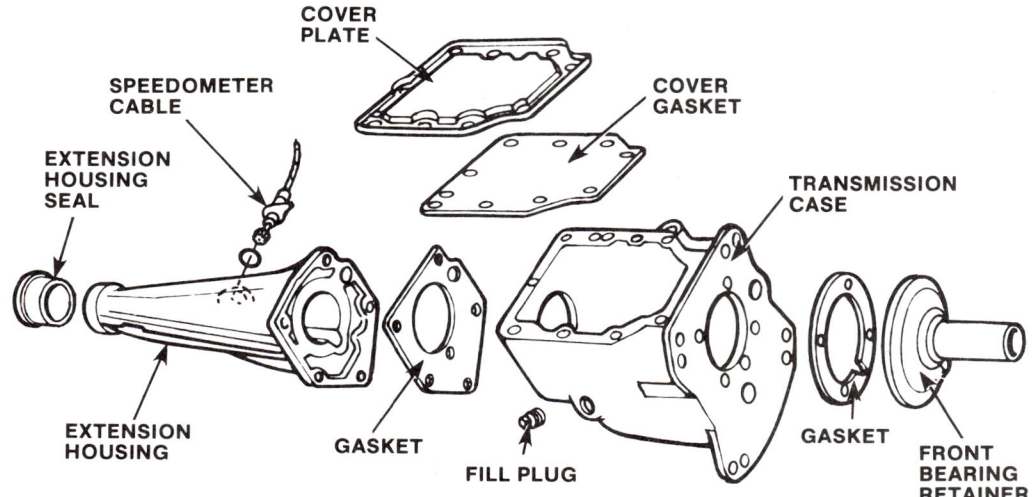

Figure 26-14 Typical four-speed manual transmission case components. *Courtesy of Ford Motor Co.*

Manual Transmissions and Transaxles

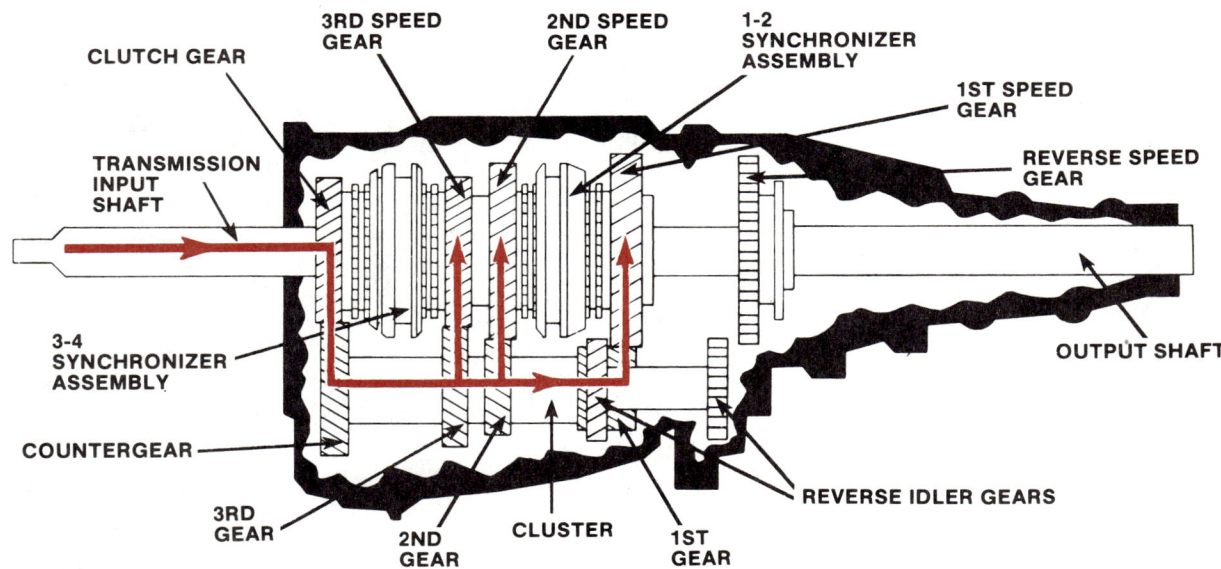

Figure 26-15 Internal parts of a four-speed transmission (shown in neutral), excluding shift forks. Power flows from the input shaft to the countershaft, and back to the mainshaft. Locking a main (speed) gear to the mainshaft or (output shaft) allows power flow through the transmission. *Courtesy of General Motors Corp.*

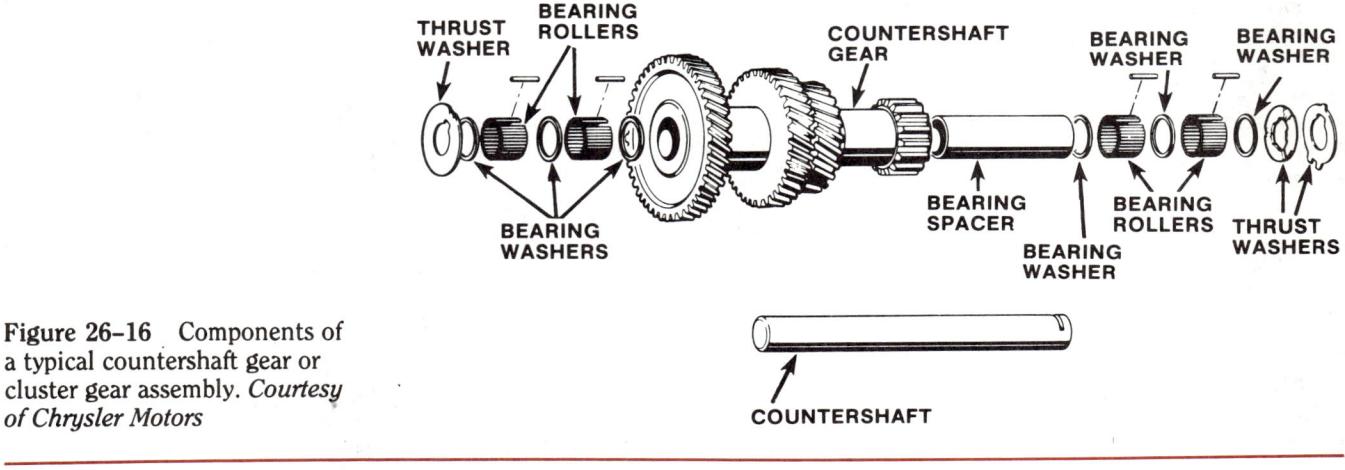

Figure 26-16 Components of a typical countershaft gear or cluster gear assembly. *Courtesy of Chrysler Motors*

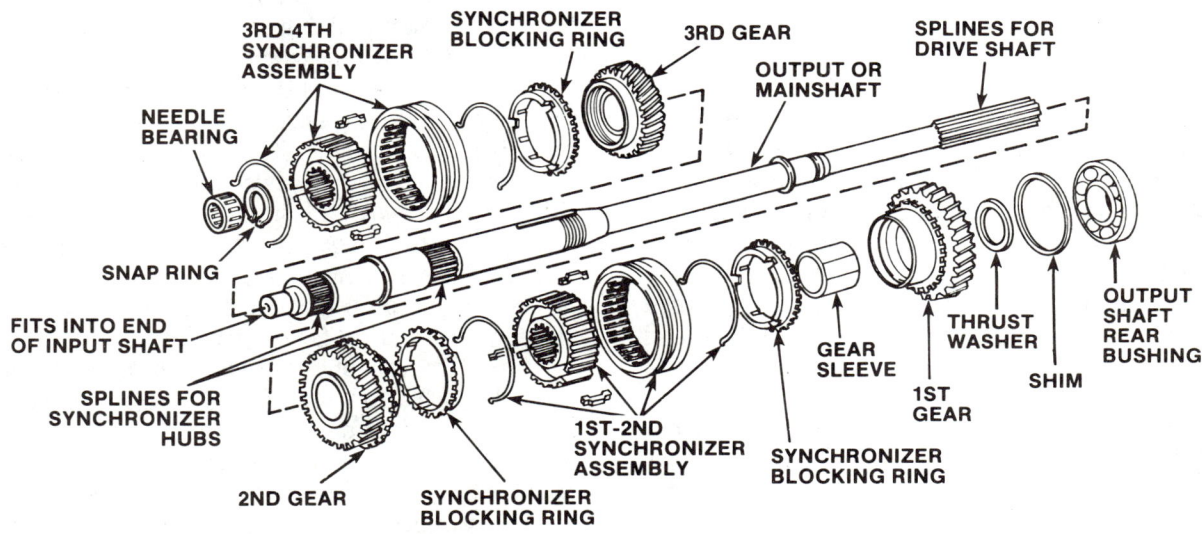

Figure 26-17 Components of a typical mainshaft or output shaft. *Courtsey of Mazda*

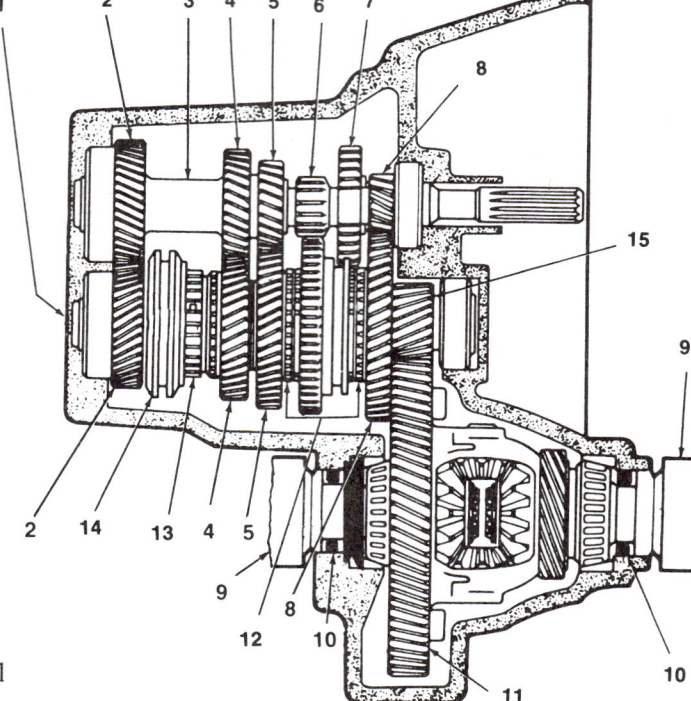

1. MAINSHAFT
2. 4TH SPEED GEARS
3. INPUT CLUSTER
4. 3RD SPEED GEARS
5. 2ND SPEED GEARS
6. REVERSE GEAR
7. REVERSE IDLER GEAR
8. 1ST SPEED GEARS
9. HALF SHAFTS
10. DIFFERENTIAL OIL SEALS
11. DIFFERENTIAL RING GEAR
12. 1ST/2ND SPEED SYNCHRONIZER BLOCKER RINGS
13. 3RD/4TH SPEED SYNCHRONIZER HUB
14. 3RD/4TH SPEED SYNCHRONIZER SLEEVE
15. PINION GEAR

Figure 26-18 Interior view of a typical four-speed manual transaxle. *Courtesy of Ford Motor Co.*

back to the mainshaft and out of the transmission to the driveline.

Transaxle Features

Transaxles use many of the design and operating principles found in transmissions. But because the transaxle also contains the differential gearing and drive axle connections, there are major differences in some areas of operation. Figure 26-18 illustrates the interior of a four-speed manual transaxle. This transaxle uses fully synchronized, constant mesh helical gears on all forward speeds and spur gears for reverse.

A transaxle has two separate shafts—an input shaft and an output shaft. The input shaft is the driving shaft. It is normally located above and parallel to the output shaft. The output shaft is the driven shaft. The transaxles main (speed) gears freewheel around the output shaft unless they are locked to the shaft by their synchronizer assembly. The main speed gears are in constant mesh with the input shaft drive gears. The drive gears turn whenever the input shaft turns.

The names used to describe transaxle shafts vary between manufacturers. The service manuals of some vehicles refer to the input shaft as the mainshaft and the output as the driven pinion or drive shaft. Others call the input shaft and its gears the input gear cluster and refer to the output shaft as the mainshaft. For clarity, this text uses the terms input gear cluster for the input shaft and its drive gears, and mainshaft for the output shaft.

A pinion gear is machined onto the end of the transaxle's mainshaft. This pinion gear is in constant mesh with the differential ring gear located in the lower portion of the transaxle housing. Because the pinion gear is part of the mainshaft, it must rotate whenever the mainshaft turns. With the pinion rotating, engine torque flows through the ring gear and differential gearing to the drive shafts and driving wheels.

☐ SYNCHRONIZERS

The synchronizer performs a number of jobs vital to transmission/transaxle operation. Its main job is to bring components that are rotating at different speeds to one synchronized speed. A synchronizer ensures that the mainshaft and the speed gear are rotating at the same speed. The second major job of the synchronizer is to actually lock these components together. The end result of these two functions is a clash-free shift. In transaxles, a synchronizer can have another important job. When spur teeth are cut into the outer sleeve of the synchronizer, the sleeve can act as a reverse idler gear and assist in producing the correct direction of rotation for reverse operation.

In modern transmissions and transaxles, all forward gears are synchronized. One synchronizer is placed between the first and second gears on the mainshaft. Another is placed between the third and fourth gears on the mainshaft. If the transmission has a fifth gear, it is also equipped with a synchronizer. Reverse gear is not normally fitted with a synchronizer. A synchronizer requires gear rotation to do its job and reverse is selected with the vehicle at a stop. In some older transmissions, or truck transmissions, both reverse and first gears may be unsynchronized.

Synchronizer Design

Figure 26-19 illustrates the most common synchronizer: a block or cone synchronizer. The synchronizer sleeve surrounds the synchronizer assembly and meshes with the external splines of the clutch hub. The clutch hub is splined to the transmission mainshaft and is held in position by a snap ring.

The synchronizer sleeve has a small internal groove and a large external groove in which the shift fork rests. Three slots are equally spaced around the outside of the clutch hub. Inserts fit into these slots and are able to slide freely back and forth. These inserts are designed with a ridge in their outer surface. Insert springs hold the ridge in contact with the synchronizer sleeve internal groove.

The synchronizer sleeve is precisely machined to slide onto the clutch hub smoothly. The sleeve and hub sometimes have alignment marks to assure proper indexing of their splines when assembling to maintain smooth operation.

Brass or bronze synchronizing blocker rings are positioned at the front and rear of each synchronizer assembly. Each blocker ring has three notches equally spaced to correspond with the three inset keys of the hub. Around the outside of each blocker ring is a set of beveled dog teeth, which is used for alignment during the shift sequence. The inside of the blocker ring is shaped like a cone. This coned surface is lined with many sharp grooves.

The cone of the blocker ring makes up only one-half of the total cone clutch. The second or mating half of the cone clutch is part of the gear to be synchronized. As shown in Figure 26-20, the shoulder of the speed gear is cone shaped to match the blocker ring. The

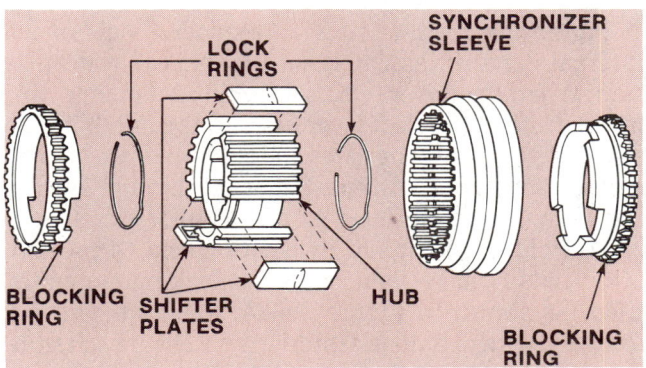

Figure 26-19 Exploded view of a blocker ring-type synchronizer assembly.

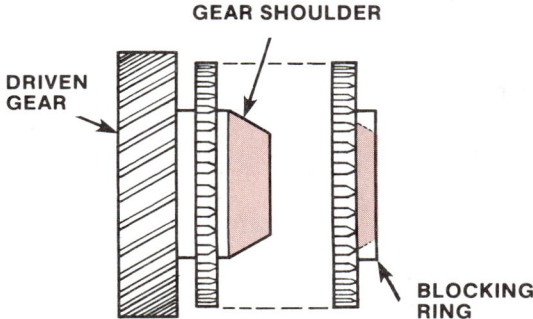

Figure 26-20 Gear shoulder and blocker ring mating surfaces.

shoulder also contains a ring of beveled dog teeth designed to align with the dog teeth on the blocker ring.

Operation

When the transmission is in neutral or reverse, the first/second and third/fourth synchronizers are in their neutral position and are not rotating with the mainshaft. Gears on the mainshaft are meshed with their countershaft partners and are freewheeling around the mainshaft at various speeds.

To shift the transmission into first gear, the clutch is disengaged and the gearshift lever is placed in first gear position. This forces the shift fork on the synchronizer sleeve toward the first speed gear on the mainshaft. As the sleeve moves, the inserts also move because the insert ridges lock the inserts to the internal groove of the sleeve.

The movement of the inserts forces the blocking ring's coned friction surface against the coned surface of the first speed gear shoulder. When the blocking ring and gear shoulder come into contact, the grooves on the blocker ring cone cut through the lubricant film on the first speed gear shoulder and a metal-to-metal contact is made (Figure 26-21). The contact generates substantial friction and heat. This is one reason bronze or brass blocker rings are used. A nonferrous metal such as bronze or brass minimizes wear on the hardened steel gear shoulder. This frictional coupling is not strong enough to transmit loads for long periods. As the components reach the same speed, the synchronizer sleeve can now slide over the external dog teeth on the blocking ring and then over the dog teeth on the first speed gear shoulder. This completes the engagement. Power flow is now from the first speed gear, to the synchronizer sleeve, to the synchronizer clutch hub, to the main output shaft, and out to the driveline.

To disengage the first speed gear from the mainshaft and shift into second speed gear, the clutch must be disengaged as the shift fork is moved to pull the synchronizer sleeve and disengage it from first gear. As the

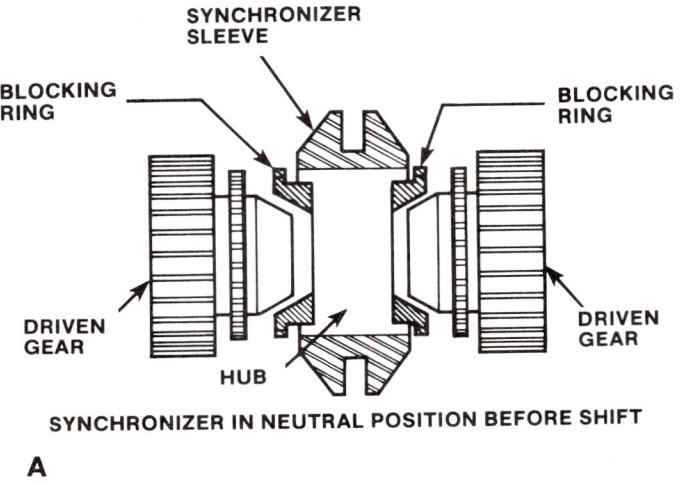
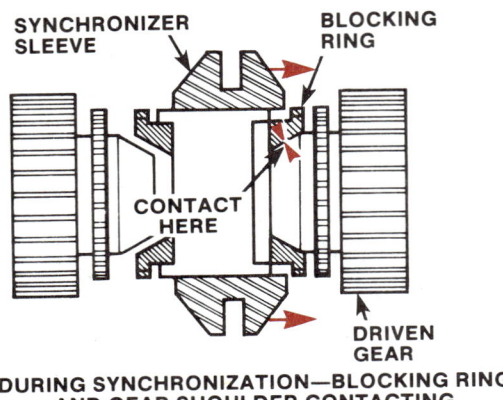

Figure 26-21 (A) Block or cone-type synchronizer in the neutral position; (B) initial contact of the blocking ring and gear shoulder; and (C) final engagement as the synchronizer sleeve locks the driven speed gear to the synchronizer hub and output shaft.

transmission is shifted into second gear, the inserts again lock into the internal groove of the sleeve. As the sleeve moves forward, the forward blocking ring is forced by the inserts against the coned friction surface on the second speed gear shoulder. Once again, the grooves on the blocker ring cut through the lubricant on the gear shoulder to generate a frictional coupling that synchronizes the gear and shaft speeds. The shift fork can then continue to move the sleeve forward until it slides over the blocker ring and gear shoulder dog teeth, locking them together. Power flow is now from the second speed gear, to the synchronizer sleeve, to the clutch hub, and out through the mainshaft.

❑ GEARSHIFT MECHANISMS

Figure 26-22 illustrates a typical transmission shift linkage for a five-speed transmission. As you can see, there are three separate shift rails and forks. Each shift rail/shift fork is used to control the movement of a synchronizer, and each synchronizer is capable of engaging and locking two speed gears to the mainshaft. The shift rails transfer motion from the driver controlled gearshift lever to the shift forks. The shift forks are semicircular castings connected to the shift rails with split pins. The shift fork rests in the groove in the synchronizer sleeve and surrounds about one-half of the sleeve circumference.

The gearshift lever is connected to the shift forks by means of a gearshift linkage. Linkage designs vary between manufacturers but can be generally classified as being internal or remote.

Internal gearshift linkage controls are positioned at the side of or on top of the transmission/transaxle housing. They are most often used in console (floor) mounted, rear-wheel-drive applications.

Internal Linkage Design

Figure 26-23 illustrates an exploded view of an internal gearshift assembly in a four-speed transmission. When the driver selects a specific gear range, the hooked end of the shift lever fits into the notch in the selected gear gate. The gates and shift forks are held to shift rails with pins. Any movement of the shift lever is transferred to the selected gate, rail, and fork.

To hold the shift rail in position and to prevent other rails from moving, a special locking system is used. As shown in Figure 26-24, the shift rails are designed with detent and interlock notches. Each shift rail has a detent ball that drops into the detent areas on the shift rail as a gear selection is made. This effectively locks the gear into position. There is also a detent

Manual Transmissions and Transaxles   651

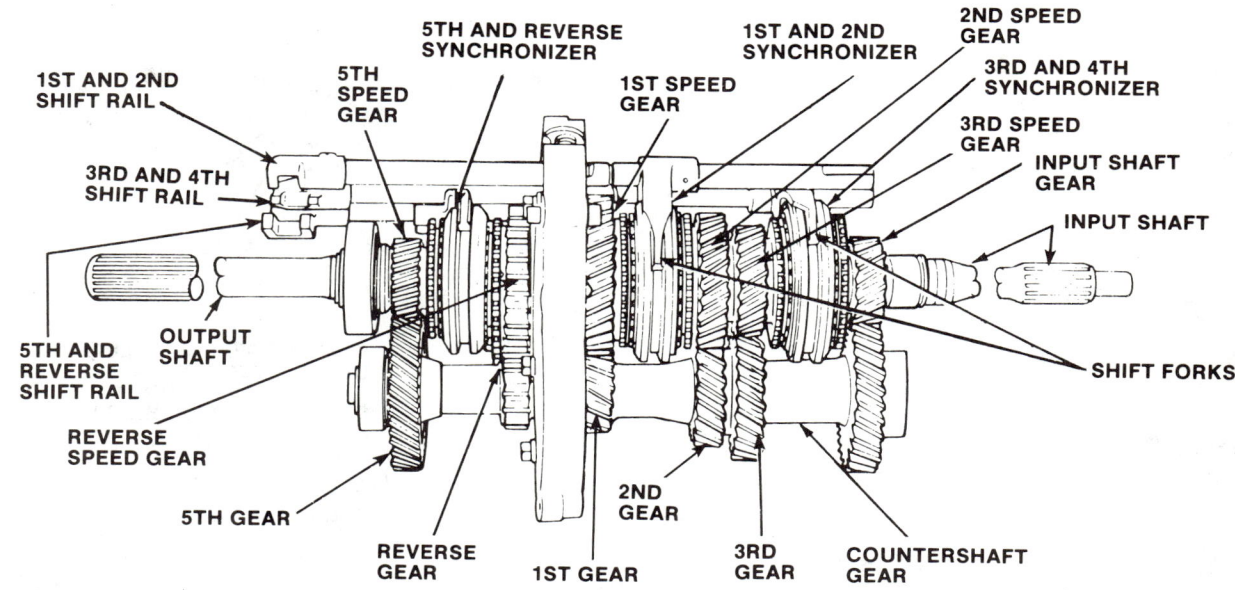

Figure 26-22 Interior view of a five-speed overdrive transmission. Three separate shift rail/shift fork/synchronizer combinations control first/second, third/fourth, and fifth/reverse shifting. *Courtesy of Ford Motor Co.*

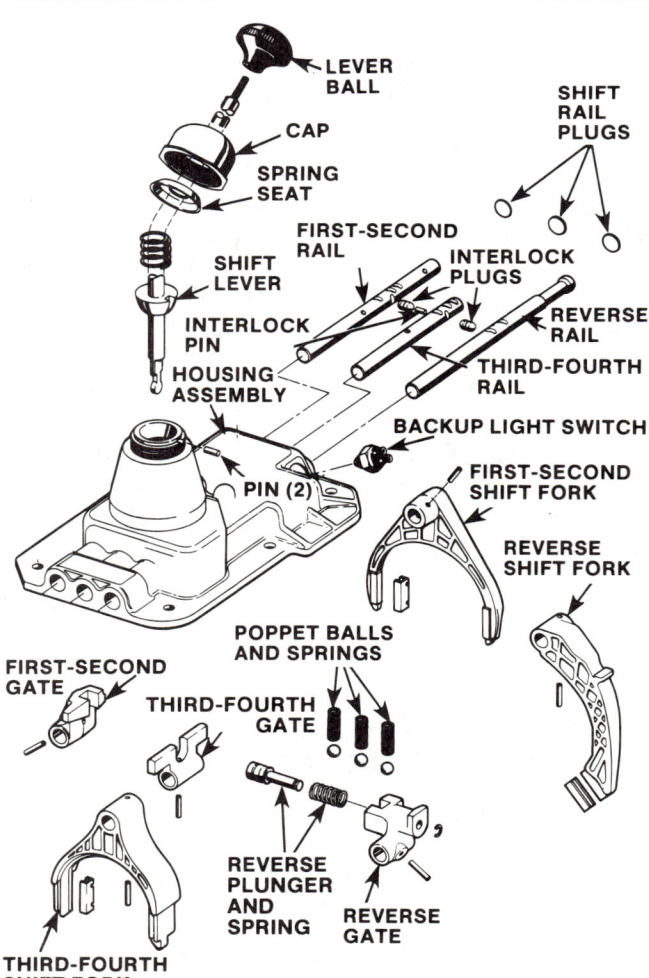

Figure 26-23 Typical internal shift linkage design. *Courtesy of Chrysler Motors*

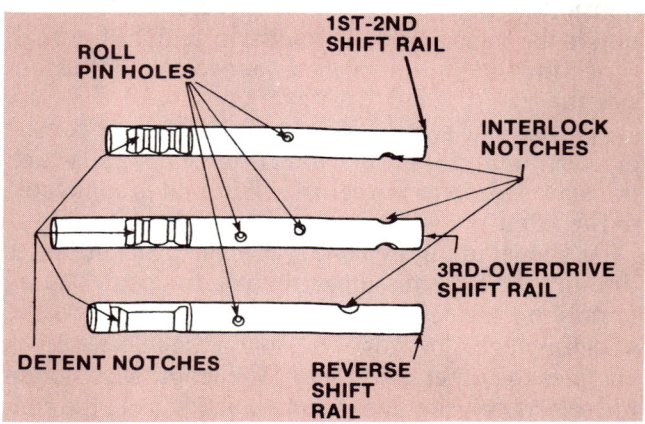

Figure 26-24 Shift rails installed on an internal linkage. *Courtesy of Ford Motor Co.*

notch for neutral. For example, when a shift from first to second gear is made, the detent ball moves from the first gear detent notch on the first/second rail to the second gear notch on the rail. A spring is used to hold the ball firmly in the notch and lock the transmission in second gear. At the same time the first to second shift is being made, the interlock pin moves out of its notch on the first/second shift rail. The interlock pin now rides on the outside diameter of the first/second rail until it is forced into the third/fourth interlock notch. The seated interlock pin holds the third/fourth rail stopping it from moving. The only way the third/fourth rail can be moved is to return the first/second rail to the neutral position. When this is done, the interlock pin drops into place, permitting third/fourth shift rail movement.

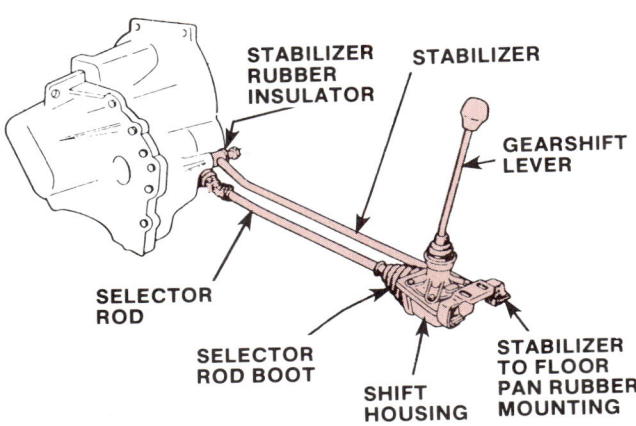

Figure 26-25 Remote gearshift showing linkage, selector rod, and stabilizer (stay bars). *Courtesy of Ford Motor Co.*

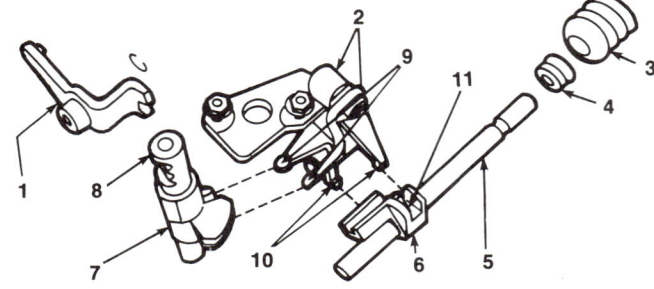

1 REVERSE GEARSHIFT LEVER
2 GUIDE LEVERS (2)
3 CONTROL SHAFT BOOT
4 CONTROL SHAFT OIL SEAL
5 CONTROL SHAFT
6 SELECTOR BLOCK
7 SELECTOR BLOCK
8 GUIDE SHAFT
9 INNER GUIDE LEVER
10 OUTER GUIDE LEVER
11 CROSS SLOT

Figure 26-27 Interior linkage components used for a remote gearshift setup. *Courtesy of Ford Motor Co.*

Remote Linkage Design

Remote gearshift linkages must be used when the shifting lever cannot or is not positioned at the transmission/transaxle location. A remote linkage can be divided into two parts: the external section required to transmit motion from the remote gearshift lever location to the transmission or transaxle, and the internal, which includes all linkage components contained inside the transmission/transaxle housing.

The external section of a remote linkage can consist of rods (Figure 26-25) or cables (Figure 26-26), which transmit motion to the control shaft that is connected to the internal components inside the housing.

As shown in Figure 26-27, the control shaft passes through the transmission/transaxle housing. The internal end of the control shaft is connected to the selector block. The crosswise slot on the selector block operates the outer guide lever. The lengthwise slot on the selector block transfers rotary action from the control shaft to the inner guide lever. The movement of these parts results in the movement of the guide shaft selector block, which engages the proper shift fork to move the required synchronizer.

☐ TRANSMISSION POWER FLOW

The following sections describe the power flow paths in a typical four-speed manual transmission.

Neutral

Neutral power flow is illustrated in Figure 26-28. The input shaft rotates at engine speed whenever the clutch is engaged. The clutch gear is mounted on the input shaft and rotates with it. The clutch gear meshes with the countershaft gear, which rotates around the countershaft.

The countershaft gear transfers power to the speed gears on the mainshaft. But since speed gears one, two, three, and four are not locked to the mainshaft when the transmission is in neutral, they cannot transfer power to the mainshaft. The mainshaft does not turn, and there is no power output to the driveline.

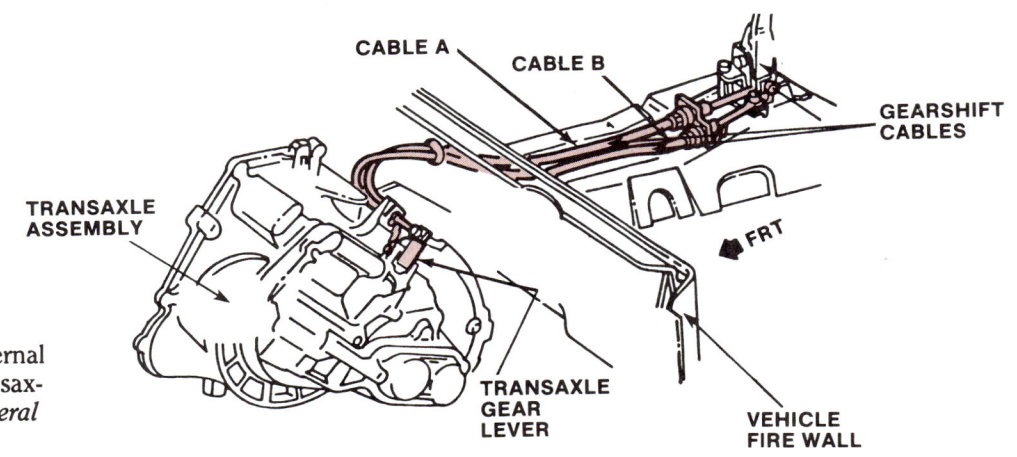

Figure 26-26 Cable-type external gearshift linkage used in a transaxle application. *Courtesy of General Motors Corp.*

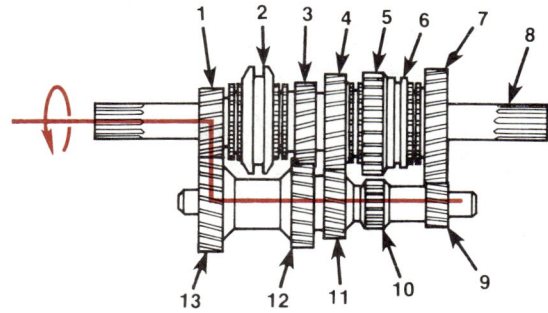

KEY
1. CLUTCH GEAR
2. 3-4 SYNCHRONIZER
3. 3RD GEAR
4. 2ND GEAR
5. 1-2 SYNCHRONIZER SLEEVE
6. 1-2 SYNCHRONIZER
7. 1ST SPEED GEAR
8. MAINSHAFT
9. COUNTERGEAR 1ST GEAR
10. COUNTERGEAR REVERSE GEAR
11. COUNTERGEAR 2ND GEAR
12. COUNTERGEAR 3RD GEAR
13. COUNTERSHAFT GEAR
14. REVERSE IDLER GEAR ASSEMBLY

Figure 26-28 Four-speed transmission power flow—neutral. *Courtesy of Volvo Car Corporation*

First Gear

First gear power flow is illustrated in Figure 26-29. Power or torque flows through the input shaft and clutch gear to the countershaft gear. The countershaft gear rotates. The first gear on the cluster drives the first speed gear on the mainshaft. When the driver selects first gear, the first/second synchronizer moves to the rear to engage the first speed gear and lock it to the mainshaft. The first speed gear drives the main (output) shaft, which transfers power to the driveline. A typical first speed gear ratio is 3:1 (three full turns of the input shaft to one full turn of the output shaft). So, if the engine torque entering the transmission is 220 foot-pounds it is multiplied three times to 660 foot-pounds by the time it is transferred to the driveline.

Second Gear

When the shift from first to second gear is made, the shift fork disengages the first/second synchronizer from the first speed gear and moves it until it locks the second speed gear to the mainshaft. Power flow is still through the input shaft and clutch gear to the countershaft gear. But now the second countergear on the cluster transfers power to the second speed gear locked on the mainshaft. Power flows from the second speed gear through the synchronizer to the mainshaft (output shaft) and driveline (Figure 26-30).

In second gear, the need for vehicle speed and acceleration is greater than the need for maximum torque multiplication. To meet these needs, the second speed gear on the mainshaft is designed slightly

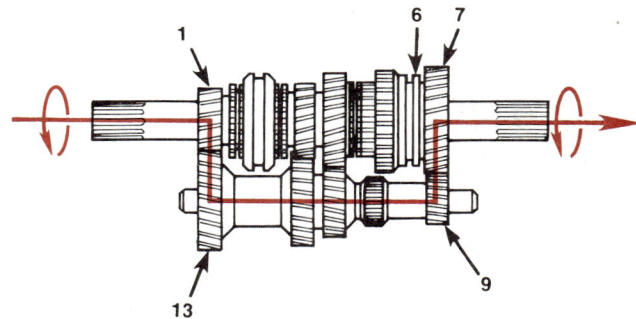

Figure 26-29 Four-speed transmission power flow—first gear. *Courtesy of Volvo Car Corporation*

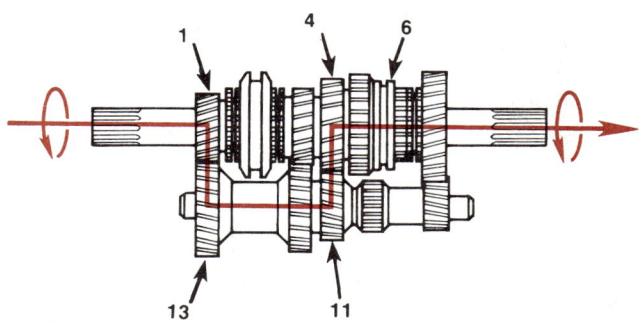

Figure 26-30 Four-speed transmission power flow—second gear. *Courtesy of Volvo Car Corporation*

smaller than the first speed gear. This results in a typical gear ratio of 2.2:1, which reflects a drop in torque and an increase in speed.

Third Gear

When the shift from second to third gear is made, the shift fork returns the first/second synchronizer to its neutral position. A second shift fork slides the third/fourth synchronizer until it locks the third speed gear to the mainshaft. Power flow now goes through the third gear of the countershaft gear to the third speed gear, through the synchronizer to the mainshaft, and driveline (Figure 26-31).

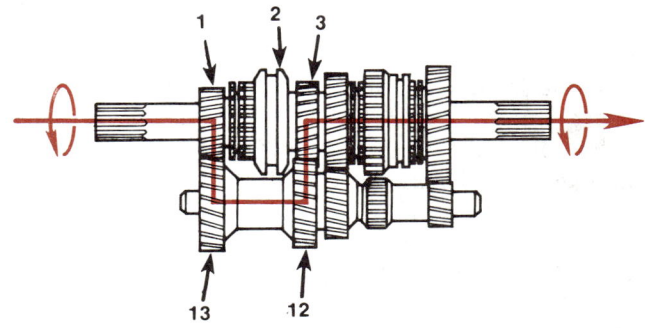

Figure 26-31 Four-speed transmission power flow—third gear. *Courtesy of Volvo Car Corporation*

654 Section 5 Manual Transmissions and Transaxles

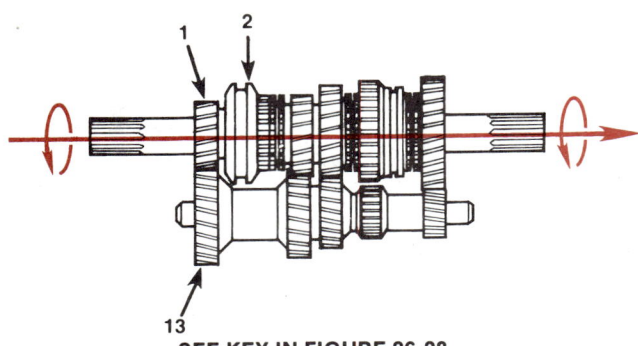

Figure 26-32 Four-speed transmission power flow—fourth gear. *Courtesy of Volvo Car Corporation*

Third gear permits a further decrease in torque and increase in speed. As you can see, the third speed gear is smaller than the second speed gear. This results in a typical gear ratio of 1.7:1.

Fourth Gear

In fourth gear, the third/fourth synchronizer is moved to lock the clutch gear on the input shaft to the mainshaft. This means power flow is directly from the input shaft to the mainshaft (output shaft) at a gear ratio of 1:1 (Figure 26-32). This ratio results in maximum speed output and no torque multiplication. Fourth gear has no torque multiplication because it is used at cruising speeds to promote maximum fuel economy. The vehicle is normally downshifted to lower gears to take advantage of torque multiplication and acceleration when passing slower vehicles or climbing grades.

Reverse

In reverse gear, it is necessary to reverse the direction of the mainshaft (output shaft). This is done by introducing a reverse idler gear into the power flow path. The idler gear is located between the countershaft reverse gear and the reverse speed gear on the mainshaft. The idler assembly is made of a short drive shaft independently mounted in the transmission case parallel to the countershaft. The idler gear may be mounted near the mid-point of the shaft (Figure 26-33).

In other transmissions, there are two separate idler gears, one near each end of the shaft. As shown in Figure 26-15, the reverse speed gear may be an independent gear located at the rear of the mainshaft. In the transmission shown in Figure 26-34, the reverse speed gear is actually the external tooth sleeve of the first-second synchronizer.

When reverse gear is selected, both synchronizers are disengaged. In the transmission shown in Figure 26-34, the shifting linkage moves the reverse idler gear

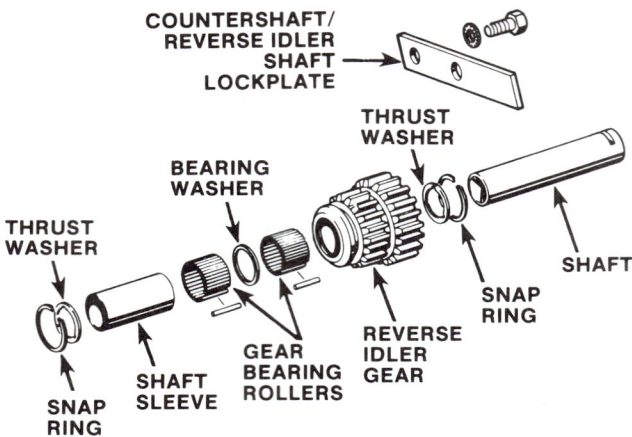

Figure 26-33 Components of a typical reverse idler gear assembly. *Courtesy of Chrysler Motors*

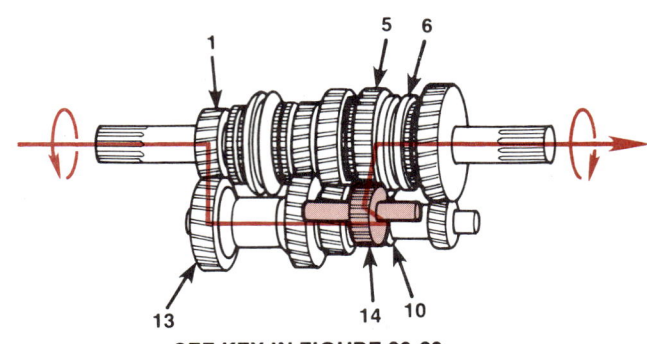

Figure 26-34 Four-speed transmission power flow—reverse gear. *Courtesy of Volvo Car Corporation*

into mesh with the first-second synchronizer sleeve. Power flows through the input shaft and clutch gear to the countershaft. From the countershaft it passes to the reverse idler gear, where it changes rotational direction. It then passes to the first-second synchronizer sleeve. Rotational direction is again reversed. From the sleeve, power passes to the mainshaft and driveline. In the transmission shown in Figure 26-15, selecting reverse slides the reverse speed gear forward until it meshes the rear idler gear. Power flows from the input shaft and clutch gear to the countershaft. It then passes through the front idler gear (direction change), rear idler gear, rear speed gear (direction change), and out through the mainshaft to the driveline.

☐ FIVE-SPEED OVERDRIVE

As discussed earlier, when a large gear drives a smaller gear, an overdrive condition occurs. The large driving gear may rotate three-quarters of a revolution while the smaller driven gear rotates one full turn. Overdrive permits an engine speed reduction at higher cruising speeds. Because the engine (rpm) is running slower, fuel economy is greater. But engine torque also drops, so power is sacrificed for better mileage.

Overdrive gears are usually located in the transmission housing. Figure 26-22 illustrates a five-speed overdrive transmission. The gear ratio of this fifth gear is 0.87:1. The reverse gear train is designed with spur type gearing. Unlike the four-speed transmission covered earlier, reverse shifting in this transmission is controlled by a synchronizer. As you can see, this synchronizer is also used to control engagement of fifth gear overdrive.

Power flows for first, second, third, fourth, and fifth gears are similar to those in the four-speed transmission described earlier. In each case, a shift fork moves the appropriate synchronizer to lock the required speed gear to the mainshaft. Power flows through the input shaft to the countershaft gear, and back through the mainshaft to the driveline.

When reverse gear is selected, the fifth/reverse synchronizer is moved by the fifth/reverse shift rail and shift fork. The synchronizer locks the reverse gear to the mainshaft. The clockwise rotation of the input shaft and clutch gear drive the countershaft gear in a counterclockwise direction. The reverse idler gearing is driven clockwise by the countershaft gear. The clockwise turning reverse idler gear drives the reverse speed gear, synchronizer, mainshaft, and driveline counterclockwise. The vehicle can then back up.

☐ TRANSAXLE POWER FLOWS

The following sections describe power flow for the gear ranges of the transaxle shown in Figure 26-16. The direction of rotation used in this example would be as viewed from the vehicle's right front fender looking into the engine compartment.

Neutral

When the transaxle is placed in neutral, the engaged clutch drives the input shaft and gear cluster assembly in a clockwise direction. The first/second and third/fourth synchronizers on the mainshaft are not engaged, so the mainshaft gears are not locked to the mainshaft. The mainshaft and the pinion gear do not turn, so there is no output to the transaxle differential ring gear.

First

In first gear, the first/second synchronizer engages the first speed gear to the mainshaft, locking it to the mainshaft. The cluster's first gear, rotating clockwise, drives the first speed gear and the mainshaft in a counterclockwise direction. The counterclockwise turning pinion on the end of the mainshaft drives the differential ring gear, differential gearing, drive shafts, and wheels in a clockwise direction (Figure 26-35).

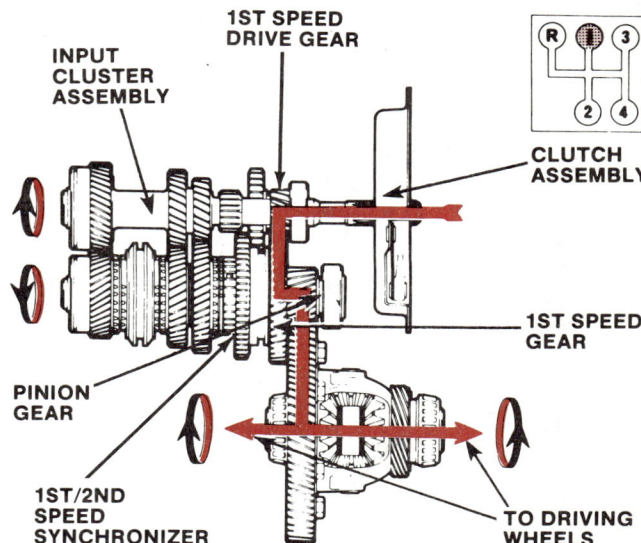

Figure 26-35 Four-speed transaxle power flow—first gear. *Courtesy of Ford Motor Co.*

Second

As the shift from first to second gear is made, the first/second synchronizer disengages the first speed gear on the mainshaft and engages the second speed gear. With the second speed gear locked to the mainshaft, power flow is as shown in Figure 26-36. As you can see, power flow and direction is similar to first gear with the exception that flow is now through the second speed gear and synchronizer to the mainshaft and pinion.

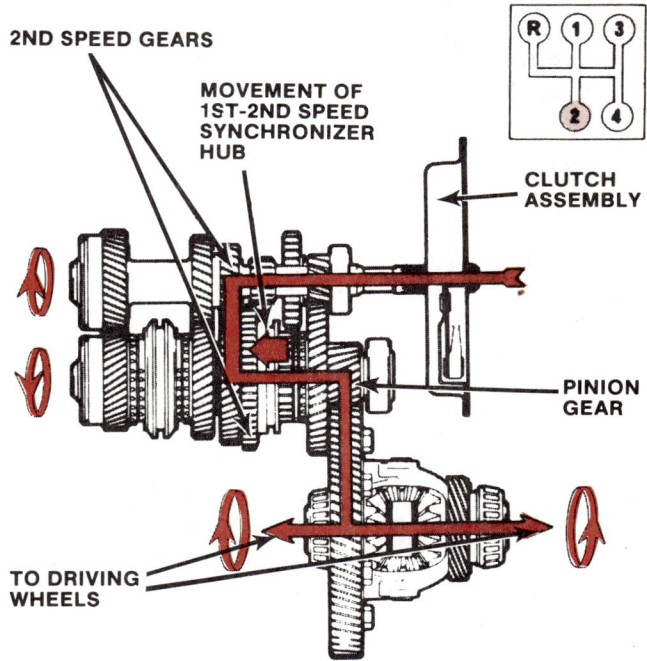

Figure 26-36 Four-speed transaxle power flow—second gear. *Courtesy of Ford Motor Co.*

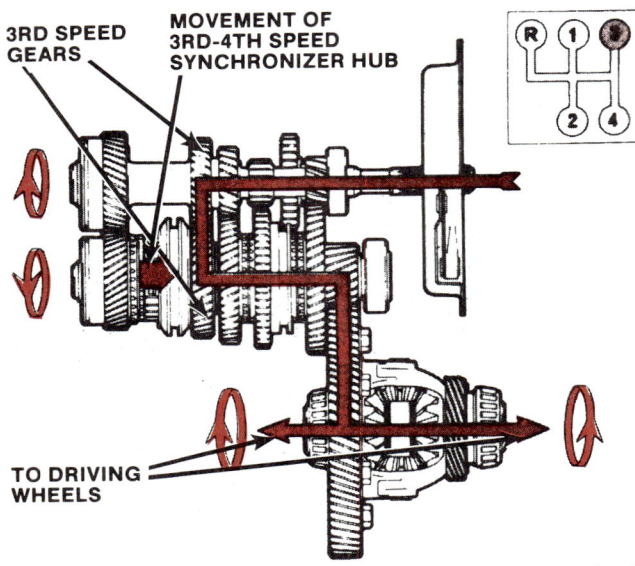

Figure 26-37 Four-speed transaxle power flow—third gear. *Courtesy of Ford Motor Co.*

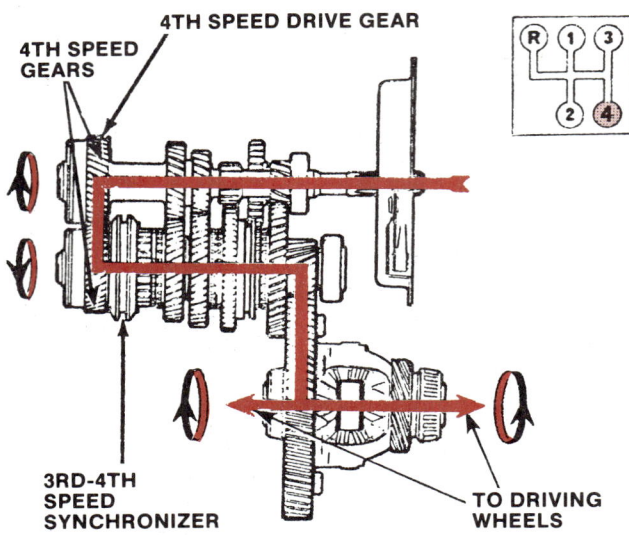

Figure 26-38 Four-speed transaxle power flow—fourth gear. *Courtesy of Ford Motor Co.*

Third

With the clutch disengaged, the first/second synchronizer sleeve disengages from the second speed gear on the mainshaft and returns to its midway or neutral position between the first and second speed gears. As the driver moves the shift lever from its second gear position through neutral to the third gear position, the gear lever inside the transaxle housing moves from the first/second synchronizer position to the third/fourth synchronizer position. It engages the third/fourth synchronizer and locks it to the third speed gear on the mainshaft. Power flow is then through the third speed gear to the synchronizer and mainshaft to the pinion gear and differential ring gear (Figure 26-37).

Fourth

The action of the shift lever moves the third/fourth synchronizer sleeve away from the mainshaft third speed gear and toward the fourth speed gear, locking it to the mainshaft. Power flow for fourth gear is shown in Figure 26-38.

Reverse

When the shift lever is placed in reverse, the reverse idler gear shifts into mesh with the input cluster reverse gear and the reverse speed gear. The reverse speed gear is the sleeve of the first/second synchronizer. To act as the reverse speed gear, the synchronizer sleeve is designed with spur teeth machined around its outside edge.

The reverse idler gear changes the direction of rotation of the mainshaft reverse speed gear so that the vehicle backs up. Reverse power flow is illustrated in Figure 26-39.

Like transmissions, some transaxles have five forward speeds. Normally, fourth and fifth gears for smaller cars have overdrive ratios. These high gear ratios compensate for very low final drive gear ratios.

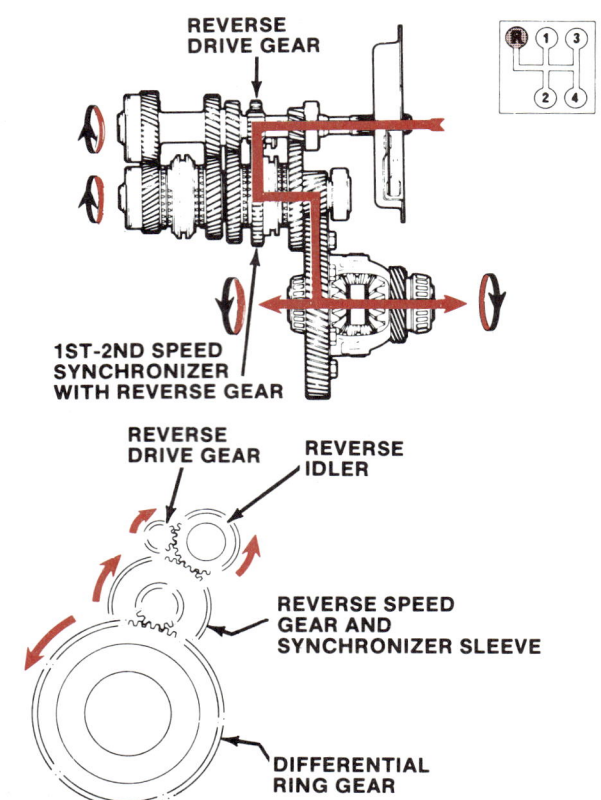

Figure 26-39 Four-speed transaxle power flow—reverse gear. *Courtesy of Ford Motor Co.*

Manual Transmissions and Transaxles

TABLE 26-1 TRANSMISSION/TRANSAXLE TROUBLESHOOTING CHART

Problem	Possible Cause	Remedy
Gear clash when shifting from one gear to another	1. Clutch adjustment incorrect 2. Clutch linkage or cable binding 3. Clutch housing misalignment 4. Lubricant level low or incorrect lubricant 5. Gearshift components or synchronizer blocker rings worn or damaged	1. Adjust clutch. 2. Lubricate or repair as necessary. 3. Check runout at rear face of clutch housing. Correct runout. 4. Drain and refill transmission/transaxle and check for lubricant leaks if level was low. Repair as necessary. 5. Remove, disassemble, and inspect transmission/transaxle. Replace worn or damaged components as necessary.
Clicking noise in any one gear range	1. Damaged teeth on input or intermediate shaft gears (transaxles) or damaged teeth on the counter gear, or cluster gear assembly, or output shaft gears (transmissions)	1. Remove, disassemble, and inspect unit. Replace worn or damaged components as necessary.
Does not shift into one gear	1. Gearshift internal linkage or shift rail assembly worn, damaged, or incorrectly assembled 2. Shift rail detent plunger worn, spring broken, or plug loose 3. Gearshift lever worn or damaged 4. Synchronizer sleeves or hubs damaged or worn	1. Remove, disassemble, and inspect transmission/transaxle cover assembly. Repair or replace components as necessary. 2. Tighten plug or replace worn or damaged components as necessary. 3. Replace gearshift lever. 4. Remove, disassemble, and inspect unit. Replace worn or damaged components.
Locked in one gear—cannot be shifted out of that gear	1. Shift rails worn or broken, shifter fork bent, setscrew loose, center detent plug missing or worn 2. Broken gear teeth on countershaft gear input shaft, or reverse idler gear 3. Gearshift lever broken or worn, shift mechanism in cover incorrectly assembled or broken, worn or damaged gear train components	1. Inspect and replace worn or damaged parts. 2. Inspect and replace damaged part. 3. Disassemble transmission/transaxle. Replace damaged parts or assemble correctly.
Slips out of gear	1. Clutch housing misaligned 2. Gearshift offset lever nylon insert worn or lever attachment nut loose 3. Gearshift mechanism, shift forks, shift rail, detent plugs, springs, or shift cover worn or damaged 4. Clutch shaft or roller bearings worn or damaged 5. Gear teeth worn or tapered, synchronizer assemblies worn	1. Check runout at rear face of clutch housing. 2. Remove gearshift lever and check for loose offset lever nut or worn insert. Repair or replace as necessary. 3. Remove, disassemble, and inspect transmission cover assembly. Replace worn or damaged components as necessary. 4. Replace clutch shaft or roller bearings as necessary. 5. Remove, disassemble, and inspect transmission/transaxle.

TABLE 26-1 TRANSMISSION/TRANSAXLE TROUBLESHOOTING CHART CONTINUED

Problem	Possible Cause	Remedy
	or damaged, excessive end play caused by worn thrust washers or output shaft gears 6. Pilot bushing worn	Replace worn or damaged components as necessary. 6. Replace pilot bushing.
Vehicle moving—rough growling noise isolated in transmission/transaxle heard in all gears	1. Intermediate shaft front or rear bearings worn or damaged (transaxle) or output shaft rear bearing worn or damaged (transmission)	1. Remove, disassemble, and inspect transmission/transaxle. Replace damaged components as necessary.
Rough growling noise when engine operating with transmission/transaxle in neutral	1. Input shaft front or rear bearings worn or damaged (transaxle) or input shaft bearing, countergear, or countershaft bearings worn or damaged (transmission)	1. Remove, disassemble, and inspect transmission/transaxle. Replace damaged components as necessary.
Vehicle moving—rough growling noise in transmission—noise heard in all gears, except direct drive	1. Output shaft pilot roller bearings	1. Remove, disassemble, and inspect transmission. Replace damaged components as needed.
Transmission/transaxle shifts hard	1. Clutch adjustment incorrect 2. Clutch linkage binding 3. Shift rail binding 4. Internal bind in transmission/transaxle caused by shift forks, selector plates, or synchronizer assemblies 5. Clutch housing misalignment 6. Incorrect lubricant	1. Adjust clutch. 2. Lubricate or repair as necessary. 3. Check for mispositioned roll pin, loose cover bolts, worn shift rail bores, worn shift rail, distorted oil seal, or extension housing not aligned with case. Repair as necessary. 4. Remove, disassemble, and inspect unit. Replace worn or damaged components as necessary. 5. Check runout at rear of clutch housing. Correct runout. 6. Drain and refill.

Low final drive ratios provide great torque multiplication, which is needed to safely accelerate with a small engine.

☐ FINAL DRIVE GEARS AND OVERALL RATIOS

All vehicles use a differential to provide an additional gear reduction (torque increase) above and beyond what the transmission or transaxle gearing can produce. This is known as the final drive gear.

In a transmission equipped vehicle, the differential gearing is located in the rear axle housing. In a transaxle, however, the final reduction is produced by the final drive gears housed in the transaxle case.

The final drive gears consist of the mainshaft pinion gear and the large differential ring gear. The fact that the driving pinion gear is much smaller than the driven ring gear leaves no doubt that there is substantial gear reduction and torque multiplication in the final drive gears. A typical final drive ratio in a transaxle is 3.78:1.

This is calculated by dividing the number of teeth on the driving ring gear (68) by the number of teeth on the driving pinion gear (18): 68 ÷ 18 = 3.78.

To obtain the overall gear ratio or the final gear reduction at the drive axles and drive wheels, the final gear ratio is multiplied by the gear ratio generated by the input cluster and mainshaft gears for each gear range.

For example, first gear cluster and mainshaft gears produce a gear ratio of 3.16:1. When multiplied by the final drive ratio of 3.78:1, the overall ratio is 3.16 × 3.78 = 11.94:1. This means driving torque at the drive axles and wheels is 11.94 times greater than engine torque at the input shaft.

Use Table 26-1 for troubleshooting transmission/transaxle problems.

CUSTOMER CARE

Just because the technician gets a little dirty in the course of a repair, does not mean the vehicle should, too. Treat every car that enters the shop with the utmost care and consideration. Scratches from belt buckles or tools and grease smears on the steering wheel, upholstery, or carpeting are inexcusible, and a sure way of losing business. Always use fender, seat, and floor covers when the job requires. Check your hands for cleanliness before driving a vehicle or operating the windows and dash controls.

CASE STUDY

Case 1

A regular customer brings a recently-purchased 1989 Mustang GT into the shop. The used car was bought just two months ago. The customer's main complaint is that the car gets extremely poor gas mileage. The customer states that the car runs well and has plenty of power, but it seems to use much more fuel than he had anticipated it would.

The technician takes the car out for a test drive. The car runs very well. In fact, the car accelerates much quicker than the technician experienced in similar cars. Knowing the customer, the technician knows the complaint is legitimate. Therefore, she begins to think of the possible causes for poor fuel mileage. Because the engine runs well, it is unlikely that an engine problem is the cause unless the engine has been modified. Another possible cause is a fuel leak. After a detailed visual inspection, the technician finds no evidence of modifications or fuel leaks.

The technician decides to road test the car again. This time she notices a problem with the speedometer. It seems to be reading much higher speeds than the car is actually travelling. To verify this, she drives the car onto the freeway and observes the odometer and the mileage markers along the side of the road. The speedometer is in error. It records speeds that are higher than actual speeds and measures a mile well before completing an actual mile.

Odometer error was causing the owner to perceive that the gas mileage was very poor. But why is the odometer in error? Another careful visual inspection is conducted. This time attention is paid to the transmission and the rear axle. Sealing compound is present around the outside of the differential housing. This indicates that the unit has been disassembled. She rotates the rear wheels while observing the drive shaft. Doing so, she is able to closely determine the final drive gear ratio. Comparing her findings to the specifications listed in the service manual, she finds that the gear ratio is much higher numerically than the standard gear ratio. She concludes that the gears had been changed for better performance and this is what caused the error in the speedometer.

The technician contacts the owner and explains what she has found. She gives the owner two options to correct the problem. Either he should replace the gears with gears of the standard ratio or have the transmission's speedometer gear replaced with one that matches the final drive gear. Because the latter is less costly, the owner elects to change the speedometer gear.

Summary

- A transmission or transaxle uses meshed gears of various sizes to give the engine a mechanical advantage over its driving wheels.
- Transaxles contain the gear train plus the differential gearing needed to produce the final gear ratios. Transaxles are commonly used on front-wheel-drive vehicles.
- Transmissions are normally used on rear-wheel-drive vehicles.
- Gears in the transmission/transaxle transfer power and motion from an input shaft to an output shaft. These shafts are mounted parallel to one another.
- Spur gears have straight cut teeth, while helical gears have teeth cut at an angle. Helical gears run without creating gear whine.
- When a small gear drives a larger gear, output speed decreases but torque (power) increases.
- When a large gear drives a smaller gear, output speed increases but torque (power) decreases.
- When two external tooth gears are meshed and turning, the driven gear rotates in the opposite direction of the driving gear.
- Synchronizers bring parts rotating at different speeds to the same speed for smooth clash-free shifting. The synchronizer also locks and unlocks the driven (speed) gears to the transmission/transaxle output shaft.
- Idler gears are used to reverse the rotational direction of the output shaft for operating the vehicle in reverse.
- In a typical five-speed transmission shift linkage, there are three separate shift rails and forks. Each shift rail/shift fork is used to control the movement of a synchronizer.
- Gear ratios indicate the number of times the input drive gear is turning for every turn of the output driven gear. Ratios are calculated by dividing the number of teeth on the driven gear by the number of teeth on the drive gear. You can also use the rpm speeds of meshed gears to calculate gear ratios.
- A gear ratio of less than 1 indicates an overdrive condition. This means the driven gear is turning faster than the drive gear. Speed is high, but output torque is low.

- All vehicles use a gearset in a differential to provide additional gear reduction (torque increase) above and beyond what the transmission or transaxle gearing can produce.

Review Questions

1. What determines whether a conventional transmission or a transaxle is used?
2. Explain the relationship between output speed and torque.
3. What is the special function the synchronizer performs in some transaxles?
4. Define final drive gear.
5. Explain the role of shift rails and shift forks in the operation of transmissions and transaxles.
6. Gears can _____.
   a. transfer speed and torque unchanged
   b. decrease speed and increase torque
   c. increase speed and decrease torque
   d. all of the above
7. The number of gear teeth per unit measurement of the gear's pitch diameter (such as teeth/inch) is known as gear _____.
   a. ratio
   b. pitch
   c. size
   d. load
8. Which of the following gear ratios shows an overdrive condition?
   a. 2.15:1
   b. 1:1
   c. 0.85:1
   d. none of the above
9. Which type of gear develops the problem of gear whine at higher speeds?
   a. spur gear
   b. helical gear
   c. both a and b
   d. all of the above
10. Technician A says that in a conventional transmission, the speed gears freewheel around the mainshaft until they are locked to it by the appropriate synchronizer. Technician B says that speed gears are an integral part of the countershaft. Who is correct?
    a. Technician A
    b. Technician B
    c. Both A and B
    d. Neither A nor B
11. When an idler gear is placed between the driving and driven gear, the driven gear _____.
    a. rotates in the same direction as the driving gear
    b. rotates in the opposite direction of the driving gear
    c. remains stationary
    d. causes the driven gear to rotate faster
12. The component used to ensure that the mainshaft (output shaft) and main (speed) gear to be locked to it are rotating at the same speed is known as a _____.
    a. synchronizer
    b. shift linkage
    c. shift fork
    d. transfer case
13. Technician A says that the countershaft gear or cluster gear is actually several gears machined out of a single piece of steel. Technician B says that the countershaft gear is driven by the clutch gear and drives the mainshaft speed gears. Who is correct?
    a. Technician A
    b. Technician B
    c. Both A and B
    d. Neither A nor B
14. In a transaxle, the pinion gear on the mainshaft meshes with the _____.
    a. reverse idler gear
    b. differential ring gear
    c. countershaft drive gear
    d. input gear
15. Which of the following gearshift linkage types mounts to the top or side of the transmission/transaxle housing?
    a. internal
    b. external
    c. remote
    d. synchronized
16. Technician A says that a gear ratio can be determined by dividing the number of teeth in the driven gear by the number of teeth in the drive gear. Technician B says the gear ratio can be determined by dividing the rpm of the driven gear by the rpm of the drive gear. Who is correct?
    a. Technician A
    b. Technician B
    c. Both A and B
    d. Neither A nor B
17. Which of following gear ratios generates the highest torque or power output?
    a. 0.85:1
    b. 2.67:1
    c. 5.23:1
    d. 11.12:1

27 MANUAL TRANSMISSION/ TRANSAXLE SERVICE

Objectives

- Perform a visual inspection of transmission/transaxle components for signs of damage or wear.
- Check transmission oil levels correctly, detect signs of contaminated oil, and change oil as needed.
- Describe the steps taken to remove and install transmissions/transaxles including the equipment used and safety precautions.
- Identify common transmission problems, and their probable causes and solutions.
- Describe the basic steps and precautions taken during transmission/transaxle disassembly, cleaning, inspection, and reassembly procedures.

When properly operated and maintained, a manual transmission/transaxle normally lasts the life of the vehicle without a major breakdown. All units are designed so that the internal parts operate in a bath of oil circulated by the motion of the gears and shafts. Some units also use a pump to circulate oil to critical wear areas that require more lubrication than the natural circulation provides.

Maintaining good internal lubrications is the key to long transmission/transaxle life. If the amount of oil falls below minimum levels, or if the oil becomes too dirty, problems result.

❏ LUBRICANT CHECK

The transmission/transaxle gear oil level should be checked at the intervals specified in the service manual. Normally, these range from every 7500 to 30,000 miles. For service convenience, many units are now designed with a dipstick and filler tube accessible from beneath the hood (Figure 27-1). Check the oil with the engine off and the vehicle resting on level grade. If the engine has been running, wait 2 to 3 minutes before checking the gear oil level.

Some vehicles have no dipstick. Instead, the vehicle must be placed on a lift, and the oil level checked through the fill plug opening on the side of the unit (Figure 27-2). Clean the area around the plug before loosening and removing it. Insert a finger or bent rod into the hole to check the level. The oil may be hot. Lubricant should be level with, or not more than 1/2 inch below the fill hole. Add the proper grade lubricant as needed using a filler pump.

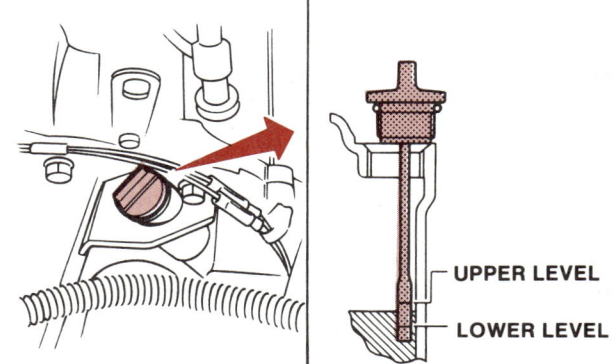

Figure 27-1 Example of typical underhood gear oil dipstick location and level readings. *Courtesy of Subaru of America*

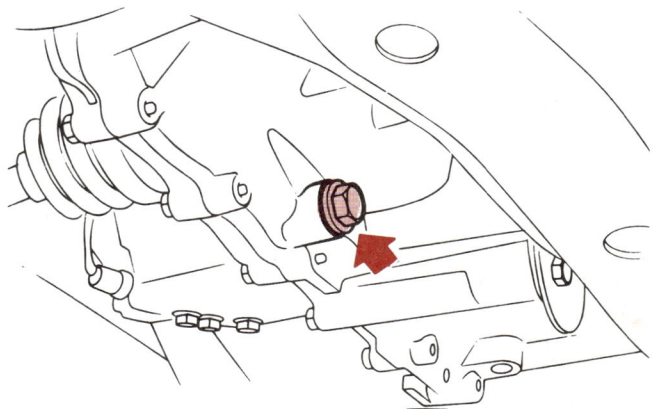

Figure 27-2 Typical drain plug location on transaxle case. *Courtesy of Subaru of America*

661

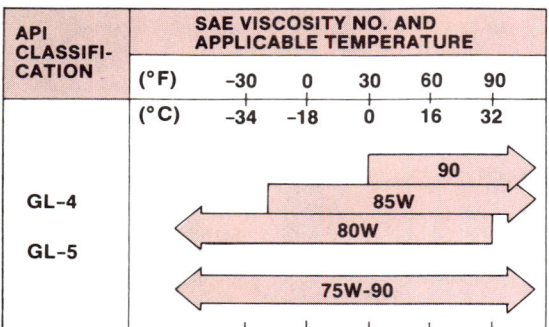

Figure 27-3 Typical transmission/transaxle gear oil classification and viscosity range data. *Courtesy of Subaru of America*

Manual transmission/transaxle lubricants in use today include single and multiple viscosity gear oils, engine oils, and automatic transmission fluid. Always refer to the service manual to determine the correct lubricant and viscosity range for the vehicle and operation conditions (Figure 27-3).

Lubricant Replacement

Transmission/transaxle lubricant should be changed at the manufacturer's specified intervals. Typical intervals are 24,000 or 30,000 miles or every two years. Vehicles used for towing trailers, off-road operation, or continuous stop-and-go driving may require shorter change intervals.

Drive the vehicle to warm the lubricant before placing the vehicle on the hoist. Clean and remove the drain plug and allow the lubricant to drain into a clean catch pan. Inspect the lubricant for metal particles, which may appear as a shiny, metallic color in the lubricant. Large amounts of metal particles indicate severe bearing, synchronizer, gear, or housing wear.

Once all lubricant has drained, replace the washer or apply a recommended sealant to the threads on the drain plug and replace it. Tighten the drain plug to the recommended torque. Fill the transmission or transaxle with the proper lubricant.

❑ DIAGNOSING PROBLEMS

Service manuals list the most common problems associated with manual transmissions and transaxles. Proper diagnosis involves locating the exact source of the problem. Many problems that seem transmission/transaxle related may actually be caused by problems in the clutch driveline or differential. Check these areas along with the transmission/transaxle, particularly if you are considering removing the transmission/transaxle for service.

Visual Inspection

Visually inspect the transmission/transaxle at regular intervals. Perform the following checks.

1. Check for lubricant leaks at all gaskets and seals. The transmission rear seal at the driveline is particularly prone to leakage.
2. Check the case body for signs of porosity that show up as leakage or seepage of lubricant.
3. Push up and down on the unit. Watch the transmission mounts to see if the rubber separates from the metal plate. If the case moves up, but not down, the mounts require replacement.
4. Move the clutch and shift linkages around and check for loose or missing components. Cable linkages should have no kinks or sharp bends and all movement should be smooth.
5. Transaxle drive axles should be checked for cracks, deformation, or damage.
6. The constant velocity joints on transaxle drive axles should be thoroughly inspected.

Transmission Noise

Most manual transmission/transaxle complaints center around noise in the unit. Once again, be certain the noise is not coming from other components in the drivetrain. Unusual noises may also be a sign of trouble in the engine or transmission mounting system. Improperly aligned engines, improperly torqued mounting bolts, damaged or missing rubber mounts, cracked brackets, or even a stone rattling around inside the engine compartment can create noises that appear to be transmission/transaxle related.

SHOP TALK

If during the test drive you hear a noise you suspect is coming from inside the transmission/transaxle, bring the vehicle to a stop. Disengage the clutch. If the noise stops with the engine at idle and the clutch disengaged, it is likely the noise is inside the unit.

Once you have eliminated all other possible sources of noise, concentrate on the transmission/transaxle unit. Noises from inside the transmission/transaxle may indicate worn or damaged bearings, gear teeth, or synchronizers. A noise that changes or disappears in different gears can indicate a specific problem area in the transmission.

CAUTION: When the transmission/transaxle is in gear and the engine is running, the driving wheels and related parts turn. Avoid touching moving parts. Severe physical injury can result from contact with spinning drive axles and wheels.

The type of noise detected may also help indicate the problem.

Rough, Growling Noise

This can be a sign of several problems in a transaxle or transmission depending on when it occurs. If the noise occurs when the transaxle is in neutral and the engine running, the problem may be the input shaft roller bearings. The input shaft is supported on either end by tapered roller bearings, and these are the only bearings in operation when the transaxle is in neutral (Figure 27-4). In early stages, the problem should not cause operational difficulties, but left uncorrected, it grows worse until the bearing race or rolling element fractures. Solving the problem involves transaxle disassembly and bearing replacement.

When the vehicle is moving, both the input and mainshaft (output shaft) are turning in the transaxle. If the noise occurs in forward and reverse gears, but not in neutral, the output or mainshaft bearings are the likely failed component. Replacement is the solution.

In transmissions, the problem is also bearing related. If the rough growling noise occurs when the engine is running, the clutch engaged, and the transmission in neutral, the front input shaft bearing is likely at fault. Rough growling when the vehicle is moving in all gears indicates faulty countergear bearings or countershaft-to-cluster assembly needle bearings. If the problem occurs in all gears except direct drive, the bearing at the rear of the transmission input shaft may be at fault. This bearing supports the pilot journal at the front of the transmission output shaft. In all forward gears except direct drive the input shaft and output shaft turn at two different speeds. In reverse, the two shafts turn in opposite directions. In direct drive, the two shafts are locked together and this bearing does not turn. If the growling noises stop during direct drive operation, the rear input shaft bearing may be at fault. Disassembly, inspection, and replacement of damaged parts is needed.

Clicking or Knocking Noise

Normally, the helical gears used in modern transmissions/transaxles are quiet because the gear teeth are constantly in contact. (When spur cut gear teeth

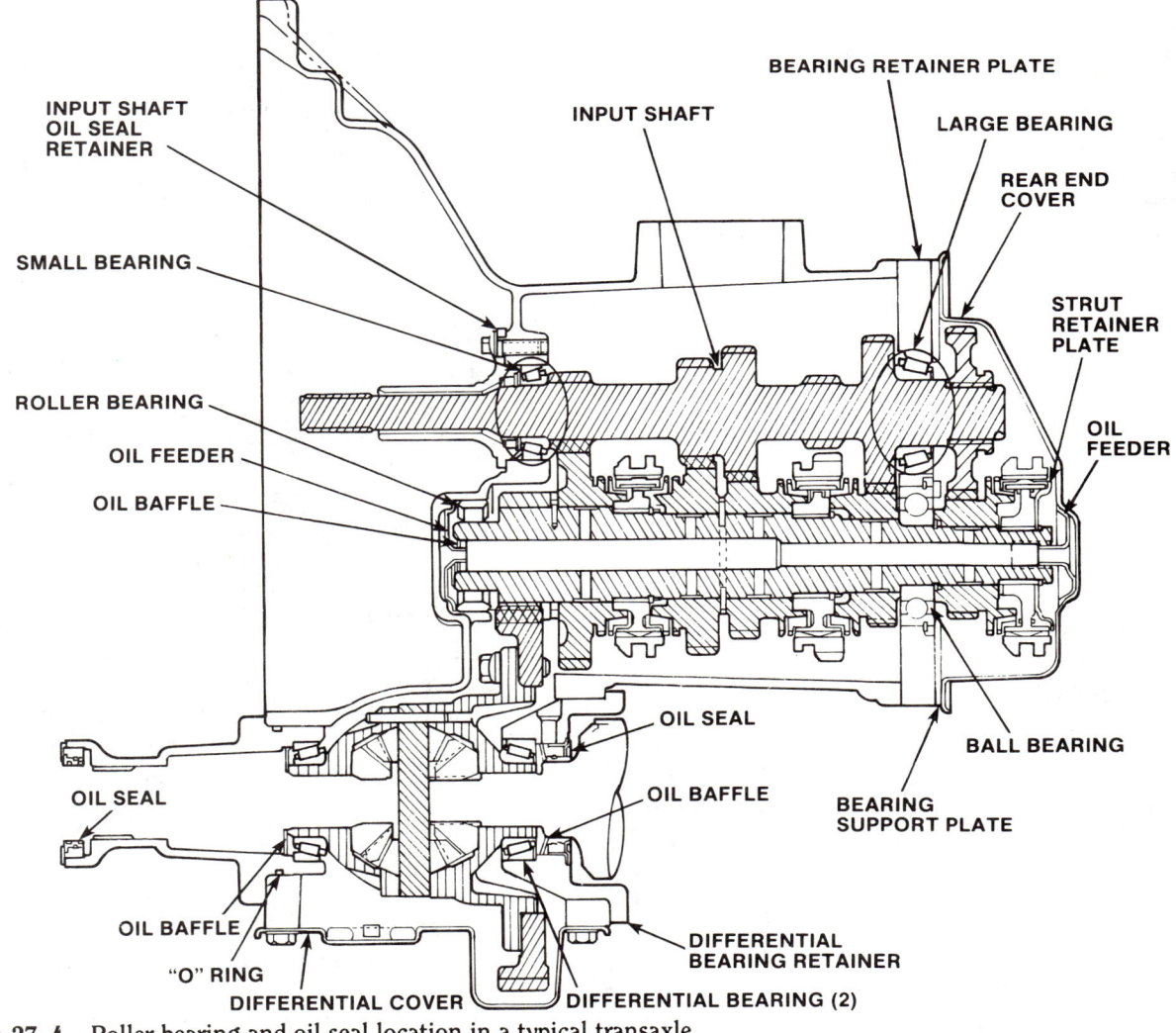

Figure 27-4 Roller bearing and oil seal location in a typical transaxle.

are found in the reverse gearing, clicking or a certain amount of gear whine is normal, particularly when backing up at faster speeds.)

Clicking or whine in forward gear ranges may indicate worn helical gear teeth. This problem may not require immediate attention.

However, chipped or broken teeth are dangerous because the loose parts can cause severe damage in other areas of the transmission/transaxle. Broken parts are usually indicated by a rhythmical knocking sound, even at low speeds. Complete disassembly, inspection, and replacement of damaged parts is the solution to this problem.

Gear Clash

Gear clash is indicated by a grinding noise during shifting. The noise is the result of one gearset remaining partly engaged while another gearset attempts to turn the mainshaft. Gear clash can be caused by incorrect clutch adjustment or binding of clutch or gearshift linkage. Damaged, worn, or defective synchronizer blocker rings can cause gear clash as can use of an improper gear lubricant.

Hard Shifting

If the shift lever is difficult to move from one gear to another, check the clutch linkage adjustment. Hard shifting also may be caused by damage inside the transmission/transaxle, or by a lubricant that is too thick. Common hard shifting includes badly worn bearings and damaged clutch gears, control rods, shift rails, shift forks, and synchronizers.

Jumping Out of Gear

If the car jumps out of gear into neutral, particularly when decelerating or going down hills, first check the shift lever and internal gearshift linkage. Excessive clearance between gears and the input shaft or badly worn bearings can cause jumping out of gear. Other internal transmission/transaxle parts to inspect are the clutch pilot bearing, gear teeth, shift forks, shift rails, and springs or detents.

Locked in Gear

If a transmission or transaxle locks in one gear and cannot be shifted, check the gearshift lever linkage for misadjustment or damage. Low lubricant level can also cause needle bearings, gears, and synchronizers to seize and lock up the transmission.

If these checks do not resolve the problem, the transmission or transaxle must be removed from the vehicle and disassembled. After disassembly, inspect the internal countershaft gear, clutch shaft, reverse idler, shift rails, shift forks, and springs or detents for damage. Also, check for worn support bearings.

> ### USING SERVICE MANUALS
> A service manual is absolutely necessary when performing any type of transmission/transaxle disassembly work. Not only does the manual clearly illustrate all components and their disassembly procedure, it also lists many vital specifications, such as shaft and gear thrust (side) clearances, synchronizer ring and cone clearances, and bolt torque values. Special service tools, such as transmission service stands, oil seal presses, bearing replacers, shaft removers, pullers, and installing tools are also illustrated and explained.

❏ TRANSMISSION/ TRANSAXLE REMOVAL

If the transmission or transaxle must be removed from the vehicle for service or overhaul, always follow the specific removal procedures listed in the vehicle service manual.

PROCEDURES
Removing the Transmission/Transaxle

1. Disconnect the ground terminal of the battery.
2. Support and raise the vehicle on a hoist or safety jack stands.
3. Drain the transmission/transaxle lubricant.
4. On transmissions, make a mark on the drive shaft-to-flange connection at the rear axle assembly. Disconnect the drive shaft at the rear axle and tape the U-joint bearings in place to prevent the loss of bearings or the entry of dirt.
5. Slide the drive shaft from the transmission output shaft and inspect.
6. On transaxles, remove the drive axles from the transaxle. This involves removing the wheel, brake, and other suspension components needed to access the drive shafts. Support the drive axles by tying them to the underbody with wire hangers.
7. Remove the rod and lever, cable, or hydraulic clutch linkage (Figure 27-5).
8. Remove the speedometer cable that connects to the transmission or transaxle. The speedometer cable housing may also be screwed or bolted to the housing. Disconnect the cable and use wire to keep it out of the way.
9. Remove all wiring, hoses, and cords from the transmission, such as the backup light switch connector near the shift lever (Figure 27-6). The ground wire, and any hoses for four-wheel-drive/front-wheel-drive changeovers. If the starter is mounted on the transmission/transaxle housing, disconnect all wiring and remove the starter.

Manual Transmission/Transaxle Service 665

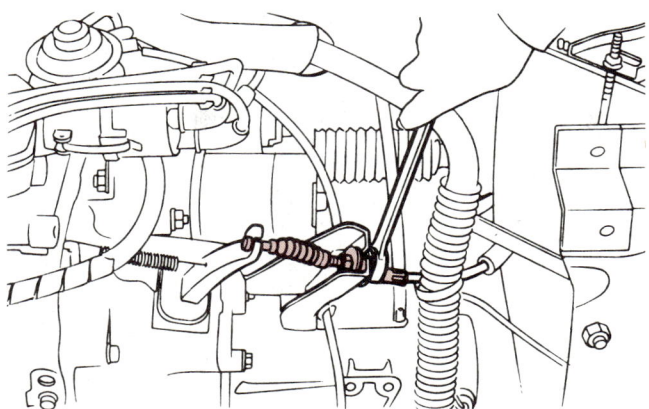

Figure 27-5 Disconnecting the clutch cable from the transaxle housing connection. *Courtesy of Subaru of America*

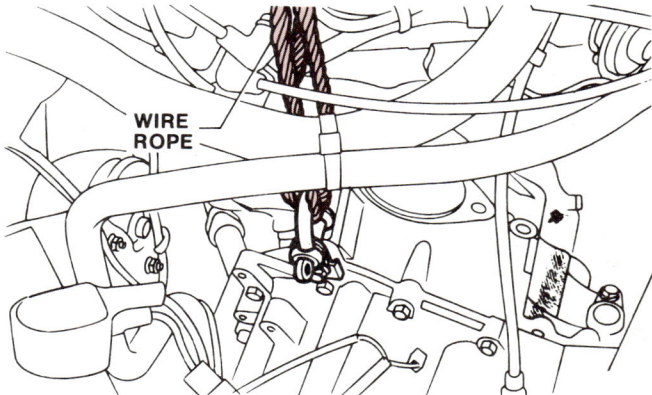

Figure 27-7 Attaching the lifting hoist cable to the lifting bracket on the transmission/transaxle. *Courtesy of Subaru of America*

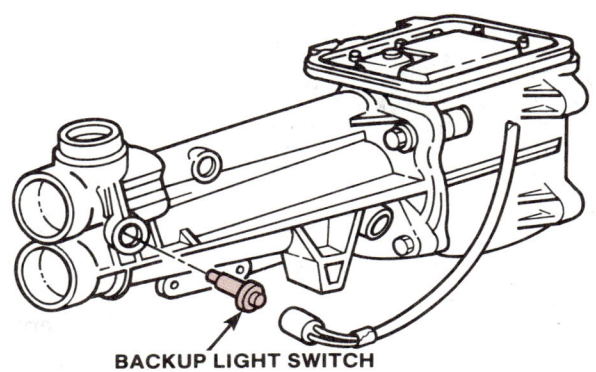

Figure 27-6 Location of typical backup light switch and wiring harness connection. *Courtesy of Ford Motor Co.*

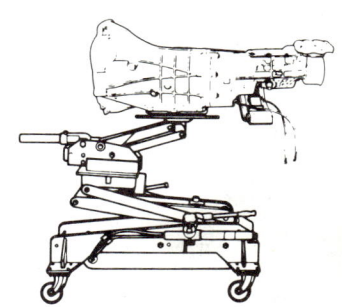

Figure 27-8 Typical transmission jack used to support the unit during removal from the vehicle. *Courtesy of Chrysler Corp.*

10. Remove the shift linkage and shift lever assembly as needed. This may require working inside and under the vehicle.
11. Remove the emergency brake linkages if they block access to the transmission.
12. With transaxles, remove any brake or suspension system parts that block access to the transaxle.
13. Remove any exhaust system components that block access to the transmission or transaxle. This may involve disconnecting the header pipe from the exhaust manifold and removing hangers and straps as needed.
14. Attach the hoist to the appropriate lifting points on the housing (Figure 27-7). In many cases a special lifting bracket is bolted to the housing to provide the point.
15. Remove the transmission cross member that supports the transmission and engine after making certain the engine and transmission are safely and securely supported with a transmission jack or jack stands (Figure 27-8).
16. Remove the transmission/transaxle attaching bolts.
17. Move the transmission/transaxle straight out of the clutch assembly.
18. Clean the excess dirt from the housing and place the transmission/transaxle on a suitable workbench.

☐ CLEANING AND INSPECTION

Disassembly and overhaul procedures can vary greatly between transmission/transaxle models, so always follow the exact steps outlined in the service manual. Figure 27-9 illustrates an exploded view of the internal components of a five-speed transaxle.

In some cases the countershaft must be removed before the input and mainshaft. In other cases the mainshaft is removed with the extension housing. It may be removed through the shift cover opening. To avoid difficulty in disassembly, follow the recommended sequence. A gear puller (Figure 27-10) or hydraulic press is often needed to remove gears and synchronizer assemblies from transmission/transaxle mainshafts.

Bearing removal and installation procedures require that the force applied to remove or install the bearing should always be placed on the tight bearing race. In some cases the inner race is tight on the shaft, while in others it is the outer race that is tight in its bore. Removal or installation force should be applied to the tight race. Serious damage to the bearing can result if this practice is not followed.

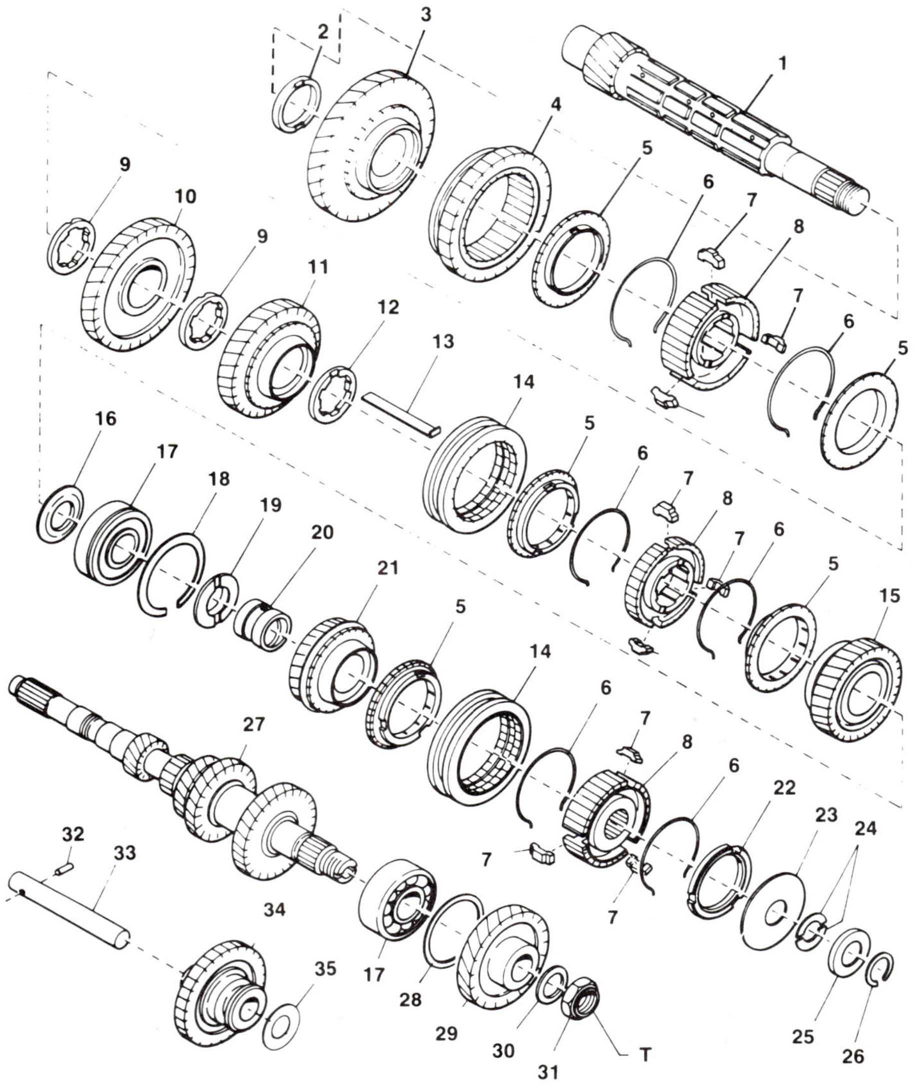

666 Section 5 Manual Transmissions and Transaxles

1. DRIVE PINION
2. WASHER
3. 1ST DRIVEN GEAR
4. REVERSE DRIVEN GEAR
5. SYNCHRONIZER RING
6. SYNCHRONIZER SPRING
7. SYNCHRONIZER HUB INSERT
8. SYNCHRONIZER HUB
9. GEAR THRUST SPACER 2
10. 2ND DRIVEN GEAR
11. 3RD DRIVEN GEAR
12. GEAR THRUST SPACER
13. GEAR THRUST SPACER KEY
14. SYNCHRONIZER SLEEVE
15. 4TH DRIVEN GEAR
16. WASHER
17. BALL BEARING
18. SNAP RING
19. 5TH DRIVEN THRUST PLATE
20. 5TH DRIVEN GEAR BUSHING
21. 5TH DRIVEN GEAR
22. INSERT GUIDE
23. WASHER
24. DRIVE PINION COTTER
25. DRIVE PINION RETAINER
26. SNAP RING OUTER
27. MAINSHAFT
28. WASHER
29. 5TH DRIVE GEAR
30. LOCK WASHER
31. LOCK NUT
32. SPRING PIN
33. REVERSE IDLER GEAR SHAFT
34. REVERSE IDLER GEAR
35. WASHER

Figure 27-9 Exploded view of typical transaxle shafts, gearsets, and synchronizer assemblies. *Courtesy of Subaru of America*

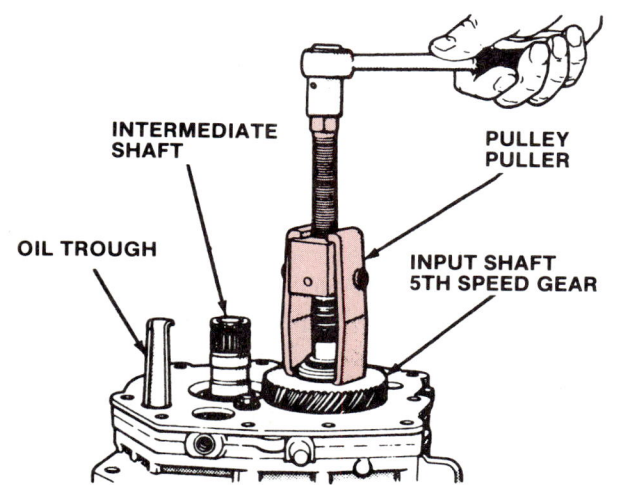

Figure 27-10 Pullers are often used to remove bearings and gears.

Use a soft-faced hammer or a brass drift and ball peen hammer if tapping is required. Never use excessive force or hammering.

During assembly of the transmission, never attempt to force parts into place by tightening the front bearing retainer bolts or extension housing bolts. All parts must be fully in place before tightening any bolts. Check for free rotation and shifting. New gaskets and seals should always be used.

The following are some general cleaning and inspection guidelines that result in quality workmanship and service.

1. Wash all parts, except sealed ball bearings and seals, in solvent. Brush or scrape all dirt from the parts. Remove all traces of old gasket. Wash roller bearings in solvent, and dry them with a clean cloth, never with compressed air.

2. Inspect the front of the transmission case for nicks or burrs that could affect its alignment with the flywheel housing. Remove all nicks and burrs with a fine stone (cast-iron casing) or fine file (aluminum casing).
3. Replace any cover that is bent or distorted. If there are vent holes in the case, make certain they are open.
4. Inspect ball bearings by holding the outer ring stationary and rotating the inner ring several times. Inspect the raceway of the inner ring from both sides for pits and spalling. Light particle indentation is acceptable wear, but all other types of wear merit replacement of the bearing assembly. Next, hold the inner ring stationary and rotate the outer ring. Examine the outer ring raceway for wear and replace as needed.
5. Examine the external surfaces of all bearings. Replace the bearings if there are radial cracks on the front and rear faces of the outer or inner rings, cracks on the outside diameter or outer ring, or deformation or cracks in the ball cage.
6. Lubricate the cleaned bearing raceways with a light coat of oil. Hold the bearing by the inner ring in a vertical position. Spin the outer ring several times by hand. If roughness or vibration is felt, or the outer ring stops abruptly, replace the bearing.
7. Replace any roller bearings that are broken, worn, or rough. Inspect their respective races. Replace them as needed.
8. Replace the countershaft (cluster) gear if its gear teeth are chipped, broken, or excessively worn. Replace the countershaft if the shaft is bent, scored, or worn.
9. Replace the reverse idler gear or sliding gear if its teeth are chipped, worn, or broken. Replace the idler gear shaft if it is bent, worn, or scored.
10. Replace the input shaft and gear if its splines are damaged or if the teeth are chipped, worn, or damaged. If the roller bearing surface in the bore of the gear is worn or rough, or if the cone surface is damaged, replace the gear and the gear rollers.
11. Replace all main or speed gears that are chipped, broken, or worn.
12. Check the synchronizer sleeves for free movement on their hubs. Alignment marks (if present) should be properly indexed (Figure 27-11).

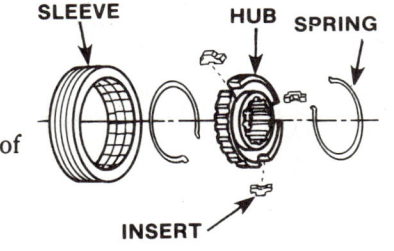

Figure 27-11 Details of typical synchronizer. *Courtesy of Subaru of America*

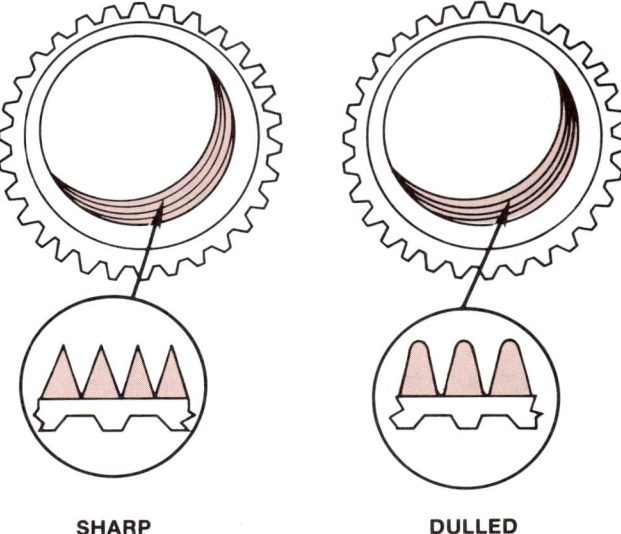

Figure 27-12 Grooves on the internal surface of the synchronizer blocker ring must be sharp.

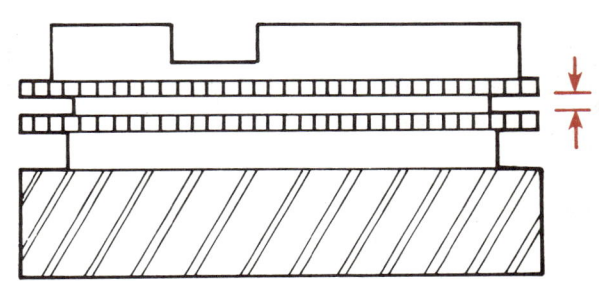

Figure 27-13 The clearance between the synchronizer blocker ring and the gear's dog teeth must meet specifications.

13. Inspect the synchronizer blocking rings for widened index slots, rounded clutch teeth, and smooth internal surfaces. Remember, the blocking rings must have machined grooves on their internal surfaces to cut through lubricant (Figure 27-12). Units with worn, flat grooves must be replaced. Also, check the clearance between the block ring and gear clog teeth against service manual specifications (Figure 27-13).
14. Replace the speedometer drive gear if its teeth are stripped or damaged. Install the correct size replacement gear.
15. Replace the output shaft if there is any sign of wear or if any of the splines are damaged.
16. Inspect the bushings and seal in the extension housing, and replace if worn or damaged. The bushing and seal should be replaced once the extension housing has been reinstalled on the transmission.
17. Replace the seal in the input shaft bearing retainer.
18. Replace the seals on the cam and shafts.

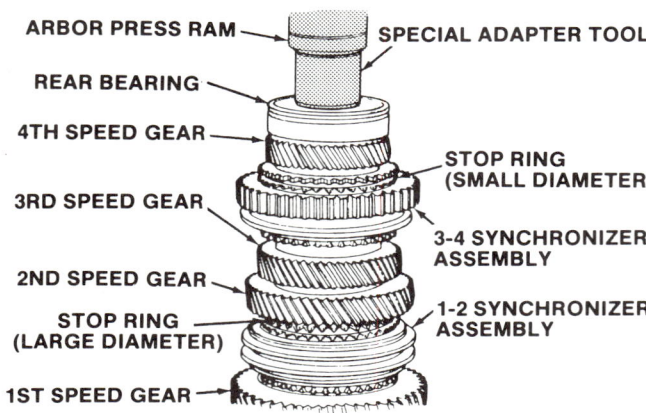

Figure 27-14 A hydraulic arbor press is often used to press gears and bearings onto the shaft during reassembly.

REASSEMBLY/REINSTALLATION OF TRANSMISSION/TRANSAXLE

Transmission/transaxle reassembly and reinstallation procedures are basically the reverse of disassembly. Once again, refer to the service manual for any special procedures. New parts are installed as needed, and new gaskets and seals are always used.

Serviceable gears are pressed onto the mainshaft using special press equipment (Figure 27-14). Separate needle bearings should be held in place with heavy grease so that shafts can be inserted into place. During reassembly, measure shaft end play. Adjust it to specifications with shims, spacers, or snap rings of different thicknesses. All fasteners are tightened to the manufacturer's torque specifications.

Soft-faced mallets can be used to tap shafts and other parts into place. After reassembly, secure the transmission to a transmission jack with safety chains and raise it into place. Before the transmission is reinstalled, inspect and service the clutch as necessary.

Reinstallation into the vehicle is basically the reverse of removal procedures outlined earlier.

CUSTOMER CARE

Lack of telephone skills costs many shops business. Every time you talk to a potential customer on the telephone, it is a one-on-one selling opportunity with no distractions. The customer is seeking professional help to solve a problem with a vehicle. Mishandling the all-important first minute of the conversation generates a bad impression of the shop and its ability to do a good job.

Always use a pleasant voice when talking on the phone. Pay attention to what the customer is saying and how he or she is saying it. The words being said and the tone of voice being used are the only contact you have with the other person. Do not allow your attention to wander.

Have a prepared response ready for the first part of the conversation. Keep an outline of this script and a sales lead sheet handy at the phone at all times. Make it a habit to pick up a pen and lead sheet whenever you answer the phone.

The following points should always be covered in any conversation.

1. Greet the customer pleasantly. State the name of the shop, your name, and ask who is calling.
2. Write down the customer's name immediately on the lead sheet. Use it frequently during the conversation.
3. Ask how you can help the customer. Find out what the vehicle seems to be doing. Find out the year and model of the car and when it was last serviced.
4. Do not make the diagnosis over the phone. You might state some general areas where the problem may be occurring, but clearly state that a thorough inspection is needed before any diagnosis or estimates can be made.
5. Ask the customer to bring the vehicle in for inspection. You want the opportunity to inspect the vehicle so you can perform all needed service.
6. Ask the customer when is a convenient time to bring in the car. Mark down the time, and repeat it to the customer so there is no misunderstanding.
7. Ask the customer if directions are needed to the shop. Give simple, complete directions if needed. Once again, it is easiest to have these written down based on some key landmarks or major streets in your area.
8. Repeat your name. Tell the customer to ask for you when bringing in the car. If you will not be available, give the name of a co-worker. Be sure to inform that person.
9. If the customer is new, ask how he or she heard of your shop. Jot the response down on the lead sheet. This data is often useful in setting up and evaluating sales programs. Thank the customer for calling.

CASE STUDY

Case 1

A customer complains his rear-wheel-drive, manual transmission vehicle is experiencing intermittent operating noise, particularly when the vehicle is "just warming up." On the test drive, the technician notices a low growling noise in the lower gear ranges. The noise disappears at cruising speeds in high (fourth) gear.

The technician returns to the shop and places the vehicle on a lift for further inspection. The driveline, differential, clutch, and wheel bearings all appear to be in good condition. This confirms that the problem is transmission related. The technician suspects a damaged bearing at the rear of the unit's input shaft. This bearing supports the pilot journal at the front of the transmission's output shaft. In all forward gear ranges except direct drive, the input and output shafts turn at different speeds. In reverse gear they turn in opposite directions. But in direct drive (fourth gear in this case), the two shafts are locked together by a synchronizer and turn at the same speed. This relieves the operating pressure placed on the input shaft rear bearing, thus eliminating the growling noise.

The only way this problem can be corrected is to disassemble the transmission, clean, examine, and replace any damaged components. The teardown confirms the technician's diagnosis. The roller bearings are cracked and disintegrating. The pilot journal on the output shaft is also slightly damaged. The shaft is sent to a machine shop where it is undercut and fitted with a press-on steel bushing to return it to the manufacturer's specified diameter. The roller bearings are then replaced and the unit reassembled. While the unit is apart, all components are cleaned and examined closely for damage and wear. The oil-cutting grooves on the first/second synchronizer are dull and flat. Although the customer has not yet experienced jumping out of gear problems in these gear ranges, the technician shows the customer the worn synchronizer and explains the problem it could cause in the near future. He strongly suggests replacement at this time and the customer agrees to this additional work.

Summary

- Proper lubrication is vital to long transmission/transaxle life. The transmission gear oil must be checked and changed at manufacturer's suggested intervals.
- Metal particles or shavings in the gear oil indicate extensive internal wear or damage.
- The first step in diagnosing transmission/transaxle problems is to confirm that the problem exists inside the unit. Clutch and driveline problems may often appear to be transmission/transaxle problems.
- The initial visual inspection should include checks for lubricant leakage at gaskets and seals, transmission mount inspection, clutch and gearshift linkage checks, and drive axle and CV joint inspection.
- Rough growling noise inside the transmission/transaxle housing is an indication of bearing problems.
- A clicking noise may indicate excessive gear tooth wear. Rhythmical knocking is a sign of loose or broken internal components.
- Gear clash occurs when one gearset remains partially engaged when a second gearset attempts to turn the mainshaft.
- Hard shifting can be caused by shift linkage problems, improper lubricant, or worn internal components such as bearings, gears, shift forks, or synchronizers.
- Jumping out of gear can be caused by a poorly adjusted shift linkage, excessive clearance between gears, or badly worn bearings.
- Low lubricant levels, poorly adjusted shift linkages, or damaged internal components can result in transmission/transaxle lockup.
- Always follow service manual recommendations for removing the transmission/transaxle from the vehicle and disassembling it.
- Use recommended bearing pullers, gear pullers, and press equipment to remove and install gears and synchronizers on shafts.
- Clean and inspect all parts carefully, replacing worn or damaged components. Never force components in place during reassembly. Follow all clearance specifications listed in the service manual.
- Always use new gaskets and seals during reassembly.

Review Questions

1. After draining gear oil from a transaxle, the technician notices the oil has shiny, metallic particles in it. What does this indicate?
2. List at least five separate checks that should be made during the visual inspection of the transmission/transaxle.
3. List at least three causes of noise that are not transmission related but may appear to be.
4. What tool is often needed to remove gears and synchronizer assemblies from the transmission/transaxle mainshaft?
5. When removing or installing bearings, where should force be applied?
6. Technician A says transmission/transaxle gaskets and seals can be reused if they show no signs of tears or excessive wear. Technician B says these items should always be replaced if the unit is disassembled. Who is correct?
   a. Technician A
   b. Technician B

c. Both A and B
d. Neither A nor B

7. Gear clash is a grinding noise that occurs most often during shifting when _____.
   a. gears involved in the shift are chipped or broken
   b. one gearset remains partially engaged while another gearset tries to turn the mainshaft
   c. there is excess clearance between the input shaft and mainshaft gears
   d. bearings seize and lock on the mainshaft

8. A rough, growling noise from a transaxle in neutral with the engine operating is a likely indication that there is a problem in the _____.
   a. transaxle input shaft bearings
   b. transaxle main (intermediate) shaft bearings
   c. first/second synchronizer assembly
   d. pinion and ring gear interaction

9. A clicking noise during transmission/transaxle operation may be an indication of _____.
   a. worn mainshaft (input shaft) bearings
   b. faulty synchronizer operation
   c. failed oil seals
   d. worn, broken, or chipped gear teeth

10. Low lubricant levels are the most likely cause of _____.
    a. gear clash
    b. hard shifting
    c. gear lockup or seizure
    d. gear jumpout

11. Using a lubricant that is thicker than service manual specifications can lead to _____.
    a. gear jumpout
    b. hard shifting
    c. gear lockup
    d. gear slippage

12. During a test drive, a noise that appears to be transmission related disappears when the driver brings the vehicle to a stop and disengages the clutch with the engine at idle. Technician A says this indicates the noise is most likely coming from inside the transmission. Technician B says the problem is most likely not transmission related. Who is correct?
    a. Technician A
    b. Technician B
    c. Both A and B
    d. Neither A nor B

13. When is gear whine or excessive clicking considered normal?
    a. at high cruising speeds
    b. when backing up at higher speeds
    c. when coasting with the clutch disengaged
    d. never

14. Technician A says spinning cleaned bearings with compressed air is a fast, convenient way of drying them. Technician B says this can damage the bearing and should never be done. Who is correct?
    a. Technician A
    b. Technician B
    c. Both A and B
    d. Neither A nor B

15. A poorly adjusted shift linkage can cause which of the following problems?
    a. gear clash
    b. hard shifting
    c. gear jumpout
    d. all of the above

16. Technician A says that the transmission rear seal at the driveline is particularly prone to leakage. When Technician B pushes up and down on the transmission, he says that the mounts require replacement because the case moves up and down. Who is correct?
    a. Technician A
    b. Technician B
    c. Both A and B
    d. Neither A nor B

17. Noise occurs in forward and reverse gears, but not in neutral. Technician A says the output shaft bearing is the likely failed component. Technician B says the mainshaft bearing is the likely failed component. Who is correct?
    a. Technician A
    b. Technician B
    c. Both A and B
    d. Neither A nor B

18. A rough growling occurs when a vehicle is moving in any gear. Technician A says the rear input shaft bearing may be at fault. Technician B says this condition indicates the countergear bearings may be faulty. Who is correct?
    a. Technician A
    b. Technician B
    c. Both A and B
    d. Neither A nor B

19. A car jumps out of gear into neutral, particularly when decelerating or going down hills. Technician A checks the shift lever and internal gearshift linkage first. Technician B says the clutch pilot bearing could be the problem. Who is correct?
    a. Technician A
    b. Technician B
    c. Both A and B
    d. Neither A nor B

28 DRIVE AXLES AND DIFFERENTIALS

Objectives

■ Name and describe the components of a front-wheel-drive axle. ■ Describe the operation of a front-wheel-drive axle. ■ Differentiate between the various types of constant velocity joints, including inboard, outboard, fixed, plunge, ball-type, and tripod. ■ Diagnose problems in CV joints. ■ Perform preventive maintenance on CV joints. ■ Explain the difference between CV joints and universal joints. ■ Name and describe the components of a rear-wheel-drive axle. ■ Describe the operation of a rear-wheel-drive axle. ■ Explain the function and operation of a differential and drive axles. ■ Describe the various differential designs including complete, integral carrier, removable carrier, and limited slip. ■ Describe the three common types of driving axles. ■ Explain the function of the main driving gears, drive pinion gear, and ring gear. ■ Describe the operation of hunting, nonhunting, and partial nonhunting gears. ■ Describe the different types of axle shafts and axle shaft bearings.

The drive axle assembly transmits torque smoothly and efficiently from the engine and transmission to drive the vehicle's wheels. The purpose of a drive axle is to change the direction of the power flow, multiply torque, and allow different speeds between the two drive wheels. Drive axles are used for both front-wheel- and rear-wheel-drive vehicles (Figure 28-1).

❏ FRONT-WHEEL-DRIVE (FWD) AXLES

Front-wheel-drive axles, also called axle shafts and front-drive shafts, transfer engine torque generally from the transaxle differential to the front wheels. One of the most important components of FWD axles is the constant velocity (CV) joint. These joints are used to transfer uniform torque and a constant speed, while operating through a wide range of angles.

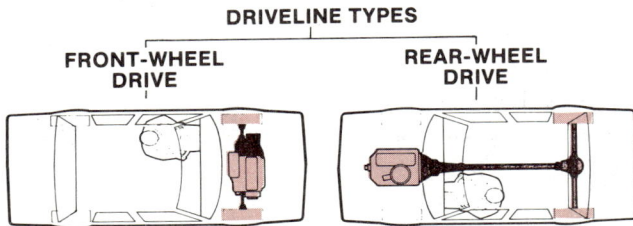

Figure 28-1 Both front-wheel- and rear-wheel-drive axles must transmit engine torque smoothly to the vehicle's driving wheels.

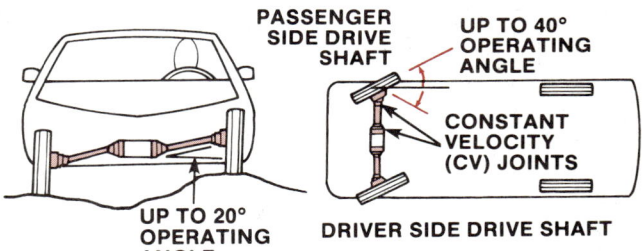

Figure 28-2 Front-wheel-drive shaft angles.

On front- or four-wheel-drive cars, operating angles of as much as 40 degrees are common (Figure 28-2). The drive axles must transmit power from the engine to front wheels that have to drive, steer, and cope with the severe angles caused by the up-and-down movement of the vehicle's suspension. To accomplish this, these cars must have a compact joint that ensures the driven shaft is rotated at a constant velocity, regardless of angle. CV joints not only need to bend, they also must permit the length of the axle assembly to change as the wheel travels up and down.

❏ TYPES OF CV JOINTS

To satisfy the needs of different applications, constant velocity (CV) joints come in a variety of styles. The different types of joints can be referred to by position (inboard or outboard), by function (fixed or plunge), or by design (ball-type or tripod).

671

Inboard and Outboard Joints

In front-wheel-drive drivetrains, two CV joints are used on each half shaft (Figure 28-3). The joint nearer the transaxle is the inner or inboard joint, and the one nearer the wheel is the outer or outboard joint. In a rear-wheel-drive vehicle with independent rear suspension (IRS), the joint nearer the differential can also be referred to as the inboard joint. The one closer to the wheel is the outboard joint.

Fixed and Plunge Joints

CV joints can also be categorized by function. They are either fixed (meaning they do not plunge in and out to compensate for changes in length) or are a plunge joint (one that is capable of in and out movement).

In front-wheel-drive applications, the inboard joint is also a plunge joint. The outboard joint is a fixed joint. Both joints do not have to plunge if one can handle the job. Further, the outer joint must also be able to handle much greater operating angles necessary for steering (up to 40 degrees).

In rear-wheel-drive applications with independent rear suspension, one joint on each axle shaft can be fixed and the other a plunge, or both can be plunge joints. Since the operating angles are not as great because the wheels do not have to steer, plunge joints can be used at either or both ends of the axle shafts.

Ball-Type Joints

CV joints are also classified by design. The two basic varieties are the ball-type and tripod-type joints. Both types are used as either inboard or outboard joints, and both are available in fixed or plunge designs.

Fixed CV Joints

The Rzeppa or fixed ball-type joint consists of an inner ball race, six balls, a cage to position the balls, and an outer housing (Figure 28-4). Tracks machined in the inner race and outer housing allow the joint to

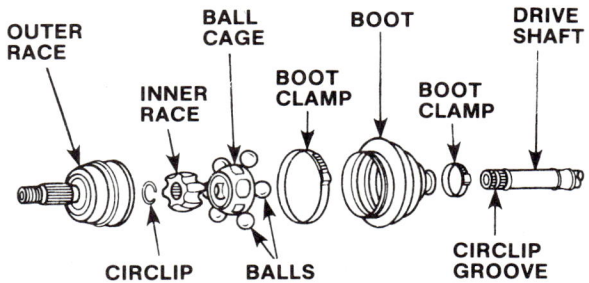

Figure 28-4 Rzeppa ball-type fixed CV joint.

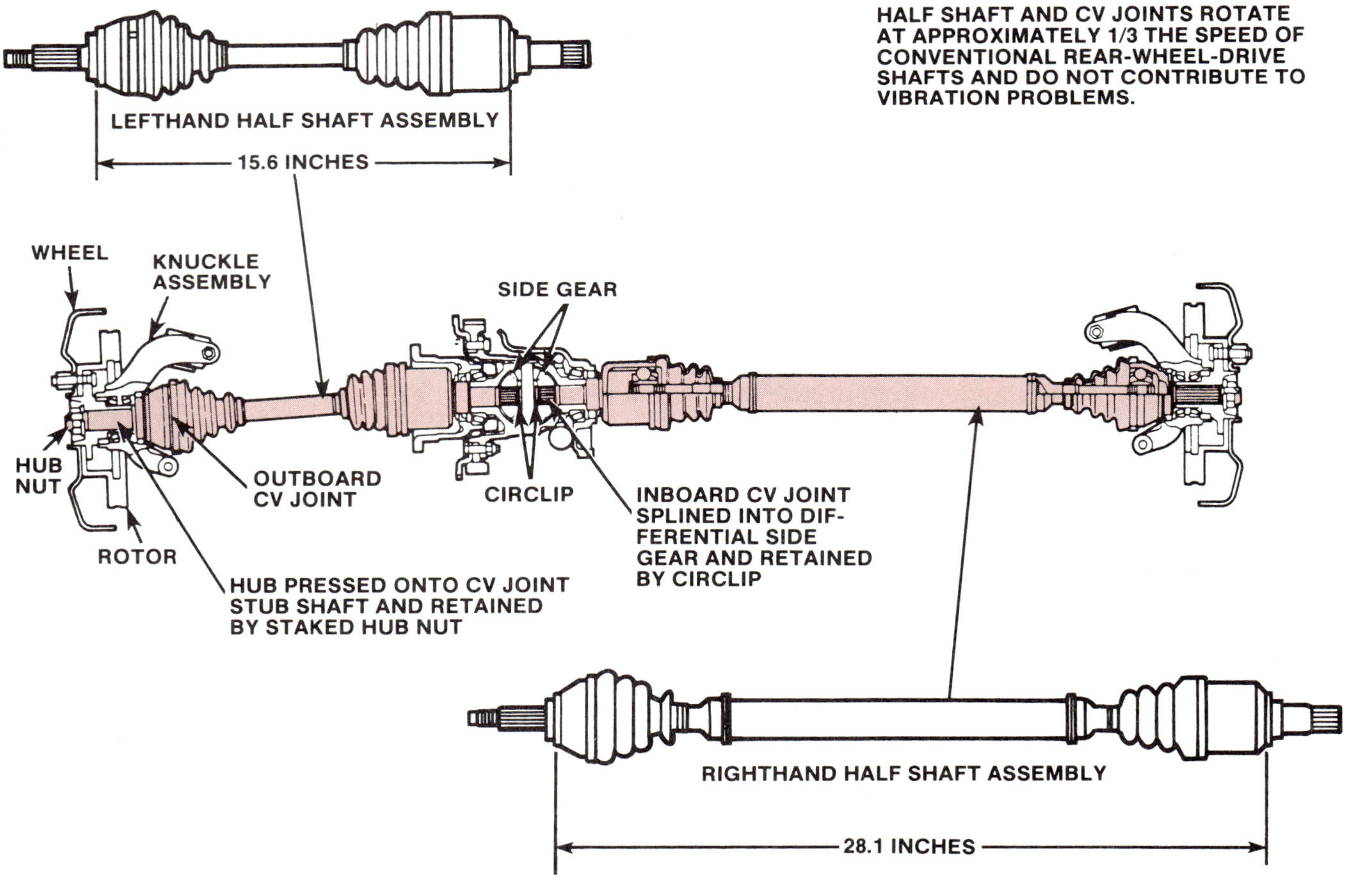

HALF SHAFT AND CV JOINTS ROTATE AT APPROXIMATELY 1/3 THE SPEED OF CONVENTIONAL REAR-WHEEL-DRIVE SHAFTS AND DO NOT CONTRIBUTE TO VIBRATION PROBLEMS.

Figure 28-3 Front-wheel-drive axles for a typical transaxle. On some vehicles, the shorter shaft is solid steel and the longer shaft is tubular.

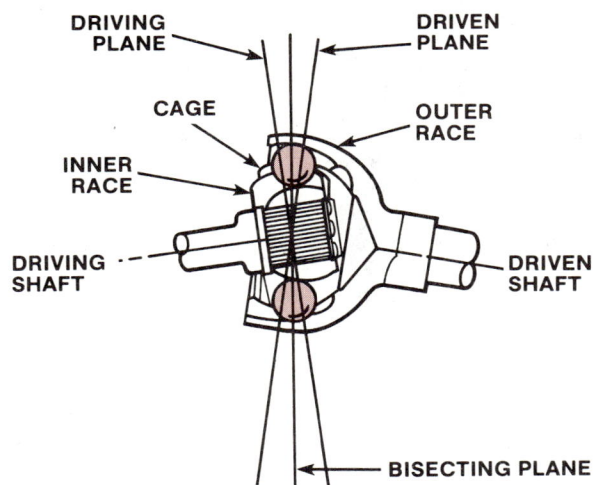

Figure 28-5 In a Rzeppa CV joint, the balls bisect the joint angle.

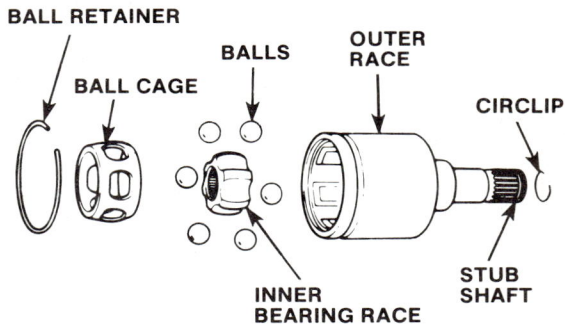

Figure 28-7 Double-offset CV joint.

flex. The inner race and outer housing form a ball-and-socket arrangement. The six balls serve both as bearings between the races and the means of transferring torque from one to the other.

If viewed from the side, the balls within the joint always bisect the angle formed by the shafts on either side of the joint regardless of the operating angle (Figure 28-5). This reduces the effective operating angle of the joint by half and virtually eliminates all vibration problems. Just as the output speed between two bevel gears is always equal, so is the output velocity of the joint—thus the description, constant velocity. The cage helps to maintain this alignment by holding the six balls snugly in its windows. If the cage windows become worn or deformed over time, the resulting play between ball and window typically results in a clicking noise when turning. It is important to note that the opposing balls in a Rzeppa CV joint always work together as a pair. Heavy wear in the tracks of one ball almost always results in identical wear in the tracks of the opposing ball.

Another ball-type joint is the disc style CV joint (Figure 28-6), which is used predominantly on Volkswagen as well as on many German rear-wheel-drive models. Its design is very similar to the Rzeppa joint.

Plunging Ball-Type Joints

There are two basic styles of plunging ball-type joints: the double-offset design that uses a cylindrical outer housing with straight grooves and the cross groove joint, which is a more compact design with a flat, doughnut-shaped outer housing and angled grooves.

The double-offset joint (Figure 28-7) is typically used in applications that require higher operating angles (up to 25 degrees) and greater plunge depth (up to 2.4 inches). This type of joint can be found at the inboard position on some front-wheel-drive half shafts as well as on the propeller shaft of some four-wheel-drive shafts.

The cross groove joint (Figure 28-8) has a much flatter design than any other plunge joint. It is used at the inboard position on front-wheel-drive half shafts or at either end of a rear-wheel-drive independent rear suspension axle shaft.

The feature that makes this joint unique is its ability to handle a fair amount of plunge (up to 1.8 inches) in a relatively short distance. The inner and outer races share the plunging motion equally so less overall depth is needed for a given amount of plunge. The cross groove can handle operating angles up to 22 degrees.

Tripod CV Joints

As with ball-type CV joints, tripod joints come in two varieties: plunge and fixed.

Tripod Plunging Joints

Tripod plunging joints (Figure 28-9) consist of a central drive part or tripod (also known as spider). This has three trunnions fitted with spherical rollers on needle bearings and an outer housing (sometimes called a tulip because of its three-lobed, flower-like

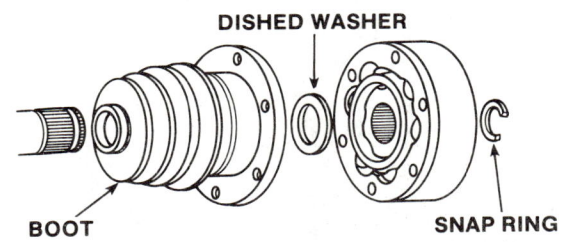

Figure 28-6 Exploded view of a disc-type CV joint.

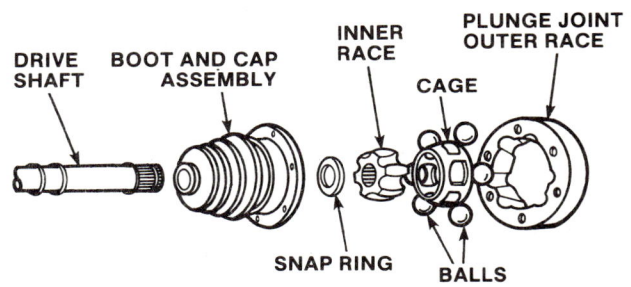

Figure 28-8 Cross groove joint.

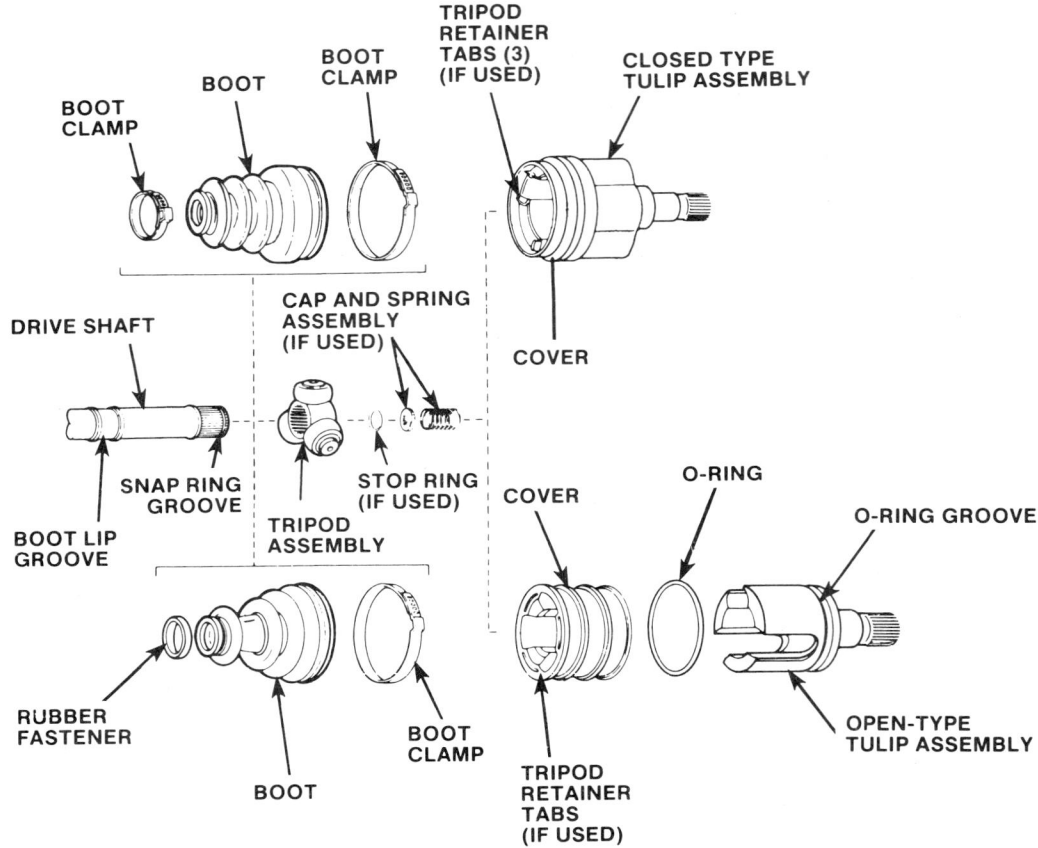

Figure 28-9 Inner tripod plunge-type joints: closed housing and open housing.

appearance). On some tripod joints, the outer housing is closed, meaning the roller tracks are totally enclosed within it. On others, the tulip is open and the roller tracks are machined out of the housing.

Tripod joints are most commonly used as front-wheel-drive inboard plunge joints. Other tripod plunge-type joints are shown in Figure 28-10.

Fixed Tripod Joints

The fixed tripod joint (Figure 28-11) is sometimes used as the outboard joint in front-wheel-drive applications. In this design, the trunnion is mounted in the outer housing and the three roller bearings turn against an open tulip on the input shaft. A steel spider holds the joint together.

The fixed tripod joint has as much angular capability. The only major difference from a service standpoint is that the fixed tripod joint cannot be removed from the drive shaft or disassembled because of the way it is manufactured. The complete joint and shaft assembly must be replaced if the joint goes bad.

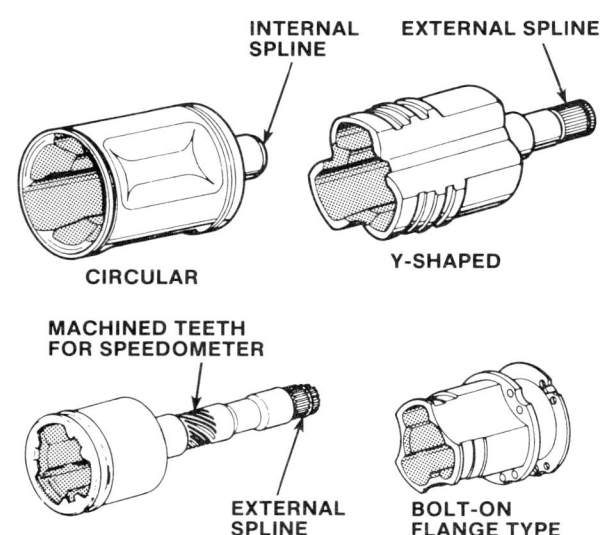

Figure 28-10 Different designs of tripod plunge joints.

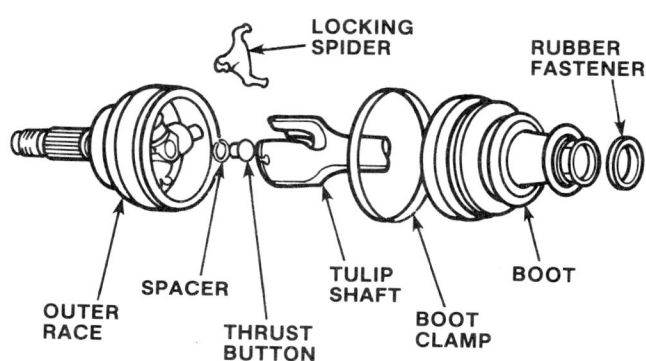

Figure 28-11 Tripod fixed CV joint.

FRONT-WHEEL-DRIVE APPLICATIONS

In a typical front-wheel-drive application, two CV joints are used on each half shaft. The outboard joints can be fixed Rzeppa or tripod, and the inner ones plunging tripod, double-offset, or cross groove joints (Figure 28-12).

Front-wheel-drive half shafts can be solid or tubular, of equal or unequal length (Figure 28-13A), and come with or without damper weights. Equal length shafts (Figure 28-13B) are used in some vehicles to help reduce torque steer (the tendency to steer to one side as engine power is applied). In these applications, an intermediate shaft is used as a link from the transaxle to one of the half shafts. This intermediate shaft can use an ordinary Cardan universal joint (described later in this chapter) to a yoke at the transaxle. At the outer end is a support bracket and bearing assembly. Looseness in the bearing or bracket can create vibrations. These items should be included in any inspection of the drivetrain components. The small damper weight that is sometimes attached to one half shaft serves to dampen harmonic vibrations in the drivetrain and to stabilize the shaft as it spins, not to balance the shaft.

Regardless of the application, outer joints typically wear at a higher rate than inner joints, because of the increased range of operating angles to which they are subjected. Inner joint angles may change only 10 to 20 degrees as the suspension travels through jounce and rebound. Outer joints can undergo changes of up to 40 degrees in addition to jounce and rebound as the wheels are steered (see Figure 28-2). That, combined with more flexing of the outer boots, is why outer joints have a higher failure rate. On average, nine outer CV joints are replaced for every inner CV joint. That does not mean the technician should overlook the inner joints. They wear too. Every time the suspension travels through jounce and rebound, the inner joints must plunge in and out to accomodate the different arcs between the driveshafts and suspension. Tripod inner joints tend to develop unique wear patterns on each of the three rollers and their respective tracks in the housing which can lead to noise and vibration problems.

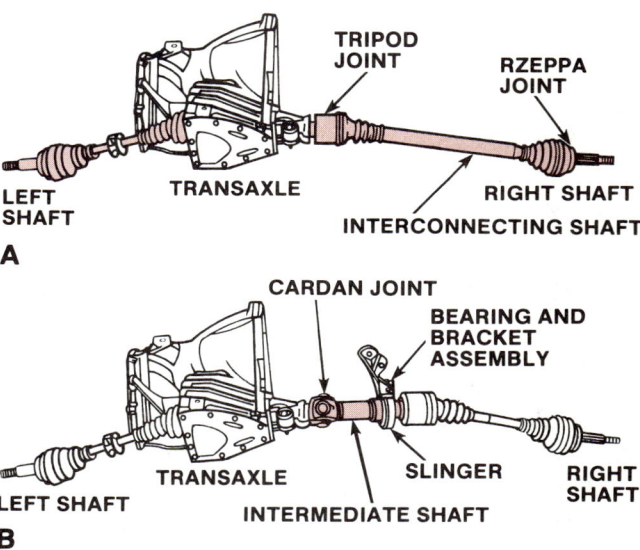

Figure 28-13 (A) Unequal length front-wheel-drive half shafts; (B) equal length front-wheel-drive half shafts with intermediate shaft.

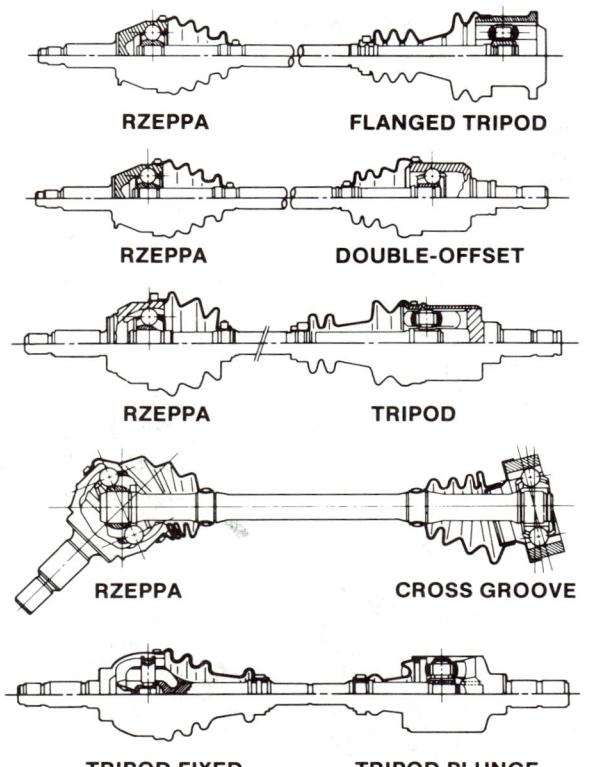

Figure 28-12 Typical CV joint combinations on front-wheel-drive half shafts.

CV JOINT SERVICE

With proper service, CV joints can have a long life, despite having to perform extremely difficult jobs in hostile environments. They must endure extreme heat and cold and survive the shock of hitting pot holes at high speeds. Fortunately, high torque loads during low-speed turns and many thousands of high-speed miles normally do not bother the CV joint. It is relatively trouble-free unless damage to the boot or joint goes unnoticed.

All CV joints are encased in a protective rubber (neoprene, natural or silicone) or thermoplastic (Hycrel) boot (Figure 28-14). The job of the boot is to retain grease and to keep dirt and water out. The importance of the boot cannot be overemphasized, because without its protection, the joint does not survive. For all practical purposes, a CV joint is lubed for life. Once packed with grease and installed, it requires

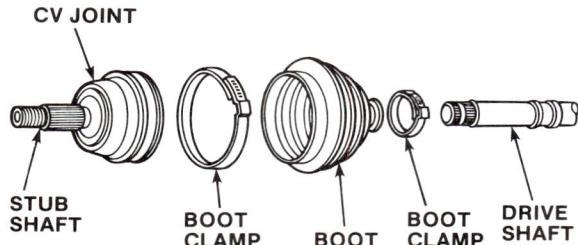

Figure 28-14 Typical CV joint boot assembly.

no further maintenance. A loose or missing boot clamp, or a slit, tear, even a small puncture in the boot itself, allows grease to leak out and water or dirt to enter. Consequently, the joint is destroyed.

Outer joints in front-wheel-drive vehicles tend to wear somewhat faster than inner joints due to the added motions of steering. By the time the outer joint produces noticeable wear symptoms, the inner joint might be on the verge of needing replacement. The decision as to whether to replace both joints when the half shaft is removed depends on the circumstances. If the vehicle has low miles and joint failure is the result of a defective boot, there is no reason to replace both joints. On a high-mileage vehicle where the bad joint has actually just worn itself out, it might be wise to save the expense and inconvenience of having the half shaft removed twice for CV joint replacement.

CV joint failure is usually preceded by various noticeable symptoms. If these signs are ignored, the results of complete failure could be very serious. For example, if an outer joint seizes due to loss of lubricant, it can cause loss of steering control. If the joint breaks, the half shaft or axle shaft could drop out of the car. Because of these possibilities, any symptom of a potential CV joint problem should be properly investigated and the appropriate service performed.

> ### CUSTOMER CARE
>
> There has been some confusion about towing a front-wheel-drive vehicle. It is correct for you to advise your customer that CV joints require only one special towing precaution. If a front-wheel-drive car requires towing, tell your customer to be sure that the tow-truck operator does not use J-hooks on the half shaft or lower control arms. The hooks can bend the half shafts or slide along the shafts or arms and rip the boots. Position the hooks on the subframe or cross member only. In fact, it is a good idea to point out these surfaces to your customer.

Diagnosis and Inspection

Any noise in the engine, drive axle, steering, or suspension is a good reason for a thorough inspection of the vehicle. A road test on a smooth surface is a good place to begin. The test should include driving at average highway speeds, some sharp turns, acceleration, and coasting. Look and listen for the following signs.

- A popping or clicking noise when turning signals a worn or damaged outer joint. The condition can be aggravated by putting the car in reverse and backing in a circle. If the noise gets louder, the outer joints should be replaced.
- A clunk during accelerating, decelerating, or putting the transaxle into drive can be caused by excessive play in the inner joint of front-wheel-drive applications, or from CV joints. A clunking noise when putting an automatic transmission into gear or when starting out from a stop usually indicates excessive play in an inner or outer joint. Be warned, though, that the same kind of noise can also be produced by excessive back-lash in the differential gears and transmission.
- A humming or growling noise is sometimes due to inadequate lubrication in either the inner or outer CV joint. It is more often due to worn or damaged wheel bearings, a bad intermediate shaft bearing on equal-length half shaft transaxles, or worn shaft bearings within the transmission.
- A shudder or vibration when accelerating is often caused by excessive play in either the inboard or outboard joints but more likely the inboard plunge joint. These kinds of vibrations can also be caused by a bad intermediate shaft bearing on transaxles with equal length half shafts. On front-wheel-drive vehicles with transverse-mounted engines, this kind of vibration can also be caused by loose or deteriorated engine/transaxle mounts. Be sure to inspect the rubber bushings in the upper torque strap on these engines to rule out this possibility. A vibration or shudder that increases with speed or comes and goes at a certain speed may be the result of excessive play in an inner or outer joint. A bent drive shaft can cause the same condition. Note, however, that some shudder could also be inherent to the vehicle.
- A cyclic vibration that comes and goes between 45 and 60 mph may lead the technician to think there is a wheel that is out of balance. Though liquid inside a tire (from using an aerosol tire sealer) can sometimes create a cyclic vibration, as a rule an out-of-balance wheel produces a continuous vibration. A more likely cause is a bad inner tripod CV joint. The vibration occurs because one of the three roller tracks has become dimpled or rough. Every time the tripod roller on the bad track hits the rough spot, it creates a little jerk in the driveline, which the driver feels as a cyclic vibration.
- If a noise is heard while driving straight ahead but it ceases while turning, the problem is usually not

a defective outer CV joint but a bad front wheel bearing. Turning changes the side load on the bearing, which may make it quieter than before.

- A vibration that increases with speed is rarely due to CV joint problems or front-wheel-drive half shaft imbalance. An out-of-balance tire or wheel, an out-of-round tire or wheel, or a bent rim are the most likely causes. It is possible that a bent half shaft, as the result of collision or towing damage, could cause the vibration. A missing damper weight could also be the culprit.

The spin test is useful for determining which of the CV joints is the problem. Put the vehicle on a lift. Make sure to raise the drive wheels clear of the rack. Support the lower control arm bushing, then spin the front tires until the noise is heard. Engine power can be used to perform this test, but the speed should never exceed 30 mph.

WARNING: Use extreme caution to avoid touching the wheels when the power is on. Also, before making a spin test, check the shop service manual. Some manufacturers do not recommend this test on their front-wheel-drive cars and rear-wheel-drive vehicles with independent rear suspensions. If the chassis is raised and the wheel spun at high speed, the joint or boot could be damaged.

Begin the CV joint inspection (Figure 28-15) by checking the condition of the boots. Splits, cracks, tears, punctures, or thin spots caused by rubbing call for immediate boot replacement. If the boot appears rotted, this indicates improper greasing or excessive heat, and it should be replaced. Squeeze all boots. If any air escapes, replace the boot. Also replace any boots that are missing.

If the inner boot appears to be collapsed or deformed, venting it (allowing air to enter) might solve the problem. Place a round-tipped rod between the boot and drive shaft. This equalizes the outside and inside air and allows the boot to return to its normal shape.

Make sure that all boot clamps are tight. Missing or loose clamps should be replaced. If the boot appears

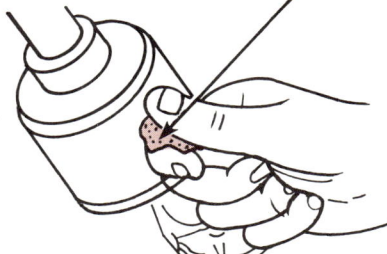

Figure 28-16 Check for contaminated grease.

loose, slide it back and inspect the grease inside for possible contamination (Figure 28-16). A milky or foamy appearance indicates water contamination. A gritty feeling when rubbed between the fingers indicates dirt. In most cases, a water- or dirt-contaminated joint should be replaced.

The drive shafts should be checked for signs of contact or rubbing against the chassis. Rubbing can be a symptom of a weak or broken spring or engine mount, as well as chassis misalignment. On front-wheel-drive transaxles with equal length half shafts, inspect the intermediate shaft U-joint, bearing, and support bracket for looseness by rocking the wheel back and forth and watching for any movement. Oil leakage around the inner CV joints indicates a faulty transaxle shaft seal. To replace the seal, the half shaft must be removed.

A quick check for possible wear in the outer joint of front-wheel-drive vehicles can be made by putting the car in reverse and driving in a circle. Clicking noises indicate worn outer joints. Alternately accelerating and decelerating in reverse while driving straight can reveal worn inner plunge joints. A bad joint clunks or shudders.

CUSTOMER CARE

The most important responsibility an automotive technician has is diagnosing problems. To

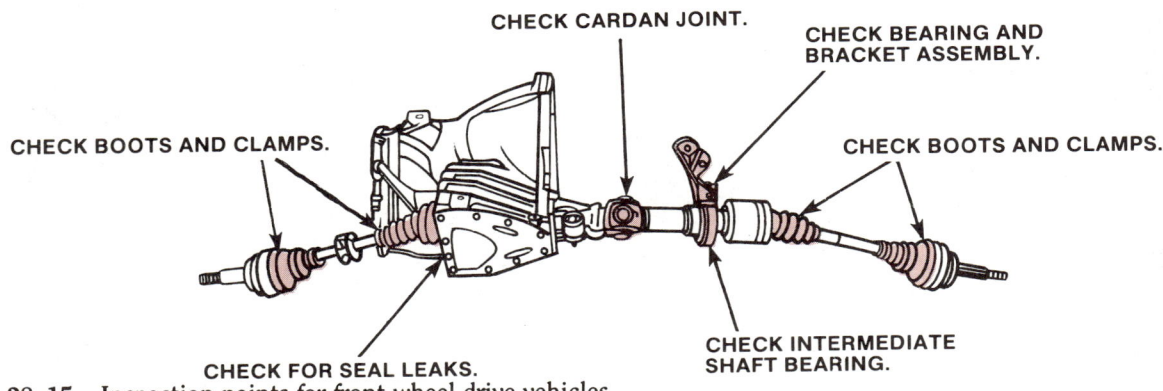

Figure 28-15 Inspection points for front-wheel-drive vehicles.

do this, you must know exactly what is wrong. Many service complaints arise when the wrong part is replaced or repaired. These problems are created when the wrong diagnosis is made. For this reason, it's important to keep in mind that the customer's complaint may be used as a very helpful guide to determine the cause of the problem.

Obtaining CV Repair Parts

CV replacement parts are available as follows.

1. Complete shaft replacement. Most aftermarket part suppliers offer a complete line of original equipment drive shafts for front-wheel-drive cars. These shafts come fully assembled and ready for installation. This repair method eliminates the need to tear down and rebuild an old shaft.
2. CV joint service kits and boot seals. Most service kits that are available from parts suppliers contain the following.
   - CV joint
   - Boot
   - Special grease for lubrication (Various joints require different amounts of grease; the correct quantity is packed in each kit.)
   - Attachment parts

Part manufacturers also produce a line of complete boot sets for each application, including all the components supplied in the service kit except the CV joint itself.

Old boots should never be reused when replacing a CV joint. In most cases, failure of the old joint is caused by some deterioration of the old boot. Reusing an old boot on a new joint usually leads to the quick destruction of the joint.

Replacement boots are packaged with new clamps and the appropriate type and amount of grease for the joint. CV joints require a special high-temperature, high-pressure grease.

Substituting any other type of grease may lead to premature failure of the joint. Be sure to use all the grease supplied in the joint or boot kit (Figure 28-17).

Figure 28-17 CV joint kit with special grease and components. *Courtesy of Perfect Circle/Dana*

The same rule applies to the clamps. Use only those clamps supplied with the replacement boot. Follow the directions for positioning and securing them. Photo Sequence 13 shows the procedure for removing a typical drive axle and replacing a CV joint boot. Always refer to the service manual for the exact service procedure.

> **USING SERVICE MANUALS**
>
> The diagnosis and service chart shown in Table 28-1 is a combination of several different service manual charts. This gives an idea of the types of front-wheel drivetrain problems that can occur. A diagnosis chart shows the technician what to look for when a certain type of problem occurs.

☐ PREVENTIVE MAINTENANCE

Lubricant is the most important key to a long life of the CV joint. Without lubrication it is rendered ineffective, just like other high-speed mechanical devices that transfer power and motion, including engines, transmissions, and axles. Any condition that starves the CV joint for lubrication causes serious failure. In addition, water entering the boot areas (due to boot breakage, punctures, or improper tightening of the clamps) can wash lubricant out of the CV joint in a short period of time.

The special grease package included with each CV joint has a three-fold purpose: to properly lubricate the joint, to protect against exposure to extreme heat and cold, and to prevent boot rot.

CV Joint Servicing

The following are some pointers that should be kept in mind when servicing CV joints.

- Never jerk or pull on the drive shaft when removing the drive shaft on a vehicle with tripod inner joints. Doing so may pull the joint apart, allowing the needle bearings to fall out of the rollers. Pull on the inner housing, and support the outer end of the shaft until the shaft is completely out.
- Always torque the hub nuts to the vehicle manufacturer's specifications. This is absolutely necessary to properly preload the wheel bearings. Do not guess. The specifications can vary from 75 to 235 foot-pounds.
- Never use an impact wrench to loosen or tighten axle hub nuts. Doing so may damage the wheel bearings as well as the CV joints.
- On vehicles with anti-lock brakes, use care to protect the wheel speed sensor and tone ring on the outer CV joint housings. If misaligned or damaged

PHOTO SEQUENCE 13

☐ REMOVING AND REPLACING A CV-JOINT BOOT

P13-1 Removing the axle from the car begins with the removal of the wheel cover and the wheel hub cover. The hub nut should be loosened before raising the car and removing the wheel and tire assembly.

P13-2 After the car is raised and the wheel is removed, the hub nut can be unscrewed from the shaft.

P13-3 The brake line holding clamp must be loosened from the suspension.

P13-4 The ball joint must be separated from the steering knuckle assembly. To do this, first remove the ball joint retaining bolt. Then, pry down on the control arm until the ball joint is free.

P13-5 The inboard joint can be pulled free from the transaxle.

P13-6 A special tool is normally needed to separate the axle shaft from the hub. This allows the axle to be removed from the car.

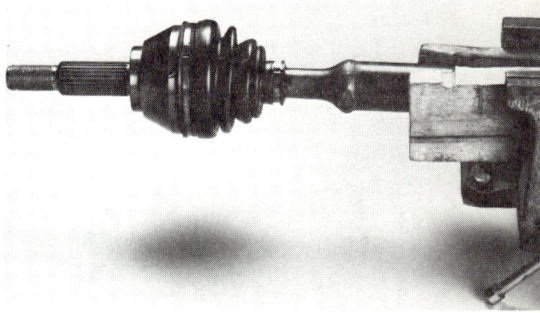

P13-7 The axle shaft should be mounted in a soft-jawed vise for work on the joint. Pieces of wood on either side of the axle works well to secure the axle without damaging it.

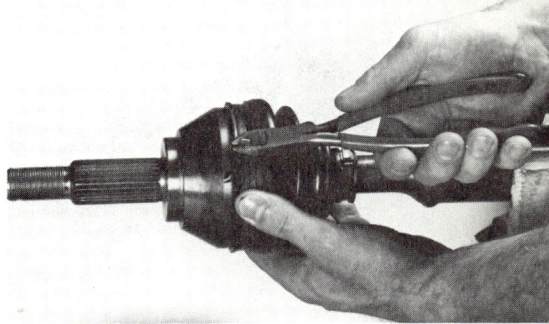

P13-8 Begin boot removal by cutting and discarding the boot clamps.

(continued)

679

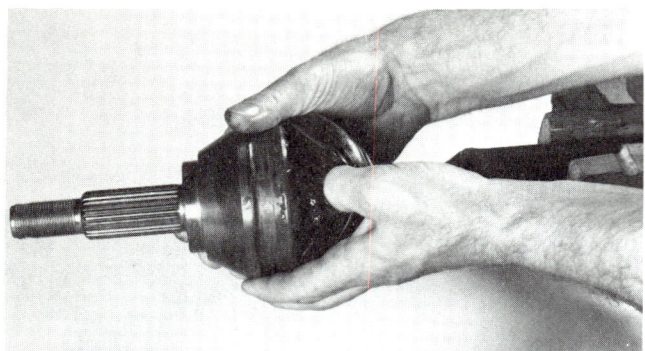

P13-9 Scribe a mark on the axle to indicate the boot's position on the shaft. Then, move the boot off the joint.

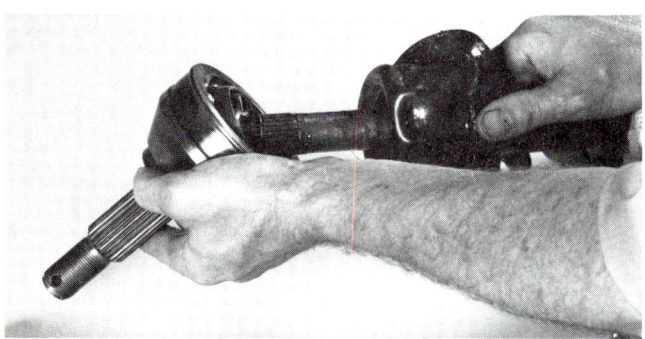

P13-10 Remove the circlip and separate the joint from the shaft.

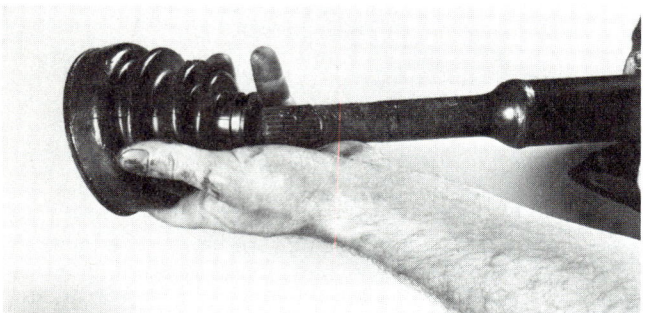

P13-11 Slide the old boot off the shaft.

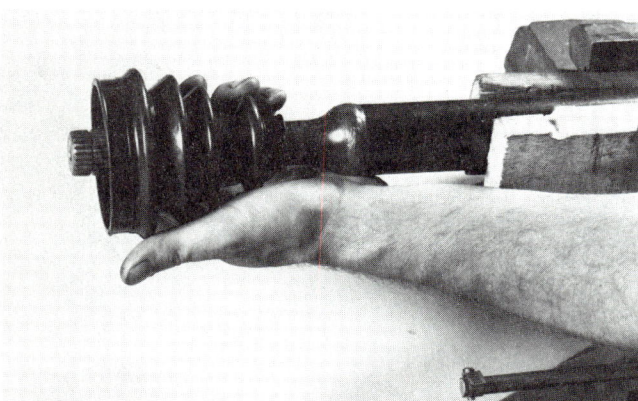

P13-12 Wipe the axle shaft clean and install the new boot onto the shaft.

P13-13 Place the boot into its proper location on the shaft and install a new clamp.

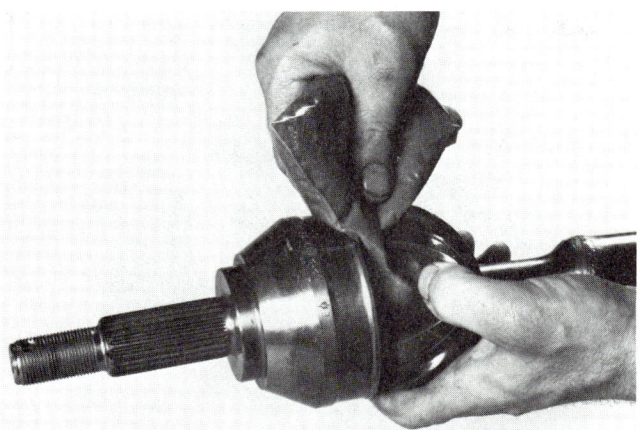

P13-14 Using a new circlip, reinstall the joint onto the shaft. Pack joint grease into the joint and boot. The entire packet of grease that comes with a new boot needs to be forced into the boot and joint.

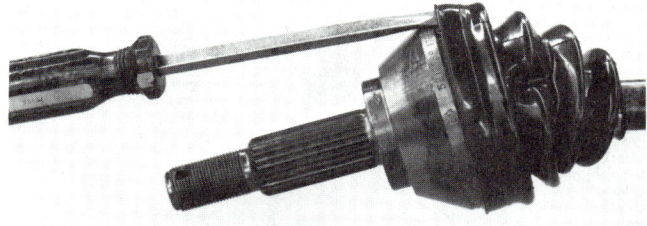

P13-15 Pull the boot over the joint and into its proper position. Use a dull screwdriver to lift the boot up, to purge it of any air that may be trapped, and to correct any collapsing of the boot.

P13-16 Install the new large boot clamp and reinstall the axle into the car. Tighten the hub nut after the wheels have been reinstalled and the car is sitting on the ground. ∎

Drive Axles and Differentials

TABLE 28-1 PROBLEM DIAGNOSIS AND SERVICE FOR FRONT-WHEEL DRIVELINE

Problem	Possible Cause	Corrective Remedy
Vibrations in steering wheel at highway speeds	Front-wheel balance	Front-wheel unbalance is felt in the steering wheel. Front wheels must be balanced.
Vibrations throughout vehicle	Worn inner CV joints	Worn parts of the inner CV joint not operating smoothly.
Vibrations throughout vehicle at low speed	Bent axle shaft	Axle shaft does not operate on center of axis, thus vibration develops.
Vibrations during acceleration	Worn or damaged outer or inner CV joints	CV joints not operating smoothly due to damage or wear on parts.
	Fatigued front springs	Sagged front springs are causing the inner CV joint to operate at too great an angle, causing vibrations.
Grease dripping on ground or sprayed on chassis parts	Ripped or torn CV joint boots	Front-wheel-drive CV joints are immersed in lubricant. If the CV joint boot has a rip or is torn, lubricant leaks out. Condition must be corrected as soon as possible.
Clicking or snapping noise heard when turning curves and corners	Worn or damaged outer CV joint	Worn parts are clicking and noisy as loading and unloading on CV joint takes place.
	Bent axle shaft	Irregular rotation of the axle shaft causing a snapping, clicking noise.

during joint replacement, it can cause wheel speed sensor problems.
- Always recheck the alignment after replacing CV joints. Marking the camber bolts is not enough, because camber can be off by as much as 3/4 degree due to differences between the size of the camber bolts and their holes.

CV Shaft and Rubber Boot Care Tips

The rubber boots need special care when you are servicing the CV joints, engine, or transaxle. The following tips might save you trouble later.

- Always support the control arm when doing on-the-car balancing of the front wheels (Figure 28-18) to avoid high-speed operation at a steep half shaft angle. Off-the-car balancing might be a wiser choice.
- Do not use half shafts as lift points for raising a car.
- Use a plastic or metal shield over rubber boots to protect them from accidental tool damage when performing other wheel, brake, suspension, or steering system maintenance.
- Clean only with soap and water.
- Avoid boot contact with gasoline, oil, or degreaser compounds.

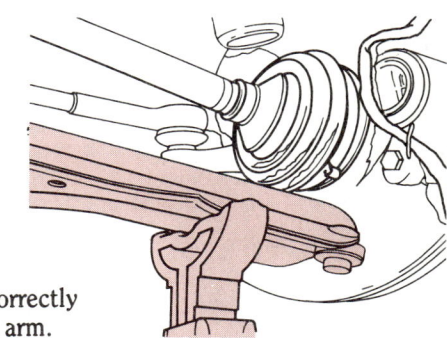

Figure 28-18 Correctly supported control arm.

USING SERVICE MANUALS

The exact procedures for performing service operations vary from vehicle to vehicle, but the included steps can be used as general guidelines. While specific installation instructions are provided with all replacement CV joints, boot kits, and drive shafts, they also can be found in the service manual as well. Figures 28-19 and 28-20 illustrate how the service manual details the assembly and disassembly procedures for both the inner and outer CV joints.

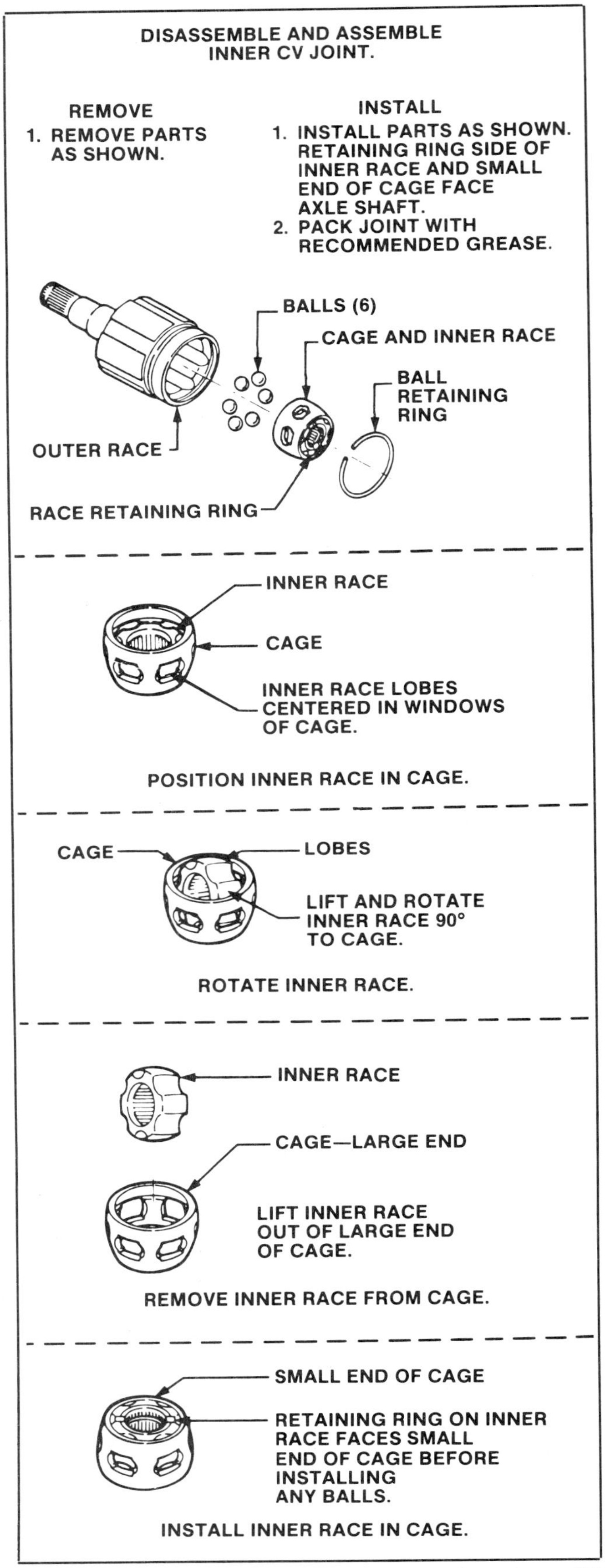

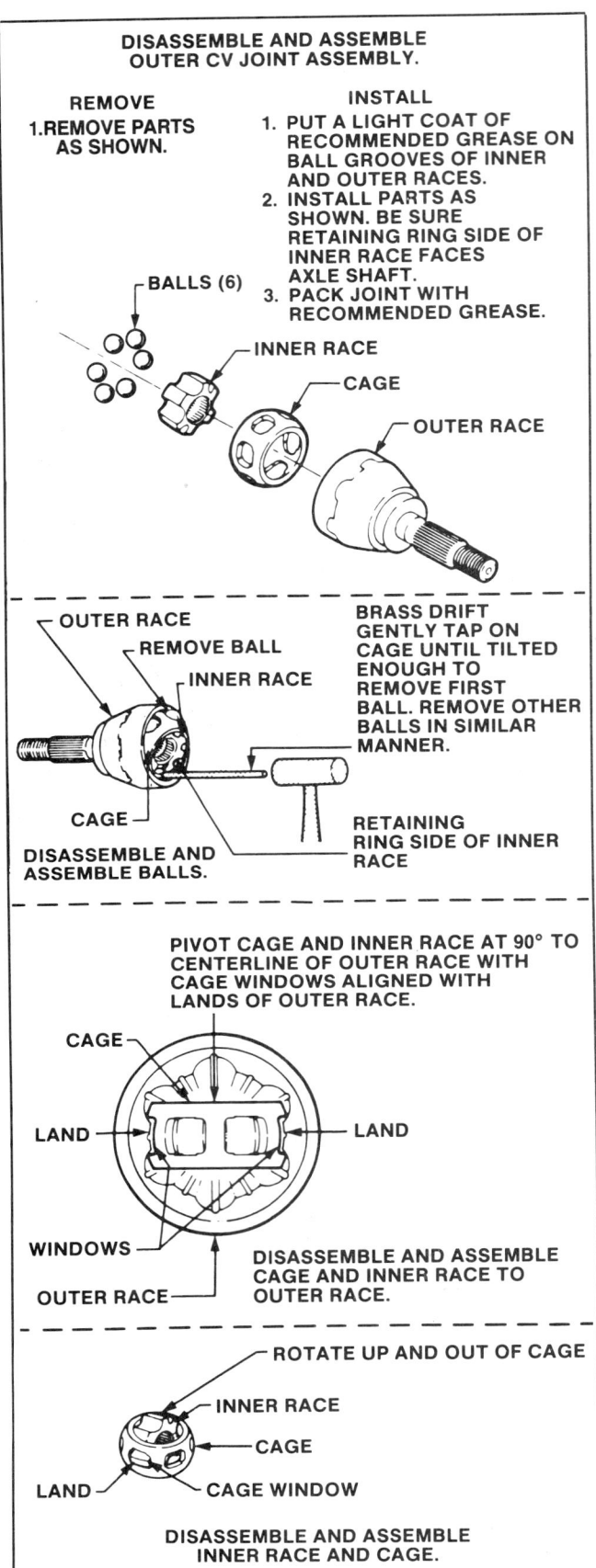

Figure 28-19 Service manual instructions for an inner CV joint. *Courtesy of Chevrolet Motor Division-GMC*

Figure 28-20 Service manual instructions for an outer CV joint. *Courtesy of Chevrolet Motor Division-GMC*

Drive Axles and Differentials 683

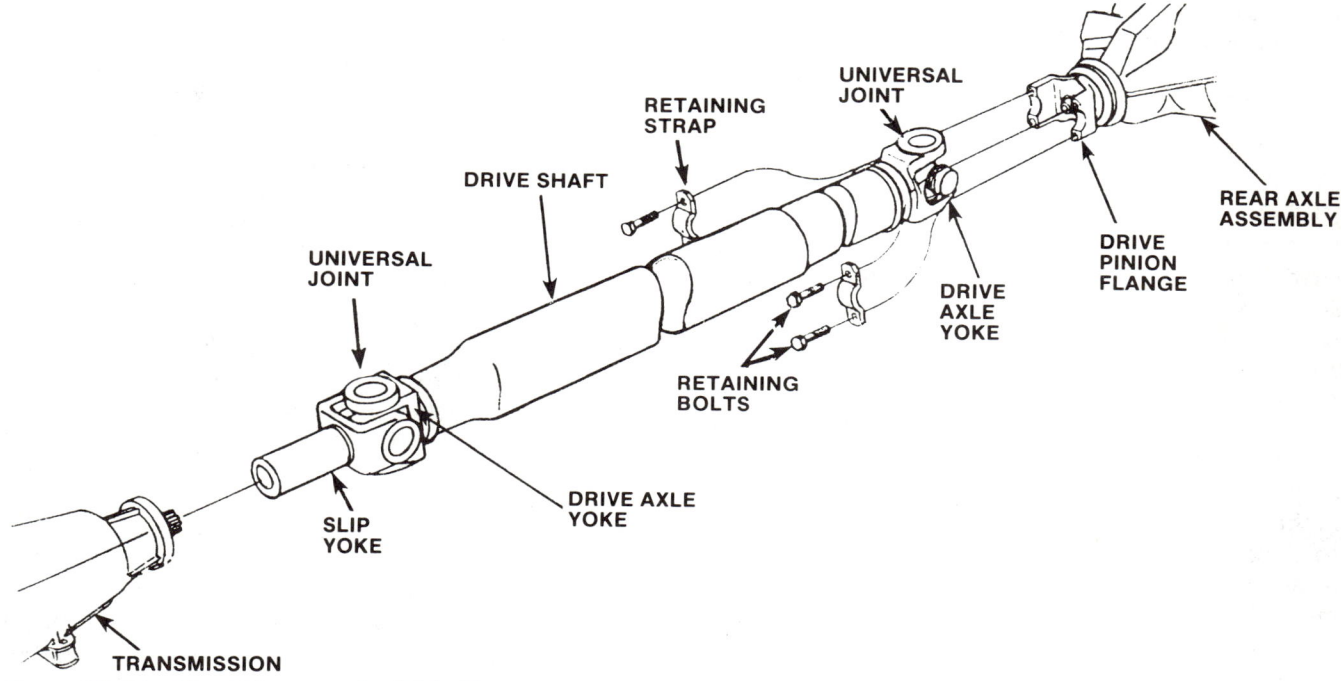

Figure 28-21 Hotchkiss rear-wheel driveline.

Rear-Wheel-Drive Axles

Starting at the front or transmission end of the rear-wheel-drive shaft, there is a slip yoke, universal joint, drive axle yoke, and drive shaft (Figure 28-21). At the rear or differential end, there is another drive axle yoke and a second universal joint connected to the differential pinion flange.

In addition to these basic components, some drivetrain systems employ a center carrier bearing for added support (Figure 28-22). Large cars with long drive shafts often use a double U-joint arrangement, called a constant velocity U-joint, to help minimize driveline vibrations. A U-joint should not be confused with the type of CV joint found on front-wheel-drive vehicles, which is described previously in this chapter. The function of these various components follows.

SLIP YOKE The most common slip or sliding yoke design (Figure 28-23) features an internally splined,

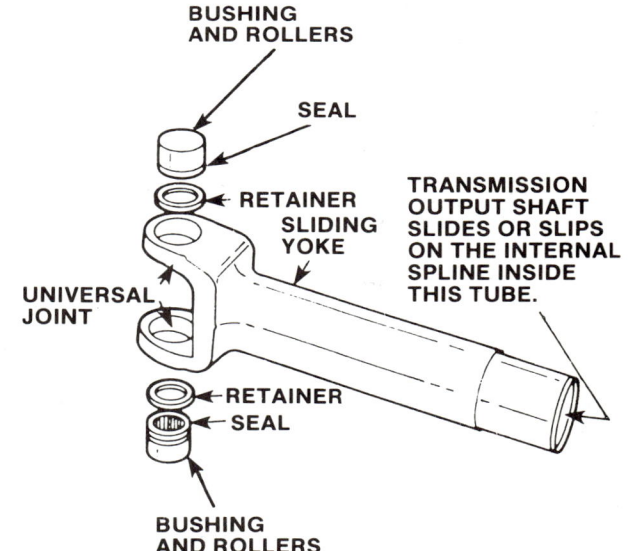

Figure 28-23 Typical slip or sliding yoke assembly.

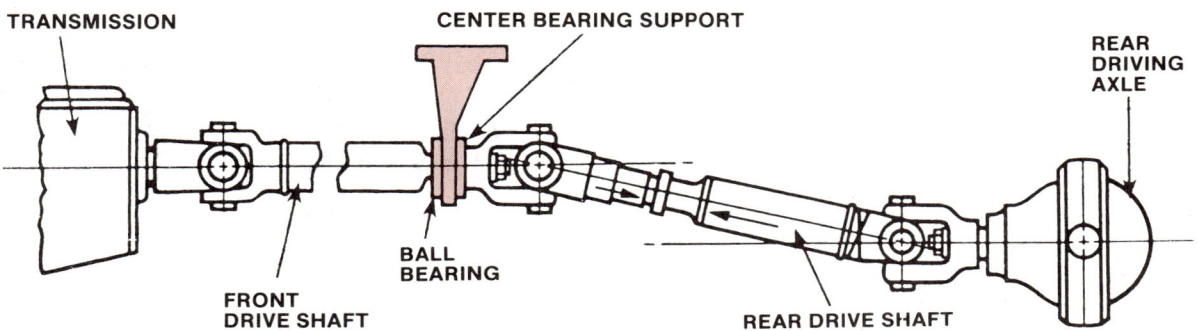

Figure 28-22 Center carrier bearing is added to a long drive shaft for additional support.

externally machined bore that lets the yoke rotate at transmission output shaft speed and slide at the same time (hence the name slip yoke). While the need for rotation is obvious, without the linear flexibility, the drive shaft would bend like a bow the first time the suspension jounced.

DRIVE SHAFT AND YOKES The drive shaft is nothing more than an extension of the transmission output shaft. The drive shaft, which is usually made from seamless steel tubing, transfers engine torque from the transmission to the rear driving axle. The yokes, which are either welded or pressed onto the shaft, provide a means of connecting two or more shafts together. At the present time, a limited number of vehicles are equipped with fiber composite—reinforced fiberglass, graphite, and aluminum—drive shafts. The advantages of the fiber composite drive shaft are weight reduction, torsional strength, fatigue resistance, easier and better balancing, and reduced interference from shock loading and torsional problems.

The drive shaft, like any other rigid tube, has a natural vibration frequency. If one end was held tightly, it would vibrate at its own frequency when deflected and released. It reaches its natural frequency at its critical speed. Critical drive shaft speed depends on the diameter of the tube and its length. Diameters are as large as possible and shafts as short as possible to keep the critical speed frequency above the driving speed range. It should be remembered that since the drive shaft generally turns three to four times faster than the tires, proper drive shaft balance is required for vibration-free operation.

Several different methods have been designed to reduce the effects of vibrations and noise transfer. One example is a drive shaft with cardboard liners that strengthen the drive shaft's axial length (Figure 28-24A). Drive shaft performance has also been improved by placing biscuits (Figure 28-24B) between the drive shaft and cardboard liner. These biscuits are simply rubber inserts that reduce noise transfer within the drive shaft. The tube-in-tube construction, illustrated in Figure 28-24C is another method of reducing drive shaft problems. This design eliminates much of the vibration and also reduces the clicking sound heard when the driveline is stressed with directional rotation changes. What makes this design different is that the input driving yoke has an input shaft that fits inside the hollow drive shaft. Rubber inserts are bonded to the outside diameter of the input shaft and to the inside diameter of the drive shaft.

As discussed later in this chapter, there are several methods of balancing drive shafts and drive axles. One of the most common techniques employed by vehicle manufacturers to reduce vibrations is to balance the drive shaft by welding balance weights to the outside diameter.

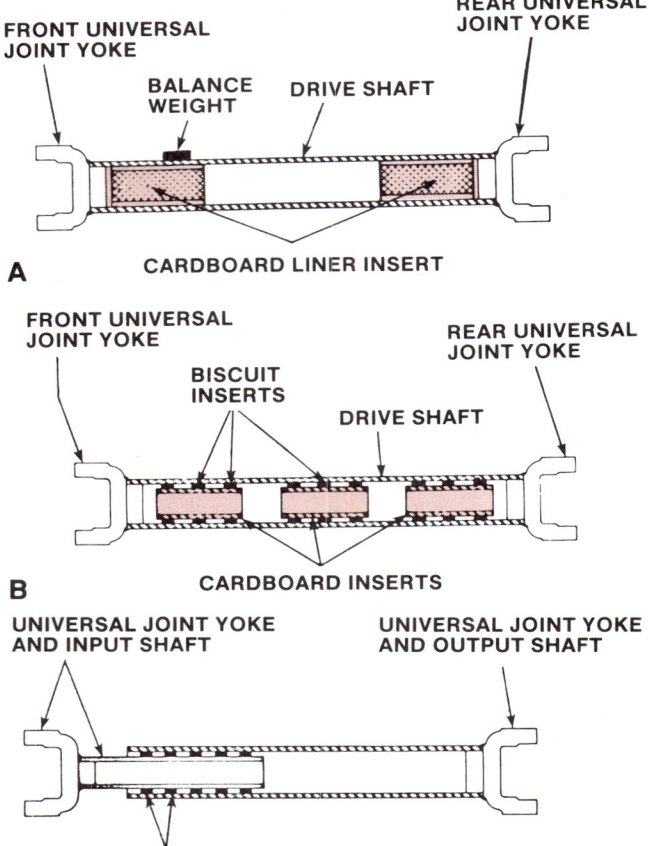

Figure 28-24 (A) Drive shaft with cardboard liner for strength; (B) drive shaft with rubber biscuit inserts to reduce noise; (C) tube-in-tube drive shaft eliminates vibration and noise.

☐ OPERATION OF U-JOINTS

The U-joint allows two rotating shafts to operate at a slight angle to each other. The original joint was developed in the sixteenth century by a French mathematician named Cardan. In 1902, Clarence Spicer modified Cardan's invention for the purpose of transmitting engine torque to an automobile's rear wheels. By joining two shafts with U-shaped forks (called yokes) to a pivoting cruciform member, the problem of torque transfer through a connection that also needed to compensate for slight angular variations was eliminated.

There are three operating U-joint considerations that automotive engineers must keep in mind when designing rear-wheel drivelines: speed variations, phasing of U-joints, and canceling angles.

Speed Variations

Although simple in appearance (Figure 28-25), the universal joint is more intricate than it seems. This is because its natural action is to speed up and slow down twice in each revolution when operating at an angle.

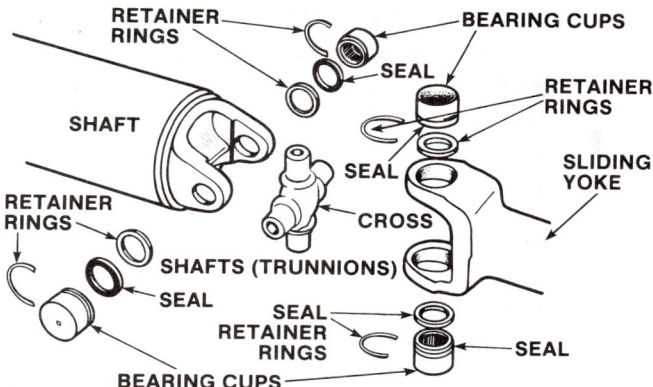

Figure 28-25 Exploded view of Cardan universal joint.

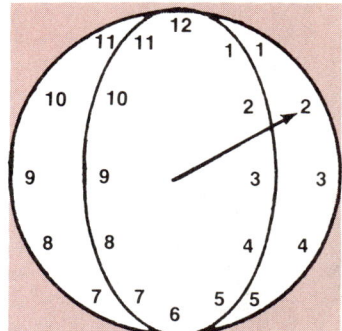

Figure 28-27 The face of a clock illustrates the elliptical action of the yokes.

The rate of speed varies, depending upon the steepness of the U-joint angle.

The universal joint operating angle is derived by taking the difference between the transmission installation angle and the drive shaft installation angle. For instance, in Figure 28-26, a true horizontal centerline is drawn through the transmission. In order to align better with the rear axle, the transmission is installed at an angle 5 degrees off the true horizontal line. The drive shaft installation angle is 8 degrees off the true horizontal. The difference between the transmission installation angle and the drive shaft installation angle is 3 degrees. Therefore, the universal joint operating angle is 3 degrees. When the universal joint is operating at an angle, the driven yoke speeds up and slows down twice during each drive shaft revolution. This acceleration and deceleration of the universal joint is known as speed variation or fluctuation.

The four speed changes are not normally visible during rotation. They might be felt as torsional vibrations due to improper installation, steep or unequal operating angles, and high speeds.

This is more easily understood after examining the universal joint action. A universal joint is a coupling between two shafts not in direct alignment, usually with changing relative positions. It would be logical to assume that the entire unit simply rotates. This is true only for the universal joint's input yoke.

An ellipse is merely a compressed form of the circle. The output yoke's circular path looks like an ellipse because it can be viewed at an angle instead of straight on. This effect can be obtained when a coin is rotated by the fingers. The height of the coin stays the same even though the sides seem to get closer together.

This might seem to be a merely visual effect, but it is more than that. The U-joint rigidly locks the circular action of the input yoke to the elliptical action of the output yoke. The result is similar to what would happen when changing a clock face from a circle to an ellipse. Figure 28-27 shows that 12, 3, 6, and 9 o'clock are the same, but in between the time reading changes. At 2 o'clock on the circle, it is 2:20 on the ellipse.

Like the hands of a clock, the input yoke turns at a constant speed in its true circular path. The output yoke, operating at an angle to the other yoke, completes its path in the same amount of time. However, its speed varies, or is not constant, compared to the input.

Speed variation is more easily visualized when looking at the travel of the yokes by 90-degree quadrants (Figure 28-28). The input yoke rotates at a steady or constant speed through the complete 360-degree turn. The output yoke quadrants alternate between shorter and longer distance travel than the input yoke quadrants. When one point of the output yoke covers the shorter distance in the same amount of time, it must travel at a slower rate. Conversely, when traveling the longer distance (but only 90 degrees) in the same amount of time, it must move faster.

Because the average speed of the output yoke through the four 90-degree quadrants (360 degrees) equals the constant speed of the input yoke during the same revolution, it is possible for the two mating yokes to travel at different speeds. The output yoke is falling behind and catching up constantly, like a racer on an irregular track. The resulting acceleration and deceleration produces a fluctuating torque and torsional vibrations. This acceleration and deceleration is characteristic of all Cardan universal joints. The steeper the U-joint angle, the greater the fluctuations in speed. Conversely, the smaller the angle, the less the speed change.

Phasing of Universal Joints

Speed variations must be canceled at exactly the same point in drive shaft rotation. The two driving yokes at opposite ends of the drive shaft must be at the same point of rotation.

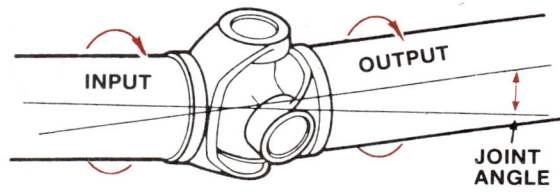

Figure 28-26 U-joint action.

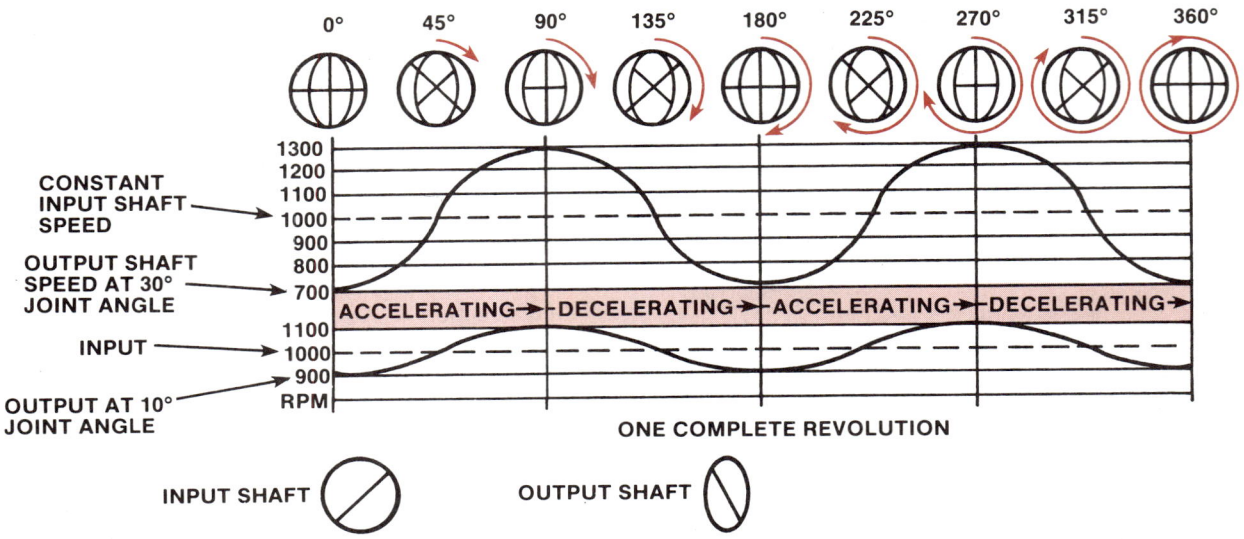

Figure 28-28 This graph shows typical yoke speed vibrations.

Single-piece drive shafts have the universal joint yokes welded into position when they are manufactured. On a two-piece drive shaft, a technician might encounter problems if care is not exercised, because the center universal joint must be disassembled to replace the center support bearing. The center driving yoke is splined to the front drive shaft. If the yoke's position on the drive shaft is not indicated in some manner, the yoke could be installed in a position that is out of phase. Manufacturers use different methods of indexing the yoke to the shaft. Some use aligning arrows (Figure 28-29). Others machine a master spline that is wider than the others. The yoke and shaft cannot be reassembled until the master spline is aligned properly. When there are no indexing marks, the technician should always index the yoke to the drive shaft before disassembling the universal joint. This saves time in the reassembly procedure. Indexing requires only a light hammer and center punch to mark the yoke and drive shaft.

Canceling Angles

Vibrations can be reduced by using canceling angles (Figure 28-30). Carefully examine the illustration, and

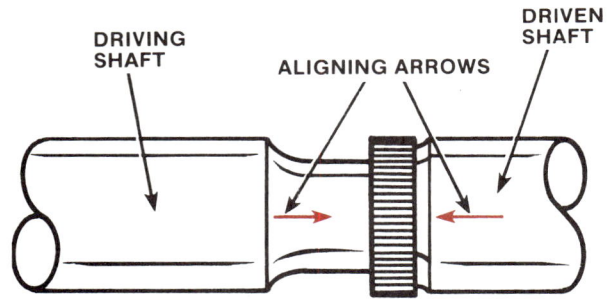

Figure 28-29 Arrows are placed on the driving and driven parts of the drive shaft to maintain alignment.

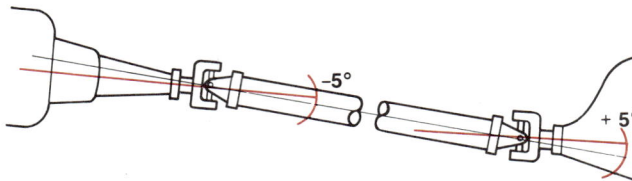

Figure 28-30 Canceling angles reduce vibrations.

note that the operating angle at the front of the drive shaft is offset by the one at the rear of the drive shaft. When the front universal joint accelerates, causing a vibration, the rear universal joint decelerates, causing a vibration. The vibrations created by the two joints oppose and dampen the vibrations from one to the other. The use of canceling angles provides a smoother drive shaft operation.

☐ TYPES OF U-JOINTS

There are three common types of U-joint designs.

1. Single U-joints retained by either an inside or outside snap ring
2. Coupled U-joints commonly called the double-Cardan constant velocity joints
3. U-joints held in the yoke by U-bolts or lock plates

Single Universal Joint

The single Cardan/Spicer universal joint is also known as the cross or four-point joint. These two names aptly describe the single Cardan, since the joint itself forms a cross, with four machined trunnions or points equally spaced around the center of the axis. Needle bearings used to abate friction and provide smoother operation are set in bearing cups. The trunnions of the cross fit into the cup assemblies and the cup assemblies fit snugly into the driving and driven

Drive Axles and Differentials 687

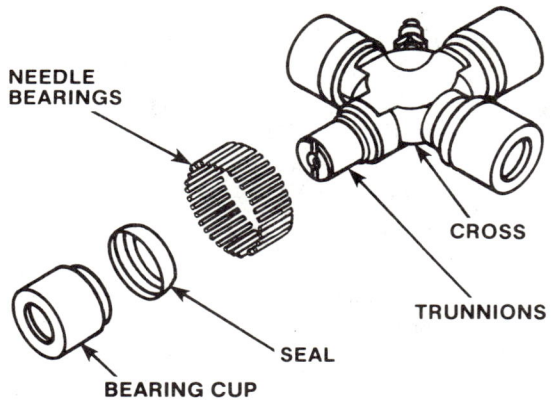

Figure 28-31 Components involved in U-joint movement.

universal joint yokes. Universal joint movement takes place between the trunnions, needle bearings, and bearing cups (Figure 28-31). No movement should take place between the bearing cup and the hole in the universal joint yoke. The fit between the hole in the yoke and the bearing cups is known as a press-fit. Retaining rings hold the bearing cups in place in the universal joint yoke.

Replacing a single U-joint requires that the technician know more than the make and model of the vehicle. It might be necessary to know the type of U-joint and the yoke span in order to obtain the proper replacement part (Figure 28-32).

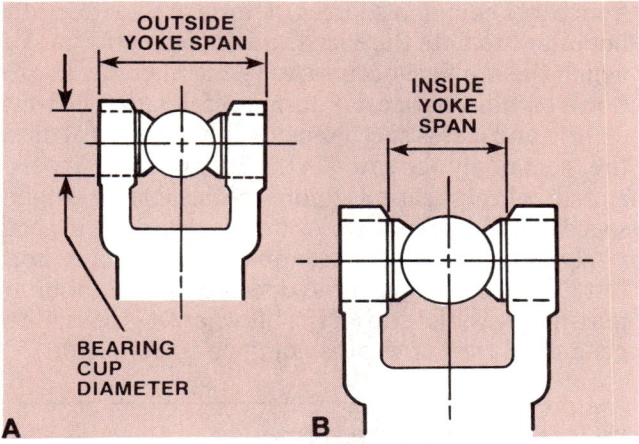

Figure 28-32 (A) Outside yoke span and (B) inside yoke span.

Spicer Style

In this single U-joint design (Figure 28-33A) an outside snap ring fits into a groove machined in the outer end of the yoke. The bearing cups for this style are machined to accommodate the snap ring.

Mechanics or Detroit/Saginaw Style

In this design (Figure 28-33B), an inside snap ring or C-clip fits into a groove machined in the bearing cup on the side closer to the grease seal. When installed, the clip rests against the machined inside portion of the yoke. The snap ring in the Detroit/Saginaw style is injected nylon. That is, the snap rings are retained by nylon injected into the retaining ring grooves.

Cleveland Style

In an attempt to combine U-joints to obtain more coverage, the Cleveland style is used for some applications. The bearing cups for this U-joint are machined to accommodate either Spicer or Mechanics style snap rings. If a replacement U-joint comes with both style clips, use the clips that pertain to your application.

> **USING SERVICE MANUALS**
>
> In addition to the technician knowing how to read a service manual, it is also important to know the ins and outs of aftermarket catalogs and similar literature. This helps to identify the correct type of joint used in a particular vehicle.

Double-Cardan Universal Joint

Most often installed in front-engine rear-wheel-drive luxury automobiles, the double-Cardan universal joint smoothly transmits torque regardless of the operating angle of the driving and driven members. It is therefore classified as a constant velocity universal joint. Observe the left and right universal joint centerlines (Figure 28-34). They bisect the angle made by the input driving and the output driven universal joint. Constant velocity operation is the result.

The double-Cardan universal joint is made up of two Cardan universal joints linked together by a coupling yoke. A centering ball socket is inside the coupling

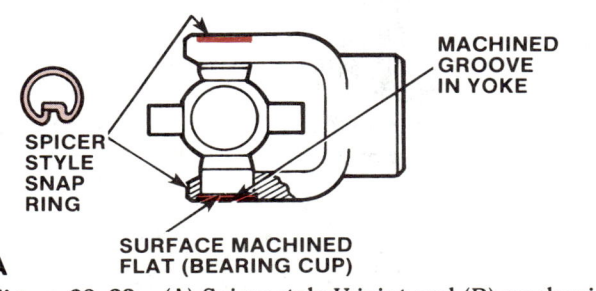 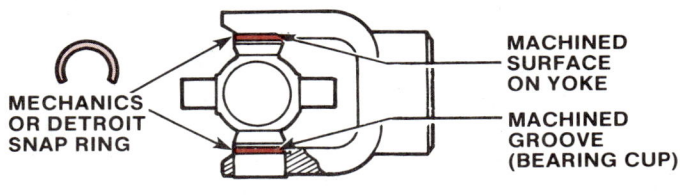

Figure 28-33 (A) Spicer style U-joint and (B) mechanics or Detroit style U-joint.

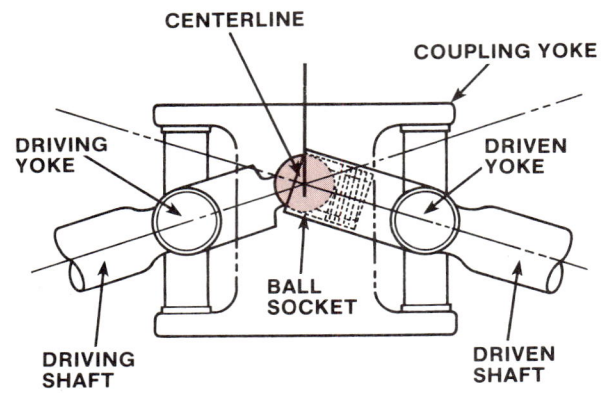

Figure 28-34 Double-Cardan constant speed universal joint's centerline bisects the angle at the ball socket.

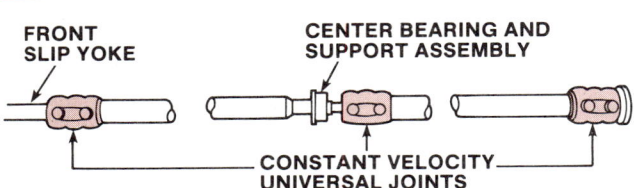

Figure 28-35 Two-piece drive shaft and double-Cardan joints.

yoke between the two universal joints. This ball and socket maintain an axial relationship between the two universal joints. The ball joint divides the universal joint operating angle into two equal parts, so that each universal joint operates at half of the operating angle. Since the two universal joints operate at the same angle, vibrations and fluctuations in speed from the front joint are nullified by the vibrations and fluctuations in speed from the rear universal joint. The canceling angles produce a smooth transfer of engine torque. The double-Cardan joint is often a vital part of a two-piece drive axle shaft (Figure 28-35).

Other U-Joint Retaining Methods

There are several methods of retaining the U-joint in its position. The methods shown in Figure 28-36 are most common.

WARNING: Extreme care should be taken when working around a rotating drive shaft. Severe injury can result from touching a moving shaft. Never attempt to stop the spinning shaft by hand. It can cause serious physical injury.

☐ DIAGNOSIS OF DRIVE SHAFT AND U-JOINT PROBLEMS

A failed U-joint or damaged drive shaft can exhibit a variety of symptoms. A clunk that is heard when the transmission is shifted into gear is the most obvious. You can also encounter unusual noise, roughness, or vibration.

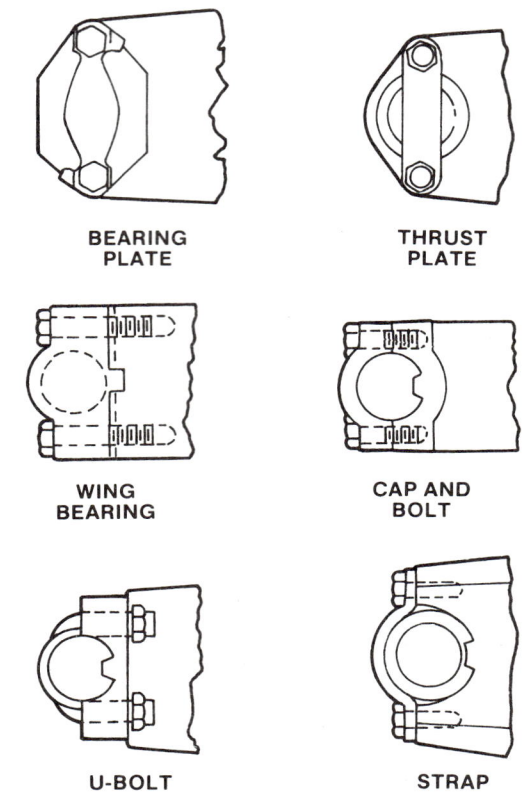

Figure 28-36 Various retaining methods for U-joints.

To help differentiate a potential drivetrain problem from other common sources of noise or vibration, it is important to note the speed and driving conditions at which the problem occurs. As a general guide, a worn U-joint is most noticeable during acceleration or deceleration and is less speed sensitive than an unbalanced tire (commonly occurring in the 30 to 60 mph range) or a bad wheel bearing (more noticeable at higher speeds). Unfortunately, it is often very difficult to accurately pinpoint drivetrain problems with only a road test. Therefore, expand the undercar investigation by putting the vehicle up on the lift where it is possible to get a good view of what is going on underneath.

CUSTOMER CARE

To some customers, a little noise might be easier to live with than the cost of a differential teardown. On the other hand, repairs now may be less extensive than later. The best method is to go over all the options in detail and let the customer decide. This goes for most other vehicle problems as well.

The first problem most likely encountered is an undercar fluid leak. If there is a lot of lube escaping from the pinion shaft seal, the drivetrain noise could be caused by a bad pinion bearing. To confirm the problem, start the engine, put the transmission in gear, and listen at the carrier. If the bearing is noisy, it is necessary to make one of those difficult judgment calls. If the bearing sounds fine but the pinion seal is still leaking, suggest an on-the-car seal replacement.

On some vehicles, seal replacement is a simple procedure that involves removing the pinion flange and replacing the seal. However, always refer to the service manual for the correct procedure and note any special precautions that may be given.

At the other end of the driveline, inspect the extension housing seal the same way. If it is leaking, the seal itself can be easily replaced. Check the extension housing bushing. That is the most likely reason the seal went bad in the first place. Once the yoke is removed, an internal expanding bearing/bushing puller makes short work of bushing replacement. Before pushing the slip yoke back in after the new seal is installed, make sure the machined surface of the bore is free of scratches, nicks, and grooves that could damage the seal. For that added margin of safety, a little transmission lube or white grease on the lip of the seal helps the parts slide in easily.

If the seals pass the test, continue driveline examination by inspecting the U-joint's grease seals for signs of rust, leakage, or lubrication breakdown. Also, check for excessive joint movement by firmly grasping and attempting to rotate the coupling yokes back and forth in opposite directions. If any perceptible trunnion-to-bearing movement is felt, the joint should be replaced.

As a final diagnosis inspection point, check the entire length of the drive shaft for excess undercoating, dents, missing weights, or other damage that could cause an imbalance and result in a vibration.

☐ DIFFERENTIALS

The differential is a geared mechanism located between the driving axles of a vehicle. Its job is to direct power flow to the driving axles. Differentials are used in all types of power trains: rear-wheel-drive, front-wheel-drive, and four-wheel-drive.

On a front-wheel-drive car or truck, the differential is normally an integral part of the transaxle assembly located at the front of the vehicle. Depending on whether the engine is mounted transversely or longitudinally, the transaxle differential design and operation vary (Figure 28-37). With a transverse mounted engine, the crankshaft centerline and drive axle are on the same plane. With a longitudinal mounted power plant, the differential must change the power flow 90 degrees.

On rear-wheel-drive vehicles, the differential is part of the rear assembly. It is located in the rear axle housing or carrier. A driveline running beneath the vehicle from front to rear connects the transmission with the differential gearing. Four-wheel-drive vehicles have differentials on both their front and rear axles. A transfer case mounted to the side or back of the transmission splits the power between two drive shafts or lines. One runs to the front drive axle and the other runs to the rear drive axle (Figure 28-38). Differentials at the front and rear axles redirect power flow to all wheels. Some full-time four-wheel-drive systems employ a third differential. This interaxle differential is located in the transfer case between the front- and rear-drive axles (Figure 28-39). The interaxle differential allows the two drivelines to rotate at different

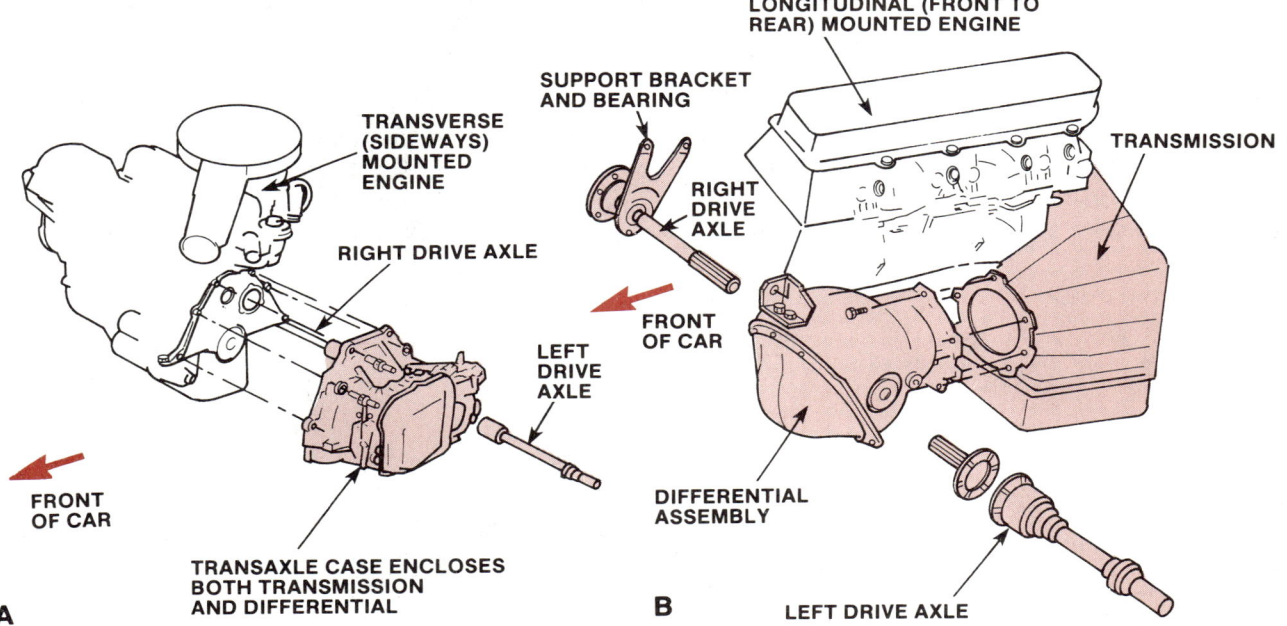

Figure 28-37 There are two basic transaxle differential design variations: (A) With transverse mounted engine, engine crankshaft centerline and axle centerline are on same plane; (B) With longitudinal mounted engine, differential must change power flow 90 degrees, as with rear-wheel drive. *Courtesy of Ford and Cadillac*

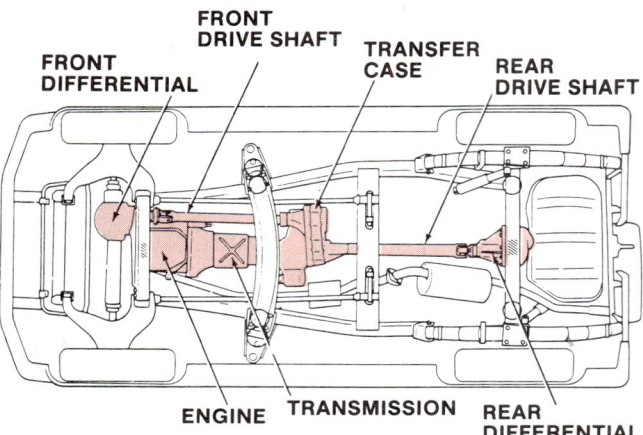

Figure 28–38 Four-wheel-drive drivetrain based on a rear-wheel-drive design. *Courtesy of Mitsubishi Motor Sales of America, Inc.*

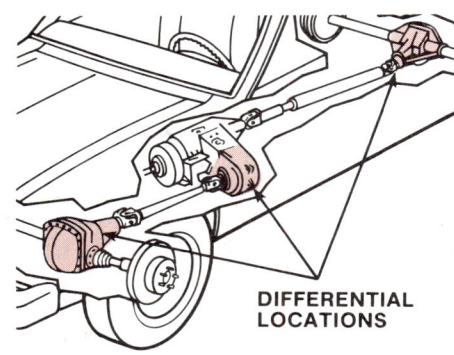

Figure 28–39 The interaxle differential is located in the transfer case between the front- and rear-drive axles.

speeds, which improves vehicle handling and reduces component wear.

Differential Functions

The differential actually performs several functions. It allows the drive wheels to rotate at different speeds when negotiating a turn or curve in the road (Figure 28-40) and redirects the engine torque from the drive shaft to the rear drive axles. The drive shaft turns in a motion that is perpendicular to the rotation of the drive wheels. The differential assembly redirects the torque so that the drive shafts turn in a motion that is parallel with the rotation of the drive wheels.

The differential also splits torque between the drive axles. Each drive wheel receives an equal amount of torque. The torque delivered to the wheels is no greater than the torque required by the wheel with the least amount of traction. If one wheel begins to slip, it requires much less torque to turn it. Less torque is then delivered to the wheel that is not slipping. In such a situation, unless the differential is a limited-slip design, the vehicle loses traction.

The drive gears of a differential are also sized to provide a gear reduction, or a torque multiplication. Differentials with a low (numerically high) gear ratio allow for fast acceleration and good pulling power. Differentials with high gear ratios allow the engine to run slower at any given speed, resulting in better fuel conservation.

Differential Components

The components of commonly used differentials are shown in Figure 28-41. There are several other basic design arrangements. However, the one most commonly used design features pinion/ring gears and a pinion shaft. The latter is a spiral bevel gear that is mounted on an input (pinion) shaft. The shaft is mounted in the front end of the carrier and supported by two or three bearings. An overhung pinion gear is supported by two tapered bearings spaced far enough apart to provide the needed leverage to rotate the ring gear and drive axles (Figure 28-42). A straddle-mounted pinion gear rests on three bearings: two tapered bearings on the front support the input shaft and one roller bearing is fitted over a short shaft extending from the rear end of the pinion gear (Figure 28-43).

The pinion gear meshes with a ring gear. The ring gear is a ring of hardened steel with curved teeth on one side and threaded holes on the other. The ring gear is bolted to the differential case. When the pinion gear is rotated by the drive shaft, the ring gear is forced to rotate, turning the differential case and axle shafts. In

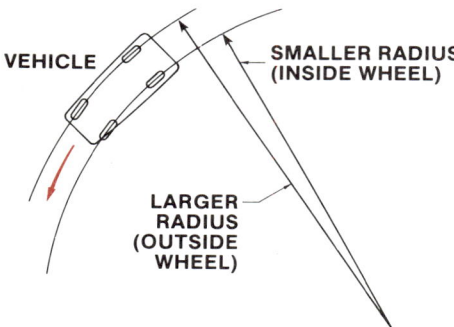

Figure 28–40 The differential is needed because the rear wheels turn at different speeds around a corner.

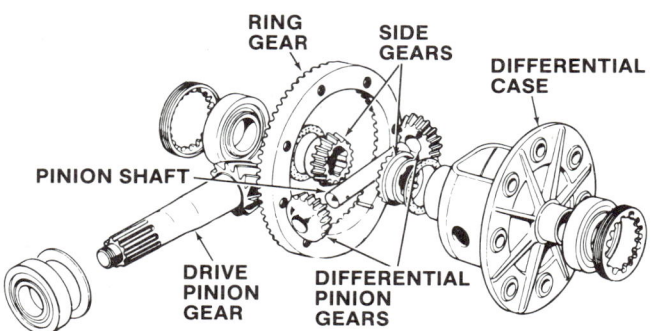

Figure 28–41 A typical differential design. *Courtesy of Toyo Kogyo Co., Ltd.*

Figure 28-42 Overhung-type of drive pinion mount.

Figure 28-43 A straddle-mounted drive pinion gear. The drive pinion is straddled between two tapered rollers and a straight roller bearing. These three bearings hold the drive pinion in mesh with the ring gear. *Courtesy of Ford Motor Co.*

most automotive applications there are two pinion gears mounted on a straight shaft. On heavier trucks, the differential contains four pinion gears mounted on a cross-shaped spider. The pinion shafts are mounted in holes in the case (or in matching grooves in the case halves) and are secured in place with a lock bolt or retaining rings.

The teeth on the drive pinion contact the ring gear at either the same, or different, places after several revolutions of the ring gear. There are three terms that describe the tooth contact.

HUNTING GEARSET When one drive pinion gear tooth contacts every ring gear tooth after several revolutions, the gearset is hunting. In other words, the drive pinion hunts out each ring gear tooth. A typical hunting gearset may have 9 drive pinion teeth and 37 ring gear teeth. The rear-axle ratio for this combination would be 4.11:1.

NONHUNTING GEARSET When one drive pinion gear tooth contacts only certain ring gear teeth, the gearset is nonhunting. A typical nonhunting gearset may have 10 drive pinion teeth and 30 ring gear teeth. The rear-axle ratio for this combination would be 3.00:1. For every revolution of the ring gear, each drive pinion tooth would contact the same 3 ring gear teeth. The drive pinion gear teeth do not hunt out all ring gear teeth.

PARTIAL NONHUNTING GEARSET The difference between nonhunting and partial nonhunting gearsets is the amount of ring gear teeth that are contacted. On a partial nonhunting gearset, one drive pinion tooth contacts six ring gear teeth instead of three. During the first revolution of the ring gear, one drive pinion tooth contacts three ring gear teeth. During the second revolution of the ring gear, the drive pinion tooth contacts three different ring gear teeth. During every other ring gear revolution, one drive pinion tooth contacts the same ring gear teeth. A typical partial nonhunting gearset may have 10 drive pinion teeth and 35 ring gear teeth. The rear-axle ratio for this combination would be 3.50:1. The number of teeth on the drive pinion and ring gear determine whether the gearset is hunting, nonhunting, or partial nonhunting. Knowing the type of gearset is important in diagnosing ring and pinion problems.

A hypoid gear is similar to a spiral bevel gear (Figure 28-44). The hypoid gear contacts more than one tooth at a time. The hypoid gear also makes contact with a sliding motion. This sliding action, however, is smoother than that of the spiral valve gear, resulting in quieter operation. The biggest difference is that, in a hypoid gear, the centerlines of the ring and pinion gears do not match. A centerline is an imaginary line that connects the axis of one part to the axis of another part. For example, when the drive pinion is set in the middle of the right gear, the centerlines of each gear meet. To determine this, draw a line from the center, or axis, of the drive-pinion-gear shaft. Then, locate the centerline of the ring gear. The centerlines should meet on spur-type bevel gears. Using hypoid gears, the drive pinion

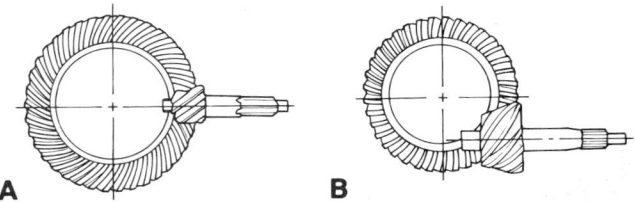

Figure 28-44 (A) Spiral bevel differential gears and (B) hypoid gears. *Courtesy of Ford Motor Co. of Canada, Ltd.*

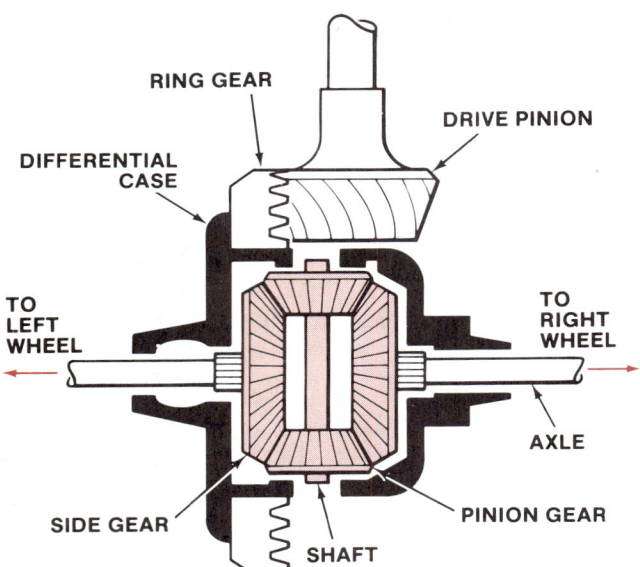

Figure 28-45 Hypoid ringer pinion assembly with side gears. *Courtesy of Ford Motor Co.*

gear is placed lower in the differential. The drive pinion meshes with the ring gear at a point below its centerline.

When hypoid gears mesh during operation, they do so with a sliding action. The teeth tend to wipe lubricant from the face of the gears, resulting in eventual damage. Differentials require the use of extreme pressure-type lubricants. The additives in this type of lubricant allow the lubricant to withstand the wiping action of the gear teeth without separating from the gear face.

The differential also contains two side gears (Figure 28-45). The inside bore of the side gears is splined and mates with splines on the ends of the drive axles. The differential pinion gears and side gears are in constant mesh. The pinion gears are mounted on a pinion gear shaft, which is mounted in the differential casing. As the casing turns with the ring gear, the pinion shaft and gears also turn. The pinion gears deliver torque to the side gears.

When the pinion and ring gear are manufactured, the faces of the gear teeth are machined to provide smooth mating surfaces. The pinion gear and ring gear are always matched to provide a good mesh. Pinion gears and the ring gear should always be installed as a set. Otherwise, a mismatched gearset might operate noisily. A matched gearset code is etched in each drive pinion and ring gearset.

Rear Axle Housing and Casing

The differential in a rear-drive vehicle is housed in the rear axle housing, or carrier. The axle housing also contains the two drive axle shafts (Figure 28-46). There are two types of axle housings found on modern automobiles: the removable carrier and the integral carrier. The removable carrier axle housing is open on the front side. Because it resembles a banjo, it is often called a banjo housing. The backside of the housing is closed to seal out dirt and contaminants and keep in the differential lubricant. The differential is mounted in a carrier assembly that can be removed as a unit from the axle housing (Figure 28-47). Removable carrier axle housings are most commonly used today on trucks and other heavy-duty vehicles.

The integral axle housing is most commonly found on late-model cars and light trucks (Figure 28-48). A cast-iron carrier forms the center of the axle housing. Steel axle tubes are pressed into both sides of the carrier to form the housing. The housing and carrier have a removable rear cover that allows access to the differential assembly. Because the carrier is not removable, the differential components must be removed and serviced separately (Figure 28-49). In addition to providing a mounting place for the differential, the axle housing also contains brackets for mounting suspension components such as control arms, leaf springs, and coil springs.

GEAR REDUCTION When a smaller gear drives a larger gear, the larger gear turns slower. This is known as speed, or gear, reduction. The smaller drive pinion gear may turn only about two-and-a-half times the ring gear speed. This difference between the speed of the drive pinion gear and the ring gear is known as the rear-axle ratio. Most rear-axle ratios appear with decimals, such as: 2.43:1, 3.08:1, or 4.11:1. In a differen-

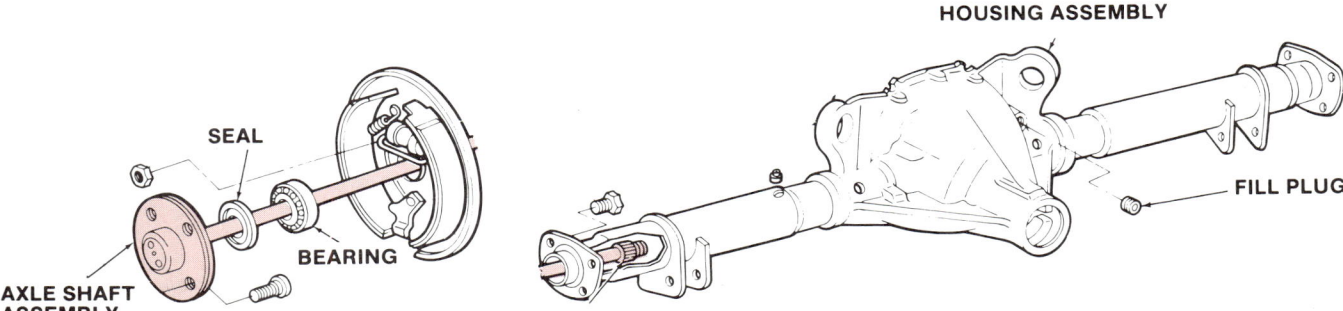

Figure 28-46 In a typical rear end, the drive axles are enclosed in metal tubes connected to the differential housing. *Courtesy of Ford Motor Co.*

Drive Axles and Differentials   693

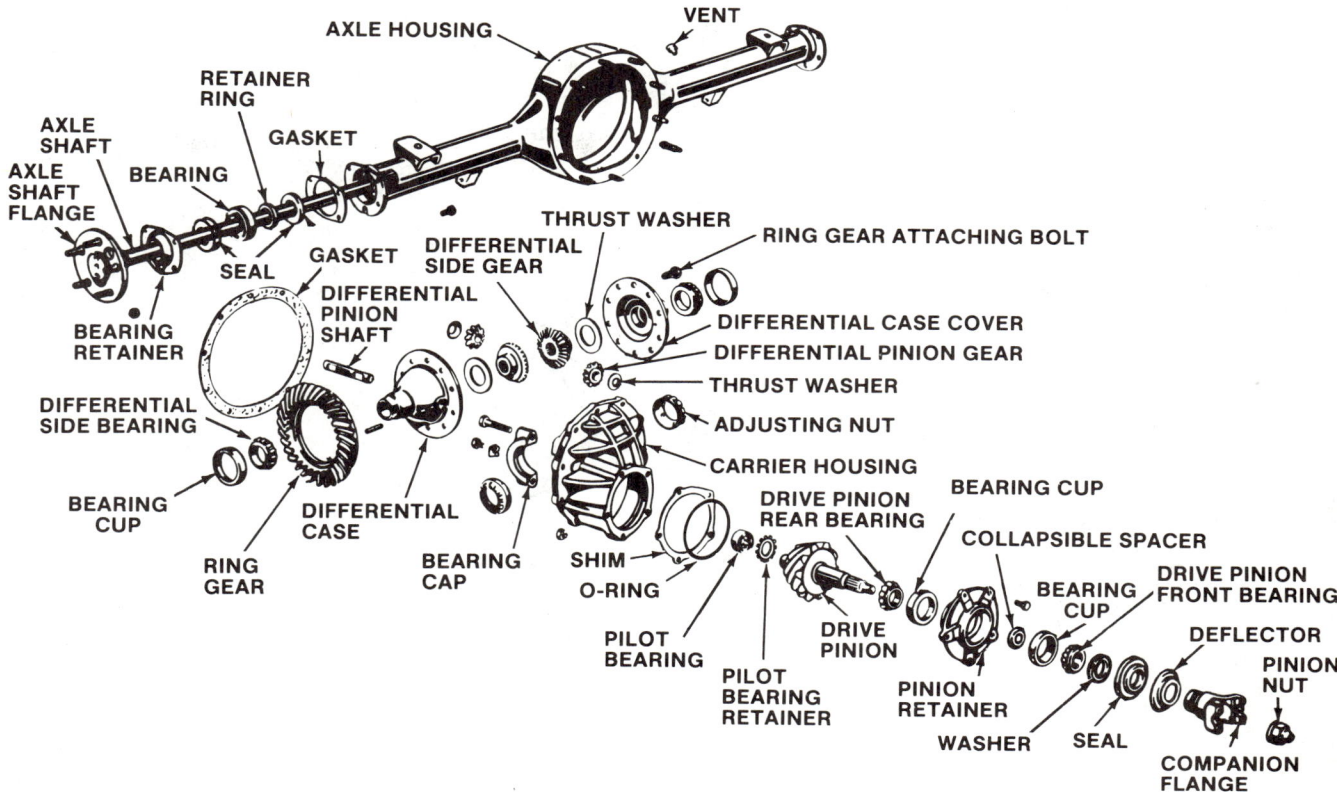

Figure 28-47 A typical removable carrier axle housing. *Courtesy of Ford Motor Co.*

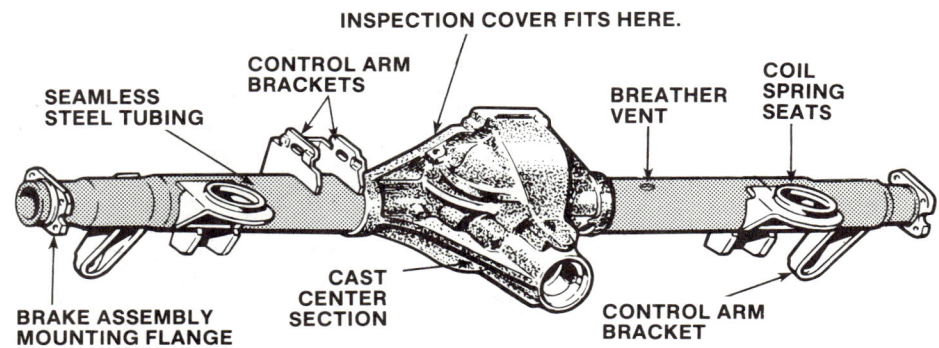

Figure 28-48 The integral axle housing is a three-piece construction where the center section is cast iron and the axle tubes are seamless steel tubing. *Courtesy of Ford Motor Co.*

tial, the smaller gear is the drive pinion gear and the larger gear is the ring gear.

INCREASING TORQUE A gear reduction increases torque.

> ### SHOP TALK
> By using the rear-axle ratio as a guideline, you can tell how much gear reduction there is. This is expressed by the torque ratio. If the rear-axle ratio is 3.00:1, the torque ratio is just the opposite, or 1:3.00. This means that the torque at the ring gear has been increased three times.

Differential Operation

The amount of power delivered to each driving wheel by differential is expressed as a percentage. When the vehicle moves straight ahead, each driving wheel rotates at 100% of the case speed. When the vehicle is turning, the inside wheel might be getting 90% of the case speed. At the same time, the outside wheel might be getting 110% of the differential action.

Power flow through the differential begins at the drive pinion yoke, or companion flange (Figure 28-50). The companion flange accepts torque from the rear U-joint. The companion flange is attached to the drive pinion gear, which transfers torque to the ring gear. As the ring gear turns, it turns the carrier and the pinion

694 Section 5 Manual Transmissions and Transaxles

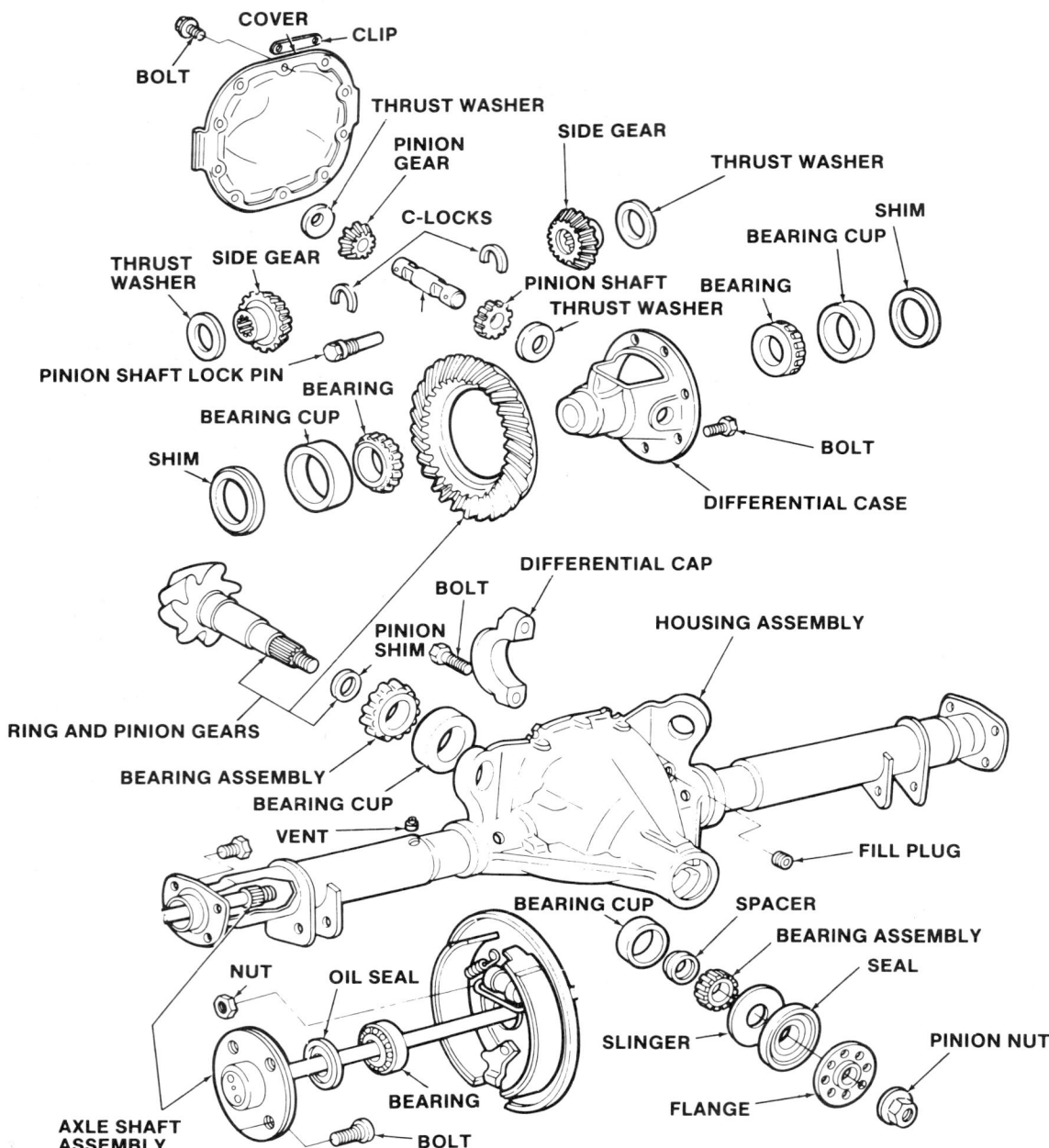

Figure 28–49 Integral-carrier differential exploded view. *Courtesy of Ford Motor Co.*

shaft. The differential pinion gears transfer torque to the side gears to turn the driving axles. The differential pinion gears determine how much torque goes to each driving axle. The pinion gears can move with the carrier, and they can rotate on the pinion shaft.

When drive shaft torque is applied to the input shaft and drive pinion, the shaft rotates in a direction that is perpendicular to the vehicle's drive axles. When this rotary motion is transferred to the ring gear, the torque flow changes direction and becomes parallel to the axles and wheels. Because the ring gear is bolted to the differential case, the case must rotate with the ring gear. The pinion gear shaft mounted in the casing must also rotate with the case and the ring gear. The pinions turn end over end. Gears do not rotate on the pinion shaft when both driving wheels are turning at the same speed. They rotate end over end as the differential case rotates. Because the pinions are meshed with both side gears, the side gears rotate and turn the axle shafts. The ring gear, differential gears, and axle shafts turn together without variation in speed as long as the vehicle is moving in a straight line.

When a vehicle turns into a curve or negotiates a turn, the wheels on the outside of the curve must travel a greater distance than the wheels on the inside of the curve. The outer wheels must then rotate faster than the inside wheels. This would be impossible if the axle shafts were locked solidly to the ring gear. However,

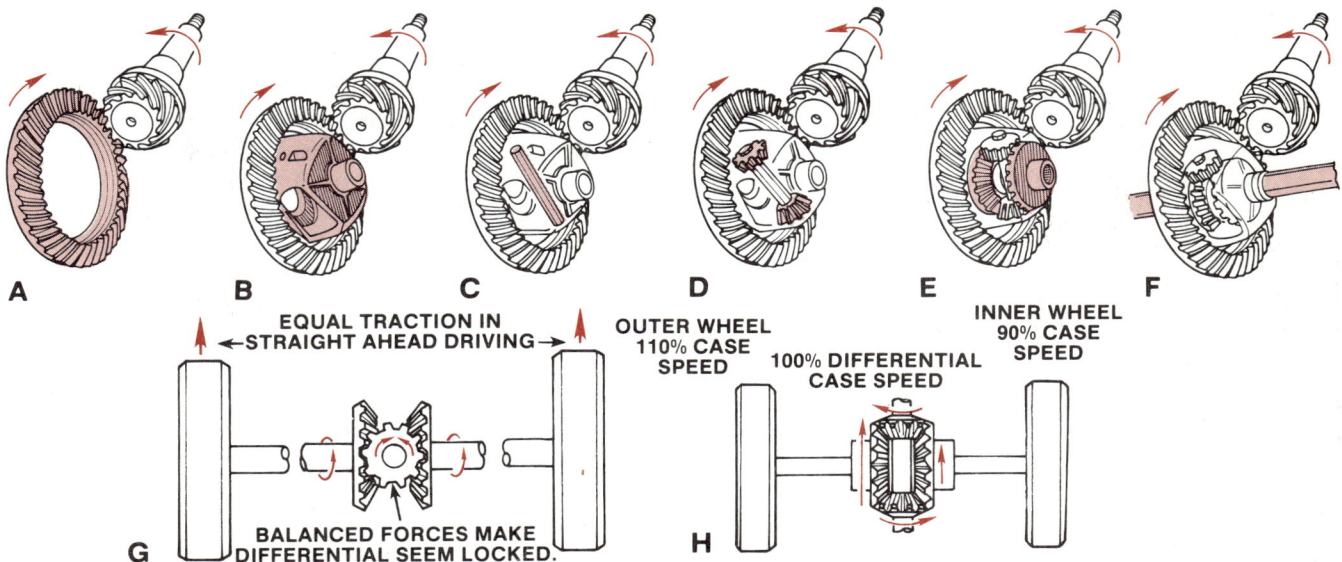

Figure 28-50 Typical differential operation. (A) The drive pinion, which is turned by the driveshaft, turns the ring gear. (B) The ring gear, which is bolted to the differential case, turns the case. (C) The pinion shaft, located in a bore in the differential case, is at right angles to the axle shafts and turns with the case. (D) The differential pinion (drive) gears are mounted on the pinion shaft and rotate with the shaft. (E) Differential side gears (driven gears) are meshed with the pinion gears and turn with the differential housing and ring gear as a unit. (F) The side gears are splined to the inner ends of the axle shafts and rotate the shafts as the housing turns. (G) Where both wheels have equal traction, the pinion gears do not rotate on the pinion shaft, since the input force of the pinion gears is divided equally between the two side gears. (H) When it is necessary to turn a corner, the differential gearing becomes effective and allows the axle shafts to rotate at different speeds. *Courtesy of General Motors Corp.*

the differential allows the outer wheels and axle shaft to increase in speed and the inner wheels and axle to slow down. This prevents the skidding and rapid tire wear that would otherwise occur. The differential action also makes the vehicle much easier to control while turning. (The differential also allows the wheels on opposite ends of the axle to rotate at different speeds to compensate for uneven road conditions and slightly mismatched tires.)

For example, when a car makes a sharp right-hand turn, the left-side wheels, axle shaft, and side gear must rotate faster than the right-side wheels, axle shaft, and side gear. The left side of the axle must speed up and the right side must slow down. This is possible because the pinions to which the side gears are meshed are free to rotate on the pinion shaft. The increased speed of the left-side wheels causes the side gear to rotate faster than the differential case. This causes the pinions to rotate and walk around the side gear. As the pinions turn to allow the left-side gear to increase speed, a reverse action—known as a reverse walking effect—is produced on the right-side gear. It slows down an amount that is inversely proportional to the increase in the left-side gear.

❏ LIMITED SLIP DIFFERENTIALS

As mentioned earlier in this chapter, driveline torque is evenly divided between the two rear drive axles by the differential. As long as the tires grip the road providing a resistance to turning, the drivetrain forces the vehicle forward. When one tire encounters a slippery spot on the road, it loses traction, resistance to rotation drops, and the wheel begins to spin. Because resistance has dropped, the torque value delivered to both drive wheels also drops. The wheel with good traction is no longer driven. If the vehicle is stationary in this situation, only the wheel over the slippery spot rotates. When this is occurring, the differential case is driving the differential pinion gears around the stationary side gear.

This situation places stress on the differential gears. When the wheel spins because of traction loss, the speed of some of the differential gears increases greatly while others remain idle. The amount of heat developed increases rapidly, lube film breaks down, metal-to-metal contact occurs, and the parts are damaged. If spinout is allowed to continue long enough, the axle could break down completely.

Other failures can occur during spinout. If a spinning wheel is subjected to grabbing on a firm surface, a shock impact occurs. If the shock is severe enough, broken gear teeth or shaft fracturing can result, a fatigue failure can start if the shock is only great enough to damage the gear or shaft material.

To overcome these problems, differential manufacturers have developed the limited slip differential (Figure 28-51). While the limited slip differentials are manufactured under such names as sure-grip, no-spin,

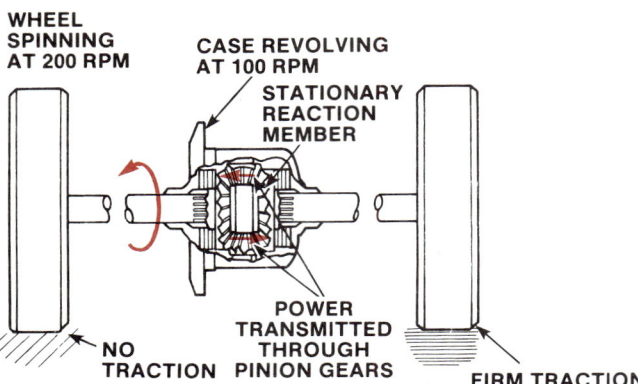

Figure 28-51 A normal differential transmits more power to the wheel with less traction.

positraction, or equal-lock, there are really only two types of these differentials: the clutch pack and the brake cone.

Clutch Packs

The clutch pack limited slip differential (Figure 28-52) uses two sets of clutch plates and friction discs to prevent normal differential action. The friction discs are steel plates with an abrasive coating on both sides. The discs are splined internally to mate with external splines on the hub of the side gears. Steel plates without friction linings are placed between the friction discs. These plates have tangs that fit into the grooves in the differential case.

When installed in the differential, the discs are connected to the side gears and the plates are locked to the case. There is one set of clutch plates between each side gear and the differential case.

Pressure is kept on the clutch packs by springs. Either an S-shaped spring or coil springs are placed between the side gears. Those differentials using coil springs also have a set of spring retainers against which the springs bear. The springs (or spring) keep pressure against the side gear and the clutch pack.

As long as the clutch friction discs maintain their grip on the steel plates, the differential side gears are locked to the differential case. The case and drive axles rotate at the same speed, which prevents one set of wheels from spinning on a slippery pavement or spinning momentarily faster when operating on uneven roads.

The clutch plates are designed to slip when a predetermined torque value is reached. This enables the car or truck to negotiate turns in a normal manner. The high torque caused by the wheels on the outside radius of a turn or curve rotating faster than the gear support case and differential causes the plates in the clutch pack to slip, allowing the side gear to increase in speed and the pinions to walk around the side gear in normal differential fashion.

Brake Cones

The most common limited slip differential in late-model vehicles employs two cone-shaped friction components to lock the side gears to the differential case (Figure 28-53). The cones are located between the side gears and the case and are splined to the side gear hubs. The exterior surface of the cones are coated with a friction material that grabs the inside surface of the case. The friction surface on the cones has a coarse

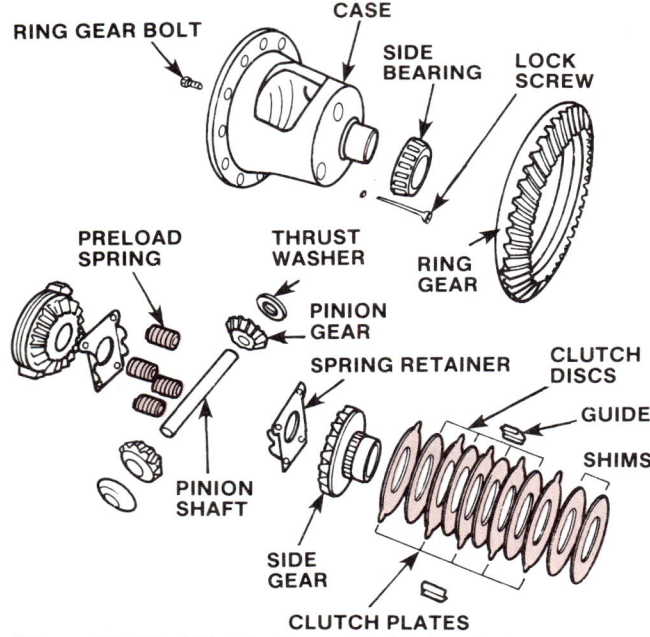

Figure 28-52 Clutch discs with friction facings are separated by steel shims in this limited slip differential. Notice the four preload springs.

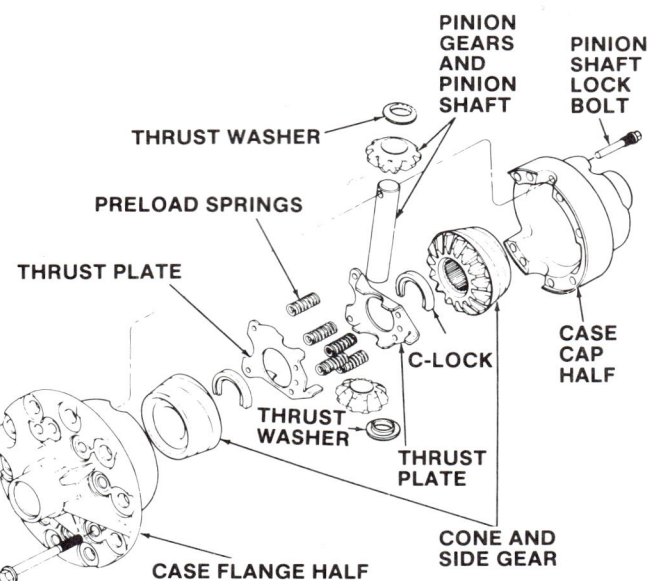

Figure 28-53 Cone-type limited slip differential. Notice the positions of the cones, thrust plates, thrust washers, and preload springs. *Courtesy of Ford Motor Co.*

spiral thread to provide a passage for lubricant. Four to six coil springs mounted in thrust plates between the side gears maintain a preload on the cones.

The operation of the cone system is essentially the same as the clutch-plate system. The cones are forced against the carrier and squeezed or compressed. At this point, the cone rotates with the carrier and locks up both axles.

Some vehicles have an antiskid sensor (part of the braking system) attached to the differential carrier for extra non-skid protection during braking (Figure 28-54).

CUSTOMER CARE

Remind your customer that the drive shaft, transmission, and rear (drive) axle should give trouble-free service if they are maintained at intervals recommended in the service manual. Be sure to check this out with your customer.

Maintenance includes inspecting the level of and changing the gear lubricant, and lubricating the universal joints if they are equipped with zerk or grease fittings (Figure 28-55). Most modern universal joints are of the extended life design, meaning that they are sealed and require no periodic lubrication. However, it is wise to inspect the joints for hidden grease plugs or fittings, initially. Also inspect the driveline for abnormal looseness, whenever the car is serviced.

In general, rear axles use either SAE 80 or 90 weight gear oil for lubrication, meeting API GL-4 or GL-5 specifications. This is stated on the top of the can. In the case of limited-slip rear axles, it is very important that the proper gear lube be used. The wrong lubricant can damage the clutch packs and cause grabbing or chattering on turns. If this condition exists, try draining the oil and refilling with the proper gear lube before having it serviced.

A common source of operation noise comes from the tires. To make sure that the noises identified during the test drive are not caused by the tire tread patterns and tread wear, drive the car on various types of road surfaces (asphalt, concrete, and packed dirt). If the noise changes with the road surfaces, it means the tires are the cause of the noise.

Another way to isolate tire noises is to coast at speeds under 30 mph. If the noise is still heard, the tires are probably the cause. Drive axle and differential noises are less noticeable at these speeds. Accelerate and compare the sounds to those made while coasting. Drive axle and differential noises change. Tire noise remains constant.

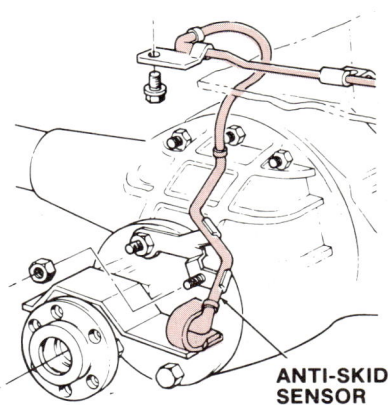

Figure 28-54 Some vehicles have an anti-skid sensor, part of a safety braking system, attached to the differential carrier. *Courtesy of Ford Motor Co.*

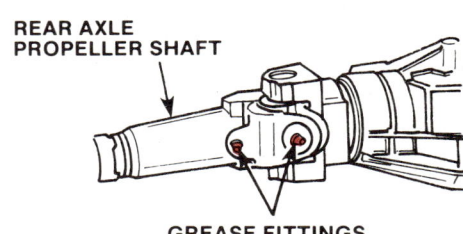

Figure 28-55 Some drive shaft U-joints are equipped with grease (zerk) fittings. Lubricate these with a grease gun.

Sometimes it is difficult to distinguish between axle bearing noises and noises coming from the differential. Differential noises often change with the driving mode whereas axle bearing noises are usually constant. The sound of the bearing noise usually increases in speed and loudness as vehicle speed increases.

AXLE SHAFTS

The purpose of the axle shaft is to transfer driving torque from the differential assembly to the vehicle's driving wheels. There are two types of axles: dead and live or drive.

DEAD AXLE This axle does not drive a vehicle. It merely supports the vehicle load and provides a mounting place for the wheels. In automotive operation, dead axles are usually on trailers and tandem-type axle vehicles.

LIVE OR DRIVE AXLE The main purpose of the drive axles is to transfer torque from the differential to each driving wheel. Depending on the design, rear axles can also help carry the weight of the vehicle or even act as part of the suspension. Most driving axles are enclosed in a housing. This housing is usually of a three-piece design. The two axle housings are pressed into the differential housing and then welded in place. Welding the three pieces together makes the axle housings and differential housing a single unit. A variation of the

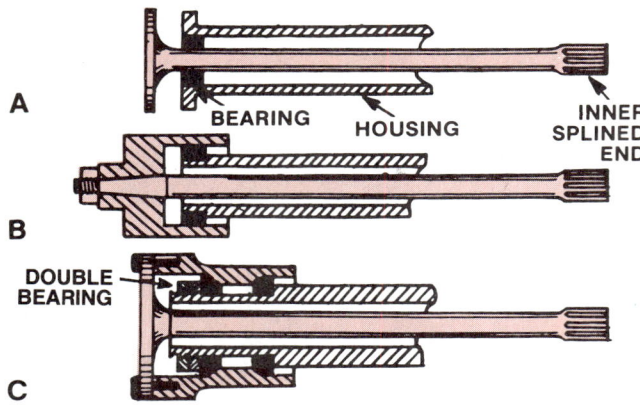

Figure 28–56 Three types of rear drive axles: (A) semifloating; (B) three-quarter floating; (C) full-floating axle assemblies.

driving axle is the open axle shaft. In this design, the axle shaft is not enclosed in a housing. Instead, the axle shaft is part of the suspension system and moves up and down with changing road conditions. Three types of driving axles are commonly used (Figure 28-56): semifloating, three-quarter floating, and full-floating.

All three use axle shafts that are splined to the differential side gears. The combination of the driving axles and the differential is known as the final drive (Figure 28-57). At the wheel ends, the axles can be attached in any one of a number of ways. This attachment depends on the type of axle that is used. The differences between the three types actually lie in the manner in which the shafts are supported on bearings and the way they are attached to the wheel hubs.

Semifloating Axle Shafts

Semifloating axles help to support the weight of the vehicle. The differential assembly is supported by

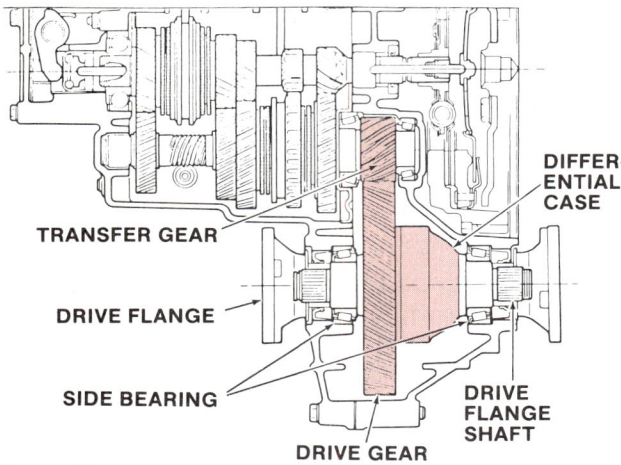

Figure 28–57 The drive pinion gear and differential drive gear are known collectively as the final drive gears. The final drive gears and differential assembly are housed in the transaxle housing. *Courtesy of Chrysler Corp.*

tapered roller bearings and the axle housing, the semifloating axle shafts are not affected by stresses associated with the differential's operation (Figure 28-58).

The inner ends of the axle shafts are splined to the axle side gears. The axle shafts transmit only driving torque and are not acted upon by other forces. Therefore, the axle shafts are said to be floating.

The driving wheels are bolted to the outer ends of the axle shafts. The outer axle bearings are located between the axle shaft and axle housing. This type of axle has a bearing pressed into the end of the axle housing. This bearing supports the axle shaft. The axle shaft is held in place with either a bearing retainer bolted to a flange on the end of the axle housing or by a C-shaped washer that fits into grooves machined in the splined end of the shaft. A flange on the wheel end of the shaft is used to attach the wheel.

Another method of holding a wheel in place in a semifloating axle is shown in Figure 28-59. The end of the axle has a key or splines that engage the axle to the hub. A key is a wedge-shaped locking device that holds two parts together.

When the semifloating axle arrangement is used to drive the vehicle, the axle shaft rotates the driving wheels. The driving wheels move ahead, while the axle shafts push on the axle shaft bearings. This places a driving force on the axle housing, springs, and vehicle chassis, moving the vehicle forward. The axle shaft takes bending stresses associated with turning corners and curves, skidding, bent, or wobbling wheels, as well as the weight of the vehicle. In the semifloating axle arrangement, if the axle shaft breaks, the driving wheel comes away from or out of the axle housing.

Three-Quarter Floating Axle

The wheel bearing on a three-quarter floating axle is on the outside of the axle housing instead of inside the housing as in the semifloating axle. The wheel hubs are bolted to the end of the axle shaft and are supported by the bearing (Figure 28-60). In this arrangement, the axle shaft does not support the weight of the vehicle. It is transferred through the wheel hub and bearing to the axle housing. Three-quarter floating axles are found on older vehicles and some trucks.

Full-Floating Axle Shafts

Most heavy commercial vehicles use a full-floating axle shaft (Figure 28-61) to accommodate the higher vehicle loads. This design is similar to the three-quarter floating axle except that two bearings rather than one are used to support the wheel hub. These are pressed over the outside of the axle housing and carry all of the stresses caused by torque loading and turning. The wheel hubs are bolted to flanges on the outer end of each axle shaft.

In operation, the axle shaft transmits only the driving torque. The driving torque from the axle shaft

Drive Axles and Differentials

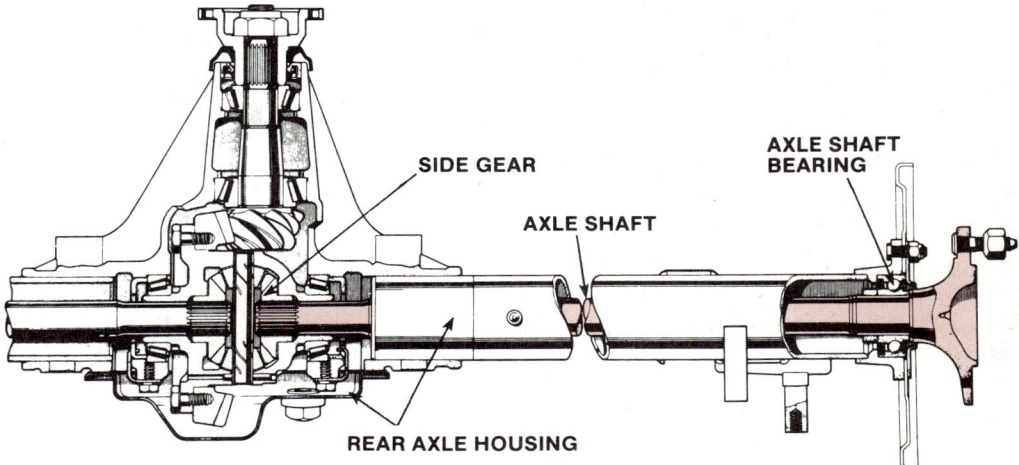

Figure 28-58 Semi-floating axle shaft in axle housing with ball-type axle bearing. If this axle shaft breaks, the axle shaft comes out of the axle housing. *Courtesy of Chrysler Corp.*

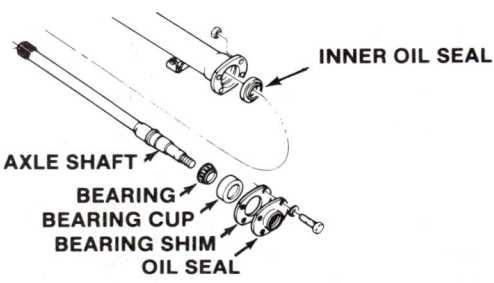

Figure 28-59 Key and spline axle assembly. *Courtesy of American Motors Corp.*

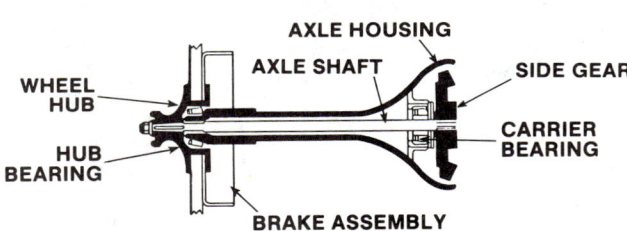

Figure 28-60 Three-quarter floating drive axle. If the axle shaft breaks, the wheel comes off the axle housing.

rotates the axle flange, wheel hub, and rear driving wheel. The wheel hub forces its bearings against the axle housing to move the vehicle. The stresses caused by turning, skidding, and bent or wobbling wheels are taken by the axle housing through the wheel bearings. If a full-floating axle shaft should break, it can be removed from the axle housing. Because the rear

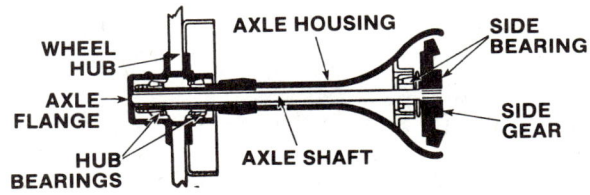

Figure 28-61 Full-floating driving axle shaft. This axle does not support vehicle weight. Therefore, it is possible to remove the axle shaft without removing the driving wheel.

wheels rotate around the rear axle housing, the disabled vehicle can be towed to a service area for replacement of the axle shaft. This is considered by many technicians to be an advantage of the full-floating axle design.

Independently Suspended Axles

This type of rear driving axle system is found mostly on European automobiles. The driving axles are usually open instead of being enclosed in an axle housing.

The two most common suspended rear driving axles are the De Dion axle system and the swing axle system.

DE DION AXLE SYSTEM This system (Figure 28-62) resembles a driveline. The driving axle resembles a drive shaft, with U-joints at each end of the axles. A slip joint is attached to the inboard, or innermost, U-joint. The outboard, or outermost, U-joint is connected to the driving wheel. This allows the driving axle to move up and down as it rotates.

SWING AXLE SYSTEM On automobiles with swing axles, the driving axles can be open or enclosed. An

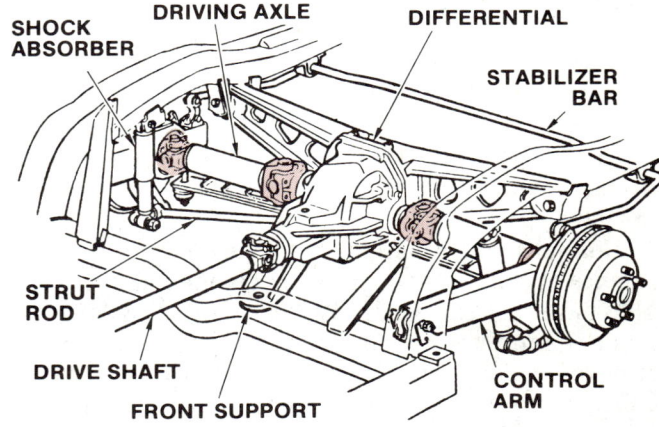

Figure 28-62 De Dion rear suspension on Chevrolet Corvette. Notice the universal joints at each end of the driving axles. *Courtesy of Chevrolet Motor Division*

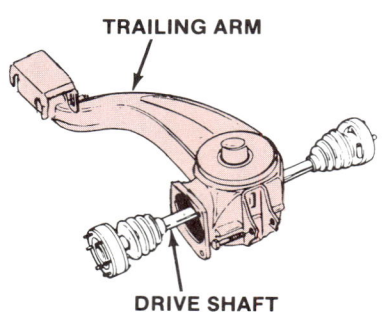

Figure 28-63 Swing axle assembly. *Courtesy of Volkswagen of America*

axle fits into the differential by way of a ball-and-socket system. The ball-and-socket system allows the axle to pivot up and down. As the axle pivots, the driving wheel swings up and down. A typical swing axle assembly is shown in Figure 28-63. This system best describes the drive axles of a front-wheel-drive vehicle.

Axle Shaft Bearings

The axle shaft bearing supports the vehicle's weight and reduces rotational friction. In an axle mount, radial and thrust loads are always present on the axle shaft bearing when the vehicle is moving. Radial bearing loads act at 90 degrees to the axle shaft's center of axis. Radial loading is always present whether or not the vehicle is moving.

Thrust loading acts on the axle bearing parallel with the center of axis. It is present on the driving wheels, axle shafts, and axle bearings when the vehicle turns corners or curves.

There are three designs of axle shaft bearings used in semifloating axles.

- Ball-type bearing (Figure 28-64A)
- Straight roller bearing (Figure 28-64B)
- Tapered roller bearing (Figure 28-64C)

The bearing load of primary concern is axle shaft end thrust. When a vehicle moves around a corner, centrifugal force acts on the vehicle body, causing it to lean to the outside of the curve. The vehicle's chassis does not lean because of the tires' contact with the road's surface. As the body leans outward, a thrust load is placed on the axle shaft and axle bearing. Each type of axle shaft bearing handles axle shaft end thrust differently.

Normally, the way the axles are held in the housing is quite obvious after the rear wheels and brake assemblies have been removed. If the axle shaft is held in by a retainer and three or four bolts, it is not necessary to remove the differential cover to remove the axle. Most ball and tapered roller bearing supported axle shafts are retained in this manner. To remove the axle, remove the bolts that hold the retainer to the backing plate, then pull the axle out. Normally, the axle shaft slides

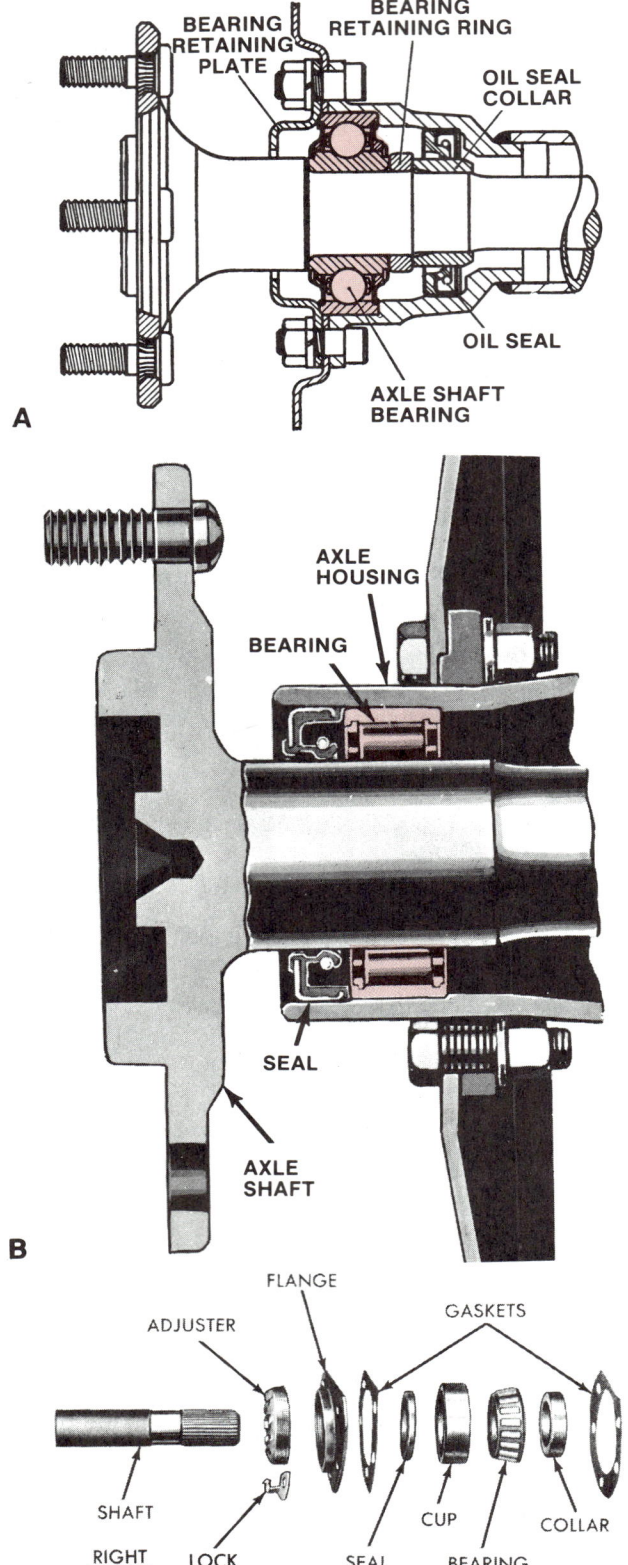

Figure 28-64 (A) Semi-floating axle shaft supported by a ball-type bearing. (Axle shaft bearing is located inside axle housing.) *Courtesy of General Motors Corp.* (B) Straight roller bearing and axle shaft installed in axle housing. *Courtesy of General Motors Corp.* (C) Tapered roller drive axle bearing and related parts. *Courtesy of Chrysler Corp.*

out without the aid of a puller. Sometimes a puller is required.

A tapered-roller bearing supported axle shaft does not use a retainer to secure it. Rather, a C-washer is used to retain the axle shaft. This C-washer is located inside the differential, and the differential cover must be removed to gain access to it. To remove this type of axle, first remove the wheel, brake drum, and differential cover. Then, remove the differential pinion shaft retaining bolt and differential pinion shaft. Now push the axle shaft in and remove the C-washer. The axle can now be pulled out of the housing.

Ball bearings are lubricated with grease packed in the bearing at the factory. An inner seal, designed to keep the gear oil from the bearing, rides on the axle shaft just in front of the retaining ring. This type of bearing also has an outer seal to prevent grease from spraying onto the rear brakes. Ball-type axle bearings are pressed on and off the axle shaft. The retainer ring is made of soft metal and is pressed onto the shaft against the wheel bearing. Never use a torch to remove the ring. Rather, drill into it or notch it in several places with a cold chisel to break the seal. The ring can then be slid off the shaft easily. Heat should not be used to remove the ring because it can take the temper out of the shaft and thereby weaken it. Likewise, a torch should never be used to remove a bearing from an axle shaft.

Roller axle bearings are lubricated by the gear oil in the axle housing. Therefore, only a seal to protect the brakes is necessary with these bearings. These bearings are typically pressed into the axle housing and not onto the axle. To remove them, the axle must first be removed and then the bearing pulled out of the housing. With the axle out, inspect the area where it rides on the bearing for pits or scores. If pits or score marks are present, replace the axle.

Tapered-roller axle bearings are not lubricated by gear oil. They are sealed and lubricated with wheel grease. This type of bearing uses two seals and must be pressed on and off the axle shaft using a press. After the bearing is pressed onto the shaft, it must be packed

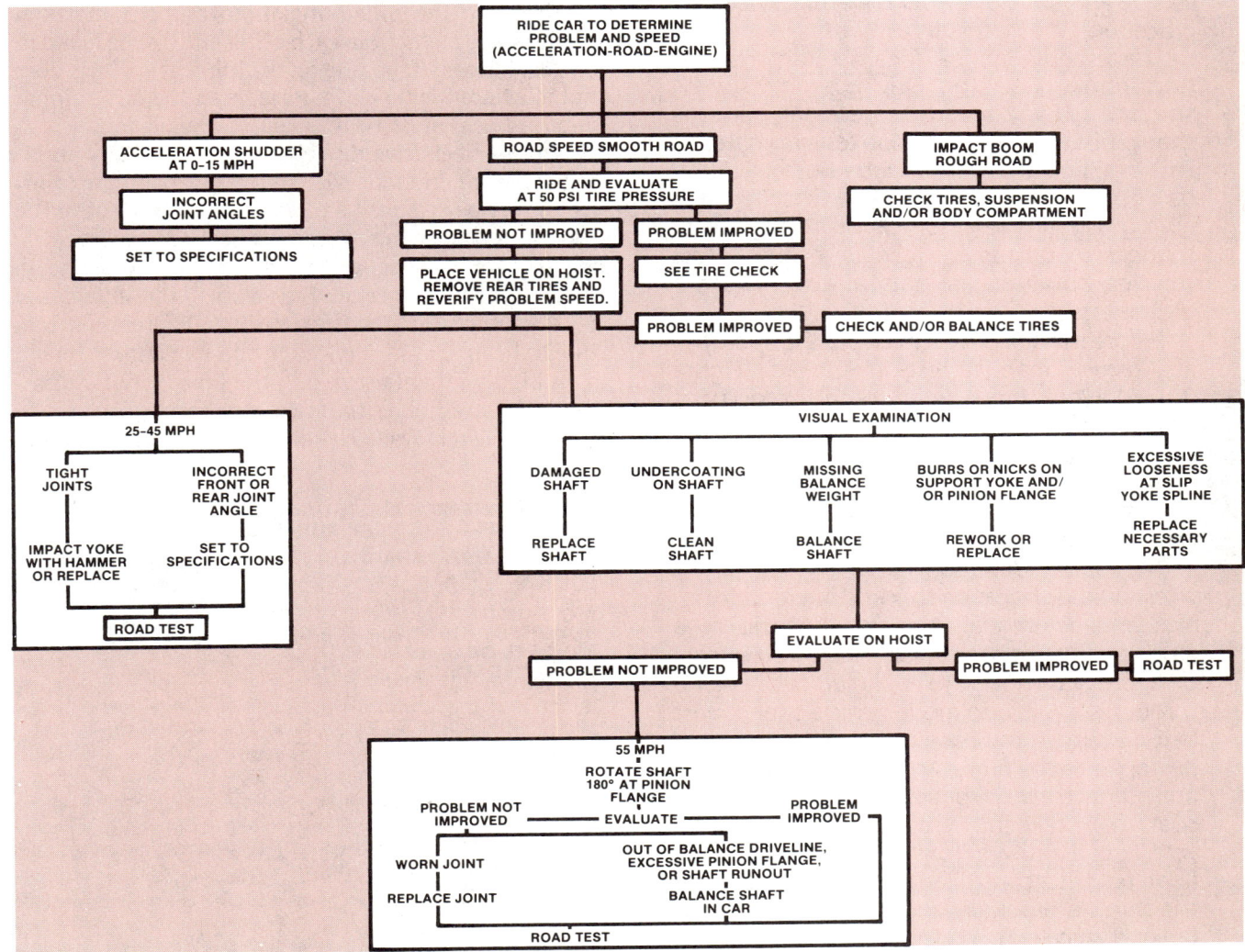

Figure 28-65 Service manual test-drive chart.

with wheel bearing grease. After packing the bearing, install the axle in the housing. Shaft endplay must be checked. Use a dial indicator and adjust the endplay to the specifications given in the service manual. If the endplay is not within specifications, change the size of the bearing shim.

The installation of new axle shaft seals is recommended whenever the axle shafts have been removed. Some axle seals are identified as being either right or left side. When installing new seals, make sure to install the correct seal in each side. Check the seals or markings of right or left or for color coding.

USING SERVICE MANUALS

The driveline can create some especially difficult diagnostic problems. The driveline easily picks up vibrations and noises from other parts of the vehicle. What may seem to be a driveline problem can actually be a suspension or wire problem. For this reason, the test drive is important. A test drive does not mean hopping into a vehicle and driving it around the block. Certain procedures are necessary.

The test drive may call for a fast start or a slow start from a dead stop. Driving at low speeds and at highway speeds is necessary. Speeds should be varied. Acceleration tests from steady cruising speeds should include both mild and hard applications of power. Note what happens during any of these speeds or during speed changes. A tachometer can be helpful. Most vehicles, however, are not equipped with tachometers.

Before the test drive, check out the appropriate service manual test-drive chart (Figure 28-65). Note that different problems occur at different speeds. Some problems that seem to come from the driveline actually come from other parts of the vehicle. Also, notice that when the problem appears at different speeds, the cause of the problem changes.

The four modes of driving given in most service manuals should be checked out for driving-axle and differential problems. For the drive mode accelerate the vehicle. The throttle must be depressed enough to apply sufficient engine torque. In the cruise mode vehicle speed must be constant. This means that the throttle must be applied at all times. The speed must be held at a predetermined rpm on a level road. For the coast mode take the foot off the throttle. Let the vehicle coast down from a specific speed. The float mode is a controlled deceleration. Back off the throttle gradually and continually. Do not brake or accelerate during this mode.

Remember that driving safely is always an important consideration. Jackrabbit starts, hard cornering, or sudden braking should be avoided. Driving conditions other than normal can worsen a problem or create a new one. Carelessness during the test drive can result in an accident. Remember, you are responsible for someone else's vehicle. Drive only in a manner that is required to diagnose the problem.

SERVICING THE DIFFERENTIAL

Problems with the differential and drive axles are usually first noticed as a leak or noise. As the problem progresses, vibrations, or a clunking noise might be felt in the various modes of operation.

Operational noises are generally caused by bearings or gears that are worn, loose, or damaged (Figure 28-66). Bearing noises might be a whine or a rumble. A whine is a high-pitched, continuous "whee" sound. A rumble sounds like distant thunder—low and rolling.

Gears can also whine or emit a howl—a very loud, continuous sound. Howling is often caused by low lubricant in the differential housing. The meshing teeth scrape metal from each other and can be heard in all gear ranges. If topping off the lubrication level does not alleviate the howling noise, then the drive pinion and ring gear must be replaced.

Front-wheel-drive differentials are normally an integral part of the transaxle. To service them, the transaxle must be removed and disassembled. Most of the procedures for servicing a rear-wheel-drive differential apply to front-wheel-drive differentials. To service a differential from a removable carrier, the differential must be removed from the housing. Differentials from integral carriers are serviced in the housing.

A highly important step in the procedure for disassembling any differential is a careful inspection of each part as it is removed. The differential bearings should

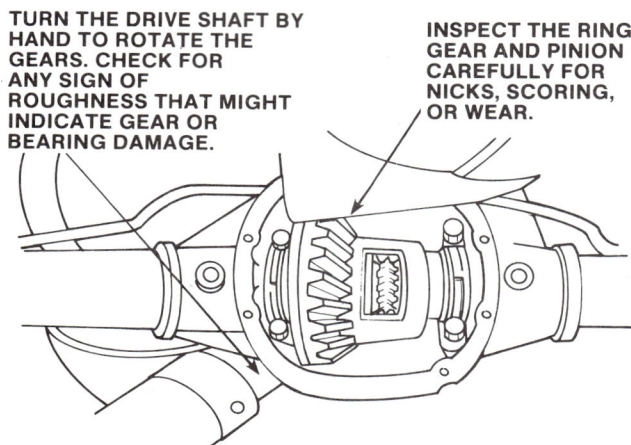

Figure 28-66 A visual inspection can verify that worn or damaged gears or bearings are the cause of abnormal noises.

be looked at and felt to determine if there are any defects or evidence of damage.

After the ring and pinion gears have been inspected and before they have been removed from the assembly, check the side play. Using a screwdriver, attempt to move the differential case assembly laterally. Any movement is evidence of side play. Side play normally indicates that as the result of loose bearing cones on the differential case hubs, the differential case must be replaced.

Prior to disassembling the differential, measure the runout of the ring gear. Excessive runout can be caused by a warped gear, worn differential side bearings, warped differential case, or particles trapped between the gear and case. Runout is checked with a dial indicator mounted on the carrier assembly (Figure 28-67). The plunger of the indicator should be set at a right angle to the gear. With the dial indicator in position and its dial set to zero, rotate the ring gear and note the highest and lowest readings. The difference between these two readings indicates the total runout of the ring gear. Normally, the maximum permissible runout is 0.004 inch.

To determine if the runout is caused by a damaged differential case, remove the ring gear and measure the runout of the ring gear mounting surface on the differential case. Runout should not exceed 0.004 inch. If runout is greater than that, the case should be replaced. If the runout was within specifications, the ring gear is probably warped and should be replaced. A ring gear is never replaced without replacing its mating pinion gear.

Some ring gear assemblies are comprised of an excitor ring, used in anti-lock brake systems. This ring is normally pressed onto the ring gear hub and can be removed after the ring gear is removed. If the ring gear assembly is equipped with an excitor ring, carefully inspect it and replace it if it is damaged.

Prior to disassembling the differential unit, the drive shaft must be removed. Before disconnecting it from the pinion's companion flange, locate the shaft to pinion alignment marks. If they are not evident, make new ones (Figure 28-68). This avoids assembling the

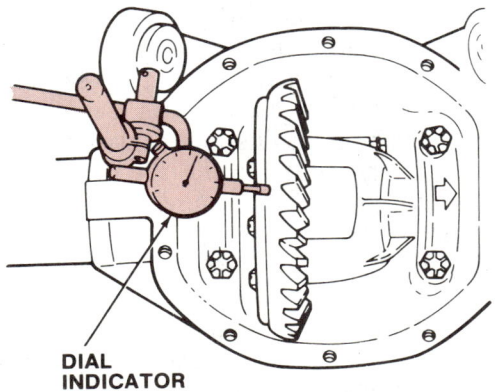

Figure 28-67 Measuring ring gear backface runout.

Figure 28-68 Marking the drive shaft and its mating flange.

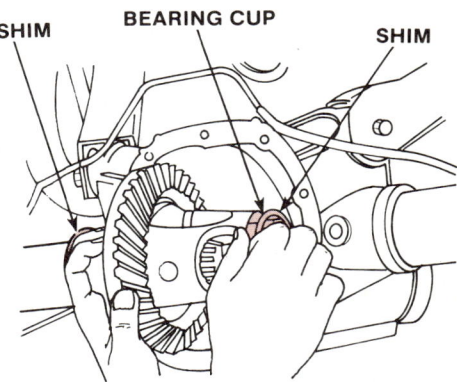

Figure 28-69 While disassembling a differential, keep all parts separated according to the side they were removed from.

unit with the wrong index, which can result in driveline vibration.

When disassembling a differential, keep the right and left differential shims, cups, and caps separated (Figure 28-69). If any of these parts are reused, they must be installed on the same side as they were originally located.

When installing a ring gear onto the differential case, make sure the bolt holes are aligned before pressing the gear in place. While pressing the gear, pressure should be evenly applied to the gear. Likewise, when tightening the bolts, always tighten them in steps and to the specified torque. These steps reduce the chances of distorting the gear.

Examine the gears to locate any timing marks on the gearset that indicate where the gears were lapped by the manufacturer. Normally, one tooth of the pinion gear is grooved and painted, while the ring gear has a notch between two painted teeth. If the paint marks are not evident, locate the notches. Proper timing of the gears is set by placing the grooved pinion tooth between the two marked ring gear teeth. Some gearsets have no timing marks. These gears are hunting gears and do not need to be timed.

Whenever the ring and pinion gears or the pinion or carrier bearings are replaced, pinion gear depth, bearing preload, and the ring and pinion gear tooth patterns must be checked and adjusted. This holds true for all types of differentials except most front-wheel-drive differentials that use helical-cut gears and taking tooth patterns is not necessary. Nearly all other final drive units use hypoid gears that must be properly adjusted to ensure a quiet operation.

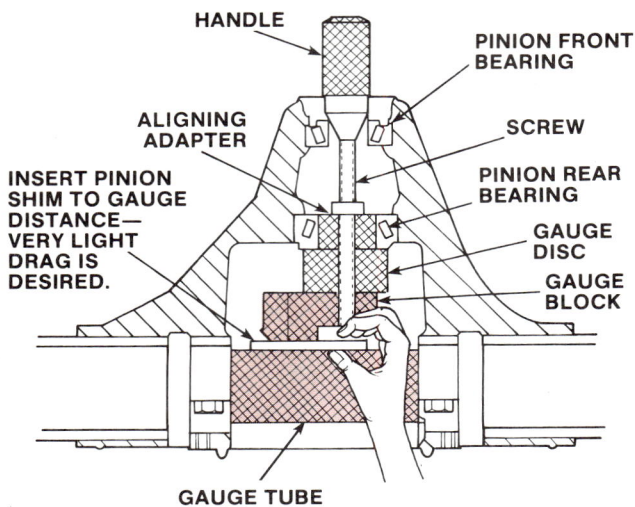

Figure 28-70 Selecting the correct pinion shim for proper pinion gear depth.

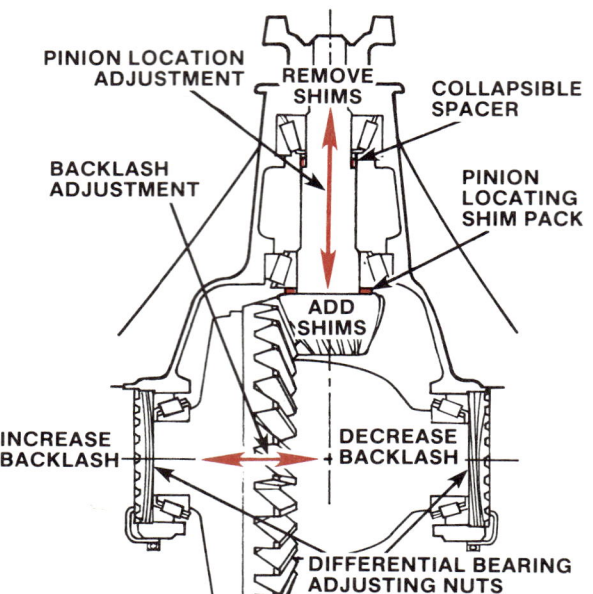

Figure 28-71 This drawing shows the direction of movement when adjusting the ring gear and pinion gear. Shims are used to position the pinion gear and bearing adjusting nuts are used to position the ring gear.

Pinion gear depth is adjusted with shims that are placed in the housing. The thickness of the drive pinion rear bearing shim controls the depth of the mesh between the pinion and ring gear. To determine and set pinion depth a special tool is normally used to select the proper pinion shim (Figure 28-70). Always follow the procedures in the service manual when setting up the tool and determining the proper shim.

Pinion bearing preload is set by tightening the pinion nut until the desired number of inch-pounds is required to turn the shaft. Tightening the nut crushes the collapsible pinion spacer, which maintains the desired preload. Never overtighten and then loosen the pinion nut to reach the desired torque reading. Tightening and loosening the pinion nut damages the collapsible spacer. It must then be replaced. For the exact procedures and specifications for bearing preload, refer to the service manual. Incorrect bearing preload can cause differential noise.

It is recommended that a new pinion seal be installed whenever the pinion shaft is removed from the differential. To install a new seal, thoroughly lubricate it and press it in place with an appropriate seal driver.

Backlash of the gearset is adjusted at the same time as the side bearing preload. Side bearing preload limits the amount the differential is able to move laterally in the axle housing. Adjusting backlash sets the depth of the mesh between the ring and pinion gears teeth. Both of these are adjusted by shim thickness or by the adjustments made by the side bearing adjusting nuts (Figure 28-71).

Always refer to the procedures given in the service manual before proceeding to adjust preload and backlash. A typical procedure for measuring and adjusting backlash and preload involves rocking the ring gear and measuring its movement with a dial indicator (Figure 28-72). Compare measured backlash with the specifications. Make the necessary adjustments. Then

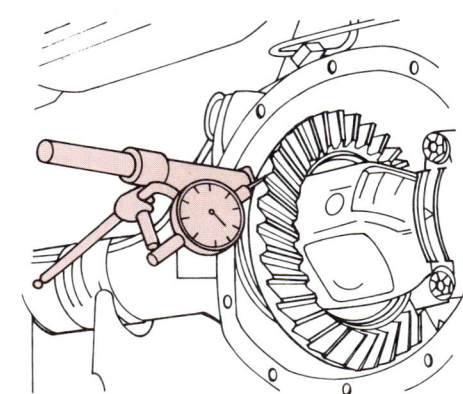

Figure 28-72 Mount a dial indicator and measure the ring gear-to-pinion backlash at three or four locations around the ring gear. The variation between readings should be no more than 0.006 inch.

recheck the backlash at four points equally spaced around the ring gear.

The pattern of gear teeth determines how quietly two meshed gears run. The pattern also describes where on the faces of the teeth the two gears mesh. The pattern should be checked during teardown for gear noise diagnosis, after adjusting backlash and side bearing preload, or after replacing the drive pinion and setting up the pinion bearing preload. The terms commonly used to describe the possible patterns on a ring gear and the necessary corrections are shown in Figure 28-73.

To check the gear tooth pattern, paint several ring gear teeth with nondrying Prussian blue, clean grease, ferric oxide, or red or white lead marking compound.

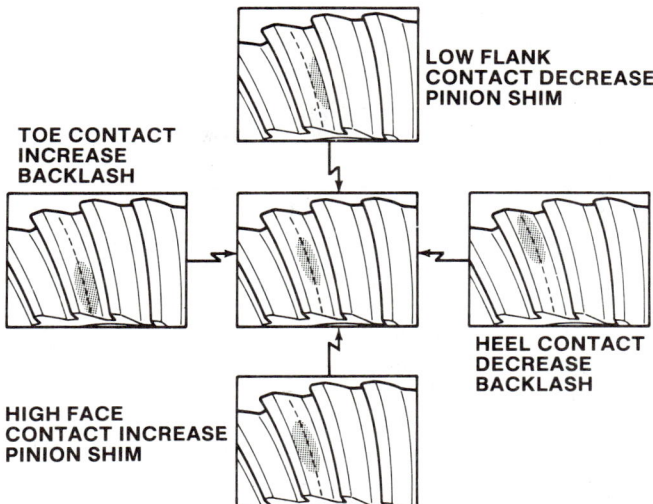

Figure 28-73 Commonly used terms describing the possible patterns on a ring gear and the necessary corrections.

White marking compound is preferred by many technicians because it tends to be more visible than the others. Use a box wrench on the ring gear bolts to rotate the ring gear so the painted teeth contact the pinion gear. Move it in both directions enough to get a clearly defined pattern (Figure 28-74). Examine the pattern on the ring gear and make the necessary corrections.

Most new gearsets purchased today come with a pattern pre-rolled on the teeth. This pattern provides the quietest operation for that gearset. Never wipe this pattern off or cover it up. When checking the pattern on a new gearset, only coat half of the ring gear with the marking compound and compare the pattern with the pre-rolled pattern.

❏ DIAGNOSING DIFFERENTIAL NOISES

If a whining is heard when turning corners or rounding curves, the problem might be damaged differential pinion gears and pinion shaft. This is caused when the inside diameter of the differential pinions and the outside diameter of the differential pinion shaft is scored and damaged. The damage is usually caused by allowing one driving wheel to revolve at high speeds while the opposite wheel remains stationary.

Another gear noise that is common in differentials is the chuckle. A chuckle is a low "heh-heh" sound that occurs when gears are worn to the point where there is excessive clearance between the pinion gear and the ring gear. Chuckle sounds occur most often in the decelerating mode—particularly below 40 mph. As the vehicle decelerates, the chuckle also slows and can be heard all the way to a stop.

A knock or clunk is caused by excessive wear or loose or broken parts. A knock is a repetitious rapping sound that occurs during all phases of driving but is most noticeable during acceleration and deceleration when the gears are loaded.

A clunk is a sharp, loud noise caused by one part hitting another. Unlike a knock, a clunk can be felt as

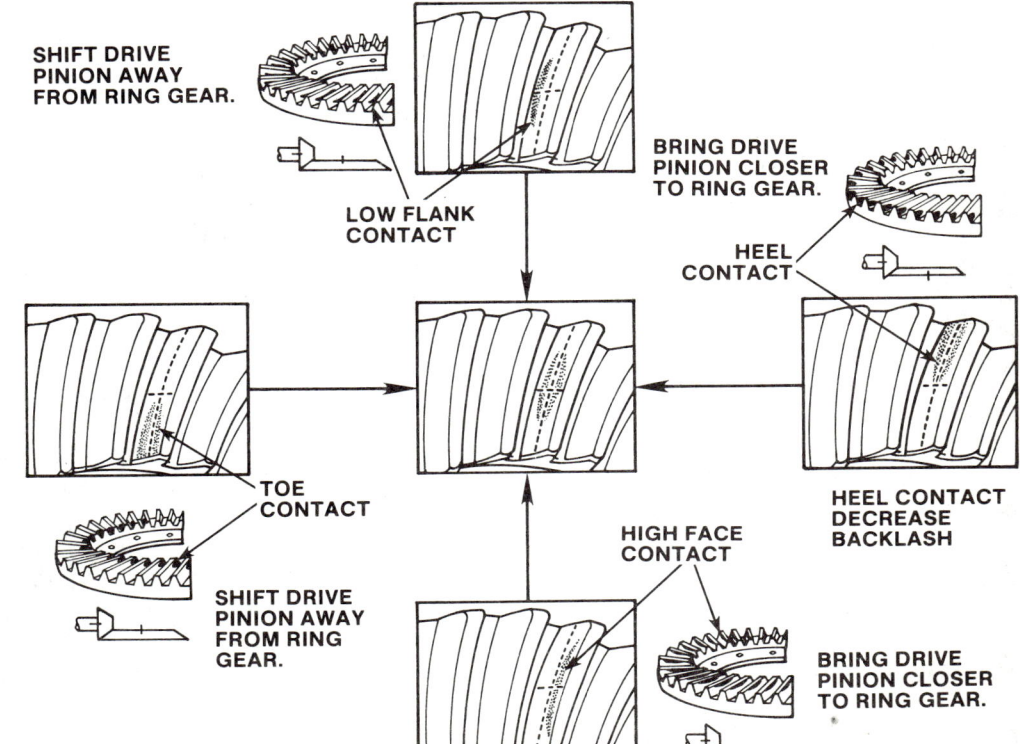

Figure 28-74 Area where grease, red lead, or ferric oxide is rubbed off ring gear is contact pattern. It must be centrally located on teeth. Note typical methods of correcting patterns. *Courtesy of General Motors Corp.*

well as heard. Clunks are generally caused by loose parts striking each other.

Limited slip clutch packs or cones that need servicing might be heard as a chatter or a rapid clicking noise that creates a vibration in the vehicle. Chattering is usually noticed when rounding a corner. A change of differential lubricant sometimes corrects this problem. After draining the oil, replace it with the manufacturer's suggested lubricant. Road test the vehicle again.

To make sure that the noise heard during the test drive is coming from the differential, stop the vehicle and shift the transmission into neutral. Run the engine at various rpm levels. If the noise is heard during this procedure, it is caused by a problem somewhere other than in the differential.

CASE STUDY

Case 1

A customer brings his subcompact, front-wheel-drive car into the shop complaining of recurring noise in the front wheels. The noise is most noticeable when the car is making turns. The owner states he had a similar complaint a few months ago and the shop had replaced an outer CV-joint. This corrected the problem until recently. The customer suspects that the same joint went bad again and demands that the shop replace it, free of charge, because it is obvious that the replacement joint was defective.

The service writer records the information from the customer and tells him that he will be notified as soon as the problem is diagnosed. As soon as the customer leaves, the service writer looks up the customer's file and finds that a CV-joint had been replaced two months ago.

The service writer gives the repair order to the technician, along with the old repair order. The technician begins the diagnostic procedure with a test drive to verify the complaint. From the test drive and a visual inspection, the technician concludes that the same CV-joint is faulty. What could cause the joint to fail so soon? Was the replacement joint defective? Was the replacement joint installed incorrectly? Is some other fault causing the joints to fail? No matter what the answer, it seems that the customer will not be charged for this repair. Also, it is likely that the technician will not get paid for the repair.

Upon disassembly of the axle, the technician finds the joint's lubricant to be contaminated with metal shavings and moisture. A thorough inspection of the boot reveals no tears or punctures. While inspecting the boot, it is noticed that the inner end of the boot moves freely on the axle shaft. The technician knows then what had caused the contamination and resulting premature failure of the joint.

When installing the replacement joint and boot, the technician failed to properly tighten the inner boot clamp. This allowed lubricant to leak from and water to enter the boot. A new joint and boot is installed on the axle. The technician verifies the repair by a test drive. The replacement joint took care of the noise. Before releasing the car back to the owner, the technician rechecks the position and tightness of the boot clamps. The customer is called and is told what had happened. Although the customer is not happy about the mistake, he appreciates the honesty of the technician. Two months later he returns to the shop for an oil change. He has been a regular customer since.

Summary

- Front-wheel-drive axles transfer engine torque generally from the transaxle differential to the front wheels.
- Constant velocity (CV) joints provide the necessary transfer of uniform torque and a constant speed while operating through a wide range of angles.
- In front-wheel-drive drivetrains, two CV joints are used on each half shaft. The different types of joints can be referred to by position (inboard or outboard), by function (fixed or plunge), or by design (ball-type or tripod).
- Front-wheel-drive half shafts can be solid or tubular, of equal or unequal length, and with or without damper weights.
- Most problems with front-wheel-drive systems are noted by noise and vibration.
- Lubricant is the most important key to a long life for the CV joint.
- The U-joint is a flexible coupling located at each end of the drive shaft between the transmission and the pinion flange on the drive axle.
- The U-joint allows two rotating shafts to operate at a slight angle to each other, which is most important in rear-wheel-drive vehicles.
- There are three common types of U-joint designs: single U-joints, coupled U-joints, and yoke U-joints.
- A failed U-joint or damaged drive shaft can exhibit a variety of symptoms. A clunk that is heard when the transmission is shifted into gear is the most obvious. You can also encounter unusual noise, roughness, or vibrations.
- A differential is a geared mechanism located between the driving axles of a vehicle. Its job is to direct power flow to the driving axles. Differentials are used in all types of power trains.
- The differential performs several functions. It allows the drive wheels to rotate at different speeds

when negotiating a turn or curve in the road, and the differential drive gears redirect the engine torque from the drive shaft to the rear-drive axles.
- While there are several basic designs of differentials, most feature pinion/ring gears and a pinion shaft.
- The differential in rear-wheel-drive vehicles is housed in the axle housing, or carrier.
- The purpose of the axle shaft is to transfer driving torque from the differential assembly to the vehicle's driving wheels.
- There are three types of driving axles commonly used: semifloating, three-quarter floating, and full-floating.
- The axle shaft bearing supports the vehicles weight and reduces rotational friction.
- Problems with the differential and drive axles are usually first noticed as a leak or noise. As the problem progresses, vibrations or a clunking noise might be felt in various modes of operation.

Review Questions

1. Name the three ways in which CV joints can be classified.
2. What type of axle housing resembles a banjo?
3. What type of axle merely supports the vehicle load and provides a mounting place for the wheels?
4. What type of floating axle has one wheel bearing per wheel on the outside of the axle housing?
5. How are problems with the differential and drive axles usually first noticed?
6. The use of constant velocity joints is restricted to _____ .
   a. front-wheel-drive vehicles
   b. rear-wheel-drive vehicles
   c. rear-wheel-drive vehicles with independent rear suspension
   d. none of the above
7. In front-wheel drivetrains, the CV joint nearer the transaxle is the _____ .
   a. inner joint
   b. inboard joint
   c. outboard joint
   d. both a and b
8. A CV joint that is capable of in and out movement is a _____ .
   a. plunge joint
   b. fixed joint
   c. inboard joint
   d. outboard joint
9. Technician A says that a gear tooth pattern identifies ring gear runout. Technician B says that gear patterns are not accurate if there is excessive ring gear runout. Who is correct?
   a. Technician A
   b. Technician B
   c. Both A and B
   d. Neither A nor B
10. The double-offset joint is typically used in applications that require _____ .
    a. higher operating angles and greater plunge depth
    b. lower operating angles and lower plunge depth
    c. higher operating angles and lower plunge depth
    d. lower operating angles and greater plunge depth
11. Which type joint has a flatter design than any other?
    a. double-offset
    b. disc
    c. cross groove
    d. fixed tripod
12. What is useful for determining which CV joint is the problem?
    a. squeeze test
    b. chassis test
    c. swerve test
    d. spin test
13. The single Cardan/Spicer universal joint is also known as the _____ .
    a. cross joint
    b. four-point joint
    c. both a and b
    d. neither a nor b
14. The drive shaft component that provides a means of connecting two or more shafts together is the _____ .
    a. pinion flange
    b. U-joint
    c. yoke
    d. biscuit
15. Large cars with long drive shafts often use a double-U-joint arrangement called a _____ .
    a. Spicer style U-joint
    b. constant velocity U-joint
    c. Cleveland style U-joint
    d. none of the above
16. Which type of driving axle supports the weight of the vehicle?
    a. semifloating
    b. three-quarter floating
    c. full-floating
    d. none of the above
17. Technician A says that limited slip differential clutch packs are designed to slip when the vehicle turns a corner. Technician B says that a special additive is placed in the hypoid gear lubricant to promote clutch pack slippage on corners. Who is correct?

a. Technician A
b. Technician B
c. Both A and B
d. Neither A nor B

18. Technician A says side bearing preload limits the amount the differential is able to move laterally in the axle housing. Technician B says that adjusting backlash sets the depth of the mesh between the ring and pinion gears' teeth. Who is correct?
    a. Technician A
    b. Technician B
    c. Both A and B
    d. Neither A nor B

19. Technician A says that a hunting gearset is one in which one drive pinion gear tooth contacts only certain ring gear teeth. Technician B says that a partial nonhunting gearset is one in which one pinion tooth contacts only six ring gear teeth. Who is correct?
    a. Technician A
    b. Technician B
    c. Both A and B
    d. Neither A nor B

20. Which of the following describes the double-Cardan universal joint?
    a. It is most often installed in front-engine rear-wheel-drive luxury automobiles.
    b. It is classified as a constant velocity U-joint.
    c. A centering ball socket is inside the coupling yoke between the two universal joints.
    d. All of the above

SECTION 6
AUTOMATIC TRANSMISSIONS AND TRANSAXLES

Chapter 29 Automatic Transmissions and Transaxles
Chapter 30 Automatic Transmission/Transaxle Service
Chapter 31 Four- and All-Wheel Drive

Many vehicles are equipped with automatic transmissions or transaxles. These systems perform the same job as standard or manual shift units, but they do so in quite a different manner. A torque converter replaces the clutch as the link between the engine and transmission/transaxle gearing. The planetary or Ravigneaux gear trains found in automatic units generate speed and torque using a completely different set of operating principles. Finally, the hydraulic and electronic control systems used to initiate shifting are unique to automatic transmissions/transaxles.

This section also covers four- and all-wheel-drive systems, which are becoming a standard feature on many vehicles.

The information found in Section 6 corresponds to materials covered on the ASE certification test on automatic transmissions/transaxles.

WE ENCOURAGE PROFESSIONALISM

THROUGH TECHNICIAN CERTIFICATION

29 AUTOMATIC TRANSMISSIONS AND TRANSAXLES

Objectives

- Explain the basic design and operation of standard and lockup torque converters. ■ Describe the design and operation of a simple planetary gearset and Simpson gear train. ■ Name the major types of planetary gear controls used on automatic transmissions and explain their basic operating principles. ■ Understand the power flow basics of the Chrysler transaxle, General Motors THM 200-4R transmission, and Ford ATX transaxle. ■ Explain the basics of hydraulic operation. ■ Describe the design and operation of the hydraulic controls and valves used in modern transmissions and transaxles. ■ Explain the role of the following components of the transmission control system: pressure regulator valve, throttle valve, governor assembly, manual valve, shift valves, and kickdown valve. ■ Identify the various pressures in the transmission, state their purpose, and tell how they influence the operation of the transmission.

Many rear-wheel-drive and four-wheel-drive vehicles are equipped with automatic transmissions (Figure 29-1). Automatic transaxles, which combine an automatic transmission and final drive assembly in a single unit, are used on front-wheel-drive, all-wheel-drive, and some rear-wheel-drive vehicles (Figure 29-2).

An automatic transmission or transaxle selects gear ratios according to engine speed, power train load, vehicle speed, and other operating factors. Little effort is needed on the part of the driver, because both upshifts and downshifts occur automatically. A driver-operated clutch is not needed to change gears, and the vehicle can be brought to a stop without shifting to neutral. This is a great convenience, particularly in stop-and-go traffic. The driver can also manually select a lower forward gear, reverse, neutral, or park. Depending on the forward range selected, the transmission can provide engine braking during deceleration.

The most widely used automatic transmissions and transaxles have three forward speeds and neutral, reverse, and park positions. Four-speed units that offer an overdrive fourth gear have become increasingly popular. Overdrive occurs when less than one full revolution of the transmission's input shaft produces one full revolution at the output shaft. The purpose of overdrive is to improve fuel economy and reduce engine speed and noise. Most new automatics also feature a lockup torque converter.

Until recently, all automatic transmissions were controlled by hydraulics. However, many new systems now feature computer-controlled operation of the torque converter and transmission. Based on input data supplied by electronic sensors and switches, the computer sets the torque converter's operating mode, controls the transmission's shifting sequence, and in some cases regulates transmission oil pressure.

❑ TORQUE CONVERTERS

Automatic transmissions use a fluid clutch known as a torque converter to transfer engine torque from the engine to the transmission.

The torque converter operates through hydraulic force provided by automatic transmission fluid often simply called transmission oil. The torque converter changes or multiplies the twisting motion of the engine crankshaft and directs it through the transmission.

The torque converter automatically engages and disengages power from the engine to the transmission in relation to engine rpm. With the engine running at the correct idle speed, there is not enough fluid flow for power transfer through the torque converter. As engine speed is increased, the added fluid flow creates sufficient force to transmit engine power through the torque converter assembly to the transmission.

Design

Torque converters, or T/Cs, are either one-piece, welded units that cannot be dismantled for repair, or

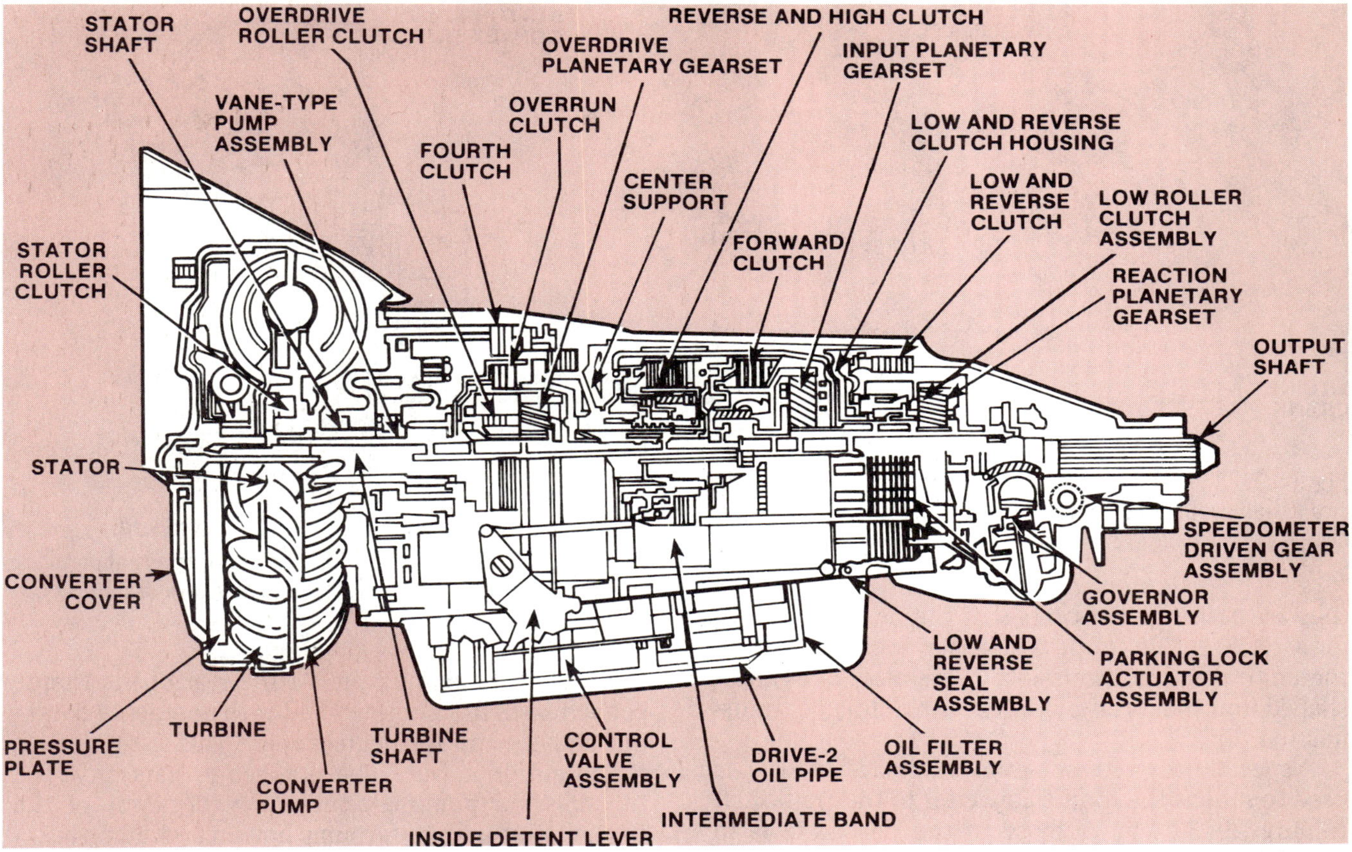

Automatic Transmissions and Transaxles 711

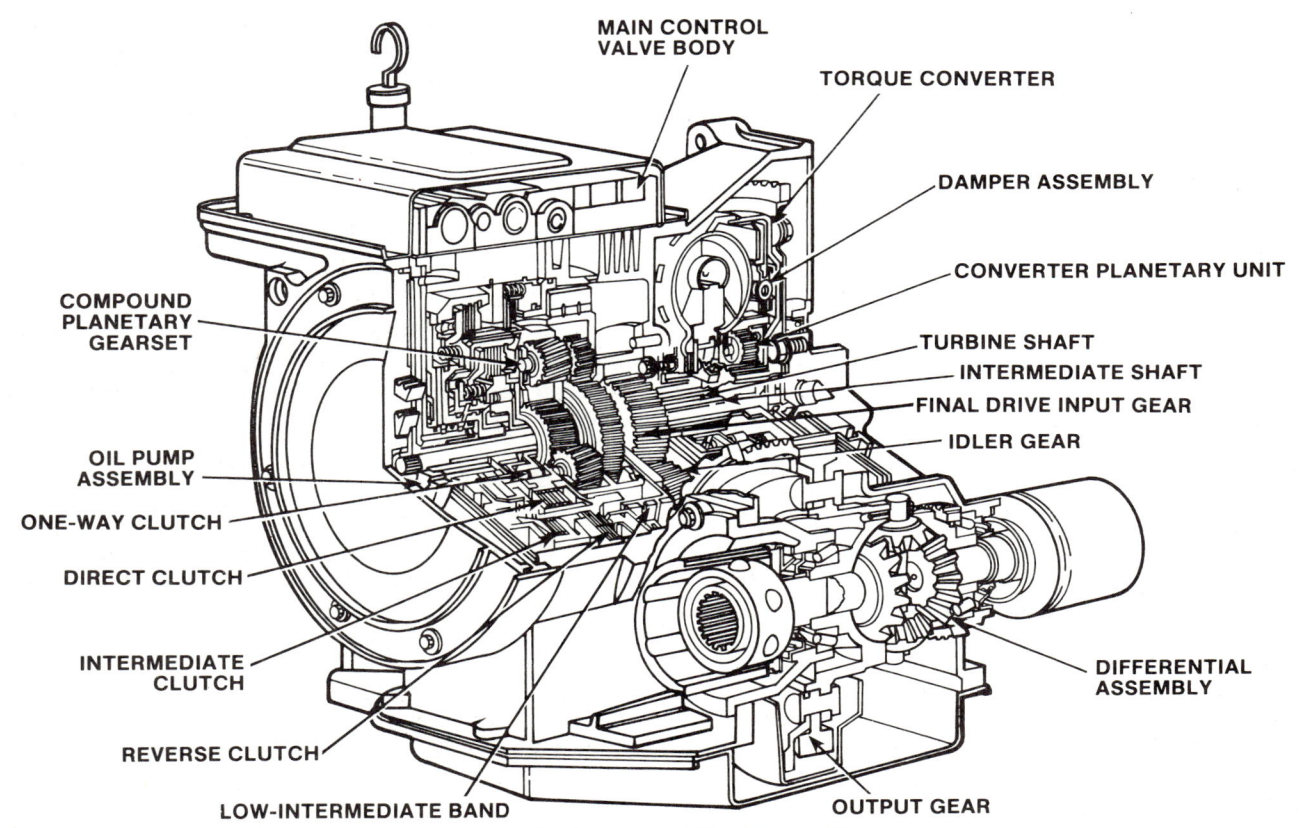

Figure 29-1 Interior view of a THM 200-4R rear-wheel-drive transmission. *Courtesy of General Motors Corp.*

Figure 29-2 Interior view of a Ford ATX transaxle. *Courtesy of Ford Motor Co.*

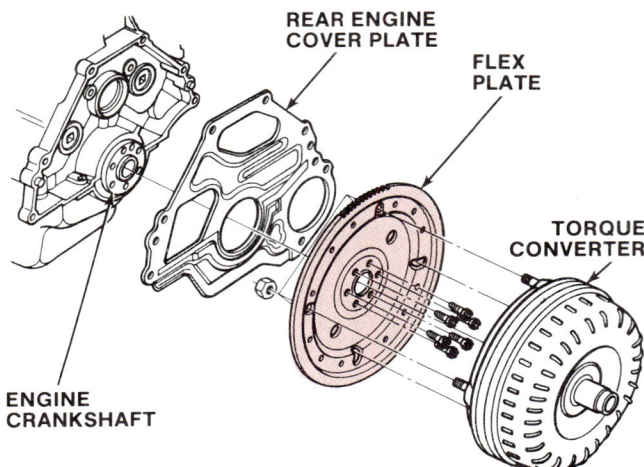

Figure 29-3 The torque converter mounts to the engine crankshaft using a flex plate or disc. *Courtesy of Ford Motor Co.*

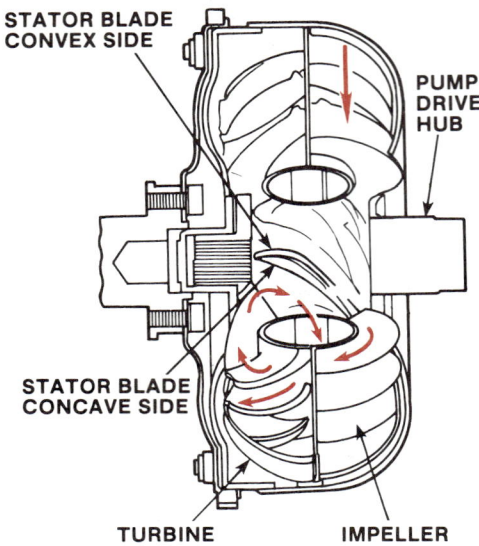

Figure 29-4 A torque converter's major internal parts are its impeller, turbine, and stator. *Courtesy of Ford Motor Co.*

they are bolt-together units that can be broken down for servicing. The torque converter, located between the engine and transmission, is a sealed, doughnut-shaped unit that is always filled with automatic transmission fluid.

A special flex plate, sometimes called a flex disc, is used to mount the torque converter to the crankshaft (Figure 29-3). The purpose of the flex plate is to transfer crankshaft rotation to the shell of the torque converter assembly. The flex plate bolts to a flange machined on the rear of the crankshaft and to mounting pads located on the front of the torque converter shell.

The flex plate also carries the starter motor ring gear. A flywheel is not required because the mass of the torque converter and flex disc acts like a flywheel to smooth out the intermittent power strokes of the engine.

Components

A standard torque converter consists of three elements (Figure 29-4): the pump assembly, often called an impeller, the stator assembly, and the turbine.

The impeller assembly is the input (drive) member. It receives power from the engine. The turbine is the output (driven) member. It is splined to the forward clutch of the transmission and to the turbine shaft assembly. The stator assembly is the reaction member or torque multiplier. The stator is supported on a roller race, which operates as an overrunning clutch and permits the stator to rotate freely in one direction and lock up in the opposite direction.

T/C EXTERIOR The exterior of the torque converter shell is shaped like two bowls standing on end, facing each other. To support the weight of the torque converter, a short stubby shaft projects forward from the front of the torque converter shell and fits into a socket at the rear of the crankshaft. At the rear of the torque converter shell is a hollow shaft with notches or flats at one end, ground 180 degrees apart. This shaft is called the pump drive hub. The notches or flats drive the transmission pump assembly. At the front of the transmission within the pump housing is a pump bushing that supports the pump drive hub and provides rear support for the torque converter assembly.

T/C INTERIOR The impeller forms one section of the torque converter shell. The impeller has numerous curved blades that rotate as a unit with the shell. It turns at engine speed, acting like a pump to start the transmission oil circulating within the torque converter shell.

While the impeller is positioned with its back facing the transmission housing, the turbine is positioned with its back to the engine. The curved blades of the turbine face the impeller assembly.

The turbine blades have a greater curve than the impeller blades. This helps eliminate oil turbulence between the turbine and impeller blades that would slow impeller speed and reduce the converter's efficiency.

The stator is located between the impeller and turbine. It redirects the oil flow from the turbine back into the impeller in the direction of impeller rotation with minimal loss of speed or force. The side of the stator blade with the inward curve is the concave side. The side with an outward curve is the convex side.

Basic Operation

Transmission oil is used as the medium to transfer energy in the T/C. Figure 29-5A illustrates the T/C impeller or pump at rest. Figure 29-5B shows it being driven. As the pump impeller rotates, centrifugal force

Automatic Transmissions and Transaxles

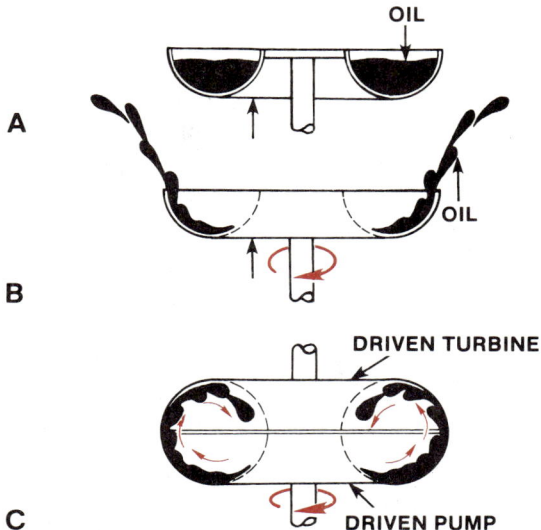

Figure 29-5 Fluid travel inside the torque converter: (A) fluid at rest in impeller/pump, (B) fluid thrown up and outward by spinning pump, and (C) fluid flow harnessed by turbine and redirected back into the pump.

throws the oil outward and upward due to the curved shape of the impeller housing.

The faster the impeller rotates, the greater the centrifugal force becomes. In Figure 29-5B, the oil is simply flying out of the housing and is not producing any work. To harness some of this energy, the turbine assembly is mounted on top of the impeller (Figure 29-5C). Now the oil thrown outward and upward from the impeller strikes the curved vanes of the turbine, causing the turbine to rotate. (There is no direct mechanical link between the impeller and turbine.) An oil pump driven by the converter shell and the engine continually delivers oil under pressure into the T/C through a hollow shaft at the center axis of the rotating torque converter assembly. A seal prevents the loss of fluid from the system.

The turbine shaft is located within this hollow shaft. As mentioned earlier, the turbine shaft is splined to the turbine and transfers power from the torque converter to the transmission's main drive shaft. Oil leaving the turbine is directed out of the torque converter to an external oil cooler and then to the transmission's oil sump or pan.

With the transmission in gear and the engine at idle, the vehicle can be held stationary by applying the brakes. At idle, engine speed is slow. Since the impeller is driven by engine speed, it turns slowly creating little centrifugal force within the torque converter. Therefore, little or no power is transferred to the transmission.

When the throttle is opened, engine speed, impeller speed, and the amount of centrifugal force generated in the torque converter increase dramatically. Oil is then directed against the turbine blades, which transfer power to the turbine shaft and transmission.

Types of Oil Flow

Two types of oil flow take place inside the torque converter: rotary and vortex flow (Figure 29-6). Rotary oil flow is the oil flow around the circumference of the torque converter caused by the rotation of the torque converter on its axis. Vortex oil flow is the oil flow occurring from the impeller to the turbine and back to the impeller.

Figure 29-7 also shows the oil flow pattern as the speed of the turbine approaches the speed of the impeller. This is known as the coupling point. The turbine and the impeller are running at essentially the same speed. They cannot run at exactly the same speed due to slippage between them. The only way they can turn at exactly the same speed is by using a lockup clutch to mechanically tie them together.

As mentioned earlier, the stator is a small, wheel-like assembly positioned between the impeller and turbine. The stator has no mechanical connection to either the impeller or turbine, but fits between the outlet of the turbine and the inlet of the impeller so that all the oil returning from the turbine to the impeller must pass through the stator.

The stator mounts through its splined center hub to a mating stator shaft, often called a ground sleeve. The stator freewheels when the impeller and turbine reach the coupling stage.

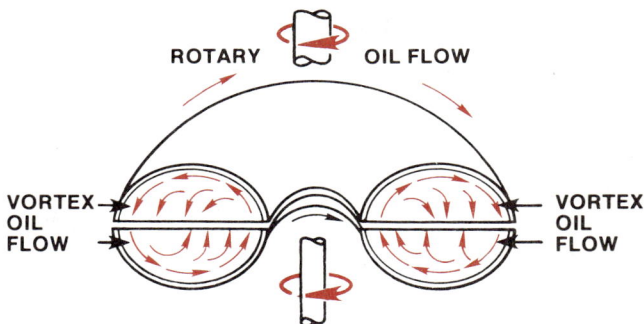

Figure 29-6 Rotary and vortex oil flow in the torque converter.

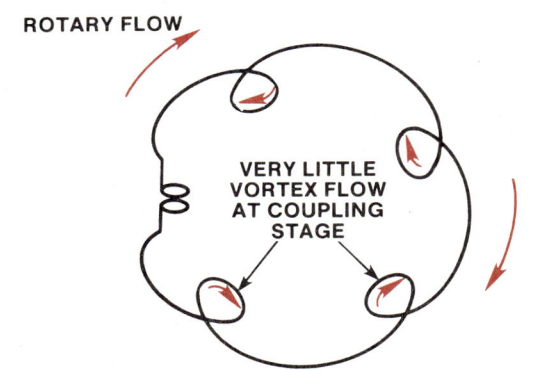

Figure 29-7 Rotary flow is at its greatest at the coupling stage.

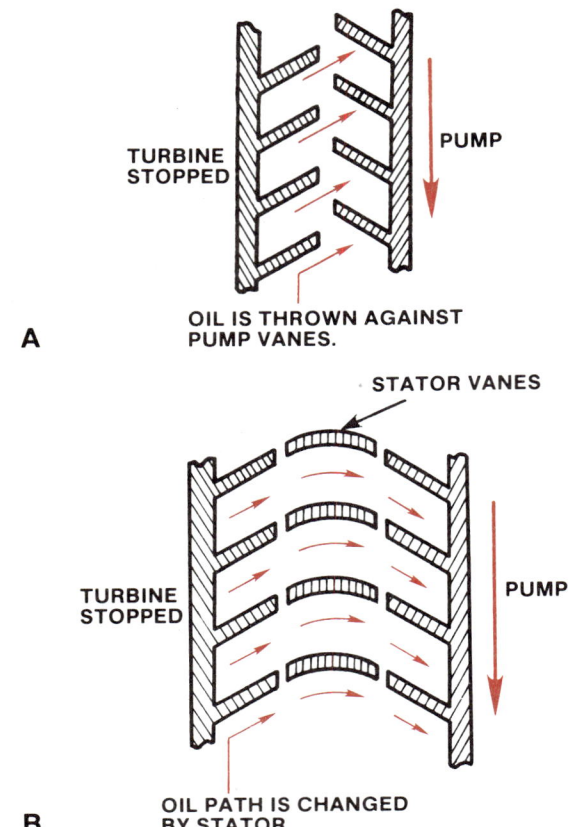

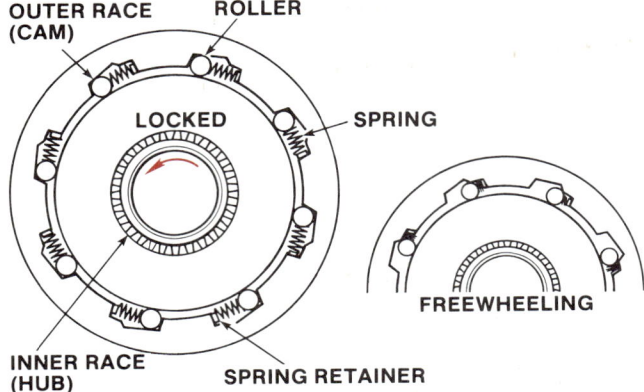

Figure 29-9 Typical roller-type overrunning clutch.

Figure 29-8 (A) Without a stator, fluid leaving the turbine works against the direction in which the impeller or pump is rotating. (B) With a stator in its locked (noncoupling) mode, fluid is directed to help push the impeller in its rotating direction.

The stator redirects the oil leaving the turbine back to the impeller, which helps the impeller rotate more efficiently (Figure 29-8). Torque converter multiplication can only occur when the impeller is rotating faster than the turbine.

A stator is either a rotating or fixed type. Rotating stators are more efficient at higher speeds because there is less slippage when the impeller and turbine reach the coupling stage.

Overrunning Clutch

An overrunning clutch keeps the stator assembly from rotating when driven in one direction and permits overrunning (rotation) when turned in the opposite direction. Rotating stators generally use a roller-type overrunning clutch that allows the stator to freewheel (rotate) when the speed of the turbine and impeller reach the coupling point.

The roller clutch (Figure 29-9) is designed with a movable inner race, rollers, accordion (apply) springs, and outer race. Around the inside diameter of the outer race are several cam-shaped pockets. The rollers and accordion springs are located in these pockets.

As the vehicle begins to move, the stator stays in its stationary or locked position because of the difference between the impeller and turbine speeds. This locking mode takes place when the inner race rotates counterclockwise. The accordion springs force the rollers down the ramps of the cam pockets into a wedging contact with the inner and outer races.

As vehicle road speed increases, turbine speed increases until it approaches impeller speed. Oil exiting the turbine vanes strikes the back face of the stator, causing the stator to rotate in the same direction as the turbine and impeller. At this higher speed, clearance exists between the inner stator race and hub. The rollers in each slot of the stator are pulled around the stator hub. The stator freewheels or turns as a unit.

If the vehicle slows, engine speed also slows along with turbine speed. This decrease in turbine speed allows the oil flow to change direction. It now strikes the front face of the stator vanes, halting the turning stator and attempting to rotate it in the opposite direction.

As this happens, the rollers jam between the inner race and hub, locking the stator in position. In a stationary position, the stator now redirects the oil exiting the turbine so that torque is again multiplied.

☐ LOCKUP TORQUE CONVERTERS

A lockup torque converter eliminates the 10% slip that takes place between the impeller and turbine at the coupling stage of operation. The engagement of a clutch between the engine crankshaft and the turbine assembly has the advantage of improving fuel economy and reducing torque converter operational heat and engine speed.

There are two types of lockup torque converters. The centrifugal lockup clutch (CLC) was installed in Ford Motor Company C-5 automatic transmissions during the early 1980s. The piston lockup clutch (PLC) is the type installed in most automatic transmissions.

Centrifugal Lockup Clutch (CLC)

As shown in Figure 29-10, the principle part added to the torque converter is the clutch and damper assembly located between the torque converter shell and turbine assembly.

The clutch and damper assembly looks like a manual transmission clutch disc. At its center is an internally splined hub meshing with an externally splined hub on the turbine assembly. The clutch and damper assembly drive the turbine when the lockup clutch is engaged. Outward from the internally splined hub is the coasting one-way overrunning clutch. This sprag-type clutch connects the clutch and damper assembly to the turbine hub when the engine is driving the vehicle. When the vehicle is decelerating or coasting, the coasting clutch overruns and disconnects the turbine from the torque converter shell. This clutch is considered a safety factor during an emergency stop because the engine will not stall.

Midway from the center of the clutch and damper assembly are six coil torsional springs that absorb the shock associated with the torque converter locking action. Collectively, the torsional coil springs are called an absorption unit. Placed around the outside edge of the clutch and damper assembly are several shoe assemblies called centrifugal clutch shoes. Each shoe is mounted on a spring sensitive to centrifugal force and faced with a friction material pad.

With the vehicle stopped, the torque converter shell drives the impeller using fluid to rotate the turbine and turbine shaft hydraulically (Figure 29-11A). As turbine speed and centrifugal force increase the centrifugal clutch, shoes are thrown outward and expand to contact the inside diameter of the torque converter shell (Figure 29-11B). Power flows from the inside surface of the torque converter shell to the expanded centrifugal clutch shoe, clutch, and damper assembly to drive the turbine hub and turbine shaft.

In the lockup mode there is no hydraulic operation. The drive is strictly mechanical. If the driver requires an increase in vehicle speed, increased impeller speed raises vortex flow and produces some torque multiplication. A friction-modified automatic transmission fluid permits the centrifugal clutch shoes to slip when extra torque is needed. When the demand for torque has been satisfied, the centrifugal clutch shoes resume driving the interior of the torque converter shell, reestablishing lockup torque converter action.

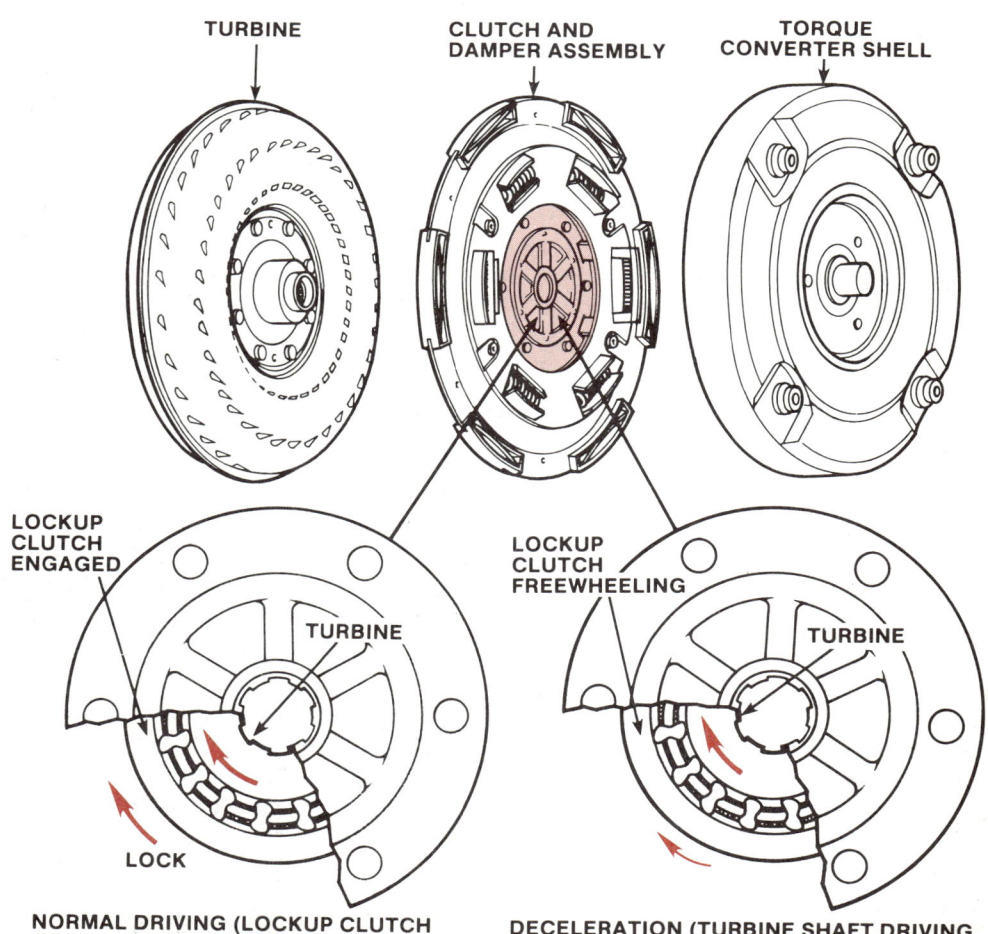

Figure 29-10 In a centrifugal lockup torque converter, a clutch and damper assembly is positioned between the turbine and the torque converter shell. It uses a coasting overrunning sprag-type clutch. *Courtesy of Ford Motor Co.*

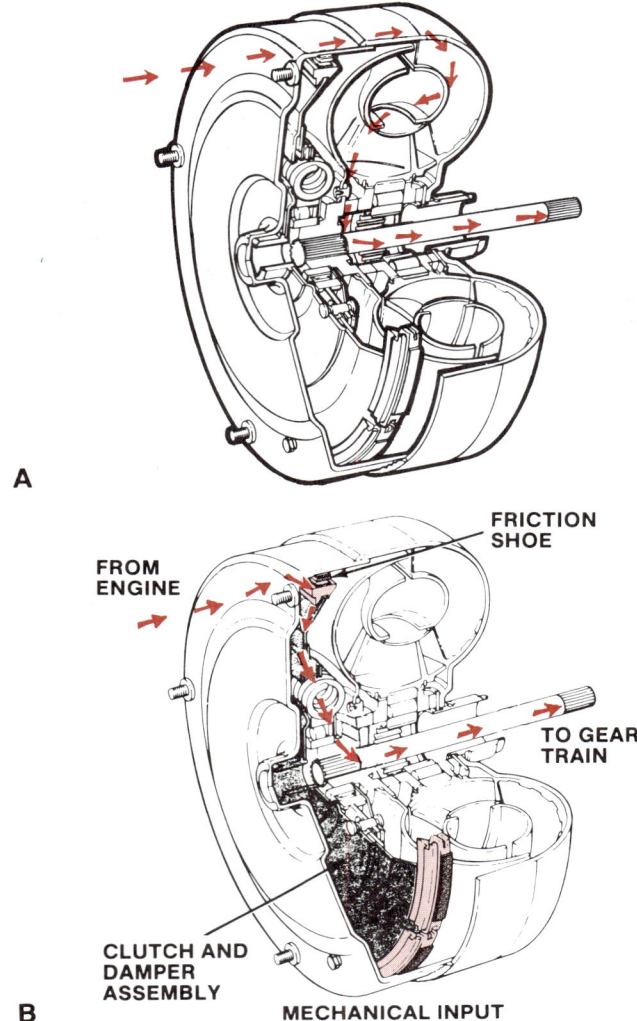

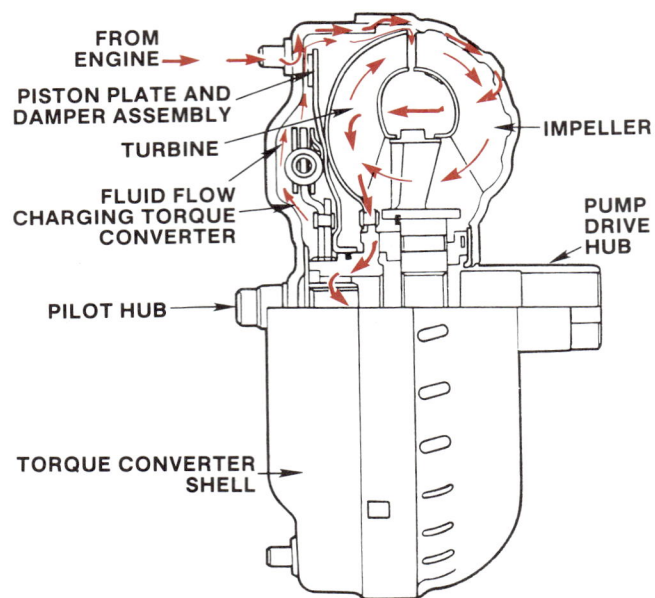

Figure 29-12 Piston lockup clutch components and oil flow. *Courtesy of Ford Motor Co.*

Figure 29-11 (A) With the vehicle stopped, the torque converter shell drives the impeller, turbine, and turbine shaft. (B) As turbine speed increases, friction shoes engage to drive the overrun clutch and turbine shaft. *Courtesy of Ford Motor Co.*

Piston Lockup Clutch (PLC)

The other type of lockup torque converter has a piston clutch located between the front of the turbine and the interior front face of the shell (Figure 29-12). Its main components are a piston plate and damper assembly and a clutch friction ring. The friction ring is bonded to the piston plate and damper assembly, in many cases. The second part of the damper assembly is made of several coil springs designed into the piston plate to transmit driving torque and absorb shock.

In piston-type lockup torque converters the front section of the turbine shaft is drilled lengthwise allowing fluids to be supplied to and drained from the chamber between the front side of the piston plate and damper assembly and torque converter shell.

Whereas a centrifugal lockup clutch is operated by engine speed, the piston lockup clutch is controlled by hydraulic valve action or, more precisely, by computer. The computer control is superior because information about the engine, fuel, ignition, vacuum, and operating temperature is fed into the computer so that engagement is closely monitored to take place at exactly the right time as it relates to engine operation.

SHOP TALK

The Chrysler lockup clutch friction facings float between the torque converter shell and the pressure plate and piston assembly. Chrysler does not have an absorption unit. It relies instead on the fluid in the torque converter to cushion lockup clutch engagement.

To provide for piston clutch control, Chrysler adds a three-valve module to its standard transmission valve body (Figure 29-13). The lockup valve is controlled by fluid pressure produced by the transmission's governor assembly called governor pressure. When vehicle road speed is high enough, governor pressure forces the lockup valve to move against coil spring tension. The moving over of the lockup valve permits fluid pressure to move to the fail-safe valve. The purpose of the fail-safe valve is to prevent lockup clutch engagement until the transmission is in third gear. Third gear fluid pressure moves the fail-safe valve, which allows fluid pressure to flow to the switch valve. The purpose of the switch valve is to direct fluid pressure, called line pressure, between the turbine shaft and the stator support to fill the torque converter. When the torque converter is filled, fluid flows out from the space around the periphery of the impeller and turbine to the

Automatic Transmissions and Transaxles 717

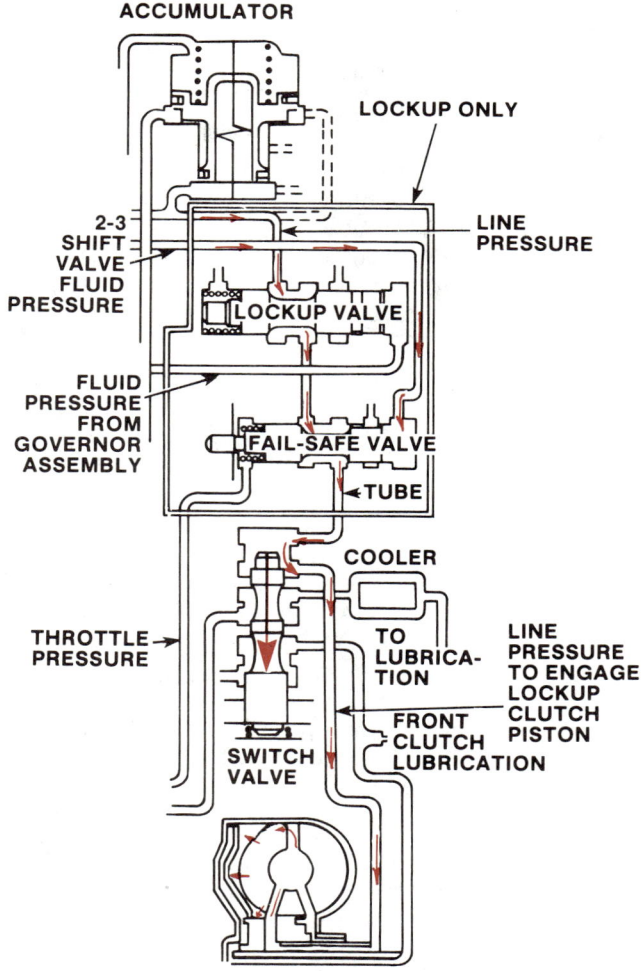

Figure 29-13 Control valve operation to produce direct lockup clutch engagement in Chrysler piston lockup torque converter. *Courtesy of Chrysler Motors*

rear of the piston plate and damper assembly. This fluid flow acts on the rear surface of the piston plate and moves it forward to bring the piston plate and friction ring into contact with the torque converter shell. When the piston plate engages, the clutch friction ring forms a fluid pressure seal with the torque converter shell. This seal stops fluid pressure from leaking to the turbine shaft. A fluid leak in this area decreases the fluid pressure that keeps the clutch engaged. The fluid in the torque converter does not circulate but remains there to act as the torque converter coolant and lubricant throughout the lockup engagement.

Forced Disengagement

While in the lockup mode, the driver might want to accelerate rapidly. By opening the throttle, pressure increases, stroking the fail-safe valve to block line pressure to the lockup valve. Spring tension moves the switch valve, directing fluid pressure to the front (disengaged) side of the piston plate and damper assembly.

The torque converter then returns to conventional operation.

❏ PLANETARY GEARS

All automatic transmissions rely on planetary gearsets to transfer power and multiply engine torque to the drive axle. Compound gearsets combine two simple planetary gearsets so that load can be spread over a greater number of teeth for strength and also to obtain the largest number of gear ratios possible in a compact area.

A simple planetary gearset consists of three parts: a sun gear, a carrier with planetary pinions mounted to it, and an internally toothed ring gear or annulus. The sun gear is located in the center of the assembly (Figure 29-14). It can be either a spur or helical gear design. It meshes with the teeth of the planetary pinion gears. Planetary pinion gears are small gears fitted into a framework called the planetary carrier. The planetary carrier can be made of cast iron, aluminum, or steel plate and is designed with a shaft for each of the planetary pinion gears. (For simplicity, planetary pinion gears are called planetary pinions.)

Planetary pinions rotate on needle bearings positioned between the planetary carrier shaft and the planetary pinions. The carrier and pinions are considered one unit—the mid-size gear member.

The planetary pinions surround the sun gear's center axis and they themselves are surrounded by the annulus or ring gear, which is the largest part of the simple gearset. The ring gear acts like a band to hold the entire gearset together and provide great strength to the unit. To help remember the design of a simple planetary gearset, use the solar system as an example. The sun is the center of the solar system with the planets rotating around it. Hence, the name planetary gearset.

How Planetary Gears Work

Each member of a planetary gearset—the sun gear, pinion gear carrier, and ring gear—can spin (revolve)

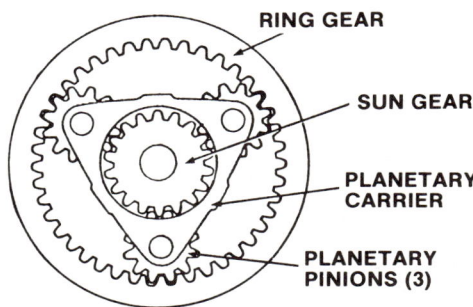

Figure 29-14 Planetary gear configuration is similar to the solar system, with the sun gear surrounded by the planetary pinion gears. The ring gear surrounds the complete gearset.

718 Section 6 Automatic Transmissions and Transaxles

TABLE 29-1 LAWS OF SIMPLE PLANETARY GEAR OPERATION

Sun Gear	Carrier	Ring Gear	Speed	Torque	Direction
1. Input	Output	Held	Maximum reduction	Increase	Same as input
2. Held	Output	Input	Minimum reduction	Increase	Same as input
3. Output	Input	Held	Maximum increase	Reduction	Same as input
4. Held	Input	Output	Minimum increase	Reduction	Same as input
5. Input	Held	Output	Reduction	Increase	Reverse of input
6. Output	Held	Input	Increase	Reduction	Reverse of input

7. When any two members are held together, speed and direction are the same as input. Direct 1:1 drive occurs.
8. When no member is held or locked together, output cannot occur. The result is a neutral condition.

or be held at rest. Power transfer through a planetary gearset is only possible when one of the members is held at rest, or if two of the members are locked together.

Any one of the three members can be used as the driving or input member. At the same time, another member might be kept from rotating and thus becomes the held or stationary member. The third member then becomes the driven or output member. Depending on which member is the driver, which is held, and which is driven, either a torque increase or a speed increase is produced by the planetary gearset. Output direction can also be reversed through various combinations.

Table 29-1 summarizes the basic laws of simple planetary gears. It indicates the resultant speed, torque, and direction of the various combinations available. Also, remember that when an external-to-external gear tooth set is in mesh, there is a change in the direction of rotation at the output (Figure 29-15A). When an external gear tooth is in mesh with an internal gear, the output rotation for both gears is the same (Figure 29-15B).

MAXIMUM FORWARD REDUCTION With the ring gear stationary and the sun gear turning clockwise, the sun gear rotates the planetary pinions counterclockwise on their shafts (Figure 29-16). The small sun gear (driving) rotates several times, driving the middle size planetary carrier one complete revolution, resulting in the most gear reduction or the maximum torque mul-

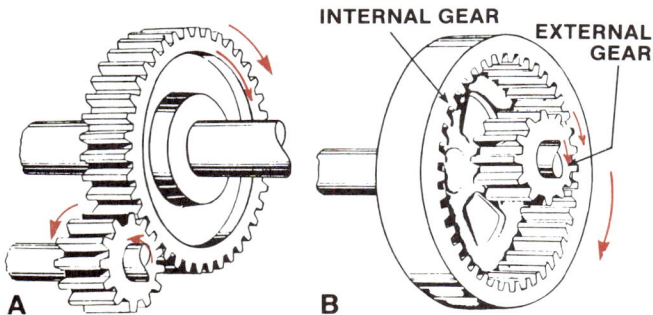

Figure 29-15 (A) With external teeth in mesh, there is a change in direction at the output. (B) When an external gear is meshed with an internal gear, both turn in the same direction.

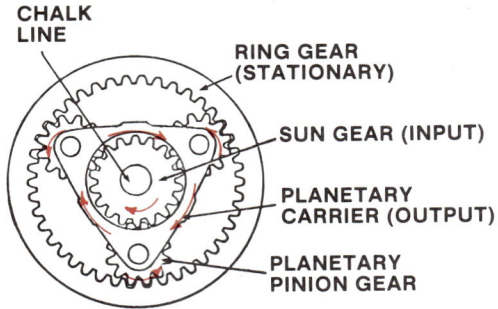

Figure 29-16 Maximum forward reduction (greatest torque, lowest speed) is produced with the sun gear as input, ring gear stationary, and carrier as output.

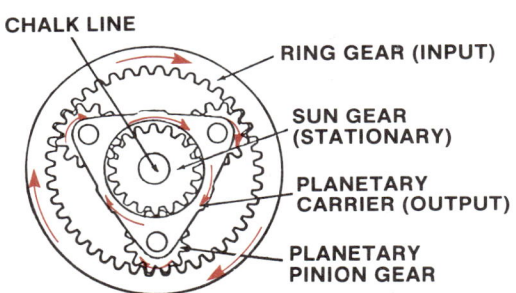

Figure 29-17 Minimum forward reduction (good torque, medium-to-high speed) is produced with the ring gear as input, the sun gear stationary, and the carrier as output.

tiplication that can be achieved in one planetary gearset. Input speed is high, but output speed is low.

MINIMUM FORWARD REDUCTION In this combination the sun gear is stationary and the ring gear rotates clockwise (Figure 29-17). The ring gear drives the planetary pinions clockwise and walks around the stationary sun gear. The planetary pinions drive the planetary carrier in the same direction as the ring gear—forward. This results in more than one turn of the input as compared to one complete revolution of the output. The result is torque multiplication. The planetary gearset is operating in a forward reduction with the large ring gear driving the small planetary carrier. Therefore, the combination produces minimum forward reduction.

Automatic Transmissions and Transaxles **719**

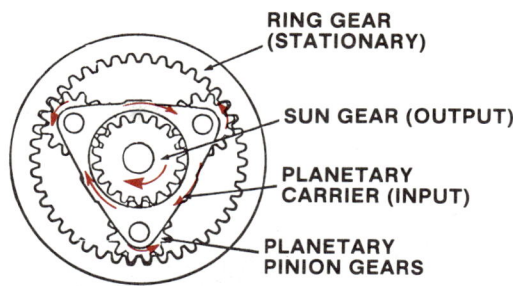

Figure 29-18 Maximum overdrive (lowest torque, greatest speed) is produced with the carrier as input, ring gear stationary, and sun gear as output.

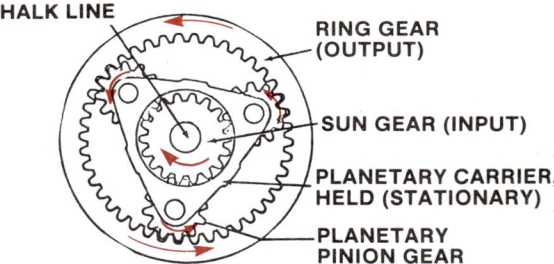

Figure 29-20 Slow reverse (opposite output direction, greatest torque, lowest speed) is produced with the sun gear as input, planetary carrier stationary, and the ring gear as output.

MAXIMUM OVERDRIVE With the ring gear stationary and the planetary carrier rotating clockwise (Figure 29-18), the three planetary pinion shafts push against the inside diameter of the planetary pinions. The pinions are forced to walk around the inside of the ring gear, driving the sun gear clockwise. In this combination, the middle size planetary carrier is rotating less than one turn and driving the smaller sun gear at a speed greater than the input speed. The result is overdrive with maximum speed increase.

SLOW OVERDRIVE In this combination, the sun gear is stationary and the carrier rotates clockwise (Figure 29-19). As the carrier rotates, the pinion shafts push against the inside diameter of the pinions and they are forced to walk around the held sun gear. This drives the ring gear faster and the speed increases. The carrier turning less than one turn causes the pinions to drive the ring gear one complete revolution in the same direction as the planetary carrier and a slow overdrive occurs.

SLOW REVERSE Here the sun gear is driving the ring gear with the planetary carrier held stationary (Figure 29-20). The planetary pinions, driven by the sun gear, rotate counterclockwise on their shafts. The planetary pinions drive the ring gear in the same direction. While the sun gear is driving, the planetary pinions are used as idler gears to drive the ring gear counterclockwise. This means the input and output shafts are operating in the opposite or reverse direction to provide a reverse

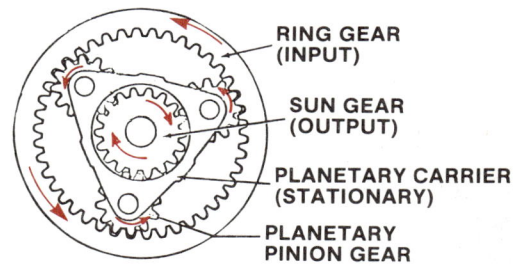

Figure 29-21 Fast reverse (opposite output direction, great torque, low speed) is produced with the ring gear as input, carrier stationary, and sun gear as output.

power flow. Since the driving sun gear is small and the driven ring gear is large, the result is slow reverse.

FAST REVERSE For fast reverse, the carrier is held, but the sun gear and ring gear reverse roles, with the ring gear now being the driving member and the sun gear driven (Figure 29-21). As the ring gear rotates counterclockwise, the pinions rotate counterclockwise as well, while the sun gear turns clockwise. In this combination, the input ring gear uses the planetary pinions to drive the output sun gear. The sun gear rotates in reverse to the input ring gear, providing fast reverse.

DIRECT DRIVE In the direct drive combination, both the ring gear and the sun gear are input members (Figure 29-22). They turn clockwise at the same speed. The internal teeth of the clockwise turning ring gear try to rotate the planetary pinions clockwise as well.

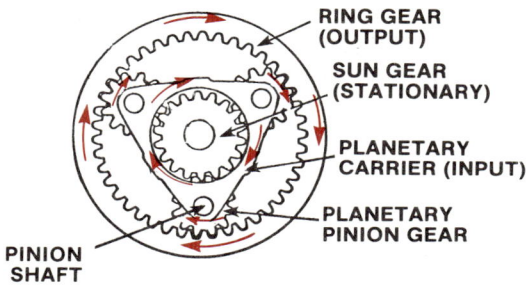

Figure 29-19 Slow overdrive (lower torque, greater speed) is produced with the carrier as input, sun gear stationary, and ring gear as output.

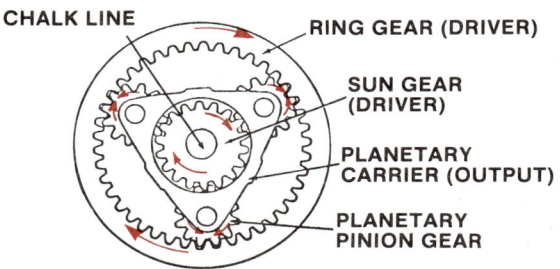

Figure 29-22 Direct drive is produced if any two gearset members are locked together.

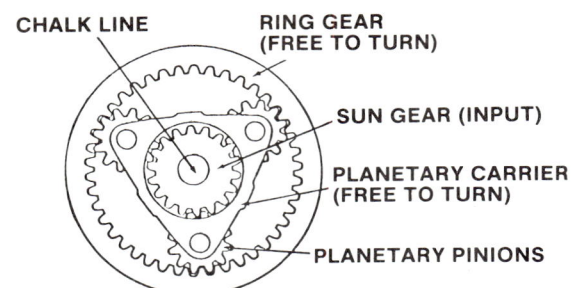

Figure 29–23 With no held or stationary member, there can be no output. The result is a neutral condition.

But the sun gear, which rotates clockwise, tries to drive the planetary pinions counterclockwise. These opposing forces lock the planetary pinions against rotation so that the entire planetary gearset rotates as one complete unit. This ties together the input and output members and provides a direct drive.

NEUTRAL OPERATION When no member is held stationary or locked, there is input into the gearset, but no output. The result is a neutral condition (Figure 29–23).

▢ PLANETARY GEAR CONTROLS

The following are helpful tips in remembering the basics of simple planetary gearset operation.

- When the planetary carrier is the drive (input) member, the gearset produces an overdrive condition. Speed increases, torque decreases.
- When the planetary carrier is the driven (output) member, the gearset produces a forward reduction. Speed decreases, torque increases.
- When the planetary carrier is held, the gearset produces a reverse.

Certain parts of the planetary gear train must be held while others must be driven to provide the needed torque multiplication and direction for vehicle operation. Planetary gear controls is the general term used to describe transmission bands, servos, and clutches.

Transmission Bands

A band is a braking assembly positioned around a stationary or rotating drum. The band brings a drum to a stop by wrapping itself around the drum and holding it. The band is hydraulically applied by a servo assembly. Connected to the drum is a member of the planetary gear train. The purpose of a band is to control the planetary gear train by holding the drum and connecting planetary gear member stationary. Bands provide excellent holding characteristics and require a minimum amount of space within the transmission housing.

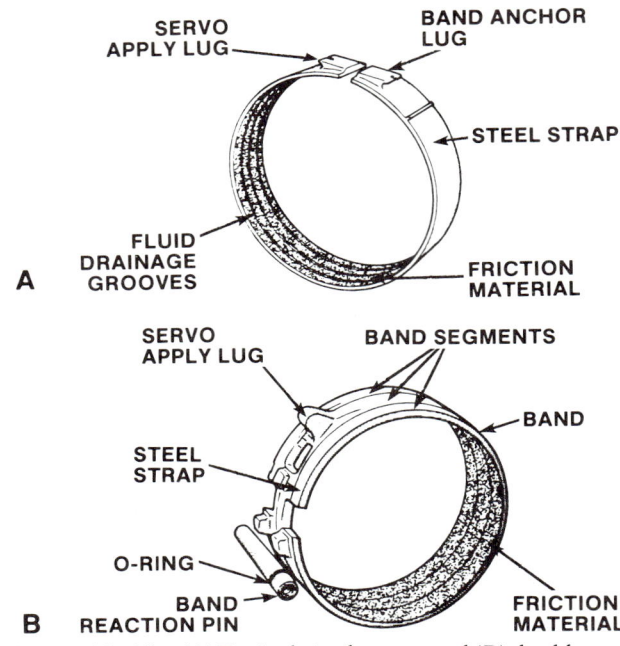

Figure 29–24 (A) Typical single-wrap and (B) double-wrap transmission band designs. *Courtesy of Chrysler Motors*

When a band closes around a rotating drum, a wedging action takes place to stop the drum from rotating. The wedging action is known as self-energizing action. It is explained later in this chapter.

There are two types of bands used in automatic transmissions: single wrap and double wrap. A thick steel single-wrap band (Figure 29–24A) is used to hold gear train components driven by high output engines. Self-energizing action is low because of the rigidity of the band's design. Thinner steel bands are not able to provide a high degree of holding power, but because of the flexibility of design, self-energizing action is stronger and provides more apply force.

Band lugs are either spot welded or cast as a part of the band assembly. The purpose of the lugs is to connect the band with the servo through the actuating (apply) linkage or the band anchor (reaction) at the opposite end.

> **SHOP TALK**
>
> A holding planetary control unit is also called a reaction unit because it holds a gear train member stationary, reacting to rotation.

The band's steel strap is designed with slots or holes to release fluid trapped between the drum and the applying band.

A typical band is designed to be larger in diameter than the drum it surrounds. This design promotes self-disengagement of the band from the drum when servo apply force is decreased to less than servo release spring tension. A friction material resembling automobile brake lining is bonded to the inside diameter of the band.

The double-wrap band is a circular external contracting band normally designed with two or three segments (parts) illustrated in Figure 29-24B. As the band closes, the segments align themselves around the drum and provide a cushion.

The steel body of the double-wrap band may be thin or thick steel strapping material. Modern automatic transmissions use thin single- or double-wrap bands for increased efficiency. Double-wrap bands made with heavy thick steel strapping are required for high output engines.

Transmission Servos

The servo assembly converts hydraulic pressure into mechanical pressure that applies the band around a drum, holding it stationary. Simple and compound servos are used to engage bands in modern transmissions.

Simple Servo

In a simple servo (Figure 29-25), the servo/piston fits into the servo cylinder and is held in the released position by a coil spring. The piston is encircled by a seal ring made of rubber, which keeps fluid pressure confined to the apply side of the servo piston.

In the illustration (but not on all servo designs), the piston pushrod is drilled through the center, which permits fluid pressure to be directed to the apply side of the servo piston. The piston pushrod locates in the band apply strut, which is indexed with the band apply lug. At the opposite end of the band is the anchor strut and adjustment screw. They receive the engagement force of a band.

To apply a band, fluid pressure is directed down the servo pushrod to the apply side of the servo piston. The servo piston strokes through the servo cylinder, compresses the servo coil spring, and develops servo apply force. As the servo piston and pushrod stroke the servo cylinder, they force the apply lever and strut against

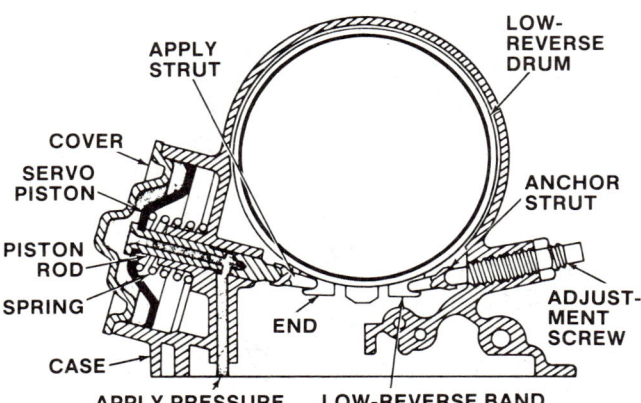

Figure 29-25 Typical simple servo design. *Courtesy of Ford Motor Co.*

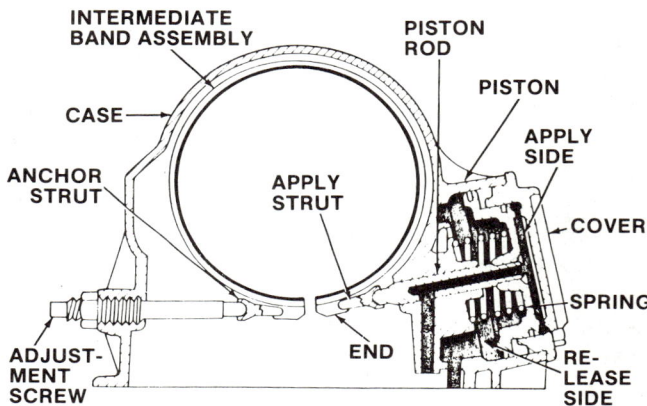

Figure 29-26 Typical compound servo design. *Courtesy of Ford Motor Co.*

the band lug. The band tightens around the rotating drum. The rotating drum comes to a stop and is held stationary by the band.

When servo apply force is released, the servo coil spring forces the servo piston to stroke back up the servo cylinder to the released position. With the servo apply force removed the band springs free and permits drum rotation.

Compound Servos

A compound servo (Figure 29-26) has a cylinder that is cast as part of the transmission housing. The servo piston located nearest the front of the transmission uses cast-iron seal rings capable of withstanding the heat generated by the torque converter and engine.

When the compound servo is applied, fluid pressure flows through the hollow piston pushrod to the apply side of the servo piston. The piston moves inward, compressing the servo coil spring and forcing the pushrod to move one end of the band toward the adjusting screw and anchor. The band tightens around the rotating drum and brings it to a stop. If the drum was stationary, the band would apply, holding the drum tight and unable to revolve. The apply of the compound servo piston is much like the simple servo, but there the similarity ends.

Fluid pressure is applied to the release side of the servo piston when the band is to be released. To release the compound servo, fluid pressure is admitted to the release side of the servo piston. Line pressure on either side of the servo piston balances out. The force of the servo spring causes the release of the servo piston.

Transmission Clutches

In contrast to a band, which can only hold a planetary gear member, transmission clutches, either overrunning or multiple-disc, are capable of both holding and driving members.

Overrunning Clutches

When applied to transmission operation, the overrunning clutch is broadened to a holder or driver. Both sprag and roller overrunning clutches can be applied to either the holding or driving application.

For example, when the turbine shaft and inner race rotate, the accordion apply springs force the rollers down their ramps and engage both the inner and outer races. Power flow passes from the inner race through the roller to the outer race, driving the low reverse sun gear and direct clutch splines at turbine shaft speed.

Should the turbine shaft decelerate and rotate slower than the driven race, the overrunning clutch rollers in an overrun mode disengage from the driving race. The low reverse sun gear and direct clutch are disengaged from the turbine shaft.

Multiple-Disc Clutches

A multiple-disc clutch uses a series of hollow friction discs to transmit torque or apply braking force. The discs have internal teeth that are sized and shaped to mesh with splines on the clutch assembly hub. In turn, this hub is connected to a planetary gear train component so gearset members receive the desired braking or transfer force when the clutch is applied or released.

DESIGN Multiple-disc clutches have a large drum-shaped housing that can be either a separate casting or part of the existing transmission housing (Figure 29-27). This drum housing holds all other clutch components: the cylinder, hub, piston, piston return springs, seals, pressure plate, clutch pack (including friction plates), and snap rings.

The cylinder in a multiple-disc clutch is very shallow when compared to an engine cylinder. The hub of the cylinder acts as a guide for piston travel.

The piston is made of cast aluminum or a steel stamping with a seal ring groove around the outside diameter. A seal ring seats in the groove. This rubber seal retains fluid pressure used to stroke the piston engaging the clutch pack. The piston return springs overcome the reduced fluid pressure in the clutch and

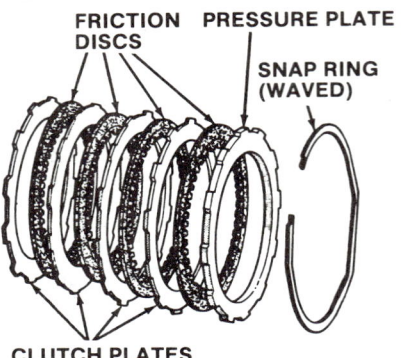

Figure 29-28 The clutch pack is made of friction discs and clutch plates. *Courtesy of Chrysler Motors*

move the piston to the disengaged position when clutch action (holding or transfer) is no longer needed.

The clutch pack consists of normal clutch plates, friction discs, and one very thick plate known as the pressure plate (Figure 29-28). The pressure plate has tabs around the outside diameter to mate with the channels in the clutch drum (Figure 29-29). It is held in place by a large snap ring. The stroking piston forces the engaging clutch pack against the fixed pressure plate. Because the pressure plate cannot move or deflect, it provides the reaction to the engaging clutch pack.

Clutch plates must be perfectly flat, and although the surface of the plate might appear smooth, it is specifically machined to promote a coefficient of friction to help transmit engine torque.

The friction discs are sandwiched between the clutch plates and pressure plate. Friction discs are designed with a steel core plate center with friction material bonded to either side. Asbestos was once the universal friction material used, but because it is hazardous to human health, cellular paper fibers, graphites, and ceramics are now being used as friction materials.

COOLING During clutch engagement, friction takes place and develops heat between the clutch plates and

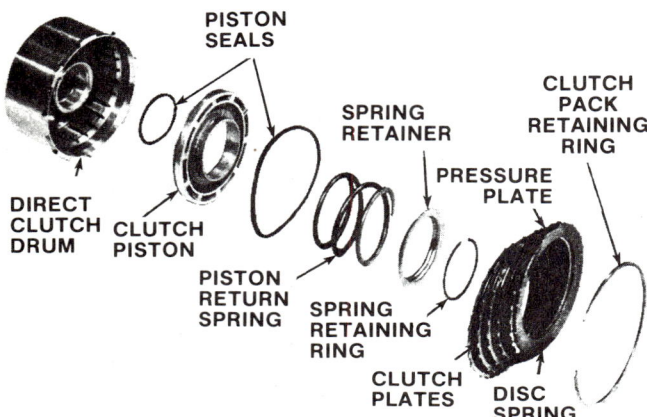

Figure 29-27 Exploded view of multiple-disc clutch assembly. *Courtesy of Ford Motor Co.*

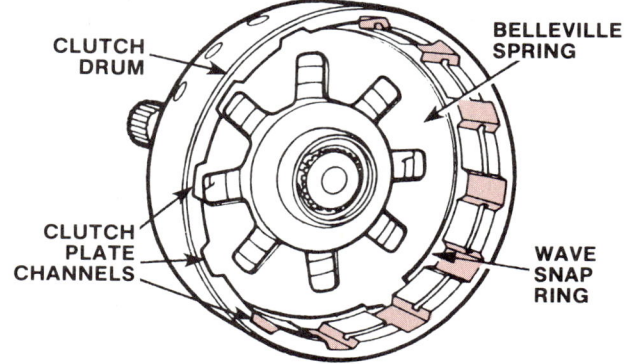

Figure 29-29 Channels in the clutch drum receive the tabs of the clutch plates. *Courtesy of Chrysler Motors*

friction discs. The transmission fluid absorbed by the paper-based friction material, transfers heat from the discs to the plates. The plates then transfer the heat to the drum housing where it can be cooled by the surrounding transmission fluid. Operating temperatures can reach 1,100 degrees Fahrenheit, so clutch disc cooling is an important design consideration in transmission manufacturing.

To help with this cooling and provide other performance advantages, friction disc surfaces are normally grooved.

Planetary Control Terminology

Table 29-2 is a crossover chart listing the names that the different manufacturers call the same planetary gear control. On some four-speed transaxles, the terminology changes because the gear train arrangement changes.

Chrysler refers to the planetary controls by their location in the transaxle or transmission housing. To help eliminate confusion, this text follows Chrysler's logical approach. Chrysler calls the clutch engaged for all forward speeds the rear clutch. The band at the front of the transaxle is the front kickdown band engaged in second gear and also in downshift from third to second gear, which is also known as the passing gear. The front clutch in the transaxle is engaged in reverse and high or third gear. The band located at the rear of the transaxle housing is known as the low and reverse band. It is engaged when the gear selector lever is placed in reverse or manually shifted to first or low gear. The overrunning clutch engages only in low gear or, if the vehicle speed is low enough, on a three to one downshift for rapid torque multiplication.

❏ PLANETARY GEAR TRAINS

Automatic transmissions use several simple planetary gearsets tied together to generate the required gear

TABLE 29-2 PLANETARY CONTROL TERMINOLOGY CROSSOVER CHART

Chrysler	Ford	General Motors
Front clutch	Reverse and high clutch	Direct clutch
Rear clutch	Forward clutch	Forward clutch
Front kickdown band	Intermediate band	Intermediate band
Low and reverse rear band	Low and reverse band or clutch	Low and reverse band or clutch
Overrunning clutch	One-way clutch	Low roller clutch

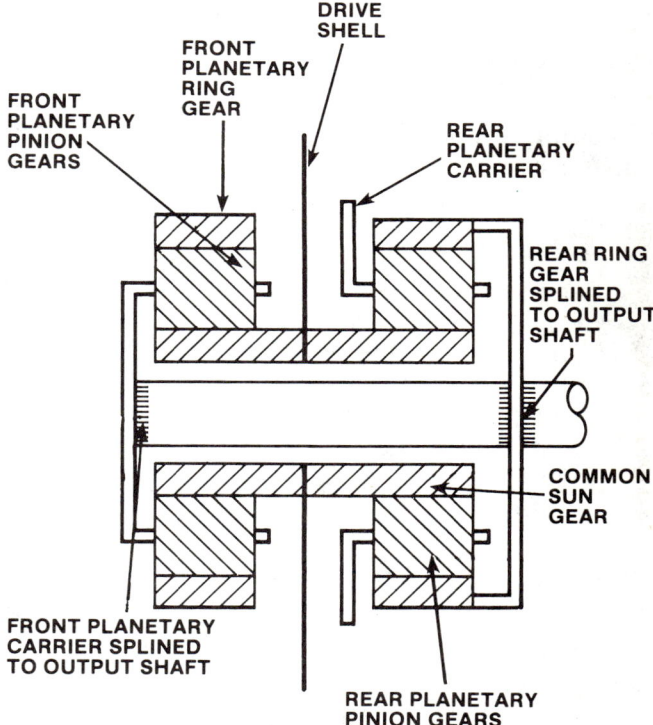

Figure 29-30 Simpson planetary gear train shown without its planetary controls.

ratios and direction needed for optimum performance. When several simple gearsets work as a unit, they are known as a gear train. The most common gear train used in automatic transmissions is the Simpson gear train.

The Simpson gear train consists of two simple planetary gearsets that share a common sun gear. This common sun gear ties the two gearsets together and allows the output of one gearset to become the input of the other (Figure 29-30).

In a Simpson gear train, both the forward ring gear and the common sun gear can be connected to the transmission input shaft using two separate multiple-disc clutches. Although the sun gear rotates around the output shaft, it is not connected to the output shaft. The sun gear and the rear carrier can be held. The sun gear is held stationary by either a band or a multiple-disc clutch, which locks the sun gear to the transmission housing.

In manually selected low gear, the rear carrier is held by either a band or multiple-disc clutch. In both cases, there is also an overrunning clutch that prevents backward rotation of the carrier while allowing forward rotation. When the drive position is selected, the overrunning clutch only holds while the transmission is in low gear.

The forward carrier and the rear ring gear are splined to the transmission output shaft. To make this connection, the output shaft extends through the hollow sun gear to reach the forward carrier.

CHRYSLER TRANSAXLE POWER FLOWS

Chrysler transaxles use a Simpson gear train. The following sections describe power flows through the transaxle.

> **SHOP TALK**
>
> In the following power flows, when a multiple-disc clutch is engaged, two horizontal lines are drawn through the clutch pack. If the horizontal lines are not shown, the clutch assembly is disengaged. An arrow shown over a band indicates band engagement. If the overrunning clutch is circled, it indicates the clutch is engaged.

Drive Range: First Gear; Gear Ratio 2.69:1
Control Units Applied: Rear Clutch; Overrunning Clutch

In Figure 29-31 the turbine shaft drives the engaged rear clutch clockwise, which rotates the front ring gear and planetary pinions in the same direction. The rear planetary pinions attempt to drive the rear planetary carrier in a counterclockwise direction, which causes the overrunning clutch to engage. The front planetary pinions drive the common sun gear counterclockwise. The sun gear drives the rear planetary pinions, ring gear, and output shaft clockwise. The ring gear drives the output shaft and gear, transfer gear and shaft, and final drive gears to move the vehicle forward.

Drive Range: Second Gear; Gear Ratio 1.55:1
Control Units Applied: Rear Clutch; Front (Kickdown) Band

Figure 29-32 illustrates the Simpson gear train with the addition of the front (kickdown) band, front clutch drum, and drive shell. With the turbine shaft driving the engaged rear clutch, front ring gear, and front planetary pinions clockwise, the front (kickdown) band is applied to hold the common sun gear stationary. The front planetary pinions walk around the held common sun gear, driving the front planetary carrier and output shaft clockwise. The output shaft and gear drive the transfer gear and shaft and final drive gears to move the vehicle forward in second gear.

Drive Range: Third Gear; Gear Ratio 1:1
Control Units Applied: Rear Clutch; Front Clutch

With two control units driving the front planetary gearset (Figure 29-33), a direct drive results from the turbine shaft to the output shaft. The rear clutch drives the front ring gear clockwise. The clockwise rotation of the ring gear drives the planetary pinions clockwise also. The engaged front clutch drives the drive shell and common sun gear clockwise. The internal front ring gear is trying to drive the front planetary pinions clockwise while the external sun gear tries to drive the pinions counterclockwise. The result is the front planetary pinions lock and direct drive results. The front planetary carrier drives the transaxle output shaft and gear in the clockwise direction, driving the transfer gear and shaft and final drive to move the vehicle forward.

Reverse Range: Reverse Gear; Gear Ratio 2.10:1
Control Units Applied: Front Clutch and Low and Reverse Rear Band

Clockwise rotation of the turbine shaft is directed through the engaged front clutch and drive shell to the common sun gear. When the front clutch is engaged, the rear section of the common sun gear (Figure

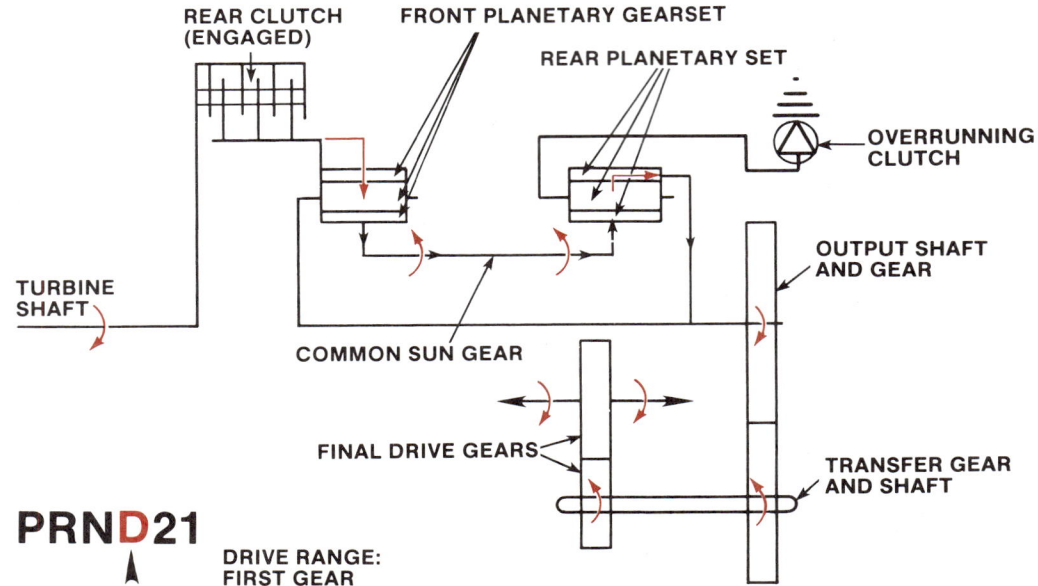

Figure 29-31 In drive range first gear, the rear clutch and overrunning clutch are engaged to drive the transfer gears and final drive assemblies.

Automatic Transmissions and Transaxles

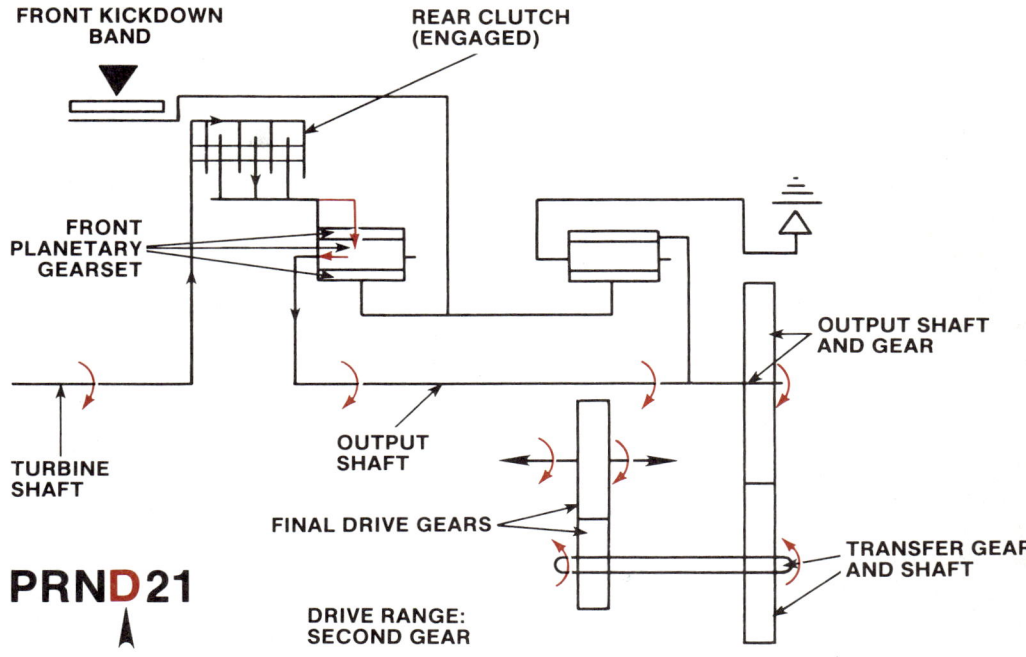

Figure 29-32 In drive range second gear, the rear clutch drives the front planetary gearset and the front kickdown band holds the common sun gear stationary.

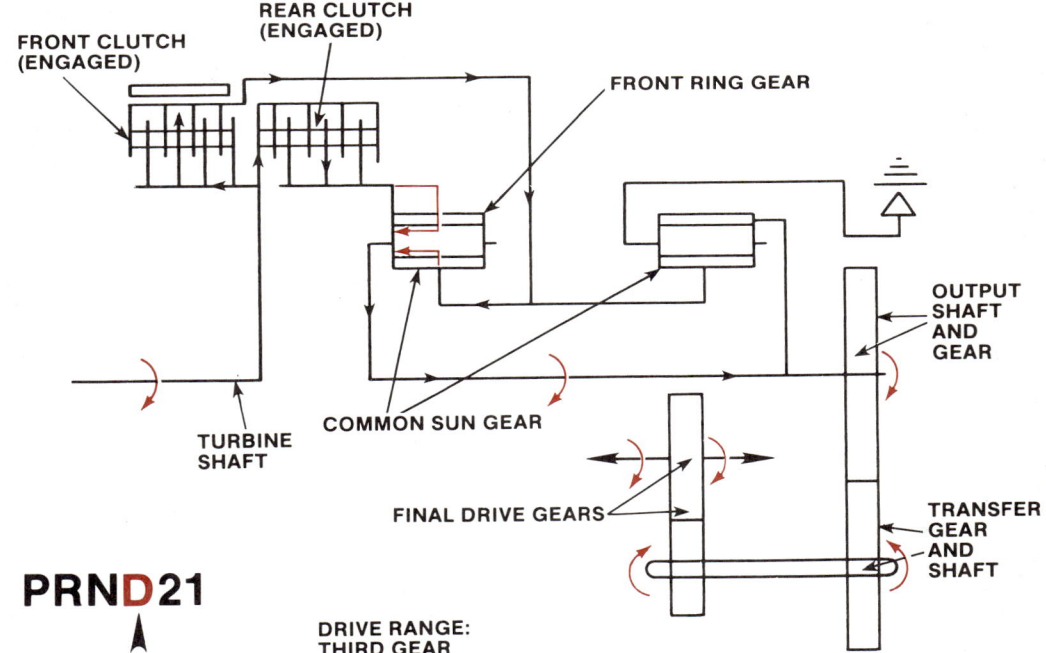

Figure 29-33 The engaged rear clutch drives the front ring gear clockwise. The engaged front clutch drives the common sun gear clockwise. The planetary pinions are locked stationary.

29-34) rotates clockwise, driving the external planetary pinions, ring gear, output shaft and gear counterclockwise. The low and reverse rear band is engaged to hold the rear planetary carrier stationary. To move the vehicle in reverse the rotation of the output shaft drives the transfer gears and shaft, final drive, and driving wheels in reverse.

**Manual Range: Manual Low Gear; Gear Ratio 2.69:1
Control Units Applied: Rear Clutch; Low and Reverse Rear Band; Overrunning Clutch (On Acceleration)**

SHOP TALK

Because there is no automatic upshift in manual low, it can be used for vehicle acceleration or deceleration. On acceleration, the engine drives the vehicle and the overrunning clutch is engaged. On deceleration, the vehicle drives the engine and the overrunning clutch overruns.

In manual low, the engine and engaged rear clutch drive the front ring and planetary pinions clockwise to

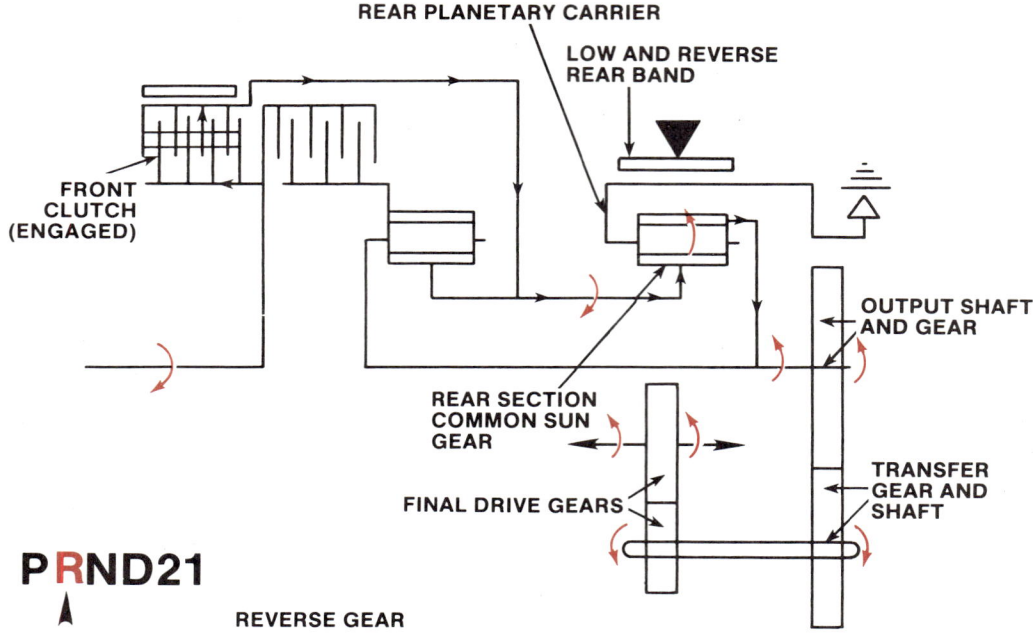

Figure 29-34 The front clutch drives the rear section of the common sun gear. The low-reverse band holds the rear planetary carrier stationary.

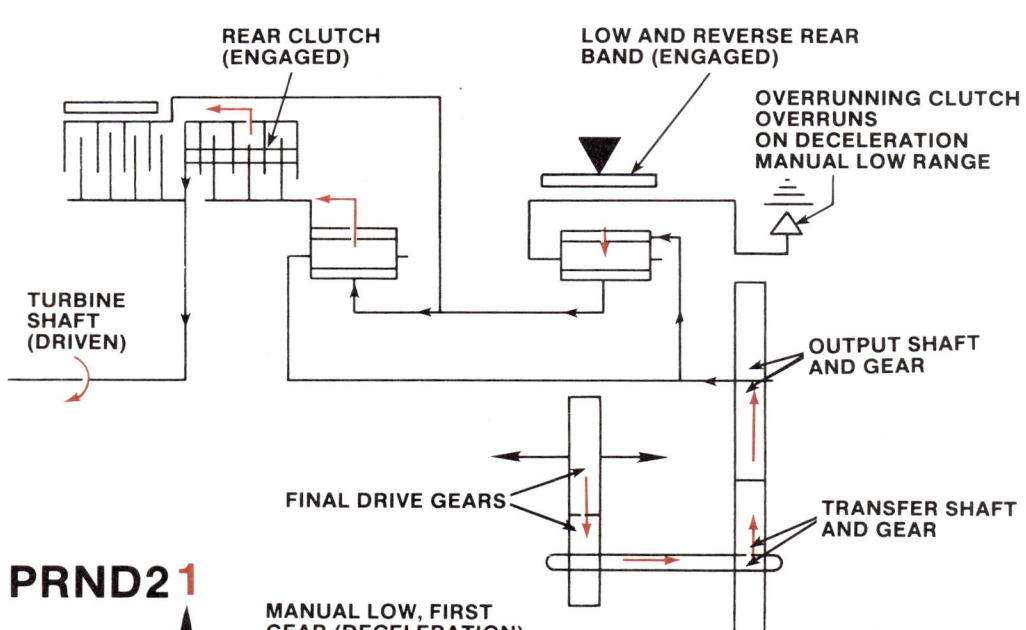

Figure 29-35 In manual low, during deceleration, the rear planetary carrier is held stationary by the low and reverse rear band.

rotate the common sun gear counterclockwise. The sun gear drives the rear planetary pinions, ring gear, output shaft, and gear. The transfer gear and shaft drive the final drive, moving the vehicle forward. The power flow is the same as drive range first gear. The overrunning clutch and low and reverse band keep the rear planetary carrier from turning counterclockwise. The main difference in the manual low range compared to drive range first gear is that the fluid pressures are increased considerably and there is no automatic upshift to second gear.

When the vehicle is operating in manual low range on deceleration, the power flow drives the final drive gears, transfer shaft and gear, and transmission output shaft and gear. The output shaft gear is splined to the output shaft acting as the driver to the Simpson gear train (Figure 29-35.)

The rear ring gear drives the rear planetary pinions, causing them to accelerate as they walk around the common sun gear. Normally, this would cause the overrunning clutch to overrun. However, to prevent overrunning action from taking place, which would place the transmission in neutral, the low and reverse rear band is applied to keep the rear planetary carrier from turning. The rear ring gear drives the rear planetary pinions and common sun gear to rotate the front planetary set, rear clutch, turbine shaft, turbine, and engine. The engine compression slows the vehicle.

Manual Range: Manual Second Gear; Gear Ratio 1.55:1
Control Units Applied: Rear Clutch; Front (Kickdown) Band

The power flow in manual second gear range is the same as in the drive range second gear with the same planetary controls engaged.

☐ GENERAL MOTORS THM 200-4R TRANSMISSION

The turbo hydra-matic (THM) 200-4R transmission is an overdrive transmission that has been used on full-size GM cars since 1982. It is used with V-6 and V-8 gasoline and V-8 diesel engines.

The THM 200-4R transmission has a fully automatic shifting program with a three-element torque converter and lockup clutch, a Simpson planetary gearset, and an overdrive planetary unit (Figure 29-36). The Simpson section planetary controls consist of three multiple-disc clutches, one overrunning clutch, and one band to hold the sun gear stationary. The overdrive planetary unit and its controls are mounted ahead of the Simpson gear train in the transmission housing with two multiple-disc clutches and one overrunning clutch. In this transmission there are five multiple-disc clutches, one band, and two overrunning clutches.

Differences

The THM 200-4R is similar in design and operation to the Chrysler transaxle in some characteristics of planetary power flow and control unit application. The addition of the overdrive unit is a major design and operational difference. Also, the low and reverse clutch assembly replaces the low and reverse rear band. In this application the low and reverse clutch acts as a holding clutch to the rear planetary carrier in reverse and manual low ranges. The rear clutch is replaced by the forward clutch. The forward clutch is engaged in all forward gear ranges. The overrunning clutch is now called the low roller clutch.

THM 200-4R Power Flows

Drive Range: First Gear; Gear Ratio 2.74:1
Control Units Applied: Overdrive Roller Clutch; Forward Clutch; Low Roller Clutch

In Figure 29-37 the turbine shaft turning clockwise drives and locks the overdrive roller clutch and overdrive sun gear, which locks the overdrive planetary gearset in a direct drive. Power flow travels from the overdrive planetary gearset to the forward clutch of the Simpson gear train section. The front ring gear causes the front planetary pinion gears to rotate clockwise on their shafts to drive the sun gear counterclockwise.

The rear section of the sun gear drives the rear planetary pinions, rear ring gear, and output shaft clockwise.

The rear planetary carrier is part of the movable inner race of the low roller clutch. When the rear planetary carrier tries to rotate counterclockwise, the low roller clutch locks, which prevents any movement.

Drive Range: Second Gear; Gear Ratio 1.57:1
Control Units Applied: Overdrive Roller Clutch; Forward Clutch; Intermediate Band

In drive range second gear, the low roller clutch disengages and the transmission upshifts automatically from first to second gear as vehicle speed increases.

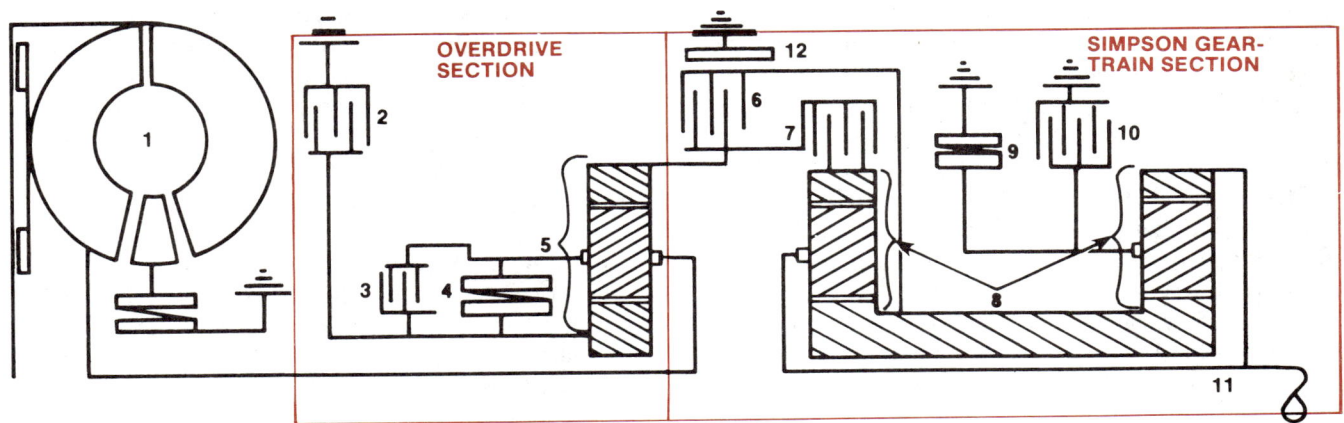

1 TORQUE CONVERTER AND LOCKUP CLUTCH
2 FOURTH CLUTCH
3 OVERRUN CLUTCH
4 OVERDRIVE ROLLER CLUTCH
5 OVERDRIVE PLANETARY GEARSET
6 REVERSE AND HIGH CLUTCH
7 FORWARD CLUTCH
8 SIMPSON PLANETARY GEARSETS
9 LOW ROLLER CLUTCH
10 LOW AND REVERSE CLUTCH
11 OUTPUT SHAFT
12 INTERMEDIATE BAND

Figure 29-36 Schematic of the THM 200-4R with its overdrive and Simpson gear train and controls.

728 Section 6 Automatic Transmissions and Transaxles

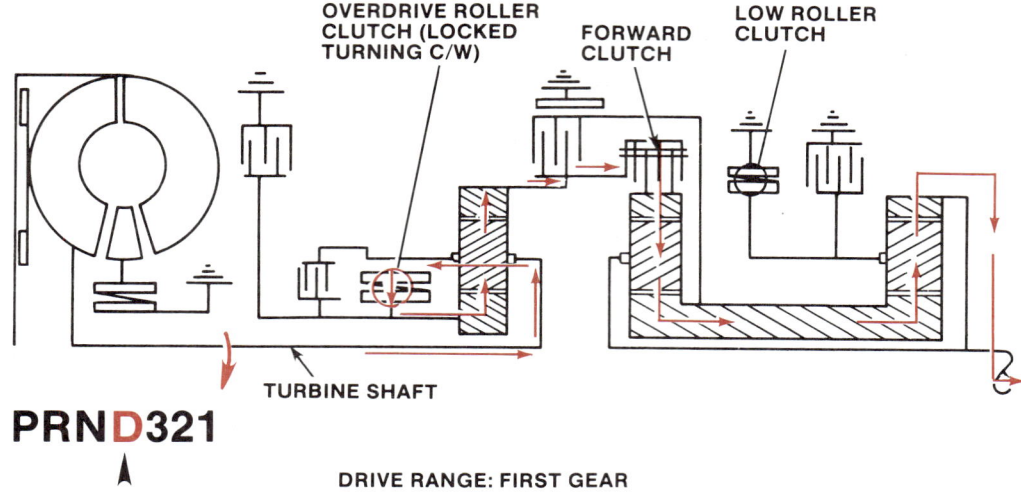

Figure 29-37 In the THM-2004R drive range first gear, the overdrive roller clutch, forward clutch, and low roller clutch are engaged.

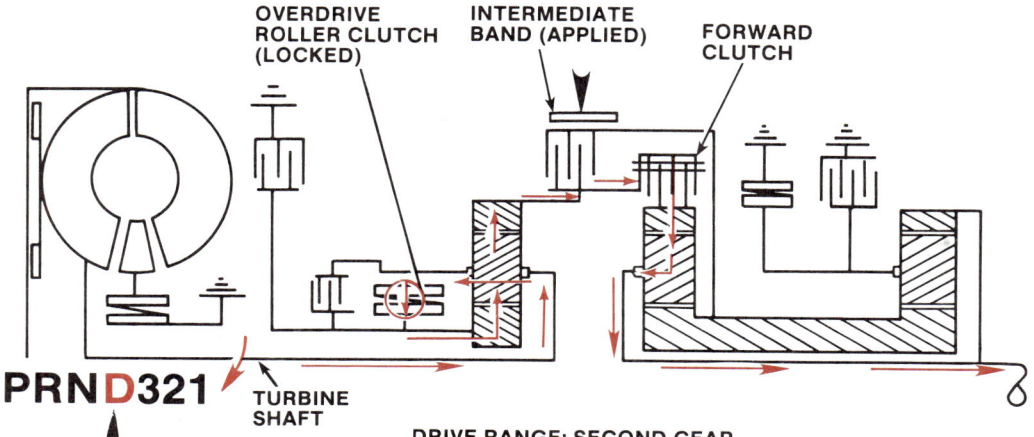

Figure 29-38 In drive range second gear, the intermediate band holds the sun gear stationary.

In Figure 29-38, the overdrive roller clutch and forward clutch remain engaged, and the arrow indicates that the intermediate band is applied.

The power flow through the overdrive planetary carrier locks the overdrive roller clutch to the overdrive sun gear. With the overdrive planetary gearset rotating clockwise in a lock mode, the forward clutch is driven clockwise. The engaged forward clutch drives the front planetary ring gear and planetary pinions clockwise.

The intermediate band is engaged, which keeps the reverse and high clutch drum, drive shell, and sun gear stationary. The sun gear acts as a reaction unit for the planetary pinions to push against as they drive the front planetary carrier. The planetary pinions walk around the held sun gear while pushing against their shafts to drive the front planetary carrier and transmission output shaft clockwise. The power flow leaves the transmission through the front planetary carrier and output shaft. The rear planetary gearset is not used in the drive second gear power flow.

Drive Range: Third Gear; Gear Ratio 1:1
Control Units Applied: Overdrive Roller Clutch; Forward Clutch; Reverse and High Clutch

In third gear the intermediate band is released and the reverse and high clutch engaged. The forward clutch remains engaged to drive the front ring gear clockwise. In the Simpson gear train, the forward, and reverse and high clutches must be applied to get direct drive (Figure 29-39). The overdrive roller clutch is locked to drive the overdrive planetary gearset in direct drive.

The locked overdrive roller clutch drives the overdrive planetary gearset in direct drive. The overdrive planetary gearset drives the engaged forward clutch, front planetary ring gear, and planetary pinions clockwise. At the same time, the reverse and high clutch is engaged to drive the reverse and high clutch drum, drive shell, and common sun gear clockwise. The front ring gear tries to drive the planetary pinions clockwise while the common sun gear tries to drive the planetary pinions counterclockwise. This results in the planetary pinions locking. Since the planetary pinions do not rotate, the whole front planetary gearset revolves as one unit, driving the output shaft clockwise.

The turbo hydra-matic 200-4R transmission is equipped with a lockup torque converter. After the transmission shifts into third gear, the lockup torque

Automatic Transmissions and Transaxles

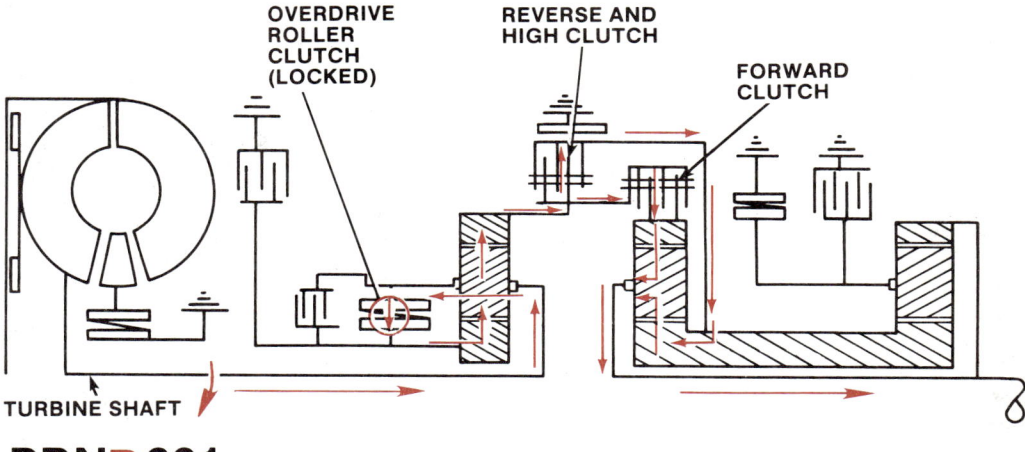

Figure 29-39 In drive range third gear with the reverse and high clutch and forward clutch engaged, the front planetary pinions are locked against rotation.

DRIVE RANGE: THIRD GEAR

converter engages and connects the engine crankshaft to the transmission output shaft.

Drive Range: Overdrive; Gear Ratio 0.667:1
Control Units Applied: Fourth Clutch; Forward Clutch; Reverse and High Clutch

To have overdrive, some additional parts must be added to the THM 200-4R transmission's design.

Overdrive Planetary Gearset and Controls

Located at the front of the Simpson gear train is the overdrive planetary set complete with ring gear, planetary pinions and carrier, and sun gear. The sun gear is driven by the overdrive roller clutch and is kept from rotating by the multiple-disc fourth clutch. When the fourth clutch is engaged, the overdrive sun gear is grounded to the transmission housing.

Overdrive Overrun Clutch

When the gear selector is placed in the manual 3, 2, or 1 position, the overrun multiple-disc clutch is engaged, which prevents the overdrive roller clutch from overrunning.

SHOP TALK

The overdrive roller clutch is engaged in all gear ranges except overdrive. The overdrive planetary carrier is rotating faster than the overdrive sun gear, which is held stationary by the fourth clutch and transmission housing. Therefore, the overdrive roller clutch is unlocked and overrunning in overdrive range.

Overdrive power flow begins with the turbine shaft driving the overdrive planetary carrier. Follow this power flow on Figure 29-40. The turbine shaft drives the overdrive planetary carrier, planetary pinions, and ring gear. The overdrive planetary set has the sun gear held, the planetary carrier as input, and the ring gear output operating in slow overdrive. The overdrive ring gear drives the engaged reverse and high clutch and the forward clutch clockwise.

SHOP TALK

The Simpson gear train is locked in direct drive because both the reverse and high clutch and the forward clutch are engaged. Therefore, the Simpson gear train transfers the overdrive power flow unchanged to the output shaft in the form of an overdrive.

Manual Shifts

Operating the THM 200-4R transmission manually enables the driver to take advantage of engine-assisted deceleration.

Manual Low Range: First Gear; Gear Ratio 2.74:1
Control Units Applied: Forward Clutch; Low and Reverse Clutch (On deceleration the low roller clutch is ineffective.)

When the transmission gear selector lever is placed in the manual low position, the gear train operates the same as in drive range first gear. The difference is that the low and reverse clutch at the rear of the transmission is engaged (Figure 29-41). The forward and low roller clutches in the Simpson section are engaged as well as the overrun clutch in the overdrive section.

Fluid pressure is increased and the hydraulically engaged control units are applied much tighter, which reduces the chance of low and reverse clutch slippage. The low and reverse multiple-disc clutch is engaged to hold the rear planetary carrier stationary.

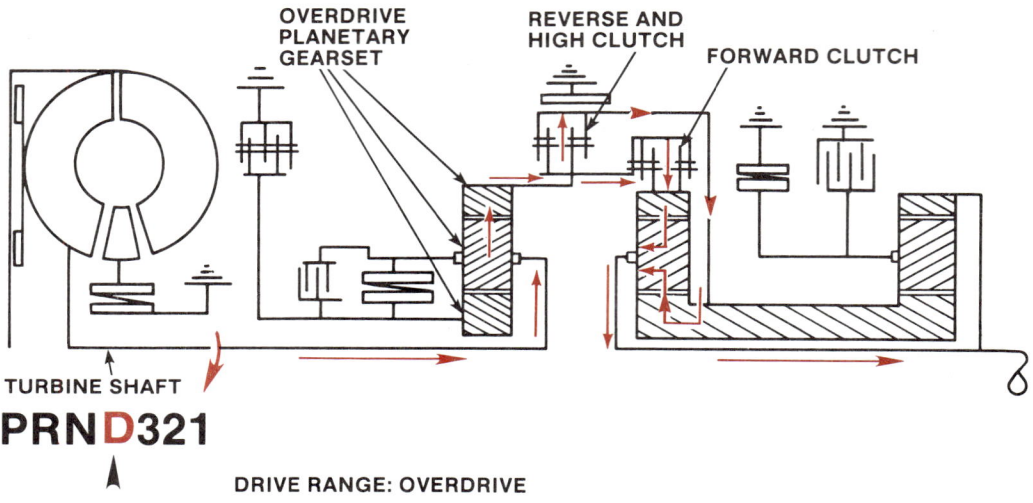

Figure 29-40 The Simpson gear train has no effect on the overdrive gear ratio.

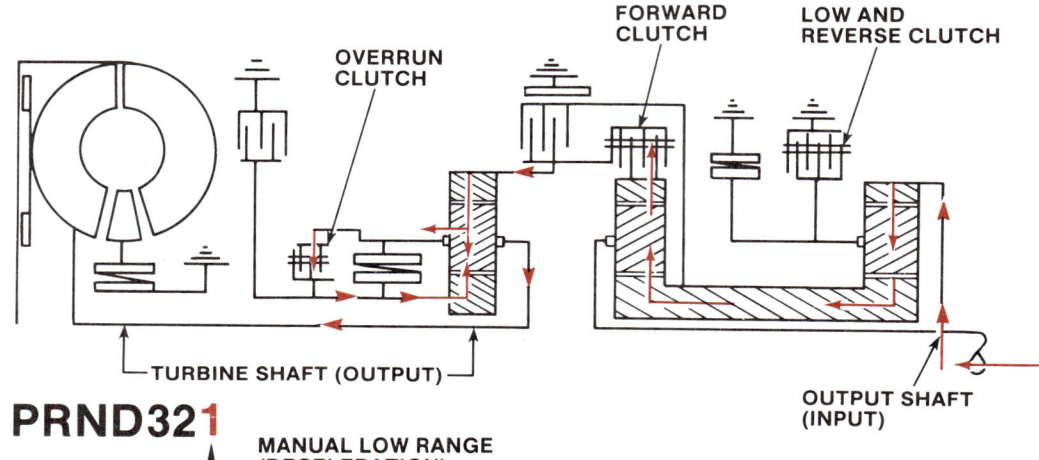

Figure 29-41 In manual low deceleration, the power flow enters the transmission by the output shaft.

In manual low range the transmission does not automatically upshift. Therefore, when the operator's foot is lifted from the throttle, engine-assisted vehicle deceleration takes place.

On deceleration, the normal transmission output shaft becomes the new input shaft. To prevent the rear planetary carrier from overrunning on the low roller clutch, the low and reverse clutch is engaged, which grounds the rear planetary carrier to the transmission housing and prevents rotation. The power flow passes through the Simpson gearset to the overdrive section and engaged overrun clutch, which drives the turbine shaft, torque converter, and engine. The engine compression acts as the braking force to slow the vehicle.

Manual Two Range: Second Gear; Gear Ratio 1.57:1
Control Units Applied: Forward Clutch; Intermediate Band; Overrun Clutch

The gear selector lever can be placed in the manual two position and the vehicle operated in either the acceleration or deceleration mode. When starting from a stop, the transmission begins in drive range first gear and automatically shifts to second gear. In the manual two position, the transmission does not shift beyond second gear until the gear selector lever is moved to a higher gear.

Since the lower roller clutch is not involved in second gear power flow, the Simpson gearset operates the same for manual second as it does for automatic second gear. In the overdrive section the overrun clutch is engaged to connect the overdrive planetary carrier to the overdrive sun gear. The overdrive planetary pinions are locked against rotation. In this range the only gear reduction involved is the Simpson front planetary gearset.

Manual Three Range: Third Gear; Gear Ratio 1:1
Control Units Applied: Forward Clutch; Reverse and High Clutch; Overrun Clutch

In this gear, the transmission starts in drive range first gear and automatically shifts to second gear and, as vehicle speed increases, to third gear. In the manual three position, the transmission does not automatically shift to overdrive.

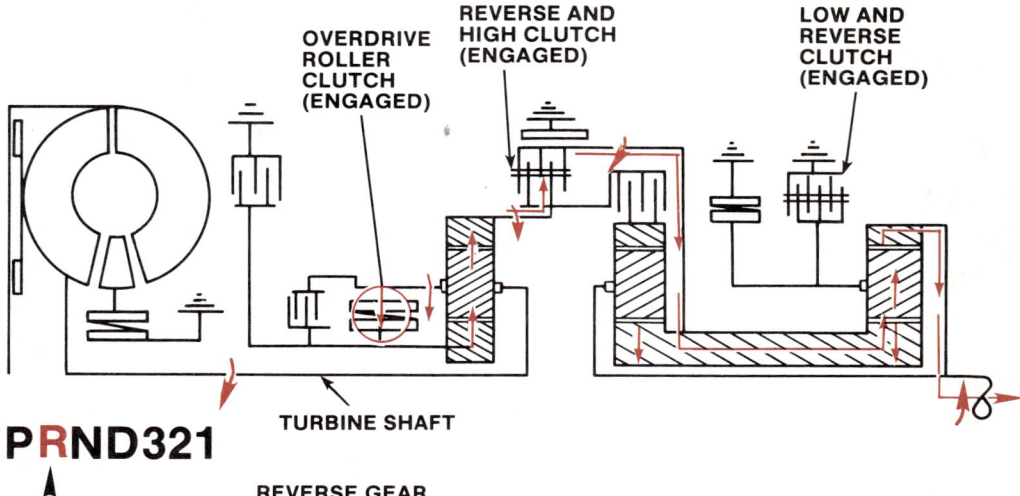

Figure 29-42 Power flow in reverse gear range.

In this range, the overrun clutch engages in the overdrive section, which connects the planetary carrier and sun gear. The overdrive planetary pinions lock against rotation. The Simpson section is in direct drive with both the reverse and high clutch and the forward clutch engaged. In all the manual selections, the engine can be used for accelerating and decelerating.

**Reverse Gear Range: Reverse Gear; Gear Ratio 2.07:1
Control Units Applied: Overdrive Roller Clutch; Reverse and High Clutch; Low and Reverse Clutch**

With the gear selector in reverse, the overdrive roller clutch again locks, preventing planetary pinion rotation. In the Simpson section (Figure 29-42) the engaged reverse and high clutch drives the reverse and high clutch drum, drive shell, and sun gear clockwise. The sun gear drives the rear planetary pinions, ring gear, and output shaft counterclockwise. The low and reverse clutch engages, grounding the rear planetary carrier to the transmission housing.

SHOP TALK

If the low and reverse clutch does not hold the rear planetary carrier stationary, the rear ring gear and output shaft remain stationary. The rear planetary carrier rotates clockwise. With the low and reverse clutch engaged, the rear planetary carrier is held stationary. The sun gear, rotating clockwise, is forced to drive the rear planetary pinions, rear ring gear, and the output shaft counterclockwise, which causes the vehicle to back up.

❑ RAVIGNEAUX GEAR TRAIN

The Ravigneaux gear train, like the Simpson gear train, provides gear reductions, overdrives, direct drive, and reverse combination. It offers the following advantages:

- Torque loading capacity is increased due to greater tooth contact area.
- It is a very compact unit in comparison to the Simpson gear train.
- It can have the large sun gear, planetary carrier, or ring gear as the output member.

Design

The Ravigneaux gear train is designed with one small and one large sun gear (Figure 29-43). There are two sets of planetary pinions—three long and three short—located in the planetary carrier. These planetary pinions revolve around their shafts, which are fastened to a common planetary carrier. The ring gear surrounds the complete assembly, holding the gears in mesh when transmitting heavy loads.

The Ravigneaux gear train is illustrated schematically in Figure 29-44. The small sun gear is meshed with the short planetary pinions, which act as idler gears to drive the long planetary pinions. The short and long

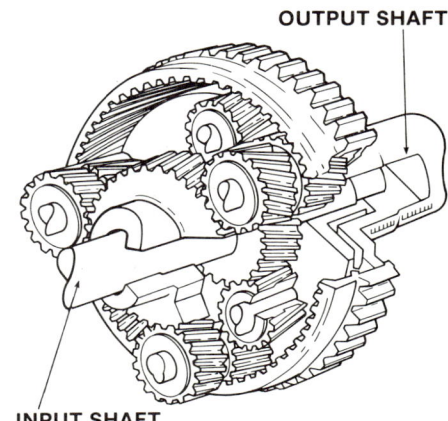

Figure 29-43 Ravigneaux gear trains have large and small sun gears.

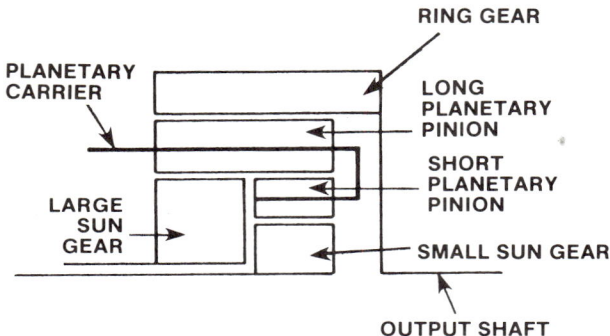

Figure 29-44 Schematic diagram of a Ravigneaux gear train.

planetary pinions rotate on separate shafts that share a common planetary carrier. The long planetary pinions mesh with the short planetary pinions, the large sun gear, and the ring gear.

☐ FORD ATX TRANSAXLE

The Ford ATX transaxle employs a Ravigneaux planetary gear train. It is one of the most compact units installed in domestic automobiles. Major components of the ATX are shown schematically in Figure 29-45. In addition to the Ravigneaux gear train, the ATX offers some unique features. One is the torque converter. It is supplied in three designs: conventional, centrifugal lockup, and split torque converter.

Another characteristic of the ATX is its overrunning clutch. All driving torque passes through the input overrunning clutch and drives the transaxle gear train. The advantage of this design is longer vehicle coastdown when the driver's foot is removed from the throttle and the vehicle decelerates. The vehicle mass driving the transaxle output shaft and planetary gear train is turning faster than the input overrunning clutch, which places the clutch in the overrun mode. As noted in earlier power flows, this overrun operation disconnects the transaxle and drivetrain from the engine compression-assisted deceleration.

In addition to the input overrunning clutch, there are two driving multiple-disc clutches, a holding clutch, and a band controlling the Ravigneaux planetary gear train.

Splitter-Type Torque Converter

The torque converter assembly is designed with a cover and damper assembly (Figure 29-46). The damper assembly is riveted to the inside of the cover. Inside the ring gear is the planetary carrier and planetary pinions. The center of the planetary carrier is splined to the intermediate shaft, which provides mechanical input to the transaxle. Central to the planetary gearset is the sun gear. The sun gear's external teeth mesh with the turbine. Internally, the sun gear is splined to drive the turbine shaft. Because the turbine is driven hydraulically, the turbine and sun gear provide the hydraulic input to the transaxle. The stator and impeller are mechanically driven and take up roles as they do in a conventional torque converter.

Gear Train

The small sun gear of the ATX Ravigneaux gear train is called the low and reverse sun gear. It is meshed with the short planetary pinions. The short planetary pinions, acting as idler gears, are meshed with the long planetary pinions. The short and long planetary pinions rotate on their own shafts sharing the planetary carrier.

In the ATX transaxle, the planetary carrier is the output member of the Ravigneaux gear train driving the final drive gear assembly. The long planetary pinions are meshed with the large sun gear known as the

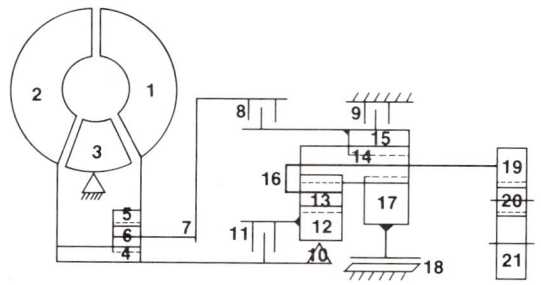

1 IMPELLER
2 TURBINE
3 STATOR
4 SPLITTER SUN GEAR
5 SPLITTER RING GEAR
6 SPLITTER PLANETARY PINIONS AND PLANETARY CARRIER
7 INTERMEDIATE SHAFT
8 INTERMEDIATE CLUTCH
9 REVERSE CLUTCH
10 INPUT ONE-WAY CLUTCH
11 DIRECT CLUTCH
12 LOW AND REVERSE SUN GEAR
13 SMALL PLANETARY PINIONS
14 LONG PLANETARY PINIONS
15 RING GEAR
16 PLANETARY CARRIER
17 FORWARD SUN GEAR
18 BAND
19 FINAL DRIVE INPUT GEAR
20 FINAL DRIVE IDLER GEAR
21 OUTPUT GEAR AND DIFFERENTIAL

Figure 29-45 Major parts of the Ford ATX transaxle.

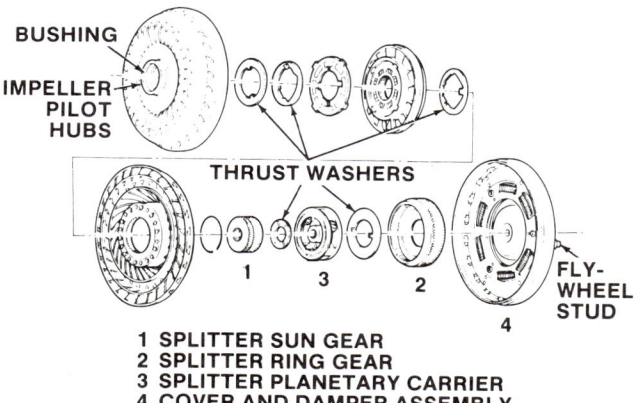

1 SPLITTER SUN GEAR
2 SPLITTER RING GEAR
3 SPLITTER PLANETARY CARRIER
4 COVER AND DAMPER ASSEMBLY

Figure 29-46 ATX torque converter using a splitter-type assembly. *Courtesy of Ford Motor Co.*

forward sun gear. The ring gear surrounds the complete planetary gear train.

> **SHOP TALK**
>
> In this application, the planetary carrier is the gear train output. In some cases the output member can be the ring gear.

Planetary Controls

The direct, intermediate, and reverse clutches are the multiple-disc type. Turbine shaft rotation drives the input one-way clutch and, if engaged, the direct clutch. Remember, a one-way clutch is the same as an overrunning clutch. Either of these planetary controls drives the reverse sun gear clockwise. The direct clutch is also engaged when the vehicle operator selects a manual shift on the gear selector. The direct clutch prevents the input one-way clutch from overrunning on deceleration. The intermediate shaft and engaged intermediate clutch drive the ring gear in drive range two and manual two selections, which provides planetary control for either acceleration or deceleration. The reverse clutch holds the ring gear stationary. The band holds the forward sun gear stationary. The forward sun gear band becomes the reaction member for the Ravigneaux gear train in drive range first and second gear ranges.

A summary of the gear train components and their operation is as follows.

- Direct clutch. Connects the turbine shaft with the reverse sun gear in direct drive and manual selections.
- Input one-way clutch. Drives the low and reverse sun gear clockwise as long as the engine is driving.
- Intermediate clutch. Driven by the torque converter planetary carrier to drive the gear train ring gear.
- Reverse clutch. Grounded to the transaxle housing. When engaged it keeps the gear train ring gear stationary.
- Band. Holds the forward sun gear stationary in drive range first and second gears.

Final Drive Assembly

The transaxle output power flow passes through a network of gears called the final drive assembly (Figure 29-47).

The Ravigneaux gear train planetary carrier drives the input gear, idler gear, and output ring gear. Riveted to the output ring gear is the differential assembly that drives the drive shafts and wheels (Figure 29-48).

FORD ATX OPERATION

Drive Range: First Gear; Gear Ratio: 2.79:1
Control Units Applied: Input One-Way Clutch; Band

In drive range first gear, the torque converter impeller operates hydraulically to drive the turbine and shaft. The turbine shaft rotation (Figure 29-49) locks the input one-way clutch to drive the low and reverse sun gear clockwise and the short planetary pinions counterclockwise. The short planetary pinions drive the long planetary pinions clockwise.

The applied band holds the forward sun gear, which becomes the reaction member to the long planetary pinions. The long planetary pinions walk around the held forward sun gear, driving the planetary carrier clockwise. The planetary carrier and final drive turn the input gear clockwise, the idler gear counterclockwise, and the output gear and differential assembly clockwise.

Drive Range: Second Gear: Gear Ratio 1.6:1
Control Units Applied: Intermediate Clutch; Band

In drive range second gear, the split torque converter planetary gearset begins mechanical operation. The input to the transaxle is 62% hydraulic and 38% mechanical. The torque converter cover and damper assembly mechanically drive the impeller and ring gear. Vortex flow between the impeller and turbine hydraulically drive the sun gear, which is meshed with the planetary pinions. The ring gear and sun gear drive the planetary pinions and planetary carrier at different speeds.

> **SHOP TALK**
>
> When the vehicle is accelerating, the impeller speed is high and turbine speed low. The torque converter sun gear has a slow input and acts as a rotating reaction unit to the planetary pinions and carrier. The cover and damper assembly drive the impeller and ring gear at engine speed. The torque converter planetary pinions and carrier blend the two speeds into one speed to drive the intermediate shaft. The intermediate shaft (Figure 29-50) drives the engaged intermediate clutch and Ravigneaux ring gear clockwise. The ring gear drives the long planetary pinions and planetary carrier clockwise. The applied band holds the forward sun gear stationary. The long planetary pinions walking around the forward sun gear, drive the planetary carrier and final drive input gear clockwise. The input gear rotates the idler gear to drive the final drive gear and differential clockwise.

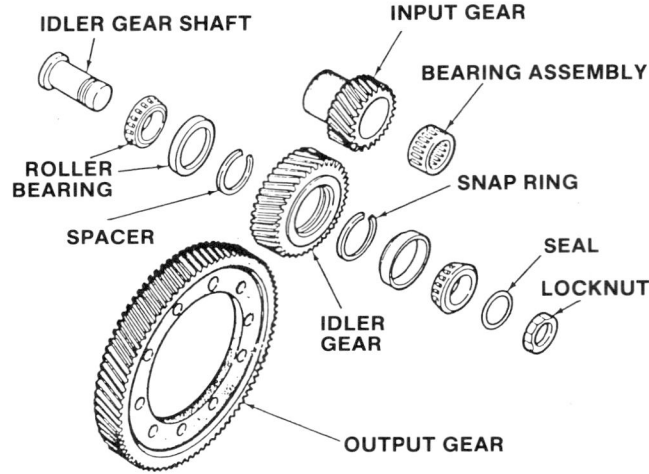

Figure 29-47 ATX transaxle final drive assembly. *Courtesy of Ford Motor Co.*

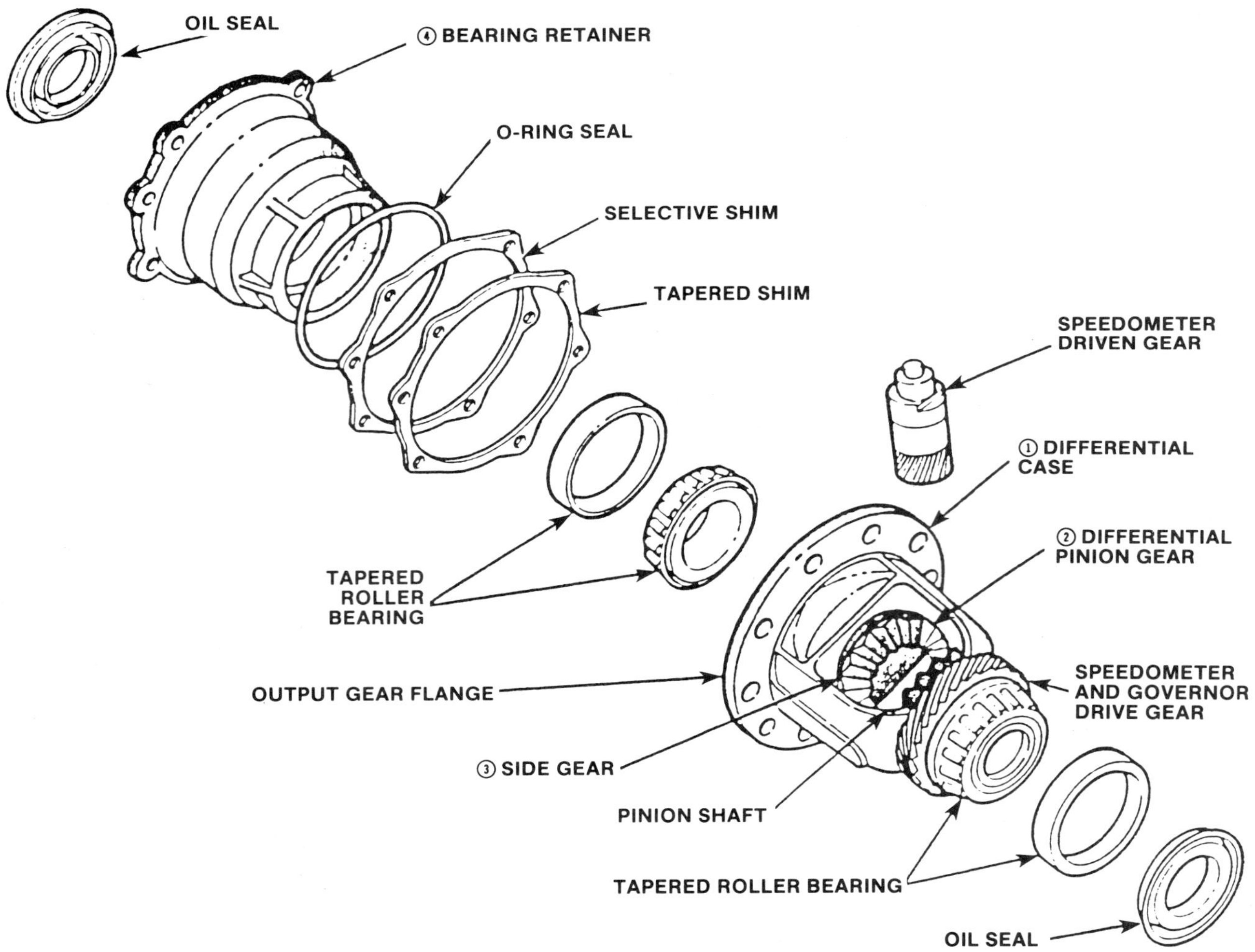

Figure 29-48 The final drive output gear is fastened to the differential case. *Courtesy of Ford Motor Co.*

Automatic Transmissions and Transaxles

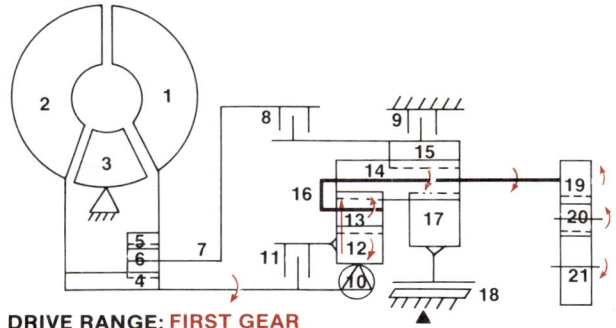

DRIVE RANGE: FIRST GEAR

1 IMPELLER
2 TURBINE
3 STATOR
4 SPLITTER SUN GEAR
5 SPLITTER RING GEAR
6 SPLITTER PLANETARY PINIONS AND PLANETARY CARRIER
7 INTERMEDIATE SHAFT
8 INTERMEDIATE CLUTCH
9 REVERSE CLUTCH
10 INPUT ONE-WAY CLUTCH
11 DIRECT CLUTCH
12 LOW AND REVERSE SUN GEAR
13 SMALL PLANETARY PINIONS
14 LONG PLANETARY PINIONS
15 RING GEAR
16 PLANETARY CARRIER
17 FORWARD SUN GEAR
18 BAND
19 FINAL DRIVE INPUT GEAR
20 FINAL DRIVE IDLER GEAR
21 OUTPUT GEAR AND DIFFERENTIAL

Figure 29-49 In drive range first gear, the input one-way clutch drives the Ravigneaux gear train. The applied band holds the forward sun gear.

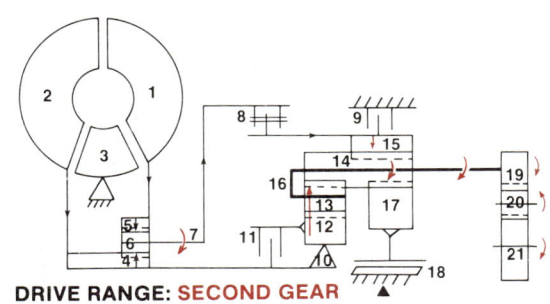

DRIVE RANGE: SECOND GEAR

1 IMPELLER
2 TURBINE
3 STATOR
4 SPLITTER SUN GEAR
5 SPLITTER RING GEAR
6 SPLITTER PLANETARY PINIONS AND PLANETARY CARRIER
7 INTERMEDIATE SHAFT
8 INTERMEDIATE CLUTCH
9 REVERSE CLUTCH
10 INPUT ONE-WAY CLUTCH
11 DIRECT CLUTCH
12 LOW AND REVERSE SUN GEAR
13 SMALL PLANETARY PINIONS
14 LONG PLANETARY PINIONS
15 RING GEAR
16 PLANETARY CARRIER
17 FORWARD SUN GEAR
18 BAND
19 FINAL DRIVE INPUT GEAR
20 FINAL DRIVE IDLER GEAR
21 OUTPUT GEAR AND DIFFERENTIAL

Figure 29-50 In drive range second gear, the intermediate shaft drives the engaged intermediate clutch and ring gear clockwise. The band holds the forward sun gear.

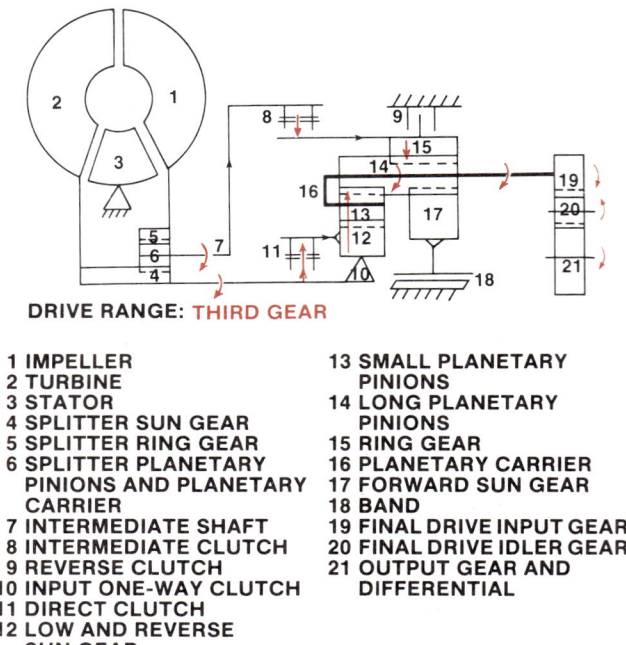

Figure 29-51 In drive range third gear, both the intermediate and direct clutches are engaged.

Drive Range: Third Gear; Gear Ratio 1:1
Control Units Applied: Intermediate Clutch; Direct Clutch

The key to understanding the split torque converter operation in drive range third gear is to realize the torque converter is operating in the coupling stage and there is very little difference in speed between the impeller and turbine. The impeller and ring gear revolve at engine speed to provide mechanical input to the torque converter planetary gearset.

The hydraulic rotary flow drives the turbine and sun gear. Since the turbine sun gear and impeller ring gear are rotating at almost the same speed, they provide a direct drive to the intermediate shaft (Figure 29-51) and engaged intermediate clutch.

The intermediate clutch drives the transaxle ring gear clockwise. The low and reverse sun gear driven by the turbine shaft rotates at transaxle ring gear speed. The Ravigneaux gear train has two inputs driving at the same speed and locking the planetary pinions against rotation. This results in direct drive.

The planetary carrier drives the final drive assembly. A 93% mechanical power flow virtually eliminates the effects of torque converter slippage at the coupling stage.

Drive Range: Reverse Gear; Gear Ratio 1.97:1
Control Units Applied: Reverse Clutch; Direct Clutch; Input One-way Clutch

The input from the torque converter to the transaxle is chiefly hydraulic. The turbine drives the turbine shaft clockwise. The direct clutch and input one-way clutch are engaged, which drives the low and reverse sun gear clockwise. The short planetary pinions turning counterclockwise, drive the long planetary pinions clockwise. The clockwise rotation of the long planetary pinions drives the planetary carrier around the inside of the held ring gear. The planetary carrier drives the final drive input counterclockwise to drive the idler gear clockwise. The final drive gear rotates counterclockwise to drive the vehicle in the reverse direction.

In reverse operation for drive and acceleration, the direct clutch and input one-way clutch are engaged. On deceleration the power flow enters through the final drive and planetary gear train, which causes the input one-way clutch to overrun. This action disconnects the transaxle gear train from engine compression, which results in a form of neutral. Therefore, in reverse range the direct clutch is engaged, which prevents the input one-way clutch from overrunning. The transaxle gear train is connected to the engine compression with the engagement of the direct clutch in reverse gear.

Manual Selections

The problem of deceleration overrun exists whenever the transaxle power flow enters the transaxle through the input one-way clutch. The direct clutch is engaged when the ATX transaxle is in the manual selection #1 position. On deceleration the input one-way clutch is prevented from overrunning by the engaged direct clutch connecting the gear train to the turbine shaft.

Automatic Transmissions and Transaxles

TABLE 29-3 PLANETARY CONTROL UNIT FOR THE FORD ATX TRANSAXLE

	Range and Gear	Band	Direct Clutch	Intermediate Clutch	Reverse Clutch	Input One-Way Clutch
	Park					Applied
	Reverse	Applied			Applied	Applied
	Neutral					Applied
D	1st	Applied				Applied
D	2nd	Applied		Applied		
D	3rd		Applied	Applied		
2	1st	Applied				Applied
2	2nd	Applied		Applied		
1	1st	Applied	Applied			Applied

Courtesy of Ford Motor Co.

Neutral and Park

In transaxles and transmissions covered previously, neutral and park have not been discussed. In conventional automatic transmissions planetary controls are not applied in the neutral and park positions. Transaxles and transmissions equipped with input one-way clutches drive the transaxle gear train when the selector lever is placed in N or P. Although there is turbine shaft rotation, the output shaft does not rotate because the planetary controls are not engaged.

Table 29-3 illustrates the complete clutch and band application chart for all gear ranges.

☐ FORD AUTOMATIC OVERDRIVE TRANSMISSION

The Ford automatic overdrive transmission (AOD) (Figure 29-52) is a rear-wheel-drive unit equipped with four multiple-disc clutches, two one-way clutches, and two bands. The gear train is the Ravigneaux type providing four forward and one reverse gear ratio. The overdrive gear ratio in this transmission is 0.667:1. This ratio decreases vehicle engine speed by approximately one-third rpm while maintaining cruising speed. In some cases with the transmission in overdrive, engine speed is reduced to less than 2000 rpm.

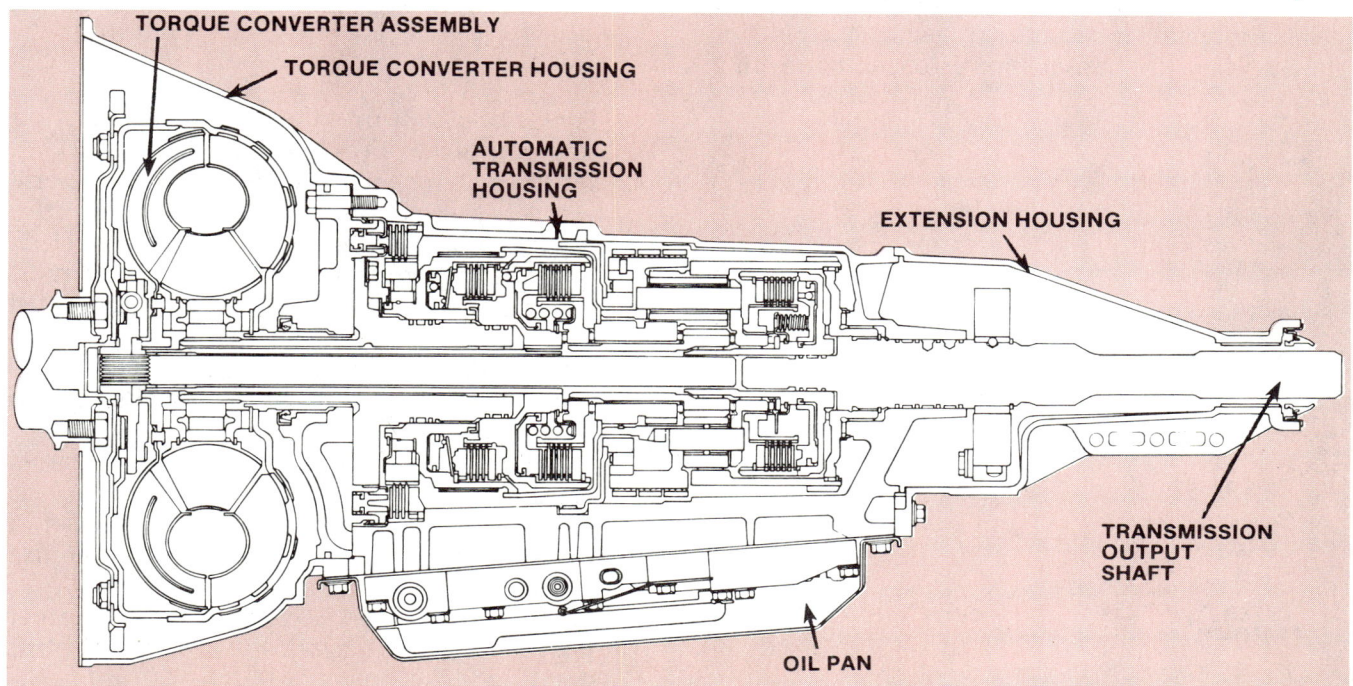

Figure 29-52 The Ford automotive overdrive transmission uses two bands, two one-way clutches, and four multiple-disc clutches. *Courtesy of Ford Motor Co.*

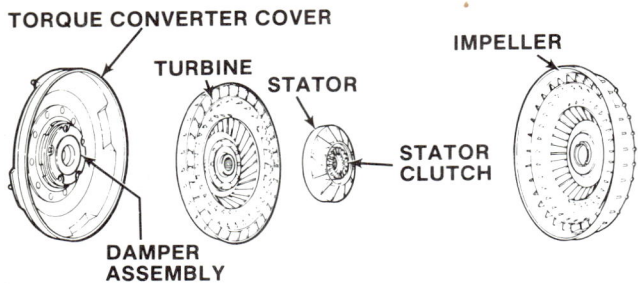

Figure 29-53 The torque converter cover and turbine drive separate the transmission input shafts. *Courtesy of Ford Motor Co.*

Torque Converter

The torque converter (Figure 29-53) is designed for conventional driving in first, second, and reverse gear. Its design is different to accommodate drive range third and overdrive ranges. The AOD transmission has two input shafts driven by the torque converter. The first input shaft is the tubular turbine shaft needed for reverse, drive range first, and second gears. The second input shaft is the solid direct input shaft connecting the torque converter shell to the direct clutch located at the rear of the transmission. The direct input shaft is splined to a reinforced insert in the pilot area of the torque converter shell. When the direct clutch is engaged, the torque converter operates like a lockup torque converter driving the Ravigneaux planetary carrier. The AOD torque converter is designed with a damper assembly to smooth out and cushion engine shocks when the transmission is operating in third gear and overdrive.

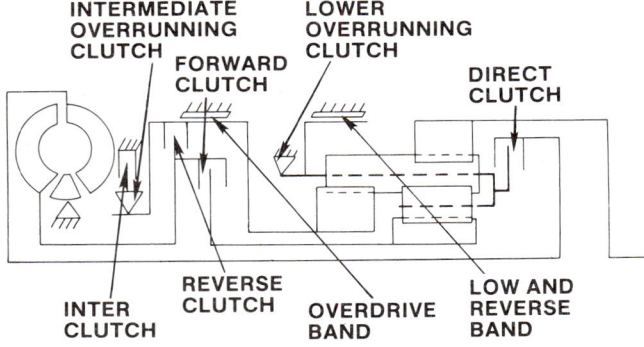

Figure 29-54 Planetary gear train controls for Ford's automatic overdrive transmission.

Planetary Gears

The Ravigneaux planetary gear train multiplies engine torque. The small sun gear is called the forward sun gear, and the large sun gear is known as the reverse sun gear. The long and short planetary pinions and ring gear's names stay the same in the AOD transmission. The planetary pinions rotate on their own shafts while sharing the common planetary carrier. In the AOD the ring gear surrounds the planetary carrier and is the output member connected to the transmission output shaft.

Planetary Controls

As shown in Figure 29-54, the forward sun gear is driven by the turbine shaft and the engaged forward clutch. If the forward clutch is disengaged, the connection between the turbine shaft and forward sun gear is broken. The large reverse sun gear is driven by the engaged reverse clutch. The overdrive band holds the reverse sun gear in overdrive range. The intermediate one-way clutch keeps the reverse sun gear from rotating counterclockwise. The intermediate multiple-disc clutch holds the intermediate one-way clutch and the reverse sun gear in second gear. The low one-way clutch is engaged in drive range first gear while the low and reverse band is engaged in manual low and reverse engagements. The shell of the torque converter drives the direct input shaft, the engaged direct clutch, and the planetary carrier.

In summary the operation of the planetary control components is as follows.

- Forward clutch. Drives the forward sun gear.
- Reverse clutch. Drives the reverse sun gear.
- Intermediate one-way clutch. Keeps the reverse sun gear from turning counterclockwise in drive range second gear on acceleration. On deceleration, the intermediate one-way clutch overruns, which results in no engine compression-assisted deceleration.
- Intermediate multiple-disc clutch. Keeps the reverse sun gear from turning counterclockwise in second gear.
- Overdrive band. Holds the reverse sun gear in overdrive operation.
- Direct clutch. Connects the direct drive shaft to the planetary carrier for direct drive and overdrive operation.
- Low one-way clutch. Keeps the planetary carrier from turning counterclockwise in drive range first gear.
- Low and reverse band. Keeps the planetary carrier stationary in manual low and reverse operation.

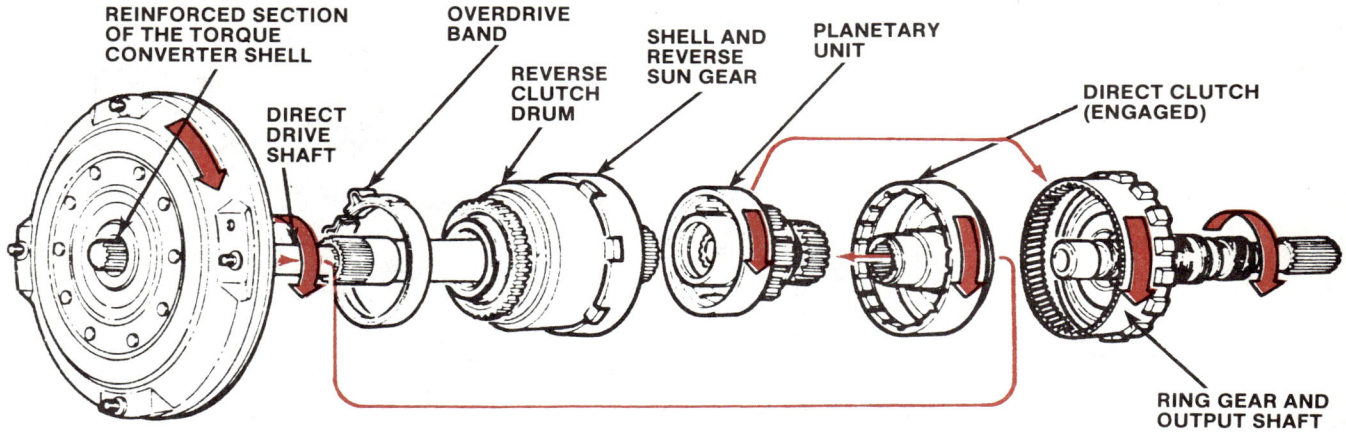

Figure 29-55 The reinforced section of the torque converter shell drives the direct drive shaft and direct clutch. *Courtesy of Ford Motor Co.*

SHOP TALK

In the AOD transmission design, when the torque converter shell rotates at engine speed, the direct drive shaft rotates at the same speed in the same direction to drive the engaged direct clutch. The result is the engine crankshaft is connected to the planetary carrier in a form of lockup clutch.

In overdrive, the direct clutch and overdrive band are applied. The torque converter shell drives the direct drive shaft (Figure 29-55) and engaged direct clutch assembly. The direct clutch drives the Ravigneaux planetary carrier clockwise.

The applied overdrive band holds the reverse clutch drum and reverse sun gear stationary. The planetary carrier driving the long planetary pinions walks around the held reverse sun gear. The long planetary pinions drive the ring gear and output shaft clockwise in a slow overdrive. The engine crankshaft, torque converter shell, and direct drive shaft turn at 0.667 of a turn to complete one turn of the transmission output shaft.

CUSTOMER CARE

Encourage your customers to have the recommended service performed at the recommended times. This usually includes changing the automatic transmission fluid, oil pan filter, and oil pan gasket.

Manual Selections

Not all gear ranges in the AOD transmissions are covered by a manual gear range selection. With the gear selector lever placed in manual #1, the low and reverse band is applied to hold the planetary carrier stationary for vehicle deceleration or acceleration. In #3 selection there is engine-assisted deceleration because the forward and direct multiple-disc clutches are engaged. In the #3 power flow there are no one-way clutches to overrun on deceleration.

☐ HYDRAULIC SYSTEMS

A hydraulic system uses a liquid to perform work. In an automatic transmission, this liquid is automatic transmission fluid (ATF). Automatic transmission fluid is one of the most complex fluids produced by the petroleum industry for the automobile.

ATF performs several jobs. It transmits engine torque as in the torque converter, controls valve body operation, and operates planetary controls such as in multiple-disc clutches, band and servo mechanisms. It also lubricates shaft bushings, thrust washers and bearings, and planetary gear train assemblies. ATF smoothly develops the action between the automatic transmission fluid and multiple-disc clutch friction discs and clutch plates, as well as between rotating drums and stationary bands. It acts as a cooling agent and transfers heat at the transmission cooler assembly while trying to operate the automatic transmission within the desired temperature range. Finally, ATF interacts with all the existing chemicals found in the automatic transmission and those developed as a result of operating extremes.

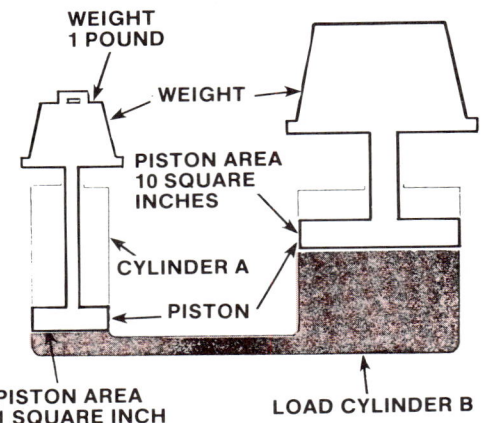

Figure 29-56 Hydraulics can be used to increase work force. *Courtesy of Chrysler Motors*

Hydraulic Principles

An automatic transmission uses ATF fluid pressure to control the action of the planetary gearsets. This fluid pressure is regulated and directed to change gears automatically through the use of various pressure regulators and control valves.

More than 300 years ago, a French scientist named Blaise Pascal discovered the basic principles that pertain to all hydraulic systems. His work resulted in Pascal's Law. It states, "Pressure exerted on a confined liquid or fluid is transmitted undiminished and equally in all directions and acts with equal force on all areas."

Figure 29-56 shows two cylinders that differ in size. In cylinder A the piston has an area of 1 square inch. The area of the piston in cylinder B is 10 square inches. The piston in cylinder A is being moved by 1 pound. A

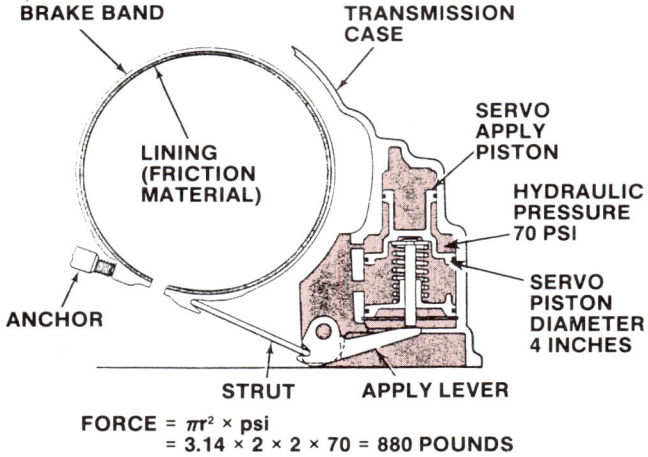

Figure 29-57 Calculating the output force developed by a servo assembly. *Courtesy of Chrysler Motors*

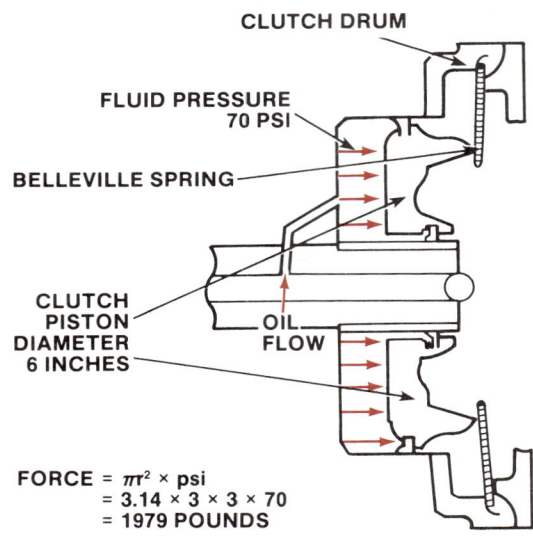

Figure 29-58 Using hydraulics to increase work in a multiple-disc clutch. *Courtesy of Chrysler Motors*

pressure of 1 pound is exerted on every square inch of the piston in cylinder B. The area of piston B is 10 square inches. Total pressure exerted on piston B is $10 \times 1 = 10$ pounds per square inch.

This example shows how fluids can be used to increase work force. Fluids work well in increasing force because they are perfect conductors of pressure. Fluids cannot be compressed. Therefore, when a piston in a cylinder moves ahead and displaces fluid, that fluid is distributed equally on the load piston's surface.

Hydraulics are used to engage planetary gear controls. A typical hydraulic application is the servo assembly (Figure 29-57). The fluid pressure in the servo is 70 psi. The output force exerted by the servo is 880 pounds. Remember this servo output force is further multiplied by the servo mechanical linkage and the natural self-energizing action of the band to stop and hold a planetary member from rotating.

A multiple-disc clutch assembly also makes use of increasing force by using hydraulics (Figure 29-58). If the fluid pressure in the automatic transmission is 70 psi, the force applying the clutch pack is 1979 pounds.

If the clutch assembly is designed with a Belleville spring having a mechanical advantage of 1.25:1, the clutch engagement force would change. The new engagement force would be $1.25 \times 1,979 = 2,474$ pounds, engaging the clutch pack.

To form a complete, working hydraulic system, the following elements are needed: fluid reservoir, pressure source, control valving, and output devices.

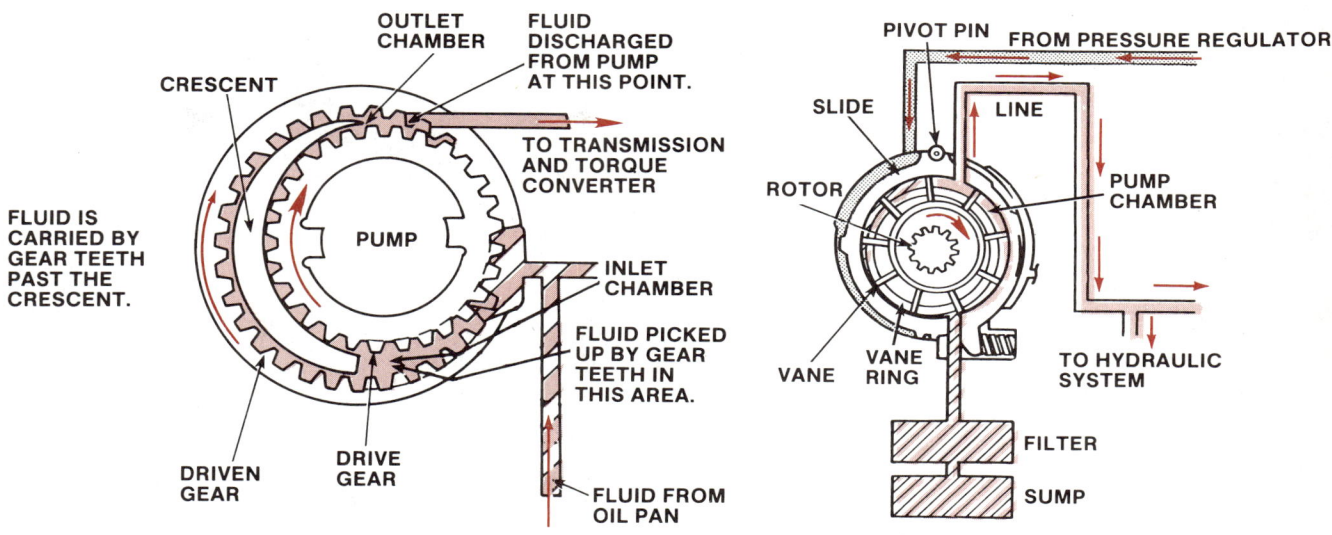

Figure 29-59 Operation of a gear-type pump.

The automatic transmission reservoir is the transmission oil pan. Transmission fluid is drawn from the pan and returned to it. The pressure source in the system is the oil pump. The valve control body contains control valving to regulate or restrict the pressure and flow of fluid within the transmission. Output devices are the servos or clutches operated by hydraulic pressure.

❏ PUMPS

The transmission pump is driven by the torque converter shell at engine speed. The purpose of the pump is to create fluid flow and pressure in the system. Pump pressure is a variable pressure, depending on engine speed from idle to full throttle. At some speeds, pump pressure exceeds transmission requirements and must be controlled by the pressure regulator valve.

Three types of oil pumps are installed in automatic transmissions: the gear, rotor, and vane. The gear type is the most popular (Figure 29-59).

Many people misunderstand the concept of how pumps move liquids. It is often thought that the action of a pump sucks liquid in, but this is not true. What actually happens during pump operation is that the liquid moves from an area of high pressure (atmospheric pressure) to an area of low pressure (below atmospheric pressure).

The spinning pump generates a low pressure area at its inlet chamber. A vent in the transmission admits atmospheric pressure to the transmission oil pan or sump. This higher atmospheric pressure acting on the transmission fluid in the oil pan forces the fluid into the low pressure area of the pump at its inlet chamber. The fluid is picked up by the pump gears, which move it to the pump's outlet chamber. Here the fluid is squeezed out of the pump.

❏ VALVE BODY

The valve body can be best understood as the control center of an automatic transmission (Figure 29-60). The purpose of the valve body is to sense the load on the vehicle's engine and drivetrain and the operator's driving requirements.

The valve body is machined from aluminum or iron castings. Many very precisely machined holes are located in the valve body to accommodate the various valves.

The valve body is made of two or three main parts. Valve bodies and related parts are bolted together and the bolts set to specifications with a torque wrench.

Some valve bodies are bolted directly to the transmission housing so that the valve body becomes a part of the housing assembly. Internally, the valve body has many fluid passages called worm tracks (Figure 29-61).

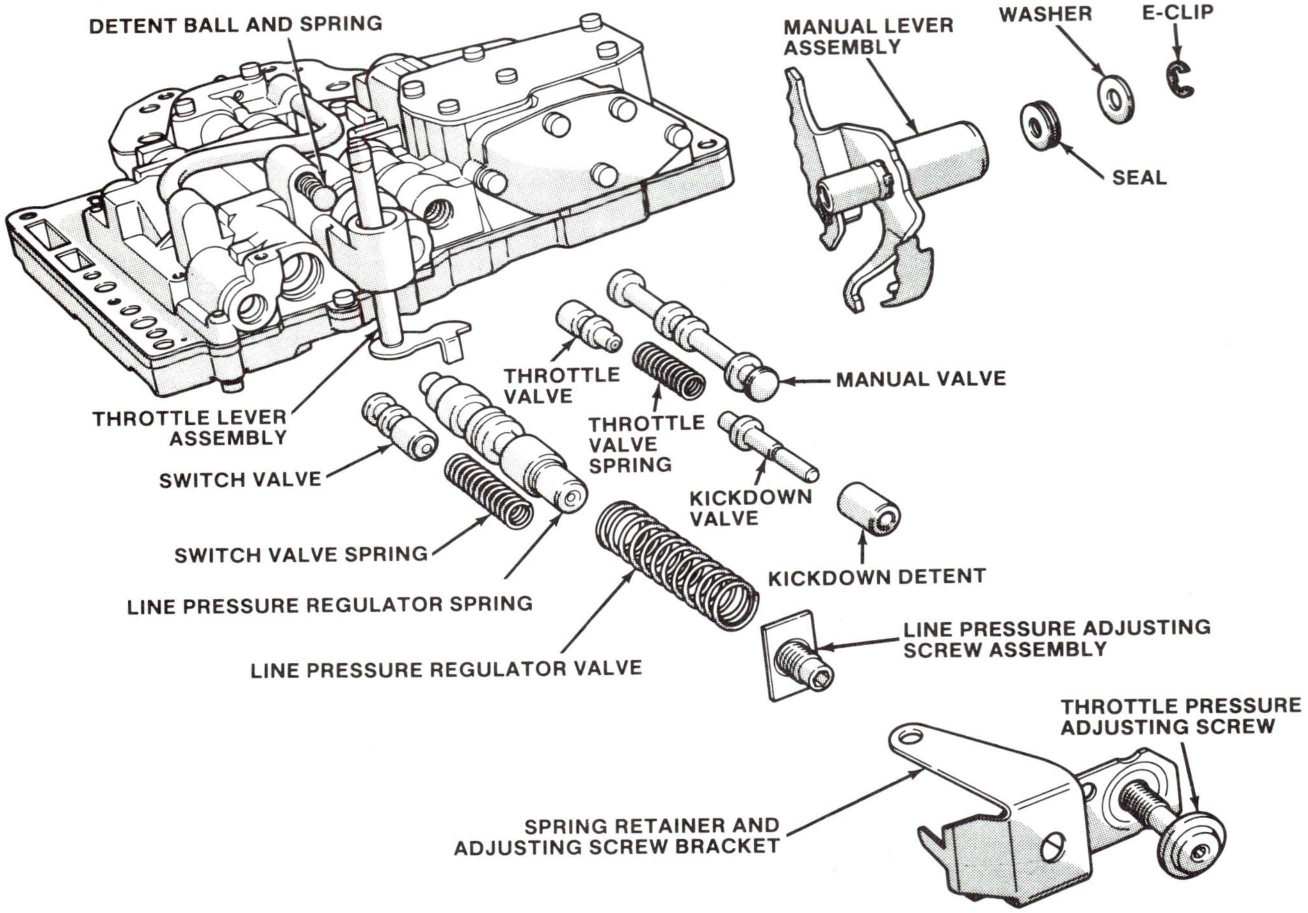

742 Section 6 Automatic Transmissions and Transaxles

Figure 29-60 Typical valve body assembly. *Courtesy of Chrysler Motors*

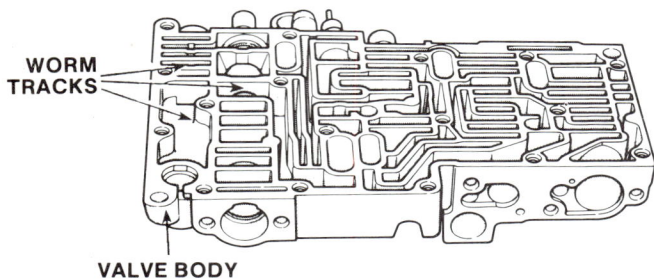

VALVE BODY

Figure 29-61 Worm tracks are the fluid passages in the valve body. *Courtesy of Chrysler Motors*

❑ VALVES

The purpose of a valve is to start, stop, or direct and regulate fluid flow. Generally in most valve bodies, three types of valves are used: check ball, poppet, and, most commonly, the spool.

Check Ball Valve

The check ball valve is a ball that operates on a seat located on the valve body. The check ball operates by having a fluid pressure or manually operated linkage force it against the ball seat to block fluid flow (Figure 29-62). Pressure on the opposite side unseats the

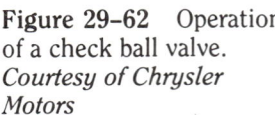

Figure 29-62 Operation of a check ball valve. *Courtesy of Chrysler Motors*

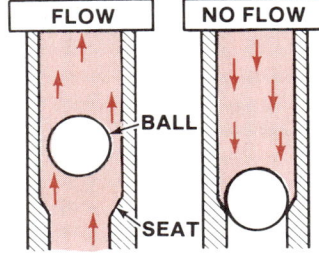

check ball. Check balls and poppet valves can be designed to be normally open, which allows free flow of fluid pressure, or normally closed. This blocks fluid pressure flow.

Check balls can be seated while directing fluid flow. Other applications of the check ball have two seats to check and direct fluid flow from two directions, being seated and unseated by pressures from either source shown in Figure 29-63.

Pressure Relief Valve

Check ball valves can be used as pressure relief valves to relieve excessive fluid pressure. The check ball is held against its seat by spring tension that is stronger than the fluid pressure. When the fluid pressure overcomes the spring tension, the check ball is

Automatic Transmissions and Transaxles

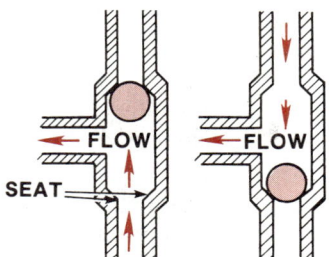

Figure 29-63 Check ball valve operating with two seats. *Courtesy of Chrysler Motors*

forced off its seat, which relieves excess pressure. As soon as the opposing fluid pressure is relieved, the spring tension forces the check ball back onto its seat.

Poppet Valve

A poppet valve (Figure 29-64) can be a ball or a flat disc. In either case the poppet valve acts to achieve its purpose, which is to block fluid flow. Often the poppet valve has a stem to guide the valve's operation. The stem normally fits into a hole acting as a guide to the valve's opening and closing. Poppet valves tend to pop open and close, hence their name.

Poppet valves close against a valve seat. In some applications fluid pressure holds the valve closed or seated. When the stem of the poppet valve is pushed, the valve pops open, permitting fluid flow. When the opening force on the stem is released, the poppet valve closes, blocking fluid flow.

Spool Valve

The most frequently used valve in the valve body is the spool valve. A spool valve (Figure 29-65) looks similar to a sewing thread spool. The large circular parts of the valve are called the spools. There are a minimum of two spools per valve. Each spool of the assembly is connected by a stem. The stem is not a precisely machined part of the valve. Adjoining spools and the valve stem form a space called the valley. Valleys form a fluid pressure chamber between the spools and valve body bore. Fluid flow can be directed into other passages depending on the spool valve and valve body design.

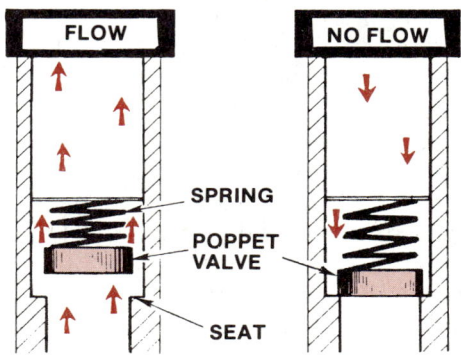

Figure 29-64 Typical poppet valve operation. *Courtesy of Chrysler Motors*

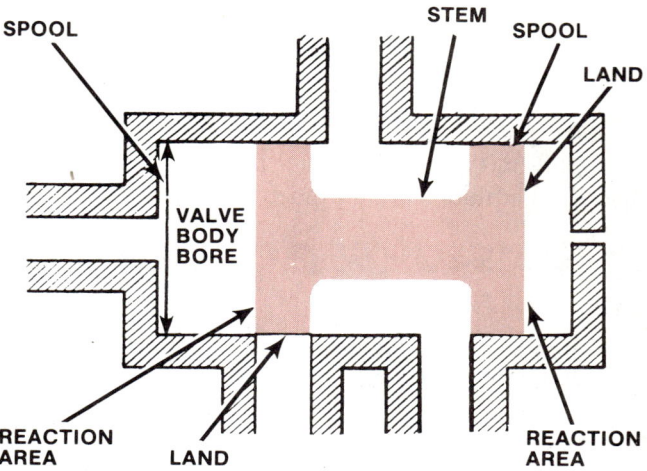

Figure 29-65 Components of a spool valve assembly. *Courtesy of Chrysler Motors*

Precisely machined around the periphery of each valve spool is the valve land. The land is the part of the spool valve assembly that rides on a very thin film of fluid in the valve body bore. The land must be treated very carefully because any damage, even a small score or scratch, can impair smooth valve operation. As the spool valve moves, the land covers (closes) or uncovers (opens) ports in the valve body.

The vertical part of each spool valve forms an area called the reaction area. Forces acting against the reaction area to move the spool valve (Figure 29-66) include spring tension, fluid pressure, or mechanical linkage.

All valve bodies are designed with ports to support spool valve operation. Each spool valve has a fluid inlet port. Aligning with the spool valve's valley, but not

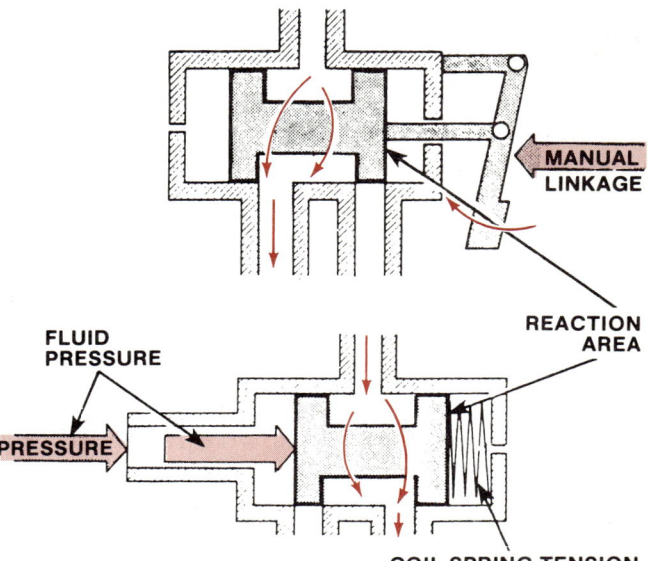

Figure 29-66 Forces acting on the reaction area of the spool valve can be mechanical linkage, spring tension, or fluid pressure. *Courtesy of Chrysler Motors*

necessarily in direct alignment with the inlet port, is the outlet port. If fluid pressure builds excessively, the spool valve moves to open the exhaust port that protects the system's parts. Each spool valve area has a vent to prevent buildup of fluid between the valve assembly and valve body. Since fluids are incompressible, fluid buildup would hinder valve travel.

❑ PRESSURE REGULATOR VALVE

When a spool valve cycles back and forth between the open and the exhaust positions it is called a regulating valve. An automatic transmission uses a positive displacement oil pump. As the pump delivers, fluid pressure rises uncontrollably until the pump stalls from extremely high pressure. This condition is aggravated by high engine speeds that drive the pump faster to deliver more fluid. To prevent this stalling, the pump has a pressure regulator valve located in the valve body. It maintains a basic fluid pressure. A simple pressure regulation circuit is illustrated in Figure 29-67. Fluid pressure flows from the pump to the pressure regulator valve, which is held in position by coil spring tension. Pressure regulator valve movement to the exhaust position is controlled by calibrated coil spring tension.

The three steps of pressure regulation operation are: charging the torque converter, exhausting fluid pressure, and establishing a balanced condition.

When fluid pressure reaches normal baseline pressure (usually about 60 psi), fluid enters at the top of the regulator valve, forcing it down against coil spring tension. The outlet port opens, which permits fluid flow to charge (fill) the torque converter. The torque converter pressure regulator valve is usually a spring-loaded spool type. Torque converter pressure is developed from line pressure at the pressure regulator valve. The torque converter pressure regulator valve has several spools and lands so when different oil pressures are applied, converter pressure varies in proportion to torque requirements. Converter pressure transmits torque and keeps transmission fluid circulating into and out of the torque converter, which reduces the formation of air bubbles and aids cooling. The exception to this is when the torque converter is operating in the lockup mode.

In the second stage, the pressure regulator valve is forced down against spring tension by fluid pressure to uncover the exhaust port. Fluid pressure not needed for transmission operation is exhausted into the pump inlet circuit.

With fluid pressure acting at one end and coil spring tension at the opposite end, the pressure regulator valve takes a balanced position. While the coil spring tension controls pressure, the valve adjusts itself automatically to the pressure, which forces it downward. The pressure regulator valve's new position might have one of the spool's lands partially covering the inlet port.

Increasing Pressure

There are times in the automatic transmission's operation when fluid pressure must be increased above its baseline pressure. This increase is needed to hold bands and clutches more tightly and to raise the point at which shifting takes place. Increasing pressure above normal line pressures allows operational load flexibility, such as when towing trailers.

There are two methods used to monitor vehicle and engine load: vacuum modulation and throttle pressure. A vacuum modulator measures fluctuating engine vacuum to sense the load placed on the engine and drivetrain. The modulator is normally a small canister that is threaded or push fit into the transmission housing. A rubber tube connects the canister to the intake manifold of the engine. The canister itself has two chambers divided by a diaphragm (Figure 29-68). The chamber closest to the transmission housing is open to atmospheric pressure, and the second chamber

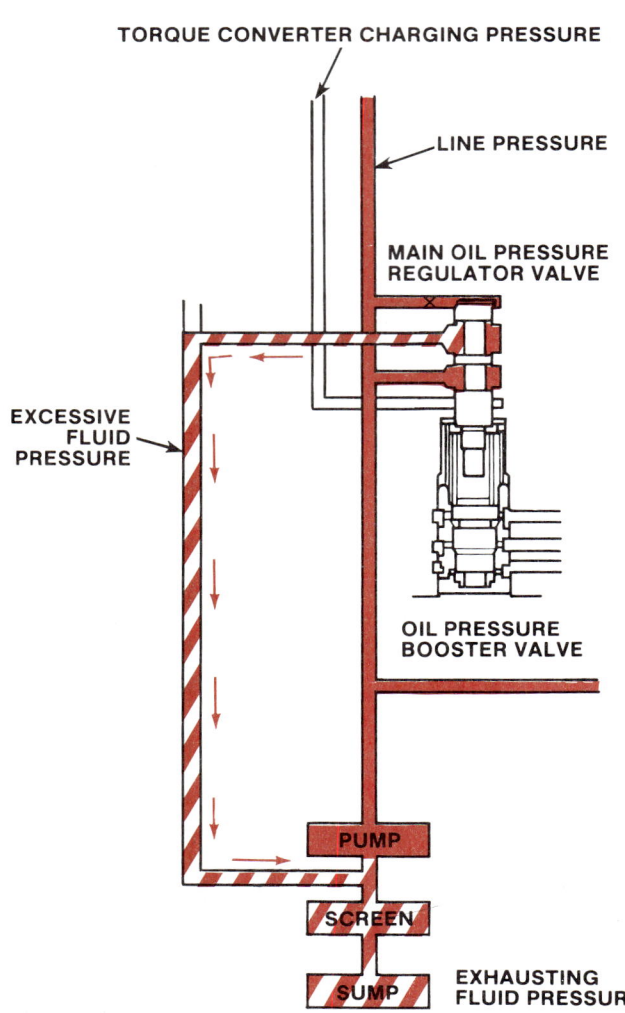

Figure 29-67 Basic pressure regulator circuit. *Courtesy of Ford Motor Co.*

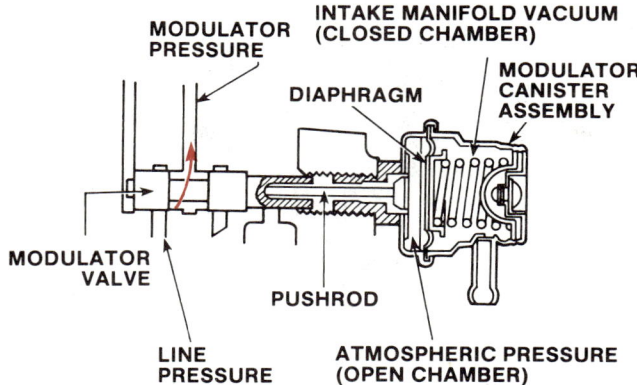

Figure 29-68 A vacuum modulator is a small canister divided into two separate chambers by a diaphragm. *Courtesy of Ford Motor Co.*

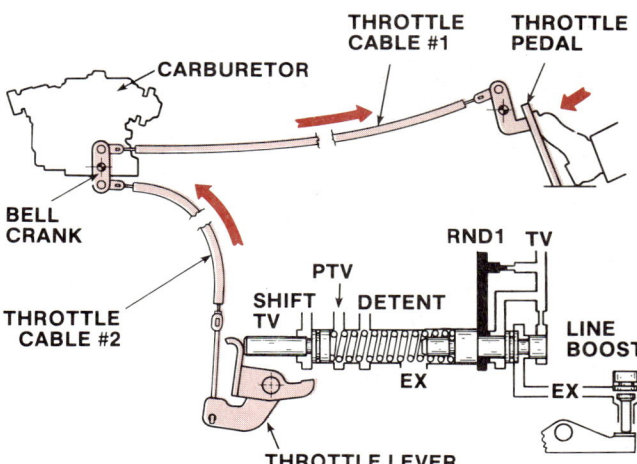

Figure 29-69 Throttle pedal movement is connected to the fuel injection or carburetor bell crank. Bell crank movement is then transferred to the transmission throttle lever by a second throttle cable. *Courtesy of General Motors Corp.*

is closed to atmospheric pressure. The closed chamber contains a coil spring trapped between the diaphragm and the end of the canister. The open chamber holds a pushrod connecting the diaphragm to the modulator valve.

Vacuum Modulator Operation

When a vehicle is placed under a heavy load, the driver opens the throttle. This reduces vacuum in the intake manifold and the closed chamber or the vacuum modulator. With reduced vacuum, the coil spring tension releases to move the diaphragm, pushrod, and modulator valve. The modulator valve opens, allowing line pressure to flow through the modulator valve to the booster valve at the pressure regulator valve. The modulator pressure acting on the booster valve assists the pressure regulator valve coil spring in pushing the regulator valve up against the line pressure at the top of the pressure regulator valve. Line pressure continues to increase until the pressure on the regulator valve overcomes the pressure regulator valve spring tension and modulator (auxiliary) pressure. The pressure regulator valve opens the exhaust port at a new boosted line pressure. This new pressure holds planetary controls tightly to resist slippage and raise automatic shift points.

Throttle Pressure

Vacuum modulators are found on older vehicles without emission controls. The effect of emission control equipment on engine vacuum is such that vacuum modulators cannot be used. Newer vehicles use throttle valve pressure to increase line pressure.

Throttle valve pressure develops when line pressure passes through the throttle valve valley to become throttle pressure. Throttle pedal movement is carried through the throttle linkage to control the operation of the throttle valve (Figure 29-69).

When the pedal is depressed (opened), the throttle valve opens to produce throttle pressure, which is directed to the pressure regulator throttle plug (Figure 29-70). It helps the pressure regulator valve spring hold the pressure regulator valve in position to close the exhaust port. This results in increased pressure.

When the pedal is released (closed), the throttle valve partially closes. This decreases throttle pressure at the throttle valve plug, resulting in a reduction of line pressure.

Relay Valve

The direction of line pressure flow is directed by a relay valve. A relay valve is a spool-type valve with several spools, lands, and reaction areas. It is held in one position in the valve body bore by coil spring tension, auxiliary fluid pressure, or a mechanical force. Auxiliary fluid pressure or mechanical force can oppose coil spring tension to move the relay valve to a new position. In the new position the valley of the relay valve aligns with interconnecting ports. Fluid pressure flows from an inlet port across the relay valve valley to the outlet port. When a relay valve is in one position, it blocks fluid flow. When moved to an alternative position, fluid is directed through to the outlet port.

Shift Valve

One application of the relay valve is a shift valve. A shift valve usually operates in one of two positions—either downshifted or upshifted. In operation, throttle pressure, which is high, is acting on one reaction area of a shift valve (Figure 29-71). Throttle pressure and light coil spring tension act and hold the valve in the downshifted position. In this position, fluid pressure is blocked from flowing to one of the planetary gear controls.

As vehicle speed increases, a device on the transmission output shaft, called the governor, develops a pressure, called governor pressure. Governor pressure is

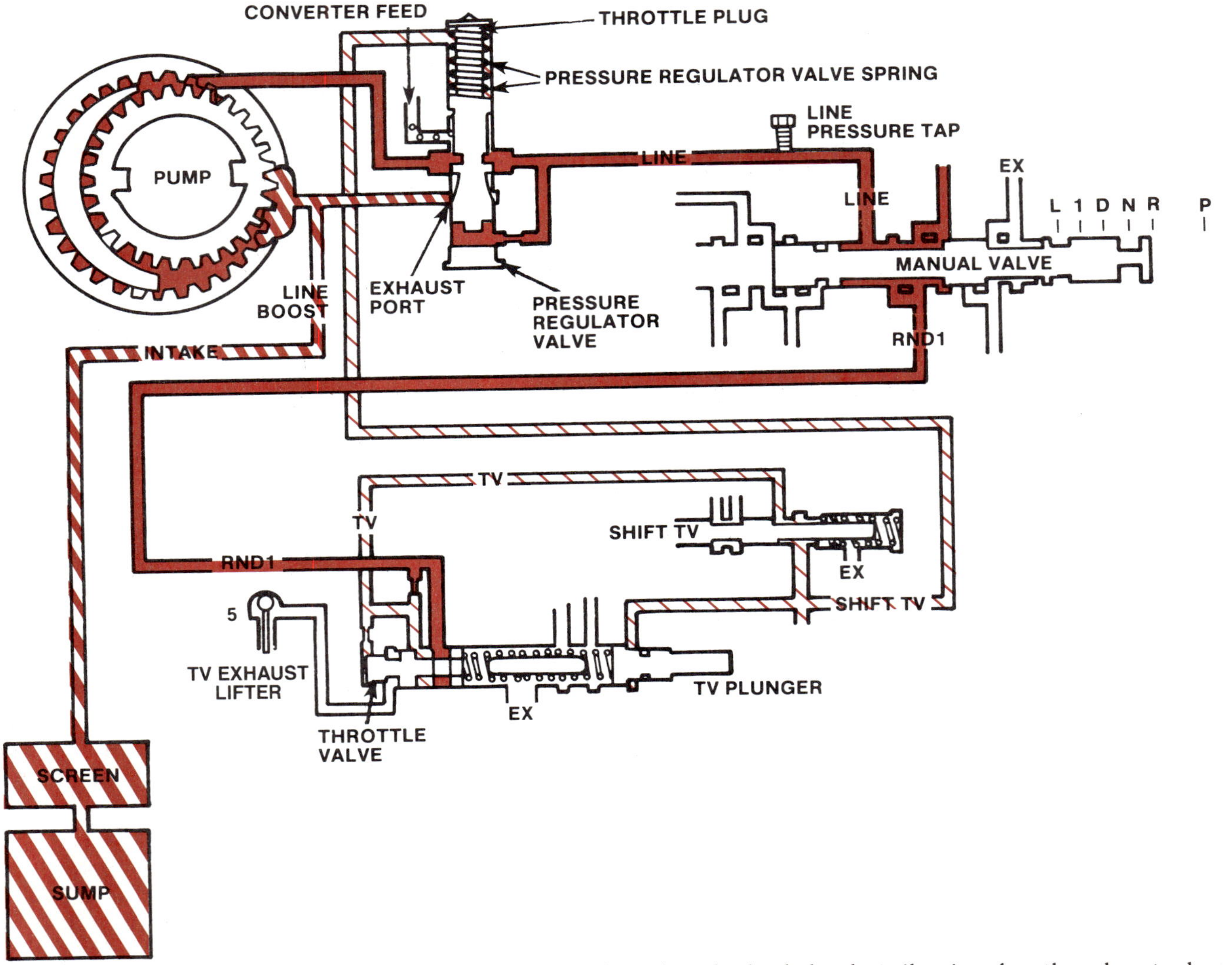

Figure 29-70 Throttle pressure directed to the pressure regulator throttle plug helps the coil spring close the exhaust valve. *Courtesy of General Motors Corp.*

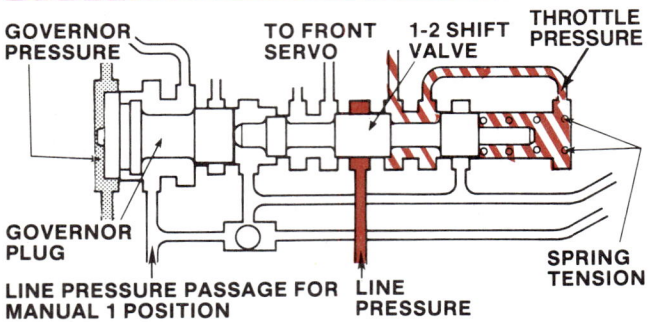

Figure 29-71 A shift valve is a relay valve. Throttle pressure and coil spring tension hold the shift valve in the downshift position. *Courtesy of Chrysler Motors*

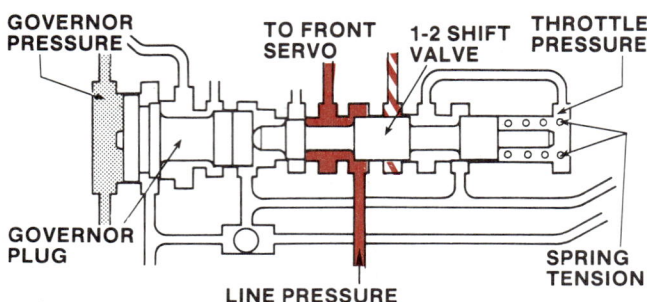

Figure 29-72 Governor pressure moves the shift valve to an upshift position. *Courtesy of Chrysler Motors*

directed to the opposite reaction area of the shift valve. With increasing vehicle speed, governor pressure increases to overcome coil spring tension and throttle pressure. Governor pressure moves the shift valve to the upshifted position. In this position (Figure 29-72) the inlet and outlet ports are in the same valley area of the shift valve. Fluid pressure flows across the shift valve valley, out of the outlet port, and through the connecting worm tracks to engage the planetary controls for the next higher gear.

If the vehicle operator pushes down on the throttle pedal, the throttle valve opens wider and throttle pressure increases. Throttle pressure is higher than gover-

Automatic Transmissions and Transaxles   747

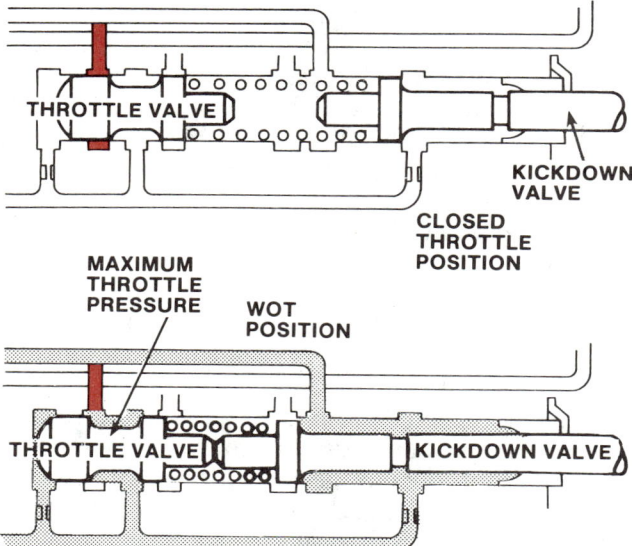

Figure 29-73 A kickdown valve is used to assist the throttle valve in making fast, smooth downshifts at WOT. *Courtesy of Chrysler Motors*

nor pressure. The high throttle pressure and coil spring tension force the shift valve to move to the downshifted position against governor pressure. The transmission automatically downshifts to the next lower gear. The shift valve blocks fluid pressure at the inlet port, which prevents the planetary controls from operating for an upshift. The automatic downshifting of the transmission is often referred to as a passing gear or kickdown. A kickdown valve (Figure 29-73) is often used to generate additional kickdown pressure from line pressure. This ensures that the downshift is made quickly and positively.

Manual Valve

The manual valve is a spool valve operated manually by the vehicle operator and gear selector linkage. When the operator selects the gear position, the gear selector linkage positions the manual valve in the valve body. The manual valve directs line pressure to the correct combination of circuits, which produces the range desired for the driver's requirements (Figure 29-74).

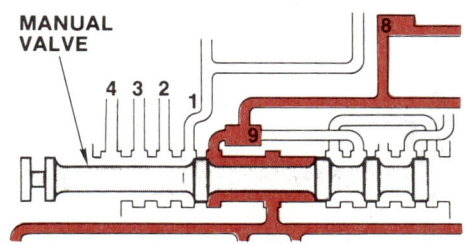

Figure 29-74 The manual valve is operated by the gear selector linkage to direct line pressure to the required circuits needed to produce the selected gear or range of gears. In this case there are four manual outlets. *Courtesy of Chrysler Motors*

For example, if the drive range is selected, the gear selector linkage is placed in a position that allows fluid pressure at the inlet port to flow across the manual valve valley passing through the outlet port to charge the forward circuit. Control areas of the forward circuit are the governor, rear clutch, and accumulator. The various transmission controls and circuitry that drive the vehicle forward make up the forward circuit. If the gear selector is moved to the reverse position, the manual valve is moved to open the reverse inlet and outlet ports to charge the rear servo and front clutch and move the vehicle in reverse.

☐ GOVERNOR ASSEMBLY

The governor assembly is a very important part of the transmission control system (Figure 29-75). The purpose of the governor assembly is to sense vehicle road speed and send a fluid pressure signal to the transmission valve body to either upshift or permit the transmission to downshift. The governor assembly is located on the transmission output shaft. It is influenced by increases and decreases in output shaft speed. When output shaft speed decreases, governor pressure decreases. Governor pressure decreases to a point less than throttle pressure and coil spring tension. As a result, high throttle pressure and coil spring tension force the shift valve to the downshifted position. Fluid inlet passages are now blocked by the 1-2 shift valve land, which stops fluid flow from stroking the 2-3 shift valve and preventing the engagement of the upshift planetary controls. The 1-2 shift valve remains in the downshifted position. With the transmission shift valve in this position, the transmission pulls away from a stop in first gear. As vehicle speed increases, the transmission output shaft speed increases, resulting in more governor pressure to automatically upshift the transmission.

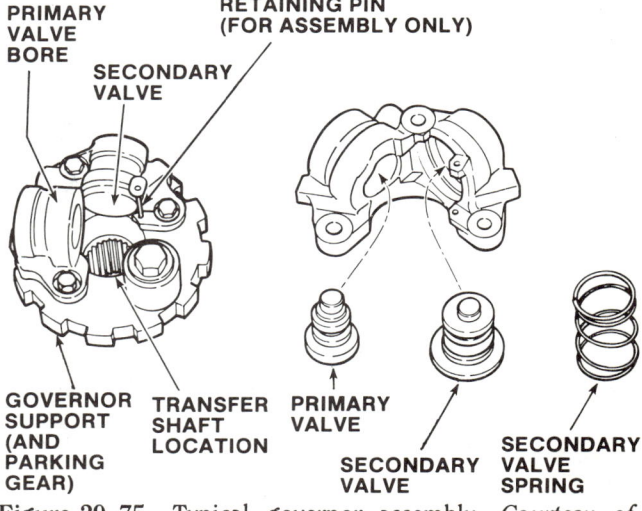

Figure 29-75 Typical governor assembly. *Courtesy of Chrysler Motors*

SHOP TALK

There are two simple rules to remember regarding throttle and governor pressures. First, throttle pressure delays the transmission upshift and forces the downshift. Secondly, governor pressure upshifts the transmission and permits the downshift.

HYDRAULIC CIRCUITS

To provide a practical review of the valve body's operation, the following sections examine the three-speed transaxle with computer-controlled lockup torque converter that is installed in Chrysler front-wheel-drive vehicles. This transaxle and valve body is not highly sophisticated, but it is a good example of general, fundamental valve body operation and the control of various fluid pressures. The hydraulic circuits for each gear selector position is explained using flow charts, accompanied by the torque converter's lockup clutch controls and operation along with schematic diagrams of transaxle power flows. The flow charts and transaxle diagrams bring together the hydraulic controls and mechanical operation that combined give transaxle operation.

Preceding the explanation for each flow chart, note the gear range, torque converter mode, planetary controls engaged, approximate vehicle speed, and throttle position. Be sure to read the flow identification and pressure chart to establish the parameters for valve body and transaxle operation.

Gear Range: Neutral and Park
Gear Selector Position: N and P
Throttle Position: 0 to 10 psi (Approximately closed)

Pump pressure leaves the transmission pump and is directed to the pressure regulator valve and manual valve (Figure 29-76). At the pressure regulator valve, pump pressure is regulated to become line pressure. Line pressure enters the pressure regulator valve and leaves as converter pressure, flowing to the switch valve. The switch valve allows line pressure to enter the torque converter. Converter pressure circulates from the switch valve to fill the torque converter and returns to the switch valve to become cooling and lubrication pressure.

From the pressure regulator valve, line pressure flows to the manual valve. From the manual valve, line pressure seats #9 check ball and flows around #8 check ball to stop at the land of the closed throttle valve. Throttle pressure is low because the throttle valve is not open. Line pressure flows to the accumulator to cushion the engagement of the planetary controls when the gear selector is moved to D or R ranges. The assumulator is basically a hydraulic shock absorber designed to absorb the shock of engaging planetary controls.

In neutral, line pressure is established by the pressure regulator valve and flows to the manual valve and throttle valve.

Gear Range: D First Gear
Selector Position: D
Torque Converter Mode: Unlock
Planetary Controls Engaged: Rear Clutch; Overrunning Clutch
Approximate Speed: 8 mph
Throttle Position: Half Throttle

In Figure 29-77, pressure between the manual valve and pressure regulator valve is considered to be line pressure. This line pressure circulates to the switch valve. Since the switch valve is held in the torque converter unlocked position line pressure flows no further.

LINE PRESSURE Beginning at the first manual valve outlet #1, line pressure seats #9 check ball flows past

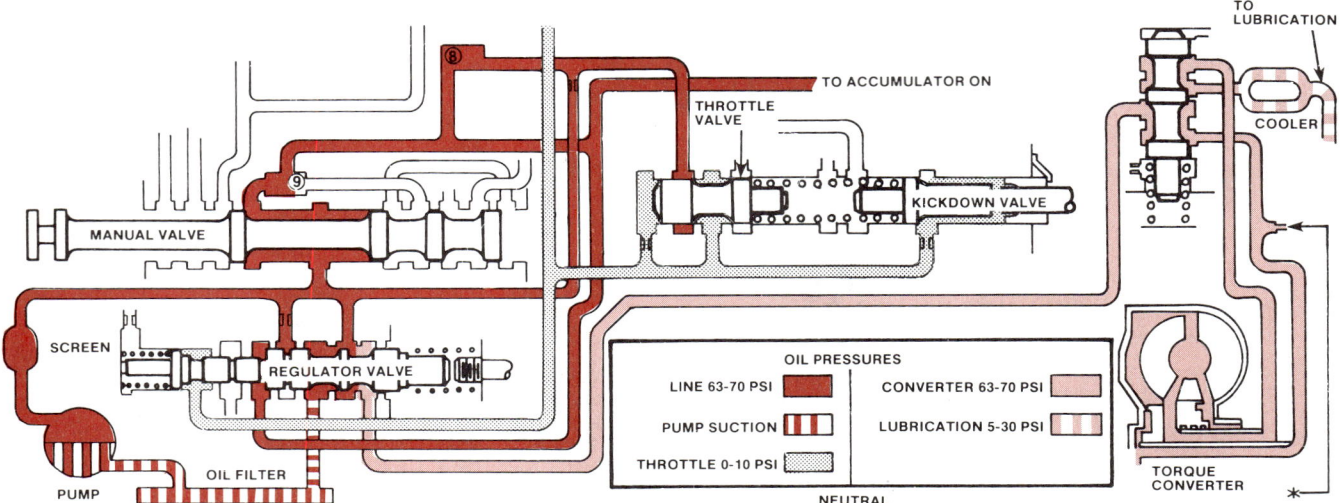

Figure 29-76 Fluid flows in the neutral gear range. *Courtesy of Chrysler Motors*

Automatic Transmissions and Transaxles

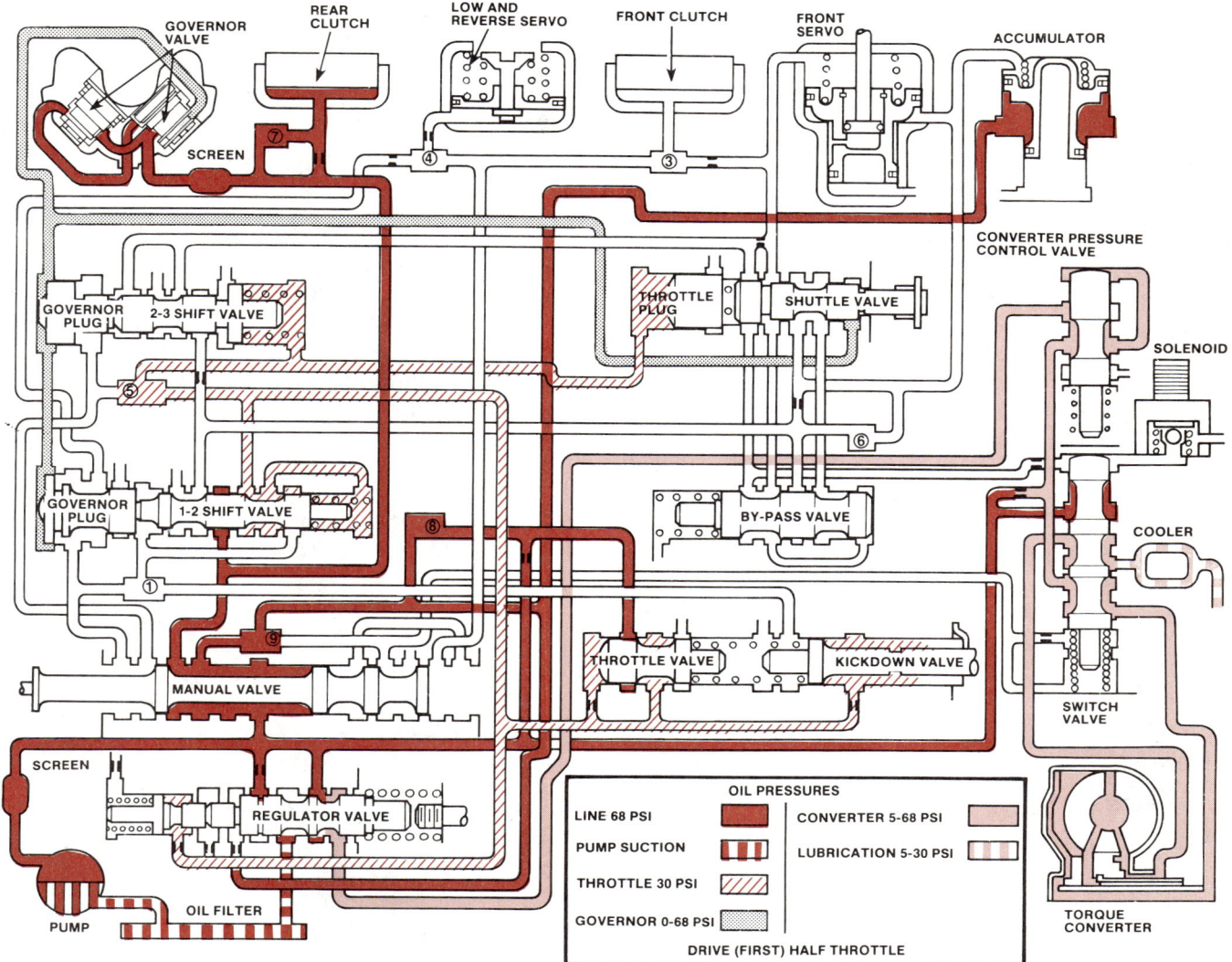

Figure 29-77 In drive range first gear the rear clutch and overrunning clutch are engaged. *Courtesy of Chrysler Motors*

#8 check ball to enter the throttle valve and establish throttle pressure. Line pressure also flows to the pressure regulator valve to regulate pressure. Line pressure strokes the accumulator piston against coil spring tension, cushioning the engagement of the rear clutch.

At outlet port #2 of the manual valve, line pressure charges (fills) the worm track, which engages the rear clutch and flows to the governor assembly. When the rear clutch is engaged and the governor assembly is filled with line pressure, the forward circuit is ready to drive the vehicle forward.

THROTTLE PRESSURE As line pressure passes through the valley of the throttle valve it becomes throttle pressure. Throttle pressure circulates around the kickdown valve valley. With throttle pressure at the kickdown valve, a very quick downshift response to full-throttle operation is provided. Throttle pressure is directed to the pressure regulator throttle plug. It acts on the throttle plug, compressing the throttle plug spring. The result is the pressure regulator valve closes the exhaust port, which results in a line pressure (boost) increase.

Throttle pressure moves to act on the spring end of the 1-2 shift valve. The throttle pressure and coil spring tension work together to hold the shift valve and governor plug in the downshifted position against governor pressure. Throttle pressure passes #5 check ball, which is acting on the spring end of the 2-3 shift valve. From the 2-3 shift valve throttle pressure flows to hold the shuttle valve throttle plug against its stop in the valve body.

GOVERNOR PRESSURE Governor pressure developed from line pressure leaves the governor assembly terminating at the shuttle valve spool land. Governor pressure also acts on the 2-3 and 1-2 shift valve governor plugs. Because the vehicle is traveling at 8 mph, governor pressure is not strong enough to overcome throttle pressure and spring tension at the opposite end of the shift valves. Therefore, the transmission stays downshifted in drive range first gear.

CONVERTER PRESSURE From the pressure regulator valve, converter pressure is directed to the converter pressure control valve. From the converter pressure control valve, converter pressure flows through the switch valve valley and enters the torque converter turbine shaft to keep the lockup piston disengaged. Converter pressure entering between the impeller and turbine fills the torque converter. Converter pressure flows back to the switch valve and enters the cooler to become cooler pressure. When cooler pressure returns to the transmission, it cools and lubricates transmission parts.

Drive Range: D Second Gear
Gear Selector Position: D
Torque Converter Mode: Unlock
Planetary Controls Engaged: Rear Clutch; Front Kickdown Band
Approximate Vehicle Speed: 15 mph
Throttle Position: Half Throttle

Line pressure leaving the area between the pressure regulator valve and manual valve develops throttle pressure and torque converter control pressure.

Referring to the manual valve (Figure 29-78), line pressure leaves the #1 outlet port, seating #9 check ball. Line pressure passing #8 check ball moves to the throttle valve to become throttle valve pressure. From the #1 outlet line pressure also flows to the pressure regulator valve, regulating line pressure. Line pressure from the same circuit flows to the accumulator, opposing line pressure and spring tension. The accumulator cushions the engagement of the intermediate band.

From the #2 manual valve outlet, fluid moves to the upshifted 1-2 shift valve. Line pressure flows to engage the rear clutch, then around the #7 check ball, through the governor screen to the governor assembly.

From the 1-2 shift valve, line pressure circulates to the shuttle valve and by-pass valve through the restriction, or around the #6 check ball to operate the front servo. When the front servo piston strokes in the cyl-

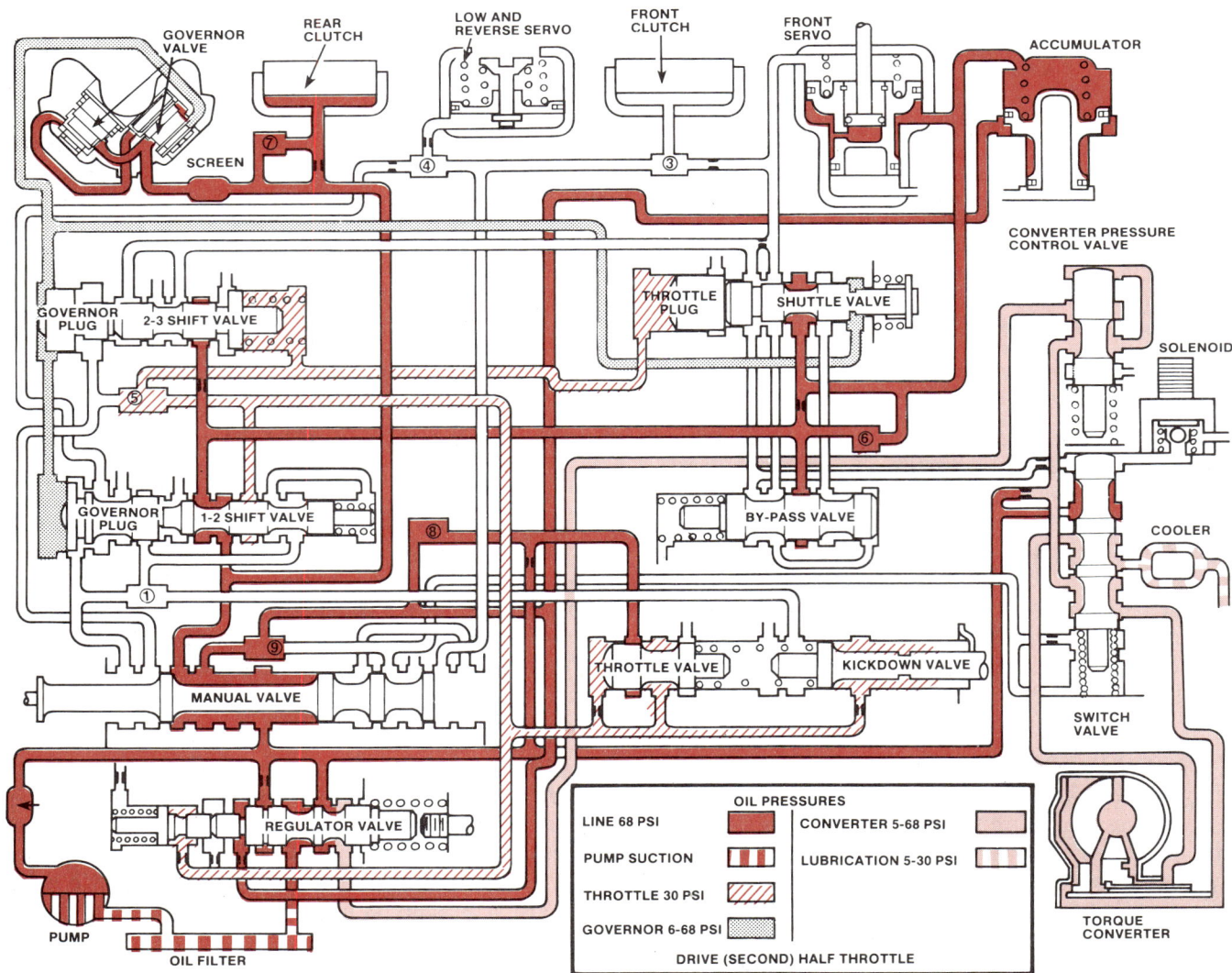

Figure 29-78 In drive range second gear, the rear clutch and front kickdown band are applied. *Courtesy of Chrysler Motors*

inder, the front kickdown band engages around the front clutch drum.

THROTTLE PRESSURE The throttle pedal is in the half-open position, developing throttle pressure, which is directed to the kickdown valve. Throttle pressure is also directed to the throttle plug of the pressure regulator valve. Throttle pressure moving the throttle plug forces it against the throttle plug spring tension. The action of the throttle plug removes some of the opposition to the pressure regulator valve spring, resulting in a boost in line pressure. Throttle pressure moves to the 1-2 shift valve where it is blocked by the upshifted valve's spool land. After seating the #5 check ball, throttle pressure and coil spring tension pushes on the 2-3 shift valve reaction area and moves it to the downshifted position against governor pressure. Throttle pressure leaves the 2-3 shift valve to hold the shuttle valve throttle plug against its seat.

> **SHOP TALK**
>
> In drive range second gear, the 1-2 shift valve is upshifted while the 2-3 shift valve is downshifted.

GOVERNOR PRESSURE Governor pressure leaves the rotating governor assembly and flows to the shuttle valve throttle plug. Governor pressure also acts on the governor plugs of the two shift valves. Vehicle speed and governor pressure are high enough to overcome throttle valve pressure and coil spring tension at the 1-2 shift valve. Governor pressure forces the 1-2 shift valve to move against throttle pressure. Therefore, throttle pressure is blocked from acting on the shift valve reaction area.

CONVERTER PRESSURE Converter pressure flow is the same as in first gear.

Drive Range: D Third Gear
Gear Selector Position: D
Torque Converter Mode: Unlock
Planetary Controls Engaged: Rear Clutch; Front Clutch
Approximate Vehicle Speed: 25 mph
Throttle Position: Half Throttle

Drive range third gear is covered in two parts. The first part explains the hydraulic operation to shift the transmission into third gear. The second part introduces the sensors and controls affiliated with engine computer operation and torque converter lockup clutch control. (To this point, in drive range first and second gears, the torque converter clutch has been unlocked.)

LINE PRESSURE Line pressure between the manual and pressure regulator valves is directed to the throttle valve and switch valve (Figure 29-79). Start at the #1 manual valve outlet where line pressure seats #9 check ball and circulates to the throttle valve. With the throttle valve open, throttle pressure is developed. In this circuit, pump pressure flows to the pressure regulator valve to develop line pressure, which, in this circuit, also operates the accumulator.

From the #2 manual valve outlet, line pressure charges the forward circuit, engages the rear clutch, and enters the governor assembly to produce governor pressure.

Line pressure also flows from the #2 manual valve outlet to circulate around the valley of the upshifted 1-2 shift valve and then around the valley of the 2-3 shift valve to the restriction above the shuttle valve. This restriction biases line pressure to the shuttle and by-pass valves. Line pressure leaves the shuttle and by-pass valve area and moves to the release side of the front servo and the front clutch. The feed line to the front clutch has a restriction that causes pressure to build on the release side of the front servo, which disengages the front kickdown band. Line pressure flowing through the front clutch feed restriction engages the front clutch for third gear direct drive operation.

THROTTLE PRESSURE With throttle valve open, throttle pressure flows to the kickdown valve, throttle plug of the pressure regulator valve, 1-2 and 2-3 shift valves, and the shuttle valve throttle plug. At the 2-3 shift valve, throttle pressure and coil spring tension are opposed by increasing governor pressure.

GOVERNOR PRESSURE Governor pressure leaves the governor to move the shuttle valve, opening line pressure circuits. The shuttle valve's movement buries the coil spring in the hollow shuttle valve throttle plug. The governor pressure has moved the 1-2 and 2-3 shift valves to the upshifted position, directing line pressure to engage the front clutch and hold the front servo released during third gear operation.

Torque Converter Controls and Pressure

The lockup torque converter clutch assembly is controlled by the engine computer. The engine computer energizes the torque converter relay, which sends 12 volts to the lockup solenoid. When the engine computer receives electronic signals from the different sensors confirming the requirements for lockup have been met, lockup clutch engagement begins.

These sensors include an engine coolant sensor, vehicle speed sensor, engine vacuum sensor, and throttle position sensor.

Lockup Relay

The lockup relay is energized when the engine computer grounds the circuit. The lockup relay sends 12 volts to energize the lockup solenoid.

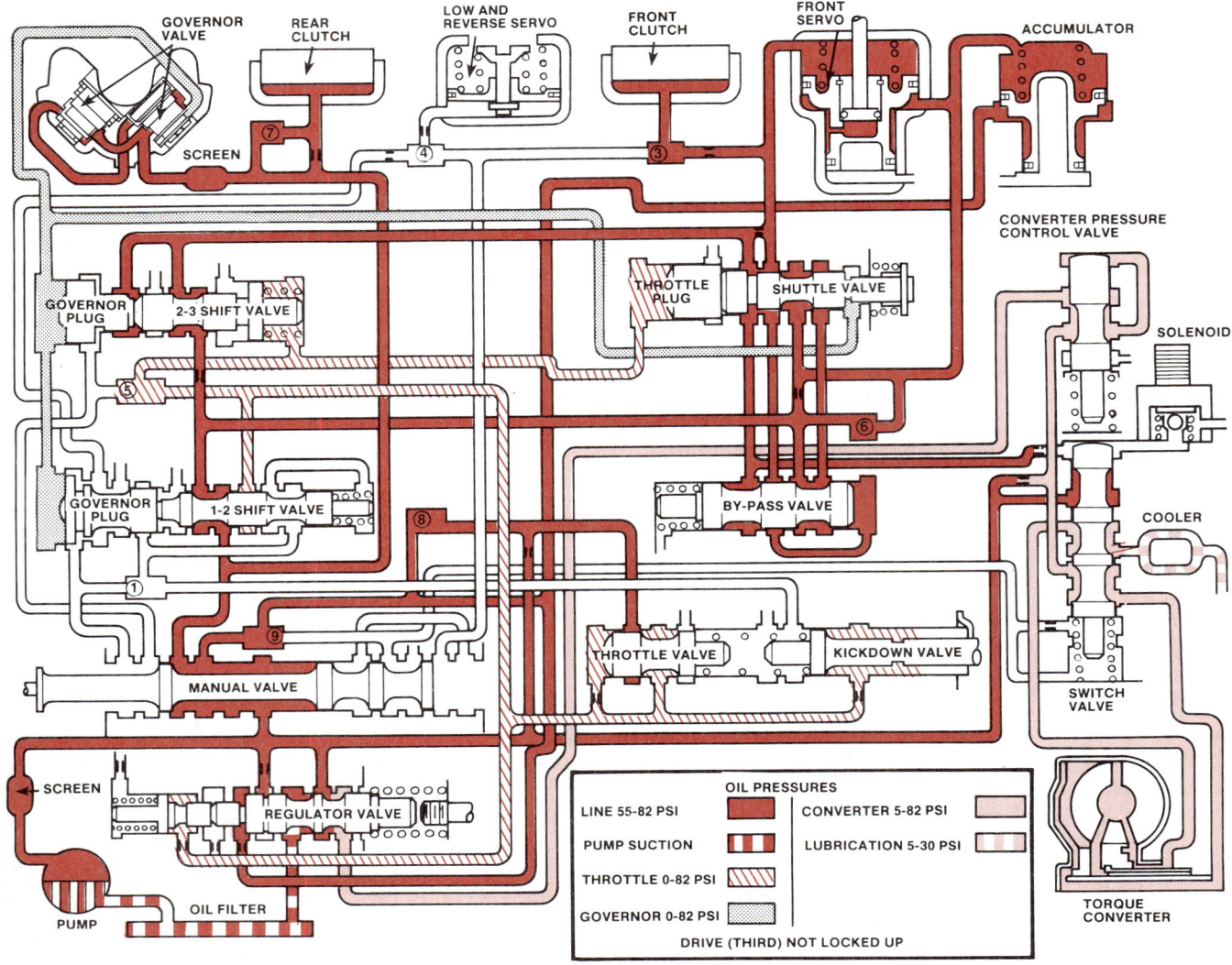

Figure 29-79 Drive range third gear with the lockup torque converter clutch disengaged and front and rear clutches engaged. *Courtesy of Chrysler Motors*

Lockup Solenoid

A solenoid is a device capable of converting electrical energy into mechanical force. When applied to the automatic transaxle lockup solenoid, the check ball is held off its seat by fluid pressure. The unseated check ball prevents line pressure from building until it is high enough to move the switch valve against switch valve spring tension.

When the lockup solenoid is electrically energized by a signal from the engine computer and lockup relay, the check ball is seated by the lockup solenoid (Figure 29-80), stopping the exhaust of line pressure. Line pressure builds up on the reaction area of the switch valve and moves it against spring tension to begin lockup engagement.

Drive Range: D Third Gear
Gear Selector Position: D
Torque Converter Mode: Locked
Planetary Controls Engaged: Rear Clutch;
Front Clutch
Approximate Vehicle Speed: 40 mph
Throttle Position: Half Throttle

In drive range third gear lockup the transaxle operates in the same manner as third gear unlock. The focus of attention is on the torque converter lockup clutch control system.

Lockup Clutch Engagement

The coolant sensor reports to the computer that the engine has reached a temperature of at least 150 degrees Fahrenheit. The vehicle speed sensor located on the speedometer cable sends an electronic signal to the computer, which reports that vehicle speed is above 40 mph. Since the vehicle is traveling at engagement speed, the throttle must be open (driver's foot on throttle). The vacuum transducer reports to the computer via electronic signal that engine vacuum is above 4 inches and within 22 inches. Based on these inputs,

Automatic Transmissions and Transaxles 753

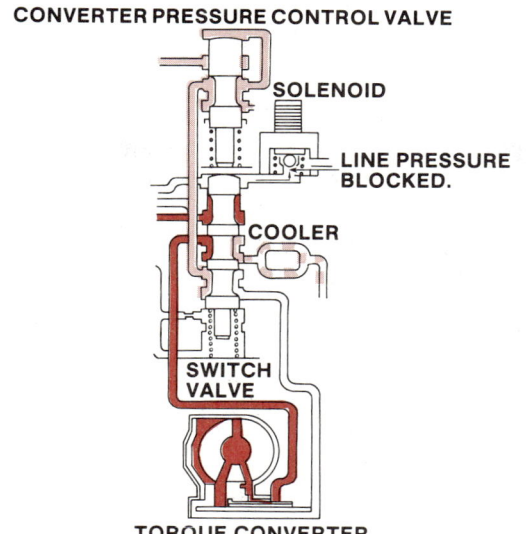

Figure 29-80 When the lockup solenoid is energized, the check ball seats and line pressure builds, forcing the switch valve into the lockup position. *Courtesy of Chrysler Motors*

the computer energizes the clutch relay and lockup solenoid to move the solenoid check ball on its seat. The lockup solenoid check ball stops the lockup solenoid from exhausting line pressure. The increasing line pressure forces the switch valve to move against coil spring tension. Line pressure from the switch valve is directed to the pump drive hub and stator support to fill the torque converter with fluid. Fluid in the torque converter during lockup operation resides there to become the cooling and lubrication pressure. Line pressure flows from the impeller and turbine to fill the space behind the torque converter clutch piston and force engagement.

Drive Range: Reverse Gear
Gear Selector Position: R
Torque Converter Mode: Unlock
Planetary Controls Engaged: Low and Reverse Rear Band; Front Clutch
Approximate Vehicle Speed: 5 mph
Throttle Position: Part Throttle

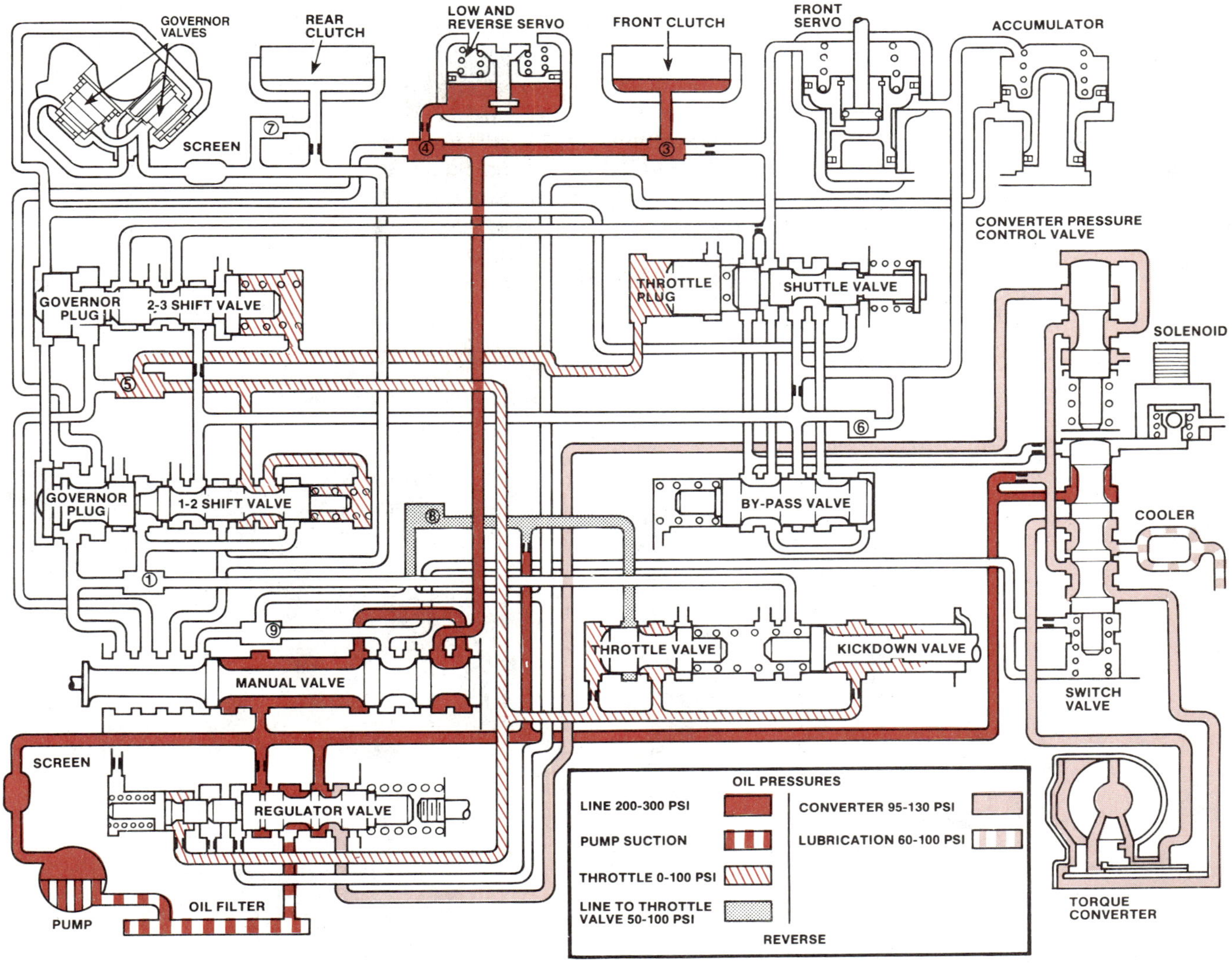

Figure 29-81 Reverse line pressure is increased to keep the front clutch, which has no Belleville spring, from slipping. The front clutch and the low reverse bands are engaged. *Courtesy of Chrysler Motors*

Line pressure from a manual valve outlet not used before circulates through a by-pass around the manual valve valley. Line pressure circulates to the low and reverse servo and front clutch (Figure 29-81). During the process of engaging the low and reverse servo and front clutch, the #4 and #3 check balls are seated by line pressure.

LINE PRESSURE Line pressure from between the pressure regulator and manual valve circulates around the pressure regulator valve. After flowing through a restriction to seat #8 check ball, line pressure enters the throttle valve, which produces line-to-throttle pressure. With the throttle valve open, throttle pressure charges the kickdown valve and strokes the throttle plug to its extreme left position at the pressure regulator valve. Line pressure from the manual valve does not flow to the pressure regulator valve to oppose spring tension. The pressure regulator valve coil spring pushes the pressure regulator valve over to close the exhaust port. Line pressure builds to approximately 200 to 300 psi. You may wonder why line pressure must be increased so much in reverse gear. The planetary control units engaged in reverse are the front clutch and the low and reverse rear band. The front clutch, unlike the rear clutch, does not have a Belleville spring. The Belleville spring multiplies clutch piston apply force on the clutch pack, which reduces possible slippage. Therefore, to keep the front clutch from slipping when moving the vehicle from a stop, reverse line pressure is increased. The concept of increasing line pressure in reverse is common in many automatic transaxles and transmissions.

THROTTLE PRESSURE Throttle pressure circulates to the shift valve area to keep both the 1-2 and 2-3 shift valves downshifted. Throttle pressure also keeps the shuttle valve throttle plug against its seat in the valve body.

CONVERTER PRESSURE In reverse, the transaxle needs the torque multiplication of vortex flow to start the vehicle moving from a stop. Therefore, the switch valve maintains the position and holds the torque converter piston in the unlocked position.

LINE-TO-THROTTLE PRESSURE This pressure is derived from line pressure and becomes the new throttle pressure.

> ### USING SERVICE MANUALS
> Before beginning to service a transaxle or transmission, have the service manual and latest service bulletins on the bench for ready reference. Many service manual publishers have complete volumes dedicated to automatic transmissions and transaxles. These volumes contain detailed information on domestic and imported transmissions and transaxles.

Electronic Controls

In many vehicles, automatic transmissions and transaxles are electronically controlled (Figure 29-82). Shifting and torque converter lockup are regulated by a computer with programmed logic and in response to

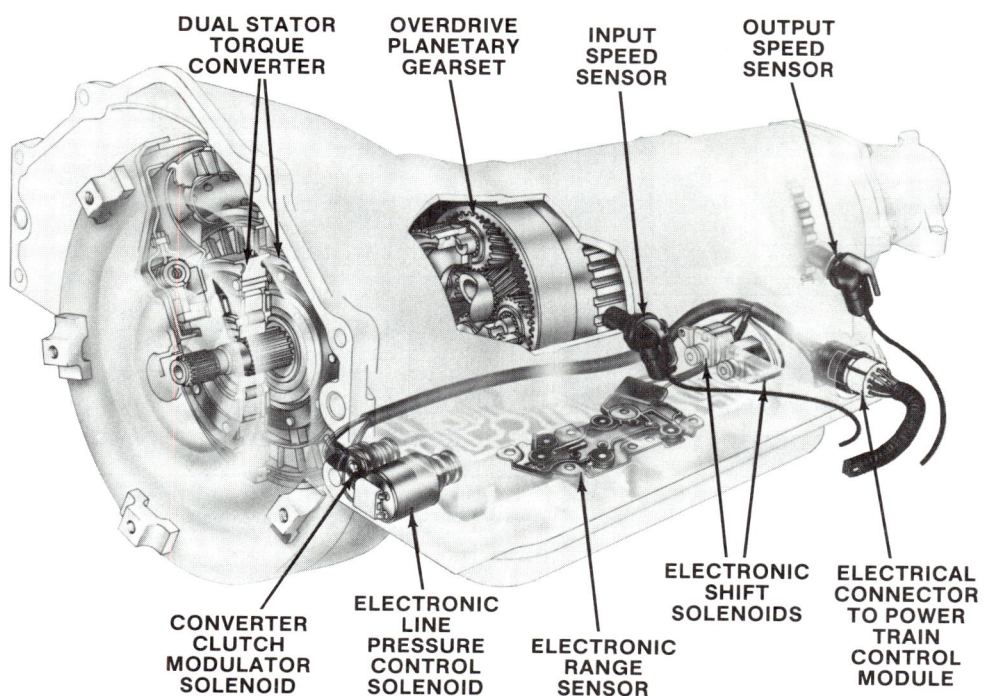

Figure 29-82 An electronic automatic transmission. *Courtesy of General Motors Corp.*

input sensors and switches. The electronic system controls these two operations by means of solenoid operated valves. The precision of this type of control produces optimum driveability. Electronic control is superior because information about the engine, fuel, ignition, vacuum, and operating temperature is fed into the computer so that shifting and lockup are closely monitored to take place at exactly the right time.

Advantages gained through electronically controlled shifting include the following.

- Automatic shifts made at precisely the right time
- Consistent shift quality
- Elimination of hunting shifts
- Engine protected by constant scanning of transaxle functions
- Improved fuel economy that meets government regulations
- Smooth, crisp, fast, reliable shifts
- Smooth response to throttle opening

The electronically controlled lockup torque converter improves fuel economy by eliminating converter slip like other lockup converters. It also prevents lockup from occurring in engine modes where noise, vibration, or harshness concerns are most evident.

One more important advantage of electronic control is access to the troubleshooting codes that are stored in the computer's memory.

Electronically Controlled Shifting

On vehicles where the shifting of the automatic transmission is controlled by computer, input signals for engine and road speed, manifold vacuum, engine operating temperature, gear selection, throttle position, and other factors are fed to the computer. The computer produces output signals that activate relays, which in turn, operate electrical solenoid valves. Instead of hydraulic pressures and springs, the motion of the solenoids controls the position of the valves. When activated, a solenoid moves its valve to control fluid pressure in a valve body.

For example, the computer shown in Figure 29-83 controls the second brake solenoid and the direct clutch solenoid. Both are responsible for operating the 1-2 and 2-3 shift valves. Feeding input to this computer are vacuum switches, the shifter lever switch, the accelerator switch, and vehicle speed-sensing switch (Figure 29-84).

Accelerator Switch

When the throttle pedal is depressed a predetermined amount, the accelerator switch opens (Figure 29-85). This tells the computer that the throttle valve is open.

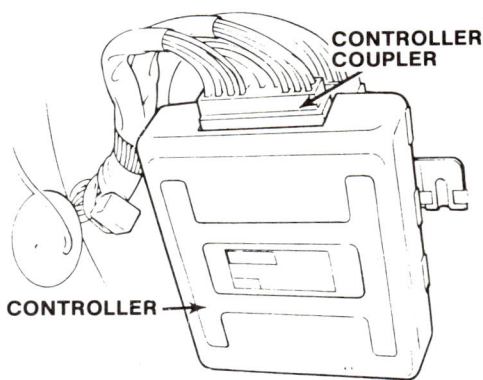

Figure 29-83 A transaxle computer. *Courtesy of General Motors Corp.*

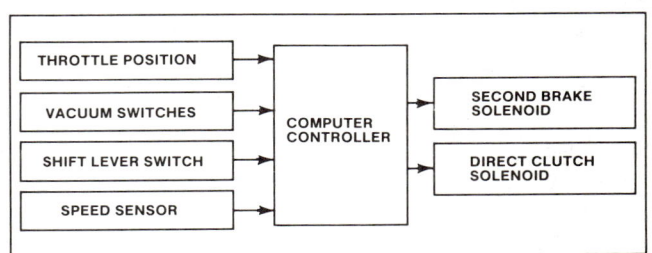

Figure 29-84 Schematic showing the relationship of input sensors to the computer controller. *Courtesy of General Motors Corp.*

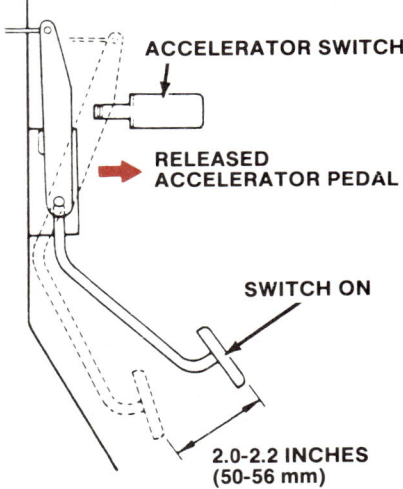

Figure 29-85 The accelerator switch indicates to the computer when the driver has moved the throttle pedal down. *Courtesy of General Motors Corp.*

Vacuum Switches

Engine vacuum is monitored by a vacuum switch (Figure 29-86). The vacuum switch has three switches each having its own range of on/off operation. The computer uses the vacuum signals and the throttle position opening to determine the load on the engine.

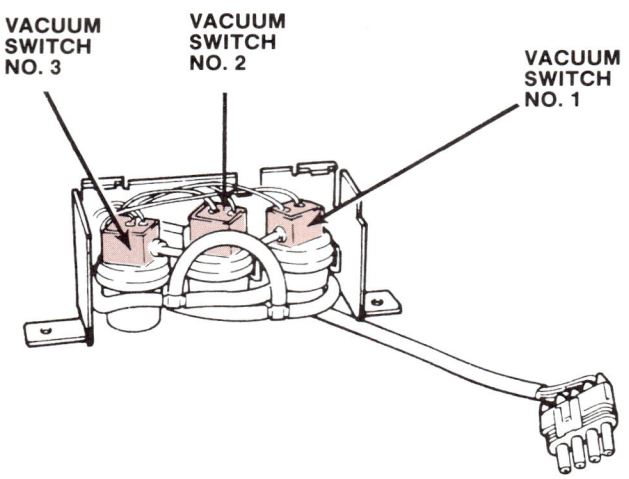

Figure 29-86 Vacuum switch assembly with its three individual switches. *Courtesy of General Motors Corp.*

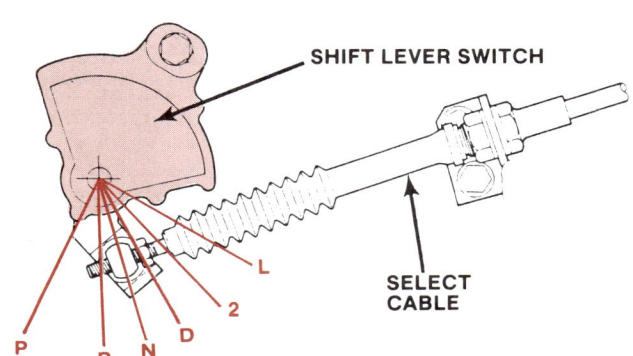

Figure 29-87 The gear selection switch must report gear range selected to the computer. *Courtesy of General Motors Corp.*

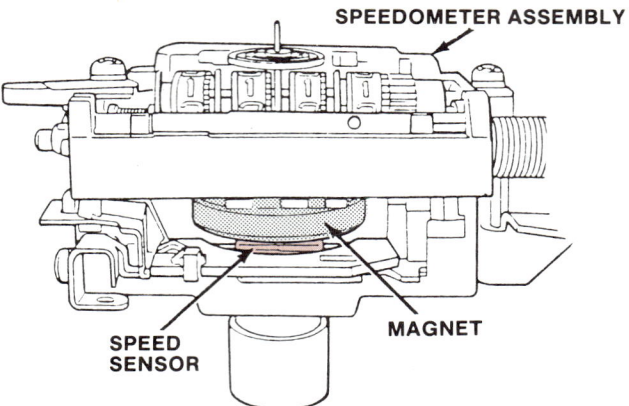

Figure 29-88 Vehicle speed sensor. *Courtesy of General Motors Corp.*

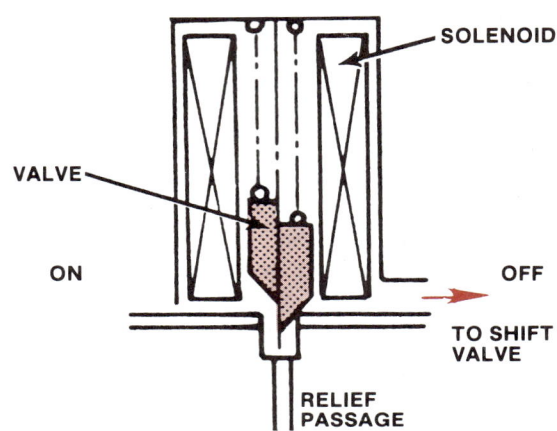

Figure 29-89 When the solenoid is on, the valve is pulled upward. When the solenoid is off, the valve moves down to block the relief passage. *Courtesy of General Motors Corp.*

Shift Lever Switch

The shift lever switch (Figure 29-87) relays the selector lever position (P-R-N-D-2-L) to the computer. The computer must know the direction of vehicle travel, forward or reverse, and the particular position the gear selector is in for forward operation. The switch's contacts in the P and N positions are connected with the starter motor circuit so that the starter motor operates in either position when the ignition key is turned to start.

Vehicle Speed Sensor

The speed sensor (Figure 29-88) consists of a lead switch and a magnet built into a speedometer assembly. As the magnet rotates driven by the speedometer cable, the magnetic force turns the lead switch on and off. As the on/off cycle frequency either increases or decreases, a voltage pulse signal sent to the computer varies accordingly. Note that a governor is not necessary when the transmission is controlled by a computer. Vehicle speed is monitored by the speed sensor.

☐ SHIFT SOLENOIDS

Figure 29-89 illustrates a typical automotive transmission solenoid. Its purpose is to convert electrical energy into a mechanical push or pull force. The system under discussion has two solenoids: the second brake (band) and the direct clutch. The two solenoids are the same in design and operation. The computer uses them at different times to control the 1-2 shift valve and the 2-3 shift valve.

When the second brake solenoid is on, the valve is pulled upward by the magnetic field around the windings and so pressure is relieved when the solenoid is off. The valve then moves down to block the relief passage. As a result, line pressure builds up, stroking the 1-2 shift valve to the upshifted position. Consequently, fluid is directed to the second brake servo to engage the brake to hold the sun gear stationary. The direct clutch solenoid operates in a similar manner to control the 2-3 shift valve and engage the direct clutch to obtain third gear operation. Table 29-4 shows the different solenoid operation cycles.

TABLE 29-4 VARIOUS SOLENOID OPERATING CYCLES

Range	D			2		L		R	P
Gear	1st	2nd	3rd	1st	2nd	1st	(2nd)	—	—
Direct Clutch Solenoid	O	O	X	X	O	X	X	X	X
2nd Brake Solenoid	O	X	X	O	X	X	O	X	X

O Operated (Solenoid valve is open.)
X Unoperated (Solenoid valve is closed.)
Courtesy of General Motors Corp.

Electronic Control of Torque Converter Lockup

To achieve better control and coordination between the engine and torque converter lockup, a computer controls the converter clutch solenoid based on the input from several sensors placed around the engine. The computer turns on the converter clutch solenoid (Figure 29-90) to move a valve that allows fluid pressure to engage the converter clutch. When the computer de-energizes the converter clutch solenoid, the converter clutch disengages.

The computer decides whether or not to energize the converter clutch solenoid on the basis of the input from several sensors and switches, among which are the vehicle speed sensor, coolant temperature sensor, throttle position sensor, gear switches, and brake switch.

The vehicle speed sensor (Figure 29-91) reports speed information to the computer. Vehicle speed must be above a certain speed before the computer energizes the converter clutch solenoid.

The coolant temperature sensor reports to the computer when the engine has warmed up sufficiently. The computer does not energize the converter clutch solenoid until the engine has reached a certain temperature.

After the converter clutch engages, the computer uses throttle position sensor information to release the converter clutch when the vehicle is accelerating or decelerating at a certain rate.

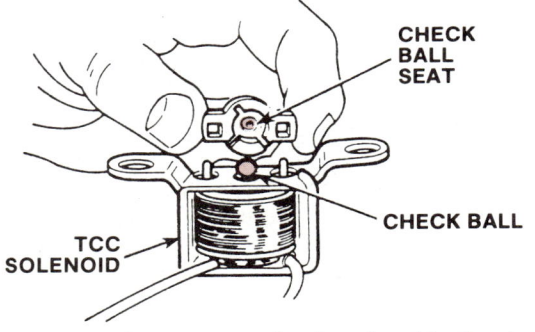

Figure 29-90 A converter clutch solenoid. *Courtesy of General Motors Corp.*

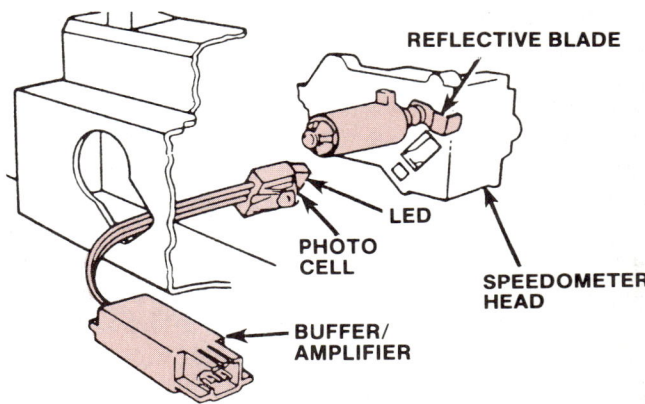

Figure 29-91 The vehicle speed sensor reports to the electronic control module when the vehicle has reached converter clutch engagement speed. *Courtesy of General Motors Corp.*

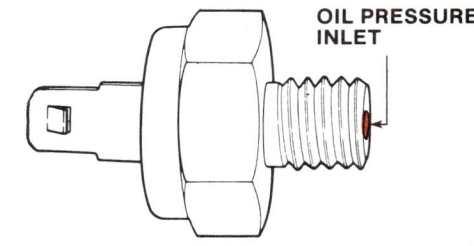

Figure 29-92 The third or fourth gear switch senses fluid pressure to determine when the third or fourth gear is engaged and sends an electrical signal to the computer. *Courtesy of General Motors Corp.*

Some transmissions use a third or fourth gear switch (Figure 29-92) to send a signal to the computer to report which gear the transmission is in. The computer uses that information to vary the conditions under which the converter clutch is applied or released.

The brake switch (Figure 29-93) is used to open the 12-volt supply to the converter clutch solenoid when the brake pedal is depressed.

The system operates in the following manner. The engine operates for more than 5 minutes and the engine coolant temperature sensor reports 150 degreees Fahrenheit. Engagement could take place if all the other sensors agree. However, the vehicle operates in congested traffic at speeds varying from 15 to 35 mph and the converted clutch engagement speed is approximately 40 mph. Under these operating conditions the vehicle speed sensor reports that the vehicle speed is

Figure 29-93 The torque converter clutch brake switch. *Courtesy of General Motors Corp.*

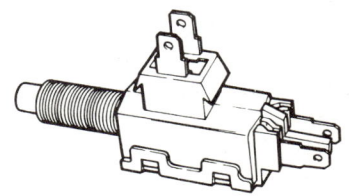

too low for clutch converter engagement. In addition, the throttle position sensor reports to the computer the unsteady, up and down movement of the throttle. The computer interprets this as a reason not to engage the converter clutch. The brake switch also opens periodically. Thus, the computer does not energize the clutch solenoid to engage the converter clutch.

If the vehicle breaks out of congested traffic and is travelling at a steady higher speed, the speed sensor reports that the vehicle is at a speed higher than converter clutch engagement speed. The throttle position sensor reports that the throttle is in a steady position in favor of engagement, and the brake switch is closed because the driver's foot is not on the brake pedal. When the computer scans all the sensors and determines that all sensor and switch signals favor engagement, it energizes the converter clutch solenoid and the converter clutch is engaged for lockup operation.

❑ CONTINUOUS VARIABLE TRANSMISSION

Stepless transmissions, also known as continuous variable transmissions (CVTs), have been around for many years but were not developed for automatic use due to technical problems. However, in recent years, automotive manufacturers such as Ford, Fiat, Subaru, Volvo, and General Motors have contributed large amounts of money to develop the stepless transmission and overcome the technical problems.

The main advantages of the CVT are maximum fuel economy and low exhaust emissions. These conditions are achieved because the engine operates in its most efficient range. The stepless gear ratio changes are very smooth compared to a conventional transmission. The stepless transmission has fewer moving parts yet maintains the efficiency of a manual shift transmission. The complete CVT is lightweight and compact. When the CVT is controlled by a computer, it is called an electronic continuous variable transmission (ECVT).

CVT Design

The CVT design is based on a system of pulleys and a drive belt. When pulleys are used to transmit power, there is a driving pulley, a V-belt, and a driven pulley. The pulleys are very simple in design. Each has two tapered sides and a hub. The tapered sides, called sheaves, in most cases, are fixed. However, the pulleys used in a CVT are adjustable. The outer sheaves of these pulleys are allowed to move in and out in order to change each pulley's outside diameter.

If the movable sheave on a pulley is moved away from the other fixed sheave, the effective diameter is reduced. The reduced diameter can be compared to a small gear. When the movable sheave is brought toward the stationary sheave, the effective diameter is increased so that it compares with a large diameter

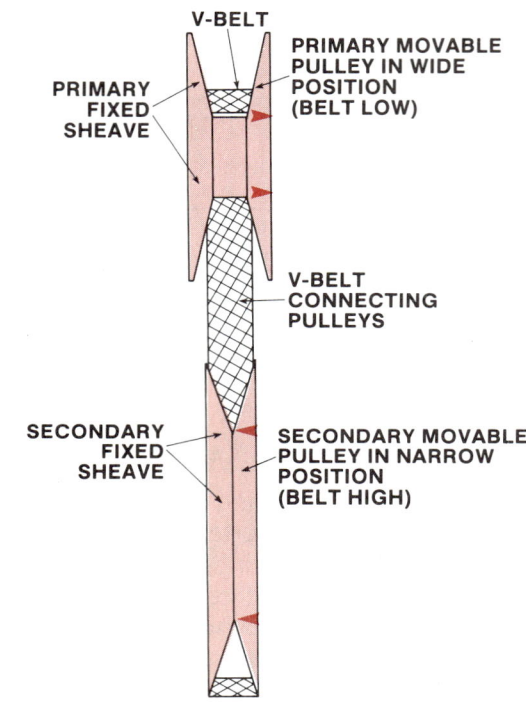

Figure 29-94 This combination of primary and secondary pulleys, used in CVT systems, is comparable to a small gear driving a large driven gear.

gear. If the diameter of one pulley increases, then the diameter of the other pulley must decrease. The belt length and the distance between the hub centers remain the same.

The operation of the CVT system is similar to that of a manual transmission gear train, only instead of switching gears to change the gear ratio, the gears themselves change. When the sheaves of the driving pulley are spread apart, and the sheaves of the driven pulley are close together (Figure 29-94), the effect is that of a small gear driving a large one. Torque multiplication occurs. When the sheaves of the driving gear move together, the driven pulley sheaves move apart (Figure 29-95), which results in a large pulley driving a small pulley, or overdrive. The result of this system is a smooth speed changing transmission operating without gears, which provides stepless ratios. The design allows for a wide, continuously variable ratio range as the belt changes position on the pulleys. Although the system looks simple in design and is economical to develop, the disadvantage is the V-belt, which is inclined to wear rapidly. As engine torque output increases, belt life decreases.

The CVT is packaged in a compact configuration making it ideal for small, front-wheel-drive vehicles. In general, the basic design of the CVT transmission is used by different manufacturers. The main difference exists in the method of transmitting engine torque to the transmission. Some manufacturers use a torque converter, but unless it is operated as a lockup, effi-

Automatic Transmissions and Transaxles

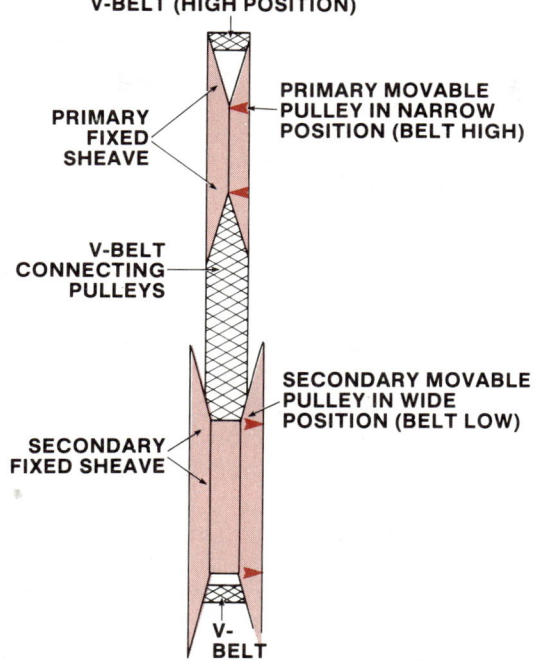

Figure 29-95 This pulley combination is comparable to a large gear driving a small gear.

ciency gained is lost. An example of a CVT that does not use a torque converter is the Subaru Justy ECVT. To transfer torque from the engine to the transmission, an electromagnetic clutch is controlled by a clutch control unit (Figure 29-96).

The clutch control unit (CCU) is located inside the passenger compartment. The transmission control unit controls the current used to energize and de-energize the electromagnetic clutch based upon reports from the various sensors. These sensors include a brake switch, accelerator pedal switches, and inhibitor switch. The brake switch de-energizes the electromagnetic clutch when the vehicle is slowing or coming to a stop. The CCU uses input from the accelerator pedal switches to vary the amount of current to the electromagnetic clutch and to signal ratio changes to the adjustable pulleys. The inhibitor switch prevents clutch engagement when the gear selector is in the P or N position.

The electromagnetic clutch drum assembly contains a fine magnetic stainless steel powder suspended in a solution. When the electromagnetic clutch is energized by the clutch control unit, engine torque is transferred to the transmission input shaft and primary pulley.

At the end of the transmission input shaft is the transmission oil pump. Pressure from the oil pump is used to control the primary and secondary pulley sheaves. The clutch control unit controls line pressure through a three-way solenoid in the transmission valve body.

Surrounding the primary and secondary pulleys is the all-important upgraded metal van Doorne belt shown in Figure 29-97. The metal drive belt operates under compression rather than tension. This endless

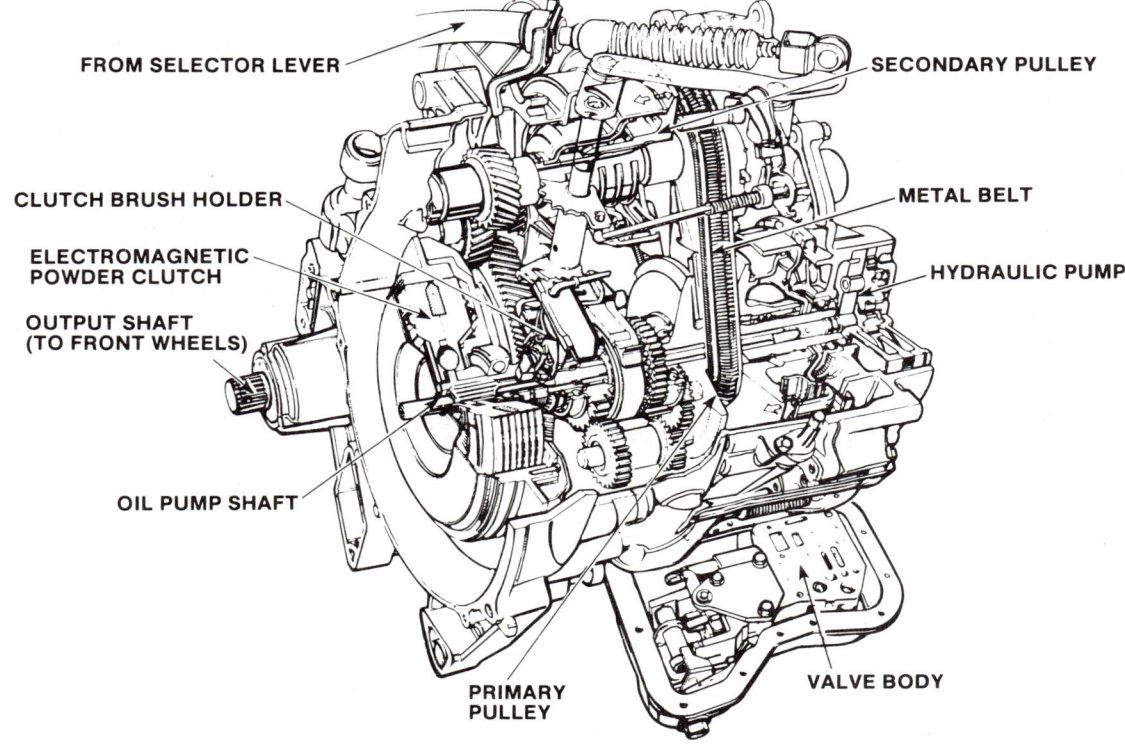

Figure 29-96 Interior view of Subaru Justy ECVT transmission. *Courtesy of Subaru of America*

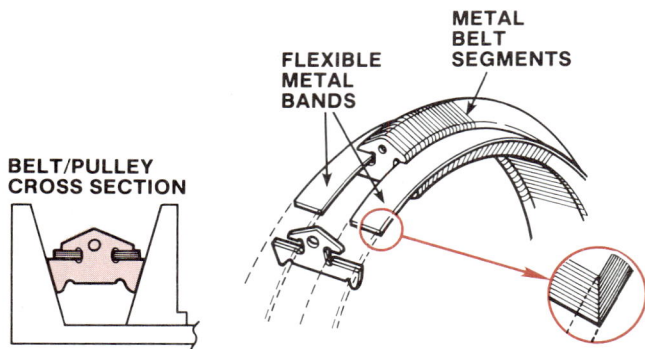

Figure 29-97 The flexible metal van Doorne belt used in the Subaru ECVT.

metal belt is made up of approximately 300 small wedge-shaped steel segments fitted on a pair of multi-layered parallel steel straps or bands. The segments are tapered to match the pulley sheave angle. The wedge-shaped segments transmit power through their edges that contact the pulley sheaves. Hydraulic pressure developed by the pump determines the driving radius and transmission ratio. The design and operation of the van Doorne metal drive belt is the secret to the CVT's success. The metal belt is very flexible, which contributes to quiet, smooth operation. The metal belt drives the secondary pulley, which drives the final drive and driven gears, differential, and front wheels.

CASE STUDY

Case 1

A "fast-lube" business has been recently faced with numerous complaints from customers who had their transmission fluid and filters changed. All of these customers owned late-model Ford products and have a common complaint of overly harsh shifting.

Concerned about these complaints, the owner reviews the files of each of these customers. He finds something else the cars have in common. All were refilled with type F transmission fluid. The owner wonders if the fluid was faulty. After doing some research, he finds that late-model Ford products call for Mercon fluid, which has special friction modifiers in it to allow for smoother shifting.

This could be the cause of the complaints. The owner contacts one of the customers and requests that the car be brought in. The fluid is drained and the Mercon fluid is put in. The car is returned to the customer. The transmission now operates normally. All of the other customers are contacted and scheduled for the same procedure. The shop owner realizes that the money saved on buying type F fluid from a surplus distributor was more than lost. Not only did he lose what he paid for the fluid, he also risked losing his customers. The correct type fluid should always be used in an automatic transmission.

Summary

- The torque converter is a fluid clutch used to transfer engine torque from the engine to the transmission. It automatically engages and disengages power transfer from the engine to the transmission in relation to engine rpm. It consists of three elements: the impeller (input), turbine (output), and stator (torque multiplier). Two types of oil flow take place inside the torque converter: rotary and vortex flow. An overrunning clutch keeps the stator assembly from rotating in one direction and permits overrunning when turned in the opposite direction.

- A lockup torque converter eliminates the 10% slip that takes place between the impeller and turbine at the coupling stage of operation. There are two types: centrifugal lockup clutch and the more popular piston lockup clutch.

- Planetary gearsets transfer power and generate torque from the engine to the drive axle. Compound gearsets combine two simple planetary gearsets so that load can be spread over a greater number of teeth for strength and also to obtain the largest number of gear ratios possible in a compact area. A simple planetary gearset consists of a sun gear, a carrier with planetary pinions mounted to it, and an internally toothed ring gear.

- Planetary gear controls include transmission bands, servos, and clutches. A band is a braking assembly positioned around a drum. There are two types: single wrap and double wrap. Simple and compound servos are used to engage bands. Transmission clutches, either overrunning or multiple-disc, are capable of both holding and driving members.

- The most common gear train used in automotive transmissions is the Simpson gear train. It consists of two simple planetary gearsets that share a common sun gear.

- Chrysler transaxles use a Simpson gear train. The General Motors THM-4R transmission also uses a Simpson gear train but it also has an overdrive planetary unit.

- Another type of gear train is the Ravigneaux gear train. It is very compact and has greater torque loading capacity compared to the Simpson gear train. It can have the large sun gear, planetary carrier, or ring gear as the output member. The Ford ATX transaxle employs a Ravigneaux gear train. The ATX may have one of the three torque converter designs: conventional, centrifugal lockup, or split torque converter. The Ford automatic overdrive transmission also uses a Ravigneaux gear train.

- An automatic transmission uses ATF fluid pressure to control the action of the planetary gearsets. This fluid pressure is regulated and directed to change gears automatically through the use of various pressure regulators and control valves. To form a complete working hydraulic system, the following elements are needed: fluid reservoir (transmission oil pan), pressure source (oil pump), control valving (valve control body), and output devices (servos and clutches).
- The transmission pump is driven by the torque converter shell at engine speed. The purpose of the pump is to create fluid flow and pressure in the system. Excessive pump pressure is controlled by the pressure regulator valve. Three types of oil pumps are installed in automatic transmissions: the gear, rotor, and vane. The gear type is the most popular.
- The valve body is the control center of the automatic transmission. It is made of two or three main parts. Internally, the valve body has many fluid passages called worm tracks.
- The purpose of a valve is to start, stop, or to direct and regulate fluid flow. Generally in most valve bodies used in automatic transmissions, three types of valves are used: check ball, poppet, and most commonly, the spool.
- To prevent stalling, the automatic transmission pump has a pressure regulator valve located in the valve body. It maintains a basic fluid pressure. The valve's movement to the exhaust position is controlled by calibrated coil spring tension. The three stages of pressure regulation are charging the torque converter, exhausting fluid pressure, and establishing a balanced position. There are times when fluid pressure must be increased above its baseline pressure.
- The purpose of the governor assembly is to sense vehicle road speed and send a fluid pressure signal to the transmission valve body to either upshift or permit the transmission to downshift. Throttle pressure delays the transmission upshift and forces the downshift.
- In many vehicles, automatic transmission/transaxle shifting and torque converter lockup are regulated by a computer with programmed logic and in response to input sensors and switches.
- Stepless transmission, or continuous variable transmissions (CVTs), resemble a manual transmission gear train, only instead of switching gears to change ratios the CVTs use variable diameter pulleys to change ratios. Their main advantages are fuel economy and low exhaust emissions.

Review Questions

1. Explain the difference between rotary and vortex fluid flow in a torque converter.
2. What component keeps the stator assembly from rotating when driven in one direction and permits rotation when turned in the opposite direction?
3. When an external gear tooth is in mesh with an internal gear, what is the direction of output rotation for one gear when the other is turned?
4. Name the two types of bands used in automatic transmissions.
5. List three purposes of automatic transmission fluid.
6. In the coupling stage of conventional torque converter operation, _____.
   a. both the impeller and turbine are turning at essentially the same speed
   b. both the stator and turbine are stationary
   c. both the stator and impeller are stationary
   d. the stator freewheels or turns as a unit
   e. both a and d
7. To achieve a slow overdrive in a simple planetary gearset, the _____.
   a. sun gear must be the input member
   b. ring gear must be the input member
   c. planetary carrier must be the input member
   d. ring gear must be held
8. In a simple planetary gearset, when the planetary carrier is held the gearset produces a _____.
   a. reverse
   b. direct drive
   c. fast overdrive
   d. forward reduction
9. Overrunning clutches are capable of _____.
   a. holding a planetary gear member stationary
   b. driving a planetary gear member
   c. both a and b
   d. neither a nor b
10. In the Ford ATX transaxle using a Ravigneaux gear train, the band holds the _____.
    a. small sun gear
    b. long planetary pinions
    c. ring gear
    d. forward sun gear
11. When the Ford AOD transmission is operating in overdrive, which planetary control units are engaged?
    a. overdrive band and forward clutch
    b. intermediate clutch and forward clutch
    c. direct clutch and forward clutch
    d. overdrive band and direct clutch
12. When the pressure regulator valve begins to operate, the first part to be charged with line pressure is the _____.
    a. torque converter
    b. forward clutch assembly
    c. manual valve
    d. governor assembly

13. To boost transmission line pressure, throttle pressure assists the _____ .
    a. pressure regulator valve coil spring
    b. pressure regulator valve
    c. modulator valve
    d. governor valve

14. What is necessary for lockup engagement to take place?
    a. The lockup solenoid check ball must be off its seat and the switch valve held up by the spring tension.
    b. The lockup solenoid must be energized with the check ball on its seat and the switch valve held down by line pressure.
    c. The lockup check ball must be off its seat and the switch valve held down by the line pressure.
    d. The solenoid must have the check ball seated and the switch valve held up by spring tension.

15. Technician A says the electronically controlled lockup torque converter improves fuel economy. Technician B says it prevents lockup from occurring during certain engine modes. Who is correct?
    a. Technician A
    b. Technician B
    c. Both A and B
    d. Neither A nor B

16. Technician A says the turbine is positioned with its back facing the transmission housing. Technician B says the turbine shaft transfers power flow to the mainshaft of the transmission. Who is correct?
    a. Technician A
    b. Technician B
    c. Both A and B
    d. Neither A nor B

17. Technician A says that rotary oil flow is the oil flow around the circumference of the torque converter caused by the rotation of the torque converter on its axis. Technician B says that the centrifugal lockup clutch is the type installed in most automatic transmissions. Who is correct?
    a. Technician A
    b. Technician B
    c. Both A and B
    d. Neither A nor B

18. Technician A says that Chrysler refers to the planetary controls by their location in the transaxle or transmission housing. Technician B says that the Simpson gear train is used in most automatic transmissions installed in North American automobiles. Who is correct?
    a. Technician A
    b. Technician B
    c. Both A and B
    d. Neither A nor B

19. Technician A says that when a Chrysler transaxle is in drive range second gear, the rear clutch and front clutch are applied. Technician B says that when it is in drive range third gear, the rear clutch and overrunning clutch are applied. Who is correct?
    a. Technician A
    b. Technician B
    c. Both A and B
    d. Neither A nor B

20. Technician A says that the Ford automatic overdrive transmission forward clutch drives the forward sun gear. Technician B says the Ford automatic overdrive transmission overdrive band drives the forward sun gear in overdrive operation. Who is correct?
    a. Technician A
    b. Technician B
    c. Both A and B
    d. Neither A nor B

30 AUTOMATIC TRANSMISSION/ TRANSAXLE SERVICE

Objectives

- Check, diagnose, and change the transmission fluid level.
- List possible causes of oil leaks.
- Explain how to check and adjust the gear selector linkage.
- Explain how to adjust the throttle cable.
- Describe the procedure for adjusting a front kickdown band.
- Explain how a vacuum modulator and governor are serviced.
- Describe how to perform a road test analysis accurately.
- Explain when and how pressure tests are performed.
- Explain the basics of computer and solenoid valve tests.

Automatic transmission diagnosis and service is a highly specialized field of automotive work. Entire books cannot cover all the variables offered by the different manufacturers. But half of all automatic transmission problems result from improper fluid levels, fluid leaks, vacuum leaks, or electrical malfunctions.

Changing fluid and filters and adjusting gear selector, throttle cable, and downshift linkages are also easily accessible service jobs that can be routinely performed by knowledgeable technicians.

Typical automatic transmission diagnostic steps may include the use of manufacturers' diagnostic guides, input from the customer, fluid and linkage checks, electrical checks, stall testing, road testing, and pressure testing.

USING SERVICE MANUALS

The diagnostic guides supplied by the automobile manufacturers provide a logical step-by-step plan to solve transmission problems. A section of a typical guide is shown in Figure 30-1.

Diagnostic sheets, such as the one shown in Figure 30-2, are extremely helpful in accurately recording all useful information during testing and troubleshooting.

CUSTOMER CARE

Before taking on the responsibility of repairing an automatic transmission, be sure that you have a competent knowledge of transmission

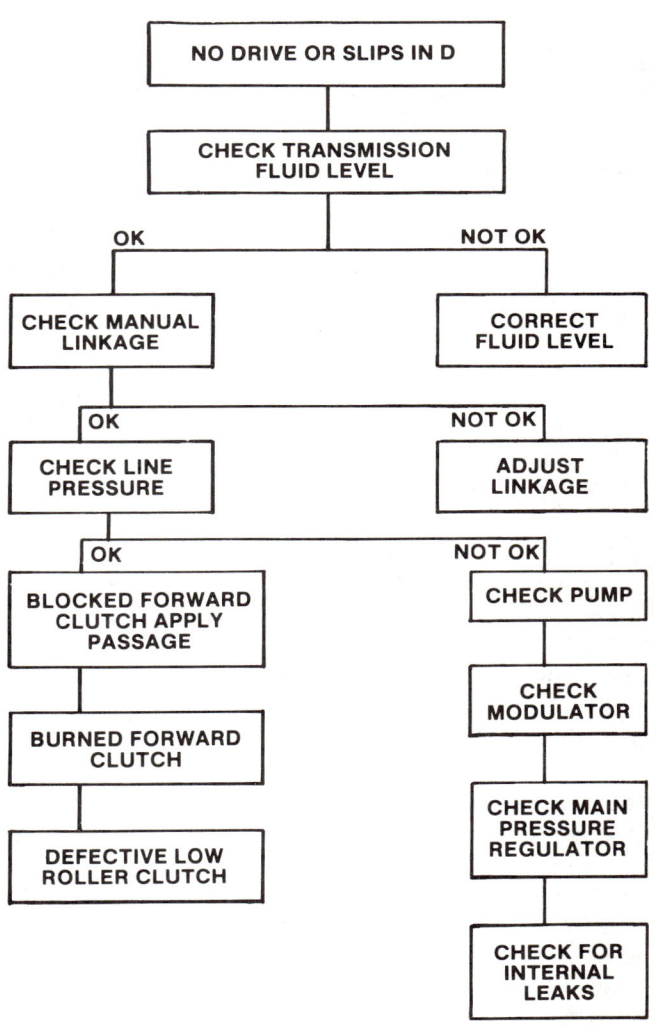

Figure 30-1 Section of a typical manufacturer's troubleshooting diagnostic chart.

MULTI-CHECK

Fluid Check

LEVEL
- ❑ OK
- ❑ Low ____
- ❑ High

CONDITION
- ❑ Normal
- ❑ Contaminated
- ❑ Varnished
- ❑ Burnt Odor

Minor Adjustment Diagnosis
- ❑ Check Shift Linkage or Cable
- ❑ Check Engine Idle Speed (RPM)
- ❑ Check Engine Performance
- ❑ Check Vacuum Hose/Cable Connections

N

Initial Engagement

Park: 3rd:
Reverse: 2nd:
Neutral: 1st:
Drive:

Driving Conditions

1st:
2nd:
3rd:
4th:
5th:
Reverse:
TCC Engagement: Passing Gear:
Noises/Vibrations:

Minor Adjustment Checks and Tests Performed
- ❑ Check Vacuum
- ❑ Check Modulator / Modulator Pin
- ❑ Check TV/ Detent Linkage or Cable
- ❑ Check Band Adjustments
- ❑ Check Shift Linkage/Cable
- ❑ Check Mounts
- ❑ Check Final Drive / Drive Axle / U Joints / CV Joints
- ❑ Fluid Retention
- ❑ Speedometer ❑ OK ❑ NG

AS REQUIRED:
- ❑ Check External Electrical Controls and Internal Solenoid(s)
- ❑ Perform Hydraulic Pressure Test

Sump: ❑ Normal ❑ EF ❑ Water ❑ EM ❑ Varnish ❑ Center Remarks

Center Remarks

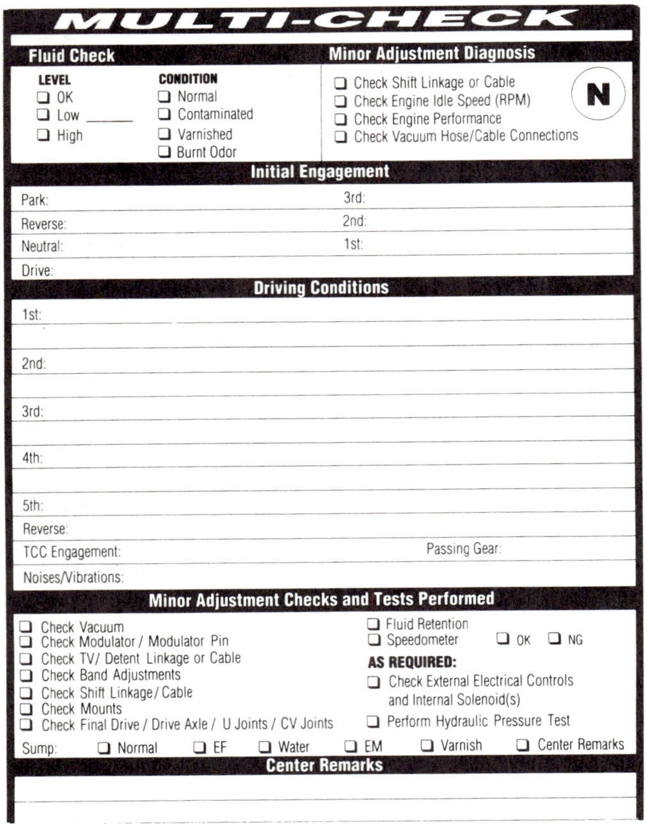

Figure 30–2 Typical transmission diagnostic checklist. *Courtesy AAMCO*

design, operation, and diagnostic procedures. There are many horror stories told by customers about dollars wasted on reconditioned transmissions when all that was needed was something as simple as topping off the transmission fluid or adjusting the gear selector linkage or throttle cable.

❑ AUTOMATIC TRANSMISSION FLUID

The ATF level should be checked at regular mileage and time intervals. The dipstick is located on the transmission housing, at the end of the engine opposite the belts and pulleys.

Make sure the vehicle is level. On most automobiles, the ATF level can be checked accurately only when the transmission is at operating temperature. For most vehicles, the engine must be running and the shift lever placed in either park or neutral, as specified by the vehicle manufacturer, with the parking brake applied. Markings on a dipstick indicate add levels, plus full levels for fluid when cool, warm, or hot (Figure 30-3).

Some dipsticks have readings on both sides. Others have readings on only one side. On some vehicles with automatic transaxles, the cold fluid level might be

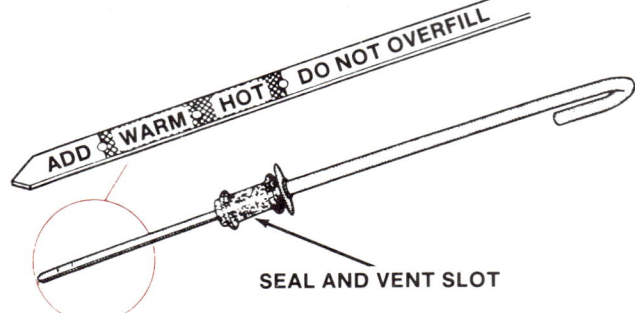

Figure 30–3 Typical transaxle dipstick indicating proper ATF levels at various operating temperatures. *Courtesy of Chrysler Motors*

higher than the hot fluid level. Refer to the manufacturer's service manual and service bulletins for specific information.

To check the fluid level, start the engine and bring it to operating temperature. Remove the dipstick and wipe it clean with a lint-free cloth or paper towel. Reinsert the dipstick fully. Remove it again and note the reading.

LOW FLUID LEVELS If the fluid level is low and off the crosshatch section of the dipstick, the problem could be external fluid leaks. Low fluid levels cause a variety of problems. The condition allows air to be drawn into the pump inlet circuit. Aeration of the fluid causes slow pressure buildup and low fluid pressures, contributing to slipping automatic shifts.

Air in the fluid pressure regulator valve can cause a buzzing action and noise as it tries to regulate pump pressure. The most probable cause of low fluid level is an external fluid leak.

HIGH FLUID LEVELS High fluid levels cause the rotating planetary gears and parts to churn up the fluid and admit air developing foam. This condition is very similar to low fluid level. Aerated fluid can cause overheating, fluid oxidation, which contributes to varnish buildup, and interference with normal spool valve, clutch, and servo operation.

Diagnosing Transmission Fluid

Uncontaminated automatic transmission fluid is pinkish or red in color. A dark brownish or blackish color or a burnt odor indicate overheating. If the fluid has overheated, the ATF and the filter must be changed and the transmission inspected. A milky color can indicate that engine coolant is leaking into the transmission cooler in the radiator outlet tank.

Bubbles on the dipstick indicate the presence of air. The bubbles usually are caused by a high-pressure leak.

Wipe the dipstick on absorbent white paper. Look at the fluid stain. Dark particles in the fluid indicate band or clutch material. Silvery metal particles indicate ex-

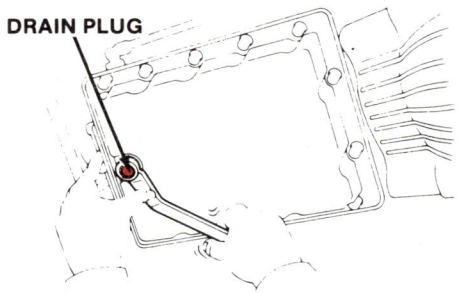

Figure 30-4 Removing transmission pan drain plug.

cessive wear on metal parts or housings. Varnish or gum deposits on a dipstick indicate the need to change the ATF and the transmission filter.

Changing Transmission/Transaxle Fluid

Change the fluid when the engine and transmission or transaxle are at normal operating temperatures. Contaminants flow out more completely when the fluid is warm.

On most units, it is necessary to remove the oil pan to drain the fluid. Some transmission pans on recent vehicles include a drain plug (Figure 30-4). After draining, the pan must be removed for inspection and to replace the filter.

Check the bottom of the oil pan for deposits and metal particles. A small amount of blackish deposits from transmission clutches and bands and a few small metal particles are normal. Large amounts of deposits or metal particles indicate major damage to friction materials or metal parts in the transmission. Clean the inside of the pan with solvent and blow it dry with compressed air.

A filter or screen is usually attached to the valve body (Figure 30-5). Filters are made of paper or fabric. A filter may be held in place by screws, clips, or bolts (Figure 30-6). A filter kit contains a new filter and a transmission pan gasket.

Screens are removed in the same way as filters. Some transmissions have valves and springs between the valve body and screen. Do not loosen or remove valves or springs. Clean the screen with fresh solvent and a stiff brush.

Remove any traces of the old gasket on the case housing and oil pan by scraping with a gasket scraper or putty knife. Do not damage the sealing surface of the housing or oil pan. Refill with the recommended type and amount of new ATF. Be careful not to overfill.

The steps involved in a typical automatic transmission fluid and filter change are illustrated in Photo Sequence 14.

SHOP TALK

Automatic transmission fluids are classified as either nonfriction modified or friction modified. Nonfriction modified fluids, such as GM's Dexron® (used in both GM and Chrysler units) and Ford's Type F are not compatible with modern lockup torque converters and automatic transmissions.

Friction modified fluids were introduced in the late 1970s and are compatible with modern transmission/transaxle designs. These include GM's Dexron® II, Ford's Mercon®, and Chrysler's ATF fluids. Ford Mercon® fluid can be used in transmissions originally designed for Ford's CJ and Type H friction modified fluids.

Always use the exact automatic transmission fluid type specified in the vehicle service manual.

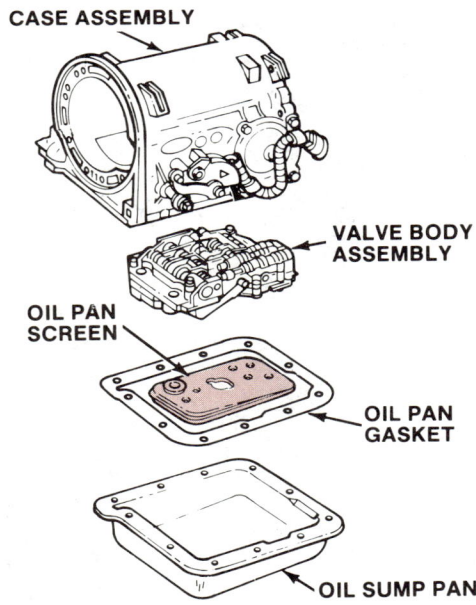

Figure 30-5 Oil screen location. *Courtesy of Ford Motor Co.*

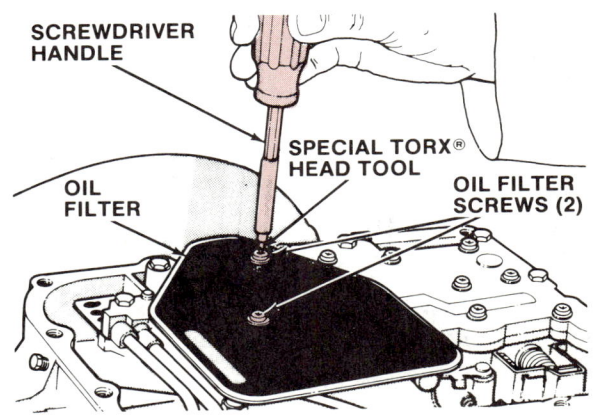

Figure 30-6 Removing a transaxle filter with a Torx® driver. *Courtesy of Chrysler Motors*

Oil Leaks

There are many possible sources for ATF leakage. One of these, the pump seal, can be replaced only if the transmission is removed from the vehicle.

Leaks caused by worn or defective gaskets or seals are repaired by replacing the defective part. The transmission need not be removed for this service. Follow the manufacturer's replacement instructions.

Case porosity, tiny holes caused by trapped air bubbles during the casting process, can occur. Leakage of ATF through the cap can be seen and felt. Case porosity may be repaired using an epoxy-type sealer. All traces of oil must be removed before attempting this repair, which may require transmission removal.

GEAR SELECTOR LINKAGE CHECK

Proper adjustment of the gear selector or manual linkage is important to have the manual valve fluid inlet and outlets properly aligned in the valve body. If the manual valve does not align with the inlet and outlets, line pressure could be lost to an open circuit.

A neutral safety switch permits starter engagement only in park or neutral gear selector positions. If the neutral safety switch is suspect, refer to the vehicle's service manual for proper testing procedures. The gear selector positions must correspond to the range selected in the transaxle.

PROCEDURES

Checking Gear Selector Linkage

1. Move the gear selector into the park position.
2. Turn the ignition key to the start position. If the starter operates in this position, the adjustment is correct.
3. Slowly move the gear selector to the neutral position and let the gear selector drop into the notch.
4. Repeat the engine start test. If the starter operates when the ignition key is in the start position, the gear selector linkage is properly adjusted. If the starter does not engage, the gear selector linkage must be adjusted.

PROCEDURES

Adjusting Gear Selector Linkage

1. Place the gear selector in the park position.
2. Loosen the clamp bolt on the gear selector cable bracket at the transaxle housing (Figure 30-7).
3. Move the transaxle shift lever to the front detent position. The shift lever is in the detent position when it clicks as the roller seats in the detent recess.
4. Move the gear selector cable to achieve the correct adjustment.

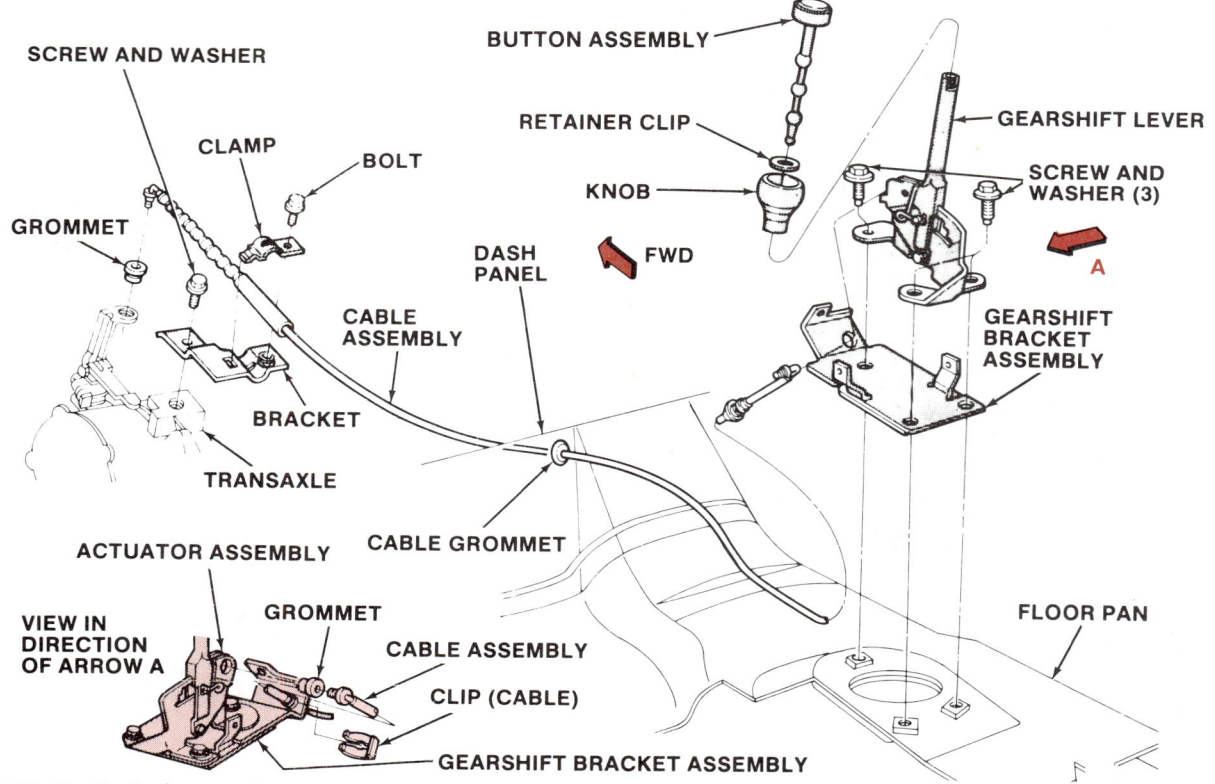

Figure 30-7 Typical gear selector control linkage for a transaxle. *Courtesy of Chrysler Motors*

PHOTO SEQUENCE 14

PERFORMING AN AUTOMATIC TRANSMISSION FLUID AND FILTER CHANGE

P14-1 To begin the procedure for changing automatic transmission fluid and filter, raise the car on a lift. Before working under the car, make sure it is safely positioned on the lift.

P14-2 Locate the transmission pan. Remove any part that may interfere with the removal of the pan.

P14-3 Position the oil drain pan under the transmission pan. A large diameter drain pan helps prevent spills.

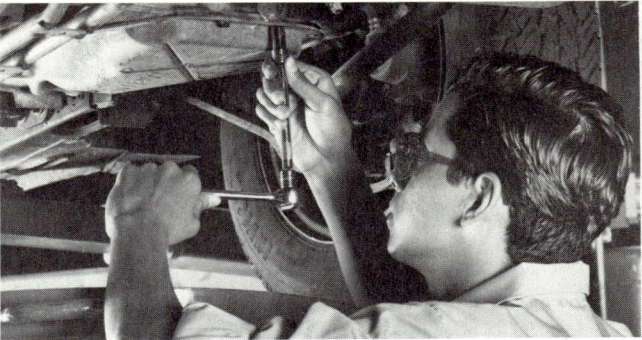

P14-4 Loosen all of the pan bolts and remove all but three. This will cause fluid to flow out around the pan into the drain pan.

P14-5 Supporting the pan with one hand, remove the remaining bolts and pour the fluid from the transmission pan into the drain pan.

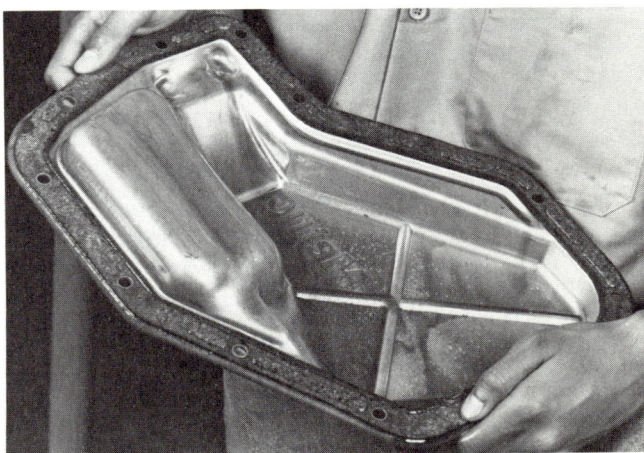

P14-6 Carefully inspect the transmission pan and the residue in it. The condition of the fluid is often an indication of the condition of the transmission and serves as a valuable diagnostic tool.

(continued)

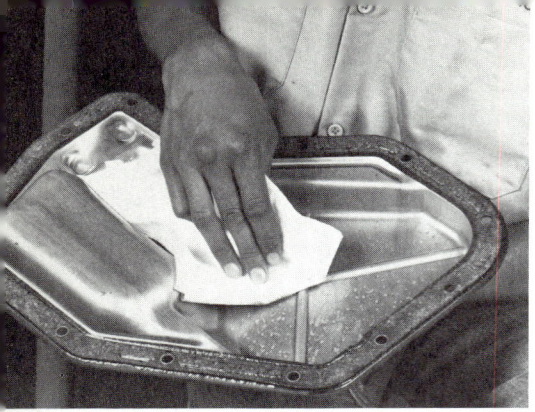

P14-7 Remove the old pan gasket and wipe the transmission pan clean with a lint-free rag.

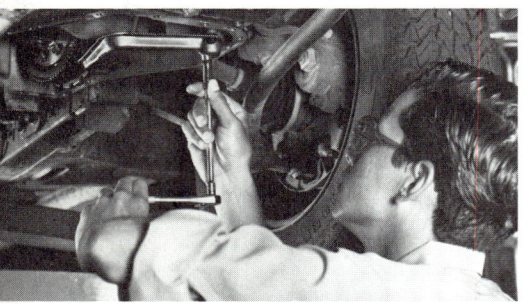

P14-8 Unbolt the fluid filter from the transmission's valve body. Keep the drain pan under the transmission while doing this. Additional fluid may leak out of the filter or valve body.

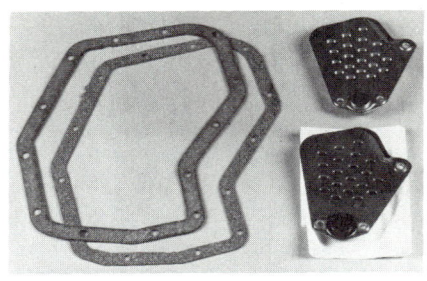

P14-9 Before continuing, compare the old filter and pan gasket with the new ones.

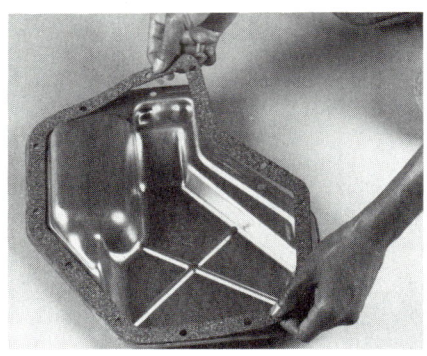

P14-10 Install the new filter onto the valve body and tighten the attaching bolts to proper specifications. Then lay the new pan gasket over the sealing surface of the pan and move the pan into place.

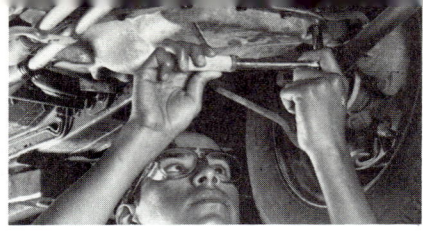

P14-11 Install the attaching bolts and tighten them to the recommended specifications. Read the specifications for installing the filter and pan carefully. Some transmissions require torque specifications of inch-pounds rather than the typical foot-pounds.

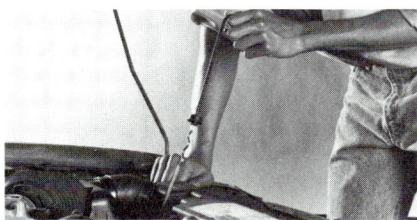

P14-12 With the pan tightened, lower the car. Start the engine, with the parking brake applied and your foot on the brake pedal. Move the shift lever through the gears. This allows the fluid to circulate throughout the entire transmission. After the engine reaches normal operating temperature, check the transmission fluid level and correct it if necessary. ■

---

5. With the gear selector cable in the cable clamp, tighten the cable clamp bolt to the manufacturer's specifications as found in the service manual.
6. Recheck the gear selector linkage adjustment. The starting motor should engage only in park and neutral positions.
7. With the ignition key turned on, place the gear selector lever in reverse. The backup lights should be on if the circuit is complete.

❑ THROTTLE CABLE LINKAGE CHECK

The throttle cable connects the throttle pedal to the transmission/transaxle valve body throttle valve, which makes throttle pressure. Throttle pressure signals the engine load and torque required and is opposed by governor pressure. Throttle pressure affects the speed at which shifting occurs.

PROCEDURES

Throttle Cable Adjustment

1. To adjust the throttle cable, the engine must be at operating temperature and off the warm-up fast idle.

2. Check engine idle speed with a reliable tachometer. Idle speed specifications are located in the vehicle service manual. Proper engine idle speed avoids harsh engagements when the gear selector is moved to reverse or drive positions. Low idle speed creates a variety of engagement problems.
3. Refer to Figure 30-8 and loosen the throttle cable bracket bolt.
4. Check the alignment of the cable bracket with the tabs to the transaxle housing.
5. Tighten the bracket bolts to manufacturer's specifications.
6. The throttle cable is held in position in the throttle cable bracket by the cross-lock, an automatic locking device that keeps the throttle cable properly adjusted. Most vehicles using throttle cables have some type of automatic cable-locking device. For the correct procedure for throttle cable adjustment and the operation of the automatic cable-locking device, refer to the vehicle's service manual.
7. To release the cross-lock's hold on the throttle cable, pull upward on the cross-lock.
8. Be sure that the throttle cable slides freely in the cross-lock.
9. With the throttle cable sliding freely in the cross-lock, hold the cable against the throttle cable

Automatic Transmission/Transaxle Service

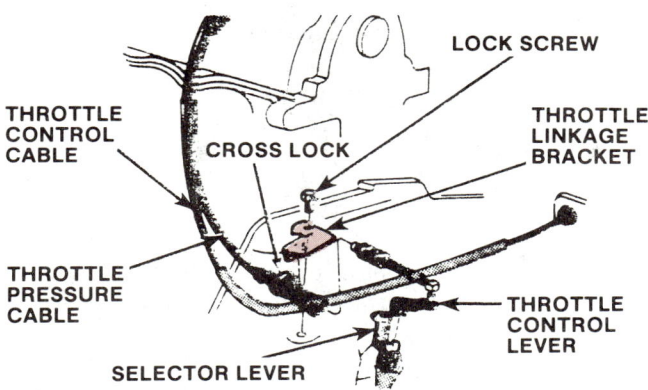

Figure 30-8 Throttle linkage adjustment bracket. *Courtesy of Chrysler Motors*

stop. With the throttle cable in contact with its stop, release the cross-lock.

10. Move the throttle control lever through its full travel from one end to the other. With the throttle lever and throttle cable moving freely, press the cross-lock down and trap the throttle cable in position. The throttle cable is now adjusted.

Figure 30-9 illustrates a typical self-adjusting throttle cable used on some front-wheel- and rear-wheel-drive vehicles.

PROCEDURES
Adjusting a Self-Adjusting Throttle Cable

1. Press in on the readjust tab.
2. Move the sliding part back through the fitting until the slider stops against the fitting.
3. Release the readjust tab.
4. Open the carburetor lever to the wide-open throttle position, which automatically adjusts the throttle cable.
5. Release the carburetor lever. The throttle cable is adjusted.

❏ BAND ADJUSTMENT

Slippage during shifting can indicate the need for band adjustment. Adjusting transmission bands may or

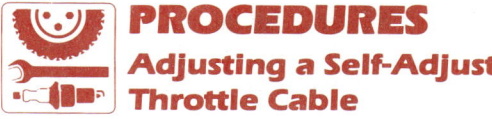
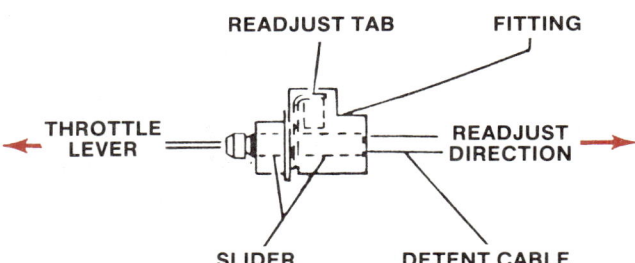

Figure 30-9 Automatic throttle cable adjuster. *Courtesy of General Motors Corp.*

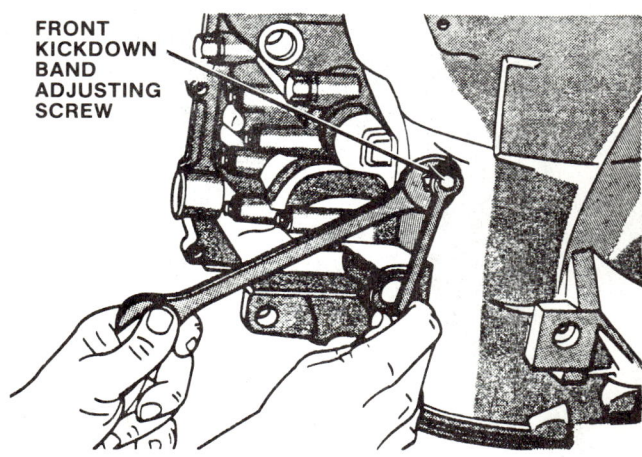

Figure 30-10 Front kickdown band adjusting screw and locknut. *Courtesy of Chrysler Motors*

may not be part of a scheduled maintenance program for the vehicle. Many transmissions have no provisions for adjusting bands. In other cases, the adjustment procedure involves draining the transmission fluid and removing the oil pan. Figure 30-10 shows a front kickdown band adjustment being made.

PROCEDURES
Adjusting the Band

1. Loosen the band adjusting bolt locknut.
2. Back off the locknut approximately five turns.
3. Rotate the adjusting screw in the transaxle housing. Be sure it is free to turn and does not interfere with the torque specification.
4. Use an inch-pound torque wrench and socket to tighten the adjusting bolt to 72 inch-pounds or the specified torque.
5. After reaching the specified torque, back out the adjusting screw the specified number of turns indicated in the vehicle's service manual for that particular model transmission/transaxle.
6. Tighten the adjuster bolt locknut.

❏ VACUUM MODULATOR SERVICE

The vacuum modulator usually is screwed or clamped into place at the side or rear of the transmission.

Improper shifting can be caused by a defective vacuum modulator or by defective or missing modulator vacuum connectors (Figure 30-11). Engine vacuum leaks can produce the same symptoms. Follow the diagnostic procedure outlined in the manufacturer's service manual to determine the exact cause.

A repeated low fluid level in the transmission with no visible external leaks and the sudden appearance of excessive blue-white smoke from the tail pipe usually

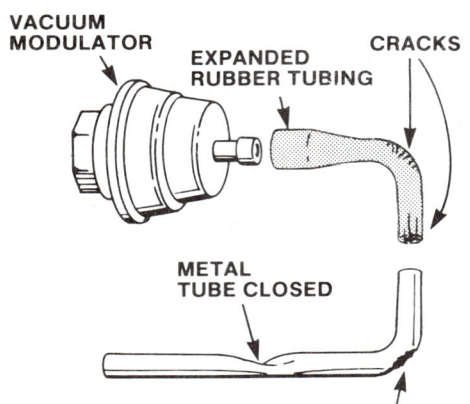

Figure 30-11 A damaged vacuum line in the modulator circuit can cause improper shifting.

indicates a ruptured diaphragm in the modulator. To check for this condition, pull the vacuum hose off the modulator connection. If ATF is present in the hose, the vacuum modulator must be replaced.

Clean the area around the modulator with solvent. Then disconnect the vacuum hose. The modulator itself is either unscrewed or unclamped from the transmission housing and removed carefully. Special tools might be necessary. Take care that the modulator valve does not fall out during this removal. Then install the new replacement unit. Refer to the manufacturer's service manual for more complete replacement procedures.

GOVERNOR SERVICE

Improper shift points can be caused by a malfunction in the governor or governor drive gear system.

Although all governors are mounted internally, some require removal of the extension housing or oil pan for access.

Another type of governor is serviced by removing an external retaining clamp and then removing the unit

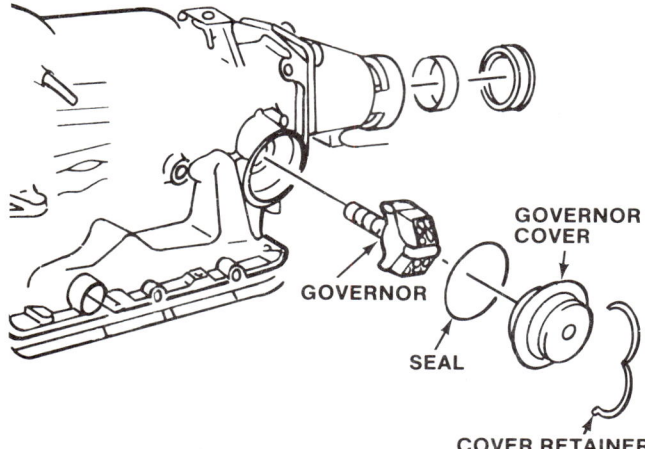

Figure 30-12 Example of governor held in place with a retaining clamp.

(Figure 30-12). Follow the manufacturer's recommended diagnostic and service procedures.

ROAD TESTING

Road testing is exceedingly important when troubleshooting automatic transaxle and transmission problems. The objective of the road test is to confirm the customer's complaint. It is always wise to have the customer accompany the diagnostician on a road test to confirm the malfunction. The road test allows for the opportunity to check the transaxle or transmission operation for slipping, harshness, incorrect upshift speeds, and incorrect downshifts.

DIAGNOSING ACCURATELY

The secret of an accurate diagnosis is knowing what planetary controls are applied in a particular gear range. The rear clutch is engaged in both D range first gear and manual first gear #1 on the gear selector. The overrunning clutch is engaged in D range first gear and the low and reverse rear band in manual first gear.

If the transaxle slips in D range first gear but not in manual first gear, the overrunning clutch must be slipping. Similarly, if the transaxle slips in any two forward gear ranges, the rear clutch is the slipping planetary control unit. Using the same procedure, the rear clutch and front clutch are engaged in D range third gear. If there is slippage in this range, either the front clutch or rear clutch is slipping. By selecting another gear range that does not use one of these two units, the planetary control slippage can be determined. If the transaxle also slips in reverse, the front clutch is slipping. If the transaxle does not slip in reverse, the rear clutch is slipping. This process of eliminating the various planetary controls can be used to detect any planetary unit that slips and to confirm proper operation of the good units.

Although road testing analysis can help to identify slipping units, the actual cause of the slip or malfunction usually cannot be decided. Nearly any slipping condition can be caused by leaking hydraulic circuits or sticking spool valves in the valve body. When hydraulic circuits leak within the transmission/transaxle housing, they are referred to as internal leaks.

PRESSURE TESTING

A road test enables the technician to determine which apply devices might not be working properly. For example, a slipping band might be detected. The next step is to find what caused the band to slip.

The problem might be mechanical—improper band adjustment or a worn friction lining. However, low hydraulic pressure could have caused the band to slip and wear out. A valve in the valve body could be stuck

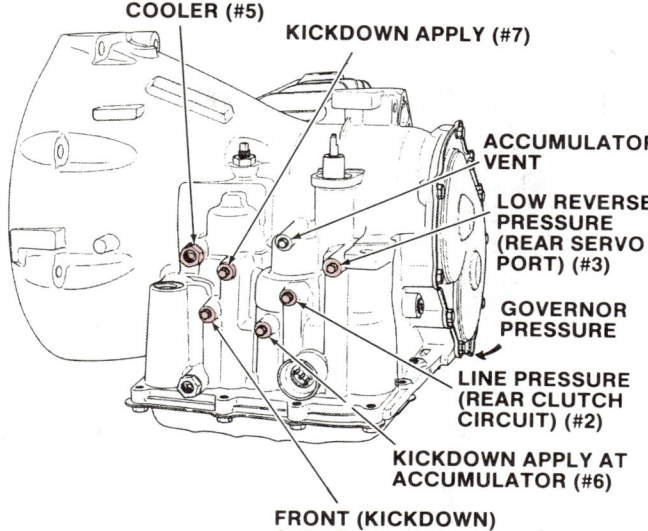

Figure 30-13 Pressure testing ports on the side of a transaxle. *Courtesy of Chrysler Motors*

or leaking. Just replacing the worn-out band would not solve the problem. If the sticking valve is not found and replaced, the new band would soon slip and wear out.

A pressure test checks hydraulic pressures in the transmission by using gauges that are attached to the transmission. The transmission is shifted into a specific gear, and the engine is run at a recommended speed while pressure readings are recorded. Pressure readings reveal possible problems in the oil pump, governor, and throttle circuits.

Pressure test openings, or ports, are located on the transmission case (Figure 30-13). After removing a plug, a fitting can be screwed into the port. The pressure gauge connects to the fitting. In addition, a tachometer and vacuum gauge might be required. The use of a combination tester, shown in Figure 30-14, makes the procedure easier. Consult the manufacturer's service manual for the recommended gauge or tester.

Procedures for pressure testing vary greatly between manufacturers. Some manufacturers' procedures call for reading more than one pressure gauge at the same time, in addition to a vacuum gauge. To perform a pressure test correctly, refer to the proper service manual.

When conducting pressure tests on different transmissions, all of the following steps might be necessary. However, some manufacturers might omit one or more of the steps. Other procedures might replace some steps with alternate, or different, ones. Additional steps might be required.

PROCEDURES

Pressure Testing

1. Start the engine and let it warm to normal operating temperature. Then shut it off.
2. Connect a tachometer to the engine according to the manufacturer's instructions.
3. Have a helper inside the vehicle start the engine and operate the transmission, accelerator, and brake controls.
4. Safely raise the vehicle on a hoist to a comfortable working height.
5. Connect pressure gauges to the specified test ports.
6. Use a T-fitting and vacuum tubing to connect a vacuum gauge with a shutoff or bleed-down valve to the vacuum modulator line.

WARNING: If the pressure test procedures or equipment require you to be under the vehicle while the test is performed, be extremely careful. The driveline and drive wheels turn for most tests. Contact with the spinning driveline or wheels can cause serious physical injury. Always wear eye protection while working under a car.

7. Start the engine. Move the selector lever to the first test position. Run the engine at the specified rpm. Take readings from the gauges, and write them down. Move the transmission controls as specified, and note the readings or change in readings. Make notes of the pressures or pressure changes.
8. Slow the engine and press gently on the service brakes to stop the spinning wheels and driveline. Shut off the engine.
9. Attach the pressure gauges and vacuum gauge to the proper pressure ports for the next test.
10. Start the engine. Move the gearshift lever to the next test position. Run the engine at the specified rpm. Take pressure readings as specified. Slow the engine, and press gently on the service brakes to stop the spinning wheels and driveline.
11. Repeat the steps for each test procedure. Make notes of all pressure readings and vacuum readings obtained for each test.

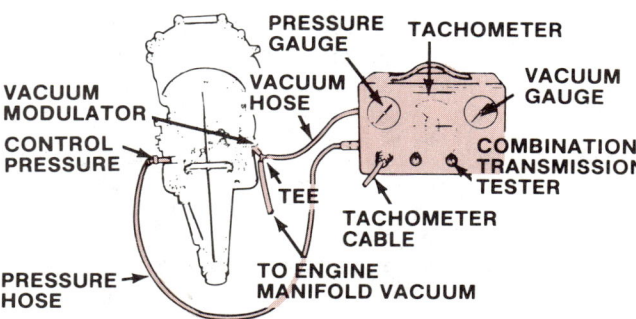

Figure 30-14 Typical combination pressure test equipment. *Courtesy of Ford Motor Co.*

Analyzing Pressure Test Readings

Charts in the manufacturers' service manual list correct specifications for the pressure tests, as well as possible causes of incorrect readings. Refer to the service manual to determine the causes of pressure readings other than as specified.

Air Pressure Tests

The source of a transmission hydraulic problem can be difficult to locate. If road testing and pressure testing have indicated a slipping clutch or band, air pressure tests can be made. Air pressure tests can determine whether the problem is in the apply device or in the valve body that supplies hydraulic pressure.

After the valve body has been removed, air pressure is applied to the case holes and passages leading to the apply devices. Correct operation of servos and clutches can be heard and felt. Air pressure tests are done during overhaul disassembly to locate leaking seals. Air pressure tests are also done during reassembly to check for proper clutch and servo operation.

Filtered, moisture-free compressed air of 40 psi is normally used for the test. Air pressure of up to 90 psi can be used if it is difficult to hear the clutches apply. An air blowgun with a conical rubber nozzle is used to apply the air pressure (Figure 30-15).

Some manufacturers recommend the use of special metal plates that bolt to the transmission to seal the case apply passages (Figure 30-16). The metal plate and gasket are bolted to the case. Identification of the holes is stamped into the plate. Air is applied through the plate holes.

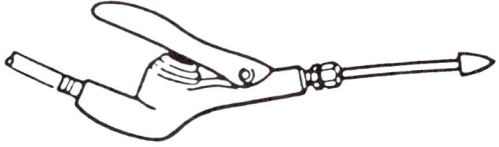

Figure 30-15 Air pressure tests are performed using an air blowgun with a conical rubber nozzle.

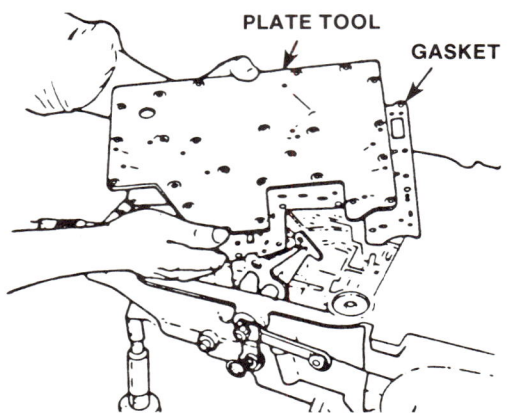

Figure 30-16 Installing the air pressure plate service tool. *Courtesy of Ford Motor Co.*

 PROCEDURES

Conducting Air Pressure Tests

1. Safely raise the vehicle on a hoist.
2. Drain the transmission oil and remove the oil pan.
3. Remove the filter.
4. Remove the valve body.
5. Refer to the manufacturer's service manual to identify the fluid passages. Attach special plates and gaskets as necessary. Torque the plate attaching screws to the manufacturer's specifications.
6. Apply air pressure to the servo and clutch apply passages and listen for 5 to 10 seconds. Listen for hissing, which indicates air leakage from faulty seals.

WARNING: Compressed air can blow liquids or metal chips into your eyes, causing serious physical injury or blindness. Always wear safety glasses or goggles when working with compressed air.

7. Release air pressure and reapply. Listen for thuds or thunks. If you cannot hear a servo operate, watch to see if the band tightens and loosens properly as air pressure is applied and released. Repair or replace apply devices during overhaul as necessary.

Computer and Solenoid Valve Tests

Refer to the manufacturer's service manual procedures for specific transmission computer tests. Be aware that improper test procedures can damage or destroy computer units immediately.

Specific tests for input and output signals are made. Special hand-held computer testers might be required. If input signals are correct and output signals are incorrect, the computer unit must be replaced.

Solenoid valves are tested by removing the electrical connector. Then the resistance of the solenoid coil can be checked between the connector and ground. Another way of testing a solenoid is to apply current with a small jumper wire to the disconnected solenoid valve. Correct operation can be heard or felt when the solenoid moves sharply. Refer to the manufacturer's service manuals and service bulletins for specific tests.

 CASE STUDY

Case 1

A customer complains of delayed and harsh shifting.

The knowledgeable technician realizes this problem results from high throttle pressure caused by a lack of engine vacuum at the vacuum modulator (closed) chamber. He seeks to determine why the engine vacuum is not reaching the modulator chamber. The technician begins by connecting a vacuum gauge to the end of the steel vacuum pipe between the intake manifold and the vacuum modulator. With the engine operating and the transmission in neutral, he checks the vacuum gauge reading. It is within specifications, so he rapidly accelerates the engine for a moment. Because the vacuum gauge needle drops rapidly at acceleration and returns immediately upon release of the throttle, the technician knows that the steel vacuum pipe is not plugged or restricted. Next, the technician uses a hand-held vacuum pump to check the steel pipe for pinholes. The hand-held pump is connected to the intake manifold end of the steel piping. The steel piping is disconnected at the vacuum modulator and the end of the steel piping is blocked. Then the technician operates the vacuum pump to pump up vacuum. Because a vacuum reading is shown on the vacuum pump and it holds steady, the technician knows that there are no pinholes in the steel piping. Finally, he examines the rubber tubing that connects the steel piping to the vacuum modulator and finds that it is porous. The technician replaces the connector tubing and the problem is corrected.

Summary

- The ATF level should be checked at regular mileage and time intervals. When the fluid is checked, the vehicle should be level and running and the transmission should be at operating temperature.
- Both low fluid levels and high fluid levels can cause aeration of the fluid, which in turn can cause a number of transmission problems.
- Uncontaminated automatic transmission fluid is pinkish or red in color and it has no dark or metallic particles suspended in it.
- The fluid should be changed when the engine and transmission or transaxle are at normal operating temperatures. After draining the fluid, the pan should be inspected and the filter replaced.
- If ATF is leaking from the pump seal, the transmission must be removed from the vehicle so that the seal can be replaced. Other worn or defective gaskets or seals can be replaced without removing the transmission. Case porosity may be repaired using an epoxy-type sealer.
- Proper adjustment of the gear selector or manual linkage is important to have the manual valve fluid inlet and outlets properly aligned in the valve body. If the manual valve does not align with the inlet and outlets, line pressure could be lost to an open circuit.
- The throttle cable connects the throttle pedal's movement to the transaxle valve body throttle valve, which produces throttle pressure. The throttle cable is held in position in the throttle cable bracket by the cross-lock, an automatic locking device that keeps the throttle cable properly adjusted.
- Slippage during shifting can indicate the need for band adjustment.
- Improper shifting can be caused by a defective vacuum modulator or by defective or missing modulator vacuum connectors. A repeated low fluid level in the transmission with no visible external leaks and the sudden appearance of excessive blue-white smoke from the tail pipe usually indicates a ruptured diaphragm in the modulator.
- Improper shift points can be caused by a malfunction in the governor or governor drive gear system.
- The road test gives the technician the opportunity to check the transaxle or transmission operation for slipping, harshness, incorrect upshift speeds, and incorrect downshift.
- Accurate diagnosis depends upon knowing what planetary controls are applied in a particular gear range. Although road testing analysis can help to diagnose slipping units, the actual cause of the slip or malfunction usually cannot be decided.
- A pressure test checks hydraulic pressures in the transmission by using gauges that are attached to the transmission. Pressure readings reveal possible problems in the oil pump, governor, and throttle circuits.
- Air pressure tests can determine whether the problem is in the apply device or in the valve body that supplies hydraulic pressure.
- If a computer's input signals are correct and its output signals are incorrect, the computer must be replaced. Solenoid valves can be checked by measuring their resistance, or by applying a current to it and listening and feeling for its movement.

Review Questions

1. What is the most probable cause of a low fluid level?
2. What does milky colored ATF indicate?
3. What does varnish or gum deposits on the dipstick indicate?
4. What switch permits starter engagement only in park or neutral gear selector positions?
5. What is a probable cause of a repeated low fluid level in the transmission with no visible external leaks and the sudden appearance of excessive blue-white smoke from the tail pipe?
6. Technician A says that automatic transmission fluid smells burned if there is a burned-out planetary control unit. Technician B says that all automatic transmission fluid smells burned after approximately 50 miles of operation. Who is correct?

a. Technician A
b. Technician B
c. Both A and B
d. Neither A nor B

7. What type of test is used to evaluate the application of servos and clutches?
   a. air pressure
   b. hydraulic pressure
   c. both a and b
   d. neither a nor b

8. Half of all automatic transmission problems result from _____ .
   a. improper fluid levels
   b. fluid leaks and vacuum leaks
   c. electrical malfunctions
   d. all of the above

9. When should the ATF level be checked on most vehicles?
   a. when the engine is cool
   b. when the engine is at operating temperature and the engine is off
   c. when the engine is at operating temperature and the engine is on
   d. it does not matter

10. Technician A says that low fluid levels can lead to aeration of the fluid. Technician B says that high fluid levels cause aeration of the fluid. Who is correct?
    a. Technician A
    b. Technician B
    c. Both A and B
    d. Neither A nor B

11. Technician A changes the ATF when the engine and transmission are cool. Technician B checks the bottom of the oil pan, finds a few small metal particles, and concludes everything is normal. Who is correct?
    a. Technician A
    b. Technician B
    c. Both A and B
    d. Neither A nor B

12. Technician A says that the pump seal can be replaced without removing the transmission from the vehicle. Technician B says that case porosity may be repaired using an epoxy-type sealer. Who is correct?
    a. Technician A
    b. Technician B
    c. Both A and B
    d. Neither A nor B

13. Technician A says that throttle pressure influences the vehicle speed at which automatic shifts take place. Technician B says that throttle pressure is opposed by governor pressure. Who is correct?
    a. Technician A
    b. Technician B
    c. Both A and B
    d. Neither A nor B

14. Which of the following is true?
    a. The cross-lock keeps the gear selector linkage properly adjusted.
    b. The cross-lock keeps the throttle cable properly adjusted.
    c. The cross-lock keeps the front kickdown band properly adjusted.
    d. none of the above

15. Technician A says that engine vacuum leaks can produce the same symptoms as a defective vacuum modulator. Technician B says that the vacuum modulator is located inside the transmission. Who is correct?
    a. Technician A
    b. Technician B
    c. Both A and B
    d. Neither A nor B

16. Improper shifting can be caused by _____ .
    a. a defective vacuum modulator
    b. a malfunction in the governor
    c. both a and b
    d. neither a nor b

17. Technician A says that a prerequisite to accurate road testing analysis is knowing what planetary controls are applied in a particular gear range. Technician B says that all slipping conditions can be traced to a leaking hydraulic circuit. Who is correct?
    a. Technician A
    b. Technician B
    c. Both A and B
    d. Neither A nor B

18. Pressure readings reveal possible problems in which of the following?
    a. oil pump
    b. governor
    c. throttle circuits
    d. all of the above

19. What level of compressed air is usually used for the air pressure test?
    a. 40 psi
    b. 60 psi
    c. 80 psi
    d. 90 psi

20. Technician A says that if input signals are correct and output signals are incorrect, the computer unit must be replaced. Technician B tests a solenoid by checking the voltage between the solenoid's connector and ground. Who is correct?
    a. Technician A
    b. Technician B
    c. Both A and B
    d. Neither A nor B

31 FOUR- AND ALL-WHEEL DRIVE

Objectives

- Identify the advantages of four- and all-wheel drive.
- Name the major components of a conventional four-wheel-drive system.
- Name the components of a transfer case.
- State the differences between the transfer, open, and limited slip differentials.
- State the major purpose of locking/unlocking hubs.
- Name the five shift lever positions on a typical 4WD vehicle.
- Understand the difference between four- and all-wheel drive.
- Know the purpose of a viscous clutch in all-wheel drive.

Four-wheel-drive (4WD) and all-wheel-drive (AWD) systems can dramatically increase a vehicle's traction and handling ability in rain, snow, and off-road driving. Consider that the vehicle's only contact with the road is the small areas of the tires. Driving and handling is vastly improved if the work load is spread out evenly among four wheels rather than two.

Factors such as the side forces created by cornering and wind gusts have less effect on vehicles with four driving wheels. The increased traction also makes it possible to apply greater amounts of energy through the drive system. Vehicles with 4WD or AWD can maintain control while transmitting levels of power that would cause two wheels to spin either on take off or while rounding a curve. The improved traction of 4WD and AWD systems allows the use of tires narrower than those used on similar 2WD vehicles. These narrow tires are less expensive. They also tend to cut through snow and water rather than hydroplane over it.

Four-wheel-drive vehicles can transfer large amounts of horsepower through the drivelines without fear of drivetrain damage. This is not necessarily true of front-wheel-drive vehicles and all-wheel-drive vehicles—both of which use transaxles.

Both 4WD and AWD systems add initial cost and weight. With most passenger cars, the weight problem is minor. A typical 4WD system adds approximately 170 pounds to a passenger car. An AWD system adds even less weight. The additional weight in larger 4WD trucks can be as much as 400 pounds or more.

The systems also add initial cost to the vehicle. Vehicles equipped with 4WD and AWD require special service and maintenance not performed on 2WD vehicles. However, the slight disadvantages of 4WD and AWD are heavily outweighed by the traction and performance these systems offer. Their popularity is increasing at a rapid rate, and technicians must be prepared to diagnose and repair these systems.

❏ 4WD VERSUS AWD

Due to the many names manufacturers give their drive systems, it is often difficult to clearly define the difference between 4WD and AWD.

In this text, 4WD systems are those having a separate transfer case (Figure 31-1A). They also give the driver the choice of operating in either 2WD or 4WD through the use of a shift lever or shift button. The locking hubs used in 4WD systems can be either manual or automatic locking. Finally, a 4WD system may or may not use an interaxle differential or viscous clutch to distribute driving power to its front and rear drivelines.

All-wheel-drive systems differ in several major ways (Figure 31-1B). They do not have a separate transfer case. All-wheel-drive systems use a front-wheel-drive transaxle equipped with a viscous clutch, center differential, or transfer clutch. The viscous clutch, center differential, or transfer clutch transfers power from the transaxle to a rear driveline and rear axle assembly. All-wheel-drive systems do not give the driver the option of selecting 2WD or 4WD modes. The system operates in continuous 4WD.

❏ FOUR-WHEEL-DRIVE SYSTEMS

The typical truck or utility 4WD vehicle contains the following components (Figure 31-2): a front-

776 Section 6 Automatic Transmissions and Transaxles

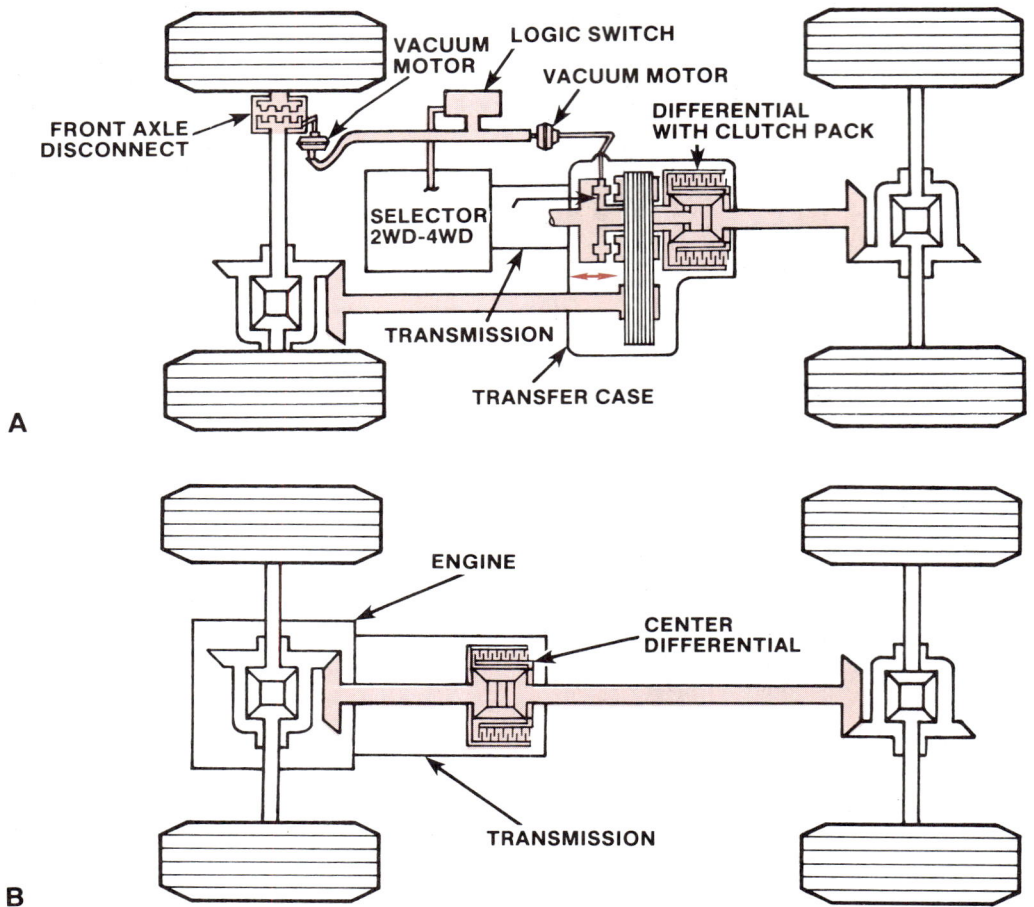

Figure 31-1 (A) Four-wheel drive compared to (B) all-wheel drive. *Courtesy of Chrysler Motors*

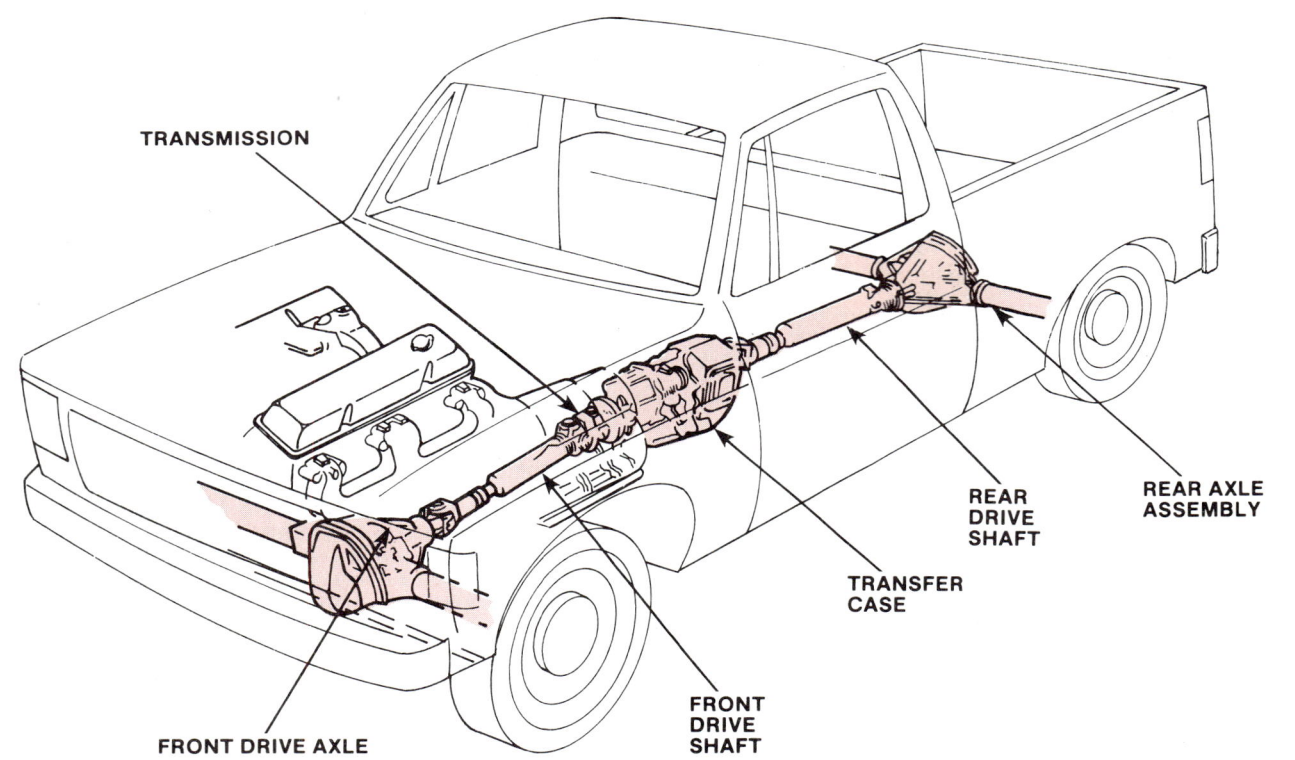

Figure 31-2 Truck-type four-wheel drivetrain based on a rear-wheel-drive design.

Four- and All-Wheel Drive   777

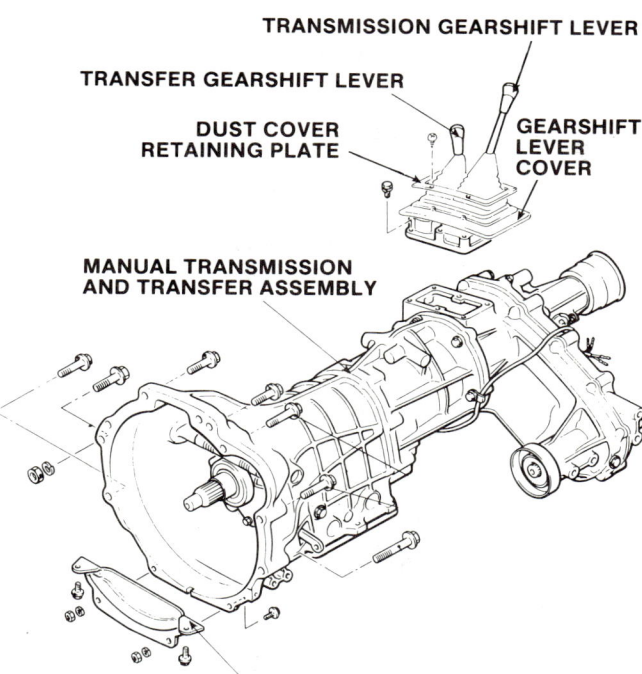

Figure 31-3 Transmission and transfer case for four-wheel drive. *Courtesy of Mitsubishi Motor Sales of America, Inc.*

mounted, longitudinally-positioned engine; the transmission (either manual or automatic); two driveline shafts (front and rear); front and rear axle assemblies; and the transfer case.

The heart of most conventional four-wheel-drive vehicles is the transfer case, which is usually mounted to the side or the back of the transmission (Figure 31-3). A chain or gear drive within the case receives the power flow from the transmission and transfers it to two separate drive shafts leading to the front and rear axles.

A selector switch or shifter located in the driving compartment (Figure 31-4) controls the transfer case so that power is directed to the axles as the driver desires. Power can be directed to all four wheels, two wheels, or no wheels (neutral). On many vehicles, the driver is also given the option of low four-wheel-drive range for extra traction in especially rough conditions, such as deep snow or mud.

The driveline from the transfer case shafts run to differentials at the front and rear axles. As on two-wheel-drive vehicles, these axle differentials are used to compensate for road and driving conditions by adjusting the rpm to opposing wheels. For example, the outer wheel must roll faster in a turn than the inner wheel during a turn because it has more ground to cover. To permit this action, the differential cuts back the power delivered to the inner wheel and boosts the amount of power delivered to the outer wheel.

U-joints are used to couple the driveline shafts with the differentials and transfer cases on all these vehicles. U-joints can also be used on some vehicles to connect the rear axle and wheels. Normally, however, rear axles are simply bolted to the wheel hubs.

The coupling between front wheels and axles is normally done with U-joints on heavy-duty vehicles and with CV (constant velocity) joints on lightweight vehicles (Figure 31-5). Generally, half axles or half shafts with CV joints are found on four-wheel-drive passenger cars. They can also be found on a number of passenger vans and on mini pickups and trucks.

On 4WD systems adapted from front-wheel-drive systems, a separate front differential and driveline are not needed. The front wheels are driven by the transaxle differential of the base model. A power takeoff is added to the transaxle to transmit power to the rear wheels in four-wheel drive. This takeoff gearing is housing in a transfer case mounted to the transaxle housing. The gearing connects to a rear driveline and rear axle assembly that includes the rear differential.

❑ TRANSFER CASE

In a 4WD vehicle, as mentioned earlier, the transfer case delivers power to both the front and rear assem-

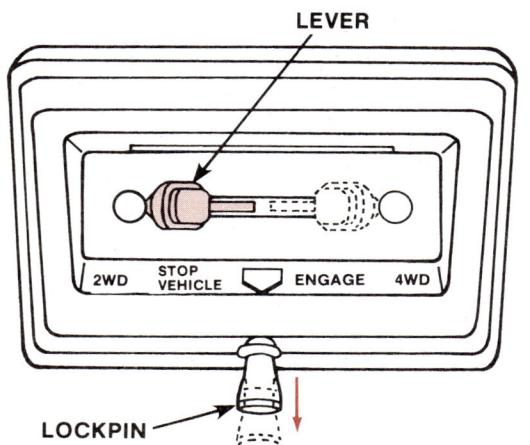

Figure 31-4 The 2WD and 4WD selector can be simply a lever on the dash to engage or disengage the four-wheel drive. *Courtesy of Chrysler Motors*

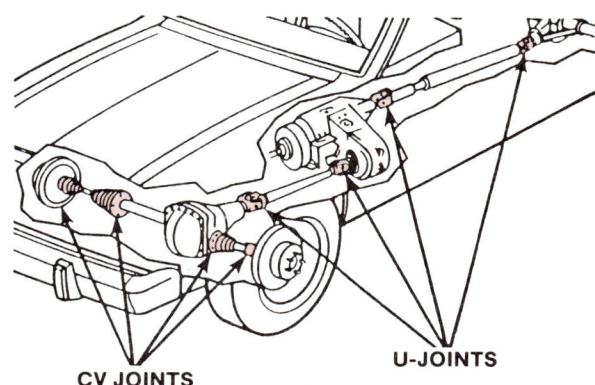

Figure 31-5 CV joint and U-joint locations on a 4WD.

blies. Two drive shafts normally operate from the transfer case, one to each drive axle.

The transfer case itself is constructed similar to a standard transmission. It uses shift forks to select the operating mode, plus splines, gears, shims, bearings, and other components found in manual and automatic transmission. The outer case of the unit is made of cast iron or aluminum. It is filled with lubricant (oil) that cuts friction on all moving parts. Seals hold the lubricant in the case and prevent leakage around shafts and yokes. Shims set up the proper clearance between the internal components and the case.

Driveline Windup

It must be kept in mind that vehicles with two driving axles have different gear ratios between the front and rear driving axles, resulting in a pull-push action. The result of having the two axle ratios is a

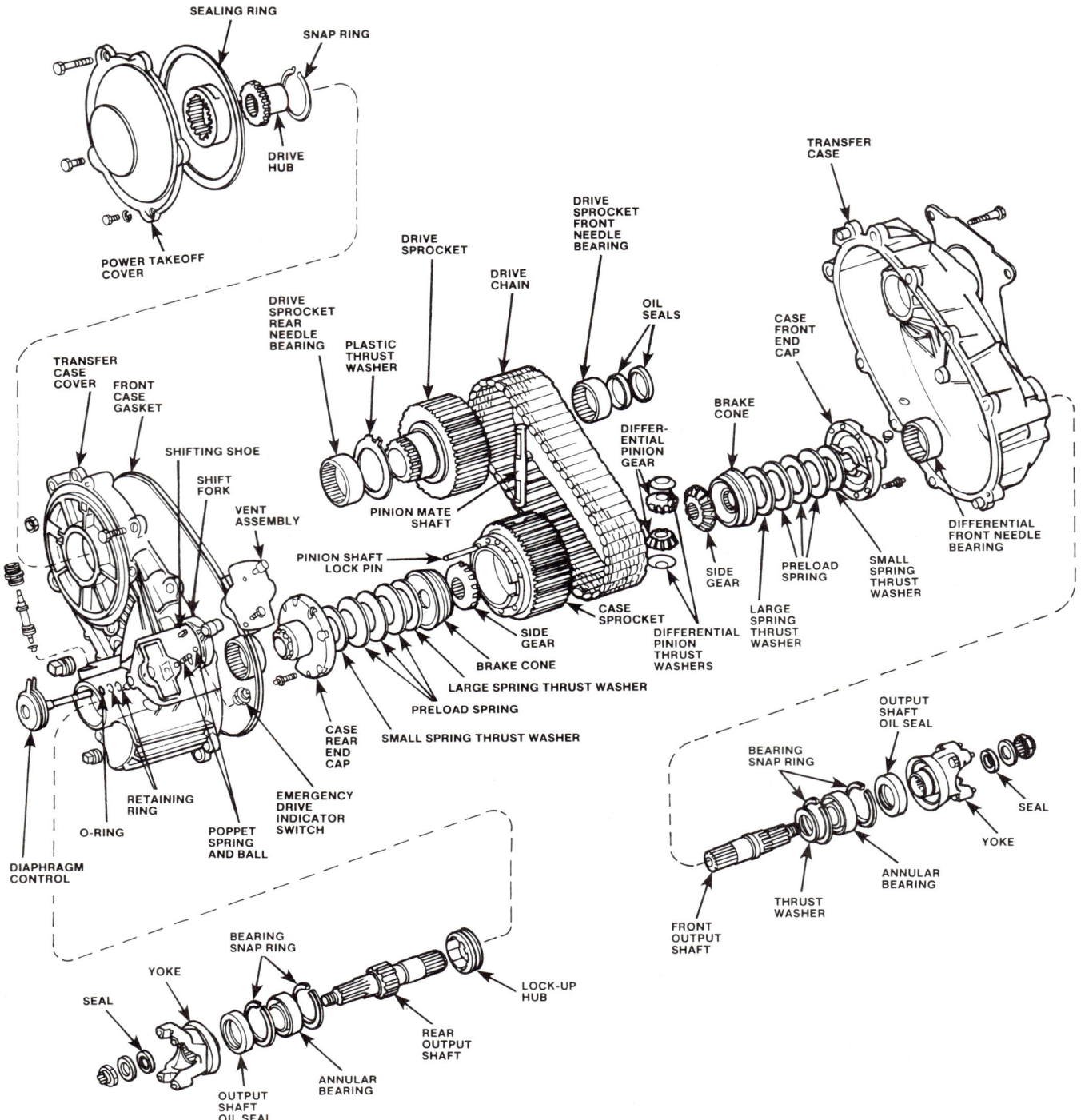

Figure 31-6 Four-wheel-drive transfer case with integral differential and cone brakes for limited slip.

phenomenon called driveline windup. Driveline windup can be explained by associating the driveline to a torsion bar. The driveline twists up when both driving axles are rotating at different speeds, pushing and pulling the vehicle on hard, dry pavement. Also remember that neither the front nor rear axle has any compensating factor for speed and gear ratio differences between the front and rear driving axles.

Driveline windup can cause handling problems, particularly when rounding turns on dry pavement. This is because the front axle wheels must travel farther than the rear axle wheels when rounding a curve. On wet or slippery roads, the front and rear wheels slide enough to prevent damage to the driveline components. However, this may not be the case on dry surfaces. This is why many older 4WD systems that do not include components to dissipate driveline windup can only be safely driven on wet or slippery surfaces.

Interaxle Differentials

The most common method of dissipating driveline windup is to include a third or interaxle differential in the transfer case gearing (Figure 31-6).

The front and rear drivelines are connected to the interaxle differential inside the transfer case. Just as a drive axle differential allows for different left and right drive axle shaft speeds, the interaxle differential allows for different front and rear driveline shaft speeds (Figure 31-7). The driveline windup, developed as a result of different front and rear axle gear ratios, is dissipated by the interaxle differential.

While the interaxle differential solves the problem of driveline windup during turns, it also lowers performance in poor traction conditions. This is because the interaxle differential will tend to deliver more power to the wheels with the least traction. The result is increased slippage, the exact opposite of what is desired.

To counteract this problem, some interaxle differentials are designed much like a limited slip differential. They use a multiple disc clutch pack to maintain a predetermined amount of torque transfer before the differential action begins to take effect. Other systems, such as the one shown in Figure 31-6, use a cone braking system rather than a clutch pack. But the end result is the same. Power is supplied to both axles regardless of the traction encountered.

Most systems also give the driver the option of locking the interaxle differential in certain operating modes. This eliminates the differential action altogether. However, the interaxle differential should only be locked while driving in slippery conditions.

❏ LOCKING/UNLOCKING HUBS

Most 4WD systems on trucks and utility vehicles use front-wheel driving hubs that can be disengaged from the front axle when the vehicle is operating in the 2WD mode. When unlocked in 2WD, the front wheels still turn, but the entire front drivetrain, including the front axles, the front differential, the front drive shaft, and certain internal transfer case components, stop turning. This helps reduce wear to these items.

The front hubs must be locked during 4WD operation. Some front hub designs lock automatically. Others require the driver to get out and turn a lever or knob at the center of each front wheel (Figure 31-8). Figures 31-9 and 31-10 illustrate the components in lock manual and automatic locking hubs. By locking the hubs, the wheels turn with the axle for the most traction. When unlocked, the wheels are free to spin at different rotational speeds, such as when cornering. The tires scrub on the pavement if the hubs are locked, causing them to wear faster, so they should only be locked when venturing off-road or under other low-traction situations, such as heavy rain, snow, or ice.

The disadvantage of the self-locking hub is that power cannot be applied to the wheels in reverse. This can be a big disadvantage if the vehicle gets stuck and backing up is the only way out. To unlock the automatic type, stop the car, disengage the four-wheel drive, and back up about 3 feet. Often these hubs unlock immediately when the four-wheel drive is disengaged, without the need to back up.

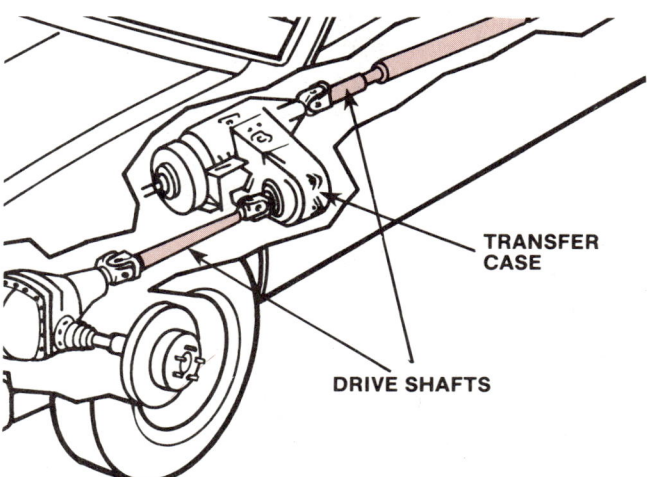

Figure 31-7 Speed of drive shaft controlled by transfer case.

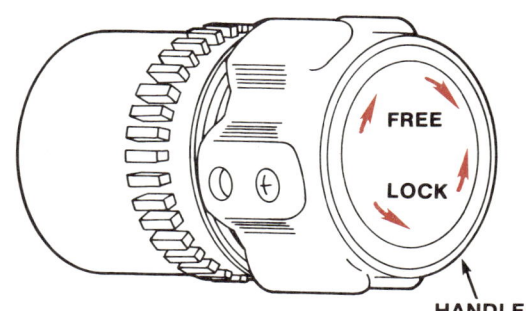

Figure 31-8 Rotating handle locks the hub.

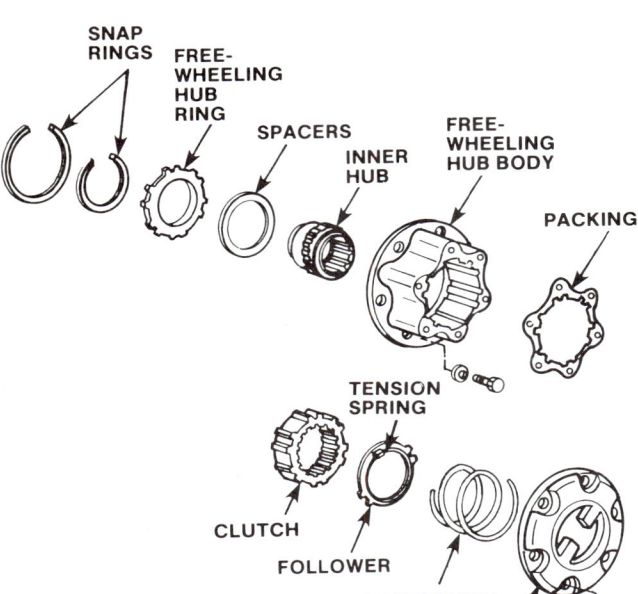

Figure 31-9 Manual locking front hub components and engagement knob. *Courtesy of Mitsubishi Motor Sales of America, Inc.*

The latest development in hubs is the fully automatic type. Once four-wheel drive is engaged, they lock automatically when power is applied, either forward or reverse. That is, power can be applied in either forward or reverse direction once locked.

Axle Disconnects

Some 4WD vehicles are equipped with ordinary front wheel hubs, but have a vacuum-operated axle disconnect shift mechanism (Figure 31-11). The vacuum motor moves a splined collar to connect or disconnect one of the front axle drive shafts from the front differential. The axle shafts and differential continue to turn. But the ring gear, pinion, and front drive axle remain stationary. This reduces wear to these major components. This system is used on both trucks and passenger cars.

☐ CONVENTIONAL 4WD OPERATING MODES

The typical five-position shift pattern of a conventional 4WD gearbox is as follows (Figure 31-12).

2WD Two-wheel-drive range. In this high-range mode, the gear ratio is at 1 to 1. Both of the output shafts revolve at the same rate as the transmission output shaft.

HI LOCK Four-wheel-drive high range with transfer case differential locked up (part-time, high-traction mode). A straight 1 to 1 gear ratio.

4WD Four-wheel-drive high range with transfer case differential not locked up (full-time, all-surface mode). A straight 1 to 1 gear ratio.

N—NEUTRAL Both front and rear axles are disengaged from the power train and the vehicle may be

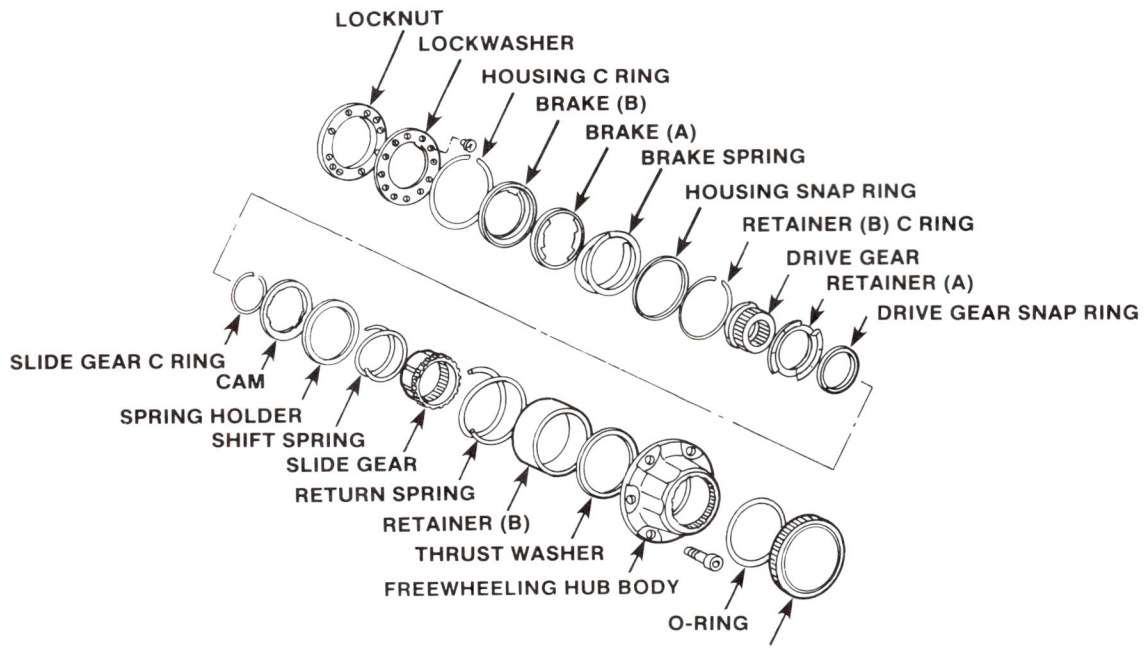

Figure 31-10 Automatic front hub components. *Courtesy of Mitsubishi Motor Sales of America, Inc.*

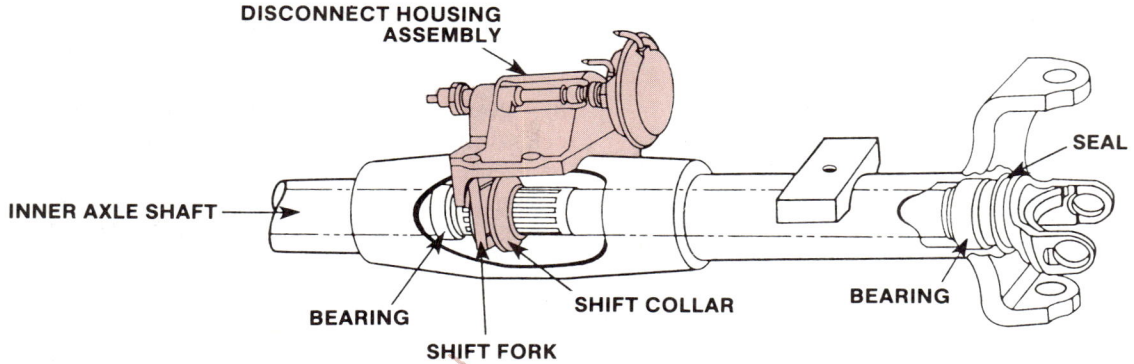

Figure 31-11 Axle disconnect mechanism using a vacuum-operated shifter. *Courtesy of Chrysler Motors*

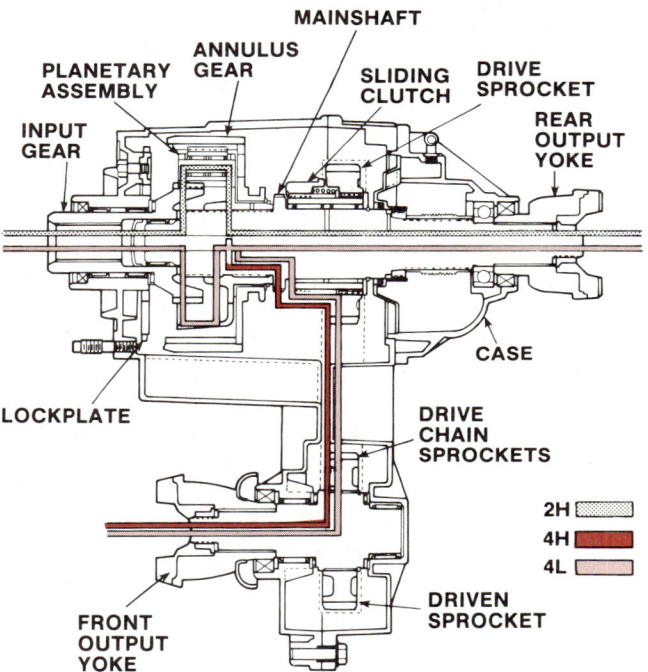

Figure 31-12 The power flow through transfer case in 2H, 4H, and 4L modes. *Courtesy of American Motors Corporation*

towed without uncoupling the propeller shafts. However, torque is not transferred to the front axle assembly.

LO LOCK Four-wheel-drive low range with transfer case differential locked up. This mode of operation has a gear ratio generally at 2 to 1 (although it may go as high as 26 to 1), which cuts the road speed in half. Thus, the vehicle can be operated in 4WD low range over difficult obstacles and through mud, snow, and sand with the engine running up in its power band but with relatively slow vehicle speed.

The transfer case shift pattern is usually marked on the shifter knob. Manufacturers use different patterns and designations for the various gear positions. On some vehicles, an indicator light is located on the dash panel to show the driver which mode of operation the vehicle is in. When the indicator lamp is not lit, it usually indicates the vehicle is 2WD or neutral.

CAUTION: Four-wheel-drive vehicles featuring high lock and lo lock should not be operated on dry, hard surfaces. Such an operation causes tire scuffing and driveline damage.

One system on the market contains a transfer case that does not have a low-range position. The transmission includes a low-geared sixth-speed position, which can only be engaged when the transfer case is in the four-wheel-drive mode. In fact, there are single-speed transfer cases available that permit the operator to employ either 2WD or 4WD through a simple gear train. In one position the gear train permits the power flow to the rear driveline only. An integral main drive gear in the transfer case (driven by the transmission output shaft) provides power to the rear driveline at all times. In addition, it is in mesh with an idler gear on a short auxiliary shaft. The idler gear, in turn, meshes with a front-axle drive gear to rotate the front driveline when in the 4WD mode. Or, the front-axle drive gear is moved out of mesh with the idler gear when the 2WD mode is desired.

On some models, particularly more recent ones, the shift to 4WD can be accomplished while the vehicle is moving (shifting on-the-fly). Most vehicles must be stopped before the change can be made. Also, the shift into a four-wheel-drive low mode normally requires that the vehicle is stopped first.

Some of the newer on-the-fly systems feature a magnetic clutch on the transfer case that speeds up the front drive shaft, differential, and axles to the same speed as the transmission (Figure 31-13). At the instant the speed is synchronized, an electric motor on the transfer case completes the shift, smoothly and quietly. The operator cannot damage the system because it does not shift until the speeds are synchronized.

The newest of all 4WD systems is the automatic design. While there are several different systems on the market, one of the more commonly used systems has a microprocessor to control the interaxle differential,

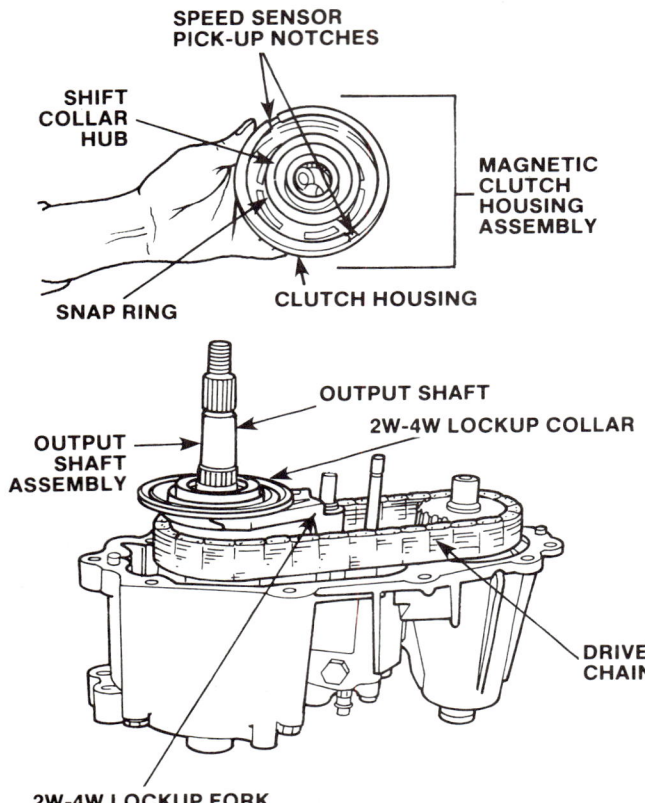

Figure 31-13 A magnetic clutch that synchronizes the shaft speeds before allowing the shift. *Courtesy of Ford Motor Co.*

thus providing varying amounts of torque to the front and rear driving wheels. That is, in a fraction of a second, a computer device senses that difference in wheel speeds and engages a clutch-type device to begin driving the rear wheels. When the wheel speeds are equal again, the system reverts to front drive.

◻ 4WD PASSENGER CARS

While most 4WD trucks and utility vehicles are design variations of most basic rear-wheel-drive vehicles, most passenger cars featuring 4WD were developed from a front-wheel-drive base model.

As mentioned at the beginning of this chapter, they feature a transaxle and differential that drive the front wheels, plus some type of mechanism for connecting the transaxle to a rear driveline. In many cases this is a simple clutch type engagement.

4WD passenger cars normally differ from heavier-duty 4WD trucks and vehicles in several other ways. First, there is no separate transfer case; any gearing needed to transfer power to the rear driveline is usually contained in the transaxle housing or small bolt on extension housing. Four-wheel-drive passenger cars do not use front wheel locking hubs. Since the cars do not have lockout hubs, traction is not quite as good in the worst conditions and tire wear not so severe should the driver forget to take the car out of four-wheel drive. Interaxle differentials are also very uncommon.

Most passenger cars with 4WD are not designed for the rigors of off-road driving, in which clearance over rocks and debris is needed. For simple road driving there is no clearance or durability problems. As with 4WD trucks, the passenger car 4WD mode should not be used on dry pavement due to increased tire and drivetrain wear.

Limited Slip and Open Differentials

To help compensate for the lack of locking hubs many 4WD passenger cars use limited slip or open differential designs for the front and rear differentials. These systems allow enough differential slippage to substantially reduce wheel scrubbing and driveline windup.

A limited slip differential uses a friction clutch to join the right and left rear axle shafts to the differential case. This system assures that most power is supplied where the traction is greatest. It permits the inner and outer wheels to rotate at different speeds when turns are made, just as in general differentials.

In addition, the LSD provides these features. When one front and one rear wheel, which are diagonal to each other, slip on snow-covered roads and driving force cannot be delivered, or when one rear wheel is caught in a ditch and runs idle, the LSD delivers strong torque to the other wheel so that the vehicle can run normally. Even if the vehicle bumps with one rear wheel off the road, such as when driving on rough terrain, gravel, or snow-covered roads, the LSD assures easy straightforward driveability by its limited differential function.

Other systems use an open differential. Here the greatest power is supplied where there is the least resistance. This is an excellent system for fuel economy and gear wear in full-time, four-wheel drive, but it does not provide the true traction advantages of four-wheel drive. For example, the greatest power would be supplied to the slipping wheels (least resistance) on icy road conditions when it is actually needed at the wheels facing the most resistance (for example, where the greatest traction is).

> **USING SERVICE MANUALS**
>
> Because of the various four-wheel-drive systems in use, it is essential that the undercar technician carefully study and understand that particular vehicle's service manual.

Systems using an open differential have a drive mode on the selector, which permits the differential to be locked up in such conditions. This causes the drivetrain to function the same as a part-time four-wheel-drive system. The power is distributed equally to all the wheels. Vehicles should not be driven in this mode, except under poor road conditions, for the same reasons that part-time systems should be used only when needed.

> **CUSTOMER CARE**
>
> Advise your customer that wear on 4WD systems is much greater than on a two-wheel-drive transaxle or transmission. This is especially true if drivers leave the four-wheel drive engaged on dry pavement. Some car makers warn that abuse of the system is not covered under the warranty.

☐ SERVICING 4WD VEHICLES

Components of 4WD vehicles can be serviced in basically the same manner as the identical components of a 2WD vehicle. Before doing any servicing, however, it is necessary to give the undercar a complete inspection. Pay particular attention to the steering dampers, steering linkage, wheel bearing, ball joints, coil springs, and radius arm bushings.

The U-joints, slip joints, or CV joints on a 4WD drivetrain that must be lubed on a regular basis are shown in Figure 31-14. To service the drive shafts on a four-wheel-drive vehicle, use the general instructions given earlier for a cross universal joint. A four-wheel-drive simply uses two drive shafts instead of one.

Servicing the Transfer Case

As with all automobile servicing procedures, be sure to check the manufacturer's service manual for specific transfer case repair and overhaul procedures. It gives details for the particular make and model of transfer case to be worked on.

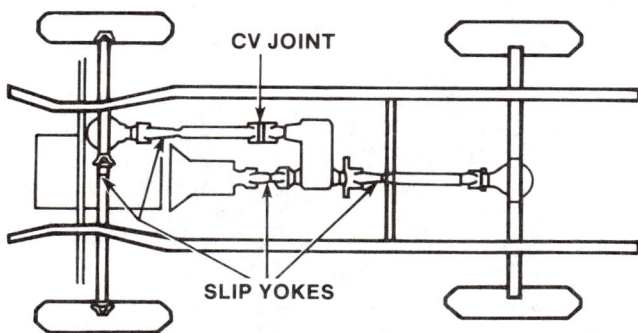

Figure 31-14   U-joints, slip joints, and CV joints on four-wheel-drive drivetrains should be lubed regularly to prevent premature failure.

CAUTION: When removing and working on a transfer case, be sure to support it on a transmission jack or safety stands. The unit is heavy and if dropped, it could cause part damage and personal injury.

When removing the transfer case, disconnect and remove all driveline or propeller shaft assemblies. Be sure to mark the parts and their relative positions on their yokes so that the proper driveline balance can be maintained when reassembled. Disconnect the linkage to the transfer case shift lever. Also disconnect wires to switches for 4WD dash indicator lights, if used. Remove all fasteners holding the case and move it away from the transaxle or transmission.

Once the transfer case has been removed from the vehicle and safely supported, take off the case cover and disconnect any electrical connections. Visually inspect for any oil leaks. Then carefully loosen and drive out the pins that hold the shift forks in place. Remove the front output shafts and chain drive or gearsets from the case. Keep in mind that some cases use chain drives while others use spur or helical cut gearsets to transfer torque from the transaxle or transmission to the output shafts. Planetary gearsets provide the necessary gear reductions in some transfer cases.

Clean and carefully inspect all parts for damage and wear. Check the slack in the chain drive by following the procedure given in the service manual (Figure 31-15). Replace any defective parts. It may be necessary to measure the shaft assembly end play. If excessive, new snap rings and shims may be used to correct the situation.

When reassembling the transfer case, the procedure is essentially the reverse of the removal. Be sure to use new gaskets between the covers when reassembling the unit.

> **CUSTOMER CARE**
>
> It is very important to remind your customers that the fluid level in a transfer case must be checked at recommended time intervals. (Check the service manual.) It is wise to show your customers where the transfer case fill plug is located and how to remove it. Also tell them that the lubricant should be almost even with the fill hole. Always refer to the service manual for recommended transfer case lubricants. Many transfer cases require extreme pressure (EP) lubricants as used in differentials and in some manual transmissions.

Upgrading 4WD Vehicles

A technician is often required to upgrade 4WD vehicles for off-road driving. The most requested upgrades by the four-wheel-drive owner are the installation of

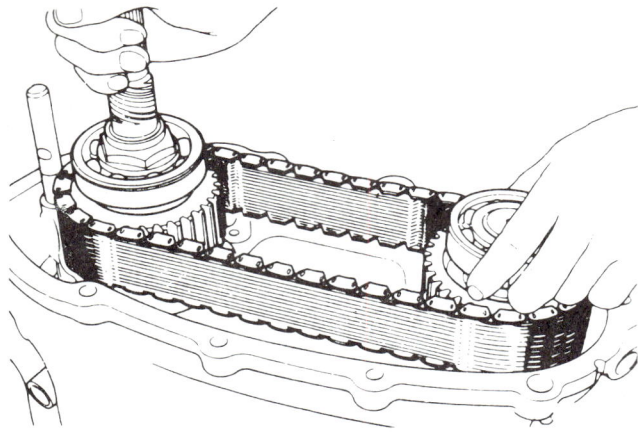

Figure 31-15 Check the chain drive for stretch. *Courtesy of Mitsubishi Motor Sales of America, Inc.*

Figure 31-16 Properly aligned lower and upper retaining bolts. *Courtesy of Moog Automotive*

cargo-type variable rate coil springs, steering damper, steering stabilizers, and helper springs; heavy-duty, trail-type shock absorbers or struts; oversized tires; and lift kits.

Heavy-Coil Installation

Extra-duty variable rate coils solve many load and ride problems. Coil spring replacement is needed on four-wheel-drive vehicles for several reasons: poor load handling capability, bottoming out, or incorrect height. The solution is replacement with extra-duty, cargo-type coil springs. The variable rate design gives additional load capacity and firmness when needed.

PROCEDURES

Replacing Coil Springs

1. Raise and support the vehicle by its frame. Remove the tires and support the axle with jack stands. Disconnect the lower shock mount.
2. Remove the two bolts holding the upper spring retainer and remove the retainer.
3. Remove the two bolts holding the lower spring retainer to the axle housing.
4. Raise the vehicle, making sure not to put strain on the brake hose, until the spring is free and can be removed.
5. Install the new cargo-type spring by properly seating the lower coil and lower retainer. Start the two lower mounting bolts, but leave them loose. Align spring to upper seat by slowly lowering the vehicle frame.
6. When properly aligned, torque the lower retainer bolts and upper retainer bolts (Figure 31-16). Connect the lower shock mount to complete the installation.

Steering Stabilizers or Damper Installation

A steering stabilizer is a shock absorber that is mounted horizontally between the frame and a part of the steering linkage. Its purpose is to absorb road shock created by pot holes or obstructions and limit its transfer back to the steering wheel. It also reduces wear and tear on other steering components. Heavy-duty units for the most severe road conditions are easily attached to four-wheel-drive vehicles (Figure 31-17).

Helper Spring Installation

Helper springs are inactive when no load is applied. When the rear end starts to sag under heavy load or impact, these springs go into action and can provide 1500 pounds of additional load handling capability. This gives the extra support needed to stop sag and bottoming out. All necessary hardware comes with the kit to make these springs an easy bolt-on addition (Figure 31-18).

PROCEDURES

Helper Spring Installation

1. Remove the rear spring U-bolts, U-bolt guides, and U-bolt retainer plate. Discard the original U-bolts because they are no longer needed.

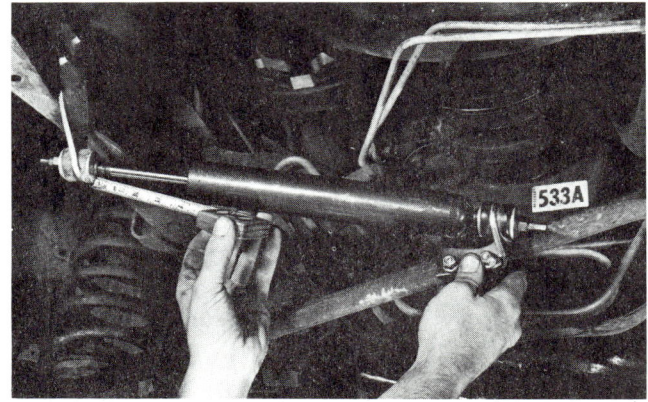

Figure 31-17 Attaching a steering damper. *Courtesy of Moog Automotive*

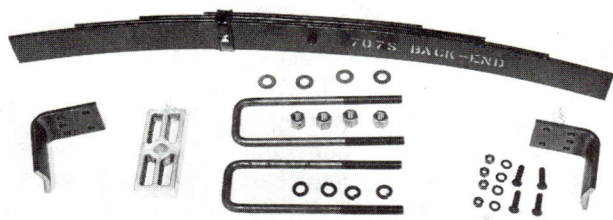

Figure 31-18 Helper spring kit. *Courtesy of Moog Automotive*

Figure 31-19 Installing helper springs. *Courtesy of Moog Automotive*

2. Place the helper spring on top of the supplied spacer block with the correct end of the spring to the rear of the truck, and with the head of the center bolt in the hole of the spacer block. Reuse the old U-bolt retainer plate and U-bolt guide. Install the new U-bolts, flat washers, lock washers, and deep nuts (Figure 31-19).
3. Install the frame brackets, using the existing holes in the frame of the clamp wedges, if supplied, on the truck frame. Center the brackets over the end of the helper spring.
4. Tighten all the U-bolts and frame the bracket nuts to specifications. Make sure the new right-hand spring is lined up properly to make contact with the brackets.

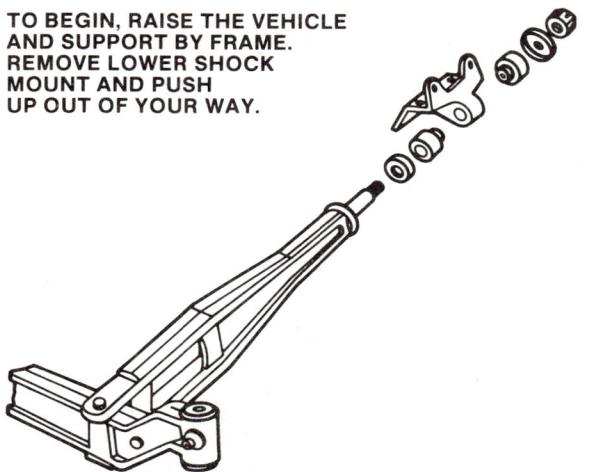

Figure 31-20 Exploded view of radius arm bushings.

 **PROCEDURES**

Radius Arm Bushing Installation

1. Raise the vehicle by the frame and remove the tires.
2. While supporting the axle with the jack stands, unbolt the lower spring seat from the radius arm. Remove the lower shock mounting bolt.
3. Unbolt the radius arm at the front and remove the nut from the rear.
4. Use a pry bar to move the axle forward to remove the radius arm. Remove the old bushing and clean the arm where the bushing mounts.
5. Install the front half of the high-performance bushing on the radius arm per instructions and reinstall the radius arm.
6. Reconnect the radius arm to the axle and leave the mounting bolts loose. Install the rear half of the bushing. Make sure the steel sleeves properly mate with the hole in the rear mounting bracket (Figure 31-20).
7. Tighten the rear radius arm nut to specification. Tighten the front bolts and line up the lower spring seat with the radius arm. Install the bolts. Reconnect the shock to complete the installation.

Oversized Tires and Lift Kits

Four-wheel-drive vehicles are widely used for the sport of off-road driving. Anybody can raise a truck suspension by using wood blocks to raise the axle, lift kits, and oversized tires. But getting a suspension to ride and handle well after it has been raised is difficult. Among the things that can be adversely affected by such suspension changes are steering, handling, ride quality, alignment, safety, stopping distance, acceleration, and reliability. For this, many off-roaders are turning to the undercar shop for proper upgrading of their 4WD vehicles for off-road use.

One consideration for raising a system is the relationship between sprung and unsprung weight. Unsprung weight is the weight of the tires, wheels, axles, control arms, and springs. In a 4WD, it is a considerable amount of mass. Anything that adds to that mass changes the way the suspension rides and responds. Oversized tires are not exactly light, and four of them can add a lot of unsprung weight. The added bulk can slow down the suspension's response to bumps, while increasing the harshness felt in the chassis and steering wheel. To compensate, stiffer shocks, springs, and a stronger steering stabilizer are needed—all of which causes a rough-riding vehicle.

Oversized tires by themselves do not alter basic suspension geometry (assuming the same sized tires are used front and rear). Even so, they can have an adverse affect on steering. Larger tires mean increased steering effort. Stability can sometimes be a problem with off-road tires that have an aggressive tread pattern. The large tires interspaced with large open areas may be excellent for traction in mud, but on dry pavement a loose tread pattern causes loose steering. Such tires can wander, vibrate, or cause a loud rumble. These are some of the trade-offs of improved off-road traction.

Conversion Kits

Conversion kits are available to change a full-time 4WD vehicle to a part-time 2WD or 4WD (Figure 31-21). Lockout hubs for the front axle to allow only two-wheel drive also require converting the transfer case.

A typical conversion kit combined with hub locks on the front-drive axle makes 4WD or 2WD optional for the driver as operating conditions change. Four-wheel drive occurs with the transfer case shift lever in high lock or low lock range and hub locks in lock or engage. Just turn the hub locks to the free position, then shift the transfer case to 2WD, hi range. All the power goes to the rear wheels. Benefits of this conversion make it very popular with 4WD vehicle owners. Two-wheel drive offers better gas mileage, less wear of front-drive components, improved front tire life, and extended life for transfer case chain. It also offers no steering wheel kickback on turns, quieter operation, and same shift patterns.

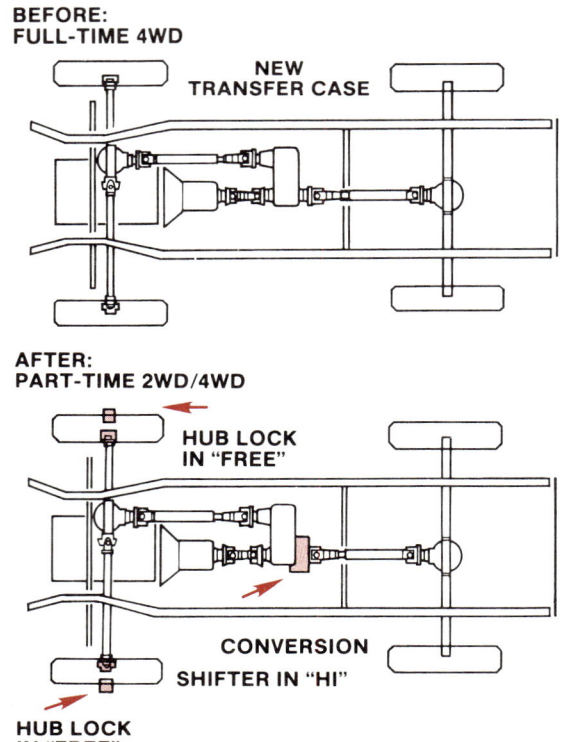

Figure 31-21 Conversion to optional four-wheel drive or two-wheel drive.

The various kits mentioned in this chapter all come with complete installation instructions that should be followed explicitly. But because of all the complexities that are involved with radical lift kits and 4WD suspension modifications, it is obviously not a job for the misinformed. It can be done, but to do the job correctly requires skill and the right parts. There is increasing opportunity for the off-road specialist who knows the profession.

☐ ALL-WHEEL-DRIVE SYSTEMS

All-wheel drive systems do not give the driver the option of 2WD or 4WD. They always drive all wheels. All-wheel-drive vehicles are usually passenger cars that are not designed for off-road operation. The all-wheel-drive vehicle is designed to increase vehicle performance in poor traction situations, such as icy or snowy roads, and in emergencies. All-wheel drive gives the vehicle operator maximum control in adverse operating conditions by biasing the driving torque to the axle with driving traction. The advantage of all-wheel drive can be compared to walking on snowshoes. Snowshoes prevent the user from sinking into the snow by spreading the body weight over a large surface. All-wheel-drive vehicles spread the driving force over four wheels when needed rather than two wheels. When a vehicle travels over the road, the driving wheels transmit a tractive force to the road's surface. The ability of each tire to transmit tractive force is a result of vehicle weight pressing the tire into the road's surface and the coefficient of friction between the tire and the road. If the road's surface is dry and the tire is dry, the coefficient of friction is high and four driving wheels are not needed. If the road's surface is wet and slippery, the coefficient of friction between the tire and road is low. The tire loses its coefficient of friction on slippery road surfaces, which could result in loss of control by the operator. Unlike a two-wheel-drive vehicle, an all-wheel-drive vehicle spreads the tractive effort to all four driving wheels. In addition to spreading the driving torque, the all-wheel-drive vehicle biases the driving torque to the axle that has the traction only when it is needed.

Viscous Clutch

The viscous clutch is used in the driveline of vehicles to drive the axle with low tractive effort, taking the place of the interaxle differential. In existence for several years, the viscous clutch is installed to improve the mobility factor under difficult driving conditions. It is similar in action to the viscous clutch described for the cooling system fan. The viscous clutch in AWD is a self-contained unit. When it malfunctions, it is simply replaced as an assembly. The viscous clutch assembly is very compact, permitting installation within a front

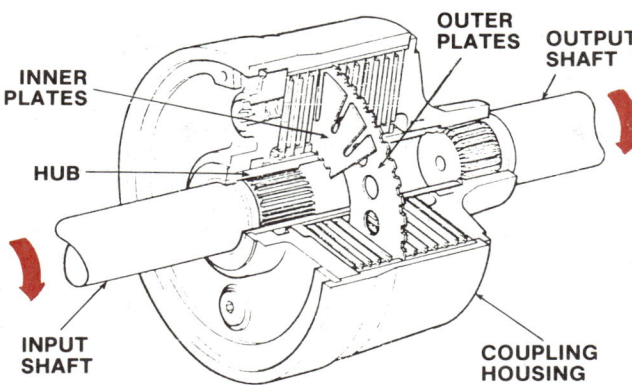

Figure 31-22 Typical viscous clutch assembly. *Courtesy of Volkswagen*

transaxle housing. Viscous clutches operate automatically while constantly transmitting power to the axle assembly as soon as it becomes necessary to improve driving wheel traction. This action is also known as biasing driving torque to the axle with tractive effort. The viscous clutch assembly is designed similarly to a multiple-disc clutch with alternating driving and driven plates (Figure 31-22).

The viscous clutch parts fit inside a drum that is completely sealed. The clutch pack is made up of alternating steel driving and driven plates. One set of steel plates is splined internally to the clutch assembly hub. The second set of clutch plates is splined externally to the clutch drum. The clutch housing is filled with a small quantity of air and special silicone fluid with the purpose of transmitting force from the driving plates to the driven plates.

Based on practical experience, vehicles operating with this clutch transmit power automatically, smoothly, and with the added benefit of the fluid being capable of dampening driveline shocks. When a difference in speed of 8% exists between the input shaft driven by the driving axle with tractive effort, the clutch plates begin shearing (cutting) the special silicone fluid. The shearing action causes heat to build within the housing very rapidly, which results in the silicone fluid stiffening. The stiffening action causes a locking action between the clutch plates to take place within approximately one-tenth second. The locking action results from the stiff silicone fluid becoming very hard for the plates to shear. The stiff silicone fluid transfers power flow from the driving to the driven plates. The driving shaft is then connected to the driven shaft through the clutch plates and stiff silicone fluid.

The viscous clutch has a self-regulating control. When the clutch assembly locks up, there is very little, if any, relative movement between the clutch plates. Because there is little relative movement, silicone fluid temperature drops, which reduces pressure within the clutch housing. But as speed fluctuates between the driving and driven members, heat increases, causing the silicone fluid to stiffen. Speed differences between the driving and driven members regulate the amount of slip in a viscous clutch driveline. The viscous clutch takes the place of the interaxle differential, biasing driving torque to the normally undriven axle during difficult driving conditions.

The viscous clutch is also used in some part-time 4WD vehicles, replacing the transfer case.

Center Differential AWD

One of the more recent AWD designs features a center differential to split the power between the front and rear axles (Figure 31-23). On the manual transmission model, the driver can lock the center differential with a switch. On the automatic transmission model, the center differential locks automatically, depending on which transaxle range the driver selects and whether or not there is any slippage between front and rear wheels.

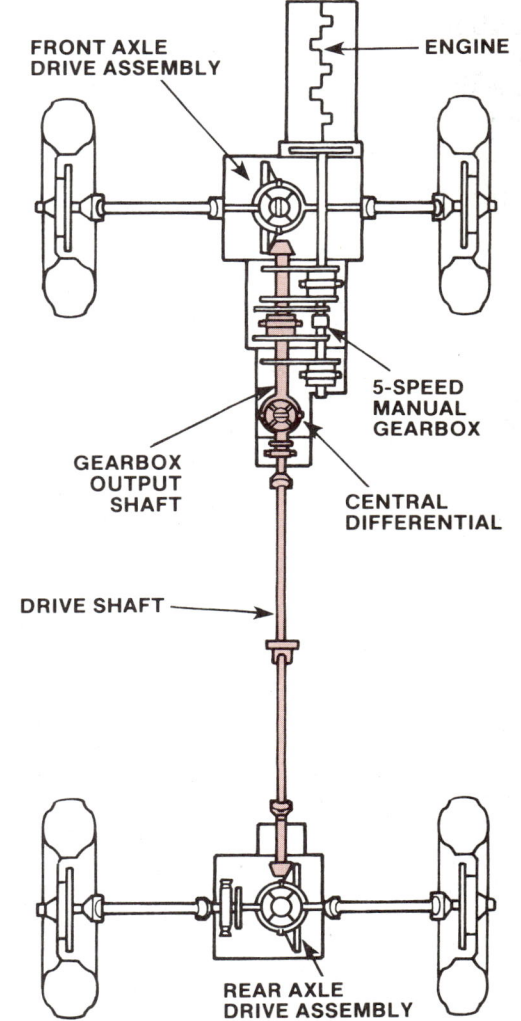

Figure 31-23 AWD system using a center differential. A conventional transfer case is not needed. *Courtesy of Porsche-Audi*

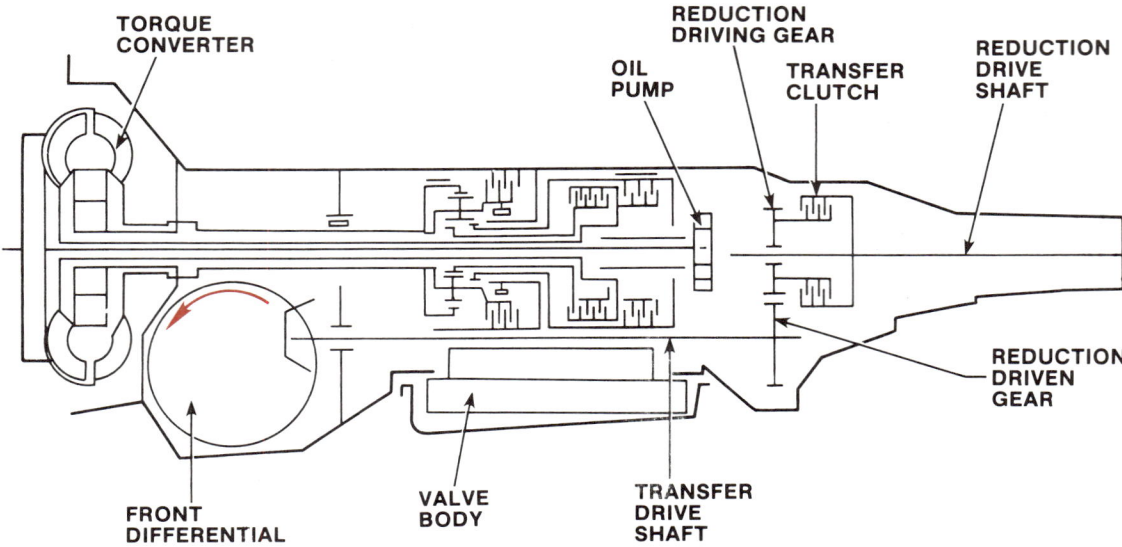

Figure 31-24 Schematic of the electrically-controlled transaxle.

Electronically-Controlled AWD

Electronically-controlled all-wheel drive is found in several import four-speed automatic overdrive transaxles designed with lockup torque converters. These vehicle drivetrains are designed with the front transaxle and two front drive shafts (each with its constant velocity universal joints). The rear drive shaft extends from the transaxle extension to the rear axle drive pinion and ring gear, two rear-drive shafts, universal joints, and driving wheels (Figure 31-24). Remember, there must be some type of interaxle differential in full-time, all-wheel drivelines.

The FWD transaxle has the same features. The torque converter is complete with impeller, turbine, stator, and lock-up clutch. The turbine shaft drives the various engaged planetary controls and planetary gears to achieve the gear range selected. The interesting area of the transaxle is the output to the rear driving axle. In this area on Figure 31-24, locate the transaxle reduction drive shaft, reduction driving gear, reduction driven gear, transfer clutch, and rear drive shaft. The reduction gearset transfers torque to the front-axle drive pinion, ring gear, differential, drive shafts, and driving wheels.

At the rear of the transaxle immediately behind the reduction gearset is the multiple-disc transfer clutch. This design of transfer clutch acts as the driveline interaxle differential, permitting the difference in front-axle and rear-axle speeds. The secret to the operation of this all-wheel-drive design is the method of controlling transfer clutch operation.

Strategically placed around the vehicle are sensors that monitor front- and rear-axle speeds, engine speed, and load on the engine and driveline. Information from the sensors is reported to the transmission computer unit called the transmission control unit (TCU). The TCU controls a solenoid called duty solenoid that operates on a duty (jitter) cycle controlling the fluid flow that engages the transfer clutch. The duty solenoid pulses, cycling on and off very rapidly, which develops a controlled slip condition. Driveline windup is dissipated when the clutch pack disengages, acting like an interaxle differential to the full-time, all-wheel driveline. The result of the operation of the transmission control unit and the duty solenoid is the transfer clutch operates like an interaxle differential to a power split from 95% front-wheel drive and 5% rear-wheel drive to 50% front-wheel drive and 50% rear-wheel drive. This power split takes place so rapidly that the vehicle operator is not aware of a traction problem.

CASE STUDY

Case 1

A four-wheel-drive pickup truck is brought into the shop. There is a severe vibration through the truck when it is travelling at road speeds. New wheels and tires were recently installed on the truck. The new wheels and tires are drastically oversized. Lift kits were installed by the owner to provide the necessary tire clearance. The owner would like the alignment checked and the wheels balanced.

The technician carefully balances and aligns the wheels. He takes the truck for a test drive to verify the repair. The truck still has a harsh vibration. It seems to get worse as speed increases. A bent wheel or bad wheel bearing or hub is suspected.

After returning to the shop, he measures the runout and checks the play of each wheel. Finding nothing wrong, he carefully checks the roundness of the tires. While doing so on the rear tires, he discovers the cause of the problem. When the lift kit was installed, the operating angle of the rear U-joint was affected. As the drive shaft turns, it hesitates slightly. This hesitation is caused by a binding of the U-joint.

The technician informs the owner of the cause and suggests that the lift kits be removed or the drive shaft operating angle be corrected.

Summary

- The importance of excellent traction and the benefits of four-wheel- and all-wheel-drive systems become readily apparent in snow or heavy rain.
- The heart of most conventional 4WD systems is the transfer case.
- One main function of the transfer case is to prevent driveline windup.
- The interaxle is placed in the transfer case to operate in the same fashion as the differentials at the axles. The only difference is that the transfer differential controls the speed of the drivelines instead of the axles.
- Many vehicles require that the front hubs be in a locked condition to operate as 4WD vehicles. This lockup may be made either manually or automatically.
- With the four-wheel drive disengaged at the transmission or transaxle, the disengaged front or rear wheels are still forced to turn the axles, differential, and drive shafts. To avoid this, hubs that lock or unlock disconnect everything from the wheels back to the transfer case.
- On 4WD vehicles with on-the-fly shifting, it is not necessary to come to a complete stop when changing operational modes.
- Components of 4WD vehicles can be serviced in basically the same manner as the identical components on a 2WD vehicle.
- All-wheel-drive vehicles use a viscous clutch, rather than a transfer case, to drive the axle with low tractive effort.
- Electronically-controlled all-wheel-drive vehicles can be found on some vehicles with four-speed automatic overdrive transaxles.

Review Questions

1. What is the main advantage of all-wheel drive?
2. Name the three main driveline components that are added to a 2WD vehicle to make it a 4WD vehicle.
3. Describe the purpose of a viscous clutch.
4. What is the purpose of the interaxle differential?
5. What is the disadvantage of the self-locking hub?
6. Tractive effort is defined as _____.
   a. driving force where a driving gear meshes with a driven gear
   b. place where the clutch disc makes contact with the flywheel and pressure plate
   c. driving force where the wheel contacts the road's surface
   d. driving force at the wheel
7. Which type of differential does not provide the true traction advantages of four-wheel drive?
   a. transfer
   b. limited slip
   c. open
   d. none of the above
8. Which shift position is used full-time for all surfaces?
   a. 4WD
   b. hi lock
   c. lo lock
   d. none of the above
9. Conversion kits offer 4WD vehicle owners which of these benefits?
   a. quieter operation
   b. better gas mileage
   c. improved front tire life
   d. all of the above
10. Coil spring replacement is needed on four-wheel-drive vehicles for which of the following reasons?
    a. poor load-handling capability
    b. bottoming out
    c. incorrect height
    d. all of the above
11. In full-time, four-wheel-drive vehicles all four wheels are _____.
    a. constantly receiving an equal amount of power
    b. constantly open to receiving power
    c. receiving power when the driver asks for it
    d. all of the above
12. Technician A says driveline windup, when referring to a four-wheel-drive vehicle, results from different gear ratios between the front and rear axles. Technician B says most 4WD vehicles use an interaxle differential in the transfer case to eliminate the problem. Who is correct?
    a. Technician A
    b. Technician B
    c. Neither A nor B
    d. Both A and B
13. The transfer clutch in the all-wheel-drive automatic transaxle takes the place of the _____.
    a. transmission
    b. reduction gears
    c. torque converter
    d. interaxle differential

14. In a typical all-wheel-drive automatic transaxle, the transfer clutch is controlled by the _____ .
    a. transmission control unit operating the pressure regulator valve
    b. engine computer controlling line pressure to the various clutches in the transmission
    c. transmission control unit and the duty solenoid
    d. front axle speed sensor and the vehicle speed sensor
15. Technician A says some AWD systems have a center differential. Technician B says some AWD vehicles have a viscous clutch. Who is correct?
    a. Technician A
    b. Technician B
    c. Neither A nor B
    d. Both A and B
16. In a viscous clutch, when the silicone fluid is heated, it _____ .
    a. becomes a very thin fluid
    b. boils to a vapor
    c. thickens to a solid mass
    d. stiffens
17. When servicing transfer cases, all of the following are correct, except _____ .
    a. it must be supported on a transmission jack or safety stands
    b. all transfer cases have both a chain drive and a planetary gearset
    c. visual inspections for leaks and damage are necessary
    d. follow the manufacturer's recommendations for lubricants
18. Which of the following is an advantage of four-wheel drive?
    a. It weighs less.
    b. It requires less maintenance.
    c. Tires cost less.
    d. None of the above.
19. The viscous clutch is used to _____ .
    a. engage engine torque to the transmission
    b. improve mobility when driving conditions become difficult
    c. drive both rear driving wheels when a vehicle is stuck
    d. drive the rear axle assembly
20. A steering stabilizer is _____ .
    a. a shock absorber
    b. used to stabilize steering under extra-heavy loads
    c. a radius arm between the frame and a part of the steering linkage
    d. all of the above
21. How is the all-wheel-drive system unique?
    a. It has a separate transfer case.
    b. All wheels are always being driven.
    c. Both a and b
    d. Neither a nor b

SECTION 7 SUSPENSIONS

Chapter 32 Tires and Wheels
Chapter 33 Suspensions
Chapter 34 Steering Systems and Wheel Alignment

A vehicle's tires, wheels, and suspension and steering systems provide the contact between the driver and the road. They allow the driver to safely maneuver the vehicle in all types of conditions as well as ride in comfort and security.

Once straightforward mechanical systems, suspension and steering systems have become increasingly sophisticated. Computer technology has made possible such features as variable ride qualities and active and adaptive suspensions. Four-wheel steering is now a reality. The electronic controls, air systems, and solenoids that operate this new technology require special servicing techniques.

The information found in Section 7 corresponds to materials covered on the ASE certification test on suspension and steering.

WE ENCOURAGE
PROFESSIONALISM

THROUGH TECHNICIAN
CERTIFICATION

32 TIRES AND WHEELS

Objectives

■ Describe basic wheel and hub design. ■ Recognize the basic parts of a tubeless tire. ■ Explain the differences between the three types of tire construction in use today. ■ Explain the tire ratings and designations in use today. ■ Describe why certain factors affect tire performance, including inflation pressure, tire rotation, and tread wear. ■ Remove and install a wheel and tire assembly. ■ Dismount and remount a tire. ■ Repair a damaged tire. ■ Describe the differences between static balance and dynamic balance. ■ Balance wheels both on and off a vehicle. ■ Describe the three popular types of wheel hub bearings.

Tire and wheel assemblies provide the only connection between the road and the vehicle. Tire design has improved dramatically during the past few years. Modern tires require increased attention to achieve their full potential of extended service and correct ride control. Tire wear that is uneven or premature is usually a good indicator of problems in the steering and suspension system. Tires, therefore, become not only a good diagnostic aid to a technician, but they also can be clear evidence to the customer for the need to service the front-end.

❑ WHEELS

Wheels are made of either stamped or pressed steel discs riveted or welded together. They are also available in the form of aluminum or magnesium rims that are die-cast or forged. Magnesium wheels are commonly referred to as mag wheels, although they are commonly made of an aluminum alloy. Aluminum wheels are lighter in weight when compared with the stamped steel type.

Near the center of the wheel are mounting holes that are tapered to fit tapered mounting nuts (lug nuts) that center the wheel over the hub. The rim has a hole for the valve stem and a drop center area designed to allow easy tire removal and installation. Wheel offset is the distance between the vertical centerline of the rim and the mounting face of the disc. The offset is considered positive if the centerline of the rim is inboard of the mounting face and negative if outboard of the mounting face. The amount and type of offset is critical because changing the wheel offset changes the loading on the front suspension loading as well as the scrub radius.

The wheel is bolted to a hub, either by lug bolts that pass through the wheel and thread into the hub, or by studs that protrude from the hub. In the case of studs, special lug nuts are required. Some vehicles employ left-hand threads (which turn counterclockwise to tighten) on the driver's side, and right-hand threads (which turn clockwise to tighten) on the passenger's side. Other cars use right-hand threads on both sides.

Wheel size is designated by rim width and rim diameter (Figure 32-1). Rim width is determined by

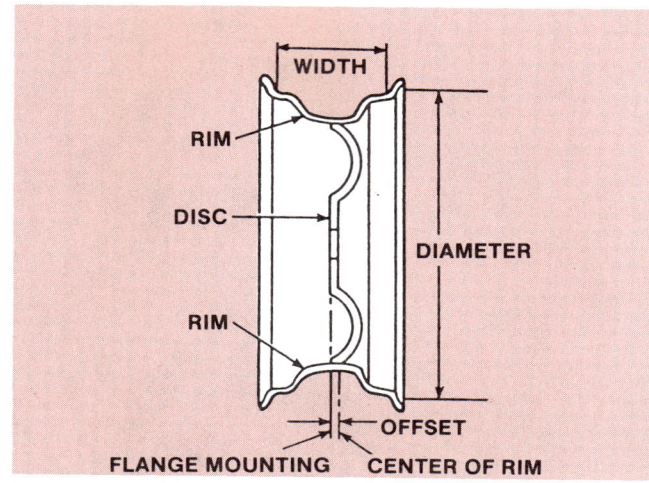

Figure 32-1 Wheel dimensions important to tire replacement.

792

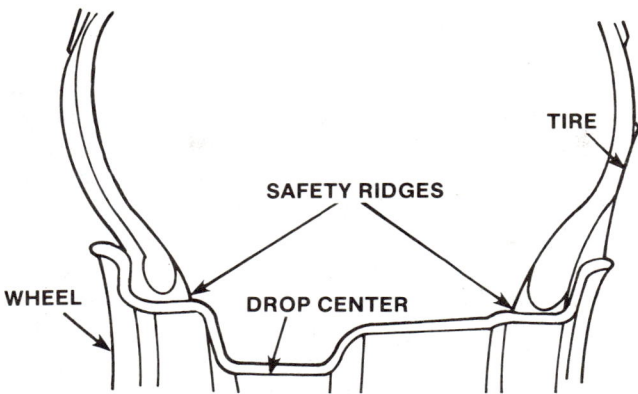

Figure 32-2 Safety rim. Note safety ridge on each side of wheel that retains tire in case of a flat or blowout (ruptured tire). *Courtesy of Chrysler Corp.*

measuring across the rim between the flanges. Rim diameter is measured across the bead seating areas from the top to the bottom of the wheel. Some rims have safety ridges near their lips. In the event of a tire blowout, these ridges tend to keep the tire from moving into the dropped center and from coming off the wheel (Figure 32-2).

Replacement wheels must be equal to the original equipment wheels in load capacity, diameter, width, offset, and mounting configuration. An incorrect wheel can affect wheel and bearing life, ground and tire clearance, or speedometer and odometer calibrations.

❏ TIRES

The primary purpose of tires is to provide traction. Tires also help the suspension absorb road shocks, but this is a side benefit. They must perform under a variety of conditions. The road might be wet or dry; paved with asphalt, concrete, or gravel; or there might be no road at all. The car might be traveling slowly on a straight road, or moving quickly through curves and over hills. All of these conditions call for special requirements that must be present, at least to some degree, in all tires.

In addition to providing good traction, tires are also designed to carry the weight of the vehicle, to withstand side thrust over varying speeds and conditions, and to transfer braking and driving torque to the road.

Tube and Tubeless Tires

Early vehicle tires were solid rubber. These were replaced with pneumatic tires, which are filled with air.

There are two basic types of pneumatic tires: those that use inner tubes and those that do not. The latter are called tubeless tires and are about the only type used on passenger cars today. A tubeless tire has a soft inner lining that keeps air from leaking between the tire and rim (Figure 32-3). This inner lining can often

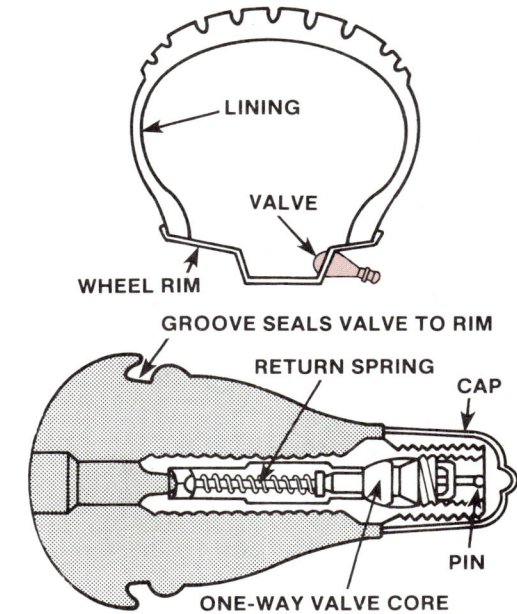

Figure 32-3 Typical tubeless tire installation and valve. *Courtesy of Chrysler Corp.*

form a seal around a nail or other object that punctures the tread. A self-sealing tire holds in air even after the object is removed. A tubeless tire air valve has a central core that is spring-loaded to allow air to pass inward only, unless the pin is depressed. If the core becomes defective, it can be unscrewed and replaced. The airtight cap on the end of the valve provides extra protection against valve leakage. A tubeless tire is mounted on a special rim that retains air between the rim and the tire casing when the tire is inflated.

Figure 32-4 shows a cutaway view of a typical tubeless tire. The basic parts are shown. The cord body or casing consists of layers of rubber-impregnated cords, called plies, that are bonded into a solid unit. Typically tires are made of 2, 4, or 8 plies; thus, the reference to 2-, 4-, and 8-ply tires. The character of the plies determines a tire's strength, handling, ride, amount of road noise, traction, and resistance to fatigue, heat, and bruises. The bead is the portion of the tire that helps keep it in contact with the rim of the wheel. It also provides the air seal on tubeless tires. The bead is constructed of a heavy band of steel wire wrapped into the inner circumference of the tire's ply structure. The tread, or crown, is the portion of the tire that comes in contact with the road surface. It is a pattern of grooves and ribs that provides traction. The grooves are designed to drain off water, while the ribs grip the road surface. Tread thickness varies with tire quality. On some tires, small cuts, called sipes, are molded into the ribs of the tread. These sipes open as the tire flexes on the road, offering additional gripping action, especially on wet road surfaces. The sidewalls are the sides of the tire body. They are constructed of thinner material than the tread to offer greater flexibility.

low in cost and give a good ride, but do not have the inherent strength needed to cope with long high-speed runs or extended periods of abusive use on rough roads. Nylon cord tires generally give a slightly harder ride than rayon—especially for the first few miles after the car has been parked—but offer greater toughness and resistance to road damage. Polyester and fiberglass tires offer many of the best qualities of rayon and nylon, but without the disadvantages. They run as smoothly as rayon tires but are much tougher. They are almost as tough as nylon, but give a much smoother ride. Steel is tougher than fiberglass or polyester, but it gives a slightly rougher ride because the steel cord does not give under impact as do fabric plies. Amarid and kevlar cords are lighter than steel cords and, pound for pound, stronger than steel.

Types of Tire Construction

There are three types of tire construction in use today (Figure 32-5).

BIAS PLY TIRES The oldest tire currently in use is the bias ply. It has a body of fabric plies that runs alternately at opposite angles to form a crisscross design. The angle varies from 30 to 38 degrees with the centerline of the tire and has an effect on high-speed stability, ride harshness, and handling. Generally speaking, the lower the cord angle, the better the high-speed stability, but also the harsher the ride. Bias ply tires usually are available in 2- or 4-ply.

BELTED BIAS PLY TIRES This type is similar to the bias ply, except that two or more belts run the circumference of the tire under the tread. This construction gives strength to the sidewall and greater stability to the tread. The belts reduce tread motion during contact with the road, thus improving tread life. Plies and belts of various combinations of rayon, nylon, polyester, fiberglass, and steel are used with belted bias con-

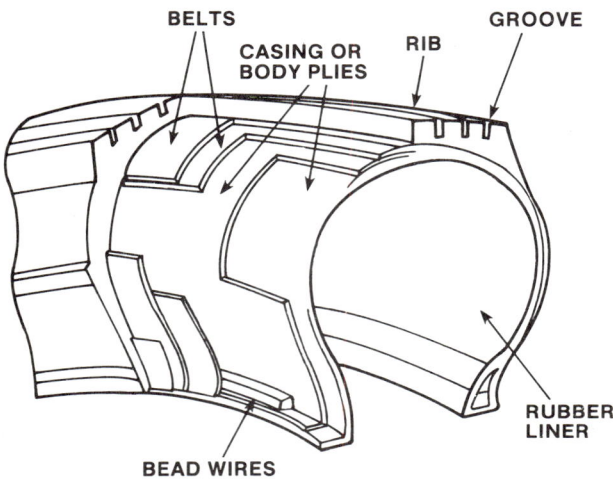

Figure 32-4 Typical tubeless tire.

The tire body and belt material can be made of rayon, nylon, polyester, fiberglass, steel, or the newest synthetics—amarid or kevlar. Each has its advantages and disadvantages. For instance, rayon cord tires are

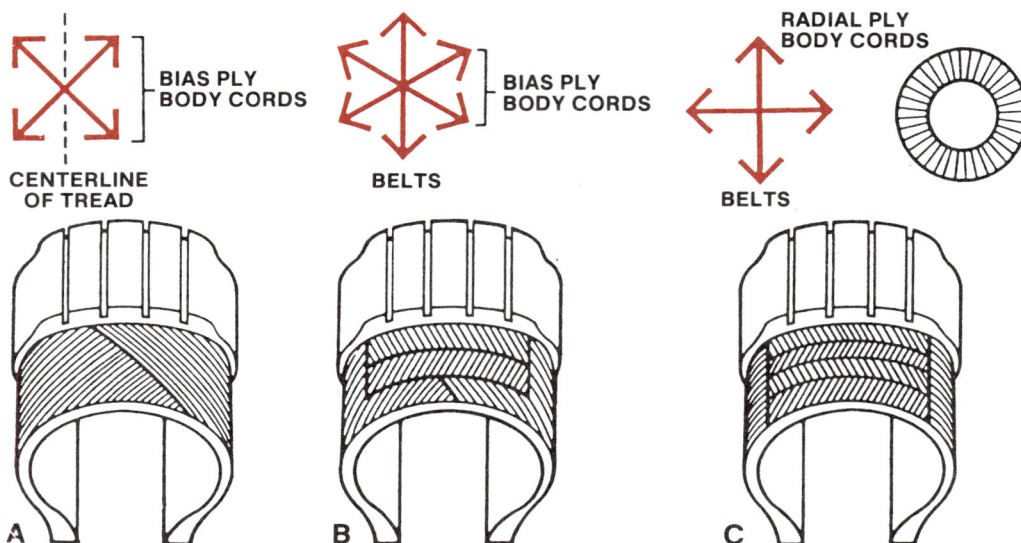

Figure 32-5 Three types of tire construction: (A) bias ply; (B) bias belted; and (C) radial ply.

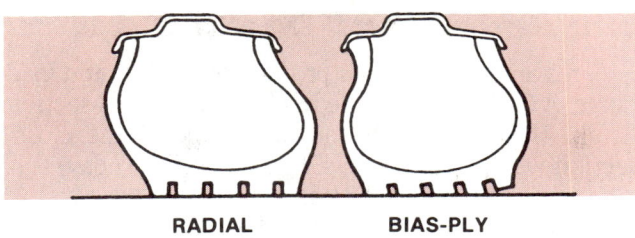

Figure 32-6 A radial tire's highly flexible sidewalls give maximum tread contact area during fast, hard turning.

struction. Belted bias ply tires generally cost more than conventional bias ply tires, but last up to 40% longer.

RADIAL PLY TIRES These have body cords that extend from bead to bead at an angle of about 90 degrees—"radial" to the tire circumferential centerline—plus two or more layers of relatively inflexible belts under the tread. This construction of various combinations of rayon, nylon, fiberglass, and steel gives greater strength to the tread area and flexibility to the sidewall (Figure 32-6). The belts restrict tread motion during contact with the road, thus improving tread life and traction. Radial ply tires also offer greater fuel economy, increased skid resistance, and more positive braking.

Although the newer synthetics are being used more frequently in radial tires, steel is still the most popular belt material. Bias ply and belted bias are available in all cord materials mentioned earlier, except amarid and kevlar. Non-radial belts are usually of the same material as the sidewalls.

Specialty Tires

Specialty tires reflect the advances made in the conventional tire field. Special snow and mud tires are available in all three construction types. Studded tires provide superior traction on ice, but are slowly disappearing from the tire market because their performance in dry weather is poor. In addition, in the last few years many states have outlawed their use because they damage roads.

The present trend in specialty tire manufacturing is toward all-season or all-weather tires. The all-season tire, however, is a compromise and might not perform as well as specialty tires under certain circumstances. Their use has not eliminated the twice-a-year tire change for many northern motorists.

> **CUSTOMER CARE**
>
> Advise your customer that the use of tire chains is not recommended by most tire manufacturers. In case of emergency, or where required by law, chains can be used if they are the proper size for the tires and are installed tightly (no slack) with their ends securely restrained. Follow the chain manufacturer's instructions. Drive slowly. If any contact of the chains against the vehicle is heard, stop and retighten the chains. Use only SAE Class S tire chains. Use of other chains can damage the vehicle.

Compact Spare Tires

A compact spare tire is designed to reduce weight and to provide more luggage room. There are several types used today.

HIGH-PRESSURE MINI SPARE The high pressure (60 psi) mini-spare tire is the one most commonly used. But this small, or temporary tire should not be used for extended mileage or for speeds above 50 mph. Check the pressure in the spare tire at least monthly. If it is in use, check the pressure when the vehicle has been stopped at least 3 hours and driven less than 1 mile. Do not reduce the pressure when the tire is hot. Use a tire gauge to check the pressure and maintain 60 psi.

SPACE-SAVER SPARE This type of tire must be blown up with a special compressor that operates off the cigarette lighter electrical circuit. Inflate the tire to 35 psi. Before installing it on the vehicle, make sure it looks like a road tire with no folds in the sidewalls.

LIGHTWEIGHT SKIN SPARE The skin spare is designed to provide additional luggage room and a lightweight, easy-to-use spare tire. This type of spare is a normal type bias ply with a reduced tread depth to provide an estimated tread life of 2,000 miles. It is for emergency use only and has a maximum speed capability of 50 mph. Maintain the cold inflation pressure as specified on the vehicle's tire pressure decal.

> **CUSTOMER CARE**
>
> Be sure to warn your customer that the mini, space-saver, skin, or similar type of compact spare should be used only temporarily for an emergency. It should never be used as a regular tire. Any continuous road use of the temporary compact spare might result in tire failure, loss of vehicle control, and injury to the vehicle's occupants.

High-Performance (Speed-Rated) Tires

In recent years, the so-called high-performance tire has made an increasing appearance on cars driven in the United States. Many drivers do not care if they actually use the speed capabilities of the tire, just as long as the performance is there. In fact, many of their cars are not capable of these higher speeds. A comparison of the Porsche 928S4 and Ford Probe GT points this out.

The Porsche has a top speed of 165 mph. The GT tops out at 120 mph. Yet, both are equipped with

TABLE 32-1 SPEED RATINGS

Symbol	Maximum Speed
F	50 mph
G	56 mph
J	62 mph
K	68 mph
L	75 mph
M	81 mph
N	87 mph
P	93 mph
Q	100 mph
R	106 mph
S	112 mph
T	118 mph
U	124 mph
H	130 mph
V	149 mph
Z	+149 mph

V-rated tires (up to 149 mph; see Table 32-1). While the Porsche can certainly use the V-rated tire, the GT is using it strictly for handling, and, of course, image.

High-performance tires, like all tires, eventually have to be replaced. In some European countries, the replacement tire must have, by law, the same speed rating as the OE tire. Although it is not the law in the United States, trading down in speed ratings would probably not be a good idea. Optimum performance and, perhaps, even safe handling might be sacrificed.

The speed ratings are currently set by the Economic Commission using the European passenger car tire regulation R-30. While United States tire makers use the testing procedures established by this association, there are no minimum standards to which they must comply.

Tire Ratings and Destinations

Tires are rated by their profile, ratio, size, and load range. A tire's profile is the relation of its cross-section height (from tread to bead) compared to the cross-section width (from sidewall to sidewall). Today, this ratio is also known as series.

For many years, the accepted profile ratio for standard bias ply passenger car tires was approximately 83. This meant the tire was 83% as high as it was wide. Since the introduction of bias belted and radial ply construction, lower profile tires with ratios of 78, 70, 60, and even 50 have become popular (Figure 32-7). The lower the number, the wider the tire. For instance, a 50-series tire is quite low and fat, being only 50% as high as it is wide. Most new cars are equipped with 80-, 78-, 75-, or 70-series tires.

Prior to 1967, tire sizes were designated by a series of numbers such as 7.75-14 or 9.50-15. The first number (9.50) referred to the cross-section width, in inches, of an inflated tire, and the second number (15) was the rim diameter. Today, three sizing systems are used: standard Alpha-numeric; all Alpha-numeric; and half Alpha-numeric, half metric.

In the standard Alpha-numeric system, the width/load letter scale starts at V and runs through Z, then takes up with A and runs through N. The V through Z ratings are uncommon. The wider the tire, the more weight it can carry. A V-rated tire can handle 650 pounds, while an N-rated one can take 1880 pounds. Table 32-2 shows the maximum weight each tire size can carry when inflated to 24 psi. As inflation is increased, so is the tire's carrying capacity up to a usual maximum of 32 psi.

In the all Alpha-numeric system, the tire letter size is followed by a number to indicate the tire's approxi-

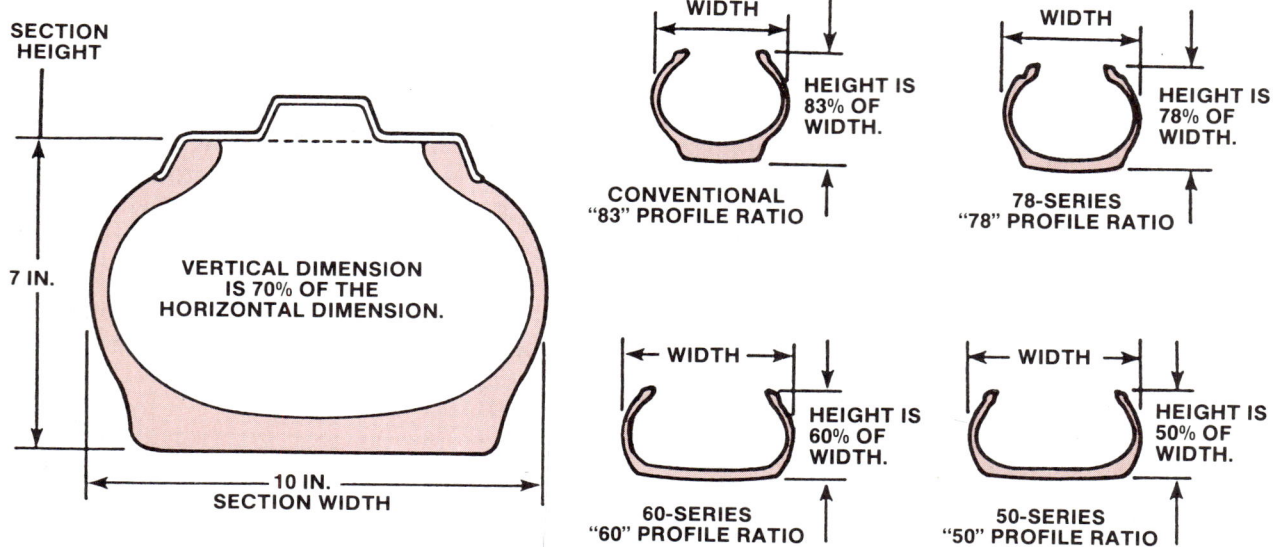

Figure 32-7 The aspect ratio (profile ratio) of a tire is its cross-sectional height compared to its cross-sectional width expressed in percentage figures.

TABLE 32-2	WIDTH/LOAD LETTER STANDARDS
	V—650 pounds
	W—710 pounds
	Y—770 pounds
	Z—830 pounds
	A—900 pounds
	B—980 pounds
	C—1050 pounds
	D—1120 pounds
	E—1190 pounds
	F—1280 pounds
	G—1380 pounds
	H—1510 pounds
	J—1580 pounds
	K—1620 pounds
	L—1680 pounds
	M—1780 pounds
	N—1880 pounds

TABLE 32-3 LOAD RANGES

Rating	Ply Rating	Maximum psi
B	4	32
C	6	36
D	8	40

mate profile ratio, followed by the rim diameter. For example, a tire designated as F78-15 means that it belongs to the 78 series and fits a 15-inch rim. Radial ply tires use the same designation but have an R inserted in the number, such as FR78-14.

The half Alpha-numeric, half metric system gives the tire's width in millimeters, but gives its rim diameter in inches, such as 195R-15. Although the profile ratio is usually omitted in part-metric designations, a few manufacturers designate the tire series, such as 185-70-14. The 70 stands for a 70-series tire. In 1977, P metric tires were introduced.

In P195/75R14, P identifies passenger car tire. If this designation is followed by M, S, or MS, the tire's tread is rated for use in mud, snow, or both. The width in millimeters is 195. The height-to-width ratio is 75. R identifies radial construction. The rim diameter is 14.

All metric system measurements are now being given along with a standard translation. A typical metric tire shows its width in millimeters, its inflation pressure in kilopascals (kPa), and its load capacity in kilograms (kg). One kilopascal equals 6.895 psi. A typical all-metric radial size is 190/65R-390. It fits a 390 mm diameter wheel.

Additionally, the letters B, C, or D, might appear on the sidewall, separate from the tire designation coding. These are holdovers from the old load-rating system, which replaced the still older ply system (Table 32-3). Load range B is the lightest design, suited to passenger car use. Load range C is in between, while load range D is heavy-duty. It is best for trucks and off-road vehicles.

The newer tires have abandoned the load range system replacing it with SL and XL for standard load and extra load. Standard load falls between load ranges B and C. XL is a little heavier duty than load range D.

Federal law requires that all tires carry designations (Figure 32-8) indicating size, load range, maximum load, maximum inflation pressure in pounds per square inch, number of plies under the tread and the sidewalls, manufacturer's name, tubeless or tube construc-

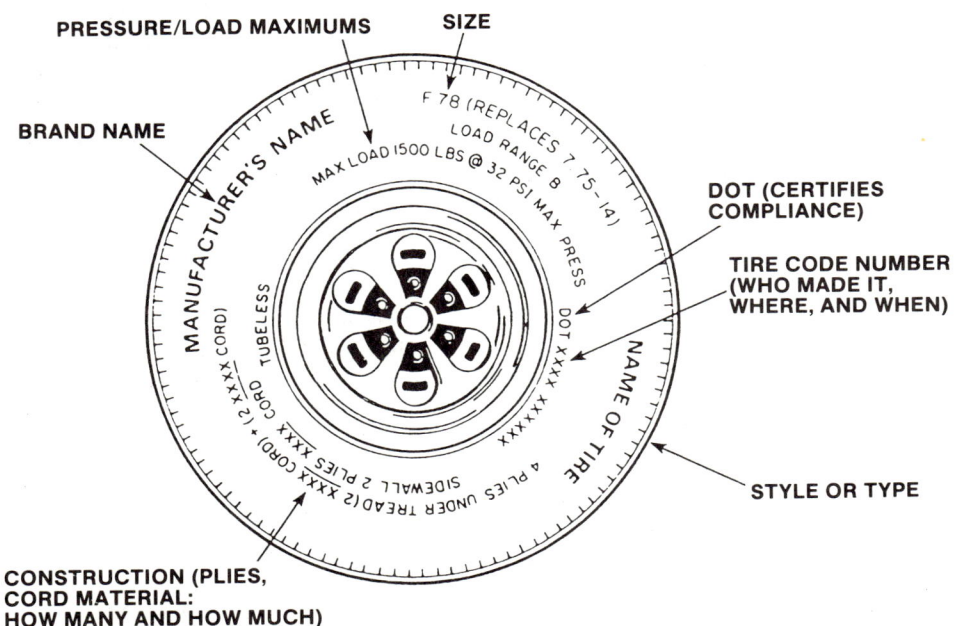

Figure 32-8 All tire sidewalls carry this information.

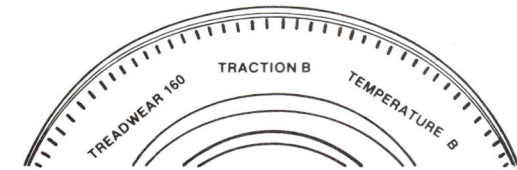

Figure 32-9 Uniform tire quality grading system.

tion, radial construction (if a radial tire), and United States Department of Transportation (DOT) symbol indicating confirmation to applicable federal standards. Adjacent to the DOT symbol is a tire identification number. The first two characters identify the tire manufacturer. The remaining characters identify size, type, date of manufacture, and whether the tires are tubeless or tube-type.

In addition, DOT requirements mandate that tires must have the uniform tire quality grading system (UTQGS) molded into their sidewalls. As shown in Figure 32-9, this consumer comparison information includes treadwear, traction, temperature, and the tire performance criteria (TPC) specification number.

TREADWEAR The treadwear grade is a comparative rating based on the wear rate of the tire when tested under controlled conditions on a specified government test course. For example, a tire graded 160 would wear twice as well on the government course as a tire graded 80.

TRACTION The wet-weather traction grades are, from highest to lowest, A, B, and C. These represent the tire's ability to stop on wet pavement as measured under controlled conditions on specified government test surfaces of asphalt and concrete. The federal government warns consumers not to choose tires that earn only a C traction rating, no matter what other ratings they have. They have poor traction on wet roads.

TEMPERATURE The resistance to high-temperature grading system also uses an A, B, and C rating. The C grade indicates that the tire meets DOT's present standards for temperature resistance and is acceptable. Tires that earn A and B temperature resistance ratings are still better.

TPC SPECIFICATION NUMBER On most vehicles equipped with radial tires, a TPC specification number is molded into the sidewall. This indicates that the tire meets rigid size and performance standards developed for that particular automobile. It assures the combination of endurance, handling, load capacity, ride, and traction on wet, dry, and snow-covered surfaces.

Tire Placard

The tire placard, or safety compliance certification label, is generally found on the driver's door jam. It includes recommended maximum vehicle load, tire

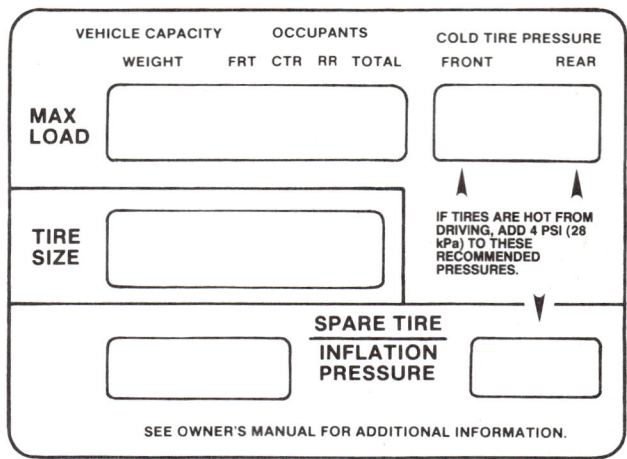

Figure 32-10 Typical tire placard. *Courtesy of General Motors Corp.*

size (including spare), and correct cold tire inflation for the specific vehicle (Figure 32-10). Never use this information for other cars.

CUSTOMER CARE

Be sure to tell your customer to stay within the gross vehicle weight rating (GVWR) and the front and rear gross axle weight rating (GAWR) when loading a vehicle. The GVWR and GAWR are shown on the safety compliance certification label or tire placard. These limits represent the designed capacity of the vehicle, not merely of the tires. When towing a trailer, the allowable passenger and cargo load must be reduced by an amount equal to the trailer tongue load on the trailer hitch. Station wagon loads should be distributed as far forward as possible. Vehicles equipped with luggage racks do not have a vehicle load capacity greater than specified on the tire placard. When carrying heavier-than-normal loads, the tire pressure should be increased, but never to an extent greater than load range.

Combining Tire Types

As a general rule, tires should be replaced with the same size designation or an approved optional size as recommended by the auto or tire manufacturer. In addition to following the vehicle manufacturer's recommendations for tire size, type, inflation pressures, and rotation patterns, the following points should be observed.

1. Never mix size or construction types on the same axle.
2. Tires on the same axle should be of approximately equal tread depth.

3. All tires on station wagons and all other vehicles used for trailer towing should be of the same size, type, and load rating.
4. On some vehicles, the use of radial tires might hinder ride quality and control due to the design of the suspension system.
5. New tires should be installed in pairs on the same axle. When replacing only one tire, it should be paired with the tire having the most tread to equalize braking traction.
6. If radial tires are used on the car, combine them with radial snow tires on the driving wheels.
7. Snow tires should be of a size and type equivalent to the other tires on the vehicle. Otherwise the safety and handling of the vehicle might be adversely affected.
8. If any doubt exists as to combining tires on the same vehicle, use Table 32-4 as a guide.

SHOP TALK

Tires larger or smaller than originally installed might affect the accuracy of the speedometer calibration. It might be necessary to change the speedometer drive gears when tire size has been changed. Check the vehicle's service manual for details.

Tire Care

To maximize tire performance, inspect for signs of improper inflation and uneven wear, which can indicate a need for balancing, rotation, or front suspension alignment. Tires should also be checked frequently for cuts, stone bruises, abrasions, blisters, and for objects that might have become imbedded in the tread. More

TABLE 32-4 TIRE COMBINATIONS

Construction		Bias on Front (Read down for rear)			Belted Bias on Front (Read down for rear)			Radial on Front (Read down for rear)			
	Series (Profile)	78 Series	70 Series	60/50 Series	78 Series	70 Series	60/50 Series	Metric	78 Series	70 Series	60/50 Series
Bias on Rear (Read across for front)	Conventional (83 Series)	A	NO	NO	A	NO	NO	NO	NO	NO	NO
	78 Series	P	A	NO	A	NO	NO	NO	NO	NO	NO
	70 Series	A	P	NO	A	A	NO	NO	NO	NO	NO
	60/50 Series	A	A	P	A	A	A	NO	NO	NO	NO
Belted Bias on Rear (Read across for front)	78 Series	A	A	NO	P	A	NO	NO	NO	NO	NO
	70 Series	A	A	NO	A	P	NO	NO	NO	NO	NO
	60/50 Series	A	A	A	A	A	P	NO	NO	NO	NO
Radial on Rear (Read across for front)	Metric	A	A	NO	A	A	NO	P	A	A	NO
	78 Series	A	A	NO	A	A	NO	A	P	A	NO
	70 Series	A	A	NO	A	A	NO	A	A	P	NO
	60/50 Series	A	A	A	A	A	A	A	A	A	P

P: Preferred applications. For best all-around car handling performance tires of the same size and construction should be used on all wheel positions.
A: Acceptable but not preferred applications. Consult the car owner's manual and do not apply if vehicle manufacturer recommends against this application.
NO: Not recommended.

Figure 32-11 Effects of inflation on tires.

TABLE 32-5	INFLATION PRESSURE CONVERSION (KILOPASCALS TO psi)		
kPa	psi	kPa	psi
140	20	215	31
145	21	220	32
155	22	230	33
160	23	235	34
165	24	240	35
170	25	250	36
180	26	275	40
185	27	310	45
190	28	345	50
200	29	380	55
205	30	415	60

Conversion: 6.9 kPa = 1 psi

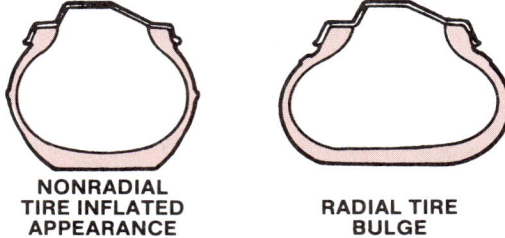

Figure 32-12 Tire profile of a nonradial tire as compared to a radial tire.

frequent inspections are recommended when rapid or extreme temperature changes occur, or where road surfaces are rough or occasionally littered with debris.

To clean tires, use a mild soap and water solution only. Rinse thoroughly with clear water. Do not use any caustic solutions or abrasive materials. Never use steel wool or wire brushes. Avoid gasoline, paint thinner, and similar materials having a mineral oil base. These materials are harmful to the tires and eventually discolor the whitewalls and raised letters.

Inflation Pressure

A properly inflated tire (Figure 32-11A) gives the best tire life, riding comfort, handling stability, and gas mileage for normal driving conditions. Too little air pressure can result in tire squeal, hard steering, excessive tire heat, abnormal tire wear, and increased fuel consumption by as much as 10%. An underinflated tire (Figure 32-11B) shows maximum wear on the outside edges of the tread. There is little or no wear in the center. Conversely, an overinflated tire (Figure 32-11C) shows its wear in the center of the tread and little wear on the outside edges. A higher tire inflation pressure than recommended can cause a hard ride, tire bruising, and rapid wear at the center of the tire.

Many inflation pressures given on OE import vehicles use kilopascals (kPa) rather than psi. Table 32-5 converts kPa to psi.

CUSTOMER CARE

Be sure to tell your customer that radial tires have a distinctive bulge (Figure 32-12) that gives the appearance of an underinflated tire. This is normal and air should not be added to make a radial tire look as inflated as a bias or bias-belted tire. Inflate a radial to the recommended pressure only. Do not overinflate.

Tire Rotation

To equalize tire wear, most car and tire manufacturers recommend that the tires be rotated. Remember that front and rear tires perform different jobs and can wear differently, depending on driving habits and the type of vehicle. In a RWD vehicle, for instance, the front tires usually wear along the outer edges, primarily because of the scuffing and slippage encountered in cornering. The rear tires wear in the center because of acceleration thrusts. To equalize wear, it is recommended that tires be rotated as illustrated in Figure 32-13. Bias ply and bias-belted tires should be rotated about every 6,000 miles. Radial tires should be initially rotated at 7,500 miles and then at least every 15,000 miles thereafter. Many auto shops keep a record of tire rotation periods so they can notify their customers when it should be done next.

When snow tires are installed, the regular tread tires on the rear should be moved to the front and the front tires stored. When snow tires are removed, install the stored tires on the rear. Do not rotate studded tires. Always remount them in their original positions.

When storing tires, lay them flat on a clean, dry, oil-free floor. Keep them away from ozone, which

Tires and Wheels   **801**

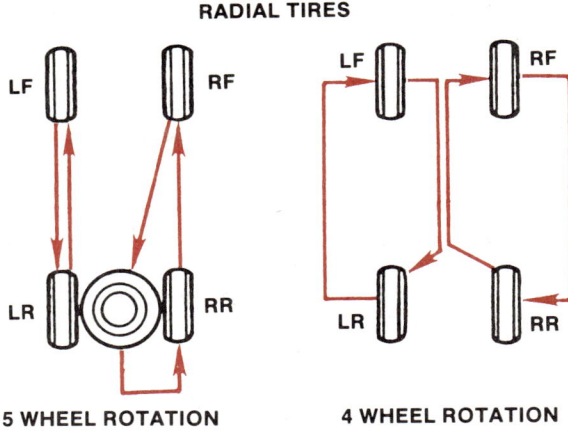

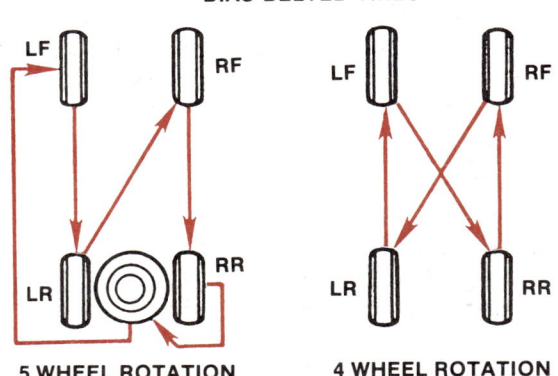

Figure 32-13 Rotation for radial and bias-belted tires.

comes from the electrical sparking frequently produced by electric motors. Store them in the dark. Direct sunlight is hard on tires.

Tread Wear

Most tires used today have built-in tread wear indicators to show when they need replacement. These indicators appear as 1/2-inch wide bands when the tire tread depth wears to 1/16 inch (Figure 32-14). When the indicators appear in two or more adjacent grooves, at three locations around the tire, or when cord or fabric is exposed, tire replacement is recommended.

If the tires do not have tread wear indicators, a tread depth indicator (Figure 32-15) quickly shows in 32nds of an inch how much tire tread is left. When only 2/32 inch is left, it is time to replace a tire.

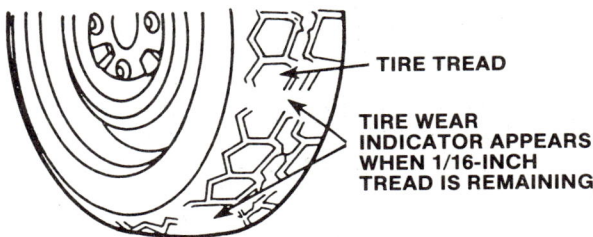

Figure 32-14 Tread wear indicators.

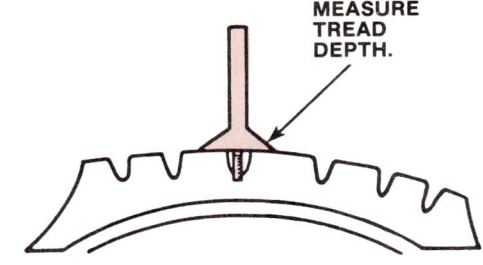

Figure 32-15 Checking tread depth.

To remove the wheels from the vehicle, it must be raised off the floor. Care must be taken when raising a vehicle. Follow the safety lifting rules given previously. Remember that incorrect hoisting can damage steering linkage and suspension components.

CUSTOMER CARE

It is good public relations to explain or, better still, to show a customer how to remove the tire/wheel assembly. This is especially true in the case of wheelcovers that are equipped with an antitheft locking system. The lock bolt for each wheelcover is located behind the hub ornament. A special key wrench is required to pry off the center hub ornament and to remove the lock bolt (Figure 32-16). To allow for service in the event the customer's key has been misplaced, a master key set is available at the new car dealership.

In recent years more and more wheels are being equipped with antitheft wheel lugs (one per wheel). The key has a circular keyway that is matched to the female slot in the antitheft wheel lug nut (Figure 32-17). To remove or install the antitheft wheel lug nut, insert the

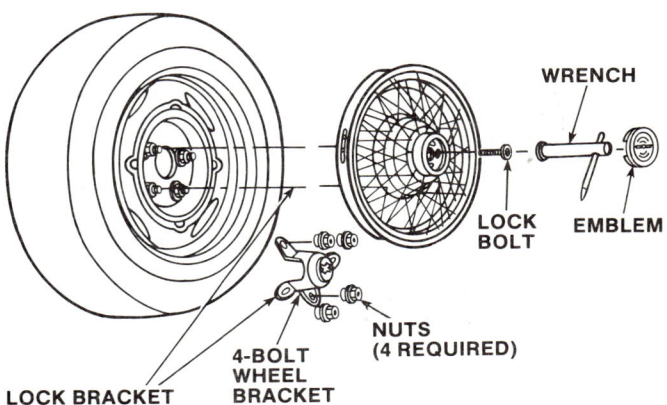

Figure 32-16 Antitheft wire wheelcovers. *Courtesy of Ford Motor Co.*

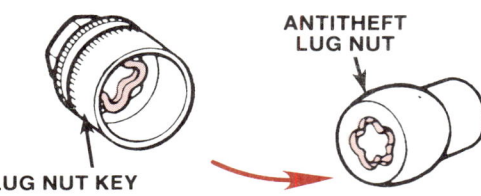

Figure 32-17 Circular keyway fits female slot of antitheft wheel lug nut. *Courtesy of Ford Motor Co.*

> special key into the slot of the lug nut. Place the lug nut wrench on the key. While applying pressure on the key, remove or install the lug nut.

Tire Repair

The most common tire repair problem is a puncture. When properly done, a repaired tire can be put back in service safely and without fear of the leak recurring. Service punctures in the tread area only (Figure 32-18). Never attempt to service punctures in the tire's shoulders or sidewalls. In addition, do not service any tire that has sustained the following damage.

- Bulges or blisters
- Ply separation
- Broken or cracked beads
- Fabric cracks or cuts
- Wear to the fabric or visible wear indicators
- Punctures larger than 1/4-inch diameter

CAUTION: *Tire sealants that are injected through the valve stem can produce wheel rust and tire imbalance.*

To locate a puncture in a tire, inflate it to the maximum inflation pressure marked on the tire. Then, submerge the tire/wheel assembly in a tank of water or sponge it with a soapy water solution. The water bubbles at the exact spot of the leak.

Mark the location of the leak with a crayon so that it can be easily found once the tire is removed from the wheel. Also place a crayon mark to identify the valve stem location so that the original tire balance and tire runout can be maintained when the tire is remounted.

The proper procedure for dismounting and remounting a tire is illustrated in Photo Sequence 15. Do not use hand tools or tire irons alone to change a tire because they might damage the beads or wheel rim. When mounting or dismounting tires on vehicles using aluminum or wire spoke wheels, it is recommended that the tire changer manufacturer be contacted about the accessories that are required to protect the wheel's finish.

Once the tire is off the wheel and the cause of the puncture is removed, the tire can be permanently serviced from the inside using a combination service plug and vulcanized patch. While the service kit manufacturer's instructions should always be followed, there are some general procedures that help to make a good, permanent patch. (Since so few vehicles still use tube-type tires, their repair is not covered in this book.)

The following methods are the most popular types of tire repair.

PLUG REPAIR The head-type plug (Figure 32-19) is the most popular method. Using a plug slightly larger than the size of the puncture hole, place it in the eye of the insertion tool. Wet both the plug and insertion tool with vulcanizing fluid.

While holding and stretching the long end of the plug, insert it into the puncture hole from inside the tire. The plug must extend above both the tread and inner liner surface. If the plug pops through, discard it and repeat the insertion procedure. Once the insertion tool has been removed, trim off the plug 1/32 inch above the inner liner surface. Do not pull on the plug while cutting.

COLD PATCH REPAIR When using a cold patch, carefully remove the backing from the patch. Spread vulcanizing fluid on the punctured area. Let it dry, then center the patch base over the punctured area. Run a stitching tool over the patch to help bind it to the tire.

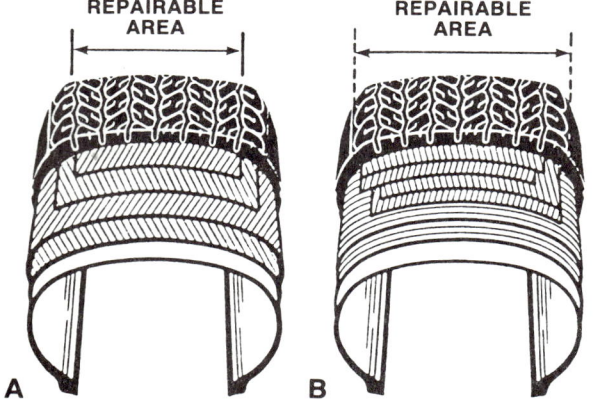

Figure 32-18 Repair areas of (A) bias and belted bias, and (B) radial.

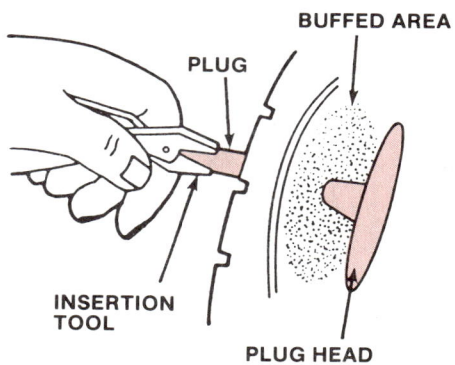

Figure 32-19 Plug for a radial tire.

PHOTO SEQUENCE 15

☐ DISMOUNTING AND MOUNTING A TIRE ON A WHEEL ASSEMBLY

P15-1 A typical tire changer.

P15-2 Dismounting the tire from the wheel begins with releasing the air, removing the air valve core, and unseating the tire from the rim. The machine does the unseating. The technician merely guides the operating lever.

P15-3 Once both sides of the tire are unseated, place the assembly onto the machine.

P15-4 Depress the pedal that clamps the wheel to the tire machine.

P15-5 Lower the machine's arm into position on the tire and wheel assembly.

P15-6 Insert the tire iron between the tire and wheel. Depress the pedal that causes the wheel to rotate. This will free the tire from the wheel.

P15-7 After the tire is totally free from the rim, remove the tire.

(continued)

P15-8 To prepare the wheel for the mounting of a new tire, use a wire brush to remove all of the dirt and rust from the sealing surface.

P15-9 Rubber compound should be liberally applied to the bead area of the new tire.

P15-10 Place the tire onto the wheel assembly and lower the arm onto the assembly. As the wheel rotates, the tire will be forced over the rim.

P15-11 After the tire is completely over the rim, install the air ring over the tire. Activate this to seat the tire against the wheel.

P15-12 Reinstall the air valve core and inflate the tire to the recommended pressure. ■

CAUTION: When repairing radial tires, use only a patch specially approved for that application. These special patches have arrows that must be lined up parallel to the radial plies.

HOT PATCH REPAIR A hot tire patch application is similar to a cold patch. The difference is that the hot patch is clamped over the puncture and heat is applied to the patch to make it adhere.

SHOP TALK

When mounting new tires, always install new valve stems. The life of tire rubber is close to the life of the valve stem rubber. Most stems are the snap-in type. These are installed from inside the wheel with a pulling tool. Make sure that the stem is properly seated. Another style of stem has a retaining nut that must be removed when pulling off the old stem. Be sure to completely tighten the new nut.

Installation of Tire/Wheel Assembly on the Vehicle

A wheel should be carefully inspected each time a tire is to be mounted on it. The major causes of wheel failure are improper maintenance, overloading, age, and accidents, including pot hole damage. Wheels must be replaced when they are bent, dented, or heavily rusted, have leaks or elongated bolt holes, and have excessive lateral or radial runout. Wheels with a lateral or radial runout greater than the recommended specification can cause high-speed vehicle vibration. Stones wedged between the wheel and disc brake rotor or drum can unbalance the wheel. Remember that wobble or shimmy caused by a damaged wheel eventually damages the wheel bearings. Also, check the lug nuts to be sure that they are set according to the torque given in the vehicle's service manual. Loose lug nuts can cause shimmy and vibration, and can also distort the stud holes in the wheels.

CAUTION: Steel wheel repairs that use welding, heating, or peening are not approved. The use of an inner tube is not an acceptable repair for leaky wheels or tubeless tires.

Before reinstalling a tire/wheel assembly on a vehicle, inspect the wheel bearings as described later in this chapter, then clean the axle/rotor flange and wheel bore with a wire brush or steel wool. Coat the axle pilot flange with disc brake caliper slide grease or an equivalent. Do not apply grease to the lug nut seats or wheel studs. Place the wheel on the hub. Install the locking

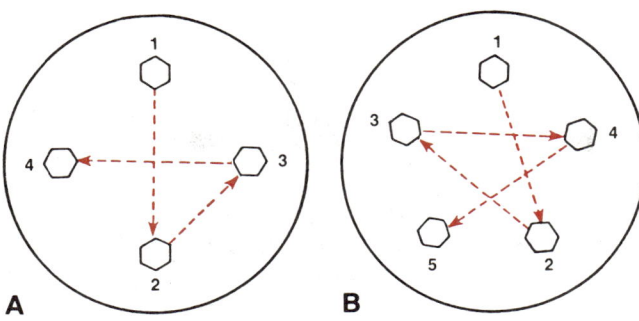

Figure 32-20 Lug nut tightening sequence for (A) four-bolt wheel and (B) five-bolt wheel.

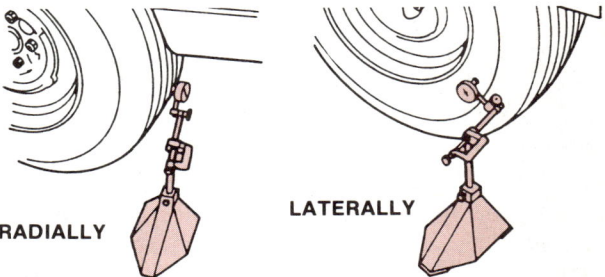

Figure 32-21 Using a dial indicator to measure tire runout.

wheelcover pedestal (if used) and lug nuts, and tighten them alternately to draw the wheel evenly against the hub. They should be tightened to a specified torque and sequence (Figure 32-20) to avoid distortion. Many tire technicians snug up the lug nuts. Then when the car is lowered to the floor, they use a torque wrench for the final tightening.

Be sure the wheels and hub are clean. To clean aluminum wheels, use a mild soap and water solution and rinse thoroughly with clear water. Do not use a steel wool abrasive cleaner or strong detergent containing high alkaline or caustic agents because they might damage the protective coating and cause discoloration. Once the vehicle is on the ground, check and adjust the air pressure in all tires.

☐ TIRE/WHEEL RUNOUT

A tire that is off center is said to run out. This is known as radial runout or eccentricity. One that wobbles side to side is said to have lateral runout. If a tire with some built-in runout is mismatched with a wheel's runout, the resulting total runout can exceed the ability of the balance weights to correct the problem. For this reason, part of a wheel balance check should be a check for excessive runout. Sometimes tires or wheels can be remounted to lessen or correct runout problems.

To avoid false readings caused by temporary flat spots in the tires, check runout only after the vehicle has been driven. Visually inspect the tire for abnormal bulges or distortions. The extent of runout should be measured with a dial indicator. All measurements should be made on the vehicle with the tires inflated to recommended load inflation pressures and with the wheel bearing adjusted to specification.

Measure tire radial runout at the center and outside ribs of the tread face (Figure 32-21). Measure tire lateral runout just above the buffing rib on the sidewall. Mark the high points of lateral and radial runout for future references. On bias or belted bias tires, radial runout must not exceed 0.104 inch and lateral runout must not exceed 0.099 inch. On radial ply tires, radial runout must not exceed 0.081 inch and lateral runout must not exceed 0.099 inch.

If total radial or lateral runout of the tire exceeds specified limits, it is necessary to check wheel runout to determine whether the wheel or tire is at fault. Wheel radial runout is measured at the wheel rim just inside the wheelcover retaining nibs. Wheel lateral runout is measured at the wheel rim bead flange just inside the curved lip of the flange. Wheel radial runout should not exceed 0.035 inch and wheel lateral runout should not exceed 0.040 inch. Mark the high points of radial and lateral runout for future reference.

If total tire runout, either lateral or radial, exceeds the specified limit but wheel runout is within the specified limit, it might be possible to reduce runout to an acceptable level. This is done by changing the position of the tire on the wheel so that the previously marked high points are 180 degrees apart.

If an air leak is suspected due to wheel damage, use the following procedure before considering wheel replacement.

PROCEDURES

Repairing Air Leaks

1. Remove the tire and wheel assembly, and inspect the wheel for structural damage. If none exists, go on to step 2. If the wheel is damaged, replace it.
2. With the tire mounted on the wheel, locate the leak as described earlier. Mark the location. Check the complete wheel for possible additional leaks. After all leaks are marked, dismount the tire.
3. On the inside of the rim, use about #80 grit sandpaper on the area of the leak, to thoroughly remove all contamination. Score the surface of the wheel to improve sealer adhesion.
4. Use a clean rag to remove all sanding dust.
5. With the wheel at room temperature, apply a generous portion of silicone rubber sealer to the leak area.
6. Use a spatula or similar tool and spread the sealer over the entire area, forming a thin coat.
7. Allow to cure for approximately 6 hours before remounting the tire.

TIRE/WHEEL ASSEMBLY SERVICE

For most tire/wheel service, the assembly must first be removed from the vehicle. The wheel and the tire must be separated whenever tires are replaced or repaired. The rear-wheel drum or disc brake rotor is usually attached to studs on the rear axle shaft hub flange. The wheel and tire mounts on the same rear axle shaft flange studs and is held against the hub and drum or rotor by the wheel nuts.

Tire/Wheel Balance

Proper front-end alignment allows the tires to roll straight without excessive tread wear. The wheels can go out of alignment from striking raised objects or pot holes. Misalignment subjects the tires to uneven and/or irregular wear. An out-of-balance condition can also cause increased wear on the ball joints, as well as deterioration of shock absorbers and other suspension components.

Should an inspection show uneven or irregular tire wear, wheel alignment and balance service is a must. Wheel balancing distributes weights along the wheel rim which counteract heavy spots in the wheels and tires and allow them to roll smoothly without vibration. There are two types of wheel imbalance: static and dynamic.

Static Balance

Static balance is the equal distribution of weight around the wheel. Wheels that are statically unbalanced cause a bouncing action called wheel tramp. This condition eventually causes uneven tire wear. As the name implies, static balance is balancing a wheel at rest. This is done by adding a compensating weight. Static balance is achieved when the wheel does not rotate by itself regardless of the position in which it is placed on its axis. This is true whether the wheel is mounted vertically, as on a spindle or balancer shaft, or horizontally, as on a bubble-type balancer.

A statically unbalanced wheel tends to rotate by itself until the heavy portion is down. To balance against the heavy portion, a weight is attached to the wheel directly opposite the heavy area. Some technicians place the weight on the inside of the wheel. Others place the weight on the outside of the wheel. Still others recommend placing two equal weights, one on each side of the wheel, opposite the heavy area.

There are many static balancers commonly used. The simplest is the bubble balancer. This design features a movable flange that rests on a point. A round sight glass filled with liquid containing a bubble rides with the flange. The bubble indicates whether the flange is level. When the tire/wheel assembly is placed on the flange, any static imbalance makes it tilt and moves the bubble off center. Lead wheel balance weights are then placed on the wheel where the bubble points to counteract the imbalance and center the bubble on the sight glass. When balance weights are used in pairs, the total balance-correcting weight is divided in half. One half is installed on the back of the wheel, the other half on the front. This weight-splitting method leaves the wheel's dynamic balance or imbalance unchanged. Many equipment manufacturers recommend static balancing a wheel at equal distances from the center of the light area. The balance weights are normally hammered on with their holding tabs between the tire bead and rim. Mag wheels require the use of tape weights to balance them.

Dynamic Balance

Dynamic balance is the equal distribution of weight on each side of the centerline. When the tire spins there is no tendency for the assembly to move from side to side. Wheels that are dynamically unbalanced can cause wheel shimmy and a wear pattern (Figure 32-22). Dynamic balance, simply stated, is balancing a wheel in motion. Once a wheel starts to rotate and is in motion, the static weights try to reach the true plane of rotation of the wheel because of the action of centrifugal force. In an attempt to reach the true plane of rotation when there is an imbalance, the static weights force the spindle to one side.

At 180 degrees of wheel rotation, static weights kick the spindle in the opposite direction. The resultant side thrusts cause the wheel assembly to wobble or wiggle (Figure 32-23). When severe enough, as already mentioned, it causes vibration and front-wheel shimmy.

To correct dynamic unbalance, equal weights are placed 180 degrees opposite each other, one on the

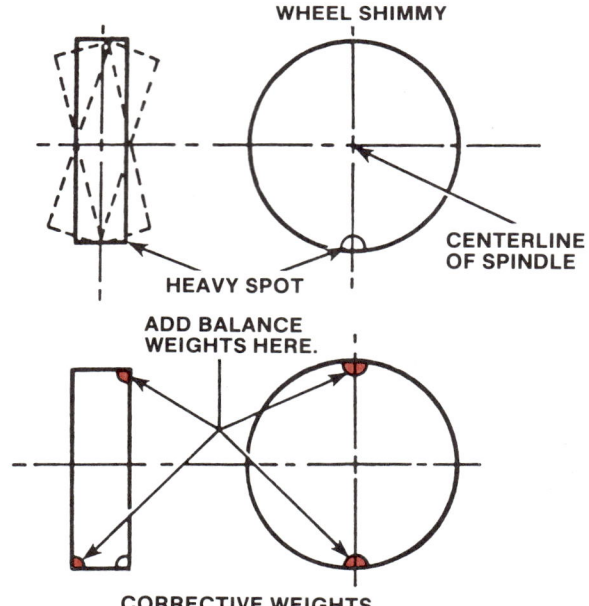

Figure 32-22 Dynamic unbalance causes wheel shimmy.

Tires and Wheels

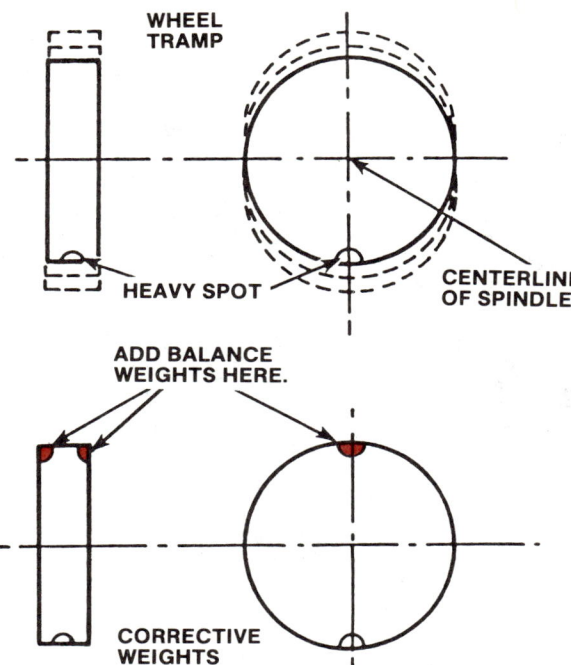

Figure 32-23 Static unbalance causes wheel tramp.

Figure 32-24 Tire/wheel assembly mounted on balancer's spindle. *Courtesy of Phonex International, Inc.*

Figure 32-25 Machine spins wheel while stroboscopic light is aimed at reference mark. *Courtesy of Hunter Engineering Co.*

inside of the wheel and one on the outside, at the point of unbalance. This corrects the couple action or wiggle of the wheel assembly. Also, note that dynamic balance is obtained, while static balance remains unaffected.

The most commonly used dynamic wheel balancer requires that the tire/wheel assembly be taken off and mounted on the balancer's spindle. The machine spins the entire assembly to indicate the heavy spot with a strobe light or other device. Two tests must be done, one for static and one for dynamic imbalance. One set of weights is placed to correct for static imbalance, and others are placed to correct for dynamic imbalance. Sometimes proper positioning of the static balance weights also corrects dynamic imbalance.

There are several electronic dynamic/static balancer units available that will permit balancing while the wheel and tire are on the car (Figure 32-24). A switch on the console sets the machine for either static or dynamic balancing. When the wheel balancing assembly is mounted for static balancing, it rotates until the heavy spot falls to the bottom. Weights are added to balance the assembly.

In the dynamic balance mode, the wheel assembly is rotated at high speed. Observing the balance scale, the operator reads out the amount of weight that has to be added and the location where the weights should be placed.

Another type of static/dynamic wheel balancing unit uses a motor to spin the wheel at a high rpm while a strobe light is aimed at a reference mark on the tire (Figure 32-25). When the heavy spot hits bottom, the light blinks and its relative position with regard to the reference mark is noted.

Wheel Bearings

There are several types of wheel bearing arrangements for both driving and nondriving wheels.

Front Wheel Hubs

Traditionally, the front wheel hub bearing for driven and nondriven wheels incorporated two bearings (Figure 32-26). They were usually of the separable type and therefore were comprised of four components. This

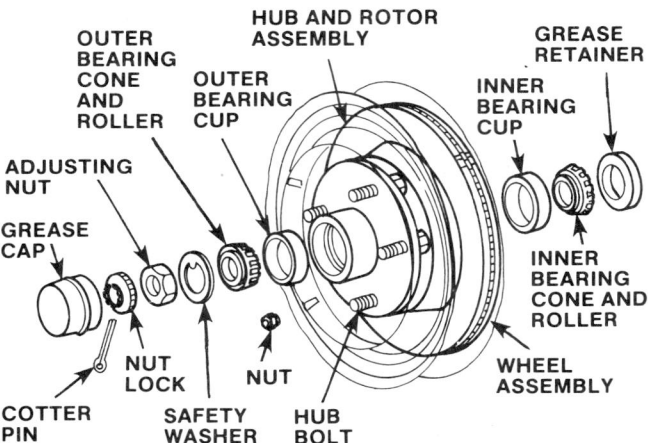

Figure 32-26 Exploded view of a typical front wheel assembly for RWD vehicle. Safety washer, used between outer bearing and spindle nut, is found on all cars. It must always be in place. *Courtesy of Ford Motor Co.*

arrangement required periodic bearing lubrication and adjustment.

In the early 1970s, the automotive industry began to show more interest in compactness and reduced mass. In order to meet future demands, especially for driven wheels, a unit in which both bearing rings were flanged was studied. The outer ring became a stiff structural member and thus permitted a simplification of the hub carrier. The hub was eliminated as the rotating inner ring flange took over its function. Design and assembly were simplified and there was a consequent savings in weight and space. Because the bearing rings are rigid, bearing geometry is precisely controlled.

There are three popular hub units (Figure 32-27).

HUB UNIT 1 This unit is a double-row, angular contact ball bearing with a two-part inner ring. The bearing has the correct axial clearance when mounted. Therefore, no adjustment is required and there is no risk of preloading the bearing. The contact angle of 32 degrees gives a large distance between the pressure centers of the bearing and reduces sensitivity to tilting movements. An added benefit is good axial carrying capacity, which is particularly important during cornering conditions. A taper roller bearing version is available for use where radial space restricts the fitting of the ball bearing type. This unit has a higher radial carrying capacity but is more sensitive to misalignment. Both ball and roller types are designed for compact FWD cars.

HUB UNIT 2 This unit is a double-row, angular contact ball bearing with a two-part inner ring and a flanged outer ring. The contact angle is 32 degrees. It is designed for outer ring rotation and incorporates the function of the wheel hub, having a spigot for centering the wheel and the brake drum or disc. Since a hub cap provides protection, there is no need for an outboard seal. This unit was designed for FWD vehicles that are somewhat larger than those using hub unit 1.

A

B

C

Figure 32-27 Examples of ready-to-mount units: (A) hub unit 1, (B) hub unit 2, and (C) hub unit 3. *Courtesy of SKF Automotive Products*

Tires and Wheels 809

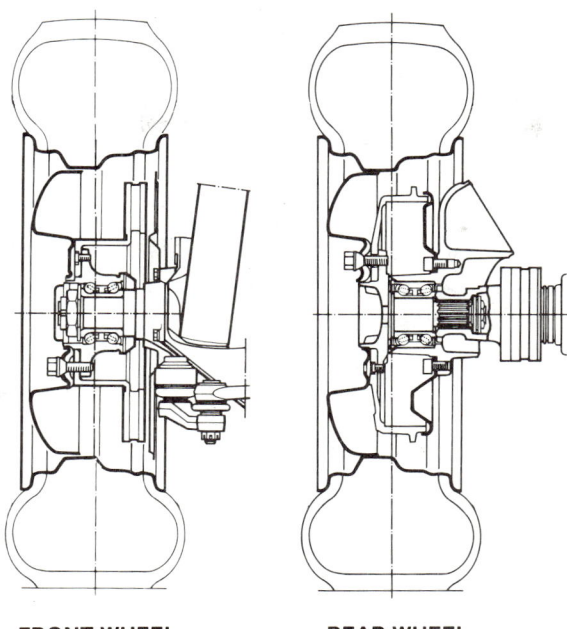

Figure 32-28 Concept 4 hub unit.

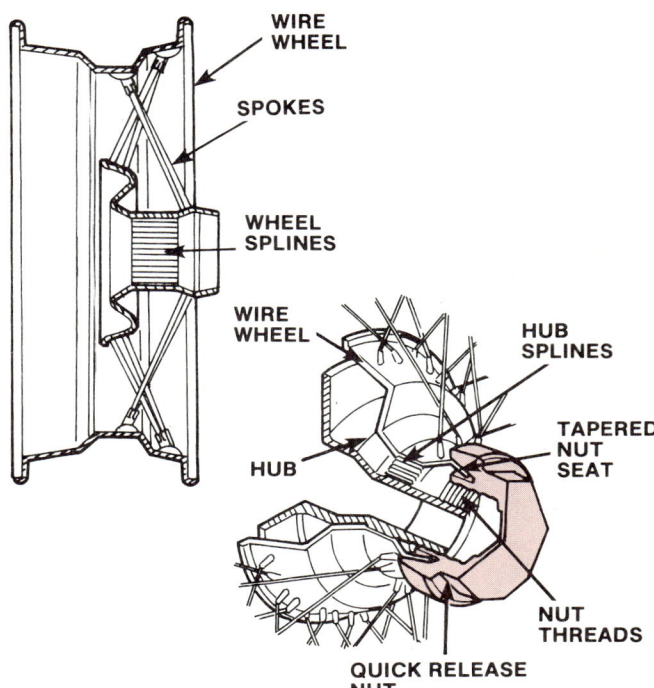

Figure 32-29 Quick-change wheel and hub assembly. A single quick release nut allows wheel removal. *Courtesy of British-Leyland*

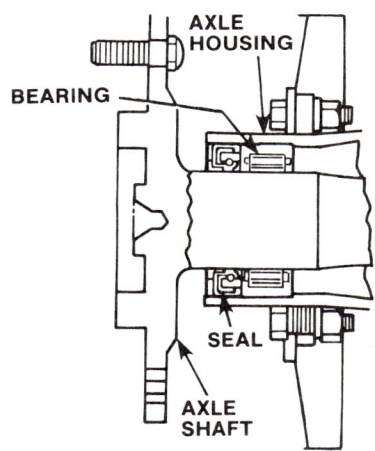

Figure 32-30 Straight roller type rear-axle bearing-and-seal arrangement. Notice the absence of a separate inner bearing race. Rollers run directly on the axle shaft. *Courtesy of General Motors Corp.*

HUB UNIT 3 This unit, designed primarily for mid-sized FWD cars, is a double-row, angular contact ball bearing with a contact angle of 32 degrees. Both inner and outer rings have been shaped to take over the functions of the other. The inner ring is extended on the outside to provide a flange and spigot. The bore is also splined, which enables hub unit 3 to completely replace the conventional driven wheel hub. The extremely stiff outer ring is also flanged and is provided with bolt holes for attachment to the steering knuckle. Therefore, it becomes a structural port of the suspension. Because the bearing outer ring is self-supporting, the steering knuckle can be designed for fatigue strength rather than for stiffness. The CV-joint shaft no longer needs to be designed to hold the bearing assembly together. Instead, its only requirement is to transmit torque, and it can be locked in the inner ring by a retaining ring.

Recently, a hub unit 4 was introduced for the larger car that has rear-wheel drive and an independent suspension on all four wheels (Figure 32-28).

Some early European sports models featured a so-called quick-change hub assembly. While this is similar to the standard disc type, it has a wire spoke center (Figure 32-29) that slides onto a splined hub and is retained by a single quick release or knock-off spinner nut. The wheel and tire assembly can be changed merely by removing this nut. The wheel then pulls off. To replace, merely reverse the procedure. This quick-change design requires special hubs.

Rear Hubs

Most RWD axle bearings are of the straight roller bearing design (Figure 32-30), in which the drive axle shaft serves as the bearing race. Some rear-wheel axle bearings are of the ball or tapered roller bearing type. Figures 32-31 and 32-32 show typical rear bearing designs.

A popular 4WD design is the so-called detachable rear axle hub (Figure 32-33). In this design, the hub is secured to the tapered axle end by means of a nut and key. The key fits into a groove cut in both the hub and axle. The key is used to prevent the hub from slipping on the axle.

810 Section 7 Suspensions

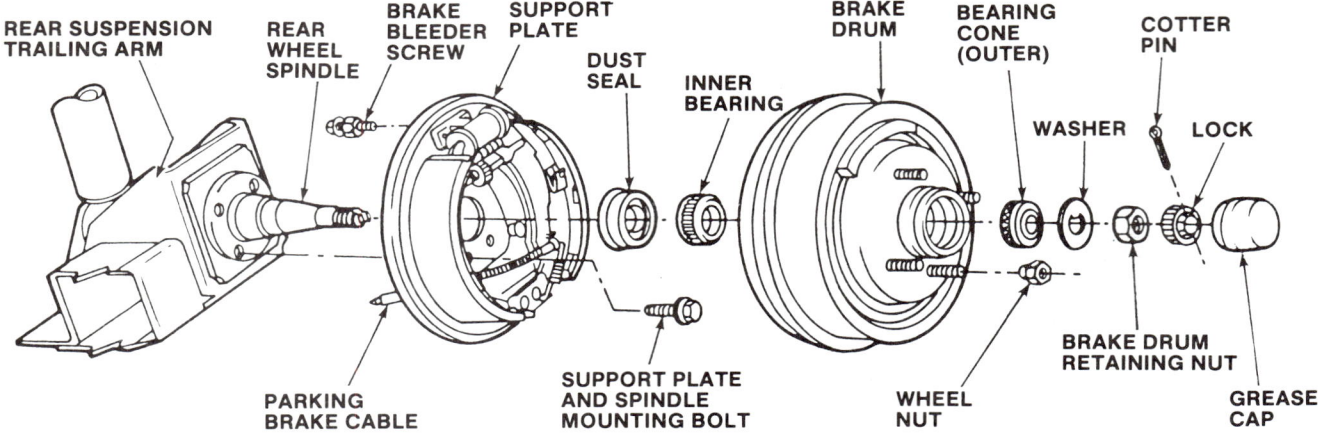

Figure 32-31 Typical rear wheel bearing assembly for a FWD vehicle. *Courtesy of Ford Motor Co.*

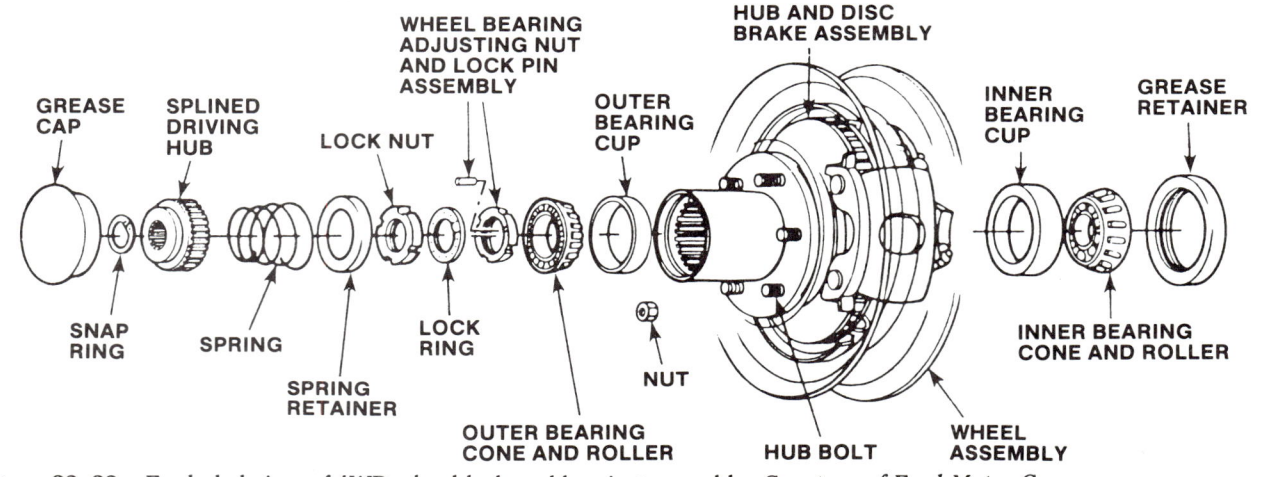

Figure 32-32 Exploded view of 4WD wheel hub and bearing assembly. *Courtesy of Ford Motor Co.*

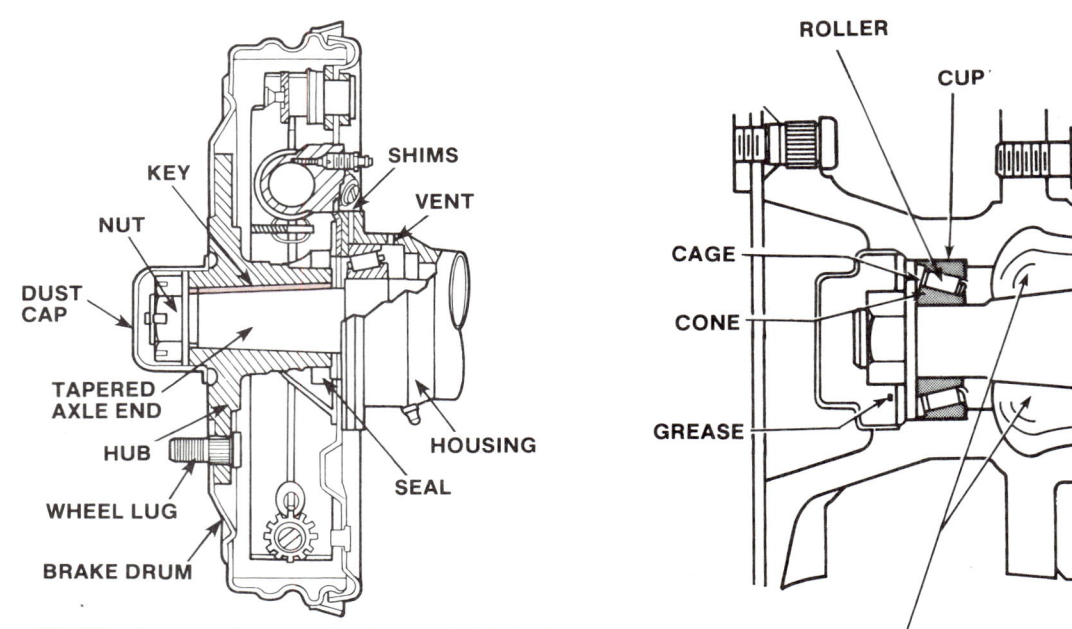

Figure 32-33 Detachable rear axle wheel hub. Hub is kept from turning on tapered axle end by a key. *Courtesy of Chrysler Motors*

Figure 32-34 Wheel bearing lubrication.

CAUTION: Never drive or move a vehicle with the wheel nuts loosened. Such an action could damage the wheel.

Wheel Bearing Grease Specification

The grease for wheel bearings should be smooth textured, consist of soaps and oils, and be free of filler and abrasives. Recommended are lithium complex (or equivalent) soaps, or solvent-refined petroleum oils. Additives could be added to inhibit corrosion and oxidation. The grease should be noncorrosive to bearing parts, with no chance of separating during storage or use.

Using the correct amount of lube is also essential. Failure to maintain proper lubrication might result in bearing damage, causing a wheel to lock (Figure 32-34). To lubricate a bearing, force grease around the outside of the bearing and between the rollers, cone, and cage. Also, pack grease into the wheel hub. The depth of the grease should be level with the inside diameter of the cup. The hub cap should also be filled with grease.

Oil Lubrication

Since it is thinner than grease, oil needs more frequent service intervals. Generally, oil is used to lubricate bearings in high-temperature and/or high-speed applications. It is primarily used on heavy-duty fleet, automotive, and agricultural vehicles.

Bearing Troubleshooting

Wheel bearings are designed for longevity. Their life expectancy, based on metal fatigue, can usually be calculated if general operating conditions are known. Bearing failures not caused by normal material fatigue are called premature failures. The causes can range from improper lubrication or incorrect mounting, to poor condition of the shaft housing or bearing surfaces.

When servicing, replacing, or installing wheel bearings, always follow the procedure given in the service manual.

CASE STUDY

Case 1

A customer wishes to purchase new tires for a sports car. The original size tire for the car is P235 VR60-15. He receives an estimate for purchasing four new tires of the same size and made by the same manufacturer. He is hesitant to spend that amount of money on replacement tires. He then asks for an estimate on a variety of alternate tires. The cost of the same tire from different tire manufacturers varies. A slightly narrower tire, e.g. P215 VR60-15, costs slightly less than the original size tire. Lower speed rated tires, e.g. H-series, cost considerably less. The customer is inclined to go with the H-series tire. Is he making the correct decision?

Although it is unlikely that the customer will travel at 150 mph, the original tires for that car were rated at these speeds. Speed ratings not only indicate the top speed that the tire can safely run at, they also indicate the amount of heat they can withstand. A tire rated at 150 mph can withstand more heat than a tire rated at 130 mph. The V-series tires would be a safer tire for that car. Therefore, if the vehicle's manufacturer installed a V-series tire, so should the customer.

This same logic is true for not changing the width of the tires. The car was built and the alignment specifications set for a particular width tire. Therefore, the customer should be advised not to switch to narrower tires.

The only possible way the customer can save money on buying replacement tires for his car is to change brands. However, all the features of the OE tires should be compared to the features and specifications of the other brands. As a technician, you should be able to give sound advice that is based on a knowledge of tires.

Summary

- Wheels are made of either stamped or pressed steel discs riveted or welded into a circular shape or are die-cast or forged aluminum or magnesium rims.
- The primary purpose of tires is to provide traction. They also are designed to carry the weight of the vehicle, to withstand side thrust over varying speeds and conditions, to transfer braking and driving torque to the road, and to absorb much of the road shock from surface irregularities.
- Pneumatic tires are of two types: those that use inner tubes and those that do not. The latter are called tubeless tires and are about the only type used on passenger cars.
- There are three types of tire construction in use today: bias ply, belted bias ply, and radial ply.
- Tires are rated by their profile, ratio, size, and load range.
- Tire construction affects both dimensions and ride characteristics, creating differences that can seriously affect vehicle handling.
- To maximize tire performance, inspect for signs of improper inflation and uneven wear, which can indicate a need for balancing, rotation, or alignment. Tires should also be checked frequently for cuts, bruises, abrasions, blisters, and for stones or other objects that might have become imbedded in the tread.
- A properly inflated tire gives the best tire life, riding comfort, handling stability, and even gas mileage during normal driving conditions.

- To equalize tire wear, most car and tire manufacturers recommend that the tires be rotated. It must be remembered that front and rear tires perform different jobs and can wear differently, depending on driving habits and the type of vehicle.
- Most tires used today have built-in tread wear indicators to show when tires need replacement.
- There are three popular methods of tire repair: head-type plug, cold patch repair, and hot patch repair.
- There are two types of wheel balancing: static balance and dynamic balance.
- The front wheel hubs on ball or tapered roller bearings are lubricated by wheel bearing grease.
- Rear wheels are bolted to integral or detachable hubs.

Review Questions

1. How is a modern tire wheel constructed? What materials are used?
2. What is the purpose of a wheel hub?
3. Define dynamic and static wheel balance.
4. How is the tire load rating designated?
5. Identify and describe the parts of a tire.
6. Which of the following statements concerning tires is incorrect?
    a. The main job of tires is to provide traction.
    b. Uneven tire wear is usually the first good indicator of alignment problems.
    c. The bead is the portion of the tire that comes in contact with the road surface.
    d. The inner tube tire was used exclusively before the 1960s.
7. Generally speaking, the lower the cord angle on a bias ply tire, the _____ .
    a. worse the high-speed stability
    b. better the high-speed stability
    c. smoother the ride
    d. b and c
8. Series is another name for a tire's _____ .
    a. size
    b. load range
    c. bead
    d. profile
9. The three belting systems available for today's tires are _____ .
    a. steel, nylon, and woven
    b. lateral, cut, and block
    c. cut, folded, and woven
    d. folded, straight ahead, and turning
10. Technician A equips a four-wheel-drive vehicle with radial tires on the rear wheels only. Technician B equips a four-wheel-drive vehicle with radial tires on all four wheels. Who is correct?
    a. Technician A
    b. Technician B
    c. Both A and B
    d. Neither A nor B
11. Which of the following statements concerning inflation pressure is incorrect?
    a. Once a tire is hot, its pressure drops 4 or more psi.
    b. All inflation pressures indicate cold inflation.
    c. A hot tire should never be held.
    d. Pressure recommendations are normally specified for light load and maximum load.
12. Where does an overinflated tire show its wear?
    a. in the center of the tread
    b. on the outside edges
    c. both a and b
    d. neither a nor b
13. Which of the following is a major cause of wheel failure?
    a. overloading
    b. age
    c. improper maintenance
    d. all of the above
14. Technician A uses tire sealant injected through the valve stem to repair a tire punctured in the tread area. Technician B uses tire sealant injected through the valve stem to repair a tire punctured in the sidewall. Who is correct?
    a. Technician A
    b. Technician B
    c. Both A and B
    d. Neither A nor B
15. Technician A says that you can drive on a temporary spare tire indefinitely, as long as you are careful. Technician B says that there are strict limitations on how fast and how far you may drive on a temporary spare tire. Who is correct?
    a. Technician A
    b. Technician B
    c. Both A and B
    d. Neither A nor B
16. Most information about a car's tires can be found on the _____ .
    a. engine block
    b. tire placard
    c. undercarriage of the vehicle
    d. steering wheel
17. A tire that wobbles from side to side is said to have _____ .
    a. radial runout
    b. lateral runout
    c. eccentric runout
    d. none of the above
18. Technician A says that tire rotation is done to even out wear on the front and rear tires. Technician B says that tire wear is always greatest on the rear wheels. Who is correct?
    a. Technician A

b. Technician B
   c. Both A and B
   d. Neither A nor B
19. When dismounting and mounting tires, use _____ .
   a. only a tire iron
   b. a tire changer
   c. only hand tools
   d. only hand tools and a tire iron
20. All of the following statements are true except _____ .
   a. a cold patch should be stitched to the inner surface of the carcass.
   b. a tread puncture that is less than 1/4 inch in diameter is repairable.
   c. wheel balancing is required only when new tires are installed.
   d. for best results, punctures should be repaired from inside the tire.
21. All of the following statements are correct except _____ .
   a. belts are reinforcing materials that encircle the tire under the tread
   b. the carcass of a tire is made up of plies, layers of cloth, and rubber
   c. most tread patterns are designed to work well on both wet and dry roads
   d. the bead is the decorative pattern at the outer edge of the tread
22. Which of the following statements about sidewall marking is correct?
   a. aspect ratio, or profile, indicates a grading for tread life.
   b. important information and safety warnings are indicated.
   c. the UTQG rating indicates maximum safe inflation pressure and load.
   d. section width is the distance between the tread and the bead.
23. All of the following statements are correct except _____ .
   a. tire inflation pressure directly affects traction
   b. recommended tire pressure for front and rear tires may be different
   c. recommended tire pressure are often lower than maximum pressures
   d. recommended maximum tire pressure is molded into the sidewall of the tire

33 SUSPENSION SYSTEMS

Objectives

- Name the different types of springs and how they operate.
- Name the advantages of ball joint suspensions.
- Explain the important differences between sprung and unsprung weight with regard to suspension control devices.
- Identify the functions of shock absorbers and struts, and describe their basic construction.
- Identify the components of a MacPherson strut system and describe their functions.
- Identify the functions of bushings and stabilizers.
- Perform a general front-suspension inspection.
- Check chassis height measurements to specifications.
- Identify the three basic types of rear suspensions and know their effects on traction and tire wear.
- Identify the various types of springs, their functions, and locations in the rear-axle housing.
- Describe the advantages and operation of the three basic electronically-controlled suspension systems: level control, adaptive, and active.
- Explain the function of electronic suspension components including air compressors, sensors, control modules, air shocks, electronic shock absorbers, and electronic struts.
- Explain the basic towing, lifting, jacking, and service precautions that must be followed when servicing air springs and other electronic suspension components.

The suspension system performs a very complicated function. It must keep the wheel lined up with the axis and direction of travel of the vehicle, provide steering control for the driver under all road conditions, and help the vehicle ride smoothly and comfortably.

In order to provide a rigid structural foundation for the vehicle body and to provide a solid anchorage for the suspension system, a frame of some type is essential. As detailed in a previous chapter, there are two basic frames in common use today.

CONVENTIONAL FRAME CONSTRUCTION In the conventional body-over-frame construction, the frame is the vehicle's foundation. The body and all major parts of a vehicle are attached to the frame. It must provide the support and strength needed by the assemblies and parts attached to it. In other words, the frame is an independent, separate component because it is not welded to any of the major units of the body shell.

UNIBODY CONSTRUCTION This type of construction has no separate frame. The body is constructed in such a manner that the body parts themselves supply the rigidity and strength required to maintain the structural integrity of the car. The unibody design significantly lowers the base weight of the car, and that in turn increases gas mileage capabilities.

☐ SUSPENSION SYSTEM COMPONENTS

Most automotive suspension systems have the same basic components and operate similarly. Their differences are found in the method in which the basic components are arranged.

Springs

The spring is the core of nearly all suspension systems. It is the component that absorbs shock forces while maintaining correct riding height. If the spring is worn or damaged, the other suspension elements shift out of their proper positions and are subject to increased wear. The increased effect of shock impairs the vehicle's handling.

Various types of springs are used in suspension systems—coil, torsion bar, leaf (both mono and multi-leaf types) (Figure 33-1) and air springs. Springs are rubber mounted to reduce road shock and noise.

Automotive springs are generally classified by the amount of deflection exhibited under a specific load. This is referred to as the spring rate. According to the law of physics, a force (weight) applied to a spring causes it to compress in direct proportion to the force applied. When that force is removed, the spring returns

Suspension Systems

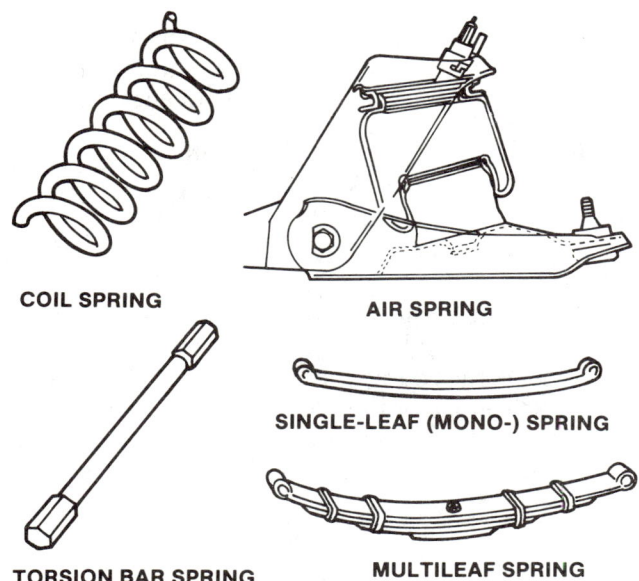

Figure 33-1 Various types of automotive springs.

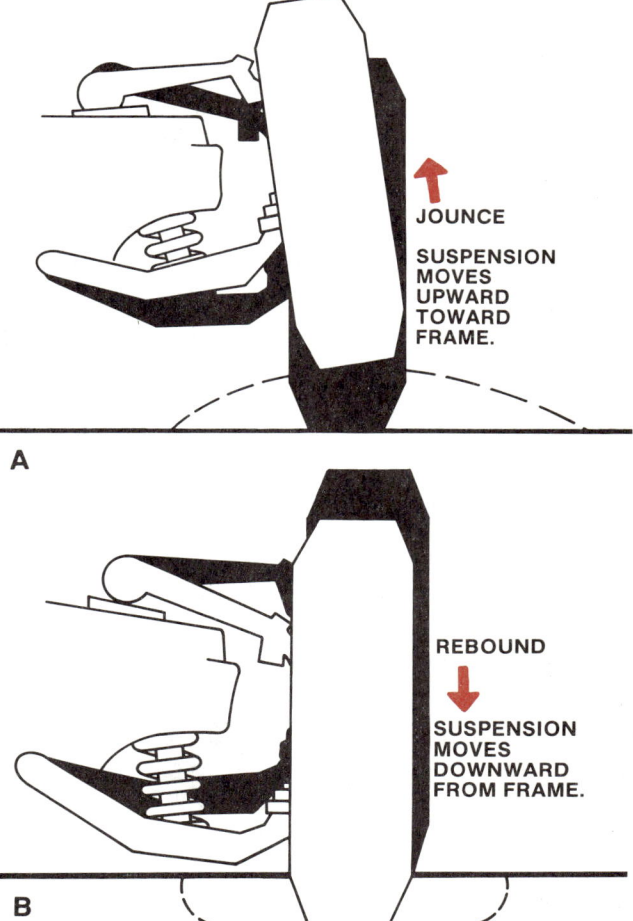

Figure 33-2 (A) Upward and (B) downward suspension movement.

to its original position if not overloaded. Remember that a heavy vehicle requires stiffer springs than a lightweight car.

The springs take care of two fundamental vertical actions: jounce and rebound. Jounce occurs when a wheel hits a bump and moves up (Figure 33-2A). When this happens, the suspension system acts to pull in the top of the wheel, maintaining an equal distance between the two front wheels and preventing a sideways scrubbing action as the wheel moves up and down. Rebound occurs when the wheel hits a dip or hole and moves downward (Figure 33-2B). In this case, the suspension system acts to move in the wheel at both the top and bottom equally, while maintaining an equal distance between the wheels.

The spring goes back and forth from jounce to rebound. Each time jounce and rebound become smaller and smaller. This is caused by friction of the spring's molecular structure and the suspension pivot joints. A shock absorber is added to each suspension to dampen and stop the motion of the spring after jounce.

All of the vehicle's weight supported by the suspension system is known as sprung weight. The weight of those components not supported by the springs is known as unsprung weight. The vehicle's body, frame, engine, transmission, and all of their components are considered sprung weight. Undercar parts classified as unsprung weight include the steering knuckles and rear axle assemblies (but not always the differentials). Keep in mind that, in general, the lower the proportion of unsprung weight to sprung weight in a vehicle, the better the ride in general.

Coil Springs

Two basic designs of coil springs are used: linear rate and variable rate. Linear rate springs characteristically have one basic shape and a consistent wire diameter. All linear rate springs are wound from a steel rod into a cylindrical shape with even spacing between the coils. As the load is increased, the spring is compressed and the coils twist (deflect). As the load is removed, the coils flex (unwind) back to the normal position. The amount of load necessary to deflect the spring 1 inch is the spring rate. On linear rate springs this is a constant rate, no matter how much the spring is compressed. For example, 250 pounds compresses the spring 1 inch and 750 pounds compresses the spring 3 inches. Spring rates for linear rate springs are normally calculated between 20 and 60% of the total spring deflection.

Since heavy-duty springs are designed to carry 3 to 5% greater loads than regular duty springs, they are somewhat different (Figure 33-3). The first difference that can be noticed is wire diameter. On heavy-duty springs, wire diameter can be up to 0.100 inch greater than the regular duty spring for the same application.

The other difference is free length. A heavy-duty spring is up to 2-1/2 inches shorter than a regular duty spring for the same application. The important factor to remember is load-carrying capabilities.

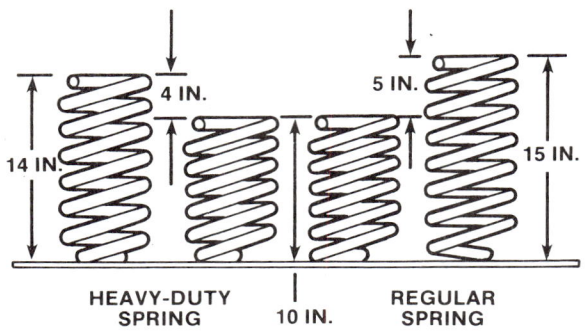

Figure 33-3 Comparison of regular and heavy duty coil springs.

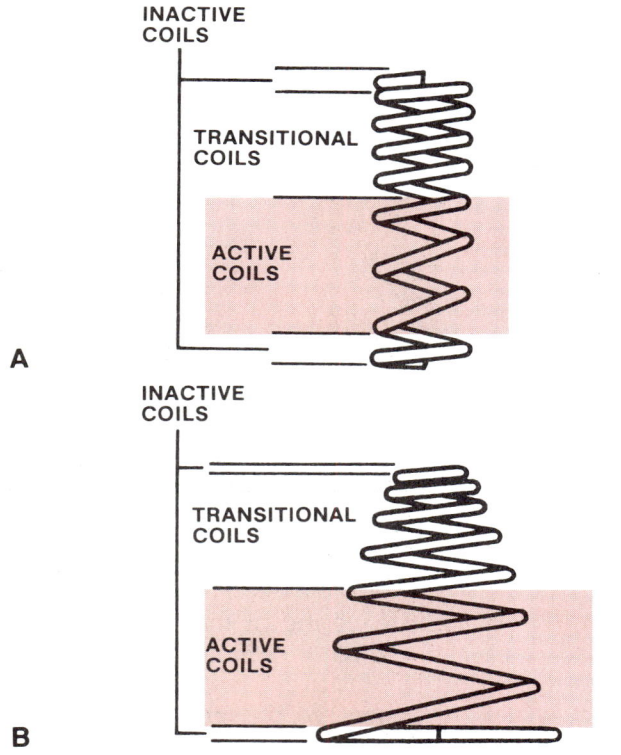

Figure 33-4 (A) Progressive rate coil; (B) cone-type variable rate coil spring.

Variable rate spring designs are characterized by a combination of wire sizes and shapes. The most commonly used variable rate springs have a consistent wire diameter, are wound in a cylindrical shape, and have unequally spaced coils. This type of spring is called a progressive rate coil spring.

The design of the coil spacing gives the spring three functional ranges of coils: inactive, transitional, and active (Figure 33-4). Inactive coils are usually the end coils and introduce force into the spring. Transitional coils become inactive as they are compressed to their point of maximum load-bearing capacity. Active coils work throughout the entire range of spring loading. Theoretically in this type of design, at stationary loads the inactive coils are supporting all of the vehicle's weight. As the loads are increased, the transitional coils take over until they reach maximum capacity. Finally, the active coils carry the remaining overload. This allows for automatic load adjustment while maintaining vehicle height.

Another common variable rate design uses tapered wire to achieve this same type of progressive rate action. In this design, the active coils have a large wire diameter and the inactive coils have a small wire diameter.

The latest designs of variable rate springs deviate from the old cylindrical shape. These include the truncated cone, the double cone, and the barrel spring. The major advantage of these designs is the ability of the coils to nest, or bottom out, within each other without touching, which lessens the amount of space needed to store the springs in the vehicle.

Unlike a linear rate spring, a variable rate spring has no predictable standard spring rate. Instead, it has an average spring rate based on the load of a predetermined spring deflection. This makes it impossible to compare a linear rate spring to a variable rate spring. Variable rate springs, however, handle loads of up to 30% over standard rate springs in some applications.

SERVICING COIL SPRINGS A technician must know how to check and replace coil springs, select the proper replacement, and recommend the proper size and type of spring to the customer.

The first step in coil spring selection is to check for the original equipment part number. This is usually on a tag wrapped around the coil. In many instances, this tag falls off before replacement is necessary. If a set of aftermarket springs has been installed, the part number might be stamped on the end of the coil. Next, check to see what type of ends the coil springs have. There are three types of ends used in automotive applications (Figure 33-5): full wire open, tapered wire closed, and pigtail. Springs with full wire open ends are cut straight off and sometimes flattened or ground into a D or square shape. Tapered wire closed ends are wound to insure squareness and ground into a taper at the ends. Pigtail ends are wound into a smaller diameter at the end.

The final step is to check the application in the catalog. To do this, it is necessary to know the make, year, model, body style, engine size (number of cylinders), and if the vehicle is equipped with air-condition-

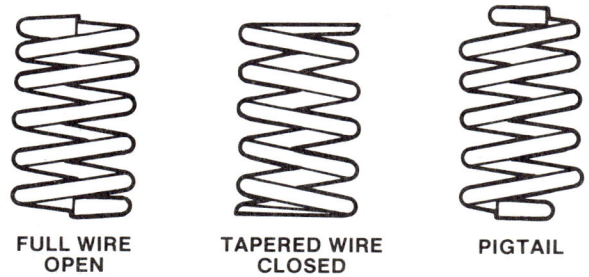

Figure 33-5 Three types of coil spring ends.

ing. In some cases, it is also good to know the type of transmission, seating capacity, and other specifics that add extra weight to the vehicle. In most catalogs, springs are listed by vehicle application in two sections: front and rear.

> ### CUSTOMER CARE
>
> When making a recommendation as to which type of spring a customer should use, keep in mind that linear rate designs are normally found in regular, heavy-duty, and sport suspension packages. Regular duty linear rate springs are a close replacement for the original spring found in the vehicle. They might replace as many as thirty different original equipment (OE) springs in the same vehicle. These are selected on the basis of tire and wheel packages, suspension packages, and optional equipment. Extra heavy-duty cargo linear rate springs offer increased load-carrying capabilities under constant loads. Two common examples of this are trailer towing and salespeople's vehicles. Variable rate designs are normally found when automatic load leveling is desired under increased loads and space savings are necessary, as in front-wheel-drive vehicles. Variable rate springs allow the suspension to maintain correct vehicle height under changing loads and give increased load-carrying capabilities over heavy-duty springs. Be sure to choose the correct spring for the intended use.

Leaf Springs

Although leaf springs were the first type of suspension spring used on automobiles, today they are generally found only on light-duty trucks, vans, and some passenger cars. There are three basic types of leaf springs: multiple leaf, monoleaf, and fiber composite.

MULTIPLE-LEAF SPRINGS Multiple-leaf springs consist of a series of flat steel leaves that are bundled together and held with clips or by a bolt placed slightly ahead of the center of the bundle (Figure 33-6). One leaf, called the main leaf, runs the entire length of the spring. The next leaf is a little shorter and attaches to the main leaf. The next leaf is shorter yet and attaches to the second leaf, and so on. This system allows almost any number of leaves to be used to support the vehicle's weight. It also gives a progressively stiffer spring. The spring easily flexes over small distances for minor bumps. The farther the spring is deflected, the stiffer it gets. The more leaves and the thicker and shorter the leaves, the stronger the spring. It must be remembered that as the spring flexes, the ends of the leaves slide over one another. This sliding could be a source of noise and can also produce friction. These problems are

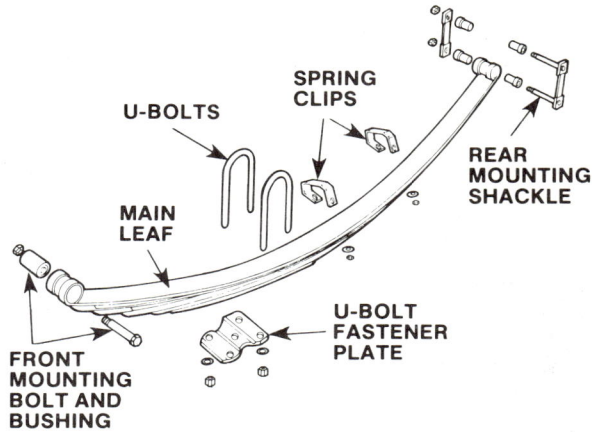

Figure 33-6 Leaf springs and related hardware.

reduced by interleaves of zinc and plastic placed between the spring's leaves. As the multiple leaves slide, friction produces a harsh ride as the spring flexes. This friction also dampens the spring motion.

Multiple-leaf springs have a curve in them. This curve, if doubled, forms an ellipse. Thus, leaf springs are sometimes called semi-elliptical or quarter-elliptical. The semi or quarter refers to how much of the ellipse the spring actually describes. The vast majority of leaf springs are semi-elliptical.

Leaf springs are commonly mounted at right angles to the axle. In addition to absorbing blows from road forces, they also serve as suspension locators by fixing the position of the suspension with respect to the front and rear of the vehicle. A centering pin is frequently used to ensure that the axle is correctly located. If a spring is broken or misplaced, the axle might be mislocated and the alignment impaired.

The front eye of the main leaf at either end of the axle is attached to a bracket on the frame of the vehicle with a bolt and bushing connection. The rear eye of the main leaf is secured to the frame with a shackle, which permits some fore and aft movement in response to physical forces of acceleration, deceleration, and braking.

MONOLEAF SPRINGS Monoleaf or single-leaf springs are usually the tapered plate type with a heavy or thick center section tapering off at both ends. This provides a variable spring rate for a smooth ride and good load-carrying ability. In addition, single-leaf springs do not have the noise and static friction characteristic of multiple-leaf type springs.

FIBER COMPOSITE SPRINGS While most leaf springs are still made of steel, recent years have shown the fiber composite types increasing in popularity. Some automotive people call them plastic springs in spite of the fact that the springs contain no plastic at all. They are made of fiberglass, laminated and bonded together by tough polyester resins. The long strands of fiberglass are saturated with resin and bundled togeth-

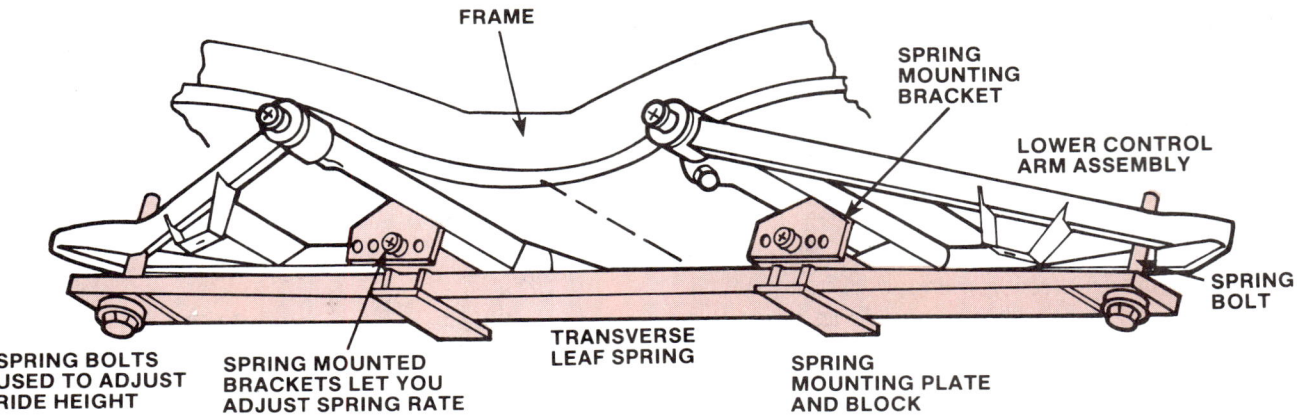

Figure 33-7 Typical transversely mounted monoleaf spring. *Courtesy Vette Brakes and Products, Inc.*

er by wrapping (a process called filament winding) or squeezed together under pressure (compression molding).

Fiber composite leaf springs are incredibly lightweight and possess some unique ride control characteristics. Conventional monoleaf steel springs are real heavyweights, tipping the scale at anywhere from 25 to 45 pounds apiece. Some multiple-leaf springs can weigh almost twice as much. A fiber composite leaf spring is a featherweight by comparison, weighing a mere eight to ten pounds. As every performance enthusiast knows, springs are dead weight. Reducing the weight of the suspension not only reduces the overall weight of the vehicle, but also reduces the sprung mass of the suspension itself. This reduces the spring effort and amount of shock control that is required to keep the wheels in contact with the road. The result is a smoother riding, better handling, and faster responding suspension—which is exactly the sort of thing every performance enthusiast wants.

Other advantages of using fiber composite springs include the following.

- A quieter ride. A fiber composite spring does not resonate or transmit sound like a steel spring. In fact, it actually dampens noise.
- A smoother ride. Because fiber composite springs use a one-piece monoleaf design, there is no rubbing friction like there is between the leafs in a multiple-leaf steel spring.
- No spring sag. All steel springs sag with age, whether leaves or coils. Spring sag affects ride height, which in turn alters wheel alignment, handling, steering, and braking. A weak spring can load the suspension unevenly, allowing the wheel under the weak spring to lose traction when accelerating or braking. But according to the manufacturers of fiber composite springs, there is no sag with age.
- Less body roll. In applications where the leaf springs are mounted sideways (transversely), the spring also acts like a sway bar to limit body sway and roll when cornering (Figure 33-7). This load transfer characteristic also permits softer than normal spring rates to be used for a smoother ride.

With fiber composite leaf springs, there is little or no danger of the spring suddenly snapping. The laminated layers create a built-in fail-safe mechanism for keeping the spring intact should a problem arise (Figure 33-8).

Air Springs

One of the latest innovations in suspension springs is the air type. Actually, it is used in an air-operated microprocessor-controlled system that replaces the conventional coil springs with air springs to provide a comfortable ride and automatic front and rear load leveling. This system, fully described later in this chapter, uses four air springs to carry the vehicle's weight.

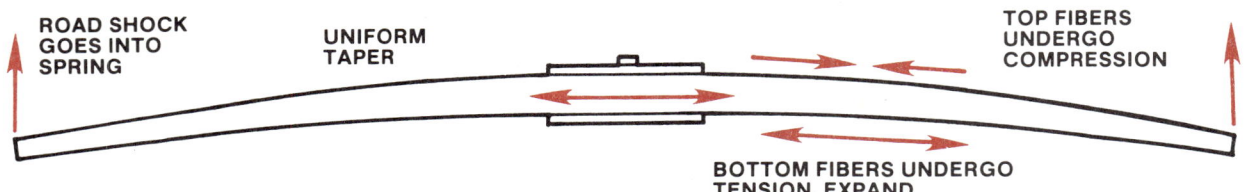

Figure 33-8 The manner in which a fiber composite spring bends dictates that there is no danger of it suddenly snapping. Laminated layers create a built-in safe mechanism for keeping the spring intact should a problem arise. *Courtesy of Vette Brakes and Products, Inc.*

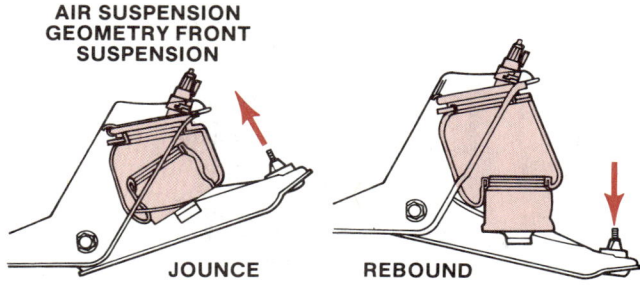

Figure 33-9 Air springs are used on some late model cars. They are especially adaptable to automatic leveling systems.

The air springs are located in the same positions as coil springs are usually found. Each spring consists of a reinforced rubber bag pressurized with air. The bottom of each air bag is attached to an inverted piston-like mount that reduces the interior volume of the air bag during jounce (Figure 33-9). This has the effect of increasing air pressure inside the spring as it is compressed, making it progressively stiffer. Thus a vehicle equipped with an electronic air suspension system is able to provide a comfortable street ride, about a third softer than conventional coil springs. At the same time, its variable spring rate helps absorb bumps and protect against bottoming.

Torsion Bar Suspension System

Torsion bars serve the same function as coil springs. In fact, they are often described as straightened-out coil springs. But instead of compressing like coil springs, a torsion bar twists and straightens out on the recoil. That is, as the bar twists, it resists up-and-down movement. One end of the bar—made of heat-treated alloy spring steel—is attached to the vehicle frame. The other end is attached to the lower control arm (Figure 33-10). When the wheel moves up and down, the lower control arm is raised and lowered. This twists the torsion bar, which causes it to absorb road shocks. The bar's natural resistance to twisting quickly restores it to its original position, returning the wheel to the road.

When torsion bars are manufactured, they are prestressed to give them fatigue strength. Because of directional prestressing, torsion bars are directional. The torsion bar is marked either right or left to identify on which side it is to be used.

A torsion bar can store a significantly higher maximum amount of energy than either an equally stressed coil or leaf spring. The shorter and thicker the rod is, the stiffer the torsion bar is. Because torsion bars use less space than either coil or leaf springs, they are usually found on the front suspension, although a few cars have them at the rear. They are easily adjusted for riding height by changing the preload at the anchored end. (Preload is the weight resting on the springs while the car is at rest.)

In a conventional torsion bar suspension, the torsion bar runs from front to rear (Figure 33-11A). Either an A-arm or a single inner bushing control arm with a strut rod is used for the lower control arm. Torsion bars can be used to adjust vehicle riding height. They are not interchangeable from side to side, because the direction of the twisting (or torsion) is different between the left and right sides.

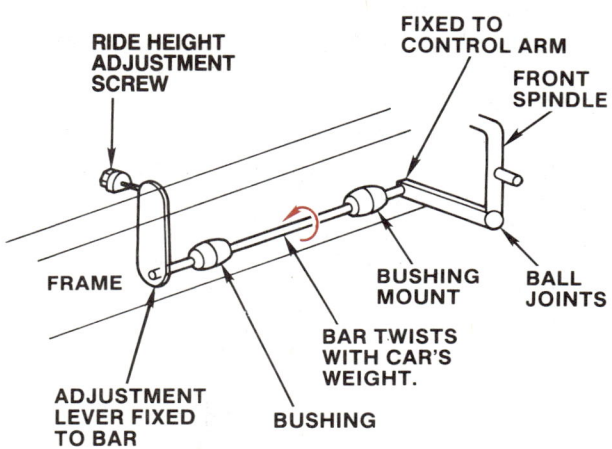

Figure 33-10 Torsion bar.

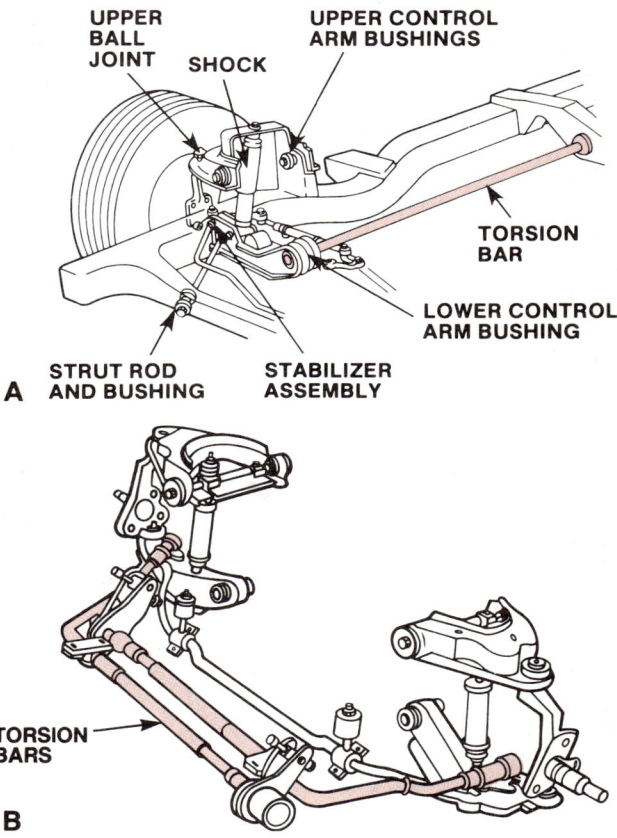

Figure 33-11 (A) Torsion bar suspension using bars mounted parallel with frame. (B) Torsion bars on this modern suspension mount crosswise in the car. Both can be adjusted to change vehicle height. *Courtesy of Moog Automotive*

In a transverse torsion bar system—the latest in torsion bar suspension—the bar is mounted from side to side and runs across the width of the chassis back to the control arm (Figure 33-11B). This eliminates the need for a strut rod or A-arm.

Because the torsion bar is connected to the lower control arm, the lower ball joint is the load carrier. A shock absorber is connected between the lower control arm and the frame to damp the twisting motion of the torsion bar.

Shock Absorbers

Shock absorbers damp or control motion in a vehicle. If unrestrained, springs continue expanding and contracting after a blow until all the energy is absorbed (Figure 33-12). Not only would this lead to a rough and unstable—perhaps uncontrollable—ride after consecutive shocks, it would also create a great deal of wear on the suspension and steering systems. Shock absorbers prevent this. Despite their name, they actually dampen spring movement instead of absorbing shock. As a matter of fact, in England and almost everywhere else but the United States, shock absorbers are referred to as dampers.

Today's conventional shock absorber is a velocity-sensitive hydraulic damping device. The faster it moves, the more resistance it has to the movement (Figure 33-13). This allows it to automatically adjust to road conditions. A shock absorber works on the principle of fluid displacement on both its compression (jounce) and extension (rebound) cycles. A typical car shock has more resistance during its extension cycle than its compression cycle. The extension cycle controls motions of the vehicle body sprung weight. The compression cycle controls the same motions of the unsprung weight. This motion energy is converted into heat energy and dissipated into the atmosphere.

Shock absorbers can be mounted either vertically or at an angle. Angle mounting of shock absorbers improves vehicle stability and dampens accelerating and braking torque.

Conventional hydraulic shocks are available in two styles: the single-tube and double-tube shock. The vast majority of domestic shocks are double tubed. While they are a little heavier and run hotter than the single-

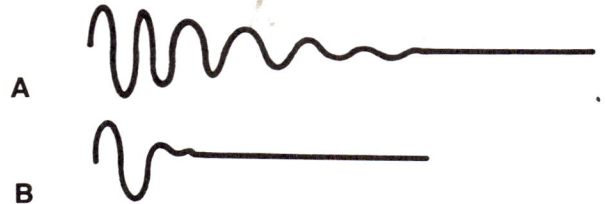

Figure 33-12 (A) Series of spring oscillations occur as shown when not controlled by the shock absorber. (B) Notice the reduced number and severity of oscillations when controlled by the shock absorber.

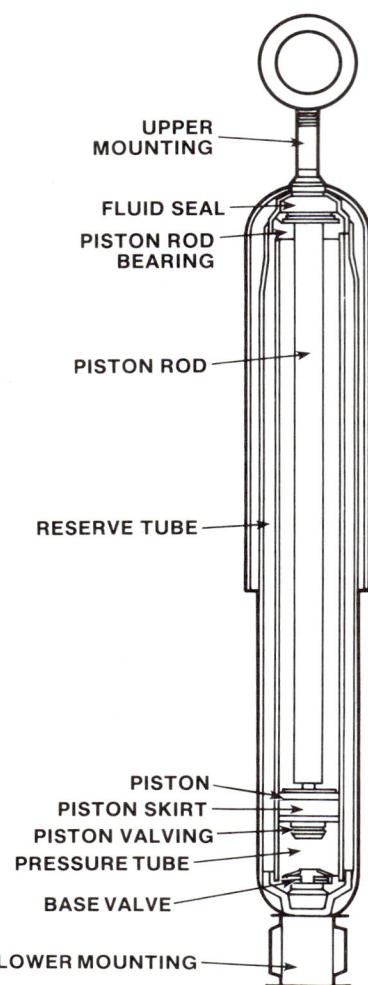

Figure 33-13 Cross section of a conventional shock absorber.

tubed type, they are easier to make. The double-tube shock has an outer tube that completely covers the inner tube. The area between the tubes is the oil reservoir. A compression valve at the bottom of the inner tube allows oil to flow between the two tubes. The piston moves up and down inside the inner tube.

In a single monoshock, there is a second floating piston near the bottom of the tube. When the fluid volume increases or decreases, the second piston moves up and down, compressing the reservoir. The fluid does not move back and forth between a reservoir and the main chamber. There are no other valves in a single-tube shock besides those in the main piston. The second piston prevents the oil from splashing around too much and getting air bubbles in it. Air in the shock oil is detrimental. Air, unlike oil, is compressible and slips past the piston easily. When this happens, the result is a shock that offers poor vehicle control on bumpy roads.

In addition to these conventional hydraulic shocks, there are a number of others that the technician may encounter.

Load-Assist Shock Absorbers

Load-assist shock absorbers can be used to increase the load carrying capacity of the springs. They are available for the front or rear suspension. They resemble a conventional shock absorber with a coil spring fitted to it. An upper spring mount if fastened to the upper shock tube and a lower spring mount is attached to the lower shock tube. The spring is mounted between. The spring is under some tension in its normal curb height position and compresses when the shock absorber compresses.

Gas-Charged Shock Absorbers

On rough roads, the passage of fluid from chamber to chamber becomes so rapid that foaming can occur. Foaming is simply the mixing of the fluid with any available air. Since aeration can cause a skip in the shock's action, engineers have sought methods of eliminating it. One is the spiral groove reservoir, the shape of which breaks up bubbles. Another is a gas-filled cell or bag (usually nitrogen) that seals air out of the reservoir so that the shock fluid can only contact the gas.

Gas-charged shock absorbers (Figure 33-14) operate on the same hydraulic fluid principle as conventional shocks do. It uses a piston and oil chamber similar to other shock absorbers. But instead of a double tube with a reserve chamber, it has a dividing piston that separates the oil chamber from the gas chamber. The oil chamber contains a special hydraulic oil, and the gas chamber contains either freon or nitrogen gas under pressure equal to approximately 25 times atmospheric pressure.

As the piston rod moves downward in the shock absorber, oil is displaced, just as it is in a double-tube shock. This oil displacement causes the divided piston to press upon the gas chamber. The gas is compressed and the chamber reduces in size. When the piston rod returns, the gas pressure returns the dividing piston to its starting piston. Whenever the static pressure of the oil column is held at approximately 100 to 360 psi (depending on the design), the pressure decreases behind the piston and, so, cannot be high enough for the gas to escape from the oil column. As a result, a gas-filled shock absorber operates without aeration.

SHOP TALK

Some high-pressure gas-charged shocks are monotube shocks with fluid and gas in separate chambers. The gas is charged to 360 psi. Its basic design does not allow the valving range needed for a more responsive ride over a broad range of road conditions. The high-pressure gas charge can provide a harsh ride under normal driving conditions and are usually found on small trucks.

Air Shock Systems

There are two basic adjustable air shock systems: manual fill (Figure 33-15) and automatic load-level-

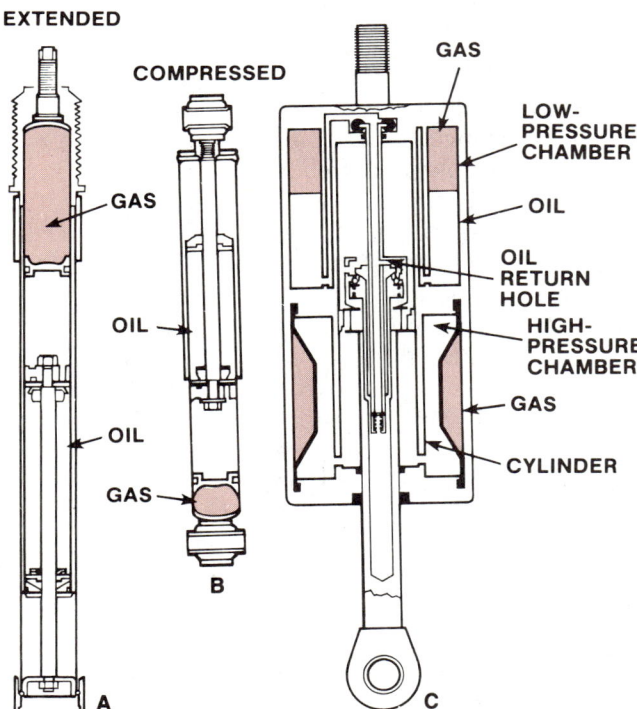

Figure 33-14 Gas-pressure damped shocks operate like conventional oil-filled shocks. Gas is used to keep oil pressurized, which reduces oil foaming and increases efficiency under severe conditions. (A) Gas-charged shock for strut. (B) Conventional style gas-charged shocks. (C) Gas-charged, self-leveling shock. *Courtesy of Volvo Corp.*

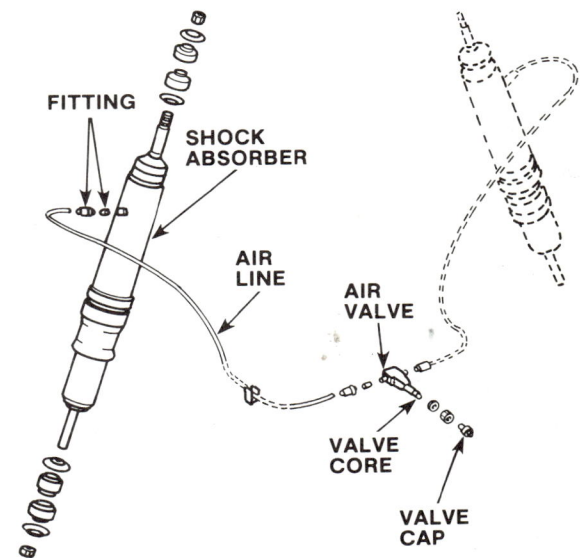

Figure 33-15 Manual level control setup. By either raising or lowering air pressure in the shocks, car level can be adjusted to desired height. *Courtesy of AMC*

ing. The manual fill system can be ordered on new vehicles or can be installed on almost any vehicle manufactured without it.

There are several different types of manual fill air shock systems available. One common manual fill air shock system uses a high-speed, direct current (DC) motor to transfer a command signal that is manually selected from the driver's seat. The selective ride feature is accomplished by the physical movement of a drive rod that can rotate approximately 90 degrees to open or close calibrated fluid passages built into the lower section of the shock body. The relative ease of installation allows the technician to find a rather straightforward approach to servicing. Basic multimeter voltage and resistance values can be adapted for use on most systems.

In another manual air system, the shock absorber is the only active part. These units are inflated through an air valve mounted at the rear of the vehicle. Air lines run between the shocks and the valve. A tire air pressure pump is used to fill the shocks to bring the rear of the vehicle to the desired height.

A two-stage vacuum-operated air compressor is sometimes used in some manual fill systems. As shown in Figure 33-16, the diaphragm forces the piston towards the reservoir. Fresh air is drawn in through check valve A. The air is compressed in the second stage cylinder and forced through check valve B, into the reservoir. The reverse stroke forces air from the first stage cylinder through the hollow cylinder into the second stage cylinder. The compressor piston cycles (moves back and forth) until the pressure built up in the reservoir is equal to the pressure generated by the piston in the second stage cylinder. When this point is reached, a balanced condition exists. The compressor does not operate until some air has been used by the system.

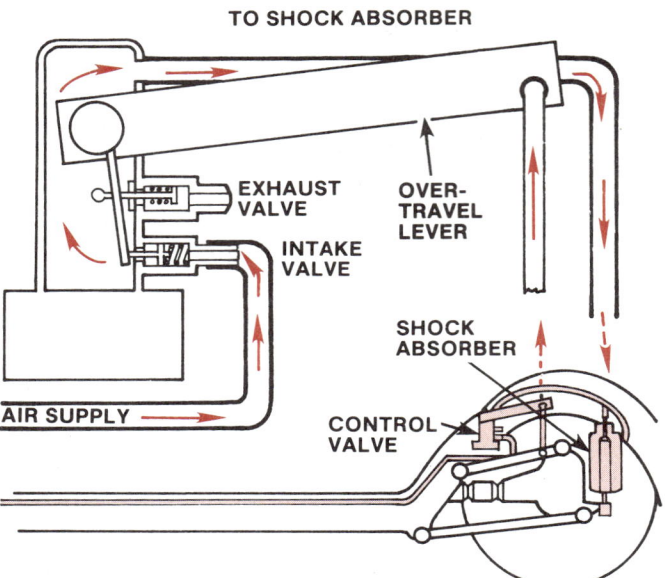

Figure 33-17 Typical lever-type shock absorber.

Some import cars use a lever-activated air shock. In this manual fill system, the piston, chamber, and reservoir are encased in a box that is fastened securely to the vehicle's body. The piston is connected to an overtravel arm extending from the box to the suspension. When the suspension moves downward, the overtravel lever opens an intake valve so compressed air can enter the shock absorber (Figure 33-17). These lever shocks help to minimize the amount of unsprung weight.

Shock Absorber Ratio

Most shock absorbers are valved to offer roughly equal resistance to suspension movement upward (jounce) and downward (rebound). The proportion of a shock absorber's ability to resist these movements is indicated by a numerical formula. The first number indicates jounce resistance. The second indicates rebound resistance. For example, passenger cars with normal suspension requirements use shock absorbers valved at 50/50 (50% jounce/50% rebound). Drag racers, on the other hand, use shocks valved at about 90/10. Small vehicles, because of their light-weight and soft springs, require more control in both jounce and rebound in the shock absorbers. Damping rates within the shock absorbers are controlled by the size of the piston, the size of the orifices, and the closing force of the valves.

It is important to keep in mind that the shock absorber ratio only describes what percent of the shock absorber's total control is compression and what percent is extension. Two shocks with the same ratio can differ greatly in their control capacity. This is one reason the technician must be sure that correct replacement shocks are installed on the vehicle.

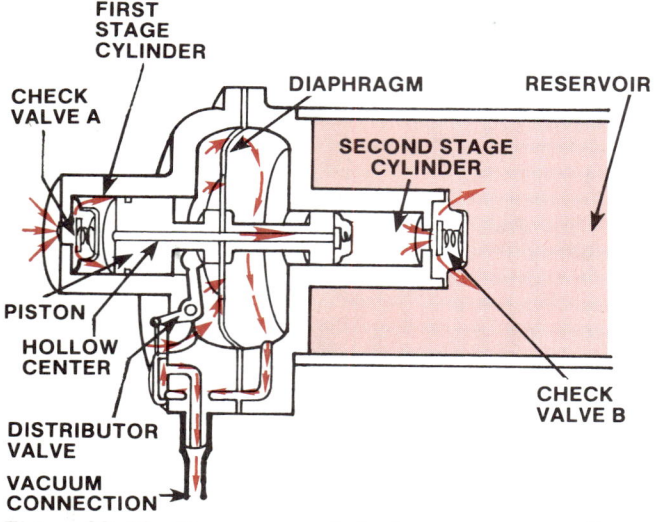

Figure 33-16 Vacuum-operated air compressor action. *Courtesy of General Motors Corp.*

ELECTRONICALLY CONTROLLED SHOCK ABSORBERS Electronically adjusted shock absorbers are one step above manually adjustable shocks. They are basically remote control shocks that allow the driver to select a soft, medium or firm ride by pressing a button on the instrument panel. When activated, variable shock damping is accomplished by varying the size of the metering orifices inside the shock absorber. This is done by rotating a control rod inside the shock by using a small electric actuator motor mounted on the tip of the shock. This control rod varies the size of the metering orifices, which in turn changes the shock rate from firm to medium to soft. The speed at which this occurs is usually less than half a second.

This type of electronically controlled shock can be used alone as a driver controlled device or it can be part of a computer controlled suspension system. In a computer controlled system, the shock is activated based on input from various vehicle sensors. Computer controlled suspensions are discussed later in this chapter.

◻ MACPHERSON STRUT SUSPENSION COMPONENTS

The MacPherson strut suspension is dramatically different in appearance from the traditional independent front suspension (Figure 33-18), but similar components operate in the same way to meet suspension demands.

The MacPherson strut suspension's most distinctive feature is the combination of the main elements into a single assembly. It typically includes the spring, upper suspension locator, and shock absorber. It is mounted vertically between the top arm of the steering knuckle and the inner fender panel (Figure 33-19).

Domestic struts have taken two forms—a concentric coil spring around the strut itself (Figure 33-20) and a spring located between the lower control arm and the frame (Figure 33-21). The location of the spring on

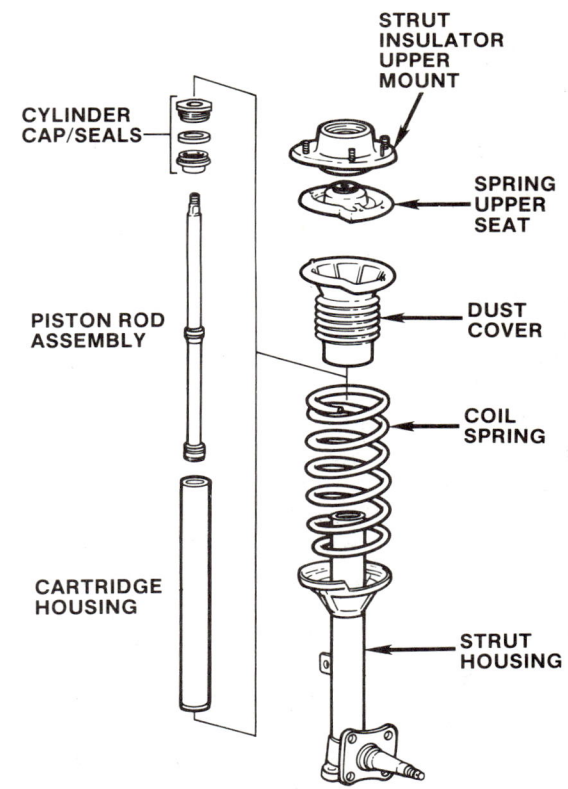

Figure 33-19 MacPherson strut with replace shock absorber (dampener) cartridge.

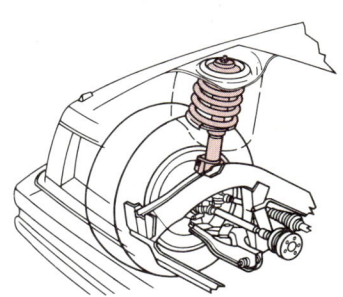

Figure 33-20 Typical MacPherson front suspension.

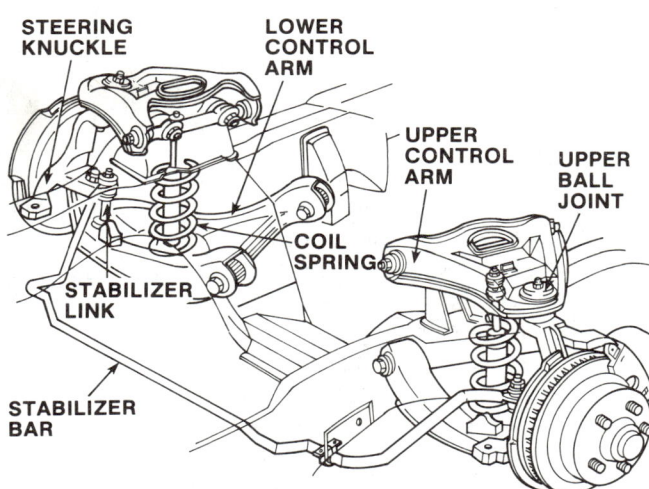

Figure 33-18 Typical coil independent front suspension (IFS) system. *Courtesy of General Motors Corp.*

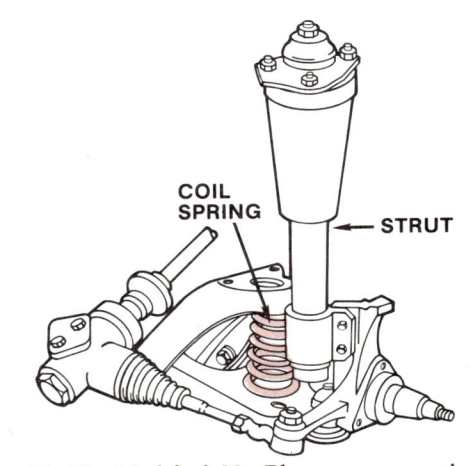

Figure 33-21 Modified MacPherson suspension has the spring mounted separately from the strut.

the lower control arm, not on the strut as in a conventional MacPherson strut system, allows minor road vibrations to be absorbed through the chassis rather than be fed back to the driver through the steering system. This sytem is called modified MacPherson suspension.

Struts

The core element of the suspension is the strut. With its cylindrical shape and protruding piston rod, it looks quite similar to the conventional shock absorber. In fact, the strut provides the damping function of the shock absorber, in addition to serving to locate the spring and to fix the position of the suspension.

The shock-damping function is accomplished differently on various types of struts. None of them use a separate shock absorber as the traditional front suspension does. Some versions are designed so that the dampener can be independently serviced.

Struts fall into two broad categories: sealed and serviceable units. A sealed strut is designed so that the top closure of the strut assembly is permanently sealed. There is no access to the shock absorber cartridge inside the strut housing and no means of replacing the cartridge. Therefore, it is necessary to replace the entire strut unit. A serviceable strut is designed so that the cartridge inside the housing, which provides the shock-absorbing function, can be replaced with a new cartridge. Serviceable struts use a threaded body nut in place of a sealed cap to retain the cartridge.

The shock absorber device inside a serviceable strut is generally wet. This means that the shock absorber contains oil that contacts and lubricates the inner wall of the strut body. The oil is sealed inside the strut by the body nut, O-ring, and piston rod seal. Servicing a wet strut with the equivalent components involves a thorough cleaning of the inside of the strut body, absolute cleanliness, and great care in reassembly.

Cartridge inserts were developed to simplify servicing wet struts. The insert is a factory-sealed replacement for the strut shock absorber. The replacement cartridge is simply substituted for the original shock absorber cartridge and retained with the body nut.

Most OE domestic struts are serviced by replacement of the entire unit. There is no strut cartridge to replace. Sealed OE units can also be serviced by replacement with an aftermarket unit that permits future servicing by cartridge replacement.

The use of the strut reduces suspension space and weight requirements. By mounting the bottom of the strut assembly to the steering knuckle, the upper control arm and ball joint of the traditional suspension are eliminated. In place of the ball joint, the upper mount, which is bolted to the fender panel, is the load-carrying member on MacPherson suspensions.

Lower Suspension Components

The suspension's lower mounting position continues to be the frame, as on the traditional suspension, because the lower control arm and ball joint are retained (Figure 33-22). As on those suspensions, the control arm serves as the lower locator for the suspension.

MacPherson strut suspensions continue to use sway, or stabilizer, bars. On models with single-bushing control arms, strut rods or the sway bar can be fastened to the control arm to provide lateral stability.

The lower ball joint is a friction or steering ball joint and is used to stabilize the steering and to retard shimmy. The only exception is on modified MacPherson suspensions. In this design, the ball joint becomes the load bearer; the upper mount becomes the steering component.

Springs

Coil springs are used on all strut suspensions. A mounting plate welded to the strut serves as the lower spring seat. The upper seat is bolted to the strut piston rod. A bearing or rubber bushing in the upper mount permits the spring and strut to turn with the motion of the wheel as it is steered.

☐ INDEPENDENT FRONT SUSPENSION

Front-suspension systems are fairly complex. They have somewhat contradictory jobs. They must keep the wheels rigidly positioned and at the same time allow them to steer right and left. In addition, because of weight transfer during braking, the front-suspension system absorbs most of the braking torque. While accomplishing this, it must provide good ride and stability characteristics.

As stated earlier in this chapter, most independent front-suspension systems have the same basic components and operate basically in the same manner as already described. These systems differ only in the way

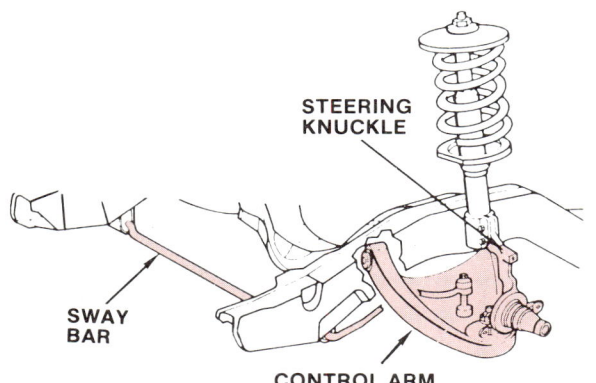

Figure 33-22 Lower suspension components.

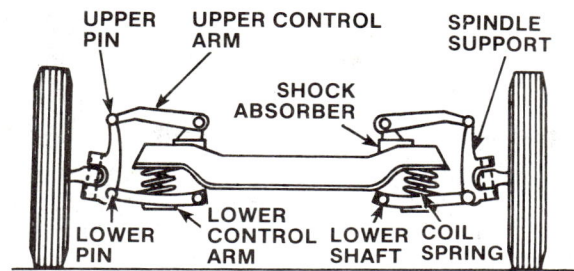

Figure 33-23 Parallelogram suspension.

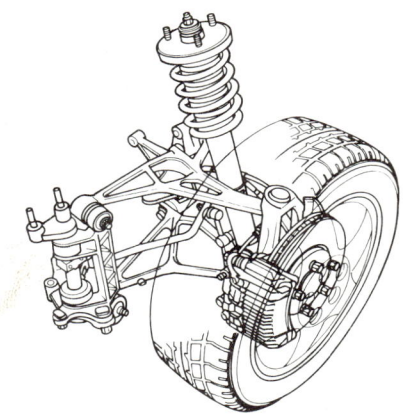

Figure 33-25 A FWD double-wishbone suspension system.

the components are arranged. The first independent system (known as knee action suspension) was the parallelogram design. It consisted of upper and lower control arms, called A arms, that were hinged to the car with pins or bushings at the frame and at the top and the bottom of the spindle support (Figure 33-23). The earlier vertical pivot pin or kingpin that enabled the wheels to turn was the only carryover from the solid conventional axle.

In the early systems, the upper and lower control arms were the same length. As the vehicle bounced along bumpy roads, this design kept wheel camber, or pitch as it was called then, at a fixed relationship. It was felt that this was necessary to maintain steering control. A detrimental side effect of this design was that the tire's contact with the road was constantly changing, causing serious tire wear problems due to the scuffing action.

A later design changed all this. In it, the upper control arm was shorter than the lower (Figure 33-24). With the upper arm pivoting in a shorter arc, the top of the wheel moved in and out slightly but the tire's road contact remained constant. Far from making the vehicle unstable, this configuration actually improved steering control. At last, independent suspension achieved both improved comfort and rideability without sacrificing tire life. The design was so successful that it was incorporated into many vehicles worldwide.

Short-Long Arm and Double-Wishbone Suspensions

The unequal length control arm or short-long arm (SLA) suspension system has been common on domestic-made vehicles for many years. Each wheel is independently connected to the frame by a steering knuckle, ball joint assemblies, and upper and lower control arms. The SLA system is often called the A-frame wishbone system.

The double-wishbone suspension system can also be used in FWD applications (Figure 33-25). The components are not subjected to the side loads that are generated by car braking, cornering, and accelerating. This means that the FWD double-wishbone can be tuned to provide firm but soft ride without taking away any of the car's built-in handling characteristics. The basic configuration of FWD double-wishbone suspension borrows heavily from the similar suspension systems used on Formula One racing cars.

The function and operation of the essential components of SLA systems are the wheel spindle assembly, control arms, ball joints, shock absorbers, and springs, among others.

A wheel spindle assembly consists of a wheel spindle and a steering knuckle (Figure 33-26). A wheel spindle is connected to the wheel through wheel bearings. The wheel spindle is the point at which the wheel hub and wheel bearings are connected. A steering knuckle is

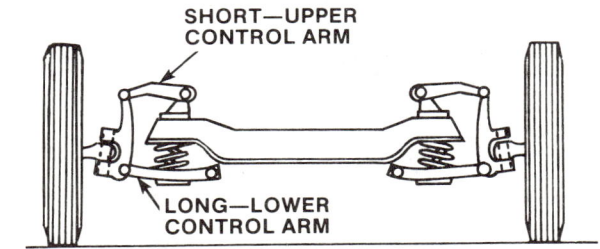

Figure 33-24 Short-long arm suspension.

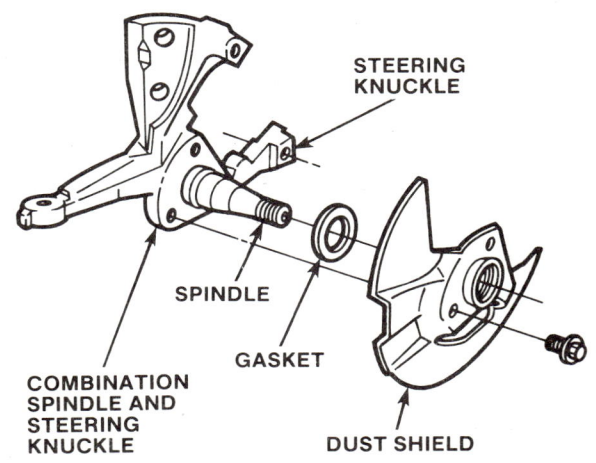

Figure 33-26 Typical wheel spindle assembly.

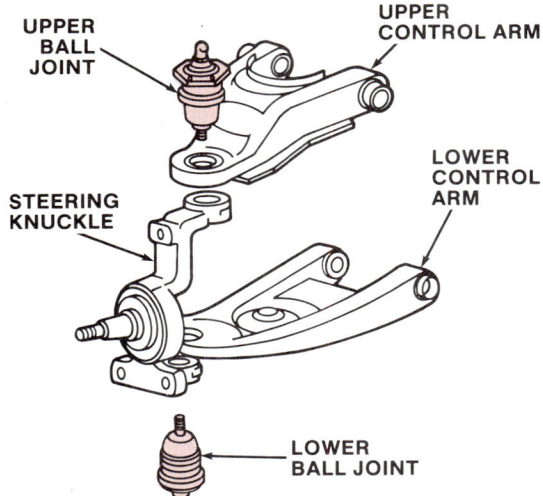

Figure 33-27 Ball joint locations. *Courtesy of Moog Automotive*

connected to control arms. In most cases, a steering knuckle and wheel spindle are forged to form a single piece.

Control Arms

The upper and lower control arms on the traditional independent front-suspension (IFS) function primarily as locators. They fix the position of the system and its components relative to the vehicle. They are attached to the frame with bushings that permit the wheel assemblies to move up and down separately in response to irregularities in the road surface. The outer ends are connected to the wheel assembly with ball joints (Figure 33-27) inserted through each arm into the steering knuckle.

There are two types of control arms: the wishbone, or double-pivot, control arm, and the single-pivot, or single-bushing, control arm (Figure 33-28). The wishbone offers greater lateral stability than the single-pivot arm. The single-pivot is lighter and requires less space than the wishbone, but also requires modifications in suspension design to compensate for the reduced lateral stability. Those modifications are discussed further later in this chapter.

Ball Joints

The ball joints connect the steering knuckle to the control arms, allowing the steering knuckle to pivot between the control arms when the car is steered. They also permit up and down movement of the control arm.

Ball joints can be grouped into two classifications: load-carrying and nonload-carrying or stabilizing type. The load-carrying or loaded ball joint supports the vehicle weight. It is mounted in the control arm of an independent front suspension system on which the coil spring is seated or to which the torsion bar spring is attached as shown in Figure 33-29. These units are designed so the weight of the vehicle holds the ball stud and its bearing surface into close contact.

Load-carrying ball joints come in two versions: compression loaded or tension loaded. Compression ball joints are designed to carry loads that bear down on top of the ball stud (Figure 33-30A). Because of this, most joint wear occurs where the head of the ball stud presses into its seat. Compression ball joints are used in suspensions, where the coil spring mounts over the upper control arm.

Tension joints carry a load that tries to pull the joint apart (Figure 33-30B). Wear occurs in this joint in the area where the shoulder of the ball stud pulls against its seat. The lower ball joint on a short-long arm suspension, where the spring sits on the lower control arm, is a tension joint. Tension joints are also found on modified MacPherson strut suspensions, where the springs sit on the lower control arm rather than the strut.

Some load-carrying ball joints have built-in wear indicators on the grease fitting. As the joint wears, the grease fitting recedes into the housing. When the shoulder of the fitting is flush with the housing, the joint needs replacing (Figure 33-31).

The nonload-carrying ball joint is used for the upper ball joint on short-long arm suspensions. The spring

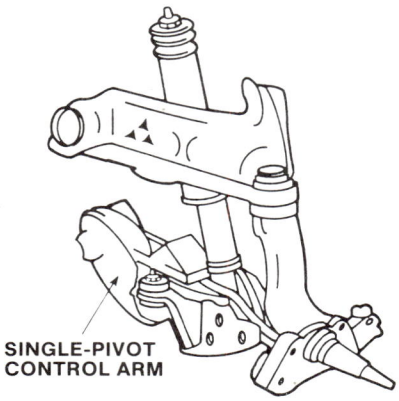

Figure 33-28 The single pivot is lighter and requires less space than the wishbone type.

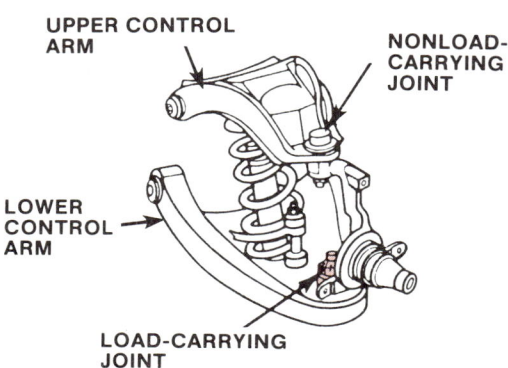

Figure 33-29 The load-carrying ball joint supports the vehicle weight.

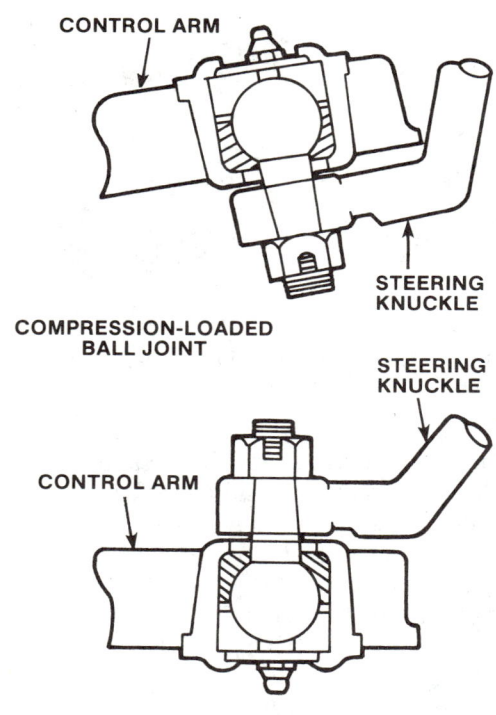

Figure 33-30 Two types of friction ball joints.

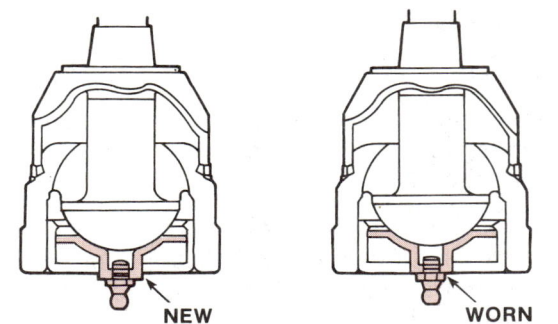

Figure 33-31 Wear-indicator load-carrying ball joints.

seats on the lower arm or the lower ball joint on suspensions in which the spring is over the upper control arm. It is also used as the lower ball joint on MacPherson strut suspensions when the spring is mounted around the strut. Because it does not carry weight, it is preloaded to keep it tight and to provide resistance for improved steering stability. Any play in a nonload-carrying ball joint means it should be replaced.

Coil Springs

As described previously in this chapter, the most commonly used spring on front suspensions is the coil spring. Most traditional suspensions have coil springs mounted between the control arms. However, some designs mount them on top of the upper control arm, seating them between the surface of the arm and a projecting arm of the frame (Figure 33-32).

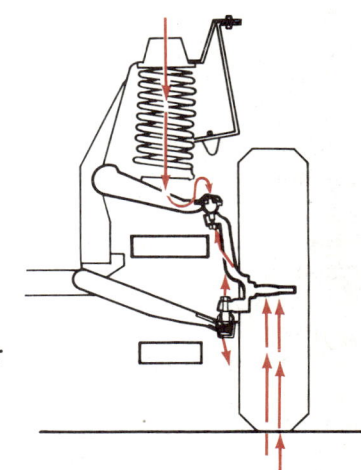

Figure 33-32 The upper ball-joint is the load-carrying joint in this system because of the position of the spring.

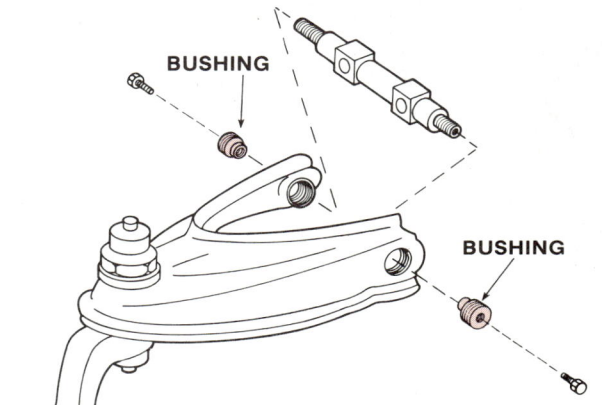

Figure 33-33 Control arm bushings.

Other Front-System Components

In addition to shock absorbers, other suspension control devices include bushings, stabilizer or sway bars, and strut rods. In the design of these suspension control devices, the difference between sprung and unsprung weight is important.

Bushings

Rubber or polyurethane bushings are found on many suspension components such as the control arms (Figure 33-33), radius arms, and strut rods (Figure 33-34). They make good suspension system pivots,

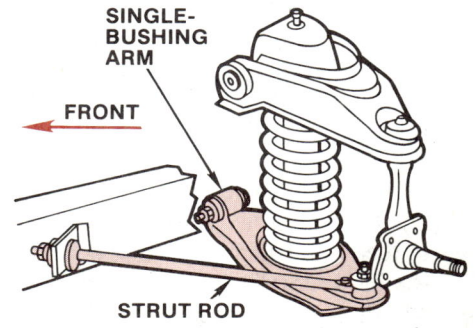

Figure 33-34 Single-bushing control arm with strut rod.

minimize the number of lubrication points, and allow for slight assembly misalignments. Bushings help to absorb road shock, allow some movement, and reduce noise entering the vehicle.

Suspension bushings can deteriorate fairly rapidly, causing tire wear. They are a common cause of misalignment. Replacement bushings come in two basic varieties: stock and performance. The latter are usually made of a high grade polyurethane material and are sold primarily as an upgrade to improve handling response and ride control.

The harder urethane bushings eliminate unwanted compliance or give in the suspension. When hard cornering overtaxes stock bushings and causes them to deflect excessively, undesirable chamber changes occur in the front wheels that result in excessive outer shoulder wear on the tires. Compliance also slows down the action of the sway bar when cornering, which has a significant impact on the vehicle's road holding ability and steering stability (especially in cross winds). Firmer bushings can also help reduce torque steer in front-wheel-drive cars. Torque steer is the tendency to pull to one side (usually to the right) under hard acceleration. It is more of a problem on FWD cars with unequal length drive shafts because the wheel with the shorter shaft (usually the left side) gets more torque than the one with the longer shaft. There is enough give in the suspension that the left wheel tries to pull ahead of the right, throwing wheel alignment off enough to make the car pull to the right.

The procedures for checking bushings and the methods for replacing them are given in service manuals.

Stabilizers

A variety of devices are used with the basic suspension components to provide additional stability. One of the most common is the sway bar—also known as the antisway bar, or stabilizer. This is a metal rod running between the opposite lower control arms. As the suspension at one wheel responds to the road surface, the sway bar transfers a similar movement to the suspension at the other wheel. For example, if the right wheel is drawn down by a dip in the road surface, the sway bar is drawn with it creating a downward draw on the left wheel as well. In this way, a more level ride is produced. Sway or lean during cornering is also reduced.

If both wheels go into a jounce, the sway bar simply rotates in its insulator bushings. It is a different matter when only one wheel goes into jounce. The stabilizer bar twists, just like a torsion bar, to lift the frame and the opposite suspension arm. This action reduces body roll.

The sway bar can be a one-piece, U-shaped rod fastened directly into the control arms with rubber bushings, or it can be attached to each control arm by a separate sway bar link (Figure 33-35). The arm is held to the links with nuts and rubber bushings and is also mounted to the frame in the center with rubber bush-

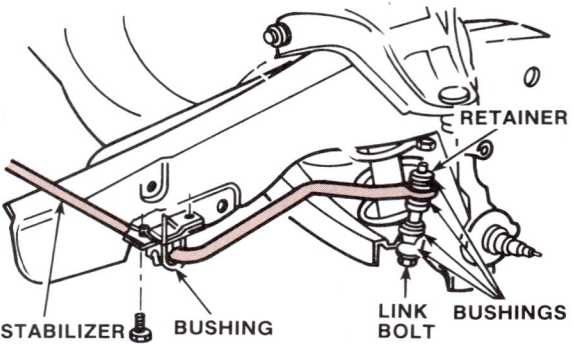

Figure 33-35 Sway bar, or stabilizer bar, controls sway and stabilizes front suspension.

ings. If the sway bar is too large, it causes the vehicle to wander. If it is too small, it has little effect on stability.

On suspensions that use single-bushing lower control arms instead of wishbone types, the sway bar can also be used to add lateral stability to the control arm. Strut rods are used on models that do not use the sway bar like this. They are attached to the arm and frame with bushings, allowing the arm a limited amount of forward and backward movement. Strut rods are directly affected by braking forces and road shocks, and their failure can quickly lead to failure of the entire suspension system.

☐ GENERAL FRONT-SUSPENSION INSPECTION

To minimize the chance of performing an unnecessary service, the following preliminary or general inspections should be made.

1. Check all tires for proper inflation pressure.
2. Check the tires for telltale indications of improper front-end alignment, wheel and tire imbalance, and physical defects or damage.
3. Check the vehicle for optional suspension equipment such as that provided for heavy-duty applications or trailer towing packages. They have a firmer ride quality.
4. Check vehicle attitude for evidence of overloading or sagging. Be sure the chassis height is correct.
5. Raise the vehicle off the floor. Grasp the upper and lower surfaces of the tire and shake each front wheel to check for worn wheel bearings.
6. Check front-suspension ball joints and mounts for looseness, wear, and damage.
7. Check the steering gear mountings, steering linkage, and steering connections for looseness, binding, or damage.
8. Check the shock absorbers or shock struts for the condition of their attaching parts.
9. Also check shocks or struts for proper action or leakage.

If, in the course of making these checks, damaged or worn parts are found, replace them.

SHOP TALK

Before visual inspection or suspension height measurements can be performed, the vehicle must be on a level surface. Tires must be at recommended pressures; gas tank must be full; and there should be no passenger or luggage compartment load. Beginning at the rear bumper, jounce the car up and down several times. Proceed to the front bumper and repeat, releasing during same cycle as rear jounce.

Chassis Height Specifications

A quick overall visual inspection detects any obvious sag from front to rear or from side to side. Under the car, at the level of the two ends of the control arms check for out-of-level, damaged, or worn rubber bumpers, or shiny or worn spring coils. All indicate weak coil springs.

A more accurate inspection reveals less obvious problems by measuring heights at specific points on each side of the suspension system.

USING SERVICE MANUALS

For the most accurate measurement of chassis height, use the service manual to check against the manufacturer's recommendations for the specific model. As can be seen in Figure 33-36, measurement points vary from one model to another manufactured by the same company. When coil spring wear is suspected, it might be necessary to load the vehicle to the manufacturer's suggested capacities and measure at the designated points.

☐ FRONT-SUSPENSION COMPONENT SERVICING

As is the case in all sections of this text, specific troubleshooting procedures are given in detail in the Tech Manual. However, following is information on servicing the major components or assemblies of front suspension systems.

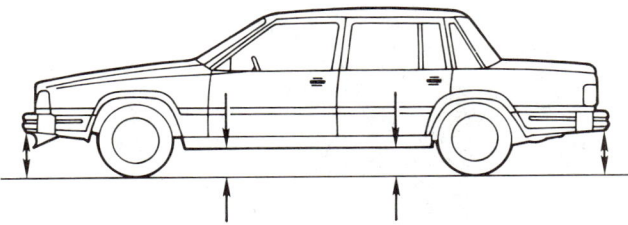

Figure 33-36 Vehicle height measurement points from manufacturer's recommendations.

Coil Springs

The never ending twisting and untwisting of the coil spring (or the torsion bar) lead to inevitable loss of elasticity and spring sag. Coil springs, then, require replacement because they sag in service. A sagged coil spring upsets vehicle trim height resulting in upset wheel alignment angles, steering angles, headlight aiming, braking distribution, riding quality, tire tread life, shock life, and U-joint life.

Coil springs also break. Downsized cars are often forced to carry the same loads as their larger counterparts, mostly because people and their hauling needs did not down-size along with the cars.

WARNING: The coil spring exerts a tremendous force on the control arm. Before you disconnect either control arm from the knuckle for any service operation, contain the spring with a spring compressor to prevent it from flying out and causing injury.

Removing a Spring

To remove a coil spring, raise and support the vehicle by its frame. Let the control arm hang free. Remove wheels, shock absorbers, and stabilizer links. Disconnect the outer tie-rod ends from their respective arms.

Unload the ball joints with a roll-around floor jack. Jack under the lower control arm from the opposite side of the vehicle. This allows the jack to roll back when the control arm is lowered. Position the jack as close to the lower ball joint as possible for maximum leverage against the spring.

The spring is ready for the installation of the spring compressor (Figure 33-37). There are many different types of spring compressors. One type uses a threaded compression rod that fits through two plates, an upper and lower ball nut, a thrust washer, and a forcing nut. The two plates are positioned at either end of the

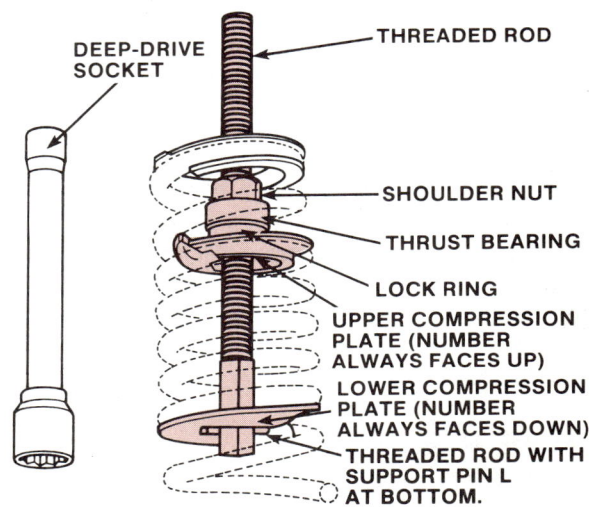

Figure 33-37 A spring compressor tool used to contain the coil spring for removal or installation. *Courtesy of Ford Motor Co.*

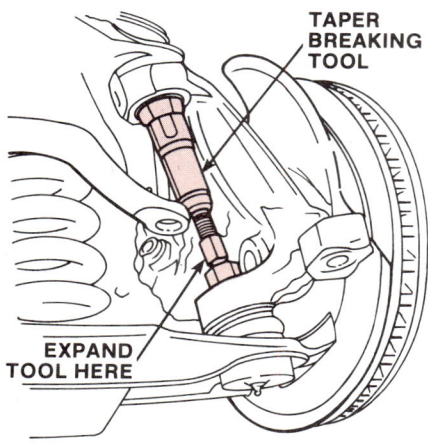

Figure 33-38 When this tool is expanded, it forces the ball joint stud out of the steering knuckle taper. *Courtesy of General Motor Corp.*

spring. The compressing rod fits through the plates with a ball nut at either end. The upper ball nut is pinned to the rod. The thrust washer and forcing nut are threaded onto the end of the rod. Turning the forcing nut draws the two plates together and compresses the spring.

In some cases, it is necessary to break the tapers of both upper and lower ball joints so that the steering knuckle can be moved to one side (Figure 33-38). If the vehicle is equipped with a strut rod, this must be disconnected at the lower control arm. Push the control arm down until the spring can be removed. If necessary, a pry bar can be used to remove the spring from its lower seat. Remove the spring and compressor.

If the same spring is to be reinstalled, leave the compressor in position. If a new spring is to be used, slowly release the pressure on the tool by backing off the forcing nut. Compress new spring prior to installing it.

Torsion Bars

Torsion bars (springs) are subjected to many of the same conditions affecting coil springs. Periodic adjustment of the torsion bars is necessary to maintain the proper height. Replacement is sometimes necessary because of breakage. It should be noted that the bars are not interchangeable from side to side.

Height inspection and measurements for vehicles with torsion bar suspensions are the same for coil springs. However, sagging can usually be corrected by adjusting the bars. Procedures for adjusting torsion bars are given in the service manual.

Ball Joints

Begin ball joint inspection by determining if the vehicle is equipped with wear indicator-type load-carrying ball joints. This information can be found in a manufacturer's ball joint specification chart or the vehicle's service manual. If the vehicle's not equipped with wear indicator-type ball joints, proceed to unload the load carriers.

When the coil spring is on the lower control arm, raise the vehicle by jacking under the control arm as close to the ball joint as possible. This gives the maximum amount of leverage against the spring. The ball joint is unloaded when the upper strike out bumper is not in contact with the control arm or frame. A quick check for looseness can be made by using a pry bar between the tire and the ground. To find out if the ball joint is loose beyond manufacturer's specifications, use an accurate measuring device. The following checking procedures demonstrate the use of a dial indicator. The dial indicator is a precision instrument and should be handled carefully to prevent damage. The mounting procedure for the checking tool might vary depending on the style of ball joint used on the vehicle. Manufacturer's tolerances can be axial (vertical), radial (horizontal), or both. To conduct these checks, follow these procedures.

TYPICAL RADIAL CHECK For a radial check, attach a dial indicator to the control arm of the ball joint being checked. Position and adjust the plunger of the dial indicator against the edge of the wheel rim nearest to the ball joint being checked. Slip the dial ring to the zero marking. Move the wheel in and out and note the amount of ball joint radial looseness registered on the dial (Figure 33-39).

TYPICAL AXIAL CHECK For an axial check, first fasten the dial indicator to the control arm, then clean off the flat on the spindle next to the ball joint stud

Figure 33-39 Typical mounting of dial indicator for a radial check. *Courtesy of Moog Automotive*

Figure 33-40 Typical mounting of dial indicator for an axial check. *Courtesy of Moog Automotive*

nut. Position the dial indicator plunger on the flat of the spindle and depress the plunger approximately 0.250 inch. Turn the lever to tighten the indicator in place. Pry the bar between the floor and tire. Record the reading (Figure 33-40).

If the ball joint looseness reading on the dial indicator exceeds manufacturer's specifications, the ball joint should be replaced.

When the load-carrying ball joints are on the upper control arm (spring mounted on the upper arm), raise the vehicle by its frame using support tools to unload the ball joints and hold them in their normal position. To determine the condition of the nonload-carrying (or follower) ball joint, vigorously push and pull on the tire, while watching the ball joint for signs of movement. Refer to the manufacturer's specifications for tolerances.

INSPECTION OF WEAR INDICATORS Wear indicator-type ball joints must remain loaded to check for wear. The vehicle should be checked with the suspension at curb height. The most common type has a small diameter boss, which protrudes from the center of the lower housing. As wear occurs internally, this boss recedes very gradually into the housing. When it is flush with the housing, the ball joint should be replaced. To remove and install a ball joint, follow the procedure given in the service manual.

Control Arm Bushings

If the bushings, which attach the arms to the frame, are not in good condition, precise wheel alignment settings cannot be maintained.

Visually inspect each rubber bushing for signs of distortion, movement, off-center condition, and presence of heavy cracking. Check metal bushings for noise and loose seals.

To remove the control arm bushings, raise the vehicle and support the frame on safety jack stands. Remove the wheel assembly. Install a spring compressor on the coil spring.

Disconnect the ball joint studs from the steering knuckle as described previously. Remove the bolts attaching the control arm assembly to the frame and remove the control arm.

Old bushings are pressed out of the control arm. A C-clamp tool can be used to remove the bushing. The C-clamp is installed over the bushing. An adapter is selected to fit on the bushing and push the bushing through the control arm. Turning the handle on the C-clamp pushes the bushing out of the control arm.

New bushings can be installed by driving or pressing. Adapters are available for the C-clamp tool to install the new bushings. After the correct adapters are selected, position the bushing and tool on the control arm as shown in Figure 33-41. Turning the C-clamp handle pushes the bushing into the control arm. When installing new bushings, make sure they are driven in straight. A poor installation could enlarge the hole in the control arm.

Some older vehicles use a bushing that is all metal instead of a metal-rubber combination. These are removed and replaced in the same way as the rubber and metal type just described.

Once the new bushings are started into the control arm, measure and mark the center between mounting holes and center the control arm. Now, alternately press in the bushings on each side, keeping the reference marks aligned. This insures that the shaft is not off center, causing binding. End cap nuts or bolts, should not be torqued until the vehicle is at curb height and the suspension has been bounced and allowed to settle out.

Rebolt the control arm and tighten the bolts to specifications, then install the coil spring into position. Install the ball joint studs into the control arms. Remove the coil spring compressor. Install the wheel assembly and lower the car. Road test the car, retighten all bolts, and set wheel alignment.

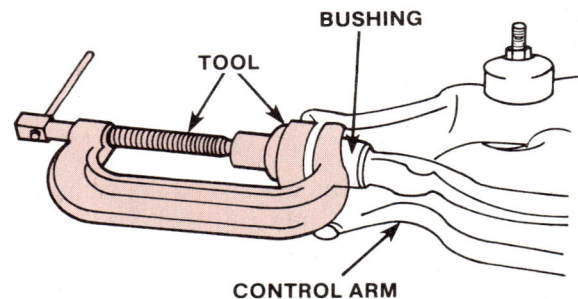

Figure 33-41 Removing a control-arm bushing. *Courtesy of Ford Motor Co.*

Strut Rod Bushings

Except in the case of accidental damage, the strut rod itself is rarely replaced. Rather, it is the bushing that wears, deteriorates, and needs replacement.

Sway Bar Bushings

These bushings anchor the sway bar securely to the vehicle frame and the control arms on each side. The condition of the bushings affects the performance of the bar. Visual inspection of mounting bushings indicates if the bushings are worn, have taken a permanent set, or are possibly missing.

Shock Absorbers

A shock absorber that is functioning properly insures vehicle stability, handling, and rideability. Most motorists fail to notice gradual changes in the operation of their car as a result of worn shock absorbers. Some common indications of shock absorber failure follow.

- Steering and handling more difficult
- Braking not smooth
- Excessive bouncing after stops
- Unusual tire wear patterns, especially cupping
- Springs bottom out

Vibrations set up by a worn shock absorber can cause premature wear in many of the undercar systems. It can cause wear in the front and rear component parts of the suspension system, the linkage component parts of the steering system, and the U-joints and motor or transmission mounts of the driveline. Also, vibrations can cause unnatural wear patterns on the tires.

A shock absorber can be bench tested. First, turn it up in the same direction it occupies in the vehicle. Then, extend it fully. Next, turn it upside down and fully compress it. Repeat this operation several times. Install a new shock absorber if a lag or skip occurs near mid-stroke of the shaft's change in travel direction, or if the shaft seizes at any point in its travel, except at the ends. Also, install a new shock absorber if noise, other than a swish or click, is encountered when the stroke is reversed rapidly, there are any leaks, or action remains erratic after purging air.

When removing and installing shock absorbers, be sure to follow the aftermarket manufacturer's instructions or those given in the service manual.

MacPherson Strut Suspension

The MacPherson strut suspension system is based on a triangular design. The strut shaft is a structural member that does away with the upper control arm bushings and the upper ball joint. Since this shaft is also the shock absorber shaft, it receives a tremendous amount of force vertically and horizontally. Therefore, this assembly should be inspected very closely for leakage, bent shaft, and poor damping.

To remove and replace the MacPherson strut, proceed as shown in Photo Sequence 16.

☐ REAR-SUSPENSION SYSTEMS

There are three basic types of rear suspensions: live-axle, semi-independent, and independent. There are distinct designs of each, but the types of components and the principles involved are the same as on front-suspension systems described earlier in this chapter. Live-axle suspensions are found on rear-wheel-drive (RWD) trucks, vans, and many four-wheel-drive (4WD) passenger cars. Semi-independent systems are used on front-wheel-drive (FWD) vehicles. Independent suspensions can be found on both RWD and FWD vehicles, as well as 4WD cars.

☐ LIVE-AXLE REAR SUSPENSION SYSTEMS

This traditional rear-suspension system consists of springs used in conjunction with a live-axle (one in which the differential axle, wheel bearings, and brakes act as a unit). The springs are either of leaf or coil type.

Leaf Spring Live-Axle System

Two springs—either multiple leaf or monoleaf—are mounted at right angles to the axle and, along with the shock absorbers, are positioned below the rear axle housing. The front of the two springs is attached to brackets on the vehicle's frame by a bolt and bushing inserted through the eyes of the springs. While the bushing allows the spring to move, it isolates the rest of the vehicle from noisy road vibrations.

The center of each leaf spring is connected to the rear axle housing with U-bolts. Rubber bumpers are located between the rear axle housing and frame or unit body to dampen severe shocks. The rear eye pivot bushings are held to the frame with shackles, which attach to the springs by a bolt and bushing (Figure 33-42).

The advantage to this live-axle suspension system is that the leaf springs act as excellent axle locators. The springs allow for the up and down movement of the axle and wheels, but, at the same time, the springs prevent them from wandering. Therefore, control arms are not required with leaf springs.

There are some disadvantages to the live-axle suspension system. First, this design has a large amount of unsprung weight. Another drawback is the instability caused by the use of a solid axle. Since both rear wheels are connected to the same axle, movement up or down by one wheel affects the other. Consequently, poor traction results because both wheels are pushed out of

PHOTO SEQUENCE 16

☐ REMOVING AND REPLACING A MACPHERSON STRUT

P16-1 The top of the strut assembly is mounted directly to the chassis of the car.

P16-2 Prior to loosening the strut to the chassis bolts, scribe alignment marks on the strut bolts and the chassis.

P16-3 With the top strut bolts or nuts removed, raise the car to a working height. It is important that the car be supported on its frame and not on its suspension components.

P16-4 Remove the wheel assembly. The strut is accessible from the wheel well after the wheel is removed.

P16-5 Remove the bolt that fastens the brake line or hose to the strut assembly.

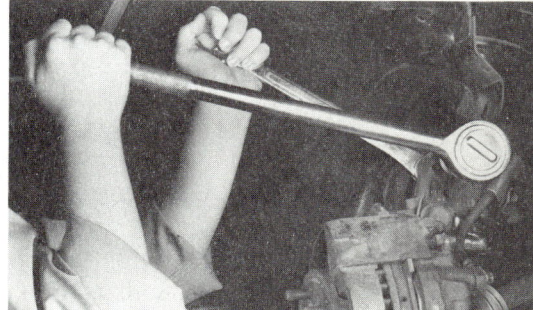

P16-6 Remove the strut to steering knuckle bolts.

(continued)

833

P16-7 Support the steering knuckle with wire and remove the strut assembly from the car.

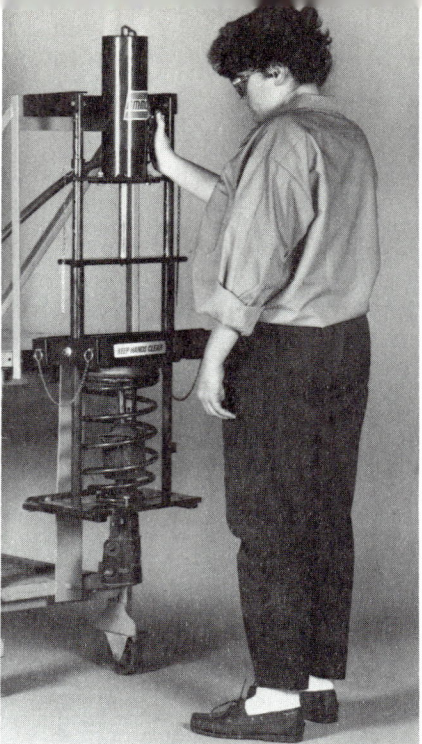

P16-8 Install the strut assembly into the proper type spring compressor. Then compress the spring until it is possible to safely loosen the retaining bolts.

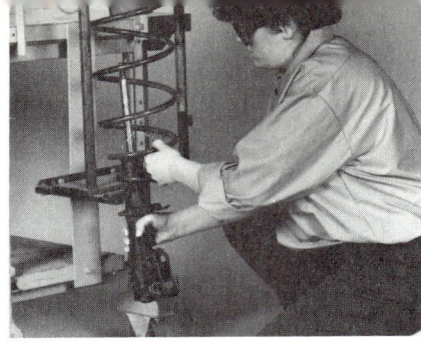

P16-9 Remove the old strut assembly from the spring and install the new strut. Compress the spring to allow for reassembly and tighten the retaining bolts.

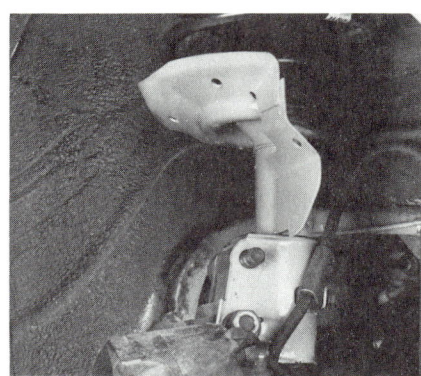

P16-10 Reinstall the strut assembly into the car. Make sure all bolts are properly tightened and in the correct locations. ■

---

alignment with the road. Under severe acceleration, this type of suspension is subject to axle tramp, a rapid up-and-down jumping of the rear axle due to the torque absorption of the leaf springs. This condition can break spring mounts and shock absorbers and cause premature wear of wheel bearings. Axle tramp is reduced by mounting shock absorbers on the opposing sides (front and back) of the axle. Some heavy-duty vehicles have two-stage springs that allow the vehicle to ride comfortably with both a light or heavy load (Figure 33-43).

Coil Spring Live-Axle System

Some vehicles use two coil springs at the rear with a live rear axle. Because coil springs can only support weight and have little axle-locating capabilities, such vehicles need forward and lateral control arms or links. This type of suspension is called the link-type rigid axle.

The coil springs, located between the brackets on the axle housing and the vehicle body or frame, are held in place by the weight of the vehicle and sometimes by the shock absorbers (Figure 33-44). The control arms are usually made of channeled steel and mounted with rubber bushings. Accelerating, driving, and braking torque are transmitted through three or four control arms, depending on the design. Two forward links are always used, but either one or two lateral links can be found on individual models. Trailing arms mount to the underside of the axle, and run forward at a 90-degree angle to the axle to brackets on the car frame. Rubber bushings are used at mounting locations to permit up-and-down movement of the arms, and to reduce noise and the effect of shock.

Some rear axle assemblies are connected to the body by two lower control arms and a tracking bar. A single torque arm is used in place of upper control arms and is rigidly mounted to the rear axle housing at the rear and through a rubber bushing to the transmission at the front.

Live-Axle Suspension System Servicing

Typical service to both coil-spring and leaf-spring systems include the replacement of shock absorbers or springs. Bushings, shackles, or control arms do not need replacement frequently. Always follow the procedures outlined in the service manual whenever servicing the rear suspension.

☐ SEMI-INDEPENDENT SUSPENSION

This system is used on many front-wheel-drive models. On some, the suspension position is fixed by an

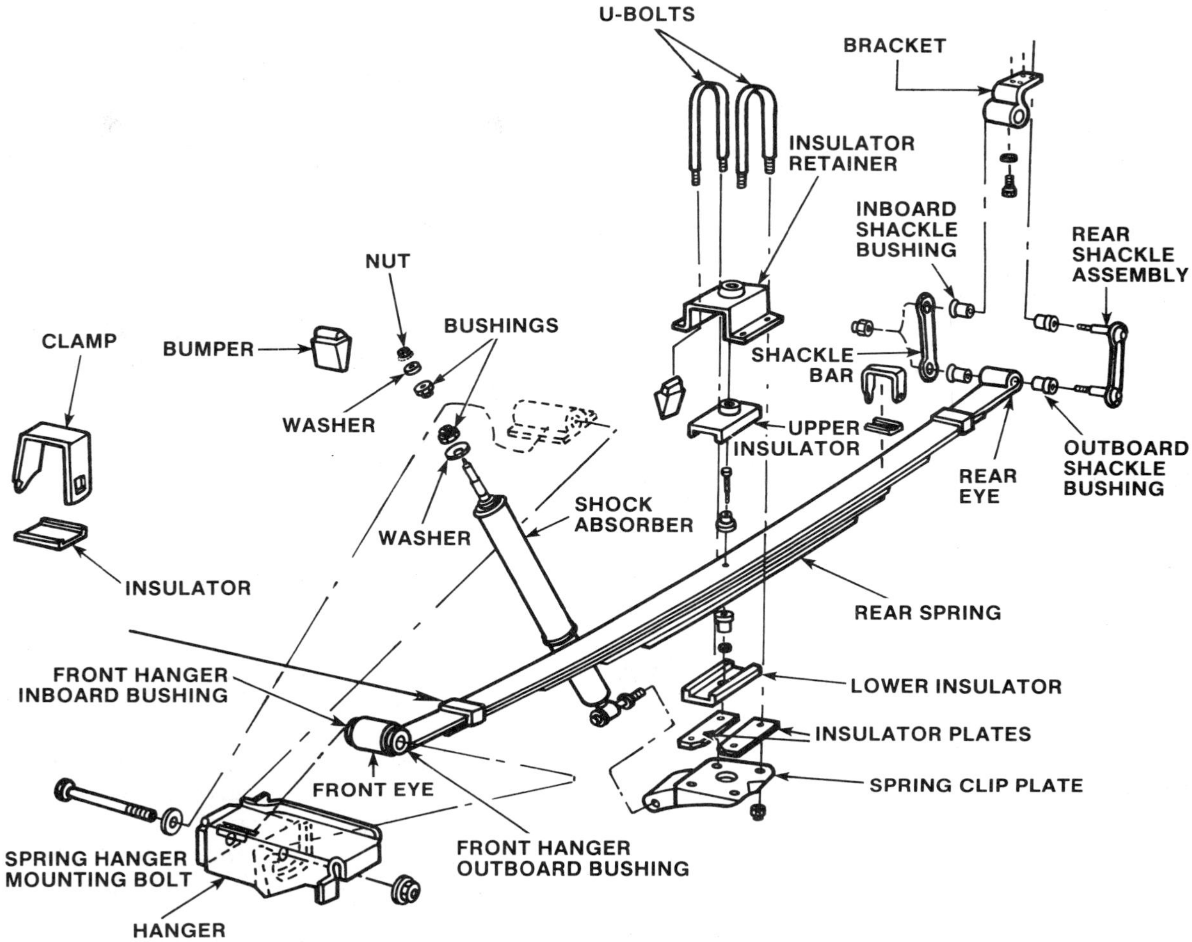

Suspension Systems   835

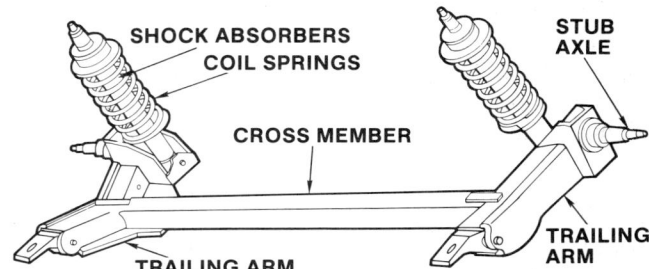

Figure 33-42 Exploded view of leaf-spring rear suspension.

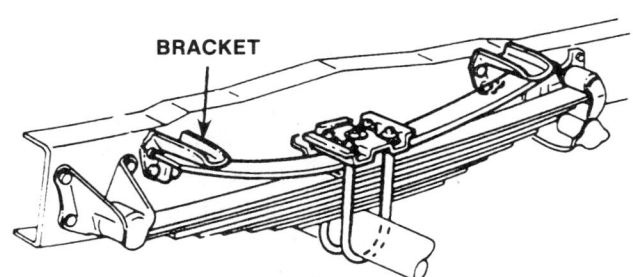

Figure 33-43 Two-stage springs. *Courtesy of Ford Motor Co.*

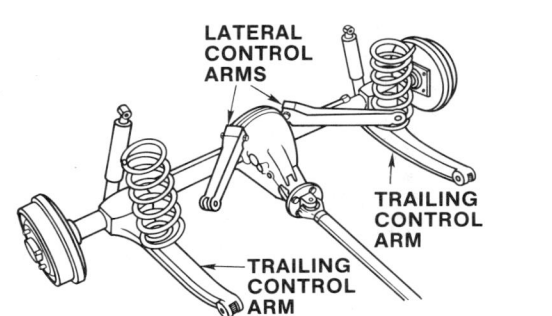

Figure 33-44 Typical live-axle suspension with coil springs.

Figure 33-45 One design of a semi-independent rear suspension.

axle beam, or cross member, running between two trailing arms (Figure 33-45). Although there is a solid connection between the two halves of the suspension because of the axle beam, the beam twists as the wheel assemblies move up and down. The twisting action not only permits semi-independent suspension movement, but it also acts as a stabilizer. Frequently, a separate shock and spring trailing arm system is also used. In either an integrated or separate shock system, each rear wheel is independently suspended by a coil spring.

A coil spring and shock absorber-strut assembly are ordinarily used with this suspension system. The bot-

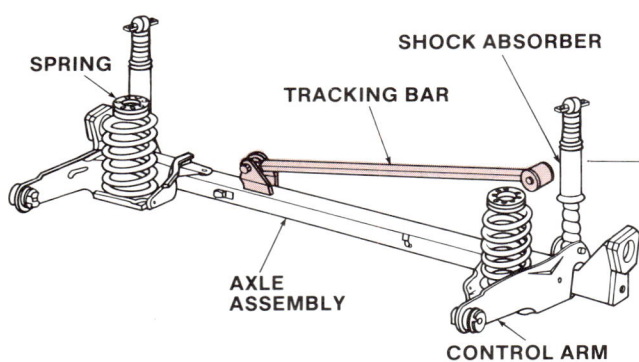

Figure 33-46 Tracking bar of rear suspension used to reduce sidesway movement.

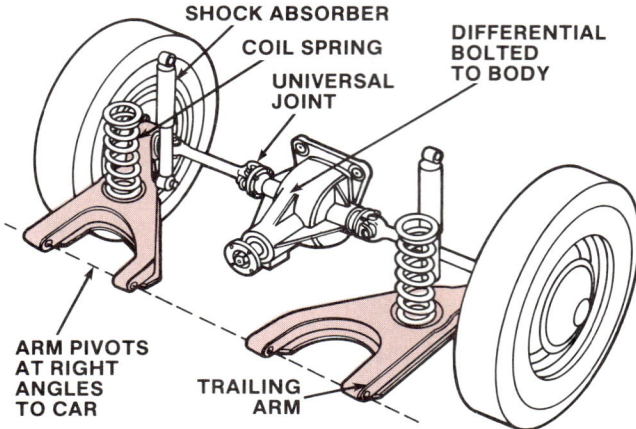

Figure 33-47 Trailing arms are often used with independent rear suspensions.

tom of the strut is mounted to the rear end of the trailing arm. The top is mounted to the reinforced inner fender panel. Braking torque is transmitted through the trailing control arms and struts. The arms and struts also maintain the force and aft, and lateral positioning of the wheels. A tracking bar is also used on some trailing arm suspension systems (Figure 33-46). The tracking bar helps to reduce sidesway movement of the axle.

Semi-Independent Suspension System Servicing

As in most rear system servicing, the first step is to remove the shock absorber. It is important to remember not to remove both shock absorbers at one time. Suspending the rear axle at full length could result in damage to the brake lines and hoses. The servicing of a semi-independent suspension system usually involves the removal and reinstallation of shock absorbers, springs, insulators, and control arm bushings. Follow the procedures given in the vehicle's service manual.

WARNING: When removing the rear springs, do not use a twin-post hoist. The swing arc tendency of the rear axle assembly when certain fasteners are removed might cause it to slip from the hoist. Perform this operation on the floor if necessary.

☐ INDEPENDENT SUSPENSION

Independent suspensions can be found in large numbers on both FWD and RWD vehicles. The introduction of independent rear suspensions was brought about by the same concerns for improved traction ride and prompted the introduction of independent front suspensions. If the wheels can move separately on the road, traction and ride is improved.

Independent coil-spring rear suspensions can have several control arm arrangements. For example, A-shaped control arms are sometimes employed. When the wide bottom of a control arm is toward the front of the car and the point turns in to meet the upright, they are called trailing arms (Figure 33-47). When the entire A-shaped control arms are mounted at an angle, they are known as semi-trailing control arms (Figure 33-48). This design is used on many sports cars. Coil springs are used between the control arm and the vehicle body. The control arms pivot on a cross member and are attached at the other end to a spindle. A shock absorber is attached to the spindle or control arm.

Some Japanese vehicles use a rear suspension system that uses a lower control arm and open driving axles. A cross member supports the control arms, while the tops of the shock absorbers are mounted to the body. The springs are set in seats at the bottom and top of the cross member.

A few European cars employ only lower control arms, but substitute a wishbone-shaped subframe for the upper control arms. Two torque arms transfer the rear-end torque to the subframe. In fact, many imports are now featuring rear double-wishbone suspension (Figure 33-49). Torque loads create bushing and control arm deflection during braking, cornering, acceler-

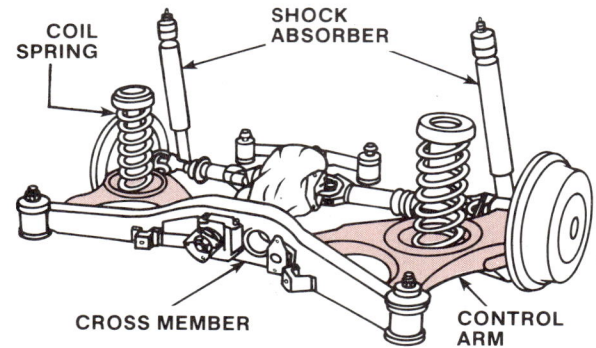

Figure 33-48 Semi-trailing control arms.

Suspension Systems   837

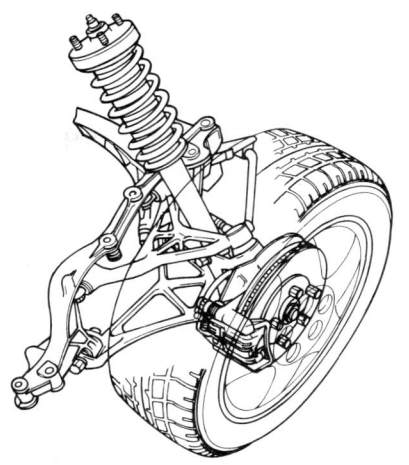

Figure 33-49   A double-wishbone type rear suspension.

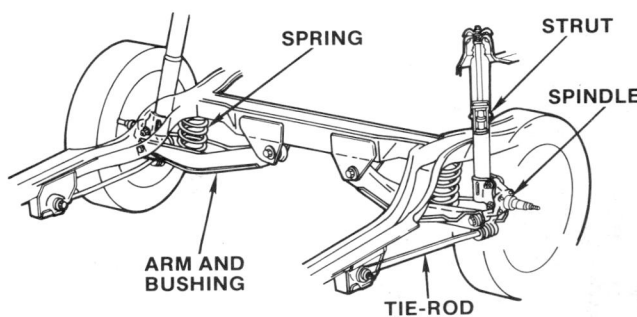

Figure 33-51   Modified MacPherson strut rear suspension.

ation, and deceleration. It is interesting to note that this rear suspension system allows for a small amount of toe-in change to enhance straight line stability. The toe-in change during cornering leads to quicker and more responsive turning. The rear suspension system can also be tuned to assure minimal dive under braking and minimal squat under acceleration.

Currently, struts are replacing conventional shock absorbers in rear independent suspension systems. One of the latest strut rear suspension designs used by car manufacturers is shown in Figure 33-50.

On this type system, the spindle is used to secure the strut, the outer ends of two of the four control arms, the rear ends of the tie-rods, and a rear wheel. The control arms contain bushings of different sizes at their outer ends. The ends with the smaller bushing attach near the body centerline. The ends with the larger bushing attach at the spindle. (When replacing control arms, it is mandatory that offsets at their outer ends and the flanges on the arms face in the direction prescribed in the manufacturer's service manual.) This system is also called the nonmodified MacPherson strut system.

The modified MacPherson strut rear suspension is very common for vehicles with front-wheel drive (Figure 33-51). Study the illustration carefully. Note the major components on each side of the vehicle are a modified MacPherson shock strut, lower control arm, tie-rod, and wheel spindle. A coil spring mounts between the lower control arm and the body cross member/side rail. The spindle, in addition to supporting the rear wheel, is used as an attaching location for the outer end of the control arm and the rear end of the tie-rod. The inner end of the control arm attaches to the cross member. The forward end of the tie-rod attaches to the side rail.

Another rear strut design uses a Chapman strut (Figure 33-52). It is similar to the modified MacPherson strut. The difference between the two struts is the MacPherson strut is involved directly in the car's steering system. The Chapman strut is not. In addition, the Chapman strut can be used with conventional springs, often a leaf-type spring. It frees the Chapman strut of load-carrying duties so it can concentrate on providing exact wheel location and shock absorbing functions.

Rear leaf-spring suspension systems are used on many vehicles with conventional rear drives. These leaf springs are generally mounted longitudinally in the same manner as described earlier in this chapter for live-axle systems. A few leaf-spring systems, however, employ springs mounted transversely. Both multiple leaf (Figure 33-53) and mono or single-leaf (Figure

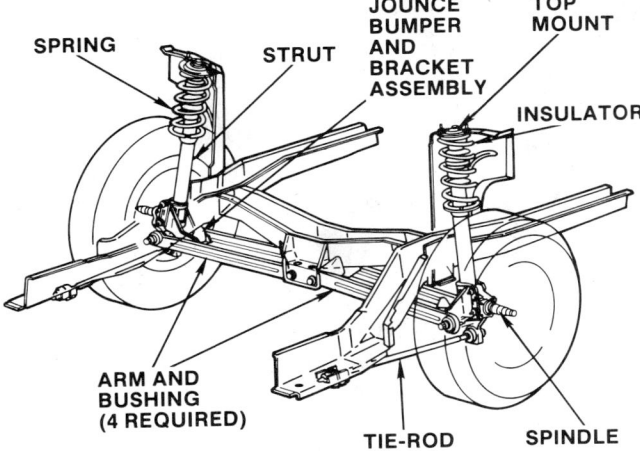

Figure 33-50   MacPherson strut rear suspension.

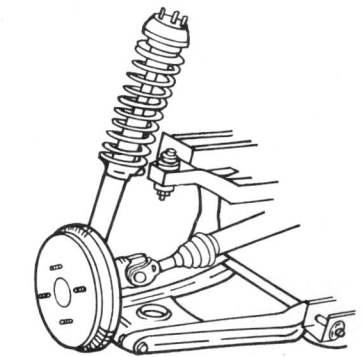

Figure 33-52   An independent rear suspension system that uses a Chapman strut.

838 Section 7   Suspensions

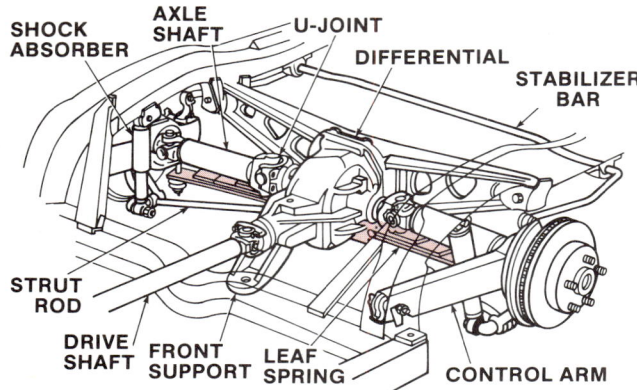

Figure 33-53 Transversely-mounted multiple-leaf rear springs.

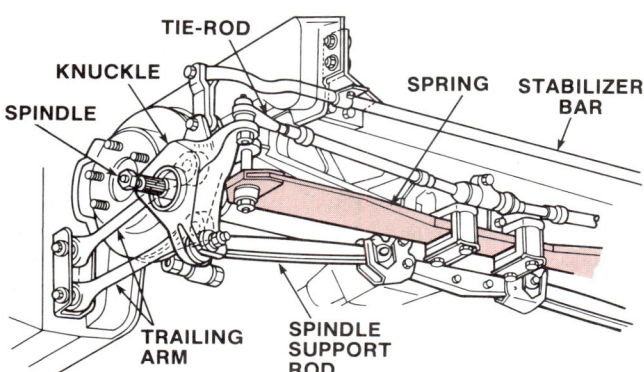

Figure 33-54 Transversely-mounted single-leaf rear spring.

33-54) can be used. The transverse leaf spring is mounted to the differential housing rather than the vehicle frame as in the longitudinal installation. The transversely-mounted spring's eyes are connected to the wheel spindle assemblies.

Rear shock absorbers or shock struts have the same service limitations as those used on the front of the vehicle. They cannot be adjusted, refilled, or repaired. The procedure for inspecting rear shocks or shock struts is similar to previously mentioned front-end parts inspection. Repetition is not necessary.

Servicing Independent Suspension Systems

Most of the servicing techniques for rear independent suspension systems—except coil, control arm, and strut removal and installation—are similar to other front and rear suspension parts. They have been covered earlier in this chapter. Of course, check the service manual for all inspection and repair techniques of the vehicle's independent rear system.

Rear Coil Spring

Raise the vehicle on a frame contact hoist or position jack stands under the frame forward of the rear axle assembly. This allows the shock absorbers to fully extend. Place a floor jack under the center of the rear axle housing and support the weight of the rear axle, but do not lift the vehicle off the jack stands. Disconnect the lower end of the shock absorber. Then, lower the floor jack until all of the coil spring force is relieved. If a coil spring positioner is used, remove it from the center of the coil spring. The coil spring can usually be removed from the vehicle at this time by lifting it from its spring seat. If the springs are to be used again, mark or tag each one so that it can be returned to its original location. When a replacement is needed, always replace coil springs in pairs. This assures equal height.

To install a spring, place the insulator on top of the coil spring and position the spring on the spring seat. The end of the top coil must be positioned to line up with the recess in the spring seat. Jack up the rear axle housing so the spring is properly seated at the lower end and the shock absorbers line up. Reconnect the shock absorbers.

There are some definite advantages to working on one spring at a time. First of all, the assembled side of the vehicle helps to support the disassembled side. It also keeps the parts aligned and eliminates the possibility of putting the parts on the wrong side of the vehicle.

Rear Control Arms

In order to remove the upper rear control arms from the vehicle, remove the bolts passing through the control arms at the frame and at the axle ends. Usually the rear coil spring does not have to be removed for this. Service one side of the vehicle at a time. This simplifies realigning the parts during assembly. On a serviceable control arm, replace the control arm bushings by removing the defective bushing with an appropriate puller. Properly position the new bushing and press it into place in the same manner it is done on front suspensions. Position the repaired control arm on the vehicle and loosely install the bolts. Repeat the service on the other control arm if necessary. Properly torque the nuts and bolts once the vehicle's entire weight is on the springs again.

The coil springs must be removed to service the lower rear control arms. Again, one side of the vehicle should be serviced at a time. Once the vehicle is properly supported and the springs are dismantled, remove the nuts and bolts that pass through the control arm. Remove the control arm from the vehicle and service it in the same way as the upper control arm.

Check the service manual to see if there is an adjustment for the driveline working angle. If none is specified, torque the control arm bolts to specification while the full vehicle weight is on the rear axle. This sets neutral bushing tension at normal curb height.

When there is a driveline working angle adjustment, adjust the angle before torquing the control arm bolts.

After the rear suspension has been serviced, always check the working angle of the universal joints on the drive shaft. This minimizes the possibility of driveline vibration.

Servicing Struts (Modified)

The independent rear suspension system shown in Figure 33-51 is a typical modified MacPherson strut design. The following applies to components that are replaced individually or as an assembly.

- The strut upper mounting is separately serviceable.
- The strut is not repairable and must be replaced as an assembly.
- Lower control arm bushings are not serviceable. They must be replaced with a lower control arm and bushing assembly.
- Tie-rod bushings can be serviced separately at both the forward and rear locations. However, if the tie-rod requires replacement, new bushings must be installed in the spindle at the same time.
- Coil springs are serviceable. If a rear coil spring is replaced, the upper spring insulator must also be replaced.

Photo Sequence #16 procedures can basically be followed when removing and installing rear struts.

☐ ELECTRONICALLY CONTROLLED SUSPENSIONS

All of the suspension systems covered up to this point are known as passive systems. Vehicle height and damping depend on fixed nonadjustable coil springs, shock absorbers, or MacPherson struts (Figure 33-55A). When weight is added, the vehicle lowers as the springs are compressed. Air adjustable shock absorbers may provide some amount of ride height and ride firmness flexibility, but there is no way to vary this setting during operation. Passive systems can be set to provide a soft, firm, or compromise ride. Vehicle body motion and tire traction vary due to road conditions and turning and braking forces. Passive systems have no way of adjusting to these changes.

Advances in electronic sensor and computer control technology have led to a new generation of suspension systems. The simplest systems are level control systems that use electronic height sensors to control an air compressor linked to air adjustable shock absorbers (Figure 33-55B).

More advanced adaptive suspensions are capable of altering shock damping and ride height continuously. Electronic sensors provide input data to a computer. The computer adjusts air spring and shock damping settings to match road and driving conditions.

The most advanced computer controlled suspension systems are true active suspensions. These systems are hydraulically, rather than air controlled. They use high

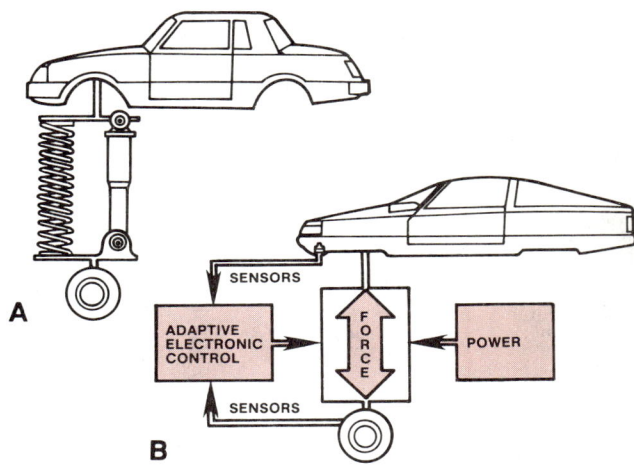

Figure 33-55 (A) Conventional passive suspension compromises handling because of static spring rates and shock valving. (B) A computer controlled adaptive suspension system constantly adapts to changing road and driving conditions.

pressure hydraulic actuators to carry the vehicle's weight rather than conventional springs or air springs.

The unique feature of an active suspension is that it can be programmed to respond almost perfectly to various operating conditions. For example, by raising the height of the outside actuators and lowering the inside actuators when going around a curve, the vehicle can be made to lean into a curve, much like a motorcycle. Active systems using hydraulic actuators are presently used on a limited number of high performance vehicles. Most manufacturers are introducing various adaptive suspension systems that rely on pneumatically actuated air springs and dampers.

Adaptive Suspensions

Adaptive suspensions use electronic shock absorbers with variable valving. In some cases, variable air spring rates are used to adapt the vehicle's ride characteristics to the prevailing road conditions or driver demands.

Electronic sensors monitor such factors as vehicle height, vehicle speed, steering angle, braking force, door position, shock damping status, engine vacuum, throttle position, and ignition switching. A computer is used to analyze this input and switch the suspension into a preset operating mode that matches exiting conditions. Some systems are fully automatic. Others allow the driver to select the ride mode.

At present, adaptive suspensions are less costly and complicated than hydraulically controlled active suspensions. However, they do have some limitations. Although they can reduce body roll, adaptive suspensions cannot eliminate it like true active systems. Adaptive systems also experience a slight delay in their reaction time, although some systems can change shock valving in as little as 150 microseconds.

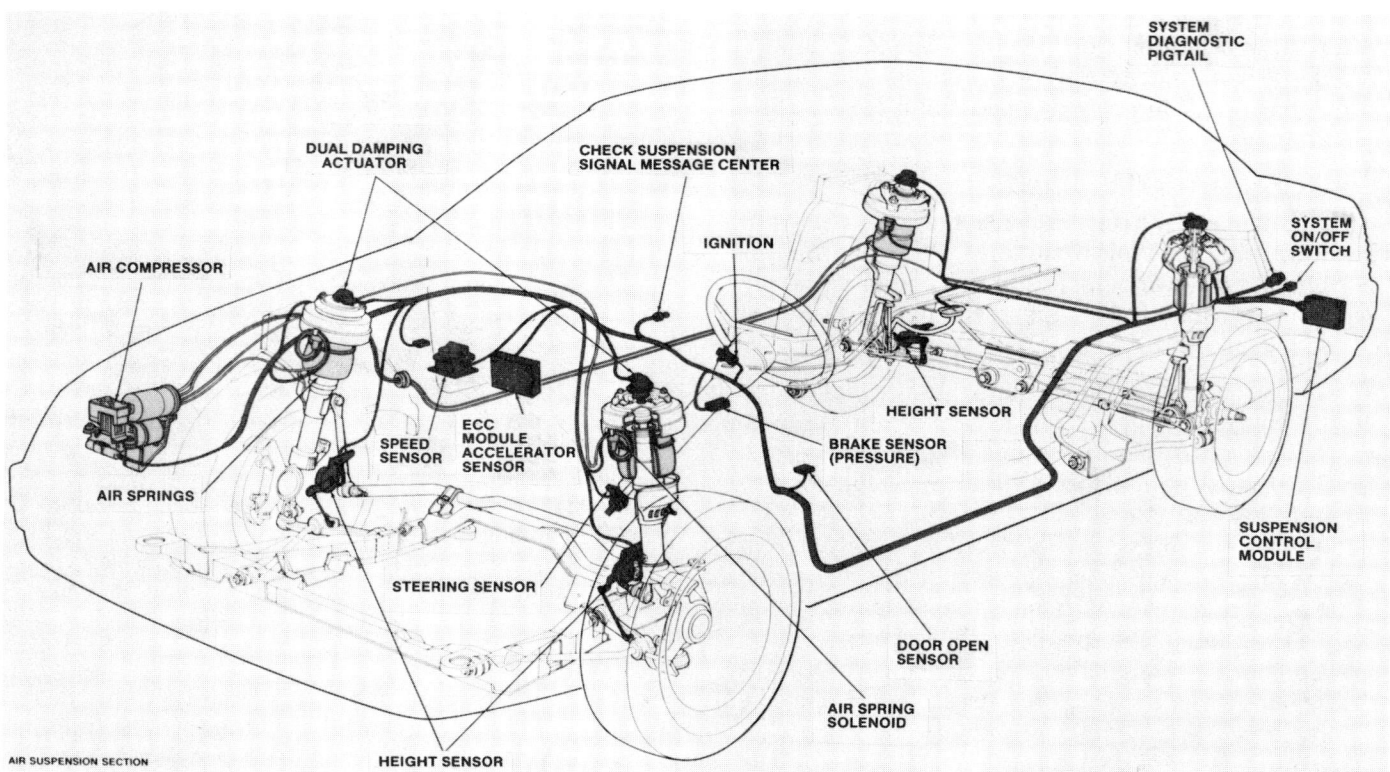

Figure 33-56 Typical electronic air suspension system. *Courtesy of Ford Motor Co.*

System Components

Although designs and components vary between manufacturers, Figure 33-56 illustrates the layout and parts of a popular adaptive suspension system. It employs four air springs that support the vehicle load at the front and rear wheels (Figure 33-57). The air spring membrane is similar to a tire in construction. A solenoid valve and filter assembly allows clean air to be added or released from the air spring. Adding or removing air changes the ride height of the vehicle.

The airflow to the springs is controlled by the interaction of the air compressor, system sensors, computer control module, and solenoid valves. All of the air operated parts of the system are connected by nylon tubing.

COMPRESSOR The compressor supplies the air pressure for operating the entire system. It is often a positive displacement single piston pump powered by a 12-volt DC motor. A regenerative air dryer is attached to the compressor output to remove moisture from the air before it is delivered to the air springs. The compressor is operated through the use of an electric relay controlled by the computer module.

SENSORS Vehicle height sensors can be rotary Hall-effect sensors that enable the computer to more accurately measure ride height as well as compensate for road variations. This prevents the vehicle from bottoming out when crossing over railroad tracks or similar road irregularities.

Advanced systems also read the steering angle by using a photo diode and shutter located inside the steering column. This allows the system to firm up the suspension when the vehicle is turning. The system also reads engine vacuum or throttle position to stiffen the suspension when the vehicle is accelerating. A brake sensor allows the system to compensate for front nose dive during hard braking. Some systems use a special G-sensor to sense sudden acceleration or braking. Other adaptive systems use a yaw sensor to pick up body roll when cornering.

ELECTRONIC SHOCK ABSORBERS Many adaptive suspension systems use electronically controlled shock absorbers that feature variable shock damping. The degree of damping is controlled by the computer based on input from the vehicle speed, steering angle, and braking sensors. As explained earlier in this chapter, variable shock damping is accomplished by varying the size of the metering orifices inside the shock. A small actuating motor mounted on top of the shock absorber rotates a control rod that alters the size of the metering orifices.

The latest advancement in adaptive suspension technology is the use of real time shock damping. These systems use solenoid-actuated shocks, rather than the motor driven shocks. Solenoids allow almost instantaneous valving changes. This means the suspension can react to bumps and body motions as they happen. Real time adaptive systems deliver most of the handling advantages of a fully active suspension with-

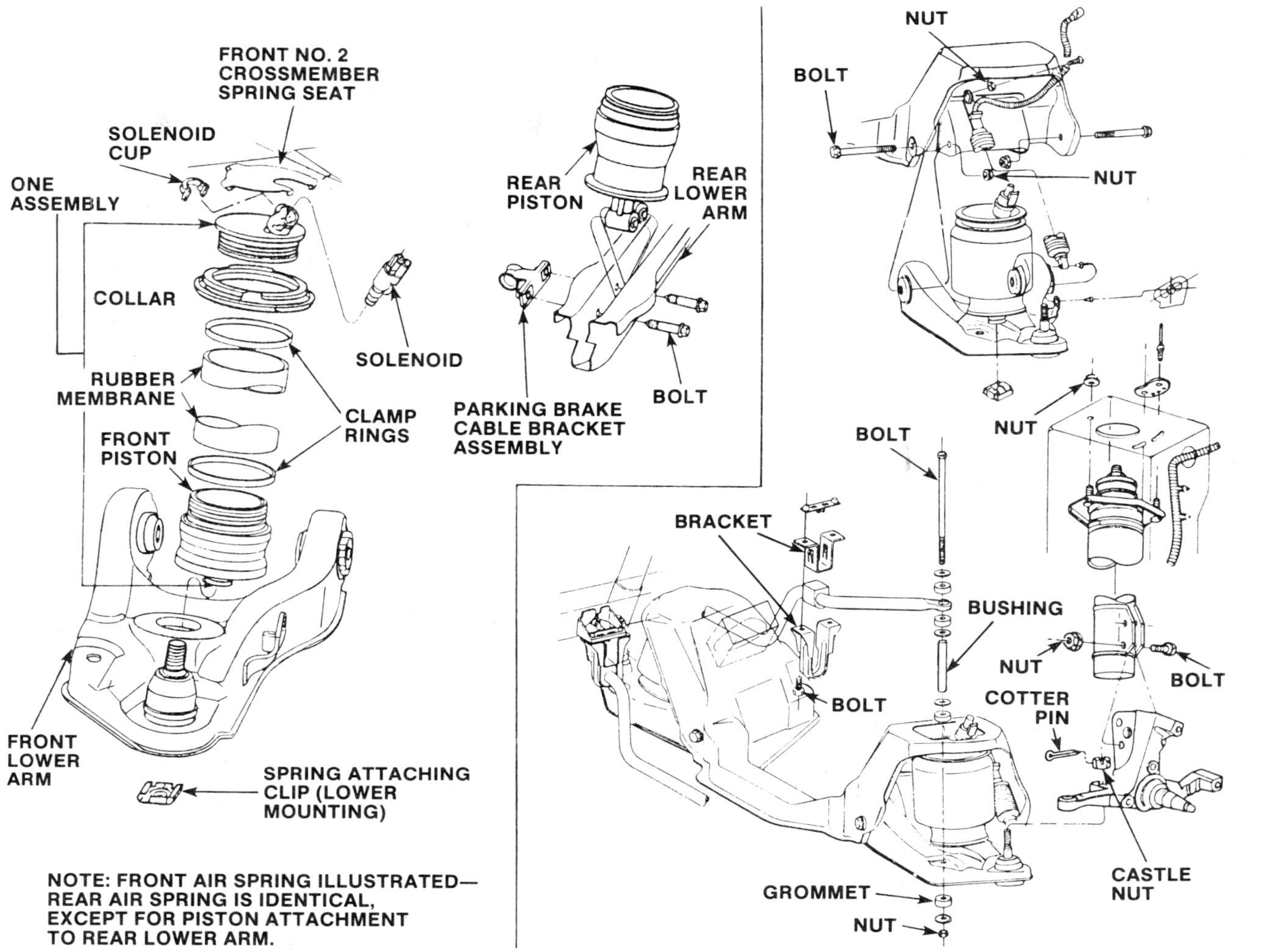

Suspension Systems

Figure 33-57 Typical components of an air spring assembly. *Courtesy of Ford Motor Co.*

out increased vehicle weight and power drain. With these systems, changes to shock valving in as little as 10 milliseconds is possible when bumps are encountered.

ELECTRONIC STRUTS Some systems use an electronically controlled strut in place of the air spring and shock absorber (Figure 33-58). Design and operation is similar to electronic shock absorbers. A valve selector or variable orifice located inside the strut controls fluid pressure in the suspension system based on input from many sensors and commands from the system's control module.

Some variable damping suspension systems use air or gas rather than a fluid. At speeds up to 40 mph, the orifice is fully open and provides full flow (Figure 33-59). From 40 to 60 mph, the orifice is in the normal position and flow is restricted. At speeds more than 60 mph, or when the vehicle is accelerating or braking, the variable orifice is shifted to the firm position.

The use of a variable orifice in the damper control, coupled with the deflected disc valving, provides opti-

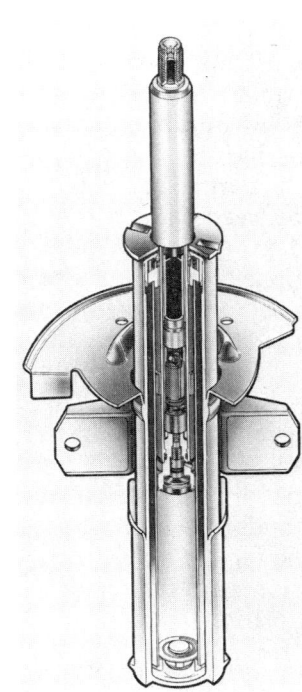

Figure 33-58 Computer command ride strut. Four electronically controlled struts are used on many adaptive suspension systems. Based on input from the computer, the valving selector shifts the variable by-pass orifice to a comfort, normal or firm setting. *Courtesy of General Motors Corp.*

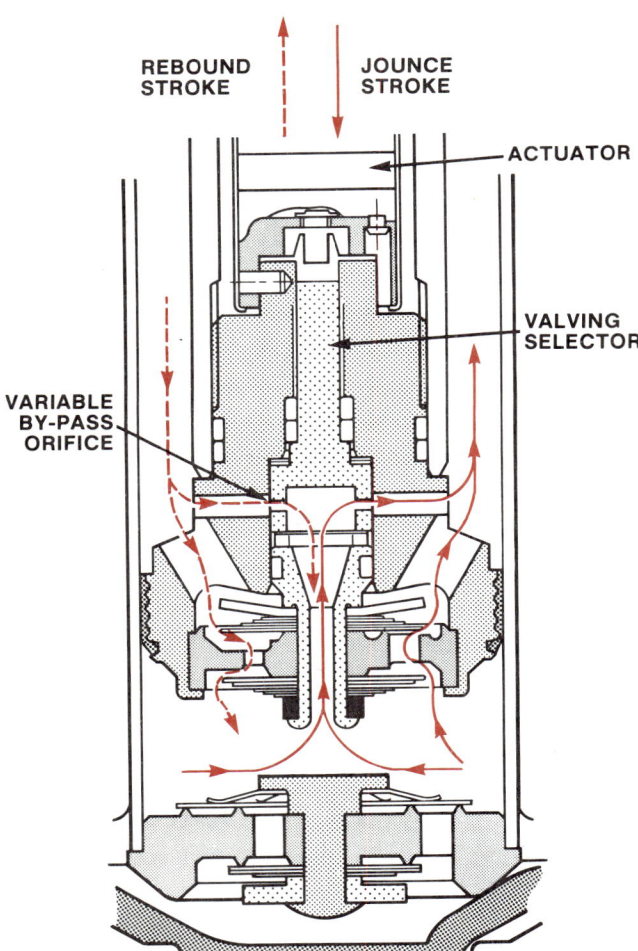

Figure 33-59 CCR damper fluid flow. The use of a variable orifice in the strut, coupled with the deflected disc valving, provides optimum fluid flow control for both rebound and jounce strokes.

mum fluid flow control for both rebound and jounce strokes. In the comfort mode, the selector is set to allow fluid flow primarily through the large selector orifice to achieve minimum damping forces. While in the normal mode, the unit is set to balance fluid flows between the small selector orifice and the deflected disc valving to provide moderate damping forces. Under conditions where the firm mode is needed, the selector is rotated to its firm or blocked position and fluid flows entirely through the deflected disc valving.

The damper control also can raise or lower the vehicle's height. This action also improves the car aerodynamic characteristics at highway speed. As speed increases, the suspension reduces the vehicle's height and the front end angles downward. This action tends to reduce wind resistance for greater stability and better gas mileage. As the vehicle slows, the suspension brings the body up to its normal height and level position.

COMPUTER CONTROL MODULE A microcomputer-based module controls the air compressor motor (through a relay), the compressor vent solenoid, and the four air spring solenoids. The computer module also controls operation of electronic shock absorber actuating motors and electronic strut valving selectors. The control module receives input from all system sensors.

The computer module also has the capability of performing diagnostic tests on the system. It has a preprogrammed routine for properly filling air springs after servicing. The module also controls the dash-mounted system warning light.

Electrical power to operate the basic air suspension system is distributed by the main body wiring harness. Each wiring harness involved has a special function in the typical air suspension system.

CAUTION: *The compressor relay, compressor vent solenoid, and all air spring solenoids have internal diodes for electrical noise supression and are polarity sensitive. Care must be taken when servicing these components not to switch the battery feed and ground circuits or component damage results. When charging the battery the ignition switch must be in the off position, if the air suspension switch is on, or damage to the air compressor relay or motor may occur. However, use of a battery charger while performing the diagnostic test or air spring fill option is acceptable. Set to a rate to maintain but not damage the vehicle battery.*

ELECTRONIC LEVELING CONTROL Adaptive suspension systems are capable of adjusting the suspension system during operation. Less complicated electronic level control systems are used on many large and mid-size vehicles.

These systems do not use a computer module. In most cases, height sensors are the only type of sensors used. These height sensors sense when passenger weight or cargo is added to or removed from the vehicle (Figure 33-60). The height sensors control two basic circuits. The compressor relay coil grounds circuits that activate the compressor. The exhaust solenoid coil grounds circuits that vent air from the system.

To prevent falsely actuating the compressor relay or exhaust solenoid circuits during normal ride motions, the sensor circuitry provides an 8- to 15-second delay before either circuit can be completed.

In addition, the typical sensor electronically limits compressor run time or exhaust solenoid energized time to a maximum of approximately 3-1/2 minutes. This time limit function is necessary to prevent continuous compressor operation in case of a solenoid malfunction. Turning the ignition off and on resets the electronic timer circuit to renew the 3-1/2 minute maximum run time. The height sensor is mounted to the frame cross member in the rear. The sensor actuator arm is attached to the rear upper control arm by a link. The link should be attached to the metal arm when making any trim adjustment.

Suspension Systems 843

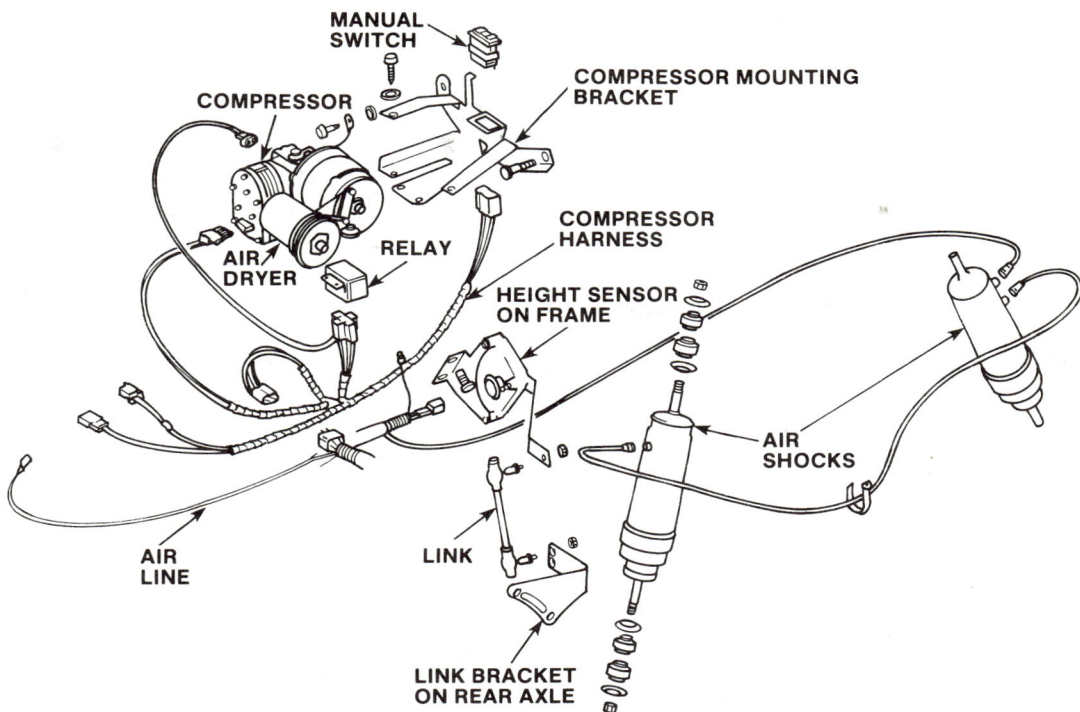

Figure 33-60 Electronic level control system. *Courtesy of Chrysler Corp.*

When the air line is attached to the shock absorber fittings or compressor dryer fitting, the retainer clip snaps into a groove in the fitting, locking the air line in position. To remove the air line, spread the retainer clip, release it from the groove, and pull on the air line.

SERVICING ELECTRONIC SUSPENSION COMPONENTS

Most electronic suspension servicing requires the removal of the component from the system, replacing or repairing it, and then reinstalling the component back into the system. Procedures for individual component replacement are covered in the vehicle's service manual. Serviceable components include the air compressor, charger, mounting brackets, height sensors, air springs, air lines and connections, gas struts, strut mounts, control arm components, shock absorbers, and stabilizer bars.

Failure to keep the following procedures in mind might result in a sudden failure of the air spring or suspension system. Suspension fasteners are important attaching parts. They could affect performance of vital components and systems or could result in major service expenses. They must be replaced with fasteners of the same part number, or with an equivalent part, if replacement becomes necessary. Do not use a replacement part of lesser quality or substitute design. Torque values must be used, as specified, during assembly to ensure proper retention of parts. New fasteners must be used in the place of the old ones whenever they are loosened or removed and when new component parts are installed.

WARNING: Do not remove an air spring under any circumstances when there is pressure in the air spring. Do not remove any components supporting an air spring without either exhausting the air or providing support for the air spring. Power to the air system must be shut off by turning the air suspension switch (in the luggage compartment) off or by disconnecting the battery when servicing any air suspension components. Most air suspension systems are equipped with a warning light. The light comes on if there is a problem, or when servicing the system.

Do not attempt to install or inflate any air spring that has become unfolded. Any spring that has unfolded must be refolded as shown in Figure 33-61 prior to being installed in a vehicle. The air spring refolding procedure should only be used to service an air spring that has never supported the vehicle's weight while in the improperly folded position. Improperly folded air springs found on vehicles during predelivery inspection or after customer mileage must be replaced. Do not attempt to inflate any air spring that has been collapsed while it is hanging from the rebound position to the jounce stop. When installing a new air spring, care must be taken not to apply a load to the suspension until springs have been inflated using air spring fill procedures. When front air springs are replaced, the height sensor must be checked and replaced if damaged.

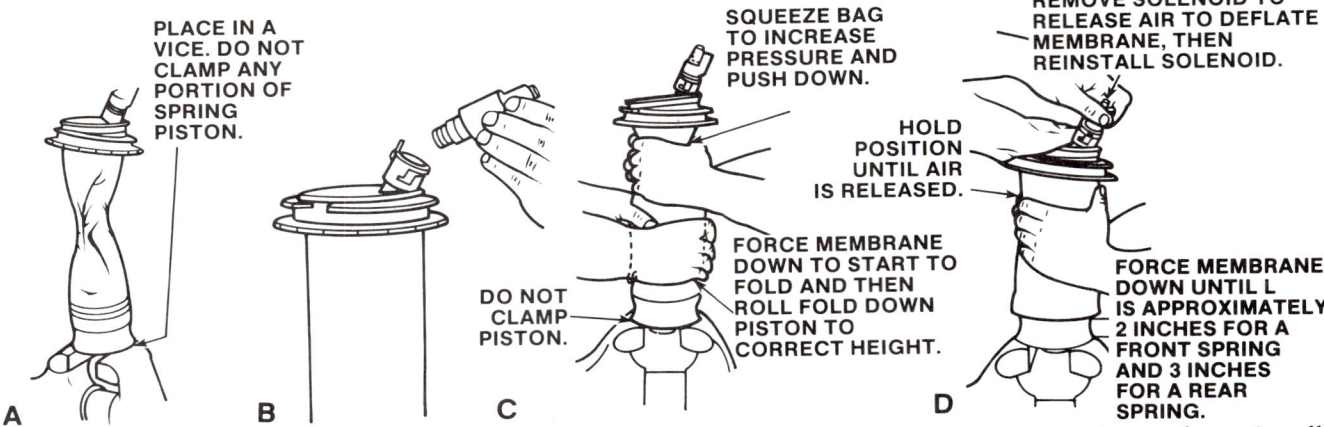

Figure 33-61 Air spring folding: (A) unroll spring membrane; (B) remove solenoid to expand membrane, then reinstall solenoid to trap air; (C) reroll spring membrane; and (D) release air to trap membrane position.

CUSTOMER CARE

Because the technician is seldom present when a vehicle requires towing, it is important to advise the customer proper procedures so the tow operator does not damage the electronic suspension system. You must also know the proper hoist lifting and jacking restrictions. While it is necessary to check the service manual for specific instructions, the following are the basics for electronic suspension.

When towing, it must be remembered that when the ignition is off, the automatic leveling suspension is still on. Before lifting the vehicle, be sure the ignition switch is turned off and the trunk switch deactivated. When towed from the front, towing should not exceed a speed of 35 mph or a distance of 50 miles. When the car is towed from the rear, speeds should not exceed 50 mph (or 35 mph on bumpy pavement).

A body hoist is usually the only type of lift recommended. In most service manuals, manufacturers warn against using a suspension hoist. The proper sequence is to position the car over the lift, shut off the ignition, then deactivate the system.

If a body hoist is not available, a floor jack and jack stands will do. Lift the car by the front cross member and the rear jacking points that are just in front of the rear wheel wells. Jack stands should be used to support the car.

In all situations, the lifting theory is the same. The suspension should be free to hang down while the car is in the air. This allows the wheels to be supported by the struts in the front and the shocks at the rear, both in their full extension (rebound) positions. Thus, the membrane of each air spring retains its proper shape while the car is in the air.

Vehicle Alignment

Aligning a vehicle with an electronic suspension system is essentially the same as the aligning procedure described in a later chapter—with one notable exception, and that is curb height.

Curb height is an important dimension because it affects the other alignment angles. Caster is the most obvious one that is affected, but front camber and toe can also be included. Curb height is especially critical when checking rear camber and toe on independent rear suspension. With electronic suspension, the ride can vary depending on various circumstances. The only way to guarantee the suspension at curb height is to preset it.

❏ ACTIVE SUSPENSIONS

Some of the advanced adaptive suspension systems may be called active suspensions. In this text, active suspensions refer to those controlled by double-acting hydraulic cylinders or solenoids (usually called actuators) that are mounted at each wheel. Each actuator maintains a sort of hydraulic equilibrium with the others to carry the vehicle's weight, while maintaining the desired body attitude. At the same time, each actuator serves as its own shock absorber, eliminating the need for yet another traditional suspension component.

In other words, each hydraulic actuator acts as both a spring (with variable-rate damping characteristics) and a variable-rate shock absorber. This is accomplished in an active suspension system by varying the hydraulic pressure within each cylinder and the rate at which it increases or decreases. By bleeding or adding hydraulic pressure from the individual actuators, each wheel can react independently to changing road conditions.

The components that make such a system possible are the actuator control valves, various sensors, and chassis computer (Figure 33-62). Feeding information

Suspension Systems 845

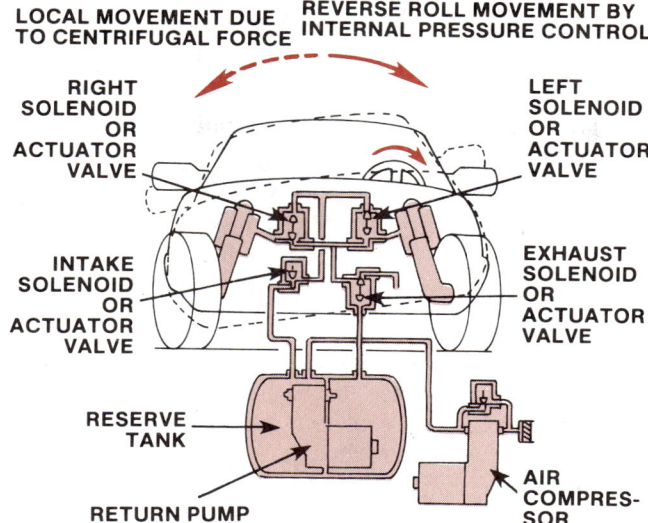

Figure 33-62 Active suspension systems counteract body roll, tilting, and leaning. This diagram shows ASC system action during left turn. *Courtesy of Mitsubishi Motor Sales of America, Inc.*

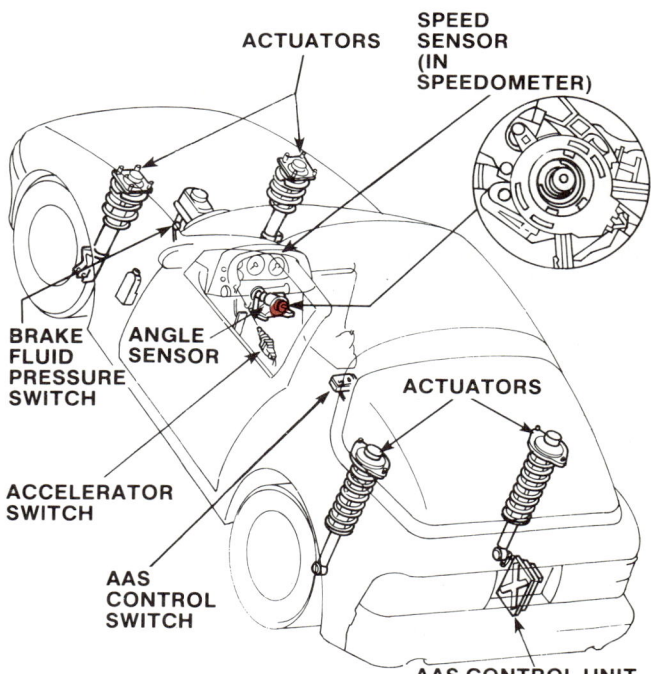

Figure 33-63 An auto adjust suspension system.

to the computer are a number of specialized sensors. Each actuator has a linear displacement sensor and an acceleration sensor to keep the computer informed about the actuator's relative position. This enables the computer to track the extension and compression of each actuator, and to know when each wheel is undergoing jounce or rebound. There are also load sensors and hub acceleration sensors in each wheel to measure how heavily each wheel is loaded.

A steering angle sensor is used to signal the computer when the vehicle is turning (Figure 33-63). To monitor body motions, a roll sensor and lateral acceleration and G-sensors are used. The computer also monitors hydraulic pressure within the system and the speed of the pump monitor.

Once it has all the necessary inputs, the computer can then regulate the flow of hydraulic pressure within each individual actuator according to any number of variables and its own built-in program. Another nice feature of a suspension such as this is that it can be programmed to behave in a variety of unique and currently impossible ways: leaning or rolling into turns, for example, or even raising a flat tire on command to change the tire without using a separate jack.

When the wheel of an active suspension hits a bump, the sensors detect the sudden upward deflection of the wheel. The computer recognizes the change as a bump, and instantly opens a control valve to bleed pressure from the hydraulic actuator. The rate at which pressure is bled from the actuator determines the cushioning of the bump and the relative harshness or softness of the ride. The rate can be varied at any point during jounce or rebound to produce a variable spring rate effect. In other words, the feel of the suspension can be programmed to respond in an almost infinite variety of ways. Once the bump has been absorbed by the actuator, pressure is forced back into it to keep the wheel in contact with the road and to maintain the suspension's desired ride height.

During hard braking with a conventional suspension system, there is a tendency for a vehicle to make a dive. The weight of the vehicle seemingly pushes the front of the car downward and back upwards. During hard braking, the active suspension increases air pressure in the front actuators and reduces air pressure in the rear actuators. These actions minimize dive to keep the vehicle level and make it easier for the driver to control. After braking, valves operate to equalize air pressures in front and rear air actuators and level the vehicle again.

Frequently, when a driver depresses the accelerator quickly during hard acceleration, the front end of the vehicle tends to lift up, while the rear end lowers. The action is known as squat. With an active suspension system, squat is controlled by the operating valve's solenoids which increase the air pressure in rear wheel actuators and reduce air pressure in front wheel actuators. When the vehicle is no longer accelerating quickly, the control system operates valves to equalize air pressures and level the vehicle. Thus, an active suspension changes the height of the front, rear, or either side of the vehicle to counteract tilting, rolling, and leaning. These active attitude control functions improve vehicle stability and increase tire traction and driver control.

The power required for a totally active system is only 3 to 5 horsepower (about the same as a typical power steering pump). Power consumption is lowest when the system is least active, as when driving on a smooth road. Rough roads and hard maneuvers, on the other hand, put more of a demand on the system. The hydraulic pump works harder and thus requires more power.

Power consumption can be reduced by going with a semi-active suspension that uses small springs with the hydraulic actuators. The springs help to support the vehicle's weight, which reduces the load on the actuators. Smaller actuators that require less hydraulic power can then be used, which reduces the bulk and weight of the system. The addition of springs also adds a certain margin of safety to the system to keep it from going flat should the hydraulics spring a leak.

Although not as widely used as electronic leveling or adaptive suspension systems, hydraulic active suspensions are sure to become more common.

☐ SONAR ROAD SURFACE SENSING

In the very near future, vehicles may be equipped with sonar sensing devices that constantly monitor the surface of the road just ahead of the vehicle. The sensor would be similar to those used on automatic-focusing 35-millimeter cameras.

The sonar sensor would mount under the front of the vehicle. Its input would enable the system computer to anticipate bumps before they are stuck, rather than react to bumps as they do in present systems.

The computer would then change the suspension settings before the bump or dip is encountered. A speed sensor would help the computer calculate the distance between the vehicle and the bump or dip. Other sensors would input steering and vehicle acceleration or braking data to help the computer make the finest adjustment possible to the suspension settings.

CASE STUDY

Case 1

An eight-year-old vehicle is brought to the shop. The customer states that the vehicle runs well, but the ride has become so bouncy he wants the shock absorbers replaced.

The work order is written and the technician replaces the shock absorbers that afternoon.

The following day, the customer returns, complaining of only a slight improvement in ride and handling. He states the shocks must be defective or mismatched to his vehicle. Faced with an angry customer, the technician now takes the time to do what he should have done the previous day. He takes the vehicle on a road test and performs a complete inspection. On checking the ride height of the vehicle, he finds the vehicle is riding extremely low. This is a sure sign the coil springs are severely weakened.

Showing the customer the ride height measurement and the factory specification for that measurement convinces the customer of the need for new coil springs.

With new coil springs and shock absorbers, ride and handling improve dramatically.

Summary

- Four types of springs are used in suspension systems: coil, leaf, torsion bar, and air.
- Springs take care of two fundamental wheel actions: jounce and rebound.
- Common coil spring materials include carbon steel, carbon boron, steel, and alloy steels. Alloy steels, such as those containing chromium and silicon, improve the coil's resistance to relaxation. Most coil springs are manufactured by either a cold coiling or a hot coiling process. Hot coiling usually requires hardening and tempering along with short peening to increase the fatigue strength of the base material.
- Two basic designs of coil springs are used in vehicles: linear rate and variable rate.
- Leaf springs are made of steel or a fiber composite.
- In torsion type suspension, the bar may either run from front to rear or side to side across the chassis.
- Air springs are generally only used in microprocessor controlled suspension systems.
- Shock absorbers damp or control motion in a vehicle. Conventional shock absorbers are a velocity-sensitive hydraulic damping device. The faster it moves, the more resistance it has to the movement.
- Shock absorbers can be mounted either vertically or at an angle. Angle mounting of shock absorbers improves vehicle stability and dampens accelerating and braking torque.
- There are two basic adjustable air shock systems. The manual fill type and the automatic or electronic load-leveling type.
- MacPherson struts provide the damping function of a shock absorber. In addition, they serve to locate the spring and to fix the position of the suspension.
- Domestic struts have taken two forms: a concentric coil spring around the strut itself and a spring located between the lower control arm and the frame.
- MacPherson suspensions use sway or stabilizer bars. Coil springs are used on all strut suspensions.
- Independent front suspension (IFS) must keep the wheels rigidly positioned and at the same time allow them to steer right and left. In addition, because of weight transfer during braking, the

front-suspension system absorbs most of the braking torque. While accomplishing this, it must provide good ride and stability characteristics.
- The unequal length arm or short-long arm (SLA) suspension system is most commonly used on domestic vehicles.
- Live-axle is the traditional rear-suspension system and consists of springs used in conjunction with a live-axle (one in which the differential axle, wheel bearings, and brakes act as a unit). The springs are either of leaf or coil type.
- Semi-independent suspension is used on many front-wheel-drive models.
- Three strut designs are frequently used in IFS systems. They are the conventional MacPherson strut, the modified MacPherson strut, and the Chapman strut.
- The two basic types of computer suspension systems are adaptive and active.
- Electronically controlled suspensions can be either simple load-leveling systems, adaptive systems, or fully active systems. Adaptive and active suspension systems are computer controlled. Most load-leveling systems do not use a computer.
- Adaptive suspensions can alter vehicle ride height and shock absorber damping while the vehicle is in motion. Such systems use air springs and electronic shock absorbers or struts.
- Active suspensions use hydraulically operated actuators to control up-and-down and side-to-side movement. They can be programmed to respond to certain road conditions and turning forces.

Review Questions

1. How does a stabilizer bar work?
2. Explain the difference between sprung and unsprung weight.
3. What is the principle of the air spring?
4. Explain the action of the conventional shock absorber on both compression (jounce) and rebound strokes.
5. Describe the action of the independent front wheel suspension system.
6. The core of any suspension system is the _____ .
   a. wheel spindle assembly
   b. spring
   c. ball joints
   d. control arm
7. What term is used to describe the action of a shock absorber when it is expanded?
   a. jounce
   b. free length
   c. deflection
   d. rebound
8. Which of the following is considered sprung weight?
   a. steering linkage
   b. tires
   c. engine
   d. all of the above
9. In an effort to improve vehicle stability, Technician A mounts the shock absorbers at an angle. Technician B mounts them vertically. Who is correct?
   a. Technician A
   b. Technician B
   c. Both A and B
   d. Neither A nor B
10. What occurs when a wheel hits a dip or hole and moves downward?
    a. jounce
    b. free length
    c. deflection
    d. rebound
11. When towing a vehicle with a computer controlled suspension system, Technician A tows from the front at speeds of less than 35 mph. Technician B tows from the rear at speeds as high as 50 mph. Who is correct?
    a. Technician A
    b. Technician B
    c. Both A and B
    d. Neither A nor B
12. Suspension ball joints can be grouped into which classifications?
    a. load-carrying or nonload-carrying
    b. load-carrying, nonload-carrying, or stabilizing
    c. load-carrying or compression
    d. load-carrying or loaded
13. Which type of electronically controlled suspension system is controlled by double-acting hydraulic cylinders or solenoids (usually called actuators)?
    a. leveling control
    b. adaptive
    c. active
    d. both b and c
14. What controls motion in a vehicle?
    a. struts
    b. shock absorbers
    c. both a and b
    d. neither a nor b
15. The coil springs of the vehicle _____ .
    a. support the weight of the vehicle
    b. provide axle location
    c. stabilize the up-and-down motion
    d. all of the above
16. Before replacing springs, vehicle height is checked on both sides of the front suspension, and tire pressure is checked. Should you check the amount of fuel in the vehicle?
    a. Yes, the fuel tank should be empty.
    b. Yes, the fuel tank should be full.

17. When servicing an air suspension component, Technician A shuts off power to the system by disconnecting the battery. Technician B shuts off power to the system by turning the air suspension switch in the luggage compartment. Who is correct?
    a. Technician A
    b. Technician B
    c. Both A and B
    d. Neither A nor B
18. The two SLA systems in common use today are _____.
    a. coil spring and strut suspension
    b. coil spring and torsion bar suspension
    c. coil spring and single control arm suspension
    d. single and double control arm suspension
19. How many coil springs are contained in a torsion bar independent front-suspension system?
    a. two
    b. none
    c. four
    d. one
20. Coil springs are used _____.
    a. on all strut suspensions
    b. on selected strut suspensions
    c. not at all on strut suspensions
    d. only on modified MacPherson suspensions
21. When the wide bottom of a control arm is toward the front of the car and the point turns in to meet the upright, it is called a(n) _____.
    a. trailing arm
    b. semi-trailing arm
    c. wishbone arm
    d. A-shaped
22. The modified MacPherson strut rear suspension is very common in _____.
    a. front-wheel-drive vehicles
    b. rear-wheel-drive vehicles
    c. pick-up trucks
    d. station wagons
23. When removing the rear leaf springs in a live-axle suspension system, Technician A would disconnect the rear shock absorbers. Technician B would not. Who is correct?
    a. Technician A
    b. Technician B
    c. Both A and B
    d. Neither A nor B
24. Leaf springs are also known as _____.
    a. quarter-elliptical
    b. semi-elliptical
    c. both a and b
    d. neither a nor b
25. Technician A says the use of firmer, urethane bushings in the suspension system improves the vehicle's road holding ability and handling. Technician B says firmer bushings also help eliminate torque steer in FWD vehicles. Who is correct?
    a. Technician A
    b. Technician B
    c. Both A and B
    d. Neither A nor B

34 STEERING SYSTEMS AND WHEEL ALIGNMENT

Objectives

- Describe the similarities and differences between parallelogram, worm and roller, and rack and pinion steering linkage systems.
- Identify the typical manual steering system components and their functions.
- Name the five basic types of steering linkage systems.
- Identify the components in a parallelogram steering linkage arrangement and describe the function of each.
- Identify the components in a manual rack and pinion steering arrangement, and describe the function of each.
- Describe the function and operation of the manual steering gearbox and the steering column.
- Explain the various manual steering service procedures.
- Describe and service conventional and nonconventional power-steering design arrangements.
- Explain the most common power-steering systems in use on passenger cars and light-duty trucks.
- Perform general conventional power-steering system checks.
- Describe the common four-wheel steering systems.
- Explain the benefits of accurate wheel alignment.
- Explain the importance of correct wheel alignment angles.
- Describe the different functions of camber and caster with regard to a vehicle's suspension.
- Identify the purposes of steering axis inclination.
- Explain why toe is the most critical tire wear factor of all the alignment angles.
- Identify the purposes of turning radius or toe-out.
- Explain the condition known as tracking.
- Understand the importance of rear-wheel alignment.
- Know the difference between two-wheel and four-wheel alignment procedures.

The purpose of the steering system is to turn the front wheels. In some cases, it also turns the rear wheels. The wheels constantly change direction, while switching lanes, rounding sharp turns, and when avoiding roadway obstacles.

Swift and sure steering responses are needed at today's driving speeds. To accomplish this, the wheels must be in alignment. Wheel alignment allows the wheels to roll without scuffing, dragging, or slipping on different types of road conditions. This gives greater safety in driving, easier steering, longer tire life, reduction in fuel consumption, and less strain on the parts that make up the front end of the vehicle.

❏ MANUAL STEERING SYSTEMS AND THEIR COMPONENTS

The steering system is composed of three major subsystems (Figure 34-1). They are the steering linkage, steering gear, and steering column and wheel. As the steering wheel is turned by the operator, the steering gear transfers this motion to the steering linkage.

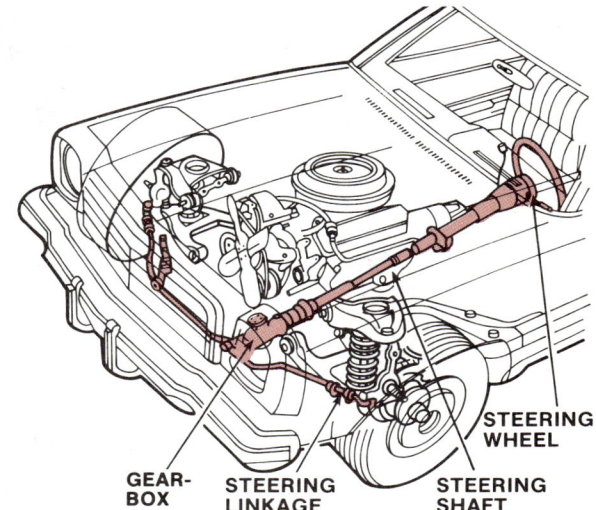

Figure 34-1 Conventional manual steering system.

The steering linkage turns the wheels to control the vehicle's direction. Although there are many variations to this system, these three major assemblies make up the steering system.

849

Steering Linkage

The term steering linkage is applied to the system of pivots and connecting parts that is placed between the steering gear and the steering arms attached to the front or rear wheels, controlling the direction of vehicle travel. The steering linkage transfers the motion of the steering gear output shaft to the steering arms, turning the wheels to maneuver the vehicle.

The type of front-wheel suspension (independent wheel suspension as compared with a solid front axle) greatly influences steering geometry. Most passenger cars, and many light trucks and recreational vehicles, have independent front-wheel suspension systems. Therefore, a steering linkage arrangement that tolerates relatively large wheel movement must be used.

Parallelogram Steering Linkage

A parallelogram type of steering linkage arrangement was at one time the most common type used on passenger cars. It is used extensively with the recirculating ball steering gear and can be classified into two distinct configurations: parallelogram steering linkage placed behind the front wheel suspension (Figure 34-2A) and parallelogram steering linkage placed ahead of the front-wheel suspension (Figure 34-2B). This type of steering linkage is most often used where motor and chassis components would interfere with normal operation of the steering linkage, if placed behind the front-wheel suspension.

These designs are the basic steering systems used in conjunction with independent front-wheel suspensions. This type of linkage also provides good steering and suspension geometry. Road vibrations and impact forces are transmitted to the linkage from the tires, causing wear and looseness in the system (Figure 34-3A). The linkage wear concentration points are shown in Figure 34-3B. This looseness permits intermittent changes in the toe setting of the front wheels, allowing further tire wear.

In a parallelogram steering linkage, the tie-rods have ball socket assemblies at each end. One end is attached to the wheel's steering arm and the other end to the center link.

The components in a parallelogram steering linkage arrangement are the pitman arm, idler arm, links, and tie-rods.

PITMAN ARM The pitman arm connects the linkage to the steering column through a steering gear located at the base of the column. It transmits the motion it receives from the gear to the linkage, causing the linkage to move left or right to turn the wheels in the appropriate direction. It also serves to maintain the height of the center link. This ensures that the tie-rods are able to be parallel to the control arm movement and

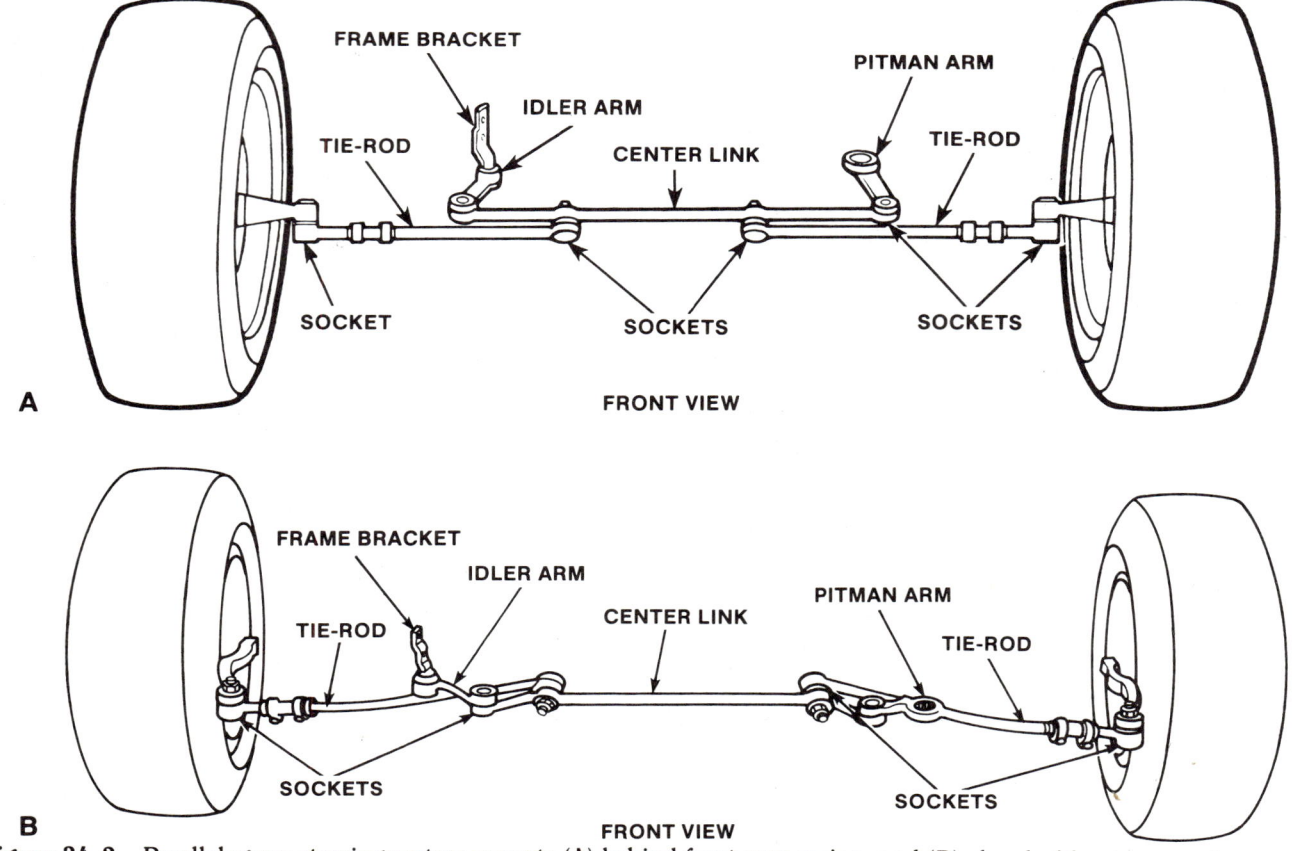

Figure 34-2 Parallelogram steering system mounts (A) behind front suspension, and (B) ahead of front suspension.

Steering Systems and Wheel Alignment 851

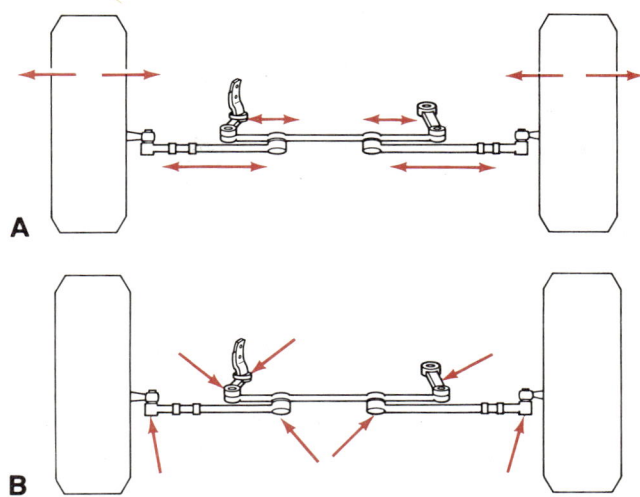

Figure 34-3 (A) Linkage force diagram and (B) linkage wear concentration points.

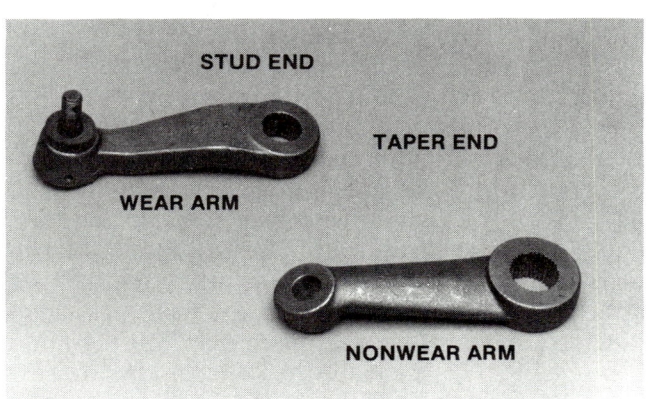

Figure 34-4 Wear and nonwear pitman arms. *Courtesy of Dana Corp.*

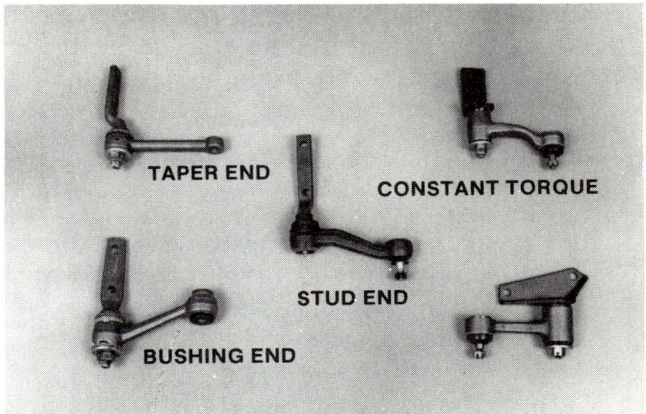

Figure 34-5 Wear on idler arms occurs at the pivot. *Courtesy of Dana Corp.*

avoid unsteady toe settings or bump steer. Toe, a critical alignment factor, is a term that defines how well the tires point to the direction of the vehicle.

There are two basic types of pitman arms: wear and nonwear (Figure 34-4). Service needs differ, depending on which type of arm is used. Nonwear arms have tapered holes at their center link ends and normally need to be replaced only if they have been damaged in an accident or have been mounted with excessive tolerance. Wear arms have studs at the center link-end and are subject to deterioration from normal operation. These arms must be inspected periodically to determine whether or not they are still serviceable.

IDLER ARM The idler arm or idler arm assembly is normally attached, on the opposite side of the center link, from the pitman arm and to the car frame, supporting the center link at the correct height. A pivot built into the arm or assembly permits sideway movement of the linkage. On some linkages, such as those on a few light-duty trucks, two idler arms are used.

Idler arms are generally more vulnerable to wear than pitman arms because of this pivot function, with wear usually showing up at the swivel point of the arm or assembly (Figure 34-5). Worn bushings or stud assemblies on idler arms permit excessive vertical movement in the idler arms.

LINKS Links, depending on the design application, can be referred to as center, drag, or steering links. Their purpose is to control sideway linkage movement, which changes the wheel directions. Because they usually are also mounting locations for tie-rods, they are very important for maintaining correct toe settings. If they are not mounted at the correct height, toe is unstable and a condition known as toe change or bump steer is produced. Center links and drag links can be used either alone or in conjunction with each other, depending on the particular steering design.

There are several common designs of center links (Figure 34-6). Like pitman arms, they can be broadly characterized as either wear or nonwear. Center links with stud or bushing ends are likely to become unserviceable from the effects of normal operation and should be inspected periodically. Links with open ta-

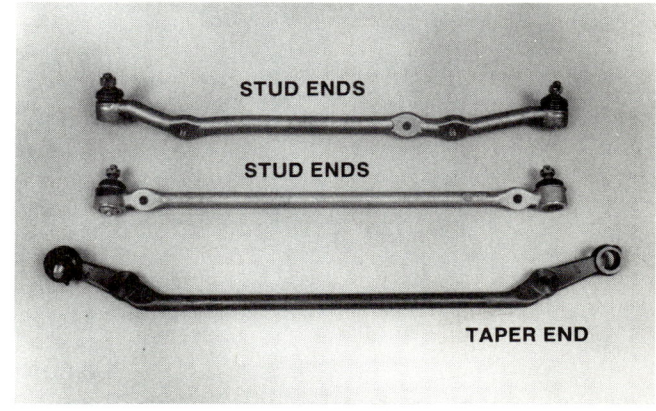

Figure 34-6 Center link designs. *Courtesy of Dana Corp.*

pers are nonwear and usually need to be replaced only if they have been damaged in an accident or through excessive tolerance at the mounting position of the idler or pitman arms.

> **SHOP TALK**
>
> If a center link is nonwear, the pitman arm is normally a wear arm. If the link is wear, the arm is usually nonwear. Idler arms or assemblies are always subject to wear.

TIE-RODS Tie-rods are actually assemblies that make the final connections between the steering linkage and steering knuckles. They consist of inner tie-rod ends, which are connected to the opposite sides of the center link, outer tie-rod ends, which connect to the steering knuckles; and adjusting sleeves or bolts, which join the inner and outer tie-rod ends, permitting the tie-rod length to be adjusted for correct toe settings (Figure 34-7).

Tie-rods are subject to wear and damage, particularly if the rubber or plastic dust boots covering the ball stud have been damaged or are missing. Contaminants such as dirt and moisture can enter and cause rapid part failure. A special bonded ball stud, in which no boot is used, is available for use on certain light-duty two-wheel-drive and four-wheel-drive trucks. An elastomer bushing bonded to the stud ball provides strong shock absorption and steering return in downsized vehicles.

Worm and Roller Steering Linkage

The components for the worm and roller steering linkage are explained later in this chapter and are basically the same as parallelogram components.

Rack and Pinion Steering Linkage

Rack and pinion is lighter in weight and has fewer components than parallelogram steering. Tie-rods are used in the same fashion on both systems, but the resemblance stops there. Steering input is received from a pinion gear attached to the steering column. This gear moves a toothed rack that is attached to the tie-rods.

In the rack and pinion steering arrangement, there is no pitman arm, idler arm assembly, or center link. The rack performs the task of the center link. Its movement pushes and pulls the tie-rods to change the wheel's direction. The tie-rods are the only steering linkage parts used in a rack and pinion system.

Most rack and pinion constructions are composed of a tube in which the steering rack can slide (Figure 34-8A). The rack is a rod with gear teeth cut along one end—spur and helical. The other end is fitted with two balls to which the ends of the divided track rods are attached. The rack meshes with the teeth of a small pinion at the end of the steering column. The two inner tie-rod ends, which are attached to the rack, are covered by rubber bellows boots that protect the rack from contamination. The inner tie-rods connect to outer tie-rod ends, which connect to the steering arms. The rack and pinion housing is fastened to the vehicle at two or three points.

In some cases, the rack and pinion steering gear on unibody cars is bolted directly to a body panel, like a cowl (Figure 34-8B). When this is done, the body panel must hold the steering gear in its correct location. The unibody structure must maintain the proper

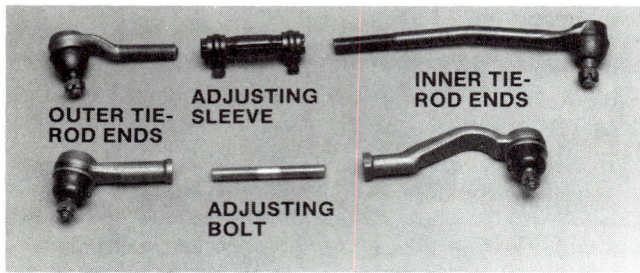

Figure 34-7 Tie-rods connect the steering linkage to the wheel assemblies and permit toe to be adjusted. *Courtesy of Dana Corp.*

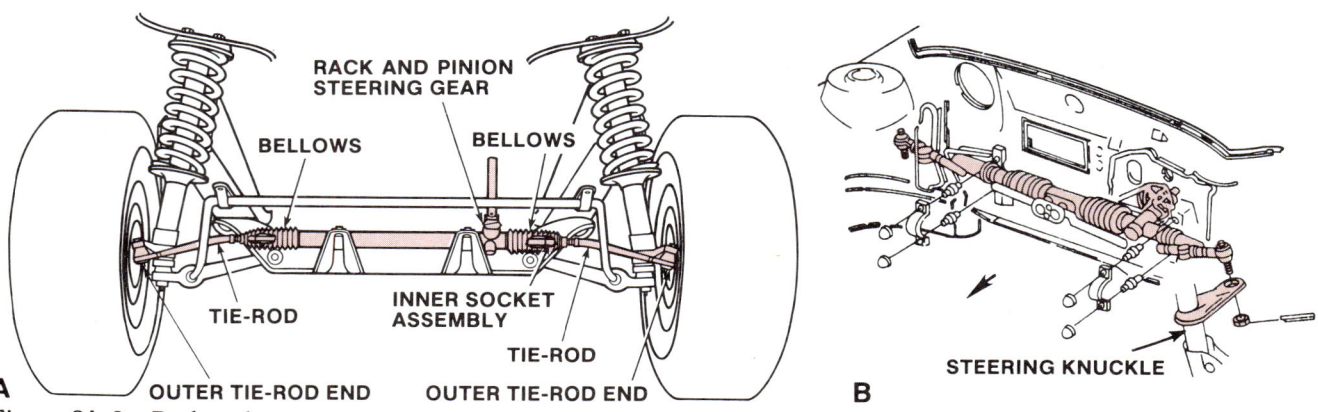

Figure 34-8 Rack and pinion steering systems (A) on conventional frame and (B) bolted to body panel of a unibody.

relationship of the steering and suspension parts to each other. Along with other advantages, the rack and pinion steering system combined with the MacPherson strut suspension system is found in most front-wheel-drive unibody vehicles because of their weight- and space-saving feature.

The vehicle operator gets a greater feeling of the road with rack and pinion because there are less friction points. This means a higher probability of car owners with steering complaints. Fewer friction points can reduce the system's total ability to isolate and dampen vibrations.

RACK The rack is a toothed bar contained in a metal housing. The rack maintains the correct height of the steering components so that the tie-rod movement is able to parallel control arm movement.

The rack is similar to the parallelogram center link in that its sideway movement in the housing is what pulls or pushes the tie-rods to change wheel directions.

PINION The pinion is a toothed or worm gear mounted at the base of the steering column assembly, where it is moved by the steering wheel. The pinion gear meshes with the teeth in the rack so that the rack is propelled sideways in response to the turning of the pinion.

YOKE ADJUSTMENT The rack-to-pinion lash, or preload, affects steering harshness, feedback, and noise. It is set according to the manufacturer's specifications. An adjustment screw, plug, or shim pack are located on the outside of the housing at the junction of the pinion and rack to correct or set the yoke lash (Figure 34-9).

TIE-RODS Tie-rods are very similar to those used on parallelogram systems. They consist of inner and outer ends and adjusting sleeves or bolts. The inner tie-rod ends on rack and pinion units are usually spring-loaded ball sockets that screw onto the rack ends (Figure 34-10). They are preloaded and protected against contaminant entry by a rubber bellows or boot.

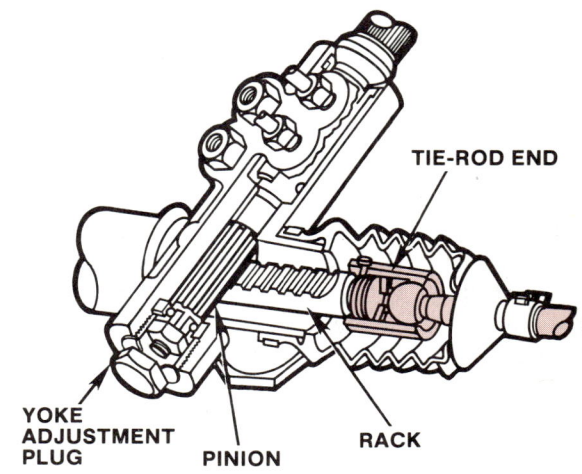

Figure 34-10 The inner tie-rod is a spring-loaded ball socket in a rack and pinion steering box.

Manual Steering Gear

The purpose of the steering gear is to change the rotational motion of the steering wheel to a reciprocating motion to move the steering linkage. There are three styles currently in use. These are the recirculating ball, worm and roller, and the rack and pinion. The latter gear assembly incorporates the already described rack and pinion linkage system and steering gear as a single unit.

The recirculating ball is generally found in larger cars, as shown in Figure 34-11. A sector shaft is supported by needle bearings in the housing and a bushing in the sector cover. A ball nut is used that has threads

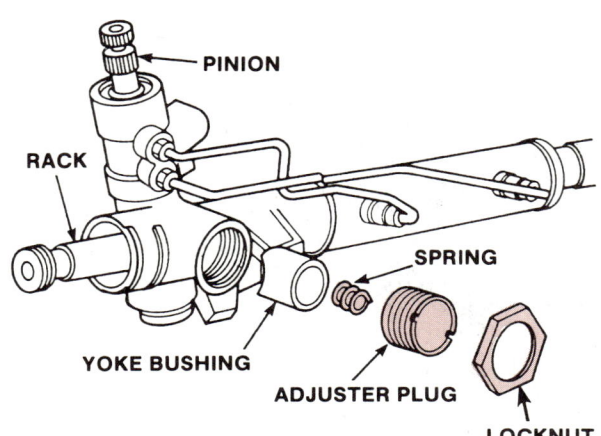

Figure 34-9 The rack preload (yoke lash) is adjusted by a screw, plug, or shim pack.

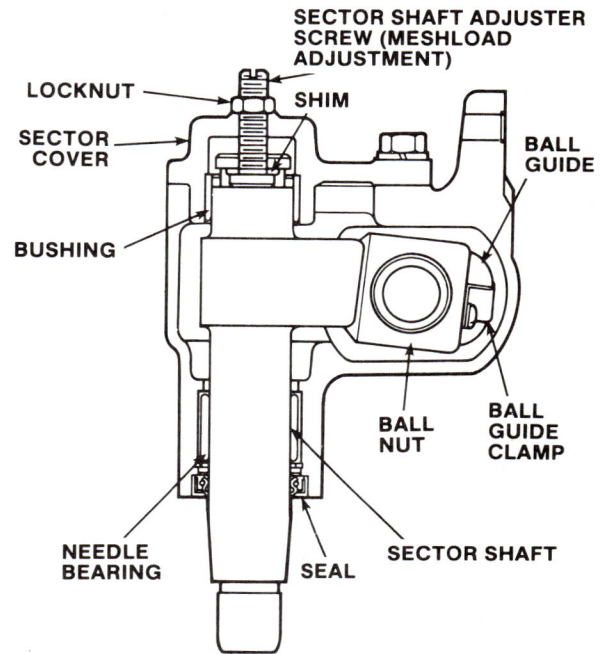

Figure 34-11 Side cutaway of a manual recirculating ball steering gear.

that mate to the threads of the wormshaft via continuous rows of ball bearings between the two. Ball bearings recirculate through two outside loops, referred to as ball return guide tubes. The ball nut has gear teeth cut on one face that mesh with gear teeth on the sector shaft. As the steering wheel is rotated, the wormshaft rotates, causing the ball nut to move up or down the wormshaft. Since the gear teeth on the ball nut are meshed with the gear teeth on the sector shaft, the movement of the nut causes the sector shaft to rotate and swing the pitman arm.

The design of two separate circuits of balls results in an almost friction-free operation of the ball nut and the wormshaft. When the steering wheel is turned, the ball bearings roll in the ball thread grooves of the wormshaft and ball nut. When the ball bearings reach the end of their respective circuit, they enter the guide tubes and are returned to the other end of the circuits.

The teeth on the sector shaft and the ball nut are designed so that an interference fit exists between the two when the front wheels are straight ahead. This interference fit eliminates gear tooth lash for a positive feel when driving straight ahead. Proper mesh engagement between the sector and ball nut is obtained by an adjusting screw that moves the sector shaft axially.

CAUTION: *Proper adjustment between the worm gear and the pitman gear is important for adequate steering response (Figure 34-12). Refer to the vehicle manual for specific adjustment procedures.*

The worm thrust bearing adjuster can be turned to provide proper preloading of the worm thrust bearings. Worm bearing preload eliminates worm end-play and is necessary to prevent steering free-play and vehicle wander.

The sector can be either constant or variable ratio (Figure 34-13). The former's teeth are all identical, while the latter has one long tooth between two shorter

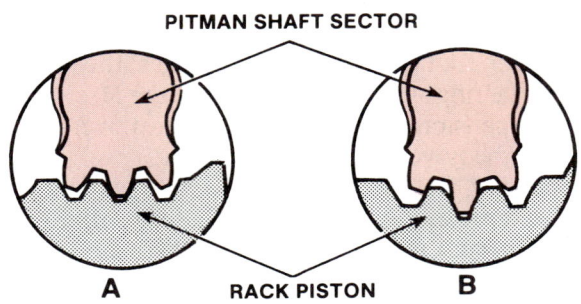

Figure 34-13 (A) Constant and (B) variable ratio.

teeth that changes the amount of mechanical advantage according to the position of the wheel. This serves to make the steering faster (maybe 13:1) in turns than in a straight direction (15 or 16:1). Variable ratio is ordinarily used only in power-steering units.

The worm and roller gearbox is similar to the recirculating ball except a single roller replaces the balls and ball nut (Figure 34-14). This reduces internal

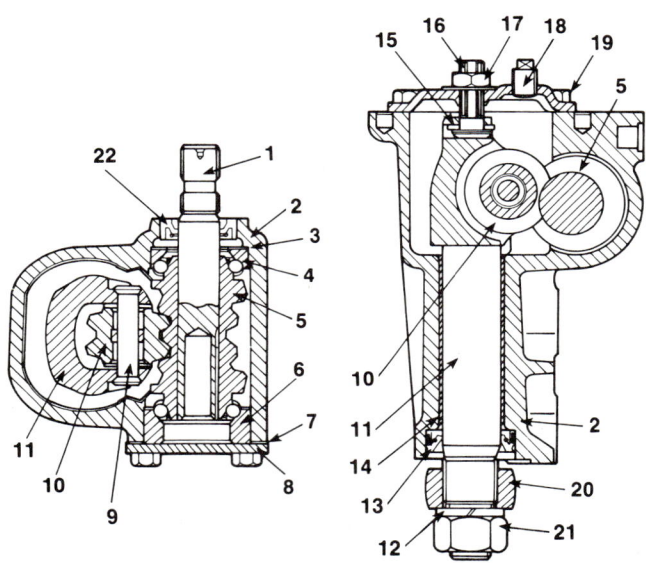

1 STEERING SHAFT
2 STEERING BOX
3 WORM UPPER BEARING SHIMS
4 REAR BALL BEARING
5 WORM
6 FRONT BALL BEARING
7 WORM LOWER BEARING SHIMS
8 WORM THRUST COVER
9 ROLLER PIN
10 ROLLER
11 ROLLER SHAFT
12 SPRING WASHER UNDER PITMAN ARM NUT
13 ROLLER SHAFT OIL SEAL
14 ROLLER SHAFT BUSHING
15 ROLLER SHAFT ADJUSTING DISC
16 ROLLER SHAFT ADJUSTING SCREW
17 LOCKNUT
18 PLUG
19 STEERING BOX COVER
20 PITMAN ARM
21 PITMAN ARM NUT
22 STEERING SHAFT OIL SEAL

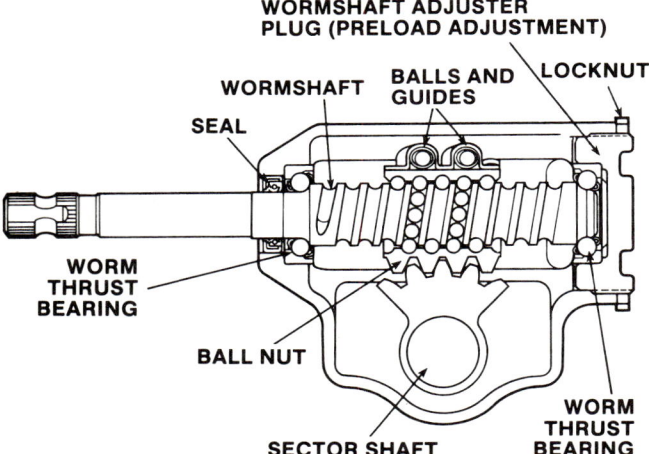

Figure 34-12 Top cutaway of a manual recirculating ball steering gear.

Figure 34-14 Worm and roller gearbox is similar to recirculating ball. *Courtesy of Fiat Corp.*

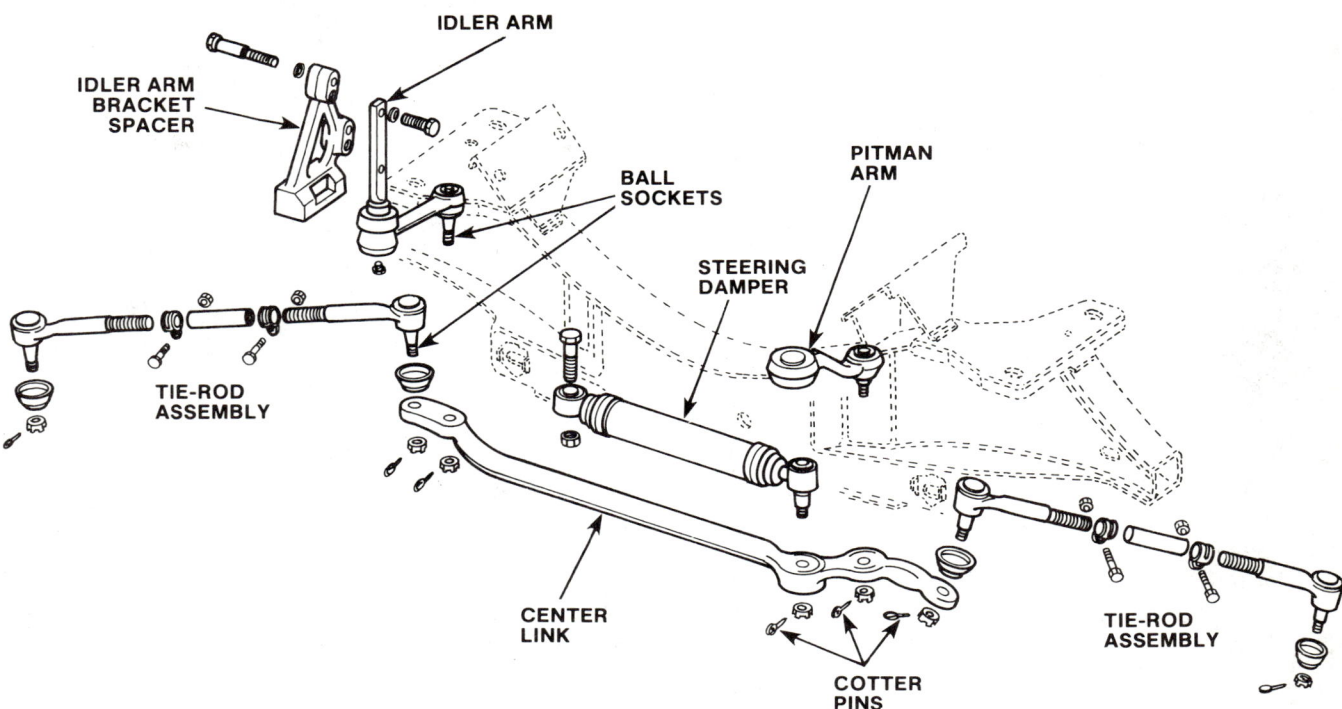

Figure 34-15 Worm and roller linkage steering. Pitman arm connects to steering gearbox. Arm swings right or left and moves other linkage components. *Courtesy of Chrysler Corp.*

friction, making it ideal for smaller cars. The steering linkage used with a worm and roller gearbox typically includes a pitman arm, center link, idler arm, and two tie-rod assemblies (Figure 34-15). The function of these components is the same as the parallelogram steering linkage earlier in this chapter.

In operation, the steering shaft rotates the worm gear. It, in turn, engages the roller, causing the roller shaft to turn. The shaft moves the pitman arm left or right to steer the vehicle.

Currently, the rack and pinion manual gear assembly is the most commonly used. When the steering shaft of the rack and pinion unit turns the pinion shaft, the pinion gear moves the rack gear. The rack then slides sideways inside the gear housing (Figure 34-16). The thrust spring preloads the rack and pinion gear teeth to prevent excessive gear backlash (play). Adjustment screws or shims may be used for setting

thrust spring tension. Either bushings or roller bearings may be used on the pinion shaft and rack. Frequently, the pinion shaft uses roller bearings and the rack uses plain bushings.

It must be noted that the steering gear does not cause the vehicle to pull to one side. Only minor pull conditions caused by the tires or suspension misalignment can be masked by setting preload and meshload specifications. Also, the steering gear does not cause road wheel shimmy.

Steering Wheel and Column

The purpose of the steering wheel and column is to produce the necessary force to turn the steering gear. The exact type of steering wheel and column depends upon the year and the car manufacturer.

Major parts of the steering wheel and column are shown in Figure 34-17. The steering wheel is used to

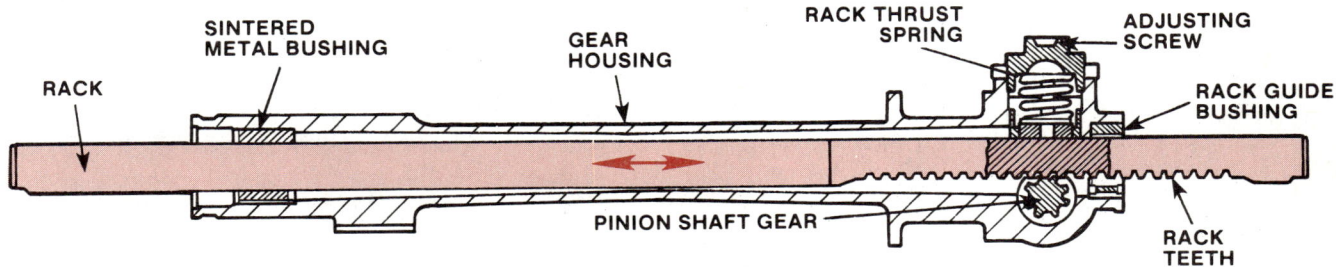

Figure 34-16 Rack slides sideways and pushes or pulls on tie-rods. This rotates the steering knuckles and front wheels. *Courtesy of Buick Corp.*

856 Section 7 Suspensions

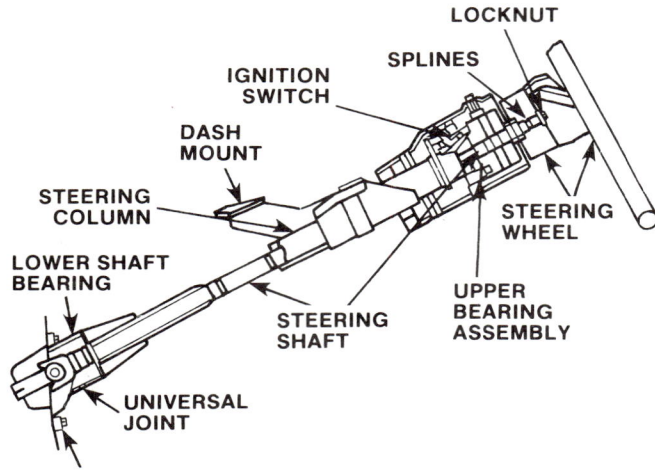

Figure 34-17 Note steering column components. Steering wheel is splined to shaft that extends through column and down to steering gearbox. *Courtesy of Toyota Corp.*

produce the turning effort. The lower and upper covers conceal parts. The universal joints rotate at angles. Support brackets are used to hold the steering column in place. Assorted screws, nuts, bolt pins, and seals are used to make the steering wheel and column perform correctly.

Differences in steering wheel and column designs include fixed column, telescoping column (Figure 34-18), tilt column, manual transmission, floor shift, and automatic transmission column shift. The tilt columns (Figure 34-19) feature at least five driving positions (two up, two down, and a center position). Both fixed and tilt columns may house an emergency warning flasher control, a turn signal switch, ignition key, lights (high/low beams), horn, windshield wipers and washers, and an anti-theft device that locks the steering system. On automatic transmission-equipped vehicles the transmisson linkage locks also. Some vehicles have steering wheels that may be pushed to the side to permit easy entrance and exit from the vehicle. (It is not possible to start the car with this feature until the steering wheel has been returned to the driving position and locked in place.)

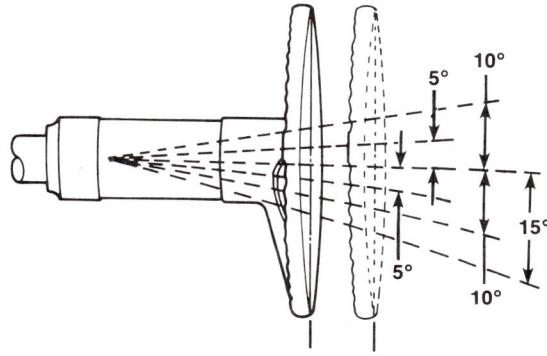

Figure 34-18 Telescoping steering operation.

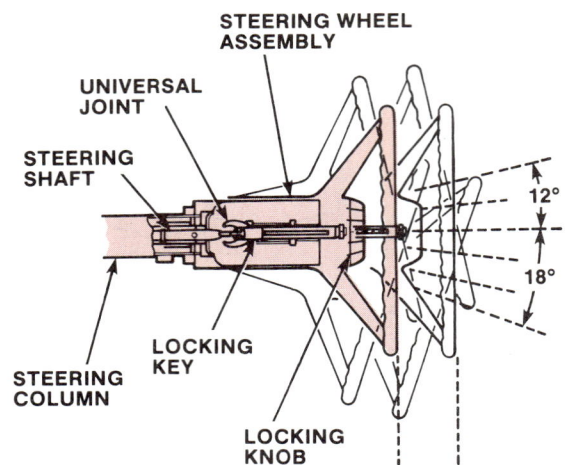

Figure 34-19 Tilt steering operation.

Most steering columns today are of the extruded absorber type. To reduce the chance of injury to the driver, automotive engineers have designed steering columns that collapse in the event of a collision. Lower steering sections are linked by two or more universal joints. These joints allow the sections to fold (Figure 34-20). The upper column normally incorporates a solid shaft and a tube. The shaft is locked to the tube and is designed to give in the event of a collision.

Methods used to lock the shaft to the tube include a breakaway plastic capsule or a series of inserts or steel balls held in a plastic retainer that allow the shaft to roll forward inside the tube. There are also collapsible steel mesh (Figure 34-21) or accordion-pleted devices that give way under pressure. After the vehicle has been in an accident, the steering column should be checked for evidence of collapse. Although the car can be steered with a collapsed column that has been pulled back, the collapsed portion must be replaced. All service manuals provide explicit instructions for doing this.

The steering wheel is usually held in place on the steering column by either a bolt or nut. When the blocked tooth on the steering gear input shaft is in the 12 o'clock position, the front wheels should be in the straight-ahead position and the steering wheel spokes

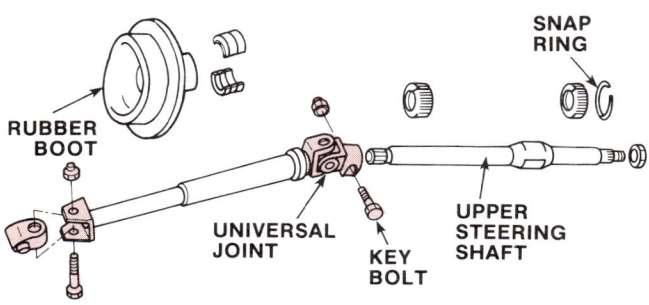

Figure 34-20 Steering shaft universal joints. *Courtesy of Chrysler Corp.*

diagnose specific problems and how to correct them, check the Tech Manual written for this book. Damaged, broken, or deformed parts must be replaced with correct replacement as described in the service manual.

Parallelogram Steering Linkage

Carefully inspect the components of parallelogram steering linkage.

PITMAN ARM Because of its function, the pitman arm is the most heavily stressed point in the system. To inspect the pitman arm, grasp it and vigorously shake it to detect any looseness. Check the socket to reveal any damage or looseness. Either conditon must be corrected by replacing the worn part.

IDLER ARM A worn or damaged idler arm can cause steering instability, uneven tire wear, front-end shimmy, hard steering, excessive play in steering, or poor returnability.

The procedure is simple for checking an idler arm for looseness or wear. The suspension should be normally loaded on the ground or on an alignment rack. When raised by a frame contact hoist, the vehicle's steering linkage is allowed to hang. Proper testing cannot be done. Check the idler arm ends for worn sockets or deteriorated bushings. Grasp the center link firmly with your hand at the idler arm end. Push up with approximately a 25-pound load. Pull down with the same load. The allowable movement of the idler arm and support assembly is ± 1/8 inch for a total acceptable movement of 1/4 inch (Figure 34-23). The load can be accurately measured by using a dial indicator or pull spring scale located as near the center link end of the idler arm as possible. Keep in mind that the test forces should not exceed 25 pounds, as even a new idler arm might be forced to show movement due to steel flexing when excessive pressure is applied. It is also necessary that a scale or ruler be rested against the frame and used to determine the amount of movement. Observers tend to overestimate the actual movement when a scale is not used. The idler arm should always

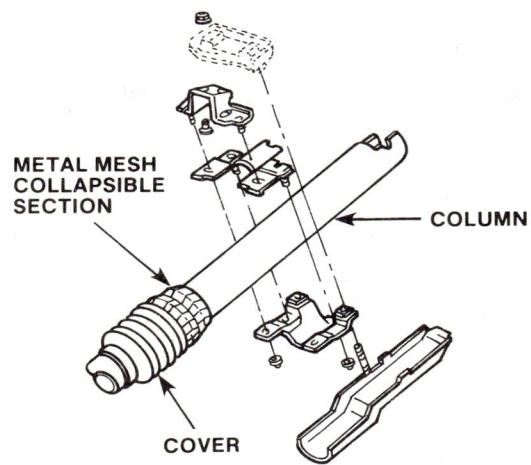

Figure 34-21 Collapsing mesh steering column. *Courtesy of Ford Motor Co.*

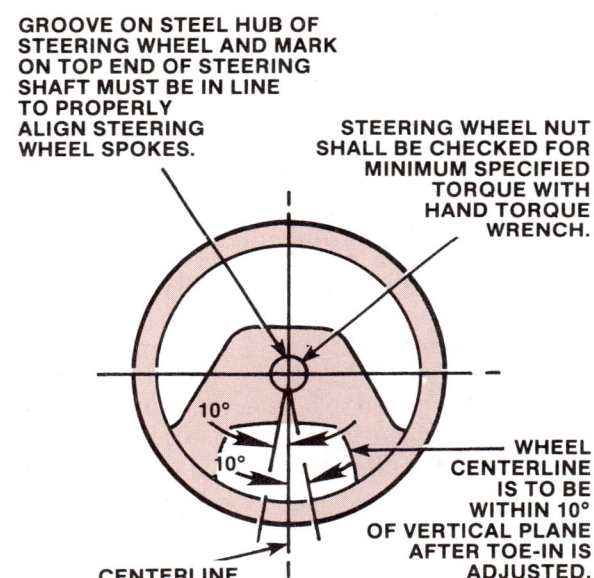

Figure 34-22 Typical acceptable steering wheel position—measured from normal spoke angle.

in their normal position (Figure 34-22). If the spokes are not in their normal position, they can be adjusted by changing the toe adjustment (as described later in this chapter). This adjustment can be made only when the steering wheel indexing mark is aligned with the steering column indexing marks. As a rule, mating flats on the wheel hub and steering shaft prevent misindexing of these components. The alignment of the notches on the steering wheel hub and steering shaft confirm correct orientation.

☐ MANUAL STEERING SERVICE PROCEDURES

In this chapter only general manual steering service procedures are covered. For more details on how to

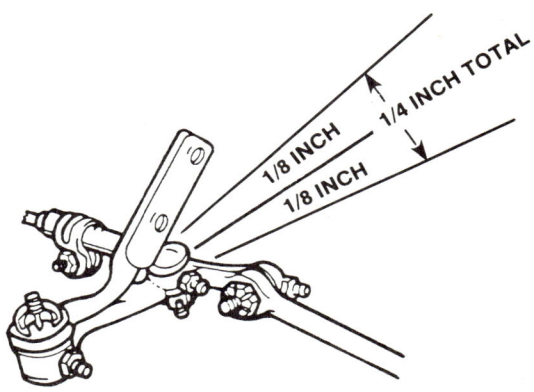

Figure 34-23 Checking idler arm movement.

be replaced if it fails this test. Jerking the right front wheel and tire assembly back and forth (causing an up and down movement in the idler arm) is not an acceptable method of checking. There is no control on the amount of force being applied.

CENTER LINK Worn or bent center links can cause front-end shimmy, vehicle pull to one side, or change in the toe setting, causing excessive tire wear.

When inspecting the center link, look closely to insure it has not been bent or damaged. Grasp the center link firmly and try moving it in all directions. Any movement, or sign of damage, is reason for replacement. Tapered openings seldom wear but should be checked for enlargement caused by a loose connection. If necessary, replace the center link.

TIE-ROD ASSEMBLY Worn tie-rod ends result in incorrect toe-in settings, scalloped and scuffed tires, wheel shimmy, understeering, or front-end noise and tire squeal on turns.

Tie-rod end and center link inspections are similar. Grasp the tie-rod end firmly. Push vertically with the stud, and inspect for movement at the joint with the steering knuckle. Any movement over 1/8 inch or observation of damaged or missing parts, such as seals, is sufficient evidence that replacement is necessary.

Adjusting sleeves resemble a piece of internally threaded pipe. They have a slot or separation that runs either their entire length or just partway. Adjusting sleeves also have two crimping or squeezing clamps located at each end to lock the toe adjustment. Badly rusted, worn, or damaged adjusting sleeves should be replaced.

An additional check of the tie-rods can be made by rotating each tie-rod end to feel for roughness or binding, which could indicate that the socket has probably rusted internally.

STEERING DAMPER The steering dampers found in some steering linkage designs are generally nonadjustable, nonrefillable, and are not repairable. At each inspection interval, make the following checks on the steering damper system.

1. Inspect damage mountings. Check the damper attachments to be sure they are properly and securely installed. Tighten, if loose. Replace the damper assembly if the rubber bushings are badly worn.
2. Inspect damage for leaks. Inspect the damper for evidence of fluid leakage. A light film of fluid is permissible on the body of the damper near the shaft seal. A dripping damper should be replaced.

DRY PARK CHECK An excellent overall check for worn or loose conventional steering components is the dry park check. With the full weight of the vehicle on the wheels, have an assistant rock the steering wheel back and forth. Start your inspection at one side to the other side. Note any looseness in tie-rod, center link,

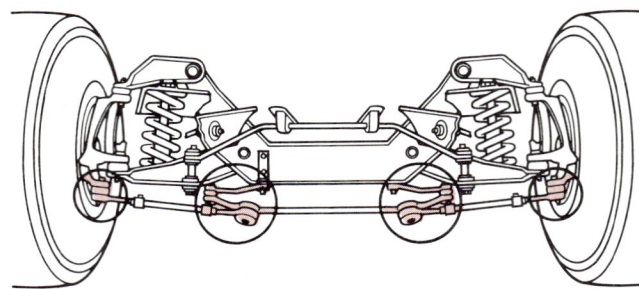

Figure 34-24 Circled areas indicate where a dry park check of steering linkage should be made.

idler arm, or pitman arm sockets (Figure 34-24). If a second person is not available, reach up under the vehicle and grasp the flexible coupling on the steering shaft. Rock the linkage.

Before assembling any steering linkage parts, thoroughly check all tapered holes for excessive out-of-round and wear. Thoroughly clean all bores that the stud tapers mount in. On new and reused parts, firmly install the tapered stud into its tapered hole. The stud must seat firmly, without rocking. Only thread should protrude from the hole. If the parts do not meet these requirements, then the mating part is worn and must be replaced, or the correct parts are not being used. Always follow the manufacturer's stud and mounting bolt torque specifications when installing chassis parts.

Worm and Roller Steering

Since the worm and roller steering linkage components are almost identical to those of a parallelogram linkage, methods of inspection are the same as given here.

> **CUSTOMER CARE**
>
> It is important for you to tell your customer that the steering linkage under normal conditions should be lubricated with any water resistant EP chassis lubricant every 7,500 miles or 6 months, whichever occurs first. Lubricate every 3,000 miles or 2 months, whichever occurs first when operating in dusty or muddy conditions or if the vehicle is used off-road. Lubrication points and additional information on the chassis lubricant recommended can be found in the vehicle's service manual.

Rack and Pinion Steering

A rack and pinion system has no idler or pitman arms and no center link. Instead, they are replaced with a rack. Because the rack has no wear points, the number of wear points on rack and pinion systems is reduced to four—each of the tie-rod ends. Tie-rod ends are also wear points on the parallelogram steering system.

In order to solve customer complaints, a very thorough inspection of the entire system is needed. Everything, including ball joints, tires, outer tie-rods, bellows boots, inner tie-rods, rack mounting bushings, steering couplings, and gearbox adjustment, must be checked. Rack and pinion steering inspection must be very thorough due to the system's sensitivity.

PROCEDURES
Rack and Pinion Steering Inspection

1. Check all working components (Figure 34-25) of the systems. Inspect the flexible steering coupling or the universal joints for wear or looseness. If any play is found, recommend replacement. Universal joints can also seize or bind. They should be checked closely.

2. Grasp the pinion gear shaft at the flexible steering coupling and try to move it in and out of the gear. If there is movement, the pinion bearing preload might need adjustment. If there is no adjustment, internal components have to be replaced.

3. Carefully inspect the rack housing. In most cases, the rack and pinion steering assemblies are mounted in rubber bushings. As the vehicle gets older, these mounting bushings deteriorate from heat, age, and oil leakage from the engine. When this happens, the housing moves within its mounting and causes loose and erratic steering. Also, be alert for excessive movement of the rack housing.

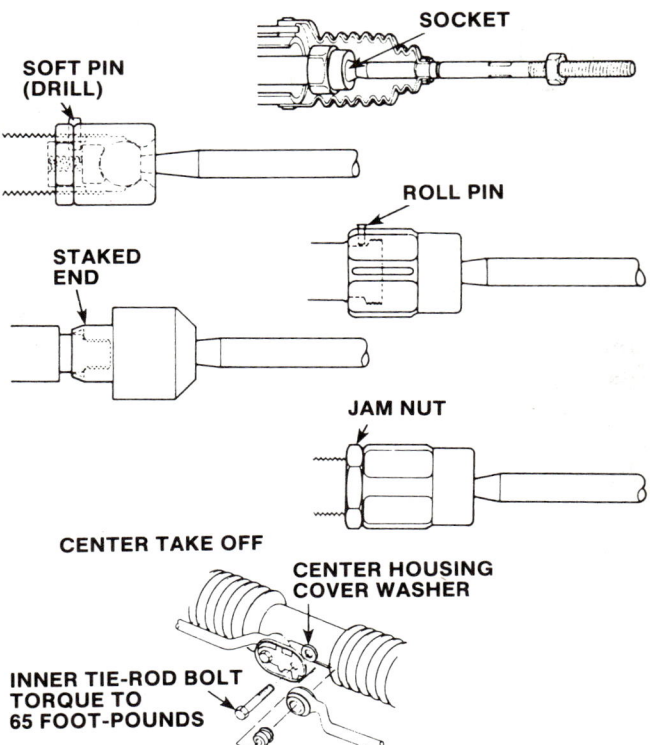

Figure 34-26 Various inner tie-rod socket assemblies.

4. Stiffness in steering can be caused by a bent rack assembly, tight yoke bearing adjustment, loose power-steering belt, weak pump, internal leaks in power-steering system, and damaged CV joints in front-wheel-drive vehicles.

5. Check the inner tie-rod socket assemblies (Figure 34-26) located inside the bellows. The most foolproof way of checking these sockets is to loosen the inner bellows clamp and pull the bellows back, giving a clear view of the socket. During the dry park check, observe any looseness. The inner tie-rod socket can also be checked by squeezing the bellows boot until the inner socket can be felt. Push and pull on the tire. If looseness is found in the tie-rod, it should be replaced. On some vehicles the boot might be made of hard plastic. For this type of boot, lock the steering wheel and push and pull on the tire. Watch for in and out movement of the tie-rod. If movement is observed, replace the inner tie-rod.

6. One fact to keep in mind is that the condition of the bellows boot determines the life of the inner socket. The bellows boot protects the rack from contamination. It might also contain fluid that helps keep the rack lubricated. If any cracks, splits, or leaks exist, the boot should be replaced. Also, be sure that clamps for the bellows are in their proper place and fastened tightly.

7. Inspect the outer tie-rod ends. In addition to the dry park check, grab each end and rotate to feel for

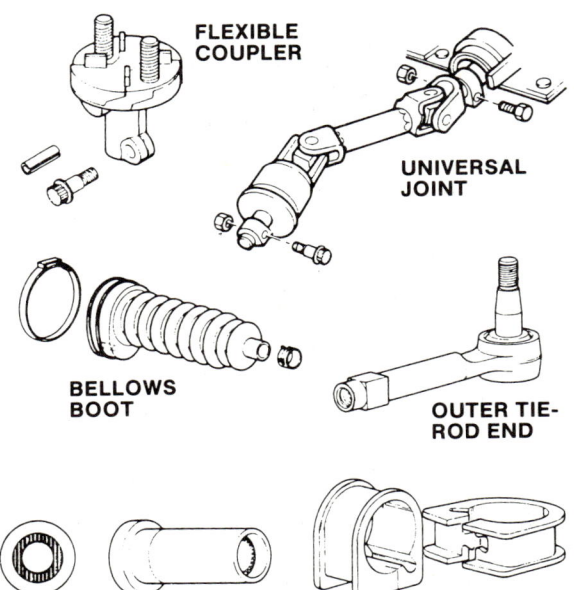

Figure 34-25 Rack and pinion steering components.

any roughness that would indicate internal rusting. Be sure to check for bent or damaged forgings and studs; split or deteriorated seals; and, damaged, out-of-round, or loose tapers. If any of these conditions exists, the parts should be replaced.

Manual Steering Gear

Before any adjustments are made or servicing procedures performed to the steering gear, a careful check should be made of front-end alignment, shock absorbers, wheel balance, and tire pressure for possible steering system problems.

Before adjusting or servicing a manual steering gear, the technician must disconnect the battery ground cable. Raise the vehicle with the front wheels in the straight-ahead position. Remove the pitman arm nut. Mark the relationship of the pitman shaft. Remove the pitman arm with a pitman arm puller. Loosen the steering gear adjuster plug lock-nut and back the adjuster plug off one-quarter turn (Figure 34-27). Remove the horn shroud or button cap. Turn the steering wheel gently in one direction until stopped by the gear; then, turn back one-half turn. Measure and record bearing drag by applying a torque wrench with a socket on the steering wheel nut and rotating through a 90-degree arc (Figure 34-28). Check the service manual for the correct amount of drag.

Once these steps are taken, the steering gear is ready for adjusting or servicing as per instructions in the vehicle's service manual.

Steering Columns

To perform service procedures on the steering column upper end components, it is not necessary to remove the column from the vehicle. The steering wheel, horn components, directional signal switch, ignition switch, and lock cylinder can be removed with the column remaining in the vehicle.

WARNING: Set the parking brake before removing the steering column. Also, remove the battery cable from the negative terminal. Remember that

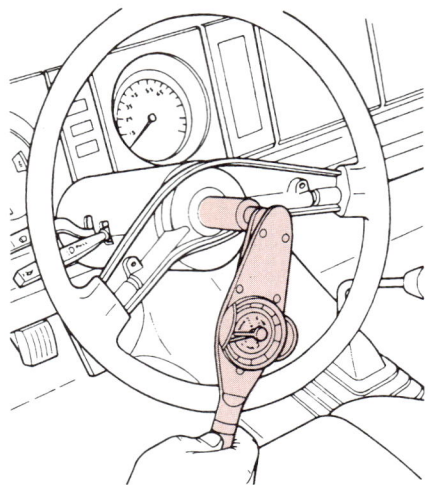

Figure 34-28 Measuring steering gear preload.

special precautions must be observed before beginning disassembly and during assembly to ensure the correct fitting together of the steering column shaft and steering gear shaft connections.

To determine if the energy-absorbing steering column components are functioning as designed, or if repairs are required, a close inspection should be made. An inspection is called for in all cases where damage is evident or whenever the vehicle is being repaired due to a front-end collision. If damage is evident, the affected parts must be replaced. Because of the differences in the steering column styles and various components, consult the service manual for more explicit inspection and servicing procedures.

CAUTION: When working on a collapsible steering column, do not hammer on or bump column components. With the column removed from the mounts, it is extremely susceptible to impact damage. A slight impact on the column end can collapse the steering shaft or loosen the plastic injections that maintain column rigidity. When removing the steering wheel, use a puller. Do not hammer or pound on any components to aid in removal.

❏ POWER STEERING

The power-steering unit is designed to reduce the amount of effort required to turn the steering wheel. It also reduces driver fatigue on long drives and makes it easier to steer the vehicle at slow road speeds, particularly during parking.

Power steering can be broken down into two design arrangements: conventional and nonconventional or electronically controlled. In the conventional arrangement, hydraulic power is used to assist the driver. In the nonconventional arrangement an electric motor and electronic controls provide power assistance in steering.

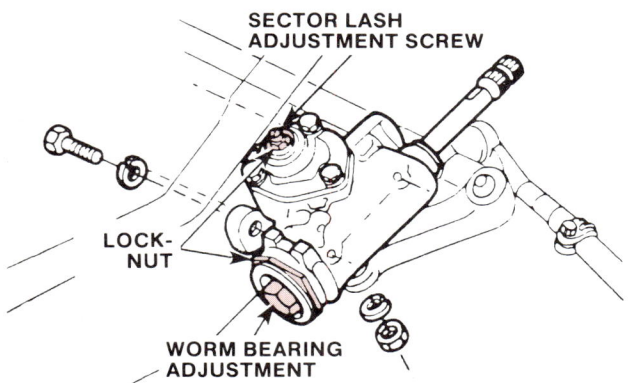

Figure 34-27 Typical steering gear adjustment points.

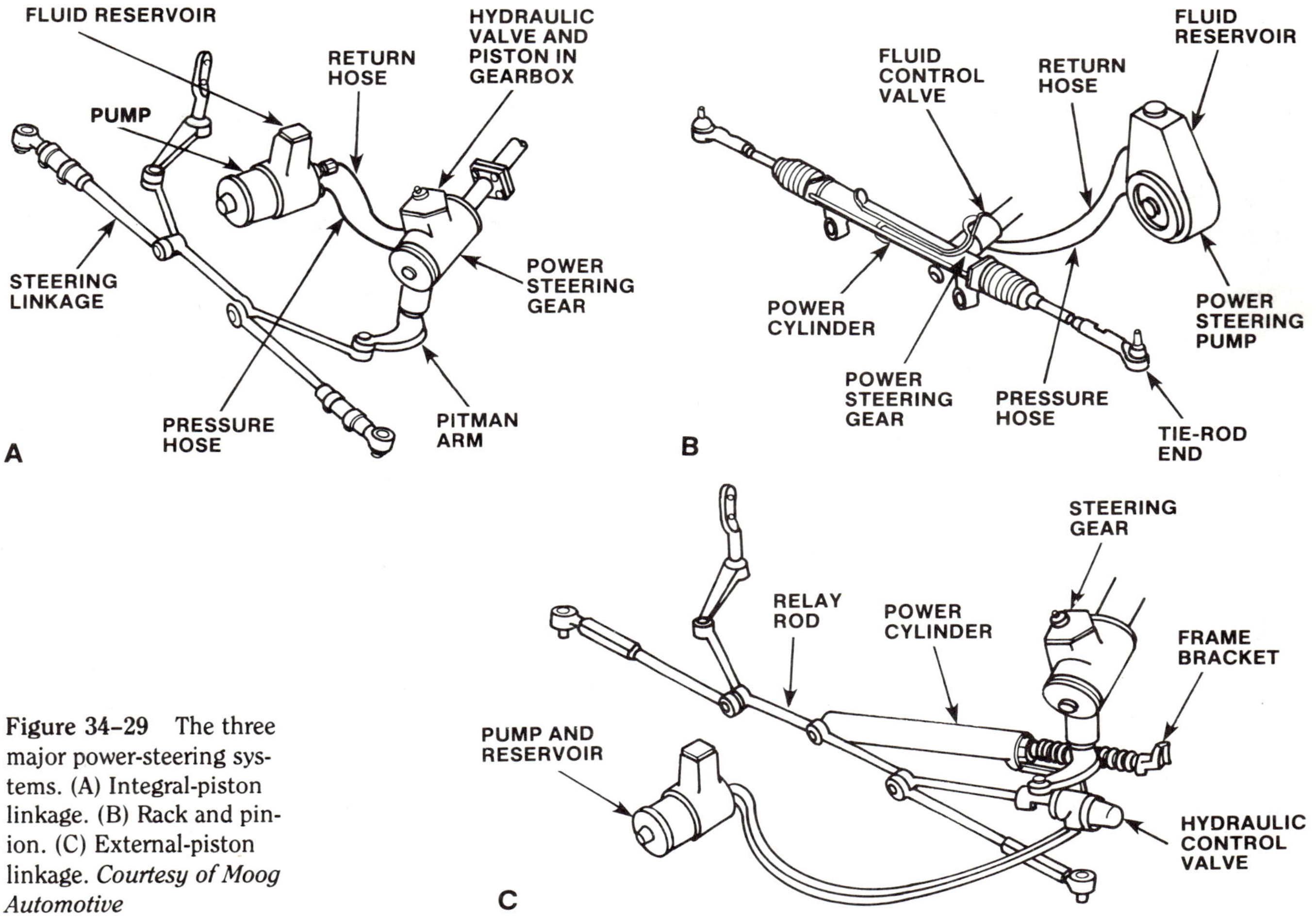

Figure 34-29 The three major power-steering systems. (A) Integral-piston linkage. (B) Rack and pinion. (C) External-piston linkage. *Courtesy of Moog Automotive*

Conventional Power Steering Systems

There are several power steering systems in use on passenger cars and light-duty trucks. The most common ones are the external-piston linkage, integral-piston, and power-assisted rack and pinion system (Figure 34-29).

External-Piston Linkage System

The external-piston linkage system, sometimes called nonintegral, is generally found on older cars. It consists of a power-steering pump and reservoir, control valve, power cylinder, and four hoses. The control valve and pressure cylinder are separate components that are not incorporated into the steering gear. The pressure hose connects the pump to the control valve and directs the pressurized fluid into the correct booster hoses to the power cylinder. The power cylinder piston provides the necessary power assistance.

Integral Piston System

The integral system is one of the most common conventional power-steering systems in use today. It consists of a power-steering pump and reservoir, power-steering pressure and return hose, and steering gear. The power cylinder and the control valve are in the same housing as the steering gear.

On some recent model cars and light trucks, instead of the conventional vacuum-assist brake booster, the hydraulic fluid from the power-steering pump is also used to actuate the brake booster. This brake system is called the hydro-boost system (Figure 34-30).

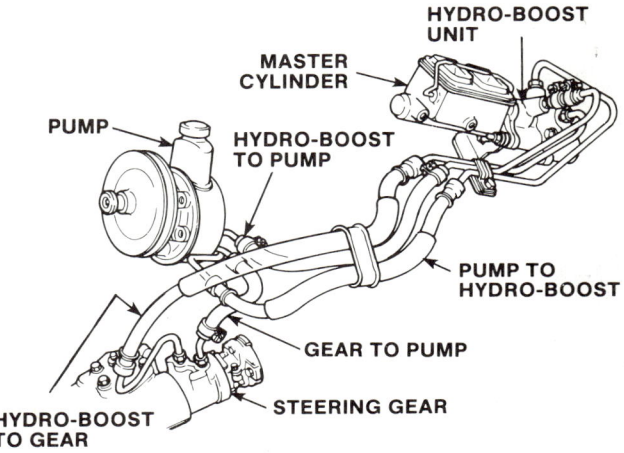

Figure 34-30 Typical hydro-boost system that uses the power-steering pump to power assist brake applications.

Power-Assisted Rack and Pinion System

The power-assisted rack and pinion system is similar to the integral system because the power cylinder and the control valve are in the same housing. The rack housing acts as the cylinder and the power piston is part of the rack. Control valve location is in the pinion housing. Turning the steering wheel moves the valve, directing pressure to either end of the rack piston. The system utilizes a pressure hose from the pump to the control valve housing and a return line to the pump reservoir. This type of steering system is common in front-wheel-drive vehicles.

Components

Several of the manual steering parts described earlier in this chapter, such as the steering linkage, are used in conventional power-steering systems. The components that have been added for power steering provide the hydraulic power that drives the system. They are the power-steering pump, flow control and pressure relief valves, reservoir, spool valves and power pistons, hydraulic hose lines, and gearbox or assist assembly on the linkage.

POWER-STEERING PUMP The steering pump is used to develop hydraulic flow, which provides the force needed to operate the steering gear. The pump is belt driven from the engine crankshaft, providing flow any time the engine is running. It is usually mounted near the front of the engine (Figure 34-31).

There are four general types of power-steering pumps: roller, vane, slipper, and gear (Figure 34-32). Functionally, all pumps operate in the same basic manner. Hydraulic fluid for the power-steering pump is stored in a reservoir. Fluid is routed to and from the pump by hoses and lines. Excessive pressure is controlled by a relief valve.

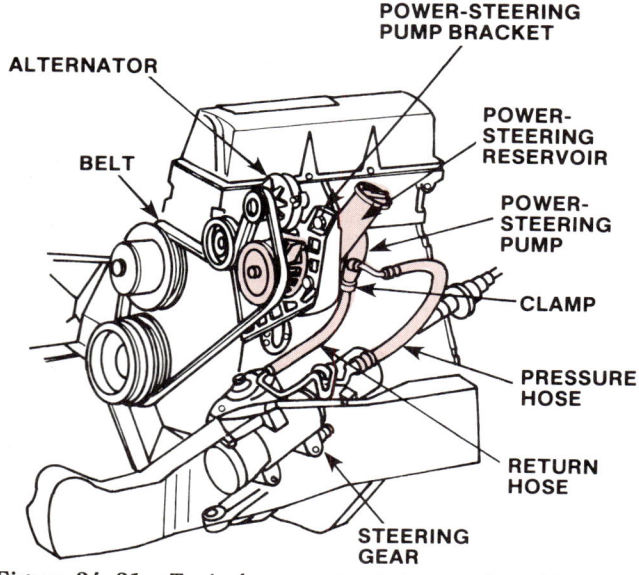

Figure 34-31 Typical power-steering pump location.

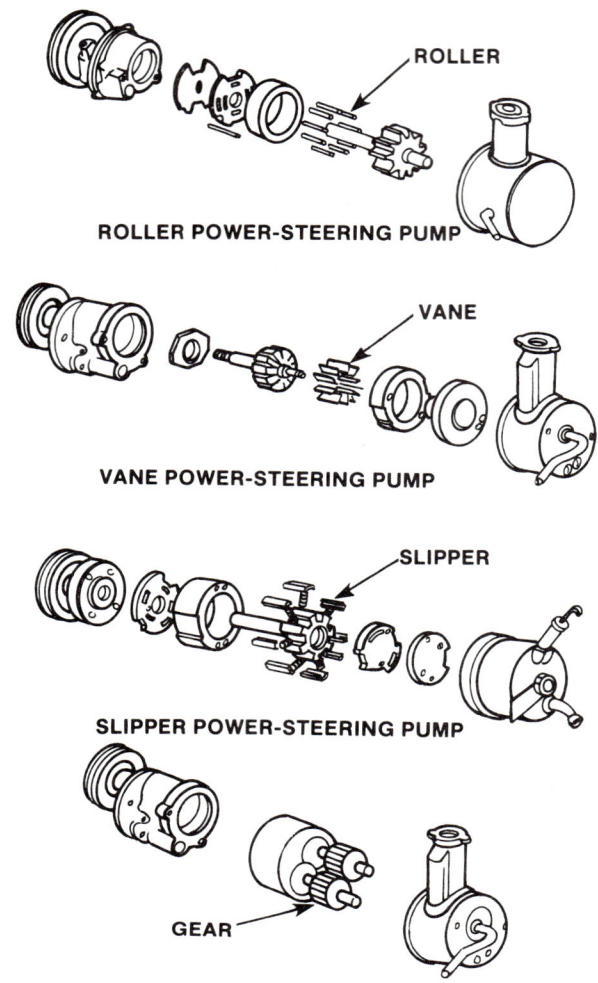

Figure 34-32 Four basic types of power-steering pumps.

FLOW CONTROL AND PRESSURE RELIEF VALVES
A pressure relief valve controls the pressure output from the pump. This valve is necessary because of the variations in engine rpm and the need for consistent steering ability in all ranges from idle to highway speeds. It is positioned in a chamber that is exposed to pump outlet pressure at one end and supply hose pressure at the other. A spring is used at the supply pressure end to help maintain a balance (Figure 34-33).

As the fluid leaves the pump rotor, it passes the end of the flow control valve and is forced through an orifice that causes a slight drop in pressure. This reduced pressure, aided by the springs, holds the flow control valve in the closed position. All pump flow is sent to the steering gear.

When engine speed increases, the pump can deliver more flow than is required to operate the system. Since the outlet orifice restricts the amount of fluid leaving the pump, the difference in pressure at the two ends of the valve becomes greater until pump outlet pressure overcomes the combined force of supply line pressure

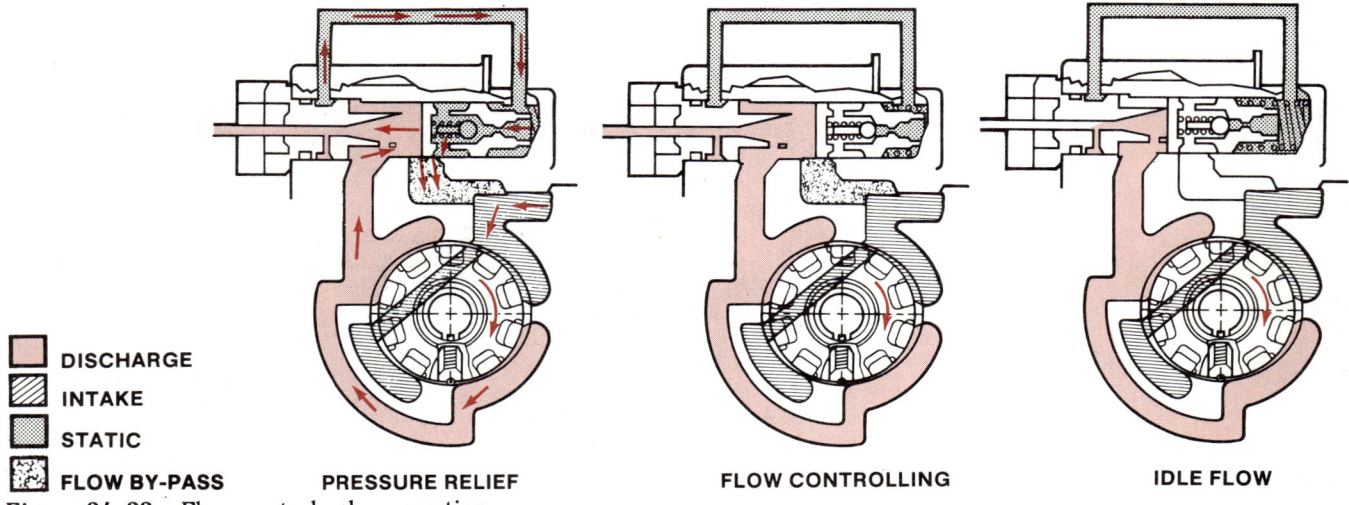

- ▨ DISCHARGE
- ▨ INTAKE
- ▨ STATIC
- ▨ FLOW BY-PASS

PRESSURE RELIEF FLOW CONTROLLING IDLE FLOW

Figure 34-33 Flow control valve operation.

and spring force. The valve is pushed down against the spring, opening a passage that returns the excess flow back to the inlet side of the pump.

A spring and ball contained inside the flow control valve are used to relieve pump outlet pressure. This is done to protect the system from damage due to excessive pressure when the steering wheel is held against the stops. Since flow in the system is severely restricted, the pump would continue to build pressure until a hose ruptured or the pump destroyed itself.

When outlet pressure reaches a preset level, the pressure relief ball is forced off its seat, creating a greater pressure differential at the two ends of the flow control valve. This allows the flow control valve to open wider, permitting more pump pressure to flow back to the pump inlet and pressure is held at a safe level.

POWER-STEERING GEARBOX A power-steering gearbox is basically the same as a manual recirculating ball gearbox with the addition of a hydraulic assist. A power-steering gearbox is filled with hydraulic fluid and uses a control valve.

In a power rack and pinion gear, the movement of the rack is assisted by hydraulic pressure. When the wheel is turned, the rotary valve changes hydraulic flow to create a pressure differential on either side of the rack. The unequal pressure causes the rack to move toward the lower pressure, reducing the effort required to turn the wheels.

The integral power steering has the spool valve and a power piston integrated with the gearbox. The spool valve directs the oil pressure to the left or right power chamber to steer the vehicle. The spool valve is actuated by a lever (Figure 34-34) or a small torsion bar (Figure 34-35).

In linkage systems, the control valve is connected directly to the steering center link and the pitman arm on the steering gear. Any movement of the steering wheel and the pitman arm compresses the centering spring and moves the valve spool. This opens and closes a series of ports directing fluid under pressure from the pump to one side, or the other, of the power cylinder piston.

The power cylinder in the linkage system is attached to the steering center link and the piston shaft is attached to the frame. As fluid under pressure is directed to one side of the piston by the control valve, power assist is provided to aid the driver in moving the steering linkage and road wheels. Two lines connect the cylinder to the control valve. Each one functions as both return line or supply line, depending on the direction of the turn.

POWER-ASSISTED RACK AND PINION STEERING Power-assisted rack and pinion components are basically the same as for manual rack and pinion steering, except for the hydraulic control housing. As mentioned earlier, the power rack and pinion steering unit may be classified as integral. The rack functions as the power piston and the spool valve is connected to the pinion gear.

In a power rack and pinion gear the piston is mounted on the rack, inside the rack housing. The rack housing is sealed on either side of the rack piston to form two separate hydraulic chambers for the left and right turn circuits. When the wheel is turned to the right, the rotary valve creates a pressure differential on either side of the rack piston. This causes the rack to move toward the lower pressure and reduces the total effort required to turn the wheels. Movement of the rack during a left and right turn is shown in Figure 34-36.

POWER-STEERING HOSES The primary purpose of power-steering hoses is to transmit power (fluid under pressure) from the pump, to the steering gearbox, and to return the fluid ultimately to the pump reservoir.

864 Section 7 Suspensions

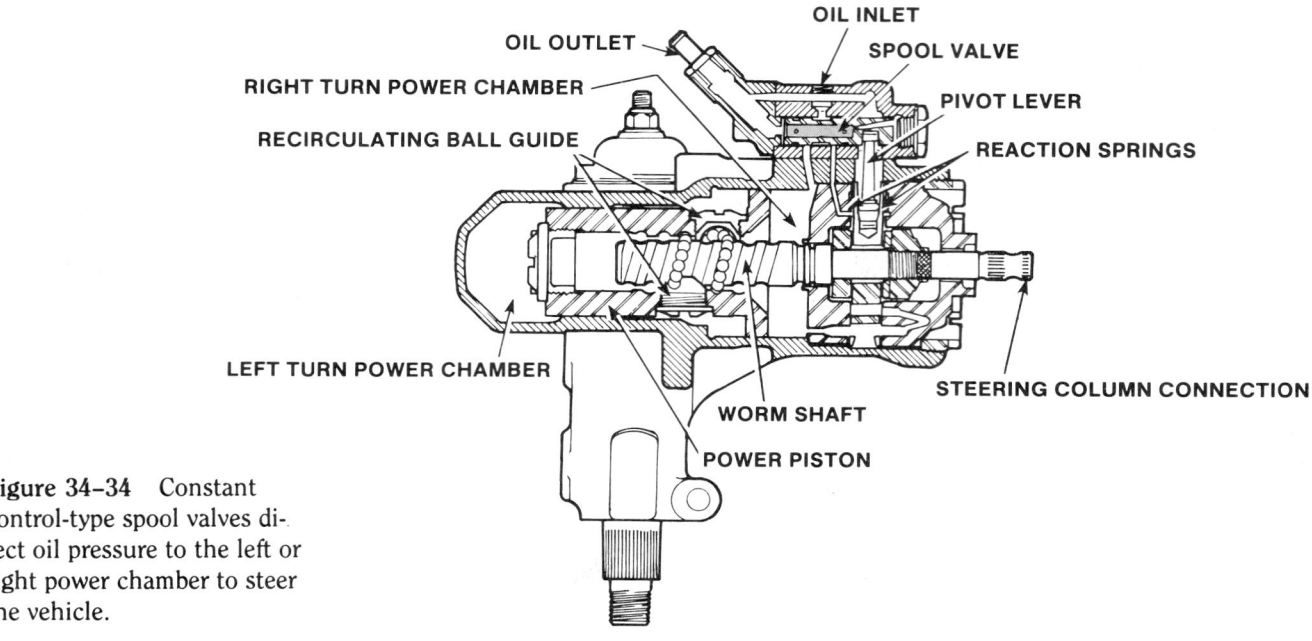

Figure 34-34 Constant control-type spool valves direct oil pressure to the left or right power chamber to steer the vehicle.

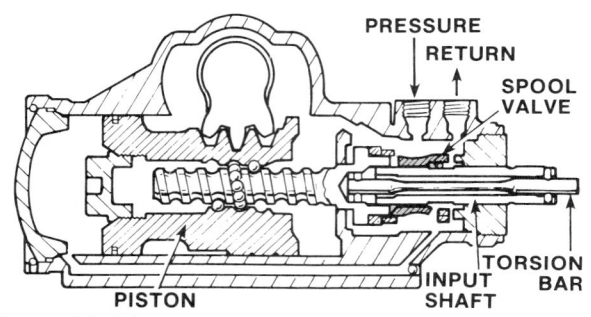

Figure 34-35 Torsion bar moves the spool valve to direct the oil flow to the piston.

Hoses also, through material and construction, function as additional reservoirs and act as sound and vibration dampers.

Hoses are generally a reinforced synthetic rubber material coupled to metal tubing at the connecting points. The pressure side must be able to handle pressures up to 1,500 psi. For that reason, wherever there is a metal tubing to a rubber connection, the connection is crimped. Pressure hoses are also subject to surges in pressure and pulsations from the pump. The reinforced construction permits the hose to expand slightly and absorb changes in pressure.

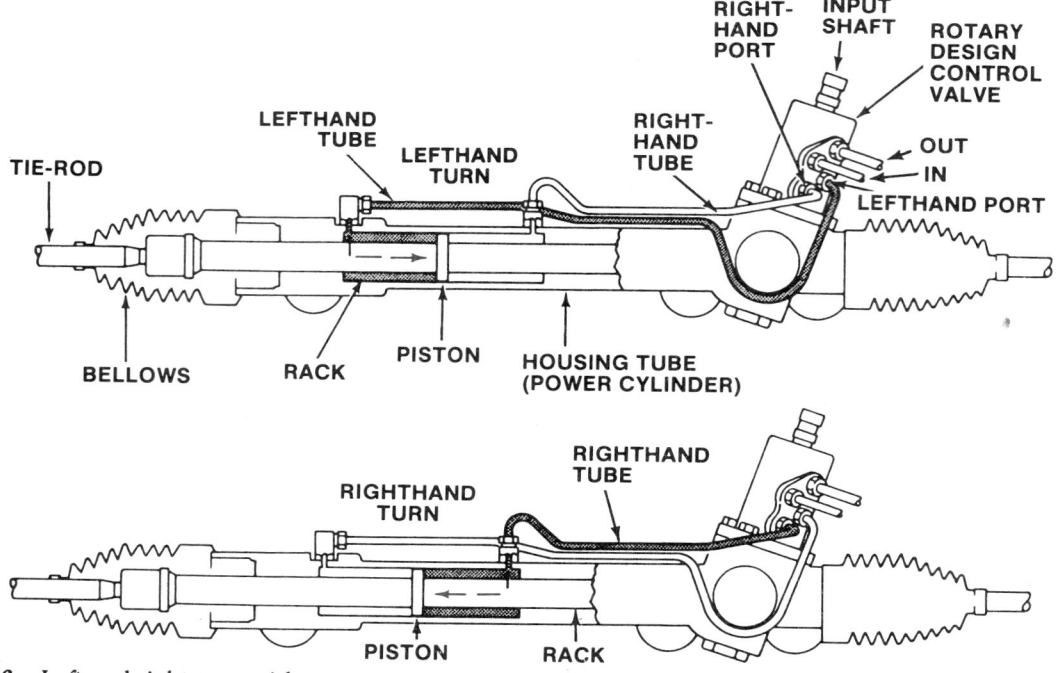

Figure 34-36 Left and right turn with power-assisted rack and pinion system. *Courtesy of Ford Motor Co.*

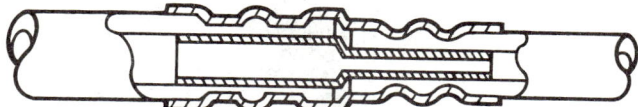

Figure 34-37 Power-steering hoses may have two internal diameters.

Where two diameters of hose (Figure 34-37) are used on the pressure side, the larger diameter or pressure hose is at the pump end. It acts as a reservoir and as an accumulator absorbing pulsations. The smaller diameter or return hose reduces the effects of kickback from the gear itself. By restricting fluid flow, it also maintains constant back pressure on the pump, which reduces pump noise. If the hose is of one diameter, the gearbox is performing the damping functions internally.

Because of working fluid temperature and adjacent engine temperatures, these hoses must be able to withstand temperatures up to 300 degrees Fahrenheit. Due to various weather conditions, they must also tolerate subzero temperatures as well. Hose material is specially formulated to resist breakdown or deterioration due to oil or temperature conditions.

CAUTION: Hoses must be carefully routed away from engine manifolds. Power-steering fluid is very flammable. If it comes in contact with hot engine parts, it could start an underhood fire.

❏ POWER-STEERING DIAGNOSIS

Because there are so many different factors that can affect a vehicle's steering, proper diagnostics is vital for locating the exact cause of a condition without performing unnecessary tests or repairs. By eliminating the simple or obvious items first, it is possible to pinpoint the condition quickly and accurately (Figure 34-38).

The first step in the diagnostic process is a thorough visual inspection. Make notes of anything that appears abnormal such as tire inflation, size, match, and general condition. Inspect the power-steering belts and hoses. Give the steering linkage special attention. In most cases an owner's concerns related to steering prove to be something relatively minor and rarely involves the steering gear or pump.

Check the fluid level in the reservoir after the engine has been run at idle for two or three minutes and the wheel has been cycled from lock to lock several times. This warms the fluid to its normal operating temperature and gives a more accurate reading.

Examine the condition of the fluid carefully. Check for evidence of contamination such as solid particles or water. If either of these conditions are present or the fluid has a burnt odor, the system should be flushed before returning to service.

If in the course of the inspection a defect is found, do not correct it until after the road test. Doing so could change the condition and make final diagnosis more difficult. The obvious exception to this would be a condition such as broken linkage or other conditions that would make driving the vehicle hazardous.

After the visual inspection is completed, a road test is necessary to verify the owner's concern. It is very important that during the road test the vehicle is driven under conditions similar to the owner's normal driving. While it may be somewhat inconvenient to seek out a particular type of road surface, this may be the only way to verify the condition. Take plenty of time since it could save hours of service time in the final diagnosis.

Once the road test has been completed and it has been determined there is an abnormal condition, certain tests are necessary to pinpoint the exact cause. In some cases partial disassembly of the system may be required to complete a test. Do not shortcut test steps to save time. Doing so can alter the results, leading to an inaccurate diagnosis and unnecessary replacement of parts. It is also vital that specifications be confirmed in the service manual. Guessing yields incorrect results.

❏ GENERAL CONVENTIONAL POWER-STEERING SYSTEM CHECKS

The steering linkage operates as a system. All components between the tires and the steering wheel can affect the way a vehicle steers. It may be that the problem is not related to the power-steering system. Therefore, first make the following checks.

TIRES Check for correct pressure, construction, size, wear, and damage, and for defects to include ply separations, sidewall knots, concentricity problems, and force problems.

TIRE AND WHEEL ASSEMBLY Check for radial and lateral runout, static, and dynamic imbalance.

WHEEL BEARINGS Check for correct adjustment.

STEERING AND SUSPENSION PIVOTS Check for wear, looseness or tightness, physical damage, and lubrication.

STEERING GEARBOX Check for loose mounting bolts and for internal maladjustment.

ALIGNMENT (FRONT AND REAR) Check for correct caster, camber, toe, toe-out on turns (turning radius), and chassis height.

When all other areas have been checked and the power-steering system is still suspect, the following checks should be made.

BELT CONDITION AND TENSION If the belt shows evidence of cracking or glazing, it should be replaced.

866 Section 7 Suspensions

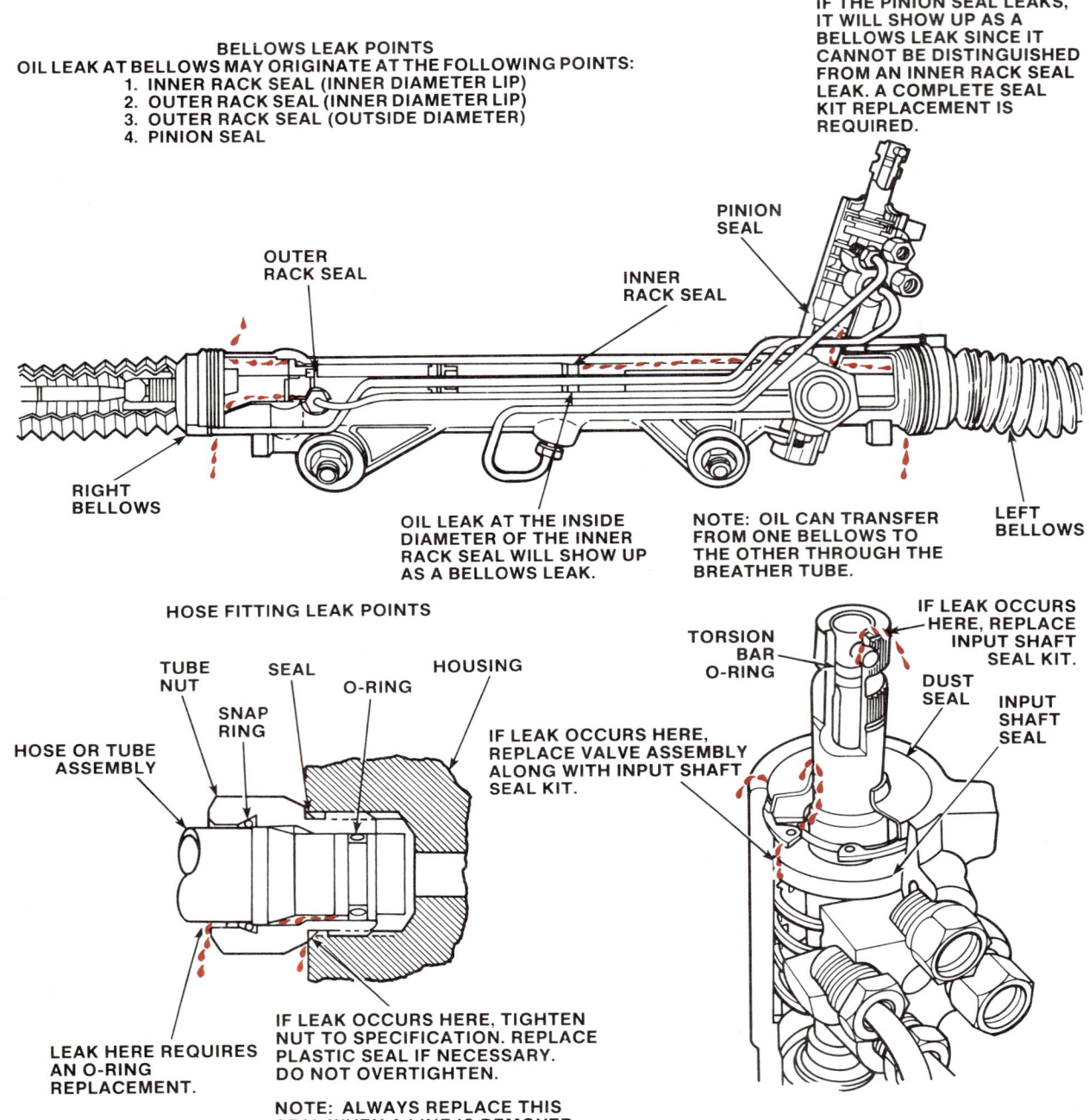

Figure 34-38 Possible leakage points on power-steering systems.

Adjust belt tension according to service manual instructions and specifications.

FLUID LEVEL The fluid is checked at the pump reservoir with a dipstick attached to the reservoir cap. However, it is not simply a matter of pulling the cap and reading the dipstick, so follow the manufacturer's procedure.

FLUID LEAKS Clean the suspected area, then cycle the wheel from lock to lock several times. If no signs of linkage are apparent, repeat the wheel cycling process and inspection several more times. Consult the appropriate section of the service manual for detailed information about the action necessary to correct any leaks.

TURNING EFFORT If an owner's concern indicates excessive turning effort, a pull scale should be used to read the actual force required to turn the wheel (Figure 34-39). Compare the test results to the specifications in the service manual. If the effort exceeds the maximum, carefully inspect the entire steering system before performing a pressure test.

TIE-ROD ARTICULATION EFFORT The effort required to move the tie-rod on its inner ball socket

Steering Systems and Wheel Alignment   867

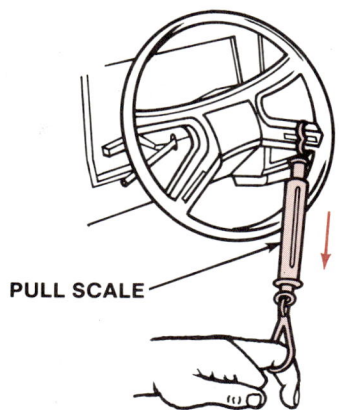

Figure 34-39 A pull scale is used to measure steering effort.

should be checked with a pull scale if excessive steering effort or looseness is noted during the road test. If the effort is not within the specified limits, the tie-rod must be replaced.

AIR IN THE SYSTEM Air in the system is usually determined during a fluid level check. If the fluid looks foamy, it is likely that air is in the system. The method of bleeding depends on the type of power-steering system. Follow the service manual procedure.

ADEQUATE PRESSURE If the preliminary tests indicate the possibility of an internal pump or gear malfunction, a steering system analyzer (Figure 34-40) provides an accurate method for evaluating the pump, rotary valve, and internal seals. The analyzer provides a direct readout of base pump pressure and flow, pump relief pressure, and steering gear seal integrity. Check the system's pressure following manufacturer's instructions.

❏ POWER-STEERING SYSTEM SERVICING

Vehicles with power-steering systems have the same types of steering linkage as manual steering. The power-steering linkage is checked and serviced as previously described. Actually, the only difference is the servicing of the hydraulic components such as the hoses, pump, and power-steering gear that are fully covered in the vehicle's service manual.

❏ ELECTRONICALLY CONTROLLED POWER-STEERING SYSTEMS

The object of power steering is to make steering easier at low speeds, especially while parking. However, higher steering efforts are desirable at higher speeds in order to provide improved down-the-road feel. The electronically controlled power-steering (EPS) systems provide both of these benefits. The hydraulic boost of these systems is tapered off by electronic control as road speed increases. Thus, these systems require well under 1 pound of steering effort at low road speeds and 3 pounds plus of steering effort at higher road speeds to enable the driver to maintain control of the steering wheel for improved high-speed handling.

Presently, true electronically controlled power-steering systems appear primarily on imported cars. One of the more popular systems uses a by-pass flow control valve in the hydraulic line (Figure 34-41). Central to this system is the speed at which the steering wheel is being turned.

A rotary valve electronic power-steering system consists of the power-steering gearbox, power-steering oil pump, pressure hose, and the return hose.

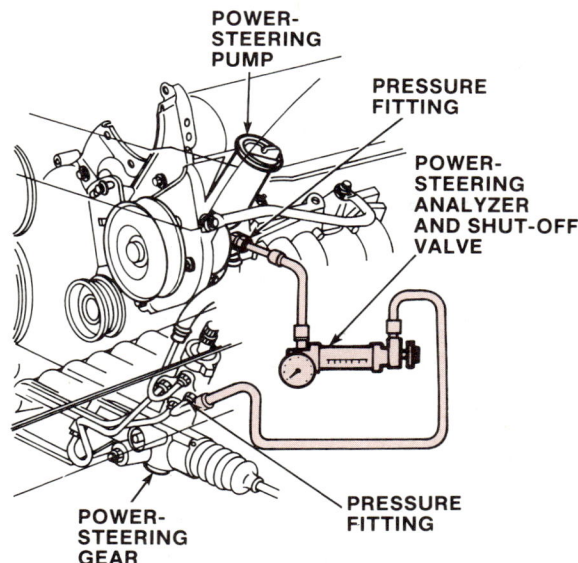

Figure 34-40 Typical power steering analyzer hookup.

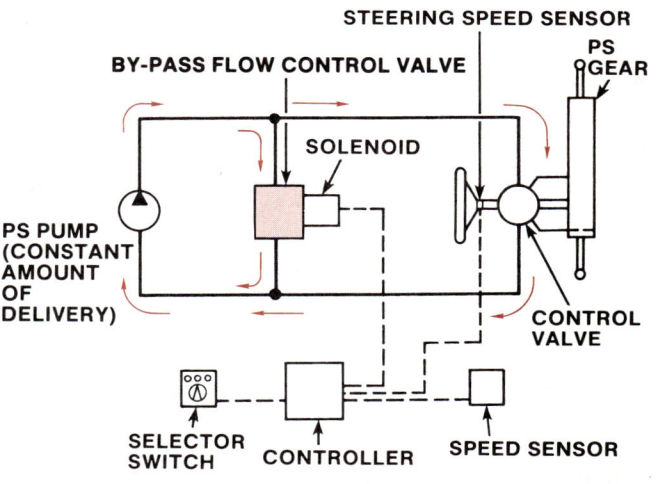

Figure 34-41 By-pass flow control valve in hydraulic line. *Courtesy of Nissan Corp.*

868 Section 7 Suspensions

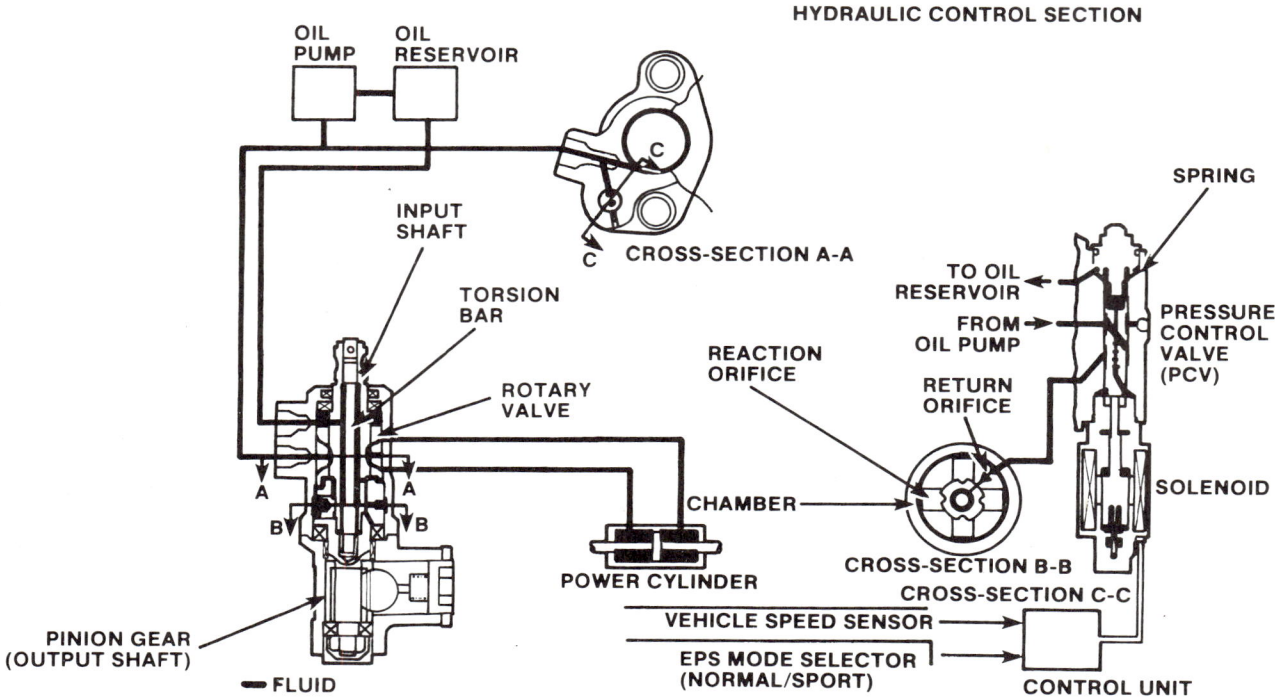

Figure 34-42 Outline of electronic power steering components. EPS PCV is exposed to spring tension and plunger force. *Courtesy of Mitsubishi Motor Sales of America, Inc.*

The amount of hydraulic fluid flow (pressure) used to boost steering is controlled by a solenoid valve that is identified as its PCV (pressure control valve).

> **SHOP TALK**
>
> The PCV (pressure control valve) is not to be confused with the PCV (positive crankcase ventilator) used with emission controls systems.

The electronic power steering (EPS) system's PCV (Figure 34-42) is exposed to spring tension on the top and plunger force on the bottom. The plunger slips inside an electromagnet. By varying the electrical current to the electromagnet, the upward force exerted by the plunger can be varied as it works against the opposing spring. Current flow to the electromagnet is variable with vehicle road speed and, therefore, provides steering to match the vehicle's road speed.

When servicing, as with any power-steering system, the first step is to look for fluid leaks, damaged components, a slipping drive belt, and so on. Only after these things have been checked and no problems have been found should the electronics be suspected as the problem. Check the appropriate service manual for the correct troubleshooting procedures of the electronics.

Electric/Electronic Rack and Pinion System

The electric/electronic rack and pinion unit replaces the hydraulic pump, hoses, and fluid associated with conventional power-steering systems with electronic controls and an electric motor located concentric to the rack itself (Figure 34-43). The design features a DC motor armature with a hollow shaft to allow passage of the rack through it (Figure 34-44). The outboard housing and rack are designed so that the rotary motion of the armature can be transferred to linear movement of the rack through a ball nut with thrust bearings. The armature is mechanically connected to the ball nut through an internal/external spline arrangement.

Essentially, the heart of the system is its ability to change the rotational direction of the electric motor, while being able to deliver the necessary amount of current to meet torque requirements at the same time. The system can deliver up to 75 amperes to the motor.

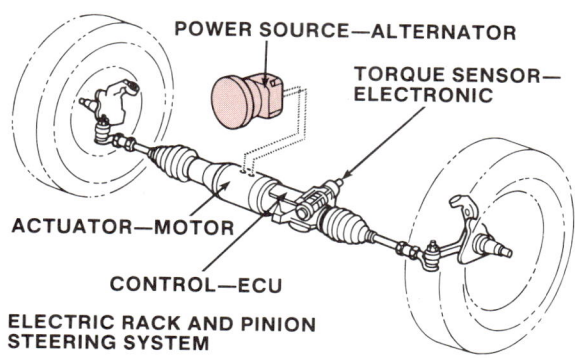

Figure 34-43 The alternator in an electronically-driven power rack and pinion system becomes the power source replacing the hydraulic pump of conventional systems.

Steering Systems and Wheel Alignment

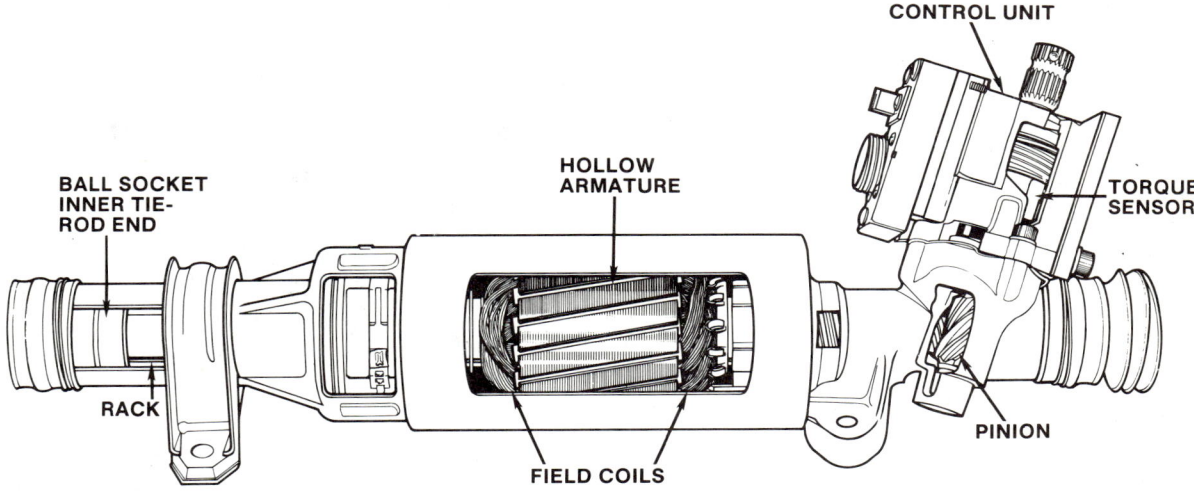

Figure 34-44 Electric/electronic rack and pinion system.

The higher the current, the greater the force exerted on the rack. The direction of the turn is controlled by changing the polarity of the signal to the motor.

The field assembly houses permanent ceramic magnets while providing structural integrity for the gear system. In essence, the electronic/electric rack design allows for a direct power source to the rack and steering linkage. The system monitors steering wheel movement through a sensor mounted on the input shaft of the rack and pinion steering gear. After receiving directional and load information from the sensor, an electronic controller activates the motor to provide power assistance.

These units are readily retrofitted to conventionally equipped vehicles. As for servicing, there are currently no replacement parts available, therefore, if the rack should become faulty, the entire unit should be replaced. Rebuilt kits, with complete installation instructions, are planned for the near future.

Unlike conventional power steering, electric/electronic units provide power assistance even when the engine stalls, since the power source is the battery rather than the engine driven pump. The feel of the steering can also be adjusted to match the particular driving characteristics of cars and drivers, from high performance to luxury touring cars. It also eliminates hydraulic oil, which means no leaks.

☐ FOUR-WHEEL STEERING SYSTEM

Four-wheel independent suspensions have been around for years and continue to be an important part of the automotive industry. Now the industry is offering four-wheel independent steering systems, where the rear wheels also help to turn the car by electrical, hydraulic, or mechanical means. Because these systems are going to be more common in the future, the automotive technician should be aware of them.

Production-built cars tend to understeer or, in a few instances, oversteer. If a car could automatically compensate for an understeer/oversteer problem, the driver would enjoy nearly neutral steering under varying operating conditions. Four-wheel steering (4WS) is a serious effort on the part of automotive design engineers to provide near-neutral steering with the following advantages.

CORNERING CAPABILITY The vehicle's cornering behavior becomes more stable and controllable at high speeds as well as on wet or slippery road surfaces (Figure 34-45).

STEERING RESPONSE The vehicle's response to steering input becomes quicker and more precise throughout the vehicle's entire speed range.

STRAIGHT-LINE STABILITY The vehicle's straight-line stability at high speeds is improved. Negative effects of road irregularities and crosswinds on the vehicle's stability are minimized.

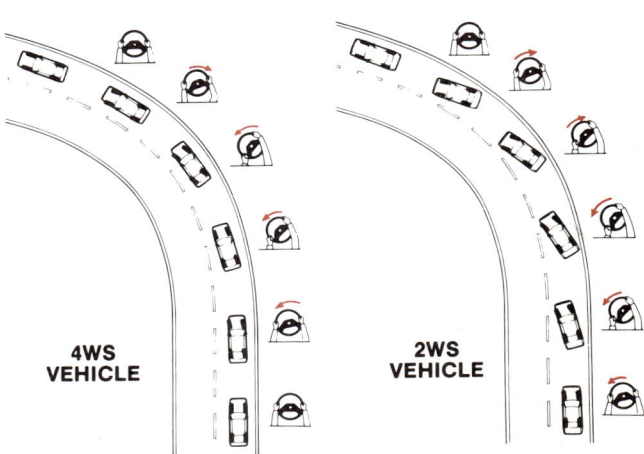

Figure 34-45 Comparison of 2WS and 4WS vehicle behavior during cornering.

LANE CHANGING Stability in lane changing at high speeds is improved. High-speed slalom-type operations become easier. The vehicle becomes less likely to go into a spin even in situations when the driver must make a sudden and relatively large change of direction.

LOW-SPEED MANEUVERABILITY By steering the rear wheels in the direction opposite the front wheels at low speeds, the vehicle's turning circle is greatly reduced. Therefore, vehicle maneuvering on narrow roads and during parking becomes easier.

To understand the advantages of four-wheel steering, it is wise to review the dynamics of typical steering maneuvers with a conventional front-steered vehicle. The tires are subject to the forces of grip, momentum, and steering input when making a movement other than straight-ahead driving. These forces compete with each other during steering manuevers. With a front-steered vehicle, the rear end is always trying to catch up to the directional changes of the front wheels. This causes the vehicle to sway. As a normal part of operating a vehicle, the driver learns to adjust to these forces without thinking about them.

When turning, the driver is putting into motion a complex series of forces. Each of these must be balanced against the others. The tires are subjected to road grip and slip angle. Grip holds the car's wheels to the road, and momentum moves the car straight ahead. Steering input causes the front wheels to turn. The car momentarily resists the turning motion, causing a tire slip angle to form (Figure 34-46). Once the vehicle begins to respond to the steering input, cornering forces are generated. The vehicle sways as the rear wheels attempt to keep up with the cornering forces already generated by the front tires. This is referred to as rear-end lag, because there is a time delay between steering input and vehicle reaction. When the front wheels are turned back to a straight-ahead position, the vehicle must again try to adjust by reversing the same forces developed by the turn. As the steering is turned, the vehicle body sways as the rear wheels again try to keep up with the cornering forces generated by the front wheels.

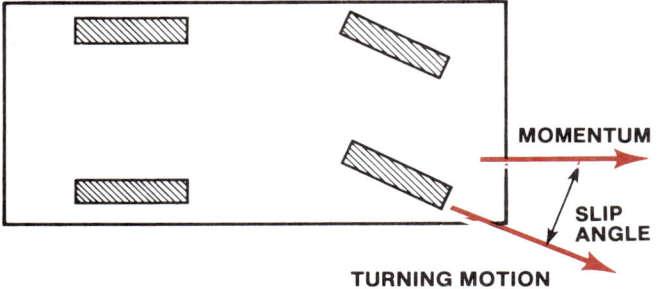

Figure 34-46 When a turn is initiated with front steering, the momentum wants to move the car forward while the steering input causes a directional change. This creates a tire slip angle as the vehicle momentarily resists turning.

The idea behind four-wheel steering is that a vehicle requires less driver input for any steering maneuver if all four wheels are steering the vehicle. As with two-wheel-steer vehicles, tire grip holds the four wheels on the road. However, when the driver turns the wheel slightly, all four wheels react to the steering input, causing slip angles to form at all four wheels. The entire vehicle moves in one direction rather than the rear half attempting to catch up to the front. There is also less sway when the wheels are turned back to a straight-ahead position. The vehicle responds more quickly to steering input because rear wheel lag is eliminated.

Currently, there are three types of production four-wheel-steering systems: mechanical, hydraulic, and electro/hydraulic designs. Since each system is unique in its construction and repair needs, the vehicle's service manual must be followed for proper diagnosis, repair, and alignment of a four-wheel system.

Mechanical 4WS

In a straight-mechanical type of 4WS, two steering gears are used—one for the front and the other for the rear wheels. A steel shaft connects the two steering gearboxes. Conventional steering linkage is used fore and aft. But, the heart of the system is the double crank. The shaft that runs from the forward steering gearbox to the rear steering gearbox terminates at an eccentric shaft. This shaft is fitted with an offset pin (Figure 34-47). This pin engages a second offset pin that fits into a planetary gear.

The planetary gear meshes with the matching teeth of an internal gear. The internal gear is secured in a fixed position to the gearbox housing. This means that the planetary gear can rotate but the internal gear cannot. The eccentric pin of the planetary gear fits into a hole in the slider that is part of the stroke rod.

A 120-degree turn of the steering wheel rotates the planetary gear to move the slider and stroke rod in the same direction that the front wheels are headed. Proportionately, the rear wheels turn the steering wheel about 1.5 to 10 degrees (Figure 34-48). Further rotation of the steering wheel, past the 120-degree point, causes the rear wheels to start straightening out due to the double-crank action (two eccentric pins) and rotation of the planetary gear. Turning the steering wheel to a greater angle, about 230 degrees, finds the rear wheels in a neutral position regarding the front wheels. Further rotation of the steering wheel results in the rear wheels going counterphase with regard to the front wheels. About 5.3 degrees maximum counterphase rear steering is possible.

Because front and rear steering systems are linked together mechanically, it stands to reason that when the front wheels are turned to make a caster check, the rear wheels are going to move as well. The same is true for checking toe out on turns.

Steering Systems and Wheel Alignment 871

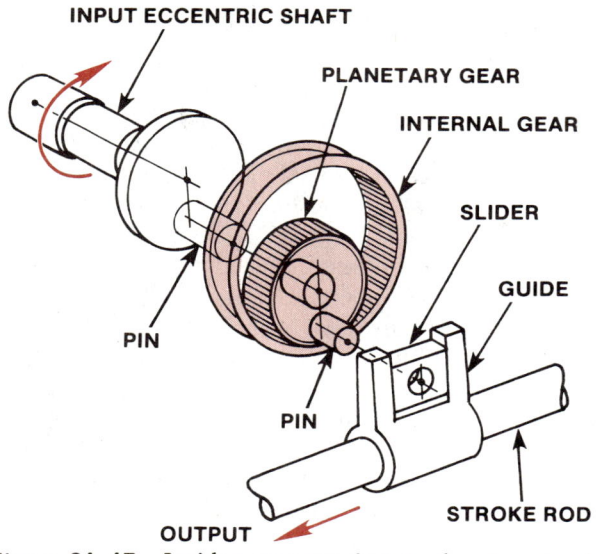

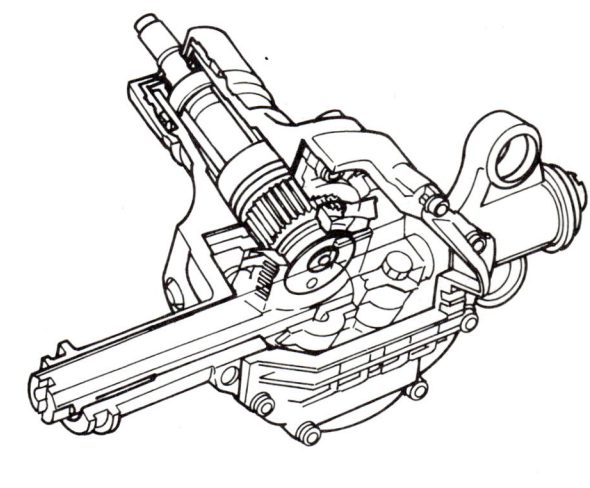

Figure 34-47 Inside a rear-steering gearbox is a simple planetary gear setup. *Courtesy of Honda Motor Corp.*

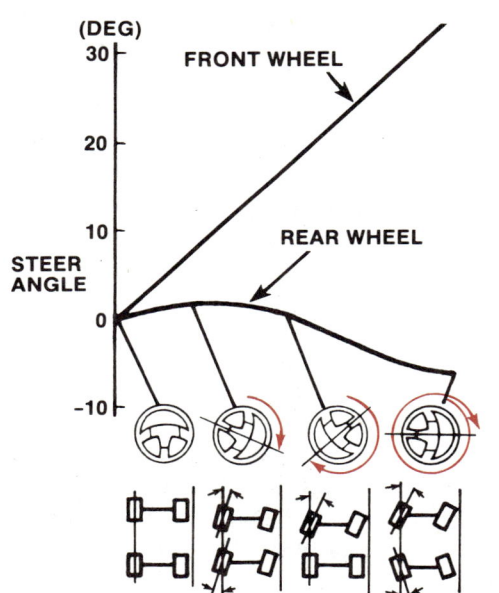

Figure 34-48 The steer angle of the rear wheels compared to the angle of the front wheels. *Courtesy of Honda Motor Corp.*

This setup makes it mandatory for all four wheels to rest on turntables or full-floating slip plates to prevent the car from crabbing to one side or the other as the front wheels are turned during wheel alignment.

Mechanical 4WS is steering angle sensitive. It is not sensitive to vehicle road speed.

Hydraulic 4WS

The hydraulically operated four-wheel-steering system shown in Figure 34-49 is a simple design, both in components and operation.

In this system, the rear wheels turn only in the same direction as the front wheel. They also turn no more than 1-1/2 degrees. The system does not use electronic sensors, a computer control module, or advanced gear-

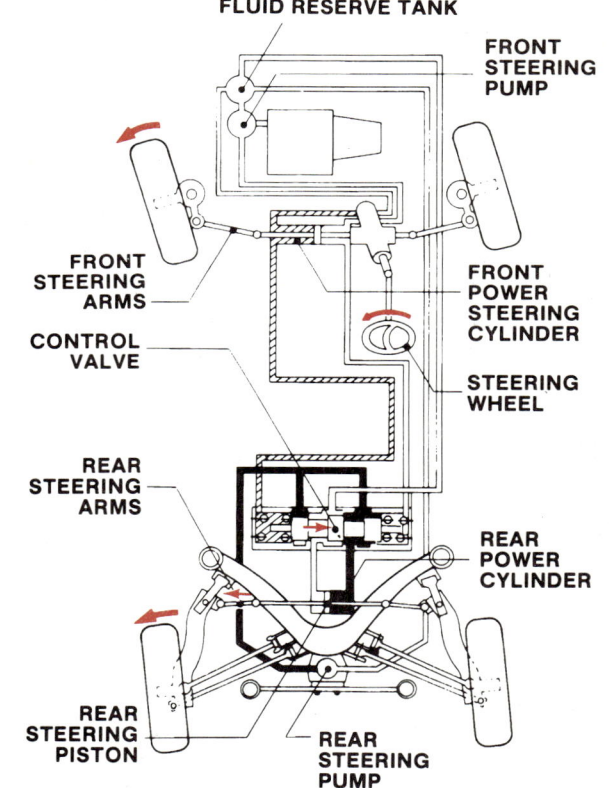

Figure 34-49 Simple hydraulic 4WS system. *Courtesy of Mitsubishi Motor Corp.*

ing mechanisms. This system only activates at speeds above 30 mph. It does not operate when the vehicle moves in reverse.

A two-way hydraulic cylinder mounted on the rear stub frame turns the wheels. Fluid for this cylinder is supplied by a rear steering pump that is driven by the differential. The pump only operates when the front wheels are turning. A tank in the engine compartment supplies the rear steering pump with fluid.

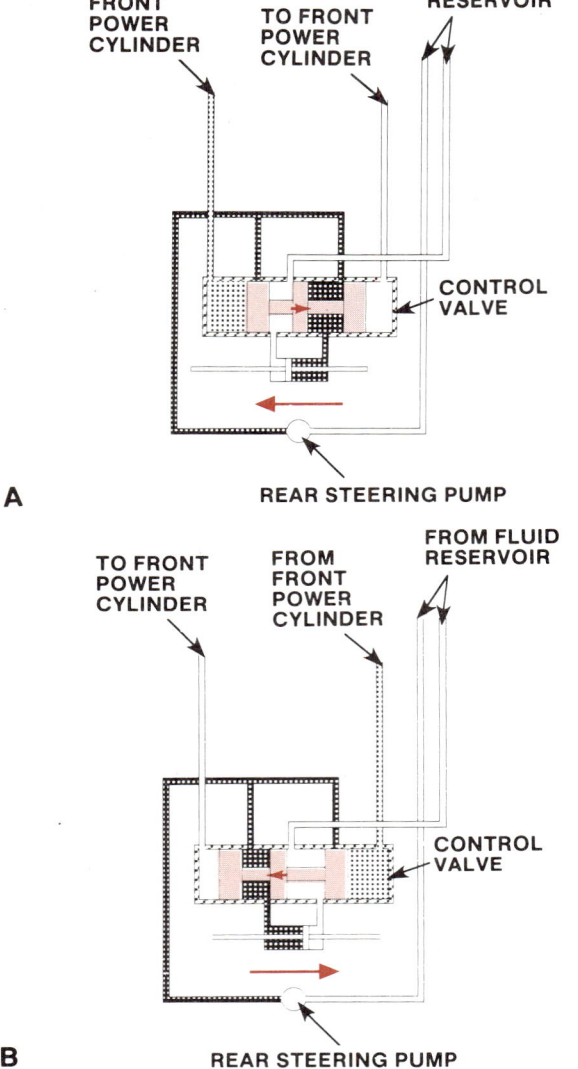

Figure 34-50 Control valve/rear steering power cylinder fluid flow for (A) left turn and (B) right turn.

When the steering wheel is turned, the front steering pump sends fluid under pressure to the rotary valve in the front rack and pinion unit. This forces fluid into the front power cylinder, and the front wheels turn in the direction steered. The fluid pressure varies with the turning of the steering wheel. The faster and farther the steering wheel is turned, the greater the fluid pressure.

The fluid is also fed under the same pressure, to the control valve where it opens a spool valve in the control valve housing (Figure 34-50). As the spool valve moves, it allows fluid from the rear steering pump to move through and operate the rear power cylinder. The higher the pressure on the spool, the farther it moves. The farther it moves, the more fluid it allows through to move the rear wheels. As mentioned earlier, this system limits rear wheel movement to 1-1/2 degrees in either the left or right direction.

Electro/Hydraulic 4WS

Several 4WS systems combine computer electronic controls with hydraulics to make the system sensitive to both steering angle and road speeds. The system shown in Figure 34-51 consists of two hydraulic pumps, a reserve tank, solenoid valve, steering angle sensor, controller (ECU), cutoff valve, vehicle speed sensor, and the power cylinder.

In this design, the speed sensor and the steering wheel angle sensor feed information to the electronic control unit (ECU). By processing the information received, the ECU commands the hydraulic system to steer the rear wheels. At low road speed, the rear wheels of this system are not considered a dynamic factor in the steering process.

At moderate road speeds, the rear wheels are steered momentarily counterphase, through neutral, then in phase with the front wheels. At high road speeds, the rear wheels turn only in phase with the front wheels.

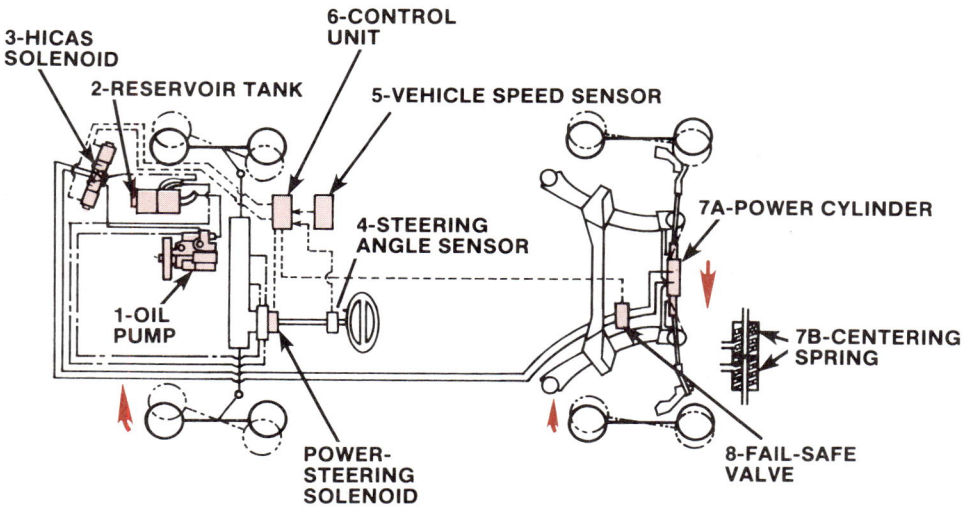

Figure 34-51 Electro/hydraulic 4WS system using an electrically controlled power cylinder. *Courtesy of Nissan Corp.*

Steering Systems and Wheel Alignment 873

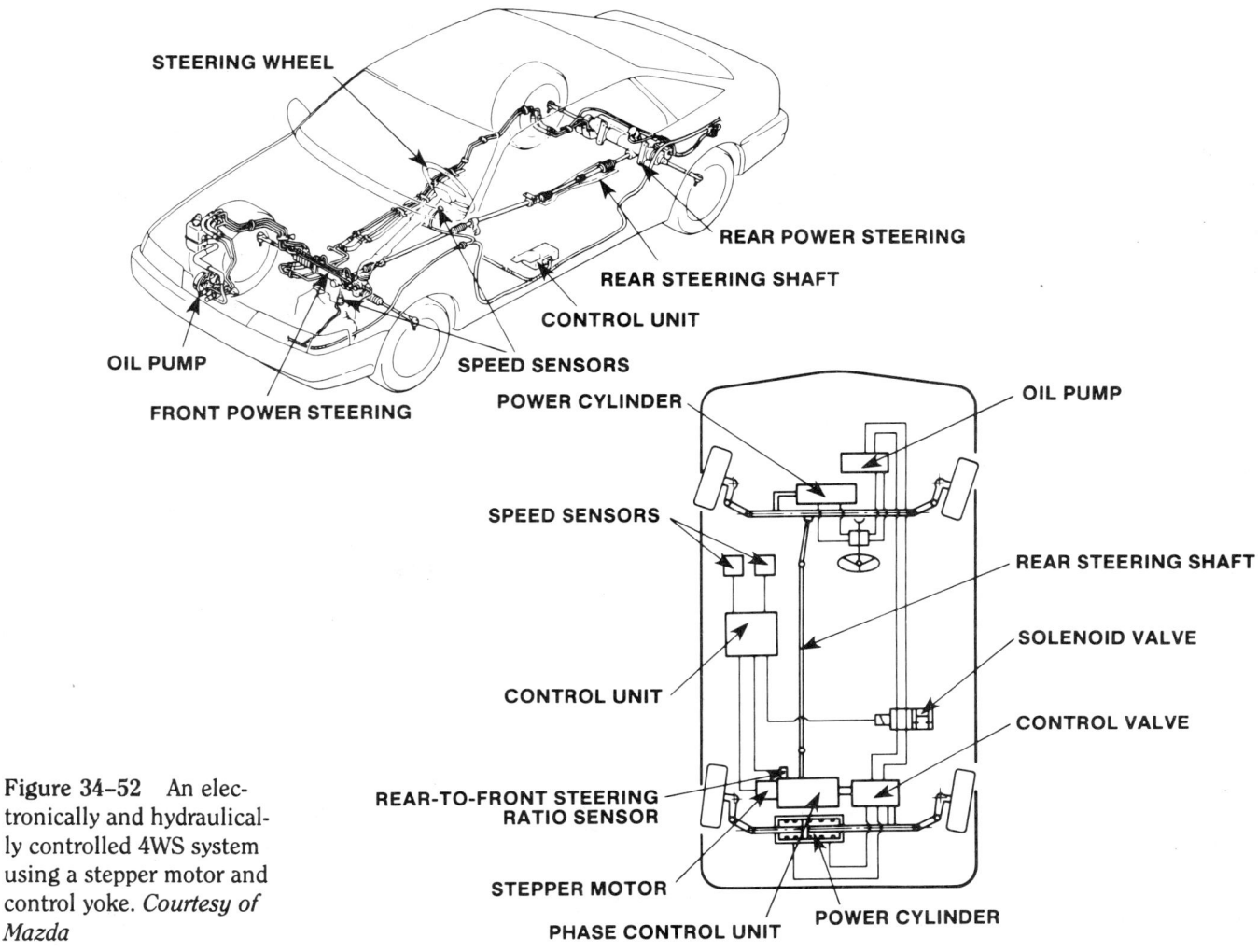

Figure 34-52 An electronically and hydraulically controlled 4WS system using a stepper motor and control yoke. *Courtesy of Mazda*

The ECU must know not only road speed, but also how much and how quickly the steering wheel is turned.

These three factors—road speed, amount of steering wheel turn, and the quickness of the steering wheel turn—are interpreted by the ECU to maintain continuous and desired steering angle of the rear wheels.

A second electro/hydraulic 4WS system is shown in Figure 34-52. The basic working elements of the design are the control unit, a stepper motor, a swing arm, a set of beveled gears, a control rod and a control valve with an output rod. Two electronic sensors tell the ECU how fast the car is going.

The control yoke is a major mechanical component of this electro/hydraulic design. The position of the control yoke varies with vehicle road speed. For example, at speeds below 22 mph, the yoke is in its downward position, which results in the rear wheels steering in the counterphase (opposite front wheels) direction. As road speeds approach and exceed 22 mph, the control yoke swings up through a neutral (horizontal) position to an up position. In the neutral position, there is no rear-wheel steer. In the yoke-up position, the rear wheels steer in phase with the front wheels.

The stepper motor moves the control yoke. A swing arm is attached to the control yoke. The position of the yoke determines the arc of the swing rod. The arc of the swing arm is transmitted through a control arm that passes through a large bevel gear. Stepper motor action eventually causes a push-or-pull movement of its output shaft to steer the rear wheels up to a maximum 5 degrees in either direction.

The electronically controlled, four-wheel steering system regulates the angle and direction of the rear wheels in response to speed and driver's steering. This speed-sensing system optimizes the vehicle's dynamic characteristics at any speed, thereby, producing enhanced stability and, within certain parameters, agility.

The actual 4WS system consists of a rack and pinion front steering that is hydraulically powered by a main twin-tandem pump. The system also has a rear steering mechanism, hydraulically powered by the main pump. The rear-steering shaft extends from the rack bar of the front steering assembly to the rear steering-phase control unit (Figure 34-53).

The rear steering is comprised of the input end of the rear-steering shaft, vehicle speed sensors, a steer-

874 Section 7 Suspensions

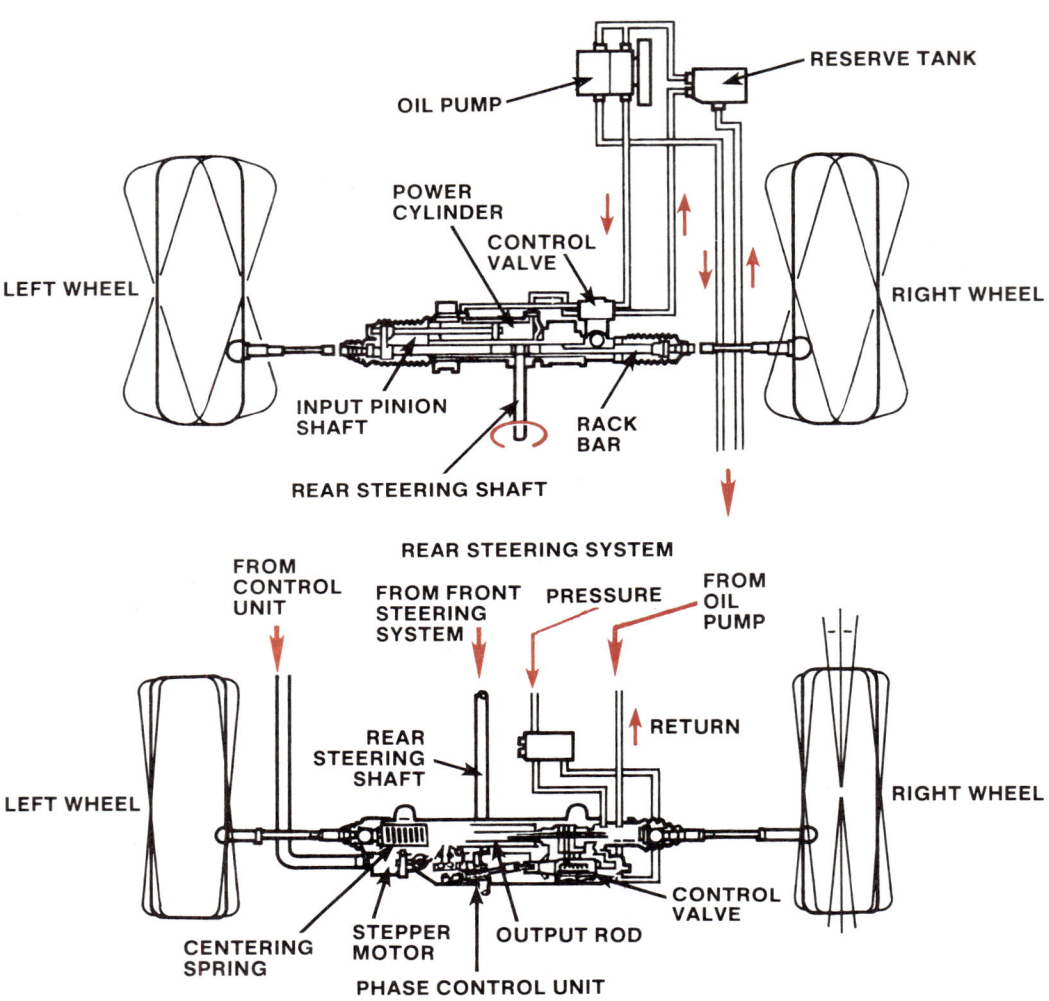

Figure 34-53 Front- and rear-steering systems. *Courtesy of Mazda*

ing-phase control unit (deciding direction and degree), a power cylinder and an output rod (Figure 34-54). A centering lock spring is incorporated, which locks the rear system in a neutral (straight-ahead) position in the event of hydraulic failure. Additionally, a solenoid valve that disengages the hydraulic boost (thereby activating the centering lock spring in case of an electrical failure) is included.

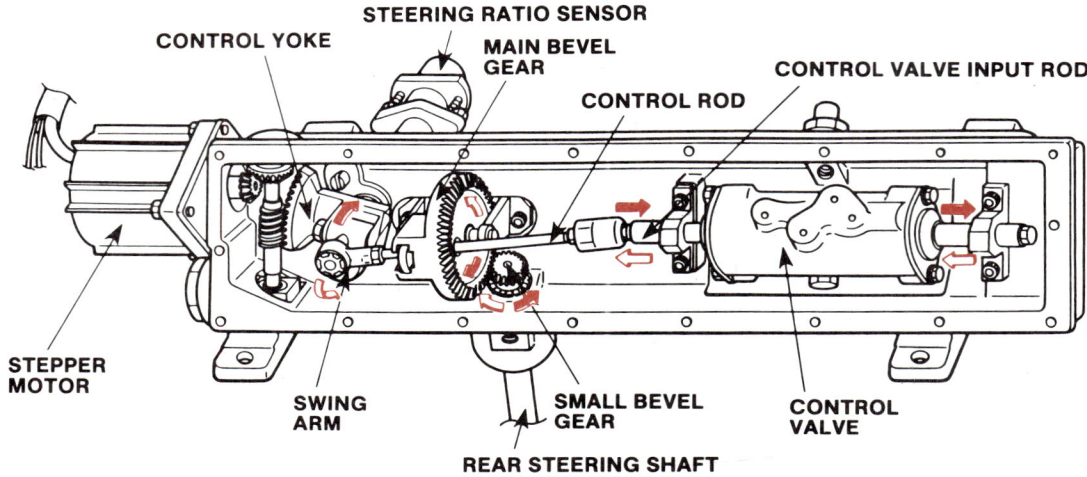

Figure 34-54 Details of a rear-steering system's control unit.

All 4WS systems have fail-safe measures. For example, with the electro/hydraulic setup, the system automatically counteracts possible causes of failure: both electronic and hydraulic, and converts the entire steering system to a conventional two-wheel steering type. Specifically, if a hydraulic defect should reduce pressure level (by a movement malfunction or a broken driving belt), the rear-wheel-steering mechanism is automatically locked in a neutral position, activating a low-level warning light.

In the event of an electrical failure, it would be detected by a self-diagnostic circuit integrated in the four-wheel-steering control unit. The control unit stimulates a solenoid valve, which neutralizes hydraulic pressure, thereby alternating the system to two-wheel steering. The failure would be indicated by the system's warning light in the main instrument display.

On any 4WS system, there must be near-perfect compliance between the position of the steering wheel, the position of the front wheels, and the position of the rear wheels. It is usually recommended that the car be driven about 20 feet in a dead-straight line. Then, the position of the front/rear wheels is checked with respect to steering wheel position. The base reference point is a strip of masking tape on the steering wheel hub and the steering column. When the wheel is positioned dead center, draw a line down the tape. Run the car a short distance straight ahead to see if the reference line holds. If not, corrections are needed, such as repositioning the steering wheel.

Even severe imbalance of a rear wheel on a speed-sensitive 4WS system can cause problems and make basic troubleshooting a bit frustrating.

❏ PRINCIPLES OF WHEEL ALIGNMENT

Proper alignment of both the front and the rear wheels ensures easy steering, comfortable ride, long tire life, and reduced road vibrations.

Steering Geometry and Alignment Angles

There is a multitude of angles and specifications that the automotive manufacturers must consider when designing a car. The multiple functions of the suspension system complicate things a great deal for design engineers. They must take into account more than basic geometry. Durability, maintenance, tire wear, available space, and production cost are all critical elements. Most elements contain a degree of compromise in order to satisfy the minimum requirements of each.

Most technicians do not need to be concerned with all of this. All they need to do is restore the vehicle to the condition the design engineer specified. To do this, however, the technician must be totally familiar with the purpose of principal alignment angles.

The alignment angles are designed in the vehicle to properly locate the vehicle's weight on moving parts and to facilitate steering. If these angles are not correct, the vehicle is misaligned. The effects of misalignment are given in Table 34-1. It is important to remember that alignment angles, when specified in the text, are those specific angles that should exist when the system is being measured under a given set of conditions. During regular performance, these angles change as the traveling surface and vehicle driving forces change.

Basic Wheel Alignment

Before making adjustments, conduct the following prealignment checks.

ROAD TEST Begin the alignment with a road test. While driving the car, check to see that the steering wheel is straight. Feel for vibration in the steering wheel as well as in the floor or seats. Notice any pulling or abnormal handling problems, such as hard steering, tire squeal while cornering, or mechanical pops or clunks. This helps find problems that must be corrected before proceeding with the alignment.

TABLE 34-1 EFFECTS OF INCORRECT ALIGNMENT

Problem	Effect
Incorrect camber setting	Tire wear Ball joint/wheel bearing wear Pull to side of most positive/least negative camber
Too much positive caster	Hard steering Excessive road shock Wheel shimmy
Too much negative caster	Wander Weave Instability at high speeds
Unequal caster	Pull to side most negative/least positive caster
Incorrect SAI	Instability Poor return Pull to side of lesser inclination Hard steering
Incorrect toe setting	Tire wear
Incorrect turning radius	Tire wear Squeal in turns

VISUAL INSPECTION This includes checking for uneven tire wear and mismatched tire sizes or types. Look for the results of collision damage and towing damage.

RIDE HEIGHT MEASUREMENT The car is designed to ride at a specific curb height. Curb height specifications are published in service manuals and in some alignment specification books. Measurements should be taken at the specific points on the chassis.

UNDER VEHICLE CHECKS With the vehicle raised, inspect all steering components such as control arm bushings, upper strut mounts, pitman arm, idler arm, center link, tie-rod ends, ball joints, and shock absorbers. Check the CV joints (if equipped) for looseness, popping sounds, binding, and broken boots. Damaged components must be repaired before adjusting alignment angles.

Angle Alignment

The proper alignment of a suspension/steering system centers around the accuracy of the following angles.

CASTER This is the angle of the steering axis of a wheel from the vertical, as viewed from the side of the vehicle. The forward or rearward tilt from the vertical line (Figure 34-55), illustrates caster. Caster is the first angle adjusted during an alignment. Tilting the wheel forward is negative caster. Tilting backward is positive caster.

Caster is designed to provide steering stability. The caster angle for each wheel on an axle should be equal. Unequal caster angles cause the vehicle to steer toward the side with less caster. Too much negative caster can cause the vehicle to have sensitive steering at high speeds. The vehicle might wander as a result of negative caster.

Caster is affected by worn or loose strut rod and control arm bushings. Caster adjustments are not possible on some strut suspension systems. Where they are provided, they can be made at the top or bottom mount of the strut suspension.

CAMBER This is the angle represented by the tilt of either the front or rear wheels inward or outward from

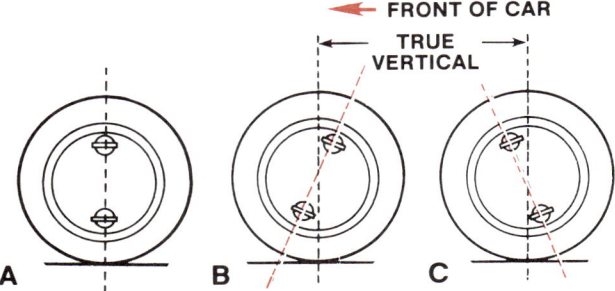

Figure 34-55 Three types of caster: (A) zero, (B) positive, and (C) negative.

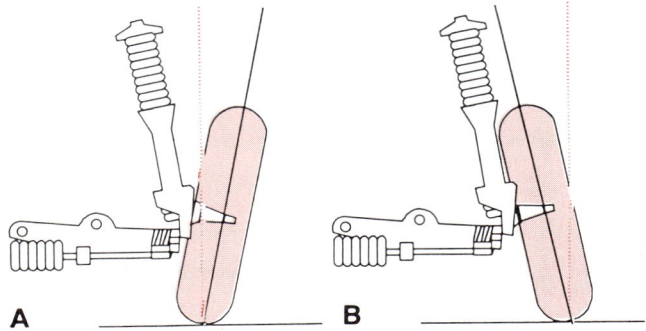

Figure 34-56 (A) Positive and (B) negative camber.

the vertical as viewed from the front of the car (Figure 34-56). Camber is designed into the vehicle to compensate for road crown, passenger weight, and vehicle weight. Camber is usually set equally for each wheel. Equal camber means each wheel is tilted outward or inward the same amount. Unequal camber causes tire wear and causes the vehicle to steer toward the side that is more positive.

Camber angle changes, through the travel of the suspension system are controlled by pivots. Camber is affected by worn or loose ball joints, control arm bushings, and wheel bearings. Anything that changes chassis height also affects camber. Camber is adjustable on most vehicles. Some manufacturers prefer to include a camber adjustment at the spindle assembly. Camber adjustments are also provided on some strut suspension systems at the top mounting position of the strut. Very little adjustment of camber (or caster) is required by strut suspensions if the tower and lower control arm positions are in their proper place. If serious camber error has occurred and the suspension mounting positions have not been damaged, it is an indication of bent suspension parts. In this case, diagnostic angle and dimensional checks should be made on the suspension parts. Damaged parts should be identified and replaced.

TOE Toe is the distance comparison between the leading edge and trailing edge of the front tires. If the leading edge distance is less, then there is toe-in. If it is greater, there is toe-out (Figure 34-57). Actually, toe is critical as a tire-wearing angle. Wheels that do not track straight ahead have to drag as they travel forward. Excessive toe measurements (in or out) cause a sawtooth edge on the tread surface from dragging the tire sideways.

Toe adjustments are made at the tie-rod. They must be made evenly on both sides of the car. If toe adjust-

Figure 34-57 Typical rear toe condition.

ments are not made evenly, the car may tend to pull due to the steering wheel being off-center. This pull condition is especially common with power-assisted rack and pinion gears. It can be corrected by making the toe adjustments equal on both sides of the car. The steering assembly must be centered before these adjustments are made. Toe is the last adjustment made in an alignment.

THRUST LINE ALIGNMENT A main consideration in any alignment is to make sure the vehicle runs straight down the road, with the rear tires tracking directly behind the front tires when the steering wheel is in the straight-ahead position. The geometric centerline of the vehicle should parallel the road direction. This is the case when rear toe is parallel to the vehicle's geometric centerline in the straight-ahead position. If rear toe does not parallel the vehicle centerline, a thrust direction to the left or right is created (Figure 34-58). This difference of rear toe from the geometric centerline is called the thrust angle. The vehicle tends to travel in the direction of the thrust line, rather than straight ahead.

To correct this problem, begin by setting individual rear wheel toe equally in reference to the geometric centerline. Four-wheel-alignment machines check individual toe on each wheel. Once the rear wheels are in alignment with the geometric centerline, set the individual front toe in reference to the thrust angle. Following this procedure assures that the steering wheel is straight ahead for straight-ahead travel. If you set the front toe to the vehicle geometric centerline, ignoring the rear toe angle, a cocked steering wheel results.

STEERING AXLE INCLINATION (SAI) This angle locates the vehicle weight to the inside or outside of the vertical centerline of the tire. The SAI is the angle between true vertical and a line drawn between the steering pivots as viewed from the front of the vehicle (Figure 34-59). It is an engineering angle designed to

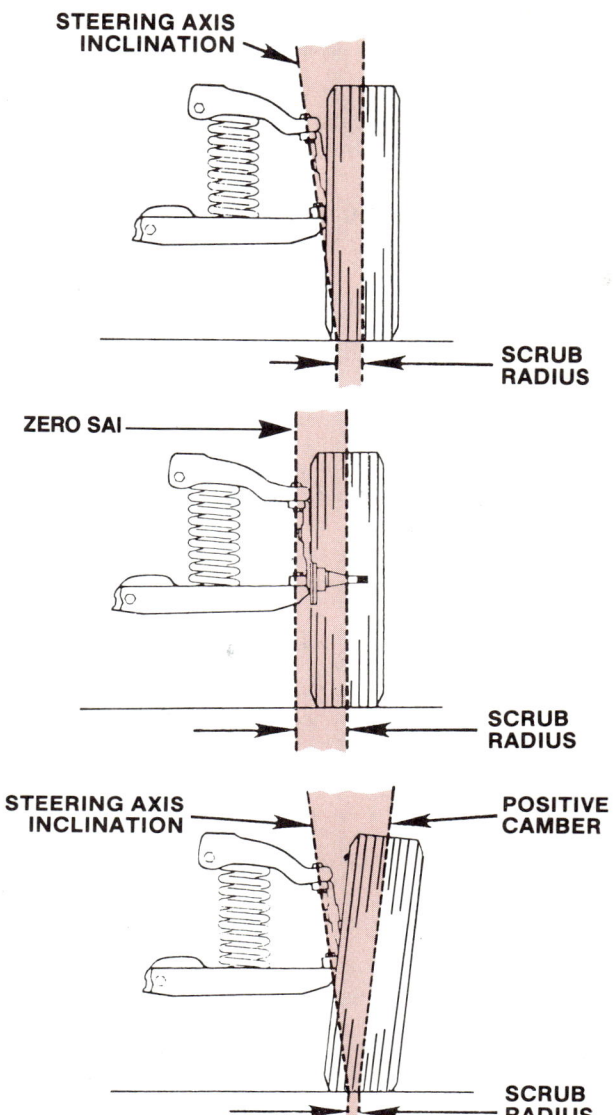

Figure 34-59 The effects of steering axis inclination changes.

project the weight of the vehicle to the road surface for stability. The SAI helps the vehicle's steering system return to straight ahead after a turn.

If the vehicle has 0 (zero) SAI, the upper and lower ball joints (or strut pivot points) would be located directly over one another. Problems associated with this simple relationship include tire scrub in turns, lack of control, and increased effort during turn recovery. If the SAI is tilted, a triangle is formed between ball joints and spindle. An arc is then formed when turning. There is a high point at straight-ahead position and a drop downward turning to each side. This motion travels through the control arms to the springs and finally to the weight of the vehicle. The forces generated in a turn are actually trying to lift the vehicle. The tilting and loading effect of SAI offsets the lifting forces and helps to pull the tires back to straight ahead when the turn is finished.

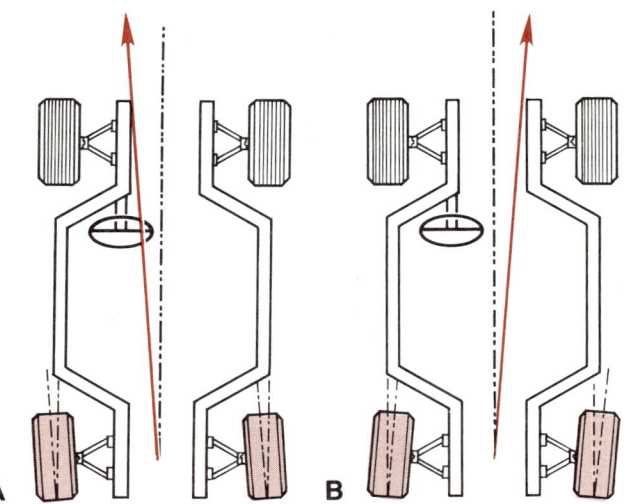

Figure 34-58 (A) Left and (B) right thrust direction.

Front-wheel drive vehicles with strut suspensions typically have a higher SAI angle (12 to 18 degrees) than a short-long arm rear-wheel-drive suspension (6 to 8 degrees). This is because the extra leverage provided by a larger angle helps directional stability.

If the SAI angles are unequal side-to-side, torque steer, brake pull, and bump steer (jerking from side to side) can occur even if static camber angles are within specifications.

Checking the SAI angle can help locate various problems that affect wheel alignment. For example, an SAI angle or SAI angle that varies from side to side may indicate an out-of-position upper strut tower, a bowed lower control arm, or a shifted center cross member.

On a short-long arm suspension, SAI is the angle between true vertical and a line drawn from the upper ball joint through the lower ball joint. In strut equipped vehicle this line is drawn through the center of the strut's upper mount down through the center of the lower ball joint.

When the camber angle is added to the SAI angle, the sum of the two is called the included angle. Comparing SAI, included, and camber angles can also help identify damaged or worn components. For example, if the SAI reading is correct, but the camber and included angles are less than specifications, the steering knuckle or strut tower may be bent. Table 34-2 summarizes the various angle combinations used to troubleshoot short-long arm, strut, and twin I-beam suspension system alignment problems.

TURNING RADIUS Turning radius or cornering angle is the amount of toe-out present in turns (Figure 34-60). As a car goes around a corner, the inside tire must travel in a smaller radius circle than the outside tire.

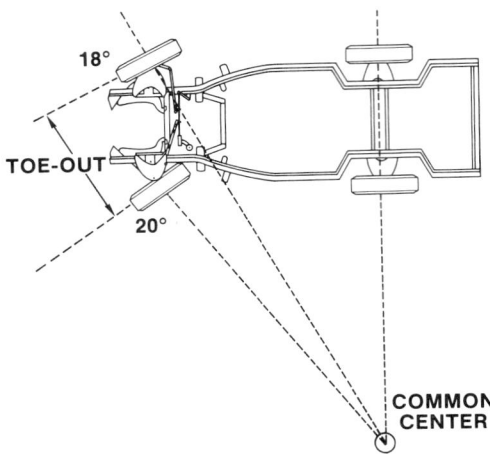

Figure 34-60 Turning radius is affected by toe-out in turns.

This is accomplished by designing the steering geometry to turn the inside wheel sharper than the outside wheel. The result can be seen as toe-out in turns. This eliminates tire scrubbing on the road surface by keeping the tires pointed in the direction they have to move.

When a car has a steering problem, the first diagnostic check should be a visual inspection of the entire vehicle for anything obvious: bent wheels, misalignment of the cradle, and so on. If there is nothing obviously wrong with the car, make a series of diagnostic checks without disassembling the vehicle. One of the most useful checks that can be made with a minimum of equipment is a jounce-rebound check.

Jounce is the motion caused by a wheel going over a bump and compressing the springs. During jounce, the

TABLE 34-2 SAI DIAGNOSTIC REFERENCE CHART				
Suspension Systems	SAI	Camber	Included Angle	Probable Cause
Short Arm/ Long Arm Suspension System	Correct	Less	Less	Bent Knuckle
	Less	Greater	Correct	Bent Lower Control Arm
	Greater	Less	Correct	Bent Upper Control Arm
	Less	Greater	Greater	Bent Knuckle
MacPherson Strut Suspension	Correct	Less	Less	Bent Knuckle and/or Bent Strut
	Correct	Greater	Greater	Bent Knuckle and/or Bent Strut
	Less	Greater	Correct	Bent Control Arm or Strut Tower (out at top)
	Greater	Less	Correct	Strut Tower (in at top)
	Greater	Greater	Greater	Strut Tower (in at top) and Spindle and/or Bent Strut
	Less	Greater	Greater	Bent Control Arm or Strut Tower (out at top) Plus Bent Knuckle and/or Bent Strut
	Less	Less	Less	Strut Tower (out at top) and Knuckle and/or Strut Bent or Bent Control Arm
Twin I Beam Suspension	Correct	Greater	Greater	Bent Knuckle
	Greater	Less	Correct	Bent I Beam
	Less	Greater	Correct	Bent I Beam
	Less	Greater	Greater	Bent Knuckle

wheel moves up toward the chassis. Jounce can be simulated by sitting on the bumper and pushing down on the car. The car should jounce equally on both sides.

Rebound is the motion caused by a wheel going into a dip or returning from a jounce and extending the spring. During rebound, the wheel moves down away from the chassis. Rebound can be simulated by lifting up on the bumper. The car should lift equally on both sides.

This jounce-rebound check determines if there is misalignment in the rack and pinion gear. For a quick check, unlock the steering wheel and see if it moves during the jounce or rebound. For a more careful check, use a pointer and a piece of chalk. Use the chalk to make a reference mark on the tire tread and place the pointer on the same line as the chalk mark. Jounce and rebound the suspension system a few times while someone watches the chalk mark and the pointer. If the mark on the wheel moves unequally in and out on both sides of the car, chances are there is a steering arm or gear out of alignment. If the mark does not move or moves equally in and out on both sides of the car, the steering arm and gear are probably all right. Each wheel or side should be checked.

TRACKING All vehicles are built around a geometric centerline that runs through the center of the chassis from the back to the front. The thrust line is the direction the rear axle would travel if unaffected by the front wheels. This condition is also called tracking. An ideal alignment has all four wheels parallel with the centerline, making the thrust line parallel with the centerline. However, the rear-wheel thrust line of a vehicle might not always be parallel to the actual centerline of the vehicle, so the angle of the thrust line must be checked first.

Rear-wheel-drive vehicles rarely need thrust line adjustment unless they have been in an accident or experienced severe usage. Independent rear suspensions can have offset thrust angles from unequal rear toe adjustments. An offset thrust angle affects handling by pulling in the direction away from the thrust line and can cause tire wear similar in pattern to that of incorrect toe settings. As a general rule, minor variations between the thrust line and centerline are not noticeable and do not cause handling problems as long as the front wheels are aligned parallel with the thrust line.

Correct tracking refers to a situation with all suspension and wheels in their correct location and condition and aligned so that the rear wheels follow directly behind the front wheels while moving in a straight line (Figure 34-61). For this to occur, all wheels must be parallel with one another and axle and spindle lines must be at 90-degree angles to the vehicle centerline. Simply stated, all four wheels should form a perfect rectangle.

LOAD DISTRIBUTION Load distribution refers to the load placed on each wheel. Every vehicle is engineered to operate at a designed curb height (also called trim height). At this height, each wheel must carry the correct amount of weight. Excessive loading to either the front, rear, or one side of the vehicle changes the curb height, upsetting vehicle balance and steering geometry.

In correct alignment, sagging springs and bent suspension parts can also change this condition, upsetting geometry and placing excessive load on only one or two wheels.

All of these elements—springs, shocks, suspension, and geometry—are engineered to work together as a balanced team to provide riding and handling. Quite naturally, if one wheel is running under a different condition of weight load and steering geometry, the vehicle does not ride and handle as it is capable.

ALIGNMENT PROCEDURES

The equipment used to check wheel alignment can vary from a simple alignment gauge to computerized four-wheel alignment systems. A typical alignment device of computerized systems gives information on a CRT screen to guide the technician step-by-step through the alignment process (Figure 34-62).

The technician selects the make of the car that is to be worked on. Then the same procedure is performed to

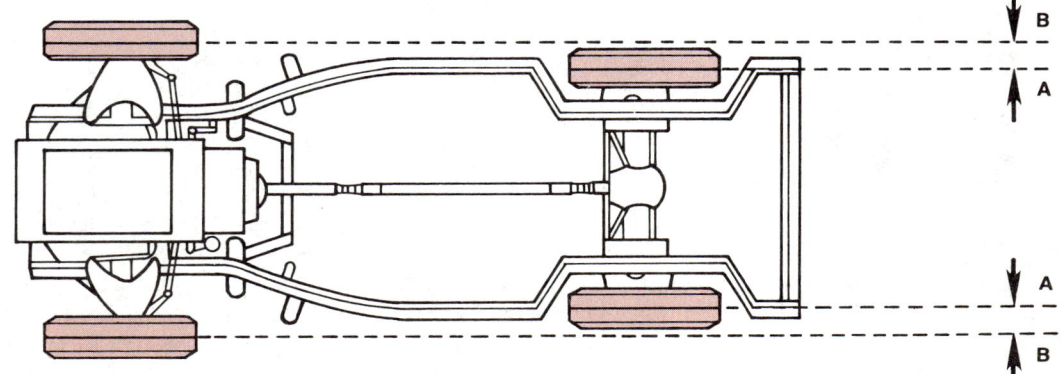

Figure 34-61 When a car is tracking correctly, its rear wheels are the same distance from the front wheels on both sides.

880 Section 7 Suspensions

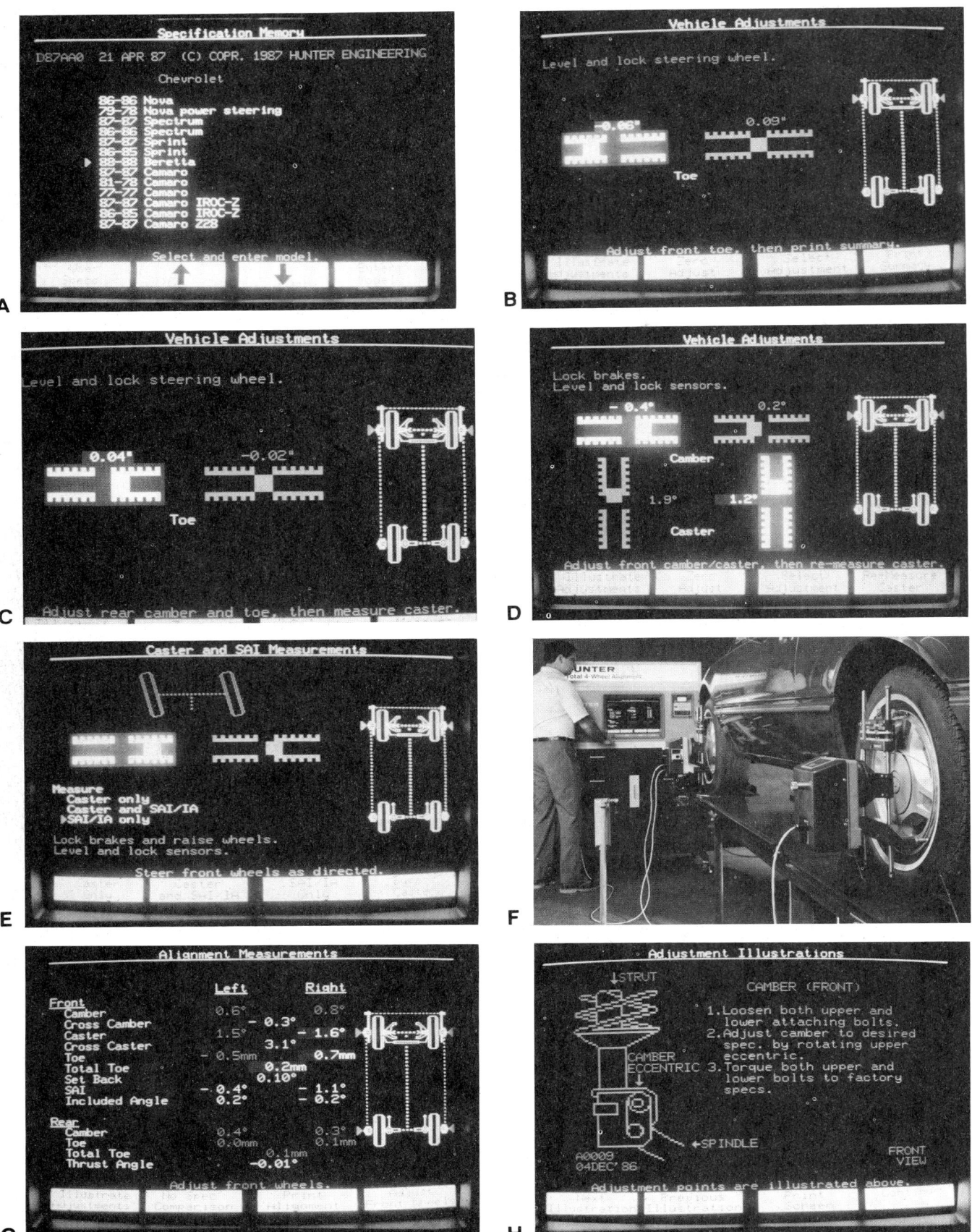

Figure 34-62 Alignment by computer: (A) Select specific year and model; (B through E) measure angles; (F and G) check specification data; (H) how and where to make adjustments are shown on screen. *Courtesy of Hunter Engineering Co.*

select the specific year and model. The electronic wheel runout compensation takes just a few seconds per wheel. When compensation is complete, alignment measurements are instantly displayed.

The CRT readings are often in color. Specification memory matches OE data including asymmetric tolerances, different left- and right-side specifications, and cross specifications (difference allowed between left and right side). Graphics and text on the screen show the technician where and how to make adjustments.

As the adjustments are made on the vehicle, the technician can observe the center block slide toward the target. When the block aligns with the target, the adjustment is within half the specified tolerance.

The computerized system for alignment, such as the one here, can perform other services. For example, it can provide an undercar checklist for the technician to use a prealignment inspection. The technician can check or by-pass any item. In addition, a printout of the inspection data can be given to the car owner as proof of the status of the vehicle.

Another popular wheel alignment system uses a combination scale as a target for a laser beam (Figure 34-63). Errors in wheel angle are shown immediately on the scale and given measurements are easily read. Measurements can be made continually while errors are being corrected. This scale/laser system makes measuring of the rear-wheel camber and toe-in as simple and exact as for the front wheels.

The technician is cautioned to follow the instructions provided by the manufacturer of the particular brand of wheel alignment equipment that is to be used. Test readings obtained from the equipment are to be compared with the vehicle manufacturer's specifications. If adjustments are necessary and can be made, proceed. Use only authorized replacement parts if a replacement should be necessary.

All wheel alignment angles are interrelated. Regardless of the make of car or the type of suspension, the same adjustment order—caster, camber, toe—should be followed, as far as the car permits such adjustments to be made. Many MacPherson suspensions do not provide for caster or camber adjustments. Additionally, adjustment methods vary from model to model and, occasionally, even in different model years.

Caster/Camber Adjustment

Although caster and camber are vital alignment angles, only conventional suspensions generally allow for their adjustment. Caster, or both caster and camber, might be preset on many MacPherson suspensions by the manufacturer and can be adjusted only by replacing either the strut assembly or control arm.

Conventional Suspension Adjustments

Several methods are used on conventional suspensions to adjust caster and camber (Figure 34-64).

Figure 34-63 (A) A typical light beam alignment machine with (B) a camber measurement fixture and (C) a caster measurement fixture. *Courtesy of Dataliner Inc.*

SHIMS Many cars use shims for adjusting caster and camber. The shims can be located between the control arm pivot shaft and the inside of the frame. Both caster and camber can be adjusted in one operation requiring the loosening of the shim bolts just once. Caster is changed by adding or subtracting shims from one end of the pivot shaft only. Then, camber is adjusted by adding or subtracting an equal amount of shims from the front and rear bolts. This procedure allows camber to change without affecting the caster setting.

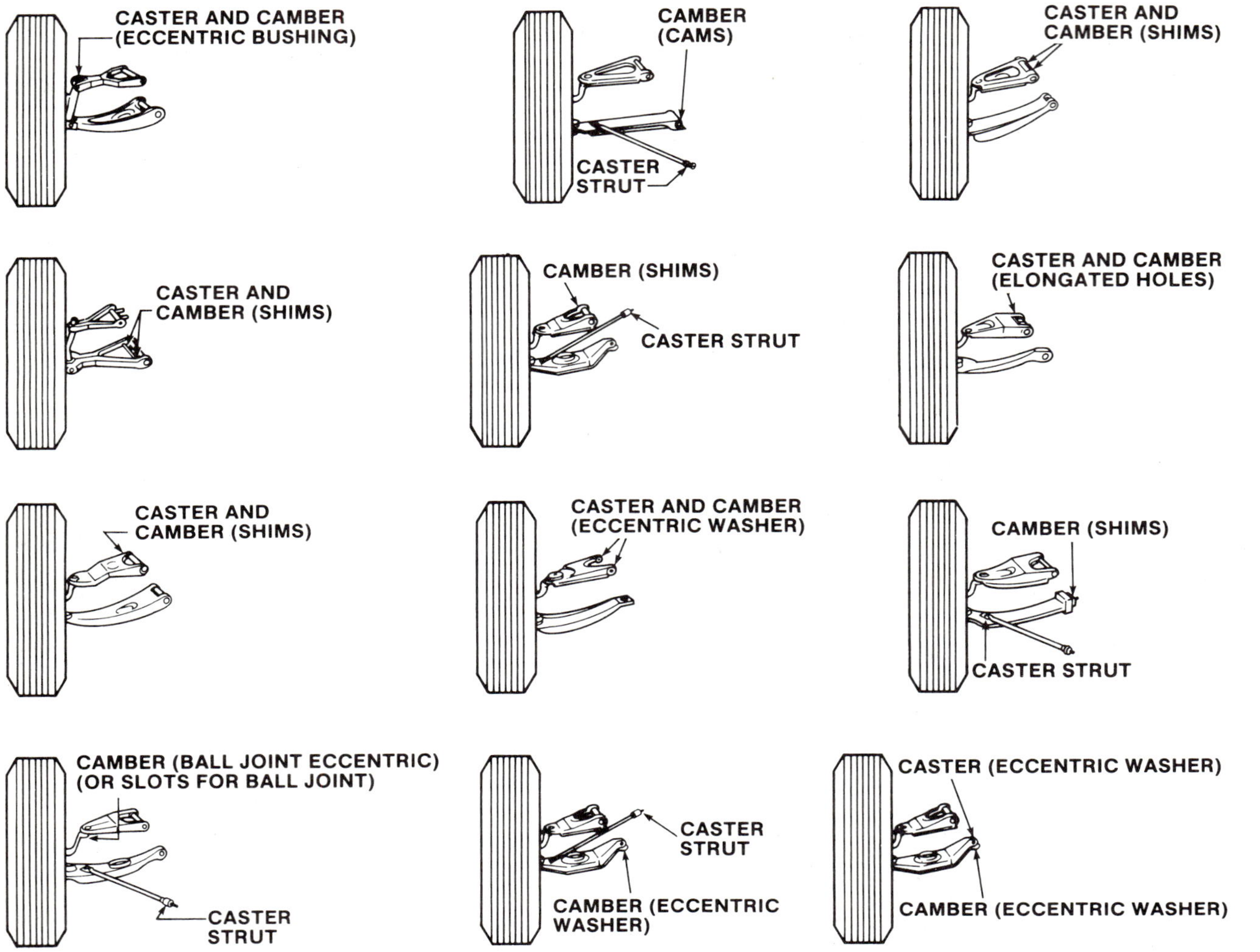

Figure 34-64 Different suspension designs showing various locations for adjusting caster and camber. *Courtesy of Snap-On Tools Corp.*

Some cars use shims located between the control arm pivot shaft and the outside of the frame. The adjustment procedure is the same as just described. Always look at the shim arrangements to determine the desired direction of change before loosening the bolts.

ECCENTRICS AND SHIMS Eccentrics and shims are used on some vehicles to adjust caster and camber. In some designs, an eccentric bolt and cam on the upper control arm adjust both caster and camber. To adjust, the nuts on the upper control arm are loosened first. Then, one eccentric bolt at a time is turned to set caster. Both bolts are turned equally to set camber.

The eccentric bolt and cam assembly (Figure 34-65) is located on the inner upper control arm. Unlike other designs, camber is adjusted first. The front lower arm pivot nut is loosened, and the cam is rotated to the proper camber setting. Caster is set by applying the same procedure to the rear cam.

Figure 34-66 shows another type of eccentric bolt and cam that is located on the lower control arm. With this type suspension, camber is corrected before caster.

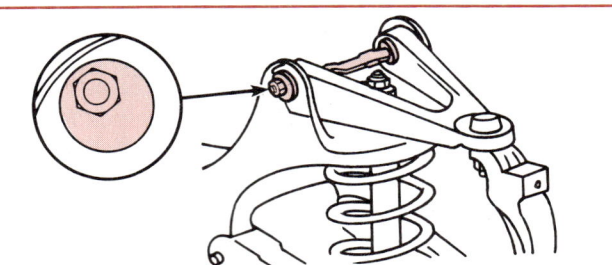

Figure 34-65 Eccentric bolt and cam (upper control arm).

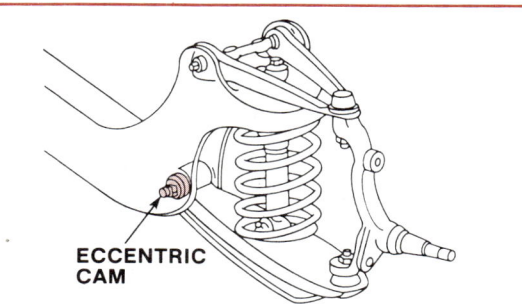

Figure 34-66 Another type of eccentric bolt and cam on a lower control arm.

Some car models have a camber eccentric in the steering knuckle of the upper support arm. A locknut is loosened, and the camber eccentric is rotated to set camber. Caster is set with an adjustable strut rod.

SLOTTED FRAME The slotted frame adjustment has slotted holes under the control arm inner shaft that allow the shaft to be repositioned to the correct caster and camber settings. Caster and camber adjusting tools help in making adjustments. One end of the shaft is moved for caster adjustment. Both ends of the shaft are moved for camber adjustment. Turning a nut on one end of the rod changes its length and adjusts caster. Camber is set by an eccentric at the inner end of the lower control arm, or by a camber eccentric in the steering knuckle of the upper support arm, as described earlier.

ROTATING BALL JOINT AND WASHERS In this design, camber is increased by disconnecting the upper ball joint, rotating it 180 degrees, and reconnecting. This positions the flat of the ball joint flange inboard and increases camber approximately 1 degree. Caster angle is changed with a kit containing two washers, one 0.12 inch thick and one 0.36 inch thick. The washers are placed at opposite ends of the locating tube between the legs of the upper control arm. Placement of the large washer at the rear leg of the control arm increases caster by 1 degree. Placement of the large washer at the front leg of the control arm decreases caster by 1 degree.

MacPherson Suspension Adjustments

Caster/camber adjustments are made only on certain models with MacPherson suspensions. There are two general OEM procedures for doing this, although aftermarket kit adapters are available for some models. Service information must be consulted for an accurate listing of models on which adjustments can be made.

In one version, a cam bolt at the base of the strut assembly is used to adjust camber (Figure 34-67). On different models, this bolt can be either the upper or the lower of the two bolts connecting the strut assembly to the steering knuckle. Both bolts must be loosened to make the adjustment, and the wheel assembly must be centered. Turn the cam bolt to reach the correct alignment, then retighten the bolts to the appropriate torque specifications. There is no caster adjustment on this version.

In the other form of kit adapter, both caster and camber are adjustable at the strut upper mount. Slots in the mounting plate permit the strut assembly to be shifted to reach the alignment specifications. To adjust caster, loosen the three locknuts on the mounting studs and relocate the plate. Do not remove the nuts (Figure 34-68). Loosen the center locknut and slide it

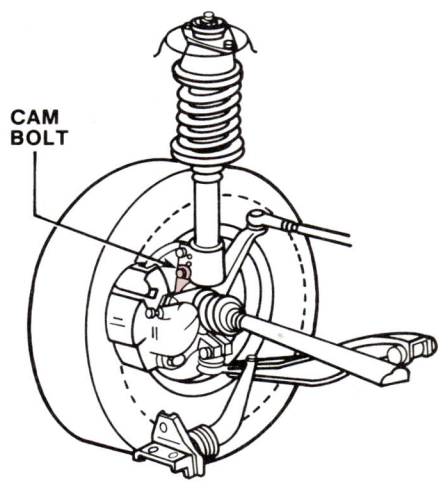

Figure 34-67 Some MacPherson suspensions use cam bolts at the connection to the steering knuckle for camber adjustments.

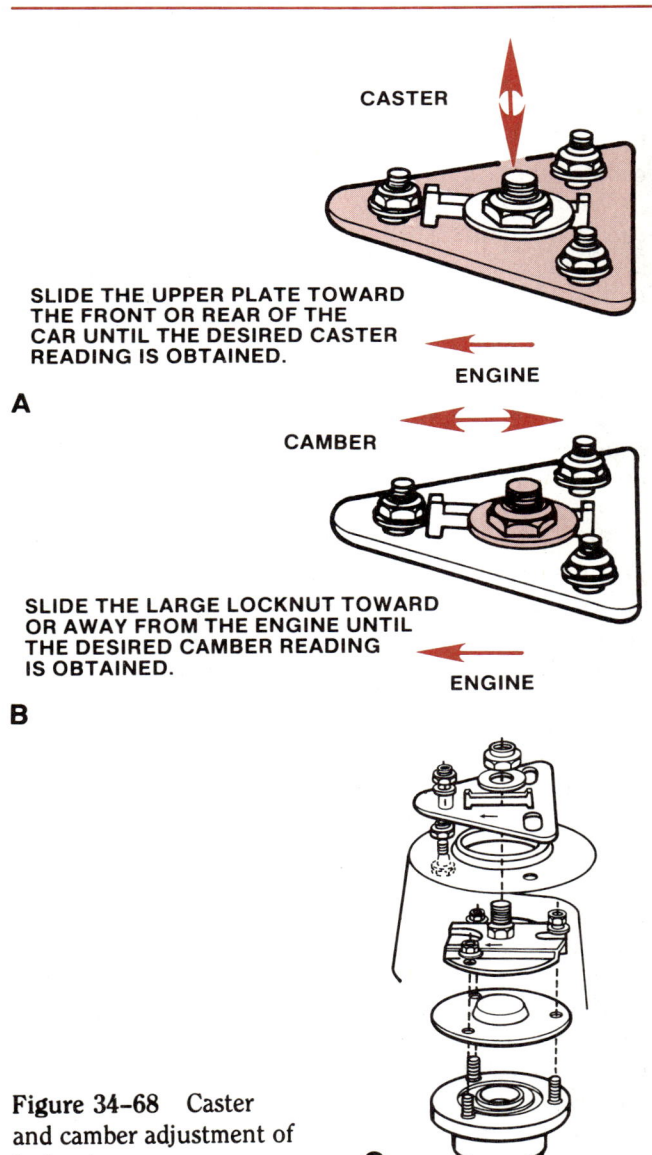

Figure 34-68 Caster and camber adjustment of locknuts.

884　Section 7　Suspensions

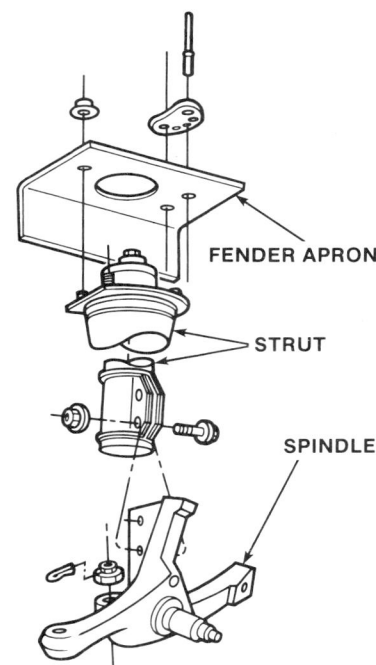

Figure 34-69　Camber adjustment—spring on single control arm with modified MacPherson strut.

Figure 34-70　Jounce and rebound camber checks.

toward or away from the engine as needed to adjust camber correctly.

While caster cannot be adjusted on many MacPherson strut front suspensions, camber can be adjusted. The camber in such an arrangement, although it is locked in place with a pop rivet, can be adjusted by removing the rivet from the camber plate and loosening the three nuts that hold the plate to the body apron (Figure 34-69). Camber is changed by moving the top of the shock strut to the position where the desired camber setting is achieved. The nuts are then tightened to specification. (It is not necessary to install a new pop rivet.)

Most suspension inspection and adjustment work is best performed on a bench or lift rack. Some camber checks, however, can be made to diagnose the condition of a strut and can be measured easily with a camber gauge. One is called a jounce-rebound camber measurement (Figure 34-70A) and can be made by loading the suspension in a similar fashion to jounce-rebound toe change and measuring the camber angle from an individual wheel.

The suspension is then unloaded as in the jounce-rebound toe check and a second camber reading of the same wheel is made (Figure 34-70B). The two readings are compared. These readings should not differ more than 2 degrees on a MacPherson strut suspension. In most cases, the readings are the same.

The jounce-rebound camber change tells the technician if the strut is bent either inboard or outboard. Check each wheel individually before deciding if that one wheel strut is bad based on the readings. If the readings differ between wheels more than 2 degrees, a bent strut is indicated.

A swing camber measurement is made by turning the front wheel in a given amount and performing a jounce-rebound camber check (Figure 34-70C).

The front wheel is then turned out the same amount and the camber angle is measured again. If the camber angle change differs more than 3 degrees from left wheel to right wheel, it is likely that either the strut is bent forward or backward of its normal position or the caster angle is incorrect. As a further test for a bent strut, perform a jounce-rebound check while the

Steering Systems and Wheel Alignment

Figure 34-71 Steering wheel holder is handy when making wheel adjustments. *Courtesy of Ammco Tools, Inc.*

wheels are turned in and while they are turned out. Check each wheel and compare the readings. These diagnostic angles are especially helpful in determining the cause of vehicle handling and tracking problems.

Toe Adjustment

Toe is the last alignment angle to be set. The same procedure is followed on all vehicles, except those with bonded ball stud sockets.

To adjust toe, start by being sure the steering wheel is centered when the front wheels point straight ahead (Figure 34-71). Then loosen the retaining bolts on the tie-rod adjusting sleeves. Turn the sleeves to move the tie-rod ends as shown in Figure 34-72.

An ideal toe condition is both wheels exactly straight ahead, which would minimize tire wear. This, however, is not possible because of the many factors affecting alignment. As a result of these numerous conditions dealing with both tire wear and handling, all suspensions are designed with a slight toe-in or toe-out.

Any misalignment of the steering linkage pivot point or control arm pivot point (such as the center link or rack and pinion out of place) causes the condition known as toe-change. Toe-change involves turning the wheels from their straight-ahead position as the suspension moves up and down.

The change might be only one wheel, both wheels in the same direction, or both wheels in the opposite direction. Regardless of the condition, any change of one or more wheels is a toe-change condition. The results are tire wear and a hard-to-handle vehicle. The poor handling effects can be to the point that the vehicle is dangerous to drive.

Toe change is not a specification, it is a condition where the toe setting constantly varies. It must be determined by equipment or a method that measures individual wheel toe at all suspension heights. There must be a change in suspension heights for any changes to occur.

Lightweight front-wheel-drive vehicles can be affected greatly by toe change. With these vehicles, the front wheels are no longer being pushed. They actually pull the vehicle forward and as a result, if the wheels are not maintaining a straight-ahead position, they affect directional control. Adverse road conditions, such as wet or icy conditions, can also increase the handling effects created by toe-change in the front-wheel-drive car.

❑ REAR ALIGNMENT

A car with a perfect front alignment can still experience poor handling and premature tire wear—particularly on front-wheel-drive cars and cars with independent rear suspensions—if the rear suspension is misaligned. Approximately 80% of today's vehicles not only have front-end alignment specifications but also require rear-wheel alignment.

REAR CAMBER Like front camber, rear camber affects both tire wear and handling. The ideal situation is to have zero running camber on all four wheels to keep the tread in full contact with the road for optimum traction and handling.

Camber is not a static angle. It changes as the suspension moves up and down. Camber also changes as the vehicle is loaded and the suspension sags under the weight.

To compensate for loading, most vehicles with in-

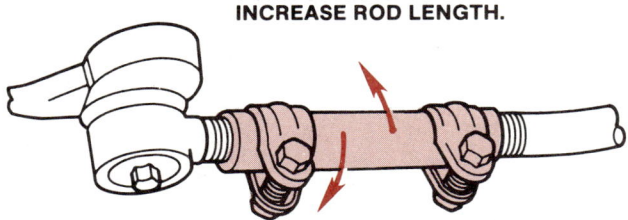
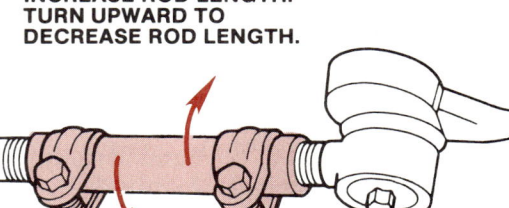

Figure 34-72 Adjusting toe.

dependent rear suspension (IRS) often call for a slight amount of positive camber, a collapsed or mislocated strut tower, bent strut, collapsed upper control arm bushing, bent upper control arm, sagging spring or an overloaded suspension. However, all can allow the rear wheels to assume a negative camber attitude. A bent spindle, strut or bowed lower control arm can cause too much positive camber. Even rigid rear axle housings in rear-wheel-drive vehicles can become bowed by excessive torque, severe overloading, or road damage.

CAUTION: *Never jack up or lift a FWD vehicle on its rear axle. The weight of the vehicle may cause the axle to bend and result in misalignment of the rear wheels. Always lift the vehicle at the recommended lifting points.*

Besides wearing the tires unevenly across the tread, uneven side-to-side camber (as when one wheel leans in and the other does not) creates a steering pull just like it does when the camber readings on the front wheels do not match. It is like leaning on a bicycle. A vehicle always pulls toward a wheel with the most positive camber. If the mismatch is at the rear wheels, the rear axle pulls toward the side with the greatest amount of positive camber. If the rear axle pulls to the right, the front of the car drifts to the left—and the result is a steering pull even though the front wheels may be perfectly aligned.

REAR TOE Rear toe, like front toe, is a critical tire rear angle. If toed-in or toed-out, the rear tires scuff just like the front ones. Either condition can also contribute to steering instability as well as reduced braking effectiveness. (Keep this in mind with antilock brake systems.)

Like camber, rear toe is not a static alignment angle. It changes as the suspension goes through jounce and rebound. It also changes in response to rolling resistance and the application of engine torque. With front-wheel-drive (FWD) vehicles, the front wheels tend to toe-in under power while the rear wheels toe-out in response to rolling resistance and suspension compliance. With rear-wheel drive (RWD), the opposite happens: the front wheels toe-out while the rear wheels on an independent suspension try to toe-in as they push the vehicle ahead.

If rear toe is not within specifications, it affects tire wear and steering stability just as much as front toe. A total toe reading that is within specifications does not necessarily mean the wheels are properly aligned—especially when it comes to rear toe measurements. If one rear wheel is toed-in while the other is toed-out by an equal amount, total toe would be within specifications. However, the vehicle would have a steering pull because the rear wheels would not be parallel to center.

Remember, the ideal situation is to have all four wheels at zero running toe when the car is traveling down the road. This is especially true with antilock brakes where improper toe can affect brakes, such a condition can affect brake balance when braking on slick or wet surfaces, causing the antilock brakes to cycle on and off to prevent a skid. Without antilock brakes, this condition may upset traction enough to cause an uncontrollable skid.

Thrust Line

If both rear wheels are square to one another and the rest of the vehicle, the thrust line is perpendicular to the rear axle and coincides with the vehicle's centerline. But if one or both rear wheels are toed in or out, or one is setback slightly with respect to the other, the thrust line is thrown off-center. This creates a thrust angle that causes a steering pull in the opposite direction. For example, a thrust line that is off-center to the right makes the car pull left.

The presence of a thrust angle can cause poor directional stability on ice, snow, or wet pavement. It can sometimes make a vehicle pull during braking or hard acceleration. It can also increase tire wear as the front wheels fight the rear ones for steering control.

The only way to eliminate the problem is to eliminate the thrust angle. The thrust line can be recentered by realigning rear toe. On most FWD applications, that can be easily done by using the factory-provided toe adjustments, by placing toe/camber shims between the rear spindles and axle (Figure 34-73), or by using eccentric bushing kits. With rear-wheel-drive vehicles that have a solid rear axle, changing rear toe is not as easy. Sometimes the floorpan or frame rails are misaligned from the factory or from collision damage. Short of pulling the chassis on a collision bench to restore the correct control arm or spring-mount geometry, the only other options are to try some type of

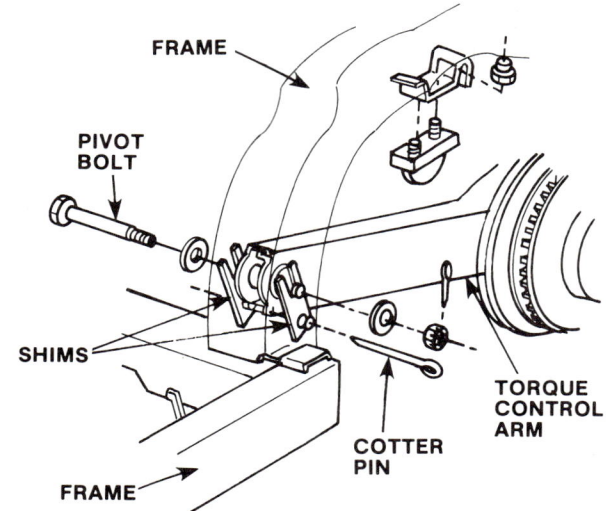

Figure 34-73 Aligning rear wheels by installing shims to eliminate an off-unit thrust angle condition. *Courtesy of General Motors Corp.*

offset trailing arm bushing with the coil springs, or to reposition the spring shackles or U-bolts with leaf springs.

If rear toe cannot be easily changed, the next best alternative is to align the front wheels to the rear axle thrust line rather than the vehicle centerline. Doing this puts the steering wheel back on center and eliminates the steering pull—but it does not eliminate dog tracking.

> ### USING SERVICE MANUALS
> Consult the appropriate service manual for details on these rear-end alignment procedures. Also, use good alignment procedures and a good alignment specifications book. Several aftermarket companies have complete and accurate specification books with front/rear-end specifications for domestic and imported cars, as well as light trucks.

☐ FOUR-WHEEL-DRIVE VEHICLE ALIGNMENT

Most aftermarket parts manufacturers have camber adjustment shims available in various thicknesses and three diameters (4-3/4 inches, 6 inches, and 6-5/8 inches) (Figure 34-74). Never stack the shims. Only one shim per side should be used.

CAUTION: Do not use shims on vehicles where brakes are mounted to the steering knuckle flange. The brakes can be misaligned and brake performance and wear can be seriously affected.

With front-wheel-drive and full-time 4WD vehicles, the front wheels are also driving wheels. As the front wheels pull the vehicle, the wheels tend to toe-in when torque is applied. To offset this tendency, the front wheels usually need less static toe-in to produce zero running toe. In fact, the preferred toe alignment specifications in this instance can be zero to slightly toed-out (1/16-inch toe-out).

It is important to note that when the front wheels of a part-time 4WD system are freewheeling, they behave the same as the front wheels in a rear-wheel-drive vehicle. That is, they roll rather than pull. The wheels tend to toe-out, so the static toe setting would have to toe-in to achieve zero running toe when driving in the two-wheel mode. The kind of tires being used can also make a difference in suspension compliance. Bias-ply tires give more than radial tires.

The tires suffer in proportion to toe misalignment. For a tire that is only 1/8-inch off (1/4 degree), the tire is scrubbed sideways 12 feet for every mile traveled. That may not sound like much, but 12 feet of sideway scrub every mile can cut a tire's life in half.

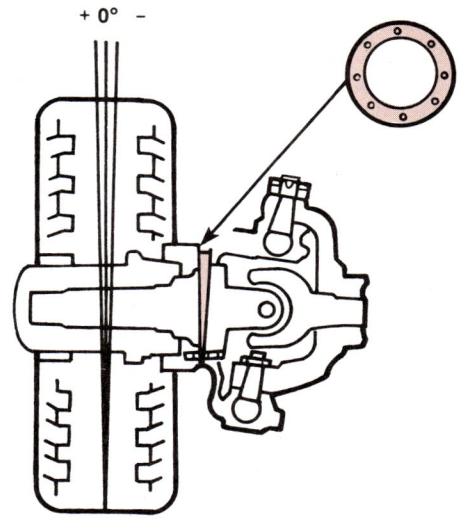

Figure 34-74 Typical camber shim used on 4WD vehicles.

If rapid tire wear seems to be the problem, look for the telltale feathered wear pattern. If the wheels are running toe-in, the feathered wear pattern leaves sharp edges on the inside edges of the tread. If the wheels are running toe-out, the sharp edges are toward the outside of the tread. It is usually easier to feel the feathered wear pattern than to see it. To tell which way the wear pattern runs, rub your fingers sideways across the tread.

Worn tie-rod ends or an idler arm are the most common causes of tire wear. A bent steering arm, which is not uncommon with off-road vehicles, causes wear. One of the most common mistakes that is made when aligning 4WD vehicles is that of aligning every vehicle to the same set of specifications. If the factory specifications do not work, chances are something is bent.

Toe alignment can also be caused by misalignment in the steering linkage. To hold the tires in the same toe position as the suspension travels through jounce and rebound, the tie-rods must be parallel to the control arms.

If the rods are not parallel to the control arms, unequal toe changes result, causing bump steer. If severe enough, bump steer can cause a noticeable jerk or pull to one side every time the vehicle hits a bump.

Bump steer can be caused by a steering rack (rack and pinion steering) or a center link (parallelogram steering) that is not level. When one side is high and the other side is low, both wheels change toe in the same direction as the suspension travels through jounce and rebound.

The parallelism of the steering linkage on an alignment rack cannot be checked unless toe measurements are compared with the suspension raised 4 inches, then lowered 4 inches.

If the amount of toe-change is not equal side-to-side, the steering linkage is misaligned. Measure the distance from each end of the steering rack or center link to the ground to see if one end is higher than the other. If it is, the chassis is probably bent and has to be tweaked to restore proper steering linkage alignment.

To align a modified 4WD vehicle that has been raised and fitted with oversized tires on off-set rims, keep in mind that off-set rims tend to increase compliance and exaggerate camber. The technician should still aim for zero running toe and a static camber setting of zero to plus 1/4 degree.

Four-Wheel Alignment

The primary objective of four-wheel (or total wheel alignment, as it is frequently called), whether front or rear drive, solid axle or independent rear suspension, is to align all four wheels so the vehicle drives and tracks straight with the steering wheel centered. To accomplish this, the wheels must be parallel to one another and perpendicular to a common centerline.

Total toe for all four wheels must be determined and rear toe adjusted where possible to bring the rear axle or wheels into square with the chassis. The front toe setting can then be adjusted to compensate for any rear alignment deviation that might persist.

Four-wheel alignment also includes checking and adjusting rear-wheel camber as well as toe, and doing all the traditional checks of front camber, toe, caster, toe-out on turns and steering axis inclination. The most important thing a four-wheel alignment job tells the technician is whether or not the rear axle or rear wheels are square with respect to the front wheels and chassis.

With two-wheel alignment equipment that aligns the front wheels to the geometric centerline, the assumption is made that the rear wheels are square with respect to the centerline. If that is true, the alignment job produces satisfactory results. If not, steering and tracking might be a problem.

Rear-wheel alignment can be checked on a two-wheel machine by simply backing the vehicle onto the rack. The rear wheels can also be checked for square by measuring the wheelbase on both sides with a track bar to make sure it is equal. The obvious drawback to this approach is that four-wheel alignment involves several extra steps. There is also the question of aligning the wheels to the centerline or thrust line.

The best approach in terms of both accuracy and completeness for wheel alignment is to reference the front wheels to the rear wheels. With this approach, individual rear toe is measured so the thrust line can be determined and the front wheels adjusted to the centerline. It also eliminates the need to back the vehicle onto the alignment machine because heads are provided for the rear wheels.

Total four-wheel alignment is measuring rear toe (and camber) and correcting any misalignment to bring the thrust line into the same plane as the centerline. This produces a vehicle that drives and tracks straight with a centered steering wheel. It minimizes rolling resistance, tire wear, and wind resistance. It improves fuel economy and tire life. In short, it does all the things a complete alignment job is supposed to do.

The actual procedure for total four-wheel alignment, as with two-wheel alignment, begins with a thorough inspection of the tires and suspension. Tires should be checked for unusual wear patterns that might indicate toe or camber misalignment, inflation pressure, or balance problems. Tires should be the same size and condition side to side, with matching tread patterns. The tires should be inflated to the recommended specifications before any measurements are taken.

All steering and suspension components, front and rear, should be visually checked for wear or obvious damage. Check ball joints, tie-rods, idler arms, pitman arm, control arms and bushings, struts, shocks, springs, sway bars and brackets, rack and pinion steering bellows, and rack mountings. (Loose or deteriorated mountings can cause steering shimmy and wander.)

Check the steering gear for play. Do not forget to check the front and rear wheel bearings. Finally, check the ride height based on the normal vehicle load.

Once the alignment heads are installed and compensated for wheel runout, read front and rear camber, front and rear toe. The thrust angle created by the rear wheels can then be determined. (Some alignment machines do this.)

Read caster by turning the front wheels side to side. Most alignment machines compensate for wheel setback. Some show how much setback is present and where.

Steering axis inclination, an angle frequently neglected on quick alignment jobs, is important to include because it can help pinpoint damaged parts. If the SAI does not match specifications, compare both sides. Problems can be caused by bent struts, control arm spindles, or steering knuckles. A mislocated strut tower or control arm anchor can also throw off the reading.

Once the basic measurements have been taken, the suspension can be adjusted. Do so in this sequence: rear camber, rear toe, caster/camber one side front, caster/camber other side front, then front toe.

Case 1

Two days after having a complete alignment performed on her late-model vehicle, a customer returns to the shop complaining of improper service. Since having the alignment work done, the vehicle now consistently pulls to the right.

The technician who performed the work road tests the vehicle and verifies that the car is drifting to the right. The technician rechecks the alignment against factory specifications. All settings appear to be within range. A check of the suspension system finds nothing wrong. Desperately trying to figure out why the vehicle is drifting, the technician reviews some notes she kept from an alignment class attended several months before. Here, she finds the answer. When setting the right wheel, she forgot to allow for road crown. The technician readjusts the right wheel to account for road crown angle and test drives the vehicle. The drifting has been eliminated.

Summary

- The components of a manual steering system include the steering linkage, steering gear, and the steering column and wheel.
- The term steering linkage is applied to the system of pivots and connecting parts that is placed between the steering gear and the steering arms attached to the front wheels, controlling the direction of vehicle travel. The steering linkage transfers the motion of the steering gear output shaft to the steering arms, turning the wheels to maneuver the vehicle.
- Basic components of a parallelogram steering linkage system include the pitman arm, idler arm, links, tie-rods, and in some designs, a steering damper.
- The worm and roller steering components are basically the same found in the parallelogram system.
- In rack and pinion steering linkage, steering input is received from a pinion gear attached to the steering column. This gear moves a toothed rack that is attached to the tie-rods that move the wheels.
- There are three types of manual steering gears in use today: recirculating ball, worm and roller, and rack and pinion.
- The steering wheel and column produces the necessary force to turn the steering gear.
- The power-steering unit is designed to reduce the amount of effort required to turn the steering wheel. It also reduces driver fatigue on long drives and makes it easier to steer the vehicle at slow road speeds, particularly during parking.
- There are several power-steering systems in use on passenger cars and light-duty trucks. The most common ones are the integral, linkage, hydroboost, and power-assisted rack and pinion systems.
- The major components of a conventional power-steering system are the steering linkage, power-steering pump, flow control and pressure relief valves, reservoir, spool valves and power pistons, hydraulic hose lines, and gearbox or assist assembly on the linkage.
- Electronic rack and pinion systems replace the hydraulic pump, hoses, and fluid associated with conventional power-steering systems with electronic controls and an electric motor located concentric to the rack itself.
- Four-wheel steering (4WS) advantages include cornering capability, steering response, straight-line stability, lane changing, and low-speed maneuverability.
- Currently there are three types of production 4WS systems: mechanical, hydraulic, and electro/hydraulic.
- Caster is the angle of the steering axis of a wheel from the vertical, as viewed from the side of the vehicle. Tilting the wheel forward is negative caster. Tilting backward is positive.
- Camber is the angle represented by the tilt of either the front or rear wheels inward or outward from the vertical as viewed from the front of the car.
- Toe is the distance comparison between the leading edge and trailing edge of the front tires. If the edge distance is less, then there is toe-in. If it is greater, there is toe-out.
- The difference of rear toe from the geometric centerline of the vehicle is called the thrust angle. The vehicle tends to travel in the direction of the thrust line, rather than straight ahead.
- Steering axis inclination (SAI) angles locate the vehicle weight to the inside or outside of the vertical centerline of the tire. The SAI is the angle between the true vertical and a line drawn between the steering pivots as viewed from the front of the vehicle.
- Turning radius or cornering angle is the amount of toe-out present on turns.
- In correct tracking all suspension and wheels are in their correct locations and conditions and are aligned so that the rear wheels follow directly behind the front wheels while moving in a straight line.
- Load distribution refers to the load placed on each wheel.
- It is important to remember that approximately 80% of today's vehicles not only have front-end alignment but require rear-wheel alignment as well.
- The primary objective of four-wheel or total-wheel alignment, whether front or rear drive, solid axle, or independent rear suspension, is to align all four wheels so the vehicle drives and tracks straight with the steering wheel centered. To accomplish this, the wheels must be parallel to one another and perpendicular to a common centerline.

Review Questions

1. Describe how a rack and pinion steering, parallelogram steering, and worm and roller system operate.
2. What checks should be made before undertaking a wheel alignment?
3. What is an integral power-steering system?
4. Define the term gearbox ratio.

5. What are the basic features of all four-wheel steering systems?
6. What is the primary purpose of power-steering hoses?
   a. to lubricate the pump
   b. to relieve pressure
   c. to transmit power through fluid under pressure
   d. none of the above
7. Which system provides power assistance even when the engine stalls?
   a. electronically controlled power steering
   b. electric/electronic rack and pinion
   c. both a and b
   d. neither a nor b
8. Technician A says that the manual steering gear is the probable cause of a shimmy. Technician B says it could be loose steering linkage. Who is correct?
   a. Technician A
   b. Technician B
   c. Both A and B
   d. Neither A nor B
9. Technician A says that adjusting the steering gear too tightly can cause hard steering. Technician B says that adjusting the steering gear too tightly can cause poor returnability. Who is correct?
   a. Technician A
   b. Technician B
   c. Both A and B
   d. Neither A nor B
10. A worn or damaged idler arm can cause _____.
    a. front-end shimmy
    b. hard steering
    c. both a and b
    d. neither a nor b
11. Worn tie-rod ends can result in _____.
    a. scalloped and scuffed tires
    b. vehicle pull to one side
    c. poor returnability
    d. all of the above
12. In a rack and pinion steering system, what protects the rack from contamination?
    a. the inner tie-rod socket
    b. the outer tie-rod socket
    c. grommets
    d. the bellows boot
13. A variable ratio can be normally found in _____.
    a. manual-steering units
    b. power-steering units
    c. both a and b
    d. neither a nor b
14. Hydro-boost provides power to the steering system and to what other system?
    a. braking
    b. electrical
    c. both a and b
    d. neither a nor b
15. All of the following angles are adjustable during wheel alignment except _____.
    a. toe-in
    b. toe-out
    c. camber
    d. steering axis inclination
16. An owner's concern indicates excessive turning effort. Technician A road tests the car to determine the actual force required to turn the wheel. Technician B uses a pull scale. Who is correct?
    a. Technician A
    b. Technician B
    c. Both A and B
    d. Neither A nor B
17. Which of the following is true of the steering linkage system?
    a. The power cylinder is integrated with the steering gear.
    b. The power cylinder has four hydraulic lines connected to it.
    c. The power cylinder is attached to the steering center link.
    d. All of the above.
18. What is another name for the circle mode of 4WS?
    a. parallel
    b. same-phase
    c. contra phase
    d. none of the above
19. Rack and pinion steering _____.
    a. is lighter in weight and has fewer components than parallelogram steering
    b. does not provide as much feel for the road as parallelogram steering
    c. does not use tie-rods in the same fashion as parallelogram steering
    d. all of the above
20. What connects the steering column to the wheels?
    a. steering shaft
    b. steering linkage
    c. gearbox
    d. pitman arm
21. Which of the following statements concerning links is correct?
    a. If a center link is nonwear, the pitman arm is normally a wear arm.
    b. Links with open tapers are nonwear.
    c. The purpose of links is to make the final connection between the steering linkage and steering knuckles.
    d. Links are important for maintaining correct toe settings.

SECTION 8 BRAKES

Chapter 35 Brake Systems
Chapter 36 Drum Brakes
Chapter 37 Disc Brakes

As with the steering and suspension systems, a properly operating brake system is vital to the safe operation and control of any vehicle. A full understanding of hydraulic principles, brake lines and hoses, and disc and drum brake components is needed to perform accurate brake service.

Anti-lock braking systems (ABS) and traction-assist systems are rapidly gaining popularity. They will soon be standard equipment on most vehicles. ABS and traction assist add yet another electronically controlled system to the increasingly complex modern vehicle.

The information found in Section 8 corresponds to materials covered on the ASE certification test on brakes.

WE ENCOURAGE PROFESSIONALISM THROUGH TECHNICIAN CERTIFICATION

35 BRAKE SYSTEMS

Objectives

■ Explain the basic principles of braking, including kinetic and static friction, friction materials, application pressure, and heat dissipation. ■ Describe the components of a hydraulic brake system and their operation, including brake lines and hoses, master cylinders, system control valves, and safety switches. ■ Perform both manual and pressure bleeding of the hydraulic system. ■ Briefly describe the operation of drum and disc brakes. ■ Inspect and service hydraulic system components. ■ Describe the operation and components of both vacuum-assist and hydraulic-assist braking units. ■ Describe the operation and components of anit-lock braking systems and automatic stability control systems.

The brake system is designed to slow and halt the motion of a vehicle. To do that, various components within a hydraulic brake system must convert the momentum of the vehicle into heat. They do so by using friction.

❑ FRICTION

Friction is the resistance to movement exerted by two objects in contact with each other. Two forms of friction play a part in controlling a vehicle (Figure 35-1): kinetic, or moving, and static, or stationary. The amount of friction, or resistance to movement, depends on the type of materials in contact, the smoothness of their rubbing surfaces, and the pressure holding them together (often gravity or weight). For example, slide your hand lightly across a polished table top. Very little effort is required because of the smooth texture of the rubbing surfaces and the small amount of pressure exerted. Now, rub your hand over a piece of sandpaper. Feel the difference in friction? The rough texture of the sandpaper resists the movement of your hand.

Rub any surface long enough or hard enough and you begin to feel heat (Figure 35-2). Friction always converts moving, or kinetic, energy into heat. The greater the friction between two moving surfaces, the greater the amount of heat produced.

As the brakes on a moving automobile are actuated, rough-textured pads or shoes are pressed against rotating parts of the vehicle—either rotors (discs) or drums (Figure 35-3). The kinetic energy, or momentum, of the vehicle is then converted into heat energy by the kinetic friction of rubbing surfaces and the car or truck slows down.

When the vehicle comes to a stop, it is held in place by static friction. The friction between the surfaces of the brakes, as well as the friction between the tires and the road, resist any movement. To overcome the static friction that holds the car motionless, the brakes are

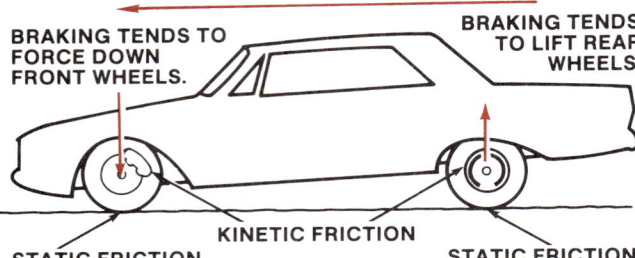

Figure 35-1 Braking action creates kinetic friction in the brakes and static friction between the tire and road to slow the vehicle. When brakes are applied, the vehicle's weight is transferred to the front wheels and is unloaded on the rear wheels.

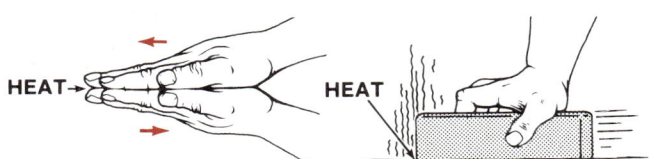

Figure 35-2 Friction produces heat.

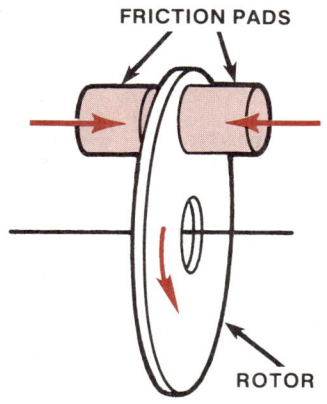

Figure 35-3 Basic disc brake operation.

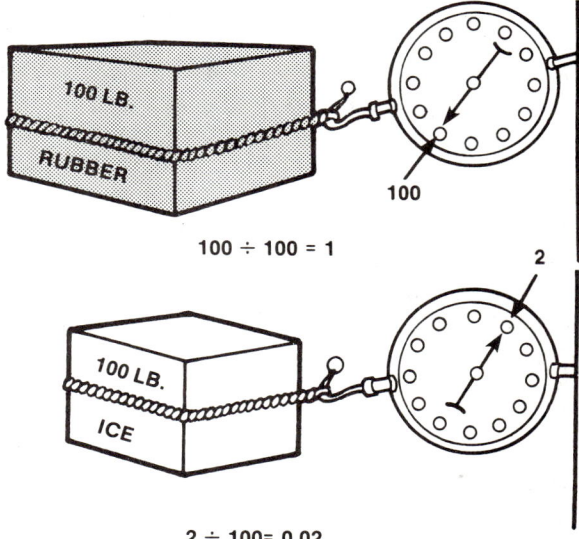

Figure 35-4 Coefficient of friction is equal to the pounds of pull divided by the weight of the object.

released. The heat energy of combustion in the engine crankcase is converted into kinetic energy by the transmission and drivetrain, and the vehicle moves.

Static friction also plays an important part in controlling a moving vehicle. The rotating tires grip the road, and the static friction between these two surfaces enables the driver to control the speed and direction of the car. When the brakes are applied, the kinetic friction of the rubbing brake components slows the rotation of the tires. This increases the static friction between the tires and the road, decreasing the motion of the car. If the kinetic or sliding friction of the brake components overcomes the static friction between the tires and road, the wheels lock up and the car begins to skid. Static friction then exists between the components in the brakes and kinetic friction between the skidding tires and the road—the car is out of control. Obviously, the most effective braking effort is achieved just below the brake component kinetic friction levels that result in wheel lockup. This is the role anti-lock braking systems play in modern vehicles. By electronically pumping the brakes on and off many times each second, anti-lock systems keep kinetic friction below the static friction between the tires and road.

Factors Governing Braking

There are four basic factors that determine the braking power of a system. The first three factors govern the generation of friction: pressure, coefficient of friction, and frictional contact surface. The fourth factor is a result of friction. It is heat, or more precisely heat dissipation.

PRESSURE The amount of friction generated between moving surfaces contacting one another depends in part on the pressure exerted on the surfaces. For example, if you slowly increase the downward pressure on the palm of your hand as you move it across a tabletop, you feel a gradual increase in friction.

In automobiles, hydraulic systems provide application pressure. Hydraulic force is used to move brake pads or brake shoes against spinning rotors or drums mounted to the wheels.

COEFFICIENT OF FRICTION The amount of friction between two surfaces is expressed as a coefficient of friction (COF). The coefficient of friction is determined by dividing the force required to pull an object across a surface by the weight of the object (Figure 35-4). For example, if it requires 100 pounds of pull to slide a 100-pound metal part across a concrete floor, the coefficient of friction is $100 \div 100$ or 1. To pull a 100-pound block of ice across the same floor might require only 2 pounds of pull. The coefficient of friction then would be only 0.02. As it applies to automotive brakes, the COF expresses the frictional relationship between pads and rotors or shoes and drums and is carefully engineered to ensure optimum performance. Therefore, when replacing pads or shoes, it is important to use replacement parts with similar COF. If, for example, the COF is too high, the brakes are too sticky to stop the car smoothly. Premature wheel lockup or grabbing would result. If the coefficient is too low, the friction material tends to slide over the machined surface of the drum or rotor rather than slowing it down. Most automotive friction materials are thus engineered with a COF of between 0.25 and 0.55, depending upon their intended application.

FRICTIONAL CONTACT SURFACE The third factor is the amount of surface, or area, which is in contact. Simply put, bigger brakes stop a car more quickly than smaller brakes used on that same car. Similarly, brakes on all four wheels slow or stop a moving vehicle faster than brakes on only two wheels, assuming the vehicles are equal in size.

HEAT DISSIPATION Any braking system must be able to effectively handle the heat created by friction within the system. The tremendous heat created by the rubbing brake surfaces must be conducted away from the pad and rotor (or shoe and drum) and be absorbed by the air. The greater the surface areas of the brake components, the faster the heat can be dissipated. Thus, the weight and potential speed of the vehicle determine the size of the braking mechanism and the friction surface area of the pad or shoe. Brakes that do not effectively dissipate heat experience brake fade during hard, continuous braking. The linings of the pad and shoe become glazed, and the rotor and drum become hardened. Therefore, the coefficient of friction is reduced and excessive foot pressure must be applied to the brake pedal to produce the desired braking effect.

Brake Lining Friction Materials

For many decades, asbestos was the standard brake lining material. It offers good friction qualities, long wear, and low noise. But new materials are being used because of the health hazards of breathing asbestos dust. In fact, the federal government has banned the use of asbestos in new vehicles and in aftermarket replacement parts.

FULLY METALLIC Fully metallic linings of sintered iron have been used for years in heavy-duty and racing applications because they have great fade resistance. However, they require very high pedal pressure and tend to quickly wear out drums and rotors.

SEMIMETALLIC Semimetallic lining materials were developed to eliminate the disadvantages of fully metallic linings. Semimetallic linings are made of iron fibers molded with an adhesive matrix. Semimetallic material offers excellent fade resistance that meets the needs of today's vehicles. It has good frictional characteristics so that only a moderate amount of application pressure is needed. Finally, semimetallic pads and shoes do not cause excessive wear on rotor or drum surfaces.

NONASBESTOS Other nonasbestos lining materials made of synthetic substances are now available. The major brake lining manufacturers are constantly experimenting with new materials that meet all established criteria for long life, friction characteristics, drum and rotor wear, and heat dissipation.

☐ PRINCIPLES OF HYDRAULIC BRAKE SYSTEMS

A hydraulic system (Figure 35-5) uses a brake fluid to transfer pressure from the brake pedal to the pads or shoes. This transfer of pressure is reliable and consistent because liquids are not compressible. That is, pressure applied to a liquid in a closed system is transmitted by that liquid equally to every other part of that system. Apply a force of 5 pounds per square inch (psi)

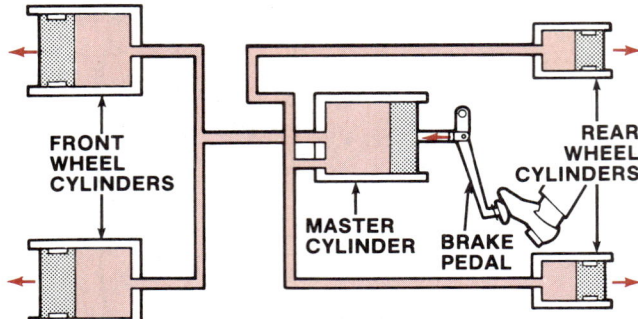

Figure 35-5 Schematic of a basic automotive hydraulic brake system.

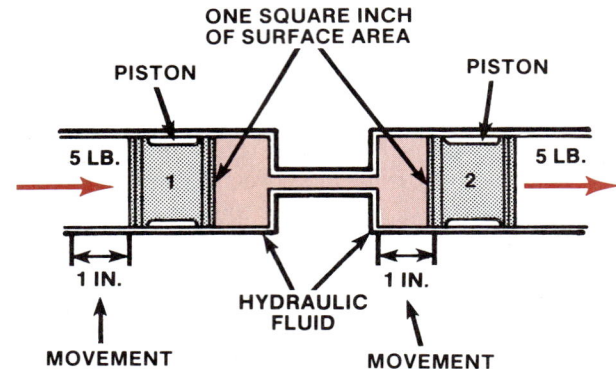

Figure 35-6 Force and movement are transmitted equally.

through the master cylinder and you can measure 5 psi anywhere in the lines and at each wheel where the brakes operate.

For example, move piston 1 a distance of 1 inch and piston 2 also moves 1 inch (Figure 35-6). The force can be increased at output (that is, at the wheel) by increasing the size of the wheel's piston, though piston travel decreases. The force at output can be decreased by decreasing the size of the wheel piston, but the piston travel increases.

Thus, to double the output force of the 5 psi at the master cylinder to 10 psi at the wheels, simply use a wheel cylinder piston with a surface area of 2 square inches (Figure 35-7). To triple the force of 100 psi, use

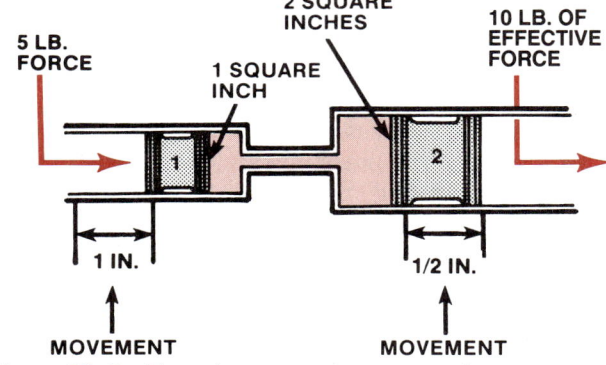

Figure 35-7 Force increases—movement decreases.

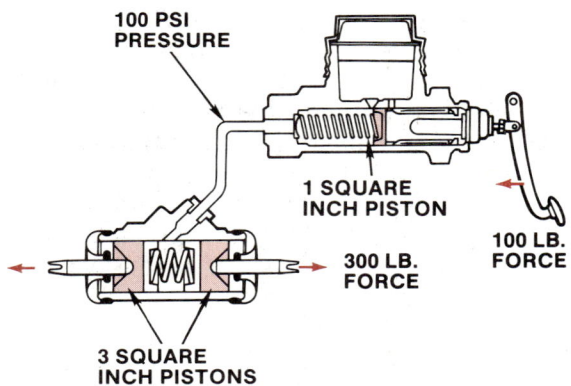

Figure 35-8 Output force increases with piston size.

a piston with 3 square inches and 300 pounds of output result (Figure 35-8). No matter what the fluid pressure is, the output force can be increased with a larger piston, though piston travel decreases proportionately. In actual practice, however, fluid movement in an automotive hydraulic brake system is very slight. In an emergency, when the pedal goes all the way to the floor, the volume of fluid displaced only amounts to about 20 cubic centimeters. About 15 cubic centimeters goes to the front discs and 5 cubic centimeters goes to the rear drums. Even under these conditions, the wheel cylinder and caliper pistons move only slightly.

Of course, the hydraulic system does not stop the car all by itself. In fact, it really just transmits the action of the driver's foot on the brake pedal out to the wheels (Figure 35-9). In the wheels, sets of friction pads are forced against rotors or drums to slow their turning and bring the car to a stop. Mechanical force (the driver stepping on the brake pedal) is changed into hydraulic pressure, which is changed back into mechanical force (brake shoes and disc pads contacting the drums and rotors). The amount of force acting upon the friction pads and shoes is equivalent to the psi applied to the pedal multiplied by the area of the piston affected. A force of 25 psi applied to the pedal times 4 square inches of piston area equals 100 pounds of pressure in the system (Figure 35-10).

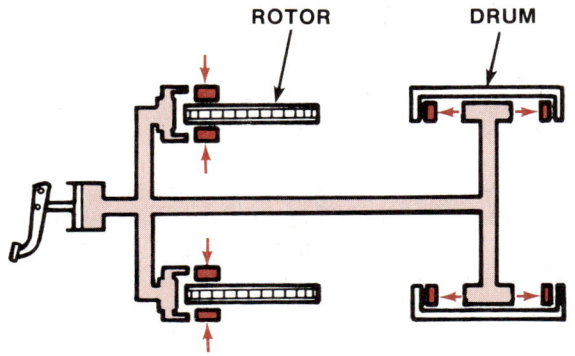

Figure 35-9 Typical hydraulic brake layout.

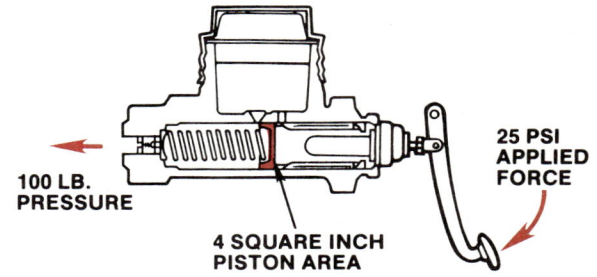

Figure 35-10 Multiplied force in a master cylinder.

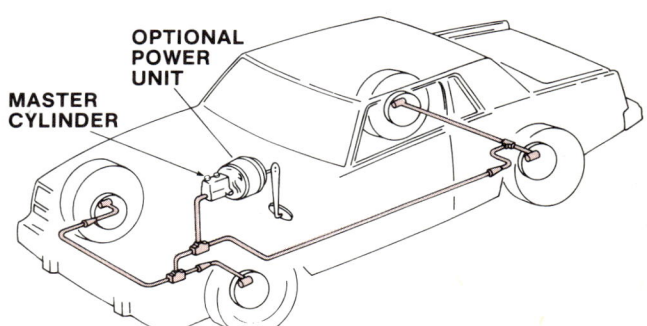

Figure 35-11 Single system braking.

Single Braking Systems

With very few exceptions, the single circuit hydraulic system (Figure 35-11) was used on cars made through 1966. This system used a master cylinder with one piston that operated the brakes on all four wheels. Later, its use was confined to trucks and industrial and construction equipment.

Dual Braking Systems

Since 1967, federal law has required that all cars be equipped with two separate brake systems. If one circuit fails, the other provides enough braking power to safely stop the car.

The dual system differs from the single system by employing a tandem master cylinder, which is essentially two master cylinders formed by installing two separate pistons and fluid reservoirs into one cylinder bore. Each piston applies hydraulic pressure to two wheels.

Front/Rear Split System

In early dual systems, the hydraulic circuits were separated front and rear (Figure 35-12). Both front wheels were on one hydraulic circuit and both rear wheels on another. If a failure occurred in one system, the other system was still available to stop the vehicle. However, the front brakes do approximately 70% of the braking work. A failure in the front brake system would only leave 20 to 40% braking power. This problem was solved, however, with the development of diagonally-split systems.

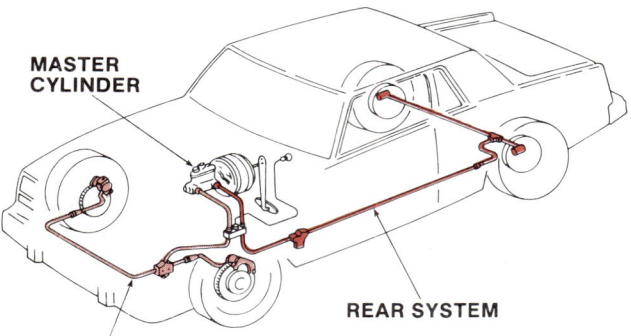

Figure 35-12 Front/rear split hydraulic system.

Diagonally-Split System

The diagonally-split system operates on the same principles as the front and rear split system. It uses primary and secondary master cylinders that move simultaneously to exert hydraulic pressure on their respective systems.

The hydraulic brake lines on this system, however, have been diagonally-split front to rear (left front to right rear and right front to left rear) (Figure 35-13). The circuit split can occur within the master cylinder or externally at a proportioning valve or pressure differential switch.

In the event of a system failure, the remaining good system would do all the braking on one front wheel and the opposite rear wheel, thus maintaining 50% of the total braking force.

❑ HYDRAULIC BRAKE SYSTEM COMPONENTS

The following sections describe the major components of a hydraulic brake system, including power-assisted systems and anti-lock braking systems.

Brake Fluid

Brake fluid is the lifeblood of any hydraulic brake system. It is what makes the system operate properly.

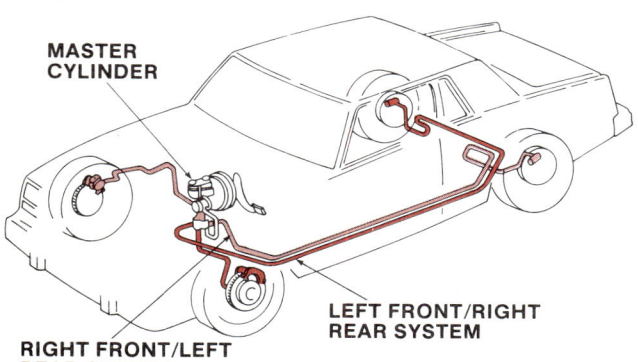

Figure 35-13 Dual diagonally-split hydraulic system.

Modern brake fluid is specially blended to enable it to perform a variety of functions. Brake fluid must be able to flow freely at extremely high temperatures (500 degrees Fahrenheit) and at very low temperatures (-104 degrees Fahrenheit). Brake fluid must also serve as a lubricant to the many parts with which it comes into contact to insure smooth and even operation. In addition, brake fluid must fight corrosion and rust in the brake lines and various assemblies and components it services. Another important property of brake fluid is that it must resist evaporation. Some of the earliest brake fluids had chemicals in them that ate away at the rubber components in the brake system (i.e., cups and seals). Modern brake fluid must be compatible with rubber to avoid damage to the cups and seals in the system. Brake fluid must provide a controlled amount of swell to the brake system cups and seals. There must be just enough swell to form a good seal. However, the swell cannot be too great. If it is, drag and poor brake response occur. Every can of brake fluid carries the identification letters of SAE and DOT. These letters (and corresponding numbers) indicate the nature, blend, and performance characteristics of that particular brand of brake fluid.

There are three basic types or classifications of hydraulic brake fluids. DOT 3 is a conventional brake fluid with a minimum dry ERBP (equilibrium reflux boiling point) of 401 degrees Fahrenheit and a minimum wet ERBP of 284 degrees Fahrenheit. It is generally recommended for most ABS systems and some power brake setups. DOT 4 is a conventional brake fluid with a minimum dry ERBP of 446 degrees Fahrenheit and a minimum wet ERBP of 356 degrees Fahrenheit. It is the most commonly used brake fluid for conventional brake systems. DOT 5 is a unique silicone-based brake fluid with a minimum dry ERBP of 500 degrees Fahrenheit and a minimum wet ERBP of 356 degrees Fahrenheit. In the last few years, DOT 5 has lost its demand by brake servicing experts. However, remember that it is best to follow the vehicle manufacturer's recommendations.

CAUTION: *Only use approved brake fluid in a brake system. Any other lubricant, such as power steering fluid, automatic transmission fluid, or engine oil, which has a petroleum base, must never be used in the brake system. Petroleum-based fluids attack the rubber components in the brake system, like the piston cups and seals, and cause them to swell and disintegrate.*

Some vehicles have brake fluid level sensors that provide the driver with an early warning message that the brake fluid in the master cylinder reservoir has dropped below the normal level.

As the brake fluid in the master cylinder reservoir drops below the designated level, the sensor closes the warning message circuit. About 15 seconds later the message "brake fluid low" appears on the instrument panel. At this time, the master cylinder reservoir should be checked and filled to the correct level with the specified brake fluid.

Brake Pedals

The brake pedal is where the brake's hydraulic system gets its start. When the brake pedal is depressed, force is applied to the master cylinder. On a basic hydraulic brake system (where there is no power assist), the force applied is transmitted mechanically. As the pedal in Figure 35-14 pivots, the force applied to it is multiplied mechanically. The force that the pushrod applies to the master cylinder piston is, therefore, much greater than the force applied to the brake pedal.

Master Cylinders

The heart of the hydraulic brake system is the master cylinder. It converts the mechanical force of the driver's foot on the brake pedal to hydraulic pressure. The master cylinder has a bore that contains a piston assembly and return spring. Seals on the piston prevent fluid leakage. A cup seal on the forward end keeps the brake fluid ahead of the piston when it is put under pressure. Although master cylinders differ in number of pistons, reservoir design, and integrated hydraulic components, the operation of all master cylinders is basically the same.

Master cylinders are generally constructed of cast iron (Figure 35-15A) with an integral fluid reservoir or weight-saving aluminum with a separate molded nylon or fiberglass reinforced plastic reservoir. Aluminum body master cylinders feature an anodized body (Figure 35-15B) to protect against corrosion and to extend bore life.

CAUTION: It is recommended that aluminum master cylinders not be rebuilt if pitting or scoring of the cylinder bore is evident. A new unit should be installed.

Single System Master Cylinders

To understand how a master cylinder works, it is easier to examine a single piston master cylinder before studying dual master cylinders. A cross section of a

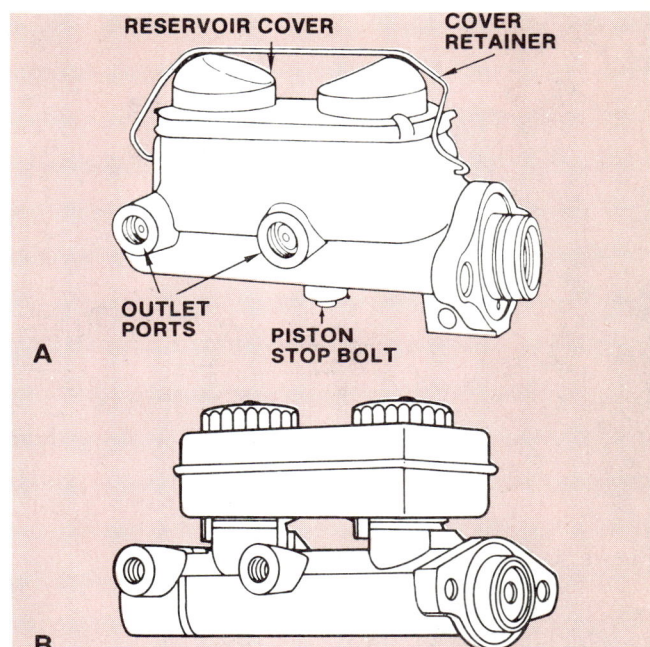

Figure 35-15 (A) Typical cast-iron dual master cylinder and (B) typical aluminum/composite dual master cylinder.

typical single piston cylinder is shown in Figure 35-16. The cylinder and the fluid reservoir are an integral unit. A vent port and compensating or replenishing port pass from the reservoir into the piston chamber. The chamber contains a piston, a return spring, and a residual pressure check valve. On the brake pedal end of the cylinder, a pushrod connects the cylinder to the power booster or brake pedal clevis. The opposite end of the cylinder contains the threaded fluid outlet to which the hydraulic line is connected.

When the brake pedal is depressed, the force from the brake pedal is transferred to the piston by a pushrod. The piston exerts pressure on the fluid, which flows out through the fluid outlet port into a single hydraulic system, serving both front and rear brakes. When the brake pedal is released, the return spring in the cylinder forces the piston back to its original position. If the piston returns too quickly, vacuum is generated in the cylinder. Fluid from the reservoir then enters the cylinder through the vent port to fill the void. As the brakes are fully released, excess fluid is returned to the reservoir through the replenishing or compensating port to relieve pressure in the system.

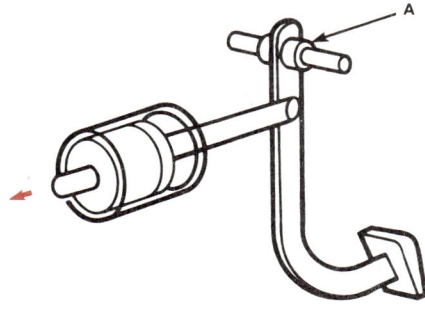

Figure 35-14 Brake pedal action.

> ### SHOP TALK
>
> Master cylinder terminology is often confusing. For example, replenishing and compensating ports are synonymous terms. That is, they serve the same function but are called different names by different manufacturers and in different parts of the country. The same is true of the master

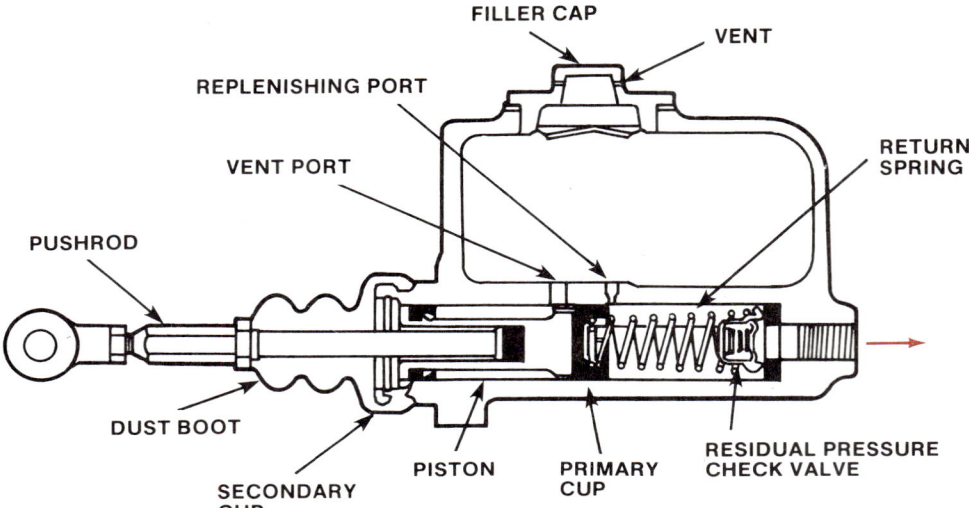

Figure 35-16 Typical single master cylinder system.

 cylinder's vent port, by-pass port, or relief passage. All these names actually perform the same function and in basically the same manner, but are called by different names.

Dual Master Cylinders

The important parts of a typical dual master cylinder are shown in Figure 35-17. Their functions are described here. The cap is also known as the bail, cover, or gasket. This part keeps an airtight seal on the master cylinder while letting it breathe. It keeps moisture from entering the system. Moisture breaks down the ability of brake fluid to lubricate properly. It also causes corrosion. The cap, or cover gasket, acts like a diaphragm. It expands and contracts as the fluid pressure rises or falls. When the brakes are applied, the demand for brake fluid could create a vacuum below the diaphragm. This would keep fluid from flowing out of the reservoir. For the gasket to expand or contract, the space between the gasket and the cover must be vented. The venting is accomplished with small grooves or drilled holes in the cap or cover. (Most seals have a bellow design. As the fluid goes down, the space above the gasket fills with air. When the brakes are released, the fluid returns to the master cylinder reservoirs and the air is forced out the vent holes.) The wire bail retainer (Figure 35-18) or a bolt is typically used to hold on the cap or cover.

Extra brake fluid is stored in two separate reservoirs. Made of either cast iron or specially blended plastic, they are designed to function independently as a protection against lost brake fluid. Without this reserve brake fluid available, the brake system functions improperly or fails. It is important to keep the reservoir filled to its proper level.

The dual master cylinder reservoir has a single piston bore that contains the two pistons (primary and secondary) lined up in tandem. Each piston has a return spring in front of it. This holds the piston cup slightly behind the replenishing port for each reservoir. In addition to keeping the replenishing ports uncovered, the return springs also return the brake pedal when the force has been removed from it. As the brakes are applied, the stiffer primary piston spring pushes the secondary piston and spring slightly. Then, the cup at the front end of the secondary piston passes and closes off the primary replenishing port on the secondary side of the master cylinder.

A retaining ring fits into a groove near the end of the bore and holds the piston.

The primary outlet (or port) is the one closer to the cowl panel. It is off the primary piston (the one which receives the initial, or primary movement).

The function of the residual check valve is to keep light (or residual) pressure in the brake lines and also at the wheel cylinders. Without residual pressure, air can be sucked past the wheel cylinder cups and into the wheel cylinders. This could occur when the brake pedal is released quickly. Residual check valves are designed to permit hydraulic fluid and pressure to flow from the master cylinder into the hydraulic lines when the pressure in the master cylinder becomes great enough to open the valve. After allowing the fluid to flow back into the master cylinder when the pedal is released, the outlet check valve spring (Figure 35-19) takes over and keeps the hydraulic lines and wheel cylinders full of fluid, ready for the next application of the brakes. On most of the newer car models, automobile manufacturers have eliminated residual pressure check valves from the brake system. Wheel cylinders are equipped with cup expanders. The cup expanders keep the cup seals tightly pressed against the cylinder walls to prevent air from entering the system.

Light residual pressure is needed for operating the drum brakes. However, when the brakes are used re-

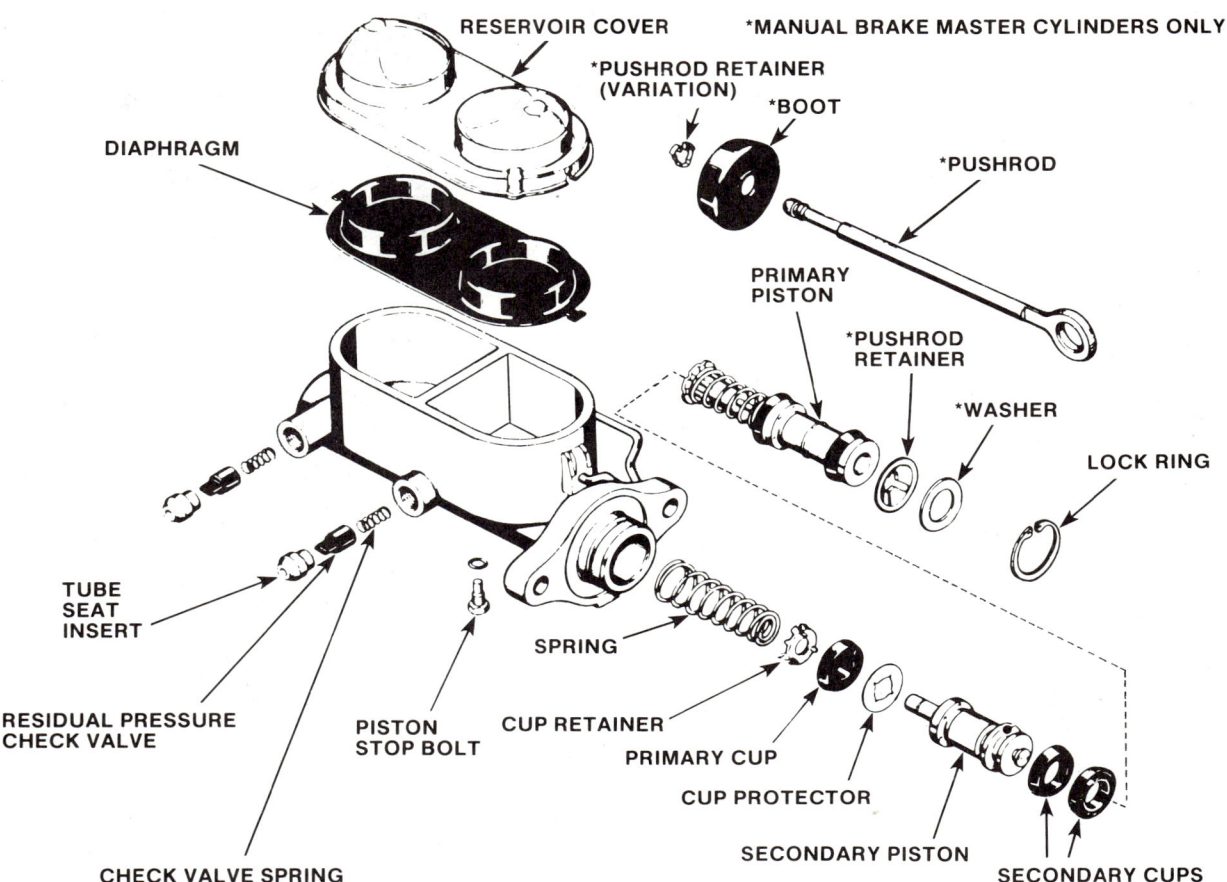

Figure 35-17 Typical Bendix dual master cylinder system—disassembled.

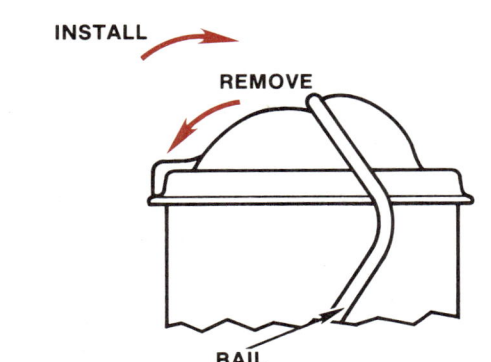

Figure 35-18 Cover and retainer bail wire.

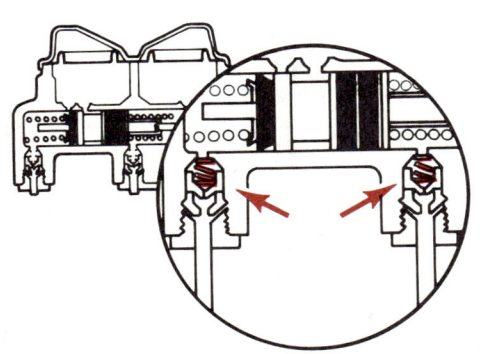

Figure 35-19 Outlet check valve springs.

peatedly, too much pressure can build up. The replenishing or compensating port (Figure 35-20) takes care of this problem. After many stops, like in city driving, the brake drums and wheel cylinders get very hot. This causes the brake fluid to heat up and expand. Such a pressure buildup can become so strong that it keeps the brake shoes from returning after releasing the brake pedal. If the brake shoes do not return properly, they might drag against the drums. This causes more heat to build up and pressure is further increased.

SHOP TALK

Extra brake fluid is forced into the hydraulic system by pumping the brakes. Pressure builds until the brake pedal is released and the piston moves back far enough to uncover the replenishing ports. This removes the excess pressure from the brake lines and wheel cylinders and allows the fluid to return to the brake master cylinder reservoir.

Vent ports help to pump up a low brake pedal by allowing more fluid in the lines. There are several reasons for a brake pedal to be lower than normal. One is that the clearance between the brake lining and the

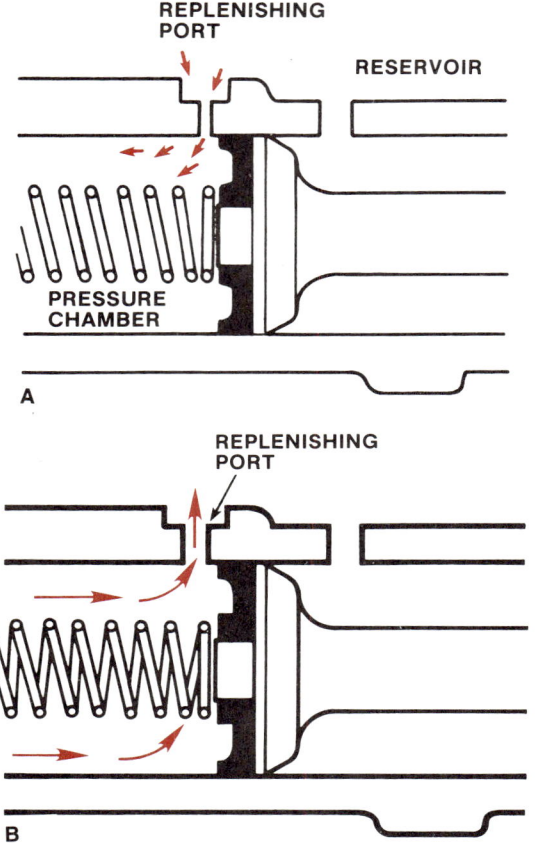

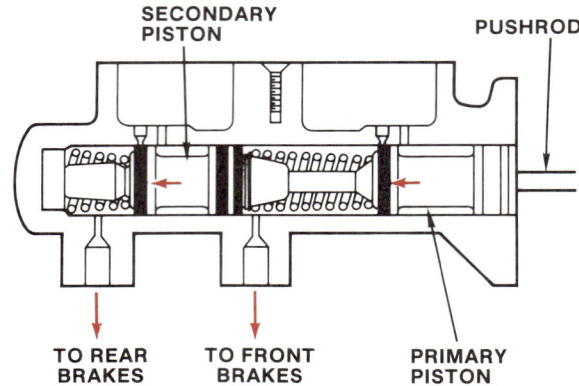

Figure 35-21 Master cylinder—brakes applied.

Figure 35-20 (A) Reservoir replenishing pressure chamber; (B) fluid returns to the reservoir.

drum is too large. This can happen when the automatic brake adjusters, if the vehicle is so equipped, are not working properly. Another reason could be the result of air leaking into the brake system. If a brake pedal is pumped too rapidly, the return springs in the master cylinder might move the pistons back very fast. At the other end of the system, the brake shoe return springs move the wheel cylinder pistons much more slowly. The flow of brake fluid from the wheel cylinders is then delayed. It cannot match the fast return of the master cylinder pistons. As a result, pressure drops in the master cylinder. The pressure in the master cylinder actually becomes lower than the pressure in the reservoir. Fluid then rushes through the vent ports, through holes in the piston, past the piston cup, and back into the area ahead of the piston cups. Vent ports are important because the replenishing ports are not large enough to handle the extra flow of fluid needed when the pedal is pumped.

OPERATION OF THE DUAL SYSTEM MASTER CYLINDER To understand the operation of a dual master cylinder, it is important to know how the various parts of the unit work together. Actually, the operation of the dual master cylinder is like that of two single piston types placed end to end in the same bore. The two pistons in the master cylinder are not rigidly connected. Each half really operates like a single system. As just mentioned, each piston has its own reservoir with vent and replenishing ports. Stepping on the brake pedal moves a pushrod forward, causing the first or primary piston to move forward. The fluid ahead of it cannot be compressed, so the secondary piston moves. As the pistons progress deeper into the cylinder bore, the brake fluid that is put under pressure transmits this force through both systems to friction pads in the wheels (Figure 35-21).

The pistons have seals at both ends: a cup seal with a one-way sealing property at the forward end and a secondary cup at the rear. Each piston has a return spring with the primary piston spring between the two pistons. On the forward stroke, the lip of each cup seal is forced against the bore wall. When the piston springs quickly back to place, the brake fluid cannot return through the lines fast enough to avoid creating a low-pressure condition ahead of it. Fluid must reach the low-pressure area in time for another stroke of the cylinder. On the return stroke, the edges of the cup pull away from the bore enough to allow fluid to pass around the piston assembly to the area of low pressure (Figure 35-22).

At the same time, the reservoir returns the small amount of fluid it had taken in during piston action (Figure 35-23). This way, the master cylinder returns

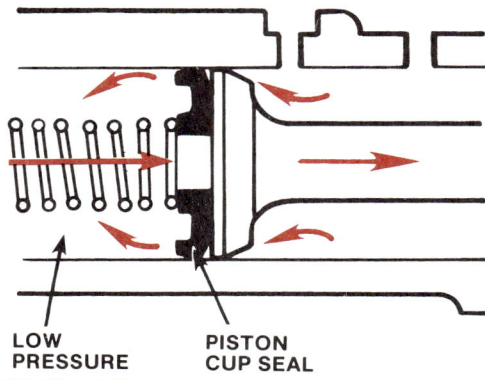

Figure 35-22 When the pedal is released, brake fluid flows around piston cup.

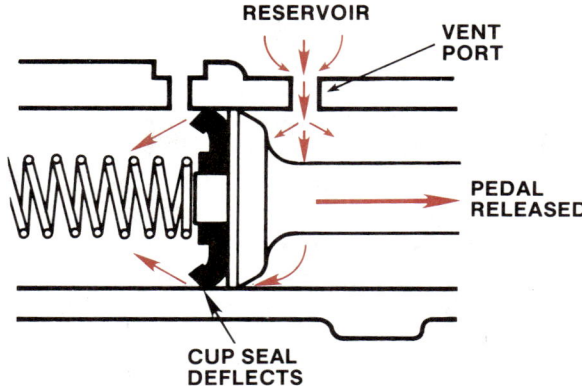

Figure 35-23 The reservoir returns fluid to the bore.

to normal before all the fluid returns from the lines. Finally, the pads and shoes return to position. That is, once the brake pedal is released and the master cylinder piston has returned to the rest position, shoe return springs (in the drum brakes) and piston seals (in the disc brakes) cause these pistons to retract.

❏ HYDRAULIC TUBES AND HOSES

Steel tubing and flexible synthetic rubber hosing serve as the arteries and veins of the hydraulic brake system. These brake lines transmit brake fluid pressure (the blood) from the master cylinder (the heart) to the wheel cylinders and calipers (the muscles and working parts) of the drum and disc brakes.

Fluid transfer from the driver-actuated master cylinder is usually routed through one or more valves and then into the steel tubing and hoses (Figure 35-24). The design of the brake lines offers quick fluid transfer response with very little friction loss. Engineering and installing the brake lines so they do not wrap around sharp curves is very important in maintaining this good fluid transfer.

BRAKE LINE TUBING Most brake line tubing consists of copper-fused double-wall steel tubing in diameters ranging from 1/8 to 3/8 inch. Some OEM brake tubing is manufactured with soft steel strips, sheathed with copper. The strips are rolled into a double-wall assembly and then bonded in a furnace at extremely high temperatures. Corrosion protection is often added by tin-plating the tubing.

FITTINGS Assorted fittings are used to connect steel tubing to junction blocks or other tubing sections. The most common fitting is the double or inverted flare style. Double flaring is important to maintain the strength and safety of the system. Single flare or sleeve compression fittings may not hold up in the rigorous operating environment of a standard vehicle brake system.

Fittings are constructed of steel or brass. The 37 degree inverted flare or standard flare fitting is the most commonly used coupling. Newer vehicles may use the ISO or metric bubble flare fitting.

Never change the style of fitting being used on the vehicle. Replace ISO fittings only with ISO fittings. Replace standard fittings with standard fittings.

The metal composition of the fittings must also match exactly. Using an aluminum-alloy fitting with steel tubing may provide a good initial seal, but the dissimilar metals create a corrosion cell that eats away the metal and reduces the connections service life.

BRAKE LINE HOSES Brake hoses offer flexible connections to wheel units so that steering and suspension members can operate without damaging the brake

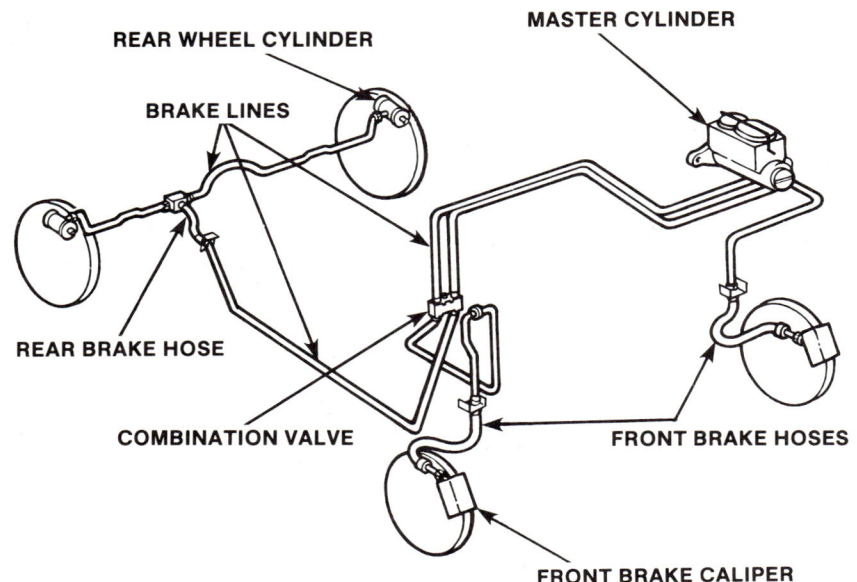

Figure 35-24 Typical hydraulic brake assembly.

902 Section 8 Brakes

system. Typical brake hoses range from 10 to 30 inches in length and are constructed of multiple layers of fabric impregnated with a synthetic rubber. Brake hose material must offer high heat resistance and withstand harsh operating conditions.

> **SHOP TALK**
>
> Many brake hose failures can be traced to errors made in the original installation or repair of the hose. Hoses that are twisted into place become stressed and are prime candidates for leaks and bursting. Most manufacturers now print a natural lay indicator or line on the hose. By making sure this line is not spiralled after fittings are tightened, you can ensure the hose is not overly stressed. Also, always use a hose of the same length and diameter as the original during servicing to maintain brake balance at all wheels.

❑ HYDRAULIC SYSTEM SAFETY SWITCHES AND VALVES

Switches and valves are installed in the brake system hydraulic lines to act as warning devices or pressure control devices.

Pressure Differential (Warning Light) Switches

A pressure differential valve is used in all dual brake systems to operate a warning light switch. Its main purpose is to tell the driver if pressure is lost in either of the two hydraulic systems. Since each brake hydraulic system functions independently, it is possible that the driver might not notice immediately that pressure and braking are lost. When a pressure loss occurs, brake pedal travel increases and a more-than-usual effort is needed for braking. Should the driver not notice the extra effort needed, the warning light is actuated by the hydraulic system safety switch.

Under normal conditions the hydraulic pressure on each side of the pressure differential valve piston is balanced. The piston is located at its center point, so that the spring-loaded warning switch plunger fits into the tapered groove of the piston. This leaves the contacts of the warning switch open. The brake warning light stays off.

If there is a leak in the front or rear braking system, the hydraulic pressure in the two systems is unequal. For example, if there is a leak in the system supplying the front brakes, there is lower pressure in the front system when the brake pedal is applied. The hydraulic pressure in the rear system then pushes the piston toward the front side, where the pressure is lower. As

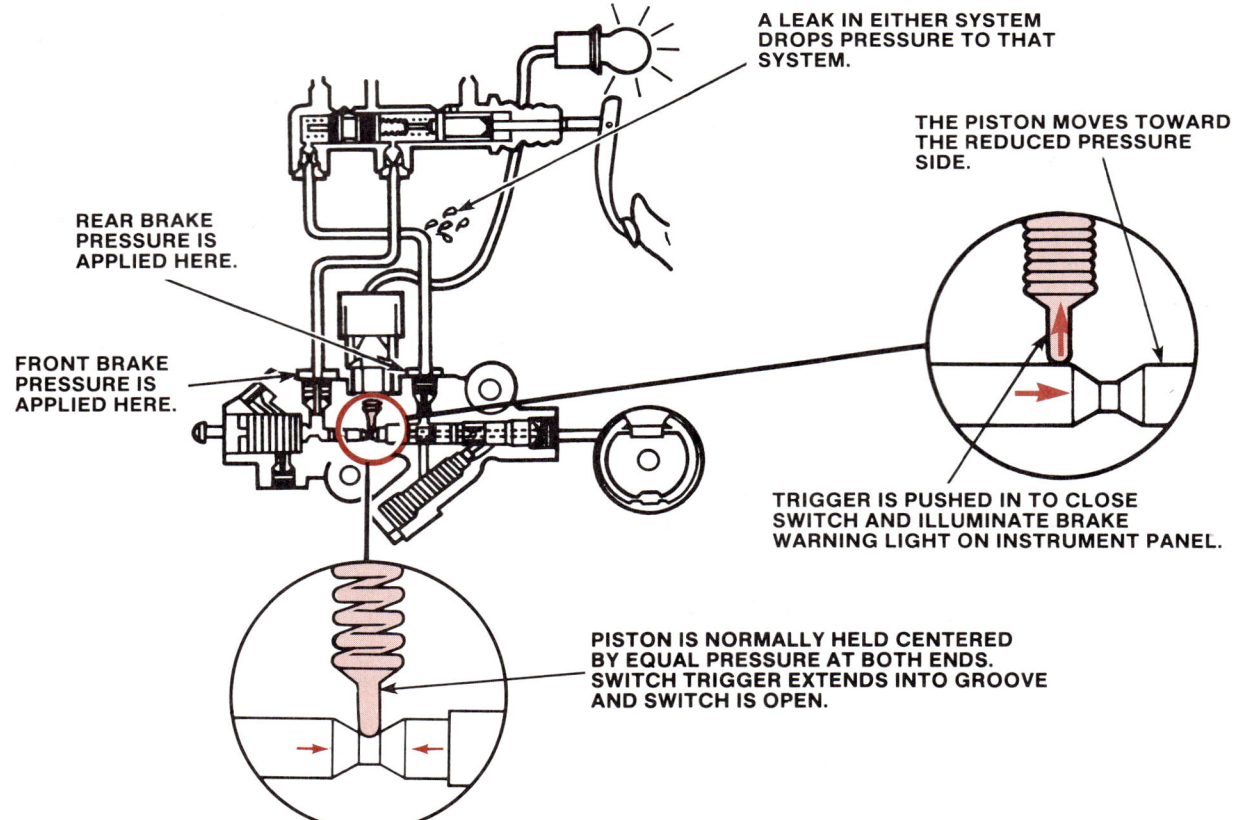

Figure 35-25 Pressure differential valve under normal conditions.

the piston moves, the plunger is pushed out (Figure 35-25). This closes the switch and illuminates the brake warning light.

While all brake warning light switches serve the same function, there are three common variations in the design of these switches. These variations include switches with centering springs, without centering springs, and with centering springs and two pistons.

Metering and Proportioning Valves

Metering and proportioning valves are used to balance the braking characteristics of disc and drum brakes.

The braking response of disc brakes is immediate when the brake pedal is applied. It is directly proportionate to the effort applied at the pedal. Drum brake response is delayed while rear brake hydraulic pressure moves the wheel cylinder pistons to overcome the force of their return springs and force the brake shoes to contact the drum. Their actions are self-energizing and tend to multiply the pedal effort.

Metering Valves

A metering valve in the front brake line holds off pressure going from the master cylinder to the front disc calipers. This delay allows pressure to build up in the rear drums first. When the rear brakes begin to take hold, the hydraulic pressure builds to the level needed to open the metering valve (Figure 35-26). When the metering valve opens, line pressure is high enough to operate the front discs. This process provides for better balance of the front and rear brakes. It also prevents lockup of the front brakes by keeping pressure from them until the rear brakes have started to operate. The metering valve has the most effect at the start of each brake operation and all during light braking conditions.

Proportioning Valves

The self-energizing action of the delayed response rear drum brakes can cause them to lock the rear

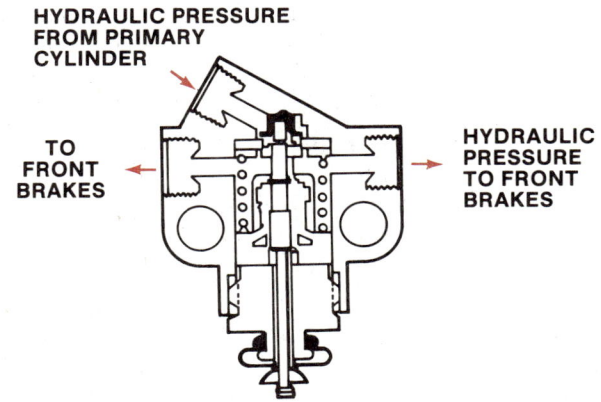

Figure 35-26 Metering valve.

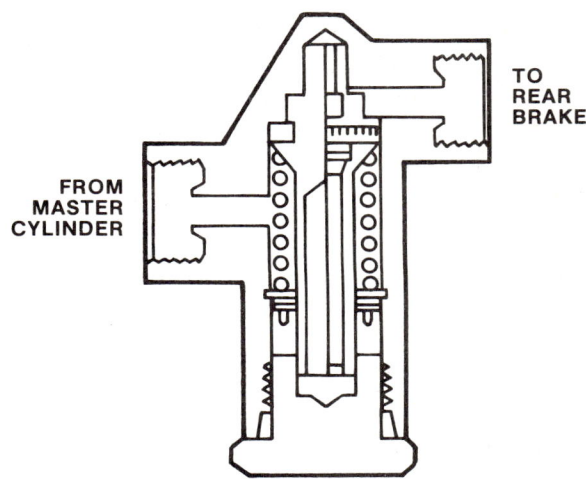

Figure 35-27 Typical proportioning valve cross section.

wheels at a lower hydraulic pressure than the front brakes. The proportioning valve is used to control rear brake pressures, particularly during hard stops. When the pressure to the rear brakes reaches a specified level, the proportioning valve overcomes the force of its spring-loaded piston, stopping the flow of fluid to the rear brakes (Figure 35-27). By doing so, it regulates rear brake system pressure and adjusts for the difference in pressure between front and rear brake systems. This keeps front and rear braking forces in balance.

SHOP TALK

Distribution of weight on some vehicles, such as station wagons, is such that a rear-to-front weight transfer does not present a similar problem. For this reason, standard proportioning valves are not required on all station wagon models.

Combination Valves

Most newer cars have a combination valve in their hydraulic system. This valve is simply a single unit that combines the metering and proportioning valves with the pressure differential valve. Combination valves are described as three-function or two-function valves, depending on the number of functions they perform in the hydraulic system.

THREE-FUNCTION VALVES This type of valve (Figure 35-28) performs the functions of the metering valve, brake warning light switch, and proportioning valve.

TWO-FUNCTION VALVES There are two variations of the two-function combination valve. One variation does the proportioning valve and brake warning light switch functions. The other performs the metering valve and brake warning light switch functions.

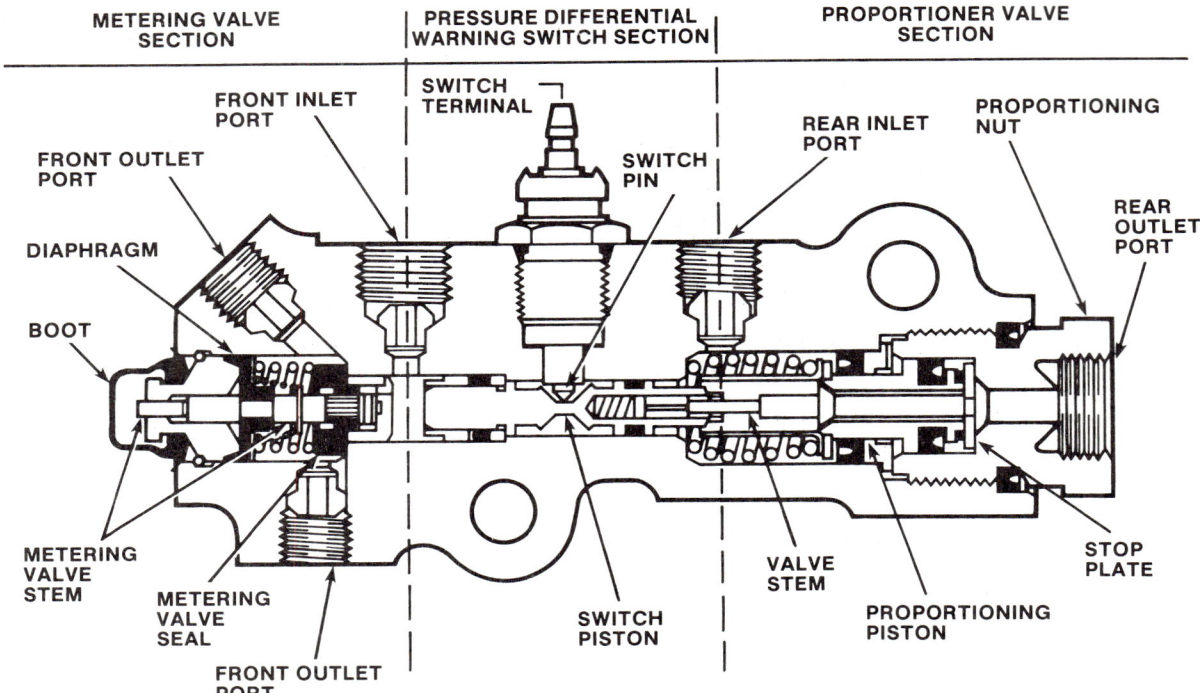

Figure 35-28 A three-function combination valve.

If any one of its several operations fails, the entire combination valve must be replaced, because these units are not repairable.

Stop Light Switch

The stop light (stop light/speed control) switch and mounting bracket assembly (Figure 35-29) is attached to the brake pedal bracket and is activated by pressing the brake pedal.

The mechanical stop light switch is operated by contact with the brake pedal or with a bracket attached to the pedal. The hydraulic switch is operated by hydraulic pressure developed in the master cylinder. In both types, the circuit through the switch is open when the brake pedal is released. When the brakes are applied, the circuit through the switch closes and causes the stop lights to come on.

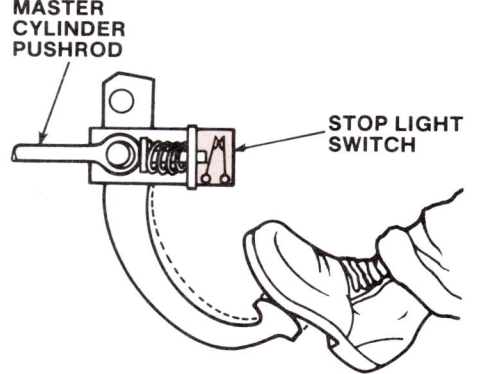

Figure 35-29 Mechanically-activated stop light switch.

☐ DRUM AND DISC BRAKE ASSEMBLIES

Although drum and disc brakes are explained in great detail in later chapters, a brief explanation of their components and operating principles is essential at this point.

Drum Brakes

A drum brake assembly consists of a cast-iron drum, which is bolted to and rotates with the vehicle's wheel, and a fixed backing plate to which are attached the shoes and other components—wheel cylinders, automatic adjusters, and linkages (Figure 35-30). Additionally, there might be some extra hardware for parking brakes. The shoes are surfaced with frictional linings, which contact the inside of the drum when the brakes are applied. The shoes are forced outward, by pistons located inside the wheel cylinder. They are actuated by hydraulic pressure. As the drum rubs against the shoes, the energy of the moving drum is transformed into heat. This heat energy is passed into the atmosphere. When the brake pedal is released, hydraulic pressure drops, and the pistons are pulled back to their unapplied position by return springs.

Disc Brakes

Disc brakes resemble the brakes on a bicycle: the friction elements are in the form of pads, which are squeezed or clamped about the edge of a rotating wheel. With automotive disc brakes, this wheel is a

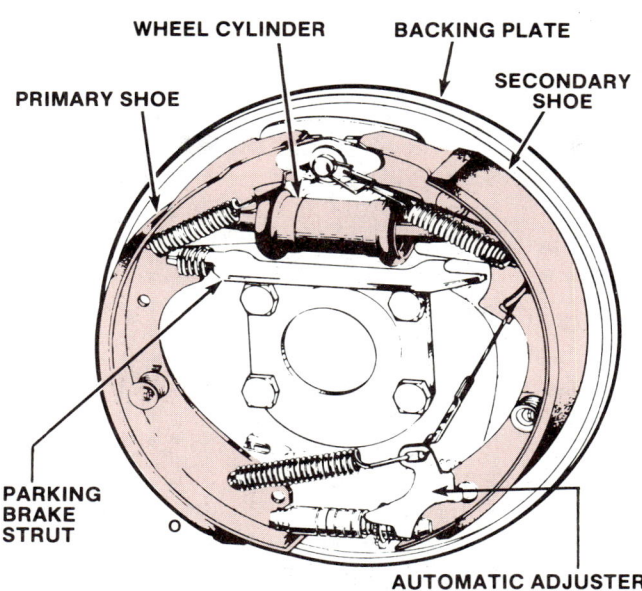

Figure 35-30 Typical drum brake.

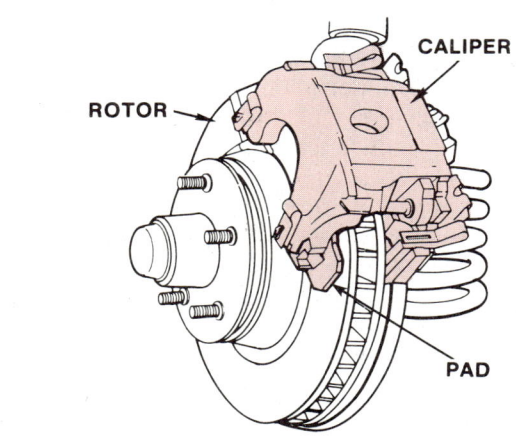

Figure 35-31 A typical disc brake.

separate unit, called a rotor, inboard of the vehicle wheel (Figure 35-31). The rotor is made of cast iron. Since the pads clamp against both sides of it, both sides are machined smooth. Usually the two surfaces are separated by a finned center section for better cooling (such rotors are called ventilated rotors). The pads are attached to metal shoes, which are actuated by pistons, the same as with drum brakes. The pistons are contained within a caliper assembly, a housing that wraps around the edge of the rotor. The caliper is kept from rotating by way of bolts holding it to the car's suspension framework.

The caliper is a housing containing the pistons and related seals, springs, and boots as well as the cylinders and fluid passages necessary to force the friction linings or pads against the rotor. The caliper resembles a hand in the way it wraps around the edge of the rotor. It is attached to the steering knuckle. Some models employ light spring pressure to keep the pads close against the rotor. In other caliper designs this is achieved by a unique type of seal that allows the piston to be pushed out the necessary amount, then retracts it just enough to pull the pad off the rotor.

Unlike shoes in a drum brake, the pads act perpendicular to the rotation of the disc when the brakes are applied. This effect is different from that produced in a brake drum, where frictional drag actually pulls the shoe into the drum. Disc brakes are said to be nonenergized, and so require more force to achieve the same braking effort. For this reason, they are ordinarily used in conjunction with a power brake unit.

☐ HYDRAULIC SYSTEM SERVICE

Hydraulic system service is relatively uncomplicated, but it is vital to the vehicle's safe operation.

Brake Fluid Inspection

The master cylinder is usually located under the hood and near the fire wall on the driver's side.

CAUTION: Clean the cover before removal to avoid dropping dirt into the reservoir.

Remove the cover and check the gasket, or diaphragm. Inspect the cover for damage or plugged vent holes. Clean the vent holes, if necessary.

Check the brake fluid level in the master cylinder. A cast-iron reservoir usually is filled to within 1/4 inch of the top. A plastic reservoir may have fluid level marks. Do not overfill a reservoir. If fluid must be added, a leak probably has developed or the shoes and/or pads are worn. Check the system carefully to locate the leak.

To check for contaminated fluid, place a small amount of brake fluid in a clear glass jar. If the fluid is dirty or separates into layers, it is contaminated. Contaminated fluid must be replaced.

Contaminated brake fluid can damage rubber parts and cause leaks. When replacing contaminated brake fluid, it is necessary to flush and refill the brake system with new fluid. Always use fluid with a DOT rating of 3 or higher. Follow manufacturer's recommendations.

Check the master cylinder for dampness and leaks around the body fittings, especially at the rear. A leak where it is mounted to the fire wall or power brake unit indicates a defective rear piston seal. The master cylinder must be rebuilt or replaced.

Brake Line Inspection

Check all tubing, hoses, and connections from under the hood to the wheels for leaks and damage (Figure 35-32). Wheels and tires also should be inspected for signs of brake fluid leaks. Check all hoses for flexibility, bulges, and cracks. Check parking brake linkage, cable, and connections for damage and wear. Replace parts where necessary.

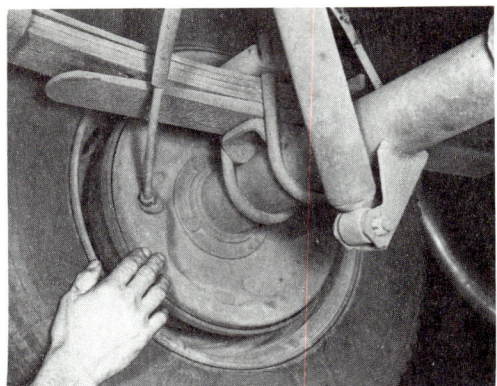

Figure 35-32 (A) Check the rear brake backing plate on each rear wheel for signs of brake fluid, leakage, or oil spray; (B) inspect all hoses and connections.

Brake Pedal Inspection

Depress and release the brake pedal several times (engine running for power brakes). Check for friction and noise. Pedal movement should be smooth, with no squeaks from the pedal or brakes. The pedal should return quickly when it is released.

When operating the engine, be sure the transmission lever is in neutral or park. Be sure the area is properly ventilated for the exhaust to escape.

Apply heavy foot pressure to the brake pedal (engine running for power brakes). Check for a spongy pedal and pedal reserve. Spongy pedal action is springy. Pedal action should feel firm. Pedal reserve is the distance between the brake pedal and the floor after the pedal has been depressed fully. The pedal should not go lower than 1 or 2 inches above the floor.

With the engine off, hold light foot pressure on the pedal for about 15 seconds. There should be no pedal movement during this time. Pedal movement indicates a leak. Repeat the procedure using heavy pedal pressure (engine running for power brakes).

If there is pedal movement, but the fluid level is not low, the master cylinder has internal leakage. It must be rebuilt or replaced. If the fluid level is low, there is an external leak somewhere in the brake system. The leak must be repaired.

Depress the pedal and check for proper stop light operation.

To check power brake operation, depress and release the pedal several times while the engine is stopped. This eliminates vacuum from the system. Hold the brake down with moderate foot pressure and start the engine. If the power unit is operating properly, the brake pedal moves downward when the engine is started.

Master Cylinder Rebuilding

A master cylinder is rebuilt to replace leaking seals or gaskets. If a more serious problem exists, the master cylinder should be replaced.

To remove a master cylinder, disconnect the brake lines at the master cylinder. Install plugs in the brake lines and master cylinder to prevent dirt from entering. Remove the nuts that attach the master cylinder to the fire wall power brake unit, and remove the cylinder.

Remove the cover and seal. Drain the master cylinder and carefully mount it in a vise. Remove the piston assembly and seals according to the manufacturer's instructions. New pistons, pushrods, and seals usually are included in rebuilding kits.

Clean master cylinder parts only with brake fluid, brake cleaning solvent, or alcohol. Do not use a solvent containing mineral oil, such as gasoline. Mineral oil is very harmful to rubber seals.

Inspect the master cylinder. Damage, cracks, porous leaks, and worn piston bores mean the master cylinder must be replaced. Check very carefully for pitting or roughness in the bore. If any is present, the cylinder must be replaced.

Reassemble, install, and bleed the master cylinder according to the manufacturer's directions.

Hydraulic System Bleeding

Fluids cannot be compressed, while gases are compressible. Any air in the brake hydraulic system is compressed as the pressure increases. This action reduces the amount of force that can be transmitted by the fluid. This is why it is very important to keep all air out of the hydraulic system. To do this, air must be bled from brakes. This procedure is called bleeding the brake system.

Bleeding is a process of forcing fluid through the brake lines and out through a bleeder valve or bleeder screw. The fluid eliminates any air that might be in the system. Bleeder screws and valves are fastened to the wheel cylinders or calipers. The bleeder must be cleaned. A drain hose then is connected from the bleeder to a glass jar (Figure 35-33).

> **CUSTOMER CARE**
>
> *Remind your customers to use only approved brake fluid in a brake system. Any other lubri-*

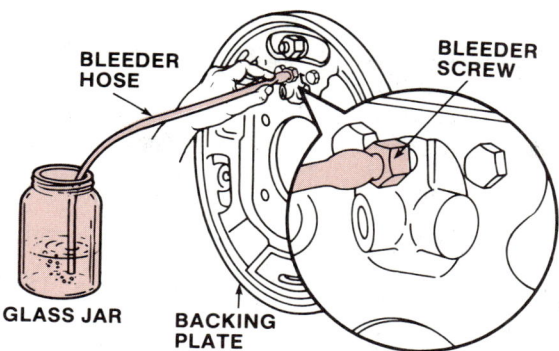

Figure 35-33 While bleeding the brake system, releasing the fluid into a glass jar will help to determine when the system is free of air.

> cant, such as power steering fluid, automatic transmission fluid, or engine oil, which has a petroleum base, must never be used in the brake system. Petroleum-based fluids attack the rubber components in the brake system, like the piston cups and seals, and cause them to swell and disintegrate. If you open a brake fluid reservoir and find that the diaphragm is swelled out of shape and it is larger than it should be, you can be sure someone has previously put some kind of petroleum-based fluid in it. Such a discovery is costly to the vehicle's owner as all rubber components in the entire brake system will need to be replaced.

Two types of brake bleeding procedures are used: manual bleeding and pressure bleeding. Always follow the manufacturer's recommendations when bleeding brakes. The sequence in which bleeding is performed can be critical. When bleeding a power brake system, remove the vacuum line from the power unit and plug the unit. To remove vacuum, the engine must be off. Pump the brake pedal several times.

CAUTION: Always use fresh brake fluid when bleeding the system. Do not use fluid that has been drained. Drained fluid may be contaminated and can damage the system.

Manual Bleeding

A manual bleeding procedure requires two people. One person operates the bleeder; the other, the brake pedal. Bleed only one wheel at a time.

CAUTION: Be sure the bleeder hose is below the surface of the liquid in the jar at all times. Do not allow the master cylinder to run out of fluid at any time. If these precautions are not followed, air can enter the system, and it must be bled again. The master cylinder cover must be kept in place.

Place the bleeder hose and jar in position. Have a helper pump the brake pedal several times and then hold it down with moderate pressure. Slowly open the bleeder valve. After fluid/air has stopped flowing, close the bleeder valve. Have the helper slowly release the pedal. Repeat this procedure until fluid that flows from the bleeder is clear and free of bubbles.

Discard all used brake fluid. Fill the master cylinder reservoirs. Check the brakes for proper operation.

CAUTION: Clean the master cylinder and cover before adding fluid. This is important for preventing dirt from entering the reservoir.

Pressure Bleeding

A pressure bleeding procedure can be done by one person. Pressure bleeding equipment uses pressurized fluid that flows through a special adapter fitted into the master cylinder (Figure 35-34).

The use of pressure bleeding equipment varies with different automobiles and different equipment makers. Always follow the automobile manufacturer's recommendations when using pressure bleeding equipment.

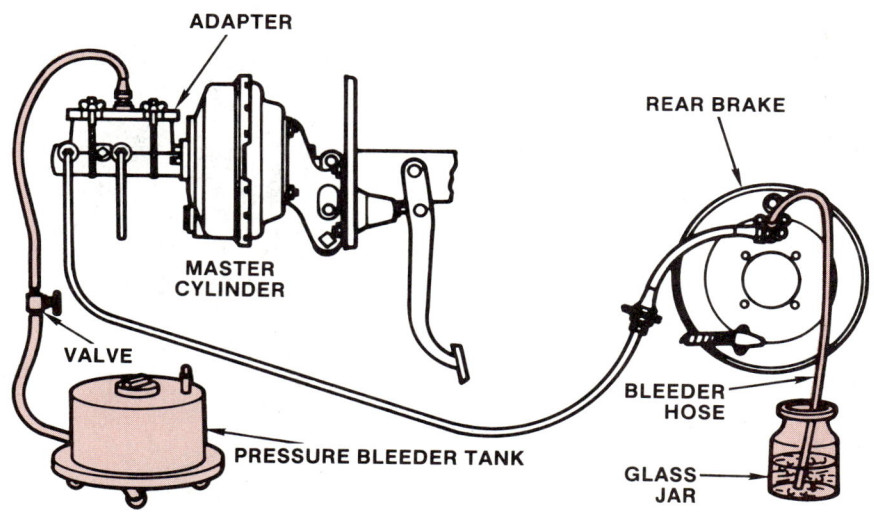

Figure 35-34 Pressure bleeding.

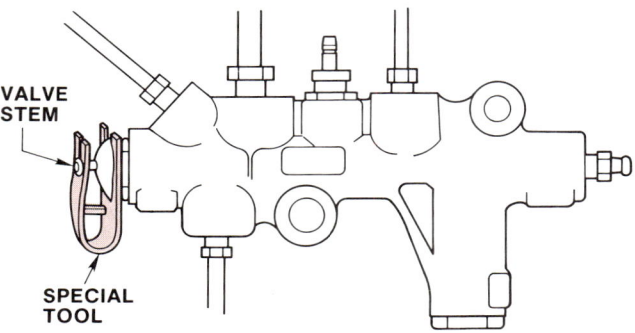

Figure 35-35 Special tool to hold the metering valve open while bleeding the system.

On automobiles with metering valves, the valve must be held open during pressure bleeding. Figure 35-35 shows a special tool used to hold open the metering section of a combination valve.

> ### USING SERVICE MANUALS
> Consult the service manual to be sure that the proper bleeding sequence is followed. If a vehicle requiring a special sequence is bled in the conventional manner, air might be chased throughout the system.

Open the bleeder valves one at a time until clear, air-free fluid is flowing. Progress from the wheel cylinder farthest from the master cylinder to the cylinder closest.

Do not exceed recommended pressure while bleeding the brakes. Always release air pressure after bleeding. Clean and fill the master cylinder after pressure bleeding. Check the brakes for proper operation. Be sure to remove the special tool used to hold the metering valve.

Power Brakes

Power brakes are nothing more than a standard hydraulic brake system with a booster unit located between the brake pedal and the master cylinder to help activate the brakes.

Two basic types of power-assist mechanisms are used. The first, is vacuum assist. These systems use engine vacuum, or sometimes vacuum pressure developed by an external vacuum pump, to help apply the brakes. The second type of power assist is hydraulic assist. It is normally found on larger vehicles. This system uses hydraulic pressure developed by the power steering pump or other external pump to help apply the brakes.

Both vacuum and hydraulic assist act to multiply the force exerted on the master cylinder pistons by the driver. This increases the hydraulic pressure delivered to the wheel cylinders or calipers while decreasing driver foot pressure.

Vacuum-Assist Power Brakes

All vacuum-assisted units are similar in design. They generate application energy by opposing engine vacuum to atmospheric pressure. A piston and cylin-

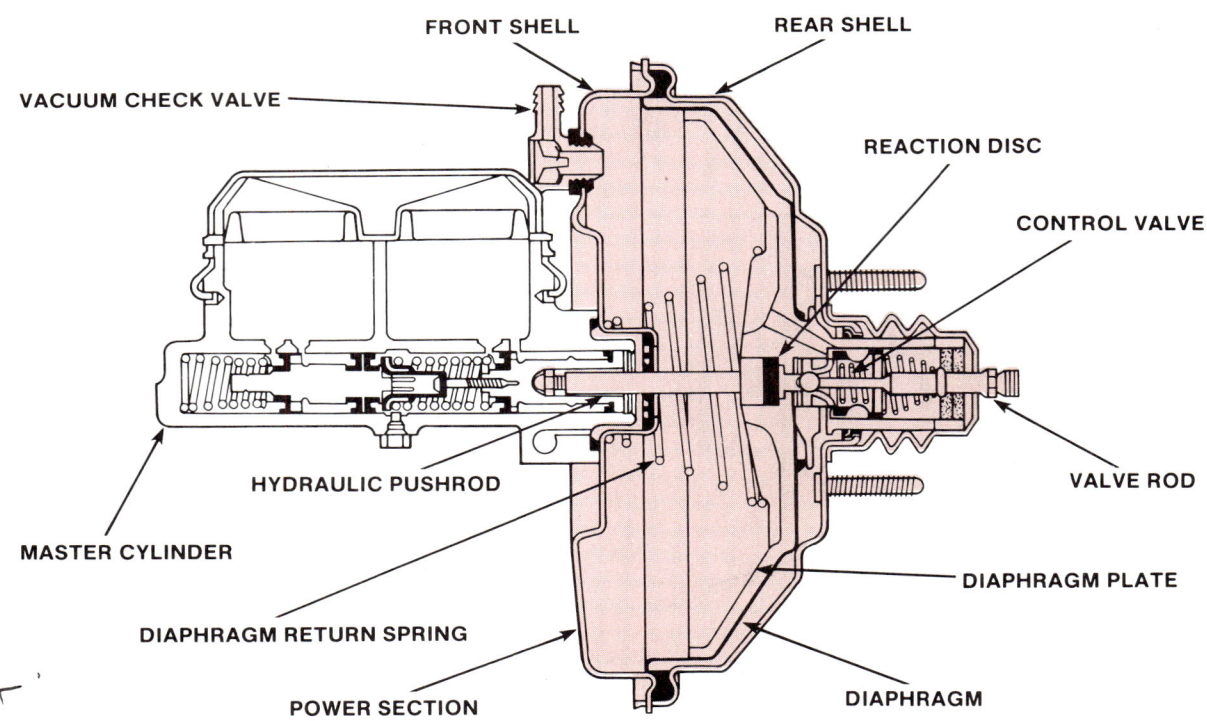

Figure 35-36 Cross section of tandem master cylinder and vacuum operated power booster.

der, flexible diaphragm or bellows use this energy to provide braking assistance.

All modern vacuum-assist units are vacuum-suspended systems. This means the diaphragm inside the unit is balanced using engine vacuum until the brake pedal is depressed. Applying the brake allows atmospheric pressure to unbalance the diaphragm and allows it to move generating application pressure.

Atmospheric pressure is normally 14 to 15 psi. So, if the diaphragm is 12 inches in diameter, it would have an area of about 113 square inches. With an atmospheric pressure of 14 psi, this results in an application force of 1552 psi.

Vacuum boosters may be single diaphragm (Figure 35-36) or tandem diaphragm (Figure 35-37). The unit consists of three basic elements which are assembled together.

The three basic elements of the single diaphragm follow.

1. A vacuum power section that includes a front and rear shell, a power diaphragm, a return spring, and a pushrod.
2. A control valve built as an integral part of the power diaphragm and connected through a valve rod to the brake pedal. It controls the degree of brake application or release in accordance with the pressure applied to the brake pedal.
3. A hydraulic master cylinder, attached to the vacuum power section that contains all the elements of the conventional brake master cylinder except for the pushrod. It supplies fluid under pressure to the wheel cylinders or calipers in proportion to the pressure applied by the brake booster.

Operation

When the brakes are applied, the valve rod and plunger move to the left in the power diaphragm. This action closes the control valve's vacuum port and opens the atmospheric port to admit air through the valve at the rear diaphragm chamber. With vacuum in the rear chamber, a force develops that moves the power diaphragm, hydraulic pushrod, and hydraulic piston or pistons to close the compensating port or ports and force fluid under pressure through the residual check valve or valves and lines into the front and rear brake assemblies.

As pressure develops in the master cylinder, a counter force acts through the hydraulic pushrod and reaction disc against the vacuum power diaphragm and valve plunger. This force tends to close the atmospheric port and reopen the vacuum port. Since this force is in opposition to the force applied to the brake pedal by the operator, it gives the operator a feel for the amount of brake applied.

Servicing Vacuum-Assist Booster Units

The fact that a vehicle's brakes still operate when the vacuum assist unit fails indicates that the hydraulic brake system and the vacuum-assist system are two separate systems. This means you should always check for faults in the hydraulic system first. If it checks out satisfactorily, start inspecting the vacuum-assist circuit.

For a fast check of vacuum-assist operation, press the brake pedal firmly and then start the engine. The pedal should fall away slightly and less pressure should be needed to maintain the pedal in any position.

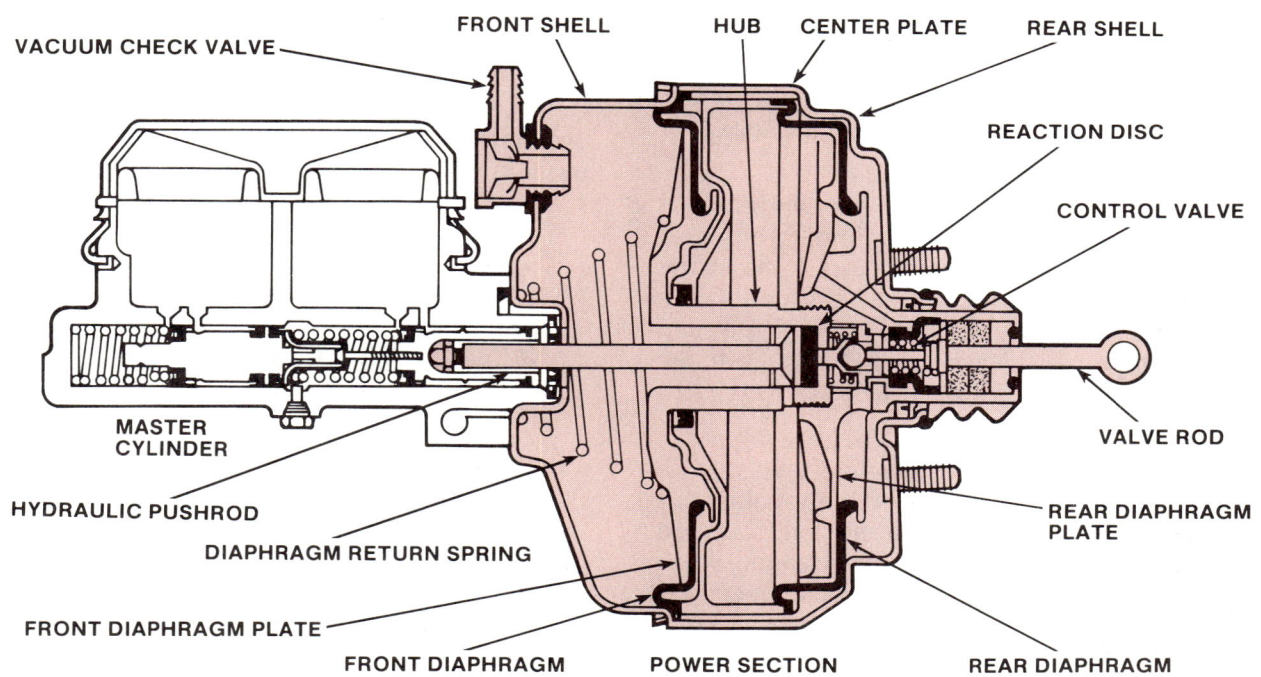

Figure 35-37 Cross section of a tandem master cylinder with a tandem diaphragm power booster.

PRESSURE CHECK Another simple check can be made by installing a suitable pressure gauge in the brake hydraulic system. Take a reading with the engine off and the power unit not operating. Maintain the same pedal height, start the engine, and read the gauge. There should be a substantial pressure increase if the vacuum assist booster is operating correctly.

PEDAL TRAVEL Pedal travel and total travel are critical on vacuum-assisted vehicles. Pedal travel should be kept strictly to specifications listed in the vehicle's service manual.

VACUUM READING If the power unit is not giving sufficient assistance, take a manifold vacuum reading. If manifold vacuum level is below specifications, tune the engine and retest the unit. Loose or damaged vacuum lines and clogged air intake filters reduce braking assistance. Most units have a check valve that retains some vacuum in the system when the engine is off. A vacuum gauge check of this valve indicates if it is restricted or stays open.

RELEASE PROBLEMS Failure of the brakes to release is often caused by a tight or misaligned connection between the power unit and the brake linkage. Broken pistons, diaphragms, bellows, or return springs can also cause this problem.

To help pinpoint the problem, loosen the connection between the master cylinder and the brake booster. If the brakes release, the problem is caused by internal binding in the vacuum unit. If the brakes do not release, look for a crimped or restricted brake line or similar problem in the hydraulic system.

HARD PEDAL Power brakes that have a hard pedal may have collapsed or leaking vacuum lines of insufficient manifold vacuum. Punctured diaphragms or bellows and leaky piston seals all lead to weak power unit operation and hard pedal. A steady hiss when the brake is held down indicates a vacuum leak that causes poor operation.

GRABBING BRAKES First, look for all the usual causes of brake grab, such as greasy linings, or scored rotors or drums. If the trouble appears to be in the power unit, check for a damaged reaction control. The reaction control is made up of a diaphragm, spring, and valve that tend to resist pedal action. It is put into the system to give the driver more brake pedal feel.

CHECK OF INTERNAL BINDING Release problems, hard pedal, and dragging (slow releasing) brakes can all be caused by internal binding. To test a vacuum unit for internal binding place the transmission/transaxle in neutral and start the engine. Increase engine speed to 1500 rpm, close the throttle, and completely depress the brake pedal. Slowly release the brake pedal and stop the engine. Remove the vacuum check valve and hose from the vacuum assist unit. Observe for backward movement of the brake pedal. If the brake pedal moves backward, there is internal binding and the unit should be replaced.

❑ PUSHROD ADJUSTMENT

Proper adjustment of the master cylinder pushrod is necessary to ensure proper operation of the power brake system. A pushrod that is too long causes the master cylinder piston to close off the replenishing port, preventing hydraulic pressure from being released and resulting in brake drag. A pushrod that is too short causes excessive brake pedal travel and causes groaning noises to come from the booster when the brakes are applied. A properly adjusted pushrod that remains assembled to the booster with which it was matched during production should not require service adjustment. However, if the booster, master cylinder, or pushrod are replaced, the pushrod might require adjustment.

There are two methods that can be used to check for proper pushrod length and installation: the gauge method and the air method.

Gauge Method

In most vacuum power units, the master cylinder pushrod length is fixed, and length is usually only checked after the unit has been overhauled or replaced. A typical adjustment using the gauge method is shown in Figure 35-38.

Air Method

The air testing method uses compressed air applied to the hydraulic outlet of the master cylinder. Air pressure is regulated to a value of approximately 5 psi to prevent brake fluid spraying from the master cylinder.

If air passes through the replenishing port, which is the smaller of the two holes in the bottom of the master cylinder reservoir, the adjustment is satisfactory. If air does not flow through the replenishing port, adjust the pushrod as required, either by means of the adjustment screw (if provided) or by adding shims between the

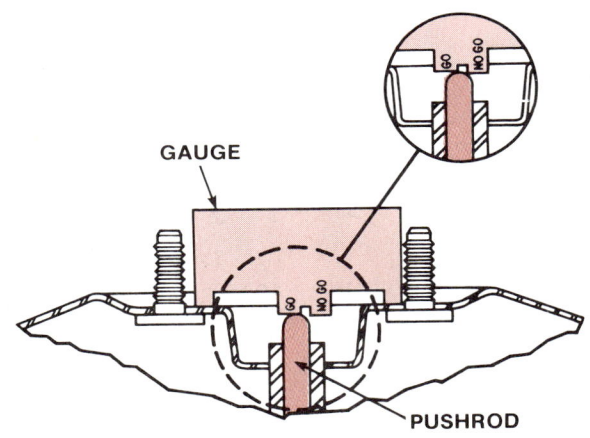

Figure 35-38 Delco-Moraine pushrod adjustment.

master cylinder and power unit shell until the air flows freely.

❏ HYDRAULIC-ASSIST POWER BRAKES

Decreases in engine size, plus the continued use of engine vacuum to operate other engine systems, such as emission control devices, led to the development of hydraulic-assist power brakes. These systems use fluid pressure, not vacuum pressure, to help apply the brakes.

The hydraulic pressure in the hydraulic booster should not be confused with the hydraulic pressure in the brake lines. Remember, they are two separate systems.

Two of the more popular hydraulic systems in use today are the hydro-boost system produced by Bendix (Figure 35-39) and the Powermaster system produced by GM.

Hydro-Boost

The hydro-boost system uses pressurized fluid from the power-steering pump to obtain its power assist. The components of a hydro-boost system are shown in Figure 35-40.

The booster assembly itself consists of an open center spool valve and sleeve assembly, a lever assembly, an input rod assembly, a power piston, an output pushrod, and the accumulator. The booster assembly is mounted on the vehicle in much the same manner as a vacuum booster. The pedal rod is connected at the booster input rod end.

A dual master cylinder is bolted to the brake booster and is operated by a pushrod projecting from the booster cylinder bore.

The power-steering pump, which is unmodified, except for a larger reservoir and an additional return port for the hydro-boost return line, supplies hydraulic pressure to the hydro-boost unit through external lines. When the engine is running, the fluid enters the unit through the pump port from which most of the fluid is directed to the gear port and then to the steering gear by an external line.

Figure 35-39 Hydro-boost power brake boosters.

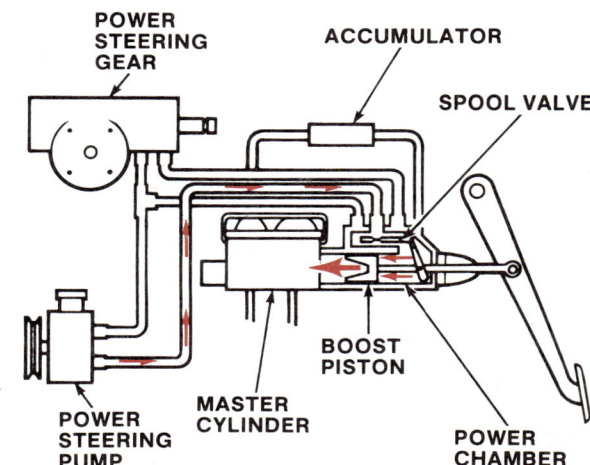

Figure 35-40 Hydro-boost components.

The small quantity of power steering fluid that does not go to the power steering gear circulates inside the hydro-boost unit and then returns to the steering pump reservoir by an external line.

Power-steering fluid flow in the hydro-boost unit is controlled by a hollow center spool valve. The spool valve has lands, annular grooves, and drilled passages. These mate with grooves and lands in the valve bore. The flow pattern of the fluid depends upon the alignment of the valve in the bore.

❏ TESTING THE HYDRO-BOOST

Any investigation of a hydro-boost complaint should begin with an inspection of the power-steering pump belt, fluid level, and hose condition and connections. Hydro-boost does not work properly if it is not supplied with a continuous supply of clean, bubble-free power-steering fluid at the proper pressure.

WARNING: Always depressurize the accumulator of any hydraulic boost system before disconnecting any brake lines or hoses. This is usually done by turning the engine off and depressing and releasing the brake pedal up to ten times.

Basic Operational Test

The basic operational test of hydro-boost is as follows. With the engine off, pump the brake pedal numerous times to bleed off the residual hydraulic pressure that is stored in the accumulator. Hold firm pressure on the brake pedal and start the engine. The brake pedal should move downward, then push up against the foot.

Accumulator Test

To be sure the accumulator is performing properly, rotate the steering wheel with the engine running until it stops and hold it in that position for no more than 5 seconds. Return the steering wheel to the center position and shut off the engine. Pump the brake pedal. You should feel two to three power-assisted strokes. Now repeat steps 1 and 2. That pressurizes the accumulator. Wait 1 hour, then pump the brake pedal. There should be two or three power-assisted strokes. If the system does not perform as just described, the accumulator is leaking and should be replaced.

Noise Troubleshooting

The hydro-boost unit is also part of another major subsystem of the vehicle, the power-steering system. Problems or malfunctions in the steering system may affect hydro-boost operation. The following are some common troubleshooting tips.

Moan or low-frequency hum usually accompanied by a vibration in the pedal or steering column might be encountered during parking or other very low-speed maneuvers. This can be caused by a low fluid level in the power-steering pump, or by air in the power-steering fluid due to holding the pump at relief pressure (steering wheel held all the way in one direction) for an excessive amount of time (more than 5 seconds). Check the fluid level and add fluid if necessary. Allow the system to sit for 1 hour with the cap removed to eliminate the air. If the condition persists, it might be a sign of excessive pump wear. Check the pump according to the vehicle manufacturer's recommended procedure.

At or near power runout (brake pedal near fully depressed position), a high-speed fluid noise (like a faucet can make) might occur. This is a normal condition and will not be heard, except in emergency braking conditions.

Whenever the accumulator pressure is used, a slight hiss is noticed. It is the sound of the hydraulic fluid escaping through the accumulator valve and is completely normal.

After the accumulator has been emptied and the engine is started again, another hissing sound might be heard during the first brake application or the first steering maneuver. This is caused by the fluid rushing through the accumulator charging orifice. It is normal and will only be heard once after the accumulator is emptied. However, if this sound continues even though no apparent accumulator pressure assist was made, it could indicate that the accumulator is not holding pressure. Check for this using the accumulator test discussed previously.

After bleeding, a gulping sound might be present during brake applications, as noted in the bleeding instructions. This is normal and should disappear with normal driving and braking.

❏ POWERMASTER HYDRAULIC BOOSTER

In 1985, General Motors introduced its Powermaster power brake system. Used primarily on full-sized passenger cars, the system incorporates a self-contained hydraulic booster that is built directly onto the master cylinder. Instead of relying on the power steering pump for hydraulic pressure as is done in the hydro-boost system, the Powermaster has its own vane pump and electric motor to provide the hydraulic pressure required for booster operation (Figure 35-41).

Pump

The vane pump is driven by an electric motor that is mounted below the master cylinder. Brake fluid is drawn through a low-pressure hose from the reservoir to the pump. There it is pressurized and exits through a high-pressure hose to the accumulator. Pump motor operation is controlled through a dual-pressure switch and relay.

Accumulator

The accumulator stores brake fluid under pressure at approximately 675 psi (maximum). It has a heavy, flexible diaphragm that separates brake fluid on one side from high-pressure nitrogen gas on the other.

Master Cylinder

In the Powermaster system, the master cylinder is similar to a conventional dual or tandem master cylinder in both design and operation.

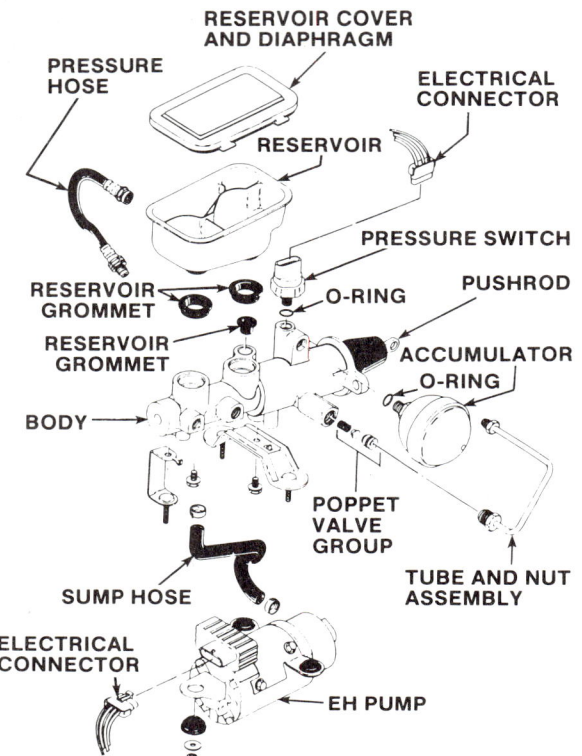

Figure 35-41 Powermaster components.

Dual-Pressure Switch

This switch controls the pump operation in conjunction with a relay attached to the pump motor. Three lead wires are attached to the switch. One leads to the pump motor relay, one leads to the brake warning light (dash mounted), and the third leads to ground. When accumulator pressure drops below 510 psi, one contact set in the switch closes, completing the ground for the relay. At this point, the relay is able to supply battery voltage to the pump motor. With the pump operating, accumulator pressure increases to approximately 675 psi. At that point, the contact set opens, breaking the ground to the relay and shutting off the pump. If accumulator pressure should drop below 400 psi, the second contact closes. This illuminates the dash-mounted brake warning light.

Reservoir

The reservoir is a removable, plastic container internally divided into three chambers. Two chambers (primary and secondary) supply the master cylinder with brake fluid as in a conventional master cylinder. Both chambers are sealed to the atmosphere. The third chamber supplies the booster pump with brake fluid and is vented to the atmosphere because of the large amount of fluid movement in this portion of the reservoir.

Booster

The booster assembly consists of a power piston, inner and outer control valves, and the reaction components. The power piston uses the high-pressure fluid from the accumulator against its large diameter to produce the force needed to apply (push) the master cylinder pistons. The reaction components fit between the power piston and master cylinder primary piston. These components consist of a reaction body group, reaction disc, and reaction piston. In operation, the reaction components provide pedal feel. The apply (outer control) valve and discharge (inner control) valve regulate fluid movement through the booster according to brake pedal movement and brake pedal pressure (force). Both valves, illustrated in Figure 35–42 are located in the power piston.

Testing the Powermaster Unit

Diagnosis and testing of the Powermaster unit requires the use of a special adapter and test gauge or aftermarket equivalents. The Powermaster pressure switch is removed and the adapter and test gauge is installed in its port. The unit can then be energized, and the switch's high pressure cut-off and low pressure turn-on points observed and checked against specifications. Follow service manual instructions for the connection and operation of the test gauge and all system test procedures.

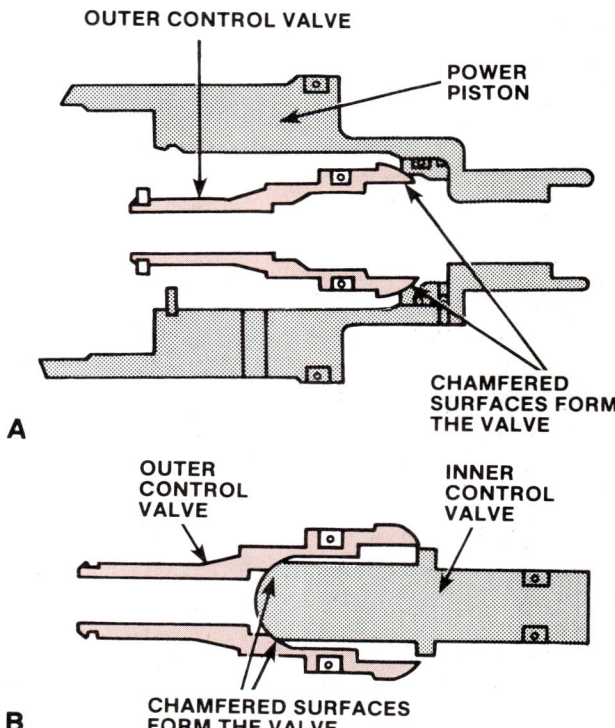

Figure 35–42 (A) Apply and (B) discharge valve in a power piston.

☐ ANTI-LOCK BRAKE SYSTEMS

Modern anti-skid brake systems can be thought of as electronic/hydraulic pumping of the brakes for straightline stopping under panic conditions (Figure 35–43). Good drivers have always pumped the brake pedal during panic stops to avoid wheel lockup and loss of steering control. Anti-skid brake systems simply get the pumping job done much faster and in a much more precise manner than the fastest human foot. Keep in mind that a tire on the verge of slipping produces more friction with respect to the road than one which is locked and skidding. Once a tire loses its grip, friction is reduced and the vehicle takes longer to stop.

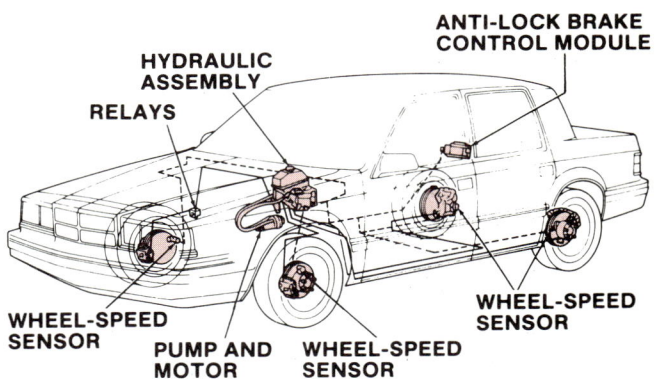

Figure 35–43 The four-wheel anti-lock braking system has few parts and operates at very high pressures.

The only exception to this rule is when a tire is on loose snow. A locked tire allows a small wedge of snow to build up ahead of it, which allows it to stop in a shorter distance than a rolling tire. That is why some car manufacturers offer an on/off switch on their ABS-equipped vehicles for deactivating the system when driving on snow.

Steering is another important consideration. As long as a tire does not slip, it only goes in the direction in which it is turned. But once it skids, it has little or no directional stability. One of the big advantages of ABS, therefore, is the ability to keep control of the vehicle under all conditions.

❏ TYPES OF ABS SYSTEMS

During normal operation, all ABS systems operate like a conventional power-assisted braking system. During heavy braking, however, the ABS system modulates hydraulic pressure to each wheel according to the wheel's speed.

The exact manner in which hydraulic pressure is controlled depends on the exact ABS design. The great majority of ABS systems are integrated systems. They combine the master cylinder, hydraulic booster, and ABS hydraulic circuitry into a single hydraulic assembly.

Other ABS systems are non-integrated. They use a conventional vacuum-assist booster and master cylinder. The system's hydraulic control unit is a separate mechanism.

In addition to being classified as integral and non-integral, ABS systems can be broken down into the level of control they provide.

TWO-WHEEL SYSTEMS These basic systems offer anti-lock brake performance to the rear wheels only. They do not provide anti-lock performance to the steering wheels. Two-wheel systems are most often found on light trucks and vans (Figure 35-44).

DIAGONALLY-SPLIT SYSTEMS This type of system uses two speed sensors to provide wheel speed data for regulation of all four wheels. One sensor has input that controls the right front wheel; the other sensor performs likewise for the left front wheel.

Brake hydraulic pressure to the opposite rear wheel is controlled simultaneously with its diagonally located front wheel. For example, the right rear wheel receives the same pumping instructions as the left front wheel.

This system is an upgrade from the two-wheel system since it does provide steering control. However, it can have shortcomings under certain operating conditions.

FULL (FOUR-WHEEL) SYSTEMS This system is the most effective ABS system available. Sensors monitor each of the four wheels. With this continuous information, the ABS electronic control module ensures each wheel receives the exact braking force it needs to maintain both anti-lock and steering control.

❏ INTEGRATED ABS SYSTEM COMPONENTS

The following sections describe the main components found in a typical four-wheel, integrated ABS system (Figure 35-45).

Hydraulic Unit

This hydraulic unit (Figure 35-46) serves the purpose of the booster and master cylinder. It contains the electrical and mechanical components needed to modulate brake fluid pressure in each hydraulic circuit while in the anti-lock mode.

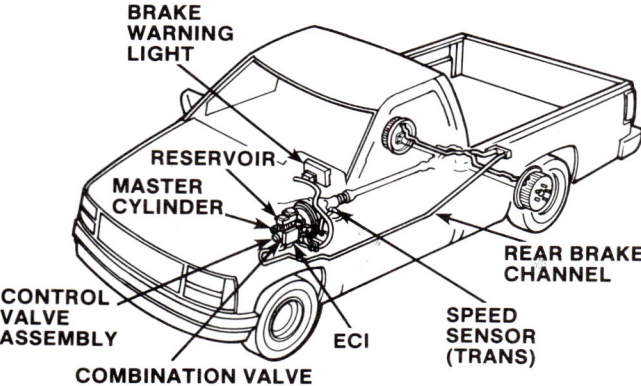

Figure 35-44 Typical two-wheel anti-lock braking system.

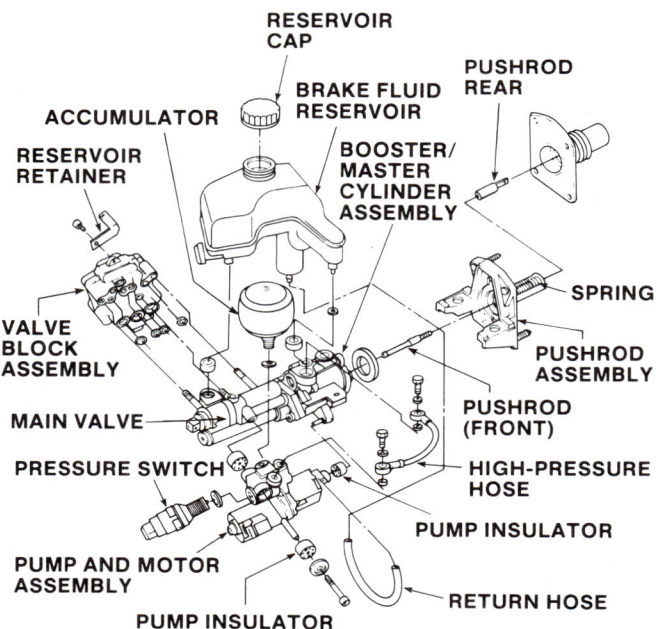

Figure 35-45 Master brake cylinder in the typical system uses an electric pump for power boost.

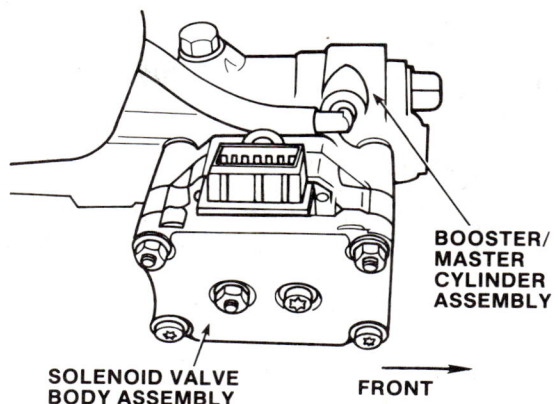

Figure 35-46 Typical ABS hydraulic control unit.

BOOSTER/MASTER CYLINDER ASSEMBLY The booster/master cylinder assembly contains the valves and pistons needed to produce hydraulic pressure in the wheel circuits during brake application. Power brake assist is provided by pressurized brake fluid supplied by the hydraulic accumulator.

VALVE BLOCK ASSEMBLY The valve block assembly attaches to the side of the booster/master cylinder and contains the hydraulic wheel circuit solenoid valves. The electronic brake control module controls the position of these solenoid valves. The valve block is serviceable separate from the booster/master cylinder but should not be disassembled. An electrical connector links the valve block to the ABS control module.

WHEEL CIRCUIT VALVES The system has three separate wheel circuits: left front, right front, and rear. Two solenoid valves are used to control each circuit. One controls the inlet valve of the circuit, the other the outlet valve.

When inlet and outlet valves of a circuit are used in combination, pressure can be increased, decreased, or held steady in the circuit. The position of each valve is determined by the control module. Outlet valves are normally closed, and inlet valves are normally open. Valves are activated when the ABS control module switches 12 volts to the circuit solenoids. During normal driving, the circuits are not activated.

MAIN VALVE This two-position valve is also controlled by the ABS control module. This valve is open only in the ABS mode. When open, pressurized brake fluid from the booster circuit is directed into the master cylinder (front brake) circuits to prevent excessive pedal travel.

PRESSURE SWITCH This switch controls pump motor operation and the low pressure warning light circuit. The pressure switch grounds the pump motor relay coil circuit, activating the pump when accumulator pressure drops below 2030 psi. The switch cuts off the motor when the pressure reaches 2610 psi. The pressure switch also contains switches to activate the dash mounted warning light if accumulator pressure drops below 1500 psi.

Pump/Motor Assembly

An integral pump/motor assembly is used to provide pressurized brake fluid to the hydraulic unit accumulator. The pump/motor is mounted on the hydraulic unit with pressure and return hoses running to the booster inlet and reservoir (Figure 35-47). The pump/motor assembly keeps the hydraulic accumulator pressure at required levels anytime the ignition switch is in the run position.

The accumulator itself is a small, sealed chamber mounted to the pump/motor assembly. It holds the highly pressurized nitrogen gas that is used to generate this charging pressure.

RESERVOIR WITH FLUID LEVEL WARNING SWITCHES The reservoir assembly is a translucent plastic container with two main chambers. Integral fluid level switches are part of the reservoir cap assembly with one electrical connector pointing forward for wire harness connections. Two low-pressure hoses lead from the reservoir. One hose attaches to the hydraulic pump assembly and the other to the master cylinder housing.

Wheel-Speed Sensors

The ABS control module continuously receives data from four wheel-speed sensors. One sensor is mounted at each wheel and generates a signal whenever the wheel turns.

The sensors use electromagnetic principles to generate a voltage pulse. Like the magnetic pulse generators discussed under ignition systems, the wheel sensor uses a toothed sensor ring that is moved past a stationary sensor (Figure 35-48). The stationary sensor consists of a permanent magnet and pickup coil. As the teeth on the ring approach and move away from the stationary sensor, they expand and contract the mag-

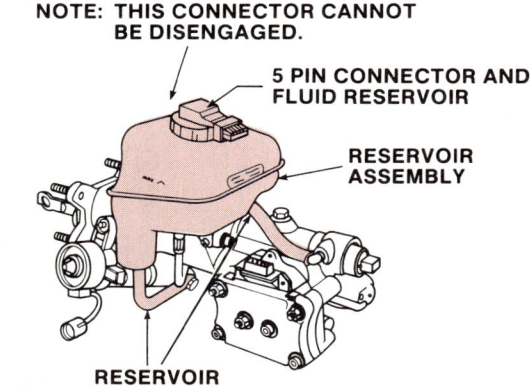

Figure 35-47 Reservoir with fluid level warning switches.

netic lines of force around the permanent magnet. This movement of magnetic force induces a voltage in the pickup coil that can be read by the ABS control module.

ABS Control Module

This small control computer is normally mounted inside the trunk on the wheel housing. It monitors system operation and controls anti-lock function when needed. The module relies on inputs from the wheel speed sensors and feedback from the hydraulic unit to determine if the anti-lock brake system is operating correctly and to determine when the anti-lock mode is required. The module has a self-diagnostic function including numerous trouble codes.

INTEGRATED SYSTEM OPERATION

When a wheel speed sensor signals the ABS control module that a high rate of deceleration is taking place at its wheel (that is, the wheel is likely to lock and skid), the controller initially signals the hydraulic unit to keep hydraulic pressure at the wheel constant. If the wheel continues to decelerate, the controller then signals the circuit valve solenoids to reduce hydraulic

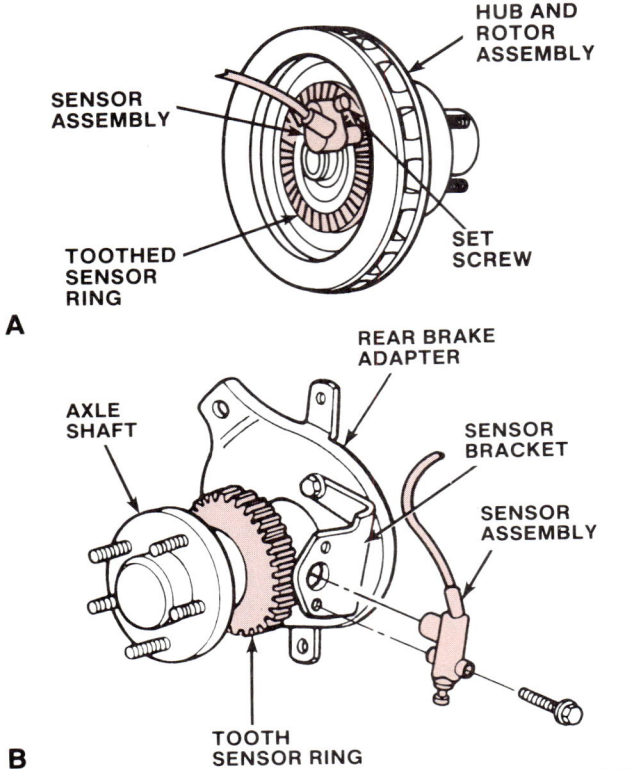

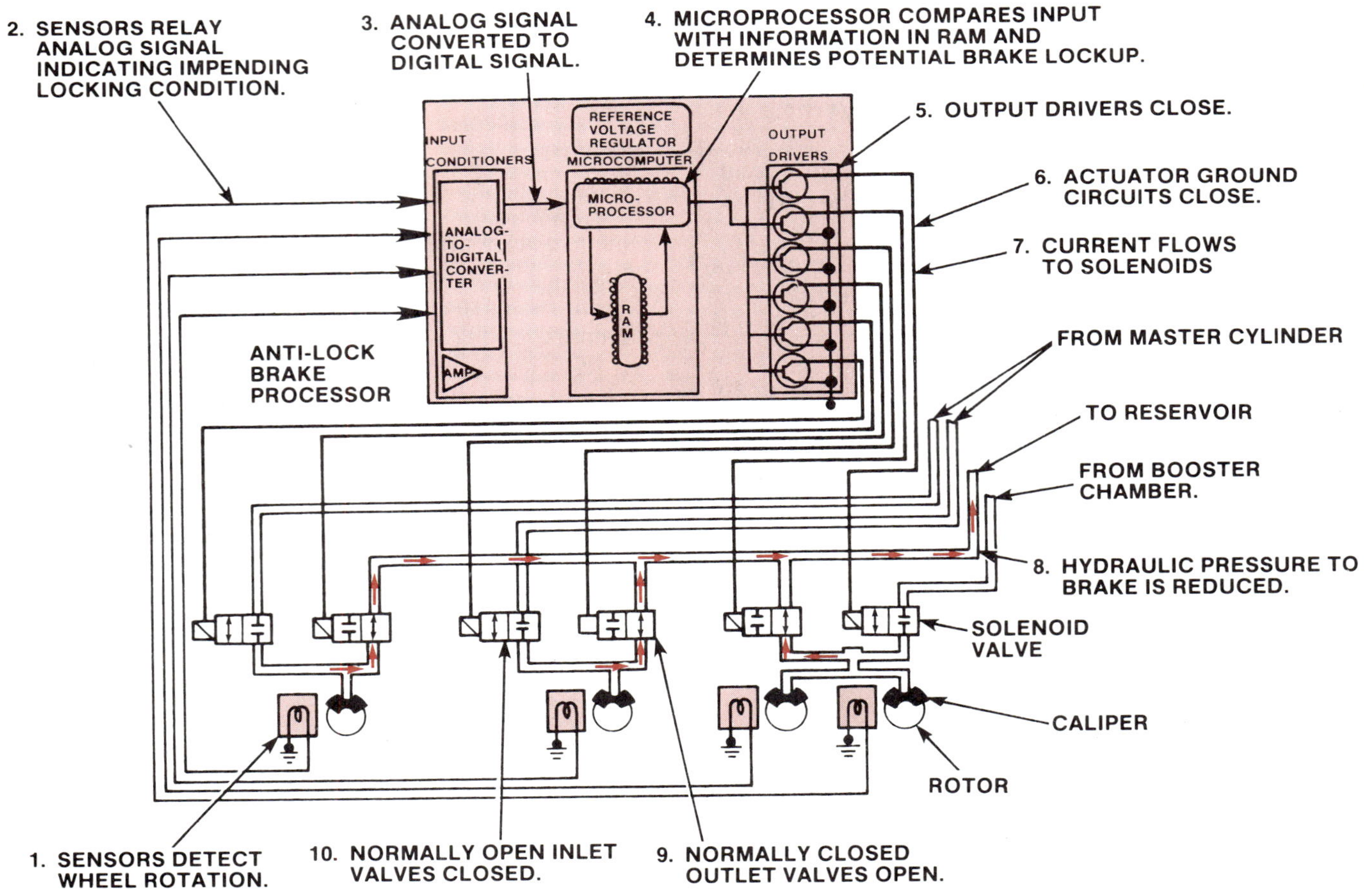

Figure 35-48 Typical ABS wheel sensors: (A) front and (B) rear wheel.

Figure 35-49 ABS operation—potential brake lock condition.

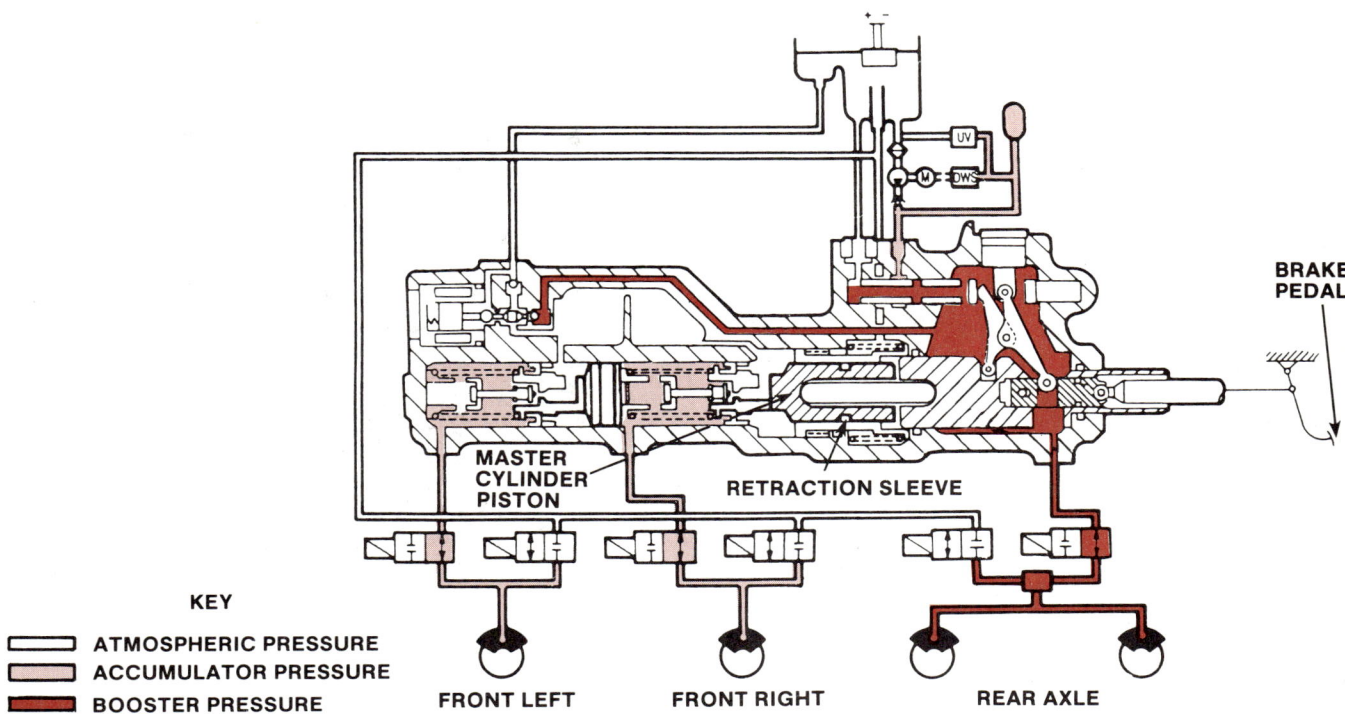

Figure 35-50   ABS operation—no braking.

pressure to the affected wheel. This reduces braking at the wheel, reducing the risk of lockup (Figure 35-49).

The wheel accelerates again as a result of the reduced braking pressure. Once a specific limit has been reached, the controller registers the fact that the wheel is not being sufficiently braked. The wheel is decelerated again by increasing the pressure, which was initially reduced. The control cycles may be executed at least four times per second depending upon the road conditions.

In operation, when the brakes are released, the piston in the master cylinder is retracted. The booster chamber is vented to the reservoir, and the fluid in the chamber is at the same low pressure as the reservoir (Figure 35-50).

When the brakes are applied, under normal conditions, the brake pedal actuates a pushrod (Figure 35-51). This operates a scissors lever, which moves a spool valve. When the spool valve moves, it closes the port from the booster chamber to the reservoir and partially opens the port from the accumulator in proportion to the pressure on the brake pedal. This allows hydraulic fluid under pressure from the accumulator to

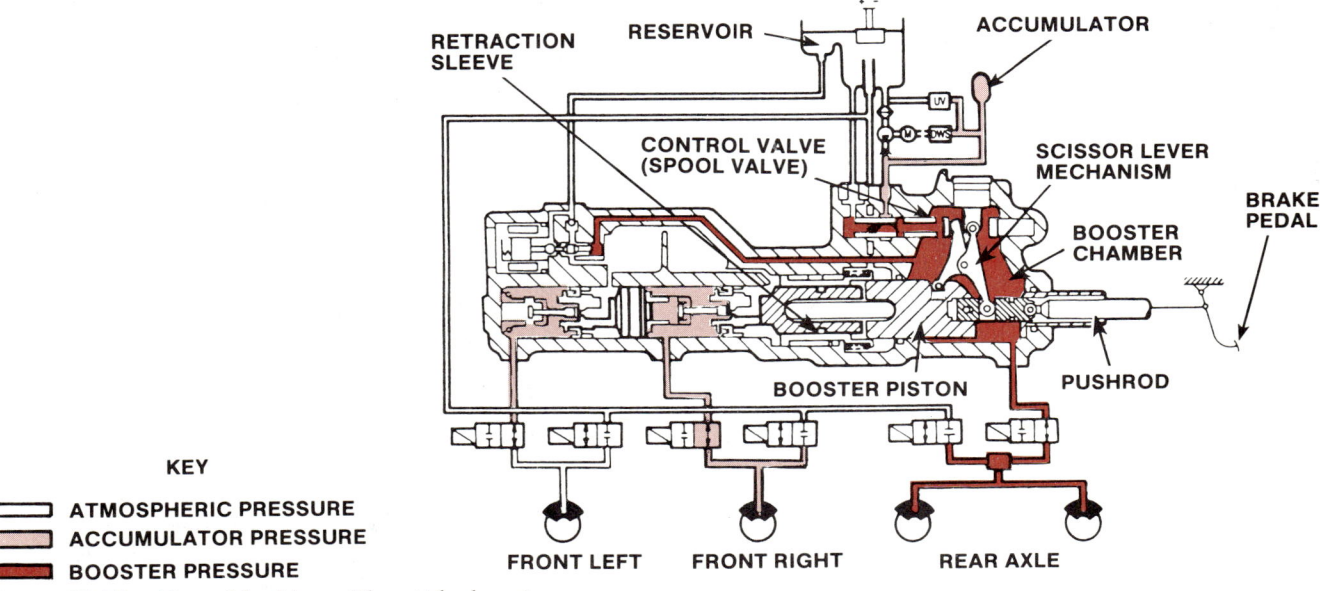

Figure 35-51   Normal braking with anti-lock system.

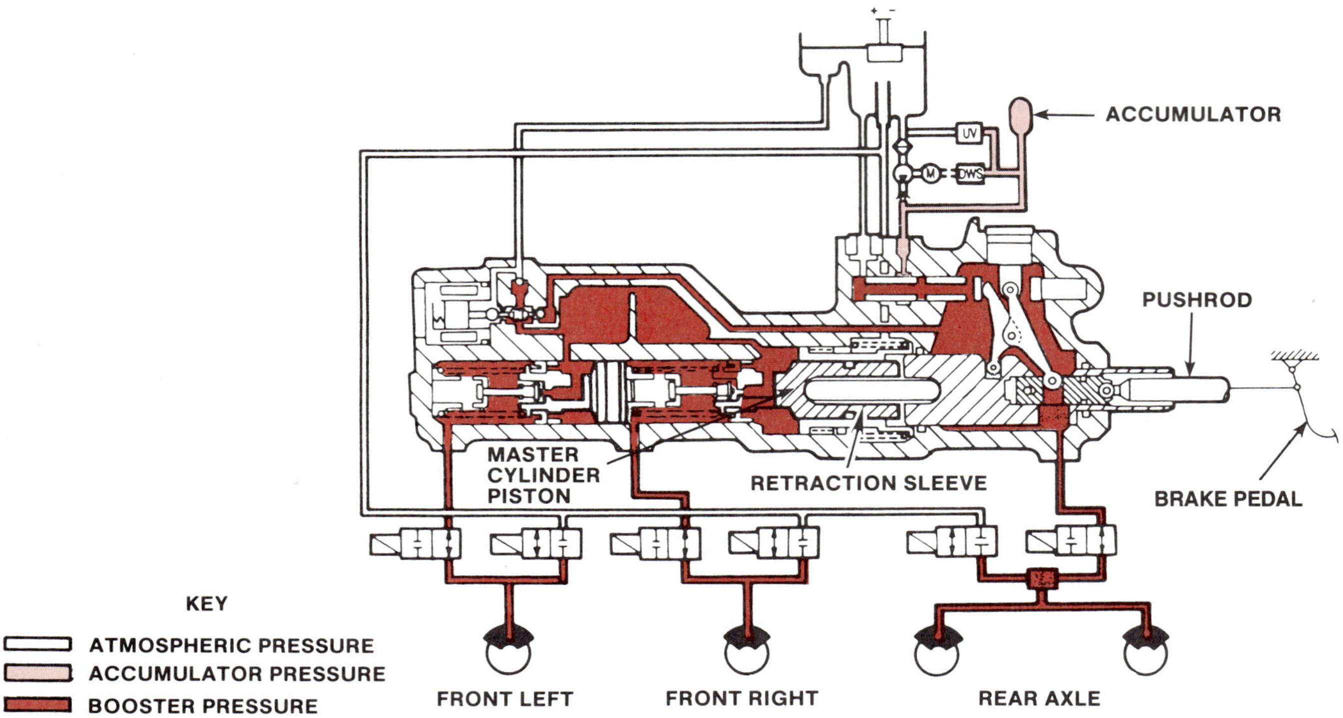

Figure 35-52 Anti-lock braking system in operation.

enter the booster chamber. As hydraulic pressure enters, it pushes the booster piston forward, providing hydraulic assist to the mechanical thrust from the pushrod.

When the controller determines that the wheels are locking up, it opens a valve that supplies one chamber between the two master cylinder pistons and another chamber between the retraction sleeve and the first master cylinder piston (Figure 35-52). The hydraulic pressure on the retraction sleeve retracts the pushrod, pushing back the brake pedal. In effect, the hydraulic pressure to the front wheels is now supplied by the accumulator, not by the brake pedal action. The controller also opens and closes the solenoid valves to cycle the brakes on the wheels that have been locking up.

When the solenoid valves are open, the master cylinder pistons supply hydraulic fluid to the front brakes and the boost pressure chamber provides hydraulic pressure to the rear. When the solenoid valves are closed, the hydraulic fluid from the master cylinder pistons and booster pressure chamber is cut off. The hydraulic fluid is returned from the brakes to the reservoir.

The electronic controller monitors the electromechanical components of the system. Malfunction of the ABS causes the electronic controller to shut off or inhibit the system. However, normal power-assisted braking remains. Malfunctions are indicated by one or two warning lights inside the vehicle. Loss of hydraulic fluid or power booster pressure disables the anti-lock brake system.

In most malfunctions in the anti-lock brake system, the check anti-lock brakes or brake light is illuminated. The sequence of illumination of these warning lights combined with the problem symptoms determine the appropriate diagnostic tests to perform. The diagnostic tests then pinpoint the exact component needing service.

◻ NON-INTEGRATED ABS SYSTEMS

These systems do not integrate the hydraulic boost, master cylinder, and ABS hydraulic valve unit into a single assembly. Instead the master cylinder and hydraulic valve unit are separate assemblies and a vacuum boost is used. In some non-integrated systems, the master cylinder supplies brake fluid to the hydraulic unit. Although the hydraulic unit is a separate assembly, it still uses a high-pressure pump/motor, accumulator, and fast-acting solenoid valves to control hydraulic pressure to the wheels. Wheel speed sensor and control module operation are also similar to integrated systems described earlier.

GM Electromagnetic ABS Systems

Beginning in 1991, General Motors began equipping certain small and mid-size vehicles with an anti-lock braking system called ABS-VI. This system is an add-on system that uses a conventional vacuum power booster and master brake cylinder. It does not use a high-pressure pump/motor and accumulator and fast-

Brake Systems 919

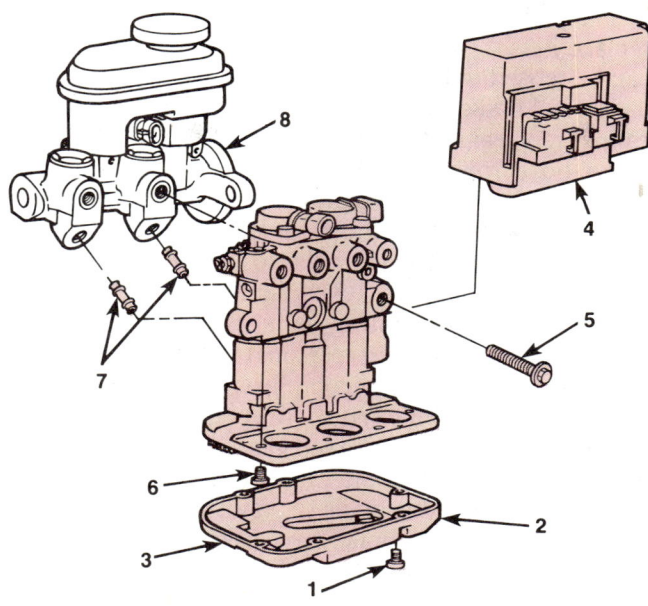

1. GEAR COVER ATTACHING SCREWS (8)
2. GEAR COVER
3. MOTOR PACK ATTACHING SCREWS (4)
4. MOTOR PACK ASSEMBLY
5. ABS HYDRAULIC VALVE BODY ASSEMBLY ATTACHING BOLTS (2)
6. ABS HYDRAULIC VALVE BODY ASSEMBLY
7. TRANSFER TUBE ASSEMBLY
8. MASTER CYLINDER

Figure 35-53 The hydraulic modulator is an add-on component to the conventional master cylinder. The electric motors can be replaced separately, as can the two solenoids.

acting solenoid valves to control hydraulic pressure. Instead, it uses a hydraulic modulator (Figure 35-53) that operates using a principle GM calls electromagnetic braking.

As in integrated systems, wheel speed is monitored using individual speed sensors. When one wheel begins to decelerate faster than the others while braking, the control module signals the hydraulic modulator assembly to reduce pressure to the affected brake.

MODULATOR OPERATION The ABS-VI modulator contains three small screw plungers—one for each front brake circuit and one for the rear brake circuit. These plungers are driven by electric motors. At the top of each plunger cavity is a check ball that controls hydraulic pressure within the brake circuit.

During normal braking conditions, each plunger is all the way up. The check ball at the top is unseated and the by-pass solenoid is normally open. This allows brake pressure from the master cylinder and vacuum power booster to apply the brakes during normal stopping.

During panic stops, the ABS mode operates. In this situation, brake pressure must be reduced to prevent wheel lockup. This is done by closing the normally open solenoid to isolate the circuit and then turning the plunger down to reduce braking pressure. As the plunger turns down, it increases the volume within the brake circuit. This causes a drop in pressure that keeps the wheel from locking. The amount of pressure applied is controlled by running the plunger up and down as required. To decrease pressure further, the plunger is run down. To reapply pressure, the plunger moves back up.

The system can cycle the brakes seven times per second. Because the system does not have a high-pressure pump and accumulator, it cannot increase brake pressure above what can be provided by the master cylinder and vacuum-assist booster.

The ABS-VI control module has five separate diagnostic modes. Data available for troubleshooting includes wheel speed sensor readings, vehicle speed, battery voltage, individual motor and solenoid command status, warning light status, and brake switch status. Numerous trouble codes are programmed into the controller to help pinpoint problems. Other diagnostic modes store past trouble codes. This data can help technicians determine if an earlier fault code, such as an intermittent wheel speed sensor, is linked to the present problem such as a completely failed wheel sensor. Another mode enables testing of individual system components.

Brake System Bleeding

The front brakes of an anti-lock brake system can be bled in the conventional manner, with or without the accumulator being charged. However, bleeding the rear brakes requires a fully-charged accumulator or a pressure bleeder attached to the reservoir cap opening, with a minimum of 35 psi.

System Bleeding with Accumulator Charged

Once accumulator pressure is available to the system, the rear brakes can be bled by opening the rear brake caliper bleeder screws for 10 seconds at a time while holding the brake pedal in the applied position with the ignition switch in the run position. Repeat until an air-free flow of brake fluid has been observed at each caliper, then close the bleeder screws. Pump the brake pedal several times to complete the bleeding procedure. Adjust the brake fluid level in the reservoir to the maximum level with a discharged accumulator.

WARNING: Care must be used when opening the rear caliper bleeder screws, due to the high pressure from a fully-charged accumulator.

System Bleeding with Pressure Bleeder

When using a pressure bleeder, it must be attached to the reservoir cap opening, and a minimum of 35 psi must be maintained on the system. With the brake pedal at rest and the ignition switch off, open the rear caliper bleeder screws for 10 seconds at a time. Once an air-free flow of brake fluid has been observed at each caliper, close the bleeder screws and place the ignition switch in the run position. Pump the brake pedal several times to complete the bleeder procedure. Siphon off the excess fluid in the reservoir to adjust the level to the maximum level with a fully-charged accumulator.

❑ DIAGNOSIS AND TESTING

Always follow the vehicle manufacturer's specified diagnostic and replacement procedures when servicing ABS systems. In general, ABS system diagnostics requires three to five different types of testing that must be performed in the specified order listed in the service manual. Types of testing may include the following.

1. Pretest checks or inspections.
2. On-board ABS control module testing (trouble code reading).
3. Warning light symptom troubleshooting.
4. Individual trouble code or component troubleshooting.

CAUTION: *Following the wrong sequence or bypassing steps may lead to unnecessary replacement of parts or incorrect resolution of the symptom. The information and procedures given in this chapter are typical of the various anti-lock systems on the market. For specific instructions, consult the vehicle's service manual.*

The prediagnosis inspection consists of a quick visual check of specific system components that could create an apparent anti-lock system malfunction. Inspecting the system before diagnosing specific symptoms can result in the detection of a simple defect, which could be the cause of an inoperative system. This inspection should be the first step in diagnosing a complaint.

If a malfunction in the ABS system occurs, be sure the control module connector is securely connected and that all ABS connectors are securely connected. Check for a blown fuse. If the malfunction is still present, refer to the procedure for reading trouble codes.

If pretest checks or inspections do not determine the problem, the ABS control module is then accessed for individual trouble codes. Some ABS systems have over fifty trouble codes, each corresponding to a different problem in the system. These codes are keyed to individual pinpoint tests and troubleshooting sequences listed in the service manual.

The brake and anti-lock warning lights are also designed to signal potential problems in the system. On/off combinations of the two lights are keyed to specific troubleshooting sequences listed in the service manual.

Many ABS components are simply remove-and-replace items. On some systems, wheel speed sensors can be reused or adjusted.

Normal brake repairs, such as replacing brake pads, caliper replacement, rotor machining or replacement, brake hose replacement, master cylinder or power booster replacement, or parking brake repair, can all be performed as usual. In other words, brake service on an ABS-equipped vehicle is similar to service on a conventional system with a few exceptions.

First, before beginning service, depressurize the accumulator to prevent personal injury from high-pressure fluid. This is accomplished by pumping the brake pedal (ignition off) until the pedal becomes hard. Air gaps between the speed sensors and toothed ring do not have to be adjusted after machining rotors if wheel bearing adjustment is made to manufacturer's specifications. Disc or drum brake service is performed as on a conventional vehicle. Always bleed the system after performing any service that allows air to enter the lines.

❑ AUTOMATIC STABILITY (TRACTION) CONTROL

Auto makers are now applying the technology used in anti-lock braking systems to design traction or automatic stability control systems. As explained earlier, ABS pumps the brakes when a braking wheel attempts to go into a locked condition. Automatic stability control systems (ASC) apply the brakes when a drive wheel attempts to spin and lose traction.

The systems work best when one drive wheel is working on a good traction surface and the other is not. The systems also work well when the vehicle is accelerating on slippery road surfaces, especially when climbing hills.

ASC is most helpful on four-wheel or all-wheel drive vehicles where loss of traction at one wheel could hamper driver control. It is also desirable on high-powered front-wheel-drive vehicles for the same reason.

During road operation, the ASC system uses an electronic control module to monitor the wheel-speed sensors. If a wheel enters a loss-of-traction situation, the module applies braking force to the wheel in trouble. Wheel spin is normally limited to a 10% slippage. Some traction control systems use separated hydraulic valve units and control modules for ABS and ASC, while others integrate both systems into one hydraulic control unit and a single control module. The pulse rings and wheel-speed sensors remain unchanged from ABS to ASC.

Some ASC systems function only at low road speeds to five to twenty miles per hour. More advanced systems work at higher speeds and usually integrate some engine control functions into the control loop. For example, if the ASC system senses a loss of traction, it not only cycles the brakes but also signals the engine control module to retard ignition timing and partially close the throttle as well. Timing and throttle reduce engine output. If wheel slippage continues, the ASC controller may also cut fuel delivery to one or more engine cylinders. This action relieves engine stress and prevents the driver from overspeeding the engine in extremely slippery conditions.

Many systems are equipped with a dash mounted warning light to alert the driver that the system is operating. There may also be a manual cut-off switch so the driver can turn off ASC operation.

CASE STUDY

Case 1

A customer brings her late-model vehicle to a brake specialty shop, complaining of occasional rear brake lockup when the brakes are lightly applied. She is nervous because she feels the vehicle is unsafe to drive. The vehicle is equipped with front disc and rear drum brakes.

A thorough road test by the technician does not verify the complaint. Talking to the customer, the technician learns the problem most often occurs in damp or cold weather, or when the vehicle has been sitting for a length of time.

The technician performs a complete visual and operational inspection. He checks the action of the brake pedal, the power brake booster, and the combination valve. All systems are working fine. He then removes the rear drums and inspects the shoes and drums. Nothing appears out of order or broken. The technician turns to his supervisor for a second opinion.

After listening to a summary of the inspection and checks made to date, the shop supervisor checks the file on factory service bulletins for that model vehicle. The answer is found in a bulletin issued about a year after the vehicle was introduced. The OEM brake shoes were found to have a tendency to swell when subjected to cold and wet. The factory recommended another type of shoe should be installed to correct the problem. Had the technician the experience to check the service bulletin file on the vehicle, valuable diagnostic time would have been saved.

The correct shoe is installed, and the vehicle is road tested. The rear brakes no longer lock up.

Summary

- The four factors that determine a vehicle's braking power are pressure, which is provided by the hydraulic system; coefficient of friction, which represents the frictional relationship between pads and rotors or shoes and drums and is engineered to ensure optimum performance; frictional contact surface, meaning that bigger brakes stop a car more quickly than smaller brakes; and head dissipation, which is necessary to prevent brake fade.
- With asbestos banned as a brake lining material, today full metallics and semi-metallics are used, as well as other nonasbestos substances.
- Since 1967, all cars have been required to have two separate brake systems. The dual brake system uses a tandem master cylinder, which is two master cylinders formed by installing two separated pistons and fluid reservoirs in one cylinder bore.
- Brake fluid is the lifeblood of any hydraulic brake system. DOT 4 is the type most commonly used on conventional systems. DOT 3 is recommended for most ABS systems and some power brake systems.
- The brake lines transmit brake fluid pressure from the master cylinder to the wheel cylinders and calipers of drum and disc brakes. Brake hoses offer flexible connections to wheel units and must offer high heat resistance.
- A pressure differential valve is used in all dual brake systems to operate a warning light switch that alerts the driver if pressure is lost in either hydraulic system.
- The metering valve, located in the front brake line, provides for better balance of the front and rear brakes, while also preventing lockup of the front brakes. The proportioning valve controls rear brake pressure, particularly during hard stops.
- Hydraulic brake system service is vital to safe vehicle operation. It includes brake fluid, brake line, and brake pedal inspection.
- Bleeding removes air from the hydraulic system.
- Power brakes can be either vacuum assist or hydraulic assist. Vacuum-assisted units use engine vacuum, or vacuum developed by an external pump, to help apply the brakes. Hydraulic-assisted units use fluid pressure.
- Modern anti-lock brake systems provide electronic/hydraulic pumping of the brakes for straight-line stopping under panic conditions.
- Integrated ABS combine the master cylinder, hydraulic booster, and hydraulic circuitry into a single assembly. The great majority of ABS systems are of this type.
- On non-integrated ABS, the master cylinder and hydraulic valve unit are separate assemblies and a vacuum boost is used. In some non-integrated systems, the master cylinder supplies brake fluid to the hydraulic unit.
- Automatic stability control (ASC) is a system that applies the brakes when a drive wheel attempts to spin and lose traction.

Review Questions

1. Explain why bleeding air out of a hydraulic system is so important.
2. Explain why modern hydraulic braking systems are dual designs, and why this is important.
3. Define the difference between an integrated and non-integrated anti-lock braking system.
4. Briefly describe the proper steps and testing needed to accurately diagnose anti-lock braking systems.
5. Describe the functions of the hydraulic system combination valve.
6. The friction that is generated between a vehicle's tires and the road when the vehicle is in a non-skidding state is called _____ friction.
    a. static
    b. kinetic
    c. heat
    d. coefficient
7. Bleeding a hydraulic system involves _____ from the system.
    a. removing water
    b. removing contaminated brake fluid
    c. removing air pockets
    d. filtering out dirt
8. The purpose of the master cylinder is to _____.
    a. generate the hydraulic pressure needed to apply the brake mechanisms
    b. automatically pump the brakes during panic stops
    c. apply braking power when wheel slippage occurs
    d. all of the above
9. After bleeding a hydraulic system, Technician A examines the brake fluid and returns it to the master cylinder if the fluid is clean. Technician B always refills the master cylinder with new brake fluid. Who is correct?
    a. Technician A
    b. Technician B
    c. Both A and B
    d. Neither A nor B
10. Which of the following can lead to brake hose failure?
    a. improperly matched fittings
    b. stressing the hose during installations
    c. deterioration from heat and contaminants
    d. all of the above
11. When the brakes are applied which type of brake offers immediate response?
    a. drum
    b. disc
    c. both A and B
    d. neither A nor B
12. Which type of brake requires greater application force and is commonly used with power-boost units?
    a. drum
    b. disc
    c. both A and B
    d. neither A nor B
13. What type of power-assist unit uses pressure developed by an external pump, such as the power steering pump?
    a. hydraulic assist
    b. vacuum assist
    c. ABS
    d. ASC
14. The power brakes in a vehicle are grabbing. Technician A immediately investigates the power unit. Technician B first checks for other causes, such as greasy lining or scored drums. Who is correct?
    a. Technician A
    b. Technician B
    c. Both A and B
    d. Neither A nor B
15. What is the name for the gas-filled pressure chamber that is part of the anti-lock braking system's pump and motor assembly?
    a. controller
    b. accumulator
    c. sensor
    d. reservoir
16. Which of the following is not a component of an anti-lock brake system?
    a. power-steering pump
    b. master cylinder
    c. solenoid valve body assembly
    d. wheel sensors
17. The metering valve portion of a combination valve fails. Technician A says that this means the entire combination valve must be replaced. Technician B says that the metering part can be repaired. Who is correct?
    a. Technician A
    b. Technician B
    c. Both A and B
    d. Neither A nor B
18. Technician A says the front brakes of an ABS system can be bled without the accumulator being charged. Technician B says that bleeding the front brakes requires a fully-charged accumulator. Who is correct?
    a. Technician A
    b. Technician B
    c. Both A and B
    d. Neither A nor B

36 DRUM BRAKES

Objectives

■ Explain how drum brakes operate. ■ Identify the major components of a typical drum brake and describe their functions. ■ Explain the difference between duo-servo and non-servo drum brakes. ■ Perform a cleaning and inspection of a drum brake assembly. ■ Recognize conditions that adversely affect the performance of drums, shoes, linings, and related hardware. ■ Reassemble a drum brake after servicing. ■ Explain how typical drum parking brakes operate. ■ Adjust a typical drum parking brake.

For many years, drum brakes were used on all four wheels on virtually every vehicle on the road. Today, disc brakes have replaced drum brakes on the front wheels of most vehicles, and some models are equipped with both front and rear disc brakes. One reason for their continued use is that drum brakes can easily handle the 20 to 40% of total braking load placed on the rear wheels. Another is that drum brakes can also be built with a simple parking brake mechanism.

☐ DRUM BRAKE OPERATION

Drum brake operation is fairly simple. The most important fact contributing to the effectiveness of the braking force supplied by the drum brake is the brake shoe pressure or force directed against the drum (Figure 36-1). With the vehicle moving in either the forward or reverse direction with the brakes on, the applied force of the brake shoe, pressing against the brake drum, increasingly multiplies itself. This is because the brake's anchor pin acts as a brake shoe stop and prohibits the brake shoe from its tendency to follow the movement of the rotating drum. The result is a wedging action between the brake shoe and brake drum. The wedging action combined with the applied brake force creates a self-multiplied brake force.

☐ DRUM BRAKE COMPONENTS

The major components of a typical drum brake are shown in Figure 36-2. The backing plate provides a

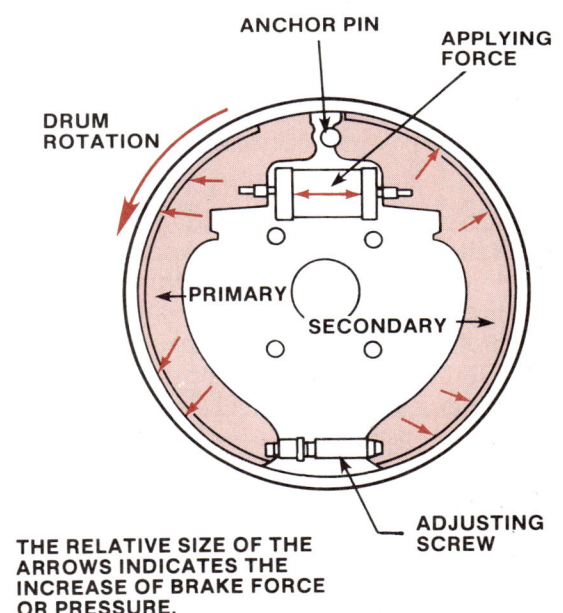

Figure 36-1 The wheel cylinder pushes the primary and secondary shoes against the inside surface of the rotating brake drum.

foundation for the brake shoes and associated hardware. The plate is secured and bolted to the axle flange or spindle. The wheel cylinder, under hydraulic pressure, forces the brake's shoes against the drum. There are also two lined brake shoes attached to the backing plate. The brake shoe is the backbone of a drum brake. The shoe must support the lining and carry it into the drum so that the pressure is distributed across the

923

924 Section 8 Brakes

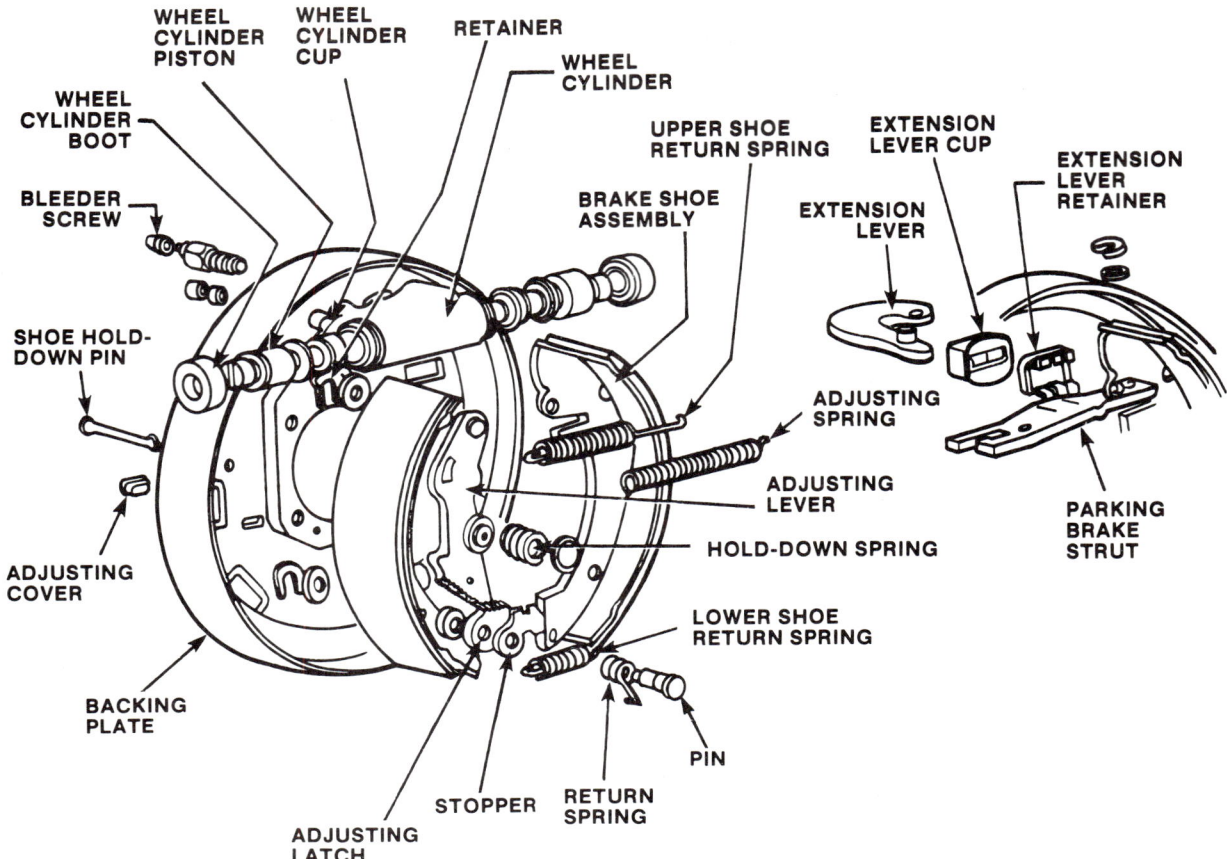

Figure 36-2 Components of a typical rear-wheel drum brake.

lining surface during brake application. Shoe return springs and shoe hold-down parts maintain the correct shoe position and clearance. Some drum brakes are self-adjusting. Others require manual adjustment mechanisms. Brake drums provide the rubbing surface area for the linings. Drums must withstand high pressures without excessive flexing and also dissipate large quantities of heat generated during brake application. Finally, the rear drum brakes on most vehicles include the parking brakes.

Wheel Cylinders

Wheel cylinders convert hydraulic pressure supplied by the master cylinder into a mechanical force at the wheel brakes. The space in the wheel cylinder bore between the cups is filled with fluid. When the brake pedal is depressed, additional brake fluid is forced into the cylinder bore. The additional fluid, which is under pressure, moves the cups and pistons outward in the bore. This piston movement forces the shoe links and brake shoes outward to contact the drum and thus apply the brakes.

Brake Shoes and Linings

The workhorse of the drum brake is the brake shoe. In the same brake sizes, there can be differences in web thickness, shape of web cutouts, and positions of any reinforcements.

The shoe rim is welded to the web to provide a table surface for the lining. The web thickness might differ to provide the stiffness or flexibility needed for a specific application. Many shoes have nibs or indented places along the edge of the rim. These nibs rest against shoe support ledges on the backing plate and keep the shoe from hanging up.

Each drum in the drum braking system contains a set of shoes. The primary (or leading) shoe is the one that is toward the front of the vehicle. The friction between the primary shoe and the brake drum forces the primary shoe to shift slightly in the direction that the drum is turning (an anchor pin permits just limited movement). The shifting of the primary shoe forces it against the bottom of the secondary shoe, which causes the secondary shoe to contact the drum. The secondary (or trailing) shoe is the one that is toward the rear of the vehicle. It comes into contact as a result of the movement and pressure from the primary shoe and wheel cylinder piston and increases the braking action.

The brake shoe lining provides friction against the drum to stop the car. It contains heat-resistant fibers. The lining is molded with a high-temperature synthetic bonding agent.

The two general methods of attaching the lining to the shoe are riveting and bonding. Regardless of the method of attachment, brake shoes are usually held in a position by spring tension. They are either held against the anchor by the shoe return springs or against the support plate pads by shoe hold-down springs. The shoe webs are linked together at the end opposite the anchor by an adjuster and a spring. The adjuster holds them apart. The spring holds them against the adjuster ends.

Mechanical Components

In the unapplied position, the shoes are held against the anchor pin by the return springs. The shoes are held to the backing plate by holddown springs or spring clips. Opposite the anchor pin, a star wheel adjuster links the shoe webs and provides a threaded adjustment that permits the shoes to be expanded or contracted. The shoes are held against the star wheel by a spring.

Shoe Return Springs

Return springs can be separately hooked into a link or a guide (Figure 36-3) or strung between the shoes. Springs are normally installed on the anchor in the order shown under each category listed in Figure 36-4.

While shoe brake springs look the same, they are usually not interchangeable. Sometimes to help distinguish between them, they are color coded. Pay close attention to the colors and the way they are hooked up.

Shoe Hold-downs

Various shoe hold-downs are illustrated in Figure 36-5. To unlock or lock the straight pin hold-downs, depress the locking cup and coil spring or the spring

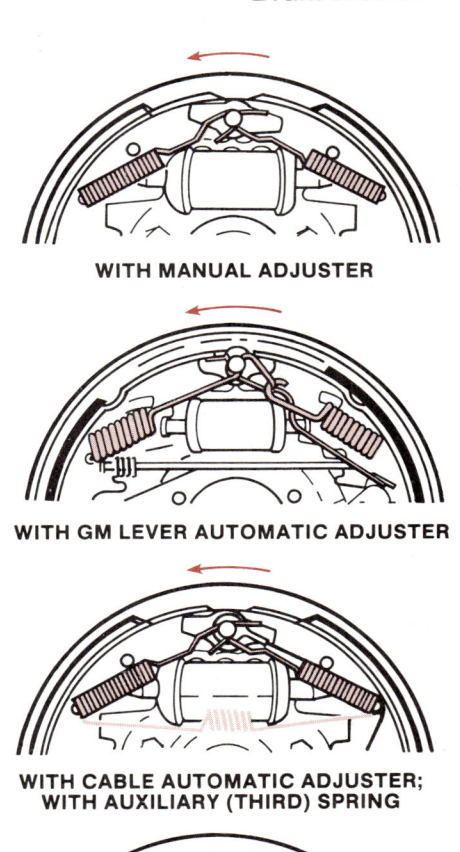

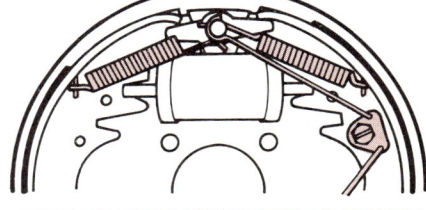

Figure 36-4 Typical brake shoe return spring anchoring points.

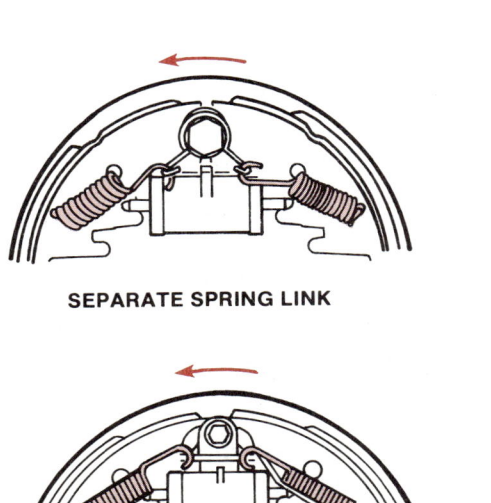

Figure 36-3 Typical brake shoe return spring alignments.

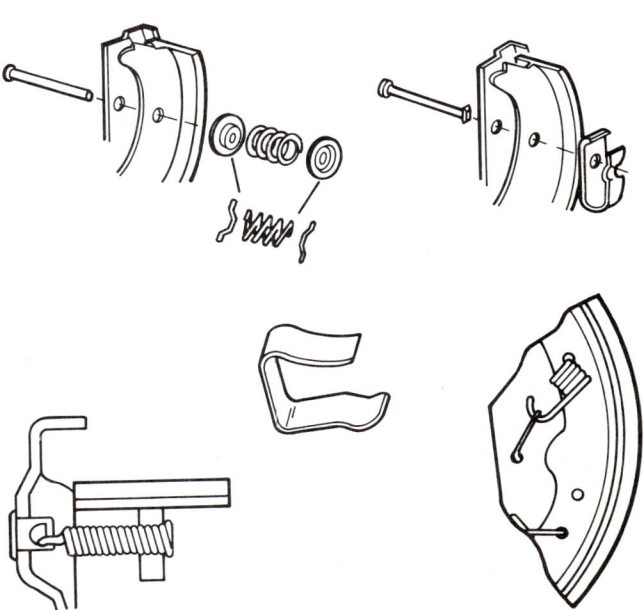

Figure 36-5 Types of brake shoe hold-downs.

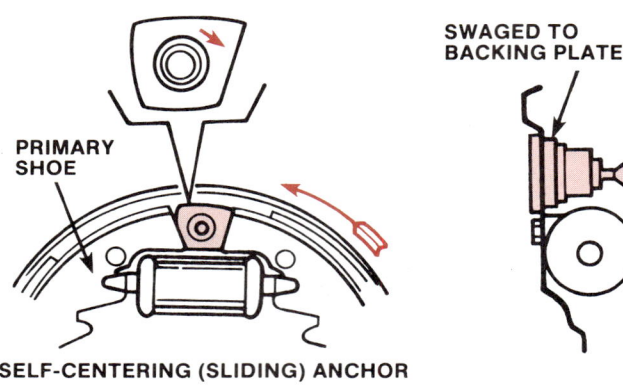

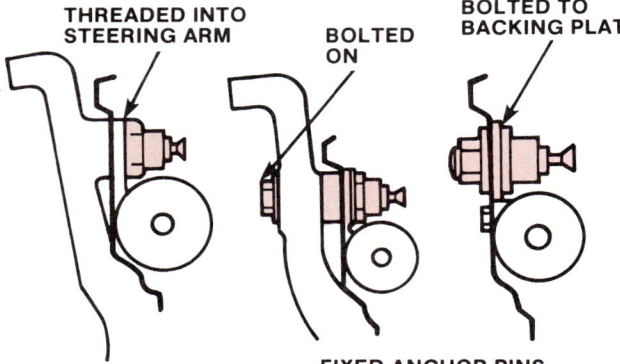

Figure 36-6 Types of brake shoe anchors.

clip, and rotate the pin or lock 90 degrees. On GM lever adjusters, the inner (bottom) cup has a sleeve that aligns the adjuster lever.

Shoe Anchors

As shown in Figure 36-6 there are various types of shoe anchors such as the fixed non-adjustable type, self-centering shoe sliding type, or, on some earlier models, adjustable fixed type providing either an eccentric or a slotted adjustment. On some front brakes, fixed anchors are threaded into or are bolted through the steering knuckle and also support the wheel cylinder.

On adjustable anchors, when it is necessary to re-center the shoes in the drum or drum gauge, loosen the locknut enough to permit the anchor to slip but not so much that it can tilt.

On eccentric anchors, tighten the star wheel to heavy brake drag (Figure 36-7). Rotate the eccentric anchor in the direction that frees the brake until drag is again encountered. Return the eccentric to the position between the two points of drag where the drum rotates freely. Repeat this sequence until drag cannot be relieved. Tighten the anchor nut. Back off the star wheel to a normal manual adjustment.

On the slotted type anchor, tighten the star wheel to heavy drag. Tap the support plate until the anchor moves and frees the brake. Repeat this sequence until drag cannot be relieved. Tighten the lock nut to 100 to 200 foot-pounds torque. Back off the star wheel to a normal manual adjustment.

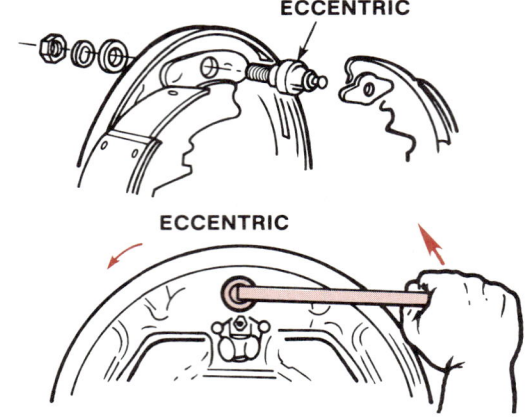

Figure 36-7 Anchor adjustment-fixed and eccentric.

Drums

Modern automotive brake drums are made of heavy cast iron (some are aluminum with an iron or steel sleeve or liner) with a machined surface inside against which the linings on the brake shoes generate friction when the brakes are applied. This results in the creation of a great deal of heat. The inability of drums to dissipate as much heat as disc brakes is one of the main reasons discs have replaced drums at the front of all late-model cars and light trucks, and at the rear of some sports and luxury cars.

Rear drums on FWD cars are usually integral with the hub, so they cannot be removed without disassembling the wheel bearing. The rear drums of most rear-wheel-drive cars are held in place by the wheel lugs, so they can be removed without tampering with the wheel bearings.

☐ DRUM BRAKE DESIGNS

There are two brake designs in common use: duo-servo (or self-energizing) drum brakes and non-servo (or leading-trailing) drum brakes.

Most large American cars use the duo-servo design of brake. However, the non-servo type has become popular as the size of cars has gotten smaller. Because the smaller cars are lighter, this type of brake helps reduce rear brake lockup without reducing breaking ability.

Duo-Servo Drum Brakes

The name duo-servo brake drum is derived from the fact that the self-energizing force is transferred from one shoe to the other with the wheel rotating in either direction. Both the primary (front) and secondary (rear) brake shoes are actuated by a double-piston wheel cylinder (Figure 36-8). The upper end of each shoe is held against a single anchor by a heavy coil return spring. An adjusting screw assembly and spring connect the lower ends of the shoes.

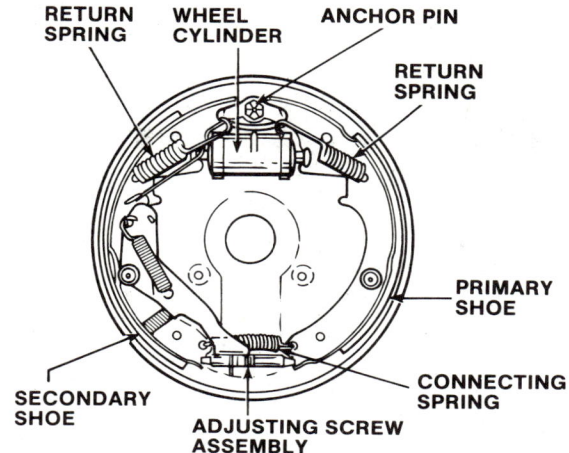

Figure 36-8 Typical duo-servo drum brake.

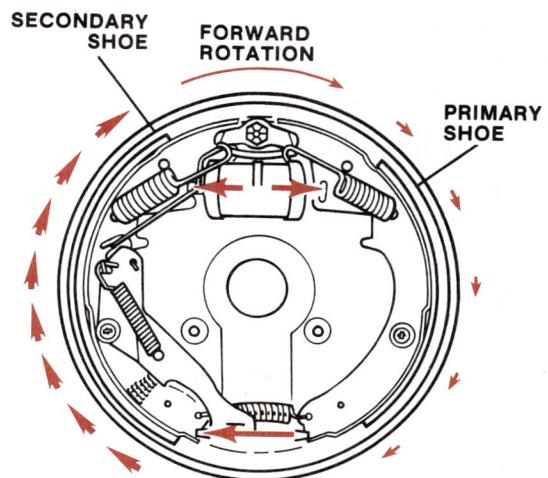

Figure 36-10 Duo-servo braking forces.

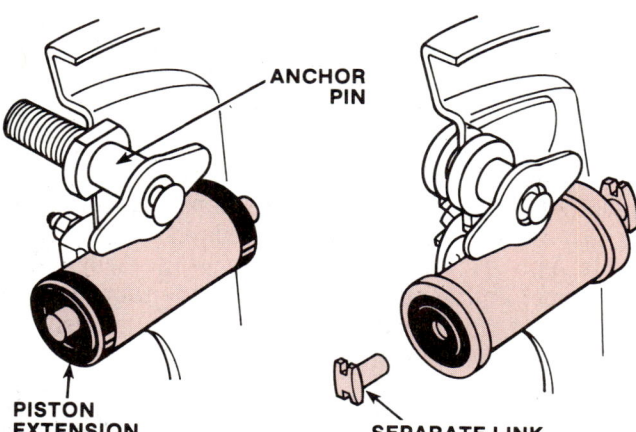

Figure 36-9 Wheel cylinder designs.

The wheel cylinder is mounted on the backing plate at the top of the brake. When the brakes are applied, hydraulic pressure behind the wheel cylinder cups forces both pistons outward causing the brakes to be applied. Some wheel cylinders have extensions on the pistons that contact the brake shoes, while others have separate links (Figure 36-9).

When the brake shoes contact the rotating drum in either direction of rotation, they tend to move with the drum until one shoe contacts the anchor and the other shoe is stopped by the star wheel adjuster link (Figure 36-10). With forward rotation, frictional forces between the lining and the drum of the primary shoe result in a force acting on the adjuster link to apply the secondary shoe. This adjuster link force into the secondary shoe is many times greater than the wheel cylinder input force acting on the primary shoe. The force of the adjuster link into the secondary shoe is again multiplied by the frictional forces between the secondary lining and rotating drum, and all of the resultant force is taken on the anchor pin. In normal forward braking, the friction developed by the secondary lining is greater than the primary lining. There-fore, the secondary brake lining is usually thicker and has more surface area. The roles of the primary and secondary linings are reversed in braking the vehicle when backing up.

Automatically Adjusted Servo Brakes

Since the early 1960s, automatic drum brake adjusters have been used on all American and most import vehicles. There are several variations of automatic adjusters used with servo brakes. The more common types available follow.

BASIC CABLE Figure 36-11 shows a typical automatic adjusting system. Adjusters, whether cable, crank, or lever, are installed on one shoe and operated whenever the shoe moves away from its anchor. The upper link, or cable eye, is attached to the anchor. As the shoe moves, the cable pulls over a guide mounted on the shoe web (the crank or lever pivots on the shoe web) and operates a lever (pawl), which is attached to the shoe so it engages a star wheel tooth. The pawl is located on the outer side of the star wheel and, on different styles, slightly above or below the wheel centerline so that it serves as a ratchet lock, which prevents the adjustment from backing off. However, whenever lining wears enough to permit sufficient shoe movement, brake application pulls the pawl high

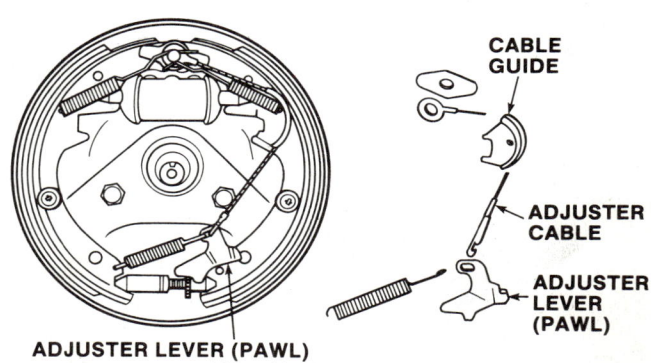

Figure 36-11 Cable self-adjusters.

enough to engage the next tooth. As the brake is released, the adjuster spring returns the pawl, thus advancing the star wheel one notch.

On most vehicles the adjuster system is installed on the secondary shoe and operates when the brakes are applied as the vehicle is backing up. On a few models, it is located on the primary shoe and operates when the brakes are applied as the vehicle is moving forward. Left-hand and right-hand threaded star wheels are used on opposite sides of the car, so parts should be kept separated. If the wrong star wheel thread is installed, the system does not adjust at all.

Another system uses a cable with downstroke pawl advance, and the left brake with right-hand threads and the right brake with left-hand threads. The first cable guide is usually retained on the shoe web by the secondary shoe return spring, and the lever-pawl engages a hole in the shoe web. The adjuster operates in either direction of vehicle movement. The cable guide is slotted and attached to the web with a screw. The guide position should be adjusted to align the pawl after the self-centering shoes are located on sliding anchors.

CABLE WITH OVERTRAVEL SPRING Figure 36-12 shows a system with an upstroke pawl advance. The left brake has left-hand threads, and the right brake has right-hand threads. The lever (pawl) is installed on a web pin with an additional pawl return mousetrap spring. The cable is hooked to the lever (pawl) by means of an overtravel spring installed in the cable hook. The overtravel spring dampens movements and prevents unnecessary adjustment should sudden hard braking cause excessive drum deflection and shoe movement.

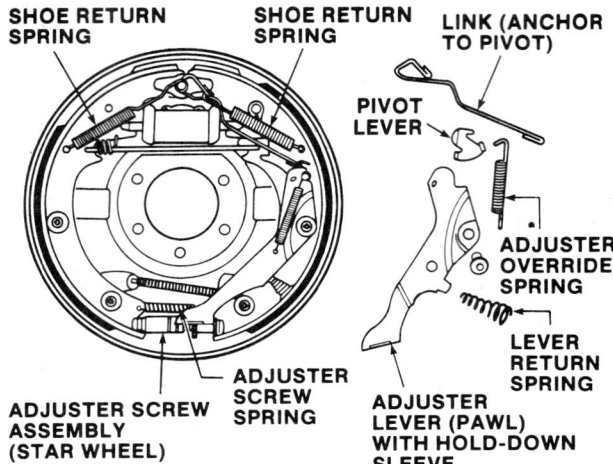

Figure 36-13 Adjusting lever with pivot and override spring.

LEVER WITH OVERRIDE The system illustrated in Figure 36-13 uses a downstroke pawl advance. The left brake has right-hand threads, and the right brake has left-hand threads.

The lever (pawl) is mounted on a shoe hold-down, pivoting on a cup sleeve. It has a separate lever-pawl return spring located between the lever and the shoe table. A pivot lever and an override spring assembled to the upper end of the main lever dampen movement, preventing unnecessary adjustment in the event of excessive drum deflection.

LEVER AND PAWL The system illustrated in Figure 36-14 uses a downstroke pawl advance. The left brake has right-hand threads, and the right break has left-

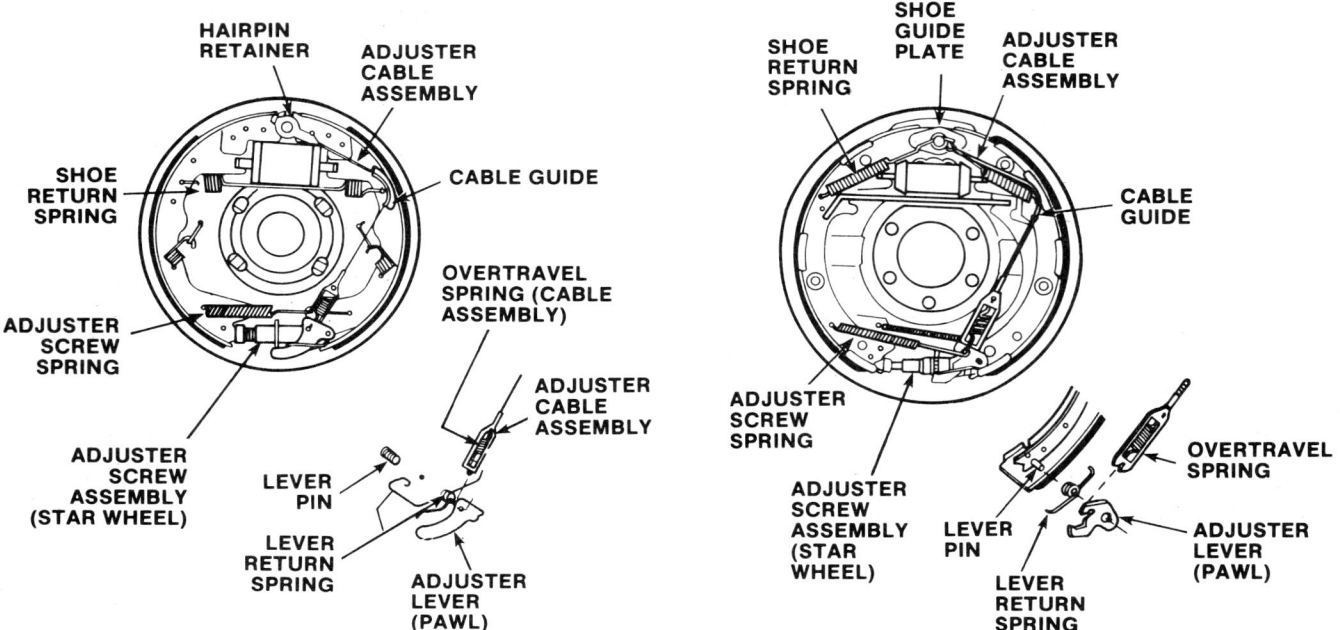

Figure 36-12 Cable automatic adjustment with overtravel springs.

Drum Brakes 929

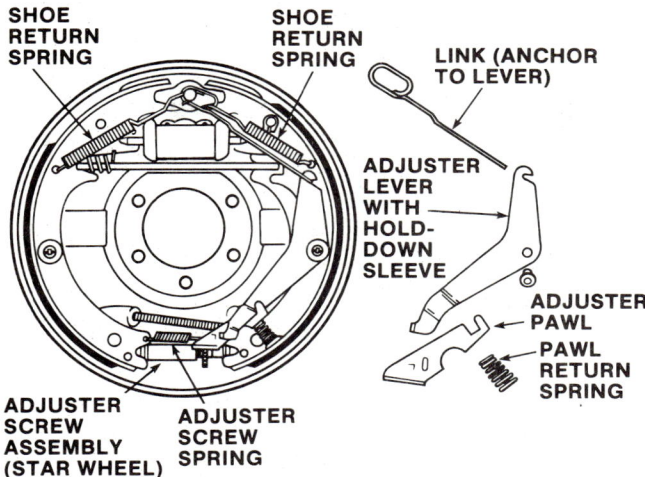

Figure 36-14 Lever and pawl automatic adjustment.

hand threads. The lever is mounted on a shoe hold-down, pivoting on a cup sleeve, and engages the pawl. A separate pawl return spring is located between the pawl and the shoe.

Non-Servo Drum Brakes

The non-servo (or as it is better known today as the leading-trailing shoe) drum brake is often used on small cars. The basic difference between this type and the duo-servo brake is that both brake shoes are held against a fixed anchor at the bottom by a retaining spring (Figure 36-15). Non-servo brakes have no servo action.

On a forward brake application, the forward (leading) shoe friction forces are developed by wheel cylinder fluid pressure forcing the lining into contact with the rotating brake drum. The shoe's friction forces work against the anchor pin at the bottom of the shoe. The trailing shoe is also actuated by wheel cylinder pressure, but can only support a friction force equal to the wheel cylinder piston forces. The trailing shoe anchor pin supports no friction load. The leading shoe in this brake is energized and does most of the braking in comparison to the non-energized trailing shoe. In reverse braking, the leading and trailing brake shoes switch functions.

> **SHOP TALK**
>
> It is important for the technician to remember that on non-servo drum systems the forward shoe is called the leading shoe and the rear one is known as the trailing shoe (when the vehicle is moving in the forward direction). On duo-servo designs, the forward shoe is the primary, and the rear is the secondary.

Non-servo, or leading-trailing shoe, drum brakes can be either manually adjusted or can have an automatic adjustment feature.

Manually Adjusted Non-Servo Drum Brakes

There are several types of manually adjusted non-servo drum brake designs available. The two most common are lockhead manual and adjustable strut adjusters.

LOCKHEED MANUAL ADJUSTER This is a very simple brake system (Figure 36-16). The shoes are located on the top and bottom rather than the sides. The shoes are held tightly against the wheel cylinder and the adjusters by two retracting springs. Each shoe has to be adjusted individually by tightening it against the drum and then backing it off until the drum turns freely.

Depending on what car this type of brake is used on, there will be differences in the brake shoes, adjusters,

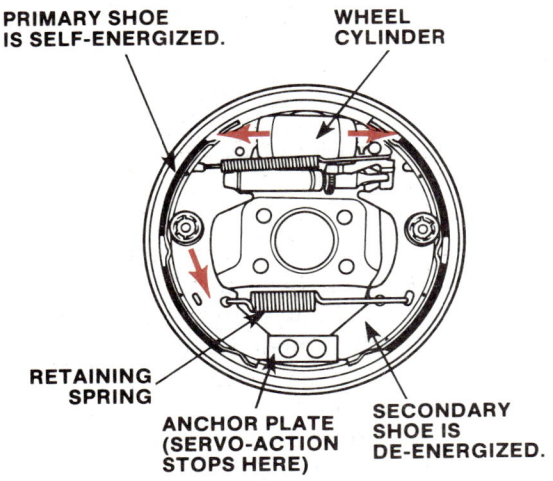

Figure 36-15 Typical non-servo drum brake.

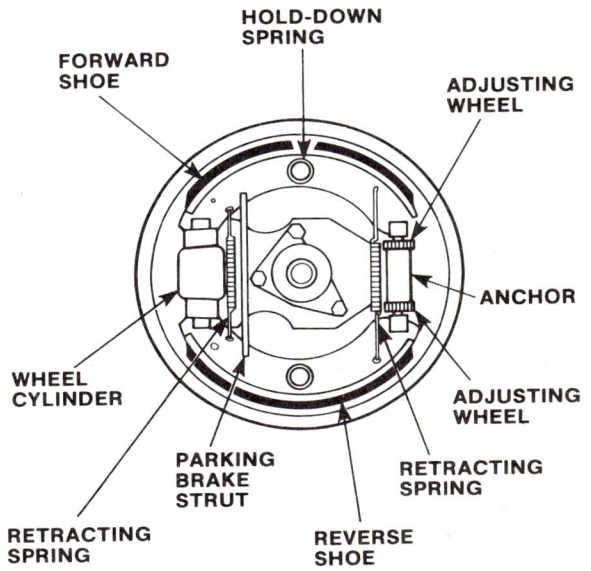

Figure 36-16 Lockheed non-servo drum brake.

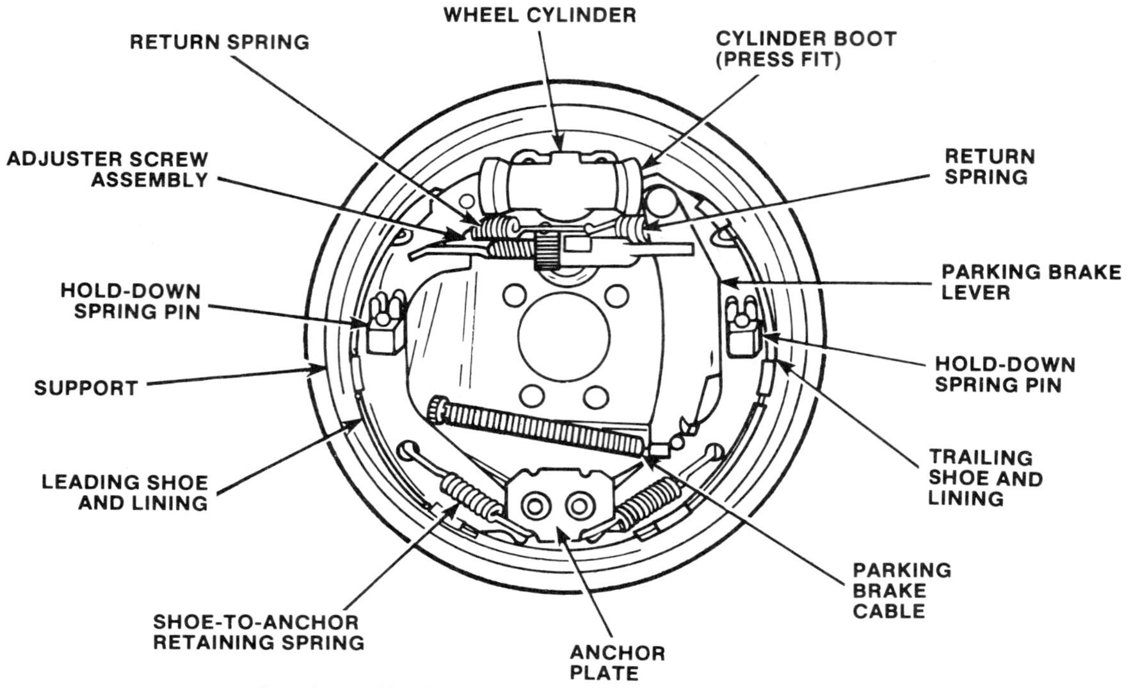

930 Section 8 Brakes

Figure 36-17 Non-servo manually adjusted brake.

anchors, wheel cylinders, or parking brake linkage. It is best to work on one wheel at a time and to use the other for reference.

ADJUSTABLE STRUT ADJUSTER On this design (Figure 36-17) the bottoms of the leading and trailing shoes are held against the anchor plate by shoe-to-anchor retaining springs. The top webs engage the wheel cylinder pistons and are straddled by a specially designed adjuster screw assembly. Return springs attached to the adjuster hole in the backing plate hold the shoes in against the adjuster screw assembly. One end engages the trailing shoe web and parking brake lever and the other end engages the leading shoe web.

The upper end of the parking brake lever is pinned to the upper end of the trailing shoe and the lower end is attached to the parking brake cable. When the cable is pulled, force is transmitted through the special adjuster assembly to the leading shoe. Shoe adjustment is done manually by inserting a thin bladed screwdriver through the hole in the backing plate and rotating the adjuster screw to spread the shoes.

Automatically Adjusted Non-Servo Brakes

While some standard automatic adjusters similar to the one already discussed are employed on small cars, some of the automatic adjuster mechanisms are unique and varied, using expanding struts between the shoes, or special ratchet adjusting mechanisms. Among the more common of these designs are automatic cam, ratchet automatic, and semi-automatic adjusters.

AUTOMATIC CAM ADJUSTERS This rear non-servo drum brake is for use with front disc brakes and has one forward acting (leading) and one reverse acting (trailing) shoe. Shoes rest against the wheel cylinder pistons at the top and are held against the anchor plate by a shoe-to-shoe pull-back spring. The anchor plate and retaining plate are riveted to the backing plate. Adjustment of the brake shoes takes place automatically as needed when the brakes are applied. The automatic cam adjusters are attached to each shoe by a pin through a slot in the shoe webbing. As the shoes move outward during application, the pin in the slot moves the cam adjuster, rotating it outward. Shoes always return enough to provide proper clearance because the pin diameter is smaller than the width of the slot (Figure 36-18).

RATCHET AUTOMATIC ADJUSTER These popular brakes are a leading-trailing shoe design with a ratchet self-adjusting mechanism. The shoes are held to the backing plate by spring and pin hold-downs. The shoes are held against the anchors at the top by a shoe-to-shoe spring. At the bottom, the shoe webs are held against the wheel cylinder piston ends by a return spring (Figure 36-19).

The self-adjusting mechanism consists of a spacer strut and a pair of toothed ratchets attached to the secondary brake shoe. The parking brake actuating lever is pivoted on the spacer strut.

The self-adjusting mechanism automatically senses the correct lining-to-drum clearance. As the linings wear, the clearance is adjusted by increasing the effective length of the spacer strut. This strut has projections to engage the inner edge of the secondary shoe via the hand brake lever and the inner edge of the large

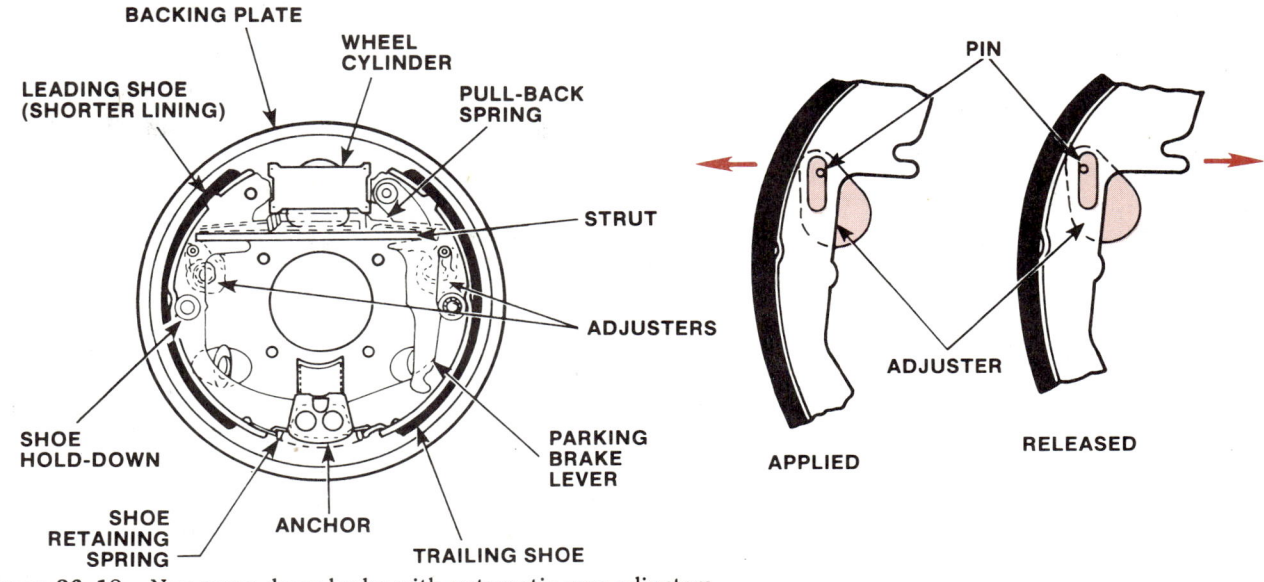

Figure 36-18 Non-servo drum brake with automatic cam adjusters.

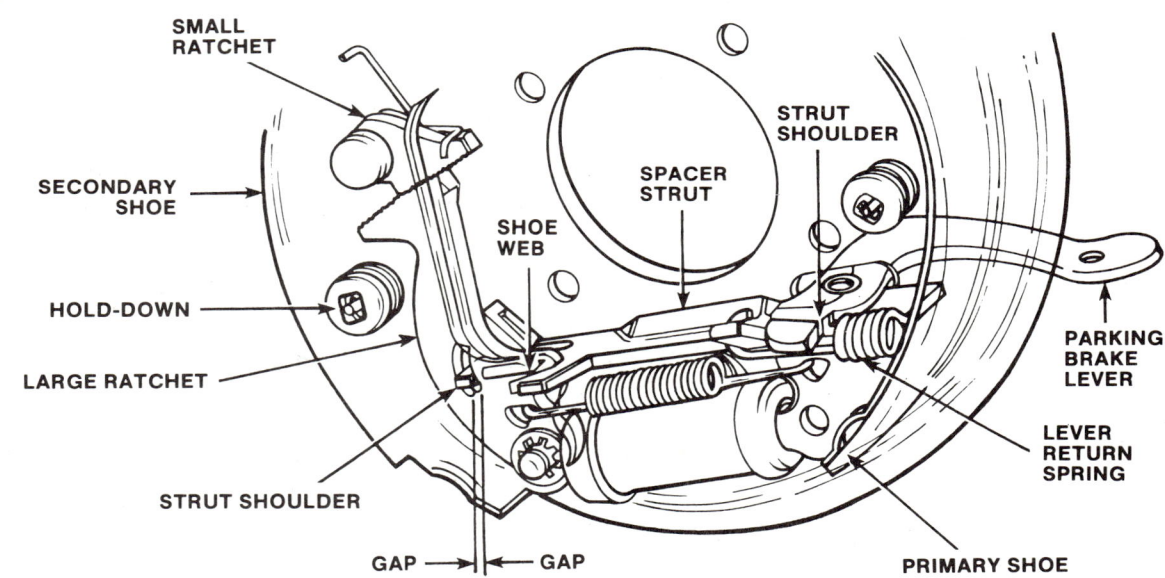

Figure 36-19 Typical non-servo self-adjusting mechanism.

ratchet on the secondary shoe. As wear on the linings increases, the movement of the shoes to bring them in contact with the drums becomes greater than the gap. The spacer strut, bearing on the shoe web, is moved together with the primary shoe to close the gap. Further movement causes the large ratchet, behind the secondary shoe, to rotate inward against the spring-loaded small ratchet, and the serrations on the mating edges maintain this new setting until further wear on the shoe results in another adjustment. On releasing brake pedal pressure, the return springs cause the shoes to move into contact with the shoulders of the spacer strut/hand brake actuating lever. This restores the clearance between the linings and the drum proportionate to the gap.

SEMI-AUTOMATIC ADJUSTER This brake was designed to be used only as a rear wheel drum for a small car with front disc brakes (Figure 36-20). It has one forward-acting and one reverse-acting shoe. A hold-down clip has replaced the hold-down spring, cup, and pin. A specially designed parking brake strut and rod assembly straddles the shoe webs just below the wheel cylinder. A shoe-to-shoe spring at the top and another at the bottom under the anchor plate hold the shoes in place.

The strut and rod assembly for the parking brake has the strut part on the forward shoe and the rod part connected to a hole in the reverse shoe. When the parking brake is applied, rear brake shoe adjustment is made. The strut and rod spread the shoes enough to

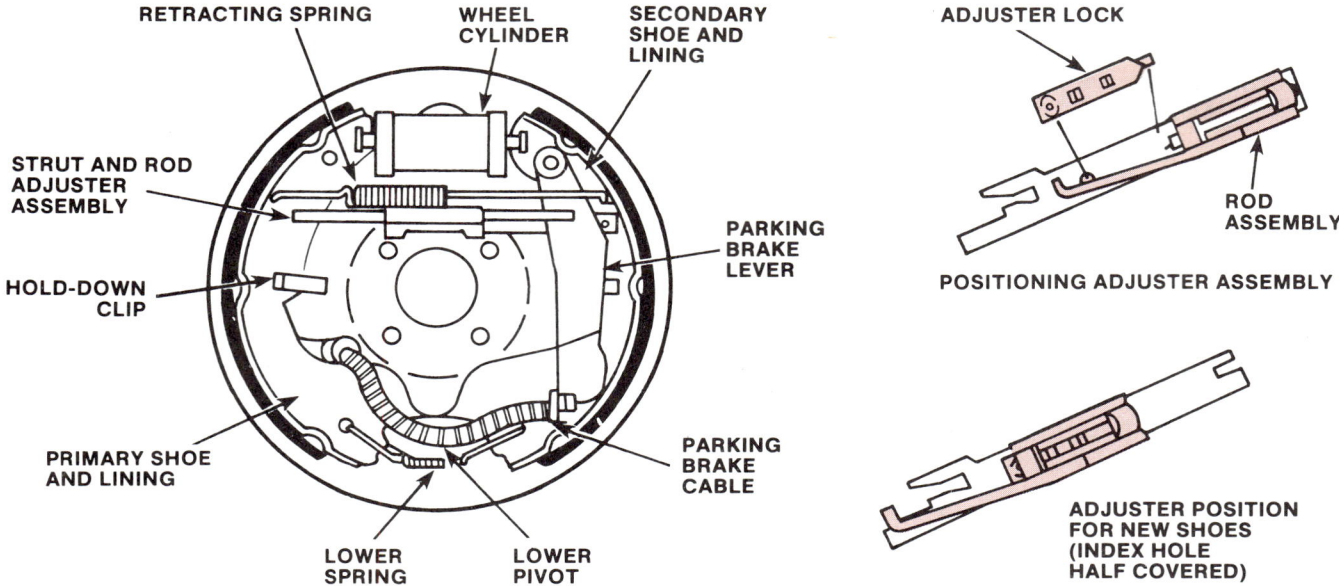

Figure 36-20 Non-servo drum brake featuring semi-automatic adjustments.

pass the spring locks mounted in the assembly. The shoes are prevented from returning to their original position. Pressure on the brake shoes is released when the rod is relaxed, providing enough clearance for the wheels to turn.

Inspection and Service

The first rule of quality brake service is to perform a complete job. For example, if new linings are installed without regard to the condition of the hydraulic system, the presence of a leaking wheel cylinder quickly ruins the new linings. Braking power and safety are also compromised.

Problems such as spongy pedal, excessive pedal travel, pedal pulsation, poor braking ability, brake drag, lock, or pulling to one side, and braking noises can be caused by trouble in the hydraulic system or the mechanical components of the brake assembly. To aid in doing a complete inspection and diagnosis, a form such as the one shown in Figure 36-21 is very helpful. Working with such a form helps the technician avoid missing any brake test and components that may be causing problems.

Brake Noise

All customer complaints related to brake performance must be carefully considered. The number one customer complaint is brake noise. Noise is often the first indication of wear or problems within the braking system, particularly in the mechanical components. Rattles, clicking, grinding, and hammering from the wheels when the brake is in the unapplied position should be carefully investigated. Be sure the noise is not caused by the bearings or various suspension parts. If the noise is coming from the brake assembly, it is most likely caused by worn, damaged, or missing brake hardware, or the poor fastening or mounting of brake components. Grinding noises usually occur when a stone or other object becomes trapped between the lining material and the rotor or drum.

When the brakes are applied, a clicking noise usually indicates play or hardware failure in the attachment of the pad or shoe. On recent systems, the noise could be caused by the lining tracking cutting tool marks in the rotor or drum. A non-directional finish on rotors eliminates this, and so does a less pointed tip on the cutting tool used to refinish drums.

Grinding noises on application can mean metal-to-metal contact, either from badly worn pads or shoes, or from a serious misalignment of the caliper, rotor, wheel cylinder, or backing plate. Wheel cylinders and calipers that are frozen due to internal corrosion can also cause grinding or squealing noises.

Other noise problems and their solutions are covered later in this chapter.

❑ ROAD TESTING BRAKES

Road testing allows the brake technician to evaluate brake performance under actual driving conditions. Whenever practical, perform the road test before beginning any work on the brake system. In every case, road test the vehicle after any brake work to make sure the brake system is working safely and properly.

WARNING: *Before test driving any car, first check the fluid level in the master cylinder. Depress the brake pedal to be sure there is adequate pedal reserve. Make a series of low-speed stops to be sure that the brakes are safe for road testing. Always make a preliminary inspection of the brake system in the shop before taking the vehicle on the road.*

Drum Brakes 933

PREBRAKE JOB INSPECTION CHECKLIST

Owner _____ Phone _____ Date _____
        LAST   FIRST
Address _____ License No. _____
Make _____ Model _____ Mileage _____ Serial No. _____ Year _____
Special Key for Hubcaps/Wheels   Location _____ Owner Use Parking Brake Yes ☐ No ☐
    4 Drum ☐ 4 Disc ☐ Disc/Drum ☐ P/B No ☐ Yes ☐ Vacuum ☐ Hydro ☐ ABS ☐
Owner Comments _____

1. CHECKS BEFORE ROAD TEST	Safe	Unsafe
Stoplight Operation		
Brake Warning Light Operation		
Master Cylinder Checks		
Fluid Level		
Fluid Contamination		
Under Hood Fluid Leaks		
Under Dash Fluid Leaks (No Power)		
Bypassing		

BRAKE PEDAL HEIGHT AND FEEL

Check One		Check One	
Low		Spongy	
Med		Firm	
High			

Power Brake Unit Checks

VACUUM	Safe	Unsafe	HYDRO	Safe	Unsafe
Vacuum Unit			Hydro Unit		
Engine Vacuum			P/S Fluid		
Vacuum Hose			P/S Belt Tension		
Unit Check Valve			P/S Belt Condition		
Reserve Braking			P/S Fluid Leaks		
			Reserve Braking		

3. In Shop Checks On Hoist	Yes	No	RF	LF	RR	LR
Brake Drag						
Intermittent Brake Drag						
Brake Pedal Linkage Binding						
Wheel Bearing Looseness						
Missing or Broken Wheel Fasteners						
Suspension Looseness						
Mark Wheels and Remove						
Caliper/Piston Stuck RF LF RR LR						
Mark Drums and Remove						
Measure Rotor Thickness or Drum Diameter.						
Measure Rotor Thickness Variation.						
Measure Rotor Runout.						
Lining Thickness						
Tubes and Hoses						
Fluid Leaks						
Broken Bleeders						
Leaky Seals						
Self-Adjuster Operation						
Parking Brake Cables and Linkage						

Tire Pressure Specs	Front	Rear
Record Pressure Found		
RF _____ LF _____ RR _____ LR _____		
Tire Condition		
RF _____ LF _____ RR _____ LR _____		

2. ROAD TEST	Yes	No	RF	LF	RR	LR
Brake Pull						
Brake Clunk						
Brake Scraping						
Brake Squeal						
Brake Grabby						
Brakes Lock Prematurely						
Wheel Bearing Noise						
Vehicle Vibrates						

STEERING WHEEL MOVEMENT WHEN STOPPING
FROM 2-3 MPH   YES/NO/RGT/LFT

	YES	NO
Does ABS Work		
Pedal Pulsation when Braking		
Steering Wheel Oscillation when Braking		
No Stopping Power		
Warning Light Comes on when Braking		
Difference in Pedal Height after Cornering		
Nose Dive		

	Front				Rear			
	Right		Left		Right		Left	
	Spec	Safe	Unsafe	Safe	Unsafe	Spec	Safe	Unsafe	Safe	Unsafe

(Self-Adjuster Operation row: Safe | Unsafe)

Figure 36-21 Sample of prebrake job inspection checklist. *Courtesy of Hennessy Industries, Inc.*

Brakes should be road tested on a dry, clean, reasonably smooth, and level roadway. A true test of brake performance cannot be made if the roadway is wet, greasy, or covered with loose dirt. All tires do not grip the road equally. Testing is also adversely affected if the roadway is crowned so as to throw the weight of the vehicle toward the wheels on one side, or if the roadway is so rough that wheels tend to bounce.

Test brakes at different speeds with both light and heavy pedal pressure. Avoid locking the wheels and sliding the tires on the roadway. There are external conditions that affect brake road-test performance. Tires having unequal contact and grip on the road cause unequal braking. Tires must be equally inflated, and the tread pattern of right and left tires must be approximately equal. When the vehicle has unequal loading, the most heavily loaded wheels require more braking power than others. A heavily loaded vehicle requires more braking effort. A loose front-wheel bearing permits the drum and wheel to tilt and have spotty contact with the brake linings, causing erratic brake action. Misalignment of the front end causes the brakes to pull to one side. Also, a loose front-wheel bearing could permit the disc to tilt and have spotty contact with brake shoe linings, causing pulsations when the brakes are applied. Faulty shock absorbers that do not prevent the car from bouncing on quick stops can give the erroneous impression that the brakes are too severe.

❏ DRUM BRAKE INSPECTION

Before inspecting drum brakes, place the vehicle in neutral, release the parking brake, and raise the vehicle on the hoist. Once the vehicle is raised, mark the wheel-to-drum and drum-to-axle positions so the components can be accurately reassembled. Relieve all tension from the parking brake cable by loosening or removing the adjusting nut at the equalizer. To access the drum brake assembly, remove the lug nuts and pull the wheel off the hub.

Shoe and Lining Removal

Several different methods are used to mount the drum to the wheel hub flange. It can be fastened with rivets or by swaging the piloting shoulders of the wheel studs, or with speed nut fasteners installed over the threads of the wheel studs.

The most common mounting method is using the tire rim and lug nuts. The drum is a slip fit over the axle flange and studs. Speed nuts are installed at the vehicle manufacturing plant for temporary retention of the drum on the assembly line until the wheel is installed.

A floating drum can be retained by a nut and cotter pin. The drum can also be secured to the axle flange by one or two bolts. Some import applications have two additional holes threaded into the drum face so that bolts can be used to press the drum from the hub or flange.

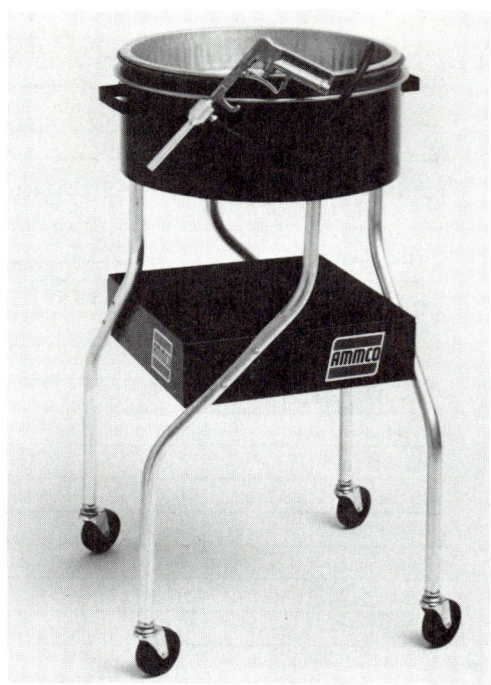

Figure 36-22 Washer used to safely remove asbestos fibers from brake surfaces. *Courtesy of Ammco Tools, Inc.*

WARNING: When servicing wheel brake parts, do not create dust by cleaning with a dry brush or with compressed air. Asbestos fibers can become airborne if dust is created during servicing. Breathing dust containing asbestos fibers can cause serious bodily harm. To clean away asbestos from brake surfaces, use an OSHA-approved washer (Figure 36-22). Follow manufacturer's instructions when using the washer.

After removing the retaining devices that hold the drum to the axle flange or hub, the drum can be removed for servicing. If the brake drum is rusted or corroded to the axle flange and cannot be removed, lightly tap the axle flange to the drum mounting surface with a plastic mallet. Remember that if the drum is worn, the brake shoe adjustment has to be backed off for the drums to clear the brake shoes. Do not force the drum or distort it. Do not allow the drum to drop.

If the brake shoes have expanded too tightly against the drum or have cut into the friction surface of the brake drum, the drums might be too tight for removal. In such a case, the shoes must be adjusted inward before the brake drum is removed. On most cars with self-adjusting mechanisms, reach through the adjusting slot with a thin screwdriver (or similar tool) and carefully push the self-adjusting lever away from the star wheel a maximum of 1/16 inch (Figure 36-23). While holding the lever back, insert a brake adjusting

Drum Brakes

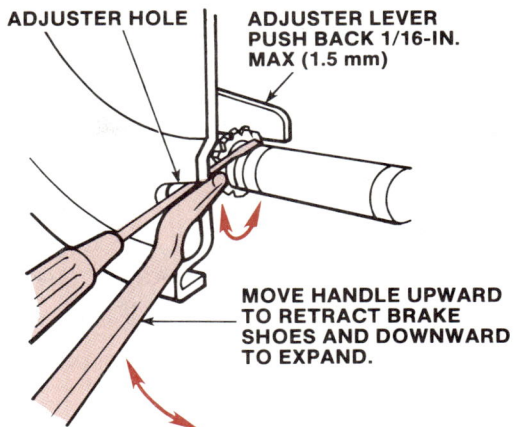

Figure 36-23 Removing brake drums equipped with self-adjusters.

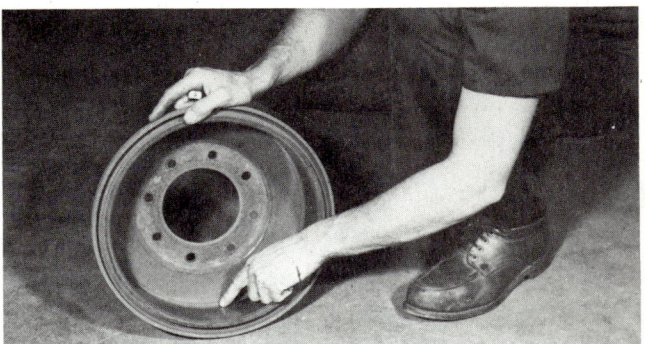

Figure 36-25 Checking the condition of the drum.

Figure 36-24 Check the wheel assembly including wheel seals and gaskets.

tool into the slot and turn the star wheel in the proper direction until the brake drum can be removed.

On cars that have the adjusting slot in the drum rather than in the backing plate, reach through the slot with a thin wire hook and pull the adjuster lever away from the star wheel while slackening the adjustment. If the slot in the drum is not open, knock out the center of the slot-shaped lanced area with a punch or chisel.

Be sure to inspect the rear wheel axle gaskets and wheel seals for leaks (Figure 36-24). Replace worn components as needed.

Drum Inspection

One of the most important safety inspections to be made is that of the brake drum (Figure 36-25). First, visually inspect the brake shoes, as installed on the car. Their condition can, many times, reveal defects in the drums. If the linings on one wheel are worn more than the others, it might indicate a rough drum. Uneven wear from side to side on any one set of shoes can be caused by a tapered drum. If some linings are worn badly at the toe or heel, it might indicate an out-of-round drum.

Thoroughly clean the drums with a water-dampened cloth or a water-based solution. Equipment for washing brake parts is commercially available. Wet cleaning methods must be used to prevent asbestos fibers from becoming airborne. If the drums have been exposed to leaking oil or grease, thoroughly clean them with a non-oil base solvent after washing to remove dust and dirt. It is important to determine the source of the oil or grease leak and correct the problem before reinstalling the drums.

Brake drums act as a heat sink. They absorb heat and dissipate it into the air. As drums wear from normal use or are machined, their cooling surface area is reduced and their operating temperatures increase. Structural strength also reduces. This leads to overdistortion, which causes some of the drum conditions covered here.

SCORED DRUM SURFACE Figure 36-26A shows a scored drum surface. The most common cause of this condition is buildup of brake dust and dirt between the brake lining and drum. A glazed brake lining, hardened by high heat or in some cases by very hard inferior grade brake lining, can also groove the drum surface. Excessive lining wear that exposes the rivet head or shoe steel will score the drum surface. If the grooves are not too deep, the drum can be turned.

BELL-MOUTHED DRUM Figure 36-26B shows a distortion due to extreme heat and braking pressure. It occurs mostly on wide drums and is caused by poor support at the outside of the drum. Full drum-to-lining contact cannot be achieved and fading can be expected. Drums must be turned.

CONCAVE DRUM Figure 36-26C shows an excessive wear pattern in the center area of the drum brake surface. Extreme braking pressure can distort the shoe platform so that braking pressure is concentrated at the center of the drum.

CONVEX DRUM This wear pattern is greater at the closed end of the drum (Figure 36-26D). It is the result of excessive heat or an oversized drum, which allows the open end of the drum to distort.

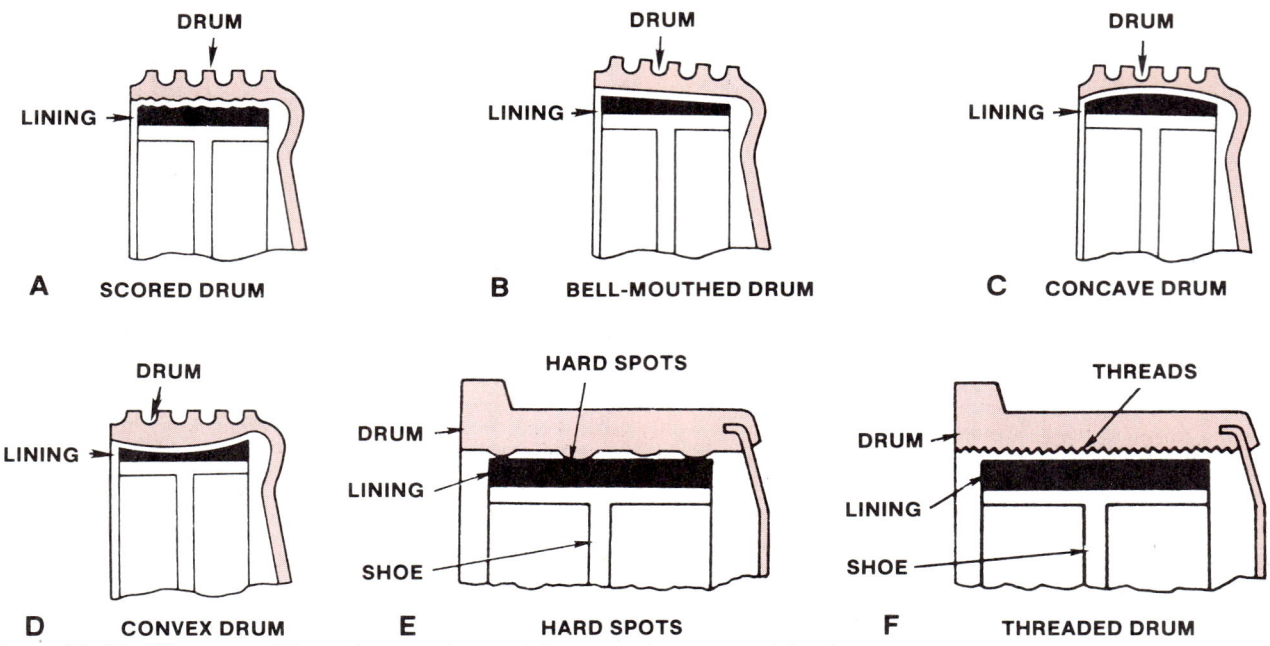

Figure 36-26 Drum conditions that require servicing or replacement of the drum.

HARD SPOTS ON THE DRUM This condition (Figure 36-26E), sometimes called chisel spots or island of steel in the cast-iron surface, results from a change in metallurgy caused by braking heat. Chatter, pulling, rapid wear, hard pedal, and noise occur. These spots can be removed by grinding. However, only the raised surfaces are removed, and they can reappear when heat is applied. The drum must be replaced.

THREADED DRUM SURFACE An extremely sharp or chipped tool bit or a lathe that turns too fast can result in a threaded drum surface (Figure 36-26F). This condition can cause a snapping sound during brake application as the shoes ride outward on the thread, then snap back. To avoid this, recondition drums using a rounded tool and proper lathe speed. Check the edge of the drum surface around the mounting flange side for tool marks indicating a previous rebore. If the drum has been rebored, it might have worn too thin for use. Check the diameter.

HEAT CHECKS Heat checks are visible, unlike hard spots that do not appear until the machining of the drum (Figure 36-27A). Extreme operating temperatures are the major cause. The drum might also show a bluish/gold tint, which is a sign of high temperatures. Hardened carbide lathe bits or special grinding attachments are available through lathe manufacturers to service these conditions. Excessive damage by heat checks or hard spots require drum replacement.

CRACKED DRUM Cracks in the cast-iron drum are caused by excessive stress (Figure 36-27B). They can be anywhere but usually are in the vicinity of the bolt circle or at the outside of the flange. Fine cracks in the drums are often hard to see and, unfortunately, often do not show up until after machining. Nevertheless, should any cracks appear, no matter how small, the drum must be replaced (Figure 36-27C).

OUT-OF-ROUND DRUMS Drums with eccentric distortion might appear good to the eye but cause pulling, grabbing, and pedal vibration or pulsation. An out-of-round or egg-shaped condition (Figure 36-28) is often caused by heating and cooling during normal brake operation. Out-of-round drums can be detected before the drum is removed by adjusting the brake to a light drag and feeling the rotation of the drum by hand. After

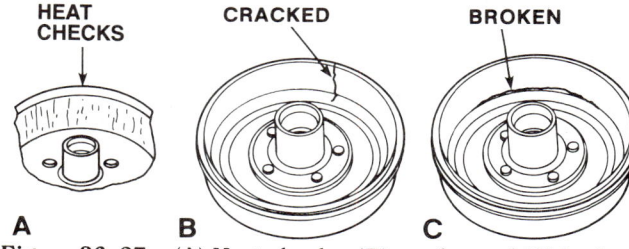

Figure 36-27 (A) Heat checks, (B) cracks, and (C) broken areas. The latter two conditions require replacement.

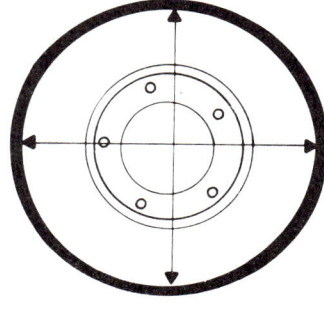

Figure 36-28 Measure the inside diameter of the drum in several spots to determine out-of-roundness.

removing the drum, gauge it to determine the amount of eccentric distortion. Drums with this defect should be machined or replaced.

Drum Measurements

Measure every drum with a drum micrometer (Figure 36-29) even if the drum passed a visual inspection to make sure that it is within the safe oversize limits. If the drum is within safe limits, even though the surface appears smooth, it should be turned to assure a true drum surface and remove any possible contamination in the surface from previous brake linings, road dust, etc. Remember that if too much metal is removed from a drum, unsafe conditions can result.

Take measurements at the open and closed edges of the friction surface and at right angles to each other. Drums with taper or out-of-roundness exceeding 0.006 inch are unfit for service and should be turned or replaced. If the maximum diameter reading (measured from the bottom of any grooves that might be present) exceeds the new drum diameter by more than 0.060 inch, the drum cannot be reworked. If the drums are smooth and true but exceed the new diameter by 0.090 inch or more, they must be replaced.

If the drums are true, smooth up any slight scores by polishing with fine emery cloth. If deep scores or grooves are present that cannot be removed by this method, the drum must be turned or replaced.

Drum Refinishing

Brake drums can be refinished either by turning or grinding on a brake lathe (Figure 36-30).

Only enough metal should be removed to obtain a true, smooth friction surface. When one drum must be machined to remove defects, the other drum on the same axle set must also be machined in the same manner and to the same diameter so that braking is equal.

Brake drums are stamped with a discard dimension (Figure 36-31). This is the allowable wear dimension

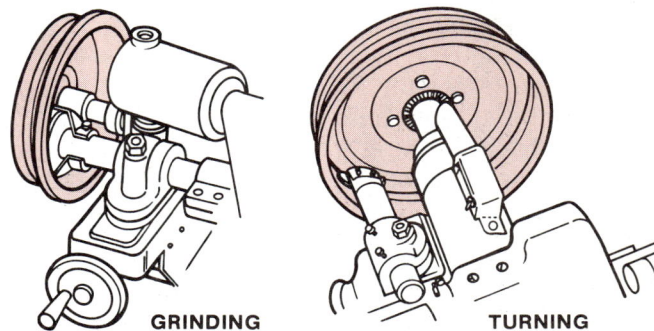

Figure 36-30 Brake drums can be remachined by grinding or turning on a brake lathe.

Figure 36-31 The drums discard diameter is stamped on the drum.

and not the allowable machining dimension. There must be 0.030 inch left for wear after turning the drums. Some states have laws about measuring the limits of a brake drum.

Machining or grinding brake drums increases the inside diameter of the drum and changes the lining-to-drum fit. When remachining a drum, follow the equipment instructions for the specific tool you are using.

Cleaning Newly Refaced Drums

The friction surface of a newly refaced drum contains millions of tiny metal particles. These particles not only remain free on the surface, they always lodge themselves in the open pores of the newly machined surface. If the metal particles are allowed to remain in the drum, they become imbedded in the brake lining. Once the brake lining gets contaminated in this manner, it acts as a fine grinding stone and scores the drum.

These metal particles must be removed by washing or cleaning the drum. Do not blow out the drum with air pressure. Either of the following methods is recommended to clean a newly refaced brake drum. The first method involves washing the brake drum thoroughly with hot water and wiping with a lint-free rag. Then, use the air pressure to thoroughly dry it. If the front hub and drums are being cleaned, be very careful to avoid contaminating the wheel bearing grease. Or, completely remove all the old grease, then regrease and repack the wheel bearing after the drum has been cleaned and dried. The wheel bearings and the grease

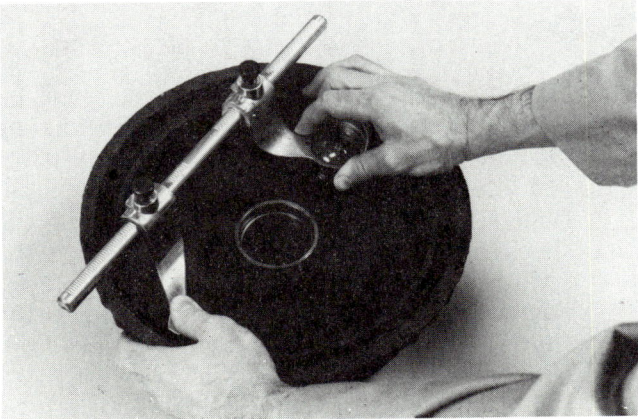

Figure 36-29 Measuring the inside diameter with a drum micrometer.

seals must be removed from the drum before cleaning. The second method involves wiping the inside of the brake drum (especially the newly machined surface) with a lint-free white cloth dipped in one of the many available brake cleaning solvents that do not leave a residue. This operation should be repeated until dirt is no longer apparent on the wiping cloth. Allow the drum to dry before reinstalling it on the vehicle.

Both of these procedures are also good for cleaning disc brake rotors.

PROCEDURES
Mechanical Component Service of Duo-servo Drum Brake

1. Disconnect the cable from the parking brake lever.
2. If required, install wheel cylinder clamps on the wheel cylinders to prevent fluid leakage or air from getting into the system while the shoes are removed. Some brakes have wheel cylinder stops; therefore, wheel cylinder clamps are not required. Regardless of whether or not the clamps are needed, do not press down on the brake pedal after shoe return springs have been removed. To prevent this, block up the brake pedal so it cannot be depressed.

> **SHOP TALK**
>
> Keep the adjusting screws and automatic adjuster parts for left and right brakes separate. These parts usually are different. For example, on many automatic adjusters, the adjusting screws on the right brakes have left-hand threads and the adjusting screws on the left brakes have right-hand threads.

3. Remove the brake shoe return springs. Use a brake spring removal and installation tool to unhook the springs from the anchor pin or anchor plate (Figure 36-32). In some cases the return springs might not be attached directly to the anchor pin. One spring might be hooked over the adjusting mechanism link, which is in turn installed over the anchor pin. Or, both springs can be hooked onto an anchor plate. Regardless of how springs are attached, carefully note the location, position, and color of all springs before removing any so that they can be reinstalled properly.

CAUTION: Do not use the brake spring tool to remove the adjusting link from the anchor pin or anchor plate.

4. Remove the shoe retaining or hold-down cups and springs. Special tools are available, but the hold-

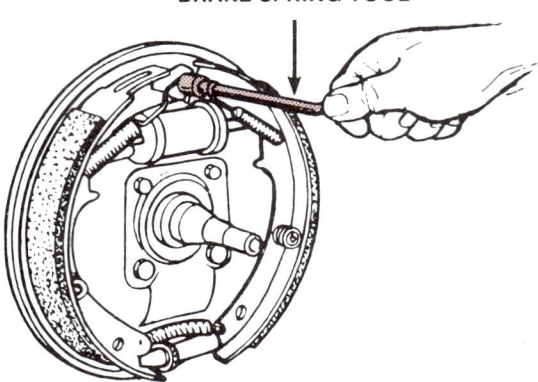

Figure 36-32 Using a spring removal tool to remove the return springs.

down springs can be removed by using pliers to compress the spring and rotating the cup with relation to the pin.
5. Self-adjuster parts can now be removed. Lift off the actuating link, lever and pivot assembly, sleeve (through lever), and return spring. No advantage is gained by disassembling the lever and pivot assembly unless one of the parts is damaged.
6. Spread the shoes slightly to free the parking brake strut and remove the strut with its spring. Disconnect the parking brake lever from the secondary shoe. It can be attached with a retaining clip, bolt, or simply hooked into the shoe.
7. Slip the anchor plate off the pin. No advantage is gained by removing the plate if it is bolted on or riveted. Spread the anchor ends of the shoes and disengage from the wheel cylinder links, if used (Figure 36-33). Remove the shoes connected at the bottom by the adjusting screw and spring, as an assembly.
8. Overlap the anchor end of the shoes to relieve spring tension. Unhook the adjusting screw spring, and remove the adjusting screw assembly.

PROCEDURES
Disassembling Non-servo or Leading-trailing Brakes (Figure 36-34)

1. Install the wheel cylinder clamp. Then unhook the adjuster spring from the parking brake strut and reverse shoe.
2. Unhook the upper shoe-to-shoe spring from the shoes and unhook the anti-noise spring from the spring bracket.
3. Remove the parking brake strut and disengage the shoe webs from the flat, clamp shoe hold-down clips.
4. Unhook the lower shoe-to-shoe spring and remove the forward shoe. Disconnect the parking brake cable, then remove the reverse shoe.

Drum Brakes 939

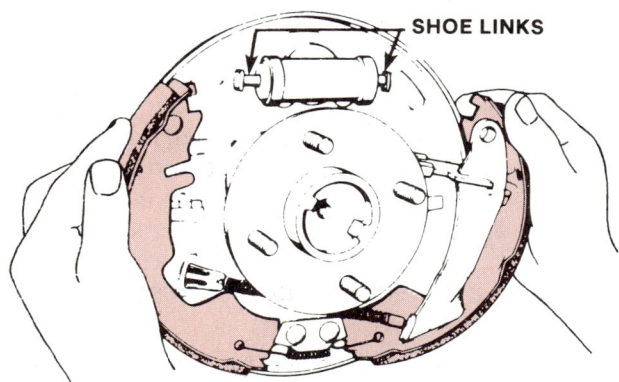

Figure 36-33 Removing the brake shoes from the backing plate.

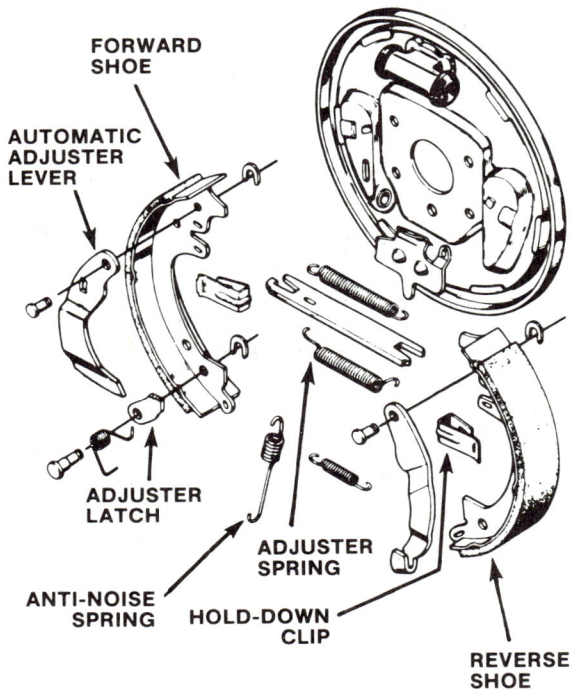

Figure 36-34 Exploded view of non-servo (leading-trailing shoe) drum brake.

5. Remove the shoe hold-down clips from the backing plate.
6. Press off the C-shaped retainers from the pins and remove the parking brake lever, automatic adjuster lever, and adjuster latch.

SHOP TALK

Mark the shoe positions if shoe and linings are to be reused. When disassembling an unfamiliar brake assembly, work on one wheel at a time and use the other wheel as a reference.

7. Remove the parking brake lever.

Cleaning, Inspecting, and Lubricating Brake Parts

WARNING: When servicing wheel brake parts, do not create dust by cleaning with a dry brush or compressed air.

 **PROCEDURES**
Cleaning and Inspecting Brake Parts

1. Clean the backing plates, struts, levers, and other metal parts to be reused using a water-dampened cloth or a water-based solution. Equipment is commercially available to perform washing functions of brake parts. Wet cleaning methods must be used to prevent asbestos fibers from becoming airborne.
2. Carefully examine the raised shoe pads on the backing plate to make sure that they are free from corrosion or other surface defects that might prevent the shoes from sliding freely. Use fine emery cloth to remove surface defects, if necessary. Clean them thoroughly.
3. At the rear wheels, look for evidence of oil or grease leakage past the wheel bearing seals. Such leakage could cause brake failure and indicates the need for additional service work.
4. Check that the backing plates are not cracked or bent. If so, they must be replaced. Make sure that backing plate bolts and bolted-on anchor pins are torqued to specifications.
5. If replacement of the wheel cylinders is needed, it should be done at this time. To determine wheel cylinder condition, carefully inspect the boots. If they are cut, torn, heat-cracked, or show evidence of excessive leakage, the wheel cylinders should be replaced. On cylinders with external boots, carefully pull back the lower edge of the boot. If more than a drop of fluid spills out, leakage is excessive and indicates that replacement is necessary. If the wheel cylinders have internal boots, carefully remove one of the wheel cylinder connecting links to check for leakage.

SHOP TALK

A slight amount of fluid behind the boot is normal. This lubricates the piston. However, if enough fluid is present to run or spill out, this indicates excessive leakage.

6. Disassemble the adjusting screw assembly (Figure 36-35) and clean the parts in a suitable solvent. Make sure that the adjusting screw threads into the pivot nut over its complete length without

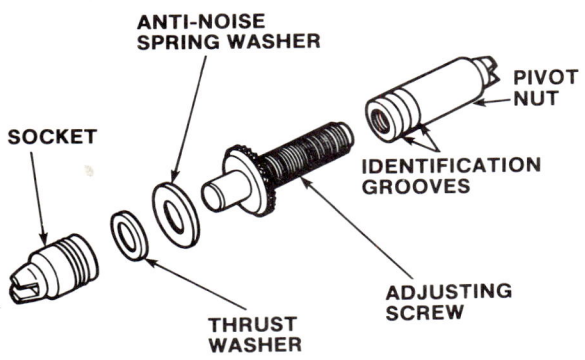

Figure 36-35 Exploded view of adjusting screw assembly.

sticking or binding. Check that none of the adjusting screw teeth are damaged, particularly on self-adjusting brakes. Lubricate the adjusting screw threads with brake lubricant, being careful not to get any on the adjusting teeth, and reassemble. Most adjusting screw assemblies use a thrust washer between the adjusting screw and socket. Some also might have the anti-noise spring washer. Thread the adjusting screw in as far as it goes.

CAUTION: Do not use ordinary grease to lubricate drum brake parts. It does not hold up under high temperatures.

7. Apply a thin film of a brake lubricant to the raised shoe pads on the backing plate lands. Check that there are no burrs on the edges of the replacement shoes where they contact the pads. On the rear brakes, lubricate the parking brake lever pivot point.

SHOP TALK

Anti-seize lubrication works very well as brake lubricant.

8. Examine the shoe anchor, support plate, and small parts for signs of looseness, wear, or damage that could cause faulty shoe alignment. Check springs for spread or collapsed coils, twisted or nicked shanks, and severe discoloration. Operate star wheel automatic adjusters by prying the shoe lightly away from its anchor or by pulling the cable to make sure the adjuster advances easily, one notch at a time. Adjuster cables tend to stretch, and star wheels and pawls become blunted after a long period of use. For rear axle parking brakes, pull on the cable and shoe linkage to make sure no binding condition is present that could cause the shoes to drag when the parking brake is released.

SHOP TALK

Some brake technicians check brake spring tension by the drop method. This method is not overly scientific and the results are not always correct. Drop the brake spring on a clean concrete floor. If it bounces with a chunky sound, it is good. If the bounced spring gives off a tinny sound, it is tired and should be replaced.

To complete the drum brake inspection, examine wheel bearings and hub grease seals for signs of damage. Service or replace, if necessary.

BRAKE SHOES AND LININGS

Lining materials influence braking operation. The use of a lining with a friction value that is too high can result in a severe grabbing condition. A friction value that is too low can make stopping difficult because of a hard pedal.

Overheating a lining accelerates wear and can result in dangerous lining fade—a friction-reducing condition that hardens the pedal and lengthens the stopping distance. Continual overheating eventually pushes the lining beyond the point of recovery into a permanent fade condition. In addition to fade, overheating can cause squeal.

Overheating is indicated by a lining that is charred or has a glass-hard glazed surface, or if severe, random cracking of the surface is present.

WARNING: Automotive friction materials often contain substantial amounts of asbestos. Studies indicate that exposure to excessive amounts of asbestos dust can be a potential health hazard. It is important that anyone handling brake linings understands this and takes the necessary precautions to avoid injury.

Inspect the linings for uneven wear, imbedded foreign material, loose rivets, and to see if they are oil soaked. If linings are oil soaked, replace them.

If linings are otherwise serviceable, tighten or replace loose rivets, remove imbedded foreign material, and clean the rivet counterbores.

If linings at any wheel show a spotty wear pattern or an uneven contact with the brake drum, it is an indication that the linings are not centered in the drums. Linings should be circle ground to provide better contact with the drum.

Brake Relining

Brake linings that are worn to within 1/32 inch of a rivet head or have been contaminated with brake fluid, grease, or oil must be replaced (Figure 36-36). Failure

Drum Brakes 941

Figure 36-36 Checking drum brake lining thickness using a depth gauge.

to replace worn linings results in a scored drum. When it is necessary to replace brake shoes, they must also be replaced on the wheel on the opposite side of the vehicle. Inspect brake shoes for distortion, cracks, or looseness. If these conditions exist, the shoe must be discarded.

Do not let brake fluid, oil, or grease touch the brake lining. If a brake lining kit is used to replace the linings, follow the instructions in the kit and install all the parts provided.

The two general methods of attaching the linings to the brake shoes are bonding and riveting (Figure 36-37). The bonded linings are fastened with a special adhesive to the shoe, clamped in place, then cured in an oven. Instead of using an adhesive, some linings are riveted to the shoe.

Sizing New Linings

Modern brake shoes are usually supplied with what is known as cam, offset, contour, or eccentric shape (Figure 36-38), which is ground in at the factory. That is, the full thickness of the lining is present at the middle of the shoe, but is ground down slightly at the heel and toe. The diameter of the circle the shoes make is slightly smaller than that of the drum. This compen-

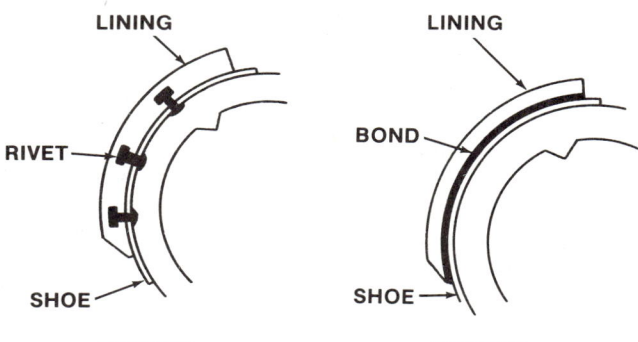

Figure 36-37 Examples of riveted and bonded brake shoe linings.

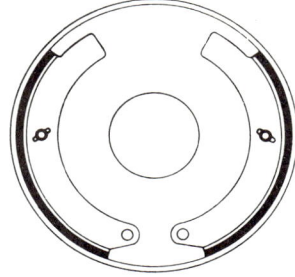

CONCENTRIC GRIND

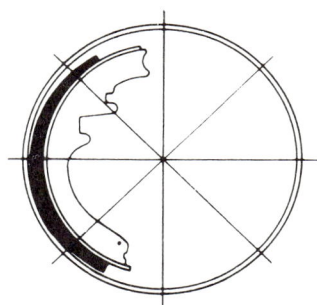

TYPICAL OEM OFFSET GRIND
(FURNISHED ON NEW VEHICLES)

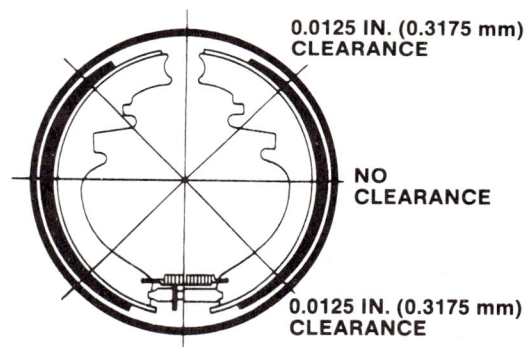

CONTOUR (ECCENTRIC) GRIND
[SERVO, 0.050 IN. (1.3 mm) UNDERSIZE]

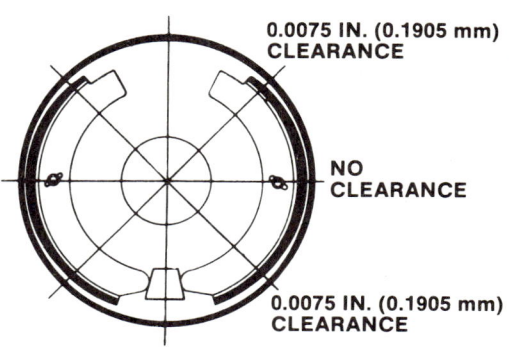

CONTOUR (ECCENTRIC) GRIND
[NON-SERVO, 0.030 IN. (0.75 mm) UNDERSIZE]

Figure 36-38 Various types of brake shoe lining grinds.

sates for the minor tolerance variations of drums and brake mountings and promotes proper wearing-in of the linings to match the drum.

> **SHOP TALK**
>
> On duo-servo shoe designs, the forward shoe is the primary and the rear, the secondary. The secondary shoe lining is longer.

Lining Adjustment

New eccentric-ground linings tolerate a closer new lining clearance adjustment than concentric ground linings. With manual adjusters, the shoes should be expanded into the drums until the linings are at the point of drag but not dragging heavily against the drum. With star wheel automatic adjusters, a drum/shoe gauge provides a convenient means of making the preliminary adjustment. This type of gauge, when set at actual drum diameter, automatically provides the working clearance of the shoes. If new linings have been concentrically ground, the initial clearance adjustment must be backed off an amount that provides sufficient working clearance.

Many technicians take pride in showing the customer a high pedal, but it should be remembered that with new linings an extremely high pedal indicates tight clearances and can cause seating problems.

Drum Shoe and Brake Installation

Before installing the shoes, be sure to sand or stone the inner edge of the shoe to dress down any slight lining or metal nicks and burrs that could interfere with the sliding upon the support pads.

A support (backing) plate must be tight on its mount and not bent. Stone the shoe support pads brightly and dress down any burrs or grooves that could cause the shoes to bind or hang up.

Using an approved lubricant, lightly coat the support pads and the threads of servo star wheel adjusters. On rear axle parking brakes, lubricate any point of potential binding in the linkage and the cable. Do not lubricate non-servo brake adjusters other than to free a frozen adjuster with penetrating oil.

Reassemble the brakes in the reverse order of disassembly. Make sure all parts are in their proper locations and that both brake shoes are properly positioned in either end of the adjuster. Also, both brake shoes should correctly engage the wheel cylinder pushrods and parking brake links. They should be centered on the backing plate. Parking brake links and levers should be in place on the rear brakes. With all of the parts in place, try the fit of the brake drum over the new shoes. If not slightly snug, pull it off and turn the star wheel until a slight drag is felt when sliding on the drum. A brake preset gauge makes this job easy and final brake adjustment simple. Then install the brake drum, wheel bearings, spindle nuts, cotter pins, dust caps, and wheel/tire assemblies, and make the final brake adjustments as specified in individual instructions in the vehicle's service manual. Torque the spindle and lug nuts to specifications.

☐ WHEEL CYLINDER INSPECTION AND SERVICING

Wheel cylinders might need replacement when the brake shoes are replaced or when they begin to leak.

Inspecting and Cleaning Wheel Cylinders

Wheel cylinder leaks reveal themselves in several ways: (1) fluid can be found when the dust boot is peeled back; (2) the cylinder, linings, and backing plate, or the inside of a tire might be wet; or (3) there might be a drop in the level of fluid in the master cylinder reservoir.

Such leaks can cause the brakes to grab or fail and should be immediately corrected. Note the amount of fluid present when the dust boot is pulled back. A small amount of fluid seepage dampening the interior of the boot is normal. A dripping boot is not.

CAUTION: Hydraulic system parts should not be allowed to come in contact with oil or grease. They should not be handled with greasy hands. Even a trace of any petroleum-based product is sufficient to cause damage to the rubber parts.

Cylinder binding can be caused by rust deposits, swollen cups due to fluid contamination, or by a cup wedged into an excessive piston clearance. If the clearance between the pistons and the bore wall exceeds allowable values, a condition called heel drag might exist. It can result in rapid cup wear and can cause the piston to retract very slowly when the brakes are released.

Typical examples of a scored, pitted, or corroded cylinder bore are a ring of hard, crystal-like substance is sometimes noticed in the cylinder bore where the piston rests after the brakes are released.

Light roughness or deposits can be removed with crocus cloth or an approved cylinder hone. While honing lightly, brake fluid can be used as a lubricant. If the bore cannot be cleaned up readily, the cylinder must be replaced.

Drum Brakes   943

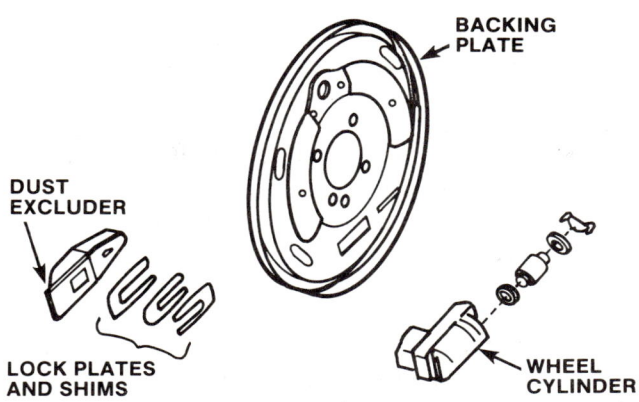

Figure 36-39   Lock plates and shims can be used to hold the wheel cylinder to the backing plate.

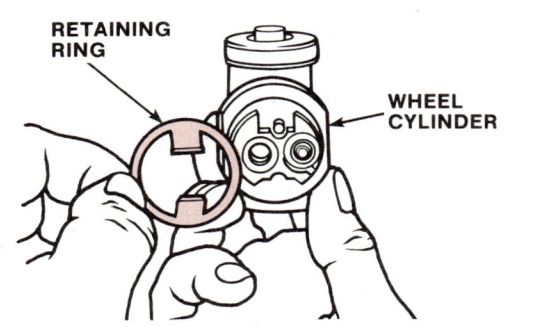

Figure 36-40   Example of a wheel cylinder retaining ring.

 **PROCEDURES**

Replacing a Wheel Cylinder

1. Since brake hoses are an important link in the hydraulic system, it is recommended that they be replaced when a new cylinder is to be installed or when the old cylinder is to be reconditioned. Remove the brake shoe assemblies from the backing plate before proceeding. The smallest amount of brake fluid contaminates the friction surface of the brake lining.

2. Using two appropriate wrenches, disconnect the hydraulic hose from the steel line located on the chassis. On solid rear axles, use the appropriate tubing wrench and disconnect the hydraulic line where it enters the wheel cylinder. Care must be exercised in removing this steel line. It might be bent at this point and be difficult to install once new wheel cylinders are mounted to the backing plate.

3. Remove the plates, shims, and bolts that hold the wheel cylinder to the backing plate (Figure 36-39). Some later designed wheel cylinders are held to the backing plate with a retaining ring (Figure 36-40) that can be removed with two small picks.

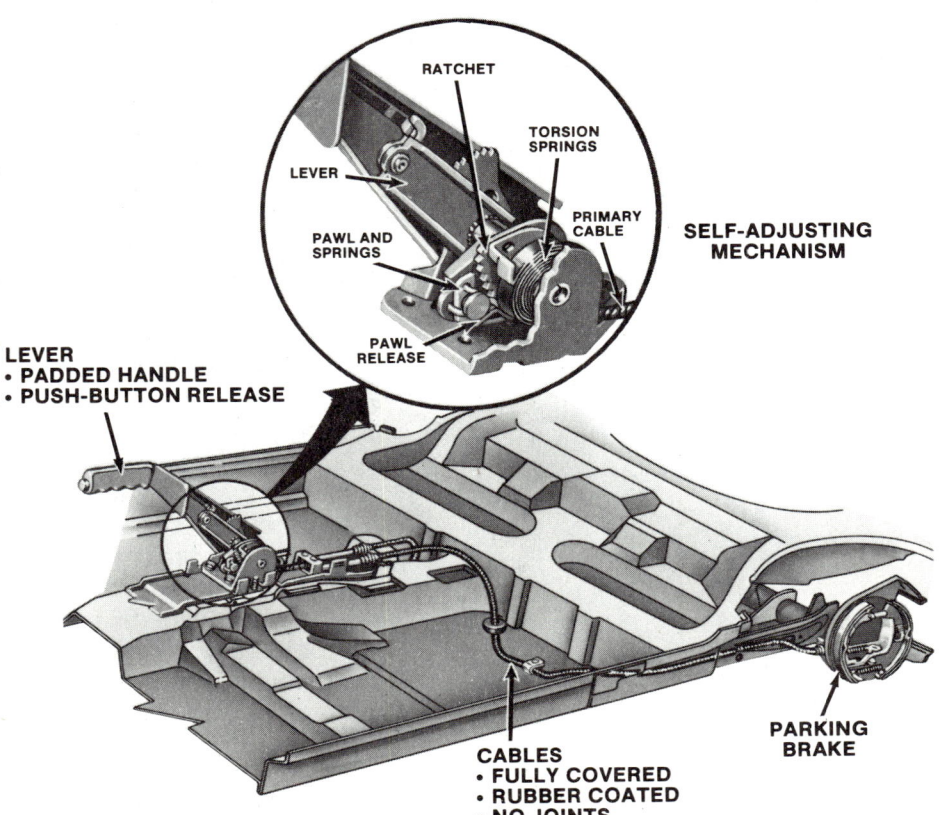

Figure 36-41   Typical center-mounted hand-operated parking brake.

4. Remove the wheel cylinder from the backing plate and clean the area with a proper cleaning solvent.

Care must be taken when installing new or reconditioned wheel cylinders on cars equipped with wheel cylinder piston stops. The rubber dust boots and the pistons must be squeezed into the cylinder before it is tightened to the backing plate. If this is not done, the pistons jam against the stops causing hydraulic fluid leaks and erratic brake performance.

DRUM PARKING BRAKES

The parking brake keeps a vehicle from rolling while it is parked. It is important to remember that the parking brake is not part of the vehicle's hydraulic braking system. It works mechanically, using a level assembly connected through a cable system to the rear drum service brakes.

Types of Parking Brake Systems

Parking brakes can be either hand or foot operated. In general, down-sized cars and light trucks use hand-operated self-adjusting lever systems (Figure 36-41). Full-size vehicles normally use a foot-operated parking brake pedal (Figure 36-42A). The pedal or lever assembly is designed to latch into an applied position and is released by pulling a brake release handle or pushing a release button.

On some vehicles, a vacuum power unit (Figure 36-42B) is connected by a rod to the upper end of the release lever. The vacuum motor is actuated to release the parking brake whenever the engine is running and the transmission is in forward driving gear. The lower end of the release lever extends down for alternate manual release in the event of vacuum power failure or for optional manual release at any time. Hoses connect the power unit and the engine manifold to a vacuum release valve on the steering column.

The starting point of a typical parking brake cable and lever system is the foot pedal (Figure 36-43) or hand lever. This assembly is a variable ratio lever mechanism that converts input effort of the operator and pedal/lever travel into output force with less travel. In the system shown in Figure 36-43, as the pedal is being depressed, the attached front cable assembly tightens increasingly as it moves a short distance (by comparison to the pedal's travel distance). Tensile force from the front cable is transmitted through the car's brake cable system to the rear brakes. This tension pulls the flexible steel cables attached to each of the rear brakes. It serves to operate the internal lever and strut mechanism of each rear brake, expanding the brake shoes against the drum. Springs return the shoes to the unapplied position when the parking brake pedal is released and tensile forces in the cable system are relaxed.

> **CUSTOMER CARE**
>
> Drivers of vehicles equipped with automatic transmission may sometimes develop the bad habit of resting their left foot on the brake pedal. The effect of this slight pressure is constant braking action that can quickly wear out components. Wear normally occurs in the brake assembly where the return springs, seals, and pistons have slightly less mechanical resistance than the other three wheels. In effect, this brake is constantly applied.
>
> On vehicles driven in stop-and-go traffic only, the weak brake assembly may be affected. In vehicles driven at constant highway speeds, all four assemblies may quickly become worn and burnt. The true danger involved is that excessive heat may lead to hydraulic fluid evaporation and brake failure.
>
> Suspect this problem when signs of accelerated wear are present. Ask the customer how often the braking system requires service. Inspect the brake pedal for signs of wear. If the left-foot brake condition is apparent, let the customer know the cause of the problem is not the quality of the replacement parts or service.

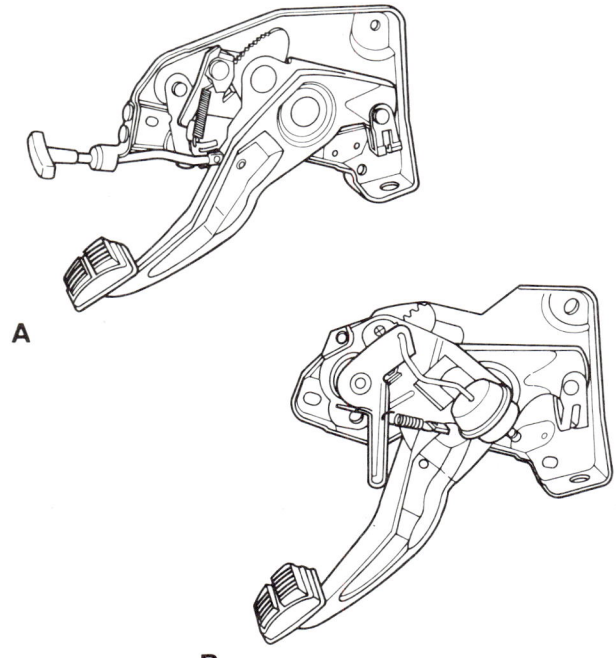

Figure 36-42 Typical pedal-operated parking brakes: (A) mechanical release and (B) vacuum release.

An electronic switch, triggered when the brake pedal is applied, lights the brake indicator in the instrument panel when the ignition is turned on. The light

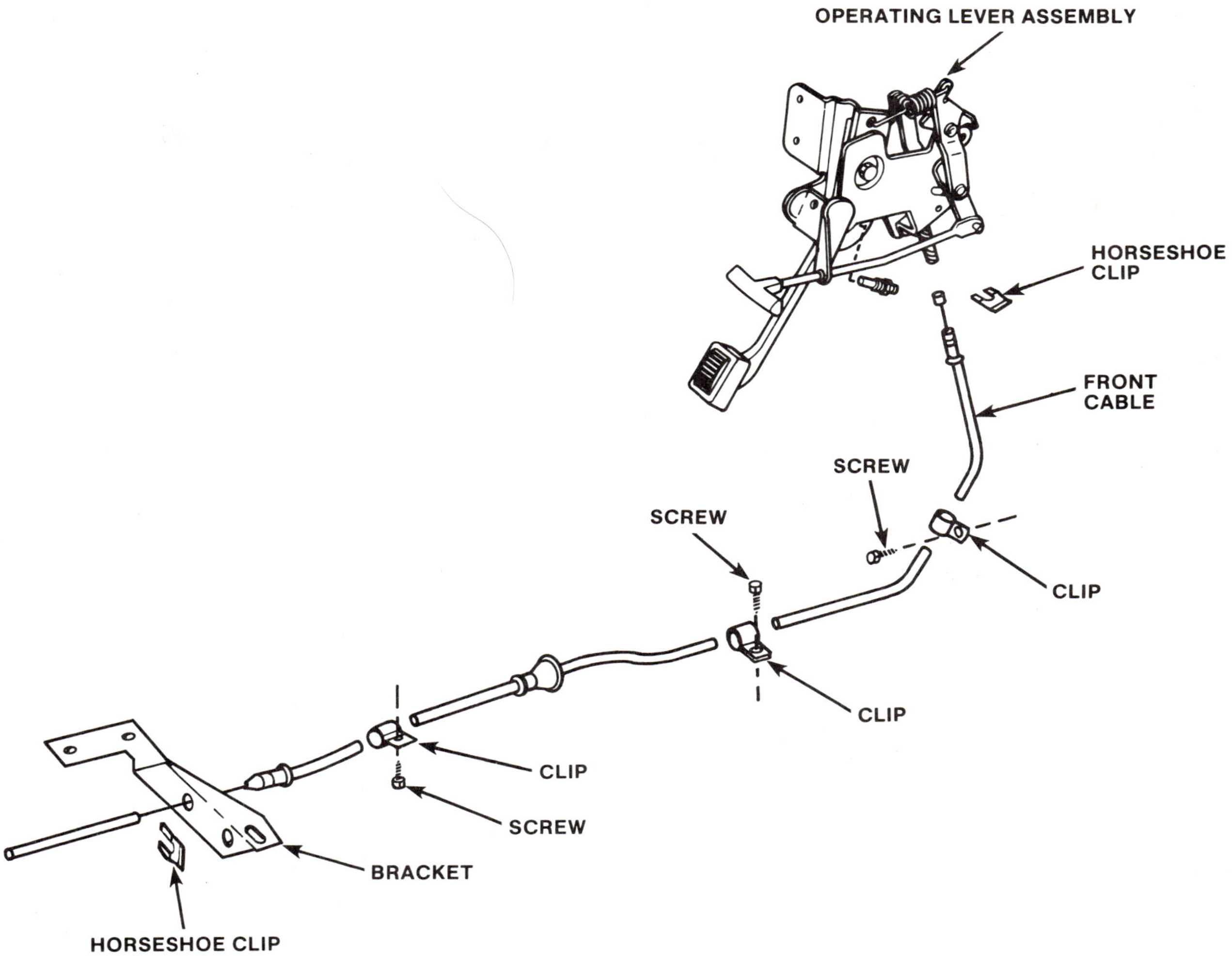

Drum Brakes 945

Figure 36-43 Typical parking brake cable and lever system.

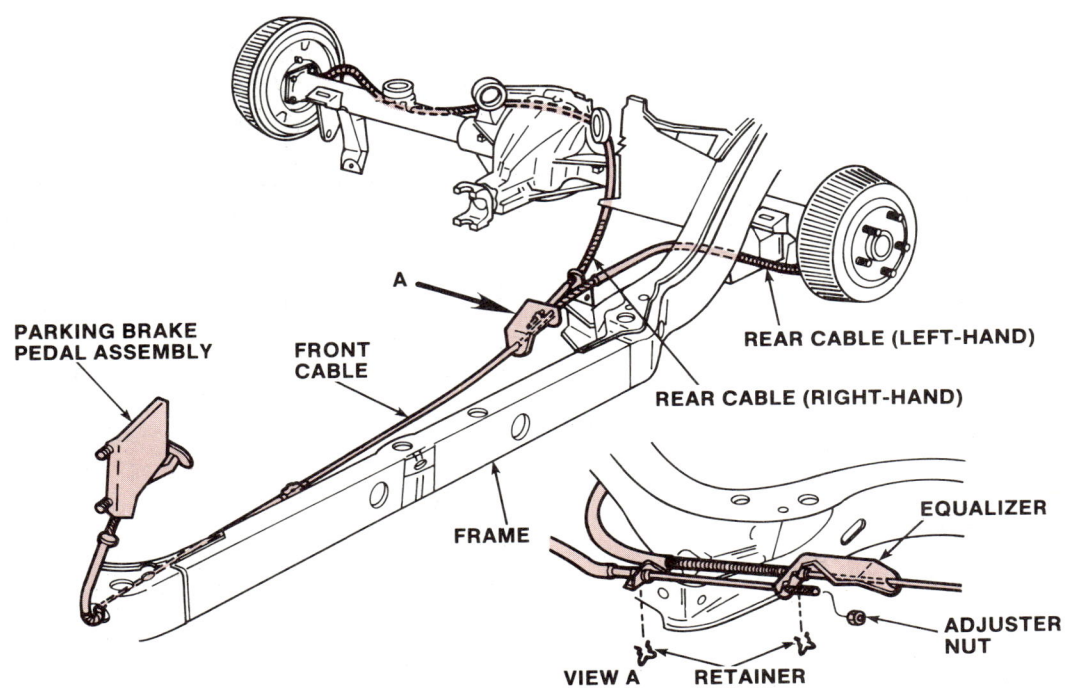

Figure 36-44 Typical parking brake routing to the rear drum brakes.

goes out when either the pedal or control is released or the ignition is turned off.

The cable/lever routing system in a typical parking brake arrangement (Figure 36-44) employs a three lever setup to multiply the physical effort of the operator. First is the pedal assembly or hand grip. When moved it multiplies the operator's effect and pulls the front cable. The front cable, in turn, pulls the equalizer lever.

The equalizer lever multiplies the effort of the pedal assembly, or hand grip, and pulls the rear cables. This pulling effort passes through an equalizer, which ensures equal pull on both rear cables. The equalizer functions by allowing the rear brake cables to slip slightly so as to balance out small differences in cable length or adjustment. Typical equalizer arrangements are shown in Figure 36-45.

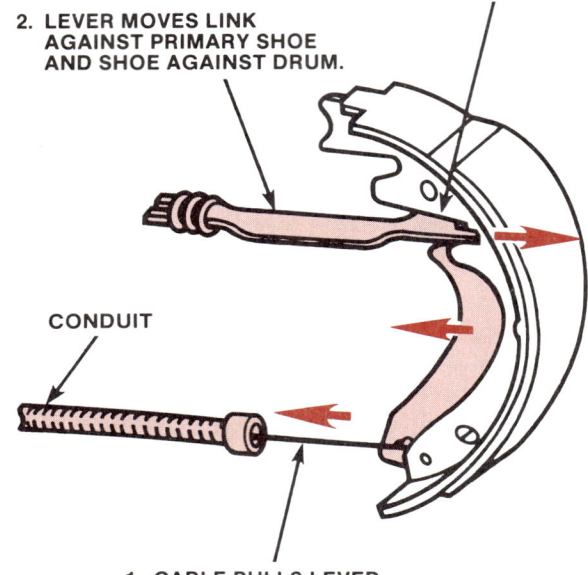

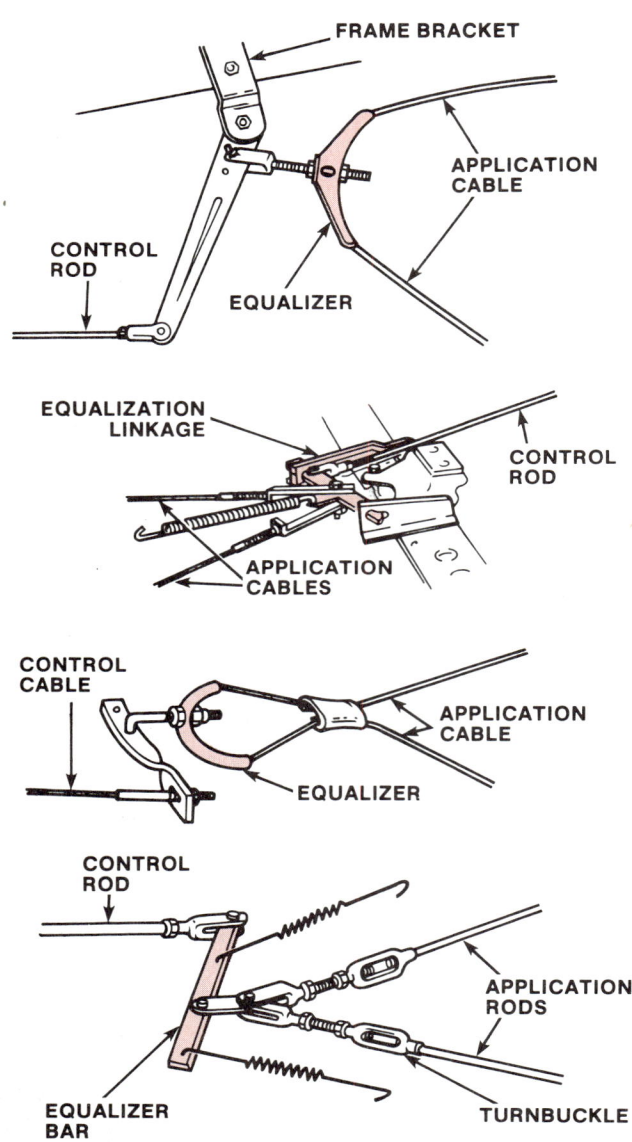

Figure 36-45 Types of equalizers used to apply even application force to each rear brake.

Figure 36-46 Integral drum brake parking brake operation.

> ### USING SERVICE MANUALS
> Service manuals list the standard brake drum inside diameter along with the discard dimension. They also state the standard and minimum lining thickness. Manual illustrations should be used to accurately identify all components plus the disassemble/reassembly procedure. Tightening torques for backing plate nuts and other components should always be followed.

The rear cables pull the parking brake levers in the drum brake assembly (Figure 36-46). As for the parking brakes themselves, there are several types in use. The integral or conventional rear drum parking brake is part of the vehicle's ordinary rear drum system. It utilizes the same friction elements as the hydraulic brakes. The transmission or drive shaft parking brake system operates independently of the rear wheel brakes. These parking brakes are known in the trade as drive shaft brakes.

❑ INTEGRAL PARKING BRAKES

Integral parking brakes are for vehicles with rear wheel drum brakes. Figure 36-47 shows a typical integral parking brake. When the parking brake pedal is applied, the cables and equalizer exert a balanced pull on the parking brake levers of both rear brakes. The levers and the parking brake struts move the shoes

PHOTO SEQUENCE 17

ADJUSTING REAR DRUM PARKING BRAKE

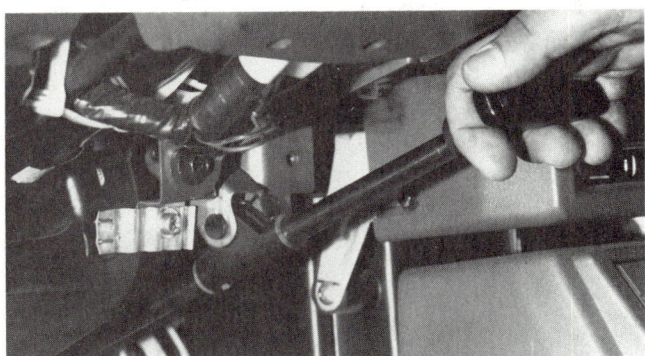

P17-1 Proper adjustment of the parking brake begins with setting the parking brake to a near full on position.

P17-2 Raise the car. Make sure it is safe to work under and that you will be able to rotate the wheels. (If the parking brake is adjusted and working properly, you should be unable to rotate the wheels.)

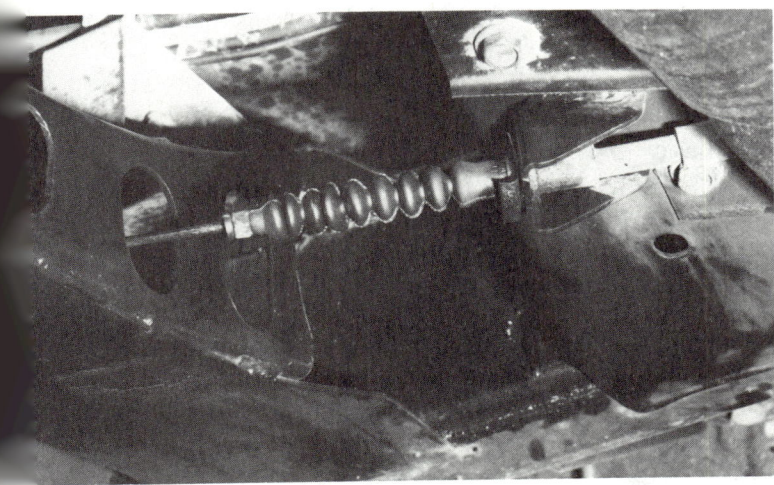

P17-3 Carefully inspect the entire length of the parking brake cable. Look for signs of fraying, breakage, and deterioration.

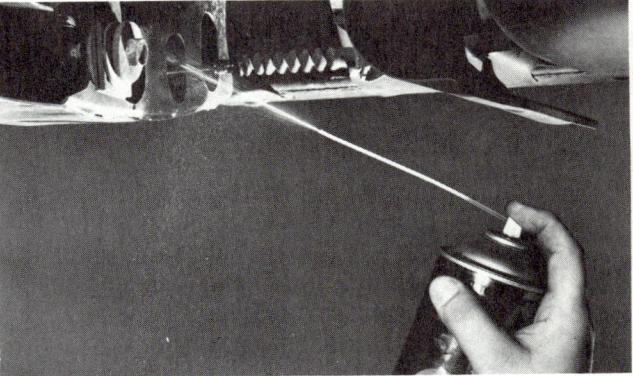

P17-4 Spray all exposed metal areas of the cable assembly with a penetrating oil. This will ensure a free-moving system.

P17-5 Inspect the adjustment mechanism. Clean off the threaded areas and make sure the tightening nuts are not damaged.

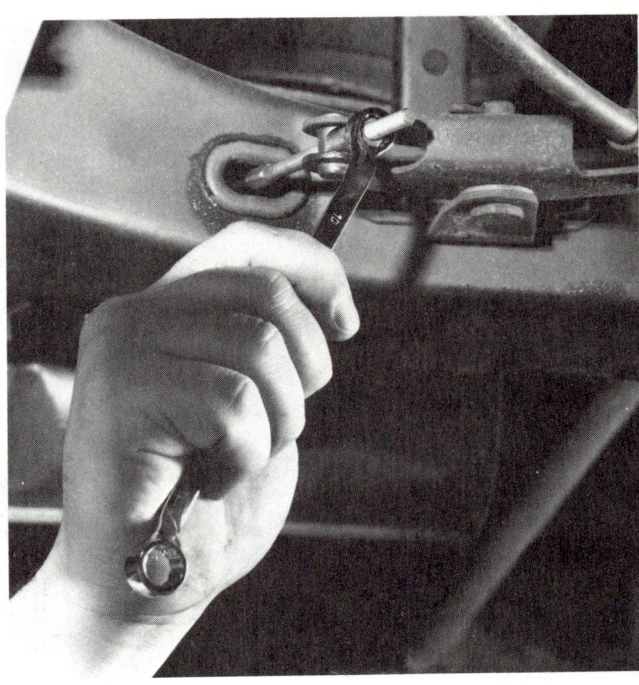

P17-6 Loosen the adjustment lock nut. Adjust the parking brake.
(continued)

947

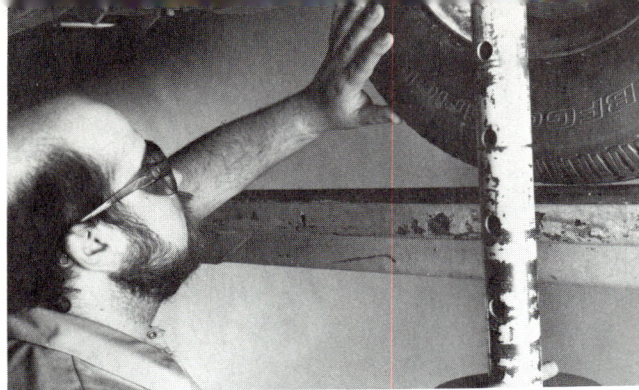

P17-7 When the wheels are unable to be turned, stop tightening the adjusting nut.

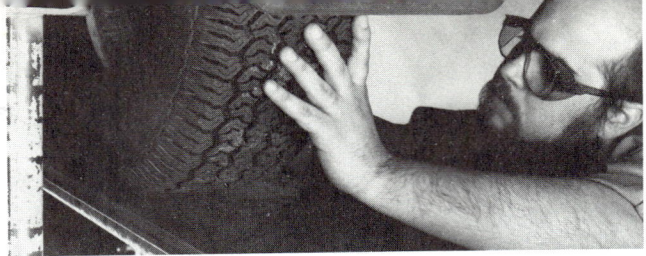

P17-9 Raise the vehicle and rotate the wheels. If the wheels turn with only a slight drag, the parking brake is properly adjusted.

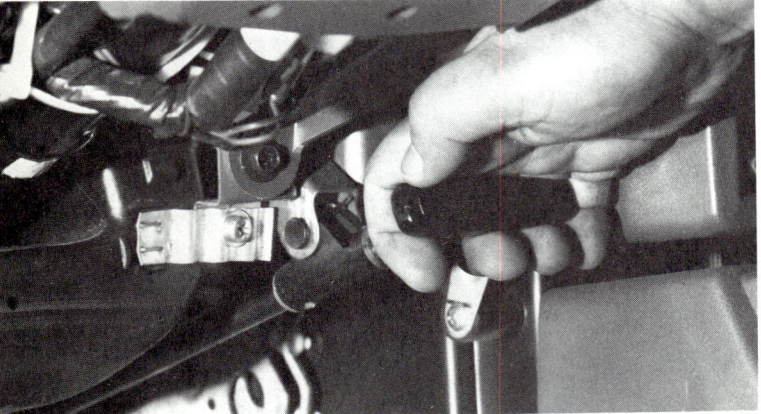

P17-8 Lower the vehicle and release the parking brake lever.

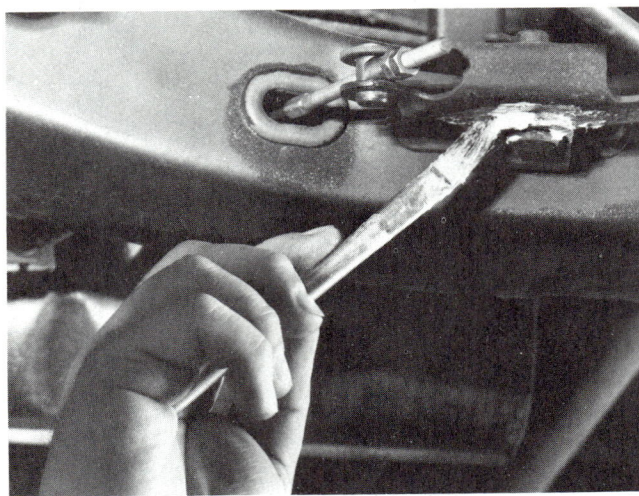

P17-10 After proper adjustment is made, tighten the adjustment lock nut. Apply a coat of white grease to all contacting surfaces of the adjustment assembly. ■

---

outward against the brake drums. The shoes are held in this position until the parking brake pedal is released. The portion of the parking brake from the equalizer on back to the rear wheel drum brake is shown in Figure 36-47. Also, the parking brake components are shown removed from the wheel brake for identification.

The rear cable enters each rear brake through a conduit (Figure 36-48). The cable end engages the lower end of the parking brake lever. This lever is hinged to the web of the secondary shoe and linked with the primary shoe by means of a strut. The lever and strut expand both shoes away from the anchor and wheel cylinder and into contact with the drum as the cable and lever are drawn forward. The shoe return springs reposition the shoes when the cable is slacked.

To remove and replace the rear brake shoes, it might be necessary to relieve the parking brake cable tension by backing off the adjusting check nuts at the equaliz-

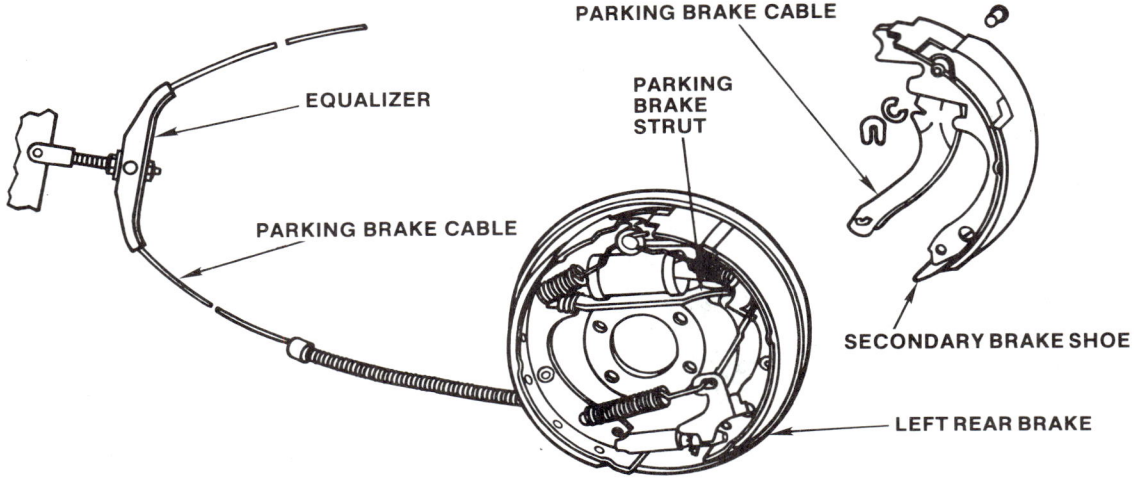

Figure 36-47 Integral parking brake components.

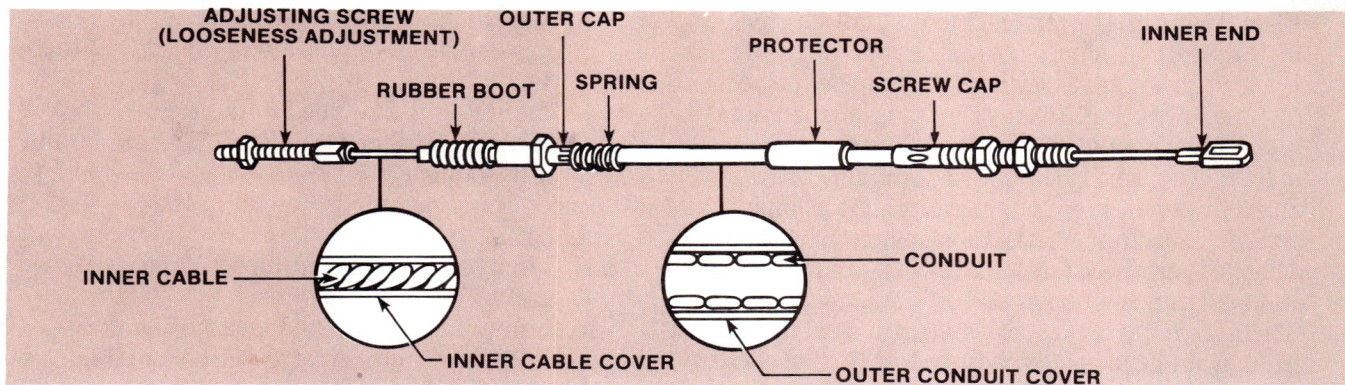

Figure 36-48 Rear cable and conduit details.

er. Count the turns backed off in order to restore the nuts to their original position.

Adjusting and Replacing Parking Brakes

Regular wheel brake service should be completed before adjusting the parking brake. Then, check the parking brake for free movement of the parking brake cables in the conduits. If necessary, apply a lubricant to free the cables. Check for worn equalizer and linkage parts. Replace any defective parts. Finally, check for broken strands in the cables. Replace any cable that has broken strands or shows signs of wear.

TESTING Test the parking brake by parking the vehicle facing up on an incline of 30 degrees or less. Set the parking brake fully and place the transmission in neutral. The vehicle should hold steady. Reverse the vehicle position so that it is facing down the incline and repeat the test. If the vehicle creeps or rolls in either case, the parking brake requires adjustment. A typical adjustment procedure is shown in Photo Sequence 17.

 CASE STUDY

Case 1

Shortly after new brake shoes and hardware were installed on a vehicle, it is returned to the shop on the rear of a tow truck. An extremely irate and distressed customer is heard throughout the entire service bay area. It seems when the customer applied the brakes while traveling at a high speed, there was a sudden loss of braking power and fine metallic grinding noise was heard. Luckily, the customer was able to control the vehicle and avoid an accident, but the situation was potentially disasterous.

The vehicle is immediately placed on a hoist and the drum brakes are disassembled. Although all the parts are new, they had failed. The shoes are pulled away from the backing plate and the holddown pins and retainers are broken.

The technician replaces all broken components with new parts from the shop's parts department. Everything appears to be installed correctly and in good working order.

The technician is reluctant to release the vehicle to the owner without uncovering the cause of the first failure. Inspecting the assembly, the technician compares the new shoes with the failed shoes. He notices the holddown pin bores on the defective shoes do not line up perfectly with the pins. More comparisons between the new and failed parts uncover slight differences. The shoes and hardware that had failed were the wrong parts for the vehicle. Although similar in many ways, these slight differences were enough to cause a major failure. The technician who had performed the original replacement should have visually compared the new parts with the old parts.

Summary

- Drum brakes are still used on the rear wheels of many cars and light trucks.
- The drum is mounted to the wheel hub. When the brakes are applied, a wheel cylinder uses hydraulic power to press two brake shoes against the inside surface of the drum. The resulting friction between the shoe's lining and drum slows the drum and wheel.
- The brake's anchor pin acts as a brake shoe stop, keeping the shoes from following the rotating drum. This creates a wedging action that multiplies braking force.
- The shoes and wheel cylinder are mounted on a backing plate. Hardware, such as shoe return springs, hold-down parts, and clearance. This hardware is a major wear item in brake service.
- The primary or leading shoe is toward the front of the vehicle while the secondary or trailing shoe is toward the rear of the vehicle.

- Brake lining can be attached to the shoes by riveting or a special adhesive bonding process.
- Brake drums act as a heat sink to dissipate the heat of braking friction. Drums can be refinished on a brake lathe provided the inside diameter is not increased above a safe limit (discard dimension).
- Servicing brakes requires performing a complete system inspection. Partial replacement of worn or damaged parts does not solve the braking problems and may ruin the new parts installed.
- When servicing brakes, extreme care must be taken to avoid generating asbestos dust.
- Wheel cylinders should be replaced if they show any signs of hydraulic fluid leakage or component wear.
- Drum brakes allow for the use of a simple parking brake mechanism that can be activated with a hand lever or foot pedal. This is a mechanical system, completely separate from the service brake hydraulic system.

Review Questions

1. Name the two methods of attaching braking lining materials to the brake shoes.
2. Explain how drum brakes create a self-multiplying brake force.
3. List at least five separate types of wear and distortion to look for when inspecting brake drums.
4. What is the job of wheel cylinder stops?
5. Explain the operation of an integral drum brake parking brake.
6. Today, the drum brake is used on _____.
    a. all four wheels of most cars and small trucks
    b. the front wheels of most cars and small trucks
    c. the rear wheels of most cars and small trucks
    d. the rear wheels of only expensive domestic or import models
7. In a typical drum brake, which component provides a foundation for the brake shoes and associated hardware?
    a. wheel cylinder
    b. drum
    c. backing plate
    d. lining
8. The function of the wheel cylinder is to _____.
    a. provide the rubbing surface area for the linings
    b. convert hydraulic pressure into a mechanical force at the wheel brakes
    c. maintain correct shoe position and clearance
    d. prohibit the shoe from following the movement of the rotating drum
9. Which of the following statements concerning drum brake shoes is incorrect?
    a. Web thickness never varies.
    b. Many shoes have nibs along the edge of the rim.
    c. The shoe rim is welded to the web.
    d. The primary shoe is the one toward the front of the vehicle.
10. Brake linings should be replaced when _____.
    a. linings are worn to within 1/32 inch of a rivet head
    b. linings are contaminated with oil or grease
    c. linings are contaminated with brake fluid
    d. all of the above
11. In the unapplied position, drum brakes shoes are held against the anchor pin by the _____.
    a. hold-down springs
    b. star wheel adjuster
    c. shoe hold-down
    d. return springs
12. Duo-servo drum brakes are also known as _____.
    a. leading-trailing brakes
    b. self-energizing brakes
    c. non-servo brakes
    d. none of the above
13. On most vehicles, the automatic adjuster system is _____.
    a. installed on the secondary shoe
    b. set up to operate when the brakes are applied as the vehicle moves forward
    c. installed on the primary shoe
    d. set up to operate when the brakes are not applied
14. When the original drum is mounted against a wheel hub flange, it can be fastened by _____.
    a. swaging the piloting shoulders of the wheel studs
    b. riveting
    c. using speed nut fasteners
    d. all of the above
15. Backing plates, struts, levers, and other metal brake parts should be _____.
    a. wet-cleaned using water or a water-based solution
    b. wet-cleaned using an alcohol-based solvent
    c. wet-cleaned using gasoline
    d. dry-cleaned only
16. A buildup of brake dust and dirt between the lining and the drum is the most common cause of _____.
    a. concave/barrel-shaped drum
    b. convex/tapered drum
    c. threaded drum surface
    d. scored drum surface

17. A drum with a taper or out-of-roundness of 0.006 inch is _____.
    a. unacceptable and should be turned
    b. unacceptable and must be replaced
    c. borderline, and probably should be turned
    d. acceptable
18. Brake drums can be refinished by _____.
    a. grinding
    b. turning
    c. grinding or turning
    d. none of the above
19. The effort of the parking brake pedal assembly or hand grip is multiplied and passed on to the rear cables by the _____.
    a. equalizer lever
    b. front cable
    c. rear disc
    d. drive shaft
20. The unit in some newer vehicles that releases the parking brake whenever the engine is running and the transmission is in forward driving gear is called a(n) _____.
    a. control assembly
    b. equalizer lever
    c. brake lever
    d. vacuum power unit
21. It has been determined that chatter and brake pull are being caused by hard spots on the brake drum. Technician A says the problem can be solved by grinding off the hard spots. Technician B says the drum must be replaced. Who is correct?
    a. Technician A
    b. Technician B
    c. Both A and B
    d. Neither A nor B
22. Technician A says the discard dimension of a brake drum is the drum's allowable machining dimension. Technician B says the discard dimension is the allowable wear dimension. There must be 0.030 inch left for wear after machining. Who is correct?
    a. Technician A
    b. Technician B
    c. Both A and B
    d. Neither A nor B
23. After resurfacing a brake drum, Technician A cleans it using hot water and a lint-free cloth. He then uses compressed air to thoroughly dry it. Technician B cleans the drum using a special brake cleaning solvent dipped in a lint-free cloth. She then allows the drum to dry before reinstallation. Who is correct?
    a. Technician A
    b. Technician B
    c. Both A and B
    d. Neither A nor B

37 DISC BRAKES

Objectives

- List the advantages of disc brakes.
- List disc brake components and describe their functions.
- Explain the difference between the three types of calipers commonly used on disc brakes.
- Describe the two types of parking brake systems used with disc brakes.
- Explain what precautions should be taken when servicing disc brake systems.
- Describe the general procedure involved in a complete caliper service or overhaul.
- List and describe five typical disc brake rotor problems.

Disc brakes resemble the brakes on a bicycle. The friction elements are in the form of pads, which are squeezed or clamped about the edge of a rotating wheel. With automotive disc brakes, this wheel is a separate unit, called a rotor, inboard of the wheel (Figure 37-1). The rotor is made of cast iron. Since the pads clamp against both sides of it, both sides are machined smooth. Usually the two surfaces are separated by a finned center section for better cooling. Such rotors are called ventilated rotors. The pads are attached to metal shoes, which are actuated by pistons, the same as with drum brakes. The pistons are contained within a caliper assembly, a housing that wraps around the edge of the rotor. The caliper is kept from rotating by way of bolts holding it to the steering knuckle.

The caliper is a housing containing the pistons and related seals, springs, and boots as well as the cylinder(s) and fluid passages necessary to force the friction linings or pads against the rotor. The caliper resembles a hand in the way it wraps around the edge of the rotor. It is attached to the steering knuckle. Some models employ light spring pressure to keep the pads close against the rotor. In other caliper designs, this is achieved by a unique seal that allows the piston to be pushed out the necessary amount, then retracts it just enough to pull the pad off the rotor.

Unlike shoes in a drum brake, the pads act perpendicular to the rotation of the disc when the brakes are applied. This effect is different from that produced in a brake drum, where frictional drag actually pulls the shoe into the drum. Disc brakes are said to be nonenergized. They require more force to achieve the same braking effort. For this reason, they are ordinarily used in conjunction with a power brake unit.

Disc brake calipers fall into two categories: fixed and moving designs. The latter includes both sliding and floating calipers.

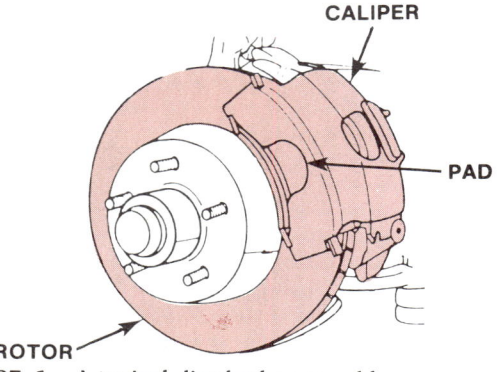

Figure 37-1   A typical disc brake assembly.

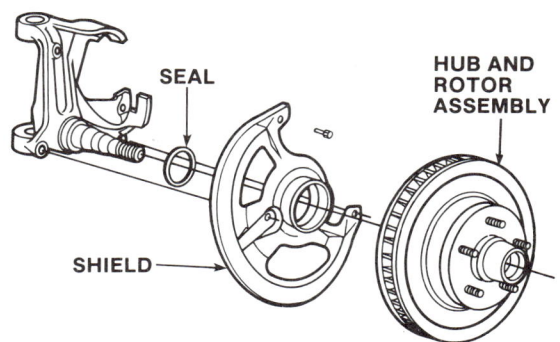

Figure 37-2   Steering knuckle, splash shield, and finned rotor for disc brake.

952

Disc brakes offer four major advantages over conventional drum brakes. They are resistant to heat fade. Disc brakes are generally more resistant to heat fade during high-speed brake stops or repeated stops. The design of the disc brake rotor exposes more surface to the air and thus dissipates heat more efficiently. They are also resistant to water fade because the rotation of the rotor tends to throw off moisture. The squeeze of the sharp edges of the pads clears the surface of water. Disc brakes perform more straight-line stops. Due to their clamping action, disc brakes are less apt to pull. Finally, disc brakes automatically adjust as pads wear.

❑ DISC BRAKE COMPONENTS AND THEIR FUNCTIONS

The disc brakes used on American cars are typically of two basic designs: fixed or floating caliper. There is also a sliding caliper, but its design is very similar to the floating caliper. The only difference is that sliding calipers slide on surfaces that have been machined smooth for this purpose, and floating calipers slide on special pins or bolts. The disc brake, regardless of its design, consists of a hub and rotor assembly, a caliper assembly, and a brake pad assembly.

Hub and Rotor Assembly

Many of the advantages of disc brakes can be attributed to the disc, or rotor, as it is more commonly called. The typical rotor is made of cast iron. Iron has a high coefficient of friction and withstands wear exceptionally well. The rotor is attached to and rotates with the hub assembly (Figure 37-2). Solid rotors are used on lightweight vehicles, but heavier automobiles, high-performance cars, and trucks generally have ventilated rotors (Figure 37-3).

Figure 37-3 (A) Downsized solid rotor; (B) full-size ventilated rotor.

The ventilated rotor is cast with a weblike construction between two friction surfaces. The webs radiate out from the center of the rotor, much like vanes or fins in a fan. As the rotor turns, air is drawn into the rotor at its center, flows between the friction surfaces, and is discharged along the outer edge. This cools the rotor very effectively, drastically reducing the incidence of brake fade, even during multiple hard stops.

Rotors are cooled by splash shields or plates. The splash shield protects the rotor and pads from road splashes and dirt. It is also shaped to channel the flow of air over the exposed rotor surfaces. As long as the car is moving, this flow of air helps to cool the rotor. The splash shield cannot be removed unless the rotor and caliper are first removed. Replacement of the splash shield is necessary only when it has been damaged or when the spindle is replaced.

Caliper Assembly

Caliper action converts hydraulic pressure into mechanical force. The caliper assembly (Figure 37-4) is composed of the following components.

Caliper Housing

The caliper housing is usually a one-piece construction of cast iron or aluminum and has an inspection hole in the top to allow for lining wear inspection. A cylinder bore is located in that portion of the casting nearest the engine. In the cylinder bore is a groove that seats a square-cut seal. This groove is tapered toward the bottom of the bore to increase the compression on the edge of the seal that is nearest hydraulic pressure. The top of the cylinder bore is also grooved as a seat for the dust boot. A fluid inlet hole is machined into the bottom of the cylinder bore and a bleeder valve outlet hole is located near the top of the casting. The caliper has inner ears with holes for mounting on the anchor plate.

Caliper Pistons

A caliper can contain one, two, or four cylinder bores and pistons that provide uniform pressure distribution against the brake's friction pads. Because there is no self-energizing action with disc brakes, the pistons are relatively large in diameter and short in stroke to provide high pressure on the friction pad assemblies with a minimum of fluid displacement.

Basically, the hydraulics of disc brakes are the same as for drum brakes, where the master cylinder piston forces the brake fluid into the wheel cylinders and against the wheel pistons.

The disc brake piston is made of either steel, aluminum, or fiberglass-reinforced phenolic resin. The steel pistons are usually nickel-chrome plated for improved durability and smoothness. The pistons usually have a larger diameter to provide the necessary braking force with little fluid movement. The top of the pistons is grooved to accept the dust boot.

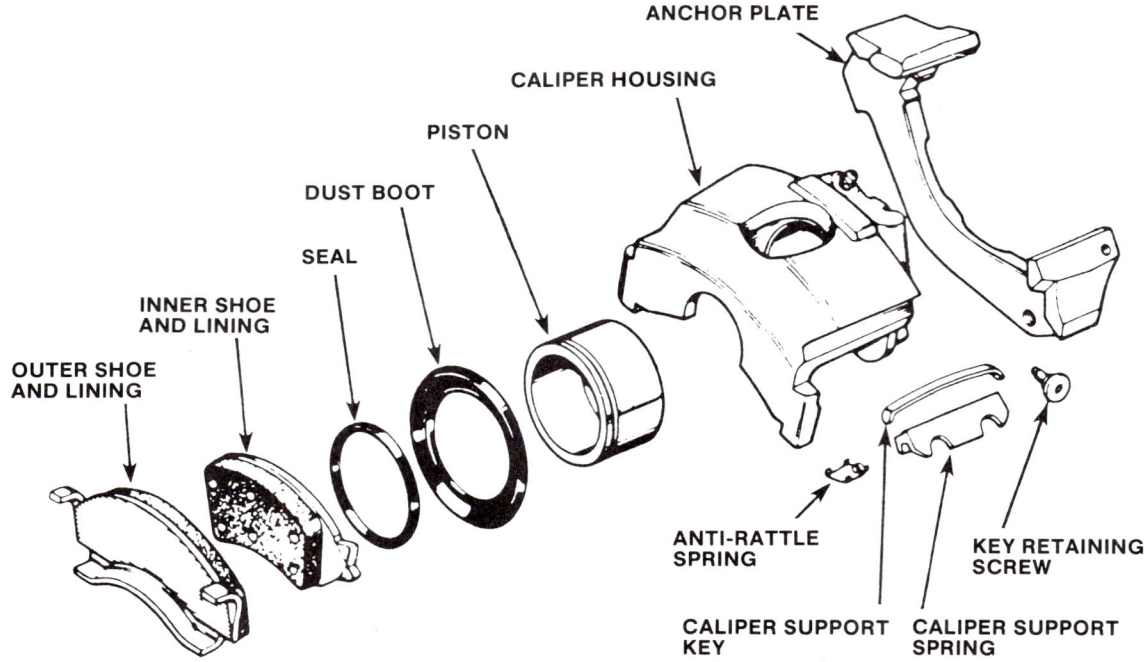

Figure 37-4 Parts of a typical sliding caliper.

Dust Boot

The dust boot seats in a groove at the top of the cylinder bore and also in a groove in the piston. The dust boot prevents moisture and road contamination from entering the bore.

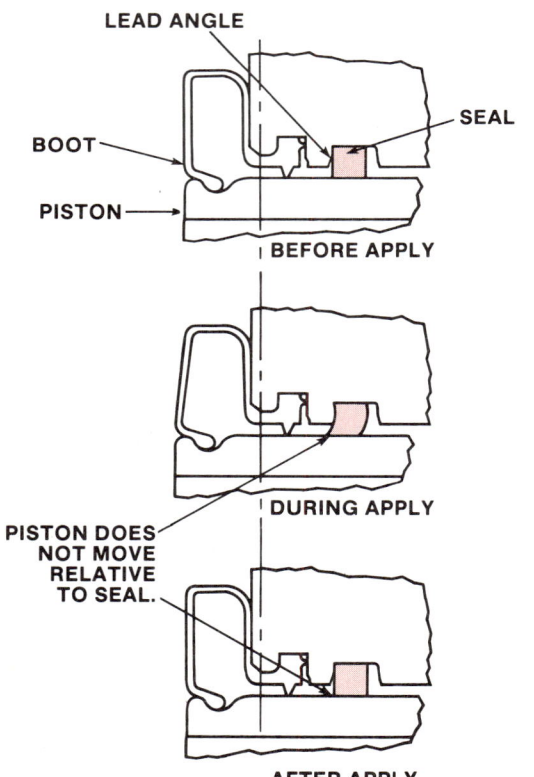

Figure 37-5 Function of a low-drag caliper seal.

Piston Hydraulic Seal

The piston hydraulic seal prevents fluid leakage between the cylinder bore wall and the piston. This rubber sealing ring also acts as a retracting mechanism for the piston when hydraulic pressure is released, causing the piston to return in its bore (Figure 37-5). The seal distorts to allow the piston to be pushed out to bring the pad into contact with the rotor. When hydraulic pressure is diminished, the seal functions as a return spring to retract the piston.

In addition, as the disc brake pads wear, the seal allows the piston to move further out to adjust automatically for the wear and to maintain the lining in proper relationship with the rotor. Additional brake fluid in the caliper bore compensates for lining wear. In this manner the caliper assembly maintains the inboard and outboard shoe and lining in the proper relationship with the rotor surface throughout the full life of the lining.

Brake Pad Assembly

Brake shoe pads with disc brakes are metal plates with the linings either riveted or bonded to them. Pads are placed one in each side of the caliper and together straddle the rotor. The inner brake pad, which is positioned against the piston, is not interchangeable with the outer brake pad (Figure 37-6). The linings are made of semimetallic or other nonasbestos material.

Disc Pad Wear Sensors

Some brake shoe pads have wear sensing indicators. The three most common design wear sensors are audible, visual, and tactile.

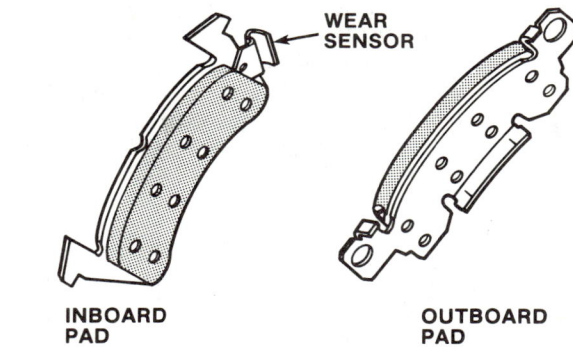

Figure 37-6 Typical pad linings.

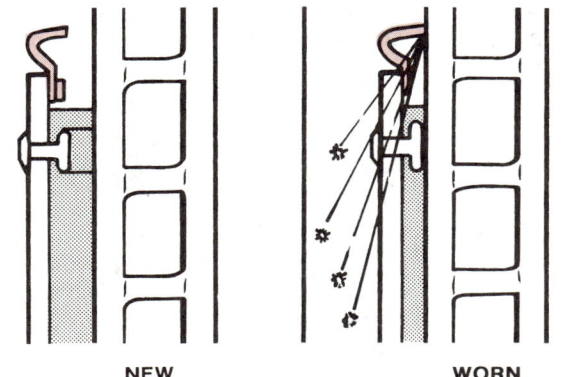

Figure 37-7 Audible disc brake wear indicator.

Audible sensors are thin, spring steel tabs that are riveted to the edge of the pad backing plate and are bent to contact the rotor when the lining wears down to a point that replacement is necessary. At that point, the sensor causes a high-pitched squeal when the brakes are applied, warning the driver that brake service is needed and perhaps saving the rotor from destruction (Figure 37-7). The tab is generally installed toward the rear of the wheel.

Visual sensors inform the driver of the need for new linings. This method employs electrical contacts recessed in the pads that touch the rotor when the linings are worn out. This completes a circuit and turns on a dashboard warning light (Figure 37-8). This system is found mostly on imports.

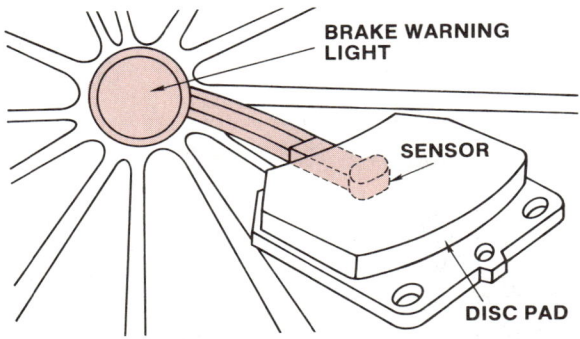

Figure 37-8 Visual sensor.

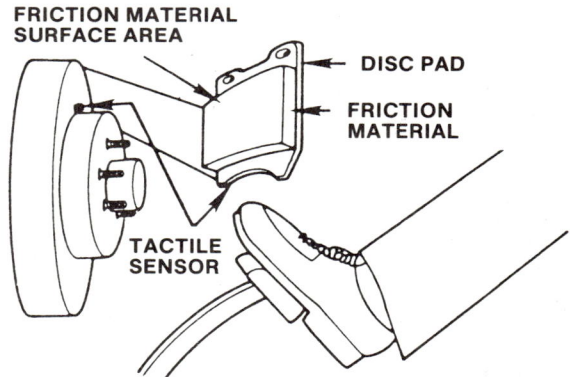

Figure 37-9 Location of the tactile sensor, which causes the brake pedal to pulsate when the brake pads are worn.

Tactile sensors create pedal pulsation as the sensor on the rotor face contacts the sensor attached to the lower portion of the disc pad (Figure 37-9).

CAUTION: As disc brake pad linings wear thin, more brake fluid is needed in the system.

CUSTOMER CARE

Excessive heat liquefies the resin binder that holds the brake pad material together. Once liquefied, the binder rises to the surface of the pad to form a glaze. A glazed pad surface may cause squealing because more heat must be created to achieve an amount of friction equal to a pad in good condition. One common cause of pad glazing is the improper break-in of the pads. Remember to inform customers that unnecessary hard braking during the first 200 miles of a pad's life can generate enough heat to glaze the pads and ruin the quality of the work just performed.

Fixed Caliper Disc Brakes

Fixed caliper disc brakes include a caliper assembly that is bolted in a fixed position and does not move when the brakes are applied. The pistons in both sides come inward to force the pads against the rotor (Figure 37-10). Import cars use the fixed caliper more widely than domestics.

Floating Caliper Disc Brakes

The Ford floating caliper disc brake shown in Figure 37-11 is a typical example of a floating caliper. The caliper on this brake is a one-piece casting that has one hydraulic cylinder and a single piston.

The caliper is attached to the spindle anchor plate with two threaded locating pins. A Teflon® sleeve separates the caliper housing from each pin. The caliper slides back and forth on the pins as the brakes are

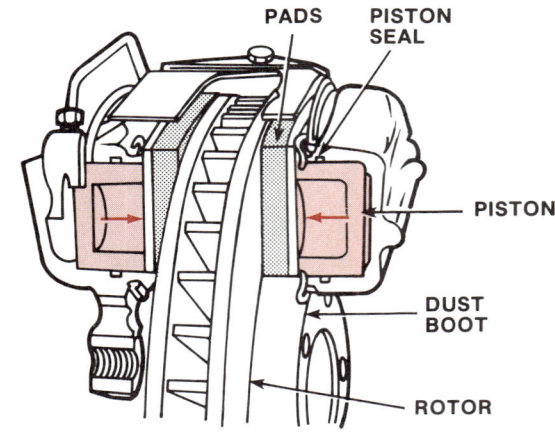

Figure 37-10 Cross section of a fixed caliper.

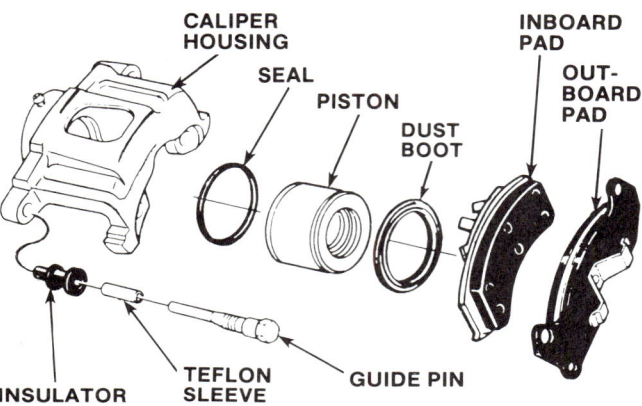

Figure 37-11 Ford/Kelsey floating caliper disc brake.

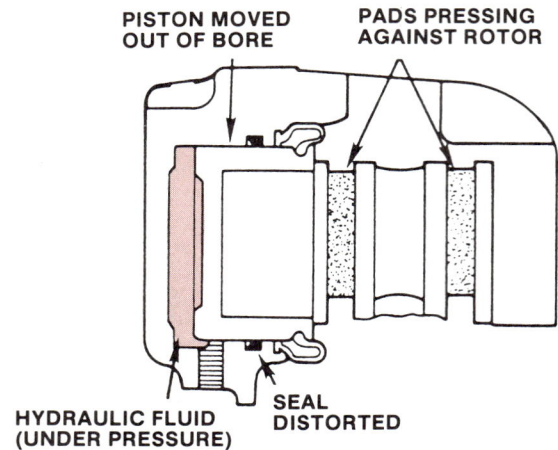

Figure 37-12 Cross section of a caliper in the applied position.

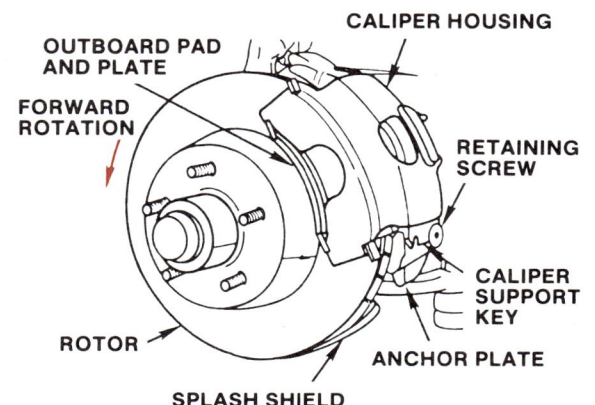

Figure 37-13 Sliding caliper disc brake.

actuated. Upon brake application, hydraulic pressure builds in the caliper cavity behind the piston and seal. Because hydraulic pressure exerts equal force in all directions, pressure against the piston is equal to that exerted against the caliper housing. The piston seal offers the point of least resistance. Initial movement is of the piston outward in the bore.

The piston presses the inboard pad against the rotor. As the pad contacts the revolving rotor, greater resistance to outward movement is increased, forcing pressure to push the caliper away from the piston. This action forces the outboard pad against the rotor (Figure 37-12). However, both pads are applied with equal pressure.

Sliding Caliper Disc Brakes

Sliding caliper disc brakes get their name from the fact that the caliper slides or moves sideways when the brakes are applied. As mentioned previously, in operation these brakes are almost identical to the floating type. Hydraulic pressure forces a piston out of its cylinder to press the inboard pad against the rotor. The caliper itself moves in the opposite direction to force the outboard pad against the opposite side of the rotor.

But unlike the floating caliper, the sliding caliper does not float on pins or bolts attached to the anchor plate. The sliding caliper has angular machined surfaces at each end that slide in mating machined surfaces on the anchor plate.

Figure 37-13 is an example of a typical sliding caliper disc brake. The caliper on this brake is a one-piece casting that has one hydraulic cylinder and a single piston. Machined surfaces on the caliper are positioned against mating machined surfaces on the anchor, which is where the caliper then slides back and forth.

☐ REAR DISC/DRUM (AUXILIARY DRUM) PARKING BRAKE

The rear disc/drum or auxiliary drum parking brake arrangement is found on some GM and Chrysler vehicles that use discs on the rear wheels. On these brakes, the inside of each rear wheel hub and rotor assembly is used as the parking brake drum. Figure 37-14 shows a typical rear disc/drum parking brake.

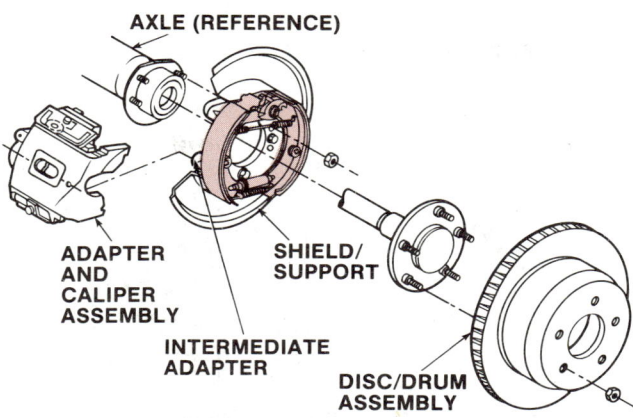

Figure 37-14 A typical parking brake that uses a drum built into the center of a rotor.

REAR DISC PARKING BRAKES

Instead of using an auxiliary drum and shoes to hold the vehicle when parked, these brakes have a mechanism that forces the pads against the rotor mechanically. One method for doing this is the ball-and-ramp arrangement. Another method, used in the GM rear calipers for E-body cars, uses a high lead thrust screw to hold the piston out and maintain contact with the pads and rotors (Figure 37-15). Other types of actuating systems for rear disc brakes include the use of a variety of cams.

SERVICE PRECAUTIONS

The following general service precautions apply to all disc brake systems and should be reviewed before studying the specific servicing techniques in this chapter.

1. Road test the vehicle to determine the condition of the brakes.
2. Be sure the vehicle is properly centered and secured on stands or a hoist.
3. Disconnect the battery ground cable.
4. Before any service is performed, inspect the wheel and brake assembly for obvious damage that could affect braking. Check the following.
   - Tires for excessive wear or improper inflation
   - Wheels for bent or warped rims
   - Wheel bearings for looseness or wear
   - Suspension components to see if worn or broken
   - Brake fluid level
   - Master cylinder, brake lines or hoses, and each wheel for leaks
5. During servicing, grease, oil, brake fluid, or any other foreign material must be kept off the brake linings, caliper, surfaces of the disc, and external surfaces of the hub. Handle the brake disc and caliper in such a way to avoid deformation of the disc and nicking or scratching brake linings.
6. Work on one wheel at a time to avoid popping pistons out of the other caliper and to allow the other caliper assembly to be used as a guide.
7. When removing wheels, be sure to avoid damage to the rotor, external lines, bleeder screws, and splash shield.
8. When a hydraulic hose is disconnected, plug it to prevent any foreign material from entering.
9. Do not attempt to remove the hub with the wheel and tire still mounted. The wheel and tire must be dismounted and the caliper removed before the hub and rotor can be dismounted.
10. Never permit the caliper assembly to hang with the weight on the brake hose. Support it on the suspension or hang it by a piece of wire (Figure 37-16).
11. Inspect the caliper for leaks. If leakage is present, the caliper must be overhauled.
12. Use crocus cloth to remove rust, corrosion, pitting, and scratches from the piston bore. If the bore cannot be cleaned with crocus cloth, light honing is permitted. Do not hone a plated bore.

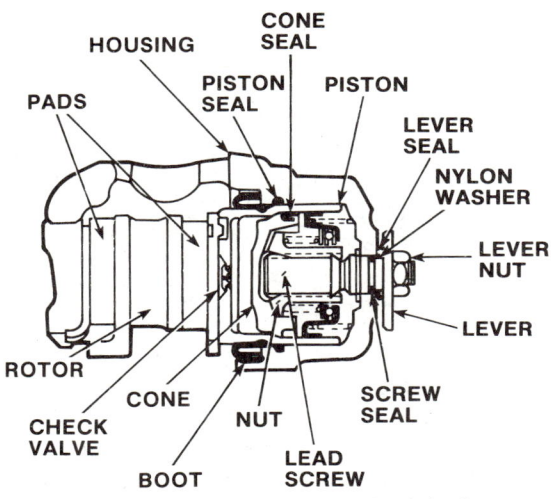

Figure 37-15 Delco-Moraine disc parking brake.

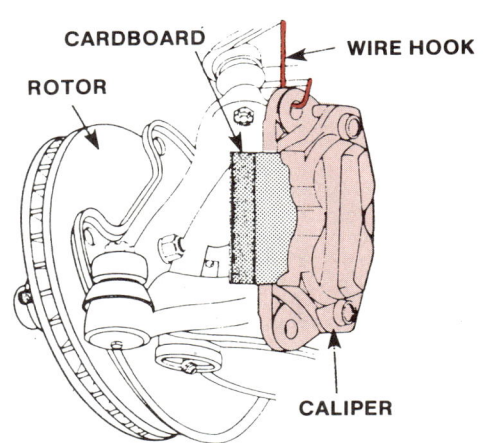

Figure 37-16 Caliper dismounted.

13. When using compressed air to remove caliper pistons, avoid high pressures. A safe pressure to use is 30 psi.
14. Clean the brake components in either denatured alcohol or clean brake fluid. Do not use mineral-based cleaning solvents such as gasoline, kerosene, carbon tetrachloride, acetone, or paint thinner to clean the caliper. It causes rubber parts to become soft and swollen in an extremely short time.
15. Lubricate any moving member such as the caliper housing or mounting bracket to assure a free-moving action. Use only recommended lubricant.
16. Before the brake pads are installed, apply a disc brake noise suppressor to the back of the pads to prevent brake squeal. For best results, follow the directions on the container.
17. The front-wheel bearing should be adjusted to the manufacturer's specifications.
18. Check the master cylinder fluid level and be sure the reservoirs are filled when the brake job is completed.
19. Obtain a firm brake pedal after servicing the brakes and before moving the vehicle. Be sure to road test the vehicle.
20. Always torque the lug nuts when installing a wheel on a vehicle with disc brakes. Never use an impact gun to tighten the lug nuts. Warpage of the rotor could result if an impact gun is used.

Before beginning brake work, remove about two-thirds of the brake fluid from the front or disc brake reservoir on a front/rear split system (Figure 37-17). On a diagonally split system, remove fluid from both reservoirs. If this is not done, the fluid could overflow and spill when the pistons are forced back into the caliper bore, possibly damaging the painted surfaces. Replace the cover. Discard old brake fluid.

Another common procedure is to open the caliper bleeder screw and run a hose down to a container to catch the fluid that is expelled when the piston is forced back into its bore. This also makes it easier to move the piston.

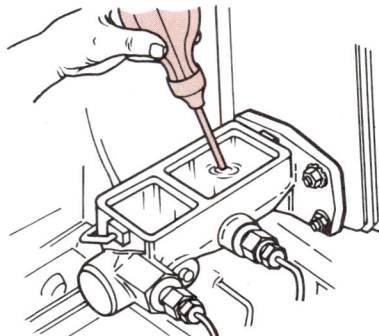

Figure 37-17 Removing brake fluid from master cylinder reservoir.

If the bleeder screws are frozen tight with corrosion, it is sometimes possible to free them using a propane torch and penetrating oil. Of course, the caliper has to be removed from the car, taken to a bench, and worked on there. If the bleeder screws cannot be loosened, they can be drilled out and the caliper retapped for an insert, or the caliper can be replaced with a new or rebuilt unit. The bleeder screw should be removed when doing an overhaul.

WARNING: *When using the propane torch to loosen a bleeder screw, use it with extreme care.*

❏ GENERAL CALIPER INSPECTING AND SERVICING

The general procedures involved in a complete caliper service or overhaul include tasks such as:

- Caliper removal
- Brake pad removal
- Caliper disassembly
- Caliper assembly
- Brake pad installation
- Caliper installation

Not all caliper work includes every one of these tasks. Frequently, caliper service involves only the removal and installation of the brake pads. However, since the new pads are thicker than the worn-out set they replace, they locate the piston farther back in the bore where dirt and corrosion might cause the seals to leak. For this reason, it is often good practice to rebuild the calipers whenever installing new pads. Of course, sometimes it might be necessary to add the task of rotor machining to do a thorough job.

When bench working a caliper assembly, use a vise that is equipped with protector jaws. Excessive vise pressure causes bore and piston distortion.

> **SHOP TALK**
>
> Some shops do not rebuild calipers. They contract them out to specialty shops. However, the brake technician must at least know how to rebuild calipers.

Caliper Removal

The first step in proper caliper service is to remove the caliper assembly from the vehicle. Depending upon the caliper design, this operation is accomplished in various ways. Specific caliper removal procedures are given in service manuals. General details of the task follow.

PROCEDURES

Removing Calipers

1. Remove the brake fluid from the master cylinder.
2. Raise the vehicle and remove the wheel and tire assembly. Use care to avoid damage to or interference with bleeder screw fitting during removal.
3. Mark the right-hand and left-hand caliper assemblies with chalk prior to removal from the vehicle, so they can be positioned correctly during installation.
4. On a sliding or floating caliper, install a C-clamp on the caliper with the solid end of the clamp on the caliper housing and the screw end on the metal portion of the outboard brake pad. Tighten the clamp until the piston bottoms in the caliper bore (Figure 37-18), then remove the clamp. Bottoming the piston allows room for the brake pad to slide over the ridge of rust that accumulates on the edge of the rotor.
5. Disconnect the brake hose from the caliper and remove the copper gasket or washer and the cap end of the brake end. If only the brake pads are to be replaced, do not disconnect the brake hose.
6. Remove the two mounting brackets to the steering knuckle bolts. Support the caliper when removing the second bolt to prevent the caliper from falling.
7. On a sliding caliper, remove the top bolts, retainer clip, and anti-rattle springs (Figure 37-19). On a floating caliper, remove the two special pins that hold the caliper to the anchor plate (Figure 37-20). On an older type fixed caliper, remove the bolts holding it to the steering knuckle. On all three types, get the caliper off by prying it straight up and lifting it clear of the rotor.

Brake Pad Removal

Disc brake linings should be checked periodically or whenever the wheels are removed. Some calipers have inspection holes in the caliper body. If they do not, the brake pads can be visually inspected from the outer ends of the caliper.

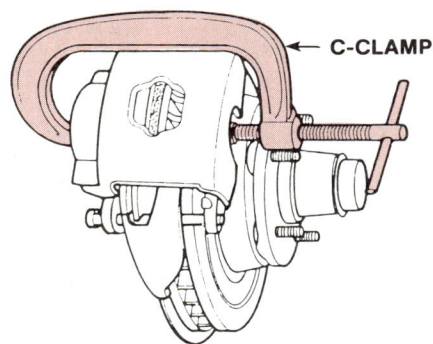

Figure 37-18 Bottoming piston in bore.

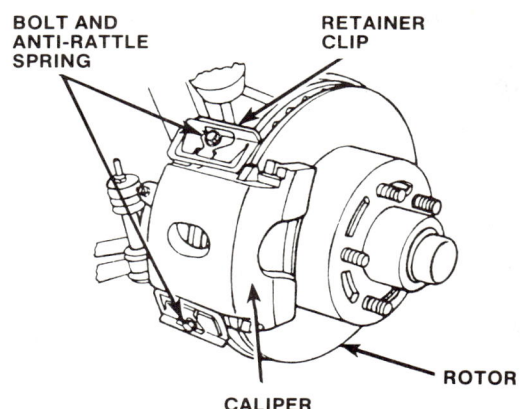

Figure 37-19 Sliding caliper removal.

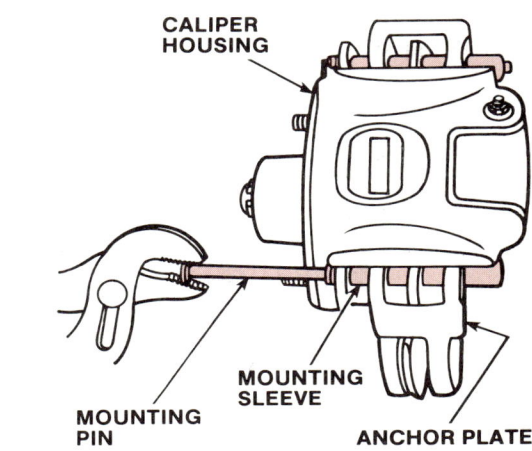

Figure 37-20 Floating caliper removal.

If the friction pads appear worn and in need of replacement, measure them at the thinnest part of the pad. Compare this measurement to the minimum brake pad lining thickness listed in the vehicle's service manual, and replace the pads if needed.

Uneven pad wear on a sliding caliper often means that the caliper is sticking and not giving equal pressure to both pads. On a sliding caliper, the problem could be that the caliper ways are not allowing a smooth sliding movement. Check these machined ways for proper clearance. A slightly tapered wear pattern on the pads of certain models is caused by caliper twist during braking. It is normal if it does not exceed 1/8-inch taper from one end of the pad to the other (Figure 37-21).

Sliding or floating calipers must always be lifted off the rotor for pad replacement. Fixed calipers might have pads that can be replaced by removing the retaining pins or clips instead of having to lift off the entire caliper. They can be held in position by retaining pins (Figure 37-22), guide pins (Figure 37-23), or a support key (Figure 37-24). Note the position of the shims, anti-rattle clips, keys, bushings, or pins during disassembly. A typical procedure for replacing brake pads is

960 Section 8 Brakes

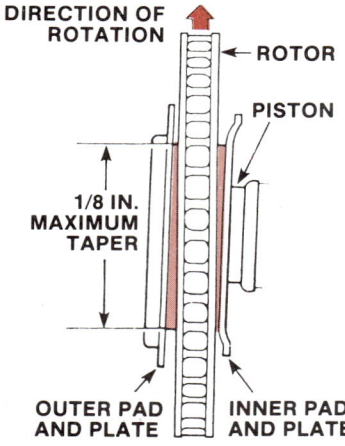

Figure 37-21 Normal pad wear pattern.

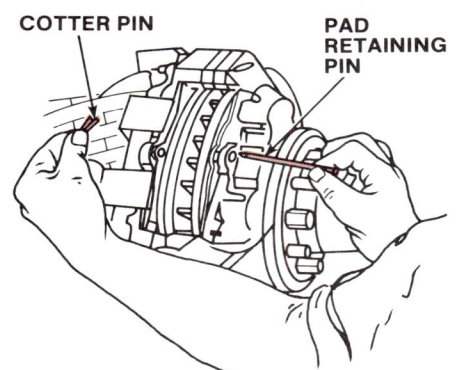

Figure 37-22 Removing brake pad retaining pins.

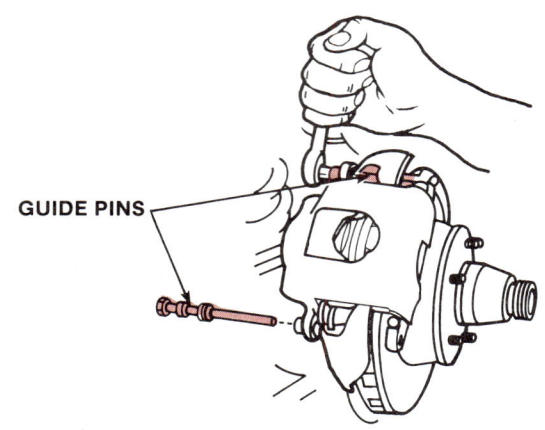

Figure 37-23 Removing guide pins.

outlined in Photo Sequence 18, included in this chapter.

If only the pads have to be replaced, lift the caliper off the rotor and hang it up by a wire. Remove the outer pad and inner pad. Remove the old sleeves and bushings and install new ones. Replace rusty pins on a floating caliper to provide for free movement. Transfer shoe retainers, which can be clips or springs, onto the new pads.

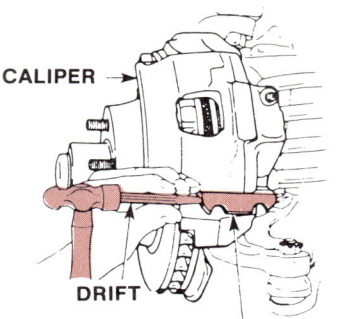

Figure 37-24 Removing caliper support key.

SHOP TALK

If new pads and plates are not to be installed immediately, insert several thicknesses of clean cardboard or plastic in the caliper. This keeps the pistons from coming out of caliper cylinders.

Caliper Disassembly

If the caliper must be rebuilt, it should be taken to the workbench for servicing. Drain any brake fluid from the caliper by way of bleeder screws. Remove the bleeder valve protector, if so equipped.

On a floating caliper, examine the mounting pins for rust that could limit travel. Most manufacturers recommend that these pins and their bushings be replaced each time the caliper is removed. This is a good idea because the pins are inexpensive and a good insurance against costly comebacks. On a fixed caliper, check the pistons for sticking and rebuild the caliper if this problem is found.

To disassemble the caliper, the piston and dust boot must first be removed. Use compressed air to pop the piston out of the bore.

 **PROCEDURES**

Disassembling a Caliper

1. Position the caliper face down on a bench (Figure 37-25).

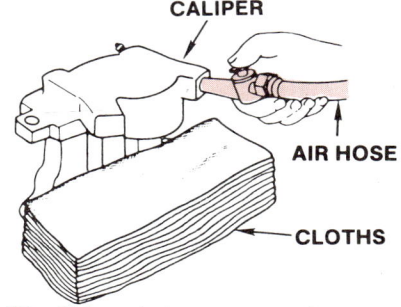

Figure 37-25 Using air to remove a piston.

PHOTO SEQUENCE 18

REMOVING AND REPLACING BRAKE PADS

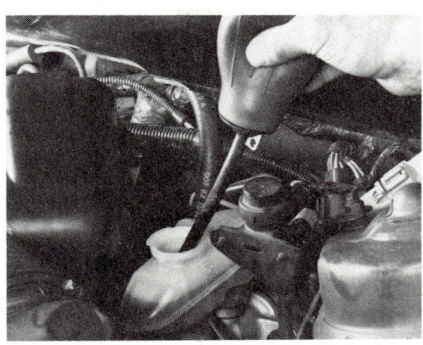

P18-1 Front brake pad replacement begins with removing brake fluid from the master cylinder reservoir. Using a siphon, remove enough fluid to cause the reservoir to be half-full.

P18-4 Loosen and remove the pad locator pins.

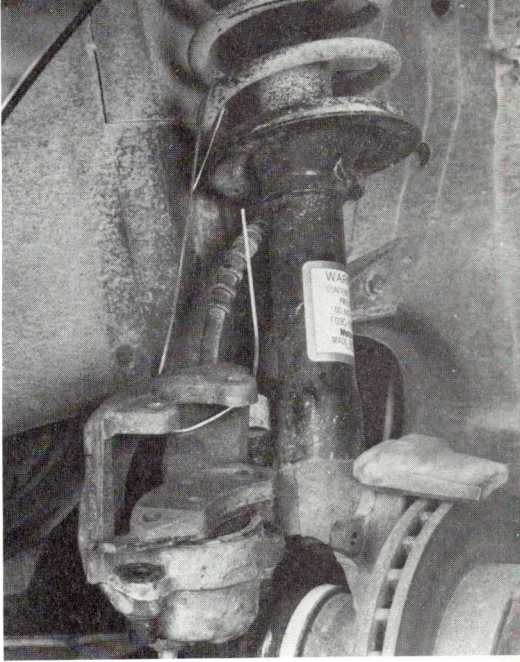

P18-7 Fasten a piece of wire to the car's frame and support the caliper with the wire.

P18-2 Raise the car. Make sure it is safely positioned on the lift. Remove its wheel assemblies.

P18-5 Lift and rotate the caliper assembly from the rotor.

P18-3 Inspect the brake assembly. Look for signs of fluid leaks, broken or cracked lines, and a damaged brake rotor. If any problem is found, correct it while installing the new brake pads.

P18-6 Remove the brake pads from the caliper assembly.

P18-8 Check the condition of the locating pin insulators and sleeves.

(continued)

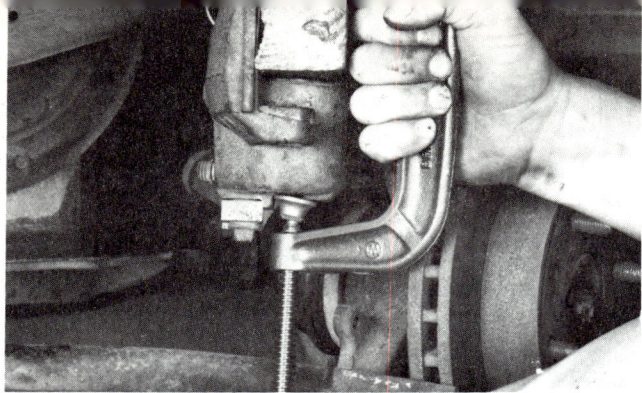

P18-9 Place a piece of wood over the caliper's piston and install a C-clamp over the wood and caliper. Tighten the clamp to force the piston back into its bore.

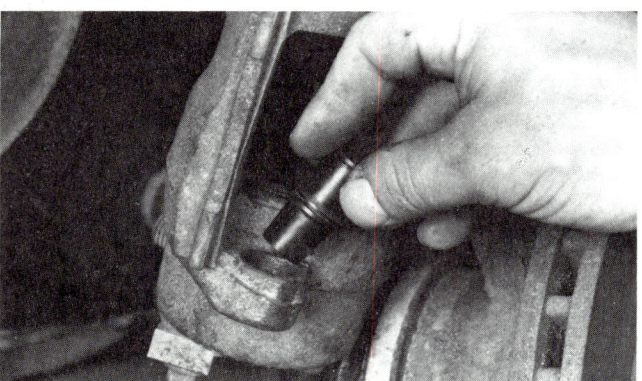

P18-10 Remove the clamp and install new locating pin insulators and sleeves, if necessary.

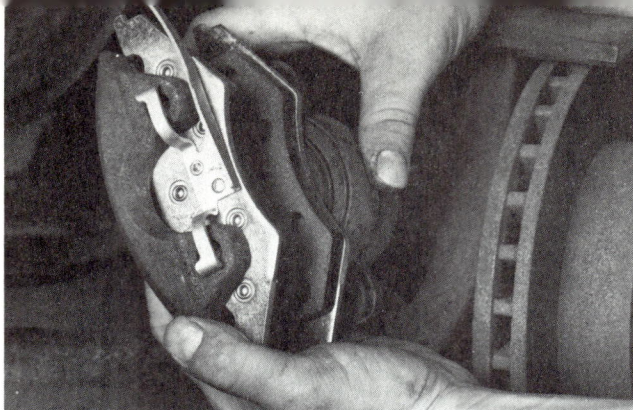

P18-11 Install the new pads into the caliper.

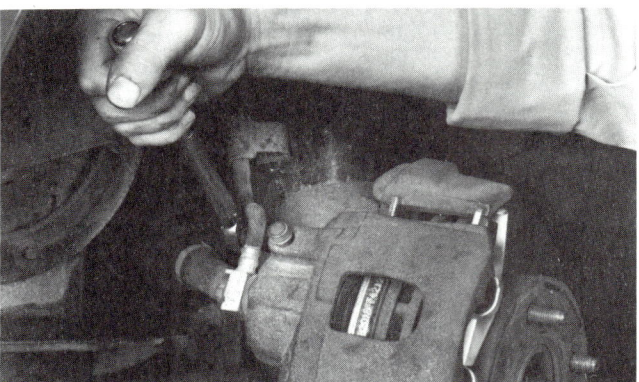

P18-12 Set caliper with pads over the rotor and install the locating pins. After the assembly is in proper position, torque the pins according to specifications. ■

2. Insert the used outer pad into the caliper. Place a folded shop towel on the face of the lining to cushion the piston.
3. Apply low air pressure (never more than 30 psi) to the fluid inlet port of the caliper to force the piston from the caliper housing.

WARNING: Be careful to apply air pressure very gradually. Be sure there are enough cloths to catch the piston when it comes out of the bore. Never place your fingers in front of the piston for any reason when applying compressed air. Personal injury could occur if the piston is popped out of the bore.

4. If a piston is frozen, release air pressure and tap the piston into its bore with a soft-headed hammer or mallet. Reapply air pressure.
5. Frozen phenolic (plastic) pistons can be broken into pieces with a chisel and hammer.

CAUTION: Protect the eyes with safety glasses. Avoid damaging the caliper bore and seal groove with the chisel.

6. Internal expanding pliers are sometimes used to remove pistons from caliper bores.

Inspect phenolic pistons for cracks, chips, or gouges (Figure 37-26). Replace the piston if any of these conditions are evident. If the plated surface of a steel piston is worn, pitted, scored, or corroded, it also should be replaced.

Dust boots vary in design depending on the type of piston and seal, but they all fit into one groove in the piston and another groove in the cylinder. One type comes out with the piston and peels off. Another type stays in place and the piston comes out through the boot, and then is removed from the cylinder (Figure 37-27). In either case, peel the boot from its groove. In some cases it might be necessary to pry out the dust boot with a screwdriver (Figure 37-28). The old boot can be discarded since it must be replaced along with the seal.

CAUTION: Be careful not to scratch the cylinder bore while prying out the dust boot.

Remove a stroking seal by prying it out of the piston with a wooden or plastic tool. Pry a fixed seal out of the cylinder with the same type of tool (Figure 37-29). Do not use a screwdriver or other metal tool. Any of these could nick the metal in the caliper bore and cause a leak. Inspect the bore for pitting or scoring. A bore that shows light scratches or corrosion can usually be cleaned with crocus cloth. However, a bore that has deep scratches or scoring must be honed, provided the diameter of the bore is not increased more than 0.002

Disc Brakes 963

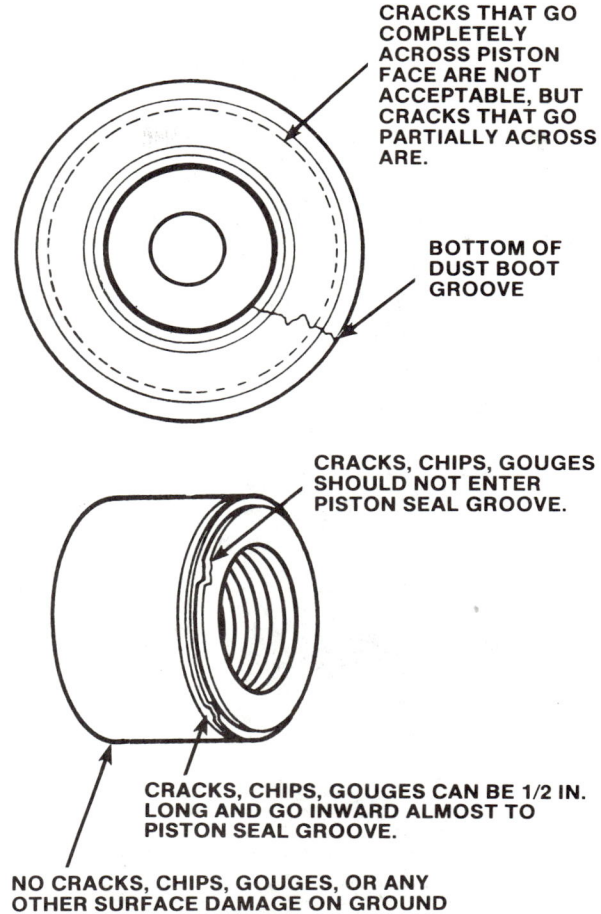

Figure 37-26 Inspect phenolic piston for surface irregularities.

Figure 37-27 Peeling off dust boot.

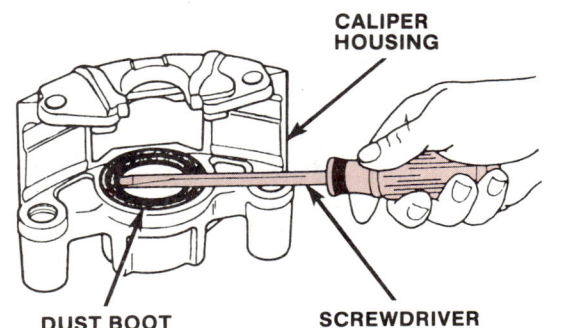

Figure 37-28 Prying out dust boot with a screwdriver.

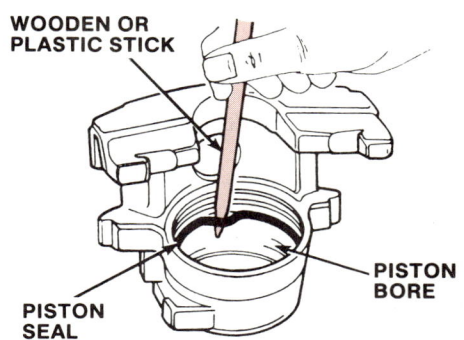

Figure 37-29 Removing piston seal with a wooden or plastic stick.

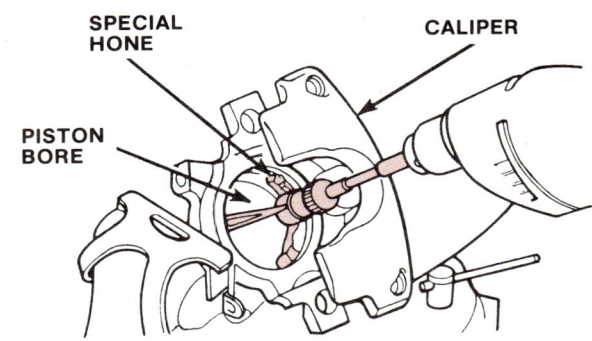

Figure 37-30 Honing caliper bore.

inch. If the bore does not clean up within this specification, a new caliper housing should be installed. Black stains on the bore walls are caused by piston seals. They do no harm.

When using a hone (Figure 37-30), be sure to install the hone baffle before honing the bore. The baffle protects the hone stones from damage. Use extreme care in cleaning the caliper after honing. Remove all dust and grit by flushing the caliper with alcohol. Wipe it dry with a clean lint-free cloth and then clean the caliper a second time in the same manner.

Loaded Calipers

There is now a trend towards installing loaded calipers, rather than overhauling calipers in the shop. Loaded calipers are completely assembled with friction pads and mounting hardware included. Besides the convenience and the savings of installation time, preassembled calipers also reduce the odds of errors in installation.

Mistakes that are frequently made when replacing calipers include forgetting to bend pad locating tabs that prevent pad vibration and noise, leaving off anti-rattle clips and pad insulators, and reusing corroded caliper mounting hardware that can cause a floating caliper to bind up and wear the pads unevenly.

One of the major causes of premature brake wear is rust. It causes improper slider and piston operation that leads to uneven pad wear. Tests have shown that when only the pads are replaced, the new pads can wear out in half the mileage as the originals when rust affects caliper operation. Installing a loaded caliper assures that all parts requiring replacement are replaced.

> **SHOP TALK**
>
> Make sure the supplier tells you what type of friction material is used on their loaded caliper assemblies. Some suppliers use lower grade friction material to keep cost down. Also, avoid mismatching friction materials from side to side. When one caliper is bad, both calipers should be replaced using the same friction material on both sides.

Caliper Assembly

Before assembling the caliper, clean all metal parts to be reused and the phenolic piston (if so equipped) in clean denatured alcohol or brake fluid. Then, clean out and dry the grooves and passageways with compressed air. Make sure that the caliper bore and component parts are thoroughly clean.

Some designs of disc brakes require that the piston-to-bore clearance be checked with a feeler gauge (Figure 37-31). If clearances exceed the limits listed in the service manual, the piston must be replaced.

To replace a typical piston seal, dust boot, and piston, first lubricate the new piston seal with clean brake fluid or assembly lubricant (usually supplied with the caliper rebuild kit). Make sure the seal is not distorted. Insert it into the groove in the cylinder bore so it does not become twisted or rolled. Install a new dust boot by setting the flange squarely in the outer groove of the caliper bore. Next, coat the piston with brake fluid or assembly lubricant and install it in the cylinder bore (Figure 37-32). Be sure to use a wood block or other flat stock when installing the piston back into the piston bore. Never apply a C-clamp directly to a phenolic piston, and be sure the pistons are not cocked. Spread the dust boot over the piston as it is installed. Seat the dust boot in the piston groove.

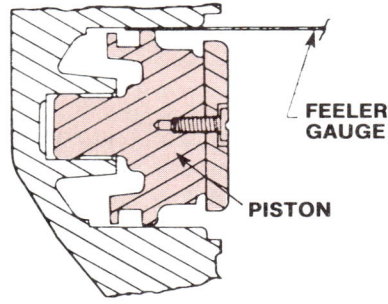

Figure 37-31 Checking piston clearance with feeler gauge.

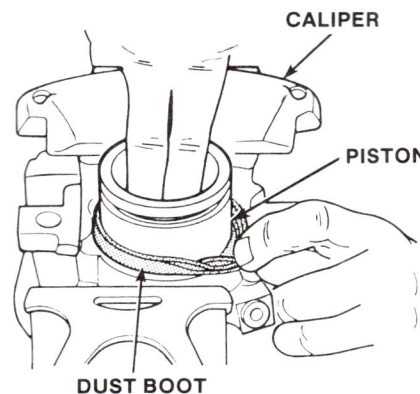

Figure 37-32 When installing a piston in a caliper bore make sure the piston is lubricated.

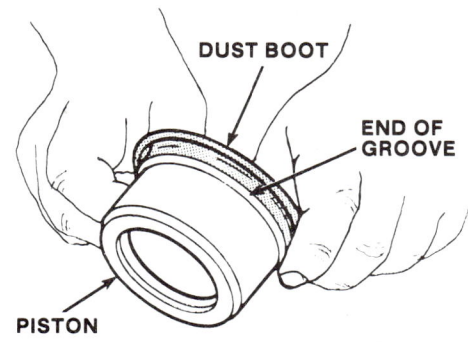

Figure 37-33 Some installation procedures require the dust boot to be pulled over the end of the piston.

With some types of boot/piston arrangements, the procedure of installation is slightly different from that already described. That is, the new dust boot is pulled over the end of the piston (Figure 37-33). Lubricate the piston with brake fluid before installing it in the caliper. Then, by hand, slip the piston carefully into the cylinder bore, pushing it straight, so the piston seal is not damaged during installation. Use an installation tool or wooden block to seat the new dust boot (Figure 37-34).

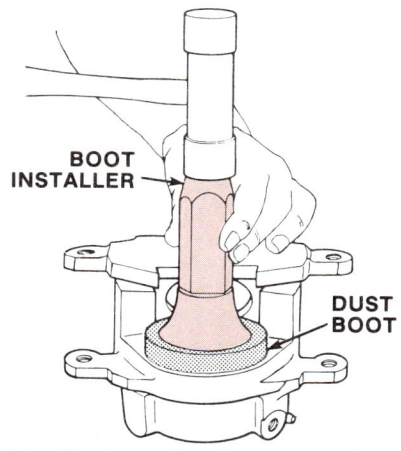

Figure 37-34 Seating a dust boot with a boot installer.

Disc Brakes 965

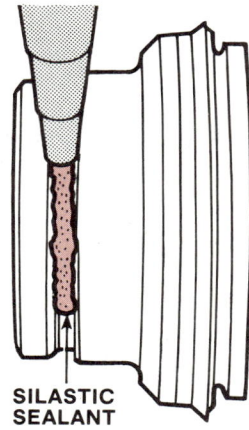

Figure 37-35 Applying sealer to dust boot groove.

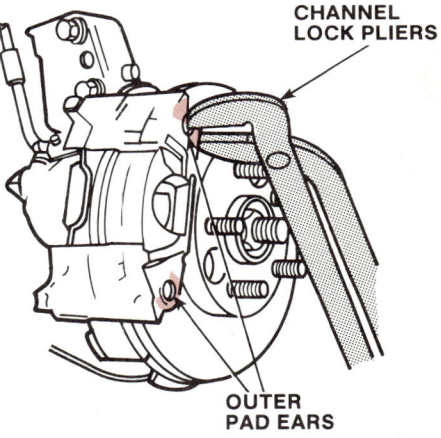

Figure 37-37 Clinching out pad ears with channel lock pliers.

The installation of some dust boots requires its groove to be filled with a bead of silicone sealer (Figure 37-35). After lubricating the dust boot, insert the piston. Bottom the piston in the cylinder bore and seat the dust boot in the recess next to the bore. Seal the area between the dust boot ring and caliper housing with a bead of silicone sealer (Figure 37-36).

CAUTION: Be sure no sealant gets between the piston and cylinder since it retards its action.

Another point to keep in mind is that some caliper designs have a slot cut in the face of the pistons that must align with an anti-squeal shim. Make sure that the piston and shim align. It might be necessary to turn the piston to achieve proper alignment.

To complete the caliper assembly job, install the bleeder screw.

CAUTION: On fixed calipers, bridge bolts are used to hold the two caliper halves together. These are high-tensile bolts ordered only by specific part number. They require accurate torque tightness to prevent leakage. Do not attempt to use standard bolts in place of bridge bolts.

Brake Pad Installation

It is a good practice to replace disc brake hardware when replacing disc brake pads. Hardware life is drastically affected by intense heat, weather conditions, abrasive particles, and normal wear. Replacement of the disc brake hardware assures proper caliper movement and brake pad retention. Hardware replacement aids in preventing brake noise and uneven brake pad wear.

Fixed Caliper Brake Pads

The designs of fixed caliper disc brakes vary slightly. Generally, to replace the pads insert new pads and plates in the caliper with the metal plates against the end of the pistons. Be sure that the plates are properly seated in the caliper. Spread the pads apart and slide the caliper into position on the rotor. With some pads, mounting bolts are used to hold them in place. These bolts are usually tightened 80 to 90 foot-pounds. On some fixed disc brakes, the pads are held in place by retaining clips or, as with some Delco-Moraine designs, both retaining pins and clips are used. Figure 37-37 shows channel lock pliers being used to clinch down the ear clips of the outer pads. Reinstall the anti-rattle spring/clips and other hardware (if so equipped).

Sliding Caliper Brake Pads

Push the piston carefully back into the bore until it bottoms. Slide a new outer pad and lining assembly into the recess of the caliper (Figure 37-38). No free play between the brake pad flanges and caliper fingers

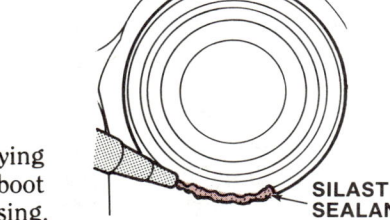

Figure 37-36 Applying sealer between dust boot ring and caliper housing.

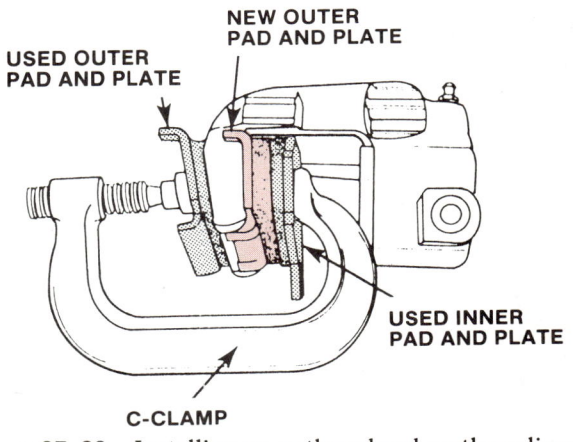

Figure 37-38 Installing an outboard pad on the caliper.

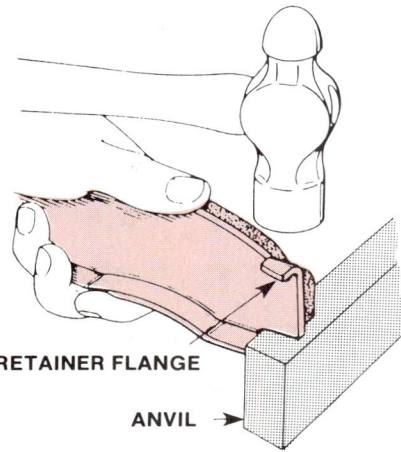

Figure 37-39 Bend the retaining flange if there is excessive free play.

should exist. If free play is found, remove the pad from the caliper and bend the flanges to eliminate all vertical free play (Figure 37-39). Install the pad.

Place the inner pad into position on the adapter with the pad flange in the adapter's machined ways. Slide the adapter assembly into position in the adapter and over the disc. Align the caliper on the adapter's ways. Do not pull the dust boot from its groove when the piston and boot slide over the inboard pad. Install the anti-rattle springs (if so equipped) on top of the retainer plate and tighten the retaining screws to specification.

Floating Caliper Brake Pads

For floating or pin caliper disc brakes, compress the flanges of the outer bushing in the caliper fingers and work them into position in the hole from the outer side of the caliper. Compress the flanges of the inner guide pin bushings and install them.

Slide the new pad and lining assemblies into position in the adapter and caliper. Be sure that the metal portion of the pad is fully recessed in the caliper and adapter and that the proper pad is on the outer side of the caliper.

Hold the outer pad and carefully slide the caliper into position in the adapter and over the disc. Align the guide pin holes of the adapter with those of the inner and outer pads. Install the guide pins through the bushings, caliper, adapter, and inner and outer pads into the outer bushings in the caliper and anti-rattle spring.

Caliper Installation

To reinstall the caliper on the vehicle, first install the caliper assembly over the rotor with the outer brake pad against the rotor's braking surface. This prevents pinching the piston boot between the inner brake pad and the piston. Make sure the correct caliper is installed on the correct anchor plate according to the way they were marked during disassembly. Next, lubricate the rubber insulators (if so equipped) with silicone dielectric compound. Install the caliper assembly back on its mounting brackets. Connect the brake hose to the caliper. If copper washers or gaskets are used, be sure to use new ones—the old ones might have taken a set and might not form a tight seal if reused. Fill the master cylinder reservoirs and bleed the hydraulic system. Check for fluid leaks under maximum pedal pressure. Lower the vehicle and road test it.

ROTOR INSPECTING AND SERVICING

The cause for braking complaints on cars equipped with drum brakes can usually be found by visually examining the brake drum. In cases where the same complaints involve disc brakes, visual inspection of the rotor does not give the answer. Tolerances on rotor thickness, parallelism, runout, flatness, and depth of scoring are very critical and must be measured with exacting gauges and micrometers. To perform a proper servicing job on rotors, accurate measuring tools and up-to-date rotor resurfacing equipment are required.

CAUTION: Never turn the rotor on one side of the vehicle and not the other.

The rotors should be inspected whenever brake pads are required and when the wheels are removed for other types of service. The following are typical disc brake rotor conditions that need careful inspection.

Lateral Runout

Excessive lateral runout is a wobbling of the rotor from side to side when it rotates. The excessive wobble knocks the pads farther back than normal, causing the pedal to pulse and vibrate during braking. Chatter can also result. It also causes excessive pedal travel because the pistons have farther to travel to reach the rotor. If runout exceeds specifications, the rotor must be turned or replaced.

Lack of Parallelism

Parallelism refers to variations in thickness of the rotor. If the rotor is out of parallel, it can cause excessive pedal travel, front end vibration, pedal pulsation, chatter, and on occasion, grabbing of the brakes. It must be resurfaced or replaced.

Scoring

Rotor wear or scoring can be caused by linings that are worn through to the rivets or backing plate or by friction material that is harsh or unkind to the mating surface. Rust, road dirt, and other contamination could also cause rotor scoring.

Light scoring (less than a depth of 0.015 inch) of the disc braking surface can occur during normal brake use. This does not affect brake operation. However, this can result in a higher-than-average brake shoe lining wear rate. But, any rotor having score marks more than 0.15 inch should be refinished or replaced.

Bluing or Heat Checking

If the lining surface is charred, blued, or hard-ended with a heavy glaze, or if the rotor is severely heat checked, machine the rotor or replace it.

Hard or chill spots of steel in a rotor cast-iron surface usually result from a change in the metallurgy caused by braking heat. Pulling, rapid wear, hard pedal, and noise occur. These spots can be removed by grinding. However, only the raised surfaces are removed, and they could reappear when heat is again encountered. The rotor must be replaced.

Rusty Rotor

If the vehicle has not been driven for a period of time, the discs rust in the area not covered by the lining and cause noise and chatter. Excessive wear and scoring of the discs and lining result. Wear ridges on the discs can cause temporary improper pad lining contact if ridges are not removed before installation of new lining. Lining deposits on the disc can cause erratic friction characteristics if a new lining is installed without resurfacing or cleaning the disc.

SHOP TALK

Specific inspection and repair procedures can be found in the service manuals. Always refer to them when performing a brake job.

CASE STUDY

Case 1

An obviously embarrassed customer explains his problem to the brake shop technician. He just finished installing new disc pads on his light truck, but the disc brakes are dragging. The young man insists he performed the work correctly and that the rest of the braking system is in fine working order.

The technician inspects the front brakes and finds that the owner cleaned all components well and installed the pads correctly. The technician checks the action of the caliper. Its piston shows no signs of sticking, but the caliper appears to be binding. Removal and inspection of the caliper locates the problem. Although the owner had carefully cleaned the slides of the caliper, he had failed to apply any lubricant to the surfaces. This was causing the calipers to bind and the brakes to drag.

Omitting the simplest of tasks when performing repairs can often lead to failure and wasted time.

Summary

- Disc brakes offer four major advantages over drum brakes: resistance to heat fade, resistance to water fade, increased straight-line stopping ability, and automatic adjustment.
- The typical rotor is attached to and rotates with the wheel hub assembly. Heavier vehicles generally use ventilated rotors. Splash shields protect the rotors and pads from road moisture and dirt.
- The caliper assembly includes cylinder bores and pistons, dust boots, and piston hydraulic seals.
- Brake pads are placed in each side of the caliper and together straddle the rotor. Some brake pads have wear sensors.
- Fixed caliper disc brakes do not move when the brakes are applied. Floating caliper disc brakes slide back and forth on pins or bolts. Sliding calipers slide on surfaces that have been machined smooth for this purpose.
- The rear disc/drum parking brake is a rear disc brake in which the inside of each rear wheel hub and rotor assembly is used as the parking brake drum.
- Rear disc parking brakes have a mechanism that forces the pads against the rotor mechanically.
- The general procedures involved in a complete caliper overhaul include tasks such as: caliper removal, brake pad removal, caliper disassembly, caliper assembly, brake pad installation, and caliper installation.
- The first step in proper caliper service is to remove the caliper assembly from the vehicle.
- Disc brake pads should be checked periodically or whenever the wheels are removed. They should be replaced if they fail to exceed minimum lining thickness as listed in the service manual.
- To disassemble the caliper, the piston and dust boot must first be removed. Compressed air is used to pop the piston out of the bore.
- Before assembling the caliper, all metal parts and the phenolic piston are cleaned in denatured alcohol or brake fluid. The grooves and passageways of the caliper are cleaned out and dried with compressed air.
- It is a good practice to replace disc brake hardware when replacing disc brake pads.
- The caliper assembly is installed over the rotor with the outer brake pad against the rotor's braking surface.
- Disc brake rotor conditions that must be corrected include lateral runout, lack of parallelism, scoring, blueing or heat checking, and rusty rotors.

Review Questions

1. Name four major advantages of disc brakes over drum brakes.
2. Name the three assemblies that make up a disc brake.
3. Name the three types of calipers used on disc brakes.
4. What type of brake uses the inside of each rear wheel hub and rotor assembly as a parking brake drum?
5. How many cylinder bores and pistons can a caliper assembly contain?
6. Which of the following statements concerning disc brakes is incorrect?
    a. Disc brakes can handle more heat than drum brakes.
    b. Disc brakes are not as likely to fade during heavy braking as are drum brakes.
    c. Disc brakes stay in adjustments automatically.
    d. Disc brakes do not tolerate water well.
7. Disc brakes are not _____ .
    a. self-adjusting
    b. rapid acting
    c. easy to reline
    d. self-energizing
8. Solid rotors are used on _____ .
    a. lightweight vehicles
    b. heavy vehicles
    c. high-performance vehicles
    d. none of the above
9. What channels the flow of air over the exposed rotor surfaces?
    a. webs
    b. hub assembly
    c. splash shield
    d. caliper assembly
10. Which of the following statements concerning the caliper assembly is incorrect?
    a. The caliper housing is usually a two-piece construction of aluminum and cast iron.
    b. Caliper action converts hydraulic pressure into mechanical force.
    c. A caliper assembly can contain as many as four cylinder bores and pistons.
    d. The caliper assembly provides a means of applying brake pads to the rotor.
11. What prevents moisture from entering the cylinder bore?
    a. phenolic piston
    b. drag caliper
    c. splash shield
    d. dust boot
12. When servicing disc brakes on a vehicle, Technician A works on one wheel before beginning work on another. Technician B uses a minimum of 50 psi of air pressure to force the piston from the caliper housing. Who is correct?
    a. Technician A
    b. Technician B
    c. Both A and B
    d. Neither A nor B
13. When examining disc brakes, Technician A visually inspects the rotor for wear. Technician B uses a propane torch and penetrating oil to free a bleeder screw frozen tight with corrosion. Who is correct?
    a. Technician A
    b. Technician B
    c. Both A and B
    d. Neither A nor B
14. What should be used to remove rust, corrosion, pitting, and scratches from the piston bore?
    a. an oily rag
    b. crocus cloth
    c. abrasive paper
    d. all of the above
15. Which term refers to variations in thickness of the rotor?
    a. torque
    b. lateral runout
    c. parallelism
    d. pedal pulsation
16. Technician A cleans brake components in denatured alcohol. Technician B cleans brake components in clean brake fluid. Who is correct?
    a. Technician A
    b. Technician B
    c. Both A and B
    d. Neither A nor B
17. Technician A states that rotor wear can be caused by worn pad linings. Technician B states that hard spots in a rotor usually result from manufacturing defects. Who is correct?
    a. Technician A
    b. Technician B
    c. Both A and B
    d. Neither A nor B
18. When replacing the brake pads, Technician A disconnects the brake hose. When removing the caliper, Technician B supports the caliper before removing the second bolt. Who is correct?
    a. Technician A
    b. Technician B
    c. Both A and B
    d. Neither A nor B
19. Technician A replaces the pads if they are 1/32-inch thick or less. Technician B says the calipers must be replaced if the pads have a slightly tapered wear pattern. Who is correct?
    a. Technician A
    b. Technician B
    c. Both A and B
    d. Neither A nor B

SECTION 9
PASSENGER COMFORT

Chapter 38 Heating and Air Conditioning
Chapter 39 Other Safety and Security Equipment

Modern vehicles are designed to provide passengers with comfort, convenience, and safety. Such accessory systems can be quite elaborate, adding electronic circuits and components to an already complex vehicle.

In addition, service to items such as air bags, passive restraint systems, and air conditioning equipment must be performed both safely and accurately. Concerns over the proper handling of air conditioning refrigerant are particularly important.

The information covered in Section 9 corresponds to materials found on the ASE certification tests on heating and air conditioning and electrical systems.

38 HEATING AND AIR CONDITIONING

Objectives

■ Identify the purpose of a ventilation system. ■ Identify the common parts of a heating system. ■ Compare the vacuum and mechanical controls of a heating system. ■ Describe how an automotive air conditioning system operates. ■ Locate, identify, and describe the function of the various air-conditioning components. ■ Understand the special handling procedures for automotive refrigerants. ■ Describe methods used to check refrigerant leaks. ■ Use approved methods and equipment to discharge, evacuate, and recharge an automotive air-conditioning system. ■ Describe the operation of the three types of air-conditioning control systems.

The discomforts of motoring's early days would daunt the toughest motorcross racer (Figure 38-1). Paper-thin tires blew out if the vehicle ran over a good-size pebble. Headlights were so dim they could barely illuminate a locomotive in their path. There was no climate control. In winter, heavy coats and blankets were all that allowed passengers to survive behind a woefully inadequate windscreen. In summer, the breeze generated by 15 mph travel was the only thing that retarded heat prostration.

Today, ventilation, heating, and air-conditioning systems are very important elements for providing passenger comfort.

☐ VENTILATION SYSTEM

The ventilation system on most vehicles is designed to supply outside air to the passenger compartment

Figure 38-1 Early model cars did not offer the conveniences of today's vehicles.

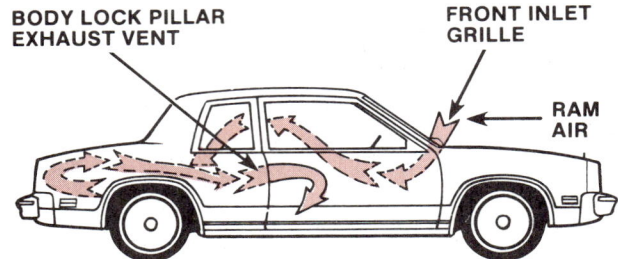

Figure 38-2 A flow-through ventilation system is used on some vehicles. Ram air is forced into the inlet grille and sent throughout the passenger and trunk compartment. The air then flows out of the vehicle through exhaust areas. *Courtesy of Chrysler Corp.*

through upper or lower vents or both. There are several systems used to vent air into the passenger compartment. The most common is the flow-through system (Figure 38-2). In this arrangement, a supply of outside air, which is called ram air, flows into the car when it is moving. When the car is not moving, a steady flow of outside air can be produced by the heater fan. In operation, ram air is forced through an inlet grille. The pressurized air then circulates throughout the passenger and trunk compartment. From there the air is forced outside the vehicle through an exhaust area.

On certain older vehicles, air is admitted by opening or closing two vent knobs under the dashboard. The left knob controls air through the left inlet. The right knob controls air through the right inlet. The air is still considered ram air and is circulated through the passenger compartment.

970

Rather than using ram air (especially if the vehicle is stopped), a ventilation fan can be used. It can be accessible from under the dashboard or from inside the engine compartment. A blower assembly is placed inside the blower housing. As the squirrel cage blower rotates, it produces a strong suction on the intake. A pressure is also created on the output. When the fan motor is energized by using the temperature controls on the dashboard, air is moved through the passenger compartment.

☐ AUTOMOTIVE HEATING SYSTEMS

The automotive heating system has been designed to work hand in hand with the cooling system to maintain proper temperatures inside the car. The heating system's primary job is to provide a comfortable passenger compartment temperature and to keep car windows clear of fog or frost. The primary components of the automotive heating system are the heater core, the heater control valve, the blower motor and the fan, and the heater and defroster duct hoses (Figure 38-3).

In the liquid-cooling system, heat from the coolant circulating inside the engine is converted to hot air, which is blown into the passenger compartment. Hot coolant from the engine is transferred by a heater hose to the heater control valve and then to the heater core inlet. As the coolant circulates through the core, heat is transferred from the coolant to the tubes and fins of the core. Air blown through the core by the blower motor and fan then picks up the heat from the surfaces of the core and transfers it into the passenger compartment of the car. After giving up its heat, the coolant is then pumped out through the heater core outlet, where it is returned to the engine to be recirculated by the water pump.

The heater core is generally designed and constructed much like a miniature radiator. It features two tanks, each with an inlet or outlet tube and a tube and fin core to facilitate coolant flow between them.

Although all heater cores basically function in the same manner, several variations in design and materials are used by different auto makers to achieve the same results. Although the core construction varies, this type has an aluminum core with plastic tanks.

Like the radiator, heater core tanks, tubes, and fins can become clogged over time by rust, scale, and mineral deposits circulated by the coolant. Heater core failures are caused generally by leakage or clogging. Feel the heater inlet and outlet hoses while the engine is idling and warm with the heater temperature control on hot. If the hose upstream of the heater valve does not feel hot, the valve is not opening.

With cable-operated control valves, check the cable for sticking, slipping (loose mounting bracket) or misadjustment. With valves that are vacuum operated, there should be no vacuum to the valve when the heater is on (except for those that are normally closed and need vacuum to open).

If the heater core appears to be plugged, the inlet hose may feel hot up to the core but the outlet hose remains cool. Reverse flushing the core with a power flusher may open up the blockage, but usually the core has to be removed for cleaning or replacement. Air pockets in the heater core can also interfere with proper coolant circulation. Air pockets form when the coolant level is low or when the cooling system is not properly filled after draining.

When the heater core leaks and must be repaired or replaced, it is a very difficult and time-consuming job, primarily because of the core's location deep within the fire wall of the car. For this reason always leak test a replacement heater core before installation. Also flush the cooling system and replace the coolant seasonally.

> ### SHOP TALK
>
> *Engines with aluminum cylinder heads or blocks sometimes lose coolant through microscopic porosity leaks in the castings. Though the amount of coolant that is lost this way is not great, over time it can contaminate the oil enough to cause premature engine wear, especially in the cylinders and bearings. Pressure testing the cooling system usually does not reveal microscopic porosity leaks because the cracks are too small to allow a noticeable pressure drop.*
>
> *Porosity leaks can be sealed by adding a hot melt sealer product to the cooling system. Some experts recommend adding stop-leak products as a preventive measure when changing the coolant in late-model engines with aluminum heads or blocks.*

Heater Control Valve

The heater control valve (sometimes called the water flow valve) controls the flow of coolant into the

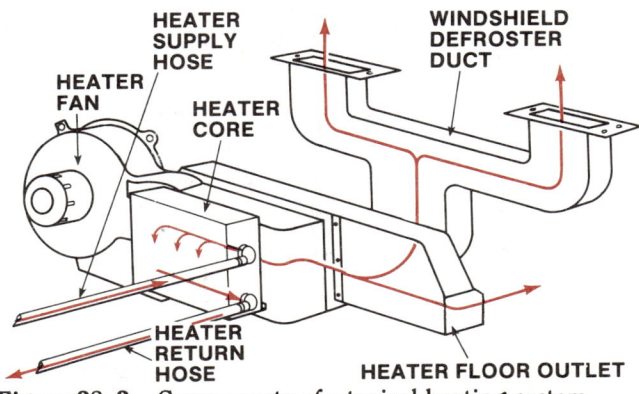

Figure 38-3 Components of a typical heating system.

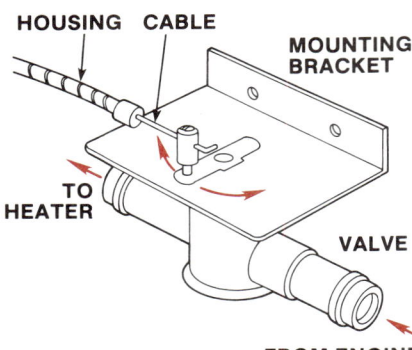

Figure 38-4 Cable-operated heater valve used to control the flow of water or coolant through the heater core.

heater core from the engine. In a closed position, the valve allows no flow of hot coolant to the heater core, keeping it cool. In an open position, the valve allows heated coolant to circulate through the heater core, maximizing heater efficiency. Heater control valves are operated in three basic ways: by cable, thermostat, or vacuum.

Cable-operated valves are controlled directly from the heater control lever on the dashboard (Figure 38-4). Thermostatically-controlled valves feature a liquid-filled capillary tube located in the discharge airstream off the heater core. This tube senses air temperature, and the valve modulates the flow of water to maintain a constant temperature, regardless of engine speed or temperature.

Most heater valves, utilized on today's cars are vacuum operated. These valves are normally located in the heater hose line or mounted directly in the engine block. When a vacuum signal reaches the valve, a diaphragm inside the valve is raised, either opening or closing the valve against an opposing spring. When the temperature selection on the dashboard is changed, vacuum to the valve is vented and the valve returns to its original position. Vacuum-actuated heater control valves are either normally open or normally closed designs.

On late-model vehicles, heater control valves are typically made of plastic for corrosion resistance and light weight. These valves feature few internal working parts and no external working parts. With the reduced weight of these valves, external mounting brackets are also not required.

The thermostat, which helps regulate the coolant temperature in the cooling system, plays a large part in the heating system. A malfunctioning thermostat can cause the engine to overheat or not reach normal operating temperature, or it can be the cause of poor heater performance.

Blower Motor

The blower motor is usually located in the heater housing assembly. It ensures that air is circulated

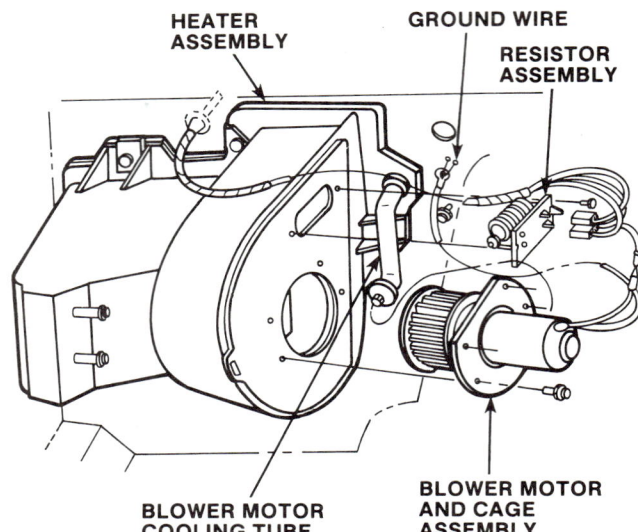

Figure 38-5 Blower motor assembly.

through the system (Figure 38-5). Its speed is controlled by a multiposition switch in the control panel. The switch works in connection with a resistor block that is usually located on the heater housing.

On some vehicles, when the engine is running, the blower motor is in constant operation at low speed. On automatic temperature control systems, the blower motor is activated only when the engine reaches a predetermined temperature. The blower motor circuit is protected by a fuse located in the fuse panel. The fuse rating is usually 20 to 30 amperes.

The blower motor resistor block is used to control the blower motor speed. The typical resistor block is composed of three or four wire resistors, in series with the blower motor, which control its voltage and current (Figure 38-6). The speed of the motor is determined by the control panel switch, which puts the resistors in series. Increasing the resistance in the system slows the blower speed.

If the blower does not operate, use a test light to make sure there is voltage on both sides of the fuse. Then, check to see if current is arriving at the motor. On cars where the blower motor is behind the inner fender shell, hunt out the wiring and check for current. If the blower motor is getting current, the problem is either a burned out blower motor, a bad ground on the

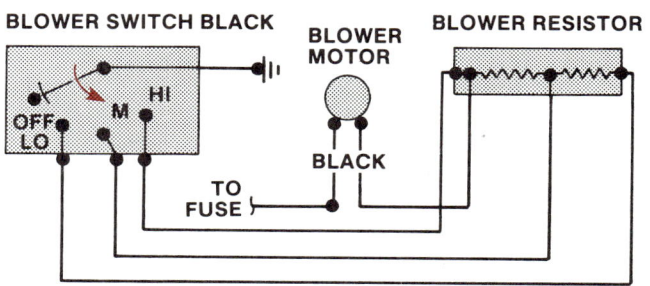

Figure 38-6 Blower motor wiring diagram.

motor, or an open-circuited radio noise capacitor at the blower motor. In situations where no current is available at the motor, backtrack to check for an open resistor. Check also for burned or corroded connections on the blower relays or bulkhead connectors. In-line fuses are another potential problem.

Sliding the heat selector control switch off on a vehicle without factory air conditioning closes a door that blocks the flow of air into the heater core. Even if the blower is turned on, no heat comes out because the air inlet is closed. On vehicles with factory air conditioning, a blend door usually routes some air through the heater core and some through the evaporator depending on the temperature range selected (Figure 38-7).

If the blower motor runs but no air comes out of the ducts, the problem is either a stuck or inoperative air-flow control or blend door. This can also affect the operation of the defrosters. These doors may be cable or vacuum operated.

Change the position of the temperature selector knob, sliding it from hot to cold. If the sound of doors opening and closing is not heard, the control cables can sometimes slip loose from the dash switch or door arm rendering the door inoperative. If this is the case, little or no resistance is felt when sliding the temperature control knob. A kinked or rusted cable can also prevent a door from working. If this is the case, resistance is felt trying to move the control knob. In either case, it is necessary to get under the dash, find the cable, and replace, reroute, or reconnect it. Doors can also be jammed by objects that have fallen down the defroster ducts. Remove the obstruction from the plenum by fishing through the heater outlet with a coat hanger or magnet, or remove the plenum.

With vacuum-controlled doors, the most common reasons for failure are leaky or loose vacuum hoses, or defective diaphragms in the little vacuum motors that move the doors. Check the vacuum by starting the

Figure 38-8 The operation of vacuum actuated valves can be checked using a hand-held vacuum pump. *Courtesy of Stant, Inc.*

engine and disconnecting the small hose that goes to the vacuum motor that works one of the doors. If you feel a vacuum or hear a hissing sound when trying different temperature settings, the vacuum source is good. If by applying vacuum to it with a hand-held pump, it moves and holds vacuum (Figure 38-8) the problem is a bad vacuum motor. If it does not, check for leaky vacuum hose connections, a defective temperature control switch, or a leaky vacuum reservoir under the dash or in the engine compartment.

A low coolant level can starve the heater resulting in little or no heat output. Check the coolant level in the radiator (not the overflow tank) to see if it is low. If low, adding coolant does not cure the problem until the problem of low coolant is found and fixed.

Air pockets can form in long heater hoses or where the heater is mounted higher than the radiator. To vent the trapped air, some vehicles have bleeder valves on the hoses. Opening the valves allows air to escape as the system is filled. The valves are then closed when coolant reaches their level. On vehicles that lack these special bleeder valves, it may be necessary to temporarily loosen the heater outlet hose so air can bleed out as the system is filled.

Heater and Defroster Duct Hoses

Transferring heated air from the heater core to passenger compartment heater and defroster outlets is the job of the heater and defroster duct hoses. These hoses vary in diameter from 1-1/2 inches to 6 inches. They are generally made by wrapping a continuous ply of elastomer (impregnated-and-coated fabric tape) and a plated reinforcing spring wire simultaneously so the

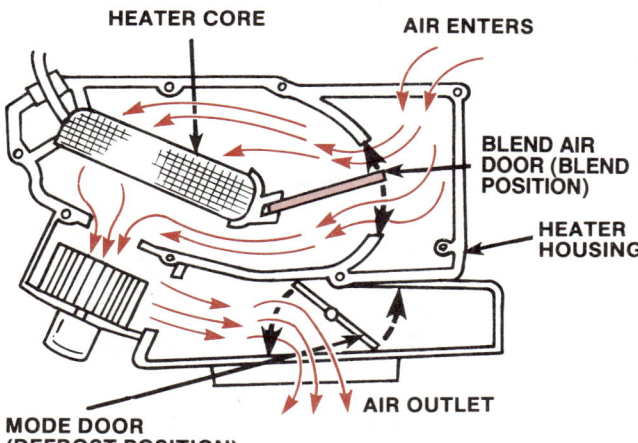

Figure 38-7 Typical blended air heater system. *Courtesy of General Motors Corp.*

wire is completely enclosed and bonded within the tape overlap. This construction improves rust protection since the wire is not exposed to condensation, and metal-to-metal contact is eliminated.

❏ HEATING SYSTEM SERVICE

When performing any checks and service procedures, always follow the procedures recommended in the manufacturer's service manual. In some cases, it is possible to make repairs to vacuum hose and electrical connections without removing the heater assembly. If it is necessary to remove the heater assembly, the cooling system must be drained before removing the heater core.

❏ THEORY OF AUTOMOTIVE AIR CONDITIONING

It is important for the technician to know the basic theory of automotive air-conditioning systems. Understanding how a system removes heat from the confined space of the passenger compartment and dissipates it into the atmosphere (Figure 38-9) will assist the technician in analyzing system failure and perform the required maintenance and service.

All air-conditioning systems are based on three fundamental laws of nature.

HEAT FLOW An air-conditioning system is designed to pump heat from one point to another. All materials or substances, as cold as -459 degrees Fahrenheit, have heat in them. Also, heat always flows from a warmer object to a colder one. For example, if one object is at 30 degrees Fahrenheit and another object at 80 degrees Fahrenheit, heat flows from the warmer object (80 degrees Fahrenheit) to the colder one (30 degrees Fahrenheit). The greater the temperature difference between the objects, the greater the amount of heat flow.

HEAT ABSORPTION Objects can be in one of three forms: solid, liquid, or gas. When objects change from one form to another, large amounts of heat can be transferred. For example, when water temperature goes below 32 degrees Fahrenheit, water changes from a liquid to a solid (ice). If the temperature of water is raised to 212 degrees Fahrenheit, the liquid turns into a gas (steam). But an interesting thing occurs when water, or any matter, changes from a solid to a liquid and then from a liquid to a gas. Additional heat is necessary to change the state of the substance, even though this heat does not register on a thermometer. For example, ice at 32 degrees Fahrenheit requires heat to change into water, which will also be at 32 degrees Fahrenheit. Additional heat raises the temperature of the water until it reaches the boiling point of 212 degrees Fahrenheit. More heat is required to change water into steam. But if the temperature of the steam was measured, it would also be 212 degrees Fahrenheit. The amount of heat necessary to change the state of a substance is called latent heat—or hidden heat—because it cannot be measured with a thermometer. This hidden heat is the basic principle behind all air-conditioning systems.

PRESSURE AND BOILING POINTS Pressure also plays an important part in air conditioning. Pressure on a substance, such as a liquid, changes its boiling point. The greater the pressure on a liquid, the higher the boiling point. If pressure is placed on a vapor, it condenses at a higher temperature. In addition, as the pressure on a substance is reduced, the boiling point can also be reduced. For example, the boiling point of water is 212 degrees Fahrenheit. The boiling point can be increased by increasing the pressure on the fluid. It can also be decreased by reducing the pressure or placing the fluid in a vacuum.

❏ THE AIR-CONDITIONING SYSTEM AND ITS COMPONENTS

An automotive air-conditioning system is a closed pressurized system. It consists of a compressor, condenser, receiver/dryer or accumulator, expansion valve or orifice tube, and an evaporator (Figure 38-10).

In a basic air-conditioning system, the heat is absorbed and transferred in the following steps (Figure 38-11).

1. Refrigerant leaves the compressor as a high-pressure, high-temperature vapor.
2. By removing heat via the condenser, the vapor becomes a high-pressure, lower-temperature liquid.

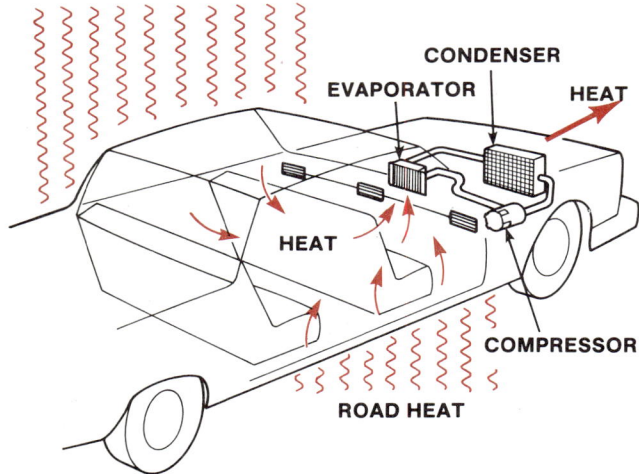

Figure 38-9 Heat flow from inside the car to outside. *Courtesy of Everco Industries, Inc.*

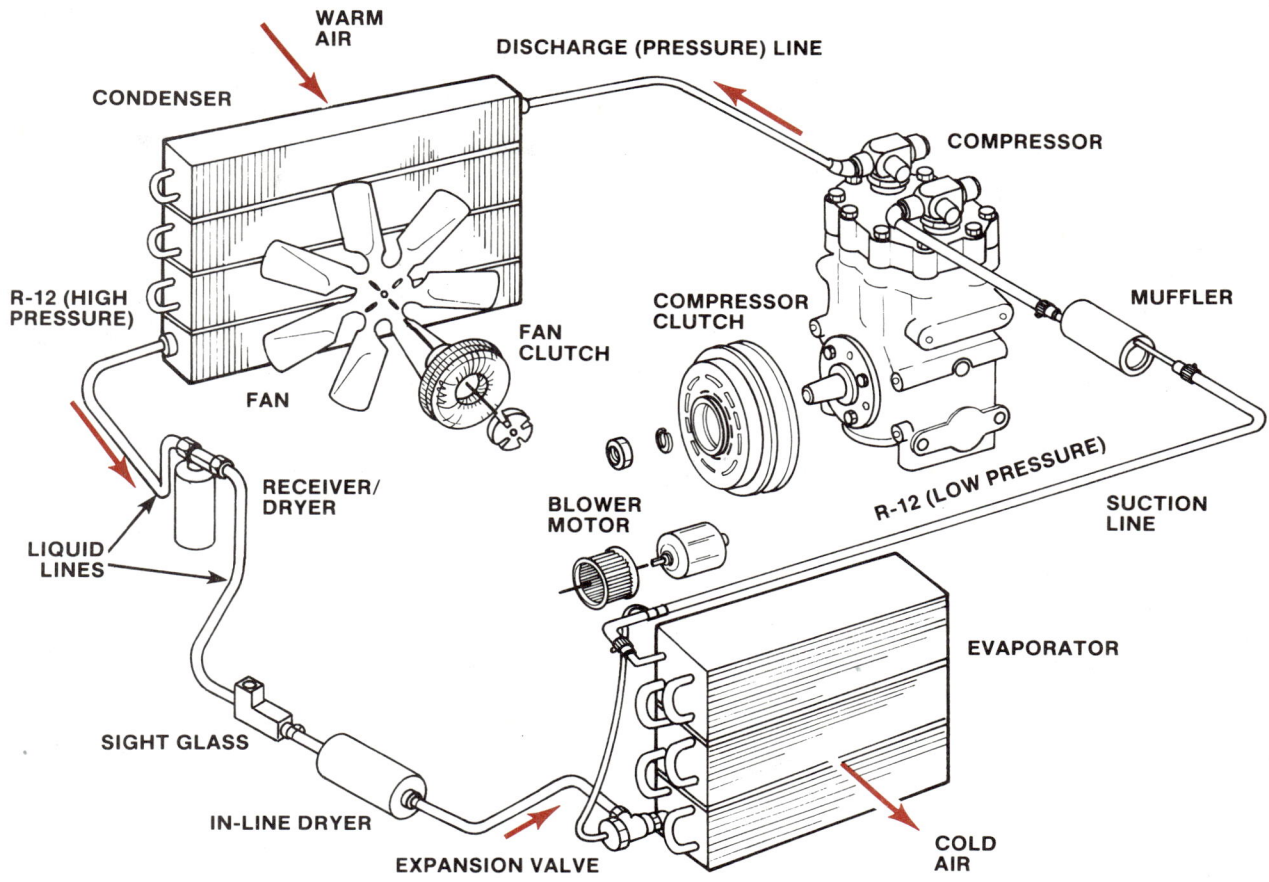

Figure 38-10 Major and secondary components of a typical air-conditioning system.

3. Moisture and contaminants are removed by the receiver/dryer, where the cleaned refrigerant is stored until it is needed.
4. The expansion valve converts the high-pressure liquid changes into a low-pressure liquid by controlling its flow into the evaporator.
5. Heat is absorbed from the air inside the passenger compartment by the low-pressure, low-temperature refrigerant, causing the liquid to vaporize.
6. The refrigerant returns to the compressor as a low-pressure, higher-temperature vapor.

To understand the operation of the five major components, remember that an air-conditioning system is divided into two sides: the high side and the low side. High side refers to the side of the system that is under high pressure and high temperature. Low side refers to the low-pressure, low-temperature side of the system.

The Compressor

The compressor is the heart of the automotive air-conditioning system. It separates the high-pressure and low-pressure sides of the system. The primary purpose of the unit is to draw the low-pressure vapor from the evaporator and compress this vapor into high-temperature, high-pressure vapor. This action results in the refrigerant having a higher temperature than surrounding air, and enables the condenser to condense the vapor back to a liquid. The secondary purpose of the compressor is to circulate or pump the refrigerant through the condenser under the different pressures required for proper operation. The compressor is located in the engine compartment.

Although there are numerous types of compressors in use today, they are usually one of two types.

PISTON COMPRESSOR This type of compressor (Figure 38-12) can have its pistons arranged in an in-line, axial, radial, or V design. It is designed to have an intake stroke and a compression stroke for each cylinder. On the intake stroke, the refrigerant from the low side of the system (evaporator) is drawn into the compressor. The intake of refrigerant occurs through intake reed valves. These one-way valves control the flow of refrigerant vapors into the cylinder. During the compression stroke, the vaporous refrigerant is compressed. This increases both the pressure and the temperature of the heat-carrying refrigerant. The outlet side (discharge) reed valves then open to allow the refrigerant to move to the condenser. The outlet reed valves are the beginning of the high side of the system. Reed valves are made of spring steel, which can be weakened or broken if improper charging procedures

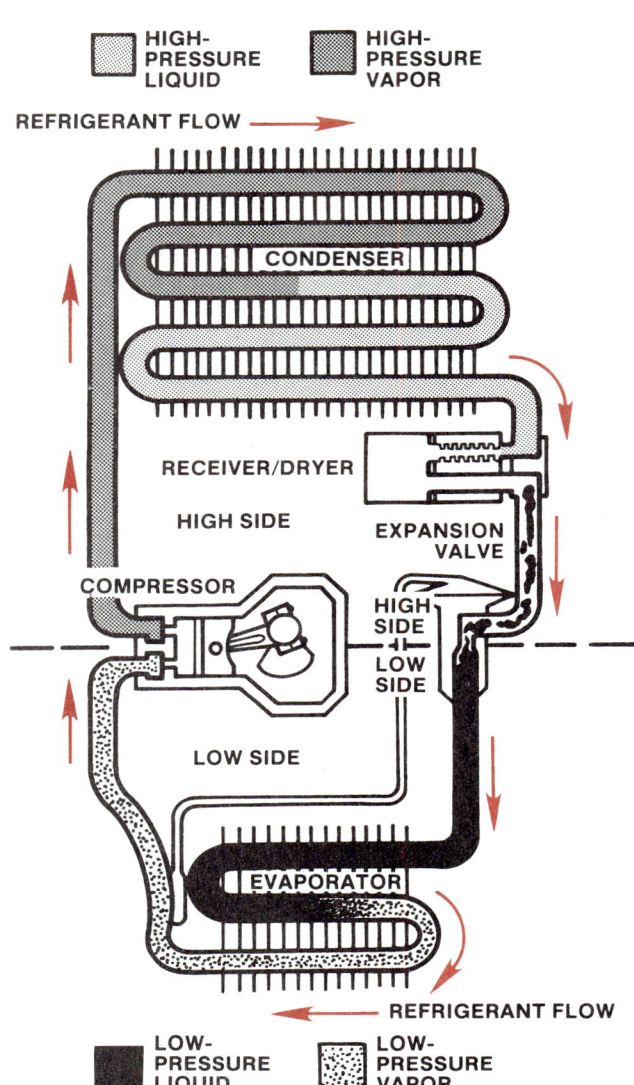

Figure 38-11 Basic refrigerant flow cycle.

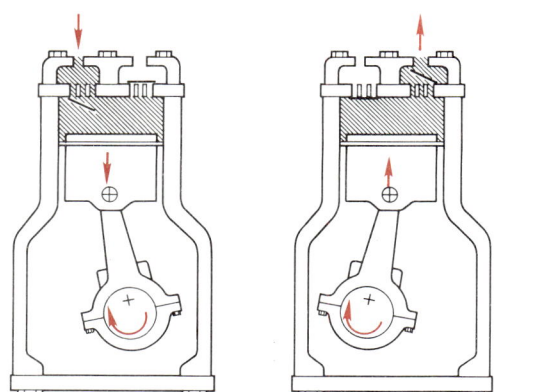

Figure 38-12 (A) Piston on the downstroke (intake) pulls low-pressure refrigerant into the cylinder cavity. The intake (suction) valve is open, and the discharge valve is closed. (B) Piston on the upstroke (discharge) compresses refrigerant vapor and forces it out through the discharge valve. The intake (suction) valve is closed, and the discharge valve is open.

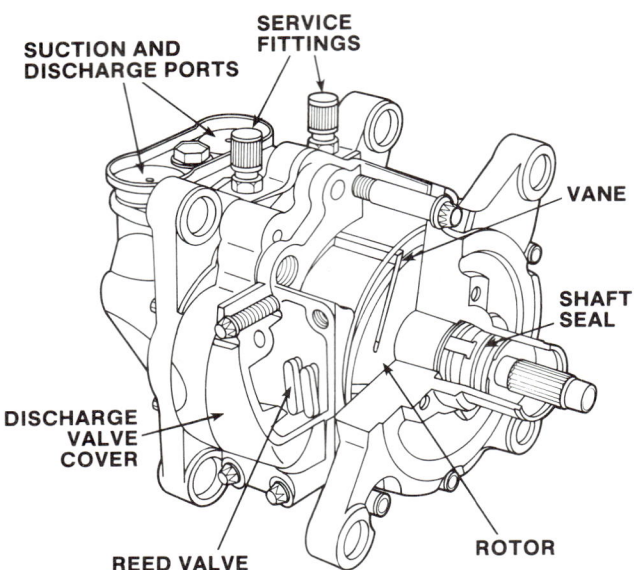

Figure 38-13 Cutaway view of a typical rotary vane compressor.

are used, such as liquid charging with the engine running.

ROTARY VANE COMPRESSOR This compressor does not have pistons (Figure 38-13). It consists of a rotor with several vanes and a carefully shaped housing. As the compressor shaft rotates, the vanes and housing form chambers. The refrigerant is drawn through the suction port into these chambers, which become smaller as the rotor turns. The discharge port is located at the point where the gas is completely compressed. No sealing rings are used in a vane compressor. The vanes are sealed against the housing by centrifugal force and lubricating oil. The oil sump is located on the discharge side, so the high pressure tends to force it around the vanes into the low-pressure side. This action ensures continuous lubrication. Because this type of compressor depends on a good oil supply, it is subject to damage if the system charge is lost. A protection device is used to disengage the clutch if pressure drops too low.

Every compressor is equipped with an electromagnetic clutch as part of the compressor pulley assembly (Figure 38-14). It is designed to engage the pulley to the compressor shaft when the clutch coil is energized. The purpose of the clutch is to transmit power from the engine to the compressor and to provide a means of engaging and disengaging the refrigeration system from engine operation.

The clutch is driven by power from the engine's crankshaft, which is transmitted through one or more belts (a few use gears) to the pulley, which is in operation whenever the engine is running. When the clutch is engaged, power is transmitted from the pulley to the compressor shaft by the clutch drive plate. When the clutch is not engaged, the compressor shaft does not rotate, and the pulley freewheels.

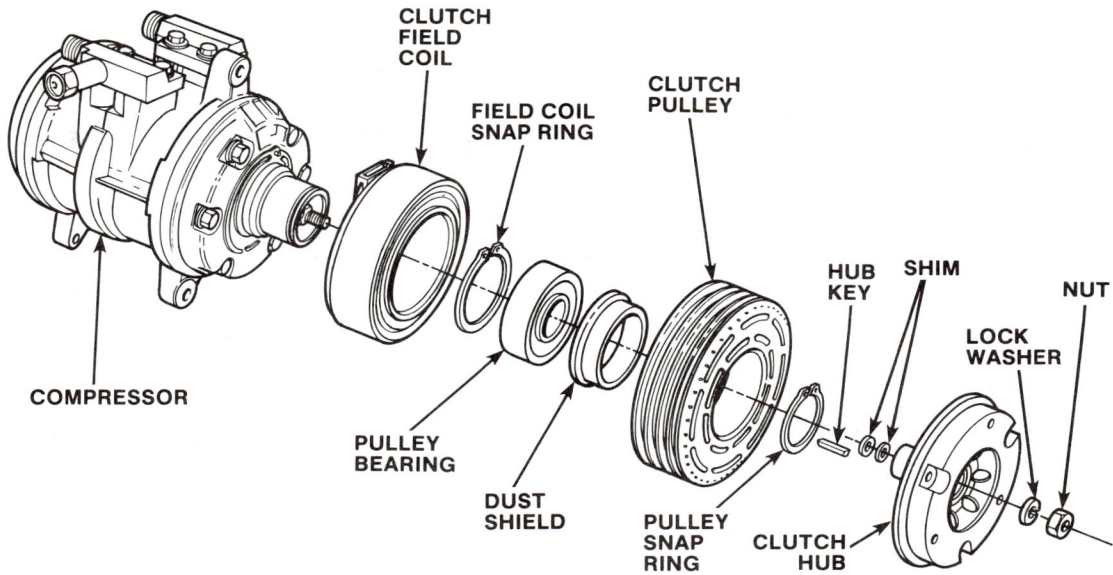

Figure 38-14 Parts of a compressor clutch assembly.

The clutch is engaged by a magnetic field and disengaged by springs when the magnetic field is broken. When the controls call for compressor operation, the electrical circuit to the clutch is completed, the magnetic clutch is energized, and the clutch engages the compressor. When the electrical circuit is opened, the clutch disengages the compressor.

Two types of electromagnetic clutches have been in use for many years. Early-model air-conditioning systems used a rotating coil clutch. The magnetic coil, which engages or disengages the compressor, is mounted within the pulley and rotates with it. Electrical connections for the clutch operation are made through a stationary brush assembly and rotating slip rings, which are part of the field coil assembly. This older rotating coil clutch, now in limited use, has been largely replaced by the stationary coil clutch.

With the stationary coil, wear has been measurably reduced, efficiency increased, and serviceability made much easier. The clutch coil does not rotate. When the driver first energizes the air-conditioning system from the passenger compartment dashboard, the pulley assembly is magnetically drawn to the stationary coil on the compressor body, thus engaging the clutch and activating the air-conditioning system. Depending on the system, the magnetic clutch is usually thermostatically controlled to cycle the operation of the compressor (depending on system temperature or pressure). In some system designs, the clutch might operate continually when the system is turned on. With stationary coil design, service is not usually necessary except for an occasional check on the electrical connections.

Condenser

The condenser (Figure 38-15) consists of a refrigerant coil tube mounted in a series of thin cooling fins to

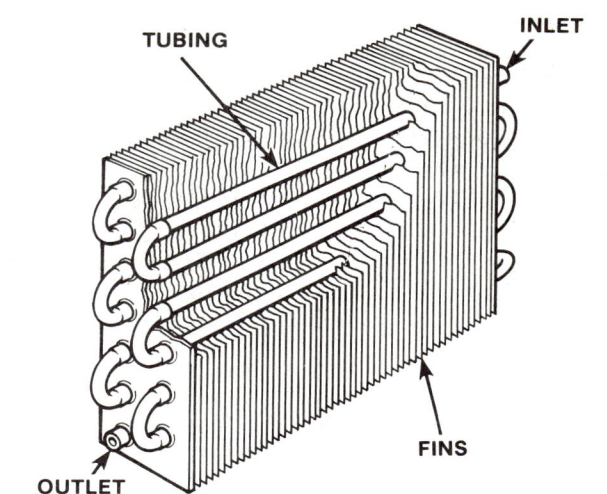

Figure 38-15 Typical condenser.

provide maximum heat transfer in a minimum amount of space. The condenser is normally mounted just in front of the vehicle's radiator. It receives the full flow of ram air from the movement of the vehicle.

The purpose of the condenser is to condense or liquefy the high-pressure hot vapor coming from the compressor. To do so, it must give up its heat. The condenser receives very hot, high-pressure refrigerant vapor from the compressor through its discharge hose. The refrigerant vapor enters the inlet at the top of the condenser and as the hot vapor passes down through the condenser coils, heat (following its natural tendencies) moves from the hot refrigerant into the cooler air as it flows across the condenser coils and fins. This process causes a large quantity of heat to be transferred to the outside air and the refrigerant to change from a high-pressure hot vapor to a high-pressure warm liquid. This high-pressure warm liquid flows from the outlet at the bottom of the condenser through a line to the receiver/dryer.

In an air-conditioning system, which is operating under an average heat load, the condenser has a combination of hot refrigerant vapor in the upper two-thirds of its coils. The lower third of the coils contains the warm liquid refrigerant, which has condensed. This high-pressure, liquid refrigerant flows from the condenser and on toward the evaporator. In effect, the condenser is a true heat exchanger.

Receiver/Dryer and Accumulator

The receiver/dryer (Figure 38-16) is a storage tank for the liquid refrigerant from the condenser, which flows into the upper portion of the receiver tank containing a bag of desiccant (moisture-absorbing material such as silica alumina, molecular sieve, or silica gel). As the refrigerant flows through an opening in the lower portion of the receiver, it is filtered through a mesh screen attached to a baffle at the bottom of the receiver. The desiccant in this assembly is to absorb any moisture that might be present that might enter the system during assembly. These features of the assembly prevent obstruction to the valves or damage to the compressor.

Depending on the manufacturer, the receiver/dryer may be known by other names such as filter, dehydrator, or accumulator. Regardless of its name, the function is the same. Included in many receiver/dryers are additional features such as a high-pressure fitting, a pressure relief valve, and a sight glass for determining the condition of the refrigerant in the system.

The receiver/dryer is often neglected when the air-conditioning system is serviced or repaired. Failure to replace it can lead to poor system performance or replacement part failure. It is recommended that the receiver/dryer or its desiccant be changed whenever a component is replaced, the system has lost the refrigerant charge, or the system has been open to the atmosphere for any length of time.

Refrigerant

R-12 is a nontoxic, nonflammable, and nonexplosive refrigerant. However, breathing large quantities of R-12 should be avoided. Doing so displaces oxygen in the lungs. Due to the fact that R-12 has a boiling point of -21.7 degrees Fahrenheit at sea level, it is necessary to contain it at pressures appreciably above atmospheric, which warrants special handling precautions.

Although R-12 is a good automotive air-conditioning refrigerant, it is apparently a major contributor to the destruction of the earth's ozone layer, the outermost shield of protection. This delicate layer protects against harmful effects of the sun's ultraviolet rays. The thinning of the ozone layer has become a worldwide concern. The ozone depletion is caused in part by release of chlorofluorocarbons (CFCs) into the atmosphere. All automotive refrigerants currently used are in the chemical family of CFCs.

Both the chemical and automotive industries have been investigating possible successors to R-12. Several ozone-safe blends that can be substituted for R-12 when an air-conditioning system is serviced are being developed.

Thermostatic Expansion Valve/Orifice Tube

The refrigerant flow to the evaporator must be controlled to obtain maximum cooling, while assuring complete evaporation of the liquid refrigerant within the evaporator. This is accomplished by a thermostatic expansion valve (TEV) or a fixed orifice tube.

The TEV is mounted at the inlet to the evaporator and separates the high-pressure side of the system from the low-pressure side. The TEV regulates refrigerant flow to the evaporator to prevent evaporator flooding. In operation, the TEV regulates the R-12 flow to the evaporator by balancing the inlet flow to the outlet temperature.

Both external and internal equalized TEVs are used in air-conditioning systems (Figure 38-17). The only difference between the two valves is that the external TEV uses an equalizer line connected to the evaporator outlet line as a means of sensing evaporator outlet pressure. The internal TEV senses evaporator inlet pressure through an internal equalizer passage. Both

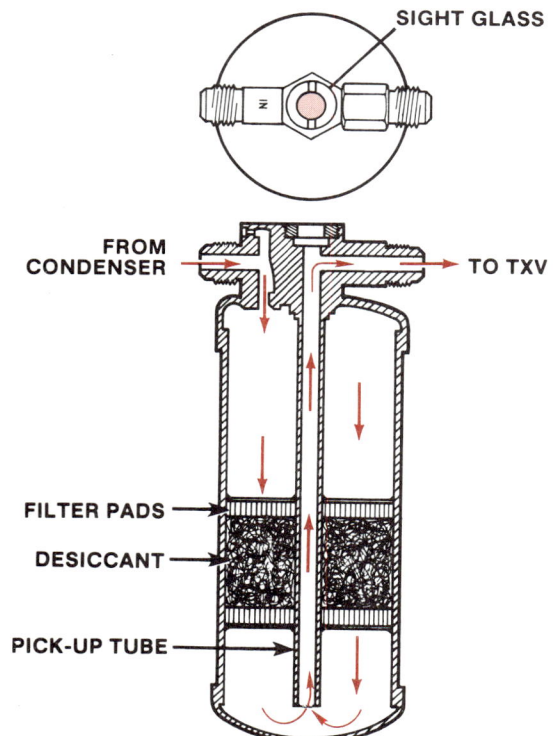

Figure 38-16 Typical receiver/dryer.

Heating and Air Conditioning 979

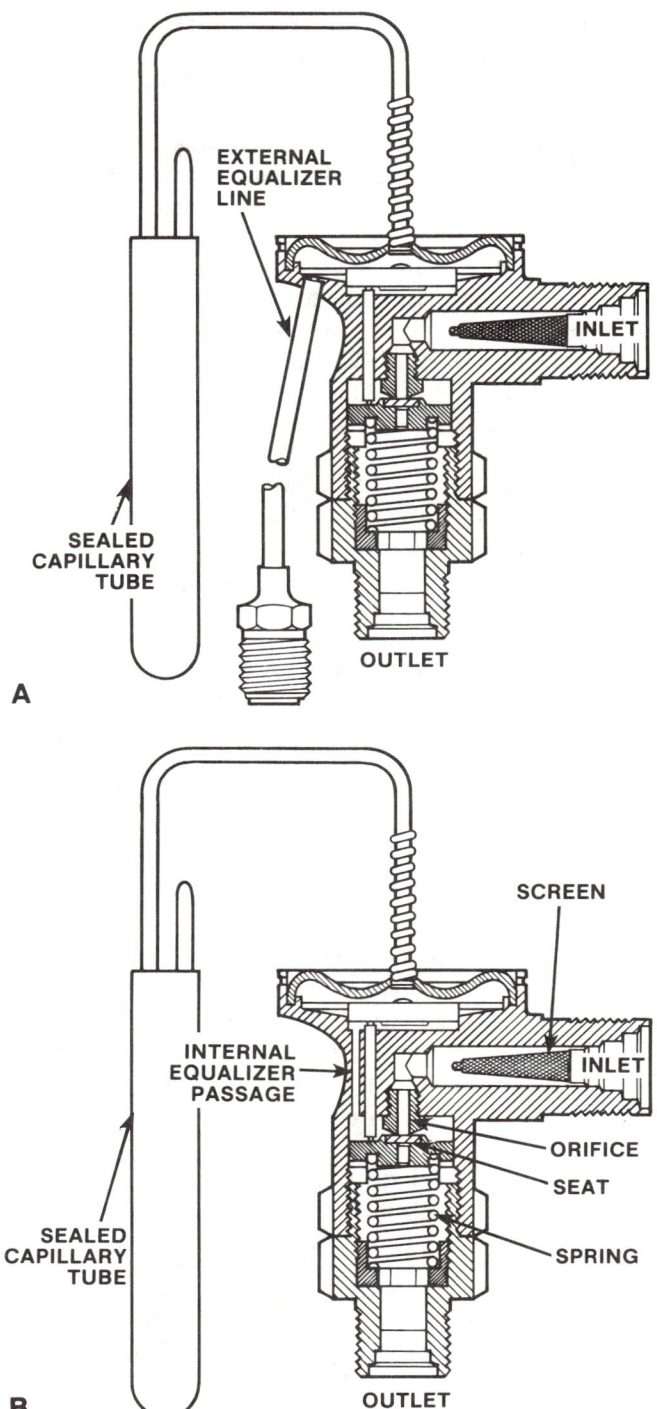

Figure 38-17 Cross-sectional views of thermostatic expansion valves: (A) externally equalized and (B) internally equalized.

valves have a capillary tube to sense evaporator outlet temperature.

During stabilized conditions (vehicle shutdown), the pressure on the bottom of the expansion valve diaphragm rises above the pressure on the top of the diaphragm. This allows the valve spring to close the valve. When the system is started, the pressure on the bottom of the diaphragm drops rapidly, allowing the valve to open and meter liquid refrigerant to the lower evaporator tubes where it begins to vaporize.

Compressor suction draws the vaporized refrigerant out of the top of the evaporator at the top tube where it passes the sealed sensing bulb. The bottom of the valve diaphragm internally senses the evaporator pressure through the internal equalization passage around the sealed sensing bulb. As evaporator pressure is increased, the diaphragm flexes upward pulling the sensing bulb and pushrod away from the ball seat of the expansion valve. The expansion valve spring forces the ball onto the tapered seat and the liquid refrigerant flow is reduced.

As the pressure is reduced due to restricted refrigerant flow, the diaphragm flexes downward again, opening the expansion valve to provide the required controlled pressure and refrigerant flow condition. The sensing bulb produces the required pressure on top of the diaphragm. As the cool refrigerant passes the body of the sensing bulb, the gas above the diaphragm contracts and allows the expansion valve spring to close the expansion valve. When heat from the passenger compartment is absorbed by the refrigerant, it causes the gas to expand. The pushrod again forces the expansion valve to open, allowing more refrigerant to flow so that more heat can be absorbed.

Like the thermostatic expansion valve, the orifice tube (Figure 38-18) is the dividing point between the high- and low-pressure parts of the system. However, its metering or flow rate control does not depend on comparing evaporator pressure and temperature. It is a fixed orifice. The flow rate is determined by pressure difference across the orifice and by subcooling. Subcooling is additional cooling of the refrigerant in the bottom of the condenser after it has changed from vapor to liquid. The flow rate through the orifice is more sensitive to subcooling than to pressure difference.

Evaporator

The evaporator, like the condenser, consists of a refrigerant coil mounted in a series of thin cooling fins (Figure 38-19). It provides a maximum amount of heat transfer in a minimum amount of space. The evaporator is usually located beneath the dashboard or instrument panel.

Upon receiving the low-pressure, low-temperature liquid refrigerant from the thermostatic expansion valve or orifice tube in the form of an atomized (or

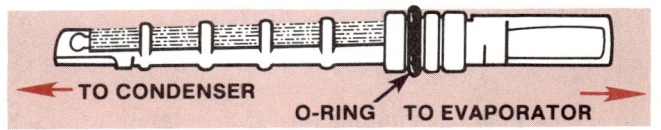

Figure 38-18 Typical orifice expansion tube.

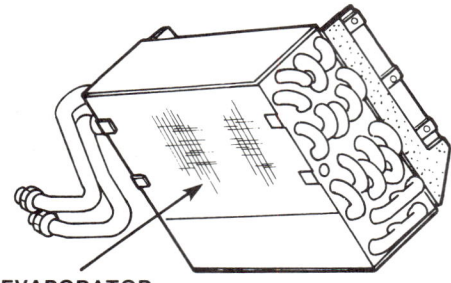

Figure 38-19 Typical evaporator.

droplet) spray, the evaporator serves as a boiler or vaporizer. This regulated flow of refrigerant boils immediately. Heat from the core surface is lost to the boiling and vaporizing refrigerant, which is cooler than the core, thereby cooling the core. The air passing over the evaporator loses its heat to the cooler surface of the core, thereby cooling the air inside the car. As the process of heat loss from air to the evaporator core surface is taking place, any moisture (humidity) in the air condenses on the outside of the evaporator core and is drained off as water. A drain tube in the bottom of the evaporator housing leads the water outside the vehicle. This dehumidification of the air is an added feature of the air-conditioning system that adds to passenger comfort. It can also be used as a means of controlling fogging of the vehicle windows. Under certain conditions, however, too much moisture can accumulate on the evaporator coils. An example would be when humidity is extremely high and the maximum cooling mode is selected. The evaporator temperature might become so low that moisture would freeze on the evaporator coils before it can drain off.

Through the metering, or controlling, action of the thermostatic expansion valve or orifice tube, greater or lesser amounts of refrigerant are provided in the evaporator to adequately cool the car under all heat load conditions. If too much refrigerant is allowed to enter, the evaporator floods. This results in poor cooling due to the higher pressure (and temperature) of the refrigerant. The refrigerant can neither boil away rapidly nor vaporize. On the other hand, if too little refrigerant is metered, the evaporator starves. Poor cooling again results because the refrigerant boils away or vaporizes too quickly before passing through the evaporator.

The temperature of the refrigerant vapor at the evaporator outlet will be approximately 4 to 16 degrees Fahrenheit higher than the temperature of the liquid refrigerant at the evaporator inlet. This temperature differential is the superheat that ensures that the vapor will not contain any droplets of liquid refrigerant that would be harmful to the compressor.

Refrigerant Lines

All the major components of the system have inlet and outlet connections that accommodate either flare or O-ring fittings. The refrigerant lines that connect between these units are made up of an appropriate length of hose or tubing with flare or O-ring fittings at each end as required. In either case the hose or tube end of the fitting is constructed with sealing beads to accommodate a hose or tube clamp connection.

There are two major refrigerant lines. Suction lines are located between the outlet side of the evaporator and the inlet (suction) side of the compressor. They carry the low-pressure, low-temperature refrigerant vapor to the compressor where it again is recycled through the system. Suction lines are always distinguished from the discharge lines by touch. They are cold to the touch. The second type of refrigerant lines is discharge lines. Beginning at the discharge outlet on the compressor, the discharge or high-pressure lines connect the compressor to the condenser, the condenser to the receiver/dryer, and the receiver/dryer to the inlet side of the expansion valve. Through these lines, the refrigerant travels in its path from a gas state (compressor outlet) to a liquid state (condenser outlet) and then to the inlet side of the expansion valve where it vaporizes on entry to the evaporator. Discharge lines are always very warm to the touch and easily distinguishable from the suction lines.

Sight Glass

The sight glass allows the technician to see the flow of refrigerant in the lines. It can be located on the receiver/dryer or in-line between the receiver/dryer and the expansion valve or tube (Figure 38-20).

To check the refrigerant, open the windows and doors, set the controls for maximum cooling, and set the blower on its highest speed. Let the system run for about five minutes. Be sure the vehicle is in a well-ventilated area, or connect an exhaust gas ventilation system.

Use care to check the sight glass while the engine is running. If oil-streaking is seen, this indicates that the

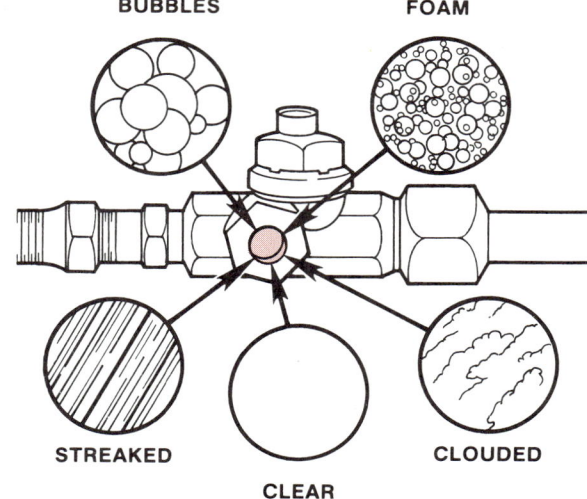

Figure 38-20 Typical sight glass location and appearances.

system is empty. Bubbles, or foam, indicate that the refrigerant is low. A sufficient level of refrigerant is indicated by what looks like a flow of clear water, with no bubbles. A clouded sight glass is an indication of desiccant breakdown with subsequent infiltration and circulation through the system.

Many newer air-conditioning systems are not equipped with a sight glass. Pressure and performance testing are the only ways to identify low refrigerant levels.

In-Line Dryer

Located between the receiver/dryer and expansion valve or tube, an in-line dryer absorbs any moisture that gets by the receiver/dryer. It also helps to prevent expansion valve or tube freeze-up.

Muffler

Some vehicle air-conditioning systems now have a muffler installed in the system. The muffler is usually located on the discharge side of the compressor. The muffler acts to reduce characteristic pumping noises of the compressor. To further reduce compressor noise transfer through the body to the passenger compartment, a sheet of soft rubber insulation is wrapped around the outside of the muffler on some models. Mufflers should be installed with inlet connection at the top and outlet connection at the bottom. This minimizes collection of oil in the unit.

Blower Motor/Fan

The blower motor/fan assembly is located in the evaporator housing. Its purpose is to increase airflow in the passenger compartment (Figure 38-21). The blower, which is basically the same type as those used in heater systems, draws warm air from the compartment, forces it over the coils and fins of the evaporator, and blows the cooled, dehumidified air into the passenger compartment. The blower motor is controlled by a fan switch.

During cold weather, the blower motor/fan assembly provides warm air to heat the passenger compartment.

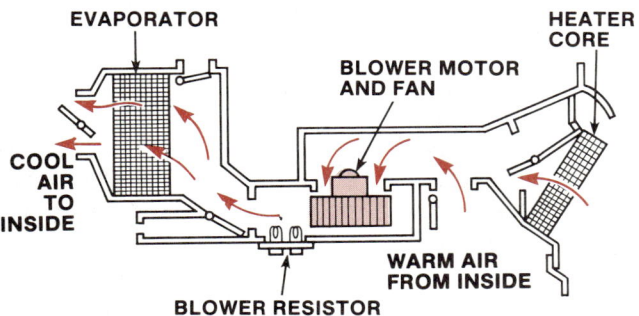

Figure 38-21 Blower fan increases airflow.

☐ AIR-CONDITIONING SYSTEMS AND CONTROLS

There are two basic types of automotive air-conditioning systems. They are classified according to the method used in obtaining temperature control and are known as a cycling clutch system or an evaporator pressure control system.

Cycling Clutch System

In every cycling clutch system, the compressor is run intermittently through controlling the application and release of its clutch by a thermostatic switch. The thermostatic switch senses the evaporator's outlet air temperature, through a capillary tube that is part of the switch assembly. With a high sensing temperature, the thermostatic switch is closed and the compressor clutch is energized. As the evaporator outlet temperature drops to a preset level, the thermostatic switch opens the circuit to the compressor clutch. The compressor then ceases to operate until such time as the evaporator temperature rises above the switch setting. From this on and off operation is derived the term cycling clutch. In effect, the thermostatic switch is calibrated to allow the lowest possible evaporator outlet temperature that prevents the freezing of condensation that might form on the evaporator.

Variations of the cycling clutch system include a system with a thermostatic expansion valve and a system with an orifice tube.

Cycling Clutch System with Thermostatic Expansion Valve

Some factory installations utilize a cycling clutch system that incorporates a TEV and receiver/dryer. The evaporator and control components are either in the engine compartment or an integral part of the cowl. In such cases there is a common blower and duct work for both heating and air-conditioning purposes. Also in these installations, the thermostatic switch has no temperature control knob and is usually mounted on the evaporator or its case. Temperature control is accomplished by using fresh or recirculating air and by reheating the cooled air in the heater core. The clutch cycles only to prevent evaporator icing.

A common form of the cycling clutch system is the field-installed (hang-on) unit. With this installation, the evaporator, the thermostatic expansion valve, and thermostatic switch are self-contained in an underdash assembly. An installation of this type operates solely on passenger compartment recirculated air. Temperature control depends on intermittent operation of the compressor. The thermostatic switch has a control knob to change its setting and allow the compressor clutch to cycle at higher temperatures when less cooling is desired.

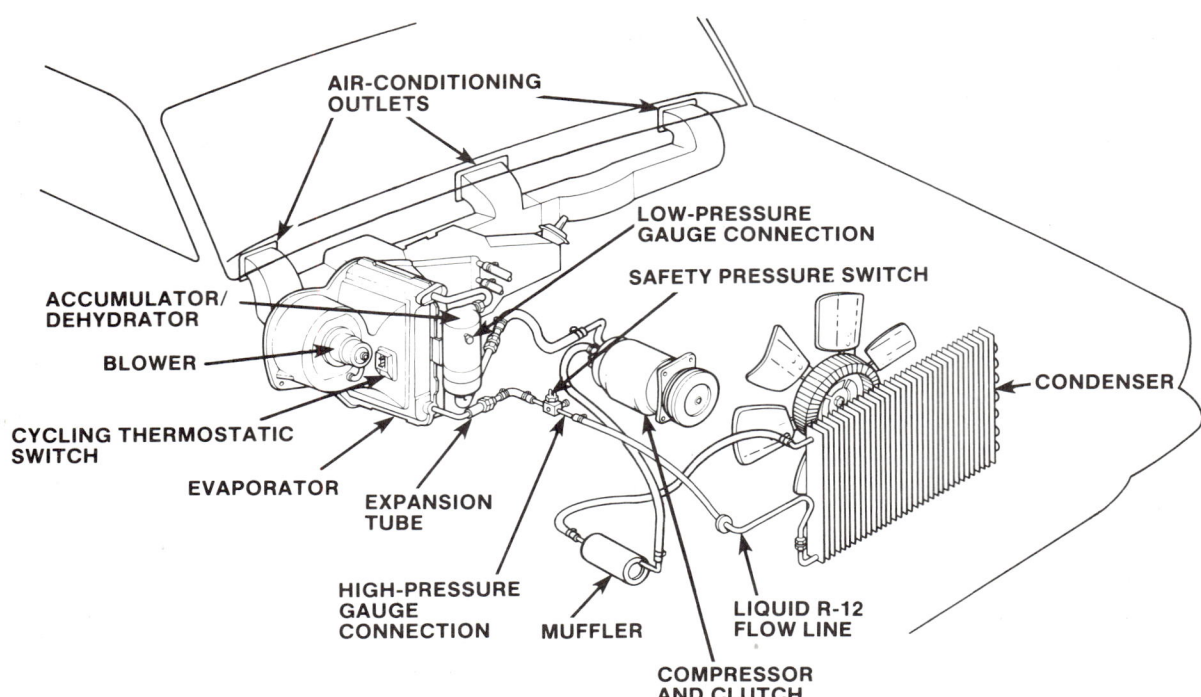

Figure 38-22 Typical cycling clutch system with expansion (orifice) tube.

Cycling Clutch System with Orifice Tube (CCOT)

A typical CCOT system is illustrated in Figure 38-22. The system is factory installed and can use a thermostatic clutch cycling switch mounted on the evaporator case or a pressure cycling switch located on the accumulator. An expansion (orifice) tube is used in place of the TEV. Also, the system has an accumulator in the evaporator outlet. The accumulator is used primarily to separate vapor from liquid refrigerant before it enters the compressor. It also contains a drying agent or desiccant to remove moisture. The CCOT system has no receiver/dryer or sight glass.

Evaporator Pressure Control System

In this type of system the compressor operates continually when dash controls are in the air-conditioning position. Evaporator outlet air temperature is automatically controlled by an evaporator pressure control valve such as the STV, POA, or EPR. This type of valve throttles the flow of refrigerant through the evaporator as required to establish a minimum evaporator pressure and thereby prevent freezing of condensation on the evaporator core. Maximum evaporator pressure is also established by this valve.

POA Valve System

Figure 38-23 shows a typical air-conditioning system that utilizes a POA valve to control evaporator temperature. In this system both evaporator and heater cores are incorporated in an air distribution duct work that is an integral part of the cowl and dash assembly. Operator controls actuate a series of air doors within the duct work that make it possible to select maximum air-conditioning or maximum heated air, as well as any combination of the two that might be desired for passenger comfort. In diagnosis work it is essential to differentiate between malfunctions that might exist in the refrigeration components and those that might be present in the air-distribution section. For comparison purposes with the cycling clutch system, remember that the compressor operates continually and that defrosting control is accomplished by the POA valve. This valve is connected in the refrigerant system between the evaporator outlet and the compressor inlet. An equalizer line (pressure sensing) connects from the POA valve to the in-line TEV. Also, an oil by-pass or liquid bleed line connects from the bottom of the evaporator to the POA valve. Its purpose is to insure sufficient oil circulation to the compressor if the POA valve sticks in a closed position. The remaining connector on the POA valve is for the purpose of taking low-pressure readings with manifold test gauges.

Valves-In-Receiver (VIR) System

This assembly incorporates the POA, TEV, and receiver/dryer into one assembly. The VIR assembly is mounted close to the evaporator and is connected to both the evaporator inlet and outlet pipes. The basic refrigeration system components for a VIR system are shown in Figure 38-24.

The TEV's equalizer function is built into the VIR assembly. The liquid bleed line (oil by-pass line) connects from the evaporator bottom to the VIR (outlet).

Heating and Air Conditioning 983

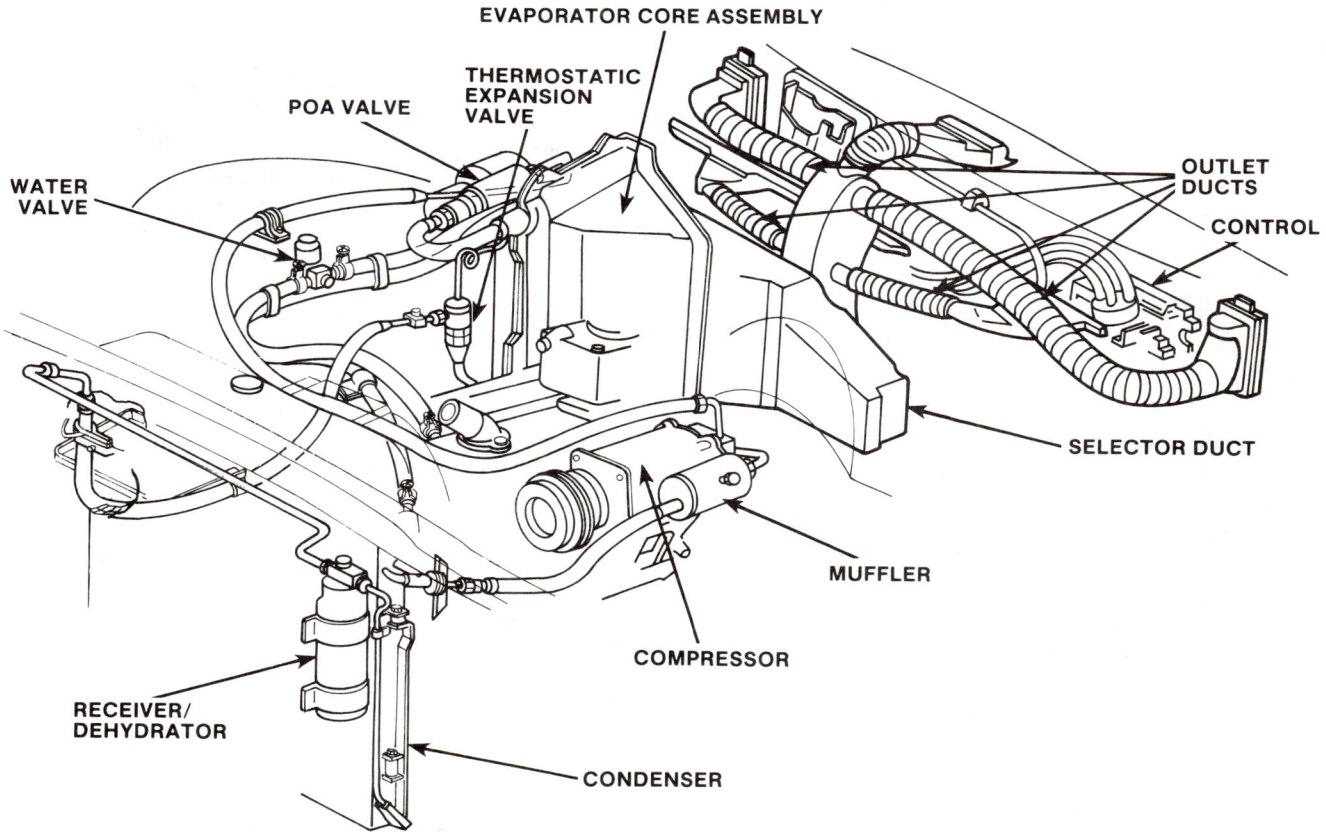

Figure 38-23 Typical evaporator pressure control system with POA valve.

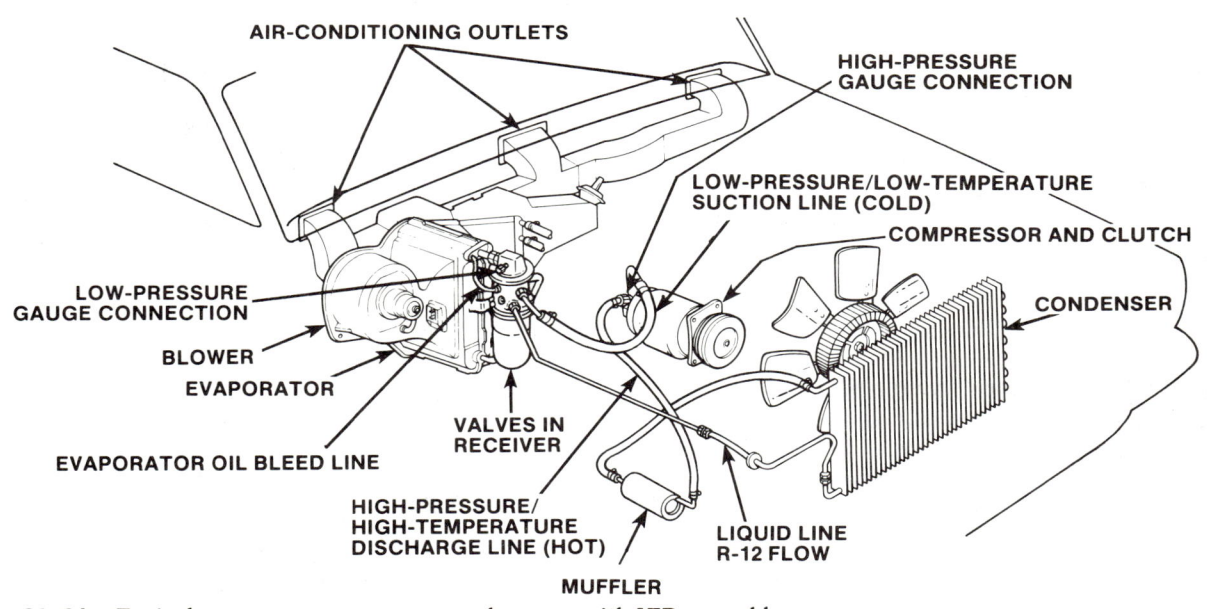

Figure 38-24 Typical evaporator pressure control system with VIR assembly.

To improve the efficiency of the compressor and evaporator, special supplemental controls are needed.

Compressor Controls

There are many controls used to monitor and maintain the compressor during its operational cycle. Each of these represents the most common protective control devices designed to ensure safe and reliable operation of the compressor.

Ambient Temperature Switch

This switch senses outside air temperature and is designed to prevent compressor clutch engagement when air conditioning is not required or when compressor operation might cause internal damage to seals and other parts.

The switch is in series with the compressor clutch electrical circuit and closes at about 37 degrees Fahrenheit. At all lower temperatures, the switch is open, preventing clutch engagement.

On some vehicles, the ambient switch is located in the air inlet duct of the air-conditioning systems that are regulated by evaporator pressure controls. Other makes have it installed near the radiator. It is not required on systems with a thermostatic switch.

Thermostatic Switch

In cycling clutch systems, the thermostatic switch is placed in series with the compressor clutch circuit so that it can turn the clutch on or off. It has two purposes. It de-energizes the clutch and stops the compressor if the evaporator is at the freezing point. On hang-on units or systems without reheat temperature control, it also controls the air temperature by turning the compressor on and off intermittently. For this purpose it has a control knob to change the switch setting.

When the temperature of the evaporator approaches the freezing point (or the low setting of the switch), the thermostatic switch opens the circuit and disengages the compressor clutch. The compressor remains inoperative until the evaporator temperature rises to the preset temperature, at which time the switch closes and compressor operation resumes.

Pressure Cycling Switch

This switch is electrically connected in series with the compressor electromagnetic clutch. Like the thermostatic switch, the turning on and off of the pressure cycling switch controls the operation of the compressor.

Low-Pressure Cutoff or Discharge Pressure Switch

This switch is located on the high side of the system and senses any low-pressure conditions (Figure 38-25). It is tied into the compressor clutch circuit, allowing it to immediately disengage the clutch when the pressure falls too low.

High-Pressure Cutout Switch

This switch, normally located in the vicinity of the compressor or discharge (high side) muffler, is wired with the compressor clutch (in series). Designed to open (cut out) and disengage the clutch at 350 to 375 psi, it again closes and normally reengages the clutch when pressure returns to 250 psi.

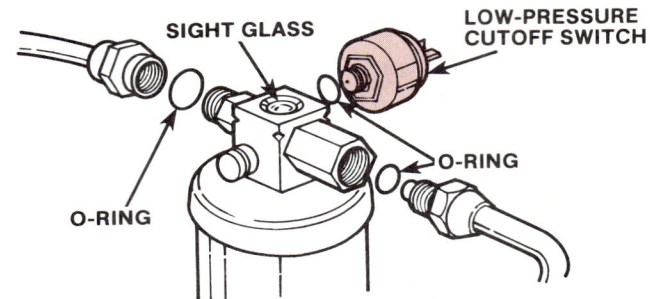

Figure 38-25 Low-pressure cutoff switch.

Thermal Limiter and Superheat Switch

A thermal limiter (fuse) and superheat switch, designed to protect the air-conditioning compressor against damage when the refrigerant charge is partially or totally lost, are incorporated in some vehicles. The thermal fuse can be found in various underhood locations. The superheat switch is located in the rear head of the compressor (Figure 38-26). The fuse and switch are connected in series by an electrical lead.

The thermal limiter on underhood applications should not be moved from its initial location because varying underhood ambients could result in improper operation of the switch.

During normal air-conditioning system operation, current flows through the control head switch, ambient switch, and thermal fuse to the clutch coil to actuate the compressor clutch. If a partial or total loss of refrigerant occurs in the system, the contacts in the superheat switch close as the switch senses low system

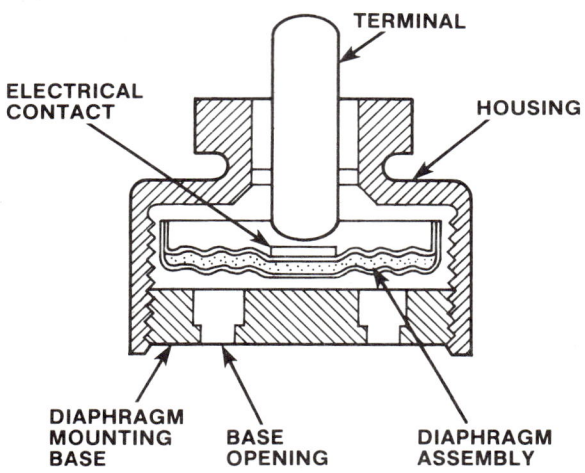

Figure 38-26 Superheat switch.

pressure and high suction gas temperature. When the contacts close, current flows to energize a resistor heater in the thermal fuse.

The resultant heat melts the fuse link, and the circuit to the compressor clutch coil opens. Compressor operation ceases and damage due to loss of refrigerant charge is prevented. Before thermal fuse replacement, the cause of the refrigerant loss must be corrected and the system charged. It is serviceable only as a unit.

The superheat switch is sealed in the rear head by means of an O-ring between the switch housing and head. A specially formed retainer ring holds the switch in place and electrically grounds the switch housing to the compressor.

High-Pressure Relief Valve

A high-pressure relief valve is incorporated into many air-conditioning systems. This valve may be installed on the receiver/dryer, compressor, or elsewhere in the high side of the system. It is a high-pressure protection device that opens to bleed off excessive pressure that might occur in the system.

Evaporator Controls

Evaporator controls maintain a back pressure in the evaporator. Because of the refrigerant temperature/pressure relationship, the effect is to regulate evaporator temperature. The temperature is controlled to a point that provides effective air cooling but prevents the freezing of moisture that condenses on the evaporator. As noted earlier, the POA valve is incorporated in the VIR assembly in some systems.

Suction Throttling Valve (STV)

The suction throttling valve determines the temperature of the evaporator core by limiting the minimum evaporator pressure. The valve in this manner also protects the core against freeze-up, which would result in a partial or complete loss of cooling capacity. While the system is in operation, the evaporator is held to a minimum pressure of 28 psi and provides maximum cooling at all times. The evaporator pressure holds at this level as long as maximum cooling is desired by the occupants of the car.

The STV valve (Figure 38-27) is located in the evaporator outlet line. It operates on a spring pressure versus evaporator pressure principle. In operation, the flow of low-pressure vapor from the evaporator to the compressor is determined and controlled by the position of the piston in the valve body, which is in turn determined by the balance of the forces applied to the diaphragm. Refrigerant vapor flows through the valve inlet, through three openings in the lower skirt of the piston, and from there through the valve outlet and the

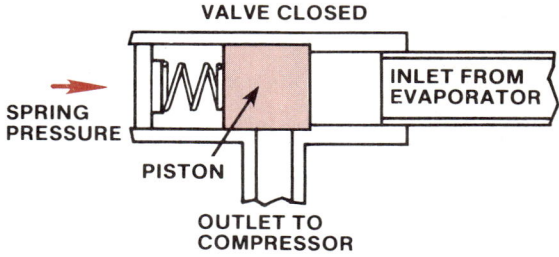

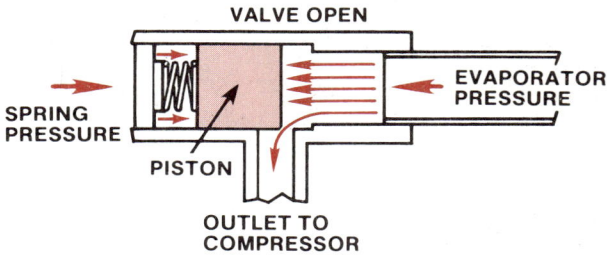

Figure 38-27 Action of a suction throttling valve (STV). Located in the evaporator outlet, it senses evaporator pressure to control R-12 flow and temperature. *Courtesy of General Motors Corp.*

suction hose to the compressor. A very small portion of the vapor flow is diverted to the interior of the piston through drilled holes in the piston wall. This pressure, transmitted to the inner side of the diaphragm, permits it to sense the actual pressure in the evaporator. Evaporator vapor pressure applied on the inner side of the diaphragm and piston assembly is balanced and opposed by spring load plus atmospheric pressure applied to the outer surface of the diaphragm. An increase of temperature and pressure in the evaporator causes the piston to move against the opposing spring pressure, opening the valve and allowing an increasing amount of vapor to flow through the valve to the compressor. This in turn lowers the evaporator pressure and allows the piston to close as required. Evaporator pressure is controlled to a predetermined setting by the action of the valve in throttling or choking off the suction line when evaporator pressure drops below the established setting. With the line restricted, the evaporator pressure rises. As the pressure rises above the valve setting, the valve is forced open as required to bring the pressure down to the proper level.

Pilot-Operated Absolute Valve (POA)

The function of the POA valve (Figure 38-28) is to control evaporator pressure. This is accomplished in the same manner as with the previously described STV valve. That is, the evaporator outlet is throttled or restricted so the pressure within the evaporator is maintained at a predetermined point. Although the end result of using this valve in the system is the same

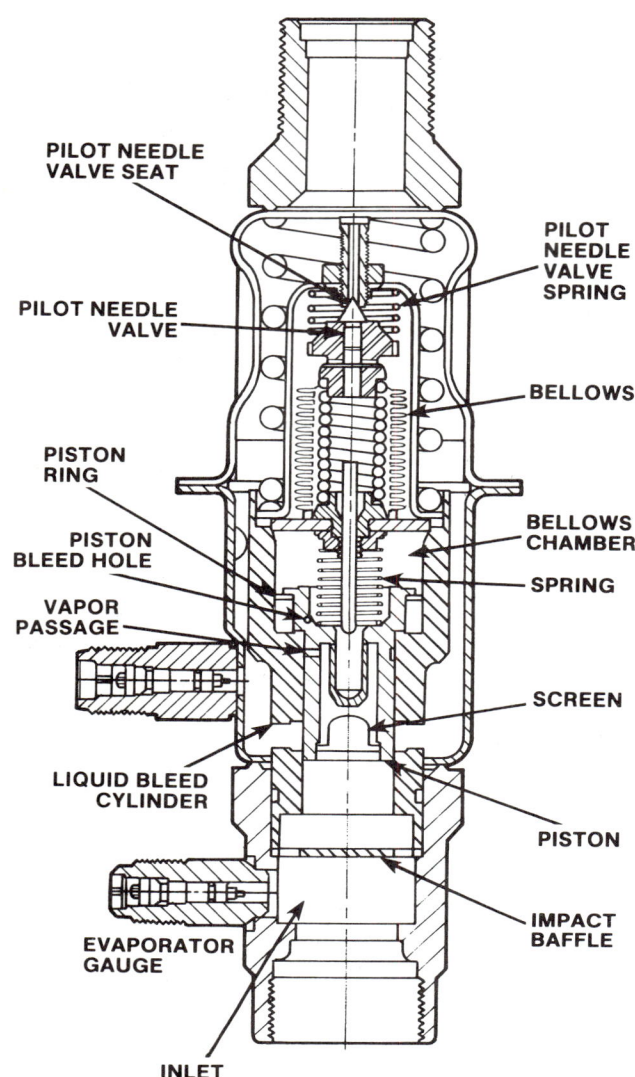

Figure 38-28 Cross section of a pilot-operated absolute (POA) valve.

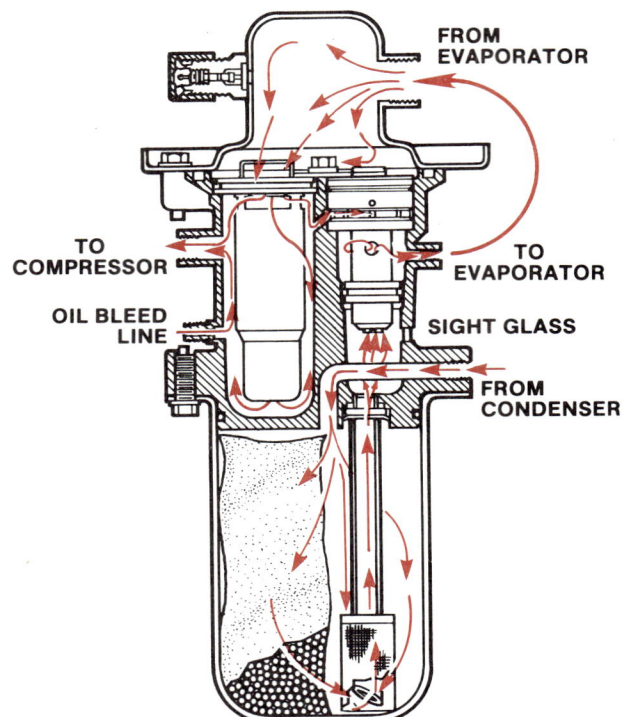

Figure 38-29 Cross section of VIR showing detail of components and direction of refrigerant flow.

as with the STV, there is no similarity in the operation of the two valves.

As its name implies, the POA valve contains a pilot valve. This valve has a bronze evacuated bellows. The POA is referenced to the nearly perfect vacuum in this bellows rather than to atmospheric pressure as in the case of the STV. The POA, therefore, requires no external altitude compensating device.

Valves-in-Receiver (VIR) Assembly

As stated earlier in this chapter, VIR is a combination of three different valves: the POA (or STV) valve, the thermostatic expansion valve, and the receiver/dryer (Figure 38-29). Early series are called simply valves-in-receiver (VIR), and later series are called evaporator equalizer valves-in-receiver (EEVIR). Both are essentially the same device. They operate and are serviced in the same manner. Replacement parts or repair kits are available.

Evaporator Pressure Regulator (EPR)

This valve is installed in the suction passage of the compressor. It is accessible after the suction line fitting is removed from the compressor. The EPR valve regulates evaporation outlet pressure to keep operation pressure between 22 to 31 psi. This valve functions the same as the STV described earlier.

❑ MAINTENANCE PRECAUTIONS

Air-conditioning systems are extremely sensitive to moisture and dirt. Therefore, clean working conditions are extremely important. The smallest particle of foreign matter in an air-conditioning system contaminates the refrigerant, causing rust, ice, or damage to the compressor. For this reason, all replacement parts are sold in vacuum-sealed containers and should not be opened until they are to be installed in the system. If, for any reason, a part has been removed from its container for any length of time, the part must be completely flushed using only recommended flush solvent to remove any dust or moisture that might have accumulated during storage. When the system has been open for any length of time, the entire system must be purged completely and a new receiver/dryer must be installed because the element of the existing unit will have become saturated and unable to remove any moisture from the system once the system is recharged.

The following general practices should be observed to insure chemical stability in the system.

> **SHOP TALK**
>
> It is important to remember that just one drop of water added to the refrigerant will start chemical changes that can result in corrosion and eventual breakdown of the chemicals in the system. Hydrochloric acid is the result of an R-12 mixture with water. The smallest amount of moist air in the refrigerant system might start reactions that can cause malfunctions.

Whenever it becomes necessary to disconnect a refrigerant connection, wipe away any dirt or oil at and near the connection to eliminate the possibility of dirt entering the system. Both sides of the connection should be immediately capped or plugged to prevent the entrance of dirt, foreign material, and moisture. It must be remembered that all air contains moisture. Air that enters any part of the system carries moisture with it, and the exposed surface collects the moisture quickly.

Keep tools clean and dry. This includes the gauge set and replacement parts. Be careful not to overtighten any connection. Overtightening results in line and flare seat distortion and a system leak.

When adding oil, the container and the transfer tube through which the oil will flow should be exceptionally clean and dry. Refrigerant oil is as moisture-free as it is possible to make it. Therefore, it quickly absorbs any moisture it contacts. For this reason, the oil container should not be opened until ready for use and then it should be capped immediately after use.

When it is necessary to open a system, have everything needed ready and handy so as little time as possible is required to perform the operation. Do not leave the system open any longer than is necessary.

Cleanliness is especially important when servicing compressors because of the very close tolerances used in these units. Consequently, repairs to the compressor itself should not be attempted unless all proper tools are at hand and a spotless work area is provided.

Any time the system has been opened and sealed again, it must be properly evacuated. Keep in mind that the complete and positive sealing of the entire system is vitally important and that this sealed condition is absolutely necessary to retain the chemicals and keep them in a pure and proper condition.

☐ REFRIGERANT SAFETY PRECAUTIONS

Whenever repairs are performed on any air-conditioner components that hold R-12, the system must be discharged, purged, or flushed (if contaminated), evacuated, charged, and leak tested. In a good system, refrigerant lines are always under pressure and should be disconnected only after the air-conditioning system has been discharged at the compressor. Never vent the refrigerant into open air. Use a recovery/recycling machine.

R-12 is safe under the right conditions. Always wear safety goggles and nonleather gloves while discharging, purging, flushing, evacuating, charging, and leak testing the system. (When R-12 gas or liquid contacts leather, the leather sticks to your skin.)

WARNING: Always wear safety goggles to protect your eyes when working with refrigerant containers and opening refrigerant connections in the air-conditioning system.

If the refrigerant gets in your eyes, do not rub your eyes. Flush them thoroughly with cold water to gradually get the temperature above the freezing point. If available, apply an antiseptic oil to the affected area. This forms a protective film over the eyeball to reduce the possibility of infection. Call an eye specialist or doctor immediately and receive medical treatment as soon as possible.

If the refrigerant should come in contact with your skin, treat it like frostbite. Do not rub or massage the affected area. Do not put a hot water bottle or any other heat application on the injury. Gradually and gently rewarm the injury using lukewarm water. Contrary to popular belief, frostbite should never be treated by rubbing the affected area with snow or ice. Call a doctor immediately.

Even though R-12 does not burn when it contacts extreme heat, such as a hot exhaust manifold or flame, poisonous phosgene gas is created. If breathed, this gas can cause severe respiratory irritation. This gas also

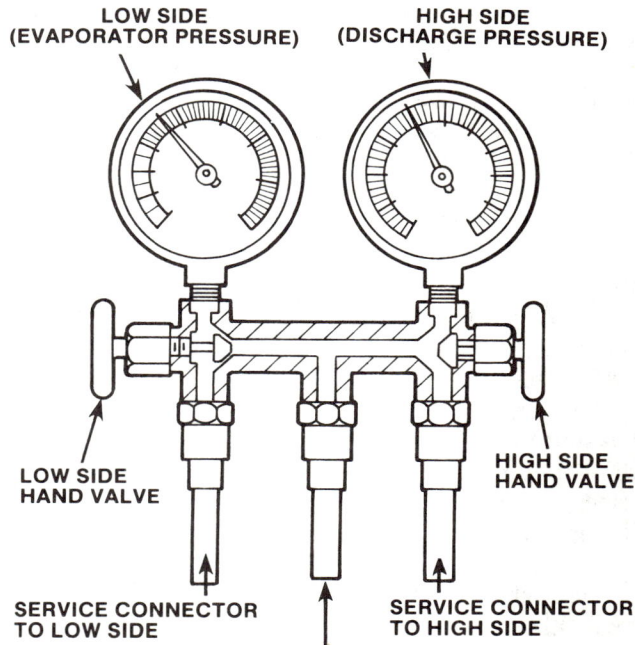

Figure 38-30 Manifold gauge set.

occurs when an open flame leak detector is used. Phosgene fumes have an acrid (bitter) smell.

R-12 comes in 30- and 60-pound cylinders. Remember that these drums are under considerable pressure and should be handled following precautions. Keep the drums in an upright position. Make sure that valves and safety plugs are protected by metal caps when the drums are not in use. Avoid dropping the drums. Handle them carefully. When transporting refrigerant, do not place containers in the vehicle's passenger compartment.

Always keep the temperature of refrigerant drums below 125 degrees Fahrenheit. Temperatures higher than this can cause the safety plug to blow or the drum to burst because of increased pressure. If you must heat a drum of refrigerant when charging a system, place the drum in water that is no hotter than 125 degrees Fahrenheit. Do not use a direct flame or heater. Attach a pressure release mechanism before heating the drum.

☐ AIR CONDITIONER TESTING AND SERVICING EQUIPMENT

There are several specially designed pieces of equipment that are required to perform test procedures. They include manifold gauge sets, service valves, vacuum pumps, charging station, charging cylinders, recovery/recycling systems, and leak-detecting devices.

Manifold Gauge Sets

The gauge set shown in Figure 38-30 is one of the most valuable air-conditioning tools. It is used when discharging, charging, evacuating, and for diagnosing trouble in the system.

The gauge illustrated on the left in Figure 38-30 is known as the low-pressure gauge. The dial is graduated into pounds of pressure from 1 to 120 (with cushion to 250) in 1-pound graduations, and, in the opposite direction, in inches of vacuum from 0 to 30. This is the gauge that should always be used in checking pressure on the low-pressure side of the system. The gauge at the right is graduated from 0 to 500 pounds pressure in 10-pound graduations. This is the high-pressure gauge that is used for checking pressure on the high-pressure side of the system.

The center manifold fitting is common to both the low and the high side and is for evacuating or adding refrigerant to the system. When this fitting is not being used, it should be capped. A test hose connected to the fitting directly under the low side gauge is used to connect the low side of the test manifold to the low side of the system. A similar connection is found on the high side.

The gauge manifold is designed to control refrigerant flow. When the manifold test set is connected into the system, pressure is registered on both gauges at all times. During all tests, both the low and high side hand valves are in the closed position (turned inward until the valve is seated).

Refrigerant flows around the valve stem to the respective gauges and registers the system's low-side pressure on the low-side gauge and the system's high-side pressure on the high-side gauge. The hand valves isolate the low and high side from the central portion of the manifold. When the gauges are first connected to the gauge fittings with the refrigeration system charged, the gauge lines should always be purged. Purging is done by cracking each valve on the gauge set to allow the pressure of the refrigerant in the refrigeration system to force the air to escape through the center gauge line. Failure to purge lines can result in air or other contaminants entering the refrigeration system.

WARNING: Do not open the low-side hand valve with the system operating and a refrigerant can connected to the center hose. The refrigerant will flow out of the system under high pressure into the can. High-side pressure is between 150 and 300 psi and will cause the refrigerant tank to burst. The only occasion for opening both hand valves at the same time would be when evacuating the system.

> **SHOP TALK**
>
> Remember that atmospheric pressure is low at elevations above sea level. The corrected gauge pressure with a closed system can be determined by subtracting the gauge altitude correction factor from the reading. This is very important when checking the system's low-side pressures.

Service Valves

System service valves, which incorporate a service gauge port for manifold gauge set connections, are provided on the low and high sides of some air-conditioning systems. When making gauge connections, purge the gauge lines first by cracking the charging valve and allowing a small amount of refrigerant to flow through the lines, then connect the lines immediately.

Two basic types of service valves are used: stem and Schrader.

Stem Service Valve

The stem valve is sometimes used on two-cylinder reciprocating-piston compressors. Access to the high-pressure and low-pressure sides of the system is provided through service valves mounted on the compressor head. The low-pressure valve is mounted at the

Heating and Air Conditioning   989

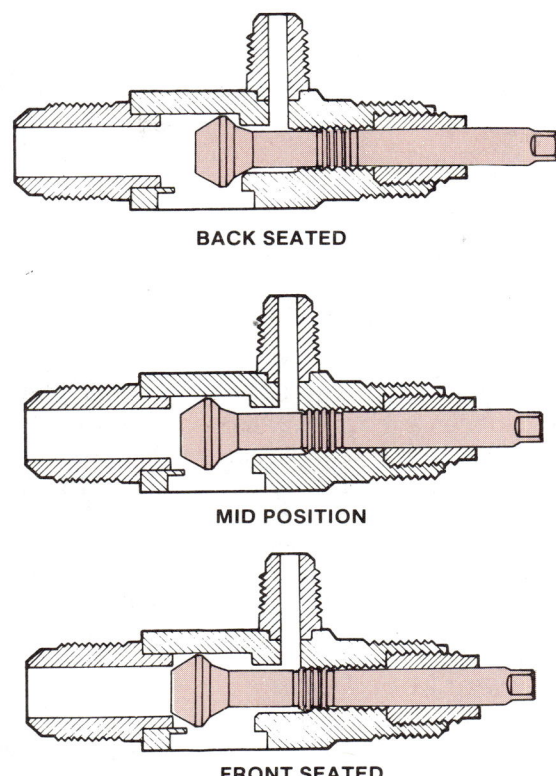

Figure 38-31 Stem service valve positions.

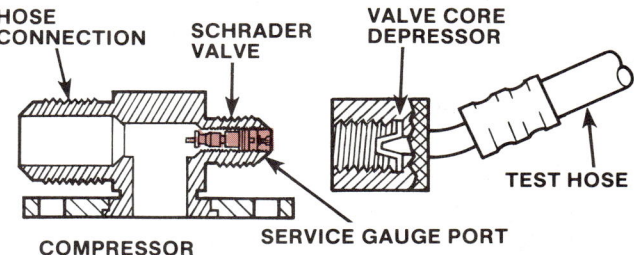

Figure 38-32 Schrader service valve.

inlet to the compressor, while the high-pressure valve is mounted at the compressor outlet. Both these valves can be used to shut off the rest of the air-conditioning system from the compressor when the compressor is being serviced. These valves have a stem under a cap (Figure 38-31) with the hose connection directly opposite.

A special wrench is used to open the valve to one of three positions. The back seated position is the normal operating position with the valve stem rotated counterclockwise to seat the rear valve face and seal off the service gauge port. The mid position is the test position with the valve stem turned clockwise (inward) 1-1/2 to 2 turns. This connects the service gauge port into the system so that gauge readings can be taken with the system operating. A service gauge hose must be connected with the valve completely back seated. In the front seated position the valve stem has been rotated clockwise to seat the front valve face and to isolate the compressor from the system. This position allows the compressor to be serviced without discharging the entire system. The front seated position is for service only. It is never used while the air conditioner is operating.

Schrader Service Valve

Systems that do not utilize stem service have Schrader service valves (Figure 38-32) in both the high and low portions of the system for test purposes. Closely resembling a tire valve, Schrader valves are usually located in the high-pressure line (from compressor to condenser) and in the low-pressure line (from evaporator to condenser) to permit checking of the high side and low side of the system. All test hoses have a Schrader core depresser in them. As the hose is threaded onto the service port, the pin in the center of the valve is depressed, allowing refrigerant to flow to the manifold gauge set. When the hose is removed, the valve closes automatically.

After disconnecting gauge lines, check the valve areas to be sure the service valves are correctly seated and the Schrader valves are not leaking.

Leak Testing A System

Testing the refrigerant system for leaks is one of the most important phases of troubleshooting. Over a period of time, all air conditioners lose or leak some refrigerant. In systems that are in good condition, R-12 losses up to a half pound per year are considered normal. Higher loss rates signal a need to locate and repair the leaks.

Leaks are most often found at the compressor hose connections and at the various fittings and joints in the system. Refrigerant can be lost through hose permeation. Leaks can also be traced to pinholes in the evaporator caused by acid, which forms when water and refrigerant mix. Since oil and refrigerant leak out together, oily spots on hoses, fittings, and components are a good indication that there is a refrigerant leak (Figure 38-33). Any suspected leak should be confirmed by using any one of the four methods of detection.

Flame (Halide) Leak Detector

The Halide leak detector (Figure 38-34) is a propane torch designed to locate a leak in any part of the system. Refrigerant gas drawn into the sampling tube attached to the torch causes the torch flame to change color in proportion to the size of the leak.

WARNING: If a flame leak detector must be used, do the work outdoors where there is a constant supply of fresh air. When in contact with extreme heat, R-12 breaks down into poisonous phosgene gas, which, if breathed, causes severe respiratory

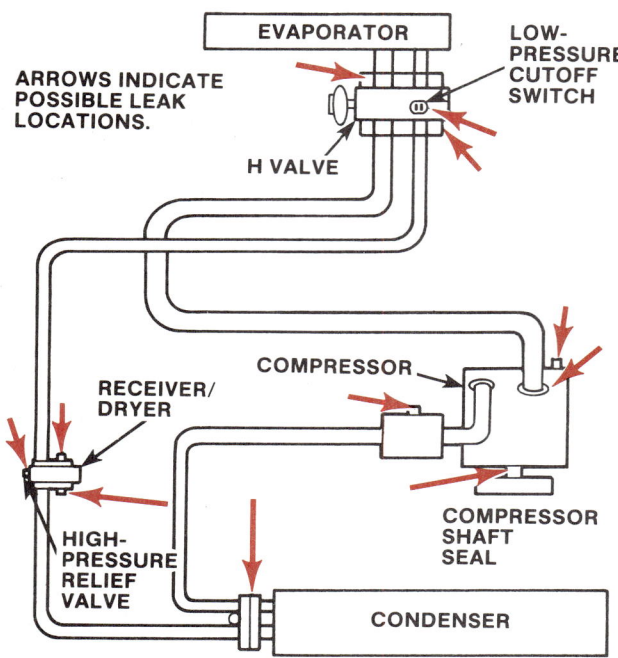

Figure 38-33 Probable refrigerant leak locations.

The following is a guide for color changes.

- Pale blue flame: no refrigerant is escaping.
- Pale yellow flame: very small amount of refrigerant is escaping.
- Bright yellow flame: small amount of refrigerant is escaping.
- Purple-tinted blue flame: large amount of refrigerant is escaping.
- Violet flame: very large amount of refrigerant is escaping.

Electronic Leak Detector

The hand-held battery-operated electronic leak detector contains a test probe that is moved about one inch per second in areas of suspected leaks. (Remember that refrigerant gas is heavier than air, thus the probe should be positioned below the test point.) An alarm or a buzzer on the detector indicates the presence of a leak. On some models, a light flashes to establish the leak. The electronic leak detector is the most sensitive of the two types.

Fluorescent Leak Tracer

To find a refrigerant leak using the fluorescent tracer system, first introduce a fluorescent dye into the air-conditioning system by means of a special infuser (Figure 38-35). Run the air conditioner for a few minutes, giving the tracer dye fluid time to circulate and penetrate. Wear the tracer protective goggles and scan the system with a black-light glow gun. Leaks in the system will shine under the black light as a luminous yellow-green.

Fluid Leak Detector

Leaks can also be located by applying leak detector fluid around areas to be tested. If a leak is present, it will form clusters of bubbles around the source. A very small leak will cause a white foam to form around the leak source within several seconds to a minute. Adequate lighting over the entire surface being tested is necessary for an accurate diagnosis.

Regardless of which type of leak detector is used, the system should have a minimum of 70 psi pressure to accurately detect a leak. Be sure to check the entire system. If a leak is found at a connection, tighten the connection carefully and recheck. If the leak is still

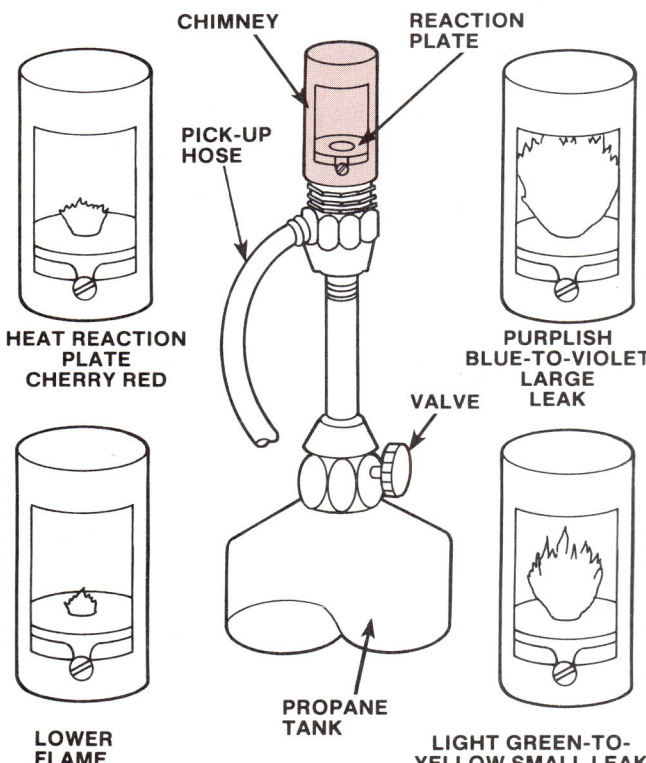

Figure 38-34 Leak testing with a halide torch.

irritation. Also, keep the flame away from all fire hazards, such as fuel lines and tanks and ether-injection starting systems. Do not use a flame leak detector inside the passenger compartment or when the engine is running.

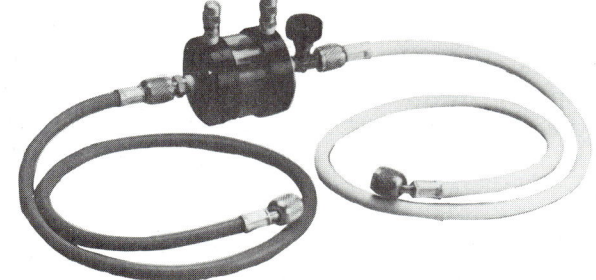

Figure 38-35 Tracer mist infuser. *Courtesy of Moog Automotive*

apparent, discharge the system as described earlier. Replace the damaged components, evacuate, charge, and test the system for leaks.

Service Procedures

To put the air conditioning in the best condition, be sure to perform the following service procedures:

- System discharging
- System flushing
- Compressor oil level checks
- Evacuation
- System charging

System Discharging

All refrigerant must be discharged from the system before repair or replacement of any component (except for compressors with stem service valves). This procedure is acccomplished through the use of a manifold gauge set, which makes it possible to control the rate of refrigerant discharge, preventing any loss of oil from the system (Figure 38-36).

Until recently, each time an air-conditioning system was serviced, the old refrigerant was vented into the atmosphere. Today, as was mentioned earlier, this practice not only depletes profits (R-12 is increasing in price), it also depletes the earth's protective ozone layer. But, with the development of recovery and recycling equipment, this wasteful and destructive practice is no longer necessary. In fact, until an ozone-safe refrigerant becomes commercially available, the Environment Protection Agency (EPA) will emphasize finding and fixing leaks in existing air-conditioning systems and recycling rather than venting refrigerant into the atmosphere when a vehicle is serviced.

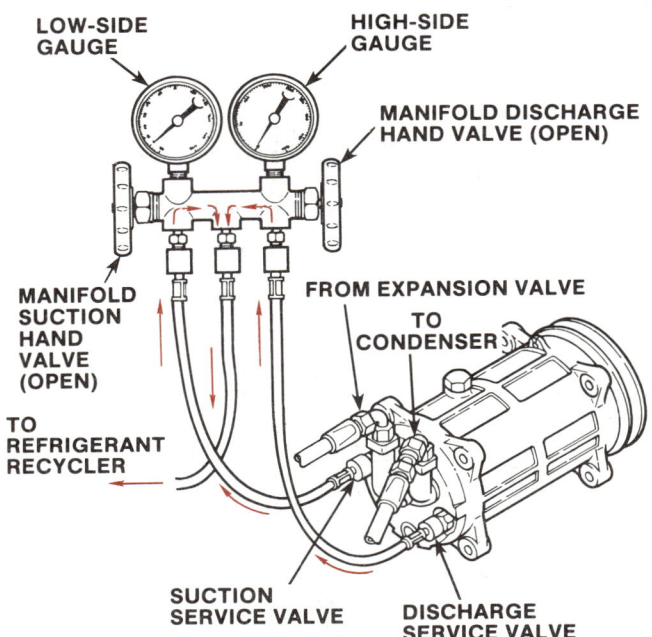

Figure 38-36 Typical discharging hookup.

In recycling, the EPA has stated that if voluntary efforts fail, it will mandate recycling equipment for all service facilities that do air-conditioning service.

When discharging a system, follow the procedure recommended in the vehicle's service manual or the equipment manufacturer's owner's guide.

System Flushing

Compressor failure causes foreign material to pass into the system. The condenser must be flushed and the receiver/dryer replaced. Filter screens sometimes are located in the suction side of the compressor and in the receiver/dryer. These screens confine foreign material to the compressor, condenser, receiver/dryer, and connecting hoses. Use only recommended flush solvents such as R113. R-12 does not usually give satisfactory results. To flush a typical system, proceed as recommended in vehicle's service manual. After the system has been flushed, be sure to oil all components that require it.

Compressor Oil Level Checks

It is not recommended that the oil level of the compressor should be checked as a matter of course. Generally, compressor oil level should be checked only where there is evidence of a major loss of system oil that could be caused by a broken refrigerant hose, severe hose fitting leak, badly leaking compressor seal, or collision damage to the system's components.

When replacing refrigerant oil, it is important to use the specific type and quantity of oil recommended by the compressor manufacturer. If there is a surplus of oil in the system, too much oil circulates with the refrigerant, causing the cooling capacity of the system to be reduced. Too little oil results in poor lubrication of the compressor. When there has been excessive leakage or it is necessary to replace a component of the refrigeration system, certain procedures must be followed to assure that the total oil charge in the system is correct after leak repair or the new part is on the car.

When the compressor is operated, oil gradually leaves the compressor and is circulated through the system with the refrigerant. Eventually a balanced condition is reached in which a certain amount of oil is retained in the compressor and a certain amount is continually circulated. If a component of the system is replaced after the system has been operated, some oil goes with it. To maintain the original total oil charge, it is necessary to compensate for this by adding oil to the new replacement part. Because of the differences in compressor designs, be sure to follow the manufacturer's instructions when adding refrigerant oil to their unit.

Evacuating and Charging the System

The system must be completely discharged before evacuation. Always wear safety goggles when working with refrigerant containers or servicing air-conditioning systems. After discharging the system, the low-pressure gauge hose remains connected to the low-pressure test fitting. Both the high- and low-pressure manifold gauge valves are closed. Then proceed as in Photo Sequence 19.

> **SHOP TALK**
>
> The importance of the correct charge cannot be stressed enough. The efficient operation of the air-conditioning system greatly depends on the correct amount of refrigerant in the system. A low charge results in inadequate cooling under high heat loads, due to a lack of reserve refrigerant, and can cause the clutch cycling switch to cycle faster than normal. An overcharge can cause inadequate cooling because of a high liquid refrigerant level in the condenser. Refrigerant controls will not operate properly and compressor damage can result. In general, an overcharge of refrigerant will cause higher than normal gauge readings and noisy compressor operation. Controls and parts of a typical charging station are shown in Figure 38-37.

Vacuum Pump

Any air or moisture that is left inside an air-conditioning system after the system has been evacuated reduces the system's efficiency and eventually leads to major problems, such as compressor failure.

Air causes excessive pressure within the system, restricting the refrigerant's ability to change its state from gas to liquid within the refrigeration cycle, which drastically reduces its heat absorbing and transferring ability. Moisture, on the other hand, can cause freeze-up at the cap tube or expansion valve, which restricts refrigerant flow or blocks it completely. Both of these problems result in intermittent cooling—or no cooling at all. Moisture also forms hydrochloric acid when mixed with refrigerant, causing internal corrosion, which is especially dangerous to the compressor.

The main function, or responsibility, of the vacuum pump is to remove the contaminating air and moisture from the system (Figure 38-38). The vacuum pump reduces system pressure in order to vaporize the mois-

Figure 38-38 Rotary vane vacuum pump. *Courtesy of Robinair Corp.*

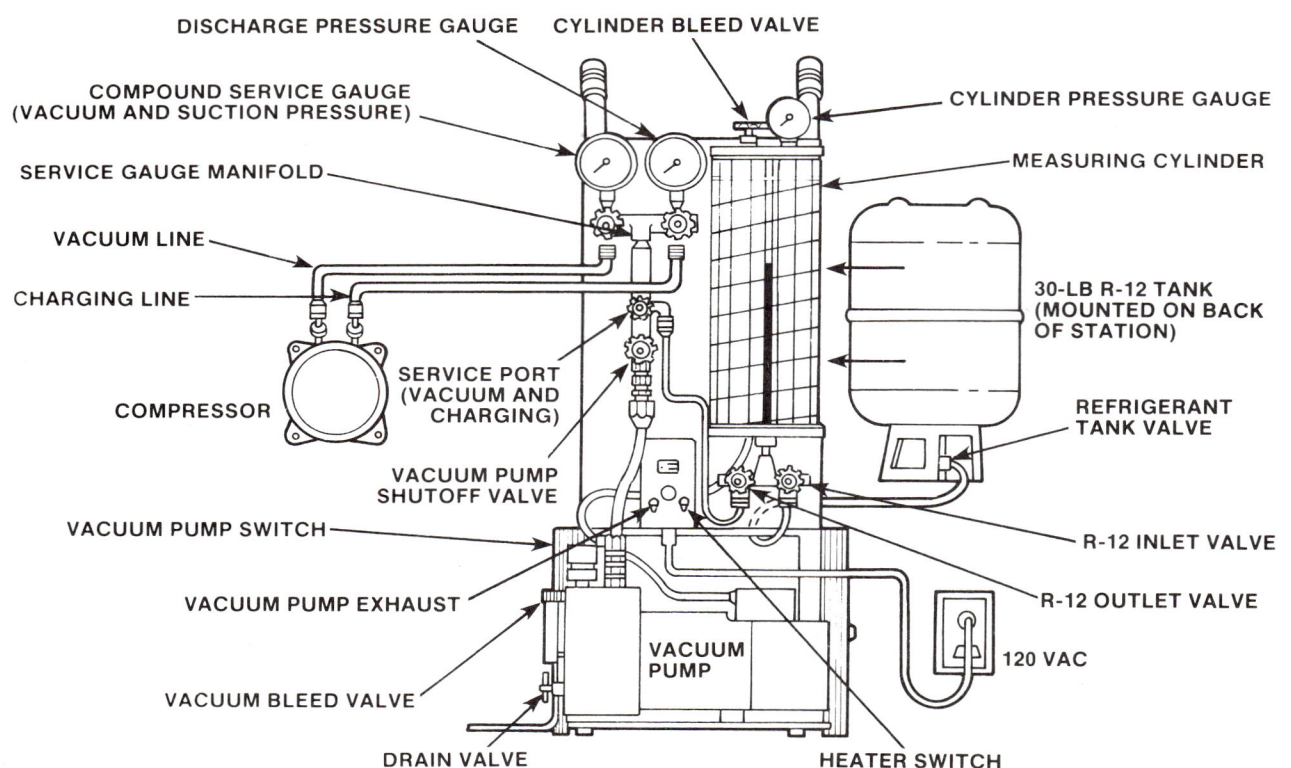

Figure 38-37 Parts and controls of a typical charging station.

PHOTO SEQUENCE 19

☐ EVACUATING AND RECHARGING AN A/C SYSTEM WITH A RECYCLING AND CHARGING STATION

P19-1 Physically locate the pressure fittings of the system you will be working with. Make sure you have the proper adapters for the fittings prior to starting any service work on air conditioning systems.

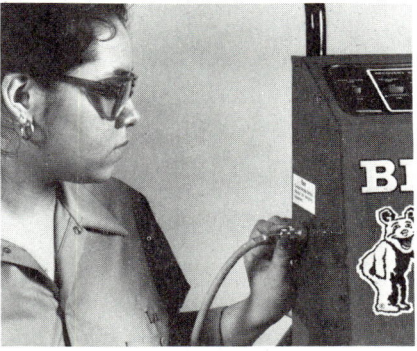

P19-4 Connect the reclaiming unit to the gauge set.

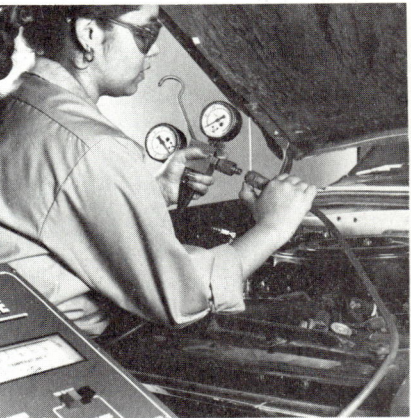

P19-7 Close the valves at the gauge set and disconnect the reclaiming machine. Connect the charging station and open the gauge set valves.

P19-2 Connect a gauge set to the system.

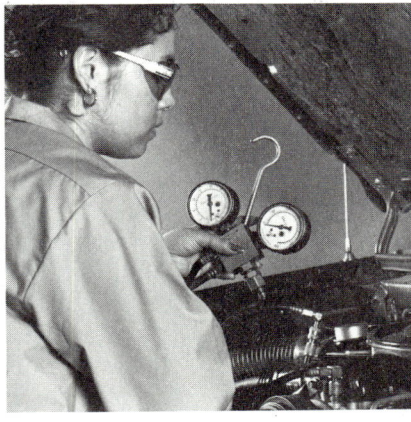

P19-5 Activate the reclaimer and allow enough time for the machine to draw a vacuum in the system. Observe the gauge set to determine when a vacuum is created.

P19-8 Allow the charging station to create 29 in. Hg of vacuum in the system. Set the unit to deliver the required amount of refrigerant for that system.

P19-3 Typical refrigerant reclaiming machine.

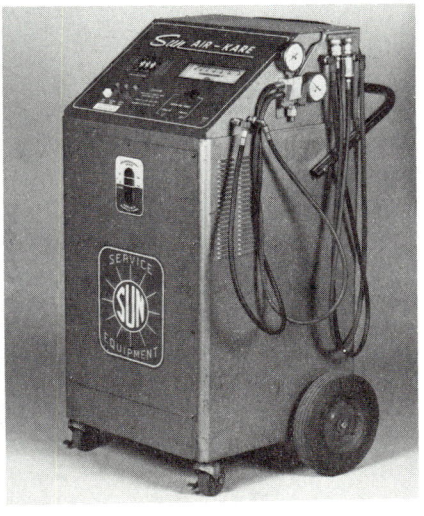

P19-6 A typical A/C charging station.

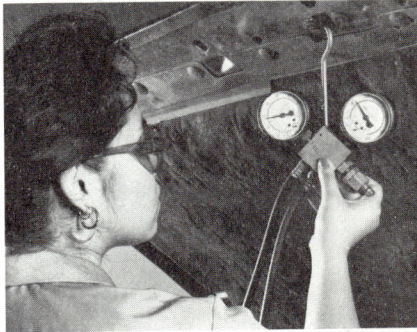

P19-9 After the system has been recharged, check the gauge readings while the system is in operation to make sure it is working properly. ■

ture and then exhausts the vapor along with all remaining air. The pump's ability to clean the system is directly related to its ability to reduce pressure—create a vacuum—low enough to boil off all the contaminating moisture.

Thermistor Vacuum Gauge

The electronic thermistor vacuum gauge (Figure 38-39) is designed to work with the vacuum pump to measure the last, most critical inch of mercury during evacuation. It constantly monitors and visually indicates the vacuum level so you know for sure when a system is free of air and moisture, eliminating guesswork and wasted time.

Charging Cylinder

With an increase in temperature in any cylinder filled with refrigerant, there is a corresponding increase in pressure and a change in the volume of liquid refrigerant in the cylinder. To measure an accurate charge by weight from a cylinder using the liquid level in a sight glass as a point of measurement, it is absolutely necessary to compensate for liquid volume variations caused by temperature variations. These temperature variations are directly related to pressure variations and accurate measurements by weight can be calibrated in relation to pressure.

The charging cylinder is designed to meter out a desired amount of a specific refrigerant by weight. Compensation for temperature variations is accomplished by reading the pressure on the gauge of the cylinder and by dialing the plastic shroud. The calibrated chart on the shroud contains corresponding pressure readings for the refrigerant being used.

When charging a refrigeration or air-conditioning system with refrigerant, often the pressure in the system reaches a point at which it is equal to the pressure in the cylinder from which the system is being charged. To get more refrigerant into the system to complete the

Figure 38-39 Thermistor vacuum gauge. *Courtesy of Robinair Corp.*

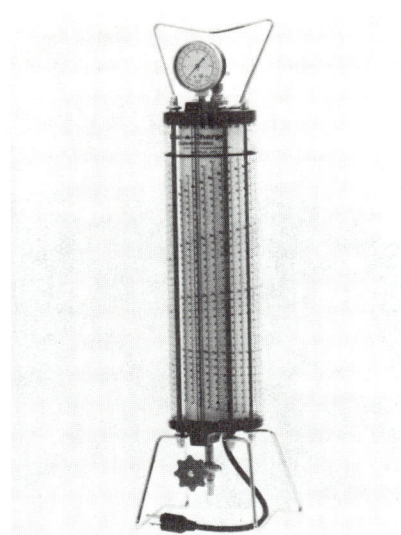

Figure 38-40 Charging cylinder. *Courtesy of Robinair Corp.*

charge, heat must be applied to the cylinder. The charging cylinder shown in Figure 38-40 eliminates the problem caused by equalization of pressure between the cylinder and the system being charged.

Performance Testing

Performance testing provides a measure of air-conditioning system operating efficiency. A manifold pressure gauge set is used to determine both high and low pressures in the refrigeration system. At the same time, a thermometer is used to determine air discharge temperature into the passenger compartment (Figure 38-41).

Before making this test, it should be established that the air distribution (air door) portion of factory-installed systems is functioning properly. This insures that all air passing through the evaporator is being routed directly to the air outlet nozzles.

 **PROCEDURES**

Performance Testing

1. Connect the manifold gauge set to the respective high- and low-pressure fittings as shown in Figure 38-42 with both valves closed. These fittings are found in various locations within the high- and low-pressure sides of the system.
2. Keep the hood open and close all the doors and windows of the car.
3. Adjust the air-conditioning controls to the maximum cooling and high blower position.
4. Idle the engine for 10 minutes in neutral or park with the brake on. For the best results, place a high volume fan in front of the radiator grille to

Heating and Air Conditioning   995

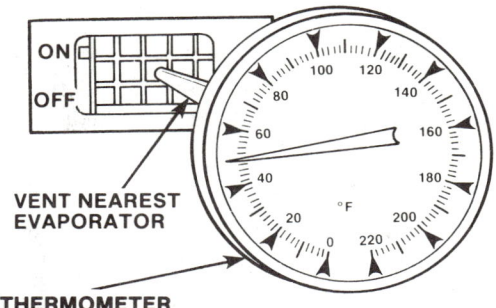

Figure 38-41 Checking outlet air temperature.

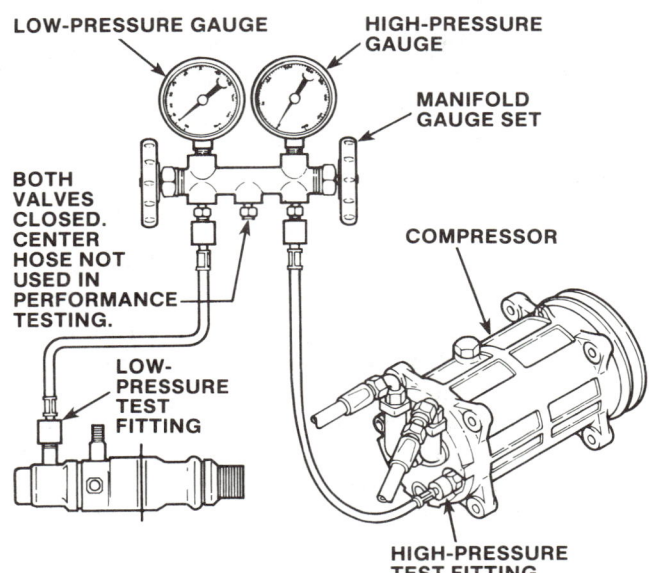

Figure 38-42 Performance testing hookup.

insure an adequate supply of airflow across the condenser.

5. Increase engine speed to 1500 to 2000 rpm.
6. Measure the temperature at the evaporator air outlet grille or air duct nozzle (35 to 40 degrees Fahrenheit).
7. Read high and low pressure, and compare to the normal range of the operating pressure given in the service manual.

Operating pressures vary with humidity as well as with outside air temperature. Accordingly, on more humid days, operating pressures will be on the high side of the range indicated in the service manual's performance chart. On less humid days, the operating pressures will read toward the lower side. If operating pressures are found to be within the normal range, the refrigeration portion of the air-conditioning system is functioning properly. This can be further confirmed with a check of evaporator outlet air temperatures.

Evaporator outlet air temperature also varies according to outside (ambient) air and humidity conditions. Further variations can be found, depending on whether the system is controlled by a cycling clutch compressor or an evaporator pressure control valve. Because of these variations, it is difficult to pinpoint what evaporator outlet air temperature should be on all applications. In general, with low outside air temperatures (70 degrees) and humidity (20%), the evaporator outlet air temperature should be in the 35- to 40-degree range. On the other extreme of 80 degrees outside air temperatures and 90% humidity condition, the evaporator air outlet temperature might be in the 55- to 60-degree range.

Since it is impractical to provide a specific performance chart for all the different types of air-conditioning systems, it is desirable to develop an experience factor for determining the correlation that can be anticipated between operating pressures and outlet air temperatures on the various systems. For example, feel the discharge line from the compressor to the condenser. The discharge line should be the same temperature along its full length. Any temperature change is a sign of restriction and the line should be flushed or replaced. Perform this test carefully because the discharge line will be hot.

There are other tests that can be performed with the engine running.

- Check the condenser by feeling up and down the face or along the return bends for a temperature change. There should be a gradual change from hot to warm as you go from the top to the bottom. Any abrupt change indicates a restriction, and the condenser has to be flushed or replaced.
- If the system has a receiver/dryer, check it. The inlet and outlet lines should be the same temperature. Any temperature difference or frost on the lines or receiver tank are signs of a restriction. The receiver/dryer must be replaced.
- If the system has a sight glass, check it as previously described.
- Feel the liquid line from the receiver/dryer to the expansion valve. The line should be warm for its entire length.
- The expansion valve should be free of frost, and there should be a sharp temperature difference between its inlet and outlet.
- The suction line to the compressor should be cool to the touch from the evaporator to the compressor. If it is covered with thick frost, this might indicate that the expansion valve is flooding the evaporator.
- On vehicles equipped with the orifice tube system, feel the liquid line from the condenser outlet to the evaporator inlet. A restriction is indicated by any temperature change in the liquid line before the crimp dimples the orifice tube in the evaporator inlet. Flush the liquid line or replace the orifice tube if restricted.

- The accumulator as well as the suction line must be cool to the touch from the evaporator outlet to the compressor.

By combining the results of both the hands-on checks and an interpretation of pressure gauge readings, the technician has a good indication that some unit in the system is malfunctioning and that further diagnosis is needed.

☐ DIAGNOSTIC AND TROUBLESHOOTING PROCEDURES

The first step in air-conditioning diagnosis—as in all automotive diagnostic work—is to get the customer's story. Is the problem no cold air, the air from the ducts never gets cold enough, or the unit only cools at certain times of the day? The complaint could also be that the system does not work at all, or that the air blows out of the wrong ducts. An accurate description of the customer's problem helps to pinpoint whether the problem is refrigerant, mechanical, or electrical related. It also reduces diagnosis time and, most important, satisfies the customer.

Because of the many construction and operational variations that exist, there is no uniform or standard diagnostic procedure applicable to all automotive air-conditioning systems. However, the information given in the Technical Manual can be used as a general guide to common air-conditioning problems and their possible remedies. For complete specific diagnostic information on a given air conditioner, check the manufacturer's service manual.

☐ TEMPERATURE CONTROL SYSTEMS

Temperature control systems for air conditioners usually are connected with heater controls. Most heater and air-conditioning systems use the same plenum chamber for air distribution. Two types of air-conditioning controls are used: manual/semiautomatic and automatic (Figure 38-43).

Manual/Semiautomatic

Air conditioner manual/semiautomatic temperature controls (MTC or SATC) operate in a manner similar to heater controls. Depending on the control setting, doors are opened and closed to direct airflow. The amount of cooling is controlled manually through the use of control settings and blower speed.

Automatic Controls

An automatic or electronic temperature control system maintains a specific temperature automatically inside the passenger compartment. To maintain a se-

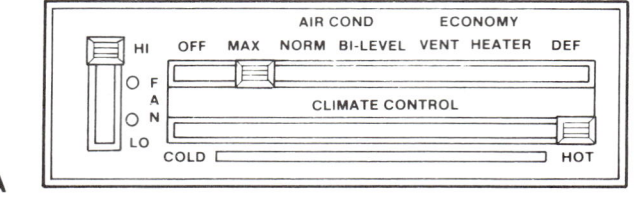
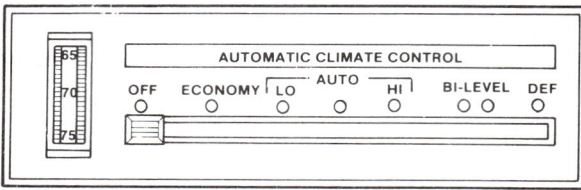

Figure 38-43 Typical air-conditioner control panels. (A) manual/semiautomatic and (B) automatic.

lected temperature, heat sensors send signals to a computer unit that controls compressor, heater valve, blower, and plenum door operation. A typical electronic control system might contain a coolant temperature sensor, in-car temperature sensor, outside temperature sensor, high-side temperature switch, low-side temperature switch, low-pressure switch, vehicle speed sensor, throttle position sensor, sunload sensor, and power steering cutout switch.

The control panel is found in the instrument panel at a convenient location for both driver and front-seat passenger access. Three types of control panels may be found: manual, push-button (Figure 38-44A), or touch

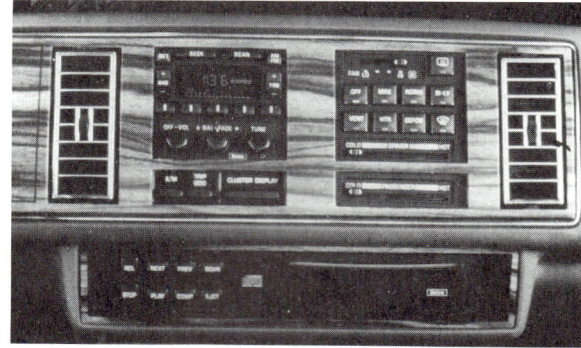

Figure 38-44 (A) Push-button control panel; (B) touch pad control panel. *Courtesy of (A) Buick Motor Division—GMC and (B) General Motors Corp.*

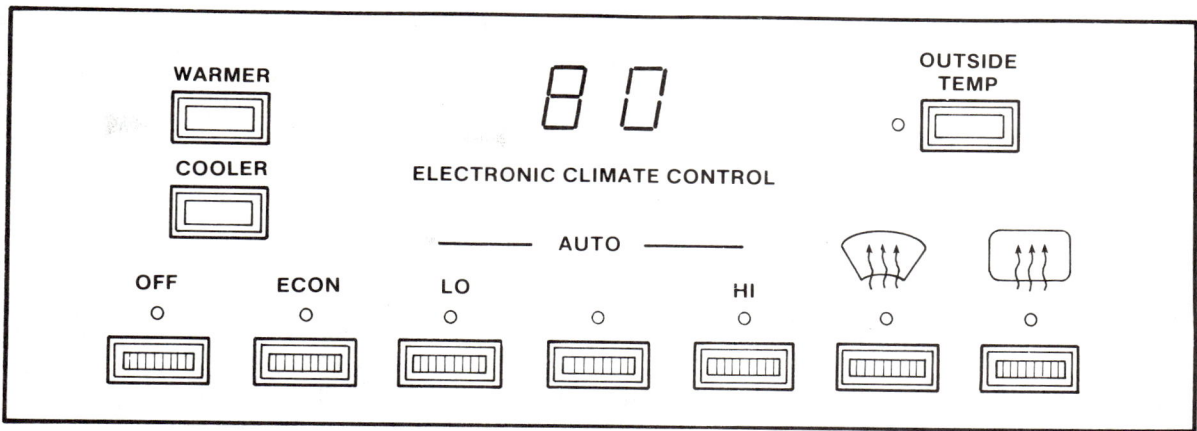

Figure 38-45 ECC digital control panel

pad (Figure 38-44B). All serve the same purpose. They provide operator input control for the air-conditioning and heating system. Some control panels have features that other panels do not have, such as provisions to display in-car and outside air temperature in degrees (Figure 38-45).

Provisions are made on the control panel for operator selection of an in-car temperature between 65 and 85 degrees Fahrenheit in one-degree increments. Some have an override feature that provides for a setting of either 60 or 90 degrees Fahrenheit. Either of these two settings overrides all in-car temperature control circuits to provide maximum cooling or heating conditions.

Usually, a microprocessor is located in the control head to input data to the programmer, based on operator-selected conditions. When the ignition switch is turned off, a memory circuit remembers the previous setting. These conditions are restored the next time the ignition switch is turned on. If the battery is disconnected, however, the memory circuit is cleared and must be reprogrammed.

Many automotive electronic temperature control systems have self-diagnostic test provisions in which an on-board microprocessor-controlled subsystem displays a code. This code (number, letter, or alphanumeric) is displayed to tell the technician the cause of the malfunction. Some systems also display a code to indicate which computer detected the malfunction. Manufacturers' specifications must be followed to identify the malfunction display codes, since they differ from car to car. For example, in some General Motors car lines ".7,0" indicates no malfunction if "no trouble" codes are stored in the computer. In some Ford car lines the no trouble code is 888.

Case/Duct Systems

A typical automotive heater/air conditioner/case and duct system is shown in Figure 38-46. The purpose of the system is twofold. It is used to house the

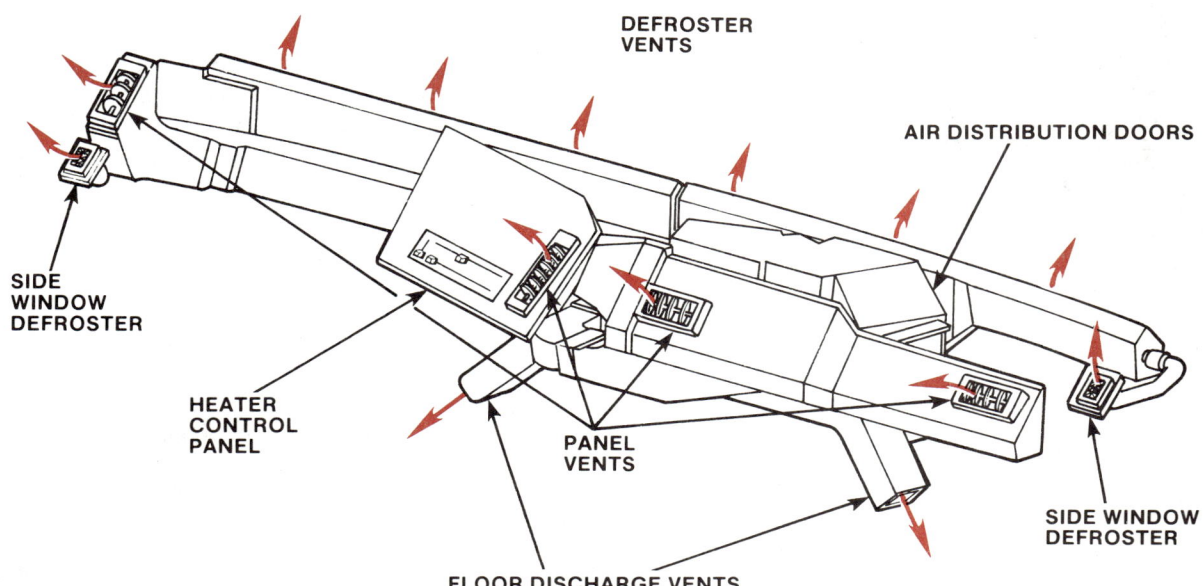

Figure 38-46 Heater/air conditioner ducts.

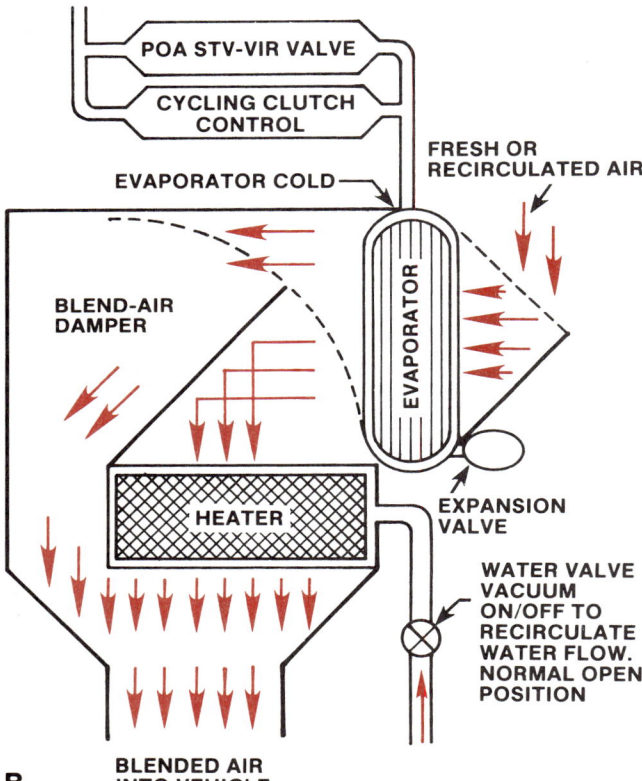

Figure 38-47 Two types of duct systems used in domestic cars: (A) stacked core reheat and (B) blend air reheat. *Courtesy of (A) Chrysler Corp. and (B) General Motors/Ford*

heater core and the air conditioner evaporator and to direct the selected supply air through these components into the passenger compartment of the vehicle. The supply air selected can be either fresh (outside) or recirculated air, depending upon the system mode. After the air is heated or cooled, it is delivered to the floor outlet, dash panel outlets, or the defrost outlets.

In domestic vehicles, there are two basic duct systems employed. In the stacked core reheat system (Figure 38-47A) the basic control is in the water valve. For maximum air the water valve is completely closed. All air enters the vehicle compartment through the heater core.

The access door, which is activated by a cable, controls only fresh or recirculated air. Recirculated air is used during maximum cold operation, the air-conditioning unit is not operative and the evaporator will not be cold. The evaporator-only is used in the max air or maximum cold position. As the control level inside the car is moved, it controls the water valve by means of a vacuum or a cable to control the amount of hot water entering the heater core and the temperature of the air at the unit outlet.

The blend air reheat system (Figure 38-47B) is found on General Motors and Ford vehicles and some truck units with factory-controlled heater system units. During heater-only operation, the air-conditioning unit is shut off, and the evaporator performs no function in air distribution or temperature control. During maximum air or extreme cold air, the air-conditioning system operates, the evaporator is cold, and the blend air door damper is completely closed. Only conditioned air enters the car.

As the control lever is moved in the vehicle from max air towards heat with the air conditioner on, the blend air door is moving. In maximum cold, it is completely shut. On maximum hot, it is completely open. The water valve on this unit is a vacuum on/off unit to regulate water flow. Normal position would be open. This type of blend air system is extremely popular and can be used with or without a water valve.

To check the proper functioning of the duct work, move the temperature control lever to see if any change occurs. If it does not, shut off the air conditioner and turn on the heater. Move the temperature control arm again to see if any change occurs. If not, check the cable and the flap door connected to the temperature control lever. You might be able to reach under the dash to reconnect the cable or free a stuck flap.

If no substantial airflow is coming out of the registers, check the fuses in the blower circuit. Remove the fan switch and test it. Check the blower motor by hot-wiring it directly to the battery with jumper cables.

USING SERVICE MANUALS

Many service manuals use block diagrams to show the component relationships and functions. Figure 38-48 illustrates such a diagram as it would pertain to typical automotive temperature control systems.

Heating and Air Conditioning   999

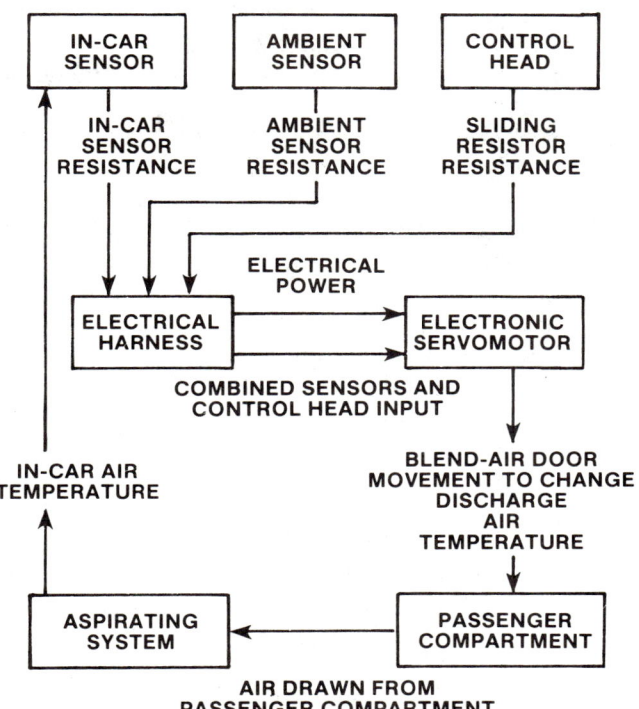

- LOW AIR TEMPERATURE AT SENSORS INCREASES RESISTANCE.
- HIGH TEMPERATURE LEVER SETTING INCREASES RESISTANCE.
- HIGH RESISTANCE CAUSES SERVOMOTOR TO MOVE BLEND-AIR DOOR TO HIGHER REHEAT POSITION.

Figure 38-48 Air-conditioning system component relationships often found in service manual.

❏ ELECTRICAL SYSTEM INSPECTION

The electrical system must be checked periodically to prevent the vehicle's air-conditioning system from failing unexpectedly. Start by checking the battery because most electrical trouble begins there (Figure 38-49). Leaky battery acid and corrosion builds up on the terminals, which can disrupt contact or eat away the terminal connections. A regular scrubbing with baking soda and water keeps the corrosion at a minimum. Check the terminal leads to be sure they are free of corrosion and make good contact with the battery terminals.

Because vehicle air-conditioning systems contain various switches, there will be times when one of them malfunctions. Sometimes this is not due to the switch itself but instead is caused by a bad connection or corrosion that has built up on the switch leads, leading to a broken contact. The switch can sometimes function intermittently because of this. It is important to check the switches from time to time and clean off the leads. Check that each switch is making good contact and is free of dirt and corrosion.

➡ CASE STUDY

Case 1

The first cold snap of winter brings a customer to the shop with the following complaint. When set on maximum, the heater does not produce sufficient heat to warm the vehicle.

First, the technician checks the coolant level. The radiator is full. She also checks the engine's operating temperature. It is normal, or more than enough to supply adequate heat.

The technician now knows the problem must be in the heating system itself. She measures the output temperature at the heater duct with the fan operating on high and the heater control positioned

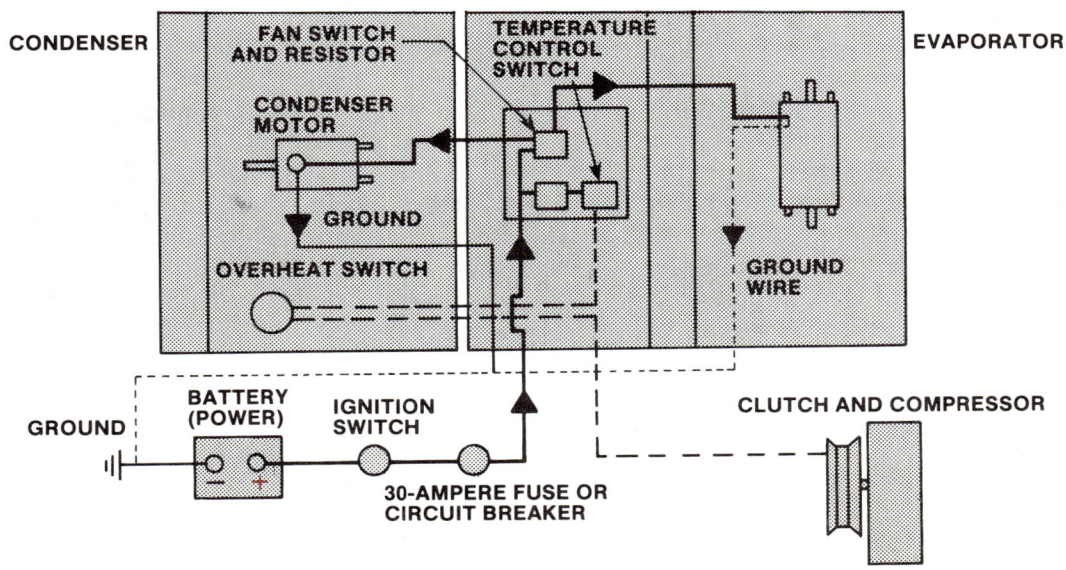

Figure 38-49 Electrical circuit inspection and checkout.

at its hottest setting. A lower-than-normal heat level is recorded. The technician checks the movement of the duct door and finds it to be open. She carefully checks the heater inlet and outlet hoses and finds them to be hot.

From these findings, the technician concludes the problem must be a plugged heater core. The core is removed and flushed, and the problem is solved.

Summary

- Ventilation, heating, and air conditioning provide the vehicle's passenger with comfort.
- The ventilation system on most vehicles is designed to supply outside air to the passenger compartment through upper or lower vents or both. There are several systems used to vent air into the passenger compartment. The most common is the flow-through system. In this arrangement, a supply of outside air, which is called ram air, flows into the car when it is moving.
- Automotive heating system has been designed to work with the cooling system to maintain proper temperature inside the car. The heating system's primary job is to provide a comfortable passenger compartment temperature and to keep car windows clear of fog or frost.
- The main components of an automotive heating system are the heater control valve, the heater core, the blower motor and fan, and heater and defroster duct hoses.
- All air-conditioning systems are based on three fundamental laws of nature: heat flow, heat absorption, and pressure and boiling points.
- The major components of an air-conditioning system are: compressor, condenser, receiver/dryer or accumulator, expansion valve or orifice tube, and evaporator.
- The compressor is the heart of an automotive air-conditioning system. It separates the high-pressure and low-pressure sides of the system. The primary purpose of the unit is to draw the low-pressure vapor from the evaporator and compress this vapor into high-temperature, high-pressure vapor. This action results in the refrigerant having a higher temperature than surrounding air, enabling the condenser to condense the vapor back to liquid.
- The secondary purpose of the compressor is to circulate or pump the refrigerant through the condenser under the different pressures required for proper operation. The compressor is located in the engine compartment.
- There are two basic types of compressors: piston and rotary vane.
- The condenser consists of a refrigerant coil tube mounted in a series of thin cooling fins to provide maximum heat transfer in a minimum amount of space. The condenser is normally mounted just in front of the vehicle's radiator.
- The receiver/dryer is a storage tank for the liquid refrigerant.
- The refrigerant flow to the evaporator must be controlled to obtain maximum cooling, while assuring complete evaporation of the liquid refrigerant within the evaporator. This is accomplished by a thermostatic expansion valve or a fixed orifice tube.
- The evaporator, like the condenser, consists of a refrigerant coil mounted in a series of thin cooling fins. It provides a maximum amount of heat transfer in a minimum amount of space. The evaporator is usually located beneath the dashboard or instrument panel.
- The refrigerant current in use in most air-conditioning systems is R-12. It is nontoxic, nonflammable, and nonexplosive. However, breathing large quantities of R-12 should be avoided, because doing so displaces oxygen in the lungs. Always wear safety glasses and nonleather gloves when handling R-12.
- There are two basic types of automotive air-conditioning systems. They are classified according to the method used in obtaining temperature control and are known as a cycling clutch system or an evaporator pressure control system.
- Evaporator controls maintain a back pressure in the evaporator. Because of the refrigerant temperature/pressure relationship, the effect is to regulate evaporator temperature. The temperature is controlled to a point that provides effective air cooling but prevents the freezing of moisture that condenses on the evaporator.
- Among the many controls used to monitor and maintain the compressor during its operational cycle within various systems are the pressure relief valve, the low- and the high-pressure cutout switches, the ambient temperature switch, and the thermostatic switch. Each of these represents the most common protective control devices designed to ensure safe and reliable operation of the compressor.
- Evaporator controls maintain a back pressure in the evaporator. Because of the refrigerant temperature/pressure relationship, the effect is to regulate evaporator temperature.
- Air-conditioning systems are extremely sensitive to moisture and dirt. Therefore, clean working conditions are extremely important. The smallest particle of foreign matter in an air-conditioning system contaminates the refrigerant, causing rust, ice, or damage to the compressor.
- Air conditioner testing and servicing equipment includes a manifold gauge set, service valves, vacuum pumps, charging station, charging cylinder,

recovery/recycling systems, and leak-detecting devices.
- To put air-conditioning systems in their best condition, the following service procedures should be performed: system discharging, system flushing, compressor oil level checks, evacuation, and system charging.
- Temperature control systems for air conditioners usually are connected with heater controls. Most heater and air-conditioner systems use the same plenum chamber for air distribution. Two types of air-conditioner controls are used: manual/semi-automatic and automatic.

Review Questions

1. What is the amount of heat necessary to change the state of a substance?
2. What type of electromagnetic clutch is used in late-model vehicles?
3. What type of valves do systems that do not utilize stem service valves use?
4. What is the name of the propane torch designed to locate a leak in any part of the air-conditioning system?
5. What causes condensed water to leak from the air-conditioning system?
6. Which of the following laws of nature is the air-conditioning system based on?
   a. heat flow
   b. heat absorption
   c. pressure and boiling points
   d. all of the above
7. Technician A says that a great amount of heat is transferred when a liquid boils or a vapor condenses. Technician B says that a change in pressure does not change the boiling point of a substance. Who is correct?
   a. Technician A
   b. Technician B
   c. Both A and B
   d. Neither A nor B
8. Which of the following statements is true?
   a. Refrigerant leaves the compressor as a high-pressure, high-temperature liquid.
   b. Refrigerant leaves the condenser as a low-pressure, low-temperature liquid.
   c. Refrigerant returns to the compressor as a low-pressure, high-temperature vapor.
   d. None of the above.
9. Which of the following types of compressors is usually used in an air-conditioning system?
   a. piston compressor
   b. rotary vane compressor
   c. both A and B
   d. neither A nor B
10. Which of the following statements is false?
    a. The condenser is normally mounted just in front of the radiator.
    b. The receiver/dryer is a storage tank for the liquid refrigerant from the condenser.
    c. An accumulator is not used in any system with a receiver/dryer.
    d. All of the above.
11. Which of the following is true of R-12?
    a. It is toxic.
    b. It is flammable.
    c. It is destructive to the earth's ozone layer.
    d. All of the above.
12. Technician A says that the thermostatic expansion valve and the fixed orifice tube perform the same function. Technician B says that heat from the evaporator core surface is lost to the boiling and vaporizing refrigerant. Who is correct?
    a. Technician A
    b. Technician B
    c. Both A and B
    d. Neither A nor B
13. Technician A says that suction lines are very warm to touch. Technician B says that discharge lines connect the compressor to the condensor. Who is correct?
    a. Technician A
    b. Technician B
    c. Both A and B
    d. Neither A nor B
14. Which of the following does not cause foaming in the receiver/dryer sight glass?
    a. insufficient refrigerant
    b. leaks in the system
    c. moisture in the system
    d. none of the above
15. Technician A says that the oil level of the compressor should be checked every year. Technician B says that the system should be charged only after it has been completely evacuated. Who is correct?
    a. Technician A
    b. Technician B
    c. Both A and B
    d. Neither A nor B
16. Technician A says that in a POA valve system, the compressor operates in on and off cycles. Technician B says that an oil by-pass line connects from the bottom of the evaporator to the POA valve. Who is correct?
    a. Technician A
    b. Technician B
    c. Both A and B
    d. Neither A nor B
17. Which of the following is electrically connected in series with the compressor electromagnetic clutch?

a. ambient temperature switch
   b. thermostatic switch
   c. pressure cycling switch
   d. none of the above
18. Which of the following determines the temperature of the evaporator core by limiting the minimum evaporator pressure?
   a. STV
   b. POA
   c. EPR
   d. all of the above
19. When is the manifold gauge set used?
   a. discharging
   b. charging
   c. evacuating
   d. all of the above
20. Which of the following does not cause excessive heat?
   a. loose or damaged control cable
   b. water flow control valve stuck open
   c. flow control valve not opening fully
   d. thermatic fan faulty
21. A heating system includes all of the following parts except a _____.
   a. heater core
   b. ventilation system
   c. receiver/dryer
   d. distribution plenum
22. All of the following statements are true except _____.
   a. the evaporator changes heated refrigerant to a liquid
   b. automatic temperature control operates to maintain a set temperature
   c. air conditioner/heater systems can be computer-controlled
   d. heaters and air conditioners use the same plenum chambers
23. A heater does not supply enough heat. The coolant level and blower are correct. Technician A says that a misadjusted heater control could be the cause. Technician B says that a bad thermostat could be the cause. Who is correct?
   a. Technician A
   b. Technician B
   c. Both A and B
   d. Neither A nor B
24. Technician A says that evacuating (pumping down) an air-conditioning system removes air and moisture from the system. Technician B says that evacuating (pumping down) an air-conditioning system removes dirt particles from the system. Who is correct?
   a. Technician A
   b. Technician B
   c. Both A and B
   d. Neither A nor B
25. To charge an air-conditioning system while it is running, the refrigerant should be added to _____.
   a. the high side
   b. the low side
   c. both the high and low sides
   d. either the high or the low side

39 OTHER SAFETY AND SECURITY EQUIPMENT

Objectives

- Identify and describe devices that contribute to automotive safety.
- Explain the difference between active and passive restraint systems.
- Identify the major parts of passive belt systems.
- Know how to service and repair passive belt systems.
- Describe the function and operation of air bags.
- Safely disarm and inspect an air bag assembly.
- Describe the purpose of energy-absorber bumpers.
- Identify the various types of energy-absorber bumpers.
- Describe the operation of keyless entry systems.
- Identify the various security disabling devices.
- Understand the operation of the various security alarms.
- Identify the components of typical radio and audio systems.
- Detail the types of safety glass.

Safety is foremost in the minds of automobile manufacturers. According to a survey by the Insurance Institute for Highway Safety, occupant protection has emerged as a leading factor in determining which car Americans will buy. According to the institute, 68% of the households surveyed ranked the "degree to which the car protects people" as a very important purchase-decision factor. While only 2% of those surveyed were driving a car with an air bag, 48% said they want one on their next car.

There are some safety technological advancements that will be available in the very near future. Traction control is already available on a few models. It keeps a wheel from spinning by reducing the power sent to the offending wheel. One manufacturer presently has taken traction control a step further by reducing the engine's power if the computer senses a certain G-force level indicating the car is going into a corner too fast. No matter how far the accelerator is depressed, the engine will not generate more than nominal power.

There will be no wire harnesses as we currently know them. Single wire multiplexing will allow a single wire, or optical fiber, to carry electrical signals to all parts of the vehicle.

Radar braking is still a ways off, but it is definitely in development. Radar, brakes, and the accelerator will be linked to determine when the brakes should be applied and then will apply them automatically. The system will take speed, weather conditions, and other factors into consideration. (The driver will still be able to apply the brakes, of course.) At a recent auto show, manufacturers showed sonar near-obstacle detection systems for parking and backing up.

Sleepy-driver alerts, already being used in trucks, will very likely begin showing up in automobiles. Communication systems will increase. Car telephones will be standard. Navigation systems using satellites will pinpoint the location of a vehicle. Signals will be transmitted from road signs to automatically display information to the driver or directly to the vehicle control system to increase driver safety.

It is important for auto technicians to keep up with all the safety developments of industry by reading trade publications and manufacturer's literature.

☐ SAFETY GLASS

Safety glass is used in all auto windows and doors. The safety glass employed in today's vehicles is of two types: laminated or tempered. These types are considered to be safety glass because of their construction. They also have government approval.

Laminated plate glass is used to make all windshields. This type of glass consists of two thin sheets of glass with a thin layer of clear plastic between them. Some glass manufacturers have increased the thickness of the plastic material for greater strength. When this type of glass is broken, the plastic material will tend to hold the shattered glass in place and prevent it from causing injury (Figure 39-1). The plastic or vinyl material is usually clear to provide an unimpeded view through the windshield from all angles.

Tempered glass is used for side and rear window glass but rarely for windshields. This type of glass is a single piece of heat-treated glass and has more resistance to impact than regular glass of the same thick-

Figure 39-1 Lamination kept windshield glass intact upon impact.

ness. The strength of tempered glass results from the high compression of its surfaces. This high compression is induced by rapidly heating the glass to approximately 1100 degrees Fahrenheit. The high temperature softens the glass. The glass is then cooled rapidly by blowing air on both flat surfaces. The resulting rapid contraction adds compressive stress to the surface of the glass, which strengthens the glass. Because of this compression, tempered glass cannot be cut, drilled, or ground after the tempering process.

When tempered glass is broken, the pieces of glass are small and have a granular texture. The shattered glass has an interlocked structure to it that obstructs visibility. This is one reason tempered glass is not used in windshields. Another reason is that this type of glass does not readily give and would, therefore, cause more severe head injuries in a collision. Tempered glass will also shatter if previously damaged or stressed. For example, a chipped edge or a stone striking it can weaken the glass so that it suddenly shatters some time after the initial defect is incurred.

Zone-tempered glass is sometimes used for windshields. Zone-tempered glass, which has a lesser degree of tempering in the area directly in front of the driver, prevents these small cracks from developing in the prescribed area in the event of glass breakage.

Antilacerative glass is similar to conventional multi-layered glass, but it has one or more additional layers of plastic affixed to the passenger compartment side of the glass. This glass is used in the front windshield only and is added protection against shattering and cuts during impact.

Tinted glass can be laminated or tempered glass. Tinted laminated glass contains a light green shade of vinyl material to filter out most of the sun's glare. This type of windshield glass is helpful in reducing eye strain, driver tension and fatigue, and prevents fading of the interior furnishings. Some windshields are shaded to reduce the sun's glare. This type uses only a dark band or section across the top part of the windshield. Tinted or shaded glass is usually recommended if the vehicle is equipped with air conditioning.

Glass can also be tinted by adding minute quantities of metal powder to the other normal ingredients of glass to give it a particular color. The addition of cobalt gives the glass a blue tint. Iron gives the glass a reddish tint. Another solar-control windshield glass has a virtually invisible layer of metal to reflect long-wavelength heat energy, reducing the solar load by 60%. Short-wavelength visible light is transmitted normally. The net result of solar safety glass is a reduced load for the air conditioner and longer life for interior trim components.

An antenna wire for radio reception is placed either between the layers of laminated glass (windshield) or printed on the surface of the glass (rear window). Some rear windows have both antenna wires and heating wires side by side. That is, before heat treatment, metal powder, which conducts electricity, is printed on the glass surface in the form of heating wires. The metal powder is baked on the surface during the tempering process. In some rear window glass, a wire grid is unobtrusively embedded in it to provide the antenna function.

There are two types of glass found in heated windshield systems. One system uses glass that contains three layers of material. That is, a plastic laminate is sandwiched between two layers of glass. A silver and zinc oxide coating is fused onto the back of the outer glass layer to carry the electrical current. This coating gives the windshield a slight gold tint. Silver busbars fused into the coating at the top and bottom of the windshield connect the coating to power and ground circuits (Figure 39-2). A sensor watches for windshield damage. The control module checks to see if there is a voltage drop across the sensor before starting the system. A voltage drop means there is an open in the windshield circuit, which may be the result of a crack in the windshield (Figure 39-3). The manufacturer recommends replacing the windshield if there is any damage at all.

The other type of glass used in heated windshields also has three layers. The inner layer is not a plastic

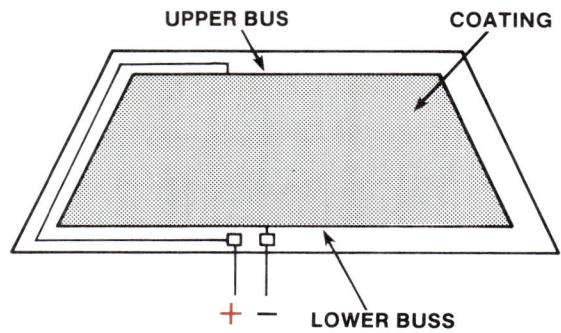

Figure 39-2 Silver busbars connect the silver and zinc oxide coating to the power and ground circuits. *Courtesy of Ford Motor Co.*

Other Safety and Security Equipment 1005

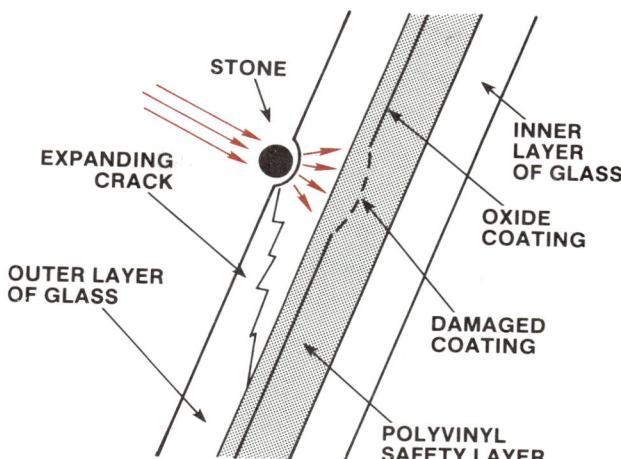

Figure 39-3 A stone hitting a heated windshield system could damage the inner silver and zinc oxide coating. This could cause an open in the circuit. *Courtesy of Ford Motor Co.*

laminate, but a thin film of resistive coating sprayed between the inner and outer windshield. The coating is transparent, so there is no tint. While there is a sense resistor in the circuit, the windshield glass does not require replacement when cracks or chips are not deep enough to break the inner coating. The standard methods of chip and "bull's eye" repair systems are given in the manufacturer's service manual.

Instructions for the replacement of cracked or broken glass can be found in the vehicle's service manual.

❏ RESTRAINT SYSTEMS

All vehicles built or sold in the United States must now have one or both of these passive restraints: automatic seat belts or air bags. Both have made a tremendous impact on driver safety over the last few years. It is very important that technicians are able to service these systems.

Seat Belts

Prior to 1990, there were two types of seat belts in common use. The active restraint system is one that a vehicle's occupant must make a manual effort to use (Figure 39-4). For example, in most vehicles the passenger must fasten the seat belts for crash protection. The passive restraint system operates automatically (Figure 39-5). No action is required of the occupant to make it functional. Federal law requires that all cars sold in the United States after 1990 be equipped with a passive restraint. In some vehicles, this means that air bags are standard equipment. In others, passive seat belts are employed.

The passive seat belt system automatically puts shoulder belts on the driver and front seat passenger (Figure 39-6). It operates by means of electric motors. The movement is accomplished with carriers and track assemblies at the top of the door frames. One end of each belt attaches to the carriers. The other ends are secured to inertia lock retractors. The retractors are mounted in the center console. When the doors are closed and the ignition turned on, the belts move rearward and secure the occupants.

The shoulder harness webbing is attached to a retractor. The retractor for the front seat is located in the B-pillar. The rear seat belt retractor is located in the C-pillar. The webbing then passes through a guide above and behind the occupant's shoulder that directs the webbing at the proper downward angle over the

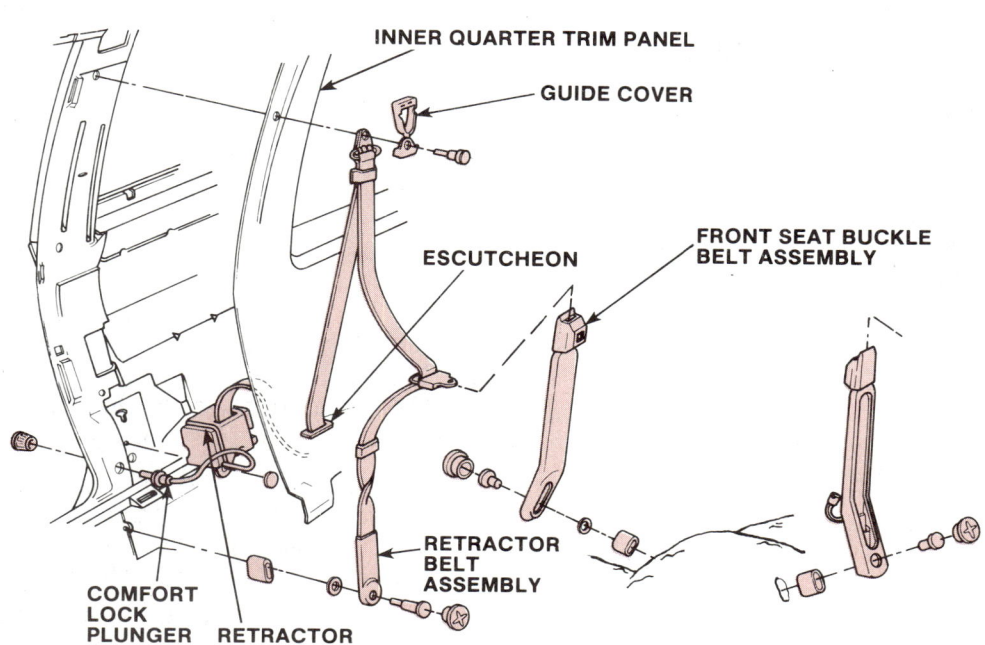

Figure 39-4 Active restraint system. *Courtesy of Ford Motor Co.*

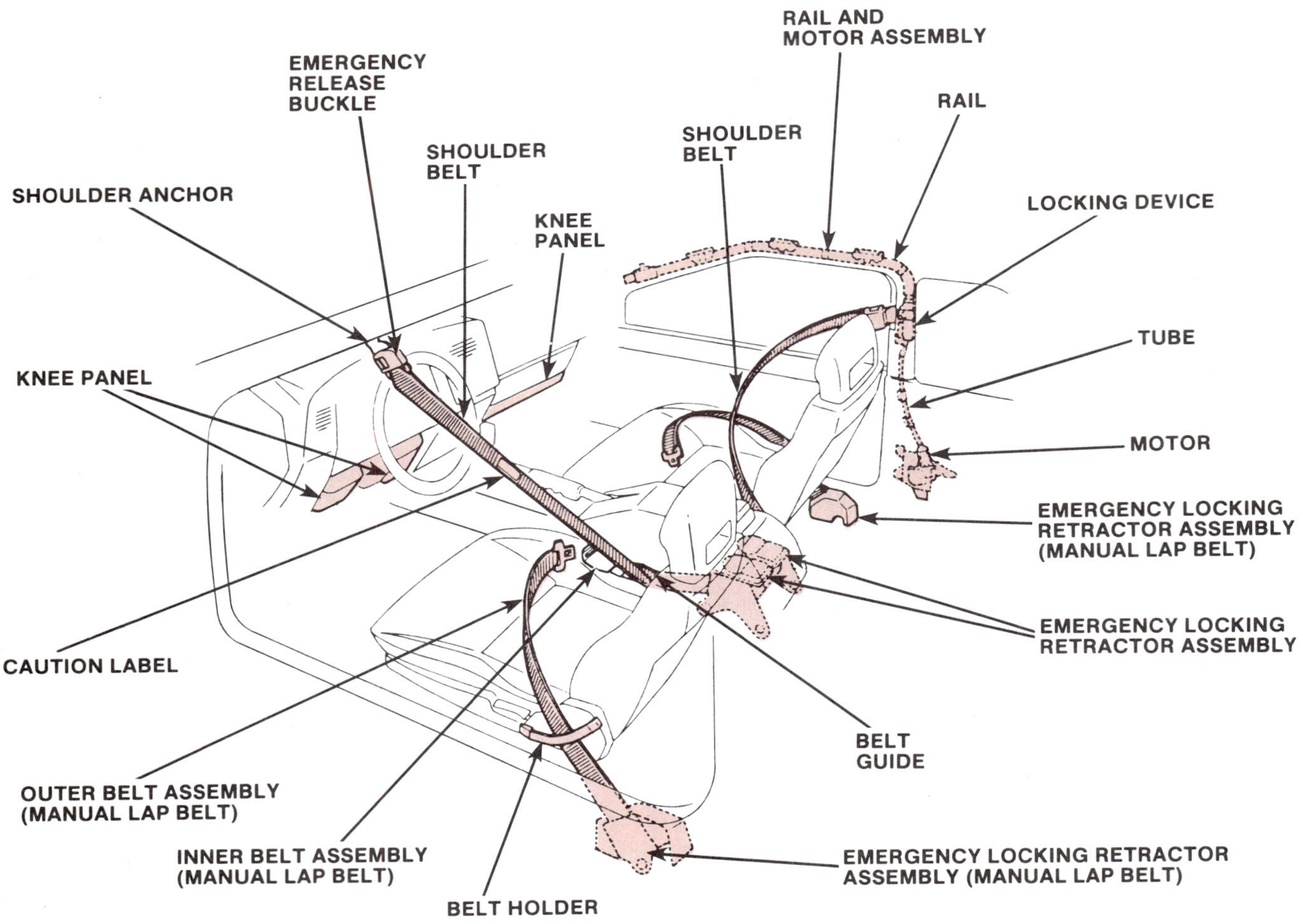

1006 Section 9 Passenger Comfort

Figure 39-5 Passive seat belt restraint system. *Courtesy of Ford Motor Co.*

Figure 39-6 Motorized seat belt in operation. *Courtesy of Ford Motor Co.*

occupant's shoulder and chest and attaches to the lap safety belt buckle. Manually operated (active) lap belts must always be used with the passive shoulder belts.

Servicing Seat Belts

When servicing or replacing lap and shoulder belts, refer to the following precautionary items.

1. Lap and shoulder belts should be serviced as follows:

- Retractor portions of front seat lap and shoulder belt for passenger and driver.
- Buckle portion of front seat lap belt for passenger and driver.
- All belts other than those mentioned will be serviced in complete sets.
- Do not intermix standard and deluxe belts on front or rear seats.

2. Keep sharp edges and damaging objects away from the belts.
3. Avoid bending or damaging any portion of the belt buckle or latch plate.
4. Do not attempt repairs on lap or shoulder belt retractor mechanisms or lap belt retractor covers. Replace them with new replacement parts.
5. Tighten all seat and shoulder belt anchor bolts as specified in the service manual.

A visual and functional inspection of the belts themselves is very important to assure maximum safety. The following inspections provide typical, detailed procedures for seat belt inspection.

Webbing Inspection

Pay special attention to where the webbing contacts maximum stress points, such as the buckle, D-ring,

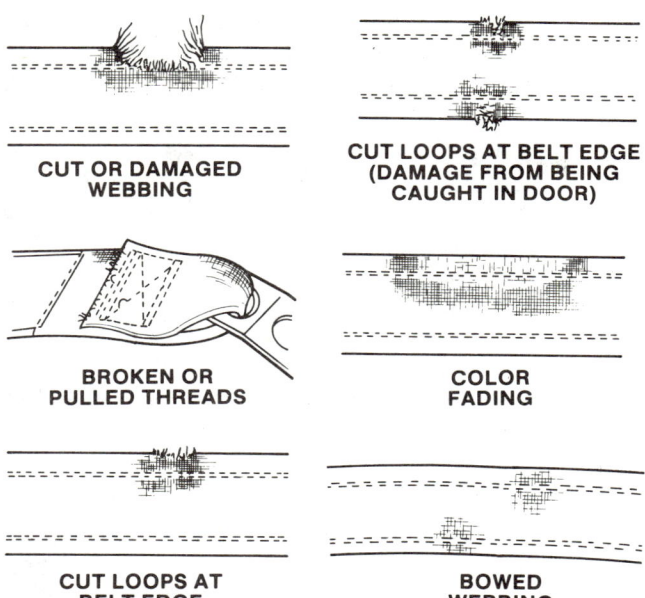

Figure 39-7 Examples of webbing defects.

and retractor. Collision forces center on these locations and can weaken the belt. Signs of damage at these points require belt replacement. Check for twisted webbing due to improper alignment when connecting the buckle. Fully extend the webbing from the retractor. Inspect the webbing and replace with a new assembly if the following conditions are noted (Figure 39-7): cut or damaged webbing, broken or pulled threads, cut loops at belt edge, color fading as a result of exposure to sun or chemical agents, or bowed webbing.

If the webbing cannot be pulled out of the retractor or will not retract to the stowed position, check for the following conditions and clean or correct as necessary: dirty webbing coated with gum, syrup, grease, or other foreign material, twisted webbing, or retractor or loop on B-pillar out of position.

SHOP TALK

Do not bleach or dye the belt webbing. Clean with a mild soap solution and water.

Buckle Inspection

The technician must find out whether or not the buckle works and if the buckle housing cover has been damaged. Insert the tongue of the seat belt into the buckle until a click is heard. Pull back on the webbing quickly to assure that the buckle is latched properly. Replace the seat belt assembly if the buckle does not latch. Depress the button on the buckle to release the belt. The belt should release with a pressure of approximately 2 pounds. Replace the seat belt assembly if the buckle cover is cracked, the push button is loose, or the pressure required to release the button is too high.

Retractor Inspection

Retractors for lap belts should lock automatically once the belt is out fully. The two types of seat belt retractors used with passive seat belt systems are either webbing sensitive or vehicle sensitive. Webbing sensitive seat belt retractors can be tested by grasping the seat belt and jerking it. The retractor should lock up. If it does not, replace the seat belt retractor.

Vehicle sensitive seat belt retractors will not lock up using the same procedure as the webbing sensitive retractors. To test these belts, a braking test is required. Perform this test in a safe place. A helper is required to check the retractors on the passenger side and in the back if the vehicle is equipped with rear lap/shoulder belts.

Do the brake test for each belt by driving the car at 5 to 8 mph and quickly applying the brakes. If a belt does not lock up, replace the seat belt assembly. During this test, it is important for the driver and helper to brace themselves in the event the retractor does not lock up. Replace any belt assembly that does not lock up. If the car is not driveable when it first comes into the shop, check the retractors after the vehicle has been repaired. Make note of their conditions on the damage report.

Most retractors are not interchangeable. That is, an R marked on the retractor tab indicates that it is for the right side only, and an L should be used on the left side only.

On some vehicles both retractor tests are required. Check the service manual.

SHOP TALK

The passive seat belt system is a part of the inertia switch circuit. During an impact, the inertia switch cuts off the power to the restraint system and the fuel pump. Reset the switch to restore operation. It is also important that both shoulder belts be replaced whenever either belt is stressed in a collision. The reason is that the dual retractor assembly might be distorted when either belt absorbs the energy of a collision.

Drive Track Assembly and Anchorage Inspection

The seat belt anchors are found where the retractors attach to the car body. High impact forces occur here during a collision; therefore, be sure to carefully inspect the anchor areas. Look for cracks and distortion in the metal where the retractors and D-rings anchor. The use of shims on the track drive assembly is not recommended. Upper body damage must be properly repaired, returning the vehicle to exact dimensional specifications, before any repairs are performed on the seat belt system. Check for cracks, distortion, and looseness in the bolts that attach the retractors to the body. These bolts are usually large, prevailing torque fasteners. Finally, look for dirt and corrosion in the anchor area.

Loose bolts should be replaced. If there is damage to the metal in the mounting area, proper repairs must be completed before reattaching the anchor. Clean the area prior to welding. Be sure to apply correct MIG welding procedures and restore corrosion protection to the area. When spraying anticorrosion materials, make sure they do not enter the retractor. This can keep it from operating properly.

The drive motor is usually located at the base of the track assembly behind the rear seat side trim panel. Its purpose is to pull the tape that positions the belt. If a check of the drive motor reveals that it is faulty, replace it. Like any motorized system, the seat belt parts need periodic lubrication.

To service the motorized seat belt system, follow the instruction given in the service manual (Figure 39-8).

Seat Belt Tensioners

Some vehicles are equipped with seat belt tensioners. These contain a small explosive charge that is detonated during a collision. This causes the seat belts to tighten during severe frontal impacts. The tensioners, located in the B-pillar, can be used on vehicles with or without air bags. Tensioners will not be deployed if the seat belt is not buckled.

To determine if the tensioner has been deployed or to replace a deployed tensioner, follow the procedures given in the service manual.

Rear Seat Restraint System

Removal and installation of a rear seat restraint system is obvious upon inspection. Check the position of the factory-installed lap belt and single loop belt anchors and reinstall and tighten the anchor plates in same position and torque as specified in the vehicle's service manual.

Some models have a rear center seat belt and a few have them in the front as well. These belts do not have a retractor. In addition to checking the webbing and anchorages, the adjustable slide locking of the belt must be checked.

Fasten the tongue to the buckle and adjust by pulling the webbing end at a right angle to the connector and buckle. Release the webbing and pull upward on the connector and buckle. If the slide lock does not hold, remove and replace the seat belt assembly.

Child Seat

There are three types of child car seats: rear facing, forward facing, or a combination. The car seat is secured with a lap and shoulder seat belt (using a locking clip provided by the car seat manufacturer) or just a lap belt (Figure 39-9). Some child safety sets provide a tether strap that goes over the back of the vehicle seat and attaches to an anchorage in the floor or panel behind the rear seat. If a tethered safety seat is installed in the front seat, the tether strap should be hooked to the rear seat lap belt tongue or the webbing of the buckled rear seat lap belt behind the child safety seat. Attachment holes (at each rear seating position) have been provided to attach the tether anchor hardware kit.

> **SHOP TALK**
>
> All vehicles built for sale in Canada include a tether anchor hardware kit for use with Canadian child safety seats.

When using any infant or child restraint system, follow the instructions provided by the manufacturer

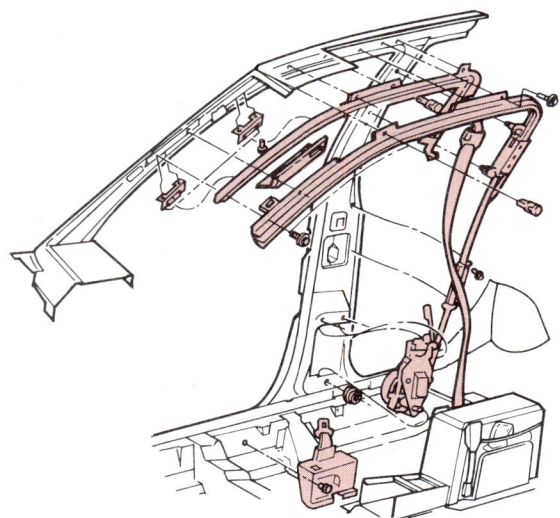

Figure 39-8 Typical motorized seat belt system. The service manual is required to dismantle the system. *Courtesy of Chrysler Corp.*

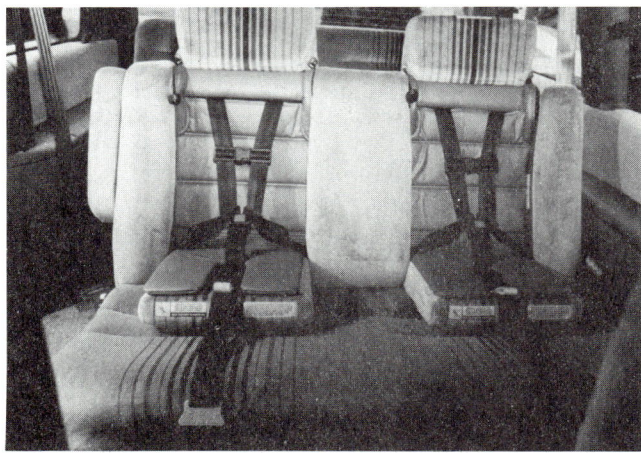

Figure 39-9 Typical integrated child seat arrangement. *Courtesy of Chrysler Corp.*

concerning its installation and use. Failure to follow each of the restraint manufacturer's instructions can result in a child striking the vehicle's interior during a sudden stop or collision.

Warning Light and Sound Systems

When the ignition is turned to the on or run position, the fasten seat belt light should come on. There should also be a buzzer or chime. In some cars there is a computerized voice that directs the occupants to fasten their seat belts. If these warning light and sound systems do not come on, check for a blown fuse or circuit breaker. If that checks out fine, and there is sound but no light, check for a damaged or burned out bulb. If the bulb lights but there is no sound, check for damaged or loose wiring, switches, or buzzer (voice module).

Running some basic electrical checks should locate the problem. Having the proper wiring diagram or service manual on hand can help (Figure 39-10).

Inspecting seat belt systems takes a systematic approach and a focus on detail. Their important function in passenger protection calls for careful attention.

Air Bags

A typical supplemental inflatable restraint (SIR) or air bag system (Figure 39-11) includes three important elements. The electrical system includes the impact sensors and the electronic control module. Its main

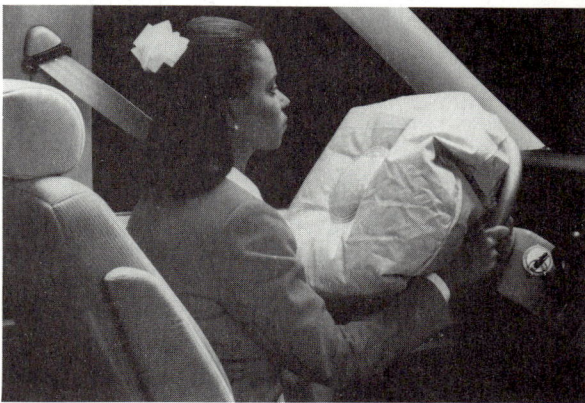

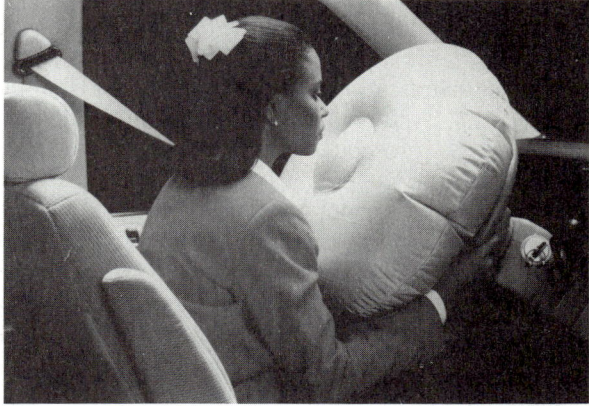

Figure 39-11 Crash sequence of a typical air bag system. *Courtesy of Chrysler Corp.*

functions are to conduct a system self-check to let the driver know that it is functioning properly, detect an impact, and to send a signal that inflates the air bag. The air bag module is located in the steering wheel. It contains the air bag and the ports that cause it to inflate. The knee diverter cushions the driver's knee from impact and helps prevent the driver from sliding under the air bag during a collision. It is located underneath the steering column and behind the steering column trim.

Electrical System Components

The electrical system generally has the following parts.

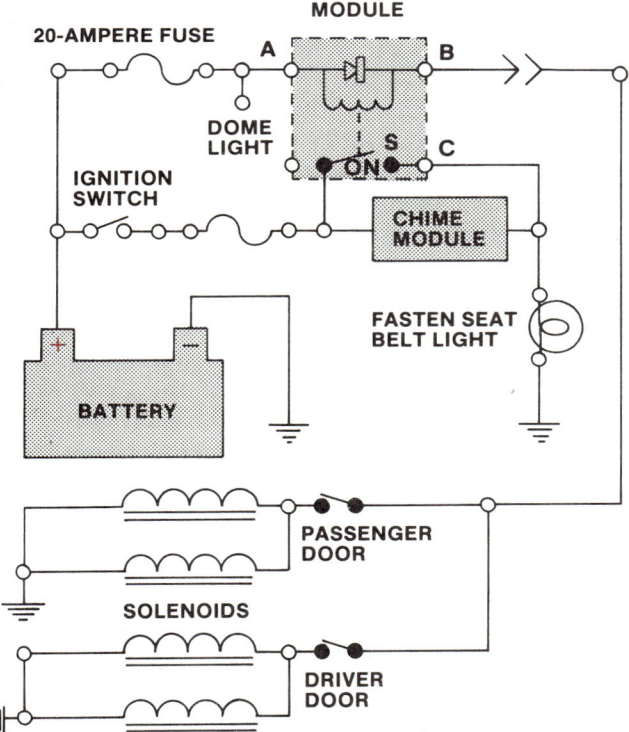

Figure 39-10 Typical seat belt alert system circuit schematic.

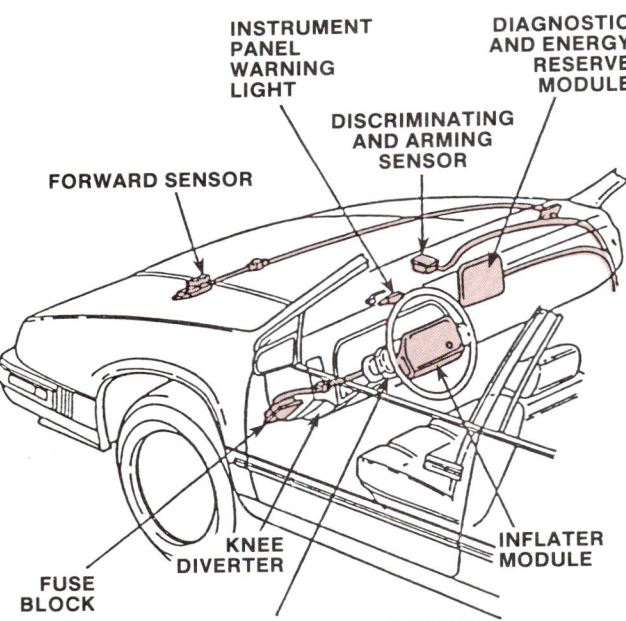

Figure 39-12 Electronic monitor assembly contains a microcomputer that monitors the electrical system components and connections. *Courtesy of Chrysler Corp.*

DIAGNOSTIC MONITOR ASSEMBLY The diagnostic monitor (Figure 39-12) contains a microcomputer that monitors the electrical system components and connections. The monitor performs a self-check of the microcomputer internal circuits and energizes the system readiness indicator during prove out and whenever a fault occurs. System electrical faults can be detected and translated into coded indicator displays. If a certain fault occurs, the microcomputer disables the system by opening a thermal fuse built into the monitor. If a system fault exists and the indicator is malfunctioning, an audible tone signals the need for service. If certain faults occur, the system is disarmed by a firing circuit disarm device incorporated within the monitor or diagnostic module.

An air bag system backup power supply is included in the diagnostic monitor to provide air bag deployment power if the battery or battery cables are damaged in an accident before the crash sensors close. The power supply depletes its stored energy approximately one minute after the positive cable of the battery is disconnected.

WARNING: The backup power supply energy must be depleted before any air bag component service is performed. To deplete the backup power supply energy, disconnect the positive battery cable and wait one minute.

SENSORS The sensors detect impact and signal the air bag to inflate (Figure 39-13). At least two sensors must be activated for the air bag to inflate. There are usually five sensors: two at the radiator support, one at the right-hand fender apron, one at the left-hand

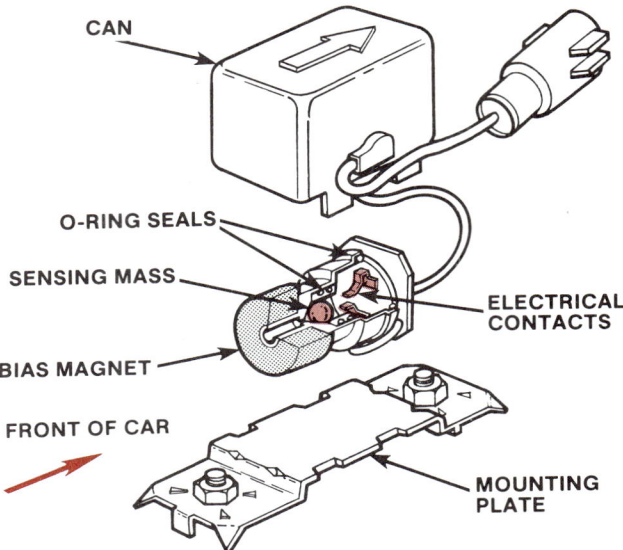

Figure 39-13 Air bag crash sensors consist of a sensing mass (either a ball or a roller) that rolls forward on impact and closes the contacts to activate the deployment circuit. *Courtesy of Chrysler Corp.*

fender apron, and one at the cowl in the passenger compartment. (A few systems use only two sensors—one in front of the radiator and another in the passenger compartment.) There is an interlock between the sensors, so that two or more must work together to trigger the system. Keep in mind that air bag systems are designed to deploy in case of frontal collisions only. While the design of individual systems varies, deployment generally occurs anywhere between 12 to 28 mph.

All the sensors use some type of inertia switching mechanism, which provides for the breakaway of a metal ball from its captive magnet. This function causes a signal to activate a portion of the deployment program set up in the control processor. The system is still capable of directly applying battery power to the squib or detonator. At least two sensors, one safing and one front crash sensor, must be activated to inflate the air bag (Figure 39-14).

An integrated version within this network includes a safing sensor, sometimes attached to the original crash sensor. This device confirms the attitude and magnitude of the frontal deceleration forces and will offer the microprocessor a second opinion before actual deployment. This is all it takes to complete the firing sequence, and the bag will deploy.

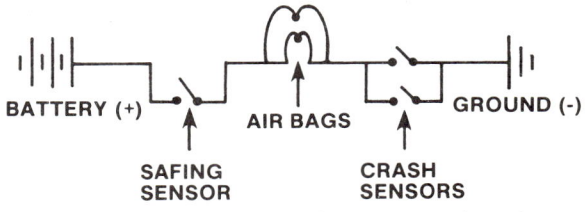

Figure 39-14 Typical air bag firing circuit diagram.

Other Safety and Security Equipment

WIRING HARNESS The harness connects all system components into a complete unit. The wires carry the electricity, which signals the air bag to inflate. The harness also passes the signals during the self-diagnostic sequence.

SIR OR AIR BAG READINESS LIGHT This light lets the driver know the air bag system is working and ready to do its job. The readiness lamp lights briefly when the driver turns the key from off to run. A malfunction in the air bag system causes the light to stay on continuously or to flash, or the light might not come on at all. Some systems have a tone generator that sounds if there is a problem in the system or if the readiness light is not functioning.

Air Bag Module

The bag itself is composed of nylon and is sometimes coated internally with neoprene. All the air bag module components are packaged in a single container, which is mounted in the center of the steering wheel. This entire assembly must be serviced as one unit when repair of the air bag system is required. The air bag module is made up of the following components (Figure 39-15).

IGNITER ASSEMBLY Inflation of the air bag is caused by an explosive release of gas. In order for the explosion to occur, a chemical reaction must be started. The igniter (Figure 39-16) does this when it receives a signal from the air bag monitor. Actually, the igniter is a two-pin bridge device. When the electrical current is applied, it arcs across the two pins creating a spark that ignites a squib or canister of gas generating zerconic potassium perchlorate (ZPP). This material ignites the propellant. Some newer-model seat bags now use solid propellent and argon. This gas has a stable structure, cools more quickly, and is inert as well as nontoxic.

INFLATER MODULE This module contains the ZPP. Once it triggers the igniter, the propellent charge is progressive burning sodium azide, which converts to nitrogen gas as it burns. It is the nitrogen gas that fills the air bag.

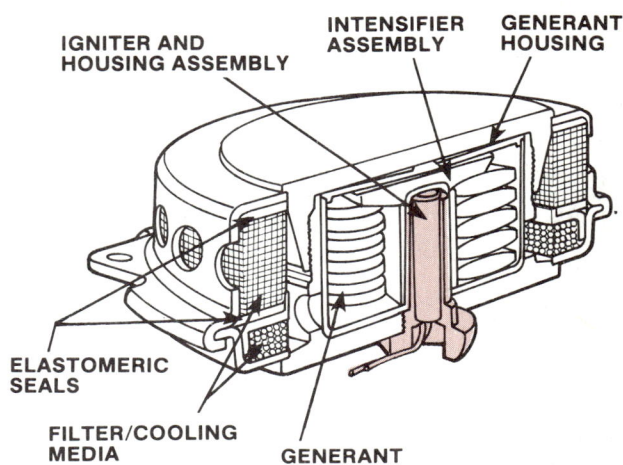

Figure 39-16 Igniter assembly holds the chemical that generates the gas as well as the mechanism that provides the electrical impulse to start the chemical reaction.

Almost as soon as the bag is filled, the gas is cooled and vented, deflating the assembly as the collision energy is absorbed. The driver is cradled in the envelope of the supplemental restraint bag instead of being propelled forward to strike the steering wheel or be otherwise injured by follow-up inertia energy from seat belt restraint systems. In addition, a certain degree of facial protection against flying objects is obtained just when it is needed.

It is important to remember that the tandem action of at least one main sensor and a safing sensor will initiate safety restraint system activation. The microcontroller also provides failure data and trouble codes for use in servicing various aspects of most systems.

MOUNTING PLATE AND RETAINER RING These attach the air bag assembly to the inflator. They also keep the entire air bag module connected to the steering wheel.

LINER AND STEERING WHEEL TRIM COVER The liner houses the air bag. The trim cover goes over the exterior of the steering wheel hub.

Passenger-side air bags are very similar in design to the driver's unit. The actual capacity of gas required to inflate the bag is much greater because the bag must span the extra distance between the occupant and the dashboard at the passenger seating location. The steering wheel and column make up this difference on the driver's side.

CAUTION: When the air bag is deployed, a great deal of heat is generated. While the heat is not harmful to passengers, it may damage or melt the clock spring electrical connector (Figure 39-17). When replacing a deployed air bag module, examine all of the electrical connections for signs of scorching or damage. If damage exists, it must be repaired.

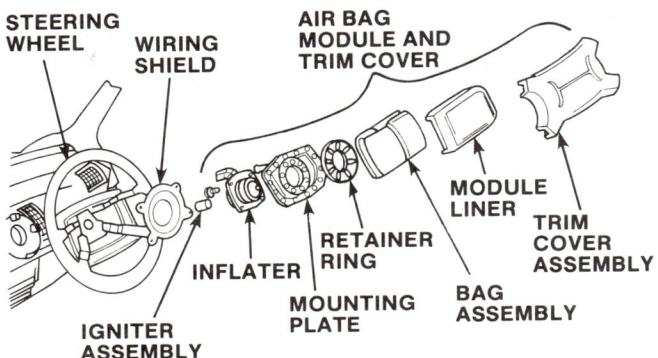

Figure 39-15 Components of a typical air bag module. The individual parts are not serviceable in the field. *Courtesy of Chrysler Corp.*

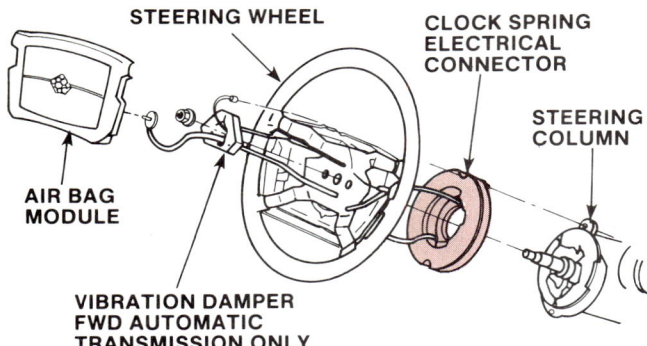

Figure 39-17 Removing the clock spring requires dismantling part of the steering column. The service manual details this procedure. *Courtesy of Chrysler Corp.*

☐ SERVICING THE AIR BAG SYSTEM

A structural service routine, beginning with a thorough visual inspection of sensor integrity, is the best place to start when diagnosing a system with a glowing light. Damage from a collision, or mishandling during a nonrelated repair, can set up a fault area, which will disarm the air bag system. If the vehicle is accessible with a service code procedure or display parameter, troubleshooting can be very straightforward.

Keep in mind that wiring difficulties of any kind call for careful removal of the air bag module and substitution of a jumper wire or special load simulator in its place. This step allows for a safe test sequence with an activated control circuit and should identify any continuity problems or short circuits.

Back-probing a live, powered-up supplemental restraint system with a self-powered multimeter or test light is a sure way to obtain a first-hand demonstration of a bag deployment. The cost involved in revitalizing this system is very expensive, so it would be prudent not to indiscriminately deploy a system.

Sodium hydroxide, a pairing chemical used with the system, can cause severe skin reactions or other more serious side effects.

The removal of the ground battery cable should precede any component service operation. On vehicles with a backup power source, the backup power pack should likewise be disconnected according to the service manual.

Even though the control processor for the air bags keeps tabs on malfunction data and possible related sensor and inertia reel data, the bag itself can be deployed at any time. This holds true because the air bag is electrically coupled directly into the battery through the detonator and the various sensors or crash detectors.

An air bag unitized module is serviced as a complete assembly in all of the available systems to date. Technicians repairing this supplemental system are also advised to service crash sensors, mercury switches, and any other related components in assembly groupings. A crash sensor that has been damaged should be replaced. It would be a good idea to replace the entire set if a failure or degradation of any single sensor is found.

Extreme care must be taken when reinstalling an air bag module. The bag modules should be stored with the horn pad facing up and the aluminum or metallic housing facing down.

The steering column clock spring or spiral wrap, used to electrically link the controller to the bag as well as the crash sensors, should be maintained in its correct index position at all times. Failure to keep the centering spring straight ahead or in the neutral position, relative to the steering wheel, can cause damage to the enclosure, wiring, or module. Any of these situations can cause the air bag system to default into a nonoperative mode.

Pulling the steering wheel to compensate for alignment variations can cause many installation errors, the first being damaging the spiral coupler or clock spring device. Another important consideration might include altering the deflection attitude of the bag for deployment. Even though the removal of the steering wheel itself is essentially similar to non-air bag vehicles, additional caution should be used when servicing these systems.

Safety precautions must be taken when working on or around air bag systems. Before beginning any kind of diagnostic procedures, repair, removal, or installation of any components of an air bag system, disconnect the battery to prevent accidental inflation of the bag. On some vehicles, wait 10 minutes for the auxiliary power supply to discharge. Check the service manual.

If you lay a module down on a surface, make sure the bag and trim cover face up to minimize a launch effect of the module if the bag suddenly inflates.

Defective, or used, air bag modules must be replaced as a whole unit. Do not attempt to service individual parts of these modules.

Wear safety glasses and protective gloves when handling inflated air bags, and wash your hands with soap and water when finished. Inflators in most cases contain irritating and toxic chemicals.

Never probe electrical connectors on an air bag module. This could set off the air bag. Never just toss out a faulty air bag module or uninflated air bag. Some manufacturers stipulate that a deployed air bag must be returned to the manufacturer. Follow specific U.S. Department of Transportation regulations when returning it.

A final inspection of the job should include checking to make sure the sensors are firmly fastened to their mounting fixtures, with the arrows on them facing forward. Be certain all the fuses are correctly rated and replaced. Make sure a final check is made for codes

NUMBER OF FLASHES	PROBABLE CAUSE
NO LIGHT	INOPERATIVE AIR BAG LAMP CIRCUIT
CONTINUOUS FLASHING	DISCONNECTED OR LOOSE MONITOR ASSEMBLY CONNECTOR
LIGHT STAYS ON/NO FLASH	DIAGNOSTIC MODULE FAULT
3	LOSS OF AIR BAG DEPLOYMENT CIRCUIT POWER
5	SHORTED FORWARD CRASH SENSOR DEPLOYMENT CIRCUIT
10	DEFECTIVE FIRING CIRCUIT DISARM DEVICE
4	POTENTIAL SHORT IN AIR BAG DEPLOYMENT CIRCUIT OR IMPROPERLY GROUNDED DASH PANEL SENSOR (MUST USE DIAGNOSTIC FLOW CHART TO TROUBLESHOOT)
6	DRIVER AIR BAG CIRCUIT INOPERATIVE
7	OPEN CIRCUIT IN MONITOR CONNECTOR
8	FORWARD CRASH SENSOR IMPROPERLY ATTACHED OR GROUNDED
9	OPEN FORWARD CRASH SENSOR DEPLOYMENT CIRCUIT
11	OPEN EXTERNAL FLASHER CIRCUIT
2	ALL FORWARD CRASH SENSORS DISCONNECTED

Figure 39-18 Typical trouble code index. For specific index, check service manual. Each number repeats itself, and then, if there is another code, it will be displayed next.

(Figure 39-18) using the approved scan tool. Carefully recheck the wire and harness routing before releasing the car.

> ### USING SERVICE MANUALS
>
> Many service manuals contain air bag testing system function diagrams similar to the two shown in Figures 39-19A and B. With the service manual in hand, connect the scan tool to the diagnostic connector jumper harness, and turn the ignition to the run position. Exit the vehicle and reconnect the battery cable disconnected earlier. The scan tool reads two types of fault codes—temporary and stored. Stored codes can only be erased with a scan tool and only after the problem has been corrected.
>
> With the scan tool attached to the diagnostic connector, begin with test 1 (Figure 39-19A). By following the chart through the steps listed, we first get a blank screen (step 8) and then a no

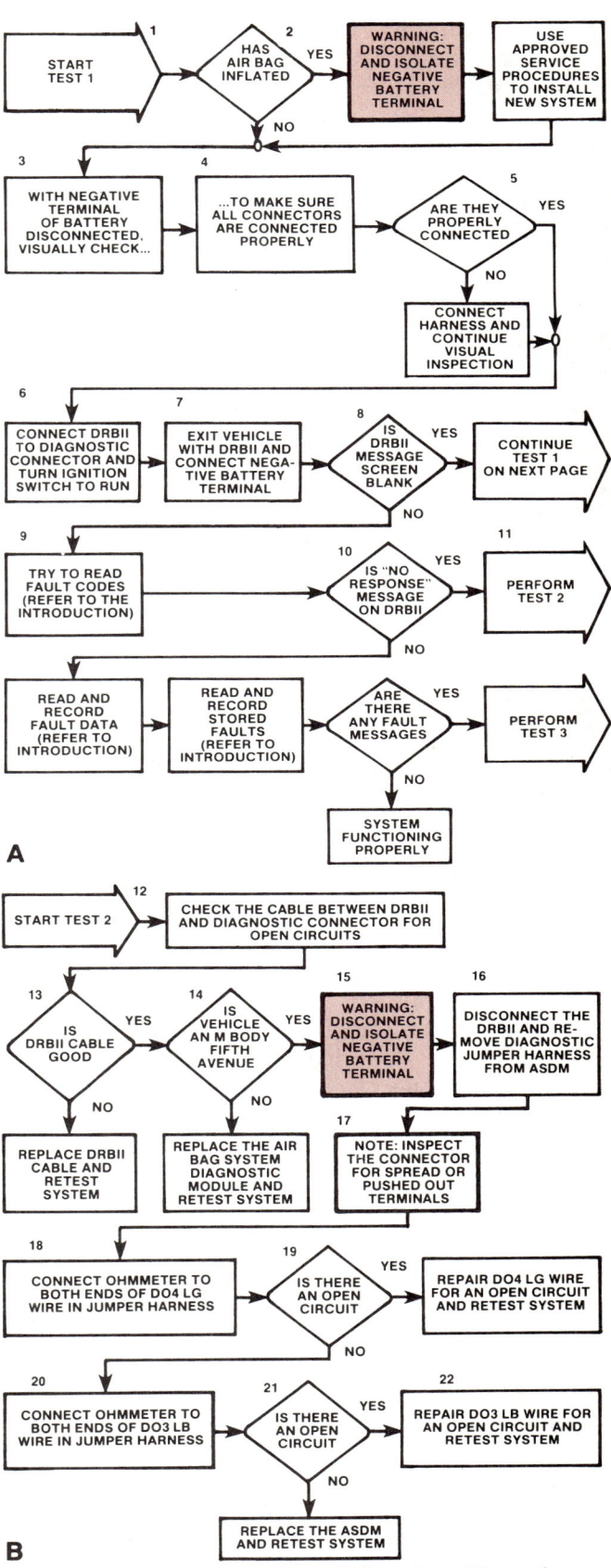

Figure 39-19 (A) Testing system function; (B) test for no response message on DRB. Test 1 is performed before proceeding. *Courtesy of Chrysler Corp.*

response message (step 9). This leads to the flow chart step that tells us to perform test 2.

For test 2 (Figure 39-19B), first check the cable between scan tool and the diagnostic circuit for damaged or open circuits. If none are found, go on. Following the chart, we find that the DRB II cable is good. Disconnect the DRB II and the diagnostic jumper harness. Check connectors for spread or damaged terminals. There are none. Connect an ohmmeter to both ends of DO4LG wire in the jumper harness. No open circuits are found.

Connect an ohmmeter to both ends of DO3LB wire in the jumper harness. There is an open circuit. This is the problem. The damaged harness is repaired or replaced, and the system is retested. This time there is no trouble code. The vehicle is ready to go.

CAUTION: The example illustrates that you are more likely to find loose connectors or damaged wiring or sensors than a faulty diagnostic module. So, do not be hasty to replace expensive parts before checking for simpler solutions. That is why following the directions in the manual is so important.

❏ ENERGY-ABSORBER SAFETY BUMPERS

Modern bumpers are designed to absorb the energy of a low-speed impact, minimizing the shock directed to the frame and to the occupants of the vehicle. Federal regulations require that automobile manufacturers equip their cars with bumpers that could withstand 5 mph collisions. In order to comply with this regulation, manufacturers fit their bumpers with energy absorbers. Most energy absorbers are mounted between the bumper face bar or bumper reinforcement and the frame (Figure 39-20).

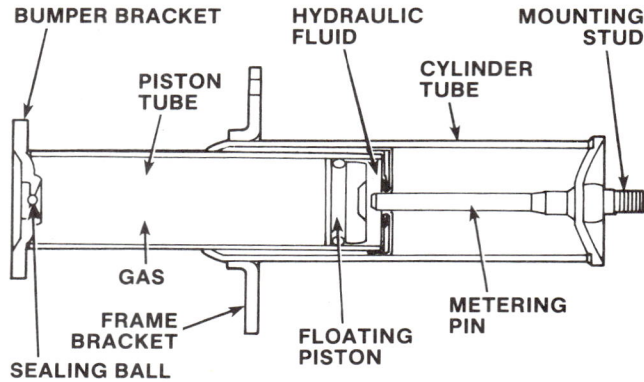

Figure 39-21 Cross section of a typical energy absorber.

There are three types of energy absorbers. The most common is similar to a shock absorber. As shown in Figure 39-21, the typical bumper shock is a cylinder filled with hydraulic fluid. Upon impact, a piston filled with inert gas is forced into the cylinder. Under pressure, the hydraulic fluid flows into the piston through a small opening. The controlled flow of fluid absorbs the energy of the impact. Fluid also displaces a floating piston within the piston tube, which compresses the inert gas. When the force of the impact is relieved, the pressure of the compressed gas forces the hydraulic fluid out of the piston. The compressed gas forces the hydraulic fluid out of the piston tube and back into the cylinder. This action forces the bumper back to its original position.

Another energy absorber design is shown in Figure 39-22. Upon impact, fluid flows from a reservoir through a metering valve into an outer cylinder. When

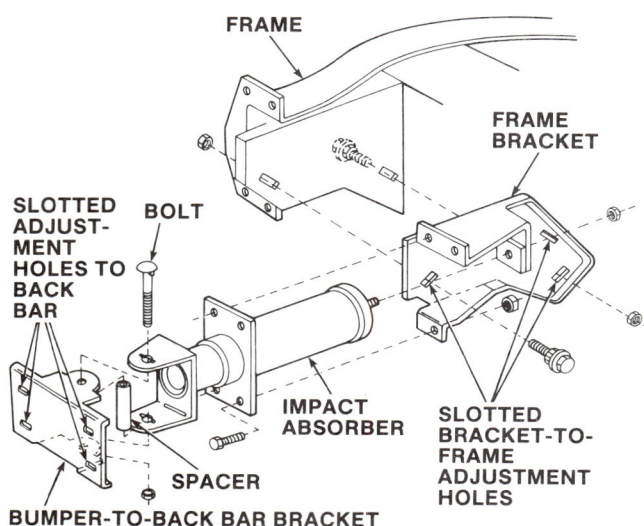

Figure 39-20 Bumper shock absorber.

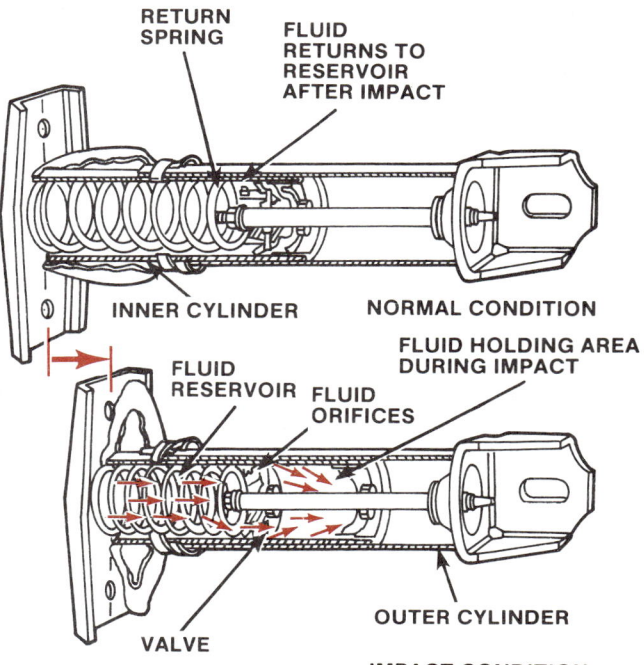

Figure 39-22 Spring-loaded bumper shocks.

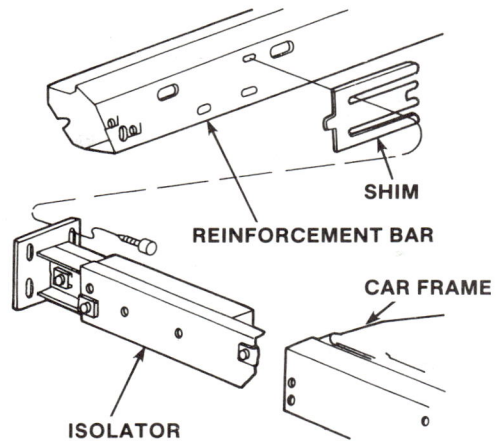

Figure 39-23 Typical bonded isolater bumper absorber.

impact forces are relieved, a spring in the absorber returns the bumper to its original position.

Another type of bumper energy absorber is the isolator (Figure 39-23). It is generally found on Ford vehicles. It works in principle like a motor mount. A rubber pad is sandwiched between the isolator and the frame. Upon impact, the isolator moves with the force, stretching the rubber pad. The give in the rubber absorbs the energy of the impact. When the force is relieved, the rubber retracts to its original shape (unless it is torn from its base by the impact), and returns the bumper to its normal position.

Another type of energy absorber is found on many light imports and sport model vehicles. Instead of shock absorbers mounted between the frame and the face bar or reinforcement bar, a thick urethane foam pad is sandwiched between an impact bar and a plastic face bar or cover. The pad is designed to give a rebound to its original shape in a 2.5 mph collision. On some vehicles the impact bar is attached to the frame with energy-absorbing bolts (Figure 39-24). The bolts and brackets are designed to deform during a collision in order to absorb some of the impact force. The brackets must be replaced in most collision repairs.

Another new bumper system is the self-restoring elastomeric energy-absorbing unit. An elastomeric polymer material gives the energy absorbers the ability to deflect and return to their original position when the car strikes a barrier at speeds up to 5 mph. The elastomer is molded into a hollow cylinder that surrounds the sliding central member of the energy absorber. When the bumper is struck, the elastomeric cylinder compresses, then buckles, providing both an energy-absorbing and an energy-storing effect. After the impact, the energy stored in the elastomeric cylinder returns the unit and the bumper to their original positions.

To replace and install a safety bumper, follow the instructions in the service manual. However, several precautions must be observed when working on bumpers with energy absorbers.

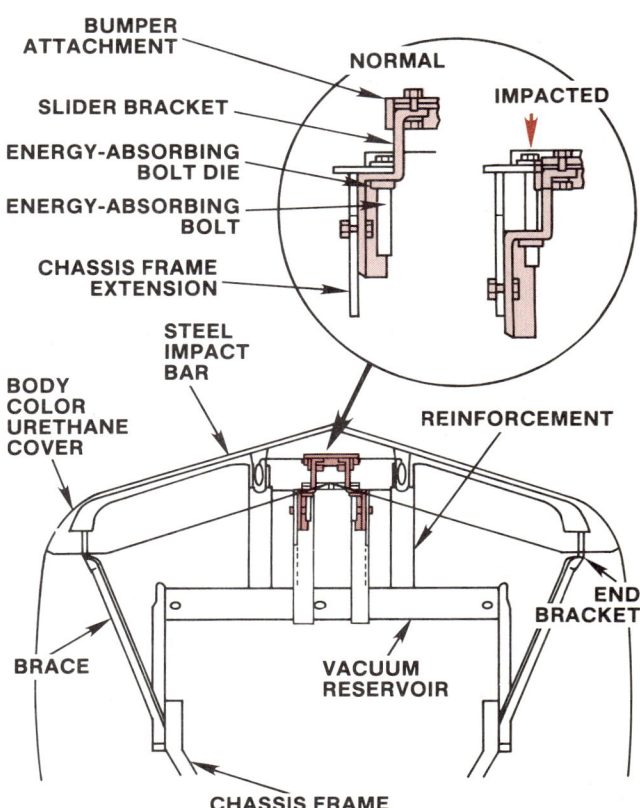

Figure 39-24 Urethane bumper with energy-absorbing bolts.

The shock-type absorber is actually a small pressure vessel. It should never be subjected to heat or bending. If the absorber is bound due to an impact, relieve the gas pressure before attempting to remove the bumper from the vehicle. Secure the bumper with a chain to prevent its sudden release and drill a hole into the front end of the piston tube to vent the pressure. Then, remove the bumper and absorber. Play it safe and wear approved safety glasses when handling, drilling into, or removing a bound energy absorber.

☐ SECURITY AND ANTITHEFT DEVICES

Every 26 seconds a car is stolen somewhere in the United States. Although more than half of the million plus cars stolen every year are luxury or sports cars, any vehicle can become a part of these statistics. However, there are some steps that can be taken to slow down thieves or even scare them off.

There are three basic types of antitheft devices available: locking devices, disabling devices, and alarm systems. Many of the devices are available as OE from the manufacturers; others are aftermarket installed. Like other electrical systems, computers control antitheft devices. The sensors and relays can be checked with a digital multimeter and a jumper wire. Read the service manual for their operation details.

Locks

A variety of locks are available that are designed to deny entry to the engine, passenger, and trunk compartments of the car as well as to prevent a thief from driving the car away. These locking systems include door and trunk locks, keyless entry systems, fuel tanks, light delay systems, and locking steering wheels. With locking steering wheels, when the ignition key is off, the steering wheel cannot be turned (Figure 39-25). A rack and sector are usually used to slide a steel pin into mesh with a slotted disc. Since the disc is splined to the steering shaft, the steering wheel does not turn.

There are both internal and external hood locks available to prevent theft of anything under the hood. These locks are especially useful on a vehicle with a battery-powered alarm system because they prevent a thief from disconnecting the power source or disabling the siren.

Many cars are equipped with special fuel filler doors that help to prevent the theft of gas from the fuel tank. Voltage is present at the fuel filler door release switch at all times. When the switch is closed, the door release solenoid is energized and the fuel door opens.

Antitheft devices are very effective in preventing tires and wheels from being stolen. A special key wrench is required to remove antitheft wheel lug nuts, and it is available only from the manufacturer (Figure 39-26). Hubcap locks (Figure 39-27) are wheelcovers equipped with an antitheft locking system. A special key wrench is required to pry off the center hub ornament and remove the lock bolt.

> **CUSTOMER CARE**
>
> When doing any wheel or tire servicing, show the customer how to change a tire if the wheel is equipped with locking hubcaps.

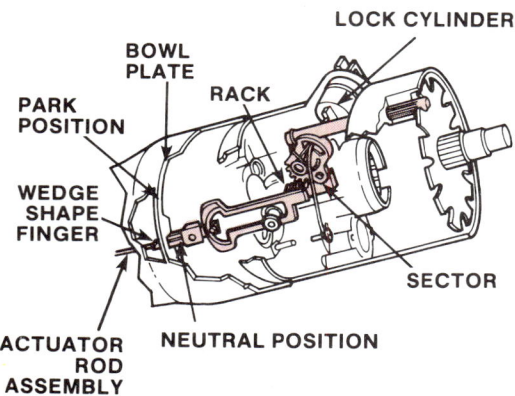

Figure 39-25 Steering wheel locking mechanism. When the ignition key is removed, the steering wheel is locked, which helps prevent theft of vehicle. *Courtesy of General Motors Corp.*

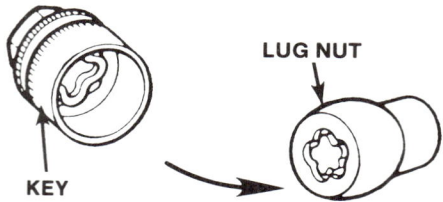

Figure 39-26 Antitheft lug nut and key.

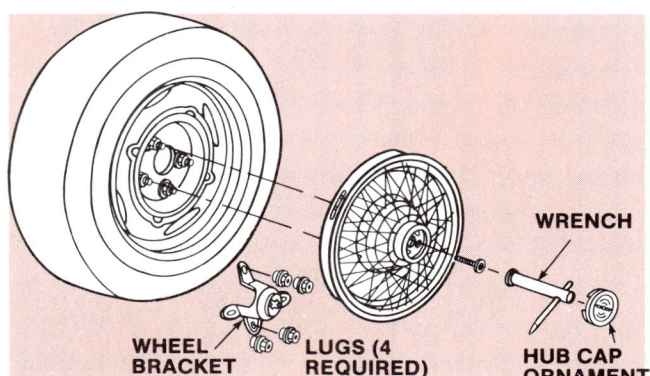

Figure 39-27 Antitheft wire hubcaps.

Some door lock systems automatically engage when vehicle speed exceeds 8 mph (manual transmissions) or when the driver shifts out of park or neutral. Also many vehicles come with child-protection rear door locks. Check the service manual for their repair or replacement.

Keyless Entry System

The keyless entry system allows the driver to unlock the doors or trunk lid from outside of the vehicle without using a key. It has two main components: an electronic control module and a coded-button keypad on the driver's door. Some keyless systems employ an illuminated entry system.

The electronic control module typically performs the following functions.

- Unlocking all doors
- Unlocking the luggage compartment
- Locking all doors
- Automatic locking of all doors when the ignition switch is in the run position, someone is seated in the driver's seat, and the transmission is shifted through the reverse position
- Turning on courtesy lamps and keypad and keyhole illumination after any button on the keypad is pushed or either front door handle is pulled

The control module also accepts and stores an owner's alternate entry code. Either code then operates the system. Wiring for a typical system is shown in Figure 39-28.

In some vehicles the backup lamp switch contacts are also part of the keyless entry system. When the

Other Safety and Security Equipment

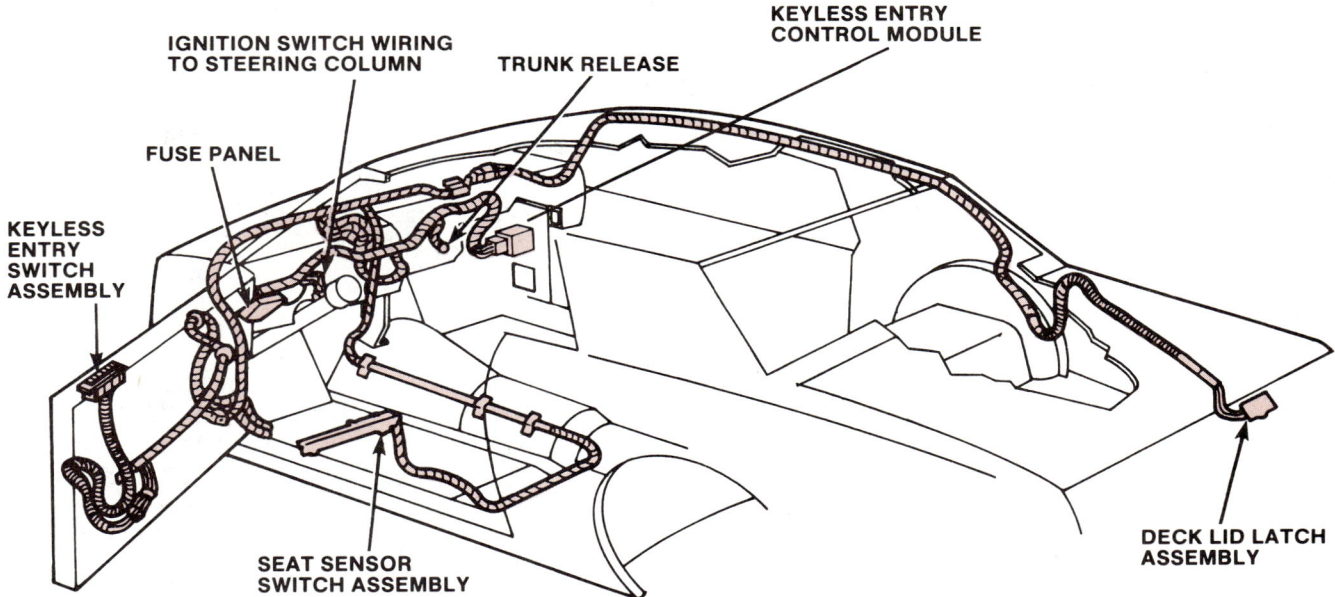

Figure 39-28 Typical keyless door entry wiring. *Courtesy of Ford Motor Co.*

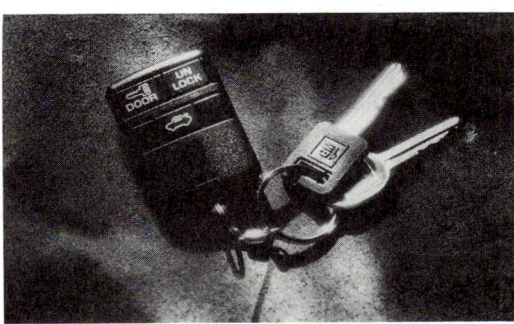

Figure 39-29 Typical remote keyless system transmitter. *Courtesy of General Motors Corp.*

transmission is shifted into or through reverse, the backup lamp switch contacts close, applying voltage to one of the pins of the keyless entry module. This prompts the module to automatically lock all doors (if other conditions are met).

Remote keyless entry systems are now available. They use a hand-held transmitter, frequently attached as part of the key fob (Figure 39-29). With a press of the unlock button on the transmitter, the interior lights turn on, the driver's door unlocks, and the theft security system is disarmed from any direction range from 25 to 50 feet, depending on the type of transmitter. The trunk can also be unlocked. When exiting the car, pressing the lock button locks all doors and arms the security system.

Disabling Devices

Disabling devices can be either actively or passively armed. Actively-armed units are controlled with either a key, a coded sequence or a digital touch-pad, or a hidden button mounted under the dash. Passive devices are part of a combination antitheft system. The more expensive models have a by-pass provision that allows the owner to leave the car at a service station or valet parking lot without telling anyone about the alarm system.

Ignition-Kill System

An ignition-kill system interferes with the ignition to such an extent that the car cannot be hot-wired. In fact, when the ignition kill is activated, not even the ignition key starts the car.

An ignition-kill system has definite advantages. There is nothing to transport, no codes to remember, and nothing visible to mar the exterior of the car or to alert a thief.

One of the latest ignition-kill systems is the pass-key arrangement (Figure 39-30). This unique system features an electronic pellet in the vehicle's ignition key. The ignition lock reads the electronic coding. Without the proper key coding, the engine does not start.

Hydraulic Lock

Hydraulic locks are permanently installed in the brake lines. They block the flow of fluid and lock up all four brakes so the car cannot move. A key lock is used to release the pressure on the brakes (Figure 39-31).

Alarm Systems

The two methods for activating alarm systems are passive and active. Passive systems switch on automatically when the ignition key is removed or the doors are locked. They are often more effective than active systems.

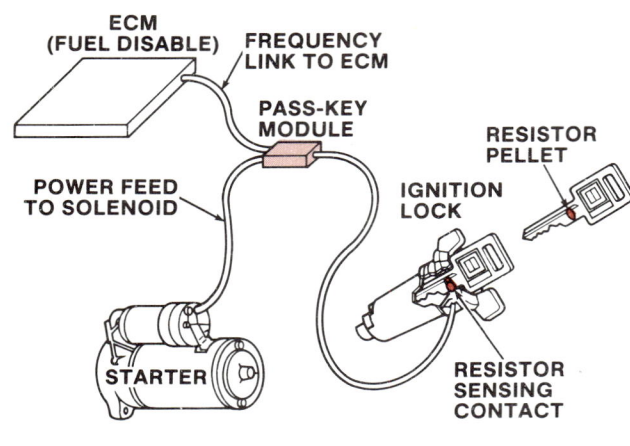

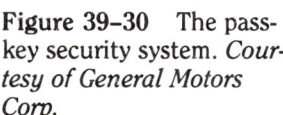

Figure 39-30 The pass-key security system. *Courtesy of General Motors Corp.*

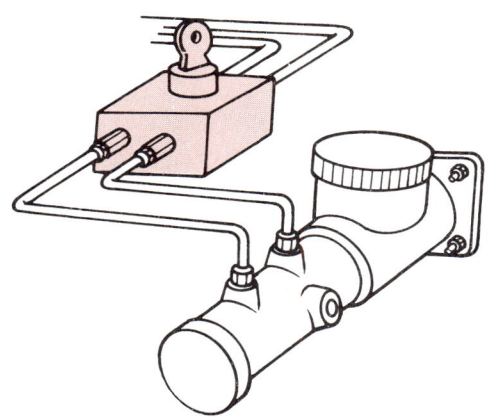

Figure 39-31 Hydraulic lock installed in brake system.

Active systems are activated manually with a key, keypad, or toggle switch. They allow the driver to leave the car at a service station or parking garage without disclosing the secrets of the system to the attendant. The disadvantage is that you must remember to turn the alarm on and off.

Among the number of devices used to trigger an alarm system, mechanical switches are similar to those used to turn on the courtesy lights as the doors are opened. When a door, hood, or trunk is opened, the switch closes and the alarm sounds. It turns itself off automatically (provided the intruder has stopped trying to enter the car) to prevent the battery from being drained. It then rearms itself automatically.

Ultrasonic sensors are like the ones used at the supermarket to open doors automatically. They sound

Figure 39-32 Ultrasonic sensor triggers the alarm when someone enters the car.

the alarm if someone tries to enter the car, either through a door or window (Figure 39-32).

Current-sensitive sensors activate the alarm if a change in current occurs within a car's electrical system. When a courtesy light goes on or the ignition starts, the alarm is activated. However, it might not be practical to use this type of sensor in a car in which the light does not turn on when the back doors are opened.

The majority of law enforcement officials recommend siren alarms over silent page alarms. A siren alarm calls attention to the car and startles the intruder. With a silent page alarm, the owner carries a pager that beeps when someone tampers with the car. However, this can be dangerous because many people recklessly confront the thief alone rather than call the police.

While increased numbers of vehicles are being equipped with security and antitheft devices, the majority of installation and repair work is done by a general auto technician. It is important for you to keep abreast of both OE and aftermarket systems for the latest information on security and antitheft equipment.

❏ OTHER ELECTRONIC EQUIPMENT

As was stated in the beginning of this chapter, there is a great deal of automobile electronic equipment at the drawing board stage. Of the important comfort and safety electronic and electrical, the most popular is the radio.

Radio and Audio Systems

Entertainment radios are available in a wide variety of models. The complexity of the system varies significantly from the basic AM radio to the compact disc (CD) player with high-power amplifiers and multiple speakers. However, the overall operation of the radio itself is electrically basically the same.

The major components in a basic AM system are a radio receiver and speaker (Figure 39-33A). In the more complex stereo systems, the major components are an AM/FM radio receiver, a stereo amplifier, sound amplifier switch, several speakers, and a power antenna system (Figure 39-33B).

Other Safety and Security Equipment 1019

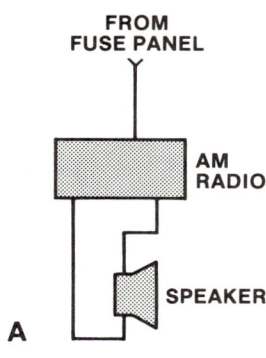
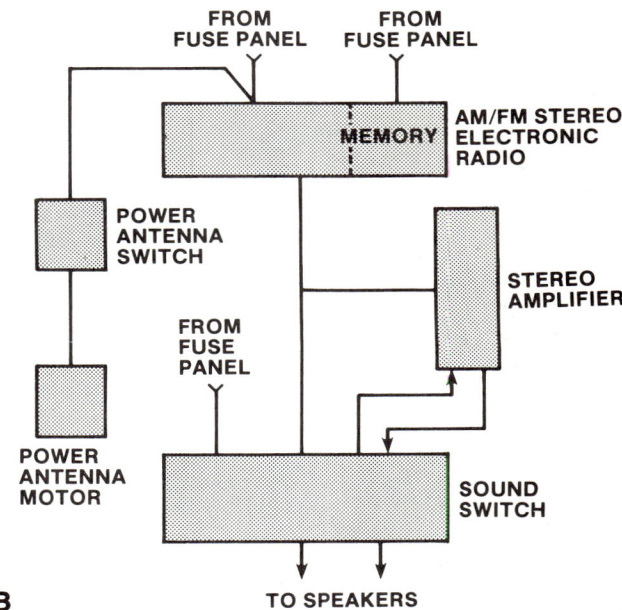

Figure 39-33 Typical radio systems: (A) AM radio and (B) AM/FM stereo electronic radio. *Courtesy of Ford Motor Co.*

Internal diagnostic examination of the radio should be left to the authorized radio service center. However, the automotive technician should be able to analyze and isolate radio reception conditions to the area or component causing the condition. All radio conditions can be isolated to one of five general areas. The trouble will be found in the antenna system, radio chassis (receiver), speaker system, radio noise suppression equipment, or sound system.

Operation of the AM radio requires only the power from the fuse panel to be available at the radio. The radio intercepts broadcast signals with its antenna and produces a corresponding input to the system speaker. In addition, some radios have built-in memory circuits to ensure that the radio returns to the previously selected station when the radio or ignition switch is turned off and back on again. Some of these memory circuits require an additional power input from the fuse panel that remains hot at all times. The current draw is very small and requires no more power than a clock. However, if battery power is removed, the memory circuit has to be reset.

The service manual and owner's guide for the vehicle contain detailed information concerning radio operation. If the radio system is not working, check the fuse. If the fuses are okay, refer to the service manual. Remember, the radio chassis (receiver) itself should only be serviced by a qualified radio technician or specialty radio service shop. If a technician determines that the radio itself is the problem, remove the radio, and send it to a qualified radio person.

Power Antenna

Over the years various methods have been made to hide the conventional mast radio antenna. The functional advantages of doing this are improved exterior appearance, elimination of one source of wind noise, and heightened resistance to antenna-snapping vandalism. As already mentioned, radio antennas are embedded into the front windshield and rear window. One of the newest hidden antennas is a special two-by-three foot plastic film that provides a ground plane for the reception of both AM and FM radio signals. This flat antenna is sandwiched unobtrusively between the headliner and roof panels.

In spite of many efforts to hide the antenna, the most popular method is still the power antenna. In addition, an auto technician can service the power antenna switch and motor. The power antenna switch is a spring-loaded switch with up, down, and center positions. In either the up or down position, power from the fuse panel is applied to the power antenna motor to move the antenna up or down as desired (Figure 39-34). The power antenna motor is a two-directional motor. It is part of the antenna assembly (Figure 39-35). It is controlled by the power antenna switch. The antenna should be in its fully extended position for the radio to work properly.

If AM reception is extremely poor and FM reception appears to have trouble holding stations, make sure the antenna and antenna connectors are properly mated. If the antenna connectors are properly mated but the reception is still poor, replace the antenna cable. If only FM reception is poor, it is unlikely that the antenna is at fault. Remove the radio chassis for service.

> **CUSTOMER CARE**
>
> Many customers do not understand the limitations of FM reception. Refer your customer to the owner's guide for information about the limitations of FM radio performance.

1020 Section 9 **Passenger Comfort**

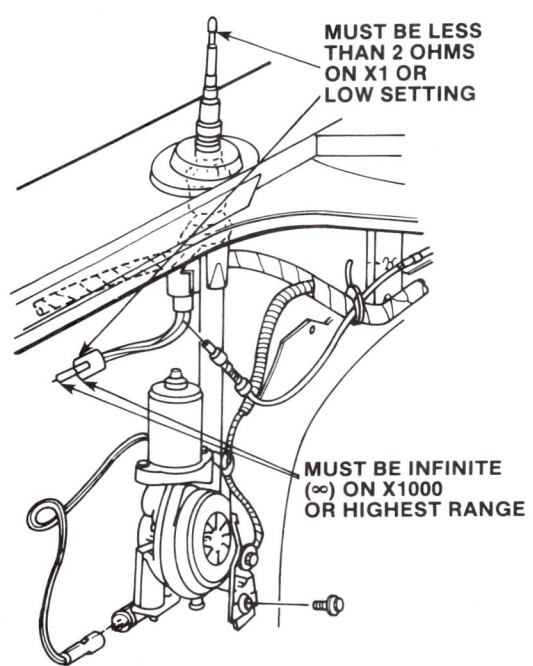

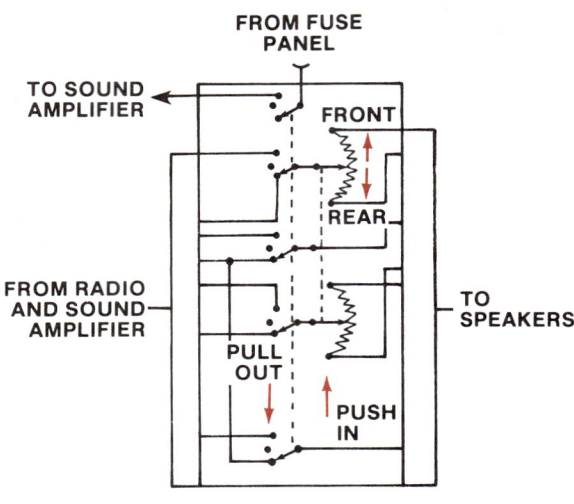

Figure 39-34 Power antenna switch. *Courtesy of Ford Motor Co.*

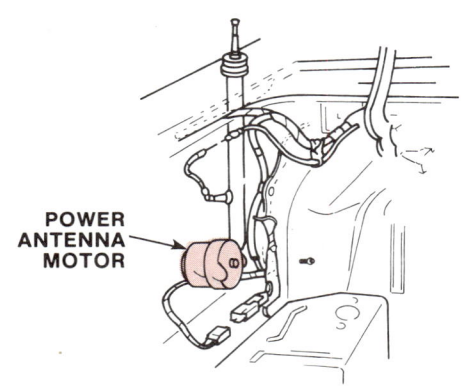

Figure 39-35 Typical power antenna motor. *Courtesy of Ford Motor Co.*

Noise Suppression

The vehicle's ignition system is a source of radio interference. This high-voltage switching system produces a radio frequency electromagnetic field that radiates at AM, FM, and CB frequencies. Although components have been designed into the vehicle to minimize this concern, the noise is more noticeable if the radio is tuned slightly off channel when listening to FM programs. Vehicle electrical accessories and owner add-on accessories may also contribute to radio interference. Furthermore, there are many noise sources that are external to the vehicle. These include power lines, communication systems, ignition systems of other vehicles, and neon signs.

The most effective method of evaluating ignition noise is to compare the radio performance with the engine on, versus engine off. To identify the source of ignition noise, check to see if the spark plug wires are suppressors and the spark plugs are the correct resistors.

Noise suppression components may be malfunctioning or missing. Check the band ground strap effectiveness. Wedge a large file between the metal parts, such as between the tailpipe and body, or between the fender and frame. This ensures a proper ground while the radio is playing and engine is running. Listen for a decrease in the objectionable radio noise. If a reduction in radio noise is noted, first try tightening body and exhaust system clamps and brackets. Then, if necessary, install a new band strap between the two metal parts to ensure proper ground.

CUSTOMER CARE

Be sure to alert your customer that before turning off the radio or the ignition of the vehicle, always eject any cassette being played. Leaving the tape mechanism stopped while a tape is engaged can result in damage to the tape, pinch roller, or capstan. Also, tell the customer not to leave a tape cassette engaged in the tape player slot when not in use. Remove it completely to permit the slot door to close and keep out airborne dirt.

Speaker and Sound Quality

Poor speaker or sound quality is usually caused by one of the following.

Experience has shown that rattles and buzzes are caused more often by loose speakers, speaker mount-

Other Safety and Security Equipment

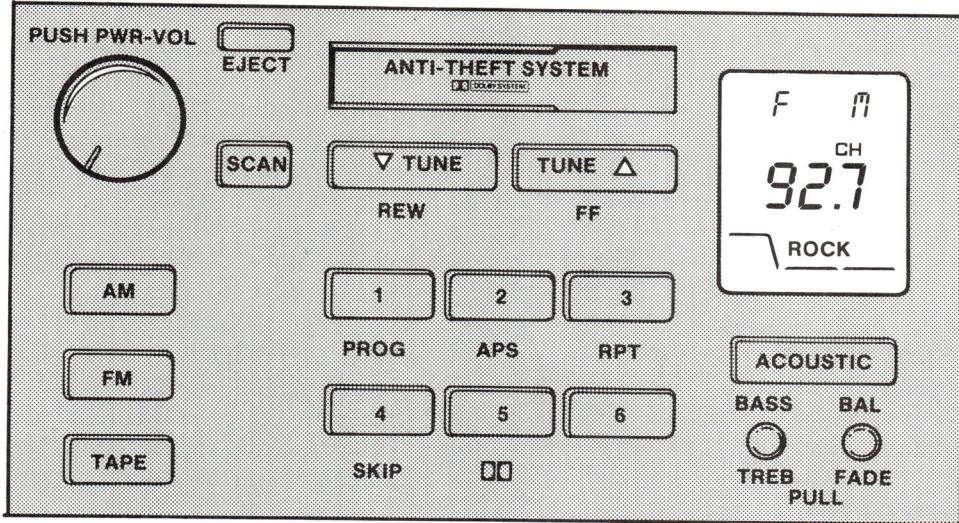

Figure 39-36 The audio antitheft display. *Courtesy of Toyota Motor Corp.*

ings, speaker grilles, or trim panels than by inoperative speakers. Check the tightness of mountings and trim pieces.

Distortion can be caused by the speaker, radio chassis, or wiring. If the concern is in the radio chassis, both speakers on the same side of the vehicle exhibit poor quality. Distortion caused by damaged wiring is most often accompanied by lower than normal sound output.

Buzzes, rattles, or distorted or weak sound from package tray speakers are often caused by bent package tray sheet metal around the speaker opening, lack of mounting brackets, or by missing or loose attaching hardware or speaker covers. Bent sheet metal should be straightened and the speaker reinstalled. Loose hardware should be finger-tightened plus approximately one full turn. Be careful not to over-tighten hardware as this may bend or deform the speaker baskets causing buzzes or distorted sound.

SHOP TALK

Antitheft audio systems (Figure 39-36) have built-in devices that make the audio system soundless if stolen. If the power source for the audio system is cut, the antitheft system operates so that even if the power source is reconnected, the audio system will not produce any sound unless the ID number selected by the customer is put in. When performing repairs on vehicles equipped with this system, before disconnecting the battery terminals or removing the audio system, the customer should be asked for the ID number so that the technician can input the ID number afterwards, or request that the customer input the ID number after the repairs are completed. With antitheft radio installation, there is a procedure in the service manual to obtain the factory back-up code using a touch tone phone if the owner's code is not available. In still other models, if the ignition key is removed and the negative battery cable is disconnected, the antitheft device is deactivated. A back-up battery in the radio keeps the code in memory allowing the radio to be removed and reinstalled. The radio becomes inoperable if the power is cut off during a collision or theft. Refer to the vehicle service manual before removing a stereo to determine if it is equipped with any antitheft devices and the procedures for removal.

Cellular phones

More and more auto manufacturers are installing cellular or mobile telephones as optional equipment (Figure 39-37). These cellular phones offer call-from-anywhere security. The service manual of such equipped vehicles contains all the necessary servicing information.

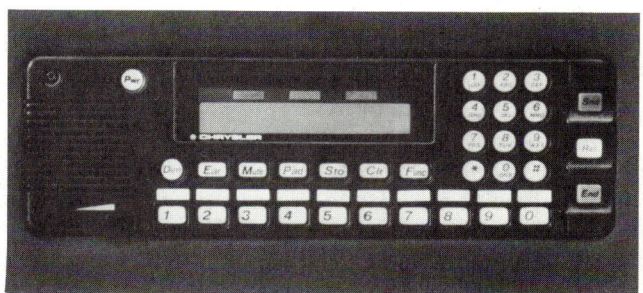

Figure 39-37 Typical of the factory-installed cellular phone. The unit shown is mounted in the back of the driver's sun visor for hands-free operation. Conventional models are floor-mounted units with hand sets. *Courtesy of Chrysler Corp.*

CASE STUDY

Case 1

A customer complains that his radio and stereo cassette player are not operating properly. The customer states they sometimes drop in volume, so low they cannot be heard. In fact, it almost seems the unit is turning itself on and off.

The technician test drives the vehicle. At first, the system operates normally, but when crossing railroad tracks, the system cuts out momentarily. The technician deliberately drives over a rough road on the way back to the shop. The intermittent volume problem repeats itself.

Back at the shop, the technician now knows the type of problem to look for. The radio unit is carefully removed from the dash. The technician inspects the wiring harness, but no loose wires are found. By checking the mounting brackets the problem is discovered. The grounding strap for the unit is not securely fastened to the metal frame. This intermittent ground was the cause of the volume cutting in and out. The unit was indeed turning itself on and off on rough roads. Securing a good ground connection solves the problem.

Summary

- Safety glass is used in all auto windows. It is of two types: laminated and tempered. Both types are available in a variety of tints.
- Laminated glass is used for windshields. The thin layer of plastic manufactured within the laminated glass keeps it from shattering when broken.
- Tempered glass is used in side and rear windows. It is harder than laminated glass, and when broken has a granular texture.
- Antenna wire for radio reception can be embedded in laminated glass or printed on the surface of tempered glass.
- A silver and zinc oxide coating fused to the glass to carry electrical current is used for some heated windshields. Others may use a laminate material capable of carrying electrical current.
- All new vehicles built or sold in the United States must have one or both types of passive restraints: seat belts or air bags.
- Seat belts are of two types: active restraint and passive restraint.
- When servicing seat belts, inspect the webbing, buckles, retractors, and anchorage.
- Child seat installation procedures vary depending on where the seat is installed.
- The main components of a typical air bag system include an electrical control system, air bag module, and knee diverter.
- An air bag electrical system consists of the monitor assembly, wire harness, and air bag readiness light.
- An air bag module consists of an igniter assembly, inflater module, mounting plate and retainer ring, and linear and steering wheel trim cover.
- Before doing any work on an air bag system, disconnect the battery.
- Care must be taken when removing a live (undeployed) air bag. Be sure the bag and trim cover are pointed away from you.
- All modern vehicle bumpers are designed to absorb the energy of a low-speed impact.
- There are three basic types of energy-absorbing bumpers, but several different designs are used.
- There are three basic types of antitheft devices available: locking devices, disabling devices, and alarm systems.
- A variety of locks are available that are designed to deny entry to the engine, passenger, and trunk compartments of the car as well as to prevent a thief from driving the car away.
- Keyless entry systems allow drivers to unlock the vehicle's door or trunk lid without using a key. There are two types: the coded-button keypad and remote keyless entry system.
- Ignition kill systems that prevent engine startup and hydraulic lock systems that lock up all four brakes are two popular disabling devices for vehicle security.
- The basic components of AM radio and audio systems are a radio receiver and speaker. In the more complex stereo systems, the major components are an AM/FM receiver, a stereo amplifier, several speakers, and a power antenna.
- Radio interference may be caused by electromagnetic fields generated by power lines, communications equipment, and some simple electrical devices.
- Radio or stereo equipment sound distortion may be caused by poor wiring, particularly if sound output is diminished.
- Cellular phones are now available as a factory-installed option.

Review Questions

1. What type of glass breaks into small pieces with a granular texture?
2. What type of glass is similar to conventional multilayered glass, but has one or more additional layers of plastic affixed to the passenger compartment side of the glass?
3. What air bag system device contains the ZPP?
4. What type of bumper is generally found on Ford vehicles?
5. What type of antitheft device is permanently installed in the brake lines?

6. What type of seat belt operates automatically, with no action required by the vehicle's occupant?
   a. passive restraint
   b. retractor
   c. active restraint
   d. anchorage
7. Technician A says that air bags are inflated by high-pressure gas stored in large steel cylinders behind the steering wheel or dash. Technician B says that air bags are inflated when chemicals combine to produce gas rapidly. Who is correct?
   a. Technician A
   b. Technician B
   c. Both A and B
   d. Neither A nor B
8. Technician A says that laminated glass is used to make windshields. Technician B says that laminated glass is a single piece of heat-treated glass and has more resistance to impact than regular glass of the same thickness. Who is correct?
   a. Technician A
   b. Technician B
   c. Both A and B
   d. Neither A nor B
9. Technician A says that tempered glass cannot be cut, drilled, or ground. Technician B says that only laminated glass can be tinted. Who is correct?
   a. Technician A
   b. Technician B
   c. Both A and B
   d. Neither A nor B
10. Technician A says seat belt webbing should be replaced if it is bowed. Technician B says that it does not need to be replaced if the color has merely faded due to exposure to the sun. Who is correct?
    a. Technician A
    b. Technician B
    c. Both A and B
    d. Neither A nor B
11. Which of the following is not an important element of a typical air bag system?
    a. electrical system
    b. air bag module
    c. knee diverter
    d. none of the above
12. Technician A says that the monitor assembly will disarm the air bag system if certain faults occur. Technician B says that at least two sensors must signal the air bag in order to trigger it. Who is correct?
    a. Technician A
    b. Technician B
    c. Both A and B
    d. Neither A nor B
13. Which of the following is false?
    a. The air bag ignitor assembly is a two-pin bridge device.
    b. The air bag ignitor assembly creates a spark that ignites a canister of gas generating zerconic potassium perchlorate.
    c. The air bag ignitor assembly is housed in the monitor assembly.
    d. None of the above.
14. Technician A checks the clock spring electrical connections for signs of damage when replacing a deployed air bag module. Technician B back probes an air bag system with a self-powered multimeter to determine if the system is in good working order. Who is correct?
    a. Technician A
    b. Technician B
    c. Both A and B
    d. Neither A nor B
15. Technician A removes the ground battery cable before servicing any component in the air bag system. Technician B wears safety glasses and protective gloves when handling inflated air bags. Who is correct?
    a. Technician A
    b. Technician B
    c. Both A and B
    d. Neither A nor B
16. Which type of energy-absorber bumper is used on many light imports and sport model vehicles?
    a. the shock absorber type
    b. isolator type
    c. urethane foam pad type
    d. none of the above
17. Which of the following is a type of antitheft device?
    a. locking devices
    b. disabling devices
    c. alarm systems
    d. all of the above
18. Technician A says that disabling devices can be either actively or passively armed. Technician B says that only the ignition key will start the car when the ignition-kill system is activated. Who is correct?
    a. Technician A
    b. Technician B
    c. Both A and B
    d. Neither A nor B
19. Technician A says that the majority of law enforcement officials recommend silent page alarms over siren alarms. Technician B says that devices used to trigger an alarm system include mechanical switches, ultrasonic sensors, and current-sensitive sensors. Who is correct?
    a. Technician A
    b. Technician B

c. Both A and B
d. Neither A nor B

20. Technician A says that air bag systems are designed to deploy in case of frontal collisions only. Technician B says that some air bag systems only have two sensors. Who is correct?
    a. Technician A
    b. Technician B
    c. Both A and B
    d. Neither A nor B

21. Technician A says some heated windshields use a silver and zinc oxide coating fused to the outer glass layer to carry the electric current needed for heating. Technician B says other heated windshields use a special laminate material in the glass that is capable of carrying the electrical current. Who is correct?
    a. Technician A
    b. Technician B
    c. Both A and B
    d. Neither A nor B

22. Technician A says that in a passive restraint system, a webbing sensitive belt retractor can be tested by grasping it and pulling on it. It should lock up. Technician B says vehicle sensitive retractors in passive systems can be tested by carefully performing a braking test on the road. Who is correct?
    a. Technician A
    b. Technician B
    c. Both A and B
    d. Neither A nor B

23. When servicing a bound shock-absorber type safety bumper, Technician A applies heat from a propane torch to expand and free the stuck piston. Technician B chains the bumper to secure it and then vents the pressure by drilling a hole in the piston tube. Who is correct?
    a. Technician A
    b. Technician B
    c. Both A and B
    d. Neither A nor B

24. Which of the following can be sources of radio interference?
    a. ignition system wiring
    b. electrical power lines
    c. neon signs
    d. all of the above

Appendix A
DECIMAL AND METRIC EQUIVALENTS

DECIMAL AND METRIC EQUIVALENTS

Fractions	Decimal (in.)	Metric (mm)	Fractions	Decimal (in.)	Metric (mm)
1/64	0.015625	0.397	33/64	0.515625	13.097
1/32	0.03125	0.794	17/32	0.53125	13.494
3/64	0.046875	1.191	35/64	0.546875	13.891
1/16	0.0625	1.588	9/16	0.5625	14.288
5/64	0.078125	1.984	37/64	0.578125	14.684
3/32	0.09375	2.381	19/32	0.59375	15.081
7/64	0.109375	2.778	39/64	0.609375	15.478
1/8	0.125	3.175	5/8	0.625	15.875
9/64	0.140625	3.572	41/64	0.640625	16.272
5/32	0.15625	3.969	21/32	0.65625	16.669
11/64	0.171875	4.366	43/64	0.671875	17.066
3/16	0.1875	4.763	11/16	0.6875	17.463
13/64	0.203125	5.159	45/64	0.703125	17.859
7/32	0.21875	5.556	23/32	0.71875	18.256
15/64	0.234275	5.953	47/64	0.734375	18.653
1/4	0.250	6.35	3/4	0.750	19.05
17/64	0.265625	6.747	49/64	0.765625	19.447
9/32	0.28125	7.144	25/32	0.78125	19.844
19/64	0.296875	7.54	51/64	0.796875	20.241
5/16	0.3125	7.938	13/16	0.8125	20.638
21/64	0.328125	8.334	53/64	0.828125	21.034
11/32	0.34375	8.731	27/32	0.84375	21.431
23/64	0.359375	9.128	55/64	0.859375	21.828
3/8	0.375	9.525	7/8	0.875	22.225
25/64	0.390625	9.922	57/64	0.890625	22.622
13/32	0.40625	10.319	29/32	0.90625	23.019
27/64	0.421875	10.716	59/64	0.921875	23.416
7/16	0.4375	11.113	15/16	0.9375	23.813
29/64	0.453125	11.509	61/64	0.953125	24.209
15/32	0.46875	11.906	31/32	0.96875	24.606
31/64	0.484375	12.303	63/64	0.984375	25.003
1/2	0.500	12.7	1	1.00	25.4

Appendix B
ABBREVIATIONS

The following abbreviations are some of the more common ones used today in the automotive industry.

A ampere
AA arithmetic average
AAS aspirator air system
AAS auto adjust suspension
AAV anti-afterburn valve
AB air bleed
ABS antilock brake system
AC alternating current
A/C air conditioning
ACC air conditioning compressor signal switch
ACCS air conditioning clutch cycling switch
ACD air conditioning demand
ACT air charge temperature
ACV air control valve
AFC airflow controlled
AFL altitude fuel limiter
AFR air/fuel ratio
AFS airflow sensor
AI air injection
AICV air injection check valve
AIR air pump
AIR-BPV air by-pass valve
AIR-CHV air check valve
AIR-DV air diverter valve
AIR-IVV air idle vacuum valve
AIR-RV air pump relief valve
AIS automatic idle speed
AIV air injection valve
ALCL assembly line communications link
ALDL assembly line diagnostic link
AMGV air management valve
ANTBV antibackfire valve
AOD automatic overdrive
APDV air pump diverter valve
API American Petroleum Institute
AS airflow sensor
ASC automatic stability control
ASD automatic shutdown
ASE automotive service excellence
ASIA Automotive Service Industry Association
ASRV air switching relief valve
ASS air switching solenoid
ASV air switching valve
A/T automatic transmission
ATDC after top dead center
ATF automatic transmission fluid
ATS air temperature sensor
ATX automatic transaxle
AWD air warning device
AWD all-wheel drive (or four-wheel drive)

BARO barometric pressure sensor
BAT− battery negative terminal
BAT+ battery positive terminal
BCDD boost controlled deceleration device
BDC bottom dead center
BHP brake horsepower
BMAPS barometric/manifold absolute pressure sensor
BOOST turbo boost actuator
BPEGR back pressure EGR
BPS barometric pressure sensor
BTDC before top dead center
BTU British thermal unit

C-3 computer command center
C-4 computer controlled catalytic converter
C-3I computer controlled ignition coil
CAFE corporate average fuel economy
CANP canister purge solenoid
CAT catalytic converter
CAV coasting air valve
CB circuit breaker
CBVV carburetor bowl vent valve
CC catalytic converter
CCC computer command control
CCEGR coolant controlled EGR
CCEVS coolant controlled engine vacuum switch
CCIE coolant controlled idle enrichment
CCO converter clutch override
CEC computerized emission control
CEL check engine light
CFI central fuel injection
CID cubic inch displacement
CIS continuous injection system
CIS mechanical control continuous injection system
CIS-E electronic control continuous injection system
CKV check valve
CLC centrifugal lockup clutch
CNG compressed natural gas
CO carbon monoxide
CO$_2$ carbon dioxide
COC conventional oxidation catalyst
COV control valve
CP crankshaft position
CPRV canister purge regulator valve
CPS canister purge solenoid
CPU central processing unit

CPV canister purge valve
CRT cathode ray tube
CSSA cold start spark advance
CSSH cold start spark hold
CT conventional thermactor
CTO coolant temperature override
CTS coolant temperature sensor
CV constant velocity (joint)
CVSCC coolant vacuum switch cold closed
CVSCO coolant vacuum switch cold open

DBC dual bed catalytic
DC direct current
DCLV deceleration valve
DCS deceleration control system
DCTO dual coolant temperature override
DEFI digital electronic fuel injection
DLV delay valve
DME digital motor electronics
DMV distributor modulator valve
DOHC dual overhead camshaft
DOT U. S. Department of Transportation
DP dashpot
DRCV distributor retard control valve
DRL daylight running lights
DS detonation sensor
DSAV deceleration spark advance
DSTVS distributor spark terminal vacuum switch
DV deceleration valve
DVCV distributor vacuum control valve
DVDV differential vacuum delay valve
DVOM digital volt-ohmmeter
DVTRV diverter valve
DVVV distributor vacuum vent valve

EAC electronic air control
EAS electronic air suspension
ECA electronic control assembly
ECC electronic controlled carburetor
ECCS electronic concentrated control system
ECI electronic controlled ignition
ECM electronic control module
ECS evaporation control system
ECT engine coolant temperature sensor
ECU electronic control unit

ECVT electronic continuous variable transmission
EEC electronic engine control
EEC evaporative emission control
EESS evaporative emission shed system
EEVIR equalizer valves-in-receiver
EFC electronic feedback carburetor
EFC electronic fuel control
EFE early fuel evaporation
EFE-TVS EFE thermal vacuum switch
EFI electronic fuel injection
EGC exhaust gas check
EGI electronic gasoline injection
EGO exhaust gas oxygen
EGOR EGO return
EGR exhaust gas recirculation
EGRC EGR controller
EGRCS EGR control solenoid
EGR-EPV EGR external pressure valve
EGR-EVR EGR electronic vacuum regulator
EGR-FDLV EGR forward delay valve
EGR-RSR EGR reservoir
EGR-TVS EGR thermal vacuum switch
EGRV EGR vent
EGR-VCV EGR vacuum control valve
EGR-VSOL EGR vacuum solenoid
EGR-VVA EGR venturi vacuum amplifier
EIS electronic ignition system
ELB electronic lean burn
ELC electronic level control
EMF electromotive force
EPA environmental protection agency
EPR-SOL exhaust pressure regulator solenoid
EPR-VLV exhaust pressure regulator valve
EPS electronic power steering
ESC electronic spark control
ESS engine speed sensor
ESSM engine speed switch module
EST electronic spark timing
ETC electronic throttle control
EVAP evaporative control system
EVCR emission vacuum control regulator
EVP EGR valve position
EVR EGR vacuum regulator
EZF performance graph ignition

FBC feedback carburetor system
FBCA feedback carburetor actuator
FCS fuel control system
FCS feedback carburetor solenoid
FES fuel evaporation system

FISR fast idle solenoid relay
4WD four-wheel drive or all-wheel drive
FP fuel pump
FSS fuel shutoff system
FVEC fuel vapor emission control
FWD front-wheel drive

GAWR gross axle weight rating
GND ground
GVWR gross vehicle weight rating

HAC high altitude compensator
HC hydrocarbon
HCV heat control valve
HEGO heat exhaust gas oxygen
HEI high energy ignition
HIC hot idle compensator
HICAS high capacity active steering
HPAA housing pressure altitude advance
HPCA housing pressure cold advance
HRV heat riser valve

IAA idle speed control
IAC idle air control
IAS inlet air solenoid
IAT intake air temperature
IC integrated circuit
ICM ignition control module
ID inside diameter
IDM ignition diagnostic monitor
IFS independent front suspension
IM ignition module
I/M inspection/maintenance
IMCO improved combustion system
IMS inferred mileage sensor
IMVC intake manifold vacuum control
IRS independent rear suspension
ISC idle speed compensator
ISC idle speed control
ISS idle speed solenoid
ITCS ignition timing control system
ITS idle tracking switch
ITVS ignition timing vacuum switch
IVR instrument voltage regulator

JAS jet air system
JCAV jet controlled air valve

KAM keep alive memory
KS knock sensor

LCV load control valve
LED light-emitting diode
LM logic module
LOS limited operational strategy
LSD limited slip differential
LUS locking upshift solenoid

MAF mass airflow
MAFTS manifold air/fuel temperature sensor
MAJC main air jet control
MAP manifold absolute pressure
MAT manifold absolute temperature
MAT manifold air temperature
M/C mixture control
MCN microprocessor control unit
MCS mixture control system
MCU microprocessor control unit
MEC motronic engine control
MFI multiport fuel injection
MHCV manifold heat control valve
MON motor octane number
MPH miles per hour
MSHA Mine Safety and Health Administration
M/T manual transmission
MTA managed thermactor air
MTC manual temperature controls

N nitrogen
N/A not applicable
NDS neutral drive switch
NGS neutral gas switch
NIASE National Institute for Automotive Service Excellence
NIOSH National Institute for Occupational Safety and Health
NO$_x$ oxides of nitrogen
NPS neutral pressure switch

O$_2$ oxygen
OC oxidation catalytic
OCC output cycling check
OD outside diameter
OE original equipment
OEM original equipment manufacturer
OHC overhead camshaft
OHV overhead valve
OS oxygen sensor
OSHA Occupational Safety and Health Administration

PA pulse air
PACV pulse air check valve
PAF pulse air feeder
PAI pulse air injection
PAS pulse air system
PCOV purge control valve
PCs personal computers
PCV positive crankcase ventilation
PCVS positive crankcase ventilation solenoid
PECV power enrichment control valve
PFE pressure feedback exhaust
PFI port fuel injection
PFI programmed fuel injection
PIP profile ignition pickup

PLC programmable logic control
PM power module
PM preventive maintenance
POT potentiometer
PPM parts per million
PROM programmable read only memory
PS power steering
PSI pounds per square inch
PSPS power steering pressure switch
PSV pulse air shutoff valve
PVCS ported vacuum control system
PVFFC pressure/vacuum fuel filler cap
PVS ported vacuum switch

R resistance
RAM random access memory
RC rear catalytic converter
RDV reverse delay valve
RMS root-mean-square
ROM read only memory
RON research octane number
RVSV rollover/vapor separator valve
RWD rear-wheel drive

SAB secondary air by-pass
SAD secondary air diverter
SAE Society of Automotive Engineers
SA-FV separator assembly-fuel vacuum
SAI steering axle inclination
SATC semiautomatic temperature controls
SBC single bed catalytic
SCC spark control computer
SCS spark control system
SCVAC speed control vacuum control
SDV spark delay valve
SEC ACT secondary actuator
SFI sequential fuel injection
SHED sealed housing evaporative determination
SI International System (actually Systeme Internationale)
SIS solenoid idle stop
SLA short-long arm
SLV solevac
SOL solenoid
SOL V EGR solenoid vacuum valve assembly

SP-CTO spark coolant temperature override
SPFI single-point fuel injection
SPOUT spark output
SPST single pole, single throw
SSD subsystem diagnostic
SSI solid state ignition
STI self-test input
STO self-test output
STRN signal return line
STV suction throttling valve
SUC shift-up control
S-V sol-vac
SVV solenoid vent valve

TAB thermactor air by-pass
TAC thermostatic air cleaner
TAD thermactor air diverter
TBI throttle body injection
TC throttle closer
T/C torque converter
TCC transmission controlled spark
TCP temperature-compensated accelerator pump
TCS transmission converter switch
TCU transmission control unit
TDC top dead center
TDS time delay solenoid
TES thermal electric switch
TEV thermostatic expansion valve
TFI thick film integrated ignition
TFI-IV thick film integrated
TGS top gear switch
TIC thermal ignition control
TIDC thermostatic ignition distributor control
TKA throttle kicker actuator
TKS throttle kicker solenoid
TP throttle position
TPC tire performance criteria
TPI tuned port injection
TPS throttle position sensor
TRC throttle return control
TSP throttle solenoid positioner
TVBV turbocharger vacuum bleed valve
TVS temperature vacuum switch
TVV thermal vent valve
TWC three-way catalyst
2WD two-wheel drive

UCS U.S. customary system

UIC universal integrated circuit
UTQGS Uniform Tire Quality Grading System

V volt
VAM vacuum advance mechanism
VAT volt/ampere tester
VAV vacuum control valve
VB vacuum break
VBAT vehicle battery voltage
VCKV vacuum check valve
VCS vacuum control switch
VCV vacuum control valve
VDV vacuum delay valve
VDV vacuum differential valve
VECI vehicle emission control information
VIN vehicle identification number
VIR valves in receiver
VMV vacuum modulator valve
VNT variable nozzle turbine
VOM volt-ohmmeter
VOTM vacuum-operated throttle modulator
VP vacuum pump
VRDV vacuum retard delay valve
VREF voltage reference
VRES vacuum reservoir
VREST vacuum restrictor
VR/S vacuum regulator solenoid
V-RSR vacuum reservoir
V-RST vacuum restrictor
VRV vacuum regulator valve
VS vacuum switch
VSA vacuum switch assembly
VSS vacuum switch solenoid
VSS vehicle speed sensor
VSV vacuum solenoid valve
VTP vacuum throttle positioner
VVA venturi vacuum amplifier
VVC variable voltage choke

WD warehouse distributor
WHMIS workplace hazardous materials information system
WOT wide-open throttle
WOTS wide-open throttle switch
WOTV wide-open throttle valve
WST waste gate
WSTC waste gate control

ZPP zirconic potassium perchlorate

GLOSSARY

Abrasion Wearing or rubbing away of a part.

Abrasive cleaning Cleaning that relies on physical abrasion, such as wire brushing and glass bead blasting.

Accumulator A device that cushions the motion of a clutch and servo action in an automatic transmission; a component used to store or hold liquid refrigerant in an air-conditioning system.

Acidity In lubrication, acidity denotes the presence of acid-type chemicals, which are identified by the acid number. Acidity within oil causes corrosion, sludges, and varnish to increase.

Ackerman principle The geometric principle used to provide toe-out on turns. The ends of the steering arms are angled so that the inside wheel turns more than the outside wheel when a car is making a turn.

Active restraint A manual seat and shoulder belt assembly that must be activated by an occupant.

Actuator A control device that delivers mechanical action in response to an electrical signal.

Additive In automotive oils, a material added to the oil to give it certain properties; for example, a material added to engine oil to lessen its tendency to congeal or thicken at low temperatures.

Adhesion The property of lubricating oil that causes it to stick or cling to a bearing surface.

Adhesive Substance that causes adjoining bodies to stick together.

Aeration The process of mixing air with a liquid. Aeration occurs in a shock absorber from rapid fluctuation in movement.

Air ducts Tubes, channels, or other tubular structures used to carry air to a specific location.

Air gap The space between spark plug electrodes, motor and generator armatures, and field shoes.

Air injection The introduction of fresh air into an exhaust manifold for additional burning and to provide oxygen to a catalytic converter.

Air lock A bubble of air trapped in a fluid circuit that interferes with normal circulation of the fluid.

Air pump A device to produce a flow of air at higher-than-atmospheric pressure. Normally referred to as a thermactor air supply pump.

Align boring A series of holes bored in a straight line.

Alignment An adjustment to a line or to bring into a line.

Alloy A mixture of different metals such as solder, which is an alloy consisting of lead and tin.

All-wheel drive System of driving all four wheels only when traction conditions dictate.

Ambient temperature Temperature of air surrounding an object.

Ammeter The instrument used to measure electrical current flow in a circuit.

Ampere The unit for measuring electrical current; usually called an amp.

Amplifier A circuit or device used to increase the voltage or current of a signal.

Amplify To enlarge or strengthen original characteristics; a term associated with electronics.

Analog A nondigital measuring method that uses a needle to indicate readings. A typical dashboard gauge with a moving needle is an analog instrument.

Analog display signal An instrument panel display in which an indicator moves in front of a fixed scale to give variable readout.

Anerobic sealer Liquid or gel that operates to bond two parts together in the absence of air.

Aneroid bellows A device that responds to atmospheric pressure and can be used to move a metering needle within a jet to automatically compensate for altitude changes.

Anodize An electrochemical process that coats and hardens the surface of aluminum.

Antifreeze A material such as alcohol or glycerin added to water to lower its freezing point.

Antilock braking system A series of sensing devices at each wheel that control braking action to prevent wheel lockup.

Antiseize compounds A type of lubrication that prevents dissimilar metals from reacting with one another and seizing.

Apply side The side of a piston on which force or pressure is exerted to move the piston to do work.

Arbor A shaft to which other parts may be attached.

Arcing Electrical energy jumping across a gap. Arcing across ignition points causes pitting and erosion.

Aspect ratio The height of a tire, from bead to tread, expressed as a percentage of the tire's section width.

Asymmetric Unequal surfaces or sizes.

Atmospheric pressure The weight of the air at sea level (about 14.7 pounds per square inch or less at higher altitudes).

Atomization The stage in which the metered air/fuel emulsion is drawn into the airstream in the form of tiny droplets.

Automotive aftermarket The network of businesses that supplies replacement parts and services to independent service shops, specialty repair shops, car and truck dealerships, fleet and industrial operations, and the general buying public.

Axial Having the same direction or being parallel to the axis or rotation.

Axial load A type of load placed on a bearing that is parallel to the axis of the rotating shaft.

Axial play Movement that is parallel to the axis or rotation.

Backlash The clearance or play between two parts, such as meshed gears.

Back pressure Pressure created by restriction in an exhaust system.

Balancer shaft A weighted shaft used on some engines to reduce vibration.

Balancing coil gauge A type of gauge that utilizes coils to create magnetic fields instead of a permanent magnet.

Ballast resistor A resistor in the primary side of the ignition system used to reduce the voltage approximately 4 to 5 volts.

Ball bearing An antifriction bearing that uses a series of steel balls held between inner and outer bearing races.

Ball joint A pivot point for turning a front wheel to the right or left. Ball joints can be considered either non-loaded or loaded when carrying the car's weight.

Barometric pressure A sensor or its signal circuit that sends a varying frequency signal to the processor relating actual barometric pressure.

Battery cell That part of a storage battery made from two dissimilar metals and an acid solution. A cell stores chemical energy for use later as electrical energy.

Bead The edge of a tire's sidewall, usually made of steel wires wrapped in rubber, used to hold the tire to the wheel.

Bearing clearance The amount of space left between a shaft and the bearing surface for lubricating oil to enter.

Bearing crush The process of compressing a bearing into place as the bearing cap is tightened.

Bearing race The machined circular surface of a bearing against which the roller or ball bearings ride.

Bearing spread The condition in which the distance across the outside parting edges of the bearing insert is slightly greater than the diameter of the housing bore.

Bellows A movable cover or seal, usually of rubber-like material, that is pleated or folded like an accordion to allow for expansion and contraction.

Bias A diagonal line of direction. In relationship to tires, bias means that belts and plies are laid diagonally or crisscrossing each other.

Blowby The unburned fuel and products of combustion that leak past the piston rings and into the crankcase during the last part of the combustion stroke.

Blower A fan that pushes, or blows, air through a ventilation, heater, or air-conditioning system.

Body-over-frame Type of vehicle construction in which the frame is the foundation, with the body and all major parts of the vehicle attached to it.

Bolt diameter The measurement across the major diameter of a bolt's threaded area, or across the bolt shank.

Bolt head The part of a bolt that the socket or wrench fits over in order to torque or tighten the bolt.

Boot Rubber protective cover with accordion pleats used to contain lubricants and exclude contaminating dirt, water, and grime. Located at each end of rack and pinion assembly and front-wheel-drive CV joints.

Bourdon tube A flexible hollow tube that uncoils and straightens as the pressure inside it is increased. A needle attached to the Bourdon tube moves over a scale to indicate the oil pressure.

Bracket An attachment used to secure parts to the body or frame.

Brake band A circle-shaped part lined with friction material that acts as a brake or holding device to stop and hold a rotating drum that has a gear train member connected to it.

Brake fade Occurs when friction surfaces become hot enough to cause the coefficient of friction to drop to a point where the application of severe pedal pressure results in little actual braking.

British thermal unit (Btu) A measurement of the amount of heat required to raise the temperature of 1 pound of water 1 degree Fahrenheit.

Buffer Any device used to reduce the shock or motion of opposing forces.

Bump steer Erratic steering that is caused from rolling over bumps, cornering, or heavy braking; same as orbital steer and roll steer.

Burnish To smooth or polish with a sliding tool under pressure.

CAFE standards Law requiring auto makers to not only manufacture clean-burning engines but also to equip vehicles with engines that burn gasoline efficiently.

Camber The attitude of a wheel and tire assembly when viewed from the front of a car. If it leans outward, away from the car at the top, the wheel is said to have positive camber. If it leans inward, it is said to have negative camber.

Capacitor A device for holding and storing a surge of current.

Carbon dioxide Compressed into solid form, this material is known as dry ice and remains at a temperature of 109 degrees. It goes directly from a solid to a vapor state.

Carbon monoxide Poisonous gas formed in engine exhaust.

Carbonize The process of carbon formation within an engine, such as on the spark plugs and within the combustion chamber.

Case harden To harden the surface of steel.

Castellated nut A nut with slots through which a cotter pin can be passed to secure the nut to its bolt or stud.

Caster Angle formed between the kingpin axis and a vertical axis as viewed from the side of the vehicle. Caster is considered positive when the top of the kingpin axis is behind the vertical axis.

Catalyst A compound or substance that can speed up or slow down the reaction of other substances without being consumed itself. In an automatic catalytic converter, special metals (for example, platinum or palladium) are used to promote more complete combustion of unburned hydrocarbons and a reduction of carbon monoxide.

C-class oil Commercial engine oil designed for use in heavy-duty commercial applications.

Center link A steering linkage component connected between the pitman and idler arm.

Center of gravity The point about which the weight of a car is evenly distributed; the point of balance.

Centrifugal force A force tending to pull an object outward when it is rotating rapidly around a center.

Chafing Damage caused by friction and rubbing.

Chamfer A bevel or taper at the edge of a hole.

Chase To straighten or repair damaged threads.

Check valve A gate of valve that allows passage of gas or fluid in one direction only.

Chemical cleaning Cleaning that relies primarily on some type of chemical action to remove dirt, grease, scale, paint, or rust.

Cherry picker A mobile crane that uses hydraulic power.

Closed loop An electronic feedback system in which the sensors provide constant information on what is taking place in the engine.

Closed-cooling systems Cooling systems with expansion tanks designed to hold any coolant that passes through the pressure cap when the engine is hot.

Clutch disc The part of a clutch that receives the driving motion from the flywheel and pressure plate assembly and transmits that motion to the transmission input shaft.

Clutch fork A forked lever that moves the clutch release bearing and hub back and forth.

Clutch release bearing A sealed, prelubricated ball bearing that moves the pressure plate release levers or diaphragm spring through the engagement and disengagement process.

Coefficient of friction A relative measurement of the friction developed between two objects in contact with each other.

Coil spring pressure plate assembly An assembly that uses weighted levers to increase or decrease the force holding the clutch disc against the flywheel according to engine speed.

Compound A mixture of two or more ingredients.

Compression ratio The ratio of the volume in the cylinder above the piston when the piston is at bottom dead center to the volume in the cylinder above the piston when the piston is at top dead center.

Compression stroke The second stroke of the four-stroke engine cycle, in which the piston moves from bottom dead center and the intake valve closes. This traps and compresses the air/fuel mixture in the cylinder.

Concentric Two or more circles have a common center.

Condensation The process of a vapor becoming a liquid; the reverse of evaporation.

Condense The process of cooling a vapor to below its boiling point. The vapor condenses into a liquid.

Continuous injection system A system that uses fuel under pressure to modulate or change the fuel injection area.

Contraction A reduction in mass or dimension; the opposite of expansion.

Control arms Suspension parts that control coil spring action as a wheel is affected by road conditions.

Convection oven Thermal cleaning oven that uses indirect heat to brake parts.

Coolant A mixture of water and ethylener glycol-based antifreeze that circulates through the engine to help maintain proper temperatures.

Cords The inner materials running through the plies that produce strength in the tire. Common cord materials are fiberglass and steel.

Core The center of the radiator, made of tubes and fins, used to transfer heat from the coolant to the air.

Corrosivity The characteristic of a material that enables it to dissolve metals and other materials or burn the skin.

Counterbore To enlarge a hole to a given depth.

Countersink To cut or form a depression to allow the head of a screw to go below the surface.

Counterweight Weight forged or cast into the crankshaft to reduce vibration.

Crank pin The machined, offset area of a crankshaft where the connecting rod journals are machined.

Crank throw The distance from the crankshaft main bearing centerline to the connecting rod journal centerline. The stroke of any engine is the crank throw.

Crank web The unmachined portion of a crankshaft that lies between two crank pins or between a crankpin and main bearing journal.

Crimp The use of pressure to force a thin holding part to clamp to, or conform to the shape of, a held part.

Crossflow radiator A radiator in which coolant enters on one side, travels through tubes, and collects on the opposite side.

Current The number of electrons flowing past a given point in a given amount of time.

Cylinder bore dial gauge Tool used to determine cylinder bore size, out-of-round, and taper.

Dampen To slow or reduce oscillations or movement.

Dead axle An axle that does not rotate but merely forms a base on which to attach the wheels.

Dead center The extreme upper or lower position of the crankshaft throw at which the piston is not moving in either direction.

Deck The top of the engine block where the cylinder head mounts.

Deflection Bending or movement away from normal due to loading.

Deflection angle The angle at which the oil is deflected inside the torque converter during operation. The greater the angle of deflection, the greater the amount of torque applied to the output shaft.

Density Compactness; relative mass of matter in a given volume.

Desiccant A special substance that absorbs moisture.

Detergent A compound of soap-like nature used in engine oil to remove engine deposits and hold them in suspension in the oil.

Detonation As used in an automobile, indicates a hasty burning or explosion of the mixture in the engine cylinders. It becomes audible through a vibration of the combustion chamber walls and is sometimes confused with a ping or spark knock.

Dial caliper Versatile measuring instrument capable of taking inside, outside, depth, and step measurements.

Dial indicator A measuring tool used to adjust small clearances up to 0.001 inch. The clearance is read on a dial.

Diaphragm A flexible, impermeable membrane on which pressure acts to produce mechanical movement.

Diaphragm spring pressure plate assembly An assembly that uses weighted levers to increase or decrease the force holding the clutch disc against the flywheel according to engine speed.

Differential A gear assembly that transmits power from the drive shaft to the wheels and allows two opposite wheels to turn at different speeds for cornering and traction.

Dilution To make thinner or weaker. Oil is diluted by the addition of fuel and water droplets.

Diode A simple semiconductor device that permits flow of electricity in one direction but not in the opposite direction.

Direct drive The downward gear engagement in which the input shaft and output shaft are locked together.

Direct ignition A distributorless ignition system in which spark distribution is controlled by the vehicle's computer.

Direct injection A diesel fuel injection system in which fuel is injected directly onto the top of the piston.

Directional stability The ability of a car to travel in a straight line with a minimum of driver control.

Disable A type of microcomputer decision that results in an automotive system being deactivated and not permitted to operate.

Displacement The volume the cylinder holds between the top dead center and bottom dead center positions of the piston.

Dowel A pin extending from one part to fit into a hole in an attached part; used for both location and retention.

Downflow radiator A radiator in which coolant enters the top of the radiator and is drawn downward by gravity.

Drive member A gear that drives, or provides power for, other gears in a planetary gearset.

Driveability The degree to which a vehicle operates properly. Includes starting, running smoothly, accelerating, and delivering reasonable fuel mileage.

Dropping resistor A device that reduces the battery voltage.

Duo-servo A drum brake design with increased stopping power due to the servo or self-energizing effect of the brake.

Duty cycle The percentage of on-time to total cycle time of fuel injectors.

Dwell time The degree of crankshaft rotation during which the primary circuit is on.

Eccentric The part of a camshaft that operates the fuel pump.

Efficiency A ratio of the amount of energy put into an engine as compared to the amount of energy coming out of the engine; a measure of the quality of how well a particular machine works.

Elasticity The principle by which a bolt can be stretched a certain amount. Each time the stretching load is reduced, the bolt returns exactly back to its original, normal size.

Electrode The firing terminals that are found in a spark plug.

Electrolysis A chemical and electrical decomposition process that can damage metals such as brass, copper, and aluminum in the cooling system.

Electrolyte A material whose atoms become ionized, or electrically charged, in solution. Automobile battery electrolyte is a mixture of sulfuric acid and water.

Electromagnet A magnet formed by electrical flow through a conductor.

Electromagnetic induction Moving a wire through a magnetic field to create current flow in the wire.

Electromechanical Refers to a device that incorporates both electronic and mechanical principles together in its operation.

Electronic Pertaining to the control of systems or devices by the use of small electrical signals and various semiconductor devices and circuits.

Embedability The ability of the bearing lining material to absorb dirt.

Emitter A portion of a transistor from which electrons are emitted, or forced out.

Emulsion The mixture of air and fuel in the carburetor.

End clearance play The extent of the possible forward and backward movement of the crankshaft, rod bearing on the crank pin, or the camshaft.

End play The amount of axial or end-to-end movement in a shaft due to clearance in the bearings.

Energy The ability to do work.

EP toxicity The characteristic of a material that enables it to leach one or more of eight heavy metals in concentrations greater than 100 times standard drinking water concentrations.

Ethanol A widely-used gasoline additive known for its abilities as an octane enhancer.

Evacuate The process of applying vacuum to a closed refrigeration system to remove air and moisture.

Evaporation A procedure by which a liquid is turned into vapor.

Excessive wear Wear caused by overloading an out-of-balance condition of a factor affecting wear, resulting in lower-than-normal life expectancy of the part or parts being subjected to the adverse operating condition.

Exhaust stroke The final stroke of the four-stroke engine cycle, in which the compressed fuel mixture is ignited in the combustion chamber.

Expansion An increase in size. For example, when a metal rod is heated, it increases in length and perhaps also in diameter; expansion is the opposite of contraction.

Fatigue Deterioration of a bearing metal under excessive intermittent loads or prolonged operation.

Ferrous metal Metal that contains iron or steel and is, therefore, subject to rust.

Field coil A coil of wire on an alternator rotor or starter motor frame that produces a magnetic field when energized.

Fillets The smooth curve where the shank flows into the bolt head.

Flange A projecting rim or collar on an object for keeping it in place.

Flare An expanded, shaped end on a metal tube or pipe.

Flat-rate manuals Literature containing figures dealing with the length of time specific repairs are supposed to require. Flat-rate manuals often contain a parts list with prices as well.

Flooding A condition in which excess, unvaporized fuel in the intake manifold prevents the engine from starting.

Flutter (bounce) As applied to engine valves, refers to a condition wherein the valve is not held tightly on its seat during the time the cam is not lifting it.

Foot-pound A unit of measurement for torque. One foot-pound is the torque obtained by a force of 1 pound applied to a wrench handle 12 inches long.

Force A push or pushing effort measured in pounds.

Forge The process of shaping metal by stamping it into a desired shape.

Free play Looseness in a linkage between the start of application and the actual movement of the device, such as the movement in the steering wheel before the wheels start to turn.

Free travel The distance a clutch pedal moves before it begins to take up slack in the clutch linkage.

Freewheeling A mechanical device that engages the driving member to impart motion to a driven member in one direction but not the other. Also known as an overrunning clutch.

Friction Resistance to motion that occurs when two objects rub against each other.

Fulcrum The support or point of rest that a lever rests on; also called the pivot point.

Galling wear Uniting two solid surfaces that are in rubbing contact; used to describe the normal wear of valve lifters.

Gear pitch The number of teeth per given unit of pitch diameter. Gear pitch is determined by dividing the number of teeth by the pitch diameter of the gear.

Gear pumps Positive displacement pumps that use two meshing external gears, one drive and one driven.

Glaze A thin residue on the cylinder walls formed by a combination heat, engine oil, and piston movement.

Grade markings Marks on fasteners that indicate strength.

Ground The negatively-charged side of a circuit. A ground can be a wire, the negative side of the battery, or even the vehicle chassis.

Gum In automotive fuels, gum refers to oxidized petroleum products that accumulate in the fuel system, carburetor, or engine parts.

Hairspring A fine wire spring.

Hand tap Tool used for hand cutting internal threads.

Hand-threading dies Tools used to cut external threads on bolts, rods, and pipes.

Hard spots Areas in the friction surface of a brake drum or rotor that have become harder than the surrounding metal; sometimes called islands of steel.

Harmonics Periods of vibration that occur when valve springs are opened and closed rapidly.

Hazardous waste Any material found on the Environmental Protection Agency list of known harmful materials. Waste is also considered hazardous if it has one or more of the following characteristics: ignitability, corrosivity, reactivity, and EP toxicity.

Heat dam The narrow groove cut into the top of the piston. It restricts the flow of heat into the piston.

Heat sink A device used to dissipate heat and protect parts.

Helical gear A gear with teeth that are cut at an angle or are spiral to the gear's axis of rotation.

Heptane A standard reference fuel with an octane number of zero, meaning that it knocks severely in an engine.

High tension High voltage. In automotive ignition systems, voltages (up to 40 kilovolts) in the secondary circuit of the system as contrasted with the low, primary circuit voltage (nominally 6 or 12 volts).

Hone An abrasive tool for correcting small irregularities or differences in diameter in a cylinder, such as an engine cylinder or brake cylinder.

Hot spot Refers to a comparatively thin section or area of the wall between the inlet and exhaust manifold of an engine, the purpose being to allow the hot exhaust gases to heat the comparatively cool incoming mixture. Also, used to designate local areas of the cooling system, which have attained above average temperatures.

Hotchkiss drive A suspension design that uses leaf springs and the frame to control rear-end torque.

Hunting gearset A differential gearset in which one drive pinion gear tooth contacts every ring gear tooth after several rotations.

Hydraulic valve lifter A lifter that provides a rigid connection between the camshaft and the valves. The hydraulic valve lifter differs from the solid type in that it uses oil to absorb the shock that results from movement of the valve train.

Hydrocarbons Particles of gasoline, present in the exhaust and in crankcase vapors, that have not been fully burned.

Hylomar A sealing supplement that never hardens, but remains soft and pliable.

Hypoid gears A type of spiral, beveled ring and pinion gearset in a differential. Hypoid gears mesh below the ring gear centerline.

Ignitability The characteristic of a solid that enables it to spontaneously ignite. Any liquid with a flash point below 140 degrees Fahrenheit is also said to possess ignitability.

Impact sockets Heavier walled sockets made of hardened steel and designed for use with an impact wrench.

Impact wrench A portable handheld reversible power wrench.

Included angle The sum of the angle of camber and steering axis inclination.

Indirect injection A diesel fuel injection system in which fuel is injected into a precombustion chamber for ignition.

Induction The process of producing electricity through magnetism rather than direct flow through a conductor.

Inertia The constant moving force applied to carry the crankshaft from one firing stroke to the next.

Inertia switch A switch that automatically shuts off the fuel pump if the vehicle is involved in a collision or rolls over.

Insert bearing A bearing made as a self-contained part and then inserted into the bearing housing.

Installed spring height The distance from the valve spring seat to the underside of the retainer when it is assembled with keepers and held in place.

Installed stem height The distance from the valve spring seat and to the stem tip.

Insulated circuit A circuit that includes all of the high current cables and connections from the battery to the starter motor.

Intake stroke The first stroke of the four-stroke engine cycle, in which the piston moves away from top dead center and the intake valve opens.

Integral Made in one piece.

Integrated circuit A large number of diodes, transistors, and other electronic components, all mounted on a single piece of semiconductor material and able to perform numerous functions.

Intercooler A device used on some turbocharged engines to cool the compressed air.

Isooctane A standard reference fuel with an octane number of 100, meaning that it does not knock in an engine.

Jam nut A locknut; one nut is tightened against another nut.

Jet A precisely sized, calibrated hole in a hollow passage through which fuel or air can pass.

Jig Device that holds the work and guides the operation.

Jounce Upward suspension movement.

Keep alive memory A series of vehicle battery-powered memory locations in the microcomputer that allow the microcomputer to store information on input failure, identified in normal operations for use in diagnostic routines. Keep alive memory adopts some calibration parameters to compensate for changes in the vehicle system.

Key A small block inserted between the shaft and hub to prevent circumferential movement.

Kinetic balance Balance of the radial forces on a spinning tire. Determined by an electronic wheel balancer.

Kinetic energy Energy in motion.

Knurling A technique used for restoring the inside diameter dimensions of a worn valve guide by plowing tiny furrows through the surface of the metal.

Lamination Thin layers of soft metal used as the core for a magnetic circuit.

Land The areas on a piston between the grooves.

Lapping The process of fitting one surface to another by rubbing them together with an abrasive material between the two surfaces.

Leakdown The relative movement of the plunger with respect to the hydraulic valve lifter body after the check valve is seated by pressurized oil. A small amount of oil leakdown is necessary for proper hydraulic valve lifter operation.

Light-emitting diode (LED) A type of digital electronic display used as either single indicator lights or grouped to show a set of letters or numbers.

Line boring An engine block machining operation in which the main bearing housing bores are rebored to standard size and in perfect alignment.

Line contact The contact made between the cylinder and the torsional rings, usually on one side of the ring. The contact made between the valve and the valve seat. When an interference angle is used, only a small line of contact is produced.

Liner Usually a thin section placed between two parts such as a replaceable cylinder liner in an engine.

Lip-type seal An assembly consisting of a metal or plastic casing, a sealing element made of rubber, and a garter spring to help hold the seal against a turning shaft.

Liquid crystal diode (LCD) A type of digital electronic display made of special glass and liquid and requiring a separate light source.

Live axle An axle on which the wheels are firmly affixed. The axle drives the wheels.

Load The work an engine must do, under which it operates more slowly and less efficiently. The load could be that of driving up a hill or pulling extra weight.

Lockup The point at which braking power overcomes the traction of the vehicle's tires and skidding occurs. The most efficient stopping occurs just before lockup is reached. Locked wheels cause loss of control, long stopping distances, and flat-spotting of the tires.

Look-up tables The part of a microcomputer's memory that indicates, in the form of calibrations and specifications, how an engine should perform.

Low and reverse band Transmission brake engaged in manual low and reverse gear ranges.

Low and reverse clutch Transmission brake device engaged in manual low and reverse ranges.

LP gas Liquified petroleum gas, often referred to as propane, which burns clean in the engine and can be precisely controlled.

Lubrication The process of reducing friction between the moving parts of an engine.

Magnet Any body with the property of attracting iron or steel.

Magnetic field The area surrounding the poles of a magnet that is affected by its attraction or repulsion forces.

Magnetic gauges Electrical analog gauges that use magnetic forces to move the needle left or right.

Magnetic pulse generator An engine position sensor used to monitor the position of the crankshaft and control the flow of current to the center base terminal of the switching transistor.

Main journal The central area of a crankshaft, where the main bearings support the shaft in the block.

Mainline pressure Pressure that is regulated in an automatic transmission hydraulic system.

Major thrust face The side of the piston to which most force is applied by side thrust.

Malleable Able to be shaped.

Manifold absolute pressure A measure of the degree of vacuum or pressure within an intake manifold; used to measure air volume flow.

MAP sensor The sensor that measures changes in the intake manifold pressure that result from changes in engine load and speed.

Margin The area between the valve face and the head of the valve.

Mass airflow sensor An EFI air intake sensor that measures the mass, not the volume, of the air flowing into the intake manifold.

Material safety data sheets Information sheets containing chemical composition and precautionary information for all products that can present a health or safety hazard.

Mechanical efficiency (engine) The ratio between the indicated horsepower and the brake horsepower of an engine.

Memory The part of a computer that stores, or holds, the programs and other data.

Mercury switch A type of switch that uses the flow of liquid metal mercury to complete the electrical circuit. Mercury switches are frequently used to control trunk and underhood lights.

Mesh To fit together, as gear teeth.

Metered To control the amount of fuel passing into an injector. Fuel is metered to obtain the correct measured quantity.

Methanol The lightest and simplest of the alcohols; also known as wood alcohol.

Microcomputer A smaller version of a computer that makes decisions based on information it receives from sensors.

Microprocessor The portion of a microcomputer that receives sensor input and handles all calculations.

Misfiring Failure of an explosion to occur in one or more cylinders while the engine is running; can be continuous or intermittent failure.

Missing A lack of power in one or more cylinders.

Monolith A single body shaped like a pillar or long tubular structure used as a catalyst in a catalytic converter.

Multimeter A tool that combines the voltmeter, ohmmeter, and ammeter together in one diagnostic instrument.

Multiviscosity oil A chemically modified oil that has been tested for viscosity at cold and hot temperatures.

Nodular iron A metal, used in pressure plates, that contains graphite, which acts as a lubricating agent.

Nonhunting gearset A differential gearset in which one drive pinion gear tooth contacts only three ring gear teeth after several rotations.

Normal wear The average expected wear when operating under normal conditions.

Normally aspirated The method by which an internal combustion engine draws air into the combustion chamber. As the piston moves downward in the cylinder, it creates a vacuum that draws air into the combustion chamber through the intake manifold.

Octane number A unit of measurement on a scale intended to indicate the tendency of a fuel to detonate or knock.

OEM parts Parts made by the original vehicle manufacturer.

Offset Placed off center. Also, the measurement between the center of the rim and the point where a wheel's center is mounted.

Ohm A unit of measured electrical resistance.

Ohm's law A basic law of electricity expressing the relationship between current, resistance, and voltage in any electrical circuit. It states that the voltage in circuit is equal to the current (in amperes) multiplied by the resistance (in ohms).

Open circuit An electrical circuit that has a break in the wire.

Open loop An electronic control system in which sensors provide information, the microcomputer gives orders, and the output actuators obey the orders without feedback to the microcomputer.

Orifice A precisely sized hole that controls fluid flow. Also, an opening.

Out-of-round An inside or outside diameter, designed to be perfectly round, having varying diameters when measured at different points across its diameter.

Overbore The dimension by which a machined hole is larger than the standard size.

Override clutch The mechanism that disengages the starter from the engine as soon as the engine turns more rapidly than the starter has cranked it.

Oxidation The combination of a substance with oxygen to produce an oxygen-containing compound. Also, the chemical breakdown of a substance or compound caused by its combination with oxygen.

Oxidation inhibitor Gasoline additives used to promote gasoline stability by controlling gum and deposit formation and staleness.

Oxidation rate Speed that oxygen is taken into a substance.

Oxides of nitrogen Various compounds of oxygen and nitrogen that are formed in the cylinders during combustion and are part of the exhaust gas.

Parallel circuit In this type of circuit, there is more than one path for the current to follow.

Peen To stretch or clinch over by pounding with the rounded end of a hammer.

Periphery The external boundary of the torque converter.

Phase Referring to the rotational positions of the various elements of a driveline.

Pick-up coil A weak permanent magnet and wire assembly that, in combination with a reluctor, forms a position sensor.

Pilot journal A mechanical journal that slides inside the pilot bearing and guides its movement.

Pinning Cold crack repair process involving the installation of tapered plugs in the crack or on either side of the crack.

Pintle The center pin used to control a fluid passing through a hole; a small pin or pointed shaft used to open or close a passageway.

Pitch The angle of the valve spring twist. A variable pitch valve spring has unevenly spaced coils.

Pitting Surface irregularities resulting from corrosion.

Play Movement between two parts.

Polarity The particular state, either positive or negative, with reference to the two poles or to electrification.

Poppet valve A valve consisting of a round head with a tapered face, an elongated stem that guides the valve, and a machined slot at the top of the stem for the valve spring retainer.

Porosity Tiny holes in a casting caused by air bubbles.

Port fuel injection A fuel injection system that uses one injector at each cylinder, thus making fuel distribution exactly equal among all of the cylinders.

Positive displacement pumps Oil pump through which a fixed volume of oil passes with each revolution of its drive shaft.

Post-combustion control systems Emission control systems that clean up the exhaust gases after the fuel has been burned.

Power A measure of work being done.

Power stroke The third stroke of the four-stroke engine cycle, in which the compressed fuel mixture is ignited in the combustion chamber.

Precombustion control system Emission control systems that prevent emissions from being created in the engine, either during or before the combustion cycle.

Preheating The application of heat as a preliminary step to some further thermal or mechanical treatment.

Preignition The process of a glowing spark or deposit igniting the air/fuel mixture before the spark plug.

Preload A thrust load applied to bearings that support a rotating part to eliminate axial play or movement.

Pressure The exertion of force upon a body in contact with it. Pressure is developed within the cooling system and is measured in pounds per square inch on a gauge.

Primary circuit The low-voltage circuit of an ignition system.

Program A set of instructions or procedures that a computer must follow when controlling a system.

Proportioning valve A pressure reduction valve used in the rear brake circuit.

Pulse width The length of time in milliseconds that an injector is energized.

Purge To separate or clean by carrying off gasoline fumes. The carbon canister has a purge line to remove impurities.

Pushrod guide plates The devices used in some engines to limit side movement of the pushrods.

Quenching The cooling of gases by pressing them into a thin area.

Race A channel in the inner or outer ring of an antifriction bearing in which the balls or roller operate.

Radial Perpendicular to the shaft or bearing bore.

Radial load A load that is applied at 90 degrees to an axis of rotation.

Radiation The transfer of heat by rays, such as heat from the sun.

Random access memory A type of memory that is used to store information temporarily.

Ratio The relation or proportion that one number bears to another.

Reactivity The characteristic of a material that enables it to react violently with water or other materials. Materials that release cyanide gas, hydrogen sulfide gas, or similar gases when exposed to low pH acid solutions are also said to possess reactivity, as are materials that generate toxic mists, fumes, vapors, and flammable gases.

Read only memory A type of memory used in automotive microcomputer to store information permanently.

Reaming A technique used to repair worn valve guides either by increasing the guide hole size to take an oversize valve stem or by restoring the guide to its original diameter.

Rebound An expansion of a suspension spring after it has been compressed as the result of jounce.

Recess A shaped hollow space on a part.

Reciprocating An up and down or back and forth motion.

Rectify To change one type of voltage to another.

Reduction The removal of oxygen from exhaust gases.

Reference voltage A voltage provided by a voltage regulator to operate potentiometers and other sensors at a constant level.

Relief The amount one surface is set below or above another surface.

Residual Remaining or left over pressure.

Residue Surplus or what remains after a separation takes place.

Resilience Elastic or rebound action.

Resistance The opposition offered by a substance or body to the passage of electric current through it.

Right-to-know laws Laws requiring employers to provide employees with a safe work place as it relates to hazardous materials.

Ring lands The high parts of a piston between the grooves.

Rolling resistance A term used to describe the amount of resistance a tire has to rolling on the road. Tires that have a lower rolling resistance usually get better gas mileage. Typically, radial tires have lower rolling resistance.

Rotary A circular motion.

Rotary flow Torque converter oil flow associated with the coupling stage of operation.

Rotor pump A type of oil pump that utilizes two rotors, a four-lobe inner and a five-lobe outer; output per revolution depends upon rotor diameter and thickness.

RTV A formed-in-place gasket product used in place of conventional paper, cork, and cork/rubber gaskets.

Runner A cast tube on an intake or exhaust manifold used to carry air in or out of the engine.

Runout Out of round or wobble.

Sampling The act of periodically collecting information, as from a sensor. A microcomputer samples input from various sensors in the process of controlling a system.

Saturation The point reached when current flowing through a coil or wire has built up the maximum magnetic field.

Scale A flaky deposit occurring on steel or iron. Ordinarily used to describe the accumulation of minerals and metals in an automobile cooling system.

Scan tool A microprocessor designed to communicate with a vehicle's on-board computer in order to perform diagnosis and troubleshooting.

Schematics Wiring diagrams used to show how circuits are constructed.

S-class oil Standard engine oil designed for use in passenger cars and light trucks.

Score A scratch, ridge, or groove marring a finished surface.

Screw pitch gauge A tool used to check the threads per inch (pitch) of a fastener.

Scuffing Scraping and heavy wear from the piston on the cylinder walls.

Seat A surface, usually machined upon which another part rests or seats; for example, the surface upon which a valve face rests.

Seize When one surface moving upon another scratches, it is said to seize. An example is a piston score or abrasion in a cylinder due to a lack of lubrication or over expansion.

Serpentine belts Multiple-ribbed belts used to drive water pumps, power steering pumps, air-conditioning compressors, alternators, and emission control pumps.

Servo The part of a cruise control system that maintains the desired car speed by receiving a controlled amount of vacuum from the transducer.

Shift forks Semicircular castings connected to the shift rails that help control the movement of the synchronizer.

Shift rails The parts of a transmission shift linkage that transfer motion from the driver controlled gear shift lever to the shift forks.

Shim Thin sheets, usually metal, which are used as spacers between two parts, such as the two halves of a journal bearing.

Short and long arm suspension (SLA) A suspension system using an upper and lower control arm. The upper arm is shorter than the lower arm. This is done to allow the wheel to deflect in a vertical direction with a minimum change in camber.

Shrink fit Where the shaft or part is slightly larger than the hole in which it is to be inserted. The outer part is heated above its normal operating temperature or the inner part chilled below its normal operating temperature and assembled in this condition. Upon cooling an exceptionally tight fit is obtained.

Shudder Momentary shake or quiver; can sometimes be severe.

Shunt More than one path for current to flow, such as a parallel part of a circuit.

Sleeving A means of reconditioning an engine by boring the cylinder oversize and installing a thin metal liner called a sleeve. The inside diameter of the sleeve is then bored, usually to the original or standard piston size.

Sliding fit Where sufficient clearance has been allowed between the shaft and journal to permit free running without overheating.

Slip A condition caused when a driving part rotates faster than a driven part.

Sludge As used in connection with automobile engines, it indicates a composition of oxidized petroleum products along with an emulsion formed by the mixture of oil and water. This forms a pasty substance and clogs oil lines and passages and interferes with engine lubrication.

Smog Air pollution created by the reaction of nitrogen oxides to sunlight.

Spark plug reach The length of the spark plug shell from the contact surface at the seat to the bottom of the shell, including both threaded and nonthreaded sections.

Speed ratio Comparison of the difference in speed between two moving parts such as impeller speed and turbine speed.

Splay To spread or move outward from a central point.

Splice To join. Electrical wires can be joined by soldering or by using crimped connectors.

Splines External or internal teeth cut into a shaft, used to keep a pulley or hub secured on a rotating shaft.

Sponginess The feel of a soft brake pedal.

Spontaneous combustion Process by which a combustible material ignites by itself and starts a fire.

Squirm To wiggle or twist about a body. When applied to tires, squirm is the wiggle or movement of the tread against the road surface. Squirm increases tire wear.

Stall speed With the engine operating at full throttle, the gear selector in D range, and the vehicle stationary, this speed can be read on a tachometer.

Stalling A condition in which the engine dies after starting.

Stamping A piece of sheet metal cut and formed into the desired shape with the use of dies.

Static balance Balance at rest, or still balance. It is the equal distribution of weight of the wheel and tire around the axis of rotation such that the wheel assembly has no tendency to rotate by itself regardless of its position.

Step ratio Transmission with steps or gear ratios. A four-speed transmission has four steps.

Step-up transformer A transformer in which the voltage created in a secondary coil is greater than the voltage in the primary, or first, coil.

Stoichiometric Chemically correct. An air/fuel mixture is considered stoichiometric when it is neither too rich nor too lean; stoichiometric ratio is 14.7 parts of air for every part of fuel.

Streamlining The practice of reducing the coefficient of drag of a vehicle's body.

Stress The force or strain to which a material is subjected.

Substrate A ceramic honeycomb grid structure coated with catalyst materials.

Suction Suction exists in a vessel when the pressure is lower than the atmospheric pressure; also, see vacuum.

Surging A condition in which the engine speeds up and slows down with the throttle held steady.

Swirl combustion A swirling of the air/fuel mixture in a corkscrew pattern. The swirling effect improves combustion.

Tang A projecting piece of metal placed on the end of the torque converter on automatic transmissions. The tangs are used to rotate the oil pump.

Tap To cut threads in a hole with a tapered, fluted, threaded tool.

Taper The difference in diameter between the cylinder bore at the bottom of the hole and the bore at the top of the hole, just below the ridge.

Telescoping gauges Tools used for measuring bore diameters and other clearances; also known as snap gauges.

Tensile strength The amount of pressure per square inch the bolt can withstand just before breaking when being pulled apart.

Tension Effort that elongates or stretches a material.

Thermal cleaning Cleaning that relies exclusively on heat to bake off or oxidize surface contaminants.

Thermo efficiency A gallon of fuel contains a certain amount of potential energy in the form of heat when burned in the combustion chamber. Some of this heat is lost and some is converted into power. The thermal efficiency is the ratio of work accomplished compared to the total quantity of heat contained in the fuel.

Thread pitch The number of threads in one inch of threaded bolt length. In the metric system, thread pitch is the distance in millimeters between two adjacent threads.

Throw With reference to an automobile engine, usually the distance from the center of the crankshaft main bearing to the center of the connecting rod journal.

Thrust line A line that divides the total toe angle of the rear wheels.

Thrust load Load placed on a part that is parallel to the center of the axis.

Tolerance A permissible variation between the two extremes of a specification or dimension.

Torque A twisting force applied to a shaft or bolt.

Torque steer A twisting axle movement in front-wheel drive automobiles that causes a pulling action under acceleration toward the side with the longer driving axle.

Tracking The travel of the rear wheels in a parallel path with the front wheels.

Traction A tire's ability to hold or grip the road surface.

Tractive effort Pushing force exerted by the vehicle's driving wheels against the road's surface.

Tramp Wheel hop caused by static balance.

Transistor An electronic device produced by joining three sections of semiconductor materials. A transistor is very useful as a switching device, functioning as either a conductor or an insulator.

Transverse Perpendicular, or at right angles, to a front-to-back centerline.

Turbo boost The positive pressure increase created by a turbocharger.

Turning torque Amount of torque required to keep a shaft or gear rotating; measured with a torque wrench.

Type A fire A fire resulting from the burning of wood, paper, textiles, and clothing.

Type B fire A fire resulting from the burning of gasoline, greases, oils, and other flammable liquids.

Type C fire A fire resulting from the burning of electrical equipment, motors, and switches.

Ultrasonic cleaning Method of cleaning that utilizes high-frequency sound waves to create microscopic bubbles that work to loosen soil from parts.

Unibody A stressed hull body structure that eliminates the need for a separate frame.

Union A hydraulic coupling used to connect two brake lines.

Universal joint A joint that allows the driveshaft to transmit torque at different angles as the suspension moves up and down.

Vacuum fluorescent A type of digital electronic display utilizing glass tubes filled with argon or neon gas; when current is passed through the tubes they glow brightly.

Valve float A condition in which the valves fail to follow the actions of the valve train and remain open.

Valve margin On a poppet valve the space or rim between the surface of the head and the surface of the valve face.

Vapor A substance in a gaseous state. Liquid becomes a vapor when they are brought above the boiling point.

Vapor lock A condition wherein the fuel boils in the fuel system forming bubbles that retard or stop the flow of fuel to the carburetor.

Vaporization The last stage of carburetion, in which a fine mist of fuel is created below the venturi in the bore.

Varnish A deposit in an engine lubrication system resulting from oxidation of the motor oil. Varnish is similar to, but softer than, lacquer.

Viscosimeter An instrument for determining the viscosity of an oil by passing a certain quantity at a definite temperature through a standard size orifice or port. The time required for the oil to pass through, which is expressed in seconds, gives the viscosity.

Viscosity A measure of a fluid's resistance to flow.

VNT The variable nozzle turbine unit designed to allow a turbocharger to accelerate quickly, thus reducing lag time.

Volatile liquid A liquid that vaporizes very quickly.

Volatility The tendency for a fluid to evaporate rapidly or pass off in the form of vapor. For example, gasoline is more volatile than kerosene because it evaporates at a lower temperature.

Volt A unit of measurement of electromotive force. One volt of electromotive force applied steadily to a conductor of one ohm resistance produces a current of one ampere.

Voltage drop Voltage lost by the passage of electrical current through resistance.

Voltmeter A tool used to measure the voltage available at any point in an electrical system.

Volume The measure of space expressed as cubic inches, cubic feet, etc.

Volumetric efficiency A measure of how well air flows in and out of an engine.

Vortex flow A swirling, twisting motion of fluid.

Vulcanized A process of heating rubber under pressure to mold it into a special shape.

Warpage Bending.

Watt's law A basic law of electricity used to find the power of an electrical circuit expressed in watts. It states that power equals the voltage multiplied by the current (in amperes).

Wheel base The distance between the center of a front wheel and the center of a rear wheel.

Whip Flexing of a shaft that occurs during rotation.

INDEX

Abrasive
  blaster, 139
  cleaners, 139-40
    media used as, *138*
Accelerator
  pump
    checking, 578-79
    circuit, 565
  switch, automatic transmissions
    and, 755
Accumulator
  air-conditioning, 978
  powermaster booster and, 912
  testing, 911-12
Active suspension systems, 844-46
Actuators, computerized engine
    controls and, 613-14
Adaptive suspension systems, 839-43
Adhesives, 307
Adjustable
  pliers, 70
  wrenches, 67
AGVs. *See* Automated guided vehicles
    (AGVs)
Air
  bags, 1009-11
    module, 1011
    readiness light, 420
    servicing, 1012-13
  by-pass valve, 596
  chisels, 75-76
  cleaners, *265*, 266-67
    thermostatic, 267-68
  control valve, 596
  drills, 74-75
  filter, 266-67
    design, 266-67
    servicing, 267
  hammer, 75-76
  induction system
    air cleaners, 266-68
    air intake, ductwork, 266
    described, 265-80
    intake manifolds and, 268-70
    vacuum systems and, 270-73
  injection
    reactor (AIR) system, hydro-
      carbons (HC), 582
    systems emissions control and,
      596-97
  intake, ductwork, 266
  management solenoids, 613
  pump, 596
  ratchet wrenches, 74
  shock systems, 821-22
  springs, 818-19
  suspension light, 420
  switching valve, 596
  systems, secondary, emissions
    control and, 597-99
  temperature sensors, 609
    fuel injection and, 525
AIR. *See* Air injection reactor (AIR)

Air-conditioning
  accumulator, 978
  ambient temperature switch, 983-84
  ASE test specifications, 12
  blower motor/fan, 981
  compressor, 975-77
    controls, 983-85
    oil level checks, 991
  condenser, 977-78
  cycling clutch, 981-82
  cylinder, charging, 994
  demand sensor, 609
  diagnostic procedures, 996
  evaporator, 979-80
    controls, 985-86
    pressure control system and, 982
    pressure regulator (EPR), 986
  high-pressure relief switch, 985
  in-line dryer, 981
  inspection, electrical system, 999
  leak testing, 989-91
  maintenance, precautions, 986-87
  manifold gauge sets, 988
  muffler, 981
  orifice tube, 978-79
  performance testing, 994
    procedure, 994-96
  pilot-operated absolute valve (POA),
    985-86
  pressure cycling switch, 984
  receiver/dryer, 978
  refrigerant, 978
    lines, 980
    safety precautions, 987-88
  service
    procedures, 991-92
    valves, 988-89
  sight glass, 980-81
  suction throttling valve (STV), 985
  superheat switch, 984-85
  system
    charging, 991-92, *993*
    evacuating, 991-92, *993*
    flushing, 991
  temperature control systems,
    996-99
  testing/service equipment, 988-94
  theory of, 974
  thermal limiter, 984-85
  thermostatic
    expansion valve, 978-79
    switch, 984
  troubleshooting, 996
  vacuum pump, 992, 994
  valves-in-receiver (VIR) assembly,
    986
Air-cooled systems, 266
Air/fuel systems, gasoline engines and,
  113
Airflow sensors
  component checks of, 536-38
  fuel injection and, 524-25
  mass, fuel injection, 525-26

Alarm systems, 1017-18
Alignment bar, 64
All-wheel drive
  center differential, 787
  electronically controlled, 788
  four wheel drive versus, 775, *776*
  viscous clutch and, 786-87
  See also Four wheel drive
Allen wrenches, 67
Alternating current
  charging systems, 380-89
  computer regulation and, 387-88
  regulator circuits and, 385
  temperature input and, 385
  voltage
    input and, 384-85
    regulation and, 384
    regulation design and, 386-87
Alternators
  construction of, 381-83
  operation of, 383
  servicing, 393-94
Aluminum
  cylinder heads, 181-82
    reconditioning, 182-83
Ambient temperature switch, 983-84
Ammeter, 84-85, 334
  charging system and, 389
Amplifier, venturi vacuum, 587
Angle alignment, 876-79
Antennas, power, 1019
Anti-icing additive, gasoline, 495
Anti-lock light, 421
Anti-locking brakes, 913-14
  bleeding, 919-20
  control module, 916
  diagnosis of, 920
  GM electromagnetic, 918-19
  hydraulic unit of, 914-15
  integrated system operation, 916-18
  non-integrated, 918-20
  pump/motor assembly of, 915
  testing of, 920
  types of, 914
  wheel-speed sensors of, 915-16
Antiseize compounds, 308
Antitheft devices, 1015-18
Armature, 369
ASE certification, 10-14
Audio systems, 1018-19
Automated guided vehicles (AGVs), 33
Automatic stability control, 920-21
Automatic transmissions
  accelerator switch and, 755
  ASE test specifications, 11
  band adjustment, 769
  centrifugal lockup clutch (CLC) and,
    715
  clutches and, 721-23
  described, 43-44
  electronic controls and, 754-55
  fluid, 764
    changing, 765, *767*

1041

diagnosing, 764-65
leaks, 766
forced disengagement of, 717
Ford, overdrive, 737-39
gear trains, planetary, 723
General Motors, 200-4R, 727-31
governor
  assembly, 747
  servicing, 770
hydraulic
  circuits and, 748-56
  systems and, 739-41
interior view of, *711*
linkage check
  gear selector, 766, 768
  throttle cable, 768-69
piston lockup clutch (PLC) and, 716-17
planetary gears of, 717-20
  controls, 720-23
  laws of, *718*
pressure testing, 770-72
road testing, 770
servos and, 721
shift lever switch and, 756
shifting, electronic, 755
solenoids, shift, 756-58
speed sensor and, 756
torque converters and,
  design of, 710, 712
  lockup, 714-17
vacuum
  modulator, servicing, 769-70
  switches and, 755
See also Transmissions
Automotive engines. See Engines
Automotive industry
  career opportunities in, 5-6
  service
    need for quality, 3-4
    on-going, 4-5
  technology advances and, 2-3
Automotive systems, 28-53
  body shapes and, 30-32
  body-over-frame construction, 30
  building, 33-34
  design evolution of, 29-30
  electronic revolution and, 32-33
  engine
    connecting rods, 35
    crankshaft, 35
    cylinder block, 34
    cylinder head, 35
    manifolds, 35
    piston, 35
    valve train, 35
  power plants, 32
  unitized construction, 30
  See also specific type of system
Automotive technician, working as, 9-10
Auxiliary air valve, idle speed control and, 529-30
Axles
  driving, described, 44
  four wheel drive, disconnects, 780
  front-wheel-drive, 671

applications of, 675
constant velocity (CV)
  joint service and, 675-82
  joint types and, 671-74
independently suspended, 699-700
rear-wheel-drive, 683-84
shafts for
  bearings for, 700-702
  dead, 697
  full-floating, 698-99
  live/drive, 697-98
  semifloating, 698
  three-quarter floating, 698
universal joints and
  canceling angles and, 686
  phasing of, 685-86
  speed variations and, 684-85
  types of, 686-87

Back pressure transduce, 588
Backup lights, 405-6
Balance test, fuel injectors, 529-40
Balancer shafts, crankshaft and, 157
Ball joints
  constant velocity (CV), 672-73
  servicing, 830-31
  suspension systems and, 826-27
Barometric pressure sensor, 609
Batteries, 351
  capacity of, 354-55
    reserve, 355
    testing, 360-61
  casing design of, 352-53
  charge, indicator light, 421
  charging of, 361-62
  cleaning of, 357-58
  cold cranking, 355
  design of, 351-53
  discharging/charging, 352
  electrolyte/specific gravity of, 352
  elements/cells of, 352
  heat shields for, 353
  hydrometers, built-in, 359-60
  inspection of, 357
  jump-starting and, 362
  life of,
    corrosion and, 355-56
    cycling and, 356
    electrolyte levels and, 355
    mounting and, 356
    overcharging and, 356
    undercharging/sulfation and, 356
  load test, 375
  maintenance, low/free, 353-54
  rating methods for, 355
  recombination, 354
  safety procedures and, 356-57
  starting system and, 366
  terminals, 353
  testing, specific gravity, 358-59
  voltage of, 354-55
    open circuit test of, 360
Bearings
  axle shafts, 700-702
  camshaft, 208
  crankshaft, 160-61

checking clearance of, *165-66*
failure, 163
installing, 163-67
rear main, oil seals for, 309-10
wheels, 807-11
Belt drives, cooling systems and, 250-51
Belted bias ply tires, 794-95
Belts, checking, 260-61
Bench grinder, 76
Bias ply tires, 794
Blaster, abrasive, 139
Bleeding
  brakes, anti-locking, 919-20
  hydraulic brake systems, 906-8
Blocks. See Cylinder, blocks
Blowgun, 76
Body shapes, 30-32
Body-over-frame construction, 30
Boiling points, pressure and, 974
Bolts, 296-98
  head sizes, *296*
  property class number, *297*
  strength markings, *297*
  See also Fasteners
Bore. See Cylinder bore
Bore and stroke, engines, 113-14
Box-end wrenches, 67
Brackets, exhaust system and, 279-80
Brakes
  anti-locking, 913-14
    bleeding, 919-20
    control module, 916
    diagnosis of, 920
    GM electromagnetic, 918-19
    hydraulic unit of, 914-15
    integrated system operation, 916-18
    non-integrated, 918-20
    pump/motor assembly of, 915
    testing of, 920
    types of, 914
    wheel-sensors of, 915-16
  ASE test specifications, 12
  cones, differentials and, 696-97
  described, 47
  disc. See Disc brakes
  drum. See Drum brakes
  factors governing, 893-94
  fluid, 896-97
    inspection of, 905
    level, warning light, 422
  hydraulic, 894-96
    bleeding, 906-8
    combination valves and, 903-4
    components of, 896-901
    metering valves, 903
    powermaster booster, 912-13
    pressure differential switches, 902-3
    proportional valves, 903
    servicing, 905-10
    stop light switch and, 904
    tubes/hoses for, 901-2
  hydro-boost, 911
    testing the, 911-12

Index **1043**

inspection checklist, *933*
line, inspection of, 905
linings, 894
master cylinders and, 897-901
on or off sensor, 609
pedal, 897
    inspection of, 906
power, 908
    hydraulic-assist, 911
    vacuum-assist, 908-10
pushrod, adjusting, 910-11
systems
    dual, 895-96
    single, 895
warning light, 422
Breaker point ignition systems, 445-46
Breaker points, inspection of, 465
Broaching machines, cylinder heads, resurfacing and, 185
Brushes, alternators and, 381-82
Bulbs, lighting fixtures and, 409-10
Bumpers, energy-absorber safety, 1014-15
Bushings
    control arm, servicing, 831
    strut rod, servicing, 832
    suspension systems and, 827-28
    sway bar, servicing, 832

Cables
    ignition, 445
    linkage of, 632
    starting system and, 366
Caliper, dial, 55-56
Cam followers, 209
Cambers
    adjusting, 881-83
    rear, adjusting, 885-86
Camshaft
    bearings, 208
    described, 207-13
    end play, 221
    inspection of, 214
    installing, 220-21
    parts of, *207*
    pushrods and, 210
        inspection of, 216-17
    rocker arms and, 210-12
        inspection of, 217-18
    timing
        component inspection, 218-20
        component installation, 223-27
        mechanisms for, 212-13
        variable valve, 213
    valve configurations and,
        flathead, 110-11
        overhead cam (OHC), 111
        overhead valve (OHV), 111
        side valve, 110-11
    valve lifters and,
        described, 209
        hydraulic, 209-10
        inspection of, 214-16
    valve operations and, 111
    valve train and,
        inspection of, 213-20
        installing, 221-23

Canister, purge solenoid, 613
Capacitors, 329
Carbon monoxide (CO), 582
Carburetion
    described, 558
    venturi, 558-60
Carburetors
    barrels and, 569
    choke
        qualifier and, 567
        unloader and, 568
    circuits
        accelerator pump, 565
        choke, 565-67
        float, 560-61
        idle, 561-62
        metering, 562-63
        power, 563-65
    dashpot and, 567
    deceleration valve and, 568
    diagnosis/adjustments of, 574-80
    draft and, 569
    feedback systems, 571-74
    HIC valve and, 567-68
    illustrated parts breakdown of, *559*
    throttle
        plate, 560
        position solenoid and, 568-69
    vacuum break, dual and, 568
    venturi, 569-70
        variable, 570-71
Career opportunities, 5-6
    classifications of, 6-8
    related, 8-9
Carrying, safe, 17-18
Casters, adjustment of, 881-83
Catalytic converters, 275-78
    emissions control and, 600
CCS. *See* Controlled combustion system (CCS)
Cellular phones, 1021
Centrifugal
    advance, 453-54
    lockup clutch (CLC), lockup torque converter and, 715
Chain
    drives, 212
    hoist, safety and, 20
    tensioners, 212
Chamber-in-piston combustion chamber, 177-78
Charge, indicator light, 421
Charging systems
    alternating current, 380-89
    alternators
        construction of, 381-83
        operation of, 383
        servicing, 393-94
    circuits
        isolated field, 385-86
        regulator, 385
        resistance, 392-93
    computer regulation and, 387-88
    described, 39-40
    direct current rectification and, 383-84

    ground, resistance, 392-93
    indicators
        ammeter and, 389
        light, 389
        voltmeter and, 389
    inspection of, 390-91
    oscilloscope and, 392
        patterns, *393*
    safety and, 390
    temperature input and, 385
    testing, 391
        current output, 391
        regulator by-pass, 391-92
    voltage
        input and, 384-85
        regulation and, 384
        regulator design, 386-87
Chassis, height specifications, 829
Check ball valves, 742-43
Chemical cleaning, engines, 134-37
Child seat, 1008-9
Chisels, 72-73
    air, 75-76
Choke
    adjustments, 576-78
    circuit, carburetors and, 565-67
    index, adjustments, 577
    pulldown adjustments, 577-78
    qualifier, 567
    unloader, 568
Chrysler transaxle, power flows through, 724-27
Cigarette lighter, 433
Circuit
    breakers, 327
    control, tests of, 379
    ground resistance test, 379
    protective devices, 324-27
    testers, 83-84
Circuits
    electrical, 322-23
        measuring, 83
        troubleshooting, 335-39
    ground, wiring connections and, 464
    hydraulic, 748-56
    isolated field, starting systems and, 385-86
    magnetic, reluctance and, 341
    regulatory, starting systems and, 385
    semiconductor, 344
    testers of, 83-84
Citrus chemicals, cleaning with, 141
Clamps, exhaust system and, 279-80
CLC. *See* Centrifugal lockup clutch (CLC)
Cleveland universal joint, 687
Clocks, 432
Clothing, protection and, 16
Clutch
    aligning, 639
    clutch disc and, 629
    described, 42
    disc, 629
    flywheel and, 629
    fork, 632

Index

installing, 314, 639
linkage, 632-34
  adjustment, 635
  hydraulic, 633-34
  lubrication of, 635-36
lockup engagement, 752-54
maintenance, 634-36
multiple disc, 722-23
operation of, 628-34
override, 372-73
overrunning
  torque converters and, 714
  transmission, 721-22
packs, differentials and, 696
pressure plate assembly, 629-31
problem diagnosis, 636-37
  chatter, 636-37
  drag/binding, 636
  noises, 637
  pedal pulsation, 637
  slippage, 636
  vibration, 637
release bearing, 631-32
removing, 637-38
self-adjusting, 632
service of, 637-38
  safety precautions, 634
transmission, 721-23
CO. *See* Carbon monoxide
Coil
  ignition, 443
  output test, 472-73
  polarity, 474
  springs, 815-16
    coil, 816-17
    live-axle systems and, 834
    rear, servicing, 838
    servicing, 829-30
    suspension systems and, 827
Cold
  patch, tire repair, 802
  start injectors, 529
Combination
  pliers, 70
  wrenches, 67
Combustion chamber
  chamber-in-piston, 177-78
  fast burn, 178
  hemispherical, 176-77
  swirl, 177
  wedge, 176
Commutator assembly, 369
Compact spare tires, 795-96
Compound servos, 721
Compressed air equipment, safety and, 18-19
Compression
  gauge, 92
    using, *93-94*
  ratio
    engines and, 114-15, 186
    rings, 168-69
Compressor
  adaptive suspension systems and, 840
  air-conditioning, 975-77
    oil level checks, 991

piston, 975-76
rotary vane, 976-77
Computer
  control modules, adaptive suspension systems and, 842
  electronic ignition systems and, 447
    operation of, 455-57
  wheel alignment and, 879, *880*, 881
Computerized engine controls. *See* Engine controls, computerized
Condenser, air-conditioning, 977-78
Conductors, electricity, described, 321-22
Connecting rods, 35
  crankshaft and, 164, 167
  installing, 169-72
Constant velocity (CV) joints
  removing/replacing, 679-80
  replacing parts, 678
  servicing, 675-82
  types of, 671-74
    ball type, 672-73
    fixed and plunge, 672
    inboard/outboard, 672
    tripod, 673-74
Continuous
  injection systems, 530-35
    checks/tests of, 544-47
  variable transmissions, 758-60
Control arm
  bushings, servicing, 831
  rear, servicing, 838-39
  suspension systems and, 826
Control modules, computer, adaptive suspensions systems and, 842-43
Controlled combustion system (CCS), 582
Controls, touch, steering wheel, 423
Convertible top, defined, 31
Coolant, 244-45
  temperature
    gauges, 419-20
    sensor, 609-10
    switch, 595
Cooling, cylinder blocks and, 147
Cooling systems
  air, 266
  described, 36, 37
  flushing, 261
  gasoline engines and, 113
  liquid, 243-55
    belt drives and, 250-51, 260-61
    coolant for, 244-45
    fan clutches and, 251-53, 259-60
    fans and, 251-53, 259-60
    heater system and, 255
    oil cooler and, 255
    pressure caps and, 246-48, 256
    radiator and, 245-46, *247*
    servicing, 255-62
    temperature indicator and, 255
    thermostat and, 249-50
    water jackets and, 253-54
    water outlet, 248-49
    water pump and, 245, 258-59

refilling/bleeding, 262
Core plugs
  cylinder blocks and, 147-48
  installing, 153-55
Corporate Average Fuel Economy (CAFE) standards, 29
Courtesy, light, 402
Cracks, repairing, 141-43
Crane, safety and, 20
Crankcase, ventilation of, 235
Cranking
  current test, 376
  test, ignition system and, 473
  voltage test, 375
Crankshaft
  balancer shafts and, 157
  bearings, 160-61
    checking clearance of, *165-66*
    failure, 163
    installing, 163-67
  clearance, checking, 160
  connecting rod, 164, 167
  described, 35
  end plan, checking, 160
  flywheel and, 157
  inspection/rebuilding of, 157-63
  oil
    clearance, 162-63
    grooves, 161
    holes, 162
  saddle alignment, checking, 158-59
  short blocks and, 155-57
  straightness, checking, 159-60
  timing, inspection of, 220
  vibration damper and, 157
Cruise control system, 433-34
Cup-type core plug, 155
Current
  cranking test, 376
  measuring, 82
  output test, charging systems and, 391
CV joint. *See* Constant velocity (CV) joint
Cycling clutch, air-conditioning, 981-82
Cylinder
  leakage tester for, 95
  power balance testing, 117-18
  sleeves, cylinder blocks and, 148
  walls, cylinder block reconditioning and, 149
Cylinder blocks, 34
  core plugs and, 147-48
  cylinder sleeves and, 148
  described, 146-47
  disassembly of, 132-34
  lubricating/cooling, 147
  reconditioning
    bore inspection and, 149-50
    cylinder walls and, 149
    deck flatness and, 148-49
  reconditioning and, cylinder walls and, 149
Cylinder bore
  boring of, 151-52
  deglazing, 151

dial gauge, 63
honing of, 152-53
inspection of, 149-50
surface finish of, 151-53
Cylinder heads, 35
   aluminum, 181-82
      reconditioning, 182-83
   assembling, 200-204
   combustion chamber. See Combustion chamber
   compression ratio and, 186
   described, 175-76
   disassembly of, 129, 131-32
   gaskets, 304-5
   installing, 221-23
   multivalve engines and, 180-81
   piston/valve interference/misalignment and, 186
   removal of, 129
   resurfacing, 183-86
   stock removal guidelines and, 185-86
   surface, finish of, 183-84
   valves
      exhaust, 178-81
      grinding, 186-88
      guide reconditioning, 188-93
      intake, 178-81
      knurling, 189-90
      seats reconditioning, 193-97
      stem seals and, 197-200

Dashpot, carburetors and, 567
De Dion axle system, 699
Dead axle, 697
Dealerships, 5
Deceleration valve, 568
Defroster
   hoses, 973-74
   warning light, 422
   window, 430-31
Deicer, gasoline, 495
Detergents, gasoline and, 496
Detroit/Saginaw universal joint, 687
Diagnostics, engine, 116-17
Diagonal cutting pliers, 70, 71
Dial
   caliper, 55-56
   indicator, 62
Dies, 71-72
Diesel
   engines, 121-22
      gasoline engines compared with, 123
      fuel injection
         components of, 548-54
         electronic control of, 554-55
         fuel lines and, 554
         governors, 550-53
         high-pressure, 547-48
         injection nozzles, 550
         starting devices and, 553
         water separators and, 554
      fuels
         cetane numbering/rating, 497
         grades, 497
         pour point, 497
         viscosity of, 496-97
         volatility of, 497
         wax appearance point (WAP), 497
Differentials
   all-wheel drive and, 787
   components of, 690-93
   described, 44, 689-90
   functions of, 690
   gear reduction and, 692
   limited slip, 695-97
   noises, diagnosing, 705-6
   operation of, 693-95
   rear axle housing and, 692
   servicing, 702-5
Dimmer switch, headlight, 399-400
Diodes, 343
   light-emitting, instrument panels and, 417
   liquid crystal, instrument panels and, 417
Dipstick, 235
Direct current, rectification of, 383-84
Disabling devices, 1017
Disc brakes, 904-5
   caliper
      assembly, 964-65
      disassembly of, 960, 962-64
      fixed, 955, 965
      floating, 955-56, 966
      inspecting/servicing, 958
      installation, 966
      removal of, 958-59
      sliding, 956, 966
   components of, 953-56
      brake pad assembly, 954-55
      caliper assembly, 953-54
      hub/rotor assembly, 953
   pads
      installation of, 965-66
      removal of, 959-60, 961-62
   parking brake, rear, 956-57
   rotor, inspection/servicing of, 966-67
   service precautions, 957-58
Disc type core plug, 154
Dished type core plug, 154
Displacement, engines and, 114
Distributor
   cap, inspection of, 464-65
   injection pump, 549-50
Diverter valve, 596
Dome/map light, 402
Door
   ajar, warning light, 422
   lock, warning light, 422
   locks, power, 426
Double-Cardan universal joint, 687-88
Double-wishbone suspensions, 825-28
Drills, air, 74-75
Drive
   axles, 697-98
      ASE test specifications, 11
   indicator light, 422
   shaft
      problem diagnosis, 688-89
      yokes, rear-wheel-drive axles and, 684

Driveline
   described, 44
   windup, 778-79
Driver, information centers, 423-24
Drivetrain, described, 41-42
Driving
   axles, described, 44
   lights, 411
Drum brakes
   components of, 904, 923-26
      cleaning, 939-40
      mechanical, 925-26
   design of, 926-32
   drums for, 926
      cleaning refaced, 937-38
      duo-servo, 926-29, 938
      inspection of, 935-37
      measurements, 937
      non-servo, 738-39, 929-32
      refinishing, 937
   inspection of, 932, 934-40
      checklist, 933
   linings for, 924-25, 940-42
      adjusting, 942
      sizing, 941-42
   operation of, 923
   parking brake, 944-46
      adjusting, 947-48, 949
      integral, 946, 948-49
   relining, 940-41
   road testing, 932, 934
   service of, 932
   shoes for, 924-25, 942
      installing, 942
      removing, 934-35
   wheel cylinders, 924
      inspecting/cleaning, 942-43
      replacing, 943-44
Dry pack check, 858
Duo-servo
   brake drums, servicing, 938
   drum brakes, 926-29
      automatic adjusted, 927-29
Dwell
   converting to milliseconds, 474
   fixed, oscilloscope pattern of, 470-71
   variable, oscilloscope pattern of, 471-72

Early fuel evaporation/thermal vacuum switch, 588, 595
Ears, protection of, 17
EEC. See Electronic engine controls (EEC)
Efficiency, engines and, 115
EGR. See Exhaust Gas Recirculating (EGR) systems
Electric
   fuel pumps, 512-14
      replacing, 514-15
   motors, 124
Electrical
   systems, 39-41
      ASE test specifications, 12
   test meters, 84-87

Electricity
    ammeters and, 334
    capacitors and, 329
    circuit breakers, 327
    circuits, 322-23
        printed, 330-31
        protective devices for, 324-27
        troubleshooting, 335-39
    conductors, described, 321-22
    flow of, 81-82
    fuses, 324-25
        links, 325-27
        maxi, 327
    jumper wires and, 335
    load, grounding, 323-24
    measuring
        circuit testers, 83-84
        circuits, 83
        current, 82
        power, 83
        pressure, 83
        resistance, 82-83
    ohmmeters and, 334
    Ohm's law, 320-21
    power and, 321
    relays and, 329
    resistors and, 324
    solenoids and, 329
    switches and, 328-29
    test lights and, 335
    volt-ohmmeter and, 334-35
        using, 337-38
    voltage, limiter, 327-28
    voltmeters and, 333-34
    wiring
        diagrams, 331, *332*
        for, 329-30
Electromagnetic interference (EMI), wiring connections and, 464
Electromagnetism, described, 339
Electronic
    engine controls (EEC), 40-41
    fuel injection, 520
        component checks of, 536-41
        system sensors for, 524-27
    fuel systems, 515-16
    idle speed control, 573-74
    ignition module tester, 91, *92*
    ignition systems, 446-47
        advantages of, 447-48
        computer controlled, 447, 455-57
        operating, 453-55
        switching systems and, 448-53
    leak detector, 990
    suspension systems, 839-43
        servicing, 843-44
    switching systems, 448-53
        engine position sensors and, 448-49
        Hall-effect sensor and, 451-53
        magnetic pulse generator and, 449-50, *451*
        metal detection sensors, 450-51
        photoelectric sensor and, 453
        timing systems, spark distribution and, 454-55

Electronics
    described, 342
    diodes and, 343
    integrated circuits, 344-45
    microprocessors
        actuators and, 349-50
        communication signals and, 347-48
        memories and, 348-49
        power supply and, 350
        sensors and, 345-47
    protecting, 350-51
    semiconductors and, 342-44
    transistors and, 343-44
EMI. *See* Electromagnetic interference (EMI)
Emissions control
    air injection systems and, 596-97
    catalytic converters and, 600
    computerized engine control and, 615
    described, 38
    evaporative emission control systems, 600-603
    exhaust gas recirculating (ERG) systems, 585-91
        diagnosis/service of, 588-91
        troubleshooting, 591
    gasoline engines and, 113
    heated air inlet and, 591-93
        inspection/performance test of, 593
    manifold, heat control valves and, 593-95
    positive crankcase ventilation (PCV) systems, 582, 583
        diagnosis of, 583-85
    secondary air system and, 597-99
        by-pass mode, 597
        downstream mode, 599
        troubleshooting, 599-600
        upstream mode, 598-99
    spark advance systems and, 595
    vacuum controls and, 270-72
Energy-absorber safety bumpers, 1014-15
Engine
    analyzer, 100-101
    bearings, oil delivery to, 235
    diagnostics, 116-17
    knock, 493-94
    measuring tools, 54-59
    position sensor, 610
    speed sensor, 610
Engine blocks
    connecting rods, installing, 169-72
    core plugs of, installing, 153-55
    crankshaft of, 155-57
        inspection/rebuilding of, 157-63
    cylinder blocks and, 146-48
        reconditioning, 148-53
    piston rings and, 168-69
    pistons, 167-68
        installing, 169-72
Engine controls
    computerized
        actuators and, 613-14

        closed loop operation mode, 614
        components of, 607-9
        emission control system and, 615
        fail safe operation mode, 614
        fuel control mode, 615
        functions of, 606-7
        limp-in operation mode, 614
        non-engine functions and, 616
        open loop operation mode, 614
        problem isolation techniques, 617-24
        sensors, 609-13
        spark control operation mode, 614-15
        spark/fuel emission control system and, 615-16
        troubleshooting, 616
Engines
    API designations, *231*
    ASE test specifications, 11
    bore and stroke of, 113-14
    break-in procedures, 316-17
    check warning light, 422
    classifications of, 105-6
    cleaning
        abrasive, 139-40
        chemicals for, 134-37, 141
        salt bath, 141
        soil contaminants and, 134
        thermal, 137-38
        ultrasonic, 140-41
    clearance volumes, stock removal guidelines and, 185
    compartment light, 402
    compression ratio and, 114-15, 186
    condition of, evaluation of, 118-19
    cooling fans, 434-35
    core plugs of, installing, 153-55
    crack repair of, 141-43
    cylinder
        block, 35, 132-34
        connecting rods and, 35
        crankshaft and, 35
        head, 35, 129, 131-32
        manifolds and, 35
        pistons and, 35
        valve train and, 35
    diesel, 121-22
    disassembled, *130*
    displacement of, 114
    efficiency of, 115
    electric, 124
    four-stroke gasoline, 106-8
        in-line, 109-10
        opposed cylinder, 110
        slant cylinder, 110
        v-type, 110
    front transverse, 112-13
    gasoline systems, 113
    horsepower of, 115-16
    identification of, 116
    installing, 315-17
    lifting an, 127-28
    location of, front longitudinal, 111-12
    mid-engine transverse, 113
    multivalve, 180-81

noise, diagnosis of, 119-21
painting, 314
performance, ASE test specifications, 12-13
position sensors and, 448-49
reassembly of, 311-15
removal preparation, 127
rotary, 122-23
stratified charge, 123-24
timing and,
   load and, 441
   RPM and, 441
torque of, 115-16
two-stroke gasoline, 108-9
valves and, arrangements of, 111
EPR. *See* Evaporator pressure regulator (EPR)
Equipment
   cleaning, safety and, 20-22
   safety and, 18-22
ERG, valve position sensor, 610
Ethanol, gasoline and, 496
Evaporative emission control systems, 600-603
   canister testing, 602-3
Evaporator
   air-conditioning, 979-80
   pressure control system and, air conditioning, 982
   pressure regulator (EPR), 986
Exhaust
   analyzer, 98-99
   manifold, 274
      installing, 314
      servicing, 281-83
   pipe/seal, 275
      servicing, 281-83
   valves, 178-81
Exhaust Gas Recirculating (EGR) systems, 583, 585-91
   delay timer control and, 587
   diagnosis/service of, 588-91
   diagnostic sensor, 610
   flow solenoids, 613
   pressure feedback, 612
   troubleshooting, 591
   vacuum diagnostic control switch, 610
Exhaust system
   components
      catalytic converters and, 275-78
      manifold, 274-75
      pipe/seal, 275
   described, 38-39
   gasoline engines and, 113
   hardware for, 279-80
   heat shields and, 279
   mufflers and, 278-79
   resonators and, 279
   service of
      component replacement, 281-83
      inspection, 280-81
   tail pipe and, 279
Expansion-type core plug, 155
Exterior lighting, rear, 403-6
Eyes, protection of, 16

F-head engines, valve arrangements and, 111
Fan
   checking, 259-60
   clutches
      checking, 259-60
      cooling system and, 251-53
   cooling system and, 251-53
   engine cooling, 434-35
Fast burn combustion chamber, 178
Fasteners
   bolts, 296-98
   described, 295-96
   threads, repair of, 300-301
   torque principles and, 298-300
   See also Bolts
Federal Clean Air Act, 582
Federal Emissions Defect Warranty, 5-6
Federal Emissions Performance Warranty, 5-6
Feedback systems, carburetors, 571-74
Feeler gauge, 61
Fiber composite springs, 817-18
Field coils, 369
Filters
   fuel, 509-96
      diesel, 554
   servicing, 508-9
Fire extinguishers
   guide to, 23
   safety and, 23-24
Fittings, brake, 901
Fixed
   caliper assembly, 955, 965
   joints, constant velocity (CV), 672
Flame (Halide) leak detector, 989-90
Flash-to-pass system, 400
Flashers, 403-4
Flex plate, installing, 314
Float
   adjustments, 579
   circuit, carburetors and, 560-61
Floating caliper assembly, 955-56, 966
Floor jack, 76
Flow control valves, power steering and, 862-63
Fluid leak detector, 990-91
Fluorescent leak detector, 990
Flywheel, 629
   crankshaft and, 157
   installing, 314
Fog lights, 411-12
Ford
   ATX transaxle, 732-33
      operation of, 733-37
   overdrive transmission, 737-39
Fouling, spark plugs, 483-84
Four stroke engines. *See* Engines, four-stroke gasoline
Four wheel drive
   alignment of, 887-88
   all-wheel drive versus, 775, 776
   described, 45-46
   hubs, locking/unlocking, 779-80
   operational modes, 780-82
   passenger cars, 782-83
   servicing, 783-86
   steering systems, 869-75
      electro/hydraulic, 872-75
      hydraulic, 871-72
      mechanical, 870-71
   systems, 775, 777
   transfer case, 777-79
      servicing, 783-84
   upgrading, 783-86
   See also All-wheel drive
Friction, 892-94
   coefficient of, 893
   contact surface and, 893
Front
   engine transverse, 112-13
   longitudinal engines, 111-12
   suspension systems
      ball joints, servicing, 830-31
      coil springs, servicing, 829-30
      control arm bushings, servicing, 831
      general, 828-29
      independent, 824-28
      torsion bars, servicing, 830
Front-wheel-drive
   axles, 671
      applications of, 675
      constant velocity (CV) joint service and, 675-82
      constant velocity (CV) joints and, 671-74
   problem diagnosis, *681*
Fuel
   alternative, 497-98
   delivery systems for, 498-515
      lines, 505-7
      tanks, 498-504
   diesel. *See* diesel fuels
   filters, 509-96
      diesel fuel injection and, 554
   gasoline
      additives, 495-96
      antiknock quality and, 493-94
      deposit control of, 495
      sulfur content of, 495
      volatility of, 494-95
   level gauge, 420
   lines, 505-7
      diesel fuel injection and, 554
   low, warning light, 422
   LP-gas, 497-98
   pressure, checking, 511
   pump
      installing, 314
      mechanical, 509-10, 512
   tanks, 498-503
      replacing, 503-4
Fuel injection
   air temperature sensors, 525
   airflow sensors, 524-25
      mass, 525-26
   computer controlled, 527
   continuous injection systems, 530-35
      checks/tests of, 544-47
   described, 519

diesel
  components of, 548-54
  electronic control of, 554-55
  fuel lines and, 554
  fuel pickup and, 553-54
  governors, 550-53
  high-pressure, 547-48
  injection nozzles, 550
  starting devices and, 553
  water separators and, 554
electronic, 520
  component checks of, 536-41
gasoline, 519-20
idle
  adjustment and, 542, 544
  speed control and, 529-30
injectors. *See* Fuel injectors
manifold absolute pressure sensor and, 526
oscilloscope checks and, 541
port fuel, 522-24
servicing, 535-36
system sensors, 524-27
throttle body (TBI), 521-22
Fuel injectors, 527-29
  checking
    balance test, 539-40
    power balance test, 540
    voltage signals, 539
  cleaner, fuel system and, 97-98
  cleaning, 541-42
  pulse tester, 98
  replacement of, 542, 543
  solenoids for, 613
Fuel system
  checking, 538-39
  described, 36-37
  electronic, 515-16
  test equipment for, 97-98
    fuel injector cleaner, 97-98
    fuel injector pulse tester, 98
    injector circuit test light, 98
    pressure gauge, 97
Full-floating axles, 698-99
Fuse links, 325-27
Fuses, 324-25
  maxi, 327

Gas
  charged shock absorbers, 821
  gauge, 420
Gaskets
  cylinder head, 304-5
  described, 301-2
  installation of, 302-4
  manifold, 305
  materials of, 302
  oil pan, 305-6
  valve cover, 305
Gasoline
  additives, 495-97
  deposit control of, 495
  engine systems, 113
    diesel engines compared with, 123
  fuel injection, 519-20
  sulfur content of, 495

volatility of, 494-95
Gauge
  coolant temperature, 419-20
  cylinder bore dial, 63
  feeler, 61
  fuel level, 420
  instrument. *See* Instrument gauges
  odometer, 418-19
  oil pressure, 419
  out-of-roundness, 64
  radius, 61
  screw pitch, 61-62
  small hole, 61
  speedometer, 418
  tachometer, 420
  telescoping, 60-61
  valve seat runout, 62-63
Gear
  and bearing puller, 73, 74
  drives, 212
  manual steering, 853-55
  trains
    planetary, 723
    Ravigneaux, 731-32
Gearbox, power-steering, 863
Gears
  idle, manual transmissions and, 643-44
  planetary
    automatic transmissions and, 717-20
    laws of, *718*
    ratios of, 644-45
    reverse, 645
  reduction of, differentials and, 692
  speed versus torque, 644-45
  teeth of, external/internal, 643
  transaxle, manual, 642-45
  transmissions, manual, 642-45
Gearsets, differentials and, 691-92
Gearshift, internal linkage, design of, 650-51
Generators, magnetic pulse, 449-50
Glass, safety, 1003-4
Glove box, light, 402
Gloves, protection and, 17
Government regulations, 24-25
Governor
  assembly
    automatic transmissions, 747
    diesel fuel injection and, 550-53
  pressure, hydraulic circuits and, 749
  servicing, 770
Graphic displays, 422-23
Grinders, bench, 76
Grinding, valves, 186-88
Ground circuits, wiring connections and, 464
Grounding, electrical load, 323-24
Guide
  integral, replacement of, 191-92
  valve
    knurling of, 189-90
    reconditioning, 188-93
    replacement of, 191-93
Gum inhibitors, gasoline, 495-96

Hair, safety and, 17
Halide leak detector, 989-90
Hall-effect sensors, 451-53
Hammers, 71, 72
  air, 75-76
  taps and dies, 71-72
Hand, cleaning parts by, 140
Handtools
  chisels, 72-73
  gear and bearing puller, 73, 74
  hammers, 71
  pliers, 70-71
  punches, 72-73
  removers, 73
  safety and, 18
  screw extractors, 73
  screwdrivers, 69-70
  tubing tools, 73, 74
  wrenches, 65-69
Hangers, exhaust system and, 279-80
Hardtop, defined, 30, *31*
Hatchback, defined, 31
Hazard warning lights, 403
HC. *See* Hydrocarbons
Head-up display (HUD), 423-24
Headlights, 397-401
  automatic, 400
  delayed-exit, 401
  dimmer switch, 399-400
  flash-to-pass system, 400
  high-beam, 420
  light bulbs, 406-7
    adjustments, 408-9
    replacement of, 407-8
  retractable, 421
  covers, 401
Heads. *See* Cylinder heads
Heat
  absorption, 974
  control valves
    manifold and, 593-95
    thermostat-operated, 595
  dissipation, braking and, 893-94
  flow of, 974
  shields, exhaust system and, 279
Heated air inlet, 591-93
  inspection/performance test of, 593
Heater
  space, safety and, 22
  system, 255
Heating
  ASE test specifications, 12
  systems, 971-74
    blower motor, 972-73
    control valve, 971-72
    duct hoses, 973-74
    servicing, 974
Helical gears, transmissions, 643
Hemispherical combustion chamber, 176-77
Heptane, engine knock and, 493
HIC valve, 567-68
High gear switch, 610
High-beam light, 420
High-performance tires, 795-96
High-pressure
  mini spare, 795

relief switch, air-conditioning, 985
Hoist, 76
    chain, safety and, 20
Horns, 431-32
Horsepower, engines and, 115-16
Hoses
    brake, 901-2
    defroster, 973-74
    heater, 973-74
    power-steering, 863-65
    water, checking/replacing, 257-58
Hot
    idle compensator valve, 567-68
    patch, tire repair, 804-5
    spray tanks, 136-37
Hubs
    four wheel drive, locking/unlocking, 779-80
    front, bearings of, 807-9
    rear, bearings of, 809-11
Hunting gearset, differentials and, 691
Hydraulic
    brakes. *See* Brakes, hydraulic
    circuits, 748-56
    clutch linkage, 633-34
    lifters, 209
        operation of, 209-10
    lock, 1017
    systems, transmissions and, 739-41
Hydraulics, principles of, 740
Hydro-boost, 911
    testing the, 911-12
Hydrocarbons (HC), 582
    air injection reactor (AIR) system and, 582
Hypereutectic pistons, 167

I-head engines, valve arrangements and, 111
Identification, engine, 116
Idle
    adjustment
        fuel injection and, 542, 544
        propane enrichment method, 575-76
    air control, valves, 529
    circuits, carburetors, 561-62
    gears, manual transmissions and, 643-44
    speed control
        actuators for, 613
        electronic, 573-74
        fuel injection and, 529-30
    tracking switch (ITS), 611
Idler arm
    steering linkage and, 851
    servicing, 857-58
Ignition, kill system, 1017
Ignition systems
    circuitry for, 441-42
    circuits, resistance, 477
    coils, output test, 472-73
    components of, 442-45
        cables, 445
        coils, 443
        spark plugs, 443-45
        testing of, 477-86

described, 39
distributorless, operation of, 457-59
electronic
    advantages of, 447-48
    computer controlled, 447, 455-57
    operating, 453-55
    spark distribution and, 454-55
    switching systems and, 448-53
gasoline engines and, 113
open circuits and, precautions, 472
oscilloscope testing of, 467-72
    current limiting and, 472
    fixed dwell patterns, 470-71
    pattern display models, 469-70
    patterns of, 468-69
    scales on, 467-68
    single cycle patterns, 470-72
    variable dwell patterns, 471-72
quick check charts, *478*
rotor
    air gap voltage drop, 474-75
    register, 475, 477
    register test, 476-77
spark duration, testing of, 473-74
spark plugs
    cold fouling, 483
    firing line diagnosis, *475*
    firing voltage, 474
    gap bridging, 484
    glazing, 484
    inspecting, 483
    overheating, 484
    removing, 482-83
    service of, 482-84
    splash fouling, 483-84
    troubleshooting, *476*
    turbulence burning, 484
    under load, 477
    wet fouling, 483
spark timing systems and, 445-47
    breaker point, 445-46
    electronic, 446-47
    solid state, 446-47
test equipment for
    compression gauge, 92, *93-94*
    cylinder leakage tester, 95
    electronic ignition module tester, 91, *92*
    magnetic timing probe, 89, *91*
    oscilloscope, 91, *92*
    tach-dwellmeter, 87
    tachometers, 87-89
    timing light, 89, *90*
    vacuum gauge, 95
    vacuum leak detector, 96
    vacuum pumps, 96
testing, 477-86
timing, 440-41
    advance, 453-54
    firing order and, 441
visual inspection of, 462-67
    breaker points, 465
    control modules, 466
    distributor cap, 464-65
    distributorless systems and, 466-67

    sensors, 466
    timing advance, 465
    wiring connections, 462-64
    See also Starting system
Impact wrenches, 74, *75*
In-carburetor filter, 508
    replacing, 509
In-line
    engines, 109-10
    filters, 508
Inboard joints, constant velocity (CV), 672
Independent
    suspended axles, 699-700
    suspension systems, 836-39
        front, 824-28
Indicators
    devices, 420-22
    dial, 62
    light, starting systems and, 389
Induced voltage, 341-42
Injection
    fuel. *See* Fuel injection
    pump
        distributor, 549-50
        timing, 549
Injector circuit test light, 98
Injectors
    cold start, 529
    fuel, 527-29
    solenoids for, 613
Insert guides, replacement of, 192-93
Instrument
    gauges
        bimetallic, 416
        described, 415
        magnetic, 415-16
        thermal, 416
    panels, 416-18
Intake
    manifold, 268-70
        installing, 313
    valves, 178-81
Integral
    guides, replacement of, 191-92
    seats, reconditioning, 195-97
Integrated circuits, 344-45
Interior lighting systems, 401-3
Isolated field circuits, starting systems and, 385-86
Isooctane, engine knock and, 493
Isopropyl alcohol, 495
ITS. *See* Idle tracking switch (ITS), 611

Jacks
    floor, 76
    safety and, 19-20
    stands for, safety and, 19-20
Jewelry, safety and, 17
Joints, constant velocity. *See* Constant velocity (CV) joint
Jump-starting, batteries and, 362
Jumper wires, electricity and, 335

Keyless entry systems, 1016-17
Knock sensor, 610-11

Knurling, valve guide and, 189-90

L-head engines, valve arrangements and, 111
Lamp-out warning light, 421-22
LCD. *See* Liquid crystal diode (LCD)
Leaf springs, 817
    exploded view of, *835*
    live-axle systems and, 832, 834
Leak testing, air-conditioning systems, 989-91
Leakage tester, cylinder, 95
LED. *See* Light-emitting diodes (LED)
Lever linkage, 632
Liftback, defined, 31
Liftgate wiper/washer system, 426
Lifting, safe, 17-18
Lifts, safety and, 19
Light
    fog, 411-12
    headlight. *See* Headlights
    trouble, 76
Light bulbs
    headlight, 406-7
        adjustments, 408-9
        replacement of, 407-8
Light-emitting diodes (LED), instrument panels and, 417
Lighting systems
    auxiliary, 410-12
    diagram of, *397*
    headlights, 397-401
    interior, 401-3
    maintenance of, 412-13
    rear, exterior, 403-6
Lightweight skin spare, 795
Limited slip differentials, 695-97
Liners, thin-wall, valve guide and, 190-91
Linkage
    clutch, 632-34
    internal, design of, 65-61
    remote, design of, 652
    steering
        parallelogram, 850-52
        worm and roller, 852, 858
Links, steering linkage and, 851-52
Liquid crystal diode (LCD), instrument panels and, 417
Live-axle
    suspension systems and, 832, 834-35
    See also Drive axles
Locking pliers, 70, *71*
Locks, 1016
Lockup
    clutch engagement, 752-54
    relay, 751
    solenoid, torque converter and, 752
    torque converter, 714-17
        centrifugal lockup clutch (CLC) and, 715
LP-gas, fuel alternatives, 497-98
Lubrication
    clutch linkage, external, 635-36
    cylinder blocks and, 147

oil types, 230-32
system
    described, 36
    gasoline engines and, 113
systems, described, 233-35

Machinist's rule, 55
MacPherson strut
    adjustments to, 883-85
    removing/replacing, *833-34*
    servicing, 832
    suspension systems, 823-24
MAF. *See* Mass inflow (MAF)
Magnetic
    circuits, reluctance and, 341
    pulse generators, 449-50, *451*
Magnetism, fundamentals of, 339-41
Main bearings
    noise, 120
    rear, oil seals for, 309-10
Maintenance schedule, preventive, *48*
Manifold
    absolute pressure (MAP) sensor, 611
        fuel injection and, 526
    described, 35
    exhaust, 274
        installing, 314
        servicing, 281-83
    gaskets, 305
    gauge sets, air-conditioning, 988
    heat control valves and, 593-95
    intake, 268-70
        installing, 313
    vacuum, checking, 588-89
Manual shift
    Ford
        ATX transaxle and, 736
        overdrive transmission and, 739
    THM 200-4R transmission and, 729-31
Manual steering, 849-60
    gear, 853-55
        servicing, 860
    linkage, parallelogram, 850-52
    parallelogram, servicing, 857-58
    rack and pinion, 852-53
        servicing, 859-60
    worm and roller, 852
        servicing, 858
Manual transaxle
    cleaning/inspection of, 665-67
    design of, 645-48
    gears, 642-45
        final drive, 658
        helical, 643
        ratios, 644-45
        reverse ratios, 645
        spur, 642-43
    gearshift, internal linkage design, 650-51
    lubrication
        check, 661-62
        replacement, 662
    manual transmissions versus, 641-42
    noise, diagnosis of, 662-64

power flow of
    first gear, 655
    fourth gear, 656
    neutral, 655
    reverse, 656
    second gear, 655
    third gear, 656
problems of, diagnosing, 662-64
reassemble/installation of, 668
removal of, 664-65
synchronizers and, 648-50
    design of, 649
    operation of, 649-50
troubleshooting chart, *657-58*
Manual transmissions
    cleaning/inspection of, 665-67
    described, 42-43
    design of, 645-48
    gears, 642-45
        final drive, 658
        helical, 643
        idle, 643-44
        ratios, 644-45
        reverse ratios, 645
        spur, 642-43
    gearshift, internal linkage design, 650-51
    lubrication
        check, 661-62
        replacement, 662
    noise, diagnosis of, 662-64
    overdrive and, 654-55
    power flow of
        first gear, 653
        fourth gear, 654
        neutral, 652
        reverse, 654
        second gear, 653
        third gear, 653-54
    problems of, diagnosing, 662-64
    reassemble/installation of, 668
    removal of, 664-65
    synchronizers and, 648-50
        design of, 649
        operation of, 649-50
    transaxle versus, 641-42
    troubleshooting chart, *657-58*
Manual valve, 747
Manufacturer's warnings, 24-25
MAP. *See* Manifold absolute pressure (MAP)
Mass inflow (MAF) sensor, 611
Master cylinder
    brakes and, 897-901
        dual, 898-900
        single system, 897
    powermaster system and, 912
    rebuilding, 906
Maxi-fuses, 327
Measuring
    systems, 54
    tools, engine, 54-59
Mechanical
    automotive systems, 36-39
    fuel pumps, 509-10, 512
Mechanics universal joint, 687
Memory, microprocessors and, 348-49

Metal
- deactivators, gasoline, 495
- detection sensors, 450-51

Metering
- rods, carburetors and, 563
- valves, hydraulic brakes and, 903

Methanol, gasoline and, 496
Methyl tertiary butyl ether (MTBE), gasoline and, 496
Microcomputer, scan tools, 99-100
Micrometers, 56-59
- depth, reading, 60
- inside using, 59-60
- outside, using, 59

Microprocessors
- actuators and, 349-50
- communication signals and, 347-48
- memories and, 348-49
- power supply and, 305
- sensors and, 345-47

Mid-engine transverse, 113
Milling machines, cylinder heads, resurfacing and, 184-86
Minicatalytic converter, 276
Mirror, power, 429-30
MON. *See* Research octane number (MON)
Monoleaf springs, 817
Monolithic catalytic converter, 276
Moon roof, 431
Motor
- mounts, installing, 315
- octane number, (MON), 493

MTBE, gasoline and, 496
Mufflers, 278-79
- air-conditioning, 981

Multi-purpose vehicles, 31-32
Multimeter, 85, *86*, 87
- testing with, *86*

Multiple
- disc clutches, 722-23
- leaf springs, 817

N-type semiconductors, 342
Natural gas, 498
Needle nose pliers, 70, *71*
Neutral drive/neutral gear switch, 611-12
Nitrogen oxides (NOx), 582
Noise
- abnormal combination, 120-21
- bearings
  - main, 120
  - thrust, 120
- diagnosis of, 119-21
- piston
  - pin knock, 120
  - slap, 120
- ridge, 120
- ring, 120
- rod-bearing, 120
- tappet, 120

Nonhunting gearset, differentials and, 691
Nose suppression, 1020-21
Nuts, strength markings, *297*

O-rings, installing, 198
Octane number, described, 493-94
Odometer, 418-19
OEM. *See* Original equipment manufacturer (OEM)
Ohmmeters, 84, 334
Ohm's law, 320-21
Oil
- changing, *49-50*
- clearance, crankshaft, 162-63
- consumption, 232-33
- control rings, 169
- coolers, 235, 255
- dipstick, 235
- engine bearings and, 235
- filters, 234-35, 238
  - changing, 49-50
- filtration systems, 238-39
- gaskets, 235
- grooves, crankshaft, 161
- holes, crankshaft, 162
- pan
  - described, 233
  - gaskets, 305-6
  - installing, 313
- passages, described, 235
- pressure
  - gauges, 419
  - indicator, 235, 237-38
  - indicator light, 421
  - regulation of, 236-37
  - testing, 117
- pumps
  - described, 233, 235-36
  - inspection/service of, 239-42
  - installation of, 242-43
  - pickup, described, 233
  - types of, 236
- seals, 235
  - rear main bearing, 309-10
  - timing cover, 309
- temperature, warning light, 421
- torque converters and, 712-13
- types of, 230-32

One-way check valve, 596
Open
- circuits, defined, 83
- end wrenches, 66-67

Opposed cylinder engines, 110
Orifice tube
- air conditioning and, 978-79
- cycling clutch system and, 982

Original equipment manufacturer (OEM), 44
Oscilloscopes, 91, *92*
- ignition testing and, 467-71

Out-of-roundness gauge, 64
Out-pump filters, 508
Outboard joints, constant velocity (CV), 672
Ovens
- pyrolytic, 137-38
- thermal cleaning, 137

Overdrive, 654-55
- overrun clutch and, 729
- planetary gearset and, 729

Override clutches, 372-73

Overrunning clutches
- torque converters and, 714
- transmission, 721-22

Oxidation inhibitors, gasoline, 495-96
Oxygen sensors, 612

P-type semiconductors, 342
Parallel circuits, 323
Parallelogram linkage, manual steering, 850-52
Parking brakes, 944-46
- adjusting, 949
- rear, *947-48*
- integral, 946, 948-49

Partial hunting gearset, differentials and, 691-92
Particulate oxidizer catalytic converter, 276-78
Parts
- manager, 8
- tumbler, 139
- washer, 135

Pascal's law, 740
Passing lights, 411
PCV. *See* Positive crankcase ventilation
Pellet catalytic converter, 276
Permanent magnetic starting motors, 372
PFE. *See* Pressure feedback EGR (PFE)
PFI. *See* Port fuel injection (PFI)
Phillips screwdrivers, 69
Photoelectric sensor, 453
Pilot-operated absolute valve (POA), 982
- air-conditioning, 985-86

Pinion, described, 853
Piston(s), 35
- compressor, 975-76
- engine blocks and, 167-68
- installing, 169-72
- lockup clutch (PLC), torque converters and, 716-17
- pin knock, 120
- power steering and,
  - integral system, 861
  - linkage system, 861
- rings, engine blocks and, 168-69
- slap, 120
- valve interference/misalignment and, 186

Pitman arm
- steering linkage and, 850-51
- servicing, 857

Planetary controls, Ford overdrive transmission and, 738-39
Planetary gears
- automatic transmissions and, 717-20
- controls, 720-23
- Ford,
  - ATX transaxle and, 733
  - overdrive transmission and, 738
- laws of, *718*
- overdrive, 729
- trains, 723

PLC. *See* Piston lockup clutch (PLC)

Index

PLC. *See* Programmable logic control (PLC)
Pliers, 70-71
Plunge joints, constant velocity (CV), 672
POA. *See* Pilot-operated absolute valve (POA)
Points, inspection of, 465
Pole shoes, 369
Poppet valve, 743
Port fuel injection (PFI), 522-24
    firing control and, 524
Ported vacuum switch (PVS), 271, 587
Positive
    crankcase ventilation (PCV) systems, 582, 583-85
        diagnosis of, 583-85
        valve, functional check of, 584-85
    engagement movable pole shoe drive, 371
    valve seats, installing, 197-98
Pour point, diesel fuels and, 497
Power
    antenna, 1019
    balance test
        cylinders, 117-18
        fuel injectors and, 540
    brakes, 908
        hydraulic-assist, 911
        vacuum-assist, 908-10
    door lock, 426
    electrical, measuring, 83
    electricity and, 321
    mirror system, 429-30
    plants, 32
    seats, 428-29
    steering, 860-65
        checks of, 865-67
        components of, 862-65
        diagnosis of, 685
        electronically controlled, 867-69
        servicing, 867
        switch, 612
    tools, 73-76
        safety and, 18
    trunk release, 426-27
    valves, carburetors and, 563-65
    windows, 427-28
Powermaster hydraulic booster, 912-13
Presses, 76
Pressure
    braking and, 893
    caps, 246-48
        testing, 256
    cycling switch, air-conditioning, 984
    electrical, measuring, 83
    feedback EGR (PFE), 612
    gauge, fuel system and, 97
    plate assembly
        coil spring, 629-30
        diaphragm spring, 630-31
        semicentrifugal, 630
    regulator valve, 744-47
    relief valves
        described, 233-34

power steering and, 862-63
testing, automatic transmissions, 770-72
Preventive maintenance, 48-51
    schedule of, *48*
Printed circuits, 330-31
Profilometer, 183
Programmable
    logic control (PLC), 33
    read only memory (PROM), 349
Proportional valves, hydraulic brakes and, 903
Pumps
    accelerator
        checking, 578-79
        circuit, 565
    power steering, 862
    transmission, 741
Punches, 72-73
Pushrods
    adjustment of, 910-11
    camshaft and, 210
    inspection of, 216-17
PVS. *See* Ported vacuum switch (PVS)
Pyrolytic ovens, 137-38

Rack, described, 853
Rack and pinion
    electric/electronic, 868-69
    power-assisted, 862, 863
    steering linkage, 852-53
Radial ply tires, 795
Radiator
    cooling system and, 245-46, *247*
    repairing, 256
Radios, 1018-19
Radius gauge, 61
Random access memory (RAM), 349
Ravigneaux gear trains, 731-32
Read only memory (ROM), 348
Rear wheel
    alignment, 885-87
    drive axles, 683-84
Refrigerant
    air-conditioning, 978
        safety precautions, 987-88
Regulator, by-pass test, charging systems and, 391-92
Relays, 329
    early fuel evaporation heater, 595
    valve, 745-47
Release bearing, clutch, 631-32
Reluctance, magnetic circuits and, 341
Removers, 73
Research octane number (RON), 493
Resistance, measuring, 82-83
Resistors, electricity and, 324
Resonators, 279
Restraint systems
    air bags, 1009-11
        module, 1011
        servicing, 1012-13
    child seat, 1008-9
    seat belts, 1005-6
        servicing, 1006-8
    sound systems and, 1009
    warning light and, 1009

Retainers, valves and, 179-80
Retaining ring pliers, 71
Ridge noise, 120
Ring noise, 120
Road testing, automatic transmissions and, 770
Rocker arms
    camshaft and, 210-12
    inspection of, 217-18
Rod-bearing noise, 120
RON. *See* Research octane number (RON)
Rotary
    engines, 122-23
    vane compressor, 976-77
Rotating release bearing, 631-32
Rotators
    valves, 180, 200
Rotor
    construction of, 381
    register, 475, 477
    register test, 476-77
    voltage drop, air gap, 474-75
Running
    gear, described, 46-48
    test, ignition test and, 473-74
Rust inhibitors, gasoline, 495

SAE, motor oil grades, *231*
Safety
    glass, 1003-4
    personal, 16-18
    work area, 22-24
Salt bath, cleaning with, 141
Scan tools, microcomputer, 99-100
Screw
    extractors, 73
    pitch gauge, 61-62
Screwdrivers, 69-70
Sealants
    anaerobic, formed-in-place, 308
    flexible, 307
    general purpose, 307
    silicone, formed-in-place, 307-8
Seals
    engine, 310-11
    oil
        rear main bearing, 309-10
        timing cover, 309
    valves and, 179-80
Seat belts, 1005-6
    servicing, 1006-8
Seats
    power, 428-29
    valve
        cutting, 196
        grinding, 195-96
        installing, 194-95
        machining, 196-97
        reconditioning, 193-97
    valves, installing umbrella type, 198
Secondary air system
    by-pass mode, 597
    downstream mode, 599
    troubleshooting, 599-600
    upstream mode, 598-99

Security devices, 1015-18
Sedan, defined, 30, *31*
Self-adjusting clutch, 632
Semi-independent suspension systems, 834-36
Semiconductors, 342-43
    circuits, 344
Semifloating axle shafts, 698
Sensors
    adaptive suspension systems and, 840
    air conditioning (A/C), 609
    barometric pressure, 609
    EGR, valve position, 610
    engine
        position, 448-49, 610
        speed, 610
    fuel injection and, 524-27
        component checks, 536-38
    Hall-effect, 451-53
    ignition system, inspection of, 466
    knock, 610-11
    manifold absolute pressure, 611
    mass airflow, 611
    metal detection, 450-51
    oxygen, 612
    photoelectric, 453
    temperature
        air, 609
        coolant, 609-10
    throttle position, 612-13
    vacuum, 613
    vehicle speed, 613
Series circuits, 322-23
Service
    manager, 8
    manuals, 76-78
    technician, 6-7
    valves, air-conditioning, 988-89
    writer, 7-8
Servos
    compound, 721
    transmission, 721
Shaft linkage, 632
Shift
    lever switch, 756
    solenoids, 756-58
    valve, 745-47
Shock absorbers, 820-23
    electronic, 840-41
    electronically controlled, 822-23
    ratios, 822-23
    servicing, 832
    shock-assist, 821
Shock-assist shock absorbers, 821
Shoe
    anchors, 926
    hold-downs, 925-26
    protection, 16-17
    return springs, 925
Shop, safety, personal, 16-18
Short-long arm suspensions, 825-28
Shorted circuit, defined, 83
Side lights, 403, *404*
Sight glass, air-conditioning, 980-81
Simpson gear train, 723
    transaxle and, Chrysler, 724
    transmissions and, General Motors, 727
Single universal joint, 686-87
Slant cylinder engines, 110
Sliding caliper assembly, 956, 966
Slip
    rings, alternators and, 381-82
    yoke, rear-wheel-drive axles and, 683-84
Small hole gauge, 61
Snap ring pliers, 71
Soak tanks, engine cleaning and, 135-36
Socket wrenches, 67-69
Solenoid, 329
    actuated gear reduction drive, 371-72
    air management, 613
    canister purge, 613
    EGR flow, 613
    lockup, 752
    mixture control, 613
    shift, 756-58
    starting system and, 366-68
    throttle position, carburetors and, 568-69
Solid
    lifters, 209
    state, ignition systems, 446-47
Solvents, safety and, 22 22-22 23
Sonar, road surface sensing and, 846
Space
    heaters, safety and, 22
    saver spare, 795
Spare tires, 795-96
Spark
    advance systems, emissions control and, 595
    distribution, electronic ignition systems and, 454-55
    plugs, 443-45
        air gap and, 445
    timing systems and, 445-47
Spark plugs
    firing line diagnosis, *475*
    fouling
        cold, 483
        splash, 483-84
        wet, 483
    gap bridging, 484
    glazing, 484
    inspecting, 483
    removing, 482-83
    servicing, 482-84
    troubleshooting, *476*
    under load, 477
Specialty
    screwdrivers, 69-70
    technician, 7
    tires, 795-96
Speed
    control system, 433-34
    rated tires, 795-96
    sensor, 756
    vehicle, sensor, 613
Speedometer, 418
Spicer universal joint, 687
Spool valve, 743-44
Sports vehicles, defined, 31-32
Springs
    air, 818-19
    coil, 815-16
        live-axle systems and, 834
        servicing, 816-17, 829-30
        spring, 838
        suspension systems and, 827
    fiber composite, 817-18
    leaf, 817
        live-axle systems and, 832, 834
    monoleaf, 817
    shoe return, 925
    struts and, 824
    suspension system, 814-19
    valves, 179-80, 198-99
        retainers/keepers and, 199-200
Spur gears, transmissions, manual, 642-43
Stabilizers, suspension systems and, 828
Standard tip screwdrivers, 69
Starting systems
    battery/cables and, 366
    control circuit, safety switch, 373, *374*
    described, 39
    drive mechanisms
        positive engagement movable pole shoe, 371
        solenoid-actuated gear reduction, 371-72
    motors, 368-70
        permanent magnet, 372
    operating principles of, 370-71
    solenoids and, 366-68
    starter
        circuit and, 365
        relays and, 368
    switches and, magnetic, 366-68
    testing of
        battery load, 375
        control circuit, 379
        cranking voltage, 375
        drive components, 380
        ground circuit resistance, 379
        insulated circuit resistance, 376
        preliminary checks, 374
        safety precautions, 374-75
        starter relay by-pass, 376, 379
        troubleshooting procedures, 375
        volt/amp tester and, 377-78
    See also Ignition system
Station wagon, defined, 31
Stator, alternators and, 382-83
Steam cleaning
    engines, 135
    safety and, 21-22
Steering, 46-47
    ASE test specifications, 11
    axle inclination, 877-78
    column, 855-57
        servicing, 860
    dampers, servicing, 858
    four-wheel, 869-75
        electro/hydraulic, 872-75

hydraulic, 871-72
manual system. *See* Manual steering
power. *See* Power steering
wheel, 855-57
  touch controls, 423
Stem seals
  valves
    described, 197
    installing positive, 197-98
Stepless transmissions, 758-60
Stethoscope, using, 119
Stock removal guidelines, cylinder heads and, 185-86
Stop light, 403, 421
  switch, 404-5
    hydraulic brakes and, 904
Stratified charge engines, 123-24
Struts
  electronic, 841-42
  rod bushings, servicing, 832
  servicing, 839
  springs and, 824
  suspension systems and, 824
STV. *See* Suction throttling valve (STV)
Suction throttling valve (STV), air-conditioning, 985
Sun roof, 431
Superchargers
  described, 288
  design of, 290-91
  operation of, 289-90
  problems of, 291-92
Superheat switch, air-conditioning, 984-85
Surface grinders, cylinder heads, resurfacing and, 185
Suspension systems
  active, 844-46
  adaptive, 839-43
  ASE test specifications, 11
  described, 46
  electronically controlled, 839-43
    servicing, 843-44
  front
    general, 828-29
    servicing, 829-34
  independent, 836-39
    front, 824-28
  live-axle systems and,
    coil springs and, 845
    servicing, 845
  MacPherson strut, 823-24
    removing/replacing, *833-34*
    servicing, 832
  rear, 832, 834-35
    live-axle, 832, 834
  semi-independent, 834-36
  shock absorbers, 820-23
    servicing, 832
  springs, 814-19
  torsion bar, 819-20
Sway bar, bushings, servicing, 832
Swing axle system, 699-700
Swirl combustion chamber, 177
Switch
  coolant temperature, 595

early fuel evaporation/thermal vacuum, 588
EGR
  diagnostic, 610
  vacuum diagnostic control, 610
electricity and, 328-29
high gear, 610
idle tracking, 611
ignition system, inspection of, 465-66
magnetic, starting system and, 366-68
neutral drive/neutral gear, 611-12
ported vacuum, 587
power steering (PS), 612
stop light, 404-5
thermal vacuum, 587, 596
Switching systems
  electronic, 448-53
    engine position sensors and, 448-49
    Hall-effect sensor and, 451-53
    magnetic pulse generator and, 449-50, *451*
    metal detection sensors, 450-51, 453

T-head engines, valve arrangements and, 111
Tach-dwellmeter, 87
Tachometers, 87-89, 420
Tail pipe, 279
Tanks
  hot spray, 136-37
  soak, 135-36
Tappets, 209
  noise and, 120
Taps, 71-72
TBI. *See* Throttle body injection
TEL. *See* Tetraethyl lead (TEL)
Telescoping gauge, 60-61
Temperature
  control, air-conditioning, 996-99
  indicator, 255
  vacuum switch (TVS), 271
Test
  lights, 335
    See also Circuit tester
  meters, electrical, 84-87
Test equipment
  ignition system
    compression gauge, 92, *93-94*
    cylinder leakage tester, 95
    electronic module tester, 91, *92*
    magnetic timing probe, 89, *91*
    oscilloscope, 91, *92*
    tach-dwellmeter, 87
    tachometers, 87-89
    timing light, 89, *90*
    vacuum gauge, 95
    vacuum leak detector, 86
    vacuum pumps, 96
  vacuum, 273
Tetraethyl lead (TEL), 495
Tetramethyl lead (TML), 495

Thermal
  cleaning, 137-38
  ovens, 137
  safety and, 21
  limiter, air-conditioning, 984-85
  vacuum switch, 587, 596
Thermostat
  installing, 313-14
  testing, 256-57
Thermostatic
  air cleaners, 267-68
  expansion valve
    air-conditioning, 978-79
    cycling clutch system and, 981
  switch, air-conditioning, 984
Thermostats, cooling systems and, 249-50
Threads, fasteners and, repair of, 300-301
Three-quarter floating axles, 698
Three-way catalytic converter, 276
Throttle
  body injection (TBI), 520-21
    advantages of, 522
    checking, 538
  cable, linkage check, 768-69
  position
    sensor (TPS), 612-13
    solenoid, carburetors and, 568-69
  wide-open valve, 588
Thrust
  bearing, noise, 120
  line alignment, 877
Tie-rods
  rack and pinion steering and, 853
  servicing, 858
Timing, 440-41
  advance, 453-54
    inspection of, 465
  belt, 212
  components installation, 223-27
  cover, installing, 312
  distributorless ignition systems and, 458-59
  gear backlash, inspection of, 218
  light, marks, *90*
  marks, 212-13
  rubber belt, inspection of, 218-20
Tires
  air leaks, repairing, 805
  balancing, 806-7
  care of, 799-802, 804-5
  described, 47-48
  destinations, 796-98
  inflation pressure, 800
  mounting/dismounting, *803-4*
  placard, 798
  ratings, 796-98
  repair of, 802, 804-5
  rotation, 800-801
  runout, 805
  specialty, 795-96
  tread wear, 801
  tube/tubeless, 793-94
  types of, 794-96
    combining, 798-99

Index

TML. *See* Tetramethyl lead (TML)
Toe
    adjustment, 885
    rear, adjusting, 886
Tools
    measuring, engine, 54–59
    safety and, 18–22
Torque
    engines and, 115–16
    fasteners and, 298–300
    indicating wrench, 65
Torque converter
    components of, 712
    controls, 751
    design of, 710, 712
    Ford overdrive transmission and, 738
    installing, 314–15
    lockup, 714–17
        electronic control of, 757–58
        solenoid, 752
    operation of, 712–13
    overrunning clutch and, 714
    pressure, 751
Torsion bars
    servicing, 830
    suspension systems, 819–20
TPS. *See* Throttle position sensor (TPS)
Traction, automatic control of, 920–21
Training
    ASE certification, 10–14
    automotive service and, 10
Transaxles
    accelerator switch and, 755
    Chrysler, power flows through, 724–27
    described, 44
    electronic controls and, 754–55
    Ford ATX, 732–33
        operation of, 733–37
    interior view of, *711*
    manual. *See* Manual transaxle
    shift lever switch and, 756
    speed sensor and, 756
    torque converter. *See* Torque converter
    vacuum switches and, 755
Transducer, back pressure, 588
Transfer case
    four wheel drive, 777–79
    servicing, 783–84
Transistors, 343–44
Transmissions
    bands, 720–21
    clutches, 721–23
    continuous variable, 758–60
    electronic controls and, 754–55
    manual. *See* Manual transmissions
    pumps and, 741
    servos, 721
    shifting, electronically, 755
    torque converter. *See* Torque converter
    See also Automatic transmissions
Tread wear, tires, 801
Tripod joints, constant velocity (CV), 673–74

Trouble light, 76
Trunk
    lid, light, 402
    release, power, 426–27
Tube tires, 793–94
Tubeless tires, 793–94
Tubes, brake, 901–2
Tubing tools, 73, 74
Tumbler, parts, 139
Turbochargers
    computer-controlled system, 285
    described, 283
    inspection of, 285–86
    intercooled, 285
    lubricating system for, 285
    operation of, 283–88
    replacing, 288
    spark-retard system, 285
    troubleshooting guide for, *287*
    turbo-lag and, 286, 288
    waste gate valve and, 285
        service for, 286
Turn, signals, 403, 421
TVS. *See* Thermal vacuum switch (TVS)
Two-stroke engines. *See* Engines, two-stroke gasoline

U-joints. *See* Universal joints
Ultrasonic cleaning, 140–41
Umbrella-type valve seats, installing, 198
Unitized construction, 30
Universal joints
    axles and, canceling angles and, 686
    phasing of, 685–86
    problem diagnosis, 688–89
    retaining methods, 688
    speed variations and, 684–85
    types of, 686–87

V-blocks, 64
V-type engines, 110
Vacuum
    advance, 454
    assist power brakes, 908–10
    break, dual, 568
    controls, increasing, 270–72
    fluorescent displays, 418
    gauge, 95
    leak detector, 96
    modulators, 745
        servicing, 769–70
    operated valve
        maintenance of, 594–95
        testing of, 594
    pumps, 96
        air-conditioning, 992, 994
    schematic, *271, 272*
    sensor, 613
    switches, automatic transmissions and, 755
    systems
        air induction system and, 270–73
        troubleshooting, 272–73
    test equipment, 273

Valve
    air
        by-pass, 596
        control, 596
        switching, 596
    cover, installing, 312–13
    diverter, 596
    lifters, camshaft and, described, 209
    one-way check, 596
    seats
        cutting, 196
        grinding, 195–96
        installing, 194–95
        machining, 196–97
        runout gauge, 62–63
    train, 35
        installing, 221–23
    wide-open throttle, 588
Valve lifters
    camshaft and
        hydraulic, 209–10
        inspection of, 214–16
Valves
    arrangement of, 111
    auxiliary air, idle speed control and, 529–30
    body of, 741
    camshaft
        flathead, 110–11
        operations and, 111
        overhead cam (OHC), 111
        overhead valve (OHV), 111
        side value, 110–11
    check ball, 742–43
    combination, hydraulic brakes and, 903–4
    cover, gaskets, 305
    deceleration, carburetors and, 568
    exhaust, 178–81
    grinding, 186–88
    guide, 179
        knurling, 189–90
        reconditioning, 188–93
        replacement of, 191–93
        thin-wall liners and, 190–91
    heat control
        manifold and, 593–95
        thermostat-operated, 595
    hot-idle compensator, 567–68
    idle air control, 529
    intake, 178–81
    manual, 747
    metering, hydraulic brakes and, 903
    oversized, 190
    piston interference/misalignment and, 186
    poppet, 743
    power, carburetors and, 563–65
    pressure
        regulator, 744–47
        relief, described, 233–34
    proportional, hydraulic brakes and, 903
    reaming, 190
    relief, 745–47
    retainers, 179–80
    rotators, 180, 200

seals, 179-80
seats
    installing umbrella type, 198
    reconditioning, 193-97
shift, 745-47
spool, 743-44
springs, 179-80, 198-99
    retainers/keepers and, 199-200
stem seals
    described, 197
    installing positive, 197-98
waste gate, turbochargers and, 285, 286
Valves-in-receiver (VIR)
    assembly, 986
    system, 982-83
Vanity, light, 402
Vehicle speed sensor, 613
Ventilation systems, 970-71
Venturi
    carburetion, 558-60
    carburetors, 569-70
        variable, 570-71
    vacuum amplifier (VVA), 587
Vibration
    cleaning, 140
    damper
        crankshaft and, 157
        installing, 312
Viscous clutch, all-wheel drive and, 786-87
Volt
    ampere tester, 85
    ohmmeter, 334-35
        using, 337-38
Voltage
    checking signals, fuel injectors and, 539
    cranking test, 375
    drop, rotor air gap, 474-75
    induced, 341-42
    input, alternating current and, 384-85

limiter, 327-28
regulation, alternating current and, 384
regulator, design of, 386-87
Voltmeter, 84, 333-34
    starting systems and, 389
VVA. *See* Venturi vacuum amplifier (VVA)

Warning
    devices
        lights, 420-22
        sound, 422
    manufacturer's, 24-25
Warranties, federal, 5-6
Washer systems, windshield, 425
Waste gate valve
    turbochargers and, 285
    service for, 286
Water
    hose, checking/replacing, 257-58
    jackets, cooling systems and, 253-54
    outlet
        cooling systems and, 248-49
        housing, installing, 313-14
    pumps, 245
        servicing, 258-59
    separators, diesel fuel injection and, 554
Wax appearance point (WAP), diesel fuels and, 497
Wedge combustion chamber, 176
Wheels, 792-93
    alignment of, 875-79
        angle, 876-79
        caster/camber adjustment and, 881-83
        effects of improper, *875*
        four-wheel drive, 887-88
        load distribution and, 879

        MacPherson suspensions and, 883-85
        procedures, 879-85
        rear, 885-87
        steering axle inclination, 877-78
        thrust line, 877, 886-87
        toe adjustment, 885
        tracking and, 879
        turning radius and, 878-79
    balancing, 806-7
    bearings
        front hubs, 807-9
        grease for, 811
        rear hubs, 809-11
    described, 47-48
    runout, 805
Wide-open throttle valve (WOT), 588
Windows
    defroster, 430-31
    power, 427-28
Windshield
    module, heated, 610
    wipers/washer system, 424-26
Wire
    color codes, *331*
    gauge sizes, *330*
    size/length, *330*
Wiring
    connections, visual inspection of, 462-64
    diagrams, electrical, 331, *332*
Work area, safety in, 22-24
Worm and roller steering, 852
    servicing, 858
WOT. *See* Wide-open throttle valve
Wrenches, 65-69
    air ratchet, 74
    impact, 74, 75
    torque-indicating, 65

Yoke adjustment, rack and pinion steering and, 853